THE

ENGLISHMAN'S

GREEK CONCORDANCE

OF THE

NEW TESTAMENT.

THE

ENGLISHMAN'S
GREEK CONCORDANCE

OF THE

NEW TESTAMENT;

BEING AN ATTEMPT AT

A VERBAL CONNEXION BETWEEN THE GREEK
AND THE ENGLISH TEXTS:

INCLUDING

A CONCORDANCE TO THE PROPER NAMES;

WITH

INDEXES,

GREEK-ENGLISH AND ENGLISH-GREEK;

AND

A CONCORDANCE OF VARIOUS READINGS.

Ninth Edition.

IN WHICH IS ADDED

A VOCABULARY OF NEW TESTAMENT GREEK.

GEORGE V. WIGRAM

**ZONDERVAN
PUBLISHING HOUSE** OF THE ZONDERVAN CORPORATION
GRAND RAPIDS, MICHIGAN 49506

Zondervan edition   1970
Eleventh printing   1979
ISBN 0-310-20320-1

Library of Congress Catalog Card Number: 71-106435

Originally published in London by Samuel Bagster & Sons in eight volumes, 1839; second edition, 1844.

George Vicesimus Wigram (1805-1879) was graduated from Queen's College, Oxford, in 1826. He later joined the Plymouth Brethren and devoted himself to exegetical writing. Besides the present volume, he produced *The Englishman's Hebrew and Chaldee Concordance of the Old Testament* and *The Hebraist's Vade Mecum*, a verbal index to the Hebrew and Aramaic Scriptures.

Printed in the United States of America

EIGHTH EDITION.

In this edition was added a CONCORDANCE OF VARIOUS READINGS from Griesbach to "the Revisers, 1881."

June, 1885.

NINTH EDITION

This edition is a careful reprint, a few errors being corrected.

A VOCABULARY OF NEW TESTAMENT GREEK is now added, with the hope that it will be found useful to the English readers.

January, 1903.

THIRD EDITION.

THE present Edition is not a mere reprint of the Editions which preceded it.

No book of reference could well be subjected to a more severe ordeal than has the "Englishman's Greek Concordance," by Mr. G. K. Gillespie,* who in an investigation of all the acceptations of each word of the Greek Testament, verified the fidelity of a great multitude of references; and, by the comparison of several thousand citations with their contexts, tested the accuracy with which the principle of putting English equivalents in italics has been carried out.

The benefit to this *Third* Edition of those his severe labours—and also his kindness and courtesy in freely communicating the fruit of them—are here thankfully acknowledged.

* Author of " The Greek Testament Roots, in a selection of texts, giving the power of reading the whole Greek Testament without difficulty."

June, 1860.

NOTA BENE.

In the present (Third) Edition, the symbol 000 . . . . . 000 has been adopted (in both the English and Greek and in the Greek and English Index) as the sign of matter which has been omitted.

When a Greek word has nothing which represents it in the translation, the mark)(has been introduced therein, to point out its place.

INTRODUCTION

TO THE FIRST EDITION.

THIS work is an attempt at a verbal connexion between the Greek and the English texts of the New Testament. Such an idea, though novel to him whose studies have been limited to the English language, is not so to the student: for it is but a modification of that developed by Marius in his Hebrew and Latin Concordance; by Kircher in his Hebrew and Greek Concordance for the LXX; by Trommius in his somewhat similar work; by Romaine in his edition of Marius; and by Taylor in his Hebrew and English Concordance.

PLAN.—The PLAN proposed was this: to present, in alphabetical succession, every word which occurs in the Greek New Testament, with the series of passages (quoted from the English translation) in which each such word occurs; the word or words exhibiting the Greek word under immediate consideration being printed in *italic* letters.

MANNER.—The MANNER in which the plan was carried into execution was simple and plain. Schmid's Concordance to the New Testament was taken as the basis. In this work we have, for the Greek New Testament, what Cruden's work was intended to be toward the whole English Bible; it is an alphabetical arrangement of each word which occurs, each word being immediately followed by the series of passages in which it occurs; this series is, of course, made up of such quotations, from the respective passages, as best exhibit the word under consideration.

It may be well to notice that the edition of Schmid used, was that printed in Glasgow, 1819. The copy used was, however, diligently corrected throughout before being accredited.*

---

* The *revision* of Schmid was thus conducted. Every word as cited in Schmid was found in a Greek New Testament, interleaved for the purpose, and therein underlined with black ink. When the whole of Schmid had thus been verified, of course it was only needful carefully to look through the Greek Testament thus marked, in order to discover *how many* words were omitted in Schmid; for if *every* word which actually occurred in Schmid was thus underlined in the New Testament, the words NOT underlined were of course not in Schmid. About 620 such were found, besides many errors, &c., &c.

A copy of Schmid's Greek Concordance was then put into the hand of a writer, with these directions :—

First. Place Schmid open before you. Write from it the first Greek heading, and under it successively all the references, *i. e.*, the books, chapters, and verses. Thus,

A, *alpha.*

Rev. 1 : 8.
      11.
  21 : 6.
  22 : 13.

Secondly. Open an interleaved Greek and English New Testament ; compare the two texts together, selecting the seven consecutive words which best illustrate the Greek word under consideration, and write them down against each reference, UNDERLINING the word which is to be put in italics. Thus,

Rev. 1 : 8 *I am Alpha and Omega, the beginning*
      11 *I am Alpha and Omega, the first and the*
  21 : 6 *I am Alpha and Omega, the beginning*
  22 : 13 *I am Alpha and Omega, the beginning*

REVISION.—When thus prepared, the manuscript was, first, examined, and each citation compared with an interleaved English and Greek Testament, in order to see that the right passage was quoted, and the right word underlined.

It was, secondly, read carefully by one accustomed to the press, and each line compared with an English Bible to verify the references (*i. e.*, books, chapters, and verses), and the spelling, capital letters, stops, &c.

Thirdly. It was compared with the corrected Schmid, and then sent to press.

When the letter-press had been *twice* carefully read with the copy, every line was

First, Again compared with an English Bible, to verify the references, spelling, capitals, stops, &c. [The Bible used in both cases was the Oxford small pica 8vo. 1836, with marginal readings, No. 8 in the Oxford Series.]

Secondly, It was then read out by one person to a second, who had Schmid before him, and read each line therein. The object of this was to see, first, that nothing was omitted ; and, secondly, that the right words were underlined.

It may be remarked here, that this is a very sure guard against the accidental quotation of a wrong part of a verse. The average number of words in each quotation in Schmid is three : now, if it be considered in how many verses in the New Testament are there three consecutive words, interchangeable, from being synonymous, with three other consecutive words, the efficiency of the guard thus provided will appear.

ITALICS.—As to the word put in ITALICS; *the general rule has* been to print in italics that word which in the English is "to the eye" equivalent to the Greek word under consideration. The exceptions are where the English contains that which is a CONVENTIONAL mark, in grammar, of something not found in the Greek text: for instance, in translating a verb, attention had not, in our authorised version, always been paid to the conventional signs of mood and tense: thus, a subjunctive is translated not "that they *might see*," but "to *see*." In the senses of the two renderings there is no difference; but observe that "to" in such cases is not put in italics, because it is the conventional sign of the infinitive mood; but the Greek verb is not the infinitive but the subjunctive.

Again, if an infinitive were translated, "that they might not *see*," "*see*" only would be in italics, because the Greek verb is in the infinitive mood, and "might" is the conventional sign of the subjunctive.

Again, if a Greek participle is translated otherwise than by an English participle, it will generally be found that there is *that, and, when,* &c. before or after the verb, by which it is expressed, in italics.

The pronouns *I, thou, he,* &c. when simply IMPLIED in the verb, are never in italics.

Where the versification of the English differs from the Greek text, both verses are placed, the English first and the Greek after it, in parentheses.

For the sake of those who cannot read Greek, the English pronunciation of the Greek word at the heading is added in English characters; *ī* has been used for ει, *ū* for ευ, *ee* for η, and *ō* for ω, when so placed as if not especially rested upon to distort the word, as *anapleeroō*; in which, without such a rest upon the second "o," the two would coalesce into a diphthong.

In order to call attention, first, to peculiar combinations of words; secondly, to the variation of government by prepositions; and, thirdly, to the different forms of the same word, conventional marks have been occasionally introduced into the headings; see αἰών, διά, ἄχρι, &c., &c. To these many other such like remarks might be added; but none of them need observation in order for the book to be used, and they will all pass before the reader's eye as he uses it. It may, however, be remarked that the sign)(has been used when there is nothing in English answering to the Greek word.

———

. Where all the occurrences of a word are not given in the body of the work, as in the case of ἀλλά, αἰτός, γάρ, a full list is given in the Appendix, in which also will be found a few remarks on δέ, καί, ὁ, and ὅς, the four words which Schmid passes by unnoticed, by reason of their too frequent occurrence.

March, 1840.

A SHORT ACCOUNT OF THE MAKING
AND PERFECTING
OF THE
ENGLISHMAN'S GREEK CONCORDANCE.

A DETAILED account of the formation, etc., of the Englishman's Greek Concordance, has been the desire of several. This I shall now endeavour to meet. The task is rather an arduous one; because, whilst the credit of exhibiting in English the exemplifications of each Greek word in the New Testament is due to another,—on myself are *supposed* to meet the offices of Corrector, Enlarger, Improver, and Editor. Simplicity, however, will pass through all difficulties, howsoever great they may seem. I would only state (as bespeaking a more favourable hearing) that my narrative will shew that the supposition, referring to myself, is without foundation. I am not Corrector, not Enlarger, not Improver, not Editor. Proprietor of the copyright, through the gift of another, I am; and mine, too, is that sort of place which belongs to one who, having the right to direct, may have chanced upon some good suggestions for the workmen.

As the book is a dry Concordance, I would crave the liberty to be as free as I can in my narrative.

My prepa-
ration for
the work. } It was in the year 1827 or 1828, that I began to prepare some Essays explanatory and illustrative of the "Terms conventional to the Scriptures;" e. g. Righteousness, Sanctification, Justification, etc. One of these I thought much of; and I may give the course pursued in the preparation of it as an explanation of my general plan. 1st. After making a list of the places (books, chapters, and verses) in which the words occurred, I carefully examined all the passages in the Greek Testament in which the word δίκη or any kindred term occurred, endeavouring to seize on the abstract thought common to all the places in which it was found. 2ndly. I considered how many English words it would be necessary to use in order to express the varieties of shades of meaning. And, 3rdly. I wrote down after each citation, either the word which would do for the translation in that place, or (where it had occurred before) some sign for it. This, when arranged, formed the skeleton of the explanation, and the object of illustration.

Mr. W. Burgh's
plan. } Full of these Essays, I spoke of them to many. In September, 1830, I went to Ireland, still labouring therein. Between that month and March, 1831, Mr. W. Burgh, till that time a perfect stranger to me, came to stay a few days at Powerscourt. In the course of a walk with him, I spoke of part of the subject then interesting me; and he, I think, in reply referred to the advantage he had found in doing much the same thing himself; only his *preparation* was better and far more simple than mine. His plan was to arrange the passages in which the word occurred, according to the order of the books in the English

Bible, from Taylor's Hebrew and Schmid's Greek Concordances, and then write after each, a quotation from the English Bible, to present the word to the eye.

The design was so novel to me, and so admirable, that it delighted me much; and I urged his devoting all his time to the accomplishment of such a work. If he would have allowed me, I should gladly have supported him while so doing; but this he positively declined. With his usual ingenuity, however, he kindly devised a manner of meeting my wishes, by offering to engage lads to do the mechanical part of the writing under him. How singular it is to look back upon the past cenes of life! My going to Ireland had been quite unexpected;—his being asked to the house at that special time;—our lighting, in a walk as perfect strangers, upon that which had occupied our minds, "how to elucidate Scripture;"—and the free blending together which followed in an effort to accomplish this object after the manner proposed by Mr. B.: and how different the motives which may operate! Mr. B.'s object I know not;—my joy in the project was the opening of a door for me, by which the plan of my Essays might be acted upon in Hebrew as well as in Greek.

Though Mr. W. B. had commenced, he says, Articles of the Greek previous to this, it was the Hebrew which, as the more difficult task, held the place of pre-eminence in his mind, and the one which he first mentioned to me. The Hebrew was arranged for between us first; (for the further account of it see that Concordance). Knowing a little of Greek (though then nothing of Hebrew), and being still labouring at my "Essays," I asked Mr. W. Burgh, whether he would permit me to adopt his plan for the Greek. Though not systematically from the beginning, yet small portions had been written out, according to his own need, perhaps, previously. To this he consented, and further agreed to endeavour to get as much of it written for me (at so many pence per page, of so many lines) as he could. About 800 pages in MS. of this was beautifully executed under his care, i.e., about 290 pages in letterpress of the 900 pages seen in the volume. Finding difficulty in proceeding with the making of the MS. further, he handed it over to me, to be continued or not, as I liked. As he had most distinctly warned me at the outset, he would not undertake to have more done than might be quite convenient to him, I of course only felt thankful for this aid, superadded to the gift of leave to do the work. For whilst he charged it only like blank paper, what it cost by the foot, to me it was the acquisition of so much "painting," for it was most accurately and beautifully done; so that it is now, though soiled by having passed through the press, MS. in a very good state of order. The 1800 remaining pages of MS. were made by various hands; some a gift, some purchased between 1831 and 1839. At Plymouth, in 1831, I gave away all that was done to a friend, in the hopes that he would correct and finish it; and from him I received it back as a present. While a lady at the same place was writing part of it for me, she complained that it would be of no use to her, unless I gave "a key" to it. "English and Greek;" this remark, repeated by several, decided me to try and make the design and plan of "A Greek and English Concordance," as opened out and given to me by Mr. Burgh, subservient to another design and plan, as expressed by the present title, "The Englishman's Greek Concordance"; by which I mean a Greek Concordance, such as one who can read English, and English only—the mere English reader—could consult. For great as the aid, to one who could read Greek, from Mr. W. B.'s Greek and English Concordance would have been, the mere English reader could not, by himself, have benefited much by it, from his want of knowing Greek.

I may give now a condensed account of—

First, Schmid's Concordance. Secondly, Mr. B.'s plan, and—Thirdly, What was afterwards added in matter and design by others.

SCHMID—

Schmid's design appears to have been to give, in alphabetical order, the whole vocabulary of the Greek Testament (some few words of minor importance being excepted), each word being followed by the series of its occurrences, books, chapters, and verses; and the citation in Greek consisting generally of three or four words.

We may suppose Schmid to have made his work, first, a vocabulary.

$$A \qquad ἀβαρής \qquad ἀββᾶ$$

2ndly, to have written down, under each, the guide to the places where it occurred, as—

A	ἀβαρής
Rev. 1: 8	2 Cor. 11 : 9
11	
21: 6	
22 : 13	

And lastly, to have written down after each such reference, the three or four Greek words in immediate connection with the word standing in the heading, thus—

$$A$$

Rev. 1 : 8. ἐγώ εἰμι τὸ A καὶ τὸ Ω
11. ἐγώ εἰμι τὸ A καὶ τὸ Ω
21 : 6. ἐγώ εἰμι τὸ A καὶ τὸ Ω
22 : 13. ἐγώ εἰμι τὸ A καὶ τὸ Ω

and so on through the whole work. This work could of course only be used by a Greek scholar, and but few know Greek enough to use it with *comfort* to themselves.

Mr. W. B.'s Plan—

Was to write down, in place of the Greek citation, the English which was equivalent to it, printing in different type (*italic* letter) the portion which translated the Greek word at the head of the article. And this, when done, made the book.

This plan was original, and clearly is such as to enable any one who knows Greek sufficiently to look at a verse in the New Testament, if he knows English *well*, to consult a Greek Concordance with as much comfort as he could Cruden.

All that was effected under my management, was—

1st. The MS. had to be made from επι, p. 231, to χρονιζω, p. 803, in the Appellatives, *i.e.* MS. for 521 pages of letter-press.

2ndly. Mistrusting Schmid's accuracy, we *re*-made a copy for ourselves thus :—

Every word, as cited by Schmid, was found in a Greek New Testament, interleaved for the purpose, and then underlined with black ink. When the whole of Schmid had thus been verified, of course it was only needful carefully to look through the Greek Testament thus marked, in order to discover how many words were omitted in Schmid, for if *every* word which actually occurred in Schmid was thus underlined in the New Testament, the words not underlined in it were of course not in Schmid. About 620 such were found, besides many errors, etc., etc. This was the kind labour of L. C. L. Brenton, in the year 1836.

3rdly. The MS. had to be lifted off its old basis, Schmid, and placed upon the larger one of the corrected Schmid.

IMPROVEMENTS.

1.—The blending into one, many words which Schmid had divided into two, making oft what was really only an adjective to be sometimes such and sometimes a substantive. A comparison of the two books will show how far this has been done.

2.—The blending of some forms, which, contrary to his principle, he had separated, as some cases in the pronouns αὐτου, αὐτην, αυτοις, etc.

3.—Sundries ; see page v. in the Introduction.

Lastly,—There were made and added,—

1.—The proper names which (though in Schmid under one alphabet with the appellatives) had been omitted in the MS., occupying from 818—872, *i.e.* 54 pages.

2.—An Index, English and Greek, which, besides its value to the mere English reader (*his* only key to the book), is a fair English and Greek Dictionary, and the best key extant to the Scripture Greek synonyms, 873—942, *i.e.* 68 pages.

3.—An Appendix I. containing the occurrences of ἀλλα, αὐτος, γαρ, and—

4.—An Appendix II. containing cursory suggestions on δε, και, ὁ, ὁς, the four words which Schmid passes by unnoticed, on account of their too frequent occurrences. The 2nd and 4th were the labours of different persons.

The greater part of this, as first published, was edited by Mr. George H. Stoddart, and under him, as corrector of the press, etc., by W. Chalk.

The printing establishment deserves my thanks for its ready aid and attention.

The only *originality*, then, in this work, is the primary design of Mr. Burgh, by a Greek and English Concordance, to enable the tyro in Greek to consult a Greek Concordance with ease; and *a secondary* design (which is really the reverse of this) the subordinating *it by the means of an English and Greek key* to the use of the mere English reader. And this is just what the title for it, "The Englishman's Greek Concordance," was meant to designate. My relation to it then is just marked by the terms Proprietor and Nursing Father. Honour or thanks I desire none. Indeed, when I think of the origin of this book; of the progress of its developement; of the innumerable difficulties which again and again threatened its destruction; and, above all, of its *tendency* (as contrasted with the now prevailing increase of Romanism); I cannot but bow my head before the God of Providence, and be ashamed at His having vouchsafed any connection with it to one so unworthy as

GEORGE V. WIGRAM.

London, March, 1844.

VOCABULARY.

This Vocabulary is added to give the English reader the meaning, in short, of each Greek word, and throw light upon the different translations of the words in the Authorised Version, as notified by *italics* in the Concordance.

Many of the Greek words are compounds of two or more words: these are shewn by the use of the hyphen.

Some of the *roots* of the words are given for the assistance of those who may wish to trace the words further, and meanings are added to those roots which do not occur in the Concordance.

Words marked with a * are those not found in the common Greek text (and therefore not in the body of the Concordance), but which have been introduced by the Editors of the various editions of the Greek Testament, most of which will be found in the Concordance of VARIOUS READINGS at the end of the volume. Some are merely variations in the spelling.

Most of the foreign words found in the Greek Testament are noted, as *Aram.* (Aramaic); *Heb.* (Hebrew), &c.

A, ἄλφα, first letter of the Greek alphabet. In composition it generally signifies *negation*. α΄=1; α,=1000.
ἀ-βαρής, not burdensome.
ἀββᾶ, father. *Aramaic.*
ἄ-βυσσος, abyss.
ἀγαθο-εργέω, to do good.
ἀγαθο-ποιέω, to do good.
ἀγαθο-ποιΐα, well doing.
ἀγαθο-ποιός, well doer.
ἀγαθός, good; τὰ ἀγαθά, goods.
*ἀγαθουργέω=ἀγαθοεργέω.
ἀγαθωσύνη, goodness.
ἀγαλλίασις, exultation: fr. ἀνάλλω, to take pride in.
ἀγαλλιάω, to exult, rejoice.
ἄ-γαμος, unmarried.
ἀγαν-ακτέω, to be carried to excess: fr. ἄγαν & ἄγω.
ἀγαν-άκτησις, indignation.
ἀγαπάω, to love.
ἀγάπη, love.
ἀγαπητός, beloved.
ἀγγαρεύω, to impress into public service. *Persian.*
ἀγγεῖον, a vessel (of any kind).
ἀγγελία, a message.
*ἀγγέλλω, to bring wood.
ἄγγελος, a messenger.
*ἄγγος=ἀγγεῖον.
ἄγε, come (now): fr. ἄγω.
ἀγέλη, a herd: *id.* [genealogy.
ἀ-γενεα-λόγητος, not reckoned by
ἀ-γενής, low-born, base: fr. γένος.
ἁγιάζω, to hallow, sanctify: ἅγιος.
ἁγιασμός, sanctification.
ἅγιον, holy (place): *neut. of* ἅγιος.
ἅγιος, holy; οἱ ἅγιοι, the saints.
ἁγιότης, holiness.
ἁγιωσύνη, holiness.
ἀγκάλαι, arms. [bending.
ἄγκιστρον, fish hook: fr. ἄγκος,
ἄγκυρα, anchor, *id.*
ἄ-γναφος, not fulled: fr. γνάπτω,
ἁγνεία, –νία, purity. [to card.
ἁγνίζω, to purify.
ἁγνισμός, purification.
ἀ-γνοέω, not to know: fr. γινώσκω.
ἀ-γνόημα, sin of ignorance, error.
ἄ-γνοια, ignorance.
ἁγνός, pure, chaste: fr. ἅγος, awe.
ἁγνότης, purity.

ἁγνῶς, purely.
ἀ-γνωσία, want of knowledge.
ἄ-γνωστος, unknown.
ἀγορά, market place, forum: fr. ἀγείρω, to gather.
ἀγοράζω, to purchase.
ἀγοραῖος, belonging to the forum (loungers there); *pl.* court days.
ἄγρα, a catch (as of fish): fr. ἄγω.
ἀ-γράμματος, without learning: fr. γράμμα, γράφω.
ἀγρ-αυλέω, to abide in the field: fr. ἀγρός & αὐλή.
ἀγρεύω, to catch, ensnare.
ἀγρι-έλαιος, wild olive tree: ἐλαία.
ἄγριος, wild.
ἀγρός, field.
ἀγρ-υπνέω, to be sleepless, watch: fr. ἀγρέω & ὕπνος, hunting after sleep.
ἀγρ-υπνία, watching.
ἄγω, to lead, bring.
ἀγωγή, manner of life.
ἀγών, contest.
ἀγωνία, contest, agony.
ἀγωνίζομαι, to contend, strive.
ἀ-δάπανος, free of charge: δαπάνη.
ἀ-δελφή, sister: fr. δελφύς, matrix.
ἀ-δελφός, brother.
ἀ-δελφότης, brotherhood.
ἄ-δηλος, uncertain.
ἀ-δηλότης, uncertainty.
ἀ-δήλως, uncertainly.
ἀδημονέω, to be sore troubled.
ᾅδης, ᾍδης, realm of the dead, Hades: fr. ἰδεῖν, ὁράω.
ἀ-διά-κριτος, impartial: fr. κρίνω.
ἀ-διά-λειπτος, unceasing: fr. λείπω.
ἀ-δια-λείπτως, unceasingly.
ἀ-δια-φθορία, uncorruptness, up-rightness: fr. φθείρω.
ἀ-δικέω, to act unjustly, injure: fr. δίκη.
ἀ-δίκημα, an act of injustice.
ἀ-δικία, unrighteousness.
ἄ-δικος, unjust, unrighteous.
ἀ-δίκως, unjustly. [fr. δέχομαι.
ἀ-δόκιμος, not approved, rejected:
ἄ-δολος, without deceit, pure.
ἁδρότης, liberality.
ἀ-δύνατέω, to be impossible.
ἀ-δύνατος, impossible, impotent.
ᾄδω, to sing.

ἀεί, always.
ἀετός, an eagle.
ἄ-ζυμος, unleavened.
ἀήρ, air.
ἀ-θανασία, non-liability to death, immortality: fr. θάνατος.
ἀ-θέμιτος, unlawful: fr. θέμις, law.
ἄ-θεος, without God.
ἄ-θεσμος, lawless: fr. τίθημι.
ἀ-θετέω, to set aside: fr. τίθημι.
ἀ-θέτησις, setting aside.
ἀθλέω, to contend (in the games).
ἄθλησις, contest: ἄθλος, combat.
*ἀθροίζω, to gather together: fr. ἄθροος, crowded.
ἀ-θυμέω, to lose heart: fr. θυμός.
ἀθῷος, ἀθῶος, innocent: fr. θωή, penalty.
αἴγειος, –γιος, of a goat: fr. αἴξ, goat.
αἰγιαλός, shore: αἴσσω, ἅλς, the sea.
ἀΐδιος, eternal: fr. ἀεί.
αἰδώς, modesty.
αἷμα, blood.
αἱματ-εκ-χυσία, blood-shedding: fr. χέω, to pour.
αἱμορ-ροέω, to have a flux of blood: αἴνεσις, praise. [fr. ῥέω.
αἰνέω, to praise: fr. αἶνος.
αἴνιγμα, enigma, riddle.
αἶνος, praise.
αἱρέομαι, to take up, choose.
αἵρεσις, choice, *hence* sect, heresy.
αἱρετίζω, to choose. [sectarian.
αἱρετικός, apt to choose, *hence*
αἴρω, to take up *or* away.
αἰσθάνομαι, to perceive.
αἴσθησις, perception.
αἰσθητήριον, organ of perception.
αἰσχρο-κερδής, eager for base gain. κέρδος.
αἰσχρο-κερδῶς, from eagerness for base gain.
αἰσχρο-λογία, foul language: λόγοι.
αἰσχρός, –όν, base, dishonourable
αἰσχρότης, baseness.
αἰσχύνη, shame.
αἰσχύνομαι, to be ashamed.
αἰτέω, to request, supplicate.
αἴτημα, a request.
αἰτία, a cause, accusation.
αἰτίαμα, an accusation.
αἴτιον, a cause, accusation.
αἴτιος, a causer, author.

*αἰτίωμα = αἰτίαμα.

αἰφνίδιος, unexpected. fr. ἄφνω.

αἰχμ-αλωσία, captivity: fr. αἰχμή, spear, & ἅλωσις.

αἰχμ-αλωτεύω, to take captive.

αἰχμ-αλωτίζω, to lead captive.

αἰχμ-άλωτος, a captive.

αἰών, age, eternity, world.

αἰώνιος, eternal.

ἀ-καθαρσία, uncleanness: καθαρός.

ἀ-καθάρτης, impurity.

ἀ-κάθαρτος, unclean. [καιρός.

ἀ-καιρέομαι, to lack opportunity: fr.

ἀ-καίρως, unopportunely.

ἄ-κακος, guileless.

ἄκανθα, thorn.

ἀκάνθινος, made of thorns.

ἄ-καρπος, unfruitful.

ἀ-κατά-γνωστος, not to be censured: γινώσκω. [τω.

ἀ-κατα-κάλυπτος, unveiled: καλύπ-

ἀ-κατά-κριτος, uncondemned: κρίνω.

ἀ-κατά-λυτος, indissoluble: λύω.

*ἀ-κατά-παστος, insatiable: πασσω, to sprinkle. [παύω.

ἀ-κατά-παυστος, unable to cease:

ἀ-κατα-στασία, instability: καθίσ-

ἀ-κατά-στατος, unstable. [τημι.

ἀ-κατά-σχετος, unrestrainable: ἔχω.

ἀ-κέραιος, harmless: fr. κεράννυμι.

ἀ-κλινής, unbending: fr. κλίνω.

ἀκμάζω, to come to a point—to fruition: fr. ἀκμή, a point.

ἀκμήν, up to this point, still.

ἀκοή, hearing, the ear. [way.

ἀκολουθέω, to follow: fr. κέλευθος, a

ἀκούω, to hear.

ἀ-κρασία, incontinence: fr. κράτος.

ἀ-κρατής, without self-control.

ἄ-κρατον, unmixed: fr. κεράννυμι.

ἀκρίβεια, exactness.

ἀκριβέστατος, most exact, suprl. of ἀκριβής, accurate.

ἀκριβέστερον, more exact, comp. of

ἀκριβόω, to enquire exactly. [id.

ἀκριβῶς, exactly.

ἀκρίς, a locust.

ἀκροατήριον, place of hearing.

ἀκροατής, a hearer.

ἀκροβυστία, uncircumcision.

ἀκρο-γωνιαῖος, chief corner (stone): γωνία, corner.

ἀκρο-θίνιον, top of a heap, spoil:

ἄκρον, extreme point. [θίς, heap.

ἀ-κυρόω, to treat as of no force: fr. κῦρος, power.

ἀ-κωλύτως, without hindrance:

ἄκων, unwilling: fr. ἑκών. [κωλύω.

*ἅλα = ἅλας.

ἀλάβαστρον, alabaster.

ἀλαζονεία, -νία, ostentation: fr. ἄλη, wandering.

ἀλαζών, ostentatious.

ἀλαλάζω, to cry aloud.

ἀ-λάλητος, unutterable: fr. λαλέω.

ἄ-λαλος, unable to speak.

ἅλας, salt.

*ἁλεεύς = ἁλιεύς.

ἀλείφω, to anoint.

ἀλεκτορο-φωνία, cock-crowing: φω-

ἀλέκτωρ, a cock. [νή.

ἄλευρον, meal: fr. ἀλήθω.

ἀλήθεια, truth.

ἀληθεύω, to speak the truth.

ἀληθής, true.

ἀληθινός, true.

ἀλήθω, to grind: fr. ἀλέω, to grind.

ἀληθῶς, truly.

ἁλιεύς, a fisherman: fr. ἅλς.

ἁλιεύω, to fish.

ἁλίζω, to salt.

ἀλίσγημα, pollution.

ἀλλά, but.

ἀλλάττω, -σσω, to alter: fr. ἄλλος.

ἀλλαχόθεν, from elsewhere.

*ἀλλαχοῦ, elsewhere.

ἀλλ-ηγορέω, to speak allegorically: ἀγορεύω, to harangue.

ἀλληλούϊα, Hallelujah. Heb.

ἀλλήλων, one another. [γένος.

ἀλλο-γενής, of another nation:

ἄλλομαι, to spring up.

ἄλλος, another, others.

ἀλλοτριο-επίσκοπος, -ριεπ-, a spy on affairs of others: σκοπέω.

ἀλλότριος, belonging to another.

ἀλλό-φυλος, one of another race:

ἄλλως, otherwise. [φυλή.

ἀλοάω, to thresh out: fr. ἀλέω, to

ἄ-λογος, irrational. [grind.

ἀλόη, the aloe.

ἅλς, salt.

ἀλυκός, saltish.

ἀ-λυπότερος, more free from grief: comp. of ἄλυπος: fr. λύπη.

ἅλυσις, a chain. [τέλος.

ἀ-λυσι-τελής, unprofitable: fr. λύω &

ἄλφα. See A.

ἅλων, a threshing floor.

ἀλώπηξ, a fox. [be taken.

ἅλωσις, capture: fr. ἁλίσκομαι, to

ἅμα, with, together with.

ἀ-μαθής, unlearned: fr. μανθάνω.

ἀ-μαράντινος, unfading: fr. μαραίνω.

ἀ-μάραντος, unfading.

ἁμαρτάνω, to miss the mark, sin.

ἁμάρτημα, a sin.

ἁμαρτία, sin, sin-offering.

ἀ-μάρτυρος, without witness.

ἁμαρτωλός, sinner.

ἄ-μαχος, not contentious: fr. μάχη.

ἀμάω, to gather, reap.

ἀ-μέθυστος, an amethyst: fr. μεθύω.

ἀ-μελέω, to disregard: fr. μέλει.

ἀ-μέμπτος, without blame: μέμφομαι.

ἀ-μέμπτως, blamelessly.

ἀ-μέριμνος, without care: μέριμνα.

ἀ-μετά-θετος, unchangeable: τίθημι.

ἀ-μετα-κίνητος, immoveable: κινέω.

ἀ-μετα-μέλητος, not to be repented of: μέλει.

ἀ-μετα-νόητος, impenitent: νοέω.

ἄ-μετρος, without measure: μέτρον.

ἀμήν, Amen, verily. Heb. ὁ ἀμήν, the Amen.

ἀ-μήτωρ, without mother: μήτηρ.

ἀ-μίαντος, undefiled: fr. μιαίνω.

ἄμμος, sand.

ἀμνός, a lamb. [change.

ἀμοιβή, requital: fr. ἀμείβω, to ex-

ἄμπελος, a vine.

ἀμπελ-ουργός, vine-dresser: ἔργον.

ἀμπελών, a vineyard.

ἀμύνομαι, to defend.

ἀμφί, in comp. around.

*ἀμφιάζω, to clothe.

*ἀμφι-βάλλω, to cast around.

ἀμφι-βληστρον, a net.

*ἀμφιέζω = ἀμφιάζω.

ἀμφι-έννυμι, to clothe.

ἄμφ-οδον, a cross-way: ὁδός.

ἀμφότερος, -ροι, both.

ἀ-μώμητος, without blame: μῶμος.

*ἄμωμον, amomum (a spice plant).

ἄ-μωμος, without blame.

ἄν (expresses possibility), may, might, &c.

*ἄν (contracted from ἐάν), if.

ἀνά, adv. (imports distribution), apiece.

ἀνά prep. upon: in comp. up, again, or it intensifies.

ἀνα-βαθμός, means of ascent: βαίνω, to go, walk.

ἀνα-βαίνω, to ascend.

ἀνα-βάλλομαι, to defer. [to go.

ἀνα-βιβάζω, to bring up: βαίνω.

ἀνα-βλέπω, to look up or again.

ἀνά-βλεψις, recovery of sight.

ἀνα-βοάω, to cry aloud.

ἀνα-βολή, delay: βάλλω.

*ἀνάγαιον = ἀνώγεον.

ἀν-αγγέλλω, to declare, report.

ἀνα-γεννάω, to beget again.

ἀνα-γινώσκω, to gather exact know-ledge, hence to read.

ἀναγκάζω, to constrain.

ἀναγκαῖος, necessary.

ἀναγκαστῶς, of necessity.

ἀνάγκη, necessity: fr. ἄγκος, en-closure.

ἀνα-γνωρίζομαι, to make known.

ἀνά-γνωσις, reading.

ἀν-άγω, to bring, lead up; pass. to put to sea.

ἀνα-δείκνυμι, to shew (by raising), display, notify.

ἀνά-δειξις, a shewing.

ἀνα-δέχομαι, to receive to oneself.

ἀνα-δίδωμι, to give up.

ἀνα-ζάω, to live again.

ἀνα-ζητέω, to search for.

ἀνα-ζώννυμι, to gird up.

ἀνα-ζω-πυρέω, to revive (as a fire): ζωός, alive, & πῦρ.

ἀνα-θάλλω, to thrive again.

ἀνά-θεμα, accursed: τίθημι.

ἀνα-θεματίζω, to bind by a curse.

ἀνα-θεωρέω, to view attentively: θεωρός, a spectator.

ἀνά-θημα, a dedicated thing.

ἀν-αίδεια, -δια, importunity: fr. αἰ-δέομαι, to reverence.

ἀν-αίρεσις, a taking away (by death).

ἀν-αιρέω, to take up, kill.

ἀν-αίτιος, guiltless.

ἀνα-καθίζω, to sit up.

ἀνα-καινίζω, to renew entirely.

ἀνα-καινόω, to renew again.

ἀνά-καίνωσις, renewing.

ἀνα-καλύπτω, to unveil.

ἀνα-κάμπτω, to return.

ἀνά-κειμαι, to recline (at table).

ἀνα-κεφαλαιόομαι, to be summed up: κεφαλή.

ἀνα-κλίνω, to make to recline.

ἀνα-κόπτω, to beat back.

ἀνα-κράζω, to cry aloud.

ἀνα-κρίνω, to investigate.

ἀνά-κρισις, investigation.

*ἀνα-κυλίω, to roll up or away.

ἀνα-κύπτω, to raise up one's self.

ἀνα-λαμβάνω, to take up.

ἀνά-ληψις, -λημψις, a taking up: λαμβάνω.

ἀν-αλίσκω, to consume.

ἀνα-λογία, analogy.

ἀνα-λογίζομαι, to well consider.

ἀν-αλος, without saltness: ἅλς.

ἀνά-λυσις, departure.

ἀνα-λύω, to depart, return.

ἀν-αμάρτητος, without sin.

ἀνα-μένω, to await.

ἀνα-μιμνήσκω, to call to mind.

ἀνά-μνησις, a calling to mind.

ἀνα-νεόω, to renew.

ἀνα-νήφω, to recover soberness.

ἀν-αντίρ-ρητος, not to be contradicted: ἐρῶ, I will speak.
ἀν-αντιρ-ρήτως, without contradiction.
ἀν-άξιος, unworthy.
ἀν-αξίως, unworthily.
ἀνά-παυσις, rest.
ἀνα-παύω, to cause to rest.
ἀνα-πείθω, to induce.
*ἀνά-πειρος = ἀνάπηρος.
ἀνα-πέμπω, to send back.
*ἀνα-πηδάω, to leap up.
ἀνά-πηρος, maimed.
ἀνα-πίπτω, to lie down.
ἀνα-πληρόω, to fill up.
ἀν-απο-λόγητος, inexcusable: λέγω.
ἀνα-πτύσσω, to unroll.
ἀν-άπτω, to kindle. [μέω.
ἀν-αρίθμητος, innumerable: ἀριθ-
ἀνα-σείω, to stir up.
ἀνα-σκευάζω, to subvert: σκεῦος.
ἀνα-σπάω, to draw up.
ἀνά-στασις, resurrection. [ἵστημι.
ἀνα-στατόω, to cause commotion :
ἀνα-σταυρόω, to crucify afresh.
ἀνα-στενάζω, to sigh deeply, groan.
ἀνα-στρέφω, to turn again ; mid.
    to live, conduct oneself.
ἀνα-στροφή, mode of life.
ἀνα-τάσσομαι, to draw up.
ἀνα-τέλλω, to rise up.
ἀνα-τίθημι, to lay before.
ἀνα-τολή, a rising: fr. ἀνατέλλω.
ἀνα-τρέπω, to overthrow.
ἀνα-τρέφω, to nourish.
ἀνα-φαίνομαι, to be brought in view.
ἀνα-φέρω, to bring up, offer up.
ἀνα-φωνέω, to cry out. [pour.
ἀνά-χυσις, a pouring out: χέω, to
ἀνα-χωρέω, to withdraw.
ἀνά-ψυξις, refreshment.
ἀνα-ψύχω, to refresh.
ἀνδραποδιστής, a man-stealer.
ἀνδρίζομαι, to act the man.
ἀνδρο-φόνος, a man-slayer. [καλέω.
ἀν-εγ-κλητος, not open to blame :
ἀν-εκ-δι-ήγητος, not to be explained :
    ἡγέομαι.
ἀν-εκ-λάλητος, unutterable.
ἀν-έκ-λειπτος, exhaustless.
ἀν-εκτότερος, more tolerable (comp.
    of ἀνεκτός): ἔχω.
ἀν-ελεήμων, unmerciful.
*ἀν-έλεος = ἀνίλεως.
ἀνεμίζομαι, be driven by the wind.
ἄνεμος, the wind. [μαι.
ἀν-έν-δεκτος, -ον, inevitable: δέχο-
ἀν-εξ-ερεύνητος, -ραν-, untraceable.
ἀνεξί-κακος, enduring: ἀνέχομαι.
ἀν-εξ-ιχνίαστος, inscrutable: ἴχνος.
ἀν-επ-αισχυντος, without cause of
    shame.
ἀν-επι-ληπτος, -λημπ-, without reproach : λαμβάνω.
ἀν-έρχομαι, to ascend.
ἄνεσις, liberty : fr. ἀνίημι.
ἀν-ετάζω, to examine strictly.
ἄνευ, without. [τίθημι.
ἀν-εύ-θετος, not commodious :
ἀν-ευρίσκω, to find by search.
ἀν-έχομαι, to bear with.
ἀνεψιός, a nephew.
ἄνηθον, anise.
ἀνήκω, to be becoming.
ἀν-ήμερος, ungentle.
ἀνήρ, a man (in contrast to woman).
ἀνθ-ίστημι, to withstand.
ἀνθ-ομο-λογέομαι, to confess in return: ὁμός, same, & λέγω.

ἄνθος, a flower.
ἀνθρακιά, heap of live coal.
ἄνθραξ, coal. [κω.
ἀνθρωπ-άρεσκος, man-pleaser: ἀρέσ-
ἀνθρώπινος, human. [to slay.
ἀνθρωπο-κτόνος, homicide: κτείνω,
ἄνθρωπος, a man, a human being.
ἀνθ-υπατεύω, to be proconsul.
ἀνθ-ύπατος, proconsul: ὑπέρ.
ἀν-ίημι, to let go.
ἀν-ίλεως, without mercy.
ἄ-νιπτος, unwashed.
ἀν-ίστημι, to raise up.
ἀ-νόητος, unwise: fr. νοεω.
ἄν-οια, folly: fr. ἄνους.
ἀν-οίγω, to open.
ἀν-οικο-δομέω, to build up again :
    οἶκος, & δέμω, to build.
ἄν-οιξις, (act of) opening.
ἀ-νομία, lawlessness.
ἄ-νομος, without law, lawless.
ἀ-νόμως, without law.
ἀν-ορθόω, to set right: ὀρθός.
ἀν-όσιος, unholy.
ἀν-οχή, forbearance: ἔχω. [ἀγών.
ἀντ-αγωνίζομαι, to contend against:
ἀντ-άλλαγμα, in exchange: ἀλλά-
ἀντ-ανα-πληρόω, to fill up. [τω.
ἀντ-απο-δίδωμι, to recompense.
ἀντ-από-δομα, a recompense.
ἀντ-από-δοσις, a recompense.
ἀντ-απο-κρίνομαι, to answer.
ἀντέπω, ἀντ-εἶπον, to gainsay.
ἀντ-έχομαι, to hold firmly.
ἀντί, instead of, for : in comp.
    against, instead of.
ἀντι-βάλλω, to throw in turn.
ἀντι-δια-τίθημι, -τιθέμενος, to place
    self in opposition: τίθεμαι.
ἀντί-δικος, legal opponent: δίκη.
ἀντί-θεσις, opposition.
ἀντι-καθ-ίστημι, to resist.
ἀντι-καλέω, to invite in turn.
ἀντί-κειμαι, to oppose.
ἀντικρύ, -ρυς, opposite to.
ἀντι-λαμβάνομαι, to aid in turn.
ἀντι-λέγω, to speak against.
ἀντί-ληψις, -λημψις, assistance :
    λαμβάνω.
ἀντι-λογία, contradiction.
ἀντι-λοιδορέω, to revile in return.
ἀντί-λυτρον, a ransom: λύω.
ἀντι-μετρέω, to measure in return.
ἀντι-μισθία, recompence: μισθός.
ἀντι-παρ-έρχομαι, to pass on the
    other side.
ἀντι-πέραν, on the opposite side.
ἀντι-πίπτω, to resist.
ἀντι-στρατεύομαι, to war against.
ἀντι-τάσσομαι, to set self against.
ἀντί-τυπος, -ον, antitypical.
ἀντί-χριστος, antichrist. [ἄντλος.
ἀντλέω, to draw (water, &c.): fr.
ἄντλημα, vessel to draw with.
ἀντ-οφθαλμέω, to direct the eye
    against, to face.
ἄν-υδρος, without water : ὕδωρ.
ἀν-υπό-κριτος, without hypocrisy.
ἀν-υπό-τακτος, non-subject.
ἄνω, above, upwards.
ἀνώγεον, -γαιον, upper room: fr.
    ἄνω & γαῖα, γῆ. [ginning.
ἄνωθεν, from above, from the be-
ἀνωτερικός, upper, i.e., inland.
ἀνώτερον, higher, above.
ἀν-ωφελής, useless : ὠφελέω.
ἀξίνη, an axe.
ἄξιος, worthy: fr. ἄγω.
ἀξιόω, to deem worthy.

ἀξίως, worthily.
ἀ-όρατος, invisible : fr. ὁράω.
ἀπ-αγγέλλω, to report. [oneself.
ἀπ-άγχομαι, to strangle or hang
ἀπ-άγω, to lead away. [παιδεύω.
ἀ-παίδευτος, uninstructed : fr.
ἀπ-αίρομαι, to be taken away.
ἀπ-αιτέω, to ask for again.
ἀπ-αλγέω, to be past feeling.
ἀπ-αλλάσσω, mid. to depart ; pass.
    to be set free. [ἀλλότριος.
ἀπ-αλλοτριόω, to alienate from :
ἁπαλός, tender, soft.
ἀπ-αντάω, to meet.
ἀπ-άντησις, a meeting.
ἅπαξ, once. [βαίνω, to move.
ἀ-παρά-βατος, untransferable :
ἀ-παρα-σκεύαστος, unprepared :
    σκεῦος.
ἀπ-αρνέομαι, to disown, deny.
ἀπ-άρτι, henceforth.
ἀπ-αρτισμός, completion.
ἀπ-αρχή, first-fruits.
ἅ-πας, all, the whole. [salute.
*ἀπ-ασπάζομαι, to take leave of,
ἀπατάω, to deceive.
ἀπάτη, deception.
ἀ-πάτωρ, without father : πατήρ.
ἀπ-αύγασμα, effulgence : αὐγή.
ἀπ-εῖδον: see ἀφοράω.
ἀ-πείθεια, unbelief, disobedience
    fr. πείθω. [obedient
ἀ-πειθέω, to refuse belief, be dis-
ἀ-πειθής, unbelieving, disobedient.
ἀπειλέω, to threaten.
ἀπειλή, threatening.
ἄπ-ειμι, to be absent.
ἄπ-ειμι, to go away.
ἀπ-ειπεῖν, to renounce. [fr. πειράζω.
ἀ-πείραστος, above being tempted :
ἄ-πειρος, inexperienced.
ἀπ-εκ-δέχομαι, to expect earnestly.
ἀπ-εκ-δύομαι, to strip off, spoil.
ἀπ-έκ-δυσις, a stripping off.
ἀπ-ελαύνω, -αύνω, to drive away.
ἀπ-ελεγμός, disrepute: ἐλέγχω.
ἀπ-ελεύθερος, a freed-man.
ἀπ-ελπίζω, to be hopeless.
ἀπ-έναντι, over against.
ἀ-πέραντος, interminable: fr. πέρας
ἀ-περι-σπάστως, without distraction : σπάω. [νω, to cut.
ἀ-περί-τμητος, uncircumcised : τέμ-
ἀπ-έρχομαι, to go or come from.
ἀπ-έχει, it is enough : fr. ἀπέχω.
ἀπ-έχομαι, to abstain from.
ἀπ-έχω, to have in full. [ful.
ἀ-πιστέω, to disbelieve, be unfaith-
ἀ-πιστία, unbelief, distrust.
ἄ-πιστος, unbelieving, distrustful.
ἁπλότης, simplicity.
ἁ-πλοῦς, simple.
ἁπλῶς, freely. [or intensifying.
ἀπό, from : in comp. away, from,
ἀπο-βαίνω, to go or come from,
    result.
ἀπο-βάλλω, to cast away.
ἀπο-βλέπω, to look, look away.
ἀπό-βλητος, to be cast away: βάλλω.
ἀπο-βολή, a casting away.
ἀπο-γενόμενος, being dead : fr.
    ἀπογίνομαι, to be dead.
ἀπο-γραφή, enrolment.
ἀπο-γράφω, to enrol.
ἀπο-δείκνυμι, to demonstrate.
ἀπό-δειξις, demonstration. [tithes
ἀπο-δεκατόω, -τεύω, to give or take
ἀπό-δεκτος, acceptable.
ἀπο-δέχομαι, to receive gladly

ἀπο-δημίω, to go or be from home.
ἀπόδημος, absent from home.
ἀπο-δίδωμι, to render (what is due).
ἀπο-δι-ορίζω, to separate.
ἀπο-δοκιμάζω, to reject.
ἀπο-δοχή, reception.
ἀπό-θεσις, a putting away.
ἀπο-θήκη, repository.
ἀπο-θησαυρίζω, to treasure up.
ἀπο-θλίβω, to press closely.
ἀπο-θνήσκω, to die.
ἀπο-καθ-ιστάω, -άνω, -ημι, restore.
ἀπο καλύπτω, to reveal.
ἀπο-κάλυψις, revelation.
ἀπο-καρα-δοκία, earnest expectation: κάρα, head, & δέχομαι.
ἀπο-κατ-αλλάσσω, -άττω, to reconcile.
ἀπο-κατά-στασις, restoration: ἵστημι.
ἀπό-κειμαι, to be reserved, laid up.
ἀπο-κεφαλίζω, to behead: κεφαλή.
ἀπο-κλείω, to shut up.
ἀπο-κόπτω, to cut off.
ἀπό-κριμα, an answer.
ἀπο-κρίνομαι, to answer.
ἀπό-κρισις, an answer.
ἀπο-κρύπτω, to conceal.
ἀπό-κρυφος, concealed.
ἀπο-κτείνω, -ταίνω, -τέννω, to kill.
ἀπο-κυέω, to bring forth.
ἀπο-κυλίζω, -λίω, to roll away.
ἀπο-λαμβάνω, to receive.
ἀπό-λαυσις, enjoyment.
ἀπο-λείπω, to leave.
ἀπο-λείχω, to lick.
ἀπ-όλλυμι, -λύω, to destroy.
ἀπο-λογέομαι, to defend oneself.
ἀπο-λογία, defence.
ἀπο-λούω, to wash away.
ἀπο-λύτρωσις, redemption: λύτρον.
ἀπο-λύω, to release.
ἀπο-μάσσομαι, to wipe off.
ἀπο-νέμω, to assign.
ἀπο-νίπτω, to wash.
ἀπο-πίπτω, to fall from.
ἀπο-πλανάω, to cause to wander.
ἀπο-πλέω, to sail away.
ἀπο-πλύνω, to wash or rinse (clothes, &c.)
ἀπο-πνίγω, to choke.
ἀ-πορέομαι, to be in doubt: fr. πόρος, passage.
ἀπορία, doubt.
ἀπορ-ρίπτω, ἀπορί-, throw aside.
ἀπ-ορφανίζομαι, to be bereaved: ὀρφανός. [σκεῦος.
ἀπο-σκευάζομαι, to pack up baggage:
ἀπο-σκίασμα, a shade: σκιά.
ἀπο-σπάω, to draw out or away.
ἀπο-στασία, defection, apostasy: ἵστημι.
ἀπο-στάσιον, divorce: id.
ἀπο-στεγάζω, to unroof: στέγη.
ἀπο-στέλλω, to send forth or away.
ἀπο-στερέω, to defraud. [ship.
ἀπο-στολή, a sending forth, apostle-
ἀπό-στολος, messenger, apostle.
ἀπο-στοματίζω, to provoke to speak: στόμα.
ἀπο-στρέφω, to turn away.
ἀπο-στυγέω, to abhor.
ἀπο-συν-άγωγος, put out of the synagogue.
ἀπο-τάσσομαι, to take leave of.
ἀπο-τελέω, to perfect.
ἀπο-τίθημι, to lay aside.
ἀπο-τινάσσω, to shake off.
ἀπο-τίνω, -τίω, to repay.
ἀπο-τολμάω, to dare.

ἀπο-τομία, severity: τέμνω, to cut.
ἀπο-τόμως, severely.
ἀπο-τρέπομαι, to turn from.
ἀπ-ουσία, absence: εἰμί.
ἀπο-φέρω, to carry away.
ἀπο-φεύγω, to flee from.
ἀπο-φθέγγομαι, to declare. [φέρω.
ἀπο-φορτίζομαι, to unlade: φορτίον.
ἀπό-χρησις, use, consumption: [χράομαι.
ἀπο-χωρέω, to go away.
ἀπο-χωρίζομαι, to separate.
ἀπο-ψύχω, to faint away.
ἀ-πρός-ιτος, unapproached: εἰμι.
ἀ-πρός-κοπος, without offence: κόπτω.
ἀ-προσωπο-λήπτως, -λήμπ-, impartially: fr. πρόσωπον & λαμβάνω.
ἄ-πταιστος, without stumbling.
ἅπτομαι, to touch.
ἅπτω, to kindle.
ἀπ-ωθέομαι, -θόμαι, to repulse.
ἀπώλεια, destruction, perdition.
ἀρά, a curse.
ἄρα, so then, thence.
ἆρα, whether? is it so? &c.
*ἀραβών = ἀρραβών.
*ἄραφος = ἄρραφος.
ἀργέω, to be unemployed.
ἀργός, not working, idle.
ἀργύρεος = ἀργυροῦς.
ἀργύριον, piece of silver, money.
ἀργυρο-κόπος, silversmith.
ἄργυρος, silver.
ἀργυροῦς, -ύρεος, made of silver.
ἀρέσκεια, -κία, desire to please.
ἀρέσκω, to please.
ἀρεστός, pleasing.
ἀρετή, goodness.
ἀρήν, a lamb.
ἀριθμέω, to number.
ἀριθμός, number. [dine.
ἀριστάω, to breakfast, (later) to
ἀριστερός, the left (hand).
ἄριστον, breakfast, dinner.
ἀρκετός, sufficient.
ἀρκέω, to be satisfied with.
ἄρκτος, ἄρκος, a bear.
ἅρμα, a chariot.
ἁρμόζω, to join together, betroth.
ἁρμός, a joint.
ἀρνέομαι, to deny.
ἀρνίον, a young lamb.
ἀρξάμενος, beginning: fr. ἄρχω.
ἀροτριάω, to plough: fr. ἀρόω, to
ἄροτρον, a plough. [plough.
ἁρπαγή, plunder.
ἁρπαγμός, rapine.
ἁρπάζω, to seize.
ἅρπαξ, rapacious.
ἀρραβών, ἀρα-, pledge. Phœnician.
ἄρ-ραφος, ἄρα-, not sewn: ῥάπτω,
ἄρρην, ἄρσην, a male. [to sew.
ἄρ-ρητος, not spoken: ἐρῶ.
ἄρ-ρωστος, infirm: ῥώννυμαι.
ἀρσενο-κοίτης, a sodomite.
ἄρσην = ἄρρην. [hang to.
ἀρτέμων, foresail: fr. ἀρτάω, to
ἄρτι, now, lately.
ἀρτι-γέννητος, new-born: γεννάω.
ἄρτιος, complete.
ἄρτος, bread, loaf.
ἀρτύω, to prepare, season.
ἀρχ-άγγελος, archangel.
ἀρχή, beginning, ruler.
ἀρχ-ηγός, beginner, prince: ἄγω.
ἀρχι-, ἀρχ-, a prefix, arch, chief, high
ἀρχ-ιερατικός, high-priestly: ἱερεύς.

ἀρχ-ιερεύς, high priest.
ἀρχι-ποίμην, chief shepherd.
ἀρχι-συν-άγωγος, ruler of a synagogue.
ἀρχι-τέκτων, architect.
ἀρχι-τελώνης, chief tax-collector: τέλος.
ἀρχι-τρί-κλινος, master of a feast: τρεῖς, τρία & κλίνη.
ἄρχομαι, to begin.
ἄρχω, to be first, to rule.
ἄρχων, chief, ruler.
ἄρωμα, an aromatic.
ἀ-σάλευτος, unshaken: fr. σάλος, tossing (as the sea). [νυμι.
ἄ-σβεστος, inextinguishable: σβέν-
ἀ-σέβεια, impiety: fr. σέβομαι.
ἀ-σεβέω, to be impious.
ἀ-σεβής, impious.
ἀ-σέλγεια, lasciviousness.
ἄ-σημος, insignificant.
ἀ-σθένεια, weakness.
ἀ-σθε-νέω, to be weak.
ἀ-σθένημα, weakness.
ἀ-σθενής, weak.
ἀ-σιτία, fasting.
ἄ-σιτος, fasting.
ἀσκέω, to exercise (self).
ἀσκός, bottle (of skin). [please.
ἀσμένως, gladly: fr. ἀνδάνω, to
ἄ-σοφος, unwise.
ἀσπάζομαι, to greet.
ἀσπασμός, greeting.
ἄ-σπιλος, without spot.
ἀσπίς, an asp. [σπένδομαι.
ἄ-σπονδος, irreconcilable: fr.
ἀσσάριον, Roman coin about ⅜d. Latin, as.
ἆσσον, nearer, comp. of ἄγχι, near.
ἀ-στατέω, to wander about: fr. ἵστημι.
ἀστεῖος, beautiful: fr. ἄστυ, a city
ἀστήρ, a star.
ἀ-στήρικτος, unstable: fr. στηρίζω.
ἄ-στοργος, without affection: fr. στέργω, to love.
ἀ-στοχέω, to deviate: fr. στόχος,
ἀστραπή, lightning. [aim.
ἀστράπτω, to lighten.
ἄστρον, a star.
ἀ-σύμ-φωνος, dissonant: φωνή.
ἀ-σύν-ετος, unintelligent: συνίημι.
ἀ-σύν-θετος, covenant breaking.
ἀ-σφάλεια, security: fr. σφάλλω, to
ἀ-σφαλής, secure. [throw down.
ἀ-σφαλίζω, to make secure.
ἀ-σφαλῶς, securely. [σχῆμα.
ἀ-σχημονέω, to act unseemly: fr.
ἀ-σχημοσύνη, unseemliness.
ἀ-σχήμων, unseemly.
ἀ-σωτία, profligacy: fr. σώζω.
ἀ-σώτως, profligately. [τάσσω.
ἀ-τακτέω, to be disorderly: fr.
ἄ-τακτος, disorderly.
ἀ-τάκτως, disorderly.
ἄ-τεκνος, childless: fr. τέκνον.
ἀ-τενίζω, to gaze upon: fr. τείνω,
ἄτερ, without. [to stretch.
ἀ-τιμάζω, to dishonour: fr. τιμή.
*ἀ-τιμάω = ἀτιμόω.
ἀτιμία, dishonour.
ἄ-τιμος, without honour.
ἀ-τιμόω, -άω, to dishonour.
ἀτμίς, vapour: fr. ἄημι, to blow.
ἄ-τομος, an atom of time: fr. τέμνω, to cut.
ἄ-τοπος, out of place, strange.
αὐγάζω, to shine upon.
αὐγή, brightness, dawn.

αὐθ-άδης, self-pleasing: fr. αὐτός & ἀνδάνω, to please.
αὐθ-αίρετος, of one's own will: αἱρέω, to choose.
αὐθεντέω, to exercise authority.
αὐλέω, to play on the flute: fr. αὐλός.
αὐλή, open place, court.
αὐλητής, flute-player: fr. αὐλός.
αὐλίζομαι, to lodge (at night): fr. αὐλή.
αὐλός, a flute: fr. ἄημι, to breathe.
αὐξάνω, αὔξω, to grow, cause to αὔξησις, growth. [grow.
αὔριον, to-morrow.
αὐστηρός, harsh: fr. αὔω, to dry.
αὐτάρκεια, sufficiency, contentment: ἀρκέω.
αὐτ-άρκης, sufficient, contented.
αὐτο-κατά-κριτος, self-condemned.
αὐτόματος, of its own accord.
αὐτ-όπτης, eye-witness: ὄψομαι, ὁράω. [noun.]
αὐτός, he, she, it (emphatic pro αὐτοῦ, here, there.
αὐτοῦ, of himself, herself, &c.
*αὐτό-φωρος, caught in the act: φώρ, thief.
αὐτό-χειρ, with one's own hands.
*αὐχέω, to boast.
αὐχμηρός, obscure.
ἀφ-αιρέω, to remove.
ἀ-φανής, out of sight: fr. φαίνομαι.
ἀ-φανίζω, to put out of sight, destroy.
ἀ-φανισμός, disappearing. [stroy.
ἄ-φαντος, invisible.
ἀφ-εδρών, a privy: ἕδρα, seat.
ἀ-φειδία, not sparing: fr. φείδομαι.
*ἀφ-εῖδον = ἀπεῖδον.
ἀ-φελότης, simplicity: fr. φελλεύς, stony ground.
ἄφ-εσις, deliverance: ἵημι, to let go.
ἀφή, a joint: fr. ἅπτομαι.
ἀ-φθαρσία, incorruption: fr. φθείρω.
ἄ-φθαρτος, incorruptible.
*ἀ-φθορία, incorruption.
ἀφ-ίημι, ἀφέω, -ίω, to let go, forgive.
ἀφ-ικνέομαι, to come to: ἵκω, to come. [φιλέω.
ἀ-φιλ-άγαθος, not a lover of good:
ἀ-φιλ-άργυρος, not fond of money.
ἄφ-ιξις, arrival, departure: ἵκω, to ἀφ-ίστημι, to draw from. [come.
ἄφνω, suddenly.
ἀ-φόβως, without fear.
ἀφ-ομοιόω, to make like. [fastly.
ἀφ-οράω, ἀπεῖδον, to look stead-
ἀφ-ορίζω, to separate from: ὅρος, boundary.
ἀφ-ορμή, occasion.
ἀφρίζω, to foam.
ἀφρός, foam.
ἀ-φροσύνη, foolishness.
ἄ-φρων, without sense. fr. φρήν.
ἀφ-υπνόω, to fall asleep: ὕπνος.
*ἀφ-υστερέω, to come too late: [ὕστερος.
ἄ-φωνος, dumb.
ἀ-χάριστος, unthankful: fr. χαρίζομαι.
ἀ-χειρο-ποίητος, not made by hands.
ἀχλύς, mist, darkness.
ἀ-χρειόομαι, to become useless.
ἀ-χρεῖος, useless: fr. χρή.
ἄ-χρηστος, useless: fr. χρίομαι.
ἄχρι, ἄχρις, to, until, while, &c.
ἄχυρον, chaff, straw.
ἀ-ψευδής, without falsehood.
ἄψινθος, wormwood.
ἄψυχος, without life: fr. ψυχή.

B, β, beta, b. β' = 2; β, = 2000.
*βαθέως, deeply. [move.
βαθμός, step, degree: fr. βαίνω, to βάθος, depth.
βαθύνω, to deepen.
βαθύς, deep.
βαΐον, a palm-branch. Coptic, bai.
βαλάντιον, βαλλ-, a purse.
βάλλω, to lay, put, cast, throw.
βαπτίζω, to dip, baptise.
βάπτισμα, baptism.
βαπτισμός, a baptism.
βαπτιστής, one who baptises.
βάπτω, to dip, dye.
βάρ, son. Chaldee.
βάρβαρος, a foreigner.
βαρέω, to weigh down.
βαρέως, heavily.
βάρος, heaviness.
βαρύνω, to make heavy.
βαρύς, heavy.
βαρύ-τιμος, precious: τιμή. [ture.)
βασανίζω, to examine (as by tor-
βασανισμός, torment.
βασανιστής, one who tortures.
βάσανος, torture.
βασιλεία, kingdom.
βασίλειον, a palace.
βασίλειος, royal, regal.
βασιλεύς, king.
βασιλεύω, to be king.
βασιλικός, royal, a courtier.
βασίλισσα, a queen.
βάσις, the foot: fr. βαίνω, to move.
βασκαίνω, to bewitch.
βαστάζω, to bear, carry.
βάτος, ἡ, ὁ, a. bush, bramble.
βάτος, ὁ, bath, a Hebrew measure (about 7½ gallons).
βάτραχος, a frog. [babble.
βαττο-λογέω, βαττα-, to stammer,
βδέλυγμα, abominable thing.
βδελυκτός, abominable.
βδελύσσομαι, to abominate. [move.
βέβαιος, firm, sure: fr. βαίνω, to βεβαιόω, to establish, confirm.
βεβαίωσις, confirmation.
βέβηλος, common, profane, 'that may be trodden.'
βεβηλόω, to profane.
*βελόνη, a point, needle: fr. βάλλω.
βέλος, a missile, dart.
βελτίον, -ων, better.
βῆμα, place stepped on, tribunal:
βήρυλλος, beryl. [fr. βαίνω, move.
βία, force.
βιάζομαι, to force, be forced.
βίαιος, violent.
βιαστής, a violent person.
βιβλαρίδιον, a little roll or book.
βιβλίον, a small book, a scroll.
βίβλος, inner rind of the papyrus used for paper: hence book.
βιβρώσκω, to eat.
βίος, life, livelihood.
βιόω, to live.
βίωσις, mode of life: fr. βίος.
βιωτικός, pertaining to life.
βλαβερός, hurtful.
βλάπτω, to hurt.
βλαστάνω, to sprout, bud.
βλασ-φημέω, to caluminate: fr. βλάπτω & φήμη.
βλασ-φημία, calumny.
βλάσ-φημος, calumnious.
βλέμμα, sight.
βλέπω, to see. [βάλλω.
βλητέος, which must be put: fr.
βοάω, to cry out.

βοή, a loud cry.
βοή-θεια, help.
βοη-θέω, to help, run at a cry.
βοη-θός, a helper.
βόθυνος, a pit, well: βαθύς.
βολή, a throw: fr. βάλλω.
βολίζω, to fathom, sound.
βολίς, a missile, dart.
βόρβορος, dirt, filth.
βορρᾶς, the north.
βόσκω, to tend, feed.
βοτάνη, herbage.
βότρυς, bunch of grapes.
βουλεύομαι, to purpose, consult
βουλευτής, a counsellor.
βουλή, counsel, purpose.
βούλημα, purpose, will.
βούλομαι, to will, be minded.
βουνός, a hill.
βοῦς, ox, cow.
βραβεῖον, award, prize.
βραβεύω, to decide, control.
βραδύνω, to delay.
βραδυ-πλοέω, to sail slowly. πλέω.
βραδύς, slow.
βραδυτής, slowness.
βραχίων, the arm.
βραχύς, short (time, distance).
βρέφος, unborn child, babe.
βρέχω, to wet, rain.
βροντή, thunder.
βροχή, rain.
βρόχος, a noose.
βρυγμός, gnashing of teeth.
βρύχω, to grash (the teeth).
βρύω, to abound, to send forth.
βρῶμα, food.
βρώσιμος, eatable. [food.
βρῶσις, the act of eating, rust,
βρώσκω = βιβρώσκω.
βυθίζω, to immerse.
βυθός, the deep. [hide.
βυρσεύς, tanner: fr. βύρσα skin,
βύσσινος, made of byssus.
βύσσος, byssus (flax or linen). Heb. bûtz.
βωμός, a raised spot, hence an altar.

Γ, γ, gamma, g (hard), γ' = 3; γ = 3000. [to eat
γάγγραινα, a gangrene: fr. γράω
γάζα, treasure. Persian.
γαζο-φυλάκιον, treasury: φυλακή.
γάλα, milk.
γαλήνη, calm.
γαμέω, to marry.
*γαμίζω, to give in marriage.
γαμίσκομαι, to be given in marriage
γάμος, a wedding.
γάρ, for.
γαστήρ, the belly. [deed, &c.
γέ (giving emphasis), at least, in-
γέ-εννα, gehenna = gê-hinnom. Heb.
γείτων, a neighbour: fr. γῆ.
γελάω, to laugh, rejoice.
γέλως, laughter.
γεμίζω, to fill.
γέμω, to be full.
γενεά, family, race, age: fr. γίνομαι
γενεα-λογέομαι, to reckon a genealogy: λέγω.
γενεα-λογία, genealogy.
γενέσια, birthday.
γένεσις, birth.
γενετή, birth.
*γένημα = γέννημα.
γεννάω, to beget.
γέννημα, γίνημα, offspring, fruit.
γέννησις, birth.

γεννητός, born.
γένος, offspring, kind, race.
γερουσία, senate.
γέρων, an old man.
γεύομαι, to taste.
γε-ωργέομαι, to till the earth.
γε-ώργιον, a (cultivated) field.
γε-ωργός, tiller of the soil: fr. γῆ & ἔργον.
γῆ, land, earth, country.
γῆρας, γῆρος, old age.
γηράσκω, to grow old. [place, exist.
γίνομαι, γίγν-, to become, take
γινώσκω, γιγν-, to know (objective
γλεῦκος, new wine. [knowledge.)
γλυκύς, sweet.
γλῶσσα, tongue, language.
γλωσσό-κομον, case (for reeds of wind instruments, &c.): κομέω, to take care of. [dress cloth.
γναφεύς, a fuller: fr. γνάπτω, to
γνήσιος, lawful, legitimate: fr.
γνησίως, sincerely. [γένος.
γνόφος, a dense cloud.
γνώμη, judgment, mind.
γνωρίζω, to make known.
γνῶσις, knowledge (objective).
γνώστης, knowing, skilful.
γνωστός, known.
γογγύζω, to murmur.
γογγυσμός, murmuring.
γογγυστής, a murmurer. [to wail.
γόης, enchanter, cheat: fr. γοάω.
γόμος, burden, wares: fr. γέμω.
γονεύς, a parent: γεννάω.
γόνυ, the knee.
γονυ-πετέω, to kneel: πεσεῖν, πίπτω.
γράμμα, a letter, learning: fr.
γραμματεύς, scribe. [γράφω.
γραπτός, written.
γραφή, a writing.
γράφω, to write, grave.
γρα-ώδης, old-womanish: fr. γραῦς, old woman, & εἶδος. [ἐγείρω.
γρηγορέω, to watch: fr. ἐγρήγορα.
γυμνάζω, to exercise (the body).
γυμνασία, bodily exercise.
γυμνητεύομαι, γυμνι-, to be naked.
γυμνός, naked.
γυμνότης, nakedness.
γυναικάριον, weak woman.
γυναικεῖος, female.
γυνή, a woman, wife.
γωνια, angle, corner: fr. γόνυ.

Δ, δ, delta, d, the fourth letter, δ'=4; δ, 4000. [demon.
δαιμονίζομαι, to be possessed by a
δαιμόνιον, demon, evil spirit.
δαιμονι-ώδης, demon-like: εἶδος.
δαίμων, demon, evil spirit.
δάκνω, to sting, bite.
δάκρυ, δάκρυον, a tear.
δακρύω, to shed tears.
δακτύλιος, a finger-ring.
δάκτυλος, a finger.
δαμάζω, to subdue.
δάμαλις, a heifer.
δανείζω, δανίζω, to lend; mid. to borrow: fr. δάνος, debt.
δάνειον, δάνιον, a loan.
δανειστής, a lender.
*δανίζω=δανείζω.
δαπανάω, to spend. [devour.
δαπάνη, expense: fr. δάπτω, to
δέ, but, moreover, &c.
δέησις, prayer: fr. δέομαι.
δεῖ, it needs, one must, &c.
δεῖγμα, that which is shewn.

δειγματίζω, to make a spectacle.
δεικνύω, -νυμι, to shew.
δειλία, timidity: fr. δέος.
δειλιάω, to be timid.
δειλός, timid.
δεῖνα, such a one.
δεινῶς, terribly.
δειπνέω, to sup. [devour.
δεῖπνον, supper: fr. δάπτω to
δεισι-δαιμονέστερος, more superstitious: fr. δείδω, to fear, & δαίμων.
δεισι-δαιμονία, fear of the gods, [religious.
δέκα, ten.
δεκα-δύο, twelve.
*δεκα-οκτώ, eighteen.
δεκα-πέντε, fifteen.
δεκα-τέσσαρες, fourteen.
δεκάτη, tithe.
δέκατος, tenth.
δεκατόω, to tithe. [δέχομαι.
δεκτός, accepted, acceptable: fr.
δελεάζω, to entrap: fr. δέλεαρ, bait.
δένδρον, a tree.
δεξιά, the right hand: see δεξιός.
δεξιο-λάβος, spearman: λαμβάνω.
δεξιός, right (hand).
δέομαι, to beseech.
*δέον, due, proper: fr. δεῖ.
*δέος, fear.
δέρμα, a skin.
δερμάτινος, leather.
δέρω, to beat (lit. to skin).
δεσμεύω, to bind: fr. δεσμός.
δεσμέω, to bind.
δέσμη, a bundle.
δέσμιος, one bound.
δεσμός, a bond: fr. δέω.
δεσμο-φύλαξ, a jailer.
δεσμωτήριον, a prison.
δεσμώτης, a prisoner.
δεσπότης, master, lord.
δεῦρο, come, hither.
δεῦτε, come, hither.
δευτεραῖος, on the second day.
δευτερό-πρωτος, lit. second-first.
δεύτερος, second.
δέχομαι, to take, accept, receive.
δέω, to bind.
δή, truly, indeed, &c.
*δηλαυγῶς, clearly.
δῆλος, plain, manifest.
δηλόω, to make manifest.
δημ-ηγορέω, to make an oration: ἀγορεύω, to harangue.
δημι-ουργός, constructor: ἔργον.
δῆμος, the people.
δημόσιος, public, common.
δηνάριον, denarius (about 7¾d.)
δή-ποτε, ever. [Latin.
δήπου, indeed, truly.
διά, with gen. through, by means of; with acc. on account of; in comp. thoroughly, asunder.
δια-βαίνω, to pass through.
δια-βάλλομαι, to be accused.
δια-βεβαιόομαι, to affirm: βέβαιος.
δια-βλέπω, to see clearly.
διάβολος, accuser, the devil: fr.
*δι-αγγέλλω, to announce. [βάλλω.
*διά-γε=διά γε.
δια-γίνομαι, to elapse.
δια-γινώσκω, to examine.
δια-γνωρίζω, to make known.
διά-γνωσις, exact knowledge.
δια-γογγύζω, to murmur greatly.
δια-γρηγορέω, to be fully awake:
δι-άγω, to lead (a life). [ἐγείρω.
δια-δέχομαι, to succeed to.
διά-δημα, diadem: δέω.

δια-δίδωμι, to distribute.
διά-δοχος, a successor: δέχομαι.
δια-ζώννυμι, -ύω, to gird up.
δια-θήκη, a covenant, disposition:
δι-αίρεσις, diversity. [τίθημι.
δι-αιρέω, to divide.
*δια-καθαίρω, to cleanse thoroughly.
δια-καθαρίζω, to cleanse thoroughly.
δια-κατ-ελέγχομαι, to refute.
διακονέω, to minister, serve.
διακονία, ministry. [διώκω.
διάκονος, minister, deacon: fr.
διακόσιοι, two hundred.
δι-ακούομαι, -ακούω, to hear fully.
δια-κρίνομαι, to judge, doubt, dispute.
διά-κρισις, discerning.
δια-κωλύω, to hinder.
δια-λαλέω, to talk, converse.
δια-λέγομαι, to discourse, reason.
δια-λείπω, to intermit.
διά-λεκτος, speech, language: λέγω.
δι-αλλάττομαι, -σσομαι, to be reconciled.
δια-λογίζομαι, to deliberate: λέγω.
δια-λογισμός, reasoning (mental).
δια-λύομαι, to disperse.
δια-μαρτύρομαι, to testify: μάρτυς.
δια-μάχομαι, to contend earnestly:
δια-μένω, to remain. [μάχη.
δια-μερίζω, to divide: μέρος.
δια-μερισμός, division.
δια-νέμομαι, to distribute.
δια-νεύω, to beckon.
διά-νόημα, thought: νοῦς.
διά-νοια, mind: νοῦς.
δι-ανοίγω, to open. [νύξ.
δια-νυκτερεύω, to pass the night:
δι-ανύω, to complete.
δια-παντός, continually.
*δια-παρα-τριβή, constant strife.
δια-περάω, to pass over.
δια-πλέω, to sail across. [πόνος.
δια-πονέομαι, to labour, be pained:
δια-πορεύομαι, to pass through.
δι-απορέω, to be in doubt: πόρος,
passage. [ing: πρᾶγμα.
δια-πραγματεύομαι, to gain by trad-
δια-πρίομαι, to be sawn asunder,
cut deeply: πρίω.
δι-αρπάζω, to plunder. [through.
διαρ-ρήγνυμι, -ρήσσω, to break
δια-σαφέω, to declare: σαφής, clear.
δια-σείω, to shake thoroughly.
δια-σκορπίζω, to disperse.
δια-σπάω, to rend asunder.
δια-σπείρω, to scatter.
δια-σπορά, a scattering.
δια-στέλλομαι, to charge, enjoin.
διά-στημα, interval: ἵστημι.
δια-στολή, distinction: στέλλω.
δια-στρέφω, to distort.
δια-σώζω, to bring safe through.
δια-ταγή, a disposition.
διά-ταγμα, an injunction.
δια-ταράττω, -σσω, to disturb.
δια-τάσσω, to arrange, order.
δια-τελέω, to continue.
δια-τηρέω, to keep carefully.
δια-τί, διὰ τί, wherefore.
δια-τίθεμαι, -θημι, to arrange.
δια-τρίβω, to wear away, spend time.
δια-τροφή, sustenance: τρέφω.
δι-αυγάζω, to shine out.
*δι-αυγής, transparent.
δια-φανής, transparent: φαίνω.
δια-φέρω, to carry different ways
δια-φεύγω, to flee, escape. [differ
δια-φημίζω, to proclaim: φήμη.

δια-φθείρω, to corrupt, destroy.
δια-φθορά, corruption.
διά-φορος, different: fr. διαφέρω.
δια-φυλάττω, -σσω, to keep carefully.
δια-χειρίζομαι, to lay hands on, kill.
*δια-χλευάζω, to deride: χλεύη, jest.
δια-χωρίζομαι, to separate.
διδακτικός, apt in teaching.
διδακτός, taught.
διδασκαλία, teaching.
διδάσκαλος, a teacher.
διδάσκω, to teach.
διδαχή, instruction.   [15½d.)
δί-δραχμον, a double drachma (abt.
δίδυμος, two-fold, twin.
δίδωμι, to give.
δι-εγείρω, to wake up.   [θυμός.
*δι-εν-θυμέομαι, to consider fully:
*δι-εξ-έρχομαι, to go out through.
δι-έξ-οδος, a way out through.
*δι-ερμηνεία, interpretation.
δι-ερμηνευτής, an interpreter.
δι-ερμηνεύω, to interpret.
δι-έρχομαι, to pass through.
δι-ερωτάω, to find by inquiry.
δι-ετής, of two years: ἔτος.
δι-ετία, space of two years.
δι-ηγέομαι, to recount fully: ἄγω.
διήγησις, a narration.   [φέρω.
δι-ηνεκής, in perpetuity: ἐνεγκεῖν.
δι-θάλασσος, washed by two seas:
    θάλασσα.   [to come.
δι-ϊκνέομαι, to pass through: ἴκω,
δι-ΐστημι, to be separated. [ἰσχυρός.
δι-ϊσχυρίζομαι, to assert strongly:
δικαιο-κρισία, just judgment.
δίκαιος, just, righteous.
δικαιοσύνη, righteousness.
δικαιόω, to justify.   [ment.
δικαίωμα, righteous act, require-
δικαίως, justly.
δικαίωσις, act of justifying.
δικαστής, a judge.
δίκη, sentence, judgment.   [cast.
δίκτυον, a fishing net: fr. δίκω, to
δί-λογος, double-tongued.
διό, wherefore, on which account.
δι-οδεύω, to travel through: ὁδός.
διό-περ, for this reason.
διο-πετής, fallen from Zeus: πίπτω.
*δι-όρθωμα, a setting right.
δι-όρθωσις, emendation: ὀρθός.
δι-ορύσσω, to dig through.
δι-ότι, for, because.
διπλοῦς, -λόος, double.
διπλόω, to double.
δίς, twice.
*δισμυριάδες, (-ριάς), two myriads.
διστάζω, to doubt, waver: fr. δίς.
δί-στομος, two-edged: στόμα.
δισ-χίλιοι, two thousand.
δι-ϋλίζω, to filter, strain. [asunder.
διχάζω, to cut into two: fr. δίχα,
διχο-στασία, division, variance:
    ἵστημι.   [to cut.
διχο-τομέω, to cut in two: τέμνω,
διψάω, to thirst, long for.
δίψος, thirst.
δί-ψυχος, double-minded.
διωγμός, persecution: διώκω.
διώκτης, a persecutor.
διώκω, to pursue, persecute.
δόγμα, a decree, ordinance. [ances.
δογματίζομαι, to be subject to ordin-
δοκέω, to seem, think.   [ances.
δοκιμάζω, to assay, test.
*δοκιμασία, a proving, testing.
δοκιμή, proof, evidence.

δοκίμιον, a test.
δόκιμος, approved.
δοκός, a beam: δέχομαι.
δόλιος, deceitful.
δολιόω, to deceive.
δόλος, deceit.
δολόω, to falsify.
δόμα, a gift: fr. δίδωμι.
δόξα, honour, glory.
δοξάζω, to glorify.
δόσις, a giving, a gift: fr. δίδωμι.
δότης, a giver.   [ἄγω.
δουλ-αγωγέω, to lead into slavery:
δουλεία, -λία, slavery.
δουλεύω, to be a slave.
δούλη, female slave.
δοῦλον, adj. enslaved.
δοῦλος, subst. a slave, bondman.
δουλόω, to lead into slavery.
δοχή, banquet: fr. δέχομαι.   [see.
δράκων, a dragon: fr. δέρκομαι, to
δράσσομαι, to seize.
δραχμή, drachm (about 7¾d.)
δρέμω, δράμω, see τρέχω.   [pluck.
δρέπανον, sickle: fr. δρέπω, to
δρόμος, course, career: fr. τρέχω.
δῦμι=δύνω.
δύναμαι, to be able.
δύναμις, power.
δυναμόω, to strengthen.
δυνάστης, a potentate.
δυνατέω, to be powerful.
δυνατός, having power.
δύνω, δῦμι, δύω, to sink.
δύο, two.
δυς, an inseparable prefix signify-
    ing difficulty, opposition, &c.
δυσ-βάστακτος, hard to bear, op-
    pressive : βαστάζω.
δυσ-εντερία, -ρίον, dysentery: ἐντός.
δυσ-ερμήνευτος, hard to interpret.
δύσ-κολος, difficult.
δυσ-κόλως, with difficulty.
δυσμή, west (setting of the sun):
    δύω, δύνω.   [νοῦς.
δυσ-νόητος, hard to be understood:
*δυσ-φημέω, to defame: φήμη.
δυσ-φημία, evil report.
δύω=δύνω.
δώδεκα, twelve.
δωδέκατος, twelfth.
δωδεκά-φυλον, twelve tribes: φυλή.
δῶμα, a house, roof: fr. δέμω, to
    build.
δωρεά, a free gift: fr. δίδωμι.
δωρεάν, freely, for nothing.
δωρέω, to give freely.
δώρημα, a free gift.
δῶρον, a gift.   [δίδωμι & φέρω.
*δωροφορία, offering of gifts: fr.

E, ε, epsilon, e, ε΄=5 ; ε,=5000.
ἔα, ha! exclamation of surprise.
ἐάν, if, ever.
ἐάν-περ, if indeed.
ἑαυτοῦ, of one-self.
ἐάω, to permit.
ἑβδομήκοντα, seventy.
ἑβδομηκοντα-ἕξ, -τα ἕξ, seventy-six.
ἑβδομηκοντάκις, seventy times.
ἕβδομος, seventh.
ἐγγίζω, to approach.
ἐγ-γράφω, ἐνγ-, to inscribe.
ἔγγυος, a surety.
ἐγγύς, near.
ἐγγύτερον, nearer.
ἐγείρω, to arouse, excite.
ἔγερσις, resurrection.
ἐγκ-=ἐνκ-.

ἐγ-κάθ-ετος, spy, foe : ἵημι, to send.
ἐγ-καίνια, dedication : καινός.
ἐγ-καινίζω, to dedicate.
*ἐγκακέω=ἐκκακέω.
ἐγ-καλέω, to call to account.
ἐγ-κατα-λείπω, to forsake.
ἐγ-κατ-οικέω, to dwell among.
*ἐγ-καυχάομαι, to boast in.
ἐγ-κεντρίζω, to insert, graft: κέντρον
ἔγ-κλημα, accusation : καλέω.
ἐγ-κομβόομαι, to tie, put on : κόμ-
    βος, knot, tie.
ἐγ-κοπή, ἐνκ-, ἐκκ-, a hindrance.
ἐγ-κόπτω, to hinder.
ἐγ-κράτεια, self-control.
ἐγ-κρατεύομαι, to restrain self.
ἐγ-κρατής, self-restrained : κράτος.
ἐγ-κρίνω, to reckon among.
ἐγ-κρύπτω, to conceal in.
ἔγ-κυος, with child.
ἐγ-χρίω, to anoint.
ἐγώ, I, pers. pron.
ἐδαφίζω, dash to the ground.
ἔδαφος, basis, ground.   [seat.
ἑδραῖος, sedentary, settled : ἕδρα,
ἑδραίωμα, basis, support.
ἐθελο-θρησκεία, -κία, self-chosen
    service : θρῆσκος.
ἐθέλω=θέλω.
ἐθίζω, to accustom.   [ἄρχω.
ἐθν-άρχης, head of a clan, governor:
ἐθνικός, Gentile, heathen.
ἐθνικῶς, like a Gentile.
ἔθνος, tribe, nation.
ἔθος, usage, custom.
ἔθω, εἴωθα, to accustom.
εἰ, a conditional particle, if ; also an
    interrogative particle, whether.
εἴγε, if indeed.
εἰ δὲ μή, but if not.
εἰ δὲ μήγε, but if not.
εἰ καί, if also, if even.
εἰ μή, only, unless.
εἰ μή τι, unless haply.
εἴ περ, εἴπερ, if on the whole.
εἴ πως, if in any way.
εἴτε . . . . εἴτε, whether . . . . or.
εἴ τις, if any one.
εἰδέα, poetical form of ἰδέα.
εἴδω, εἴδω, οἶδα, to perceive, (con-
    scious knowledge).
εἶδος, form, figure, kind.
εἴδω=εἰδέω.
εἰδωλεῖον, -λῖον, idol temple. [θύω.
εἰδωλό-θυτον, -ος, sacrificed to idols.
εἰδωλο-λατρεία, -ρία, worship of
    idols : λάτρις, servant.
εἰδωλο-λάτρης, idolater.
εἴδωλον, image, idol.
εἴην, εἴης, εἴη, see εἰμί.
εἰ-καί, see after εἰ.
εἰκῇ, εἰκῆ, without purpose.
εἴκοσι, twenty.
εἴκω, to yield.
εἴκω, ἔοικα, to resemble.
εἰκών, image, likeness.
εἰλι-κρίνεια, -νία, clearness, sin-
    cerity : κρίνω.
εἰλι-κρινής, spotless.
εἰλίσσω, ἑλ-, to roll up.
εἰ-μή, see after εἰ.
εἰμί, to exist, to happen.
*εἶμι, to go.
εἵνεκεν=ἕνεκα.
εἴ-περ, see after εἰ.
εἶπον, to say, answer.
εἰ-πως, see after εἰ.
εἰρηνεύω, to be at peace.
εἰρήνη, peace : fr. εἴρω, to join.

εἰρηνικός, peaceable.
εἰρηνο-ποιέω, to make peace.
εἰρηνο-ποιός, peace-maker.
εἴρω = ἐρέω. [towards.
εἰς, into, even to. *In comp.* into,
εἷς, μία, ἕν, one.
εἰς καθ' εἷς, one by one, every one.
εἰσ-άγω, to lead in.
εἰσ-ακούω, to hearken to.
εἰσ-δέχομαι, to receive into favour.
εἴσ-ειμι, to go into.
εἰς-έρχομαι, to go or come into.
εἰσ-καλέω, to call in.
εἰσ-οδος, an entrance.
εἰς πηδάω, to spring in.
εἰς-πορεύομαι, to go in.
εἰσ-τρέχω, to run in.
εἰσ-φέρω, to bring in.
εἶτα, then.
εἶτε, see after εἰ.
εἴτις, see after εἰ.
εἴωθα = ἔθω.
ἐκ, ἐξ, from, out from. *In comp.*
  removal, continuance, *or inten-*
  sities.
ἕκαστος, each one, every one.
ἑκάστοτε, always.
ἑκατόν, a hundred. [ἔτος.
ἑκατοντα-έτης, a hundred years old:
ἑκατοντα-πλασιων, a hundredfold.
ἑκατοντ-άρχης, a centurion: ἄρχω.
ἑκατόντ-αρχος, a centurion.
*ἐκ-βαίνω, to go out.
ἐκ-βάλλω, to cast *or* put forth.
ἔκ-βασις, a way out: βαίνω, go.
ἐκ-βολή, a casting out: βάλλω.
ἐκ-γαμίζω, to give in marriage:
  γάμος.
ἐκ-γαμίσκομαι, to give in marriage.
ἔκ-γονα, -νος, offspring: γίνομαι.
ἐκ-δαπανάω, to spend, exhaust:
  δάπτω, to devour.
ἐκ-δέχομαι, to receive, wait for.
ἔκ-δηλος, manifest.
ἐκ-δημέω, to go abroad: δῆμος.
ἐκ-δίδωμι, to deliver up, let out.
ἐκ-δι-ηγέομαι, to rehearse.
ἐκ-δικέω, to vindicate.
ἐκ-δίκησις, an avenging.
ἔκ-δικος, an avenger.
ἐκ-διώκω, to persecute, expel.
ἔκ-δοτος, delivered up: δίδωμι.
ἐκ-δοχή, expectation: δέχομαι.
ἐκ-δύω, to strip off.
ἐκεῖ, there.
ἐκεῖθεν, thence. [those (*emphatic*).
ἐκεῖνος, -η, -ο, he, she, it, they, that,
ἐκεῖσε, thither.
ἐκ-ζητέω, to seek out.
*ἐκ-ζήτησις, a seeking out.
ἐκ-θαμβέω, to terrify.
ἐκ..μβος, amazed.
*ἐκ-θαυμάζω, to marvel greatly.
ἔκ-θετος, exposed: τίθημι.
ἐκ-καθαίρω, to purge out.
ἐκ-καίομαι, to burn out.
ἐκ-κακέω, ἐγκ-, to faint, despond.
ἐκ-κεντέω, to pierce through.
ἐκ-κλάζω, -άω, to break off.
ἐκ-κλείω, to shut out.
ἐκ-κλησία, an assembly: καλέω.
ἐκ-κλίνω, to turn away.
ἐκ-κολυμβάω, to swim out of:
  κόλυμβος, diver.
ἐκ-κομίζω, to carry out.
ἐκ-κόπτω, to cut off.
*ἐκ-κράζω, to cry out.
ἐκ-κρέμαμαι, -μομαι, to hang upon.
*ἐκ-λαλέω, to speak out.

ἐκ-λάμπω, to shine forth.
ἐκ-λανθάνομαι, to forget entirely.
ἐκ-λέγομαι, to choose out.
ἐκ-λείπω, to fail, die.
ἐκ-λεκτός, chosen, elect.
ἐκ-λογή, choice: λέγω.
ἐκ-λύω, to loose, become weary.
ἐκ-μάσσω, to wipe off. [the nose.)
ἐκ-μυκτηρίζω, to mock (turn up
ἐκ-νεύω, to withdraw.
*ἐκ-νέω, to swim away, escape.
ἐκ-νήφω, to become sober.
ἑκούσιος, spontaneous: ἑκών.
ἑκουσίως, spontaneously.
ἐκ-πάλαι, of old, long since.
ἐκ-πειράζω, to try, prove.
ἐκ-πέμπω, to send out.
*ἐκ-περισσῶς, exceedingly.
ἐκ-πετάννυμι, to stretch forth.
*ἐκ-πηδάω, to spring forth.
ἐκ-πίπτω, to fall from, fail.
ἐκ-πλέω, to sail out. [πλήρης.
ἐκ-πληρόω, to fulfil completely:
ἐκ-πλήρωσις, fulfilment.
ἐκ-πλήσσω, -ττω, to strike with
  astonishment.
ἐκ-πνέω, to expire, die.
ἐκ-πορεύομαι, to go from or out.
ἐκ-πορνεύω, to be given to lewdness.
ἐκ-πτύω, to loathe, reject.
ἐκ-ριζόω, to root up *or* out.
ἔκ-στασις, ecstacy, amazement.
ἐκ-στρέφομαι, to be perverted.
*ἐκ-σώζω, to save from.
ἐκ-ταράσσω, to disturb.
ἐκ-τείνω, to stretch out.
ἐκ-τελέω, to complete. [stretch.
ἐκ-τένεια, intentness: τείνω, to
ἐκ-τενέστερον, more intently.
ἐκ-τενής, intense.
ἐκ-τενῶς, intensely.
ἐκ-τίθημι, to place out, tell out.
ἐκ-τινάσσω, to shake off.
ἕκτος, sixth.
ἐκτός, without, except.
ἐκ-τρέπομαι, to turn from, forsake.
ἐκ-τρέφω, to nourish, bring up.
ἐκ-τρωμα, an abortion: τραῦμα.
ἐκ-φέρω, to bring forth.
ἐκ-φεύγω, to flee from, escape.
ἐκ-φοβέω, to terrify.
ἔκ-φοβος, terrified.
ἐκ-φύω, to put forth.
ἐκ-χέω, to pour out.
ἐκ-χύνω, -χύννω = ἐκ-χέω.
ἐκ-χωρέω, to go out, flee.
ἐκ-ψύχω, to breathe out, die.
ἑκών, willing.
ἐλαία, an olive tree.
ἔλαιον, olive oil.
ἐλαιών, olive garden.
ἐλάσσων, -ττων, less, inferior.
ἐλαττονέω, to receive less.
ἐλαττόω, to make less, inferior.
ἐλαύνω, to urge forward, drive.
ἐλαφρία, lightness, levity.
ἐλαφρός, light in weight.
ἐλάχιστος, smallest, least.
ἐλαχιστότερος, less than the least.
ἐλάω = ἐλαύνω.
ἐλεάω = ἐλεέω.
*ἐλεγμός, correction, conviction.
ἔλεγξις, conviction.
ἔλεγχος, conviction, proof.
ἐλέγχω, to convict.
ἐλεεινός, ἐλει-, pitiable.
ἐλεέω, ἐλεάω, to pity, have mercy.
ἐλεημοσύνη, pity, alms.
ἐλεήμων, pitiful.

ἔλεος, ὁ, τό, pity, mercy.
ἐλευθερία, liberty: fr. ἦλθον, ἔρχομα.
ἐλεύθερος, free.
ἐλευθερόω, to set free. [ἔρχομαι.
ἔλευσις, a coming: fr. ἐλεύσομαι,
ἐλεφάντινος, of ivory: fr. ἐλέφας,
*ἕλιγμα, a roll. [elephant.
ἑλίσσω, to roll up.
ἑλκόομαι, to be ulcerated.
ἕλκος, an ulcer, sore.
ἑλκύω, to draw.
ἕλκω, to draw.
ἐλ-λογέω, -άω, to charge to.
ἐλπίζω, to hope for.
ἐλπίς, hope.
Ἐλωΐ, my God. *Aram.*
ἐμ- in comp. the same as ἐν-.
ἐμαυτοῦ, -τῷ, -τόν, myself.
ἐμ-βαίνω, to go upon, into.
ἐμ-βάλλω, to cast into.
ἐμ-βάπτω, to immerse.
ἐμ-βατεύω, to enter or pry into.
ἐμ-βιβάζω, to cause to enter.
ἐμ-βλέπω, to view, look on.
ἐμ-βριμάομαι, to be moved with
  indignation: βρίμη, expression
ἐμέω, to vomit. [of anger.
ἐμ-μαίνομαι, to be mad against.
ἐμ-μένω, ἐνμ-, to persevere in.
ἐμός, mine.
*ἐμ-παιγμονή, mockery: παῖς.
ἐμ-παιγμός, mockery.
ἐμ-παίζω, to mock.
ἐμ-παῖκται, (-της), mockers.
ἐμ-περι-πατέω, ἐνπ-, to walk in:
  πάτος, path. [fill up.
ἐμ-πιπλάω, -πίμπλημι, ἐμπλήθω, to
*ἐμ-πιπράω, -ημι, to kindle.
ἐμ-πίπτω, to fall into.
ἐμ-πλέκω, to intertwine.
ἐμ-πλήθω = ἐμπιπλάω.
ἐμ-πλοκή, braiding: πλέκω.
ἐμ-πνέω, ἐνπ, to breathe out.
ἐμ-πορεύομαι, to trade. [traverse.
ἐμ-πορία, merchandise: περάω,
ἐμ-πόριον, a market.
ἐμ-πορος, a merchant. [to burn.
ἐμ-πρήθω, to set fire to: πίπρημι,
ἔμ-προσθεν, before.
ἐμ-πτύω, to spit upon.
ἐμ-φανής, manifest: φαίνω.
ἐμ-φανίζω, to make manifest.
ἔμ-φοβος, afraid.
ἐμ-φυσάω, to breathe upon.
ἔμ-φυτος, engrafted: φύω.
ἐν, in, among. *In comp.* (*changing*
  to ἐμ- and ἐγ-), in, into, upon.
ἐν-αγκαλίζομαι, to take into one's
  arms: ἀγκάλη, an arm.
ἐν-άλιος, marine: ἅλς.
ἔν-αντι, in presence of.
ἐν-αντίον, before.
ἐν-αντίος, over against.
ἐν-άρχομαι, to begin.
ἔνατος = ἔννατος. [lack.
ἐν-δεής, in want, needy: δέω, to
ἔν-δειγμα, proof.
ἐν-δείκνυμι, to manifest.
ἔνδειξις, manifestation.
ἔνδεκα, eleven.
ἐνδέκατος, eleventh.
ἐν-δέχεται, -χομαι, to be possible.
ἐν-δημέω, to be at home: δῆμος,
ἐν-διδύσκομαι, to be clothed. [land.
ἐν-δικος, just, righteous.
ἐν-δόμησις, ἐνδώ-, a building:
  δέμω, to build.
ἐν-δοξάζομαι, to be glorified.
ἔν-δοξος, glorious.

ἐν-δυμα, clothing.
ἐν-δυναμόω, to strengthen.
ἐν-δύνω, to clothe, creep into.
ἔν-δυσις, a wearing of clothes.
ἐν-δύω, to put on.
ἐνδώμησις=ἐνδόμησις.
ἐνέγκω=φέρω.
ἐν-έδρα, -ρον, an ambush.
ἐν-εδρεύω, to lie in ambush.
ἐν-ειλέω, to envelope.
ἔν-ειμι, to be in.   [by reason of.
ἕνεκα, ἕνεκεν, εἵνεκεν, in respect of,
ἐνενήκοντα see ἐννενήκοντα.
ἐνεός=ἐννεός.
ἐν-έργεια, working, efficiency: ἔργον.
ἐν-εργέω, to work effectually.
ἐν-έργημα, thing effected.
ἐν-εργής, efficient.
ἐν-εστώς=ἐνίστημι.   [λόγος.
ἐν-ευ-λογέομαι, to be blessed in:
ἐν-έχω, to coerce.
ἔνθα-δε, hither, here.
*ἔνθεν, hence.
ἐν-θυμέομαι, to meditate on.
ἐν-θύμησις, thought, reflection.
ἔνι, there is in: contracted from
ἐνιαυτός, a year.   [ἔνεστι.
ἐν-ίστημι, to place in or among.
ἐν-ισχύω, to strengthen.
ἔννατος, ἔνα-, ninth.
ἐννέα, nine.
ἐνενηκοντα-εννέα, ninety-nine.
ἐννεός, ἐνεός, speechless.
ἐν-νεύω, to nod, beckon.
ἔν-νοια, notion, idea: νοῦς.
ἔν-νομος, duly subject.
ἔν-νυχος, -ον, -χα, nocturnal: νύξ.
ἐν-οικέω, to inhabit.
ἐνόντα see ἔνειμι.
*ἐν-ορκίζω, to adjure.
ἐνότης, unity, concord: fr. εἷς.
ἐν-οχλέω, to occasion tumult.
ἔν-οχος, bound, subject to: ἔχω.
ἔν-ταλμα, commandment: fr. ἐντέλλομαι.   [τάφος.
ἐν-ταφιάζω, to prepare for burial:
ἐν-ταφιασμός, preparation for
ἐν-τέλλομαι, to command.   [burial.
ἐντεῦθεν, hence.
ἔν-τευξις, intercession: τυγχάνω.
ἔν-τιμος, held in renown: τιμή.
ἐντολή, precept, commandment:
fr. ἐντέλλομαι.
ἐν-τόπιος, inhabitant: τόπος.
ἐντός, within.   [to respect.
ἐν-τρέπω, to put to shame; mid.
ἐν-τρέφομαι, to be nourished.
ἔν-τρομος, terrified.
ἐν-τροπή, shame, reproach.   [τρυφή.
ἐν-τρυφάω, to live luxuriously:
ἐν-τυγχάνω, to fall in with.
ἐν-τυλίττω, -σσω, to enwrap.
ἐν-τυπόω, to engrave: τύπος.
ἐν-υβρίζω, to contemn.
ἐν-υπνιάζομαι, to dream: ὕπνος.
ἐν-ύπνιον, a dream.   [ὤψ, face.
ἐν-ώπιον, before, in presence of:
ἐν-ωτίζομαι, to give ear, listen: οὖς.
ἐξ see ἐκ.
ἔξ, six.
ἐξ-αγγέλλω, to announce abroad.
ἐξ-αγοράζω, to buy from, redeem:
ἐξ-άγω, to lead forth.   [ἀγορά.
ἐξ-αιρέω, to take to or for (self).
ἐξ-αίρω, to take up, remove.
ἐξ-αιτέομαι, to claim, ask for.
ἐξ-αίφνης, ἐξέφνης, suddenly: ἄφνω.
ἐξ-ακολουθέω, to follow.
ἐξακόσιοι, six hundred.

ἐξ-αλείφω, to efface, annul.
ἐξ-άλλομαι, to spring up or forth.
ἐξ-ανά-στασις, a resurrection:
ἐξ-ανα-τέλλω, to spring up. [ἵστημι.
ἐξ-αν-ίστημι, to cause to rise up.
ἐξ-απατάω, to deceive.
ἐξάπινα, unexpectedly: ἄφνω.
ἐξ-απορέομαι, to be in utter perplexity.
ἐξ-απο-στέλλω, to send forth.
ἐξ-αρτίζω, to perfect: ἄρω, to fit.
ἐξ-αστράπτω, to glitter.
ἐξ-αυτῆς, on the instant.
ἐξ-εγείρω, to arouse, raise up.
ἔξ-ειμι, to go out.
ἐξ-ελέγχω, to convince of error.
ἐξ-έλκομαι, to draw out.
ἐξέλω see ἐξαιρέω.
ἐξ-έραμα, vomit.   [diligently.
ἐξ-ερευνάω, ἐξεραυνάω, to search
ἐξ-έρχομαι, to depart.
ἔξεστι, it is lawful.
ἐξ-ετάζω, to examine strictly.
ἐξ-έφνης=ἐξαίφνης.
ἐξ-ηγέομαι, to declare fully.
ἑξήκοντα, sixty.
ἑξῆς, next in order.
ἐξ-ηχέομαι, to sound forth: ἦχος.
ἕξις, habit, use: ἔχω.   [contracted.
ἐξ-ίστημι, τάω, -τάνω, to amaze, be
ἐξ-ισχύω, to be fully able.
ἔξ-οδος, a going out.
ἐξ-ολοθρεύομαι, ἐξολε-, to destroy
utterly: ὄλεθρος, ὄλλυμι, to
destroy.   [give thanks.
ἐξ-ομο-λογέομαι, to confess fully,
ἐξόν, it is possible: fr. ἔξεστι.
ἐξ-ορκίζω, to adjure: ὅρκος.
ἐξ-ορκιστής, exorcist: id.
ἐξ-ορύττω, -σσω, to dig out or
*ἐξ-ουδενέω=ἐξουδενόω.   [through.
ἐξ-ουδενόω, to set at nought: οὐδέν,
nothing.
ἐξ-ουθενέω, *-νόω, to set at nought.
ἐξ-ουσία, authority, power: fr. ἔξεστι.
ἐξ-ουσιάζω, to exercise authority.
ἐξ-οχή, eminence: fr. ἔχω.
ἐξ-υπνίζω, to awake from sleep.
ἔξ-υπνος, awake from sleep.
ἔξω, without, outside.
ἔξωθεν, from without.
ἐξ ωθῶ, -θέω, to drive out.
ἐξώτερος, outer.
ἔοικα see εἴκω.
ἑορτάζω, to keep a feast.
ἑορτή, feast, festival.   [mise.
ἐπ-αγγελία, announcement, pro-
ἐπ-αγγέλλομαι, to announce, pro-
ἐπ-άγγελμα, a promise.   [mise.
ἐπ-άγω, to bring upon.
ἐπ-αγωνίζομαι, to contend earnestly.
ἐπ-αθροίζομαι, to gather together:
ἀθρόος, assembled.
ἐπ-αινέω, to approve, praise.
ἔπ-αινος, approbation, praise.
ἐπ-αίρω, to lift, raise up.
ἐπ-αισχύνομαι, to be ashamed of.
ἐπ-αιτέω, to beg, ask alms.
ἐπ-ακολουθέω, to follow.
ἐπ-ακούω, to listen.
ἐπ-ακροάομαι, to hear.
ἐπάν, if, whenever.   [cessity.
ἐπ-άναγκες, compulsory, of ne-
ἐπ-αν-άγω, to put out, lead back.
ἐπ-ανα-μιμνήσκω, to remind.
ἐπ-ανα-παύομαι, to rest upon.
ἐπ-αν-έρχομαι, to return.
ἐπ-αν-ίσταμαι, -ίστημι, to rise up
against.

ἐπ-αν-όρθωσις, restoration to a
right state: ὀρθός.
ἐπ-άνω, above, more than.
*ἐπ-άρατος, accursed: ἀρά.
ἐπ-αρκέω, give relief to.   [xxv. 1.
*ἐπ-άρχειος, province: Ti. in Acts
ἐπ-αρχία, -χεία, province: ἀρχή.
ἐπ-αυλις, cottage, dwelling.
ἐπ-αύριον, the morrow.
ἐπ-αυτο-φώρω, in the act (of
stealing): φώρ, thief.
ἐπ-αφρίζω, to foam out.
ἐπ-εγείρω, to raise up against.
ἐπεί, when, since, because.
ἐπει-δή, since, inasmuch as.
ἐπει-δή-περ, since, because.
ἐπ-εῖδω, -εῖδον=ἐφοράω.
ἐπ-ειμι=ἐπίειμι.
ἐπεί-περ, since indeed.
ἐπ-εισ-αγωγή, a bringing in.
*ἐπ-εισ-έρχομαι, to come in upon.
ἔπ-ειτα, thereupon, next.
ἐπ-έκεινα, beyond.
ἐπ-εκ-τείνομαι, to stretch towards.
ἐπ-εν-δύομαι, to put on over.
ἐπ-εν-δύτης, an upper garment.
ἐπ-έρχομαι, to come upon.
ἐπ-ερωτάω, to interrogate.
ἐπ-ερώτημα, demand.
ἐπ-έχω, to fix (the mind) on.
ἐπ-ηρεάζω, to injure: ἀρά.
ἐπί, on, upon, towards, &c. In
comp. upon, &c., signifying
addition, renewal, &c.
ἐπι-βαίνω, to go upon.
ἐπι-βάλλω, to cast on or over.
ἐπι-βαρέω, to burden.
ἐπι-βιβάζω, to cause to ascend:
βαίνω: to go.   [favour.
ἐπι-βλέπω, to look upon (with
ἐπί-βλημα, that which is added:
ἐπι-βοάω, to cry out.   [βάλλω.
ἐπι-βουλή, a design against.
ἐπι-γαμβρεύω, to marry as next of
kin: γαμβρός, brother-in-law.
ἐπί-γειος, earthly: γῆ.
ἐπι-γίνομαι, to come on, spring up.
ἐπι-γινώσκω, to know well, re-
cognise.   [tive).
ἐπί-γνωσις, full knowledge (objec-
ἐπι-γραφή, an inscription.
ἐπι-γράφω, to inscribe.
ἐπι-δείκνυμι, to shew plainly.
ἐπι-δέχομαι, to welcome.
ἐπι-δημέω, to sojourn (as a
foreigner): δῆμος.   [mands.
ἐπι-δια-τάσσομαι, to superadd com-
ἐπι-δίδωμι, to give, deliver.
ἐπι-δι-ορθόω, to put in order: ὀρθός.
ἐπι-δύω, to go down.   [εἴκω.
ἐπι-είκεια, -κία, gentleness: ἔοικα,
ἐπι-εικής, gentle.
ἐπίειμι see ἐπιοῦσα.
ἐπι-ζητέω, to seek earnestly.
ἐπι-θανάτιος, doomed to death.
ἐπί-θεσις, a laying on (of hands):
τίθημι.
ἐπι-θυμέω, to desire earnestly.
ἐπι-θυμητής, one who longs for.
ἐπι-θυμία, earnest desire.
ἐπι-καθ-ίζω, to seat or sit upon.
ἐπι-καλέομαι, to call upon, surname.
ἐπι-κάλυμμα, veil, cloak.
ἐπι-καλύπτω, to cover over.
ἐπι-κατ-άρατος, accursed: ἀρά.
ἐπί-κειμαι, to press upon.
*ἐπι-κέλλω, to run aground.
ἐπι-κουρία, assistance: κόρος, a lad.
ἐπι-κρίνω, to give judgment.

ἐπι-λαμβάνομαι, to take hold of.
ἐπι-λανθάνομαι, to forget, neglect.
ἐπι-λέγομαι, to be called, to choose.
ἐπι-λείπω, to fail.
*ἐπι-λείχω, to lick over. [to forget.
ἐπι-λησμονή, forgetfulness: λήθω.
ἐπί-λοιπος, remaining.
ἐπί-λυσις, solution, interpretation.
ἐπι-λύω, to solve, interpret.
ἐπι-μαρτυρέω, to testify, affirm.
ἐπι-μέλεια, care for, attention.
ἐπι-μελέομαι, to take care of.
ἐπι-μελῶς, carefully, diligently.
ἐπι-μένω, to remain, persist in.
ἐπι-νεύω, to nod, assent (by nodding).
ἐπί-νοια, thought, purpose: νοῦς.
ἐπι-ορκέω, to swear falsely.
ἐπί-ορκος, a perjurer.
ἐπ-ιοῦσα, following.
ἐπ-ιούσιος, sufficient (for the day).
ἐπι-πίπτω, to fall upon.
ἐπι-πλήττω, -σσω, to reprove.
ἐπι-ποθέω, to desire earnestly.
ἐπι-πόθησις, earnest desire.
ἐπι-πόθητος, greatly desired.
ἐπι-ποθία, -πόθεια, earnest desire.
ἐπι-πορεύομαι, to come to.
ἐπι-ῤῥάπτω, to sew to or upon.
ἐπι-ῤῥίπτω, to cast upon. [σημεῖον.
ἐπί-σημος, marked, noted: σῆμα,
ἐπι-σιτισμός, provision: σῖτος, food.
ἐπι-σκέπτομαι, to inspect, look after.
*ἐπι-σκευάζομαι, to get ready: σκεῦος. [σκῆνος.
ἐπι-σκηνόω, to dwell, tabernacle:
ἐπι-σκιάζω, to overshadow: σκιά.
ἐπι-σκοπέω, to oversee: σκέπτομαι.
ἐπι-σκοπή, overseership. [to survey.
ἐπί-σκοπος, overseer.
ἐπι-σπάομαι, to be uncircumcised.
*ἐπι-σπείρω, to sow upon.
ἐπί-σταμαι, to know well.
*ἐπί-στασις, a stopping, checking.
ἐπι-στάτης, master.
ἐπι-στέλλω, to instruct by letter.
ἐπι-στήμων, intelligent, skilful.
ἐπι-στηρίζω, to stand firmly.
ἐπι-στολή, an epistle. [στόμα.
ἐπι-στομίζω, to stop the mouth of:
ἐπι-στρέφω, to turn to, to turn one-
ἐπι-στροφή, a turning. [self.
ἐπι-συν-άγω, to gather together.
ἐπι-συν-αγωγή, a gathering together.
ἐπι-συν-τρέχω, to run together.
ἐπι-σύ-στασις, a crowding, concourse. [perilous.
ἐπι-σφαλής, easily overthrown,
ἐπι-σχύω, to strengthen, grow
ἐπι-σωρεύω, to heap up. [stronger.
ἐπι-ταγή, a precept, injunction.
ἐπι-τάσσω, to enjoin upon.
ἐπι-τελέω, to bring to an end.
ἐπιτήδειος, fit, suitable.
ἐπι-τίθημι, to place upon.
ἐπι-τιμάω, to reprove, rebuke.
ἐπι-τιμία, rebuke.
ἐπι-τρέπω, to permit, intrust.
ἐπι-τροπή, commission.
ἐπί-τροπος, one in charge.
ἐπι-τυγχάνω, to light upon, attain.
ἐπι-φαίνω, to bring to light.
ἐπι-φάνεια, appearance.
ἐπι-φανής, illustrious, glorious.
ἐπι-φαύω, -φαύσκω, to shine upon.
ἐπι-φέρω, to bring upon.
ἐπι-φωνέω, -ῶ, to cry aloud.
ἐπι-φώσκω, to shine upon, dawn.
ἐπι-χειρέω, to take in hand.

ἐπι-χέω, to pour upon.
ἐπι-χορ-ηγέω, to supply: χορός,
choir, & ἡγέομαι, to lead, hence,
to furnish a choir.
ἐπι-χορ-ηγία, supply, assistance.
ἐπι-χρίω, to spread on, anoint.
ἐπ-οικο-δομέω, to build upon: οἶκος,
& δέμω, to build.
ἐπ-οκέλλω, to drive upon.
ἐπ-ονομάζομαι, to be named.
ἐπ-οπτεύω, to be witness of:
ὄπτομαι, ὁράω.
ἐπ-όπτης, an eye-witness.
ἔπος, a word.
ἐπ-ουράνιος, heavenly: οὐρανός.
ἑπτά, seven.
ἑπτάκις, seven times.
ἑπτακισ-χίλιοι, seven thousand.
ἔπω, to say.
ἐργάζομαι, to work, accomplish.
ἐργασία, business, profit.
ἐργάτης, a worker.
ἔργον, work. [voke.
ἐρεθίζω, to stir up, stimulate, pro-
ἐρείδω, to fix firmly.
ἐρεύγομαι, to pour out (words).
ἐρευνάω, ἐραυ-, to investigate.
ἐρέω=ἐρῶ: see εἶπον.
ἐρημία, uninhabited tract.
ἔρημος, ἡ, a desert.
ἔρημος, adj. solitary.
ἐρημόω, to make desolate.
ἐρήμωσις, desolation.
ἐρίζω, to contend.
ἐριθεία, θία, contention.
ἔριον, wool.
ἔρις, contention.
ἐρίφιον, a goat, kid.
ἔριφος, a goat, kid.
ἑρμηνεία, -νία, interpretation.
*ἑρμηνευτής, interpreter.
ἑρμηνεύω, to interpret.
ἑρπετόν, a reptile: fr. ἕρπω, to creep.
ἔρχομαι, to come: ὁ ἐρχόμενος, the
ἐρῶ see εἶπον. [coming one.
ἐρωτάω, to ask. [clothe.
ἐσθής, a robe, vestment: fr. ἕννυμι,
ἔσθησις, raiment.
ἐσθίω, ἔσθω, to eat.
ἔσ-οπτρον, semi-transparent me-
dium: ὄπτομαι, ὁράω.
ἑσπέρα, evening.
ἔσχατος, extreme, last.
ἐσχάτως, in extremity.
ἔσω, in, within.
ἔσωθεν, from within.
ἐσώτερος, inner, interior.
ἑταῖρος, a companion.
ἑτερό-γλωσσος, one of another
tongue: γλῶσσα.
ἑτερο-διδασκαλέω, to teach otherwise: διδάσκαλος. [ζυγός.
ἑτερο-ζυγέω, to be diversely yoked:
ἕτερος, other, another.
ἑτέρως, otherwise.
ἔτι, yet, still, even, &c.
ἑτοιμάζω, to make ready.
ἑτοιμασία, state of preparation.
ἕτοιμος, prepared, ready.
ἑτοίμως, in readiness.
ἔτος, a year. [fairly.
εὖ, well, good. In comp. well,
εὐ-αγγελίζω, -ομαι, to bring glad
εὐ-αγγέλιον, glad tidings. [tidings.
εὐ-αγγελιστής, an evangelist.
εὐ-αρεστέω, to be well pleasing.
εὐ-άρεστος, well pleasing: ἀρέσκω.
εὐ-αρέστως, acceptably.
*εὖ-γε, well done.

εὐγενής, well-born, noble: γένος.
εὐ-δία, fair weather: δῖος, heavenly,
εὐ-δοκέω, to think well of.
εὐ-δοκία, delight, pleasure.
εὐ-εργεσία, a good deed: ἔργον.
εὐ-εργετέω, to do good.
εὐ-εργέτης, a benefactor.
εὔ-θετος, useful, fit: τίθημι.
εὐ-θέως, immediately.
εὐθυ-δρομέω, to go in a straight
course: δρομέω see τρέχω.
εὐ-θυμέω, to be cheerful.
εὔ-θυμος, cheerful.
εὐ-θυμότερον, more cheerfully.
*εὐ-θύμως, cheerfully.
εὐθύνω, to make straight.
εὐθύς, adj. straight, right.
εὐθύς, adv. straightway, forthwith.
εὐθύτης, rectitude.
εὐ-καιρέω, to have leisure.
εὐ-καιρία, convenient opportunity.
εὔ-καιρος, well-timed, convenient.
εὐ-καίρως, opportunely.
εὐ-κοπώτερος, easier: κόπος.
εὐ-λάβεια, reverence, godly fear.
εὐ-λαβέομαι, to be cautious, afraid.
εὐ-λαβής, cautious, god-fearing,
pious: λαμβάνω.
εὐ-λογέω, -ῶ, to bless, praise.
εὐ-λογία, blessing, praise. [δίδωμι
εὐ-λογητός, blessed, worthy of
praise.
εὐ-μετά-δοτος, ready to impart
εὐ-νοέω, to be well affected to.
εὔ-νοια, good will: νοῦς.
εὐνουχίζω, to castrate.
εὐνοῦχος, one emasculated: εὐνή,
bed, & ἔχω.
εὐ-οδοῦμαι, to be prospered.
*εὐ-πάρ-εδρος, assiduous: ἕδος, seat.
εὐ-πειθής, easily intreated.
εὐ-περι-στατος, easily besetting:
εὐ-ποιία, well-doing. [ἵστημι.
εὐ-πορέομαι, to be well-off.
εὐ-πορία, wealth. [be becoming.
εὐ-πρέπεια, gracefulness: πρέπω, to
εὐ-πρόσ-δεκτος, acceptable: δέχομαι,
εὐ-πρόσ-εδρος, assiduous: ἕδος, seat.
εὐ-προσ-ωπέω, to make a fair
appearance: ὤψ, face.
*εὐρακύλων see εὐροκλύδων.
εὑρίσκω, to discover.
εὐρο-κλύδων, an eastern hurricane:
κλύζω, to wash away.
εὐρύ-χωρος, broad.
εὐ-σέβεια, piety, devotion.
εὐ-σεβέω, to exercise piety.
εὐ-σεβής, pious, devout.
εὐ-σεβῶς, piously.
εὔ-σημος, well marked, clear.
εὔ-σπλαγχνος, tender hearted.
εὐ-σχημόνως, becomingly.
εὐ-σχημοσύνη, seemliness.
εὐ-σχήμων, decorous: σχῆμα.
εὐ-τόνως, strenuously: τείνω, to
stretch. [turn aside.
εὐ-τραπελία, jesting talk: τρέπω, to
εὐ-φημια, good report.
εὔ-φημος, of good report: φήμη.
εὐ-φορέω, to bear well: φέρω.
εὐ-φραίνω, -ομαι, to gladden: φρήν,
εὐ-φροσύνη, gladness. [mind.
εὐ-χαριστέω, to give thanks: χάρις.
εὐ-χαριστία, thanksgiving.
εὐ-χάριστος, grateful.
εὐχή, prayer, vow.
εὔχομαι, to pray, wish for.
εὐ-χρηστος, highly useful. [ψυχή.
εὐ-ψυχέω, to be in good spirits.

εὐ-ωδία, good odour: ὄζω.
εὐώνυμος, the left (hand): ὄνομα.
ἐφ-άλλομαι, to spring upon.
ἐφ-άπαξ, once for all.
ἐφ-ευρετής, an inventor.
ἐφ-ημερια, daily service: ἡμέρα.
ἐφ-ήμερος, daily.
ἐφ-ικνέομαι, to come to. [hand.
ἐφ-ίστημι, to stand by, to be at
ἐφ-οράω, to look upon.
*ἐφνίδιος = αἰφνίδιος.
ἐφφαθά, be opened. Aram.
*ἐχθές = χθές.
ἐχθρα, enmity.
ἐχθρός, hated, an enemy.
ἐχιδνα, a viper.
ἔχω, to possess (in any sense).
ἕως, until, up to.

ζ, Z, zeta, the sixth letter. ζ' = 7; ζ, = 7,000.
ζάω, to live: ὁ ζῶν, the living One.
ζβέννυμι = σβέννυμι.
ζεστός, hot.
ζεῦγος, yoke, pair.
ζευκτηρία, a fastening.
ζέω, to be hot, fervent.
*ζηλεύω, to be zealous.
ζῆλος, fervour, heat, zeal.
ζηλόω, to desire earnestly.
ζηλωτής, a zealot.
ζημία, damage, loss.
ζημιόω, to inflict loss.
ζητέω, to seek for.
ζήτημα, a question.
ζήτησις, question, debate.
ζιζάνια, -νιον, darnel.
ζόφος, thick darkness.
ζυγός, a yoke, balance.
ζύμη, leaven.
ζυμόω, to leaven.
ζω-γρέω, to take alive: ἀγρεύω.
ζωή, life, state of being.
ζώνη, zone, belt.
ζωννύω, -νυμι, to gird.
ζωο-γονέω, preserve alive.
ζῶον, ζῷον, a living creature.
ζωο-ποιέω, to impart life.

η, H, eta, the seventh letter. η' = 8; η, = 8000.
ἤ, or, whether, than, &c.
ἤ μήν, surely.
ἡγεμονεύω, to be governor: fr. ἄγω.
ἡγεμονια, government.
ἡγεμών, governor.
ἡγέομαι, -οῦμαι, to lead.
ἡδέως. ἥδιστα, with pleasure: fr. ἥδομαι, to delight.
ἤδη, now, already.
ἥδιστα see ἡδέως.
ἡδονή, pleasure.
ἡδύ-οσμον, -ος, mint: ὄζω, smell.
ἦθος, character, manner: fr. ἔθω.
ἥκω, to have come.
Ἠλί, Ἐλωΐ, my God. Aram.
ἡλικία, age, growth: fr. ἧλιξ, of the
ἡλίκος, how large, great. [same age.
ἥλιος, the sun.
ἧλος, a nail.
ἡμᾶς see ἐγώ.
ἡμεῖς see ἐγώ.
ἡμέρα, a day.
ἡμέτερος, our.
ἥ μην, see after ἤ.
ἡμι-θανής, half dead: θνήσκω.
ἥμισυ, -συς, half.
ἡμι-ώριον, -ρον, a half-hour: ὥρα.
ἡνίκα, when.

ἤπερ, than.
ἤπιος, placid, mild.
ἤρεμος, quiet, tranquil.
ἡσσάομαι = ἡττάομαι.
ἥσσων = ἥττων, ἧττον.
ἡσυχάζω, to rest.
ἡσυχία, quiet, tranquil.
ἡσύχιος, quiet, gentle.
ἤτοι, whether. [fr. ἥττων.
ἡττάομαι, ἡσσά-, to be less, inferior:
ἥττημα, inferior condition.
ἥττον, ἥττων, inferior.
ἠχέω, to sound, roar.
ἦχος ὁ, sound, report.
*ἦχος, τό, sound, noise.
*ἠχώ, an echo.

θ, Θ, theta. θ' = 9; θ, = 9000.
θάλασσα, the sea: perhaps fr. ταράσσω.
θάλπω, to warm, cherish.
θαμβέομαι, to be astonished.
θάμβος, astonishment.
θανάσιμος, deadly: fr. θνήσκω.
θανατη-φόρος, death bringing: φέρω.
θάνατος, death.
θανατόω, to put to death.
θάπτω, to bury: fr. τάφος.
θαρρέω, to be of good courage.
θαρσέω, to be of good courage.
θάρσος, courage. [gaze at.
θαῦμα, wonder: fr. θεάομαι, to
θαυμάζω, to wonder, admire.
θαυμάσιος, wonderful.
θαυμαστός, wonderful.
θεά, a goddess.
θεάομαι, to witness, gaze upon.
θεατρίζομαι, to be exposed (as in a
θέατρον, a theatre. [theatre].
θεῖον, sulphur.
θεῖος, divine.
θειότης, divinity.
θει-ώδης, sulphureous: εἶδος.
θέλημα, will, desire.
θέλησις, will, pleasure.
θέλω, ἐθέλω, to desire, will.
θεμέλιον, -ος, foundation: fr. τίθημι.
θεμελιόω, to lay a foundation.
θεο-δίδακτος, taught of God: διδάσκω.
θεο-λόγος, one who speaks of God (in the title of the Rev.)
θεο-μαχέω, to fight against God: μάχη.
θεο-μάχος, a fighter against God.
θεό-πνευστος, God-breathed: πνέω.
θεός, God, a god.
θεο-σέβεια, worship of God: σέβομαι.
θεο-σεβής, God-fearing, devout.
θεο-στυγής, hateful to God: στυγέω.
θεότης, divinity, Godhead. [to hate.
θεραπεία, service, household.
θεραπεύω, to serve, minister to.
θεράπων, a servant.
θερίζω, to reap or gather: fr. θέρος.
θερισμός, harvest.
θεριστής, a harvester.
θερμαίνομαι, to warm oneself.
θέρμη, warmth.
θέρος, summer: fr. θέρω, to warm.
θεωρέω, to be a spectator: fr.
θεωρία, a spectacle. [θεάομαι.
θήκη, receptacle: fr. τίθημι.
θηλάζω, to suck, give suck: fr. θηλή, breast.
θήλεια, -λυς, -λυ, female.
θήρα, hunting: hence a snare: fr. θήρ, wild beast.
θηρεύω, to hunt. [beasts: μάχη.
θηριο-μαχέω, to fight with wild

θηρίον, a wild beast.
θησαυρίζω, to treasure up. [τίθημι.
θησαυρός, treasure, wealth: fr.
θίγω, θιγγάνω, to touch.
θλίβω, to press upon.
θλίψις, pressure, affliction.
θνήσκω, to die.
θνητός, mortal.
*θορύβαζω, to confuse by noise; pass. to be troubled.
θορυβέω, to disturb, make a noise.
θόρυβος, noise, uproar.
θραύω, to bruise, oppress.
θρέμμα, flock, cattle: fr. τρέφω.
θρηνέω, to lament: fr. θρέομαι, to
θρῆνος, lamentation. [cry aloud.
θρησκεια, -κία, religion, piety.
θρῆσκος, θρησκός, religious, pious.
θριαμβεύω, to triumph over.
θρίξ, τριχός, hair.
θροέομαι, to be disturbed.
θρόμβος, large drop (as of blood):
θρόνος, a throne. [fr. τρέφω.
θυγάτηρ, a daughter.
θυγάτριον, a little daughter.
θύελλα, a tempest: fr. θύω, B.
θύϊνος, made of the thyine tree: fr. θύα, perhaps juniper.
θυμίαμα, incense: fr. θύω, A.
θυμιατήριον, a censer.
θυμιάω, to burn incense.
θυμο-μαχέω, to be highly hostile.
θυμόομαι, to be provoked to anger.
θυμός, anger.
θύρα, a door.
θυρεός, (door-shaped) shield.
θυρίς, an opening. [care.
θυρ-ωρός, a door-keeper: fr. ὥρα.
θυσία, sacrifice: fr. θύω, A.
θυσιαστήριον, an altar.
θύω, A. to slay, sacrifice; B. rush.
θώραξ, breast, breastplate.

ι, ι, iota, i, ι' = 10; ι, = 10,000.
ἴαμα, healing.
ἰάομαι, -ῶμαι, to heal.
ἴασις, healing.
ἴασπις, jasper.
ἰατρός, a physician: fr. ἰάομαι.
ἴδε, ἰδέ, behold.
ἰδέα, εἰδέα, aspect.
ἴδιος, one's own. [person.
ἰδιώτης, an unlearned, ignorant
ἰδού, lo! see!
ἱδρώς, sweat.
ἱερατεία, -τία, office of a priest.
ἱεράτευμα, priesthood.
ἱερατεύω, to act as priest.
ἱερεύς, a priest. [θύω, A
*ἱερό-θυτος, offered in sacrifice: fr.
ἱερόν, the temple (buildings in general).
ἱερο-πρεπής, befitting sacred ones: πρέπω, to be becoming.
ἱερός, sacred.
ἱερο-συλέω, to despoil temples.
ἱερό-συλος, robbing temples.
ἱερ-ουργέω, to minister in sacred things: ἔργον.
ἱερωσύνη, priesthood.
ἱκανός, sufficient: fr. ἵκω, to come.
ἱκανότης, sufficiency.
ἱκανόω, -ῶ, to make sufficient.
ἱκετηρία, supplication: fr. ἵκω, to
ἱκμάς, moisture. [come.
ἱλαρός, cheerful: fr. ἵλαος, gracious.
ἱλαρότης, cheerfulness.
ἱλάσκομαι, to make propitiation.
ἱλασμός, propitiation.

ἱλαστήριον, -ος, mercy-seat.
ἵλεως, propitious.
ἱμάς, thong (of a shoe).
ἱματίζομαι, to be clothed: εἷμα, ἔννυμι, to put on.
ἱμάτιον, clothing.
ἱματισμός, clothes.   [longing.
ἱμείρομαι, to yearn over: fr. ἵμερος,
ἵνα, that, in order that.
ἱνατί, ἵνα τί, why? to what end?
ἰός, poison, rust.
Ἰουδαΐζω, to Judaise.
Ἰουδαϊσμός, Judaism.
ἱππεύς, a horse soldier: fr. ἵππος.
ἱππικόν, cavalry.
ἵππος, a horse.
ἶρις, a rainbow.
ἰσ-άγγελος, equal to angels.
ἴσημι, I know, see οἷδα.
ἴσος, ἶσος, like, equal to.
ἰσότης, equality.
ἰσό-τιμος, of like value: τιμή.
ἰσό-ψυχος, like-minded: ψυχή.
ἴστημι, ἱστάω, ἱστάνω, to stand, weigh, hold fast.
ἱστορέω, to examine: fr. ἵστωρ.
ἰσχυρός, strong.   [judge.
ἰσχύς, strength: fr. ἴσχω, ἔχω.
ἰσχύω, to be strong.
ἴσως, equally, probably.
ἰχθύδιον, a small fish.
ἰχθύς, a fish.
ἴχνος, footstep.
ἰῶτα, ἰότα, yod, smallest letter of the Hebrew alphabet.

Κ, κ, kappa, k, κʹ = 20; κͺ = 20,000.
κἀγώ, κἀμοί, κἀμέ, I also.
καθ = κατά.
καθά (καθ' ἅ), according as.
καθ-αίρεσις, overthrowing.
καθ-αιρέω, to overthrow. [καθαρός.
καθαίρω, to purge, cleanse: fr.
καθ-άπερ, as, even as.
καθ-άπτω, to lay hold of.
καθαρίζω, to cleanse.
καθαρισμός, cleansing.
κάθαρμα see περικάθαρμα.
καθαρός, pure, clean.
καθαρότης, purity.
καθ-έδρα, a seat: ἕδος, a seat.
καθ-έζομαι, to sit down.
καθ-εἷς, καθ' εἷς, one by one.
καθ-εξῆς, in succession: ἔχω.
καθ-εύδω, to sleep.
καθ-ηγητής, a leader: ἡγέομαι.
καθ-ῆκον, -κω, becoming.
κάθ-ημαι, to sit down.
καθ' ἡμέραν, daily.
κσθ-ημερινός, daily.
καθίζω, to cause to sit down.
καθ-ίημι, to let down.
καθ-ίστημι, to place, appoint.
καθ-ό, according as.
καθολικός, universal (in the title of the catholic epistles).
καθ-όλου, entirely, at all.
καθ-οπλίζομαι, to arm fully.
καθ ὁράω, -ῶ, to look down on.
καθ-ότι, as, because.
καθ-ώς, according as, even as.
*καθ-ώς-περ, even as, just as.
καί, and, also, even.
καίγε, and at least.   [kind.)
καινός, new (absolutely, of another
καινότης, newness.
και περ, although.
καιρός measure of time, season.
καί-τοι, καί-τοι-γε, though indeed.

καίω, to burn.
κἀκεῖ, and there.
κἀκεῖθεν, and thence.
κἀκεῖνος, and he, she, it, that one.
κακία, worthlessness.
κακο-ήθεια, -θία, malevolence: ἦθος.
κακο-λογέω, ῶ, to speak evil of: λέγω.
κακο-πάθεια, -θία, suffering of evil.
κακο-παθέω, -ῶ, to suffer evil:
κακο-ποιέω, -ῶ, to do evil. [πάσχω.
κακο-ποιός, an evil-doer.   [ness.
κακός, wicked; τὸ κακόν, wicked-
κακ-οῦργος, an evil-doer: ἔργον.
κακ-ουχούμενος, -χέω, ill-treated:
κακόω, to ill-treat.   [ἔχω.
κακῶς, badly, miserably, wrongly.
κάκωσις, ill-treatment.
καλάμη, straw.
κάλαμος, a stalk, reed.
καλέω, to call.
καλλι-έλαιος, a good olive tree.
κάλλιον see καλῶς.
καλλίων see καλός.   [is good.
καλο-διδάσκαλος, a teacher of what
καλο-ποιῶν, well-doing.
καλός, beautiful, good.
κάλυμμα, a covering, veil.
καλύπτω, to cover.
καλῶς & κάλλιον, well, better.
κάμέ see κἀγώ.
κάμηλος, a camel.
κάμινος, a furnace.   [μύω, close.
καμ-μύω, to shut (the eyes): κατα-
κάμνω, to be weary, sick.
κάμοί see κἀγώ.
κάμπτω, to bend (the knee).
κἄν (καὶ ἐάν), and if, if only. [reed.
κανών, a measure rule: κάννα,
καπηλεύω, to make gain by corrupt-ing: fr. κάπηλος, a hawker.
καπνός, smoke.
καρδία, the heart.   [the heart.
καρδιο-γνώστης, one who knows
καρπός, fruit, offspring.
καρπο-φορέω, to bear fruit: φέρω.
καρπο-φόρος, fruitful.
καρτερέω, to endure: κάρτος, κράτος.
κάρφος, dry stubble.
κατά, down, against, according to, &c. In comp. similar meanings.
κατα-βαίνω, to descend.
κατα-βάλλω, to cast down, lay.
κατα-βαρέω, to bear down.
*κατα-βαρύνω, to weigh down.
κατά-βασις, descent: βαίνω, to move.   [descend.
κατα-βιβάζομαι, to be caused to
κατα-βολή, a laying down, found-ing: βάλλω.   [βραβεύς, judge.
κατα-βραβεύω, to defraud of a prize:
κατ-αγγελεύς, an announcer.
κατ-αγγέλλω, to announce.
κατα-γελάω, to deride.
κατα-γινώσκω, to condemn.
κατ-άγνυμι, to break.
*κατα-γράφω, to delineate.
κατ-άγω, to lead down.
κατ-αγωνίζομαι, to overcome.
κατα-δέω, to bind up.
κατά-δηλος, manifest.
κατα-δικάζω, to condemn.
*κατα-δίκη, condemnation.
κατα-διώκω, to pursue.
κατα-δουλόω, to enslave.
κατα-δρέμω see κατατρέχω.   [της.
κατα-δυναστεύω, to oppress: δυνάσ-
*κατά-θεμα, a curse: τίθημι.
*κατα-θεματίζω, to curse.

κατ-αισχύνω, to shame.
κατα-καίω, to burn up.
κατα-καλύπτομαι, to be veiled.
κατα-καυχάομαι, to glory against.
κατά-κειμαι, to lie down.   [pieces.
κατα-κλάω, -κλάζω, to break in
κατα-κλείω, to shut up.   [δίδωμι.
κατα-κληρο-δοτέω, to divide by lot
*κατα-κληρο-νομέω, to allot (as an inheritance).
κατα-κλίνω, to cause to lie down.
κατα-κλύζομαι, to be submerged.
κατα-κλυσμός, deluge.
κατ-ακολουθέω, to follow after.
κατα-κόπτω, to cut to pieces, bruise.
κατα-κρημνίζω, to cast down head-long: κρημνός.
κατά-κριμα, condemnation.
κατα-κρίνω, to condemn.
κατά-κρισις, condemnation.
*κατα-κύπτω, to bend down.
κατα-κυριεύω, to overcome: κύριος.
κατα-λαλέω, to speak against.
κατα-λαλιά, evil-speaking.
κατά-λαλος, an evil-speaker.
κατα-λαμβάνω, to seize upon.
κατα-λέγομαι, to enroll.
κατά-λειμμα, a remnant.
κατα-λειπω, to leave behind.
κατα-λιθάζω, to stone.
κατ-αλλαγή, reconciliation.
κατ-αλλάσσω, to reconcile.
κατά-λοιπος, the residue.
κατά-λυμα, a lodging-place.
κατα-λύω, A. to lodge; B. to destroy.
κατα-μανθάνω, to learn well.
κατα-μαρτυρέω, to witness against.
κατα-μένω, to remain.
κατα-μόνας, κατὰ μόνας, alone.
κατ-ανά-θεμα, a curse: τίθημι.
κατ-ανα-θεματίζω, to curse.
κατ-αν-αλίσκω, to consume. [some.
κατα-ναρκέω, to be torpid, burden-
κατα-νεύω, to nod, make signs.
κατα-νοέω, to perceive.
κατ-αντάω, to arrive at.
κατά-νυξις, deep sleep.
κατα-νύσσω, to prick, pierce.
κατ-αξιόομαι, to be accounted worthy.
κατα-πατέω, to tread down.
κατά-παυσις, repose.
κατα-παύω, to cause to rest.
κατα-πέτασμα, veil, curtain.
κατα-πίνω, to drink up.
κατα-πίπτω, to fall down.
κατα-πλέω, to sail to.
κατα-πονέομαι, to be oppressed.
κατα-ποντίζομαι, to sink down: πόντος, the deep.
κατ-άρα, an execration.
κατ-αράομαι, to execrate.
κατ-αργέω, to render useless.
κατ-αριθμέομαι, to be numbered with: ἀριθμός.
κατ-αρτίζω, to restore, unite.
κατ-άρτισις, perfecting.
κατ-αρτισμός, perfecting.
κατα-σείω, to shake, beckon. [down.
κατα-σκάπτω, to dig down, break
κατα-σκευάζω, to prepare, erect.
κατα-σκηνόω, to pitch one's tent.
κατα-σκήνωσις, tent, roost.
κατα-σκιάζω, to overshadow: σκιά.
κατα-σκοπέω, to inspect.
κατά-σκοπος, a spy.   [σοφός.
κατα-σοφίζομαι, to circumvent:
κατα-στέλλω, to repress.
κατά-στημα, deportment: ἵστημι.

καταστολή, dress.
κατα-στρέφω, to overturn.
κατα-στρηνιάζω, -άω, to grow wanton against.
κατα-στροφή, overthrow.
κατα-στρώννυμι, to prostrate.
κατα-σύρω, to drag along.
κατα-σφάττω, -άζω, to kill off.
κατα-σφραγίζομαι, to seal up.
κατά-σχεσις, possession: ἔχω.
κατα-τίθημι, to lay down, lay up for oneself. [cut.
κατα-τομή, mutilation: τέμνω, to
κατα-τοξεύομαι, to shoot through.
κατα-τρέχω, to hasten down.
κατα-φάγω, κατεσθίω, to eat up.
κατα-φέρω, to bear down.
κατα-φεύγω, to flee away.
κατα-φθείρω, to corrupt, destroy.
κατα-φιλέω, to kiss repeatedly.
κατα-φρονέω, to contemn.
κατα-φρονητής, a despiser.
κατα-χέω, to pour upon. [earth.
κατα-χθόνιος, subterranean: χθών,
κατα-χράομαι, to use immoderately.
κατα-ψύχω, to cool.
κατ-είδωλος, full of idols: εἶδος.
κατ-έν-αντι, over against. [face.
κατ-εν-ώπιον, in presence of: ὤψ,
κατ-εξ-ουσιάζω, to exercise authority: ἔξειμι.
κατ-εργάζομαι, to work out: ἔργον.
κατ-έρχομαι, to descend.
κατ-εσθίω, to eat up.
κατ-ευθύνω, to direct.
*κατ-ευ-λογέω, to bless much: λέγω.
κατ-εφ-ίστημι, to set up against.
κατ-έχω, to hold fast. [speak.
κατ-ηγορέω, to accuse: ἀγορεύω, to
κατ-ηγορία, accusation.
κατ-ήγορος, an accuser.
*κατ-ήγωρ, an accuser. Heb.
κατήφεια, dejection.
κατ-ηχέω, to instruct.
κατ' ἰδίαν=κατά & ἰδίος.
κατ-ιόομαι, to rust over: ἰός.
κατ-ισχύω, to be strong against.
κατ-οικέω, to dwell in. [ἰσχύω, ἔχω.
κατ-οίκησις, a dwelling.
κατ-οικητήριον, a dwelling.
κατ-οικία, habitation.
*κατ-οικίζω, to cause to dwell.
κατ-οπτρίζομαι, to behold as in a mirror: ὄψομαι, ὁράω.
κατ-όρθωμα, a right action: ὀρθός.
κάτω, κατωτέρω, downwards.
κατώτερος, lower.
κατωτέρω see κάτω.
καῦμα, heat, scorching: fr. καίω.
καυματίζω, to burn, scorch.
καῦσις, burning.
καυσόω, to burn up.
καύσων, burning heat.
καυτηριάζομαι, καυστ-, to brand.
καυχάομαι, to glory.
καύχημα, glorying, boasting.
καύχησις, act of glorying.
κεῖμαι, to lie, be set.
κειρίαι, bandages, graveclothes.
κείρω, to cut off.
κέλευσμα, a word of command.
κελεύω, to command.
κενο-δοξία, vainglory.
κενό-δοξος, vainglorious.
κενός, empty, vain. [φωνή.
κενο-φωνία, empty discussion:
κενόω, to make empty, void.
κέντρον, a sting. [centurio.
κεντυρίων, a centurion. Latin,

κενῶς, in vain.
κεραία, κερέα, point (on Heb. letters).
κεραμεύς, a potter.
κεραμικός, made by a potter.
κεράμιον, an earthen vessel.
κέραμος, potters' clay.
κεράννυμι, -νυω, κεράω, to mix.
κέρας, a horn.
κεράτιον, pod of the carob tree.
κερδαίνω, to gain, win.
κέρδος, gain.
κερέα see κεραία.
κέρμα, small coin: κείρω.
κερματιστής, money-changer.
κεφάλαιον, chief point. [head.
κεφαλαιόω, -λιόω, to smite on the
κεφαλή, the head.
κεφαλίς, roll, chapter.
*κημόω, to muzzle. [census.
κῆνσος, registration, tax. Latin,
κῆπος, a garden. [watcher.
κηπ-ουρός, a gardener: οὖρος, a
κηρίον, honeycomb: κηρός, beeswax.
κήρυγμα, a preaching.
κῆρυξ, κῆ-, a herald.
κηρύσσω, to proclaim.
κῆτος, a sea monster.
κιβωτός, a hollow vessel, ark.
κιθάρα, a harp.
κιθαρίζω, to play on a harp.
κιθαρ-ῳδός, a harper: ἀοιδός, a singer.
κινάμωμον, κιννα-, cinnamon. Heb.
κινδυνεύω, to be in danger.
κίνδυνος, danger.
κινέω, to move, stir.
κίνησις, a moving.
κίχρημι=χράω.
κλάδος, a branch, shoot.
κλάζω, κλάω, to break.
κλαίω, to weep, lament.
κλάσις, a breaking.
κλάσμα, a fragment.
κλαυθμός, lamentation.
κλάω see κλάζω.
κλείς, a key.
κλείω, to close, shut up.
κλέμμα, stealing.
κλέος, glory, praise.
κλέπτης, a thief.
κλέπτω, to steal.
κλῆμα, branch, shoot: κλάω.
κληρο-νομέω, to inherit: νέμω, to distribute.
κληρο-νομία, an inheritance.
κληρο-νόμος, an heir.
κληρόομαι, to cast lots, assign.
κλῆρος, a lot, possession.
κλῆσις, an invitation, a calling.
κλητός, invited.
κλίβανος, an oven.
κλίμα, a region.
*κλινάριον, a small bed.
κλίνη, a bed.
κλινίδιον, a small bed.
κλίνω, to recline.
κλισία, company, reclining.
κλοπή, theft. [wash.
κλύδων, wave, surge: fr. κλύζω, to
κλυδωνίζομαι, to be tossed.
κνήθω, to scratch, titillate: fr. κνάω, to tickle.
κοδράντης, the fourth of an as (about 3/16d.) Latin, quadrans.
κοιλία, the belly.
κοιμάομαι, to fall asleep: fr. κεῖμαι.
κοιμάω, a reposing. [σύν.
κοινός, common, unclean: fr ξύν,
κοινόω, to make common.

κοινωνέω, to partake in.
κοινωνία, fellowship.
κοινωνικός, sociable.
κοινωνός, a participator. [tion.
κοίτη, bed, marriage bed, cohabita-
κοιτών, a bed-chamber. [scarlet.
κόκκινος, τὸ κόκκινον, crimson,
κόκκος, seed, grain.
κολάζομαι, to punish.
κολακεία, κια, flattery.
κόλασις, punishment.
κολαφίζω, to buffet.
κολλάω, to adhere.
κολλούριον, κολλύ-, eye-salve.
κολλυβιστής, money changer.
κολοβόω, to cut off or shorten.
κόλπος, the bosom.
κολυμβάω, to swim.
κολυμβήθρα, swimming-pool.
κολωνία, a colony. Latin, colonia.
κομάω, to have long hair.
κόμη, hair, head of hair.
κομίζω, to receive back.
κομψότερον, better. [dust.
κονιάω, to whitewash: fr. κόνις,
κονι-ορτός, dust: ὄρνυμι, to raise up.
κοπάζω, to rest, abate.
κοπετός, lamentation: κόπτω.
κοπή, a cutting in pieces.
κοπιάω, to grow weary.
κόπος, weariness, trouble.
κοπρία, dung.
*κόπριος, full of dung, filthy.
κόπτω, to cut, cut off; mid. to mourn.
κόραξ, a raven.
κοράσιον, a girl, maiden.
κορβᾶν, κορβανᾶν, corban, gift (to God). Heb.
κορέννυμι, to satisfy. [Heb. cor.
κόρος, dry measure (abt. 64½ gall.)
κοσμέω, to set in order.
κοσμικός, of this world.
κόσμιος, decorous.
κοσμο-κράτωρ, a world-ruler: κρατέω.
κόσμος, the world (as well arranged)
κούμ, κούμι, κούμ, arise: Aram.
κουστωδία, guard, watch. Latin, custodia.
κουφίζω, to lighten: κοῦφος, light.
κόφινος, hand basket.
κράββατος, κράβαττος, a light bed.
κράζω, to cry aloud.
κραιπάλη, κρε-, excess.
κρανίον, a skull.
κράσπεδον, fringe, tassel.
κραταιός, strong.
κραταιόω, to strengthen.
κρατέω, to subdue.
κράτιστος, most noble.
κράτος, power, dominion.
κραυγάζω, to cry out.
κραυγή, an outcry.
κρέας, meat, flesh.
κρεῖσσον, better.
κρείσσων, -ττων, stronger, better.
κρέμαμαι, κρεμάω, κρεμάννυμι, κρεμαννύω, to hang up, depend.
κρημνός, a precipice.
κριθή, barley.
κρίθινος, made of barley.
κρίμα, κρῖμα, decree, judgment.
κρίνον, a lily. [suit.
κρίνω, to try, judge, have a law-
κρίσις, judgment, condemnation, law, justice.
κριτήριον, tribunal, suit.
κριτής, a judge.
κριτικός, apt at judging.
κρούω, to knock.

*κρύπτη, κρυπτή, crypt, vault.
κρυπτός, hidden, secret.
κρύπτω, to hide, conceal.
κρυσταλλίζω, to be clear.
κρύσταλλος, crystal.
*κρυφαῖος, secret, hidden.
κρυφῇ, in secret.
κτάομαι, to acquire, possess.
κτῆμα, possession.
κτῆνος, beast of burden.
κτήτωρ, a possessor.
κτίζω, to create.
κτίσις, creature, creation.
κτίσμα, a creature.
κτιστής, the Creator.
κυβεία, κυβία, sleight, cheating.
κυβέρνησις, government.
κυβερνήτης, steersman.
*κυκλεύω, to encircle.
κυκλόθεν, all round.
κυκλόω, to encircle.
κύκλῳ (-λος), in a circle.
κυλίομαι, to be rolled.
κύλισμα, a wallowing place.
*κυλισμός, a rolling.
κυλλός, crooked, maimed.
κῦμα, wave (of the sea).
κύμβαλον, a cymbal.
κύμινον, cummin.
κυνάριον, a little dog.
κύπτω, to stoop down.   [Cyria).
κυρία, a lady (or a proper name,
κυριακός, of the Lord.
κυριεύω, to be lord of.
κύριος, sir, lord.
κυριότης, lordship.
κυρόω, to confirm.
κύων, a dog.
κῶλον, a limb.
κωλύω, to impede.
κώμη, a village.
κωμό-πολις, large village, town.
κῶμος, nocturnal revel.
κώνωψ, a gnat.   [κόπτω.
κωφός, blunted, dumb, deaf: fr.

Λ, λ, lambda, l, λ´=30; λ=30,000.
λαγχάνω, to obtain by lot.
λάθρα, -ρᾳ, secretly.
λαῖλαψ, a whirlwind.
λακέω, to burst with a loud report.
λακτίζω, to kick: fr. λάξ, with the
λαλέω, to speak.   [foot.
λαλιά, speech.
λαμά, λαμμᾶ, why? Aram.
λαμβάνω, to take.
λαμπάς, lamp, torch.
λαμπρός, shining.
λαμπρότης, brightness.
λαμπρῶς, brightly.
λάμπω, to shine.
λανθάνω, to be hidden.
λα-ξευτός, cut out of stone: fr. λᾶς,
  stone, & ξύω, to plane.
λαός, people, nation.
λάρυγξ, the throat.
λάσκω see λακέω.
λα-τομέω, to hew stones: fr. λᾶς,
  stone, & τέμνω, to cut.
λατρεία, service (to God).
λατρεύω, to worship, serve.
λάχανον, garden-herbs.
λεγεών, a legion. Lat. legio.
λέγω, to speak, say; pass. to be
λεῖμμα, a remnant. [called, chosen.
λεῖος, smooth, level.
λείπω, to leave, forsake, be wanting.
λειτ-ουργέω, to serve, minister: fr.
  λαός, & ἔργον.

λειτ-ουργία, service.
λειτ-ουργικός, rendering service.
λειτ-ουργός, public servant.
λέντιον, a linen cloth. Lat. linteum.
λεπίς, a scale or crust: fr. λέπω,
λέπρα, leprosy.   [to strip off.
λεπρός, a leper.
λεπτόν, a mite (about 3/32d.)
λευκαίνω, to make white.
λευκός, white, bright.
λέων, a lion.
λήθη, forgetfulness: fr. λανθάνω.
ληνός, a wine-press.
λῆρος, idle talk.   [carry off.
λῃστής, a robber: fr. λῄζομαι, to
λῆψις, λῆμψις, a receiving: fr.
λίαν, very much.   [λαμβάνω.
λίβανος, frankincense.
λιβανωτός, -ον, frankincense.
λιβερτῖνος, one liberated. Lat.
λιθάζω, to stone.   [libertinus.
λίθινος, of stone.
λιθο-βολέω, to stone: βάλλω.
λίθος, a stone.   [στρώννυμι.
λιθό-στρωτος, paved with stones:
λικμάω, to scatter, winnow, grind
  to powder.
λιμήν, port, haven.
λίμνη, a lake.
λιμός, hunger, famine.
λίνον, linen, flax.
λιπαρός, fat, dainty: fr. λίπος, lard.
λίτρα, a pound (12 ounces).
λίψ, south-west wind.
λογία, a collection (as of money):
  fr. λέγω, to collect.
λογίζομαι, to compute.
λογικός, rational, mental.
λόγιον (divine) oracle.
λόγιος, eloquent, learned.
λογισμός, a reasoning.
λογο-μαχέω, to contend about
  words: μάχη.   [words.
λογο-μαχία, contention about
λόγος, word, saying, discourse,
  doctrine, reason, account. ὁ λόγος, the Word.
λόγχη, a spear, lance.
λοιδορέω, to revile.
λοιδορία, reviling.
λοίδορος, a reviler.
λοιμός, pestilence.
λοιπόν, τὸ λοιπόν, ὁ λοιπόν, now, for
  the rest, henceforth: fr. λείπω.
λοιπός, the remaining.
  τοῦ λοιποῦ, from henceforth.
λουτρόν, a bathing: fr. λούω.
λούω, to wash, cleanse.
λύκος, a wolf.   [ruin.
λυμαίνομαι, to ravage: fr. λύμη,
λυπέω, to grieve.
λύπη, grief, pain.
λύσις, a loosening, divorce.
λυσι-τελεῖ, it is profitable: τελέω.
λύτρον, a ransom.
λυτρόω, to ransom.
λύτρωσις, redemption.
λυτρωτής, a redeemer.
λυχνία, a lamp-stand.
λύχνος, a lamp.   [dismiss.
λύω, to loosen, nullify, destroy,

M, μ, mu, m, μ´=40; μ=40,000.
μαγεία, -γία, magic.
μαγεύω, to be a magician.
μάγος, a magus, sorcerer. [Lchm.
*μαζός, the breast: Rev. i. 13,
μαθητεύω, to make a disciple, to
μαθητής, a disciple.   [teach.

μαθήτρια, a female disciple. [sire.
μαίνομαι, to be mad: fr. μάω, to de-
μακαρίζω, to pronounce blessed.
μακάριος, happy, blessed.
μακαρισμός, declaration of blessing.
μάκελλον, meat-market. Lat. ma-
μακράν, far, far off.   [cellum.
μακρόθεν, from afar.
μακρο-θυμέω, to be patient: θυμός.
μακρο-θυμία, patience, long-suffer-
μακρο-θύμως, patiently.   [ing.
μακρός, long, remote.
μακρο-χρόνιος, long-lived: χρόνος.
μαλακία, softness, infirmity.
μαλακός, soft, effeminate.
μάλιστα, most of all.
μᾶλλον, more, rather.
μάμμη, mother, grandmother.
μαμμωνᾶς, μαμωνᾶς, mammon. A-
μανθάνω, to learn. [ram. wealth.
μανία, madness: fr. μάω, to desire.
μάννα, manna: Exo. xvi. 15. Heb.
μαντεύομαι, to divine: fr. μάντις,
μαραίνομαι, to wither.   [seer.
μαρὰν ἀθά, the Lord cometh. Aram.
μαργαρίτης, a pearl. Persian.
μάρμαρον, marble.
μάρτυρ, μάρτυς, a witness, martyr.
μαρτυρέω, -έομαι, to be a witness.
μαρτυρία, a bearing witness.
μαρτύριον, testimony.
μαρτύρομαι, to call to witness.
μάρτυς see μάρτυρ.   [Tdf.
*μασθός, the breast. Rev. i. 13.
μασσάομαι, μασά-, to bite, gnaw.
μαστιγόω, to scourge.
μαστίζω, to scourge.
μάστιξ, a whip, scourge.
μαστός, the breast.   [folly.
ματαιο-λογία, vain talk: μάτη, a
ματαιο-λόγος, vain talker.
ματαιόομαι, to become vain.
μάταιος, vain, empty.
ματαιότης, vanity.
μάτην, in vain.
μάχαιρα, large knife, sword.
μάχη, contention.
μάχομαι, to contend.
μεγαλ-αυχέω, to boast greatly.
μεγαλεῖα, -λεῖος, magnificent.
μεγαλειότης, magnificence.
μεγαλο-πρεπής, magnificent: πρέπω,
μεγαλύνω, to enlarge. [to beseem.
μεγάλως, greatly.
μεγαλωσύνη, greatness.
μέγας, great.
μέγεθος, greatness.
μεγιστᾶνες (-τάν), great men.
μέγιστος, greatest.   [terpret.
μεθ-ερμηνεύομαι, to translate, in-
μέθη, intoxication.
μεθ-ιστάνω, μεθ-ίστημι, to remove.
μεθ-οδεία: artifice: ὁδός.
μεθ-όρια (-ριος, -ριον), borders:
  ὅρος, a boundary.
μεθύσκομαι, to be intoxicated.
μέθυσος, intoxicated.
μεθύω, to be intoxicated.
μεῖζον see μείζων.
μειζότερος, greater.
μείζων, μεῖζον, greater, elder.
μέλαν, ink.
μέλας, black.
μέλει, it concerns.
μελετάω, to think upon.   [a bee.
μέλι, honey.
μελίσσιος, made by bees: μέλισσα,
μέλλω, to be about (to do, come, &c.)
μέλος, member, limb.

μεμβράνα, parchment. *Lat. membrana.*
μέμφομαι, to complain. [fate.
μεμψί-μοιρος, complaining: μοῖρα,
μέν, truly, indeed (*a particle of affirmation*).
*μεν-οῦν, moreover, therefore.
μεν-οῦν-γε, yes indeed, nay but.
μέν-τοι, yet still.
μένω, to remain. [μείρομαι, share.
μερίζω, to divide, bestow: fr.
μέριμνα, care, burden.
μεριμνάω, to care for.
μερίς, a part.
μερισμός, a division.
μεριστής, a divider.
μέρος, a portion.
μεσ-ημβρία, mid-day: ἡμέρα.
μεσιτεύω, to mediate, interpose.
μεσίτης, a mediator.
μεσο-νύκτιον, midnight: νύξ.
μέσος, middle.
μεσό-τοιχον, middle wall: τοῖχος.
μεσ-ουράνημα, mid-heaven: οὐρανός.
μεσόω, to be midway.
μεστός, full.
μεστόω, to fill.
μετά, in, with, &c.: *in comp. denotes participation, succession. Lat.*
μετα-βαίνω, to depart, pass.
μετα-βάλλομαι, to change (one's mind).
μετ-άγω, to turn about.
μετα-δίδωμι, to impart, share.
μετά-θεσις, transfer, change: τίθημι.
μετ-αίρω, to go away.
μετα-καλέομαι, to call for.
μετα-κινέω, to remove.
μετα-λαμβάνω, to partake of.
μετά-ληψις, a taking, participation.
μετ-αλλάσσω, -ττω, to exchange.
μετα-μέλομαι, to repent. [μορφή.
μετα-μορφόομαι, be changed in form:
μετα-νοέω, to change one's mind, repent.
μετά-νοια, repentance. [repent.
μετα-ξύ, between: ξύν, σύν, in the midst.
μετα-πέμπω, to send for.
μετα-στρέφω, to turn, change.
μετα-σχηματίζω, to transfer, transform: σχῆμα.
μετα-τίθημι, to transpose.
*μετα-τρέπω, to turn back, change.
μετ-έπειτα, afterwards.
μετ-έχω, to partake.
μετ-εωρίζομαι, to be raised up (by false hopes), unsettled.
μετ-οικεσία, change of abode: οἰκία.
μετ-οικίζω, to cause to remove.
μετοχή, a partaking: ἔχω.
μέτοχος, companion, partaker.
μετρέω, to measure.
μετρητής, a measure (abt. 8¾ gall.)
μετριο-παθέω, to forbear, bear with.
μετρίως, moderately.
μέτρον, a measure. [eye.
μέτ-ωπον, the forehead: ὤψ, the
μέχρι, μέχρις, unto, until.
μή, not: *in comp. a particle of negation.*
ἐὰν μή, unless, if not. [negation.
ἵνα μή, that not, lest.
οὐ μή, not at all.
μή-γε see εἰ δὲ μήγε.
μηδαμῶς, by no means.
μηδέ, but not, and not.
μηδείς, μηδεμία, μηδέν, not one, no one, nothing.
μηδέ-ποτε, never. [one, nothing.
μηδέ-πω, not yet.
*μηθείς, μηθέν, no one, none.
μηκέτι, no more, no further.
μῆκος, length: fr. μακρός.

μηκύνομαι, to lengthen. [sheep.
μηλωτή, a sheepskin: fr. μῆλον, a
μήν, a month.
μήν, truly (*a strengthening particle with* ἤ). [sire.
μηνύω, to disclose: fr. μάω, to de-
μὴ οὐκ (*an interrogative negative particle*).
μή-ποτε, lest ever, no longer.
*μή-που, lest anywhere = μή που.
μή-πω, not yet.
μή-πως, lest in any way.
μηρός, the thigh.
μήτε, neither, nor.
μήτηρ, a mother. [gative particle.)
μήτι, whether at all? (*an interro-*
μήτιγε, how much more.
μῆτις, (has) any one.
μήτρα, the womb. [ἀλοάω, to beat.
μητρ-αλῴης, -ολῴης, a matricide:
μια see εἰς.
μιαίνω, to dye, pollute.
μίασμα, pollution.
μιασμός, pollution.
μίγμα, a mixture.
μίγνυμι, to mix.
μικρός, -όν, little, small.
μίλιον, a mile (about 1,618 yards). *Lat. milliarium.*
μιμέομαι, to imitate.
μιμητής, an imitator.
μιμνήσκομαι, to remember.
μισέω, to hate.
μισθ-απο-δοσία, recompense: δίδωμι.
μισθ-απο-δότης, a rewarder.
μίσθιος, a hired servant.
μισθόομαι, to hire.
μισθός, wages, recompense.
μίσθωμα, hire, rent, what is let.
μισθωτός, a hired servant.
μνᾶ, a coin and weight (about £3. 4s. 7d.) *Heb. maneh.*
μνάομαι, to remember.
μνεία, remembrance.
μνῆμα, a memorial, tomb.
μνημεῖον, a memorial, grave.
μνήμη, remembrance.
μνημονεύω, to remember.
μνημόσυνον, a memorial in thought.
μνηστεύομαι, to be betrothed.
μογι-λάλος, μογγι-, speaking with difficulty: λαλέω.
μόγις, with difficulty.
μόδιος, a dry measure (abt. 2 galls.) *Lat. modius.*
μοιχαλίς, an adulteress.
μοιχάομαι, to commit adultery.
μοιχεία, adultery.
μοιχεύω, to commit adultery.
μοιχός, an adulterer.
μόλις, with difficulty.
μολύνω, to pollute.
μολυσμός, pollution.
μομφή, complaint: fr. μέμφομαι.
μονή, an abode: fr. μένω.
μονο-γενής, only begotten: fr. γίνομαι.
μόνον see μόνος.
μονόομαι, to be left alone.
μόνος, only, alone.
μον-όφθαλμος, having but one eye.
μορφή, form, shape.
μορφόομαι, to be formed, fashioned.
μόρφωσις, formation, semblance.
μοσχο-ποιέω, to form (an image of) a calf.
μόσχος, a calf, young bullock.
μουσικός, a musician.
μόχθος, toil, distress.
μυελός, marrow.

μυέομαι, to be initiated.
μῦθος, a word, speech, fable.
μυκάομαι, to low, bellow.
μυκτηρίζω, -ομαι, to turn up the nose at, mock: fr. μυκτήρ, the nose.
μυλικός, belonging to a mill: fr. μύλη, a mill.
*μύλινος, made of mill-stones.
μύλος, a mill-stone.
μυλών, mill-house.
μυριάς, a myriad (10,000).
μυρίζω, to anoint. [merable.
μυρίοι (-ος), ten thousand, innu-
μύρον, an ointment. *Heb. mor.*
μυστήριον, a mystery: μυέομαι.
μυ-ωπάζω, to see dimly: ὤψ, the
μώλωψ, a stripe, bruise. [eye.
μωμάομαι, to blame.
μῶμος, spot, blemish.
μωραίνω, to make foolish, insipid.
μωρία, folly.
μωρο-λογία, foolish talking: λέγω.
μωρός, stupid, foolish.

N, ν, *nu, n,* ν´ = 50; ν, = 50,000.
ναί, yes. [to dwell.
ναός, temple (the house): fr. ναίω,
νάρδος, spikenard.
ναυ-αγέω, to make shipwreck: ἄγνυμι, to break.
ναύ-κληρος, ship-master.
ναῦς, a ship.
ναύτης, a seaman.
νεανίας, a young man: fr. νέος.
νεανίσκος, a young man.
νεκρός, dead, dead body.
νεκρόω, to put to death.
νέκρωσις, death.
*νεομηνία = νουμηνία.
νέος, νεώτερος, new, younger.
νεοσσός, νος-, a young bird.
νεότης, youth. [φύω.
νεό-φυτος, newly-planted, a novice:
νεύω, to nod, beckon.
νεφέλη, a cloud.
νέφος, a cloud.
νεφρός, a kidney.
νεω-κόρος, temple-guardian.
νεωτερικός, youthful.
νεώτερος see νέος.
νή, by (in asseverations).
νήθω, to spin.
νηπιάζω, to be a babe.
νήπιος, an infant.
νησίον, a small island.
νῆσος, an island.
νηστεία, a fast, fasting.
νηστεύω, to fast.
νῆστις, fasting.
νηφάλεος, -λιος, sober.
νήφω, to be sober, sober-minded.
νικάω, to conquer.
νίκη, victory.
νῖκος, victory. [&c.)
νιπτήρ, basin (for washing hands,
νίπτω, to wash (hands or feet).
νοέω, to weigh in the mind, think.
νόημα, thought, the mind.
νόθος, a bastard.
νομή, pasturage: fr. νέμω, to graze.
νομίζω, to do by custom, to reckon.
νομικός, a teacher of the law.
νομίμως, lawfully.
νόμισμα, lawful coin, &c. [law.
νομο-διδάσκαλος, a teacher of the
νομο-θεσία, legislation: τίθημι.
νομο-θετέω, to enact laws.
νομο-θέτης, a lawgiver.
νόμος, law, custom.

νόος = νοῦς.
νοσέω, to be sick.
νόσημα, disease, sickness.
νόσος, disease, sickness.
νοσσιά, a brood of birds.
νοσσίον, young of birds.
νοσσός see νεοσσός.
νοσφίζομαι, to separate, embezzle.
νότος, the south wind.
νου-θεσία, admonition : τίθημι.
νου-θετέω, to admonish.
νου-μηνία, νεομ-, new moon : μήν.
νουν-εχῶς, wisely : ἔχω.
νοῦς, mind, intellect, faculty.
νύμφη, bride, daughter-in-law.
νυμφίος, bridegroom.
νυμφών, bride-chamber.
νῦν, now.
   τὰ νῦν, τανῦν, the present.
νυνί, now.
νύξ, night.
νυστάζω, to sleep, delay.
νύττω, νύσσω, to pierce, stab.
νυχθ-ήμερον, a night and day: ἡμέρα.
νωθρός, slow, slothful.
νῶτος, the back.

Ξ, ξ, xi, x, ξ´=60 ; ξ,=60,000.
ξενία, a lodging.
ξενίζω, to entertain.
ξενο-δοχέω, to entertain : δέχομαι.
ξένος, A. strange, foreign ; B. a host.
ξέστης, a measure (nearly a pint).
   Sextarius, Lat.
ξηραίνω, to dry, dry up.
ξηρός, dry, withered.
ξύλινος, wooden.
ξύλον, cut wood : hence cross, &c.
ξυράω, to shear, shave : fr. ξυρόν, a razor.

O, o, omicron, o, o´=70 ; o,=70,000.
ὅ ἐστι, which is.
ὀγδοήκοντα, eighty.
ὄγδοος, eighth.   [ἤνεγκον, φέρω.
ὄγκος, weight, encumbrance : fr.
ὅδε, ἥδε, τόδε, this that ; he, she.
ὁδεύω, to travel.
ὁδ-ηγέω, to lead, guide : ἄγω.
ὁδ-ηγός, leader, guide.
ὁδοι-πορέω, to travel : πόρος, way.
ὁδοι-πορία, a journeying.
*ὁδο-ποιέω, to level, open a road.
ὁδός, a way, road.
ὀδούς, a tooth.
ὀδυνάομαι, to be in agony.
ὀδύνη, pain, distress.
ὀδυρμός, a lamentation.
ὄζω, to stink, be offensive.
ὅθεν, whence, wherefore.
ὀθόνη, linen cloth.
ὀθόνιον, a linen bandage.
οἶδα see εἴδέω.
οἰκεῖος, belonging to a household.
*οἰκετεία, a household.
οἰκέτης, a household servant.
οἰκέω, to dwell in.
οἴκημα, a dwelling, prison.
οἰκητήριον, a dwelling.
οἰκία, a house, family.
οἰκιακός, a domestic.
οἰκο-δεσποτέω, to rule a house.
οἰκο-δεσπότης, master of a house.
οἰκο-δομέω, to build : δέμω, to build.
οἰκο-δομή, a building.
*οἰκο-δομία building up, edification
*οἰκο-δόμος, a builder.
οἰκο-νομέω, to be a steward : νέμω,
   to dispense.

οἰκο-νομία, stewardship.
οἰκο-νόμος, a steward.
οἶκος, a house.
οἰκουμένη, the habitable earth.
*οἰκ-ουργός, a worker at home:
   ἔργον.
οἰκ-ουρός, a keeper at home : ὁράω. B.
οἰκτείρω, -ρέω, to be compassionate.
οἰκτιρμός, compassion.
οἰκτίρμων, compassionate.
οἶμαι, οἴομαι, to think.   [πίνω.
οἰνο-πότης, one given to wine :
οἶνος, wine.   [boil over.
οἰνο-φλυγία, drunkenness : φλύω, to
οἴομαι see οἶμαι.
οἷος, what, such as.   [v. 4, Lach.
*οἰοσδηποτοῦν, whatsoever.   John
οἴσω see φέρω.
ὀκνέω, to be slothful.
ὀκνηρός, slothful.
ὀκτα-ήμερος, of the eighth day.
ὀκτώ, eight.
*ὀλεθρεύω see ὀλοθρεύω.
*ὀλέθριος, destructive, deadly.
ὄλεθρος, destruction : ὄλλυμι, to
   destroy.
*ὀλιγο-πιστία, little faith : πείθω.
ὀλιγό-πιστος, of little faith.
ὀλίγος, little, small.
ὀλιγό-ψυχος, faint-hearted : ψυχή.
ὀλιγ-ωρέω, to make little of: ὥρα.
*ὀλίγως, just, scarcely.   [care.
ὀλοθρευτής, a destroyer.
ὀλοθρεύω, ὀλεθ-, to destroy. [καίω.
ὁλο-καύτωμα, whole burnt-offering:
ὁλο-κληρία, perfect soundness.
ὁλό-κληρος, whole, sound.
ὀλολύζω, to howl, wail.
ὅλος, all, the whole.
ὁλο-τελής, perfect, complete: τελέω.
ὄλυνθος, an unripe fig.
ὅλως, wholly.
ὄμβρος, a shower, rain.
*ὁμείρομαι, to long for.
ὁμ-ιλέω, to associate with.
ὁμ-ιλία, intercourse: fr. ὁμός, same,
ὅμ-ιλος, company.   [& ἴλη, troop.
*ὁμίχλη, ὁ-, a mist, fog.
ὄμμα, an eye: fr. ὄψομαι, ὁράω.
ὄμνυμι, ὀμνύω, to swear.
ὁμο-θυμαδόν, with one mind : θυμός.
ὁμοιάζω, to be like.   [πάσχω.
ὁμοιο-παθής, of like affections:
ὅμοιος, like, similar.
ὁμοιότης, likeness.
ὁμοιόω, to make like.
ὁμοίωμα, likeness.
ὁμοίως, likewise.
ὁμοίωσις, likeness.   [λέγω.
ὁμο-λογέω, to promise, confess:
ὁμο-λογία, profession.
ὁμο-λογουμένως, confessedly.
ὁμό-τεχνος, of the same trade:
ὁμοῦ, together.   [τέχνη.
ὁμό-φρων, of one mind : φρήν.
ὁμόω see ὄμνυμι.
ὅμως, even, yet.
ὄναρ, a dream.
ὀνάριον, a young ass : fr. ὄνος.
ὀνειδίζω, to reproach.
ὀνειδισμός, a reproach.
ὄνειδος, reproach.
ὀνίνημι, ὀναίμην see ὀνίνημι.
ὀνικός, worked by an ass : fr. ὄνος.
ὀνίνημι, to profit.   [γινώσκω.
ὄνομα, name, reputation : fr.
ὀνομάζω, to name, call upon the
ὄνος, an ass.   [name.
ὄντα, ὄντας, &c., see under ὤν.

ὄντως, really, truly.
ὄξος, vinegar, sour wine.
ὀξύς, sharp, swift.
ὀπή, an opening.
ὄπισθεν, from behind.
ὀπίσω, back, behind.
ὅπλα see ὅπλον.
ὁπλίζομαι, to furnish with arms.
ὅπλον, ὅπλα, an instrument, arms :
   fr. ἕπω, to handle.
ὁποῖος, of what sort.
ὁπότε, when.
ὅπου, where.
ὀπτάνομαι, to be seen.
ὀπτασία, a vision.
ὄπτομαι (ὁράω), to see, behold.
ὀπτός, cooked, broiled.
ὀπ-ώρα, autumn, fruits : ὥρα.
ὅπως, how, so that.
ὅραμα, a sight, vision.
ὅρασις, appearance, aspect.
ὁρατός, visible.   [for.
ὁράω, ὄψομαι, A. to see ; B. to care
ὀργή, anger, indignation.
ὀργίζομαι, to be angry.
ὀργίλος, prone to anger.
ὀργυιά, a fathom (length from
   finger ends with arms stretched
   out, abt. 2 yards: fr. ὀρέγομαι.
ὀρέγομαι, to stretch out.
ὀρεινός, ὀρι-, hilly : fr. ὄρος.
ὄρεξις, desire, lust.   [πούς.
ὀρθο-ποδέω, to walk uprightly :
ὀρθός, upright, straight. [to cut.
ὀρθο-τομέω, to cut straight : τέμνω,
ὀρθρίζω, to rise early.
ὀρθρινός, early.
ὄρθριος, early.
ὄρθρος, daybreak.
ὀρθῶς, rightly.
ὅρια (ὅριον), boundaries.
ὀρινός see ὀρεινός.
ὁρίζω, to define, determine.
ὁρκίζω, to adjure.   [strain.
ὅρκος, an oath : fr. εἴργω, to re-
ὁρκ-ωμοσία, an oath : ὄμνυμι.
ὁρμάω, to incite, start.
ὁρμή, impulse, assault.
ὅρμημα, impulse.
ὄρνεον, a bird, fowl.
*ὄρνιξ = ὄρνις.   Luke xiii. 34, Tdf.
ὄρνις, a fowl.
ὀρο-θεσία, boundary.
ὄρος, a mountain.
ὀρύσσω, to dig.
ὀρφανός, bereaved.
ὀρχέομαι, to dance.
ὅς, ἥ, ὅ, who, which.
ὁσάκις, as often as.
ὅσγε, ὅς γε, precisely he who.
ὅσιος, holy.
ὁσιότης, holiness.
ὁσίως, holily.
ὀσμή, an odour, savour : fr. ὄζω.
ὅσος, how much, how long. [who.
ὅσ-περ, ἥ-περ, ὅ-περ, the very one
ὀστέον, a bone.
ὅσ-τις, ἥ-τις, ὅτι, whosoever, what-
ὀστράκινος, earthen.   [soever.
ὄσφρησις, the sense of smelling:
   ὀσφραίνομαι, to scent.
ὀσφύς, the loins.
ὅταν, when, whenever.
ὅτε, when.
ὅτι, that, because.
ὅτου see ὅστις.
οὗ, where, whither.
οὐ, οὐκ, οὐχ, no, not.
οὐά, οὐά, ah ! aha !

οὐαί, woe! alas!
οὐδαμῶς, by no means.
οὐ-δέ, neither, nor. [nothing.
οὐδ-είς, οὐδε-μία, οὐδ-έν, no one,
οὐδέ-ποτε, never.
οὐδέ-πω, not yet.
οὐθείς, οὐθέν, no one, nothing.
οὐκ see οὐ.
οὐκ-έτι, οὐκ ἔτι, no more, no further.
οὐκ-οῦν, not therefore.
οὐ μή see under μή.
οὖν, therefore, then.
οὔ-πω, not yet.
οὐρά, a tail.
οὐράνιος, heavenly.
οὐρανόθεν, from heaven.
οὐρανός, heaven.
οὖς, the ear.
οὖσα, οὔσῃ, &c., see ὤν.
οὐσία, substance, property: fr. εἰμί.
οὔ-τε, neither, nor.
οὗτοι, these.
οὗτος, αὕτη, τοῦτο, this.
οὕτω, οὕτως, thus, so.
οὐχ see οὐ.
οὐχί, by no means.
ὀφειλέτης, a debtor.
ὀφειλή, a debt, duty.
ὀφείλημα, a debt.
ὀφείλω, to owe.
ὄφελον, O that! I wish.
ὄφελος, profit. [δοῦλος.
ὀφθαλμο-δουλεία, -λία, eye-service:
ὀφθαλμός, the eye (of the mind),
ὄφις, a serpent. [understanding.
ὀφρύς, the eyebrow, a projection.
ὀχλέομαι, to be disturbed, vexed.
ὀχλο-ποιέω, to gather a crowd.
ὄχλος, a crowd.
ὀχύρωμα, a fortress: fr. ἔχω.
ὀψάριον, a little fish.
ὀψέ, late, at the end of.
ὄψιμος, latter.
ὄψιος, ὀψία, late, evening.
ὄψις, the face, aspect.
ὀψώνιον, wages, recompense.

Π, π, pi, p, π´ = 80; π, = 80,000.
παγιδεύω, to ensnare.
παγίς, a snare, trap: πήγνυμι.
πάθημα, suffering, affliction.
παθητός, destined to suffer.
πάθος, suffering, emotion: πάσχω.
παιδ-αγωγός, a tutor, pædagogue:
παιδάριον, a boy, lad. [ἄγω.
παιδεία, -δια, training, correction.
παιδευτής, preceptor.
παιδεύω, to train, discipline.
παιδιόθεν, from childhood.
παιδίον, a child, infant.
παιδίσκη, a bondmaid.
παίζω, to play, dance.
παῖς, child, servant.
παίω, to strike.
πάλαι, of old, long ago.
παλαιός, old, former.
παλαιότης, old, oldness.
παλαιόω, to make old.
πάλη, a contest. [tion: γίνομαι.
παλιγ-γενεσία, παλιγγ-, regenera-
πάλιν, again. [πλῆθος.
παμ-πληθεί, πανπ-, all together:
πάμ-πολυς, very great.
παν, in comp. wholly, complete.
παν-δοχεῖον, -κιον, a khan, inn:
δέχομαι.
παν-δοχεύς, -κεύς, inn-keeper.
παν-ήγυρις, a general convocation:
ἀγείρω, to collect.

παν-οικί, with the whole household:
οἶκος.
παν-οπλία, panoply, armour:
ὅπλον, a weapon.
παν-ουργία, shrewdness: ἔργον.
παν-οῦργος, shrewd, crafty.
*παν-πληθεί = παμπληθεί.
*πανταχῇ, -ῇ, everywhere.
πανταχόθεν, from all sides.
πανταχοῦ, everywhere. [τελέω.
παν-τελές (-λής), perfect, complete:
πάντῃ, -η, wholly.
πάντοθεν, from all parts.
παντο-κράτωρ, almighty: κράτος.
πάντοτε, always.
πάντως, wholly.
παρά, beside, beyond, on account
of. In comp. besides, to the
side, amiss, change. [gress.
παρα-βαίνω, to go aside from, trans-
παρα-βάλλω, to compare, pass over.
παρά-βασις, transgression.
παρα-βάτης, a transgressor.
παρα-βιάζομαι, to constrain. [λω.
*παρα-βολεύομαι, to venture: βάλ-
παρα-βολή, comparison, simile.
παρα-βουλεύομαι, to expose oneself
to danger.
παρ-αγγελία, a charge, command.
παρ-αγγέλλω, to charge, command.
παρα-γίνομαι, to come near, arrive.
παρ-άγω, to pass away.
παρα-δειγματίζω, to make an example of: δεῖγμα. [Persian.
παράδεισος, park, garden, Paradise,
παρα-δέχομαι, to receive, approve.
παρα-δια-τριβή, useless occupation:
τρίβω, to rub, waste.
παρα-δίδωμι, to deliver over. [δοκέω.
παρά-δοξος, unexpected, strange:
παρά-δοσις, a giving over (as by
tradition): δίδωμι.
παρα-ζηλόω, to provoke: ζῆλος.
παρα-θαλάσσιος, by the seaside:
θάλασσα.
παρα-θεωρέω, to overlook, slight.
παρα-θήκη, a deposit: τίθημι.
παρ-αινέω, to exhort.
παρ-αιτέομαι, to refuse, make ex-
cuses: αἰτέω.
*παρα-καθέζομαι, to sit down near.
παρα-καθίζω, to sit down near.
παρα-καλέω, to invite, exhort,
encourage, beseech.
παρα-καλύπτω, to cover over, veil.
παρα-κατα-θήκη, a trust, deposit.
παρά-κειμαι, to be present with.
παρά-κλησις, encouragement, comfort: καλέω. [καλέω.
παρά-κλητος, paraclete, advocate:
παρ-ακοή, disobedience: ἀκούω.
παρ-ακολουθέω, to follow closely:
κέλευθος, a way.
παρ-ακούω, to disregard.
παρα-κύπτω, to stoop to examine.
παρα-λαμβάνω, to take, receive.
παρα-λέγομαι, to skirt, coast.
παρ-άλιος, near the sea: ἅλς.
παρ-αλλαγή, change: ἀλλάττω.
παρα-λογίζομαι, to deceive: λέγω.
παρα-λύομαι, to be enfeebled, para-
παρα-λυτικός, palsied. [lysed.
παρα-μένω, to remain by.
παρα-μυθέομαι, to comfort.
παρα-μυθία, comfort: μῦθος.
παρα-μύθιον, comfort.
παρα-νομέω, to break the law.
παρα-νομία, transgression.
παρα-πικραίνω, to provoke: πικρός.

παρα-πικρασμός, provocation.
παρα-πίπτω, to fall away.
παρα-πλέω, to sail past.
παρα-πλήσιον, near to.
παρα-πλησίως, in like manner.
παρα-πορεύομαι, to pass by.
παρά-πτωμα, a falling away, transgression: πίπτω.
παρα-ρρυέω, -ρέω, to slip away.
παρά-σημος, noted, marked: σῆμα.
παρα-σκευάζω, to prepare. [token
παρα-σκευή, a preparation.
παρα-τείνω, to extend.
παρα-τηρέω, to examine well.
παρα-τήρησις, observation.
παρα-τίθημι, to place by the side.
παρα-τυγχάνω, to fall in with.
παρ-αυτίκα, immediately.
παρα-φέρω, to bear aside or away.
παρα-φρονέω, to be beside oneself:
φρήν. [φρήν
παρα-φρονία, being beside oneself.
παρα-χειμάζω, to winter: χειμών.
παρα-χειμασία, spending the winter
παρα-χρῆμα, immediately.
πάρδαλις, a leopard, panther.
*παρ-εδρεύω, to sit by, serve.
πάρ-ειμι, to be present.
παρ-εισ-άγω, to bring in by stealth.
παρ-εισ-ακτος, brought in by stealth.
παρ-εισ-δύνω, -δύω, to come in by
stealth. [bye.
παρ-εισ-έρχομαι, to come in by the
παρ-εισ-φέρω, to bring in besides.
παρ-εκτός, without, except.
*παρ-εμβάλλω, to put in beside.
παρ-εμ-βολή, camp, army: βάλλω.
παρ-εν-οχλέω, to cause trouble.
παρ-επί-δημος, a foreigner.
παρ-έρχομαι, to pass by.
πάρ-εσις, remission, passing over
παρ-έχω, to furnish [ἵημι, to send
παρ-ηγορία, consolation: ἀγορεύω,
to speak to.
παρθενία, -νεία, virginity.
παρθένος, a virgin.
παρ-ίεμαι, -ίημι, to let pass, relax.
παρ-ιστάνω, to place near, present
παρ-ίστημι, to stand near, help.
πάρ-οδος, a passing near.
παρ-οικέω, to dwell as a stranger.
παρ-οικία, a sojourning.
πάρ-οικος, a stranger. [way
παρ-οιμία, simile, proverb: οἶμος.
πάρ-οινος, given to wine.
παρ-οίχομαι, to pass by.
παρ-ομοιάζω, to resemble.
παρ-όμοιος, resembling. [irritated
παρ-οξύνομαι, to be sharpened
παρ-οξυσμός, irritation, incite-
παρ-οργίζω, to irritate. [ment.
παρ-οργισμός, irritation.
παρ-οτρύνω, to incite.
παρ-ουσία, presence, advent.
παρ-οψίς, a side dish, dish.
παρ-ρησία, speaking freely: ῥῆσις,
a speech.
παρ-ρησιάζομαι, to speak freely.
πᾶς, πᾶσα, πᾶν, any, of every kind,
the whole. [Heb.
πάσχα, a passing over, the Passover
πάσχω, to experience, suffer.
πατάσσω, to strike, smite.
πατέω, to trample on.
πατήρ, a father.
πατρ-αλῴης, -ας, a parricide:
ἀλοιάω, to strike.
πατριά, ancestry, family.
πατρι-άρχης, a patriarch: ἄρχω.

πατρικός, of a father, ancestral.
πατρίς, one's native country.
*πατρολῴας = πατραλῴης.
πατρο-παρά-δοτος, handed down from forefathers.
πατρῷος, hereditary.
παύομαι, to cease, restrain. [dull.
παχύνομαι, to become gross: παχύς,
πέδη, a fetter, shackle.
πεδινός, level, plain.
πεζεύω, to travel on foot.
πεζῇ, on foot or by land.
*πεζός, on foot, walking.
πειθ-αρχέω, to obey.
πειθός, πι-, persuasion.
πείθω, πέποιθα, to persuade, trust.
πεινάω, to hunger.
πεῖρα, experiment, attempt.
πειράζω, to make trial of, test.
πειρασμός, temptation, trial.
πειράω, to tempt, try.
πεισμονή, persuasion: fr. πείθω.
πέλαγος, the deep, the sea.
πελεκίζομαι, to be beheaded: fr. πέ-
πέμπτος, fifth. [λεκυς, an axe.
πέμπω, to send, dismiss. [need.
πένης, poor: fr. πένομαι, to be in
πενθερά, a mother-in-law.
πενθερός, a father-in-law.
πενθέω, to mourn.
πένθος, mourning: fr. πάθος.
πενιχρός, needy, poor: fr. πένομαι, to be in need.
πεντάκις, five times.
πεντακια-χίλιοι, five thousand.
πεντακόσιοι, five hundred.
πέντε, five.
πεντε-και-δέκατος, fifteenth.
πεντήκοντα, fifty.
πεντηκοστή, fiftieth, Pentecost.
πέποιθα see πείθω.
πεποίθησις, trust, confidence.
περ, *an enclitic particle signifying intensity.*
*περαιτέρω, further, more.
πέραν, beyond.
πέρας, limit, bound.
περί, about, around. *In comp.* around, above, beyond.
περι-άγω, to lead around.
περι-αιρέω, to make away with.
*περι-άπτω, to fasten round.
περι-αστράπτω, to flash around.
περι-βάλλω, to put around.
περι-βλέπω, to look around.
περι-βόλαιον, that which is thrown around, covering: βάλλω.
περι-δέομαι, to bind around.
περι-δρέμω see περιτρέχω.
περι-εῖλον, -ελών see περιαιρέω.
περι-εργάζομαι, to be a busybody.
περί-εργος, a busybody.
περι-έρχομαι, to go about.
περι-έχω, to encompass.
περι-ζώννυμι, to gird around.
περί-θεσις, a putting around.
περι-ίστημι, to place around; mid. turn oneself, avoid.
περι-κάθαρμα, off-scouring: καθαρός.
*περι-καθ-ίζω, to sit around: Luke xxii. 55. Lch.
περι-καλύπτω, to cover around.
περί-κειμαι, to lie around.
περι-κεφαλαία, a helmet: κεφαλή.
περι-κρατής, being master of:
περι-κρύπτω, to conceal. [κράτος.
περι-κυκλόω, to compass about: κύκλος, a circle.
περι-λάμπω, to shine around.

περι-λείπομαι, to remain over.
περί-λυπος, greatly grieved: λύπη.
περι-μένω, to wait for.
πέριξ, round about.
περι-οικέω, to dwell around.
περί-οικος, a neighbour.
περι-ούσιος, especial, peculiar: εἰμί.
περι-οχή, compass, portion: ἔχω.
περι-πατέω, to walk, behave, live.
περι-πείρω, to pierce through.
περι-πίπτω, to encounter.
περι-ποιέομαι, to acquire for self.
περι-ποίησις, an acquisition.
*περιρ-ραίνω, to besprinkle.
περιρ-ρήγνυμι, to break off.
περι-σπάομαι, to be distracted.
περισσεία, abundance.
περίσσευμα, superfluity.
περισσεύω, to abound.
περισσός, -ότερος, abundant, more abundant.
περισσότερον, more abundantly.
περισσοτέρως, more abundantly.
περισσῶς, exceedingly.
περιστερά, a dove, pigeon.
περι-τέμνω, to circumcise.
περι-τίθημι, to place around.
περι-τομή, circumcision.
περι-τρέπω, to turn about.
περι-τρέχω, to run round.
περι-φέρω, to carry round.
περι-φρονέω, to contemn: φρήν.
περί-χωρος, surrounding country.
περί-ψημα, off-scouring: ψάω, to wipe.
περπερεύομαι, to boast one's self.
πέρυσι, a year ago.
πετάομαι, -ῶμαι, to fly.
πετεινόν, a bird, fowl.
πέτομαι, to fly.
πέτρα, a rock, cliff.
πέτρος, a stone.
πετρ-ώδης, stony: εἶδος.
πήγανον, rue.
πηγή, a fountain.
πήγνυμι, to fix.
πηδάλιον, a rudder.
πηλίκος, how great, large.
πηλός, clay, mire.
πήρα, a bag, satchel.
πῆχυς, a cubit (from the elbow to the tip of the middle finger, abt. 18in.)
πιάζω, to lay hold of.
πιέζω, to press down. [πείθω.
πιθανο-λογία, a plausible speech:
πικραίνω, to embitter.
πικρία, bitterness.
πικρός, bitter.
πικρῶς, bitterly.
πίμπλημι see πλήθω.
πιμπράμαι, to be inflamed.
πινακίδιον, a small table or tablet.
πίναξ, a plate, dish.
πίνω, πίω, πίομαι, to drink.
πιότης, richness.
πιπράσκω, to sell: fr. περάω, to sell.
πίπτω, ἔπεσον, to fall.
πιστεύω, to believe.
πιστικός, pure.
πίστις, faith.
πιστός, faithful.
πιστόω, to make faithful, assure.
πλανάω, to lead astray.
πλάνη, wandering.
πλανήτης, wandering.
πλάνος, wandering, a deceiver.
πλάξ, a tablet. [vessel.
πλάσμα, thing formed, earthen
πλάσσω, to form, fashion.

πλαστός, well-turned, **false.**
πλατεῖα, a broad way.
πλάτος, breadth.
πλατύνω, to enlarge.
πλατύς, broad, wide.
πλέγμα, a plait, braid.
πλείων, πλεῖον, or πλέον, πλεῖστος, more, most.
πλέκω, to weave, braid.
πλέον see πλείων.
πλεονάζω, to superabound. [ἔχω.
πλεον-εκτέω, to excel, overreach:
πλεον-έκτης, greedy, covetous.
πλεον-εξία, covetousness.
πλευρά, side (of the body).
πλέω, to sail.
πληγή, a stroke, wound: fr. πλήσσω.
πλῆθος, a multitude: fr. πίμπλημι.
πληθύνω, to increase.
πλήθω, πίμπλημι, to fill.
πλήκτης, a striker.
πλημμύρα, a flood: πίμπλημι.
πλήν, except, howbeit.
πλήρης, full.
πληρο-φορέω, to render full: φέρω.
πληρο-φορία, full assurance.
πληρόω, to fill, fulfil, complete.
πλήρωμα, whole, fulness.
πλησίον, near, near by: ὁ πλησίον, a neighbour.
πλησμονή, repletion: πίμπλημι.
πλήσσω, to smite.
πλοιάριον, a small ship, boat.
πλοῖον, a ship: πλέω.
πλόος, sailing, voyage.
πλούσιος, rich: πλοῦτος.
πλουσίως, richly.
πλουτέω, to be rich.
πλουτίζω, to make rich.
πλοῦτος, riches, wealth.
πλύνω, to wash (as garments).
πνεῦμα, spirit, the Spirit.
πνευματικός, spiritual.
πνευματικῶς, spiritually.
πνέω, to breathe, blow.
πνίγω, to strangle.
πνικτός, strangled.
πνοή, breath, a blowing.
ποδ-ήρης, a long robe: fr. πούς & ἀραρίσκω, to fit.
πόθεν, whence.
ποία, grass, herbage; *read by some interpreters in Jas. iv. 14, instead of from ποῖος.*
ποιέω, to do, practise.
ποίημα, workmanship.
ποίησις, a doing.
ποιητής, a maker, doer.
ποικίλος, various.
ποιμαίνω, to feed, tend.
ποιμήν, a shepherd.
ποίμνη, a flock.
ποίμνιον, a little flock.
ποῖος, what, of what kind, &c.
πολεμέω, to go to war.
πόλεμος, war, strife.
πόλις, a city.
πολιτ-άρχης, ruler of a city, 'poli-
πολιτεία, citizenship. [tarch.'
πολίτευμα, commonwealth. [one.
πολιτεύομαι, to be a citizen, act as
πολίτης, a citizen, fellow-citizen.
πολλά see πολύς.
πολλάκις, often.
πολλα-πλασίων, manifold.
*πολυ-εύ-σπλαγχνος, very tender-hearted (Jas. v. 11 in a few MSS).
πολυ-λογία, much speaking: λόγος.
πολυ-μερῶς, in many parts: μέρος.

πολυ-ποίκιλος manifold, variegated.
πολύς, many, much. [σπλάγχνα.
πολύ-σπλαγχνος, very merciful:
πολυ-τελής, very costly: τελέω.
πολύ-τιμος, very costly: τιμή.
πολυ-τρόπως, in various ways:
πόμα, drink: πίνω. [τρόπος.
πονηρία, wickedness: πένομαι, to
toil, be in need.
πονηρός, evil, the wicked one.
πόνος, labour, pain.
πορεία, a way, course of life: fr.
περάω, to pass. [journey.
πορεύομαι, to proceed, set out,
πορθέω, to lay waste: fr. πέρθω,
to waste. [source.
πορισμός, gain: fr. πόρος, a re-
πορνεία, fornication (figuratively
of idolatry).
πορνεύω, to commit fornication.
πόρνη, a harlot: fr. πέρνημι, to sell.
πόρνος, a fornicator.
πόρρω, πορρωτέρω (-ρον), far off:
fr. πρό, πρόσω, further.
πόρρωθεν, at a distance. [ment.
πορφύρα, purple or crimson gar-
πορφυρέος,-ρυῦς, purple or crimson.
πορφυρό-πωλις, seller of purple
fabrics: πωλέω. [often.
ποσάκις, how many times, how
πόσις, drink: πίνω.
πόσος, how much, how great.
ποταμός, river, torrent.
ποταμο-φόρητος, carried away by a
stream: φέρω.
ποταπός, of what nature?
ποτέ, at some time.
πότε, when.
πότερον, whether.
ποτήριον, a drinking vessel, the
portion which God allots: fr.
ποτίζω, to cause to drink. [πίνω.
πότος, a drinking bout.
που, somewhere.
ποῦ, where, whither.
πούς, the foot.
πρᾶγμα, deed, work. [tion.
πραγματεία,-τία, business, occupa-
πραγματεύομαι, to carry on a
business. [torian camp. Lat.
πραιτώριον, prætor's palace, præ-
πράκτωρ, officer who inflicts pun-
πρᾶξις, mode of action. [ishment.
πρᾶος, meek, gentle.
πρᾳότης, meekness.
πρασιά, plot of ground, a company:
fr. πράσον, a leek.
πράσσω, ττω, to practise, perform.
*πραϋπάθεια,-θία, gentleness.
πραῦς, meek, gentle.
πραϋτης, meekness.
πράω see πιπράσκω.
πρέπει, it is fitting.
πρεσβεία, an embassy. [bassador.
πρεσβεύω, to be aged, be an am-
πρεσβυτέριον, body of elders, presbytery. [the elders.
πρεσβύτερος,-τέρα, elder (of two),
πρεσβύτης, an old man.
πρεσβῦτις, an old woman.
πρηνής, headlong.
πρίζω, to saw asunder. [fr. πρό.
πρίν, before; πρὶν ἤ, sooner than:
πρίω see πρίζω. [before.
πρό before (in any sense). In comp.
προ ἄγω, to lead forth, to go before.
προ-αιρέομαι, to prefer, purpose.
προ-αιτιάομαι, to bring a charge
previously.

προ-ακούω to hear before.
προ-αμαρτάνω, to sin before.
προ-αύλιον, forecourt, porch.
προ-βαίνω, to go forward.
προ-βάλλω, to put forth.
προβατικός, pertaining to sheep.
*προβάτιον, a little sheep.
πρόβατον, a sheep: βαίνω, to move.
προ-βιβάζω, to put forward: βαίνω,
προ-βλέπω, to foresee. [to move.
προ-γίνομαι, to happen before.
προ-γινώσκω, to know beforehand.
πρό-γνωσις, foreknowledge.
πρό-γονοι (-ος), ancestors: γίνομαι.
προ-γράφω, to write before, mark
προ-δηλος, evident, manifest. [out.
προ-δίδωμι, to give before, betray.
προ-δότης, a betrayer.
προδρέμω see προτρέχω.
πρό-δρομος, a forerunner.
προ-ειδέω, [-δον], to foresee. [fore.
προ-εῖπον,-ερῶ,-είρηκα, to say be-
προ-ελπίζω, to hope before.
προέπω see προεῖπον.
προ-εν-άρχομαι, to begin before.
προ-επ-αγγέλλομαι, to promise be-
προερέω see προεῖπον. [fore.
προ-έρχομαι, to go forward, go
before. [hand.
προ-ετοιμάζω, to prepare before-
προ-ευ-αγγελίζομαι, to announce
glad tidings beforehand.
προ-έχομαι, to advance, go before.
προ-ηγέομαι, to take the lead: ἄγω.
πρό-θεσις, a setting forth, purpose:
τίθημι. [beforehand.
προ-θεσμία,-ος, time appointed
προ-θυμία, readiness, zeal.
πρό-θυμος, ready, zealous.
προ-θύμως, readily.
πρόϊμος see πρώϊμος.
προ-ΐστημι, to set or place before.
προ-καλέομαι, to call forth, irritate.
προ-κατ-αγγέλλω, to pre-announce,
promise. [hand: ἄρω, to fit.
προ-κατ-αρτίζω, to prepare before-
πρό-κειμαι, to be set before.
προ-κηρύσσω,-ττω, to announce
beforehand.
προ-κοπή, progress, advancement.
προ-κόπτω, to go forward.
πρό-κριμα, pre-judgment, prejudice.
προ-κυρόομαι, to ratify beforehand:
κῦρος, confirmation.
προ-λαμβάνω, to anticipate.
προ-λέγω, to tell beforehand.
προ-μαρτύρομαι, to testify beforehand.
προ-μελετάω, to premeditate: με-
λέτη, practice.
προ-μεριμνάω, to be solicitous beforehand: μέριμνα.
προ-νοέω, to provide beforehand.
πρό-νοια, forethought, care for.
προ-οράω, to foresee.
προ-ορίζω, to pre-determine.
προ-πάσχω, to suffer before.
*προ-πάτωρ, a forefather.
προ-πέμπω, to send forward.
προ-πετής, rash, precipitate: πίπτω.
προ-πορεύομαι, to precede.
πρός, towards, at, near. In comp.
towards, near, at, besides, &c.
προ-σάββατον, πρὸς σάβ-. Heb.
the day before the sabbath.
προσαγορεύομαι, to call, designate.
προσ-άγω, to bring.
προσαγωγή, approach, access.
προσ-αιτέω,-ῶ, to beg.

*προσ-αίτης, a beggar.
προσ-ανα-βαίνω, to ascend.
προσ-αναλίσκω, to expend besides.
προσ-ανα-πληρόω, to fill up by
adding.
προσ-ανα-τίθημι, to confer.
προσ-απειλέομαι, to add threats.
προσ-δαπανάω, to spend besides.
προσ-δέομαι, to stand in need.
προσ-δέχομαι, to receive, expect.
προσ-δοκάω, to look for.
προσ-δοκία, expectation.
προσ-δρέμω see προστρέχω.
προσ-εαω,-ῶ, to permit more.
προσ-εγγίζω, to approach to.
προσ-εδρεύω, to minister to: ἕδρα,
a seat; ἕζω, to sit. [ἔργον.
προσ-εργάζομαι, to earn besides:
προσ-έρχομαι, to approach, assent
προσ-ευχή, prayer, an oratory. [to.
προσ-εύχομαι, to offer prayer.
προσ-έχω, to fix the mind on.
προσ-ηλόω, to fix with nails: ἧλος.
προσ-ήλυτος, a proselyte: ἦλθον,
πρός-καιρος, temporary. [ἔρχομαι.
προσ-καλέομαι, to call, invite.
προσ-καρτερέω, to give attention to.
προσ-καρτέρησις, perseverance.
προσ-κεφάλαιον, a pillow: κεφαλή.
προσ-κληρόομαι, to be attached to:
κλῆρος. [21. Lch.
*πρόσ-κλησις, invitation, 1 Tim. v.
*προσ-κλίνω, to incline to.
πρός-κλισις, leaning towards.
προσ-κολλάομαι, to join self with:
κόλλα, glue. [offence.
πρόσ-κομμα, a stumbling-block,
προσ-κοπή, occasion of offence.
προσ-κόπτω, to strike against.
προσ-κυλίω, to roll to or upon.
προσ-κυνέω, to do homage to.
προσ-κυνητής, a worshipper.
προσ-λαλέω, to converse with.
προσ-λαμβάνω, to take to self.
πρόσ-ληψις,-λημψις, a receiving.
προσ-μένω, to remain with.
προσ-ορμίζομαι, to come to land.
προσ-οφείλω, to owe besides.
προσ-οχθίζω, to be grieved with:
ὀχθέω, to be angry.
*προσ-παίω, to strike against.
Mat. vii. 25. Lch. [hunger.
πρόσ-πεινος, very hungry: πεῖνα,
προσ-πήγνυμι, to affix to.
προσ-πίπτω, to fall towards or upon.
προσ-ποιέομαι, to conform self to.
προσ-πορεύομαι, to approach to.
προσ-ρήγνυμι, to dash against.
προσ-τάσσω, to enjoin upon.
προσ-στάτις, a helper: ἵστημι.
προσ-τίθημι, to place near, add.
προσ-τρέχω, to run to.
προσ-φάγιον, food eaten with bread:
ἔφαγον see ἐσθίω. [slay.
πρόσ-φατος, new made: φένω, to
προσ-φάτως, lately. [before.
προσ-φέρω, προσ-ήνεγκα, to bring
προσ-φιλής, pleasing: φιλος. [φέρω.
προσ-φορά, an offering, sacrifice:
προσ-φωνέω, to call to, summon:
φωνή. [γέω, to pour.
πρόσ-χυσις, an affusion, sprinkling:
προσ-ψαύω, to touch.
προσωπο-ληπτέω,-λημπ-, to shew
favour: λαμβάνω.
προσωπο-λήπτης,-λήμπ-, a respecter of persons.
προσωπο-ληψια,-λημψ-, respect
of persons.

προσ-ωπον, face, countenance: ὤψ, the eye.

προ-τάσσομαι, be appointed before.

προ-τείνω, to stretch forth.

πρότερον, former, τὸ πρότερον, formerly: fr. πρό, comparative.

πρότερος, former: id.

προ-τίθημι, to place before.

προ-τρέπομαι, to exhort.

προ-τρέχω, to run before.

προ-ὑπ-άρχω, to be before.

πρό-φασις, pretext: φημί.

προ-φέρω, to bring forth.

πρό-φημι=προερέω.

προ-φητεία, prophecy: φημί.

προ-φητεύω, to prophesy.

προ-φήτης, a prophet.

προ-φητικός, prophetic.

προ-φῆτις, a prophetess.

προ-φθάνω, to anticipate.

προ-χειρίζομαι, to appoint.

προ-χειρο-τονέομαι, to fore-appoint: χείρ, τείνω, to stretch.

πρύμνα, the stern (of a ship).

πρωΐ, early.

πρωΐα, πρώϊος, early.

πρώϊμος, πρόϊ-, early, former.

πρωϊνός, of the morning.

πρώϊος=πρωΐα.

πρώρα, the prow (of a ship): fr. πρό.

πρωτεύω, to be chief. [to sit.

πρωτο-καθ-εδρία, a chief seat: ἕζω.

πρωτο-κλισία, a chief place: κλίνω.

πρῶτον, first; τὸ πρῶτον, at the first: fr. πρό, superlative.

πρῶτος, first: id.

πρωτο-στάτης, a leader: ἵστημι.

πρωτο-τόκια, birth-right: τίκτω.

πρωτό-τοκος, first-born.

*πρώτως, first.

πταίω, to stumble, fall into misery.

πτέρνα, the heel.

πτερύγιον, little wing, pinnacle.

πτέρυξ, a wing, pinion: fr. πέτομαι.

πτηνόν, winged; τὰ πτηνά, birds: πτοέομαι, to be terrified. [fr. πέτομαι.

πτόησις, terror.

πτύον, a winnowing shovel.

πτύρομαι, to terrify.

πτύσμα, spittle.

πτύσσω, to fold up.

πτύω, to spit.

πτῶμα, a corpse: fr. πίπτω.

πτῶσις, a fall: id. [cringe.

πτωχεία, poverty: fr. πτώσσω, to

πτωχεύω, to be in poverty.

πτωχός, poor.

πυγμή, the fist.

πυκνός, compact, frequent.

πυκτεύω, to box.

πύλη, a door, gate.

πυλών, gateway, porch.

πυνθάνομαι, to ask, enquire.

πῦρ, fire, hence trial.

πυρά, a fire.

πύργος, fortress, tower.

πυρέσσω, to have a fever.

πυρετός, a fever.

πυρινός, fiery.

πυρόομαι, to be set on fire.

πυρράζω, to grow red, glow.

πυρρός, fiery-red.

πύρωσις, a burning.

πώ, even yet (enclitic particle, used only in composition).

πωλέω, to sell.

πῶλος, a colt.

πώ-ποτε, at any time.

πωρόω, to harden: fr. πῶρος, stone

πώρωσις, hardness.

πώς, by any means.

πῶς, how? why?

P, ρ, rho, r, ρ'=100; ρ,=100,000.

ῥαββί, ῥαββεί, rabbi, my master, teacher. Heb.

ῥαββονί, -ουνί, -ουνεί, rabboni. id.

ῥαβδίζω, to beat with rods.

ῥάβδος, a wand, rod.

ῥαβδ-οῦχος, one who holds the rods, a lictor: ἔχω.

ῥαδι-ούργημα, villany: fr. ῥᾴδιος, easy, & ἔργον.

ῥαδι-ουργία, temerity.

ῥακά, ῥαχά, empty (term of contempt). Heb. [ῥήγνυμι.

ῥάκος, a piece torn off, cloth: fr.

ῥαντίζω, to sprinkle, purify.

ῥαντισμός, sprinkling, purification.

ῥαπίζω, to smite with the hand: fr. ῥαπίς, rod.

ῥάπισμα, a blow with the hand.

ῥαφίς, a needle: ῥάπτω, to sew.

ῥαχά=ῥακά.

ῥέδα, ῥέδη, a chariot. Lat., rheda.

ῥέω A, to flow: John vii. 38.

ῥέω B, to say; ἐρῶ as future of φημί.

ῥῆγμα, a crash, ruin.

ῥήγνυμι, ῥήσσω, to break forth.

ῥῆμα, a word, utterance: fr. ῥέω B.

ῥήσσω see ῥήγνυμι.

ῥήτωρ, an orator: fr. ῥέω B.

ῥητῶς, expressly.

ῥίζα, a root, descendant.

ῥιζόομαι, to be rooted, fixed.

ῥιπή, a jerk, twinkle: fr. ῥίπτω.

ῥιπίζομαι, to be moved, agitated.

ῥίπτω, -τέω, to throw, throw off.

ῥμδ', 144, Rev. vii. 4.

ῥοιζηδόν, with a rushing noise: fr. ῥοῖζος, a rushing, whistling ῥομφαία, a sword. [sound.

ῥύμη, narrow street, lane: fr. ῥέω A.

ῥύομαι, to rescue.

*ῥυπαίνω, to make filthy.

*ῥυπαρεύομαι, to be filthy.

ῥυπαρία, filth.

ῥυπαρός, filthy.

ῥύπος, filth.

ῥυπόω, to be filthy.

ῥύσις, a flux, issue: fr. ῥέω A.

ῥυτίς, a wrinkle, defect.

ῥώννυμαι, -μι, to render firm.

Σ, σ, final ς, sigma, s, σ'=200; σ,=200,000. [me. Aram.

σαβαχθανί,-νεί, thou hast forsaken

σαβαώθ, armies. Heb.

σαββατισμός, a keeping sabbath, rest. Heb. [week. Heb.

σάββατον, -τα, sabbath, rest, a

σαγήνη, a seyne, drag net.

σαίνω, to agitate, disturb.

σάκκος, sackcloth.

σαλεύω, to shake.

σάλος, swell of the sea.

σάλπιγξ, a trumpet.

σαλπίζω, to sound a trumpet.

σαλπιστής, a trumpeter.

σανδάλιον, a sandal. Persian.

σανίς, a board, plank.

σαπρός, rotten, corrupt.

σάπφειρος, a sapphire.

σαργάνη, a basket.

σάρδινος, sardius, sardian.

σάρδιον, -ου, sardius.

σαρδ-όνυξ, -διόνυξ, sardonyx.

σαρκικός, fleshly, carnal.

σάρκινος, fleshy, fleshly. [creature.

σάρξ, flesh, the body, living

σαρόω, to sweep, cleanse: fr. σαίρω, to sweep. [and a half).

σάτον, Heb. measure (abt. a peck

σαυτοῦ, ῷ, όν see σεαυτοῦ.

σβέννυμι, to extinguish, restrain.

σεαυτοῦ, thyself, of or to thyself.

σεβάζομαι, to adore, worship.

σέβασμα, object of worship.

σεβαστός, venerable.

σέβομαι, to reverence, worship.

σειρά, a rope, chain.

*σειρός, σιρός, a pit, cavern.

σεισμός, a shaking, earthquake.

σείω, to shake, agitate.

σελήνη, the moon.

σεληνιάζομαι, to be lunatic.

σεμίδαλις, flour. [σέβομαι.

σεμνός, venerable, honourable: fr.

σεμνότης, dignity, gravity.

σημαίνω, to signify: fr. σῆμα, a sign.

σημεῖον, a sign, token.

σημειόομαι, to mark, note.

σήμερον, to-day.

σήπω, to corrupt.

σηρικόν, σιρικόν, silk, silken.

σής, a moth. [to eat.

σητό-βρωτος moth-eaten: βιβρώσκω,

σθενόω, to strengthen.

σιαγών, cheek, jaw-bone.

σιγάω, to keep silence, conceal.

σιγή, silence.

σιδήρεος, -οῦς, made of iron.

σίδηρος, iron.

σικάριος, an assassin. Lat., sicarius.

σίκερα, strong drink. Heb.

σιμικίνθιον, ση-, an apron. Lat., semicinctium.

σίναπι, mustard seed.

σινδών, a linen cloth. [sieve.

σινιάζω, to sift by trials: fr. σινίον,

σιρικόν see σηρικόν.

σιρός=σειρός.

σιτευτός, fed with corn, fattened.

*σιτίον, corn, grain.

σιτιστός, a fatling.

σιτο-μέτριον, a corn ration: μέτρον.

σῖτος, wheat, corn.

σιωπάω, to be silent, still.

σκανδαλίζω, to stumble, grieve.

σκάνδαλον, a snare, cause of

σκάπτω, to dig. [stumbling.

σκάφη, a boat.

σκέλος, the leg. [cover.

σκέπασμα, clothing: fr. σκέπω, to

σκευή, equipment, utensils.

σκεῦος, a vessel, implement.

σκηνή, a tent, tabernacle.[πήγνυμι

σκηνο-πηγία, feast of tabernacles:

σκηνο-ποιός, a tent-maker.

σκῆνος, a tabernacle.

σκηνόω, to fix one's tabernacle.

σκήνωμα, a tent, tabernacle.

σκιά, a shadow.

σκιρτάω, to leap.

σκληρο-καρδία, hardness of heart.

σκληρός, stern, violent.

σκληρότης, hardness, obduracy.

σκληρο-τράχηλος, stiff-necked.

σκληρύνω, to harden.

σκολιός, crooked, perverse.

σκόλοψ, a thorn, infliction.

σκοπέω, to mark, take heed.

σκοπός, mark, goal.

σκορπίζω, to disperse.

σκορπίος, a scorpion.

σκοτεινός, -τινός, full of darkness.

σκοτια, darkness.

σκοτίζομαι, to be darkened.
σκοτόομαι, to be darkened.
σκότος, darkness.
σκύβαλον, refuse, dregs.
σκυθρ-ωπός, of a sad countenance.
σκύλλω, to vex, harass.
σκῦλον, a skin, spoils.
σκωληκό-βρωτος, eaten of worms : βιβρώσκω, to eat.
σκώληξ, a worm.
σμαράγδινος, made of emerald.
σμάραγδος, an emerald. *Sanscrit.*
σμύρνα, myrrh. *Phœnician.*
σμυρνίζομαι, to be mingled with
σορός, a bier, coffin. [myrrh.
σός, σή, σόν, thy, thine.
σουδάριον, a napkin. *Lat. sudarium.*
σοφία, wisdom.
σοφίζω, to make wise. [clear.
σοφός, wise, profound : fr. σαφής.
σπαράσσω, -ττω, to convulse, tear.
σπαργανόω, to swathe : fr. σπάργω.
σπάομαι, to draw. [to wrap.
σπαταλάω, to live luxuriously.
σπεῖρα, a cohort (of soldiers).
σπείρω, to sow.
σπεκουλάτωρ, a spy, scout, a body-guard. *Lat., speculator.*
σπένδομαι, to be poured out.
σπέρμα, seed, offspring : fr. σπείρω.
σπερμο-λόγος, empty talker. [ly.
σπεύδω, to hasten, to desire earnest-
σπήλαιον, a cave : fr. σπέος, cave.
σπιλάς, a hidden rock.
σπίλος, a blot, stain.
σπιλόω, to stain.
σπλαγχνίζομαι, to feel compassion.
σπλάγχνον, -να, bowels, heart.
σπόγγος, a sponge.
σποδός, ashes.
σπορά, a sowing : fr. σπείρω.
σπόριμος, sown ; τὰ σπόριμα, sown
σπόρος, a sowing, seed. [fields.
σπουδάζω, to be in earnest : σπεύδω.
σπουδαῖος, earnest, diligent.
σπουδαιότερος, more earnest.
σπουδαίως, -οτέρως, earnestly, dili-
σπουδή, diligence. [gently.
σπυρίς, σφυρίς, basket, hamper.
στάδιον, -ος, race-course, a stadium (abt. 607 feet).
στάμνος, an urn, vase : ἵστημι.
*στασιαστής, an insurgent.
στάσις, a standing, sedition.
στατήρ, a stater (abt. 2s. 7d.)
σταυρός, a stake, cross.
σταυρόω, to crucify.
σταφυλή, a bunch of grapes.
στάχυς, an ear (of corn) : fr. ἵστημι.
στέγη, cover, roof.
στέγω, to cover, endure.
στεῖρα, barren.
στέλλομαι, to withdraw, avoid.
στέμμα, a garland : fr. στέφω, to encircle. [to groan.
στεναγμός, a groaning : fr. στένω.
στενάζω, to sigh, groan.
στενός, narrow, strait.
στενο-χωρέομαι, to be straitened : χῶρος, a place.
στενο-χωρία, a narrow place.
στερεός, firm, stable.
στερεόω, to make firm. [fastness.
στερέωμα, solidity, firmness, sted-
στέφανος, a crown, honour : fr. στέφω, to encircle.
στεφανόω, to crown (as victor).
στῆθος, the breast : fr. ἵστημι (con-veying firmness)

στήκω, to stand firm : fr. ἕστηκα,
στηριγμός, firmness. [ἵστημι.
στηρίζω, to fix firmly.
*στιβάς, bed of leaves, straw, &c. : fr. στείβω, to tread on. [mark.
στίγμα, brand, mark : fr. στίζω, to
στιγμή, an instant : id.
στίλβω, to shine.
στοά, a portico.
στοιβάς (properly στι-), bough, branch. [στείχω, to walk.
στοιχεῖον, element, rudiment : fr.
στοιχέω, to walk : id.
στολή, a long garment : fr. στέλλω,
στόμα, the mouth. [to place.
στόμαχος, the stomach.
στρατεία, warfare : fr. στρατός.
στράτευμα, armed forces
στρατεύομαι, to serve as a soldier.
στρατ-ηγός, ruler, captain : ἄγω.
στρατιά, army, host.
στρατιώτης, a soldier.
στρατο-λογέω, to enlist troops λέγω, to gather.
στρατο-πεδ-άρχης, a prefect : ἄρχω.
στρατό-πεδον, an encamped army : πέδον, the ground. [στρέφω.
στρεβλόω, to rack, distort : fr.
στρέφω, to turn, convert.
στρηνιάω, to live voluptuously.
στρῆνος arrogance, voluptuousness.
στρουθίον, a small bird, sparrow : fr. στρουθός, a sparrow.
στρωννύω, -υμι, to strew, furnish.
στυγνητός, hateful : fr. στυγέω, to
στυγνάζω, to be sad, gloomy. [hate.
στύλος, a pillar, column.
στωϊκός, a stoic : fr. στοά.
συγ = συν-.
συγ-γένεια, kindred, family : γίνομαι.
συγ-γενής, a kinsman.
*συγ-γενίς, a kinswoman.
συγ-γνώμη, consent : γινώσκω.
συγ-κάθ-ημαι, to be seated with.
συγ-καθ-ίζω, to company with.
συγ-κακο-παθέω, to suffer evils with : πάσχω. [with : ἔχω.
συγ-κακ-ουχίομαι, to suffer hardship
συγ-καλέω, to call together.
συγ-καλύπτομαι, to conceal.
συγ-κάμπτω, to oppress, bow down.
συγ-κατα-βαίνω, to descend with.
συγ-κατά-θεσις, agreement.
συγ-κατα-τίθημι, to consent to.
συγ-κατα-ψηφίζομαι, to be classed with : ψῆφος.
συγ-κεράννυμι, to mix with.
συγ-κινέω, to move together, excite.
συγ-κλείω, to enclose.
συγ-κληρο-νόμος, a joint-heir : νέμω, to distribute.
συγ-κοινωνέω, to partake with.
συγ-κοινωνός, an associate.
συγ-κομίζω, to bear away together.
συγ-κρίνω, to combine, compare.
συγ-κύπτω, to be bowed together.
συγ-κυρία, a concurrence : κυρέω, to meet with.
συγ-χαίρω, to rejoice with.
συγ-χέω, -χύνω, -ύννω, to excite.
συγ-χράομαι, to associate with.
συγ-χύνω, -ννω = συγχέω.
σύγ-χυσις, confusion.
συ-ζάω, to live with.
συ-ζεύγνυω, -μι, to unite together.
συ-ζητέω, to discuss, dispute.
συ-ζήτησις, disputation.
συ-ζητητής, a disputant.
σύ-ζυγος, a yoke-fellow.

συ-ζωο-ποιέω, to quicken together with.
συκάμινος, a sycamine tree (mul-
συκῆ, a fig-tree. [berry.
συκο-μωραία, -ρέα, -μορέα, a syca-more, a fig. [more tree.
συκο-φαντέω, to defraud : φαίνω, to
συλ- = συν-. [make clear.
συλ-αγωγέω, to spoil, rob : ἄγω.
συλάω, to rob, plunder.
συλ-λαλέω, to converse with.
συλ-λαμβάνω, to seize, conceive,
συλ-λέγω, to gather. [assist.
συλ-λογίζομαι, to reckon, reason.
συλ-λυπέομαι, to be distressed.
συμ- = συν-.
συμ-βαίνω, to happen, befall.
συμ-βάλλω, to confer, combat, to help.
συμ-βασιλεύω, to reign together.
συμ-βιβάζω, to unite, gather, to teach : βαίνω, to move.
συμ-βουλεύω, to consult together.
συμ-βούλιον, a council.
σύμ-βουλος, a counsellor.
συμ-μαθητής, a fellow-disciple.
συμ-μαρτυρέω, to testify together.
συμ-μερίζομαι, to partake with : μέρος, part.
συμ-μέτ-οχος, joint partaker : ἔχω.
συμ-μιμητής, joint imitator : μῖμος, mimic. [able.
*συμ-μορφίζω, to make conform-
συμ-μορφόομαι, to be conformed to.
σύμ-μορφος, conformed to : μορφή.
συμ-παθέω, to sympathise with : ἔπαθον, πάσχω.
συμ-παθής, sympathetic.
συμ-παρα-γίνομαι, to stand by one.
συμ-παρα-καλέομαι, to be comforted with.
συμ-παρα-λαμβάνω, to take with.
συμ-παρα-μένω, to remain with.
συμ-πάρ-ειμι, to be present with.
συμ-πάσχω, to suffer with.
συμ-πέμπω, to send with.
συμ-περι-λαμβάνω, to embrace.
συμ-πίνω, to drink with. [gether.
*συμ-πίπτω, to coincide, fall to-
συμ-πληρόω, to fill up.
συμ-πνίγω, to suffocate.
συμ-πολίτης, a fellow-citizen.
συμ-πορεύομαι, to go with.
συμ-πόσιον, a drinking party : πίνω.
συμ-πρεσβύτερος, a fellow elder.
συμ-φαγεῖν see συνεσθίω.
συμ-φέρω, to bring together, to be σύμ-φημι, to assent to. [expedient.
*σύμ-φορος, profitable.
συμ-φυλέτης, a fellow countryman :
συμ-φύομαι, to grow with. [φυλή.
σύμ-φυτος, grown up with.
συμ-φωνέω, to agree with.
συμ-φώνησις, unison, accord.
συμ-φωνία, symphony, music.
σύμ-φωνος, harmonious : φωνή.
συμ-ψηφίζω, to reckon together : ψῆφος.
σύμ-ψυχος, like-minded : ψυχή.
σύν, with. *In comp.* with, *or it intensifies: the ν changes to γ, λ, μ, and is dropped before σ or ζ.*
συν-άγω, to bring together, be hospitable. [gogue.
συναγωγή, a congregation, syna-
συν-αγωνίζομαι, to strive together.
συν-αθλέω, to contend with.
συν-αθροίζω, to collect together.
συν-αίρω, to take account with.

συν-αιχμ-άλωτος, a fellow-prisoner.
συν-ακολουθέω, to accompany.
συν-αλίζομαι, to associate: ἁλίς, crowded.   [reconcile.
*συν-αλλάσσω, to commune with,
συν-ανα-βαίνω, to ascend with.
συν-ανά-κειμαι, to recline with.
συν-ανα-μίγνυμι, to mingle with.
συν-ανα-παύομαι, to be refreshed
συν-αντάω, to meet with.   [with.
συν-άντησις, a meeting with.
συν-αντι-λαμβάνομαι, to join in helping.
συν-απ-άγομαι, to be led away with.
συν-απο-θνήσκω, to die with.
συν-απ-όλλυμαι, –μι, to perish with.
συν-απο-στέλλω, to send together.
συν-αρμο-λογέομαι, to be framed together: ἁρμός.
συν-αρπάζω, to seize.
συν-αυξάνομαι, to grow together.
συν-δέομαι, to be bound with.
σύν-δεσμος, a bond, band.
συν-δοξάζομαι, to be glorified with.
σύν-δουλος, a fellow-slave. [τρέχω.
συν-δρομή, a concourse: ἔδραμον.
συν-εγείρω, to raise with.
συν-έδριον, any assembly, council, sanhedrin: ἕζομαι, to sit.
συν-ειδέω, –δον, to be conscious, aware.
συν-είδησις, consciousness, the conscience.
σύν-ειμι, to be with.   [science.
σύν-ειμι, to come together.
συν-εις-έρχομαι, to enter with.
συν-έκ-δημος, a fellow-traveller.
συν-εκλεκτός, chosen with.
συν-ελαύνω, to drive together.
συν-επι-μαρτυρέω, to bear joint witness.
*συν-επι-τίθημι, to join in attack.
συν-έπομαι, to follow with.
συν-εργέω, to work with.
συν-εργός, fellow-workman: ἔργον.
συν-έρχομαι, to come together.
συν-εσθίω, to eat with.
σύν-εσις, understanding: fr. συνίημι.
συν-ετός, wise, intelligent: id.
συν-ευ-δοκέω, to consent to.
συν-ευ-ωχέομαι, to feast with; ἔχω.
συν-εφ-ίστημι, to rise against.
συν-έχω, to hold together, urge, [oppress.
συν-ήδομαι, to delight in.
συν-ήθεια, custom, habit: ἔθω, to be wont.   [ἥλιξ, of same age.
συν-ηλικιώτης, one of equal age:
συν-θάπτομαι, to be buried with.
συν-θλάομαι, to be broken.
συν-θλίβω, to press upon.
συν-θρύπτω, to break, crush.
συν-ίημι, –ιέω, to consider, be wise.
συν-ιστάνω = συνιστάω.
συν-ιστάω, –ίστημι, to commend, establish, hold together.
συν-οδεύω, to journey with: ὁδός.
συν-οδία, a caravan.
συνοιδα see συνειδέω.
συν-οικέω, to dwell together.
συν-οικο-δομέομαι, to be built together: δέμω, to build. [band.
συν-ομ-ιλέω, to talk with: ἴλη, a
συν-ομ-ορέω, to adjoin: ὁμός, common, & ὅρος, boundary.
συν-οχή, distress: ἔχω.
συν-τάσσω, to arrange, appoint.
συν-τέλεια, a finishing.
συν-τελέω, to accomplish.
συν-τέμνω, to cut short.   [mind.
συν-τηρέω, to preserve, keep in

συν-τίθημι, to place together.
συν-τόμως, concisely: τέμνω, to cut.
συν-τρέχω, to run together.
συν-τρίβω, to break, bruise.
σύν-τριμμα, a breaking, ruin.
σύν-τροφος, foster-brother: τρέφω.
συν-τυγχάνω, to meet with.
συν-υπο-κρίνομαι, to dissemble with.
συν-υπ-ουργέω, to help together: ἔργον.
συν-ωδίνω, to travail together.
συν-ωμοσία, a conspiracy: ὄμνυμι.
σύρτις, a quicksand. Lat., syrtis.
σύρω, to draw, drag.
συ-σπαράσσω, to convulse. [sign.
σύσ-σημον, a sign, signal: σῆμα,
σύσ-σωμος, in the same body: σῶμα.
συ-στασιαστής, fellow-insurgent: στάσις.
συ-στατικός, commendatory: ἴστημι.
συ-σταυρόω, to crucify with.
συ-στέλλω, to enshroud, shorten.
συ-στενάζω, to groan together.
συ-στοιχέω, to march together: στεῖχω, to move.
συ-στρατιώτης, a fellow-soldier.
συ-στρέφω, to gather together.
συ-στροφή, a concourse, conspiracy.
συ-σχηματίζομαι, to be conformed:
σφαγή, slaughter.   [σχῆμα.
σφάγιον, victim (for sacrifice).
σφάζω, –άττω, to kill, slaughter.
σφόδρα, vehemently.
σφοδρῶς, vehemently.
σφραγίζω, to seal, accredit.
σφραγίς, a seal, signet.
*σφυδρόν = σφυρόν.
σφυρίς = σπυρίς.
σφυρόν, the ankle.
σχεδόν, nearly: fr. ἔχω.
σχῆμα, fashion, habit: fr. ἔχω.
σχίζω, to divide.
σχίσμα, a division.
σχοινίον, a cord, rope.
σχολάζω, to be at leisure. [stop.
σχολή, leisure, a school: fr. ἔχω, to
σώζω, to heal, save: fr. σάω, to
σῶμα, the body.   [keep.
σωματικός, pertaining to the body.
σωματικῶς, bodily.
σωρεύω, to heap up.
σωτήρ, a saviour: fr. σώζω.
σωτηρία, deliverance, salvation.
σωτήριον, safety, salvation.
σωτήριος, saving.
σω-φρονέω, to be sober-minded: fr. σῶς, sound, & φρήν.
σω-φρονίζω, to admonish.
σω-φρονισμός, wise discretion.
σω-φρόνως, soberly.
σω-φροσύνη, soberness of mind.
σώ-φρων, sober-minded.

T, τ, tau, t. τ′ = 300; ͵τ = 300,000.
ταβέρναι, taverns. Lat., tabernae.
τάγμα, rank, order.
τακτός, appointed: τάσσω.
ταλαιπωρέω, to be miserable.
ταλαιπωρία, misery.
ταλαίπωρος, miserable: fr. τάλας, wretched.
ταλαντιαῖος, of a talent weight.
τάλαντον, a talent (abt. £200).
ταλιθά, ταλει–, a maiden. Aram.
ταμεῖον, ταμιεῖον, a storehouse: fr.
τανῦν, now.   [τέμνω, to cut.
τάξις, arrangement, style.
ταπεινός, humble.
ταπεινο-φροσύνη, lowliness of mind.

*ταπεινό-φρων, lowly in mind: φρήν, φρονέω.
ταπεινόω, to be humbled.
ταπείνωσις, humiliation.
ταράσσω, to agitate.
ταραχή, agitation.
τάραχος, a commotion.   [tarus.
ταρταρόω, to thrust down to Tartάσσω, to appoint.
ταῦρος, a bull.
ταυτά, τὰ αὐτά, the same things.
ταῦτα, &c., from οὖτος.
ταφή, a burial: θάπτω.
τάφος, a burial-place.
τάχα, peradventure.
*τάχειον = τάχιον.
ταχέως, soon, quickly.
ταχινός, swift, impending.
τάχιον, –χειον, more swiftly.
τάχιστα, very quickly.
τάχος, quickness, speed.
ταχύ, speedily.
ταχύς, quick.
τέ, and, both.
τεῖχος, a wall.
τεκμήριον, a sign, proof.
τεκνίον, a little child: fr. τίκτω.
τεκνο-γονέω, to bear children: fr. τίκτω, & γονή, γίνομαι.
τεκνο-γονία, child-bearing.
τέκνον, a child.   [τρέφω.
τεκνο-τροφέω, to bring up children:
τέκτων, a carpenter.
τέλειος, complete, mature: fr. τέλος.
τελειότης, maturity, completeness.
τελειόω, to make perfect.
τελείως, perfectly.
τελείωσις, perfection.
τελειωτής, one who makes perfect.
τελεσ-φορέω, to bring to maturity:
τελευτάω, to finish, die.   [φέρω.
τελευτή, end, death.
τελέω, to bring to an end, pay.
τέλος, an end, terminus, tax.
τελ-ώνης, a tax-collector: ὠνός,
τελ-ώνιον, a tax-office. [purchase.
τέρας, a wonder.
τεσσαράκοντα, τεσσε–, forty. [years.
τεσσαρακοντα-ετής, τεσσε–, of 40
τεσσαρακοντα-τέσσαρες, τεσσε–forty-τέσσαρες, –ρα, τέσσε–, four. [four.
τεσσερ-και-δέκατος, fourteenth.
τεσσερ– see τεσσαρ–.
τεταρταῖος, on the fourth day.
τέταρτος, fourth.
τετρά-γωνος, four-cornered: γωνία.
τετράδιον, a quaternion, four men.
τετρακισ-χίλιοι, four thousand.
τετρακόσιοι, –σια, four hundred.
τετρά-μηνον, –νος, four months:
τετρα-πλόος, –πλοῦς, four-fold. [μήν.
τετρά-πους, four-footed.
τετρ-αρχέω, to be a tetrarch: ἄρχω.
τετρ-άρχης, –ράρ–, a tetrarch.
τεύχω see τυγχάνω. [τέφρα, ashes.
τεφρόω, to reduce to ashes: fr.
τέχνη, skill, craft.
τεχνίτης, a workman.
τήκομαι, to melt.   [& αὐγή.
τηλ-αυγῶς, clearly: fr. τῆλε, afar,
τηλικ-οῦτος, so great.
τηρέω, to keep, guard.
τήρησις, keeping, a prison.
τίθημι, ἔθηκα, ἐθίμην, θῶ, &c., to place, put aside, make, constitute, determine, &c.
τίκτω, ἔτεκον, to bring forth.
τίλλω, to pluck off.
τιμάω, to estimate, **honour**.

τιμή, price, value, honour.
τίμιος, in honour.
τιμιότης, preciousness.
τιμ-ωρέω, to punish: οὖρος, ὁράω.
τιμ-ωρία, punishment.
τίνω = τίω.
τις, any one, some one.
τίς, who, which, what. [titulus.
τίτλος, title, inscription. Lat.,
τίω, to honour, pay justice, suffer
τοι, truly, indeed. [penalty.
τοι-γαρ-οῦν, consequently.
τοί-νυν, now, therefore.
τοιόσ-δε, of this kind.
τοιοῦτος, such like.
τοῖχος, wall of a house.
τόκος, interest: fr. τίκτω.
τολμάω, to have courage: fr. τλάω,
  to venture.
τολμηρότερον, more boldly.
*τολμηροτερῶς, more boldly.
τολμητής, presumptuous.
τομώτερος, keener: fr. τέμνω, to cut.
τόξον, a bow: fr. τυχεῖν, τυγχάνω.
τοπάζιον, the topaz.
τόπος, place, opportunity.
τοσοῦτος, so much, so many.
τότε, then.
τοῦ, his (gen. of ὁ).
τοὐναντίον, on the contrary.
τοὔνομα, the name.
τουτέστι, τοῦτ᾽ ἔστι, that is.
τούτο, &c., from οὗτος.
τράγος, a he-goat: fr. τρώγω.
τράπεζα, table: fr. τέτρα, four, &
  πέζα, foot. [changer.
τραπεζίτης, -ζείτης, a money-
τραῦμα, a wound: fr. τείρω, to wear
τραυματίζω, to wound. [out.
τραχηλίζομαι, to be exposed.
τράχηλος, the neck.
τραχύς, rugged.
τρεῖς, τρία, three.
τρέμω, to tremble.
τρέφω, to bring up.
τρέχω, to run. [out.
*τρῆμα, a hole: fr. τείρω, to wear
τριάκοντα, thirty.
τρια-κόσιοι, three hundred.
τρί-βολος, a thistle: fr. βάλλω.
τρίβος, a road, way: fr. τρίβω, to
  rub. [ἔτος.
τρι-ετία, a space of three years:
τρίζω, to grate, gnash.
τρί-μηνον, a space of three months:
τρίς, thrice. [μήν.
τρί-στεγον, a third floor: στέγω,
  to cover.
τρισ-χίλιοι, three thousand.
τρίτος, the third.
τρίχινος, made of hair.
τριχός see θρίξ.
τρόμος, a trembling: fr. τρέμω.
τροπή, a turning: fr. τρέπω, to turn.
τρόπος, manner, character: id.
τροπο-φορέω, to bear one's manners:
  φέρω.
τροφή, food, nourishment: fr.
  τρέφω.
τροφός, a nurse. [ment.
*τροφο-φορέω, -ῶ, to bring nourish-
τροχιά, the track of a wheel: fr.
τροχός, a wheel, circle. [τρέχω.
τρύβλιον, a dish, platter.
τρυγάω, to gather grapes.
τρυγών, a turtle-dove: fr. τρύζω,
  to murmur. [to rub down.
τρυμαλιά, eye of a needle: fr. τρύω,
τρύπημα, a hole, eye of a needle.

τρυφάω, to live in pleasure.
τρυφή, luxury.
τρώγω, to eat. [happen.
τυγχάνω, τεύξω, to obtain, to
τυμπανίζομαι, to be tortured: fr.
  τύμπανον, a stake.
*τυπικῶς, typically.
τύπος, figure, form, type.
τύπτω, to beat, strike.
τυρβάζομαι, to be agitated: fr.
  τύρβη, tumult.
τυφλός, blind, ignorant.
τυφλόω, to make blind.
τύφομαι, to smoke.
τυφόομαι, to be puffed up.
τυφωνικός, tempestuous: fr. τυφώς.
τυχόν, it may be. [whirlwind.

Υ, υ, upsilon, u, υʹ = 400; υ, =
  400,000.
ὑακίνθινος, resembling a jacinth.
ὑάκινθος, a jacinth.
ὑάλινος, glassy, transparent.
ὕαλος, crystal. [shamefully.
ὑβρίζω, to be insolent, treat
ὕβρις, insolence, injury.
ὑβριστής, an insolent person.
ὑγιαίνω, to be in health.
ὑγιής, sound, in health.
ὑγρός, moist, green.
ὑδρία, a water-pot.
ὑδρο-ποτέω, to drink water: πίνω.
ὑδρωπικός, dropsical.
ὕδωρ, water.
ὑετός, rain: fr. ὕω, to rain.
υἱο-θεσία, sonship: τίθημι.
υἱός, a son.
ὕλη, wood, fuel.
ὑμέτερος, your.
ὑμνέω, to sing praise.
ὕμνος, hymn.
ὑπ-άγω, to go away.
ὑπ-ακοή, obedience.
ὑπ-ακούω, to listen, obey.
ὕπ-ανδρος, married: ἀνήρ. [face.
ὑπ-αντάω, to meet: ἄντα, face to
ὑπ-άντησις, a meeting.
ὕπαρξις, property.
ὑπάρχοντα, property.
ὑπ-άρχω, to be, subsist.
ὑπ-είκω, to yield.
ὑπ-εν-αντίος, adverse, an adversary:
  ἄντα, face to face.
ὑπέρ, for, instead of, over, above:
  in comp. denotes superiority or in
  aid of. [elated.
ὑπερ-αίρομαι, to exalt self, be
ὑπέρ-ακμος, past the flower of life:
  ἀκμή, prime of life.
ὑπερ-άνω, far above. [ly.
ὑπερ-αυξάνω, to increase exceeding-
ὑπερ-βαίνω, to go beyond. [λω.
ὑπερ-βαλλόντως, exceedingly. βάλ-
ὑπερ-βάλλω, to surpass.
ὑπερ-βολή, excess, pre-eminence.
*ὑπερ-εγώ = ὑπὲρ ἐγώ.
ὑπερ-εῖδον, -ίδω, to overlook, bear
  with: fr. ὑπεροράω, to overlook.
ὑπερ-έκεινα, beyond. [measure.
*ὑπερ-εκ-περισσοῦ, -σῶς, beyond
ὑπερ-εκ-τείνω, to stretch beyond.
ὑπερ-εκ-χύνομαι, to overflow: χέω,
  to pour.
ὑπερ-εν-τυγχάνω, to intercede for.
ὑπερ-έχω, to excel, surpass.
ὑπερ-ηφανία, pride: φαίνω.
ὑπερ-ήφανος, proud.
*ὑπερ-λίαν, very much.
ὑπερ-νικάω, to gain a victory.

ὑπέρ-ογκος, immoderate.
ὑπερ-οχή, pre-eminence: ἔχω.
ὑπερ-περισσεύω, to superabound.
ὑπερ-περισσῶς, superabundantly.
ὑπερ-πλεονάζω, to superabound.
ὑπερ-υψόω, to highly exalt.
ὑπερ-φρονέω, to think highly of
  self: φρήν.
ὑπερῷον, an upper room.
ὑπ-έχω, to place under.
ὑπ-ήκοος, submissive: ἀκοή.
ὑπ-ηρετέω, to assist, serve: ἐρέσσω,
  to row. [id.
ὑπ-ηρέτης, an appointed servant:
ὕπνος, sleep.
ὑπό, under, by. In comp. ὑπό
  denotes subjection, diminution,
  concealment.
ὑπο-βάλλω, to instigate, suborn.
ὑπο-γραμμός, copy to write from:
  γράφω.
ὑπό-δειγμα, a copy, example.
ὑπο-δείκνυμι, to shew, point out.
ὑπο-δέομαι, to bind on sandals.
ὑπο-δέχομαι, to receive hospitality.
ὑπό-δημα, a sandal, shoe.
ὑπό-δικος, under judgment: δίκη.
ὑπο-ζύγιον, a beast of burden:
  ζυγόν, yoke.
ὑπο-ζώννυμι, to undergird.
ὑπο-κάτω, underneath.
ὑπο-κρίνομαι, to pretend.
ὑπό-κρισις, dissimulation.
ὑπο-κριτής, a dissembler.
ὑπο-λαμβάνω, to take up, assume.
*ὑπό-λειμμα, -λιμμα, a remnant.
ὑπο-λείπομαι, to be left behind.
ὑπο-λήνιον, a wine-vat: ληνός.
ὑπο-λιμπάνω, to leave behind:
  λείπω.
ὑπο-μένω, to endure, remain.
ὑπο-μιμνήσκω, to remind, call to
  mind. [desire.
ὑπόμνησις, recollection: μάω, to
ὑπο-μονή, patient endurance: μένω.
ὑπο-νοέω, to conjecture: νοῦς.
ὑπό-νοια, a surmising.
ὑπο-πλέω, to sail under shelter.
ὑπο-πνέω, to blow gently.
ὑπο-πόδιον, a footstool: πούς.
ὑπό-στασις, assurance, substance:
ὑπο-στέλλω, to draw back. [ἵστημι.
ὑπο-στολή, a drawing back.
ὑπο-στρέφω, to turn back.
ὑπο-στρώννυμι, -ύω, to strew under.
ὑπο-ταγή, subjection.
ὑπο-τάσσω, to subject.
ὑπο-τίθημι, to lay down, suggest.
ὑπο-τρέχω, to sail under. [τύπος.
ὑπο-τύπωσις, outline, delineation:
ὑπο-φέρω, to bear up under.
ὑπο-χωρέω, to withdraw.
ὑπ-ωπιάζω, to bruise, weary out:
ὗς, ὑός, a hog, sow. [ὤψ, face.
ὕσσωπος, hyssop. Heb.
ὑστερέω, to come short.
ὑστέρημα, deficiency, poverty.
ὑστέρησις, poverty.
ὕστερον, afterwards.
ὕστερος, latter.
*ὑφαίνω, to weave.
ὑφαντός, woven.
ὑψηλός, elevated: fr. ὕψι, aloft.
ὑψηλο-φρονέω, to be high-minded:
  φρήν. [aloft.
ὕψιστος, most elevated: fr. ὕψι,
ὕψος, exaltation: id.
ὑψόω, to elevate.
ὕψωμα, an elevation.

Ψ, φ, *phi, ph*, φ´ = 500; φ, = 500,000.
φάγος, a glutton.
φάγω see ἐσθίω.
φαιλόνης, φελ- (*better* φαινόλης), a cloak. *Latin, paenula.* [shine.
φαίνω, to shine, appear: φάω, to
φανερός, manifest, clear: φαίνω.
φανερόω, to manifest.
φανερῶς, manifestly.
φανέρωσις, manifestation.
φανός, torch, light: φαίνω.
φαντάζομαι, to appear: *id.*
φαντασία, show, display: *id.*
φάντασμα, a phantom, an appari-
φάραγξ, valley, gorge. [tion: *id.*
φαρμακεία, magic, enchantment.
φαρμακεύς, a magician.
*φάρμακον, a drug, enchantment: Rev. ix. 21, WH.
φαρμακός, a magician.
φάσις, report, disclosure: φημί.
φάσκω, to assert, profess.
φάτνη, a manger, crib: fr. πατέομαι.
φαῦλος, vile, wicked. [to eat.
φέγγος, brightness, splendour.
φείδομαι, to spare, forbear.
φειδομένως, sparingly.
φελόνης see φαιλόνης. [hold.
φέρω, οἴσω, ἤνεγκα, to bring, up-
φεύγω, to flee.
φήμη, a voice, rumour.
φημί, to say.
*φημίζω, to speak, report.
φθάνω, to precede.
φθαρτός, corruptible.
φθέγγομαι, to speak aloud.
φθείρω, to corrupt.
φθιν-οπωρινός, autumnal: fr. φθίνω, to waste, & ὀπώρα.
φθόγγος, a sound: fr. φθέγγομαι.
φθονέω, to envy.
φθόνος, envy.
φθορά, corruption: fr. φθείρω.
φιάλη, a bowl, goblet.
φιλ-άγαθος, loving, goodness.
φιλ-αδελφία, brotherly love.
φιλ-άδελφος, loving brother or sister. [ἀνήρ.
φίλ-ανδρος, loving one's husband:
φιλ-ανθρωπία, philanthropy.
φιλ-ανθρώπως, benevolently.
φιλ-αργυρία, love of money.
φιλ-άργυρος, money-loving: ἀργός.
φίλ-αυτος, self-loving. [white.
φιλέω, to love, kiss.
φίλη, a female friend: see φίλος.
φιλ-ήδονος, pleasure-loving: ἡδονή.
φίλημα, a kiss.
φιλία, friendship.
φιλό-θεος, a lover of God.
φιλο-νεικία, love of dispute: νεικέω, to wrangle.
φιλό-νεικος, strife-loving.
φιλο-ξενία, hospitality.
φιλό-ξενος, hospitable.
φιλο-πρωτεύω, to love pre-eminence: [πρῶτος.
φίλος, loving, a friend.
φιλο-σοφία, love of wisdom.
φιλό-σοφος, wisdom-loving.
φιλό-στοργος, tenderly loving: στέργω, to love.
φιλό-τεκνος, child-loving.
φιλο-τιμέομαι, to be ambitious.
φιλο-φρόνως, in a friendly manner.
φιλό-φρων, friendly, kind: φρήν.
φιμόω, to put to silence: fr. φιμός, muzzle. [burn.
φλογίζω, to inflame: fr. φλέγω, to
φλ ξ, a flame.

φλυαρέω, to talk folly.
φλύαρος, an idle talker.
φοβέομαι, to be afraid: fr. φέβομαι,
φοβερός, fearful. [to be afraid.
φόβητρον, -ηθρον, a terror.
φόβος, fear.
φοῖνιξ, a palm-branch. [slay.
φονεύς, -έως, a murderer: fr. φένω, to
φονεύω, to murder.
φόνος, murder. [φέρω.
φορέω, to bear about, wear: fr.
φόρος, tribute, tax.
φορτίζω, to load.
φορτίον, a load.
φόρτος, load, cargo. [flagellum.
φραγέλλιον, a whip, scourge. *Latin,*
φραγελλόω, to whip, scourge. *Latin, flagello.*
φραγμός, a hedge, fence: fr. φράσσω.
φράζω, to tell, expound.
φράσσω, to fence, stop.
φρέαρ, a pit, well.
φρεν-απατάω, to deceive: ἀπάτη.
φρεν-απάτης, a deceiver.
φρένες (φρήν), the midriff, mind.
φρήν see φρένες.
φρίσσω, to shudder.
φρονέω, to think, judge: fr. φρήν.
φρόνημα, thought, care for.
φρόνησις, understanding, wisdom.
φρόνιμος, intelligent: fr. φρήν.
φρονίμως, prudently.
φροντίζω, to think, be careful.
φρουρέω, to guard: fr. πρό, ὁράω.
φρυάσσω, to behave arrogantly.
φρύγανον, a dry twig; fr. φρύγω,
φυγή, flight. [to parch.
φυλακή, guard, watch.
φυλακίζω, to imprison.
φυλακτήριον, an amulet, phylactery.
φύλαξ, a keeper, guard. [keep self.
φυλάσσω, to keep, guard: *mid.* to
φυλή, a tribe: fr. φύω.
φύλλον, a leaf: fr. φλέω, to abound.
φῦμι see φύω. [to mix.
φύραμα, a kneaded mass: fr. φύρω,
φυσικός, according to nature.
φυσικῶς, naturally. [bellows.
φυσιόω, to inflate, puff up: fr. φῦσα,
φύσις, nature, birth, propensity, custom.
φυσίωσις, inflation of mind.
φυτεία, a plant.
φυτεύω, to plant.
φύω, to produce.
φωλεός, den, lair. [φωνή.
φωνέω, to sound, call, name: fr.
φωνή, a sound, voice.
φῶς, light: fr. φάω, to shine.
φωστήρ, light-bearer.
φωσ-φόρος, the day-star: φέρω.
φωτεινός, -τινός, full of light.
φωτίζω, to enlighten.
φωτισμός, radiance, shining.

X, χ, *chi, ch*, χ´ = 600; χ, = 600,000.
χαίρω, to rejoice, hail.
χάλαζα, hailstorm, hailstones.
χαλάω, to let down.
χαλεπός, hard, harsh.
χαλιν-αγωγέω, to bridle, curb: ἄγω.
χαλινός, a bridle. [copper.
χάλκεος, -οῦς, made of brass or
χαλκεύς, coppersmith.
χαλκηδών, χαλκε-, a chalcedony.
χαλκίον, a brazen vessel.
χαλκο-λίβανον, fine brass.
χαλκός, copper, brass.
χαμαί, on *or* to the ground.

χαρά, joy, gladness: fr. χαίρω.
χάραγμα, a stamp, sculpture: fr. χαράσσω, to engrave.
χαρακτήρ, impress, likeness.
χάραξ, a palisade: fr. χαράσσω, to make pointed.
χαρίζομαι, to gratify, bestow, forgive.
χάριν, for the sake of, because of.
χάρις, grace: fr. χαίρω.
χάρισμα, a gift.
χαριτόω, to take into favour.
χάρτης, paper. *Latin, charta.*
χάσμα, chasm, gulf: fr. χάσκω, to yawn.
χεῖλος, a lip, language: *fig.* shore.
χειμάζομαι, to be tempest-tossed: fr. χεῖμα, cold, storm.
χείμαρ-ρος, a winter-torrent: ῥέω.
χειμών, winter, foul weather.
χείρ, a hand. [ἄγω.
χειρ-αγωγέω, to lead by the hand.
χειρ-αγωγός, a leader by the hand.
χειρό-γραφον, hand-writing, obligation: γράφω. [ποιέω.
χειρο-ποίητος, made by hands:
χειρο-τονέω, to choose by vote, appoint: τείνω, to stretch out.
χείρων, -ρον, inferior.
*χερουβίμ, -βείν, cherubim. *Heb.*
χήρα, a widow.
χθές, ἐχθές, yesterday.
χιλιάδες (χιλιάς), thousands.
χιλί-αρχος (*lit.* ruler of 1,000 men), a military tribune: ἄρχω.
χιλιάς, a thousand. (subst.)
χίλιοι, a thousand. (adj.)
χιτών, a tunic, vest.
χιών, snow.
χλαμύς, a robe, cloak. [a jest.
χλευάζω, to scoff, deride: fr. χλεύη,
χλιαρός, lukewarm.
χλωρός, green, yellowish, pale: fr. χλόη, young grass.
χξς´, six hundred and sixty six.
χοϊκός, made of earth: fr. χόος, dust.
χοῖνιξ, a choenix (abt. 2 pints).
χοῖρος, a pig, swine.
χολάω, to be enraged.
χολή, gall, bitter wrath.
χόος, χοῦς, dust: fr. χέω, to pour.
χορ-ηγέω, to supply: ἄγω.
χορός, a dance with singing,
χορτάζω, to satiate.
χόρτασμα, food, sustenance.
χόρτος, grass, herbage.
χοῦς see χόος.
χράομαι, to make use of.
χράω, to lend.
χρεία, need, business. [debtor.
χρε-ωφειλέτης, χρεοφ-, χρεοφιλ-, a
χρή, it is meet.
χρῄζω, to have need.
χρῆμα, money, wealth: χράομαι.
χρηματίζω, to instruct (divinely), to be named.
χρηματισμός, an oracle.
χρήσιμος, profitable.
χρῆσις, manner of using.
χρηστεύομαι, to be kind.
χρηστο-λογία, kind words.
χρηστός, good, goodness: fr. χράομαι.
χρηστότης, goodness.
χρῖσμα, χρί-, an unction: fr. χρίω.
χριστιανός, a Christian.
ὁ χριστός, the anointed One.
χρίω, to anoint.
χρονίζω, to linger.
χρόνος, time, delay.

χρονο-τριβέω, to spend time: τρίβω, to wear away.

χρύσεος, -οῦς, golden.

χρυσίον, gold, things made of gold.

χρυσο-δακτύλιος, wearing gold rings: δάκτυλος.

χρυσό-λιθος, a chrysolite.

χρυσό-πρασος, a chrysoprase: πράσον, a leek.

χρυσός, gold.

χρυσοῦς see χρύσεος.

χουσόω, to adorn with gold: to gild.

χρώς, the skin: fr. χοάω, to graze.

χωλός, lame, crippled.

χώρα, country, land, fields.

χωρέω, to give place, receive.

χωριζω, to separate.

χωρίον, a field, possession.

χωρίς, apart from, besides. [corus.

χῶρος, north-west wind.   Latin.

Ψ, ψ, psi, ps, ψ' = 700; ψ, = 700,000.

ψάλλω, to sing (to a harp): fr. ψάω, to touch lightly.

ψαλμός, a psalm.

ψευδ-άδελφος, a false brother.

ψευδ-απόστολος, a false apostle.

ψευδής, false, lying.

ψευδο-διδάσκαλος, a false teacher.

ψυδο-λόγος, false-speaking.

ψεύδομαι, to speak falsely.

ψευδο-μάρτυρ (or -τυς), a false witness.   [witness.

ψευδο-μαρτυρέω, to bear false

ψευδο-μαρτυρία, false testimony.

ψευδο-προ-φήτης, a false prophet.

ψεῦδος, falsehood, lying.

ψευδό-χριστος, a false Christ.

ψευδ-ώνυμος, falsely called: ὄνομα.

ψεῦσμα, falsehood.

ψεύστης, a deceiver.

ψηλαφάω, to touch, feel after.

ψηφίζω, to calculate.

ψῆφος, a pebble, hence a vote.

ψιθυρισμός, a whispering, scandal.

ψιθυριστής, a whisperer.

ψιχίον, a crumb: fr. ψίξ, a morsel.

ψυχή, life, soul, person: fr ψύχω, to breathe.

ψυχικός, animal, natural.

ψύχομαι, to grow cold.

ψῦχος, cold.   (subst.)

ψυχρός, cold, cool. (adj.) [crumble.

ψωμίζω, to feed : fr. ψάω, to

ψωμίον, bit, morsel.

ψώχω, to rub in pieces.

Ω, ω, omega, o, ω' = 800; ω, = 800,000. τὸ Ω, the Omega.

ὦ, O ! | oh !

ὧδε, here, herein.

ᾠδή, an ode, song : fr. ἀείδω, to sing.

ὠδίν, pangs, labour.

ὠδίνω, to be in travail.

ὦμος, a shoulder.

ὠνέομαι, to buy.

ὠόν, ᾠόν, an egg.

ὥρα, hour, time.

ὡραῖος, ripe, mature, beautiful.

ὠρύομαι, to roar.

ὡς, as, as if, how, when.   [Heb.

ὡσαννά, ὡ-, Hosanna, save now !

ὡσ-αύτως, likewise.

ὡσ-εί, as it were, about.

ὥσ-περ, as, just as.

ὡσ-περ-εί, as if, as it were.

ὥσ-τε, so that, therefore.

*ὠτάριον, a (small) ear: fr. οὖς.

ὠτίον, the ear : id.

ὠφέλεια, -λία, usefulness, profit fr. ὀφέλλω, to increase.

ὠφελέω, to benefit.

ὠφέλιμος, profitable.

THE
ENGLISHMAN'S GREEK CONCORDANCE.

A, *alpha.*

Rev. 1: 8. I am *Alpha* and Omega, the beginning
  11. I am *Alpha* and Omega, the first and the
  21: 6. I am *Alpha* and Omega, the beginning
  22:13. I am *Alpha* and Omega, the beginning

ἀϐαρής, *abarees.*

2Co.11: 9. kept myself *from being burdensome*

ἀϐϐᾶ, *abba.*

Mar 14:36. And he said, *Abba,* Father,
Ro. 8:15. whereby we cry, *Abba,* Father.
Gal. 4: 6. into your hearts, crying, *Abba,* Father.

ἄϐυσσος, *abussos.*

Lu. 8:31. command them to go out into the *deep.*
Ro. 10: 7. Who shall descend into the *deep?*
Rev. 9: 1. the key of the *bottomless* pit.
  2. And he opened the *bottomless* pit ;
  11. the angel of the *bottomless pit,*
  11: 7. that ascendeth out of the *bottomless pit*
  17: 8. shall ascend out of the *bottomless pit,*
  20: 1. having the key of the *bottomless pit*
  3. cast him into the *bottomless pit,*

ἀγαθοεργέω, *agathoergeo.*

1Ti. 6:18. *That* they *do good,* that they be rich in

ἀγαθοποιέω, *agathopoyeo.*

Mar. 3: 4. *to do good* on the sabbath days,
Lu. 6: 9. on the sabbath days *to do good,*
  33. ye *do good* to them *which do good*
  35. and *do good,* and lend,
Acts 14:17. in that he *did good,* and gave us
1Pet 2:15. *with well doing* ye may put to silence
  20. *when* ye *do well,* and suffer (for it),
  3: 6. as long as ye *do well,* and are not afraid
  17. ye suffer for *well doing,* than for evil
3 Joh. 11. He *that doeth good* is of God:

ἀγαθοποιΐα, *agathopoiya.*

1Pet. 4:19. their souls (to him) in *well doing,*

ἀγαθοποιός, *agathopoyos.*

1Pet. 2:14. for the praise of them *that do well.*

ἀγαθός, *agathos.*

Mat. 5:45. to rise on the evil and on the *good,*
  7:11. give *good* gifts unto your children,
  — which is in heaven give *good things*
  17. every *good* tree bringeth forth good fruit ;
  18. A *good* tree cannot bring forth evil
  12:34. ye, being evil, speak *good things?*
  35. A *good* man out of the *good* treasure of
   the heart bringeth forth *good things :*
  19:16. *Good* Master, what *good thing* shall I do,
  17. Why callest thou me *good?* (there is)
   none *good*
  20:15. Is thine eye evil, because I am *good?*
  22:10. many as they found, both bad and *good:*
  25:21. Well done, (thou) *good* and faithful
  23. Well done, *good* and faithful servant;
Mar 10:17. *Good* Master, what shall I do that I
  18. Why callest thou me *good?* (there is)
   none *good*
Lu. 1:53. hath filled the hungry with *good things;*
  6:45. A *good* man out of the *good* treasure of
   his heart bringeth forth that which is
   good ;
  8: 8. And other fell on *good* ground,
  15. which in an honest and *good* heart,
  10:42. Mary hath chosen that *good* part,
  11:13. know how to give *good* gifts unto your
  12:18. will I bestow all my fruits and my *goods.*
  19. Soul, thou hast much *goods* laid up
  16:25. thy lifetime receivedst thy *good things,*
  18:18. *Good* Master, what shall I do to inherit
  19. Why callest thou me *good?* none (is)
   good,
  19:17. Well, thou *good* servant: because thou
  23:50. (he was) a *good* man, and a just:
Joh. 1:46(47). Can there any *good thing* come out
  5:29. they that have done *good,* unto the
  7:12. some said, He is a *good* man: others
Acts 9:36. this woman was full of *good works*
  11:24. For he was a *good* man, and full of the
  23: 1. I have lived in all *good* conscience
Ro. 2: 7. by patient continuance *in well* doing
  10. peace, to every man that worketh *good,*
  3: 8. Let us do evil, that *good* may come ?
  5: 7. for a *good* man some would even dare
  7:12. commandment holy, and just, and *good.*
  13. Was then that which is *good* made death
  — working death in me by that which is *good ;*
  18. in my flesh, dwelleth no *good thing :*

Ro. 7:19. For the *good* that I would I do not:
    8:28. all things work together for *good*
    9:11. neither having done any *good* or evil,
    10:15. and bring glad tidings of *good things!*
    12: 2. ye may prove what (is) that *good*, and
      9. cleave to that which is *good*.
      21. overcome evil with *good*.
    13: 3. rulers are not a terror to *good* works,
      — do that which is *good*,
      4. the minister of God to thee for *good*.
    14:16. Let not then your *good* be evil spoken of:
    15: 2. please (his) neighbour for (his) *good* to
    16:19. wise unto that which is *good*,
2Co. 5:10. whether (it be) *good* or bad.
    9: 8. may abound to every *good* work:
Gal. 6: 6. him that teacheth in all *good things*.
    10. let us do *good* unto all (men),
Eph. 2:10. created in Christ Jesus unto *good* works,
    4:28. with (his) hands the thing which is *good*,
    29. but that which is *good* to the use
    6: 8. whatsoever *good* thing any man doeth,
Phi. 1: 6. he which hath begun a *good* work
Col. 1:10. being fruitful in every *good* work,
1Th. 3: 6. ye have *good* remembrance of us
    5:15. ever follow that which is *good*,
2Th. 2:16. consolation and *good* hope through grace,
    17. stablish you in every *good* word and work.
1Ti. 1: 5. a pure heart, and (of) a *good* conscience,
    19. Holding faith, and a *good* conscience,
    2:10. professing godliness with *good* works.
    5:10. have diligently followed every *good* work.
2 Ti. 2:21. (and) prepared unto every *good* work.
    3:17. throughly furnished unto all *good* works.
Tit. 1:16. and unto every *good* work reprobate.
    2: 5. keepers at home, *good*, obedient to
    10. shewing all *good* fidelity ;
    3: 1. to be ready to every *good* work,
Philem. 6. the acknowledging of every *good thing*
    14. that thy *benefit* should not be as
Heb. 9:11. an high priest of *good things* to come,
    10: 1. having a shadow of *good things* to come,
    13:21. Make you perfect in every *good* work
Jas. 1:17. Every *good* gift and every perfect gift
    3:17. full of mercy and *good* fruits,
1 Pet. 2:18. not only to the *good* and gentle,
    3:10. he that will love life, and see *good* days
    11. Let him eschew evil, and do *good ;*
    13. be followers of that which is *good ?*
    16. Having a *good* conscience ; that,
    — falsely accuse your *good* conversation
    21. the answer of a *good* conscience toward
3 Joh. 11. but that which is *good*.

ἀγαθωσύνη, *agathōsunee*.

Ro. 15:14. ye also are full of *goodness*, filled
Gal. 5:22. longsuffering, gentleness, *goodness*, faith,
Eph. 5: 9. the fruit of the Spirit (is) in all *goodness*
2 Th. 1:11. all the good pleasure of (his) *goodness*,

ἀγαλλίασις, *agalliasis*.

Luke 1:14. thou shalt have joy and *gladness ;*
    44. the babe leaped in my womb for *joy*.
Acts 2:46. with *gladness* and singleness of heart,
Heb. 1: 9. hath anointed thee with the oil of *gladness*
Jude 24. presence of his glory with *exceeding joy*,

ἀγαλλιάω, *agalliao*.

Mat. 5:12. Rejoice, and *be exceeding glad :* for great

Lu. 1:47. my spirit *hath rejoiced* in God my Saviour.
    10:21. In that hour Jesus *rejoiced* in spirit,
Joh. 5:35. willing for a season *to rejoice* in his light.
    8:56. Your father Abraham *rejoiced* to see my
Acts 2:26. heart rejoice, and my tongue *was glad ;*
    16:34. set meat before them, and *rejoiced*,
1Pet.1: 6. Wherein ye *greatly rejoice*, though now for
      a season,
    8. ye *rejoice* with joy unspeakable and
    4:13. ye may be glad also *with exceeding joy*.
Rev.19: 7. *Let* us be glad and *rejoice*, and give

ἄγαμος, *agamos*.

1Cor.7: 8. I say therefore to the *unmarried* and
    11. if she depart, let her remain *unmarried*,
    32. He that is *unmarried* careth for
    34. The *unmarried* woman careth for the

ἀγανακτέω, *aganakteo*.

Mat.20:24. they *were moved with indignation* against
    21:15. they *were sore displeased*,
    26: 8. they *had indignation*, saying, To what
Mar 10:14. Jesus saw (it), he *was much displeased*,
    41. they began *to be much displeased*
    14: 4. some *that had indignation* within
Lu. 13:14. answered *with indignation*, because

ἀγανάκτησις, *aganakteesis*.

2Cor.7:11. yea, (what) *indignation*, yea, (what) fear,

ἀγαπάω, *agapao*.

Mat. 5:43. Thou shalt *love* thy neighbour, and
    44. I say unto you, *Love* your enemies,
    46. For if ye *love* them *which love* you,
    6:24. will hate the one, and *love* the other ;
    19:19. Thou shalt *love* thy neighbour as thyself.
    22:37. Thou shalt *love* the Lord thy God with all
      thy heart,
    39. Thou shalt *love* thy neighbour as
Mar 10:21. Jesus beholding him *loved* him, and
    12:30. thou shalt *love* the Lord thy God with
    31. Thou shalt *love* thy neighbour as thyself.
    33. *to love* him with all the heart, and
    — *to love* (his) neighbour as himself, is
Lu. 6:27. you which hear, *Love* your enemies,
    32. if ye *love* them *which love* you, what
    — sinners also *love* those *that love* them.
    35. *love* ye your enemies, and do good,
    7: 5. he *loveth* our nation, and he hath
    42. which of them *will love* him most ?
    47. are forgiven ; for she *loved* much :
    — little is forgiven, (the same) *loveth* little.
    10:27. Thou shalt *love* the Lord thy God with
    11:43. for ye *love* the uppermost seats in
    16:13. will hate the one, and *love* the other ;
Joh. 3:16. For God so *loved* the world, that he gave
    19. men *loved* darkness rather than light,
    35. The Father *loveth* the Son, and hath
    8:42. If God were your Father, ye would *love* me :
    10:17. Therefore *doth* my Father *love* me,
    11: 5. Now Jesus *loved* Martha, and her
    12:43. they *loved* the praise of men more
    13: 1. *having loved* his own which were in the
      world, he *loved* them unto the end.
    23. one of his disciples, whom Jesus *loved*.

Joh. 13:34. That ye *love* one another; as I *have loved* you, that ye also *love* one another.

14:15. If ye *love* me, keep my commandments.

21. he it is *that loveth* me: and he *that loveth* me *shall be loved* of my Father, and I *will love* him,

23. If a man *love* me, he will keep my words: and my Father *will love* him,

24. He *that loveth* me not keepeth not

28. If ye *loved* me, ye would rejoice,

31. world may know that I *love* the Father;

15: 9. As the Father *hath loved* me, so *have* I *loved* you: continue ye

12. my commandment, That ye *love* one another, as I *have loved* you.

17. I command you, that *ye love* one another.

17:23. *hast loved* them, as thou *hast loved* me.

24. thou *lovedst* me before the foundation

26. the love wherewith thou *hast loved* me

19:26. the disciple standing by, whom he *loved,*

21: 7. that disciple whom Jesus *loved* saith

15. (son) of Jonas, *lovest* thou me more than

16. Simon, (son) of Jonas, *lovest* thou me?

20. the disciple whom Jesus *loved* following;

Ro. 8:28. for good to them *that love* God,

37. than conquerors through him *that loved* us.

9:13. As it is written, Jacob *have* I *loved,*

25. her *beloved,* which was not *beloved.*

13: 8. to *love* one another: for he *that loveth* another

9. Thou *shalt love* thy neighbour as thyself.

1Co. 2: 9. prepared for them *that love* him.

8: 3. if any man *love* God, the same is

2Co. 9: 7. for God *loveth* a cheerful giver.

11:11. Wherefore? because I *love* you not?

12:15. abundantly I *love* you, the less I *be loved.*

Gal. 2:20. the Son of God, who *loved* me, and

5:14. Thou *shalt love* thy neighbour as thyself.

Eph. 1: 6. hath made us accepted in the *beloved.*

2: 4. his great love wherewith he *loved* us, ·

5: 2. walk in love, as Christ also *hath loved* us,

25. Husbands, *love* your wives, even as Christ also *loved* the church,

28. So ought men *to love* their wives as

— He *that loveth* his wife *loveth* himself.

33. so *love* his wife even as himself;

6:24. with all them *that love* our Lord Jesus

Col. 3:12. the elect of God, holy and *beloved,*

19. Husbands, *love* (your) wives, and

1Th. 1: 4. Knowing, brethren *beloved,* your

4: 9. taught of God *to love* one another.

2Th. 2:13. for you, brethren *beloved* of the Lord,

16. even our Father, which *hath loved* us,

2Ti. 4: 8. unto all them also *that love* his appearing.

10. *having loved* this present world,

Heb. 1: 9. Thou *hast loved* righteousness, and

12: 6. For whom the Lord *loveth* he chasteneth,

Jas. 1:12. hath promised to them *that love* him.

2: 5. hath promised to them *that love* him?

8. Thou *shalt love* thy neighbour as

1Pet. 1: 8. Whom having not seen, ye *love ;*

22. (see that ye) *love* one another with a

2:17. *Love* the brotherhood. Fear God.

3:10. For he that will *love* life, and see

2Pet. 2:15. who *loved* the wages of unrighteousness;

1Joh. 2:10. He *that loveth* his brother abideth

15. *Love* not the world, neither the

— If any man *love* the world, the

3:10. neither he *that loveth* not his brother.

11. that we *should love* one another.

14. because we *love* the brethren. He *that loveth* not (his) brother

1Joh. 3:18. little children, *let* us not *love* in word,

23. his Son Jesus Christ, and *love* one another,

4: 7. Beloved, *let* us *love* one another:

— every one *that loveth* is born of God,

8. He *that loveth* not knoweth not God ;

10. Herein is love, not that we *loved* God, but that he *loved* us, and sent his Son

11. Beloved, if God so *loved* us, we ought also *to love* one another.

12. If we *love* one another, God dwelleth

19. We *love* him, because he first *loved* us.

20. If a man say, I *love* God, and

— for he *that loveth* not his brother

— how can he *love* God whom he

21. That he *who loveth* God *love* his brother

5:1. every one *that loveth* him that begat *loveth* him also that is begotten

2. we know that we *love* the children of God, when we *love* God,

2 Joh. 1. her children, whom I *love* in the truth ;

5. from the beginning, that we *love* one

3 Joh. 1. wellbeloved Gaius, whom I *love* in the truth.

Rev. 1: 5. Unto him *that loved* us, and

3: 9. to know that I *have loved* thee.

12:11. they *loved* not their lives unto the

20: 9. the saints about, and the *beloved* city:

ἀγάπη, *agapee.*

Mat. 24:12. the *love* of many shall wax cold.

Lu. 11:42. pass over judgment and the *love* of God:

Joh. 5:42. ye have not the *love* of God in you.

13:35. if ye have *love* one to another.

15: 9. I *loved* you: continue ye in my *love.*

10. ye shall abide in my *love ;*

— commandments, and abide in his *love.*

13. Greater *love* hath no man than this,

17:26. the *love* wherewith thou hast loved

Ro. 5: 5. because the *love* of God is shed

8. God commendeth his *love* toward us,

8:35. separate us from the *love* of Christ?

39. to separate us from the *love* of God,

12: 9. (Let) *love* be without dissimulation.

13:10. *Love* worketh no ill to his neighbour: therefore *love* (is) the fulfilling of the law.

14:15. now walkest thou not *charitably.*

15:30. Christ's sake, and for the *love* of the Spirit,

1Cor. 4:21. with a rod, or in *love,* and (in) the

8: 1. Knowledge puffeth up, but *charity* edifieth.

13: 1. of angels, and have not *charity,* I

2. remove mountains, and have not *charity,*

3. body to be burned, and have not *charity,*

4. *Charity* suffereth long, (and) is kind ; *charity* envieth not ; *charity* vaunteth not itself, is not

8. *Charity* never faileth: but whether

13. now abideth faith, hope, *charity,*

— the greatest of these (is) *charity.*

14: 1. Follow after *charity,* and desire spiritual

16:14. Let all your things be done with *charity.*

24. My *love* (be) with you all in Christ Jesus.

2Cor. 2: 4. that ye might know the *love* which I

8. confirm (your) *love* toward him.

5:14. For the *love* of Christ constraineth us;

6: 6. by the Holy Ghost, by *love* unfeigned,

8: 7. (in) all diligence, and (in) your *love* to us.

8. to prove the sincerity of your *love.*

24. before the churches, the proof of your *love,*

13:11. the God of *love* and peace shall be

14(13). and the *love* of God, and the

Gal. 5: 6. faith which worketh by *love*.
     13. but by *love* serve one another.
     22. the fruit of the Spirit is *love*, joy, peace,
Eph. 1: 4. without blame before him in *love* :
     15. faith in the Lord Jesus, and *love* unto all
     2: 4. for his great *love* wherewith he
     3:17(18). being rooted and grounded in *love*,
     19. to know the *love* of Christ, which
     4: 2. forbearing one another in *love* ;
     15. speaking the truth in *love*, may
     16. the edifying of itself in *love*.
     5: 2. walk in *love*, as Christ also hath
     6:23. to the brethren, and *love* with faith,
Phil. 1: 9. that your *love* may abound yet
     17. the other of *love*, knowing that
     2: 1. in Christ, if any comfort of *love*,
     2. be likeminded, having the same *love*,
Col. 1: 4. of the *love* (which ye have) to all the
     8. Who also declared unto us your *love*
     13. kingdom of his *dear* Son: (lit. Son of his *love*)
     2: 2. be comforted, being knit together in *love*,
     3:14. above all these things (put on) *charity*,
1Th. 1: 3. work of faith, and labour of *love*,
     3: 6. good tidings of your faith and *charity*,
     12. abound in *love* one toward another,
     5: 8. putting on the breastplate of faith and *love* ;
     13. highly in *love* for their work's sake.
2Th. 1: 3. the *charity* of every one of you all
     2:10. they received not the *love* of the truth,
     3: 5. direct your hearts into the *love* of God,
1Ti. 1: 5. the commandment is *charity* out of a
     14. abundant with faith and *love* which
     2:15. in faith and *charity* and holiness
     4:12. in conversation, in *charity*, in spirit,
     6:11. faith, *love*, patience, meekness.
2Ti. 1: 7. of power, and of *love*, and of a sound
     13. in faith and *love* which is in Christ
     2:22. follow righteousness, faith, *charity*,
     3:10. faith, longsuffering, *charity*, patience,
Tit. 2: 2. sound in faith, in *charity*, in patience.
Philem. 5. Hearing of thy *love* and faith,
     7. great joy and consolation in thy *love*,
     9. for *love's* sake I rather beseech
Heb. 6:10. to forget your work and labour of *love*,
     10:24. to provoke unto *love* and to good
1Pet. 4: 8. have fervent *charity* among yourselves: for *charity* shall cover the multitude
     5:14. Greet ye one another with a kiss of *charity*.
2 Pet 1: 7. to brotherly kindness *charity*.
1Joh 2: 5. verily is the *love* of God perfected :
     15. the *love* of the Father is not in him.
     3: 1. what manner of *love* the Father hath
     16. Hereby perceive we the *love* (of God)
     17. how dwelleth the *love* of God in him ?
     4: 7. love one another: for *love* is of God ;
     8. knoweth not God ; for God is *love*.
     9. manifested the *love* of God toward us,
     10. Herein is *love*, not that we loved God,
     12. his *love* is perfected in us.
     16. *love* that God hath to us. God is *love* ; and he that dwelleth in *love* dwelleth in God,
     17. Herein is our *love* made perfect,
     18. There is no fear in *love* ; but perfect *love* casteth out fear :
     — feareth is not made perfect in *love*.
     5: 3. this is the *love* of God, that we
2 Joh. 3. the Son of the Father, in truth and *love*.
     6. this is *love*, that we walk after
3 Joh. 6. have borne witness of thy *charity*
Jude 2. Mercy unto you, and peace, and *love*,
     12. spots in your *feasts of charity*,

Jude 21. Keep yourselves in the *love* of God,
Rev. 2: 4. thou hast left thy first *love*.
     19. I know thy works, and *charity*,

ἀγαπητός, agapeetos.

Mat. 3:17. saying, This is my *beloved* Son,
     12:18. whom I have chosen ; my *beloved*,
     17: 5. which said, This is my *beloved* Son,
Mar. 1:11. (saying), Thou art my *beloved* Son,
     9: 7. saying, This is my *beloved* Son :
     12: 6. one son, his *wellbeloved*, he sent
Lu. 3:22. which said, Thou art my *beloved* Son ;
     9:35. saying, This is my *beloved* Son :
     20:13. I will send my *beloved* son :
Acts15:25. chosen men unto you with our *beloved*
Rom. 1: 7. To all that be in Rome, *beloved* of God,
     11:28. touching the election, (they are) *beloved*
     12:19. *Dearly beloved*, avenge not yourselves,
     16: 5. Salute my *wellbeloved* Epenetus,
     8. Greet Amplias my *beloved* in the Lord.
     9. Salute Urbane,...and Stachys my *beloved*.
     12. Salute the *beloved* Persis, which laboured
1Cor 4:14. as my *beloved* sons I warn (you).
     17. who is my *beloved* son, and
     10:14. Wherefore, my *dearly beloved*, flee from idolatry.
     15:58. Therefore, my *beloved* brethren,
2Cor 7: 1. *dearly beloved*, let us cleanse ourselves
     12:19. (we do) all things, *dearly beloved*,
Eph. 5: 1. followers of God, as *dear* children ;
     6:21. a *beloved* brother and faithful
Phil. 2:12. Wherefore, my *beloved*, as ye have
     4: 1. my brethren *dearly beloved* and longed for,
     — stand fast in the Lord, (my) *dearly beloved*.
Col. 1: 7. our *dear* fellowservant, who is
     4: 7. unto you, (who is) a *beloved* brother,
     9. a faithful and *beloved* brother,
     14. Luke, the *beloved* physician, and Demas,
1Th. 2: 8. because ye were *dear* unto us.
1Ti. 6: 2. because they are faithful and *beloved*,
2Ti. 1: 2. To Timothy, (my) *dearly beloved* son :
Philem. 1. unto Philemon our *dearly beloved*, and
     2. to (our) *beloved* Apphia, and Archippus
     16. above a servant, a brother *beloved*,
Heb. 6: 9. *beloved*, we are persuaded better things
Jas. 1:16. Do not err, my *beloved* brethren.
     19. Wherefore, my *beloved* brethren, let every
     2: 5. Hearken, my *beloved* brethren,
1Pet. 2:11. *Dearly beloved*, I beseech (you) as strangers
     4:12. *Beloved*, think it not strange
2Pet. 1:17. This is my *beloved* Son, in whom
     3: 1. This second epistle, *beloved*, I now write
     8. *beloved*, be not ignorant of this
     14. Wherefore, *beloved*, seeing that ye look
     15. even as our *beloved* brother Paul
     17. Ye therefore, *beloved*, seeing ye know
1Joh. 3:2. *Beloved*, now are we the sons of God,
     21. *Beloved*, if our heart condemn us not,
     4: 1. *Beloved*, believe not every spirit,
     7. *Beloved*, let us love one another:
     11. *Beloved*, if God so loved us,
3 Joh. 1. The elder unto the *wellbeloved* Gaius,
     2. *Beloved*, I wish above all things
     5. *Beloved*, thou doest faithfully
     11. *Beloved*, follow not that which is evil,
Jude 3. *Beloved*, when I gave all diligence
     17. *beloved*, remember ye the words
     20. But ye, *beloved*, building up yourselves

ἀγγαρεύω, angaruo.

Mat 5:41. whosoever *shall compel* thee *to go* a mile,

Mat 27:32. him they *compelled* to bear his cross.
Mar 15:21. they *compel* one Simon a Cyrenian,

ἀγγεῖον, *angīon.*

Mat 13:48. gathered the good into *vessels,* but
25: 4. But the wise took oil in their *vessels*

ἀγγελία, *angelia.*

1Joh. 3:11. For this is the *message* that ye heard

ἄγγελος, *angelos.*

Mat. 1:20. the *angel* of the Lord appeared unto
24. did as the *angel* of the Lord had bidden
2:13. *angel* of the Lord appeareth to Joseph
19. behold, an *angel* of the Lord appeareth
4: 6. He shall give his *angels* charge
11. behold, *angels* came and ministered
11:10. Behold, I send my *messenger*
13:39. and the reapers are the *angels.*
41. The Son of man shall send forth his *angels,*
49. the *angels* shall come forth, and sever
16:27. the glory of his Father with his *angels;*
18:10. That in heaven their *angels* do
22:30. are as the *angels* of God in heaven.
24:31. And he shall send his *angels* with
36. no, not the *angels* of heaven,
25:31. all the holy *angels* with him,
41. prepared for the devil and his *angels:*
26:53. more than twelve legions of *angels?*
28: 2. for the *angel* of the Lord descended
5. the *angel* answered and said
Mar. 1: 2. Behold, I send my *messenger* before
13. and the *angels* ministered unto him.
8:38. of his Father with the holy *angels.*
12:25. are as the *angels* which are in heaven.
13:27. then shall he send his *angels,*
32. not the *angels* which are in heaven,
Lu. 1:11. appeared unto him an *angel* of the
13. the *angel* said unto him, Fear not,
18. Zacharias said unto the *angel,*
19. the *angel* answering said unto him,
26. the sixth month the *angel* Gabriel
28. And the *angel* came in unto her,
30. *angel* said unto her, Fear not, Mary:
34. Then said Mary unto the *angel,*
35. the *angel* answered and said unto her,
38. And the *angel* departed from her.
2: 9. the *angel* of the Lord came upon them,
10. the *angel* said unto them, Fear not:
13. with the *angel* a multitude of
15. as the *angels* were gone away
21. which was so named of the *angel*
4:10. He shall give his *angels* charge over thee,
7:24. when the *messengers* of John were departed,
27. Behold, I send my *messenger* before
9:26. (in his) Father's, and of the holy *angels.*
52. And sent *messengers* before his face:
12: 8. confess before the *angels* of God:
9. denied before the *angels* of God.
15:10. in the presence of the *angels* of God
16:22. carried by the *angels* into Abraham's bosom:
22:43. there appeared an *angel* unto him
24:23. had also seen a vision of *angels,*
Joh. 1:51. (52) the *angels* of God ascending and
5: 4. For an *angel* went down at
12:29. others said, An *angel* spake to him.
20:12. seeth two *angels* in white sitting,

Acts 5:19. the *angel* of the Lord by night
6:15. as it had been the face of an *angel.*
7:30. mount Sina an *angel* of the Lord in
35. by the hand of the *angel* which
38. with the *angel* which spake to him
53. the law by the disposition of *angels,*
8:26. *angel* of the Lord spake unto Philip,
10: 3. an *angel* of God coming in to him,
7. when the *angel* which spake unto Cornelius
22. warned from God by an holy *angel*
11:13. had seen an *angel* in his house,
12: 7. the *angel* of the Lord came upon
8. the *angel* said unto him, Gird thyself,
9. which was done by the *angel;*
10. forthwith the *angel* departed
11. the Lord hath sent his *angel,*
15. said they, It is his *angel.*
23. the *angel* of the Lord smote him,
23: 8. no resurrection, neither *angel,* nor spirit:
9. if a spirit or an *angel* hath spoken
27:23. by me this night the *angel* of God,
Rom 8:38. nor life, nor *angels,* nor principalities,
1Co 4: 9. the world, and to *angels,* and to men.
6: 3. Know ye not that we shall judge *angels?*
11:10. on (her) head because of the *angels.*
13: 1. the tongues of men and of *angels,*
2Co 11:14. transformed into an *angel* of light.
12: 7. in the flesh, the *messenger* of Satan
Gal 1: 8. we, or an *angel* from heaven,
3:19. (and it was) ordained by *angels* in
4:14. received me as an *angel* of God,
Col. 2:18. humility and worshipping of *angels;*
2Th. 1: 7. from heaven with his mighty *angels*
1Ti. 3:16. in the Spirit, seen of *angels,*
5:21. Jesus Christ, and the elect *angels,*
Heb. 1: 4. made so much better than the *angels,*
5. unto which of the *angels* said he
6(7). let all the *angels* of God worship him.
7. *angels* he saith, Who maketh his *angels*
13. to which of the *angels* said he at
2: 2. if the word spoken by *angels* was stedfast,
5. unto the *angels* hath he not put
7. a little lower than the *angels;*
9. made a little lower than the *angels*
16. not on (him the nature of) *angels;*
12:22. an innumerable company of *angels,*
13: 2. some have entertained *angels* unawares.
Jas. 2:25. she had received the *messengers,*
1Pet.1:12. which things the *angels* desire to look into.
3:22. *angels* and authorities and powers
2Pet.2: 4. spared not the *angels* that sinned,
11. Whereas *angels,* which are greater
Jude 6. the *angels* which kept not their
Rev. 1: 1. he sent and signified (it) by his *angel*
20. the *angels* of the seven churches:
2: 1. Unto the *angel* of the church of Ephesus
8. unto the *angel* of the church
12. to the *angel* of the church in Pergamos
18. unto the *angel* of the church
3: 1. unto the *angel* of the church
5. my Father, and before his *angels.*
7. to the *angel* of the church in
14. unto the *angel* of the church
5: 2. I saw a strong *angel* proclaiming
11. I heard the voice of many *angels*
7: 1. I saw four *angels* standing
2. I saw another *angel* ascending
— a loud voice to the four *angels,*
11. all the *angels* stood round
8: 2. I saw the seven *angels* which
3. another *angel* came and stood at the altar
4. before God out of the *angel's* hand.

Rev. 8: 5. the *angel* took the censer, and filled
6. seven *angels* which had the seven trumpets
7. The first *angel* sounded, and there followed
8. the second *angel* sounded, and as it were
10. the third *angel* sounded, and there fell
12. the fourth *angel* sounded, and the third part
13. heard an *angel* flying through the midst
— the trumpet of the three *angels*,
9: 1. the fifth *angel* sounded, and I saw
11. (which is) the *angel* of the bottomless pit,
13. And the sixth *angel* sounded,
14. Saying to the sixth *angel* which had the trumpet, Loose the four *angels*
15. And the four *angels* were loosed,
10: 1. And I saw another mighty *angel*
5. the *angel* which I saw stand
7. of the voice of the seventh *angel*,
8. open in the hand of the *angel*
9. I went unto the *angel*, and said
10. the little book out of the *angel's* hand,
11: 1. and the *angel* stood, saying, Rise,
15. And the seventh *angel* sounded;
12: 7. Michael and his *angels* fought against the dragon ; and the dragon fought and his *angels*,
9. his *angels* were cast out with him.
14: 6. I saw another *angel* fly in the
8. And there followed another *angel*, saying,
9. the third *angel* followed them,
10. in the presence of the holy *angels*,
15. another *angel* came out of the temple,
17. another *angel* came out of the temple
18. another *angel* came out from the altar,
19. the *angel* thrust in his sickle
15: 1. seven *angels* having the seven last plagues ;
6. the seven *angels* came out of
7. gave unto the seven *angels*
8. plagues of the seven *angels* were fulfilled.
16: 1. saying to the seven *angels*,
3. the second *angel* poured out his vial
4. the third *angel* poured out his vial
5. I heard the *angel* of the waters
8. the fourth *angel* poured out his vial
10. the fifth *angel* poured out his vial
12. the sixth *angel* poured out his vial
17. the seventh *angel* poured out his vial
17: 1. one of the seven *angels* which
7. And the *angel* said unto me,
18: 1. I saw another *angel* come down
21. a mighty *angel* took up a stone
19:17. I saw an *angel* standing in the sun;
20: 1. And I saw an *angel* come down
21: 9. one of the seven *angels* which
12. at the gates twelve *angels*,
17. measure of a man, that is, of the *angel*.
22: 6. sent his *angel* to shew unto
8. before the feet of the *angel*
16. have sent mine *angel* to testify

ἄγε, *age,* adv.

Jas. 4:13. *Go to* now, ye that say, To day
5: 1. *Go to* now, (ye) rich men, weep

ἀγέλη, *agelee.*

Mat. 8:30. an *herd* of many swine feeding.
31. go away into the *herd* of swine.

Mat. 8:32. they went into the *herd* of swine: and, behold, the whole *herd* of swine ran
Mar 5:11. a great *herd* of swine feeding.
13. the *herd* ran violently down
Lu. 8:32. an *herd* of many swine feeding
33. the *herd* ran violently down a steep

ἀγενεαλόγητος, *agenealogeetos.*

Heb 7: 3. father, without mother, *without descent,*

ἀγενής, *agenees.*

1Co. 1:28. *base things* of the world, and things

ἀγιάζω, *hagiazo.*

Mat. 6: 9. in heaven, *Hallowed be* thy name.
23:17. or the temple *that sanctifieth* the gold ?
19. or the altar *that sanctifieth* the gift ?
Lu. 11: 2. in heaven, *Hallowed be* thy name.
Joh.10:36. whom the Father *hath sanctified,*
17:17. *Sanctify* them through thy truth:
19. for their sakes I *sanctify* myself, that they also might be *sanctified* through the
Acts20:32. among all them *which are sanctified.*
26:18. among them *which are sanctified*
Ro. 15:16. *being sanctified* by the Holy Ghost.
1Co. 1: 2. *that are sanctified* in Christ Jesus,
6:11. are washed, but ye *are sanctified,*
7:14. husband *is sanctified* by the wife, and the unbelieving wife *is sanctified*
Eph 5:26. That he *might sanctify* and cleanse
1Th. 5:23. God of peace *sanctify* you wholly ;
1Ti. 4: 5. it *is sanctified* by the word of God
2Ti. 2:21. unto honour, *sanctified,* and meet
Heb 2:11. *that sanctifieth* and they *who are sanctified*
9:13. unclean, *sanctifieth* to the purifying
10:10. By the which will we are *sanctified*
14. for ever them *that are sanctified.*
29. the covenant, wherewith he *was sanctified,*
13:12. that he *might sanctify* the people
1Pet 3:15. *sanctify* the Lord God in your hearts:
Jude 1. them that are *sanctified* by God
Rev.22:11. that is holy, *let* him *be holy* still.

ἀγιασμός, *hagiasmos.*

Ro. 6:19. servants to righteousness unto *holiness.*
22. ye have your fruit unto *holiness,*
1Co. 1:30. and *sanctification,* and redemption:
1Th. 4: 3. will of God, (even) your *sanctification,*
4. his vessel in *sanctification* and honour ;
7. unto uncleanness, but unto *holiness.*
2Th. 2:13. through *sanctification* of the Spirit
1Ti. 2:15. charity and *holiness* with sobriety.
Heb 12:14. peace with all (men), and *holiness,*
1Pet.1: 2. through *sanctification* of the Spirit,

ἄγιον, *hagion.*

Observe. † Holies(pl). § Holy (sing.) of Holies(pl).

Heb 8: 2. A minister of the *sanctuary,*† and
9: 1. divine service, and a worldly *sanctuary.*
2. which is called the *sanctuary.*
3. which is called the *Holiest of all ;*§
8. the way into the *holiest of all*† was
12. entered in once into the *holy place,*†
24. into the *holy places*† made with hands,
25. into the *holy place*† every year

Heb 10:19. to enter Into the *holiest*† by the blood
13:11. brought into the *sanctuary*† by the

ἅγιος, *hagios.*

Mat. 1:18. found with child of the *Holy* Ghost.
    20. in her is of the *Holy* Ghost.
  3:11. baptize you with the *Holy* Ghost,
  4: 5. him up into the *holy* city,
  7: 6. Give not that which is *holy* unto
12:32. speaketh against the *Holy* Ghost,
24:15. the prophet, stand in the *holy* place,
25:31. all the *holy* angels with him,
27:52. bodies of the *saints* which slept arose,
    53. and went into the *holy* city,
28:19. of the Son, and of the *Holy* Ghost:
Mar. 1: 8. baptize you with the *Holy* Ghost.
    24. thou art, the *Holy One* of God.
  3:29. blaspheme against the *Holy* Ghost
  6:20. was a just man and an *holy*,
  8:38. his Father with the *holy* angels.
12:36. himself said by the *Holy* Ghost,
13:11. not ye that speak, but the *Holy* Ghost.
Lu. 1:15. be filled with the *Holy* Ghost,
    35. The *Holy* Ghost shall come upon thee,
  — also that *holy thing* which shall
    41. filled with the *Holy* Ghost:
    49. great things; and *holy* (is) his name.
    67. was filled with the *Holy* Ghost,
    70. the mouth of his *holy* prophets,
    72. to remember his *holy* covenant;
  2:23. shall be called *holy* to the Lord;
    25. and the *Holy* Ghost was upon him.
    26. unto him by the *Holy* Ghost,
  3:16. baptize you with the *Holy* Ghost
    22. the *Holy* Ghost descended in
  4: 1. Jesus being full of the *Holy* Ghost
    34. thou art; the *Holy One* of God.
  9:26. (in his) Father's, and of the *holy* angels.
11:13. Father give the *Holy* Spirit to them
12:10. blasphemeth against the *Holy* Ghost
    12. For the *Holy* Ghost shall teach
Joh. 1:33. which baptizeth with the *Holy* Ghost.
  7:39. for the *Holy* Ghost was not yet
14:26. the Comforter, (which is) the *Holy* Ghost,
17:11. I come to thee. *Holy* Father, keep
20:22. unto them, Receive ye the *Holy* Ghost:
Acts 1: 2. that he through the *Holy* Ghost
    5. be baptized with the *Holy* Ghost
    8. that the *Holy* Ghost is come upon
    16. which the *Holy* Ghost by the mouth
  2: 4. were all filled with the *Holy* Ghost,
    33. the promise of the *Holy* Ghost,
    38. shall receive the gift of the *Holy* Ghost.
  3:14. ye denied the *Holy One* and the Just,
    21. the mouth of all his *holy* prophets
  4: 8. filled with the *Holy* Ghost,
    27. against thy *holy* child Jesus,
    30. name of thy *holy* child Jesus.
    31. they were all filled with the *Holy* Ghost,
  5: 3. heart to lie to the *Holy* Ghost,
    32. (so is) also the *Holy* Ghost,
  6: 3. full of the *Holy* Ghost and wisdom,
    5. of faith and of the *Holy* Ghost,
    13. words against this *holy* place,
  7:33. where thou standest is *holy* ground.
    51. ye do always resist the *Holy* Ghost:
    55. being full of the *Holy* Ghost,
  8:15. that they might receive the *Holy* Ghost:
    17. they received the *Holy* Ghost.
    18. the *Holy* Ghost was given,

Acts 8:19. he may receive the *Holy* Ghost.
  9:13. he hath done to thy *saints* at
    17. be filled with the *Holy* Ghost.
    31. in the comfort of the *Holy* Ghost,
    32. came down also to the *saints*
    41. when he had called the *saints*
10:22. warned from God by an *holy* angel
    38. with the *Holy* Ghost and with power:
    44. the *Holy* Ghost fell on all them
    45. poured out the gift of the *Holy* Ghost.
    47. have received the *Holy* Ghost as
11:15. the *Holy* Ghost fell on them,
    16. be baptized with the *Holy* Ghost.
    24. full of the *Holy* Ghost and of faith:
13: 2. the *Holy* Ghost said, Separate me
    4. sent forth by the *Holy* Ghost,
    9. filled with the *Holy* Ghost, set
    52. with joy, and with the *Holy* Ghost.
15: 8. giving them the *Holy* Ghost,
    28. seemed good to the *Holy* Ghost,
16: 6. were forbidden of the *Holy* Ghost
19: 2. Have ye received the *Holy* Ghost
  — whether there be any *Holy* Ghost.
    6. the *Holy* Ghost came on them;
20:23. Save that the *Holy* Ghost witnesseth
    28. the *Holy* Ghost hath made you
21:11. Thus saith the *Holy* Ghost,
    28. and hath polluted this *holy* place.
26:10. many of the *saints* did I shut up
28:25. Well spake the *Holy* Ghost by Esaias
Ro. 1: 2. his prophets in the *holy* scriptures,
    7. beloved of God, called (to be) *saints:*
  5: 5. our hearts by the *Holy* Ghost
  7:12. the law (is) *holy*, and the commandment
    holy,
  8:27. he maketh intercession for the *saints*
  9: 1. me witness in the *Holy* Ghost,
11:16. For if the firstfruit (be) *holy*,
  — if the root (be) *holy*, so (are)
12: 1. a living sacrifice, *holy*, acceptable
    13. to the necessity of *saints ;*
14:17. peace, and joy in the *Holy* Ghost.
15:13. through the power of the *Holy* Ghost.
    16. sanctified by the *Holy* Ghost.
    25. Jerusalem to minister unto the *saints.*
    26. for the poor *saints* which are
    31. may be accepted of the *saints ;*
16: 2. in the Lord, as becometh *saints,*
    15. all the *saints* which are with them.
    16. Salute one another with an *holy* kiss.
1Co. 1: 2. called (to be) *saints,* with all
  2:13. which the *Holy* Ghost teacheth;
  3:17. for the temple of God is *holy*,
  6: 1. and not before the *saints*?
    2. that the *saints* shall judge the world?
    19. is the temple of the *Holy* Ghost
  7:14. unclean; but now are they *holy*.
    34. may be *holy* both in body and
12: 3. is the Lord, but by the *Holy* Ghost.
14:33. in all churches of the *saints.*
16: 1. concerning the collection for the *saints*
    15. to the ministry of the *saints,*
    20. Greet ye one another with an *holy* kiss.
2Co. 1: 1. with all the *saints* which are
  6: 6. by kindness, by the *Holy* Ghost,
  8: 4. of the ministering to the *saints.*
  9: 1. the ministering to the *saints,*
    12. supplieth the want of the *saints,*
13:12. Greet one another with an *holy* kiss.
13(12). All the *saints* salute you.
14(13). communion of the *Holy* Ghost,
Eph. 1: 1. to the *saints* which are at Ephesus,

Eph. 1: 4. we should be *holy* and without
13. with that *holy* Spirit of promise,
15. and love unto all the *saints*,
18. his inheritance in the *saints*,
2:19. fellowcitizens with the *saints*,
21. groweth unto an *holy* temple
3: 5. unto his *holy* apostles and prophets
8. less than the least of all *saints*,
18. to comprehend with all *saint*
4:12. For the perfecting of the *saints*,
30. grieve not the *holy* Spirit
5: 3. among you, as becometh *saints ;*
27. be *holy* and without blemish.
6:18. supplication for all *saints ;*
Phil. 1: 1. to all the *saints* in Christ Jesus
4:21. Salute every *saint* in Christ Jesus.
22. All the *saints* salute you,
Col. 1: 2. To the *saints* and faithful
4. (which ye have) to all the *saints*,
12. the inheritance of the *saints* in light:
22. through death, to present you *holy*
26. made manifest to his *saints :*
3:12. elect of God, *holy* and beloved,
1Th. 1: 5. in power, and in the *Holy* Ghost,
6. with joy of the *Holy* Ghost:
3:13. Jesus Christ with all his *saints.*
4: 8. given unto us his *holy* Spirit.
5:26. Greet all the brethren with an *holy* kiss.
27. unto all the *holy* brethren.
2Th. 1:10. to be glorified in his *saints,*
1Ti. 5:10. if she have washed the *saints'* feet,
2Ti. 1: 9. called (us) with an *holy* calling,
14. by the *Holy* Ghost which dwelleth
Tit. 3: 5. and renewing of the *Holy* Ghost;
Philem. 5. Lord Jesus, and toward all *saints ;*
7. the bowels of the *saints* are
Heb 2: 4. miracles, and gifts of the *Holy* Ghost,
3: 1. Wherefore, *holy* brethren, partakers
7. as the *Holy* Ghost saith, To day
6: 4. made partakers of the *Holy* Ghost,
10. have ministered to the *saints,*
9: 8. The *Holy* Ghost this signifying,
10:15. the *Holy* Ghost also is a witness
13:24. over you, and all the *saints.*
1Pet 1:12. with the *Holy* Ghost sent down
15. called you is *holy*, so be ye *holy*
16. Be ye *holy ;* for I am *holy.*
2: 5. spiritual house, an *holy* priesthood,
9. a royal priesthood, an *holy* nation,
3: 5. in the old time the *holy* women
2Pet 1:18. with him in the *holy* mount.
21. *holy* men of God spake (as they were) moved by the *Holy* Ghost.
2:21. from the *holy* commandment delivered
3: 2. spoken before by the *holy* prophets,
11. in (all) *holy* conversation and
1Joh.2:20. have an unction from the *Holy* One,
5: 7. the Word, and the *Holy* Ghost:
Jude 3. once delivered unto the *saints.*
14. with ten thousands of his *saints,*
20. on your *most holy* faith, praying in the *Holy* Ghost,
Rev. 3: 7. saith he that is *holy*, he that
4: 8. and night, saying, Holy, holy, holy,
5: 8. which are the prayers of *saints.*
6:10. How long, O Lord, *holy* and true,
8: 3. with the prayers of all *saints* upon
4. with the prayers of the *saints,*
11: 2. the *holy* city shall they tread under
18. the prophets, and to the *saints,*
13: 7. to make war with the *saints,*
10. patience and the faith of the *saints.*

Rev.14:10. the presence of the *holy* angels,
12. Here is the patience of the *saints:*
15: 3. (are) thy ways, thou King of *saints.*
16: 6. they have shed the blood of *saints*
17: 6. drunken with the blood of the *saints,*
18:20. (ye) *holy* apostles and prophets;
24. blood of prophets, and of *saints,*
19: 8. fine linen is the righteousness of *saints.*
20: 6. Blessed and *holy* (is) he that
9. compassed the camp of the *saints*
21: 2. And I John saw the *holy* city,
10. great city, the *holy* Jerusalem,
22: 6. God of the *holy* prophets sent his angel
11. that is *holy*, let him be holy still.
19. of life, and out of the *holy* city,

ἁγιότης, *hagiotees.*

Heb 12:10. might be partakers of his *holiness.*

ἁγιωσύνη, *hagiosunee.*

Ro. 1: 4. according to the spirit of *holiness,*
2Co. 7: 1. perfecting *holiness* in the fear of God.
1Th. 3:13. unblameable in *holiness* before

ἀγκάλαι, *ankalai.*

Lu. 2:28. took he him up in his *arms,*

ἄγκιστρον, *ankistron.*

Mat.17:27. go thou to the sea, and cast an *hook,*

ἄγκυρα, *ankura.*

Acts27:29. they cast four *anchors* out of the stern,
30. would have cast *anchors* out
40. they had taken up the *anchors,*
Heb 6:19. Which (hope) we have as an *anchor*

ἄγναφος, *agnaphos.*

Mat. 9:16. a piece of *new* cloth unto an old garment,
Mar 2:21. a piece of *new* cloth on an old garment:

ἁγνεία, *hagnia.*

1Ti. 4:12. in spirit, in faith, in *purity.*
5: 2. the younger as sisters, with all *purity.*

ἁγνίζω, *hagnizo.*

Joh.11:55. the passover, to *purify* themselves.
Acts21:24. Them take, and *purify thyself*
26. next day *purifying himself* with them
24:18. found me *purified* in the temple,
Jas. 4: 8. (ye) sinners; and *purify* (your) hearts,
1Pet.1:22. Seeing ye have *purified* your souls
1Joh.3: 3. *purifieth* himself, even as he

ἁγνισμός, *hagnismos.*

Acts21:26. of the days of *purification,* until

ἀγνοέω, *agnoeo.*

Mar 9:32. they *understood not* that saying,

Lu. 9:45. they *understood not* this saying,
Acts13:27. *because* they *knew* him *not*,
　17:23. Whom therefore ye *ignorantly* worship,
Ro. 1:13. Now I would not have you *ignorant*,
　2: 4. *not knowing* that the goodness
　6: 3. *Know* ye *not*, that so many of
　7: 1. *Know* ye *not*, brethren, for I speak
　10: 3. For they *being ignorant* of God's
　11:25. that ye *should be ignorant* of this
1Co.10: 1. not that ye *should be ignorant*,
　12: 1. I would not have you *ignorant*.
　14:38. *be ignorant, let* him *be ignorant*.
2Co. 1: 8. not, brethren, have you *ignorant* of
　2:11. for we *are* not *ignorant* of his devices.
　6: 9. As *unknown*, and (yet) well known;
Gal. 1:22. was *unknown* by face unto the
1Th. 4:13. not have you *to be ignorant*,
1Ti. 1:13. I did (it) *ignorantly* in unbelief.
Heb. 5: 2. have compassion on the *ignorant*,
2Pet.2:12. things that they *understand not ;*

ἀγνόημα, *agnoeema*.

Heb. 9: 7. himself, and (for) the *errors* of the people:

ἄγνοια, *agnoia*.

Acts 3:17. I wot that through *ignorance* ye did
　17:30. the times of this *ignorance* God
Eph 4:18. through the *ignorance* that is in
1Pet.1:14. former lusts in your *ignorance :*

ἀγνός, *hagnos*.

2Co. 7:11. yourselves to be *clear* in this matter.
　11: 2. present (you as) a *chaste* virgin
Phil. 4: 8. (are) just, whatsoever things (are) *pure*,
1Ti. 5:22. keep thyself *pure*.
Tit. 2: 5. discreet, *chaste*, keepers at home,
Jas. 3:17. from above is first *pure*,
1Pet.3: 2. behold your *chaste* conversation
1Joh.3: 3. purifieth himself, even as he is *pure*.

ἀγνότης, *hagnotees*.

2Co. 6: 6. By *pureness*, by knowledge, by

ἀγνῶς, *hagnōs*.

Phil. 1:16. preach Christ of contention, not *sincerely*,

ἀγνωσία, *agnōsia*.

1Co.15:34. some have *not the knowledge* of God:
1 Pet.2:15. silence the *ignorance* of foolish men:

ἄγνωστος, *agnōstos*.

Acts17:23. To The *Unknown* God.

ἀγορά, *agora*.

Mat.11:16. children sitting in the *markets*,
　20: 3. standing idle in the *marketplace*,
　23: 7. greetings in the *markets*, and
Mar. 6:56. they laid the sick in the *streets*,
　7: 4. (when they come) from the *market*

Mar.12:38. salutations in the *marketplaces*,
Lu. 7:32. children sitting in the *marketplace*,
　11:43. and greetings in the *markets*.
　20:46. love greetings in the *markets*,
Acts16:19. drew (them) into the *marketplace*
　17:17. in the *market* daily with them

ἀγοράζω, *agorazo*.

Mat.13:44. that he hath, and *buyeth* that field.
　46. all that he had, and *bought* it.
　14:15. villages, and *buy* themselves victuals.
　21:12. sold and *bought* in the temple,
　25: 9. that sell, and *buy* for yourselves.
　10. while they went *to buy*, the
　27: 7. *bought* with them the potter's field,
Mar. 6:36. villages, and *buy* themselves bread:
　37. go and *buy* two hundred pennyworth
　11:15. sold and *bought* in the temple,
　15:46. he *bought* fine linen, and
　16: 1. *had bought* sweet spices, that they
Lu. 9:13. we *should* go and *buy* meat for
　14:18. I *have bought* a piece of ground,
　19. I *have bought* five yoke of oxen,
　17:28(27). did eat, they drank, they *bought*,
　19:45. sold therein, and them *that bought ;*
　22:36. sell his garment, and *buy* one.
Joh. 4: 8. away unto the city to *buy* meat.
　6: 5. Whence *shall* we *buy* bread,
　13:29. *Buy* (those things) that we have
1Co. 6:20. For ye *are bought* with a price.
　7:23. Ye *are bought* with a price ;
　30. they *that buy*, as though they
2Pet. 2: 1. denying the Lord *that bought* them,
Rev. 3:18. I counsel thee *to buy* of me gold tried
　5: 9. *redeemed* us to God by thy blood
　13:17. that no man might *buy* or sell,
　14: 3. which *were redeemed* from the earth.
　4. These *were redeemed* from among men,
　18:11. for no man *buyeth* their merchandise

ἀγοραῖος, *agoraios*.

Acts17: 5. certain lewd fellows of the *baser sort*,
　19:38. against any man, the *law* is open,

ἄγρα, *agra*.

Lu. 5: 4. let down your nets for a *draught*.
　9. at the *draught* of the fishes which

ἀγράμματος, *agrammatos*.

Acts 4:13. they were *unlearned* and ignorant men,

ἀγραυλέω, *agrauleo*.

Lu. 2: 8. shepherds *abiding in the field*,

ἀγρεύω, *agrūo*.

Mar.12:13. *to catch* him in (his) words.

ἀγριέλαιος, *agrielaios*.

Ro. 11:17. thou, being a *wild olive tree*,
　24. cut out of the *olive tree which is wild*

ἄγριος, agrios.

Mat. 3: 4. meat was locusts and *wild* honey.
Mar. 1: 6. did eat locusts and *wild* honey;
Jude 13. *Raging* waves of the sea, foaming

ἀγρός, agros.

Mat. 6:28. Consider the lilies of the *field*, how
   30. so clothe the grass of the *field*, which
  13:24. which sowed good seed in his *field:*
   27. sow good seed in thy *field ?*
   31. took, and sowed in his *field:*
   36. parable of the tares of the *field.*
   38. The *field* is the world; the good
   44. like unto treasure hid in a *field;*
   — he hath, and buyeth that *field.*
  19:29. or wife, or children, or *lands,*
  22: 5. went their ways, one to his *farm,*
  24:18. let him which is in the *field*
   40. Then shall two be in the *field;*
  27: 7. bought with them the potter's *field,*
   8. that *field* was called, The *field*
   10. gave them for the potter's *field,*
Mar. 5:14. in the city, and in the *country.*
  6:36. go into the *country* round about,
   56. into villages, or cities, or *country,*
  10:29. or wife, or children, or *lands,* for
   30. mothers, and children, and *lands,*
  13:16. let him that is in the *field* not
  15:21. coming out of the *country,* the father
  16:12. walked, and went into the *country.*
Lu. 8:34. in the city and in the *country.*
  9:12. into the towns and *country* round
  12:28. which is to day in the *field,*
  14:18. I have bought a *piece of ground,*
  15:15. sent him into his *fields* to feed
  25. his elder son was in the *field:*
  17: 7. when he is come from the *field,*
   31. he that is in the *field,* let
   36. Two (men) shall be in the *field;*
  23:26. coming out of the *country,*
Acts 4:37. Having *land,* sold (it), and brought

ἀγρυπνέω, agrupneo.

Mar.13:33. Take ye heed, *watch* and pray:
Lu. 21:36. *Watch* ye therefore, and pray always,
Eph. 6:18. and *watching* thereunto with all
Heb.13:17. for they *watch* for your souls,

ἀγρυπνία, agrupnia.

2Co. 6: 5. in tumults, in labours, in *watchings,*
  11:27. painfulness, in *watchings* often,

ἄγω, ago.

Mat.10:18. ye *shall be brought* before governors
  14: 6. when Herod's birthday *was kept,*
  21: 2. loose (them), and *bring* (them) unto me.
   7. *brought* the ass, and the colt,
  26:46. Rise, *let* us *be going:* behold, he
Mar. 1:38. *Let* us *go* into the next towns.
  11: 2. never man sat; loose him, and *bring*
   (him).
   7. they *brought* the colt to Jesus,
  13:11. when they *shall lead* (you),
  14:42. Rise up, *let* us *go;* lo, he that
Lu. 4: 1. *was led* by the Spirit into the

Lu. 4: 9. And he *brought* him to Jerusalem,
   29. *led* him unto the brow of the hill
   40. diseases *brought* them unto him ;
  10:34. *brought* him to an inn, and
  18:40. commanded him *to be brought* unto him:
  19:27. reign over them, *bring* hither, and
   30. loose him, and *bring* (him hither).
   35. And they *brought* him to Jesus:
  21:12. *being brought* before kings and rulers
  22:54. Then took they him, and *led* (him),
  23: 1. of them arose, and *led* him unto Pilate.
   32. malefactors, *led* with him to be put
  24:21. to day *is* the third day since these
Joh. 1:42(43). he *brought* him to Jesus.
  7:45. Why *have* ye not *brought* him ?
  8: 3. the scribes and Pharisees *brought* unto
  9:13. They *brought* to the Pharisees him
  10:16. of this fold: them also I must *bring,*
  11: 7. *Let* us *go* into Judæa again.
   15. nevertheless *let* us *go* unto him.
   16. *Let* us also *go,* that we may die
  14:31. Arise, *let* us *go* hence.
  18:28. Then *led* they Jesus from Caiaphas
  19: 4. Behold, I *bring* him forth to you,
   13. he *brought* Jesus forth, and sat down
Acts 5:21. to the prison *to have* them *brought.*
   26. the officers, and *brought* them without
   27. And *when* they *had brought* them,
  6:12. caught him, and *brought* (him)
  8:32. He *was led* as a sheep to the
  9: 2. he *might bring* them bound
   21. he *might bring* them bound
   27. took him, and *brought* (him) to
  11:26(25). had found him, he *brought* him
  17: 5. sought *to bring* them out to the
   15. conducted Paul *brought* him unto Athens:
   19. took him, and *brought* him unto
  18:12. against Paul, and *brought* him
  19:37. For ye *have brought* hither these men,
   38. against any man, the law *is open,*
  20:12. they *brought* the young man alive,
  21:16. *brought* with them one Mnason
   34. commanded him *to be carried*
  22: 5. *to bring* them which were there **bound**
   24. commanded him *to be brought*
  23:10. *to bring* (him) into the castle.
   18. took him, and *brought* (him) to
   — *to bring* this young man unto thee,
   31. took Paul, and *brought* (him) by night
  25: 6. commanded Paul *to be brought.*
   17. commanded the man *to be brought forth.*
   23. commandment Paul *was brought forth.*
Ro. 2: 4. God *leadeth* thee to repentance ?
  8:14. many as *are led* by the Spirit of God,
1Co.12: 2. dumb idols, even as ye *were led.*
Gal. 5:18. if ye *be led* of the Spirit, ye are not
1 Th.4:14. in Jesus *will* God *bring* with him.
2 Ti. 3: 6. *led away* with divers lusts,
  4:11. Take Mark, and *bring* him with thee.
Heb. 2:10. *bringing* many sons unto glory,

ἀγωγή, agōgee.

2 Ti. 3:10. my doctrine, *manner of life,* purpose,

ἀγών, agōn.

Phil. 1:30. Having the same *conflict* which ye saw
Col. 2: 1. what great *conflict* I have for you,
1Th. 2: 2. gospel of God with much *contention.*
1 Ti. 6:12. Fight the good *fight* of faith,

2 Ti. 4: 7. I have fought a good *fight*, I have
Heb.12: 1. the *race* that is set before us,

ἀγωνία, *agōnia*.

Lu. 22:44. being in an *agony* he prayed

ἀγωνίζομαι, *agōnizomai*.

Lu. 13:24. *Strive* to enter in at the strait
Joh.18:36. then *would* my servants *fight*,
1Co. 9:25. And every man *that striveth* for
Col. 1:29. *striving* according to his working,
     4:12. *labouring fervently* for you in prayers,
1 Ti. 6:12. *Fight* the good fight of faith,
2 Ti. 4: 7. I *have fought* a good fight,

ἀδάπανος, *adapanos*.

1Co. 9:18. the gospel of Christ *without charge*,

ἀδελφή, *adelphee*.

Mat.12:50. the same is my brother, and *sister*,
  13:56. his *sisters*, are they not all with us?
  19:29. forsaken houses, or brethren, or *sisters*
Mar. 3:35. is my brother, and my *sister*,
   6: 3. are not his *sisters* here with us?
  10:29. house, or brethren, or *sisters*, or father,
     30. houses, and brethren, and *sisters*,
Lu. 10:39. she had a *sister* called Mary,
     40. not care that my *sister* hath left
  14:26. children, and brethren, and *sisters*,
Joh.11: 1. town of Mary and her *sister* Martha.
     3. Therefore his *sisters* sent unto him,
     5. loved Martha, and her *sister*,
    28. called Mary her *sister* secretly,
    39. the *sister* of him that was dead,
  19:25. his mother, and his mother's *sister*,
Acts23:16. when Paul's *sister's* son heard of
Ro. 16: 1. I commend unto you Phebe our *sister*,
    15. and Julia, Nereus, and his *sister*,
1Co. 7:15. A brother or a *sister* is not under
   9: 5. to lead about a *sister*, a wife,
1 Ti. 5: 2. as mothers; the younger as *sisters*,
Jas. 2:15. If a brother or *sister* be naked,
2 Joh. 13. The children of thy elect *sister* greet

ἀδελφός, *adelphos*.

Mat. 1: 2. begat Judas and his *brethren*;
    11. begat Jechonias and his *brethren*,
   4:18. the sea of Galilee, saw two *brethren*,
      Simon called Peter, and Andrew his
      brother,
    21. he saw other two *brethren*, James (the
      son) of Zebedee, and John his *brother*,
   5:22. whosoever is angry with his *brother*
     — whosoever shall say to his *brother*,
    23. that thy *brother* hath ought against thee;
    24. first be reconciled to thy *brother*,
    47. if ye salute your *brethren* only,
   7: 3. the mote that is in thy *brother's* eye,
     4. wilt thou say to thy *brother*,
     5. mote out of thy *brother's* eye.
  10: 2. called Peter, and Andrew his *brother*;
    –(3). (son) of Zebedee, and John his *brother*;
    21. And the *brother* shall deliver up the
      brother to

Mat.12:46. (his) mother and his *brethren*
    47. thy mother and thy *brethren*
    48. and who are my *brethren*?
    49. Behold my mother and my *brethren*!
    50. the same is my *brother*, and sister,
  13:55. his *brethren*, James, and Joses,
  14: 3. Herodias' sake, his *brother* Philip's wife.
  17: 1. James, and John his *brother*,
  18:15. if thy *brother* shall trespass
     — thou hast gained thy *brother*,
    21. how oft shall my *brother* sin
    35. forgive not every one his *brother* their
  19:29. houses, or *brethren*, or sisters,
  20:24. indignation against the two *brethren*.
  22:24. his *brother* shall marry his wife, and raise
      up seed unto his *brother*.
    25. there were with us seven *brethren*:
     — left his wife unto his *brother*:
  23: 8. (even) Christ; and all ye are *brethren*.
  25:40. the least of these my *brethren*,
  28:10. go tell my *brethren* that they go
Mar. 1:16. saw Simon and Andrew his *brother*
    19. (son) of Zebedee, and John his *brother*,
   3:17. and John the *brother* of James;
    31. There came then his *brethren* and
    32. thy mother and thy *brethren* without
    33. Who is my mother, or my *brethren*?
    34. Behold my mother and my *brethren*!
    35. will of God, the same is my *brother*,
   5:37. and John the *brother* of James.
   6: 3. son of Mary, the *brother* of James,
    17. Herodias' sake, his *brother* Philip's wife:
    18. for thee to have thy *brother's* wife.
  10:29. left house, or *brethren*, or sisters,
    30. houses, and *brethren*, and sisters,
  12:19. If a man's *brother* die, and leave
     — that his *brother* should take his wife, and
      raise up seed unto his *brother*.
    20. Now there were seven *brethren*:
  13:12. the *brother* shall betray the *brother*
Lu. 3: 1. and his *brother* Philip tetrarch of
    19. for Herodias his *brother* Philip's wife,
   6:14. named Peter, and Andrew his *brother*,
    41. mote that is in thy *brother's* eye,
    42. say to thy *brother*, *Brother*, let me
     — mote that is in thy *brother's* eye.
   8:19. (his) mother and his *brethren*,
    20. Thy mother and thy *brethren*
    21. My mother and my *brethren* are
  12:13. Master, speak to my *brother*, that
  14:12. not thy friends, nor thy *brethren*,
    26. children, and *brethren*, and sisters,
  15:27. said unto him, Thy *brother* is come;
    32. for this thy *brother* was dead, and
  16:28. For I have five *brethren*; that
  17: 3. If thy *brother* trespass against thee,
  18:29. house, or parents, or *brethren*, or wife,
  20:28. If any man's *brother* die, having
     — that his *brother* should take his wife, and
      raise up seed unto his *brother*.
    29. There were therefore seven *brethren*:
  21:16. by parents, and *brethren*, and kinsfolks,
  22:32. art converted, strengthen thy *brethren*.
Joh. 1:40(41). was Andrew, Simon Peter's *brother*.
    41(42). findeth his own *brother* Simon,
   2:12. his mother, and his *brethren*,
   6: 8. Andrew, Simon Peter's *brother*, saith
   7: 3. His *brethren* therefore said unto him,
     5. neither did his *brethren* believe
    10. But when his *brethren* were gone up, then
  11: 2. whose *brother* Lazarus was sick.
    19. to comfort them concerning their *brother*.

Joh.11:21. been here, my *brother* had not died.
23. Thy *brother* shall rise again.
32. been here, my *brother* had not died.
20:17. go to my *brethren*, and say unto them,
21:23. saying abroad among the *brethren*,
Acts 1:14. of Jesus, and with his *brethren*.
16. Men (and) *brethren*, this scripture
2:29. Men (and) *brethren*, let me freely
37. Men (and) *brethren*, what shall we do?
3:17. now, *brethren*, I wot that through
22. unto you of your *brethren*, like
6: 3. Wherefore, *brethren*, look ye out among
7: 2. said, Men, *brethren*, and fathers,
13. was made known to his *brethren ;*
23. to visit his *brethren* the children
25. his *brethren* would have understood
26. saying, Sirs, ye are *brethren ;*
37. unto you of your *brethren*, like
9:17. said, *Brother* Saul, the Lord, (even)
30. (Which) when the *brethren* knew,
10:23. certain *brethren* from Joppa accompanied
11: 1. the apostles and *brethren* that
12. these six *brethren* accompanied me,
29. to send relief unto the *brethren* which
12: 2. he killed James the *brother* of John
17. unto James, and to the *brethren*.
13:15. saying, (Ye) men (and) *brethren*,
26. Men (and) *brethren*, children of
38. unto you therefore, men (and) *brethren*,
14: 2. minds evil affected against the *brethren*.
15: 1. from Judæa taught the *brethren*,
3. caused great joy unto all the *brethren*.
7. said unto them, Men (and) *brethren*,
13. Men (and) *brethren*, hearken
22. chief men among the *brethren :*
23. and elders and *brethren* (send) greeting unto the *brethren*.
32. exhorted the *brethren* with many words,
33. from the *brethren* unto the apostles.
36. go again and visit our *brethren*
40. being recommended by the *brethren*
16: 2. reported of by the *brethren* that were
40. and when they had seen the *brethren*,
17: 6. they drew Jason and certain *brethren*
10. the *brethren* immediately sent away Paul
14. the *brethren* sent away Paul
18:18. then took his leave of the *brethren*,
27. the *brethren* wrote, exhorting the
20:32. now, *brethren*, I commend you
21: 7. saluted the *brethren*, and abode with them one day.
17. the *brethren* received us gladly.
20. Thou seest, *brother*, how many thousands
22: 1. Men, *brethren*, and fathers, hear ye
5. I received letters unto the *brethren*,
13. *Brother* Saul, receive thy sight.
23: 1. Men (and) *brethren*, I have lived
5. I wist not, *brethren*, that he was
6. Men (and) *brethren*, I am a Pharisee,
28:14. Where we found *brethren;* and were
15. And from thence, when the *brethren*
17. Men (and) *brethren*, though I have
21. any of the *brethren* that came
Ro. 1:13. not have you ignorant, *brethren*,
7: 1. Know ye not, *brethren*, for I speak
4. Wherefore, my *brethren*, ye also are
8:12. Therefore, *brethren*, we are debtors,
29. the firstborn among many *brethren*.
9: 3. accursed from Christ for my *brethren*,
10: 1. *Brethren*, my heart's desire and prayer
11: 25. *brethren*, that ye should be ignorant
12: 1. I beseech you therefore, *brethren*,

Ro. 14:10. why dost thou judge thy *brother ?* or why dost thou set at nought thy *brother ?*
13. to fall in (his) *brother's* way.
15. if thy *brother* be grieved with
21. (any thing) whereby thy *brother* stumbleth
15:14. persuaded of you, my *brethren*,
15. *brethren*, I have written the more
30. Now I beseech you, *brethren*,
16:14. the *brethren* which are with them.
17. I beseech you, *brethren*, mark them
23. saluteth you, and Quartus a *brother*.
1Co. 1: 1. will of God, and Sosthenes (our) *brother*,
10. I beseech you, *brethren*, by the name
11. declared unto me of you, my *brethren*,
26. ye see your calling, *brethren*,
2: 1. I, *brethren*, when I came to you,
3: 1. I, *brethren*, could not speak unto you
4: 6. And these things, *brethren*, I have
5:11. that is called a *brother* be a
6: 5. be able to judge between his *brethren ?*
6. *brother* goeth to law with *brother*,
8. defraud, and that (your) *brethren*,
7:12. If any *brother* hath a wife that
15. A *brother* or a sister is not under
24. *Brethren*, let every man, wherein
29. this I say, *brethren*, the time (is)
8:11. shall the weak *brother* perish, for
12. ye sin so against the *brethren*,
13. meat make my *brother* to offend,
— lest I make my *brother* to offend.
9: 5. (as) the *brethren* of the Lord, and
10: 1. *brethren*, I would not that ye should
11: 2. I praise you, *brethren*, that ye
33. Wherefore, my *brethren*, when ye come
12: 1. Now concerning spiritual (gifts), *brethren*,
14: 6. Now, *brethren*, if I come unto you
20. *Brethren*, be not children in underst.:
26. How is it then, *brethren ?* when
39. Wherefore, *brethren*, covet to prophesy,
15: 1. Moreover, *brethren*, I declare unto you
6. above five hundred *brethren* at once ;
50. this I say, *brethren*, that flesh and
58. Therefore, my beloved *brethren*,
16:11. I look for him with the *brethren*.
12. As touching (our) *brother* Apollos,
— unto you with the *brethren*:
15. I beseech you, *brethren*, ye know
20. All the *brethren* greet you.
2Co. 1: 1. will of God, and Timothy (our) *brother*,
8. not, *brethren*, have you ignorant of
2:13. I found not Titus my *brother*:
8: 1. Moreover, *brethren*, we do you to wit
18. have sent with him the *brother*,
22. have sent with them our *brother*,
23. or our *brethren* (be enquired of),
9: 3. Yet have I sent the *brethren*,
5. necessary to exhort the *brethren*,
11: 9. the *brethren* which came from
12:18. with (him) I sent a *brother*.
13:11. Finally, *brethren*, farewell. Be perfect,
Gal. 1: 2. all the *brethren* which are with me,
11. I certify you, *brethren*, that the gospel
19. save James the Lord's *brother*.
3:15. *Brethren*, I speak after the manner
4:12. *Brethren*, I beseech you, be as I (am) ;
28. Now we, *brethren*, as Isaac was,
31. So then, *brethren*, we are not children
5:11. And I, *brethren*, if I yet preach
13. For, *brethren*, ye have been called
6: 1. *Brethren*, if a man be overtaken
18. *Brethren*, the grace of our Lord
Eph. 6:10. Finally, my *brethren*, be strong

Eph. 6:21. a beloved *brother* and faithful minister
23. Peace (be) to the *brethren*, and love
Phil. 1:12. ye should understand, *brethren*,
14. many of the *brethren* in the Lord,
2:25. send to you Epaphroditus, my *brother*,
3: 1. Finally, my *brethren*, rejoice in
13. *Brethren*, I count not myself to
17. *Brethren*, be followers together
4: 1. my *brethren* dearly beloved and
8. Finally, *brethren*, whatsoever things
21. The *brethren* which are with me
Col. 1: 1. will of God, and Timotheus (our) *brother*,
2. saints and faithful *brethren*
4: 7. you (who is) a beloved *brother*,
9. a faithful and beloved *brother*,
15. Salute the *brethren* which are
1 Th. 1: 4. Knowing, *brethren* beloved, your
2: 1. For yourselves, *brethren*, know
9. ye remember, *brethren*, our
14. For ye, *brethren*, became followers
17. we, *brethren*, being taken from
3: 2. sent Timotheus, our *brother*,
7. Therefore, *brethren*, we were comforted
4: 1. we beseech you, *brethren*, and
6. defraud his *brother* in (any) matter:
10. toward all the *brethren* which
— we beseech you, *brethren*, that
13. not have you to be ignorant, *brethren*,
5: 1. the times and the seasons, *brethren*,
4. ye, *brethren*, are not in darkness,
12. we beseech you, *brethren*, to know
14. we exhort you, *brethren*, warn
25. *Brethren*, pray for us.
26. Greet all the *brethren* with
27. read unto all the holy *brethren*.
2Th. 1: 3. thank God always for you, *brethren*,
2: 1. we beseech you, *brethren*, by
13. for you, *brethren* beloved of the
15. Therefore, *brethren*, stand fast,
3: 1. Finally, *brethren*, pray for us,
6. we command you, *brethren*,
— from every *brother* that walketh
13. ye, *brethren*, be not weary in
15. admonish (him) as a *brother*.
1Ti. 4: 6. put the *brethren* in remembrance
5: 1. the younger men as *brethren*;
6: 2. because they are *brethren*;
2Ti. 4.21. Claudia, and all the *brethren*.
Philem. 1. Timothy (our) *brother*, unto
7. the saints are refreshed by thee, *brother*.
16. above a servant, a *brother* beloved,
20. Yea, *brother*, let me have
Heb. 2:11. not ashamed to call them *brethren*,
12. declare thy name unto my *brethren*,
17. made like unto (his) *brethren*,
3: 1. Wherefore, holy *brethren*,
12. Take heed, *brethren*, lest there
7: 5. that is, of their *brethren*,
8:11. neighbour, and every man his *brother*,
10:19. Having therefore, *brethren*, boldness
13:22. I beseech you, *brethren*, suffer
23. Know ye that (our) *brother*
Jas. 1: 2. My *brethren*, count it all joy
9. Let the *brother* of low degree
16. Do not err, my beloved *brethren*.
19. Wherefore, my beloved *brethren*,
2: 1. My *brethren*, have not the faith
5. Hearken, my beloved *brethren*,
14. What (doth it) profit, my *brethren*,
15. If a *brother* or sister be naked,
3: 1. My *brethren*, be not many masters,
10. My *brethren*, these things ought

Jas. 3:12. Can the figtree, my *brethren*,
4:11. of another, *brethren*. He that speaketh
evil of (his) *brother*, and judgeth his *brother*,
5: 7. Be patient therefore, *brethren*,
9. Grudge not one against another, *brethren*,
10. Take, my *brethren*, the prophets,
12. above all things, my *brethren*,
19. *Brethren*, if any of you do err
1Pet. 5:12. a faithful *brother* unto you,
2Pet. 1:10. the rather, *brethren*, give diligence
3:15. as our beloved *brother* Paul also
1Joh.2: 7. *Brethren*, I write no new commandment
9. in the light, and hateth his *brother*,
10. He that loveth his *brother* abideth
11. he that hateth his *brother*
3:10. that loveth not his *brother*.
12. wicked one, and slew his *brother*.
— works were evil, and his *brother's* righteous.
13. Marvel not, my *brethren*, if
14. because we love the *brethren*. He that
loveth not (his) *brother* abideth
15. Whosoever hateth his *brother*
16. (our) lives for the *brethren*.
17. seeth his *brother* have need,
4:20. hateth his *brother*, he is a liar: for he that
loveth not his *brother*
21. loveth God love his *brother* also.
5:16. If any man see his *brother* sin
3Joh. 3. when the *brethren* came and
5. thou doest to the *brethren*, and
10. he himself receive the *brethren*,
Jude 1. of Jesus Christ, and *brother* of James,
Rev. 1: 9. I John, who also am your *brother*,
6:11. fellowservants also and their *brethren*,
12:10. the accuser of our *brethren* is cast
19:10. of thy *brethren* that have the
22: 9. of thy *brethren* the prophets, and

ἀδελφότης, *adelphotees*.

1Pet.2:17. Love the *brotherhood*. Fear God.
5: 9. accomplished in your *brethren*

ἄδηλος, *adeelos*.

Lu. 11:44. are as graves which *appear not*,
1Co.14: 8. the trumpet give an *uncertain* sound,

ἀδηλότης, *adeelotees*.

1Ti. 6:17. nor trust in *uncertain* riches,

ἀδήλως, *adeelōs*.

1Co. 9:26. so run, not as *uncertainly*,

ἀδημονέω, *adeemoneo*.

Mat.26:37. to be sorrowful and *very heavy*.
Mar 14:33. sore amazed, and *to be very heavy*;
Phil. 2:26. after you all, and was *full of heaviness*,

ᾅδης, *hadees*.

Mat.11:23. shalt be brought down to *hell*:
16:18. the gates of *hell* shall not prevail
Lu. 10:15. shalt be thrust down to *hell*.
16:23. in *hell* he lift up his eyes,

Acts 2:27. wilt not leave my soul in *hell*,
    31. his soul was not left in *hell*,
1 Co.15:55. O *grave*, where (is) thy victory?
Rev. 1:18. have the keys of *hell* and of death.
    6: 8. was Death, and *Hell* followed
   20:13. death and *hell* delivered up the
    14. death and *hell* were cast into

ἀδιάκριτος, *adiakritos.*

Jas. 3:17. *without partiality*, and without hypocrisy.

ἀδιάλειπτος, *adialiptos.*

Ro. 9: 2. great heaviness and *continual* sorrow
2 Ti. 1: 3. that *without ceasing* I have

ἀδιαλείπτως, *adialīptōs.*

Ro. 1: 9. that *without ceasing* I make mention
1 Th. 1: 3. Remembering *without ceasing*
   2:13. thank we God *without ceasing*,
   5:17. Pray *without ceasing*.

ἀδιαφθορία, *adiaphthoria.*

Tit. 2: 7. in doctrine (shewing) *uncorruptness*,

ἀδικέω, *adikeo.*

Mat.20:13. Friend, I *do* thee no *wrong* :
Lu. 10:19. nothing *shall* by any means *hurt* you.
Acts 7:24. seeing one (of them) *suffer wrong*,
   26. why *do ye wrong* one to another ?
   27. he *that did* his neighbour *wrong*
  25:10. to the Jews have I *done* no *wrong*,
   11. For if I *be an offender*, or have
1 Co. 6: 7. Why *do ye* not rather *take wrong* ?
   8. Nay, ye *do wrong*, and defraud,
2 Co. 7: 2. we *have wronged* no man,
   12. his cause *that had done the wrong*, nor for
    his cause *that suffered wrong*,
Gal. 4:12. ye *have* not *injured* me at all.
Col. 3:25. he *that doeth wrong* shall receive for the
    wrong which he *hath done:*
Philem 18. If he *hath wronged* thee, or oweth
Rev. 2:11. *shall* not *be hurt* of the second
   6: 6. (see) thou *hurt* not the oil and
   7: 2. it was given *to hurt* the earth
   3. Saying, *Hurt* not the earth, neither
   9: 4. *should* not *hurt* the grass of
   10. (was) *to hurt* men five months.
   19. with them they *do hurt*.
  11: 5. if any man will *hurt* them,
   — and if any man will *hurt* them,
  22:11. He *that is unjust, let* him *be unjust*

ἀδίκημα, *adikeema.*

Acts18:14. If it were a *matter of wrong* or
  24:20. found any *evil doing* in me,
Rev.18: 5. God hath remembered her *iniquities.*

ἀδικία, *adikia.*

Lu. 13:27. from me, all (ye) workers of *iniquity.*
  16: 8. commended the *unjust* steward,

Lu. 16: 9. of the mammon of *unrighteousness;*
  18: 6. Hear what the *unjust* judge saith.
Joh. 7:18. no *unrighteousness* is in him.
Acts 1:18. with the reward of *iniquity ;*
  8:23. (in) the bond of *iniquity.*
Ro. 1:18. ungodliness and *unrighteousness* of men,
    who hold the truth in *unrighteousness ;*
   29. filled with all *unrighteousness,*
   2: 8. the truth, but obey *unrighteousness,*
   3: 5. if our *unrighteousness* commend the
   6:13. instruments of *unrighteousness* unto
   9:14. (Is there) *unrighteousness* with God ?
1 Co.13: 6. Rejoiceth not in *iniquity*, but
2 Co.12:13. forgive me this *wrong.*
2 Th. 2:10. deceivableness of *unrighteousness* in
   12. had pleasure in *unrighteousness.*
2 Ti. 2:19. name of Christ depart from *iniquity.*
Heb. 8:12. merciful to their *unrighteousness,*
Jas. 3: 6. tongue (is) a fire, a world of *iniquity :*
2 Pet.2:13. the reward of *unrighteousness,*
   15. loved the wages of *unrighteousness ;*
1 Joh.1: 9. cleanse us from all *unrighteousness.*
   5:17. All *unrighteousness* is sin:

ἄδικος, *adikos.*

Mat. 5:45. rain on the just and on the *unjust.*
Lu. 16:10. he that is *unjust* in the least is *unjust*
   11. faithful in the *unrighteous* mammon,
  18:11. extortioners, *unjust*, adulterers, or
Acts24:15. both of the just and *unjust.*
Ro. 3: 5. (Is) God *unrighteous* who taketh
1 Co. 6: 1. go to law before the *unjust*, and
   9. the *unrighteous* shall not inherit the
Heb. 6:10. For God (is) not *unrighteous* to forget
1 Pet.3:18. for sins, the just for the *unjust*,
2 Pet.2: 9. to reserve the *unjust* unto the day

ἀδίκως, *adikōs.*

1 Pet.2:19. endure grief, suffering *wrongfully.*

ἀδόκιμος, *adokimos.*

Ro. 1:28. gave them over to a *reprobate* mind,
1 Co. 9:27. I myself should be *a castaway.*
2 Co.13: 5. Christ is in you, except ye be *reprobates ?*
   6. that we are not *reprobates.*
   7. though we be as *reprobates.*
2 Ti. 3: 8. *reprobate* concerning the faith.
Tit. 1:16. unto every good work *reprobate.*
Heb. 6: 8. beareth thorns and briers (is) *rejected,*

ἄδολος, *adolos.*

1 Pet.2: 2. desire the *sincere* milk of the word,

ἁδρότης, *hadrotees.*

2 Co. 8:20. blame us in this *abundance*

ἀδυνατέω, *adunateo.*

Mat.17:20. nothing *shall be impossible* unto
Lu. 1:37. with God nothing *shall be impossible.*

ἀδύνατος, adunatos.

Mat.19:26. With men this is *impossible;*
Mar 10:27. With men (it is) *impossible,*
Lu. 18:27. things which are *impossible* with
Acts 14: 8. man at Lystra, *impotent* in his feet,
Ro. 8: 3. For what the law *could not do,*
15: 1. bear the infirmities of the *weak,*
Heb. 6: 4. For (it is) *impossible* for those
18. in which (it was) *impossible* for
10: 4. (it is) *not possible* that the blood
11: 6. without faith (it is) *impossible* to

ᾄδω, ado.

Eph. 5:19. *singing* and making melody
Col. 3:16. *singing* with grace in your
Rev. 5: 9. they *sung* a new song, saying,
14: 3. they *sung* as it were a new
15: 3. they *sing* the song of Moses

ἀεί, aï.

Mar 15: 8. as he had *ever* done unto them.
Acts 7:51. ye do *always* resist the Holy Ghost:
2Co. 4:11. we which live are *alway* delivered
6:10. As sorrowful, yet *alway* rejoicing ;
Tit. 1:12. The Cretians (are) *alway* liars,
Heb. 3:10. They do *alway* err in (their) heart ;
1Pet. 3:15. (be) ready *always* to (give) an
2Pet. 1:12. to put you *always* in remembrance

ἀετός, aetos.

Mat.24:28. there will the *eagles* be gathered
Lu. 17:37. thither will the *eagles* be gathered
Rev. 4: 7. fourth beast (was) like a flying *eagle.*
12:14. given two wings of a great *eagle,*

ἄζυμος, azumos.

Mat.26:17. the (feast of) *unleavened bread*
Mar.14: 1. the passover, and of *unleavened bread:*
12. the first day of *unleavened bread,*
Lu. 22: 1. Now the feast of *unleavened bread*
7. came the day of *unleavened bread,*
Acts 12: 3. were the days of *unleavened bread.*
20: 6. after the days of *unleavened bread,*
1Co. 5: 7. a new lump, as ye are *unleavened.*
8. *unleavened* (bread) of sincerity and

ἀήρ, aeer.

Acts 22:23. (their) clothes, and threw dust into the *air,*
1Co. 9:26. not as one that beateth the *air:*
14: 9. for ye shall speak into the *air.*
Eph. 2: 2. prince of the power of the *air,*
1 Th. 4.17. to meet the Lord in the *air:* and
Rev. 9: 2. the sun and the *air* were darkened
16:17. poured out his vial into the *air;*

ἀθανασία, athanasia.

1Co.15:53. this mortal (must) put on *immortality.*
54. shall have put on *immortality,*
1Ti. 6:16. Who only hath *immortality,*

ἀθέμιτος, athemitos.

Acts 10:28. it is an *unlawful thing* for a
1Pet. 4: 3. banquetings, and *abominable* idolatries:

ἄθεος, atheos.

Eph. 2:12. no hope, and *without God* in the world:

ἄθεσμος, athesmos.

2 Pet. 2: 7. filthy conversation of the *wicked:*
3:17. with the error of the *wicked,*

ἀθετέω, atheteo.

Mar. 6:26. he would not *reject* her.
7: 9. ye *reject* the commandment of
Lu. 7:30. lawyers *rejected* the counsel of
10:16. he *that despiseth* you *despiseth* me; and he *that despiseth* me *despiseth* him that sent me.
Joh. 12:48. He *that rejecteth* me, and receiveth
1Co. 1:19. *will bring to nothing* the understanding
Gal. 2:21. I do not *frustrate* the grace of God:
3:15. confirmed, no man *disannulleth,*
1Th. 4: 8. therefore *that despiseth, despiseth* not man,
1Ti. 5:12. they *have cast off* their first faith.
Heb 10:28. He *that despised* Moses' law
Jude 8. defile the flesh, *despise* dominion,

ἀθέτησις, atheteesis.

Heb. 7:18. verily a *disannulling* of the
9:26. to *put away* sin by the sacrifice

ἀθλέω, athleo.

2Ti. 2: 5. if a man also *strive* for
— except he *strive* lawfully.

ἄθλησις, athleesis.

Heb 10:32. endured a great *fight* of afflictions;

ἀθυμέω, athumeo.

Col. 3:21. (to anger), lest they *be discouraged.*

ἀθῶος, athōos.

Mat.27: 4. I have betrayed the *innocent* blood.
24. I am *innocent* of the blood of

αἴγειος, aigīos.

Heb 11:37. about in sheepskins and *goat*skins ;

αἰγιαλός, aigialos.

Mat.13: 2. whole multitude stood on the *shore.*
48. was full, they drew to *shore,*
Joh.21: 4. Jesus stood on the *shore:*
Acts 21: 5. kneeled down on the *shore,* and prayed.
27:39. discovered a certain creek with a *shore,*
40. to the wind, and made toward *shore.*

ἀΐδιος, aïdios.

Rom. 1:20. (even) his *eternal* power and
Jude 6. reserved in *everlasting* chains

αἰδώς, aidōs.

1Ti. 2: 9. with *shamefacedness* and sobriety;
Heb12:28. acceptably with *reverence* and godly fear:

αἷμα, haima.

Mat.16:17. for flesh and *blood* hath not
23:30. in the *blood* of the prophets.
35. the righteous *blood* shed upon the earth,
from the *blood* of righteous Abel
— unto the *blood* of Zacharias son of
26:28. For this is my *blood* of the new
27: 4. I have betrayed the innocent *blood.*
6. because it is the price of *blood.*
8. was called, The field of *blood,*
24. I am innocent of the *blood* of this
25. His *blood* (be) on us, and on our
Mar. 5:25. which had an issue of *blood*
29. the fountain of her *blood* was
14:24. This is my *blood* of the new
Lu. 8:43. having an issue of *blood* twelve
44. her issue of *blood* stanched.
11:50. the *blood* of all the prophets,
51. From the *blood* of Abel unto the *blood* of Zacharias,
13: 1. whose *blood* Pilate had mingled
22:20. new testament in my *blood,*
44. great drops of *blood* falling down
Joh. 1:13. Which were born, not of *blood,* nor
6:53. Son of man, and drink his *blood,*
54. eateth my flesh, and drinketh my *blood,*
55. my *blood* is drink indeed.
56. eateth my flesh, and drinketh my *blood,*
19:34. came thereout *blood* and water.
Acts 1:19. to say, The field of *blood.*
2:19. *blood,* and fire, and vapour of
20. into darkness, and the moon into *blood,*
5:28. bring this man's *blood* upon us.
15:20. things strangled, and (from) *blood.*
29. offered to idols, and from *blood,*
17:26. hath made of one *blood* all nations
18: 6. Your *blood* (be) upon your own
20:26. from the *blood* of all (men).
28. purchased with his own *blood.*
21:25. from *blood,* and from strangled,
22:20. when the *blood* of thy martyr
Ro. 3:15. Their feet (are) swift to shed *blood:*
25. through faith in his *blood,* to
5: 9. being now justified by his *blood,*
1Co.10.16. communion of the *blood* of Christ?
11:25. the new testament in my *blood:*
27. the body and *blood* of the Lord.
15:50. that flesh and *blood* cannot
Gal. 1:16. I conferred not with flesh and *blood:*
Eph. 1: 7. have redemption through his *blood,*
2:13. nigh by the *blood* of Christ.
6:12. wrestle not against flesh and *blood,*
Col. 1:14. redemption through his *blood,*
20. peace through the *blood* of his
Heb 2:14. partakers of flesh and *blood,* he
9: 7. once every year, not without *blood,*
12. Neither by the *blood* of goats and calves, but by his own *blood*
13. For if the *blood* of bulls and of
14. more shall the *blood* of Christ,

Heb. 9:18. (testament) was dedicated without *blood.*
19. he took the *blood* of calves and
20. Saying, This (is) the *blood* of the
21. sprinkled with *blood* both the tabernacle,
22. are by the law purged with *blood*
25. every year with *blood* of others:
10: 4. that the *blood* of bulls and of
19. the holiest by the *blood* of Jesus,
29. counted the *blood* of the covenant,
11:28. the passover, and the sprinkling of *blood,*
12: 4. not yet resisted unto *blood,*
24. to the *blood* of sprinkling, that
13:11. those beasts, whose *blood* is
12. sanctify the people with his own *blood,*
20. through the *blood* of the everlasting
1Pet. 1: 2. sprinkling of the *blood* of Jesus Christ:
19. with the precious *blood* of Christ,
1Joh.1: 7. the *blood* of Jesus Christ his Son
5: 6. came by water and *blood,* (even) Jesus Christ: not by water only, but by water and *blood.*
8. the spirit, and the water, and the *blood:*
Rev. 1: 5. from our sins in his own *blood,*
5: 9. redeemed us to God by thy *blood*
6:10. not judge and avenge our *blood*
12. the moon became as *blood;*
7:14. white in the *blood* of the Lamb.
8: 7. hail and fire mingled with *blood,*
8. part of the sea became *blood;*
11: 6. over waters to turn them to *blood,*
12:11. by the *blood* of the Lamb, and
14:20. *blood* came out of the winepress,
16: 3. it became as the *blood* of a dead
4. of waters; and they became *blood.*
6. shed the *blood* of saints and prophets, and thou hast given them *blood* to drink;
17: 6. drunken with the *blood* of the saints, and with the *blood* of the martyrs of Jesus:
18:24. was found the *blood* of prophets,
19: 2. avenged the *blood* of his servants
13. with a vesture dipped in *blood:*

αἱματεκχυσία, haimatekkusia.

Heb 9:22. without *shedding of blood* is no

αἱμορροέω, haimorroeo.

Mat. 9:20. *diseased with an issue of blood* twelve

αἴνεσις, ainesis.

Heb13:15. let us offer the sacrifice *of praise* to

αἰνέω, aineo.

Lu. 2:13. the heavenly host, *praising* God,
20. glorifying and *praising* God for
19:37. to rejoice and *praise* God with a
24:53. *praising* and blessing God.
Acts 2:47. *Praising* God, and having favour
3: 8. walking, and leaping, and *praising* God,
9. saw him walking and *praising* God:
Ro. 15:11. again, *Praise* the Lord, all ye
Rev.19: 5. saying, *Praise* our God, all ye

αἴνιγμα, ainigma.

1Co.13:12. now we see through a glass, *darkly;*

αἶνος, ainos.

Mat.21:16. thou hast perfected *praise?*
Lu. 18:43. saw (it), gave *praise* unto God.

αἱρέομαι, haireomai.

Phil. 1:22. what I *shall choose* I wot not.
2 Th. 2:13. from the beginning *chosen* you
Heb 11:25. *Choosing* rather to suffer

αἵρεσις, hairesis.

Acts 5:17. which is the *sect* of the Sadducees
15: 5. certain of the *sect* of the Pharisees
24: 5. of the *sect* of the Nazarenes:
14. the way which they call *heresy,*
26: 5. straitest *sect* of our religion
28:22. for as concerning this *sect,*
1Co.11:19. there must be also *heresies*
Gal. 5:20. strife, seditions, *heresies,*
2Pet.2: 1. shall bring in damnable *heresies,*

αἱρετίζω, hairetizo.

Mat.12:18. my servant, whom I *have chosen;*

αἱρετικός, hairetikos.

Tit. 3:10. A man that is an *heretick*

αἴρω, airo.

Mat. 4: 6. in (their) hands they *shall bear* thee *up*
9: 6. Arise, *take up* thy bed, and go
16. to fill it up *taketh* from the garment,
11:29. *Take* my yoke upon you, and
13:12. from him *shall be taken away*
14:12. came, and *took up* the body,
20. they *took up* of the fragments
15:37. they *took up* of the broken (meat)
16:24. *take up* his cross, and follow me.
17:27. *take up* the fish that first
20:14. *Take* (that) thine (is), and go thy
21:21. *Be* thou *removed,* and be thou cast into
43. of God *shall be taken* from you,
22:13. hand and foot, and *take* him *away,*
24:17. *to take* any thing out of his house:
18. return back *to take* his clothes.
39. came, and *took* them all *away;*
25:28. *Take* therefore the talent from him,
29. that hath not *shall be taken away*
27:32. they compelled *to bear* his cross.
Mar 2: 3. which was *borne* of four.
9. Arise, and *take up* thy bed,
11. Arise, and *take up* thy bed,
12. he arose, *took up* the bed, and went
. 21. filled it up *taketh away* from the
4:15. *taketh away* the word that was
25. from him *shall be taken* even
6: 8. they *should take* nothing for
29. they came and *took up* his corpse,
43. they *took up* twelve baskets full
8: 8. they *took up* of the broken (meat)
19. baskets full of fragments *took* ye *up?*
20. baskets full of fragments *took* ye *up?*
34. deny himself, and *take up* his cross,
10:21. come, *take up* the cross, and follow
11:23. *Be* thou *removed,* and be thou cast into
13:15. *to take* anything out of his house:

Mar 13:16. for *to take up* his garment.
15:21. of Alexander and Rufus, to *bear* his cross.
24. what every man *should take.*
16:18. They *shall take up* serpents ;
Lu. 4:11. in (their) hands they *shall bear* thee *up,*
5:24. Arise, and *take up* thy couch, and go
25. before them, and *took up* that whereon
6:29. him *that taketh away* thy cloke
30. of him *that taketh away* thy goods
8:12. the devil, and *taketh away* the word out
18. from him *shall be taken* even that
9: 3. *Take* nothing for (your) journey, neither
17. there *was taken up* of fragments
23. deny himself, and *take up* his cross daily,
11:22. he *taketh* from him all his armour
52. ye *have taken away* the key of knowledge:
17:13. they *lifted up* (their) voices, and said,
31. let him not come down *to take* it *away:*
19:21. thou *takest up* that thou layedst
22. *taking up* that I laid not down,
24. *Take* from him the pound, and
26. that he hath *shall be taken away*
22:36. that hath a purse, *let* him *take* (it),
23:18. saying, *Away with* this (man),
Joh. 1:29. Lamb of God, which *taketh away*
2:16. *Take* these things hence ; make
5: 8. Rise, *take up* thy bed, and walk.
9. was made whole, and *took up* his bed,
10. not lawful for thee *to carry* (thy) bed.
11. said unto me, *Take up* thy bed,
12. said unto thee, *Take up* thy bed, and
8:59. Then *took* they *up* stones to cast
10:18. No man *taketh* it from me, but
24. How long dost thou make us to doubt? (lit. *suspend* our souls)
11:39. Jesus said, *Take* ye *away* the stone.
41. Then they *took away* the stone (from)
— Jesus *lifted up* (his) eyes, and said,
48. Romans shall come and *take away* both
15: 2. beareth not fruit he *taketh away:*
16:22. your joy no man *taketh* from you.
17:15. that thou *shouldest take* them out
19:15. cried out, *Away with* (him), *away with* (him),
31. (that) they *might be taken away.*
38. *might take away* the body of Jesus:
— came therefore, and *took* the body of Jesus.
20: 1. the stone *taken away* from the
2. They *have taken away* the Lord
13. they *have taken away* my Lord,
15. laid him, and I *will take* him *away.*
Acts 4:24. they *lifted up* their voice to
8:33. his judgment *was taken away:*
— his life *is taken* from the earth.
20: 9. the third loft, and *was taken up* dead.
21:11. come unto us, he *took* Paul's girdle,
36. followed after, crying, *Away with* him.
22:22. said, *Away with* such a (fellow)
27:13. *loosing* (thence), they sailed close
17. Which when they *had taken up,*
1Co. 6:15. shall I then *take* the members
Eph. 4:31. evil speaking, *be put away* from you,
Col. 2:14. contrary to us, and *took* it out of the way,
1Joh.3: 5. was manifested *to take away* our sins;
Rev.10: 5. *lifted* up his hand to heaven,
18:21. a mighty angel *took up* a stone

αἰσθάνομαι, aisthanomai.

Lu. 9:45. hid from them, that they *perceived* it not ;

αἴσθησις, aistheesis.

Phil. 1: 9. in knowledge and (in) all *judgment;*

αἰσθητήριον, aistheeteerion.

Heb. 5:14. have their *senses* exercised to

αἰσχροκερδής, aiskrokerdees.

1Ti. 3: 3. no striker, not *greedy of filthy lucre;*
8. to much wine, not *greedy of filthy lucre;*
Tit. 1: 7. no striker, not *given to filthy lucre;*

αἰσχροκερδῶς, aiskrokerdos.

1Pet.5: 2. willingly; not *for filthy lucre,*

αἰσχρολογία, aiskrologia.

Col. 3: 8. *filthy communication* out of your

αἰσχρόν, aiskron.

1Co.11: 6. if it be a *shame* for a woman to
14:35. for it is. a *shame* for women to
Eph. 5:12. For it is a *shame* even to speak

αἰσχρός, aiskros.

Tit. 1:11. ought not, for *filthy* lucre's sake.

αἰσχρότης, aiskrotees.

Eph. 5: 4. Neither *filthiness,* nor foolish talking,

αἰσχύνη, aiskunee.

Lu. 14: 9. thou begin with *shame* to take
2Co. 4: 2. the hidden things of *dishonesty,*
Phil. 3:19. (whose) glory (is) in their *shame,*
Heb 12: 2. endured the cross, despising the *shame,*
Jude 13. foaming out their own *shame;*
Rev. 3:18. the *shame* of thy nakedness do

αἰσχύνομαι, aiskunomai.

Lu. 16: 3. I cannot dig; to beg I am *ashamed.*
2Co.10: 8. your destruction, I *should* not be *ashamed:*
Phil. 1:20. in nothing I *shall be ashamed,*
1Pet.4:16. a Christian, *let* him not *be ashamed;*
1Joh.2:28. not *be ashamed* before him

αἰτέω, aiteo.

Mat. 5:42. Give to him *that asketh* thee, and
6: 8. have need of, before ye *ask* him.
7: 7. *Ask,* and it shall be given you;
8. every one *that asketh* receiveth;
9. if his son *ask* bread, will he
10. Or if he *ask* a fish, will he give
11. good things to them *that ask* him?
14: 7. give her whatsoever she *would ask.*
18:19. any thing that they *shall ask,*
20:20. *desiring* a certain thing of him.
22. said, Ye know not what ye *ask.*

Mat.21:22. whatsoever ye *shall ask* in prayer
27:20. that they *should ask* Barabbas.
58. to Pilate, and *begged* the body of Jesus.
Mar. 6:22. *Ask* of me whatsoever thou wilt;
23. Whatsoever thou *shalt ask* of me,
24. unto her mother, What *shall I ask?*
25. unto the king, and *asked,* saying,
10:35. for us whatsoever we *shall desire.*
38. Ye know not what ye *ask:*
11:24. What things soever ye *desire,* when
15: 6. one prisoner, whomsoever they *desired.*
8. began *to desire* (him to do) as he
43. unto Pilate, and *craved* the body of Jesus.
Lu. 1:63. he *asked* for a writing table, *and* wrote,
6:30. Give to every man *that asketh* of thee;
11: 9. *Ask,* and it shall be given you;
10. every one *that asketh* receiveth;
11. If a son *shall ask* bread of any
12. Or if he *shall ask* an egg, will
13. Holy Spirit to them *that ask* him?
12:48. of him they *will ask* the more.
23:23. *requiring* that he might be
25. into prison, whom they *had desired;*
52. unto Pilate, and *begged* the body of Jesus.
Joh. 4: 9. being a Jew, *askest* drink of me,
10. thou *wouldest have asked* of him,
11:22. whatsoever thou *wilt ask* of God,
14:13. whatsoever ye *shall ask* in my
14. If ye *shall ask* any thing in
15: 7. abide in you, ye *shall ask* what
16. whatsoever ye *shall ask* of the
16:23. Whatsoever ye *shall ask* the Father
24. ye *asked* nothing in my name: *ask,*
26. At that day ye *shall ask* in my
Acts 3: 2. *to ask* alms of them that entered
14. the Just, and *desired* a murderer to
7:46. *desired* to find a tabernacle for
9: 2. *desired* of him letters to Damascus
12:20. their friend, *desired* peace; because
13:21. afterward they *desired* a king:
28. yet *desired* they Pilate that he
16:29. Then he *called for* a light, and sprang
25: 3. *desired* favour against him, that
15. *desiring* (to have) judgment against
1Co. 1:22. For the Jews *require* a sign, and
Eph. 3:13. I *desire* that ye faint not at my
20. above all that we *ask* or think,
Col. 1: 9. to *desire* that ye might be filled
Jas. 1: 5. you lack wisdom, *let* him *ask* of God,
6. But *let* him *ask* in faith, nothing
4: 2. ye have not, because ye *ask* not.
3. Ye *ask,* and receive not, because ye *ask*
amiss, that ye may
1Pet.3:15. every man *that asketh* you a
1Joh.3:22. whatsoever we *ask,* we receive
5:14. if we *ask* any thing according
15. we *ask,* we know that we have the petitions that we *desired* of him.
16. not unto death, he *shall ask,* and

αἴτημα, aiteema.

Lu. 23:24. it should be as they *required.* (lit. their *request*)
Phil. 4: 6. let your *requests* be made known
1Joh.5:15. we have the *petitions* that we

αἰτία, aitia.

Mat.19: 3. to put away his wife for every *cause?*
10. If the *case* of the man be so with

Mat.27:37. over his head his *accusation* written,
Mar 15:26. his *accusation* was written over,
Lu. 8:47. for what *cause* she had touched
Joh.18:38. I find in him no *fault* (at all).
   19: 4. I find no *fault* in him.
    6. for I find no *fault* in him.
Acts10:21. what (is) the *cause* wherefore
   13:28. they found no *cause* of death (in)
   22:24. he might know *where*fore (lit. for what *cause*) they
   23:28. I would have known the *cause*
   25:18. they brought none *accusation* of
    27. the *crimes* (laid) against him.
   28:18. there was no *cause* of death in me.
    20. For this *cause* therefore have I
2Ti. 1: 6. *Wherefore* (lit. for which *cause*) I put thee in remembrance
    12. For the which *cause* I also suffer
Tit. 1:13. witness is true. *Where*fore rebuke
Heb.2:11. for which *cause* he is not ashamed

αἰτίαμα, *aitiama.*

Acts25: 7. many and grievous *complaints* against

αἴτιον, *aition.*

Lu. 23: 4. I find no *fault* in this man.
   14. have found no *fault* in this man
   22. I have found no *cause* of death in
Acts19:40. there being no *cause* whereby

αἴτιος, *aitios.*

Heb. 5: 9. he became the *author* of eternal

αἰφνίδιος, *aiphnidios.*

Lu. 21:34. that day come upon you *unawares.*
1Th. 5: 3. then *sudden* destruction cometh

αἰχμαλωσία, *aikmalōsia.*

Eph. 4: 8. he led *captivity* captive, and gave
Rev.13:10. He that leadeth into *captivity* shall go into *captivity* :

αἰχμαλωτεύω, *aikmalotĕuo.*

Eph. 4: 8. up on high, he *led* captivity *captive,*
2Ti. 3: 6. *lead* captive silly women laden

αἰχμαλωτίζω, *aikmalotizo.*

Lu. 21:24. *shall be led away* captive into
Ro. 7:23. *bringing* me into *captivity* to
2Co.10: 5. *bringing into captivity* every

αἰχμάλωτος, *aikmalōtos.*

Lu. 4:18(19). to preach deliverance to the *captives,*

αἰών, *aiōn.*

Note.—[1] εις τον α. [2] εις τους α. [3] εις τ8ς α. των α.

Mat. 6:13. the power, and the glory, for *ever.* [2]

Mat.12:32. forgiven him, neither in this *world,*
   13:22. heareth the word ; and the care of this *world,*
    39. the harvest is the end of the *world ;*
    40. it be in the end of this *world.*
    49. So shall it be at the end of the *world :*
   21:19. grow on thee benceforward for *ever.* [1]
   24: 3. thy coming, and of the end of the *world ?*
   28:20. (even) unto the end of the *world.*
Mar. 3:29. against the Holy Ghost hath never (lit. not for *ever*)[1]
   4:19. the cares of this *world,* and the
   10:30. in the *world* to come eternal life.
   11:14. No man eat fruit of thee hereafter for *ever.*[1]
Lu. 1:33. over the house of Jacob for *ever ;*[2] and
    55. to Abraham, and to his seed for *ever.* [1]
    70. which have been since the *world began :* (lit. from *ever*) (απ' αιωνος)
   16: 8. the children of this *world* are in
   18:30. in the *world* to come life
   20:34. The children of this *world* marry,
    35. worthy to obtain that *world,* and
Joh. 4:14. shall give him shall never thirst ; (lit. not for *ever*)[1]
   6:51. of this bread, he shall live for *ever :*[1]
    58. eateth of this bread shall live for *ever.* [1]
   8:35. abideth not in the house for *ever :*[1] (but) the Son abideth for *ever.*[1]
    51. my saying, he shall never see death. (lit. not for *ever*)[1]
    52. my saying, he shall never taste of (lit. not for *ever*)[1]
   9:32. Since the *world began* was it (εκ τ8 α.)
   10:28. they shall never perish, neither (lit. not for *ever*)[1]
   11:26. believeth in me shall never die. (lit. not for *ever*)[1]
   12:34. that Christ abideth for *ever :*[1]
   13: 8. Thou shalt never wash my feet. (lit. not for *ever*)[1]
   14:16. he may abide with you for *ever ;*[1]
Acts 3:21. holy prophets since the *world began.* (lit. from *ever*) (απ' αιωνος)
   15:18. from the *beginning of the world.* (απ' αιωνος)
Ro. 1:25. the Creator, who is blessed for *ever.*[2]
   9: 5. is over all, God blessed for *ever.*[2]
   11:36. to whom (be) glory for *ever.*[2]
   12: 2. be not conformed to this *world :*
   16:27. (be) glory through Jesus Christ for *ever.*[2]
1Co. 1:20. where (is) the disputer of this *world ?*
   2: 6. yet not the wisdom of this *world,* nor of the princes of this *world,*
    7. God ordained before the *world* (προ των)
    8. none of the princes of this *world* knew :
   3:18. seemeth to be wise in this *world,*
   8:13. no flesh *while the world standeth,* (lit. *for ever*)[1]
   10:11. the ends of the *world* are come. (των α.)
2Co. 4: 4. the god of this *world* hath blinded
   9: 9. his righteousness remaineth for *ever.*[1]
   11:31. Christ, which is blessed for *evermore,*[2]
Gal. 1: 4. deliver us from this present evil *world,*
    5. To whom (be) glory for *ever* and *ever.*[3]
Eph. 1:21. named, not only in this *world,*
   2: 2. according to the *course* of this world,
    7. That in the *ages* to come he might
   3: 9. the *beginning of the world* (απο των α.)
    11. According to the *eternal* purpose (των α.)
    21. throughout all ages, *world* without *end* (τ8 α. των α.)
   6:12. of the darkness of this *world,*

Phi. 4:20. our Father (be) glory for *ever* and *ever*.[3]

Col. 1:26. hid from *ages* and from generations, (απο των α.)

1Ti. 1:17. Now unto the King *eternal*, (των α.)
— (be) honour and glory for *ever* and *ever*.[3]
6:17. that are rich in this *world*,

2Ti. 4:10. having loved this present *world*,
18. to whom (be) glory for *ever* and *ever*.[3]

Tit. 2:12. godly, in this present *world* ;

Heb 1: 2. by whom also he made the *worlds* ;
8. Thy throne, O God, (is) for *ever* and *ever*: (του α. τε α.)
5: 6. Thou (art) a priest for *ever*[1] after
6: 5. the powers of the *world* to come,
20. made an high priest for *ever*[1] after
7:17. Thou (art) a priest for *ever*[1] after
21. Thou (art) a priest for *ever*[1] after
24. this (man), because he continueth *ever*,[1]
28. Son, who is consecrated for *evermore*.[1]
9:26. now once in the end of the *world* (των α.)
11: 3. the *worlds* were framed by the
13: 8. yesterday, and to day, and for *ever*.[2]
21. to whom (be) glory for *ever* and *ever*.[3]

1Pet. 1:23. which liveth and abideth for *ever*.[1]
25. word of the Lord endureth for *ever*.[1]
4:11. praise and dominion for *ever* and *ever*.[3]
5:11. (be) glory and dominion for *ever* and *ever*.[3]

2Pet. 2:17. of darkness is reserved for *ever*. (εις αιωνα)
3:18. (be) glory both now and for *ever*. (εις (ημεραν αιωνος)

1Joh. 2:17. the will of God abideth for *ever*.[1]

2Joh. 2. shall be with us for *ever*.[1]

Jude 13. the blackness of darkness for *ever*.[1]
25. both now and *ever*. (εις παντας τες α.)

Rev. 1: 6. (be) glory and dominion for *ever* and *ever*.[3]
18. behold, I am alive for *evermore*,[3]
4: 9. who liveth for *ever* and *ever*,[3]
10. worship him that liveth for *ever* and *ever*,[3]
5:13. unto the Lamb for *ever* and *ever*.[3]
14. worshipped him that liveth for *ever* and *ever*.[3]
7:12. might, (be) unto our God for *ever* and *ever*.[3]
10: 6. sware by him that liveth for *ever* and *ever*,[3]
11:15. he shall reign for *ever* and *ever*.[3]
14:11. their torment ascendeth up for *ever* and *ever* : (εις αιωνας αιωνων)
15: 7. God, who liveth for *ever* and *ever*.[3]
19: 3. her smoke rose up for *ever* and *ever*.[3]
20:10. tormented day and night for *ever* and *ever*.[3]
22: 5. they shall reign for *ever* and *ever*.[3]

αἰώνιος, *aiōnios*.

Mat.18: 8. to be cast into *everlasting* fire.
19:16. that I may have *eternal* life?
29. shall inherit *everlasting* life.
25:41. ye cursed, into *everlasting* fire,
46. go away into *everlasting* punishment: but the righteous into life *eternal*.

Mar 3:29. in danger of *eternal* damnation:
10:17. that I may inherit *eternal* life?
30. in the world to come *eternal* life.

Lu. 10:25. what shall I do to inherit *eternal* life?
16: 9. receive you into *everlasting* habitations.
18:18. what shall I do to inherit *eternal* life?
30. in the world to come life *everlasting*.

Joh. 3:15. not perish, but have *eternal* life.
16. not perish, but have *everlasting* life.
36. believeth on the Son hath *everlasting* life.

Joh. 4:14. springing up into *everlasting* life.
36. gathereth fruit unto life *eternal* :
5:24. that sent me, hath *everlasting* life,
39. ye think ye have *eternal* life:
6:27. which endureth unto *everlasting* life,
40. on him, may have *everlasting* life:
47. believeth on me hath *everlasting* life.
54. drinketh my blood, hath *eternal* life;
68. thou hast the words of *eternal* life.
10:28. I give unto them *eternal* life ;
12:25. shall keep it unto life *eternal*.
50. his commandment is life *everlasting* :
17: 2. he should give *eternal* life to as
3. this is life *eternal*, that they

Acts13:46. unworthy of *everlasting* life, lo,
48. as many as were ordained to *eternal* life

Ro. 2: 7. honour and immortality, *eternal* life:
5:21. through righteousness unto *eternal* life
6:22. unto holiness, and the end *everlasting* life.
23. the gift of God (is) *eternal* life
16:25. kept secret since the *world* began, (χρονοις αιωνιοις)
26. commandment of the *everlasting* God,

2Co. 4:17. exceeding (and) *eternal* weight of glory ;
18. things which are not seen (are) *eternal*.
5: 1. with hands, *eternal* in the heavens.

Gal. 6: 8. shall of the Spirit reap life *everlasting*.

2Th. 1: 9. be punished with *everlasting* destruction
2:16. hath given (us) *everlasting* consolation

1Ti. 1:16. believe on him to life *everlasting*.
6:12. lay hold on *eternal* life, whereunto
16. (be) honour and power *everlasting*.
19. they may lay hold on *eternal* life.

2Ti. 1: 9. in Christ Jesus before the *world* began ; (προ χρονων αιωνιων)
2:10. in Christ Jesus with *eternal* glory.

Tit. 1: 2. hope of *eternal* life, which God, that cannot lie, promised before the *world* began ; (προ χρ. αι.)
3: 7. to the hope of *eternal* life.

Philem.15. thou shouldest receive him *for ever* ;

Heb 5: 9. the author of *eternal* salvation
6: 2. the dead, and of *eternal* judgment.
9:12. having obtained *eternal* redemption
14. who through the *eternal* Spirit offered
15. the promise of *eternal* inheritance.
13:20. blood of the *everlasting* covenant,

1Pet. 5:10. called us unto his *eternal* glory

2Pet. 1:11. into the *everlasting* kingdom of our

1Joh.1: 2. shew unto you that *eternal* life,
2:25. promised us, (even) *eternal* life.
3:15. no murderer hath *eternal* life
5:11. God hath given to us *eternal* life,
13. know that ye have *eternal* life,
20. the true God, and *eternal* life.

Jude 7. suffering the vengeance of *eternal* fire.
21. Lord Jesus Christ unto *eternal* life.

Rev.14: 6. having the *everlasting* gospel to

ἀκαθαρσία, *akatharsia*.

Mat.23:27. dead (men's) bones, and of all *uncleanness*.

Ro. 1:24. gave them up to *uncleanness* through
6:19. your members servants to *uncleanness*

2Co.12:21. have not repented of the *uncleanness*

Gal. 5:19. Adultery, fornication, *uncleanness*,

Eph. 4:19. to work all *uncleanness* with greediness.
5: 3. fornication, and all *uncleanness*, or

Col. 3: 5. upon the earth ; fornication, *uncleanness*,

1Th. 2: 3. not of deceit, nor of *uncleanness*, nor
4: 7. God hath not called us unto *uncleanness*,

ἀκαθάρτης, akathartees.

Rev.17: 4. abominations and *filthiness* of her fornication:

ἀκάθαρτος, akathartos.

Mat.10: 1. power (against) *unclean* spirits,
   12:43. When the *unclean* spirit is gone
Mar 1:23. a man with an *unclean* spirit ;
   26. when the *unclean* spirit had torn
   27. commandeth he even the *unclean* spirits,
   3:11. *unclean* spirits, when they saw
   30. said, He hath an *unclean* spirit.
   5: 2. a man with an *unclean* spirit,
   8. Come out of the man, (thou) *unclean*
      spirit.
   13. the *unclean* spirits went out,
   6: 7. gave them power over *unclean* spirits ;
   7:25. young daughter had an *unclean* spirit,
   9:25. he rebuked the *foul* spirit, saying
Lu. 4:33. had a spirit of an *unclean* devil,
   36. he commandeth the *unclean* spirits,
   6:18. that were vexed with *unclean* spirits:
   8:29. had commanded the *unclean* spirit
   9:42. Jesus rebuked the *unclean* spirit,
   11:24. When the *unclean* spirit is gone
Acts 5:16. which were vexed with *unclean* spirits:
   8: 7. For *unclean* spirits, crying with
   10:14. any thing that is common or *unclean.*
   28. not call any man common or *unclean.*
   11: 8. nothing common or *unclean* hath at
1Co. 7:14. else were your children *unclean ;*
2Co. 6:17. touch not the *unclean* (thing) ;
Eph. 5: 5. nor *unclean* person, nor covetous man,
Rev.16:13. I saw three *unclean* spirits like
   18: 2. the hold of every *foul* spirit, and a cage of
      every *unclean* and hateful bird.

ἀκαιρέομαι, akaireomai.

Phil. 4:10. careful, but ye *lacked opportunity.*

ἀκαίρως, akairōs.

2Ti. 4: 2. be instant in season, *out of season ;*

ἄκακος, akakos.

Ro. 16:18. deceive the hearts of the *simple.*
Heb 7:26. (who is) holy, *harmless,* undefiled,

ἄκανθα, akantha

Mat. 7:16. Do men gather grapes of *thorns,* or figs
   13: 7. some fell among *thorns ;* and the *thorns*
   22. seed among the *thorns* is he that
   27:29. had platted a crown of *thorns,*
Mar 4: 7. some fell among *thorns,* and the *thorns*
   18. they which are sown among *thorns ;*
Lu. 6:44. For of *thorns* men do not gather
   8: 7. some fell among *thorns ;* and the *thorns*
      sprang up with it, and
   14. that which fell among *thorns* are
Joh.19: 2. the soldiers platted a crown of *thorns,*
Heb 6: 8. that which beareth *thorns* and

ἀκάνθινος, akanthinos.

Mar 15:17. platted a crown *of thorns,* and put it
Joh.19: 5. wearing the crown *of thorns,* and the

ἄκαρπος, akarpos.

Mat.13:22. choke the word, and he becometh *un-*
      fruitful.
Mar 4:19. the word, and it becometh *unfruitful.*
1Co.14:14. my understanding is *unfruitful.*
Eph. 5:11. with the *unfruitful* works of
Tit. 3:14. that they be not *unfruitful.*
2Pet.1: 8. neither (be) barren nor *unfruitful* in
Jude 12. whose fruit withereth, *without fruit,*

ἀκατάγνωστος, akatagnōstos.

Tit. 2: 8. Sound speech, that *cannot be condemned ;*

ἀκατακάλυπτος, akatakaluptos.

1Co.11: 5. prophesieth with (her) head *uncovered*
   13. that a woman pray unto God *uncovered ?*

ἀκατάκριτος, akatakritos.

Acts16:37. have beaten us openly *uncondemned,*
   22:25. a man that is a Roman, and *uncondemned ?*

ἀκατάλυτος, akatalutos.

Heb 7:16. after the power of an *endless* life.

ἀκατάπαυστος, akatapaustos.

2Pet. 2:14. that *cannot cease* from sin ; beguiling

ἀκαταστασία, akatastasia.

Lu. 21: 9. shall hear of wars and *commotions,*
1Co.14:33. God is not (the author) of *confusion,*
2Co. 6: 5. in imprisonments, in *tumults,* in
   12:20. whisperings, swellings, *tumults :*
Jas. 3:16. there (is) *confusion* and every evil work.

ἀκατάστατος, akatastatos.

Jas. 1: 8. A double minded man (is) *unstable* in

ἀκατάσχετος, akatasketos.

Jas. 3: 8. (it is) an *unruly* evil, full of deadly

ἀκέραιος, akeraios.

Mat.10:16. wise as serpents, and *harmless* as doves.
Ro. 16:19. is good, and *simple* concerning evil.
Phil. 2:15. ye may be blameless and *harmless,*

ἀκλινής, aklinees.

Heb 10:23. profession of (our) faith *without wavering ;*

ἀκμάζω, akmazo.

Rev.14:18. for her grapes *are fully ripe.*

ἀκμήν, akmeen.

Mat.15:16. Are ye also *yet* without understanding?

ἀκοή, akoee.

Mat. 4:24. his *fame* went throughout all Syria:
13:14. By *hearing* ye shall hear, and
14: 1. heard of the *fame* of Jesus,
24: 6. hear of wars and *rumours* of wars:
Mar 1:28. immediately his *fame* spread
7:35. straightway his *ears* were opened,
13: 7. hear of wars and *rumours* of wars,
Lu. 7: 1. sayings in the *audience* of the people,
Joh.12:38. who hath believed our *report?*
Acts17:20. certain strange things to our *ears :*
28:26. *Hearing* ye shall hear, and shall not
Ro. 10:16. who hath believed our *report?*
17. faith (cometh) by *hearing,* and *hearing*
1Co.12:17. the *hearing?* If the whole (were) *hearing,* where
Gal. 3: 2. or by the *hearing* of faith?
5. the law, or by the *hearing* of faith?
1Th. 2:13. the word of God *which ye heard* of us, ye
2Ti. 4: 3. to themselves teachers, having itching
ears ;
4. shall turn away (their) *ears* from
Heb 4: 2. the word *preached* did not profit
5:11. seeing ye are dull of *hearing.*
2Pet:2: 8. among them, in seeing and *hearing,*

ἀκολουθέω, akoloutheo.

Mat. 4:20. left (their) nets, and *followed* him.
22. left the ship and their father, and *followed* him.
25. there *followed* him great multitudes
8: 1. great multitudes *followed* him.
10. said to them *that followed,* Verily
19. I *will follow* thee whithersoever
22. Jesus said unto him, *Follow* me ;
23. into a ship, his disciples *followed* him.
9: 9. *Follow* me. And he arose, and *followed*
19. Jesus arose, and *followed* him,
27. two blind men *followed* him, crying,
10:38. taketh not his cross, and *followeth* after me, is not worthy
12:15. great multitudes *followed* him,
14:13. they *followed* him on foot out of the
16:24. take up his cross, and *follow* me.
19: 2. great multitudes *followed* him ;
21. treasure in heaven: and come (and) *follow* me.
27. have forsaken all, and *followed* thee ;
28. That ye which *have followed* me,
20:29. a great multitude *followed* him,
34. received sight, and they *followed* him.
21: 9. multitudes that went before, and *that followed,*
26:58. Peter *followed* him afar off unto
27:55. which *followed* Jesus from Galilee,
Mar 1:18. forsook their nets, and *followed* him.
2:14. *Follow* me. And he arose and *followed*
15. there were many, and they *followed* him.
3: 7. a great multitude from Galilee *followed*

Mar 5:24. with him ; and much people *followed* him,
6: 1. own country ; and his disciples *follow* him.
8:34. take up his cross, and *follow* me.
9:38. in thy name, and he *followeth* not us: and we forbad him, because he *followeth* not
10:21. take up the cross, and *follow* me.
28. have left all, and *have followed* thee.
32. *as they followed,* they were afraid.
52. received his sight, and *followed* Jesus
11: 9. went before, and they *that followed,*
14:13. bearing a pitcher of water: *follow* him.
51. there *followed* him a certain young
54. Peter *followed* him afar off, even
15:41. he was in Galilee, *followed* him, and
Lu. 5:11. they forsook all, and *followed* him.
27. custom: and he said unto him, *Follow* me.
28. he left all, rose up, and *followed* him.
7: 9. unto the people *that followed* him,
9:11. when they knew (it), *followed* him:
23. take up his cross daily, and *follow* me.
49. because he *followeth* not with us.
57. I *will follow* thee whithersoever
59. he said unto another, *Follow* me.
61. also said, Lord, I *will follow* thee ;
18:22. treasure in heaven: and come, *follow* me.
28. we have left all, and *followed* thee.
43. received his sight, and *followed* him,
22:10. *follow* him into the house where
39. his disciples also *followed* him.
54. priest's house. And Peter *followed* afar off.
23:27. there *followed* him a great company
Joh. 1:37. heard him speak, and they *followed*
38. Jesus turned, and saw them *following,*
40 (41) heard John (speak), and *followed* him,
43 (44) findeth Philip, and saith unto him, *Follow* me.
6: 2. a great multitude *followed* him,
8:12. he *that followeth* me shall not
10: 4. before them, and the sheep *follow* him:
5. a stranger *will* they not *follow,*
27. I know them, and they *follow* me:
11:31. up hastily and went out, *followed* her,
12:26. If any man serve me, *let* him *follow* me ;
13:36. not *follow* me now ; but thou *shalt follow*
37. why cannot I *follow* thee now?
18:15. Simon Peter *followed* Jesus, and (so)
20: 6. cometh Simon Peter *following* him,
21:19. he saith unto him, *Follow* me.
20. disciple whom Jesus loved *following ;*
22. what (is that) to thee? *follow* thou me.
Acts12: 8. thy garment about thee, and *follow* me.
9. he went out, and *followed* him ;
13:43. religious proselytes *followed* Paul and
21:36. the multitude of the people *followed* after,
1Co 10: 4. spiritual Rock *that followed* them:
Rev. 6: 8. was Death, and Hell *followed* with him.
14: 4. are they which *follow* the Lamb
8. there *followed* another angel, saying,
9. the third angel *followed* them,
13. their works *do follow* them.
18: 5. her sins *have reached* unto heaven,
19:14. *followed* him upon white horses,

ἀκούω, akouo.

Mat. 2: 3. *When* Herod the king *had heard* (these things)
9. *When* they *had heard* the king, they
18. In Rama *was* there a voice *heard,*
22. *when* he *heard* that Archelaus did
4:12. *when* Jesus *had heard* that John

Mat. 5:21. Ye *have heard* that it was said
27. Ye *have heard* that it was said
33. Ye *have heard* that it hath been
38. Ye *have heard* that it hath been said
43. Ye *have heard* that it hath been
7:24. whosoever *heareth* these sayings
26. every one *that heareth* these sayings
8:10. *When* Jesus *heard* (it), he marvelled,
9:12. *when* Jesus *heard* (that), he said
10:14. not receive you, nor *hear* your words,
27. what ye *hear* in the ear, (that) preach
11: 2. *when* John *had heard* in the prison
4. things which ye *do hear* and see:
5. lepers are cleansed, and the deaf *hear*, the
15. He that hath ears *to hear, let* him *hear.*
12:19. *shall* any man *hear* his voice in
24. *when* the Pharisees *heard* (it), they
42. *to hear* the wisdom of Solomon; and,
13: 9. Who hath ears *to hear, let* him *hear.*
13. seeing, see not; and *hearing* they *hear* not,
14. By hearing ye *shall hear*, and shall
15. (their) ears are dull of *hearing*, and
— with (their) eyes, and *hear* with (their) ears,
16. they see: and your ears, for they *hear.*
17. *to hear* (those things) which ye *hear*, and *have* not *heard* them.
18. *Hear* ye therefore the parable of
19. *When* any one *heareth* the word
20. same is he *that heareth* the word,
22. is he *that heareth* the word; and the
23. good ground is he *that heareth* the
43. Who hath ears *to hear, let* him *hear.*
14: 1. Herod the tetrarch *heard* of the fame
13. *When* Jesus *heard* (of it), he departed
— *when* the people *had heard* (thereof),
15:10. said unto them, *Hear*, and understand:
12. offended, *after they heard* this saying?
17: 5. I am well pleased; *hear* ye him.
6. *when* the disciples *heard* (it), they
18:15. if he *shall hear* thee, thou hast gained
16. if he *will* not *hear* (thee, then) take
19:22. *when* the young man *heard* that
25. *When* his disciples *heard* (it), they
20:24. *when* the ten *heard* (it), they were
30. *when* they *heard* that Jesus passed
21:16. said unto him, *Hearest* thou what
33. *Hear* another parable: There was
45. *when* the chief priests and Pharisees *had heard*
22: 7. *when* the king *heard* (thereof), he
22. *When* they *had heard* (these words),
33. *when* the multitude *heard* (this),
34. *when* the Pharisees *had heard*
24: 6. ye shall *hear* of wars and rumours
26:65. now ye *have heard* his blasphemy.
27:13. *Hearest* thou not how many things
47. *when* they *heard* (that), said,
28:14. if this *come to* the governor's ears, (lit. be *heard* by)
Mar 2: 1. it *was noised* that he was in
17. *When* Jesus *heard* (it), he saith
3: 8. *when* they *had heard* what great
21. *when* his friends *heard* (of it),
4: 3. *Hearken;* Behold, there went out
9. that hath ears *to hear, let* him *hear.*
12. *hearing* they *may hear*, and not
15. when they *have heard*, Satan
16. who, when they *have heard* the
18. among thorns; such *as hear* the word,
20. such as *hear* the word, and receive

Mar 4:23. have ears *to hear, let* him *hear.*
24. Take heed what ye *hear :* with
— unto you *that hear* shall more
33. as they were able *to hear* (it).
5:27. *When* she *had heard* of Jesus, came
36. As soon as Jesus *heard* the word
6: 2. many *hearing* (him) were astonished,
11. shall not receive you, nor *hear* you,
14. king Herod *heard* (of him); for
16. *when* Herod *heard* (thereof), he said,
20. *when* he *heard* him, he did many things, and *heard* him gladly.
29. *when* his disciples *heard* (of it), they
55. were sick, where they *heard* he was.
7:14. *Hearken* unto me every one (of you),
16. If any man have ears *to hear, let* him *hear.*
25. had an unclean spirit, *heard* of him,
37. he maketh both the deaf *to hear*, and
8:18. see ye not? having ears, *hear* ye not?
9: 7. This is my beloved Son: *hear* him.
10:41. *when* the ten *heard* (it), they began
47. *when* he *heard* that it was Jesus
11:14. hereafter for ever. And his disciples *heard* (it).
18. the scribes and chief priests *heard* (it),
12:28. *having heard* them reasoning
29. *Hear*, O Israel; The Lord our God is
37. the common people *heard* him gladly.
13: 7. ye *shall hear* of wars and rumours of wars,
14:11. *when* they *heard* (it), they were glad,
58. We *heard* him say, I will destroy
64. Ye *have heard* the blasphemy:
15:35. *when* they *heard* (it), said, Behold,
16:11. *when* they *had heard* that he was
Lu. 1:41. when Elisabeth *heard* the salutation
58. her cousins *heard* how the Lord
66. all they *that heard* (them) laid
2:18. all they *that heard* (it) wondered
20. things that they *had heard* and seen,
46. both *hearing* them, and asking them
47. all *that heard* him were astonished
4:23. whatsoever we *have heard* done
28. *when* they *heard* these things, were
5: 1. upon him *to hear* the word of God,
15. great multitudes came together *to hear* and to be healed
6:17(18). which came *to hear* him, and to be
27. I say unto you *which hear*, Love your
47. cometh to me, and *heareth* my sayings,
49. he *that heareth*, and doeth not, is like
7: 3. *when* he *heard* of Jesus, he sent
9. *When* Jesus *heard* these things,
22. what things ye have seen and *heard;*
— lepers are cleansed, the deaf *hear*,
29. all the people *that heard* (him),
8: 8. He that hath ears *to hear, let* him *hear.*
10. *hearing* they might not understand.
12. by the way side are they *that hear;*
13. which, when they *hear*, receive the
14. which, *when* they *have heard*, go
15. *having heard* the word, keep (it),
18. Take heed therefore how ye *hear:*
21. are these *which hear* the word of God,
50. *when* Jesus *heard* (it), he answered
9: 7. Herod the tetrarch *heard* of all that
9. who is this, of whom I *hear* such things?
35. This is my beloved Son: *hear* him.
10:16. He *that heareth* you *heareth* me;
24. *to hear* those things which ye *hear*, and *have* not *heard* (them).
39. sat at Jesus' feet, and *heard* his word.
11:28. blessed (are) they *that hear* the word

Lu. 11:31. *to hear* the wisdom of Solomon ;
12: 3. in darkness *shall be heard* in the
14:15. at meat with him *heard* these things,
35. He that hath ears *to hear, let* him *hear*.
15: 1. publicans and sinners for *to hear* him.
25. he *heard* musick and dancing.
16: 2. How is it that I *hear* this of thee ?
14. were covetous, *heard* all these things:
29. Moses and the prophets; *let* them *hear* them.
31. If they *hear* not Moses and the prophets,
18: 6. *Hear* what the unjust judge saith.
22. *when* Jesus *heard* these things,
23. *when* he *heard* this, he was very
26. they *that heard* (it) said, Who then
36. *hearing* the multitude pass by,
19:11. *as* they *heard* these things, he added
48. people were very attentive to *hear* him.
20:16. *when* they *heard* (it), they said,
45. *in the audience of* all the people
21: 9. ye *shall hear* of wars and commotions,
38. in the temple, for *to hear* him.
22:71. ourselves *have heard* of his own
23: 6. *When* Pilate *heard* of Galilee, he
8. he had *heard* many things of him ;
Joh. 1:37. the two disciples *heard* him speak,
40(41). One of the two *which heard* John
3: 8. thou *hearest* the sound thereof,
29. which standeth and *heareth* him,
32. what he hath seen and *heard*, that
4: 1. the Pharisees *had heard* that Jesus
42. for we *have heard* (him) ourselves,
47. *When* he *heard* that Jesus was
5:24. He *that heareth* my word, and believeth
25. when the dead *shall hear* the voice
— they *that hear* shall live.
28. in the graves *shall hear* his voice,
30. as I *hear*, I judge: and my judgment
37. Ye *have* neither *heard* his voice
6:45. Every man therefore that *hath heard*,
60. *when* they *had heard* (this),
— an hard saying ; who can *hear* it ?
7:32. The Pharisees *heard* that the people
40. *when* they *heard* this saying,
51. judge (any) man, before it *hear* him,
8: 9. they *which heard* (it), being convicted
26. things which I *have heard* of him.
40. the truth, which I *have heard* of God:
43. because ye cannot *hear* my word.
47. He that is of God *heareth* God's words: ye therefore *hear* (them) not,
9:27. told you already, and ye *did* not *hear:* wherefore would ye *hear* (it) again?
31. we know that God *heareth* not sinners:
— doeth his will, him he *heareth*.
32. *was* it not *heard* that any man
35. Jesus *heard* that they had cast
40. Pharisees which were with him *heard*
10: 3. the sheep *hear* his voice: and he calleth
8. the sheep *did* not *hear* them.
16. they *shall hear* my voice ; and there
20. a devil, and is mad ; why *hear* ye him ?
27. My sheep *hear* my voice, and I know
11: 4. *When* Jesus *heard* (that), he said,
6. When he *had heard* therefore that
20. as soon as she *heard* that Jesus
29. As soon as she *heard* (that), she
41. I thank thee that thou *hast heard* me.
42. I knew that thou *hearest* me always:
12:12. *when* they *heard* that Jesus was
18. for that they *heard* that he had
29. that stood by, and *heard* (it), said

Joh.12:34. We *have heard* out of the law
47. if any man *hear* my words,
14:24. the word which ye *hear* is not
28. Ye *have heard* how I said unto
15:15. things that I *have heard* of my
16:13. whatsoever he *shall hear*, that
18:21. ask them *which heard* me,
37. Every one that is of the truth *heareth*
19: 8. When Pilate therefore *heard* that
13. *When* Pilate therefore *heard* that
21: 7. *when* Simon Peter *heard* that it was
Acts 1: 4. which, (saith he), ye *have heard* of me.
2: 6. every man *heard* them speak in
8. how *hear* we every man in our
11. we *do hear* them speak in our
22. men of Israel, *hear* these words;
33. which ye now see and *hear*.
37. *when* they *heard* (this), they were
3:22. him *shall* ye *hear* in all things
23. which *will* not *hear* that prophet,
4: 4. many of them *which heard* the
19. in the sight of God *to hearken* unto
20. things which we have seen and *heard*.
24. *when* they *heard* that, they lifted
5: 5. Ananias *hearing* these words
— on all them *that heard* these things.
11. upon as many *as heard* these things.
21. *when* they *heard* (that), they entered
24. the chief priests *heard* these things,
33. *When* they *heard* (that), they were
6:11. We *have heard* him speak blasphemous
14. For we *have heard* him say, that
7: 2. Men, brethren, and fathers, *hearken ;*
12. *when* Jacob *heard* that there was
34. I *have heard* their groaning, and am
37. like unto me ; him *shall* ye *hear*.
54. *When* they *heard* these things, they
8: 6. Philip spake, *hearing* and seeing the
14. at Jerusalem *heard* that Samaria
30. *heard* him read the prophet Esaias,
9: 4. fell to the earth, and *heard* a voice saying
7. stood speechless, *hearing* a voice, but
13. I *have heard* by many of this man,
21. all *that heard* (him) were amazed,
38. the disciples had *heard* that Peter
10:22. into his house, and *to hear* words of thee.
33. *to hear* all things that are commanded
44. fell on all them *which heard* the word.
46. For they *heard* them speak with tongues,
11: 1. in Judæa *heard* that the Gentiles
7. I *heard* a voice saying unto me,
18. *When* they *heard* these things, they
22. Then tidings of these things *came* unto
13: 7. desired *to hear* the word of God.
16. ye that fear God, *give audience*.
44. together, *to hear* the word of God.
48. *when* the Gentiles *heard* this, they
14: 9. The same *heard* Paul speak: who
14. Barnabas and Paul, *heard* (of), they rent
15: 7. should *hear* the word of the gospel,
12. *gave audience to* Barnabas and Paul,
13. Men (and) brethren, *hearken* unto me:
24. as we *have heard*, that certain which
16:14. which worshipped God, *heard* (us):
38. *when* they *heard* that they were Romans.
17: 8. *when* they *heard* these things.
21. to tell, or to *hear* some new thing.
32. *when* they *heard* of the resurrection
— We *will hear* thee again of this
18: 8. the Corinthians *hearing* believed,
26. *when* Aquila and Priscilla *had heard*,
19: 2. We *have* not so much as *heard* whether

Acts19: 5. *When* they *heard* (this), they were
10. in Asia *heard* the word of the Lord
26. ye see and *hear*, that not alone
28. *when* they *heard* (these sayings),
21:12. when we *heard* these things, both
20. *when* they *heard* (it), they glorified
22. for they *will hear* that thou art
22: 1. brethren, and fathers, *hear* ye my defence
2. *when* they *heard* that he spake
7. *heard* a voice saying unto me,
9. they *heard* not the voice of him
14. shouldest *hear* the voice of his
15. of what thou hast seen and *heard.*
22. they *gave* him *audience* unto
26. *When* the centurion *heard* (that), he went
23:16. *when* Paul's sister's son *heard* of their lying
24: 4. thou wouldest *hear* us of thy clemency
22. *when* Felix *heard* these things, having
24. sent for Paul, and *heard* him concerning
25:22. I would also *hear* the man myself. To
morrow, said he, thou *shalt hear* him.
26: 3. I beseech thee *to hear* me patiently.
14. I *heard* a voice speaking unto me,
29. also all *that hear* me this day,
28:15. *when* the brethren *heard* of us,
22. we desire *to hear* of thee what thou
26. Hearing ye *shall hear*, and shall not
27. their ears are dull of *hearing*, and their
— see with (their) eyes, and *hear* with (their)
ears,
28. unto the Gentiles, and (that) they *will
hear* it.
Ro. 10:14. of whom they *have* not *heard?* and how
shall they *hear* without a preacher?
18. I say, *Have* they not *heard?* Yes verily,
11: 8. ears that they should not *hear;* unto
15:21. they that *have* not *heard* shall
1Co. 2: 9. Eye hath not seen, nor ear *heard*,
5: 1. It *is reported* commonly (that there)
11:18. I *hear* that there be divisions among
14: 2. for no man *understandeth* (him);
2Co.12: 4. into paradise, and *heard* unspeakable
6. seeth me (to be), or (that) he *heareth* of
me.
Gal. 1:13. ye *have heard* of my conversation
23. they had *heard* only, That he
4:21. under the law, *do* ye not *hear* the law?
Eph. 1:13. *after that* ye *heard* the word of truth,
15. *after* I *heard* of your faith in the Lord
3: 2. If ye *have heard* of the dispensation
4:21. If so be that ye *have heard* him,
29. may minister grace unto the *hearers.*
Phi. 1:27. I *may hear* of your affairs, that ye
30. saw in me, (and) now *hear* (to be) in me.
2:26. because that ye *had heard* that he
4: 9. both learned, and received, and *heard*, and
seen
Col. 1: 4. *Since* we *heard* of your faith in
6. since the day ye *heard* (of it), and knew
9. we also, since the day we *heard* (it),
23. the gospel, which ye *have heard*,
2Th. 3:11. For we *hear* that there are some
1Ti. 4:16. save thyself, and them *that hear* thee.
2Ti. 1:13. words, which thou *hast heard* of me,
2: 2. things that thou *hast heard* of me
14. to the subverting of the *hearers.*
4:17. (that) all the Gentiles *might hear:*
Philem. 5. *Hearing* of thy love and faith, which thou
Heb. 2: 1. to the things *which we have heard*,
3. unto us by them *that heard* (him);
3: 7. To day if ye *will hear* his voice,
15. To day if ye *will hear* his voice,

Heb 3:16. some, *when* they *had heard*, did
4: 2. with faith in them *that heard* (it).
7. To day if ye *will hear* his voice,
12:19. which (voice) they *that heard*
Jas. 1:19. let every man be swift *to hear*,
2: 5. *Hearken*, my beloved brethren, Hath
5:11. Ye *have heard* of the patience of Job,
2Pet. 1:18. voice which came from heaven we *heard*,
1Joh 1: 1. which we *have heard*, which we
3. That which we have seen and *heard*
5. the message which we *have heard*
2: 7. the word which ye *have heard* from
18. as ye *have heard* that antichrist
24. which ye *have heard* from the beginning.
If that which ye *have heard* from
3:11. the message that ye *heard* from
4: 3. ye *have heard* that it should come;
5. of the world, and the world *heareth* them.
6. he that knoweth God *heareth* us; he that
is not of God *heareth* not us.
5:14. according to his will, he *heareth* us:
15. if we know that he *hear* us,
2Joh. 6. as ye *have heard* from the beginning,
3Joh. 4. I have no greater joy than to *hear*
Rev. 1: 3. they *that hear* the words of this prophecy,
10. *heard* behind me a great voice,
2: 7. He that hath an ear, *let him hear*
11. He that hath an ear, *let him hear*
17. He that hath an ear, *let him hear*
29. He that hath an ear, *let him hear*
3: 3. how thou hast received and *heard*,
6. He that hath an ear, *let* him *hear*
13. He that hath an ear, *let* him *hear*
20. if any man *hear* my voice, and open
22. He that hath an ear, *let him hear*
4: 1. the first voice which I *heard* (was)
5:11. I *heard* the voice of many angels
13. that are in them, *heard* I saying,
6: 1. I *heard*, as it were the noise of
3. I *heard* the second beast say, Come
5. I *heard* the third beast say, Come and see.
6. I *heard* a voice in the midst of
7. I *heard* the voice of the fourth beast
7: 4. I *heard* the number of them which
8:13. I beheld, and *heard* an angel flying
9:13. I *heard* a voice from the four horns
16. I *heard* the number of them.
20. neither can see, nor *hear*, nor walk:
10: 4. I *heard* a voice from heaven saying
8. the voice which I *heard* from heaven
11:12. they *heard* a great voice from heaven
12:10. I *heard* a loud voice saying in
13: 9. If any man have an ear, *let* him *hear.*
14: 2. I *heard* a voice from heaven, as the
— I *heard* the voice of harpers harping
13. I *heard* a voice from heaven
16: 1. I *heard* a great voice out of the
5. I *heard* the angel of the waters say,
7. I *heard* another out of the altar say,
18: 4. I *heard* another voice from heaven,
22. trumpeters, *shall be heard* no more
— the sound of a millstone *shall be heard* no
more
23. the bride *shall be heard* no more
19: 1. I *heard* a great voice of much people
6. I *heard* as it were the voice of a
21: 3. I *heard* a great voice out of heaven
22: 8. I John saw these things, and *heard* (them).
And when I *had heard* and seen,
17. let him *that heareth* say, Come.
18. every man *that heareth* the words of the
prophecy of this book,

ἀκρασία, akrasia.

Mat.23:25. they are full of extortion and *excess*.
1Co. 7: 5. tempt you not for your *incontinency*.

ἀκρατής, akratees.

2Ti. 3: 3. false accusers, *incontinent*, fierce,

ἄκρατον, akraton.

Rev.14:10. which is poured out *without mixture*

ἀκρίβεια, akribīa.

Acts22: 3. according to the *perfect manner* of the

ἀκριβέστατος, akribestatos.

Acts26: 5. after the *most straitest* sect of our

ἀκριβέστερον, akribesteron, adv.

Acts18:26. him the way of God *more perfectly*.
   23:15. enquire something *more perfectly*
   20. enquire somewhat of him *more perfectly*.
   24:22. having *more perfect* knowledge

ἀκριβόω, akriboō.

Mat. 2: 7. *enquired* of them *diligently* what
   16. he *had diligently enquired* of the wise

ἀκριβῶς, akribōs.

Mat. 2: 8. Go and search *diligently* for the young
Lu. 1: 3. having had *perfect* understanding of all
Acts18:25. he spake and taught *diligently* the things
Eph. 5:15. that ye walk *circumspectly*, not
1Th. 5: 2. yourselves know *perfectly* that the

ἀκρίς, akris.

Mat. 3: 4. his meat was *locusts* and wild honey.
Mar. 1: 6. he did eat *locusts* and wild honey;
Rev. 9: 3. out of the smoke *locusts* upon the
   7. the shapes of the *locusts* (were) like unto

ἀκροατήριον, akroateerion.

Acts25:23. was entered into the *place of hearing*,

ἀκροατής, akroatees.

Ro. 2:13. For not the *hearers* of the law (are) just
Jas. 1:22. doers of the word, and not *hearers* only,
   23. if any be a *hearer* of the word, and not
   25. he being not a forgetful *hearer*, but

ἀκροβυστία, akrobustīa.

Acts11: 3. Thou wentest in to men uncircumcised,
   (lit. having *uncircumcision*)

Ro. 2:25. thy circumcision is made *uncircumcision*.
   26. if the *uncircumcision* keep the
   — shall not his *uncircumcision* be
   27. shall not *uncircumcision* which is
   3:30. by faith, and *uncircumcision* through
   4: 9. or upon the *uncircuncision* also ?
   10. in circumcision, or in *uncircumcision* ?
     Not in circumcision, but in *uncircumcision*.
   11. (he had yet) being uncircumcised: (lit. in *uncircumcision*)
   — though they be *not circumcised*; that
   12. (he had) being (yet) *uncircumcised*.
1Co. 7:18. Is any called in *uncircumcision* ?
   19. *uncircumcision* is nothing, but
Gal. 2: 7. gospel of the *uncircumcision* was
   5: 6. any thing, nor *uncircumcision*;
   6:15. nor *uncircumcision*, but a new creature.
Eph. 2:11. who are called *Uncircumcision* by
Col. 2:13. the *uncircumcision* of your flesh,
   3:11. circumcision nor *uncircumcision*,

ἀκρογωνιαῖος, akrogōniaios.

Eph. 2:20. Christ himself being the *chief corner* (stone;)
1Pet.2: 6. I lay in Sion a *chief corner* stone, elect,

ἀκροθίνιον, akrothinion.

Heb. 7: 4. Abraham gave the tenth *of the spoils*.

ἄκρον, akron.

Mat.24:31. from *one end* of heaven to the *other*.
Mar.13:27. from the *uttermost part* of the earth to the *uttermost part* of heaven.
Lu. 16:24. may dip the *tip* of his finger in water,
Heb 11:21. (leaning) upon the *top* of his staff.

ἀκυρόω, akuroō.

Mat.15: 6. Thus have ye *made* the commandment of God *of none effect*
Mar. 7:13. *Making* the word of God *of none effect*
Gal. 3:17. years after, cannot *disannul*, that

ἀκωλύτως, akōlutōs.

Acts28:31. all confidence, *no man forbidaing him*.

ἄκων, akōn.

1Co. 9:17. if *against my will*, a dispensation

ἀλάβαστρον, alabastron.

Mat.26: 7. having an *alabaster box* of very
Mar14: 3. having an *alabaster box* of ointment
   — she brake the *box*, and poured (it) on
Lu. 7:37. brought an *alabaster box* of ointment,

ἀλαζονεία, alazonīa.

Jas. 4:16. now ye rejoice in your *boastings*:
1Joh.2:16. lust of the eyes, and the *pride* of life,

ἀλαζών, alazōn.

Ro. 1:30. spiteful, proud, *boasters*, inventors
2Ti. 3: 2. covetous, *boasters*, proud, blasphemers,

ἀλαλάζω, alalazo.

Mar. 5:38. them that wept and *wailed* greatly.
1Co 13: 1. (as) sounding brass, or a *tinkling* cymbal.

ἀλάλητος, alaleetos.

Ro. 8:26. with groanings *which cannot be uttered*.

ἄλαλος, alalos.

Mar. 7:37. the deaf to hear, and the *dumb* to speak.
9:17. my son, which hath a *dumb* spirit ;
25. (Thou) *dumb* and deaf spirit, I charge thee,

ἄλας, halas.

Mat. 5.13. Ye are the *salt* of the earth: but if the *salt* have lost his savour,
Mar. 9:50. *Salt* (is) good: but if the *salt* have
— Have *salt* in yourselves, and have
Lu. 14:34. *Salt* (is) good: but if the *salt* have
Col. 4: 6. grace, seasoned with *salt*, that ye

ἀλείφω, alīpho.

Mat. 6:17. *anoint* thine head, and wash thy face ;
Mar. 6:13. *anointed* with oil many that were
16: 1. they might come and *anoint* him.
Lu. 7:38. *anointed* (them) with the ointment.
46. My head with oil thou *didst* not *anoint:* but this woman *hath anointed* my feet
Joh. 11: 2. Mary *which anointed* the Lord
12: 3. *anointed* the feet of Jesus, and wiped
Jas. 5:14. *anointing* him with oil in the

ἀλεκτοροφωνία, alektorophōnia.

Mar 13:35. at midnight, or at the *cockcrowing*,

ἀλέκτωρ, alektōr.

Mat. 26:34. this night, before the *cock* crow,
74. I know not the man. And immediately the *cock* crew.
75. Before the *cock* crow, thou shalt deny
Mar 14:30. before the *cock* crow twice, thou
68. into the porch ; and the *cock* crew.
72. the second time the *cock* crew.
— Before the *cock* crow twice, thou
Lu. 22:34. the *cock* shall not crow this day,
60. while he yet spake, the *cock* crew.
61. Before the *cock* crow, thou shalt deny
Joh. 13:38. The *cock* shall not crow, till thou
18:27. denied again: and immediately the *cock* crew.

ἄλευρον, alūron.

Mat. 13:33. hid in three measures of *meal*, till
Lu. 13:21. took and hid in three measures of *meal*,

ἀλήθεια, aleethīa.

Mat. 22:16. teachest the way of God in *truth*,
Mar. 5:33. before him, and told him all the *truth*.
12:14. teachest the way of God in *truth :*
32. Master, thou hast said the *truth :*
Lu. 4:25. I tell you of a *truth*, many widows
20:21. teachest the way of God truly: (lit. in *truth*)
22:59. Of a *truth* this (fellow) also was
Joh. 1:14. of the Father, full of grace and *truth*.
17. grace and *truth* came by Jesus Christ.
3:21. he that doeth *truth* cometh to the
4:23. worship the Father in spirit and in *truth :*
24. worship (him) in spirit and in *truth*.
5:33. he bare witness unto the *truth*.
8:32. ye shall know the *truth*, and the *truth* shall make you free.
40. a man that hath told you the *truth*,
44. abode not in the *truth*, because there is no *truth* in him.
45. because I tell (you) the *truth*, ye
46. if I say the *truth*, why do ye not
14: 6. I am the way, the *truth*, and the life:
17. (Even) the Spirit of *truth ;* whom the
15:26. (even) the Spirit of *truth*, which
16: 7. Nevertheless I tell you the *truth ;*
13. when he, the Spirit of *truth*, is come, he will guide you into all *truth :*
17:17. Sanctify them through thy *truth :* thy word is *truth*.
19. be sanctified through the *truth*.
18:37. I should bear witness unto the *truth*. Every one that is of the *truth* heareth
38. Pilate saith unto him, What is *truth ?*
Acts 4:27. For of a *truth* against thy holy
10:34. said, Of a *truth* I perceive that
26:25. the words of *truth* and. soberness.
Ro. 1:18. who hold the *truth* in unrighteousness ;
25. Who changed the *truth* of God into
2: 2. judgment of God is according to *truth*
8. contentious, and do not obey the *truth*,
20. knowledge and of the *truth* in the law.
3: 7. For if the *truth* of God hath more
9: 1. I say the *truth* in Christ, I lie not,
15: 8. circumcision for the *truth* of God,
1Co. 5: 8. unleavened (bread) of sincerity and *truth*.
13: 6. in iniquity, but rejoiceth in the *truth ;*
2Co. 4: 2. by manifestation of the *truth*
6: 7. By the word of *truth*, by the power
7:14. we spake all things to you in *truth*,
— (I made) before Titus, is found a *truth*.
11:10. As the *truth* of Christ is in me,
12: 6. for I will say the *truth :* but (now)
13: 8. we can do nothing against the *truth*, but for the *truth*.
Gal. 2: 5. that the *truth* of the gospel might
14. according to the *truth* of the gospel,
3: 1. that ye should not obey the *truth*,
5: 7. that ye should not obey the *truth ?*
Eph. 1:13. after that ye heard the word of *truth*,
4:21. taught by him, as the *truth* is in Jesus:
24. created in righteousness and *true* holiness.
25. speak every man *truth* with his neighbour:
5: 9. in all goodness and righteousness and *truth ;*
6:14. your loins girt about with *truth*,
Phi. 1:18. whether in pretence, or in *truth*,
Col. 1: 5. the word of the *truth* of the gospel ;
6. knew the grace of God in *truth :*
2Th. 2:10. received not the love of the *truth*,

2Th. 2:12. damned who believed not the *truth,*
　　　 13. of the Spirit and belief of the *truth:*
1Ti. 2: 4. unto the knowledge of the *truth.*
　　　 7. I speak the *truth* in Christ, (and) lie not;
　　　　　 a teacher of the Gentiles in faith and
　　　　　 verity.
　　 3:15. the pillar and ground of the *truth.*
　　 4: 3. which believe and know the *truth.*
　　 6: 5. corrupt minds, and destitute of the *truth,*
2Ti. 2: 15. rightly dividing the word of *truth.*
　　　 18. Who concerning the *truth* have erred,
　　　 25. to the acknowledging of the *truth ;*
　　 3: 7. come to the knowledge of the *truth.*
　　　 8. so do these also resist the *truth:*
　　 4: 4. turn away (their) ears from the *truth,*
Tit. 1: 1. the acknowledging of the *truth* which
　　 14. men, that turn from the *truth.*
Heb 10:26. received the knowledge of the *truth,*
Jas. 1:18. begat he us with the word of *truth,*
　　 3:14. glory not, and lie not against the *truth.*
　　 5:19. if any of you do err from the *truth,*
1Pet.1:22. purified your souls in obeying the *truth*
2Pet.1:12. be established in the present *truth.*
　　 2: 2. the way of *truth* shall be evil spoken
1Joh.1: 6. we lie, and do not the *truth :*
　　　 8. ourselves, and the *truth* is not in us.
　　 2 : 4. is a liar, and the *truth* is not in him.
　　　 21. the *truth,* but because ye know it, and
　　　　　 that no lie is of the *truth.*
　　 3:18. neither in tongue ; but in deed and in
　　　　　 truth.
　　　 19. we know that we are of the *truth,*
　　 4: 6. Hereby know we the Spirit of *truth,*
　　 5: 6. witness, because the Spirit is *truth.*
2 Joh. 1. her children, whom I love in the *truth ;*
　　 — they that have known the *truth ;*
　　 2. For the *truth*'s sake, which dwelleth
　　 3. Son of the Father, in *truth* and love.
　　 4. of thy children walking in *truth,*
3 Joh. 1. Gaius, whom I love in the *truth.*
　　 3. testified of the *truth* that is in thee, even
　　　　　 as thou walkest in the *truth.*
　　 4. that my children walk in *truth.*
　　 8. might be fellowhelpers to the *truth.*
　　 12. report of all (men), and of the *truth*
　　　　　 itself:

ἀληθεύω, *aleethūo.*

Gal. 4:16. your enemy, *because* I *tell* you *the truth?*
Eph. 4:15. *speaking the truth* in love, may

ἀληθής, *aleethees.*

Mat22:16. Master, we know that thou art *true,*
Mar12:14. Master, we know that thou art *true,*
Joh. 3:33. set to his seal that God is *true.*
　　 4:18. hast is not thy husband: in that saidst thou
　　　　　 truly.
　　 5:31. of myself, my witness is not *true.*
　　　 32. which he witnesseth of me is *true.*
　　 7:18. glory that sent him, the same is *true,*
　　 8:13. of thyself; thy record is not *true.*
　　 14. of myself, (yet) my record is *true:*
　　 16. if I judge, my judgment is *true :*
　　 17. the testimony of two men is *true.*
　　 26. he that sent me is *true ;* and I speak
　 10:41. that John spake of this man were *true.*
　 19:35. he knoweth that he saith *true,*
　 21:24. we know that his testimony is *true.*

Acts12: 9. wist not that it was *true* which
Ro. 3: 4. yea, let God be *true,* but every man
2Co. 6: 8. as deceivers, and (yet) *true ;*
Phi. 4: 8. brethren, whatsoever things are *true,*
Tit. 1:13. This witness is *true.* Wherefore
1Pet.5:12. this is the *true* grace of God wherein
2Pet.2:22. according to the *true* proverb,
1Joh.2: 8. which thing is *true* in him and in you:
　　 27. of all things, and is *truth,* and is no lie,
3 Joh. 12. ye know that our record is *true.*

ἀληθινός, *aleethinos.*

Lu. 16:11. commit to your trust the *true* (riches)?
Joh. 1: 9. (That) was the *true* Light, which lighteth
　　 4:23. when the *true* worshippers shall
　　 37. herein is that saying *true,* One
　　 6:32. my Father giveth you the *true* bread
　　 7:28. he that sent me is *true,* whom
　 15: 1. I am the *true* vine, and my Father
　 17: 3. might know thee the only *true* God,
　 19:35. bare record, and his record is *true :*
1Th. 1: 9. to serve the living and *true* God ;
Heb. 8: 2. the sanctuary, and of the *true* tabernacle,
　　 9:24. (which are) the figures of the *true ;*
　 10:22. Let us draw near with a *true* heart
1Joh 2: 8. darkness is past, and the *true* light now
　　 5:20. we may know him that is *true,* and we
　　　　　 are in him that is *true,*
　　 — This is the *true* God, and eternal life.
Rev. 3: 7. he that is holy, he that is *true,*
　　 14. the faithful and *true* witness, the
　　 6:10. How long, O Lord, holy and *true,*
　　 15: 3. just and *true* (are) thy ways, thou
　　 16: 7. *true* and righteous (are) thy judgments.
　　 19: 2. *true* and righteous (are) his judgments
　　 9. These are the *true* sayings of God.
　　 11. sat upon him (was) called Faithful and
　　　　　 True,
　　 21: 5. these words are *true* and faithful.
　　 22: 6. These sayings (are) faithful and *true*

ἀλήθω, *aleetho.*

Mat.24:41. Two (women shall be) *grinding* at the
Lu. 17:35. Two (women) shall be *grinding* together ;

ἀληθῶς, *aleethōs.*

Mat.14:33. *Of a truth* thou art the Son of God.
　 26:73. *Surely* thou also art (one) of them ;
　 27:54. *Truly* this was the Son of God.
Mar 14:70. *Surely* thou art (one) of them: for
　 15:39. *Truly* this man was the Son of God.
Lu. 9:27. I tell you *of a truth,* there be some
　 12:44. *Of a truth* I say unto you, that he
　 21: 3. *Of a truth* I say unto you, that this
Joh. 1:47(48). Behold an Israelite *indeed,* in
　　 4:42. this is *indeed* the Christ, the Saviour
　　 6:14. This is *of a truth* that prophet that
　　 55. For my flesh is meat *indeed,* and my blood
　　　　　 is drink *indeed.*
　　 7:26. Do the rulers know *indeed* that this is the
　　　　　 very Christ ?
　　 40. *Of a truth* this is the prophet.
　　 8:31. (then) are ye my disciples *indeed ;*
　 17: 8. have known *surely* that I came
Acts12:11. I know *of a surety,* that the Lord
1Th. 2:13. as it is *in truth,* the word of God,
1Joh.2: 5. in him *verily* is the love of God

ἁλιεύς, haliūs.

Mat. 4:18. a net into the sea: for they were *fishers*.
19. I will make you *fishers* of men.
Mar 1:16. a net into the sea: for they were *fishers*.
17. make you to become *fishers* of men.
Lu. 5: 2. but the *fishermen* were gone out

ἁλιεύω, haliūo.

Joh. 21: 3. Peter saith unto them, I go *a fishing*.

ἁλίζω, halizo.

Mat. 5:13. lost his savour, wherewith *shall* it *be salted*?
Mar 9:49. every one *shall be salted* with fire, and every sacrifice *shall be salted* with salt.

ἀλίσγημα, alisgeema.

Acts15:20. abstain from *pollutions* of idols, and

ἀλλά, alla.

Mat. 4: 4. *but* by every word that proceedeth out of
5:15. under a bushel, *but* on a candlestick:
17. not come to destroy, *but* to fulfil.
&c. &c.
Note.—It is always rendered in E. T. " *but*," with the exception of the following passages. :—
Mat.19:11. *save* (they) to whom it is given.
Mar 9: 8. they saw no man any more, *save* Jesus
14:29. all shall be offended, *yet* (will) not I.
36. cup from me: *nevertheless* not what I will,
Lu. 16:21. moreover (lit. *but* even) the dogs came and licked
17: 8. *And* will not rather say
23:15. *No*, nor yet Herod: for I sent you
24:21. and (αλλα γε) beside all this
22. *Yea*, and certain women also of our
Joh. 7:27. *Howbeit* we know this man whence he is:
11:15. *nevertheless* let us go unto him.
16: 2. *yea*, the time cometh, that whosoever
7. *Nevertheless* I tell you the truth ;
Acts 7:48. *Howbeit* the most High dwelleth
10:20. Arise *therefore*, and get thee down,
19: 2. We have not so much as heard (αλλ' ουδε)
Ro. 3:31. God forbid: *yea*, we establish the law.
5:14. *Nevertheless* death reigned from Adam
6: 5. we shall be also (αλλα και)
7: 7. *Nay*, I had not known sin, but
8:37. *Nay*, in all these things we are more
1Co. 3: 2. neither (αλλ' ουτε) yet now are ye able.
4: 3. *yea*, I judge not mine own self.
4. *yet* am I not hereby justified:
15. instructers in Christ, *yet* (have ye) not
6: 8. *Nay*, ye do wrong, and defraud,
8: 7. *Howbeit* (there is) not in every man
9: 2. unto others, *yet* doubtless I am to you:
12. *Nevertheless* we have not used this power ;
12:22. *Nay*, much more those members of
14:19. *Yet* in the church I had rather speak
20. *howbeit* in malice be ye children,
15:46. *Howbeit* that (was) not first which is
2Co. 1:13. unto you, than (αλλ' η) what ye read or
4: 8. troubled on every side, *yet* not distressed ;
16. our outward man perish, *yet* the inward
5:16. *yet* now henceforth know we (him) no

2Co. 7: 6. *Nevertheless* God, that comforteth those
11. *yea*, (what) clearing of yourselves, *yea*, (what) indignation, *yea*, (what) fear, *yea*, (what) vehement desire, *yea*, (what) zeal, *yea*, (what) revenge !
8: 7. *Therefore*, as ye abound in every (thing),
11: 1. in (my) folly: and *indeed* bear with me.
6. rude in speech, *yet* not in knowledge ;
12:16. *nevertheless*, being crafty, I caught you
13: 4. crucified through weakness, *yet* he liveth
Gal. 4: 8. *Howbeit* then, when ye knew not
17. *yea*, they would exclude you, that ye
30. *Nevertheless* what saith the scripture ?
Eph. 5:24. *Therefore* as the church is subject unto Christ,
Phi. 1:18. therein do rejoice, *yea*, and will rejoice.
2:17. *Yea*, and if I be offered upon the
3: 8. *Yea* doubtless, and I count all things
Col. 2: 5. absent in the flesh, *yet* am I with you
1Ti. 1:16. *Howbeit* for this cause I obtain mercy,
2Ti. 1:12. *nevertheless* I am not ashamed:
Heb 3:16. *howbeit* not all that came out of Egypt
Jas. 2:18. *Yea*, a man may say, Thou hast faith,
Rev. 2: 4. *Nevertheless* I have (somewhat) against thee,
20. *Notwithstanding* I have a few things

ἀλλάττω, allatto.

Acts 6:14. *shall change* the customs which
Ro. 1:23. *changed* the glory of the uncorruptible
1Co.15:51. all sleep, but we *shall all be changed*,
52. incorruptible, and we *shall be changed*.
Gal. 4:20. with you now, and *to change* my voice ;
Heb 1:12. fold them up, and they *shall be changed :*

ἀλλαχόθεν, allakothen.

Joh. 10: 1. sheepfold, but climbeth up *some other way*,

ἀλληγορέω, alleegoreō.

Cal. 4:24. Which things are an allegory (lit. *allegorized*): for these

---

ἀλληλούια, alleelouya.

Rev.19: 1. much people in heaven, saying, *Alleluia ;*
3. again they said, *Alleluia*. And her
4. on the throne, saying, Amen ; *Alleluia*.
6. of mighty thunderings, saying, *Alleluia :*

ἀλλήλων, alleelōn.

Mat.24:10. offended, and shall betray *one another*, and shall hate *one another*.
25:32. shall separate them *one* from *another*,
Mar 4:41. feared exceedingly, and said *one* to *another*,
8:16. they reasoned among *themselves*, saying,
9:34. they had disputed among *themselves*,
50. have peace *one* with *another*.
15:31. mocking said among *themselves* with
Lu. 2:15. the shepherds said *one* to *another*,
4:36. all amazed, and spake among *themselves*,
6:11. communed *one* with *another* what
7:32. in the marketplace, and calling *one* to *another*,
8:25. wondered, saying *one* to *another*, What

Lu. 12: 1. that they trode *one* upon *another*, he
23:12. Pilate and Herod were made friends *together:*
24:14. they talked *together* of all these things
17. these that ye have *one* to *another*, as
32. they said *one* to *another*, Did not our
Joh. 4:33. said the disciples *one* to *another*,
5:44. which receive honour *one* of *another*,
6:43. Murmur not among *yourselves.*
52. The Jews therefore strove among *themselves*,
11:56. spake among *themselves*, as they
13:14. ought to wash *one another's* feet.
22. the disciples looked *one* on *another*,
34. unto you, That ye love *one another* ; as I have loved you, that ye also love *one another.*
35. if ye have love *one* to *another.*
15:12. That ye love *one another*, as I have
17. I command you, that ye love *one another.*
16:17. his disciples among *themselves*, What
19. Do ye enquire among *yourselves* of
19:24. said therefore among *themselves*,
Acts 2: 7. marvelled, saying *one* to *another*,
4:15. they conferred among *themselves*,
7:26. why do ye wrong *one* to *another ?*
15:39. departed asunder *one* from the *other:*
19:38. deputies: let them implead *one another.*
21: 6. had taken our leave *one* of *another*,
26:31. they talked between *themselves*,
28: 4. they said among *themselves*, No doubt
25. when they agreed not among *themselves*,
Ro. 1:12. by the *mutual* faith both of you and me.
27. in their lust *one* toward *another* ;
2:15. accusing or else excusing *one another* ;
12: 5. every one members *one* of *another.*
10. affectioned *one* to *another* with brotherly love ; in honour preferring *one another* ;
16. (Be) of the same mind *one* toward *another.*
13: 8. to love *one another:* for he that loveth
14:13. not therefore judge *one another* any more:
19. things wherewith *one* may edify *another.*
15: 5. be likeminded *one* toward *another*
7. Wherefore receive ye *one another*, as
14. able also to admonish *one another.*
16:16. Salute *one another* with an holy kiss.
1Co. 7: 5. Defraud ye not *one* the *other*, except
11:33. together to eat, tarry *one* for *another.*
12:25. have the same care *one* for *another.*
16:20. Greet ye *one another* with an holy kiss.
2Co. 13:12. Greet *one another* with an holy kiss.
Gal. 5:13. by love serve *one another.*
15. if ye bite and devour *one another*, take heed that ye be not consumed *one* of *another.*
17. these are contrary the *one* to the *other:*
26. provoking *one another*, envying *one another.*
6: 2. Bear ye *one another's* burdens, and so
Eph 4: 2. forbearing *one another* in love ;
25. for we are members *one* of *another.*
32. ye kind *one* to *another*, tenderhearted,
5:21. Submitting yourselves *one* to *another*
Phi. 2: 3. let *each* esteem *other* better than
Col. 3: 9. Lie not *one* to *another*, seeing that
13. Forbearing *one another*, and forgiving one
1Th. 3:12. abound in love *one* toward *another*,
4: 9. are taught of God to love *one another.*
18. comfort *one another* with these words.
5:11. Wherefore comfort yourselves *together*,
15. both among *yourselves*, and to all (men).
2Th. 1: 3. you all toward *each other* aboundeth ;
Tit. 3: 3. envy, hateful, (and) hating *one another.*

Heb 10:24. let us consider *one another* to provoke
Jas. 4:11. Speak not evil *one* of *another*, brethren.
5: 9. Grudge not *one* against *another*, brethren,
16. Confess (your) faults *one* to *another*, and pray *one* for *another*, that ye may
1Pet. 1:22. (see that ye) love *one another* with
4: 9. Use hospitality *one* to *another* without
5: 5. all (of you) be subject *one* to *another*,
14. Greet ye *one another* with a kiss of
1Joh. 1: 7. we have fellowship *one* with *another*,
3:11. that we should love *one another.*
23. love *one another*, as he gave us
4: 7. Beloved, let us love *one another:*
11. we ought also to love *one another.*
12. If we love *one another*, God dwelleth
2Joh. 5. the beginning, that we love *one another.*
Rev. 6: 4. that they should kill *one another:*
11:10. shall send gifts *one* to *another* ;

ἀλλογενής, *allogenees.*

Lu. 17:18. to give glory to God, save this *stranger.*

ἄλλομαι, *hallomai.*

Joh. 4:14. water *springing up* into everlasting life.
Acts 3: 8. into the temple, walking, and *leaping*, and
14:10. on thy feet. And he *leaped* and walked.

ἄλλος, *allos.*

Mat. 2:12. into their own country *another* way.
4:21. he saw *other* two brethren, James
5:39. right cheek, turn to him the *other* also.
8: 9. he goeth ; and to *another*, Come, and he cometh ;
10:23. persecute you in this city, flee ye into *another:*
12:13. restored whole, like as the *other.*
13: 5. *Some* fell upon stony places, where
7. *some* fell among thorns ; and the
8. *other* fell into good ground, and
24. *Another* parable put he forth unto
31. *Another* parable put he forth unto
33. *Another* parable spake he unto them ;
16:14. John the Baptist: *some*, Elias ; and others,
19: 9. fornication, and shall marry *another*,
20: 3. saw *others* standing idle in the
6. found *others* standing idle, and saith
21: 8. *others* cut down branches from the
33. Hear *another* parable: There was a
36. Again, he sent *other* servants more
41. (his) vineyard unto *other* husbandmen,
22: 4. Again, he sent forth *other* servants,
25:16. made (them) *other* five talents.
17. (received) two, he also gained *other* two.
20. brought *other* five talents, saying,
— gained beside them five talents *more.*
22. I have gained two *other* talents
26:71. into the porch, *another* (maid) saw
27:42. He saved *others* ; himself he cannot
61. Mary Magdalene, and the *other* Mary,
28: 1. came Mary Magdalene and the *other* Mary
Mar. 3: 5. hand was restored whole as the *other.*
4: 5. *some* fell on stony ground, where
7. *some* fell among thorns, and the
8. *other* fell on good ground, and did
36. were also with him *other* little ships.

Mar. 6:15. *Others* said, That it is Elias. And *others* said, That it is a prophet,

7: 4. many *other* things there be, which
8. many *other* such like things ye
8:28. *some* (say), Elias ; and *others*, One of the
10:11. put away his wife, and marry *another*,
12. her husband, and be married to *another*,
11: 8. *others* cut down branches off the
12: 4. he sent unto them *another* servant ;
5. again he sent *another ;* and him they killed, and many *others ;*
9. will give the vineyard unto *others*.
31. There is none *other* commandment
32. one God ; and there is none *other* but he :
14:19. (Is) it I? and *another* (said), (Is) it I ?
58. three days I will build *another*
15:31. He saved *others ;* himself he cannot
41. many *other* women which came
Lu. 5:29. publicans and of *others* that sat down
6:10. was restored whole as the *other*.
29. on the (one) cheek offer also the *other ;*
7: 8. to *another*, Come, and he cometh ;
19. that should come ? or look we for *another?*
20. that should come ? or look we for *another?*
9: 8. that Elias had appeared ; and of *others*,
19. *some* (say), Elias ; and *others* (say),
20:16. shall give the vineyard to *others*.
22:59. one hour after *another* confidently
23:35. He saved *others ;* let him save
Joh. 4:37. true, *One* soweth, and *another* reapeth.
38. *other* men laboured, and ye are
5: 7. *another* steppeth down before me.
32. There is *another* that beareth witness
43. if *another* shall come in his
6:22. there was none *other* boat there,
23. there came *other* boats from
7:12. He is a good man: *others* said,
41. *Others* said, This is the Christ. But *some* said, Shall Christ come
9: 9. *Some* said, This is he : *others* (said),
16. *Others* said, How can a man
10:16. *other* sheep I have, which are
21. *Others* said, These are not the words
12:29. *others* said, An angel spake to him.
14:16. he shall give you *another* Comforter,
15:24. works which none *other* man did,
18:15. followed Jesus, and (so did) *another* disciple :
16. Then went out that *other* disciple,
34. or did *others* tell it thee of me ?
19:18. crucified him, and two *other* with him,
32. the first, and of the *other* which was
20: 2. to the *other* disciple, whom Jesus loved,
3. went forth, and that *other* disciple,
4. the *other* disciple did outrun Peter,
8. Then went in also that *other* disciple,
25. The *other* disciples therefore said
30. many *other* signs truly did Jesus
21: 2. the (sons) of Zebedee, and two *other* of his
8. the *other* disciples came in a little
18. *another* shall gird thee, and carry (thee)
25. there are also many *other* things
Acts 2:12. were in doubt, saying *one to another*,
4:12. Neither is there salvation in any *other :*
15: 2. Paul and Barnabas, and certain *other* of them,
19:32. *Some* therefore cried one thing, and some *another :*
21:34. *some* cried one thing, some *another*,
1Co. 1:16. whether I baptized any *other*.
3:10. foundation, and *another* buildeth thereon.

1Co. 3:11. For *other* foundation can no man
9: 2. If I be not an apostle unto *others*,
12. If *others* be partakers of (this) power
27. when I have preached to *others*,
10:29. my liberty judged of *another* (man's)
12: 8. to *another* the word of knowledge
9. to *another* the gifts of healing by
10. To *another* the working of miracles ; to *another* prophecy ; to *another* discerning of spirits ;
— to *another* the interpretation of tongues :
14:19. (by my voice) I might teach *others*
29. two or three, and let the *other* judge.
30. revealed to *another* that sitteth by,
15:39. *one* (kind of) flesh of men, *another* flesh of beasts, *another* of fishes, (and) *another* of birds.
41. *one* glory of the sun, and *another* glory of the moon, and *another* glory of the stars :
2Co. 1:13. For we write none *other* things
8:13. (I mean) not that *other* men be
11: 4. if he that cometh preacheth *another*
8. I robbed *other* churches, taking
Gal. 1: 7. Which is not *another ;* but there
5:10. ye will be none *otherwise* minded :
Phi. 3: 4. If any *other* man thinketh that
1Th. 2: 6. neither of you, nor (yet) of *others*,
Heb. 4: 8. afterward have spoken of *another* day.
11:35. *others* were tortured, not accepting
Jas. 5:12. by the earth, neither by any *other* oath :
Rev. 2:24. I will put upon you none *other* burden.
6: 4. there went out *another* horse
7: 2. I saw *another* angel ascending
8: 3. *another* angel came and stood at
10: 1. I saw *another* mighty angel
12: 3. there appeared *another* wonder in
13:11. I beheld *another* beast coming
14: 6. I saw *another* angel fly in the
8. there followed *another* angel, saying,
15. *another* angel came out of the
17. *another* angel came out of the
18. *another* angel came out from
15: 1. I saw *another* sign in heaven,
16: 1. I heard *another* out of the altar
17:10. one is, (and) the *other* is not yet come ;
18: 1. I saw *another* angel come down
4. I heard *another* voice from heaven,
20:12. *another* book was opened, which

ἀλλοτριοεπίσκοπος, *allotrioepiskopos*.

1Pet. 4:15. or as a busybody in *other men's matters*.

ἀλλότριος, *allotrios*.

Mat.17:25. of their own children, or of *strangers?*
26. Peter saith unto him, Of *strangers*.
Lu. 16:12. faithful in that which is *another man's*,
Joh.10: 5. *a stranger* will they not follow,
— they know not the voice of *strangers*.
Acts 7: 6. should sojourn in a *strange* land ;
Ro. 14: 4. that judgest *another man's* servant?
15:20. build upon *another man's* foundation.
2Co.10:15. (that is), of *other men's* labours ;
16. not to boast in *another man's* line
1Ti. 5:22. neither be partaker of *other men's* sins :
Heb. 9:25. every year with blood of *others ;*
11: 9. land of promise, as (in) a *strange* country,
34. to flight the armies of the *aliens*.

ἀλλόφυλος, allophulos.

Acts10:28. or come unto *one of another nation ;*

ἄλλως, allōs.

1Ti. 5:25. they that are *otherwise* cannot be hid.

ἀλοάω, aloaō.

1Co. 9: 9. of the ox that *treadeth out the corn.*
　　　10. that he that *thresheth* in hope should
1Ti. 5:18. the ox that *treadeth out the corn.*

ἄλογος, alogos.

Acts 25:27. For it seemeth to me *unreasonable* to
2Pet. 2:12. these, as natural *brute* beasts, made
Jude　10. know naturally, as *brute* beasts, in

ἀλόη, aloee.

Joh.19:39. brought a mixture of myrrh and *aloes,*

ἄλς, hals.

Mar. 9:49. every sacrifice shall be salted with *salt.*

ἀλυκός, halukos.

Jas. 3:12. no fountain both yield *salt* water and
　　　fresh.

ἀλυπότερος, alupoteros.

Phil. 2:28. that I may be the *less sorrowful.*

ἄλυσις, halusis.

Mar. 5: 3. could bind him, no, not with *chains:*
　　　4. often bound with fetters and *chains,* and
　　　　the *chains* had been plucked asunder
Lu. 8:29. he was kept bound with *chains* and
Acts12: 6. bound with two *chains:* and the
　　　7. his *chains* fell off from (his) hands.
　　21:33. (him) to be bound with two *chains;*
　　28:20. of Israel I am bound with this *chain.*
Eph. 6:20. For which I am an ambassador in *bonds:*
2Ti. 1:16. was not ashamed of my *chain:*
Rev.20: 1. bottomless pit and a great *chain* in his
　　　hand.

ἀλυσιτελής, alusitelecs.

Heb 13:17. for that (is) *unprofitable* for you.

ἄλων, halōn.

Mat. 3:12. he will throughly purge his *floor,* and
Lu. 3:17. he will throughly purge his *floor,*

ἀλώπηξ, alōpeex.

Mat. 8:20. The *foxes* have holes, and the birds of the
Lu. 9:58. Jesus said unto him, *Foxes* have holes,
　　13:32. Go ye, and tell that *fox,* Behold, I cast

ἅλωσις, halōsis.

2Pet. 2:12. beasts, made to *be taken* and destroyed,
　　　(lit. for *capture*)

ἅμα, hama.

Mat.13:29. ye root up also the wheat *with* them.
　　20: 1. which went out early (lit. *with* the early
　　　　dawn) in the morning
Acts24:26. He hoped *also* that money should
　　27:40. unto the sea, *and* loosed the rudder bands,
Ro. 3:12. they are *together* become unprofitable ;
Col. 4: 3. *Withal* praying also for us, that God
1Th. 4:17. shall be caught up *together* with
　　5:10. we should live *together* with him.
1Ti. 5:13. *withal* they learn (to be) idle,
Philem.22. *withal* prepare me also a lodging:

ἀμαθής, amathees.

2Pet. 3:16. which they that are *unlearned* and

ἀμαράντινος, amarantinos.

1Pet.5: 4. a crown of glory *that fadeth not away.*

ἀμάραντος, amarantos.

1Pet. 1: 4. undefiled, and *that fadeth not away,*

ἁμαρτάνω, hamartano.

Mat.18:15. if thy brother *shall trespass* against
　　21. how oft *shall* my brother *sin* against
　　27: 4. I *have sinned* in that I have
Lu. 15:18. Father, I *have sinned* against heaven,
　　21. Father, I *have sinned* against heaven,
　　17: 3. If thy brother *trespass* against thee,
　　4. if he *trespass* against thee seven times
Joh. 5:14. thou art made whole: *sin* no more,
　　8:11. condemn thee: go, and *sin* no more.
　　9: 2. Master, who *did sin,* this man, or
　　3. Neither *hath* this man *sinned,* nor
Acts25: 8. *have* I *offended* any thing at all.
Ro. 2:12. as many as *have sinned* without law
　　— as many as *have sinned* in the law
　　3:23. For all *have sinned,* and come short
　　5:12. upon all men, for that all *have sinned.*
　　14. them *that had* not *sinned* after
　　16. not as (it was) by one *that sinned,*
　　6:15. shall we *sin,* because we are not
1Co. 6:18. fornication *sinneth* against his own
　　7:28. if thou marry, thou *hast* not *sinned ;* and
　　　if a virgin marry, she *hath* not *sinned.*
　　36. do what he will, he *sinneth* not:
　　8:12. ye *sin* so against the brethren, and wound
　　　their weak conscience, ye *sin* against
　　　Christ.

1Co.15:34. Awake to righteousness, and *sin* not;
Eph. 4:26. Be ye angry, and *sin* not: let not
1Ti. 5:20. Them that *sin* rebuke before all,
Tit. 3:11. is subverted, and *sinneth*, being condemned
Heb. 3:17. with them *that had sinned*,
10:26. For if we *sin* wilfully after that
1Pet.2:20. if, when ye be buffeted *for your faults*, (lit. *having sinned*)
2Pet. 2: 4. spared not the angels *that sinned*,
1Joh.1:10. If we say that we *have* not *sinned*,
2: 1. that ye *sin* not. And if any man *sin*,
3: 6. Whosoever abideth in him *sinneth* not: whosoever *sinneth* hath not seen him,
8. for the devil *sinneth* from the
9. he cannot *sin*, because he is
5:16. see his brother *sin* a sin (which)
— them *that sin* not unto death.
18. whosoever is born of God *sinneth* not;

ἁμάρτημα, *hamarteema.*

Mar. 3:28. All *sins* shall be forgiven unto
4:12. (their) *sins* should be forgiven them.
Ro. 3:25. for the remission of *sins* that are
1Co.6:18. Every *sin* that a man doeth is

ἁμαρτία, *hamartia.*

Mat. 1:21. shall save his people from their *sins*.
3: 6. in Jordan, confessing their *sins*.
9: 2. good cheer ; thy *sins* be forgiven thee.
5. to say, (Thy) *sins* be forgiven thee ;
6. hath power on earth to forgive *sins*,
12:31. All manner of *sin* and blasphemy
26:28. for many for the remission of *sins*.
Mar. 1: 4. repentance for the remission of *sins*.
5. river of Jordan, confessing their *sins*.
2: 5. Son, thy *sins* be forgiven thee.
7. who can forgive *sins* but God
9. (Thy) *sins* be forgiven thee ; or to
10. hath power on earth to forgive *sins*,
Lu. 1:77. by the remission of their *sins*,
3: 3. repentance for the remission of *sins* ;
5:20. Man, thy *sins* are forgiven thee.
21. Who can forgive *sins*, but God
23. to say, Thy *sins* be forgiven thee ;
24. hath power upon earth to forgive *sins*,
7:47. Her *sins*, which are many, are
48. said unto her, Thy *sins* are forgiven.
49. Who is this that forgiveth *sins* also ?
11: 4. forgive us our *sins* ; for we also
24:47. repentance and remission of *sins*
Joh. 1:29. which taketh away the *sin* of the world.
8:21. seek me, and shall die in your *sins* :
24. that ye shall die in your *sins* :
— I am (he), ye shall die in your *sins*.
34. Whosoever committeth *sin* is the servant of *sin*.
46. Which of you convinceth me of *sin* ?
9:34. Thou wast altogether born in *sins*,
41. ye should have no *sin* : but now ye say, We see ; therefore your *sin* remaineth.
15:22. unto them, they had not had *sin* : but now they have no cloke for their *sin*.
24. man did, they had not had *sin* :
16: 8. he will reprove the world of *sin*, and
9. Of *sin*, because they believe not
19:11. unto thee hath the greater *sin*.
20:23. Whose soever *sins* ye remit, they

Acts 2:38. for the remission of *sins*, and ye
3:19. that your *sins* may be blotted out,
5:31. repentance to Israel, and **forgiveness of** *sins*.
7:60. lay not this *sin* to their charge.
10:43. shall receive remission of *sins*.
13:38. unto you the forgiveness of *sins* :
22:16. be baptized, and wash away thy *sins*,
26:18. they may receive forgiveness of *sins*,
Ro. 3: 9. that they are all under *sin* ;
20. by the law (is) the knowledge of *sin*.
4: 7. forgiven, and whose *sins* are covered.
8. to whom the Lord will not impute *sin*.
5:12. by one man *sin* entered into the world, and death by *sin* ; and so death
13. until the law *sin* was in the world : but *sin* is not imputed when
20. where *sin* abounded, grace did
21. That as *sin* hath reigned
6: 1. Shall we continue in *sin*, that grace
2. shall we, that are dead to *sin*, live
6. the body of *sin* might be destroyed, that henceforth we should not serve *sin*.
7. he that is dead is freed from *sin*.
10. he died unto *sin* once : but in
11. to be dead indeed unto *sin*, but alive
12. Let not *sin* therefore reign in your
13. instruments of unrighteousness unto *sin* :
14. For *sin* shall not have dominion
16. whether of *sin* unto death, or of
17. that ye were the servants of *sin*,
18. Being then made free from *sin*,
20. when ye were the servants of *sin*,
22. now being made free from *sin*,
23. For the wages of *sin* (is) death ;
7: 5. the motions of *sins*, which were by
7. we say then ? (Is) the law *sin* ?
— I had not known *sin*, but by
8. *sin*, taking occasion by the
— For without the law *sin* (was) dead.
9. *sin* revived, and I died.
11. For *sin*, taking occasion by the
13. *sin*, that it might appear *sin*,
— that *sin* by the commandment
14. I am carnal, sold under *sin*.
17. *sin* that dwelleth in me.
20. I that do it, but *sin* that dwelleth
23. to the law of *sin* which is in
25. but with the flesh the law of *sin*.
8: 2. free from the law of *sin* and death.
3. likeness of *sinful* flesh, and for *sin*, condemned *sin* in the flesh :
10. the body (is) dead because of *sin* ;
11:27. when I shall take away their *sins*.
14:23. whatsoever (is) not of faith is *sin*.
1Co.15: 3. that Christ died for our *sins*
17. ye are yet in your *sins*.
56. The sting of death (is) *sin* ; and the strength of *sin* (is) the law.
2Co. 5:21. hath made him (to be) *sin* for us, who knew no *sin* ;
11: 7. Have I committed an *offence* in
Gal. 1: 4. Who gave himself for our *sins*,
2:17. (is) therefore Christ the minister of *sin* ?
3:22. scripture hath concluded all under *sin*,
Eph. 2: 1. were dead in trespasses and *sins* ;
Col. 1:14. his blood, (even) the forgiveness of *sins*.
2:11. the body of the *sins* of the flesh by
1Th. 2:16. to fill up their *sins* alway: for
2Th. 2: 3. that man of *sin* be revealed, the
1Ti. 5:22. partaker of other men's *sins*: keep
24. Some men's *sins* are open beforehand,

2Ti. 3: 6. captive silly women laden with *sins*,
Heb. 1: 3. had by himself purged our *sins*,
  2:17. reconciliation for the *sins* of the
  3:13. through the deceitfulness of *sin*.
  4:15. like as (we are, yet) without *sin*.
  5: 1. both gifts and sacrifices for *sins* :
    3. also for himself, to offer for *sins*.
  7:27. sacrifice, first for his own *sins*,
  8:12. their *sins* and their iniquities will
  9:26. to put away *sin* by the sacrifice
    28. offered to bear the *sins* of many ;
    — second time without *sin* unto
 10: 2. had no more conscience of *sins*.
    3. again (made) of *sins* every year.
    4. bulls and of goats should take away *sin*.
    6. (sacrifices) for *sin* thou hast
    8. (offering) for *sin* thou wouldest not,
   11. which can never take away *sins* :
   12. had offered one sacrifice for *sins*,
   17. their *sins* and iniquities will I
   18. (there is) no more offering for *sin*.
   26. remaineth no more sacrifice for *sins*,
 11:25. the pleasures of *sin* for a season ;
 12: 1. the *sin* which doth so easily beset
    4. unto blood, striving against *sin*.
 13:11. by the high priest for *sin*, are
Jas. 1:15. it bringeth forth *sin* : and *sin*, when
  2: 9. respect to persons, ye commit *sin*,
  4:17. doeth (it) not, to him it is *sin*.
  5:15. if he have committed *sins*,
    20. shall hide a multitude of *sins*.
1Pet.2:22. Who did no *sin*, neither was
    24. Who his own self bare our *sins* in
    — that we, being dead to *sins*,
  3:18. hath once suffered for *sins*,
  4: 1. in the flesh hath ceased from *sin* ;
    8. shall cover the multitude of *sins*.
2Pet.1: 9. was purged from his old *sins*.
  2:14. that cannot cease from *sin* ;
1Joh.1: 7. his Son cleanseth us from all *sin*.
    8. If we say that we have no *sin*,
    9. If we confess our *sins*, he is faithful and
      just to forgive us (our) *sins*,
  2: 2. he is the propitiation for our *sins* :
   12. because your *sins* are forgiven
  3: 4. Whosoever committeth *sin*
    — *sin* is the transgression of the law.
    5. manifested to take away our *sins* ; and in
      him is no *sin*.
    8. He that committeth *sin* is of the
    9. born of God doth not commit *sin* ;
  4:10. the propitiation for our *sins*.
  5:16. see his brother sin a *sin* (which)
    — There is a *sin* unto death : I do
   17. All unrighteousness is *sin* : and there is
      a *sin* not unto death.
Rev. 1: 5. washed us from our *sins* in his
 18: 4. ye be not partakers of her *sins*,
    5. For her *sins* have reached unto

ἀμάρτυρος, *amarturos*.

Acts14:17. he left not himself *without witness*,

ἀμαρτωλός, *hamartōlos*.

Mat. 9:10. many publicans and *sinners* came and
   11. your Master with publicans and *sinners* ?
   13. the righteous, but *sinners* to repentance.
 11:19. a friend of publicans and *sinners*.

Mat.26:45. is betrayed into the hands of *sinners*.
Mar. 2:15. many publicans and *sinners* sat also
   16. eat with publicans and *sinners*, they
    — eateth and drinketh with publicans and
      sinners ?
   17. the righteous, but *sinners* to repentance.
  8:38. this adulterous and *sinful* generation ;
 14:41. is betrayed into the hands of *sinners*.
Lu. 5: 8. for I am a *sinful* man, O Lord.
   30. eat and drink with publicans and *sinners* ?
   32. the righteous, but *sinners* to repentance.
  6:32. for *sinners* also love those that
   33. for *sinners* also do even the same.
   34. for *sinners* also lend to *sinners*,
  7:34. a friend of publicans and *sinners* !
   37. a woman in the city, which was a *sinner*,
   39. toucheth him : for she is a *sinner*.
 13: 2. were *sinners* above all the Galilæans,
 15: 1. the publicans and *sinners* for to hear
    2. This man receiveth *sinners*, and
    7. over one *sinner* that repenteth,
   10. over one *sinner* that repenteth.
 18:13. God be merciful to me a *sinner*.
 19: 7. guest with a man that is a *sinner*.
 24: 7. into the hands of *sinful* men,
Joh. 9:16. can a man that is a *sinner* do
   24. we know that this man is a *sinner*.
   25. Whether he be a *sinner* (or no), I
   31. that God heareth not *sinners* :
Ro. 3: 7. am I also judged as a *sinner* ?
  5: 8. that, while we were yet *sinners*,
   19. disobedience many were made *sinners*,
  7:13. might become exceeding *sinful*.
Gal. 2:15. Jews by nature, and not *sinners* of
   17. we ourselves also are found *sinners*,
1Ti. 1: 9. for the ungodly and for *sinners*, for
   15. into the world to save *sinners* ;
Heb. 7:26. undefiled, separate from *sinners*,
 12: 3. such contradiction of *sinners* against
Jas. 4: 8. Cleanse (your) hands, (ye) *sinners* ;
  5:20. which converteth the *sinner*
1Pet.4:18. where shall the ungodly and the *sinner*
      appear ?
Jude 15. which ungodly *sinners* have

ἄμαχος, *amakos*.

1Ti. 3: 3. patient, *not a brawler*, not covetous ;
Tit. 3: 2. evil of no man, to be *no brawlers*, (but)

ἀμάω, *amao*.

Jas. 5: 4. the labourers *who have reaped down*

ἀμέθυστος, *amethustos*.

Rev 21:20. a jacinth ; the twelfth, *an amethyst*.

ἀμελέω, *ameleo*.

Mat.22: 5. they *made light of* (it), and went their
1Ti. 4:14. *Neglect* not the gift that is in thee,
Heb.2: 3. if we *neglect* so great salvation ; which
  8: 9. I *regarded* them *not*, saith the Lord.
2Pet.1:12. I *will* not *be negligent* to put you

ἄμεμπτος, *amemptos*.

Lu. 1: 6. ordinances of the Lord *blameless*.

Phil. 2:15. That ye may be *blameless* and
    3: 6. which is in the law, *blameless.*
1Th. 3:13. stablish your hearts *unblameable* in
Heb. 8: 7. that first (covenant) had been *faultless,*

ἀμέμπτως, *amemptōs.*

1Th. 2:10. justly and *unblameably* we behaved
    5:23. be preserved *blameless* unto the

ἀμέριμνος, *amerimnos.*

Mat.28:14. we will persuade him, and secure (lit.
    make *without care*) you.
1Co. 7:32. I would have you *without carefulness.*

ἀμετάθετος, *ametathetos.*

Heb.6:17. the *immutability* of his counsel,
    18. That by two *immutable* things,

ἀμετακίνητος, *ametakineetos.*

1Co.15:58. be ye stedfast, *unmoveable,* always

ἀμεταμέλητος, *ametameleetos.*

Ro. 11:29. gifts and calling of God (are) *without*
    repentance.
2Co. 7:10. to salvation *not to be repented of:*

ἀμετανόητος, *ametanoeetos.*

Ro. 2: 5. thy hardness and *impenitent* heart

ἄμετρος, *ametros*

2Co.10:13. boast of *things without* (our) *measure,*
    15. Not boasting of *things without* (our) *mea-*
    sure,

ἀμήν, *ameen.*

Mat. 5:18. For *verily* I say unto you, Till heaven
    26. *Verily* I say unto thee, Thou shalt
    6: 2. *Verily* I say unto you, They have their
    reward.
    5. *Verily* I say unto you, They have
    13. the power, and the glory, for ever. *Amen.*
    16. *Verily* I say unto you, They have
    8:10. *Verily* I say unto you, I have not
    10:15. *Verily* I say unto you, It shall be
    23. for *verily* I say unto you, Ye shall
    42. *verily* I say unto you, he shall in
    11:11. *Verily* I say unto you, Among them that
    13:17. For *verily* I say unto you, That many
    16:28. *Verily* I say unto you, There be some
    17:20. for *verily* I say unto you, If ye
    18: 3. And said, *Verily* I say unto you,
    13. And if so be that he find it, *verily*
    18. *Verily* I say unto you, Whatsoever
    19:23. *Verily* I say unto you, That a rich man
    28. *Verily* I say unto you, That ye which

Mat.21:21. *Verily* I say unto you, If ye have faith,
    31. *Verily* I say unto you, That the publicans
    23:36. *Verily* I say unto you, All these things
    24: 2. See ye not all these things? *verily* I say
    34. *Verily* I say unto you, This generation
    47. *Verily* I say unto you, That he
    25.12. *Verily* I say unto you, I know you not.
    40. King shall answer and say unto them,
    Verily
    45. shall he answer them, saying, *Verily*
    26:13. *Verily* I say unto you, Wheresoever this
    gospel
    21. *Verily* I say unto you, that one of you
    34. *Verily* I say unto thee, That this night,
    28:20. (even) unto the end of the world. *Amen.*
Mar 3:28. *Verily* I say unto you, All sins shall
    6:11. *Verily* I say unto you, It shall be more
    8:12. seek after a sign? *verily* I say unto you,
    9: 1. *Verily* I say unto you, That there be some
    41. because ye belong to Christ, *verily* I say
    unto
    10:15. *Verily* I say unto you, Whosoever
    29. *Verily* I say unto you, There is no man
    11:23. For *verily* I say unto you, That whosoever
    12:43. *Verily* I say unto you, That this poor
    widow
    13:30. *Verily* I say unto you, that this generation
    14: 9. *Verily* I say unto you, Wheresoever
    18. *Verily* I say unto you, One of you which
    25. *Verily* I say unto you, I will drink
    30. *Verily* I say unto thee, That this day,
    16:20. confirming the word with signs follow-
    ing. *Amen.*
Lu. 4:24. *Verily* I say unto you, No prophet is
    12:37. shall find watching: *verily* I say unto you,
    13:35. left unto you desolate: and *verily* I say
    18:17. *Verily* I say unto you, Whosoever
    29. *Verily* I say unto you, There is no
    21.32. *Verily* I say unto you, This generation
    23:43. *Verily* I say unto thee, To day shalt thou
    24:53. in the temple, praising and blessing God.
    Amen.
Joh. 1:51(52). *Verily, verily,* I say unto you, Here-
    after ye shall
    3: 3. *Verily, verily,* I say unto thee, Except a
    5. *Verily, verily,* I say unto thee, Except a
    11. *Verily, verily,* I say unto thee, We speak
    5:19. *Verily, verily,* I say unto you, The Son
    24. *Verily, verily,* I say unto you, He that
    25. *Verily, verily,* I say unto you, The
    6:26. *Verily, verily,* I say unto you, Ye seek
    32. *Verily, verily,* I say unto you, Moses gave
    47. *Verily, verily,* I say unto you, He
    53. *Verily, verily,* I say unto you, Except
    8:34. *Verily, verily,* I say unto you, Whosoever
    51. *Verily, verily,* I say unto you, If a
    58. *Verily, verily,* I say unto you, Before
    10: 1. *Verily, verily,* I say unto you, He
    7. *Verily, verily,* I say unto you,
    12:24. *Verily, verily,* I say unto you, Except
    13:16. *Verily, verily,* I say unto you, The servant
    20. *Verily, verily,* I say unto you, He
    21. testified, and said, *Verily, verily,* I say
    38. for my sake? *Verily, verily,* I say unto
    14:12. *Verily, verily,* I say unto you,
    16:20. *Verily, verily,* I say unto you, That
    23. ask me nothing. *Verily, verily,* I say unto
    21:18. *Verily, verily,* I say unto thee, When
    25. contain the books that should be written.
    Amen.
Ro. 1:25. the Creator, who is blessed for ever. *Amen.*
    9: 5. over all, God blessed for ever. **Amen.**

Ro. 11:36. to whom (be) glory for ever. *Amen.*
15:33. God of peace (be) with you all. *Amen.*
16:24. Jesus Christ (be) with you all. *Amen.*
27. glory through Jesus Christ for ever. *Amen.*
1Co.14:16. unlearned say *Amen* at thy giving of thanks,
16:24. you all in Christ Jesus. *Amen.*
2Co. 1:20. (are) yea, and in him *Amen,* unto the
13:14(13). of the Holy Ghost, (be) with you all. *Amen.*
Gal. 1: 5. (be) glory for ever and ever. *Amen.*
6:18. Christ (be) with your spirit. *Amen.*
Eph. 3:21. throughout all ages, world without end. *Amen.*
6:24. Jesus Christ in sincerity. *Amen.*
Phi. 4:20. (be) glory for ever and ever. *Amen.*
23. (be) with you all. *Amen.*
Col. 4:18. Remember my bonds. Grace (be) with you. *Amen.*
1Th. 5:28. Christ (be) with you. *Amen.*
2Th. 3:18. Christ (be) with you all. *Amen.*
1Ti. 1:17. and glory for ever and ever. *Amen.*
6:16. (be) honour and power everlasting. *Amen.*
21. Grace (be) with thee. *Amen.*
2Ti. 4:18. to whom (be) glory for ever and ever. *Amen.*
22. Grace (be) with you. *Amen.*
Tit. 3:15. Grace (be) with you all. *Amen.*
Philem.25. Christ (be) with your spirit. *Amen.*
Heb 13:21. to whom (be) glory for ever and ever. *Amen.*
25. Grace (be) with you all. *Amen.*
1Pet.4:11. be praise and dominion for ever and ever. *Amen.*
5:11. glory and dominion for ever and ever. *Amen.*
14. all that are in Christ Jesus. *Amen.*
2Pet.3:18. (be) glory both now and for ever. *Amen.*
1Joh.5:21. Little children, keep yourselves from idols. *Amen.*
2Joh. 13. of thy elect sister greet thee. *Amen.*
Jude 25. dominion and power, both now and ever. *Amen.*
Rev. 1: 6. and dominion for ever and ever. *Amen.*
7. shall wail because of him. Even so, *Amen.*
18. I am alive for evermore, *Amen ;*
3:14. These things saith the *Amen,*
5:14. And the four beasts said, *Amen.*
7:12. Saying, *Amen :* Blessing, and glory,
— might, (be) unto our God for ever and ever. *Amen.*
19: 4. sat on the throne, saying, *Amen ;* Alleluia.
22:20. *Amen.* Even so, come, Lord Jesus.
21. Jesus Christ (be) with you all. *Amen.*

ἀμήτωρ, *ameetor.*

Heb 7: 3. Without father, *without mother,*

ἀμίαντος, *amiantos.*

Heb 7:26. (who is) holy, harmless, *undefiled,*
13: 4. honourable in all, and the bed *undefiled :*
Jas. 1:27. Pure religion and *undefiled* before God
1Pet.1: 4. an inheritance incorruptible, and *undefiled,*

ἄμμος, *ammos.*

Mat. 7:26. which built his house upon the *sand :*

Ro. 9:27. Israel be as the *sand* of the sea,
Heb 11:12. as the *sand* which is by the sea shore
Rev.13: 1(12:18). I stood upon the *sand* of the sea,
20: 8. number of whom (is) as the *sand* of the sea.

ἀμνός, *amnos.*

Joh. 1:29. Behold the *Lamb* of God, which
36. he saith, Behold the *Lamb* of God !
Acts 8:32. like a *lamb* dumb before his shearer,
1Pet.1:19. blood of Christ, as of a *lamb* without

ἀμοιβή, *amoibee.*

1Ti. 5: 4. piety at home, and to requite (lit. return *recompences* to) their parents:

ἄμπελος, *ampelos.*

Mat.26:29. of this fruit of the *vine,* until that
Mar 14:25. drink no more of the fruit of the *vine,*
Lu. 22:18. I will not drink of the fruit of the *vine,*
Joh.15: 1. I am the true *vine,* and my Father is
4. except it abide in the *vine ;* no more
5. I am the *vine,* ye (are) the branches:
Jas. 3:12. bear olive berries ? either a *vine,* figs ?
Rev.14:19. gathered the *vine* of the earth, and cast

ἀμπελουργός, *ampelourgos.*

Lu. 13: 7. said he unto the *dresser of his vineyard,*

ἀμπελών, *ampelon.*

Mat.20: 1. to hire labourers into his *vineyard.*
2. he sent them into his *vineyard.*
4. Go ye also into the *vineyard,* and
7. Go ye also into the *vineyard ;* and
8. the lord of the *vineyard* saith
21:28. work to day in my *vineyard.*
33. housholder, which planted a *vineyard,*
39. cast (him) out of the *vineyard,* and
40. the lord therefore of the *vineyard*
41. will let out (his) *vineyard* unto
Mar 12: 1. A (certain) man planted a *vineyard,*
2. of the fruit of the *vineyard.*
8. cast (him) out of the *vineyard.*
9. therefore the lord of the *vineyard* do ?
— will give the *vineyard* unto others.
Lu. 13: 6. had a fig tree planted in his *vineyard ;*
20: 9. A certain man planted a *vineyard,*
10. give him of the fruit of the *vineyard :*
13. said the lord of the *vineyard,*
15. they cast him out of the *vineyard,*
— shall the lord of the *vineyard* do
16. shall give the *vineyard* to others.
1Co. 9: 7. who planteth a *vineyard,* and eateth

ἀμύνομαι, *amunomai.*

Acts 7:24. suffer wrong, he *defended* (him), and

ἀμφίβληστρον, *amphibleestron.*

Mat. 4:18. casting a *net* into the sea: for they

Mar 1:16. Andrew his brother casting a *net* into the sea:

ἀμφιέννυμι, *amphiennumi.*

Mat. 6:30. if God so *clothe* the grass of the field,
  11: 8. A man *clothed* in soft raiment?
Lu. 7:25. A man *clothed* in soft raiment?
  12:28. If then God so *clothe* the grass,

ἄμφοδον, *amphodon.*

Mar 11: 4. in a place *where two ways met;*

ἀμφότερος, *amphoteros.*

Mat. 9:17. into new bottles, and *both* are preserved.
  13:30. Let *both* grow together until the
  15:14. *both* shall fall into the ditch.
Lu. 1: 6. they were *both* righteous before God,
    7. they *both* were (now) well stricken
  5: 7. they came, and filled *both* the ships,
    38. into new bottles; and *both* are preserved.
  6:39. shall they not *both* fall into the
  7:42. he frankly forgave them *both.*
Acts 8:38. went down *both* into the water,
  23: 8. angel, nor spirit: but the Pharisees confess *both.*
Eph. 2:14. our peace, who hath made *both* one,
  16. he might reconcile *both* unto God
  18. through him we *both* have access

ἀμώμητος, *amōmeetos.*

Phi. 2:15. the sons of God, *without rebuke,*
2Pet. 3:14. in peace, without spot, and *blameless.*

ἄμωμος, *amōmos.*

Eph. 1: 4. *without blame* before him in love:
  5:27. that it should be holy and *without blemish.*
Col. 1:22. to present you holy and *unblameable*
Heb 9:14. offered himself *without spot* to God,
1Pet. 1:19. as of a lamb *without blemish* and
Jude   24. to present (you) *faultless* before the
Rev.14: 5. for they are *without fault* before the

ἄν, *an.*

Observe.—The place where, ἄν stands is marked thus)(

Mat. 2:13. and be thou there until)(I bring thee word:
  5:18. Till)(heaven and earth pass, one jot or one tittle shall in no wise pass from the law, till)(all be fulfilled.
  19. whosoever)(shall do and teach (them),
  21. and whosoever)(shall kill shall be in danger
  22. and whosoever)(shall say to his brother, Raca,
  — but whosoever)(shall say, Thou fool, shall be
  26. come out thence, till)(thou hast paid
  31. said, Whosoever)(shall put away his wife,

Mat. 5:32. whosoever)(shall put away his wife, saving
  6: 5. the streets, that)(they may be seen
  7:12. all things whatsoever)(ye would that men
  10:11. whatsoever)(city or town ye shall enter, — and there abide till)(ye go thence.
  23. Israel, till)(the Son of man be come.
  33. But whosoever)(shall deny me before men,
  11:21. Sidon, they would have repented long ago)(in sackcloth
  23. Sodom, it would have remained)(until this day.
  12: 7. sacrifice,)(ye would not have condemned
  20. not quench, till)(he send forth judgment
  32. whosoever)(speaketh a word against the Son
  — but whosoever)(speaketh against the Holy Ghost,
  50. whosoever)(shall do the will of my
  15: 5. Whosoever)(shall say to (his) father
  16:25. whosoever)(will save his life shall lose it: and whosoever)(will lose his life
  28. death, till)(they see the Son of man
  18: 6. But whoso)(shall offend one of these
  19: 9. Whosoever)(shall put away his wife,
  21:22. all things, whatsoever)(ye shall ask
  44. on whomsoever)(it shall fall, it will
  22: 9. as many as)(ye shall find, bid to
  44. right hand, till)(I make thine enemies
  23: 3. All therefore whatsoever)(they bid you observe,
  16. Whosoever)(shall swear by the temple, it is nothing; but whosoever)(shall swear by the gold
  18. but whosoever)(sweareth by the gift
  30. we)(would not have been partakers with them
  39. henceforth, till)(ye shall say,
  24:22. shortened, there)(should no flesh be saved:
  34. shall not pass, till)(all these things
  43. he)(would have watched, and)(would not have suffered his house
  25:27. coming I)(should have received mine
  26:48. Whomsoever I)(shall kiss, that same is he:
Mar 3:28. blasphemies wherewith soever)(they shall blaspheme:
  29. But he that)(shall blaspheme against the
  35. For whosoever)(shall do the will of God,
  4:25. For he that)(hath, to him shall be
  6:10. there abide till)(ye depart from that place.
  11. And whosoever)(shall not receive you,
  56. And whithersoever)(he entered, into villages,
  — as many as)(touched him were made whole.
  8:35. For whosoever)(will save his life shall lose it; but whosoever)(shall lose his
  38. Whosoever therefore)(shall be ashamed of me
  9: 1. death, till)(they have seen the kingdom
  18. wheresoever)(he taketh him, he teareth him:
  41. For whosoever)(shall give you a cup
  42. And whosoever)(shall offend one of (these)
  10:44. And whosoever of you)(will be the chiefest,
  11:23. whosoever)(shall say unto this mountain,
  24. What things soever)(ye desire, when ye pray,

Mar 12:36. right hand, till)(I make thine enemies

13:20. those days, no flesh)(should be saved:

14: 9. Wheresoever this gospel)(shall be preached

44. Whomsoever)(I shall kiss, that same is he;

Lu. 1:62. father, how)(he would have him called.

2:35. thoughts of many hearts)(may be revealed.

6:11. communed one with another what)(they might do

7:39. a prophet,)(would have known who

8:18. for whosoever)(hath, to him shall be given ; and whosoever)(hath not, from him shall

9: 4. And whatsoever)(house ye enter into,

5. And whosoever)(will not receive you,

24. For whosoever)(will save his life shall lose it: but whosoever)(will lose his life

26. For whosoever)(shall be ashamed of me

27. till)(they see the kingdom of God.

46. which of them)(should be greatest.

57. I will follow thee whithersoever)(thou goest.

10: 5. whatsoever)(house ye enter, first say, Peace

8. And into whatsoever)(city ye enter,

10. But into whatsoever)(city ye enter, and

13. they had)(a great while ago repented, sitting

35. and whatsoever)(thou spendest more, when I

12: 8. Whosoever)(shall confess me before men,

39. thief would come, he)(would have watched, and)(not have suffered his house

13:25. When once the master of the house)(is risen up,

35. not see me, until)((the time) come when

17: 6. faith as a grain of mustard seed,)(ye might say unto

— planted in the sea ; and)(it should obey you.

19:23. coming)(I might have required mine own

20:18. on whomsoever)(it shall fall, it will

43. Till)(I make thine enemies thy footstool.

21:32. not pass away, till)(all be fulfilled.

Joh. 1:33. Upon whom)(thou shalt see the Spirit descending,

2: 5. Whatsoever)(he saith unto you, do (it).

4:10. thou)(wouldest have asked of him, and)(he would have given thee living water.

14. But whosoever)(drinketh of the water

5:19. what things soever)(he doeth, these also

46. believed Moses, ye would have believed)(me:

8:19. me,)(ye should have known my Father

39. Abraham's children,)(ye would do the works

42. your Father, ye)(would love me:

9:41. If ye were blind, ye)(should have no sin:

11:21. hadst been here, my brother)(had not died.

22. whatsoever)(thou wilt ask of God, God

32. if thou hadst been here, my brother)(had

13:24. ask who)(it should be of whom

14: 2. if (it were) not (so),)(I would have

7. If ye had known me,)(ye should have known

13. whatsoever)(ye shall ask in my name,

28. If ye loved me,)(ye would rejoice,

15:16. whatsoever)(ye shall ask of the Father

Joh. 15:19. of the world, the world)(would love

16:13. but whatsoever)(he shall hear, (that) shall

23. Whatsoever)(ye shall ask the Father in

18:30. not a malefactor,)(we would not have delivered

36. if my kingdom were of this world, then)(would my servants fight,

20:23. Whose soever sins)(ye remit, they are remitted unto them ; (and) whose soever (sins))(ye retain,

Acts 2:12. What)(meaneth this?

21. whosoever)(shall call on the name

35. Until)(I make thy foes thy footstool.

39. as many as)(the Lord our God shall

45. to all (men), as)(every man had need.

3:19. blotted out, when)(the times of refreshing shall come

22. in all things whatsoever)(he shall say

23. soul, which)(will not hear that prophet,

4:35. unto every man according as)(he had

5:24. doubted of them whereunto this)(would grow.

7: 3. into the land which)(I shall shew thee.

8:19. power, that on)(whomsoever I lay hands,

31. How)(can I, except some man should guide

10:17. what this vision which he had seen)(should mean,

15:17. That the residue of men)(might seek after

17:18. some said, What)(will this babbler say?

20. know therefore what these things)(mean.

18:14. reason would that)(I should bear with you:

21:33. and demanded who)(he was, and what

26:29. And Paul said, I would)(to God, that not

Ro. 3: 4. That)(thou mightest be justified in thy sayings,

9:15. mercy on whom)(I will have mercy, and I will have compassion on whom)(I will

29. had left us a seed,)(we had been as Sodoma, and)(been made like unto

10:13. For whosoever)(shall call upon the name

16: 2. whatsoever business)(she hath need of you:

1Co. 2: 8. had they known (it), they)(would not have

4: 5. before the time, until)(the Lord come,

7: 5. not one the other, except (it))((be) with consent

11:25. this do ye, as oft as)(ye drink (it), in

26. For as often as)(ye eat this bread, and

— shew the Lord's death till)(he come.

27. Wherefore whosoever)(shall eat this bread,

31. judge ourselves, we)(should not be judged.

34. the rest will I set in order when)(I come.

12: 2. dumb idols, even as)(ye were led.

15:25. For he must reign, till he)(hath put all

16: 2. in store, as (God))(hath prospered him,

2Co. 3:16. when it)(shall turn to the Lord,

10: 9. not seem as if I)(would terrify

11:21. Howbeit whereinsoever any)(is bold,

Gal. 1:10. men, I)(should not be the servant of Christ.

3:21. righteousness)(should have been by the law.

4:15. out your own eyes, and)(have given them

Gal. 5:10. shall bear his judgment, whosoever)(he be.

17. cannot do the things that ye)(would.

Phi. 2:23. so soon as I)(shall see how it will

Col. 3:17. And whatsoever)(ye do in word or deed,

1Th. 2: 7. among you, even as a nurse)(cherisheth

Heb 1:13. right hand, until)(I make thine enemies

4: 8. then)(would he not afterward have spoken

8: 4. on earth, he)(should not be a priest,

7. faultless, then)(should no place have been sought for the second.

10: 2. For then)(would they not have ceased to

11:15. came out, they)(might have had opportunity

Jas. 3: 4. whithersoever)(the governor listeth.

4: 4. whosoever)(therefore will be a friend

5: 7. patience for it, until)(he receive the early

1Joh.2: 5. But whoso)(keepeth his word, in him

19. of us, they)(would (no doubt) have continued

3:17. whoso)(hath this world's good,

4:15. Whosoever)(shall confess that Jesus is the Son

5:15. whatsoever)(we ask, we know that we

Rev. 2:25. which ye have (already) hold fast till)(I come.

13:15. that as many as)(would not worship

14: 4. the Lamb whithersoever)(he goeth.

ἀνά, ana. adv.

Mat.20: 9. they received *every man* a penny.

10. likewise received *every man* a penny.

Mar. 6:40. in ranks, *by* hundreds, and *by* fifties.

Lu. 9: 3. money; neither have two coats *apiece.*

14. sit down *by* fifties in a company.

10: 1. sent them two *and* two before

Joh. 2: 6. containing two or three firkins *apiece.*

Rev. 4: 8. the four beasts had *each* of them

21:21. **every *several*gate was of one pearl**:

ἀνά, ana. prep.

Mat.13:25. sowed tares among (lit. *in* the midst of) the wheat,

Mar. 7:31. *through* the midst of the coasts

1Co. 6: 5. to judge between (lit. *in* the midst of) his brethren?

14:27. most (by) three, and (that) *by* course;

Rev. 7:17. the Lamb which is *in* the midst

ἀναϐαθμός, anabathmos.

Acts21:35. when he came upon the *stairs,* so

40. Paul stood on the *stairs,* and beckoned

ἀναϐαίνω, anabaino.

Mat. 3:16. *went up* straightway out of the water,

5: 1. he *went up* into a mountain: and

13: 7. the thorns *sprung up,* and choked them:

14:23. he *went up* into a mountain apart

15:29. *went up* into a mountain, and sat

17:27. the fish that first *cometh up ;* and

20:17. Jesus *going up* to Jerusalem

18. Behold, we *go up* to Jerusalem ;

Mar. 1:10. straightway *coming up* out of the water,

3:13. he *goeth up* into a mountain, and

4: 7. the thorns *grew up,* and choked it,

8. fruit *that sprang up* and increased ;

32. when it is sown, it *groweth up,*

6:51. he *went up* unto them into the ship ;

10:32. in the way *going up* to Jerusalem ;

33. Behold, we *go up* to Jerusalem ;

Lu. 2: 4. Joseph also *went up* from Galilee,

42. they *went up* to Jerusalem after

5:19. they *went up*on the housetop, and let

9:28. *went up* into a mountain to pray.

18:10. Two men *went up* into the temple

31. Behold, we *go up* to Jerusalem, and

19: 4. *climbed up* into a sycomore tree

28. he went before, *ascending up* to

24:38. why do thoughts *arise* in your hearts?

Joh. 1:51(52). the angels of God *ascending* and

2:13. was at hand, and Jesus *went up* to Jerusalem,

3:13. no man *hath ascended up* to heaven,

5: 1. of the Jews; and Jesus *went up* to Jerusalem.

6:62. ye shall see the Son of man *ascend up*

7: 8. *Go* ye *up* unto this feast: I *go* not *up* yet unto this feast ;

10. when his brethren *were gone up*, then *went* he also *up* unto the feast,

14. Jesus *went up* into the temple,

10: 1. *climbeth up* some other way, the

11:55. *went* out of the country *up* to Jerusalem

12:20. Greeks among them *that came up* to

20:17. for I am not yet *ascended* to my

— I *ascend* unto my Father, and your

21: 3. They went forth, and *entered* into a ship

11. Simon Peter *went up*, and drew the

Acts 1:13. they *went up* into an upper room,

2:34. For David is not *ascended* into the

3: 1. Peter and John *went up* together into

7:23. it *came* into his heart to visit his

8:31. that he would *come up* and sit with him.

39. *were come up* out of the water,

10: 4. thine alms *are come up* for a

9. Peter *went up* upon the housetop

11: 2. when Peter *was come up* to Jerusalem,

15: 2. should *go up* to Jerusalem unto

18:22. landed at Cæsarea, *and gone up*, and saluted

20:11. therefore *was come up* again, and had

21: 4. he should not *go up* to Jerusalem.

12. besought him not *to go up* to Jerusalem.

15. our carriages, and *went up* to Jerusalem.

31. tidings *came* unto the chief captain

24:11. since I *went up* to Jerusalem for

25: 1. he *ascended* from Cæsarea to Jerusalem.

9. said, Wilt thou *go up* to Jerusalem,

Ro. 10: 6. Who shall *ascend* into heaven?

1Co. 2: 9. neither *have entered* into the heart

Gal. 2: 1. I *went up* again to Jerusalem

2. I *went up* by revelation, and

Eph 4: 8. When he *ascended up* on high,

9. Now that he *ascended*, what is

10. the same also *that ascended up*

Rev. 4: 1. which said, Come *up* hither, and I will

7: 2. another angel *ascending* from the

8: 4. *ascended up* before God out of

9: 2. there *arose* a smoke out of the pit,

11: 7. the beast *that ascendeth* out of the

12. saying unto them, Come *up* hither. And they *ascended up* to heaven in a

13: 1. saw a beast *rise up* out of the sea,

11. another beast *coming up* out of

14:11. their torment *ascendeth up* for ever

Rev 17: 8. shall *ascend* out of the bottomless
19: 3. her smoke *rose up* for ever and
20: 9. they *went up* on the breadth of

ἀναϐάλλομαι, *anaballomai.*

Acts24:22. of (that) way, he *deferred* them, and

ἀναϐιϐάζω, *anabibazo.*

Mat.13:48. they *drew* to shore, *and* sat down,

ἀναϐλέπω, *anablepo.*

Mat.11: 5. The blind *receive* their *sight,* and
14:19. *looking up* to heaven, he blessed,
20:34. their eyes *received sight,* and they
Mar. 6:41. he *looked up* to heaven, *and* blessed,
7:34. *looking up* to heaven, he sighed,
8:24. he *looked up, and* said, I see men
25. upon his eyes, and made him *look up:*
10:51. Lord, that I *might receive* my *sight.*
52. immediately he *received* his *sight,*
16: 4. when they *looked,* they saw that
Lu. 7:22. how that the blind *see,* the lame
9:16. *looking up* to heaven, he blessed
18:41. Lord, that I *may receive* my *sight.*
42. said unto him, *Receive* thy *sight:*
43. immediately he *received* his *sight,*
19: 5. came to the place, he *looked up, and*
21: 1. he *looked up, and* saw the rich men
Joh. 9:11. I went and washed, and I *received sight.*
15. how he *had received* his *sight.*
18. had been blind, and *received* his *sight,*
— of him *that had received* his *sight.*
Acts 9:12. that he *might receive* his *sight.*
17. that thou *mightest receive* thy *sight,*
18. he *received sight* forthwith, and arose,
22:13. Brother Saul, *receive* thy *sight.* And the
same hour I *looked up* upon him.

ἀνάϐλεψις, *anablepsis.*

Lu. 4:18. *recovering of sight* to the blind,

αναϐοάω, *anaboao.*

Mat.27:46. Jesus *cried* with a loud voice,
Mar.15: 8. the multitude *crying aloud*
Lu. 9:38. a man of the company *cried out,*

ἀναϐολή, *anabolee.*

Acts25:17. without any *delay* on the morrow

ἀναγγέλλω, *anangello.*

Mar. 5:14. *told* (it) in the city, and in the country.
19. *tell* them how great things the
Joh. 4:25. he *will tell* us all things.
5:15. *told* the Jews that it was Jesus,
16:13. he *will shew* you things to come.
14. of mine, and *shall shew* (it) unto you.
15. mine, and *shall shew* (it) unto you.

Joh 16:25. I *shall shew* you plainly of the
Acts14:27. they *rehearsed* all that God
15: 4. they *declared* all things that
16:38. the serjeants *told* these words unto
19:18. came, and confessed, and *shewed* their
deeds.
20:20. have *shewed* you, and have taught you
27. to *declare* unto you all the counsel
Ro. 15:21. To whom he *was* not *spoken* of, they
2Co. 7: 7. when he *told* us your earnest desire,
1Pet. 1:12. things, which *are* now *reported* unto you
1Joh.1: 5. *declare* unto you, that God is light,

ἀναγεννάω, *anagennao.*

1Pet. 1: 3. which...hath *begotten* us *again* unto a lively
23. *Being born again,* not of corruptible

ἀναγινώσκω, *anaginōsko.*

Mat.12: 3. *Have* ye not *read* what David did, when
5. Or *have* ye not *read* in the law, how
19: 4. *Have* ye not *read,* that he which made
21:16. *have* ye never *read,* Out of the mouth of
42. *Did* ye never *read* in the scriptures,
22:31. *have* ye not *read* that which was
24:15. whoso *readeth,* let him understand:
Mar. 2:25. *Have* ye never *read* what David did,
12:10. *have* ye not *read* this scripture ; The
26. *have* ye not *read* in the book of Moses,
13:14. let him *that readeth* understand,
Lu. 4:16. sabbath day, and stood up for *to read.*
6: 3. *Have* ye not *read* so much as this,
10:26. What is written in the law? how *readest*
thou ?
Joh.19:20. This title then *read* many of the Jews:
Acts 8:28. in his chariot *read* Esaias the prophet.
30. heard him *read* the prophet Esaias, and
said, Understandest thou what thou
readest ?
32. the scripture which he *read* was this,
13:27. the prophets *which are read* every sabbath
15:21. *being read* in the synagogues every
31. (Which) *when* they *had read,* they rejoiced
23:34. *when* the governor *had read* (the letter),
2Co. 1:13. than what ye *read* or acknowledge ;
3: 2. in our hearts, known and *read* of all men:
15. unto this day, when Moses *is read,*
Eph 3: 4. *when* ye *read,* ye may understand
Col. 4:16. when this epistle *is read* among you, cause
that it *be read* also in the church
— that ye likewise *read* the (epistle)
1Th. 5:27. that this epistle *be read* unto all
Rev. 1: 3. Blessed (is) he *that readeth,* and they that
5: 4. worthy to open and *to read* the book,

ἀναγκάζω, *anankazo.*

Mat.14:22. Jesus *constrained* his disciples to get
Mar. 6:45. he *constrained* his disciples to get
Lu. 14:23. *compel* (them) to come in, that my
Acts26:11. *compelled* (them) to blaspheme ;
28:19. I *was constrained* to appeal unto
2Co.12:11. a fool in glorying ; ye *have compelled* me:
Gal. 2: 3. being a Greek, *was compelled* to be
14. why *compellest* thou the Gentiles
6:12. they *constrain* you to be circumcised ;

ἀναγκαῖος, anankaios.

Acts10:24. together his kinsmen and *near* friends.
13:46. It was *necessary* that the word of
1Co.12:22. seem to be more feeble, are *necessary:*
2Co. 9: 5. Therefore I thought it *necessary* to exhort
Phi. 1:24. in the flesh (is) *more needful* for you.
2:25. Yet I supposed it *necessary* to send
Tit. 3:14. maintain good works for *necessary* uses,
Heb 8: 3. (it is) of *necessity* that this man have

ἀναγκαστῶς, anankastōs.

1Pet.5: 2. not *by constraint*, but willingly;

ἀνάγκη, anankee.

Mat.18: 7. for it *must needs* be that offences
Lu. 14:18. ground, and I *must needs* go and see it:
21:23. there shall be great *distress* in the land,
23:17. For of *necessity* he must release one
Ro. 13: 5. (ye) *must needs* be subject, not
1Co. 7:26. this is good for the present *distress,*
37. in his heart, having no *necessity,*
9:16. for *necessity* is laid upon me; yea,
2Co. 6: 4. much patience, in afflictions, in *neces-sities,*
9: 7. not grudgingly, or of *necessity:* for
12:10. in reproaches, in *necessities,* in persecu-tions,
1Th. 3: 7. in all our affliction and *distress* by
Philem.14. not be as it were of *necessity,* but
Heb. 7:12. there is made of *necessity* a change
27. Who *needeth* not daily, as those
9:16. there must also of *necessity* be the
23. therefore *necessary* that the patterns
Jude 3. it was *needful* for me to write unto

ἀναγνωρίζομαι, anagnōrizomai.

Acts 7:13. Joseph *was made known* to his

ἀνάγνωσις, anagnōsis.

Acts13:15. after the *reading* of the law and the
2Co. 3:14. in the *reading* of the old testament;
1Ti. 4:13. give attendance *to reading*, to exhortation,

ἀνάγω, anago.

Mat. 4: 1. Then *was* Jesus *led up* of the spirit into
Lu. 2:22. they *brought* him to Jerusalem,
4: 5. the devil, *taking* him *up* into an
8:22. And they *launched forth.*
22:66. *led* him into their council, saying,
Acts 7:41. *offered* sacrifice unto the idol, and
9:39. they *brought* him into the upper
12: 4. after Easter *to bring* him *forth* to the
13:13. *when* Paul and his company *loosed* from Paphos,
16:11. Therefore *loosing* from Troas, we came
34. *when* he *had brought* them into
18:21. if God will. And he *sailed* from Ephesus.
20: 3. he was about *to sail* into Syria, he
13. to ship, and *sailed* unto Assos, there
21: 1. after we were gotten from them and *had launched,*

ἀναδείκνυμι, anadīknumi.

Lu. 10: 1. the Lord *appointed* other seventy
Acts 1:24. *shew* whether of these two thou

ἀνάδειξις, anadīxis.

Lu. 1:80. till the day of his *shewing* unto Israel.

ἀναδέχομαι, anadekomai.

Acts28: 7. name was Publius; who *received* us, *and*
Heb11:17. he *that had received* the promises

ἀναδίδωμι, anadidōmi.

Acts23:33. when...*delivered* the epistle to the governor,

ἀναζάω, anazao.

Lu. 15:24. my son was dead, and *is alive again;*
32. thy brother was dead, and *is alive again;*
Ro. 7: 9. the commandment came, sin *revived,*
14: 9. Christ both died, and rose, and *revived,* that
Rev.20: 5. rest of the dead *lived not again* until

ἀναζητέω, anazęeteo.

Lu. 2:44. they *sought* him among (their)
Acts11:25. Barnabas to Tarsus, for *to seek* Saul:

ἀναζώννυμι, anazōnnumi.

1Pet. 1:13. Wherefore *gird up* the loins of your

ἀναζωπυρέω, anazōpureo.

2Ti. 1: 6. that thou *stir up* the gift of God,

ἀναθάλλω, anathallo.

Phi. 4:10. your care of me hath *flourished again;*

ἀνάθεμα, anathema.

Acts23:14. We have bound ourselves under a *great curse,* (lit. under a curse *by a curse*)
Ro. 9: 3. that myself were *accursed* from
1Co.12: 3. calleth Jesus *accursed:* and (that) no
16:22. let him be *Anathema* Maran-atha.
Gal. 1: 8. preached unto you, let him be *accursed.*
9. have received; let him be *accursed.*

ἀναθεματίζω, anathematizo.

Mar 14:71. he began *to curse* and to swear, (saying),
Acts23:12. *bound* themselves *under a curse,*
　　14. *bound* ourselves *under a great curse,*
　　21. *have bound* themselves *with an oath,*

ἀναθεωρέω, anatheōreo.

Acts17:23. *as* I passed by, and *beheld* your devotions,
Heb13: 7. *considering* the end of (their) conversation:

ἀνάθημα, anatheema.

Lu. 21: 5. was adorned with goodly stones and *gifts,*

ἀναίδεια, anaidia.

Lu. 11: 8. because of his *importunity* he will rise

ἀναίρεσις, anairesis.

Acts 8: 1. Saul was consenting unto his *death.*
　　22:20. standing by, and consenting unto his *death,*

ἀναιρέω, anaireo.

Mat. 2:16. sent forth, and *slew* all the children that
Lu. 22: 2. sought how they *might kill* him ;
　　23:32. led with him *to be put to death.*
Acts 2:23. by wicked hands have crucified and *slain :*
　　5:33. took counsel *to slay* them.
　　36. who *was slain ;* and all, as many as
　　7:21. Pharaoh's daughter *took* him *up,* and
　　28. Wilt thou *kill* me, as thou *diddest* (lit. *killedst*) the Egyptian
　　9:23. the Jews took counsel *to kill* him:
　　24. watched the gates day and night to *kill* him.
　　29. they went about *to slay* him.
　　10:39. whom they *slew* and hanged on a tree:
　　12: 2. he *killed* James the brother of John
　　13:28. that he should *be slain.*
　　16:27. his sword, and would *have killed* himself,
　　22:20. the raiment of them *that slew* him.
　　23:15. he come near, are ready *to kill* him.
　　21. nor drink till they *have killed* him:
　　27. should **have** *been killed* of them:
　　25: 3. laying wait in the way *to kill*
　　26:10. *when* they *were put to death,* I gave
Heb 10: 9. He *taketh away* the first, that he

ἀναίτιος, anaitios.

Mat.12: 5. profane the sabbath, and are *blameless ?*
　　7. would not have condemned the *guiltless.*

ἀνακαθίζω, anakathizo.

Lu. 7:15. he that was dead *sat up,* and began
Acts 9:40 when she saw Peter, she *sat up.*

ανακαινίζω, anakainizo.

Heb.6: 6. *to renew* them again unto repentance ;

ἀνακαινόω, anakainoō.

2Co. 4:16. the inward (man) *is renewed* day by day.
Col. 3:10. *which is renewed* in knowledge

ἀνακαίνωσις, anakainōsis.

Ro. 12: 2. transformed by the *renewing* of your
Tit. 3: 5. regeneration, and *renewing* of the Holy Ghost ;

ἀνακαλύπτω, anakalupto.

2Co. 3:14. remaineth the same vail un*taken away*
　　18. we all, with *open* face beholding as

ἀνακάμπτω, anakampto.

Mat. 2:12. that they should not *return* to Herod,
Lu. 10: 6. if not, it *shall turn* to you again.
Acts18:21. I *will return* again unto you,
Heb11:15. had opportunity *to have returned.*

ἀνάκειμαι, anakīmai.

Mat. 9:10. *as* Jesus *sat at meat* in the house,
　　22:10. the wedding was furnished with *guests.*
　　11. the king came in to see the *guests,*
　　26: 7. on his head, *as* he *sat* (at meat).
　　20. he *sat* down with the twelve.
Mar.5:40. entereth in where the damsel was *lying.*
　　14:18. *as* they *sat* and did eat, Jesus said,
　　16:14. the eleven *as* they *sat at meat,*
Lu. 7:37. knew that (Jesus) *sat at meat* in
　　22:27. (is) greater, he *that sitteth at meat,*
　　— (is) not he *that sitteth at meat?*
Joh. 6:11. disciples to them *that were set down ;*
　　13:23. there was *leaning* on Jesus' bosom
　　28. no man *at the table* knew for (lit. *of those reclining*)

ἀνακεφαλαιόομαι, anakephalaio-omai.

Ro. 13: 9. it *is briefly comprehended* in this saying,
Eph. 1:10. he might *gather together in one* all

ἀνακλινῶ, anaklino.

Mat. 8:11. *shall sit down* with Abraham, and
　　14:19. commanded the multitude *to sit down*
Mar. 6:39. *to make* all *sit down* by companies
Lu. 2: 7. laid him in a manger ; because
　　7:30. Pharisee's house, and *sat down* to meat.
　　9:15. they did so, and *made* them all *sit down.*
　　12:37. *make* them *to sit down* to meat, and will
　　13:29. *shall sit down* in the kingdom of God.

ἀνακόπτω, anakopto.

Gal. 5: 7. who *did hinder* you that ye should

ἀνακράζω, anakrazo.

Mar. 1:23. with an unclean spirit ; and he *cried out,*
　　6:49. it had been a spirit, and *cried out :*

Lu. 4:33. unclean devil, and *cried out* with a loud voice,
    8:28. When he saw Jesus, he *cried out, and* fell
  23:18. they *cried out* all at once, saying,

ἀνακρίνω, anakrino.

Lu. 23:14. I, *having examined* (him) before
Acts 4: 9. If we this day *be examined* of the
  12:19. him not, he *examined* the keepers, *and*
  17:11. *searched* the scriptures daily, whether
  24: 8. *by examining* of whom thyself
  28:18. Who, *when* they *had examined* me,
1Co. 2:14. because they *are* spiritually *discerned*.
    15. he that is spiritual *judgeth* all things, yet he himself *is judged* of no man.
  4: 3. that I *should be judged* of you,
    — yea, I *judge* not mine own self.
    4. he *that judgeth* me is the Lord.
  9: 3. to them *that do examine* me is this,
  10:25. *asking* no *question* for conscience
    27. eat, *asking* no *question* for conscience
  14:24. convinced of all, he *is judged* of all:

ἀνάκρισις, anakrisis.

Acts25:26. that, after *examination* had, I might

ἀνακύπτω, anakupto.

Lu. 13:11. could in no wise *lift up* (herself).
  21:28. then *look up*, and lift up your heads
Joh. 8: 7. he *lifted up* himself, *and* said unto
    10. *When* Jesus *had lifted up* himself, and

ἀναλαμβάνω, analambano.

Mar 16:19. he *was received up* into heaven,
Acts 1: 2. the day in which he *was taken up*,
    11. Jesus, which *is taken up* from you
    22. day that he *was taken up* from us,
  7:43. Yea, ye *took up* the tabernacle of
  10:16. the vessel *was received up* again
  20:13. there intending *to take in* Paul: for
    14. we *took* him *in*, and came to Mitylene.
  23:31. *took* Paul, *and* brought (him) by night
Eph. 6:13. *take unto* you the whole armour of
    16. *taking* the shield of faith, wherewith
1Ti. 3:16. in the world, *received up* into glory.
2Ti. 4:11. *Take* Mark, *and* bring him with thee:

ἀνάληψις, analeepsis.

Lu. 9:51. *that* he *should be received up*, (lit. of his *taking up*)

ἀναλίσκω, analisko.

Lu. 9:54. come down from heaven, and *consume* them,
Gal. 5:15. that ye *be* not *consumed* one of
2Th. 2: 8. whom the Lord *shall consume* with

ἀναλογία, analogia.

Ro. 12: 6. according to the *proportion* of faith ;

ἀναλογίζομαι, analogizomai.

Heb 12: 3. For *consider* him that endured

ἄναλος, analos.

Mar. 9:50. if the salt have *lost* his *saltness*,

ἀνάλυσις, analusis.

2Ti. 4: 6. the time of my *departure* is at hand.

ἀναλύω, analuo.

Lu. 12:36. when he *will return* from the wedding ;
Phil. 1:23. having a desire *to depart*, and to be with

ἀναμάρτητος, anamarteetos.

Joh. 8: 7. He *that is without sin* among you,

ἀναμένω, anameno.

1Th. 1:10. *to wait* for his Son from heaven,

ἀναμιμνήσκω, anamimneesko.

Mar 11:21. Peter *calling to remembrance* saith
  14:72. Peter *called to mind* the word that
1Co. 4:17. *bring* you *into remembrance* of my
2Co. 7:15. he *remembereth* the obedience of
2Ti. 1: 6. I *put* thee *in remembrance* that
Heb 10:32. *call to remembrance* the former

ἀνάμνησις, anamneesis.

Lu. 22:19. this do in *remembrance* of me.
1Co.11:24. this do in *remembrance* of me.
    25. drink (it), in *remembrance* of me.
Heb 10: 3. (there is) a *remembrance again* (made)

ἀνανεόω, ananeoō.

Eph. 4:23. *be renewed* in the spirit of your

ἀνανήφω, ananeepho.

2Ti. 2:26. they *may recover* themselves out of

ἀναντίῤῥητος, anantirreetos.

Acts19:36. these things *cannot be spoken against*,

ἀναντιρρήτως, anantirreetos.

Acts10:29. came I (unto you) *without gainsaying,*

ἀνάξιος, anaxios.

1Co. 6: 2. are ye *unworthy* to judge the smallest

ἀναξίως, anaxios.

1Co.11:27. cup of the Lord, *unworthily,* shall be
29. he that eateth and drinketh *unworthily,*

ἀνάπαυσις, anapausis.

Mat.11:29. ye shall find *rest* unto your souls.
12:43. through dry places, seeking *rest,* and
Lu. 11:24. through dry places, seeking *rest ;* and
Rev. 4: 8. they *rest* not day and night, saying,
14:11. they have no *rest* day nor night, who

ἀναπαύω, anapauo.

Mat.11:28. are heavy laden, and I *will give* you *rest.*
26:45. Sleep on now, and *take* (your) *rest :* behold,
Mar. 6:31. into a desert place, and *rest* a while:
14:41. Sleep on now, and *take* (your) *rest :* it is
Lu. 12:19. *take* thine *ease,* eat, drink, (and)
1Co.16:18. they *have refreshed* my spirit and your's:
2Co. 7:13. his spirit *was refreshed* by you all.
Philem. 7. bowels of the saints *are refreshed* by thee,
20. *refresh* my bowels in the Lord.
1Pet.4:14. of glory and of God *resteth* upon you:
Rev. 6:11. they *should rest* yet for a little
14:13. that they *may rest* from their labours ;

ἀναπείθω, anapitho.

Acts18:13. This (fellow) *persuadeth* men to worship

ἀναπέμπω, anapempo.

Lu. 23: 7. he *sent* him to Herod, who himself
11. a gorgeous robe, and *sent* him *again* to Pilate.
15. nor yet Herod: for I *sent* you to him ;
Philem 12. Whom I *have sent again :* thou

ἀνάπηρος, anapeeros.

Lu. 14:13. call the poor, the *maimed,* the lame,
21. hither the poor, and the *maimed,* and the

ἀναπίπτω, anapipto.

Mat.15:35. the multitude *to sit down* on the
Mar. 6:40. they *sat down* in ranks, by hundreds,
8: 6. the people *to sit down* on the ground:
Lu. 11:37. he went in, and *sat down* to meat.
14:10. go and *sit down* in the lowest room ;
17: 7. Go and *sit down to meat ?*
22:14. he *sat down,* and the twelve apostles
Joh. 6:10. Jesus said, Make the men *sit down.*

Joh. 6:10. So the men *sat down,* in number
13:12. his garments, *and was set down* again,
21:20. which also *leaned* on his breast

ἀναπληρόω, anapleeroo.

Mat.13:14. in them is *fulfilled* the prophecy
1Co.14:16. shall he *that occupieth* the room
16:17. lacking on your part they *have supplied.*
Gal. 6: 2. so *fulfil* the law of Christ.
Phi. 2:30. to *supply* your lack of service
1Th. 2:16. *to fill up* their sins alway: for

ἀναπολόγητος, anapologeetos.

Ro. 1:20. so that they are *without excuse :*
2: 1. Therefore thou art *inexcusable,*

ἀναπτύσσω, anaptusso.

Lu. 4:17. *when* he *had opened* the book,

ἀνάπτω, anapto.

Lu. 12:49. will I, if it be already *kindled ?*
Acts28: 2. for they *kindled* a fire, *and* received
Jas. 3: 5. how great a matter a little fire *kindleth !*

ἀναρίθμητος, anarithmeetos.

Heb 11:12. sand which is by the sea shore *innumerable.*

ἀνασείω, anasio.

Mar 15:11. the chief priests *moved* the people,
Lu. 23: 5. saying, He *stirreth up* the people,

ἀνασκευάζω, anaskuazo.

Acts15:24. with words, *subverting* your souls,

ἀνασπάω, anaspao.

Lu. 14: 5. straightway *pull him out* on the sabbath
Acts11:10. all *were drawn up* again into heaven.

ἀνάστασις, anastasis.

Mat.22:23. which say that there is no *resurrection,*
28. in the *resurrection* whose wife
30. For in the *resurrection* they neither
31. touching the *resurrection* of the
Mar 12:18. which say there is no *resurrection ;*
23. In the *resurrection* therefore,
Lu. 2:34. for the fall and *rising again* of many
14:14. at the *resurrection* of the just.
20:27. deny that there is any *resurrection ;*
33. Therefore in the *resurrection* whose
35. that world, and the *resurrection* from
36. being the children of the *resurrection.*
Joh. 5:29. the *resurrection* of life ; and they that
have done evil, unto the *resurrection*

Joh.11:24. rise again in the *resurrection* at
25. I am the *resurrection*, and the life:
Acts 1:22. a witness with us of his *resurrection*.
2:31. spake of the *resurrection* of Christ,
4: 2. through Jesus the *resurrection* from
33. the *resurrection* of the Lord Jesus:
17:18. unto them Jesus, and the *resurrection*.
32. heard of the *resurrection* of the dead,
23: 6. of the hope and *resurrection* of the dead
8. say that there is no *resurrection*,
24:15. there shall be a *resurrection* of the
21. Touching the *resurrection* of the dead
26:23. the first *that should rise* (lit. of *the res.*)
from the dead,
Ro. 1: 4. by the *resurrection* from the dead:
6: 5. (in the likeness) of (his) *resurrection :*
1Co.15:12. there is no *resurrection* of the dead?
13. if there be no *resurrection* of the
21. also the *resurrection* of the dead.
42. So also (is) the *resurrection* of the dead.
Phi. 3:10. the power of his *resurrection*, and
2Ti. 2:18. that the *resurrection* is past already;
Heb. 6: 2. of *resurrection* of the dead, and of
11:35. their dead *raised to life again:* (lit.
from *res.*)
— might obtain a better *resurrection :*
1Pet.1: 3. hope by the *resurrection* of Jesus Christ
3:21. by the *resurrection* of Jesus Christ:
Rev 20: 5. This (is) the first *resurrection*.
6. hath part in the first *resurrection :*

ἀναστατόω, *anastatoō.*

Acts17: 6. *that have turned* the world *upside down*
21:38. before these days *madest an uproar,*
Gal. 5:12. were even cut off *which trouble* you.

ἀνασταυρόω, *anastauroō.*

Heb. 6: 6. seeing they *crucify* to themselves the Son
of God *afresh,*

ἀναστενάζω, *anastenazo.*

Mar. 8:12. he *sighed deeply* in his spirit, *and*

ἀναστρέφω, *anastrepho.*

Mat.17:22. *while* they *abode* in Galilee, Jesus
Joh. 2:15. changers' money, and *overthrew* the tables;
Acts 5:22. not in the prison, they *returned, and*
15:16. After this I *will return,* and will build
2Co. 1:12. *had* our *conversation* in the world,
Eph. 2: 3. we all *had* our *conversation* in
1Ti. 3:15. *to behave* thy*self* in the house of God,
Heb10:33. whilst ye became companions of them
that were so used.
13:18. in all things willing *to live* honestly.
1Pet.1:17. *pass* the time of your sojourning
2Pet.2:18. from them *who live* in error.

ἀναστροφή, *anastrophee.*

Gal. 1:13. ye have heard of my *conversation* in
Eph.4:22. concerning the former *conversation*
1Ti. 4:12. in word, in *conversation,* in charity,

Heb13: 7. the end of (their) *conversation :*
Jas. 3:13. shew out of a good *conversation* his
1Pet.1:15. holy in all manner of *conversation ;*
18. from your vain *conversation*
2:12. Having your *conversation* honest
3: 1. won by the *conversation* of the wives;
2. they behold your chaste *conversation*
16. your good *conversation* in Christ.
2Pet.2: 7. the filthy *conversation* of the wicked:
3:11. in (all) holy *conversation* and godliness,

ἀνατάσσομαι, *anatassomai.*

Lu. 1: 1. *to set forth in order* a declaration of

ἀνατέλλω, *anatello.*

Mat. 4:16. shadow of death light *is sprung up.*
5:45. *maketh* his sun *to rise* on the evil and on
13: 6. *when* the sun *was up,* they were scorched;
Mar. 4: 6. *when* the sun *was up,* it was scorched;
16: 2. unto the sepulchre *at the rising of* the sun.
Lu. 12:54. When ye see a cloud *rise* out of the west,
Heb. 7:14. our Lord *sprang* out of Juda ; of
Jas. 1:11. For the sun is no sooner *risen* with
2Pet.1:19. the day star *arise* in your hearts:

ἀνατίθημι, *anatitheemi.*

Acts25:14. Festus *declared* Paul's cause unto
Gal. 2: 2. *communicated* unto them that

ἀνατολή, *anatolee.*

Mat. 2: 1. wise men from the *east* to Jerusalem,
2. we have seen his star in the *east,*
9. the star, which they saw in the *east,*
8:11. shall come from the *east* and west, and
24:27. the lightning cometh out of the *east,*
Lu. 1:78. the *dayspring* from on high hath
13:29. they shall come from the *east,* and
Rev. 7: 2. angel ascending from the east, (from) (lit.
the *rising* of the sun)
16:12. the way of the kings of the east (lit.
from the *rising* of the sun) might
21:13. On the *east* three gates; on the north

ἀνατρέπω, *anatrepo.*

2Ti. 2:18. *overthrow* the faith of some.
Tit. 1:11. who *subvert* whole houses, teaching

ἀνατρέφω, *anatrepho.*

Acts 7:20. *nourished up* in his father's house
21. *nourished* him for her own son.
22: 3. yet *brought up* in this city at the

ἀναφαίνομαι, *anaphainomai.*

Lu. 19:11. kingdom of God should immediately
appear.
Acts21: 3. *when* we *had discovered* Cyprus,

ἀναφέρω, anaphero.

Mat.17: 1. *bringeth* them *up* into an high
Mar. 9: 2. *leadeth* them *up* into an high
Lu. 24:51. from them, and *carried up* into heaven.
Heb. 7:27. those high priests, *to offer up* sacrifice,
   — when he *offered up* himself.
   9:28. once offered *to bear* the sins of many ;
  13:15. *let* us *offer* the sacrifice of praise
Jas. 2:21. when he *had offered* Isaac his son upon
1Pet.2: 5. *to offer up* spiritual sacrifices,
   24. his own self *bare* our sins in

ἀναφωνέω, anaphōneo.

Lu. 1:42. she *spake out* with a loud voice,

ἀνάχυσις, anakusis.

1Pet.4: 4. to the same *excess* of riot, speaking

ἀναχωρέω, anakōreo.

Mat. 2:12. they *departed* into their own country
   13. when they *were departed*, behold,
   14. by night, and *departed* into Egypt :
   22. he *turned aside* into the parts
  4:12. into prison, he *departed* into Galilee ;
  9:24. He said unto them, *Give place :*
  12:15. he *withdrew* himself from thence.
  14:13. he *departed* thence by ship into a
  15:21. *departed* into the coasts of Tyre and
     Sidon.
   27: 5. in the temple, and *departed*, and went
Mar. 3: 7. Jesus *withdrew* himself with his
Joh. 6:15. he *departed* again into a mountain
Acts23:19. *went* (with him) *aside* privately, and
  26:31. when they *were gone aside*, they

ἀνάψυξις, anapsuxis.

Acts 3:19(20). the times of *refreshing* shall

ἀναψύχω, anapsuko.

2Ti. 1:16. for he oft *refreshed* me, and was not

ἀνδραποδιστής, andrapodistees.

1Ti. 1:10. for *menstealers*, for liars, for perjured

ἀνδρίζομαι, andrizomai.

1Co.16:13. *quit* you *like men*, be strong.

ἀνδροφόνος, androphonos.

1Ti. 1: 9. murderers of mothers, for *manslayers*,

ἀνέγκλητος, anenkleetos.

1Co.1: 8. (that ye may be) *blameless* in the
Col. 1:22. holy and unblameable and *unreprovable*

1Ti. 3:10. office of a deacon, being (found) *blameless.*
Tit. 1: 6. If any be *blameless*, the husband
   7. For a bishop must be *blameless,*

ἀνεκδιήγητος, anekdieegeetos.

2Co. 9:15. Thanks (be) unto God for his *unspeakable*
   gift.

ἀνεκλάλητος, aneklaleetos.

1Pet.1: 8. with joy *unspeakable* and full of glory :

ἀνέκλειπτος, anekliptos.

Lu. 12:33. treasure in the heavens *that faileth not,*

ἀνεκτότερος, anektoteros.

Mat.10:15. It shall be *more tolerable* for the
  11:22. It shall be *more tolerable* for Tyre and
   24. it shall be *more tolerable* for the land.
Mar. 6:11. It shall be *more tolerable* for Sodom
Lu. 10:12. it shall be *more tolerable* in that day
   14. it shall be *more tolerable* for Tyre and

ἀνελεήμων, anele-eemōn.

Ro. 1:31. natural affection, implacable, *unmerciful :*

ἀνεμίζομαι, anemizomai.

Jas. 1: 6. *driven with the wind* and tossed.

ἄνεμος, anemos.

Mat. 7:25. floods came, and the *winds* blew,
   27. the floods came, and the *winds* blew, and
  8:26. rebuked the *winds* and the sea ;
   27. that even the *winds* and the sea obey him !
  11: 7. A reed shaken with the *wind?*
  14:24. for the *wind* was contrary.
   30. when he saw the *wind* boisterous,
   32. come into the ship, the *wind* ceased.
  24:31. his elect from the four *winds,*
Mar. 4:37. there arose a great storm of *wind,*
   39. he arose, and rebuked the *wind,*
   — the *wind* ceased, and there was a
   41. that even the *wind* and the sea obey
  6:48. for the *wind* was contrary unto
   51. into the ship ; and the *wind* ceased :
  13:27. his elect from the four *winds,*
Lu. 7:24. A reed shaken with the *wind?*
  8:23. there came down a storm of *wind*
   24. he arose, and rebuked the *wind* and the
   25. commandeth even the *winds* and water,
Joh. 6:18. by reason of a great *wind* that blew.
Acts27: 4. because the *winds* were contrary.
   7. the *wind* not suffering us, we
   14. arose against it a tempestuous *wind,*
   15. could not bear up into the *wind,*
Eph. 4:14. carried about with every *wind*
Jas. 3: 4. (are) driven of fierce *winds*, yet
Jude 12. without water, carried about of *winds ;*

Rev. 6:13. when she is shaken of a mighty *wind*.

7: 1. holding the four *winds* of the earth, that the *wind* should not blow

---

ἀνένδεκτον, *anendekton*.

Lu. 17: 1. It is *impossible* but that offences

ἀνεξερεύνητος, *anexerūneetos.*

Ro. 11:33. how *unsearchable* (are) his judgments,

ἀνεξίκακος, *anexikakos*.

2Ti. 2:24. gentle unto all (men), apt to teach, *patient,*

ἀνεξιχνίαστος, *anexikniastos*.

Ro. 11:33. his ways *past finding out!*

Eph. 3: 8. the *unsearchable* riches of Christ;

ἀνεπαίσχυντος, *anepaiskuntos*.

2Ti. 2:15. a workman *that needeth not to be ashamed,*

ἀνεπίληπτος, *anepileeptos*.

1Ti. 3: 2. A bishop then must be *blameless,*

5: 7. that they may be *blameless.*

6:14. without spot, *unrebukeable*, until

ἀνέρχομαι, *anerkomai*.

Joh. 6: 3. Jesus *went up* into a mountain,

Gal. 1:17. Neither *went I up* to Jerusalem to

18. after three years I *went up* to Jerusalem

ἄνεσις, *anesis*.

Acts24:23. to let (him) have *liberty*, and that he

2Co. 2:13. I had no *rest* in my spirit,

7: 5. our flesh had no *rest*, but we were

8:13. (I mean) not that other men be *eased*,

2Th. 1: 7. you who are troubled *rest* with us,

ἀνετάζω, *anetazo*.

Acts22:24. should *be examined* by scourging;

29. which should *have examined* him:

ἄνευ, *anū*.

Mat.10:29. fall on the ground *without* your Father.

1Pet.3: 1. may *without* the word be won

4: 9. hospitality one to another *without* grudging.

ἀνεύθετος, *anūthetos*.

Acts27:12. the haven was *not commodious* to

ἀνευρίσκω, *anūrisko*.

Lu. 2:16. with haste, and *found* Mary, and Joseph,

Acts21: 4. *finding* disciples, we tarried there

ἀνέχομαι, *anekomai*.

Mat.17:17. how long *shall I suffer* you?

Mar. 9:19. how long *shall I suffer* you?

Lu. 9:41. shall I be with you, and *suffer* you?

Acts18:14. would that I *should bear with* you:

1Co. 4:12. being persecuted, we *suffer* it:

2Co.11: 1. could *bear with* me a little in (my) folly: and indeed *bear with* me.

4. ye might well *bear with* (him).

19. For ye *suffer* fools gladly, seeing

20. For ye *suffer*, if a man bring

Eph. 4: 2. *forbearing* one another in love;

Col. 3:13. *Forbearing* one another, and forgiving

2Th. 1: 4. persecutions and tribulations that ye *endure:*

2Ti. 4: 3. when they *will* not *endure* sound

Heb13:22. brethren, *suffer* the word of exhortation:

ἀνεψιός, *anepsios*.

Col. 4:10. Marcus, *sister's son* to Barnabas,

ἄνηθον, *aneethon*.

Mat.23:23. tithe of mint, and *anise* and cummin,

ἀνήκω, *anecko*.

Eph. 5: 4. nor jesting, which are not *convenient:*

Col. 3:18. own husbands, as *it is fit* in the Lord.

Philem. 8. injoin thee that *which is convenient,*

ἀνήμερος, *aneemeros*.

2Ti. 3: 3. false accusers, incontinent, *fierce,*

ἀνήρ, *aneer*.

Mat. 1:16. begat Joseph the *husband* of Mary,

19. Then Joseph her *husband*, being

7:24. I will liken him unto a wise *man,*

26. be likened unto a foolish *man,*

12:41. The *men* of Nineveh shall rise

14:21. were about five thousand *men,*

35. when the *men* of that place had

15:38. that did eat were four thousand *men,*

Mar. 6:20. that he was a just *man* and an holy,

44. were about five thousand *men*.

10: 2. Is it lawful for a *man* to put

12. a woman shall put away her *husband,*

Lu. 1:27. espoused to a *man* whose name

34. this be, seeing I know not a *man?*

2:36. lived with an *husband* seven

5: 8. for I am a sinful *man*, O Lord.

12. behold a *man* full of leprosy:

18. behold, *men* brought in a bed

7:20. When the *men* were come unto

8:27. a certain *man*, which had devils

38. Now the *man* out of whom the

41. there came a *man* named Jairus,

9:14. were about five thousand *men*.

Lu. 9:30. there talked with him two *men*,
32. the two *men* that stood with him.
38. behold, a *man* of the company
11:31. with the *men* of this generation,
32. The *men* of Nineve shall rise
14:24. none of those *men* which were
16:18. is put away from (her) *husband*
17:12. ten *men* that were lepers, which
19: 2. (there was) a *man* named Zacchæus,
7. guest with a *man* that is a sinner.
22:63. the *men* that held Jesus mocked
23:50. (there was) a *man* named Joseph, (and he
was) a good *man*, and a just:
24: 4. two *men* stood by them in
19. which was a prophet mighty in (lit. a
man, a prophet)
Joh. 1:13. nor of the will of *man*, but of God.
30. After me cometh a *man* which
4:16. Go, call thy *husband*, and come
17. answered and said, I have no *husband*.
— hast well said, I have no *husband:*
18. For thou hast had five *husbands;* and he
whom thou now hast is not thy *husband:*
6:10. So the *men* sat down, in number
Acts 1:10. two *men* stood by them in white
11. Ye *men* of Galilee, why stand ye
16. *Men* (and) brethren, this scripture
21. these *men* which have companied
2: 5. Jews, devout *men*, out of every nation
14. Ye *men* of Judæa, and all (ye) that dwell
22. Ye *men* of Israel, hear these words; Jesus
of Nazareth, a *man* approved of God
29. *Men* (and) brethren, let me freely
37. *Men* (and) brethren, what shall we do?
3: 2. a certain *man* lame from his
12. Ye *men* of Israel, why marvel
14. desired a murderer (lit. a *man* a murderer)
to be granted
4: 4. the number of the *men* was about
5: 1. a certain *man* named Ananias,
9. have buried thy *husband* (are)
10. buried (her) by her *husband*.
14. multitudes both of *men* and women.
25. the *men* whom ye put in prison
35. Ye *men* of Israel, take heed to
36. to whom a number of *men*, about
6: 3. seven *men* of honest report,
5. a *man* full of faith and of the Holy
11. Then they suborned *men*, which
7: 2. *Men*, brethren, and fathers, hearken;
26. saying, *Sirs*, ye are brethren; why
8: 2. devout *men* carried Stephen
3. haling *men* and women committed
9. was a certain *man*, called Simon,
12. were baptized, both *men* and women.
27. behold, a *man* of Ethiopia,
9: 2. whether they were *men* or women,
7. the *men* which journeyed
12. a *man* named Ananias coming
13. heard by many of this *man*,
38. they sent unto him two *men*,
10: 1. There was a certain *man* in
5. now send *men* to Joppa, and call
17. the *men* which were sent from
19. Behold, three *men* seek thee.
21. down to the *men* which were sent
22. the centurion, a just *man*, and one
28. for a *man* that is a Jew to keep
30. behold, a *man* stood before me
11: 3. in to *men* uncircumcised,
11. there were three *men* already come
12. we entered into the *man's* house:

Acts 11:13. said unto him, Send *men* to Joppa,
20. were *men* of Cyprus and Cyrene, which,
24. he was a good *man*, and full of the Holy
13: 7. Sergius Paulus, a prudent *man ;* who
15. saying, (Ye) *men* (and) brethren,
16. said, *Men* of Israel, and ye that fear God,
21. a *man* of the tribe of Benjamin,
22. a *man* after mine own heart,
26. *Men* (and) brethren, children of the
38. therefore, *men* (and) brethren, that
14: 8. there sat a certain *man* at Lystra,
15. *Sirs*, why do ye these things?
15: 7. said unto them, *Men* (and) brethren,
13. *Men* (and) brethren, hearken unto
22. to send chosen *men* of their own
— chief *men* among the brethren:
25. to send chosen *men* unto you
16: 9. There stood a *man* of Macedonia,
17: 5. certain lewd *fellows* of the baser
12. were Greeks, and of *men*, not a few.
22. said, (Ye) *men* of Athens, I perceive
31. by (that) *man* whom he hath
34. certain *men* clave unto him, and
18:24. an eloquent *man*, (and) mighty
19: 7. all the *men* were about twelve.
25. *Sirs*, ye know that by this
35. he said, (Ye) *men* of Ephesus,
37. ye have brought hither these *men*,
20:30. of your own selves shall *men* arise,
21:11. bind the *man* that owneth this
23. We have four *men* which have a
26. Then Paul took the *men*, and the
28. Crying out, *Men* of Israel, help:
38. four thousand *men* that were
22: 1. *Men*, brethren, and fathers, hear ye
3. I am verily a *man* (which am) a Jew,
4. into prisons both *men* and women.
12. a devout *man* according to the law,
23: 1. said, *Men* (and) brethren, I have
6. *Men* (and) brethren, I am a Pharisee,
21. of them more than forty *men*,
27. This *man* was taken of the Jews,
30. the Jews laid wait for the *man*,
24: 5. we have found this *man* (a)
25: 5. with (me), and accuse this *man*, if
14. There is a certain *man* left in
17. commanded the *man* to be brought
23. chief captains, and principal *men*
24. all *men* which are here present
27:10. *Sirs*, I perceive that this voyage
21. *Sirs*, ye should have hearkened
25. Wherefore, *sirs*, be of good cheer:
28:17. *Men* (and) brethren, though I have
Ro. 4: 8. Blessed (is) the *man* to whom the
7: 2. by the law to (her) *husband* so long
— if the *husband* be dead, she is loosed from
the law of (her) *husband*.
3. if, while (her) *husband* liveth, she be
married to another *man*,
— if her *husband* be dead, she is
— she be married to another *man*.
11: 4. to myself seven thousand *men*,
1Co. 7: 2. let every woman have her own *husband*.
3. Let the *husband* render unto the
— also the wife unto the *husband*.
4. of her own body, but the *husband :* and
likewise also the *husband* hath not power
10. Let not the wife depart from (her) *husband;*
11. or be reconciled to (her) *husband:* and let
not the *husband* put away (his) wife.
13. the woman which hath an *husband*
14. the unbelieving *husband.* is

1Co. 7:14. wife is sanctified by the *husband:*
16. whether thou shalt save (thy) *husband?*
or how knowest thou, O *man,* whether
34. how she may please (her) *husband.*
39. as long as her *husband* liveth; but if her *husband* be dead,
11: 3. the head of every *man* is Christ; and the head of the woman (is) the *man;*
4. Every *man* praying or prophesying,
7. For a *man* indeed ought not to
— woman is the glory of the *man.*
8. For the *man* is not of the woman; but the woman of the *man.*
9. Neither was the *man* created for the woman; but the woman for the *man.*
11. neither is the *man* without the woman, neither the woman without the *man,*
12. as the woman (is) of the *man,* even so (is) the *man* also by the
14. that, if a *man* have long hair, it
13:11. when I became a *man,* I put away
14:35. let them ask their *husbands* at home:
2Co.11: 2. I have espoused you to one *husband,*
Gal. 4:27. than she which hath an *husband.*
Eph. 4:13. unto a perfect *man,* unto the measure
5:22. yourselves unto your own *husbands,*
23. the *husband* is the head of the wife,
24. (be) to their own *husbands* in every
25. *Husbands,* love your wives, even
28. So ought *men* to love their wives
33. that she reverence (her) *husband.*
Col. 3:18. yourselves unto your own *husbands,*
19. *Husbands,* love (your) wives, and
1Ti. 2: 8. that *men* pray every where, lifting
12. nor to usurp authority over the *man,*
3: 2. the *husband* of one wife, vigilant,
12. be the *husbands* of one wife, ruling
5: 9. having been the wife of one *man,*
Tit. 1: 6. the *husband* of one wife, having
2: 5. good, obedient to their own *husbands,*
Jas. 1: 8. A double minded *man* (is) unstable
12. Blessed (is) the *man* that endureth
20. the wrath of *man* worketh not the
23. he is like unto a *man* beholding
2: 2. assembly a *man* with a gold ring,
3: 2. the same (is) a perfect *man,* (and)
1Pet.3: 1. in subjection to your own *husbands;*
5. subjection unto their own *husbands:*
7. Likewise, ye *husbands,* dwell with
Rev.21: 2. as a bride adorned for her *husband.*

ἀνθίστημι, anthisteemi.

Mat. 5:39. unto you, That ye *resist* not evil:
Lu. 21:15. not be able to gainsay nor *resist.*
Acts 6:10. were not able *to resist* the wisdom
13: 8. *withstood* them, seeking to turn
Ro. 9:19. For who *hath resisted* his will?
13: 2. *resisteth* the ordinance of God: and they *that resist* shall receive
Gal. 2:11. I *withstood* him to the face,
Eph. 6:13. able *to withstand* in the evil day,
2Ti. 3: 8. Jannes and Jambres *withstood* Moses,
— *do* these also *resist* the truth:
4:15. he hath greatly *withstood* our words.
Jas. 4: 7. *Resist* the devil, and he will flee
1Pet.5: 9. Whom *resist* stedfast in the faith,

ἀνθομολογέομαι, anthomologeomai.

Lu. 2:38. *gave thanks* likewise unto the Lord,

ἄνθος, anthos.

Jas. 1:10. because as the *flower* of the grass
11. the grass, and the *flower* thereof falletl
1Pet.1:24. the glory of man as the *flower* of grass.
— the *flower* thereof falleth away:

ἀνθρακιά, anthrakia.

Joh.18:18. who had made a *fire of coals;* for
21: 9. they saw a *fire of coals* there, and fish

ἄνθραξ, anthrax.

Ro. 12:20. thou shalt heap *coals of fire* on his

ἀνθρωπάρεσκος, anthrōpareskos.

Eph. 6: 6. Not with eyeservice, as *menpleasers;*
Col. 3:22. not with eyeservice, as *menpleasers;*

ἀνθρώπινος, anthrōpinos.

Ro. 6:19. I speak *after the manner of men*
1Co. 2: 4. with enticing words *of man's wisdom,*
13. not in the words which *man's* wisdom
4: 3. of you, or of *man's* judgment:
10:13. such as is *common to man:*
Jas. 3: 7. hath been tamed of mankind: (lit. **human** nature)
1Pet.2:13. to every ordinance *of man* for the

ἀνθρωποκτόνος, anthrōpoktonos.

Joh. 8:44. He was a *murderer* from the beginning,
1Joh.3:15. hateth his brother is a *murderer:* and ye know that no *murderer* hath eternal life

ἄνθρωπος, anthrōpos.

Mat. 4: 4. *Man* shall not live by bread
19. I will make you fishers of *men.*
5:13. to be trodden under foot of *men.*
16. Let your light so shine before *men,*
19. shall teach *men* so, he shall be
6: 1. do not your alms before *men,*
2. that they may have glory of *men.*
5. that they may be seen of *men.*
14. if ye forgive *men* their trespasses,
15. if ye forgive not *men* their trespasses,
16. that they may appear unto *men*
18. That thou appear not unto *men*
7: 9. what *man* is there of you, whom
12. ye would that *men* should do to you,
8: 9. For I am a *man* under authority,
20. the Son of *man* hath not where
27. the *men* marvelled, saying,
9: 6. know that the Son of *man* hath
8. had given such power unto *men.*
9. he saw a *man,* named Matthew,
32. brought to him a dumb *man*
10:17. beware of *men:* for they will deliver
23. till the Son of *man* be come.
32. shall confess me before *men,*
33. shall deny me before *men,* him
35. to set a *man* at variance against
36. a *man's* foes (shall be) they of

Mat.11: 8. A *man* clothed in soft raiment?
19. The Son of *man* came eating and drinking, and they say, Behold a *man* gluttonous,
12: 8. For the Son of *man* is Lord even
10. behold, there was a *man* which
11. What *man* shall there be among
12. then is a *man* better than a sheep?
13. Then saith he to the *man*, Stretch
31. blasphemy shall be forgiven unto *men* :
— shall not be forgiven unto *men*.
32. speaketh a word against the Son of *man*,
35. A good *man* out of the good
— an evil *man* out of the evil
36. idle word that *men* shall speak,
40. so shall the Son of *man* be three
43. unclean spirit is gone out of a *man*,
45. the last (state) of that *man* is
13:24. is likened unto a *man* which
25. while *men* slept, his enemy
28. unto them, An (lit. a *man* an) enemy hath done this.
31. which a *man* took, and sowed in
37. soweth the good seed is the Son of *man* ;
41. The Son of *man* shall send forth
44. which when a *man* hath found,
45. is like unto a merchant *man*,
52. like unto a *man* (that is) an
15: 9. doctrines the commandments of *men*.
11. goeth into the mouth defileth a *man* ;
— out of the mouth, this defileth a *man*.
18. the heart ; and they defile the *man*.
20. defile a *man* : but to eat with unwashen hands defileth not a *man*.
16:13. Whom do *men* say that I the Son of *man* am ?
23. of God, but those that be of *men*.
26. For what is a *man* profited, if
— or what shall a *man* give in
27. For the Son of *man* shall come
28. till they see the Son of *man*
17: 9. until the Son of *man* be risen
12. shall also the Son of *man* suffer
14. came to him a (certain) *man*,
22. The Son of *man* shall be betrayed into the hands of *men* :
18: 7. woe to that *man* by whom the
11. For the Son of *man* is come to
12. if a *man* have an hundred
23. heaven likened unto a *certain* king,
19: 3. Is it lawful for a *man* to put
5. this cause shall a *man* leave
6. together, let not *man* put asunder.
10. If the case of the *man* be so with
12. which were made eunuchs of *men* :
26. With *men* this is impossible;
28. when the Son of *man* shall sit
20: 1. like unto a *man* (that is) an
18. the Son of *man* shall be betrayed
28. Even as the Son of *man* came not
21:25. from heaven, or of *men* ? And
26. if we shall say, Of *men* ; we fear
28. A (certain) *man* had two sons;
33. There was a certain (lit. a certain *man* a) housholder,
22: 2. heaven is like unto a *certain* king,
11. saw there a *man* which had not
16. regardest not the person of *men*.
23: 4. lay (them) on *men's* shoulders ;
5. they do for to be seen of *men* :
7. to be called of *men*, Rabbi, Rabbi.
13(14). the kingdom of heaven against *men* :
28. appear righteous unto *men*, but
24:27. the coming of the Son of *man* be.

Mat.24:30. sign of the Son of *man* in heaven.
— shall see the Son of *man* coming
37. the coming of the Son of *man* be.
39. the coming of the Son of *man* be.
44. the Son of *man* cometh.
25:13. wherein the Son of *man* cometh.
14. as a *man* travelling into a far
24. that thou art an hard *man*,
31. When the Son of *man* shall come
26: 2. the Son of *man* is betrayed to be
24. Son of *man* goeth as it is written of him: but woe unto that *man* by whom the Son of *man* is betrayed ! it had been good for that *man* if he had not
45. the Son of *man* is betrayed into
64. shall ye see the Son of *man* sitting
72. with an oath, I do not know the *man*.
74. (saying), I know not the *man*.
27:32. they found a *man* of Cyrene,
57. there came a rich *man* of
Mar. 1:17. you to become fishers of *men*.
23. a *man* with an unclean spirit;
2:10. that the Son of *man* hath power
27. The sabbath was made for *man*, and not *man* for the sabbath:
28. the Son of *man* is Lord also of
3: 1. there was a *man* there which
3. he saith unto the *man* which
5. he saith unto the *man*, Stretch
28. forgiven unto the sons of *men*,
4:26. as if a *man* should cast seed
5: 2. out of the tombs a *man* with an
8. said unto him, Come out of the *man*,
7: 7. doctrines the commandments of *men*.
8. ye hold the tradition of *men*,
11. If a *man* shall say to his father
15. There is nothing from without a *man*,
— are they that defile the *man*.
18. without entereth into the *man*,
20. That which cometh out of the *man*, that defileth the *man*.
21. out of the heart of *men*, proceed evil
23. from within, and defile the *man*.
8:24. said, I see *men* as trees, walking.
27. Whom do *men* say that I am ?
31. that the Son of *man* must suffer
33. the things that be of *men*.
36. For what shall it profit a *man*,
37. what shall a *man* give in exchange
38. of him also shall the Son of *man* be
9: 9. till the Son of *man* were risen from
12. it is written of the Son of *man*, that
31. The Son of *man* is delivered into the hands of *men*,
10: 7. this cause shall a *man* leave his
9. together, let not *man* put asunder.
27. With *men* (it is) impossible, but not
33. the Son of *man* shall be delivered
45. For even the Son of *man* came
11: 2. a colt tied, whereon never *man* sat;
30. was (it) from heaven, or of *men* ?
32. if we shall say, Of *men* ; they
12: 1. A (certain) *man* planted a vineyard,
14. regardest not the person of *men*, but
13:26. shall they see the Son of *man* coming
34. (Son of man is) as a *man* taking a far
14:13. there shall meet you a *man* bearing
21. The Son of *man* indeed goeth,
— woe to that *man* by whom the Son of *man* is betrayed ! good were it for that *man* if he
41. the Son of *man* is betrayed into
62. ye shall see the Son of *man* sitting

Mar.14:71. I know not this *man* of whom
  15:39. Truly this *man* was the Son of God.
Lu. 1:25. take away my reproach among *men*.
  2:14. peace, good will toward *men*.
    15. the (lit. the *men* the) shepherds said one to another,
    25. there was a *man* in Jerusalem,
    — the same *man* (was) just and devout,
    52. stature, and in favour with God and *man*.
  4: 4. That *man* shall not live by bread
    33. there was a *man*, which had a
  5:10. henceforth thou shalt catch *men*.
    18. brought in a bed a *man* which
    20. said unto him, *Man*, thy sins are
    24. that the Son of *man* hath power
  6: 5. That the Son of *man* is Lord also
    6. there was a *man* whose right hand
    8. said to the *man* which had the
    10. he said unto the *man*, Stretch
    22. Blessed are ye, when *men* shall
    — as evil, for the Son of *man's* sake.
    26. when all *men* shall speak well
    31. as ye would that *men* should do
    45. A good *man* out of the good treasure
    — an evil *man* out of the evil treasure
    48. He is like a *man* which built
    49. is like a *man* that without a foundation
  7: 8. I also am a *man* set under authority,
    25. A *man* clothed in soft raiment?
    31. shall I liken the *men* of this generation?
    34. The Son of *man* is come eating
    — Behold a gluttonous *man*, and a
  8:29. spirit to come out of the *man*.
    33. Then went the devils out of the *man*,
    35. came to Jesus, and found the *man*,
  9:22. The Son of *man* must suffer
    25. For what is a *man* advantaged, if
    26. of him shall the Son of *man* be
    44. for the Son of *man* shall be delivered into the hands of *men*.
    56. For the Son of *man* is not come to destroy *men's* lives,
    58. the Son of *man* hath not where
  10:30. A certain (*man*) went down from
  11:24. unclean spirit is gone out of a *man*,
    26. the last (state) of that *man* is worse
    30. so shall also the Son of *man* be to this
    44. the *men* that walk over (them) are
    46. (ye) lawyers! for ye lade *men* with
  12: 8. Whosoever shall confess me before *men*, him shall the Son of *man* also
    9. he that denieth me before *men*
    10. a word against the Son of *man*,
    14. said unto him, *Man*, who made me
    16. The ground of a certain rich *man*
    36. ye yourselves like unto *men* that
    40. for the Son of *man* cometh at
  13: 4. they were sinners above all *men*
    19. mustard seed, which a *man* took,
  14: 2. there was a certain *man* before
    16. A certain *man* made a great supper,
    30. Saying, This *man* began to build,
  15: 4. What *man* of you, having an
    11. he said. A certain *man* had two
  16: 1. There was a certain rich *man*,
    15. which justify yourselves before *men* ;
    — esteemed among *men* is abomination
    19. There was a certain rich *man*,
  17:22. one of the days of the Son of *man*,
    24. so shall also the Son of *man* be
    26. in the days of the Son of *man*.
    30. when the Son of *man* is revealed.

Lu. 18: 2. feared not God, neither regarded *man* :
    4. I fear not God, nor regard *man* ;
    8. when the Son of *man* cometh,
    10. Two *men* went up into the temple
    11. that I am not as other *men* (are),
    27. which are impossible with *men* are
    31. concerning the Son of *man* shall
  19:10. For the Son of *man* is come to seek
    12. A certain noble*man* went into
    21. because thou art an austere *man* :
    22. knewest that I was an austere *man*,
    30. whereon yet never *man* sat:
  20: 4. was it from heaven, or of *men* ?
    6. if we say, Of *men* ; all the people
    19. A certain *man* planted a vineyard,
  21:26. *Men's* hearts failing them for fear,
    27. see the Son of *man* coming in a cloud
    36. to stand before the Son of *man*.
  22:10. there shall a *man* meet you, bearing
    22. Son of *man* goeth, as it was determined: but woe unto that *man* by whom
    48. betrayest thou the Son of *man*
    58. Peter said, *Man*, I am not.
    60. Peter said, *Man*, I know not what
    69. shall the Son of *man* sit on the
  23: 4. I find no fault in this *man*.
    6. whether the *man* were a Galilæan.
    14. Ye have brought this *man* unto me,
    — have found no fault in this *man*
    47. Certainly this was a righteous *man*.
  24: 7. The Son of *man* must be delivered into the hands of sinful *men*,
Joh. 1: 4. the life was the light of *men*.
    6. There was a *man* sent from God,
    9. which lighteth every *man* that
    51(52) descending upon the Son of *man*.
  2:10. Every *man* at the beginning doth
    25. that any should testify of *man* : for he knew what was in *man*.
  3: 1. There was a *man* of the Pharisees,
    4. How can a *man* be born when
    13. (even) the Son of *man* which is
    14. so must the Son of *man* be
    19. *men* loved darkness rather than
    27. A *man* can receive nothing,
  4:28. into the city, and saith to the *men*,
    29. Come, see a *man*, which told me
    50. the *man* believed the word that
  5: 5. a certain *man* was there, which
    7. Sir, I have no *man*, when the
    9. immediately the *man* was made
    12. What *man* is that which said
    15. The *man* departed, and told the
    27. because he is the Son of *man*.
    34. I receive not testimony from *man* :
    41. I receive not honour from *men*.
  6:10. Said, Make the *men* sit down.
    14. Then those *men*, when they had
    27. which the Son of *man* shall
    53. the flesh of the Son of *man*, and
    62. ye shall see the Son of *man* ascend
  7:22. ye on the sabbath day circumcise a *man*.
    23. If a *man* on the sabbath day receive
    — I have made a *man* every whit
    46. Never *man* spake like this *man*.
    51. Doth our law judge (any) *man*, before
  8:17. the testimony of two *men* is true.
    28. have lifted up the Son of *man*,
    40. a *man* that hath told you the
  9: 1. he saw a *man* which was blind
    11. A *man* that is called Jesus
    16. This *man* is not of God, because

Joh. 9:16. Others said, How can a *man* that
24. again called they the *man*
— we know that this *man* is a
30. The *man* answered and said unto
10:33. thou, being a *man*, makest
11:47. this *man* doeth many miracles.
50. that one *man* should die for
12:23. that the Son of *man* should be
34. The Son of *man* must be lifted up? who
is this Son of *man*?
43. loved the praise of *men* more
13:31. Now is the Son of *man* glorified,
16:21. for joy that a *man* is born into
17: 6. manifested thy name unto the *men*
18:14. that one *man* should die for the
17. also (one) of this *man's* disciples?
29. accusation bring ye against this *man*?
19: 5. saith unto them, Behold the *man*!
Acts 4: 9. deed done to the impotent *man*,
12. given among *men*, whereby we
13. were unlearned and ignorant *men*,
14. beholding the *man* which was
16. What shall we do to these *men*?
17. henceforth to no *man* in this
22. the *man* was above forty years
5: 4. thou hast not lied unto *men*, but
28. to bring this *man's* blood upon us.
29. to obey God rather than *men*.
35. to do as touching these *men*.
38. Refrain from these *men*, and let them
— counsel or this work be of *men*,
6:13. This *man* ceaseth not to speak
7:56. the Son of *man* standing on the
9:33. he found a certain *man* named
10:26. Stand up ; I myself also am a *man*.
28. should not call any *man* common
12:22. voice of a god, and not of a *man*.
14:11. down to us in the likeness of *men*.
15. We also are *men* of like passions
15:17. the residue of *men* might seek
26. *Men* that have hazarded their
16:17. These *men* are the servants of
20. saying, These *men*, being Jews,
35. saying, Let those *men* go.
37. uncondemned, being Romans, (lit. Roman
men) and
17:25. Neither is worshipped with *men's* hands,
26. made of one blood all nations of *men*
29. graven by art and *man's* device.
30. commandeth all *men* every where
18:13. This (fellow) persuadeth *men* to
19:16. the *man* in whom the evil spirit
35. what *man* is there that knoweth
21:28. This is the *man*, that teacheth all
39. Paul said, I am a *man* (which am)
22:15. shalt be his witness unto all *men*
25. scourge a *man* that is a Roman,
26. thou doest: for this *man* is a Roman.
23: 9. We find no evil in this *man*:
24:16. offence toward God, and (toward) *men*.
25:16. to deliver any *man* to die, before
22. I would also hear the *man* myself.
26:31. This *man* doeth nothing worthy
32. This *man* might have been set
28: 4. No doubt this *man* is a murderer,
Ro. 1:18. ungodliness and unrighteousness of *men*,
23. image made like to corruptible *man*,
2: 1. inexcusable, O *man*, whosoever
3. thinkest thou this, O *man*, that
9. every soul of *man* that doeth evil,
16. shall judge the secrets of *men*
29. whose praise (is) not of *men*, but of God.

Ro. 3: 4. God be true, but every *man* a liar;
5. taketh vengeance? I speak as a *man*
28. that a *man* is justified by faith
4: 6. the blessedness of the *man*, unto whom
5:12. as by one *man* sin entered into
— so death passed upon all *men*,
15. gift by grace, (which is) by one *man*,
18. (judgment came) upon all *men*
— (the free gift came) upon all *men* unto
19. as by one *man's* disobedience many
6: 6. that our old *man* is crucified
7: 1. dominion over a *man* as long as
22. law of God after the inward *man*:
24. O wretched *man* that I am !
9:20. O *man*, who art thou that repliest
10: 5. the *man* which doeth those things
12:17. honest in the sight of all *men*.
18. live peaceably with all *men*.
14:18. acceptable to God, and approved of *men*.
20. (it is) evil for that *man* who eateth
1Co. 1:25. foolishness of God is wiser than *men*; and
the weakness of God is stronger than *men*.
2: 5. not stand in the wisdom of *men*,
9. entered into the heart of *man*, the
11. what *man* knoweth the things of a *man*,
save the spirit of *man*
14. the natural *man* receiveth not
3: 3. are ye not carnal, and walk as *men*?
21. Therefore let no man glory in *men*.
4: 1. Let a *man* so account of us, as
9. unto the world, and to angels, and to *men*.
6:18. Every sin that a *man* doeth is
7: 1. (It is) good for a *man* not to touch
7. I would that all *men* were even
23. be not ye the servants of *men*.
26. (it is) good for a *man* so to be.
9: 8. Say I these things as a *man*?
11:28. let a *man* examine himself,
13: 1. with the tongues of *men* and of angels
14: 2. speaketh not unto *men*, but unto
3. speaketh unto *men* (to) edification,
15:19. we are of all *men* most miserable.
21. since by *man* (came) death, by *man* (came)
also the resurrection
32. If after the manner of *men* I have
39. (there is) one (kind of) flesh of *men*,
45. The first *man* Adam was made
47. The first *man* (is) of the earth, earthy: the
second *man* (is) the Lord
2Co. 3: 2. known and read of all *men*:
4: 2. to every *man's* conscience in
16. though our outward *man* perish,
5:11. we persuade *men*; but we are
8:21. also in the sight of *men*.
12: 2. I knew a *man* in Christ about
3. I knew such a *man*, whether
4. is not lawful for a *man* to utter.
Gal. 1: 1. Paul, an apostle, not of *men*, neither by *man*,
10. For do I now persuade *men*, or God? or
do I seek to please *men*? for if I yet
pleased *men*, I
11. preached of me is not after *man*.
12. I neither received it of *man*,
2: 6. God accepteth no *man's* person:
16. a *man* is not justified by the
3:12. The *man* that doeth them shall
15. I speak after the manner of *men*; Though
(it be) but a *man's* covenant,
5: 3. I testify again to every *man*
6: 1. if a *man* be overtaken in a
7. for whatsoever a *man* soweth,
Eph. 2:15. himself of twain one new *man*,

Eph. 3: 5. known unto the sons of *men*,
    16. by his Spirit in the inner *man* ;
  4: 8. captivity captive, and gave gifts unto *men*.
    14. by the sleight of *men*, (and) cunning
    22. the old *man*, which is corrupt
    24. that ye put on the new *man*,
  5: 31. shall a *man* leave his father
  6: 7. as to the Lord, and not to *men*:
Phi. 2: 7. was made in the likeness of *men*:
    8. being found in fashion as a *man*,
  4: 5. moderation be known unto all *men*.
Col. 1: 28. Whom we preach, warning every *man*,
     and teaching every *man* in all wisdom ;
     that we may present every *man*
  2: 8. vain deceit, after the tradition of *men*,
    22. commandments and doctrines of *men* ?
  3: 9. ye have put off the old *man* with
    23. to the Lord, and not unto *men* ;
1Th. 2: 4. not as pleasing *men*, but God,
    6. Nor of *men* sought we glory, neither
    13. received (it) not (as) the word of *men*,
    15. please not God, and are contrary to all
     men :
  4: 8. despiseth not *man*, but God,
2Th. 2: 3. that *man* of sin be revealed, the
  3: 2. from unreasonable and wicked *men* :
1Ti. 2: 1. of thanks, be made for all *men* ;
    4. Who will have all *men* to be saved,
    5. one mediator between God and *men*, the
     man Christ Jesus ;
  4: 10. who is the saviour of all *men*,
  5: 24. Some *men's* sins are open beforehand,
  6: 5. disputings of *men* of corrupt minds,
    9. which drown *men* in destruction
    11. But thou, O *man* of God, flee
    16. whom no *man* hath seen, nor
2Ti. 2: 2. commit thou to faithful *men*,
  3: 2. For *men* shall be lovers of their
    8. *men* of corrupt minds, reprobate
    13. evil *men* and seducers shall wax
    17. That the *man* of God may be
Tit. 1: 14. commandments of *men*, that
  2: 11. salvation hath appeared to all *men*,
  3: 2. shewing all meekness unto all *men*.
    8. are good and profitable unto *men*.
    10. A *man* that is an heretick after
Heb 2: 6. What is *man*, that thou art
    — or the son of *man*, that thou
  5: 1. priest taken from among *men* is ordained
     for *men* in things
  6: 16. For *men* verily swear by the greater:
  7: 8. here *men* that die receive tithes ;
    28. maketh *men* high priests which
  8: 2. the Lord pitched, and not *man*.
  9: 27. as it is appointed unto *men*
  13: 6. I will not fear what *man* shall
Jas. 1: 7. let not that *man* think that he
    19. let every *man* be swift to hear,
  2: 20. wilt thou know, O vain *man*,
    24. that by works a *man* is justified,
  3: 8. the tongue can no *man* tame ;
    9. therewith curse we *men*, which
  5: 17. Elias was a *man* subject to like
1Pet. 1: 24. all the glory of *man* as the flower
  2: 4. disallowed indeed of *men*, but
    15. silence the ignorance of foolish *men* :
  3: 4. the hidden *man* of the heart,
  4: 2. in the flesh to the lusts of *men*,
    6. according to *men* in the flesh,
2Pet. 1: 21. not in old time by the will of *man*: but
     holy *men* of God spake (as they were)
  2: 16. dumb ass speaking with *man's* voice

2Pet. 3: 7. judgment and perdition of ungodly *men*.
1Joh. 5: 9. If we receive the witness of *men*,
Jude   4. there are certain *men* crept-in
Rev. 1: 13. (one) like unto the Son of *man*,
  4: 7. third beast had a face as a *man*,
  8: 11. many *men* died of the waters,
  9: 4. only those *men* which have not
    5. a scorpion, when he striketh a *man*.
    6. those days shall *men* seek death,
    7. faces (were) as the faces of *men*.
    10. their power (was) to hurt *men*
    15. to slay the third part of *men*.
    18. was the third part of *men* killed,
    20. the rest of the *men* which were
 11: 13. were slain of *men* seven thousand:
 13: 13. on the earth in the sight of *men*,
    18. for it is the number of a *man* ;
 14: 4. were redeemed from among *men*,
    14. sat like unto the Son of *man*,
 16: 2. grievous sore upon the *men*
    8. unto him to scorch *men* with fire.
    9. *men* were scorched with great
    18. as was not since *men* were
    21. there fell upon *men* a great hail
    — and *men* blasphemed God
 18: 13. chariots, and slaves, and souls of *men*.
 21: 3. tabernacle of God (is) with *men*,
    17. (according to) the measure of a *man*,

ἀνθυπατεύω, *anthupatŭo*.

Acts 18: 12. *when* Gallio *was the deputy* of

ἀνθύπατος, *anthupatos*.

Acts 13: 7. was with the *deputy* of the country,
    8. to turn away the *deputy* from the
    12. Then the *deputy*, when he saw
 19: 38. the law is open, and there are *deputies* :

ἀνίημι, *anieemi*.

Acts 16: 26. every one's bands *were loosed*.
  27: 40. *loosed* the rudder bands, and hoised
Eph. 6: 9. unto them, *forbearing* threatening:
Heb 13: 5. he hath said, I *will* never *leave* thee,

ἀνίλεως, *anileōs*.

Jas. 2: 13. shall have judgment *without mercy*,

ἄνιπτος, *aniptos*.

Mat. 15: 20. to eat with *unwashen* hands
Mar 7: 2. to say, with *unwashen*, hands,
    5. eat bread with *unwashen* hands ?

ἀνίστημι, *anisteemi*.

Mat. 9: 9. Follow me. And he *arose, and* followed
     him.
 12: 41. men of Nineveh *shall rise* in
 17: 9. the Son of man *be risen again* from
 20: 19. the third day he *shall rise again*.
 22: 24. *raise up* seed unto his brother.
 26: 62. the high priest *arose, and* said
Mar 1: 35. *rising up* a great while before

Mar. 2:14. Follow me. And he *arose and* followed
3:26. if Satan *rise up* against himself,
5:42. the damsel *arose*, and walked ;
7:24. from thence he *arose, and* went into
8:31. after three days *rise again.*
9: 9. the Son of man *were risen* from the
10. what the *rising* from the dead (lit. *to rise*)
27. lifted him up ; and he *arose.*
31. he *shall rise* the third day.
10: 1. he *arose* from thence, *and* cometh
34. the third day he *shall rise again.*
50. *rose,* and came to Jesus.
12:23. therefore, when they *shall rise,*
25. when they *shall rise* from the
14:57. there *arose* certain, *and* bare false
60. priest *stood up* in the midst, and
16: 9. when (Jesus) *was risen* early
Lu. 1:39. Mary *arose* in those days, *and*
4:16. sabbath day, and *stood up* for to read,
29. *rose up,* and thrust him out of the
38. he *arose* out of the synagogue, *and*
39. she *arose and* ministered unto them.
5:25. immediately he *rose up* before them, *and*
28. he left all, *rose up, and* followed him.
6: 8. he *arose and* stood forth.
8:55. came again, and she *arose* straightway :
9: 8. one of the old prophets *was risen again.*
19. one of the old prophets *is risen again.*
10:25. behold, a certain lawyer *stood up,*
11: 7. I cannot *rise and* give thee.
8. Though he will not *rise and* give him,
32. *shall rise up* in the judgment
15:18. I will *arise and* go to my father,
20. he *arose, and* came to his father.
16:31. though one *rose* from the dead.
17:19. said unto him, *Arise,* go thy way:
18:33. the third day he *shall rise again.*
22:45. when he *rose up* from prayer,
46. *rise and* pray, lest ye enter into
23: 1. whole multitude of them *arose, and*
24: 7. the third day *rise again.*
12. Then *arose* Peter, *and* ran unto the
33. they *rose up* the same hour, *and*
46. *to rise* from the dead the third day:
Joh. 6:39. should *raise* it *up again* at the
40. I *will raise* him *up* at the last
44. I *will raise* him *up* at the last day.
54. I *will raise* him *up* at the last day.
11:23. Thy brother *shall rise again.*
24. I know that he *shall rise again*
31. that she *rose up* hastily and went
20: 9. that he must *rise again* from the
Acts 1:15. Peter *stood up* in the midst of...*and*
2:24. Whom God *hath raised up,* having
30. he would *raise up* Christ to sit
32. This Jesus *hath* God *raised up,*
3:22. your God *raise up* unto you of your
26. God, *having raised up* his Son
5: 6. the young men *arose,* wound...*and*
17. Then the high priest *rose up, and*
34. *Then stood* there *up* one in the
36. before these days *rose up* Theudas,
37. After this man *rose up* Judas
6: 9. Then there *arose* certain of the
7:18. Till another king *arose,* which
37. A prophet *shall* the Lord your God *raise up*
8:26. *Arise,* and go toward the south
27. he *arose and* went: and, behold, a
9: 6. *Arise,* and go into the city, and it shall
11. *Arise, and* go into the street which
18. *arose, and* was baptized.
34. *arise,* and make thy bed. And he *arose*

Acts 9:39. *Then* Peter *arose* and went with them.
40. the body said, Tabitha, *arise.*
41. her (his) hand, and *lifted* her *up,*
10:13. *Rise,* Peter ; kill, and eat.
20. *Arise* therefore, and get thee down,
26. saying, *Stand up;* I myself also
41. after he *rose* from the dead.
11: 7. *Arise,* Peter ; slay and eat.
28. there *stood up* one of them...*and*
12: 7. raised him up, saying, *Arise up*
13:16. *Then* Paul *stood up,* and beckoning
33(32). he *hath raised up* Jesus *again;*
34. he *raised* him *up* from the dead,
14:10. *Stand* upright on thy feet.
20. he *rose up,* and came into the city:
15: 7. Peter *rose up,* and said unto them,
17: 3. suffered, and *risen again* from the dead ;
31. he *hath raised* him from the dead.
20:30. of your own selves *shall* men *arise,*
22:10. said unto me, *Arise, and* go into
16. *arise, and* be baptized, and wash
23: 9. of the Pharisees' part *arose, and*
26:16. *rise,* and stand upon thy feet:
30. the king *rose up,* and the governor,
Ro. 14: 9. Christ both died, and *rose,* and revived,
15:12. he *that shall rise* to reign over
1Co.10: 7. eat and drink, and *rose up* to play.
Eph. 5:14. *arise* from the dead, and Christ shall
1Th. 4:14. Jesus died *and rose again,* even so
16. the dead in Christ *shall rise* first:
Heb 7:11. another priest should *rise* after
15. there *ariseth* another priest,

ἀνόητος, anoeetos.

Lu. 24:25. O *fools,* and slow of heart to believe
Ro. 1:14. both to the wise, and to the *unwise.*
Gal. 3: 1. O *foolish* Galatians, who hath
3. Are ye so *foolish ?* having begun
1Ti. 6: 9. (into) many *foolish* and hurtful
Tit. 3: 3. ourselves also were sometimes *foolish,*

ἄνοια, anoia.

Lu. 6:11. they were filled with *madness;*
2Ti. 3: 9. their *folly* shall be manifest

ἀνοίγω, anoigo.

Mat. 2:11. when they *had opened* their treasures,
3:16. the heavens *were opened* unto him,
5: 2. he *opened* his mouth, *and* taught
7: 7. knock, and it *shall be opened* unto you:
8. that knocketh, it *shall be opened.*
9:30. their eyes *were opened ;* and Jesus
13:35. I *will open* my mouth in parables;
17:27. when thou *hast opened* his mouth,
20:33. Lord, that our eyes *may be opened.*
25:11. saying, Lord, Lord, *open* to us.
27:52. the graves *were opened ;* and many
Lu. 1:64. his mouth *was opened* immediately,
3:21. praying, the heaven was *opened,*
11: 9. knock, and it *shall be opened* unto you.
10. that knocketh it *shall be opened.*
12:36. they *may open* unto him immediately
13:25. saying, Lord, Lord, *open* unto us ;
Joh. 1:51(52). ye shall see heaven *open,* and
9:10. How *were* thine eyes *opened ?*
14. Jesus made the clay, and *opened* his eyes.
17. that he *hath opened* thine eyes ?

Joh. 9:21. or who *hath opened* his eyes,
26. how *opened* he thine eyes?
30. (yet) he *hath opened* mine eyes.
32. that any man *opened* the eyes
10: 3. To him the porter *openeth*; and
21. Can a devil *open* the eyes of the
11:37. *which opened* the eyes of the blind,
Acts 5:19. by night *opened* the prison doors,
23. *when* we *had opened*, we found
7:56. Behold, I see the heavens *opened*,
8:32. so *opened* he not his mouth:
35. Then Philip *opened* his mouth, *and*
9: 8. *when* his eyes *were opened*, he
40. she *opened* her eyes: and when
10:11. saw heaven *opened*, and a certain
34. *Then* Peter *opened* (his) mouth, *and*
12:10. which *opened* to them of his
14. she *opened* not the gate for gladness,
16. *when* they *had opened* (the door),
14:27. how he *had opened* the door of
16:26. all the doors *were opened*, and every
27. seeing the prison doors *open*,
18:14. was now about *to open* (his) mouth,
26:18. *To open* their eyes, (and) to turn
Ro. 3:13. Their throat (is) an *open* sepulchre;
1Co.16: 9. a great door and effectual *is opened* unto
2Co. 2:12. when...a door *was opened* unto me of the
6:11. our mouth *is open* unto you, our
Col. 4: 3. that God *would open* unto us a door
Rev. 3: 7. he *that openeth*, and no man shutteth; and
shutteth, and no man *openeth*;
8. I have set before thee an *open* door,
20. hear my voice, and *open* the door,
4: 1. a door (was) *opened* in heaven:
5: 2. Who is worthy *to open* the book, and
3. was able *to open* the book, neither
4. found worthy *to open* and to read the
5. hath prevailed *to open* the book,
9. *to open* the seals thereof: for thou
6: 1. when the Lamb *opened* one of the
3. when he *had opened* the second
5. when he *had opened* the third
7. when he *had opened* the fourth
9. when he *had opened* the fifth
12. when he *had opened* the sixth
8: 1. when he *had opened* the seventh
9: 2. he *opened* the bottomless pit;
10: 2. in his hand a little book *open*:
8. take the little book which is *open*
11:19. temple of God *was opened* in
12:16. the earth *opened* her mouth, and
13: 6. he *opened* his mouth in blasphemy
15: 5. the testimony in heaven *was opened*:
19:11. I saw heaven *opened*, and behold
20:12. the books *were opened*: and another book
was *opened*, which is

ἀνοικοδομέω, *anoikodomeō.*

Acts15:16. *will build again* the tabernacle
— I *will build again* the ruins thereof,

ἄνοιξις, *anoixis.*

Eph. 6:19. that I may open (lit. in the *opening* of)
my mouth boldly,

ἀνομία, *anomia.*

Mat. 7:23. depart from me, ye that work *iniquity.*

Mat.13:41. that offend, and them which do *iniquity*;
23:28. are full of hypocrisy and *iniquity.*
24:12. because *iniquity* shall abound,
Ro. 4: 7. they whose *iniquities* are forgiven,
6:19. servants to uncleanness and *to iniquity*
unto *iniquity*;
2Co. 6:14. hath righteousness with *unrighteousness*?
2Th. 2: 7. the mystery of *iniquity* doth already
Tit. 2:14. might redeem us from all *iniquity*,
Heb 1: 9. loved righteousness, and hated *iniquity*;
8:12. their *iniquities* will I remember no
10:17. their sins and *iniquities* will I remember
1Joh.3: 4. Whosoever committeth sin transgresseth
also (lit. commits *transgression of*) the
law: for sin is the *transgression of the
law.*

ἄνομος, *anomos.*

Mar 15:28. numbered with the *transgressors.*
Lu. 22:37. reckoned among the *transgressors*:
Acts 2:23. by *wicked* hands have crucified
1Co. 9:21. that are *without law*, as *without law*, being
not *without law* to God,
— gain them that are *without law.*
2Th. 2: 8. then shall that *Wicked* be revealed,
1Ti. 1: 9. for the *lawless* and disobedient,
2Pet.2: 8. to day with (their) *unlawful* deeds;

ἀνόμως, *anomōs.*

Ro. 2:12. as many as have sinned *without law* shall
also perish *without law*:

ἀνορθόω, *anorthoō.*

Lu. 13:13. she *was made straight*, and
Acts15:16. the ruins thereof, and I *will set* it *up*:
Heb 12:12. *lift up* the hands which hang

ἀνόσιος, *anosios.*

1Ti. 1: 9. for *unholy* and profane, for
2Ti. 3: 2. disobedient to parents, unthankful, *unholy*,

ἀνοχή, *anokee.*

Ro. 2: 4. riches of his goodness and *forbearance*
3:25(26). through the *forbearance* of God;

ἀνταγωνίζομαι, *antagōnizomai.*

Heb 12: 4. unto blood, *striving against* sin.

ἀντάλλαγμα, *antallagma.*

Mat.16:26. what shall a man give *in exchange*
Mar. 8:37. shall a man give *in exchange* for

ἀνταναπληρόω, *antanapleeroō.*

Col. 1:24. *fill up* that which is behind of the

ἀνταποδίδωμι, antapodidomi.

Lu. 14:14. they cannot *recompense* thee: for thou
shalt *be recompensed*
Ro. 11:35. it *shall be recompensed* unto him
12:19. I *will repay*, saith the Lord.
1Th. 3: 9. what thanks can we *render* to God
2Th. 1: 6. with God *to recompense* tribulation
Heb 10:30. I *will recompense*, saith the Lord.

ἀνταπόδομα, antapodoma.

Lu. 14:12. again, and a *recompence* be made thee.
Ro. 11: 9. a stumblingblock, and a *recompence* unto

ἀνταπόδοσις, antapodosis.

Col. 3:24. ye shall receive the *reward* of the inheritance:

ἀνταποκρίνομαι, antapokrinomai.

Lu. 14: 6. could not *answer* him *again* to
Ro. 9:20. thou *that repliest against* God?

ἀντέπω, antepo.

Lu. 21:15. shall not be able *to gainsay* nor
Acts 4:14. they could *say* nothing *against it*.

ἀντέχομαι, antekomai.

Mat. 6:24. or else he *will hold to* the one, and
Lu. 16:13. or else he *will hold to* the one, and despise
1Th. 5:14. *support* the weak, be patient
Tit. 1: 9. *Holding fast* the faithful word

ἀντί, anti.

Mat. 2:22. *in the room* of his father Herod,
5:38. An eye *for* an eye, and a tooth *for*
17:27. give unto them *for* me and thee.
20:28. give his life a ransom *for* many.
Mar 10:45. to give his life a ransom *for* many.
Lu. 1:20. because (lit. *for* that) thou believest not
my words,
11:11. will he *for* a fish give him a
12: 3. Therefore (lit. *for* that) whatsoever ye have
spoken
19:44. because (lit. *for* that) thou knewest not
the
Joh. 1:16. all we received, and grace *for* grace.
Acts 12:23. because (lit. *for* that) he gave not God
the glory:
Ro. 12:17. Recompense to no man evil *for* evil.
1Co 11:15. (her) hair is given her *for* a covering.
Eph. 5:31. *For* this cause shall a man leave
1Th. 5:15. none render evil *for* evil unto any
2Th. 2:10. because (lit. *for* that) they received not
the love
Heb 12: 2. who *for* the joy that was set
16. who *for* one morsel of meat sold
Jas. 4:15. *For* that ye (ought) to say, If the
1Pet.3: 9. Not rendering evil *for* evil, or railing *for*
railing:

ἀντιβάλλω, antiballo.

Lu. 24:17. (are) these *that* ye *have* one to another,

ἀντιδιατιθέμενος, antidiatithemenos.

2Ti. 2:25. instructing those *that oppose themselves;*

ἀντίδικος, antidikos.

Mat. 5:25. Agree with thine *adversary* quickly,
— at any time the *adversary* deliver
Lu. 12:58. goest with thine *adversary* to the
18: 3. saying, Avenge me of mine *adversary*.
1Pet.5: 8. because your *adversary* the devil,

ἀντίθεσις, antithesis.

1Ti. 6:20. *oppositions* of science falsely so called:

ἀντικαθίστημι, antikathisteemi.

Heb 12: 4. Ye *have* not yet *resisted* unto blood,

ἀντικαλέω, antikaleō.

Lu. 14:12. lest they also *bid* thee *again*, and

ἀντίκειμαι, antikimai.

Lu. 13:17. all his *adversaries* were ashamed:
21:15. which all your *adversaries* shall
1Co 16: 9. unto me, and (there are) many *adversaries*.
Gal. 5:17. these *are contrary* the one to the other:
Phi. 1:28. nothing terrified by your *adversaries:*
2Th. 2: 4. Who *opposeth* and exalteth himself
1Ti. 1:10. that *is contrary* to sound doctrine;
5:14. give none occasion to the *adversary*

ἀντικρύ, antikru.

Acts 20:15. came the next (day) *over against* Chios;

ἀντιλαμβάνομαι, antilambanomai.

Lu. 1:54. He *hath holpen* his servant Israel,
Acts 20:35. ye ought *to support* the weak, and
1Ti. 6: 2. beloved, *partakers* of the benefit.

ἀντιλέγω, antilego.

Lu. 2:34. a sign *which shall be spoken against;*
20:27. *which deny* that there is any resurrection;
Joh. 19:12. himself a king *speaketh against* Cæsar.
Acts 13:45. *spake against* those things which were
spoken by Paul, *contradicting* and blaspheming.
28:19. *when* the Jews *spake against* (it),
22. every where it *is spoken against*.
Ro. 10:21. a disobedient and *gainsaying* people.
Tit. 1: 9. exhort and to convince the *gainsayers.*
2: 9. well in all (things); not *answering again;*

ἀντίληψις, antileepsis.

1Co.12:28. gifts of healings, *helps*, governments,

ἀντιλογία, antilogia.

Heb. 6:16. (is) to them an end of all *strife*.
   7: 7. without all *contradiction* the less is
  12: 3. endured such *contradiction* of
Jude 11. perished in the *gainsaying* of Core.

ἀντιλοιδορέω, antiloidoreo.

1Pet.2:23. when he was reviled, *reviled* not *again ;*

ἀντίλυτρον, antilutron.

1Ti. 2: 6. Who gave himself a *ransom* for all,

ἀντιμετρέω, antimetreo.

Mat. 7: 2. it *shall be measured* to you *again*.
Lu. 6:38. it *shall be measured* to you *again*.

ἀντιμισθία, antimisthia.

Ro. 1:27. that *recompence* of their error which
2Co. 6:13. Now for a *recompence* in the same,

ἀντιπαρέρχομαι, antiparerkomai.

Lu. 10:31. he *passed by on the other side*.
     32. looked (on him), and *passed by on the other side*.

ἀντιπέραν, antiperan.

Lu. 8:26. Gadarenes, which is *over against* Galilee.

ἀντιπίπτω, antipipto.

Acts 7:51. ye *do* always *resist* the Holy Ghost:

ἀντιστρατεύομαι, antistratuomai.

Ro. 7:23. *warring against* the law of my mind,

ἀντιτάσσομαι, antitassomai.

Acts18: 6. *when* they *opposed* themselves, and
Ro. 13: 2. Whosoever therefore *resisteth* the power,
Jas. 4: 6. he saith, God *resisteth* the proud, but
   5: 6. the just; (and) he *doth* not *resist* you.
1Pet.5: 5. for God *resisteth* the proud, and giveth

ἀντίτυπον, antitupon.

Heb. 9:24. (which are) the *figures* of the true ;
1Pet.3:21. The *like figure whereunto,* (even) baptism

ἀντιχρίστος, antikristos.

1Joh 2:18. have heard that *antichrist* shall come, even
        now are there many *antichrists ;*
   22. He is *antichrist,* that denieth the Father
   4: 3. this is that (spirit) of *antichrist,* whereof
2Joh. 7. This is a deceiver and an *antichrist.*

ἀντλέω, antleo.

Joh. 2: 8. saith unto them, *Draw out* now, and bear unto
   9. the servants *which drew* the water knew ;
   4: 7. cometh a woman of Samaria *to draw* water:
  15. I thirst not, neither come hither *to draw.*

ἄντλημα, antleema.

Joh. 4:11. Sir, thou hast no*thing to draw with,*

ἀντοφθαλμέω, antophthalmeo.

Acts27:15. could not *bear up into* the wind,

ἄνυδρος, anudros.

Mat.12:43. he walketh through *dry* places, seeking
Lu. 11:24. walketh through *dry* places, seeking rest ;
2Pet.2:17. These are wells *without water,* clouds
Jude 12. clouds (they are) *without water,*

ἀνυπόκριτος, anupokritos.

Ro. 12: 9. (Let) love be *without dissimulation.*
2Co. 6: 6. by the Holy Ghost, by love *unfeigned,*
1Ti. 1: 5. a good conscience, and (of) faith *un-feigned:*
2Ti. 1: 5. the *unfeigned* faith that is in thee,
1Pet.1:22. unto *unfeigned* love of the brethren,
Jas. 3:17. without partiality, and *without hypocrisy.*

ἀνυπότακτος, anupotaktos.

1Ti. 1: 9. for the lawless and *disobedient,* for the
Tit. 1: 6. not accused of riot, or *unruly.*
  10. there are many *unruly* and vain
Heb. 2: 8. nothing (*that is*) not *put under* him.

ἄνω, ano.

Joh. 2: 7. they filled them up to *the brim.*
  8:23. Ye are from beneath ; I am from *above:*
  11:41. Jesus lifted *up* (his) eyes, and said,
Acts 2:19. I will shew wonders in heaven *above,*
Gal. 4:26. Jerusalem which is *above* is free,
Phi. 3:14. prize of the *high* calling of God
Col. 3: 1. seek those things which are *above,*
   2. Set your affection on things *above,*
Heb 12:15. of bitterness springing *up* trouble (you),

ἀνώγεον, anōgeon.

Mar 14:15. shew you a large *upper room* furnished
Lu. 22:12. shew you a large *upper room* furnished:

ἄνωθεν, anōthen.

Mat.27:51. in twain from *the top* to the bottom ;
Mar 15:38. in twain from *the top* to the bottom.
Lu. 1: 3. of all things *from the very first,*
Joh. 3: 3. Except a man be born *again,*
     7. Ye must be born *again.*
     31. He that cometh *from above* is
     19:11. except it were given thee *from above:*
     23. woven from the *top* throughout.
Acts26: 5. knew me *from the beginning,*
Gal. 4: 9. ye desire *again* (lit. a second time *again*
     παλιν ανωθεν) to be in bondage?
Jas. 1:17. every perfect gift is *from above,*
     3:15. descendeth not *from above,* but
     17. the wisdom that is *from above* is

ἀνωτερικός, anōterikos.

Acts19: 1. having passed through the *upper* coasts

ἀνώτερον, anōteron.

Lu. 14:10. say unto thee, Friend, go up *higher:*
Heb 10: 8. *Above* when he said, Sacrifice and

ανωφελής, anōphelees.

Tit. 6: 9. for they are *unprofitable* and vain.
Heb. 7:18. the weakness and *unprofitableness* thereof.

ἀξίνη, axinee.

Mat. 3:10. now also the *ax* is laid unto the root
Lu. 3: 9. now also the *axe* is laid unto the root

ἄξιος, axios.

Mat. 3: 8. therefore fruits *meet* for repentance:
     10:10. the workman is *worthy* of his meat.
     11. enquire who in it is *worthy; * and there
     13. if the house be *worthy,* let your peace
     — if it be not *worthy,* let your peace return
     37. more than me is not *worthy* of me:
     — than me is not *worthy* of me.
     38. followeth after me, is not *worthy* of me.
     22: 8. they which were bidden were not *worthy.*
Lu. 3: 8. therefore fruits *worthy* of repentance,
     7: 4. That he was *worthy* for whom he
     10: 7. for the labourer is *worthy* of his hire.
     12:48. did commit things *worthy* of stripes,
     15:19. am no more *worthy* to be called
     21. am no more *worthy* to be called thy
     23:15. nothing *worthy* of death is done unto
     41. for we receive the *due reward* of our
Joh. 1:27. shoe's latchet I am not *worthy* to unloose.
Acts13:25. of (his) feet I am not *worthy* to loose.
     46. judge yourselves un*worthy* of
     23:29. laid to his charge *worthy* of death
     25:11. committed any thing *worthy* of death,
     25. committed nothing *worthy* of death,
     26:20. do works *meet* for repentance.
     31. doeth nothing *worthy* of death or of
Ro. 1:32. such things are *worthy* of death,
     8:18. present time (are) not *worthy* (to be)
1Co16: 4. if it be *meet* that I go also, they shall
2Th. 1: 3. for you, brethren, as it is *meet,* because

1Ti. 1:15. faithful saying, and *worthy* of all accep-
     tation,
     4: 9. This (is) a faithful saying and *worthy*
     of all
     5:18. The labourer (is) *worthy* of his reward.
     6: 1. their own masters *worthy* of all
Heb 11:38. Of whom the world was not *worthy:*
Rev. 3: 4. in white: for they are *worthy.*
     4:11. Thou art *worthy,* O Lord, to receive
     5: 2. Who is *worthy* to open the book,
     4. no man was found *worthy* to open
     9. Thou art *worthy* to take the book,
     12. *Worthy* is the Lamb that was slain
     16: 6. blood to drink ; for they are *worthy.*

ἀξιόω, axioō.

Lu. 7: 7. neither *thought* I myself *worthy* to
Acts15:38. Paul *thought* not *good* to take him
     28:22. we *desire* to hear of thee what thou
2Th. 1:11. God *would count* you *worthy* of (this)
1Ti. 5:17. be counted *worthy* of double honour,
Heb. 3: 3. was counted *worthy* of more glory,
     10:29. shall he be thought *worthy,* who hath

ἀξίως, axiōs.

Ro. 16: 2. her in the Lord, *as becometh* saints,
Eph. 4: 1. that ye walk *worthy* of the vocation
Phil. 1:27. be *as it becometh* the gospel of Christ.
Col. 1:10. might walk *worthy* of the Lord unto
1Th. 2:12. That ye would walk *worthy* of God,
3 Joh. 6. their journey after a godly sort, (lit.
     worthily of God) thou

ἀόρατος, aoratos.

Ro. 1:20. For the *invisible things* of him from
Col. 1:15. Who is the image of the *invisible* God,
     16. that are in earth, visible and *invisible,*
1Ti. 1:17. the King eternal, immortal, *invisible,*
Heb11:27. as seeing him who is *invisible.*

ἀπαγγέλλω, apangello.

Mat. 2: 8. *bring me word again,* that I may
     8:33. into the city, and *told* every thing,
     11: 4. Go and *shew* John *again* those things
     12:18. he *shall shew* judgment to the
     14:12. buried it, and went and *told* Jesus.
     28: 8. did run *to bring* his disciples *word.*
     9. And as they went *to tell* his disciples,
     10. go *tell* my brethren that they go
     11. *shewed* unto the chief priests all
Mar. 6:30. *told* him all things, both what
     16:10. she went and *told* them that had
     13. they went and *told* (it) unto the residue:
Lu. 7:18. *shewed* him of all these things.
     22. Go your way, and *tell* John what things
     8:20. it *was told* him (by certain) which
     34. went and *told* (it) in the city and in the
     36. which saw (it) *told* them by what
     47. she *declared* unto him before
     9:36. kept (it) close, and *told* no man in those
     13: 1. some *that told* him of the Galilæans,
     14:21. came, and *shewed* his lord these things.
     18:37. they *told* him, that Jesus of
     24: 9. *told* all these things unto the

Joh. 4:51. his servants met him, and *told* (him),
20:18. came *and told* the disciples that
Acts 4:23. *reported* all that the chief priests
5:22. not in the prison, they returned, and *told*,
25. Then came one and *told* them, saying,
11:13. he *shewed* us how he had seen
12:14. ran in, and *told* how Peter stood before
17. Go *shew* these things unto James,
15:27. *who shall* also *tell* (you) the same
16:36. keeper of the prison *told* this saying
22:26. he went and *told* the chief captain,
23:16. entered into the castle, and *told* Paul.
17. he hath a certain thing *to tell* him.
19. What is that thou hast *to tell* me?
26:20. *shewed* first unto them of Damascus,
28:21. that came *shewed* or spake any
1Co.14:25. *and report* that God is in you of a truth.
1Th. 1: 9. themselves *shew* of us what
Heb. 2:12. I *will declare* thy name unto
1Joh.1: 2. bear witness, and *shew* unto you that
3. seen and heard *declare* we unto you,

ἀπάγχομαι, *apankomai̇́*.

Mat.27: 5. departed, and went and *hanged himself.*

ἀπάγω, *apago.*

Mat. 7:13. the way, *that leadeth* to destruction,
14. narrow (is) the way, *which leadeth* unto
26:57. laid hold on Jesus *led* (him) *away*
27: 2. bound him, they *led* (him) *away,*
31. *led* him *away* to crucify (him).
Mar 14:44. take him, and *lead* (him) *away* safely.
53. they *led* Jesus *away* to the high
15:16. the soldiers *led* him *away* into
Lu. 13:15. from the stall, and *lead* (him) *away* to
23:26. as they *led* him *away,* they laid
Joh. 18:13. *led* him *away* to Annas first;
19:16. they took Jesus, and *led* (him) *away.*
Acts12:19. commanded that (they) should *be put to
death.*
23:17. *Bring* this young man unto the
24: 7. *took* (him) *away* out of our hands,
1Co 12: 2. *carried away* unto these dumb idols, even

ἀπαίδευτος, *apaidūtos.*

2Ti. 2:23. foolish and *unlearned* questions avoid,

ἀπαίρομαι, *apairomai.*

Mat. 9:15. bridegroom *shall be taken* from them,
Mar. 2:20. bridegroom *shall be taken away* from
Lu. 5:35. bridegroom *shall be taken away* from

ἀπαιτέω, *apaiteo.*

Lu. 6:30. away thy goods *ask* (them) not *again.*
12:20. thy soul *shall be required* of thee:

ἀπαλγέω, *apalgeo.*

Eph. 4:19. Who *being past feeling* have given

ἀπαλλάσσω, *apallasso.*

Lu. 12:58. that thou mayest *be delivered* from him;
Acts19:12. the diseases *departed* from them,
Heb. 2:15. and *deliver* them who through fear of

ἀπαλλοτριόω, *apallotrioō.*

Eph. 2:12. *being aliens* from the commonwealth
4:18. being *alienated* from the life of
Col. 1:21. that were sometime *alienated*

ἀπαλός, *hapalos.*

Mat.24:32. When his branch is yet *tender,*
Mar 13:28. When her branch is yet *tender,*

ἀπαντάω, *apantao.*

Mat.28: 9. behold, Jesus *met* them, saying,
Mar. 5: 2. there *met* him out of the tombs a
14:13. there *shall meet* you a man bearing
Lu. 14:31. *to meet* him that cometh against
17:12. there *met* him ten men that were
Joh. 4:51. his servants *met* him, and told (him),
Acts16:16. with a spirit of divination *met* us,

ἀπάντησις, *apanteesis.*

Mat.25: 1. went forth to *meet* (lit. the *meeting* of) the
bridegroom.
6. bridegroom cometh; go ye out to *meet*
him.
Acts28:15. they came to *meet* us as far as
1Th. 4:17. to *meet* the Lord in the air: and

ἅπαξ, *hapax.*

2Co 11:25. beaten with rods, *once* was I stoned,
Phi. 4:16. ye sent *once* and again unto my
1Th. 2:18. come unto you, even I Paul, *once* and
again;
Heb. 6: 4. those who were *once* enlightened,
9: 7. the high priest alone *once* every year,
26. now *once* in the end of the world
27. it is appointed unto men *once* to die,
28. Christ was *once* offered to bear the
10: 2. worshippers *once* purged should
12:26. Yet *once* more I shake not the
27. this (word) Yet *once* more, signifieth
1Pet.3:18. Christ also hath *once* suffered for sins,
20. when *once* the longsuffering of God
Jude 3. faith which was *once* delivered
5. though ye *once* knew this, how that

ἀπαράβατος, *aparabatos.*

Heb. 7:24. hath an *unchangeable* priesthood.

ἀπαρασκεύαστος, *aparaskūastos.*

2Co. 9: 4. with me, and find you *unprepared,*

ἀπαρνέομαι, *aparneomai̇́.*

Mat.16:24. come after me, *let* him *deny* himself,

Mat.26:34. cock crow, thou *shalt deny* me thrice.
  35. yet *will* I not *deny* thee.
  75. cock crow, thou *shalt deny* me thrice.
Mar. 8:34. *let* him *deny* himself, and take
 14:30. crow twice, thou *shalt deny* me thrice.
  31. I *will* not *deny* thee in any wise.
  72. twice, thou *shalt deny* me thrice.
Lu. 9:23. come after me, *let* him *deny* himself,
 12: 9. *shall be denied* before the angels
 22:34. thou *shalt* thrice *deny* that thou
  61. cock crow, thou *shalt deny* me thrice.
Joh.13:38. crow, till thou *hast denied* me

ἀπάρτι, *aparti.*

Rev.14:13. die in the Lord *from henceforth :*
For other occurrences of ἀπ' ἄρτι see under ἀπο,
  p. 63, and ἄρτι, p. 82.

ἀπαρτισμός, *apartismos.*

Lu. 14:28. whether he have (sufficient) to finish (it)?
  (lit. the *finishing*)

ἀπαρχή, *aparkee.*

Ro. 8:23. which have the *firstfruits* of the Spirit,
 11:16. For if the *firstfruit* (be) holy, the
 16: 5. who is the *firstfruits* of Achaia
1Co.15:20. become the *firstfruits* of them that
  23. Christ the *firstfruits ;* afterward
 16:15. that it is the *firstfruits* of Achaia,
Jas. 1:18. a kind of *firstfruits* of his creatures.
Rev.14: 4. (being) the *firstfruits* unto God and

ἄπας, *hapas.*

Mat. 6:32. ye have need of *all* these things.
 24:39. the flood came, and took them *all* away ;
 28:11. unto the chief priests *all* the things that
Mar. 5 40. when he had put them *all* out, he
 8:25. restored, and saw *every* man clearly.
 11:32. for *all* (men) counted John, that he was
 16:15. Go ye into *all* the world, and preach
Lu. 2:39. had performed *all things* according
 3:16. John answered, saying unto (them) *all,*
 21. when *all* the people were baptized,
 4: 6. *All* this power will I give thee,
 5:11. they forsook *all,* and followed him.
 26. they were *all* amazed, and they glorified
 28. he left *all,* rose up, and followed him.
 7:16. there came a fear on *all :* and they
 8:37. Then the *whole* multitude of the
 9:15. they did so, and made them *all* sit
 15:13. younger son gathered *all* together,
 17:27. the flood came, and destroyed them *all.*
 29. from heaven, and destroyed (them) *all.*
 19: 7. when they saw (it), they *all* murmured,
 37. the *whole* multitude of the disciples
 48. for *all* the people were very attentive
 21: 4. For *all* these have of their abundance
 — hath cast in *all* the living that
 12. before *all* these, they shall lay
 23: 1. the *whole* multitude of them arose,
Acts 2: 1. they were *all* with one accord in
 4. they were *all* filled with the Holy
 14. *all* (ye) that dwell at Jerusalem,
 44. together, and had *all* things common ;
 4:31. they were *all* filled with the Holy
 32. they had *all* things common.
 5:12. they were *all* with one accord in

Acts 5:16. they were healed *every one.*
 6:15. *all* that sat in the council, looking
 10: 8. he had declared *all* (these) *things*
 11:10. *all* were drawn up again into heaven.
 13:29. had fulfilled *all* that was written
 16: 3. they knew *all* that his father was
 28. Do thyself no harm : for we are *all* here.
 27:33. Paul besought (them) *all* to take
Eph 6:13. having done *all,* to stand.
Jas. 3: 2. in many things we offend *all.*

ἀπατάω, *apatao.*

Eph. 5: 6. *Let* no man *deceive* you with
1Ti. 2:14. Adam *was* not *deceived,* but the woman
  being deceived was in the
Jas. 1:26. his tongue, but *deceiveth* his own

ἀπάτη, *apatee.*

Mat.13:22. the *deceitfulness* of riches, choke
Mar. 4:19. the *deceitfulness* of riches, and the
Eph. 4:22. corrupt according to the *deceitful*
Col. 2: 8. through philosophy and vain *deceit,*
2Th. 2:10. with all *deceivableness* of
Heb 3:13. through the *deceitfulness* of sin.
2Pet.2:13. with their own *deceivings* while

ἀπάτωρ, *apator.*

Heb 7: 3. *Without father,* without mother,

ἀπαύγασμα, *apaugasma.*

Heb 1: 3. Who being the *brightness* of (his)

ἀπείθεια, *apithia.*

Ro. 11:30. obtained mercy through their *unbelief :*
 32. concluded them all in *unbelief,*
Eph. 2: 2. in the children of *disobedience :*
 5: 6. upon the children of *disobedience*
Col. 3: 6. on the children of *disobedience :*
Heb 4: 6. entered not in because of *unbelief :*
 11. the same example of *unbelief.*

ἀπειθέω, *apitheo.*

Joh. 3:36. he *that believeth not* the Son shall
Acts14: 2. the *unbelieving* Jews stirred up the
 17: 5. the Jews *which believed not,* moved
 19: 9. divers were hardened, and *believed not,*
Ro. 2: 8. *do not obey* the truth, but obey
 10:21. unto a *disobedient* and gainsayir.g people.
 11:30. in times past *have not believed* God,
 31. have these also now *not believed,*
 15:31. from them *that do not believe* in
Heb 3:18. to them *that believed not ?*
 11:31. not with them *that believed not,*
1Pet.2: 7. unto them *which be disobedient,* the
 8. stumble at the word, *being disobedient :*
 3: 1. that, if any *obey not* the word, they
 20. Which sometime *were disobedient,*
 4:17. them *that obey not* the gospel of God ?

ἀπειθής, apīthees.

Lu. 1:17. the *disobedient* to the wisdom of the just;
Acts26:19. I was not *disobedient* unto the heavenly
Ro. 1:30. of evil things, *disobedient* to parents,
2Ti. 3: 2. blasphemers, *disobedient* to parents,
Tit. 1:16. being abominable, and *disobedient*, and
　　 3: 3. were sometimes foolish, *disobedient*,

ἀπειλέω, apīleo.

Acts 4:17. *let* us straitly *threaten* them, that they
1Pet. 2:23. when he suffered, he *threatened* not;

ἀπειλή, apīlee.

Acts 4:17. let us *straitly* (lit. with *threatening*) threaten
　　　　 them, that .
　　 29. Lord, behold their *threatenings* :
　 9: 1. breathing out *threatenings*, and
Eph. 6: 9. unto them, forbearing *threatening* :

ἄπειμι, apīmi.

1Co. 5: 3. For I verily, as *absent* in body, but
2Co.10: 1. *being absent* am bold toward you:
　　 11. by letters when we *are absent*, such
　　 13: 2. *being absent* now I write to them
　　 10. I write these things *being absent*,
Phi. 1:27. I come and see you, or else *be absent*,
Col. 2: 5. though I *be absent* in the flesh;

ἄπειμι, apīmi.

Acts17:10. *went* into the synagogue of the Jews.

ἀπειπεῖν, apīpīn.

2Co. 4: 2. *have renounced* the hidden things

ἀπείραστος, apīrastos.

Jas. 1:13. for God *cannot be tempted* with

ἄπειρος, apīros.

Heb. 5:13. (is) *unskilful* in the word of

ἀπεκδέχομαι, apekdekomai.

Ro. 8:19. *waiteth for* the manifestation of the
　　 23. ourselves, *waiting for* the adoption,
　　 25. (then) do we with patience *wait for* (it).
1Co. 1. 7. *waiting for* the coming of our
Gal. 5: 5. *wait for* the hope of righteousness
Phi. 3:20. whence also we *look for* the Saviour,
Heb 9:28. unto them *that look for* him shall

ἀπεκδύομαι, apekduomai.

Col. 2:15. *having spoiled* principalities and
　　 3: 9. that ye *have put off* the old man

ἀπέκδυσις, apekdusis.

Col. 2:11. in *putting off* the body of the sins

ἀπελάω, apelao.

Acts18:16. he *drave* them from the judgment seat.

ἀπελεγμός, apelegmos.

Acts19:27. our craft is in danger to be set at *nought*;

ἀπελεύθερος, apelutheros.

1Co. 7:22. (being) a servant, is the Lord's *freeman* :

ἀπελπίζω, apelpizo.

Lu. 6:35. lend, *hoping for* nothing *again*;

ἀπέναντι, apenanti.

Mat.21: 2. Go into the village *over against* you,
　 27:24. washed (his) hands *before* the multitude,
　　 61. sitting *over against* the sepulchre.
Acts 3:16. soundness *in the presence* of you all.
　 17: 7. these all do *contrary* to the decrees of
Ro. 3:18. no fear of God *before* their eyes.

ἀπέραντος, aperantos.

1Ti. 1: 4. to fables and *endless* genealogies, which

ἀπερισπάστως, aperispastos.

1Co. 7:35. upon the Lord *without distraction*.

ἀπερίτμητος, aperitmeetos.

Acts 7:51. stiffnecked and *uncircumcised* in heart

ἀπέρχομαι, aperkomai.

Mat. 2:22. he was afraid *to go* thither:
　 4:24. his fame *went* throughout all Syria:
　 8:18. commandment *to depart* unto the
　　 19. will follow thee whithersoever thou *goest*.
　　 21. suffer me first *to go* and bury my father.
　　 31. suffer us *to go away* into the herd
　　 32. they *went* into the herd of swine:
　　 33. fled, and *went* their *ways* into the city, and
　 9: 7. he arose, and *departed* to his house.
　 10: 5. *Go* not into the way of the Gentiles,
　 13:25. tares among the wheat, and *went* his *way*.
　　 28. that we *go and* gather them up ?
　　 46. *went and* sold all that he had, and
　 14:15. that they *may go* into the villages, *and*
　　 16. said unto them, They need not *depart* ;
　　 25. Jesus *went* unto them, walking
　 16: 4. he left them, and *departed*.
　　 21. how that he must *go* unto Jerusalem,
　 18:30. *went and* cast him into prison, till
　 19:22. that saying, he *went away* sorrowful:

Mat.20: 4(5). And they *went* their way.
21:29. afterward he repented, and *went*.
30. said, I (go), Sir: and *went* not.
22: 5. *went* their *ways*, one to his farm,
22. left him, and *went* their way.
25:10. *while* they *went* to buy, the bridegroom
18. *went and* digged in the earth, and hid
25. *went and* hid thy talent in the earth:
46. these *shall go away* into everlasting
26:36. Sit ye here, while I *go and* pray yonder.
42. He *went away* again the second time, *and*
44. he left them, *and went away* again,
27: 5. departed, and *went and* hanged himself.
60. the door of the sepulchre, and *departed*.
28:10. my brethren that they *go* into
Mar 1:20. the hired servants, and *went* after him.
35. he went out, and *departed* into a
42. the leprosy *departed* from him,
3:13. whom he would: and they *came* unto
5:17. to pray him *to depart* out of their
20. he *departed*, and began to publish
24. (Jesus) *went* with him ; and much
6:27(28). he *went and* beheaded him in
32. they *departed* into a desert place
36. that they *may go* into the country
37. Shall we *go and* buy two hundred
46. he *departed* into a mountain
7:24. he arose, and *went* into the borders
30. *when* she *was come* to her
8:13. again *departed* to the other side.
9:43. having two hands *to go* into hell,
10:22. sad at that saying, and *went away*
11: 4. they *went* their *way*, and found
12:12. they left him, and *went* their *way*.
14:10. one of the twelve, *went* unto the
12. Where wilt thou *that* we *go and*
39. again he *went away, and* prayed
16:13. they *went and* told (it) unto the
Lu. 1:23. he *departed* to his own house.
38. the angel *departed* from her.
2:15. as the angels *were gone away* from
5:13. the leprosy *departed* from him.
14. *go, and* shew thyself to the priest,
25. *departed* to his own house,
7:24. *when* the messengers of John were *departed,*
8:31. command them *to go out* into
34. *went and* told (it) in the city and in
37. besought him *to depart* from them ;
39. he *went* his *way*, and published
9:12. that they may *go* into the towns...*and*
57. I will follow thee whithersoever thou *goest.*
59. suffer me first *to go* and bury my father.
60. *go* thou *and* preach the kingdom of God.
10:30. *departed*, leaving (him) half dead.
17:23. *go* not after (them), nor follow (them).
19:32. that were sent *went* their *way*,
22: 4. he *went* his *way, and* communed
13. they *went, and* found as he had
23:33. when they *were come* to the place,
24:12. clothes laid by themselves, and *departed,*
24. *went* to the sepulchre, and found
Joh. 4: 3. He left Judæa, and *departed* again into
8. For his disciples *were gone away*
28. *went* her *way* into the city, and
43. after two days he *departed* thence
47. he *went* unto him, and besought
5:15. The man *departed*, and told the Jews
6: 1. Jesus *went* over the sea of Galilee,
22. (that) his disciples *were gone away*
66. many of his disciples *went back*,
68. Lord, to whom *shall* we *go* ?
9: 7. He *went* his *way* therefore, and

Joh. 9:11. I *went and* washed, and I received sight.
10:40. *went away* again beyond Jordan
11:28. had so said, she *went* her *way,*
46. some of them *went* their *ways* to the
54. *went* thence unto a country
12:19. behold, the world *is gone* after him.
36. These things spake Jesus, and *departed,* and
16: 7. expedient for you that I *go away :* for if I *go* not *away,*
18: 6. they *went* backward, and fell to
20:10. the disciples *went away* again
Acts 4:15. commanded them *to go aside* out
5:26. **Then** *went* the captain with
9:17. Ananias *went* his *way*, and entered
10: 7. spake unto Cornelius *was departed,*
28:29. the Jews *departed*, and had great
Ro. 15:28. I *will come* by you into Spain.
Gal. 1:17. I *went* into Arabia, and returned
Jas. 1:24. beholdeth himself, and *goeth* his *way,*
Jude 7. *going* after strange flesh, are
Rev. 9:12. One woe *is past ;* (and), behold,
10: 9. I *went* unto the angel, and said unto
11:14. The second woe *is past ;* (and), behold,
12:17. *went* to make war with the
16: 2. the first *went*, and poured out his
18:14. lusted after *are departed* from thee,
— goodly *are departed* from thee, and
21: 4. the former things *are passed away.*

ἀπέχει, apekī.

Mar.14:41. *it is enough*, the hour is come ;

ἀπέχομαι, apekŏmai.

Acts15:20. that they *abstain* from pollutions
29. That ye *abstain* from meats offered
1Th. 4: 3. that ye should *abstain* from fornication:
5:22. *Abstain* from all appearance of evil.
1Ti. 4: 3. (commanding) *to abstain* from meats,
1Pet. 2:11. *abstain* from fleshly lusts, which

ἀπέχω, apeko.

Mat. 6: 2. I say unto you, They *have* their reward.
5. I say unto you, They *have* their reward.
16. I say unto you, They *have* their reward.
15: 8. their heart *is* far from me.
Mar. 7: 6. their heart *is* far from me.
Lu. 6:24. ye *have received* your consolation.
7: 6. *when* he *was* now not far from the house,
15:20. *when* he *was* yet a great way off,
24:13. *which was* from Jerusalem (about)
Phi. 4:18. But I *have* all, and abound :
Philem.15. that thou *shouldest receive* him for

ἀπιστέω, apisteo.

Mar.16:11. had been seen of her, *believed not.*
16. he *that believeth not* shall be damned.
Lu. 24:11. as idle tales, and they *believed* them *not.*
41. *while* they yet *believed not* for joy, and
Acts28:24. were spoken, and some *believed not.*
Ro. 3: 3. what if some *did not believe ?*
2Ti. 2:13. If we *believe not*, (yet) he abideth

ἀπιστία, apistia.

Mat.13:58. works there because of their *unbelief*.
17:20. said unto them, Because of your *unbelief:*
Mar. 6: 6. he marvelled because of their *unbelief*.
9:24. I believe; help thou mine *unbelief*.
16:14. upbraided them with their *unbelief*
Ro. 3: 3. shall their *unbelief* make the
4:20. promise of God through *unbelief;*
11:20. because of *unbelief* they were broken
23. if they abide not in *unbelief,*
1Ti. 1:13. I did (it) ignorantly in *unbelief*.
Heb. 3:12. you an evil heart of *unbelief,*
19. not enter in because of *unbelief*.

ἄπιστος, apistos.

Mat.17:17. O *faithless* and perverse generation,
Mar. 9:19. O *faithless* generation, how long shall
Lu. 9:41. O *faithless* and perverse generation,
12:46. his portion with the *unbelievers*.
Joh.20:27. be not *faithless*, but believing.
Acts26: 8. thought a *thing incredible* with you,
1Cor.6: 6. that before the *unbelievers*.
7:12. hath a wife *that believeth not*,
13. hath an husband *that believeth not,*
14. For the *unbelieving* husband
— the *unbelieving* wife is sanctified
15. if the *unbelieving* depart, let him
10:27. If any of them *that believe not*
14:22. to them *that believe not:* but
— not for them *that believe not,*
23. (that are) unlearned, or *unbelievers,*
24. there come in one *that believeth not,*
2Co. 4: 4. minds of them *which believe not,*
6:14. yoked together with *unbelievers:*
15. hath he that believeth with an *infidel?*
1Ti. 5: 8. is worse than an *infidel.*
Tit. 1:15. defiled and *unbelieving* (is) nothing
Rev.21: 8. But the fearful, and *unbelieving,*

ἀπλότης, haplotees.

Ro. 12:8. (let him do it) with *simplicity;*
2Co. 1:12. that in *simplicity* and godly sincerity
8: 2. unto the riches of their *liberality.*
9:11. in every thing to all *bountifulness,*
13. for (your) *liberal* distribution unto
11: 3. from the *simplicity* that is in Christ.
Eph. 6: 5. in *singleness* of your heart, as
Col. 3:22. in *singleness* of heart, fearing God:

ἀπλοῦς, haplous.

Mat. 6:22. if therefore thine eye be *single,*
Lu. 11:34. therefore when thine eye is *single,*

ἀπλῶς, haplōs.

Jas. 1: 5. that giveth to all (men) *liberally,*

ἀπό, apo.

NOTE.—Only with a genitive.

Mat. 1:17. the generations *from* Abraham
— *from* David until the carrying
— *from* the carrying away into

Mat. 1:21. shall save his people *from* their sins.
24. Then Joseph being raised *from* sleep
2: 1. came wise men *from* the east
16. *from* two years old and under, according
3: 4. had his raiment *of* camel's hair,
7. to flee *from* the wrath to come?
13. cometh Jesus *from* Galilee to Jordan
16. went up straightway *out of* the water:
4:17. *From* that time Jesus began to
25. multitudes of people *from* Galilee, and
5:18. shall in no wise pass *from* the law,
29. pluck it out, and cast (it) *from* thee:
30. cut it off, and cast (it) *from* thee: for
42. from him that would borrow *of* thee
6:13. temptation, but deliver us *from* evil:
7: 4. pull out the mote *out of* thine eye;
15. Beware *of* false prophets, which come
16. Ye shall know them *by* their fruits. Do
men shall gather grapes *of* thorns, or figs *of*
thistles?
20. Wherefore *by* their fruits ye shall
23. depart *from* me, ye that work iniquity.
8: 1. was come down *from* the mountain,
11. many shall come *from* the east and
30. a good way off *from* them an herd
34. he would depart *out of* their coasts.
9:15. bridegroom shall be taken *from* them,
16. to fill it up taketh *from* the garment,
22. was made whole *from* that hour.
10:17. But beware *of* men: for they will
28. fear not them (lit. *for* them) which kill
the body,
11:12. *from* the days of John the Baptist
19. wisdom is justified *of* her children.
25. hast hid these things *from* the wise
29. my yoke upon you, and learn *of* me;
12:38. we would see a sign *from* thee.
43. the unclean spirit is gone *out of* a man,
13: 1. same day went Jesus *out of* the house,
12. *from* him shall be taken away
35. kept secret *from* the foundation of
44. *for* joy thereof goeth and selleth all
14: 2. he is risen *from* the dead; and
13. followed him on foot *out of* the cities.
26. they cried out *for* fear.
29. Peter was come down *out of* the ship,
15: 1. which were *of* Jerusalem, saying,
8. their heart is far *from* me.
22. came *out of* the same coasts, and
27. dogs eat *of* the crumbs which fall *from*
28. made whole *from* that very hour.
16: 6. beware *of* the leaven of the Pharisees
11. ye should beware *of* the leaven of
12. bade (them) not beware *of* the leaven of
bread, but *of* the doctrine of the Pharisees,
21. *From* that time forth began Jesus
— suffer many things *of* the elders
17: 9. as they came down *from* the mountain,
18. the devil; and he departed *out of* him: and
the child was cured *from* that very
25. *of* whom do the kings of the earth
— *of* their own children, or *of* strangers?
26. Peter saith unto him, *Of* strangers.
18: 7. Woe unto the world *because of* offences!
8. cut them off, and cast (them) *from* thee:
9. pluck it out, and cast (it) *from* thee:
35. if ye *from* your hearts forgive not
19: 1. he departed *from* Galilee, and came
4. which made (them) *at* the beginning
8. *from* the beginning it was not so.
20: 8. beginning *from* the last unto the
29. as they departed *from* Jericho,

Mat.21: 8. cut down branches *from* the trees,
     11. the prophet *of* Nazareth of Galilee.
     43. shall be taken *from* you, and given
  22:46. durst any (man) *from* that day
  23:33. can ye escape (lit. *from*) the damnation of hell?
     34. persecute (them) *from* city to city:
     35. *from* the blood of righteous Abel unto
     39. Shall not see me hence*forth*, till ye
  24: 1. went out, and departed *from* the temple:
     21. not *since* the beginning of the world
     27. lightning cometh *out of* the east,
     29. the stars shall fall *from* heaven,
     31. *from* one end of heaven to the other
     32. Now learn a parable *of* the fig tree;
  25:28. Take therefore the talent *from* him,
     29. *from* him that hath not shall be taken away (lit. *from* him) even
     32. separate them one *from* another, as a shepherd divideth (his) sheep *from* the goats:
     34. *from* the foundation of the world:
     41. Depart *from* me, ye cursed, into
  26:16. *from* that time he sought opportunity
     29. I will not drink hence*forth* of this
     39. let this cup pass *from* me: nevertheless
     42. cup may not pass away *from* me,
     47. *from* the chief priests and elders of
     58. Peter followed him afar *off* (lit. *from* far)
     64. Here*after* shall ye see the Son of man
  27: 9. they *of* the children of Israel did
     21. Whether *of* the twain will ye that
     24. I am innocent *of* the blood of
     40. come down *from* the cross.
     42. now come down *from* the cross,
     45. Now *from* the sixth hour there
     51. rent in twain *from* the top to the
     55. were there beholding afar *off*, which followed Jesus *from* Galilee,
     57. came a rich man *of* Arimathæa,
     64. He is risen *from* the dead: so the
  28: 2. rolled back the stone *from* the
     4. *for* fear of him the keepers did
     7. that he is risen *from* the dead;
     8. departed quickly *from* the sepulchre

Mar. 1: 9. that Jesus came *from* Nazareth
     10. coming up *out of* the water, he saw
     42. the leprosy departed *from* him,
   2:20. shall be taken away *from* them,
   3: 7. a great multitude *from* Galilee followed him, and *from* Judæa,
     8. *from* Jerusalem, and *from* Idumæa,
     22. scribes which came down *from* Jerusalem
   4:25. *from* him shall be taken even that
   5: 6. when he saw Jesus afar *off*, he
     17. him to depart *out of* their coasts.
     29. that she was healed *of* that plague.
     34. in peace, and be whole *of* thy plague.
     35. there came *from* the ruler of the
   6.33. ran afoot thither *out of* all cities, and
     43. of the fragments, and *of* the fishes.
   7: 1. scribes, which came *from* Jerusalem.
     4. (when they come) *from* the market,
     6. their heart is far *from* me.
     15. but the things which come *out of* him,
     17. entered into the house *from* the people,
     28. under the table eat *of* the children's
     33. he took him aside *from* the multitude,
   8:11. seeking of him a sign *from* heaven,
     15. beware *of* the leaven of the Pharisees,
     31. be rejected *of* the elders, and (of) the chief
   9: 9. as they came down *from* the mountain,
  10: 6. *from* the beginning of the creation

Mar.10:46. as he went *out of* Jericho with his
  11:12. when they were come *from* Bethany,
  12: 2. *of* the fruit of the vineyard.
     34. not far *from* the kingdom of God.
     38. Beware *of* the scribes, which love
  13:19. as was not *from* the beginning of
     27. *from* the uttermost part of the
     28. Now learn a parable *of* the fig tree;
  14:35. the hour might pass *from* him.
     36. take away this cup *from* me:
     52. linen cloth, and fled *from* them naked.
     54. Peter followed him afar *off*, even
  15:21. who passed by, coming *out of* the country,
     30. Save thyself, and come down *from* the cross.
     32. descend now *from* the cross, that
     38. rent in twain *from* the top to the
     40. also women looking on afar *off*:
     43. Joseph *of* Arimathæa, an
     45. when he knew (it) *of* the centurion,
  16: 8. out quickly, and fled *from* the sepulchre;
     9. Mary Magdalene, *out of* whom he

Lu. 1: 2. which *from* the beginning were
     38. the angel departed *from* her.
     48. *from* henceforth all generations shall
     52. put down the mighty *from* (their) seats,
     70. which have been *since* the world began:
   2: 4. Joseph also went up *from* Galilee,
     15. were gone away *from* them into
     36. seven years *from* her virginity;
     37. which departed not *from* the temple,
   3: 7. to flee *from* the wrath to come?
   4: 1. returned *from* Jordan, and was led
     13. he departed *from* him for a season.
     35. in the midst, he came *out of* him,
     41. devils also came *out of* many,
     42. that he should not depart *from* them.
   5: 2. the fishermen were gone *out of* them,
     3. thrust out a little *from* the land.
     8. saying, Depart *from* me; for
     10. *from* henceforth thou shalt catch
     13. immediately the leprosy departed *from* him.
     15. healed by him *of* their infirmities.
     35. shall be taken away *from* them,
     36. that was (taken) *out of* the new agreeth
   6:13. *of* them he chose twelve, whom
     17. multitude of people *out of* all Judæa
     — to be healed *of* their diseases.
     29. and him (lit. *from* him) that taketh away thy cloke
     30. *of* him that taketh away thy goods
   7: 6. was now not far *from* the house,
     21. cured many *of* (their) infirmities and
     35. wisdom is justified *of* all her children.
     45. this woman, *since* the time I came
   8: 2. had been healed *of* evil spirits and
     — *out of* whom went seven devils,
     3. ministered unto him *of* their substance.
     12. the word *out of* their hearts, lest
     18. *from* him shall be taken even
     29. the unclean spirit to come *out of* the
     33. Then went the devils *out of* the man,
     35. *out of* whom the devils were
     37. besought him to depart *from* them;
     38. the man *out of* whom the devils
     43. an issue of blood twelve (lit. *from* twelve) years,
     46. I perceive that virtue is gone *out of* me.
   9: 5. when ye go *out of* that city, shake off the very dust *from* your feet
     22. be rejected *of* the elders and chief priests

Lu. 9:33. as they departed *from* him,
    37. they were come down *from* the
    38. behold, a man *of* the company
    39. bruising him hardly departeth *from* him.
    45. it was hid *from* them, that they
    54. fire to come down *from* heaven,
  10.21. hid these things *from* the wise and
    30. went down *from* Jerusalem to Jericho,
    42. shall not be taken away *from* her.
  11: 4. temptation ; but deliver us *from* evil.
    24. the unclean spirit is gone *out of* a
    50. was shed *from* the foundation of the world,
        may be required *of* this generation ;
    51. *From* the blood of Abel unto the
    — be required *of* this generation.
  12: 1. Beware ye *of* the leaven of the Pharisees,
     4. Be not afraid *of* them that kill
    15. Take heed, and beware *of* covetousness:
    20. thy soul shall be required *of* thee:
    52. For *from* henceforth there shall be
    54. When ye see a cloud rise *out of* the west,
    57. why even *of* yourselves judge ye
    58. thou mayest be delivered *from* him ;
  13:15. loose his ox or (his) ass *from* the stall,
    16. be loosed *from* this bond on the
    25. When once (lit. *from* when) the master of
        the house
    27. depart *from* me, all (ye) workers
    29. they shall come *from* the east, and (from)
        the west, and *from* the north,
  14:18. all *with* one (consent) began to make
  15:16. filled his belly *with* the husks that
  16: 3. taketh away *from* me the stewardship:
    16. *since* that time the kingdom of
    18. that is put away *from* (her) husband
    21. *with* the crumbs which fell *from* the
    23. seeth Abraham afar *off*, and
    30. went unto them *from* the dead,
  17:25. be rejected *of* this generation.
    29. day that Lot went *out of* Sodom it rained
        fire and brimstone *from* heaven,
  18: 3. Avenge me *of* mine adversary.
    34. this saying was hid *from* them,
  19: 3. could not *for* the press, because he
    24. Take *from* him the pound, and give
    26. *from* him that hath not, even
    — shall be taken away *from* him.
    39. Pharisees *from* among the multitude
    42. now they are hid *from* thine eyes.
  20:10. should give him *of* the fruit of the
    46. Beware *of* the scribes, which desire
  21:11. signs shall there be *from* heaven.
    26. Men's hearts failing them *for* fear,
    30. know *of* your own selves that summer
  22:18. not drink *of* the fruit of the vine,
    41. he was withdrawn *from* them about
    42. remove this cup *from* me:
    43. an angel unto him *from* heaven,
    45. when he rose up *from* prayer,
    — found them sleeping *for* sorrow,
    69. Here*after* shall the Son of man
    71. ourselves have heard *of* his own mouth.
  23: 5. beginning *from* Galilee to this place.
    26. coming *out of* the country, and on him
    49. women that followed him *from* Galilee,
    51. (he was) *of* Arimathæa, a city of the
  24: 2. stone rolled away *from* the sepulchre.
     9. returned *from* the sepulchre, and
    13. which was *from* Jerusalem
    21. third day *since* these things were
    27. beginning *at* Moses and (lit. and *at*) all
        the

Lu. 24:31. he vanished *out of* their sight.
    41. they yet believed not *for* joy, and
    42. broiled fish, and *of* an honeycomb.
    47. all nations, beginning *at* Jerusalem.
    51. he was parted *from* them, and carried
Joh. 1:44(45). Philip was *of* Bethsaida, the
    45(46). Jesus *of* Nazareth the son of Joseph.
    51(52). Here*after* ye shall see heaven open,
  3: 2. thou art a teacher come *from* God:
  5:19. The Son can do nothing *of* himself,
    30. I can *of* mine own self do nothing:
  7:17. or (whether) I speak *of* myself.
    18. He that speaketh *of* himself seeketh
    28. I am not come *of* myself, but he
    42. *out of* the town of Bethlehem, where
  8: 9. beginning *at* the eldest, (even)
    28. (that) I do nothing *of* myself, but
    42. neither came I *of* myself, but he
    44. He was a murderer *from* the beginning,
  10: 5. not follow, but will flee *from* him:
    18. No man taketh it *from* me, but I lay it
        down *of* myself. I have
  11: 1. (named) Lazarus, *of* Bethany, the
    18. unto Jerusalem, about fifteen furlongs *off:*
    51. this spake he not *of* himself: but
    53. Then *from* that day forth they took
  12:21. which (was) *of* Bethsaida of Galilee,
    36. departed, and did hide himself *from* them.
  13: 3. that he was come *from* God, and
    19. Now (lit. *from* now) I tell you before it
        come,
  14: 7. *from* henceforth ye know him,
    10. unto you I speak not *of* myself:
  15: 4. the branch cannot bear fruit *of* itself,
    27. been with me *from* the beginning.
  16:13. for he shall not speak *of* himself ;
    22. your joy no man taketh *from* you.
    30. that thou camest forth *from* God.
  18:28. led they Jesus *from* Caiaphas unto
    34. Sayest thou this thing *of* thyself,
  19:27. *from* that hour that disciple took
    38. after this Joseph *of* Arimathæa,
  21: 2. Nathanael *of* Cana in Galilee, and
     6. to draw it *for* the multitude of fishes.
     8. they were not far *from* land, but as it
        were two hundred cubits, (lit. *off*)
    10. Bring *of* the fish which ye have now
Acts 1: 4. should not depart *from* Jerusalem,
     9. a cloud received him *out of* their sight.
    11. is taken up *from* you into heaven,
    12. *from* the mount called Olivet,
    22. Beginning *from* the baptism of
    — that he was taken up *from* us,
  2: 5. *out of* every nation under heaven.
    17. I will pour out *of* my Spirit upon
    18. in those days *of* my Spirit ; and
    22. a man approved *of* God among
    40. yourselves *from* this untoward generation.
  3:19. *from* the presence of the Lord ;
    21. holy prophets *since* the world began.
    24. all the prophets *from* Samuel
    26. every one of you *from* his iniquities.
  5: 2. kept back (part) *of* the price, his
     3. to keep back (part) *of* the price of the
    38. Refrain *from* these men, and let
    41. departed *from* the presence of the
  6: 9. Alexandrians, and *of* them *of* Cilicia
  7:45. God drave out *before* the face of
  8:10. *from* the least to the greatest,
    22. Repent therefore *of* this thy wickedness,
    26. that goeth down *from* Jerusalem
    33. his life is taken *from* the earth.

Acts 8:35. began *at* the same scripture, and
9: 3. round about him a light *from* heaven:
8. Saul arose *from* the earth ; and when
13. I have heard *by* many of this man,
18. there fell *from* his eyes as it had
10:17. men which were sent *from* Cornelius
21. were sent unto him *from* Cornelius ;
23. certain brethren *from* Joppa
30. Four days *ago* I was fasting until
37. all Judæa, and began *from* Galilee,
38. God anointed Jesus *of* Nazareth
11:11. I was, sent *from* Cæsarea unto me.
19. Now they which were scattered abroad *upon* the
27. came prophets *from* Jerusalem
12: 1. to vex certain *of* the church.
10. the angel departed *from* him.
14. opened not the gate *for* gladness,
19. he went down *from* Judæa to
20. was nourished *by* the king's
13: 8. turn away the deputy *from* the faith.
13. his company loosed *from* Paphos,
— John departing *from* them
14. when they departed *from* Perga,
23. *Of* this man's seed hath God
29. they took (him) down *from* the tree
31. with him *from* Galilee to
39. *from* which ye could not be
50. expelled them *out of* their coasts.
14:15. should turn *from* these vanities
19. thither (certain) Jews *from* Antioch
15: 1. men which came down *from*
5. certain *of* the sect of the Pharisees
7. how that a good while *ago*
18. *from* the beginning of the world.
19. which *from* among the Gentiles
20. that they abstain *from* pollutions
33. *from* the brethren unto the apostles.
38. departed *from* them *from* Pamphylia,
39. departed asunder one *from* the other:
16:11. Therefore loosing *from* Troas,
18. to come *out of* her. And he
33. of the night, and washed (their) (lit. *from* their) stripes;
17: 2. with them *out of* the scriptures,
13. when the Jews *of* Thessalonica had
27. he be not far *from* every one of us:
18: 2. lately come *from* Italy, with his
5. Timotheus were come *from* Macedonia,
6. *from* henceforth I will go unto
16. drave them *from* the judgment seat.
21. if God will. And he sailed *from* Ephesus.
19: 9. he departed *from* them, and separated
12. So that *from* his body were brought
— the diseases departed *from* them, and the evil spirits went *out of* them.
13. Then certain *of* the vagabond Jews,
20: 6. we sailed away *from* Philippi
9. *with* sleep, and fell down *from* the third loft, and
17. *from* Miletus he sent to Ephesus,
18. know, *from* the first day that (lit. *from* which) I
26. that I (am) pure *from* the blood of
21: 1. after we were gotten *from* them,
7. we had finished (our) course *from* Tyre,
10. there came down *from* Judæa
16. (certain) of the disciples *of* Cæsarea,
21. the Gentiles to forsake Moses, (lit. apostasy *from*)
27. the Jews which were *of* Asia, when
22:11. I could not see *for* the glory of

Acts 22:22. **Away with such a (fellow) *from* the earth:**
29. straightway they departed *from* him
30. he loosed him *from* (his) bands,
23:21. looking for a promise *from* thee.
23. *at* the third hour of the night;
34. he understood that (he was) *of* Cilicia ;
24:11. twelve days since (lit. *from* that) I went up to
18. certain Jews *from* Asia found
25: 1. he ascended *from* Cæsarea to
7. Jews which came down *from*
26: 4. from my youth, which was *at* the first
18. to turn (them) *from* darkness to
27:21. not have loosed *from* Crete, and
44. some on (broken pieces) *of* the ship.
28:21. neither received letters *out of* Judæa
23. both *out of* the law of Moses, and
— *from* morning till evening.
Ro. 1: 7. Grace to you and peace *from* God
18. revealed *from* heaven against
20. of him *from* the creation of the world
5: 9. we shall be saved *from* wrath
14. death reigned *from* Adam to Moses,
6: 7. he that is dead is freed *from* sin.
18. Being then made free *from* sin,
22. now being made free *from* sin,
7: 2. she is loosed *from* the law of
3. she is free *from* that law ;
6. now we are delivered *from* the law,
8: 2. free *from* the law of sin and death.
21. delivered *from* the bondage of
35. separate us *from* the love of Christ ?
39. able to separate us *from* the love of
9: 3. myself were accursed *from* Christ
11:25. blindness *in* part is happened
26. turn away ungodliness *from* Jacob:
13: 1. For there is no power but *of* God:
15:15. more boldly unto you *in* some sort,
19. so that *from* Jerusalem, and round
23. a great desire these (lit. *from*) many years
24. somewhat (lit. *in* part) filled with your (company).
31. be delivered *from* them that do not
16:17. ye have learned; and avoid (lit. bend *from*) them.
1 Co. 1: 3. Grace (be) unto you, and peace, *from* God
30. who *of* God is made unto us wisdom,
4: 5. shall every man have praise *of* God.
6:19. which ye have *of* God, and ye are
7:10. not the wife depart *from* (her) husband:
27. Art thou loosed *from* a wife? seek
10:14. my dearly beloved, flee *from* idolatry.
11:23. For I have received *of* the Lord that
14:36. came the word of God out *from* you ?
2 Co. 1: 2. Grace (be) to you and peace *from* God our
14. ye have acknowledged us *in* part,
16. to come again *out of* Macedonia unto
2: 3. sorrow (from them) *of* whom I ought
5. he hath not grieved me, but *in* part:
3: 5. to think any thing as *of* ourselves ;
18. into the same image *from* glory to glory, (even) as *by* the Spirit of the Lord.
5: 6. we are absent *from* the Lord:
16. Wherefore hence*forth* know we no
7: 1. cleanse ourselves *from* all filthiness
13. his spirit was refreshed *by* you all.
8:10. also to be forward a year *ago*.
9: 2. that Achaia was ready a year *ago* ;
10: 7. let him *of* himself think this again,

2Co.11: 3. corrupted *from* the simplicity
9. brethren which came *from* Macedonia
12: 8. that it might depart *from* me.
Gal. 1: 1. Paul, an apostle, not *of* men,
3. Grace (be) to you and peace *from* God the
6. so soon removed *from* him that called
2: 6. *of* those who seemed to be somewhat,
12. before that certain came *from* James,
3: 2. This only would I learn *of* you,
4: 24. the one *from* the mount Sinai,
5: 4. Christ is become of no effect (lit. ye cease *from* Christ) unto you,
Eph. 1: 2. Grace (be) to you, and peace, *from* God
3: 9. *from* the beginning of the world
4: 31. evil speaking, be put away *from* you,
6: 23. love with faith, *from* God the Father
Phi. 1: 2. Grace (be) unto you, and peace, *from* God our
5. the gospel *from* the first day until
28. to you of salvation, and that *of* God.
4: 15. when I departed *from* Macedonia,
Col. 1: 2. Grace (be) unto you, and peace, *from* God
6. *since* the day ye heard (of it),
7. As ye also learned *of* Epaphras
9. we also, *since* the day we heard (it),
23. moved away *from* the hope of the
26. been hid *from* ages and *from* generations,
2: 20. with Christ *from* the rudiments
3: 24. that *of* the Lord ye shall receive
1Th. 1: 1. Grace (be) unto you, and peace, *from* God
8. For *from* you sounded out the word
9. how ye turned to God *from* idols
10. which delivered us *from* the wrath to
2: 6. neither *of* you, nor (yet) *of* others, when
17. being taken *from* you for a short
3: 6. Timotheus came *from* you unto us,
4: 3. ye should abstain *from* fornication:
16. shall descend *from* heaven with a
5: 22. Abstain *from* all appearance of evil.
2Th. 1: 2. Grace unto you, and peace, *from* God our
7. shall be revealed *from* heaven with
9. destruction *from* the presence of the Lord, and *from* the glory of his power;
2: 2. That ye be not soon shaken *in* mind,
13. God hath *from* the beginning chosen
3: 2. delivered *from* unreasonable and
3. stablish you, and keep (you) *from* evil.
6. *from* every brother that walketh disorderly,
1Ti. 1: 2. Grace, mercy, (and) peace, *from* God
3: 7. a good report *of* them which are without;
6: 5. *from* such withdraw thyself.
10. they have erred *from* the faith,
2Ti. 1: 2. Grace, mercy, (and) peace, *from* God
3. I serve *from* (my) forefathers with
2: 19. name of Christ depart *from* iniquity.
21. If a man therefore purge himself *from* these,
3: 15. that *from* a child thou hast known
4: 4. turn away (their) ears *from* the truth,
18. deliver me *from* every evil work,
Tit. 1: 4. Grace, mercy, (and) peace, *from* God the
2: 14. might redeem us *from* all iniquity,
Philem. 3. Grace to you, and peace, *from* God our
Heb 3: 12. in departing *from* the living God.
4: 3. finished *from* the foundation of
4. the seventh day *from* all his works.
10. hath ceased *from* his own works, as God (did) *from* his.
5: 7. was heard *in* that he feared;
8. *by* the things which he suffered;
6: 1. of repentance *from* dead works,
7. receiveth blessing *from* God:

Heb 7: 1. returning *from* the slaughter
2. Abraham gave a tenth part *of* all;
13. *of* which no man gave attendance at
26. undefiled, separate *from* sinners,
8: 11. *from* the least to the greatest.
9: 14. purge your conscience *from* dead works
26. *since* the foundation of the world:
10: 22. sprinkled *from* an evil conscience,
11: 12. Therefore sprang there even *of* one,
15. that (country) *from* whence they came
34. *out of* weakness were made strong,
12: 15. lest any man fail *of* the grace of God;
25. away from him that (speaketh) *from* heaven:
13: 24. They *of* Italy salute you.
Jas. 1: 13. tempted, I am tempted *of* God:
17. cometh down *from* the Father of
27. himself unspotted *from* the world.
4: 7. Resist the devil, and he will flee *from* you.
5: 4. which is *of* you kept back by fraud,
19. any of you do err *from* the truth,
1Pet. 1: 12. Holy Ghost sent down *from* heaven;
3: 10. let him refrain his tongue *from* evil,
11. Let him eschew (lit. depart *from*) evil, and do good;
4: 17. must begin *at* the house of God: and if (it) first (begin) *at* us, what shall
2Pet. 3: 4. for since (lit *from* that) the fathers fell asleep,
— *from* the beginning of the creation.
1Joh. 1: 1. which was *from* the beginning,
5. message which we have heard *of* him,
7. his Son cleanseth us *from* all sin.
9. to cleanse us *from* all unrighteousness.
2: 7. which ye had *from* the beginning.
— ye have heard *from* the beginning.
13. (that is) *from* the beginning.
14. him (that is) *from* the beginning.
20. have an unction *from* the Holy One,
24. heard *from* the beginning. If that which ye have heard *from* the beginning
27. which ye have received *of* him
28. ashamed *before* him at his coming.
3: 8. the devil sinneth *from* the
11. that ye heard *from* the beginning,
17. shutteth up his bowels (of compassion) *from*
4: 21. commandment have we *from* him,
5: 21. children, keep yourselves *from* idols.
2Joh. 5. which we had *from* the beginning,
6. ye have heard *from* the beginning,
3Joh. 7. taking nothing *of* the Gentiles.
Jude 14. Enoch also, the seventh *from* Adam,
23. the garment spotted *by* the flesh.
Rev. 1: 4. *from* him which is, and which was,
— *from* the seven spirits which
5. *from* Jesus Christ, (who is) the
— washed us *from* our sins in his
2: 17. I give to eat *of* the hidden manna,
3: 12. down out of heaven *from* my God:
6: 4. to take peace *from* the earth, and
10. avenge our blood *on* them that
16. hide us *from* the face of him
— *from* the wrath of the Lamb:
7: 2. angel ascending *from* the east,
17. wipe away all tears *from* their eyes.
9: 6. death shall flee *from* them.
12: 6. she hath a place prepared *of* God,
14. *from* the face of the serpent.
13: 8. slain *from* the foundation of the
14: 3. which were redeemed *from* the earth.
4. These were redeemed *from* among

Rev.14:20. *by the space of* a thousand (and)
16:12. the way of the kings *of* the east
  17. voice *out of* the temple of heaven, *from*
      the throne,
  18. such as was not since (lit. *from* that) men
      were
17: 8. life *from* the foundation of the world,
18:10. Standing afar *off* for the fear of
  14. lusted after are departed *from* thee,
  — and goodly are departed *from* thee,
  15. *by* her, shall stand afar *off* for the fear
  17. as trade by sea, stood afar *off*,
20: 9. fire came down *from* God out of
  11. *from* whose face the earth and the
21: 2. coming down *from* God out of
  4. wipe away all tears *from* their eyes ;
  10. descending out of heaven *from* God,
  13. *On* the east three gates ; *on* the north
     three gates ; *on* the south three gates ;
     and *on* the west three gates.
22:19. shall take away *from* the words
  — away his part *out of* the book of

ἀποϐαίνω, apobaino.

Lu. 5: 2. the fishermen *were gone out* of them, *and*
21:13. it *shall turn* to you for a testimony.
Joh.21: 9. then as they *were come* to land,
Phi. 1:19. that this *shall turn* to my salvation

ἀποϐάλλω, apoballo.

Mar 10:50. he, *casting away* his garment,
Heb 10:35. *Cast* not *away* therefore your

ἀποϐλέπω, apoblepo.

Heb 11:26. for he *had respect* unto the

ἀπόϐλητος, apobleetos.

1Ti. 4: 4. nothing *to be refused*, if it be received

ἀποϐολή, apobolee.

Acts 27:22. there shall be no *loss* of (any man's) life
Ro. 11:15. For if the *casting away* of them (be)

ἀπογενόμενος, apogenomenos.

1Pet.2:24. that we, *being dead* to sins, should

ἀπογραφή, apographee.

Lu. 2: 2. this *taxing* was first made when
Acts 5:37. in the days of the *taxing*, and drew

ἀπογράφω, apographo.

Lu. 2: 1. that all the world should *be taxed*.
  3. all went *to be taxed*, every one into
  5. *To be taxed* with Mary his espoused
Heb 12:23. firstborn, *which are written* in heaven

ἀποδείκνυμι, apodiknumi.

Acts 2:22. a man *approved* of God among you
  25: 7. against Paul, which they could not *prove*.
1Co. 4: 9. that God hath *set forth* us the apostles
2Th. 2: 4. *shewing* himself that he is God.

ἀπόδειξις, apodixis.

1Co. 2: 4. in *demonstration* of the Spirit and of

ἀποδεκατόω, apodekatoö,

Mat.23:23. for ye *pay tithe* of mint and anise
Lu. 11:42. for ye *tithe* mint and rue and all manner
18:12. I *give tithes* of all that I possess.
Heb. 7: 5. *to take tithes* of the people according

ἀπόδεκτος, apodektos.

1Ti. 2: 3. For this (is) good and *acceptable* in the
  5: 4. good and *acceptable* before God.

ἀποδέχομαι, apodekomai.

Lu. 8:40. the people gladly *received* him:
Acts 2:41. they *that* gladly *received* his word
  15: 4. they *were received* of the church,
  18:27. exhorting the disciples *to receive* him:
  24: 3. We *accept* (it) always, and in all
  28:30. *received* all that came in unto

ἀποδημέω, apodeemeö.

Mat.21:33. *went into a far country:*
  25:14. a man *travelling into a far country*,
    15. ability; and straightway *took his journey*.
Mar 12: 1. husbandmen, and *went into a far country*.
Lu. 15:13. *took* his *journey* into a far country,
  20: 9. *went into a far country* for a long

ἀπόδημος, apodeemos.

Mar 13:34. as a man *taking a far journey*,

ἀποδίδωμι, apodidōmi.

Mat. 5:26. till thou *hast paid* the uttermost
  33. *shalt perform* unto the Lord
  6: 4. himself *shall reward* thee openly.
  6. seeth in secret *shall reward* thee openly.
  18. in secret, *shall reward* thee openly.
  12:36. they *shall give* account thereof
  16:27. then he *shall reward* every man
  18:25. forasmuch as he had not *to pay*,
  — that he had, and *payment to be made*.
  26. with me, and I *will pay* thee all.
  28. saying, *Pay* me that thou owest.
  29. patience with me, and I *will pay* thee all.
  30. till he *should pay* the debt.
  34. till he *should pay* all that was
  20: 8. Call the labourers, and *give* them (their)
    hire,
  21:41. which *shall render* him the
  22:21. *Render* therefore unto Cæsar the

Mat.27:58. commanded the body *to be delivered.*
Mar 12:17. *Render* to Cæsar the things that
Lu. 4:20. he *gave* (it) *again* to the minister, *and*
     7:42. when they had nothing *to pay,*
     9:42. *delivered* him *again* to his father.
    10:35. I come again, I *will repay* thee.
    12:59. till thou *hast paid* the very
    16: 2. *give* an account of thy stewardship ;
    19: 8. accusation, I *restore* (him) fourfold.
    20:25. *Render* therefore unto Cæsar the
Acts 4:33. *gave* the apostles witness of the
     5: 8. whether ye *sold* the land for
     7: 9. with envy, *sold* Joseph into Egypt:
    19:40. we may *give* an account of
Ro. 2: 6. Who *will render* to every man
    12:17. *Recompense* to no man evil
    13: 7. *Render* therefore to all their dues:
1Co. 7: 3. *Let* the husband *render* unto the
1Th. 5:15. See that none *render* evil for evil
1Ti. 5: 4. piety at home, and to requite (lit. *to render*
           recompence *to*) their parents:
2Ti. 4: 8. *shall give* me at that day:
    14. the Lord *reward* him according
Heb 12:11. afterward it *yieldeth* the peaceable
    16. morsel of meat *sold* his birthright.
    13:17. as they *that* must *give* account,
1Pet.3: 9. Not *rendering* evil for evil, or
     4: 5. Who *shall give* account to him
Rev.18: 6. *Reward* her even as she *rewarded*
    22: 2. *yielded* her fruit every month:
    12. *to give* every man according

ἀποδιορίζω, *apodiorizo.*

Jude   19. These be they *who separate* themselves,

ἀποδοκιμάζω, *apodokimazo.*

Mat.21:42. The stone which the builders *rejected,*
Mar. 8:31. *be rejected* of the elders, and (of) the
    12:10. The stone which the builders *rejected*
Lu. 9:22. *be rejected* of the elders and chief
    17:25. *be rejected* of this generation.
    20:17. The stone which the builders *rejected,*
Heb 12:17. inherited the blessing, he *was rejected*:
1Pet.2: 4. *disallowed* indeed of men, but
     7. the stone which the builders *disallowed,*

ἀποδοχή, *apodokee.*

1Ti. 1:15. worthy of all *acceptation,* that
     4: 9. saying and worthy of all *acceptation.*

ἀπόθεσις, *apothesis.*

1Pet.3:21. not the *putting away* of the filth
2Pet.1:14. I must put off (this) my tabernacle, (lit.
           my *putting off* of)

ἀποθήκη, *apotheekee.*

Mat. 3:12. gather his wheat into the *garner ;*
     6:26. do they reap, nor gather into *barns ;*
    13:30. gather the wheat into my *barn.*
Lu. 3:17. gather the wheat into his *garner ;*
    12:18. I will pull down my *barns,*
    24. which neither have storehouse nor *barn ;*

ἀποθησαυρίζω, *apotheesaurizo.*

1Ti. 6:19. *Laying up in store* for themselves

ἀποθλίβω, *apothlibo.*

Lu. 8:45. the multitude throng thee and *press*
          (thee),

ἀποθνήσκω, *apothneesko.*

Mat. 8:32. into the sea, and *perished* in the waters.
     9:24. for the maid *is* not *dead,* but sleepeth.
    22:24. Master, Moses said, If a man *die,*
    27. last of all the woman *died* also.
    26:35. Though I should *die* with thee, yet
Mar. 5:35. which said, Thy daughter *is dead:*
    39. the damsel *is* not *dead,* but sleepeth.
     9:26. that many said, He *is dead.*
    12:19. If a man's brother *die,* and leave (his)
    20. took a wife, and *dying* left no seed.
    21. the second took her, and *died,* neither
    22. last of all the woman *died* also.
    15:44. he asked him whether he *had been* **any**
           while *dead.*
Lu. 8:42. twelve years of age, and she *lay a dying.*
    52. Weep not ; she *is* not *dead,* but sleepeth.
    53. knowing that she *was dead.*
    16:22. it came to pass, that the beggar *died,*
    — the rich man also *died,* and was
    20:28. If any man's brother *die,* having a wife,
           and he *die* without children, that his
    29. took a wife, and *died* without children.
    30. her to wife, and he *died* childless.
    31. they left no children, and *died.*
    32. Last of all the woman *died* also.
    36. Neither can they *die* any more:
Joh. 4:47. for he was at the point *of death.*
    49. Sir, come down ere my child *die.*
     6:49. eat manna in the wilderness, and *are*
           dead.
    50. a man may eat thereof, and not *die.*
    58. fathers did eat manna, and *are dead:*
     8:21. shall seek me, and *shall die* in your
    24. that ye *shall die* in your sins:
    — ye *shall die* in your sins:
    52. Abraham *is dead,* and the prophets;
    53. which *is dead?* and the prophets *are*
           dead:
    11:14. unto them plainly, Lazarus *is dead*
    16. that we *may die* with him.
    25. though he *were dead,* yet shall
    26. believeth in me *shall* never *die.*
    32. been here, my brother *had* not *died.*
    37. this man should not *have died?*
    50. one man *should die* for the people,
    51. that Jesus should *die* for that
    12:24. of wheat fall into the ground and *die,*
           it abideth alone: but if it *die,* it
    33. signifying what death he should *die.*
    18:32. what death he should *die.*
    19: 7. by our law he ought *to die,*
    21:23. that disciple *should* not *die :* yet Jesus
           said not unto him, He *shall* not *die ;*
Acts 7: 4. thence, when his father was *dead,*
     9:37. that she was sick, and *died :*
    21:13. also *to die* at Jerusalem for the
    25:11. worthy of death, I refuse not *to die :*
Ro. 5: 6. in due time Christ *died* for the
     7. for a righteous man *will* one *die :*

Ro. 5: 7. some would even dare *to die.*
8. yet sinners, Christ *died* for us.
15. the offence of one many *be dead,*
6: 2. How shall we, that *are dead* to sin,
7. For he that *is dead* is freed from
8. Now if we *be dead* with Christ,
9. raised from the dead, *dieth* no more ;
10. For in that he *died,* he *died* unto
7: 2. if the husband *be dead,* she is
3. if her husband *be dead,* she is
6. that *being dead* wherein we
9(10)sin revived, and I *died.*
8:13. live after the flesh, ye shall *die:*
34. (It is) Christ *that died,* yea rather,
14: 7. no man *dieth* to himself.
8. whether we *die,* we *die* unto
— live therefore, or *die,* we are the Lord's.
9. to this end Christ both *died,* and rose,
15. thy meat, for whom Christ *died.*
1Co. 8:11. brother perish, for whom Christ *died ?*
9:15. better for me *to die,* than that any
15: 3. how that Christ *died* for our sins
22. For as in Adam all *die,* even so
31. Jesus our Lord, I *die* daily.
32. eat and drink ; for to morrow we *die.*
36. is not quickened, except it *die:*
2Co. 5:14(15). that if one *died* for all, then were all
dead: (lit. *died*)
15. (that) he *died* for all, that they
— unto him *which died* for them,
6: 9. as *dying,* and, behold, we live ;
Gal. 2:19. I through the law am *dead* to
21. then Christ *is dead* in vain.
Phi. 1:21. to live (is) Christ, and *to die* (is) gain.
Col. 2:20. if ye *be dead* with Christ from
3: 3. For ye *are dead,* and your life is hid
1Th. 4:14. that Jesus *died* and rose again, even
5:10. *Who died* for us, that, whether we
Heb. 7: 8. here men *that die* receive tithes ;
9:27. it is appointed unto men once *to die,*
10:28. despised Moses' law *died* without
11: 4. by it he *being dead* yet speaketh.
13. These all *died* in faith, not having
21. Jacob, when he was *a dying,*
37. were slain with (lit. *died by* the death of)
the sword:
Jude 12. without fruit, twice *dead,* plucked
Rev. 3: 2. remain, that are ready *to die:*
8: 9. in the sea, and had life, *died;*
11. many men *died* of the waters,
9: 6. not find it ; and shall desire *to die,*
14:13. Blessed (are) the dead *which die* in the
Lord
16: 3. every living soul *died* in the sea.

ἀποκαθιστ-άω, -άνω, -ημι,
apokathist-ao, -ano, -eemi.

Mat.12:13. it *was restored* whole, like as the other.
17:11. first come, and *restore* all things.
Mar. 3: 5. his hand *was restored* whole as
8:25. he *was restored,* and saw every man
9:12. cometh first, and *restoreth* all things ;
Lu. 6:10. his hand *was restored* whole as the
Acts 1: 6. at this time *restore again* the kingdom
Heb 13:19. that I *may be restored* to you the

ἀποκαλύπτω, apokalupto.

Mat.10:26. that *shall* not *be revealed;* and

Mat.11:25. *hast revealed* them unto babes.
27. to whomsoever the Son will *reveal* (him).
16:17. flesh and blood *hath* not *revealed* (it)
unto
Lu. 2:35. of many hearts may *be revealed.*
10:21. *hast revealed* them unto babes:
22. (he) to whom the Son will *reveal* (him).
12: 2. covered, that *shall* not *be revealed;*
17:30. when the Son of man *is revealed.*
Joh.12:38. arm of the Lord *been revealed ?*
Ro. 1:17. *is* the righteousness of God *revealed* from
18. the wrath of God *is revealed* from
8:18. glory which shall *be revealed* in us.
1Co. 2:10. God *hath revealed* (them) unto us
3:13. because it *shall be revealed* by fire ;
14:30. If (any thing) *be revealed* to another
Gal. 1:16. *To reveal* his son in me, that
3:23. which should afterwards *be revealed.*
Eph.3: 5. as it *is* now *revealed* unto his holy
Phi. 3:15. God *shall reveal* even this unto you.
2Th. 2: 3. that man of sin *be revealed,* the
6. that he *might be revealed* in his
8. then *shall* that Wicked *be revealed,*
1Pet.1: 5. ready *to be revealed* in the last
12. Unto whom it *was revealed,* that
5: 1. the glory that shall *be revealed:*

ἀποκάλυψις, apokalupsis.

Lu. 2:32. A light *to lighten* the Gentiles, and
Ro. 2: 5. *revelation* of the righteous judgment
8:19. *manifestation* of the sons of God.
16:25. according to the *revelation* of the mystery,
1Co. 1: 7. waiting for the *coming* of our Lord
14: 6. speak to you either by *revelation,*
26. hath a tongue, hath a *revelation,*
2Co.12: 1. to visions and *revelations* of the Lord.
7. the abundance of the *revelations,*
Gal. 1:12. by the *revelation* of Jesus Christ.
2: 2. I went up by *revelation,* and
Eph. 1:17. the spirit of wisdom and *revelation*
3: 3. How that by *revelation* he made
2Th. 1: 7. *when* the Lord Jesus *shall be revealed* (lit.
in the *revelation* of &c.) from
1Pet.1: 7. glory at the *appearing* of Jesus
13. at the *revelation* of Jesus Christ ;
4:13. *when* his glory *shall be revealed,*
Rev. 1: 1. The *Revelation* of Jesus Christ,

ἀποκαραδοκία, apokaradokia.

Ro. 8:19. the *earnest expectation* of the
Phi. 1:20. According to my *earnest expectation*

ἀποκαταλλάττω, apokatallatto.

Eph.2:16. that he *might reconcile* both unto
Col. 1:20. by him *to reconcile* all things unto
21. yet now *hath* he *reconciled*

ἀποκατάστασις, apokatastasis.

Acts 3:21. the times of *restitution* of all things,

ἀπόκειμαι, apokīmai.

Lu. 19:20. which I have kept *laid up* in

Col. 1: 5. the hope *which is laid up* for you
2Ti. 4: 8. there *is laid up* for me a crown of
Heb. 9:27. as it *is appointed* unto men

ἀποκεφαλίζω, *apokephalizo.*

Mat.14:10. he sent, and *beheaded* John in
Mar. 6:16. It is John, whom I *beheaded :*
     27(28). he went and *beheaded* him in the
Lu. 9: 9. Herod said, John *have* I *beheaded :*

ἀποκλείω, *apoklio.*

Lu. 13:25. is risen up, and *hath shut to* the door,

ἀποκόπτω, *apokopto.*

Mar. 9:43. if thy hand offend thee, *cut it off :*
     45. if thy foot offend thee, *cut it off :*
Joh. 18:10. priest's servant, and *cut off* his right ear.
     26. (his) kinsman whose ear Peter *cut off,*
Acts27:32. the soldiers *cut off* the ropes of
Gal. 5:12. I would they were even *cut off*

ἀπόκριμα, *apokrima.*

2Co. 1: 9. we had the *sentence* of death in

ἀποκρίνομαι, *apokrinomai.*

Mat. 3:15. Jesus *answering* said unto him,
   4: 4. he *answered and* said, It is written,
   8: 8. The centurion *answered and* said,
  11: 4. Jesus *answered and* said unto them,
     25. At that time Jesus *answered and*
  12:38. scribes and of the Pharisees *answered,*
     39. he *answered and* said unto them,
     48. he *answered and* said unto him
  13:11. He *answered and* said unto them,
     37. He *answered and* said unto them,
  14:28. Peter *answered* him *and* said, Lord,
  15: 3. he *answered and* said unto them,
     13. he *answered and* said, Every plant,
     15. Then *answered* Peter *and* said unto
     23. he *answered* her not a word.
     24. he *answered and* said, I am not sent
     26. he *answered and* said, It is not meet
     28. Then Jesus *answered and* said unto her,
  16: 2. He *answered and* said unto them,
     16. Simon Peter *answered and* said,
     17. Jesus *answered and* said unto him,
  17: 4. Then *answered* Peter, *and* said unto
     11. Jesus *answered and* said unto them,
     17. Then Jesus *answered and* said,
  19: 4. he *answered and* said unto them,
     27. Then *answered* Peter *and* said unto
  20:13. he *answered* one of them, *and* said,
     22. Jesus *answered and* said, Ye know
  21:21. Jesus *answered and* said unto them,
     24. Jesus *answered and* said unto them,
     27. they *answered* Jesus, *and* said,
     29. He *answered and* said, I will not:
     30. he *answered and* said, I (go), sir:
  22: 1. Jesus *answered and* spake unto
     29. Jesus *answered and* said unto them,
     46. no man was able *to answer* him
  24: 4. Jesus **answered and** said unto them,

Mat.25: 9. the **wise** *answered,* saying, (Not so) ;
     12. he *answered and* said, Verily I say
     26. His lord *answered and* said unto
     37. Then *shall* the righteous *answer* him,
     40. the King shall *answer and* say unto
     44. Then *shall* they also *answer* him,
     45. Then *shall* he *answer* them,
  26:23. he *answered and* said, He that
     25. which betrayed him, *answered and* said,
     33. Peter *answered and* said unto him,
     62. unto him, *Answerest thou* nothing ?
     63. the high priest *answered and* said
     66. They *answered and* said, He is guilty
  27:12. priests and elders, he *answered* **nothing**
     14. he *answered* him to never a
     21. The governor *answered and* said
     25. Then *answered* all the people, *and*
  28: 5. the angel *answered and* said
Mar. 3:33. he *answered* them, saying,
   5: 9. he *answered,* saying, My name
   6:37. He *answered and* said unto them,
   7: 6. He *answered and* said unto them,
     28. she *answered and* said unto him,
   8: 4. his disciples *answered* him,
     28. they *answered,* John the Baptist:
     29. Peter *answereth and* saith unto him,
   9: 5. Peter *answered and* said to Jesus,
     12. he *answered and* told them, Elias
     17. one of the multitude *answered and*
     19. He *answereth* him, *and* saith,
     38. John *answered* him, saying,
  10: 3. he *answered and* said unto them,
     5. Jesus *answered and* said unto
     20. he *answered and* said unto him,
     24. Jesus *answereth* again, *and* saith
     29. Jesus *answered and* said, Verily
     51. Jesus *answered and* said unto him,
  11:14. Jesus *answered and* said unto it,
     22. Jesus *answering* saith unto
     29. Jesus *answered and* said unto
     — ask of you one question, and *answer* me,
     30. from heaven, or of men ? *answer* me.
     33. they *answered and* said unto Jesus,
     — Jesus *answering* saith unto
  12:17. Jesus *answering* said unto them,
     24. Jesus *answering* said unto
     28. that he *had answered* them well,
     29. Jesus *answered* him, The first
     34. saw that he *answered* discreetly,
     35. Jesus *answered and* said, while
  13: 2. Jesus *answering* said unto him,
     5. Jesus *answering* them began
  14:20. he *answered and* said unto them,
     40. wist they what to *answer* him.
     48. Jesus *answered and* said unto
     60. saying, *Answerest thou* nothing ?
     61. held his peace, and *answered* nothing.
  15: 2. he *answering* said unto him,
     4. saying, *Answerest thou* nothing ?
     5. Jesus yet *answered* nothing ;
     9. Pilate *answered* them, saying,
     12. Pilate *answered and* said again
Lu.   1:19. the angel *answering* said unto
     35. the angel *answered and* said unto
     60. his mother *answered and* said,
   3:11. He *answereth and* saith unto them,
     16. John *answered,* saying unto (them)
   4: 4. Jesus *answered* him, saying,
     8. Jesus *answered and* said unto him,
     12. Jesus *answering* said unto him,
   5: 5. Simon *answering* said unto him,
     22. he *answering* said unto them,

Lu. 5:31. Jesus *answering* said unto them,
6: 3. Jesus *answering* them said,
7:22. Then Jesus *answering* said unto
40. Jesus *answering* said unto him,
43. Simon *answered* and said, I, suppose
8:21. he *answered and* said unto them,
50. he *answered* him, saying, Fear not:
9:19. They *answering* said, John the
20. Peter *answering* said, The Christ
41. Jesus *answering* said, O faithless
49. John *answered* and said, Master,
10:27. he *answering* said, Thou shalt
28. unto him, Thou *hast answered* right:
41. Jesus *answered* and said unto her,
11: 7. from within shall *answer and* say,
45. Then *answered* one of the lawyers, *and*
13: 2. Jesus *answering* said unto them
8. he *answering* said unto him,
14. the ruler of the synagogue *answered...and*
15. The Lord then *answered* him,
25. he shall *answer and* say unto you,
14: 3. Jesus *answering* spake unto the
5. *answered* them, saying, Which
15:29. he *answering* said to (his) father,
17:17. Jesus *answering* said, Were there
20. he *answered* them and said,
37. they *answered and* said unto him,
19:40. he *answered and* said unto them,
20: 3. he *answered and* said unto them,
7. they *answered*, that they could
24. They *answered and* said, Cæsar's.
34. Jesus *answering* said unto them,
39. certain of the scribes *answering*
22:51. Jesus *answered* and said, Suffer
68. ye *will* not *answer* me, nor let
23: 3. he *answered* him *and* said,
9. he *answered* him nothing.
40. the other *answering* rebuked him,
24:18. Cleopas, *answering* said unto him,
Joh. 1:21. Art thou that prophet ? And he *answered*, No.
26. John *answered* them, saying,
48(49) Jesus *answered* and said unto him,
49(50) Nathanael *answered* and saith
50(51) Jesus *answered* and said unto
2:18. Then *answered* the Jews and said
19. Jesus *answered* and said unto them,
3: 3. Jesus *answered* and said unto him,
5. Jesus *answered*, Verily, verily,
9. Nicodemus *answered* and said
10. Jesus *answered* and said unto
27. John *answered* and said, A man
4:10. Jesus *answered* and said unto her,
13. Jesus *answered* and said unto her,
17. The woman *answered* and said,
5: 7. The impotent man *answered*
11. He *answered* them, He that
17. Jesus *answered* them, My Father
19. Then *answered* Jesus and said
6: 7. Philip *answered* him, Two
26. Jesus *answered* them and said,
29. Jesus *answered* and said unto them,
43. Jesus therefore *answered* and said
68. Then Simon Peter *answered* him,
70. Jesus *answered* them, Have not
7:16. Jesus *answered* them, and said,
20. The people *answered* and said,
21. Jesus *answered* and said unto them,
46. The officers *answered*, Never man
47. Then *answered* them the Pharisees,
52. They *answered* and said unto him,
8:14. Jesus *answered* and said unto him,
19. Jesus *answered*, Ye neither know

Joh. 8:33. They *answered* him, We be Abraham's
34. Jesus *answered* them, Verily,
39. They *answered* and said unto him,
48. Then *answered* the Jews, and said
49. Jesus *answered*, I have not a devil ;
54. Jesus *answered*, If I honour
9: 3. Jesus *answered*, Neither hath this
11. He *answered* and said, A man that
20. His parents *answered* them
25. He *answered* and said, Whether he
27. He *answered* them, I have told
30. The man *answered* and said unto
34. They *answered* and said unto him,
36. He *answered* and said, Who is he,
10:25. Jesus *answered* them, I told you,
32. Jesus *answered* them, Many
33. The Jews *answered* him, saying,
34. Jesus *answered* them, Is it not
11: 9. Jesus *answered*, Are there not
12:23. Jesus *answered* them, saying,
30. Jesus *answered* and said, This voice
34. The people *answered* him,
13: 7. Jesus *answered* and said unto him,
8. Jesus *answered* him, If I wash
26. Jesus *answered*, He it is, to whom
36. Jesus *answered* him, Whither
38. Jesus *answered* him, Wilt thou
14:23. Jesus *answered* and said unto him,
16:31. Jesus *answered* them, Do ye now
18: 5. They *answered* him, Jesus of Nazareth.
8. Jesus *answered*, I have told you
20. Jesus *answered* him, I spake
22. *Answerest* thou the high priest so?
23. Jesus *answered* him, If I have
30. They *answered* and said unto him,
34. Jesus *answered* him, Sayest
35. Pilate *answered*, Am I a Jew ?
36. Jesus *answered*, My kingdom
37. Jesus *answered*, Thou sayest
19: 7. The Jews *answered* him, We have
11. Jesus *answered*, Thou couldest
15. The chief priests *answered*, We
22. Pilate *answered*, What I have
20:28. Thomas *answered* and said unto
21: 5. They *answered* him, No.
Acts 3:12. he *answered* unto the people,
4:19. Peter and John *answered and* said unto
5: 8. Peter *answered* unto her, Tell me
29. Peter and the (other) apostles *answered and*
8:24. Then *answered* Simon, *and* said,
34. the eunuch *answered* Philip, *and*
37. he *answered and* said, I believe
9:13. Then Ananias *answered*, Lord,
10:46. magnify God. Then *answered* Peter,
11: 9. the voice *answered* me again
15:13. James *answered*, saying, Men
19:15. the evil spirit *answered and* said,
21:13. Then Paul *answered*, What mean
22: 8. I *answered*, Who art thou, Lord?
28. the chief captain *answered*, With
24:10. *answered*, Forasmuch as I know
25. Felix trembled, and *answered*,
25: 4. Festus *answered*, that Paul
9. *answered* Paul, *and* said, Wilt thou
12. *answered*, Hast thou appealed
16. To whom I *answered*, It is not
Col. 4: 6. how ye ought *to answer* every
Rev. 7:13. one of the elders *answered*, saying

ἀπόκρισις, *apokrisis.*

Lu. 2:47. at his understanding and *answers.*
20:26. they marvelled at his *answer*,

Joh. 1:22. that we may give an *answer*
19: 9. Jesus gave him no *answer*.

ἀποκρύπτω, apokrupto.

Mat. 11:25. because thou *hast hid* these things
25:18. in the earth, and *hid* his lord's money
Lu. 10:21. that thou *hast hid* these things
1Co. 2: 7. (even) the *hidden* (wisdom), which
Eph. 3: 9. *hath been hid* in God, who
Col. 1:26. which *hath been hid* from ages

ἀπόκρυφος, apokruphos.

Mar. 4:22. neither was any thing **kept** *secret*,
Lu. 8:17. neither (any thing) *hid*, that shall
Col. 2: 3. In whom are *hid* all the treasures

ἀποκτείνω, apoktino.

Mat. 10:28. fear not them *which kill* the body, but are
  not able *to kill* the soul:
14: 5. he would *have put* him *to death*,
16:21. *be killed*, and be raised again the
17:23. they *shall kill* him, and the third
21:35. beat one, and *killed* another, and stoned
38. come, *let* us *kill* him, and let us
39. out of the vineyard, and *slew* (him).
22: 6. entreated (them) spitefully, and *slew*
  (them).
23:34. (some) of them ye *shall kill* and crucify ;
37. (thou) *that killest* the prophets, and
24: 9. to be afflicted, and *shall kill* you:
26: 4. take Jesus by subtilty, and *kill* (him)
Mar. 3: 4. to save life, or *to kill?* But they
6:19. would *have killed* him ; but
8:31. chief priests, and scribes, and *be killed*,
9:31. they *shall kill* him ; and *after that* he *is killed*,
10:34. spit upon him, and *shall kill* him:
12: 5. him they *killed*, and many others ; beating
  some, and *killing* some.
7. come, *let* us *kill* him, and
8. they took him, and *killed* (him),
14: 1. by craft, and *put* (him) *to death*.
Lu. 9:22. *be slain*, and be raised the third
11:47. prophets, and your fathers *killed* them.
48. for they indeed *killed* them, and
49. (some) of them they *shall slay* and
12: 4. afraid of them *that kill* the body,
5. after he *hath killed* hath power
13: 4. fell, and *slew* them, think ye that
31. for Herod will *kill* thee.
34. Jerusalem, *which killest* the prophets,
18:33. scourge (him), and *put* him *to death*:
20:14. come, *let* us *kill* him, that the
15. out of the vineyard, and *killed* (him).
Joh. 5:16. persecute Jesus, and sought *to slay* him,
18. sought the more *to kill* him,
7: 1. the Jews sought *to kill* him.
19. Why go ye about *to kill* me ?
20. who goeth about *to kill* thee ?
25. he, whom they seek *to kill?*
8:22. *Will* he *kill* himself? because
37. ye seek *to kill* me, because
40. now ye seek *to kill* me, a man
11:53. together for *to put* him *to death*.
12:10. *might put* Lazarus also *to death*;
16: 2. that whosoever *killeth* you will

Joh. 18:31. for us *to put* any man *to death*:
Acts 3:15. and *killed* the Prince of life, whom
7:52. they *have slain* them which
21:31. they went about *to kill* him,
23:12. till they *had killed* Paul.
14. nothing until we *have slain* Paul.
27:42. counsel was to *kill* the prisoners,
Ro. 7:11. deceived me, and by it *slew* (me).
11: 3. Lord, they *have killed* thy prophets,
2Co. 3: 6. for the letter *killeth*, but the spirit
Eph. 2:16. *having slain* the enmity thereby:
1Th. 2:15. *Who* both *killed* the Lord Jesus,
Rev. 2:13. who *was slain* among you,
23. I *will kill* her children with
6: 8. *to kill* with sword, and with hunger,
11. that should *be killed* as they
9: 5. that they *should* not *kill* them,
15. for to *slay* the third part of men.
18. *was* the third part of men *killed*,
20. men which *were* not *killed* by these
11: 5. he must in this manner *be killed*.
7. shall overcome them, and *kill* them
13. *were slain* of men seven thousand:
13:10. he that *killeth* with the sword must *be killed*
  with the sword.
15. image of the beast *should be killed*.
19:21. the remnant *were slain* with

ἀποκυέω, apokueo.

Jas. 1:15. is finished, *bringeth forth* death.
18. Of his own will *begat* he us with

ἀποκυλίζω, apokulizo.

Mat. 28: 2. came and *rolled back* the stone
Mar 16: 3. Who *shall roll* us *away* the stone
4. that the stone *was rolled away*:
Lu. 24: 2. found the stone *rolled away* from

ἀπολαμβάνω, apolambano.

Mar. 7:33. *took* him aside from the multitude, *and*
Lu. 6:34. of whom ye hope *to receive*, what
— lend to sinners, *to receive* as much
15:27. because he *hath received* him
16:25. in thy lifetime *receivedst* thy
18:30. Who *shall* not *receive* manifold
23:41. for we *receive* the due reward
Ro. 1:27. *receiving* in themselves that
Gal. 4: 5. that we *might receive* the
Col. 3:24. ye *shall receive* the reward of the
2Joh. 8. that *we receive* a full reward.
3Joh. 8. We therefore ought *to receive* such,

ἀπόλαυσις, apolausis.

1Ti. 6:17. to us richly all things to enjoy; (lit. for
  enjoyment)
Heb 11:25. than *to enjoy* the pleasures of sin

ἀπολείπω, apolipo.

2Ti. 4:13. The cloke that I *left* at Troas with
20. Trophimus *have* I *left* at Miletum
Heb. 4: 6. Seeing therefore it *remaineth* that
9. There *remaineth* therefore a rest to
10:26. there *remaineth* no more sacrifice
Jude 6. but *left* their own habitation, he hath

ἀπολείχω, apoliko.

Lu. 16:21. the dogs came and *licked* his sores.

ἀπόλλυμι, apollumi.

Mat. 2:13. the young child *to destroy* him.
　5:29. one of thy members *should perish*,
　30. one of thy members *should perish*,
　8:25. Lord, save us: *we perish*.
　9:17. wine runneth out, and the bottles *perish*:
　10: 6. go rather to the *lost* sheep of the house
　28. able *to destroy* both soul and body in hell.
　39. that findeth his life *shall lose* it: and he
　　　that loseth his life for my sake
　42. *shall* in no wise *lose* his reward.
　12:14. how they *might destroy* him.
　15:24. unto the *lost* sheep of the house
　16:25. will save his life *shall lose* it: and whoso-
　　　ever *will lose* his life
　18:11. come to save that *which was lost*.
　14. of these little ones *should perish*.
　21:41. *will* miserably *destroy* those wicked
　22: 7. *destroyed* those murderers, and
　26:52. *shall perish* with the sword.
　27:20. ask Barabbas, and *destroy* Jesus.
Mar. 1:24. art thou come *to destroy* us?
　2:22. the bottles *will be marred*:
　3: 6. how they *might destroy* him.
　4:38. carest thou not that we *perish*?
　8:35. will save his life *shall lose* it; but whoso-
　　　ever *shall lose* his life
　9:22. into the waters, to *destroy* him:
　41. he *shall* not *lose* his reward.
　11:18. how they *might destroy* him:
　12: 9. will come and *destroy* the husbandmen,
Lu. 4:34. art thou come *to destroy* us?
　5:37. spilled, and the bottles *shall perish*.
　6: 9. to save life, or *to destroy* (it)?
　8:24. saying, Master, master, we *perish*.
　9:24. will save his life *shall lose* it: but whoso-
　　　ever *will lose* his life for my
　25. *and lose* himself, or be cast away
　56. not come *to destroy* men's lives,
　11:51. *which perished* between the altar
　13: 3. ye *shall* all likewise *perish*.
　5. ye *shall* all likewise *perish*.
　33. that a prophet *perish* out of Jerusalem.
　15: 4. *if he lose* one of them, doth not
　　 — go after that *which is lost*, until
　6. found my sheep *which was lost*.
　8. if she *lose* one piece, doth not
　9. found the piece which I *had lost*.
　17. to spare, and I *perish* with hunger!
　24. he was *lost*, and is found.
　32. and was *lost*, and is found.
　17:27. flood came, and *destroyed* them all.
　29. from heaven, and *destroyed* (them) all.
　33. to save his life *shall lose* it; and whosoever
　　　shall lose his life
　19:10. to save that *which was lost*.
　47. people sought *to destroy* him,
　20:16. come and *destroy* these husbandmen,
　21:18. not an hair of your head *perish*.
Joh. 3:15. believeth in him *should* not *perish*,
　16. believeth in him *should* not *perish*,
　6:12. that remain, that nothing *be lost*.
　27. for the meat *which perisheth*,
　39. given me I *should lose* nothing,
　10:10. for to steal, and to kill, and to *destroy*:
　28. they *shall* never *perish*, neither

Joh. 11:50. that the whole nation *perish* not.
　12:25. that loveth his life *shall lose* it;
　17:12. I have kept, and none of them *is lost*,
　18: 9. thou gavest me have I *lost* none.
　14. one man should *die* for the people.
Acts 5:37. he also *perished*; and all, (even) as
Ro. 2:12. *shall* also *perish* without law:
　14:15. *Destroy* not him with thy meat,
1Co. 1:18. to them *that perish* foolishness;
　19. I *will destroy* the wisdom of the
　8:11. *shall* the weak brother *perish*,
　10: 9. tempted, and *were destroyed* of serpents.
　10. *were destroyed* of the destroyer.
　15:18. fallen asleep in Christ *are perished*.
2Co. 2:15. are saved, and in them *that perish*:
　4: 3. it is hid to them *that are lost*:
　9. cast down, but not *destroyed*;
2Th. 2:10. unrighteousness in them *that perish*;
Heb. 1:11. They *shall perish*; but thou remainest;
Jas. 1:11. grace of the fashion of it *perisheth*:
　4:12. is able to save and *to destroy*:
1Pet. 1: 7. precious than of gold *that perisheth*,
2Pet. 3: 6. being overflowed with water, *perished*:
　9. not willing that any should *perish*,
2Joh. 8. that we *lose* not those things
Jude 5. afterward *destroyed* them that
　11. *perished* in the gainsaying of Core.

ἀπολογέομαι, apologeomai.

Lu. 12:11. how or what thing ye *shall answer*,
　21:14. meditate before what ye shall *answer*:
Acts 19:33. would *have made* his *defence* unto
　24:10. more cheerfully *answer* for myself
　25: 8. *While* he *answered* for him*self*,
　26: 1. the hand, and *answered* for himself:
　2. I shall *answer* for myself this
　24. *as* he thus *spake* for himself,
Ro. 2:15. accusing or else *excusing* one another
2Co. 12:19. that we *excuse* ourselves unto you?

ἀπολογία, apologia.

Acts 22: 1. hear ye my *defence*, (which I make)
　25:16. have licence *to answer* for himself
1Co. 9: 3. Mine *answer* to them that
2Co. 7:11. yea, (what) *clearing of* yourselves,
Phi. 1: 7. in the *defence* and confirmation
　17. for the *defence* of the gospel.
2Ti. 4:16. At my first *answer* no man
1Pet. 3:15. to (give) an *answer* to every

ἀπολούω, apolouō.

Acts 22:16. be baptized, and *wash away* thy sins,
1Co. 6:11. ye *are washed*, but ye are sanctified,

ἀπολύτρωσις, apolutrōsis.

Lu. 21:28. for your *redemption* draweth nigh.
Ro. 3:24. through the *redemption* that is in
　8:23. the *redemption* of our body.
1Co. 1:30. sanctification, and *redemption*:
Eph. 1: 7. In whom we have *redemption*
　14. until the *redemption* of the
　4:30. unto the day of *redemption*.
Col. 1:14. In whom we have *redemption*

Heb. 9:15. for the *redemption* of the transgressions
11:35. tortured, not accepting *deliverance;*

ἀπολύω, apoluo.

Mat. 1:19. was minded *to put* her *away* privily.
5:31. Whosoever *shall put away* his wife,
32. whosoever *shall put away* his wife,
— shall marry her *that is divorced*
14:15. *send* the multitude *away,* that
22. while he *sent* the multitudes *away.*
23. *when* he *had sent* the multitudes *away,*
15:23. saying, Send her *away;* for she
32. I will not *send* them *away* fasting,
39. he *sent away* the multitude, *and*
18:27. *loosed* him, and forgave him the
19: 3. for a man *to put away* his wife
7. divorcement, and *to put* her *away?*
8. you *to put away* your wives:
'9. Whosoever *shall put away* his wife,
— marrieth her *which is put away*
27:15. was wont *to release* unto the people
17. Whom will ye that I *release* unto you?
21. will ye that I *release* unto you?
26. Then *released* he Barabbas unto
Mar. 6:36. Send them *away,* that they may
45. while he *sent away* the people.
8: 3. if I *send* them *away* fasting
9. he *sent* them *away.*
10: 2. for a man *to put away* (his) wife?
4. divorcement, and *to put* (her) *away.*
11. Whosoever *shall put away* his wife,
12. if a woman *shall put away* her
15: 6. he *released* unto them one prisoner,
9. Will ye that I *release* unto you
11. he *should* rather *release* Barabbas
15. *released* Barabbas unto them,
Lu. 2:29. *lettest* thou thy servant *depart* in
6:37. *forgive,* and ye shall be *forgiven:*
8:38. Jesus *sent* him *away,* saying,
9:12. *Send* the multitude *away,* that
13:12. thou *art loosed* from thine infirmity.
14: 4. healed him, and *let* him *go;*
16:18. Whosoever *putteth away* his wife,
— marrieth her *that is put away* from
22:68. ye will not answer me, nor *let* (me) *go.*
23:16. therefore chastise him, and *release* (him).
17. he must *release* one unto them
18. *release* unto us Barabbas:
20. therefore, willing *to release* Jesus,
22. chastise him, and *let* (him) *go.*
25. he *released* unto them him
Joh. 18:39. that I *should release* unto you
— that I *release* unto you the King
19:10. have power *to release* thee?
12. Pilate sought *to release* him:
— If thou *let* this man *go,* thou art
Acts 3:13. determined *to let* (him) *go.*
4:21. they *let* them *go,* finding nothing
23. *being let go,* they went to their
5:40. the name of Jesus, and *let* them *go.*
13: 3. on them, they *sent* (them) *away.*
15:30. *when* they *were dismissed,* they
33. they *were let go* in peace from
16:35. saying, Let those men *go.*
36. have sent *to let* you *go:* now
17: 9. of the other, they *let* them *go.*
19:41. thus spoken, he *dismissed* the assembly.
23:22. *let* the young man *depart,* and
26:32. might *have been set at liberty,*
28:18. would *have let* (me) *go,* because

Acts 28:25. among themselves, they *departed,*
Heb 13:23. brother Timothy *is set at liberty;*

ἀπομάσσομαι, apomassomai.

Lu. 10:11. we *do wipe off* against you:

ἀπονέμω, aponemo.

1Pet. 3: 7. *giving* honour unto the wife, as

ἀπονίπτω, aponipto.

Mat. 27:24. *washed* (his) hands before the

ἀποπίπτω, apopipto.

Acts 9:18. there *fell from* his eyes as it had

ἀποπλανάω, apoplanao.

Mar 13:22. *to seduce,* if (it were) possible,
1Ti. 6:10. they *have erred* from the faith,

ἀποπλέω, apopleo.

Acts 13: 4. from thence they *sailed* to Cyprus.
14:26. thence *sailed* to Antioch, from
20:15. we *sailed* thence, *and* came the
27: 1. that we should *sail* into Italy,

ἀποπλύνω, apopluno.

Lu. 5: 2. *were washing* (their) nets.

ἀποπνίγω, apopnigo.

Mat. 13: 7. the thorns sprung up, and *choked* them:
Lu. 8:33. place into the lake, and *were choked.*

ἀπορέομαι, aporeomai.

Joh. 13:22. another, *doubting* of whom he spake.
Acts 25:20. because I *doubted* of such manner
2Co. 4: 8. (we are) *perplexed,* but not in despair;
Gal. 4:20. for I *stand in doubt* of you.

ἀπορία, aporia.

Lu. 21:25. distress of nations, with *perplexity;*

ἀπορρίπτω, aporipto.

Acts 27:43. should *cast* (themselves) first

ἀπορφανίζομαι, aporphanizomai.

1Th. 2:17. *being taken* from you for a short

ἀποσκευάζομαι, aposkŭazomai.

Acts21:15. we *took up our carriages* (lit. *made* ourselves
　　　　ready), *and* went up

ἀποσκίασμα, aposkiasma.

Jas. 1:17. variableness, neither *shadow* of turning.

ἀποσπάω, apospao.

Mat.26:51. *drew* his sword, and struck a servant
Lu. 22:41. he *was withdrawn* from them
Acts20:30. *to draw away* disciples after them.
　　21: 1. *after* we *were gotten* from them,

ἀποστασία, apostasia.

Acts21:21. among the Gentiles *to forsake* Moses,
2Th. 2: 3. except there come a *falling away* first,

ἀποστάσιον, apostasion.

Mat. 5:31. give her a *writing of divorcement* :
　　19: 7. to give a writing of *divorcement*,
Mar10: 4. to write a bill of *divorcement*, and

ἀποστεγάζω, apostegazo.

Mar 2: 4. they *uncovered* the roof where

ἀποστέλλω, apostello.

Mat. 2:16. *sent forth, and* slew all the children
　　10: 5. These twelve Jesus *sent forth*,
　　16. I *send* you *forth* as sheep in the
　　40. receiveth him *that sent* me.
　　11:10. I *send* my messenger before thy
　　13:41. The Son of man *shall send forth*
　　14:35. they *sent out* into all the country
　　15:24. I *am* not *sent* but unto the
　　20: 2. he *sent* them into his vineyard.
　　21: 1. then *sent* Jesus two disciples,
　　3. straightway he *will send* them.
　　34. he *sent* his servants to the
　　36. he *sent* other servants more
　　37. last of all he *sent* unto them
　　22: 3. *sent forth* his servants to call
　　4. Again, he *sent forth* other servants,
　　16. they *sent out* unto him their
　　23:34. I *send* unto you prophets, and wise
　　37. stonest them *which are sent* unto
　　24:31. he *shall send* his angels with
　　27:19. his wife *sent* unto him, saying,
Mar 1: 2. I *send* my messenger before thy
　　3:14. that he *might send them forth*
　　31. standing without, *sent* unto him,
　　4:29. immediately he *putteth* in the sickle,
　　5:10. that he *would* not *send* them away
　　6: 7. began *to send* them *forth* by two and two ;
　　17. *had sent forth* and laid hold upon
　　27. the king *sent* an executioner, *and*
　　8:26. he *sent* him *away* to his house,
　　9:37. not me, but him *that sent* me.
　　11: 1. he *sendeth forth* two of his disciples,
　　3. straightway he *will send* him

Mar12: 2. he *sent* to the husbandmen a
　　3. beat him, and *sent* (him) *away* empty.
　　4. he *sent* unto them another
　　— *sent* (him) *away* shamefully
　　5. again he *sent* another; and
　　6. he *sent* him also last unto them,
　　13. they *send* unto him certain
　　13:27. then *shall* he *send* his angels,
　　14:13. he *sendeth forth* two of his disciples,
Lu. 1:19. *am sent* to speak unto thee,
　　26. the angel Gabriel *was sent* from
　　4:18. he *hath sent* me to heal the
　　— *to set* at liberty them that are
　　43. for therefore *am* I *sent*.
　　7: 3. he *sent* unto him the elders of
　　20. John Baptist *hath sent* us unto
　　27. I *send* my messenger before thy
　　9: 2. he *sent* them to preach the
　　48. receiveth him *that sent* me:
　　52. *sent* messengers before his face:
　　10: 1. *sent* them two and two before
　　3. I *send* you *forth* as lambs among
　　16. despiseth him *that sent* me.
　　11:49. I *will send* them prophets and
　　13:34. stonest them *that are sent* unto
　　14:17. *sent* his servant at supper time
　　32. he *sendeth* an ambassage, *and*
　　19:14. *sent* a message after him, saying,
　　29. he *sent* two of his disciples,
　　32. they *that were sent* went their
　　20:10. he *sent* a servant to the husbandmen,
　　20. *sent forth* spies, which should
　　22: 8. he *sent* Peter and John, saying, Go
　　35. When I *sent* you without purse,
　　24:49. I *send* the promise of my Father
Joh. 1: 6. There was a man *sent* from God,
　　19. when the Jews *sent* priests and
　　24. they *which were sent* were of the
　　3:17. For God *sent* not his Son into the
　　28. that I am *sent* before him.
　　34. he whom God *hath sent* speaketh
　　4:38. I *sent* you to reap that whereon
　　5:33. Ye *sent* unto John, and he bare witness
　　36. that the Father *hath sent* me.
　　38. for whom he *hath sent*, him
　　6:29. on him whom he *hath sent*.
　　57. As the living Father *hath sent* me,
　　7:29. from him, and he *hath sent* me.
　　32. chief priests *sent* officers to take
　　8:42. came I of myself, but he *sent* me.
　　9: 7. which is by interpretation, *Sent*.
　　10:36. sanctified, and *sent* into the world,
　　11: 3. Therefore his sisters *sent* unto him,
　　42. believe that thou *hast sent* me.
　　17: 3. Jesus Christ, whom thou *hast sent*.
　　8. that thou *didst send* me.
　　18. As thou *hast sent* me into the world, even
　　　　so *have* I also *sent* them into
　　21. believe that thou *hast sent* me.
　　23. know that thou *hast sent* me,
　　25. have known that thou *hast sent* me.
　　18:24. Now Annas *had sent* him bound
　　20:21. as (my) Father *hath sent* me, even
Acts 3:20. he *shall send* Jesus Christ, which
　　26. *sent* him to bless you, in turning
　　5:21. *sent* to the prison to have them
　　7:14. Then *sent* Joseph, *and* called his
　　34. I *will send* thee into Egypt.
　　35. the same *did* God *send* (to be)
　　8:14. they *sent* unto them Peter and John:
　　9:17. *hath sent* me, that thou mightest
　　38. they *sent* unto him two men,

Acts10: 8. he *sent* them to Joppa.
　　17. the men *which were sent* from
　　20. for I *have sent* them.
　　21. to the men *which were sent* unto
　　36. The word which (God) *sent* unto
　11:11. *sent* from Cæsarea unto me.
　　13. *Send* men to Joppa, and call for
　　30. *and sent* it to the elders by the hands
　13:15. rulers of the synagogue *sent* unto
　　26. the word of this salvation *sent*.
　15:27. We *have sent* therefore Judas
　16:35. the magistrates *sent* the serjeants,
　　36. The magistrates *have sent* to let
　19:22. *So* he *sent* into Macedonia two
　26:17. unto whom now I *send* thee,
　28:28. salvation of God *is sent* unto the
Ro. 10:15. preach, except they *be sent?*
1Co. 1:17. For Christ *sent* me not to baptize,
2Co.12:17. of them whom I *sent* unto you?
2Ti. 4:12. Tychicus *have* I *sent* to Ephesus.
Heb 1:14. *sent forth* to minister for them
1Pet. 1:12. Holy Ghost *sent* down from heaven;
1Joh.4: 9. God *sent* his only begotten Son
　　10. he loved us, and *sent* his Son (to be)
　　14. that the Father *sent* the Son
Rev. 1: 1. he *sent and* signified (it) by his
　5: 6. *sent forth* into all the earth.
　22: 6. *sent* his angel to shew unto

ἀποστερέω, apostereo.

Mar 10:19. *Defraud* not, Honour thy father
1Co. 6: 7. rather (suffer yourselves to) *be defrauded?*
　8. Nay, ye do wrong, and *defraud,*
　7: 5. *Defraud* ye not one the other,
1Ti. 6: 5. corrupt minds, and *destitute* of the truth,
Jas. 5: 4. which *is* of you *kept back by fraud,*

ἀποστολή, apostolee.

Acts 1:25. of this ministry and *apostleship,*
Ro. 1: 5. received grace and *apostleship,* for
1Co. 9: 2. the seal of mine *apostleship* are
Gal. 2: 8. to the *apostleship* of the circumcision,

ἀπόστολος, apostolos.

Mat.10: 2. the names of the twelve *apostles*
Mar 6:30. the *apostles* gathered themselves
Lu. 6:13. whom also he named *apostles;*
　9:10. the *apostles,* when they were
　11:49. send them prophets and *apostles*
　17: 5. the *apostles* said unto the Lord,
　22:14. the twelve *apostles* with him.
　24:10. told these things unto the *apostles.*
Joh.13:16. neither *he that is sent* greater
Acts 1: 2. commandments unto the *apostles*
　26. numbered with the eleven *apostles.*
　2:37. Peter and to the rest of the *apostles,*
　42. in the *apostles'* doctrine and fellowship,
　43. were done by the *apostles.*
　4:33. gave the *apostles* witness of the
　35. laid (them) down at the *apostles'* feet:
　36. who by the *apostles* was surnamed
　37. laid (it) at the *apostles'* feet.
　5: 2. laid (it) at the *apostles'* feet.
　12. by the hands of the *apostles* were
　18. laid their hands on the *apostles,*
　29. Peter and the (other) *apostles* answered

Acts 5:34. to put the *apostles* forth a little
　40. they had called the *apostles,*
　6: 6. Whom they set before the *apostles:*
　8: 1. Judæa and Samaria, except the *apostles.*
　14. Now when the *apostles* which
　18. laying on of the *apostles'* hands
　9:27. brought (him) to the *apostles,* and
　11: 1. the *apostles* and brethren that were
　14: 4. with the Jews, and part with the *apostles.*
　14. (Which) when the *apostles,* Barnabas
　15: 2. unto the *apostles* and elders about
　4. (of) the *apostles* and elders, and they
　6. the *apostles* and elders came together
　22. Then pleased it the *apostles* and
　23. The *apostles* and elders and brethren
　33. the brethren unto the *apostles.*
　16: 4. were ordained of the *apostles* and
Ro. 1: 1. called (to be) an *apostle,* separated
　11:13. as I am the *apostle* of the Gentiles,
　16: 7. are of note among the *apostles,*
1Co. 1: 1. called (to be) an *apostle* of Jesus
　4: 9. set forth us the *apostles* last,
　9: 1. Am I not an *apostle?* am I not
　2. If I be not an *apostle* unto others,
　5. as well as other *apostles,* and
　12:28. first *apostles,* secondarily
　29. (Are) all *apostles?* (are) all
　15: 7. of James; then of all the *apostles.*
　9. I am the least of the *apostles,* that am not
　　meet to be called an *apostle,*
2Co. 1: 1. Paul, an *apostle* of Jesus Christ
　8:23. (they are) the *messengers* of the
　11: 5. behind the very chiefest *apostles.*
　13. themselves into the *apostles* of Christ.
　12:11. the very chiefest *apostles,*
　12. the signs of an *apostle* were
Gal. 1: 1. Paul, an *apostle,* not of men,
　17. to them which were *apostles*
　19. others of the *apostles* saw I none,
Eph. 1: 1. Paul, an *apostle* of Jesus Christ
　2:20. the foundation of the *apostles* and
　3: 5. revealed unto his holy *apostles* and
　4:11. he gave some, *apostles;* and some,
Phi. 2:25. your *messenger,* and he that
Col. 1: 1. Paul, an *apostle* of Jesus Christ
1Th. 2: 6. as the *apostles* of Christ.
1Ti. 1: 1. Paul, an *apostle* of Jesus Christ
　2: 7. ordained a preacher, and an *apostle,*
2Ti. 1: 1. Paul, an *apostle* of Jesus Christ
　11. appointed a preacher, and an *apostle,*
Tit. 1: 1. an *apostle* of Jesus Christ,
Heb 3: 1. consider the *apostle* and high priest
1Pet. 1: 1. Peter, an *apostle* of Jesus Christ, to
2Pet. 1: 1. a servant and an *apostle* of Jesus
　3: 2. of us the *apostles* of the Lord and Saviour:
Jude 17. before of the *apostles* of our Lord
Rev. 2: 2. them which say they are *apostles,*
　18:20. (ye) holy *apostles* and prophets;
　21:14. the names of the twelve *apostles*

ἀποστοματίζω, apostomatizo.

Lu. 11:53. *to provoke* him *to speak* of many things:

ἀποστρέφω, apostrepho.

Mat. 5:42. borrow of thee *turn* not thou *away.*
　26:52. *Put up again* thy sword into his
　27: 3. *brought again* the thirty pieces
Lu. 23:14. as one *that perverteth* the people:
Acts 3:26. in *turning away* every one of you

Ro. 11:26. *shall turn away* ungodliness from
2Ti. 1:15. in Asia *be turned away* from me;
4: 4. they *shall turn away* (their) ears
Tit. 1:14. men, *that turn from* the truth.
Heb12:25. if we *turn away from* him that

ἀποστυγέω, apostugeo.

Ro. 12: 9. *Abhor* that which is evil; cleave

ἀποσυνάγωγος, aposunagōgos.

Joh. 9:22. be *put out of the synagogue.*
12:42. should be *put out of the synagogue :*
16: 2. shall put you *out of the synagogues :*

ἀποτάσσομαι, apotassomai.

Mar 6:46. when he *had sent* them *away,*
Lu. 9:61. let me first go *bid* them *farewell,*
14:33. that *forsaketh* not all that he hath,
Acts18:18. *then took* his *leave* of the brethren,
21. *bade* them *farewell,* saying, I
2Co. 2:13. *taking* my *leave* of them, I went

ἀποτελέω, apoteleo.

Jas. 1:15. sin, *when* it is *finished,* bringeth

ἀποτίθημι, apotitheemi.

Acts 7:58. the witnesses *laid down* their clothes
Ro. 13:12. therefore *cast off* the works of darkness,
Eph. 4:22. That ye *put off* concerning the former
25. Wherefore *putting away* lying, speak
Col. 3: 8. now ye also *put off* all these; anger,
Heb12: 1. let us *lay aside* every weight, and
Jas. 1:21. Wherefore *lay apart* all filthiness
1Pet.2: 1. Wherefore *laying aside* all malice,

ἀποτινάσσω, apotinasso.

Lu. 9: 5. *shake off* the very dust from your
Acts28: 5. he *shook off* the beast into the fire,

ἀποτίω, apotio.

Philem.19. with mine own hand, I *will repay* (it):

ἀποτολμάω, apotolmaō.

Ro. 10:20. Esaias *is very bold,* and saith,

ἀποτομία, apotomia.

Ro. 11:22. therefore the goodness and *severity* of
God: on them which fell, *severity* ; but

ἀποτόμως, apotomōs.

2Co. 13:10. being present I should use *sharpness,*
Tit. 1:13. Wherefore rebuke them *sharply,*

ἀποτρέπομαι, apotrepomai.

2Ti. 3: 5. power thereof. from such *turn away.*

ἀπουσία, apousia.

Phi. 2:12. now much more in my *absence,*

ἀποφέρω, apophero.

Mar15: 1. bound Jesus, and *carried* (him) *away,*
Lu. 16:22. was *carried* by the angels into
1Co.16: 3. them will I send *to bring* your
Rev.17: 3. So he *carried* me *away* in the spirit
21:10. he *carried* me *away* in the spirit

ἀποφεύγω, apophūgo.

2Pet.1: 4. *having escaped* the corruption
2:18. *that were* clean *escaped* from them
20. For if *after* they *have escaped* the

ἀποφθέγγομαι, apophthengomai.

Acts 2: 4. as the Spirit gave them *utterance.*
14. lifted up his voice, and *said* unto them,
26:25. *speak forth* the words of truth

ἀποφορτίζομαι, apophortizomai.

Acts21: 3. the ship was to *unlade* her burden.

ἀπόχρησις, apokreesis.

Col. 2:22. all are to perish with the *using;*

ἀποχωρέω, apokōreo.

Mat. 7:23. *depart* from me, ye that work
Lu. 9:39. him hardly *departeth* from him.
Acts13:13. John *departing* from them

ἀποχωρίζομαι, apokōrizomai.

Acts15:39. they *departed asunder* one from
Rev. 6:14. the heaven *departed* as a scroll

ἀποψύχω, apopsuko.

Lu. 21:26. Men's *hearts failing* them for fear,

ἀπρόσιτος, aprositos.

1Ti. 6:16. the light *which no man can approach*

ἀπρόσκοπος, aproskopos.

Acts24:16. a conscience *void of offence* toward
1Co.10:32. Give *none offence,* neither to the Jews,
Phi. 1:10. *without offence* till the day of Christ;

ἀπροσωπολήπτως, aprosōpoleeptōs.

1Pet. 1:17. who *without respect of persons* judgeth

ἄπταιστος, aptaistos.

Jude 24. is able to keep you *from falling,*

ἄπτομαι, haptomai.

Mat. 8: 3. Jesus put forth (his) hand, and *touched* him,
15. he *touched* her hand, and the fever
9:20. *touched* the hem of his garment:
21. If I *may* but *touch* his garment,
29. Then *touched* he their eyes,
14:36. *might* only *touch* the hem of his garment: and as many as *touched* were made
17: 7. Jesus came and *touched* them, and said,
20:34. compassion (on them), and *touched* their eyes:
Mar. 1:41. *touched* him, and saith unto him,
3:10. upon him for to *touch* him,
5:27. behind, and *touched* his garment.
28. If I *may touch* but his clothes,
30. said, Who *touched* my clothes?
31. sayest thou, Who *touched* me?
6:56. that they *might touch* if it were
— as many as *touched* him were
7:33. he spit, and *touched* his tongue;
8:22. besought him to *touch* him.
10:13. that he *should touch* them:
Lu. 5:13. put forth (his) hand, and *touched* him,
6:19. multitude sought *to touch* him:
7:14. he came and *touched* the bier:
39. woman (this is) that *toucheth* him:
8:44. *touched* the border of his garment:
45. Jesus said, Who *touched* me?
— sayest thou, Who *touched* me?
46. Jesus said, Somebody *huth touched* me:
47. what cause she *had touched* him,
18:15. that he *would touch* them:
22:51. he *touched* his ear, and healed him.
Joh.20:17. *Touch* me not; for I am not
1Co. 7: 1. for a man not *to touch* a woman.
2Co. 6:17. *touch* not the unclean (thing);
Col. 2:21. *Touch* not; taste not; handle not;
1Joh.5:18. that wicked one *toucheth* him not.

ἅπτω, hapto.

Lu. 8:16. No man, *when he hath lighted* a
11:33. No man, *when he hath lighted* a
15: 8. *doth* not *light* a candle, and sweep
22:55. *when* they *had kindled* a fire in

ἀπωθέομαι, apōtheomai.

Acts13:46. seeing ye *put* it *from* you, and judge

ἀπώθομαι, apōthomai

Acts 7:27. his neighbour wrong *thrust* him *away,*
39. not obey, but *thrust* (him) *from* them,
Ro. 11: 1. *Hath* God *cast away* his people?
2. God *hath* not *cast away* his people
1Ti. 1:19. which some *having put away*

ἀπώλεια, apōlia.

Mat. 7:13. that leadeth to *destruction,* and
26: 8. To what purpose (is) this *waste?*
Mar.14: 4. Why was this *waste* of the ointment
Joh.17:12. the son of *perdition;* that the
Acts 8:20. Thy money perish (lit. be to *destruction*) with thee,
25:16. Romans to deliver any man to *die,*
Ro. 9:22. vessels of wrath fitted to *destruction:*
Phi. 1:28. an evident token of *perdition,* but
3:19. Whose end (is) *destruction,* whose
2Th. 2: 3. be revealed, the son of *perdition;*
1Ti. 6: 9. drown men in destruction and *perdition.*
Heb10:39. who draw back unto *perdition;* but
2Pet 2: 1. shall bring in *damnable* heresies,
— upon themselves swift *destruction.*
2. shall.follow their *pernicious ways;*
3. their *damnation* slumbereth not.
3: 7. judgment and *perdition* of ungodly
16. unto their own *destruction.*
Rev.17: 8. bottomless pit, and go into *perdition:*
11. is of the seven, and goeth into *perdition.*

ἀρά, ara.

Ro. 3:14. Whose mouth (is) full of *cursing* and bitterness:

ἄρα, ara. γε[2]

Mat. 7:20. *Wherefore* by their fruits ye shall[2]
12:28. *then* the kingdom of God is come
17:26. unto him, *Then* are the children free.[2]
18: 1. Who (lit. who *then*) is the greatest in the kingdom of
19:25. saying, Who *then* can be saved?
27. what shall we have *therefore?*
24:45. Who *then* is a faithful and wise
Mar. 4:41. What *manner of man* is this,
11:13. if *haply* he might find any thing
Lu. 1:66. What *manner* of child shall this be!
8:25. What *manner of man* is this!
11:20. *no doubt* the kingdom of God is
48. *Truly* ye bear witness that ye
12:42. Who *then* is that faithful and wise
22:23. which (lit. which *then*) of them it was that should
Acts 7: 1. priest, Are these things so? (lit. *indeed* so)
8:22. if *perhaps* the thought of thine
11:18. *Then* hath God also to the Gentiles[2]
12:18. what (lit. what *indeed*) was become of Peter.
17:27. if *haply* they might feel after[2]
21:38. Art not thou (lit. thou *then*) that Egyptian, which
Ro. 5:18. *Therefore* as by the offence of one
7: 3. So *then* if, while (her) husband
21. I find *then* a law, that,
25. So *then* with the mind I myself
8: 1. (There is) *therefore* now no condemnation
12. *Therefore,* brethren, we are
9:16. So *then* (it is) not of him that
18. *Therefore* hath he mercy on whom
10:17. So *then* faith (cometh) by hearing,
14:12. So *then* every one of us shall
19. Let us *therefore* follow after the
1Co. 5:10. for *then* must ye needs go out

1Co. 7:14. else (lit. else *indeed*) were your children unclean;

15:14. *then* (is) our preaching vain, and
15. if *so be* that the dead **rise not.**
18. *Then* they also which are fallen

2Co. 1:17. thus minded, did I (lit. I *indeed*) use lightness?
5:14(15). died for all, *then* were all dead:
7:12. *Wherefore*, though I wrote unto you,

Gal. 2:21. *then* Christ is dead in vain.
3: 7. Know ye *therefore* that they
29. *then* are ye Abraham's seed,
4:31. So *then*, brethren, we are not
5:11. *then* is the offence of the cross
6:10. As we have *therefore* opportunity,

Eph. 2:19. Now *therefore* ye are no more

1Th. 5: 6. *Therefore* let us not sleep, as

2Th. 2:15. *Therefore*, brethren, stand fast,

Heb 4: 9. There remaineth *therefore* a
12: 8. *then* are ye bastards, and not sons.

ἄρα, ara, adv. whether,

Lu. 18: 8.)(shall he find faith on the earth?
Acts 8:30.)(Understandest thou what thou readest?
Gal. 2:17. (is) *therefore* Christ the minister

ἀργέω, argeo.

2Pet. 2: 3. of a long time *lingereth* not,

ἀργός, argos.

Mat.12:36. That every *idle* word that men
20: 3. saw others standing *idle* in the
6. standing *idle*, and saith unto them, Why stand ye here all the day *idle?*

1Ti. 5:13. withal they learn (to be) *idle*,
— not only *idle*, but tattlers also

Tit. 1:12. alway liars, evil beasts, *slow* bellies.

2Pet. 1: 8. neither (be) *barren* nor unfruitful

ἀργύριον, argurion.

Mat.25:18. in the earth, and hid his lord's *money*.
27. therefore to have put my *money*
26:15. for thirty *pieces of silver.*
27: 3. the thirty *pieces of silver* to the
5. he cast down the *pieces of silver* in
6. chief priests took the *silver pieces*,
9. took the thirty *pieces of silver*,
28:12. they gave large *money* unto the
15. So they took the *money*, and did

Mar.14:11. promised to give him *money*.

Lu. 9: 3. neither bread, neither *money*;
19:15. to whom he had given the *money*,
23. gavest not thou my *money* into
22: 5. covenanted to give him *money*.

Acts 3: 6. *Silver* and gold have I none; but
7:16. Abraham bought for a sum of *money*
8:20. Thy *money* perish with thee,
19:19. fifty thousand (pieces) *of silver.*
20:33. I have coveted no man's *silver*,

1Pet. 1:18. corruptible things, (as) *silver* and gold,

ἀργυροκόπος, argurokopos.

Acts19:24. Demetrius, a *silversmith*, which

ἄργυρος, arguros.

Mat.10: 9. Provide neither gold, nor *silver*,
Acts17:29. like unto gold, or *silver*, or stone,
1Co. 3:12. this foundation gold, *silver*,
Jas. 5: 3. Your gold and *silver* is cankered;
Rev.18:12. merchandise of gold, and *silver*,

ἀργυροῦς, argurous.

Acts19:24. which made *silver* shrines for
2Ti. 2:20. not only vessels of gold and *of silver*,
Rev. 9:20. idols of gold, and *silver*, and brass, and stone,

ἀρέσκεια, areskĭa.

Col. 1:10. worthy of the Lord unto all *pleasing*,

ἀρέσκω, aresko.

Mat.14: 6. danced before them, and *pleased* Herod.
Mar. 6:22. danced, *and pleased* Herod and them that
Acts 6: 5. the saying *pleased* the whole multitude :
Ro. 8: 8. they that are in the flesh cannot *please* God.
15: 1. the weak, and not *to please* ourselves.
2. *Let* every one of us *please* (his) neighbour
3. even Christ *pleased* not himself;
1Co. 7:32. how he may *please* the Lord:
33. how he may *please* (his) wife.
34. how she may *please* (her) husband.
10:33. as I *please* all (men) in all (things),
Gal. 1:10. do I seek *to please* men? for if I yet *pleased* men, I should
1Th. 2: 4. not as *pleasing* men, but God
15. have persecuted us; *and* they *please* not God,
4: 1. how ye ought to walk and *to please* God,
2Ti. 2: 4. that he may *please* him who hath

ἀρεστός, arestos.

Joh. 8:29. I do always those *things that please* him.
Acts 6: 2. It is not *reason* that we should
12: 3. because he saw it *pleased* the Jews,
1Joh 3:22. *things that are pleasing* in his sight.

ἀρετή, aretee.

Phi. 4: 8. if (there be) any *virtue*, and if (there be) any praise,
1Pet. 2: 9. shew forth the *praises* of him who
2Pet. 1: 3. hath called us to glory and *virtue :*
5. add to your faith *virtue ;* and to *virtue* knowledge ;

ἀρήν, areen.

Lu. 10: 3. I send you forth as *lambs* among wolves.

ἀριθμέω, arithmeo.

Mat 10:30. hairs of your head are all *numbered*
Lu. 12: 7. hairs of your head *are* all *numbered.*
Rev. 7: 9. multitude, which no man could *number*,

ἀριθμός, arithmos.

Lu. 22: 3. being of the *number* of the twelve.
Joh. 6:10. in *number* about five thousand.
Acts 4: 4. the *number* of the men was about
    5:36. a *number* of men, about four hundred,
    6: 7. the *number* of the disciples multiplied
  11:21. a great *number* believed, and turned
  16: 5. in the faith, and increased in *number* daily.
Ro. 9:27. Though the *number* of the children
Rev. 5:11 & 7: 4. the *number* of them
  9:16. the *number* of the army of the
    — I heard the *number* of them.
  13:17. name of the beast, or the *number* of his
    name.
    18. count the *number* of the beast: for it is
    the *number* of a man; and his *number* is
    (χξϛ')
  15: 2. over the *number* of his name,
  20: 8. the *number* of whom (is) as the sand

ἀριστάω, aristaō.

Lu. 11:37. besought him to *dine* with him:
Joh.21:12. Jesus saith unto them, Come (and) *dine*.
  15. So when they *had dined*, Jesus

ἀριστερός, aristeros.

Mat. 6: 3. let not thy *left* hand know what
Lu. 23:33. one on the right hand, and the other on
  the *left*.
2Co. 6: 7. on the right hand and on the *left*,

ἄριστον, ariston.

Mat.22: 4. Behold, I have prepared my *dinner:*
Lu. 11:38. had not first washed before *dinner*.
  14:12. When thou makest a *dinner* or a supper,

ἀρκετός, arketos.

Mat. 6:34. *Sufficient* unto the day (is) the evil thereof.
  10:25. It is *enough* for the disciple that he
1Pet.4: 3. the time past of (our) life may *suffice* us

ἀρκέω, arkeo.

Mat.25: 9. lest there *be* not *enough* for us and you:
Lu. 3:14. *be content* with your wages.
Joh. 6: 7. of bread *is* not *sufficient* for them,
  14: 8. shew us the Father, and it *sufficeth* us.
2Co12: 9. My grace *is sufficient* for thee:
1 Ti. 6: 8. food and raiment *let us be* therewith *content*.
Heb13: 5. (be) *content* with such things as ye have:
3Joh. 10. malicious words: and not *content* therewith,

ἄρκτος, arktos.

Rev.13: 2. his feet were as (the feet) of a *bear*,

ἅρμα, harma.

Acts 8:28. returning, and sitting in his *chariot*
  29. Go near, and join thyself to this *chariot*.
  38. he commanded the *chariot* to stand
Rev. 9: 9. as the sound of *chariots* of many

ἁρμός, harmos.

Heb. 4:12. of the *joints* and marrow, and (is)

ἁρμόζω, harmozo.

2Co.11: 2. for I *have espoused* you to one husband,

ἀρνέομαι, arneomai.

Mat 10:33. whosoever *shall deny* me before men, him
    will I also *deny* before my Father
  26:70. he *denied* before (them) all,
    72. again he *denied* with an oath,
Mar 14:68. he *denied*, saying, I know not,
    70. he *denied* it again.   And a little
Lu. 8:45. *When* all *denied*, Peter and they
  12: 9. he *that denieth* me before men
  22:57. he *denied* him, saying, Woman,
Joh. 1:20. he confessed, and *denied* not; but
  18:25. He *denied* (it), and said, I am not.
  27. Peter then *denied* again:
Acts 3:13. *denied* him in the presence of Pilate,
  14. ye *denied* the Holy One and the Just,
  4:16. in Jerusalem; and we cannot *deny* (it).
  7:35. Moses whom they *refused*, saying,
1 Ti. 5: 8. he *hath denied* the faith, and is
2 Ti. 2:12. if we *deny* (him), he also *will deny* us:
  13. he cannot *deny* himself.
  3: 5. form of godliness, but *denying* the power
Tit. 1:16. in works they *deny* (him),
  2:12. *denying* ungodliness and worldly lusts,
Heb11:24. *refused* to be called the son of
2Pet. 2: 1. even *denying* the Lord that bought
1Joh 2:22. he *that denieth* that Jesus is the Christ?
  — *that denieth* the Father and the Son.
  23. Whosoever *denieth* the Son, the
Jude 4. *denying* the only Lord God, and our
Rev. 2:13. *hast* not *denied* my faith,
  3: 8. *hast* not *denied* my name.

ἀρνίον, arnion.

Joh.21:15. He saith unto him, Feed my *lambs*.
Rev. 5: 6. in the midst of the elders, stood a *Lamb*
  8. elders fell down before the *Lamb*,
  12. Worthy is the *Lamb* that was slain
  13. upon the throne, and unto the *Lamb* for
    ever
  6: 1. when the *Lamb* opened one of the seals,
  16. from the wrath of the *Lamb:*
  7: 9. before the *Lamb*, clothed with white
  10. upon the throne, and unto the *Lamb*.
  14. white in the blood of the *Lamb*.
  17. For the *Lamb* which is in the
  12:11. by the blood of the *Lamb*, and by the
  13: 8. book of life of the *Lamb* slain
  11. he had two horns like a *lamb*,
  14: 1. lo, a *Lamb* stood on the mount
  4. they which follow the *Lamb*
  — the firstfruits unto God and to the *Lamb*.
  10. in the presence of the *Lamb:*
  15: 3. of God, and the song of the *Lamb*, saying,
  17:14. These shall make war with the *Lamb*, and
    the *Lamb* shall overcome them:
  19: 7. the marriage of the *Lamb* is come,
  9. unto the marriage supper of the *Lamb*.
  21: 9. shew thee the bride, the *Lamb's* wife.
  14. the twelve apostles of the *Lamb*.
  22. Lord God Almighty, and the *Lamb*

Rev 21:23. the *Lamb* (is) the light thereof.
    27. written in the *Lamb's* book of life.
22: 1. the throne of God and of the *Lamb*.
    3. the throne of God and of the *Lamb*

ἀρξάμενος, arxamenos.

Lu. 24:47. among all nations, *beginning* at Jerusalem.
Acts 10:37. *and began* from Galilee, after the

ἀροτριάω, arotriao.

Lu. 17: 7. which of you, having a servant *plowing*
1Co. 9:10. he *that ploweth* should *plow* in hope ;

ἄροτρον, arotron.

Lu. 9:62. having put his hand to the *plough*,

ἁρπαγή, harpagee.

Mat. 23:25. are full of *extortion* and excess.
Lu. 11:39. inward part is full of *ravening* and
Heb 10:34. took joyfully the *spoiling* of your goods,

ἁρπαγμός, harpagmos.

Phil. 2: 6. thought it not *robbery* to be equal with God :

ἁρπάζω, harpazo.

Mat 11:12. the violent *take* it by force.
    13:19. cometh the wicked (one), and *catcheth away*
Joh. 6:15. would come and *take* him *by force*,
    10:12. the wolf *catcheth* them, and scattereth
    28. any (man) *pluck* them out of my hand.
    29. *to pluck* (them) out of my Father's hand.
Acts 8:39. Spirit of the Lord *caught away* Philip,
    23:10. *to take* him *by force* from among
2Co 12: 2. such an one *caught up* to the third heaven.
    4. that he *was caught up* into paradise,
1Th. 4:17. *shall be caught up* together with
Jude 23. with fear, *pulling* (them) out of the fire ;
Rev 12: 5. her child *was caught up* unto God,

ἅρπαξ, harpax.

Mat. 7:15. inwardly they are *ravening* wolves.
Lu. 18:11. as other men (are), *extortioners*, unjust,
1Co. 5:10. with the covetous, or *extortioners*, or
    11. a railer, or a drunkard, or an *extortioner ;*
    6:10. revilers, nor *extortioners*, shall inherit

ἀῤῥαβών, arrabon..

2 Co. 1:22. given the *earnest* of the Spirit in
    5: 5. hath given unto us the *earnest* of the Spirit.
Eph. 1:14. Which is the *earnest* of our inheritance

ἄῤῥαφος, arraphos.

Joh 19:23. now the coat was *without seam*,

ἄῤῥην, arreen.

Ro. 1:27. likewise also the *men*, leaving

Rev 12: 5. she brought forth a *man* child,
    13. woman which brought forth the *man*
    (child).

ἄῤῥητος, arreetos.

2Co 12: 4. into paradise, and heard *unspeakable* words,

ἄῤῥωστος, arrōstos.

Mat 14:14. toward them, and he healed their *sick*.
Mar. 6: 5. laid his hands upon a few *sick folk*,
    13. anointed with oil many *that were sick*,
    16:18. they shall lay hands on the *sick*, and
1Co 11:30. many (are) weak and *sickly* among you,

ἀρσενοκοίτης, arsenokoitees.

1Co 6: 9. effeminate, nor *abusers of* themselves *with*
    mankind,
1Ti. 1:10. *that defile* themselves *with mankind*,

ἄρσην, arseen.

Mat 19: 4. made them *male* and female,
Mar 10: 6. God made them *male* and female.
Lu. 2:23. Every *male* that openeth the womb
Ro. 1:27. *men* with *men* working that
Gal. 3:28. there is neither *male* nor female :

ἀρτέμων, artemōn.

Acts 27:40. hoised up the *mainsail* to the wind,

ἄρτι, arti.

Mat. 3:15. Suffer (it to be so) *now :* for thus it
    9:18. My daughter is *even now* dead.
    11:12. until *now* the kingdom of heaven
    23:39. Ye shall not see me *henceforth*, till
    26:29. I will not drink *henceforth* of this fruit
    53. that I cannot *now* pray to my Father,
    64. *Hereafter* shall ye see the Son of man
Joh. 1:51(52). *Hereafter* ye shall see heaven open,
    2:10. hast kept the good wine until *now*.
    5:17. My Father worketh *hitherto*, and I work.
    9:19. how then doth he *now* see ?
    25. whereas I was blind, *now* I see.
    13: 7. What I do thou knowest not *now ;*
    19. *Now* (lit. *henceforth*) I tell you before it
    come,
    33. cannot come ; so *now* I say to you.
    37. why cannot I follow thee *now ?*
    14: 7. from *henceforth* ye know him,
    16:12. ye cannot bear them *now*.
    24. *Hitherto* have ye asked nothing
    31. Jesus answered them, Do ye *now* believe
1Co. 4:11. Even unto this *present* hour we both
    13. the offscouring of all things unto *this*
    day.
    8: 7. conscience of the idol unto *this hour*
    13:12. For *now* we see through a glass,
    — *now* I know in part ; but then
    15: 6. greater part remain unto *this present*,
    16: 7. I will not see you *now* by the way ;
Gal. 1: 9. we said before, so say I *now* again,

Gal. 1:10. For do I *now* persuade men, or God?
    4:20. I desire to be present with you *now*,
1Th. 3: 6. *now* when Timotheus came
2Th. 2: 7. only he who *now* letteth, (will let),
1Pet.1: 6. though *now* for a season, if need be,
     8. whom, though *now* ye see (him) not,
1Joh.2: 9. is in darkness even until *now*.
Rev.12:10. *Now* is come salvation, and strength,

ἀρτιγέννητος, artigenneetos.

1Pet.2: 2. As *newborn* babes, desire the

ἄρτιος, artios.

2Ti. 3:17. That the man of God may be *perfect*,

ἄρτος, artos.

Mat. 4: 3. command that these stones be made *bread*.
    4. Man shall not live by *bread* alone,
  6:11. Give us this day our daily *bread*.
  7: 9. whom if his son ask *bread*, will
12: 4. did eat the shew*bread*, which
14:17. We have here but five *loaves*,
  19. took the five *loaves*, and the two fishes,
  — gave the *loaves* to (his) disciples,
15: 2. their hands, when they eat *bread*.
  26. not meet to take the children's *bread*,
  33. should we have so much *bread*
  34. How many *loaves* have ye?
  36. he took the seven *loaves* and the fishes,
16: 5. they had forgotten to take *bread*.
  7. because we have taken no *bread*.
  8. because ye have brought no *bread?*
  9. neither remember the five *loaves*
  10. Neither the seven *loaves* of the
  11. not to you concerning *bread*,
  12. not beware of the leaven of *bread*,
26:26. Jesus took *bread*, and blessed (it),
Mar. 2:26. did eat the shew*bread*, which
  3:20. could not so much as eat *bread*.
  6: 8. no scrip, no *bread*, no money
  36. into the villages, and buy themselves *bread :*
  37. two hundred pennyworth of *bread*,
  38. How many *loaves* have ye?
  41. when he had taken the five *loaves*
  — blessed, and brake the *loaves*,
  44. they that did eat of the *loaves*
  52. not (the miracle) of the *loaves:*
  7: 2. saw some of his disciples eat *bread*
  5. eat *bread* with unwashen hands?
  27. not meet to take the children's *bread*,
  8: 4. satisfy these (men) with *bread*
  5. How many *loaves* have ye?
  6. he took the seven *loaves*, and
  14. (disciples) had forgotten to take *bread*,
  — with them more than one *loaf.*
  16. because we have no *bread*.
  17. because ye have no *bread?*
  19. When I brake the five *loaves*
14:22. Jesus took *bread*, and blessed,
Lu. 4: 3. this stone that it be made *bread*.
  4. man shall not live by *bread* alone,
  6: 4. did take and eat the shew*bread*,
  7:33. neither eating *bread* nor drinking

Lu. 9: 3. nor scrip, neither *bread*, neither
  13. We have no more but five *loaves*
  16. Then he took the five *loaves* and
11: 3. Give us day by day our daily *bread*.
  5. Friend, lend me three *loaves ;*
  11. If a son shall ask *bread* of any
14: 1. to eat *bread* on the sabbath day,
  15. he that shall eat *bread* in the
15:17. servants of my father's have *bread*,
22:19. he took *bread*, and gave thanks,
24:30. he took *bread*, and blessed (it),
  35. known of them in breaking of *bread*.
Joh. 6: 5. Whence shall we buy *bread*,
  7. Two hundred pennyworth of *bread*
  9. which hath five barley *loaves*,
  11. Jesus took the *loaves ;* and when
  13. fragments of the five barley *loaves*,
  23. place where they did eat *bread*,
  26. because ye did eat of the *loaves*,
  31. He gave them *bread* from heaven
  32. Moses gave you not that *bread*
  — my Father giveth you the true *bread*,
  33. For the *bread* of God is he which
  34. Lord, evermore give us this *bread*.
  35. I am the *bread* of life: he that
  41. I am the *bread* which came down
  48. I am that *bread* of life.
  50. This is the *bread* which cometh
  51. I am the living *bread* which
  — if any man eat of this *bread*,
  — the *bread* that I will give
  58. This is that *bread* which came
  — he that eateth of this *bread* shall
13:18. He that eateth *bread* with me
21: 9. fish laid thereon, and *bread*.
  13. Jesus then cometh, and taketh *bread*,
Acts 2:42. in breaking of *bread*, and in prayers.
  46. breaking *bread* from house to house,
20: 7. came together to break *bread*,
  11. had broken *bread*, and eaten,
27:35. he took *bread*, and gave thanks
1Co.10.16. The *bread* which we break, is it
  17. we, (being) many are one *bread*, (and)
  — all partakers of that one *bread*.
11:23. in which he was betrayed took *bread:*
  26. as often as ye eat this *bread*,
  27. whosoever shall eat this *bread*,
  28. so let him eat of (that) *bread*,
2Co. 9:10. minister *bread* for (your) food,
2Th. 3: 8. Neither did we eat any man's *bread*
  12. they work, and eat their own *bread*.
Heb. 9: 2. the table, and the shew*bread ;*

ἀρτύω, artuo.

Mar. 9:50. wherewith *will* ye *season* it?
Lu. 14:34. wherewith *shall* it *be seasoned?*
Col. 4: 6. alway with grace, *seasoned* with salt,

ἀρχάγγελος, arkangelos.

1Th. 4:16. with the voice of the *archangel*,
Jude   9. Yet Michael the *archangel*,

ἀρχαῖος. arkaios.

Mat. 5:21. was said by *them of old time*,
  27. was said by *them of old time*,
  33. been said by **them of old time**,

Lu. 9: 8. one of the *old* prophets was risen
    19. one of the *old* prophets is risen
Acts15: 7. how that a good while ago (lit. from days *of old*)
    21. For Moses of *old* time hath in
  21:16. one Mnason of Cyprus, an *old* disciple
2Co. 5:17. *old* things are passed away ;
2Pet.2: 5. spared not the *old* world, but
Rev.12: 9. that *old* serpent, called the Devil,
    20: 2. that *old* serpent, which is the devil,

ἀρχή, *arkee.*

Mat.19: 4. which made (them) at the *beginning*
    8. from the *beginning* it was not so.
  24: 8. these (are) the *beginning* of sorrows.
    21. since the *beginning* of the world
Mar. 1: 1. The *beginning* of the gospel of
  10: 6. from the *beginning* of the creation
  13: 8(9). these (are) the *beginnings* of sorrows.
    19. as was not from the *beginning*
Lu. 1: 2. from the *beginning* were eyewitnesses,
  12:11. unto the synagogues, and (unto) *magistrates,*
  20:20. might deliver him unto the *power* and authority of the governor.
Joh. 1: 1. In the *beginning* was the Word,
    2. The same was in the *beginning*
  2:11. This *beginning* of miracles did
  6:64. Jesus knew from the *beginning* who
  8:25. I said unto you from the *beginning.*
    44. was a murderer from the *beginning,*
  15:27. with me from the *beginning.*
  16: 4. not unto you at the *beginning,*
Acts10:11. knit at the four *corners,* and let
  11: 5. down from heaven by four *corners ;*
    15. as on us at the *beginning.*
  26: 4. which was at *the first* among
Ro. 8:38. nor *principalities,* nor powers, nor
1Co.15:24. have put down all *rule* and all
Eph. 1:21. above all *principality,* and power,
  3:10. now unto the *principalities* and
  6:12. against *principalities,* against powers,
Phil.4:15. that in the *beginning* of the gospel,
Col. 1:16. dominions, or *principalities,* or
    18. who is the *beginning,* the
  2:10. the head of all *principality* and
    15. having spoiled *principalities* and
2Th. 2:13. God hath from the *beginning* chosen
Tit. 3: 1. subject to *principalities* and powers,
Heb. 1:10. Thou, Lord, in the *beginning*
  2: 3. which *at the first* began to
  3:14. if we hold the *beginning* of
  5:12. the *first* principles of the oracles
  6: 1. leaving the *principles* of the doctrine
  7: 3. having neither *beginning* of days,
2Pet.3: 4. from the *beginning* of the creation.
1Joh.1: 1. which was from the *beginning,*
  2: 7. which ye had from the *beginning.*
    — ye have heard from the *beginning.*
    13. him (that is) from the *beginning.*
    14. known him (that is) from the *beginning.*
    24. have heard from the *beginning.*
    — ye have heard from the *beginning*
  3: 8. the devil sinneth from the *beginning.*
    11. that ye heard from the *beginning,*
2Joh. 5. which we had from the *beginning,*
    6. as ye have heard from the *beginning,*
Jude 6. angels which kept not their *first estate,*
Rev.1: 8. the *beginning* and the ending,
  3:14. the *beginning* of the creation of God ;

Rev.21: 6. the *beginning* and the end. I will
  22:13. Alpha and Omega, the *beginning* and the end,

ἀρχηγός, *arkeegos.*

Acts 3:15. killed the *Prince* of life, whom
  5:31. (to be) a *Prince* and a Saviour, for to
Heb. 2:10. to make the *captain* of their salvation
  12: 2. Jesus the *author* and finisher of (our) faith ;

ἀρχιερατικός, *arkieratikos.*

Acts 4: 6. of the kindred *of the high priest,*

ἀρχιερεύς, *arkierŭs.*

Mat. 2: 4. gathered all the *chief priests* and
  16:21. the elders and *chief priests* and scribes,
  20:18. betrayed unto the *chief priests*
  21:15. when the *chief priests* and scribes
    23. the *chief priests* and the elders of the
    45. the *chief priests* and Pharisees had
  26: 3. assembled together the *chief priests,*
    — unto the palace of the *high priest,*
    14. Iscariot, went unto the *chief priests,*
    47. from the *chief priests* and elders of
    51. struck a servant of the *high priest's,*
    57. away to Caiaphas the *high priest,*
    58. unto the *high priest's* palace, and
    59. Now the *chief priests,* and elders, and all
    62. the *high priest* arose, and said
    63. the *high priest* answered and said
    65. the *high priest* rent his clothes,
  27: 1. all the *chief priests* and elders of
    3. silver to the *chief priests* and elders,
    6. the *chief priests* took the silver
    12. he was accused of the *chief priests*
    20. the *chief priests* and elders persuaded
    41. also the *chief priests* mocking (him),
    62. the *chief priests* and Pharisees came
  28:11. shewed unto the *chief priests* all
Mar. 2:26. days of Abiathar the *high priest,*
  8:31. (of) the *chief priests,* and scribes,
  10:33. be delivered unto the *chief priests,*
  11:18. the scribes and *chief priests* heard
    27. there come to him the *chief priests,*
  14: 1. the *chief priests* and the scribes sought
    10. went unto the *chief priests,* to
    43. from the *chief priests* and the scribes
    47. smote a servant of the *high priest,*
    53. led Jesus away to the *high priest:*
    — assembled all the *chief priests* and the
    54. into the palace of the *high priest:*
    55. the *chief priests* and all the council
    60. the *high priest* stood up in the
    61. Again the *high priest* asked him,
    63. the *high priest* rent his clothes,
    66. one of the maids of the *high priest:*
  15: 1. the *chief priests* held a consultation
    3. the *chief priests* accused him
    10. the *chief priests* had delivered him
    11. the *chief priests* moved the people,
    31. also the *chief priests* mocking
Lu. 3: 2. Annas and Caiaphas being the *high priests,*
  9:22. *chief priests* and scribes, and be slain,
  19:47. the *chief priests* and the scribes
  20: 1. the *chief priests* and the scribes

Lu. 20:19. the *chief priests* and the scribes the
22: 2. the *chief priests* and scribes sought
4. communed with the *chief priests*
50. smote the servant of the *high priest,*
52. Jesus said unto the *chief priests,*
54. into the *high priest's* house.
66. the *chief priests* and the scribes
23: 4. said Pilate to the *chief priests*
10. the *chief priests* and scribes stood
13. together the *chief priests* and the rulers
23. of them and of the *chief priests*
24:20. how the *chief priests* and our rulers
Joh. 7:32. the Pharisees and the *chief priests*
45. came the officers to the *chief priests*
11:47. gathered the *chief priests* and the
49. being the *high priest* that same
51. being *high priest* that year,
57. both the *chief priests* and the Pharisees
12:10. the *chief priests* consulted that
18: 3. from the *chief priests* and Pharisees,
10. smote the *high priest's* servant,
13. was the *high priest* that same year.
15. known unto the *high priest,* and
— into the palace of the *high priest.*
16. known unto the *high priest,*
19. The *high priest* then asked Jesus
22. Answerest thou the *high priest* so?
24. bound unto Caiaphas the *high priest.*
26. the servants of the *high priest,*
35. Thine own nation and the *chief priests*
19: 6. the *chief priests* therefore and officers
15. The *chief priests* answered,
21. Then said the *chief priests* of the
Acts 4: 6. Annas the *high priest,* and Caiaphas;
23. the *chief priests* and elders had said
5:17. the *high priest* rose up, and all they
21. the *high priest* came, and they that
24. the *chief priests* heard these things,
27. the *high priest* asked them,
7: 1. Then said the *high priest,* Are
9: 1. went unto the *high priest,*
14. authority from the *chief priests*
21. bound unto the *chief priests?*
19:14. a Jew, (and) *chief of the priests,*
22: 5. also the *high priest* doth bear
30. commanded the *chief priests* and
23: 2. the *high priest* Ananias commanded
4. Revilest thou God's *high priest?*
5. that he was the *high priest:*
14. they came to the *chief priests*
24: 1. Ananias the *high priest* descended
25: 2. the *high priest* and the chief of the
15. the *chief priests* and the elders of
26:10. authority from the *chief priests;*
12. commission from the *chief priests,*
Heb 2:17. merciful and faithful *high priest*
3: 1. apostle and *high priest* of our
4:14. we have a great *high priest,* that
15. we have not an *high priest* which
5: 1. every *high priest* taken from
5. to be made an *high priest;*
10. Called of God an *high priest*
6:20. made an *high priest* for ever
7:26. For such an *high priest* became
27. not daily, as those *high priests,*
28. maketh men *high priests* which
8: 1. We have such an *high priest,*
3. For every *high priest* is ordained
9: 7. (went) the *high priest* alone once
11. Christ being come an *high priest*
25. as the *high priest* entereth into
13:11. by the *high priest* for sin, are

ἀρχιποίμην, *arkipoimeen.*

1Pet.5: 4. when the *chief Shepherd* shall

ἀρχισυνάγωγος, *arkisunagōgos.*

Mar. 5:22. one of the *rulers of the synagogue,*
35. from the *ruler of the synagogue's* (house)
36. unto the *ruler of the synagogue,*
38. house of the *ruler of the synagogue,*
Lu. 8:49. from the *ruler of the synagogue's* (house)
13:14. the *ruler of the synagogue* answered
Acts13:15. the *rulers of the synagogue* sent
18: 8. the *chief ruler of the synagogue,*
17. the *chief ruler of the synagogue,*

ἀρχιτέκτων, *arkitektōn.*

1Co. 3:10. as a wise *masterbuilder,* I have

ἀρχιτελώνης, *arkitelōnees.*

Lu. 19: 2. was the *chief* among the publicans,

ἀρχιτρίκλινος, *arkitriklinos.*

Joh. 2: 8. bear unto the *governor of the feast.*
9. When the *ruler of the feast* had
— the *governor of the feast* called the

ἄρχομαι, *arkomai.*

Mat. 4:17. Jesus *began* to preach, and to say,
11: 7. Jesus *began* to say unto the
20. Then *began* he to upbraid the
12: 1. *began* to pluck the ears of corn,
14:30. *beginning* to sink, he cried,
16:21. *began* Jesus to shew unto his
22. *began* to rebuke him, saying,
18:24. *when* he had *begun* to reckon,
20: 8. *beginning* from the last unto
24:49. *shall begin* to smite (his)
26:22. *began* every one of them to say
37. *began* to be sorrowful and very heavy.
74. Then *began* he to curse and to swear,
Mar. 1:45. *began* to publish (it) much,
2:23. his disciples *began,* as they went,
4: 1. he *began* again to teach by the
5:17. they *began* to pray him to depart
20. *began* to publish in Decapolis
6: 2. he *began* to teach in the synagogue:
7. *began* to send them forth by two
34. *began* to teach them many things.
55. *began* to carry about in beds
8:11. *began* to question with him,
31. he *began* to teach them, that
32. Peter took him, and *began* to rebuke
10:28. Then Peter *began* to say unto him,
32. *began* to tell them what things
41. they *began* to be much displeased
47. he *began* to cry out, and say, Jesus,
11:15. *began* to cast out them that sold
12: 1. he *began* to speak unto them
13: 5. Jesus answering them *began* to say,
14:19. they *began* to be sorrowful, and to
33. *began* to be sore amazed, and to be
65. some *began* to spit on him,

Mar.14:69. *began* to say to them that stood by,
    71. he *began* to curse and to swear, (saying,)
  15: 8. crying aloud, *began* to desire (him)
    18. *began* to salute him, Hail,
Lu. 3: 8. *begin* not to say within yourselves,
    23. Jesus himself began (lit. was *beginning*) to be about
  4:21. he *began* to say unto them, This
  5:21. scribes and the Pharisees *began* to reason,
  7:15. he that was dead sat up, and *began* to
    24. he *began* to speak unto the people
    38. *began* to wash his feet with tears,
    49. *began* to say within themselves,
  9:12. when the day *began* to wear away,
  11:29. gathered thick together, he *began* to say,
    53. scribes and the Pharisees *began* to
  12: 1. he *began* to say unto his disciples
    45. *shall begin* to beat the menservants
  13:25. ye *begin* to stand without, and to knock
    26. Then *shall* ye *begin* to say, We
  14: 9. thou *begin* with shame to take
    18. with one (consent) *began* to make excuse.
    29. behold (it) *begin* to mock him,
    30. Saying, This man *began* to build,
  15:14. he *began* to be in want.
    24. they *began* to be merry.
  19:37. multitude of the disciples *began* to
    45. *began* to cast out them that sold
  20: 9. Then *began* he to speak to the people
  21:28. *when* these things *begin* to come
  22:23. they *began* to enquire among
  23: 2. they *began* to accuse him, saying,
    5. *beginning* from Galilee to this
    30. Then *shall* they *begin* to say to
  24:27. *beginning* at Moses and all the
Joh. 8: 9. *beginning* at the eldest, (even)
  13: 5. *began* to wash the disciples' feet,
Acts 1: 1. all that Jesus *began* both to do and teach,
    22. *Beginning* from the baptism of
  2: 4. *began* to speak with other tongues,
  8:35. *began* at the same scripture, *and*
  11: 4. *rehearsed* (the matter) *from the beginning*, and
    15. as I *began* to speak, the Holy
  18:26. he *began* to speak boldly in the
  24: 2. Tertullus *began* to accuse (him),
  27:35. had broken (it), he *began* to eat.
2Co. 3: 1. *Do* we *begin* again to commend
1Pet.4:17. judgment must *begin* at the house

ἄρχω, *arho*.

Mar.10:42. accounted *to rule over* the Gentiles
Ro. 15:12. he that shall rise *to reign over* the

ἄρχων, *arkōn*.

Mat. 9:18. there came a certain *ruler*,
    23. Jesus came into the *ruler's* house,
    34. through the *prince* of the devils.
  12:24. by Beelzebub the *prince* of the devils.
  20:25. the *princes* of the Gentiles exercise
Mar. 3:22. by the *prince* of the devils casteth
Lu. 8:41. he was a *ruler* of the synagogue:
  11:15. through Beelzebub the *chief* of the devils.
  12:58. with thine adversary to the *magistrate*,
  14: 1. house of one of the *chief* Pharisees
  18:18. a certain *ruler* asked him,
  23:13. chief priests and the *rulers* and the people,
    35. the *rulers* also with them derided (him),

Lu. 24:20. the chief priests and our *rulers* delivered
Joh. 3: 1. Nicodemus, a *ruler* of the Jews:
  7:26. Do the *rulers* know indeed that
    48. Have any of the *rulers* or of the
  12:31. now shall the *prince* of this world
    42. among the *chief rulers* also
  14:30. the *prince* of this world·cometh,
  16:11. the *prince* of this world is judged.
Acts 3:17. ye did (it) as (did) also your *rulers*.
  4: 5. that their *rulers*, and elders, and scribes,
    8. Ye *rulers* of the people, and elders
    26. the *rulers* were gathered together
  7:27. Who made thee a *ruler* and a judge
    35. Who made thee a *ruler* and a judge?
    — God send (to be) a *ruler* and a
  13:27. dwell at Jerusalem, and their *rulers*,
  14: 5. also of the Jews with their *rulers*,
  16:19. into the marketplace unto the *rulers*,
    23: 5. not speak evil of the *ruler* of thy
Ro. 13: 3. For *rulers* are not a terror to good
1Co. 2: 6. nor of the *princes* of this world,
    8. none of the *princes* of this world
Eph. 2: 2. the *prince* of the power of the air,
Rev. 1: 5. the *prince* of the kings of the earth.

ἄρωμα, *arōma*.

Mar.16: 1. bought *sweet spices*, that they
Lu. 23:56. prepared *spices* and ointments;
  24: 1. bringing the *spices* which they
Joh.19:40. in linen clothes with the *spices*,

ἀσάλευτος, *asalūtos*.

Acts27:41. stuck fast, and remained *unmoveable*,
Heb 12:28. a kingdom *which cannot be moved*,

ἄσβεστος, *asbestos*.

Mat. 3:12. the chaff with *unquenchable* fire.
Mar. 9:43. fire that *never shall be quenched:*
    45. fire that *never shall be quenched:*
Lu. 3:17. will burn with fire *unquenchable*.

ἀσέβεια, *asebĭa*.

Ro. 1:18. against all *ungodliness* and
  11:26. shall turn away *ungodliness*
2Ti. 2:16. will increase unto more *ungodliness*.
Tit. 2:12. denying *ungodliness* and worldly
Jude 15. their *ungodly* deeds which they have
    18. after their own *ungodly* lusts.

ἀσεβέω, *asebeo*.

2Pet.2: 6. that after should *live ungodly*;
Jude 15. deeds which they *have ungodly committed*,

ἀσεβής, *asebēs*.

Ro. 4: 5. him that justifieth the *ungodly*,
  5: 6. Christ died for the *ungodly*.
1Ti. 1: 9. for the *ungodly* and for sinners, for
1Pet.4:18. where shall the *ungodly* and the
2Pet.2: 5. upon the world of the *ungodly*;

2Pet.3: 7. judgment and perdition of *ungodly* men.
Jude   4. *ungodly men*, turning the grace
      15. convince all *that are ungodly*
      — which *ungodly* sinners have

ἀσέλγεια, *aselgïa*.

Mar. 7:22. deceit, *lasciviousness*, an evil eye,
Ro. 13:13. not in chambering and *wantonness*,
2Co.12:21. *lasciviousness* which they have
Gal. 5:19. fornication, uncleanness, *lasciviousness*,
Eph. 4:19. themselves over unto *lasciviousness*,
1Pet.4: 3. we walked in *lasciviousness*,
2Pet.2: 7. vexed with the *filthy* conversation of
      18. (through much) *wantonness*, those
Jude   4. grace of our God into *lasciviousness*,

ἄσημος, *aseemos*.

Acts21:39. in Cilicia, a citizen of no *mean* city:

ἀσθένεια, *asthenïa*.

Mat. 8:17. Himself took our *infirmities*, and
Lu. 5:15. healed by him of their *infirmities*.
  8: 2. healed of evil spirits and *infirmities*,
  13:11. which had a spirit of *infirmity*
    12. thou art loosed from thine *infirmity*.
Joh. 5: 5. had an *infirmity* thirty and eight years.
  11: 4. This *sickness* is not unto death,
Acts28: 9. which had *diseases* in the island,
Ro. 6:19. because of the *infirmity* of your flesh:
  8:26. the Spirit also helpeth our *infirmities*:
1Co. 2: 3. I was with you in *weakness*, and in
  15:43. it is sown in *weakness*; it is raised
2Co.11:30. things which concern mine *infirmities*.
  12: 5. not glory, but in mine *infirmities*.
    9. is made perfect in *weakness*.
    — I rather glory in my *infirmities*,
    10. I take pleasure in *infirmities*,
  13: 4. he was crucified through *weakness*,
Gal. 4:13. through *infirmity* of the flesh
1Ti. 5:23. stomach's sake and thine often *infirmities*.
Heb. 4:15. with the feeling of our *infirmities*;
  5: 2. also is compassed with *infirmity*.
  7:28. high priests which have *infirmity*;
  11:34. out of *weakness* were made strong,

ἀσθενέω, *astheneo*.

Mat.10: 8. Heal the *sick*, cleanse the lepers,
  25:36. I *was sick*, and ye visited me:
Mar. 6:56. they laid the *sick* in the streets,
Lu. 4.40. all they that had any *sick* with
  7:10. servant whole *that had been sick*.
  9: 2. kingdom of God, and to heal the *sick*.
Joh. 4:46. whose son *was sick* at Capernaum.
  5: 3. a great multitude of *impotent folk*,
    7. The *impotent man* answered him,
  6: 2. did on them *that were diseased*.
  11: 1. Now a certain (man) was *sick*,
    2. whose brother Lazarus *was sick*.
    3. he whom thou lovest is *sick*.
    6. heard therefore that he *was sick*,
Acts 9:37. that she *was sick, and* died:
  19:12. were brought unto the *sick*
  20:35. ye ought to support the *weak*,

Ro. 4:19. *being* not *weak* in faith, he
  8: 3. that it *was weak* through the flesh
  14: 1. Him *that is weak* in the faith
    2. another, *who is weak*, eateth herbs.
    21. is offended, or *is made weak*.
1Co. 8: 9. stumblingblock to them *that are weak*.
    11. shall the *weak* brother perish,
    12. wound their *weak* conscience
2Co.11:21. as though we *had been weak*.
    29. Who *is weak*, and I *am* not *weak*?
  12:10. for when I *am weak*, then am
  13: 3. to you-ward *is* not *weak*, but
    4. For we also *are weak* in him,
    9. we are glad, when we *are weak*,
Phil. 2:26. heard that he *had been sick*.
    27. he *was sick* nigh unto death:
2Ti. 4:20. Trophimus have I left at Miletum *sick*.
Jas. 5:14. *Is* any *sick* among you ? let

ἀσθένημα, *astheneema*.

Ro. 15: 1. to bear the *infirmities* of the weak,

ἀσθενής, *asthenees*.

Mat.25:39. Or when saw we thee *sick*, or in
    43. *sick*, and in prison, and ye visited
    44. naked, or *sick*, or in prison, and
  26:41. willing, but the flesh (is) *weak*.
Mar 14:38. ready, but the flesh (is) *weak*.
Lu. 10: 9. heal the *sick* that are therein,
Acts 4: 9. done to the *impotent* man,
  5:15. brought forth the *sick* into the
    16. bringing *sick* folks, and them
Ro. 5: 6. we were yet *without strength*,
1Co. 1:25. the *weakness* of God is stronger
    27. the *weak things* of the world
  4:10. we (are) *weak*, but ye (are) strong;
  8: 7. their conscience being *weak*
    10. conscience of him which is *weak*
  9:22. To the *weak* became I as *weak*, that I
    might gain the *weak*
  11:30. many (are) *weak* and sickly among
  12:22. which seem to be *more feeble*,
2Co.10:10. (his) bodily presence (is) *weak*,
Gal. 4: 9. to the *weak* and beggarly elements,
1Th. 5:14. support the *weak*, be patient
Heb. 7:18. for the *weakness* and unprofitableness
1Pet.3: 7. as unto the *weaker* vessel, and

ἀσιτία, *asitïa*.

Acts27:21. after long *abstinence* Paul stood

ἄσιτος, *asitos*.

Acts27:33. ye have tarried and continued *fasting*,

ἀσκέω, *askeo*.

Acts24:16. herein *do* I *exercise* myself, to

ἀσκός, *askos*.

Mat. 9:17. put new wine into old *bottles*;
    — else the *bottles* break, and the wine

Mat. 9:17. wine runneth out, and the *bottles* perish:
— put new wine into new *bottles*,
Mar. 2:22. putteth new wine into old *bottles:*
— new wine doth burst the *bottles*,
— the *bottles* will be marred:
— wine must be put into new *bottles*.
Lu. 5:37. putteth new wine into old *bottles;*
— new wine will burst the *bottles*,
— spilled, and the *bottles* shall perish.
38. new wine must be put into new *bottles;*

ἀσμένως, asmenōs.

Acts 2:41. they that *gladly* received his word
21:17. the brethren received us *gladly.*

ἄσοφος, asophos.

Eph. 5:15. circumspectly, not as *fools*, but as wise,

ἀσπάζομαι, aspazomai.

Mat. 5:47. if ye *salute* your brethren
10:12. when ye come into an house, *salute* it.
Mar. 9:15. running to (him) *saluted* him.
15:18. began *to salute* him, Hail,
Lu. 1:40. house of Zacharias, and *saluted* Elisabeth.
10: 4. *salute* no man by the way.
Acts 18:22. when...gone up, and *saluted* the church,
20: 1. the disciples, and *embraced* (them),
21: 6. when we *had taken* our *leave* one of another,
7. *saluted* the brethren, *and* abode
19. when he *had saluted* them,
25:13. came unto Cæsarea, to *salute* Festus.
Ro. 16: 3. *Greet* Priscilla and Aquila my
5. *Salute* my wellbeloved Epenetus,
6. *Greet* Mary ; who bestowed much
7. *Salute* Andronicus and Junia,
8. *Greet* Amplias my beloved
9. *Salute* Urbane, our helper
10. *Salute* Apelles, approved in Christ. *Salute* them which are of
11. *Salute* Herodion my kinsman. *Greet* them that be of the (houshold)
12. *Salute* Tryphena and Tryphosa,
— *Salute* the beloved Persis, which
13. *Salute* Rufus chosen in the
14. *Salute* Asyncritus, Phlegon,
15. *Salute* Philologus, and Julia,
16. *Salute* one another with an holy kiss. The churches of Christ *salute* you.
21. Jason, and Sosipater, my kinsmen, *salute* you.
22. I, Tertius, who wrote (this) epistle, *salute* you
23. the whole church, *saluteth* you.
— chamberlain of the city *saluteth* you,
1Co.16:19(18). The churches of Asia *salute* you.
— Aquila and Priscilla *salute* you
20. All the brethren *greet* you. *Greet* ye one another with an
2Co.13:12. *Greet* one another with an holy kiss.
13(12). All the saints *salute* you.
Phi. 4:21. *Salute* every saint in Christ Jesus. The brethren which are with me *greet* you.
22. All the saints *salute* you,
Col. 4:10. my fellowprisoner *saluteth* you,
12. a servant of Christ, *saluteth* you,
14. beloved physician, and Demas, *greet* you.

Col. 4:15. *Salute* the brethren which are
1Th. 5:26. *Greet* all the brethren with an
2Ti. 4:19. *Salute* Prisca and Aquila, and the
21. Eubulus *greeteth* thee, and Pudens,
Tit. 3:15(14). All that are with me *salute* thee.
Greet them that love us in the
Philem 23. There *salute* thee Epaphras, my
Heb 11:13. *embraced* (them), and confessed that
13:24. *Salute* all them that have
— They of Italy *salute* you.
1Pet. 5:13. elected together with (you), *saluteth* you;
14. *Greet* ye one another with a
2Joh. 13. children of thy elect sister *greet* thee.
3Joh. 14(15). (Our) friends *salute* thee.
—(—) *Greet* the friends by name.

ἀσπασμός, aspasmos.

Mat.23: 7. *greetings* in the markets, and to be
Mar 12:38. *salutations* in the marketplaces,
Lu. 1:29. what manner of *salutation* this
41. when Elisabeth heard the *salutation* of
44. the voice of thy *salutation* sounded
11:43. *greetings* in the markets.
20:46. love *greetings* in the markets,
1Co.16:21. The *salutation* of (me) Paul with
Col. 4:18. The *salutation* by the hand of
2Th. 3:17. The *salutation* of Paul with mine

ἄσπιλος, aspilos.

1Ti. 6:14. (this) commandment *without spot*,
Jas. 1:27. to keep himself *unspotted* from
1Pet.1:19. a lamb without blemish and *without spot:*
2Pet.3:14. in peace, *without spot*, and blameless.

ἀσπίς, aspis.

Ro. 3:13. the poison of *asps* (is) under their lips:

ἄσπονδος, aspondos.

Ro. 1:31. without natural affection, *implacable*,
2Ti. 3: 3. Without natural affection, *trucebreakers*,

ἀσσάριον, assarion.

Mat.10:29. two sparrows sold for a *farthing ?*
Lu. 12: 6. five sparrows sold for two *farthings*,

ἄσσον, asson.

Note.—Considered by Stephens as a proper name.
Acts27:13. they sailed *close* by Crete.

ἀστατέω, astateo.

1Co. 4:11. *have no certain dwellingplace ;*

ἀστεῖος, astīos.

Acts 7:20. Moses was born, and was exceeding *fair;*
Heb 11:23. they saw (he was) a *proper* child ;

ἀστήρ, asteer.

Mat. 2: 2. we have seen his *star* in the east,
     7. what time the *star* appeared.
     9. lo, the *star*, which they saw in the east,
    10. When they saw the *star*, they
   24:29. the *stars* shall fall from heaven,
Mar 13:25. the *stars* of heaven shall fall,
1Co.15:41. another glory of the *stars:* for (one) *star*
         differeth from (another) *star* in glory.
Jude   13. wandering *stars*, to whom is
Rev. 1:16. had in his right hand seven *stars:*
    20. The mystery of the seven *stars*
    — The seven *stars* are the angels
   2: 1. that holdeth the seven *stars* in
   28. I will give him the morning *star.*
   3: 1. Spirits of God, and the seven *stars;*
   6:13. the *stars* of heaven fell unto
   8:10. there fell a great *star* from heaven,
   11. the name of the *star* is called
   12. the third part of the *stars ;* so as
   9: 1. I saw a *star* fall from heaven
  12: 1. upon her head a crown of twelve *stars:*
   4. the third part of the *stars* of heaven,
  22:16. the bright and morning *star.*

ἀστήρικτος, asteeriktos.

2Pet. 2:14. beguiling *unstable* souls: an
   3:16. they that are unlearned and *unstable*

ἄστοργος, astorgos.

Ro.   1:31. *without natural affection*, implacable,
2Ti. 3: 3. *Without natural affection*, truce-breakers,

ἀστοχέω, astokeo.

1Ti. 1: 6. From which some *having swerved*
   6:21. *have erred* concerning the faith.
2Ti. 2:18. Who concerning the truth *have erred,*

ἀστραπή, astrapee.

Mat.24:27. For as the *lightning* cometh
   28: 3. His countenance was like *lightning,*
Lu. 10:18. I beheld Satan as *lightning* fall
   11:36. as when the *bright shining* of a
   17:24. For as the *lightning*, that lighteneth
Rev. 4: 5. proceeded *lightnings* and thunderings
   8: 5. thunderings, and *lightnings*, and an
   11:19. there were *lightnings*, and voices,
   16:18. voices, and thunders, and *lightnings*

ἀστράπτω, astrapto.

Lu. 17:24. the lightning, *that lighteneth* out
   24: 4. stood by them in *shining* garments:

ἄστρον, astron.

Lu. 21:25. in the moon, and in the *stars ;* and upon
Acts 7:43. the *star* of your god Remphan,
   27:20. when neither sun nor *stars* in
Heb 11:12. as the *stars* of the sky in multitude,

ἀσύμφωνος, asumphōnos.

Acts28:25. when they *agreed not* among themselves,

ἀσύνετος, asunetos.

Mat.15:16. Are ye also yet *without understanding ?*
Mar. 7:18. Are ye so *without understanding*
Ro.   1:21. their *foolish* heart was darkened.
     31. *Without understanding*, covenantbreakers,
  10:19. by a *foolish* nation I will anger you.

ἀσύνθετος, asunthetos.

Ro.   1:31. *covenantbreakers*, without natural affec-
     tion,

ἀσφάλεια, asphalia.

Lu.   1: 4. know the *certainty* of those things,
Acts 5:23. found we shut with all *safety,*
1Th. 5: 3. when they shall say, Peace and *safety;*

ἀσφαλής, asphalees.

Acts21:34. could not know the *certainty* for
   22:30. he would have known the *certainty*
   25:26. Of whom I have no *certain* thing
Phi. 3: 1. not grievous, but for you (it is) *safe,*
Heb. 6:19. the soul, both *sure* and stedfast,

ἀσφαλίζω, asphalizo.

Mat.27:64. the sepulchre *be made sure*
   65. *make* (it) as *sure* as ye can.
   66. they went, and *made* the sepulchre *sure,*
Acts16:24. *made* their feet *fast* in the stocks.

ἀσφαλῶς, asphalōs.

Mar 14:44. take him, and lead (him) away *safely.*
Acts 2:36. house of Israel know *assuredly,*
   16:23. the jailor to keep them *safely :*

ἀσχημονέω, askeemoneo.

1Co. 7:36. he *behaveth* himself *uncomely*
   13: 5. *Doth* not *behave* itself *unseemly,*

ἀσχημοσύνη, askeemosunee.

Ro.   1:27. men working *that which is unseemly,*
Rev.16:15. walk naked, and they see his *shame.*

ἀσχήμων, askeemōn.

1Co.12:23. our *uncomely* (parts) have more

ἀσωτία, asōtia.

Eph. 5:18. drunk with wine, wherein is *excess;*
Tit.   1: 6. not accused of *riot*, or unruly,
1Pet. 4: 4. to the same excess of *riot*, speaking

ἀσώτως, asōtōs.

Lu. 15:13. wasted his substance with *riotous* living.

ἀτακτέω, atakteo.

2Th. 3: 7. *behaved* not ourselves *disorderly*

ἄτακτος, ataktos.

1Th. 5:14. warn them that are *unruly*,

ἀτάκτως, ataktōs.

2Th. 3: 6. every brother that walketh *disorderly*,
11. which walk among you *disorderly*,

ἄτεκνος, ateknos.

Lu. 20:28. he die *without children*, that
29. took a wife, and died *without children*.
30. to wife, and he died *childless*.

ἀτενίζω, atenizo.

Lu. 4:20. eyes of all them that...were *fastened* on
him.
22:56. *earnestly looked* upon him, *and* said,
Acts 1:10. they *looked stedfastly* toward
3: 4. Peter, *fastening* his *eyes* upon him
12. why *look* ye so *earnestly* on us,
6:15. *looking stedfastly* on him, saw
7:55. *looked* up *stedfastly* into heaven, *and*
10: 4. *when* he *looked* on him, he was
11: 6. *when* I had *fastened* mine *eyes*,
13: 9. *Then*...*set* his *eyes* on him,
14: 9. who *stedfastly beholding* him,
23: 1. Paul, *earnestly beholding* the council,
2Co. 3: 7. could not *stedfastly behold* the
13. could not *stedfastly look* to the

ἄτερ, ater.

Lu. 22: 6. *in the absence* of the multitude.
35. When I sent you *without* purse,

ἀτιμάζω, atimazo.

Lu. 20:11. *entreated* (him) *shamefully, and* sent
Joh. 8:49. I honour my Father, and ye *do dishonour*
me.
Acts 5:41. worthy *to suffer shame* for his name.
Ro. 1:24. *to dishonour* their own bodies
2:23. the law *dishonourest* thou God?
Jas. 2: 6. ye *have despised* the poor. Do not

ἀτιμία, atimia.

Ro. 1:26. God gave them up unto *vile* affections:
9:21. honour, and another unto *dishonour*?
1Co.11:14. long hair, it is a *shame* unto him?
1Co.15:43. It is sown in *dishonour;* it is
2Co. 6: 8. By honour and *dishonour*, by evil
11:21. I speak as concerning *reproach*,
2Ti. 2:20. some to honour, and some to *dishonour*.

ἄτιμος, atimos.

Mat.13:57. A prophet is not *without honour*,
Mar 6: 4. A prophet is not *without honour*,
1Co. 4:10. honourable, but we (are) *despised*.
12:23. we think to be *less honourable*,

ἀτιμόω, atimoó.

Mar 12: 4. sent (him) away *shamefully handled*.

ἀτμίς, atmis.

Acts 2:19. blood, and fire, and *vapour* of smoke:
Jas. 4:14. It is even a *vapour*, that appeareth

ἄτομος, atomos.

1Co 15:52. In a *moment*, in the twinkling

ἄτοπος, atopos.

Lu. 23:41. this man hath done nothing *amiss*.
Acts28: 6. saw no *harm* come to him, they
2Th. 3: 2. from *unreasonable* and wicked men:

αὐγάζω, augazo.

2Co. 4: 4. should *shine* unto them.

αὐγή, augee.

Acts20:11. a long while, even till *break of day*,

αὐθάδης, authadees.

Tit. 1: 7. not *selfwilled*, not soon angry,
2Pet. 2:10. Presumptuous (are they), *selfwilled*,

αὐθαίρετος, authairetos.

2Co. 8: 3. (they were) *willing of* them*selves;*
17. of his *own accord* he went unto you.

αὐθεντέω, authenteo.

1Ti. 2:12. nor *to usurp authority* over the man,

αὐλέω, auleo.

Mat 11:17. We *have piped* unto you, and ye have
Lu. 7:32. We *have piped* unto you, and ye
1Co 14: 7. known *what is piped* or harped?

αὐλή, aulee.

Mat 26: 3. unto the *palace* of the high priest,
58. unto the high priest's *palace*,
69. Peter sat without in the *palace:*
Mar14:54. into the *palace* of the high priest:

Mar 14:66. Peter was beneath in the *palace*,
   15:16. into the *hall*, called Prætorium ;
Lu. 11:21. man armed keepeth his *palace*,
   22:55. a fire in the midst of the *hall*,
Joh.10: 1. the door into the sheep*fold*,
   16. which are not of this *fold :*
   18:15. into the *palace* of the high priest.
Rev 11: 2. the *court* which is without the

αὐλητής, *auleetees*.

Mat. 9:23. saw the *minstrels* and the people
Rev 18:22. harpers, and musicians, and of *pipers*,

αὐλίζομαι, *aulizomai*.

Mat 21:17. into Bethany; and he *lodged* there.
Lu. 21:37. he went out, and *abode* in the mount

αὐλός, *aulos*.

1Co 14: 7. whether *pipe* or harp, except they

αὐξάνω & αὔξω, *auxano & auxo*.

Mat. 6:28. lilies of the field, how they *grow ;*
   13:32. when it *is grown*, it is the greatest
Mar 4: 8. fruit that sprang up and *increased ;*
Lu. 1:80. the child *grew*, and waxed strong
   2:40. the child *grew*, and waxed strong
   12:27. Consider the lilies how they *grow :*
 • 13:19. it *grew*, and waxed a great tree ;
Joh. 3:30. He must *increase*, but I (must)
Acts 6: 7. the word of God *increased ;*
   7:17. the people *grew* and multiplied
   12:24. the word of God *grew* and multiplied.
   19:20. So mightily *grew* the word of God
1Co. 3: 6. God *gave the increase*.
   7. God *that giveth the increase*.
2Co. 9:10. *increase* the fruits of your
   10:15. *when* your faith *is increased*,
Eph. 2:21. *groweth* unto an holy temple
   4:15. *may grow up* into him in all
Col. 1:10. *increasing* in the knowledge of God ;
   2:19. *increaseth* with the increase of God.
1Pet. 2: 2. the word, that ye *may grow* thereby:
2Pet. 3:18. *grow* in grace, and (in) the knowledge

αὔξησις, *auxeesis*.

Eph. 4:16. maketh *increase* of the body
Col. 2:19. increaseth with the *increase* of God.

αὔριον, *aurion*.

Mat. 6:30. *to morrow* is cast into the oven,
   34. no thought for the *morrow :* for the *morrow*
     shall take thought
Lu. 10:35. on the *morrow* when he departed,
   12:28. *to morrow* is cast into the oven ;
   13:32. I do cures to day and *to morrow*, and
   33. I must walk to day, and *to morrow*,
Acts 4: 3. in hold unto the *next day :*
   5. it came to pass on the *morrow*,
   23:15. him down unto you *to morrow*,
   20. bring down Paul *to morrow*

Acts25:22. *To morrow*, said he, thou shalt
1Co 15:32. eat and drink ; for *to morrow* we die.
Jas. 4:13. To day or *to morrow* we will go
   14. what (shall be) on the *morrow*.

αὐστηρός, *austeeros*.

Lu. 19:21. because thou art an *austere* man:
   22. that I was an *austere* man,

αὗται & αὕτη see οὗτος.

αὐτάρκεια, *autarkīa*.

2Co. 9: 8. having all *sufficiency* in all
1Ti. 6: 6. godliness with *contentment* is

αὐτάρκης, *autarkees*.

Phi. 4:11. state I am, (therewith) to be *content*.

αὐτοκατάκριτος, *autokatakritos*.

Tit. 3:11. sinneth, being *condemned of* himself.

αὐτόματος, *automatos*.

Mar 4:28. earth bringeth forth fruit of her*self ;*
Acts12:10. opened to them *of* his *own* accord :

αὐτόπτης, *autoptees*.

Lu. 1: 2. beginning were *eyewitnesses*,

αὐτός, *autos*.

[2] marks those combined with the definite article.
Mat. 1:20. that which is conceived in *her* is
   2:16. and in all the coasts *thereof,*
   3: 5. Then went out to *him*
   7. He said unto *them,*
   5: 3. for *their's* is the kingdom
   4. for *they* shall be comforted.
   10. for *their's* is the kingdom
   7:13. many there be that go in *there*at:
   10:11. enquire who in *it* is worthy ;
   13: 2. so that *he* went into a ship,
   4. And when *he* sowed,
   16:21. how that *he* must go unto Jerusalem,
   17:18. Jesus rebuked the devil (lit. *him*); and *he*
     (lit. the devil) departed
   21:19. and found nothing *there*on, but leaves
   41. destroy *those* wicked men,
   24:32. fig tree ; When *his* branch is
   25:16. went and traded with *the same,*
Mar 1:19. who (lit. and *they*) also were in the ship
   2:15. that, as Jesus (lit. *he*) sat at meat in *his*
   6:22. daughter of the *said* Herodias[2]
   31. Come ye your*selves* apart
   7:25. whose young (lit. of whom *her*) daughter
   12:37. David therefore him*self* calleth *him* Lord ;
   44. of *their* abundance ;
   13:28. fig tree : When *her* branch is yet
   16:14. as *they* sat at meat,
Lu. 1:57. time came that *she* should be delivered ;
   2:22. the days of her (lit. *their*) purification

Lu. 2:35. through thy *own* soul also,[2]

    38. she coming in *that* instant gave thanks[2]

    6:42. when thou thy*self* beholdest not

    7:12. mother, and *she* was a widow:

    21. And in *that same* hour he cured[2]

    10: 9. heal the sick that are *therein,*

    10. into the streets of *the same,*

    11: 4. for we (lit. we our*selves*) also forgive

    14:32. while *the other* is yet a great way

    19:23. have required *mine own* (lit. *it*) with

    21:21. countries enter *there*into.

    24:18. which are come to pass there (lit. in *it*)

    39. that it is I my*self* :

Joh.11: 4. might be glorified *thereby.*

    12: 7. burying hath she kept *this.*

    14:17. because it seeth *him* not,

    15: 2. he taketh (lit. taketh *it*) away:

    17:11. *those* whom thou hast given me,

    18:28. and they them*selves* went not into

Acts 3:12. had made *this man* to walk ?

    9:37. whom (lit. and *her*) when they had washed,

    11:22. Then tidings of *these things*

Ro. 8:16. The Spirit *itself* beareth[2]

    9:17. for this *same* purpose

    13: 6. upon this *very* thing.

2Co. 2: 3. I wrote this *same* unto you,

    5: 5. for the self*same* thing (is) God,

    13:11. be of one mind, (lit. think the *same* thing[2])

1Th. 5:23. And the *very* God of peace[2]

Heb 3: 3. who hath builded the house (lit. *it*) hath more honour than the house.

    9:19. both the book, (lit. both the book *itself*[2])

    10: 1. not the *very* image of the things,[2]

Jas. 3: 9. *There*with bless we God, even the Father;

1Pet.1:12. unto us they did minister the *things,*

    2:24. Who his own *self* bare our sins

    4:14. on *their* part he is evil spoken of,

2Pet. 1: 5. And beside this (Gr. Even this *very* thing),

3Joh. 12. and of the truth *itself* :[2]

Rev.17: 9. on *which* the woman sitteth.

       &c. &c.

OBSERVE the meaning of ἐπι & κατα...το αὐτο.

Mat.22:34. were gathered *together.*

Lu. 17:35. Two (women) shall be grinding *together ;*

Acts14: 1. they went both *together*

       &c. &c.

αὐτοῦ, *autou,* adv.

Mat.26:36. Sit ye *here,* while I go and pray

Acts15:34. it pleased Silas to abide *there* still.

    18:19. to Ephesus, and left them *there :*

    21: 4. we tarried *there* seven days:

αὐτοῦ, *hautou.*

Mat. 1:21. he shall save *his* people from

    24. took unto him *his* wife:

    25. brought forth *her* firstborn son:

    2:11. they had opened *their* treasures,

    12. departed into *their own* country

    18. Rachel weeping (for) *her* children,

    3: 4. had *his* raiment of camel's hair, and a leathern girdle about *his* loins;

    6. in Jordan, confessing *their* sins,

    7. Sadducees come to *his* baptism,

    12. he will throughly purge *his* floor, and gather *his* wheat into the garner;

    4: 6. He shall give *his* angels charge

    21. in a ship with Zebedee *their* father,

Mat. 4:22. left the ship and *their* father, and

    5: 2. he opened *his* mouth, and taught

    22. is angry with *his* brother without

    — whosoever shall say to *his* brother,

    28. adultery with her already in *his* heart.

    31. Whosoever shall put away *his* wife,

    32. whosoever shall put away *his* wife,

    45. he maketh *his* sun to rise on

    6: 2. They have *their* reward.

    5. I say unto you, They have *their* reward.

    16. for they disfigure *their* faces,

    — I say unto you, They have *their* reward.

    27. add one cubit unto *his* stature ?

    29. Solomon in all *his* glory was

    7: 6. trample them under *their* feet,

    24. which built *his* house upon a rock:

    26. which built *his* house upon the sand:

    8:18. Jesus saw great multitudes about *him,*

    9: 7. he arose, and departed to *his* house.

    37. Then saith he unto *his* disciples,

    38. send forth labourers into *his* harvest.

    10:10. workman is worthy of *his* meat.

    17. scourge you in *their* synagogues ;

    24. nor the servant above *his* lord.

    38. he that taketh not *his* cross, and

    39. He that findeth *his* life shall

    — he that loseth *his* life for my

    42. shall in no wise lose *his* reward.

    11: 1. of commanding *his* twelve disciples,

    2. he sent two of *his* disciples,

    16. calling unto *their* fellows,

    19. wisdom is justified of *her* children.

    12:49. forth *his* hand toward *his* disciples,

    13:15. *their* eyes they have closed; lest

    24. which sowed good seed in *his* field:

    31. a man took, and sowed in *his* field:

    41. shall send forth *his* angels, and

    43. in the kingdom of *their* Father.

    52. bringeth forth out of *his* treasure

    54. he was come into *his* own country,

    57. save in *his* own country, and in *his* own house.

    14: 2. said unto *his* servants, This is

    3. Herodias' sake, *his* brother Philip's wife.

    8. before instructed of *her* mother,

    11. she brought (it) to *her* mother.

    22. Jesus constrained *his* disciples

    15: 2. they wash not *their* hands

    6(5). and honour not *his* father or *his* mother

    8. nigh unto me with *their* mouth,

    27. fall from *their* master's table.

    32. Then Jesus called *his* disciples

    36. brake (them), and gave to *his* disciples,

    16:13. he asked *his* disciples, saying,

    20. Then charged he *his* disciples

    21. to shew unto *his* disciples, how that

    24. Then said Jesus unto *his* disciples,

    — take up *his* cross, and follow me.

    25. whosoever will save *his* life shall

    — whosoever will lose *his* life for my

    26. whole world, and lose *his own* soul?

    — give in exchange for *his* soul?

    27. come in the glory of *his* Father

    28. Son of man coming in *his* kingdom.

    17: 6. they fell on *their* face, and were

    8. they had lifted up *their* eyes,

    25. of *their own* children, or of strangers?

    18:23. would take account of *his* servants.

    28. found one of *his* fellowservants,

    31. came and told unto *their* lord all

    35. every one *his* brother their trespasses.

    19: 3. a man to put away *his* wife for

Mat.19: 5. shall cleave to *his* wife. and they
9. Whosoever shall put away *his* wife,
23. Then said Jesus unto *his* disciples,
28. shall sit in the throne of *his* glory,
20: 1. to hire labourers into *his* vineyard.
2. he sent them into *his* vineyard.
8. saith unto *his* steward, Call the
20. of Zebedee's children with *her* sons,
28. to give *his* life a ransom for many.
21: 7. put on them *their* clothes, and
34. he sent *his* servants to the
37. he sent unto them *his* son, saying,
22: 2. which made a marriage for *his* son,
3. sent forth *his* servants to call
5. his farm, another to *his* merchandise:
7. he sent forth *his* armies, and destroyed
8. Then saith he to *his* servants, The
16. sent out unto him *their* disciples
24. raise up seed unto *his* brother.
25. left *his* wife unto *his* brother:
23: 1. the multitude, and to *his* disciples,
4. move them with one of *their* fingers.
5. all *their* works they do for to
— they make broad *their* phylacteries,
— the borders of *their* garments,
37. them which are sent unto *thee*,
24: 17. take any thing out of *his* house:
18. return back to take *his* clothes,
29. the moon shall not give *her* light,
31. he shall send *his* angels with
43. have suffered *his* house to be
45. made ruler over *his* household,
47. ruler over all *his* goods.
48. evil servant shall say in *his* heart,
25: 1. ten virgins, which took *their* lamps,
4. the wise took oil in *their* vessels with *their* lamps.
7. virgins arose, and trimmed *their* lamps.
14. delivered unto them *his* goods.
18. in the earth, and hid *his* lord's money.
31. Son of man shall come in *his* glory,
— sit upon the throne of *his* glory:
33. set the sheep on *his* right hand,
34. say unto them on *his* right hand,
26: 1. he said unto *his* disciples,
39. a little farther, and fell on *his* face,
45. Then cometh he to *his* disciples,
51. drew *his* sword, and struck a
65. the high priest rent *his* clothes,
27: 39. reviled him, wagging *their* heads,
60. laid it in *his own* new tomb,
Mar. 1: 5. of Jordan, confessing *their* sins.
6. a girdle of a skin about *his* loins;
18. straightway they forsook *their* nets,
20. they left *their* father Zebedee
27. they questioned among *themselves*,
2: 6. reasoning in *their* hearts,
8. Jesus perceived in *his* spirit that
3: 7. himself with *his* disciples to the sea:
9. he spake to *his* disciples, that a
34. on them which sat about *him*,
4: 2. said unto them in *his* doctrine,
34. expounded all things to *his* disciples.
5: 30. that virtue had gone out of *him*,
6: 1. came into *his* own country: and his
4. without honour, but in *his* own country,
— own kin, and in *his own* house.
17. Herodias' sake, *his* brother Philip's wife:
21. that Herod on *his* birth day made a supper to *his* lords, high captains,
24. went forth, and said unto *her* mother,
28. the damsel gave it to *her* mother.

Mar. 6: 41. gave (them) to *his* disciples to set
45. he constrained *his* disciples to get
7: 12. to do ought for *his* father or *his*
26. the devil out of *her* daughter.
30. when she was come to *her* house,
33. put *his* fingers into his ears, and he
8: 1. Jesus called *his* disciples (unto him),
3. fasting to *their* own houses,
6. gave to *his* disciples to set before
10. entered into a ship with *his* disciples,
12. sighed deeply in *his* spirit, and saith,
27. by the way he asked *his* disciples,
33. turned about, and looked on *his* disciples,
34. with *his* disciples also, he said
— take up *his* cross, and follow me.
35. whosoever will save *his* life shall
— whosoever shall lose *his* life for
36. whole world, and lose *his own* soul?
37. a man give in exchange for *his* soul?
38. cometh in the glory of *his* Father
9: 16. What question ye with *them*?
18. he foameth, and gnasheth with *his* teeth,
31. For he taught *his* disciples, and said
41. He shall not lose *his* reward.
10: 7. shall a man leave *his* father and mother, and cleave to *his* wife;
11. Whosoever shall put away *his* wife,
12. a woman shall put away *her* husband,
23. saith unto *his* disciples, How
45. to give *his* life a ransom for many.
50. he, casting away *his* garment,
11: 1. he sendeth forth two of *his* disciples,
7. cast *their* garments on him;
8. many spread *their* garments in
23. shall not doubt in *his* heart, but
12: 6. one son, *his* wellbeloved, he sent
19. raise up seed unto *his* brother.
38. said unto them in *his* doctrine,
43. he called (unto him) *his* disciples,
44. she of *her* want did cast in all that she had, (even) all *her* living.
13: 15. to take any thing out of *his* house:
16. for to take up *his* garment.
24. the moon shall not give *her* light,
27. then shall he send *his* angels, and shall gather together *his* elect from
34. taking a far journey, who left *his* house, and gave authority to *his* servants, and to every man *his* work, and commanded
14: 13. sendeth forth two of *his* disciples,
32. he saith to *his* disciples, Sit ye here,
46. they laid *their* hands on him,
63. the high priest rent *his* clothes,
15: 29. railed on him, wagging *their* heads,
Lu. 1: 7. were (now) well stricken in years. (lit. in *their* days)
15. even from *his* mother's womb.
18. wife well stricken in years. (lit. in *her* days)
23. he departed to *his own* house.
36. conceived a son in *her* old age.
48. the low estate of *his* handmaiden:
51. hath shewed strength with *his* arm;
54. He hath holpen *his* servant Israel,
56. returned to *her own* house.
58. had shewed great (lit. *his own*) mercy upon her;
66. laid (them) up in *their* hearts,
68. hath visited and redeemed *his* people,
69. in the house of *his* servant David;
70. by the mouth of *his* holy prophets,
72. to remember *his* holy covenant;
2: 7. brought forth *her* firstborn son,

Lu. 2: 8. keeping watch over *their* flock
19. pondered (them) in *her* heart.
28. took he him up in *his* arms,
36. seven years from *her* virginity;
39. to *their* own city Nazareth.
51. all these sayings in *her* heart.
3:15. all men mused in *their* hearts
17. and he will throughly purge *his* floor, and will gather the wheat into *his* garner;
4:10. He shall give *his* angels charge
24. is accepted in *his* own country.
5:15. healed by him of *their* infirmities.
25. departed to *his* own house,
29. a great feast in *his* own house:
6:13. he called (unto him) *his* disciples:
17. and to be healed of *their* diseases;
20. he lifted up *his* eyes on *his* disciples,
40. The disciple is not above *his* master:
45. the good treasure of *his* heart
— out of the evil treasure of *his* heart
7: 1. he had ended all *his* sayings in
3. would come and heal *his* servant.
12. the only son of *his* mother, and she
16. God hath visited *his* people.
19. calling (unto him) two of *his* disciples
35. wisdom is justified of all *her* children.
38. wipe (them) with the hairs of *her* head,
44. wiped (them) with the hairs of *her* head.
8: 5. A sower went out to sow *his* seed:
41. that he would come into *his* house:
9: 1. Then he called *his* twelve disciples
14. he said to *his* disciples, Make
23. take up *his* cross daily, and follow me.
24. whosoever will save *his* life
— whosoever will lose *his* life
26. he shall come in *his* own glory,
43. he said unto *his* disciples,
51. set *his* face to go to Jerusalem,
52. sent messengers before *his* face:
62. having put *his* hand to the plough,
10: 1. two and two before *his* face into
2. send forth labourers into *his* harvest.
7. the labourer is worthy of *his* hire.
38. Martha received him into *her* house.
11: 1. as John also taught *his* disciples.
12: 1. began to say unto *his* disciples
22. he said unto *his* disciples,
25. can add to *his* stature one cubit?
27. Solomon in all *his* glory was
39. not have suffered *his* house
42. make ruler over *his* houshold,
44. ruler over all that he hath. (lit. is *his*)
45. that servant say in *his* heart,
53. against *her* daughter in law,
— against *her* mother in law.
13: 6. a fig tree planted in *his* vineyard;
15. on the sabbath loose *his* ox or
34. stonest them that are sent unto *thee;*
14:17. sent *his* servant at supper
21. shewed *his* lord these things.
— being angry, said to *his* servant,
27. whosoever doth not bear *his* cross,
15:13. there wasted *his* substance with
15. he sent him into *his* fields to
16. have filled *his* belly with the husks
22. the father said to *his* servants,
16: 1. he said also unto *his* disciples,
18. Whosoever putteth away *his* wife,
23. in hell he lift up *his* eyes, being
24. may dip the tip of *his* finger in
17:24. the Son of man be in *his* day.
33. shall seek to save *his* life shall

Lu. 18: 7. shall not God avenge *his own* elect,
13. smote upon *his* breast, saying,
14. This man went down to *his* house
40. him to be brought unto *him :*
19:15. servants to be called unto *him,*
29. he sent two of *his* disciples,
36. spread *their* clothes in the way.
20:28. raise up seed unto *his* brother.
45. he said unto *his* disciples,
21: 1. casting *their* gifts into the treasury.
4. she of *her* penury hath cast
12. shall lay *their* hands on you,
22:36. let him sell *his* garment, and buy
23:11. Herod with *his* men of war set
24:26. to enter into *his* glory?
50. he lifted up *his* hands, and blessed
Joh. 1:47(48). Jesus saw Nathanael coming to *him,*
2:11. manifested forth *his* glory; and
21. he spake of the temple of *his* body.
3: 4. second time into *his* mother's womb,
16. gave *his* only begotten Son, that
17. God sent not *his* Son into the
4: 5. Jacob gave to *his* son Joseph.
28. The woman then left *her* waterpot,
5: 9. took up *his* bed, and walked:
6: 3. there he sat with *his* disciples.
5. a great company come unto *him,*
12. he said unto *his* disciples,
22. Jesus went not with *his* disciples
7:53. every man went unto *his own* house.
9:21. he shall speak for *himself.*
10:11. the good shepherd giveth *his* life
11: 2. wiped his feet with *her* hair,
28. called Mary *her* sister secretly,
54. there continued with *his* disciples.
12: 3. wiped his feet with *her* hair:
25. He that loveth *his* life shall lose it; and he that hateth *his* life in this
13:12. had taken *his* garments, and was
16. servant is not greater than *his* lord;
18. lifted up *his* heel against me.
15:13. a man lay down *his* life for *his* friends.
20. servant is not greater than *his* lord.
22. have no cloke for *their* sin.
17: 1. lifted up *his* eyes to heaven,
13. my joy fulfilled in *themselves.*
18: 1. he went forth with *his* disciples
2. resorted thither with *his* disciples.
19:12. whosoever maketh *himself* a king
17. he bearing *his* cross went forth
26. he saith unto *his* mother, Woman,
20:20. shewed unto them (his) hands and *his* side.
30. in the presence of *his* disciples,
21:14. Jesus shewed himself to *his* disciples,
Acts 2:14. lifted up *his* voice, and said unto them,
3: 2. lame from *his* mother's womb
13. hath glorified *his* Son Jesus;
18. by the mouth of all *his* prophets,
21. by the mouth of all *his* holy prophets
26. God, having raised up *his* Son Jesus,
5: 1. Ananias, with Sapphira *his* wife,
18. laid *their* hands on the apostles,
31. God exalted with *his* right hand
37. drew away much people after *him :*
7:10. over Egypt and all *his* house.
13. was made known to *his* brethren;
14. sent Joseph, and called *his* father Jacob
— all *his* kindred, threescore and fifteen
19. cast out *their* young children,
20. nourished up in *his* father's house
23. to visit *his* brethren the children
25. he supposed *his* brethren would

Acts 7:39. in *their* hearts turned back again
41. in the works of *their own* hands.
54. they were cut to the (lit. *their*) heart, and
57. stopped *their* ears, and ran upon
58. witnesses laid down *their* clothes
8: 28. returning, and sitting in *his* chariot
32. so opened he not *his* mouth:
35. Then Philip opened *his* mouth,
39. he went on *his* way rejoicing.
9: 4. heard a voice saying unto *him*,
8. when *his* eyes were opened, he
40. she opened *her* eyes: and when
10: 2. feared God with all *his* house,
7. called two of *his* houshold servants,
22. to send for thee into *his* house, and
24. had called together *his* kinsmen
12:11. the Lord hath sent *his* angel,
13:36. was laid unto *his* fathers,
42. might be preached to *them* the next sabbath.
50. expelled them out of *their* coasts.
51. shook off the dust of *their* feet
14: 3. unto the word of *his* grace,
8. a cripple from *his* mother's womb,
11. they lifted up *their* voices, saying
14. they rent *their* clothes, and ran in
16. to walk in *their own* ways.
15:14. out of them a people for *his* name.
18. Known unto God are all *his* works
26. hazarded *their* lives for the name of
16: 3. Paul have to go forth with *him;*
16. brought *her* masters much gain
19. the hope of *their* gains was gone,
34. he had brought them into *his* house,
18: 8. on the Lord with all *his* house;
19:18. confessed, and shewed *their* deeds.
20:30. to draw away disciples after *them.*
36. he kneeled (lit. bending *his* knees) down,
21:11. bound *his own* hands and feet,
22:14. that thou shouldest know *his* will,
22. (then) lifted up *their* voices, and said,
23: 2. them that stood by *him* to
24:24. Felix came with *his* wife
25:21. I commanded *him* to be kept till
27:27. *they* drew near to some country;
28:27. *their* eyes have they closed; lest
Ro. 1: 2. promised afore by *his* prophets
3. Concerning *his* Son Jesus Christ
21. became vain in *their* imaginations,
27. burned in *their* lust one toward
— recompence of *their* error which
2:15. the law written in *their* hearts,
3:13. with *their* tongues they have
25. to declare *his* righteousness for
8:29. conformed to the image of *his* Son,
9:22. to make *his* power known,
23. the riches of *his* glory on the
11: 1. Hath God cast away *his* people?
2. God hath not cast away *his* people
1Co. 2:10. revealed (them) unto us by *his* Spirit:
6: 5. to judge between *his* brethren?
14. also raise up us by *his own* power.
7:36. himself uncomely toward *his* virgin,
37. hath so decreed in *his* heart
9:10. should be partaker of *his* hope.
11: 4. covered, dishonoureth *his* head.
15:25. all enemies under *his* feet.
2Co. 2:14. the savour of *his* knowledge
11: 3. beguiled Eve through *his* subtilty,
Gal. 1:15. called (me) by *his* grace,
16. To reveal *his* Son in me, that
4: 4. God sent forth *his* Son, made
6. sent forth the Spirit of *his* Son
25. is in bondage with *her* children.

Eph. 1: 5. by Jesus Christ to *himself,* according to the good pleasure of *his* will,
6. the praise of the glory of *his* grace,
9. unto us the mystery of *his* will, according to *his* good pleasure which he hath purposed in *himself:*
11. after the counsel of *his own* will:
17. revelation in the knowledge *of him:*
20. set (him) at *his own* right hand
2: 4. for *his* great love wherewith he
7. the exceeding riches of *his* grace
15. Having abolished in *his* flesh the
3:16. according to the riches of *his* glory,
— by *his* Spirit in the inner man;
4:17. in the vanity of *their* mind,
25. speak every man truth with *his* neighbour:
5:31. shall a man leave *his* father and mother, and shall be joined unto *his* wife,
Phi. 4:19. according to *his* riches in glory
Col. 1:13. into the kingdom of *his* dear Son:
20. to reconcile all things unto *himself;*
22. In the body of *his* flesh through
— unreprovable in *his* sight:
2:18. puffed up by *his* fleshly mind,
1Th. 2:16. to fill up *their* sins alway:
4: 6. defraud *his* brother in (any) matter;
8. given unto us *his* holy Spirit.
2Th. 1: 7. from heaven with *his* mighty angels,
10. to be glorified in *his* saints,
2: 8. consume with the spirit of *his* mouth,
— with the brightness of *his* coming:
1Ti. 5:18. The labourer (is) worthy of *his* reward.
2Ti. 2:19. The Lord knoweth them that are *his.*
4: 1. at *his* appearing and *his* kingdom;
18. preserve (me) unto *his* heavenly kingdom:
Tit. 1: 3. manifested *his* word through preaching,
3: 5. according to *his* mercy he saved us,
Heb. 1: 3. all things by the word of *his* power,
7. Who maketh *his* angels spirits, and *his* ministers a flame of fire.
2: 4. according to *his* own will?
3: 6. Christ as a son over *his own* house;
18. should not enter into *his* rest,
4: 4. seventh day from all *his* works.
10. hath ceased from *his own* works,
5: 7. Who in the days of *his* flesh, when
6:17. the immutability of *his* counsel,
7: 5. to the law, that is, of *their* brethren,
8:11. not teach every man *his* neighbour, and every man *his* brother, saying,
9:26. by the sacrifice *of himself.*
10:20. the veil, that is to say, *his* flesh;
30. The Lord shall judge *his* people.
11: 7. an ark to the saving of *his* house;
22. commandment concerning *his* bones.
23. was hid three months of *his* parents,
35. Women received *their* dead raised
12: 2. the joy that was set before *him*
3. contradiction of sinners against *himself,*
10. chastened (us) after *their own* pleasure;
16. morsel of meat sold *his* birthright.
13:21. which is wellpleasing in *his* sight,
Jas. 1: 8. A double minded man (is) unstable in all *his* ways.
9. rejoice in that he is exalted: (lit in *his* exaltation)
10. the rich, in that he is made low: (lit. in *his,* &c.)
11. rich man fade away in *his* ways.
18. a kind of firstfruits of *his* creatures.
23. a man beholding *his* natural face
25. shall be blessed in *his* deed.

Jas. 1:26. bridleth not *his* tongue, but deceiveth *his* own heart, this

2:21. he had offered Isaac *his* son upon

3:13. *his* works with meekness of wisdom.

4:11. judgeth *his* brother, speaketh evil

5:18. the earth brought forth *her* fruit.

1Pet. 1: 3. according to *his* abundant mercy

2: 9. into *his* marvellous light:

24. bare our sins in *his own* body

3:10. let him refrain *his* tongue from evil, and *his* lips that they speak no guile:

5:10. called us unto *his* eternal glory

2Pet. 1: 9. was purged from *his* old sins.

2:12. perish in *their* own corruption;

13. with *their* own deceivings while

3: 3. walking after *their* own lusts,

16. unto *their* own destruction.

1Joh. 2: 9. hateth *his* brother, is in darkness

10. He that loveth *his* brother abideth

11. he that hateth *his* brother is in

3:10. he that loveth not *his* brother.

12. that wicked one, and slew *his* brother.

15. Whosoever hateth *his* brother is

16. he laid down *his* life for us:

17. seeth *his* brother have need, and shutteth up *his* bowels (of compassion)

4: 9. God sent *his* only begotten Son

10. sent *his* Son (to be) the propitiation

13. he hath given us of *his* Spirit.

20. I love God, and hateth *his* brother,

— he that loveth not *his* brother

21. who loveth God love *his* brother also.

5: 9. he hath testified of *his* Son.

10. record that God gave of *his* Son.

16. If any man see *his* brother sin

Jude 14. with ten thousands of *his* saints,

16. walking after *their own* lusts;

24. before the presence of *his* glory

Rev. 1: 1. to shew unto *his* servants things

— sent and signified (it) by *his* angel unto *his* servant John:

5. from our sins in *his own* blood,

6. priests unto God and *his* Father;

16. he had in *his* right hand seven

— as the sun shineth in *his* strength.

17. he laid *his* right hand upon me,

2: 1. seven stars in *his* right hand,

18. who hath *his* eyes like unto a flame

21. to repent of *her* fornication;

22. except they repent of *their* deeds.

3: 4. have not defiled *their* garments;

4: 4. had on *their* heads crowns of gold.

10. cast *their* crowns before the throne,

6: 5. a pair of balances in *his* hand.

13. a fig tree casteth *her* untimely figs,

14. were moved out of *their* places.

7:11. before the throne on *their* faces,

14. have washed *their* robes, and made them (lit. *their* robes) white in the blood

8:12. shone not for a third part *of it*,

9: 4. seal of God in *their* foreheads.

11. they had a king over *them*,

20. not of the works of *their* hands,

21. Neither repented they of *their* murders, nor of *their* sorceries, nor of *their* fornication, nor of *their* thefts.

10: 2. he had in *his* hand a little book open: and he set *his* right foot upon the sea,

5. lifted up *his* hand to heaven,

11: 7. shall have finished *their* testimony,

11. they stood upon *their* feet; and

16. sat before God on *their* seats, fell upon *their* faces, and worshipped

Rev 12: 3. seven crowns upon *his* heads.

11. by the word of *their* testimony; and they loved not *their* lives unto

14. into *her* place, where she is

15. the serpent cast out of *his* mouth

16. the earth opened *her* mouth,

— the dragon cast out of *his* mouth.

13: 2. the dragon gave him *his* power, and *his* seat,

6. he opened *his* mouth in blasphemy

14: 1. name written in *their* foreheads.

2. harpers harping with *their* harps:

8. the wrath of *her* fornication.

9. mark in *his* forehead, or in *his* hand,

13. they may rest from *their* labours;

14. having on *his* head a golden crown, and in *his* hand a sharp sickle.

16. thrust in *his* sickle on the earth;

19. the angel thrust in *his* sickle

16: 2. poured out *his* vial upon the earth;

3. poured out *his* vial upon the sea;

4. poured out *his* vial upon the rivers

8. poured out *his* vial upon the sun;

10. poured out *his* vial upon the seat

— they gnawed *their* tongues for pain,

11. because of *their* pains and *their* sores, and repented not of *their* deeds.

12. poured out *his* vial upon the great river

15. watcheth, and keepeth *his* garments,

17. poured out *his* vial into the air;

19. wine of the fierceness of *his* wrath.

17: 4. a golden cup in *her* hand full

— filthiness of *her* fornication:

5. upon *her* forehead (was) a name

17. in their hearts to fulfil *his* will,

— give *their* kingdom unto the beast,

18: 7. for she saith in *her* heart,

19. they cast dust on *their* heads,

19: 2. the earth with *her* fornication,

— avenged the blood of *his* servants

16. on *his* thigh a name written,

20: 1. a great chain in *his* hand.

4. mark upon *their* foreheads, or in *their* hands;

7. Satan shall be loosed out of *his* prison,

21: 2. a bride adorned for *her* husband.

24. bring *their* glory and honour into it.

22: 2. yielded *her* fruit every month:

6. sent *his* angel to shew unto *his* servants

αὐτόχειρ, autokīr.

Acts 27:19. we cast out *with* our *own hands*

αὐχμηρός, aukmeeros.

2Pet. 1:19. light that shineth in a *dark* place,

ἀφαιρέω, aphaireo.

Mat 26:51. high priest's, and *smote off* his ear.

Mar 14:47. high priest, and *cut off* his ear.

Lu. 1:25. *to take away* my reproach among men.

10:42. *shall not be taken away* from her.

16: 3. my lord *taketh away* from me

22:50. high priest, and *cut off* his right ear.

Ro. 11:27. when I *shall take away* their sins,

Heb 10: 4. should *take away* sins.

Rev 22:19. if any man *shall take away*

— God *shall take away* his part

ἀφανής, aphanees.

Heb. 4:13. *that is not manifest* in his sight:

ἀφανίζω, aphanizo.

Mat. 6:16. for they *disfigure* their faces,
 19. where moth and rust *doth corrupt*,
 20. neither moth nor rust *doth corrupt*,
Acts13:41. Behold, ye despisers, and wonder, and *perish :*
Jas. 4:14. a little time, and then *vanisheth away.*

ἀφανισμός, aphanismos.

Heb. 8:13. waxeth old (is) ready *to vanish away.*

ἄφαντος, aphantos.

Lu. 24:31. he (lit. he was) *vanished out of* their sight.

ἀφεδρών, aphedrōn.

Mat 15:17. is cast out into the *draught?*
Mar. 7:19. goeth out into the *draught*, purging

ἀφειδία, aphidia.

Col. 2:23. humility, and *neglecting* of the body ;

ἀφελότης, aphelotees.

Acts 2:46. with gladness and *singleness* of heart,

ἄφεσις, aphesis.

Mat 26:28. for many for the *remission* of sins.
Mar. 1: 4. repentance for the *remission* of sins.
 3:29. hath never *forgiveness*, but is in
Lu. 1:77. by the *remission* of their sins,
 3: 3. repentance for the *remission* of sins ;
 4:18(19). to preach *deliverance* to the captives,
 —(—). to set at *liberty* them that are bruised,
 24:47. repentance and *remission* of sins
Acts 2:38. for the *remission* of sins, and ye
 5:31. repentance to Israel, and *forgiveness* of sins.
 10:43. shall receive *remission* of sins.
 13:38. unto you the *forgiveness* of sins:
 26:18. may receive *forgiveness* of sins,
Eph. 1: 7. the *forgiveness* of sins, according
Col. 1:14. (even) the *forgiveness* of sins:
Heb. 9:22. without shedding of blood is no *remission.*
 10:18. Now where *remission* of these (is),

ἀφή, haphee

Eph. 4:16. that which every *joint* supplieth,
Col. 2:19. all the body by *joints* and bands

ἀφθαρσία, aphtharsia.

Ro. 2: 7. glory and honour and *immortality,*
1 Co 15:42. it is raised in *incorruption :*
 50. doth corruption inherit *incorruption.*

1 Co 15:53. must put on *incorruption*, and
 54. shall have put on *incorruption,*
Eph. 6:24. love our Lord Jesus Christ in *sincerity.*
2 Ti. 1:10. brought life and *immortality* to
Tit. 2: 7. uncorruptness, gravity, *sincerity,*

ἄφθαρτος, aphthartos.

Ro. 1:23. the glory of the *uncorruptible* God
1 Co. 9:25. crown; but we an *incorruptible.*
 15:52. dead shall be raised *incorruptible,*
1 Ti. 1:17. unto the King eternal, *immortal,*
1 Pet 1: 4. To an inheritance *incorruptible,*
 23. *incorruptible*, by the word of God,
 3: 4. that which is *not corruptible,*

ἀφίημι, aphieemi.

Mat. 3:15. *Suffer* (it to be so) now:' for thus it
 — Then he *suffered* him.
 4:11. Then the devil *leaveth* him,
 20. they straightway *left* (their) nets, *and*
 22. they immediately *left* the ship *and*
 5:24. *Leave* there thy gift before the
 40. *let* him have (thy) cloke also.
 6:12. *forgive* us our debts, as we *forgive* our debtors.
 14. For if ye *forgive* men their trespasses, your heavenly Father *will* also *forgive* you:
 15. if ye *forgive* not men their
 — *will* your Father *forgive* your trespasses.
 7: 4. *Let* me pull out the mote out of
 8:15. the fever *left* her: and she arose,
 22. *let* the dead bury their dead.
 9: 2. of good cheer; thy sins *be forgiven* thee.
 5. to say (Thy) sins *be forgiven* thee ;
 6. power on earth *to forgive* sins,
 12:31. blasphemy *shall be forgiven*
 — *shall* not *be forgiven* unto men
 32. it *shall be forgiven* him:
 — it *shall* not *be forgiven* him,
 13:30. *Let* both grow together until the
 36. Jesus *sent* the multitude *away, and*
 15:14. *Let* them alone: they be blind
 18:12. *doth* he not *leave* the ninety and
 21. sin against me, and I *forgive* him?
 27. loosed him, and *forgave* him the
 32. I *forgave* thee all that debt,
 35. *forgive* not every one his brother
 19:14. *Suffer* little children, and forbid them not,
 27. Behold, we *have forsaken* all,
 29. every one that *hath forsaken* houses,
 22:22. *left* him, *and* went their way.
 25. *left* his wife unto his brother:
 23:13(14) neither *suffer* ye them that
 23. *have omitted* the weightier
 — not *to leave* the other undone.
 38. your house *is left* unto you desolate.
 24: 2. There *shall* not *be left* here one
 40. one shall be taken, and the other *left.*
 41. one shall be taken, and the other *left.*
 26:44. he *left* them, *and* went away
 56. the disciples *forsook* him, *and* fled.
 27:49. The rest said, *Let be*, let us see
 50. a loud voice, *yielded up* the ghost.
Mar. 1:18. straightway they *forsook* their nets, *and*
 20. they *left* their father Zebedee...*and*
 31. immediately the fever *left* her,
 34. *suffered* not the devils to speak,
 2: 5. Son, thy sins *be forgiven* thee.

Mar. 2: 7. who can *forgive* sins but God
9. (Thy) sins *be forgiven* thee ; or to say,
10. power on earth *to forgive* sins,
3:28. All sins *shall be forgiven* unto
4:12. (their) sins *should be forgiven* them.
36. *when* they *had sent away* the multitude,
5:19. Howbeit Jesus *suffered* him not,
37. he *suffered* no man to follow
7: 8. *laying aside* the commandment
12. ye *suffer* him no more to do
27. *Let* the children first be filled:
8:13. he *left* them, *and* entering into
10:14. *Suffer* the little children *to come*
28. Lo, we *have left* all, and have folk *ved*
29. no man that *hath left* house, or
11: 6. commanded: and they *let* them *go*.
16. *would* not *suffer* that any man
25. *forgive*, if ye have ought against
— *may forgive* you your trespasses,
26. if ye *do* not *forgive*, neither
— in heaven *forgive* your trespasses.
12:12. they *left* him, *and* went their way.
19. wife (behind him), and *leave* no children,
20. dying *left* no seed.
21. neither *left* he any seed: and
22. the seven had her, and *left* no seed:
13: 2. there *shall* not *be left* one stone
34. who *left* his house, *and* gave
14: 6. Jesus said, *Let* her *alone ;*
50. they all *forsook* him, *and* fled.
15:36. saying, *Let alone ;* let us see
37. Jesus *cried* with a loud voice, *and* gave up
the ghost.
Lu. 4:39. rebuked the fever; and it *left* her:
5:11. they *forsook* all, *and* followed him.
20. Man, thy sins *are forgiven* thee.
21. Who can *forgive* sins, but God
23. Thy sins *be forgiven* thee ; or
24. power upon earth *to forgive* sins,
6:42. Brother, *let* me pull out the mote
7:47. Her sins, which are many, *are forgiven ;*
— to whom little *is forgiven*,
48. said unto her, Thy sins *are forgiven*.
49. Who is this that *forgiveth* sins also?
8:51. he *suffered* no man to go in,
9:60. *Let* the dead bury their dead:
10:30. departed, *leaving* (him) half dead.
11: 4. *forgive* us our sins ; for we also *forgive*
every one
42. not *to leave* the other undone.
12:10. it *shall be forgiven* him: but
— it *shall* not *be forgiven*.
39. not *have suffered* his house to be
13: 8. Lord, *let* it *alone* this year also,
35. your house *is left* unto you desolate:
17: 3. if he repent, *forgive* him.
4. saying, I repent ; thou *shalt forgive* him.
34. taken, the other *shall be left*.
35. one shall be taken, and the other *left*.
36. one shall be taken, and the other *left*.
18:16. *Suffer* little children to come unto me,
28. Peter said, Lo, we *have left* all,
29. no man that *hath left* house,
19:44. they *shall* not *leave* in thee one stone
21: 6. there *shall* not *be left* one stone
23:34. said Jesus, Father, *forgive* them ;
Joh. 4: 3. He *left* Judæa, and departed again
28. The woman then *left* her waterpot,
52. the seventh hour the fever *left* him.
8:29. the Father *hath* not *left* me alone ;
10:12. *leaveth* the sheep, and fleeth:
11:44. Loose him, and *let* him go.

Joh. 11:48. If we *let* him thus *alone*, all (men)
12: 7. Then said Jesus, *Let* her *alone :*
14:18. I *will* not *leave* you comfortless:
27. Peace I *leave* with you, my peace
16:28. again, I *leave* the world, and go to
32. *shall leave* me alone: and yet I
18: 8. *let* these go their way:
20:23. sins ye *remit*, they *are remitted*
Acts 8:22. of thine heart *may be forgiven* thee.
14:17. he *left* not himself without witness,
Ro. 1:27. *leaving* the natural use of the woman,
4: 7. they whose iniquities *are forgiven*,
1Co. 7:11. let not the husband *put away* (his) wife.
12. *let* him not *put* her *away*.
13. dwell with her, *let* her not *leave* him.
Heb. 2: 8. he *left* nothing (that is) not put
6: 1. *leaving* the principles of the doctrine
Jas. 5:15. they *shall be forgiven* him.
1 Joh 1: 9. faithful and just to *forgive* us (our) sins,
2:12. because your sins *are forgiven*
Rev. 2: 4. thou *hast left* thy first love.
11: 9. *shall* not *suffer* their dead

ἀφικνέομαι, *aphikneomai*.

Ro. 16:19. your obedience *is come abroad*

ἀφιλάγαθος, *aphilagathos*.

2Ti. 3: 3. *despisers of those that are good*,

ἀφιλάργυρος, *aphilarguros*.

1Ti. 3: 3. not a brawler, *not covetous ;*
Heb 13: .5. conversation (be) *without covetousness ;*

ἄφιξις, *aphixis*.

Acts20:29. I know this, that after my *departing*

ἀφίστημι, *aphisteemi*.

Lu. 2:37. which *departed* not from the temple,
4:13. he *departed* from him for a season.
8:13. in time of temptation *fall away*.
13:27. *depart* from me, all (ye) workers of
iniquity.
Acts 5:37. *drew away* much people after him:
38. *Refrain* from these men, and let them
12:10. the angel *departed* from him.
15:38. *who departed* from them from
19: 9. he *departed* from them, *and* separated
22:29. straightway they *departed* from him
2Co 12: 8. that it *might depart* from me.
1Ti. 4: 1. some *shall depart* from the faith,
6: 5. from such *withdraw thyself*.
2Ti. 2:19. name of Christ *depart* from iniquity.
Heb. 3:12. in *departing* from the living God.

ἄφνω, *aphno*.

Acts 2: 2. *suddenly* there came a sound
16:26. *suddenly* there was a great earthquake,
28: 6. swollen, or fallen down dead *suddenly :*

ἀφόβως, aphobōs.

Lu. 1:74. might serve him *without fear,*
1Co 16:10. he may be with you *without fear:*
Phi. 1:14. bold to speak the word *without fear.*
Jude 12. feeding themselves *without fear:*

ἀφομοιόω, aphomoi-oō.

Heb. 7: 3. *made like* unto the Son of God;

ἀφοράω, aphoraō.

Phi. 2:23. so soon as *I shall see*
Heb12: 2. *Looking* unto Jesus the author and

ἀφορίζω, aphorizo.

Mat 13:49. *sever* the wicked from among the just,
25:32. he *shall separate* them one from another,
as a shepherd *divideth* (his) sheep
Lu. 6:22. when they *shall separate* you (from)
Acts13: 2. *Separate* me Barnabas and Saul for
19: 9. from them, and *separated* the disciples,
Ro. 1: 1. *separated* unto the gospel of God,
2Co. 6:17. *be* ye *separate,* saith the Lord,
Gal. 1:15. *who separated* me from my mother's
2:12. he withdrew and *separated* himself,

ἀφορμή, aphormee.

Ro. 7: 8. taking *occasion* by the commandment,
11. taking *occasion* by the commandment,
2Co. 5:12. give you *occasion* to glory on our behalf,
11:12. that I may cut off *occasion* from them
which desire *occasion;*
Gal. 5:13. (use) not liberty for an *occasion* to
1Ti. 5:14. give none *occasion* to the adversary

ἀφρίζω, aphrizo.

Mar. 9:18. he *foameth,* and gnasheth with his teeth,
20. fell on the ground, and wallowed *foaming.*

ἀφρός, aphros.

Lu. 9:39. teareth him that he foameth again, (lit.
with *foaming*)

ἀφροσύνη, aphrosunee.

Mar. 7:22. blasphemy, pride, *foolishness:*
2Co.11: 1. bear with me a little in (my) *folly:*
17. as it were foolishly (lit. in *folly*), in this
confidence
21. I speak *foolishly,* I am bold also.

ἄφρων, aphrōn.

Lu. 11:40. (Ye) *fools,* did not he that made
12:20. (Thou) *fool,* this night thy soul
Ro. 2:20. An instructor of the *foolish,* a
1Co.15:36. (Thou) *fool,* that which thou sowest
2Co.11:16. Let no man think me a *fool;*

2Co.11:16. yet as a *fool* receive me,
19. For ye suffer *fools* gladly, seeing
12: 6. I shall not be a *fool;* for I
11. I am become a *fool* in glorying;
Eph. 5:17. Wherefore be ye not *unwise,*
1Pet.2:15. silence the ignorance of *foolish* men:

ἀφυπνόω, aphupnoō.

Lu. 8:23. as they sailed he *fell asleep:*

ἄφωνος, aphōnos.

Acts 8:32. like a lamb *dumb* before his shearer,
1Co.12: 2. carried away unto these *dumb* idols,
14:10. none of them (is) *without signification.*
2Pet.2:16. the *dumb* ass speaking with man's voice

ἀχάριστος, akaristos.

Lu. 6:35. he is kind unto the *unthankful* and (to)
2Ti. 3: 2. disobedient to parents, *unthankful,*

ἀχειροποίητος, akīropoi-eetos.

Mar 14:58. will build another *made without hands.*
2Co. 5: 1. an house *not made with hands,*
Col. 2:11. the circumcision *made without hands,*

ἀχλύς, aklus.

Acts13:11. there fell on him a *mist* and a

ἀχρειόομαι, akrīo-omai.

Ro. 3:12. they *are* together *become unprofitable;*

ἀχρεῖος, akrīos.

Mat.25:30. cast ye the *unprofitable* servant
Lu. 17:10. say, We are *unprofitable* servants:

ἄχρηστος, akreestos.

Philem 11. in time past was to thee *unprofitable,*

ἄχρι & ἄχρις, akri & akris.

Observe.—Those marked [2] are αχρις.
Mat.24:38. *until* the day that Noe entered
Lu. 1:20. *until* the day that these things
4:13. departed from him *for a season.*
17:27. *until* the day that Noe entered
21:24. *until* the times of the Gentiles
Acts 1: 2. *Until* the day in which he was
2:29. his sepulchre is with us *unto* this day.
3:21. *until* the times of restitution of
7:18. *Till* another king arose, which knew[2]
11: 5. four corners; and it came *even to* me:
13: 6. through the isle *unto* Paphos,
11. not seeing the sun *for a season.*

Acts20: 4. there accompanied him *into* Asia
    6. unto them to Troas *in* five days ;²
    11. even *till* break of day, so he departed. ²
  22: 4. I persecuted this way *unto* the death,
    22. gave him audience *unto* this word,
  23: 1. conscience before God *until* this day.
  26:22. I continue *unto* this day, witnessing
  27:33. *while* the day was coming on,
  28:15. to meet us *as far as* Appii forum,²
Ro. 1:13. come unto you, but was let hither*to*,
  5:13. For *until* the law sin was in
  8:22. travaileth in pain together *until* now.
  11:25. *until* the fulness of the Gentiles be²
1Co. 4:11. Even *unto* this present hour we
  11:26. shew the Lord's death *till* he come. ²
  15:25. *till* he hath put all enemies under²
2Co. 3:14. for *until* this day remaineth the
  10:13. a measure to reach even *unto* you.
  14. we are come *as far as to* you also in
Gal. 3:19. *till* the seed should come to whom²
  4: 2. *until* the time appointed of the father.
  19. *until* Christ be formed in you,²
Phi. 1: 5. from the first day *until* now ;
  6. *until* the day of Jesus Christ:²
Heb.3:13. *while* it is called To day ;²
  4:12. even *to* the dividing asunder of soul
  6:11. full assurance of hope *unto* the end:
Rev. 2:10. be thou faithful *unto* death,
  25. have (already) hold fast *till* I come:²
  26. keepeth my works *unto* the end,
  7: 3. *till* we have sealed the servants²
  12:11. loved not their lives *unto* the death.
  14:20. even *unto* the horse bridles,
  15: 8. *till* the seven plagues of the seven
  17:17. *until* the words of God shall
  18: 5. her sins have reached *unto* heaven,
  20: 3. *till* the thousand years should

ἄχυρον, *akuron.*

Mat. 3:12. he will burn up the *chaff* with
Lu. 3:17. the *chaff* he will burn with fire

ἀψευδής, *apsūdees.*

Tit. 1: 2. which God, *that cannot lie,* ·

ἄψινθος, *apsinthos.*

Rev. 8:11. third part of the waters became *wormwood ;*

ἄψυχος, *apsukos.*

1Co.14: 7. things *without life* giving sound,

βαθμός, *bathmos.*

1Ti. 3:13. purchase to themselves a good *degree,*

βάθος, *bathos.*

Mat.13: 5. they had no *deepness* of earth:

Mar. 4: 5. because it had no *depth* of earth:
Lu. 5: 4. Launch out into the *deep,* and let
Ro. 8:39. Nor height, nor *depth,* nor any other
  11:33. O the *depth* of the riches both of
1Co. 2:10. yea, the *deep things* of God.
2Co. 8: 2. their *deep* poverty abounded
Eph. 3:18. the breadth, and length, and *depth,* and
Rev. 2:24. have not known the *depths* of Satan,

βαθύνω, *bathuno.*

Lu. 6:48. which built an house, and digged *deep*
  (lit. and *deepened*)

βαθύς, *bathus.*

Lu. 24: 1. *very early* in the morning, they came
Joh. 4:11. to draw with, and the well is *deep:*
Acts20: 9. being fallen into a *deep* sleep:

βαΐον, *bai-on.*

Joh.12:13. Took *branches* of palm-trees, and went

βαλάντιον, *balantion.*

Lu. 10: 4. Carry neither *purse,* nor scrip,
  12:33. provide yourselves *bags* which wax not old,
  22:35. I sent you without *purse,* and scrip,
  36. he that hath a *purse,* let him take (**it**),

βάλλω, *ballo.*

Mat. 3:10. hewn down, and *cast* into the fire.
  4: 6. the Son of God, *cast* thyself down:
  18. *casting* a net into the sea: for
  5:13. good for nothing, but *to be cast* out,
  25. to the officer, and thou *be cast* into prison.
  29. pluck it out, and *cast* (it) from thee:
  — whole body *should be cast* into hell.
  30. cut it off, and *cast* it from thee:
  — whole body *should be cast* into hell.
  6:30. to morrow is *cast* into the oven,
  7: 6. neither *cast* ye your pearls before swine,
  19. hewn down, and *cast* into the fire.
  8: 6. my servant *lieth* at home sick
  14. he saw his wife's mother *laid,* and sick
  9: 2. sick of the palsy, *lying* on a bed:
  17. Neither do men *put* new wine into
  — they *put* new wine into new bottles,
  10:34. that I am come *to send* peace on earth:
    I come not *to send* peace,
  13:42. *shall cast* them into a furnace
  47. a net, that was *cast* into the sea,
  48. good into vessels, but *cast* the bad away.
  50. *shall cast* them into the furnace
  15:26. children's bread, and *to cast* (it) to dogs.
  17:27. go thou to the sea, and *cast* an hook,
  18: 8. cut them off, and *cast* (them) from thee
  — *to be cast* into everlasting fire.
  9. pluck it out, and *cast* (it) from thee:
  — two eyes *to be cast* into hell fire.
  30. went and *cast* him into prison,
  21:21. *be* thou *cast* into the sea ;
  25:27. therefore *to have put* my money
  26:12. *in that* she hath *poured* this

Mat.27: 6. for *to put* them into the treasury,
    35. parted his garments, *casting* lots:
    — upon my vesture *did* they *cast* lots.
Mar. 1:16. *casting* a net into the sea:
    2:22. no man *putteth* new wine into
    4:26. a man *should cast* seed into the ground;
    7:27. children's bread, and *to cast* (it) unto the dogs.
    30. her daughter *laid* upon the bed.
    33. *put* his fingers into his ears, and
    9:22. it *hath cast* him into the fire,
    42. his neck, and he *were cast* into the sea.
    45. two feet *to be cast* into hell,
    47. two eyes *to be cast* into hell fire:
   11:23. removed, and *be* thou *cast* into the sea;
   12:41. people *cast* money into the treasury: and many that were rich *cast* in much.
    42. she *threw* in two mites, which make
    43. this poor widow hath *cast* more in, than all they which *have cast* into
    44. (they) *did cast* in of their abundance; but she of her want *did cast* in all
   14:65. the servants *did strike* him
   15:24. parted his garments, *casting* lots
Lu. 3: 9. is hewn down, and *cast* into the fire.
   4: 9. *cast* thyself down from hence:
   5:37. no man *putteth* new wine into
   12:28. to morrow is *cast* into the oven ;
    49. I am come *to send* fire on the earth ;
    58. the officer *cast* thee into prison.
   13: 8. till I shall dig about it, and dung (it): (lit. *cast in* dung)
    19. a man took, and *cast* into his garden ;
   14:35. for the dunghill ; (but) men *cast* it out.
   16:20. Lazarus, which *was laid* at his gate,
   21: 1. the rich men *casting* their gifts
    2. a certain poor widow *casting* in
    3. this poor widow *hath cast* in more
    4. of their abundance *cast* in unto
    — she of her penury *hath cast* in
   23:19. for murder, was *cast* into prison.
    25. for sedition and murder was *cast* into prison,
    34. parted his raiment, and *cast* lots.
Joh. 3:24. John was not yet *cast* into prison.
   5: 7. to *put* me into the pool: but while
   8: 7. *let* him first *cast* a stone at her.
    59. took they up stones to *cast* at him:
   12: 6. the bag, and bare *what was put* therein.
   13: 2. devil *having* now *put* into the heart
    5. he *poureth* water into a bason,
   15: 6. he *is cast* forth as a branch, and is
    — *cast* (them) into the fire, and they are
   18:11. *Put up* thy sword into the sheath:
   19:24. and for my vesture they *did cast* lots.
   20:25. *put* my finger into the print of the nails, and *thrust* my hand into his side,
    27. *thrust* (it) into my side: and be
   21: 6. *Cast* the net on the right side of
    — They *cast* therefore, and now they
    7. *did cast* himself into the sea.
Acts16:23. they *cast* (them) into prison,
    24. *thrust* them into the inner prison,
    37. *have cast* (us) into prison; and now
   22:23. *as* they...*cast* (off) their clothes, and *threw* dust into the air,
   27:14. there *arose* against it a tempestuous wind,
Jas. 3: 3. *we put* bits in the horses' mouths,
1Joh.4:18. perfect love *casteth out* fear:
Rev. 2:10. the devil shall *cast* (some) of you
    14. Balac *to cast* a stumbling-block
    22. Behold, I *will cast* her into a bed,

Rev. 2:24. I *will put* upon you none other
   4:10. *cast* their crowns before the throne,
   6:13. as a fig tree *casteth* her untimely figs,
   8: 5. *cast* (it) into the earth: and there were
    7. they *were cast* upon the earth:
    8. with fire *was cast* into the sea:
   12: 4. stars of heaven, and *did cast* them to the earth:
    9. the great dragon *was cast out*,
    — he *was cast out* into the earth, and his angels *were cast out* with him.
    13. dragon saw that he *was cast* unto
    15. the serpent *cast* out of his mouth
    16. the dragon *cast* out of his mouth.
   14:16. *thrust* in his sickle on the earth ;
    19. the angel *thrust* in his sickle
    — *cast* (it) into the great wine-press
   18:19. they *cast* dust on their heads,
    21. millstone, and *cast* (it) into the sea,
    — great city Babylon *be thrown down*,
   19:20. These both *were cast* alive into
   20: 3. *cast* him into the bottomless pit,
    10. *was cast* into the lake of fire and
    14. death and hell *were cast* into the lake
    15. *was cast* into the lake of fire.

βαπτίζω, baptizo.

Mat. 3: 6. *were baptized* of him in Jordan,
    11. I indeed *baptize* you with water
    — he *shall baptize* you with the
    13. unto John, *to be baptized* of him.
    14. I have need *to be baptized* of thee,
    16. Jesus, *when* he *was baptized*,
   20:22. *to be baptized*, with the baptism that I *am baptized* with ?
    23. and *be baptized* with the baptism that I *am baptized* with:
   28:19. *baptizing* them in the name
Mar. 1: 4. John *did baptize* in the wilderness,
    5. *were* all *baptized* of him in the
    8. I indeed *have baptized* you with water: but he *shall baptize* you with the
    9. *was baptized* of John in Jordan.
   6:14. That John the *Baptist* was risen
   7: 4. except they *wash*, they eat not.
   10:38. and *be baptized* with the baptism that I am baptized with ?
    39. and with the baptism that I *am baptized* withal *shall* ye *be baptized*:
   16:16. He that believeth and is *baptized* shall
Lu. 3: 7. came forth *to be baptized* of him,
    12. came also publicans *to be baptized*,
    16. I indeed *baptize* you with water ;
    — he *shall baptize* you with the
    21. when all the people were *baptized*, it came to pass, that Jesus also *being baptized*,
   7:29. *being baptized* with the baptism
    30. themselves, *being* not *baptized* of him.
   11:38. *had* not first *washed* before dinner.
   12:50. I have a baptism *to be baptized* with;
Joh. 1:25. said unto him, Why *baptizest* thou then,
    26. saying, I *baptize* with water:
    28. Jordan, where John was *baptizing*.
    31. therefore am I come *baptizing* with
    33. sent me *to baptize* with water,
    — which *baptizeth* with the Holy Ghost.
   3:22. there he tarried with them, and *baptized*
    23. John also was *baptizing* in Ænon
    — they came, and *were baptized*.
    26. behold, the same *baptizeth*, and all

Joh. 4: 1. that Jesus made and *baptized* more disciples
2. Though Jesus himself *baptized* not,
10:40. place where John at first *baptized;*
Acts 1: 5. John truly *baptized* with water;
— ye *shall be baptized* with the Holy Ghost
2:38. Repent, and *be baptized* every one of you
41. received his word *were baptized:*
8:12. *were baptized,* both men and women.
13. *when he was baptized,* he continued
16. only they were *baptized* in the name
36. what doth hinder me *to be baptized?*
38. Philip and the eunuch; and he *baptized*
him.
9:18. forthwith, and arose, and *was baptized.*
10:47. that these should not *be baptized,*
48. commanded them *to be baptized*
11:16. John indeed *baptized* with water;
— ye *shall be baptized* with the Holy Ghost.
16:15. when she *was baptized,* and her
33. *was baptized,* he and all his,
18: 8. hearing believed, and *were baptized.*
19: 3. Unto what then *were ye baptized?*
4. John verily *baptized* with the
5. they *were baptized* in the name
22:16. arise, and *be baptized,* and wash away
Ro. 6: 3. so many of us as *were baptized* into Jesus
Christ *were baptized* into his death?
1Co. 1:13. *were ye baptized* in the name
14. that I *baptized* none of you,
15. that I *had baptized* in mine own name.
16. I *baptized* also the houshold of Stephanas:
besides, I know not whether I *baptized*
any other.
17. Christ sent me not *to baptize,*
10: 2. were all *baptized* unto Moses
12:13. by one Spirit *are* we all *baptized*
15:29. which are *baptized* for the dead,
— why *are* they then *baptized* for
Gal. 3:27. *have been baptized* into Christ

βάπτισμα, baptisma.

Mat. 3: 7. Pharisees and Sadducees come to his
baptism,
20:22. the *baptism* that I am baptized with?
23. with the *baptism* that I am
21:25. The *baptism* of John, whence was it?
Mar. 1: 4. preach the *baptism* of repentance
10:38. the *baptism* that I am baptized with?
39. with the *baptism* that I am
11:30. The *baptism* of John, was (it) from
Lu. 3: 3. preaching the *baptism* of repentance
7:29. baptized with the *baptism* of John.
12:50. I have a *baptism* to be baptized
20: 4. The *baptism* of John, was it from
Acts 1:22. Beginning from the *baptism* of John,
10:37. the *baptism* which John preached;
13:24. the *baptism* of repentance to all
18:25. knowing only the *baptism* of John.
19: 3. they said, Unto John's *baptism.*
4. with the *baptism* of repentance,
Ro. 6: 4. with him by *baptism* into death:
Eph. 4: 5. One Lord, one faith, one *baptism,*
Col. 2:12. Buried with him in *baptism,*
1Pet.3:21. (even) *baptism,* doth also now save us

βαπτισμός, baptismos.

Mar. 7: 4. (as) the *washing* of cups, and pots,

Mar. 7: 8. (as) the *washing* of pots and cups:
Heb. 6: 2. Of the doctrine of *baptisms,* and of
9:10. meats and drinks, and divers *washings,*

βαπτιστής, baptistees.

Mat. 3: 1. In those days came John the *Baptist,*
11:11. a greater than John the *Baptist:*
12. from the days of John the *Baptist*
14: 2. This is John the *Baptist;*
8. Give me here John *Baptist's* head
16:14. (that thou art) John the *Baptist:*
17:13. spake unto them of John the *Baptist.*
Mar. 6:24. The head of John the *Baptist.*
25. the head of John the *Baptist.*
8:28. they answered, John the *Baptist:*
Lu. 7:20. John *Baptist* hath sent us
28. a greater prophet than John the *Baptist:*
33. John the *Baptist* came neither
9:19. answering said, John the *Baptist;*

βάπτω, bapto.

Lu. 16:24. that he *may dip* the tip of his finger
Joh. 13:26. shall give a sop *when I have dipped* (it).
Rev.19:13. clothed with a vesture *dipped* in blood:

βάρ€αρος, barbaros.

Acts28: 2. the *barbarous* people shewed us
4. when the *barbarians* saw the (venomous)
Ro. 1:14. to the Greeks, and to the *Barbarians;*
1Co.14:11. unto him that speaketh a *barbarian,*
— (shall be) a *barbarian* unto me.
Col. 3:11. *Barbarian,* Scythian, bond (nor) free:

βαρέω, bareo.

Mat.26:43. asleep again: for their eyes were *heavy.*
Mar.14:40. asleep again: for their eyes were *heavy,*
Lu. 9:32. were with him were *heavy* with sleep:
2Co. 1: 8. we *were pressed* out of measure,
5: 4. do groan, *being burdened:* not
1Ti. 5:16. let not the church *be charged;*

βαρέως, bareōs.

Mat.13:15. (their) ears are *dull* of hearing,
Acts28:27. their ears are *dull* of hearing, and their

βάρος, baros.

Mat.20:12. have borne the *burden* and heat of the day.
Acts15:28. upon you no greater *burden* than
2Co. 4:17. exceeding (and) eternal *weight* of glory;
Gal. 6: 2. Bear ye one another's *burdens,*
1Th. 2: 6. we might have been *burdensome,* as
Rev. 2:24. put upon you none other *burden.*

βαρύνω, baruno.

Lu. 21:34. your hearts *be overcharged* with

βαρύς, barus.

Mat.23: 4. For they bind *heavy* burdens and

Mat.23:23. omitted the *weightier* (matters) of the law,
Acts20:29. shall *grievous* wolves enter in among
    25: 7. laid many and *grievous* complaints
2Co.10:10. letters, say they, (are) *weighty* and power-
    ful;
1Joh.5: 3. his commandments are not *grievous*.

βαρύτιμος, *barutimos*.

Mat.26: 7. box of *very precious* ointment, and

βασανίζω, *basanizo*.

Mat. 8: 6. sick of the palsy, grievously *tormented*.
    29. art thou come hither *to torment* us
14:24. midst of the sea, *tossed* with waves:
Mar. 5: 7. that thou *torment* me not.
    6:48. he saw them *toiling* in rowing,
Lu. 8:28. I beseech thee, *torment* me not.
2Pet.2: 8. *vexed* (his) righteous soul from
Rev. 9: 5. *should be tormented* five months:
    11:10. these two prophets *tormented* them
    12: 2. in birth, *and pained* to be delivered.
    14:10. he *shall be tormented* with fire
    20:10. *shall be tormented* day and night

βασανισμός, *basanismos*.

Rev. 9: 5. their *torment* (was) as the *torment* of
14:11. the smoke of their *torment* ascendeth
18: 7. so much *torment* and sorrow give her:
    10. afar off for the fear of her *torment*,
    15. for the fear of her *torment*, weeping

βασανιστής, *basanistees*.

Mat.18:34. delivered him to the *tormentors*,

βάσανος, *basanos*.

Mat. 4:24. taken with divers diseases and *torments*,
Lu. 16:23. he lift up his eyes, being in *torments*,
    28. also come into this place of *torment*.

βασιλεία, *basilīa*.

Mat. 3: 2. for the *kingdom* of heaven is at hand.
    4: 8. all the *kingdoms* of the world,
    17. for the *kingdom* of heaven is at hand.
    23. preaching the gospel of the *kingdom*,
    5: 3. their's is the *kingdom* of heaven.
    10. for their's is the *kingdom* of heaven.
    19. least in the *kingdom* of heaven:
    — called great in the *kingdom* of heaven.
    20. enter into the *kingdom* of heaven.
    6:10. Thy *kingdom* come. Thy will be
    13. For thine is the *kingdom*, and the
    33. seek ye first the *kingdom* of God,
    7:21. shall enter into the *kingdom* of heaven;
    8:11. Isaac, and Jacob, in the *kingdom* of heaven.
    12. the children of the *kingdom* shall
    9:35. preaching the gospel of the *kingdom*,
    10: 7. The *kingdom* of heaven is at hand.
    11:11. least in the *kingdom* of heaven
    12. until now the *kingdom* of heaven

Mat.12:25. Every *kingdom* divided against
    26. how shall then his *kingdom* stand?
    28. then the *kingdom* of God is come
13:11. mysteries of the *kingdom* of heaven
    19. any one heareth the word of the **kingdom,**
    24. the *kingdom* of heaven is likened
    31. The *kingdom* of heaven is like
    33. The *kingdom* of heaven is like
    38. are the children of the *kingdom;*
    41. shall gather out of his *kingdom*
    43. in the *kingdom* of their Father.
    44. the *kingdom* of heaven is like
    45. Again, the *kingdom* of heaven is
    47. the *kingdom* of heaven is like
    52. instructed unto the *kingdom* of heaven
16:19. the keys of the *kingdom* of heaven:
    28. Son of man coming in his *kingdom*.
18: 1. greatest in the *kingdom* of heaven?
    3. shall not enter into the *kingdom* of heaven
    4. greatest in the *kingdom* of heaven.
    23. Therefore is the *kingdom* of heaven
19:12. for the *kingdom* of heaven's sake.
    14. for of such is the *kingdom* of heaven.
    23. hardly enter into the *kingdom* of heaven.
    24. a rich man to enter into the *kingdom* of
    God.
20: 1. For the *kingdom* of heaven is
    21. the other on the left, in thy *kingdom*.
21:31. go into the *kingdom* of God before you.
    43. The *kingdom* of God shall be taken
22: 2. The *kingdom* of heaven is like
23:13(14). ye shut up the *kingdom* of heaven
24: 7. nation, and *kingdom* against *kingdom:*
    14. this gospel of the *kingdom* shall
25: 1. Then shall the *kingdom* of heaven
    34. inherit the *kingdom* prepared for
26:29. with you in my Father's *kingdom*.
Mar 1:14. the gospel of the *kingdom* of God,
    15. the *kingdom* of God is at hand:
    3:24. if a *kingdom* be divided against itself, that
    kingdom cannot stand.
    4:11. the mystery of the *kingdom* of God:
    26. So is the *kingdom* of God, as if a
    30. shall we liken the *kingdom* of God?
    6:23. unto the half of my *kingdom*.
    9: 1. have seen the *kingdom* of God
    47. to enter into the *kingdom* of God
10:14. for of such is the *kingdom* of God.
    15. shall not receive the *kingdom* of **God**
    23. enter into the *kingdom* of God!
    24. to enter into the *kingdom* of God!
    25. to enter into the *kingdom* of God.
11:10. Blessed (be) the *kingdom* of our **father**
12:34. not far from the *kingdom* of God.
13: 8. *kingdom* against *kingdom:* and
14:25. I drink it new in the *kingdom* of God.
15:43. also waited for the *kingdom* of God,
Lu. 1:33. of his *kingdom* there shall be no end.
    4: 5. all the *kingdoms* of the world
    43. I must preach the *kingdom* of God
    6:20. for your's is the *kingdom* of God.
    7:28. he that is least in the *kingdom* of God
    8: 1. glad tidings of the *kingdom* of God:
    10. the mysteries of the *kingdom* of God:
    9: 2. to preach the *kingdom* of God
    11. spake unto them of the *kingdom* of **God,**
    27. till they see the *kingdom* of God.
    60. preach the *kingdom* of God.
    62. is fit for the *kingdom* of God.
10: 9. The *kingdom* of God is come nigh
    11. the *kingdom* of God is come nigh unto
    you.

Lu. 11: 2. Thy *kingdom* come. Thy will
17. Every *kingdom* divided against
18. how shall his *kingdom* stand ?
20. the *kingdom* of God is come upon you.
12:31. seek ye the *kingdom* of God ;
32. pleasure to give you the *kingdom*.
13:18. what is the *kingdom* of God like ?
20. shall I liken the *kingdom* of God ?
28. the prophets, in the *kingdom* of God,
29. shall sit down in the *kingdom* of God.
14:15. eat bread in the *kingdom* of God.
16:16. the *kingdom* of God is preached,
17:20. when the *kingdom* of God should come,
— The *kingdom* of God cometh not
21. the *kingdom* of God is within you.
18:16. of such is the *kingdom* of God.
17. shall not receive the *kingdom* of God
24. enter into the *kingdom* of God !
25. enter into the *kingdom* of God.
29. for the *kingdom* of God's sake,
19:11. thought that the *kingdom* of God
12. to receive for himself a *kingdom*,
15. returned, having received the *kingdom*,
21:10. nation, and *kingdom* against *kingdom* :
31. the *kingdom* of God is nigh at hand.
22:16. fulfilled in the *kingdom* of God.
18. until the *kingdom* of God shall come.
29. I appoint unto you a *kingdom*, as
30 drink at my table in my *kingdom*,
23:42. when thou comest into thy *kingdom*.
51. waited for the *kingdom* of God.
Joh. 3: 3. cannot see the *kingdom* of God.
5. enter into the *kingdom* of God.
18:36. My *kingdom* is not of this world: if my
kingdom were of this world,
— now is my *kingdom* not from hence.
Acts 1: 3. pertaining to the *kingdom* of God:
6. restore again the *kingdom* to Israel ?
8:12. concerning the *kingdom* of God,
14:22. enter into the *kingdom* of God.
19: 8. concerning the *kingdom* of God.
20:25. gone preaching the *kingdom* of God.
28:23. testified the *kingdom* of God,
31. Preaching the *kingdom* of God,
Ro. 14:17. For the *kingdom* of God is not
1Co. 4:20. the *kingdom* of God (is) not in word,
6: 9. shall not inherit the *kingdom* of God ?
10. shall inherit the *kingdom* of God.
15:24. delivered up the *kingdom* to God,
50. cannot inherit the *kingdom* of God ;
Gal. 5:21. shall not inherit the *kingdom* of God.
Eph. 5: 5. inheritance in the *kingdom* of Christ
Col. 1:13. into the *kingdom* of his dear Son:
4:11. into the *kingdom* of God, which
1Th. 2:12. called you unto his *kingdom* and glory.
2Th. 1: 5. worthy of the *kingdom* of God,
2Ti. 4: 1. at his appearing and his *kingdom* ;
18. unto his heavenly *kingdom* :
Heb 1: 8. righteousness (is) the sceptre of thy
kingdom.
11:33. through faith subdued *kingdoms*,
12:28. receiving a *kingdom* which cannot
Jas. 2: 5. heirs of the *kingdom* which he
2Pet. 1:11. the everlasting *kingdom* of our Lord
Rev. 1: 9. in the *kingdom* and patience of
11:15. The *kingdoms* of this world are
12:10. strength, and the *kingdom* of our God,
16:10. his *kingdom* was full of darkness ;
17:12. have received no *kingdom* as yet ;
17. give their *kingdom* unto the beast,
18. which reigneth (lit. having *dominion*)
over the kings of the earth.

βασίλειον, *basilion*.

Lu. 7:25. live delicately, are in *kings' courts*.

βασίλειος, *basilios*.

1Pet. 2: 9. a *royal* priesthood, an holy nation,

βασιλεύς, *basilus*.

Mat. 1: 6. Jesse begat David the *king*; and David
the *king* begat Solomon of her
2: 1. in the days of Herod the *king*.
2. he that is born *King* of the Jews ?
3. When Herod the *king* had heard
9. When they had heard the *king*,
5:35. for it is the city of the great *King*.
10:18. before governors and *kings* for my sake,
11: 8. soft (clothing) are in *kings'* houses.
14: 9. the *king* was sorry: nevertheless
17:25. the *kings* of the earth take custom
18:23. likened unto a certain *king*, ..nich
21: 5. Behold. thy *King* cometh unto thee,
22: 2. like unto a certain *king*, which
7. when the *king* heard (thereof), he
11. when the *king* came in to see
13. Then said the *king* to the servants,
25:34. Then shall the *King* say unto them
40. the *King* shall answer and say
27:11. Art thou the *king* of the Jews ?
29. saying, Hail, *king* of the Jews !
37. THIS IS JESUS THE *KING* OF THE
JEWS.
42. If he be the *King* of Israel,
Mar 6:14. *king* Herod heard (of him); for
22. the *king* said unto the damsel,
25. with haste unto the *king*, and asked
26. the *king* was exceeding sorry ;
27. immediately the *king* sent an
13: 9. before rulers and *kings* for my sake,
15: 2. Art thou the *King* of the Jews ?
9. I release unto you the *King* of the Jews ?
12. whom ye call the *King* of the Jews ?
18. salute him, Hail, *King* of the Jews !
26. written over, THE *KING* OF THE
JEWS.
32. Let Christ the *King* of Israel
Lu. 1: 5. days of Herod, the *king* of Judæa,
10:24. many prophets and *kings* have
14:31. Or what *king*, going to make war against
another *king*,
19:38. Blessed (be) the *King* that cometh
21:12. before *kings* and rulers for my name's
sake.
22:25. The *kings* of the Gentiles exercise
23: 2. that he himself is Christ a *King*.
3. Art thou the *King* of the Jews ?
37. If thou be the *King* of the Jews,
38. THIS IS THE *KING* OF THE JEWS.
Joh. 1:49(50). thou art the *King* of Israel.
6:15. by force, to make him a *king*,
12:13. Blessed (is) the *King* of Israel
15. thy *King* cometh, sitting on an ass's colt.
18:33. Art thou the *King* of the Jews ?
37. said unto him, Art thou a *king* then ?
Jesus answered, Thou sayest that I am
a *king*.
39. release unto you the *King* of the Jews ?
19: 3. said, Hail, *King* of the Jews !
12. whosoever maketh himself a *king*

Joh. 19:14. saith unto the Jews, Behold your *King!*
15. Shall I crucify your *King?*
— We have no *king* but Cæsar.
19. JESUS OF NAZARETH THE *KING* OF THE JEWS.
21. Write not, The *King* of the Jews ; but that he said, I am *King* of the Jews.
Acts 4:26. The *kings* of the earth stood up,
7:10. sight of Pharaoh *king* of Egypt ;
18. Till another *king* arose, which
9:15. my name before the Gentiles, and *kings,*
12: 1. Herod the *king* stretched forth
20. Blastus the *king's* chamberlain
13:21. afterward they desired a *king :*
22. unto them David to be their *king ;*
17: 7. saying that there is another *king,*
25:13. *king* Agrippa and Bernice came
14. declared Paul's cause unto the *king,*
24. Festus said, *King* Agrippa, and all
26. before thee, O *king* Agrippa,
26: 2. I think myself happy, *king* Agrippa,
7. For which hope's sake, *king* Agrippa,
13. At midday, O *king,* I saw in
19. Whereupon, O *king* Agrippa,
26. the *king* knoweth of these things,
27. *King* Agrippa, believest thou
30. the *king* rose up, and the governor,
2Co.11:32. the governor under Aretas the *king*
1Ti. 1:17. Now unto the *King* eternal,
2: 2. For *kings,* and (for) all that are in
6:15. the *King* of kings, and Lord of lords ;
Heb 7: 1. Melchisedec, *king* of Salem,
— from the slaughter of the *kings,*
2. interpretation *King* of righteousness, and after that also *King* of Salem, which is, *King* of peace ;
11:23. afraid of the *king's* commandment.
27. fearing the wrath of the *king :* for
1Pet.2:13. whether it be to the *king,* as supreme ;
17. Fear God. Honour the *king.*
Rev. 1: 5. the prince of the *kings* of the earth.
6. hath made us *kings* and priests unto
5:10. made us unto our God *kings* and priests:
6:15. the *kings* of the earth, and the great
9:11. they had a *king* over them, (which is)
10:11. peoples, and nations, and tongues, and *kings.*
15: 3. true (are) thy ways, thou *King* of saints.
16:12. the way of the *kings* of the east might
14. go forth unto the *kings* of the earth
17: 2. With whom the *kings* of the earth
10. there are seven *kings :* five are fallen,
12. horns which thou sawest are ten *kings,*
— receive power as *kings* one hour
14. Lord of lords, and *King* of kings:
18. reigneth over the *kings* of the earth.
18: 3. the *kings* of the earth have committed
9. the *kings* of the earth, who have
19:16. written, *KING* OF *KINGS,* AND LORD OF LORDS.
18. That ye may eat the flesh of *kings,*
19. I saw the beast, and the *kings* of the earth,
21:24. the *kings* of the earth do bring their

βασιλεύω, *basilūo.*

Mat. 2:22. that Archelaus *did reign* in Judæa
Lu. 1:33. he *shall reign* over the house of Jacob
19:14. We will not have this (man) *to reign* over us.
27. not that I should *reign* over them, .

Ro. 5:14. death *reigned* from Adam to Moses,
17. by one man's offence death *reigned*
— *shall reign* in life by one, Jesus Christ.
21. as sin *hath reigned* unto death, even so might grace *reign* through
6:12. *Let* not sin therefore *reign* in
1Co. 4: 8. ye *have reigned* as kings without us: and I would to God ye *did reign,*
15:25. For he must *reign,* till he hath put
1Ti. 6:15. the King of *kings* (lit. of *them that reign*), and Lord of lords ;
Rev. 5:10. we *shall reign* on the earth.
11:15. his Christ ; and he *shall reign* for ever and ever.
17. to thee thy great power, and *hast reigned.*
19: 6. the Lord God omnipotent *reigneth.*
20: 4. they lived and *reigned* with Christ
6. *shall reign* with him a thousand years.
22: 5. they *shall reign* for ever and ever.

βασιλικός, *basilikós.*

Joh. 4:46. there was a certain *nobleman,* whose
49. The *nobleman* saith unto him,
Acts12:20. was nourished by the *king's* (country).
21. Herod, arrayed in *royal* apparel, sat
Jas. 2: 8. If ye fulfil the *royal* law according

βασίλισσα, *basilissa.*

Mat 12:42. The *queen* of the south shall rise
Lu. 11:31. The *queen* of the south shall rise up
Acts 8:27. under Candace *queen* of the Ethiopians,
Rev 18: 7. she saith in her heart, I sit a *queen,*

βάσις, *basis.*

Acts 3: 7. his *feet* and ancle bones received strength.

βασκαίνω, *baskaino.*

Gal. 3: 1. O foolish Galatians, who *hath bewitched* you,

βαστάζω, *bastazo.*

Mat. 3:11. whose shoes I am not worthy *to bear :*
8:17. our infirmities, and *bare* (our) sicknesses.
20:12. *which have borne* the burden and heat
Mar 14:13. a man *bearing* a pitcher of water:
Lu. 7:14. they *that bare* (him) stood still.
10: 4. *Carry* neither purse, nor scrip, nor shoes:
11:27. Blessed (is) the womb *that bare* thee,
14:27. whosoever *doth* not *bear* his cross,
22:10. a man meet you, *bearing* a pitcher
Joh. 10:31. the Jews *took up* stones again to stone him.
12: 6. had the bag, and *bare* what was put
16:12. ye cannot *bear* them now.
19:17. he *bearing* his cross went forth
20:15. Sir, if thou *have borne* him (hence),
Acts 3: 2. from his mother's womb *was carried,*
9:15. *to bear* my name before the Gentiles,
15:10. our fathers nor we were able *to bear*
21:35. that he was *borne* of the soldiers
Ro. 11:18. thou *bearest* not the root, but the
15: 1. ought *to bear* the infirmities of the
Gal. 5:10. *shall bear* his judgment, whosoever
6: 2. *Bear* ye one another's burdens,
5. every man *shall bear* his own burden

Gal. 6:17. for I *bear* in my body the marks
Rev. 2: 2. how thou canst not *bear* them
  3. *hast borne*, and hast patience, and for
17: 7. the woman, and of the beast *that carrieth* her,

ὁ βάτος, *batos*, m.

Lu. 16: 6. he said, An hundred *measures* of oil.

ἡ βάτος, *batos*, f.

Mar 12:26. how in the *bush* God spake unto him,
Lu. 6:44. nor of a *bramble bush* gather they grapes.
  20:37. even Moses shewed at the *bush*,
Acts 7:30. in a flame of fire in a *bush*.
  35. which appeared to him in the *bush*.

βάτραχος, *batrakos*.

Rev 16:13. I saw three unclean spirits like *frogs*

βαττολογέω, *battologeo*.

Mat. 6: 7. when ye pray, *use not vain repetitions*,

βδέλυγμα, *bdelugma*.

Mat 24:15. see the *abomination* of desolation,
Mar 13:14. shall see the *abomination* of desolation,
Lu. 16:15. is *abomination* in the sight of God.
Rev 17: 4. full of *abominations* and filthiness of
  5. MOTHER OF HARLOTS AND *ABO-MINATIONS* OF THE EARTH.
  21:27. (whatsoever) worketh *abomination*,

βδελυκτός, *bdeluktos*.

Tit. 1:16. being *abominable*, and disobedient,

βδελύσσομαι, *bdelussomai*.

Ro. 2:22. thou that *abhorrest* idols, dost thou
Rev 21: 8. unbelieving, and the *abominable*, and

βέβαιος, *bebaios*.

Ro. 4:16. the promise might be *sure* to all
2Co. 1: 7(6). our hope of you (is) *stedfast*, knowing,
Heb. 2: 2. word spoken by angels was *stedfast*,
  3: 6. rejoicing of the hope *firm* unto the end.
  14. our confidence *stedfast* unto the end;
  6:19. anchor of the soul, both sure and *stedfast*,
  9:17. a testament (is) *of force* after men
2Pet.1:10. make your calling and election *sure*:
  19. also a *more sure* word of prophecy;

βεβαιόω, *bebaioō*.

Mar 16:20. *confirming* the word with signs
Ro. 15: 8. to *confirm* the promises (made)
1Co. 1: 6. testimony of Christ *was confirmed*
  8. Who *shall* also *confirm* you unto
2Co. 1:21. he which *stablisheth* us with you

Col. 2: 7. *stablished* in the faith, as ye
Heb. 2: 3. *was confirmed* unto us by them
  13: 9. the heart be *established* with grace;

βεβαίωσις, *bebaiōsis*.

Phi. 1: 7. defence and *confirmation* of the gospel,
Heb. 6:16. an oath for *confirmation* (is) to them

βέβηλος, *bebeelos*.

1Ti. 1: 9. sinners, for unholy and *profane*,
  4: 7. refuse *profane* and old wives' fables,
  6:20. avoiding *profane* (and) vain babblings,
2Ti. 2:16. shun *profane* (and) vain babblings:
Heb 12:16. any fornicator, or *profane person*,

βεβηλόω, *bebeeloō*.

Mat 12: 5. priests in the temple *profane* the sabbath,
Acts 24: 6. hath gone about *to profane* the temple:

βέλος, *belos*.

Eph. 6:16. to quench all the fiery *darts* of the wicked.

βέλτιον, *beltion*.

2Ti. 1:18. at Ephesus, thou knowest *very well*.

βῆμα, *beema*.

Mat 27:19. was set down on the *judgment seat*,
Joh. 19:13. sat down in the *judgment seat*
Acts 7: 5. no, not (so much as) *to set his foot* on:
  (lit. foot-*room*)
  12:21. sat upon his *throne*, and made an
  18:12. brought him to the *judgment seat*,
  16. drave them from the *judgment seat*.
  17. beat (him) before the *judgment seat*.
  25: 6. next day sitting on the *judgment seat*
  10. I stand at Cæsar's *judgment seat*,
  17. I sat on the *judgment seat*, and
Ro. 14:10. before the *judgment seat* of Christ.
2Co. 5:10. before the *judgment seat* of Christ;

βήρυλλος, *becrullos*.

Rev 21:20. seventh, chrysolite; the eighth, *beryl*;

βία, *bia*.

Acts 5:26. brought them without *violence*:
  21:35. for the *violence* of the people.
  24: 7. with great *violence* took (him)
  27:41. with the *violence* of the waves.

βιάζομαι, *biazomai*.

Mat 11:12. kingdom of heaven *suffereth violence*,
Lu. 16:16. preached, and every man *presseth* into it.

βίαιος, *biaios*.

Acts 2: 2. as of a rushing *mighty* wind,

βιαστής, *biastees.*

Mat 11:12. the *violent* take it by force.

βιελαρίδιον, *biblaridion.*

Rev 10: 2. had in his hand a *little book* open:
　　　 8. Go (and) take the *little book* which is open
　　　 9. said unto him, Give me the *little book.*
　　　 10. I took the *little book* out of the angel's hand,

βιελίον, *biblion.*

Mat 19: 7. to give a *writing* of divorcement,
Mar 10: 4. to write a *bill* of divorcement, and to
Lu. 4:17. delivered unto him the *book* of the prophet
　　　　　 Esaias. And when he had opened the
　　　　　 book, he
　　　 20. he closed the *book,* and he gave (it) again
Joh. 20:30. which are not written in this *book :*
　　　 21:25. could not contain the *books* that
Gal. 3:10. all things which are written in the *book*
2Ti. 4:13. bring (with thee), and the *books,* (but)
Heb. 9:19. sprinkled both the *book,* and all the people,
　　 10: 7. in the volume of the *book* it is written
Rev. 1:11. What thou seest, write in a *book,*
　　 5: 1. on the throne a *book* written within
　　　 2. Who is worthy to open the *book,* and
　　　 3. was able to open the *book,* neither
　　　 4. worthy to open and to read the *book,*
　　　 5. hath prevailed to open the *book,*
　　　 7. he came and took the *book* out of the
　　　 8. when he had taken the *book,* the
　　　 9. Thou art worthy to take the *book,*
　　 6:14. the heaven departed as a *scroll* when
　　 17: 8. whose names were not written in the *book*
　　 20:12. the *books* were opened: and another *book*
　　　　　 was opened, which
　　　 — which were written in the *books,*
　　 21:27. written in the Lamb's *book* of life.
　　 22: 7. sayings of the prophecy of this *book.*
　　　 9. which keep the sayings of this *book :*
　　　 10. sayings of the prophecy of this *book :*
　　　 18. words of the prophecy of this *book,*
　　　 — plagues that are written in this *book :*
　　　 19. things which are written in this *book.*

βιελος, *biblos.*

Mat. 1: 1. The *book* of the generation of Jesus Christ,
Mar 12:26. have ye not read in the *book* of Moses,
Lu. 3: 4. As it is written in the *book* of the words
　　 20:42. David himself saith in the *book* of Psalms,
Acts 1:20. it is written in the *book* of Psalms,
　　 7:42. written in the *book* of the prophets,
　　 19:19. brought their *books* together, and burned
Phi. 4: 3. whose names (are) in the *book* of life.
Rev. 3: 5. blot out his name out of the *book* of life.
　　 13: 8. not written in the *book* of life of
　　 20:15. found written in the *book* of life
　　 22:19. take away from the words of the *book*
　　　 — take away his part out of the *book* of life,

βίος, *bios.*

Mar 12:44. all that she had, (even) all her *living.*
Lu. 8:14. riches and pleasures of (this) *life,*
　　 43. spent all her *living* upon physicians,

Lu. 15:12. he divided unto them (his) *living.*
　　　 30. hath devoured thy *living* with harlots,
　　 21: 4. cast in all the *living* that she had,
1Ti. 2: 2. a quiet and peaceable *life* in all
2Ti. 2: 4. himself with the affairs of (this) *life ;*
1Pet. 4: 3. the time past of (our) *life* may
1Joh. 2:16. the pride of *life,* is not of the Father,
　　 3:17. whoso hath this world's *good,*

βιόω, *bioō.*

1Pet. 4: 2. should *live* the rest of (his) time in

βίωσις, *biōsis.*

Acts 26: 4. My *manner of life* from my youth,

βιωτικός, *biōtikos.*

Lu. 21:34. drunkenness, and cares *of this life,*
1Co. 6: 3. *things that pertain to this life ?*
　　　 4. ***things pertaining to this life,***

βλαεερός, *blaberos.*

1Ti. 6: 9. (into) many foolish and *hurtful* lusts,

βλάπτω, *blapto.*

Mar 16:18. deadly thing, it *shall* not *hurt* them ;
Lu. 4:35. he came out of him, and *hurt* him not.

βλαστάνω, *blastano.*

Mat 13:26. when the blade *was sprung up,*
Mar 4:27. the seed *should spring* and grow up,
Heb. 9: 4. Aaron's rod *that budded,* and the tables
Jas. 5:18. the earth *brought forth* her fruit.

βλασφημέω, *blaspheemeo.*

Mat. 9: 3. within themselves, This (man) *blasphemeth.*
　　 26:65. saying, He *hath spoken blasphemy ;*
　　 27:39. they that passed by *reviled* him,
Mar. 3:28. wherewith soever they *shall blaspheme :*
　　　 29. he that *shall blaspheme* against
　　 15:29. they that passed by *railed on* him,
Lu. 12:10. unto him that *blasphemeth* against
　　 22:65. *blasphemously* spake they against him.
　　 23:39. which were hanged *railed on* him,
Joh. 10:36. Thou *blasphemest ;* because I said,
Acts 13:45. contradicting and *blaspheming.*
　　 18: 6. *when* they opposed themselves, and *blas-*
　　　　　 phemed,
　　 19:37. nor yet *blasphemers* of your goddess.
　　 26:11. compelled (them) *to blaspheme ;*
Ro. 2:24. the name of God *is blasphemed*
　　 3: 8. as we *be slanderously reported,*
　　 14:16. *Let* not then your good *be evil spoken of*
1Co. 4:13. *Being defamed,* we intreat: we
　　 10:30. why *am* I *evil spoken of* for that
1Ti. 1:20. that they may learn not *to blaspheme.*
　　 6: 1. (his) doctrine *be* not *blasphemed.*
Tit. 2: 5. the word of God *be* not *blasphemed.*
　　 3: 2. *To speak evil of* no man, to be no

Jas. 2: 7. *Do* not they *blaspheme* that worthy
1Pet.4: 4. excess of riot, *speaking evil* of (you):
   14. on their part he *is evil spoken of,*
2Pet.2: 2. the way of truth *shall be evil spoken of.*
   10. are not afraid *to speak evil of* dignities.
   12. *speak evil of* the things that they
Jude   8. despise dominion, and *speak evil of*
   10. these *speak evil of* those things
Rev13: 6. *to blaspheme* his name, and his
16: 9. *blasphemed* the name of God,
   11. *blasphemed* the God of heaven
   21. men *blasphemed* God because

βλασφημία, *blaspheemia.*

Mat.12:31. All manner of sin and *blasphemy*
   — the *blasphemy (against)* the (Holy)
  15:19. thefts, false witness, *blasphemies;*
  26:65. now ye have heard his *blasphemy.*
Mar. 2: 7. doth this (man) thus speak *blasphemies?*
   3:28. *blasphemies* wherewith soever
   7:22. an evil eye, *blasphemy,* pride,
  14:64. Ye have heard the *blasphemy:*
Lu.   5:21. Who is this which speaketh *blasphemies?*
Joh.10:33. for *blasphemy;* and because that
Eph.4:31. clamour, and *evil speaking,* be put away
Col. 3: 8. anger, wrath, malice, *blasphemy,*
1Ti. 6: 4. whereof cometh envy, strife, *railings,*
Jude   9. against him a *railing* accusation,
Rev. 2: 9. (I know) the *blasphemy* of them
  13: 1. upon his heads the name of *blasphemy.*
    5. speaking great things and *blasphemies;*
    6. opened his mouth in *blasphemy*
  17: 3. full of names of *blasphemy,*

βλάσφημος, *blaspheemos.*

Acts 6:11. heard him speak *blasphemous* words
   13. to speak *blasphemous* words
1Ti. 1:13. Who was before a *blasphemer,*
2Ti. 3: 2. covetous, boasters, proud, *blasphemers,*
2Pet.2:11. bring not *railing* accusation

βλέμμα, *blemma.*

2Pet.2: 8. among them, in *seeing* and hearing,

βλέπω. *blepo.*

Mat. 5:28. whosoever *looketh on* a woman to lust
   6: 4. thy Father *which seeth* in secret
    6. thy Father *which seeth* in secret
   18. thy Father, *which seeth* in secret,
   7: 3. why *beholdest* thou the mote that
  11: 4. things which ye do hear and *see:*
  12:22. blind and dumb both spake and *saw.*
  13:13. because they *seeing see* not;
   14. *seeing ye shall see,* and shall not
   16. blessed (are) your eyes, for they *see :*
   17. desired to see (those things) which ye *see,*
  14:30. *when* he *saw* the wind boisterous,
  15:31. *when* they *saw* the dumb to speak,
   — lame to walk, and the blind to *see :*
  18:10. do always *behold* the face of my Father
  22:16. for thou *regardest* not the person
  24: 2. *See* ye not all these things?
    4. *Take heed* that no man deceive
Mar. 4:12. That *seeing* they *may see,* and not
   24. *Take heed* what ye hear: with what
   5:31. Thou *seest* the multitude thronging

Mar. 8:15. Take heed, *beware* of the leaven of
   18. Having eyes, *see* ye not? and having
   23. he asked him if he *saw* ought.
   24. said, I *see* men as trees, walking.
  12:14. for thou *regardest* not the person
   38. *Beware* of the scribes, which love
  13: 2. *Seest* thou these great buildings?
    5. *Take heed* lest any (man) deceive
    9. *take heed* to yourselves: for they
   23. *take* ye *heed :* behold, I have
   33. *Take* ye *heed,* watch and pray:
Lu.   6:41. why *beholdest* thou the mote
   42. *when* thou thyself *beholdest* not the beam
   7:21. many (that were) blind he gave *sight.*
   44. said unto Simon, *Seest* thou this woman?
   8:10. that *seeing* they *might* not *see,*
   16. which enter in may *see* the light.
   18. *Take heed* therefore how ye hear:
   9:62. hand to the plough, and *looking* back,
  10:23. Blessed (are) the eyes *which see* the
       things that ye *see :*
   24. to see those things which ye *see,*
  11:33. which come in may *see* the light.
  21: 8. *Take heed* that ye be not deceived:
   30. ye *see and* know of your own selves
  24:12. he *beheld* the linen clothes
Joh. 1:29. John *seeth* Jesus coming unto
   5:19. what he *seeth* the Father do:
   9: 7. therefore, and washed, and came *seeing.*
   15. clay upon mine eyes, and I washed, and
       do see.
   19. how then *doth* he now *see?*
   21. by what means he now *seeth,* we
   25. whereas I was blind, now I *see.*
   39. that they *which see* not *might see;* and that
       they *which see* might be made blind.
   41. now ye say, We *see ;* therefore
  11: 9. because he *seeth* the light of this
  13:22. the disciples *looked* one on another,
  20: 1. *seeth* the stone taken away from
    5. *saw* the linen clothes lying ;
  21: 9. they *saw* a fire of coals there,
   20. *seeth* the disciple whom Jesus loved
Acts 1: 9. *while* they *beheld,* he was taken up;
   2:33. which ye now *see* and hear.
   3: 4. upon him with John, said, *Look* on us.
   4:14. *beholding* the man which was
   8: 6. *seeing* the miracles which he did.
   9: 8. eyes were opened, he *saw* no man:
    9. days without sight, (lit. not *seeing*)
  12: 9. the angel ; but thought he *saw* a vision.
  13:11. blind, not *seeing* the sun for a season.
   40. *Beware* therefore, lest that come
  27:12. *lieth* toward the south west and
  28:26. *seeing* ye *shall see,* and not perceive:
Ro.   7:23. I *see* another law in my members,
   8:24. hope *that is seen* is not hope: for what a
       man *seeth,* why doth
   25. if we hope for that we *see* not, (then)
  11: 8. eyes that they should not see, (lit. *of* not
       seeing)
   10. darkened, that they may not *see,*
1Co. 1:26. For ye *see* your calling, brethren,
   3:10. *let* every man *take heed* how he
   8: 9. *take heed* lest by any means this
  10:12. *let...*standeth *take heed* lest he fall.
   18. *Behold* Israel after the flesh:
  13:12. For now we *see* through a glass,
  16:10. *see* that he may be with you
2Co. 4:18. *which are seen,* but at the things *which are*
       not *seen:* for the things *which are seen*
       (are) temporal; but the things *which are*
       not *seen* (are) eternal.

2Co. 7: 8. for I *perceive* that the same epistle
 10: 7. *Do* ye *look on* things after the outward
 12: 6. that which he *seeth* me (to be), or
Gal. 5:15. *take heed* that ye be not consumed
Eph.5:15. *See* then that ye walk circumspectly,
Phi. 3:-2. *Beware* of dogs, *beware* of evil workers,
  beware of the concision.
Col. 2: 5. joying and *beholding* your order,
  8. *Beware* lest any man spoil you
 4:17. *Take heed* to the ministry which
Heb. 2: 9. we *see* Jesus, who was made a
 3:12. *Take heed*, brethren, lest there be
 19. So we *see* that they could not enter
 10:25. more, as ye *see* the day approaching.
 11: 1. the evidence of things not *seen*.
  3. things *which are seen* were not
  7. of things not *seen* as yet, moved
 12:25. *See* that ye refuse not him that
Jas. 2:22. *Seest* thou how faith wrought
2Joh. 8. *Look to* yourselves, that we lose
Rev. 1:11. What thou *seest*, write in a book,
 12: 1. I turned *to see* the voice that
 3:18. with eyesalve, that thou *mayest see*.
 5: 3. open the book, neither *to look* thereon.
  4. the book, neither *to look* thereon.
 6: 1. four beasts saying, Come and *see*.
  3. second beast say, Come and *see*.
  5. the third beast say, Come and *see*.
  7. the fourth beast say, Come and *see*.
 9:20. which neither can *see*, nor hear,
 11: 9. nations *shall see* their dead bodies
 16:15. lest he walk naked, and they *see*
 17: 8. *when* they *behold* the beast that was,
 18: 9. when they *shall see* the smoke of her
 22: 8. I John *saw* these things, *and* heard (them).
  And when I had heard and *seen*, I fell

βλητέος, *bleeteos.*

Mar. 2:22. new wine *must be put* into new bottles.
Lu. 5:38. new wine *must be put* into new

βοάω, *boao.*

Mat. 3: 3. The voice of one *crying* in the wilderness,
Mar. 1: 3. The voice of one *crying* in the wilderness,
 15:34. ninth hour Jesus *cried* with a loud voice,
Lu. 3: 4. The voice of one *crying* in the wilderness,
 18: 7. his own elect, *which cry* day and night
 38. he *cried*, saying, Jesus, (thou) son of
  David,
Joh. 1:23. the voice of one *crying* in the wilderness,
Acts 8: 7. unclean spirits, *crying* with loud voice,
 17: 6. unto the rulers of the city, *crying*,
 21:34. some *cried* one thing, some another,
Gal. 4:27. break forth and *cry* thou that travailest

βοή, *boee.*

Jas. 5: 4. the *cries* of them which have reaped

βοήθεια, *boeethia.*

Acts27:17. had taken up, they used *helps*,
Heb. 4:16. find grace *to help* in time of need. (lit. for
  seasonable *help*)

βοηθέω, *boeetheo.*

Mat.15:25. worshipped him, saying, Lord, *help* me.
Mar. 9:22. have compassion on us, and *help* us.
 24. I believe ; *help* thou mine unbelief.
Acts16: 9. Come over into Macedonia, and *help* us.
 21:28. Crying out, Men of Israel, *help:*
2Co. 6: 2. in the day of salvation *have* I *succoured*
  thee :
Heb. 2:18. he is able *to succour* them that are
Rev.12:16. the earth *helped* the woman, and the

βοηθός, *boeethos.*

Heb13: 6. The Lord (is) my *helper*, and I will

βόθυνος, *bothunos.*

Mat.12:11. if it fall into a *pit* on the sabbath day,
 15:14. the blind, both shall fall into the *ditch*.
Lu. 6:39. shall they not both fall into the *ditch?*

βολή, *bolee.*

Lu. 22:41. withdrawn from them about a stone's
  cast,

βολίζω, *bolizo.*

Acts27:28. *sounded, and* found (it) twenty fathoms:
 — gone a little further, they *sounded* again,
  and

βολίς, *bolis.*

Heb 12:20. stoned, or thrust through with a *dart:*

βόρβορος, *borboros.*

2Pet.2:22. to her wallowing in the *mire.*

βορράς, *borras.*

Lu. 13:29. from the *north*, and (from) the south,
Rev.21:13. on the *north* three gates ; on the south

βόσκω, *bosko.*

Mat. 8:30. an herd of many swine *feeding*.
 33. they *that kept* them fled, *and* went
Mar. 5:11. a great herd of swine *feeding*.
 14. they *that fed* the swine fled, and told
Lu. 8:32. an herd of many swine *feeding* on
 34. they *that fed* (them) saw what was done,
 15:15. he sent him into his fields *to feed* swine.
Joh.21:15. He saith unto him, *Feed* my lambs.
 17. Jesus saith unto him, *Feed* my sheep.

βοτάνη, *botance.*

Heb. 6: 7. bringeth forth *herbs* meet for them

βότρυς, *botrus.*

Rev.14:18. gather the *clusters of the vine* of the
  earth ;

βουλεύομαι, bouluomai.

Lu. 14:31. consulteth whether he be able with
Joh. 12:10. the chief priests consulted that
Acts 5:33. took counsel to slay them.
    15:37. Barnabas determined to take
    27:39. a shore, into the which they were minded,
2Co. 1:17. When I therefore was thus minded,
   — that I purpose, do I purpose according

βουλεύτης, boulutees.

Mar 15:43. Joseph of Arimathæa, an honourable counsellor,
Lu. 23:50. (there was) a man named Joseph, a counsellor;

βουλή, boulee.

Lu. 7:30. lawyers rejected the counsel of God
   23:51. consented to the counsel and deed of them;
Acts 2:23. by the determinate counsel and
   4:28. to do whatsoever thy hand and thy counsel
   5:38. for if this counsel or this work be
  13:36. by the will of God, fell on sleep,
  20:27. unto you all the counsel of God.
  27:12. the more part advised (lit. gave counsel) to depart
    42. the soldiers' counsel was to kill
1Co. 4: 5. manifest the counsels of the hearts:
Eph. 1:11. after the counsel of his own will:
Heb. 6:17. the immutability of his counsel,

βούλημα, bouleema.

Acts 27:43. kept them from (their) purpose;
Ro. 9:19. For who hath resisted his will?

βούλομαι, boulomai.

Mat. 1:19. was minded to put her away privily.
  11:27. to whomsoever the Son will reveal (him).
Mar 15:15. Pilate, willing to content the people,
Lu. 10:22. (he) to whom the Son will reveal (him).
  22:42. Father, if thou be willing, remove
Joh. 18:39. will ye therefore that I release
Acts 5:28. intend to bring this man's blood upon us.
  12: 4. intending after Easter to bring
  17:20. we would know therefore what
  18:15. for I will be no judge of such
    27. when he was disposed to pass
  19:30. when Paul would have entered
  22:30. because he would have known the
  23:28. when I would have known the cause
  25:20. I asked (him) whether he would go to
   22. I would also hear the man myself.
  27:43. the centurion, willing to save Paul,
  28:18. would have let (me) go, because
1Co. 12:11. to every man severally as he will.
2Co. 1:15. I was minded to come unto you
Phi. 1:12. I would ye should understand,
1Ti. 2: 8. I will therefore that men pray
  5:14. I will therefore that the younger
  6: 9. they that will be rich fall into temptation
Tit. 3: 8. these things I will that thou affirm
Philem 13. Whom I would have retained with me,
Heb. 6:17. God, willing more abundantly to shew

Jas. 1:18. Of his own will begat he us with the
  3: 4. whithersoever the governor listeth.
  4: 4. whosoever therefore will be a friend of
2Pet. 3: 9. not willing that any should perish,
2Joh. 12. I would not (write) with paper and ink:
3Joh. 10. forbiddeth them that would, and casteth
Jude 5. I will therefore put you in remembrance,

βουνός, bounos.

Lu. 3: 5. every mountain and hill shall be brought
  23:30. Fall on us; and to the hills, Cover us.

βοῦς, bous.

Lu. 13:15. loose his ox or (his) ass from the stall,
  14: 5. have an ass or an ox fallen into a pit,
  19. I have bought five yoke of oxen,
Joh. 2:14. those that sold oxen and sheep and doves,
  15. out of the temple, and the sheep, and the oxen;
1Co. 9: 9. not muzzle the mouth of the ox that
  — Doth God take care for oxen?
1Ti. 5:18. Thou shalt not muzzle the ox that

βραβεῖον, brabion.

1Co. 9:24. run all, but one receiveth the prize?
Phi. 3:14. I press toward the mark for the prize

βραβεύω, brabuo.

Col. 3:15. the peace of God rule in your hearts,

βραδύνω, braduno.

1Ti. 3:15. if I tarry long, that thou mayest
2Pet. 3: 9. The Lord is not slack concerning

βραδυπλοέω, braduploeō.

Acts 27: 7. when we had sailed slowly many days,

βραδύς, bradus.

Lu. 24:25. O fools, and slow of heart to believe all
Jas. 1:19. swift to hear, slow to speak, slow to wrath:

βραδυτής, bradutees.

2Pet. 3: 9. as some men count slackness;

βραχίων, brakiōn.

Lu. 1:51. He hath shewed strength with his arm;
Joh. 12:38. to whom hath the arm of the Lord been
Acts 13:17. with an high arm brought he

βραχύς, brakus.

Lu. 22:58. after a little while another saw him,
Joh. 6: 7. every one of them may take a little.
Acts 5:34. to put the apostles forth a little space;
  27:28. when they had gone a little further,

Heb. 2: 7. madest him a *little* lower than the angels ;
    9. made a *little* lower than the angels
13:22. written a letter unto you in *few words.*

βρέφος, *brephos.*

Lu. 1:41. the *babe* leaped in her womb ;
    44. the *babe* leaped in my womb
  2:12. the *babe* wrapped in swaddling clothes,
    16. Mary, and Joseph, and the *babe* lying in a
18:15. they brought unto him also *infants,*
Acts 7:19. they cast out their *young children,*
2Ti. 3:15. from a *child* thou hast known
1Pet.2: 2. As newborn *babes,* desire the sincere

βρέχω, *breko.*

Mat. 5:45. *sendeth rain* on the just and on the
Lu. 7:38. began *to wash* his feet with tears,
    44. she *hath washed* my feet with tears,
17:29. it *rained* fire and brimstone from
Jas. 5:17. that it might not *rain:* and it *rained* not
Rev 11: 6. that it *rain* not in the days of

βροντή, *brontee.*

Mar. 3:17. which is, The sons of *thunder :*
Joh. 12:29. heard (it), said that it thundered: (lit.
    that there was *thunder*)
Rev. 4: 5. lightnings and *thunderings* and voices:
    6: 1. as it were the noise of *thunder,*
    8: 5. voices, and *thunderings,* and lightnings.
    10: 3. seven *thunders* uttered their voices.
    4. when the seven *thunders* had uttered
    — things which the seven *thunders* uttered,
11:19. lightnings, and voices, and *thunderings,*
14: 2. as the voice of a great *thunder :*
16:18. were voices, and *thunders,* and lightnings ;
19: 6. as the voice of mighty *thunderings,*

βροχή, *brokee.*

Mat. 7:25. the *rain* descended, and the floods came,
    27. the *rain* descended, and the floods came,

βρόχος, *brokos.*

1Co. 7:35. not that I may cast a *snare* upon you,

βρυγμός, *brugmos.*

Mat. 8:12. shall be weeping and *gnashing* of teeth.
13:42. shall be wailing and *gnashing* of teeth.
    50. shall be wailing and *gnashing* of teeth.
22:13. shall be weeping and *gnashing* of teeth.
24:51. shall be weeping and *gnashing* of teeth.
25:30. shall be weeping and *gnashing* of teeth.
Lu. 13:28. shall be weeping and *gnashing* of teeth,

βρύχω, *bruko.*

Acts 7:54. they *gnashed* on him with (their) teeth.

βρύω, *bruo.*

Jas. 3:11. Doth a fountain *send forth* at the

βρῶμα, *brōma.*

Mat.14:15. the villages, and buy themselves *victuals.*
Mar. 7:19. into the draught, purging all *meats ?*

Lu. 3:11. he that hath *meat,* let him do likewise.
  9:13. except we should go and buy *meat* for
Joh. 4:34. My *meat* is to do the will of him
Ro. 14:15. brother be grieved with (thy) *meat,*
    — Destroy not him with thy *meat,*
    20. For *meat* destroy not the work of God.
1Co. 3: 2. fed you with milk, and not with *meat:*
  6:13. *Meats* for the belly, and the belly for
    meats:
  8: 8. *meat* commendeth us not to God:
    13. if *meat* make my brother to offend,
  10: 3. did all eat the same spiritual *meat ;*
1Ti. 4: 3. (commanding) to abstain from *meats,*
Heb. 9:10. (Which stood) only in *meats* and drinks,
  13: 9. not with *meats,* which have not

βρώσιμος, *brōsimos.*

Lu. 24:41. said unto them, Have ye here any *meat ?*
    (lit. *thing eatable*)

βρῶσις, *brōsis.*

Mat. 6:19. where moth and *rust* doth corrupt,
    20. where neither moth nor *rust* doth corrupt,
Joh. 4:32. I have *meat* to eat that ye know
  6:27. Labour not for the *meat* which perisheth,
    but for that *meat* which endureth
    55. For my flesh is *meat* indeed,
Ro. 14:17. the kingdom of God is not *meat* and
1Co. 8: 4. the *eating* of those things that are
2Co. 9:10. both minister bread for (your) *food,*
Col. 2:16. no man therefore judge you in *meat,*
Heb 12:16. for one *morsel of meat* sold his birthright.

βρώσκω, *brōsko.*

Joh. 6:13. over and above unto them *that had eaten.*

βυθίζω, *buthizo.*

Lu. 5: 7. the ships, so that they *began to sink.*
1Ti. 6: 9. which *drown* men in destruction

βυθός, *buthos.*

2Co.11:25. night and a day I have been in the *deep ;*

βυρσεύς, *bursūs.*

Acts 9:43. days in Joppa with one Simon a *tanner.*
  10: 6. He lodgeth with one Simon a *tanner,*
    32. in the house of (one) Simon a *tanner*

βύσσινος, *bussinos.*

Rev.18:16. city, that was clothed in *fine linen,*
  19: 8. she should be arrayed in *fine linen,* clean
    and white: for the *fine linen* is the
    14. clothed in *fine linen,* white and clean.

βύσσος, *bussos.*

Lu. 16:19. was clothed in purple and *fine linen,*
Rev.18:12. pearls, and *fine linen,* and purple, and

βωμός, bōmos.

Acts17:23. I found an *altar* with this inscription.

γάγγραινα, gangraina.

2Ti. 2:17. their word will eat as doth a *canker:*

γάζα, gaza.

Acts 8:27. had the charge of all her *treasure,*

γαζοφυλάκιον, gazophulakion.

Mar 12:41. Jesus sat over against the *treasury,*
— people cast money into the *treasury:*
43. which have cast into the *treasury :*
Lu. 21: 1. casting their gifts into the *treasury.*
Joh. 8:20. These words spake Jesus in the *treasury,*

γάλα, gala.

1Co. 3: 2. I have fed you with *milk,* and not with
9: 7. eateth not of the *milk* of the flock ?
Heb. 5:12. become such as have need of *milk,*
13. For every one that useth *milk* (is)
1Pet.2: 2. desire the sincere *milk* of the word,

γαλήνη, galeenee.

Mat. 8.26. the sea; and there was a great *calm.*
Mar. 4:39. wind ceased, and there was a great *calm.*
Lu. 8:24. they ceased, and there was a *calm.*

γαμέω, gameo.

Mat. 5:32. whosoever *shall marry* her that
19: 9. *shall marry* another, committeth adultery: and *whoso marrieth* her which
10. with (his) wife, it is not good *to marry.*
22:25. the first, *when* he *had married a wife,*
30. in the resurrection they neither *marry,*
24:38. *marrying* and giving in marriage,
Mar. 6:17. Philip's wife: for he *had married* her.
10:11. whosoever shall put away his wife, and *marry*
12. her husband, and *be married* to another,
12:25. they neither *marry,* nor are given in
Lu. 14:20. another said, I *have married* a wife,
16:18. putteth away his wife, and *marrieth*
— whosoever *marrieth* her that is put away
17:27. they drank, they *married wives,* they
20:34. The children of this world *marry,*
35. neither *marry,* nor are given in
1Co. 7: 9. if they cannot contain, *let* them *marry:*
for it is better *to marry* than to burn.
10. unto the *married* I command,
28. if thou *marry,* thou hast not sinned; and
if a virgin *marry,* she hath not sinned.
33. he *that is married* careth for the
34. she *that is married* careth for the
36. he sinneth not: *let* them *marry.*
39. she is at liberty *to be married* to whom
1Ti. 4: 3. Forbidding *to marry,* (and commanding)
5:11. wanton against Christ, they will *marry ;*
14. therefore that the younger women *marry,*

γαμίσκομαι, gamiskomai.

Mar.12:25. neither marry, nor *are given in marriage;*

γάμος, gamos.

Mat.22: 2. a certain king, which made a *marriage*
3. them that were bidden to the *wedding :*
4. (are) ready: come unto the *marriage.*
8. The *wedding* is ready, but they which
9. shall find, bid to the *marriage.*
10. the *wedding* was furnished with guests.
11. which had not on a *wedding* garment:
12. in hither not having a *wedding* garment?
25:10. went in with him to the *marriage :*
Lu. 12:36. when he will return from the *wedding ;*
14: 8. bidden of any (man) to a *wedding,*
Joh. 2: 1. the third day there was a *marriage*
2. called, and his disciples, to the *marriage.*
Heb 13: 4. *Marriage* (is) honourable in all, and the
Rev.19: 7. for the *marriage* of the Lamb is come,
9. unto the *marriage* supper of the Lamb.

γάρ, gar.

Mat. 1:20. *for* that which is conceived in her
&c. &c.

Note.—Always rendered " *for,*" except in,

Mat. 1:18. When *as* his mother Mary was
15:27. Truth, Lord: yet (και γαρ) the dogs
27:23. *Why,* what evil hath he done ?
Mar 7:28. yet (και γαρ) the dogs under
8:38. Whosoever *therefore* shall be ashamed
15:14. *Why,* what evil
Lu. 12:58. When)(thou goest with thine adversary
20:36. Neither)(can they die any more:
23:22. *Why,* what evil hath he done ?
Joh. 3:19. *because* their deeds were evil.
4:37. *And* herein is that saying true,
7:41. Shall)(Christ come
8:42. neither)(came I of myself,
9:30. *Why* herein is a marvellous thing,
10:26. *because* ye are not of my sheep, as
Acts 2:15. *seeing* it is (but) the third hour
4:34. Neither)(was there any among them
8:31. said, How)(can I,
39. *and* he went on his way rejoicing.
16:37. nay *verily ;* but let them come
19:35. what)(man is there that knoweth not
28:20. *because that* for the hope of Israel
Ro. 3: 2. chiefly,)(because that unto them were
4:15. *Because* the law worketh wrath:
5: 7. *yet* peradventure for a good man some
8: 7. law of God, neither *indeed* can be.
15: 2. Let)(every one of us please (his)
27. It hath pleased them *verily ;* and their
1Co. 9:10. For our sakes, *no doubt,* (this) is written:
11: 9. Neither)(was the man created for the
22. *What ?* have ye not houses to eat
2Co.12: 1. I)(will come to visions and revelations
Phi. 1:18. What *then ?* notwithstanding, every
2: 5. Let)(this mind be in you, which was
1Th. 4:10. And *indeed* ye do it toward all the
2Ti. 2: 7. *and* the Lord give thee understanding
Jas. 4:14. It is *even* a vapour, that appeareth for
1Pet.4:15. *But* let none of you suffer as a
2Pet.1: 9. *But* he that lacketh these things
3Joh. 7. *Because that* for his name's sake they

γαστήρ, gasteer.

Mat. 1:18. she was found with child (lit. having in
the *womb*)
23. Behold, a virgin shall be with child, (lit.
having &c.)
24:19. woe unto them that are with child, (lit.
having &c.)
Mar 13:17. woe to them that are with child, (lit. ...)
Lu. 1:31. thou shalt conceive in thy *womb*,
21:23. woe unto them that are with child, (lit.
having &c.)
1Th. 5: 3. as travail upon a woman with child; (lit.
having &c.)
Tit. 1:12. alway liars, evil beasts, slow *bellies*.
Rev.12: 2. she being with child (lit. ...) cried, travailing

γέ, ge.

See also ἄραγε, εἴγε, εἰ δὲ μήγε, καίτοιγε, μενοῦνγε.

Lu. 11: 8. *yet* because of his importunity he
18: 5. *Yet* because this widow troubleth
19:42. even thou, *at least* in this thy day,
24:21. *and beside* (ἀλλα γε) all this, to day is the
third
Acts 2:18. and)(on my servants and on my
8:30.)(Understandest thou what thou
11:18. Then hath)(God also to the Gentiles
Ro. 8:32. He that)(spared not his own Son,
1Co. 4: 8. I would)(to God ye did reign,
6: 3. how much more)(things that pertain
9: 2. apostle unto others, yet *doubtless* I am to
you:

γέεννα, ge-enna.

Mat. 5:22. shall be in danger of *hell* fire.
29. whole body should be cast into *hell*.
30. whole body should be cast into *hell*.
10:28. to destroy both soul and body in *hell*.
18: 9. two eyes to be cast into *hell* fire.
23:15. more the child of *hell* than yourselves.
33. can ye escape the damnation of *hell?*
Mar 9:43. having two hands to go into *hell*,
45. having two feet to be cast into *hell*,
47. having two eyes to be cast into *hell* fire:
Lu. 12: 5. hath power to cast into *hell;*
Jas. 3: 6. of nature; and it is set on fire of *hell*.

γείτων, gīton.

Lu. 14:12. thy kinsmen, nor (thy) rich *neighbours;*
15: 6. calleth together (his) friends and *neighbours,*
9. calleth (her) friends and (her) *neighbours*
Joh. 9: 8. The *neighbours* therefore, and they which

γελάω, gelao.

Lu. 6:21. (ye) that weep now: for ye *shall laugh.*
25. Woe unto you *that laugh* now!

γέλως, gelōs.

Jas. 4: 9. let your *laughter* be turned to

γεμίζω, gemizo.

Mar 4:37. into the ship, so that it *was now full.*
15:36. one ran and *filled* a spunge *full of*
Lu. 14:23. that my house *may be filled.*
15:16. he would fain *have filled* his belly
Joh. 2: 7. *Fill* the waterpots with water. And they
filled them up to the brim.
6:13. *filled* twelve baskets with the
Rev. 8: 5. *filled* it with fire of the altar, and cast (it)
15: 8. the temple *was filled* with smoke

γέμω, gemo.

Mat.23:25. within they *are full* of extortion
27. *are* within *full* of dead (men's) bones,
Lu. 11:39. your inward part *is full* of ravening
Ro. 3:14. Whose mouth (*is*) *full* of cursing
Rev. 4: 6. *full* of eyes before and behind.
8. (they were) *full* of eyes within: and they
5: 8. harps, and golden vials *full* of odours,
15: 7. *full* of the wrath of God, who liveth
17: 3. *full* of names of blasphemy,
4. cup in her hand *full* of abominations
21: 9. seven vials *full* of the seven last plagues,

γενεά, genea.

Mat. 1:17. all the *generations* from Abraham to David
(are) fourteen *generations;*
— into Babylon (are) fourteen *generations;*
— unto Christ (are) fourteen *generations.*
11:16. whereunto shall I liken this *generation?*
12:39. An evil and adulterous *generation*
41. in judgment with this *generation,*
42. in the judgment with this *generation,*
45. also unto this wicked *generation.*
16: 4. A wicked and adulterous *generation*
17:17. O faithless and perverse *generation,*
23:36. shall come upon this *generation.*
24:34. This *generation* shall not pass,
Mar 8:12. Why doth this *generation* seek
— no sign be given unto this *generation.*
38. this adulterous and sinful *generation;*
9:19. O faithless *generation,* how long
13:30. that this *generation* shall not pass,
Lu. 1:48. all *generations* shall call me blessed.
50. from *generation* to *generation.*
7:31. liken the men of this *generation?*
9:41. O faithless and perverse *generation,*
11:29. to say, This is an evil *generation:*
30. Son of man be to this *generation.*
31. with the men of this *generation,*
32. in the judgment with this *generation,*
50. may be required of this *generation;*
51. It shall be required of this *generation.*
16: 8. are in their *generation* wiser than
17:25. be rejected of this *generation.*
21:32. This *generation* shall not pass
Acts 2:40. yourselves from this untoward *generation.*
8:33. who shall declare his *generation?*
13:36. he had served his own *generation*
14:16. Who in *times* past suffered all
15:21. For Moses of old *time* hath in
Eph. 3: 5. Which in other *ages* was not made known
21. throughout all *ages,* world without end.
Phi. 2:15. in the midst of a crooked and perverse
nation,

Col. 1:26. hid from ages and from *generations*,
Heb 3:10. I was grieved with that *generation*,

γενεαλογέομαι, *genealogeomai*.

Heb 7: 6. whose *descent is* not *counted* from them

γενεαλογία, *genealogia*.

1Ti. 1: 4. heed to fables and endless *genealogies*,
Tit. 3: 9. avoid foolish questions, and *genealogies*,

γενέσια, *genesia*.

Mat. 14: 6. when Herod's *birthday* was kept,
Mar 6:21. Herod on his *birthday* made a supper

γένεσις, *genesis*.

Mat. 1: 1. The book of the *generation* of Jesus Christ,
Jas. 1:23. a man beholding his *natural* face in a
 glass:
 3: 6. setteth on fire the course of *nature*;

γενετή, *genetee*.

Joh. 9: 1. a man which was blind from (his) *birth*.

γεννάω, *gennao*.

Mat. 1: 2. Abraham *begat* Isaac; and Isaac *begat*
 Jacob; and Jacob *begat* Judas
 3. Judas *begat* Phares...and Phares *begat*
 Esrom; and Esrom *begat* Aram;
 4. Aram *begat* Aminadab; and Aminadab
 begat Naasson; and Naasson *begat* Salmon;
 5. Salmon *begat* Booz...Booz *begat* Obed of
 Ruth; and Obed *begat* Jesse;
 6. Jesse *begat* David
 — David the king *begat* Solomon
 7. Solomon *begat* Roboam; and Roboam
 begat Abia; and Abia *begat* Asa;
 8. Asa *begat* Josaphat; and Josaphat *begat*
 Joram; and Joram *begat* Ozias;
 9. Ozias *begat* Joatham; and Joatham *begat*
 Achaz; and Achaz *begat* Ezekias;
 10. Ezekias *begat* Manasses; and Manasses
 begat Amon; and Amon *begat* Josias;
 11. Josias *begat* Jechonias
 12. Jechonias *begat* Salathiel; and Salathiel
 begat Zorobabel;
 13. Zorobabel *begat* Abiud; and Abiud *begat*
 Eliakim; and Eliakim *begat* Azor;
 14. Azor *begat* Sadoc; and Sadoc *begat* Achim;
 and Achim *begat* Eliud;
 15. Eliud *begat* Eleazar; and Eleazar *begat*
 Matthan; and Matthan *begat* Jacob;
 16. Jacob *begat* Joseph the husband of Mary,
 of whom *was born* Jesus, who is
 20. that which is *conceived* in her is
 2: 1. *when* Jesus *was born* in Bethlehem
 4. where Christ *should be born*.

Mat. 19:12. which *were* so *born* from (their) mother's
 womb:
 26:24. that man if he *had* not *been born*.
Mar 14:21. that man if he *had* never *been born*.
Lu. 1:13. thy wife Elisabeth *shall bear* thee a son,
 35. that holy thing which *shall be born*
 57. delivered; and she *brought forth* a son.
 23:29. barren, and the wombs that never *bare*,
Joh. 1:13. Which *were born*, not of blood, nor of
 3: 3. Except a man *be born* again, he
 4. How can a man be *born* when he is old?
 — into his mother's womb, and be *born*?
 5. Except a man *be born* of water
 6. That *which is born* of the flesh is flesh;
 and that *which is born* of the Spirit is
 spirit.
 7. Ye must *be born* again.
 8. every one *that is born* of the Spirit.
 8:41. We *be* not *born* of fornication; we
 9: 2. or his parents, that he *was born* blind?
 19. your son, who ye say *was born* blind?
 20. our son, and that he *was born* blind:
 32. the eyes of one *that was born* blind.
 34. Thou *wast* altogether *born* in sins,
 16:21. as soon as she *is delivered of* the child,
 — that a man *is born* into the world.
 18:37. To this end *was* I *born*, and for this cause
Acts 2: 8. our own tongue, wherein we *were born*?
 7: 8. so (Abraham) *begat* Isaac, and circumcised
 20. In which time Moses *was born*,
 29. Madian, where he *begat* two sons.
 13:33. my Son, this day *have* I *begotten* thee.
 22: 3. a man (which am) a Jew, *born* in Tarsus,
 28. Paul said, But I *was* (free) *born*.
Ro. 9:11. For (the children) *being* not yet *born*,
1Co. 4:15. I *have begotten* you through the gospel.
Gal. 4:23. bondwoman *was born* after the flesh;
 24. *which gendereth* to bondage, which
 29. he *that was born* after the flesh
2Ti. 2:23. knowing that they *do gender* strifes.
Philem. 10. whom I *have begotten* in my bonds:
Heb 1: 5. my Son, this day *have* I *begotten* thee?
 5: 5. my Son, to day *have* I *begotten* thee.
 11:12. Therefore *sprang* there even of one, and
 him
 23. By faith Moses, when he *was born*,
2Pet. 2:12. beasts, *made* to be taken and destroyed,
1Joh. 2:29. doeth righteousness *is born* of him.
 3: 9. Whosoever is *born* of God doth not
 — because he *is born* of God.
 4: 7. every one that loveth *is born* of God.
 5: 1. Jesus is the Christ *is born* of God: and
 every one that loveth him *that begat*
 loveth him also *that is begotten* of him.
 4. For whatsoever is *born* of God
 18. whosoever is *born* of God sinneth not;
 but he that is *begotten* of God keepeth

γέννημα, *genneema*.

Mat. 3: 7. O *generation* of vipers, who hath
 12:34. O *generation* of vipers, how can ye,
 23:33. (Ye) serpents, (ye) *generation* of vipers,
 26:29. henceforth of this *fruit* of the vine,
Mar 14:25. drink no more of the *fruit* of the vine,
Lu. 3: 7. O *generation* of vipers, who hath
 12:18. there will I bestow all my *fruits* and
 22:18. I will not drink of the *fruit* of the vine,
2Co. 9:10. increase the *fruits* of your righteousness;

γέννησις, genneesis.

Mat. 1:18. Now the *birth* of Jesus Christ was on
Lu. 1:14. gladness; and many shall rejoice at his *birth*.

γεννητός, genneetos.

Mat.11:11. Among *them that are born* of women
Lu. 7:28. Among *those that are born* of women

γένος, genos.

Mat.13:47. into the sea, and gathered of every *kind:*
17:21. Howbeit this *kind* goeth not out
Mar. 7:26. a Greek, a Syrophenician by *nation;*
9:29. This *kind* can come forth by nothing,
Acts 4: 6. of the *kindred* of the high priest,
36. a Levite, (and) of the *country* of Cyprus,
7:13. Joseph's *kindred* was made known
19. same dealt subtilly with our *kindred,*
13:26. children of the *stock* of Abraham,
17:28. For we are also his *offspring.*
29. then as we are the *offspring* of God,
18: 2. Aquila, *born* in (lit. by *birth* of) Pontus,
24. Jew named Apollos, *born* at Alexandria,
1Co.12:10. to another (divers) *kinds* of tongues;
28. governments, *diversities* of tongues.
14:10. many *kinds* of voices in the world,
2Co.11:26. (in) perils by (mine own) *countrymen,*
Gal. 1:14. many my equals in mine own *nation,*
Phi. 3: 5. of the *stock* of Israel, (of) the tribe of
1Pet.2: 9. ye (are) a chosen *generation,* a royal
Rev.22:16. I am the root and the *offspring* of David,

γερουσία, gerousia.

Acts 5:21. all the *senate* of the children of Israel,

γέρων, geron.

Joh. 3: 4. can a man be born when he is *old?*

γεύομαι, gūomai.

Mat.16:28. which *shall* not *taste* of death, till
27:34. *when* he *had tasted* (thereof), he would
Mar. 9: 1. here, which *shall* not *taste* of death,
Lu. 9:27. *shall* not *taste* of death, till they see
14:24. were bidden *shall taste* of my supper.
Joh. 2: 9. ruler of the feast *had tasted* the water
8:52. saying, he *shall* never *taste* of death.
Acts10:10. very hungry, and would *have eaten:*
20:11. had broken bread, and *eaten,* and talked
23:14. that we will *eat* nothing until we
Col. 2:21. Touch not; *taste* not; handle not;
Heb. 2: 9. *should taste* death for every man.
6: 4. *have tasted* of the heavenly gift, and were
5. *have tasted* the good word of God,
1Pet.2: 3. If so be ye *have tasted* that the Lord

γεωργέομαι, geōrgeomai.

Heb. 6: 7. for them by whom it *is dressed,* receiveth

γεώργιον, geōrgion.

1Co. 3: 9. with God: ye are God's *husbandry,*

γεωργός, geōrgos.

Mat.21:33. let it out to *husbandmen,* and went
34. sent his servants to the *husbandmen,*
35. the *husbandmen* took his servants,
38. when the *husbandmen* saw the son,
40. will he do unto those *husbandmen?*
41. (his) vineyard unto other *husbandmen,*
Mar.12: 1. let it out to *husbandmen,* and went
2. he sent to the *husbandmen*
— might receive from the *husbandmen*
7. those *husbandmen* said among
9. will come and destroy the *husbandmen,*
Lu. 20: 9. a vineyard, and let it forth to *husbandmen,*
10. sent a servant to the *husbandmen,*
— the *husbandmen* beat him,
14. when the *husbandmen* saw him,
16. shall come and destroy these *husbandmen,*
Joh.15: 1. my Father is the *husbandman.*
2Ti. 2: 6. The *husbandman* that laboureth
Jas. 5: 7. the *husbandman* waiteth for the

γῆ, gee.

Mat. 2: 6. thou Bethlehem, (in) the *land* of Juda,
20. go into the *land* of Israel: for they
21. came into the *land* of Israel.
4:15. The *land* of Zabulon, and the *land* of N.
5: 5. the meek: for they shall inherit the *earth.*
13. Ye are the salt of the *earth:* but if
18. Till heaven and *earth* pass, one jot or
35. Nor by the *earth;* for it is his footstool:
6:10. Thy will be done in *earth,* as (it is)
19. for yourselves treasures upon *earth,*
9: 6. man hath power on *earth* to forgive
26. fame hereof went abroad into all that *land.*
31. abroad his fame in all that *country.*
10:15. for the *land* of Sodom and Gomorrha in
29. shall not fall on the *ground* without
34. I am come to send peace on *earth:*
11:24. more tolerable for the *land* of Sodom
25. O Father, Lord of heaven and *earth,*
12:40. three nights in the heart of the *earth.*
42. from the uttermost parts of the *earth* to
13: 5. where they had not much *earth:*
— they had no deepness of *earth:*
8. other fell into good *ground,*
23. received seed into the good *ground*
14:34. came into the *land* of Gennesaret.
15:35. multitude to sit down on the *ground.*
16:19. whatsoever thou shalt bind on *earth*
— whatsoever thou shalt loose on *earth*
17:25. of whom do the kings of the *earth* take
18:18. Whatsoever ye shall bind on *earth*
— whatsoever ye shall loose on *earth*
19. if two of you shall agree on *earth* as
23: 9. call no (man) your father upon the *earth:*
35. righteous blood shed upon the *earth,*
24:30. then shall all the tribes of the *earth*
35. Heaven and *earth* shall pass away,
25:18. received one went and digged in the *earth,*
25. went and hid thy talent in the *earth.*
27:45. there was darkness over all the *land*
51. the *earth* did quake, and the rocks rent;
28:18. given unto me in heaven and in *earth.*
Mar. 2:10. Son of man hath power on *earth* to

Mar. 4: 1. multitude was by the sea on the *land*.
5. where it had not much *earth ;*
— because it had no depth of *earth :*
8. other fell on good *ground*, and did
20. which are sown on good *ground ;*
26. should cast seed into the *ground ;*
28. the *earth* bringeth forth fruit of herself ;
31. when it is sown in the *earth*, is less than all the seeds that be in the *earth :*
6:47. the sea, and he alone on the *land*.
53. came into the *land* of Gennesaret,
8: 6. people to sit down on the *ground*.
9: 3. as no fuller on *earth* can white them.
20. he fell on the *ground*, and wallowed
13:27. from the uttermost part of the *earth*
31. Heaven and *earth* shall pass away :
14:35. fell on the *ground*, and prayed that,
15:33. there was darkness over the whole *land*
Lu. 2:14. on *earth* peace, good will toward men.
4:25. famine was throughout all the *land ;*
5: 3. thrust out a little from the *land*.
11. had brought their ships to *land*,
24. Son of man hath power upon *earth*
6:49. built an house upon the *earth ;*
8: 8. other fell on good *ground*, and sprang
15. that on the good *ground* are they,
27. when he went forth to *land*, there met
10:21. O Father, Lord of heaven and *earth*, that
11: 2. be done, as in heaven, so in *earth*.
31. from the utmost parts of the *earth*
12:49. I am come to send fire on the *earth ;*
51. come to give peace on *earth ?* I tell
56. ye can discern the face of the sky and of the *earth ;* but how
13: 7. why cumbereth it the *ground ?*
14:35. It is neither fit for the *land*, nor
16:17. easier for heaven and *earth* to pass,
18: 8. shall he find faith on the *earth ?*
21:23. shall be great distress in the *land*,
25. upon the *earth* distress of nations,
33. Heaven and *earth* shall pass away :
35. dwell on the face of the whole *earth*.
22:44. of blood falling down to the *ground*.
23:44. there was a darkness over all the *earth*
24: 5. bowed down (their) faces to the *earth*,
Joh. 3:22. his disciples into the *land* of Judæa ;
31. he that is of the *earth* is *earthly*, and speaketh of the *earth :*
6:21. the ship was at the *land* whither
8: 6. with (his) finger wrote on the *ground*,
8. he stooped down, and wrote on the *ground*.
12:24. a corn of wheat fall into the *ground* and die,
32. if I be lifted up from the *earth*,
17: 4. I have glorified thee on the *earth :*
21: 8. they were not far from *land*, but
9. then as they were come to *land*,
11. drew the net to *land* full of great
Acts 1: 8. unto the uttermost part of the *earth*.
2:19. signs in the *earth* beneath ;
3:25. the kindreds of the *earth* be blessed.
4:24. which hast made heaven, and *earth*,
26. The kings of the *earth* stood up,
7: 3. Get thee out of thy *country*,
— come into the *land* which I shall
4. Then came he out of the *land*
— he removed him into this *land*,
6. seed should sojourn in a strange *land ;*
11. a dearth over all the *land* of Egypt
29. was a stranger in the *land* of Madian,
33. where thou standest is holy *ground*.
36. signs in the *land* of Egypt, and in

Acts 7:40. brought us out of the *land* of Egypt,
49. my throne, and *earth* (is) my footstool :
8:33. his life is taken from the *earth*.
9: 4. he fell to the *earth*, and heard a voice
8. Saul arose from the *earth ;* and when
10:11. four corners, and let down to the *earth :*
12. fourfooted beasts of the *earth*,
11: 6. saw fourfooted beasts of the *earth*,
13:17. as strangers in the *land* of Egypt,
19. seven nations in the *land* of Chanaan, he divided their *land* to them by lot.
47. salvation unto the ends of the *earth*.
14:15. God, which made heaven, and *earth*,
17:24. he is Lord of heaven and *earth*, dwelleth
26. to dwell on all the face of the *earth*,
22:22. Away with such a (fellow) from the *earth :*
26:14. when we were all fallen to the *earth*,
27:39. was day, they knew not the *land :*
43. first (into the sea), and get to *land :*
44. that they escaped all safe to *land*.
Ro. 9:17. be declared throughout all the *earth*.
28. will the Lord make upon the *earth*.
10:18. their sound went into all the *earth*,
1Co. 8: 5. whether in heaven or in *earth*,
10:26. For the *earth* (is) the Lord's, and the fulness
28. for the *earth* (is) the Lord's, and the fulness
15:47. The first man (is) of the *earth*, earthy :
Eph. 1:10. are in heaven, and which are on *earth ;*
3:15. the whole family in heaven and *earth* is named,
4: 9. into the lower parts of the *earth ?*
6: 3. thou mayest live long on the *earth*.
Col. 1.16. are in heaven, and that are in *earth*,
20. whether (they be) things in *earth*, or
3: 2. things above, not on things on the *earth*.
5. your members which are upon the *earth ;*
Heb 1:10. hast laid the foundation of the *earth ;*
6: 7. For the *earth* which drinketh in
8: 4. For if he were on *earth*, he should
9. to lead them out of the *land* of Egypt ;
11: 9. he sojourned in the *land* of promise,
13. were strangers and pilgrims on the *earth*.
38. (in) dens and caves of the *earth*.
12:25. refused him that spake on *earth*,
26. Whose voice then shook the *earth :*
— once more I shake not the *earth* only,
Jas. 5: 5. Ye have lived in pleasure on the *earth*,
7. the precious fruit of the *earth*,
12. neither by heaven, neither by the *earth*,
17. it rained not on the *earth* by the
18. the *earth* brought forth her fruit.
2Pet.3: 5. the *earth* standing out of the water
7. the heavens and the *earth*, which are
10. the *earth* also and the works that
13. for new heavens and a new *earth*,
1Joh.5: 8. there are three that bear witness in *earth*,
Jude 5. the people out of the *land* of Egypt,
Rev. 1: 5. prince of the kings of the *earth*.
7. all kindreds of the *earth* shall
3:10. them that dwell upon the *earth*.
5: 3. nor in *earth*, neither under the *earth*,
5. of God sent forth into all the *earth*.
10. we shall reign on the *earth*.
13. on the *earth*, and under the *earth*,
6: 4. to take peace from the *earth ;* and that
8. over the fourth part of the *earth*,
— death, and with the beasts of the *earth*.
10. on them that dwell on the *earth ?*
13. the stars of heaven fell unto the *earth*,
15. the kings of the *earth*, and the great men,

Rev. 7: 1. standing on the four corners of the *earth*,
    holding the four winds of the *earth*, that
    the wind should not blow on the *earth*,
  2. it was given to hurt the *earth*
  3. Saying, Hurt not the *earth*, neither
  8: 5. cast (it) into the *earth:* and there were
    7. blood, and they were cast upon the *earth:*
    13. woe, to the inhabiters of the *earth* by
  9: 1. a star fall from heaven unto the *earth:*
    3. of the smoke locusts upon the *earth:*
    — as the scorpions of the *earth* have power.
    4. should not hurt the grass of the *earth*,
 10: 2. (his) left (foot) on the *earth*,
    5. stand upon the sea and upon the *earth*
    6. the *earth*, and the things that therein are,
    8. standeth upon the sea and upon the *earth*.
 11: 4. standing before the God of the *earth*.
    6. to smite the *earth* with all plagues,
    10. they that dwell upon the *earth* shall
    — tormented them that dwelt on the *earth*.
    18. destroy them which destroy the *earth*.
 12: 4. did cast them to the *earth:*
    9. he was cast out into the *earth:*
    12. Woe to the inhabiters of the *earth*
    13. saw that he was cast unto the *earth*,
    16. the *earth* helped the woman, and the *earth*
    opened her mouth,
 13: 3. all the *world* wondered after
    8. all that dwell upon the *earth*
    11. beast coming up out of the *earth;*
    12. causeth the *earth* and them which
    13. from heaven on the *earth* in the
    14. deceiveth them that dwell on the *earth*
 14: 3. which were redeemed from the *earth*.
    6. unto them that dwell on the *earth*,
    7. him, that made heaven, and *earth*,
    15. for the harvest of the *earth* is ripe.
    16. thrust in his sickle on the *earth;* and the
    earth was reaped.
    18. the clusters of the vine of the *earth;*
    19. angel thrust in his sickle into the *earth*,
    and gathered the vine of the *earth*,
 16: 1. the wrath of God upon the *earth*.
    2. poured out his vial upon the *earth;*
    14. unto the kings of the *earth* and of
    18. not since men were upon the *earth*,
 17: 2. With whom the kings of the *earth*
    — the inhabitants of the *earth* have
    5. OF HARLOTS AND ABOMINATIONS
    OF THE *EARTH*
    8. they that dwell on the *earth* shall
    18. reigneth over the kings of the *earth*.
 18: 1. the *earth* was lightened with his glory.
    3. the kings of the *earth* have committed
    — the merchants of the *earth* are waxed
    9. the kings of the *earth*, who have
    11. the merchants of the *earth* shall weep
    23. were the great men of the *earth;* for
    24. all that were slain upon the *earth*.
 19: 2. which did corrupt the *earth* with
    19. the beast, and the kings of the *earth*,
 20: 8. in the four quarters of the *earth*,
    9. up on the breadth of the *earth*,
    11. the *earth* and the heaven fled away;
 21: 1. I saw a new heaven and a new *earth:* for
    the first heaven and the first *earth* were
    24. the kings of the *earth* do bring their

γῆρας, *geeras.*

Lu. 1:36. also conceived a son in her *old age:*

γηράσκω, *geerasko.*

Joh. 21:18. when thou *shalt be old*, thou shalt
Heb. 8:13. that which decayeth and *waxeth old*

γίνομαι, *ginomai.*

Mat. 1:22. Now all this *was done*, that it
  4: 3. command that these stones *be made* bread.
  5:18. from the law, till all *be fulfilled*.
    45. ye *may be* the children of your Father
  6:10. Thy will *be done* in earth, as (it is)
    16. when ye fast, *be* not, as the hypocrites,
  7:28. it *came to pass*, when Jesus had
  8:13. thou hast believed, (so) *be* it *done* unto
    thee.
    16. *When* the even *was come*, they brought
    24. *there arose* a great tempest in the sea,
    26. the sea ; and there *was* a great calm.
  9:10. it *came to pass*, as Jesus sat at
    16. the garment, and the rent *is made* worse.
    29. According to your faith *be* it unto you.
 10:16. *be* ye therefore wise as serpents,
    25. the disciple that he *be* as his master,
 11: 1. it *came to pass*, when Jesus had made
    20. most of his mighty works *were done*,
    21. the mighty works, *which were done* in you,
    had been done in Tyre
    23. mighty works, *which have been done* in thee,
    had been done in Sodom,
    26. for so it *seemeth* good in thy sight.
 12:45. the last (state) of that man *is* worse
 13:21. *when* tribulation or persecution *ariseth*
    22. choke the word, and he *becometh* unfruitful.
    32. greatest among herbs, and *becometh* a tree,
    53. it *came to pass*, (that) when Jesus
 14:15. *when* it *was* evening, his disciples
    23. *when* the evening *was come*, he was
 15:28. *be* it unto thee even as thou wilt.
 16: 2. said unto them, *When* it *is* evening,
 17: 2. his raiment *was* white as the light.
 18: 3. converted, and *become* as little children,
    12. if a man *have* an hundred sheep,
    13. if so *be* that he find it, verily I say
    19. it *shall be done* for them of my Father
    31. his fellowservants saw *what was done*,
    — unto their lord all *that was done*.
 19: 1. it *came to pass*, (that) when Jesus
    8. from the beginning it *was* not so.
 20: 8. So *when* even *was come*, the lord of
    26. whosoever will *be* great among you,
 21: 4. All this *was done*, that it might
    19. *Let* no fruit *grow* on thee henceforward
    21. thou cast into the sea ; it *shall be done*.
    42. the same *is become* the head of the corner:
    this *is* the Lord's *doing*, and it is mar-
    vellous
 23:15. when he *is made*, ye make him
    26. the outside of them *may be* clean also.
 24: 6. (these things) must *come to pass*,
    20. that your flight *be* not in the winter,
    21. such as *was* not since the beginning
    — to this time, no, nor ever *shall be*.
    32. When his branch *is* yet tender,
    34. till all these things *be fulfilled*.
    44. Therefore *be* ye also ready: for in
 25: 6. at midnight there *was* a cry *made*,
 26: 1. it *came to pass*, when Jesus had
    2. after two days *is* (the feast of) the
    5. lest there *be* an uproar among the people.
    6. *when* Jesus *was* in Bethany, in the
    20. Now *when* the even *was come*,

Mat.26:42. except I drink it, thy will *be done*.
   54. scriptures be fulfilled, that thus it must *be?*
   56. all this *was done*, that the scriptures
27: 1. *When* the morning *was come*,
   24. (that) rather a tumult *was made*,
   45. there *was* darkness over all the land
   54. those things *that were done*, they
   57. *When* the even *was come*, there
28: 2. behold, there *was* a great earthquake:
   4. keepers did shake, and *became* as dead (men).
   11. all the things *that were done*.
Mar. 1: 4. John *did* baptize in the wilderness
   9. it *came to pass* in those days,
   11. there *came* a voice from heaven,
   17. I will make you *to become* fishers of men.
   32. at (lit. *when* it *was*) even, when the sun
2:15. it *came to pass*, that, as Jesus sat
   21. the rent *is made* worse.
   23. it *came to pass*, that he went
   27. The sabbath *was made* for man,
4: 4. it *came to pass*, as he sowed, some
   10. when he *was* alone, they that were
   11. all (these) things *are done* in parables:
   17. *when* affliction or persecution *ariseth* for
   19. choke the word, and it *becometh* unfruitful.
   22. neither *was* any thing *kept* secret,
   32. *becometh* greater than all herbs,
   35. same day, *when* the even *was come*,
   37. there *arose* a great storm of wind,
   39. wind ceased, and there *was* a great calm.
5:14. to see what it was *that was done*.
   16. *befell* to him that was possessed with the
   33. knowing what *was done* in her,
6: 2. *when* the sabbath day *was come*,
   — mighty works *are wrought* by his hands?
   14. for his name *was* spread abroad:
   21. *when* a convenient day *was come*,
   26. the king *was* exceeding sorry; (yet)
   35. *when* the day *was* now far spent,
   47. *when* even *was come*, the ship
9: 3. his raiment *became* shining,
   7. there *was* a cloud that overshadowed
   21. since this *came* unto him? And he said,
   26. out of him: and he *was* as one dead;
   33. *being* in the house he asked them,
   50. if the salt have lost his saltness, (lit. *be saltless*)
10:43. whosoever will *be* great among you,
   44. whosoever of you will *be* the chiefest,
11:19. when even *was come*, he went out
   23. things which he saith *shall come to pass;*
12:10. *is become* the head of the corner:
   11. This *was* the Lord's *doing*, and it is
13: 7. for (such things) must needs *be;*
   18. that your flight *be* not in the winter.
   19. such as *was* not from the beginning
   — unto this time, neither *shall be*.
   28. When her branch *is* yet tender,
   29. shall see these things *come to pass*,
   30. till all these things *be done*.
14: 4. Why *was* this waste of the ointment *made?*
   17. in the evening (lit. *when* it *was*) he cometh with
15:33. *when* the sixth hour *was come*, there *was*
   42. now *when* the even *was come*,
16:10. them that *had been* with him, as
Lu. 1: 2. *which* from the beginning *were*
   5. There *was* in the days of Herod, the
   8. it *came to pass*, that while he
   20. these things *shall be performed*,
   23. it *came to pass*, that, as soon as the

Lu. 1:38. *be* it unto me according to thy word.
   41. it *came to pass*, that, when Elisabeth
   44. as soon as the voice...sounded (lit. *was*) in mine ears,
   59. it *came to pass*, that on the eighth
   65. fear *came* on all that dwelt round
2: 1. it *came to pass* in those days, that
   2. this taxing *was first made*
   6. so it *was*, that, while they were there,
   13. suddenly there *was* with the angel
   15. it *came to pass*, as the angels were
   — this thing *which is come to pass*,
   42. when he *was* twelve years old, they
   46. it *came to pass*, that after three days
3: 2. the word of God *came* unto John the
   21. it *came to pass*, that Jesus also being
   22. a voice *came* from heaven, which said,
4: 3. this stone that it be *made* bread.
   23. we have heard *done* in Capernaum,
   25. great famine *was* throughout all the land;
   36. they *were* all amazed, and spake among
   42. *when* it *was* day, he departed and went
5: 1. it *came to pass*, that, as the people pressed
   12. it *came to pass*, when he was in a
   17. it *came to pass* on a certain day, as he was
6: 1. it *came to pass* on the second sabbath
   6. it *came to pass* also on another sabbath,
   12. it *came to pass* in those days, that he
   13. when it *was* day, he called (unto him)
   16. Judas Iscariot, which also *was* the traitor.
   36. *Be* ye therefore merciful, as your Father
   48. *when* the flood *arose*, the stream beat
   49. the ruin of that house *was* great.
7:11. it *came to pass* the day after, that
8: 1. it *came to pass* afterward, that he
   17. that *shall* not *be made* manifest;
   22. Now it *came to pass* on a certain day,
   24. they ceased, and there *was* a calm.
   34. that fed (them) saw *what was done*,
   35. they went out to see *what was done;*
   40. it *came to pass*, that, when Jesus
   56. should tell no man *what was done*.
9: 7. heard of all *that was done* by him:
   18. it *came to pass*, as he was alone
   28. it *came to pass* about an eight days
   29. as he prayed, the fashion of his countenance *was*
   33. it *came to pass*, as they departed from him,
   34. there *came* a cloud, and overshadowed them:
   35. there *came* a voice out of the cloud,
   36. when the voice *was* past, Jesus
   37. it *came to pass*, that on the next day,
   51. it *came to pass*, when the time was come
   57. it *came to pass*, that, as they went
10:13. the mighty works *had been done* in Tyre and Sidon, *which have been done* in you,
   21. for so it seemed (lit. *was*) good in thy
   32. a Levite, *when* he *was* at the place,
   36. *was* neighbour unto him that fell
   38. it *came to pass*, as they went, that
11: 1. it *came to pass*, that, as he was
   2. Thy will *be done*, as in heaven, so in earth.
   14. it *came to pass*, when the devil was
   26. last (state) of that man *is* worse than the first.
   27. it *came to pass*, as he spake these
   30. as Jonas *was* a sign unto the Ninevites,
12:40. *Be* ye therefore ready also: for the Son of
   54. ye say, There cometh a shower; and so it *is*.

Lu. 12:55. There will be heat; and it *cometh to pass.*
13: 2. *were* sinners above all the Galilæans,
　　4. think ye that they *were* sinners above
　　17. glorious things *that were done* by him.
　　19. it grew, and *waxed* a great tree; and the
14: 1. it *came to pass,* as he went into the
　　12. bid thee again, and a recompence *be made* thee.
　　22. Lord, it *is done* as thou hast commanded,
15:10. there *is* joy in the presence of the angels
　　14. there *arose* a mighty famine in that
16:11. If therefore ye *have* not *been* faithful in
　　12. if ye *have* not *been* faithful in that
　　22. it *came to pass,* that the beggar died,
17:11. it *came to pass,* as he went to
　　14. it *came to pass,* that, as they went,
　　26. as it *was* in the days of Noe, so shall
　　28. also as it *was* in the days of Lot;
18:23. heard this, he *was* very sorrowful:
　　24. Jesus saw *that* he *was* very sorrowful,
　　35. it *came to pass,* that as he was come
19: 9. This day *is* salvation *come* to this house,
　　15. it *came to pass,* that when he was
　　17. because thou *hast been* faithful
　　19. *Be* thou also over five cities.
　　29. it *came to pass,* when he was come
20: 1. it *came to pass,* (that) on one of those
　　14. that the inheritance *may be* our's.
　　16. they heard (it), they said, God forbid. (lit. *be it* not)
　　17. the same *is become* the head of the
　　33. whose wife of them *is* she? for
21: 7. when these things shall *come to pass?*
　　9. these things must first *come to pass;*
　　28. these things begin to *come to pass,*
　　31. see these things *come to pass,* know
　　32. not pass away, till all *be fulfilled.*
　　36. these things that shall *come to pass,*
22:14. when the hour *was* come, he sat down,
　　24. there *was* also a strife among them,
　　26. *let* him *be* as the younger; and he
　　40. *when* he *was* at the place, he said
　　42. not my will, but thine, *be done.*
　　44. *being* in an agony he prayed more earnestly: and his sweat *was* as it were great drops
　　66. as soon. as it *was* day, the elders
23: 8. have seen some miracle *done* by him.
　　12. Pilate and Herod *were made* friends together:
　　19. a certain sedition *made* in the city,
　　24. that it should *be* as they required.
　　31. what *shall be done* in the dry?
　　44. there *was* a darkness over all the earth
　　47. the centurion saw *what was done,*
　　48. beholding the things *which were done,*
24: 4. it *came to pass,* as they were much
　　5. *as* they *were* afraid, and bowed down
　　12. at that *which was come to pass.*
　　15. it *came to pass,* that, while they communed
　　18. things *which are come to pass* there
　　19. which *was* a prophet mighty in deed
　　21. third day since these things *were done.*
　　22. *which were* early at the sepulchre; •
　　30. it *came to pass,* as he sat at meat
　　31. he vanished out of their sight. (lit. he *was* vanished)
　　37. they *were* terrified and affrighted, *and*
　　51. it *came to pass,* while he blessed
Joh. 1: 3. All things *were made* by him; .... *was* not any thing *made* that *was made.*

Joh. 1: 6. There *was* a man sent from God,
　　10. the world *was made* by him, and the
　　12. power *to become* the sons of God,
　　14. the Word *was made* flesh, and dwelt
　　15. after me *is preferred* before me:
　　17. grace and truth *came* by Jesus Christ.
　　27. coming after me *is preferred* before me,
　　28. These things *were done* in Bethabara
　　30. a man which *is preferred* before me,
2: 1. the third day there *was* a marriage
　　9. tasted the water *that was made* wine,
3: 9. unto him, How can these things *be?*
　　25. there *arose* a question between (some)
4:14. *shall be* in him a well of water
5: 4. *was made* whole of whatsoever disease
　　6. unto him, Wilt thou *be made* whole?
　　9. immediately the man *was made* whole,
　　14. Behold, thou *art made* whole: sin no more, lest a worse thing *come* unto thee.
6:16. when even *was* (now) *come,* his
　　17. it *was* now dark, and Jesus was not
　　19. on the sea, and *drawing* nigh unto the ship:
　　21. immediately the ship *was* at the land
　　25. Rabbi, when *camest* thou hither?
7:43. there *was* a division among the people
8:33. sayest thou, Ye *shall be made* free?
　　58. Before Abraham *was,* I am.
9:22. he *should be* put out of the synagogue.
　　27. will ye also *be* his disciples?
　　39. they which see *might be made* blind.
10:16. there *shall be* one fold, (and) one shepherd.
　　19. There *was* a division therefore again
　　22. it *was* at Jerusalem the feast of
　　35. unto whom the word of God *came,*
12:29. heard (it), said that it thundered: (lit. that there *was* thunder)
　　30. This voice *came* not because of me,
　　36. that ye *may be* the children of light.
　　42. lest they *should be* put out of the
13: 2. supper *being ended,* the devil having
　　19. Now I tell you before it *come,* that, when it *is come to pass,* ye may
14:22. Lord, how *is* it that thou wilt manifest
　　29. I have told you before it *come to pass,* that, when it *is come to pass,* ye might
15: 7. it *shall be done* unto you.
　　8. so *shall* ye *be* my disciples.
16:20. your sorrow *shall be turned* into joy.
19:36. these things *were done,* that the
20:27. *be* not faithless, but believing.
21: 4. *when* the morning *was* now *come,*
Acts 1:16. Judas, *which was* guide to them
　　18. *falling* headlong, he burst asunder
　　19. it *was* known unto all the dwellers
　　20. *Let* his habitation *be* desolate, and let
　　22. must one *be ordained to be* a witness
2: 2. suddenly there *came* a sound from
　　6. *when* this *was* noised abroad, the
　　43. fear *came* upon every soul: and many wonders and signs *were done* by the apostles.
4: 4. the number of the men *was* about
　　5. it *came to pass* on the morrow,
　　11. *which is become* the head of the corner.
　　16. miracle *hath been done* by them
　　21. glorified God for that *which was done.*
　　22. this miracle of healing *was shewed.*
　　28. counsel determined before *to be done.*
　　30. signs and wonders may *be done* by the

Acts 5: 5. great fear *came* on all them
7. it *was* about the space of three hours
— not knowing *what was done,*
11. great fear *came* upon all the church,
12. *were* many signs and wonders *wrought*
24. of them whereunto this *would grow.*
36. were scattered, *and brought* to nought.
6: 1. there *arose* a murmuring of the
7:13. Joseph's kindred *was made* known
29. *was* a stranger in the land of Madian,
31. voice of the Lord *came* unto him,
32. Then Moses trembled (lit. *was* trembling), *and* durst not behold.
38. This is he, *that was* in the church
39. To whom our fathers would not obey, (lit. *be* obedient)
40. we wot not what *is become* of him.
52. of whom ye *have been* now the betrayers
8: 1. at that time there *was* a great
8. there *was* great joy in that city.
13. the miracles and signs *which were done.*
9: 3. as he journeyed,)(**he came near**
19. Then *was* Saul certain days with
32. it *came to pass,* as Peter passed
37. it *came to pass* in those days,
42. it *was* known throughout all Joppa;
43. it *came to pass,* that he tarried many
10: 4. when he looked on him, he *was* afraid, *and*
10. he *became* very hungry, and would
13. there *came* a voice to him, Rise.
16. This *was done* thrice: and the vessel
25. as Peter *was* coming in, Cornelius
37. *which was published* throughout
40. third day, and shewed him openly; (lit. made him *to be* manifest)
11:10. this *was done* three times: and all
19. scattered abroad upon the persecution *that arose* about Stephen
26. it *came to pass,* that a whole year
28. which *came to pass* in the days of
12: 5. prayer was *made* without ceasing
9. *which was done* by the angel;
11. *when* Peter *was come* to himself,
18. *as soon as* it *was* day, there was
— the soldiers, what *was become* of Peter.
23. he *was* eaten of worms, *and* gave up the ghost.
13: 5. *when* they *were* at Salamis, they
12. when he saw *what was done,* believed,
22. the promise *which was made*
14: 1. it *came to pass* in Iconium, that
3. signs and wonders *to be done* by their hands.
5. there *was* an assault *made* both of the
15: 2. *When* therefore Paul and Barnabas *had* no small
7. *when* there *had been* much disputing,
25. *being assembled* with one accord,
39. the contention *was* so sharp between
16:16. it *came to pass,* as we went to prayer,
26. suddenly there *was* a great earthquake,
27. keeper of the prison awaking (lit. *being* awaked) out of his sleep,
29. sprang in, and *came* trembling, *and*
35. *when* it *was* day, the magistrates
19: 1. it *came to pass,* that, while Apollos
10. this *continued* by the space of two years;
17. this *was* known to all the Jews
21. After I *have been* there, I must
23. same time there *arose* no small
26. no gods, *which are made* with hands:
28. they *were* full of wrath, and cried out,

Acts19:34. was a Jew, all with one voice...cried out, (lit. there *was* from all &c.)
20: 3. when the Jews laid wait for him, (lit. *when* there *was* a laying in wait)
— he purposed (lit. there *was* the purpose) to return through
16. he *would* not spend the time in
— *to be* at Jerusalem the day of
18. I *have been* with you at all seasons,
37. they all wept (lit. there *was* a weeping sore,
21: 1. it *came to pass,* that after we were
5. when we (lit. it *was* that we) had accomplished those
14. The will of the Lord *be done.*
17. *when* we *were come* to Jerusalem,
30. city was moved, and the people ran (lit. there *was* a concourse) together:
35. when he *came* upon the stairs,
40. *when* there *was made* a great silence,
22: 6. it *came to pass,* that, as I made my
9. saw indeed the light, and *were* afraid;
17. it *came to pass,* that, when I was
— in the temple, I *was* in a trance;
23: 7. there *arose* a dissension between the
9. there *arose* a great cry: and the scribes
10. *when* there *arose* a great dissension,
12. *when* it *was* day, certain of the Jews
24: 2. very worthy deeds are *done* unto this
25. Felix trembled (lit. *having become* alarmed), and answered, Go thy way
25:15. About whom, *when* I *was* at Jerusalem,
26. *after* examination *had,* I might
26: 4. *which was* at the first among mine
6. hope of the promise *made* of God
19. I *was* not disobedient unto the
22. prophets and Moses did say should *come:*
28. thou persuadest me *to be* a Christian.
29. *were* both almost, and altogether such as I am,
27: 7. scarce *were come* over against Cnidus,
16. much work *to come* by the boat:
27. when the fourteenth night *was come,*
29. of the stern, and wished for (lit. it *to be*) the day.
33. while the day was coming on, (lit. about *to be*)
36. *Then were* they all of good cheer,
39. when it *was* day, they knew not
42. the soldiers' counsel *was* to kill
44. so it *came to pass,* that they
28: 6. saw no harm *come* to him,
8. it *came to pass,* that the father
9. So *when* this *was done,* others also,
17. it *came to pass,* that after three
Ro. 1: 3. *which was made* of the seed of David
2:25. thy circumcision *is made* uncircumcision.
3: 4. God forbid (lit. *let* it not *be*): *let* God be true, but every man a liar;
6. God forbid (lit. *let &c.*): for then how
19. all the world *may become* guilty
31. God forbid (lit. *let &c.*): yea, we establish
4:18. that he might *become* the father
6: 2. God forbid (lit. *let &c.*). How shall we, that
.. if we have been planted together
15. but under grace? God forbid. (lit. *let &c.*)
7: 3. she *be married* to another man,
— *though* she *be married* to another
4. that ye should *be married* to another,
7. (Is) the law sin? God forbid. (lit. *let &c.*)
13. *made* death unto me? God forbid. (lit. *let &c.*)

Ro. 7:13. *might become* exceeding sinful.
  9:14. unrighteousness with God? God forbid. (lit. *may* it not *be*)
    29. we *had been* as Sodoma,
 10:20. I *was made* manifest unto them
 11: 1. God cast away his people? God forbid. (lit. *may, &c.*)
    5. there *is* a remnant according
    6. otherwise grace *is* no more grace.
    9. *Let* their table *be made* a snare, and a
   11. stumbled that they should fall? God forbid: (lit. *may, &c.*)
   17. and with them partakest (lit. *be* partaker) of the root
   25. blindness in part *is happened* to Israel,
   34. or who *hath been* his counsellor?
 12:16. *Be* not wise in your own conceits.
 15: 8. Jesus Christ *was* a minister of the
   16. offering up of the Gentiles *might be*
   31. *may be* accepted of the saints ;
 16: 2. she *hath been* a succourer of many,
    7. who also *were* in Christ before me.
1Co. 1:30. who of God *is made* unto us wisdom,
  2: 3. I *was* with you in weakness, and in
  3:13. Every man's work *shall be made*
   18. let him *become* a fool, that he *may be* wise.
  4: 5. then *shall* every man *have* praise
    9. we *are made* a spectacle unto the
   13. we *are made* as the filth of the world,
   16. I beseech you, *be* ye followers of me.
  6:15. the members of an harlot? God forbid. (lit. *may, &c.*)
  7:21. if thou mayest *be made* free,
   23. *be* not ye the servants of men.
   36. need so require, (lit. it so *to be*) let him do what
  8: 9. *become* a stumblingblock to them
  9:15. that it *should be* so *done* unto me:
   20. unto the Jews I *became* as a Jew,
   22. To the weak *became* I as weak,
   — I *am made* all things to all
   23. that I *might be* partaker thereof
   27. I myself *should be* a castaway.
 10: 6. these things *were* our examples,
   7. Neither *be* ye idolaters, as (were)
   20. ye should have fellowship (lit. *be* partakers) of
   32. Give none offence (lit. *be* without offence), neither to the Jews,
 11: 1. *Be* ye followers of me, even as
   19. *may be made* manifest among you.
 13: 1. I *am become* (as) sounding brass,
   11. when I *became* a man, I put
 14:20. *be* not children in understanding:
   — in understanding *be* men.
   25. *are* the secrets of his heart *made* manifest;
   26. *Let* all things *be done* unto edifying.
   40. *Let* all things *be done* decently
 15:10. (bestowed) upon me *was* not in vain ;
   20. (and) *become* the firstfruits of them
   37. thou sowest not that body *that shall be*,
   45. Adam *was made* a living soul ;
   54. then *shall be brought to pass* the
   58. my beloved brethren, *be* ye stedfast,
 16: 2. that there *be* no gatherings when
   10. that he *may be* with you without
   14. *Let* all your things *be done* with charity.
2Co. 1: 8. trouble *which came* to us in Asia,
   18. our word toward you *was* not yea and nay.
   19. *was* not yea and nay, but in him *was* yea.
  3: 7. written ·(and) engraven in stones, *was* glorious,
  5:17. behold, all things *are become* new.

2Co. 5:21. we *might be made* the righteousness
  6:14. *Be* ye not unequally yoked together
  7:14. which (I made) before Titus, *is found* a truth.
  8:14. that their abundance also *may be*
   — that there *may be* equality:
 12:11. I *am become* a fool in glorying;
Gal. 2:17. minister of sin? God forbid. (lit. *may, &c.*)
  3:13. *being made* a curse for us: for it is
   14. blessing of Abraham *might come* on the
   17. the law, *which was* four hundred
   21. against the promises of God? God forbid: (lit. *may, &c.*)
   24. the law *was* our schoolmaster
  4: 4. his Son, *made* of a woman, *made* under
   12. Brethren, I beseech you, *be* as I (am);
   16. *Am* I therefore *become* your enemy,
  5:26. *Let* us not *be* desirous of vain glory,
  6:14. God forbid (lit. *may* it not *be*) that I should glory,
Eph. 2:13. *are made* nigh by the blood of Christ.
  3: 7. Whereof I *was made* a minister,
  4:32. *be* ye kind one to another, tenderhearted,
  5: 1. *Be* ye therefore followers of God, as
   7. *Be* not ye therefore partakers with
   12. those things *which are done* of them
   17. Wherefore *be* ye not unwise, but
  6: 3. That it *may be* well with thee,
Phi. 1:13. my bonds in Christ *are* manifest
  2: 7. *and was made* in the likeness of men:
   8. *and became* obedient unto death,
   15. That ye *may be* blameless and harmless,
  3: 6. which is in the law,)(blameless.
   17. Brethren, *be* followers together of me,
   21. that it may *be* fashioned like unto
Col. 1:18. he *might have* the preeminence.
   23. whereof I Paul *am made* a minister ;
   25. Whereof I *am made* a minister,
  3:15. called in one body ; and *be* ye thankful.
  4:11. which *have been* a comfort unto me.
1Th. 1: 5. our gospel *came* not unto you
   — what manner of men we *were*
   6. ye *became* followers of us, and of the
   7. So that ye *were* ensamples to all
  2: 1. unto you, that it *was* not in vain:
   5. at any time used we (lit. *were* we in) flattering words,
   7. we *were* gentle among you,
   8. because ye *were* dear unto us.
   10. unblameably we *behaved ourselves*
   14. ye, brethren, *became* followers of the
  3: 4. even as it *came to pass*, and ye know.
   5. tempted you, and our labour *be* in vain.
2Th. 2: 7. until he *be taken* out of the way.
1Ti. 2:14. deceived *was* in the transgression.
  4:12. *be* thou an example of the believers,
  5: 9. *having been* the wife of one man,
  6: 4. strifes of words, whereof *cometh* envy, strife,
2Ti. 1:17. *when* he *was* in Rome, he sought me
  2:18. that the resurrection is *past* already ;
  3: 9. manifest unto all (men), as their's also *was*.
   11. afflictions, which *came* unto me at Antioch,
Tit. 3: 7. we *should be made* heirs according
Philem. 6. thy faith *may become* effectual by
Heb 1: 4. *Being made* so much better than
  2: 2. word spoken by angels *was* stedfast,
   17. that he *might be* a merciful and faithful
  3:14. we *are made* partakers of Christ,
  4: 3. although the works *were finished* from
  5: 5. himself *to be made* an high priest;

Heb 5: 9. he *became* the author of eternal
11. seeing ye *are* dull of hearing.
12. *are become* such as have need of milk,
6: 4. *were made* partakers of the Holy Ghost,
12. That ye *be* not slothful, but followers
20. Jesus, *made* an high priest for ever
7:12. there *is made* of necessity a change
16. Who *is made*, not after the law of a
18. For there *is* verily a disannulling of
21(20). those priests *were made* without an oath;
22. By so much *was* Jesus *made* a surety
23. they truly were. (lit. are *made*) many priests,
26. *made* higher than the heavens;
9:15. that by means of death (lit. death *having taken place*), for the
22. without shedding of blood *is* no remission.
10:33. *whilst* ye *became* companions of
11: 3. *were* not *made* of things which do appear.
6. he *is* a rewarder of them that
7. *became* heir of the righteousness
24. Moses, *when* he *was come* to years,
34. made strong, *waxed* valiant in fight,
12: 8. whereof all *are* partakers, then
Jas. 1:12. for *when* he *is* tried, he shall receive
22. *be* ye doers of the word, and not hearers
25. he *being* not a forgetful hearer,
2: 4. *are become* judges of evil thoughts?
10. in one (point), he *is* guilty of all.
11. thou *art become* a transgressor of the law.
3: 1. My brethren, *be* not many masters,
9. *which are made* after the similitude
10. these things ought not so to *be*.
5: 2. your garments *are* motheaten.
1Pet.1:15. so *be* ye holy in all manner of
16. Because it is written, *Be* ye holy;
2: 7. the same *is made* the head of the
3: 6. whose daughters ye *are*, as long
13. if ye *be* followers of that which is good?
4:12. the fiery trial *which is* to try you,
5: 3. *being* ensamples to the flock.
2Pet.1: 4. by these ye *might be* partakers of the
16. *were* eyewitnesses of his majesty.
20. no prophecy of the scripture *is* of any private
2: 1. there *were* false prophets also among
20. the latter end *is* worse with them
1Joh.2:18. even now *are* there many antichrists;
3Joh. 8. that we *might be* fellowhelpers
Rev. 1: 1. things which must shortly *come to pass*,
9. *was* in the isle that is called Patmos,
10. I *was* in the Spirit on the Lord's day,
18. (I am) he that liveth, and *was* dead;
19. the things which shall *be* hereafter;
2: 8. which *was* dead, and is alive;
10. *be* thou faithful unto death, and I will
3: 2. *Be* watchful, and strengthen the things
4: 1. things which must *be* hereafter.
2. immediately I *was* in the spirit:
6:12. *there was* a great earthquake; and the sun *became* black as sackcloth of hair, and the moon *became* as blood;
8: 1. there *was* silence in heaven about
5. there *were* voices, and thunderings,
7. there *followed* hail and fire mingled
8. third part of the sea *became* blood;
11. part of the waters *became* wormwood;
11:13. same hour *was* there a great earthquake,
— the remnant *were* affrighted,
15. there *were* great voices in heaven, saying, The kingdoms of this world *are become*

Rev.11:19. there *were* lightnings, and voices,
12: 7. there *was* war in heaven:
10. Now *is come* salvation, and strength,
16: 2. there *fell* a noisome and grievous
3. it *became* as the blood of a dead (man):
4. fountains of waters; and they *became* blood.
10. his kingdom *was* full of darkness;
17. from the throne, saying, It *is done*.
18. there *were* voices, and thunders,
— there *was* a great earthquake, such as *was* not since men *were* upon the earth,
19. the great city *was divided* into
18: 2. *is become* the habitation of devils,
21: 6. he said unto me, It *is done*.
22: 6. things which must shortly *be done*.

γινώσκ-ω & -ομαι, *ginōsk-ō* & -*omai*.

Mat. 1:25. *knew* her not till she had brought
6: 3. *let* not thy left hand *know* what
7:23. profess unto them, I never *knew* you:
9:30. saying, See (that) no man *know* (it).
10:26. hid, that *shall* not *be known*.
12: 7. if ye *had known* what (this) meaneth,
15. *when* Jesus *knew* (it), he withdrew
33. the tree *is known* by (his) fruit.
13:11. given unto you *to know* the mysteries
16: 3. ye can (lit. *know* how to) discern the face of the sky;
8. (Which) *when* Jesus *perceived*, he said
21:45. they *perceived* that he spake of them.
22:18. Jesus *perceived* their wickedness, *and*
24:32. ye *know* that summer (is) nigh:
33. these things, *know* that it is near,
39. *knew* not until the flood came,
43. *know* this, that if the goodman
50. in an hour that he *is* not *aware of*,
25:24. Lord, I *knew* thee that thou art an
26:10. *When* Jesus *understood* (it), he said
Mar 4:11. *to know* the mystery of the kingdom
13. how then *will* ye *know* all parables?
5:29. she *felt* in (her) body that she was
43. that no man *should know* it;
6:38. And *when* they *knew*, they say, Five,
7:24. would have no man *know* (it):
8:17. *when* Jesus *knew* (it), he saith unto
9:30. that any man *should know* (it).
12:12. they *knew* that he had spoken the
13:28. ye *know* that summer is near:
29. come to pass, *know* that it is nigh,
15:10. he *knew* that the chief priests
45. *when* he *knew* (it) of the centurion,
Lu. 1:18. Whereby *shall* I *know* this?
34. this be, seeing I *know* not a man?
2:43. Joseph and his mother *knew* not (of it).
6:44. every tree *is known* by his own
7:39. would *have known* who and what
8:10. Unto you it is given *to know*
17. that *shall* not *be known* and come
46. for I *perceive* that virtue is gone
9:11. the people, *when* they *knew* (it),
10:11. *be* ye sure of this, that the kingdom
22. no man *knoweth* who the Son is,
12: 2. neither hid, that *shall* not *be known*.
39. this *know*, that if the goodman
46. at an hour when he *is* not *aware*,
47. servant, *which knew* his lord's will,
48. he *that knew* not, and did commit
16: 4. I *am resolved* what to do,
15. God *knoweth* your hearts: for

Lu. 18:34. neither *knew* they the things which
  19:15. that he *might know* how much
    42. Saying, If thou *hadst known,*
    44. thou *knewest* not the time of thy
  20:19. they *perceived* that he had spoken
  21:20. then *know* that the desolation
    30. ye see and *know* of your own selves
    31. *know* ye that the kingdom of God
  24:18. *hast* not *known* the things
    35. how he *was known* of them in
Joh. 1:10. the world *knew* him not.
    48(49). unto him, Whence *knowest* thou me ?
  2:24. unto them, because he *knew* all
    25. for he *knew* what was in man.
  3:10. a master of Israel, and *knowest* not these
      things ?
  4: 1. When therefore the Lord *knew* how
    53. So the father *knew* that (it was)
  5: 6. and *knew* that he had been now a
    42. I *know* you, that ye have not
  6:15. *When* Jesus therefore *perceived* that
    69. we believe and *are sure* that thou
  7:17. he *shall know* of the doctrine,
    26. Do the rulers *know* indeed that
    27. no man *knoweth* whence he is.
    49. this people *who knoweth* not the law
    51. before it hear him, and *know*
  8:27. They *understood* not that he
    28. then *shall ye know* that I am
    32. ye *shall know* the truth, and the truth
    43. Why do ye not *understand* my speech ?
    52. Now we *know* that thou hast a devil.
    55. Yet ye *have* not *known* him ;
  10: 6. they *understood* not what things
    14. *know* my (sheep) and *am known* of mine.
    15. As the Father *knoweth* me, even so *know* I
      the Father:
    27. I *know* them, and they follow me:
    38. believe the works: that ye *may know,*
  11:57. if any man *knew* where he were,
  12: 9. of the Jews therefore *knew* that he
    16. These things *understood* not his disciples
  13: 7. thou *shalt know* hereafter.
    12. *Know* ye what I have done
    28. no man at the table *knew*
    35. this *shall* all (men) *know* that
  14: 7. If ye *had known* me, ye should *have known*
      my Father also: and from henceforth ye
      know him,
    9. *hast* thou not *known* me,
    17. neither *knoweth* him: but ye *know*
    20. At that day ye *shall know* that
    31. that the world *may know* that
  15:18. ye *know* that it hated me
  16: 3. they *have* not *known* the Father,
    19. Jesus *knew* that they were desirous
  17: 3. that they *might know* thee the only true
    7. they *have known* that all things
    8. and *have known* surely that I
    23. that the world *may know* that
    25. the world *hath* not *known* thee: but I *have*
      known thee, and these *have known* that
  19: 4. that ye *may know* that I find no fault
  21:17. thou *knowest* that I love thee.
Acts 1: 7. not for you *to know* the times
  2:36. *let* all the house of Israel *know* assuredly,
  8:30. *Understandest* thou what thou
  9:24. their laying await *was known*
  17:13. Jews of Thessalonica *had knowledge*
    19. May we *know* what this new
    20. we would *know* therefore what these
  19:15. evil spirit answered and said, Jesus I
    know,

Acts19:35. that *knoweth* not how that the city
  20:34. ye yourselves *know,* that these hands
  21:24. all *may know* that those things,
    34. when he could not *know* the certainty
    37. Who said, *Canst* thou *speak* Greek?
  22:14. that thou shouldest *know* his will,
    30. would *have known* the certainty
  23: 6. *when* Paul *perceived* that the one
    28. when I would *have known* the cause
  24:11. Because that thou mayest *understand,*
Ro. 1:21. *when* they *knew* God, they glorified
  2:18. *knowest* (his) will, and approvest the
  3:17. way of peace *have* they not *known:*
  6: 6. *Knowing* this, that our old man
  7: 1. I speak to them *that know* the law,
    7. I *had* not *known* sin, but by the
    15. that which I do I *allow* not: for what
  10:19. I say, *Did* not Israel *know ?*
  11:34. who *hath known* the mind of the Lord ?
1Co. 1:21. the world by wisdom *knew* not God,
  2: 8. none of the princes of this world *knew:*
    for *had* they *known* (it) they would not
    14. neither can he *know* (them), because
    16. who *hath known* the mind of the Lord,
  3:20. The Lord *knoweth* the thoughts of
  4:19. *will know,* not the speech of them
  8: 2. he *knoweth* nothing yet as he ought *to*
    know.
    3. the same *is known* of him.
  13: 9. For we *know* in part, and we prophesy
    12. now I *know* in part ; but then
  14: 7. how *shall* it *be known* what
    9. how *shall* it *be known* what is
2Co. 2: 4. that ye *might know* the love
    9. that I *might know* the proof of
  3: 2. *known* and read of all men:
  5:16. though we *have known* Christ after the
    flesh, yet now henceforth *know* we (him)
    no more.
    21. *who knew* no sin; that we
  8: 9. ye *know* the grace of our Lord
  13: 6. I trust that ye *shall know* that
Gal. 2: 9. *when...perceived* the grace that was
  3: 7. *Know* ye therefore that they which
  4: 9. *after* that ye *have known* God, or rather
    are known of God,
Eph. 3:19. *to know* the love of Christ, which
  5: 5. this ye *know,* that no whoremonger,
  6:22. that ye *might know* our affairs,
Phi. 1:12. I would ye should *understand,*
  2:19. good comfort, *when* I *know* your state.
    22. ye *know* the proof of him, that,
  3:10. That I may *know* him, and the
  4: 5. *Let* your moderation *be known*
Col. 4: 8. that he *might know* your estate,
1Th. 3: 5. I sent *to know* your faith, lest by
2Ti. 1:18. at Ephesus, thou *knowest* very well.
  2:19. The Lord *knoweth* them that are his.
  3: 1. This *know* also, that in the last
Heb. 3:10. they *have* not *known* my ways.
  8:11. his brother, saying, *Know* the Lord:
  10:34. *knowing* in yourselves that ye have
  13:23. *Know* ye that (our) brother Timothy
Jas. 1: 3. *Knowing* (this), that the trying of
  2:20. wilt thou *know,* O vain man,
  5:20. *Let* him *know,* that he which
2Pet. 1:20. *Knowing* this first, that no prophecy
  3: 3. *Knowing* this first, that there shall
1Joh.2: 3. we *do know* that we *know*(lit. *have* kn.)him,
    4. He that saith, I *know* (lit. *have* kn.) him,
    5. hereby *know* we that we are in him.
    13. because ye *have known* him

1Joh.2:13. because ye *have known* the Father.
14. because ye *have known* him (that is)
18. we *know* that it is the last time.
29. ye *know* that every one that doeth
3: 1. the world *knoweth* us not, because it *knew* him not.
6. not seen him, neither *known* him.
16. Hereby *perceive* (lit. *have perceived*) we the love (of God),
19. hereby we *know* that we are of
20. than our heart, and *knoweth* all things.
24. hereby we *know* that he abideth
4: 2. Hereby *know* ye the Spirit of God:
6. he *that knoweth* God heareth us;
— Hereby *know* we the spirit of truth,
7. is born of God, and *knoweth* God.
8. He that loveth not *knoweth* (lit. *hath known*) not God;
13. Hereby *know* we that we dwell
16. we *have known* and believed the
5: 2. By this we *know* that we love
20. that we *may know* him that is true,
2Joh. 1. they *that have known* the truth;
Rev. 2:17. which no man *knoweth* saving
23. all the churches *shall know*
24. which *have* not *known* the depths
3: 3. thou shalt not *know* what hour
9. and to *know* that I have loved thee.

γλεῦκος, *glukos.*

Acts 2:13. These men are full of *new wine.*

γλυκύς, *glukus.*

Jas. 3:11. the same place *sweet* (water) and bitter?
12. fountain both yield salt water and *fresh.*
Rev.10: 9. be in thy mouth *sweet* as honey.
10. it was in my mouth *sweet* as honey:

γλῶσσα, *glōssa.*

Mar. 7:33. he spit, and touched his *tongue*;
35. the string of his *tongue* was loosed,
16:17. they shall speak with new *tongues*;
Lu. 1:64. his *tongue* (loosed), and he spake, and
16:24. his finger in water, and cool my *tongue*;
Acts 2: 3. there appeared unto them cloven *tongues*
4. began to speak with other *tongues*,
11. hear them speak in our *tongues* the
26. heart rejoice, and my *tongue* was glad;
10:46. they heard them speak with *tongues*
19: 6. they spake with *tongues*, and prophesied.
Ro. 3:13. with their *tongues* they have used deceit;
14:11. every *tongue*·shall confess to God.
1Co.12:10. to another (divers) kinds of *tongues*; to another the interpretation of *tongues*:
28. governments, diversities of *tongues*:
30. do all speak with *tongues*? do all
13: 1. I speak with the *tongues* of men and of
8. whether (there be) *tongues*, they shall
14: 2. he that speaketh in an (unknown) *tongue*
4. He that speaketh in an (unknown) *tongue*
5. that ye all spake with *tongues*,
— than he that speaketh with *tongues*,
6. if I come unto you speaking with *tongues*,
9. except ye utter by the *tongue* words
13. that speaketh in an (unknown) *tongue*

1Co.14:14. if I pray in an (unknown) *tongue*,
18. I speak with *tongues* more than
19. thousand words in an (unknown) *tongue*.
22. Wherefore *tongues* are for a sign,
23. all speak with *tongues*, and there
26. hath a doctrine, hath a *tongue*,
27. any man speak in an (unknown) *tongue*,
39. forbid not to speak with *tongues*.
Phi. 2:11. (that) every *tongue* should confess
Jas. 1:26. bridleth not his *tongue*, but
3: 5. so the *tongue* is a little member,
6. the *tongue* (is) a fire, a world of iniquity: so is the *tongue* among our members,
8. the *tongue* can no man tame;
1Pet.3:10. let him refrain his *tongue* from evil,
1Joh.3:18. not love in word, neither in *tongue*;
Rev. 5: 9. out of every kindred, and *tongue*, and
7: 9. kindreds, and people, and *tongues*, stood
10:11. many peoples, and nations, and *tongues*,
11: 9. kindreds and *tongues* and nations shall
13: 7. over all kindreds, and *tongues*, and nations.
14: 6. to every nation, and kindred, and *tongue*,
16:10. they gnawed their *tongues* for pain,
17:15. multitudes, and nations, and *tongues*.

γλωσσόκομον, *glōssokomon.*

Joh.12: 6. he was a thief, and had the *bag*,
13:29. thought, because Judas had the *bag*,

γναφεύς, *gnaphŭs.*

Mar. 9: 3. so as no *fuller* on earth can white them.

γνήσιος, *gneesios.*

2Co. 8: 8. to prove the *sincerity* of your love.
Phi. 4: 3. I intreat thee also, *true* yokefellow,
1Ti. 1: 2. Unto Timothy, (my) *own* son in the faith:
Tit. 1: 4. Titus, (mine) *own* son after the common

γνησίως, *gneesiōs.*

Phi. 2:20. who will *naturally* care for your state. (lit. *sincerely* or *truly*)

γνόφος, *gnophos.*

Heb 12:18. nor unto *blackness*, and darkness, and

γνώμη, *gnōmee.*

Acts20: 3. he purposed (lit. it *was his purpose*) to return
1Co. 1:10. same mind and in the same *judgment.*
7:25. yet I give my *judgment*, as one
40. if she so abide, after my *judgment*:
2Co. 8:10. herein I give (my) *advice*: for
Philem 14. without thy *mind* would I do
Rev.17:13. These have one *mind*, and shall
17. in their hearts to fulfil his *will*, and to agree (lit. to form one *judgment*)

γνωρίζω, gnōrizo.

Lu. 2:15. which the Lord *hath made known* unto us.
Joh 15:15. I *have made known* unto you.
17:26. I *have declared* unto them thy name, and *will declare* (it) :
Acts 2:28. Thou *hast made known* to me the
Ro. 9:22. *to make* his power *known,* endured
23. that he *might make known* the riches
16:26. *made known* to all nations for
1Co 12: 3. Wherefore I *give* you *to understand,*
15: 1. brethren, I *declare* unto you the gospel
2Co. 8: 1. we *do* you *to wit* of the grace of God
Gal. 1:11. I *certify* you, brethren, that the
Eph. 1: 9. *Having made known* unto us
3: 3. he *made known* unto me the mystery ;
5. *was* not *made known* unto the sons
10. *might be known* by the church
6:19. *to make known* the mystery of
21. *shall make known* to you all things:
Phi. 1:22. what I shall choose I *wot* not.
4: 6. *let* your requests *be made known* unto God.
Col. 1:27. To whom God would *make known*
4: 7. *shall* Tychicus *declare* unto you,
9. They *shall make known* unto you
2Pet. 1:16. when we *made known* unto you

γνῶσις, gnōsis.

Lu. 1:77. To give *knowledge* of salvation
11:52. have taken away the key of *knowledge:*
Ro. 2:20. which hast the form of *knowledge*
11:33. of the wisdom and *knowledge* of God !
15:14. filled with all *knowledge,* able
1Co. 1: 5. all utterance, and (in) all *knowledge ;*
8: 1. we know that we all have *knowledge.*
Knowledge puffeth up, but charity edifieth.
7. not in every man that *knowledge:*
10. see thee which hast *knowledge* sit
11. through thy *knowledge* shall the
12: 8. to another the word of *knowledge*
13: 2. all mysteries, and all *knowledge ;*
8. whether (there be) *knowledge,* it
14: 6. either by revelation, or by *knowledge,*
2Co. 2:14. manifest the savour of his *knowledge*
4: 6. the light of the *knowledge* of the glory
6: 6. by *knowledge,* by longsuffering, by kindness,
8: 7. (in) faith, and utterance, and *knowledge,*
10: 5. against the *knowledge* of God,
11: 6. rude in speech, yet not in *knowledge ;*
Eph. 3:19. love of Christ, which passeth *knowledge,*
Phi. 3: 8. excellency of the *knowledge* of Christ
Col. 2: 3. treasures of wisdom and *knowledge.*
1Ti. 6:20. oppositions of *science* falsely so called:
1Pet. 3: 7. dwell with (them) according to *knowledge,*
2Pet. 1: 5. your faith, virtue ; and to virtue *knowledge ;*
6. to *knowledge* temperance ; and to
3:18. (in) the *knowledge* of our Lord and Saviour

γνώστης, gnōstees.

Acts 26: 3. to be *expert* in all customs and questions

γνωστός, gnōstos.

Lu. 2:44. among (their) kinsfolk and *acquaintance.*
23:49. all his *acquaintance,* and the women
Joh. 18:15. that disciple was *known* unto the
16. which was *known* unto the high priest,
Acts 1:19. it was *known* unto all the dwellers
2:14. be this *known* unto you, and hearken
4:10. Be it *known* unto you all, and to all
16. a *notable* miracle hath been done
9:42. it was *known* throughout all Joppa ;
13:38. Be it *known* unto you therefore, men
15:18. *Known* unto God are all his works
19:17. this was *known* to all the Jews
28:22. we *know* that every where it is spoken
28. Be it *known* therefore unto you,
Ro. 1:19. that *which may be known* of God

γογγύζω, gonguzo.

Mat. 20:11. they *murmured* against the goodman
Lu. 5:30. their scribes and Pharisees *murmured*
Joh. 6:41. The Jews then *murmured* at him,
43. *Murmur* not among yourselves.
61. that his disciples *murmured* at it,
7:32. Pharisees heard that the people *murmured*
1Co. 10:10. Neither *murmur* ye, as some of them also *murmured,* and were destroyed of

γογγυσμός, gongusmos.

Joh. 7:12. there was much *murmuring* among
Acts 6: 1. there arose a *murmuring* of the Grecians
Phi. 2:14. Do all things without *murmurings*
1Pet. 4: 9. hospitality one to another without *grudging.*

γογγυστής, gongustees.

Jude. 16. These are *murmurers,* complainers,

γόης, goees.

2Ti. 3:13. evil men and *seducers* shall wax worse

γόμος, gomos.

Acts 21: 3. the ship was to unlade her *burden.*
Rev. 18:11. no man buyeth their *merchandise*
12. The *merchandise* of gold, and silver,

γονεύς, gonŭs.

Mat. 10:21. children shall rise up against (their) *parents,*
Mar 13:12. children shall rise up against (their) *parents,*
Lu. 2:27. when the *parents* brought in the
41. his *parents* went to Jerusalem every
8:56. her *parents* were astonished: but he
18:29. hath left house, or *parents,* or brethren,
21:16. shall be betrayed both by *parents,* and
Joh. 9: 2. who did sin, this man, or his *parents,*
3. this man sinned, nor his *parents :*
18. they called the *parents* of him that

Joh. 9:20. His *parents* answered them and said,
    22. These (words) spake his *parents*,
    23. Therefore said his *parents*, He is of age;
Ro. 1:30. evil things, disobedient to *parents*,
2Co.12:14. ought not to lay up for the *parents*, but
    the *parents* for the children.
Eph. 6: 1. obey your *parents* in the Lord:
Col. 3:20. obey (your) *parents* in all things:
2Ti. 3: 2. blasphemers, disobedient to *parents*,

γόνυ, *gonu.*

Mar 15:19. bowing (their) *knees* worshipped him.
Lu. 5: 8. he fell down at Jesus' *knees*, saying,
    22:41. stone's cast, and *kneeled* (lit. placing the
    knees) down,
Acts 7:60. he *kneeled* down, and cried with a
    9:40. put them all forth, and *kneeled* down,
    20:36. he *kneeled* down, and prayed with
    21: 5. we *kneeled* down on the shore,
Ro. 11: 4. who have not bowed the *knee* to
    14:11. every *knee* shall bow to me,
Eph. 3:14. I bow my *knees* unto the Father
Phi. 2:10. name of Jesus every *knee* should bow,
Heb12:12. hands which hang down, and the feeble
    knees;

γονυπετέω, *gonupeteo.*

Mat.17:14. a (certain) man, *kneeling down*
    27:29. they *bowed the knee* before him, *and*
Mar. 1:40. beseeching him, and *kneeling down*
    10:17. running, and *kneeled* to him, *and* asked

γράμμα, *gramma.*

Lu. 16: 6. he said unto him, Take thy *bill*,
    7. he said unto him, Take thy *bill*,
    23:38. written over him in *letters* of Greek,
Joh. 5:47. if ye believe not his *writings*,
    7:15. How knoweth this man *letters*,
Acts26:24. much *learning* doth make thee mad.
    28:21. We neither received *letters* out of Judæa
Ro. 2:27. who by the *letter* and circumcision
    29. in the spirit, (and) not in the *letter*;
    7: 6. not (in) the oldness of the *letter*.
2Co. 3: 6. not of the *letter*, but of the spirit: for the
    letter killeth, but the spirit
    7. written (lit. in *letters*,) (and) engraven in
    stones,
Gal. 6:11. Ye see how large a *letter* I have
2Ti. 3:15. thou hast known the holy *scriptures*,

γραμματεύς, *grammatūs.*

Mat. 2: 4. chief priests and *scribes* of the people
    5:20. (righteousness) of the *scribes* and Phari-
    sees,
    7:29. having authority, and not as the *scribes*.
    8:19. a certain *scribe* came, and said unto
    9: 3. behold, certain of the *scribes* said
    12:38. certain of the *scribes* and of the Pha-
    risees
    13:52. every *scribe* (which is) instructed
    15: 1. came to Jesus *scribes* and Pharisees,
    16:21. the elders and chief priests and *scribes*,
    17:10. Why then say the *scribes* that
    20:18. the chief priests and unto the *scribes*,

Mat.21:15. when the chief priests and *scribes* saw
    23: 2. The *scribes* and the Pharisees sit in
    13. woe unto you, *scribes* and Pharisees,
    14. Woe unto you, *scribes* and Pharisees,
    15. Woe unto you, *scribes* and Pharisees,
    23. Woe unto you, *scribes* and Pharisees,
    25. Woe unto you, *scribes* and Pharisees,
    27. Woe unto you, *scribes* and Pharisees,
    29. Woe unto you, *scribes* and Pharisees,
    34. unto you prophets, and wise men, and
    scribes:
    26: 3. the chief priests, and the *scribes*, and the
    57. where the *scribes* and the elders were
    27:41. with the *scribes* and elders, said,
Mar. 1:22. had authority, and not as the *scribes*.
    2: 6. certain of the *scribes* sitting there,
    16. when the *scribes* and Pharisees saw
    3:22. the *scribes* which came down
    7: 1. certain of the *scribes*, which came
    5. the Pharisees and *scribes* asked him,
    8:31. (of) the chief priests, and *scribes*, and be
    9:11. Why say the *scribes* that Elias
    14. the *scribes* questioning with them.
    16. he asked the *scribes*, What question
    10:33. the chief priests, and unto the *scribes*;
    11:18. the *scribes* and chief priests heard (it),
    27. the chief priests, and the *scribes*, and the
    12:28. one of the *scribes* came, and having
    32. the *scribe* said unto him, Well,
    35. How say the *scribes* that Christ
    38. Beware of the *scribes*, which love
    14: 1. the chief priests and the *scribes* sought
    43. from the chief priests and the *scribes*
    53. chief priests and the elders and the
    scribes.
    15: 1. the elders and *scribes*, and the whole
    council,
    31. said among themselves with the *scribes*,
Lu. 5:21. the *scribes* and the Pharisees began to
    reason,
    30. their *scribes* and Pharisees murmured
    6: 7. the *scribes* and Pharisees watched him,
    9:22. the elders and chief priests and *scribes*,
    11:44. Woe unto you, *scribes* and Pharisees,
    53. the *scribes* and the Pharisees began
    15: 2. the Pharisees and *scribes* murmured,
    19:47. the chief priests and the *scribes* and the
    20: 1. the chief priests and the *scribes* came
    19. the chief priests and the *scribes* the same
    39. certain of the *scribes* answering said,
    46. Beware of the *scribes*, which desire to
    22: 2. the chief priests and *scribes* sought
    66. the chief priests and the *scribes* came to-
    gether,
    23:10. the chief priests and *scribes* stood
Joh. 8: 3. the *scribes* and Pharisees brought unto
Acts 4: 5. that their rulers, and elders, and *scribes*,
    6:12. the elders, and the *scribes*, and came upon
    (him),
    19:35. when the *townclerk* had appeased the
    23: 9. the *scribes* (that were) of the Pharisees,
1Co. 1:20. Where (is) the wise? where (is) the
    scribe?

γραπτός, *graptos.*

Ro. 2:15. the work of the law *written* in their

γραφή, *graphee.*

Mat.21:42. Did ye never read in the *scriptures*,

Mat.22:29. Ye do err, not knowing the *scriptures,*
26:54. shall the *scriptures* be fulfilled,
56. that the *scriptures* of the prophets
Mar 12:10. have ye not read this *scripture ;*
24. because ye know not the *scriptures,*
14:49. the *scriptures* must be fulfilled.
15:28. the *scripture* was fulfilled, which saith,
Lu. 4:21. This day is this *scripture* fulfilled
24:27. in all the *scriptures* the things
32. he opened to us the *scriptures ?*
45. they might understand the *scriptures,*
Joh. 2:22. they believed the *scripture,* and the
5:39. Search the *scriptures ;* for in them
7:38. as the *scripture* hath said, out of
42. Hath not the *scripture* said,
10:35. the *scripture* cannot be broken ;
13:18. that the *scripture* may be fulfilled,
17:12. that the *scripture* might be fulfilled.
19:24. that the *scripture* might be fulfilled,
28. that the *scripture* might be fulfilled,
36. that the *scripture* should be fulfilled,
37. again another *scripture* saith,
20: 9. as yet they knew not the *scripture,*
Acts 1:16. this *scripture* must needs have
8:32. The place of the *scripture* which
35. began at the same *scripture,*
17: 2. reasoned with them out of the *scriptures,*
11. searched the *scriptures* daily,
18:24. eloquent man, (and) mighty in the *scriptures,*
28. shewing by the *scriptures* that
Ro. 1: 2. by his prophets in the holy *scriptures,*
4: 3. For what saith the *scripture ?*
9:17. For the *scripture* saith unto Pharaoh,
10:11. For the *scripture* saith, Whosoever
11: 2. Wot ye not what the *scripture* saith
15: 4. through patience and comfort of the *scriptures*
16:26. by the *scriptures* of the prophets,
1Co.15: 3. for our sins according to the *scriptures ;*
4. the third day according to the *scriptures :*
Gal. 3: 8. the *scripture,* foreseeing that God
22. the *scripture* hath concluded all
4:30. Nevertheless what saith the *scripture ?*
1Ti. 5:18. For the *scripture* saith, Thou shalt
2Ti. 3:16. All *scripture* (is) given by inspiration
Jas. 2: 8. according to the *scripture,* Thou shalt love
23. the *scripture* was fulfilled which
4: 5. Do ye think that the *scripture* saith in
1Pet.2: 6. also it is contained in the *scripture,*
2Pet.1:20. that no prophecy of the *scripture* is of
3:16. as (they do) also the other *scriptures,*

γράφω, *grapho.*

Mat. 2: 5. for thus it *is written* by the prophet,
4: 4. he answered and said, It *is written,*
6. cast thyself down : for it *is written,*
7. Jesus said unto him, It *is written* again,
10. Get thee hence, Satan : for it *is written,*
11:10. this is (he), of whom it *is written,*
21:13. It *is written,* My house shall be called
26:24. as it *is written* of him : but woe
31. for it *is written,* I will smite the
27:37. over his head his accusation *written,*
Mar 1: 2. As it *is written* in the prophets,
7: 6. of you hypocrites, as it *is written,*
9:12. how it *is written* of the Son of man,
13. whatsoever they listed, as it *is written*
10: 4. *to write* a bill of divorcement,
5. he *wrote* you this precept.

Mar 11:17. saying unto them, *Is* it not *written,*
12:19. Master, Moses *wrote* unto us,
14:21. indeed goeth, as it *is written* of him :
27. it *is written,* I will smite the shepherd,
Lu. 1: 3. from the very first, *to write* unto thee
63. *wrote,* saying, His name is John.
2:23. it *is written* in the law of the Lord,
3: 4. it *is written* in the book of the words
4: 4. It *is written,* That man shall not live
8. it *is written,* Thou shalt worship the Lord
10. it *is written,* He shall give his angels
17. the place where it was *written,*
7:27. This is (he), of whom it *is written,*
10:20. your names *are written* in heaven.
26. What *is written* in the law ? how readest thou ?
16; 6. sit down quickly, and *write* fifty.
7. Take thy bill, and *write* fourscore.
18:31. all things *that are written* by the
19:46. Saying unto them, It *is written,*
20:17. What is this then *that is written,*
28. Saying, Master, Moses *wrote* unto us,
21:22. all things *which are written*
22:37. this *that is written* must yet be
23:38. a superscription also was *written*
24:44. must be fulfilled, *which were written*
46. said unto them, Thus it *is written,*
Joh. 1:45(46). in the law, and the prophets, *did write,*
2:17. remembered that it was *written,*
5:46. have believed me : for he *wrote* of me.
6:31. as it is *written,* He gave them bread
45. It *is written* in the prophets, And
8: 6. with (his) finger *wrote* on the ground,
8. stooped down, and *wrote* on the ground.
17. It *is* also *written* in your law,
10:34. Is it not *written* in your law,
12:14. sat thereon ; as it is *written,*
16. these things were *written* of him,
15:25. fulfilled *that is written* in their law,
19:19. Pilate *wrote* a title, and put (it) on the cross. And the *writing* was, JESUS OF NAZARETH
20. it was *written* in Hebrew, (and) Greek,
21. *Write* not, The King of the Jews ;
22. What I *have written* I *have written.*
20:30. which are not *written* in this book :
31. these *are written,* that ye might
21:24. and *wrote* these things : and we know
25. if they *should be written* every one,
— the books *that should be written.*
Acts 1:20. it *is written* in the book of Psalms,
7:42. it *is written* in the book of the prophets,
13:29. all *that was written* of him,
33. it *is* also *written* in the second
15:15. words of the prophets ; as it *is written,*
23. *And* they *wrote* (letters) by them after
18:27. the brethren *wrote,* exhorting the
23: 5. for it *is written,* Thou shalt not
25. *And* he *wrote* a letter after this manner :
24:14. all things *which are written* in
25:26. I have no certain thing *to write*
— I might have somewhat *to write.*
Ro. 1:17. as it *is written,* The just shall live
2:24. through you, as it *is written.*
3: 4. every man a liar ; as it *is written,*
10. as it *is written,* There is none righteous
4:17. as it *is written,* I have made thee
23. it was not *written* for his sake
8:36. as it *is written,* For thy sake we are
9:13. as it *is written,* Jacob have I loved,
33. as it *is written,* Behold, I lay in Sion

Ro. 10: 5. Moses *describeth* the righteousness
15. as it *is written*, How beautiful are
11: 8. According as it *is written*, God hath
26. as it *is written*, There shall come
12:19. it *is written*, Vengeance (is) mine;
14:11. For it *is written*, (As) I live, saith
15: 3. as it *is written*, The reproaches of
9. as it *is written*, For this cause I will
15. I *have written* the more boldly
21. as it *is written*, To whom he was
16:22. I Tertius, *who wrote* (this) epistle,
1Co. 1:19. For it *is written*, I will destroy the
31. according as it *is written*, He that
2: 9. as it *is written*, Eye hath not seen,
3:19. For it *is written*, He taketh the wise
4: 6. above that which *is written*, that no
14. I *write* not these things to shame you,
5: 9. I *wrote* unto you in an epistle
11. now I *have written* unto you
7: 1. things whereof ye *wrote* unto me:
9: 9. it *is written* in the law of Moses,
10. For our sakes, no doubt, (this) *is written*:
15. neither *have* I *written* these things,
10: 7. as it *is written*, The people sat
11. they *are written* for our admonition,
14:21. In the law it *is written*, With (men)
37. the things that I *write* unto you
15:45. so it *is written*, The first man
54. to pass the saying *that is written*,
2Co. 1:13. we *write* none other things unto you,
2: 3. I *wrote* this same unto you, lest,
4. I *wrote* unto you with many tears ;
9. to this end also *did* I *write*, that
4:13. according *as it is written*, I believed,
7:12. Wherefore, though I *wrote* unto you,
8:15. As it *is written*, He that (had **gathered**)
9: 1. superfluous for me *to write* to you:
9. As it *is written*, He hath dispersed
13: 2. being absent now I *write* to them
10. I *write* these things being absent,
Gal. 1:20. the things which I *write* unto you,
3:10. for it *is written*, Cursed (is) every
— things *which are written* in the book
13. for it *is written*, Cursed (is) every one
4:22. For it *is written*, that Abraham had
27. For it *is written*, Rejoice, (thou) barren
6:11. I *have written* unto you with
Phi. 3: 1. *To write* the same things to you,
1Th. 4: 9. need not that I *write* unto you:
5: 1. have no need that I *write* unto you.
2Th. 3:17. token in every epistle: so I *write*.
1Ti. 3:14. These things *write* I unto thee,
Philem.19. I Paul *have written* (it) with
21. I *wrote* unto thee, knowing that
Heb 10: 7. in the volume of the book it *is written*
1Pet.1:16. Because it *is written*, Be ye holy;
5:12. I *have written* briefly, exhorting,
2Pet.3: 1. beloved, I now *write* unto you;
15. given unto him *hath written* unto you;
1Joh.1: 4. these things *write* we unto you,
2: 1. these things *write* I unto you,
7. I *write* no new commandment
8. a new commandment I *write* unto you,
12. I *write* unto you, little children,
13. I *write* unto you, fathers, because **ye**
— I *write* unto you, young men, because
— I *write* unto you, little children,
14. I *have written* unto you, fathers,
— I *have written* unto you, young men,
21. I *have* not *written* unto you because
26. These (things) *have* I *written* unto you
5:13. These things *have* I *written* unto you

2Joh. 5. as *though* I *wrote* a new commandment
12. Having many things *to write* unto you,
3Joh. 9. I *wrote* unto the church: but Diotrephes,
13. I had many things *to write*, but I will not
with ink and pen *write* unto thee:
Jude 3. *to write* unto you of the common
— needful for me *to write* unto you,
Rev: 1: 3. those things *which are written* therein:
11. What thou seest, *write* in a book,
19. *Write* the things which thou hast
2: 1. angel of the church of Ephesus *write ;*
8. angel of the church in Smyrna *write ;*
12. angel of the church in Pergamos *write ;*
17. in the stone a new name *written*,
18. angel of the church in Thyatira *write ;*
3: 1. angel of the church in Sardis *write ;*
7. angel of the church in Philadelphia *write ;*
12. I *will write* upon him the name
14. angel of the church of the Laodiceans
write ;
5: 1. a book *written* within and on the backside,
10: 4. their voices, I was about to *write :*
— thunders uttered, and *write* them not.
13: 8. names *are* not *written* in the book
14: 1. his Father's name *written* in their foreheads.
13. *Write*, Blessed (are) the dead which
17: 5. upon her forehead (was) a name *written*,
8. whose names *were* not *written*
19: 9. he saith unto me, *Write*, Blessed (are)
12. he had a name *written*, that no
16. on his thigh a name *written*,
20:12. out of those things *which were written*
15. not found *written* in the book of life
21: 5. he said unto me, *Write :* for these
27. they *which are written* in the Lamb's
22:18. plagues *that are written* in this book:
19. things *which are written* in this

γραώδης, *graōdees.*

1Ti. 4: 7. refuse profane and *old wives'* fables,

γρηγορέω, *greegoreo.*

Mat.24:42. *Watch* therefore: for ye know not what
43. he would *have watched*, and would not
have
25:13. *Watch* therefore, for ye know neither the
26:38. tarry ye here, and *watch* with me.
40. could ye not *watch* with me one hour ?
41. *Watch* and pray, that ye enter not into
Mar 13:34. commanded the porter to *watch*.
35. *Watch* ye therefore: for ye know not
37. unto you I say unto all, *Watch*.
14:34. tarry ye here, and *watch*.
37. couldest not thou *watch* one hour ?
38. *Watch* ye and pray, lest ye enter into
Lu. 12:37. when he cometh shall find *watching :*
39. would come, he would *have watched*,
Acts20:31. Therefore *watch*, and remember, that
1Co.16:13. *Watch* ye, stand fast in the faith,
Col. 4: 2. *and watch* in the same with thanksgiving;
1Th. 5: 6. *let* us *watch* and be sober.
10. whether we *wake* or sleep, we should
1Pet.5: 8. Be sober, *be vigilant ;* because your
Rev. 3: 2. Be *watchful*, and strengthen the things
3. If therefore thou *shalt* not *watch*,
16:15. Blessed (is) he *that watcheth*, and keepeth

γυμνάζω, *gumnazo*.

1Ti. 4: 7. *exercise* thyself (rather) unto godliness.
Heb 5:14. have their senses *exercised* to discern
   12:11. unto them *which are exercised* thereby.
2Pet.2:14. an heart they have *exercised* with

γυμνασία, *gumnasia*.

1Ti. 4: 8. For bodily *exercise* profiteth little:

γυμνητεύομαι, *gumneetŭomai*.

1Co. 4:11. we both hunger, and thirst, and *are naked*,

γυμνός, *gumnos*.

Mat.25:36. *Naked*, and ye clothed me: I was sick,
     38. took (thee) in? or *naked*, and clothed
       (thee)?
     43. *naked*, and ye clothed me not: sick,
     44. a stranger, or *naked*, or sick, or in prison,
Mar14:51. a linen cloth cast about (his) *naked* (body);
     52. linen cloth, and fled from them *naked*.
Joh.21: 7. for he was *naked*, and did cast himself
Acts19:16. out of that house *naked* and wounded.
1Co.15:37. body that shall be, but *bare* grain,
2Co. 5: 3. we shall not be found *naked*
Heb 4:13. all things (are) *naked* and opened unto
Jas. 2:15. If a brother or sister be *naked*, and
Rev. 3:17. miserable, and poor, and blind, and
       naked :
   16:15. lest he walk *naked*, and they see his shame.
   17:16. shall make her desolate and *naked*,

γυμνότης, *gumnotees*.

Ro. 8:35. famine, or *nakedness*, or peril, or sword?
2Co.11:27. fastings often, in cold and *nakedness*.
Rev. 3:18. the shame of thy *nakedness* do not appear ;

γυναικάριον, *gunaikarion*.

2Ti. 3: 6. lead captive *silly women* laden with

γυναικεῖος, *gunaikīos*.

1Pet.3: 7. giving honour unto the **wife**, as unto the

γυνή, *gunee*.

Mat. 1:20. to take unto thee Mary thy *wife* :
     24. bidden him, and took unto him his *wife* :
   5:28. whosoever looketh on a *woman* to lust
     31. Whosoever shall put away his *wife*, let
     32. That whosoever shall put away his *wife*,
   9:20. behold, a *woman*, which was diseased
     22. the *woman* was made whole from
   11:11. them that are born of *women* there
   13:33. leaven, which a *woman* took, and hid
   14: 3. Herodias' sake, his brother Philip's *wife*.
     21. five thousand men, beside *women*
   15:22. behold, a *woman* of Canaan came
     28. O *woman*, great (is) thy faith:

Mat.15:38. four thousand men, beside *women*
   18:25. to be sold, and his *wife*, and children,
   19: 3. lawful for a man to put away his *wife*
      5. shall cleave to his *wife:* and they
      8. suffered you to put away your *wives :*
      9. Whosoever shall put away his *wife*,
     10. case of the man be so with (his) *wife*,
     29. father, or mother, or *wife*, or children,
   22:24. his brother shall marry his *wife*
     25. left his *wife* unto his brother :
     27. last of all the *woman* died also.
     28. whose *wife* shall she be of the seven ?
   26: 7. There came unto him a *woman*
     10. Why trouble ye the *woman* ? for she
   27:19. his *wife* sent unto him, saying,
     55. many *women* were there beholding
   28: 5. angel answered and said unto the *women*,
Mar. 5:25. a certain *woman*, which had an
     33. the *woman* fearing and trembling,
   6:17. Herodias' sake, his brother Philip's *wife:*
     18. for thee to have thy brother's *wife*.
   7:25. For a (certain) *woman*, whose young
     26. The *woman* was a Greek, a Syrophenician
   10: 2. for a man to put away (his) *wife* ?
      7. father and mother, and cleave to his *wife:*
     11. Whosoever shall put away his *wife*,
     12. if a *woman* shall put away her husband,
     29. or father, or mother, or *wife*, or children,
   12:19. die, and leave (his) *wife* (behind him),
   — his brother should take his *wife*,
     20. the first took a *wife*, and dying left no
      seed.
     22. last of all the *woman* died also.
     23. whose *wife* shall she be of them? for the
      seven had her to *wife*.
   14: 3. there came a *woman* having an
   15:40. There were also *women* looking on
Lu. 1: 5. his *wife* (was) of the daughters of Aaron,
     13. thy *wife* Elisabeth shall bear
     18. man, and my *wife* well stricken in years
     24. those days his *wife* Elisabeth conceived,
     28. blessed (art) thou among *women*.
     42. said, Blessed (art) thou among *women*,
   2: 5. taxed with Mary his espoused *wife*,
   3:19. Herodias his brother Philip's *wife*,
   4:26. unto a *woman* (that was) a widow.
   7:28. Among those that are born of *women*
     37. behold, a *woman* in the city,
     39. who and what manner of *woman*
     44. he turned to the *woman*, and said unto
      Simon, Seest thou this *woman* ?
     50. he said to the *woman*, Thy faith
   8: 2. certain *women*, which had been
      3. Joanna the *wife* of Chuza
     43. a *woman* having an issue of blood
     47. when the *woman* saw that she
   10:38. a certain *woman* named Martha
   11:27. a certain *woman* of the company
   13:11. there was a *woman* which had a
     12. *Woman*, thou art loosed from thine
     21. like leaven, which a *woman* took
   14:20. another said, I have married a *wife*,
     26. his father, and mother, and *wife*, and
      children,
   15: 8. what *woman* having ten pieces
   16:18. Whosoever putteth away his *wife*,
   17:32. Remember Lot's *wife*.
   18:29. left house, or parents, or brethren, or
      wife,
   20:28. If any man's brother die, having a *wife*,
   — his brother should take his *wife*,
     29. seven brethren: and the first took a *wife*,

Lu. 20:30. the second took her to *wife*,
    32. Last of all the *woman* died also.
    33. whose *wife* of them is she? for seven had her to *wife*.
22:57. saying, *Woman*, I know him not.
23:27. a great company of people, and of *women*,
    49. the *women* that followed him
    55. the *women* also, which came with him
24:22. certain *women* also of our company
    24. even so as the *women* had said:
Joh. 2: 4. *Woman*, what have I to do with thee?
  4: 7. There cometh a *woman* of Samaria
    9. Then saith the *woman* of Samaria
    — which am a *woman* of Samaria?
    11. The *woman* saith unto him, Sir,
    15. The *woman* saith unto him, Sir,
    17. The *woman* answered and said, I have
    19. The *woman* saith unto him, Sir,
    21. Jesus saith unto her, *Woman*, believe me,
    25. The *woman* saith unto him, I know
    27. that he talked with the *woman*:
    28. The *woman* then left her waterpot,
    39. the saying of the *woman*, which testified,
    42. said unto the *woman*, Now we believe,
  8: 3. brought unto him a *woman* taken
    4. this *woman* was taken in adultery,
    9. the *woman* standing in the midst.
    10. and saw none but the *woman*, he said
    — *Woman*, where are those thine accusers?
16:21. A *woman* when she is in travail hath
19:26. his mother, *Woman*, behold thy son!
20:13. they say unto her, *Woman*, why weepest thou?
    15. *Woman*, why weepest thou? whom
Acts 1:14. prayer and supplication, with the *women*,
  5: 1. Ananias, with Sapphira his *wife*,
    2. his *wife* also being privy (to it),
    7. his *wife*, not knowing what was
    14. multitudes both of men and *women*.
  8: 3. haling men and *women* committed
    12. were baptized, both men and *women*.
  9: 2. whether they were men or *women*,
13:50. the devout and honourable *women*,
16: 1. the son of a certain *woman*,
    13. spake unto the *women* which
    14. a certain *woman* named Lydia,
17: 4. of the chief *women* not a few.
    12. also of honourable *women* which were
    34. a *woman* named Damaris, and others
18: 2. from Italy, with his *wife* Priscilla;
21: 5. on our way, with *wives* and children,
22: 4. into prisons both men and *women*.
24:24. Felix came with his *wife* Drusilla,
Ro. 7: 2. the *woman* which hath an husband
1Co. 5: 1. that one should have his father's *wife*.
  7: 1. good for a man not to touch a *woman*.
    2. let every man have his own *wife*,
    3. Let the husband render unto the *wife*
    — also the *wife* unto the husband.
    4. The *wife* hath not power of her own body,
    — power of his own body, but the *wife*.
    10. Let not the *wife* depart from (her) husband:
    11. let not the husband put away (his) *wife*.
    12. If any brother hath a *wife* that believeth not,
    13. the *woman* which hath an husband
    14. husband is sanctified by the *wife*, and the unbelieving *wife* is sanctified by
    16. For what knowest thou, O *wife*,
    — whether thou shalt save (thy) *wife*?
    27. Art thou bound unto a *wife*?

1Co. 7:27. Art thou loosed from a *wife*? seek not a *wife*.
    29. they that have *wives* be as though
    33. how he may please (his) *wife*.
    34. difference (also) between a *wife* and a virgin.
    39. The *wife* is bound by the law
  9: 5. to lead about a sister, a *wife*, as
 11: 3. the head of the *woman* (is) the man;
    5. every *woman* that prayeth or
    6. if the *woman* be not covered,
    — a shame for a *woman* to be shorn
    7. the *woman* is the glory of the man.
    8. the man is not of the *woman*; but the *woman* of the man.
    9. created for the *woman*; but the *woman* for
    10. For this cause ought the *woman*
    11. neither is the man without the *woman*, neither the *woman* without the man,
    12. as the *woman* (is) of the man, even so (is) the man also by the *woman*;
    13. that a *woman* pray unto God uncovered?
    15. if a *woman* have long hair, it is
14:34. Let your *women* keep silence in
    35. a shame for *women* to speak in the church.
Gal. 4: 4. sent forth his Son, made of a *woman*,
Eph 5:22. *Wives*, submit yourselves unto
    23. the husband is the head of the *wife*,
    24. so (let) the *wives* (be) to their own
    25. Husbands, love your *wives*, even
    28. So ought men to love their *wives*
    — He that loveth his *wife* loveth himself.
    31. shall be joined unto his *wife*,
    33. so love his *wife* even as himself; and the *wife* (see) that she reverence
Col. 3:18. *Wives*, submit yourselves unto
    19. Husbands, love (your) *wives*, and be not
1Ti. 2: 9. that *women* adorn themselves in
    10. which becometh *women* professing
    11. Let the *woman* learn in silence
    12. I suffer not a *woman* to teach,
    14. the *woman* being deceived was
  3: 2. the husband of one *wife*, vigilant,
    11. Even so (must their) *wives* (be) grave,
    12. deacons be the husbands of one *wife*,
  5: 9. having been the *wife* of one man,
Tit. 1: 6. be blameless, the husband of one *wife*,
Heb 11:35. *Women* received their dead raised to
1Pet.3: 1. ye *wives*, (be) in subjection to your own
    — won by the conversation of the *wives*;
    5. the holy *women* also, who trusted in God,
Rev. 2:20. thou sufferest that *woman* Jezebel,
  9: 8. they had hair as the hair of *women*,
12: 1. a *woman* clothed with the sun,
    4. the dragon stood before the *woman*
    6. the *woman* fled into the wilderness,
    13. he persecuted the *woman* which brought
    14. to the *woman* were given two wings
    15. water as a flood after the *woman*,
    16. the earth helped the *woman*, and the
    17. the dragon was wrpth with the *woman*,
14: 4. they which were not defiled with *women*;
17: 3. I saw a *woman* sit upon a scarlet coloured beast,
    4. the *woman* was arrayed in purple
    6. I saw the *woman* drunken with the
    7. tell thee the mystery of the *woman*,
    9. seven mountains, on which the *woman* sitteth.
    18. the *woman* which thou sawest
19: 7. his *wife* hath made herself ready.
21: 9. I will shew thee the bride, the Lamb's *wife*.

γωνία, gōnia.

Mat. 6: 5. in the *corners* of the streets, that they
21:42. is become the head of the *corner* :
Mar.12:10. is become the head of the *corner* :
Lu. 20:17. same is become the head of the *corner* ?
Acts 4:11. which is become the head of the *corner*.
26:26. for this thing was not done in a *corner*.
1Pet.2: 7. same is made the head of the *corner*,
Rev. 7: 1. standing on the four *corners* of the earth,
20: 8. which are in the four *quarters* of the earth,

δαιμονίζομαι, daimonizomai.

Mat. 4:24. those which were *possessed with devils*,
8:16. many that were *possessed with devils* :
28. there met him two *possessed with devils*,
33. befallen to the *possessed of the devils*.
9:32. a dumb man *possessed with a devil*.
12:22. one *possessed with a devil*, blind, and dumb :
15:22. my daughter *is* grievously *vexed with a devil*.
Mar. 1:32. them *that were possessed with devils*.
5:15. him *that was possessed with the devil*,
16. to him *that was possessed with the devil*,
18. he *that had been possessed with the devil*
Lu. 8:36. he *that was possessed of the devils*
Joh.10:21. not the words of him *that hath a devil*.

δαιμόνιον, daimonion.

Mat. 7:22. in thy name have cast out *devils* ?
9:33. when the *devil* was cast out, the
34. Pharisees said, He casteth out *devils* through the prince of the *devils*.
10: 8. raise the dead, cast out *devils :*
11:18. nor drinking, and they say, He hath a *devil*.
12:24. This (fellow) doth not cast out *devils*, but by Beelzebub the prince of the *devils*.
27. if I by Beelzebub cast out *devils*,
28. if I cast out *devils* by the Spirit
17:18. Jesus rebuked the *devil* ; and he departed
Mar. 1:34. divers diseases, and cast out many *devils ;* and suffered not the *devils* to speak,
39. throughout all Galilee, and cast out *devils*.
3:15. to heal sicknesses, and to cast out *devils :*
22. by the prince of the *devils* casteth he out *devils*.
6:13. they cast out many *devils*, and anointed
7:26. that he would cast forth the *devil*
29. the *devil* is gone out of thy daughter.
30. she found the *devil* gone out,
9:38. we saw one casting out *devils*
16: 9. out of whom he had cast seven *devils*.
17. In my name shall they cast out *devils;*
Lu. 4:33. which had a spirit of an unclean *devil*,
35. when the *devil* had thrown him
41. *devils* also came out of many,
7:33. ye say, He hath a *devil*.
8: 2. out of whom went seven *devils*,
27. a certain man, which had *devils*
30. because many *devils* were entered
33. Then went the *devils* out of the man,
35. out of whom the *devils* were departed,
38. the man out of whom the *devils* were

Lu. 9: 1. power and authority over all *devils*,
42. the *devil* threw him down, and tare (him).
49. Master, we saw one casting out *devils*
10:17. Lord, even the *devils* are subject unto us
11:14. he was casting out a *devil*, and it was
— when the *devil* was gone out,
15. He casteth out *devils* through Beelzebub the chief of the *devils*.
18. that I cast out *devils* through Beelzebub.
19. if I by Beelzebub cast out *devils*,
20. with the finger of God cast out *devils*,
13:32. Behold, I cast out *devils*, and I do cures
Joh. 7:20. people answered and said, Thou hast a *devil*.
8:48. thou art a Samaritan, and hast a *devil* ?
49. Jesus answered, I have not a *devil ;*
,52. Now we know that thou hast a *devil*.
10:20. many of them said, He hath a *devil*.
21. Can a *devil* open the eyes of the blind ?
Acts17:18. to be a setter forth of strange *gods :*
1Co.10:20. they sacrifice to *devils*, and not to God:
— that ye should have fellowship with *devils*.
21. cup of the Lord, and the cup of *devils :*
— the Lord's table, and of the table of *devils*.
1Ti. 4: 1. heed to seducing spirits, and doctrines of *devils ;*
Jas. 2:19. the *devils* also believe, and tremble.
Rev. 9:20. that they should not worship *devils*,

δαιμονιώδης, daimoniōdees.

Jas. 3:15. not from above, but (is) earthly, sensual, *devilish*.

δαίμων, daimōn.

Mat. 8:31. So the *devils* besought him, saying,
Mar. 5:12. all the *devils* besought him, saying,
Lu. 8:29. was driven of the *devil* into the wilderness.
Rev.16:14. For they are the spirits of *devils*,
18: 2. is become the habitation of *devils*,

δάκνω, dakno.

Gal. 5:15. if ye *bite* and devour one another,

δάκρυ & δάκρυον, dakru & dakruon.

Note.—[2] marks those which are obvious from δακρυον

Mar. 9:24. said with *tears*, Lord, I believe ;
Lu. 7:38. began to wash his feet with *tears*,
44. she hath washed my feet with *tears*,
Acts20:19. humility of mind, and with many *tears*,
31. warn every one night and day with *tears*.
2Co. 2: 4. I wrote unto you with many *tears ;*
2Ti. 1: 4. being mindful of thy *tears*, that
Heb. 5: 7. supplications with strong crying and *tears*
12:17. though he sought it carefully with *tears*.
Rev. 7:17. God shall wipe away all *tears*[2]
21: 4. God shall wipe away all *tears* from[2]

δακρύω, dakruo.

Joh.11:35. Jesus *wept*.

δακτύλιος, *daktulios.*

Lu. 15:22. put a *ring* on his hand, and shoes on

δάκτυλος, *daktulos.*

Mat.23: 4. move them with one of their *fingers.*
Mar. 7:33. put his *fingers* into his ears, and he spit,
Lu. 11:20. if I with the *finger* of God cast out
    46. the burdens with one of your *fingers.*
  16:24. may dip the tip of his *finger* in water,
Joh. 8: 6. with (his) *finger* wrote on the ground,
  20:25. put my *finger* into the print of the nails,
    27. Reach hither thy *finger,* and behold

δαμάζω, *damazo.*

Mar. 5: 4. neither could any (man) *tame* him.
Jas. 3: 7. things in the sea, *is tamed,* and *hath been tamed* of mankind:
    8. the tongue can no man *tame;* (it is)

δάμαλις, *damalis.*

Heb. 9:13. the ashes of an *heifer* sprinkling

δανείζω, *danizo.*

Mat. 5:42. from him that would *borrow* of thee
Lu. 6:34. if ye *lend* (to them) of whom ye hope
    — for sinners also *lend* to sinners,
    35. do good, and *lend,* hoping for nothing

δάνειον, *danion.*

Mat.18:27. loosed him, and forgave him the *debt.*

δανειστής, *danistees.*

Lu. 7:41. There was a certain *creditor* which

δαπανάω, *dapanav.*

Mar. 5:26. *had spent* all that she had, and was
Lu. 15:14. *when* he *had spent* all, there arose
Acts21:24. *be at charges* with them, that they
2Co.12:15. I *will* very gladly *spend* and be spent
Jas. 4: 3. that ye *may consume* (it) upon your lusts.

δαπάνη, *dapanee.*

Lu. 14:28. sitteth not down first, and counteth the *cost,*

δέ, see Appendix.

δέησις, *de-cesis.*

Lu. 1:13. Zacharias: for thy *prayer* is heard;
  2:37. served (God) with fastings and *prayers* night and day.
  5:33. disciples of John fast often, and make *prayers,*

Acts 1:14. with one accord in prayer and *supplication,*
Ro. 10: 1. my heart's desire and *prayer* to God for
2Co. 1:11. helping together by *prayer* for us,
  9:14. by their *prayer* for you, which long
Eph. 6:18. Praying always with all prayer and *supplication*
    — perseverance and *supplication* for all saints;
Phil. 1: 4. Always in every *prayer* of mine for you all making *request* with joy,
    19. to my salvation through your *prayer,*
  4: 6. every thing by prayer and *supplication*
1Ti. 2: 1. that, first of all, *supplications,*
    5: 5. continueth in *supplications* and prayers
2Ti. 1: 3. of thee in my *prayers* night and day;
Heb. 5: 7. when he had offered up *prayers* and
Jas. 5:16. fervent *prayer* of a righteous man
1Pet.3:12. his ears (are open) unto their *prayers:*

δεῖ, *dī,* an impersonal verb.

Mat.16:21. how that he *must* go unto Jerusalem,
  17:10. that Elias *must* first come?
  18:33. *Shouldest* not thou also have had
  23:23. these *ought* ye to have done, and not
  24: 6. all (these things) *must* come to pass,
  25:27. Thou *oughtest* therefore to have put
  26:35. Though I *should* die with thee,
    54. scriptures be fulfilled, that thus it *must* be?
Mar. 8:31. the Son of man *must* suffer many
  9:11. the scribes that Elias *must* first come?
  13: 7. for (such things) *must* needs be;
    10. the gospel *must* first be published
    14. standing where it *ought* not,
  14:31. If I *should* die with thee, I will not
Lu. 2:49. I *must* be about my Father's business?
  4:43. I *must* preach the kingdom of God
  9:22. The Son of man *must* suffer many things,
  11:42. these *ought* ye to have done, and not to
  12:12. in the same hour what ye *ought* to say.
  13:14. six days in which men *ought* to work:
    16. *ought* not this woman, being a
    33. Nevertheless I *must* walk to day,
  15:32. It *was meet* that we should make merry,
  17:25. first *must* he suffer many things,
  18: 1. that men *ought* always (to) pray,
  19: 5. to day I *must* abide at thy house.
  21: 9. these things *must* first come to pass;
  22: 7. when the passover *must* be killed.
    37. that is written *must* yet be accomplished
  24: 7. The Son of man *must* be delivered into
    26. *Ought* not Christ to have suffered these
    44. that all things *must* be fulfilled,
    46. thus it *behoved* Christ to suffer,
Joh. 3: 7. Ye *must* be born again.
    14. so *must* the Son of man be lifted up:
    30. He *must* increase, but I (must) decrease.
  4: 4. he *must* needs go through Samaria.
    20. place where men *ought* to worship.
    24. *must* worship (him) in spirit and in truth.
  9: 4. I *must* work the works of him that
  10:16. them also I *must* bring, and they
  12:34. The Son of man *must* be lifted up?
  20: 9. that he *must* rise again from the dead.
Acts 1:16. scripture *must* needs have been fulfilled,
  22(21). *must* one be ordained
  3:21. Whom the heaven *must* receive until
  4:12. among men, whereby we *must* be saved.
  5:29. We *ought* to obey God rather than men.
  9: 6. shall be told thee what thou *must* do.
    16. he *must* suffer for my name's sake.

Acts10: 6. tell thee what thou *oughtest* to do.
14:22. we *must* through much tribulation
15: 5. That it was *needful* to circumcise
16:30. Sirs, what *must* I do to be saved?
17: 3. that Christ *must needs* have suffered,
18:21. I *must* by all means keep this feast
19:21. been there, I *must* also see Rome.
    36. ye *ought* to be quiet, and to do nothing rashly.
20:35. labouring ye *ought* to support the weak,
21:22. multitude *must* needs come together :
23:11. so *must* thou bear witness also at Rome.
24:19. Who *ought* to have been here before
25:10. where I *ought* to be judged:
    24. crying that he *ought* not to live
26: 9. that I *ought* to do many things
27:21. Sirs, ye *should* have hearkened unto me,
    24. thou *must* be brought before Cæsar:
    26. we *must* be cast upon a certain island.
Ro. 1:27. recompence of their error which *was meet.*
8:26. what we should pray for as we *ought :*
12: 3. more highly than he *ought* to think ;
1Co. 8: 2. nothing yet as he *ought* to know.
11:19. For there *must* be also heresies among
15:25. For he *must* reign, till he hath put all
    53. this corruptible *must* put on incorruption,
2Co. 2: 3. from them of whom I *ought* to rejoice ;
5:10. we *must* all appear before the judgment seat
11:30. If I *must needs* glory, I will glory of the
Eph. 6:20. may speak boldly, as I *ought* to speak.
Col. 4: 4. manifest, as I *ought* to speak.
    6. how ye *ought* to answer every man.
1Th. 4: 1. how ye *ought* to walk and to please
2Th. 3: 7. know how ye *ought* to follow us:
1Ti. 3: 2. A bishop then *must* be blameless,
    7. Moreover he *must* have a good report
    15. how thou *oughtest* to behave thyself
5:13. speaking things which they *ought* not.
2Ti. 2: 6. that laboureth *must* be first partaker
    24. the servant of the Lord *must* not strive ;
Tit. 1: 7. For a bishop *must* be blameless.
    11. Whose mouths *must* be stopped,
    — teaching things which they *ought* not,
Heb. 2: 1. we *ought* to give the more earnest heed
9:26. then *must* he often have suffered
11: 6. he that cometh to God *must* believe
1Pet.1: 6. though now for a season, if *need* be,
2Pet.3:11. what manner (of persons) *ought* ye to be
Rev. 1: 1. things which *must* shortly come to pass ;
4: 1. things which *must* be hereafter.
10:11. said unto me, Thou *must* prophesy
11: 5. he *must* in this manner be killed.
13:10. *must* be killed with the sword.
17:10. he *must* continue a short space.
20: 3. after that he *must* be loosed a little
22: 6. the things which *must* shortly be done.

δεῖγμα, *dīgma.*

Jude   7. are set forth for an *example,* suffering

δειγματίζω, *dīgmatizo.*

Col. 2:15. he *made a shew* of them openly,

δεικνύ-ω & -υμι, *dīknu-o* & *-umi.*

Mat. 4: 8. *sheweth* him all the kingdoms of the

Mat. 8: 4. go thy way, *shew* thyself to the priest,
16:21. began Jesus *to shew* unto his disciples,
Mar. 1:44. go thy way, *shew* thyself to the priest,
14:15. he *will shew* you a large upper room
Lu. 4: 5. *shewed* unto him all the kingdoms
5:14. go, and *shew* thyself to the priest, and offer
22:12. he *shall shew* you a large upper room
Joh. 2:18. What sign *shewest* thou unto us,
5:20. *sheweth* him all things that himself doeth: and he *will shew* him greater works than
10:32. Many good works *have* I *shewed* you
14: 8. Lord, *shew* us the Father, and it sufficeth
    9. sayest thou (then), *Shew* us the Father?
20:20. he *shewed* unto them (his) hands
Acts 7: 3. into the land which I *shall shew* thee.
10:28. God *hath shewed* me that I should
1Co.12:31. *shew* I unto you a more excellent way.
1Ti. 6:15. Which in his times he *shall shew,*
Heb. 8: 5. the pattern *shewed* to thee in the mount.
Jas. 2:18. *shew* me thy faith without thy works, and I *will shew* thee my faith by my
3:13. *let* him *shew* out of a good conversation
Rev. 1: 1. *to shew* unto his servants things
4: 1. I *will shew* thee things which must
17: 1. I *will shew* unto thee the judgment
21: 9. I *will shew* thee the bride, the Lamb's
    10. *shewed* me that great city, the holy
22: 1. he *shewed* me a pure river of water
    6. *to shew* unto his servants the things
    8. the angel *which shewed* me these things.

δειλία, *dīlia.*

2Ti. 1: 7. God hath not given us the spirit of *fear ;*

δειλιάω, *dīliao.*

Joh.14:27. heart be troubled, neither *let* it *be afraid.*

δειλός, *dīlos.*

Mat. 8:26. Why are ye *fearful,* O ye of little faith?
Mar. 4:40. said unto them, Why are ye so *fearful?*
Rev.21: 8. the *fearful,* and unbelieving, and the abominable,

---

δεῖνα, *dīna.*

Mat.26:18. Go into the city to *such a man,*

δεινῶς, *dīnōs.*

Mat. 8: 6. of the palsy, *grievously* tormented.
Lu. 11:53. Pharisees began to urge (him) *vehemently,*

δειπνέω, *dīpneo.*

Lu. 17: 8. Make ready wherewith I *may sup,*
22:20. Likewise also the cup after *supper,* (lit. the *supping)*
1Co.11:25. (took) the cup, when he *had supped,*
Rev. 3:20. *will sup* with him, and he with me.

δεῖπνον, dipnon.

Mat.23: 6. love the uppermost rooms at *feasts,*
Mar. 6:21. made a *supper* to his lords, high captains,
    12:39. the uppermost rooms at *feasts:*
Lu. 14:12. When thou makest a dinner or a *supper,*
    16. A certain man made a great *supper,*
    17. sent his servant at *supper* time
    24. were bidden shall taste of my *supper.*
    20:46. the chief rooms at *feasts;*
Joh.12: 2. There they made him a *supper;*
    13: 2. *supper* being ended, the devil having
      4. He riseth from *supper,* and laid aside his
    21:20. also leaned on his breast at *supper,*
1Co.11:20. (this) is not to eat the Lord's *supper.*
    21. one taketh before (other) his own *supper:*
Rev.19: 9. unto the marriage *supper* of the Lamb.
    17. unto the *supper* of the great God;

δεισιδαιμονέστερος, disidaimonesteros.

Acts17:22. in all things ye are *too superstitious.*

δεισιδαιμονία, disidaimonia.

Acts25:19. questions against him of their own *super-stition,*

δέκα, deka.

Mat.20:24. when the *ten* heard (it), they were
    25: 1. heaven be likened unto *ten* virgins,
    28. and give (it) unto him which hath *ten* talents.
Mar10:41. when the *ten* heard (it), they began
Lu. 13: 4. Or those eighteen (lit. eight and *ten*), upon whom the
    11. a spirit of infirmity eighteen (lit. eight &c.) years,
    16. whom Satan hath bound, lo, these eighteen (lit. eight &c.) years,
    14:31. be able with *ten* thousand to meet him
    15: 8. what woman having *ten* pieces of silver,
    17:12. there met him *ten* men that were lepers,
    17. said, Were there not *ten* cleansed?
    19:13. he called his *ten* servants, and delivered them *ten* pounds, and said unto them,
    16. Lord, thy pound hath gained *ten* pounds.
    17. have thou authority over *ten* cities.
    24. give (it) to him that hath *ten* pounds.
    25. said unto him, Lord, he hath *ten* pounds.
Acts25: 6. tarried among them more than *ten* days,
Rev. 2:10. ye shall have tribulation *ten* days:
    12: 3. red dragon, having seven heads and *ten*
    13: 1. out of the sea, having seven heads and *ten* horns, and upon his horns *ten* crowns, and upon
    17: 3. blasphemy, having seven heads and *ten* horns.
    7. which hath the seven heads and *ten* horns.
    12. the *ten* horns which thou sawest are *ten* kings, which have received
    16. the *ten* horns which thou sawest

δεκαδύο, dekaduo.

Acts19: 7. all the men were about *twelve.* (lit. *ten* (&) *two*)
    24:11. *twelve* days since I went up to (lit. *ten* &c.)

δεκαπέντε, dekapente.

Joh.11:18. nigh unto Jerusalem, about *fifteen* furlongs
Acts27:28. sounded again, and found (it) *fifteen* fathoms.
Gal. 1:18. to see Peter, and abode with him *fifteen* days.

δεκατέσσαρες, dekatessares.

Mat. 1.17. Abraham to David (are) *fourteen* (lit. *four* (&) *ten*) generations;
    — Babylon (are) *fourteen* generations;
    — unto Christ (are) *fourteen* generations.
2Co.12: 2. a man in Christ about *fourteen* years ago,
Gal. 2: 1. *fourteen* years after I went up again

δεκάτη, dekatee, subst.

Heb. 7: 2. Abraham gave a *tenth part* of all;
    4. Abraham gave the *tenth* of the spoils.
    8. here men that die receive *tithes;*
    9. Levi also, who receiveth *tithes,*

δέκατος, dekatos.

Joh. 1:39(40). for it was about the *tenth* hour.
Rev 11:13. the *tenth* part of the city fell,
    21:20. ninth, a topaz; the *tenth,* a chrysoprasus;

δεκατόω, dekatoō.

Heb. 7: 6. *received tithes* of Abraham, and blessed
    9. Levi also, who receiveth tithes, *payed tithes*

δεκτός, dektos.

Lu. 4:19. To preach the *acceptable* year of the Lord.
    24. No prophet is *accepted* in his own country.
Acts10:35. worketh righteousness, is *accepted*
2Co. 6: 2. I have heard thee in a time *accepted,*
Phi. 4:18. a sweet smell, a sacrifice *acceptable,*

δελεάζω, deleazo.

Jas. 1:14. drawn away of his own lust, and *enticed.*
2Pet.2:14. *beguiling* unstable souls: an heart
    18. they *allure* through the lusts of the flesh,

δένδρον, dendron.

Mat. 3:10. the ax is laid unto the root of the *trees:* therefore every *tree* which bringeth not
    7:17. every good *tree* bringeth forth good fruit; but a corrupt *tree* bringeth forth evil
    18. A good *tree* cannot bring forth evil fruit, neither (can) a corrupt *tree* bring forth
    19. Every *tree* that bringeth not forth
    12:33. Either make the *tree* good, and his fruit good; or else make the *tree* corrupt, and
    — for the *tree* is known by (his) fruit.
    13:32. greatest among herbs, and becometh a *tree,*

Mat.21: 8. others cut down branches from the *trees*,
Mar. 8:24. said, I see men as *trees*, walking.
    11: 8. others cut down branches off the *trees*,
Lu. 3: 9. the axe is laid unto the root of the *trees:*
       every *tree* therefore which bringeth not
    6:43. a good *tree* bringeth not forth corrupt
       fruit ; neither doth a corrupt *tree* bring
       forth
    44. every *tree* is known by his own fruit.
    13:19. it grew, and waxed a great *tree ;*
    21:29. Behold the fig tree, and all the *trees ;*
Jude   12. *trees* whose fruit withereth, without
Rev. 7: 1. nor on the sea, nor on any *tree.*
    3. the earth, neither the sea, nor the *trees,*
    8: 7. the third part of *trees* was burnt
    9: 4. neither any green thing, neither any *tree;*

δεξιολάϬος, *dexiolabos.*

Acts23:23. *spearmen* two hundred, at the third

δεξιός, *dexios.*

[2] marks those which have χεῖρ understood and
[3] those which have μέρη understood.

Mat. 5:29. if thy *right* eye offend thee, pluck
    30. if thy *right* hand offend thee,
    39. shall smite thee on thy *right* cheek,
    6: 3. know what thy *right hand* doeth:[2]
    20:21. may sit, the one on thy *right hand,*[3]
    23. to sit on my *right hand,* and on my left,[3]
    22:44. Sit thou on my *right hand,* till I make[3]
    25:33. set the sheep on his *right hand,*[3]
    34. say unto them on his *right hand,*[3]
    26:64. sitting on the *right hand* of power,[3]
    27:29. a reed in his *right hand :* and they[2]
    38. one on the *right hand,* and another on[3]
Mar 10:37. we may sit, one on thy *right hand,*[3]
    40. to sit on my *right hand* and on my left[3]
    12:36. Sit thou on my *right hand,* till I make[3]
    14:62. sitting on the *right hand* of power,[3]
    15:27. the one on his *right hand,* and the other[3]
    16: 5. a young man sitting on the *right side,*[3]
    19. sat on the *right hand* of God.[3]
Lu. 1:11. standing on the *right side* of the altar[3]
    6: 6. a man whose *right* hand was withered.
    20:42. Sit thou on my *right hand,*[3]
    22:50. cut off his *right* ear.
    69. sit on the *right hand* of the power of God.[3]
    23:33. one on the *right hand,* and the other on[3]
Joh.18:10. priest's servant, and cut off his *right* ear.
    21: 6. Cast the net on the *right* side of the ship,
Acts 2:25. for he is on my *right hand,* that[3]
    33. being by the *right hand* of God[2]
    34. Sit thou on my *right hand,*[3]
    3: 7. he took him by the *right* hand,
    5:31. Him hath God exalted with his *right hand*[2]
    7:55. Jesus standing on the *right hand* of God,[3]
    56. standing on the *right hand* of God.[3]
Ro. 8:34. even at the *right hand* of God,[2]
2Co. 6: 7. on the *right hand* and on the left,[3]
Gal. 2: 9. the *right hands* of fellowship; that[2]
Eph.1:20. set (him) at his own *right hand*[2]
Col. 3: 1. Christ sitteth on the *right hand* of God.[2]
Heb. 1: 3. the *right hand* of the Majesty on high ;[2]
    13. Sit on my *right hand,* until I make[3]
    8: 1. set on the *right hand* of the throne[2]
    10:12. sat down on the *right hand* of God ;[2]
    12: 2. is set down at the *right hand* of the[2]
1Pet.3:22. is on the *right hand* of God ;[2]

Rev. 1:16. he had in his *right* hand seven stars:
    17. he laid his *right* hand upon me,
    20. which thou sawest in my *right hand,*[2]
    2: 1. the seven stars in his *right hand,*[2]
    5: 1. I saw in the *right hand* of him[2]
    7. took the book out of the *right hand*[2]
    10: 2. he set his *right* foot upon the sea,
    13:16. to receive a mark in their *right* hand,

δέομαι, *deomai.*

Mat. 9:38. *Pray* ye therefore the Lord of the harvest,
Lu. 5:12. seeing Jesus fell on(his) face, and *besought*
       him, saying,
    8:28. I *beseech* thee, torment me not.
    38. *besought* him that he might be
    9:38. I *beseech* thee, look upon my son:
    40. I *besought* thy disciples to cast him out;
    10: 2. *pray* ye therefore the Lord of the harvest,
    21:36. Watch ye therefore, and *pray* always,
    22:32. I *have prayed* for thee, that thy faith
Acts 4:31. *when* they *had prayed,* the place
    8:22. *pray* God, if perhaps the thought
    24. *Pray* ye to the Lord for me, that none
    34. I *pray* thee, of whom speaketh the
    10: 2. alms to the people, and *prayed to* God
       alway.
    21:39. I *beseech* thee, suffer me to speak
    26: 3. I *beseech* thee to hear me patiently
Ro. 1:10. *Making request,* if by any means
2Co. 5:20. we *pray* (you) in Christ's stead,
    8: 4. *Praying* us with much intreaty
    10: 2. I *beseech* (you), that I may not
Gal. 4:12. Brethren, I *beseech* you, be as I (am);
1Th. 3:10. Night and day *praying* exceedingly

δέρμα, *derma.*

Heb 11:37. wandered about in sheepskins and goat-
       skins;

δερμάτινος, *dermatinos.*

Mat. 3: 4. a *leathern* girdle about his loins ;
Mar. 1: 6. with a girdle *of a skin* about his loins ;

δέρω, *dero.*

Mat.21:35. husbandmen took his servants, and *beat*
       one,
Mar 12: 3. they caught (him), and *beat* him,
    5. many others; *beating* some, and killing
       some.
    13: 9. in the synagogues ye *shall be beaten:*
Lu. 12:47. *shall be beaten* with many (stripes).
    48. *shall be beaten* with few (stripes).
    20:10. the husbandmen *beat* him, and
    11. another servant: *and* they *beat* him also,
    22:63. that held Jesus mocked him, *and smote*
       (him).
Joh.18:23. if well, why *smitest* thou me ?
Acts 5:40. called the apostles, *and beaten* (them),
    16:37. They *have beaten* us openly uncondemned,
       ...*and*
    22:19. imprisoned *and beat* in every synagogue
1Co. 9:26. not as *one that beateth* the air:
2Co.11:20. if a man *smite* you on the face.

δεσμεύω, desmūo.

Mat.23: 4. For they *bind* heavy burdens
Acts22: 4. *binding* and delivering into prisons

δεσμέω, desmeo.

Lu. 8:29. he *was* kept *bound* with chains

δέσμη, desmee.

Mat.13:30. bind them in *bundles* to burn

δέσμιος, desmios.

Mat.27:15. to release unto the people a *prisoner,*
16. they had then a notable *prisoner,*
Mar.15: 6. he released unto them one *prisoner,*
Acts16:25. praises unto God: and the *prisoners* heard them.
27. supposing that the *prisoners* had been fled.
23:18. Paul the *prisoner* called me unto (him),
25:14. a certain man left *in bonds* by Felix:
27. unreasonable to send a *prisoner,*
28:16. the centurion delivered the *prisoners*
17. yet was I delivered *prisoner* from
Eph. 3: 1. I Paul, the *prisoner* of Jesus Christ
4: 1. I therefore, the *prisoner* of the Lord,
2Ti. 1: 8. of our Lord, nor of me his *prisoner:*
Philem. 1. Paul, a *prisoner* of Jesus Christ,
9. now also a *prisoner* of Jesus Christ.
Heb 13: 3. Remember them *that are in bonds,*

ὁ δεσμὸς & τὰ δεσμά,
ho desmos & ta desma.

Always masculine in the singular. In the plural, the masculine and neuter forms are found: Those obviously neuter are thus marked [3].

Mar. 7:35. the *string* of his tongue was loosed,
Lu. 8:29. he brake the *bands,* and was driven[3]
13:16. be loosed from this *bond* on the
Acts16:26. every one's *bands* were loosed.[3]
20:23. saying that *bonds* and afflictions abide me.[3]
22:30. he loosed him from (his) *bands,*
23:29. worthy of death or of *bonds.*
26:29. such as I am, except these *bonds.*
31. nothing worthy of death or of *bonds.*
Phi. 1: 7. inasmuch as both in my *bonds,*
13. So that my *bonds* in Christ are
14. waxing confident by my *bonds,*
16. to add affliction to my *bonds:*
Col. 4:18. Remember my *bonds.* Grace (be) with you.
2Ti. 2: 9. as an evil doer, (even) unto *bonds;*
Philem.10. whom I have begotten in my *bonds:*
13. have ministered unto me in the *bonds*
Heb 10:34. had compassion of me in my *bonds,*
11:36. moreover of *bonds* and imprisonment.
Jude 6. hath reserved in everlasting *chains*

δεσμοφύλαξ, desmophulax.

Acts16:23. charging the *jailor* to keep them safely:
27. the *keeper of the prison* awaking out
36. the *keeper of the prison* told this saying

δεσμωτήριον, desmōteerion.

Mat.11: 2. when John had heard in the *prison*
Acts 5:21. sent to the *prison* to have them brought.
23. The *prison* truly found we shut
16:26. foundations of the *prison* were shaken:

δεσμότης, desmotees.

Acts27: 1. delivered Paul and certain other *prisoners*
42. soldiers' counsel was to kill the *prisoners,*

δεσπότης, despotees.

Lu. 2:29. *Lord,* now lettest thou thy servant
Acts 4:24. *Lord,* thou (art) God, which hast made
1Ti. 6: 1. their own *masters* worthy of all honour,
2. they that have believing *masters,*
2Ti. 2:21. sanctified, and meet for the *master's* use,
Tit. 2: 9. to be obedient unto their own *masters,*
1Pet.2:18. (be) subject to (your) *masters* with all fear;
2Pet.2: 1. denying the *Lord* that bought them,
Jude 4. denying the only *Lord* God, and our
Rev. 6:10. How long, O *Lord,* holy and true, dost

δεῦρο, dūro.

Mat.19:21. treasure in heaven: and *come* (and) follow me.
Mar.10:21. *come,* take up the cross, and follow me.
Lu. 18:22. treasure in heaven: and *come,* follow me.
Joh.11:43. with a loud voice, Lazarus, *come* forth.
Acts 7: 3. *come* into the land which I shall
34. now *come,* I will send thee into Egypt.
Ro. 1:13. come unto you, but was let *hitherto,*
Rev.17: 1. *Come hither;* I will shew unto
21: 9. *Come hither,* I will shew thee the bride,

δεῦτε, dūte.

Mat. 4:19. he saith unto them, Follow (lit. *come* after) me,
11:28. *Come* unto me, all (ye) that labour
21:38. *come,* let us kill him, and let us
22: 4. things (are) ready: *come* unto the marriage.
25:34. *Come,* ye blessed of my Father, inherit
28: 6. *Come,* see the place where the Lord lay
Mar. 1:17. *Come* ye after me, and I will make
6:31. *Come* ye yourselves apart into a
12: 7. the heir; *come,* let us kill him,
Lu. 20:14. the heir; *come,* let us kill him,
Joh. 4:29. *Come,* see a man, which told me
21:12. Jesus saith unto them, *Come* (and) dine.
Rev.19:17. *Come* and gather yourselves together

δευτεραῖος, dūteraios.

Acts28:13. we came the *next day* to Puteoli:

δευτερόπρωτος, duteroprōtos.

Lu. 6: 1. it came to pass on the *second* sabbath, *after the first,*

δεύτερος, dūteros.

Mat.21:30. he came to the *second*, and said
   22:26. Likewise the *second* also, and the third,
      39. the *second* (is) like unto it, Thou
   26:42. He went away again the *second time*,
Mar 12:21. the *second* took her, and died,
      31. the *second* (is) like, (namely) this,
   14:72. the *second time* the cock crew.
Lu. 12:38. he shall come in the *second* watch,
   19:18. the *second* came, saying, Lord,
   20:30. the *second* took her to wife, and he died
Joh. 3: 4. can he enter the *second time* into his
   4:54. This (is) again the *second* miracle
   9:24. Then *again* called they the man
   21:16. He saith to him again the *second time*,
Acts 7:13. at the *second* (time) Joseph was
   10:15. (spake) unto him again the *second time*,
   11: 9. voice answered me *again* from heaven,
   12:10. past the first and the *second* ward,
   13:33. also written in the *second* psalm,
1Co.12:28. first apostles, *secondarily* prophets,
   15:47. the *second* man (is) the Lord
2Co. 1:15. that ye might have a *second* benefit;
   13: 2. as if I were present, the *second time*;
Tit. 3:10. after the first and *second* admonition
Heb 8: 7. have been sought for the *second*.
   9: 3. after the *second* veil, the tabernacle
     7. into the *second* (went) the high priest
    28. shall he appear the *second time*
   10: 9. that he may establish the *second*.
2Pet.3: 1. This *second* epistle, beloved, I now
Jude   5. *afterward* destroyed them that
Rev. 2:11. shall not be hurt of the *second* death.
   4: 7. the *second* beast like a calf,
   6: 3. when he had opened the *second* seal, I
        heard the *second* beast say, Come and
        see.
   8: 8. the *second* angel sounded, and as it
   11:14. The *second* woe is past; (and), behold,
   16: 3. the *second* angel poured out his vial
   19: 3. *again* they said, Alleluia.
   20: 6. the *second* death hath no power,
    14. This is the *second* death.
   21: 8. fire and brimstone: which is the *second*
        death.
    19. foundation (was) jasper; the *second*,

δέχομαι, dekomai.

Mat.10:14. whosoever shall not *receive* you,
    40. He *that receiveth* you *receiveth* me, and he
        that receiveth me *receiveth* him that sent
        me.
    41. He *that receiveth* a prophet in the
     — he *that receiveth* a righteous man
   11:14. if ye will *receive* (it), this is Elias,
   18: 5. whoso shall *receive* one such little child in
        my name *receiveth* me.
Mar. 6:11. whosoever shall not *receive* you,
   9:37. Whosoever shall *receive* one of such chil-
        dren in my name, *receiveth* me: and
        whosoever shall *receive* me, *receiveth*
   10:15. Whosoever shall not *receive* the kingdom
Lu. 2:28. Then *took* he him up in his arms,
   8:13. when they hear, *receive* the word with joy;
   9: 5. whosoever will not *receive* you,
    11. he *received* them, *and* spake unto them
    48. Whosoever shall *receive* this child in my
        name *receiveth* me: and whosoever shall
        receive me *receiveth* him that sent me:

Lu. 9:53. they *did* not *receive* him, because
   10: 8. whatsoever city ye enter, and they *receive*
        you,
    10. city ye enter, and they *receive* you not,
   16: 4. they *may receive* me into their houses.
    6. he said unto him, Take thy bill,
    7. Take thy bill, and write fourscore.
    9. they *may receive* you into everlasting
   18:17. Whosoever shall not *receive* the
   22:17. he *took* the cup, *and* gave thanks,
Joh. 4:45. the Galilæans *received* him, having
Acts 3:21. Whom the heaven must *receive*
   7:38. who *received* the lively oracles
    59. saying, Lord Jesus, *receive* my spirit.
   8:14. that Samaria *had received* the word
   11: 1. Gentiles *had* also *received* the word
   17:11. in that they *received* the word
   21:17. the brethren *received* us gladly.
   22: 5. from whom also I *received* letters...*and*
   28:21. We neither *received* letters out of
1Co. 2:14. the natural man *receiveth* not
2Co. 6: 1. *receive* not the grace of God in vain.
   7:15. with fear and trembling ye *received* him.
   8: 4. that we would *receive* the gift,
    17. For indeed he *accepted* the exhortation;
   11: 4. gospel, which ye *have* not *accepted*,
    16. yet as a fool *receive* me, that I
Gal. 4:14. *received* me as an angel of God,
Eph. 6:17. *take* the helmet of salvation, and the
Phi. 4:18. *having received* of Epaphroditus
Col. 4:10. if he come unto you, *receive* him;
1Th. 1: 6. *having received* the word in much
   2:13. ye *received* (it) not (as) the word of men,
2Th. 2:10. they *received* not the love of the truth,
Heb 11:31. *when* she *had received* the spies with peace.
Jas. 1:21. *receive* with meekness the engrafted word,

δέω, deo.

Mat.12:29. except he first *bind* the strong man
   13:30. *bind* them in bundles to burn
   14: 3. laid hold on John, and *bound* him,
   16:19. whatsoever thou shalt *bind* on earth shall
        be *bound* in heaven:
   18:18. Whatsoever ye shall *bind* on earth shall be
        bound in heaven:
   21: 2. straightway ye shall find an ass *tied*,
   22:13. *Bind* him hand and foot, *and* take
   27: 2. *when* they *had bound* him,
Mar. 3:27. except he will first *bind* the strong
   5: 3. no man could *bind* him, no,
    4. had been often *bound* with fetters
   6:17. laid hold upon John, and *bound* him
   11: 2. ye shall find a colt *tied*, whereon
    4. found the colt *tied* by the door
   15: 1. *bound* Jesus, *and* carried (him) away,
    7. Barabbas, (which lay) *bound* with
Lu. 13:16. whom Satan *hath bound*, lo, these
   19:30. ye shall find a colt *tied*, whereon
Joh. 11:44. *bound* hand and foot with graveclothes:
   18:12. the Jews took Jesus, and *bound* him,
    24. Now Annas had sent him *bound*
   19:40. *wound* it in linen clothes
Acts 9: 2. bring them *bound* unto Jerusalem.
    14. to *bind* all that call on thy name.
    21. he might bring them *bound*
   10:11. a great sheet *knit* at the four corners,
   12: 6. *bound* with two chains: and the
   20:22. I go *bound* in the spirit unto
   21:11. *bound* his own hands and feet, *and*

Acts21:11. Jews at Jerusalem *bind* the man
　　13. I am ready not *to be bound* only,
　　33. commanded (him) *to be bound* with
22: 5. *bound* unto Jerusalem, for to be punished.
　　29. because he had *bound* him.
24:27. the Jews a pleasure, left Paul *bound*.
Rom.7: 2. which hath an husband *is bound* by
1Co 7:27. *Art* thou *bound* unto a wife?
　　39. The wife *is bound* by the law as
Col. 4: 3. for which I *am* also *in bonds:*
2Ti. 2: 9. the word of God *is* not *bound*.
Rev. 9:14. Loose the four angels *which are bound*
　　20: 2. Satan, and *bound* him a thousand years,

δή, *dee*.

Mat.13:23. which *also* beareth fruit, and bringeth
Lu. 2:15. Let us *now* go even unto Bethlehem,
Acts13: 2. Separate)(me Barnabas and Saul
　　15:36. Let us go again *and* visit our brethren
1Co. 6:20. *therefore* glorify God in your body,
2Co.12: 1. not expedient for me *doubtless* to glory.

δῆλος, *deelos*.

Mat.26:73. thy speech bewrayeth thee. (lit. maketh
　　thee *manifest*)
1Co.15:27. (it is) *manifest* that he is excepted,
Gal. 3:11. (it is) *evident:* for, The just shall live
1Ti. 6: 7. (it is) *certain* we can carry nothing out.

δηλόω, *deeloō*.

1Co. 1:11. it hath *been declared* unto me
　　3:13. for the day *shall declare* it, because
Col. 1: 8. *Who* also *declared* unto us your love
Heb 9: 8. The Holy Ghost this *signifying*,
　　12:27. *signifieth* the removing of those
1Pet.1:11. which was in them *did signify*,
2Pet.1:14. our Lord Jesus Christ hath *shewed* me.

δημηγορέω, *deemeegoreo*

Acts12:21. sat upon his throne, and *made an oration*

δημιουργός, *deemiouryos*.

Heb11:10. hath foundations, whose builder and
　　maker (is) God.

δῆμος, *deemos*.

Acts12:22. the *people* gave a shout, (saying),
　　17: 5. to bring them out to the *people*.
　　19:30. have entered in unto the *people*,
　　33. have made his defence unto the *people*.

δημόσιος, *deemosios*.

In the passages marked [2] δημοσια (χωρα *in a place*,
　　being understood) is used as an adverb.

Acts 5:18. put them in the *common* prison.

Acts16:37. They have beaten us *openly* [2]
　　18:28. convinced the Jews, (and that) *publickly*,[2]
　　20:20. have taught you *publickly*, and from [2]

δηνάριον, *deenarion*.

Mat.18:28. which owed him an hundred *pence:*
　　20: 2. agreed with the labourers for a *penny* a day,
　　9. they received every man a *penny*.
　　10. likewise received every man a *penny*.
　　13. didst not thou agree with me for a *penny?*
　　22:19. they brought unto him a *penny*.
Mar. 6:37. buy two hundred *penny*worth of bread,
　　12:15. bring me a *penny*, that I may see (it).
　　14: 5. sold for more than three hundred *pence*,
Lu. 7:41. the one owed five hundred *pence*,
　　10:35. he took out two *pence*, and gave (them)
　　to the
　　20:24. Shew me a *penny*. Whose image
Joh. 6: 7. Two hundred *penny*worth of bread
　　12: 5. ointment sold for three hundred *pence*,
Rev. 6: 6. A measure of wheat for a *penny*, and
　　three measures of barley for a *penny;*

δήποτε, *deepote*.

Joh. 5: 4. made whole of whatso*ever* disease

δήπου, *deepou*.

Heb. 2:16. For *verily* he took not on (him)

Followed by an accusative and a genitive ;—the cases
in which it is followed by a genitive are marked
with a *g*.

Mat. 1:22. spoken of the Lord *by* the prophet,
　　saying,*g*
　　2: 5. for thus it is written *by* the prophet,*g*
　　12. into their own country another (lit. *by*
　　another) way.*g*
　　15. spoken of the Lord *by* the prophet, saying,*g*
　　23. which was spoken *by* the prophets,*g*
　　4: 4. proceedeth out *of* the mouth of God.*g*
　　14. which was spoken *by* Esaias the prophet,*g*
　　6:25. *Therefore* I say unto you, Take no
　　7:13. Enter ye in *at* the strait gate:*g*
　　— many there be which go in thereat :*g*
　　8:17. which was spoken *by* Esaias the prophet,*g*
　　28. no man might pass *by* that way.*g*
　　10:22. hated of all (men) *for* my name's sake:
　　12: 1. on the sabbath day *through* the corn ;*g*
　　17. which was spoken *by* Esaias the prophet,*g*
　　27. *therefore* they shall be your judges.
　　31. Wherefore I say unto you, All manner
　　43. he walketh *through* dry places, seeking
　　rest,*g*
　　13: 5. *because* they had no deepness of earth:
　　6. *because* they had no root, they withered
　　13. There*fore* speak I to them in parables:
　　21. persecution ariseth *because of* the word,
　　35. which was spoken *by* the prophet,*g*
　　52. There*fore* every scribe (which is) in-
　　structed
　　58. works there, *because of* their unbelief.

Mat.14: 2. ther*efore* mighty works do shew forth

3. put (him) in prison *for* Herodias' *sake*,

9. nevertheless *for* the oath's *sake*,

15: 3. of God *by* your tradition?

6. of none effect *by* your tradition.

17:20. said unto them, *Because of* your unbelief:

18: 7. that man *by* whom the offence cometh!ᵍ

10. their angels do always (lit. *through* all (time)) behold the faceᵍ

23. Therefore is the kingdom of heaven

19:12. *for* the kingdom of heaven's sake.

24. a camel to go *through* the eye of a needle,ᵍ

21: 4. which was spoken *by* the prophet,ᵍ

43. Ther*efore* say I unto you, The kingdom

23:14(13). ther*efore* ye shall receive the greater

34. Wher*efore*, behold, I send unto you

24: 9. hated of all nations *for* my name's sake.

12. *because* iniquity shall abound,

15. spoken of *by* Daniel the prophet, standᵍ

22. *for* the elect's *sake* those days shall

44. Therefore be ye also ready: for in such

26:24. *by* whom the Son of man is betrayed !ᵍ

61. to build it *in* three days.ᵍ

27: 9. that which was spoken *by* Jeremy the prophet,ᵍ

18. he knew that *for* envy they had deliveredᵍ

19. this day in a dream *because of* him.

Mar. 2: 1. into Capernaum *after* (some) days ;ᵍ

4. come nigh unto him *for* the press,

23. that he went *through* the corn fieldsᵍ

27. The sabbath was made *for* man, and not man *for* the sabbath:

3: 9. wait on him *because of* the multitude,

4: 5. *because* it had no depth of earth:

6. *because* it had no root, it withered

17. persecution ariseth *for* the word's *sake*,

5: 4. *Because* that he had been often bound

6: 2. mighty works are wrought *by* his hands?ᵍ

6. he marvelled *because of* their unbelief.

14. ther*efore* mighty works do shew forth

17. in prison *for* Herodias' *sake*,

26. (yet) *for* his oath's *sake*, and for their

7:29. *For* this saying go thy way; the

9:30. departed thence, and passed *through* Galilee ;ᵍ

10: 1. Judæa *by* the farther side of Jordan:ᵍ

25. a camel to go *through* the eye of a needle,ᵍ

11:16. should carry (any) vessel *through* the temple.ᵍ

24. Therefore I say unto you, What

12:24. Do ye not ther*efore* err, because ye

13:13. hated of all (men) *for* my name's *sake* :

20. *for* the elect's *sake*, whom he hath

14:21. *by* whom the Son of man is betrayed !ᵍ

58. *within* three days I will build another ᵍ

15:10. chief priests had delivered him *for* envy.

16:20. confirming the word *with* signs following.ᵍ

Lu. 1:70. spake *by* the mouth of his holy prophets,ᵍ

78. *Through* the tender mercy of our God ;

2: 4. *because* he was of the house and lineage

4:30. he passing *through* the midst of them ᵍ

5: 5. Master, we have toiled all (lit. *through* all) the night,ᵍ

19. could not find *by* ᵍ what (way) they might bring him in *because of* the multitude,

— let him down *through* the tiling ᵍ

6: 1. that he went *through* the corn fields ;ᵍ

8: 4. of every city, he spake *by* a parable:ᵍ

6. withered away, *because* it lacked moisture.

19. could not come at him *for* the press.

47. *for* what cause she had touched him,

9: 7. *because* that it was said of some, that

Lu. 11: 8. give him, *because* he is his friend, yet *because of* his importunity he

19. ther*efore* shall they be your judges.

24. he walketh *through* dry places, seeking ᵍ

49. Therefore also said the wisdom of God,

12:22. Therefore I say unto you, Take no thought

13:24. Strive to enter in *at* the strait gate:ᵍ

14:20. a wife, and ther*efore* I cannot come.

17: 1. woe (unto him), *through* whom they come !ᵍ

11. passed *through* the midst of Samaria ᵍ

18: 5. Yet *because* this widow troubleth me,

25. a camel to go *through* a needle's eye,ᵍ

31. things that are written *by* the prophetsᵍ

19: 4. for he was to pass)(that (way),ˢ

11. *because* he was nigh to Jerusalem,

21:17. hated of all (men) *for* my name's *sake*.

22:22. that man *by* whom he is betrayed !ᵍ

23: 8. *because* he had heard many things

19. Who *for* a certain sedition made in

25. him that *for* sedition and murder was

Joh. 1: 3. All things were made *by* him ;ᵍ

7. all (men) *through* him might believe ᵍ

10. the world was made *by* him, and the ᵍ

17. For the law was given *by*ᵍ Moses, (but) grace and truth came *by* ᵍ Jesus Christ.

31. ther*efore* am I come baptizing with

2:24. unto them, *because* he knew all (men),

3:17. the world *through* him might be saved.ᵍ

29. *because of* the bridegroom's voice:

4: 4. he must needs go *through* Samaria.ᵍ

39. *for* the saying of the woman, which

41. more believed *because of* his own word;

42. we believe, not *because of* thy saying:

5:16. ther*efore* did the Jews persecute Jesus,

18. Therefore the Jews sought the more

6:57. sent me, and I live *by* the Father:

— eateth me, even he shall live *by* me.

65. Therefore said I unto you, that no

7:13. openly of him *for* fear of the Jews.

22. Moses ther*efore* gave unto you circumcision ;

43. a division among the people *because of*

8:47. ye ther*efore* hear (them) not, because ye

59. going *through* the midst of them,ᵍ

9:23. Therefore said his parents, He is of age :

10: 1. He that entereth not *by* the door into theᵍ

2. he that entereth in *by* the door is theᵍ

9. *by* me if any man enter in, he shallᵍ

17. Therefore doth my Father love me,

19. among the Jews *for* these sayings.

32. *for* which of those works do ye stone me?

11: 4. Son of God might be glorified ther*eby*.ᵍ

15. I am glad *for* your *sakes* that I was

42. *because of* the people which stand by

12: 9. they came not *for* Jesus' *sake* only,

11. Because that *by reason of* him many

18. *For* this *cause* the people also met him,

27. *for* this *cause* came I unto this hour.

30. This voice came not *because of* me, but *for* your *sakes*.

39. Ther*efore* they could not believe,

42. *because of* the Pharisees they did not

13:11. ther*efore* said he, Ye are not all clean.

14: 6. no man cometh unto the Father, but *by* me.ᵍ

11. believe me *for* the very works' *sake*.

15: 3. Now ye are clean *through* the word

19. ther*efore* the world hateth you.

21. do unto you *for* my name's *sake*,

16:15. ther*efore* said I, that he shall take

21. *for* joy that a man is born into

Joh.17:20. believe on me *through* their word ;*g*
19:11. there*fore* he that delivered me unto
23. woven from the top *through*out.*g*
38. secretly *for* fear of the Jews, besought
42. *because of* the Jews' preparation (day) ;
20:19. were assembled *for* fear of the Jews,
Acts 1: 2. he *through* the Holy Ghost had given*g*
3. being seen of them (lit. *through*) forty days,*g*
16. *by* the mouth of David spake before*g*
2:16. which was spoken *by* the prophet Joel ; *g*
22. which God did *by* him in the *g*
23. *by* wicked hands have crucified*g*
25. the Lord always (lit. *through* all (time)) before my face,*g*
26. There*fore* did my heart rejoice,
43. wonders and signs were done *by* the apostles. *g*
3:16. the faith which is *by* him hath given*g*
18. *by* the mouth of all his prophets,*g*
21. *by* the mouth of all his holy prophets*g*
4: 2. grieved *that* (lit. *because that*) they taught the people,
16. miracle hath been done *by* them*g*
21. punish them, *because of* the people:
25. *by* the mouth of thy servant David *g*
30. *by* the name of thy holy child Jesus. *g*
5:12. *by* the hands of the apostles were many*g*
19. Lord *by* night opened the prison doors,*g*
7:25. God *by* his hand would deliver them:*g*
8:11. *because that* of long time he had
18. *through* laying on of the apostles' hands*g*
20, may be purchased *with* money. *g*
9:25. let (him) down *by* the wall, in a basket.*g*
32. Peter passed *through*out all (quarters),*g*
10:21. what (is) the cause where*fore* ye are come ?
36. preaching peace *by* Jesus Christ:*g*
43. *through* his name whosoever believeth*g*
11:28. signified *by* the spirit that there *g*
30. *by* the hands of Barnabas and Saul.*g*
12: 9. which was done *by* the angel ;*g*
20. *because* their country was nourished
13:38. *through* this man is preached unto *g*
49. published *through*out all the region.*g*
14: 3. wonders to be done *by* their hands. *g*
22. we must *through* much tribulation*g*
15: 7. the Gentiles *by* my mouth should*g*
11. *through* the grace of the Lord Jesus*g*
12. wrought among the Gentiles *by* them.*g*
23. they wrote (letters) *by* them after this*g*
27. tell (you) the same things *by* mouth.*g*
32. exhorted the brethren *with* many words,*g*
16: 3. circumcised him *because of* the Jews
9. a vision appeared to Paul *in* the night ;*g*
17:10. Paul and Silas *by* night unto Berea:*g*
18: 2. *because that* Claudius had commanded
3. *because* he was of the same craft,
9. to Paul in the night *by* a vision,*g*
27. which had believed *through* grace:*g*
28. shewing *by* the scriptures that *g*
19:11. miracles *by* the hands of Paul:*g*
26. no gods, which are made *with* hands:*g*
20: 3. purposed to return *through* Macedonia.*g*
28. hath purchased *with* his own blood.*g*
21: 4. who said to Paul *through* the Spirit,*g*
19. among the Gentiles *by* his ministry.*g*
34. not know the certainty *for* the tumult,
35. *for* the violence of the people.
22:24. might know where*fore* they cried so
23:28. the cause where*fore* they accused him,
31. brought (him) *by* night to Antipatris.*g*

Acts 24: 2. Seeing that *by* thee we enjoy great*g*
— unto this nation *by* thy providence,*g*
17. Now *after* many years I came *g*
27: 4. *because* the winds were contrary.
9. *because* the fast was now already
28: 2. *because of* the present rain, and *because of* the cold.
18. *because* there was no cause of death
20. *For* this cause therefore have I called
25. Well spake the Holy Ghost *by* Esaias the prophet *g*
Ro. 1: 2. had promised afore *by* his prophets*g*
5. *By* whom we have received grace *g*
8. I thank my God *through* Jesus Christ *g*
12. *by* the mutual faith both of you and me.*g*
26. *For* this cause God gave them up
2:12. shall be judged *by* the law ;*g*
16. judge the secrets of men *by* Jesus Christ
23. *through* breaking the law dishonourest*g*
24. blasphemed among the Gentiles *through*
27. who *by* the letter and circumcision dost *g*
3:20. for *by* the law (is) the knowledge of sin.*g*
22. (which is) *by* faith of Jesus Christ *g*
24. *through* the redemption that is in *g*
25. *through* faith in his blood,*g*
— *For* the remission of sin.
27. It is excluded. *By* what law ?*g*
— *by* the law of faith. *g*
30. uncircumcision *through* faith. *g*
31. make void the law *through* faith?*g*
4:11. though*g* they be not circumcised ; (lit. *through g* uncircumcision)
13. or to his seed, *through g* the law, but *through g* the righteousness of faith.
16. Therefore (it is) of faith, that (it might be)
23. not written *for* his sake alone,
24. *for* us also, to whom it shall be
25. Who was delivered *for* our offences, and was raised again *for* our justification.
5: 1. *through* our Lord Jesus Christ:*g*
2. *By* whom also we have access*g*
5. in our hearts *by* the Holy Ghost *g*
9. shall be saved from wrath *through* him.*g*
10. reconciled to God *by* the death of his Son,*g*
11. *through g* our Lord Jesus Christ, *by g* whom we have now received
·12. Where*fore*,· as *by g* one man sin entered into the world, and death *by g* sin ;
16. not as (it was) *by* one that sinned,*g*
17. one man's offence death reigned *by* one ;*g*
— shall reign in life *by* one, Jesus Christ.*g*
18. as *by* the offence of one (judgment) *g*
— even so *by* the righteousness of one*g*
19. as *by* one man's disobedience*g*
so *by* the obedience of one shall *g*
21. *through g* righteousness unto eternal life *by g* Jesus Christ our Lord.
6: 4. buried with him *by* baptism into*g*
— from the dead *by* the glory of the Father,*g*
19. *because of* the infirmity of your flesh:
7: 4. dead to the law *by* the body of Christ ;*g*
5. which were *by* the law,*g*
7. had not known sin, but *by* the law :*g*
8. taking occasion *by* the commandment,*g*
11. taking occasion *by g* the commandment, deceived me, and *by g* it slew (me).
13. death in me *by g* that which is good ; that sin *by g* the commandment might
25. *through* Jesus Christ our Lord.*g*
8: 3. that it was weak *through* the flesh,*g*
10. the body (is) dead *because of* sin ; but the Spirit (is) life *because of* righteousness

Ro. 8:11. *by* his Spirit that dwelleth in you.
20. *by reason of* him who hath subjected
25. do we *with* patience wait for (it).ᵍ
37. conquerors *through* him that loved us.ᵍ
10:17. hearing *by* the word of God.ᵍ
11:28. (they are) enemies *for* your *sakes:*
— (they are) beloved *for* the fathers' *sakes.*
36. For of him, and *through* him, and to him,ᵍ
12: 1. brethren, *by* the mercies of God, thatᵍ
3. *through* the grace given unto me,ᵍ
13: 5. be subject, not only *for* wrath, but also *for* conscience *sake.*
6. For *for* this cause pay ye tribute
14:14. (there is) nothing unclean *of* itself:ᵍ
15. thy brother be grieved *with* (thy) meat,
20. that man who eateth *with* offence.ᵍ
15: 4. that we *through* patience and comfortᵍ
9. *For* this cause I will confess to thee
15. *because of* the grace that is given
18. which Christ hath not wrought *by* me,ᵍ
28. I will come *by* you into Spain.ᵍ
30. *for*ᵍ the Lord Jesus Christ's sake, and *for*ᵍ the love of the Spirit, that ye
32. with joy *by* the will of God,ᵍ
16:18. *by* good words and fair speeches deceiveᵍ
26. *by* the scriptures of the prophets,ᵍ
27. (be) glory *through* Jesus Christ for ever.ᵍ
1Co. 1: 1. *through* the will of God,ᵍ
9. *by* whom ye were called untoᵍ
10. *by* the name of our Lord Jesus Christ,ᵍ
21. the world *by*ᵍ wisdom knew not God, it pleased God *by*ᵍ the foolishness of
2:10. revealed (them) unto us *by* his Spirit:ᵍ
3: 5. ministers *by* whom ye believed,ᵍ
15. shall be saved; yet so as *by* fire.ᵍ
4: 6. to myself and (to) Apollos *for* your *sakes;*
10. We (are) fools *for* Christ's sake,
15. I have begotten you *through* the gospel.ᵍ
17. *For* this cause have I sent unto you
6:14. raise up us *by* his own power.ᵍ
7: 2. Nevertheless, (to avoid) (lit. *on account of*) fornication,
5. Satan tempt you not *for* your incontinency.
26. this is good *for* the present distress,
8: 6. Jesus Christ, *by*ᵍ whom (are) all things, and we *by*ᵍ him.
11. brother perish, *for* whom Christ died?
9:10. saith he (it) altogether *for* our *sakes? For* our *sakes,* no doubt,
23. this I do *for* the gospel's *sake,*
10: 1. all passed *through* the sea;ᵍ
25. asking no question *for* conscience *sake:*
27. asking no question *for* conscience *sake.*
28. eat not *for* his *sake* that shewed it,
11: 9. Neither was the man created *for* the woman; but the woman *for* the man.
10. *For* this *cause* ought the woman to have power on (her) head *because of* the angels.
12. so (is) the man also *by* the woman;ᵍ
30. *For* this *cause* many (are) weak
12: 8. *by* the Spirit the word of wisdom;ᵍ
13:12. For now we see *through* a glass, darkly;ᵍ
14: 9. except ye utter *by* the tongue wordsᵍ
19. rather speak five words *with* myᵍ
15: 2. *By* which also ye are saved, if yeᵍ
21. For since *by*ᵍ man (came) death, *by*ᵍ man (came) also the resurrection
57. victory *through* our Lord Jesus Christ. ᵍ
16: 3. whomsoever ye shall approve *by* (your)ᵍ
2Co. 1: 1. of Jesus Christ *by* the will of God,ᵍ
4. *by* the comfort, wherewith we ourselvesᵍ

2Co. 1: 5. consolation also aboundeth *by* Christ.ᵍ
11. thanks may be given *by* many onᵍ
16. to pass *by* you into Macedonia, and toᵍ
19. who was preached among you *by*ᵍ us, (even) *by*ᵍ me and Silvanus and
20. unto the glory of God *by* us.ᵍ
2: 4. I wrote unto you *with* many tears;ᵍ
10. *for* your *sakes* (forgave I it) in the
14. his knowledge *by* us in every place.ᵍ
3: 4. such trust have we *through* Christᵍ
7. *for* the glory of his countenance;
11. that which is done away (was) glorious,ᵍ (lit. *through* glory)
4: 1. There*fore* seeing we have this ministry,
5. your servants *for* Jesus' sake.
11. delivered unto death *for* Jesus' sake,
14. shall raise up us also *by* Jesus,ᵍ
15. all things (are) *for* your *sakes,*
— *through* the thanksgiving of manyᵍ
5: 7. For we walk *by*ᵍ faith, not *by*ᵍ sight:
10. receive the things (done) *in* (his) body,ᵍ
18. reconciled us to himself *by* Jesus Christ,ᵍ
20. as though God did beseech (you) *by* us:ᵍ
6: 7. *by* the armour of righteousnessᵍ
8. *By*ᵍ honour and dishonour, *by*ᵍ evil
7:13. There*fore* we were comforted in your
8: 5. unto us *by* the will of God.ᵍ
8. *by occasion of* the forwardness of others,ᵍ
9. yet *for* your *sakes* he became poor,
18. the gospel *throughout* all the churches;ᵍ
9:11. causeth *through* us thanksgivingᵍ
12. *by* many thanksgivings unto God;ᵍ
13. Whiles *by* the experiment of thisᵍ
14. *for* the exceeding grace of God
10: 1. *by* the meekness and gentleness of Christ,ᵍ
9. as if I would terrify you *by* letters.ᵍ
11. *by* letters when we are absent,ᵍ
11:33. *through*ᵍ a window in a basket was I let down *by*ᵍ the wall, and escaped
12:17. *by* any of them whom I sent unto you?ᵍ
13:10. There*fore* I write these things being
Gal 1: 1. not of men, neither *by*ᵍ man, but *by*ᵍ Jesus Christ, and God the Father,
12. *by* the revelation of Jesus Christ.ᵍ
15. mother's womb, and called (me) *by* his grace,ᵍ
2: 1. Then fourteen years *after* I went upᵍ
4. that *because of* false brethren unawares
16. *by* the faith of Jesus Christ, even weᵍ
19. For I *through* the law am dead to the law,ᵍ
21. for if righteousness (come) *by* the law,ᵍ
3:14. the promise of the Spirit *through* faith.ᵍ
18. God gave (it) to Abraham *by* promise.ᵍ
19. ordained *by* angels in the hand ofᵍ
26. children of God *by* faith in Christ Jesus.ᵍ
4: 7. then an heir of God *through* Christ.ᵍ
13. Ye know how *through* infirmity of
23. he of the freewoman (was) *by* promise.ᵍ
5: 6. faith which worketh *by* love.ᵍ
13. *by* love serve one another.ᵍ
6:14. Jesus Christ, *by* whom the world is crucifiedᵍ
Eph. 1: 1. apostle of Jesus Christ *by* the will of God,ᵍ
5. adoption of children *by* Jesus Christᵍ
7. we have redemption *through* his blood,ᵍ
15. Where*fore* I also, after I heard of
2: 4. *for* his great love wherewith he loved us,
8. by grace are ye saved *through* faith;ᵍ
16. unto God in one body *by* the cross,ᵍ
18. For *through* him we both haveᵍ
3: 6. of his promise in Christ *by* the gospel:ᵍ
9. who created all things *by* Jesus Christ:ᵍ
10. might be known *by* the churchᵍ

Eph. 3:12. with confidence *by* the faith of him.�

16. be strengthened with might *by* his Spirit ᵍ

17. Christ may dwell in your hearts *by* faith;ᵍ

4: 6. who (is) above all, and *through* all,ᵍ

16. *by* that which every joint supplieth,ᵍ

18. *through* the ignorance that is in them, *because of* the blindness of their heart:

5: 6. for *because of* these things cometh

17. Where*fore* be ye not unwise,

6:13. Where*fore* take unto you the whole

18. Praying always *with* all prayer ᵍ

Phil. 1: 7. *because* I have you in my heart;

11. which are *by* Jesus Christ, unto the ᵍ

15. preach Christ even *of* envy and strife ; and some also *of* good will:

19. to my salvation *through* your prayer,ᵍ

20. whether (it be) *by*ᵍ life, or *by*ᵍ death.

24. in the flesh (is) more needful *for* you.

26. *by* my coming to you again.ᵍ

2:30. Because *for* the work of Christ

3: 7. those I counted loss *for* Christ.

8. *for* the excellency of the knowledge

— *for* whom I have suffered the loss

9. which is *through* the faith of Christ,ᵍ

Col. 1: 1. of Jesus Christ *by* the will of God,ᵍ

5. *For* the hope which is laid up for

9. *For* this cause we also, since the

14. we have redemption *through* his blood,ᵍ

16. all things were created *by* him, and for him:ᵍ

20. peace *through*ᵍ the blood of his cross, *by*ᵍ him to reconcile all things unto himself; *by*ᵍ him, (I say), whether (they be)

22. In the body of his flesh *through* death,ᵍ

2: 8. lest any man spoil you *through* philosophyᵍ

12. *through* the faith of the operation ofᵍ

19. from which all the body *by* jointsᵍ

3: 6. *For* which things' *sake* the wrath of

17. thanks to God and the Father *by* him.ᵍ

4: 3. *for* which I am also in bonds:

1Th. 1: 5. we were among you *for* your *sake*.

2:13. *For* this *cause* also thank we God

3: 5. *For* this *cause*, when I could no longer

7. Therefore, brethren, we were comforted

— affliction and distress *by* your faith:ᵍ

9. we joy *for* your *sakes* before our God;

4: 2. we gave you *by* the Lord Jesus.ᵍ

14. them who also sleep *in* Jesusᵍ

5: 9. obtain salvation *by* our Lord Jesus Christ,ᵍ

13. highly in love *for* their work's *sake*.

2Th. 2: 2. be troubled, neither *by*ᵍ spirit, nor *by*ᵍ word, nor *by*ᵍ letter as *from*ᵍ us, as that the day of

11. *for* this *cause* God shall send them

14. Whereunto he called you *by* our gospel,ᵍ

15. whether *by*ᵍ word, or (lit. or *by*ᵍ) our epistle.

3:12. exhort *by* our Lord Jesus Christ,ᵍ

14. obey not our word *by* this epistle,ᵍ

16. you peace always (lit. *through*ᵍ all time) by all means.

1Ti. 1:16. *for* this *cause* I obtained mercy,

2:10. professing godliness *with* good works.ᵍ

15. she shall be saved *in* childbearing,ᵍ

4: 5. sanctified *by* the word of Godᵍ

14. which was given thee *by* prophecy,ᵍ

5:23. a little wine *for* thy stomach's *sake*

2Ti. 1: 1. *by* the will of God, according to ᵍ

6. Where*fore* I put thee in remembrance

— *by* the putting on of my hands.ᵍ

10. *by* the appearing of our Saviour ᵍ

— immortality to light *through* the gospel:ᵍ

2Ti. 1:12. *For* the which cause I also suffer

14. keep *by* the Holy Ghost which ᵍ

2: 2. heard of me *among* many witnesses,

10. Therefore I endure all things *for* the elect's sakes,

3:15. *through* faith which is in Christ Jesus.ᵍ

4:17. that *by* me the preaching mightᵍ

Tit. 1:13. Where*fore* rebuke them sharply,

3: 5. *by* the washing of regeneration,ᵍ

6. *through* Jesus Christ our Saviour ; ᵍ

Philem. 7. saints are refreshed *by* thee, brother.ᵍ

9. Yet *for* love's *sake* I rather beseech (thee),

15. For perhaps he therefore departed for

22. I trust that *through* your prayers ᵍ

Heb. 1: 2. *by* whom also he made the worlds ;ᵍ

3. when he had *by* himself purged our sins,ᵍ

9. therefore God, (even) thy God, hath

14. sent forth to minister *for* them

2: 1. Therefore we ought to give the more

2. For if the word spoken *by* angels ᵍ

3. began to be spoken *by* the Lord,ᵍ

9. *for* the suffering of death, crowned

10. *for* whom (are) all things, and *by*ᵍ whom

— their salvation perfect *through* sufferings ᵍ

11. *for* which cause he is not ashamed to

14. that *through* death he might destroy ᵍ

15. through fear of death were all (lit. *through*ᵍ all) their lifetime

3:16. all that came out of Egypt *by* Moses.ᵍ

19. could not enter in *because of* unbelief.

4: 6. entered not in *because of* unbelief:

5: 3. *by reason hereof* he ought, as for the

12. *for* the time ye ought to be teachers,

14. those who *by reason of* use have

6: 7. meet for them *by* whom it is dressed,

12. them who *through* faith and patience ᵍ

18. That *by* two immutable things,ᵍ

7: 9. receiveth tithes, payed tithes *in* Abraham.ᵍ

11. perfection were *by* the Leviticalᵍ

18. *for* the weakness and unprofitableness

19. *by* the which we draw nigh unto God.ᵍ

21. *by* him that said unto him,ᵍ

23. to continue *by reason of* death:

24. this (man), *because* he continueth

25. that come unto God *by* him,ᵍ

9:11. *by* a greater and more perfect tabernacle,ᵍ

12. Neither *by*ᵍ the blood of goats and calves, but *by*ᵍ his own blood he entered in

14. who *through* the eternal Spirit ᵍ

15. *for* this *cause* he is the mediator

26. *by* the sacrifice of himself.ᵍ

10: 2. *because* that the worshippers

10. *through* the offering of the body ofᵍ

20. consecrated for us, *through* the veil,ᵍ

11: 4. *by* which he obtained witness ᵍ

— *by* it he being dead yet speaketh.ᵍ

7. *by* the which he condemned the world,ᵍ

29. through the Red sea as *by* dry (land):ᵍ

33. Who *through* faith subdued kingdoms,ᵍ

39. obtained a good report *through* faith,ᵍ

12: 1. let us run *with* patience the race ᵍ

11. them which are exercised thereby.ᵍ

15. thereby many be defiled ;ᵍ

28. let us have grace, whereby we may serve ᵍ

13: 2. for thereby some have entertained ᵍ

11. into the sanctuary *by* the high priestᵍ

12. sanctify the people *with* his own blood,ᵍ

15. *By* him therefore let us offer ᵍ

21. in his sight, *through* Jesus Christ ;ᵍ

22. written a letter unto you *in* few words.ᵍ

Jas. 2:12. be judged *by* the law of liberty.ᵍ

4: 2. ye have not, *because* ye ask not.

1Pet.1: 3. *by* the resurrection of Jesus Christ*s*
 5. *through* faith unto salvation*s*
 7. though it be tried *with* fire, might*s*
 12. *by* them that have preached the gospel*s*
 20. manifest in these last times *for* you,
 21. Who *by* him do believe in God, that*s*
 22. obeying the truth *through* the Spirit *s*
 23. *by* the word of God, which liveth*s*
 2: 5. acceptable to God *by* Jesus Christ.*s*
 13. ordinance of man *for* the Lord's *sake :*
 14. unto them that are sent *by* him*s*
 19. a man *for* conscience toward God
 3: 1. won *by* the conversation of the wives ;*s*
 14. if ye suffer *for* righteousness' *sake,*
 20. eight souls were saved *by* water.*s*
 21. *by* the resurrection of Jesus Christ:*s*
 4:11. may be glorified *through* Jesus Christ,*s*
 5:12. *By* Silvanus, a faithful brother *s*
 — I have written briefly (lit. *with s* a few
  words), exhorting,
2Pet. 1: 3. *through s* the knowledge of him that hath
  called us to*s* glory and virtue:
 4. Whereby are given unto us exceeding*s*
 — that *by* these ye might be*s*
 2: 2. *by reason of* whom the way of truth
 3: 5. out of the water and *in* the water:*s*
 6. Where*by* the world that then*s*
 12. where*in* the heavens being on fire
1Joh.2:12. forgiven you *for* his name's *sake.*
 3: 1. there*fore* the world knoweth us
 4: 5. there*fore* speak they of the world,
 9. that we might live *through* him.*s*
 5: 6. is he that came *by* water and blood.
2Joh. 2. *For* the truth's *sake,* which dwelleth
 12. I would not (write) *with* paper and ink:*s*
3Joh. 10. Where*fore,* if I come, I will remember
 13. I will not *with* ink and pen write *s*
Rev. 1: 1. sent and signified (it) *by* his angel*s*
 9. called Patmos, *for* the word of God, and
  for the testimony
 2: 3. hast patience, and *for* my name's *sake*
 4:11. *for* thy pleasure they are and were
 6: 9. were slain *for* the word of God, and *for*
  the testimony which they held:
 7:15. There*fore* are they before the throne
 12:11. overcame him *by* the blood of the Lamb,
  and *by* the word of their testimony ;
 12. There*fore* rejoice, (ye) heavens, and ye
 13:14. *by* (the means of) those miracles
 18: 8. There*fore* shall her plagues come
 10. afar off *for* the fear of her torment,
 15. afar off *for* the fear of her torment,
 20: 4. were beheaded *for* the witness of Jesus,
  and *for* the word of God, and which had

διαβαίνω, *diabaino.*

Lu. 16:26. they which would *pass* from hence
Acts16: 9. saying, *Come over* into Macedonia, *and*
Heb 11:29. By faith they *passed through* the Red sea

διαβάλλομαι, *diaballomai.*

Lu. 16: 1. the same *was accused* unto him

διαβεβαιόομαι, *diabebaio-omai.*

1Ti. 1: 7. what they say, nor whereof they *affirm.*
Tit. 3: 8. things I will that thou *affirm constantly,*

διαβλέπω, *diablepo.*

Mat. 7: 5. then *shalt* thou *see clearly* to cast
Lu. 6:42. then *shalt* thou *see clearly* to pull

διάβολος, *diabolos.*

Mat. 4: 1. to be tempted of the *devil.*
 5. Then the *devil* taketh him up into
 8. Again the *devil* taketh him up
 11. Then the *devil* leaveth him,
 13:39. The enemy that sowed them is the *devil ;*
 25:41. prepared for the *devil* and his angels:
Lu. 4: 2. Being forty days tempted of the *devil.*
 3. the *devil* said unto him, If thou
 5. the *devil,* taking him up into
 6. the *devil* said unto him, All this
 13. when the *devil* had ended all
 8:12. then cometh the *devil,* and taketh
Joh. 6:70. you twelve, and one of you is a *devil?*
 8:44. Ye are of (your) father the *devil,*
 13: 2. the *devil* having now put into
Acts10:38. all that were oppressed of the *devil ;*
 13:10. (thou) child of the *devil,* (thou) enemy
Eph. 4:27. Neither give place to the *devil.*
 6:11. to stand against the wiles of the *devil.*
1Ti. 3: 6. the condemnation of the *devil.*
 7. reproach and the snare of the *devil.*
 11. wives (be) grave, not *slanderers,* sober,
2Ti. 2:26. out of the snare of the *devil,* who
 3: 3. trucebreakers, *false accusers,* incontinent,
Tit. 2: 3. not *false accusers,* not given to much wine,
Heb 2:14. power of death, that is, the *devil ;*
Jas. 4: 7. Resist the *devil,* and he will flee
1Pet.5: 8. because your adversary the *devil,*
1Joh.3: 8. He that committeth sin is of the *devil ;*
  for the *devil* sinneth from the beginning.
 — might destroy the works of the *devil.*
 10. manifest, and the children of the *devil :*
Jude 9. when contending with the *devil*
Rev. 2:10. the *devil* shall cast (some) of you
 12: 9. that old serpent, called the *Devil,*
 12. the *devil* is come down unto you,
 20: 2. that old serpent, which is the *devil,*
 10. the *devil* that deceived them was

διαγγέλλω, *diangello.*

Lu. 9:60. go thou and *preach* the kingdom of God.
Acts21:26. to *signify* the accomplishment of the
Ro. 9:17. that my name *might be declared*

διαγίνομαι, *diaginomai.*

Mar.16: 1. *when* the sabbath *was past,*
Acts25:13. *after* (lit. *when were past*) certain days
  king Agrippa
 27: 9. Now *when* much time *was spent,*

διαγινώσκω, *diaginōsko.*

Acts23:15. ye would *enquire* something more perfectly
 24:22. I *will know the uttermost* of your matter.

διαγνωρίζω, diagnōrizo.

Lu. 2:17. they *made known* abroad the

διάγνωσις, diagnōsis.

Acts25:21. reserved unto the *hearing* of Augustus,

διαγογγύζω, diagonguzo.

Lu. 15: 2. the Pharisees and scribes *murmured*,
19: 7. when they saw (it), they all *murmured*,

διαγρηγορέω, diagreegoreo.

Lu. 9:32. *when* they *were awake*, they saw

διάγω, diago.

1Ti. 2: 2. that we *may lead* a quiet and peaceable life
Tit. 3: 3. *living* in malice and envy, hateful,

διαδέχομαι, diadekomai.

Acts 7:45. also our fathers *that came after*

διάδημα, diadeema.

Rev.12: 3. seven *crowns* upon his heads.
13: 1. upon his horns ten *crowns*, and upon
19:12. on his head (were) many *crowns;*

διαδίδωμι, diadidōmi.

Lu. 11:22. wherein he trusted, and *divideth* his spoils.
18:22. *distribute* unto the poor, *and* thou shalt
Joh. 6:11. he *distributed* to the disciples, and the
Acts 4:35. *distribution was made* unto every
Rev.17:13. shall *give* their power and strength

διάδοχος, diadokos.

Acts24:27. Porcius Festus came into Felix' *room:*
(lit. Felix received a *successor* Porcius Festus)

διαζώννυμι, diazōnnumi.

Joh.13: 4. took a towel, and *girded* himself.
5. the towel wherewith he was *girded.*
21: 7. he *girt* (his) fisher's coat (unto him),

διαθήκη, diatheekee.

Mat.26:28. my blood of the new *testament*,
Mar.14:24. my blood of the new *testament*,
Lu. 1:72. to remember his holy *covenant ;*
22:20. This cup (is) the new *covenant* in
Acts 3:25. of the *covenant* which God made
7: 8. he gave him the *covenant* of
Ro. 9: 4. the glory, and the *covenants*, and the giving

Ro. 11:27. this (is) my *covenant* unto them,
1Co.11:25. This cup is the new *testament* in
2Co. 3: 6. able ministers of the new *testament;*
14. in the reading of the old *testament;*
Gal. 3:15. Though (it be) but a man's *covenant*,
17. the *covenant*, that was confirmed
4:24. for these are the two *covenants;*
Eph. 2:12. strangers from the *covenants* of
Heb 7:22. made a surety of a better *testament.*
8: 6. the mediator of a better *covenant*,
8. when I will make a new *covenant*
9. Not according to the *covenant* that
— they continued not in my *covenant*,
10. this (is) the *covenant* that I will make
9: 4. the ark of the *covenant* overlaid
— the tables of the *covenant;*
15. the mediator of the new *testament*,
— (that were) under the first *testament*,
16. For where a *testament* (is), there must
17. For a *testament* (is) of force after
20. This (is) the blood of the *testament*
10:16. This (is) the *covenant* that I will make
29. counted the blood of the *covenant*,
12:24. the mediator of the new *covenant*,
13:20. the blood of the everlasting *covenant*,
Rev.11:19. his temple the ark of his *testament:*

διαίρεσις, dīairesis.

1Co.12: 4. Now there are *diversities* of gifts,
5. there are *differences* of administrations,
6. there are *diversities* of operations,

διαιρέω, diaireo.

Lu. 15:12. he *divided* unto them (his) living.
1Co.12:11. *dividing* to every man severally as

διακαθαρίζω, diakatharizo.

Mat. 3:12. he *will throughly purge* his floor,
Lu. 3:17. he *will throughly purge* his floor,

διακατελέγχομαι, diakatelenkomai.

Acts18:28. For he mightily *convinced* the Jews,

διακονέω, diakoneo.

Mat. 4:11. angels came and *ministered unto* him.
8:15. she arose, and *ministered unto* them.
20:28. came not *to be ministered unto*, but *to minister*, and to give his life a
25:44. in prison, and *did not minister unto* thee?
27:55. from Galilee, *ministering unto* him:
Mar. 1:13. the angels *ministered unto* him.
31. left her, and she *ministered unto* them.
10:45. not *to be ministered unto*, but *to minister*,
15:41. followed him, and *ministered unto* him;
Lu. 4:39. she arose and *ministered unto* them.
8: 3. others, which *ministered unto* him
10:40. my sister hath left me *to serve* alone?
12:37. will come forth and *serve* them.
17: 8. I may sup, and gird thyself, and *serve* me,
22:26. he that is chief, as he *that doth serve.*
27. that sitteth at meat, or he *that serveth?*

Lu. 22:27. I am among you as he *that serveth.*
Joh. 12: 2. made him a supper; and Martha *served:*
26. If any man *serve* me, let him follow me;
— if any man *serve* me, him will (my)
Acts 6: 2. leave the word of God, and *serve* tables.
19:22. two of them *that ministered unto* him,
Ro. 15:25. unto Jerusalem to *minister unto* the saints.
2Co. 3: 3. the epistle of Christ *ministered* by us,
8:19. which is *administered* by us to the
20. which is *administered* by us:
1Ti. 3:10. *let them use the office of a deacon,*
13. For they *that have used the office of a deacon*
well
2Ti. 1:18. how many things he *ministered unto*
Philem.13. he *might have ministered unto* me
Heb. 6:10. *in that* ye *have ministered to* the saints,
and do *minister.*
1Pet.1:12. unto us they *did minister* the things,
4:10. (even so) *minister* the same one to
another,
11. if any man *minister,* (let him do it)

διακονία, *diakonia.*

Lu. 10:40. Martha was cumbered about much *serving,*
Acts 1:17. had obtained part of this *ministry.*
25. he may take part of this *ministry*
6: 1. neglected in the daily *ministration.*
4. to prayer, and to the *ministry* of the word.
11:29. determined to send *relief* unto the
12:25. they had fulfilled (their) *ministry,*
20:24. the *ministry,* which I have received
21:19. among the Gentiles by his *ministry.*
Ro. 11:13. I magnify mine *office:*
12: 7. Or *ministry,* (let us wait) on (our) *minis-*
tering:
15:31. that my *service* which (I have)
1Co.12: 5. are differences of *administrations,*
16:15. themselves to the *ministry* of the saints,
2Co. 3: 7. if the *ministration* of death, written
8. shall not the *ministration* of the spirit
9. if the *ministration* of condemnation
— doth the *ministration* of righteousness
4: 1. seeing we have this *ministry,*
5:18. to us the *ministry* of reconciliation;
6: 3. that the *ministry* be not blamed:
8: 4. the fellowship of the *ministering* to
9: 1. touching the *ministering* to the saints,
12. For the *administration* of this service
13. by the experiment of this *ministration*
11: 8. wages (of them), to *do you service.* (lit.
for *ministering* to you)
Eph. 4:12. for the work of the *ministry,*
Col. 4:17. Take heed to the *ministry* which
1Ti. 1:12. putting me into the *ministry;*
2Ti. 4: 5. make full proof of thy *ministry.*
11. profitable to me for the *ministry.*
Heb. 1:14. spirits, sent forth to *minister* for them
Rev. 2:19. I know thy works, and charity, and *ser-*
vice,

διάκονος, *diakonos.*

Mat.20:26. let him be your *minister;*
22:13. Then said the king to the *servants,*
23:11. greatest among you shall be your *servant.*
Mar. 9:35. be last of all, and *servant* of all.
10:43. among you, shall be your *minister:*
Joh. 2: 5. His mother saith unto the *servants,*
9. the *servants* which drew the water

Joh. 12:26. there shall also my *servant* be:
Ro. 13: 4. For he is the *minister* of God to thee
— he is the *minister* of God, a revenger
15: 8. a *minister* of the circumcision for
16: 1. Phebe our sister, which is a *servant*
1Co. 3: 5. *ministers* by whom ye believed,
2Co. 3: 6. also hath made us able *ministers*
6: 4. ourselves as the *ministers* of God,
11:15. if his *ministers* also be transformed as the
ministers of righteousness;
23. Are they *ministers* of Christ?
Gal. 2:17. (is) therefore Christ the *minister* of sin?
Eph 3: 7. Whereof I was made a *minister,*
6:21. beloved brother and faithful *minister*
Phi. 1: 1. with the bishops and *deacons:*
Col. 1: 7. for you a faithful *minister* of Christ;
23. I Paul am made a *minister;*
25. Whereof I am made a *minister,*
4: 7. a faithful *minister* and fellowservant
1Th. 3: 2. Timotheus, our brother, and *minister* of
God,
1Ti. 3: 8. Likewise (must) the *deacons* (be) grave,
12. *deacons* be the husbands of one wife,
4: 6. thou shalt be a good *minister* of

διακόσιοι, *diakosioi.*

Mar. 6:37. two *hundred* pennyworth of bread,
Joh. 6: 7. *Two hundred* pennyworth of bread
21: 8. as it were *two hundred* cubits,
Acts23:23. Make ready *two hundred* soldiers
— spearmen *two hundred,* at the third
27:37. *two hundred* threescore and sixteen
Rev.11: 3. a thousand *two hundred* (and) threescore
12: 6. a thousand *two hundred* (and) threescore
days.

διακούομαι, *diakou-omai.*

Acts23:35. I *will hear* thee, said he, when

διακρίνω, *diakrino.*

Mat.16: 3. ye can *discern* the face of the sky;
21:21. If ye have faith, and *doubt* not, ye
Mar.11:23. shall not *doubt* in his heart,
Acts10:20. go with them, *doubting* nothing:
11: 2. of the circumcision *contended* with him,
12. bade me go with them, nothing *doubting.*
15: 9. *put* no *difference* between us and them,
Ro. 4:20. He *staggered* not at the promise of God
14:23. he *that doubteth* is damned if he eat,
1Co. 4: 7. For who *maketh* thee to *differ*
6: 5. able *to judge* between his brethren?
11:29. not *discerning* the Lord's body.
31. For if we would *judge* ourselves,
14:29. speak two or three, and *let* the other *judge.*
Jas. 1: 6. nothing *wavering.* For he that *wavereth*
2: 4. Are ye not then *partial* in yourselves,
Jude 9. when *contending* with the devil
22. of some have compassion, *making a*
difference:

διάκρισις, *diakrisis.*

Ro. 14: 1. not to doubtful *disputations.*
1Co.12:10. to another *discerning* of spirits; to
Heb 5:14. exercised to *discern* both good and evil.

L

διακωλύω, diakōluo.

Mat. 3:14. John *forbad* him, saying, I have

διαλαλέω, dialaleo.

Lu. 1:65. these sayings *were noised abroad*
6:11. *communed* one with another what

διαλέγομαι, dialegomai.

Mar 9:34. they *had disputed* among themselves,
Acts17: 2. *reasoned with* them out of the scriptures,
17. Therefore *disputed* he in the synagogue
18: 4. he *reasoned* in the synagogue every
19. the synagogue, and *reasoned* with the Jews.
19: 8. three months, *disputing* and persuading
9. *disputing* daily in the school
20: 7. Paul *preached unto* them, ready
9. *as* Paul *was* long *preaching*, he sunk
24:12. in the temple *disputing* with any man,
25. *as* he *reasoned* of righteousness,
Heb12: 5. which *speaketh* unto you as unto
Jude 9. he *disputed* about the body of Moses,

διαλείπω, dialīpo.

Lu. 7:45. *hath* not *ceased* to kiss my feet.

διάλεκτος, dialektos.

Acts 1:19. field is called in their proper *tongue*,
2: 6. heard them speak in his own *language*.
8. hear we every man in our own *tongue*,
21:40. spake unto (them) in the Hebrew *tongue*,
22: 2. he spake in the Hebrew *tongue* to them,
26:14. saying in the Hebrew *tongue*, Saul,

διαλλάττομαι, diallattomai.

Mat. 5:24. first *be reconciled* to thy brother,

διαλογίζομαι, dialogizomai.

Mat.16: 7. they *reasoned* among themselves,
8. why *reason* ye among yourselves,
21:25. they *reasoned* with themselves, saying,
Mar 2: 6. sitting there, and *reasoning* in their hearts,
8. that they so *reasoned* within themselves,
— Why *reason* ye these things in your
8:16. they *reasoned* among themselves,
17. Why *reason* ye, because ye have no bread?
9:33. that ye *disputed* among yourselves
Lu. 1:29. *cast in* her *mind* what manner
3:15. And *as*...all men *mused* in their hearts
5:21. scribes and the Pharisees began *to reason*,
22. What *reason* ye in your hearts?
12:17. he *thought* within himself, saying,
20:14. they *reasoned* among themselves,
Joh.11:50. Nor *consider* that it is expedient

διαλογισμός, dialogismos.

Mat.15:19. out of the heart proceed evil *thoughts*,

Mar 7:21. heart of men, proceed evil *thoughts*,
Lu. 2:35. that the *thoughts* of many hearts
5:22. when Jesus perceived their *thoughts*,
6: 8. he knew their *thoughts*, and said to
9:46. there arose a *reasoning* among them,.
47. perceiving the *thought* of their heart,
24:38. why do *thoughts* arise in your hearts?
Ro. 1:21. became vain in their *imaginations*,
14: 1. not to *doubtful* disputations.
1Co. 3:20. The Lord knoweth the *thoughts* of
Phi. 2:14. Do all things without murmurings and *disputings*:
1Ti. 2: 8. holy hands, without wrath and *doubting*.
Jas. 2: 4. become judges of evil *thoughts*?

διαλύομαι, dialuomai.

Acts 5:36. *were scattered*, and brought to nought.

διαμαρτύρομαι, diamarturomai.

Lu. 16:28. that he *may testify unto* them,
Acts 2.40. many other words *did* he *testify* and exhort,
8:25. *when* they *had testified* and preached
10:42. *to testify* that it is he which was
18: 5. *and testified* to the Jews (that) Jesus (was) Christ.
20:21 *Testifying* both to the Jews, and also to
23. Holy Ghost *witnesseth* in every city,
24. *to testify* the gospel of the grace of God.
23:11. for as thou *hast testified* of me in
28:23. expounded *and testified* the kingdom of God,
1Th. 4: 6. have forewarned you and *testified*.
1Ti. 5:21. I *charge* (thee) before God, and the Lord
2Ti. 2:14. *charging* (them) before the Lord that
4: 1. I *charge* (thee) therefore before God,
Heb 2: 6. one in a certain place *testified*, saying,

διαμάχομαι, diamakomai.

Acts23: 9. the Pharisees' part arose, and *strove*, saying,

διαμένω, diameno.

Lu. 1:22. beckoned unto them, and *remained* speechless.
22:28. they *which have continued* with me
Gal. 2: 5. the truth of the gospel *might continue*
Heb 1:11. They shall perish ; but thou *remainest* ;
2Pet.3: 4. all things *continue* as (they were)

διαμερίζω, diamerizo.

Mat.27:35. *parted* his garments, casting lots:
— They *parted* my garments among
Mar15:24. they *parted* his garments, casting lots
Lu. 11:17. Every kingdom *divided* against itself
18. If Satan also *be divided* against himself,
12:52. shall be five in one house *divided*,
53. The father *shall be divided* against
22:17. Take this, and *divide* (it) among yourselves:
23:34. they *parted* his raiment, *and* cast lots.
Joh.19:24. They *parted* my raiment among them,

Acts 2: 3. appeared unto them *cloven* tongues
45. *parted* them to all (men), as every

διαμερισμός, *diamerismos.*

Lu. 12:51. I tell you, Nay ; but rather *division* .

διανέμομαι, *dianemomai.*

Acts 4:17. that it *spread* no further among the people,

διανεύω, *dianuo.*

Lu. 1:22. for he beckoned (lit. was *beckoning*) unto
them, and remained

διανόημα, *dianoeema.*

Lu. 11:17. he, knowing their *thoughts*, said

διάνοια, *dianoya.*

Mat.22:37. with all thy soul, and with all thy *mind*.
Mar 12:30. all thy soul, and with all thy *mind*,
Lu. 1:51. in the *imagination* of their hearts.
10:27. all thy strength, and with all thy *mind*;
Eph. 1:18. The eyes of your *understanding* being
2: 3. desires of the flesh and of the *mind*;
4:18. Having the *understanding* darkened,
Col. 1:21. enemies in (your) *mind* by wicked
Heb 8:10. I will put my laws into their *mind*,
10:16. in their *minds* will I write them ;
1Pet.1:13. gird up the loins of your *mind*,
2Pet.3: 1. I stir up your pure *minds* by way
1Joh.5:20. hath given us an *understanding*,

διανοίγω, *dianoigo.*

Mar 7:34. saith unto him, Ephphatha, that is, *Be opened*.
35. straightway his ears *were opened*,
Lu. 2:23. Every male *that openeth* the womb
24:31. their eyes *were opened*, and they knew him ;
32. while he *opened* to us the scriptures ?
45. Then *opened* he their understanding,
Acts16:14. whose heart the Lord *opened*, that
17: 3. *Opening* and alledging, that Christ

διανυκτερεύω, *dianukteruo.*

Lu. 6:12. *continued all night* in prayer to God.

διανύω, *dianuo.*

Acts21: 7. *when we had finished* (our) course

διαπαντός, *diapantos.*

Mar 5: 5. *always*, night and day, he was in
Lu. 24:53. were *continually* in the temple,

Acts10: 2. alms to the people, and prayed to God
alway.
24:16. to have *always* a conscience void of
Ro. 11:10. bow down their back *alway*.
Heb 9: 6. the priests went *always* into the first tabernacle,
13:15. sacrifice of praise to God *continually*,

διαπεράω, *diaperao.*

Mat. 9: 1. he entered into a ship, and *passed over*,
14:34. *when they were gone over*, they
Mar 5:21. *when* Jesus *was passed over* again
6:53. *when they had passed over*, they came
Lu. 16:26. neither *can* they *pass* to us, that (would
come)
Acts21: 2. finding a ship *sailing over* unto

διαπλέω, *diapleo.*

Acts27: 5. *when* we *had sailed over* the sea of

διαπονέομαι, *diaponeomai.*

Acts 4: 2. *Being grieved* that they taught the people,
16:18. Paul, *being grieved*, turned and said

διαπορεύομαι, *diaporuomai.*

Lu. 6: 1. that he *went through* the corn fields ;
13:22. he *went through* the cities and villages,
18:36. hearing the multitude *pass by*,
Acts16: 4. as they *went through* the cities,
Ro. 15:24. for I trust to see you *in my journey*,

διαπορέω, *diaporeo.*

Lu. 9: 7. he *was perplexed*, because that it was
24: 4. as they were *much perplexed* thereabout,
Acts 2:12. they were all amazed, and *were in doubt*,
5:24. they *doubted* of them whereunto
10:17. while Peter *doubted* in himself what

διαπραγματεύομαι, *diapragmatuomai.*

Lu. 19:15. how much every man *had gained by
trading*.

διαπρίομαι, *diapriomai.*

Acts 5:33. heard (that), they *were cut* (to the heart),
7:54. they *were cut* to the heart, and they

διαρπάζω, *diarpazo*

Mat.12:29. into a strong man's house, and *spoil* his
goods,
— then he *will spoil* his house.
Mar 3:27. a strong man's house, and *spoil* his goods,
— then he *will spoil* his house.

διαρρήσσω & διαρρήγνυμι, diarreesso & diarreegnumi.

Mat.26:65. Then the high priest *rent* his clothes,
Mar 14:63. Then the high priest *rent* his clothes, *and*
Lu. 5: 6. multitude of fishes: and their net *brake*.
     8:29. he *brake* the bands, *and* was driven
Acts14:14. they *rent* their clothes, *and* ran in

διασαφέω, diasapheo.

Mat.18:31. came and *told unto* their lord all that

διασείω, diasio.

Lu. 3:14. *Do violence to* no man, neither accuse

διασκορπίζω, diaskorpizo.

Mat 25:24. gathering where thou *hast* not *strawed*
     26. gather where I *have* not *strawed* :
     26:31. the flock *shall be scattered abroad*.
Mar 14:27. the shepherd, and the sheep *shall be scattered*.
Lu. 1:51. he *hath scattered* the proud in the
     15:13. there *wasted* his substance with
     16: 1. that he had *wasted* his goods.
Joh. 11:52. children of God *that were scattered abroad*.
Acts 5:37. as many as obeyed him, *were dispersed*.

διασπάω, diaspao.

Mar 5: 4. the chains had been *plucked asunder*
Acts23:10. lest Paul *should have been pulled in pieces*

διασπείρω, diaspiro.

Acts 8: 1. they *were* all *scattered abroad* throughout
     4. they *that were scattered abroad* went
     11:19. they *which were scattered abroad* upon

διασπορά, diaspora.

Joh. 7:35. unto the *dispersed* (lit. the *dispersion*)
     among the Gentiles,
Jas. 1: 1. twelve tribes *which are scattered abroad*,
1Pet.1: 1. strangers *scattered* throughout Pontus,

διαστέλλομαι, diastellomai.

Mat 16:20. Then *charged* he his disciples
Mar 5:43. he *charged* them straitly that no
     7:36. he *charged* them that they should
     — the more he *charged* them, so much
     8:15. he *charged* them, saying, Take heed,
     9: 9. he *charged* them that they should
Acts15:24. we *gave* no (such) *commandment* :
Heb 12:20. not endure *that which was commanded*,

διάστημα, diasteema.

Acts 5: 7. it was about the *space* of three hours

διαστολή, diastolee.

Ro. 3:22. for there is no *difference* :
     10:12. no *difference* between the Jew and the
1Co.14: 7. except they give a *distinction* in the
     sounds,

διαστρέφω, diastrepho.

Mat.17:17. O faithless and *perverse* generation, how
Lu. 9:41. O faithless and *perverse* generation, how
     23: 2. We found this (fellow) *perverting* the nation,
Acts13: 8. seeking *to turn away* the deputy from
     10. cease to *pervert* the right ways of the Lord ?
     20:30. men arise, speaking *perverse* things,
Phi. 2:15. midst of a crooked and *perverse* nation,

διασώζω, diasozo.

Mat.14:36. many as touched *were made perfectly whole*.
Lu. 7: 3. that he would come and *heal* his servant.
Acts23:24. bring (him) *safe* unto Felix the governor.
     27:43. the centurion, willing *to save* Paul,
     44. that they *escaped* all *safe* to land.
     28: 1. *when* they *were escaped*, then they
     4. *though* he *hath escaped* the sea, yet
1Pet.3:20. eight souls *were saved* by water.

διαταγή, diatagee.

Acts 7:53. the law by the *disposition* of angels,
Ro. 13: 2. resisteth the *ordinance* of God: and they

διάταγμα, diatagma.

Heb 11:23. not afraid of the king's *commandment*.

διαταράττω, diataratto.

Lu. 1:29. she *was troubled* at his saying, and cast

διατάσσω, diatasso.

Mat.11: 1. of *commanding* his twelve disciples,
Lu. 3:13. than that which *is appointed* you.
     8:55. he *commanded* to give her meat.
     17: 9. things *that were commanded* him ?
     10. those things *which are commanded* you,
Acts 7:44. as he *had appointed*, speaking
     18: 2. Claudius *had commanded* all
     20:13. for so had he *appointed*, minding
     23:31. the soldiers, as it *was commanded*
     24:23. he *commanded* a centurion to keep
1Co. 7:17. so *ordain* I in all churches.
     9:14. Even so hath the Lord *ordained*
     11:34. the rest *will* I *set in order* when
     16: 1. as I *have given order* to the churches
Gal. 3:19. (it was) *ordained* by angels in
Tit. 1: 5. as I *had appointed* thee:

διατελέω, diateleo.

Acts27:33. *continued* fasting, having taken nothing.

διατηρέω, diateereo.

Lu. 2:51. his mother *kept* all these sayings in
Acts15:29. from which *if* ye *keep* yourselves, ye

διατί, diati.

Mat. 9:11. *Why* eateth your Master with publicans
      14. *Why* do we and the Pharisees fast oft,
   13:10. *Why* speakest thou unto them in parables?
   15: 2. *Why* do thy disciples transgress
       3. *Why* do ye also transgress the
   17:19. *Why* could not we cast him out?
   21:25. *Why* did ye not then believe him?
Mar. 2:18. *Why* do the disciples of John and of the
    7: 5. *Why* walk not thy disciples according
   11:31. *Why* then did ye not believe him?
Lu. 5:30. *Why* do ye eat and drink with publicans
     33. *Why* do the disciples of John fast often,
   19:23. *Wherefore* then gavest not thou my
     31. ask you, *Why* do ye loose (him)?
   20: 5. *Why* then believed ye him not?
   24:38. *why* do thoughts arise in your hearts?
Joh. 7:45. *Why* have ye not brought him?
    8:43. *Why* do ye not understand my speech?
     46. *why* do ye not believe me?
   12: 5. *Why* was not this ointment sold
   13:37. Lord, *why* cannot I follow thee now?
Acts 5: 3. *why* hath Satan filled thine heart
Ro. 9:32. *Wherefore?* Because (they sought it)
1Co. 6: 7. *Why* do ye not rather take wrong? *why* do
        ye not rather (suffer yourselves)
2Co.11:11. *Wherefore?* because I love you not?
Rev.17: 7. *Wherefore* didst thou marvel?

διατίθεμαι, diatithemai.

Lu. 22:29. I *appoint* unto you a kingdom, as my
       Father *hath appointed* unto me ;
Acts 3:25. the covenant which God *made*
Heb. 8:10. the covenant that I *will make* with
    9:16. be the death of the *testator.*
     17. strength at all while the *testator* liveth.
   10:16. the covenant that I *will make* with

διατρίβω, diatribo.

Joh. 3:22. there he *tarried* with them, and baptized.
   11:54. there *continued* with his disciples.
Acts12:19. from Judæa to Cæsarea, and (there) *abode.*
   14: 3. Long time therefore *abode* they speaking
     28. there they *abode* long time with
   15:35. Paul also and Barnabas *continued* in
       Antioch,
   16:12. we were in that city *abiding* certain days.
   20: 6. where we *abode* seven days.
   25: 6. And *when* he *had tarried* among them
     14. when they *had been* there many days,

διατροφή, diatrophee.

1Ti. 6: 8. having *food* and raiment let us be

διαυγάζω, diaugazo.

2Pet. 1:19. until the day *dawn*, and the day star

διαφανής, diaphanees.

Rev.21:21. as it were *transparent* glass.

διαφέρω, diaphero.

Mat. 6:26. *Are* ye not much *better* than they?
   10:31. ye *are of more value* than many sparrows.
   12:12. How much then *is* a man *better* than a
       sheep?
Mar11:16. that any man *should carry* (any) vessel
Lu. 12: 7. ye *are of more value* than many sparrows.
     24. more *are* ye *better* than the fowls?
Acts13:49. word of the Lord *was published* through-
       out
   27:27. *as* we *were driven up and down* in
Ro. 2:18. the things *that are more excellent,*
1Co.15:41. for (one) star *differeth from* (another)
Gal. 2: 6. it *maketh* no *matter* to me:
    4: 1. *differeth* nothing *from* a servant,
Phi. 1:10. ye may approve things *that are excellent ;*

διαφεύγω, diaphūgo.

Acts27:42. any of them should swim out, and *escape.*

διαφημίζω, diapheemizo.

Mat. 9:31. *spread abroad* his *fame* in all that country.
   28:15. this saying *is commonly reported* among
Mar. 1:45. *to blaze abroad* the matter, insomuch

διαφθείρω, diaphthiro.

Lu. 12:33. no thief approacheth, neither moth *cor-*
       rupteth.
2Co. 4:16. though our outward man *perish,*
1Ti. 6: 5. disputings of men of *corrupt* minds,
Rev. 8: 9. third part of the ships *were destroyed.*
   11:18. shouldest *destroy* them *which destroy* the
       earth.

διαφθορά, diaphthora.

Acts 2:27. suffer thine Holy One to see *corruption.*
     31. neither his flesh did see *corruption.*
   13:34. no more to return to *corruption,*
     35. suffer thine Holy One to see *corruption.*
     36. laid unto his fathers, and saw *corruption:*
     37. God raised again, saw no *corruption.*

διάφορος, diaphoros.

Ro. 12: 6. gifts *differing* according to the grace
Heb. 1: 4. obtained a *more excellent* name
    8: 6. obtained a *more excellent* ministry,
    9:10. in meats and drinks, and *divers* washings,

διαφυλάττω, diaphulatto.

Lu. 4:10. his angels charge over thee, *to keep* thee;

διαχειρίζομαι, diakirizomai.

Acts 5:30. Jesus, whom ye *slew* and hanged on a tree.
26:21. the temple, and went about *to kill* (me).

διαχωρίζομαι, diakōrizomai.

Lu. 9:33. as they *departed* from him, Peter said

διδακτικός, didaktikos.

1Ti. 3: 2. given to hospitality, *apt to teach ;*
2Ti. 2:24. gentle unto all (men), *apt to teach,*

διδακτός, didaktos.

Joh. 6:45. they shall be all *taught* of God.
1Co. 2:13. words *which* man's wisdom *teacheth,* but *which* the Holy Ghost *teacheth ;*

διδασκαλία, didaskalia.

Mat.15: 9. teaching (for) *doctrines* the commandments
Mar. 7: 7. teaching (for) *doctrines* the commandments of men.
Ro. 12: 7. or he that teacheth, on *teaching ;*
15: 4. aforetime were written for our *learning,*
Eph. 4:14. about with every wind of *doctrine,*
Col. 2:22. the commandments and *doctrines* of men?
1Ti. 1:10. that is contrary to sound *doctrine ;*
4: 1. to seducing spirits, and *doctrines* of devils;
6. words of faith and of good *doctrine,*
13. to reading, to exhortation, to *doctrine.*
16. Take heed unto thyself, and unto. the
doctrine ;
5:17. who labour in the word and *doctrine.*
6: 1. the name of God and (his) *doctrine* be
3. to the *doctrine* which is according
2Ti. 3:10. thou hast fully known my *doctrine,*
16. profitable for *doctrine,* for reproof,
4: 3. will not endure sound *doctrine ;*
Tit. 1: 9. may be able by sound *doctrine*
2: 1. things which become sound *doctrine:*
7. in *doctrine* (shewing) uncorruptness,
10. may adorn the *doctrine* of God

διδάσκαλος, didaskalos.

Mat. 8:19. said unto him, *Master,* I will
9:11. Why eateth your *Master* with publicans
10:24. The disciple is not above (his) *master,*
25. the disciple that he be as his *master,*
12:38. *Master,* we would see a sign from thee.
17:24. Doth not your *master* pay tribute?
19:16. Good *Master,* what good thing
22:16. *Master,* we know that thou art true,
24. Saying, *Master,* Moses said, If a
36. *Master,* which (is) the great command
ment
26:18. say unto him, The *Master* saith,
Mar. 4:38. *Master,* carest thou not that we perish?
5:35. why troublest thou the *Master*
9:17. said, *Master,* I have brought
38. *Master,* we saw one casting out
10:17. Good *Master,* what shall I do
20. *Master,* all these have I observed

Mar.10:35. saying, *Master,* we would that
12:14. they say unto him, *Master,* we know
19. *Master,* Moses wrote unto us,
32. Well, *master,* thou hast said the
13: 1. *Master,* see what manner of stones
14:14. The *master* saith, Where is the
Lu. 2:46. sitting in the midst of the *doctors,*
3:12. *Master,* what shall we do ?
6:40. The disciple is not above his *master:*
— perfect shall be as his *master.*
7:40. he saith, *Master,* say on.
8:49. is dead ; trouble not the *Master.*
9:38. saying, *Master,* I beseech thee,
10:25. *Master,* what shall I do to inherit
11:45. said unto him, *Master,* thus saying
12:13. said unto him, *Master,* speak
18:18. saying, Good *Master,* what shall
19:39. said unto him, *Master,* rebuke thy disciples.
20:21. *Master,* we know that thou sayest
28. Saying, *Master,* Moses wrote unto us,
39. said, *Master,* thou hast well said.
21: 7. saying, *Master,* but when shall
22:11. The *Master* saith unto thee, Where
Joh. 1:38(39). to say, being interpreted, *Master.*
3: 2. we know that thou art a *teacher*
10. Art thou a *master* of Israel,
8: 4. They say unto him, *Master,* this
11:28. saying, The *Master* is come,
13:13. Ye call me *Master* and Lord: and ye
14. If I then, (your) Lord and *Master,*
20:16. Rabboni ; which is to say, *Master.*
Acts13: 1. at Antioch certain prophets and *teachers ;*
Ro. 2:20. a *teacher* of babes, which hast the
1Co.12:28. secondarily prophets, thirdly *teachers,*
29. (are) all prophets? (are) all *teachers?*
Eph. 4:11. evangelists ; and some, pastors and
teachers ;
1Ti. 2: 7. a *teacher* of the Gentiles in faith
2Ti. 1:11. an apostle, and a *teacher* of the Gentiles.
4: 3. they heap to themselves *teachers,*
Heb. 5:12. for the time ye ought to be *teachers,*
Jas. 3: 1. My brethren, be not many *masters,*

διδάσκω, didasko.

Mat. 4:23. *teaching* in their synagogues, and preaching
5: 2. he opened his mouth, and *taught* them,
19. shall *teach* men so, he shall be
— whosoever shall do and *teach* (them),
7:29. he taught (lit. was *teaching*) them as (one)
having authority,
9:35. *teaching* in their synagogues,
11: 1. to *teach* and to preach in their cities.
13:54. he *taught* them in their synagogue,
15: 9. *teaching* (for) doctrines the commandments
21:23. came unto him as he *was teaching,*
22:16. and *teachest* the way of God in truth,
26:55. with you *teaching* in the temple,
28:15. did as they *were taught:* and this
20. *Teaching* them to observe all things
Mar. 1:21. entered into the synagogue, and *taught.*
22. for he taught (lit. was *teaching*) them as
one that had
2:13. resorted unto him, and he *taught* them.
4: 1. he began again to *teach* by the
2. he *taught* them many things
6: 2. began to *teach* in the synagogue:
6. round about the villages, *teaching.*

Mar. 6:30. had done, and what they *had taught.*
   34. he began *to teach* them many things.
   7: 7. *teaching* (for) doctrines the commandments
   8:31. he began *to teach* them, that the
   9:31. For he *taught* his disciples, and said
   10: 1. as he was wont, he *taught* them
   1:17. he *taught*, saying unto them,
   12:14. but *teachest* the way of God in truth:
   35. *while* he *taught* in the temple,
   14:49. daily with you in the temple *teaching*,
Lu. 4:15. he *taught* in their synagogues,
   31. taught (lit. was *teaching*) them on the sabbath days.
   5: 3. *taught* the people out of the ship.
   17. on a certain day, as he was *teaching*,
   6: 6. entered into the synagogue and *taught:*
   11: 1. said unto him, Lord, *teach* us to pray, as John also *taught* his disciples.
   12:12. the Holy Ghost *shall teach* you in the
   13:10. he was *teaching* in one of the synagogues
   22. went through the cities and villages, *teaching*,
   26. thou *hast taught* in our streets.
   19:47. he taught (lit. was *teaching*) daily in the temple.
   20: 1. *as* he *taught* the people in the temple,
   21. we know that thou sayest and *teachest* rightly.
   — *teachest* the way of God truly:
   21:37. in the day time he was *teaching* in the
   23: 5. *teaching* throughout all Jewry,
Joh. 6:59. as he *taught* in Capernaum.
   7:14. Jesus went up into the temple, and *taught.*
   28. cried Jesus in the temple as he *taught*,
   35. among the Gentiles, and *teach* the Gentiles?
   8: 2. he sat down, and *taught* them.
   20. *as* he *taught* in the temple: and no
   28. as my Father *hath taught* me, I
   9:34. born in sins, and dost thou *teach* us?
   14:26. he *shall teach* you all things,
   18:20. I ever *taught* in the synagogue,
Acts 1: 1. Jesus began both to do and *teach*,
   4: 2. grieved that they *taught* the people,
   18. not to speak at all nor *teach* in
   5:21. early in the morning, and *taught.*
   25. in the temple, and *teaching* the people.
   28. ye should not *teach* in this name?
   42. they ceased not to *teach* and preach
   11:26. with the church, and *taught* much people.
   15: 1. down from Judæa *taught* the brethren,
   35. *teaching* and preaching the word
   18:11. *teaching* the word of God among them.
   25. he spake and *taught* diligently the
   20:20. have shewed you, and *have taught* you
   21:21. that thou *teachest* all the Jews
   28. This is the man, *that teacheth* all
   28:31. *teaching* those things which
Ro. 2:21. Thou therefore *which teachest* another, *teachest* thou not thyself?
   12: 7. or he *that teacheth*, on teaching;
1Co. 4:17. as I *teach* every where in every church.
   11:14. Doth not even nature itself *teach* you,
Gal. 1:12. neither *was* I *taught* (it), but by
Eph. 4:21. heard him, and *have been taught* by him,
Col. 1:28. *teaching* every man in all wisdom;
   2: 7. as ye *have been taught*, abounding
   3:16. *teaching* and admonishing one another
2Th. 2:15. traditions which ye *have been taught*,
1Ti. 2:12. I suffer not a woman *to teach*,
   4:11. These things command and *teach.*
   6: 2. These things *teach* and exhort.

2Ti. 2: 2. who shall be able *to teach* others also.
Tit. 1:11. *teaching* things which they ought not,
Heb. 5:12. ye have need that one *teach* you
   8:11. they shall not *teach* every man
1Joh. 2:27. ye need not that any man *teach* you:
   — the same anointing *teacheth* you
   — even as it *hath taught* you, ye
Rev. 2:14. who *taught* Balac to cast a stumblingblock
   20. *to teach* and to seduce my servants

διδαχή, *didakee.*

Mat. 7:28. were astonished at his *doctrine:*
   16:12. of the *doctrine* of the Pharisees and of
   22:33. they were astonished at his *doctrine.*
Mar. 1:22. they were astonished at his *doctrine:*
   27. what new *doctrine* (is) this? for
   4: 2. said unto them in his *doctrine*,
   11:18. the people was astonished at his *doctrine.*
   12:38. he said unto them in his *doctrine*,
Lu. 4:32. they were astonished at his *doctrine:*
Joh. 7:16. My *doctrine* is not mine, but his
   17. he shall know of the *doctrine*,
   18:19. of his disciples, and of his *doctrine.*
Acts 2:42. in the apostles' *doctrine* and fellowship,
   5:28. filled Jerusalem with your *doctrine*,
   13:12. astonished at the *doctrine* of the Lord.
   17:19. what this new *doctrine*, whereof
Ro. 6:17. form of *doctrine* which was delivered
   16:17. offences contrary to the *doctrine*
1Co.14: 6. or by prophesying, or by *doctrine?*
   26. hath a psalm, hath a *doctrine*,
2Ti. 4: 2. with all longsuffering and *doctrine.*
Tit. 1: 9. Holding fast the faithful word as he *hath been taught*,
Heb. 6: 2. Of the *doctrine* of baptisms, and of
   13: 9. about with divers and strange *doctrines.*
2Joh. 9. abideth not in the *doctrine* of Christ,
   — He that abideth in the *doctrine* of Christ,
   10. bring not this *doctrine*, receive him
Rev. 2:14. that hold the *doctrine* of Balaam,
   15. that hold the *doctrine* of the Nicolaitanes,
   24. as many as have not this *doctrine*,

δίδραχμον, *didrakmon.*

Mat.17:24. they that received *tribute* (money)
   — Doth not your master pay *tribute?*

δίδωμι, *didōmi.*

Mat. 4: 9. All these things *will* I *give* thee,
   5:31. *let* him *give* her a writing of divorcement:
   42. *Give* to him that asketh thee,
   6:11. *Give* us this day our daily bread.
   7: 6. *Give* not that which is holy unto
   7. Ask, and it *shall be given* you;
   11. know how to *give* good gifts unto
   — *shall* your Father which is in heaven *give*
   9: 8. which *had given* such power unto men.
   10: 1. he *gave* them power (against) unclean
   8. freely ye have received, freely *give.*
   19. it *shall be given* you in that same
   12:39. there *shall* no sign *be given* to it,
   13: 8. into good ground, and *brought forth* fruit,
   11. Because it *is given* unto you to know
   — to them it *is not given.*
   12. whosoever hath, to him *shall be given*,

Mat.14: 7. *to give* her whatsoever she would ask.
8. *Give* me here John Baptist's head
9. he commanded (it) *to be given* (her).
11. in a charger, and *given* to the damsel:
16. need not depart; *give* ye them to eat.
19. *gave* the loaves to (his) disciples,
15:36. brake (them), and *gave* to his disciples,
16: 4. there *shall* no sign *be given* unto it,
19. I *will give* unto thee the keys of the
26. what *shall* a man *give* in exchange
17:27. that take, and *give* unto them for me and thee.
19: 7. command *to give* a writing of divorcement,
11. save (they) to whom it *is given*.
21. *give* to the poor, and thou shalt have
20: 4. whatsoever is right I *will give* you.
14. I will *give* unto this last, even
23. on my left, is not mine *to give*,
28. *to give* his life a ransom for many.
21:23. who *gave* thee this authority?
43. shall be taken from you, and *given* to
22:17. Is it lawful *to give* tribute unto
24:24. *shall shew* great signs and wonders;
29. the moon *shall* not *give* her light,
45. *to give* them meat in due season?
25: 8. *Give* us of your oil; for our lamps
15. unto one he *gave* five talents,
28. *give* (it) unto him which hath ten
29. every one that hath *shall be given*,
35. an hungred, and ye *gave* me meat:
42. an hungred, and ye *gave* me no meat:
26: 9. sold for much, and *given* to the poor.
15. said (unto them), What will ye *give* me,
26. brake (it), and *gave* (it) to the disciples,
27. gave thanks, and *gave* (it) to them, saying,
48. he that betrayed him *gave* them
27:10. *gave* them for the potter's field,
34. They *gave* him vinegar to drink
28:12. they *gave* large money unto
18. All power *is given* unto me in heaven
Mar. 2:26. *gave* also to them which were with him?
4: 7. choked it, and it *yielded* no fruit.
8. *did yield* fruit that sprang up
11. Unto you it *is given* to know the
25. he that hath, to him *shall be given:*
5:43. something should *be given* her to eat.
6: 2. this *which is given* unto him,
7. *gave* them power over unclean spirits;
22. whatsoever thou wilt, and I *will give* (it)
23. I *will give* (it) thee, unto the half
25. I will that thou *give* me by and by
28. in a charger, and *gave* it to the damsel: and the damsel *gave* it to her mother.
37. *Give* ye them to eat. And they
— of bread, and *give* them to eat?
41. *gave* (them) to his disciples to set
8: 6. brake, and *gave* to his disciples to set
12. There *shall* no sign *be given* unto
37. what *shall* a man *give* in exchange
10:21. *give* to the poor, and thou shalt have
37. *Grant* unto us that we may sit,
40. is not mine *to give;* but (it shall be)
45. *to give* his life a ransom for many.
11:28. who *gave* thee this authority to do
12: 9. *will give* the vineyard unto others.
14. Is it lawful *to give* tribute to Cæsar,
15(14). Shall we *give*, or shall we not *give?*
13:11. shall *be given* you in that hour,
22. *shall shew* signs and wonders, to
24. the moon *shall* not *give* her light,
34. *gave* authority to his servants,

Mar 14: 5. and *have been given* to the poor.
11. promised *to give* him money.
22. brake (it), and *gave* to them, and said,
23. had given thanks, he *gave* (it) to them;
44. betrayed him *had given* them a
15:23. they *gave* him to drink wine
Lu. 1:32. the Lord God *shall give* unto him the
74(73). That he would *grant* unto us,
77. *To give* knowledge of salvation
2:24. *to offer* a sacrifice according to that
4: 6. All this power *will* I *give* thee,
— to whomsoever I will I *give* it.
6: 4. *gave* also to them that were with him;
30. *Give* to every man that asketh of thee;
38. *Give*, and it *shall be given* unto you;
— *shall* men *give* into your bosom.
7:15. he *delivered* him to his mother.
44. thou *gavest* me no water for my feet:
45. Thou *gavest* me no kiss: but this
8:10. Unto you it *is given* to know the
18. whosoever hath, to him *shall be given;*
55. he commanded *to give* her meat.
9: 1. *gave* them power and authority over all
13. said unto them, *Give* ye them to eat.
16. *gave* to the disciples to set before
10:19. I *give* unto you power to tread on
35. two pence, and *gave* (them) to the host,
11: 3. *Give* us day by day our daily bread.
7. I cannot rise and *give* thee.
8. Though he will not rise and *give* him,
— he will rise and *give* him as many
9. Ask, and it *shall be given* you; seek,
13. *to give* good gifts unto your children:
— *shall* (your) heavenly Father *give* the
29. there *shall* no sign *be given* it, but
41. rather *give* alms of such things
12:32. your Father's good pleasure *to give* you
33. Sell that ye have, and *give* alms;
42. *to give* (them their) portion of meat
48. unto whomsoever much *is given*, of
51. that I am come *to give* peace on earth?
58. *give* diligence that thou mayest be
14: 9. say to thee, *Give* this man place;
15:12. Father, *give* me the portion of goods
16. no man *gave* unto him.
22. *put* a ring on his hand, and shoes on
29. yet thou never *gavest* me a kid,
16:12. who *shall give* you that which is
17:18. that returned *to give* glory to God,
18:43. when they saw (it), *gave* praise unto God.
19: 8. my goods I *give* to the poor;
13. *delivered* them ten pounds, and said
15. to whom he *had given* the money,
23. Wherefore then *gavest* not thou my
24. *give* (it) to him that hath ten pounds.
26. unto every one which hath *shall be given;*
20: 2. who is he *that gave* thee this authority?
10. they *should give* him of the fruit
16. *shall give* the vineyard to others.
22. Is it lawful for us *to give* tribute
21:15. For I *will give* you a mouth
22: 5. covenanted *to give* him money.
19. brake (it), and *gave* unto them, saying, This is my body *which is given* for you:
23: 2. forbidding *to give* tribute to Cæsar,
Joh. 1:12. to them *gave* he power to become
17. the law *was given* by Moses,
22. that we *may give* an answer to
3:16. that he *gave* his only begotten Son,
27. except it be *given* him from heaven.
34. God *giveth* not the Spirit by measure
35. *hath given* all things into his hand.

Joh. 4: 5. that Jacob *gave* to his son Joseph.
    7. Jesus saith unto her, *Give* me to drink.
    10. saith to thee, *Give* me to drink ;
    — he would *have given* thee living water.
    12. Jacob, which *gave* us the well,
    14. the water that I *shall give* him
    — the water that I *shall give* him shall
    15. Sir, *give* me this water, that I thirst not,
  5:22. *hath committed* all judgment unto
    26. so *hath* he *given* to the Son to have
    27. *hath given* him authority to execute
    36. which the Father *hath given* me
  6:27. the Son of man *shall give* unto you:
    31. He *gave* them bread from heaven
    32. Moses *gave* you not that bread
    — my Father *giveth* you the true
    33. *giveth* life unto the world.
    34. Lord, evermore *give* us this bread.
    37. All that the Father *giveth* me
    39. of all which he *hath given* me
    51. bread that I *will give* is my flesh, which I
        will give for the life of the world.
    52. How can this man *give* us (his) flesh
    65. were *given* unto him of my Father.
  7:19. *Did* not Moses *give* you the law,
    22. Moses therefore *gave* unto you circum-
        cision;
  9:24. said unto him, *Give* God the praise:
 10:28. I *give* unto them eternal life ;
    29. My Father, which *gave* (them) me,
 11:22. God *will give* (it) thee.
    57. the Pharisees *had given* a commandment,
 12: 5. three hundred pence, and *given* to the
        poor?
    49. he *gave* me a commandment,
 13: 3. the Father *had given* all things into
    15. For I *have given* you an example,
    26. the sop, he *gave* (it) to Judas Iscariot,
    29. that he *should give* something to
    34. A new commandment I *give* unto you,
 14:16. he *shall give* you another Comforter,
    27. my peace I *give* unto you : not as the world
        giveth, *give* I unto you.
 15:16. in my name, he *may give* it you.
 16:23. in my name, he *will give* (it) you.
 17: 2. As thou *hast given* him power
    — that he *should give* eternal life to as many
        as thou *hast given* him.
    4. work which thou *gavest* me to do.
    6. which thou *gavest* me out of the world : thine
        they were, and thou *gavest* them me ;
    7. whatsoever thou *hast given* me
    8. I *have given* unto them the words which
        thou *gavest* me ;
    9. for them which thou *hast given* me ;
    11. those whom thou *hast given* me,
    12. those that thou *gavest* me I have kept,
    14. I *have given* them thy word ; and the
    22. the glory which thou *gavest* me I *have*
        given them ;
    24. they also, whom thou *hast given* me,
    — my glory, which thou *hast given* me :
 18: 9. Of them which thou *gavest* me have I
    11. cup which my Father *hath given* me,
    22. struck Jesus (lit. *gave* a blow to) with the
        palm of his hand,
 19: 3. they *smote* him with their hands.
    9. Jesus *gave* him no answer.
    11. except it were *given* thee from above:
 21:13. taketh bread, and *giveth* them, and fish
Acts 1:26. they *gave* forth their lots ; and the lot
  2: 4. as the Spirit *gave* them utterance.

Acts 2:19. I *will shew* wonders in heaven above,
    27. neither *wilt* thou *suffer* thine Holy
  3: 6. such as I have *give* I thee: In the
    16. *hath given* him this perfect soundness
  4:12. name under heaven *given* among men,
    29. *grant* unto thy servants, that with
  5:31. for *to give* repentance to Israel,
    32. whom God *hath given* to them that
  7: 5. he *gave* him none inheritance in it,
    — promised that he would *give* it to him
    8. he *gave* him the covenant of circumcision:
    10. *gave* him favour and wisdom in the sight
    25. God by his hand would deliver (lit. *give*
        salvation to) them:
    38. the lively oracles *to give* unto us:
  8:18. the Holy Ghost *was given*, he offered
    19. Saying, *Give* me also this power, that
  9:41. he *gave* her (his) hand, *and* lifted her
 10:40. the third day, and shewed him openly ;
        (lit. *gave* him to be manifested)
 11:17. as God *gave* them the like gift as
    18. to the Gentiles *granted* repentance
 12:23. because he *gave* not God the glory:
 13:20. after that he *gave* (unto them) judges
    21. God *gave* unto them Saul the son of Cis,
    34. I *will give* you the sure mercies of David.
    35. *shalt* not *suffer* thine Holy One to see
 14: 3. and *granted* signs and wonders to be done
    17. *and gave* us rain from heaven, and fruitful
 15: 8. *giving* them the Holy Ghost, even
 17:25. *seeing* he *giveth* to all life, and breath,
 19:31. not *adventure* himself into the theatre.
 20:32. *to give* you an inheritance among
    35. It is more blessed *to give* than to receive.
 24:26. money should *have been given* him
Ro. 4:20. strong in faith, *giving* glory to God ;
  5: 5. Holy Ghost *which is given* unto us.
 11: 8. God *hath given* them the spirit of
 12: 3. through the grace *given* unto me,
    6. the grace *that is given* to us, whether
    19. *give* place unto wrath: for it is written,
 14:12. *shall give* account of himself to God.
 15: 5. *grant* you to be likeminded one
    15. the grace *that is given* to me of God,
1Co. 1: 4. the grace of God *which is given*
  3: 5. even as the Lord *gave* to every man?
    10. grace of God *which is given* unto me,
  7:25. yet I *give* my judgment, as one
  9:12. lest we should hinder (lit. *give* any hin-
        drance to) the gospel
 11:15. hair *is given* her for a covering.
 12: 7. manifestation of the Spirit *is given* to
        every
    8. to one *is given* by the Spirit the word
    24. *having given* more abundant honour
 14: 7. things without life *giving* sound,
    — except they *give* a distinction in the
    8. if the trumpet *give* an uncertain sound,
    9. except ye *utter* by the tongue words easy
 15:38. God *giveth* it a body as it hath pleased
    57. God, *which giveth* us the victory through
2Co. 1:22. and *given* the earnest of the Spirit
  5: 5. *who* also *hath given* unto us the earnest
    12. *give* you occasion to glory on our behalf,
    18. and *hath given* to us the ministry of
  6: 3. *Giving* no offence in any thing,
  8: 1. grace of God *bestowed* on the churches
    5. first *gave* their own selves to the Lord,
    10. herein I *give* (my) advice: for this
    16. God, *which put* the same earnest care
  9: 9. he *hath given* to the poor: his
 10: 8. the Lord *hath given* us for edification,

2Co.12: 7. there *was given* to me a thorn in
13:10. power which the Lord *hath given* me
Gal. 1: 4. *Who gave* himself for our sins,
2: 9. the grace *that was given* unto me, they
gave to me and Barnabas the
3:21. if there *had been* a law *given* which
22. *might be given* to them that believe.
4:15. your own eyes, and *have given* them to me.
Eph. 1:17. *may give* unto you the spirit of
22. *gave* him (to be) the head over all
3: 2. *which is given* me to you-ward:
7. the grace of God *given* unto me by
8. *is* this grace *given*, that I should
16. That he *would grant* you, according
4: 7. unto every one of us *is given* grace
8. captivity captive, and *gave* gifts unto men.
11. he *gave* some, apostles ; and some,
27. Neither *give* place to the devil.
29. that it *may minister* grace unto
6:19. that utterance *may be given* unto me,
Col. 1:25. *which is given* to me for you,
1Th. 4: 2. we *gave* you by the Lord Jesus.
8. *who hath* also *given* unto us his holy
Spirit.
2Th. 1: 8. *taking* vengeance on them that
2:16. and *hath given* (us) everlasting consolation
3: 9. to *make* ourselves an ensample
16. *give* you peace always by all means.
1Ti. 2: 6. *Who gave* himself a ransom for
4:14. which *was given* thee by prophecy,
5:14. *give* none occasion to the adversary
2Ti. 1: 7. God *hath* not *given* us the spirit of fear ;
9. grace, *which was given* us in Christ
16. The Lord *give* mercy unto the house
18. The Lord *grant* unto him that he
2: 7. the Lord *give* thee understanding
25. if God peradventure will *give* them
Tit. 2:14. *Who gave* himself for us, that he
Heb 2:13. the children which God *hath given* me.
7: 4. Abraham *gave* the tenth of the spoils.
8:10. I will *put* my laws into their mind,
10:16. I will *put* my laws into their hearts,
Jas. 1: 5. ask of God, *that giveth* to all (men)
— upbraideth not ; and it *shall be given* him.
2:16. notwithstanding ye *give* them not
4: 6. he *giveth* more grace. Wherefore
— *giveth* grace unto the humble.
5:18. the heaven *gave* rain, and the earth
1Pet.1:21. from the dead, and *gave* him glory ;
5: 5. *giveth* grace to the humble.
2Pet.3:15. according to the wisdom *given* unto him
1Joh.3: 1. of love the Father *hath bestowed* upon us,
23. as he *gave* us commandment.
24. by the Spirit which he *hath given* us.
4:13. because he *hath given* us of his Spirit.
5:11. God *hath given* to us eternal life,
16. he *shall give* him life for them
20. *hath given* us an understanding,
Rev. 1: 1. which God *gave* unto him, to shew
2: 7. *will* I *give* to eat of the tree of life,
10. I *will give* thee a crown of life.
17. To him that overcometh *will* I *give* to eat
— and *will give* him a white stone,
21. I *gave* her space to repent of her
23. I *will give* unto every one of you
26. to him *will* I *give* power over
28. I *will give* him the morning star.
3: 8. I *have set* before thee an open door,
9. Behold, I will *make* them of the
21. that overcometh *will* I *grant* to sit
4: 9. when those beasts *give* glory
6: 2. a crown *was given* unto him:

Rev. 6: 4. (power) *was given* to him that sat
— there *was given* unto him a great sword.
8. power *was given* unto them over
11. white robes *were given* unto every
7: 2. to whom it *was given* to hurt
8: 2. to them *were given* seven trumpets.
3. there *was given* unto him much incense,
that he *should offer* (it) with the prayers
9: 1. to him *was given* the key of the
3. unto them *was given* power, as the
5. to them it *was given* that they
10: 9. said unto him, *Give* me the little book.
11: 1. there *was given* me a reed like
2. for it *is given* unto the Gentiles:
3. I *will give* (power) unto my two
13. *gave* glory to the God of heaven.
18. that thou shouldest *give* reward
12:14. to the woman *were given* two wings
13: 2. the dragon *gave* him his power,
4. which *gave* power unto the beast:
5. there *was given* unto him a mouth
— power *was given* unto him to continue
7. it *was given* unto him to make war
— power *was given* him over all
14. miracles which he *had power* to do
15. he had power (lit. it *was given* him) *to*
give life unto the image of
16. to receive (lit. that he *should give* them) a
mark in their right hand,
14: 7. Fear God, and *give* glory to him ;
15: 7. *gave* unto the seven angels seven
16: 6. thou *hast given* them blood to drink ;
8. power *was given* unto him to scorch
9. they repented not *to give* him glory.
19. *to give* unto her the cup of the wine
17:17. For God *hath put* in their hearts to
— and *give* their kingdom unto the beast,
18: 7. so much torment and sorrow *give* her:
19: 7. be glad and rejoice, and *give* honour to
him:
8. to her *was granted* that she should
20: 4. judgment *was given* unto them:
13. the sea *gave up* the dead which
— death and hell *delivered up* the dead which
21: 6. I *will give* unto him that is athirst

διεγείρω, *diegiro.*

Mat. 1:24. Then Joseph *being raised* from sleep
Mar 4:38. they *awake* him, and say unto him,
39. he *arose, and* rebuked the wind,
Lu. 8:24. they came to him, and *awoke* him,
Joh. 6:18. the sea *arose* by reason of a great
2Pet.1:13. in this tabernacle, *to stir* you *up*
3: 1. I *stir up* your pure minds by

διέξοδος, *diexodos.*

Mat.22: 9. Go ye therefore into the *highways,*

διερμηνευτής, *diermeenutees.*

1Co.14:28. if there be no *interpreter,* let him

διερμηνεύω, *diermeenŭo.*

Lu. 24:27. he *expounded* unto them in all

Acts 9:36. which *by interpretation* is called
1Co.12:30. do all speak with tongues? *do all interpret?*
    14: 5. except he *interpret*, that the church
    13. pray that he *may interpret*.
    27. (that) by course ; and *let one interpret*.

διέρχομαι, dierkomai.

Mat.12:43. he *walketh through* dry places, seeking rest,
    19:24. easier for a camel *to go through* the eye
Mar 4:35. *Let us pass over* unto the other side.
Lu. 2:15. *Let us* now *go* even unto Bethlehem,
    35. a sword *shall pierce through* thy
    4:30. he *passing through* the midst of them
    5:15. the more *went* there a fame *abroad*
    8:22. *Let us go over* unto the other side
    9: 6. they departed, and *went through* the towns,
    11:24. he *walketh through* dry places, seeking
    17:11. he *passed through* the midst of Samaria
    19: 1. (Jesus) entered and *passed through* Jericho.
    4. for he was *to pass* that (way).
Joh. 4: 4. he must needs *go through* Samaria.
    8:59. *going through* the midst of them,
Acts 8: 4. *went every where* preaching the word.
    40. *passing through* he preached in all
    9:32. as Peter *passed through* out all (quarters),
    38. would not delay *to come* to them.
    10:38. who *went about* doing good, and healing
    11:19. *travelled* as far as Phenice, and Cyprus,
    22. that he should *go* as far as Antioch.
    12:10. When they *were past* the first and the second
    13: 6. when they *had gone through* the isle
    14. when they *departed* from Perga,
    14:24. after they *had passed throughout* Pisidia,
    15: 3. they *passed through* Phenice,
    41. he *went through* Syria and Cilicia,
    16: 6. when they *had gone throughout* Phrygia
    17:23. For as I *passed by*, and beheld your
    18:23. and *went over* (all) the country of Galatia
    27. when he was disposed *to pass* into Achaia,
    19: 1. Paul *having passed through* the
    21. when he *had passed through* Macedonia
    20: 2. when he *had gone over* those parts,
    25. among whom I *have gone* preaching
Ro. 5:12. so death *passed* upon all men,
1Co.10: 1. all *passed through* the sea;
    16: 5. when I shall *pass through* Macedonia: for I *do pass through* Macedonia.
2Co. 1:16. *to pass* by you into Macedonia,
Heb 4:14. high priest, *that is passed* into the heavens,

διερωταω, dierōtao.

Acts10:17. *had made enquiry for* Simon's house, *and*

διετης, dietees.

Mat. 2:16. from *two years old* and under, according

διετία, dietia.

Acts24:27. after *two years* Porcius Festus came
    28:30. Paul dwelt *two whole years* in his own

διηγέομαι, dieegeomai.

Mar 5:16. they that saw (it) *told* them how it
    9: 9. that they *should tell* no man what
Lu. 8:39. *shew* how great things God hath done
    9:10. *told* him all that they had done.
Acts 8:33. who *shall declare* his generation ?
    9:27. *declared* unto them how he had seen
    12:17. *declared* unto them how the Lord
Heb 11:32. the time would fail me to *tell of*

διήγησις, dieegeesis.

Lu. 1: 1. to set forth in order a *declaration*

(εἰς τὸ) διηνεκές, dieenekes.

Heb 7: 3. of God; abideth a priest *continually*.
    10: 1. offered year by year *continually* make
    12. *for ever* sat down on the right hand
    14. he hath perfected *for ever* them that

διθάλασσος, dithalassos.

Acts27:41. falling into a place *where two seas met*,

διϊκνέομαι, diikneomai.

Heb 4:12. *piercing* even to the dividing asunder

διΐστημι, diisteemi.

Lu. 22:59. about the space of one hour after (lit. about one hour *having intervened*)
    24:51. he *was parted* from them, and carried
Acts27:28. when they *had gone* a little *further*,

διϊσχυρίζομαι, diiskurizomai.

Lu. 22:59. another *confidently affirmed*, saying,
Acts12:15. she *constantly affirmed* that it was

δικαιοκρισία, dikaiokrisia.

Ro. 2: 5. revelation of the *righteous judgment* of God ;

δίκαιος, dikaios.

Mat. 1:19. Joseph her husband, being a *just* (man),
    5:45. sendeth rain on the *just* and on the unjust.
    9:13. not come to call the *righteous*, but sinners
    10:41. he that receiveth a *righteous* man in the name of a *righteous* man shall receive a *righteous* man's reward
    13:17. many prophets and *righteous* (men) have
    43. Then shall the *righteous* shine forth
    49. sever the wicked from among the *just*,
    20: 4. whatsoever is *right* I will give you.
    7. whatsoever is *right*, (that) shall ye receive.
    23:28. outwardly appear *righteous* unto men,
    29. garnish the sepulchres of the *righteous*,
    35. the *righteous* blood shed upon the earth, from the blood of *righteous* Abel unto
    25:37. Then shall the *righteous* answer him,

Mat.25:46. the *righteous* into life eternal.
27:19. nothing to do with that *just* man:
24. innocent of the blood of this *just* person:
Mar. 2:17. I came not to call the *righteous*, but
6:20. knowing that he was a *just* man
Lu. 1: 6. they were both *righteous* before God,
17. disobedient to the wisdom of the *just;*
2:25. the same man (was) *just* and devout,
5:32. I came not to call the *righteous*, but
12:57. yourselves judge ye not what is *right?*
14:14. at the resurrection of the *just.*
15: 7. more than over ninety and nine *just* persons,
18: 9. in themselves that they were *righteous*,
20:20. which should feign themselves *just* men,
23:47. Certainly this was a *righteous* man.
50. (he was) a good man, and a *just:*
Joh. 5:30. my judgment is *just;* because I
7:24. appearance, but judge *righteous* judgment.
17:25. O *righteous* Father, the world hath
Acts 3:14. ye denied the Holy One and the *Just*,
4:19. Whether it be *right* in the sight
7:52. of the coming of the *Just* One ;
10:22. Cornelius the centurion, a *just* man,
22:14. know his will, and see that *Just* One,
24:15. of the dead, both of the *just* and unjust.
Ro. 1:17. written, The *just* shall live by faith.
2:13. hearers of the law (are) *just* before God,
3:10. There is none *righteous*, no, not one:
26. might be *just*, and the justifier
5: 7. scarcely for a *righteous* man will one die:
19. shall many be made *righteous*.
7:12. the commandment holy, and *just*, and good.
Gal. 3:11. The *just* shall live by faith.
Eph. 6: 1. in the Lord: for this is *right*.
Phi. 1: 7. Even as it is *meet* for me to think
4: 8. whatsoever things (are) *just*, whatsoever
Col. 4: 1. that which is *just* and equal ;
2Th. 1: 5. of the *righteous* judgment of God,
6. Seeing (it is) a *righteous* thing
1Ti. 1: 9. law is not made for a *righteous* man,
2Ti. 4: 8. which the Lord, the *righteous* judge,
Tit. 1: 8. a lover of good men, sober, *just*, holy,
Heb 10:38. Now the *just* shall live by faith:
11: 4. obtained witness that he was *righteous*,
12:23. to the spirits of *just* men made perfect,
Jas. 5: 6. have condemned (and) killed the *just;*
16. prayer of a *righteous* man availeth much.
1Pet. 3:12. eyes of the Lord (are) over the *righteous*,
18. suffered for sins, the *just* for the unjust,
4:18. if the *righteous* scarcely be saved,
2Pet. 1:13. Yea, I think it *meet*, as long as I am
2: 7. delivered *just* Lot, vexed with the filthy
8. For that *righteous* man dwelling
— vexed (his) *righteous* soul from day
1Joh.1: 9. he is faithful and *just* to forgive us
2: 1. with the Father, Jesus Christ the *righteous:*
29. If ye know that he is *righteous*,
3: 7. is *righteous*, even as he is *righteous*.
12. works were evil, and his brother's *righteous*.
Rev.15: 3. *just* and true (are) thy ways, thou King
16: 5. Thou art *righteous*, O Lord, which art,
7. true and *righteous* (are) thy judgments.
19: 2. true and *righteous* (are) his judgments:
22:11. he that is *righteous*, let him be righteous

δικαιοσύνη, *dikaiosunee.*

Mat. 3:15. becometh us to fulfil all *righteousness*.

Mat. 5: 6. do hunger and thirst after *righteousness:*
10. persecuted for *righteousness'* sake:
20. except your *righteousness* shall exceed
6:33. kingdom of God, and his *righteousness;*
21:32. in the way of *righteousness*,
Lu. 1:75. In holiness and *righteousness* before him,
Joh.16: 8. of *righteousness*, and of judgment:
10. Of *righteousness*, because I go to
Acts10:35. feareth him, and worketh *righteousness*,
13:10. (thou) enemy of all *righteousness*,
17:31. will judge the world in *righteousness*
24:25. as he reasoned of *righteousness*,
Ro. 1:17. therein is the *righteousness* of God
3: 5. commend the *righteousness* of God,
21. now the *righteousness* of God
22. Even the *righteousness* of God (which)
25. to declare his *righteousness* for
26. at this time his *righteousness:*
4: 3. counted unto him for *righteousness*.
5. his faith is counted for *righteousness*.
6. God imputeth *righteousness* without works,
9. reckoned to Abraham for *righteousness*.
11. a seal of the *righteousness* of the
— that *righteousness* might be imputed
13. through the *righteousness* of faith.
22. was imputed to him for *righteousness*.
5:17. of the gift of *righteousness*
21. might grace reign through *righteousness*
6:13. instruments of *righteousness* unto God.
16. or of obedience unto *righteousness?*
18. became the servants of *righteousness*.
19. your members servants to *righteousness*
20. ye were free from *righteousness*.
8:10. Spirit (is) life because of *righteousness*.
9:28. cut (it) short in *righteousness:*
30. which followed not after *righteousness*, have attained to *righteousness*, even *righteousness* which is of faith.
31. followed after the law of *righteousna* hath not attained to the law of *right. ousness*.
10: 3. being ignorant of God's *righteousness*, and going about to establish their own *righteousness*, have not submitted themselves unto the *righteousness* of God.
4. of the law for *righteousness* to
5. Moses describeth the *righteousness*
6. the *righteousness* which is of faith
10. man believeth unto *righteousness;*
14:17. but *righteousness*, and peace, and joy in
1Co. 1:30. made unto us wisdom, and *righteousness*,
2Co. 3: 9. the ministration of *righteousness*
5:21. be made the *righteousness* of God in him.
6: 7. by the armour of *righteousness* on
14. what fellowship hath *righteousness* with
9: 9. his *righteousness* remaineth for ever.
10. increase the fruits of your *righteousness;*
11:15. as the ministers of *righteousness;*
Gal. 2:21. for if *righteousness* (come) by the law,
3: 6. was accounted to him for *righteousness*.
21. verily *righteousness* should have been
5: 5. the hope of *righteousness* by faith.
Eph. 4:24. created in *righteousness* and true holiness.
5: 9. in all goodness and *righteousness*
6:14. the breastplate of *righteousness;*
Phi. 1:11. filled with the fruits of *righteousness*,
3: 6. touching the *righteousness* which
9. not having mine own *righteousness*,
— *righteousness* which is of God by faith:
1Ti. 6:11. follow after *righteousness*, godliness,
2Ti. 2:22. follow *righteousness*, faith, charity
3:16. for instruction in *righteousness:*

2Ti. 4: 8. for me a crown of *righteousness*,
Tit. 3: 5. Not by works of *righteousness* which
Heb 1: 9. Thou hast loved *righteousness*,
    5:13. unskilful in the word of *righteousness:*
    7: 2. King of *righteousness*, and after that
   11: 7. the *righteousness* which is by faith.
    33. wrought *righteousness*, obtained
   12:11. the peaceable fruit of *righteousness*
Jas. 1:20. worketh not the *righteousness* of God.
   2:23. imputed unto him for *righteousness:*
   3:18. the fruit of *righteousness* is sown
1Pet. 2:24. should live unto *righteousness:*
   3:14. if ye suffer for *righteousness'* sake,
2Pet. 1: 1. through the *righteousness* of God
   2: 5. a preacher of *righteousness*, bringing
   21. known the way of *righteousness.*
   3:13. wherein dwelleth *righteousness.*
1Joh. 2:29. every one that doeth *righteousness*
   3: 7. he that doeth *righteousness* is
   10. whosoever doeth not *righteousness*
Rev. 19:11. in *righteousness* he doth judge and make
   war.

δικαιόω, *dikaioō.*

Mat.11 :19. wisdom *is justified* of her children.
   12:37. by thy words thou *shalt be justified,*
Lu. 7:29. the publicans, *justified* God, being
   35. wisdom *is justified* of all her children.
   10:29. he, willing *to justify* himself, said
   16:15. Ye are they *which justify* yourselves
   18:14. went down to his house *justified*
Acts13 :39. by him all that believe *are justified*
   — ye could not *be justified* by the
Ro. 2:13. the doers of the law *shall be justified.*
   3: 4. That thou *mightest be justified* in
   20. there *shall* no flesh *be justified* in his
   24. *Being justified* freely by his grace
   26. the *justifier* of him which believeth
   28. that a man is *justified* by faith
   30. one God, which *shall justify* the
   4: 2. if Abraham *were justified* by works,
   5. believeth on him that *justifieth* the
   5: 1. Therefore *being* (lit. *having been*) *justified*
   by faith,
   9. *being* now *justified* (lit. *having been j.*) by
   his blood,
   6: 7. he that is dead *is freed* (lit. *is justified*),
   from sin.
   8:30. whom he called, them he also *justified:*
   and whom he *justified*, them he also glorified.
   33. of God's elect? (It is) God *that justifieth.*
1Co. 4: 4. yet *am* I not hereby *justified:*
   6:11. ye *are* (lit. *have been*) *justified* in the name
   of
Gal. 2:16. a man *is* not *justified* by the works
   — that we *might be justified* by the
   — *shall* no flesh *be justified.*
   17. while we seek *to be justified* by Christ,
   3: 8. that God *would justify* the heathen
   11. no man *is justified* by the law
   24. that we *might be justified* by faith.
   5: 4. whosoever of you *are justified* by
1Ti. 3:16. was manifest in the flesh, *justified* in the
   Spirit,
Tit. 3: 7. That *being justified* (lit. *having been j.*) by
   his grace,
Jas. 2:21. *Was* not Abraham our father *justified* by
   works,
   24. that by works a man *is justified,*

Jas. 2:25. *was* not Rahab the harlot *justified* by works,
Rev.22:11. righteous, *let* him *be righteous* still:

δικαίωμα, *dikaiōma.*

Lu. 1: 6. commandments and *ordinances* of the
   Lord
Ro. 1:32. Who knowing the *judgment* of God,
   2:26. keep the *righteousness* of the law,
   5:16. of many offences unto *justification.*
   18. by the *righteousness* of one
   8: 4. That the *righteousness* of the law
Heb. 9: 1. had also *ordinances* of divine service,
   10. divers washings, and carnal *ordinances,*
Rev.15: 4. thy *judgments* are made manifest.
   19: 8. fine linen is the *righteousness* of saints.

δικαίως, *dikaiōs.*

Lu. 23:41. we indeed *justly;* for we receive
1Co.15:34. Awake *to righteousness,* and sin not;
1Th. 2:10. how holily and *justly* and unblameably we
Tit. 2:12. we should live soberly, *righteously,* and
1Pet.2:23. to him that judgeth *righteously:*

δικαίωσις, *dikaiōsis.*

Ro. 4:25. was raised again for our *justification.*
   5:18. upon all men unto *justification* of life.

δικαστής, *dikastees.*

Lu. 12:14. who made me a *judge* or a divider
Acts 7:27. Who made thee a ruler and a *judge* over
   us?
   35. Who made thee a ruler and a *judge?*

δίκη, *dikee.*

Acts25:15. (to have) *judgment* against him.
   28: 4. yet *vengeance* suffereth not to live.
2Th. 1: 9. Who shall be punished (lit. suffer *ven-*
   geance) with
Jude 7. suffering the *vengeance* of eternal fire.

δίκτυον, *diktuon.*

Mat. 4:20. they straightway left (their) *nets,*
   21. mending their *nets;* and he called them.
Mar. 1:18. straightway they forsook their *nets,*
   19. in the ship mending their *nets.*
Lu. 5: 2. were washing (their) *nets.*
   4. let down your *nets* for a draught.
   5. at thy word I will let down the *net.*
   6. of fishes: and their *net* brake.
Joh.21: 6. Cast the *net* on the right side
   8. dragging the *net* with fishes.
   11. drew the *net* to land full of
   — yet was not the *net* broken.

δίλογος, *dilogos.*

1Ti. 3: 8. not *doubletongued,* not given to

διό, dio.

Mat.27: 8. *Wherefore* that field was called,
Lu.　1:35. *therefore* also that holy thing which
　　　 7: 7. *Wherefore* neither thought I myself
Acts10:29. *Therefore* came I (unto you) without
　　　13:35. *Wherefore* he saith also in another
　　　15:19. *Wherefore* my sentence is, that we
　　　20:26. *Wherefore* I take you to record this
　　　　31. *Therefore* watch, and remember, that
　　　24:26. *wherefore* he sent for him the oftener,
　　　25:26. *Wherefore* I have brought him
　　　26: 3. *wherefore* I beseech thee to hear me
　　　27:25. *Wherefore*, sirs, be of good cheer:
　　　　34. *Wherefore* I pray you to take (some)
Ro.　1:24. *Wherefore* God also gave them up to
　　　 2: 1. *Therefore* thou art inexcusable, O man,
　　　 4:22. *therefore* it was imputed to him
　　　13: 5. *Wherefore* (ye) must needs be subject,
　　　15: 7. *Wherefore* receive ye one another,
　　　　22. *For which cause* also I have been
1Co.12: 3. *Wherefore* I give you to understand,
2Co. 2: 8. *Wherefore* I beseech you that ye
　　　 4:13. I believed, *and therefore* have I spoken;
　　　— we also believe, and *therefore* speak;
　　　　16. *For which cause* we faint not;
　　　 5: 9. *Wherefore* we labour, that, whether
　　　 6:17. *Wherefore* come out from among them,
　　　12:10. *Therefore* I take pleasure in infirmities,
Eph. 2:11. *Wherefore* remember, that ye (being)
　　　 3:13. *Wherefore* I desire that ye faint not
　　　 4: 8. *Wherefore* he saith, When he
　　　　25. *Wherefore* putting away lying,
　　　 5:14. *Wherefore* he saith, Awake thou that
Phi.　2: 9. *Wherefore* God also hath highly
1Th. 2:18. *Wherefore* we would have come unto
　　　 3: 1. *Wherefore* when we could no longer
　　　 5:11. *Wherefore* comfort yourselves
Philem. 8. *Wherefore*, though I might be much
Heb. 3: 7. *Wherefore* as the Holy Ghost saith,
　　　　10. *Wherefore* I was grieved with that
　　　 6: 1. *Therefore* leaving the principles
　　　10: 5. *Wherefore* when he cometh into
　　　11:12. *Therefore* sprang there even of one,
　　　　16. *wherefore* God is not ashamed to
　　　12:12. *Wherefore* lift up the hands which
　　　　28. *Wherefore* we receiving a kingdom
　　　13:12. *Wherefore* Jesus also, that he might
Jas.　1:21. *Wherefore* lay apart all filthiness
　　　 4: 6. *Wherefore* he saith, God resisteth
1Pet.1:13. *Wherefore* gird up the loins of your
　　　 2: 6. *Wherefore* also it is contained in
2Pet.1:10. *Wherefore* the rather, brethren,
　　　　12. *Wherefore* I will not be negligent
　　　 3:14. *Wherefore*, beloved, seeing that ye

διοδεύω, dioduo

Lu.　8: 1. he *went throughout* every city and village,
Acts17: 1. *when* they *had passed through* Amphipolis

διόπερ, dioper.

1Co. 8:13. *Wherefore*, if meat make my
　　　10:14. *Wherefore*, my dearly beloved, flee
　　　14:13. *Wherefore* let him that speaketh

διοπετής, diopetees.

Acts19:35. the (image) *which fell down from Jupiter*?

διόρθωσις, diorthōsis.

Heb. 9:10. until the time of *reformation*.

διορύσσω, diorusso.

Mat. 6:19. where thieves *break through* and steal:
　　　　20. where thieves *do* not *break through* nor
　　　　steal:
　　　24:43. suffered his house *to be broken up*.
Lu.　12:39. suffered his house *to be broken through*.

διότι, dioti.

Lu.　1:13. *for* thy prayer is heard; and thy wife
　　　 2: 7. *because* there was no room for them
　　　21:28. *for* your redemption draweth nigh.
Acts10:20. doubting nothing: *for* I have sent them.
　　　17:31. *Because* he hath appointed a day,
　　　18:10. *For* I am with thee, and no man
　　　— *for* I have much people in this city.
　　　22:18. *for* they will not receive thy testimony
Ro.　1:19. *Because* that which may be known
　　　　21. *Because that*, when they knew God,
　　　 3:20. *Therefore* (lit. *because*) by the deeds of the
　　　　law there
　　　 8: 7. *Because* the carnal mind (is) enmity
1Co.15: 9. *because* I persecuted the church of God.
Gal. 2:16. *for* by the works of the law shall no
Phi. 2:26. *because that* ye had heard that he
1Th. 2: 8. *because* ye were dear unto us.
　　　 4: 6. *because that* the Lord (is) the avenger
Heb11: 5. *because* God had translated him:
　　　　23. *because* they saw (he was) a proper
Jas.　4: 3. receive not, *because* ye ask amiss,.
1Pet.1:16. *Because* it is written, Be ye holy;
　　　　24. *For* all flesh (is) as grass, and all

διπλοῦς, diplous.

Mat.23:15. *twofold more* the child of hell than
1Ti.　5:17. be counted worthy of *double* honour,
Rev.18: 6. *double* unto her *double* according to
　　　— which she hath filled fill to her *double*.

διπλόω, diploō.

Rev.18: 6. *double* unto her double according to

δίς, dis.

Mar.14:30. this night, before the cock crow *twice*,
　　　　72. Before the cock crow *twice*, thou shalt
Lu.　18:12. I fast *twice* in the week, I give
Phi.　4:16. sent once and *again* unto my necessity.
1Th. 2:18. even I Paul, once and *again*;
Jude　12. without fruit, *twice* dead, plucked up

διστάζω, distazo.

Mat.14:31. wherefore *didst* thou *doubt*?
　　　28:17. they worshipped him: but some *doubted*.

δίστομος, distomos.

Heb. 4:12. sharper than any *twoedged* sword,

Rev. 1:16. went a sharp *twoedged* sword:
2:12. hath the sharp sword *with two edges ;*

διςχίλιοι, *diskilioi.*

Mar. 5:13. they were about *two thousand ;*

διϋλίζω, *diulizo.*

Mat.23:24. (Ye) blind guides, which *strain at* a gnat,
(lit. *strain out*)

διχάζω, *dikazo.*

Mat.10:35. *to set* a man *at variance* against

διχοστασία, *dikostasia.*

Ro. 16:17. mark them which cause *divisions*
1Co. 3: 3. among you envying, and strife, and *divisions,*
Gal. 5:20. emulations, wrath, strife, *seditions,*

διχοτομέω, *dikotomeo.*

Mat.24:51. *shall cut* him *asunder,* and appoint
Lu. 12:46. *will cut* him *in sunder,* and will appoint

διψάω, *dipsao.*

Mat. 5: 6. which do hunger and *thirst* after righteousness:
25:35. I *was thirsty,* and ye gave me drink:
37. fed (thee)? or *thirsty,* and gave (thee) drink *?*
42. I *was thirsty,* and ye gave me no drink:
44. Lord, when saw we thee an hungred, or *athirst,*
Joh. 4:13. drinketh of this water *shall thirst* again:
14. water that I shall give him *shall* never *thirst ;*
15. give me this water, that I *thirst* not,
6:35. believeth on me shall never *thirst.*
7:37. If any man *thirst,* let him come unto me,
19:28. scripture might be fulfilled, saith, I *thirst.*
Ro. 12:20. feed him ; if he *thirst,* give him drink:
1Co. 4:11. both hunger, and *thirst,* and are naked,
Rev. 7:16. hunger no more, neither *thirst* any more ;
21: 6. I will give unto him *that is athirst*
22:17. let him *that is athirst* come.

δίψος, *dipsos.*

2Co.11:27. in watchings often, in hunger and *thirst,*

δίψυχος, *dipsukos.*

Jas. 1: 8. A *double minded* man (is) unstable
4: 8. purify (your) hearts, (ye) *double minded.*

διωγμός, *diōgmos.*

Mat.13:21. or *persecution* ariseth because of the word,
Mar. 4:17. or *persecution* ariseth for the word's sake,

Mar 10:30. children, and lands, with *persecutions ;*
Acts 8: 1. a great *persecution* against the church
13:50. raised *persecution* against Paul and
Ro. 8:35. distress, or *persecution,* or famine,
2Co.12:10. in necessities, in *persecutions,* in distresses
2Th. 1: 4. faith in all your *persecutions* and tribulations
2Ti. 3:11. *Persecutions,* afflictions, which came
— at Lystra.; what *persecutions* I endured:

διώκτης, *diōktces.*

1Ti. 1:13. a blasphemer, and a *persecutor,* and injurious:

διώκω, *diōko.*

Mat. 5:10. *which* are persecuted for righteousness' sake:
11. when (men) shall revile you, and *persecute* (you),
12. for so *persecuted* they the prophets
44. despitefully use you, and *persecute* you ;
10:23. when they *persecute* you in this city,
23:34. and *persecute* (them) from city to city:
Lu. 17:23. go not after (them), nor *follow* (them).
21:12. lay their hands on you, and *persecute* (you),
Joh. 5:16. therefore did the Jews *persecute* Jesus,
15:20. If they *have persecuted* me, they *will* also *persecute* you ;
Acts 7:52. *have* not your fathers *persecuted ?*
9: 4. Saul, Saul, why *persecutest* thou me?
5. I am Jesus whom thou *persecutest :*
22: 4. I *persecuted* this way unto the death,
7. Saul, Saul, why *persecutest* thou me?
8. Jesus of Nazareth, whom thou *persecutest.*
26:11. I *persecuted* (them) even unto strange cities.
14. Saul, Saul, why *persecutest* thou me?
15. I am Jesus whom thou *persecutest.*
Ro. 9:30. *which followed* not *after* righteousness,
31. Israel, *which followed after* the law
12:13. necessity of saints ; *given to* hospitality.
14. Bless them *which persecute* you:
14:19. therefore *follow after* the things which
1Co. 4:12. *being persecuted,* we suffer it:
14: 1. *Follow after* charity, and desire spiritual
15: 9. because I *persecuted* the church of God
2Co. 4: 9. *Persecuted,* but not forsaken ; cast
Gal. 1:13. beyond measure I *persecuted* the church
23. he *which persecuted* us in times past
4:29. *persecuted* him (that was born) after
5:11. why do I yet *suffer persecution ?*
6:12. should *suffer persecution* for the cross
Phi. 3: 6. Concerning zeal, *persecuting* the church ;
12. I *follow after,* if that I may
14. I *press toward* the mark for the
1Th. 5:15. ever *follow* that which is good.
1Ti. 6:11. *follow after* righteousness, godliness,
2Ti. 2:22. *follow* righteousness, faith, charity,
3:12. in Christ Jesus *shall suffer persecution.*
Heb 12:14. *Follow* peace with all (men), and holiness,
1Pet.3:11. let him seek peace, and *ensue* it.
Rev.12:13. he *persecuted* the woman which

δόγμα, *dogma.*

Lu. 2: 1. there went out a *decree* from Cæsar

Acts16: 4. they delivered them the *decrees* for
17: 7. all do contrary to the *decrees* of Cæsar,
Eph. 2:15. commandments(contained)in *ordinances;*
Col. 2:14. the handwriting of *ordinances* that

δογματίζομαι, *dogmatizomai.*

Col. 2:20. in the world, *are ye subject to ordinances,*

δοκέω, *dokeo.*

NOTE.—In many of the passages the form is that of
the impersonal verb.

Mat. 3: 9. *think* not to say within yourselves,
6: 7. for they *think* that they shall be heard
17:25. saying, What *thinkest* thou, Simon?
18:12. How *think* ye? if a man have
21:28. what *think* ye? A (certain) man had
22:17. Tell us therefore, What *thinkest* thou?
42. Saying, What *think* ye of Christ?
24:44. in such an hour as ye *think* not
26:53. *Thinkest* thou that I cannot now
66. What *think* ye? They answered and said,
Mar. 6:49. they *supposed* it had been a spirit,
10:42. they *which are accounted* to rule over
Lu. 1: 3. It *seemed good* to me also, having
8:18. even that which he *seemeth* to have.
10:36. Which now of these three, *thinkest* thou,
12:40. at an hour when ye *think* not.
51. *Suppose* ye that I am come to give
13: 2. *Suppose* ye that these Galilæans were
4. *think* ye that they were sinners
17: 9. were commanded him? I *trow* not.
19:11. they *thought* that the kingdom of God
22:24. of them *should be accounted* the greatest.
24:37. *supposed* that they had seen a spirit.
Joh. 5:39. in them ye *think* ye have eternal life:
45. Do not *think* that I will accuse
11:13. they *thought* that he had spoken
56. What *think* ye, that he will not come
13:29. For some (of them) *thought,* because
16: 2. *will think* that he doeth God service.
20:15. She, *supposing* him to be the gardener,
Acts12: 9. by the angel; but *thought* he saw a vision.
15:22. Then *pleased* it the apostles
25. It *seemed good* unto us, being
28. For it *seemed good* to the Holy Ghost,
34. it *pleased* Silas to abide there still.
17:18. He *seemeth* to be a setter forth of
25:27. For it *seemeth* to me unreasonable
26: 9. I verily *thought* with myself,
27:13. *supposing* that they had obtained
1Co. 3:18. *seemeth* to be wise in this world,
4: 9. For I *think* that God hath set
7:40. I *think* also that I have the Spirit
8: 2. if any man *think* that he knoweth
10:12. let him *that thinketh* he standeth
11:16. if any man *seem* to be contentious,
12:22. members of the body, *which seem* to be
23. which we *think* to be less honourable,
14:37. If any man *think* himself to be
2Co.10: 9. That I *may* not *seem* as if I would
11:16. *Let* no man *think* me a fool;
12:19. *think* ye that we excuse ourselves
Gal. 2: 2. to them *which were of reputation,*
6. of those *who seemed* to be somewhat,
— for they *who seemed* (to be somewhat)
9. *who seemed* to be pillars, perceived
6: 3. if a man *think* himself to be something,

Phi. 3: 4. If any other man *thinketh* that he
Heb. 4: 1. any of you *should seem* to come
10:29. how much sorer punishment, *suppose* ye,
12:10. chastened (us) after their *own pleasure*
11. the present *seemeth* to be joyous,
Jas. 1:26. If any man among you *seem* to be
4: 5. *Do* ye *think* that the scripture saith

δοκιμάζω, *dokimazo.*

Lu. 12:56. ye can *discern* the face of the sky and
— that ye *do* not *discern* this time?
14:19. five yoke of oxen, and I go *to prove* them:
Ro. 1:28. they *did* not *like* to retain God in (their)
2:18. *approvest* the things that are more
12: 2. that ye may *prove* what (is) that good,
14:22. in that thing which he *alloweth.*
1Co. 3:13. the fire *shall try* every man's work
11:28. *let* a man *examine* himself,
16: 3. whomsoever ye shall *approve* by
2Co. 8: 8. to *prove* the sincerity of your love.
22. whom we *have* oftentimes *proved*
13: 5. in the faith; *prove* your own selves.
Gal. 6: 4. *let* every man *prove* his own work,
Eph. 5:10. *Proving* what is acceptable unto the Lord.
Phi. 1:10. That ye may *approve* things that
1Th. 2: 4. as we *were allowed* of God to be
— God, *which trieth* our hearts.
5:21. *Prove* all things; hold fast that
1Ti. 3:10. *let* these also first *be proved;*
Heb. 3: 9. your fathers tempted me *proved* me,
1Pet.1: 7. *though* it *be tried* with fire,
1Joh.4: 1. *try* the spirits whether they are

δοκιμή, *dokimee.*

Ro. 5: 4. *experience;* and *experience,* hope:
2Co. 2: 9. I might know the *proof* of you,
8: 2. that in a great *trial* of affliction
9:13. by the *experiment* of this ministration
13: 3. Since ye seek a *proof* of Christ
Phi. 2:22. ye know the *proof* of him,

δοκίμιον, *dokimion.*

Jas. 1: 3. the *trying* of your faith worketh
1Pet.1: 7. That the *trial* of your faith, being

δόκιμος, *dokimos.*

Ro. 14:18. acceptable to God, and *approved* of men.
16:10. Salute Appelles *approved* in Christ.
1Co.11:19. they *which are approved* may be
2Co.10:18. he that commendeth himself is *approved,*
13: 7. not that we should appear *approved,*
2Ti. 2:15. Study to shew thyself *approved* unto God,
Jas. 1:12. for when he is *tried,* he shall receive

δοκός, *dokos.*

Mat. 7: 3. considerest not the *beam* that is in
4. behold, a *beam* (is) in thine own eye?
5. first cast out the *beam* out of thine
Lu. 6:41. perceivest not the *beam* that is in
42. beholdest not the *beam* that is in
— cast out first the *beam* out of thine

δόλιος, dolios.

2Co.11:13. false apostles, *deceitful* workers,

δολιόω, dolioō.

Ro.　3:13. with their tongues they *have used deceit;*

δόλος, dolos.

Mat.26: 4. they might take Jesus by *subtilty,*
Mar. 7:22. wickedness, *deceit,* lasciviousness,
　　14: 1. they might take him by *craft,*
Joh. 1:47(48)Israelite indeed, in whom is no *guile!*
Acts13:10. O full of all *subtilty* and all mischief,
Ro.　1:29. full of envy, murder, debate, *deceit,*
2Co.12:16. being crafty, I caught you with *guile.*
1Th. 2: 3. nor of uncleanness, nor in *guile:*
1Pet.2: 1. laying aside all malice, and all *guile,*
　　22. neither was *guile* found in his mouth:
　3:10. his lips that they speak no *guile:*
Rev.14. 5. in their mouth was found no *guile:*

δολόω, doloō.

2Co. 4: 2. nor *handling* the word of God *deceitfully;*

δόμα, doma.

Mat. 7:11. know how to give good *gifts* unto
Lu. 11:13. to give good *gifts* unto your children:
Eph. 4: 8. captivity captive, and gave *gifts* unto men.
Phil. 4:17. Not because I desire a *gift:*

δόξα, doxa.

Mat. 4: 8. of the world, and the *glory* of them;
　6:13. the power, and the *glory,* for ever.
　29. even Solomon in all his *glory* was
　16:27. in the *glory* of his Father with
　19:28. shall sit in the throne of his *glory,*
　24:30. with power and great *glory.*
　25:31. Son of man shall come in his *glory,*
　— sit upon the throne of his *glory:*
Mar. 8:38. cometh in the *glory* of his Father
　10:37. on thy left hand, in thy *glory.*
　13:26. in the clouds with great power and *glory.*
Lu.　2: 9. the *glory* of the Lord shone round
　14. *Glory* to God in the highest, and on
　32. the *glory* of thy people Israel.
　4: 6. will I give thee, and the *glory* of them:
　9:26. when he shall come in his own *glory,*
　31. Who appeared in *glory,* and spake of his
　32. they saw his *glory,* and the two men
　12:27. Solomon in all his *glory* was not
　14:10. then shalt thou have *worship* in the
　17:18. returned to give *glory* to God, save
　19:38. peace in heaven, and *glory* in the highest.
　21:27. in a cloud with power and great *glory.*
　24:26. to enter into his *glory?*
Joh. 1:14. we beheld his *glory,* the *glory* as of the
　2:11. Galilee, and manifested forth his *glory;*
　5:41. I receive not *honour* from men.
　44. which receive *honour* one of another,
　— the *honour* that (cometh) from God only?
　7:18. himself seeketh his own *glory:* ɒut he that
　seeketh his *glory* that sent him,

Joh. 8:50. I seek not mine own *glory:*
　54. If I honour myself, my *honour* is nothing:
　9:24. said unto him, Give God the *praise:*
　11: 4. for the *glory* of God, that the Son
　40. thou shouldest see the *glory* of God?
　12:41. said Esaias, when he saw his *glory,*
　43. they loved the *praise* of men more than the
　praise of God.
　17: 5. with the *glory* which I had
　22. the *glory* which thou gavest me
　24. that they may behold my *glory,*
Acts 7: 2. The God of *glory* appeared unto
　55. saw the *glory* of God, and Jesus
　12:23. because he gave not God the *glory:*
　22:11. for the *glory* of that light, being
Ro.　1:23. the *glory* of the uncorruptible God
　2: 7. in well doing seek for *glory* and honour
　10. *glory,* honour, and peace, to every man
　3: 7. through my lie unto his *glory;*
　23. come short of the *glory* of God;
　4:20. was strong in faith, giving *glory* to God;
　5: 2. rejoice in hope of the *glory* of God.
　6: 4. by the *glory* of the Father,
　8:18. the *glory* which shall be revealed
　21. into the *glorious* liberty (lit. liberty of the
　glory) of the children of God.
　9: 4. the adoption, and the *glory,* and the
　covenants,
　23. make known the riches of his *glory* on
　— had afore prepared unto *glory,*
　11:36. to whom (be) *glory* for ever.
　15: 7. received us to the *glory* of God.
　16:27. To God only wise, (be) *glory* through
1Co. 2: 7. before the world unto our *glory:*
　8. not have crucified the Lord of *glory.*
　10:31. do all to the *glory* of God.
　11: 7. as he is the image and *glory* of God: but
　the woman is the *glory* of the man.
　15. have long hair, it is a *glory* to her:
　15:40. the *glory* of the celestial (is) one, and the
　41. one *glory* of the sun, and another *glory* of
　— another *glory* of the stars: for (one) star
　differeth from (another) star in *glory.*
　43. sown in dishonour; it is raised in *glory:*
2Co. 1:20. unto the *glory* of God by us.
　3: 7. engraven in stones, was *glorious,* (lit. in
　glory)
　— for the *glory* of his countenance;
　8. ministration of the spirit be rather *glorious?*
　(lit. in *glory*)
　9. ministration of condemnation (be) *glory,*
　— of righteousness exceed in *glory.*
　10. by reason of the *glory* that excelleth.
　11. which is done away (was) *glorious* (lit.
　through *glory*), much more that which
　remaineth (is) *glorious.* (lit. in *glory*)
　18. as in a glass the *glory* of the Lord,
　— the same image from *glory* to *glory,*
　4: 4. the light of the *glorious* gospel of Christ,
　(lit. gospel of the *glory*)
　6. the knowledge of the *glory* of God
　15. redound to the *glory* of God.
　17. exceeding (and) eternal weight of *glory;*
　6: 8. By *honour* and dishonour, by evil
　8:19. to the *glory* of the same Lord,
　23. messengers of the churches, (and) the
　glory of Christ.
Gal. 1: 5. To whom (be) *glory* for ever and ever.
Eph. 1: 6. To the praise of the *glory* of his grace,
　12. should be to the praise of his *glory,*
　14. unto the praise of his *glory.*
　17. the Father of *glory,* may give unto

Eph. 1:18. the riches of the *glory* of his inheritance

3:13. tribulations for you, which is your *glory*.

16. according to the riches of his *glory*,

21. Unto him (be) *glory* in the church

Phi. 1:11. unto the *glory* and praise of God.

2:11. to the *glory* of God the Father.

3:19. (whose) *glory* (is) in their shame,

21. fashioned like unto his *glorious* body, (lit. the body of his *glory*)

4:19. his riches in *glory* by Christ Jesus.

20. our Father (be) *glory* for ever and ever.

Col. 1:11. according to his *glorious* power, (lit. power of his *glory*)

27. the riches of the *glory* of this mystery

— Christ in you, the hope of *glory*:

3: 4. shall ye also appear with him in *glory*.

1Th. 2: 6. Nor of men sought we *glory*,

12. called you unto his kingdom and *glory*.

20. For ye are our *glory* and joy.

2Th. 1: 9. from the *glory* of his power;

2:14. the *glory* of our Lord Jesus Christ.

1Ti. 1:11. According to the *glorious* gospel (lit. gospel of the *glory*) of

17. (be) honour and *glory* for ever and ever.

3:16. in the world, received up into *glory*.

2Ti. 2:10. in Christ Jesus with eternal *glory*.

4:18. to whom (be) *glory* for ever and ever.

Tit. 2:13. the *glorious* appearing (lit. appearing of the *glory*) of the great God

Heb. 1: 3. Who being the brightness of (his) *glory*,

2: 7. thou crownedst him with *glory*

9. the suffering of death, crowned with *glory*,

10. in bringing many sons unto *glory*,

3: 3. counted worthy of more *glory* than Moses,

9: 5. over it the cherubims of *glory*

13:21. to whom (be) *glory* for ever and ever.

Jas. 2: 1. our Lord Jesus Christ, (the Lord) of *glory*,

1Pet. 1: 7. praise and honour and *glory* at the appearing

11. the *glory* (lit. *glories*) that should follow

21. up from the dead, and gave him *glory*;

24. the *glory* of man as the flower of grass.

4:11. to whom be *praise* and dominion for ever

13. when his *glory* shall be revealed,

14. for the spirit of *glory* and of God resteth

5: 1. a partaker of the *glory* that shall be

4. ye shall receive a crown of *glory*

10. hath called us unto his eternal *glory*

11. To him (be) *glory* and dominion for ever

2Pet. 1: 3. hath called us to *glory* and virtue:

17. from God the Father honour and *glory*,

— a voice to him from the excellent *glory*,

2:10. not afraid to speak evil of *dignities*.

3:18. To him (be) *glory* both now and for ever.

Jude 8. speak evil of *dignities*.

24. faultless before the presence of his *glory*

25. God our Saviour, (be) *glory* and majesty,

Rev. 1: 6. to him (be) *glory* and dominion for ever

4: 9. when those beasts give *glory* and honour

11. to receive *glory* and honour and power:

5:12. strength, and honour, and *glory*, and blessing.

13. Blessing, and honour, and *glory*, and power,

7:12. Saying, Amen: Blessing, and *glory*,

11:13. gave *glory* to the God of heaven.

14: 7. Fear God, and give *glory* to him;

15: 8. with smoke from the *glory* of God,

16: 9. they repented not to give him *glory*.

18: 1. the earth was lightened with his *glory*.

19: 1. Salvation, and *glory*, and honour, and power,

7. be glad and rejoice, and give *honour* to him:

Rev. 21:11. Having the *glory* of God: and her

23. the *glory* of God did lighten it,

24. do bring their *glory* and honour into it.

26. they shall bring the *glory* and honour

δοξάζω, *doxazo*.

Mat. 5:16. may see your good works, and *glorify*

6: 2. that they *may have glory* of men.

9: 8. they marvelled, and *glorified* God,

15:31. they *glorified* the God of Israel.

Mar. 2:12. were all amazed, and *glorified* God,

Lu. 2:20. *glorifying* and praising God for all

4:15. *being glorified* of all.

5:25. to his own house, *glorifying* God.

26. were all amazed, and they *glorified* God,

7:16. they *glorified* God, saying,

13:13. she was made straight, and *glorified* God.

17:15. *and* with a loud voice *glorified* God,

18:43. followed him, *glorifying*:

23:47. saw what was done, he *glorified* God,

Joh. 7:39. because that Jesus *was* not yet *glorified*.

8:54. If I *honour* myself, my honour is nothing: it is my Father *that honoureth* me;

11: 4. the Son of God *might be glorified*

12:16. when Jesus *was glorified*, then

23. the Son of man *should be glorified*.

28. Father, *glorify* thy name.

— I *have* both *glorified* (it), and *will glorify* (it)

13:31. Now *is* the Son of man *glorified*, and God *is glorified* in him.

32. If God *be glorified* in him, God *shall* also *glorify* him in himself, and *shall* straightway *glorify* him.

14:13. the Father *may be glorified* in the Son.

15: 8. Herein *is* my Father *glorified*,

16:14. He *shall glorify* me: for he

17: 1. *glorify* thy Son, that thy Son also *may glorify* thee:

4. I *have glorified* thee on the earth:

5. O Father, *glorify* thou me with

10. I *am glorified* in them.

21:19. by what death he should *glorify* God.

Acts 3:13. *hath glorified* his Son Jesus;

4:21. for all (men) *glorified* God for that

11:18. held their peace, and *glorified* God,

13:48. *glorified* the word of the Lord:

21:20. they *glorified* the Lord, and said

Ro. 1:21. they *glorified* (him) not as God,

8:30. justified, them he also *glorified*.

11:13. I *magnify* mine office:

15: 6. with one mind (and) one mouth *glorify* God,

9. the Gentiles might *glorify* God

1Co. 6:20. therefore *glorify* God in your body,

12:26. or one member *be honoured*, all

2Co. 3:10. that *which was made glorious had* no glory in this respect,

9:13. *Whiles*...they *glorify* God for your professed

Gal. 1:24. they *glorified* God in me.

2Th. 3: 1. *be glorified*, even as (it is) with you:

Heb 5: 5. Christ *glorified* not himself

1Pet. 1: 8. joy unspeakable and *full of glory*:

2:12. they *may*...*glorify* God in the day of visitation.

4:11. *may be glorified* through Jesus Christ,

14. on your part he *is glorified*.

16. *let* him *glorify* God on this behalf.

Rev. 15: 4. Who shall not fear thee, O Lord, and *glorify* thy name?

Rev.18: 7. How much she *hath glorified* herself,

δόσις, *dosis.*

Phi. 4:15. concerning *giving* and receiving, but
Jas. 1:17. Every good *gift* (lit. *giving*) and every
　　　　perfect gift is

δότης, *dotees.*

2Co. 9: 7. for God loveth a cheerful *giver.*

δουλαγωγέω, *doulagōgeo.*

1Co. 9:27. under my body, and *bring* (it) *into subjection:*

δουλεία, *doulīa.*

Ro. 8:15. received the spirit of *bondage* again
　　21. shall be delivered from the *bondage* of
Gal. 4:24. which gendereth to *bondage,*
　　5: 1. again with the yoke of *bondage.*
Heb 2:15. all their lifetime subject to *bondage.*

δουλεύω, *doulŭo.*

Mat. 6:24. No man can *serve* two masters:
　　　— Ye cannot *serve* God and mammon.
Lu. 15:29. these many years *do* I *serve* thee,
　　16:13. No servant can *serve* two masters:
　　　— Ye cannot *serve* God and mammon.
Joh. 8:33. *were* never *in bondage* to any
Acts 7: 7. to whom they *shall be in bondage*
　　20:19. *Serving* the Lord with all humility
Ro. 6: 6. henceforth we should not *serve* sin.
　　7: 6. we should *serve* in newness of spirit,
　　25. I myself *serve* the law of God;
　　9:12. The elder *shall serve* the younger.
　　12:11. fervent in spirit; *serving* the Lord;
　　14:18. *that* in these things *serveth* Christ
　　16:18. such *serve* not our Lord Jesus Christ,
Gal. 4: 8. ye *did service* unto them which
　　9. ye desire again *to be in bondage?*
　　25. *is in bondage* with her children.
　　5:13. by love *serve* one another.
Eph. 6: 7. With good will *doing service,* as to
Phi. 2:22. he *hath served* with me in the gospel.
Col. 3:24. for ye *serve* the Lord Christ.
1Th. 1: 9. *to serve* the living and true God;
1Ti. 6: 2. *let* them not...but rather *do* (them) *service,*
Tit. 3: 3. *serving* divers lusts and pleasures, living

δούλη, *doulee.*

Lu. 1:38. Behold the *handmaid* of the Lord;
　　48. regarded the low estate of his *handmaiden*:
Acts 2:18. on my servants and on my *handmaidens*

δοῦλον, *doulon.*

Ro. 6:19. yielded your members *servants* to
　　　— your members *servants* to righteousness

δοῦλος, *doulos.*

Mat. 8: 9. to my *servant,* Do this, and he doeth (it).
　　10:24. nor the *servant* above his lord.
　　25. as his master, and the *servant* as his lord.
　　13:27. the *servants* of the housholder came
　　28. The *servants* said unto him, Wilt thou
　　18:23. which would take account of his *servants*
　　26. The *servant* therefore fell down,
　　27. the lord of that *servant* was moved
　　28. the same *servant* went out, and found
　　32. O thou wicked *servant,* I forgave thee
　　20:27. chief among you, let him be your *servant*:
　　21.34. sent his *servants* to the husbandmen,
　　35. the husbandmen took his *servants,*
　　36. Again, he sent other *servants* more
　　22: 3. sent forth his *servants* to call
　　4. Again, he sent forth other *servants,*
　　6. the remnant took his *servants,*
　　8. Then saith he to his *servants,*
　　10. those *servants* went out into the
　　24:45. Who then is a faithful and wise *servant,*
　　46. Blessed (is) that *servant,* whom his lord
　　48. if that evil *servant* shall say
　　50. The lord of that *servant* shall come
　　25:14. called his own *servants,* and delivered
　　19. the lord of those *servants* cometh,
　　21. Well done, (thou) good and faithful *servant*:
　　23. Well done, good and faithful *servant*;
　　26. (Thou) wicked and slothful *servant,*
　　30. cast ye the unprofitable *servant* into
　　26:51. drew his sword, and struck a *servant*
Mar 10:44. the chiefest, shall be *servant* of all.
　　12: 2. sent to the husbandmen a *servant,*
　　4. he sent unto them another *servant*;
　　13:34. gave authority to his *servants,*
　　14:47. smote a *servant* of the high priest,
Lu. 2:29. now lettest thou thy *servant* depart in peace,
　　7: 2. a certain centurion's *servant,* who was
　　3. that he would come and heal his *servant.*
　　8. to my *servant,* Do this, and he doeth (it).
　　10. found the *servant* whole that had
　　12:37. Blessed (are) those *servants,* whom
　　38. find (them) so, blessed are those *servants.*
　　43. Blessed (is) that *servant,* whom his
　　45. if that *servant* say in his heart,
　　46. The lord of that *servant* will come
　　47. that *servant,* which knew his lord's will,
　　14:17. sent his *servant* at supper time
　　21. So that *servant* came, and shewed his lord
　　　— said to his *servant,* Go out quickly into
　　22. the *servant* said, Lord, it is done
　　23. the lord said unto the *servant,*
　　15:22. the father said to his *servants,*
　　17: 7. which of you, having a *servant* plowing
　　9. Doth he thank that *servant* because
　　10. say, We are unprofitable *servants*:
　　19:13. he called his ten *servants,* and delivered
　　15. commanded these *servants* to be called
　　17. said unto him, Well, thou good *servant*:
　　22. will I judge thee, (thou) wicked *servant.*
　　20:10. sent a *servant* to the husbandmen,
　　11. again he sent another *servant*:
　　22:50. smote the *servant* of the high priest,
Joh. 4:51. going down, his *servants* met him,
　　8:34. Whosoever committeth sin is the *servant*
　　35. the *servant* abideth not in the house
　　13:16. The *servant* is not greater than his lord;
　　15:15. I call you not *servants*; for the *servant*

Joh.15:20. The *servant* is not greater than his lord.
18:10. drew it, and smote the high priest's *servant*,
— The *servant's* name was Malchus.
18. the *servants* and officers stood there,
26. One of the *servants* of the high priest,
Acts 2:18. on my *servants* and on my handmaidens.
4:29. grant unto thy *servants*, that with
16:17. the *servants* of the most high God,
Ro. 1: 1. Paul, a *servant* of Jesus Christ, called
6:16. yield yourselves *servants* to obey, his *servants* ye are to whom ye obey;
17. that ye were the *servants* of sin,
20. when ye were the *servants* of sin,
1Co. 7:21. Art thou called (being) a *servant?*
22. (being) a *servant*, is the Lord's freeman:
— (being) free, is Christ's *servant*.
23. be not ye the *servants* of men.
12:13. whether (we be) *bond* or free; and have
2Co. 4: 5. ourselves your *servants* for Jesus' sake.
Gal. 1:10. I should not be the *servant* of Christ.
3:28. there is neither *bond* nor free, there
4: 1. a child, differeth nothing from a *servant*,
7. Wherefore thou art no more a *servant*,
Eph. 6: 5. *Servants*, be obedient to them that
6. as the *servants* of Christ, doing the
8. whether (he be) *bond* or free.
Phi. 1: 1. the *servants* of Jesus Christ, to all
2: 7. took upon him the form of a *servant*,
Col. 3:11. Barbarian, Scythian, *bond* (nor) free:
22. *Servants*, obey in all things (your)
4: 1. give unto (your) *servants* that which
12. a *servant* of Christ, saluteth you,
1Ti. 6: 1. many *servants* as are under the yoke
2Ti. 2:24. the *servant* of the Lord must not strive;
Tit. 1: 1. Paul, a *servant* of God, and an apostle
2: 9. (Exhort) *servants* to be obedient
Philem.16. Not now as a *servant*, but above a *servant*,
Jas. 1: 1. a *servant* of God and of the Lord Jesus Christ,
1Pet.2:16. but as the *servants* of God.
2Pet.1: 1. a *servant* and an apostle of Jesus Christ,
2:19. themselves are the *servants* of corruption:
Jude 1. Jude, the *servant* of Jesus Christ,
Rev. 1: 1. to shew unto his *servants* things
— by his angel unto his *servant* John:
2:20. to teach and to seduce my *servants*
6:15. the mighty men, and every *bondman*,
7: 3. have sealed the *servants* of our God
10: 7. declared to his *servants* the prophets.
11:18. shouldest give reward unto thy *servants*
13:16. rich and poor, free and *bond*, to receive
15: 3. the song of Moses the *servant* of God,
19: 2. avenged the blood of his *servants* at
5. Praise our God, all ye his *servants*,
18. flesh of all (men, both) free and *bond*,
22: 3. his *servants* shall serve him:
6. to shew unto his *servants* the things

δουλόω, douloō.

Acts 7: 6. they should *bring* them *into bondage*,
Ro. 6:18. ye *became* the *servants* of righteousness.
22. and *become servants* to God, ye have
1Co. 7:15. *is* not *under bondage* in such (cases):
9:19. have I *made* myself *servant* unto all,
Gal. 4: 3. were *in bondage* under the elements
Tit. 2: 3. not *given* to much wine, teachers
2Pet. 2:19. of the same *is* he *brought in bondage*.

δοχή, dokee.

Lu. 5:29. Levi made him a great *feast* in his
14:13. when thou makest a *feast*, call the poor,

δράκων, drakōn.

Rev.12: 3. behold a great red *dragon*, having
4. the *dragon* stood before the woman
7. his angels fought against the *dragon*; and the *dragon* fought and his angels,
9. the great *dragon* was cast out, that
13. when the *dragon* saw that he was
16. the flood which the *dragon* cast out
17. the *dragon* was wroth with the woman,
13: 2. the *dragon* gave him his power,
4. they worshipped the *dragon* which
11. like a lamb, and he spake as a *dragon*.
16:13. out of the mouth of the *dragon*,
20: 2. he laid hold on the *dragon*, that old

δράσσομαι, drassomai.

1Co. 3:19. He *taketh* the wise in their own craftiness.

δραχμή, drakmee.

Lu. 15: 8. what woman having ten *pieces of silver*, if she lose one *piece*, (lit. *drachma*)
9. I have found the *piece* which I had lost.

δρέμω see τρέχω.

δρέπανον, drepanon.

Mar 4:29. immediately he putteth in the *sickle*,
Rev.14:14. in his hand a sharp *sickle*.
15. Thrust in thy *sickle*, and reap:
16. thrust in his *sickle* on the earth;
17. he also having a sharp *sickle*.
18. to him that had the sharp *sickle*, saying, Thrust in thy sharp *sickle*,
19. the angel thrust in his *sickle*

δρόμος, dromos.

Acts13:25. as John fulfilled his *course*, he said,
20:24. that I might finish my *course* with joy,
2Ti. 4: 7. I have finished (my) *course*, I have

δῦμι see δύνω.

δύναμαι, dunamai.

Mat. 3: 9. God *is able* of these stones to raise up
5:14. A city that is set on an hill *cannot* be hid.
36. thou *canst* not make one hair white
6:24. No man *can* serve two masters:
— Ye *cannot* serve God and mammon.
27. by taking thought *can* add one cubit
7:18. A good tree *cannot* bring forth evil
8: 2. if thou wilt, thou *canst* make me clean.

Mat. 9:15. *Can* the children of the bridechamber
28. Believe ye that I *am able* to do this?
10:28. but *are* not *able* to kill the soul:
— fear him *which is able* to destroy both
12:29. how *can* one enter into a strong man's
34. how *can* ye, being evil, speak good things?
16: 3. *can* ye not (discern) the signs of the times?
17:16. thy disciples, and they *could* not cure him.
19. Why *could* not we cast him out?
19:12. He *that is able* to receive (it), let him
25. saying, Who then *can* be saved?
20:22. *Are* ye *able* to drink of the cup that
— They say unto him, We *are able.*
22:46. no man *was able* to answer him
26: 9. this ointment *might* have been sold
42. if this cup *may* not pass away from me,
53. that I *cannot* now pray to my Father,
61. said, I *am able* to destroy the temple
27:42. He saved others; himself he *cannot* save.
Mar 1:40. If thou wilt, thou *canst* make me clean.
45. that Jesus *could* no more openly enter
2: 4. *when* they *could* not come nigh unto
7. who *can* forgive sins but God only?
19. *Can* the children of the bridechamber
— bridegroom with them, they *cannot* fast.
3:20. they *could* not so much as eat bread.
23. How *can* Satan cast out Satan?
24. that kingdom *cannot* stand.
25. against itself, that house *cannot* stand.
26. he *cannot* stand, but hath an end.
27. No man *can* enter into a strong
4:32. the fowls of the air *may* lodge under
33. as they *were able* to hear (it).
5: 3. no man *could* bind him, no,
6: 5. he *could* there do no mighty work,
19. would have killed him; but she *could* not:
7:15. that entering into him *can* defile him:
18. into the man, (it) *cannot* defile him;
24. know (it): but he *could* not be hid.
8: 4. whence *can* a man satisfy these
9: 3. as no fuller on earth *can* white them.
22. if thou *canst do* any thing, have
23. If thou *canst* believe, all things
28. Why *could* not we cast him out?
29. This kind *can* come forth by nothing,
39. that *can* lightly speak evil of me.
10:26. Who then *can* be saved?
38. *can* ye drink of the cup that I
39. they said unto him, We *can.*
14: 5. it *might* have been sold for
7. whensoever ye will ye *may* do them good:
15:31. He saved others; himself he *cannot* save.
Lu. 1:20. thou shalt be dumb, *and* not *able* to speak,
22. he *could* not speak unto them:
3: 8. God *is able* of these stones to raise up
5:12. if thou wilt, thou *canst* make me clean.
21. Who *can* forgive sins, but God alone?
34. *Can* ye make the children of the
6:39. *Can* the blind lead the blind?
42. how *canst* thou say to thy brother,
8:19. *could* not come at him for the press.
9:40. to cast him out; and they *could* not.
11: 7. I *cannot* rise and give thee.
12:25. taking thought *can* add to his stature
26. If ye then *be* not *able* to do that
13:11. and *could* in no wise lift up (herself).
14:20. married a wife, and therefore I *cannot* come.
26. own life also, he *cannot* be my disciple.
27. come after me, *cannot* be my disciple.
33. he hath, he *cannot* be my disciple.

Lu. 16: 2. for thou *mayest* be no longer steward.
13. No servant *can* serve two masters:
— Ye *cannot* serve God and mammon.
26. so that they which would pass...*cannot;*
18:26. Who then *can* be saved?
19: 3. *could* not for the press, because he
20:36. Neither *can* they die any more:
21:15. shall *not be able* to gainsay nor resist.
Joh. 1:46(47). *Can* there any good thing come
3: 2. for no man *can* do these miracles
3. he *cannot* see the kingdom of God.
4. How *can* a man be born when he is old?
can he enter the second time into
5. he *cannot* enter into the kingdom of God.
9. How *can* these things be?
27. A man *can* receive nothing, except it be
5:19. The Son *can* do nothing of himself,
30. I *can* of mine own self do nothing:
44. How *can* ye believe, which receive
6:44. No man *can* come to me, except
52. How *can* this man give us (his) flesh
60. an hard saying; who *can* hear it?
65. that no man *can* come unto me,
7: 7. The world *cannot* hate you; but me
34. where I am, (thither) ye *cannot* come.
36. where I am, (thither) ye *cannot* come?
8:21. whither I go, ye *cannot* come.
22. saith, Whither I go, ye *cannot* come.
43. because ye *cannot* hear my word.
9: 4. night cometh, when no man *can* work.
16. How *can* a man that is a sinner do
33. were not of God, he *could* do nothing.
10:21. *Can* a devil open the eyes of the blind?
29. no (man) *is able* to pluck (them) out of
35. the scripture *cannot* be broken;
11:37. *Could* not this man, which opened
12:39. Therefore they *could* not believe,
13:33. Whither I go, ye *cannot* come;
36. Whither I go, thou *canst* not follow me
37. Lord, why *cannot* I follow thee now?
14: 5. how *can* we know the way?
17. whom the world *cannot* receive,
15: 4. the branch *cannot* bear fruit of itself,
5. without me ye *can* do nothing.
16:12. ye *cannot* bear them now.
Acts 4:16. in Jerusalem; and we *cannot* deny (it).
20. For we *cannot* but speak the things
5:39. be of God, ye *cannot* overthrow it; lest
8:31. How *can* I, except some man should
10:47. *Can* any man forbid water, that
13:39. from which ye *could* not be justified by
15: 1. the manner of Moses, ye *cannot* be saved.
17:19. *May* we know what this new
19:40. we *may* give an account of this concourse.
20:32. to the word of his grace, *which is able* to
21:34. *when* he *could* not know the certainty
24: 8. thyself *mayest* take knowledge of all
11. *Because that* thou *mayest* understand,
13. Neither *can* they prove the things
25:11. no man *may* deliver me unto them.
26:32. This man *might* have been set at liberty,
27:12. if by any means they *might* attain
15. *And when* the ship...*could* not bear up
31. abide in the ship, ye *cannot* be saved.
39. if it *were possible,* to thrust in the ship.
43. they *which could* swim should
Ro. 8: 7. law of God, neither indeed *can* be.
8. they that are in the flesh *cannot* please
39. creature, *shall be able* to separate
15:14. *able* also to admonish one another.
16:25. to him *that is of power* to stablish you

1Co. 2:14. neither *can* he know (them), because
3: 1. I, brethren, *could* not speak unto you
  2. hitherto ye *were* ·not *able* (to bear it),
     neither yet now *are* ye *able*.
  11. other foundation *can* no man lay
6: 5. not one that *shall be able* to judge
7:21. if thou *mayest* be made free,
10:13. tempted above that ye *are able;*
  — that ye may *be able* to bear (it).
  21. Ye *cannot* drink the cup of the Lord,
  — ye *cannot* be partakers of the Lord's table,
12: 3. (that) no man *can* say that Jesus
  21. the eye *cannot* say unto the hand,
14:31. ye *may* all prophesy one by one,
15:50. flesh and blood *cannot* inherit the
2Co. 1: 4. we may *be able* to comfort them
3: 7. *could* not stedfastly behold the face
13: 8. we *can do* nothing against the truth
Gal. 3:21. a law given *which could* have given
Eph. 3: 4. when ye read, ye *may* understand
  20. Now unto him *that is able* to do
6:11. that ye may *be able* to stand against
  13. that ye *may* be *able* to withstand in
  16. wherewith ye *shall be able* to quench
Phi. 3:21. whereby he *is able* even to subdue all
1Th. 2: 6. *when* we *might* have been burdensome,
3: 9. what thanks *can* we render to God
1Ti. 5:25. they that are otherwise *cannot* be hid.
6: 7. certain we *can* carry nothing out.
  16. whom no man hath seen, nor *can* see:
2Ti. 2:13. faithful: he *cannot* deny himself.
3: 7. and never *able* to come to the knowledge
  15. scriptures, *which are able* to make thee
     wise
Heb. 2:18. he *is able* to succour them that are
3:19. we see that they *could* not enter in
4:15. an high priest *which cannot* be touched
5: 2. *Who can* have compassion on the
  7. unto him *that was able* to save him
7:25. Wherefore he *is able* also to save them to
9: 9. sacrifices, *that could* not make him that
10: 1. *can* never with those sacrifices
  11. which *can* never take away sins:
Jas. 1:21. word, *which is able* to save your souls.
2:14. have not works? *can* faith save him?
3: 8. the tongue *can* no man tame;
  12. *Can* the fig tree, my brethren,
4: 2. desire to have, and *cannot* obtain:
  12. lawgiver, *who is able* to save and to
1Joh.3: 9. he *cannot* sin, because he is born of God.
4:20. how *can* he love God whom he
Jude   24. Now unto him *that is able* to keep
Rev. 2: 2. how thou *canst* not bear them
3: 8. an open door, and no man *can* shut it:
5: 3. *was able* to open the book, neither
6:17. who shall be *able* to stand?
7: 9. multitude, which no man *could* number,
9:20. which neither *can* see, nor hear,
13: 4. who *is able* to make war with him?
  17. that no man *might* buy or sell,
14: 3. no man *could* learn that song
15: 8. no man *was able* to enter into

δύναμις, *dunamis.*

Mat. 6:13. thine is the kingdom, and the *power,*
7:22. in thy name done many *wonderful works?*
11:20. most of his *mighty works* were done,
  21. for if the *mighty works,* which were
  23. if the *mighty works,* which have been

Mat.13:54. this wisdom, and (these) *mighty works?*
  58. he did not many *mighty works* there be-
     cause of their unbelief.
14: 2. therefore *mighty works* do shew forth
22:29. the scriptures, nor the *power* of God.
24:29. the *powers* of the heavens shall be shaken:
  30. with *power* and great glory.
25:15. according to his several *ability;*
26:64. sitting on the right hand of *power,*
Mar. 5:30. that *virtue* had gone out of him,
6: 2. even such *mighty works* are wrought
  5. could there do no *mighty work,*
  14. therefore *mighty works* do shew forth
9: 1. kingdom of God come with *power.*
  39. no man which shall do a *miracle*
12:24. the scriptures, neither the *power* of God?
13:25. the *powers* that are in heaven shall
  26. in the clouds with great *power* and glory.
14:62. sitting on the right hand of *power,*
Lu. 1:17. in the spirit and *power* of Elias, to
  35. the *power* of the Highest shall overshadow
     thee:
4:14. Jesus returned in the *power* of the Spirit
  36. with authority and *power* he commandeth
5:17. the *power* of the Lord was (present) to
     heal
6:19. for there went *virtue* out of him,
8:46. I perceive that *virtue* is gone out of me.
9: 1. gave them *power* and authority over all
10:13. if the *mighty works* had been done
  19. over all the *power* of the enemy:
19:37. the *mighty works* that they had seen;
21:26. the *powers* of heaven shall be shaken.
  27. in a cloud with *power* and great glory.
22:69. the right hand of the *power* of God.
24:49. until ye be endued with *power*
Acts 1: 8. ye shall receive *power,* after that
2:22. by *miracles* and wonders and signs,
3:12. as though by our own *power* or
4: 7. By what *power,* or by what name,
  33. with great *power* gave the apostles
6: 8. Stephen, full of faith and *power,*
8:10. This man is the great *power* of God.
  13. the *miracles* and signs which were done.
10:38. with the Holy Ghost and with *power:*
19:11. God wrought special *miracles*
Ro. 1: 4. (to be) the Son of God with *power,*
  16. for it is the *power* of God unto
  20. (even) his eternal *power* and Godhead;
8:38. nor principalities, nor *powers,*
9:17. that I might shew my *power*
15:13. through the *power* of the Holy Ghost.
  19. through mighty (lit. by the *power* of)
     signs and wonders, by the *power* of
1Co. 1:18. saved it is the *power* of God.
  24. Christ the *power* of God, and the wisdom
2: 4. demonstration of the Spirit and of *power:*
  5. in the *power* of God.
4:19. which are puffed up, but the *power.*
  20. not in word, but in *power.*
5: 4. with the *power* of our Lord Jesus Christ,
6:14. raise up us by his own *power.*
12:10. To another the working of *miracles;*
  28. thirdly teachers, after that *miracles,*
  29. (are) all *workers of miracles?*
14:11. know not the *meaning* of the voice,
15:24. all rule and all authority and *power.*
  43. in weakness; it is raised in *power:*
  56. the *strength* of sin (is) the law.
2Co. 1: 8. pressed out of measure, above *strength,*
4: 7. excellency of the *power* may be of God,
6: 7. word of truth, by the *power* of God,

2Co. 8: 3. For to (their) *power*, I bear record, yea, and beyond (their) *power* (they were) willing of themselves;

12: 9. for my *strength* is made perfect

— the *power* of Christ may rest upon me.

12. signs, and wonders, and *mighty deeds*.

13: 4. he liveth by the *power* of God.

— by the *power* of God toward·you.

Gal. 3: 5. worketh *miracles* among you,

Eph. 1:19. the exceeding greatness of his *power*

21. all principality, and power, and *might*,

3: 7. the effectual working of his *power*.

16. be strengthened with *might* by

20. according to the *power* that worketh

Phi. 3:10. the *power* of his resurrection, and the

Col. 1:11. Strengthened with all *might*,

29. which worketh in me *mightily*.

1Th. 1: 5. in word only, but also in *power*,

2Th. 1: 7. from heaven with his *mighty* angels, (lit. angels of *power* of him)

11. the work of faith with *power*:

2: 9. with all *power* and signs and lying

2Ti. 1: 7. of *power*, and of love, and of a sound mind.

8. according to the *power* of God;

3: 5. godliness, but denying the *power*

Heb. 1: 3. all things by the word of his *power*,

2: 4. signs and wonders, and with divers *miracles*,

6: 5. the *powers* of the world to come,

7:16. after the *power* of an endless life.

11:11. received *strength* to conceive seed,

34. Quenched the *violence* of fire,

1Pet.1: 5. Who are kept by the *power* of God

3:22. authorities and *powers* being made

2Pet.1: 3. According as his divine *power*

16. the *power* and coming of our Lord

2:11. which are greater in power and *might*,

Rev. 1:16. as the sun shineth in his *strength*.

3: 8. for thou hast a little *strength*,

4:11. to receive glory and honour and *power*:

5:12. to receive *power*, and riches, and wisdom,

7:12. honour, and *power*, and might, (be) unto

11:17. hast taken to thee thy great *power*,

12:10. Now is come salvation, and *strength*,

13: 2. the dragon gave him his *power*,

15: 8. the glory of God, and from his *power*;

17:13. shall give their *power* and strength unto

18: 3. the *abundance* of her delicacies.

19: 1. honour, and *power*, unto the Lord our God:

δυναμόω, *dunamoō*.

Col. 1:11. *Strengthened* with all might,

δυνάστης, *dunastees*.

Lu. 1:52. hath put down the *mighty* from (their) seats,

Acts 8:27. an eunuch *of great authority* under Candace

1Ti. 6:15. (who is) the blessed and only *Potentate*,

δυνατέω, *dunateo*.

2Co.13: 3. is not weak, but *is mighty* in you.

δυνατός, *dunatos*.

Mat.19:26. with God all things are *possible*.

24:24. insomuch that, if (it were) *possible*,

26:39. O my Father, if it be *possible*, let this

Mar. 9:23. all things (are) *possible* to him that believeth.

10:27. with God all things are *possible*.

13:22. if (it were) *possible*, even the elect.

14:35. if it were *possible*, the hour might pass

36. Father, all things (are) *possible* unto thee;

Lu. 1:49. he *that is mighty* hath done to me

14:31. whether he be *able* with ten thousand

18:27. impossible with men are *possible* with God.

24:19. a prophet *mighty* in deed and word

Acts 2:24. it was not *possible* that he should

7:22. was *mighty* in words and in deeds.

11:17. that I *could* (lit. should be *able*) withstand God?

18:24. an eloquent man, (and) *mighty* in the scriptures,

20:16. he hasted, if it were *possible* for him,

25: 5. said he, which among you are *able*,

Ro. 4:21. promised, he was *able* also to perform.

9:22. (his) wrath, and to make his *power* known,

11:23. for God is *able* to graff them in again.

12:18. if it be *possible*, as much as lieth in you,

14: 4. for God is *able* to make him stand.

15: 1. We then that are *strong* ought to

1Co. 1:26. not many *mighty*, not many noble,

2Co. 9: 8. God (is) *able* to make all grace abound

10: 4. *mighty* through God to the pulling down

12:10. for when I am weak, then am I *strong*.

13: 9. when we are weak, and ye are *strong*:

Gal. 4:15. that, if (it had been) *possible*, ye would

2Ti. 1:12. persuaded that he is *able* to keep

Tit. 1: 9. he may be *able* by sound doctrine

Heb 11:19. that God (was) *able* to raise (him) up,

Jas. 3: 2. *able* also to bridle the whole body.

Rev. 6:15. the chief captains, and the *mighty men*,

δύνω & δῦμι, *duno* & *dumi*.

Mar. 1:32. at even, when the sun *did set*,

Lu. 4:40. Now *when* the sun *was setting*, all they

δύο, *duo*.

Mat. 4:18. saw *two* brethren, Simon called Peter,

21. from thence, he saw other *two* brethren,

5:41. compel thee to go a mile, go with him *twain*.

6:24. No man can serve *two* masters:

8:28. there met him *two* possessed with devils,

9:27. *two* blind men followed him, crying,

10:10. neither *two* coats, neither shoes,

29. Are not *two* sparrows sold for a farthing?

11: 2. he sent *two* of his disciples,

14:17. We have here but five loaves, and *two* fishes.

19. took the five loaves, and the *two* fishes,

18: 8. having *two* hands or *two* feet to be

9. having *two* eyes to be cast into hell fire.

16. (then) take with thee one or *two* more, that in the mouth of *two* or three witnesses

19. if *two* of you shall agree on earth as

20. where *two* or three are gathered

19: 5. they *twain* shall be one flesh?

6. Wherefore they are no more *twain*,

Mat.20:21. Grant that these my *two* sons may
24. with indignation against the *two* brethren.
30. *two* blind men sitting by the way side,
21: 1. then sent Jesus *two* disciples,
28. A (certain) man had *two* sons;
31. Whether of them *twain* did the
22:40. On these *two* commandments
24:40. Then shall *two* be in the field;
41. *Two* (women shall be) grinding at
25:15. to another *two*, and to another one;
17. (had received) *two*, he also gained other *two*.
22. He also that had received *two* talents
— thou deliveredst unto me *two* talents: behold, I have gained *two* other talents beside them.
26: 2. Ye know that after *two* days is
37. with him Peter and the *two* sons of Zebedee,
60. At the last came *two* false witnesses,
27:21. Whether of the *twain* will ye that I
38. *two* thieves crucified with him,
51. the temple was rent in *twain*
Mar. 6: 7. to send them forth by *two* and *two*;
9. shod with sandals; and not put on *two* coats.
38. they say, Five, and *two* fishes.
41. taken the five loaves and the *two* fishes,
— the *two* fishes divided he among them all.
9:43. having *two* hands to go into hell,
45. having *two* feet to be cast into hell,
47. having *two* eyes to be cast into hell fire:
10: 8. they *twain* shall be one flesh: so then they are no more *twain*,
11: 1. he sendeth forth *two* of his disciples,
12:42. poor widow, and she threw in *two* mites,
14: 1. After *two* days was (the feast of) the
13. he sendeth forth *two* of his disciples,
15:27. with him they crucify *two* thieves;
38. the veil of the temple was rent in *twain*
16:12. in another form unto *two* of them,
Lu. 2:24. pair of turtledoves, or *two* young pigeons.
3:11. He that hath *two* coats, let him impart
5: 2. saw *two* ships standing by the lake:
7:19. John calling (unto him) *two* of his disciples
41. a certain creditor which had *two* debtors:
9: 3. neither have *two* coats apiece.
13. no more but five loaves and *two* fishes;
16. took the five loaves and the *two* fishes,
30. behold, there talked with him *two* men,
32. the *two* men that stood with him.
10: 1. sent them *two* and *two* (lit. by *twos*) before his face
35. when he departed, he took out *two* pence,
12: 6. five sparrows sold for *two* farthings,
52. three against *two*, and *two* against three.
15:11. he said, A certain man had *two* sons:
16;13. No servant can serve *two* masters:
17:34. there shall be *two* (men) in one bed;
35. *Two* (women) shall be grinding together;
36. *Two* (men) shall be in the field;
18:10. *Two* men went up into the temple
19:29. he sent *two* of his disciples,
21: 2. poor widow casting in thither *two* mites.
22:38. Lord, behold, here (are) *two* swords.
23:32. there were also *two* other, malefactors,
24: 4. *two* men stood by them in shining garments:
13. *two* of them went that same day
Joh. 1:35. John stood, and *two* of his disciples;
37. the *two* disciples heard him speak,

Joh. 1:40. One of the *two* which heard John
2: 6. containing *two* or three firkins
4:40. with them: and he abode there *two* days.
43. after *two* days he departed thence,
6: 9. five barley loaves, and *two* small fishes:
8:17. that the testimony of *two* men is true.
11: 6. he abode *two* days still in the same
19:18. crucified him, and *two* other with him,
20: 4. So they ran *both* together: and the
12. seeth *two* angels in white sitting,
21: 2. the (sons) of Zebedee, and *two* other his disciples.
Acts 1:10. *two* men stood by them in white apparel
23. they appointed *two*, Joseph called
24. whether of these *two* thou hast chosen,
7:29. land of Madian, where he begat *two* sons.
9:38. they sent unto him *two* men,
10: 7. called *two* of his houshold servants,
12: 6. Peter was sleeping between *two* soldiers, bound with *two* chains: and the keepers
19:10. continued by the space of *two* years;
22. he sent into Macedonia *two* of them that
34. about the space of *two* hours cried out,
21:33. to be bound with *two* chains;
23:23. he called unto (him) *two* centurions,
1Co. 6:16. for *two*, saith he, shall be one flesh.
14:27. (let it be) by *two*, or at the most (by) three,
29. Let the prophets speak *two* or three, and let
2Co.13: 1. In the mouth of *two* or three witnesses
Gal. 4:22. that Abraham had *two* sons,
24. for these are the *two* covenants; the
Eph. 2:15. to make in himself of *twain* one new man,
5:31. they *two* shall be one flesh
Phi. 1:23. For I am in a strait betwixt *two*,
1Ti. 5:19. before *two* or three witnesses.
Heb 6:18. That by *two* immutable things,
10:28. without mercy under *two* or three witnesses:
Rev. 9:12. there come *two* woes more hereafter.
16. *two* hundred thousand thousand:
11: 2. tread under foot forty (and) *two* months.
3. (power) unto my *two* witnesses,
4. the *two* olive trees, and the *two* candlesticks
10. these *two* prophets tormented them
12:14. to the woman were given *two* wings of a great eagle,
13: 5. to continue forty (and) *two* months.
11. he had *two* horns like a lamb,
19:20. These *both* were cast alive into a lake

δυσϐάστακτος, *dusbastaktos*.

Mat.23: 4. heavy burdens and *grievous to be borne*,
Lu. 11:46. with burdens *grievous to be borne*,

δυσεντερία, *dusenteria*.

Acts28: 8. sick of a fever and of a *bloody flux:* (lit. a *dysentery*)

δυσερμήνευτος, *dusermecnūtos*.

Heb 5:11. things to say, and *hard to be uttered*, seeing

δύσκολος, duskolos.

Mar.10:24. how *hard* is it for them that trust

δυσκόλως, duskolōs.

Mat.19:23. a rich man shall *hardly* enter into
Mar.10:23. How *hardly* shall they that have riches
Lu. 18:24. How *hardly* shall they that have riches

δυσμή, dusmee.

Mat. 8:11. many shall come from the east and *west*,
    (lit. *setting*)
24:27. shineth even unto the *west;* so
Lu. 12:54. When ye see a cloud rise out of the *west*,
13:29. come from the east, and (from) the *west*,
Rev.21:13. on the *west* three gates.

δυσνόητος, dusnoeetos.

2Pet.3:16. are some things *hard to be understood*,

δυσφημία, duspheemia.

2Co. 6: 8. by *evil report* and good report: as

δώδεκα, dōdeka.

Mat. 9:20. with an issue of blood *twelve* years,
10: 1. called unto (him) his *twelve* disciples,
2. the names of the *twelve* apostles are
5. These *twelve* Jesus sent forth,
11: 1. of commanding his *twelve* disciples,
14:20. fragments that remained *twelve* baskets
    full.
19:28. ye also shall sit upon *twelve* thrones, judg-
    ing the *twelve* tribes of Israel.
20:17. took the *twelve* disciples apart
26:14. Then one of the *twelve*, called
20. he sat down with the *twelve*.
47. lo, Judas, one of the *twelve*, came,
53. more than *twelve* legions of angels?
Mar. 3:14. he ordained *twelve*, that they
4:10. were about him with the *twelve*
5:25. had an issue of blood *twelve* years,
42. she was (of the age) of *twelve* years.
6: 7. he called (unto him) the *twelve*,
43. they took up *twelve* baskets full
8:19. They say unto him, *Twelve*.
9:35. he sat down, and called the *twelve*,
10:32. he took again the *twelve*, and began
11:11. went out unto Bethany with the *twelve*.
14:10. Judas Iscariot, one of the *twelve*,
17. in the evening he cometh with the *twelve*.
20. (It is) one of the *twelve*, that dippeth
43. cometh Judas, one of the *twelve*,
Lu. 2:42. when he was *twelve* years old,
6:13. of them he chose *twelve*, whom
8: 1. the *twelve* (were) with him,
42. one only daughter, about *twelve* years
43. having an issue of blood *twelve* years,
9: 1. he called his *twelve* disciples together,
12. then came the *twelve*, and said unto him,
17. that remained to them *twelve* baskets.
18:31. Then he took (unto him) the *twelve*,
22: 3. being of the number of the *twelve*.

Lu. 22:14. sat down, and the *twelve* apostles with
    him.
30. judging the *twelve* tribes of Israel.
47. called Judas, one of the *twelve*, went
Joh. 6:13. filled *twelve* baskets with the fragments
67. Then said Jesus unto the *twelve*,
70. Have not I chosen you *twelve*,
71. betray him, being one of the *twelve*.
11: 9. Are there not *twelve* hours in the day?
20:24. Thomas, one of the *twelve*, called
Acts 6: 2. Then the *twelve* called the multitude
7: 8. Jacob (begat) the *twelve* patriarchs.
1Co.15: 5. seen of Cephas, then of the *twelve*:
Jas. 1: 1. to the *twelve* tribes which are
Rev. 7: 5. of Juda (were) sealed *twelve* thousand.
— of Reuben (were) sealed *twelve* thousand.
— of Gad (were) sealed *twelve* thousand.
6. of Aser (were) sealed *twelve* thousand.
— of Nepthalim (were) sealed *twelve* thou-
    sand. Of the tribe of Manasses (were)
    sealed *twelve* thousand.
7. of Simeon (were) sealed *twelve* thousand.
— of Levi (were) sealed *twelve* thousand.
— of Issachar (were) sealed *twelve* thousand.
8. of Zabulon (were) sealed *twelve* thou-
    sand.
— of Joseph (were) sealed *twelve* thousand.
— of Benjamin (were) sealed *twelve* thou-
    sand.
12: 1. upon her head a crown of *twelve* stars:
21:12. high, (and) had *twelve* gates, and at the
    gates *twelve* angels, and names
— the *twelve* tribes of the children of Israel:
14. wall of the city had *twelve* foundations,
— the names of the *twelve* apostles
16. with the reed, *twelve* thousand furlongs.
21. the *twelve* gates (were) *twelve* pearls;
22: 2. which bare *twelve* (manner of) fruits,

δωδέκατος, dōdekatos.

Rev.21:20. the *twelfth*, an amethyst.

δωδεκάφυλον, dōdekaphulon.

Acts26: 7. Unto which (promise) our *twelve tribes*,

δῶμα, dōma.

Mat.10:27. (that) preach ye upon the *housetops*.
24:17. him which is on the *housetop* not
Mar.13:15. let him that is on the *housetop* not
Lu. 5:19. they went upon the *housetop*,
12: 3. shall be proclaimed upon the *housetops*.
17:31. he which shall be upon the *housetop*,
Acts10: 9. Peter went up upon the *housetop*

δωρεά, dōrea.

Joh. 4:10. If thou knewest the *gift* of God,
Acts 2:38. ye shall receive the *gift* of the Holy
    Ghost.
8:20. hast thought that the *gift* of God may
10:45. poured out the *gift* of the Holy Ghost.
11:17. as God gave them the like *gift* as
Ro. 5:15. the grace of God, and the *gift* by grace,
17. of the *gift* of righteousness shall

2Co. 9:15. Thanks (be) unto God for his unspeak-
able *gift*.
Eph. 3: 7. according to the *gift* of the grace of
    4: 7. the measure of the *gift* of Christ.
Heb. 6: 4. have tasted of the heavenly *gift*,

δωρεάν, *dōrean*.

Mat.10: 8. *freely* ye have received, *freely* give
Joh.15:25. They hated me *without a cause*.
Ro. 3:24. Being justified *freely* by his grace
2Co.11: 7. to you the gospel of God *freely?*
Gal. 2:21. the law, then Christ is dead *in vain*.
2Th. 3: 8. did we eat any man's bread *for nought;*
Rev.21: 6. fountain of the water of life *freely*.
    22:17. let him take the water of life *freely*.

δωρέω, *dōreo*.

Mar.15:45. he *gave* the body to Joseph.
2Pet.1: 3. his divine power hath *given* unto us
    4. Whereby *are given* unto us exceeding

δώρημα, *dōreema*.

Ro. 5:16. by one that sinned, (so is) the *gift:*
Jas. 1:17. Every good gift and every perfect *gift*

δῶρον, *dōron*.

Mat. 2:11. They presented unto him *gifts;*
    5:23. if thou bring thy *gift* to the altar,
    24. Leave there thy *gift* before the altar,
    — then come and offer thy *gift*.
    8: 4. offer the *gift* that Moses commanded,
    15: 5. (It is) a *gift*, by whatsoever thou
    23:18. whosoever sweareth by the *gift* that
    19. whether (is) greater, the *gift*, or the altar
        that sanctifieth the *gift?*
Mar. 7:11. Corban, that is to say, a *gift*, by whatso-
    ever
Lu. 21: 1. casting their *gifts* into the treasury.
    4. cast in unto the *offerings* of God:
Eph. 2: 8. not of yourselves: (it is) the *gift* of God:
Heb. 5: 1. may offer both *gifts* and sacrifices for
    8: 3. to offer *gifts* and sacrifices: wherefore
    4. there are priests that offer *gifts*
    9: 9. were offered both *gifts* and sacrifices,
    11: 4. God testifying of his *gifts:* and by it
Rev.11:10. shall send *gifts* one to another;

ἔα, *ea*.

Mar. 1:24. Saying, *Let* (us) *alone;* what have we
Lu. 4:34. Saying, *Let* (us) *alone;* what have we

ἐάν, *ean*.

NOTE.—Those in which it is combined with μή, &
is mostly rendered *except*, or lit. *if...not*, are
marked thus [2].

Mat. 4: 9. *if* thou wilt fall down and worship me.

Mat. 5:13. but *if* the salt have lost his savour,
    19. Who*soever* therefore shall break one
    20. *except*[2] your righteousness shall exceed
    23. *if* thou bring thy gift to the altar,
    32. who*soever* shall marry her that is
    46. For *if* ye love them which love you,
    47. *if* ye salute your brethren only,
    6:14. For *if* ye forgive men their trespasses,
    15. *if*[2] ye forgive not men their trespasses,
    22. *if* therefore thine eye be single, thy
    23. But *if* thine eye be evil, thy whole
    7: 9. whom *if* his son ask bread, will he
    10. Or *if* he ask a fish, will he give him
    8: 2. Lord, *if* thou wilt, thou canst make me
        clean.
    19. follow thee whither*soever* thou goest.
    9:21. *If* I may but touch his garment,
    10:13. *if* the house be worthy, let your
    — but *if*[2] it be not worthy, let your peace
    14. who*soever*[2] shall not receive you,
    42. who*soever* shall give to drink unto one
    11: 6. who*soever*[2] shall not be offended in me.
    27. to whom*soever* the Son will reveal (him).
    12:11. *if* it fall into a pit on the sabbath day,
    29. *except*[2] he first bind the strong man?
    36. every idle word that)(men shall speak,
    14: 7. to give her what*soever* she would ask.
    15: 5. by what*soever* thou mightest be profited
    14. *if* the blind lead the blind, both
    16:19. what*soever* thou shalt bind on earth
    — what*soever* thou shalt loose on earth
    26. *if* he shall gain the whole world,
    17:20. *If* ye have faith as a grain of mustard
    18: 3. *Except*[2] ye be converted, and become as
    5. who*so* shall receive one such little child
    12. *if* a man have an hundred sheep,
    13. *if so* be that he find it, verily I say
    15. *if* thy brother shall trespass against thee,
    — *if* he shall hear thee, thou hast gained
    16. But *if*[2] he will not hear (thee, then) take
    17. And *if* he shall neglect to hear them,
    — but *if* he neglect to hear the church,
    18. What*soever* ye shall bind on earth
    — what*soever* ye shall loose on earth
    19. That *if* two of you shall agree on earth as
        touching anything that)(they shall ask,
    35. *if*[2] ye from your hearts forgive not
    20: 4. what*soever* is right I will give you.
    7. what*soever* is right, (that) shall ye receive.
    26. who*soever* will be great among you,
    27. who*soever* will be chief among you,
    21: 3. *if* any (man) say ought unto you,
    21. *If* ye have faith, and doubt not, ye
    24. one thing, which *if* ye tell me, I in
    25. *If* we shall say, From heaven; he
    26. But *if* we shall say, Of men; we fear
    22:24. *If* a man die, having no children,
    23:18. Who*soever* shall swear by the altar,
    24:23. *if* any man shall say unto you,
    26. Wherefore *if* they shall say unto you,
    28. For where*soever* the carcase is, there
    48. But and *if* that evil servant shall say in
    26:13. Where*soever* this gospel shall be preached
    42. *except*[2] I drink it, thy will be done.
    28:14. *if* this come to the governor's ears,
Mar. 1:40. *If* thou wilt, thou canst make me clean.
    3:24. *if* a kingdom be divided against itself,
    25. *if* a house be divided against itself,
    27. *except*[2] he will first bind the strong
    4:22. which)([2]shall not be manifested;
    26. as *if* a man should cast seed into
    6:10. In what place *soever* ye enter into

Mar 6:22. Ask of me what*soever* thou wilt,
23. What*soever* thou shalt ask of me,
7: 3. *except*² they wash (their) hands oft,
4. *except*² they wash, they eat not.
11. *If* a man shall say to his father or
— by what*soever* thou mightest be profited
8: 3. *if* I send them away fasting to their
36. *if* he shall gain the whole world,
9:37. Who*soever* shall receive one of such
— who*soever* shall receive me, receiveth
43. *if* thy hand offend thee, cut it off:
45. *if* thy foot offend thee,
47. *if* thine eye offend thee, pluck it out:
50. but *if* the salt have lost his saltness,
10:11. Who*soever* shall put away his wife,
12. *if* a woman shall put away her husband,
15. Who*soever*² shall not receive the kingdom
30. *But*² he shall receive an hundredfold
35. do for us what*soever* we shall desire.
43. who*soever* will be great among you,
11: 3. *if* any man say unto you,
23. he shall have what*soever* he saith.
31. saying, *If* we shall say, From heaven;
32. But *if* we shall say, Of men; they
12:19. *If* a man's brother die, and leave
13:11. what*soever* shall be given you in
21. And then *if* any man shall say to you,
14:14. where*soever* he shall go in, say ye
31. *If* I should die with thee, I will not deny
Lu. 4: 6. to whom*soever* I will give it.
7. *If* thou therefore wilt worship me,
5:12. *if* thou wilt, thou canst make me clean.
6:33. *if* ye do good to them which do good
34. *if* ye lend (to them) of whom ye hope
7:23. who*soever*² shall not be offended in me.
9:48. Who*soever* shall receive this child
— who*soever* shall receive me receiveth
10: 6. *if* the son of peace be there, your peace
22. to *whom*)(the Son will reveal (him).
11:12. Or *if* he shall ask an egg, will he
12:38. *if* he shall come in the second watch,
45. But *and if* that servant say in his heart,
13: 3. *except*² ye repent, ye shall all likewise perish.
5. but, *except*² ye repent, ye shall all
14:34. but *if* the salt have lost his savour,
15: 8. *if* she lose one piece, doth not
16:30. *if* one went unto them from the dead,
31. *though* (lit. *if*) one rose from the dead.
17: 3. *If* thy brother trespass against thee,
— *if* he repent, forgive him.
4. *if* he trespass against thee seven times
33. Who*soever* shall seek to save his life
— who*soever* shall lose his life shall
18:17. Who*soever*² shall not receive the
19:31. *if* any man ask you, Why do ye
40. *if* these should hold their peace,
20: 5. *If* we shall say, From heaven;
6. But *and if* we say, Of men; all the people
28. *If* any man's brother die, having
22:67. *If* I tell you, ye will not believe:
68. *if* I also ask (you), ye will not
Joh. 3: 2. *except*² God be with him.
3. *Except*² a man be born again,
5. *Except*² a man be born of water
12. *if* I tell you (of) heavenly things?
27. *except*² it be given him from heaven.
4:48. *Except*² ye see signs and wonders, ye
5:19. *but*² what he seeth the Father do:
31. *If* I bear witness of myself, my
43. *if* another shall come in his own
6:44. can come to me, *except*² the Father

Joh. 6:51. *if* any man eat of this bread,
53. *Except*² ye eat the flesh of the Son of man,
62. (What) *and if* ye shall see the Son of man
65. *except*² it were given unto him
7:17. *If* any man will do his will,
37. *If* any man thirst, let him come
51. judge (any) man, before it (lit. *unless*² it previously) hear him,
8:16. yet *if* I judge, my judgment is
24. *if*² ye believe not that I am (he),
31. *If* ye continue in my word,
36. *If* the Son therefore shall make
51. *If* a man keep my saying, he shall
52. thou sayest, *If* a man keep my saying,
54. *If* I honour myself, my honour is nothing:
55. *if* I should say, I know him not,
9:22. that *if* any man did confess that
31. but *if* any man be a worshipper of God,
10: 9. by me *if* any man enter in, he
11: 9. *If* any man walk in the day, he
10. But *if* a man walk in the night, he
40. *if* thou wouldest believe, thou shouldest
48. *If* we let him thus alone, all (men)
57. that, *if* any man knew where he were,
12:24. *Except*² a corn of wheat fall into the
— *if* it die, it bringeth forth much fruit.
26. *If* any man serve me, let him follow
— *if* any man serve me, him will
32. *if* I be lifted up from the earth, will
47. *if* any man hear my words, and believe
13: 8. *If*² I wash thee not, thou hast no
17. happy are ye *if* ye do them.
20. He that receiveth whom*soever* I send
35. *if* ye have love one to another.
14: 3. *if* I go and prepare a place for you, I will
14. *If* ye shall ask any thing in my name,
15. *If* ye love me, keep my commandments.
23. *If* a man love me, he will keep my words:
15: 4. *except*² it abide in the vine; no more can ye, *except*² ye abide in me.
6. *If*² a man abide not in me, he is
7. *If* ye abide in me, and my words abide in you, ye shall ask what)(ye will, and it shall
10. *If* ye keep my commandments,
14. *if* ye do whatsoever I command you.
16: 7. for *if*² I go not away, the Comforter
— but *if* I depart, I will send him unto you.
19:12. saying, *If* thou let this man go,
20:25. *Except*² I shall see in his hands the
21:22. *If* I will that he tarry till I come,
23. *If* I will that he tarry till I come,
25. which, *if* they should be written
Acts 5:38. for *if* this counsel or this work be
7: 7. the nation to whom)(they shall be
8:31. *except*² some man should guide me?
9: 2. that *if* he found any of this way,
13:41. *though* a man declare it unto you.
15: 1. *Except*² ye be circumcised after the
26: 5. *if* they would testify, that after the
27:31. *Except*² these abide in the ship,
Ro. 2:25. profiteth, *if* thou keep the law: but *if* thou be a breaker of the law,
26. Therefore *if* the uncircumcision keep
7: 2. but *if* the husband be dead, she is
3. *if*, while (her) husband liveth, she be
— but *if* her husband be dead, she is free
9:27. *Though* the number of the children
10: 9. *if* thou shalt confess with thy mouth
15. shall they preach, *except*² they be sent?
11:22. *if* thou continue in (his) goodness:
23. *if*² they abide not in unbelief, shall

Ro. 12:20. *if* thine enemy hunger, feed him ; *if* he thirst, give him drink:

13: 4. But *if* thou do that which is evil, be afraid;

14: 8. For *whether* we live, we live unto the Lord ; and *whether* we die, we die unto the Lord: *whether* we live therefore, *or* die, we are the Lord's.

23. he that doubteth is damned *if* he eat,

15:24. Whensoever I take my journey into

— *if* first I be somewhat filled with

1Co. 4:15. *though* ye have ten thousand instructers

19. come to you shortly, *if* the Lord will,

5:11. *if* any man that is called a brother

6: 4. *If* then ye have judgments of things

18. Every sin that)(a man doeth is without

7: 8. for them *if* they abide even as I.

11. But and *if* she depart, let her remain

28. But and *if* thou marry, thou hast not sinned; and *if* a virgin marry, she hath not sinned.

36. *if* she pass the flower of (her) age,

39. but *if* her husband be dead, she is at

40. she is happier *if* she so abide,

8: 8. neither, *if* we eat, are we the better; neither, *if*[2] we eat not, are we the worse.

10. For *if* any man see thee which

9:16. *though* I preach the gospel, I have

— woe is unto me, *if*[2] I preach not the gospel!

10:28. *if* any man say unto you, This

11:14. that, *if* a man have long hair, it is

15. But *if* a woman have long hair, it is

12:15. *If* the foot shall say, Because I am

16. *If* the ear shall say, Because I am

13: 1. *Though* I speak with the tongues

2. *though* I have (the gift of) prophecy,

— *though* I have all faith, so that I

3. *though* I bestow all my goods

— *though* I give my body to be burned,

14: 6. *if* I come unto you speaking

— *except*[2] I shall speak to you either

7. *except*[2] they give a distinction in

8. *if* the trumpet give an uncertain

9. *except*[2] ye utter by the tongue words

11. Therefore *if*[2] I know not the meaning

14. For *if* I pray in an (unknown) tongue,

16. *when* thou shalt bless with the spirit,

23. *If* therefore the whole church be come

24. But *if* all prophesy, and there come in one

28. But *if*[2] there be no interpreter, let him

30. *If* (any thing) be revealed to another

15:36. is not quickened, *except*[2] it die:

16: 3. whomso*ever* ye shall approve by

4. *if* it be meet that I go also, they shall

6. on my journey whitherso*ever* I go.

7. a while with you, *if* the Lord permit.

10. *if* Timotheus come, see that he may

2Co. 5: 1. we know that *if* our earthly house

8:12. accepted according to that)(a man hath,

9: 4. *if* they of Macedonia come with me,

10: 8. For *though* I should boast somewhat

12: 6. For *though* I would desire to glory,

13: 2. that, *if* I come again, I will not spare:

Gal. 1: 8. *though* (lit. even *if*) we, or an angel from heaven,

2:16. but (lit. *if*[2] not) by the faith of Jesus Christ,

5: 2. that *if* ye be circumcised, Christ

6: 1. *if* a man be overtaken in a fault,

7. whatso*ever* a man soweth, that shall

Eph. 6: 8. whatso*ever* good thing any man doeth,

Col. 3: 13. *if* any man have a quarrel against

23. whatso*ever* ye do, do (it) heartily,

4:10. *if* he come unto you, receive him ;

1Th. 3: 8. we live, *if* ye stand fast in the Lord.

2Th. 2: 3. *except*[2] there come a falling away first,

1Ti. 1: 8. law (is) good, *if* a man use it lawfully ;

2:15. *if* they continue in faith and charity

3:15. But *if* I tarry long, that thou mayest

2Ti. 2: 5. *if* a man also strive for masteries,

— *except*[2] he strive lawfully.

21. *If* a man therefore purge himself

Heb. 3: 6. *if* we hold fast the confidence and the

7. To day *if* ye will hear his voice,

14. *if* we hold the beginning of our

15. To day *if* ye will hear his voice,

4: 7. To day *if* ye will hear his voice,

6: 3. this will we do, *if* God permit.

10:38. *if* (any man) draw back, my

13:23. *if* he come shortly, I will see

Jas. 2: 2. For *if* there come unto your

14. *though* a man say he hath faith,

15. *If* a brother or sister be naked,

17. faith, *if*[2] it hath not works, is dead,

4:15. *If* the Lord will, we shall live,

5:19. *if* any of you do err from the truth,

1Pet.3:13. *if* ye be followers of that which is good?

1Joh.1: 6. *If* we say that we have fellowship

7. But *if* we walk in the light, as he is

8. *If* we say that we have no sin,

9. *If* we confess our sins, he is faithful

10. *If* we say that we have not sinned,

2: 1. *if* any man sin, we have an advocate

3. *if* we keep his commandments.

15. *If* any man love the world, the

24. *If* that which ye have heard from

29. *If* ye know that he is righteous,

3: 2. we know that, *when* he shall appear,

20. For *if* our heart condemn us,

21. *if*[2] our heart condemn us not,

22. whatso*ever* we ask, we receive of him,

4:12. *If* we love one another, God dwelleth in us,

20. *If* a man say, I love God, and hateth

5:14. *if* we ask any thing according to his

15. *if* we know that he hear us,

16. *If* any man see his brother sin

3Joh. 5. whatso*ever* thou doest to the brethren,

10. Wherefore, *if* I come, I will remember

Rev. 2: 5. out of his place, *except*[2] thou repent.

22. *except*[2] they repent of their deeds.

3: 3. *If*[2] therefore thou shalt not watch,

19. As many as)(I love, I rebuke

20. *if* any man hear my voice, and open

11: 6. all plagues, as often as)(they will.

22:18. *If* any man shall add unto these

19. And *if* any man shall take away

ἑαυτ-οῦ, -ῷ, -ὸν, &c, *heaut-ou*, *-o*, *-on*, &c.

Note.—See also the contracted form of this word under αὐτοῦ.

Mat. 3: 9. think not to say within *yourselves*,

6:34. take thought for the things of *itself*.

8:22. let the dead bury *their* dead.

9: 3. the scribes said within *themselves*,

21. For she said within *herself*, If I may

12:25. Every kingdom divided against *itself*

— or house divided against *itself*

26. he is divided against *himself*;

45. taketh with *himself* seven other spirits more wicked than *himself*,

Mat.13:21. Yet hath he not root in *himself*,
14:15. villages, and buy *themselves* victuals.
15:30. having with *them* (those that were) lame,
16: 7. they reasoned among *themselves*,
8. why reason ye among *yourselves*,
24. let him deny *himself*, and take up
18: 4. Whosoever therefore shall humble *himself*
19:12. have made *themselves* eunuchs for
21: 8. spread *their* garments in the way;
25. they reasoned with *themselves*, saying,
38. they said among *themselves*,
23:12. whosoever shall exalt *himself* shall
— he that shall humble *himself* shall
31. ye be witnesses unto *yourselves*, that
37. as a hen gathereth *her* chickens under
25: 3. They that (were) foolish took *their* lamps,
and took no oil with *them*:
9. them that sell, and buy for *yourselves*.
26:11. ye have the poor always with *you*;
27:35. parted my garments among *them*,
42. He saved others; *himself* he cannot save.
Mar. 2: 8. they so reasoned within *themselves*,
19. they have the bridegroom with *them*,
3:24. if a kingdom be divided against *itself*,
25. if a house be divided against *itself*,
26. if Satan rise up against *himself*,
4:17. have no root in *themselves*, and so
5: 5. crying, and cutting *himself* with stones.
26. had spent all that she had (lit. all things
from *herself*), and was nothing.
30. Jesus, immediately knowing in *himself*
6:36. villages, and buy *themselves* bread: for
51. they were sore amazed in *themselves*
8:14. with *them* more than one loaf.
34. let him deny *himself*, and take up
9: 8. save Jesus only with *themselves*.
10. they kept that saying with *themselves*,
33. that ye disputed among *yourselves*
50. Have salt in *yourselves*, and have peace
10:26. saying among *themselves*, Who then
11:31. they reasoned with *themselves*, saying
12: 7. husbandmen said among *themselves*,
33. to love (his) neighbour as *himself*,
13: 9. take heed to *yourselves*: for they shall
14: 4. that had indignation within *themselves*,
7. ye have the poor with *you* always,
33. he taketh with *him* Peter and James
15:31. He saved others; *himself* he cannot save.
16: 3. they said among *themselves*, Who shall
Lu. 1:24. hid *herself* five months, saying,
3: 8. begin not to say within *yourselves*,
7:30. the counsel of God against *themselves*,
39. he spake within *himself*, saying,
49. began to say within *themselves*,
9:23. let him deny *himself*, and take up
25. gain the whole world, and lose *himself*,
47. took a child, and set him by *him*,
60. Let the dead bury *their* dead:
10:29. he, willing to justify *himself*,
11:17. Every kingdom divided against *itself*
18. If Satan also be divided against *himself*,
21. man armed keepeth *his* palace,
26. other spirits more wicked than *himself*;
12: 1. Beware ye)(of the leaven of the Pharisees,
17. he thought within *himself*, saying,
21. that layeth up treasure for *himself*,
33. provide *yourselves* bags which
36. like unto men that wait for *their* lord,
47. servant, which knew *his* lord's will,
57. why even of *yourselves* judge ye
13:19. a man took, and cast into *his* garden;

Lu. 13:34. as a hen (doth gather) *her* brood
14:11. whosoever exalteth *himself* shall
— he that humbleth *himself* shall
26. come to me, and hate not *his* father,
— yea, and *his own* life also, he cannot
33. forsaketh not all that he hath (lit. all the
things of *himself*), he
15: 5. he layeth (it) on *his* shoulders, rejoicing.
17. when he came to *himself*, he said,
20. he arose, and came to *his* father. But
when
16: 3. Then the steward said within *himself*,
5. called every one of *his* lord's debtors
8. are in *their* generation wiser than the
children
9. Make to *yourselves* friends of the mammon
15. Ye are they which justify *yourselves*
17: 3. Take heed to *yourselves*: If thy brother
14. Go shew *yourselves* unto the priests.
18: 4. afterward he said within *himself*,
9. certain which trusted in *themselves*
11. stood and prayed thus with *himself*,
14. every one that exalteth *himself* shall be
— he that humbleth *himself* shall be
19:12. to receive for *himself* a kingdom,
13. he called *his* ten servants, and delivered
35. they cast *their* garments upon the colt,
20: 5. they reasoned with *themselves*, saying,
14. they reasoned among *themselves*,
20. which should feign *themselves* just
21:30. ye see and know of *your own selves* that
34. take heed to *yourselves*, lest at any
22:17. divide (it) among *yourselves*:
23. began to enquire among *themselves*,
66. led him into *their* council, saying,
23: 2. saying that *he himself* is Christ
12. at enmity between *themselves*.
28. weep for *yourselves*, and for your children.
35. He saved others; let him save *himself*,
48. smote *their* breasts, and returned.
24:12. departed, wondering in *himself* at
27. the scriptures the things concerning *himself*.
Joh. 2:24. Jesus did not commit *himself* unto
5:18. making *himself* equal with God.
19. Son can do nothing of *himself*,
26. as the Father hath life in *himself*;
— the Son to have life in *himself*;
42. ye have not the love of God in *you*.
6:53. his blood, ye have no life in *you*.
61. When Jesus knew in *himself* that
7:18. He that speaketh of *himself* seeketh
35. said the Jews among *themselves*,
8:22. said the Jews, Will he kill *himself*?
11:33. groaned in the spirit, and was troubled,
(lit. disturbed *himself*)
38. therefore again groaning in *himself*
51. this spake he not of *himself*: but
55. before the passover, to purify *themselves*.
12: 8. the poor always ye have with *you*;
19. Pharisees therefore said among *themselves*
13: 4. took a towel, and girded *himself*.
32. God shall also glorify him in *himself*,
15: 4. the branch cannot bear fruit of *itself*,
16:13. for he shall not speak of *himself*,
18:34. Sayest thou this thing of *thyself*,
19: 7. he made *himself* the Son of God.
24. They parted my raiment among *them*,
20:10. went away again unto their own home.
(lit. to *themselves*)
21: 1. Jesus shewed *himself* again to the

Joh.21: 7. did cast *himself* into the sea.
Acts 1: 3. To whom also he shewed *himself* alive
  5:35. take heed to *yourselves* what ye intend
  36. Theudas, boasting *himself* to be somebody;
  7:21. nourished him for *her own* son.
  8: 9. that *himself* was some great one:
  34. of *himself*, or of some other man?
  10:17. while Peter doubted in *himself*
  12:11. when Peter was come to *himself*,
  13:46. judge *yourselves* unworthy of everlasting
     life,
  14:17. he left not *himself* without witness,
  15:29. from which if ye keep *yourselves*,
  16:27. would have killed *himself*,
  19:31. not adventure *himself* into the theatre.
  20:28. Take heed therefore unto *yourselves*,
  21:23. men which have a vow on *them* ;
  23:12. bound *themselves* under a curse,
  14. We have bound *ourselves* under a
  21. which have bound *themselves* with
  25: 4. that *he himself* would depart shortly
  28:16. Paul was suffered to dwell by *himself*
  29. had great reasoning among *themselves*.
Ro. 1:24. their own bodies between *themselves*:
  27. receiving in *themselves* that recompence
  2:14. are a law unto *themselves*:
  4:19. considered not *his own* body now dead,
  5: 8. God commendeth *his* love toward us,
  6:11. reckon ye also *yourselves* to be dead
  13. yield *yourselves* unto God, as
  16. to whom ye yield *yourselves* servants
  8: 3. God sending *his own* Son in the
  23. we ourselves groan within *ourselves*,
  11:25. should be wise in your own conceits; (lit.
     in or by *yourselves*)
  12:16. Be not wise in your own conceits. (lit. in
     or by *yourselves*)
  19. Dearly beloved, avenge not *yourselves*,
  13: 2. shall receive to *themselves* damnation.
  9. Thou shalt love thy neighbour as *thyself*.
  14: 7. none of us liveth to *himself*, and no man
     dieth to *himself*.
  12. shall give account of *himself* to God.
  14. (there is) nothing unclean of *itself*:
  22. he that condemneth not *himself*
  15: 1. and not to please *ourselves*.
  3. For even Christ pleased not *himself*;
  16: 4. laid down *their own* necks:
  18. *their own* belly; and by good words
1Co. 3:18. Let no man deceive *himself*.
  6: 7. ye go to law *one* with *another*.
  19. have of God, and ye are not *your own*?
  7: 2. let every man have *his own* wife,
  37. in his heart that he will keep *his* virgin,
  10:24. Let no man seek *his own*, but
  29. Conscience, I say, not *thine own*, but
  11: 5. head uncovered dishonoureth *her* head:
  28. let a man examine *himself*, and so
  29. eateth and drinketh damnation to *himself*,
  31. if we would judge *ourselves*, we
  13: 5. seeketh not *her own*, is not easily
  14: 4. in an (unknown) tongue edifieth *himself*;
  28. Let him speak to *himself*, and to God.
  16: 2. every one of you lay by *him* in store,
  15. they have addicted *themselves* to the
2Co. 1: 9. the sentence of death in *ourselves*, that we
     should not trust in *ourselves*,
  3: 1. Do we begin again to commend *ourselves*?
  5. Not that we are sufficient of *ourselves* to
     think any thing as of *ourselves* ;
  13. (which) put a vail over *his* face,
  4: 2. commending *ourselves* to every man's

2Co. 4: 5. For we preach not *ourselves*, but Christ
  — *ourselves* your servants for Jesus' sake.
  5:12. For we commend not *ourselves* again
  15. not henceforth live unto *themselves*,
  18. reconciled us to *himself* by Jesus
  19. reconciling the world unto *himself*,
  6: 4. approving *ourselves* as the ministers
  7: 1. let us cleanse *ourselves* from all
  11. ye have approved *yourselves* to be
  8: 5. first gave *their own selves* to the Lord,
  10: 7. If any man trust to *himself* that
  — let him of *himself* think this again,
  12. or compare *ourselves* with some that com-
     mend *themselves* : but they measuring
     themselves by *themselves*, and comparing
     themselves among *themselves*,
  14. we stretch not *ourselves* beyond
  18. not he that commendeth *himself*
  13: 5. Examine *yourselves*, whether ye be in the
     faith; prove *your own selves*. Know ye
     not *your own selves*,
Gal. 1: 4. Who gave *himself* for our sins,
  2:12. he withdrew and separated *himself*,
  20. loved me, and gave *himself* for me.
  5:14. Thou shalt love thy neighbour as *thyself*.
  6: 3. he is nothing, he deceiveth *himself*.
  4. let every man prove *his own* work,
  — have rejoicing in *himself* alone,
  8. he that soweth to *his* flesh shall
Eph. 2:15. for to make in *himself* of twain
  4:16. unto the edifying of *itself* in love.
  19. have given *themselves* over unto
  32. tenderhearted, forgiving *one another*,
  5: 2. hath given *himself* for us an offering
  19. Speaking to *yourselves* in psalms
  25. Husbands, love *your* wives, even
  — loved the church, and gave *himself* for it;
  27. present it to *himself* a glorious church,
  28. So ought men to love *their* wives as *their
     own* bodies. He that loveth *his* wife
     loveth *himself*.
  29. no man ever yet hated *his own* flesh;
  33. in particular so love *his* wife even as *him-
     self*; and the wife
Phi. 2: 3. esteem other better than *themselves*.
  4. Look not every man on *his own* things,
  7. made *himself* of no reputation,
  8. he humbled *himself*, and became obedient
  12. work out *your own* salvation with fear
  21. For all seek *their own*, not the things
  3:21. to subdue all things unto *himself*.
Col. 3:13. forgiving *one another*, if any man
  16. teaching and admonishing *one another* in
1Th. 2: 7. as a nurse cherisheth *her* children:
  8. also *our own* souls, because ye were
  11. as a father (doth) *his* children,
  12. hath called you unto *his* kingdom
  4: 4. know how to possess *his* vessel in
  5:13. be at peace among *yourselves*.
2Th. 2: 4. shewing *himself* that he is God.
  6. might be revealed in *his* time.
  3: 9. to make *ourselves* an ensample
  12. they work, and eat *their own* bread.
1Ti. 2: 6. Who gave *himself* a ransom for all,
  9. women adorn *themselves* in modest
  3:13. purchase to *themselves* a good degree,
  6:10. pierced *themselves* through with
  19. Laying up in store for *themselves*
2Ti. 2:13. faithful: he cannot deny *himself*.
  21. If a man therefore purge *himself*
  4: 3. they heap to *themselves* teachers,
Tit. 2:14. Who gave *himself* for us, that he

Tit. 2:14. purify unto *himself* a peculiar people,
Heb. 1: 3. had by *himself* purged our sins,
    3:13. exhort *one another* daily, while
    5: 3. so also for *himself*, to offer for sins.
      4. no man taketh this honour unto *himself*,
      5. Christ glorified not *himself*
    6: 6. crucify to *themselves* the Son of God
     13. by no greater, he sware by *himself*,
    7:27. when he offered up *himself*.
    9: 7. which he offered for *himself*,
     14. offered *himself* without spot
     25. that he should offer *himself* often,
   10:25. the assembling of *ourselves* together,
     34. knowing in *yourselves* that ye
Jas. 1:22. hearers only, deceiving *your own selves*.
     24. For he beholdeth *himself*, and goeth
     27. to keep *himself* unspotted from the world.
    2: 4. Are ye not then partial in *yourselves*,
     17. faith,...is dead, being alone. (lit. by *itself*)
1Pet. 1:12. that not unto *themselves*, but unto
    3: 5. adorned *themselves*, being in
    4: 8. have fervent charity among *yourselves*:
     10. minister the same *one to another*,
     19. commit the keeping of *their* souls
2Pet. 2: 1. bring upon *themselves* swift destruction.
1Joh. 1: 8. have no sin, we deceive *ourselves*,
    3: 3. purifieth *himself*, even as he is pure.
    5:10. hath the witness in *himself*:
     18. begotten of God keepeth *himself*,
     21. Little children, keep *yourselves* from idols.
2Joh.   8. Look to *yourselves*, that we lose not
Jude   6. angels which kept not *their* first estate,
     12. feeding *themselves* without fear:
     13. foaming out *their own* shame;
     18. walk after *their own* ungodly lusts.
     20. building up *yourselves* on your
     21. Keep *yourselves* in the love of God,
Rev. 2: 9. of them which say *they* are Jews,
     20. which calleth *herself* a prophetess,
    3: 9. which say *they* are Jews, and are not,
    4: 8. beasts had each of them (lit. each by *itself*) six wings
   6:15. hid *themselves* in the dens
   8: 6. prepared *themselves* to sound.
  10: 3. seven thunders uttered *their* voices.
     4. seven thunders had uttered *their* voices,
     7. declared to *his* servants the prophets.
  17:13. shall give *their* power and strength
  18: 7. How much she hath glorified *herself*,
  19: 7. his wife hath made *herself* ready.

ἐάω, eao.

Mat. 24:43. would not *have suffered* his
Lu. 4:41. *suffered* them not to speak:
  22:51. *Suffer* ye thus far.   And he touched
Acts 5:38. Refrain from these men, and *let* them *alone:*
  14:16. *suffered* all nations to walk in
  16: 7. the Spirit *suffered* them not.
  19:30. the disciples *suffered* him not.
  23:32. they *left* the horsemen to go with him, *and*
  27:32. ropes of the boat, and *let* her fall off.
    40. they *committed* (themselves) unto the sea,
  28: 4. yet vengeance *suffereth* not to live.
1Co. 10:13. who *will* not *suffer* you to be tempted
Rev. 2:20. because thou *sufferest* that woman Jezebel, which calleth

---

ἐϐδομήκοντα, hebdomeekonta

Lu. 10: 1. the Lord appointed other *seventy*
     17. the *seventy* returned again with joy, saying, Lord, even the devils
Acts 7:14. kindred, threescore and fifteen (lit. *seventy* five) souls.
  23:23. horsemen *threescore and ten*, and spearmen
  27:37. threescore and sixteen (lit. *seventy* six) souls.

ἐϐδομηκοντάκις, hebdomeekontakis.

Mat. 18:22. Until seven times: but, Until *seventy times* seven.

ἔϐδομος, hebdomos.

Joh. 4:52. Yesterday at the *seventh* hour the fever left him.
Heb 4: 4. of the *seventh* (day) on this wise, and God did rest the *seventh* day from all his works.
Jude 14. Enoch also, the *seventh* from Adam
Rev. 8: 1. when he had opened the *seventh* seal,
  10: 7. the days of the voice of the *seventh* angel, when he shall begin to sound,
  11:15. the *seventh* angel sounded; and there
  16:17. the *seventh* angel poured out his vial
  21:20. the *seventh*, chrysolite; the eighth, beryl, the ninth, a topaz;

ἐϐραϊκός, hebraikos.

See among Proper Names.

ἐϐραΐς, hebrais.

See among Proper Names.

ἐϐραϊστί, hebraisti.

See among Proper Names.

ἐγγίζω, engizo.

Mat. 3: 2. for the kingdom of heaven *is at hand*.
  4:17. for the kingdom of heaven *is at hand*.
  10: 7. The kingdom of heaven *is at hand*.
  15: 8. *draweth nigh* unto me with their mouth,
  21: 1. when they *drew nigh* unto Jerusalem,
    34. when the time of the fruit *drew near*,
  26:45. behold, the hour *is at hand*, and the
    46. he *is at hand* that doth betray me.
Mar. 1:15. the kingdom of God *is at hand:*
  11: 1. when they *came nigh* to Jerusalem,
  14:42. lo, he that betrayeth me *is at hand*.
Lu. 7:12. when he *came nigh* to the gate of the city,
  10: 9. The kingdom of God *is come nigh* unto you.
    11. the kingdom of God *is come nigh* unto
  12:33. where no thief *approacheth*, neither
  15: 1. Then *drew near* unto him all the
  25. as he came and *drew nigh* to the house,
  18:35. as he was *come nigh* unto Jericho

Lu. 18:40. *when* he *was come near*, he asked him,
  19:29. when he *was come nigh* to Bethphage
    37. *when* he *was come nigh*, even now
    41. when he *was come near*, he beheld
  21: 8. the time *draweth near:* go ye not
    20. that the desolation thereof *is nigh*.
    28. for your redemption *draweth nigh*.
  22: 1. the feast of unleavened bread *drew nigh*,
    47. *drew near* unto Jesus to kiss him.
  24:15. Jesus himself *drew near, and* went with them.
    28. they *drew nigh* unto the village,
Acts 7:17. the time of the promise *drew nigh*,
    9: 3. as he journeyed, he *came near* Damascus:
  10: 9. *as* they went...and *drew nigh* unto the city,
  21:33. chief captain *came near, and* took him,
  22: 6. *as* I made my journey, and *was come nigh*
  23:15. we, or ever he *come near*, are ready
Ro. 13:12. night is far spent, the day *is at hand:*
Phi. 2:30. work of Christ he *was nigh* unto death,
Heb. 7:19. by the which we *draw nigh* unto God.
  10:25. the more, as ye see the day *approaching*.
Jas. 4: 8. *Draw nigh* to God, and he will *draw nigh*
   5: 8. the coming of the Lord *draweth nigh*.
1Pet.4: 7. the end of all things *is at hand:*

ἐγγράφω, *engrapho*.

2Co. 3: 2. Ye are our epistle *written in* our hearts,
    3. ministered by us, *written* not with ink,

ἔγγυος, *enguos*.

Heb. 7:22. Jesus made a *surety* of a better testament.

ἐγγύς, *engus*.

Mat.24:32. ye know that summer (is) *nigh:*
    33. know that it is *near*, (even) at the doors.
  26:18. The Master saith, My time is *at hand;*
Mar.13:28. ye know that summer is *near:*
    29. know that it is *nigh*, (even) at the doors.
Lu. 19:11. because he was *nigh* to Jerusalem,
  21:30. that summer is now *nigh at hand*.
    31. kingdom of God is *nigh at hand*.
Joh. 2:13. the Jews' passover was *at hand*,
   3:23. was baptizing in Ænon *near* to Salim,
   6: 4: the passover, a feast of the Jews, was *nigh*.
    19. on the sea, and drawing *nigh* unto the ship:
    23. *nigh* unto the place where they
   7: 2. Jews' feast of tabernacles was *at hand*.
  11:18. Bethany was *nigh* unto Jerusalem,
    54. unto a country *near* to the wilderness,
    55. the Jews' passover was *nigh at hand:*
  19:20. was crucified was *nigh* to the city:
    42. the sepulchre was *nigh at hand*.
Acts 1:12. *from* Jerusalem a sabbath day's journey.
   9:38. as Lydda was *nigh* to Joppa,
  27: 8. *nigh* whereunto was the city (of) Lasea.
Ro. 10: 8. The word is *nigh* thee, (even) in thy
Eph. 2:13. are made *nigh* by the blood of Christ.
    17. were afar off, and to them that were *nigh*.
Phi. 4: 5. unto all men. The Lord (is) *at hand*.
Heb. 6: 8. rejected, and (is) *nigh unto* cursing;
   8:13. waxeth old (is) *ready* to vanish away.
Rev. 1: 3. for the time (is) *at hand*.
  22:10. for the time is *at hand*.

ἐγγύτερον, *enguteron*.

Ro. 13:11. now (is) our salvation *nearer*

ἐγείρω, *egiro*.

Mat. 2:13. *Arise, and* take the young child
    14. *When* he *arose*, he took the young
    20. *Arise, and* take the young child
    21. he *arose, and* took the young child
   3: 9. *to raise up* children unto Abraham.
  8:15. she *arose, and* ministered unto them.
    25. *awoke* him, saying, Lord, save us:
    26. Then he *arose, and* rebuked the winds
   9: 5. or to say, *Arise*, and walk?
    6. *Arise*, take up thy bed, and go unto
    7. he *arose, and* departed to his house.
    19. Jesus *arose, and* followed him,
    25. took her by the hand, and the maid *arose*.
  10: 8. *raise* the dead, cast out devils:
  11: 5. the dead *are raised up*, and the poor
    11. there *hath* not *risen* a greater than John
  12:11. will he not lay hold on it, and *lift* (it) out?
    42. The queen of the south *shall rise up* in
  14: 2. John the Baptist; he *is risen* from the dead;
  16:21. and *be raised again* the third day.
  17: 7. said, *Arise*, and be not afraid.
    23. the third day he *shall be raised again*.
  24: 7. nation *shall rise* against nation,
    11. many false prophets *shall rise*,
    24. For there *shall arise* false Christs,
  25: 7. Then all those virgins *arose*, and trimmed
  26:32. after I *am risen again*, I will go
    46. *Rise*, let us be going: behold, he is
  27:52. bodies of the saints which slept *arose*,
    63. After three days I will *rise again*.
    64. He *is risen* from the dead: so the
  28: 6. He is not here: for he *is risen*, as he said.
    7. tell his disciples that he *is risen* from
Mar. 1:31. by the hand, and *lifted* her up;
  2: 9. or to say, *Arise*, and take up thy bed,
    11. I say unto thee, *Arise*, and take up thy bed,
    12. immediately he *arose*, took up the bed,
  3: 3. had the withered hand, *Stand* forth.
  4:27. should sleep, and *rise* night and day,
  5:41. Damsel, I say unto thee, *arise*.
  6:14. That John the Baptist *was risen*
    16. he *is risen* from the dead.
  9:27. *lifted* him *up;* and he arose.
  10:49. Be of good comfort, *rise;* he calleth thee.
  12:26. as touching the dead, that they *rise:*
  13: 8. nation *shall rise* against nation,
    22. false Christs and false prophets *shall rise*,
  14:28. after that I *am risen*, I will go
    42. *Rise up*, let us go; lo, he that
  16: 6. he *is risen;* he is not here:
    14. had seen him *after* he *was risen*.
Lu. 1:69. *hath raised up* an horn of salvation
   3: 8. *to raise up* children unto Abraham.
  5:23. or to say, *Rise up* and walk?
    24. I say unto thee, *Arise*, and take up
  6: 8. *Rise up*, and stand forth in the midst.
  7:14. Young man, I say unto thee, *Arise*.
    16. a great prophet *is risen up* among us;
    22. the deaf hear, the dead *are raised*,
  8:24. Then *he arose, and* rebuked the wind
    54. called, saying, Maid, *arise*.
  9: 7. that John *was risen* from the dead;

Lu. 9:22. and *be raised* the third day.
11: 8. he will not *rise and* give him as many
31. The queen of the south *shall rise up*
13:25. the master of the house *is risen up*,
20:37. Now that the dead *are raised*,
21:10. Nation *shall rise* against nation,
24: 6. He is not here, but *is risen:*
34. Saying, The Lord *is risen* indeed,
Joh. 2:19. in three days I *will raise* it up.
20. *wilt* thou *rear* it *up* in three days?
22. When therefore he *was risen* from the dead,
5: 8. Jesus saith unto him, *Rise,* take up
21. as the Father *raiseth up* the dead,
7:52. for out of Galilee *ariseth* no prophet.
11:29. she *arose* quickly, and came unto him.
12: 1. whom he *raised* from the dead.
9. whom he *had raised* from the dead.
17. *raised* him from the dead, bare record.
13: 4. He *riseth* from supper, and laid aside his
14:31. even so I do. *Arise,* let us go hence.
21:14. *after that* he *was risen* from the dead.
Acts 3: 6. name of Jesus Christ of Nazareth *rise up* and walk.
7. by the right hand, and *lifted* (him) *up:*
15. whom God *hath raised* from the dead;
4:10. whom God *raised* from the dead,
5:30. The God of our fathers *raised up* Jesus,
9: 8. Saul *arose* from the earth; and when
10:26. Peter *took* him *up,* saying, Stand up;
40. Him God *raised up* the third day,
12: 7. *raised* him *up,* saying, Arise up
13:22. he *raised up* unto them David
23. *raised* unto Israel a Saviour, Jesus:
30. God *raised* him from the dead:
37. he, whom God *raised again,* saw no
26: 8. that God should *raise* the dead?
Ro. 4:24. we believe on him *that raised up* Jesus
25. and *was raised again* for our justification.
6: 4. as Christ *was raised up* from the dead
9. Christ *being raised* from the dead
7: 4. to him *who is raised* from the dead
8:11. Spirit of him *that raised up* Jesus
— he *that raised up* Christ from the dead
34. yea rather, *that is risen again,*
10: 9. God *hath raised* him from the dead,
13:11. high time *to awake* out of sleep:
1Co. 6:14. God *hath* both *raised up* the Lord,
15: 4. that he *rose again* the third day
12. preached that he *rose* from the dead,
13. then *is* Christ not *risen:*
14. if Christ *be* not *risen,* then
15. of God that he *raised up* Christ: whom he *raised* not *up,* if so be that the dead *rise* not.
16. For if the dead *rise* not, then *is* not Christ *raised:*
17. if Christ *be* not *raised,* your faith
20. now *is* Christ *risen* from the dead,
29. for the dead, if the dead *rise* not at all?
32. advantageth it me, if the dead *rise* not?
35. How *are* the dead *raised up?*
42. it *is raised* in incorruption:
43. sown in dishonour; it *is raised* in glory: it is sown in weakness; it *is raised* in power:
44. it *is raised* a spiritual body.
52. the dead *shall be raised* incorruptible,
2Co. 1: 9. in God *which raiseth* the dead:
4:14. he *which raised up* the Lord Jesus *shall raise up* us also by Jesus,
5:15. unto him *which* died for them, and *rose again.*

Gal. 1: 1. the Father, *who raised* him from the dead ;
Eph. 1:20. *when* he *raised* him from the dead,
5:14. he saith, *Awake* thou that sleepest,
Col. 2:12. of God, *who hath raised* him from the dead.
1Th. 1:10. whom he *raised* from the dead,
2Ti. 2: 8. was *raised* from the dead according to
Heb 11:19. that God (was) able *to raise* (him) *up,*
Jas. 5:15. the Lord *shall raise* him *up;*
1Pet. 1:21. God, *that raised* him *up* from the dead,
Rev. 11: 1. *Rise,* and measure the temple of God,

ἔγερσις, *egersis.*

Mat. 27:53. came out of the graves after his *resurrection,*

ἐγκάθετος, *enkathetos.*

Lu. 20:20. they watched (him), and sent forth *spies,*

ἐγκαίνια, *enkainia.*

Joh. 10:22. at Jerusalem the *feast of the dedication,*

ἐγκαινίζω, *enkainizo.*

Heb. 9:18. (testament) *was dedicated* without blood.
10:20. way, which he *hath consecrated* for us,

ἐγκαλέω, *enkaleo.*

Acts 19:38. *let* them *implead* one another.
40. we are in danger *to be called in question*
23:28. the cause wherefore they *accused* him,
29. to be *accused* of questions of their law,
26: 2. the things whereof I *am accused* of the Jews:
7. king Agrippa, I *am accused* of the Jews.
Ro. 8:33. Who *shall lay* any thing *to the charge* of God's elect?

ἐγκαταλείπω, *enkatalipo.*

Mat. 27:46. my God, why *hast* thou *forsaken* me?
Mar 15:34. my God, why *hast* thou *forsaken* me?
Acts 2:27. thou *wilt* not *leave* my soul in hell,
Ro. 9:29. the Lord of Sabaoth *had left* us a seed,
2Co. 4: 9. Persecuted, but not *forsaken;* cast
2Ti. 4:10. For Demas *hath forsaken* me,
16. with me, but all (men) *forsook* me:
Heb 10:25. Not *forsaking* the assembling of ourselves together,
13: 5. I will never leave thee, nor *forsake* thee.

ἐγκατοικέω, *enkatoikeo.*

2Pet. 2: 8. that righteous man *dwelling among* them,

ἐγκεντρίζω, *enkentrizo.*

Ro. 11:17. *wert graffed in* among them,
19. broken off, that I *might be graffed in.*
23. abide not in unbelief, *shall be graffed in.* for God is able *to graff* them *in* again.

Ro. 11:24. and *wert graffed* contrary to nature *into* a
— *shall* these...*be graffed into* their own olive
tree ?

ἔγκλημα, *enkleema.*

Acts23:29. to have nothing *laid to* his *charge* worthy
25:16. concerning the *crime laid against* him.

ἐγκομβόομαι, *enkombo-omai.*

1Pet.5: 5. *be clothed with* humility: for God

ἐγκοπή, *enkopee.*

1Co. 9:12. lest we should hinder (lit. give any *hin-drance*) the gospel of Christ.

ἐγκόπτω, *enkopto.*

Acts24: 4. that I *be* not further *tedious unto* thee,
Ro. 15:22. I *have been* much *hindered* from coming
Gal. 5: 7. Ye did run well; who *did hinder* (lit. *hath hindered*) you
1Th. 2:18. once and again; but Satan *hindered* us.
1Pet.3: 7. that your prayers *be* not *hindered*.

ἐγκράτεια, *enkratia.*

Acts24:25. reasoned of righteousness, *temperance,*
Gal. 5:23. Meekness, *temperance:* against such
2Pet. 1: 6. to knowledge *temperance;* and to *temper-ance*

ἐγκρατεύομαι, *enkratuomai.*

1Co. 7: 9. if they *cannot contain,* let them marry:
9:25. striveth for the mastery *is temperate* in

ἐγκρατής, *enkratees.*

Tit. 1: 8. sober, just, holy, *temperate;*

ἐγκρίνω, *enkrino.*

2Co.10:12. we dare not *make* ourselves *of the number,*

ἐγκρύπτω, *enkrupto.*

Mat.13:33. took, and *hid in* three measures of meal,
Lu. 13:21. took and *hid in* three measures of meal,

ἔγκυος, *enkuos.*

Lu. 2: 5. his espoused wife, being *great with child.*

ἐγχρίω, *enkrio.*

Rev. 3:18. *anoint* thine eyes with eyesalve, that

ἐγώ, *ego.*

Mat. 3:11. *I* indeed baptize you with water
14. *I* have need to be baptized of thee,
5:22. *I* say unto you, That whosoever
28. *I* say unto you, That whosoever
32. *I* say unto you, That whosoever
34. *I* say unto you, Swear not at all ;
39. *I* say unto you, That ye resist not evil:
44. *I* say unto you, Love your enemies.
8: 7. unto him, *I* will come and heal him.
9. For *I* am a man under authority,
10:16. Behold, *I* send you forth as sheep in
11:10. Behold, *I* send my messenger before
12:27. if *I* by Beelzebub cast out devils,
28. if *I* cast out devils by the Spirit of God,
14:27. Be of good cheer ; it is *I;* be not afraid.
18:33. even as *I* had pity on thee ?
20:15. Is thine eye evil, because *I* am good ?
22. the cup that *I* shall drink of,
— the baptism that *I* am baptized with ?
23. the baptism that *I* am baptized with:
21:27. Neither tell *I* you by what authority
30. he answered and said, *I* (go), sir:
22:32. *I* am the God of Abraham,
23:34. behold, *I* send unto you prophets,
24: 5. in my name, saying, *I* am Christ ;
25:27. *I* should have received mine own
26:22. to say unto him, Lord, is it *I?*
25. answered and said, Master, is it *I?*
33. (yet) will *I* never be offended.
39. not as *I* will, but as thou (wilt).
28:20. lo, *I* am with you alway,
Mar 1: 2. Behold, *I* send my messenger
8. *I* indeed have baptized you with water:
6:16. It is John, whom *I* beheaded:
50. Be of good cheer: it is *I;* be not afraid.
9:25. *I* charge thee, come out of him,
10:38. drink of the cup that *I* drink of ?
— the baptism that *I* am baptized with ?
39. drink of the cup that *I* drink of; and
with the baptism that *I* am baptized
withal
11:33. Neither do *I* tell you by what
12:26. saying, *I* (am) the God of Abraham,
13: 6. in my name, saying, *I* am (Christ) ;
14:19. (Is) it *I?* and another (said), (Is) it *I?*
29. be offended, yet (will) not *I.*
36. not what *I* will, but what thou wilt.
58. *I* will destroy this temple that is
62. Jesus said, *I* am: and ye shall see
Lu. 1:18. for *I* am an old man, and my wife
19. said unto him, *I* am Gabriel,
3:16. *I* indeed baptize you with water ;
7: 8. For *I* also am a man set under
27. Behold, *I* send my messenger before
8:46. for *I* perceive that virtue is gone out of
me.
9: 9. Herod said, John have *I* beheaded:
— of whom *I* hear such things ?
10: 3. behold, *I* send you forth as lambs
35. when I come again, *I* will repay thee.
11:19. if *I* by Beelzebub cast out devils,
15:17. to spare, and *I* perish with hunger !
19:22. Thou knewest that *I* was an austere man,
23. *I* might have required mine own
20: 8. Neither tell *I* you by what authority
21: 8. in my name, saying, *I* am (Christ) ;
15. For *I* will give you a mouth and wisdom,
22:27. *I* am among you as he that serveth.
32. *I* have prayed for thee, that thy
70. said unto them, Ye say that *I* am.

Lu. 23:14. *I*, having examined (him) before you,
24:39. that it is *I* myself: handle me,
49. *I* send the promise of my Father
Joh. 1:20. confessed, *I* am not the Christ.
23. *I* (am) the voice of one crying in the
26. saying, *I* baptize with water:
27. *I* am not worthy to unloose.
30. This is he of whom *I* said, After
31. am *I* come baptizing with water.
3:28. said, *I* am not the Christ, but that
4:14. of the water that *I* shall give him
26. *I* that speak unto thee am (he).
32. *I* have meat to eat that ye
38. *I* sent you to reap that whereon ye
5: 7. while *I* am coming, another steppeth
30. *I* can of mine own self do nothing:
31. If *I* bear witness of myself, my
34. *I* receive not testimony from man:
36. *I* have greater witness than (that)
— the same works that *I* do, bear
43. *I* am come in my Father's name,
45. Do not think that *I* will accuse you
6:20. he saith unto them, It is *I*; be not
35. *I* am the bread of life: he that
40. *I* will raise him up at the last day.
41. *I* am the bread which came down
44. *I* will raise him up at the last day.
48. *I* am that bread of life.
51. *I* am the living bread which
— bread that *I* will give is my flesh, which *I*
will give for the life of
54. *I* will raise him up at the last day.
63. the words that *I* speak unto you,
70. Have not *I* chosen you twelve,
7: 7. me it hateth, because *I* testify of it,
8. *I* go not up yet unto this feast ;
17. or (whether) *I* speak of myself.
29. *I* know him: for I am from him,
34. where *I* am, (thither) ye cannot come.
36. where *I* am, (thither) ye cannot come ?
8:11. Neither do *I* condemn thee:
12. *I* am the light of the world: he
14. Though *I* bear record of myself,
15. after the flesh; *I* judge no man.
16. yet if *I* judge, my judgment
— *I* and the Father that sent me
18. *I* am one that bear witness
21. *I* go my way, and ye shall seek me,
— whither *I* go, ye cannot come.
22. Whither *I* go, ye cannot come.
23. Ye are from beneath; *I* am from above:
— *I* am not of this world.
24. if ye believe not that *I* am (he),
28. then shall ye know that *I* am (he),
29. for *I* do always those things that
38. *I* speak that which I have seen with
42. for *I* proceeded forth and came from
God ;
45. because *I* tell (you) the truth, ye
49. Jesus answered, *I* have not a devil ;
50. *I* seek not mine own glory:
54. If *I* honour myself, my honour
55. *I* know him: and if I should say,
58. Before Abraham was, *I* am.
9: 9. like him: (but) he said, *I* am (he).
39. *I* am come into this world,
10: 7. *I* am the door of the sheep.
9. *I* am the door: by me if any
10. *I* am come that they might
11. *I* am the good shepherd: the
14. *I* am the good shepherd, and know
17. because *I* lay down my life,

Joh. 10:18. *I* lay it down of myself. I have
25. works that *I* do in my Father's name,
30. *I* and (my) Father are one.
34. in your law, *I* said, Ye are gods ?
11:25. *I* am the resurrection, and the life:
27. *I* believe that thou art the Christ,
42. *I* knew that thou hearest me
12:26. where *I* am, there shall also
46. *I* am come a light into the world,
47. believe not, *I* judge him not:
49. *I* have not spoken of myself;
50. whatsoever *I* speak therefore, even
13: 7. What *I* do thou knowest not now;
14. If *I* then (your) Lord and Master,
15. that ye should do as *I* have done to you.
18. *I* know whom I have chosen:
19. ye may believe that *I* am (he).
26. *I* shall give a sop, when I have dipped (it).
33. Whither *I* go, ye cannot come ;
14: 3. that where *I* am, (there) ye may
4. whither *I* go ye know, and the way
6. *I* am the way, the truth, and the life:
10. Believest thou not that *I* am in the Father,
— the words that *I* speak unto you
11. Believe me that *I* (am) in the Father,
12. works that *I* do shall he do also;
— because *I* go unto my Father.
14. any thing in my name, *I* will do (it).
16. *I* will pray the Father, and he shall
19. because *I* live, ye shall live also.
20. know that *I* (am) in my Father,
21. *I* will love him, and will manifest
27. not as the world giveth, give *I* unto you.
28. Ye have heard how *I* said unto you,
15: 1. *I* am the true vine, and my Father
5. *I* am the vine, ye (are) the branches:
10. even as *I* have kept my Father's
14. if ye do whatsoever *I* command you.
16. *I* have chosen you, and ordained you,
19. *I* have chosen you out of the world,
20. Remember the word that *I* said
26. whom *I* will send unto you
16: 4. remember that *I* told you of them.
7. Nevertheless *I* tell you the truth ; It is
expedient for you that *I* go away:
16. because *I* go to the Father.
17. Because *I* go to the Father ?
26. not unto you, that *I* will pray
27. believed that *I* came out from God.
33. *I* have overcome the world.
17: 4. *I* have glorified thee on the earth:
9. *I* pray for them: I pray not for
11. in the world, and *I* come to thee.
12. *I* kept them in thy name:
14. *I* have given them thy word ;
— even as *I* am not of the world.
16. even as *I* am not of the world.
19. for their sakes *I* sanctify myself,
22. thou gavest me *I* have given them ;
23. *I* in them, and thou in me,
24. be with me where *I* am ;
25. *I* have known thee, and these have
18: 5. Jesus saith unto them, *I* am (he).
6. as he had said unto them, *I* am (he),
8. *I* have told you that *I* am (he):
20. *I* spake openly to the world ; *I* ever taught
in the synagogue,
21. behold, they know what *I* said.
26. Did not *I* see thee in the garden
35. Pilate answered, Am *I* a Jew ?
37. Thou sayest that *I* am a king. To this
end was *I* born, and for this

Joh.18:38. *I* find in him no fault (at all).
   19: 6. for *I* find no fault in him.
Acts 7: 7. shall be in bondage will *I* judge,
   32. (Saying), *I* (am) the God of thy fathers,
  9: 5. *I* am Jesus whom thou persecutest:
  10. he said, Behold, *I* (am here), Lord.
  16. *I* will shew him how great things
 10:20. for *I* have sent them.
  21. *I* am he whom ye seek:
 11: 5. *I* was in the city of Joppa praying:
  17. what was *I* that I could withstand God?
 13:25. *I* am not (he). But, behold, there
  33. my Son, this day have *I* begotten thee.
  41. *I* work a work in your days,
 15:19. Wherefore my sentence is (lit. *I* judge),
    that we
 17: 3. Jesus, whom *I* preach unto you,
  him declare *I* unto you.
 18: 6. *I* (am) clean: from henceforth I will go
  10. For *I* am with thee, and no man shall
  15. for *I* will be no judge of such (matters).
 20:22. *I* go bound in the spirit unto Jerusalem,
  25. now, behold, *I* know that ye all,
  26. that *I* (am) pure from the blood
  29. For *I* know this, that after my departing
 21:13. for *I* am ready not to be bound only,
  39. *I* am a man (which am) a Jew,
 22: 3. *I* am verily a man (which am) a Jew,
  8. *I* answered, Who art thou, Lord? and he
    said unto me, *I* am Jesus of Nazareth,
  19. they know that *I* imprisoned and beat
  21. for *I* will send thee far hence
  28. With a great sum obtained *I* this freedom.
    And Paul said, But *I* was (free) born.
 23: 1. *I* have lived in all good conscience
  6. Men (and) brethren, *I* am a Pharisee,
  — of the dead *I* am called in question.
 24:21. *I* am called in question by you this day.
 25:18. of such things as *I* supposed:
  20. because *I* doubted of such manner
  25. when *I* found that he had committed
 26: 9. *I* verily thought with myself, that
  10. the saints did *I* shut up in prison,
  15. *I* said, Who art thou, Lord? And he said,
    I am Jesus whom thou persecutest.
 28:17. nothing...yet was *I* delivered prisoner
Ro. 7: 9. *I* was alive without the law once:
  — but...sin revived, and *I* died.
  14. *I* am carnal, sold under sin.
  17. then it is no more *I* that do it,
  20. if I do that *I* would not, it is no more *I*
    that do it, but sin
  24. O wretched man that *I* am!
  25. *I* myself serve the law of God;
 9: 3. For I could wish that)(myself
 10:19. *I* will provoke you to jealousy by
 11: 1. For *I* also am an Israelite,
  13. as *I* am the apostle of the Gentiles,
  19. that *I* might be graffed in.
 12:19. *I* will repay, saith the Lord.
 14:11. (As) *I* live, saith the Lord, every
 15:14. *I* myself also am persuaded of you,
 16: 4. unto whom not only *I* give thanks,
  22. *I* Tertius, who wrote (this) epistle,
1Co. 1:12. *I* am of Paul; and *I* of Apollos; and *I*
    of Cephas; and *I* of Christ.
 2: 3. *I* was with you in weakness,
 3: 1. *I*, brethren, could not speak unto you
  4. while one saith, *I* am of Paul; and an-
    other, *I* (am) of Apollos;
  6. *I* have planted, Apollos watered;
 4:15. *I* have begotten you through the gospel.

1Co. 5: 3. For *I* verily, as absent in body,
 6:12. *I* will not be brought under the power
 7:10. *I* command, (yet) not *I*, but the Lord,
  12. to the rest speak *I*, not the Lord:
  28. in the flesh: but *I* spare you.
 9: 6. Or *I* only and Barnabas, have not we
  15. *I* have used none of these things:
  26. *I* therefore so run, not as uncertainly;
 10:30. For if *I* by grace be a partaker,
  — that for which *I* give thanks?
 11:23. *I* have received of the Lord
 15: 9. For *I* am the least of the apostles,
  10. yet not *I*, but the grace of God
  11. Therefore whether (it were) *I* or they,
 16:10. the work of the Lord, as *I* also (do).
2Co. 1:23. Moreover *I* call God for a record
 2: 2. For if *I* make you sorry, who
  10. *I* (forgive) also: for if *I* forgave any
 10: 1. Now *I* Paul myself beseech you
 11:23. I speak as a fool *I* (am) more;
  29. who is offended, and *I* burn not?
 12:11. *I* ought to have been commended
  13. that *I* myself was not burdensome
  15. *I* will very gladly spend and be
  16. be it so, *I* did not burden you:
Gal. 1:12. For *I* neither received it of man,
 2:19. For *I* through the law am dead
  20. nevertheless I live; yet not *I*,
 4:12. Brethren, I beseech you, be as *I* (am);
 5: 2. Behold, *I* Paul say unto you.
  10. *I* have confidence in you
  11. *I*, brethren, if I yet preach
 6:17. *I* bear in my body the marks
Eph. 3: 1. For this cause *I* Paul, the prisoner
 4: 1. *I* therefore, the prisoner of the Lord,
 5:32. *I* speak concerning Christ and the church.
Phi. 3: 4. Though *I* might also have
  — might trust in the flesh, *I* more:
  13. *I* count not myself to have apprehended:
 4:11. for *I* have learned, in whatsoever
Col. 1:23. whereof *I* Paul am made a minister;
  25. Whereof *I* am made a minister,
1Th. 2:18. even *I* Paul, once and again;
1Ti. 1:11. which was committed to *my* trust.
  15. to save sinners; of whom *I* am chief.
 2: 7. Whereunto *I* am ordained a preacher,
2Ti. 1:11. Whereunto *I* am appointed a preacher,
 4: 1. *I* charge (thee) therefore before God,
  6. *I* am now ready to be offered,
Tit. 1: 3. preaching, which is committed unto *me*
  5. in every city, as *I* had appointed thee:
Philem 13. Whom *I* would have retained with me,
  19. *I* Paul have written (it) with mine
  — *I* will repay (it): albeit I do not
  20. let *me* have joy of thee in the Lord:
Heb. 1: 5. this day have *I* begotten thee? And again,
    I will be to him a Father,
 2:13. again, *I* will put my trust in him.
  — Behold *I* and the children which God
 5: 5. my Son, to day have *I* begotten thee.
 10:30. *I* will recompense, saith the Lord.
 12:26. *I* shake not the earth only,
1Pet.1:16. Be ye holy; for *I* am holy.
2Pet.1:17. in whom *I* am well pleased.
2Joh. 1. whom *I* love in the truth; and not *I* only
    but also all they
3Joh. 1. Gaius, whom *I* love in the truth.
Rev. 1: 8. *I* am Alpha and Omega, the
  9. *I* John, who also am your brother,
  11. Saying, *I* am Alpha and Omega,
  17. Fear not; *I* am the first and the last:
 2:22. Behold, *I* will cast her into a bed,

Rev. 2:23. that *I* am he which searcheth the
    3: 9. to know that *I* have loved thee.
    19. As many as I love, *I* rebuke and chasten:
    5: 4. *I* wept much, because no man
    17: 7. *I* will tell thee the mystery of the
    21: 2. *I* John saw the holy city, new Jerusalem,
    6. *I* am Alpha and Omega, the beginning
    — *I* will give unto him that is athirst
    22: 8. *I* John saw these things, and heard
    13. *I* am Alpha and Omega, the beginning and the end,
    16. *I* Jesus have sent mine angel
    — *I* am the root and the offspring of David,

See also in κἀγώ.

ἐδαφίζω, edaphizo.

Lu. 19:44. *shall lay* thee *even with the ground,*

ἔδαφος, edaphos.

Acts22: 7. I fell unto the *ground,* and heard

ἑδραῖος, hedraios.

1Co. 7:37. he that standeth *stedfast* in his heart,
    15:58. my beloved brethren, be ye *stedfast,*
Col. 1:23. continue in the faith grounded and *settled,*

ἑδραίωμα, hedraiōma.

1 Ti. 3:15. the pillar and *ground* of the truth.

ἐθελοθρησκεία, ethelothreeskia.

Col. 2:23. a shew of wisdom in *will worship,*

ἐθέλω see ϑέλω.

ἐθίζω, ethizo.

Lu. 2:27. to do for him after the *custom* of the law, (lit. *that which was wont to be done*)

ἐθνάρχης, ethnarkees.

2Co.11:32. the *governor* under Aretas the king

ἐθνικός, ethnikos.

Mat. 6: 7. use not vain repetitions, as the *heathen*
    18:17. let him be unto thee as an *heathen man*

ἐθνικῶς, ethnikōs.

Gal. 2:14. livest *after the manner of Gentiles,*

ἔθνος, ethnos.

Mat. 4:15. beyond Jordan, Galilee of the *Gentiles:*

Mat. 6:32. after all these things do the *Gentiles* seek:
    10: 5. Go not into the way of the *Gentiles,*
    18. a testimony against them and the *Gentiles.*
    12:18. shall shew judgment to the *Gentiles.*
    21. in his name shall the *Gentiles* trust.
    20:19. shall deliver him to the *Gentiles*
    25. the princes of the *Gentiles* exercise dominion
    21:43. given to a *nation* bringing forth the
    24: 7. For *nation* shall rise against *nation,*
    9. ye shall be hated of all *nations* for
    14. for a witness unto all *nations;*
    25:32. before him shall be gathered all *nations:*
    28:19. Go ye therefore, and teach all *nations,*
Mar 10:33. shall deliver him to the *Gentiles:*
    42. accounted to rule over the *Gentiles*
    11:17. called of all *nations* the house of prayer?
    13: 8. For *nation* shall rise against *nation,*
    10. first be published among all *nations.*
Lu: 2:32. A light to lighten the *Gentiles,*
    7: 5. For he loveth our *nation,* and he hath
    12:30. do the *nations* of the world seek after:
    18:32. he shall be delivered unto the *Gentiles,*
    21:10. *Nation* shall rise against *nation,*
    24. led away captive into all *nations:*
    — shall be trodden down of the *Gentiles,* until the times of the *Gentiles* be fulfilled.
    25. upon the earth distress of *nations,*
    22:25. The kings of the *Gentiles* exercise lordship
    23: 2. We found this (fellow) perverting the *nation,*
    24:47. preached in his name among all *nations,*
Joh.11:48. take away both our place and *nation.*
    50. that the whole *nation* perish not.
    51. that Jesus should die for that *nation;*
    52. not for that *nation* only, but that
    18:35. Thine own *nation* and the chief priests
Acts 2: 5. out of every *nation* under heaven.
    4:25. Why did the *heathen* rage, and the people
    27. with the *Gentiles,* and the people of Israel,
    7: 7. the *nation* to whom they shall be
    45. into the possession of the *Gentiles,*
    8: 9. bewitched the *people* of Samaria,
    9:15. to bear my name before the *Gentiles,*
    10:22. among all the *nation* of the Jews,
    35. in every *nation* he that feareth him,
    45. on the *Gentiles* also was poured out
    11: 1. the *Gentiles* had also received the word
    18. hath God also to the *Gentiles* granted
    13:19. when he had destroyed seven *nations*
    42. the *Gentiles* besought that these words
    46. lo, we turn to the *Gentiles.*
    47. thee to be a light of the *Gentiles,*
    48. when the *Gentiles* heard this, they
    14: 2. the unbelieving Jews stirred up the *Gentiles,*
    5. of the *Gentiles,* and also of the Jews
    16. all *nations* to walk in their own ways.
    27. the door of faith unto the *Gentiles.*
    15: 3. declaring the conversion of the *Gentiles:*
    7. that the *Gentiles* by my mouth should hear
    12. wrought among the *Gentiles* by them.
    14. did visit the *Gentiles,* to take out of
    17. all the *Gentiles,* upon whom my name
    19. which from among the *Gentiles* are
    23. the brethren which are of the *Gentiles*
    17:26. made of one blood all *nations* of men
    18: 6. I will go unto the *Gentiles.*
    21:11. into the hands of the *Gentiles.*
    19. God had wrought among the *Gentiles*
    21. the Jews which are among the *Gentiles*
    25. As touching the *Gentiles* which believe,

Acts 22:21. send thee far hence unto the *Gentiles*.
24: 2. worthy deeds are done unto this *nation*
10. many years a judge unto this *nation*,
17. I came to bring alms to my *nation*,
26: 4. among mine own *nation* at Jerusalem,
17. from the people, and (from) the *Gentiles*,
20. (then) to the *Gentiles*, that they should repent
23. light unto the people, and to the *Gentiles*.
28:19. had ought to accuse my *nation* of.
28. salvation of God is sent unto the *Gentiles*,
Ro. 1: 5. to the faith among all *nations*,
13. even as among other *Gentiles*.
2:14. the *Gentiles*, which have not the law,
24. God is blasphemed among the *Gentiles*
3:29. also of the *Gentiles?* Yes, of the *Gentiles* also:
4:17. made thee a father of many *nations*,
18. become the father of many *nations*,
9:24. Jews only, but also of the *Gentiles?*
30. That the *Gentiles*, which followed not
10:19. no *people*, (and) by a foolish *nation* I will
11:11. salvation (is come) unto the *Gentiles*,
12. diminishing of them the riches of the *Gentiles;*
13. For I speak to you *Gentiles*, inasmuch as I am the apostle of the *Gentiles*,
25. until the fulness of the *Gentiles* be
15: 9. that the *Gentiles* might glorify God
— I will confess to thee among the *Gentiles*,
10. he saith, Rejoice, ye *Gentiles*,
11. Praise the Lord, all ye *Gentiles;*
12. shall rise to reign over the *Gentiles;* in him shall the *Gentiles* trust.
16. minister of Jesus Christ to the *Gentiles*,
— the offering up of the *Gentiles* might
18. to make the *Gentiles* obedient,
27. if the *Gentiles* have been made partakers
16: 4. all the churches of the *Gentiles*.
26. made known to all *nations* for
1Co. 5: 1. not so much as named among the *Gentiles*,
10:20. the things which the *Gentiles* sacrifice,
12: 2. Ye know that ye were *Gentiles*,
2Co.11:26. (in) perils by the *heathen*, (in) perils
Gal. 1:16. I might preach him among the *heathen;*
2: 2. gospel which I preach among the *Gentiles*,
8. mighty in me toward the *Gentiles:*
9. we (should go) unto the *heathen*,
12. he did eat with the *Gentiles:*
14. the *Gentiles* to live as do the Jews?
15. not sinners of the *Gentiles*,
3: 8. that God would justify the *heathen*
— In thee shall all *nations* be blessed.
14. might come on the *Gentiles* through
Eph. 2:11. ye (being) in time past *Gentiles* in
3: 1. prisoner of Jesus Christ for you *Gentiles*,
6. That the *Gentiles* should be fellowheirs,
8. I should preach among the *Gentiles*
4:17. walk not as other *Gentiles* walk,
Col. 1:27. this mystery among the *Gentiles;*
1Th. 2:16. Forbidding us to speak to the *Gentiles*
4: 5. as the *Gentiles* which know not God:
1Ti. 2: 7. a teacher of the *Gentiles* in faith
3:16. preached unto the *Gentiles*, believed
2Ti. 1:11. an apostle, and a teacher of the *Gentiles*.
4:17. (that) all the *Gentiles* might hear:
1Pet.2: 9. a royal priesthood, an holy *nation*,
12. conversation honest among the *Gentiles:*
4: 3. wrought the will of the *Gentiles*,
3Joh. 7. taking nothing of the *Gentiles*.
Rev. 2:26. to him will I give power over the *nations:*

Rev. 5: 9. every kindred, and tongue, and people and *nation;*
7: 9. no man could number, of all *nations*,
10:11. before many peoples, and *nations*, and tongues,
11: 2. for it is given unto the *Gentiles:*
9. people and kindreds and tongues and *nations*
18. the *nations* were angry, and thy wrath
12: 5. was to rule all *nations* with a rod of iron:
13: 7. over all kindreds, and tongues, and *nations*.
14: 6. to every *nation*, and kindred, and tongue,
8. she made all *nations* drink of the wine
15: 4. all *nations* shall come and worship
16:19. the cities of the *nations* fell:
17:15. peoples, and multitudes, and *nations*,
18: 3. For all *nations* have drunk of the wine
23. by thy sorceries were all *nations* deceived.
19:15. with it he should smite the *nations:*
20: 3. should deceive the *nations* no more,
8. shall go out to deceive the *nations*
21:24. the *nations* of them which are saved
26. glory and honour of the *nations* into it.
22: 2. (were) for the healing of the *nations*.

ἔθος, ethos.

Lu. 1: 9. According to the *custom* of the priest's office,
2:42. after the *custom* of the feast.
22:39. came out, and went, as he *was wont*,
Joh.19:40. as the *manner* of the Jews is to bury.
Acts 6:14. change the *customs* which Moses delivered us.
15: 1. circumcised after the *manner* of Moses,
16:21. teach *customs*, which are not lawful for us
21:21. neither to walk after the *customs*.
25:16. It is not the *manner* of the Romans
26: 3. to be expert in all *customs* and questions
28:17. against the people, or *customs* of our fathers,
Heb 10:25. as the *manner* of some (is);

ἔθω, εἴωθα, etho, iōtha.

Mat 27:15. the governor *was wont* to release unto
Mar 10: 1. as he *was wont*, he taught them again.
Lu. 4:16. as his *custom was*, he went into the
Acts17: 2. Paul, as his *manner was*, went in

εἶ, from εἰμί, i, from imi.

Mat. 2: 6. *art* not the least among the princes
4: 3. If thou *be* the Son of God, command
6. If thou *be* the Son of God, cast thyself down:
5:25. whiles thou *art* in the way with him;
11: 3. *Art* thou he that should come, or do
14:28. Lord, if it *be* thou, bid me come
33. Of a truth thou *art* the Son of God.
16:16. Thou *art* the Christ, the Son of the living God.
17. Blessed *art* thou, Simon Bar-jona:
18. I say also unto thee, That thou *art* Peter,
23. thou *art* an offence unto me: for thou
22:16. Master, we know that thou *art* true,
25:24. I knew thee that thou *art* an hard man,

Mat.26:63. whether thou *be* the Christ, the Son of God.

73. Surely thou also *art* (one) of them ;

27:11. saying, *Art* thou the King of the Jews ?

40. If thou *be* the Son of God, come down

Mar. 1:11. Thou *art* my beloved Son, in whom

24. I know thee who thou *art*, the Holy One of God

3:11. saying, Thou *art* the Son of God.

8:29. saith unto him, Thou *art* the Christ.

12:14. Master, we know that thou *art* true,

34. Thou *art* not far from the kingdom of God.

14:61. *Art* thou the Christ, the Son of the Blessed?

70. to Peter, Surely thou *art* (one) of them : for thou *art* a Galilæan, and thy speech

15: 2. *Art* thou the King of the Jews ?

Lu. 3:22. which said, Thou *art* my beloved Son ;

4: 3. If thou *be* the Son of God, command this

9. If thou *be* the Son of God, cast thyself down

34. who thou *art ;* the Holy One of God.

41. Thou *art* Christ the Son of God.

7:19. saying, *Art* thou he that should come ?

20. saying, *Art* thou he that should come ?

15:31. unto him, Son, thou *art* ever with me,

19:21. because thou *art* an austere man:

22:58. saw him, and said, Thou *art* also of them.

67(66). *Art* thou the Christ ? tell us.

70. *Art* thou then the Son of God ?

23: 3. *Art* thou the King of the Jews ?

37. If thou *be* the king of the Jews, save thyself.

39. If thou *be* Christ, save thyself and us.

40. seeing thou *art* in the same condemnation ?

Joh. 1:19. from Jerusalem to ask him, Who *art* thou ?

21. What then ? *Art* thou Elias ?

— *Art* thou that prophet ? And he answered, No.

22. said they unto him, Who *art* thou ?

25. if thou *be* not that Christ, nor Elias,

42(43). Thou *art* Simon the son of Jona:

49(50). Rabbi, thou *art* the Son of God ; thou *art* the King of Israel.

3:10. *Art* thou a master of Israel,

4:12. *Art* thou greater than our father Jacob,

19. I perceive that thou *art* a prophet.

6:69. are sure that thou *art* that Christ,

7:52. said unto him, *Art* thou also of Galilee ?

8:25. said they unto him, Who *art* thou ?

48. that thou *art* a Samaritan, and hast a devil ?

53. *Art* thou greater than our father Abraham,

9:28. reviled him, and said, Thou *art* his disciple ;

10:24. If thou *be* the Christ, tell us plainly.

11:27. I believe that thou *art* the Christ,

18:17. *Art* not thou also (one) of this man's

25. *Art* not thou also (one) of his disciples ?

33. *Art* thou the King of the Jews ?

37. said unto him, *Art* thou a king then ?

19: 9. saith unto Jesus, Whence *art* thou ?

12. thou *art* not Cæsar's friend:

21:12. durst ask him, Who *art* thou ?

Acts 9: 5. he said, Who *art* thou, Lord ?

13:33. in the second psalm, Thou *art* my Son,

21:38. *Art* not thou that Egyptian,

22: 8. I answered, Who *art* thou, Lord ?

27. Tell me, *art* thou a Roman ?

26:15. I said, Who *art* thou, Lord ?

Ro. 2: 1. Therefore thou *art* inexcusable, O man,

9:20. who *art* thou that repliest against God ?

14: 4. Who *art* thou that judgest another

Gal. 4: 7. Wherefore thou *art* no more a servant,

Heb 1: 5. Thou *art* my Son, this day have I

12. thou *art* the same, and thy years

5: 5. said unto him, Thou *art* my Son,

Jas. 4:11. thou *art* not a doer of the law,

12. who *art* thou that judgest another ?

Rev. 2: 9. tribulation, and poverty, but thou *art* rich

3: 1. hast a name that thou livest, and *art* dead.

15. that thou *art* neither cold nor hot:

16. So then because thou *art* lukewarm,

17. knowest not that thou *art* wretched,

4:11. Thou *art* worthy, O Lord, to receive glory

5: 9. Thou *art* worthy to take the book,

16: 5. Thou *art* righteous, O Lord, which art.

εἰ, ἰ, conj.

Mat. 4: 3. *If* thou be the Son of God, command

6. *If* thou be the Son of God, cast thyself down:

5:29. And *if* thy right eye offend thee, pluck

30. *if* thy right hand offend thee,

6:23. *If* therefore the light that is in thee

30. Wherefore, *if* God so clothe the grass

7:11. *If* ye then, being evil, know how

8:31. *If* thou cast us out, suffer us to go

10:25. *If* they have called the master of

11:14. And *if* ye will receive (it), this is Elias,

21. for *if* the mighty works, which were

23. for *if* the mighty works, which have

12: 7. But *if* ye had known what (this) meaneth,

10.)(Is it lawful to heal on the sabbath

26. *if* Satan cast out Satan, he is divided

27. *if* I by Beelzebub cast out devils,

28. But *if* I cast out devils by the Spirit of God,

14:28. Lord, *if* it be thou, bid me come

17: 4. *if* thou wilt, let us make here three

18: 8. Wherefore *if* thy hand or thy foot offend thee,

9. *if* thine eye offend thee, pluck it out,

19: 3.)(Is it lawful for a man to put away

10. *If* the case of the man be so with (his) wife,

17. *if* thou wilt enter into life, keep the

21. *If* thou wilt be perfect, go (and) sell that

22:45. *If* David then call him Lord,

23:30. *If* we had been in the days of our fathers,

24:24. *if* (it were) possible, they shall deceive

43. *if* the goodman of the house had known

26:24. *if* he had not been born.

39. O my Father, *if* it be possible, let

42. *if* this cup may not pass away

63. tell us *whether* thou be the Christ,

27:40. save thyself. *If* thou be the Son of God,

42. *If* he be the King of Israel, let

43. deliver him now, *if* he will have him:

49. let us see *whether* Elias will come

Mar. 3: 2. *whether* he would heal him on the sabbath day ;

26. *if* Satan rise up against himself,

8:12. There shall no sign be given (lit *if* a sign shall be given)

9:23. *If* thou canst believe, all things (are)

42. that (lit. *if*) a millstone were hanged

10: 2.)(Is it lawful for a man to put away

11:13. *if* haply he might find any thing

25. forgive, *if* ye have ought against any:

26. But *if* ye do not forgive, neither will

13:22. to seduce, *if* (it were) possible, even the elect.

14:21. that man *if* he had never been born.

29. *Although* all shall be offended,

Mar 14:35. prayed that, *if* it were possible,

    15:36. let us see *whether* Elias will come

    44. marvelled *if* he were already dead:

Lu. 4: 3. *If* thou be the Son of God, command

    9. *If* thou be the Son of God, cast

    6: 7. *whether* he would heal on the sabbath day ;

    32. For *if* ye love them which love you,

    7:39. This man, *if* he were a prophet,

    9:23. *If* any (man) will come after me,

    10:13. *if* the mighty works had been done

    11:13. *If* ye then, being evil, know how

    18. *If* Satan also be divided

    19. *if* I by Beelzebub cast out devils,

    20. But *if* I with the finger of God

    36. *If* thy whole body therefore (be) full

    12:26. *If* ye then be not able to do that

    28. *If* then God so clothe the grass,

    39. that *if* the goodman of the house

    49. what will I, *if* it be already kindled ?

    13:23. Lord,)(are there few that be saved ?

    14: 3.)(Is it lawful to heal on the sabbath day ?

    28. *whether* he have (sufficient) to finish (it) ?

    31. *whether* he be able with ten thousand

    16:11. *If* therefore ye have not been faithful

    12. *if* ye have not been faithful in that

    31. *If* they hear not Moses and the prophets,

    17: 2. that (lit. *if*) a millstone were hanged

    6. *If* ye had faith as a grain of mustard seed,

    19:42. *If* thou hadst known, even thou,

    22:42. *if* thou be willing, remove this cup

    49. Lord,)(shall we smite with the sword ?

    67.)(Art thou the Christ ? tell us.

    23: 6. *whether* the man were a Galilæan.

    31. *if* they do these things in a green tree,

    35. *if* he be Christ, the chosen of God.

    37. *If* thou be the king of the Jews,

    39. *If* thou be Christ, save thyself and us.

Joh. 1:25. Why baptizest thou then, *if* thou be not

    3:12. *If* I have told you earthly things,

    4:10. *If* thou knewest the gift of God,

    5:46. For)(had ye believed Moses, ye

    47. *if* ye believe not his writings, how

    7: 4. *If* thou do these things, shew thyself

    23. *If* a man on the sabbath day

    8:19. *if* ye had known me, ye should

    39. *If* ye were Abraham's children,

    42. *If* God were your Father,

    46. *if* I say the truth, why do ye not believe

    9:25. *Whether* he be a sinner (or no),

    41. *If* ye were blind, ye should have no sin:

    10:24. *If* thou be the Christ, tell us plainly.

    35. *If* he called them gods, unto whom

    37. *If* I do not the works of my Father,

    38. But *if* I do, though ye believe not me,

    11:12. Lord, *if* he sleep, he shall do well.

    21. Lord, *if* thou hadst been here,

    32. Lord, *if* thou hadst been here,

    13:14. *If* I then, (your) Lord and Master,

    17. *If* ye know these things, happy

    32. *If* God be glorified in him,

    14: 7. *If* ye had known me, ye should

    28. *If* ye loved me, ye would rejoice,

    15:18. *If* the world hate you, ye know that

    19. *If* ye were of the world, the world

    20. *If* they have persecuted me, they

    — *if* they have kept my saying, they will

    18: 8. *if* therefore ye seek me, let these go

    23. Jesus answered him, *If* I have spoken evil,

    — but *if* well, why smitest thou me ?

    36. *if* my kingdom were of this world,

    20:15. Sir, *if* thou have borne him hence,

Acts 1: 6.)(wilt thou at this time restore again

Acts 4: 9. *If* we this day be examined of the

    19. *Whether* it be right in the sight of God

    5: 8. *whether* ye sold the land for so much ?

    39. But *if* it be of God, ye cannot overthrow

    7: 1. said the high priest,)(Are these things

    8:22. *if* perhaps the thought of thine heart

    37. *If* thou believest with all thine heart,

    10:18. *whether* Simon, which was surnamed

    11:17. *Forasmuch* then *as* God gave them

    13:15. *if* ye have any word of exhortation

    16:15. *If* ye have judged me to be faithful

    17:11. *whether* those things were so.

    27. *if* haply they might feel after him,

    18:14. *If* it were a matter of wrong or

    15. But *if* it be a question of words

    19: 2.)(Have ye received the Holy Ghost

    — *whether* there be any Holy Ghost.

    38. Wherefore *if* Demetrius, and the craftsmen

    39. But *if* ye enquire any thing concerning

    20:16. he hasted, *if* it were possible for him,

    21:37.)(May I speak unto thee ?

    22:25.)(Is it lawful for you to scourge a man

    27. Tell me,)(art thou a Roman ?

    23: 9. *if* a spirit or an angel hath spoken

    25:11. For *if* I be an offender, or have committed

    — but *if* there be none of these things

    20. *whether* he would go to Jerusalem,

    26: 8. incredible with you, *that* God should raise the dead ?

    23. *That* Christ should suffer, (and) *that* he should be the first that should rise

    27:39. *if* it were possible, to thrust in the ship.

Ro. 3: 3. For what *if* some did not believe ?

    5. But *if* our unrighteousness commend

    7. *if* the truth of God hath more abounded

    4: 2. For *if* Abraham were justified by works,

    14. *if* they which are of the law (be) heirs,

    5:10. For *if*, when we were enemies,

    15. *If* through the offence of one many

    17. For *if* by one man's offence death

    6: 5. For *if* we have been planted together

    8. Now *if* we be dead with Christ,

    7:16. *If* then I do that which I would not,

    20. Now *if* I do that I would not,

    8: 9. *if* any man have not the Spirit of Christ,

    10. *if* Christ (be) in you, the body (is)

    11. *if* the Spirit of him that raised up

    13. For *if* ye live after the flesh, ye shall die: but *if* ye through the Spirit do mortify

    17. *if* children, then heirs ; heirs of God,

    25. *if* we hope for that we see not,

    31. *If* God (be) for us, who (can be) against us ?

    9:22. *if* God, willing to shew (his) wrath,

    11: 6. *if* by grace, then (is it) no more of works:

    — But *if* (it be) of works, then is it no more grace:

    12. Now *if* the fall of them (be) the riches

    15. For *if* the casting away of them

    16. For *if* the firstfruit (be) holy, the

    — *if* the root (be) holy, so (are) the branches.

    17. *if* some of the branches be broken off,

    18. *if* thou boast, thou bearest not the root,

    21. *if* God spared not the natural branches,

    24. For *if* thou wert cut out of the olive tree,

    12:18. *If* it be possible, as much as lieth in you,

    14:15. *if* thy brother be grieved with (thy) meat,

    15:27. For *if* the Gentiles have been made

1Co. 2: 8. for)(had they known (it), they would not

    3:12. *if* any man build upon this foundation

1Co. 4: 7. now *if* thou didst receive (it), why dost
6: 2. *if* the world shall be judged by you,
7: 9. *if* they cannot contain, let them
15. *if* the unbelieving depart, let him depart.
16. *whether* thou shalt save (thy) husband?
— *whether* thou shalt save (thy) wife?
21. *if* thou mayest be made free,
36. *if* any man think that he
8: 2. *if* any man think that he knoweth
3. *if* any man love God, the same
13. *if* meat make my brother to offend,
9: 2. *If* I be not an apostle unto others,
11. *If* we have sown unto you spiritual
— *if* we shall reap your carnal things?
12. *If* others be partakers of (this) power
17. For *if* I do this thing willingly,
— *if* against my will, a dispensation
10:27. *If* any of them that believe not
30. For *if* I by grace be a partaker,
11: 6. For *if* the woman be not covered,
— *if* it be a shame for a woman to
16. *if* any man seem to be contentious,
31. For *if* we would judge ourselves,
34. *if* any man hunger, let him eat at home;
12:17. *If* the whole body (were) an eye,
— *If* the whole (were) hearing, where
19. *if* they were all one member,
14:10. There are,)(it may be, so many kinds
35. *if* they will learn any thing,
38. *if* any man be ignorant, let him
15: 2. *if* ye keep in memory what I preached
12. Now *if* Christ be preached that he rose
13. But *if* there be no resurrection of the dead,
14. *if* Christ be not risen, then (is) our
16. *if* the dead rise not, then is not Christ
raised:
17. *if* Christ be not raised, your faith (is) vain;
19. *If* in this life only we have hope in Christ,
29. *if* the dead rise not at all? why are
32. *If* after the manner of men I have
— what advantageth it me, *if* the dead rise not?
37.)(it may chance of wheat, or of some
2Co. 2: 2. For *if* I make you sorry, who is he
5. *if* any have caused grief, he hath
9. *whether* ye be obedient in all things.
3: 7. *if* the ministration of death,
9. *if* the ministration of condemnation
11. For *if* that which is done away
5:14(15). that *if* one died for all,
8:12. For *if* there be first a willing mind,
11: 4. For *if* he that cometh preacheth another
6. though (lit. *if* even) (I be) rude in speech,
yet
30. *If* I must needs glory, I will glory
13: 4. For *though* he was crucified through
weakness,
5. Examine yourselves, *whether* ye be in
Gal. 1:10. for *if* I yet pleased men, I should not
2:14. *If* thou, being a Jew, livest after
17. *if*, while we seek to be justified
18. For *if* I build again the things
21. for *if* righteousness (come) by the law
3:18. For *if* the inheritance (be) of the law,
21. for *if* there had been a law given
29. *if* ye (be) Christ's, then are ye
4: 7. *if* a son, then an heir of God
15. *if* (it had been) possible, ye would
5:11. brethren, *if* I yet preach circumcision,
15. But *if* ye bite and devour one another,
18. But *if* ye be led of the Spirit, ye are not
25. *If* we live in the Spirit, let us also
6: 3. *if* a man think himself to be something,

Phi . 1:22. *if* I live in the flesh, this (is) the fruit
Col. 2: 5. For *though* I be absent in the flesh,
20. Wherefore *if* ye be dead with Christ
3: 1. *If* ye then be risen with Christ,
1Th. 4:14. For *if* we believe that Jesus died
2Th. 3:14. *if* any man obey not our word
1Ti. 3: 5. For *if* a man know not how to
5: 4. *if* any widow have children or
8. *if* any provide not for his own,
10. *if* she have brought up children, *if* she have
lodged strangers, *if* she have washed the
saints' feet, *if* she have relieved the
afflicted, *if* she have diligently followed
2Ti. 2:11. For *if* we be dead with (him), we
12. *If* we suffer, we shall also reign with
(him): *If* we deny (him), he also will
deny us:
13. *If* we believe not, (yet) he abideth
faithful:
Philem 17. *If* thou count me therefore a partner
18. *If* he hath wronged thee,
Heb. 2: 2. For *if* the word spoken by angels
3:11. They shall not (lit. *if* they shall) enter
into my rest.
4: 3. *if* they shall enter into my rest:
5. *If* they shall enter into my rest.
8. For *if* Jesus had given them rest,
7:11. *If* therefore perfection were by the
15. for that (lit. *if*) after the similitude of
8: 4. For *if* he were on earth, he should not
7. For *if* that first (covenant) had been
9:13. For *if* the blood of bulls and of goats,
11:15. truly, *if* they had been mindful
12: 7. *If* ye endure chastening, God dealeth
8. But *if* ye be without chastisement,
25. For *if* they escaped not who refused
Jas. 1: 5. *If* any of you lack wisdom, let him
26. *If* any man among you seem to
2: 8. *If* ye fulfil the royal law according
9. *if* ye have respect to persons, ye commit
11. Now *if* thou commit no adultery, yet
3:14. But *if* ye have bitter envying
4:11. *if* thou judge the law, thou art not
1Pet.1: 6. though now for a season, *if* need be,
17. *if* ye call on the Father, who without
2:19. *if* a man for conscience toward
20. *if*, when ye be buffeted for your faults,
— but *if*, when ye do well, and suffer (for it),
3:14. But and *if* ye suffer for righteousness'
sake,
17. *if* the will of God be so, that ye
4:14. *If* ye be reproached for the name
16. Yet *if* (any man suffer) as a Christian,
17. *if* (it) first (begin) at us, what shall
18. *if* the righteous scarcely be saved,
2Pet.2: 4. For *if* God spared not the angels
20. For *if* after they have escaped the
1Joh.2:19. for *if* they had been of us, they would
3:13. my brethren, *if* the world hate you.
4: 1. the spirits *whether* they are of God:
11. *if* God so loved us, we ought also
5: 9. *If* we receive the witness of men,

εἴγε, ige.

2Co. 5: 3. *If so be that* being clothed we
Gal. 3: 4. many things in vain? *if* (it be) *yet* in vain.
Eph. 3: 2. *If* ye have heard of the dispensation
4:21. *If so be that* ye have heard him,
Col. 1:23. *If* ye continue in the faith

εἰ δὲ μή, & εἰ δὲ μήγε,
i de mee, & *ī de meege.*

Mat. 6: 1. *otherwise* ye have no reward of your
9:17. *else* the bottles break, and the wine runneth out,
Mar. 2:21. *else* the new piece that filled it up
22. *else* the new wine doth burst the bottles,
Lu. 5:36. *if otherwise,* then both the new maketh
37. *else* the new wine will burst the
10: 6. *if not,* it shall turn to you again.
13: 9. if it bear fruit, (well): *and if not,* (then)
14:32. *Or else,* while the other is yet a great
Joh.14: 2. *if* (it were) *not* (so), I would have told you.
11. *or else* believe me for the very works' sake.
2Co.11:16. *if otherwise,* yet as a fool receive me,
Rev. 2: 5. *or else* I will come unto thee quickly,
16. Repent; *or else* I will come unto thee

εἰ καὶ, *ī kai.*

Mat.26:33. *Though* all (men) shall be offended
Lu. 11: 8. *Though* he will not rise and give him,
18: 4. *Though* I fear not God, nor regard man;
2Co. 4: 3. But *if* our gospel be hid, it is hid to them
16. *though* our outward man perish,
5:16. yea, *though* we have known Christ after
7: 8. For *though* I made you sorry with a letter,
I do not repent, *though* I did repent:
— *though* (it were) but for a season.
12. Wherefore, *though* I wrote unto you,
11:15. *if* his ministers also be transformed
12:11. chiefest apostles, *though* I be nothing.
15. *though* the more abundantly I love you,
Phi. 2:17. Yea, *and if* I be offered upon the sacrifice
3:12. *if that* I may apprehend that
Heb. 6: 9. accompany salvation, *though* we thus speak.

εἰ μὴ, *ī mee.*

Mat. 5:13. good for nothing, *but* to be cast out,
11:27. knoweth the Son, *but* the Father; neither knoweth any man the Father, *save* the Son,
12: 4. with him, *but* only for the priests?
24. *but* by Beelzebub the prince of the devils.
39. *but* the sign of the prophet Jonas:
13:57. without honour, *save* in his own country,
14:17. We have here *but* five loaves,
15:24. I am not sent *but* unto the lost sheep
16: 4. *but* the sign of the prophet Jonas.
17: 8. they saw no man, *save* Jesus only.
21. goeth not out *but* by prayer and fasting.
19: 9. *except* (it be) for fornication,
17. (there is) none good *but* one, (that is), God:
21:19. found nothing thereon, *but* leaves only,
24:22. *except* those days should be shortened,
36. of heaven, *but* my Father only.
Mar 2: 7. who can forgive sins *but* God only?
26. not lawful to eat *but* for the priests,
5:37. suffered no man to follow him, *save* Peter,
6: 4. without honour, *but* in his own country,
5. *save that* he laid his hands upon a
8. nothing for (their) journey, *save* a staff
8:14. with them *more than* one loaf.
9: 9. till (lit. *except* when) the Son of man were risen

Mar 9:29. by nothing, *but* by prayer and fasting.
10:18. (there is) none good *but* one, (that is), God.
11:13. he found nothing *but* leaves;
13:20. *except that* the Lord had shortened
32. neither the Son, *but* the Father.
Lu. 4:26. was Elias sent, *save* unto Sarepta,
27. was cleansed, *saving* Naaman the Syrian.
5:21. Who can forgive sins, *but* God alone?
6: 4. not lawful to eat *but* for the priests alone?
8:51. no man to go in, *save* Peter, and James, and John,
10:22. knoweth who the Son is, *but* the Father; and who the Father is, *but* the Son,
11:29. *but* the sign of Jonas the prophet.
17:18. to give glory to God, *save* this stranger.
18:19. none (is) good, *save* one, (that is), God.
Joh. 3:13. *but* he that came down from heaven,
6:22. *save* that one whereinto his disciples
46. *save* he which is of God, he hath
9:33. *If* this man were *not* of God, he
10:10. The thief cometh not, *but* for to steal,
14: 6. no man cometh unto the Father, *but* by me.
15:22. *If* I had *not* come and spoken unto them,
24. *If* I had *not* done among them the
17:12. is lost, *but* the son of perdition;
18:30. *If* he were *not* a malefactor, we
19:11. *except* it were given thee from above:
15. We have no king *but* Cæsar.
Acts11:19. to none *but* unto the Jews only.
21:25. *save only that* they keep themselves
26:32. *if* he had *not* appealed unto Cæsar.
Ro. 7: 7. I had not known sin, *but* by the law:
— *except* the law had said, Thou
9:29. *Except* the Lord of Sabaoth had
11:15. (of them be), *but* life from the dead?
13: 1. For there is no power *but* of God:
8. any thing, *but* to love one another:
14:14. *but* to him that esteemeth any
1Co. 1:14. none of you, *but* Crispus and Gaius;
2: 2. *save* Jesus Christ, and him crucified.
11. *save* the spirit of man which is
— knoweth no man, *but* the Spirit of God.
7:17. *But* as God hath distributed to every man,
8: 4. (there is) none other God *but* one.
10:13. *but* such as is common to man:
12: 3. *but* by the Holy Ghost.
14: 5. *except*)(he interpret, that the church
15: 2. *unless*)(ye have believed in vain.
2Co. 2: 2. *but* the same which is made sorry
3: 1. or need we (lit. *if* we need *not*), as some (others), epistles
12: 5. I will not glory, *but* in mine infirmities.
13. *except* (it be) that I myself was not
Gal 1: 7. *but* there be some that trouble you,
19. saw I none, *save* James the Lord's brother.
6:14. that I should glory, *save* in the cross of
Eph. 4: 9. what is it *but* that he also descended
Phi. 4:15. concerning giving and receiving, *but* ye only.
1Ti. 5:19. but (lit. *unless with this exception*) before two or three witnesses.
Heb. 3:18. *but* to them that believed not?
1Joh.2:22. Who is a liar *but* he that denieth
5: 5. *but* he that believeth that Jesus is
Rev. 2:17. no man knoweth *saving* he that
9: 4. *but* only those men which have not
13:17. buy or sell, *save* he that had the mark,
14: 3. *but* the hundred (and) forty (and) four thousand,
19:12. that no man knew, *but* he himself.

Rev.21:27. *but* they which are written in the Lamb's book

εἰ μή τι, *ī mee ti.*

Lu. 9:13. *except* we should go and buy meat
1Co. 7:· 5. *except* (it be) with consent for a time,
2Co.13: 5. Christ is in you, *except* ye be reprobates?

εἰ περ, *ī per.*

Ro. 8: 9. *if so be that* the Spirit of God dwell in you.
      17. *if so be that* we suffer with (him),
1Co. 8: 5. For *though* there be that are called gods,
     15:15. *if* so be *that* the dead rise not.
2Th. 1: 6. *Seeing* (it is) a righteous thing with God
1Pet.2: 3. *If so be* ye have tasted that the Lord

εἰ πως, *ī pōs.*

Acts27:12. *if by any means* they might attain
Ro. 1:10. *if by any means* now at length
     11:14. *If by any means* I may provoke to
Phi. 3:11. *If by any means* I might attain unto

εἴτε, *īte.*

Ro. 12: 6. *whether* prophecy, (let us prophesy) according
       7. *Or* ministry, (let us wait) on (our) ministering: *or* he that teacheth, on teaching;
       8. *Or* he that exhorteth, on exhortation:
1Co. 3:22. *Whether* Paul, *or* Apollos, *or* Cephas, *or* the world, *or* life, *or* death, *or* things present, *or* things to come;
     8: 5. *whether* in heaven *or* in earth,
    10:31. *Whether* therefore ye eat, *or* drink, *or* whatsoever
    12:13. *whether* (we be) Jews *or* Gentiles, *whether* (we be) bond *or* free;
       26. *whether* one member suffer, all the members suffer with it; *or* one member be honoured,
    13: 8. *whether* (there be) prophecies, they shall fail; *whether* (there be) tongues, they shall cease; *whether* (there be) knowledge, it shall
    14: 7. *whether* pipe *or* harp, except they give
       27. *If* any man speak in an (unknown) tongue,
    15:11. Therefore *whether* (it were) I *or* they, so
2Co. 1: 6. And *whether* we be afflicted, (it is) for your
      — *or whether* we be comforted, (it is) for your
     5: 9. *whether* present *or* absent, we may be
       10. hath done, *whether* (it be) good *or* bad.
       13. *whether* we be beside ourselves, (it is) to God, *or whether* we be sober,
     8:23. *Whether* (any do enquire) of Titus,
      — *or* our brethren (be enquired of),
    12: 2. *whether* in the body, I cannot tell; *or whether*
       3. *whether* in the body, or out of the body,
Eph. 6: 8. of the Lord, *whether* (he be) bond *or* free.
Phi. 1:18. *whether* in pretence, *or* in truth,
       20. *whether* (it be) by life, *or* by death.
       27. *whether* I come and see you, *or* else be absent,

---

Col. 1:16. *whether* (they be) thrones, *or* dominions, *or* principalities, *or* powers:
       20. *whether* (they be) things in earth, *or* things
1Th. 5:10. *whether* we wake *or* sleep, we should
2Th. 2:15. taught, *whether* by word, *or* our epistle.
1Pet. 2:13. *whether* it be to the king, as supreme;
        14. *Or* unto governors, as unto them that

εἴ τις, *ī tis.*

Mat.16:24. *If any* (man) will come after me,
Mar. 4:23. *If any* man have ears to hear,
     7:16. *If any* man have ears to hear,
     8:23. he asked him *if* he saw *ought.*
     9:22. *if* thou canst do *any thing,* have compassion
       35. *If any* man desire to be first,
Lu. 14:26. *If any* (man) come to me, and hate not
     19: 8. *if* I have taken any thing *from any* man
Acts24:19. *if* they had *ought* against me.
       20. *if* they have found *any* evil doing in me,
     25: 5. *if* there be *any* wickedness in him.
Ro. 13: 9. *if* (there be) *any* other commandment,
1Co. 1:16. I know not *whether* I baptized *any* other.
      3:14. *If any* man's work abide which
       15. *If any* man's work shall be burned,
       17. *If any* man defile the temple of God,
       18. *If any* man among you seemeth to be
      7:12. *If any* brother hath a wife that believeth not,
     14:37. *If any* man think himself to be a prophet,
     16:22. *If any* man love not the Lord Jesus Christ,
2Co. 2:10. for *if* I forgave *any thing,* to whom
      5:17. Therefore *if any* man (be) in Christ,
      7:14. *if* I have boasted *any thing* to him
     10: 7. *If any* man trust to himself
     11:20. *if a man* bring you into bondage, *if a man* devour (you), *if a man* take (of you), *if a man* exalt himself, *if a man* smite
Gal. 1: 9. *If any* (man) preach any other gospel
Eph. 4:29. but that which (lit. *if any*) is good to the use of
Phi. 2: 1. *If* (there be) therefore *any* consolation in Christ, *if any* comfort of love, *if any* fellowship of the Spirit, *if any* bowels and mercies,
      3: 4. *If any* other man thinketh that
       15. *if* in *any thing* ye be otherwise
      4: 8. *if* (there be) *any* virtue, and *if* (there be) *any* praise,
2Th. 3:10. that *if any* would not work,
1Ti. 1:10. *if* there be *any* other thing that
      3: 1. *If a man* desire the office of a bishop,
      5:16. *If any* man or woman that
      6: 3. *If any* man teach otherwise,
Tit. 1: 6. *If any* be blameless, the husband
Jas. 1:23. For *if any* be a hearer of the word,
     3: 2. *If any* man offend not in word,
1Pet.3: 1. that, *if any* obey not the word, they
     4:11. *If any* man speak, (let him speak)
      — *if any* man minister, (let him do it)
2Joh. 10. *If* there come *any* unto you, and bring
Rev.11: 5. *if any* man will hurt them, fire
      — *if any* man will hurt them, he must
     13: 9. *If any* man have an ear, let him hear.
       10. He that (lit. *if any*) leadeth into captivity shall go into captivity: he that (lit. *if any*) killeth with the sword
     14: 9. *If any* man worship the beast
       11. *whosoever* receiveth the mark of his name.
     20:15. *whosoever* was not found written

εἰδέω, εἴδω, οἶδα,
ideo, ido, oida.

Mat. 2: 2. for we *have seen* his star in the east,
　　 9. the star, which they *saw* in the east,
　　 10. *When* they *saw* the star, they rejoiced
　　 16. Herod, *when* he *saw* that he was
　 3: 7. *when* he *saw* many of the Pharisees
　　 16. he *saw* the spirit of God descending
　 4:16. which sat in darkness *saw* great light;
　　 18. by the sea of Galilee, *saw* two brethren,
　　 21. from thence, he *saw* other two brethren,
　 5: 1. *seeing* the multitudes, he went up
　　 16. that they *may see* your good works,
　 6: 8. your Father *knoweth* what things
　　 32. your heavenly Father *knoweth* that ye
　 7:11. If ye then,...*know* how to give good
　 8:14. he *saw* his wife's mother laid, and sick
　　 18. Now *when* Jesus *saw* great multitudes
　　 34. *when* they *saw* him, they besought
　 9: 2. Jesus *seeing* their faith said unto
　　 4. said, Jesus *knowing* their thoughts said,
　　 6. that ye *may know* that the Son of man
　　 8. But *when* the multitudes *saw* (it), they
　　 9. he *saw* a man, named Matthew,
　　 11. And *when* the Pharisees *saw* (it), they
　　 22. and *when* he *saw* her, he said, Daughter,
　 ·23. and *saw* the minstrels and the people
　　 36. But *when* he *saw* the multitudes, he was
　11: 8. what went ye out *for to see?* A man
　　 9. what went ye out *for to see?* A prophet?
　12: 2. But *when* the Pharisees *saw* (it), they said
　　 25. Jesus *knew* their thoughts, *and* said
　　 38. Master, we would *see* a sign from thee.
　13:14. ye shall see, and shall not *perceive:*
　　 15. lest at any time they *should see* with
　　 17. righteous (men) have desired *to see* (those
　　　　 things) which ye see, and *have* not *seen*
　　　　 (them);
　14:14. Jesus went forth, and *saw* a great
　　 26. And *when* the disciples *saw* him walking
　15:12. *Knowest* thou that the Pharisees were
　16:28. till they *see* the Son of man coming
　17: 8. they *saw* no man, save Jesus only.
　18:31. So *when* his fellowservants *saw* what
　20: 3. and *saw* others standing idle in the
　　 22. said, Ye *know* not what ye ask.
　　 25. Ye *know* that the princes of the Gentiles
　21:15. And *when* the chief priests and scribes *saw*
　　 19. And *when* he *saw* a fig tree in the way,
　　 20. And *when* the disciples *saw* (it) they
　　　　 marvelled,
　　 27. they answered Jesus, and said, We can-
　　　　 not *tell.*
　　 32. ye, *when* ye *had seen* (it), repented not
　　 38. But *when* the husbandmen *saw* the son,
　22:11. he *saw* there a man which had not
　　 16. Master, we *know* that thou art true,
　　 29. Ye do err, not *knowing* the scriptures,
　23:39. Ye shall not *see* me henceforth, till
　24:15. shall *see* the abomination of desolation,
　　 33. when ye shall *see* all these things,
　　 36. of that day and hour *knoweth* no (man),
　　 42. ye *know* not what hour your Lord
　　 43. man of the house *had known* in what
　25:12. Verily I say unto you, I *know* you not.
　　 13. ye *know* neither the day nor the hour
　　 26. thou *knewest* that I reap where
　　 37. Lord, when *saw* we thee an hungred,
　　 38. When *saw* we thee a stranger,
　　 39. Or when *saw* we thee sick, or in prison,

Mat.25:44. Lord, when *saw* we thee an hungred,
　26: 2. Ye *know* that after two days is (the feast)
　　 8. But *when* his disciples *saw* (it), they had
　　 58. sat with the servants, *to see* the end.
　　 70. I *know* not what thou sayest.
　　 71. another (maid) *saw* him, and said
　　 72. I *do* not *know* the man.
　　 74. to swear, (saying), I *know* not the man.
　27: 3. *when* he *saw* that he was condemned,
　　 18. For he *knew* that for envy they had
　　 24. *When* Pilate *saw* that he could prevail
　　 49. *let* us *see* whether Elias will come
　　 54. *saw* the earthquake, and those things
　　 65. make (it) as sure as ye *can.* (lit. *know*)
　28: 5. for I *know* that ye seek Jesus,
　　 6. Come, *see* the place where the Lord lay.
　　 17. And *when* they *saw* him, they worshipped
Mar. 1:10. he *saw* the heavens opened, and the
　　 16. he *saw* Simon and Andrew his brother
　　 19. he *saw* James the (son) of Zebedee,
　　 24. I *know* thee who thou art, the
　　 34. devils to speak, because they *knew* him.
　 2: 5. *When* Jesus *saw* their faith, he said
　　 10. that ye *may know* that the Son of man
　　 12. saying, We never *saw* it on this fashion.
　　 14. he *saw* Levi the (son) of Alphæus
　　 16. And *when* the scribes and Pharisees *saw*
　 4:12. they may see, and not *perceive;*
　　 13. *Know* ye not this parable? and how
　　 27. grow up, he *knoweth* not how.
　 5: 6. But *when* he *saw* Jesus afar off, he ran
　　 14. they went out *to see* what it was
　　 16. they *that saw* (it) told them how it
　　 22. and *when* he *saw* him, he fell at his feet,
　　 32. he looked round about *to see* her that
　　 33. *knowing* what was done in her,
　 6:20. *knowing* that he was a just man
　　 33. the people *saw* them departing,
　　 34. And Jesus, when he came out, *saw*
　　 38. How many loaves have ye? go and *see.*
　　 48. he *saw* them toiling in rowing;
　　 49. But *when* they *saw* him walking upon
　　 50. For they all *saw* him, and were troubled.
　 7: 2. And *when* they *saw* some of his disciples
　 8:33. when he had turned about and *looked* on
　 9: 1. till they *have seen* the kingdom of God
　　 6. For he *wist* not what to say; for they
　　 8. they *saw* no man any more, save Jesus
　　 9. tell no man what things they *had seen,*
　　 14. he *saw* a great multitude about them,
　　 15. the people, *when* they *beheld* him,
　　 20. and *when* he *saw* him, straightway the
　　 25. *When* Jesus *saw* that the people came
　　 38. we *saw* one casting out devils in thy name,
　10:14. But *when* Jesus *saw* (it), he was much
　　 19. Thou *knowest* the commandments,
　　 38. Ye *know* not what ye ask:
　　 42. Ye *know* that they which are accounted
　11:13. *seeing* a fig tree afar off having leaves,
　　 20. they *saw* the fig tree dried up
　　 33. answered and said unto Jesus, We *cannot*
　　　　 tell.
　12:14. Master, we *know* that thou art true,
　　 15. he, *knowing* their hypocrisy,
　　 — bring me a penny, that I *may see* (it).
　　 24. *because* ye *know* not the scriptures,
　　 28. *perceiving* that he had answered
　　 34. *when* Jesus *saw* that he answered discreetly,
　13:14. when ye shall *see* the abomination of
　　 29. when ye shall *see* these things come to pass,
　　 32. But of that day and (that) hour *knoweth* no
　　 33. for ye *know* not when the time is.

Mar 13:35. ye *know* not when the master of the house

14:40. neither *wist* they what to answer him.

67. *when* she *saw* Peter warming himself,

68. he denied, saying, I *know* not, neither

69. a maid *saw* him again, *and* began

71. I *know* not this man of whom ye speak.

15:32. that we *may see* and believe.

36. *let* us *see* whether Elias will come

39. *when* the centurion...*saw* that he so cried out,

16: 5. they *saw* a young man sitting on the

Lu. 1:12. *when* Zacharias *saw* (him), he was

29. *when* she *saw* (him), she was troubled

2:15. Let us now go...and *see* this thing which is come to pass,

17. *when* they *had seen* (it), they made

20. things that they had heard and *seen*,

26. that he should not *see* death, before he *had seen* the Lord's Christ.

30. For mine eyes *have seen* thy salvation,

48. *when* they *saw* him, they were amazed:

49. *wist* ye not that I must be about

4:34. I *know* thee who thou art; the Holy

41. for they *knew* that he was Christ.

5: 2. *saw* two ships standing by the lake:

8. *When* Simon Peter *saw* (it), he fell down

12. who *seeing* Jesus fell on (his) face,

20. *when* he *saw* their faith, he said

24. that ye *may know* that the Son of man

26. We *have seen* strange things to day.

6: 8. he *knew* their thoughts, and said to the man

7:13. *when* the Lord *saw* her, he had compassion

22. tell John what things ye *have seen*

25. what went ye out *for to see?*

26. what went ye out *for to see?* A prophet?

39. Now *when* the Pharisee...*saw* (it),

8:20. stand without, desiring *to see* thee.

28. *When* he *saw* Jesus, he cried out,

34. *When* they that fed (them) *saw* what

35. they went out *to see* what was done;

36. They also *which saw* (it) told them

47. *when* the woman *saw* that she was not hid,

53. *knowing* that she was dead.

9: 9. he desired *to see* him.

27. till they *see* the kingdom of God.

32. they *saw* his glory, and the two men

33. one for Elias: not *knowing* what he said.

47. Jesus, *perceiving* the thought of their heart,

49. we *saw* one casting out devils in thy name;

54. *when* his disciples James and John *saw*

55. Ye *know* not what manner of spirit

10:24. kings have desired *to see* those things which ye see, and *have* not *seen* (them);

31. *when* he *saw* him, he passed by on the

32. came and *looked* (on him), *and* passed by

33. *when* he *saw* him, he had compassion (on him),

11:13. *know* how to give good gifts unto

17. he, *knowing* their thoughts, said

38. And *when* the Pharisee *saw* (it), he

44. that walk over (them) *are* not *aware* (of them).

12:30. and your Father *knoweth* that ye have need

39. goodman of the house *had known* what

54. When ye *see* a cloud rise out of the west,

56. ye *can* discern the face of the sky and of the earth;

13:12. *when* Jesus *saw* her, he called (her to him),

25. I *know* you not whence ye are;

27. I *know* you not whence ye are; depart

35. say unto you, Ye shall not *see* me, until

14:18. I must needs go and *see* it: I pray thee

Lu. 15:20. his father *saw* him, and had compassion,

17:14. *when* he *saw* (them), he said unto them,

15. *when* he *saw* that he was healed,

22. ye shall desire *to see* one of the days of

18:15. *when* (his) disciples *saw* (it), they rebuked

20. Thou *knowest* the commandments,

24. *when* Jesus *saw* that he was very

43. all the people, *when* they *saw* (it),

19: 3. he sought *to see* Jesus who he was;

4. up into a sycomore tree to *see* him:

5. he looked up, and *saw* him, and said

7. *when* they *saw* (it), they all murmured,

22. Thou *knewest* that I was an austere man

37. the mighty works that they *had seen;*

41. he *beheld* the city, *and* wept over it,

20: 7. that they could not *tell* whence (it was).

13. reverence (him) *when* they *see* him.

14. *when* the husbandmen *saw* him,

21. we *know* that thou sayest and teachest

21: 1. And he looked up, and *saw* the rich

2. he *saw* also a certain poor widow

20. when ye shall *see* Jerusalem compassed

29. *Behold* the fig tree, and all the trees;

31. *when* ye *see* these things come to pass,

22:34. shalt thrice deny that thou *knowest me.*

49. *When* they which were about him *saw*

56. a certain maid *beheld* him...*and* said,

57. saying, Woman, I *know* him not.

58. another *saw* him, *and* said,

60. Man, I *know* not what thou sayest.

23: 8. And *when* Herod *saw* Jesus, he

— was desirous *to see* him of a long (season),

— he hoped *to have seen* some miracle

34. for they *know* not what they do.

47. *when* the centurion *saw* what was done,

24:24. had said: but him they *saw* not.

39. *Behold* my hands and my feet, that it is I myself: handle me, and *see;*

Joh. 1:26. one among you, whom ye *know* not;

31. I *knew* him not: but that he should

33. I *knew* him not: but he that sent

— Upon whom thou shalt *see* the Spirit

39(40). He saith unto them, Come and *see.* They came and *saw* where he dwelt,

46(47). Philip saith unto him, Come and *see.*

47(48). Jesus *saw* Nathanael coming to him,

48(49). thou wast under the fig tree, I *saw* thee.

50(51). I *saw* thee under the fig tree,

2: 9. *knew* not whence it was: but the servants which drew the water *knew;*

3: 2. we *know* that thou art a teacher

3. he cannot *see* the kingdom of God.

8. *canst* not *tell* whence it cometh,

11. We speak that we *do know,* and testify

4:10. If thou *knewest* the gift of God, and who

22. Ye worship ye *know* not what: we *know* what we worship:

25. I *know* that Messias cometh, which is

29. Come, *see* a man, which told me

32. meat to eat that ye *know* not *of.*

42. we have heard (him) ourselves, and *know*

48. Except ye *see* signs and wonders, ye will

5: 6. *When* Jesus *saw* him lie, and knew that

13. he that was healed *wist* not who it was:

32. I *know* that the witness which he

6: 6. he himself *knew* what he would do.

14. *when* they *had seen* the miracle

22. *when* the people...*saw* that there was

24. the people therefore *saw* that Jesus was

26. not because ye *saw* the miracles,

30. that we *may see,* and believe thee?

Joh. 6:42. whose father and mother we *know*?
61. *When* Jesus *knew* in himself that
64. For Jesus *knew* from the beginning
7:15. saying, How *knoweth* this man letters,
27. we *know* this man whence he is:
28. Ye both *know* me, and ye *know* whence I am:
— sent me is true, whom ye *know* not.
29. I *know* him: for I am from him,
52. Search, and *look:* for out of Galilee ariseth no prophet.
8:14. I *know* whence I came, and whither I go; but ye *cannot tell* whence
19. Ye neither *know* me, nor my Father:
— if ye *had known* me, ye should *have known* my Father also.
37. I *know* that ye are Abraham's seed ;
55. I *know* him: and if I should say, I *know* him not,
— I *know* him, and keep his saying.
56. Abraham rejoiced to *see* my day: and he *saw* (it), and was glad.
9: 1. he *saw* a man which was blind from
12. Where is he? He said, I *know* not.
20. We *know* that this is our son,
21. what means he now seeth, we *know* not; or who hath opened his eyes, we *know* not:
24. we *know* that this man is a sinner.
25. I *know* not: one thing I *know*, that,
29. We *know* that God spake unto Moses:
— we *know* not from whence he is.
30. that ye *know* not from whence he is,
31. we *know* that God heareth not sinners:
10: 4. sheep follow him: for they *know* his voice.
5. they *know* not the voice of strangers.
11:22. I *know*, that even now, whatsoever
24. I *know* that he shall rise again
31. *when* they *saw* Mary, that she rose
32. was come where Jesus was, *and saw* him,
33. When Jesus therefore *saw* her weeping,
34. said unto him, Lord, come and *see*.
42. I *knew* that thou hearest me always:
49. Ye *know* nothing at all,
12: 9. that they *might see* Lazarus also,
21. saying, Sir, we would *see* Jesus.
35. in darkness *knoweth* not whither he
40. that they *should* not *see* with
41. when he *saw* his glory, and spake of him.
50. I *know* that his commandment
13: 1. *when* Jesus *knew* that his hour
3. Jesus *knowing* that the Father had
7. What I do thou *knowest* not now ;
11. For he *knew* who should betray him ;
17. If ye *know* these things, happy are ye if
18. I *know* whom I have chosen:
14: 4. whither I go ye *know*, and the way ye *know*.
5. Lord, we *know* not whither thou goest ; and how can we *know* the way?
15:15. the servant *knoweth* not what his lord doeth:
21. they *know* not him that sent me.
16:18. we *cannot tell* what he saith.
30. Now *are* we *sure* that thou *knowest* all
18: 2. Judas also, which betrayed him, *knew*
4. *knowing* all things that should come
21. behold, they *know* what I said.
26. Did not I *see* thee in the garden
19: 6. priests therefore and officers *saw* him,
10. *knowest* thou not that I have power
26. *When* Jesus therefore *saw* his mother,
28. Jesus *knowing* that all things were
33. *saw* that he was dead already,
35. he *knoweth* that he saith true,

Joh. 20: 2. we *know* not where they have laid him.
8. to the sepulchre, and he *saw*, and believed.
9. as yet they *knew* not the scripture,
13. I *know* not where they have laid him.
14. *knew* not that it was Jesus.
20. disciples glad, *when* they *saw* the Lord.
25. Except I shall *see* in his hands the
27. Reach hither thy finger, and *behold* my hands;
29. they *that have* not *seen*, and (yet)
21: 4. disciples *knew* not that it was Jesus.
12. *knowing* that it was the Lord.
15. Lord; thou *knowest* that I love thee.
16. Yea, Lord; thou *knowest* that I love thee.
17. Lord, thou *knowest* all things ;
21. Peter *seeing* him saith to Jesus,
24. we *know* that his testimony is true.
Acts 2:22. as ye yourselves also *know:*
27. thine Holy One *to see* corruption.
30. *knowing* that God had sworn with
31. neither his flesh *did see* corruption.
3: 3. Who *seeing* Peter and John about to go
9. all the people *saw* him walking
12. *when* Peter *saw* (it), he answered
16. this man strong, whom ye see and *know:*
17. I *wot* that through ignorance ye did (it),
4:20. things which we *have seen* and heard.
5: 7. his wife, not *knowing* what was done,
6:15. *saw* his face as it had been the face
7:18. another king arose, which *knew* not Joseph.
24. *seeing* one (of them) suffer wrong,
31. *When* Moses *saw* (it), he wondered
34. I have seen, I *have seen* (lit. *seeing* I *have seen*) the affliction of my people
40. we *wot* not what is become of him.
55. *saw* the glory of God, and Jésus standing
8:39. that the eunuch *saw* him no more:
9:12. *hath seen* in a vision a man
27. how he *had seen* the Lord in the way,
35. all that dwelt at Lydda and Saron *saw*
40. *when* she *saw* Peter, she sat up.
10: 3. He *saw* in a vision evidently
17. what this vision which he *had seen*
37. That word, (I say,) ye *know*,
11: 5. in a trance I *saw* a vision,
6. I considered, and *saw* fourfooted
13. he *had seen* an angel in his house,
23. *when* he came, and *had seen* the grace
12: 3. *because* he *saw* it pleased the Jews,
9. *wist* not that it was true which
11. Now I *know* of a surety, that the Lord
16. had opened (the door), and *saw* him,
13:12. the deputy, *when* he *saw* what was done,
35. thine Holy One *to see* corruption.
36. laid unto his fathers, and *saw* corruption:
37. God raised again, *saw* no corruption.
41. *Behold*, ye despisers, and wonder, and perish:
45. *when* the Jews *saw* the multitudes,
14: 9. *perceiving* that he had faith to be healed,
11. *when* the people *saw* what Paul had done,
15: 6. came together for *to consider* of this matter.
16: 3. they *knew* all that his father was a Greek.
10. after he *had seen* the vision, immediately
19. And *when* her masters *saw* that the hope
27. *seeing* the prison doors open, he drew
40. *when* they *had seen* the brethren,
19:21. I have been there, I must also *see* Rome.
32. the more part *knew* not wherefore
20:22. not *knowing* the things that shall
25. now, behold, I *know* that ye all,
29. I *know* this, that after my departing

Acts21:32. *when* they *saw* the chief captain
22:14. know his will, and *see* that Just One,
   18. And *saw* him saying unto me, Make
23: 5. Then said Paul, I *wist* not, brethren,
24:22. *having* more perfect *knowledge* of (that) way,
26:13. I *saw* in the way a light from heaven,
   16. these things which thou *hast seen,*
   27. I *know* that thou believest.
28: 4. when the barbarians *saw* the
   15. whom *when* Paul *saw,* he thanked God,
   20. *to see* (you), and to speak with (you):
   26. seeing ye shall see, and not *perceive:*
   27. lest they *should see* with (their) eyes,
Ro. 1:11. For I long *to see* you, that I may
2: 2. we *are sure* that the judgment
3:19. Now we *know* that what things
5: 3. *knowing* that tribulation worketh patience;
6: 9. *Knowing* that Christ being raised
   16. *Know* ye not, that to whom ye yield
7: 7. for I *had* not *known* lust, except
   14. we *know* that the law is spiritual:
   18. For I *know* that in me that is,
8:22. we *know* that the whole creation
   26. we *know* not what we should pray
   27. *knoweth* what (is) the mind of the Spirit,
   28. we *know* that all things work together
11: 2. *Wot* ye not what the scripture saith
   22. *Behold* therefore the goodness and severity
13:11. *knowing* the time, that now (it is)
14:14. I *know,* and am persuaded by the Lord Jesus,
15:29. I *am sure* that, when I come
1Co. 1:16. I *know* not whether I baptized any other.
2: 2. not *to know* any thing among you,
9. Eye *hath* not *seen,* nor ear heard,
   11. what man *knoweth* the things of
— the things of God *knoweth* no man,
   12. that we *might know* the things
3:16. *Know* ye not that ye are the temple
5: 6. *Know* ye not that a little leaven
6: 2. *Do* ye not *know* that the saints shall
3. *Know* ye not that we shall judge angels?
9. *Know* ye not that the unrighteous
   15. *Know* ye not that your bodies are
   16. *know* ye not that he which is joined
   19. *know* ye not that your body is the temple
7:16. For what *knowest* thou, O wife,
— or how *knowest* thou, O man, whether
8: 1. we *know* that we all have knowledge.
2. if any man think that he *knoweth* any
4. we *know* that an idol (is) nothing
   10. if any man *see* thee which hast knowledge
9:13. *Do* ye not *know* that they which
   24. *Know* ye not that they which run
11: 3. I would have you *know,* that the
12: 2. Ye *know* that ye were Gentiles,
13: 2. though I have...prophecy, and *understand*
14:11. if I *know* not the meaning of the voice,
   16. he *understandeth* not what thou sayest?
15:58. *forasmuch as* ye *know* that your labour
16: 7. I will not *see* you now by the way;
   15. ye *know* the house of Stephanas,
2Co. 1: 7. *knowing,* that as ye are partakers
4:14. *Knowing* that he which raised up
5: 1. we *know* that if our earthly house
6. *knowing* that, whilst we are at home
   11. *Knowing* therefore the terror of the Lord,
   16. henceforth *know* we no man after the flesh:
9: 2. I *know* the forwardness of your mind,
11:11. because I love you not? God *knoweth.*

2Co.11:31. *knoweth* that I lie not.
12: 2. I *knew* a man in Christ about
— in the body, I *cannot tell;* or whether out of the body, I *cannot tell :* God *knoweth ;*
3. I *knew* such a man, whether in
— I *cannot tell :* God *knoweth ;*
Gal. 1:19. other of the apostles *saw* I none,
2: 7. when they *saw* that the gospel of
   14. when I *saw* that they walked not uprightly
   16. *Knowing* that a man is not justified
4: 8. then, *when* ye *knew* not God,
   13. Ye *know* how through infirmity
6:11. Ye *see* how large a letter I have written
Eph. 1:18. that ye may *know* what is the hope
6: 8. *Knowing* that whatsoever good thing
9. *knowing* that your Master also is
   21. that ye also *may know* my affairs,
Phi. 1:17. *knowing* that I am set for the defence
   19. For I *know* that this shall turn
   25. I *know* that I shall abide and continue
   27. that whether I come and *see* you, or
   30. the same conflict which ye *saw* in me,
2:28. *when* ye *see* him again, ye may rejoice,
4: 9. received, and heard, and *seen* in me, do:
   12. I *know* both how to be abased, and I *know*
   15. Now ye Philippians *know* also,
Col. 2: 1. I would that ye *knew* what great
3:24. *Knowing* that of the Lord ye shall
4: 1. *knowing* that ye also have a Master
6. that ye may *know* how ye ought
1Th. 1: 4. *Knowing,* brethren beloved, your
5. ye *know* what manner of men we were
2: 1. yourselves, brethren, *know* our entrance
2. were shamefully entreated, as ye *know,*
5. used we flattering words, as ye *know,*
   11. As ye *know* how we exhorted
   17. *to see* your face with great desire.
3: 3. yourselves *know* that we are appointed
4. even as it came to pass, and ye *know.*
6. desiring greatly *to see* us, as we also
   10. that we might *see* your face, and might
4: 2. ye *know* what commandments we gave
4. That every one of you should *know* how
5. the Gentiles *which know* not God:
5: 2. yourselves *know* perfectly that the *day* of the Lord
   12. *to know* them which labour among you,
2Th. 1: 8. vengeance on them *that know* not God,
2: 6. now ye *know* what withholdeth
3: 7. yourselves *know* how ye ought to follow us:
1Ti. 1: 8. we *know* that the law (is) good, if a
9. *Knowing* this, that the law is not made for
3: 5. if a man *know* not how to rule his
   15. that thou *mayest know* how thou oughtest
6:16. whom no man *hath seen,* nor can *see :*
2Ti. 1: 4. Greatly desiring *to see* thee, being
   12. for I *know* whom I have believed,
   15. This thou *knowest,* that all they
2:23. *knowing* that they do gender strifes,
3:14. *knowing* of whom thou hast learned
   15. thou *hast known* the holy scriptures,
Tit. 1:16. They profess that they *know* God ;
3:11. *Knowing* that he that is such
Philem.21. *knowing* that thou wilt also do
Heb 3: 9. proved me, and *saw* my works forty years.
8:11. for all *shall know* me, from the least
10:30. For we *know* him that hath said,
11: 5. translated that he should not *see* death;
   13. *having seen* them afar off, and were
   23. because they *saw* (he was) a proper child;
Jas. 3: 1. *knowing* that we shall receive the

Jas. 4: 4. *know* ye not that the friendship of
17. to him *that knoweth* to do good,
5:11. *have seen* the end of the Lord; that
1Pet.1: 8. Whom *having* not *seen*, ye love;
18. *Forasmuch as* ye *know* that ye were not
3: 9. *knowing* that ye are thereunto called,
10. he that will love life, and *see* good days,
5: 9. *knowing* that the same afflictions
2Pet.1:12. these things, though ye *know* (them),
14. *Knowing* that shortly I must put
2: 9. The Lord *knoweth* how to deliver the
1Joh.2:11. *knoweth* not whither he goeth, because
20. from the Holy One, and ye *know* all things.
21. ye *know* not the truth, but because ye *know*
29. If ye *know* that he is righteous,
3: 1. *Behold*, what manner of love the
2. we *know* that, when he shall appear,
5. ye *know* that he was manifested to
14. We *know* that we have passed from
15. ye *know* that no murderer hath eternal life
5:13. that ye *may know* that ye have eternal life,
15. if we *know* that he hear us,
— we *know* that we have the petitions
16. If any man *see* his brother sin a sin
18. We *know* that whosoever is born of God
19. we *know* that we are of God, and the whole
20. we *know* that the Son of God is come,
3Joh. 12. ye *know* that our record is true.
14. I trust I shall shortly *see* thee,
Jude 5. *though* ye once *knew* this, how that
10. those things which they *know* not:
Rev. 1: 2. of all things that he *saw*.
12. being turned, I *saw* seven golden candlesticks;
17. when I *saw* him, I fell at his feet
19. Write the things which thou *hast seen*,
20. the seven stars which thou *sawest* in my
— the seven candlesticks which thou *sawest*
2: 2. I *know* thy works, and thy labour,
9. I *know* thy works, and tribulation,
13. I *know* thy works, and where thou dwellest,
19. I *know* thy works, and charity, and service,
3: 1. I *know* thy works, that thou hast a
8. I *know* thy works: behold, I have
15. I *know* thy works, that thou art
17. *knowest* not that thou art wretched,
4: 1. After this I *looked*, and, behold, a
4. I *saw* four and twenty elders sitting,
5: 1. I *saw* in the right hand of him
2. I *saw* a strong angel proclaiming
6. I *beheld*, and, lo, in the midst of
11. I *beheld*, and I heard the voice of
6: 1. I *saw* when the Lamb opened one
2. I *saw*, and behold a white horse:
5. I *beheld*, and lo a black horse;
8. I *looked*, and behold a pale horse:
9. I *saw* under the altar the souls
12. I *beheld* when he had opened the sixth
7: 1. after these things I *saw* four angels
2. I *saw* another angel ascending from
9. After this I *beheld*, and, lo, a great
14. I said unto him, Sir, thou *knowest*.
8: 2. I *saw* the seven angels which stood
13. I *beheld*, and heard an angel flying
9: 1. I *saw* a star fall from heaven
17. thus I *saw* the horses in the vision,
10: 1. I *saw* another mighty angel come down
5. the angel which I *saw* stand upon the sea
12:12. *because* he *knoweth* that he hath but
13. when the dragon *saw* that he was cast
13: 1. *saw* a beast rise up out of the sea,
2. the beast which I *saw* was like unto

Rev.13: 3. I *saw* one of his heads as it were wounded
11. I *beheld* another beast coming
14: 1. I *looked*, and, lo, a Lamb stood on
6. I *saw* another angel fly in the midst
14. I *looked*, and behold a white cloud,
15: 1. I *saw* another sign in heaven,
2. I *saw* as it were a sea of glass
5. after that I *looked*, and, behold, the temple
16:13. I *saw* three unclean spirits like frogs
17: 3. I *saw* a woman sit upon a scarlet coloured
beast,
6. I *saw* the woman drunken with
— when I *saw* her, I wondered with
8. The beast that thou *sawest* was, and is
12. the ten horns which thou *sawest* are
15. The waters which thou *sawest*,
16. the ten horns which thou *sawest* upon
18. the woman which thou *sawest* is
18: 1. after these things I *saw* another angel
7. am no widow, and shall *see* no sorrow.
19:11. I *saw* heaven opened, and behold
12. that no man *knew*, but he himself.
17. I *saw* an angel standing in the sun;
19. I *saw* the beast, and the kings of the earth,
20: 1. I *saw* an angel come down from heaven,
4. I *saw* thrones, and they sat upon them,
11. I *saw* a great white throne, and him
12. I *saw* the dead, small and great,
21: 1. I *saw* a new heaven and a new earth:
2. I John *saw* the holy city, new Jerusalem,
22. I *saw* no temple therein: for the

See also *ἴδε* and *ἰδού* for passages where used
adverbially.

εἶδος, *idos.*

Lu. 3:22. in a bodily *shape* like a dove
9:29. the *fashion* of his countenance was
Joh. 5:37. at any time, nor seen his *shape*.
2Co. 5: 7. For we walk by faith, not by *sight:*
1Th. 5:22. Abstain from all *appearance* of evil.

εἴδω see εἰδέω.

εἰδωλεῖον, *idolion.*

1Co. 8:10. sit at meat in the *idol's temple*, shall

εἰδωλόθυτον, *idolothutcn.*

Acts15:29. abstain from *meats offered to idols*,
21:25. from (things) *offered to idols*, and from
blood,
1Co. 8: 1. as touching *things offered unto idols*,
4. eating of those *things that are offered in
sacrifice unto idols*,
7. eat (it) as a *thing offered unto an idol;*
10. to eat those *things which are offered to idols;*
10:19. or that *which is offered in sacrifice to idols*
is any thing?
28. This is *offered in sacrifice unto idols*,
Rev. 2:14. to eat *things sacrificed unto idols*,
20. to eat *things sacrificed unto idols*.

εἰδωλολατρεία, *idololatria.*

1Co.10:14. my dearly beloved, flee from *idolatry.*

Gal. 5:20. *Idolatry*, witchcraft, hatred, variance,
Col. 3: 5. and covetousness, which is *idolatry:*
1Pet.4: 3. banquetings, and abominable *idolatries:*

εἰδωλολάτρης, *īdŏlolatrees.*

1Co. 5:10. or extortioners, or with *idolaters ;*
　　11. a fornicator, or covetous, or an *idolater,*
　6: 9. neither fornicators, nor *idolaters,* nor
　　　　adulterers,
　10: 7. Neither be ye *idolaters,* as (were) some
Eph. 5: 5. nor covetous man, who is an *idolater,*
Rev.21: 8. *idolaters,* and all liars, shall have their part
　22:15. and murderers, and *idolaters,*

εἴδωλον, *īdŏlon.*

Acts 7:41. offered sacrifice unto the *idol,*
　15:20. that they abstain from pollutions of *idols,*
Ro. 2:22. thou that abhorrest *idols,* dost thou
1Co. 8: 4. we know that an *idol* (is) nothing
　　7. with conscience of the *idol* unto this hour
　10:19. that the *idol* is any thing,
　12: 2. carried away unto these dumb *idols,*
2Co. 6:16. hath the temple of God with *idols?*
1Th. 1: 9. how ye turned to God from *idols*
1Joh.5:21. Little children, keep yourselves from *idols.*
Rev. 9:20. *idols* of gold, and silver, and brass,

εἴην, εἴης, εἴη, &c. *īeen, īees, īee.* optat. from εἰμί.

Lu. 1:29. what manner of salutation this *should be.*
　3:15. whether he *were* the Christ, or not ;
　8: 9. saying, What *might* this parable *be?*
　9:46. which of them *should be* greatest.
　15:26. asked what these things *meant.*
　18:36. pass by, he asked what it *meant.*
　22:23. which of them it *was* that should do
Joh.13:24. who it *should be* of whom he spake.
Acts 8:20. Thy money *perish* (lit. *be* to destruction)
　　　　with thee, because
　10:17. this vision which he had seen *should mean,*
　21:33. demanded who he *was,* and what he
Rev. 3:15. I would thou *wert* cold or hot.

εἰ καὶ.

See after εἰ.

εἰκῆ, *īkee.*

Mat. 5:22. angry with his brother *without a cause*
Ro. 13: 4. he beareth not the sword *in vain:*
1Co.15: 2. unless ye have believed *in vain.*
Gal. 3: 4. so many things *in vain?* if (it be) yet *in vain.*
　4:11. bestowed upon you labour *in vain.*
Col. 2:18. *vainly* puffed up by his fleshly mind,

εἴκοσι, *īkosi.*

Lu. 14:31. cometh against him with *twenty* thousand ?
Jon. 6:19. about five and *twenty* or thirty furlongs,
Acts 1:15. were about an hundred and *twenty,*
　27:28. sounded, and found (it) *twenty* fathoms :

1Co.10: 8. fell in one day three and *twenty* thousand.
Rev. 4: 4. the throne (were) four and *twenty* seats:
　　— I saw four and *twenty* elders sitting,
　10. The four and *twenty* elders fall down
　5: 8. four (and) *twenty* elders fell down before
　14. the four (and) *twenty* elders fell down
　11:16. the four and *twenty* elders, which sat
　19: 4. four and *twenty* elders and the four beasts

εἴκω, *īko.*

Gal. 2: 5. To whom we *gave place* by subjection,

εἴκω, *īko.*

Jas. 1: 6. he that wavereth, *is like* a wave of the sea
　23. he *is like* unto a man beholding his

εἰκών, *īkōn.*

Mat.22:20. Whose (is) this *image* and superscription ?
Mar.12:16. Whose (is) this *image* and superscription ?
Lu. 20:24. Whose *image* and superscription hath it ?
Ro. 1:23. into an *image* made like to corruptible man,
　8:29. conformed to the *image* of his Son,
1Co.11: 7. as he is the *image* and glory of God:
　15:49. have borne the *image* of the earthy, we shall
　　　　also bear the *image* of the heavenly.
2Co. 3:18. into the same *image* from glory to glory,
　4: 4. of Christ, who is the *image* of God,
Col. 1:15. Who is the *image* of the invisible God,
　3:10. the *image* of him that created him:
Heb 10: 1. not the very *image* of the things,
Rev.13:14. should make an *image* to the beast,
　15. to give life unto the *image* of the beast,
　　　　that the *image* of the beast
　　— as would not worship the *image*
　14: 9. worship the beast and his *image,*
　11. who worship the beast and his *image,*
　15: 2. victory over the beast, and over his *image,*
　16: 2. them which worshipped his *image.*
　19:20. them that worshipped his *image.*
　20: 4. not worshipped the beast, neither his *image,*

εἰλικρίνεια, *īlikrinīa.*

1Co. 5: 8. with the unleavened (bread) of *sincerity*
2Co. 1:12. that in simplicity and godly *sincerity,*
　2:17. as of *sincerity,* but as of God, in the

εἰλικρινής, *īlikrinees.*

Phi. 1:10. that ye may be *sincere* and without offence
2Pet.3: 1. in (both) which I stir up your *pure* minds

εἱλίσσω, *īlisso.*

Rev. 6:14. as a scroll *when* it is *rolled* together ;

εἰ μή.

See after εἰ.

εἰμί, ĭmi.

Mat. 3:11. whose shoes I *am* not worthy to bear:
　　8: 8. Lord, I *am* not worthy that thou
　　　9. For I *am* a man under authority,
　11:29. for I *am* meek and lowly in heart:
　14:27. Be of good cheer; it is I (lit. I *am*); be not afraid.
　18:20. there *am* I in the midst of them.
　20:15. Is thine eye evil, because I *am* good?
　22:32. I *am* the God of Abraham, and the God
　24: 5. in my name, saying, I *am* Christ;
　26:22. to say unto him, Lord, is it I? (lit. *am* I)
　　25. answered and said, Master, is it I? (lit. *am* I)
　27:24. I *am* innocent of the blood of this just person:
　　43. for he said, I *am* the Son of God.
　28:20. I *am* with you alway, (even) unto the end
Mar. 1: 7. I *am* not worthy to stoop down and unloose.
　6:50. Be of good cheer: it is I (lit. I *am*); be not afraid.
　13: 6. in my name, saying, I *am* (Christ);
　14:62. Jesus said, I *am* : and ye shall see
Lu. 1:18. for I *am* an old man, and my wife
　　19. answering said unto him, I *am* Gabriel,
　3:16. whose shoes I *am* not worthy to unloose:
　5: 8. for I *am* a sinful man, O Lord.
　7: 6. I *am* not worthy that thou shouldest
　　8. For I also *am* a man set under authority,
　15:19. *am* no more worthy to be called thy son:
　　21. *am* no more worthy to be called thy son.
　18:11. that I *am* not as other men (are),
　19:22. Thou knewest that I *was* an austere man,
　21: 8. in my name, saying, I *am* (Christ);
　22:27. I *am* among you as he that serveth.
　　33. Lord, I *am* ready to go with thee,
　　58. Peter said, Man, I *am* not.
　　70. he said unto them, Ye say that I *am*.
　24:39. that it is I myself (lit. I *am* myself): handle me,
Joh. 1:20. confessed, I *am* not the Christ.
　　21. Art thou Elias? And he saith, I *am* not.
　　27. whose shoe's latchet I *am* not worthy to unloose.
　3:28. that I said, I *am* not the Christ, but that I *am* sent before him.
　4:26. I that speak unto thee *am* (he).
　6:20. saith unto them, It is I; (lit. I *am*)
　　35. said unto them, I *am* the bread of life:
　　41. I *am* the bread which came down
　　48. I *am* that bread of life.
　　51. I *am* the living bread which came
　7:28. know me, and ye know whence I *am* :
　　29. I know him: for I *am* from him,
　　33. Yet a little while *am* I with you,
　　34. where I *am*, (thither) ye cannot come.
　　36. where I *am*, (thither) ye cannot come?
　8:12. saying, I *am* the light of the world:
　　16. for I *am* not alone, but I and the Father
　　18. I *am* one that bear witness of myself,
　　23. Ye are from beneath; I *am* from above: — I *am* not of this world.
　　24. If ye believe not that I *am* (he),
　　28. then shall ye know that I *am* (he),
　　58. Before Abraham was, I *am*.
　9: 5. I *am* the light of the world.
　　9. He is like him: (but) he said, I *am* (he).
　10: 7. I say unto you, I *am* the door of the sheep.
　　9. I *am* the door: by me if any man
　　11. I *am* the good shepherd: the good

Joh. 10:14. I *am* the good shepherd, and know
　　36. because I said, I *am* the Son of God?
　11:25. I *am* the resurrection, and the life:
　12:26. where I *am*, there shall also my servant
　13:13. ye say well; for (so) I *am*.
　　19. ye may believe that I *am* (he).
　　33. yet a little while I *am* with you.
　14: 3. that where I *am*, (there) ye may be also.
　　6. I *am* the way, the truth, and the life:
　　9. *Have* I *been* so long time with you,
　15: 1. I *am* the true vine, and my Father
　　5. I *am* the vine, ye (are) the branches:
　16:32. yet I *am* not alone, because the Father
　17:11. now I *am* no more in the world,
　　14. even as I *am* not of the world.
　　16. even as I *am* not of the world.
　　24. be with me where I *am* ; that they
　18: 5. Jesus saith unto them, I *am* (he).
　　6. as he had said unto them, I *am* (he),
　　8. I have told you that I *am* (he):
　　17. this man's disciples? He saith, I *am* not.
　　25. He denied (it), and said, I *am* not.
　　35. Pilate answered, *Am* I a Jew?
　　37. Thou sayest that I *am* a king.
　19:21. that he said, I *am* King of the Jews.
Acts 9: 5. I *am* Jesus whom thou persecutest:
　10:21. Behold, I *am* he whom ye seek:
　　26. Stand up; I myself also *am* a man.
　13:25. I *am* not (he). But, behold, there cometh — shoes of (his) feet I *am* not worthy to loose.
　18:10. For I *am* with thee, and no man shall
　21:39. I *am* a man (which am) a Jew of
　22: 3. I *am* verily a man (which am) a Jew,
　　8. I *am* Jesus of Nazareth, whom thou
　23: 6. Men (and) brethren, I *am* a Pharisee,
　25:10. I stand (lit. *am* standing) at Cæsar's judgment seat,
　26:15. I *am* Jesus whom thou persecutest.
　　29. almost, and altogether such as I *am*,
　27:23. of God, whose I *am*, and whom I serve,
Ro. 1:14. I *am* debtor both to the Greeks,
　7:14. I *am* carnal, sold under sin.
　11: 1. For I also *am* an Israelite,
　　13. as I *am* the apostle of the Gentiles,
1Co. 1:12. every one of you saith, I *am* of Paul;
　3: 4. while one saith, I *am* of Paul;
　9: 1. *Am* I not an apostle? *am* I not free?
　　2. If I be not an apostle unto others, yet doubtless I *am* to you:
　12:15. Because I *am* not the hand, I *am* not of
　　16. Because I *am* not the eye, I *am* not of
　13: 2. have not charity, I *am* nothing.
　15: 9. For I *am* the least of the apostles, that *am* not meet to be called an apostle,
　　10. by the grace of God I *am* what I *am* :
2Co.12:10. when I am weak, then *am* I strong.
　　11. chiefest apostles, though I *be* nothing.
Phi. 4:11. in whatsoever state I *am*,
Col. 2: 5. yet *am* I with you in the spirit,
1Ti. 1:15. to save sinners; of whom I *am* chief.
Heb 12:21. Moses said, I exceedingly fear (lit. 1 *am* exceedingly afraid) and quake:
1Pet. 1:16. Be ye holy; for I *am* holy.
2Pet. 1:13. as long as I *am* in this tabernacle,
Rev. 1: 8. I *am* Alpha and Omega, the
　　11. Saying, I *am* Alpha and Omega,
　　17. Fear not; I *am* the first and the last:
　　18. behold, I *am* alive for evermore,
　2:23. I *am* he which searcheth the reins
　3:17. Because thou sayest, I *am* rich,
　18: 7. *am* no widow, and shall see no sorrow.

Rev.19:10. I *am* thy fellowservant, and of thy brethren
21: 6. It is done.   I *am* Alpha and Omega,
22: 9. for I *am* thy fellowservant, and of
13. I *am* Alpha and Omega, the beginning
16. I *am* the root and the offspring of David,

See persons and tenses from this verb severally arranged under—

Εἶ, ἐστί, ἐσμέν, ἐστέ, εἰσί.

Ἧν, ἧς, ἧσθα, ἦν, &c. *Imp.*

Ἤμην, ἦσο, ἦτο, &c. *Plup.*

Ἔσομαι, ἔση, ἔσται, &c. *Fut.*

Ἔστω, ἔστε, ἔστωσαν, ἴσθι, ἤτω.

Ἔιην, εἴης, εἴη.

Ὦ, ἧς, ἦ, ὦμεν, ἦτε, ὦσι.

Εἶναι, ἔσεσθαι, ἐσόμενος.

εἶναι, ῑναῑ, from εἰμί.

Mat.16:13. Whom do men say that I the Son of man
am ?
15. whom say ye that I *am* ?
17: 4. Lord, it is good for us *to be* here:
19:21. If thou wilt *be* perfect, go (and) sell
20:27. whosoever will *be* chief among you,
22:23. which say that there *is* no resurrection,
Mar. 6:49. they supposed it *had been* a spirit,
8:27. Whom do men say that I *am* ?
29. whom say ye that I *am* ?
9: 5. Master, it is good for us *to be* here:
35. If any man desire *to be* first,
12:18. which say there *is* no resurrection;
14:64. condemned him *to be* guilty of death.
Lu. 2: 4. because he *was* of the house and lineage
6. so it was, that, while they *were* there,
44. supposing him *to have been* in the company,
49. that I must *be* about my Father's business?
4:41. for they knew that he *was* Christ.
5:12. when he *was* in a certain city,
8:38. besought him that he might *be* with him :
9:18. came to pass, as he *was* alone praying,
— Whom say the people that I *am* ?
20. whom say ye that I *am* ?
33. it is good for us *to be* here:
11: 1. as he *was* praying in a certain place,
8. give him, because he *is* his friend,
14:26. own life also, he cannot *be* my disciple.
27. come after me, cannot *be* my disciple.
33. that he hath, he cannot *be* my disciple.
19:11. because he *was* nigh to Jerusalem,
20: 6. they be persuaded that John *was* a prophet.
20. should feign themselves)(just men,
27. which deny that there *is* any resurrection;
41. How say they that Christ *is* David's son ?
22:24. should be accounted)(the greatest.
23: 2. that he himself *is* Christ a King.
Joh. 1:46(47). Can there any good thing *come* out
7: 4. himself seeketh *to be* known openly.
17: 5. I had with thee before the world *was*.
Acts 2:12. saying one to another, What meaneth this?
(lit. might this *be*)
4:32. which he possessed *was* his own ;
5:36. Theudas, boasting himself *to be* somebody;
8: 9. that himself *was* some great one:
37. I believe that Jesus Christ *is* the Son of
God.

Acts13:25. he said, Whom think ye that I *am* ?
47. that thou *shouldest be* for salvation
16:13. where prayer was wont *to be made* ;
15. judged me *to be* faithful to the Lord,
17: 7. saying that there *is* another king,
18. He seemeth *to be* a setter forth of strange
20. therefore what these things mean. (lit.
would *be*)
29. that the Godhead *is* like unto gold,
18: 3. because he *was* of the same craft,
15. for I will *be* no judge of such (matters).
28. by the scriptures that Jesus *was* Christ.
19: 1. that, while Apollos *was* at Corinth,
23: 8. say that there *is* no resurrection,
27: 4. because the winds *were* contrary.
28: 6. said that he *was* a god.
Ro. 1:20. so that they *are* without excuse:
22. Professing themselves *to be* wise,
2:19. thou thyself *art* a guide of the blind,
3: 9. that they *are* all under sin ;
26. that he might *be* just, and the justifier
4:11. that he might *be* the father of all
13. that he should *be* the heir of the world,
16. the promise might *be* sure to all the seed,
6:11. yourselves *to be* dead indeed unto sin,
7: 3. so that she *is* no adulteress, though
8:29. that he might *be* the firstborn among
9: 3. I could wish that myself *were* accursed from
14:14. esteemeth any thing *to be* unclean,
15:16. That I should *be* the minister of Jesus
16:19. yet I would have you)(wise unto that
1Co. 3:18. seemeth *to be* wise in this world,
7: 7. I would that all men *were* even as I myself.
25. obtained mercy of the Lord *to be* faithful.
26. that (it is) good for a man so *to be*.
32. I would have you)(without carefulness.
10: 6. we should not lust after (lit. *be* desirers)
11:16. if any man seem *to be* contentious,
19. there must *be* also heresies among you,
12:23. which we think *to be* less honourable,
14:37. If any man think himself *to be* a prophet,
2Co. 5: 9. or absent, we may *be* accepted of him.
7:11. have approved yourselves *to be* clear
9: 5. that the same might *be* ready, as
10: 7. trust to himself that he *is* Christ's,
11:16. Let no man think me)(a fool;
Gal. 2: 6. of those who seemed *to be* somewhat,
9. Cephas, and John, who seemed *to be* pillars,
4:21. ye that desire *to be* under the law,
6: 3. if a man think himself *to be* something,
Eph. 1: 4. that we should *be* holy and without blame
12. we should *be* to the praise of his glory,
3: 6. That the Gentiles should *be* fellowheirs,
Phi. 1:23. a desire to depart, and *to be* with Christ ;
2: 6. not robbery *to be* equal with God:
3: 8. I count all things)((but) loss for the
— do count them)((but) dung, that I
4:11. whatsoever state I am, (therewith) *to be*
content.
1Th. 2: 6. when we might *have been* burdensome,
1Ti. 1: 7. Desiring *to be* teachers of the law;
2:12. over the man, but *to be* in silence.
3: 2. A bishop then must *be* blameless,
6: 5. supposing that gain *is* godliness:
18. ready to distribute, (lit. *to be* distributors)
2Ti. 2:24. not strive; but *be* gentle unto all (men),
Tit. 1: 7. For a bishop must *be* blameless,
2: 2. That the aged men *be* sober, grave,
4. to love their husbands, (lit. *to be* loving
their husbands)
9. to please (them) well (lit. *to be* well pleasing) in all (things);

Tit. 3: 1. *to be* ready to every good work,
  2. *to be* no brawlers, (but) gentle,
Heb 5:12. when for the time ye ought *to be* teachers,
  11: 4. obtained witness that he *was* righteous,
  12:11. for the present seemeth *to be* joyous,
Jas. 1:18. we should *be* a kind of firstfruits
  26. man among you seem *to be* religious,
  4: 4. will *be* a friend of the world
1Pet.1:21. your faith and hope might *be* in God.
  5:12. that this *is* the true grace of God
1Joh.2: 9. He that saith he *is* in the light,
Rev. 2: 2. them which say they *are* apostles,
  9. of them which say they *are* Jews,
  3: 9. which say they *are* Jews, and are not,

εἴνεκεν see ἕνεκα.

εἶπα, εἶπον, see ἔπω.

εἴπερ.

See after εἰ.

εἴπως.

See after εἰ.

εἰρηνεύω, *ireenüo*.

Mar. 9:50. *have peace* one with another.
Ro. 12:18. *live peaceably* with all men.
2Co.13:11. be of one mind, *live in peace ;*
1Th. 5:13. *be at peace* among yourselves.

εἰρήνη, *ireenee*.

Mat.10:13. let your *peace* come upon it: but if it be
  not worthy, let your *peace* return to
  you.
  34. *peace* on earth: I came not to send *peace*,
Mar. 5:34. go in *peace*, and be whole of thy plague.
Lu. 1:79. to guide our feet into the way of *peace*.
  2:14. on earth *peace*, good will toward men.
  29. lettest thou thy servant depart in *peace*,
  7:50. Thy faith hath saved thee; go in *peace*.
  8:48. thy faith hath made thee whole; go in
  peace.
  10: 5. first say, *Peace* (be) to this house.
  6. And if the son of *peace* be there, your
  peace shall rest upon it:
  11:21. his goods are in *peace :*
  12:51. I am come to give *peace* on earth?
  14:32. an ambassage, and desireth conditions of
  peace.
  19:38. *peace* in heaven, and glory in the highest.
  42. things (which belong) unto thy *peace !*
  24:36. saith unto them, *Peace* (be) unto you.
Joh.14:27. *Peace* I leave with you, my *peace* I give
  16:33. that in me ye might have *peace*.
  20:19. saith unto them, *Peace* (be) unto you.
  21. to them again, *Peace* (be) unto you:
  26. said, *Peace* (be) unto you.
Acts 7:26. would have set them at *one* again,

Acts 9:31. Then had the churches *rest*
  10:36. preaching *peace* by Jesus Christ:
  12:20. their friend, desired *peace ;*
  15:33. they were let go in *peace* from the
  16:36. now therefore depart, and go in *peace*.
  24: 2. by thee we enjoy great *quietness*,
Ro. 1: 7. Grace to you and *peace* from God
  2:10. glory, honour, and *peace*, to every man
  3:17. the way of *peace* have they not known:
  5: 1. by faith, we have *peace* with God
  8: 6. spiritually minded (is) life and *peace*.
  10:15. them that preach the gospel of *peace*,
  14:17. righteousness, and *peace*, and joy in the
  19. the things which make for *peace*,
  15:13. with all joy and *peace* in believing,
  33. the God of *peace* (be) with you all.
  16:20. the God of *peace* shall bruise Satan
1Co. 1: 3. Grace (be) unto you, and *peace*,
  7:15. God hath called us to *peace*.
  14:33. not (the author) of confusion, but of
  peace,
  16:11. conduct him forth in *peace*, that
2Co. 1: 2. Grace (be) to you and *peace* from God
  13:11. the God of love and *peace* shall be with
  you.
Gal. 1: 3. Grace (be) to you and *peace* from God the
  5:22. love, joy, *peace*, longsuffering, gentleness,
  6:16. *peace* (be) on them, and mercy, and upon
Eph. 1: 2. Grace (be) to you, and *peace*, from God
  2:14. For he is our *peace*, who hath made
  15. one new man, (so) making *peace ;*
  17. came and preached *peace* to you
  4: 3. unity of the Spirit in the bond of *peace*.
  6:15. the preparation of the gospel of *peace ;*
  23. *Peace* (be) to the brethren, and love with
  faith,
Phi. 1: 2. Grace (be) unto you, and *peace*, from
  God
  4: 7. the *peace* of God, which passeth all
  9. the God of *peace* shall be with you.
Col. 1: 2. Grace (be) unto you, and *peace*, from God
  3:15. let the *peace* of God rule in your hearts,
1Th. 1: 1. Grace (be) unto you, and *peace*, from
  God
  5: 3. when they shall say, *Peace* and safety;
  23. the very God of *peace* sanctify you
2Th. 1: 2. Grace unto you, and *peace*, from God
  3:16. the Lord of *peace* himself give you *peace*
1Ti. 1: 2. Grace, mercy, (and) *peace*, from God
2Ti. 1: 2. Grace, mercy, (and) *peace*, from God
  2:22. follow righteousness, faith, charity, *peace*,
Tit. 1: 4. Grace, mercy, (and) *peace*, from God
Philem. 3. Grace to you, and *peace*, from God
Heb 7: 2. King of Salem, which is, King of *peace ;*
  11:31. she had received the spies with *peace*.
  12:14. Follow *peace* with all (men), and holiness,
  13:20. the God of *peace*, that brought again
Jas. 2:16. say unto them, Depart in *peace*,
  3:18. fruit of righteousness is sown in *peace* of
  them that make *peace*.
1Pet.1: 2. Grace unto you, and *peace*, be multiplied.
  3:11. let him seek *peace*, and ensue it.
  5:14. *Peace* (be) with you all that are in Christ
  Jesus.
2Pet.1: 2. Grace and *peace* be multiplied unto you
  3:14. ye may be found of him in *peace*,
2Joh. 3. Grace be with you, mercy, (and) *peace*,
3Joh. 14(15). *Peace* (be) to thee. (Our) friends
  salute thee.
Jude 2. Mercy unto you, and *peace*, and love,
Rev. 1: 4. Grace (be) unto you, and *peace*, from him
  6: 4. to take *peace* from the earth,

εἰρηνικός, ĭreenikos.

Heb 12:11. the *peaceable* fruit of righteousness unto
Jas.　3:17. first pure, then *peaceable*, gentle,

εἰρηνοποιέω, ĭreenopoyeō.

Col.　1:20. *having made peace* through the blood

εἰρηνοποιός, ĭreenopoyos.

Mat. 5: 9. Blessed (are) the *peacemakers :* for they

εἴρω, see ἐρέω.

εἰς, īs.

Mat. 2: 1. came wise men from the east *to* Jerusalem,
　　 8. he sent them *to* Bethlehem, and said,
　　11. when they were come *into* the house,
　　12. they departed *into* their own country
　　13. flee *into* Egypt, and be thou there until
　　14. by night, and departed *into* Egypt:
　　20. go *into* the land of Israel:
　　21. came *into* the land of Israel.
　　22. he turned aside *into* the parts of Galilee:
　　23. came and dwelt *in* a city called Nazareth:
　3:10. hewn down, and cast *into* the fire.
　　11. baptize you with water *unto* repentance:
　　12. gather his wheat *into* the garner ;
　4: 1. led up of the spirit *into* the wilderness
　　 5. devil taketh him up *into* the holy city,
　　 8. up *into* an exceeding high mountain,
　　12. he departed *into* Galilee ;
　　13. he came and dwelt *in* Capernaum,
　　18. casting a net *into* the sea: for they
　　24. his fame went *throughout* (lit. *into*) all
　　　　Syria:
　5: 1. he went up *into* a mountain:
　　13. it is thenceforth good *for* nothing,
　　20. enter *into* the kingdom of heaven.
　　22. shall be in danger *of* (lit. *unto*) hell fire.
　　25. the officer, and thou be cast *into* prison.
　　29. thy whole body should be cast *into* hell.
　　30. thy whole body should be cast *into* hell.
　　35. neither *by* Jerusalem ; for it is
　6: 6. when thou prayest, enter *into* thy closet,
　　13. lead us not *into* temptation,
　　— the power, and the glory, *for* ever.
　　26. Behold)(the fowls of the air:
　　— reap, nor gather *into* barns ;
　　30. to morrow is cast *into* the oven,
　　34. therefore no thought *for* the morrow:
　7:13. the way, that leadeth *to* destruction,
　　14. the way, which leadeth *unto* life,
　　19. is hewn down, and cast *into* the fire.
　　21. shall enter *into* the kingdom of heaven ;
　8: 4. *for* a testimony unto them.
　　 5. when Jesus was entered *into* Capernaum,
　　12. shall be cast out *into* outer darkness:
　　14. when Jesus was come *into* Peter's house,
　　18. to depart *unto* the other side.
　　23. when he was entered *into* a ship,
　　28. *to* the other side *into* the country of the
　　31. to go away *into* the herd of swine.
　　32. they went *into* the herd of swine:

Mat. 8:32. ran violently down a steep place *into* the
　　　　sea,
　　33. went their ways *into* the city, and told
　　34. the whole city came out *to* meet Jesus:
　9: 1. he entered *into* a ship, and passed over,
　　　　and came *into* his own city.
　　 6. take up thy bed, and go *unto* thine house.
　　 7. he arose, and departed *to* his house.
　　13. the righteous, but sinners *to* repentance.
　　17. do men put new wine *into* old bottles:
　　— they put new wine *into* new bottles,
　　23. when Jesus came *into* the ruler's house,
　　26. fame hereof went abroad *into* all that land.
　　28. when he was come *into* the house,
　　38. send forth labourers *into* his harvest.
　10: 5. Go not *into* the way of the Gentiles, and
　　　　into (any) city of the Samaritans
　　 9. nor silver, nor brass *in* your purses,
　　10. Nor scrip *for* (your) journey, neither
　　11. *into* whatsoever city or town ye shall
　　　　enter,
　　12. when ye come *into* an house, salute it.
　　17. will deliver you up *to* the councils,
　　18. *for* a testimony against them
　　21. shall deliver up the brother *to* death,
　　22. he that endureth *to* the end shall
　　23. this city, flee ye *into* another:
　　27. what ye hear *in* the ear, (that)
　　41. receiveth a prophet *in* the name of a
　　　　prophet
　　— *in* the name of a righteous man
　　42. (water) only *in* the name of a disciple,
　11: 7. What went ye out *into* the wilderness to
　　　　see ?
　12: 4. he entered *into* the house of God,
　　 9. he went *into* their synagogue:
　　11. if it fall *into* a pit on the sabbath day,
　　18. *in* whom my soul is well pleased:
　　20. till he send forth judgment *unto* victory.
　　29. can one enter *into* a strong man's house,
　　41. they repented *at* the preaching of Jonas ;
　　44. I will return *into* my house
　13: 2. so that he went *into* a ship, and sat ;
　　22. He also that received seed *among* the
　　　　thorns
　　30. bind them *in* bundles to burn them: but
　　　　gather the wheat *into* my barn.
　　33. hid *in* three measures of meal,
　　36. multitude away, and went *into* the house:
　　42. shall cast them *into* a furnace of fire:
　　47. a net, that was cast *into* the sea,
　　48. gathered the good *into* vessels,
　　50. shall cast them *into* the furnace of fire:
　　52. instructed *unto* the kingdom of heaven
　　54. he was come *into* his own country,
　14:13. by ship *into* a desert place apart:
　　15. that they may go *into* the villages,
　　19. looking up *to* heaven, he blessed,
　　22. his disciples to get *into* a ship, and to go
　　　　before him *unto* the other side,
　　23. he went up *into* a mountain apart
　　31. where*fore* didst thou doubt ?
　　32. when they were come *into* the ship,
　　34. they came *into* the land of Gennesaret.
　　35. they sent out *into* all that country
　15:11. Not that which goeth *into* the mouth
　　14. both shall fall *into* the ditch.
　　17. entereth *in* at the mouth goeth *into* the
　　　　belly, and is cast out *into* the draught ?
　　21. departed *into* the coasts of Tyre and Sidon.
　　24. I am not sent but *unto* the lost sheep
　　29. went up *into* a mountain,

Mat.15:39. took ship (lit. entered *into* a ship), and came *into* the coasts

16: 5. his disciples were come *to* the other side,
13. Jesus came *into* the coasts of Cæsarea
21. that he must go *unto* Jerusalem,

17: 1. up *into* an high mountain apart,
15. falleth *into* the fire, and oft *into* the water.
22. shall be betrayed *into* the hands of men:
24. when they were come *to* Capernaum,
25. when he was come *into* the house,
27. go thou *to* the sea, and cast an hook,

18: 3. ye shall not enter *into* the kingdom of heaven.
6. of these little ones which believe *in* me,
8. better for thee to enter *into* life halt
— to be cast *into* everlasting fire.
9. thee to enter *into* life with one eye,
— having two eyes to be cast *into* hell fire.
15. thy brother shall trespass *against* thee,
20. are gathered together *in* my name,
21. how oft shall my brother sin *against* me,
29. his fellowservant fell down *at* his feet,
30. went and cast him *into* prison,

19: 1. came *into* the coasts of Judæa
5. they twain shall be)(one flesh?
17. if thou wilt enter *into* life,
23. hardly enter *into* the kingdom of heaven.
24. to enter *into* the kingdom of God.

20: 1. to hire labourers *into* his vineyard.
2. he sent them *into* his vineyard,
4. Go ye also *into* the vineyard,
7. Go ye also *into* the vineyard;
17. Jesus going up *to* Jerusalem
18. Behold, we go up *to* Jerusalem;
19. to the Gentiles)(to mock, and to scourge,

21: 1. when they drew nigh *unto* Jerusalem, and were come *to* Bethphage,
2. Go *into* the village over against you,
10. when he was come *into* Jerusalem,
12. Jesus went *into* the temple of God,
17. went out of the city *into* Bethany;
18. as he returned *into* the city,
19. no fruit grow on thee henceforward *for* ever.
21. be thou cast *into* the sea; it shall be done.
23. when he was come *into* the temple,
31. go *into* the kingdom of God before you.
42. same is become)(the head of the corner:

22: 3. that were bidden *to* the wedding:
4. all things (are) ready: come *unto* the marriage.
5. one *to* his farm, another *to* his merchandise:
9. as ye shall find, bid *to* the marriage.
10. servants went out *into* the highways,
13. cast (him) *into* outer darkness;
16. thou regardest not)(the person of men.

23:34. persecute (them) from city *to* city:

24: 9. deliver you up to be afflicted, (lit. *unto* affliction)
13. he that shall endure *unto* the end,
14. *for* a witness unto all nations;
38. the day that Noe entered *into* the ark,

25: 1. went forth to meet (lit. *unto* the meeting) the bridegroom.
6. go ye out to meet him. (lit. *unto* &c.)
10. went in with him *to* the marriage:
21. enter thou *into* the joy of thy lord.
23. enter thou *into* the joy of thy lord.
30. unprofitable servant *into* outer darkness.
41. ye cursed, *into* everlasting fire;
46. go away *into* everlasting punishment: but the righteous *into* life eternal.

Mat.26: 2. Son of man is betrayed *to* be crucified.
3. *unto* the palace of the high priest,
8. *To* what purpose (is) this waste?
10. she hath wrought a good work *upon* me.
13. be told *for* a memorial of her.
18. Go *into* the city to such a man,
28. shed for many *for* the remission of sins.
30. they went out *into* the mount of Olives.
32. I will go before you *into* Galilee.
36. *unto* a place called Gethsemane.
41. that ye enter not *into* temptation:
45. betrayed *into* the hands of sinners.
52. Put up again thy sword *into* his place:
67. Then did they spit *in* his face,
71. when he was gone out *into* the porch,

27: 6. to put them *into* the treasury,
7. the potter's field, to bury strangers in. (lit. *for* the burial of strangers)
10. gave them *for* the potter's field,
27. took Jesus *into* the common hall,
30. they spit *upon* him, and took the reed, and smote him *on* the head.
31. led him away)(to crucify (him).
33. were come *unto* a place called Golgotha,
51. the veil of the temple was rent *in* twain
53. went *into* the holy city, and appeared

28: 1. as it began to dawn *toward* the first
7. he goeth before you *into* Galilee;
10. tell my brethren that they go *into* Galilee,
11. some of the watch came *into* the city,
16. went away *into* Galilee, *into* a mountain,
19. baptizing them *in* the name of the Father,

Mar. 1: 4. repentance *for* the remission of sins.
9. was baptized of John *in* Jordan.
12. the spirit driveth him *into* the wilderness.
14. Jesus came *into* Galilee, preaching
21. they went *into* Capernaum;
— he entered *into* the synagogue, and taught.
28. *throughout* all the region round about
29. they entered *into* the house of Simon
35. departed *into* a solitary place,
38. Let us go *into* the next towns,
— for there*for* came I forth.
39. *throughout* all Galilee, and cast out devils.
44. *for* a testimony unto them.
45. no more openly enter *into* the city,

2: 1. again he entered *into* Capernaum
— it was noised that he was *in* the house.
11. go thy way *into* thine house.
17. the righteous, but sinners *to* repentance.
22. no man putteth new wine *into* old bottles.
— new wine must be put *into* new bottles.
26. How he went *into* the house of God

3: 1. he entered again *into* the synagogue;
3. withered hand, Stand forth. (lit. *into* the midst)
13. he goeth up *into* a mountain,
19(20). they went *into* an house.
27. No man can enter *into* a strong
29. shall blaspheme *against* the Holy Ghost
— hath never (εις τον αιωνα) forgiveness, but is in danger of eternal damnation:

4: 1. so that he entered *into* a ship,
7. some fell *among* thorns,
8. other fell *on* good ground, and did
18. they which are sown *among* thorns;
22. that it should come abroad. (lit. *unto* manifestation)
35. Let us pass over *unto* the other side.
37. the waves beat *into* the ship,

5: 1. *unto* the other side of the sea, *into* the

Mar. 5:12. *into* the swine, that we may enter *into* them.
13. went out, and entered *into* the swine:
— down a steep place *into* the sea,
14. told (it) *in* the city, and *in* the country.
18. when he was come *into* the ship,
19. Go home *to* thy friends, and tell them
21. over again by ship *unto* the other side,
26. nothing bettered, but rather grew)(worse,
34. go *in* peace, and be whole of thy plague.
38. he cometh *to* the house of the ruler
6: 1. came *into* his own country;
8. should take nothing *for* (their) journey,
— no bread, no money *in* (their) purse:
10. what place soever ye enter *into* an house,
11. *for* a testimony against them.
31. ye yourselves apart *into* a desert place,
32. they departed *into* a desert place
36. that they may go *into* the country
41. he looked up *to* heaven, and blessed,
45. to get *into* the ship, and to go *to* the other side
46. he departed *into* a mountain to pray.
51. he went up unto them *into* the ship;
56. whithersoever he entered, *into* villages,
7:15. that entering *into* him can defile him:
17. when he was entered *into* the house
18. entereth *into* the man, (it) cannot defile him;
19. it entereth not *into* his heart, but *into* the belly, and goeth out *into* the draught,
24. went *into* the borders of Tyre
— entered *into* an house, and would have
30. when she was come *to* her house,
33. put his fingers *into* his ears,
34. looking up *to* heaven, he sighed,
8: 3. away fasting *to* their own houses,
10. straightway he entered *into* a ship
— came *into* the parts of Dalmanutha.
13. entering *into* the ship again departed *to* the
19. I brake the five loaves *among* five thousand.
20. when the seven *among* four thousand,
22. he cometh *to* Bethsaida; and they
23. when he had spit *on* his eyes, and put
26. *to* his house, saying, Neither go *into* the town,
27. *into* the towns of Cæsarea Philippi:
9: 2. leadeth them up *into* an high mountain
22. cast him *into* the fire, and *into* the waters,
25. enter no more *into* him.
28. when he was come *into* the house,
31. delivered *into* the hands of men,
33. he came *to* Capernaum:
42. (these) little ones that believe *in* me,
— he were cast *into* the sea.
43. for thee to enter *into* life maimed,
— to go *into* hell, *into* the fire that
45. better for thee to enter halt *into* life,
— to be cast *into* hell, *into* the fire that
47. to enter *into* the kingdom of God
— having two eyes to be cast *into* hell fire:
10: 1. cometh *into* the coasts of Judæa
8. they twain shall be)(one flesh!
15. he shall not enter there*in*.
17. when he was gone forth *into* the way,
23. enter *into* the kingdom of God !
24. in riches to enter *into* the kingdom of God !
25. a rich man to enter *into* the kingdom of God.
32. in the way going up *to* Jerusalem;
33. Behold, we go up *to* Jerusalem;
46. they came *to* Jericho: and as he went
11: 1. they came nigh *to* Jerusalem, *unto* Beth-phage

Mar.11: 2. Go your way *into* the village
— as soon as ye be entered *into* it,
8. many spread their garments *in* the way:
— branches off the trees, and strawed (them) *in* the way.
11. Jesus entered *into* Jerusalem, and *into* the temple:
— he went out *unto* Bethany with
14. No man eat fruit of thee hereafter *for* ever.
15. they come *to* Jerusalem : and Jesus went *into* the
23. removed, and be thou cast *into* the sea;
27. they come again *to* Jerusalem:
12:10. is become)(the head of the corner:
14. thou regardest not)(the person of men,
41. people cast money *into* the treasury:
43. which have cast *into* the treasury:
13: 3. as he sat *upon* the mount of Olives
9. deliver you up to councils; and *in* the synagogues (lit. *unto* the synagogues)
— *for* a testimony against them.
10. first be published *among* all nations.
12. brother shall betray the brother *to* death,
13. he that shall endure *unto* the end,
14. in Judæa flee *to* the mountains:
15. not go down *into* the house,
16. him that is *in* the field not turn)(back
14: 4. Why (lit. *for* what) was this waste of the
6. she hath wrought a good work *on* me.
8. to anoint my body *to* the burying.
9. preached *throughout* the whole world,
— spoken of *for* a memorial of her.
13. saith unto them, Go ye *into* the city,
16. disciples went forth, and came *into* the city,
20. that dippeth with me *in* the dish.
26. they went out *into* the mount of Olives.
28. I will go before you *into* Galilee.
32. they came *to* a place which was
38. lest ye enter *into* temptation.
41. is betrayed *into* the hands of sinners.
54. even *into* the palace of the high priest:
55.)(to put him to death; and found none.
60. the high priest stood up *in* the midst,
68. he went out *into* the porch;
15:34. why (lit. *for* what) hast thou forsaken me?
38. the veil of the temple was rent *in* twain
41. came up with him *unto* Jerusalem.
16: 5. entering *into* the sepulchre,
7. that he goeth before you *into* Galilee:
12. as they walked, and went *into* the country.
15. Go ye *into* all the world,
19. he was received up *into* heaven,
Lu. 1: 9. he went *into* the temple of the Lord.
20. which shall be fulfilled *in* their season.
23. he departed *to* his own house.
26. sent from God *unto* a city of Galilee,
33. reign over the house of Jacob *for* ever;
39. went *into* the hill country with haste, *into* a city of Juda;
40. entered *into* the house of Zacharias,
44. thy salutation sounded *in* mine ears,
50. from generation to generation. (lit. *unto* generations of g.)
55. to Abraham, and to his seed *for* ever.
56. three months, and returned *to* her own house.
79. to guide our feet *into* the way of peace.
2: 3. every one *into* his own city.
4. *into* Judæa, *unto* the city of David,
15. gone away from them *into* heaven,
22. they brought him *to* Jerusalem,

Lu. 2:27. he came by the Spirit *into* the temple:
    28. took he him up *in* his arms,
    32. A light to lighten (lit. *toward* the enlightening) the Gentiles,
    34. *for* the fall and rising again of many
    — *for* a sign which shall be spoken against;
    39. returned *into* Galilee, *to* their own city
    41. his parents went *to* Jerusalem
    42. they went up *to* Jerusalem
    45. they turned back again *to* Jerusalem,
    51. with them, and came *to* Nazareth,
3: 3. came *into* all the country about Jordan,
    — repentance *for* the remission of sins ;
    5. crooked shall be made straight, (lit. *into*) and the rough ways (shall be) made smooth ; (lit. *into* smooth ways)
    9. hewn down, and cast *into* the fire.
    17. gather the wheat *into* his garner ;
4: 1. led by the Spirit *into* the wilderness,
    5. taking him up *into* an high mountain,
    9. he brought him *to* Jerusalem,
    14. in the power of the Spirit *into* Galilee:
    16. he came *to* Nazareth, where he
    — he went *into* the synagogue
    26. save *unto* Sarepta, (a city) of Sidon,
    29. that they might cast him down headlong. (lit. *for* to cast &c.)
    31. came down *to* Capernaum,
    35. had thrown him *in* the midst,
    37. *into* every place of the country
    38. entered *into* Simon's house.
    42. went *into* a desert place:
    43. for *therefore* am I sent.
5: 3. he entered *into* one of the ships.
    4. Launch out *into* the deep, and let down your nets *for* a draught.
    14. *for* a testimony unto them.
    17. was (present) to heal them. (lit. *for* their being healed)
    19. *into* the midst before Jesus.
    24. go *unto* thine house.
    25. departed *to* his own house,
    32. righteous, but sinners *to* repentance.
    37. new wine *into* old bottles ;
    38. new wine must be put *into* new bottles ;
6: 4. he went *into* the house of God,
    6. he entered *into* the synagogue
    8. stand forth *in* the midst.
    12. he went out *into* a mountain
    20. he lifted up his eyes *on* his disciples,
    38. shall men give *into* your bosom.
    39. both fall *into* the ditch ?
7: 1. *in* the audience of the people, he entered *into* Capernaum.
    10. returning *to* the house, found
    11. he went *into* a city called Nain ;
    24. What went ye out *into* the wilderness
    30. counsel of God *against* themselves, (lit. *towards* themselves.)
    36. he went *into* the Pharisee's house,
    44. I entered *into* thine house, thou
    50. faith hath saved thee ; go *in* peace.
8:14. that which fell *among* thorns
    17. be known and come abroad. (lit. *unto* manifestation)
    22. he went *into* a ship with his disciples:
    — Let us go over *unto* the other side
    23. a storm of wind *on* the lake;
    26. *at* the country of the Gadarenes,
    29. driven of the devil *into* the wilderness.
    30. many devils were entered *into* him.
    31. to go out *into* the deep.

Lu. 8:32. suffer them to enter *into* them.
    33. entered *into* the swine:
    — down a steep place *into* the lake,
    34. told (it) *in* the city and *in* the country.
    37. he went up *into* the ship,
    39. Return *to* thine own house,
    41. that he would come *into* his house:
    43. spent all her living *upon* physicians,
    48. made thee whole ; go *in* peace.
    51. when he came *into* the house,
9: 3. Take nothing *for* (your) journey,
    4.)(whatsoever house ye enter into,
    5. *for* a testimony against them.
    10. aside privately *into* a desert place
    12. that they may go *into* the towns
    13. buy meat *for* all this people.
    16. looking up *to* heaven, he
    28. went up *into* a mountain *to* pray.
    34. as they entered *into* the cloud.
    44. these sayings sink down *into* your ears.
    — delivered *into* the hands of men.
    51. set his face to go *to* Jerusalem,
    52. *into* a village of the Samaritans,
    53. though he would go *to* Jerusalem.
    56. they went *to* another village.
    61. which are at home *at* my house.
    62. hand to the plough, and looking)(back, is fit *for* the kingdom of God.
10: 1. *into* every city and place, whither
    2. send forth labourers *into* his harvest.
    5. *into* whatsoever house ye enter,
    7. Go not from house *to* house.
    8. *into* whatsoever city ye enter,
    10. *into* whatsoever city ye enter,
    — go your ways out *into* the streets
    30. down from Jerusalem *to* Jericho,
    34. brought him *to* an inn,
    36. him that fell *among* the thieves?
    38. he entered *into* a certain village:
    — Martha received him *into* her house.
11: 4. lead us not *into* temptation;
    7. my children are with me *in* bed ;
    24. I will return *unto* my house whence
    32. they repented *at* the preaching of
    33. putteth (it) *in* a secret place,
    49. I will send)(them prophets and apostles,
12: 5. hath power to cast *into* hell;
    10. speak a word *against* the Son of man,
    — blasphemeth *against* the Holy Ghost
    19. goods laid up *for* many years ;
    21. is not rich *toward* God.
    28. to morrow is cast *into* the oven;
    49. come to send fire *on* the earth;
    58. the officer cast thee *into* prison.
13: 9. if not, (then) after that (lit. *for* afterwards) thou shalt cut it down.
    11. bowed together, and could *in* no wise lift up (herself).
    19. took, and cast *into* his garden ; and it grew, and waxed)(a great tree;
    21. hid *in* three measures of meal,
    22. teaching, and journeying *toward* Jerusalem.
14: 1. as he went *into* the house of one
    5. an ass or an ox fallen *into* a pit,
    8. bidden of any (man) *to* a wedding, sit not down *in* the highest
    10. sit down *in* the lowest room;
    21. Go out quickly *into* the streets
    23. Go out *into* the highways and hedges,
    31. to make war (lit. to enter *upon* war) against another king,
    35. fit *for* the land, nor yet *for* the dunghill ,

Lu. 15: 6. when he cometh)(home, he calleth
13. took his journey *into* a far country,
15. he sent him *into* his fields to feed swine.
17. when he came *to* himself,
18. I have sinned *against* heaven,
21. I have sinned *against* heaven,
22. put a ring *on* his hand, and shoes *on* (his)
feet:
16: 4. may receive me *into* their houses.
8. are *in* (lit. *towards*) their generation
wiser
9. receive you *into* everlasting habitations.
16. every man presseth *into* it.
22. by the angels *into* Abraham's bosom:
27. send him *to* my father's house:
28. come *into* this place of torment.
17: 2. about his neck, and he cast *into* the sea,
3. If thy brother trespass *against* thee,
4. if he trespass *against* thee seven
11. as he went *to* Jerusalem, that
12. he entered *into* a certain village,
24. shineth *unto* the other (part) under
27. that Noe entered *into* the ark,
31. let him likewise not return)(back.
18: 5. by her continual coming (lit. coming *for*
ever) she weary me.
10. Two men went up *into* the temple to pray ;
13. so much as (his) eyes *unto* heaven, but
smote *upon* his breast, saying,
14. this man went down *to* his house
17. shall in no wise enter there*in*.
24. enter *into* the kingdom of God !
25. a rich man to enter *into* the kingdom
31. Behold, we go up *to* Jerusalem,
35. he was come nigh *unto* Jericho,
19: 12. nobleman went *into* a far country
28. ascending up *to* Jerusalem,
29. he was come nigh *to* Bethphage
30. Go ye *into* the village over against
45. he went *into* the temple, and began
20: 17. the same is become)(the head of the
20. that so they might deliver (lit. *for* to
deliver) him unto the
21: 1. casting their gifts *into* the treasury.
4. cast *in* unto the offerings of God:
12. *to* the synagogues, and into prisons,
13. it shall turn to you *for* a testimony.
14. Settle (it) therefore *in* your hearts,
21. in Judæa flee *to* the mountains ;
— are in the countries enter there*into*.
24. led away captive *into* all nations:
37. went out, and abode *in* the mount
22: 3. Then entered Satan *into* Judas
10. when ye are entered *into* the city,
— follow him *into* the house
19. this do *in* (lit. *unto*) remembrance of me.
33. both *into* prison, and *to* death.
39. *to* the mount of Olives ;
40. that ye enter not *into* temptation.
46. lest ye enter *into* temptation.
54. him *into* the high priest's house.
65. blasphemously spake they *against* him.
66. led him *into* their council,
23: 19. for murder, was cast *into* prison.
25. for sedition and murder was cast *into*
prison,
46. *into* thy hands I commend my
24: 5. down (their) faces *to* the earth,
7. delivered *into* the hands of sinful men,
13. went that same day *to* a village
20. delivered him *to* be condemned to death,
26. and to enter *into* his glory ?

Lu. 24: 28. they drew nigh *unto* the village,
33. returned *to* Jerusalem, and found
47. in his name *among* all nations,
50. led them out as far as *to* Bethany,
51. from them, and carried up *into* heaven.
52. returned *to* Jerusalem with great joy :
Joh. 1: 7. The same came *for* a witness,
9. that cometh *into* the world.
11. He came *unto* his own,
12. them that believe *on* his name:
18. which is *in* the bosom of the Father,
43(44). Jesus would go forth *into* Galilee,
2: 2. called, and his disciples, *to* the marriage.
11. his disciples believed *on* him.
12. he went down *to* Capernaum,
13. Jesus went up *to* Jerusalem,
23. many believed *in* his name,
3: 4. second time *into* his mother's womb,
5. enter *into* the kingdom of God.
13. no man hath ascended up *to* heaven,
15. That whosoever believeth *in* him
16. that whosoever believeth *in* him
17. sent not his Son *into* the world to
18. He that believeth *on* him is not
— hath not believed *in* the name of
19. that light is come *into* the world,
22. his disciples *into* the land of Judæa ;
24. John was not yet cast *into* prison.
36. He that believeth *on* the Son hath
4: 3. departed again *into* Galilee.
5. Then cometh he *to* a city of Samaria,
8. gone away *unto* the city to buy
14. I shall give him shall never (lit. not *for*
ever) thirst ;
— springing up *into* everlasting life.
28. went her way *into* the city,
36. gathereth fruit *unto* life eternal :
38. ye are entered *into* their labours.
39. believed *on* him for the saying
43. went *into* Galilee.
45. when he was come *into* Galilee,
— they also went *unto* the feast.
46. So Jesus came again *into* Cana
47. was come out of Judæa *into* Galilee,
54. was come out of Judæa *into* Galilee.
5: 1. Jesus went up *to* Jerusalem.
7. to put me *into* the pool:
24. shall not come *into* condemnation ; but
is passed from death *unto* life.
29. *unto* the resurrection of life ;
— *unto* the resurrection of damnation.
45. (even) Moses, *in* whom ye trust.
6: 3. Jesus went up *into* a mountain,
9. what are they *among* so many ?
14. that should come *into* the world.
15. he departed again *into* a mountain
17. entered *into* a ship, and went over the sea
toward Capernaum.
21. received him *into* the ship:
— at the land whither (lit. *unto* which) they
went.
22. where*into* his disciples were entered,
— with his disciples *into* the boat,
24. took shipping (lit. entered *into* ships), and
came *to* Capernaum,
27. endureth *unto* everlasting life,
29. believe *on* him whom he hath sent.
35. he that believeth *on* me shall never thirst.
40. seeth the Son, and believeth *on* him,
47. He that believeth *on* me hath
51. he shall live *for* ever: and the bread
58. eateth of this bread shall live *for* ever.

Joh. 6:66. many of his disciples went)(back,

7: 3. Depart hence, and go *into* Judæa,
5. neither did his brethren believe *in* him.
8. Go ye up *unto* this feast: I go not up yet *unto* this feast;
10. went he also up *unto* the feast,
14. Jesus went up *into* the temple,
31. many of the people believed *on* him,
35. will he go *unto* the dispersed among
38. He that believeth *on* me, as the
39. they that believe *on* him should
48. the Pharisees believed *on* him?
53. every man went *unto* his own house.

8: 1. Jesus went *unto* the mount of Olives.
2. he came again *into* the temple,
6. with (his) finger wrote *on* the ground,
8. stooped down, and wrote *on* the ground.
26. I speak *to* (lit. *into*) the world those things
30. many believed *on* him.
35. abideth not in the house *for* ever: (but) the Son abideth)(ever.
51. he shall never see death. (εις τον αιωνα)
52. he shall never taste of death. (εις &c.)

9: 7. Go, wash *in* the pool of Siloam,
11. Go *to* the pool of Siloam, and wash:
35. Dost thou believe *on* the Son of God?
36. that I might believe *on* him?
39. *For* judgment I am come *into* this

10: 1. by the door *into* the sheepfold,
28. shall never perish, (εισ τον αιωνα)
36. sanctified, and sent *into* the world,
40. *into* the place where John at first
42. many believed *on* him there.

11: 7. Let us go *into* Judæa again.
25. he that believeth *in* me,
26. whosoever liveth and believeth *in* me shall never die. (εις τον αιωνα)
27. which should come *into* the world.
30. Jesus was not yet come *into* the town,
31. She goeth *unto* the grave to weep
32. she fell down *at* his feet, saying
38. himself cometh *to* the grave.
45. which Jesus did, believed *on* him.
48. all (men) will believe *on* him:
52. he should gather together *in* one
54. went thence *unto* a country near
— *into* a city called Ephraim,
55. up *to* Jerusalem before the passover,
56. that he will not come *to* the feast?

12: 1. before the passover came *to* Bethany,
7. *against* the day of my burying
11. went away, and believed *on* Jesus.
12. people that were come *to* the feast,
— that Jesus was coming *to* Jerusalem,
13. went forth to meet (lit. *to* the meeting) him, and cried,
24. a corn of wheat fall *into* the ground
25. shall keep it *unto* life eternal.
27. for this cause came I *unto* this hour.
34. that Christ abideth *for* ever:
36. believe *in* the light, that ye may
37. yet they believed not *on* him:
42. rulers also many believed *on* him;
44. believeth *on* me, believeth not *on* me, but *on* him that sent me.
46. I am come a light *into* the world, that whosoever believeth *on* me

13: 1. he loved them *unto* the end.
2. put *into* the heart of Judas Iscariot,
3. had given all things *into* his hands,
5. he poureth water *into* a bason,
8. Thou shalt never (lit. not *for* ever) wash

Joh. 13:22. disciples looked one *on* another,
27. after the sop Satan entered *into* him.
29. we have need of *against* the feast;

14: 1. believe *in* God, believe also *in* me.
12. He that believeth *on* me, the works
16. he may abide with you *for* ever;

15: 6. cast (them) *into* the fire, and they

16: 9. because they believe not *on* me;
13. he will guide you *into* all truth:
20. your sorrow shall be turned *into* joy.
21. that a man is born *into* the world.
28. am come *into* the world:
32. scattered, every man *to* his own,

17: 1. lifted up his eyes *to* heaven,
18. thou hast sent me *into* the world,
— I also sent them *into* the world.
20. which shall believe *on* me through
23. they may be made perfect *in* one;

18: 1. a garden, *into* the which he entered,
6. they went back*ward*, and fell to the
11. Put up thy sword *into* the sheath:
15. *into* the palace of the high priest.
28. *unto* the hall of judgment:
— went not *into* the judgment hall,
33. Pilate entered *into* the judgment hall
37. *To* this end was I born, and *for* this

19: 9. went again *into* the judgment hall,
13. *in* a place that is called the Pavement,
17. went forth *into* a place called
27. took her *unto* his own (home).
37. They shall look *on* him whom

20: 1. *unto* the sepulchre, and seeth the
3. that other disciple, and came *to* the sepulchre.
4. came first *to* the sepulchre.
6. went *into* the sepulchre,
7. wrapped together *in* a place by itself.
8. came first *to* the sepulchre,
11. (looked) *into* the sepulchre,
14. she turned herself)(back, and saw
19. came Jesus and stood *in* the midst,
25. my finger *into* the print of the nails, and thrust my hand *into* his side,
26. stood *in* the midst, and said,
27. thrust (it) *into* my side: and be

21: 3. entered *into* a ship immediately;
4. Jesus stood *on* the shore.
6. Cast the net *on* the right side of the
7. did cast himself *into* the sea.
9. then as they were come *to* land,
23. this saying abroad *among* the brethren,

Acts 1:10. looked stedfastly *toward* heaven
11. why stand ye gazing up *into* heaven?
— is taken up from you *into* heaven,
— have seen him go *into* heaven.
12. returned they *unto* Jerusalem
13. they went up *into* an upper room,
25. he might go *to* his own place.

2:20. The sun shall be turned *into* darkness, and the moon *into* blood,
22. a man approved of God *among* you by miracles
25. David speaketh *concerning* him,
27. thou wilt not leave my soul *in* hell,
31. his soul was not left *in* hell,
34. not ascended *into* the heavens:
38. *for* the remission of sins,
39. to all that are afar off, (lit. *at* a distance)

3: 1. up together *into* the temple
2. them that entered *into* the temple;
3. Peter and John about to go *into* the temple
4. fastening his eyes *upon* him with John, said, Look *on* us.

Acts 3: 8. entered with them *into* the temple,
19. that your sins may be blotted out, (lit. *unto* your sins being blotted out)
4: 3. put (them) *in* hold *unto* the next day:
6. gathered together *at* Jerusalem.
11, is become)(the head of the corner.
17. spread no further *among* the people,
30. stretching forth thine hand to heal; (lit. *to* the healing)
5: 16. round about *unto* Jerusalem,
21. they entered *into* the temple
— sent *to* the prison to have them
36. were scattered, and brought *to* nought.
6: 11. blasphemous words *against* Moses,
12. brought (him) *to* the council,
15. looking stedfastly *on* him,
7: 3. come *into* the land which I
4. he removed him *into* this land, where*in* ye now dwell
5. give it to him *for* a possession,
9. with envy, sold Joseph *into* Egypt:
15. Jacob went down *into* Egypt,
16. were carried over *into* Sychem,
19. *to the end* they might not live.
21. nourished him *for* her own son.
26. have set them *at* one again,
34. I will send thee *into* Egypt.
39. hearts turned back again *into* Egypt,
53. *by* the disposition of angels,
55. looked up stedfastly *into* heaven,
8: 3. committed (them) *to* prison.
5. Philip went down *to* the city of Samaria,
16. *in* the name of the Lord Jesus.
20. Thy money perish (lit. be *unto* destruction) with thee,
23. thou art *in* the gall of bitterness,
25. the Lord, returned *to* Jerusalem,
26. down from Jerusalem *unto* Gaza,
27. had come *to* Jerusalem for to
38. went down both *into* the water,
40. Philip was found *at* Azotus:
— till he came *to* Cæsarea.
9: 1. *against* the disciples of the Lord,
2. desired of him letters *to* Damascus
— bring them bound *unto* Jerusalem.
6. Arise, and go *into* the city, and it
8. brought (him) *into* Damascus.
17. went his way, and entered *into* the house;
21. came hither *for* that *intent*, that he
26. when Saul was come *to* Jerusalem,
30. *to* Cæsarea, and sent him forth *to* Tarsus.
39. brought him *into* the upper chamber:
10: 4. are come up *for* a memorial
5. now send men *to* Joppa,
8. unto them, he sent them *to* Joppa.
16. was received up again *into* heaven.
22. to send for thee *into* his house,
24. after they entered *into* Cæsarea.
32. Send therefore *to* Joppa, and call
43. whosoever believeth *in* him
11: 2. when Peter was come up *to* Jerusalem,
6. *Upon* the which when I had fastened
8. at any time entered *into* my mouth.
10. all were drawn up again *into* heaven.
12. we entered *into* the man's house:
13. Send men *to* Joppa, and call
18. granted repentance *unto* life.
20. when they were come *to* Antioch,
22. came *unto* the ears of the church
25. Then departed Barnabas *to* Tarsus,
26(25). he brought him *unto* Antioch.
27. prophets from Jerusalem *unto* Antioch.

Acts 11: 29. to send)(relief unto the brethren
12: 4. put (him) *in* prison, and delivered
10. gate that leadeth *unto* the city;
17. departed, and went *into* another place.
19. went down from Judæa *to* Cæsarea,
13: 2. *for* the work whereunto I have
4. departed *unto* Seleucia; and from thence they sailed *to* Cyprus.
9. Holy Ghost, set his eyes *on* him,
13. they came *to* Perga in Pamphylia:
— from them returned *to* Jerusalem.
14. they came *to* Antioch in Pisidia, and went *into* the synagogue on the
22. raised up unto them David *to* be their king; (lit. *for* a king)
29. laid (him) *in* a sepulchre.
31. with him from Galilee *to* Jerusalem,
34. no more to return *to* corruption,
42. preached to them)(the next sabbath.
46. lo, we turn *to* the Gentiles.
47. I have set thee to be a light (lit. *for* a light)
— that thou shouldest be *for* salvation unto
48. as were ordained *to* eternal life
51. against them, and came *unto* Iconium.
14: 1. *into* the synagogue of the Jews,
6. fled *unto* Lystra and Derbe, cities of
14. ran *in among* the people, crying
20. rose up, and came *into* the city:
— he departed with Barnabas *to* Derbe.
21. they returned again *to* Lystra,
22. enter *into* the kingdom of God.
23. the Lord, *on* whom they believed.
24. they came *to* Pamphylia.
25. they went down *into* Attalia:
26. thence sailed *to* Antioch,
— *for* the work which they fulfilled.
15: 2. should go up *to* Jerusalem
4. when they were come *to* Jerusalem
22. of their own company *to* Antioch
30. were dismissed, they came *to* Antioch:
38. went not with them *to* the work.
39. took Mark, and sailed *unto* Cyprus;
16: 1. Then came he *to* Derbe and Lystra:
8. by Mysia came down *to* Troas.
9. saying, Come over *into* Macedonia,
10. to go *into* Macedonia,
11. with a straight course *to* Samothracia, and the next (day) *to* Neapolis;
12. from thence *to* Philippi,
15. come *into* my house, and abide
16. came to pass, as we went *to* prayer,
19. drew (them) *into* the marketplace
23. they cast (them) *into* prison,
24. thrust them *into* the inner prison, and made their feet fast *in* the stocks.
34. had brought them *into* his house,
37. have cast (us) *into* prison;
40. entered *into* (the house of) Lydia:
17: 1. they came *to* Thessalonica,
5. to bring them out *to* the people.
10. Paul and Silas by night *unto* Berea:
— *into* the synagogue of the Jews.
20. certain strange things *to* our ears:
21. spent their time *in* nothing else,
18: 1. departed from Athens, and came *to* Corinth;
6. I will go *unto* the Gentiles.
7. entered *into* a certain (man's) house,
18. sailed thence *into* Syria:
19. he came *to* Ephesus, and left them
— himself entered *into* the synagogue,
21. this feast that cometh *in* Jerusalem:

Acts18:22. when he had landed *at* Cæsarea,
— he went down *to* Antioch.
24. mighty in the scriptures, came *to* Ephesus.
27. was disposed to pass *into* Achaia,
19: 1. through the upper coasts came *to* Ephesus:
3. *Unto* what then were ye baptized? and they said, *Unto* John's baptism.
4. believe *on* him which should come after him, that is, *on* Christ Jesus.
5. *in* the name of the Lord Jesus.
8. he went *into* the synagogue,
21. to go *to* Jerusalem, saying,
22. So he sent *into* Macedonia two
— he himself stayed *in* Asia
27. in danger to be set at nought ; (lit. should come *into* reprobation)
— goddess Diana should be despised, (lit. be reckoned *for* nothing)
29. rushed with one accord *into* the theatre.
30. entered *in unto* the people,
31. not adventure himself *into* the theatre.
20: 1. for to go *into* Macedonia.
2. he came *into* Greece,
3. was about to sail *into* Syria,
6. came unto them *to* Troas
13. before to ship, and sailed *unto* Assos,
14. when he met with us *at* Assos, we took him in, and came *to* Mitylene.
15. next (day) we arrived *at* Samos,
— next (day) we came *to* Miletus.
16. for him, to be *at* Jerusalem
17. from Miletus he sent *to* Ephesus,
18. the first day that I came *into* Asia,
21. repentance *toward* God, and faith
22. bound in the spirit *unto* Jerusalem,
29. grievous wolves enter *in among* you,
38. they accompanied him *unto* the ship.
21: 1. course *unto* Coos, and the (day) following *unto* Rhodes, and from thence *unto* Patara:
2. a ship sailing over *unto* Phenicia,
3. sailed *into* Syria, and landed *at* Tyre:
4. should not go up *to* Jerusalem.
6. leave one of another, we took (lit. embarked *into*) ship ; and they returned)(home again.
7. from Tyre, we came *to* Ptolemais,
8. *unto* Cæsarea: and we entered *into* the house
11. *into* the hands of the Gentiles.
12. not to go up *to* Jerusalem.
13. also to die *at* Jerusalem for the
15. went up *to* Jerusalem.
17. when we were come *to* Jerusalem,
26. with them entered *into* the temple,
28. brought Greeks also *into* the temple,
29. Paul had brought *into* the temple.
34. to be carried *into* the castle,
37. Paul was to be led *into* the castle,
38. leddest out *into* the wilderness
22: 4. delivering *into* prisons both men
5. unto the brethren, and went *to* Damascus,
— were there bound *unto* Jerusalem,
7. I fell *unto* the ground, and heard
10. Arise, and go *into* Damascus ;
11. with me, I came *into* Damascus.
13. same hour I looked up *upon* him.
17. when I was come again *to* Jerusalem,
21. send thee far hence *unto* the Gentiles.
23. threw dust *into* the air,
24. to be brought *into* the castle,
30. set him *before* them.

Acts23:10. to bring (him) *into* the castle.
11. hast testified of me *in* Jerusalem,
— must thou bear witness also *at* Rome.
16. went and entered *into* the castle,
20. to morrow *into* the council,
28. I brought him forth *into* their council:
30. the Jews laid wait *for* the man,
31. by night *to* Antipatris.
32. with him, and returned *to* the castle:
33. when they came *to* Cæsarea,
24:15. have hope *toward* God, which
17. to bring alms *to* my nation,
24. concerning the faith *in* Christ
25: 1. ascended from Cæsarea *to* Jerusalem.
3. send for him *to* Jerusalem,
6. he went down *unto* Cæsarea ;
8. *against* the law of the Jews, neither *against* the temple, nor yet *against* Cæsar,
9. Wilt thou go up *to* Jerusalem,
13. Agrippa and Bernice came *unto* Cæsarea
15. when I was *at* Jerusalem,
16. to deliver any man to die, (lit. *unto* death)
20. I doubted of such manner *of* questions, (lit. *as to* the investigation about this)
— whether he would go *to* Jerusalem,
21. *unto* the hearing of Augustus,
23. entered *into* the place of hearing,
26: 7. *Unto* which (promise) our twelve
11. even *unto* strange cities.
12. as I went *to* Damascus with
14. we were all fallen *to* the earth,
16. appeared unto thee *for* this *purpose*,
17. *unto* whom now I send thee,
18. turn (them) from darkness *to* light,
— sanctified by faith that is *in* me.
20. *throughout* all the coasts of Judæa,
24. much learning doth make thee mad. (lit. perverts thee *to* madness)
27: 1. that we should sail *into* Italy,
3. next (day) we touched *at* Sidon.
5. we came *to* Myra, (a city) of Lycia.
6. ship of Alexandria sailing *into* Italy ; and he put us therein.
8. came *unto* a place which is called
12. they might attain *to* Phenice,
17. should fall *into* the quicksands,
26. must be cast *upon* a certain island.
29. should have fallen *upon* rocks,
30. let down the boat *into* the sea,
38. cast out the wheat *into* the sea.
39. *into* the which they were minded,
40. committed (themselves) *unto* the sea,
— to the wind, and made *toward* shore.
41. *into* a place where two seas met,
28: 5. shook off the beast *into* the fire,
6. saw no harm come *to* him,
12. landing *at* Syracuse, we
13. fetched a compass, and came *to* Rhegium:
— we came the next day *to* Puteoli,
14. so we went *toward* Rome.
15. they came to meet (lit. *unto* the meeting) us as far
16. when we came *to* Rome,
17. *into* the hands of the Romans.
23. came many to him *into* (his) lodging ;
Ro. 1: 1. separated *unto* the gospel of God,
5. *for* obedience to the faith
11. *to* the end ye may be established ;
16. *unto* salvation to every one
17. revealed from faith *to* faith:
20. so *that* they are without excuse:
24. gave them up *to* uncleanness

Ro. 1:25. who is blessed *for* ever.
26. them up *unto* vile affections:
— *into* that which is against nature:
27. lust one *toward* another;
28. over *to* a reprobate mind,
2: 4. God leadeth thee *to* repentance?
26. be counted *for* circumcision?
3: 7. through my lie *unto* his glory;
22. *unto* all and upon all them
25. to declare (lit. *unto* the demonstration of) his righteousness
26. that he might be (lit. *unto* his being) just,
4: 3. counted unto him *for* righteousness.
5. faith is counted *for* righteousness.
9. reckoned to Abraham *for* righteousness.
11. that he might be the father (lit. *unto* his being the father)
— that righteousness might be imputed (lit. *unto* righteousness being imputed)
16. *to the end* the promise might be
18. that he might become the father (lit. *unto* his becoming)
20. staggered not *at* the promise of God
22. imputed to him *for* righteousness.
5: 2. access by faith *into* this grace
8. commendeth his love *toward* us,
12. sin entered *into* the world,
— so death passed *upon* (lit. towards) all men,
15. hath abounded *unto* many.
16. (was) by one *to* condemnation,
— of many offences *unto* justification.
18. *upon* all men *to* condemnation;
— *upon* all men *unto* justification
21. through righteousness *unto* eternal life
6: 3. baptized *into* Jesus Christ were baptized *into* his death?
4. with him by baptism *into* death:
12. that ye should obey it (lit. *unto* obeying it)
16. servants to obey, (lit. *unto* obedience)
— whether of sin *unto* death, or of obedience *unto* righteousness?
17. that form of doctrine which was delivered you. (lit. *unto* which you were delivered)
19. uncleanness and to iniquity *unto* iniquity;
— servants to righteousness *unto* holiness.
22. have your fruit *unto* holiness,
7: 4. that ye should be married to another, (lit. *unto* your becoming another's)
5. to bring (lit. *unto* bringing) forth fruit *unto* death.
10. which (was ordained) to life (lit. *unto* life), I found (to be) *unto* death.
8: 7. carnal mind (is) enmity *against* God:
15. spirit of bondage again *to* (lit. *unto*) fear;
18. which shall be revealed *in* us.
21. *into* the glorious liberty of the
28. all things work together *for* good
29. that he might be (lit. *unto* his being) the firstborn
9: 5. over all, God blessed *for* ever.
8. the children of the promise are counted *for* the seed.
17. Even *for* this same *purpose* have I raised
21. *unto* honour, and another *unto* dishonour?
22. of wrath fitted *to* (lit. *unto*) destruction;
23. had afore prepared *unto* glory,
31. *to* the law of righteousness.
10: 1. that they might be saved. (lit. is *unto* their salvation)
4. the law *for* righteousness to every
6. Who shall ascend *into* heaven?
7. Who shall descend *into* the deep?

Ro. 10:10. man believeth *unto* righteousness;
— confession is made *unto* salvation.
12. rich *unto* all that call upon him.
14. *in* whom they have not believed?
18. their sound went *into* all the earth,
— words *unto* the ends of the world.
11: 9. their table be made)(a snare, and)(a trap, and)(a stumblingblock, and)(a recompence
11. *for* to provoke them to jealousy.
24. *into* a good olive tree:
32. hath concluded them all *in* unbelief,
36. through him, and *to* (lit. *for* or *unto*) him, (are) all things: to whom (be) glory *for* ever.
12: 2. that ye may prove (lit. *unto* your proving)
3. to think soberly, (lit. *unto* being soberminded)
10. kindly affectioned one *to* another
16. the same mind one *toward* another.
13: 4. minister of God to thee *for* good.
— a revenger *to* (execute) wrath upon him
6. attending continually *upon* this
14. for the flesh, to (fulfil) the lusts (lit. *unto* lusts)
14: 1. not *to* doubtful disputations.
9. For *to* this *end* Christ both died,
19. wherewith one may edify another. (lit. of edification *towards* each other)
15: 2. *for* (his) good to edification.
4. were written *for* our learning,
7. received us *to* the glory of God.
8. to confirm (lit. *unto* confirming) the promises (made)
13. that ye may abound (lit. *unto* your abounding) in hope,
16. That I should be (lit. *unto* my being) the minister of Jesus Christ *to* the Gentiles,
18. to make the Gentiles obedient, (lit. *unto* the obedience of the Gentiles)
24. I take my journey *into* Spain,
25. now I go *unto* Jerusalem
26. contribution *for* the poor saints
28. I will come by you *into* Spain.
31. my service which (I have) *for* Jerusalem
16: 5. the firstfruits of Achaia *unto* Christ.
6. bestowed much labour *on* us.
19. obedience is come abroad *unto* all
— wise *unto* that which is good, and simple concerning evil. (lit. *unto* that which is evil)
26. known *to* all nations *for* the obedience of faith:
27. glory through Jesus Christ *for* ever.
1Co. 1: 9. *unto* the fellowship of his Son
13. baptized *in* the name of Paul?
15. baptized *in* mine own name.
2: 7. before the world *unto* our glory:
4: 3. with me it is)(a very small thing
6. transferred *to* myself and (to) Apollos
5: 5. *for* the destruction of the flesh,
6:16. for two, saith he, shall be)(one flesh.
18. sinneth *against* his own body.
8: 6. (are) all things, and we *in* him;
10. to eat (lit. *unto* eating) those things which are offered to idols;
12. ye sin so *against* the brethren,
— ye sin *against* Christ.
13. no flesh while the world standeth, (εἰς τον αιωνα)
9:18. *that* I abuse not my power
10: 2. were all baptized *unto* Moses

1Co.10: 6. *to the intent* we should not lust
11. *upon* whom the ends of the world
31. do all *to* the glory of God.
11:17. not *for* the better, but *for* the worse.
22. houses to eat and to drink in? (lit. *for* eating and drinking)
24. this do *in* (lit. *unto*) remembrance of me.
25. drink (it), *in* (lit. *unto*) remembrance of me.
33. when ye come together *to* eat,
34. not together *unto* condemnation.
12:13. all baptized *into* one body,
— made to drink *into* one Spirit.
14: 8. prepare himself *to* the battle?
9. for ye shall speak *into* the air.
22. Wherefore tongues are *for* a sign,
36. or came it *unto* you only?
15:10. his grace which was (bestowed) *upon* me
45. Adam was made)(a living soul ;
— (was made))(a quickening spirit.
54. Death is swallowed up *in* victory.
16: 1. the collection *for* the saints,
3. bring your liberality *unto* Jerusalem.
15. *to* the ministry of the saints,
2Co. 1: 4. that we may be able (lit. *unto* our being able) to comfort
5. as the sufferings of Christ abound *in* us,
10. *in* whom we trust that he will
11. *upon* us by the means of many
16. to pass by you *into* Macedonia,
— brought on my way *toward* Judæa.
21. stablisheth us with you *in* Christ,
23. I came not as yet *unto* Corinth.
2: 4. have more abundantly *unto* you.
8. confirm (your) love *toward* him.
9. *to* this end also did I write,
— ye be obedient *in* all things.
12. when I came *to* Troas to (preach) Christ's gospel, (lit. *for* the gospel of)
13. I went from thence *into* Macedonia.
16. the savour of death *unto* death;
— the savour of life *unto* life.
3: 7. stedfastly behold)(the face of Moses
13. *to* the end of that which is abolished:
18. same image from glory *to* glory,
4: 4. lest the light...should shine unto them. (lit. *unto* the light...not shining unto them)
11. delivered *unto* death for Jesus' sake,
15. redound *to* the glory of God.
17. worketh for us a far more exceeding (lit. according to excess *unto* excess)
5: 5. *for* the selfsame thing (is) God,
6: 1. receive not the grace of God *in* vain.
18. will be)(a Father unto you, and ye shall be my sons (lit. to me *for* sons)
7: 3. to die and live with (you). (lit. *unto* dying together and living with you)
5. when we were come *into* Macedonia,
9. that ye sorrowed *to* repentance:
10. worketh repentance *to* salvation
15. affection is more abundant *toward* you,
8: 2. poverty abounded *unto* the riches
4. the ministering *to* the saints.
6. *Insomuch that* we desired Titus,
— finish *in* you the same grace also.
14(13). (may be a supply) *for* their want,
— may be (a supply) *for* your want:
22. confidence which (I have) *in* you.
23. partner and fellowhelper *concerning* you:
24. *to* them, and *before* (lit. *unto* the face of) the churches,
9: 1. the ministering *to* the saints,

2Co. 9: 5. they would go before *unto* you,
8. all grace abound *toward* you;
— may abound *to* every good work
9. his righteousness remaineth *for* ever.
10. both minister bread *for* (your) food,
11. every thing *to* all bountifulness,
13. subjection *unto* the gospel of Christ,
— distribution *unto* them, and *unto* all
10: 1. being absent am bold *toward* you:
5. *to* the obedience of Christ;
8. *for* edification, and not *for* your destruction,
13. not boast *of* things without (our) measure,
14. though we reached not *unto* you:
15. boasting *of* things without (our) measure,
— according to our rule abundant*ly*,
16. the gospel *in* the (regions) beyond you,
— *of* things made ready to our hand.
11: 3. the simplicity that is *in* Christ.
6. manifest *among* you in all things.
10. no man shall stop me of this boasting (lit. this boasting shall not be stopped *unto* me)
13. themselves *into* the apostles of Christ.
14. transformed *into* an angel of light.
20. if a man smite you *on* the face.
31. Christ, which is blessed *for* evermore,
12: 1. I will come *to* visions and revelations
4. he was caught up *into* paradise,
6. should think *of* me above that
13: 2. that, if I come again, (lit. *to* a return)
3. which *to* you-*ward* is not weak,
4. by the power of God *toward* you.
10. *to* edification, and not *to* destruction.
Gal. 1: 5. To whom (be) glory *for* ever and ever.
6. grace of Christ *unto* another gospel:
17. Neither went I up *to* Jerusalem
— I went *into* Arabia, and returned again *unto* Damascus.
18. I went up *to* Jerusalem to see
21. I came *into* the regions of Syria
2: 1. I went up again *to* Jerusalem
2. I should run, or had run, *in* vain.
8. in Peter *to* the apostleship
— mighty in me *toward* the Gentiles:
9. (should go) *unto* the heathen, and they *unto* the circumcision
11. when Peter was come *to* Antioch,
16. we have believed *in* Jesus Christ,
3: 6. accounted to him *for* righteousness.
14. might come *on* the Gentiles
17. confirmed before of God *in* Christ,
— that it should make (lit. *unto* making) the promise of none effect.
23. shut up *unto* the faith which
24. schoolmaster (to bring us) *unto* Christ,
27. have been baptized *into* Christ
4: 6. Spirit of his Son *into* your hearts,
11. bestowed *upon* you labour in vain.
24. which gendereth *to* bondage,
5:10. I have confidence *in* you through
13. liberty *for* an occasion to the flesh,
6: 4. have rejoicing *in* himself alone, and not *in* another.
8. he that soweth *to* his flesh
— he that soweth *to* the Spirit
Eph. 1: 5. *unto* the adoption of children...*to* himself,
6. *To* the praise of the glory of his
8. hath abounded *toward* us
10. That *in* the dispensation of the
12. That we should be (lit. *unto* our being) *to* the praise of his glory,
14. *until* the redemption of the purchased

Eph. 1:14. *unto* the praise of his glory.
15. love *unto* all the saints,
18. *that* ye may know what is the
19. greatness of his power *to* us-*ward*
2:15. of twain)(one new man, (so)
21. *unto* an holy temple in the Lord:
22. *for* an habitation of God
3: 2. which is given me *to* you-*ward:*
16. *his* Spirit *in* the inner man;
19. *with* (lit. *into*) all the fulness of God.
21. *throughout* all ages, world without end.
4: 8. When he ascended up *on* high,
9. descended first *into* the lower
12. *for* the work of the ministry, *for* the edifying
13. all come *in* the unity of the faith,
— *unto* a perfect man, *unto* the measure
15. may grow up *into* him in all
16. *unto* the edifying of itself in love.
19. *to* work (lit. *unto* working) all uncleanness
30. sealed *unto* the day of redemption.
32. be ye kind one *to* another,
5: 2. *for* a sweetsmelling savour.
31. they two shall be)(one flesh.
32. I speak *concerning* Christ and)(the church.
6:18. watching there*unto* with all
22. I have sent unto you *for* the same
Phi. 1: 5. For your fellowship *in* the gospel
10. *That* ye may approve things
— *till* the day of Christ;
11. *unto* the glory and praise of God.
12. *unto* the furtherance of the gospel;
17. *for* the defence of the gospel.
19. this shall turn *to* my salvation
23. having a desire to depart, (lit. *for* departing)
25. *for* your furtherance and joy of faith;
29. not only to believe *on* him,
2:11. *to* the glory of God the Father.
16. that I may rejoice (lit. *for* a rejoicing to me) *in* the day of Christ, that I have not run *in* vain, neither laboured *in* vain.
22. hath served with me *in* the gospel.
3:11. *unto* the resurrection of the dead.
16. Nevertheless, where*to* we have already
21. that it may be (lit. *unto* being) fashioned like unto his glorious body,
4:15. *as* concerning (lit. *to* account of) giving and receiving,
16. once and again *unto* my necessity.
17. that may abound *to* your account.
20. (be) glory *for* ever and ever.
Col. 1: 4. love (which ye have) *to* all the saints,
6. Which is come *unto* you, as (it is) in
10. worthy of the Lord *unto* all pleasing,
— increasing *in* the knowledge of God;
11. *unto* all patience and longsuffering
12. to be partakers of (lit. *unto* the sharing) the inheritance
13. *into* the kingdom of his dear Son:
16. were created by him, and *for* him.
20. to reconcile all things *unto* himself;
25. which is given to me *for* you,
29. Where*unto* I also labour, striving
2: 2. *unto* all riches of the full assurance
— *to* the acknowledgement of the
5. stedfastness of your faith *in* Christ.
22. Which all are to perish (lit. *unto* perishing) with the using;
3: 9. Lie not one *to* another, seeing

Col. 3:10. renewed *in* knowledge after
15. *to* the which also ye are called
4: 8. *for* the same *purpose*, that he
11. fellowworkers *unto* the kingdom of God,
1Th. 1: 5. came not *unto* you in word only,
2: 9. we preached *unto* you the gospel
12. That ye would walk (lit. *unto* your walking) worthy of God, who hath called you *unto* his kingdom
16. to fill up (lit. *unto* filling up) their sins — come upon them *to* the uttermost.
3: 2. *to* establish you, and to comfort you
3. that we are appointed there*unto*.
5. I sent *to* know your faith,
— our labour be *in* vain.
10. *that* we might see your face,
12. in love one *toward* another, and *toward* all (men), even as we (do) *toward* you:
13. *To* the end he may stablish
4: 8. also given *unto* us his holy Spirit.
9. taught of God *to* love one another.
10. do it *toward* all the brethren
15. remain *unto* the coming of the Lord
17. to meet (lit. *unto* meeting) the Lord *in* the air:
5: 9. appointed us *to* wrath, but to obtain salvation (lit. *unto* acquisition of salvation)
15. both *among* yourselves, and *to* all
18. in Christ Jesus *concerning* you.
2Th. 1: 3. of you all *toward* each other aboundeth;
5. *that* ye may be counted worthy
11. Where*fore* also we pray always
2: 2. *That* ye be not soon shaken in
4. sitteth *in* the temple of God,
6. *that* he might be revealed in his time.
10. that they might be (lit. *unto* their being) saved.
11. *that* they should believe a lie:
13. chosen you *to* salvation through
14. Where*unto* he called you by our gospel, *to* the obtaining of the glory of our
3: 5. *into* the love of God, and *into* the patient
9. an ensample unto you *to* follow us.
1Ti. 1: 3. when I went *into* Macedonia,
6. turned aside *unto* vain jangling;
12. putting me *into* the ministry;
15. came *into* the world to save sinners;
16. believe on him *to* life everlasting.
17. (be) honour and glory *for* ever and ever.
2: 4. to come *unto* the knowledge of the
7. Where*unto* I am ordained a preacher,
3: 6. *into* the condemnation of the devil.
7. lest he fall *into* reproach and the
4: 3. created to be (lit. *unto* being) received with thanksgiving
10. For there*fore* we both labour and suffer
5:24. going before *to* judgment;
6: 7. we brought nothing *into* (this) world,
9. fall *into* temptation and a snare,
— which drown men *in* destruction
12. where*unto* thou art also called,
17. giveth us richly all things *to* enjoy;
19. *against* the time to come,
2Ti. 1:11. Where*unto* I am appointed a
12. committed unto him *against* that day
2:14. strive not about words *to* no profit,
20. some *to* honour, and some *to* dishonour.
21. he shall be a vessel *unto* honour
— prepared *unto* every good work.
25. *to* the acknowledging of the truth;
26. taken captive by him *at* his will.
3: 6. they which creep *into* houses,

2Ti. 3: 7. never able to come *to* the knowledge
15. to make thee wise *unto* salvation
4:10. is departed *unto* Thessalonica ; Crescens *to* Galatia, Titus *unto* Dalmatia.
11. profitable to me *for* the ministry.
12. Tychicus have I sent *to* Ephesus.
18. *unto* his heavenly kingdom: to whom (be) glory *for* ever and ever.
Tit. 3:12. to come unto me *to* Nicopolis:
14. maintain good works *for* necessary uses,
Philem 5. the Lord Jesus, and *toward* all saints ;
6. which is in you *in* Christ Jesus.
Heb. 1: 5. to him)(a Father, and he shall be to me)(a Son?
6. the firstbegotten *into* the world,
8. Thy throne, O God, (is) *for* ever and ever:
14. sent forth *to* minister (lit. *unto* ministering)
2: 3. was confirmed *unto* us by them
10. bringing many sons *unto* glory,
17. to make (lit. *unto* making) reconciliation
3: 5. *for* a testimony of those things
11. They shall not enter *into* my rest.
18. they should not enter *into* his rest,
4: 1. of entering *into* his rest, any of
3. have believed do enter *into* rest,
— if they shall enter *into* my rest:
5. If they shall enter *into* my rest.
6. that some must enter *therein*,
10. he that is entered *into* his rest,
11. labour therefore to enter *into* that rest,
16. grace to (lit. *unto*) help in time of need.
5: 6. Thou (art) a priest *for* ever after
6: 6. renew them again *unto* repentance ;
8. end (is) to be burned: (lit. *unto* burning)
10. ye have shewed *toward* his name,
16. an oath *for* confirmation (is) to them
19. entereth *into* that within the veil ;
20. made an high priest *for* ever
7: 3. abideth a priest continually. (lit. *for* a continuance)
14. *of* which tribe Moses spake nothing
17. Thou (art) a priest *for* ever after the
21. Thou (art) a priest *for* ever after
24. because he continueth)(ever,
25. to save them *to* the uttermost
— *to* make intercession for them.
28. who is consecrated *for* evermore.
8: 3. high priest is ordained *to* offer gifts
10. will put my laws *into* their mind,
— I will be to them)(a God, and they shall be to me)(a people:
9: 6. went always *into* the first tabernacle,
7. *into* the second (went) the high priest
9. a figure *for* the time then present,
12. entered in once *into* the holy place,
14. *to* serve the living God ?
15. *for* the redemption of the transgressions
24. not entered *into* the holy places made
— *into* heaven itself, now to appear
25. entereth *into* the holy place every
26. *to* put away (lit. *unto* the putting away)sin
28. offered *to* bear the sins of many ;
— without sin *unto* salvation.
10: 1. offered year by year continual*ly*
5. when he cometh *into* the world,
12. *for* ever sat down on the right
14. perfected *for* ever them that
19. boldness *to* enter into the holiest
24. *to* provoke unto love and to good works:
31. to fall *into* the hands of the living God.
39. who draw back *unto* perdition ;

Heb 10:39. believe *to* the saving of the soul.
11: 3. *so that* things which are seen
7. an ark *to* the saving of his house ;
8. called to go out *into* a place which
— after receive *for* an inheritance,
9. sojourned *in* the land of promise,
11. received strength *to* conceive seed,
26. had respect *unto* the recompence
12: 2. Looking *unto* Jesus the author and
3. contradiction of sinners *against* himself,
10. *that* (we) might be partakers of
13: 8. same yesterday, and to day, and *for* ever.
11. blood is brought *into* the sanctuary
21. every good work *to* do his will,
— to whom (be) glory *for* ever and ever.
Jas. 1:18. *that* we should be a kind of
19. swift *to* hear, slow *to* speak, slow *to* wrath:
25. whoso looketh *into* the perfect law
2: 2. if there come *unto* your assembly
6. draw you *before* the judgment seats?
23. imputed unto him *for* righteousness:
3: 3. we put bits *in* the horses' mouths,
4: 9. your laughter be turned *to* mourning, and (your) joy *to* heaviness.
13. we will go *into* such a city,
5: 3. shall be)(a witness against you,
4. entered *into* the ears of the Lord
12. lest ye fall *into* condemnation.
1Pet.1: 2. *unto* obedience and sprinkling
3. again *unto* a lively hope by the
4. *To* an inheritance incorruptible,
— reserved in heaven *for* you,
5. through faith *unto* salvation
7. be found *unto* praise and honour
8. *in* whom, though now ye see (him) not,
10. grace (that should come) *unto* you:
11. Searching)(what, or)(what manner of time
— testified beforehand the sufferings *of* Christ,
12. which things the angels desire to look *into*.
21. Who by him do believe *in* God,
— your faith and hope might be *in* God.
22. *unto* unfeigned love of the brethren,
23. which liveth and abideth *for* ever.
25. word of the Lord endureth *for* ever
— the gospel is preached *unto* you.
2: 7. the same is made)(the head of the
8. where*unto* also they were appointed.
9. a peculiar people ; (lit. a people *unto* acquisition)
— of darkness *into* his marvellous light:
14. *for* the punishment of evildoers,
21. For even here*unto* were ye called:
3: 7. *that* your prayers be not hindered.
9. that ye are there*unto* called,
12. his ears (are open) *unto* their prayers:
20. where*in* few, that is, eight souls
21. of a good conscience *toward* God,
22. Who is gone *into* heaven, and is on
4: 2. *That* he no longer should live
4. run not with (them) *to* the same excess
6. For *for* this cause was the gospel
7. therefore sober, and watch *unto* prayer.
8. fervent charity *among* yourselves:
9. Use hospitality one *to* another
10. minister the same one *to* another,
11. praise and dominion *for* ever and ever
5:10. called us *unto* his eternal glory
11. glory and dominion *for* ever and ever.
12. grace of God where*in* ye stand.
2Pet. 1: 8. *in* the knowledge of our Lord Jesus

2 Pet.1:11. *into* the everlasting kingdom of
17. *in* whom I am well pleased.
2: 4. to be reserved *unto* judgment;
9. *unto* the day of judgment to
12. made *to* be taken and destroyed,
17. darkness is reserved *for* ever.
22. *to* her wallowing in the mire.
3: 7. *against* the day of judgment
9. is longsuffering *to* us-*ward*,
— that all should come *to* repentance.
18. To him (be) glory both now and *for* ever.
1Joh.2:17. the will of God abideth *for* ever.
3: 8. *For* this *purpose* the Son of God was
14. have passed from death *unto* life,
4: 1. are gone out *into* the world.
9. only begotten Son *into* the world,
5: 8. these three agree *in* one.
10. He that believeth *on* the Son
— believeth not)(the record that God
13. believe *on* the name of the Son
— believe *on* the name of the Son of God.
2Joh. 2. shall be with us *for* ever.
7. deceivers are entered *into* the world,
10. receive him not *into* (your) house,
3Joh. 5. doest *to* the brethren, and *to* strangers ;
Jude 4. ordained *to* this condemnation,
— grace of our God *into* lasciviousness,
6. *unto* the judgment of the great day.
13. the blackness of darkness *for* ever.
21. *unto* eternal life.
25. and power, both now and)(ever.
Rev. 1: 6. glory and dominion *for* ever and ever.
11. What thou seest, write *in* a book,
— *unto* Ephesus, and *unto* Smyrna, and *unto*
Pergamos, and *unto* Thyatira, and *unto*
Sardis, and *unto* Philadelphia, and *unto*
Laodicea.
18. behold, I am alive *for* evermore,
2:10. shall cast (some) of you *into* prison,
22. Behold, I will cast her *into* a bed,
— with her *into* great tribulation,
4: 9. who liveth *for* ever and ever,
10. worship him that liveth *for* ever
5: 6. sent forth *into* all the earth.
13. unto the Lamb *for* ever and ever.
14. him that liveth *for* ever and ever.
6:13. stars of heaven fell *unto* the earth,
15. *in* the dens and *in* the rocks of the
7:12. unto our God *for* ever and ever.
8: 5. of the altar, and cast (it) *into* the earth:
7. they were cast *upon* the earth:
8. with fire was cast *into* the sea :
11. part of the waters became)(wormwood ;
9: 1. a star fall from heaven *unto* the earth:
3. of the smoke locusts *upon* the earth:
7. like unto horses prepared *unto* battle ;
9. of many horses running *to* battle.
15. were prepared *for* an hour, and a day,
10: 5. lifted up his hand *to* heaven,
6. by him that liveth *for* ever and ever,
11: 6. over waters to turn them *to* blood,
9. suffer their dead bodies to be put *in* graves.
12. they ascended up *to* heaven in
15. he shall reign *for* ever and ever.
12: 4. did cast them *to* the earth:
6. the woman fled *into* the wilderness,
9. he was cast out *into* the earth,
13. that he was cast *unto* the earth,
14. fly *into* the wilderness, *into* her place,
13: 3. as it were wounded *to* death;
6. *in* blasphemy against God,
10. shall go *into* captivity:

Rev.13:13. down from heaven *on* the earth
14:11. ascendeth up *for* ever and ever:
19. thrust in his sickle *into* the earth,
— and cast (it) *into* the great winepress
15: 7. God, who liveth *for* ever and ever.
8. was able to enter *into* the temple,
16: 1. the wrath of God *upon* the earth.
2. grievous sore *upon* the men
3. poured out his vial *upon* the sea ;
4. poured out his vial *upon* the rivers and)(
fountains of waters ;
14. *to* the battle of that great day
16. together *into* a place called in
17. poured out his vial *into* the air;
19. city was divided *into* three parts,
17: 3. in the spirit *into* the wilderness:
8. go *into* perdition: and they that
11. of the seven, and goeth *into* perdition.
17. God hath put *in* their hearts
18:21. a great millstone, and cast (it) *into* the sea,
19: 3. her smoke rose up *for* ever and ever.
9. called *unto* the marriage supper
17. *unto* the supper of the great God ;
20. both were cast alive *into* a lake
20: 3. cast him *into* the bottomless pit,
8. to gather them together *to* battle:
10. was cast *into* the lake of fire
— day and night *for* ever and ever.
14. death and hell were cast *into* the lake
15. was cast *into* the lake of fire.
21:24. bring their glory and honour *into* it.
26. glory and honour of the nations *into* it.
27. shall in no wise enter *into* it
22: 2. *for* the healing of the nations.
5. they shall reign *for* ever and ever.
14. in through the gates *into* the city.

εἷς, ἕν, *hīs, hen.*

(μία, see in its place.)

Mat. 5:18. *one* jot or one tittle shall in no wise
29. that *one* of thy members should perish,
30. that *one* of thy members should
41. shall compel thee to go *a* mile
6:24. for either he will hate the *one*,
— or else he will hold to the *one*,
27. can add *one* cubit unto his stature ?
29. was not arrayed like *one* of these.
8:19. *a certain* scribe came, and said
10:29. *one* of them shall not fall on the
42. unto *one* of these little ones a cup
12:11. that shall have *one* sheep, and if it
13:46. when he had found *one* pearl
16:14. Jeremias, or *one* of the prophets.
18: 5. shall receive *one* such little child
6. shall offend *one* of these little ones
10. despise not *one* of these little ones;
12. *one* of them be gone astray,
14. that *one* of these little ones should
16. take with thee *one* or two more,
24. *one* was brought unto him,
28. found *one* of his fellowservants,
19:16. behold, *one* came and said unto him,
17. none good but *one*, (that is), God:
20:13. he answered *one* of them, and said,
21. the *one* on thy right hand, and the *other*
21:24. I also will ask you *one* thing,
22:35. Then *one* of them, (which was) a lawyer.
23: 8. for *one* is your Master, (even) Christ ;

Mat.23: 9. for *one* is your Father, which is
10. for *one* is your Master, (even) Christ.
15. sea and land to make *one* proselyte,
24:40. the *one* shall be taken, and the *other* left.
25:15. to another two, and to another *one* ;
18. he that had received *one* went
24. he which had received the *one*
40. unto *one* of the least of these
45. to *one* of the least of these, ye did
26:14. Then *one* of the twelve, called
21. that *one* of you shall betray me.
47. lo, Judas, *one* of the twelve, came,
51. *one* of them which were with Jesus
27:14. answered him to never *a* word ;
15. release unto the people *a* prisoner,
38. *one* on the right hand, and *another*
48. straightway *one* of them ran,
Mar. 2: 7. who can forgive sins but God *only ?*
4: 8. *some* (lit. *one*) thirty, and *some* sixty, and
some an
20. *some* thirtyfold, *some* sixty, and *some*
5:22. there cometh *one* of the rulers of
6:15. a prophet, or as *one* of the prophets.
8:14. with them more than *one* loaf.
28. others, *One* of the prophets.
9:17. *one* of the multitude answered
37. shall receive *one* of such children
42. whosoever shall offend *one* of (these)
10:17. there came *one* running, and kneeled
18. none good but *one*, (that is), God.
21. said unto him, *One* thing thou lackest:
37. *one* on thy right hand, and the *other*
11:29. I will also ask of you *one* question,
12: 6. Having yet therefore *one* son,
28. *one* of the scribes came, and having heard
29. The Lord our God is *one* Lord:
32. for there is *one* God; and there is none
other but he:
13: 1. *one* of his disciples saith unto him,
14:10. Judas Iscariot, *one* of the twelve,
18. *One* of you which eateth with me
20. (It is) *one* of the twelve, that dippeth
43. cometh Judas, *one* of the twelve,
47. *one* of them that stood by drew
51. followed him *a* certain young man,
15: 6. he released unto them *one* prisoner,
27. *one* on his right hand, and the *other*
36. *one* ran and filled a spunge full
Lu. 4:40. laid his hands on every *one* of them,
5: 3. he entered into *one* of the ships,
7:41. the *one* owed five hundred pence,
9: 8. that *one* of the old prophets was
10:42. *one* thing is needful: and Mary
11:46. with *one* of your fingers.
12: 6. not *one* of them is forgotten before God ?
25. can add to his stature *one* cubit ?
27. was not arrayed like *one* of these.
52. there shall be five in *one* house
15: 4. if he lose *one* of them, doth not
7. over *one* sinner that repenteth,
10. over *one* sinner that repenteth.
15. joined himself to *a* citizen (lit. *one* of the
citizens)
19. as *one* of thy hired servants.
26. he called *one* of the servants,
16: 5. every *one* of his lord's debtors
13. for either he will hate the *one*,
— or else he will hold to the *one*,
17: 2. should offend *one* of these little ones.
15. *one* of them, when he saw
34. the *one* shall be taken, and the other
18:10. the *one* a Pharisee, and the other a

Lu. 18:19. none (is) good, save *one*, (that is), **God.**
22. Yet lackest thou *one* thing:
20: 3. I will also ask you *one* thing ;
22:47. Judas, *one* of the twelve, went
50. *one* of them smote the servant
23:17. he must release *one* unto them
39. *one* of the malefactors which were
24:18. the *one* of them, whose name was
Joh. 1: 3. was not *any* thing made that was
40(41). *One* of the two which heard John
6: 8. *One* of his disciples, Andrew,
9. There is *a* lad here, which hath
22. save that *one* whereinto his disciples
70. *one* of you is a devil ?
71. betray him, being *one* of the twelve.
7:21. I have done *one* work, and ye all
50. to Jesus by night, being *one* of them,
8:41. we have *one* Father, (even) God.
9:25. *one* thing I know, that, whereas
10:16. shall be one fold, (and) *one* shepherd.
30. I and (my) Father are *one*.
11:49. *one* of them, (named) Caiaphas,
50. that *one* man should die for the
52. together in *one* the children of God
12: 2. Lazarus was *one* of them that sat
4. Then saith *one* of his disciples,
13:21. that *one* of you shall betray me.
23. on Jesus' bosom *one* of his disciples,
17:11. that they may be *one*, as we (are).
21. That they all may be *one* ;
— that they also may be *one* in us:
22. they may be *one*, even as we are *one* :
23. may be made perfect in *one* ;
18:14. *one* man should die for the people.
22. *one* of the officers which stood by
26. *One* of the servants of the high priest,
39. release unto you *one* at the passover:
19:34. *one* of the soldiers with a spear
20: 7. together in a place by itself. (lit. *one*
place)
12. the *one* at the head, and the *other* at the
feet,
24. Thomas, *one* of the twelve,
21:25. if they should be written every *one*,
Acts 1:22. must *one* be ordained to be
24. shew whether of these two (lit. out of these
two *one* which) thou
2: 3. it sat upon each)(of them.
6. because that every *man* (lit. *one*) heard
4:32. neither said *any* (of them) that
11:28. there stood up *one* of them
17:26. hath made of *one* blood all
27. not far from every *one* of us:
20:31. to warn every *one* night and day
21:19. he declared particularly (lit. by each *one*)
what things
26. offered for every *one* of them.
23: 6. that the *one* part were Sadducees,
17. Paul called *one* of the centurions
28:25. after that Paul had spoken *one* word,
Ro. 3:10. There is none righteous, no, not *one* :
12. none that doeth good, no, not *one*.
30. Seeing (it is) *one* God, which shall
5:12. as by *one* man sin entered into
15. if through the offence of *one* many
— (which is) by *one* man, Jesus Christ,
16. not as (it was) by *one* that sinned,
— the judgment (was) by *one* to
17. For if by *one* man's offence death reigned
by *one* ;
— shall reign in life by *one*, Jesus Christ.
18. as by the offence of *one* (or, by *one* offence)

Ro. 5:18. by the righteousness of *one* (or, by *one* righteousness)
  19. as by *one* man's disobedience
  — so by the obedience of *one* shall
  9:10. Rebecca also had conceived by *one*,
  12: 4. have many members in *one* body,
    5. (being) many, are *one* body in Christ,
  15: 6. may with one mind (and) *one* mouth
1Co. 3: 8. planteth and he that watereth are *one :*
  4: 6. no *one* of you be puffed up for *one*
  6: 5. not *one* that shall be able
    16. joined to an harlot is *one* body ?
    17. joined unto the Lord is *one* spirit.
  8: 4. (there is) none other God but *one*.
    6. to us (there is but) *one* God,
    — *one* Lord Jesus Christ, by whom
  9:24. run all, but *one* receiveth the prize ?
  10:17. (being) many are *one* bread, (and) *one* body: for we are all partakers of that *one* bread.
  11: 5. for that is even all *one* as if
  12:11. that *one* and the selfsame Spirit,
    12. For as the body is *one*,
    — the members of that *one* body, being many, are *one* body:
    13. For by *one* Spirit are we all baptized into *one* body, whether
    — all made to drink into *one* Spirit.
    14. the body is not *one* member,
    18. every *one* of them in the body,
    19. if they were all *one* member,
    20. many members, yet but *one* body.
    26. whether *one* member suffer,
    — or *one* member be honoured,
  14:27. by course ; and let *one* interpret.
    31. ye may all prophesy one by *one*,
2Co. 5:14(15). that if *one* died for all, then
  11: 2. have espoused you to *one* husband,
Gal. 3:16. as of many ; but as of *one*,
  20. not (a mediator) of *one*, but God is *one*.
  28. ye are all *one* in Christ Jesus.
  4:22. the *one* by a bondmaid, the *other* by
  5:14. the law is fulfilled in *one* word,
Eph. 2:14. who hath made both *one*, and hath
  15. in himself of twain *one* new man,
  16. both unto God in *one* body by
  18. by *one* Spirit unto the Father.
  4: 4. (There is) *one* body, and *one* Spirit,
    5. *One* Lord, one faith, *one* baptism,
    6. *One* God and Father of all, who
    7. unto every *one* of us is given grace
    16. working in the measure of every)(part,
  5:33. every *one* of you in particular (lit. you one by one)
Phi. 1:27. that ye stand fast in *one* spirit,
  2: 2. (being) of one accord, of *one* mind.
  3:13(14). (this) *one* thing (I do), forgetting
Col. 3:15. also ye are called in *one* body ;
  4: 6. to answer every *man*. (lit. *one*)
1Th. 2:11. comforted and charged every *one* of you,
  5:11. edify *one another*, even as also ye do.
2Th. 1: 3. the charity of every *one* of you
1Ti. 2: 5. (there is) *one* God, and *one* mediator
  5: 9. having been the wife of *one* man,
Heb. 2:11. who are sanctified (are) all of *one :*
  11:12. Therefore sprang there even of *one*,
Jas. 2:10. yet offend in *one* (point), he is
  19. Thou believest that there is *one* God ;
  4:12. There is *one* lawgiver, who is
    13. continue there *a* year, and buy and sell,
2Pet. 3: 8. be not ignorant of this *one* thing,
1Joh. 5: 7. these three are *one*.

1Joh. 5: 8. these three agree in *one*.
Rev. 4: 8. the four beasts had each of them (lit. *one* by itself)
  5: 5. *one* of the elders saith unto me,
  6: 1. *one* of the four beasts saying,
  7:13. *one* of the elders answered, saying
  8:13. heard *an* angel flying through
  15: 7. *one* of the four beasts gave unto
  17: 1. there came *one* of the seven angels
    10. five are fallen, and *one* is,
  18:21. *a* mighty angel took up a stone
  19:17. I saw *an* angel standing in
  21: 9. came unto me *one* of the seven
    21. every)(several gate was of *one* pearl:
  22: 2. yielded her fruit every)(month:

εἷς καθ’ εἷς, *his kath his.*

Mar 14:19. to say unto him *one by one*,
Joh. 8: 9. went out *one by one*, beginning

εἰσάγω, *isago.*

Lu. 2:27. when the parents *brought in* the
  14:21. *bring in* hither the poor, and the
  22:54. *brought* him *into* the high priest's
Joh. 18:16. the door, and *brought in* Peter.
Acts 7:45. Which also our fathers...*brought in* with Jesus
  9: 8. *brought* (him) *into* Damascus.
  21:28. *brought* Greeks also *into* the temple,
    29. Paul had *brought into* the temple.
    37. as Paul was *to be led into* the castle,
Heb. 1: 6. when he *bringeth in* the firstbegotten

εἰσακούω, *isakouo.*

Mat. 6: 7. they think that they *shall be heard*
Lu. 1:13. for thy prayer *is heard ;* and thy
Acts 10:31. said, Cornelius, thy prayer *is heard,*
1Co. 14:21. for all that *will* they not *hear* me,
Heb. 5: 7. *was heard* in that he feared ;

εἰσδέχομαι, *isdekomai.*

2Co. 6:17. unclean (thing) ; and I *will receive* you,

εἴσειμι, *isimi.*

Acts 3: 3. Peter and John about *to go into* the temple
  21:18. Paul *went in* with us unto James ;
    26. with them *entered into* the temple,
Heb. 9: 6. the priests *went* always *into* the first

εἰσέρχομαι, *iserhomai.*

Mat. 5:20. ye shall in no case *enter into*
  6: 6. when thou prayest, *enter into* thy
  7:13. *Enter* ye *in* at the strait gate ·
    — many there be *which go in* thereat:
    21. *shall enter into* the kingdom of heaven ;
  8: 5. *when* Jesus *was entered into* Capernaum,
    8. thou *shouldest come* under my roof:
  9:25. put forth, he *went in, and* took her
  10: 5. city of the Samaritans *enter* ye not:
    11. whatsoever city or town ye shall *enter,*

Mat.10:12. *when* ye *come into* an house,

12: 4. How he *entered into* the house of God,

29. how can one *enter into* a strong

45. *they enter in and* dwell there:

15:11. Not that *which goeth into* the mouth

17:25. when he *was come into* the house,

18: 3. ye shall not *enter into* the kingdom

8. *to enter into* life halt or maimed,

9. *to enter into* life with one eye,

19:17. if thou wilt *enter into* life,

23. *shall* hardly *enter into* the kingdom

24. *to enter into* the kingdom of God.

21:10. *when* he *was come into* Jerusalem,

12. Jesus *went into* the temple of God,

22:11. *when* the king *came in* to see the

12. Friend, how *camest* thou *in* hither

23:13. ye neither *go in* (yourselves), neither suffer
ye them *that are entering* to *go in.*

24:38. day that Noe *entered into* the ark,

25:10. *went in* with him to the marriage:

21. *enter* thou into the joy of thy lord.

23. *enter* thou into the joy of thy lord.

26:41. that ye *enter* not into temptation:

58. high priest's palace, and *went in, and*

27:53. *went into* the holy city, and appeared

Mar. 1:21. he *entered into* the synagogue, *and*

45. no more openly *enter into* the city,

2: 1. again he *entered into* Capernaum

26. How he *went into* the house of God

3: 1. he *entered* again *into* the synagogue;

27. can *enter into* a strong man's house, *and*

5:12. that we *may enter into* them.

13. went out, and *entered into* the swine:

39. *when* he *was come in,* he saith

6:10. place soever ye *enter into* an house,

22. *when* the daughter of the said .H...*came in,*

25. *came in* straightway with haste...*and*

7:17. when he *was entered into* the house

24. *entered into* an house, *and* would

8:26. Neither *go into* the town, nor tell (it)

9:25. *enter* no more *into* him.

28. *when* he *was come into* the house,

43. *to enter into* life maimed,

45. for thee *to enter* halt *into* life,

47. *to enter into* the kingdom of God

10:15. he shall not *enter* therein.

23. *shall...enter into* the kingdom of God

24. *to enter into* the kingdom of God !

25. a camel *to go through* the eye of a needle,

— *to enter into* the kingdom of God.

11:11. Jesus *entered into* Jerusalem,

15. Jesus *went into* the temple, *and*

13:15. neither *enter* (therein), to take any

14:14. wheresoever he shall *go in,* say

38. lest ye *enter into* temptation.

15:43. came, and *went in* boldly unto Pilate,

16: 5. *entering into* the sepulchre,

Lu. 1: 9. *when* he *went into* the temple of the Lord.

28. the angel *came in* unto her, *and*

40. *entered into* the house of Zacharias,

4:16. he *went into* the synagogue

38. *entered into* Simon's house.

6: 4. How he *went into* the house of God,

6. that he *entered into* the synagogue

7: 1. he *entered into* Capernaum.

6. thou *shouldest enter* under my roof:

36. *went into* the Pharisee's house, *and*

44. I *entered into* thine house,

45. since the time I *came in*

8:30. many devils *were entered into* him.

32. suffer them *to enter into* them.

33. *entered into* the swine: and the herd

Lu. 8:41. that he would *come into* his house:

51. *when* he *came into* the house, he suffered
no man *to go in,*

9: 4. whatsoever house ye *enter into,*

34. feared as they *entered into* the cloud.

46. there *arose* a reasoning among them,

52. they went, and *entered into* a village

10: 5. into whatsoever house ye *enter,*

8. into whatsoever city ye *enter,*

10. into whatsoever city ye *enter,*

38. he *entered into* a certain village:

11:26. they *enter in,* and dwell there:

37. he *went in,* and sat down to meat.

52. ye *entered* not *in* yourselves, and them
that were entering in ye hindered.

13:24. Strive *to enter in* at the strait gate:

— will seek *to enter in,* and shall not

14:23. compel (them) *to come in,* that my

15:28. was angry, and would not *go in:*

17: 7. *when* he *is come* from the field,

12. *as* he *entered into* a certain village,

27. that Noe *entered into* the ark,

18:17. shall in no wise *enter* therein.

24. *shall* they that have riches *enter into* the

25. a camel *to go* through a needle's eye,

— *to enter into* the kingdom of God.

19: 1. (Jesus) *entered and* passed through

7. he *was gone* to be guest with a

45. he *went into* the temple, *and* began

21:21. *let* not them that are in the countries *enter*
thereinto.

22: 3. Then *entered* Satan into Judas

10. *when* ye *are entered* into the city,

40. that ye *enter* not into temptation.

46. lest ye *enter* into temptation.

24: 3. they *entered in,* and found not **the**

26. *to enter into* his glory ?

29. he *went in* to tarry with them.

Joh. 3: 4. can he *enter* the second time into

5. he cannot *enter into* the kingdom

4:38. ye *are* (lit. *have*) *entered into* their labours.

10: 1. He *that entereth* not by the door

2. he *that entereth in* by the door

9. by me if any man *enter in,*

— shall *go in* and out, and find pasture.

13:27. Satan *entered into* him.

18: 1. a garden, into the which he *entered,*

28. *went* not *into* the judgment hall,

33. Pilate *entered into* the judgment hall

19: 9. *went* again *into* the judgment hall,

20: 5. clothes lying; yet *went* he not *in.*

6. *went into* the sepulchre,

8. *went in* also that other disciple,

Acts 1:13. when they *were come in,* they went

21. the Lord Jesus *went in* and out among us,

3: 8. *entered* with them *into* the temple,

5: 7. not knowing what was done, *came in.*

10. the young men *came in,* and found

21. they *entered into* the temple early

9: 6. Arise, and *go into* the city, and it shall

12. a man named Ananias *coming in,*

17. *went* his way, and *entered into* the house

10: 3. an angel of God *coming in* to him,

24. after they *entered into* Cæsarea.

25. as Peter **was** *coming in,*

27. talked with him, he *went in,*

11: 3. Thou *wentest in* to men uncircumcised,

8. at any time *entered into* my mouth.

12. we *entered into* the man's house:

20. *when* they *were come* to Antioch,

13:14. *went into* the synagogue...and sat

14: 1. that they *went* both together *into* the

Acts14:20. he rose up, and *came into* the city:
22. *enter into* the kingdom of God.
16:15. *come into* my house, *and* abide (there).
40. *entered into* (the house of) Lydia:
17: 2. as his manner was, *went in* unto them,
18:19. *entered into* the synagogue, *and*
19: 8. he *went into* the synagogue, *and* spake
30. have *entered in* unto the people,
20:29. *shall* grievous wolves *enter in*
21: 8. we *entered into* the house...*and*
23:16. *entered into* the castle, *and*
33. Who, *when* they *came* to Cæsarea,
25:23. *when...was entered into* the place of hearing,
28: 8. to whom Paul *entered in,...and* healed him.
Ro. 5:12. sin *entered into* the world,
11:25. fulness of the Gentiles *be come in*.
1Co.14:23. there *come in* (those that are) unlearned,
24. there *come in* one that believeth not,
Heb. 3:11. They *shall* not *enter into* my rest,
18. should not *enter into* his rest,
19. that they could not *enter in*
4: 1. left (us) of *entering into* his rest,
3. have believed *do enter into* rest,
— if they *shall enter into* my rest:
5. If they *shall enter into* my rest.
6. that some must *enter* therein,
— *entered* not *in* because of unbelief:
10. he *that is entered into* his rest,
11. therefore *to enter into* that rest,
6:19. and *which entereth into* that within
20. the forerunner *is* for us *entered,*
9:12. *entered in* once into the holy place,
24. For Christ *is* not *entered into* the holy
25. as the high priest *entereth into* the
10: 5. *when* he *cometh into* the world,
Jas. 2: 2. if there *come* unto your assembly
— there *come in* also a poor man
5: 4. *are entered into* the ears of the Lord
2Joh. 7. deceivers *are entered into* the world,
Rev. 3:20. open the door, I *will come in* to him,
11:11. life from God *entered* into them,
15: 8. was able *to enter into* the temple,
21:27. shall in no wise *enter into* it
22:14. *may enter in* through the gates into

εἰσί, *isi,* from εἰμί.

Mat. 2:18. comforted, because they *are* not.
7:13. many there *be* which go in thereat:
14. few there *be* that find it.
15. inwardly they *are* ravening wolves.
10:30. hairs of your head *are* all numbered.
11: 8. wear soft (clothing) *are* in kings' houses.
12: 5. profane the sabbath, and *are* blameless?
48. who *are* my brethren?
13:38. the good seed *are* the children of the
— the tares *are* the children of the
39. the reapers *are* the angels.
56. *are* they not all with us?
15:14. they *be* blind leaders of the blind.
16:28. There *be* some standing here, which
17:26. Then *are* the children free.
18:20. two or three *are* gathered together
19: 6. Wherefore they *are* no more twain,
12. For there *are* some eunuchs,
— and there *are* some eunuchs, which
— and there *be* eunuchs, which have
20:16. for many *be* called, but few chosen.
22:14. many *are* called, but few (are) chosen.

Mat.22:30. *are* as the angels of God in **heaven.**
Mar. 4:15. these *are* they by the way side,
16. these *are* they likewise which
17. endure but for a time: (lit. *are* temporary)
18. these *are* they which are sown among
thorns;)(such as hear the word,
20. these *are* they which are sown on good
6: 3. *are* not his sisters here with us?
9: 1. there *be* some of them that stand
10: 8. then they *are* no more twain,
12:25. *are* as the angels which are in
Lu. 7:25. live delicately, *are* in kings' courts.
31. to what *are* they like?
32. They *are* like unto children
8:12. by the way side *are* they that hear;
14. which fell among thorns *are* they, which,
15. that on the good ground *are* they,
21. *are* these which hear the word
9:13. We have no (lit. There *are* not to us) more
27. there *be* some standing here,
11: 7. my children *are* with me in bed;
12:38. so, blessed *are* those servants.
13:14. There *are* six days in which men
30. there *are* last which shall be first, and
there *are* first which shall be last.
16: 8. *are* in their generation wiser than
18: 9. that they *were* righteous, and despised
20:36. they *are* equal unto the angels; and *are*
the children of God, being
21:22. these *be* the days of vengeance,
Joh. 4:35. for they *are* white already to harvest.
5:39. they *are* they which testify of me.
6:64. there *are* some of you that believe not.
— who they *were* that believed not,
7:49. who knoweth not the law *are* cursed.
8:10. where *are* those thine accusers?
10: 8. came before me *are* thieves and robbers:
12. whose own the sheep *are* not,
11: 9. *Are* there not twelve hours in the day?
14: 2. In my Father's house *are* many mansions:
17: 9. given me; for they *are* thine.
11. these *are* in the world, and I come
14. they *are* not of the world,
16. They *are* not of the world, even as
Acts 2: 7. *are* not all these which speak
13. These men *are* full of new wine.
4:13. that they *were* unlearned and ignorant
5:25. *are* standing in the temple,
13:31. who *are* his witnesses unto the people.
16:17. *are* the servants of the most high God,
38. they heard that they *were* Romans.
19:26. that they *be* no gods, which
38. law is open, and there *are* deputies:
21:20. thousands of Jews there *are* which
23. We have (lit. There *are* to us) four men
23:21. now *are* they ready, looking for
24:11. there *are* yet but twelve days
Ro. 1:32. such things *are* worthy of death,
2:14. *are* a law unto themselves:
8:14. they *are* the sons of God.
9: 4. Who *are* Israelites; to whom
7. they *are* the seed of Abraham,
13: 1. powers that be *are* ordained of God.
3. rulers *are* not a terror to good works,
6. for they *are* God's ministers,
15:27. their debtors they *are*.
16: 7. who *are* of note among the apostles,
1Co. 1:11. there *are* contentions among you.
3: 8. planteth and he that watereth *are* one:
20. thoughts of the wise, that they *are* vain.
8: 5. there *be* that are called gods,
— as there *be* gods many, and lords

1Co.10:18. *are* not they which eat of the sacrifices
partakers of the altar?
12: 4. there *are* diversities of gifts,
5. there *are* differences of administrations,
6. there *are* diversities of operations,
14:22. Wherefore tongues *are* for a sign,
37. *are* the commandments of the Lord.
2Co.11:22, *Are* they Hebrews? so (am) I. *Are* they
Israelites? so (am) I. *Are* they the seed
of Abraham?
23. *Are* they ministers of Christ?
Gal. 1: 7. there *be* some that trouble you,
3: 7. same *are* the children of Abraham.
10. as many as *are* of the works of the law
are under the curse: for it is
4:24. for these *are* the two covenants;
Eph. 5:16. because the days *are* evil.
Col. 2: 3. In whom *are* hid all the treasures
1Ti. 5:24. Some men's sins *are* open beforehand,
6: 1. as many servants as *are* under
2. because they *are* brethren; but rather do
(them) service, because they *are* faithful
2Ti. 3: 6. For of this sort *are* they which
Tit. 1:10. there *are* many unruly and vain
3: 9. for they *are* unprofitable and vain.
Heb 1:10. the heavens *are* the works of thine
14. *Are* they not all ministering
7:21 priests *were* made without an oath;
23. they truly *were* many priests,
11:13. they *were* strangers and pilgrims on the
2Pet.2:17. These *are* wells without water,
3: 7. by the same word *are* kept in store,
1Joh.2:19. that they *were* not all of us.
4: 5. They *are* of the world: therefore speak
they of the world,
5: 3. his commandments *are* not grievous.
7. there *are* three that bear record
— these three *are* one.
8. there *are* three that bear witness
— and these three *agree* in one.
Jude   12. These *are* spots in your feasts
16. These *are* murmurers,
19. These *be* they who separate
Rev. 1:19. the things which *are*, and the
20. The seven stars *are* the angels
— *are* the seven churches.
2: 2. say they are apostles, and *are* not,
9. which say they are Jews, and *are* not,
3: 4. in white: for they *are* worthy.
9. which say they are Jews, and *are* not,
4: 5. which *are* the seven Spirits of God.
11. and for thy pleasure they *are*
5: 6. which *are* the seven Spirits of God
8. which *are* the prayers of saints.
7:13. What *are* these which are arrayed
14. These *are* they which came
15. Therefore *are* they before the throne of
God,
9:19. their power *is* in their mouth,
11: 4. These *are* the two olive trees,
14: 4. These *are* they which were not defiled
with women; for they *are* virgins.
These *are* they which follow the Lamb
5. for they *are* without fault before
16: 6. blood to drink; for they *are* worthy.
14. they *are* the spirits of devils,
17: 9. The seven heads *are* seven mountains,
10. there *are* seven kings: five
12. which thou sawest *are* ten kings,
15. *are* peoples, and multitudes, and nations,
19: 9. These *are* the true sayings of God.
21: 5. these words *are* true and faithful.

εἰσκαλέω, *iskaleo.*

Acts10:23. Then *called* he them *in, and* lodged

εἴσοδος, *īsodos.*

Acts13:24. had first preached before his *coming*
1Th. 1: 9. what manner of *entering in* we
2: 1. know our *entrance in* unto you,
Heb 10:19. boldness to *enter into* (lit. for *entrance
into*) the holiest
2Pet.1:11. an *entrance* shall be ministered

εἰσπηδάω, *ispeedao.*

Acts14:14. *ran in* among the people, crying
16:29. called for a light, and *sprang in,*

εἰσπορεύομαι, *isporūomai.*

Mat.15:17. *what*soever *entereth in* at the mouth
Mar. 1:21. they *went into* Capernaum;
4:19. the lusts of other things *entering in,*
5:40. *entereth in* where the damsel
6:56. whithersoever he *entered,*
7:15. *that entering into* him can defile
18. *what*soever thing from without *entereth
into*
19. it *entereth* not *into* his heart,
11: 2. as soon as ye *be entered into* it,
Lu. 8:16. they *which enter in* may see
11:33. they *which come in* may see
19:30. in the which *at* your *entering*
22:10. the house where he *entereth in.*
Acts 3: 2. of them *that entered into* the temple;
8: 3. As for Saul,...*entering into* every house,
9:28. he was with them *coming in*
28:30. received all *that came in* unto him,

εἰστρέχω, *istreko.*

Acts12:14. she opened not...but *ran in, and* told

εἰσφέρω, *isphero.*

Mat. 6:13. *lead* us not *into* temptation,
Lu. 5:18. sought (means) *to bring* him *in,*
19. they *might bring* him *in* because
11: 4. *lead* us not *into* temptation;
Acts17:20. *bringest* certain strange things to
1Ti. 6: 7. we *brought* nothing *into* (this)
Heb 13:11. whose blood *is brought into* the

εἶτα, *īta.*

Mar. 4:17. *afterward,* when affliction or persecution
28. *then* the ear, *after that* the full
8:25. *After that* he put (his) hands again
Lu. 8:12. *then* cometh the devil, and taketh
Joh.13: 5. *After that* he poureth water into
19:27. *Then* saith he to the disciple,
20:27. *Then* saith he to Thomas, Reach
1Co.12:28. *then* gifts of healings, helps,
15: 5. seen of Cephas, *then* of the twelve.
7. *then* of all the apostles.
24. *Then* (cometh) the end, when he

1Ti. 2:13. Adam was first formed, *then* Eve.
  3:10. *then* let them use the office of a
Heb 12: 9. *Furthermore* we have had fathers
Jas. 1:15. *Then* when lust hath conceived,

εἴτε, *ite.*
See after εἰ.

εἴ τις.
See after εἰ.

εἴωθα see ἔθω

ἐκ, ἐξ, *ek, ex.*

Mat. 1: 3. Judas begat Phares and Zara *of* Thamar;
  5. Salmon begat Booz *of* Rachab ; and Booz
    begat Obed *of* Ruth ;
  6. the king begat Solomon *of* her
  16. *of* whom was born Jesus,
  18. with child *of* the Holy Ghost.
  20. in her is *of* the Holy Ghost.
  2: 6. for *out of* thee shall come a
  15. *Out of* Egypt have I called my son.
  3: 9. God is able *of* these stones to
  17. lo a voice *from* heaven, saying,
  5:37. more than these cometh *of* evil.
  6:27. Which *of* you by taking thought
  7: 5. the beam *out of* thine own eye ;
  — the mote *out of* thy brother's eye.
  9. Or what man is there *of* you,
  8:28. devils, coming *out of* the tombs,
  10:29. one *of* them shall not fall on the
  12:11. What man shall there be *among*
  33. the tree is known *by* (his) fruit.
  34. *out of* the abundance of the heart
  35. *out of* the good treasure of the heart
  — evil man *out of* the evil treasure
  37. *by* thy words thou shalt be justified, and
    by thy words thou shalt be condemned.
  42. *from* the uttermost parts of the earth
  13:41. *out of* his kingdom all things
  47. gathered *of* every kind:
  49. the wicked *from* among the just,
  52. *out of* his treasure (things) new
  15: 5. thou mightest be profited *by* me ;
  11. that which cometh *out of* the mouth,
  18. which proceed *out of* the mouth come forth
    from the heart ;
  19. *out of* the heart proceed evil thoughts,
  16: 1. shew them a sign *from* heaven.
  17: 5. behold a voice *out of* the cloud,
  9. be risen again *from* the dead.
  18:12. one *of* them be gone astray, doth
  19:12. so born *from* (their) mother's womb
  20. have I kept *from* my youth *up :*
  20: 2. with the labourers *for* a penny a day,
  21. the one *on* my right...the other *on* the left,
  23. to sit *on* my right hand, and *on* my
  21:16. *Out of* the mouth of babes and
  19. *on* thee henceforward for ever.
  25. *from* heaven, or *of* men ?
  — If we shall say, *From* heaven ;
  26. if we shall say, *Of* men ;
  31. Whether *of* them twain did

Mat.22:35. Then one *of* them, (which was)
  44. Sit thou *on* my right hand,
  23:25. are full *of* extortion and excess.
  34. (some) *of* them ye shall kill
  — (Some) *of* them shall ye scourge
  24:17. take any thing *out of* his house:
  31. his elect *from* the four winds,
  25: 2. five *of* them were wise, and five
  8. Give us *of* your oil ; for our
  33. sheep *on* his right hand, but the goats *on*
    the left.
  34. unto them *on* his right hand,
  41. unto them *on* the left hand,
  26:21. that one *of* you shall betray me.
  27. Saying, Drink ye all *of* it ;
  29. henceforth *of* this fruit of the vine,
  42. went away again)(the second time,
  44. prayed)(the third time, saying
  64. sitting *on* the right hand of power,
  73. Surely thou also art (one) *of* them ;
  27: 7. bought *with* them the potter's field,
  29. they had platted a crown *of* thorns,
  38. one *on* the right hand, and another *on* the left.
  48. straightway one *of* them ran,
  53. came *out of* the graves after his
  28: 2. descended *from* heaven, and came
Mar. 1:11. there came a voice *from* heaven,
  25. Hold thy peace, and come *out of* him.
  26. he came *out of* him.
  29. were come *out of* the synagogue,
  5: 2. when he was come *out of* the ship, imme-
    diately there met him *out of* the tombs
  8. Come *out of* the man,
  30. that virtue had gone *out of* him,
  6:14. the Baptist was risen *from* the dead,
  16. he is risen *from* the dead.
  51. amazed in themselves *beyond* (lit. *out of*)
    measure,
  54. they were come *out of* the ship,
  7:11. mightest be profited *by* me ;
  20. That which cometh *out of* the man,
  21. *out of* the heart of men, proceed
  26. the devil *out of* her daughter.
  29. devil is gone *out of* thy daughter.
  31. departing *from* the coasts of Tyre
  9: 7. a voice came *out of* the cloud,
  9. were risen *from* the dead.
  10. rising *from* the dead should mean.
  17. one *of* the multitude answered
  25. I charge thee, come *out of* him,
  10:20. these have I observed *from* my youth.
  37. one *on* my right hand, and the other *on*
    thy left
  40. to sit *on* my right hand and *on* my left
  11: 8. cut down branches *off* the trees,
  14. No man eat fruit *of* thee hereafter
  20. fig tree dried up *from* the roots.
  30. *from* heaven, or *of* men ?
  31. If we shall say, *From* heaven ;
  32. if we shall say, *Of* men ;
  12:25. when they shall rise *from* the dead,
  30. thou shalt love the Lord thy God *with* all
    thy heart, and *with* all thy soul, and *with*
    all thy mind, and *with* all thy strength:
  33. And to love him *with* all the heart, and
    with all the understanding, and *with* all
    the soul, and *with* all the strength,
  36. Sit thou *on* my right hand,
  44. did cast in *of* their abundance ; but she *of*
    her want did cast in
  13: 1. as he went *out of* the temple,
  15. take any thing *out of* his house:

Mar 13:27. his elect *from* the four winds,
14:18. One *of* you which eateth with
20. one *of* the twelve, that dippeth
23. they all drank *of* it.
25. I will drink no more *of* the fruit
31. he spake the more vehemently, (lit. *of* excess)
62. sitting *on* the right hand of power,
69. that stood by, This is (one) *of* them.
70. Surely thou art (one) *of* them:
72.)(the second time the cock crew.
15:27. one *on* his right hand, and the other *on*
39. which stood over against (lit. *on* the opposite) him,
46. hewn *out of* a rock,
16: 3. roll us away the stone *from* the door
12. in another form unto two *of* them,
19. sat *on* the right hand of God.
Lu. 1: 5. Zacharias, *of* the course of Abia: and his wife (was) *of* the daughters of Aaron,
11. *on* the right side of the altar
15. even *from* his mother's womb.
27. was Joseph, *of* the house of David ;
35. which shall be born *of* thee
71. saved *from* our enemies, and *from* the hand
74. *out of* the hand of our enemies
78. the dayspring *from* on high
2: 4. *out of* the city of Nazareth,
— *of* the house and lineage of David:
35. that the thoughts *of* many hearts
36. of Phanuel, *of* the tribe of Aser:
3: 8. God is able *of* these stones to raise
22. a voice came *from* heaven,
4:22. proceeded *out of* his mouth.
35. Hold thy peace, and come *out of* him.
38. he arose *out of* the synagogue.
5: 3. taught the people *out of* the ship.
17. *out of* every town of Galilee,
6:42. the beam *out of* thine own eye,
44. tree is known *by* his own fruit. For *of* thorns men do not gather figs, nor *of* a bramble bush gather
45. *out of* the good treasure of his
— evil man *out of* the evil treasure
— for *of* the abundance of the heart
8:27. there met him *out of* the city
— which had devils)(long time,
9: 7. that John was risen *from* the dead;
35. there came a voice *out of* the cloud,
10: 7. Go not *from* house to house.
11. the very dust *of* your city,
18. Satan as lightning fall *from* heaven.
27. *with* all thy heart, and *with* all thy soul, and *with* all thy strength, and *with* all
11: 5. Which *of* you shall have a friend,
6. a friend of mine *in* his journey
13. (your) heavenly Father (lit. your Father *from* heaven)
15. some *of* them said, He casteth
16. sought of him a sign *from* heaven.
27. a certain woman *of* the company
31. *from* the utmost parts of the earth
49. (some) *of* them they shall slay
54. something *out of* his mouth,
12: 6. not one *of* them is forgotten
13. one *of* the company said unto
15. in the abundance *of* the things which he possesseth.
25. which *of* you with taking thought
36. he will return *from* the wedding ;
14:28. which *of* you, intending to build
33. whosoever he be *of* you that forsaketh

Lu. 15: 4. What man *of* you, having an hundred sheep, if he lose one *of* them,
16: 9. *of* the mammon of unrighteousness ;
31. though one rose *from* the dead.
17: 7. which *of* you, having a servant
— when he is come *from* the field,
15. one *of* them, when he saw
24. *out of* the one (part) under heaven,
18:21. these have I kept *from* my youth *up.*
19:22. *Out of* thine own mouth will I
20: 4. was it *from* heaven, or *of* men?
5. If we shall say, *From* heaven ;
6. if we say, *Of* men ;
35. the resurrection *from* the dead,
42. Sit thou *on* my right hand,
21: 4. these have *of* their abundance
— she *of* her penury hath cast in
16. (some) *of* you shall they cause to be
18. not an hair *of* your head perish.
22: 3. being *of* the number of the twelve.
16. I will not any more eat there*of,*
23. which *of* them it was that should
50. one *of* them smote the servant
58. Thou art also *of* them.
69. the Son of man sit *on* the right hand
23: 7. he belonged *unto* Herod's jurisdiction,
8. desirous to see him *of* a long (season),
33. one *on* the right hand, and the other *on* the
55. which came with him *from* Galilee,
24:13. two *of* them went that same day
22. certain women also *of* our company
46. to rise *from* the dead the third day:
49. endued with power *from* on high.
Joh. 1:13. Which were born, not *of* blood, nor *of* the will of the flesh, nor *of* the will of man, but *of* God.
16. *of* his fulness have all we
19. sent priests and Levites *from* Jerusalem
24. sent were *of* the Pharisees,
32. descending *from* heaven like
35. John stood, and two *of* his disciples ;
40(41). One *of* the two which heard
44(45). the city (lit. *of* the city) of Andrew
46(47). thing come *out of* Nazareth?
2:15. made a scourge *of* small cords, he drove them all *out of* the temple,
22. he was risen *from* the dead,
3: 1. There was a man *of* the Pharisees,
5. Except a man be born *of* water
6. That which is born *of* the flesh
— that which is born *of* the Spirit
8. every one that is born *of* the Spirit.
13. he that came down *from* heaven,
25. question between (some) *of* John's disciples and (lit. *of* John's disciples with)
27. it be given him *from* heaven.
31. he that is *of* the earth is *earthly,* (lit. *of* the earth) and speaketh *of* the earth: he that cometh *from* heaven
34. giveth not the Spirit *by* measure
4: 6. being wearied *with* (his) journey,
7. There cometh a woman *of* Samaria
12. the well, and drank there*of* himself,
13. Whosoever drinketh *of* this water
14. whosoever drinketh *of* the water
22. for salvation is *of* the Jews.
30. Then they went *out of* the city,
39. the Samaritans *of* that city believed
47. come *out of* Judæa into Galilee,
54. when he was come *out of* Judæa
5:24. is passed *from* death unto life.
6: 8. One *of* his disciples, Andrew,

Joh. 6:11. likewise *of* the fishes as much
13. fragments *of* the five barley loaves,
23. came other boats *from* Tiberias
26. because ye did eat *of* the loaves,
31. gave them bread *from* heaven to eat.
32. that bread *from* heaven; but my Father
    giveth you the true bread *from* heaven.
33. he which cometh down *from* heaven,
38. For I came down *from* heaven,
39. given me I should lose nothing, (lit. not
    lose *of* it)
41. which came down *from* heaven.
42. saith, I came down *from* heaven ?
50. bread which cometh down *from* heaven,
    that a man may eat there*of*
51. came down *from* heaven: if any man eat
    of this
58. bread which came down *from* heaven:
60. Many therefore *of* his disciples,
64. some *of* you that believe not. For Jesus
    knew *from* the beginning
65. given unto him *of* my Father.
66. *From* that (time) many of his
70. one *of* you is a devil ?
71. being one *of* the twelve.
7:17. whether it be *of* God, or
19. none *of* you keepeth the law ?
22. not because it is *of* Moses, but *of* the
    fathers ;
25. some *of* them of Jerusalem,
31. many *of* the people believed
38. *out of* his belly shall flow rivers
40. Many *of* the people therefore,
41. Shall Christ come *out of* Galilee ?
42. cometh *of* the seed of David,
44. some *of* them would have taken
48. Have any *of* the rulers or *of* the Pharisees
    believed on him ?
50. to Jesus by night, being one *of* them,
52. Art thou also *of* Galilee?
— *out of* Galilee ariseth no prophet.
8:23. Ye are *from* beneath ; I am *from* above:
    ye are *of* this world; I am not *of* this
    world.
41. We be not born *of* fornication ;
42. proceeded forth and came *from* God ;
44. Ye are *of* (your) father the devil,
— he speaketh *of* his own:
46. Which *of* you convinceth me of sin ?
47. He that is *of* God heareth God's words:
— because ye are not *of* God.
59. went *out of* the temple, going
9: 1. which was blind *from* (his) birth.
6. made clay *of* the spittle, and he
16. said some *of* the Pharisees,
24. Then again (lit. *of* a second time) called
32. *Since* the world began (εκ του αιωνος) was
    it not heard that
40. (some) *of* the Pharisees which were
10:16. which are not *of* this fold:
20. many *of* them said, He hath
26. because ye are not *of* my sheep,
28. pluck them *out of* my hand.
29. *out of* my Father's hand.
32. I shewed you *from* my Father ;
39. he escaped *out of* their hand,
11: 1. of Bethany,)(the town of Mary
19. many *of* the Jews came to
37. some *of* them said, Could not
45. many *of* the Jews which came
46. some *of* them went their ways
49. one *of* them, (named) Caiaphas.

Joh. 11:55. many went *out of* the country
12: 1. whom he raised *from* the dead.
3. *with* the odour of the ointment.
4. Then saith one *of* his disciples,
9. Much people *of* the Jews
— he had raised *from* the dead.
17. called Lazarus *out of* his grave, and raised
    him *from* the dead,
20. Greeks *among* them that came up to
27. Father, save me *from* this hour:
28. came there a voice *from* heaven,
32. if I be lifted up *from* the earth,
34. We have heard *out of* the law
42. *among* the chief rulers also many
49. I have not spoken *of* myself;
13:. 1. should depart *out of* this world
4. He riseth *from* supper, and laid
21. that one *of* you shall betray me.
15:19. If ye were *of* the world, the
— because ye are not *of* the world, but I
    have chosen you *out of* the world,
16: 4. I said not unto you *at* the beginning,
5. none *of* you asketh me,
14. for he shall receive *of* mine,
15. that he shall take *of* mine,
17. Then said (some) *of* his disciples
17: 6. gavest me *out of* the world:
12. none *of* them is lost, but the
14. they are not *of* the world, even as I am
    not *of* the world.
15. take them *out of* the world,
— shouldest keep them *from* the evil.
16. They are not *of* the world, even as I am
    not *of* the world.
18: 3. *from* the chief priests and Pharisees,
9. *Of* them which thou gavest me
17. also (one) *of* this man's disciples ?
25. Art not thou also (one) *of* his disciples ?
26. One *of* the servants of the high priest,
36. My kingdom is not *of* this world: if my
    kingdom were *of* this world,
37. Every one that is *of* the truth
19: 2. soldiers platted a crown *of* thorns,
12. *from* thenceforth Pilate sought
23. woven *from* the top throughout.
20: 1. stone taken away *from* the sepulchre.
2. the Lord *out of* the sepulchre,
9. he must rise again *from* the dead.
24. Thomas, one *of* the twelve,
21: 2. two other *of* his disciples.
14. that he was risen *from* the dead.
Acts 1:18. *with* the reward of iniquity;
24. shew whether *of* these two. thou
25. *from* which Judas by transgression
2: 2. there came a sound *from* heaven
25. for he is *on* my right hand,
30. that *of* the fruit of his loins,
34. Sit thou *on* my right hand,
3: 2. lame *from* his mother's womb
15. God hath raised *from* the dead ;
22. raise up unto you *of* your brethren,
23. destroyed *from among* the people.
4: 2. the resurrection *from* the dead.
6. *of* the kindred of the high priest,
10. whom God raised *from* the dead,
5:38. counsel or this work be *of* men,
39. if it be *of* God, ye cannot
6: 3. look ye *out among* you seven men
9. arose certain *of* the synagogue, which
7: 3. Get thee *out of* thy country, and *from*
    thy kindred,
4. *out of* the land of the Chaldæans,

Acts 7:10. *out of* all his afflictions,
37. unto you *of* your brethren,
40. *out of* the land of Egypt,
55. standing *on* the right hand of God,
56. standing *on* the right hand of God.
8:37. believest *with* all thine heart,
39. were come up *out of* the water,
9:33. had kept his bed)(eight years,
10: 1. a centurion *of* the band called
15. unto him again)(the second time,
41. after he rose *from* the dead.
45. they *of* the circumcision which
11: 2. they that were *of* the circumcision
5. a great sheet, let down *from* heaven
9. answered me again (lit. *of* a second time) *from* heaven,
20. some *of* them were men of Cyprus
28. there stood up one *of* them named
12: 7. his chains fell *off from* (his) hands.
11. *out of* the hand of Herod, and (from)
17. had brought him *out of* the prison.
25. Barnabas and Saul returned *from* Jerusalem,
13:17. brought he them *out of* it.
21. a man *of* the tribe of Benjamin,
30. God raised him *from* the dead:
34. he raised him up *from* the dead,
42. were gone *out of* the synagogue,
14: 8. a cripple *from* his mother's womb,
15: 2. certain other *of* them, should go up
14. take *out of* them (lit. *out of* the nations)
21. Moses *of* old time hath in every
22. to send chosen men *of* their own
23. which are *of* the Gentiles in Antioch
24. certain which went *out from* us
29. *from* which if ye keep yourselves,
16:40. they went *out of* the prison,
17: 3. suffered, and risen again *from* the dead;
4. some *of* them believed, and consorted
12. Therefore many *of* them believed;
26. hath made *of* one blood all nations
31. he hath raised him *from* the dead.
33. Paul departed *from* among them.
18: 1. Paul departed *from* Athens, and came
2. all Jews to depart *from* Rome:
19:16. fled *out of* that house
25. ye know that *by* this craft
33. drew Alexander *out of* the multitude,
34. all with one voice (lit. one voice *from* all)
20:30. Also *of* your own selves shall
21: 8. which was (one) *of* the seven ;
22: 6. there shone *from* heaven a great
14. hear the voice *of* (lit. *from*) his mouth.
18. get thee quickly *out of* Jerusalem:
23:10. by force *from* among them,
21. *of* them more than forty men,
34. asked *of* what province he was.
24: 7. took (him) away *out of* our hands,
10. thou hast been *of* many years
26: 4. My manner of life *from* my youth,
17. Delivering thee *from* the people,
23. first that should rise from the dead, (lit. first *from* the resurrection of the dead)
27:22. no loss of (any man's) life *among* you,
29. four anchors *out of* the stern,
30. about to flee *out of* the ship,
— cast anchors *out of* the foreship,
34. not an hair fall *from* the head
28: 3. came a viper *out of* the heat,
4. beast hang *on* his hand,
— though he hath escaped)(the sea,
17. was I delivered prisoner *from* Jerusalem

Ro. 1: 3. made *of* the seed of David
4. *by* the resurrection from the dead:
17. revealed *from* faith to faith:
— The just shall live *by* faith.
2: 8. unto them that *are* contentious, (lit. *of* contention)
18. being instructed *out of* the law ;
27. uncircumcision which is *by* nature,
29. whose praise (is) not *of* men, but *of* God.
3:20. *by* the deeds of the law there shall
26. justifier of him which believeth (lit. him *of* faith)
30. justify the circumcision *by* faith,
4: 2. if Abraham were justified *by* works,
12. not *of* the circumcision only,
14. they which are *of* the law
16. Therefore (it is) *of* faith, that
— not to that only which is *of* the law, but to that also which is *of* the faith of A. ;
24. raised up Jesus our Lord *from* the dead ;
5: 1. Therefore being justified *by* faith.
16. the judgment (was) *by* one to
— the free gift (is) *of* many offences
6: 4. Christ was raised up *from* the dead
9. Christ being raised *from* the dead
13. those that are alive *from* the dead,
17. ye have obeyed *from* the heart
7: 4. him who is raised *from* the dead,
24. deliver me *from* the body of this death?
8:11. raised up Jesus *from* the dead
— that raised up Christ *from* the dead
9: 5. Whose (are) the fathers, and *of* whom
6. not all Israel, which are *of* Israel:
10. Rebecca also had conceived *by* one,
11. not *of* works, but *of* him that calleth ;
21. *of* the same lump to make
24. not *of* the Jews only, but also *of* the Gentiles?
30. righteousness which is *of* faith.
32. not *by* faith, but as it were *by* the
10: 5. righteousness which is *of* the law,
6. righteousness which is *of* faith
7. bring up Christ again *from* the dead.
9. hath raised him *from* the dead,
17. So then faith (cometh) *by* hearing,
11: 1. *of* the seed of Abraham,
6. then (is it) no more *of* works:
— if (it be) *of* works, then is it
14. might save some *of* them.
15. but life *from* the dead ?
24. *out of* the olive tree which is wild
26. There shall come *out of* Sion the
36. For *of* him, and through him,
12:18. as much as lieth in you, (lit. as is *of* you)
13: 3. thou shalt have praise *of* the same:
11. time to awake *out of* sleep:
14:23. because (he eateth) not *of* faith: for whatsoever (is) not *of* faith is sin.
16:10. which are *of* Aristobulus' (houshold).
11. be *of* the (houshold) of Narcissus,
1Co. 1:30. *of* him are ye in Christ Jesus,
2:12. the spirit which is *of* God ;
5: 2. be taken away *from* among you.
10. needs go *out of* the world.
13. put away *from among* yourselves
7: 5. except (it be) *with* consent for a time,
7. hath his proper gift *of* God,
8: 6. the Father, *of* whom (are) all things,
9: 7. eateth not *of* the fruit thereof?
— eateth not *of* the milk of the flock ?
13. live (of the things) *of* the temple ?
14. should live *of* the gospel.

1Co. 9:19. though I be free *from* all (men),
10: 4. they drank *of* that spiritual Rock
17. all partakers *of* that one bread.
11: 8. man is not *of* the woman ; but the woman *of* the man.
12. as the woman (is) *of* the man,
— by the woman ; but all things *of* God.
28. eat *of* (that) bread, and drink *of* (that) cup.
12:15. I am not *of* the body ; is it therefore not *of* the body ?
16. not the eye, I am not *of* the body ; is it therefore not *of* the body?
27. body of Christ, and members *in* particular.
13: 9. we know *in* part, and we prophesy *in* part.
10. then that which is *in* part
12. now I know *in* part ;
15: 6. *of* whom the greater part remain
12. that he rose *from* the dead,
20. now is Christ risen *from* the dead,
47. The first man (is) *of* the earth, earthy: the second man (is) the Lord *from* heaven.
2Co. 1:10. delivered us *from* so great a death,
11. *by the means of* many persons
2: 2. same which is made sorry *by* me ?
4. For *out of* much affliction and
17. as *of* sincerity, but as *of* God,
3: 1. (letters) of commendation *from* you ?
5. think any thing as *of* ourselves ; but our sufficiency (is) *of* God ;
4: 6. the light to shine *out of* darkness,
7. may be of God, and not *of* us.
5: 1. we have a building *of* God,
2. our house which is *from* heaven:
8. rather to be absent *from* the body,
18. all things (are) *of* God, who hath
6:17. come out *from* among them,
7: 9. receive damage *by* us in nothing.
8: 7. and (in) your love (lit. love *from* you) to us,
11. a performance also *out of* that
14(13). *by* an equality, (that) now
9: 2. your zeal (lit. the zeal *of* you) hath provoked
7. not grudgingly (lit. *of* grief), or *of* necessity:
11:26. (in) perils *by* (mine own) countrymen, (in) perils *by* the heathen,
12: 6. or (that) he heareth *of* me.
13: 4. he was crucified *through* weakness, yet he liveth *by* the power of God.
— live with him *by* the power of God
Gal. 1: 1. who raised him *from* the dead;
4. *from* this present evil world,
8. though we, or an angel *from* heaven,
15. separated me *from* my mother's womb,
2:12. which were *of* the circumcision.
15. not sinners *of* the Gentiles,
16. not justified *by* the works of the law, but by the faith of Jesus Christ,
— that we might be justified *by* the faith of Christ, and not *by* the works of the law: for *by* the works of the law shall no
3: 2. the Spirit *by* the works of the law, or *by* the hearing of faith ?
5. *by* the works of the law, or *by* the
7. that they which are *of* faith,
8. justify the heathen *through* faith,
9. then they which be *of* faith
10. as are *of* the works of the law
11. The just shall live *by* faith.
12. the law is not *of* faith:

Gal. 3:13. hath redeemed us *from* the curse
18. if the inheritance (be) *of* the law, (it is) no more *of* promise:
21. should have been *by* the law.
22. the promise *by* faith of Jesus Christ
24. we might be justified *by* faith.
4: 4. his Son, made *of* a woman,
22. one *by* a bondmaid, the other *by* a freewoman.
23. he (who was) *of* the bondwoman
— he *of* the freewoman (was) by
5: 5. hope of righteousness *by* faith.
8. (cometh) not *of* him that calleth you.
6: 8. shall *of* the flesh reap corruption ;
— shall *of* the Spirit reap life
Eph. 1:20. he raised him *from* the dead,
2: 8. that not *of* yourselves:
9. Not *of*·works, lest any man should
3:15. *Of* whom the whole family
20. exceeding abundantly (lit. *of* abundance) above all that
4:16. *From* whom the whole body
29. proceed *out of* your mouth,
5:14. that sleepest, and arise *from* the dead,
30. For we are members of his body, *of* his flesh, and *of* his bones.
6: 6. the will of God *from* the heart;
Phil. 1:16. one preach Christ *of* contention,
17. the other *of* love, knowing that
23. I am in a strait *betwixt* two, (lit. am held in a strait *by* the two)
3: 5. *of* the stock of Israel,
— an Hebrew *of* the Hebrews ;
9. righteousness, which is *of* the law,
— righteousness which is *of* God
20. *from* whence also we look for
4:22. they that are *of* Cæsar's houshold.
Col. 1:13. delivered us *from* the power of
18. the firstborn *from* the dead;
2:12. hath raised him *from* the dead.
14. took it *out of* the way, nailing it
19. *from* which all the body by
3: 8. filthy communication *out of* your mouth.
23. ye do, do (it) heartily, (lit. *from* the heart)
4: 9. beloved brother, who is (one) *of* you.
11. who are *of* the circumcision.
12. who is (one) *of* you, a servant of Christ,
16. read the (epistle) *from* Laodicea.
1Th. 1:10. to wait for his Son *from* heaven, whom he raised *from* the dead,
2: 3. (was) not *of* deceit, nor *of* uncleanness,
6. Nor *of* men sought we glory,
3:10. praying exceedingly (lit. above *of* excess)
5:13. esteem them very highly (lit. above *of* excess) in love
2Th. 2: 7. until he be taken *out of* the way.
1Ti. 1: 5. charity *out of* a pure heart,
6: 4. of words, whereof cometh envy,
2Ti. 2: 8. Jesus Christ *of* the seed of David was raised *from* the dead according
22. on the Lord *out of* a pure heart.
26. *out of* the snare of the devil,
3: 6. For *of* this sort are they which
11. *out of* (them) all the Lord delivered me.
4:17. delivered *out of* the mouth of the lion.
Tit. 1:10. specially they *of* the circumcision:
12. One *of* themselves, (even) a prophet
2: 8. he that is *of* the contrary part
3: 5. Not *by* works of righteousness
Heb. 1:13. Sit *on* my right hand, until
2:11. sanctified (are) all *of* one:
3:13. lest any *of* you be hardened

Heb 3:16. not all that came *out of* Egypt
4: 1. any *of* you should seem to come
5: 1. high priest taken *from among* men
7. able to save him *from* death,
7: 4. Abraham gave)(the tenth of the spoils.
5. they that are *of* the sons of Levi,
— come *out of* the loins of Abraham:
6. descent is not counted *from* them
12. there is made *of* necessity a change
14. our Lord sprang *out of* Juda ;
8: 9. to lead them *out of* the land of Egypt ;
9:28. shall he appear)(the second time
10:38. the just shall live *by* faith:
11: 3. not made *of* things which do appear.
19. to raise (him) up, even *from* the dead ;
35. received their dead raised to life again:
(lit. their dead *of* or by resurrection)
13:10. where*of* they have no right to eat
20. *from* the dead our Lord Jesus,
Jas. 2:16. one *of* you say unto them,
18. shew me thy faith *without* thy works, and
I will shew thee my faith *by* my works.
21. Abraham our father justified *by* works,
22. *by* works was faith made perfect ?
24. see then how that *by* works a man is justified, and not *by* faith only.
25. Rahab the harlot justified *by* works,
3:10. *Out of* the same mouth proceedeth
11. send *forth at* the same place
13. shew *out of* a good conversation
4: 1. *of* your lusts that war in your
5:20. the sinner *from* the error of his way shall
save a soul *from* death,
1Pet.1: 3. of Jesus Christ *from* the dead,
18. *from* your vain conversation
21. that raised him up *from* the dead,
22. love one another *with* a pure heart
23. not *of* corruptible seed, but of
2: 9. hath called you *out of* darkness
12. they may *by* (your) good works,
4:11. as *of* the ability which God giveth:
2Pet.1:18. this voice which came *from* heaven
2: 8. soul from day to day (lit. day *after* day)
9. deliver the godly *out of* temptations,
21. turn *from* the holy commandment
3: 5. earth standing *out of* the water
1Joh.2:16. is not *of* the Father, but is *of* the world.
19. They went out *from* us, but they were not
of us ; for if they had been *of* us,
— that they were not all *of* us.
21. that no lie is *of* the truth.
29. doeth righteousness is born *of* him.
3: 8. that committeth sin is *of* the devil ;
9. Whosoever is born *of* God doth
— because he is born *of* God.
10. doeth not righteousness is not *of* God,
12. Cain, (who) was *of* that wicked one,
14. passed *from* death unto life,
19. we know that we are *of* the truth,
24. *by* the Spirit which he hath given us.
4: 1. whether they are *of* God:
2. come in the flesh is *of* God:
3. in the flesh is not *of* God:
4. Ye are *of* God, little children,
5. They are *of* the world: therefore speak
they *of* the world,
6. We are *of* God: he that knoweth
— he that is not *of* God heareth not us.
Hereby know we the spirit of
7. love one another: for love is *of* God ; and
every one that loveth is born *of* God,
13. he hath given us *of* his Spirit.

1Joh.5: 1. Jesus is the Christ is born *of* God:
— also that is begotten *of* him.
4. whatsoever is born *of* God
18. whosoever is born *of* God sinneth not ;
but he that is begotten *of* God keepeth
19. we know that we are *of* God,
2Joh. 4. that I found *of* thy children
3Joh. 10. casteth (them) *out of* the church.
11. He that doeth good is *of* God:
Jude 5. people *out of* the land of Egypt,
23. pulling (them) *out of* the fire ;
Rev. 1: 5. the first begotten *of* the dead,
16. *out of* his mouth went a sharp
2: 5. thy candlestick *out of* his place,
7. to eat *of* the tree of life, which is
10. the devil shall cast (some) *of* you
11. shall not be hurt *of* the second death.
17. I give to eat *of* the hidden manna,
21. to repent *of* her fornication ;
22. except they repent *of* their deeds.
3: 5. his name *out of* the book of life,
9. them *of* the synagogue of Satan,
10. thee *from* the hour of temptation,
12. which cometh down *out of* heaven
16. I will spue thee *out of* my mouth.
18. buy of me gold tried *in* the fire,
4: 5. *out of* the throne proceeded lightnings
5: 5. one *of* the elders saith unto me,
— the Lion *of* the tribe of Juda,
7. *out of* the right hand of him
9. *out of* every kindred, and tongue,
6: 1. the Lamb opened one *of* the seals,
— one *of* the four beasts saying,
14. were moved *out of* their places
7: 4. *of* all the tribes of the children
5. *Of* the tribe of Juda (were) sealed
— *Of* the tribe of Reuben... *Of* the tribe of
Gad
6. *Of* the tribe of Aser... *Of* the tribe of
Nepthalim... *Of* the tribe of Manasses
7. *Of* the tribe of Simeon... *Of* the tribe of
Levi... *Of* the tribe of Issachar
8. *Of* the tribe of Zabulon... *Of* the tribe of
Joseph... *Of* the tribe of Benjamin
9. *of* all nations, and kindreds, and people,
13. one *of* the elders answered,
14. came *out of* great tribulation,
8: 4. *out of* the angel's hand.
5. filled it *with* fire of the altar,
10. fell a great star *from* heaven,
11. many men died *of* the waters,
13. *by reason of* the other voices
9: 1. I saw a star fall *from* heaven
2. there arose a smoke *out of* the pit,
— *by reason of* the smoke of the pit.
3. there came *out of* the smoke
13. I heard a voice *from* the four horns
17. *out of* their mouths issued fire
18. *by* the fire, and *by* the smoke, and *by* the
brimstone, which issued *out of* their
mouths.
20. repented not *of* the works of their
21. repented they *of* their murders, nor *of*
their sorceries, nor *of* their fornication,
nor *of* their thefts.
10: 1. angel come down *from* heaven,
4. I heard a voice *from* heaven
8. the voice which I heard *from* heaven
10. little book *out of* the angel's hand,
11: 5. fire proceedeth *out of* their mouth,
7. *out of* the bottomless pit
9. they *of* the people and kindreds

Rev.11:11. the Spirit of life *from* God
    12. they heard a great voice *from* heaven
12:15. the serpent cast *out of* his mouth
    16. the dragon cast *out of* his mouth.
13: 1. a beast rise up *out of* the sea,
    11. coming up *out of* the earth;
    13. maketh fire come down *from* heaven
14: 2. I heard a voice *from* heaven,
    8. made all nations drink *of* the wine
    10. same shall drink *of* the wine of
    13. I heard a voice *from* heaven
    — they may rest *from* their labours;
    15. angel came *out of* the temple,
    17. another angel came *out of* the temple
    18. angel came out *from* the altar,
    20. blood came *out of* the winepress,
15: 2. *over* the beast, and *over* his image, and
      over his mark (and) *over* the number of
    6. seven angels came *out of* the temple,
    7. one *of* the four beasts gave unto
    8. *from* the glory of God, and *from* his power;
16: 1. a great voice *out of* the temple
    7. I heard another *out of* the altar
    10. they gnawed their tongues *for* pain,
    11. because *of* their pains and)(their sores,
      and repented not *of* their deeds.
    13. *out of* the mouth of the dragon, and *out of*
      the mouth of the beast, and *out of* the
      mouth of the false prophet.
    21. a great hail *out of* heaven,
    — *because of* the plague of the hail;
17: 1. came one *of* the seven angels
    2. *with* the wine of her fornication.
    6. *with* the blood of the saints, and *with* the
      blood of the martyrs of Jesus:
    8. ascend *out of* the bottomless pit,
    11. is *of* the seven, and goeth into
18: 1. another angel come down *from* heaven,
    — was lightened *with* his glory.
    3. have drunk *of* the wine of the
    — *through* the abundance of her
    4. I heard another voice *from* heaven, saying,
      Come *out of* her, my people,
    — receive not *of* her plagues.
    12. vessels *of* most precious wood,
    19. *by reason of* her costliness!
    20. God hath avenged you *on* (lit. *of*) her.
19: 2. blood of his servants *at* her hand.
    5. a voice came *out of* the throne,
    15. *out of* his mouth goeth a sharp
    21. (sword) proceeded *out of* his mouth: and
      all the fowls were filled *with* their flesh.
20: 1. an angel come down *from* heaven,
    7. shall be loosed *out of* his prison,
    9. down from God *out of* heaven,
    12. judged *out of* those things which were
21: 2. down from God *out of* heaven,
    3. I heard a great voice *out of* heaven
    6. *of* the fountain of the water of life
    10. descending *out of* heaven from God,
    21. every several gate was *of* one pearl:
22: 1. proceeding *out of* the throne
    19. *out of* the holy city, and (from) the

ἕκαστος, *hekastos.*

Mat.16:27. shall reward *every* man according
    18:35. forgive not *every one* his brother
    25:15. to *every* man according to his
    26:22. began *every one* of them to say

Mar 13:34. to *every* man his work,
Lu. 2: 3. *every one* into his own city.
    4:40. his hands on *every* one of them,
    6:44. For *every* tree is known by
   13:15. doth not *each one* of you on the
   16: 5. called *every* one of his lord's debtors
Joh. 6: 7. that *every one* of them may take
    7:53. *every man* went unto his own house.
   16:32. scattered, *every man* to his own,
   19:23. four parts, to *every* soldier a part;
Acts 2: 3. it sat upon *each* of them.
    6. *every* man heard them speak
    8. how hear we *every man* in our
    38. be baptized *every one* of you
   3:26. turning away *every one* of you
   4:35. made unto *every* man according
   11:29. *every* man according to his ability,
   17:27. not far from *every* one of us:
   20:31. to warn *every* one night and day
   21:19. he declared *particularly* (lit. by *each*
      one)
    26. offered for *every* one of them.
Ro. 2: 6. render to *every* man according
   12: 3. as God hath dealt to *every* man
   14: 5. Let *every* man be fully persuaded
    12. So then *every one* of us shall
   15: 2. Let *every one* of us please
1Co. 1:12. that *every one* of you saith,
   3: 5. as the Lord gave to *every* man?
    8. *every* man shall receive his own
    10. let *every* man take heed how
    13. *Every man's* work shall be
    — fire shall try *every man's* work
   4: 5. *every* man have praise of God.
   7: 2. let *every man* have his own wife, and let
      every woman have her own husband.
    7. *every* man hath his proper gift
    17. hath distributed to *every* man, as the Lord
      hath called *every* one,
    20. Let *every* man abide in the same
    24. let *every* man, wherein he is called,
  10:24. *every* man another's (wealth).
  11:21. in eating *every one* taketh before
  12: 7. given to *every* man to profit
    11. dividing to *every* man severally
    18. *every* one of them in the body,
  14:26. *every one* of you hath a psalm,
  15:23. *every* man in his own order:
    38. to *every* seed his own body.
  16: 2. let *every one* of you lay by him
2Co. 5:10. that *every one* may receive the
  9: 7. *Every* man according as he purposeth
Gal. 6: 4. let *every* man prove his own work,
    5. *every* man shall bear his own burden.
Eph. 4: 7. unto *every* one of us is given grace
    16. in the measure of *every* part,
    25. speak *every* man truth with
   5:33. let *every one* of you in particular
   6: 8. good thing *any* man doeth,
Phi. 2: 4. Look not *every* man on his own things,
      but *every* man also on the things
Col. 4: 6. ought to answer *every* man.
1Th. 2:11. charged *every* one of you,
  4: 4. That *every one* of you should
2Th. 1: 3. the charity of *every* one of you
Heb. 3:13. exhort one another daily,(lit. on *every* day)
  6:11. we desire that *every* one of you
  8:11. teach *every* man his neighbour, and *every*
      man his brother,
  11:21. blessed *both* (lit. *each* of) the sons of
      Joseph;
Jas. 1:14. *every* man is tempted, when

1Pet.1:17. according to *every man's* work,
   4:10. As *every* man hath received the
Rev. 2:23. I will give unto *every one* of you
   5: 8. having *every one* of them harps,
   6:11. given unto *every one* of them ;
  20:13. they were judged *every* man
  21:21. *every* several gate was of one
  22: 2. yielded her fruit *every* month:
    12. to give *every* man according

ἑκάστοτε, *hekastote.*

2Pet.1:15. able...to have these things *always* in re-
    membrance.

ἑκατόν, *hekaton.*

Mat.13: 8. some an *hundred*fold, some
   23. bringeth forth, some an *hundred*fold,
  18:12. if a man have an *hundred* sheep,
   28. owed him an *hundred* pence:
Mar. 4: 8. some sixty, and some an *hundred.*
   20. some sixty, and some an *hundred.*
   6:40. by *hundreds,* and by fifties.
Lu. 15: 4. having an *hundred* sheep,
  16: 6. An *hundred* measures of oil.
    7. An *hundred* measures of wheat.
Joh.19:39. about an *hundred* pound (weight).
  21:11. fishes, an *hundred* and fifty and three:
Acts 1:15. about an *hundred* and twenty,
Rev. 7: 4. sealed an *hundred* (and) forty (and) four
  14: 1. an *hundred* forty (and) four thousand,
    3. the *hundred* (and) forty (and) four thou-
    sand,
  21:17. an *hundred* (and) forty (and) four cubits,

ἑκατονταέτης, *hekatontaetees.*

Ro. 4:19. was about an *hundred years old,*

ἑκατονταπλασίων, *hekatontaplasiōn.*

Mat.19:29. shall receive an *hundred*fold,
Mar 10:30. he shall receive an *hundred*fold
Lu. 8: 8. bare fruit an *hundred*fold.

ἑκατοντάρχης, *hekatontarkees.*

Acts10: 1. a *centurion* of the band called
   22. they said, Cornelius the *centurion,*
  24:23. commanded a *centurion* to
  27: 1. a *centurion* of Augustus' band.
   31. Paul said to the *centurion*

ἑκατόνταρχος, *hekatontarkos.*

Mat. 8: 5. there came unto him a *centurion,*
   8. The *centurion* answered and said,
   13. Jesus said unto the *centurion,*
  27:54. when the *centurion,* and they that
Lu. 7: 2. a certain *centurion's* servant,
   6. the *centurion* sent friends to him,
  23:47. when the *centurion* saw what
Acts21:32. immediately took soldiers and *centurions,*
  22:25. Paul said unto the *centurion*

Acts22:26. When the *centurion* heard (that),
  23:17. Paul called one of the *centurions*
   23. he called unto (him) two *centurions,*
  27: 6. there the *centurion* found a ship
   11. the *centurion* believed the master
   43. the *centurion,* willing to save Paul,
  28:16. the *centurion* delivered the prisoners

ἐκβάλλω, *ekballo.*

Mat. 7: 4. Let me *pull out* the mote out of
   5. first *cast out* the beam out of
  — see clearly *to cast out* the mote out of
   22. in thy name *have cast out* devils ?
  8:12. *shall be cast out* into outer darkness:
   16. he *cast out* the spirits with (his) word,
   31. saying, If thou *cast us out,*
  9:25. when the people *were put forth,*
   33. *when* the devil *was cast out,*
   34. He *casteth out* devils through
   38. that he will *send forth* labourers
  10: 1. unclean spirits, *to cast* them *out,*
   8. raise the dead, *cast out* devils:
  12:20. till he *send forth* judgment unto
   24. *doth* not *cast out* devils,
   26. if Satan *cast out* Satan, he is
   27. if I by Beelzebub *cast out* devils,
  — *do* your children *cast* (them) *out?*
   28. if I *cast out* devils by the Spirit
   35. *bringeth forth* good things:
  — *bringeth forth* evil things.
  13:52. *bringeth forth* out of his treasure
  15:17. *is cast out* into the draught?
  17:19. Why could not we *cast* him *out?*
  21:12. *cast out* all them that sold
   39. they caught him, and *cast* (him) out
  22:13. *cast* (him) into outer darkness;
  25:30. *cast* ye the unprofitable servant into outer
Mar. 1:12. *driveth* him into the wilderness.
   34. and *cast out* many devils ;
   39. throughout all Galilee, and *cast out* devils.
   43. forthwith *sent* him *away;*
  3:15. *to cast out* devils:
   22. of the devils *casteth* he *out* devils.
   23. How can Satan *cast out* Satan ?
  5:40. *when* he *had put* them all *out,*
  6:13. they *cast out* many devils,
  7:26. he *would cast forth* the devil
  9:18. that they *should cast* him *out ;*
   28. Why could not we *cast* him *out ?*
   38. we saw one *casting out* devils
   47. thine eye offend thee, *pluck* it *out:*
  11:15. began *to cast out* them that
  12: 8. *cast* (him) out of the vineyard.
  16: 9. out of whom he had *cast* seven devils.
   17. *shall* they *cast out* devils;
Lu. 4:29. *thrust* him out of the city,
  6:22. shall reproach (you), and *cast out* your
    name
   42. let me *pull out* the mote
  — *cast out* first the beam out of
  — see clearly *to pull out* the mote
  8:54. *put* them all *out,* and took her by the hand,
    and
  9:40. thy disciples to *cast* him *out ;*
   49. we saw one *casting out* devils
  10: 2. that he *would send forth* labourers into his
    harvest.
   35. he *took out* two pence, *and* gave
  11:14. he was *casting out* a devil,
   15. He *casteth out* devils through

Lu. 11:18. I *cast out* devils through Beelzebub.
19. if I by Beelzebub *cast out* devils, by whom *do* your sons *cast* (them) *out?*
20. But if I with the finger of God *cast out*
13:28. you (yourselves) *thrust* out.
32. Behold, I *cast out* devils,
19:45. to *cast out* them that sold therein,
20:12. wounded him also, and *cast* (him) *out*.
15. *cast* him out of the vineyard, *and*
Joh. 2:15. he *drove* them all *out* of the temple,
6:37. I *will* in no wise *cast out*.
9:34. thou teach us? And they *cast* him *out*.
35. that they *had cast* him *out;*
10: 4. he *putteth forth* his own sheep,
12:31. *shall* the prince of this world *be cast out*.
Acts 7:58. *cast* (him) out of the city, *and*
9:40. *put* them all *forth*, and kneeled down, *and*
13:50. *expelled* them out of their coasts.
16:37. now do they *thrust* us *out* privily?
27:38. and cast *out* the wheat into the sea.
Gal. 4:30. *Cast out* the bondwoman
Jas. 2:25. and *had sent* (them) *out* another way?
3Joh. 10. *casteth* (them) *out* of the church.
Rev.11: 2. without the temple *leave* out,

ἔκϐασις, *ekbasis*.

1Co.10:13. also make a *way to escape*,
Heb 13: 7. considering the *end* of (their) conversation:

ἐκϐολή, *ekbolee*.

Acts27:18. next (day) they lightened the ship; (lit. they made a *casting out*)

ἐκγαμίζω, *ekgamizo*.

Mat.22:30. neither marry, nor *are given in marriage*,
24:38. marrying and *giving in marriage*,
Lu. 17:27. they *were given in marriage*,
1Co. 7:38. he *that giveth* (her) *in marriage* doeth well; but he *that giveth* (her) not *in marriage*

ἐκγαμίσκομαι, *ekgamiskomai*.

Lu. 20:34. marry, and *are given in marriage:*
35. neither marry, nor *are given in marriage:*

ἔκγονα, *ekgona*.

1Ti. 5: 4. have children or *nephews*, (lit. *descendants*)

ἐκδαπανάω, *ekdapanao*.

2Co.12:15. I will very gladly spend and *be spent*

ἐκδέχομαι, *ekdekomai*.

Joh. 5: 3. withered, *waiting for* the moving
Acts17:16. *while* Paul *waited for* them at Athens,
1Co.11:33. to eat, *tarry* one *for* another.

1Co.16:11. I *look for* him with the brethren.
Heb 10:13. *expecting* till his enemies be
11:10. he *looked for* a city which hath
Jas. 5: 7. the husbandman *waiteth for* the
1Pet.3:20. *waited* in the days of Noah,

ἔκδηλος, *ekdeelos*.

2Ti. 3: 9. folly shall be *manifest* unto all

ἐκδημέω, *ekdeemeo*.

2Co. 5: 6. we *are absent* from the Lord:
8. rather *to be absent* from the body,
9. that, whether present or *absent,*

ἐκδίδωμι, *ekdidōmi*.

Mat.21:33. built a tower, and *let it out* to
41. *will let out* (his) vineyard unto
Mar 12: 1. *let it out* to husbandmen,
Lu. 20: 9. *let* it *forth* to husbandmen,

ἐκδιηγέομαι, *ekdieegeomai*.

Acts13:41. though a man *declare* it unto you.
15: 3. *declaring* the conversion of the

ἐκδικέω, *ekdikeo*.

Lu. 18: 3. saying, *Avenge* me of mine adversary.
5. I *will avenge* her, lest by her
Ro. 12:19. Dearly beloved, *avenge* not yourselves,
2Co.10: 6. to *revenge* all disobedience,
Rev. 6:10. dost thou not judge and *avenge* our blood
19: 2. hath *avenged* the blood of his

ἐκδίκησις, *ekdikeesis*.

Lu. 18: 7. shall not God *avenge* (lit. make *vengeance for*) his own
8. that he will *avenge* (lit. make, &c.) them speedily.
21:22. these be the days of *vengeance*,
Acts 7:24. *avenged* (lit. made *v. &c.*) him that was oppressed,
Ro. 12:19. it is written, *Vengeance* (is) mine;
2Co. 7:11. (what) zeal, yea, (what) *revenge!*
2Th. 1: 8. taking *vengeance* on them that
Heb 10:30. said, *Vengeance* (belongeth) unto me,
1Pet.2:14. for the *punishment* of evildoers,

ἔκδικος, *ekdikos*.

Ro. 13: 4. a *revenger* to (execute) wrath upon
1Th. 4: 6. the Lord (is) the *avenger* of all such,

ἐκδιώκω, *ekdioko*.

Lu. 11:49. them they shall slay and *persecute:*
1Th. 2:15. own prophets, and *have persecuted* us;

ἔκδοτος, *ekdotos.*

Acts 2:23. being *delivered* by the determinate

ἐκδοχή, *ekdokee.*

Heb 10:27. a certain fearful *looking for* of judgment

ἐκδύω, *ekduo.*

Mat.27:28. they *stripped* him, *and* put on him
31. they *took* the robe *off from* him,
Mar 15:20. they *took off* the purple *from* him,
Lu. 10:30. which *stripped* him...*and* departed,
2Co. 5: 4. that we would *be unclothed,*

ἐκεῖ, *ekī.*

Mat. 2:13. be thou *there* until I bring thee word:
15. was *there* until the death of Herod:
22. he was afraid to go *thither:*
5:24. Leave *there* thy gift before the
6:21. *there* will your heart be also.
8:12. *there* shall be weeping and gnashing
12:45. they enter in and dwell *there:*
13:42. *there* shall be wailing and gnashing
50. *there* shall be wailing and gnashing
58. did not many mighty works *there*
14:23. evening was come, he was *there* alone.
15:29. into a mountain, and sat down *there.*
17:20. Remove hence *to yonder place;*
18:20. *there* am I in the midst of them.
19: 2. he healed them *there.*
21:17. into Bethany; and he lodged *there.*
22:11. he saw *there* a man which had
13. *there* shall be weeping and gnashing
24:28. *there* will the eagles be gathered
51. *there* shall be weeping and gnashing
25:30. *there* shall be weeping and gnashing
26:36. while I go and pray *yonder.*
71. said unto them that were *there,*
27:36. they watched him *there;*
47. Some of them that stood *there,*
55. many women were *there*
61. *there* was Mary Magdalene,
28: 7. *there* shall ye see him:
Mar 1:13. he was *there* in the wilderness
2: 6. certain of the scribes sitting *there,*
3: 1. there was a man *there* which
5:11. Now there was *there* nigh unto
6: 5. could *there* do no mighty work,
10. *there* abide till ye depart from
33. ran afoot *thither* out of all cities,
55. where they heard he was)(.
11: 5. them that stood *there* said
13:21. Lo, here (is) Christ; or, lo, (he is) *there;*
14:15. *there* make ready for us.
16: 7. *there* shall ye see him, as he said
Lu. 2: 6. that, while they were *there,*
6: 6. *there* was a man whose right
8:32. there was *there* an herd of many
9: 4. *there* abide, and thence depart.
10: 6. if the son of peace be *there,*
11:26. they enter in, and dwell *there:*
12:18. *there* will I bestow all my
34. *there* will your heart be also.
13:28. *There* shall be weeping and gnashing
15:13. *there* wasted his substance
17:21. Lo here! or, lo *there!*

Lu. 17:23. See here; or, see *there:*
37. *thither* will the eagles be gathered
21: 2. casting in *thither* two mites.
22:12. room furnished: *there* make ready.
23:33. *there* they crucified him,
Joh. 2: 1. the mother of Jesus was *there:*
6. were set *there* six waterpots
12. they continued *there* not many
3:22. *there* he tarried with them,
23. there was much water *there:*
4: 6. Now Jacob's well was *there.*
40. he abode *there* two days.
5: 5. a certain man was *there,*
6: 3. *there* he sat with his disciples.
22. was none other boat *there,*
24. saw that Jesus was not *there,*
10:40. first baptized; and *there* he abode.
42. many believed on him *there.*
11: 8. goest thou *thither* again?
15. that I was not *there,* to the
31. unto the grave to weep *there.*
12: 2. *There* they made him a supper;
9. knew that he was *there:*
26. *there* shall also my servant be:
18: 2. Jesus ofttimes resorted *thither*
3. cometh *thither* with lanterns
19:42. *There* laid they Jesus therefore
Acts 9:33. *there* he found a certain man
14:28. *there* they abode long time with
16: 1. a certain disciple was *there,*
17:14. Timotheus abode *there* still.
19:21. After I have been *there,*
25: 9. *there* be judged of these things
14. they had been *there* many days,
Ro. 9:26. *there* shall they be called the
15:24. brought on my way *thitherward*
2Co. 3:17. Spirit of the Lord (is), *there* (is) liberty.
Tit. 3:12. I have determined *there* to winter.
Heb. 7: 8. *there* he (receiveth them), of whom
Jas. 2: 3. to the poor, Stand thou *there,*
3:16. *there* (is) confusion and every evil work.
4:13. continue *there* a year, and buy and sell,
Rev. 2:14. thou hast *there* them that hold
12: 6. they should feed her *there*
14. where she is nourished)(for
21:25. there shall be no night *there.*
22: 5. there shall be no night *there;*

See also κἀκεῖ.

ἐκεῖθεν, *ekīthen.*

Mat. 4:21. going on *from thence,* he saw
5:26. by no means come out *thence,*
9: 9. as Jesus passed forth *from thence,*
27. when Jesus departed *thence,*
11: 1. he departed *thence* to teach
12: 9. when he was departed *thence,*
15. he withdrew himself *from thence:*
13:53. finished these parables, he departed *thence.*
14:13. he departed *thence* by ship
15:21. went *thence,* and departed into
29. Jesus departed *from thence,*
19:15. hands on them, and departed *thence.*
Mar. 1:19. had gone a little farther *thence,*
6: 1. he went out *from thence,*
10. till ye depart *from that place.*
11. when ye depart *thence,* shake
7:24. *from thence* he arose, and went
9:30. they departed *thence,* and passed
Lu. 9: 4. there abide, and *thence* depart.

Lu. 12:59. thou shalt not depart *thence*,
16:26. that (would come) from *thence*.
Joh. 4:43. after two days he departed *thence*,
11:54. went *thence* unto a country near
Acts13: 4. *from thence* they sailed to Cyprus,
16:12. *from thence* to Philippi, which
18: 7. he departed *thence*, and entered
20:13. *there* (lit. *thence*) intending to take in Paul :

See also κἀκεῖθεν.

ἐκεῖνος, *ekīnos.*

Mat. 3: 1. In *those* days came John the Baptist,
7:22. Many will say to me in *that* day,
25. winds blew, and beat upon *that* house ;
27. winds blew, and beat upon *that* house ;
8:13. healed in the *selfsame* hour.
28. no man might pass by *that* way.
9:22. was made whole from *that* hour.
26. went abroad into all *that* land.
31. abroad his fame in all *that* country.
10:14. depart out of *that* house or city,
15. than for *that* city.
19. be given you in *that* same hour
11:25. At *that* time Jesus answered
12: 1. At *that* time Jesus went on the
45. the last (state) of *that* man
13: 1. *The same* day went Jesus out
11. to *them* it is not given.
44. that he hath, and buyeth *that* field.
14: 1. At *that* time Herod the tetrarch
35. when the men of *that* place
— sent out into all *that* country
15:22. came out of *the same* coasts,
28. made whole from *that very* hour.
17:18. child was cured from *that very* hour.
27. *that* take, and give unto them
18: 1. At *the same* time came the
7. woe to *that* man by whom
27. Then the lord of *that* servant
28. *the same* servant went out,
32. I forgave thee all *that* debt,
21:40. do unto *those* husbandmen?
22: 7. destroyed *those* murderers,
10. So *those* servants went out
23. *The same* day came to him
46. from *that* day forth ask him
24:19. them that give suck in *those* days !
22. except *those* days should be shortened,
— elect's sake *those* days shall be shortened.
29. the tribulation of *those* days
36. of *that* day and hour knoweth
43. know *this*, that if the goodman
46. Blessed (is) *that* servant, whom
48. if *that* evil servant shall say
50. The lord of *that* servant shall
25: 7. Then all *those* virgins arose,
19. the lord of *those* servants cometh,
26:24. woe unto *that* man by whom
— it had been good for *that* man
29. until *that* day when I drink it
55. In *that same* hour said Jesus
27: 8. Wherefore *that* field was called,
19. nothing to do with *that* just man :
63. we remember that *that* deceiver said,
Mar. 1: 9. it came to pass in *those* days,
2:20. shall they fast in *those* days.
3:24. *that* kingdom cannot stand.
25. *that* house cannot stand.
4:11. unto *them* that are without,
35. *the same* day, when the even

Mar. 6:11. judgment, than for *that* city.
55. ran through *that* whole region
7:15. *those* are they that defile the man.
20. *that* defileth the man.
8: 1. In *those* days the multitude being
12: 7. *those* husbandmen said among
13:11. shall be given you in *that* hour,
17. that give suck in *those* days !
19. (in) *those* days shall be affliction,
24. in *those* days, after *that* tribulation, the
32. of *that* day and (that) hour knoweth
14:21. woe to *that* man by whom
— good were it for *that* man
25. until *that* day that I drink it
16:10. *she* went and told them that had
13. neither believed they *them*.
20. *they* went forth, and preached
Lu. 2: 1. it came to pass in *those* days,
4: 2. in *those* days he did eat nothing:
5:35. shall they fast in *those* days.
6:23. Rejoice ye in *that* day, and leap
48. beat vehemently upon *that* house,
49. the ruin of *that* house was great.
8:32. suffer them to enter into *them*.
9: 5. when ye go out of *that* city,
34. as *they* entered into the cloud.
36. told no man in *those* days
10:12. more tolerable in *that* day for Sodom,
than for *that* city.
31. came down a certain priest *that* way:
11:26. the last (state) of *that* man
12:37. Blessed (are) *those* servants, whom
38. blessed are *those* servants.
43. Blessed (is) *that* servant, whom
45. if *that* servant say in his heart, My lord
delayeth his coming ;
46. The lord of *that* servant will
47. *that* servant, which knew his
13: 4. Or *those* eighteen, upon whom
14:21. So *that* servant came, and shewed
24. none of *those* men which were
15:14. a mighty famine in *that* land ;
15. to a citizen of *that* country ;
17: 9. Doth he thank *that* servant
31. In *that* day, he which shall be
18: 3. there was a widow in *that* city ;
14. justified (rather) than *the other* :
19: 4. for he was to pass *that* (way).
27. *those* mine enemies, which
20: 1. on one of *those* days, as he taught
18. Whosoever shall fall upon *that* stone
35. worthy to obtain *that* world,
21:23. that give suck, in *those* days !
34. (so) *that* day come upon you unawares.
22:22. woe unto *that* man by whom
Joh. 1: 8. *He* was not that Light, but (was)
18. of the Father, *he* hath declared (him).
33. *the same* said unto me,
39(40). abode with him *that* day :
2:21. *he* spake of the temple of his body.
3:28. that I am sent before *him*.
30. *He* must increase, but I (must)
4:25. when *he* is come, he will tell
39. the Samaritans of *that* city
53. at *the same* hour, in the which
5: 9. on *the same* day was the sabbath.
11. *the same* said unto me,
19. for what things soever *he* doeth,
35. *He* was a burning and a shining light,
38. for whom *he* hath sent,
39. *they* are they which testify of me.
43. his own name, *him* ye will receive.

Joh. 5:46. for *he* wrote of me.
  47. if ye believe not *his* writings,
6:22. save *that* one whereinto his
  29. believe on him whom *he* hath sent.
7:11. said, Where is *he*?
  45. *they* said unto them,
8:10. where are *those* thine accusers?
  42. neither came I of myself, but *he* sent me.
  44. *He* was a murderer from the
9: 9. *he* said, I am (he).
  11. *He* answered and said, A man
  12. said they unto him, Where is *he*?
  25. *He* answered and said, Whether
  28. said, Thou art *his* disciple;
  36. *He* answered and said, Who is he,
  37. it is *he* that talketh with thee.
10: 1. *the same* is a thief and a robber.
  6. *they* understood not what
  35. If he called *them* gods, unto
11:13. *they* thought that he had spoken
  29. As soon as *she* heard (that),
  49. the high priest *that same* year,
  51. being high priest *that* year,
  53. Then from *that* day forth they
12:48. *the same* shall judge him in
13: 6. Peter (lit. *he*) saith unto him, Lord,
  25. *He* then lying on Jesus' breast
  26. *He* it is, to whom I shall give
  27. Satan entered into *him*.
  30. *He* then having received the sop
14:20. At *that* day ye shall know
  21. *he* it is that loveth me:
  26. *he* shall teach you all things,
15:26. *he* shall testify of me:
16: 8. when *he* is come, *he* will reprove
  13. Howbeit when *he*, the Spirit of truth,
  14. *He* shall glorify me: for he shall
  23. in *that* day ye shall ask me
  26. At *that* day ye shall ask in my
18:13. the high priest *that same* year.
  15. *that* disciple was known unto
  17. *He* saith, I am not.
  25. *He* denied (it), and said, I am not.
19:21. that *he* said, I am King of the Jews.
  27. from *that* hour their disciple took
  31. for *that* sabbath day was an high day,
20:13. *they* say unto her, Woman,
  15. *She*, supposing him to be the
  16. *She* turned herself, and saith unto
  19. *the same* day at evening,
21: 3. *that* night they caught nothing.
  7. *that* disciple whom Jesus loved
  23. that *that* disciple should not die:
Acts 1:19. *that* field is called in their
  2:18. I will pour out in *those* days
  41. *the same* day there were added
  3:13. *he* was determined to let (him) go.
  23. which will not hear *that* prophet,
  7:41. they made a calf in *those* days,
  8: 1. at *that* time there was a great
  8. there was great joy in *that* city.
  9:37. it came to pass in *those* days,
10: 9. as *they* went on their journey,
  10. while *they* made ready, he
12: 1. Now about *that* time Herod
  6. *the same* night Peter was sleeping
14:21. preached the gospel to *that* city,
16: 3. which were in *those* quarters:
  33. *the same* hour of the night,
  35. saying, Let *those* men go.
19:16. they fled out of *that* house
  23. *the same* time there arose no

Acts20: 2. he had gone over *those* parts,
  21: 6. *they* returned home again.
  22:11. for the glory of *that* light, being
  28: 7. In *the same* quarters were
Ro. 6:21. the end of *those* things (is) death.
  11:23. *they* also, if they abide not in
  14:14. to *him* (it is) unclean.
  15. Destroy not *him* with thy meat,
1Co. 9:25. *they* (do it) to obtain a corruptible
  10:11. these things happened unto *them*
  28. for *his* sake that shewed it,
  15:11. whether (it were) I or *they*, so we
2Co. 7: 8. I perceive that *the same* epistle
  8: 9. that ye through *his* poverty might
  14(13). (be a supply) for *their* want,
  — *their* abundance also may be
  10:18. not *he* that commendeth himself is
Eph. 2:12. That at *that* time ye were
2Th. 1:10. was believed in *that* day.
2Ti. 1:12. unto him against *that* day.
  18. mercy of the Lord in *that* day:
  2:13. believe not, (yet) *he* abideth faithful:
  26. taken captive by him at *his* will.
  3: 9. unto all (men), as *their's* also was.
  4: 8. shall give me at *that* day:
Tit. 3: 7. being justified by *his* grace,
Heb. 3:10. I was grieved with *that* generation,
  4: 2. but the word preached did not profit *them*.
  11. to enter into *that* rest, lest
  6: 7. herbs meet for *them* by whom
  8: 7. if *that* first (covenant) had been
  10. after *those* days, saith the Lord;
  10:16. after *those* days, saith the Lord,
  11:15. if they had been mindful of *that* (country)
  12:25. For if *they* escaped not who
Jas. 1: 7. let not *that* man think
  4:15. we shall live, and do this, or *that*
2Pet.1:16. were eyewitnesses of *his* majesty.
1Joh.2: 6. even as *he* walked.
  3: 3. himself, even as *he* is pure.
  5. ye know that *he* was manifested
  7. righteous, even as *he* is righteous.
  16. *he* laid down his life for us:
  4:17. because as *he* is, so are we in
  5:16. I do not say that he shall pray for *it*.
Rev. 9: 6. in *those* days shall men seek
  11:13. *the same* hour was there a
  16:14. to the battle of *that* great day

  See also κἀκεῖνος.

ἐκεῖσε, *ekise.*

Acts21: 3. for *there* the ship was to unlade
  22: 5. to bring them which were *there*

ἐκζητέω, *ekzeteo.*

Lu. 11:50. *may be required* of this generation;
  51. It *shall be required* of this generation.
Acts15:17. men *might seek* after the Lord,
Ro. 3:11. none *that seeketh* after God.
Heb11: 6. them *that diligently seek* him.
  12:17. though he *sought* it *carefully*
1Pet.1:10. *have enquired* and searched diligently

ἐκθαμβέω, *ekthambeo.*

Mar. 9:15. when they beheld him, *were greatly amazed*,
  14:33. began *to be sore amazed*,

Mar 16: 5. they *were affrighted.*
6. he saith unto them, *Be not affrighted:*

ἔκθαμβος, *ekthambos.*

Acts 3:11. is called Solomon's, *greatly wondering.*

ἔκθετος, *ekthetos.*

Acts 7:19. cast out their young children, (lit. in making their young children *exposed*)

ἐκκαθαίρω, *ekkathairo.*

1Co. 5: 7. *Purge out* therefore the old leaven,
2Ti. 2:21. If a man therefore *purge* himself

ἐκκαίομαι, *ekkaiomi.*

Ro. 1:27. *burned* in their lust one toward another ;

ἐκκακέω, *ekkakeo.*

Lu. 18: 1. ought always (to) pray, and not *to faint ;*
2Co. 4: 1. received mercy, we *faint* not ;
16. For which cause we *faint* not ;
Gal. 6: 9. *let* us not *be weary* in well doing :
Eph. 3:13. I desire that ye *faint* not
2Th. 3:13. *be* not *weary* in well doing.

ἐκκεντέω, *ekkenteo.*

Joh. 19:37. look on him whom they *pierced.*
Rev. 1: 7. they (also) which *pierced* him:

ἐκκλάζω, *ekklazo.*

Ro. 11:17. if some of the branches *be broken off,*
19. The branches *were broken off*,
20. of unbelief they *were broken off,*

ἐκκλείω, *ekkleio.*

Ro. 3:27. Where (is) boasting then? It *is excluded.*
Gal. 4:17. yea, they would *exclude* you,

ἐκκλησία, *ekkleesia.*

Mat. 16:18. I will build my *church ;*
18:17. tell (it) unto the *church:* but if he neglect to hear the *church,*
Acts 2:47. the Lord added to the *church* daily
5:11. fear came upon all the *church,*
7:38. he, that was in the *church*
8: 1. the *church* which was at Jerusalem ;
3. he made havock of the *church,*
9:31. Then had the *churches* rest
11:22. the *church* which was in Jerusalem:
26. assembled themselves with the *church,*
12: 1. to vex certain of the *church.*
5. without ceasing of the *church* unto God
13: 1. Now there were in the *church*
14:23. elders in every *church,* and had
27. had gathered the *church* together,

Acts 15: 3. on their way by the *church,*
4. they were received of the *church,*
22. elders, with the whole *church,*
41. confirming the *churches.*
16: 5. so were the *churches* established
18:22. gone up, and saluted the *church,*
19:32. for the *assembly* was confused ;
39. determined in a lawful *assembly.*
41. thus spoken, he dismissed the *assembly.*
20:17. called the elders of the *church.*
28. to feed the *church* of God,
Ro. 16: 1. is a servant of the *church*
4. all the *churches* of the Gentiles.
5. the *church* that is in their house.
16. The *churches* of Christ salute you.
23. mine host, and of the whole *church,*
1Co. 1: 2. Unto the *church* of God which
4:17. I teach every where in every *church.*
6: 4. least esteemed in the *church.*
7:17. so ordain I in all *churches.*
10:32. nor to the *church* of God:
11:16. neither the *churches* of God.
18. come together in the *church,*
22. or despise ye the *church* of God,
12:28. God hath set some in the *church,*
14: 4. that prophesieth edifieth the *church.*
5. the *church* may receive edifying.
12. to the edifying of the *church.*
19. in the *church* I had rather speak
23. the whole *church* be come together
28. keep silence in the *church ;*
33. as in all *churches* of the saints.
34. keep silence in the *churches :*
35. for women to speak in the *church.*
15: 9. I persecuted the *church* of God.
16: 1. to the *churches* of Galatia,
19. The *churches* of Asia salute you.
— with the *church* that is in their house.
2Co. 1: 1. unto the *church* of God which
8: 1. on the *churches* of Macedonia;
18. gospel throughout all the *churches*
19. was also chosen of the *churches*
23. the messengers of the *churches,*
24. to them, and before the *churches,*
11: 8. I robbed other *churches,* taking
28. the care of all the *churches.*
12:13. were inferior to other *churches,*
Gal. 1: 2. unto the *churches* of Galatia:
13. I persecuted the *church* of God
22. unto the *churches* of Judæa
Eph. 1:22. gave him (to be) the head over all (things) to the *church,*
3:10. might be known by the *church*
21. glory in the *church* by Christ Jesus
5:23. Christ is the head of the *church:*
24. the *church* is subject unto Christ,
25. as Christ also loved the *church,*
27. to himself a glorious *church,*
29. even as the Lord the *church:*
32. concerning Christ and the *church.*
Phi. 3: 6. Concerning zeal, persecuting the *church ;*
4:15. no *church* communicated with me
Col. 1:18. the head of the body, the *church :*
24. body's sake, which is the *church:*
4:15. the *church* which is in his house.
16. in the *church* of the Laodiceans ;
1Th. 1: 1. unto the *church* of the Thessalonians
2:14. followers of the *churches* of God
2Th. 1: 1. unto the *church* of the Thessalonians
4. in you in the *churches* of God
1Ti. 3: 5. take care of the *church* of God ?
15. the *church* of the living God,

1Ti. 5:16. let not the *church* be charged;
Philem 2. to the *church* in thy house:
Heb. 2:12. in the midst of the *church*
    12:23. assembly and *church* of the firstborn,
Jas. 5:14. call for the elders of the *church* ;
3Joh. 6. thy charity before the *church*:
    9. I wrote unto the *church*:
    10. casteth (them) out of the *church*.
Rev. 1: 4. John to the seven *churches*
    11. unto the seven *churches* which
    20. the angels of the seven *churches*:
    — are the seven *churches*.
  2: 1. the angel of the *church* of Ephesus
    7. the Spirit saith unto the *churches* ;
    8. the angel of the *church* in Smyrna
    11. the Spirit saith unto the *churches*;
    12. to the angel of the *church* in Pergamos
    17. the Spirit saith unto the *churches* ;
    18. the angel of the *church* in Thyatira
    23. all the *churches* shall know
    29. the Spirit saith unto the *churches*.
  3: 1. angel of the *church* in Sardis
    6. the Spirit saith unto the *churches*.
    7. to the angel of the *church* in
    13. the Spirit saith unto the *churches*.
    14. unto the angel of the *church* of
    22. the Spirit saith unto the *churches*.
  22:16. these things in the *churches*.

ἐκκλίνω, *ekklino*.

Ro. 3:12. They *are all gone out of the way*,
  16:17. which ye have learned ; and *avoid* them.
1Pet. 3:11. Let him *eschew* evil, and do good ;

ἐκκολυμβάω, *ekkolumbao*.

Acts27:42. lest any of them should *swim out, and*

ἐκκομίζομαι, *ekkomizomai*.

Lu. 7:12. there *was* a dead man *carried out*,

ἐκκόπτω, *ekkopto*.

Mat. 3:10. *is hewn down*, and cast into the fire.
  5:30. *cut it off*, and cast (it) from thee:
  7:19. *is hewn down*, and cast into the fire.
  18: 8. *cut them off*, and cast (them) from thee:
Lu. 3: 9. *is hewn down*, and cast into the fire.
  13: 7. find none: *cut it down* ;
    9. after that thou *shalt cut* it down.
Ro. 11:22. thou also *shalt be cut off*.
    24. *wert cut out* of the olive tree
2Co.11:12. that I *may cut off* occasion
1Pet.3: 7. your prayers *be not hindered*.
    Some read here εγκοπτ.

ἐκκρέμαμαι, *ekkremamai*.

Lu. 19:48. were very attentive to hear (lit. *hung* on
    him hearing) him.

ἐκλαλέω, *eklaleo*.

Acts23:22. *tell* no man that thou hast

ἐκλάμπω, *eklampo*.

Mat.13:43. Then *shall* the righteous *shine forth* as the

ἐκλανθάνομαι, *eklanthanomai*.

Heb.12: 5. ye *have forgotten* the exhortation

ἐκλέγομαι, *eklegomai*.

Mar.13:20. elect's sake, whom he *hath chosen*,
Lu. 6:13. of them he *chose* twelve, whom
  10:42. Mary *hath chosen* that good part,
  14: 7. they *chose out* the chief rooms ;
Joh. 6:70. *Have* not I *chosen* you twelve,
  13:18. I know whom I *have chosen :*
  15:16. Ye *have* not *chosen* me, but I *have chosen*
    you, and
    19. I *have chosen* you out of the world,
Acts 1: 2. the apostles whom he *had chosen :*
    24. of these two thou *hast chosen*,
  6: 5. they *chose* Stephen, a man full
  13:17. *chose* our fathers, and exalted the
  15: 7. God *made choice* among us,
    22. to send *chosen* men of their own
    25. to send *chosen* men unto you
1Co. 1:27. God *hath chosen* the foolish things of
    — and God *hath chosen* the weak
    28. which are despised, *hath* God *chosen*,
Eph. 1: 4. as he *hath chosen* us in him
Jas. 2: 5. *Hath* not God *chosen* the poor of

ἐκλείπω, *eklipo*.

Lu. 16: 9. that, when ye *fail*, they may
  22:32. for thee, that thy faith *fail* not:
Heb. 1:12. thy years *shall* not *fail*.

ἐκλέκτος, *eklektos*.

Mat.20:16. many be called, but few *chosen*.
  22:14. many are called, but few (are) *chosen*.
  24:22. for the *elect's* sake those days
    24. shall deceive the very *elect*.
    31. shall gather together his *elect*
Mar.13:20. for the *elect's* sake, whom he hath
    22. if (it were) possible, even the *elect*.
    27. shall gather together his *elect*
Lu. 18: 7. shall not God avenge his own *elect*,
  23:35. if he be Christ, the *chosen* of God.
Ro. 8:33. to the charge of God's *elect* ?
  16:13. Salute Rufus *chosen* in the Lord,
Col. 3:12. therefore, as the *elect* of God,
1Ti. 5:21. Jesus Christ, and the *elect* angels,
2Ti. 2:10. all things for the *elect's* sakes,
Tit. 1: 1. to the faith of God's *elect*,
1Pet.1: 2. *Elect* according to the foreknowledge
  2: 4. *chosen* of God, (and) precious,
    6. a chief corner stone, *elect*, precious:
    9. ye (are) a *chosen* generation,
2Joh. 1. The elder unto the *elect* lady
    13. The children of thy *elect* sister
Rev.17:14. (are) called, and *chosen*, and faithful.

ἐκλογή, *eklogee*.

Acts 9:15. he is a chosen vessel (lit. a vessel of *election*) unto me,

Ro. 9:11. purpose of God according to *election*
    11: 5. according to the *election* of grace.
      7. the *election* hath obtained it,
     28. as touching the *election*,
1Th. 1: 4. beloved, your *election* of God.
2Pet. 1:10. your calling and *election* sure:

ἐκλύω, *ekluo.*

Mat. 9:36. because they fainted (lit. were *faint*), and
   15:32. lest they *faint* in the way.
Mar. 8: 3. they *will faint* by the way:
Gal. 6: 9. we shall reap, *if* we *faint* not.
Heb 12: 3. wearied *and faint* in your minds.
     5. nor *faint* when thou art rebuked

ἐκμάσσω, *ekmasso.*

Lu. 7:38. *did wipe* (them) with the hairs of
    44. *wiped* (them) with the hairs of her head.
Joh. 11: 2. and *wiped* his feet with her hair,
   12: 3. *wiped* his feet with her hair:
   13: 5. *to wipe* (them) with the towel

ἐκμυκτηρίζω, *ekmukteerizo.*

Lu. 16:14. all these things: and they *derided* him.
   23:35. rulers also with them *derided* (him),

ἐκνεύω, *eknuo.*

Joh. 5:13. Jesus *had conveyed himself away*,

ἐκνήφω, *ekneepho.*

1Co.15:34. *Awake* to righteousness, and sin not;

ἑκούσιος, *hekousios.*

Philem.14. it were of necessity, but willingly. (lit.
    according to *willing*)

ἑκουσίως, *hekousiōs.*

Heb 10:26. For if we sin *wilfully* after
1Pet.5: 2. not by constraint, but *willingly*;

ἔκπαλαι, *ekpalai.*

2Pet.2: 3. whose judgment now *of a long time*
   3: 5. the heavens were *of old*, and the

ἐκπειράζω, *ekpīrazo.*

Mat. 4: 7. Thou *shalt* not *tempt* the Lord
Lu. 4:12. Thou *shalt* not *tempt* the Lord
   10:25. stood up, *and tempted* him, saying,
1Co.10: 9. Neither *let* us *tempt* Christ,

ἐκπέμπω, *ekpempo.*

Acts13: 4. So they, *being sent forth* by the Holy Ghost,
   17:10. *sent away* Paul and Silas by night

ἐκπετάννυμι, *ekpetannumi.*

Ro. 10:21. I *have stretched forth* my hands

ἐκπίπτω, *ekpipto.*

Mar.13:25. the stars of heaven shall *fall*,
Acts12: 7. his chains *fell off* from (his) hands.
   27:17. lest they should *fall* into the
     26. we must *be cast* upon a certain island.
     29. lest we *should have fallen* upon rocks,
     32. of the boat, and let her *fall off*.
Ro. 9: 6. word of God *hath taken none effect*.
1Co.13: 8. Charity never *faileth :* but whether
Gal. 5: 4. ye *are fallen* from grace.
Jas. 1:11. the flower thereof *falleth*,
1Pet.1:24. the flower thereof *falleth away :*
2Pet.3:17. lest ye also,...*fall* from your
Rev. 2: 5. from whence thou *art fallen*,

ἐκπλέω, *ekpleo.*

Acts15:39. took Mark, and *sailed* unto Cyprus ;
   18:18. *sailed thence* into Syria,
   20: 6. we *sailed away* from Philippi

ἐκπληρόω, *ekpleeroō.*

Acts13:33(32). God *hath fulfilled* the same

ἐκπλήρωσις, *ekpleerōsis.*

Acts21:26. the *accomplishment* of the days

ἐκπλήσσω, *ekpleesso.*

Mat. 7:28. the people *were astonished* at
   13:54. insomuch that they were astonished, (lit.
     so as for them *to be astonished*)
   19:25. they *were* exceedingly *amazed*,
   22:33. they *were astonished* at his doctrine.
Mar. 1:22. they *were astonished* at his doctrine:
    6: 2. many hearing (him) *were astonished*,
    7:37. *were* beyond measure *astonished*,
   10:26. they *were astonished* out of measure,
   11:18. the people *was astonished* at his
Lu. 2:48. saw him, they *were amazed :*
   4:32. they *were astonished* at his doctrine:
   9:43. they *were* all *amazed* at the
Acts13:12. *being astonished* at the doctrine

ἐκπνέω, *ekpneo.*

Mar.15:37. with a loud voice, and *gave up the ghost*.
    39. so cried out, and *gave up the ghost*,
Lu. 23:46. said thus, he *gave up the ghost*.

ἐκπορεύομαι, *ekporuomai.*

Mat. 3: 5. Then *went out* to him Jerusalem,
   4: 4. every word *that proceedeth out of* the
   15:11. that *which cometh out of* the mouth,
     18. *which proceed out of* the mouth
   17:21. this kind *goeth* not *out* but by
   20:29. as they *departed* from Jericho,

Mar. 1: 5. there *went out* unto him all the
6:11. *when* ye *depart* thence, shake off
7:15. the things *which come out of* him,
19. *goeth out* into the draught,
20. That *which cometh out of* the man,
21. of men, *proceed* evil thoughts,
23. these evil things *come* from within;
10:17. *when* he *was gone forth* into
46. *as* he *went out of* Jericho with
11:19. he *went out of* the city.
13: 1. *as* he *went* out of the temple,
Lu. 3: 7. to the multitude *that came forth*
4:22. *which proceeded out of* his mouth.
37. the fame of him *went out* into every place
of the country
Joh. 5:29. *shall come forth* ; they that have
15:26. which *proceedeth* from the Father,
Acts 9:28. he was with them coming in and *going out*
at Jerusalem.
25: 4. he himself would *depart* shortly
Eph. 4:29. *Let* no corrupt communication *proceed* out
of your mouth,
Rev. 1:16. out of his mouth went (lit. *coming forth*)
a sharp twoedged sword :
4: 5. out of the throne *proceeded* lightnings
9:17. out of their mouths *issued* fire
18. *which issued* out of their mouths.
11: 5. fire *proceedeth* out of their mouth,
16:14. (which) *go forth* unto the kings
19:15. out of his mouth *goeth* a sharp
21. *which* (sword) *proceeded* out of his mouth:
22: 1. clear as crystal, *proceeding* out of the throne
of God

ἐκπορνεύω, *ekpornūo.*

Jude 7. in like manner, *giving themselves over to
fornication,*

ἐκπτύω. *ekptuo.*

Gal. 4:14. ye despised not, nor *rejected* ;

ἐκριζόω, *ekrizoō.*

Mat. 13:29. lest...ye *root up* also the wheat
15:13. hath not planted, *shall be rooted up.*
Lu. 17: 6. *Be* thou *plucked up by the root,*
Jude 12. twice dead, *plucked up by the roots* ;

ἔκστασις, *ekstasis.*

Mar. 5:42. astonished with a great *astonishment.*
16: 8. and were amazed: (lit. *astonishment* took
them)
Lu. 5:26. were all amazed, (lit. *amazement* took them)
Acts 3:10. filled with wonder and *amazement*
10:10. made ready, he fell into a *trance,* (lit. a
trance fell upon him)
11: 5. in a *trance* I saw a vision,
22:17. in the temple, I was in a *trance* ;

ἐκστρέφομαι, *ekstrephomai.*

Tit. 3:11. he that is such *is subverted,*

ἐκταράσσω, *ektarasso.*

Acts 16:20. *do exceedingly trouble* our city,

ἐκτείνω, *ektino.*

Mat. 8: 3. Jesus *put forth* (his) hand, *and*
12:13. *Stretch forth* thine hand. And he *stretched*
(it) *forth* ;
49. he *stretched forth* his hand toward his
disciples, *and*
14:31. Jesus *stretched forth* (his) hand, *and*
26:51. *stretched out* (his) hand, *and drew*
Mar. 1:41. *put forth* (his) hand, *and* touched
3: 5. *Stretch forth* thine hand. And he *stretched*
(it) *out :*
Lu. 5:13. he *put forth* (his) hand, *and* touched
6:10. *Stretch forth* thy hand.
22:53. ye *stretched forth* no hands against
Joh. 21:18. thou *shalt stretch forth* thy hands,
Acts 4:30. By *stretching forth* thine hand
26: 1. Then Paul *stretched forth* the hand, *and*
27:30. as though they would have cast anchors
out (lit. were about *to cast* out a.)

ἐκτελέω, *ekteleo.*

Lu. 14:29. is not able *to finish* (it),
30. was not able *to finish.*

ἐκτένεια, *ektenia.*

Acts 26: 7. *instantly* (lit. in *intensity*) serving, (God)
day and night,

ἐκτενέστερον, *ektenesteron.*

Lu. 22:44. he prayed *more earnestly:*

ἐκτενής, *ektenees.*

Acts 12: 5. prayer was made *without ceasing* (lit. *intense*)
1 Pet. 4: 8. *fervent* charity among yourselves:

ἐκτενῶς, *ektenōs.*

1 Pet. 1:22. with a pure heart *fervently:*

ἐκτίθημι, *ektitheemi.*

Acts 7:21. *when* he *was cast out,* Pharaoh's daughter
11: 4. and *expounded* (it) by order unto them,
18:26. and *expounded* unto him the way of God
28:23. to whom he *expounded* and testified

ἐκτινάσσω, *ektinasso.*

Mat. 10:14. *shake off* the dust of your feet.
Mar. 6:11. *shake off* the dust under your feet
Acts 13:51. they *shook off* the dust of their feet against
them, *and*
18: 6. he *shook* (his) raiment, *and* said

ἔκτος, hektos.

Mat.20: 5. about the *sixth* and ninth hour,
27:45. from the *sixth* hour there was
Mar.15:33. when the *sixth* hour was come,
Lu. 1:26. in the *sixth* month the angel
36. this is the *sixth* month with her,
23:44. it was about the *sixth* hour,
Joh. 4: 6. it was about the *sixth* hour.
19:14. about the *sixth* hour: and he saith
Acts10: 9. to pray about the *sixth* hour:
Rev. 6:12. he had opened the *sixth* seal,
9:13. the *sixth* angel sounded,
14. Saying to the *sixth* angel which
16:12. the *sixth* angel poured out his vial
21:20. fifth, sardonyx ; the *sixth*, sardius ;

ἐκτός, ektos.

Mat.23:26. that the *outside* of them may be
Acts26:22. none *other* things *than* those which the
prophets and Moses
1Co. 6:18. that a man doeth is *without* the body ;
14: 5. with tongues, except (lit. *unless* with the
exception that) he interpret,
15: 2. *unless* ye have believed in vain.
27. that he is excepted (lit. that this is *with
the exception* of him), which did put
2Co.12: 2. or whether *out of* the body, I cannot tell:
3. in the body, or *out of* the body,
1Ti. 5:19. but (lit. *unless* with the exception) before
two or three witnesses.

ἐκτρέπομαι, ektrepomai.

1Ti. 1: 6. have *turned aside* unto vain
5:15. some *are* already *turned aside*
6:20. *avoiding* profane (and) vain babblings,
2Ti. 4: 4. and *shall be turned* unto fables.
Heb 12:13. lest that which is lame *be turned out of the
way ;*

ἐκτρέφω, ektrepho.

Eph. 5:29. *nourisheth* and cherisheth it, even as the
6: 4. *bring them up* in the nurture and

ἔκτρωμα, ektrōma.

1Co.15: 8. seen of me also, as of one *born out of due
time.*

ἐκφέρω, ekphero.

Lu. 15:22. *Bring forth* the best robe,
Acts 5: 6. *carried* (him) *out,* and buried (him).
9. at the door, and *shall carry* thee *out.*
10. *carrying* (her) *forth,* buried (her)
15. they *brought forth* the sick into
1Ti. 6: 7. certain we can *carry* nothing *out.*
Heb. 6: 8. that *which beareth* thorns

ἐκφεύγω, ekphŭgo.

Lu. 21:36. worthy *to escape* all these things
Acts16:27. that the prisoners had been fled. (lit. *to
have escaped*)

Acts19:16. they *fled* out of that house naked
Ro. 2: 3. that thou *shalt escape* the judgment of
God ?
2Co.11:33. was I let down by the wall, and *escaped*
his hands.
1Th. 5: 3. with child ; and they shall not *escape.*
Heb. 2: 3. How *shall* we *escape,* if we neglect

ἐκφοβέω, ekphobeo.

2Co.10: 9. as if I would *terrify* you by letters.

ἔκφοβος, ekphobos.

Mar. 9: 6. for they were *sore afraid.*
Heb.12:21. said, I exceedingly fear (lit. am *exceedingly fearful*) and quake:

ἐκφύω, ekphuo.

Mat.24:32. When his branch is yet tender, and *putteth
forth* leaves,
Mar.13:28. yet tender, and *putteth forth* leaves,

ἐκχέω, ekkeo.

Mat. 9:17. bottles break, and the wine *runneth out,*
Mar. 2:22. the wine *is spilled,*
Joh. 2:15. *poured out* the changers' money,
Acts 2:17. I *will pour out* of my Spirit
18. I *will pour out* in those days
33. he *hath shed forth* this, which
22:20. blood of thy martyr Stephen *was shed,*
Ro. 3:15. Their feet (are) swift *to shed* blood:
Tit. 3: 6. Which he *shed* on us abundantly
Rev.16: 1. *pour out* the vials of the wrath
2. *poured out* his vial upon the earth ;
3. second angel *poured out* his vial
4. third angel *poured out* his vial
6. they *have shed* the blood of saints
8. fourth angel *poured out* his vial
10. fifth angel *poured out* his vial
12. sixth angel *poured out* his vial
17. seventh angel *poured out* his vial

ἐκχύνω, ekkuno.

Mat.23:35. righteous blood *shed* upon the earth,
26:28. *which is shed* for many for
Mar.14:24. blood of the new testament, *which is shed*
for many
Lu. 5:37. will burst the bottles, and *be spilled,*
11:50. prophets, *which was shed* from the foundation
22:20. my blood, *which is shed* for you.
Acts 1:18. all his bowels *gushed out.*
10:45. on the Gentiles also *was poured out* the
gift of the Holy Ghost.
Ro. 5: 5. the love of God *is shed abroad*
Jude 11. and *ran greedily* after the error of

ἐκχωρέω, ekhōreo.

Lu. 21:21. *let* them which are in the midst of it *depart out ;*

ἐκψύχω, ekpsuko.

Acts 5: 5. fell down, and *gave up the ghost:*
10. at his feet, and *yielded up the ghost:*
12:23. eaten of worms, and *gave up the ghost.*

ἑκών, hekōn.

Ro. 8:20. subject to vanity, not willingly, (lit. not *willing*)
1Co. 9:17. if I do this thing *willingly,*

ἐλαία, elaia.

Mat.21: 1. unto the mount of *Olives,*
24: 3. he sat upon the mount of *Olives,*
26:30. went out into the mount of *Olives.*
Mar.11: 1. at the mount of *Olives,* he sendeth
13: 3. as he sat upon the mount of *Olives*
14:26. went out into the mount of *Olives.*
Lu. 19:29. called (the mount) of *Olives,*
37. the descent of the mount of *Olives,*
21:37. that is called (the mount) of *Olives.*
22:39. to the mount of *Olives;*
Joh. 8: 1. Jesus went unto the mount of *Olives.*
Ro. 11:17. root and fatness of the *olive tree;*
24. graffed into their own *olive tree?*
Jas. 3:12. fig tree, my brethren, bear *olive berries?*
Rev.11: 4. These are the two *olive trees,*

ἔλαιον, elaion.

Mat.25: 3. took no *oil* with them:
4. the wise took *oil* in their vessels
8. Give us of your *oil;* for our lamps
Mar. 6:13. anointed with *oil* many that
Lu. 7:46. My head with *oil* thou didst
10:34. pouring in *oil* and wine,
16: 6. An hundred measures of *oil.*
Heb. 1: 9. with the *oil* of gladness above
Jas. 5:14. anointing him with *oil* in the name
Rev. 6: 6. hurt not the *oil* and the wine.
18:13. wine, and *oil,* and fine flour,

ἐλαιών, elaiōn.

Acts 1:12. from the mount called *Olivet,*

ἐλάσσων, & ἐλάττων, elassōn, & elattōn.

Joh. 2:10. then that which is *worse:*
Ro. 9:12. The elder shall serve the *younger.*
1Ti. 5: 9. into the number *under* threescore years
Heb. 7: 7. the *less* is blessed of the better.

ἐλαττονέω, elattoneo.

2Co. 8:15. he that (had gathered) little *had* no *lack.*

ἐλαττόω, elattoō.

Joh. 3:30. He must increase, but I (must) *decrease.*

Heb. 2: 7. Thou *madest* him a little *lower*
9. Jesus, *who was made* a little *lower*

ἐλαύνω, elauno.

Mar 6:48. he saw them toiling in *rowing;*
Lu. 8:29. *was driven* of the devil into the
Joh. 6:19. *when* they *had rowed* about five
Jas. 3: 4. (are) *driven* of fierce winds, yet
2Pet.2:17. clouds *that are carried* with a tempest;

ἐλαφρία, elaphria.

2Co. 1:17. thus minded, did I use *lightness?*

ἐλαφρός, elaphros.

Mat.11:30. easy, and my burden is *light.*
2Co. 4:17. For our *light* affliction, which is but for a moment,

ἐλάχιστος, elakistos.

Mat. 2: 6. art not the *least* among the
5:19. one of these *least* commandments,
— he shall be called the *least* in the
25:40. the *least* of these my brethren,
45. to one of the *least* of these,
Lu. 12:26. to do that thing which is *least,*
16:10. faithful in that which is *least*
— he that is unjust in the *least*
19:17. thou hast been faithful in a *very little,*
1Co. 4: 3. with me it is a *very small* thing
6: 2. to judge the *smallest* matters?
15: 9. I am the *least* of the apostles,
Jas. 3: 4. turned about with a *very small* helm,

ἐλαχιστότερος, elakistoteros.

Eph. 3: 8. who am *less than the least* of all saints,

ἐλάω, see ἐλαύνω.

ἔλεγξις, elenxis.

2Pet.2:16. But was rebuked (lit. had *rebuke*) for his

ἔλεγχος, elenkos.

2Ti. 3:16. for doctrine, for *reproof,* for
Heb11: 1. the *evidence* of things not seen.

ἐλέγχω, elenko.

Mat.18:15. go and *tell* him his *fault* between
Lu. 3:19. *being reproved* by him for Herodias
Joh. 3:20. lest his deeds *should be reproved.*
8: 9. *being convicted* by (their own)
46. Which of you *convinceth* me of sin?
16: 8. he *will reprove* the world of sin,
1Co.14:24. unlearned, he *is convinced* of all,
Eph. 5:11. of darkness, but rather *reprove* (them).

Eph. 5:13. all things *that are reproved* are
1Ti. 5:20. Them that sin *rebuke* before all,
2Ti. 4: 2. *reprove*, rebuke, exhort with all
Tit. 1: 9. to exhort and *to convince* the gainsayers.
       13. Wherefore *rebuke* them sharply,
     2:15. *rebuke* with all authority.
Heb 12: 5. *when* thou *art rebuked* of him:
Jas. 2: 9. *and are convinced* (lit. *being convicted*) of
       the law as transgressors.
Rev. 3:19. As many as I love, I *rebuke*

ἐλεεινός, *ele-īnos*.

1Co.15:19. we are of all men most miserable. (lit.
       more miserable than all)
Rev. 3:17. thou art wretched, and *miserable*,

ἐλεέω, *eleëo*.

Mat. 5: 7. for they *shall obtain mercy*.
     9:27. son of David, *have mercy on* us.
   15:22. *Have mercy on* me, O Lord,
   17:15. Lord, *have mercy on* my son:
   18:33. Shouldest not thou also *have had compas-
       sion on* thy fellowservant, even as I *had
       pity on* thee ?
   20:30. *Have mercy on* us, O Lord,
       31. saying, *Have mercy on* us, O Lord,
Mar 5:19. and *hath had compassion on* thee.
   10:47. son of David, *have mercy on* me.
       48. son of David, *have mercy on* me.
Lu. 16:24. Father Abraham, *have mercy on* me,
   17:13. Master, *have mercy on* us.
   18:38. son of David, *have mercy on* me.
       39. son of David, *have mercy on* me.
Ro. 9:15. I will *have mercy on* whom I *will have
       mercy,*
       16. of God *that sheweth mercy*.
       18. Therefore *hath* he *mercy on* whom he will
       (have mercy)
   11:30. yet *have* now *obtained mercy*
       31. they also *may obtain mercy*.
       32. that he *might have mercy upon* all.
   12: 8. he *that sheweth mercy*, with
1Co. 7:25. as one *that hath obtained mercy*
2Co. 4: 1. as we *have received mercy*,
Phi. 2:27. God *had mercy on* him ;
1Ti. 1:13. I *obtained mercy*, because I did
       16. for this cause I *obtained mercy*,
1Pet.2:10. *which had* not *obtained mercy*, but now
       have obtained mercy.
Jude 22. *of* some *have compassion*,

ἐλεημοσύνη, *ele-eemosunee*.

Mat. 6: 1. do not your *alms* before men,
       2. Therefore when thou doest (thine) *alms*,
       3. when thou doest *alms*, let not
       4. That thine *alms* may be in secret:
Lu. 11:41. rather give *alms* of such things
   12:33. Sell that ye have, and give *alms ;*
Acts 3: 2. to ask *alms* of them that entered
       3. into the temple asked an *alms*.
      10. it was he which sat for *alms*
   9:36. full of good works and *almsdeeds*
   10: 2. gave much *alms* to the people,
       4. Thy prayers and thine *alms* are come

Acts 10:31. thine *alms* are had in remembrance
   24:17. I came to bring *alms* to my nation,

ἐλεήμων, *ele-eemōn*.

Mat. 5: 7. Blessed (are) the *merciful :* for they
Heb. 2:17. a *merciful* and faithful high priest

ἔλεος, *eleos*.

Generally neuter, but those marked [2] are masculine.

Mat. 9:13. I will have *mercy*,[2] and not sacrifice:
   12: 7. I will have *mercy*,[2] and not sacrifice,
   23:23. judgment, *mercy*,[2] and faith:
Lu. 1:50. his *mercy* (is) on them that fear him
       54. in remembrance of (his) *mercy ;*
       58. shewed great *mercy* upon her;
       72. To perform the *mercy* (promised)
       78. the tender *mercy* of our God;
   10:37. He that shewed *mercy* on him.
Ro. 9:23. glory on the vessels of *mercy*,
   11:31. that through your *mercy* they
   15: 9. might glorify God for (his) *mercy ;*
Gal. 6:16. peace (be) on them, and *mercy*,
Eph. 2: 4. God, who is rich in *mercy*,
1Ti. 1: 2. Grace, *mercy*, (and) peace, from
2Ti. 1: 2. Grace, *mercy*, (and) peace, from God
       16. The Lord give *mercy* unto the
       18. may find *mercy* of the Lord
Tit. 1: 4. Grace, *mercy*, (and) peace, from God
   3: 5. according to his *mercy*[2] he saved
Heb. 4:16. that we may obtain *mercy*,[2]
Jas. 2:13. that hath shewed no *mercy ;* and *mercy*
       rejoiceth against judgment.
   3:17. full of *mercy* and good fruits,
1Pet.1: 3. according to his abundant *mercy*
2Joh. 3. Grace be with you, *mercy*, (and) peace,
Jude 2. *Mercy* unto you, and peace, and love,
      21. the *mercy* of our Lord Jesus Christ

ἐλευθερία, *elūtheria*.

Ro. 8:21. glorious *liberty* of the children of God.
1Co.10:29. why is my *liberty* judged of
2Co. 3:17. the Lord (is), there (is) *liberty*.
Gal. 2: 4. to spy out our *liberty* which we
   5: 1. in the *liberty* wherewith Christ
      13. ye have been called unto *liberty;* only
       (use) not *liberty* for an occasion
Jas. 1:25. the perfect law of *liberty*,
   2:12. judged by the law of *liberty*.
1Pet.2:16. free, and not using (your) *liberty*
2Pet.2:19. While they promise them *liberty*,

ἐλεύθερος, *elūtheros*.

Mat.17:26. Then are the children *free*.
Joh. 8:33. sayest thou, Ye shall be made *free ?*
      36. ye shall be *free* indeed.
Ro. 6:20. ye were *free* from righteousness.
   7: 3. she is *free* from that law ;
1Co. 7:21. if thou mayest be made *free*,
      22. he that is called, (being) *free*,
      39. she is *at liberty* to be married
   9: 1. an apostle? am I not *free ?*
      19. though I be *free* from all (men),
   12:13. whether (we be) bond or *free ;*

Gal. 3:28. there is neither bond nor *free*,
    4:22. the other by a *freewoman*.
    23. he of the *freewoman* (was) by
    26. Jerusalem which is above is *free*,
    30. with the son of the *freewoman*.
    31. bondwoman, but of the *free*.
Eph. 6: 8. whether (he be) bond or *free*.
Col. 3:11. Barbarian, Scythian, bond (nor) *free* :
1Pet.2:16. As *free*, and not using (your) liberty
Rev. 6:15. every bondman, and every *free man*,
   13:16. rich and poor, *free* and bond, to receive
   19:18. all (men, both) *free* and bond,

ἐλευθερόω, *elūtheroō.*

Joh. 8:32. the truth *shall make* you *free.*
    36. the Son therefore *shall make* you *free,*
Ro. 6:18. *Being* then *made free* from sin,
    22. now *being made free* from sin,
   8: 2. *hath made* me *free* from the law
   21. *shall be delivered* from the bondage
Gal. 5: 1. wherewith Christ *hath made* us *free,*

ἔλευσις, *elūsis.*

Acts 7:52. of the *coming* of the Just One ;

ἐλεφάντινος, *elephantinos.*

Rev.18:12. all manner vessels *of ivory,*

ἑλίσσω, *helisso.*

Heb. 1:12. as a vesture *shalt* thou *fold them up,*

ἑλκύομαι, *helko-omai.*

Lu. 16:20. laid at his gate, *full of sores,*

ἕλκος, *helkos.*

Lu. 16:21. the dogs came and licked his *sores.*
Rev.16: 2. fell a noisome and grievous *sore*
    11. because of their pains and their *sores,*

ἑλκύω, *helkuo.*

Joh. 6:44. which hath sent me *draw* him :
  12:32. *will draw* all (men) unto me.
  18:10. Peter having a sword *drew* it,
   21: 6. they were not able *to draw* it
    11. Peter went up, and *drew* the net to land
Acts16:19. they caught...and *drew* (them) into

ἕλκω, *helko.*

Acts21:30. they took Paul, and *drew* him out of the
Jas. 2: 6. Do not rich men...and *draw* you before

ἐλλογέω, *ellogeo.*

Ro. 5:13. sin is not *imputed* when there
Philem 18. *put that on* mine *account ;*

ἐλπίζω, *elpizo.*

Mat.12:21. in his name *shall* the Gentiles *trust.*
Lu. 6:34. of whom ye *hope* to receive,
   23: 8. he *hoped* to have seen some miracle
   24:21. we *trusted* that it had been
Joh. 5:45. (even) Moses, in whom ye *trust.*
Acts24:26. He *hoped* also that money should
   26: 7. serving (God) day and night, *hope* to
    come.
Ro. 8:24. why doth he yet *hope for* ?
    25. if we *hope for* that we see not,
   15:12. in him *shall* the Gentiles *trust.*
    24. for I *trust* to see you in my
1Co.13: 7. believeth all things, *hopeth* all things,
   15:19. only we have hope (lit. are *hoping*) in
    Christ,
   16: 7. I *trust* to tarry a while with you,
2Co. 1:10. in whom we *trust* that he will
   13. I *trust* ye shall acknowledge
   5:11. I *trust* also are made manifest
   8: 5. not as we *hoped,* but first gave their own
    selves to the Lord,
   13: 6. I *trust* that ye shall know
Phi. 2:19. I *trust* in the Lord Jesus
   23. Him therefore I *hope* to send
1Ti. 3:14. *hoping* to come unto thee shortly:
   4:10. because we *trust* in the living God,
   5: 5. *trusteth* in God, and continueth
   6:17. nor *trust* in uncertain riches,
Philem 22. for I *trust* that through your
Heb 11: 1. substance of *things hoped for,*
1Pet.1:13. *hope* to the end for the grace
   3: 5. women also, *who trusted* in God,
2Joh. 12. I *trust* to come unto you,
3Joh. 14. I *trust* I shall shortly see thee,

ἐλπίς, *elpis.*

Acts 2:26. also my flesh shall rest in *hope:*
  16:19. the *hope* of their gains was gone,
  23: 6. of the *hope* and resurrection of the
  24:15. have *hope* toward God, which
  26: 6. for the *hope* of the promise made
    7. For which *hope's* sake, king
  27:20. all *hope* that we should be
  28:20. that for the *hope* of Israel
Ro. 4:18. Who against *hope* believed in *hope,*
   5: 2. rejoice in *hope* of the glory of God.
    4. experience ; and experience, *hope* :
    5. *hope* maketh not ashamed ;
   8:20. subjected (the same) in *hope,*
    24. we are saved by *hope:* but *hope* that is seen
    is not *hope* :
  12:12. Rejoicing in *hope ;* patient in
  15: 4. of the scriptures might have *hope.*
   13. Now the God of *hope* fill you with
   — that ye may abound in *hope,* through the
    power of the Holy Ghost.
1Co. 9:10. should plow in *hope ;* and that he that
    thresheth in *hope* should be partaker of
    his *hope.*
  13:13. now abideth faith, *hope,* charity,
2Co. 1: 7(6). our *hope* of you (is) stedfast,
   3:12. Seeing then that we have such *hope,*
  10:15. having *hope,* when your faith is
Gal. 5: 5. through the Spirit wait for the *hope* of
    righteousness by faith.
Eph. 1:18. what is the *hope* of his calling,
   2:12. having no *hope,* and without God
   4: 4. called in one *hope* of your calling ;

Phi. 1:20. earnest expectation and (my) *hope*
Col. 1: 5. the *hope* which is laid up for you
23. from the *hope* of the gospel,
27. Christ in you, the *hope* of glory:
1Th. 1: 3. and patience of *hope* in our Lord Jesus Christ,
2:19. For what (is) our *hope*, or joy,
4:13. even as others which have no *hope*.
5: 8. an helmet, the *hope* of salvation.
2Th. 2:16. consolation and good *hope* through grace,
1Ti. 1: 1. Jesus Christ, (which is) our *hope*;
Tit. 1: 2. In *hope* of eternal life, which
2:13. Looking for that blessed *hope*, and the glorious appearing
3: 7. to the *hope* of eternal life.
Heb. 3: 6. the confidence and the rejoicing of the *hope* firm unto
6:11. full assurance of *hope* unto the end:
18. upon the *hope* set before us:
7:19. bringing in of a better *hope*
10:23. the profession of (our) *faith*
1Pet.1: 3. a lively *hope* by the resurrection
21. your faith and *hope* might be in God.
3:15. a reason of the *hope* that is in you
1Joh.3: 3. every man that hath this *hope* in him purifieth himself,

---

Ἔλω, Ἔλομαι, helo, helomai.

See in αἱρέομαι.

Ἐλωΐ, Elōi.

Mar 15:34. *Eloi, Eloi*, lama sabachthani ?

ἐμαυτοῦ, -τῷ, -τὸν, emautou, -to, -ton.

Mat. 8: 9. having soldiers under *me:* (lit. *myself*)
Lu. 7: 7. neither thought I *myself* worthy
8. having under *me* soldiers,
Joh. 5:30. I can of *mine own self* do nothing:
31. If I bear witness of *myself*,
7:17. or (whether) I speak of *myself*.
28. I am not come of *myself*, but he
8:14. Though I bear record of *myself*,
18. I am one that bear witness of *myself*,
28. (that) I do nothing of *myself*;
42. neither came I of *myself*,
54. answered, If I honour *myself*,
10:18. I lay it down of *myself*.
12:32. will draw all (men) unto *me*.
49. I have not spoken of *myself*;
14: 3. again, and receive you unto *myself*;
10. I speak not of *myself:* but the
21. will manifest *myself* to him.
17:19. for their sakes I sanctify *myself*,
Acts 20:24. count I my life dear unto *myself*,
24:10. more cheerfully answer for *myself*:
26: 2. I think *myself* happy, king
9. I verily thought with *myself*,
Ro. 11: 4. I have reserved to *myself* seven
1Co. 4: 3. yea, I judge not *mine own self*.
4. For I know nothing by *myself*;
6. in a figure transferred to *myself*
7: 7. all men were even as *I myself*.
9:19. have I made *myself* servant
10:33. not seeking *mine own* profit,
2Co. 2: 1. I determined this with *myself*,
11: 7. in abasing *myself* that ye

2Co.11: 9. I have kept *myself* from being
12: 5. yet of *myself* I will not glory,
Gal. 2:18. I make *myself* a transgressor.
Phi. 3:13. I count not *myself* to have
Philem 13. Whom I would have retained with *me*,

ἐμβαίνω, embaino.

Mat. 8:23. when he *was entered* into a ship,
9: 1. he *entered into* a ship, *and* passed
13: 2. so that he *went into* a ship, *and* sat;
14:22. his disciples *to get into* a ship,
32. when they *were come into* the ship,
15:39. took ship, (lit. *entered* into a ship)
Mar. 4: 1. so that he *entered* into a ship, *and* sat
5:18. when he *was come into* the ship,
6:45. his disciples *to get into* the ship,
8:10. he *entered* into a ship with his...*and*
13. *entering* into the ship again
Lu. 5: 3. he *entered* into one of the ships, which was Simon's, *and*
8:22. that he *went into* a ship with
37. he *went up into* the ship, *and*
Joh. 5: 4. whosoever then first after...*stepped in*
6:17. *entered* into a ship, *and* went over
22. whereinto his disciples *were entered*,
24. took shipping, (lit. *entered* into ships)

ἐμβάλλω, emballo.

Lu. 12: 5. hath power *to cast into* hell;

ἐμβάπτω, embapto.

Mat.26:23. He *that dippeth* (his) hand with
Mar.14:20. *that dippeth* with me in the dish.
Joh.13:26. when he *had dipped* the sop,

ἐμβατεύω, embatŭo.

Col. 2:18. *intruding into* those things which he hath not seen,

---

ἐμβιβάζω, embibazo.

Acts27: 6. sailing into Italy; and he *put* us *therein*. (lit. *caused* us *to enter* into it)

ἐμβλέπω, emblepo.

Mat. 6:26. *Behold* the fowls of the air: for they
19:26. Jesus *beheld* (them), *and* said unto
Mar. 8:25. *saw* every man clearly.
10:21. Jesus *beholding* him loved him, and said
27. Jesus *looking upon* them
14:67. she *looked upon* him, *and* said,
Lu. 20:17. he *beheld* them, *and* said,
22:61. the Lord turned, and *looked upon* Peter.
Joh. 1:36. *looking upon* Jesus as he walked,
42(43). when Jesus *beheld* him,
Acts 1:11. why stand ye *gazing up* into heaven?
22:11. when I *could* not *see* for the glory

ἐμβριμάομαι, embrimaomai.

Mat. 9:30. Jesus *straitly charged* them,

Mar. 1:43. he *straitly charged* him, *and* forthwith
14: 5. they *murmured against* her.
Joh.11:33. *he groaned* in the spirit, and was troubled,
38. therefore again *groaning* in himself

ἐμέ, eme, from ἐγώ.

Mat.10:37. loveth father or mother more than *me*
— loveth son or daughter more than *me*
40. He that receiveth you receiveth *me*, and he
that receiveth *me*
18: 5. in my name receiveth *me*.
6. little ones which believe in *me*,
21. shall my brother sin against *me*,
26:10. hath wrought a good work upon *me*.
11. *me* ye have not always.
Mar. 9.37. in my name, receiveth *me*: and whosoever
shall receive *me*, receiveth not *me*, but
him that sent me.
42. little ones that believe in *me*,
14: 6. hath wrought a good work on *me*.
7. *me* ye have not always.
Lu. 4:18. The Spirit of the Lord (is) upon *me*,
9:48. in my name receiveth *me*: and whosoever
shall receive *me*
10:16. despiseth you despiseth *me*; and he that
despiseth *me* despiseth
22:53. stretched forth no hands against *me*:
23:28. weep not for *me*, but weep for
24:39. as ye see *me* have.
Joh. 3:30. He must increase, but *I* (must) decrease.
6:35. he that believeth on *me* shall
37. giveth me shall come to *me*;
47. He that believeth on *me* hath
57. even he shall live by *me*.
7: 7. *me* it hateth, because I testify of it,
38. He that believeth on *me*, as the
8:19. Ye neither know *me*, nor my Father:
if ye had known *me*, ye should
42. ye would love *me*:
9: 4. *I* must work the works of him
11:25. he that believeth in *me*, though
26. whosoever liveth and believeth in *me*
12: 8. *me* ye have not always.
30. This voice came not because of *me*,
44. He that believeth on *me*, believeth not on
me, but on
45. he that seeth *me* seeth him that
46. that whosoever believeth on *me*
48. He that rejecteth *me*, and receiveth not
13:18. lifted up his heel against *me*.
20. whomsoever I send receiveth *me*; and he
that receiveth *me* receiveth
14: 1. believe also in *me*.
9. he that hath seen *me* hath
12. He that believeth on *me*,
15:18. ye know that it hated *me*
20. If they have persecuted *me*,
23. He that hateth *me* hateth
24. hated both *me* and my Father.
16: 3. not known the Father, nor *me*.
9. because they believe not on *me*;
14. He shall glorify *me*: for he
23. in that day ye shall ask *me* nothing,
27. because ye have loved *me*
32. shall leave *me* alone:
17:18. As thou hast sent *me* into
20. them also which shall believe on *me* through
their word;
23. loved them, as thou hast loved *me*.
18: 8. if therefore ye seek *me*, let

Acts 3:22. of your brethren, like unto *me*;
7:37. of your brethren, like unto *me*;
8:24. ye have spoken come upon *me*.
13:25. there cometh one after *me*,
22: 6. a great light round about *me*.
26:18. inheritance among them which are sanctified by faith that is in *me*.
Ro. 1:15. So, as much as in *me* is,
10:20. of them that sought *me* not;
— them that asked not after *me*.
15: 3. that reproached thee fell on *me*
1Co. 9: 3. to them that do examine *me*
15:10. grace which (was bestowed) upon *me*
2Co. 2: 5. he hath not grieved *me*,
11:10. no man shall stop *me* of this
12: 6. lest any man should think of *me*
9. power of Christ may rest upon *me*.
Eph. 6:21. ye also may know my affairs, (lit. the
things as to *me*)
Phi. 1:12. things (which happened) unto *me* (lit.
the &c.)
2:23. see how it will go with *me*.
27. not on him only, but on *me* also,
Col. 4: 7. All *my* state (lit. the &c.) shall Tychicus
2Ti. 1: 8. nor of *me* his prisoner:
Philem 17. If thou count *me* therefore a partner, receive him as *myself*.
Rev. 1:17. laid his right hand upon *me*,

ἐμέω, emeo.

Rev. 3:16. I will *spue* thee out of my mouth.

ἐμμαίνομαι, emmainomai.

Acts26:11. *being* exceedingly *mad against* them,

ἐμμένω, emmeno.

Acts14:22. *to continue* in the faith,
Gal. 3:10. every one that *continueth* not in
Heb. 8: 9. they *continued* not in my covenant,

ἐμοί, emoi, from ἐγώ.

Mat.10:32. Whosoever therefore shall confess *me*
11: 6. shall not be offended in *me*.
18:26. Lord, have patience with *me*,
29. saying, Have patience with *me*,
25:40. ye have done (it) unto *me*.
45. ye did (it) not to *me*.
26:31. shall be offended because of *me*
Mar. 5: 7. What have *I* to do with thee,
14:27. shall be offended because of *me*
Lu. 4: 6. for that is delivered unto *me*;
7:23. shall not be offended in *me*.
8:28. What have *I* to do with thee, Jesus,
12: 8. Whosoever shall confess *me* before
15:29. yet thou never gavest *me* a kid,
22:37. must yet be accomplished in *me*,
Joh. 2: 4. what have *I* to do with thee?
5:46. ye would have believed *me*:
6:56. dwelleth in *me*, and I in him.
7:23. are ye angry at *me*, because
8:12. he that followeth *me* shall not
10:38. though ye believe not *me*,
— believe, that the Father (is) in *me*,
12:26. If any man serve *me*, let him follow *me*;
— if any man serve *me*, him

Joh.14:10. and the Father in *me*? the words
— the Father that dwelleth in *me*,
11. the Father in *me*: or else
20. in my Father, and ye in *me*,
30. cometh, and hath nothing in *me*.
15: 2. Every branch in *me* that beareth not
4. Abide in *me*, and I in you.
— except ye abide in *me*.
5. He that abideth in *me*, and I in him,
6. If a man abide not in *me*,
7. If ye abide in *me*, and my words
16:33. that in *me* ye might have peace.
17: 6. thou gavest them *me*;
21. as thou, Father, (art) in *me*,
23. I in them, and thou in *me*,
18:35. have delivered thee unto *me*:
19:10. Speakest thou not unto *me*?
Acts10:28. God hath shewed *me* that I
11:12. these six brethren accompanied *me*,
22: 9. they that were with *me* saw
24:20. found any evil doing in *me*,
26:13. them which journeyed with *me*.
28:18. there was no cause of death in *me*.
Ro. 7: 8. wrought in *me* all manner of
13. made death unto *me*?
17. sin that dwelleth in *me*.
18. For I know that in *me* that
20. sin that dwelleth in *me*.
21. when *I* would do good, evil is present
with *me*.
12:19. Vengeance (is) *mine*; (lit. to *me*)
14:11. every knee shall bow to *me*,
1Co. 4: 3. with *me* it is a very small thing
9:15. should be so done unto *me*:
14:11. (shall be) a barbarian unto *me*.
15:10. grace of God which was with *me*.
16: 4. they shall go with *me*.
2Co. 1:17. that with *me* there should be
9: 4. they of Macedonia come with *me*,
11:10. the truth of Christ is in *me*,
13: 3. a proof of Christ speaking in *me*,
Gal. 1: 2. the brethren which are with *me*,
16. To reveal his Son in *me*,
24. they glorified God in *me*.
2: 3. neither Titus, who was with *me*,
6. in conference added nothing to *me*:
8. mighty in *me* toward the Gentiles:
9. they gave to *me* and Barnabas
20. not I, but Christ liveth in *me*:
6:14. God forbid that *I* should glory, (lit. be it
not to *me* to glory)
the world is crucified unto *me*,
Eph. 3: 8. Unto *me*, who am less than the least
Phi. 1: 7. as it is meet for *me* to think this
21. For to *me* to live (is) Christ,
26. abundant in Jesus Christ for *me*
30. same conflict which ye saw in *me*, (and)
now hear (to be) in *me*.
2:16. *I* may rejoice in the day of Christ,
22. served with *me* in the gospel.
3: 1. to *me* indeed (is) not grievous,
4: 9. heard, and seen in *me*, do:
21. The brethren which are with *me*
Col. 1:29. which worketh in *me* mightily.
1Ti. 1:16. that in *me* first Jesus Christ
2Ti. 4: 8. not to *me* only, but unto all them
Philem 11. profitable to thee and to *me*:
16. a brother beloved, specially to *me*,
18. put that on mine account; (lit. on account
to *me*)
Heb 10:30. Vengeance (belongeth) unto *me*,
13: 6. The Lord (is) *my* helper, and I will

ἐμός, *emos.*

Mat.18:20. gathered together in *my* name,
20:15. do what I will with *mine own*?
23. is not *mine* to give, but (it)
25:27. received *mine own* with usury.
Mar. 8:38. ashamed of me and of *my* words
10:40. is not *mine* to give;
Lu. 9:26. ashamed of me and of *my* words,
15:31. all that I have (lit. *mine*) is thine.
22:19. this do in remembrance *of me*.
Joh. 3:29. this *my* joy therefore is fulfilled.
4:34. *My* meat is to do the will of him
5:30. I judge: and *my* judgment is just; because I seek not *mine own* will,
47. how shall ye believe *my* words?
6:38. not to do *mine own* will,
7: 6. *My* time is not yet come:
8. for *my* time is not yet full come.
16. *My* doctrine is not *mine*,
8:16. I judge, *my* judgment is true:
31. If ye continue in *my* word,
37. *my* word hath no place in you.
43. do ye not understand *my* speech? (even)
because ye cannot hear *my* word.
51. If a man keep *my* saying,
56. Abraham rejoiced to see *my* day:
10:14. know *my* (sheep), and am known of *mine*.
26. ye are not of *my* sheep,
27. *My* sheep hear my voice, and I know
12:26. there shall also *my* servant be:
13:35. that ye are *my* disciples,
14:15. keep *my* commandments.
24. word which ye hear is not *mine*,
27. *my* peace I give unto you:
15: 8. so shall ye be *my* disciples.
9. continue ye in *my* love.
11. that *my* joy might remain in you, (lit.
that *my* joy in you might remain)
12. This is *my* commandment,
16:14. for he shall receive of *mine*,
15. that the Father hath are *mine*:
— that he shall take of *mine*,
17:10. all *mine* are thine, and thine are *mine*;
13. *my* joy fulfilled in themselves.
24. they may behold *my* glory,
18:36. *My* kingdom is not of this world: if *my*
kingdom were of this world, then would
my servants fight,
— but now is *my* kingdom not from hence.
Ro. 3: 7. through *my* lie unto his glory;
10: 1. *my* heart's desire and prayer to God
1Co. 1:15. had baptized in *mine own* name.
5: 4. gathered together, and *my* spirit,
7:40. so abide, after *my* judgment:
9: 2. the seal of *mine* apostleship are
3. *Mine* answer...that do examine me
11:24. this do in remembrance *of me*.
25. new testament in *my* blood:
— in remembrance *of me*.
16:18. have refreshed *my* spirit and your's:
21. Paul with *mine own* hand.
2Co. 1:23. for a record upon *my* soul,
2: 3. that *my* joy is (the joy) of you all.
8:23. *my* partner and fellowhelper
Gal. 1:13. have heard of *my* conversation
6:11. unto you with *mine own* hand.
Phi. 1:26. by *my* coming to you again.
3: 9. not having *mine own* righteousness,
Col. 4:18. by the hand *of me* Paul.
2Th. 3:17. of Paul with *mine own* hand,
2Ti. 4: 6. the time of *my* departure is

Philem.10. I beseech thee for *my* son
    12. that is, *mine own* bowels:
    19. written (it) with *mine own* hand,
2Pet.1:15. may be able after *my* decease
3Joh.   4. that *my* children walk in truth.
Rev. 2:20. to teach and to seduce *my* servants

ἐμοῦ, emou, from ἐγώ.

Mat. 5:11. against you falsely, for *my* sake. (lit. on
      account of *me*)
    7:23. depart from *me*, ye that work
   10:18. kings for *my* sake, (lit. on account of *me*)
    39. loseth his life for *my* sake shall
   11:29. my yoke upon you, and learn of *me ;*
   12:30. He that is not with *me* is against *me;* and
      he that gathereth not with *me*
   15: 5. mightest be profited by *me ;*
    8. their heart is far from *me*.
   16:25. will lose his life for *my* sake
   17:27. give unto them for *me* and thee.
   25:41. Depart from *me*, ye cursed, into
   26:23. dippeth (his) hand with *me* in the
    38. tarry ye here, and watch with *me*.
    39. let this cup pass from *me*
    40. could ye not watch with *me* one hour?
    42. may not pass away from *me*,
Mar. 7: 6. their heart is far from *me*.
    11. thou mightest be profited by *me ;*
  8:35. shall lose his life for *my* sake and the
      gospel's, (lit. on account of *me* and)
   10:29. for *my* sake, and the gospel's,
   13: 9. before rulers and kings for *my* sake,
   14:18. One of you which eateth with *me*.
    20. that dippeth with *me* in the dish.
    36. take away this cup from *me:*
Lu. 5: 8. saying, Depart from *me ;*
   8:46. that virtue is gone out of *me*.
   9:24. will lose his life for *my* sake,
   10:16. He that heareth you heareth *me ;*
   11: 7. my children are with *me* in bed ;
    23. He that is not with *me* is against *me:* and
      he that gathereth not with *me* scattereth.
   12:13. divide the inheritance with *me*.
   13:27. depart from *me*, all (ye) workers
   15:31. Son, thou art ever with *me*,
   16: 3. my lord taketh away from *me*
   22:21. with *me* on the table.
    28. which have continued with *me*
    37. for the things concerning *me*
    42. remove this cup from *me:*
   23:43. shalt thou be with *me* in paradise.
   24:44. (in) the psalms, concerning *me*.
Joh. 4: 9. askest drink of *me*, which am
   5: 7. another steppeth down before *me*.
    32. another that beareth witness of *me;*
    — which he witnesseth of *me*
    36. that I do, bear witness of *me*
    37. hath borne witness of *me*.
    39. they are they which testify of *me*.
    46. for he wrote of *me*.
   8:18. that sent me beareth witness of *me*.
    29. he that sent me is with *me:*
   10: 8. All that ever came before *me*
    9. by *me* if any man enter in,
    18. No man taketh it from *me*,
    25. they bear witness of *me*.
   13: 8. thou hast no part with *me*.
    18. He that eateth bread with *me* hath
    38. down thy life for *my* sake? (lit. for *me*)
   14: 6. cometh unto the Father, but by *me*.

Joh.15: 5. without *me* ye can do nothing.
    26. he shall testify of *me:*
    27. ye have been with *me* from the beginning.
   16:32. because the Father is with *me*.
   17:24. be with *me* where I am ;
   18:34. did others tell it thee of *me ?*
   19:11. no power (at all) against *me*,
Acts 8:24. Pray ye to the Lord for *me*,
   11: 5. it came even to *me:*
   20:34. to them that were with *me*.
   22:18. receive thy testimony concerning *me*.
   23:11. hast testified of *me* in Jerusalem,
   25: 9. judged of these things before *me ?*
Ro. 1:12. mutual faith both of you and *me*.
   11:27. this (is) *my* covenant unto them,
   15:18. Christ hath not wrought by *me*,
    30. in (your) prayers to God for *me ;*
   16: 2. of many, and of *myself* also.
    7. also were in Christ before *me*.
    13. his mother and *mine*.
2Co. 1:19. by *me* and Silvanus and Timotheus,
   2: 2. which is made sorry by *me ?*
   7: 7. your fervent mind toward *me ;*
   12: 6. or (that) he heareth of *me*.
    8. that it might depart from *me:*
Gal. 1:11. which was preached of *me*
    17. which were apostles before *me;*
   2:20. loved me, and gave himself for *me*.
Eph. 6:19. for *me*, that utterance may
Phil. 4:10. at the last your care of *me*
2Ti. 1:13. which thou hast heard of *me*,
   2: 2. that thou hast heard of *me*
   4:11. Only Luke is with *me*.
    17. that by *me* the preaching might
Tit. 3:15. All that are with *me* salute thee.
Heb 10: 7. the book it is written of *me*,
Rev. 1:12. the voice that spake with *me*.
   3: 4. shall walk with *me* in white:
    18. I counsel thee to buy of *me* gold
    20. will sup with him, and he with *me*.
    21. to sit with *me* in my throne,
   4: 1. of a trumpet talking with *me ;*
   10: 8. spake unto *me* again, and said,
   17: 1. talked with *me*, saying unto me,
   21: 9. talked with *me*, saying, Come
    15. he that talked with *me* had
   22:12. my reward (is) with *me*, to give

ἐμπαιγμός, empaigmos.

Heb 11:36. trial of (cruel) *mockings* and scourgings,

ἐμπαίζω, empaizo.

Mat. 2:16. he *was mocked* of the wise men,
   20:19. deliver him to the Gentiles *to mock*,
   27:29. before him, and *mocked* him, saying,
    31. after that they *had mocked* him,
    41. the chief priests *mocking* (him),
Mar 10:34. they *shall mock* him, and shall
   15:20. when they *had mocked* him,
    31. also the chief priests *mocking*
Lu. 14:29. that behold (it) begin *to mock* him,
   18:32. *shall be mocked*, and spitefully
   22:63. men that held Jesus *mocked* him,
   23:11. set him at nought, and *mocked* (him),
    36. the soldiers also *mocked* him,

ἐμπαῖκται, empaiktai.

2Pet.3: 3. shall come in the last day *scoffers*,
Jude 18. should be *mockers* in the last time,

ἐμπεριπατέω, emperipateo.

2Co. 6:16. I will dwell in them, and *walk in* (them);

ἐμπιπλάω, empiplao.

Acts14:17. *filling* our hearts with food and

ἐμπίπτω, empipto.

Mat.12:11. if it *fall into* a pit on the sabbath day,
Lu. 10:36. unto him *that fell among* the thieves?
14: 5. an ass or an ox fallen into (lit. *shall fall into*) a pit,
1Ti. 3: 6. he *fall into* the condemnation
7. lest he *fall into* reproach
6: 9. *fall into* temptation and a snare,
Heb 10:31. *to fall into* the hands of the

ἐμπλέκω, empleko.

2Ti. 2: 4. *entangleth himself with* the
2Pet.2:20. they are again *entangled* therein; and

ἐμπλήθω, empleetho.

Lu. 1:53. He *hath filled* the hungry with
6:25. Woe unto you *that are full!*
Joh. 6:12. When they *were filled*, he said
Ro. 15:24. somewhat *filled* with your (company).

ἐμπλοκή, emplokee.

1Pet.3: 3. (adorning) of *plaiting* the hair,

ἐμπνέω, empneo.

Acts 9: 1. Saul, yet *breathing* out threatenings

ἐμπορεύομαι, emporŭomai.

Jas. 4:13. and *buy and sell*, and get gain:
2Pet. 2: 3. *shall* they...*make merchandise of* you:

ἐμπορία, emporia.

Mat.22: 5. another to his *merchandise*:

ἐμπορίον, emporion.

Joh. 2:16. Father's house an house of *merchandise*.

ἔμπορος, emporos.

Mat.13:45. like unto a *merchant* man,

Rev.18: 3. the *merchants* of the earth are
11. the *merchants* of the earth shall
15. The *merchants* of these things,
23. thy *merchants* were the great men

ἐμπρήθω, empreetho.

Mat.22: 7. those murderers, and *burned up* their city.

ἔμπροσθεν, emprosthen.

Mat. 5:16. Let your light so shine *before* men,
24. Leave there thy gift *before* the altar,
6: 1. do not your alms *before* men,
2. do not sound a trumpet *before* thee,
7: 6. cast ye your pearls *before* swine,
10:32. shall confess me *before* men, him will I confess also *before* my Father
33. shall deny me *before* men, him will I also deny *before* my
11:10. shall prepare thy way *before* thee.
26. it seemeth good *in* thy *sight*.
17: 2. was transfigured *before* them:
18:14. it is not the will *of* (lit. *before*) your Father
23:13(14). the kingdom of heaven *against* (lit. *before*) men:
25:32. *before* him shall be gathered all
26:70. he denied *before* (them) all,
27:11. Jesus stood *before* the governor:
29. they bowed the knee *before* him,
Mar. 1: 2. shall prepare thy way *before* thee.
9: 2. he was transfigured *before* them.
Lu. 5:19. into the midst *before* Jesus.
7:27. shall prepare thy way *before* thee.
10:21. so it seemed good *in* thy *sight*.
12: 8. shall confess me *before* men, him shall the Son of man also confess *before* the angels of God:
14: 2. there was a certain man *before* him
19: 4. he ran *before*, and climbed up
27. bring hither, and slay (them) *before* me.
28. had thus spoken, he went *before*,
21:36. to stand *before* the Son of man.
Joh. 1:15. after me is preferred *before* me:
27. coming after me is preferred *before* me,
30. a man which is preferred *before* me:
3:28. that I am sent *before* him.
10: 4. he goeth *before* them, and the sheep
12:37. done so many miracles *before* them,
Acts18:17. beat (him) *before* the judgment seat.
2Co. 5:10. all appear *before* the judgment seat
Gal. 2:14. I said unto Peter *before* (them) all,
Phi. 3:13(14). unto those things which are *before*,
1Th. 1: 3. *in the sight of* God and our Father;
2:19. *in the presence of* our Lord Jesus
3: 9. for your sakes *before* our God;
13. unblameable in holiness *before* God,
1Joh.3:19. shall assure our hearts *before* him.
Rev. 4: 6. full of eyes *before* and behind.
19:10. I fell *at* his feet to worship
22: 8. *before* the feet of the angel

ἐμπτύω, emptuo.

Mat.26:67. Then *did* they *spit* in his face,
27:30. they *spit upon* him, *and* took

Mar 10:34. scourge him, and *shall spit upon* him,
　　14:65. some began *to spit on* him,
　　15:19. *did spit upon* him, and bowing
Lu. 18:32. shall be mocked, and spitefully entreated,
　　　　and *spitted on:*

ἐμφανής, *emphanees.*

Acts10:40. shewed him *openly;* (lit. gave him to be
　　manifest)
Ro. 10:20. I was made *manifest* unto them

ἐμφανίζω, *emphanizo.*

Mat.27:53. into the holy city, and *appeared* unto
Joh.14:21. *will manifest* myself to him.
　　22. that thou wilt *manifest* thyself
Acts23:15. *signify* to the chief captain
　　22. thou *hast shewed* these things to me.
　24: 1. who *informed* the governor against Paul.
　25: 2. the Jews *informed* him against Paul,
　　15. elders of the Jews *informed* (me),
Heb 9:24. now *to appear* in the presence of
　　11:14. *declare plainly* that they seek a country.

ἔμφοβος, *emphobos.*

Lu. 24: 5. as they were *afraid,* and bowed down
　　37. they were terrified and *affrighted,*
Acts10: 4. looked on him, he was *afraid,*
　22: 9. saw indeed the light, and were *afraid;*
　24:25. Felix trembled, and (lit. becoming *afraid*)
　　answered,
Rev.11:13. the remnant were *affrighted,*

ἐμφυσάω, *emphusao.*

Joh.20:22. said this, he *breathed on* (them),

ἔμφυτος, *emphutos.*

Jas. 1:21. with meekness the *engrafted* word,

ἐν, *en.*

Mat. 1:18. she was found with child (lit. having *in*
　　the womb) of the
　　20. that which is conceived *in* her is
　　23. a virgin shall be with child, (lit. shall have
　　in the womb)
　2: 1. born *in* Bethlehem of Judæa *in* the days
　　of Herod
　　2. have seen his star *in* the east,
　　5. *In* Bethlehem of Judæa:
　　6. not the least *among* the princes
　　9. which they saw *in* the east,
　　16. children that were *in* Bethlehem, and *in*
　　all the coasts thereof,
　　18. *In* Rama was there a voice
　　19. in a dream to Joseph *in* Egypt,
　3: 1. *In* those days came John the Baptist,
　　preaching *in* the wilderness of
　　3. of one crying *in* the wilderness, Prepare
　　6. baptized of him *in* Jordan,
　　9. think not to say *within* yourselves,
　　11. I indeed baptize you *with* water

Mat. 3:11. baptize you *with* the Holy Ghost,
　　12. Whose fan (is) *in* his hand,
　　17. *in* whom I am well pleased.
　4:13. *in* the borders of Zabulon
　　16. people which sat *in* darkness
　　— *in* the region and shadow of death
　　21. *in* a ship with Zebedee their
　　23. teaching *in* their synagogues,
　　— all manner of disease *among* the people.
　5:12. for great (is) your reward *in* heaven:
　　13. where*with* shall it be salted?
　　15. unto all that are *in* the house.
　　16. your Father which is *in* heaven.
　　19. least *in* the kingdom of heaven:
　　— great *in* the kingdom of heaven.
　　25. whiles thou art *in* the way with
　　28. with her already *in* his heart.
　　34. Swear not at all; neither *by* heaven;
　　35. Nor *by* the earth; for it is his
　　36. Neither shalt thou swear *by* thy head,
　　45. your Father which is *in* heaven:
　　48. Be ye therefore perfect, even as your
　　Father which is *in* heaven
　6: 1. your Father which is *in* heaven.
　　2. *in* the synagogues and *in* the streets,
　　4. alms may be *in* secret: and thy Father
　　which seeth *in* secret himself shall
　　reward thee open*ly.* (lit. *in* open way)
　　5. *in* the synagogues and *in* the corners of
　　6. thy Father which is *in* secret; and thy
　　Father which seeth *in* secret shall reward
　　thee open*ly.*
　　7. be heard *for* their much speaking.
　　9. Our Father which art *in* heaven,
　　10. in earth as (it is) *in* heaven.
　　18. thy Father which is *in* secret: and thy
　　Father, which seeth *in* secret, shall
　　reward thee open*ly.*
　　20. for yourselves treasures *in* heaven,
　　23. the light that is *in* thee be
　　29. even Solomon *in* all his glory
　7: 2. *with* what judgment ye judge,
　　— *with* what measure ye mete,
　　3. mote that is *in* thy brother's eye,
　　— beam that is *in* thine own eye?
　　4. a beam (is) *in* thine own eye?
　　6. they trample them *under* their feet,
　　11. your Father which is *in* heaven
　　15. come to you *in* sheep's clothing,
　　21. my Father which is *in* heaven,
　　22. Many will say to me *in* that day,
　8: 6. my servant lieth *at* home sick
　　10. so great faith, no, not *in* Israel.
　　11. *in* the kingdom of heaven.
　　13. was healed *in* the selfsame hour.
　　24. there arose a great tempest *in* the sea,
　　32. into the sea, and perished *in* the waters.
　9: 3. the scribes said *within* themselves,
　　4. think ye evil *in* your hearts?
　　10. Jesus sat at meat *in* the house,
　　21. For she said *within* herself,
　　31. his fame *in* all that country.
　　33. It was never so seen *in* Israel.
　　34. *through* the prince of the devils.
　　35. teaching *in* their synagogues,
　　— every disease *among* the people.
　10:11. enquire who *in* it is worthy;
　　15. *in* the day of judgment,
　　16. as sheep *in* the midst of wolves:
　　17. will scourge you *in* their synagogues;
　　19. be given you *in* that same hour
　　20. your Father which speaketh *in* you.

Mat. 10:23. when they persecute you *in* this city,
27. What I tell you *in* darkness, (that) speak ye *in* light:
28. destroy both soul and body *in* hell.
32. shall confess)(me before men,)(him will I confess also before my Father which is *in* heaven.
33. my Father which is *in* heaven.
11: 1. to preach *in* their cities.
2. John had heard *in* the prison
6. shall not be offended *in* me.
8. A man clothed *in* soft raiment?
— soft (clothing) are *in* kings' houses.
11. *Among* them that are born of women
— he that is least *in* the kingdom
16. children sitting *in* the markets,
20. where*in* most of his mighty works
21. works, which were done *in* you, had been done *in* Tyre and Sidon, they would have repented long ago *in* sackcloth
22. *at* the day of judgment,
23. works, which have been done *in* thee, had been done *in* Sodom, it would
24. *in* the day of judgment, than for thee.
25. *At* that time Jesus answered and said,
12: 1. *At* that time Jesus went on the
2. to do *upon* the sabbath day.
5. have ye not read *in* the law,
— the priests *in* the temple profane
19. hear his voice *in* the streets.
21. *in* his name shall the Gentiles trust.
24. *by* Beelzebub the prince of the devils.
27. if I *by* Beelzebub cast out devils, *by* whom do your children cast
28. cast out devils *by* the Spirit of God,
32. neither *in* this world, neither *in* the (world) to come.
36. *in* the day of judgment.
40. three nights *in* the whale's belly;
— three nights *in* the heart of the earth.
41. shall rise *in* judgment with
42. shall rise up *in* the judgment
50. my Father which is *in* heaven,
13: 1.)(The same day went Jesus out
3. many things unto them *in* parables,
4. when he sowed, (lit. *in* his sowing)
10. speakest thou unto them *in* parables?
13. speak I to them *in* parables.
19. which was sown *in* his heart.
21. Yet hath he not root *in* himself,
24. sowed good seed *in* his field:
25. while men slept (lit. *in* men's sleeping), his enemy
27. sow good seed *in* thy field?
30. *in* the time of harvest I will say to the
31. a man took, and sowed *in* his field:
32. lodge *in* the branches thereof.
34. unto the multitude *in* parables;
35. I will open my mouth *in* parables;
40. shall it be *in* the end of this world.
43. *in* the kingdom of their Father.
44. like unto treasure hid *in* a field;
49. *at* the end of the world:
54. taught them *in* their synagogue,
57. they were offended *in* him.
— without honour, save *in* his own country, and *in* his own house.
14: 1. *At* that time Herod the tetrarch
2. do shew forth themselves *in* him.
3. put (him) *in* prison for Herodias' sake,
6. danced before them (lit. *in* the midst), and pleased Herod.

Mat. 14:10. beheaded John *in* the prison.
13. he departed thence *by* ship into
33. they that were *in* the ship came
15:32. lest they faint *in* the way.
33. so much bread *in* the wilderness,
16: 7. they reasoned *among* themselves,
8. why reason ye *among* yourselves,
17. but my Father which is *in* heaven.
19. shall be bound *in* heaven:
— shall be loosed *in* heaven.
27. For the Son of man shall come *in* the glory of his Father with
28. Son of man coming *in* his kingdom.
17: 5. This is my beloved Son, *in* whom I am well pleased;
12. have done *unto* him whatsoever
21. goeth not out but *by* prayer
22. while they abode *in* Galilee,
18: 1. *At* the same time came the
— greatest *in* the kingdom of heaven?
2. set him *in* the midst of them,
4. greatest *in* the kingdom of heaven.
6. drowned *in* the depth of the sea.
10. *in* heaven their angels do always
— my Father which is *in* heaven.
14. your Father which is *in* heaven,
18. Whatsoever ye shall bind on earth shall be bound *in* heaven:
— shall be loosed *in* heaven.
19. my Father which is *in* heaven.
20. am I *in* the midst of them.
19:21. and thou shalt have treasure *in* heaven:
28. *in* the regeneration when the Son of man shall sit in the throne
20: 3. standing idle *in* the marketplace,
15. what I will *with* mine own?
17. twelve disciples apart *in* the way,
21. on the left, *in* thy kingdom.
26. it shall not be so *among* you: but whosoever will be great *among* you,
27. whosoever will be chief *among* you,
21: 8. spread their garments *in* the way;
— strawed (them) *in* the way.
9. Blessed (is) he that cometh *in* the name of the Lord; Hosanna *in* the highest.
12. that sold and bought *in* the temple,
14. blind and the lame came to him *in* the temple;
15. children crying *in* the temple,
19. came to it, and found nothing there*on*,
22. whatsoever ye shall ask *in* prayer
23. *By* what authority doest thou these
24. will tell you *by* what authority
27. Neither tell I you *by* what authority
28. work to day *in* my vineyard.
32. *in* the way of righteousness,
33. digged a winepress *in* it, and built
38. they said *among* themselves,
41. render him the fruits *in* their seasons.
42. Did ye never read *in* the scriptures,
— it is marvellous *in* our eyes?
22: 1. spake unto them again *by* parables,
15. might entangle him *in* (his) talk.
16. teachest the way of God *in* truth,
23.)(The same day came to him the
28. Therefore *in* the resurrection
30. For *in* the resurrection they neither
— as the angels of God *in* heaven.
36. the great commandment *in* the law?
37. *with* all thy heart, and *with* all thy soul, and *with* all thy mind.
40. *On* these two commandments

Mat.22:43. How then doth David *in* spirit call
23: 6. the uppermost rooms *at* feasts, and the
    chief seats *in* the synagogues,
  7. greetings *in* the markets, and to be
  9. your Father, which is *in* heaven.
 16. Whosoever shall swear *by* the temple,
 — whosoever shall swear *by* the gold
 18. Whosoever shall swear *by* the altar,
 — whosoever sweareth *by* the gift
 20. shall swear *by* the altar, sweareth *by* it,
    and *by* all
 21. whoso shall swear *by* the temple, sweareth
    by it, and *by* him
 22. he that shall swear *by* heaven, sweareth *by*
    the throne of God, and *by* him
 30. If we had been *in* the days
 — *in* the blood of the prophets.
 34. scourge *in* your synagogues,
 39. shall say, Blessed (is) he that cometh *in*
    the name of the Lord.
24:14. be preached *in* all the world
 15. stand *in* the holy place,
 16. let them which be *in* Judæa
 18. let him which is *in* the field
 19. woe unto them that are with child (lit.
    have *in* the womb),and to them that give
    suck *in* those days !
 20. neither *on* the sabbath day:
 26. Behold, he is *in* the desert ;
 — (he is) *in* the secret chambers;
 30. And then shall appear the sign of the Son
    of man *in* heaven:
 38. For as *in* the days that were before the
    flood they
 40. Then shall two be *in* the field ;
 41. (shall be) grinding *at* the mill ;
 45. to give them meat *in* due season ?
 48. evil servant shall say *in* his heart,
 50. The lord of that servant shall come *in* a
    day when he looketh not for (him), and
    in an hour
25: 4. the wise took oil *in* their vessels
 13. where*in* the Son of man cometh
 16. went and traded *with* the same,
 18. went and digged *in* the earth,
 25. went and hid thy talent *in* the earth:
 31. When the Son of man shall come *in* his
    glory, and all the
 36. I was *in* prison, and ye came unto me.
 39. when saw we thee sick, or *in* prison,
 43. sick, and *in* prison, and ye visited me not.
 44. or naked, or sick, or *in* prison,
26: 5. they said, Not *on* the feast (day), lest there
    be an uproar *among* the people.
 6. when Jesus was *in* Bethany, *in* the house
    of Simon
 13. be preached *in* the whole world,
 23. (his) hand with me *in* the dish.
 29. with you *in* my Father's kingdom.
 31. All ye shall be offended *because of* me
)(this night:
 33. shall be offended *because of* thee, (lit. *in*
    thee)
 34. That)(this night, before the cock crow,
 52. shall perish *with* the sword.
 55. *In* that same hour said Jesus
 — with you teaching *in* the temple,
 69. Peter sat without *in* the palace:
27: 5. the pieces of silver *in* the temple,
 12. when he was accused (lit. *in* his being
    acc.) of the chief priests
 40. buildest (it) *in* three days,

Mat.27:56. *Among* which was Mary Magdalene,
 60. laid it *in* his own new tomb, which he had
    hewn out *in* the rock:
28:18. power is given unto me *in* heaven and in
Mar. 1: 2. As it is written *in* the prophets,
 3. voice of one crying *in* the wilderness,
 4. John did baptize *in* the wilderness,
 5. *in* the river of Jordan,
 8. have baptized you *with* water:
 — baptize you *with* the Holy Ghost.
 9. it came to pass *in* those days,
 11. *in* whom I am well pleased.
 13. he was there *in* the wilderness
 15. repent ye, and believe)(the gospel.
 16. casting a net *into* the sea:
 19. *in* the ship mending their nets.
 20. *in* the ship with the hired
 23. there was *in* their synagogue a man *with*
    an unclean spirit ;
 39. he preached *in* their synagogues
 45. was without *in* desert places:
2: 6. reasoning *in* their hearts,
 8. they so reasoned *within* themselves,
 — reason ye these things *in* your hearts?
 15. it came to pass, that, as Jesus sat (lit. *in*
    his sitting) at meat *in* his house,
 19. while (lit. *in* which time) the bridegroom
    is with
 20. then shall they fast *in* those days.
 23. through the corn fields *on* the sabbath day;
 24. why do they *on* the sabbath day
3:22. *by* the prince of the devils casteth
 23. said unto them *in* parables,
4: 1. entered into a ship, and sat *in* the sea;
 2. taught them many things *by* parables,
    and said unto them *in* his doctrine,
 4. it came to pass, as he sowed, (lit. *in*
    sowing)
 11. things are done *in* parables:
 15. that was sown *in* their hearts.
 17. have no root *in* themselves,
 24. *with* what measure ye mete,
 28. after that the full corn *in* the ear.
 30. or *with* what comparison shall
 35. And)(the same day, when
 36. even as he was *in* the ship.
5: 2. a man *with* an unclean spirit,
 3. had (his) dwelling *among* the tombs ;
 5. he was *in* the mountains, and *in*
 13. were choked *in* the sea.
 20. began to publish *in* Decapolis
 21. was passed over again *by* ship
 25. which had (lit. being *in*) an issue of blood
 27. came *in* the press behind,
 30. immediately knowing *in* himself
 — turned him about *in* the press,
6: 2. to teach *in* the synagogue:
 3. they were offended *at* him.
 4. *in* his own country, and *among* his own
    kin, and *in* his own house.
 11. *in* the day of judgment,
 14. do shew forth themselves *in* him.
 17. upon John, and bound him *in* prison
 27(28). beheaded him *in* the prison,
 29. his corpse, and laid it *in* a tomb.
 47. ship was *in* the midst of the sea,
 48. he saw them toiling *in* rowing ;
 51. were sore amazed *in* themselves
 56. they laid the sick *in* the streets,
8: 1. *In* those days the multitude
 3. they will faint *by* the way:
 14. neither had they *in* the ship

Mar. 8:26. nor tell (it) to any *in* the town.
27. *by* the way he asked his disciples,
38. *in* this adulterous and sinful generation ;
— cometh *in* the glory of his Father
9: 1. kingdom of God come *with* power.
29. come forth *by* nothing, but *by* prayer
33. being *in* the house he asked them,
— disputed among yourselves *by* the way?
34. *by* the way they had disputed
36. set him *in* the midst of them:
41. water to drink *in* my name,
50. where*with* will ye season it? Have salt *in* yourselves, and have peace one with an-other. (lit. *in* one another)
10:10. *in* the house his disciples asked
21. thou shalt have treasure *in* heaven:
30. hundredfold now *in* this time,
— in the world to come eternal life.
32. they were *in* the way going up
37. on thy left hand, *in* thy glory.
43. so shall it not be *among* you: but whoso-ever will be great *among* you,
52. followed Jesus *in* the way.
11: 9. cometh *in* the name of the Lord:
10. cometh *in* the name of the Lord: Hosanna *in* the highest.
13. he might find any thing there*on:*
15. that sold and bought *in* the temple,
23. shall not doubt *in* his heart,
25. your Father also which is *in* heaven
26. your Father which is *in* heaven
27. as he was walking *in* the temple,
28. *By* what authority doest thou
29. I will tell you *by* what authority
33. *by* what authority I do these things.
12: 1. to speak unto them *by* parables.
11. it is marvellous *in* our eyes ?
23. *In* the resurrection therefore,
25. as the angels which are *in* heaven.
26. not read *in* the book of Moses,
35. while he taught *in* the temple,
36. himself said *by* the Holy Ghost,
38. said unto them *in* his doctrine,
— which love to go *in* long clothing, and (love) salutations *in* the marketplaces,
39. chief seats *in* the synagogues, and the uppermost rooms *at* feasts:
13:11. shall be given you *in* that hour,
14. let them that be *in* Judæa flee
17. woe to them that are with child (lit. have *in* the womb), and to them that give suck *in* those days !
24. *in* those days, after that tribulation,
25. the powers that are *in* heaven
26. Son of man coming *in* the clouds
32. not the angels which are *in* heaven,
14: 1. might take him *by* craft,
2. they said, Not *on* the feast (day)
3. being *in* Bethany *in* the house
25. new *in* the kingdom of God.
27. offended *because of* (lit. *in*) me)(this night:
30. this day, (even) *in* this night,
49. I was daily with you *in* the temple
66. Peter was beneath *in* the palace,
15: 7. committed murder *in* the insurrection.
29. buildest (it) *in* three days,
40. *among* whom was Mary
41. Who also, when he was *in* Galilee,
46. laid him *in* a sepulchre
16: 5. a young man sitting *on* the right side,
12. he appeared *in* another form

Mar.16:17. *In* my name shall they cast
Lu. 1: 1. are most surely believed *among* us,
5. *in* the days of Herod, the king
6. walking *in* all the commandments
7. were.(now) well stricken *in* years.
8. that while he executed the priest's office (lit. *in* his executing, &c,) before God *in* the order of his course,
17. *in* the spirit and power of Elias,
— disobedient *to* the wisdom of the just ;
18. my wife well stricken *in* years.
21. that he tarried (lit. *at* his tarrying) so long *in* the temple.
22. had seen a vision *in* the temple:
25. *in* the days wherein he looked on (me), to
— take away my reproach *among* men.
26. *in* the sixth month the angel
28. blessed (art) thou *among* women,
31. thou shalt conceive *in* thy womb,
36. conceived a son *in* her old age:
39. Mary arose *in* those days,
41. the babe leaped *in* her womb ;
42. Blessed (art) thou *among* women,
44. the babe leaped *in* my womb *for* joy.
51. hath shewed strength *with* his arm ;
59. that *on* the eighth day they came
61. There is none *of* thy-kindred that
65. *throughout* all the hill country
66. laid (them) up *in* their hearts,
69. *in* the house of his servant David ;
75. *In* holiness and righteousness before
77. *by* the remission of their sins,
78. where*by* the dayspring from on
79. to them that sit *in* darkness
80. was *in* the deserts till the day
2: 1. it came to pass *in* those days,
6. while they were (lit. *in* their being) there,
7. laid him *in* a manger ; because there was no room for them *in* the inn.
8. there were *in* the same country
11. this day *in* the city of David a Saviour,
12. lying *in* a manger.
14. Glory to God *in* the highest,
— peace, good will *toward* men.
16. the babe lying *in* a manger.
19. pondered (them) *in* her heart.
21. he was conceived *in* the womb.
23. written *in* the law of the Lord,
24. is said *in* the law of the Lord,
25. there was a man *in* Jerusalem,
27. he came *by* the Spirit into
— when the parents brought in (lit. *on the* parents bringing in) the child Jesus,
29. thy servant depart *in* peace,
34. rising again of many *in* Israel ;
36. she was of a great (lit. advanced *in*) age,
38. looked for redemption *in* Jerusalem.
43. as they returned (lit. *in* their ret.), the child Jesus tarried behind *in* Jerusalem ;
44. to have been *in* the company,
— *among* (their) kinsfolk and)(acquaint-ance.
46. *in* the temple, sitting *in* the midst
49. I must be *about* my Father's business ?
51. kept all these sayings *in* her heart.
3: 1. Now *in* the fifteenth year of the
2. of Zacharias *in* the wilderness.
4. As it is written *in* the book of the
— one crying *in* the wilderness,
8. begin not to say *within* yourselves,
15. all men mused *in* their hearts
16. *with* the Holy Ghost and with fire:

Lu. 3:17. Whose fan (is) *in* his hand,
20. that he shut up John *in* prison.
21. when all the people were baptized, (lit. *in* all, &c. being baptized)
22. *in* thee I am well pleased.
4: 1. was led *by* the Spirit into the
2. *in* those days he did eat nothing:
5. the world *in* a moment of time.
14. Jesus returned *in* the power of the
15. he taught *in* their synagogues,
16. *on* the sabbath day, and stood
18(19). to set *at* liberty them that are
20. that were *in* the synagogue
21. this scripture fulfilled *in* your ears.
23. have heard done *in* Capernaum, do also here *in* thy country.
24. accepted *in* his own country.
25. many widows were *in* Israel *in* the days of Elias,
27. many lepers were *in* Israel
28. all they *in* the synagogue,
31. taught them *on* the sabbath days.
32. for his word was *with* power.
33. *in* the synagogue there was a man,
36. for *with* authority and power
44. he preached *in* the synagogues
5: 1. it came to pass, that, as the people pressed (lit. *in* the p. pressing)
7. which were *in* the other ship,
12. came to pass, when he was (lit. *in* his being) *in* a certain city,
16. withdrew himself *into* the wilderness,
17. came to pass *on* a certain day,
22. What reason ye *in* your hearts?
29. a great feast *in* his own house:
34. while (lit. *in* which time) the bridegroom is with them?
35. shall they fast *in* those days.
6: 1. came to pass *on* the second sabbath
2. to do *on* the sabbath days?
6. came to pass also *on* another
7. would heal *on* the sabbath day;
12. came to pass *in* those days,
— continued all night *in* prayer
23. Rejoice ye *in* that day, and leap
— your reward (is) great *in* heaven:
41. mote that is *in* thy brother's eye,
— beam that is *in* thine own eye?
42. the mote that is *in* thine eye,
— beam that is *in* thine own eye?
— mote that is *in* thy brother's eye.
7: 9. so great faith, no, not *in* Israel.
11. it came to pass)(the day after,
16. prophet is risen up *among* us;
17. went forth *throughout* all Judæa, and *throughout* all the region round
21. *in* the same hour he cured many
23. shall not be offended *in* me.
25. A man clothed in soft raiment?
— which are gorgeously apparelled (lit. *in* gorgeous apparel), and live delicately, are *in* kings' courts.
28. *Among* those that are born of women
— least *in* the kingdom of God
32. sitting *in* the marketplace,
37. behold, a woman *in* the city,
— sat at meat *in* the Pharisee's house,
39. he spake *within* himself, saying,
49. began to say *within* themselves,
8: 1. it came to pass afterward, (lit. *in* after time)
5. as he sowed (lit. *in* his sowing), some fell

Lu. 8: 7. some fell *among* thorns; and the
10. to others *in* parables; that seeing
13. *in* time of temptation fall away.
15. that *on* the good ground are they, which *in* an honest and good heart, having
— bring forth fruit *with* patience.
22. came to pass *on* a certain day,
27. neither abode *in* (any) house, but *in* the tombs.
32. swine feeding *on* the mountain:
40. came to pass, that, when Jesus was returned, (lit. *on* Jesus's having returned)
42. as he went (lit. *in* his going) the people thronged
43. having (lit. being *in*))(an issue of blood
9:12. we are here *in* a desert place.
18. as he was alone (lit. *in* his being alone)
26. he shall come *in* his own glory,
29. as he prayed, (lit. *in* his praying)
31. Who appeared *in* glory, and spake
— should accomplish *at* Jerusalem.
33. came to pass, as they departed (lit. *in* their departure)
34. they feared as they entered (lit. *in* their entering)
36. when the voice was past, (lit. *in* the &c.)
— told no man *in* those days
37. came to pass, that *on* the next
46. arose a reasoning *among* them,
48. that is least *among* you all,
51. came to pass, when the time was come (lit. *in* the, &c.)
57. as they went *in* the way,
10: 3. forth as lambs *among* wolves.
7. *in* the same house remain,
9. heal the sick that are ther*ein*,
12. more tolerable *in* that day for
13. had been done *in* Tyre and Sidon, which have been done *in* you, they had...repented, sitting *in* sackcloth and
14. Tyre and Sidon *at* the judgment,
17. subject unto us *through* thy name.
20. *in* this rejoice not, that the spirits
— your names are written *in* heaven.
21. *In* that hour Jesus rejoiced in spirit,
26. What is written *in* the law?
31. came down a certain priest)(that way:
35. when I come again (lit. *in* my coming again), I will repay thee.
38. it came to pass, as they went, (lit. *in* their going)
11: 1. that, as he was praying (lit. *in* his being praying) *in* a certain place,
2. Our Father which art *in* heaven,
— Thy will be done, as *in* heaven,
15. *through* Beelzebub the chief of the
18. I cast out devils *through* Beelzebub.
19. if I *by* Beelzebub cast out devils, *by* whom do your sons cast (them)
20. if I *with* the finger of God cast
21. his goods are *in* peace:
27. it came to pass, as he spake (lit. *in* his, &c.)
31. shall rise up *in* the judgment
32. shall rise up *in* the judgment
35. the light which is *in* thee be not
37. as he spake (lit. *in* his, &c.), a certain
43. uppermost seats *in* the synagogues, and greetings *in* the markets.
12: 1. *In* the mean time, when there
3. ye have spoken *in* darkness shall be heard *in* the light;
— have spoken in the ear *in* closets

Lu. 12: 8. Whosoever shall confess)(me before men,)(him shall the Son of man

12. shall teach you *in* the same hour

15. not *in* the abundance of the

17. he thought *within* himself,

27. Solomon *in* all his glory was

28. which is to day *in* the field,

33. a treasure *in* the heavens

38. shall come *in* the second watch, or come *in* the third

42. portion of meat *in* due season?

45. if that servant say *in* his heart,

46. will come *in* a day when...and *at* an hour

51. come to give peace *on* earth?

52. there shall be five *in* one house

58. (as thou art) *in* the way, give

13: 1. There were present *at* that season

4. the tower *in* Siloam fell,

— men that dwelt *in* Jerusalem?

6. a fig tree planted *in* his vineyard; and he came and sought fruit there*on*,

7. seeking fruit *on* this fig tree,

10. teaching *in* one of the synagogues *on* the sabbath.

14. six days *in* which men ought to work: *in* them therefore come

19. lodged *in* the branches of it.

26. thou hast taught *in* our streets.

28. prophets, *in* the kingdom of God,

29. sit down *in* the kingdom of God.

31.)(The same day there came certain

35. cometh *in* the name of the Lord.

14: 1. it came to pass, as he went (lit. *in* his going) into

5. pull him out *on* the sabbath day?

14. *at* the resurrection of the just.

15. *in* the kingdom of God.

31. be able *with* ten thousand

34. where*with* shall it be seasoned?

15: 4. the ninety and nine *in* the wilderness,

7. likewise joy shall be *in* heaven

25. his elder son was *in* the field:

16: 3. the steward said *within* himself,

10. faithful *in* that which is least is faithful also *in* much: and he that is unjust *in* the least is unjust also *in* much.

11. *in* the unrighteous mammon,

12. have not been faithful *in* that which is

15. highly esteemed *among* men

23. *in* hell he lift up his eyes, being *in* torments, and seeth Abraham afar off, and Lazarus *in* his bosom.

24. I am tormented *in* this flame.

25. remember that thou *in* thy lifetime

17: 6. be thou planted *in* the sea;

11. came to pass, as he went (lit. *in* his &c.)

14. pass, that, as they went, (lit. *in* their &c.)

24. the Son of man be *in* his day.

26. as it was *in* the days of Noe,

— *in* the days of the Son of man.

28. as it was *in* the days of Lot;

31. *In* that day, he which shall

— his stuff *in* the house,

— he that is *in* the field, let him

36. Two (men) shall be *in* the field;

18: 2. There was *in* a city a judge,

3. there was a widow *in* that city;

4. afterward he said *within* himself,

8. he will avenge them speedi*ly*.

22. thou shalt have treasure *in* heaven:

30. more *in* this present time, and *in* the world to come

Lu. 18:35. it came to pass, that as he was come nigh (lit. *in* his coming nigh)

19: 5. I must abide *at* thy house

15. it came to pass, that when he was returned, (lit. *on* his returning)

17. hast been faithful *in* a very little,

20. have kept laid up *in* a napkin:

30. *in* the which at your entering

36. spread their clothes *in* the way.

38. cometh *in* the name of the Lord: peace *in* heaven, and glory *in* the highest.

42. at least *in* this thy day,

44. thy children *within* thee; and they shall not leave *in* thee

45. cast out them that sold there*in*,

47. he taught daily *in* the temple.

20: 1. (that) *on* one of those days, as he taught the people *in* the temple,

2. *by* what authority doest thou

8. *by* what authority I do these

10. *at* the season he sent a servant

19. and the scribes)(the same hour sought

33. Therefore *in* the resurrection whose

42. saith *in* the book of Psalms,

46. desire to walk *in* long robes, and love greetings *in* the markets, and the highest seats *in* the synagogues, and the chief rooms *at* feasts;

21: 6. *in* the which there shall not be

19. *In* your patience possess ye your

21. them which are *in* Judæa flee

— them which are *in* the midst of it

— them that are *in* the countries

23. unto them that are with child (lit. have *in* the womb), and to them that give suck, *in* those days!

— wrath *upon* this people.

25. shall be signs *in* the sun, and

— distress of nations, *with* perplexity;

27. coming *in* a cloud with power

34. be overcharged *with* surfeiting,

36. Watch ye therefore, and pray always, (lit. *at* all times)

37. he was teaching *in* the temple;

38. to him *in* the temple, for to hear

22: 7. when (lit. *in* which) the passover must be killed.

16. fulfilled *in* the kingdom of God.

20. new testament *in* my blood,

24. was also a strife *among* them,

26. he that is greatest *among* you,

27. I am *among* (lit. *in* the midst of) you as he that serveth.

28. with me *in* my temptations.

30. at my table *in* my kingdom,

37. must yet be accomplished *in* me,

44. being *in* an agony he prayed

49. shall we smite *with* the sword?

53. daily with you *in* the temple,

55. a fire *in* the midst of the hall,

— Peter sat down *among* (lit. *in* the midst of) them.

23: 4. I find no fault *in* this man.

7. was *at* Jerusalem *at* that time.

9. questioned with him *in* many words;

12. And)(the same day Pilate and Herod were made friends together: for before they were *at* enmity

14. found no fault *in* this man

19. sedition made *in* the city,

22. found no cause of death *in* him:

29. *in* the which they shall say,

Lu. 23:31. do these things *in* a green tree, what shall
be done *in* the dry?
40. art *in* the same condemnation?
42. thou comest into (lit. *in*) thy kingdom.
43. shalt thou be with me *in* paradise.
53. laid it *in* a sepulchre that was hewn
24: 4. it came to pass, as they were much perplexed (lit. *in* their being per.)
— stood by them *in* shining garments:
6. when he was yet *in* Galilee,
13. went)(that same day to a village
15. it came to pass, that, while they communed
(lit. *in* their c.)
18. thou only a stranger *in* Jerusalem,
— come to pass there (lit. *in* it) *in* these
days ?
19. a prophet mighty *in* deed and word
27. unto them *in* all the scriptures
30. it came to pass, as he sat (lit. *in* his
sitting) at meat
32. our heart burn *within* us, while he talked
with us *by* the way,
35. things (were done) *in* the way,
— of them *in* breaking of bread.
36. stood *in* the midst of them,
38. do thoughts arise *in* your hearts?
44. written *in* the law of Moses,
49. tarry ye *in* the city of Jerusalem,
51. came to pass, while he blessed (lit. *in* his
blessing) them,
53. were continually *in* the temple,
Joh. 1: 1. *In* the beginning was the Word,
2. The same was *in* the beginning
4. *In* him was life ; and the life
5. the light shineth *in* darkness ;
10. He was *in* the world, and the
14. was made flesh, and dwelt *among* us,
23. of one crying *in* the wilderness,
26. saying, I baptize *with* water:
28. These things were done *in* Bethabara
31. I come baptizing *with* water.
33. sent me to baptize *with* water,
— baptizeth *with* the Holy Ghost.
45(46). of whom Moses *in* the law,
47(48). *in* whom is no guile !
2: 1. a marriage *in* Cana of Galilee;
11. did Jesus *in* Cana of Galilee,
14. found *in* the temple those
19. *in* three days I will raise it up.
20. thou rear it up *in* three days?
23. when he was *in* Jerusalem *at* the passover,
in the feast
25. for he knew what was *in* man.
3:13. Son of man which is *in* heaven.
14. the serpent *in* the wilderness,
21. that they are wrought *in* God.
23. also was baptizing *in* Ænon
35. given all things *into* his hand.
4:14. shall be *in* him a well of water
20. Our fathers worshipped *in* this
— that *in* Jerusalem is the place
21. neither *in* this mountain, nor yet *at*
Jerusalem,
23. worship the Father *in* spirit and
24. worship (him) *in* spirit and in truth.
31. *In* the mean while his disciples
37. here*in* is that saying true,
44. no honour *in* his own country.
45. he did *at* Jerusalem *at* the feast:
46. whose son was sick *at* Capernaum.
52. the hour when (lit. *in* which) he began
to amend.

Joh. 4:53. *at* the same hour, *in* the which
5: 2. Now there is *at* Jerusalem
3. *In* these lay a great multitude
4. at a certain season *into* the pool,
5. had an infirmity (lit. having *in* infirmity)
thirty and eight years.
7. while (lit. *in* which time) I am coming,
9. and *on* the same day was the sabbath.
13. a multitude being *in* (that) place.
14. Jesus findeth him *in* the temple,
16. had done these things *on* the sabbath day.
26. the Father hath life *in* himself ;
— the Son to have life *in* himself ;
28. *in* the which all that are *in* the
35. a season to rejoice *in* his light.
38. his word abiding *in* you:
39. *in* them ye think ye have eternal
42. have not the love of God *in* you.
43. I am come *in* my Father's name,
— shall come *in* his own name,
6:10. there was much grass *in* the place.
31. did eat manna *in* the desert ;
39. raise it up again *at* the last day.
45. It is written *in* the prophets,
49. did eat manna *in* the wilderness,
53. ye have no life *in* you.
56. dwelleth *in* me, and I *in* him.
59. *in* the synagogue, as he taught *in*
61. When Jesus knew *in* himself
7: 1. Jesus walked *in* Galilee: for he would not
walk *in* Jewry,
4. doeth any thing *in* secret,
— seeketh to be known open*ly.*
9. he abode (still) *in* Galilee.
10. as it were *in* secret.
11. Jews sought him *at* the feast,
12. murmuring *among* the people
18. no unrighteousness is *in* him.
22. ye *on* the sabbath day circumcise
23. If a man *on* the sabbath day
— whole *on* the sabbath day ?
28. Then cried Jesus *in* the temple
37. *In* the last day, that great (day)
43. was a division *among* the people
8: 3. a woman taken *in* adultery ; and when
they had set her *in* the midst,
5. Moses *in* the law commanded
9. the woman standing *in* the midst.
12. shall not walk *in* darkness,
17. It is also written *in* your law,
20. spake Jesus *in* the treasury, as he taught
in the temple:
21. shall die *in* your sins:
24. die *in* your sins: for if ye believe not that
I am (he), ye shall die *in* your sins.
31. If ye continue *in* my word,
35. servant abideth not *in* the house
37. my word hath no place *in* you.
44. abode not *in* the truth, because there is
no truth *in* him.
9: 3. be made manifest *in* him.
5. As long as I am *in* the world,
16. there was a division *among* them.
30. Why here*in* is a marvellous thing,
34. wast altogether born *in* sins,
10:19. again *among* the Jews for these
22. it was *at* Jerusalem the feast
23. *in* the temple *in* Solomon's porch.
25. that I do *in* my Father's name,
34. Is it not written *in* your law,
38. that the Father (is) *in* me, and I *in* him.
11: 6. two days still *in* the same place

Joh. 11: 9. If any man walk *in* the day,
10. if a man walk *in* the night,
— because there is no light *in* him.
17. *in* the grave four days already.
20. Mary sat (still) *in* the house.
24. *in* the resurrection *at* the last day.
30. was *in* that place where
31. were with her *in* the house,
38. again groaning *in* himself
54. no more openly *among* the Jews ;
56. as they stood *in* the temple,
12: 13. cometh *in* the name of the Lord.
20. came up to worship *at* the feast:
25. hateth his life *in* this world
35. he that walketh *in* darkness
46. should not abide *in* darkness.
48. shall judge him *in* the last day.
13: 1. his own which were *in* the world,
23. there was leaning *on* Jesus' bosom
31. God is glorified *in* him.
32. If God be glorified *in* him, God shall also glorify him *in* himself,
35. *By* this shall all (men) know
— if ye have love one *to* another.
14: 2. *In* my Father's house are
10. that I am *in* the Father, and the Father *in* me?
— the Father that dwelleth *in* me,
11. I (am) *in* the Father, and the Father *in* me:
13. ye shall ask *in* my name,
— Father may be glorified *in* the Son.
14. ask any thing *in* my name,
17. dwelleth with you, and shall be *in* you.
20. *At* that day ye shall know that I (am) *in* my Father, and ye *in* me, and I *in* you.
26. Father will send *in* my name,
30. cometh, and hath nothing *in* me.
15: 2. Every branch *in* me that
4. Abide *in* me, and I *in* you.
— except it abide *in* the vine ;
— except ye abide *in* me.
5. He that abideth *in* me, and I *in* him,
6. If a man abide not *in* me,
7. If ye abide *in* me, and my words abide *in* you, ye
8. Here*in* is my Father glorified,
9. continue ye *in* my love.
10. ye shall abide *in* my love ;
— abide *in* his love
11. my joy might remain *in* you,
16. ask of the Father *in* my name,
24. If I had not done *among* them
25. that is written *in* their law,
16: 23. *in* that day ye shall ask me
— ask the Father *in* my name,
24. ye asked nothing *in* my name:
25. have I spoken unto you *in* proverbs:
— no more speak unto you *in* proverbs,
26. *At* that day ye shall ask *in* my
30. *by* this we believe that thou
33. *in* me ye might have peace. *In* the world ye shall have tribulation:
17: 10. I am glorified *in* them.
11. I am no more *in* the world, but these are *in* the world,
— keep *through* thine own name
12. I was with them *in* the world, I kept them *in* thy name:
13. these things I speak *in* the world,
— my joy fulfilled *in* themselves.
17. Sanctify them *through* thy truth:

Joh. 17: 19. be sanctified *through* the truth.
21. thou, Father, (art) *in* me, and I *in* thee, that they also may be one *in* us:
23. I *in* them, and thou *in* me,
26. may be *in* them, and I *in* them.
18: 20. *in* the synagogue, and *in* the temple,
— *in* secret have I said nothing.
26. thee *in* the garden with him ?
38. I find *in* him no fault (at all).
39. release unto you one *at* the passover:
19: 4. that I find no fault *in* him.
6. for I find no fault *in* him.
31. upon the cross *on* the sabbath day,
41. Now *in* the place where he was
— *in* the garden a new sepulchre, where*in* was never man yet laid.
20: 12. seeth two angels *in* white sitting,
25. Except I shall see *in* his hands
30. are not written *in* this book:
31. have life *through* his name.
21: 3. and)(that night they caught nothing.
20. leaned on his breast *at* supper,
Acts 1: 3. *by* many infallible proofs,
5. baptized *with* the Holy Ghost
6. wilt thou *at* this time restore
7. hath put *in* his own power.
8. *in* Jerusalem, and *in* all Judæa,
10. stood by them *in* white apparel ;
15. *in* those days Peter stood up *in* the midst of the disciples,
20. written *in* the book of Psalms,
— let no man dwell there*in*:
21. all the time that (lit. *in* all the time *in* which) the Lord Jesus
2: 1. when the day of Pentecost was fully come, (lit. *in* the day of P. being fully come)
5. were dwelling *at* Jerusalem
8. where*in* we were born ?
17. come to pass *in* the last days,
18. I will pour out *in* those days
19. shew wonders *in* heaven above,
22. by him *in* the midst of you,
29. his sepulchre is *with* us unto
46. with one accord *in* the temple,
— did eat their meat *with* gladness
3: 6. *In* the name of Jesus Christ
26. *in* turning away every one of you
4: 2. *through* Jesus the resurrection
7. had set them *in* the midst, they asked, *By* what power, or *by* what name,
9. *by* what means he is made whole;
10. *by* the name of Jesus Christ of
— *by* him doth this man stand
12. is there salvation *in* any other:
— given *among* men, where*by* we
24. the sea, and all that *in* them is:
30. *By* stretching forth thine hand
31. where (lit. *in* which) they were assembled together;
34. any *among* them that lacked:
5: 4. was it not *in* thine own power ?
— this thing *in* thine heart ?
12. wrought *among* the people;
— one accord *in* Solomon's porch.
18. put them *in* the common prison.
20. stand and speak *in* the temple,
22. found them not *in* the prison,
23. shut *with* all safety,
25. whom ye put *in* prison are standing *in* the temple,
27. set (them) *before* the council:
34. stood there up one *in* the council,

Acts 5:37. *in* the days of the taxing,
42. daily *in* the temple,
6: 1. *in* those days, when the number
— neglected *in* the daily ministration.
7. multiplied *in* Jerusalem
8. wonders and miracles *among* the people.
15. all that sat *in* the council,
7: 2. when he was *in* Mesopotamia, before he dwelt *in* Charran,
4. dwelt *in* Charran: and from
5. none inheritance *in* it,
6. should sojourn *in* a strange land;
7. serve me *in* this place.
12. that there was corn *in* Egypt,
13. *at* the second (time) Joseph was
14)(threescore and fifteen souls.
16. laid *in* the sepulchre that Abraham
17. grew and multiplied *in* Egypt,
20. *In* which time Moses was born,
— nourished up *in* his father's house
22. mighty *in* words and *in* deeds.
29. fled Moses *at* this saying, and was a stranger *in* the land of Madian,
30. *in* the wilderness of mount Sina
— *in* a flame of fire *in* a bush.
33. the place where (lit. *in* which) thou standest
34. my people which is *in* Egypt,
35. *by* the hand of the angel which appeared to him *in* the bush.
36. *in* the land of Egypt, and *in* the Red sea, and *in* the wilderness
38. *in* the church *in* the wilderness
— spake to him *in* the mount Sina,
41. made a calf *in* those days,
— rejoiced *in* the works of their own
42. written *in* the book of the prophets,
— forty years *in* the wilderness?
44. Our fathers had the tabernacle of witness (lit. the tab. &c. was *among* our fathers)
45. *into* the possession of the Gentiles,
48. not *in* temples made with hands;
8: 1. *at* that time there was a great
— church which was *at* Jerusalem;
6.)(hearing and seeing the miracles
8. there was great joy *in* that city.
9. beforetime *in* the same city
14. apostles which were *at* Jerusalem
21. part nor lot *in* this matter:
33. *In* his humiliation his judgment
9: 3. as he journeyed, (lit. *in* his journeying)
10. a certain disciple *at* Damascus,
— said the Lord *in* a vision,
11. enquire *in* the house of Judas
12. hath seen *in* a vision a man
13. to thy saints *at* Jerusalem:
17. *in* the way as thou camest,
19. disciples which were *at* Damascus.
20. preached Christ *in* the synagogues,
21. called on this name *in* Jerusalem,
22. Jews which dwelt *at* Damascus,
25. down by the wall *in* a basket.
27. had seen the Lord *in* the way,
— preached boldly *at* Damascus *in* the name of Jesus.
28. coming in and going out *at* Jerusalem.
29(28). And he spake boldly *in* the name of the Lord Jesus,
36. there was *at* Joppa a certain
37. it came to pass *in* those days,
— laid (her) *in* an upper chamber.
38. heard that Peter was there, (lit. *in* it)

Acts 9:43. he tarried many days *in* Joppa
10: 1. a certain man *in* Cæsarea
3. He saw *in* a vision evidently
12. Wherein were all manner of
17. while Peter doubted *in* himself
30. I prayed *in* my house,
— before me *in* bright clothing,
32. he is lodged *in* the house of (one)
35. *in* every nation he that feareth
39. *in* the land of the Jews, and *in* Jerusalem;
48. *in* the name of the Lord.
11: 5. I was *in* the city of Joppa praying: and *in* a trance I saw a vision,
11. unto the house where (lit. *in* which) I
13. seen an angel *in* his house,
14. where*by* thou and all thy house
15. as I began (lit. *on* my beginning) to speak, the Holy Ghost fell on them, as on us *at* the beginning.
16. baptized *with* the Holy Ghost.
22. church which was *in* Jerusalem:
26. assembled themselves *with* the church,
— called Christians first *in* Antioch.
27. *in* these days came prophets
29. brethren which dwelt *in* Judæa:
12: 5. Peter therefore was kept *in* prison:
7. a light shined *in* the prison:
— saying, Arise up quickly.
11. when Peter was come *to* himself,
18. no small stir *among* the soldiers,
13: 1. church that was *at* Antioch
5. when they were *at* Salamis,
— *in* the synagogues of the Jews:
15. if ye have (lit. if there is *in* you) any
17. when they dwelt as strangers (lit. *in* the sojourning) *in* the land of Egypt,
18. their manners *in* the wilderness.
19. *in* the land of Chanaan,
26. whosoever *among* you feareth
27. they that dwell *at* Jerusalem,
33. written *in* the second psalm,
35. he saith also *in* another (psalm),
39. *by* him all that believe are
— justified *by* the law of Moses.
40. spoken of *in* the prophets;
41. I work a work *in* your days,
14: 1. it came to pass *in* Iconium,
8. sat a certain man *at* Lystra,
15. all things that are there*in* :
16. Who *in* times past suffered
25. preached the word *in* Perga,
15: 7. God made choice *among* us,
12. had wrought *among* the Gentiles
21. being read *in* the synagogues
22. chief men *among* the brethren:
35. Barnabas continued *in* Antioch,
36. every city where (lit. *in* which) we have
16: 2. brethren that were *at* Lystra
3. which were *in* those quarters:
4. elders which were *at* Jerusalem.
6. to preach the word *in* Asia,
12. we were *in* that city abiding
18. *in* the name of Jesus Christ
32. all that were *in* his house.
33.)(the same hour of the night,
36. therefore depart, and go *in* peace.
17: 11. than those *in* Thessalonica,
13. was preached of Paul *at* Berea,
16. Paul waited for them *at* Athens, his spirit was stirred *in* him,
17. *in* the synagogue with the Jews,
— *in* the market daily with them

Acts17:22. Paul stood *in* the midst of
23. an altar with this inscription, (lit. *on* which was inscribed)
24. the world and all things there*in*,
— not *in* temples made with hands;
28. For *in* him we live, and move,
31. a day, *in* the which he will judge the world *in* righteousness *by* (that) man
34. *among* the which (was) Dionysius
18: 4. he reasoned *in* the synagogue
9. *in* the night by a vision,
10. I have much people *in* this city.
11. the word of God *among* them.
18. having shorn (his) head *in* Cenchrea:
24. mighty *in* the scriptures,
26. to speak boldly *in* the synagogue:
19: 1. that, while Apollos was (lit. *in* Apollos's being) *at* Corinth,
9. disputing daily *in* the school
16. the man *in* whom the evil
21. Paul purposed *in* the spirit,
39. determined *in* a lawful assembly.
20: 5. tarried for us *at* Troas.
7. *upon* the first (day) of the week,
8. many lights *in* the upper chamber,
10. for his life is *in* him.
15. tarried *at* Trogyllium; and the
16. not spend the time *in* Asia:
19. *by* the lying in wait of the Jews:
22. that shall befall me there: (lit. *in* it)
25. *among* whom I have gone
26. I take you to record)(this day,
28. *over* the which the Holy Ghost
32. an inheritance *among* all them
21:11. So shall the Jews *at* Jerusalem
19. had wrought *among* the Gentiles
27. they saw him *in* the temple,
29. before with him *in* the city
34. some another, *among* the multitude:
22: 3. a Jew, born *in* Tarsus,
— yet brought up *in* this city
17. *in* the temple, I was *in* a trance;
18. quick*ly* out of Jerusalem:
23: 6. he cried out *in* the council,
9. We find no evil *in* this man:
35. kept *in* Herod's judgment hall.
24:11. since I went up *to* Jerusalem for to worship. (lit. I went up to worship *in* Jerusalem)
12. neither found me *in* the temple
— neither *in* the synagogues,
14. in the law and *in* the prophets:
16. here*in* do I exercise myself,
18. Where*upon* certain Jews from Asia found me purified *in* the temple,
20. found any evil doing *in* me,
21. I cried standing *among* them,
25: 4. Paul should be kept *at* Cæsarea, and that he himself would depart short*ly*
5. which *among* you are able, go
— if there be any wickedness *in* him.
6. he had tarried *among* them
24. both *at* Jerusalem, and (also) here,
26: 4. *among* mine own nation *at* Jerusalem,
7. instant*ly* (lit. *in* intensity) serving (God) day and night,
10. I also did *in* Jerusalem:
12. Where*upon* as I went to Damascus
18. inheritance *among* them which
20. first *unto* them of Damascus,
21. the Jews caught me *in* the temple,
26. was not done *in* a corner.

Acts26:28. Almost (lit. *in* part) thou persuadest me to be a Christian.
29. were both almost, and altogether such (lit. both *in* part, and *in* whole)
27: 7. when we had sailed slowly)(many days,
21. Paul stood forth *in* the midst
27. driven up and down *in* Adria,
31. Except these abide *in* the ship,
37. we were in all *in* the ship
28: 7. *In* the same quarters were
9. which had diseases *in* the island,
11. we departed *in* a ship of Alexandria, which had wintered *in* the isle,
18. was no cause of death *in* me.
29. great reasoning *among* themselves.
30. *in* his own hired house,
Ro. 1: 2. prophets *in* the holy scriptures,
4. the Son of God *with* power,
5. to the faith *among* all nations,
6. *Among* whom are ye also the
7. To all that be *in* Rome,
8. *throughout* the whole world.
9. *with* my spirit *in* the gospel
10. *by* the will of God to come
12. together *with* you by the mutual faith (lit. by the faith *in* the one and the other)
13. *among* you also, even as *among* other
15. to you that are *at* Rome also.
17. For there*in* is the righteousness
18. hold the truth *in* unrighteousness;
19. of God is manifest *in* them;
21. became vain *in* their imaginations,
23. *into* an image made like to
24. *through* the lusts of their own
— their own bodies *between* themselves:
25. the truth of God *into* a lie,
27. burned *in* their lust one toward another; men *with* men working that
— receiving *in* themselves that
28. to retain God *in* (their) knowledge,
2: 1. for where*in* thou judgest another,
5. wrath *against* the day of wrath
12. as have sinned *in* the law
15. the law written *in* their hearts,
16. *In* the day when God shall judge
17. makest thy boast *of* God,
19. of them which are *in* darkness,
20. of the truth *in* the law.
23. makest thy boast *of* the law,
24. blasphemed *among* the Gentiles
28. which is one outward*ly;*
— which is outward (lit. *in* outward manifestation) *in* the flesh:
29. a Jew, which is one inward*ly;*
— of the heart, *in* the spirit, (and) not
3: 4. justified *in* thy sayings, and mightest overcome when thou art judged. (lit. *in* being judged)
7. *through* my lie unto his glory;
16. misery (are) *in* their ways:
19. them who are *under* the law:
24. redemption that is *in* Christ Jesus:
25. through faith *in* his blood,
—(26). *through* the forbearance of God;
26. *at* this time his righteousness:
4:10. *in* circumcision, or *in* uncircumcision? Not *in* circumcision, but *in* uncircumcision
11. (yet) being uncircumcised: (lit. *in* unc.)
12. which (he had) being (yet) uncircumcised. (lit. *in* uncircumcision)

Ro. 5: 2. this grace where*in* we stand,
    3. we glory *in* tribulations also:
    5. shed abroad *in* our hearts
    9. now justified *by* his blood,
    10. we shall be saved *by* his life.
    11. we also joy *in* God through
    13. sin was *in* the world:
    15. the gift *by* grace, (which is)
    17. shall reign *in* life by one,
    21. as sin hath reigned *unto* (lit. *in*) death,
   6: 2. live any longer there*in* ?
    4. should walk *in* newness of life.
    11. *through* Jesus Christ our Lord.
    12. reign *in* your mortal body, that ye should obey it *in* the lusts thereof.
    23. the gift of God (is) eternal life *through* Jesus Christ our Lord.
   7: 5. when we were *in* the flesh,
    — did work *in* our members
    6. dead where*in* we were held ;
    — serve *in* newness of spirit,
    8. wrought *in* me all manner
    17. sin that dwelleth *in* me.
    18. *in* me that is, *in* my flesh,
    20. sin that dwelleth *in* me.
    23. another law *in* my members,
    — of sin which is *in* my members.
   8: 1. them which are *in* Christ Jesus,
    2. Spirit of life *in* Christ Jesus
    3. *in* that it was weak through
    — *in* the likeness of sinful flesh, and for sin, condemned sin *in* the flesh:
    4. law might be fulfilled *in* us,
    8. they that are *in* the flesh cannot
    9. ye are not *in* the flesh, but *in* the Spirit,
    — the Spirit of God dwell *in* you.
    10. if Christ (be) *in* you, the body
    11. dwell *in* you, he that raised
    — his Spirit that dwelleth *in* you.
    15. where*by* we cry, Abba, Father.
    23. ourselves groan *within* ourselves,
    29. firstborn *among* many brethren.
    34. *at* the right hand of God,
    37. *in* all these things we are more
    39. which is *in* Christ Jesus our Lord.
   9: 1. I say the truth *in* Christ,
    — me witness *in* the Holy Ghost,
    7. *In* Isaac shall thy seed be called.
    17. I might shew my power *in* thee,
    — declared *throughout* all the earth.
    22. endured *with* much longsuffering
    25. As he saith also *in* Osee,
    26. *in* the place where it was said
    28. cut (it) short *in* righteousness:
    33. I lay *in* Sion a stumblingstone
  10: 5. those things shall live *by* them.
    6. Say not *in* thine heart,
    8. *in* thy mouth, and *in* thy heart:
    9. shalt confess *with* thy mouth the Lord Jesus, and shalt believe *in* thine heart
  11: 2. the scripture saith *of* Elias ?
    5. so then *at* this present time
    17. wert graffed in *among* them,
  12: 3. to every man that is *among* you,
    4. have many members *in* one body,
    5. are one body *in* Christ,
    7. (let us wait) *on* (our) ministering: or he that teacheth, *on* teaching ;
    8. that exhorteth, *on* exhortation: he that giveth, (let him do it) *with* simplicity ; he that ruleth, *with* diligence ; he that sheweth mercy, *with* cheerfulness.

Ro. 12:21. overcome evil *with* good.
  13: 9. comprehended *in* this saying, namely (lit *in* this), Thou shalt love thy
    13. Let us walk honestly, as *in* the day ;
  14: 5. fully persuaded *in* his own mind.
    14. persuaded *by* the Lord Jesus,
    17. peace, and joy *in* the Holy Ghost.
    18. *in* these things serveth Christ
    21. where*by* thy brother stumbleth,
    22. *in* that thing which he alloweth.
  15: 5. likeminded one toward another (lit. *toward* one another)
    6. with one mind (and))(one mouth
    9. to thee *among* the Gentiles,
    13. all joy and peace *in* believing,
    — abound *in* hope, *through* the power
    16. sanctified *by* the Holy Ghost.
    17. I may glory *through* Jesus Christ
    19. *Through* mighty signs and wonders, *by* the power of the Spirit of God ;
    23. no more place *in* these parts,
    26. saints which are *at* Jerusalem.
    27. minister unto them *in* carnal things.
    29. *in* the fulness of the blessing
    30. together with me *in* (your) prayers
    31. that do not believe *in* Judæa ;
    32. *with* joy by the will of God,
  16: 1. church which is *at* Cenchrea:
    2. That ye receive her *in* the Lord,
    — *in* whatsoever business she hath
    3. my helpers *in* Christ Jesus:
    7. are of note *among* the apostles, who also were *in* Christ before me.
    8. my beloved *in* the Lord.
    9. Urbane, our helper *in* Christ,
    10. Salute Apelles approved *in* Christ.
    11. which are *in* the Lord.
    12. who labour *in* the Lord.
    — laboured much *in* the Lord.
    13. Rufus chosen *in* the Lord,
    16. Salute one another *with* an holy kiss.
    20. under your feet short*ly*.
    22. salute you *in* the Lord.
1Co. 1: 2. church of God which is *at* Corinth,
    — sanctified *in* Christ Jesus,
    — that *in* every place call upon
    4. is given you *by* Jesus Christ ;
    5. *in* every thing ye are enriched *by* him, *in* all utterance,
    6. was confirmed *in* you:
    7. ye come behind *in* no gift ;
    8. *in* the day of our Lord Jesus
    10. no divisions *among* you ;
    — *in* the same mind and *in* the same judgment.
    11. there are contentions *among* you.
    17. not *with* wisdom of words,
    21. *in* the wisdom of God
    30. of him are ye *in* Christ Jesus,
    31. let him glory *in* the Lord.
   2: 2. to know any thing *among* you,
    3. with you *in* weakness, and *in* fear, and *in* much trembling.
    4. *with* enticing words of man's wisdom, but *in* demonstration of the Spirit
    5. not stand *in* the wisdom of men, but *in* the power of God.
    6. wisdom *among* them that are perfect:
    7. wisdom of God *in* a mystery,
    11. spirit of man which is *in* him ?
    13. not *in* the words which man's
    — but which (lit. *in* the which) the Holy Ghost teacheth ;

1Co. 3: 1. as unto babes *in* Christ.
    3. *among* you envying, and strife,
   13. it shall be revealed *by* fire;
   16. Spirit of God dwelleth *in* you?
   18. If any man *among* you seemeth to be wise *in* this world,
   19. the wise *in* their own craftiness.
   21. let no man glory *in* men.
  4: 2. it is required *in* stewards,
    4. yet am I not here*by* justified:
    6. that ye might learn *in* us
   10. ye (are) wise *in* Christ;
   15. ten thousand instructers *in* Christ,
   — for *in* Christ Jesus I have begotten
   17. faithful *in* the Lord, who shall
   — my ways which be *in* Christ, as I teach every where *in* every church.
   20. not *in* word, but *in* power.
   21. unto you *with* a rod, or *in* love, and
  5: 1. (there is) fornication *among* you,
   — as named *among* the Gentiles,
   4. *In* the name of our Lord Jesus
   5. saved *in* the day of the Lord Jesus.
   8. not *with* old leaven, neither *with* the leaven of malice and wickedness; but *with* the unleavened (bread) of
   9. I wrote unto you *in* an epistle
  6: 2. shall be judged *by* you,
   4. least esteemed *in* the church.
   5. is not a wise man *among* you?
   7. utterly a fault *among* you,
   11. *in* the name of the Lord Jesus, and *by* the Spirit
   19. the Holy Ghost (which is) *in* you,
   20. glorify God *in* your body, and *in* your spirit, which are God's.
  7:14. is sanctified *by* the wife,
   — wife is sanctified *by* the husband:
   15. under bondage *in* such (cases): but God hath called us *to* peace.
   17. so ordain I *in* all churches.
   18. Is any called *in* uncircumcision?
   20. Let every man abide *in* the same calling wherein he was called. (lit. Let every man *in* the calling wherein he was called remain *in* the same)
   22. he that is called *in* the Lord,
   24. every man, wherein he is called, there*in* abide
   37. standeth stedfast *in* his heart,
   — hath so decreed *in* his heart
   39. whom she will; only *in* the Lord.
  8: 4. an idol (is) nothing *in* the world,
   5. whether *in* heaven or in earth,
   7. not *in* every man that knowledge:
   10. at meat *in* the idol's temple,
  9: 1. are not ye my work *in* the Lord?
   2. are ye *in* the Lord.
   9. written *in* the law of Moses,
   15. that it should be so done *unto* me:
   18. not my power *in* the gospel.
   24. they which run *in* a race run
 10. 2. *in* the cloud and *in* the sea;
   5. *with* many of them God was not
   — overthrown *in* the wilderness.
   8. fell *in* one day three and twenty thousand.
   25. is sold *in* the shambles,
 11:11. without the man, *in* the Lord.
   13. Judge *in* yourselves: is it comely
   18. come together *in* the church,
   — there be divisions *among* you;
   19. be also heresies *among* you,

1Co.11:19. be made manifest *among* you.
   21. For *in* eating every one taketh before
   22. shall I praise you *in* this?
   23.)(the (same) night in which he was betrayed
   25. new testament *in* my blood:
   30. many (are) weak and sickly *among* you,
   34. let him eat *at* home;
  12: 3. speaking *by* the Spirit of God
   — but *by* the Holy Ghost.
   6. God which worketh all *in* all.
   9. faith *by* the same Spirit; to another the gifts of healing *by* the same Spirit;
   13. For *by* one Spirit are we all
   18. every one of them *in* the body,
   25. be no schism *in* the body;
   28. God hath set some *in* the church,
 13:12. we see through a glass, dark*ly*;
 14: 6. either *by* revelation, or *by* knowledge, or *by* prophesying, or *by* doctrine?
   10. many kinds of voices *in* the world,
   11. (shall be) a barbarian *unto* me.
   19. Yet *in* the church I had rather
   — words *in* an (unknown) tongue.
   21. *In* the law it is written, *With* (men of) other tongues and)(other lips will I
   25. that God is *in* you of a truth.
   28. keep silence *in* the church;
   33. as *in* all churches of the saints.
   34. women keep silence *in* the churches:
   35. ask their husbands *at* home:
   — women to speak *in* the church.
 15: 1. have received, and where*in* ye stand;
   3. I delivered unto you first of all (lit. *in the* first)
   12. how say some *among* you
   17. ye are yet *in* your sins.
   18. which are fallen asleep *in* Christ
   19. If *in* this life only we have hope *in* Christ, we are of all men most miserable.
   22. For as *in* Adam all die, even so *in* Christ shall all be made alive.
   23. every man *in* his own order:
   — that are Christ's *at* his coming.
   28. that God may be all *in* all.
   31. which I have *in* Christ Jesus
   32. I have fought with beasts *at* Ephesus,
   41. for (one) star differeth from (another) star *in* glory.
   42. sown *in* corruption; it is raised *in* incorruption:
   43. sown *in* dishonour; it is raised *in* glory: it is sown *in* weakness; it is raised *in* power:
   52. *In* a moment, *in* the twinkling of an eye, *at* the last trump:
   58. *in* the work of the Lord,
   — labour is not in vain *in* the Lord.
 16: 7. will not see you now *by* the way;
   8. I will tarry *at* Ephesus until
   11. but conduct him forth *in* peace,
   13. stand fast *in* the faith,
   14. your things be done *with* charity.
   19. salute you much *in* the Lord,
   20. one another *with* an holy kiss.
   24. with you all *in* Christ Jesus.
2Co. 1: 1. church of God which is *at* Corinth, with all the saints which are *in* all Achaia:
   4. them which are *in* any trouble
   6. *in* the enduring of the same
   8. which came to us *in* Asia,
   9. sentence of death *in* ourselves,

2Co. 1:12. *in* simplicity and godly sincerity, not
with fleshly wisdom, but *by* the grace
of God, we have had our conversation
in the world,
14. *in* the day of the Lord Jesus.
19. who was preached *among* you
— not yea and nay, but *in* him was yea.
20. *in* him (are) yea, and, *in* him Amen,
22. of the Spirit *in* our hearts.
2: 1. come again to you *in* heaviness.
10. *in* the person of Christ ;
12. opened unto me *of* the Lord,
14. causeth us to triumph *in* Christ,
— by us *in* every place.
15. *in* them that are saved, and *in* them
17. speak we *in* Christ.
3: 2. epistle written *in* our hearts,
3. not *in* tables of stone, but *in*
7. ministration of death, written (and) engraven *in* stones, was glorious, (lit. *in*
letters, engraven *in* stones, was *in* glory)
8. the spirit be rather)(glorious ? (lit. *in* g.)
9. righteousness exceed *in* glory.
10. had no glory *in* this respect,
11. that which remaineth (is) glorious. (lit.
that which remaineth *in* glory)
14. is done away *in* Christ.
4: 2. not walking *in* craftiness,
3. it is hid *to* them that are lost:
4. *In* whom the god of this world
6. hath shined *in* our hearts,
— *in* the face of Jesus Christ.
7. this treasure *in* earthen vessels,
8. (We are) troubled *on* every side,
10. bearing about *in* the body
— be made manifest *in* our body.
11. manifest *in* our mortal flesh.
12. death worketh *in* us, but life *in* you.
5: 1. eternal *in* the heavens.
2. For *in* this we groan, earnestly
4. we that are *in* (this) tabernacle
6. we are at home *in* the body,
11. made manifest *in* your consciences
12. which glory *in* appearance,
17. if any man (be) *in* Christ,
19. that God was *in* Christ, reconciling
— hath committed *unto* us the word
21. righteousness of God *in* him.
6: 2. *in* the day of salvation have I
3. Giving no offence *in* any thing,
4. *in* all (things) approving ourselves
— *in* much patience, *in* afflictions, *in* necessities, *in* distresses,
5. *In* stripes, *in* imprisonments, *in* tumults,
in labours, *in* watchings, *in* fastings;
6. *By* pureness, *by* knowledge, *by* longsuffering, *by* kindness, *by* the Holy
Ghost, *by* love unfeigned,
7. *By* the word of truth, *by* the power of
12. not straitened *in* us, but ye are straitened
in your own bowels.
16. God hath said, I will dwell *in* them,
7: 1. holiness *in* the fear of God.
3. that ye are *in* our hearts to die
5. we were troubled *on* every side ;
6. *by* the coming of Titus ;
7. not *by* his coming only, but *by* the consolation wherewith
8. I made you sorry *with* a letter,
9. receive damage by us *in* nothing.
11. *In* all (things) ye have approved yourselves to be clear *in* this matter.

2Co. 7:14. spake all things to you *in* truth,
16. confidence *in* you *in* all (things).
8: 1. bestowed *on* the churches of
2. *in* a great trial of affliction
7. as ye abound *in* every (thing),
— diligence, and (in) your love *to* us, (see)
that ye abound *in* this grace also.
10. herein I give (my) advice :
14(13). *at* this time your abundance
16. *into* the heart of Titus for you.
18. whose praise (is) *in* the gospel
20. blame us *in* this abundance
22. proved diligent *in* many things,
9: 3. be in vain *in* this behalf ;
4. should be ashamed *in* this
8. always having all sufficiency *in* all (things),
11. Being enriched *in* every thing
10: 1. in presence (am) base *among* you,
3. though we walk *in* the flesh,
6. having *in* a readiness to revenge
12. measuring themselves *by* themselves,
14. *in* (preaching) the gospel of Christ:
15. Not boasting...*of* other men's labours ;
— we shall be enlarged *by* you
16. not to boast *in* another man's
17. let him glory *in* the Lord.
11: 3. beguiled Eve *through* his subtilty,
6. we have been through*ly* made manifest
among you *in* all things.
9. *in* all (things) I have kept myself from
10. the truth of Christ is *in* me,
— boasting *in* the regions of Achaia.
12. that wherein they glory,
17. as it were foolish*ly*, *in* this confidence
21. where*in*soever any is bold, I speak foolish*ly*, I am bold also.
23. *in* labours more abundant, *in* stripes above
measure, *in* prisons more frequent, *in*
deaths oft.
25. I have been *in* the deep;
26. perils *in* the city, (in) perils *in* the wilderness, (in) perils *in* the sea, (in)
perils *among* false brethren ;
27. *In* weariness and painfulness, *in* watchings often, *in* hunger and thirst, *in* fastings often, *in* cold and nakedness.
32. *In* Damascus the governor under
33. through a window *in* a basket
12: 2. I knew a man *in* Christ about
— whether *in* the body, I cannot tell ;
3. whether *in* the body, or out of the
5. not glory, but *in* mine infirmities.
9. is made perfect *in* weakness.
— I rather glory *in* my infirmities,
10. I take pleasure *in* infirmities, *in* reproaches, *in* necessities, *in* persecutions, *in* distresses for Christ's sake:
12. *among* you *in* all patience, *in* signs, and
wonders, and mighty deeds.
19. we speak before God *in* Christ:
13: 3. of Christ speaking *in* me,
— not weak, but is mighty *in* you.
4. we also are weak *in* him,
5. whether ye be *in* the faith ;
— that Jesus Christ is *in* you,
12. Greet one another *with* an holy kiss.
Gal. 1: 6. *into* the grace of Christ unto
13. in time past *in* the Jews' religion,
14. profited *in* the Jews' religion above many
my equals *in* mine own nation,
16. To reveal his Son *in* me, that I might
preach him *among* the

Gal. 1:22. churches of Judæa which were *in* Christ:
24. they glorified God *in* me.
2: 2. which I preach *among* the Gentiles,
4. which we have *in* Christ Jesus,
17. seek to be justified *by* Christ,
20. not I, but Christ liveth *in* me: and the life which I now live *in* the flesh I live *by* the faith of the Son of God,
3: 1. set forth, crucified *among* you?
5. worketh miracles *among* you,
8. *In* thee shall all nations be blessed.
10. *in* all things which are written *in* the book
11. no man is justified *by* the law
12. doeth them shall live *in* them.
14. on the Gentiles *through* Jesus Christ;
19. *in* the hand of a mediator.
26. by faith *in* Christ Jesus.
28. ye are all one *in* Christ Jesus.
4:14. which was *in* my flesh
18. affected always *in* (a) good (thing), and not only when I am present with you. (lit. *in* my being present with you)
19. until Christ be formed *in* you,
20. for I stand in doubt *of* you.
25. Agar is mount Sinai *in* Arabia,
5: 4. are justified *by* the law;
6. For *in* Jesus Christ neither
10. confidence in you *through* the Lord,
14. law is fulfilled *in* one word, (even) *in* this;
6: 1. a man be overtaken *in* a fault,
— *in* the spirit of meekness;
6. teacheth *in* all good things.
12. to make a fair shew *in* the flesh,
13. that they may glory *in* your flesh.
14. save *in* the cross of our Lord
15. For *in* Christ Jesus neither
17. I bear *in* my body the marks
Eph. 1: 1. which are *at* Ephesus, and to the faithful *in* Christ Jesus:
3. *with* all spiritual blessings *in* heavenly (places) *in* Christ:
4. he hath chosen us *in* him
— without blame before him *in* love:
6. where*in* he hath made us accepted *in* the beloved.
7. *In* whom we have redemption
8. *in* all wisdom and prudence;
9. he hath purposed *in* himself:
10. all things *in* Christ, both which are *in* heaven, and which are on earth; (even) *in* him:
11. *In* whom also we have obtained
12. who first trusted *in* Christ.
13. *In* whom ye also (trusted),
— *in* whom also after that ye
15. your faith *in* the Lord Jesus,
17. *in* the knowledge of him:
18. his inheritance *in* the saints,
20. Which he wrought *in* Christ,
— *at* his own right hand *in* the heavenly
21. not only *in* this world, but also *in*
23. of him that filleth all *in* all.
2: 2. Where*in* in time past ye walked
— *in* the children of disobedience:
3. *Among* whom also we all had
— *in* the lusts of our flesh,
4. God, who is rich *in* mercy,
6. *in* heavenly (places) *in* Christ Jesus:
7. That *in* the ages to come he
— *in* (his) kindness toward us *through* Christ Jesus.
10. created *in* Christ Jesus unto

Eph. 2:10. that we should walk *in* them.
11. in time past Gentiles *in* the flesh,
— Circumcision *in* the flesh made
12. That *at* that time ye were
— without God *in* the world:
13. now *in* Christ Jesus ye who
— nigh *by* the blood of Christ.
15. Having abolished *in* his flesh the enmity, (even) the law of commandments (contained) *in* ordinances; for to make *in* himself of twain one new man,
16. both unto God *in* one body
— having slain the enmity there*by:*
18. have access *by* one Spirit unto
21. *In* whom all the building
— unto an holy temple *in* the Lord:
22. *In* whom ye also are builded
— habitation of God *through* the Spirit.
3: 3. as I wrote afore *in* few words,
4. *in* the mystery of Christ
5. Which *in* other ages was not
— apostles and prophets *by* the Spirit;
6. his promise *in* Christ by the gospel:
8. I should preach *among* the Gentiles
9. hath been hid *in* God, who
10. powers *in* heavenly (places) might
11. which he purposed *in* Christ Jesus
12. *In* whom we have boldness and access *with* confidence by the
13. faint not *at* my tribulations for you,
15. the whole family *in* heaven
17. Christ may dwell *in* your hearts by faith;
—(18). that ye, being rooted and grounded *in* love,
20. the power that worketh *in* us,
21. glory *in* the church *by* Christ Jesus
4: 1. the prisoner *of* the Lord,
2. forbearing one another *in* love;
3. Spirit *in* the bond of peace.
4. as ye are called *in* one hope
6. through all, and *in* you all.
14. *by* the sleight of men, (and) cunning craftiness, (lit. *in* cunning craftiness)
15. speaking the truth *in* love,
16. *in* the measure of every part,
— the edifying of itself *in* love.
17. testify *in* the Lord, that ye
— *in* the vanity of their mind,
18. the ignorance that is *in* them,
19. all uncleanness *with* greediness.
21. have been taught *by* him, as the truth is *in* Jesus:
24. which after God is created *in* righteousness and
30. where*by* ye are sealed unto
32. as God *for* Christ's *sake* hath
5: 2. walk *in* love, as Christ also
3. not be once named *among* you,
5. inheritance *in* the kingdom of
8. now (are ye) light *in* the Lord:
9. *in* all goodness and righteousness
18. drunk with wine, where*in* is excess; but be filled *with* the Spirit;
19. melody *in* your heart to the Lord;
20. *in* the name of our Lord Jesus
21. one to another *in* the fear of God.
24. own husbands *in* every thing.
26. washing of water *by* the word,
6: 1. obey your parents *in* the Lord:
2. first commandment *with* promise
4. *in* the nurture and admonition
5. *in* singleness of your heart,

Eph. 6: 9. your Master also is *in* heaven
10. be strong *in* the Lord, and *in* the power of
12. spiritual wickedness *in* high (places).
13. to withstand *in* the evil day,
14. your loins girt about *with* truth,
15. shod *with* the preparation of the
16. where*with* ye shall be able to
18. Praying always (lit. *in* all times) with all
prayer and supplication *in* the Spirit,
— *with* all perseverance and supplication
19. that I may open (lit. *in* the opening of)
my mouth bold*ly*,
20. an ambassador *in* bonds: that there*in* I
may speak boldly,
21. faithful minister *in* the Lord,
24. love our Lord Jesus Christ *in* sincerity.
Phi. 1: 1. to all the saints *in* Christ Jesus which are
at Philippi,
4. Always *in* every prayer of mine
6. begun a good work *in* you
7. I have you *in* my heart; inasmuch as
both *in* my bonds,
8. *in* the bowels of Jesus Christ.
9. yet more and more *in* knowledge
13. my bonds *in* Christ are manifest *in* all the
palace,
14. many of the brethren *in* the Lord,
18. I there*in* do rejoice. yea, and will
20. *in* nothing I shall be ashamed, but (that)
with all boldness,
— be magnified *in* my body,
22. if I live *in* the flesh, this
24. to abide *in* the flesh (is) more
26. abundant *in* Jesus Christ *for* me
27. that ye stand fast *in* one spirit,
28. *in* nothing terrified by your
30. ye saw *in* me, (and) now hear (to be) *in*
me.
2: 1. any consolation *in* Christ,
5. this mind be *in* you, which was also *in*
6. being *in* the form of God,
7. was made *in* the likeness of men:
10. *at* the name of Jesus every
12. not as *in* my presence only, but now much
more *in* my absence,
13. God which worketh *in* you
15. *in* the midst of a crooked
— *among* whom ye shine as lights *in* the
world;
19. I trust *in* the Lord Jesus to send
24. I trust *in* the Lord that I
29. *in* the Lord with all gladness;
3: 1. rejoice *in* the Lord.
3. rejoice *in* Christ Jesus, and have no confidence *in* the flesh.
4. have confidence *in* the flesh.
— he might trust *in* the flesh,
6. righteousness which is *in* the law,
9. be found *in* him, not having
14. calling of God *in* Christ Jesus.
19. (whose) glory (is) *in* their shame,
20. our conversation is *in* heaven;
4: 1. so stand fast *in* the Lord,
2. of the same mind *in* the Lord.
3. laboured with me *in* the gospel,
— names (are) *in* the book of life.
4. Rejoice *in* the Lord alway:
6. *in* every thing by prayer and
7. hearts and minds *through* Christ Jesus.
9. heard, and seen *in* me, do:
10. I rejoiced *in* the Lord greatly,
11. *in* whatsoever state I am,

Phi. 4: 12. every where (lit. *in* all) and *in* all things
13. Christ which strengtheneth (lit. *in* Christ
strengthening) me.
15. that *in* the beginning of the gospel,
16. For even *in* Thessalonica ye
19. riches *in* glory *by* Christ Jesus.
21. Salute every saint *in* Christ Jesus.
Col. 1: 2. brethren *in* Christ which are *at* Colosse:
4. your faith *in* Christ Jesus,
5. laid up for you *in* heaven,
— before *in* the word of the truth
6. as (it is) *in* all the world;
— as (it doth) also *in* you, since the
— the grace of God *in* truth:
8. your love *in* the Spirit.
9. *in* all wisdom and spiritual understanding;
10. fruitful *in* every good work,
11. Strengthened *with* all might,
12. inheritance of the saints *in* light:
14. *In* whom we have redemption
16. *by* him were all things created, that are
in heaven,
17. *by* him all things consist.
18. that *in* all (things) he might have
19. *in* him should all fulness dwell;
20. in earth, or things *in* heaven.
21. in (your) mind *by* wicked works,
22. *In* the body of his flesh through
23. was preached *to* every creature
24. now rejoice *in* my sufferings
— *in* my flesh for his body's sake, which is the
church:
27. mystery *among* the Gentiles; which is
Christ *in* you,
28. teaching every man *in* all wisdom;
— every man perfect *in* Christ Jesus:
29. which worketh *in* me mighti*ly*.
2: 1. (for) them *at* Laodicea,
— not seen my face *in* the flesh;
2. being knit together *in* love,
3. *In* whom are hid all the
4. beguile you *with* enticing words.
6. the Lord, (so) walk ye *in* him:
7. Rooted and built up *in* him, and stablished
in the faith,
— abounding there*in* *with* thanksgiving.
9. For *in* him dwelleth all
10. ye are complete *in* him,
11. *In* whom also ye are circumcised
— *in* putting off the body of the
— *by* the circumcision of Christ:
12. Buried with him *in* baptism, where*in*
13. you, being dead *in* your sins
15. made a shew of them open*ly* triumphing
over them *in* it.
16. *in* meat, or *in* drink, or *in* respect
18. *in* a voluntary humility and
20. as though living *in* the world,
23. shew of wisdom *in* will worship,
— not *in* any honour to the satisfying
3: 1. sitteth *on* the right hand of God.
3. life is hid with Christ *in* God.
4. ye also appear with him *in* glory.
7. *In* the which ye also walked some time,
when ye lived *in* them.
11. Christ (is) all, and *in* all.
15. peace of God rule *in* your hearts,
— ye are called *in* one body,
16. dwell *in* you richly *in* all wisdom;
— *with* grace *in* your hearts to the Lord.
17. *in* word or)(deed, (do) all *in* the name
18. as it is fit *in* the Lord.

Col. 3:22. not *with* eyeservice, as
— *in* singleness of heart, fearing God:
4: 1. ye also have a Master *in* heaven.
   2. watch *in* the same *with* thanksgiving;
   5. Walk *in* wisdom toward them
   6. your speech (be) alway *with* grace,
   7. fellowservant *in* the Lord.
  12. labouring fervently for you *in* prayers,
— complete *in* all the will of God.
  13. *in* Laodicea, and them *in* Hierapolis.
  15. the brethren which are *in* Laodicea,
  16. *in* the church of the Laodiceans ;
  17. thou hast received *in* the Lord,
1Th. 1: 1. *in* God the Father and (in) the Lord
   5. not unto you *in* word only, but also *in*
     power, and *in* the Holy Ghost, and *in*
     much assurance ;
— we were *among* you for your sake.
   6. the word *in* much affliction,
   7. to all that believe *in* Macedonia
   8. not only *in* Macedonia and Achaia, but
     also *in* every place your faith
2: 2. as ye know, *at* Philippi, we were bold *in*
     our God to speak unto you the gospel
     of God *with* much contention.
   3. nor of uncleanness, nor *in* guile:
   5. at any time used we flattering words (lit.
     were we *in* fl. w.), as ye know, nor a
     cloke (lit. *in* a cloke) of covetous-
     ness ;
  6(7). we might have been burdensome, (lit.
     in or *for* a burden)
   7. we were gentle *among* you,
  13. worketh also *in* you that believe.
  14. which *in* Judæa are *in* Christ Jesus:
  17. to see your face *with* great desire.
  19. Lord Jesus Christ *at* his coming?
3: 1. to be left *at* Athens alone;
   2. labourer *in* the gospel of Christ,
   3. moved *by* these afflictions:
   8. if ye stand fast *in* the Lord.
  13. unblameable *in* holiness before
— *at* the coming of our Lord Jesus
4: 1. exhort (you) *by* the Lord Jesus,
   4. *in* sanctification and honour ;
   5. Not *in* the lust of concupiscence,
   6. defraud his brother *in* (any) matter:
   7. unto uncleanness, but *unto* holiness.
  10. which are *in* all Macedonia:
  15. unto you *by* the word of the Lord,
  16. *with* a shout, *with* the voice of the arch-
     angel, and *with* the trump of God: and
     the dead *in* Christ shall rise first:
  17. together with them *in* the clouds,
  18. comfort one another *with* these words.
5: 2. cometh as a thief *in* the night.
   3. as travail upon a woman with child; (lit.
     having *in* the womb)
   4. But ye, brethren, are not *in* darkness,
  12. *among* you, and are over you *in* the Lord,
  13. *in* love for their work's sake. (And) be
     at peace *among* yourselves.
  18. *In* every thing give thanks: for this is the
     will of God *in* Christ Jesus
  23. *unto* the coming of our Lord Jesus
  26. all the brethren *with* an holy kiss.
2Th. 1: 1. *in* God our Father and the Lord
   4. glory *in* you *in* the churches
— faith *in* all your persecutions
   7. when the Lord Jesus shall be revealed
     (lit. *in* the revelation of the Lord Jesus)
   8. *In* flaming fire taking vengeance

2Th. 1:10. to be glorified *in* his saints, and to be
     admired *in* all them that believe
— was believed *in* that day.
  11. the work of faith *with* power:
  12. glorified *in* you, and ye *in* him,
2: 6. might be revealed *in* his time.
   9. *with* all power and signs
  10. *with* all deceivableness of unrighteousness
     in them that perish ;
  12. had pleasure *in* unrighteousness.
  13. *through* sanctification of the
  16. consolation and good hope *through* grace,
  17. stablish you *in* every good word
3: 4. we have confidence *in* the Lord
   6. *in* the name of our Lord Jesus
   7. not ourselves disorderly *among* you;
   8. wrought *with* labour and travail
  11. which walk *among* you disorderly, .
  16. peace always *by* all means.
  17. is the token *in* every epistle:
1Ti. 1: 2. (my) own son *in* the faith :
   3. thee to abide still *at* Ephesus,
   4. godly edifying which is *in* faith:
  13. I did (it) ignorantly *in* unbelief.
  14. love which is *in* Christ Jesus.
  16. that *in* me first Jesus Christ
  18. that thou *by* them mightest
2: 2. (for) all that are *in* authority ; ·
— *in* all godliness and honesty.
   7. I speak the truth *in* Christ,
— a teacher of the Gentiles *in* faith
   8. that men pray every where, (lit. *in* every
     place)
   9. adorn themselves *in* modest apparel,
— not *with* broidered hair, or gold,
  11. learn *in* silence *with* all subjection.
  12. over the man, but to be *in* silence.
  14. was *in* the transgression.
  15. if they continue *in* faith and charity
3: 4. having his children *in* subjection
   9. the faith *in* a pure conscience.
  11. sober, faithful *in* all things.
  13. *in* the faith which is *in* Christ Jesus.
  15. behave thyself *in* the house of God,
  16. God was manifest *in* the flesh, justified *in*
     the Spirit,
— preached *unto* the Gentiles, believed on
     in the world, received up *into* glory.
4: 1. that *in* the latter times some shall
   2. Speaking lies *in* hypocrisy ;
  12. *in* word, *in* conversation, *in* charity, *in*
     spirit, *in* faith, *in* purity.
  14. the gift that is *in* thee, which
  15. give thyself wholly *to* them (lit. be *in*
     them); that thy profiting may appear
     to all.
5: 2. younger as sisters. *with* all purity.
  10. Well reported of *for* good works;
  17. they who labour *in* the word
6:17. that are rich *in* this world,
— *in* the living God, who giveth
  18. that they be rich *in* good works,
2Ti. 1: 1. life which is *in* Christ Jesus,
   3. *with* pure conscience, that
— *in* my prayers night and day;
   5. unfeigned faith that is *in* thee, which
     dwelt first *in* thy grandmother
— I am persuaded that *in* thee also.
   6. the gift of God, which is *in* thee
   9. was given us *in* Christ Jesus
  13. *in* faith and love which is *in* Christ
  14. Holy Ghost which dwelleth *in* us.

2Ti. 1:15. all they which are *in* Asia
17. when he was *in* Rome,
18. mercy of the Lord *in* that day:
— ministered unto me *at* Ephesus,
2: 1. *in* the grace that is *in* Christ Jesus.
7. understanding *in* all things.
9. Where*in* I suffer trouble,
10. salvation which is *in* Christ Jesus
20. *in* a great house there are not
25. *In* meekness instructing those
3: 1. that *in* the last days perilous
11. unto me *at* Antioch, *at* Iconium, *at* Lystra;
12. will live godly *in* Christ Jesus
14. *in* the things which thou hast
15. faith which is *in* Christ Jesus.
16. for instruction *in* righteousness:
4: 2. *with* all longsuffering and doctrine.
5. watch thou *in* all things,
8. shall give me *at* that day:
13. The cloke that I left *at* Troas
16. *At* my first answer no man
20. Erastus abode *at* Corinth: but Trophimus have I left *at* Miletum
Tit. 1: 3. manifested his word *through* preaching,
5. this cause left I thee *in* Crete,
6. not accused (lit. not *in* accusation) of riot, or unruly.
9. may be able *by* sound doctrine
13. they may be sound *in* the faith ;
2: 3. *in* behaviour as becometh holiness,
7. *in* doctrine (shewing) uncorruptness,
9. to please (them) well *in* all (things);
10. God our Saviour *in* all things.
12. righteously, and godly, *in* this present world ;
3: 3. living *in* malice and envy, hateful,
5. Not by works *of* righteousness which
15. them that love us *in* the faith.
Philem. 6. *by* the acknowledging of every good thing which is *in* you
8. might be much bold *in* Christ
10. whom I have begotten *in* my bonds:
13. *in* the bonds of the gospel:
16. both *in* the flesh, and *in* the Lord ?
20. have joy of thee *in* the Lord: refresh my bowels *in* the Lord.
23. my fellowprisoner *in* Christ Jesus ;
Heb. 1: 1. unto the fathers *by* the prophets,
2(1). spoken unto us *by* (his) Son,
3. *on* the right hand of the Majesty *on* high;
2: 8. For *in* that he put all
12. *in* the midst of the church
16. For *in* that he himself hath
3: 2. Moses (was faithful) *in* all his house.
5. faithful *in* all his house,
8. as *in* the provocation, in the day of temptation *in* the wilderness ;
11. So I sware *in* my wrath,
12. lest there be *in* any of you
— *in* departing from the living God.
15. While it is said (lit. *in* its being said), To day if ye
— as *in* the provocation.
17. carcases fell *in* the wilderness ?
4: 3. As I have sworn *in* my wrath,
4. God did rest)(the seventh day
5. *in* this (place) again, If they
7. a certain day, saying *in* David,
11. *after* the same example of unbelief.
5: 6. he saith also *in* another (place),
7. Who *in* the days of his flesh,
6:17. Where*in* God, willing more

Heb 6:18. *in* which (it was) impossible
7:10. yet *in* the loins of his father,
8: 1. who is set *on* the right hand
— of the Majesty *in* the heavens ;
5. shewed to thee *in* the mount.
9. *in* the day when I took them
— they continued not *in* my covenant,
13. *In* that he saith, A new (covenant),
9: 2. where*in* (was) the candlestick,
4. where*in* (was) the golden pot that
22. by the law purged *with* blood ;
23. patterns of things *in* the heavens
25. every year *with* blood of others ;
10: 3. *in* those (sacrifices there is) a remembrance
7. *in* the volume of the book it is
10. *By* the which will we are sanctified
12. *on* the right hand of God ;
19. the holiest *by* the blood of Jesus,
22. *in* full assurance of faith,
29. where*with* he was sanctified,
32. the former days, *in* which, after
34. knowing *in* yourselves that ye have *in* heaven a better and an
38. shall have no pleasure *in* him.
11: 2. For *by* it the elders obtained
9. dwelling *in* tabernacles
18. *in* Isaac shall thy seed be called:
19. he received him *in* a figure.
26. than the treasures *in* Egypt:
34. made strong, waxed valiant *in* fight,
37. were slain *with* the sword: (lit. died *in* the slaughter of the sword)
— *in* sheepskins (and))(goatskins;
38. they wandered *in* deserts,
12: 2. set down *at* the right hand
23. which are written *in* heaven,
13: 3. being yourselves also *in* the body.
4. Marriage (is) honourable *in* all,
9. that have been occupied there*in*.
18. *in* all things willing to live
20. *through* the blood of the everlasting
21. perfect *in* every good work to do his will, working *in* you that which
Jas. 1: 1. tribes which are scattered abroad, (lit. *in* the dispersion)
4. perfect and entire, wanting)(nothing.
6. let him ask *in* faith, nothing wavering:
8. unstable *in* all his ways.
9. rejoice in that he is exalted: (lit. *in* his exaltation)
10. in that he is made low: (lit. *in* his humiliation)
11. the rich man fade away *in* his ways.
21. receive *with* meekness the
23. beholding his natural face *in* a glass:
25. shall be blessed *in* his deed.
26. If any man *among* you seem
27. fatherless and widows *in* their affliction,
2: 1. *with* respect of persons.
2. with a gold ring, *in* goodly apparel,
— also a poor man *in* vile raiment ;
4. not then partial *in* yourselves,
5. poor of this world rich *in* faith,
10. yet offend *in* one (point),
16. say unto them, Depart *in* peace,
3: 2. If any man offend not *in* word,
6. so is the tongue *among* our members,
9. There*with* bless we God, even the Father; and there*with* curse we men,
13. endued with knowledge *among* you ?
— *with* meekness of wisdom.
14. envying and strife *in* your hearts,

Jas. 3:18. righteousness is sown *in* peace
4: 1. wars and fightings *among* you?
— lusts that war *in* your members?
3. may consume (it) *upon* your lusts.
5. The spirit that dwelleth *in* us
16. ye rejoice *in* your boastings:
5: 3. treasure together *for* the last days.
5. as *in* a day of slaughter.
13. Is any *among* you afflicted?
14. Is any sick *among* you?
— *in* the name of the Lord:
19. if any *of* you do err from the truth,
1Pet. 1: 2. *through* sanctification of the Spirit,
4. reserved *in* heaven for you,
5. kept *by* the power of God
— to be revealed *in* the last time.
6. Where*in* ye greatly rejoice, though
— in heaviness *through* manifold temptations:
7. *at* the appearing of Jesus Christ:
11. which was *in* them did signify,
12. unto you *with* the Holy Ghost
13. *at* the revelation of Jesus Christ;
14. former lusts *in* your ignorance:
15. holy *in* all manner of conversation;
17. of your sojourning (here) *in* fear:
22. purified your souls *in* obeying the
2: 2. that ye may grow there*by:*
6. it is contained *in* the scripture, Behold, I lay *in* Sion a chief
12. honest *among* the Gentiles: that, whereas (lit. *in* that which) they speak against
— glorify God *in* the day of visitation.
18. subject to (your) masters *with* all fear;
22. was guile found *in* his mouth:
24. bare our sins *in* his own body
3: 2. conversation (coupled) *with* fear.
4. *in* that which is not corruptible,
15. sanctify the Lord God *in* your
— of the hope that is *in* you
16. whereas (lit. *in* that which) they speak evil of you,
— your good conversation *in* Christ.
19. *By* which also he went and preached unto the spirits *in* prison;
20. waited *in* the days of Noah,
22. is *on* the right hand of God
4: 1. hath suffered *in* the flesh
2. rest of (his) time *in* the flesh
3. we walked *in* lasciviousness,
4. Where*in* they think it strange
11. that God *in* all things may be
12. strange concerning the fiery trial which is to try you, (lit. the fiery trial *in* you which is to try you)
13. when his glory shall be revealed, (lit. *in* the revelation of his glory)
14. reproached *for* the name of Christ,
16. glorify God *on* this behalf.
19. (to him) *in* well doing,
5: 1. The elders which are *among* you
2. flock of God which is *among* you,
6. he may exalt you *in* due time:
9. your brethren that are *in* the world.
10. his eternal glory *by* Christ Jesus,
13. The (church that is) *at* Babylon,
14. one another *with* a kiss of charity.
— all that are *in* Christ Jesus.
2Pet. 1: 1. *through* the righteousness of God
2. *through* the knowledge of God,
4. that is *in* the world *through* lust.
5. add *to* your faith virtue; and *to* virtue

2Pet. 1: 6. *to* knowledge temperance; and *to* temperance patience; and *to* patience
7. *to* godliness brotherly kindness; and *to* brotherly kindness charity.
12. established *in* the present truth.
13. as long as I am *in* this tabernacle,
— *by* putting (you) in remembrance;
18. with him *in* the holy mount.
19. a light that shineth *in* a dark place,
— the day star arise *in* your hearts:
2: 1. there were false prophets also *among* the people, even as there shall be false teachers *among* you,
3. *through* covetousness shall they
7. vexed *with* the filthy conversation
8. righteous man dwelling *among* them,
10. *in* the lust of uncleanness,
12. speak evil *of* the things that they understand not; and shall utterly perish *in* their own corruption;
13. to riot *in* the day time.
— *with* their own deceivings
16. speaking *with* man's voice
18. they allure *through* the lusts of the
— from them who live *in* error.
20. *through* the knowledge of the Lord
3: 1. *in* (both) which I stir up your pure minds *by* way of remembrance;
10. as a thief *in* the night; *in* the which the heavens
— the works that are there*in*
11. *in* (all) holy conversation
13. where*in* dwelleth righteousness.
14. ye may be found of him *in* peace,
16. *in* all (his) epistles, speaking *in* them of these things; *in* which are some things hard
18. grow *in* grace, and (in) the knowledge
1 Joh. 1: 5. *in* him is no darkness
6. with him, and walk *in* darkness,
7. walk *in* the light, as he is *in*
8. the truth is not *in* us.
10. his word is not *in* us.
2: 3. here*by* we do know that we
4. the truth is not *in* him.
5. *in* him verily is the love of God perfected: here*by* know we that we are *in* him.
6. that saith he abideth *in* him
8. is true *in* him and *in* you:
9. that saith he is *in* the light,
— is *in* darkness even until now.
10. abideth *in* the light, and there is none occasion of stumbling *in* him.
11. is *in* darkness, and walketh *in* darkness,
14. word of God abideth *in* you,
15. things (that are) *in* the world.
— the Father is not *in* him.
16. For all that (is) *in* the world,
24. Let that therefore abide *in* you,
— shall remain *in* you, ye also shall continue *in* the Son, and *in* the Father.
27. received of him abideth *in* you,
— ye shall abide *in* him.
28. little children, abide *in* him;
— ashamed before him *at* his coming
3: 5. and *in* him is no sin.
6. Whosoever abideth *in* him sinneth not:
9. his seed remaineth *in* him:
10. *In* this the children of God are manifest,
14. not (his) brother abideth *in* death.
15. hath eternal life abiding *in* him.
16. Here*by* perceive we the love

1Joh. 3:17. the love of God *in* him?

19. here*by* we know that we are

24. dwelleth *in* him, and he *in* him. And here*by* we know that he abideth *in* us,

4: 2. Here*by* know ye the Spirit

— come *in* the flesh is of God:

3. come *in* the flesh is not of God:

— now already is it *in* the world.

4. greater is he that is *in* you, than he that is *in* the world.

9. *In* this was manifested the love of God *toward* us,

10. Here*in* is love, not that we

12. God dwelleth *in* us, and his love is perfected *in* us.

13. Here*by* know we that we dwell *in* him, and he *in* us,

15. God dwelleth *in* him, and he *in* God.

16. the love that God hath *to* us.

— he that dwelleth *in* love dwelleth *in* God, and God *in* him.

17. Here*in* is our love made perfect,

— boldness *in* the day of judgment:

— so are we *in* this world.

18. There is no fear *in* love:

— is not made perfect *in* love.

5: 2. *By* this we know that we

6. not *by* water only, but *by* water and blood.

7. three that bear record *in* heaven,

8. three that bear witness *in* earth,

10. hath the witness *in* himself:

11. this life is *in* his Son.

19. whole world lieth *in* wickedness.

20. we are *in* him that is true, (even) *in* his Son Jesus Christ.

2Joh. 1. whom I love *in* the truth;

2. truth's sake, which dwelleth *in* us,

3. the Father, *in* truth and love.

4. thy children walking *in* truth,

6. ye should walk *in* it.

7. Jesus Christ is come *in* the flesh.

9. abideth not *in* the doctrine of

— He that abideth *in* the doctrine

3 Joh. 1. whom I love *in* the truth.

3. as thou walkest *in* the truth.

4. that my children walk *in* truth.

Jude 1. sanctified *by* God the Father,

10. as brute beasts, *in* those things they corrupt themselves.

12. These are spots *in* your feasts of

14. the Lord cometh *with* ten thousands

18. be mockers *in* the last time,

20. praying *in* the Holy Ghost,

21. Keep yourselves *in* the love of God,

23. And others save *with* fear,

24. before the presence of his glory *with* exceeding joy,

Rev. 1: 1. must short*ly* come to pass;

3. things which are written there*in:*

4. churches which are *in* Asia:

5. from our sins *in* his own blood,

9. companion *in* tribulation, and *in* the

— was *in* the isle that is called

10. I was *in* the Spirit *on* the Lord's day,

11. seven churches which are *in* Asia;

13. *in* the midst of the seven

15. as if they burned *in* a furnace,

16. he had *in* his right hand

— as the sun shineth *in* his strength.

2: 1. seven stars *in* his right hand, who walketh *in* the midst of

Rev. 2: 7. *in* the midst of the paradise

12. the church *in* Pergamos write;

13. even *in* those days where*in*

14. who taught)(Balac to cast a stumbling-block

16. *with* the sword of my mouth.

18. of the church *in* Thyatira write;

23. I will kill her children *with* death;

24. unto the rest *in* Thyatira,

27. rule them *with* a rod of iron;

3: 1. of the church *in* Sardis write;

4. hast a few names even *in* Sardis

— shall walk with me *in* white:

5. shall be clothed *in* white raiment;

7. of the church *in* Philadelphia

12. a pillar *in* the temple of my God,

21. to sit with me *in* my throne,

— with my Father *in* his throne.

4: 1. a door (was) opened *in* heaven:

2. immediately I was *in* the spirit: and, behold, a throne was set *in* heaven,

4. sitting, clothed *in* white raiment;

6. *in* the midst of the throne,

5: 3. no man *in* heaven, nor

6. *in* the midst of the throne

— *in* the midst of the elders,

9. redeemed us to God *by* thy blood

13. which is *in* heaven, and *on* the earth,

— the sea, and all that are *in* them,

6: 5. a pair of balances *in* his hand.

6. *in* the midst of the four beasts

8. *with* sword, and *with* hunger, and *with* death,

7: 9. palms *in* their hands;

14. white *in* the blood of the Lamb.

15. day and night *in* his temple:

8: 1. there was silence *in* heaven

9. creatures which were *in* the sea,

13. *through* the midst of heaven,

9: 6. *in* those days shall men seek

10. there were stings *in* their tails:

11. *in* the Greek tongue hath (his)

17. thus I saw the horses *in* the vision,

19. power is *in* their mouth, and in their

— *with* them they do hurt.

20. were not killed *by* these plagues

10: 2. he had *in* his hand a little book

6. sware *by* him that liveth for ever and ever, who created heaven, and the things that there*in* are, and the earth, and the things that there*in* are, and the sea, and the things which are there*in*,

7. *in* the days of the voice

8. open *in* the hand of the angel

9. it shall be *in* thy mouth sweet

10. it was *in* my mouth sweet

11: 1. them that worship there*in*.

6. *in* the days of their prophecy:

12. ascended up to heaven *in* a cloud;

13.)(the same hour was there a great earthquake,

— *in* the earthquake were slain

15. there were great voices *in* heaven,

19. temple of God was opened *in* heaven, and there was seen *in* his temple

12: 1. appeared a great wonder *in* heaven;

2. she being with child (lit. having *in* the womb) cried, travailing

3. another wonder *in* heaven;

5. all nations *with* a rod of iron;

7. there was war *in* heaven:

8. found any more *in* heaven.

Rev.12:10. a loud voice saying *in* heaven,
12. ye that dwell *in* them.
13: 3. all the world wondered after (lit. *in* all the world it was wondered)
6. them that dwell *in* heaven.
8. written *in* the book of life
10. he that killeth *with* the sword must be killed *with* the sword.
12. them which dwell there*in*
14: 2. harpers harping *with* their harps:
5. *in* their mouth was found no
6. fly *in* the midst of heaven,
7. Saying *with* a loud voice,
9. saying *with* a loud voice,
10. *into* the cup of his indignation;
— tormented *with* fire and brimstone
13. the dead which die *in* the Lord
14. *in* his hand a sharp sickle.
15. crying *with* a loud voice to him
17. the temple which is *in* heaven,
15: 1. I saw another sign *in* heaven,
— *in* them is filled up the wrath
5. the testimony *in* heaven was
16: 3. every living soul died *in* the sea.
8. to scorch men *with* fire.
17: 3. carried me away *in* the spirit
4. having a golden cup *in* her hand
16. eat her flesh, and burn her *with* fire.
18: 2. cried mightily *with* a strong voice,
6. *in* the cup which she hath filled
7. for she saith *in* her heart,
8. her plagues come *in* one day,
— shall be utterly burned *with* fire:
10. *in* one hour is thy judgment come.
16. purple, and scarlet, and decked *with* gold,
19. where*in* were made rich all that had ships *in* the sea by
22. heard no more at all *in* thee;
— shall be found any more *in* thee;
— shall be heard no more at all *in* thee;
23. shine no more at all *in* thee;
— heard no more at all *in* thee:
— for *by* thy sorceries were all
24. *in* her was found the blood
19: 1. voice of much people *in* heaven,
2. corrupt the earth *with* her fornication,
11. *in* righteousness he doth judge
14. the armies (which were) *in* heaven
15. *with* it he should smite the nations : and he shall rule them *with* a rod of iron:
17. an angel standing *in* the sun;
— fowls that fly *in* the midst of heaven,
20. *with* which he deceived them
— lake of fire burning *with* brimstone.
21. remnant were slain *with* the sword
20: 6. hath part *in* the first resurrection:
8. which are *in* the four quarters
12. which were written *in* the books,
13. the dead which were *in* it;
— the dead which were *in* them:
15. found written *in* the book of life
21: 8. shall have their part *in* the lake
10. he carried me away *in* the spirit
14. *in* them the names of the twelve
22. I saw no temple there*in* :
23. the moon, to shine *in* it:
24. shall walk *in* the light of it:
27. are written *in* the Lamb's book
22: 2. *In* the midst of the street of it,
3. the Lamb shall be *in* it;
6. things which must short*ly* be done.
18. that are written *in* this book:

Rev.22:19. which are written *in* this book.

ἐναγκαλίζομαι, enankalizomai.

Mar. 9:36. *when* he had *taken* him *in* his *arms*,
10:16. he *took* them *up in* his *arms*, put (his) hands upon them, *and* blessed them.

ἐνάλιος, enalios.

Jas. 3: 7. and of *things in the sea*, is tamed,

ἔναντι, enanti.

Lu. 1: 8. *before* God in the order of his course,

ἐναντίον, enantion.

Mar. 2:12. went forth *before* them all;
Lu. 20:26. his words *before* the people:
24:19. *before* God and all the people:
Acts 7:10. wisdom *in the sight of* Pharaoh
8:32. like a lamb dumb *before* his shearer,

ἐναντίος, enantios.

Mat.14:24. for the wind was *contrary*.
Mar. 6:48. for the wind was *contrary* unto
15:39. which stood *over against* him, (lit. from or on the *opposite* side)
Acts26: 9. many things *contrary* to the name of Jesus
27: 4. because the winds were *contrary*.
28:17. committed nothing *against* the people,
1Th. 2:15. are *contrary* to all men:
Tit. 2: 8. he that is of the *contrary* part

ἐνάρχομαι, enarkomai.

Gal. 3: 3. *having begun* in the Spirit,
Phi. 1: 6. that he *which hath begun* a good work in you

ἐνδεής, ende-ees.

Acts 4:34. any among them that lacked: (lit. *needy*)

ἔνδειγμα, endīgma.

2Th. 1: 5. a *manifest token* of the righteous

ἐνδείκνυμι, endīknumi.

Ro. 2:15. Which *shew* the work of the law
9:17. that I *might shew* my power
22. willing *to shew* (his) wrath,
2Co. 8:24. Wherefore *shew* ye to them,
Eph. 2: 7. he *might shew* the exceeding riches
1Ti. 1:16. Jesus Christ *might shew forth*
2Ti. 4:14. the coppersmith *did* me much evil:
Tit. 2:10. *shewing* all good fidelity;
3: 2. *shewing* all meekness unto all men.
Heb. 6:10. ye *have shewed* toward his name,
11. desire that every one of you *do shew* the same diligence

ἔνδειξις, endīxis.

Ro. 3:25. to declare (lit. for *declaration* of) his righteousness
     26. To declare (lit. for *declaration* &c.), (I say), at this time
2Co. 8:24. the *proof* of your love, and of our
Phi. 1:28. to them an *evident token* of perdition,

ἔνδεκα, hendeka.

Mat.28:16. Then the *eleven* disciples went away
Mar 16:14. he appeared unto the *eleven*
Lu. 24: 9. told all these things unto the *eleven*,
     33. found the *eleven* gathered together,
Acts 1:26. numbered with the *eleven* apostles.
     2:14. Peter, standing up with the *eleven*,

ἐνδέκατος, hendekatos.

Mat.20: 6. about the *eleventh* hour he
     9. (were hired) about the *eleventh* hour,
Rev.21:20. the *eleventh*, a jacinth;

ἐνδέχεται, endeketai.

Lu. 13:33. for it *cannot* be that a prophet

ἐνδημέω, endeemeo.

2Co. 5: 6. *whilst* we *are at home* in the
     8. *to be present* with the Lord.
     9. that, whether *present* or absent, we may

ἐνδιδύσκομαι, endiduskomai.

Lu. 8:27. long time, and *ware* no clothes,
     16:19. which *was clothed in* purple

ἔνδικος, endikos.

Ro. 3: 8. whose damnation is *just*.
Heb. 2: 2. received a *just* recompence

ἐνδόμησις, endomeesis.

Rev.21:18. the *building* of the wall of it

ἐνδοξάζομαι, endoxazomai.

2Th. 1:10. he shall come *to be glorified* in
     12. That the name of our Lord Jesus Christ *may be glorified*

ἔνδοξος, endoxos.

Lu. 7:25. they which are *gorgeously* apparelled,
     13:17. for all the *glorious* things that were done by him.
1Co. 4:10. ye (are) strong; ye (are) *honourable*,
Eph. 5:27. That he might present it to himself a *glorious* church,

ἔνδυμα, enduma.

Mat. 3: 4. John had his *raiment* of camel's hair,
     6:25. than meat, and the body than *raiment?*
     28. why take ye thought for *raiment?*
     7:15. come to you in sheep's *clothing,*
     22:11. had not on a wedding *garment:*
     12. not having a wedding *garment?*
     28: 3. his *raiment* white as snow:
Lu. 12:23. the body (is more) than *raiment.*

ἐνδυναμόω, endunamoō.

Acts 9:22. Saul *increased* the more *in strength,*
Ro. 4:20. *was strong* in faith, giving glory
Eph. 6:10. brethren, *be strong* in the Lord,
Phi. 4:13. Christ which *strengtheneth* me.
1Ti. 1:12. Jesus our Lord, *who hath enabled* me,
2Ti. 2: 1. my son, *be strong* in the grace that
     4:17. with me, and *strengthened* me;
Heb 11:34. out of weakness *were made strong,*

ἐνδύνω, enduno.

2Ti. 3: 6. they which *creep* into houses,

ἔνδυσις, endusis.

1Pet. 3: 3. or of *putting on* of apparel;

ἐνδύω, enduo.

Mat. 6:25. your body, what ye *shall put on.*
     22:11. a man *which had* not *on* a wedding garment:
     27:31. and *put* his own raiment *on* him,
Mar. 1: 6. John was *clothed with* camel's hair,
     6: 9. not *put on* two coats.
     15:17. they *clothed* him with purple,
     20. *put* his own clothes *on* him,
Lu. 12:22. the body, what ye *shall put on.*
     15:22. the best robe, and *put* (it) *on* him;
     24:49. until ye *be endued* with power
Acts12:21. Herod, *arrayed* in royal apparel,
Ro. 13:12. let us *put on* the armour of light.
     14. *put* ye *on* the Lord Jesus Christ,
1Co.15:53. For this corruptible must *put on* incorruption,
     — (must) *put on* immortality.
     54. shall have *put on* incorruption,
     — shall have *put on* immortality,
2Co. 5: 3. If so be that *being clothed*
Gal. 3:27. into Christ have *put on* Christ.
Eph. 4:24. that ye *put on* (lit. *have put on*) the new man,
     6:11. *Put on* the whole armour of God,
     14. *having on* the breastplate of
Col. 3:10. *have put on* the new (man),
     12. *Put on* therefore, as the elect of God,
1Th. 5: 8. *putting on* the breastplate of faith
Rev. 1:13. *clothed with* a garment down to the foot,
     15: 6. *clothed in* pure and white linen,
     19:14. *clothed in* fine linen, white and clean.

ἐνέγκω see φέρω.

ἐνέδρα & -δρον, enedra & -dron.

Acts 23:16. heard of their *lying in wait*,
    25: 3. laying wait (lit. making a *lying in wait*)
      in the way to kill him.

ἐνεδρεύω, enedrŭo.

Lu. 11:54. *Laying wait for* him, and seeking
Acts 23:21. for there *lie in wait for* him

ἐνειλέω, enīleo.

Mar 15:46. and *wrapped* him *in* the linen,

ἔνειμι, enīmi.

Lu. 11:41. But rather give alms of *such things as ye have ;* (lit. but as to *things that are in*)

ἕνεκα, ἕνεκεν, εἵνεκεν,
heneka, heneken, hīneken.

Mat. 5:10. persecuted *for* righteousness' *sake :*
    11. against you falsely, *for* my *sake.*
   10:18. *for* my *sake,* for a testimony against
    39. loseth his life *for* my *sake* shall
   16:25. will lose his life *for* my *sake*
   19: 5. *For* this *cause* shall a man
    29. *for* my name's *sake,* shall receive
Mar. 8:35. shall lose his life *for* my *sake*
   10: 7. *For* this *cause* shall a man leave
    29. *for* my *sake,* and the gospel's,
    13: before rulers and kings *for* my *sake,*
Lu. 4:18. *because* (or lit. *in* that) he hath anointed
   6:22. *for* the Son of man's *sake.*
   9:24. will lose his life *for* my *sake,*
   18:29. *for* the kingdom of God's *sake,*
   21:12. *for* my name's *sake.*
Acts 19:32. knew not where*fore* they were come
   26:21. *For* these *causes* the Jews caught me
   28:20. because that *for* the hope of Israel
Ro. 8:36. *For* thy *sake* we are killed all the day
   14:20. *For* meat destroy not the work of God.
2Co. 3:10. *by reason of* the glory that excelleth.
   7:12. not *for* his *cause* that had done the wrong,
    nor *for* his *cause* that suffered wrong,
    but *that* (lit. *for that*) our care

ἐνέργεια, energīa.

Eph. 1:19. the *working* of his mighty power,
   3: 7. by the *effectual working* of his power.
   4:16. the *effectual working* in the
Phi. 3:21. according to the *working* whereby
Col. 1:29. striving according to his *working,*
   2:12. through the faith of the *operation* of
2Th. 2: 9. is after the *working* of Satan
   11. shall send them strong delusion, (lit. *working* of error)

ἐνεργέω, energeo.

Mat. 14: 2. works *do shew forth* themselves in him.
Mar. 6:14. mighty works *do shew forth* them*selves*
Ro. 7: 5. *did work* in our members
1Co. 12: 6. God *which worketh* all in all.

ICo. 12:11. all these *worketh* that one and the self-
    same Spirit,
2Co. 1: 6. *which is effectual* (lit. *that worketh*) in the enduring
   4:12. So then death *worketh* in us,
Gal. 2: 8. For he *that wrought effectually in* Peter
    — the same *was mighty in* me
   3: 5. and *worketh* miracles among you,
   5: 6. faith *which worketh* by love.
Eph. 1:11. of him *who worketh* all things
    20. Which he *wrought* in Christ,
   2: 2. the spirit *that* now *worketh in*
   3:20. the power *that worketh in* us,
Phi. 2:13. God *which worketh in* you both to will and to do of (his) good
Col. 1:29. *which worketh in* me mightily.
1Th. 2:13. which *effectually worketh* also *in* you
2Th. 2: 7. mystery of iniquity *doth* already *work:*
Jas. 5:16. The *effectual fervent* prayer of a righteous man availeth much.

ἐνέργημα, energeema.

1Co. 12: 6. there are diversities of *operations,*
    10. To another the *working* of miracles ;

ἐνεργής, energees.

1Co. 16: 9. a great door and *effectual* is opened
Philem 6. become *effectual* by the acknowledging
Heb. 4:12. word of God (is) quick, and *powerful,*

ἐνεστῶτα see ἐνίστημι.

ἐνευλογέομαι, enŭlogeomai.

Acts 3:25. in thy seed *shall* all the kindreds of the earth *be blessed.*
Gal. 3: 8. In thee *shall* all nations *be blessed.*

ἐνέχω, eneko.

Mar. 6:19. Herodias *had a quarrel against* him,
Lu. 11:53. began *to urge* (him) vehemently,
Gal. 5: 1. *be* not *entangled* again *with* the

ἐνθάδε, enthade.

Lu. 24:41. Have ye *here* any meat?
Joh. 4:15. neither come *hither* to draw.
    16. call thy husband, and come *hither.*
Acts 10:18. Peter, were lodged *there.*
   16:28. for we are all *here.*
   17: 6. are come *hither* also ;
   25:17. when they were come *hither,*
    24. both at Jerusalem, and (also) *here,*

ἐνθυμέομαι, enthumeomai.

Mat. 1:20. *while* he *thought* on these things,
   9: 4. Wherefore *think* ye evil in your
Acts 10:19. *While* Peter *thought* on the vision,

ἐνθύμησις, enthumeesis.

Mat. 9: 4. Jesus knowing their *thoughts*
　　12:25. Jesus knew their *thoughts*,
Acts17:29. graven by art and man's *device*.
Heb. 4:12. a discerner of the *thoughts* and intents

ἔνι for ἔνεστι.

Gal. 3:28. *There is* neither Jew nor Greek, *there is*
　　　　neither bond nor free, *there is* neither
　　　　male nor female:
Col. 3:11. Where *there is* neither Greek nor Jew,
Jas. 1:17. with whom *is* no variableness,

ἐνιαυτός, eniautos.

Lu. 4:19. the acceptable *year* of the Lord.
Joh. 11:49. the high priest that same *year*,
　　　　51. being high priest that *year*,
　　18:13. the high priest that same *year*.
Acts11:26. a whole *year* they assembled
　　18:11. continued (there) a *year* and six months,
Gal. 4:10. days, and months, and times, and *years*.
Heb. 9: 7. high priest alone once every *year*,
　　　　25. into the holy place every *year*
　　10: 1. they offered year by *year*
　　　　3. again (made) of sins every *year*.
Jas. 4:13. continue there a *year*, and buy
　　5:17. by the space of three *years*
Rev. 9:15. an hour, and a day, and a month, and a
　　　　year,

ἐνίστημι, enisteemi.

Ro. 8:38. nor powers, nor things *present*,
1Co. 3:22. things *present*, or things to come ;
　　7:26. good for the *present* distress,
Gal. 1: 4. from this *present* evil world,
2Th. 2: 2. the day of Christ *is at hand*.
2Ti. 3: 1. perilous times *shall come*.
Heb.9: 9. for the time then *present*,

ἐνισχύω, eniskuo.

Lu. 22:43. from heaven, *strengthening* him.
Acts 9:19. received meat, he *was strengthened*.

ἔννατος, ennatos.

Mat.20: 5. about the sixth and *ninth* hour,
　　27:45. all the land unto the *ninth* hour.
　　　　46. about the *ninth* hour Jesus cried
Mar.15:33. whole land until the *ninth* hour.
　　　　34. at the *ninth* hour Jesus cried
Lu. 23:44. all the earth until the *ninth* hour.
Acts 3: 1. (being) the *ninth* (hour).
　　10: 3. about the *ninth* hour of the day
　　　　30. at the *ninth* hour I prayed
Rev.21:20. the *ninth*, a topaz ; the tenth, a

ἐννέα, ennea.

Lu. 17:17. where (are) the *nine?*

ἐννενηκονταεννέα, enneneekontaennea.

Mat.18:12. doth he not leave the *ninety* and *nine*,

Mat.18:13. the *ninety* and *nine* which went not
Lu. 15: 4. doth not leave the *ninety* and *nine*
　　　　7. than over *ninety* and *nine* just persons,

ἐννεός, enneos.

Acts 9: 7. stood *speechless*, hearing a voice,

ἐννεύω, ennuo.

Lu. 1:62. they *made signs* to his father,

ἔννοια, ennoia.

Heb. 4:12. thoughts and *intents* of the heart.
1Pet.4: 1. arm yourselves likewise with the same
　　　　mind:

ἔννομος, ennomos.

Acts19:39. determined in a *lawful* assembly.
1Co. 9:21. but *under* the *law* to Christ,

ἔννυχον, ennukon.

Mar. 1:35. in the morning, rising up a great while
　　　　before day, (lit. while yet much *in the
　　　　night*)

ἐνοικέω, enoikeo.

Ro. 8:11. his Spirit that *dwelleth in* you.
2Co. 6:16. God hath said, I *will dwell in* them,
Col. 3:16. *Let* the word of Christ *dwell in* you
2Ti. 1: 5. which *dwelt* first *in* thy grandmother
　　　　14. Holy Ghost which *dwelleth in* us.

ἐνόντα see ἔνειμι.

ἑνότης, henotees.

Eph. 4: 3. to keep the *unity* of the Spirit
　　　　13. come in the *unity* of the faith,

ἐνοχλέω, enokleo.

Heb12:15. lest any root of bitterness springing up
　　　　trouble

ἔνοχος, enokos.

Mat. 5:21. shall be *in danger of* the judgment:
　　　　22. shall be *in danger of* the judgment:
　　　　— shall be *in danger of* the council:
　　　　— shall be *in danger of* hell fire.
　　26:66. said, He is *guilty of* death.
Mar. 3:29. is *in danger of* eternal damnation:
　　14:64. condemned him to be *guilty of* death.
1Co.11:27. shall be *guilty of* the body and blood
Heb. 2:15. their lifetime *subject* to bondage.
Jas. 2:10. offend in one (point), he is *guilty of* all.

ἔνταλμα, entalma.

Mat.15: 9. the *commandments* of men.
Mar. 7: 7. the *commandments* of men.
Col. 2:22. the *commandments* and doctrines of men ?

ἐνταφιάζω, entaphiazo.

Mat.26:12. she did (it) for my burial. (lit. unto
    burying me)
Joh.19:40. manner of the Jews is *to bury.*

ἐνταφιασμός, entaphiasmos.

Mar 14: 8. to anoint my body to the *burying.*
Joh.12: 7. against the day of my *burying*

ἐντέλλομαι, entellomai.

Mat. 4: 6. He *shall give* his angels *charge* concerning
    thee:
  15: 4. For God *commanded*, saying,
  17: 9. Jesus *charged* them, saying,
  19: 7. Why *did* Moses then *command* to
  28:20. whatsoever I *have commanded* you:
Mar 10: 3. What did Moses *command* you?
  11: 6. even as Jesus *had commanded:*
  13:34. *commanded* the porter to watch.
Lu. 4:10. He *shall give* his angels *charge* over thee,
Joh. 8: 5. Moses in the law *commanded* us,
  14:31. the Father *gave* me *commandment,*
  15:14. do whatsoever I *command* you.
  17. These things I *command* you,
Acts 1: 2. *after that* he...*had given commandments*
    unto the apostles
  13:47. the Lord *commanded* us,
Heb. 9:20. which God *hath injoined* unto you.
  11:22. *gave commandment* concerning his bones.

ἐντεῦθεν, entūthen.

Mat.17:20. Remove *hence* to yonder place ;
Lu. 4: 9. cast thyself down *from hence:*
  13:31. Get thee out, and depart *hence:*
  16:26. would pass *from hence* to you
Joh. 2:16. Take these things *hence* ;
  7: 3. Depart *hence*, and go into Judæa,
  14:31. Arise, let us go *hence.*
  18:36. my kingdom not *from hence.*
  19:18. two other with him, on either side (lit.
    hence and *hence*)
Jas. 4: 1. (come they) not *hence*, (even) of
Rev.22: 2. *on* either side (lit. *hence* &c.) of the river,
    (was there)

ἔντευξις, entūxis.

1Ti. 2: 1. *intercessions*, (and) giving of thanks,
  4: 5. sanctified by the word of God and *prayer.*

ἔντιμος, entimos

Lu. 7: 2. who was *dear* unto him,
  14: 8. lest a *more honourable* man
Phi. 2:29. hold such *in reputation:*
1Pet.2: 4. chosen of God, (and) *precious*,
  6. a chief corner stone, elect, *precious:*

ἐντολή, entolée.

Mat. 5:19. one of these least *commandments,*
  15: 3. transgress the *commandment*
    6. made the *commandment* of God
  19:17. keep the *commandments.*
  22:36. which (is) the great *commandment*
    38. first and great *commandment.*
    40. On these two *commandments*
Mar. 7: 8. laying aside the *commandment*
  9. ye reject the *commandment*
  10: 5. he wrote you this *precept.*
  19. Thou knowest the *commandments,*
  12:28. the first *commandment* of all?
  29. first of all the *commandments*
  30. this (is) the first *commandment.*
  31. none other *commandment* greater
Lu. 1: 6. in all the *commandments*
  15:29. at any time thy *commandment:*
  18:20. Thou knowest the *commandments,*
  23:56. according to the *commandment.*
Joh.10:18. This *commandment* have I
  11:57. had given a *commandment,*
  12:49. he gave me a *commandment,*
  50. his *commandment* is life
  13:34. A new *commandment* I give
  14:15. keep my *commandments.*
  21. that hath my *commandments,*
  15:10. If ye keep my *commandments,*
  — my Father's *commandments,*
  12. This is my *commandment,*
Acts17:15. receiving a *commandment*
Ro. 7: 8. occasion by the *commandment,*
  9. when the *commandment* came,
  10. the *commandment*, which
  11. occasion by the *commandment,*
  12. the *commandment* holy, and just,
  13. sin by the *commandment* might
  13: 9. any other *commandment*, it
1Co. 7:19. keeping of the *commandments*
  14:37. the *commandments* of the Lord.
Eph. 2:15. the law of *commandments*
  6: 2. which is the first *commandment*
Col. 4:10. ye received *commandment:*
1Ti. 6:14. keep (this) *commandment* without
Tit. 1:14. *commandments* of men, that
Heb 7: 5. have a *commandment* to take
  16. law of a carnal *commandment,*
  18. of the *commandment* going before
  9:19. Moses had spoken every *precept*
2Pet.2:21. to turn from the holy *commandment*
  3: 2. the *commandment* of us the
1Joh.2: 3. if we keep his *commandments.*
  4. keepeth not his *commandments,*
  7. I write no new *commandment* unto you,
    but an old *commandment*
  — The old *commandment* is the
  8. a new *commandment* I write
  3:22. we keep his *commandments,*
  23. this is his *commandment,*
  — as he gave us *commandment*
  24. keepeth his *commandments*
  4:21. this *commandment* have we
  5: 2. keep his *commandments.*
  3. that we keep his *commandments:* and his
    commandments are not grievous.
2Joh. 4. have received a *commandment*
  5. not as though I wrote a new *command-*
    ment
  6. walk after his *commandments.* This is the
    commandment, That,
Rev.12:17. keep the *commandments* of God

Rev.14:12. keep the *commandments* of God.
22:14. that do his *commandments,*

ἐντόπιος, *entopios*

Acts21:12. both we, and they *of that place,*

ἐντός, *entos.*

Mat.23:26. that (which is) *within* the cup
Lu. 17:21. kingdom of God is *within* you.

ἐντρέπω, -ομαι, *entrepo, -omai.*

Mat.21:37. saying, They *will reverence* my son.
Mar.12: 6. saying, They *will reverence* my son.
Lu. 18: 2. which feared not God, neither *regarded*
　　　　　man:
　　　4. I fear not God, nor *regard* man ;
　20:13. may be they *will reverence* (him)
1Co. 4:14. I write not these things to *shame* you,
2Th. 3:14. that he *may be ashamed.*
Tit. 2: 8. of the contrary part *may be ashamed,*
Heb12: 9. we *gave* (them) *reverence:*

ἐντρέφομαι, *entrephomai.*

1Ti. 4: 6. *nourished up in* the words of faith

ἐντρομος, *entromos.*

Acts 7:32. Then Moses *trembled* (lit. being *trembling*),
　　　　　and durst not
　16:29. sprang in, and came *trembling,*
Heb12:21. I exceedingly fear and *quake :* (lit. am fear-
　　　　　ful and *quaking*)

ἐντροπή, *entropee.*

1Co. 6: 5. I speak to your *shame.* Is it so,
　15:34. I speak (this) to your *shame.*

ἐντρυφάω, *entruphao.*

2Pet.2:13. *sporting themselves* with their own

ἐντυγχάνω, *entunkano.*

Acts25:24. the Jews *have dealt* with me,
Ro. 8:27. *maketh intercession* for the saints
　　34. also *maketh intercession* for us.
　11: 2. he *maketh intercession* to God
Heb 7:25. *to make intercession* for them.

ἐντυλίττω, *entulitto.*

Mat.27:59. he *wrapped* it *in* a clean linen cloth,
Lu. 23:53. *wrapped* it *in* linen, and laid it in
Joh.20: 7. *wrapped together* in a place by itself.

ἐντυπόω, *entupoō.*

2Co. 3: 7. written (and) *engraven* in stones,

ἐνυβρίζω, *enubrizo.*

Heb 10:29. and *hath done despite unto* the Spirit

ἐνυπνιάζομαι, *enupniazomai.*

Acts 2:17. your old men *shall dream* dreams:
Jude 8. Likewise also these (filthy) *dreamers* defile
　　　　the flesh,

ἐνύπνιον, *enupnion.*

Acts 2:17. your old men shall dream *dreams :*

ἐνώπιον, *enōpion.*

Lu. 1: 6. were both righteous *before* God,
　　15. great *in the sight of* the Lord,
　　17. shall go *before* him in the spirit
　　19. that stand *in the presence of* God ;
　　75. In holiness and righteousness *before* him,
　4: 7. If thou therefore wilt worship)(me,
　5:18. to lay (him) *before* him.
　　25. he rose up *before* them, and took
　8:47. unto him *before* all the people
　12: 6. of them is forgotten *before* God?
　　9. he that denieth me *before* men shall be
　　　　denied *before* the angels of God.
　13:26. have eaten and drunk *in* thy *presence,*
　14:10. *in the presence of* them that sit
　15:10. joy *in the presence of* the angels
　　18. sinned against heaven, and *before* thee,
　　21. against heaven, and *in* thy *sight,*
　16:15. which justify yourselves *before* men;
　— abomination *in the sight of* God.
　23:14. having examined (him) *before* you
　24:11. their words seemed *to* them
　　43. did eat *before* them.
Joh.20:30. *in the presence of* his disciples,
Acts 2:25. the Lord always *before* my face,
　4.10. stand here *before* you whole.
　　19. be right *in the sight of* God
　6: 5. saying pleased)(the whole multitude:
　　6. Whom they set *before* the apostles:
　7:46. Who found favour *before* God,
　8:21. not right *in the sight of* God.
　9:15. my name *before* the Gentiles,
　10: 4. up for a memorial *before* God.
　　30. a man stood *before* me in bright clothing,
　　31. remembrance *in the sight of* God
　　33. we all here present *before* God,
　19: 9. that way *before* the multitude,
　　19. burned them *before* all (men):
　27:35. to God *in presence of* them all:
Ro. 3:20. no flesh be justified *in* his *sight :*
　12:17. honest *in the sight of* all men.
　14:22. have (it) to thyself *before* God.
1Co. 1:29. no flesh should glory *in* his *presence.*
2Co. 4: 2. conscience *in the sight of* God.
　7:12. for you *in the sight of* God
　8:21. only *in the sight of* the Lord, but also *in*
　　　　　the sight of men.
Gal. 1:20. behold, *before* God, I lie not.
1Ti. 2: 3. *in the sight of* God our Saviour;
　5: 4. good and acceptable *before* God.
　　20. Them that sin rebuke *before* all,
　　21. I charge (thee) *before* God, and the
　6:12. profession *before* many witnesses.

1Ti. 6:13. charge *in the sight of* God,
2Ti. 2:14. charging (them) *before* the Lord
    4: 1. therefore *before* God, and the Lord Jesus
Heb. 4:13. is not manifest *in* his *sight :*
   13:21. is wellpleasing *in* his *sight,*
Jas. 4:10. *in the sight of* the Lord,
1Pet.3: 4. which is *in the sight of* God
1Joh.3:22. that are pleasing *in* his *sight.*
3Joh. 6. of thy charity *before* the church:
Rev. 1: 4. which are *before* his throne;
   2:14. *before* the children of Israel,
   3: 2. thy works perfect *before* God.
    5. *before* my Father, and *before* his angels.
    8. set *before* thee an open door,
    9. come and worship *before* thy feet,
   4: 5. burning *before* the throne,
    6. *before* the throne (there was) a sea
   10. elders fall down *before* him
   — their crowns *before* the throne,
   5: 8. fell down *before* the Lamb,
   7: 9. *before* the throne, and *before* the Lamb,
   11. fell *before* the throne on their faces,
   15. they *before* the throne of God,
   8: 2. angels which stood *before* God;
    3. which was *before* the throne.
    4. ascended up *before* God out of
   9:13. golden altar which is *before* God,
11: 4. *before* the God of the earth.
   16. sat *before* God on their seats,
12: 4. the dragon stood *before* the woman
   10. accused them *before* our God
13:12. the first beast *before* him,
   13. on the earth *in the sight of* men,
   14. to do *in the sight of* the beast ;
14: 3. *before* the throne, and *before* the four
   5. without fault *before* the throne of God.
   10. *in the presence of* the holy angels, and *in
   the presence of* the Lamb:
15: 4. shall come and worship *before* thee ;
16:19. came in remembrance *before* God,
19:20. that wrought miracles *before* him,
20:12. small and great, stand *before* God ;

ἐνωτίζομαι, enōtizomai.

Acts 2:14. unto you, and *hearken to* my words:

ἐξ see above ἐκ.

ἕξ, hex.

Mat.17: 1. after *six* days Jesus taketh Peter,
Mar 9: 2. after *six* days Jesus taketh
Lu. 4:25. shut up three years and *six* months,
  13:14. There are *six* days in which men
Joh. 2: 6. were set there *six* waterpots
   20. Forty and *six* years was this temple
  12: 1. *six* days before the passover
Acts11:12. these *six* brethren accompanied
  18:11. continued (there) a year and *six* months,
  27:37. two hundred threescore and *six*teen (lit.
  seventy *six*)
Jas. 5:17. space of three years and *six* months.
Rev. 4: 8. each of them *six* wings about
  13:18. Six hundred threescore (and) *six*.

ἐξαγγέλλω, exangello.

1Pet.2: 9. ye *should shew forth* the praises

ἐξαγοράζω, exagorazo.

Gal. 3:13. Christ *hath redeemed* us from the
   4: 5. To *redeem* them that were under the law,
Eph 5:16. *Redeeming* the time, because
Col. 4: 5. *redeeming* the time.

ἐξάγω, exago.

Mar 8:23. and *led* him *out* of the town ;
  15:20. *led* him *out* to crucify him.
Lu. 24:50. he *led* them *out* as far as to Bethany,
Joh. 10: 3. by name, and *leadeth* them *out.*
Acts 5:19. *brought* them *forth, and* said,
   7:36. He *brought* them *out,* after that
   40. Moses, which *brought* us *out* of the
  12:17. the Lord *had brought* him *out* of the prison.
  13:17. *brought* he them *out* of it.
  16:37. let them come themselves and *fetch* us
   out.
   39. *brought* (them) *out, and* desired
  21:38. *which* before...*leddest out* into the wilderness
Heb 8: 9. *to lead* them *out* of the land of Egypt ;

ἐξαιρέω, exaireo.

Mat. 5:29. *pluck* it *out,* and cast (it) from thee:
  18: 9. *pluck* it *out,* and cast (it) from thee:
Acts 7:10. And *delivered* him out of all his afflictions,
  34. am come down *to deliver* them.
  12:11. *hath delivered* me out of the hand
  23:27. came I with an army and *rescued* him,
  26:17. *Delivering* thee from the people,
Gal. 1: 4. that he *might deliver* us from

ἐξαίρω, exairo.

1Co. 5: 2. *might be taken away* from among you.
  13. *put away* from among yourselves

ἐξαιτέομαι, exaiteomai.

Lu. 22:31. Satan *hath desired* (to have) you,

ἐξαίφνης, exaiphnees.

Mar.13:36. Lest coming *suddenly* he find
Lu. 2:13. *suddenly* there was with the angel
  9:39. he *suddenly* crieth out;
Acts 9: 3. *suddenly* there shined round about
  22: 6. *suddenly* there shone from heaven

ἐξακολουθέω, exakoloutheo.

2Pet.1:16. For we *have* not *followed* cunningly devised
  fables, *when*
  2: 2. many *shall follow* their pernicious
  15. *following* the way of Balaam

ἑξακόσιοι, hexakosioi.

Rev.13:18. *Six hundred* threescore (and) six.
    14:20. a thousand (and) *six hundred* furlongs.

ἐξαλείφω, exalīpho.

Acts 3:19. your sins may *be blotted out*,
Col. 2:14. *Blotting out* the handwriting of
Rev. 3: 5. I *will* not *blot out* his name
    7:17. God *shall wipe away* all tears
   21: 4. God *shall wipe away* all tears

ἐξάλλομαι, exallomai.

Acts 3: 8. he *leaping up* stood, and walked,

ἐξανάστασις, exanastasis.

Phi. 3:11. unto the *resurrection* of the dead.

ἐξανατέλλω, exanatello.

Mat.13: 5. forthwith they *sprung up*,
Mar. 4: 5. immediately it *sprang up*,

ἐξανίστημι, exanisteemi.

Mar 12:19. should take his wife, and *raise up* seed
Lu. 20:28. and *raise up* seed unto his brother.
Acts15: 5. there *rose up* certain of the sect

ἐξαπατάω, exapatao.

Ro. 7:11. *deceived* me, and by it slew (me).
  16:18. *deceive* the hearts of the simple.
1Co. 3:18. *Let* no man *deceive* himself.
2Co.11: 3. as the serpent *beguiled* Eve
2Th. 2: 3. Let no man *deceive* you by any

ἐξάπινα, exapina.

Mar. 9: 8. *suddenly*, when they had looked

ἐξαπορέομαι, exaporeomai.

2Co. 1: 8. that we *despaired* even of life:
   4: 8. perplexed, but not *in despair ;*

ἐξαποστέλλω, exapostello

Lu. 1:53. the rich he *hath sent* empty *away.*
  20:10. beat him, and *sent* (him) *away* empty.
    11. shamefully, and *sent* (him) *away* empty.
Acts 7:12. he *sent out* our fathers first.
   9:30. *sent* him *forth* to Tarsus.
  11:22. they *sent forth* Barnabas, that
  12:11. the Lord *hath sent* his angel,
  17:14. the brethren *sent away* Paul
  22:21. for I *will send* thee far hence
Gal. 4: 4. God *sent forth* his Son,
   6. God *hath sent forth* the Spirit of

ἐξαρτίζω, exartizo.

Acts21: 5. when we *had accomplished* those days,
2Ti. 3:17. *throughly furnished* unto all good

ἐξαστράπτω, exastrapto.

Lu. 9:29. his raiment (was) white (and) *glistering.*

ἐξαυτῆς, exautees.

Mar. 6:25. that thou give me *by and by* in a
Acts10:33. *Immediately* therefore I sent to thee;
  11:11. *immediately* there were three men
  21:32. Who *immediately* took soldiers
  23:30. I sent *straightway* to thee, and gave
Phi. 2:23. therefore I hope to send *presently*

ἐξεγείρω, exegīro.

Ro. 9:17. same purpose *have* I *raised* thee *up,*
1Co. 6:14. *will* also *raise up* us by his own power.

ἔξειμι, exīmi.

Acts13:42. when the Jews *were gone out* of the
  17:15. with all speed, they *departed.*
  20: 7. ready *to depart* on the morrow;
  27:43. first (into the sea), and *get* to land:

ἐξελέγχω, exelenko.

Jude   15. *to convince* all that are ungodly

ἐξέλκομαι, exelkomai.

Jas. 1:14. when he *is drawn away* of his own

ἐξέλω see ἐξαιρέω.

ἐξέραμα, exerama.

2Pet. 2:22. turned to his own *vomit* again ;

ἐξερευνάω, exerūnao.

1Pet.1:10. have enquired and *searched diligently,*

ἐξέρχομαι, exerkomai.

Mat. 2: 6. out of thee *shall come* a Governor,
   5:26. shalt by no means *come out*
   8:28. *coming out* of the tombs,
    32. when they *were come out*, they went
    34. city, *came out* to meet Jesus:
   9:26. fame hereof *went abroad* into
    31. when they *were departed,*
    32. As they *went out*, behold, they
  10:11. there abide till ye *go thence.*
    14. when ye *depart out of* that house
  11: 7. What *went* ye *out* into the wilderness

Mat.11: 8. what *went* ye *out* for to see?
    9. what *went* ye *out* for to see?
  12:14. Then the Pharisees *went out, and*
    43. unclean spirit *is gone out* of a man,
    44. from whence I *came out ;*
  13: 1. same day *went* Jesus *out* of the house, *and*
    3. a sower *went forth* to sow ;
    49. the angels *shall come forth,*
  14:14. Jesus *went forth, and* saw a great
  15:18. *come forth* from the heart ;
    19. For out of the heart *proceed* evil
    21. Then Jesus *went* thence, *and*
    22. a woman of Canaan *came out of* the same
      coasts, *and* cried
  17:18. he *departed out of* him :
  18:28. the same servant *went out, and* found
  20: 1. which *went out* early in the morning
    3. he *went out* about the third hour, *and*
    5. Again he *went out...and* did
    6. the eleventh hour he *went out,, and* found
  21:17. *went out of* the city into Bethany ;
  22:10. those servants *went out...and* gathered
  24: 1. Jesus *went out, and* departed from
    26. he is in the desert; *go* not *forth :*
    27. lightning *cometh out of* the east,
  25: 1. *went forth* to meet the bridegroom.
    6. *go* ye *out* to meet him.
  26:30. they *went out* into the mount
    55. *Are* ye *come out* as against a thief
    71. *when* he *was gone out* into the
    75. he *went out, and* wept bitterly.
  27:32. *as* they *came out,* they found
    53. *came out* of the graves...*and* went
  28: 8. they *departed...and* did run
Mar 1:25. Hold thy peace, and *come out of* him.
    26. he *came out of* him.
    28. his fame *spread abroad* throughout
    29. *when* they *were come out* of the synagogue,
    35. before day, he *went out,*
    38. for therefore *came* I *forth.*
    45. he *went out, and* began to publish
  2:12. *went forth* before them all ;
    13. he *went forth* again by the sea side ;
  3: 6. the Pharisees *went forth, and* straightway
    21. they *went out* to lay hold on him :
  4: 3. there *went out* a sower to sow :
  5: 2. *when* he *was come out* of the ship,
    8. *Come out* of the man, (thou) unclean
    13. the unclean spirits *went out, and*
    14. they *went out* to see what it was
    30. *that* virtue *had gone out* of him,
  6: 1. he *went out* from thence,
    10. till ye *depart* from that place.
    12. they *went out, and* preached that
    24. she *went forth, and* said unto her
    34. Jesus, *when* he *came out,* saw
    54. *when* they *were come out* of the
  7:29. the devil *is gone out* of thy daughter.
    30. she found the devil *gone out,*
    31. again, *departing* from the coasts
  8:11. the Pharisees *came forth,*
    27. Jesus *went out,* and his disciples,
  9:25. I charge thee, *come out of* him,
    26. rent him sore, and *came out of* him :
    29. This kind can *come forth* by nothing,
    30. they *departed* thence, *and* passed
  11:11. he *went out* unto Bethany with
    12. *when* they *were come* from Bethany,
  14:16. his disciples *went forth,* and came
    26. sung an hymn, they *went out* into
    48. *Are* ye *come out,* as against
    68. he *went out* into the porch ;

Mar 16: 8. they *went out* quickly, *and* fled
    20. they *went forth, and* preached every where,
Lu. 1:22. *when* he *came out,* he could
  2: 1. that there *went out* a decree
  4:14. there *went out* a fame of him
    35. Hold thy peace, and *come out* of him.
    — he *came out* of him, and hurt him not.
    36. unclean spirits, and they *come out.*
    41. devils also *came out of* many,
    42. was day, he *departed and* went into
  5: 8. saying, *Depart* from me ;
    27. after these things he *went forth,*
  6:12. he *went out* into a mountain
    19. there *went* virtue *out of* him,
  7:17. this rumour of him *went forth*
    24. What *went* ye *out* into the
    25. what *went* ye *out* for to see?
    26. what *went* ye *out* for to see?
  8: 2. *out* of whom *went* seven devils,
    5. A sower *went out* to sow his seed :
    27. *when* he *went forth* to land,
    29. *to come out* of the man.
    33. *went* the devils *out* of the man, *and*
    35. they *went out* to see what was
    — out of whom, the devils *were departed,*
    38. out of whom the devils *were departed*
    46. *that* virtue *is gone out* of me.
  9: 4. there abide, and thence *depart.*
    5. *when* ye *go out* of that city,
    6. they *departed, and* went through
  10:10. *go* your ways *out* into the streets of the
      same, *and*
    35. on the morrow *when* he *departed,*
  11:14. *when* the devil *was gone out,*
    24. unclean spirit *is gone out* of a man,
    — unto my house whence I *came out.*
  12:59. thou *shalt* not *depart* thence,
  13:31. *Get* thee *out,* and depart hence :
  14:18. I must needs *go* and see it :
    21. *Go out* quickly into the streets
    23. *Go out* into the highways and hedges,
  15:28. therefore *came* his father *out, and* intreated
      him.
  17:29. same day that Lot *went out* of Sodom
  21:37. at night he *went out,* and abode
  22:39. he *came out, and* went, as he was wont,
    52. *Be* ye *come out,* as against·a thief,
    62. Peter *went out, and* wept bitterly.
Joh. 1:43(44). Jesus would *go forth* into Galilee,
  4:30. Then they *went out* of the city,
    43. after two days he *departed* thence,
  8: 9. *went out* one by one,
    42. I *proceeded forth* and came from God ;
    59. and *went out* of the temple,
  10: 9. *shall go* in and *out,* and find pasture.
    39. he *escaped* out of their hand,
  11:31. she rose up hastily and *went out,*
    44. he that was dead *came forth,*
  12:13. and *went forth* to meet him,
  13: 3. that he *was come* from God,
    30. the sop *went* immediately *out :*
    31(30). Therefore, when he *was gone out,*
  16:27. that I *came out* from God.
    28. I *came forth* from the Father,
    30. that thou *camest forth* from God.
  17: 8. that I *came out* from thee,
  18: 1. he *went forth* with his disciples
    4. *went forth, and* said unto them,
    16. Then *went out* that other disciple,
    29. Pilate then *went out* unto them,
    38. he *went out* again unto the Jews,
  19: 4. Pilate therefore *went forth* again,

Joh.19: 5. **Then** *came* Jesus forth, wearing
    17. *went forth* into a place called
    34. forthwith *came* thereout blood and water.
20: 3. Peter therefore *went forth*,
21: 3. They *went forth*, and entered into
    23. Then *went* this saying *abroad*
Acts 1:21. *went* in and *out* among us,
    7: 3. *Get* thee *out* of thy country,
    4. Then *came* he *out* of the land...*and*
    7. after that *shall* they *come forth*,
    8: 7. *came out* of many that were
10:23. Peter *went away* with them,
11:25. Then *departed* Barnabas to Tarsus,
12: 9. he *went out*, and followed him;
    10. they *went out*, and passed on through
    17. he *departed,* and went into another
14:20. he *departed* with Barnabas to Derbe.
15:24. certain *which went out* from us have
    40. Paul chose Silas, and *departed*,
16: 3. Paul have *to go forth* with him ;
    10. *to go* into Macedonia,
    13. on the sabbath we *went out* of the city
    18. in the name of Jesus Christ *to come out* of
    her. And he *came out*
    19. hope of their gains *was gone*,
    36. therefore *depart, and* go in peace.
    39. *to depart out* of the city.
    40. they *went out* of the prison, *and* entered
    — they comforted them, and *departed.*
17:33. Paul *departed* from among them.
18:23. he *departed,* and went over (all)
19:12. the evil spirits *went out* of them.
20: 1. *departed* for to go into Macedonia.
    11. break of day, so he *departed.*
21: 5. we *departed and* went our way ;
    8. were of Paul's company *departed, and*
    came unto
22:18. *get* thee quickly *out* of Jerusalem:
28: 3. *came* a viper *out* of the heat, *and*
    15. they *came* to meet us as far
Ro. 10:18. their sound *went* into all the
1Co. 5:10. needs *go out* of the world.
14:36. *came* the word of God *out* from
2Co. 2:13. I *went* from thence into Macedonia.
6:17. *come out* from among them,
8:17. his own accord he *went* unto you.
Phi. 4:15. when I *departed* from Macedonia,
1Th. 1: 8. faith to God-ward *is spread abroad ;*
Heb. 3:16. howbeit not all *that came out* of Egypt by
Moses.
7: 5. though they *come out* of the loins of
11: 8. he was called *to go out* into a
    — he *went out*, not knowing whither
    15. from whence they *came out,*
13:13. *Let* us *go forth* therefore unto
Jas. 3:10. *proceedeth* blessing and cursing.
1Joh.2:19. They *went out* from us,
4: 1. false prophets *are gone out* into
3Joh. 7. for his name's sake they *went forth,*
Rev. 3:12. he *shall go* no more *out :*
6: 2. he *went forth* conquering, and to conquer.
    4. there *went out* another horse
9: 3. there *came out* of the smoke locusts
14:15. another angel *came out* of the temple,
    17. And another angel *came out* of the
    18. another angel *came out* from the
    20. blood *came out* of the winepress,
15: 6. seven angels *came out* of the temple,
16:17. *came* a great voice *out* of the temple
18: 4. saying, *Come out* of her,
19: 5. a voice *came out* of the throne,
20: 8. *shall go out* to deceive the nations

ἔξεστι, exesti.

Mat.12: 2. that which *is* not *lawful* to do
    4. was not *lawful* for him to eat,
    10. *Is* it *lawful* to heal on the sabbath
    12. Wherefore it *is lawful* to do well
14: 4. It *is* not *lawful* for thee to have her.
19: 3. *Is* it *lawful* for a man to put
20:15. *Is* it not *lawful* for me to do
22:17. *Is* it *lawful* to give tribute
27: 6. It *is* not *lawful* for to put them
Mar. 2:24. that which *is* not *lawful ?*
    26. which *is* not *lawful* to eat
3: 4. *Is* it *lawful* to do good on the
6:18. It *is* not *lawful* for thee to have
10: 2. *Is* it *lawful* for a man to put
12:14. *Is* it *lawful* to give tribute
Lu. 6: 2. that which *is* not *lawful* to do
    4. which it *is* not *lawful* to eat
    9. *Is* it *lawful* on the sabbath days
14: 3. *Is* it *lawful* to heal on the
20:22. *Is* it *lawful* for us to give tribute
Joh. 5:10. it *is* not *lawful* for thee to carry
18:31. It *is* not *lawful* for us to put
Acts 2:29. let me freely speak unto you (lit. it *being*
permitted me to freely speak)
8:37. all thine heart, thou mayest. (lit. it *is*
permitted)
16:21. which *are* not *lawful* for us to receive,
21:37. May I speak (lit. *Is* it *permitted* me to
speak) unto thee?
22:25. *Is* it *lawful* for you to scourge
1Co. 6:12. All things *are lawful* unto me, but all
    — all things *are lawful* for me, but I
10:23. All things *are lawful* for me,
    — all things *are lawful* for me, but all
2Co.12: 4. which it *is* not *lawful* for a man

ἐξετάζω, exetazo.

Mat. 2: 8. *search* diligently for the young child ;
10:11. *enquire* who in it is worthy;
Joh.21:12. none of the disciples durst *ask* him,

ἐξηγέομαι, exeegeomai.

Lu. 24:35. they *told* what things (were done)
Joh. 1:18. of the Father, he *hath declared* (him).
Acts10: 8. *when* he *had declared* all
15:12. *declaring* what miracles and wonders
    14. Simeon *hath declared* how
21:19. he *declared* particularly what

ἐξήκοντα, hexeekonta.

Mat.13: 8. some *sixty*fold, some thirtyfold.
    23. some an hundredfold, some *sixty,*
Mar. 4: 8. some thirty, and some *sixty,*
    20. some thirtyfold, some *sixty,*
Lu. 24:13. from Jerusalem (about) *threescore* furlongs.
1Ti. 5: 9. number under *threescore* years old,
Rev.11: 3. a thousand two hundred (and) *threescore*
12: 6. a thousand two hundred (and) *threescore*
13:18. Six hundred *threescore* (and) six.

ἐξῆς, hexees.

Lu. 7:11. it came to pass *the* day *after,*
9:37. it came to pass, that on *the next* day,

Acts21: 1. the (day) *following* unto Rhodes,
25:17. *on the morrow* I sat on the
27:18. *the next* (day) they lightened the

ἐξηχέομαι, *exeekeomai.*

1Th. 1: 8. from you *sounded out* the word

ἕξις, *hexis.*

Heb. 5:14. those who by reason of *use*

ἐξίστημι, *existeemi.*

Mat.12:23. all the people *were amazed,*
Mar. 2:12. that they *were* all *amazed,*
     3:21. they said, He *is beside himself.*
     5:42. they *were astonished* with a great astonishment.
     6:51. they *were* sore *amazed*
Lu.   2:47. *were astonished* at his understanding
     8:56. her parents *were astonished :*
     24:22. *made* us *astonished,* which were early
Acts 2: 7. they *were* all *amazed*
     12. they *were* all *amazed,*
     8: 9. *bewitched* the people of Samaria,
     11. he *had bewitched* them with
     13. *wondered,* beholding the miracles
     9:21. all that heard (him) *were amazed,*
     10:45. *were astonished,* as many as
     12:16. saw him, they *were astonished.*
2Co. 5:13. whether we *be beside ourselves,*

ἐξισχύω, *exiskuo.*

Eph. 3:18. *May be able* to comprehend

ἔξοδος, *exodos.*

Lu.   9:31. spake of his *decease* which he
Heb 11:22. the *departing* of the children of Israel;
2Pet.1:15. may be able after my *decease*

ἐξολοθρεύομαι, *exolothruomai.*

Acts 3:23. *shall be destroyed* from among

ἐξομολογέομαι, *exomologeomai.*

Mat. 3: 6. in Jordan, *confessing* their sins.
     11:25. said, I *thank* thee, O Father,
Mar. 1: 5. of Jordan, *confessing* their sins.
Lu. 10:21. said, I *thank* thee, O Father,
     22: 6. he *promised,* and sought opportunity
Acts19:18. came, *and confessed,* and shewed
Ro. 14:11. every tongue *shall confess* to God.
     15: 9. I *will confess* to thee among the Gentiles,
Phi. 2:11. every tongue *should confess* that
Jas.   5:16. *Confess* (your) faults one to another,
Rev. 3: 5. I *will confess* his name before

ἐξόν see in ἔξεστι.

ἐξορκίζω, *exorkizo.*

Mat.26:63. I *adjure* thee by the living God,

ἐξορκιστής, *exorkistees.*

Acts19:13. of the vagabond Jews, *exorcists,*

ἐξορύττω, *exorutto.*

Mar. 2: 4. *when* they *had broken* (it) *up,*
Gal. 4:15. ye *would have plucked out* your own eyes, *and*

ἐξουδενόω, *exoudenoō.*

Mar. 9:12. that he must suffer many things, and *be set at nought.*

ἐξουθενέω, *exoutheneo.*

Lu. 18: 9. were righteous, and *despised* others:
     23:11. *set* him *at nought,* and mocked
Acts 4:11. the stone *which was set at nought* of you builders,
Ro. 14: 3. *Let* not him that eateth *despise*
     10. why dost thou *set at nought* thy brother ?
1Co. 1:28. things *which are despised,* hath God chosen,
     6: 4. set them to judge *who are least esteemed* in the church.
     16:11. Let no man therefore *despise* him:
2Co.10:10. (his) speech *contemptible.*
Gal. 4:14. in my flesh ye *despised* not, nor
1Th. 5:20. *Despise* not prophesyings.

ἐξουσία, *exousia.*

Mat. 7:29. as (one) having *authority,*
     8: 9. For I am a man under *authority,*
     9: 6. Son of man hath *power* on earth
     8. had given such *power* unto men.
     10: 1. he gave them *power* (against)
     21:23. By what *authority* doest thou these things? and who gave thee this *authority?*
     24. by what *authority* I do these things.
     27. by what *authority* I do these things.
     28:18. All *power* is given unto me
Mar. 1:22. as one that had *authority,*
     27. for with *authority* commandeth
     2:10. Son of man hath *power* on earth
     3:15. to have *power* to heal sicknesses,
     6: 7. gave them *power* over unclean spirits ;
     11:28. By what *authority* doest thou these things: and who gave thee this *authority*
     29. by what *authority* I do these things.
     33. by what *authority* I do these things.
     13:34. gave *authority* to his servants,
Lu.   4: 6. All this *power* will I give thee,
     32. for his word was with *power.*
     36. for with *authority* and power
     5:24. the Son of man hath *power*
     7: 8. am a man set under *authority,*
     9: 1. gave them power and *authority*
     10:19. I give unto you *power* to tread
     12: 5. hath *power* to cast into hell ;
     11. (unto) magistrates, and *powers,*

Lu. 19:17. have thou *authority* over ten cities.
  20: 2. by what *authority* doest thou these
      things? or who is he that gave thee
      this *authority?*
      8. by what *authority* I do these things.
      20. power and *authority* of the governor.
  22:53. your hour, and the *power* of darkness.
  23: 7. belonged unto Herod's *jurisdiction,*
Joh. 1:12. to them gave he *power* to become
  5:27. hath given him *authority* to
  10:18. I have *power* to lay it down, and I have
      power to take it again.
  17: 2. hast given him *power* over all flesh.
  19:10. I have *power* to crucify thee, and have
      power to release thee?
      11. Thou couldest have no *power*
Acts 1: 7. Father hath put in his own *power.*
  5: 4. was it not in thine own *power?*
  8:19. Give me also this *power,*
  9:14. here he hath *authority* from
  26:10. having received *authority* from
      12. with *authority* and commission from
      18. (from) the *power* of Satan unto God,
Ro. 9:21. Hath not the potter *power* over
  13: 1. be subject unto the higher *powers.* For
      there is no *power* but of God: the
      powers that be are ordained
      2. Whosoever therefore resisteth the *power,*
      3. not be afraid of the *power?*
1Co. 7:37. hath *power* over his own will,
  8: 9. lest by any means this *liberty*
  9: 4. Have we not *power* to eat and to drink?
      5. Have we not *power* to lead about
      6. have not we *power* to forbear
      12. partakers of (this) *power* over you,
      — we have not used this *power;*
      18. that I abuse not my *power*
  11:10. the woman to have *power*
  15:24. all rule and all *authority* and power.
2Co. 10: 8. somewhat more of our *authority,*
  13:10. according to the *power* which
Eph. 1:21. all principality, and power, and might,
  2: 2. prince of the *power* of the air,
  3:10. principalities and *powers* in heavenly
  6:12. against principalities, against *powers,*
Col. 1:13. from the *power* of darkness,
      16. dominions, or principalities, or *powers :*
  2:10. head of all principality and *power :*
      15. spoiled principalities and *powers,*
2Th. 3: 9. Not because we have not *power,*
Tit. 3: 1. subject to principalities and *powers,*
Heb 13:10. whereof they have no *right* to eat
1Pet. 3:22. *authorities* and powers being made
Jude 25. majesty, dominion and *power,*
Rev. 2:26. will I give *power* over the nations:
  6: 8. *power* was given unto them
  9: 3. unto them was given *power,* as the scorpions
      of the earth have *power,*
      10. their *power* (was) to hurt men
      19. their *power* is in their mouth,
  11: 6. These have *power* to shut heaven,
      — have *power* over waters to turn
  12:10. the *power* of his Christ: for the
  13: 2. his seat, and great *authority.*
      4. which gave *power* unto the beast:
      5. *power* was given unto him
      7. *power* was given him over all
      12. he exerciseth all the *power* of
  14:18. which had *power* over fire ;
  16: 9. hath *power* over these plagues
  17:12. receive *power* as kings one hour
      13. shall give their *power* and *strength*

Rev. 18: 1. from heaven, having great *power ;*
  20: 6. second death hath no *power,*
  22:14. that they may have *right* to the tree of life

ἐξουσιάζω, exousiazo.

Lu. 22:25. they *that exercise authority upon* them
1Co. 6:12. I *will* not *be brought under the power* of
  7: 4. *hath* not *power of* her own body,
      — the husband *hath* not *power of* his own
      body,

ἐξοχή, exokee.

Acts 25:23. and principal men (lit. the men which
      were of *eminence*) of the city,

ἐξυπνίζω, exupnizo.

Joh. 11:11. that I *may awake* him *out of sleep.*

ἔξυπνος, exupnos.

Acts 16:27. awaking (lit. being *awakened*) *out of* his
      sleep, and seeing

ἔξω, exo.

Mat. 5:13. for nothing, but to be cast *out,*
  12:46. his brethren stood *without,*
      47. thy brethren stand *without,*
  13:48. but cast the bad *away.*
  21:17. went *out of* the city into Bethany ;
      39. cast (him) *out of* the vineyard,
  26:69. Peter sat *without* in the palace:
      75. he went *out,* and wept bitterly.
Mar. 1:45. was *without* in desert places:
  3:31. standing *without,* sent unto him,
      32. thy brethren *without* seek for thee.
  4:11. unto them that are *without,*
  5:10. send them away *out of* the country.
  8:23. led him *out of* the town ;
  11: 4. tied by the door *without*
      19. he went *out of* the city.
  12: 8. cast (him) *out of* the vineyard.
  14:68. he went *out* into the porch ;
Lu. 1:10. the people were praying *without*
  4:29. thrust him *out of* the city,
  8:20. thy brethren stand *without,*
      54. he put them all *out,* and took
  13:25. ye begin to stand *without,*
      28. you (yourselves) thrust *out.*
      33. a prophet perish *out of* Jerusalem.
  14:35. men cast it *out.*
  20:15. they cast him *out of* the vineyard,
  22:62. Peter went *out,* and wept bitterly.
  24:50. he led them *out* as far as
Joh. 6:37. I will in no wise cast *out.*
  9:34. And they cast him *out.*
      35. that they had cast him *out;*
  11:43. loud voice, Lazarus, come *forth.*
  12:31. prince of this world be cast *out.*
  15: 6. he is cast *forth* as a branch,
  18:16. Peter stood at the door *without.*
  19: 4. Pilate therefore went *forth* again,
      — I bring him *forth* to you,
      5. Then came Jesus *forth,*
      13. he brought Jesus *forth,*

Joh.20:11. Mary stood *without* at the sepulchre
Acts 4:15. aside *out of* the council,
　　5:23. the keepers standing *without*
　　34. to put the apostles *forth* a little
　　7:58. cast (him) *out of* the city,
　　9:40. Peter put them all *forth*,
　　14:19, drew (him) *out of* the city,
　　16:13. we went *out of* the city
　　30. brought them *out*, and said,
　　21: 5. till (we were) *out of* the city:
　　30. drew him *out of* the temple:
　　26:11. even unto strange cities. (lit. cities *without*)
1Co. 5:12. judge them also that are *without?*
　　13. them that are *without* God judgeth.
2Co. 4:16. though our *outward* man perish,
Col. 4: 5. toward them that are *without*,
1Th. 4:12. toward them that are *without*,
Heb 13:11. are burned *without* the camp.
　　12. suffered *without* the gate.
　　13. unto him *without* the camp,
1Joh.4:18. perfect love casteth *out* fear:
Rev. 3:12. he shall go no more *out:*
　　11: 2. which is without the temple leave *out*,
　　14:20. was trodden *without* the city,
　　22:15. For *without* (are) dogs,

ἔξωθεν, exōthen.

NOTE. — In Rev. xi. 2, ἐσωθεν is the common reading.

Mat.23:25. ye make clean the *outside* of the
　　27. which indeed appear beautiful *outward*,
　　28. Even so ye also *outwardly* appear
Mar. 7:15. nothing *from without* a man,
　　18. whatsoever thing *from without*
Lu. 11:39. the *outside* of the cup and the platter;
　　40. made that which is *without*
2Co. 7: 5. *without* (were) fightings, within
1Ti. 3: 7. of them which are *without;*
1Pet.3: 3. adorning let it not be that *outward*
Rev.11: 2. the court which is *without* the

ἐξωθῶ, exōtho.

Acts 7:45. whom God *drave out* before
　　27:39. were possible, *to thrust in* the ship.

ἐξώτερος, exōteros.

Mat. 8:12. be cast out into *outer* darkness:
　　22:13. cast (him) into *outer* darkness;
　　25:30. unprofitable servant into *outer* darkness:

ἑορτάζω, heortazo.

1Co. 5: 8. Therefore *let us keep the feast*,

ἑορτή, heortee.

Mat.26: 5. they said, Not on the *feast* (day),
　　27:15. at (that) *feast* the governor was
Mar 14: 2. they said, Not on the *feast* (day),
　　15: 6. Now at (that) *feast* he released unto

Lu. 2:41. at the *feast* of the passover.
　　42. after the custom of the *feast*.
　　22: 1. the *feast* of unleavened bread
　　23:17. release one unto them at the *feast*.
Joh. 2:23. at the passover, in the *feast* (day),
　　4:45. at Jerusalem at the *feast*: for they also went unto the *feast*.
　　5: 1. there was a *feast* of the Jews;
　　6: 4. a *feast* of the Jews, was nigh.
　　7: 2. the Jews' *feast* of tabernacles was
　　8. Go ye up unto this *feast*: I go not up yet unto this *feast;*
　　10. went he also up unto the *feast*,
　　11. Jews sought him at the *feast*,
　　14. about the midst of the *feast*
　　37. that great (day) of the *feast*,
　　11:56. he will not come to the *feast?*
　　12:12. were come to the *feast*,
　　20. to worship at the *feast:*
　　13: 1. before the *feast* of the passover,
　　29. need of against the *feast;*
Acts18:21. by all means keep this *feast*
Col. 2:16. or in respect of an *holyday*,

ἐπαγγελία, epangelia.

Lu. 24:49. I send the *promise* of my Father
Acts 1: 4. for the *promise* of the Father,
　　2:33. the *promise* of the Holy Ghost,
　　39. the *promise* is unto you,
　　7:17. the time of the *promise* drew nigh,
　　13:23. according to (his) *promise*
　　32. the *promise* which was made
　　23:21. looking for a *promise* from thee.
　　26: 6. for the hope of the *promise* made
Ro. 4:13. For the *promise*, that he should
　　14. the *promise* made of none effect:
　　16. the *promise* might be sure to
　　20. not at the *promise* of God
　　9: 4. service (of God), and the *promises;*
　　8. the children of the *promise*
　　9. this (is) the word of *promise*,
　　15: 8. to confirm the *promises* (made)
2Co. 1:20. For all the *promises* of God
　　7: 1. Having therefore these *promises*,
Gal. 3:14. the *promise* of the Spirit through
　　16. were the *promises* made.
　　17. make the *promise* of none effect.
　　18. (it is) no more of *promise*: but God gave (it) to Abraham by *promise*.
　　21. against the *promises* of God?
　　22. that the *promise* by faith of Jesus
　　29. heirs according to the *promise*.
　　4:23. the freewoman (was) by *promise*.
　　28. are the children of *promise*.
Eph. 1:13. that holy Spirit of *promise*,
　　2:12. from the covenants of *promise*,
　　3: 6. partakers of his *promise* in Christ
　　6: 2. first commandment with *promise;*
1Ti. 4: 8. having *promise* of the life
2Ti. 1: 1. according to the *promise* of life
Heb. 4: 1. lest, a *promise* being left
　　6:12. faith and patience inherit the *promises*.
　　15. he obtained the *promise*.
　　17. unto the heirs of *promise*
　　7: 6. blessed him that had the *promises*.
　　8: 6. established upon better *promises*.
　　9:15. might receive the *promise*
　　10:36. ye might receive the *promise*.
　　11: 9. sojourned in the land of *promise*,

Heb 11: 9. of the same *promise* :
13. not having received the *promises,*
17. that had received the *promises*
33. obtained *promises,* stopped the
39. received not the *promise:*
2Pet.3: 4. Where is the *promise* of his coming?
9. not slack concerning his *promise,*
1Joh. 1: 5. This then is the *message* which
2:25. this is the *promise* that he

ἐπαγγέλλομαι, *epangellomai.*

Mar 14:11. they were glad, and *promised* to give
Acts 7: 5. he *promised* that he would give
Ro. 4:21. that, what he *had promised,*
Gal. 3:19. to whom the *promise was made ;*
1Ti. 2:10. women *professing* godliness
6:21. Which some *professing* have
Tit. 1: 2. which God, that cannot lie, *promised*
Heb. 6:13. *when* God *made promise* to Abraham,
10:23. he (is) faithful *that promised;*
11:11. him faithful *who had promised.*
12:26. now he *hath promised,* saying,
Jas. 1:12. which the Lord *hath promised*
2: 5. which he *hath promised* to them
2Pet.2:19. *While* they *promise* them liberty,
1Joh.2:25. that he *hath promised* us,

ἐπάγγελμα, *epangelma.*

2Pet.1: 4. exceeding great and precious *promises:*
3:13. according to his *promise,*

ἐπάγω, *epago.*

Acts 5:28. *to bring* this man's blood *upon* us.
2Pet.2: 1. *and bring upon* themselves swift
5. *bringing in* the flood *upon* the

ἐπαγωνίζομαι, *epagōnizomai.*

Jude 3. should *earnestly contend for* the faith

ἐπαθροίζομαι, *epathro-izomai.*

Lu. 11:29. *when* the people *were gathered thick together,*

ἐπαινέω, *epaineo.*

Lu. 16: 8. the lord *commended* the unjust
Ro. 15:11. *laud* him, all ye people.
1Co.11: 2. Now I *praise* you, brethren,
17. I *praise* (you) not, that ye come together
22. shall I *praise* you in this? I *praise* (you) not.

ἔπαινος, *epainos.*

Ro. 2:29. whose *praise* (is) not of men,
13: 3. thou shalt have *praise* of the same:
1Co. 4: 5. every man have *praise* of God.
2Co. 8:18. whose *praise* (is) in the gospel

Eph. 1: 6. To the *praise* of the glory of his
12. to the *praise* of his glory,
14. unto the *praise* of his glory.
Phi. 1:11. the glory and *praise* of God.
4: 8. if (there be) any *praise,*
1Pet.1: 7. be found unto *praise* and honour
2:14. the *praise* of them that do well.

ἐπαίρω, *epairo.*

Mat.17: 8. *when* they *had lifted up* their eyes,
Lu. 6:20. he *lifted up* his eyes on his disciples, *and*
11:27. *lifted up* her voice, *and* said
16:23. *lift up* his eyes, being in torments, *and*
18:13. would not *lift up* so much as
21:28. *lift up* your heads ; for your redemption
24:50. *lifted up* his hands, *and* blessed them.
Joh. 4:35. *Lift up* your eyes, and look on the
6: 5. *When* Jesus then *lifted up* (his) eyes,
13:18. *hath lifted up* his heel against me.
17: 1. *lifted up* his eyes to heaven,
Acts 1: 9. he *was taken up ;* and a cloud
2:14. *lifted up* his voice, and said
14:11. they *lifted up* their voices,
22:22. and (then) *lifted up* their voices,
27:40. *hoised up* the mainsail to the wind, *and*
2Co.10: 5. every high thing *that exalteth itself*
11:20. if a man *exalt himself,*
1Ti. 2: 8. *lifting up* holy hands,

ἐπαισχύνομαι, *epaiskunomai.*

Mar. 8:38. therefore *shall be ashamed* of me
— *shall* the Son of man *be ashamed,*
Lu. 9:26. whosoever *shall be ashamed* of me
— of him *shall* the Son of man *be ashamed,*
Ro. 1:16. For I *am* not *ashamed* of the
6:21. whereof ye *are* now *ashamed?*
2Ti. 1: 8. *Be* not thou therefore *ashamed*
12. nevertheless I *am* not *ashamed:*
16. and *was* not *ashamed* of my chain:
Heb. 2:11. *is* not *ashamed* to call them brethren,
11:16. God *is not ashamed* to be called

ἐπαιτέω, *epaiteo.*

Lu. 16: 3. *to beg* I am ashamed.

ἐπακολουθέω, *epakoloutheo.*

Mar.16:20. the word with signs *following.*
1Ti. 5:10. if she have diligently *followed* every
24. some (men) they *follow after.*
1Pet.2:21. that ye *should follow* his steps:

ἐπακούω, *epakouo.*

2Co. 6: 2. I *have heard* thee in a time

ἐπακροάομαι, *epakroaomai.*

Acts16:25. the prisoners *heard* them.

ἐπάν, epan.

Mat. 2: 8. *when* ye have found (him),
Lu. 11:22. *when* a stronger than he shall
    34. *when* (thine eye) is evil, thy

ἐπάναγκες, epanankes.

Acts15:28. than these *necessary* things;

ἐπανάγω, epanago.

Mat.21:18. *as* he *returned* into the city,
Lu. 5: 3. that he would *thrust out* a little
    4. *Launch out* into the deep,

ἐπαναμιμνήσκω, epanamimneesko.

Ro. 15:15. as *putting* you *in mind*, because

ἐπαναπαύομαι, epanapauomai.

Lu. 10: 6. your peace *shall rest upon* it:
Ro. 2:17. a Jew, and *restest in* the law,

ἐπανέρχομαι, epanerkomai.

Lu. 10:35. when I *come again*, I will repay thee.
  19:15. that when he was *returned*,

ἐπανίσταμαι, epanistamai.

Mat.10:21. the children *shall rise up against*
Mar.13:12. children *shall rise up against* (their)
    parents,

ἐπανόρθωσις, epanorthōsis

2Ti. 3:16. for reproof, for *correction*,

ἐπάνω, epano.

Mat. 2: 9. stood *over* where the young
  5:14. A city that is set *on* an hill
  21: 7. put *on* them their clothes, and they set
    (him) there*on*.
  23:18. by the gift that is *upon* it,
    20. by all things there*on*.
    22. by him that sitteth there*on*.
  27:37. set up *over* his head his
  28: 2. from the door, and sat *upon* it.
Mar.14: 5. *more than* three hundred pence,
Lu. 4:39. he stood *over* her, and rebuked
  10:19. to tread *on* serpents and scorpions,
  11:44. the men that walk *over* (them)
  19:17. have thou authority *over* ten cities.
    19. Be thou also *over* five cities.
Joh. 3:31. cometh from above is *above* all:
  — cometh from heaven is *above* all.
1Co.15: 6. seen of *above* five hundred brethren
Rev. 6: 8. his name that sat *on* him
  20: 3. set a seal *upon* him,

ἐπαρκέω, eparkeo.

1Ti. 5:10. if she *have relieved* the afflicted,

1Ti. 5:16. *let* them *relieve* them,
  — that it *may relieve* them that are widows
    indeed.

ἐπαρχία, eparkia.

Acts23:34. he asked of what *province* he was.
  25: 1. Festus was come into the *province*,

ἔπαυλις, epaulis.

Acts 1:20. Let his *habitation* be desolate,

ἐπαύριον, epaurion.

Mat.27:62. Now the *next day*, that followed
Mar 11:12. on the *morrow*, when they were
Joh. 1:29. The *next day* John seeth Jesus
    35. the *next day after* John stood,
    43(44). The *day following* Jesus would
  6:22. The *day following*, when the people
  12:12. On the *next day* much people that
Acts10: 9. On the *morrow*, as they went
    23. on the *morrow* Peter went away
    24. the *morrow* after they entered
  14:20. the *next day* he departed with
  20: 7. ready to depart on the *morrow;*
  21: 8. the *next* (day) we that were
  22:30. On the *morrow*, because he
  23:32. On the *morrow* they left the
  25: 6. the *next day* sitting on the
    23. on the *morrow*, when Agrippa

ἐπαυτοφώρω, epautophōro.

Joh. 8: 4. taken in adultery, *in the very act*.

ἐπαφρίζω, epaphrizo.

Jude 13. *foaming out* their own shame;

ἐπεγείρω, epegiro.

Acts13:50. and *raised* persecution against Paul
  14: 2. Jews *stirred up* the Gentiles,

ἐπεί, epī.

Mat.18:32. *because* thou desiredst me:
  27: 6. *because* it is the price of blood.
Mar 15:42. *because* it was the preparation,
Lu. 1:34. *seeing* I know not a man?
  7: 1. *when* he had ended all his
Joh.13:29. *because* Judas had the bag,
  19:31. *because* it was the preparation,
Ro. 3: 6. *for then* how shall God judge
  11: 6. *otherwise* grace is no more grace.
  — *otherwise* work is no more work.
    22. *otherwise* thou also shalt be cut off.
1Co. 5:10. *for then* must ye needs go out of
  7:14. *else* were your children unclean;
  14:12. *forasmuch as* ye are zealous of
    16. *Else* when thou shalt bless
  15:29. *Else* what shall they do which

2Co.11:18. *Seeing that* many glory after the
13: 3. *Since* ye seek a proof of Christ
Heb 2:14. *Forasmuch* then *as* the children
4: 6. *Seeing* therefore it remaineth that *some*
5: 2. *for that* he himself also is compassed
11. *seeing* ye are dull of hearing.
6:13. *because* he could swear by no
9:17. *otherwise* it is of no strength
26. *For then* must he often have
10: 2. *For then* would they not have
11:11. *because* she judged him faithful

ἐπείπερ, *epīper.*

Ro. 3:30. *Seeing* (it is) one God, which

ἐπειδή, *epīdee.*

Mat.21:46. *because* they took him for a
Lu. 11: 6. *For* a friend of mine in his
Acts13:46. *seeing* ye put it from you,
14:12. *because* he was the chief speaker.
15:24. *Forasmuch as* we have heard,
1Co. 1:21. For *after that* in the wisdom
22. *For* the Jews require a sign,
14:16. *seeing* he understandeth not what
15:21. For *since* by man (came) death,
2Co. 5: 4. not *for that* we would be unclothed,
Phi. 2:26. *For* he longed after you all,

ἐπειδήπερ, *epīdeeper.*

Lu. 1: 1. *Forasmuch as* many have

ἐπείδω see ἐφοράω.

ἐπεισαγωγή, *epīsagogee.*

Heb 7:19. the *bringing in* of a better hope

ἔπειτα, *epīta.*

Mar 7: 5. *Then* the Pharisees and scribes asked
Lu. 16: 7. *Then* said he to another,
Joh.11: 7. *Then* after that saith he to (his)
1Co.12:28. *after that* miracles, then gifts
15: 6. *After that,* he was seen of above five
hundred
7. *After that,* he was seen of James ;
23. *afterward* they that are Christ's
46. *afterward* that which is spiritual.
Gal. 1:18. *Then* after three years I went up
21. *Afterwards* I came into the regions
2: 1. *Then* fourteen years after I went
1Th. 4:17. *Then* we which are alive (and) remain
Heb 7: 2. *after that* also King of Salem,
27. for his own sins, and *then* for the people's:
Jas. 3:17. is first pure, *then* peaceable,
4:14. a little time, and *then* vanisheth away.

ἐπέκεινα, *epekīna.*

Acts 7:43. carry you away *beyond* Babylon.

ἐπεκτείνομαι, *epektīnomai.*

Phi. 3:13(14). *reaching forth unto* those things

ἐπενδύομαι, *ependuomai.*

2Co. 5: 2. earnestly desiring *to be clothed upon*
4. would be unclothed, but *clothed upon,*

ἐπενδύτης, *ependutees.*

Joh.21: 7. he girt (his) *fisher's coat* (unto him),

ἐπέρχομαι, *eperkomai.*

Lu. 1:35. The Holy Ghost *shall come upon* thee,
11:22. he shall *come upon* him *and* overcome
21:26. looking after those things *which are coming
on* the earth:
35. as a snare *shall* it *come on* all
Acts 1: 8. *after that* the Holy Ghost *is come upon* you:
8:24. which ye have spoken *come upon* me.
13:40. lest that *come upon* you, which
14:19. there *came* thither (certain) Jews
Eph. 2: 7. in the ages *to come* he might
Jas. 5: 1. miseries *that shall come upon* (you).

ἐπερωτάω, *eperōtao.*

Mat.12:10. they *asked* him, saying,
16: 1. *desired* him that he would
17:10. his disciples *asked* him, saying,
22:23. is no resurrection, and *asked* him,
35. a lawyer, *asked* (him a question),
41. gathered together, Jesus *asked* them,
46. durst any (man) from that day forth *ask*
27:11. the governor *asked* him, saying,
Mar 5: 9. he *asked* him, What (is) thy name ?
7: 5. Pharisees and scribes *asked* him,
17. his disciples *asked* him
8: 5. he *asked* them, How many loaves
23. he *asked* him if he saw ought.
27. by the way he *asked* his disciples,
9:11. they *asked* him, saying, Why say the scribes
16. he *asked* the scribes, What question ye
21. he *asked* his father, How long is it ago
28. his disciples *asked* him privately,
32. were afraid *to ask* him.
33. in the house he *asked* them,
10: 2. came to him, and *asked* him,
10. his disciples *asked* him again
17. kneeled to him, and *asked* him,
11:29. I *will* also *ask* of you one question.
12:18. they *asked* him, saying,
28. *asked* him, Which is the first
34. no man after that durst *ask* him
13: 3. John and Andrew *asked* him
14:60. in the midst, and *asked* Jesus,
61. Again the high priest *asked* him,
15: 2. Pilate *asked* him, Art thou
4. Pilate *asked* him again,
44. he *asked* him whether he had been
Lu. 2:46. hearing them, and *asking* them *questions.*
3:10. the people *asked* him, saying,
14. soldiers likewise *demanded* of him,
6: 9. I *will ask* you one thing ;
8: 9. his disciples *asked* him,
30. Jesus *asked* him, saying,

Lu. 9:18. he *asked* them, saying,
   17:20. *when he was demanded* of
   18:18. a certain ruler *asked* him,
     40. was come near, he *asked* him,
   20:21. they *asked* him, saying, Master,
     27. and they *asked* him,
     40. they durst not *ask* him
   21: 7. they *asked* him, saying,
   22:64. struck him on the face, and *asked* him.
   23: 3. Pilate *asked* him, saying,
     6. he *asked* whether the man
     9. he *questioned* with him in many words ;
Joh. 18: 7. Then *asked* he them again,
     21. Why *askest* thou me ? *ask* them which heard
Acts 1: 6. they *asked* of him, saying, Lord.
   5:27. the high priest *asked* them,
   23:34. he *asked* of what province he was.
Ro. 10:20. unto them *that asked* not *after* me.
1Co.14:35. *let* them *ask* their husbands at home:

ἐπερώτημα, *eperoteema.*

1Pet.3:21. the *answer* of a good conscience

ἐπέχω, *epeko.*

Lu. 14: 7. *when* he *marked* how they chose
Acts 3: 5. he *gave heed unto* them,
   19:22. he himself *stayed* in Asia
Phi. 2:16. *Holding forth* the word of life ;
1Ti. 4:16. *Take heed unto* thyself, and unto

ἐπηρεάζω, *epeereazo.*

Mat. 5:44. pray for them *which despitefully use* you,
Lu. 6:28. for them *which despitefully use* you.
1Pet.3:16. ashamed *that falsely accuse* your good

ἐπί, *epi.*

Followed by a genitive, a dative, or an accusative ; which are severally distinguished by ᵍ, ᵈ, ᵃ.

Mat. 1:11. *about the time*ᵍ they were carried away to Babylon:
   2:22. Archelaus did reign *in*ᵍ Judæa
   3: 7. Sadducees come *to*ᵃ his baptism,
     13. cometh Jesus from Galilee *to*ᵃ Jordan
     16. like a dove, and lighting *upon*ᵃ him:
   4: 4. Man shall not live *by*ᵈ bread alone, but *by*ᵈ every word that proceedeth
     5. *on*ᵃ a pinnacle of the temple,
     6. *in*ᵍ (their) hands they shall bear
   5:15. under a bushel, but *on*ᵃ a candlestick ;
     23. bring thy gift *to*ᵃ the altar,
     39. smite thee *on*ᵃ thy right cheek,
     45. his sun to rise *on*ᵍ the evil and on the good, and sendeth rain *on*ᵃ the just and on the unjust.
   6:10. Thy will be done *in*ᵍ earth, as
     19. for yourselves treasures *upon*ᵍ earth,
     27. add one cubit *unto*ᵃ his stature ?
   7:24. built his house *upon*ᵃ a rock:
     25. for it was founded *upon*ᵃ a rock.
     26. built his house *upon*ᵃ the sand:
     28. astonished *at*ᵈ his doctrine:
   9: 2. sick of the palsy, lying *on*ᵍ a bed:

Mat. 9: 6. hath power *on*ᵍ earth to forgive
     9. sitting *at*ᵃ the receipt of custom:
     15. as long as (lit. *for*ᵃ as long as) the bridegroom is
     16. new cloth *unto*ᵈ an old garment,
     18. lay thy hand *upon*ᵍ her, and she
   10:13. let your peace come *upon*ᵃ it:
     18. brought *before*ᵃ governors and kings
     21. children shall rise up *against*ᵃ (their)
     27. preach ye *upon*ᵍ the housetops.
     29. shall not fall *on*ᵃ the ground
     34. come to send peace *on*ᵃ earth:
   11:29. Take my yoke *upon*ᵃ you, and learn
   12:18. I will put my spirit *upon*ᵃ him,
     26. he is divided *against*ᵃ himself ;
     28. kingdom of God is come *unto*ᵃ you.
     49. forth his hand *toward*ᵃ his disciples,
   13: 2. whole multitude stood *on*ᵃ the shore
     5. Some fell *upon*ᵃ stony places,
     7. some fell *among*ᵃ thorns ;
     8. other fell *into*ᵃ good ground,
     14. *in*ᵈ them is fulfilled the prophecy
     20. received the seed *into*ᵃ stony places,
     23. received seed *into*ᵃ the good ground
     48. they drew *to*ᵃ shore, and sat down,
   14: 8. John Baptist's head *in*ᵈ a charger.
     11. head was brought *in*ᵈ a charger,
     14. with compassion *toward*ᵃ them,
     19. to sit down *on*ᵃ the grass,
     25. went unto them, walking *on*ᵍ the sea.
     26. saw him walking *on*ᵍ the sea,
     28. come unto thee *on*ᵃ the water.
     29. he walked *on*ᵃ the water,
   15:32. I have compassion *on*ᵃ the multitude,
     35. to sit down *on*ᵃ the ground.
   16:18. *upon*ᵈ this rock I will build·
     19. thou shalt bind *on*ᵍ earth
     — thou shalt loose *on*ᵍ earth
   17: 6. they fell *on*ᵃ their face,
   18: 5. such little child *in*ᵈ my name
     6. were hanged *about*ᵃ his neck,
     12. goeth *into*ᵃ the mountains,
     13. he rejoiceth more *of*ᵈ that (sheep), than *of*ᵈ the ninety and nine
     16. that *in*ᵍ the mouth of two or three
     18. Whatsoever ye shall bind *on*ᵍ earth
     — whatsoever ye shall loose *on*ᵍ earth
     19. two of you shall agree *on*ᵍ earth
     26. Lord, have patience *with*ᵈ me,
     29. saying, Have patience *with*ᵈ me,
   19: 9. except (it be) *for*ᵈ fornication,
     28. shall sit *in*ᵍ the throne of his glory, ye also shall sit *upon*ᵃ twelve thrones,
   21: 5. meek, and sitting *upon*ᵃ an ass,
     19. And when he saw a fig tree *in*ᵍ the way, he came *to*ᵃ it,
     44. whosoever shall fall *on*ᵃ this stone
     — *on*ᵃ whomsoever it shall fall,
   22: 9. therefore *into*ᵃ the highways,
     33. were astonished *at*ᵈ his doctrine.
   23: 2. the Pharisees sit *in*ᵍ Moses' seat:
     4. lay (them) *on*ᵃ men's shoulders;
     9. call no (man) your father *upon*ᵍ the earth:
     35. That *upon*ᵃ you may come all the righteous blood shed *upon*ᵍ the earth,
     36. shall come *upon*ᵃ this generation.
   24: 2. one stone *upon*ᵃ another,
     3. sat *upon*ᵍ the mount of Olives,
     5. many shall come *in*ᵈ my name,
     7. nation shall rise *against*ᵃ nation, and kingdom *against*ᵃ kingdom:
     16. flee *into*ᵃ the mountains:

Mat.24:17. him which is on ^{g} the housetop
   30. coming in ^{g} the clouds of heaven
   33. it is near, (even) at ^{d} the doors.
   45. hath made ruler over ^{g} his houshold,
   47. make him ruler over ^{d} all his goods.
  25:20. I have gained beside ^{d} them five
   21. faithful over ^{a} a few things, I will make
      thee ruler over ^{g} many things:
   22. two other talents beside ^{d} them.
   23. faithful over ^{a} a few things, I will make
      thee ruler over ^{g} many things:
   31. sit upon ^{g} the throne of his glory:
   40. Inasmuch ^{a} as ye have done (it)
   45. Inasmuch ^{a} as ye did (it) not
  26: 7. poured it on ^{a} his head, as he sat
   12. poured this ointment on ^{g} my body,
   39. fell on ^{a} his face, and prayed,
   50. wherefore ^{d} art thou come?
   — laid hands on ^{a} Jesus, and took him.
   55. come out as against ^{a} a thief,
   64. coming in ^{g} the clouds of heaven.
  27:19. set down on ^{g} the judgment seat,
   25. and said, His blood (be) on ^{a} us, and on ^{a}
      our children.
   27. gathered unto ^{a} him the whole
   29. they put (it) upon ^{a} his head, and a reed
      in ^{a} his right hand:
   35. upon ^{a} my vesture did they cast
   43. He trusted in ^{a} God; let him
   45. darkness over ^{a} all the land
  28:14. if this come to ^{g} the governor's ears,
   18. unto me in heaven and in ^{g} earth.
Mar. 1:10. like a dove descending upon ^{a} him:
   22. were astonished at ^{d} his doctrine.
  2: 4. the bed wherein ^{d} the sick of the palsy
   10. power on ^{g} earth to forgive sins,
   14. sitting at ^{a} the receipt of custom,
   21. new cloth on ^{d} an old garment:
   26. in the days of ^{g} Abiathar
  3: 5. grieved for ^{d} the hardness of their hearts,
   24. kingdom be divided against ^{a} itself,
   25. a house be divided against ^{a} itself,
   26. if Satan rise up against ^{a} himself,
  4: 1. was by the sea on ^{g} the land.
   5. some fell on ^{a} stony ground,
   16. which are sown on ^{a} stony ground;
   20. are sown on ^{a} good ground;
   21. not to be set on ^{a} a candlestick?
   26. should cast seed into ^{g} the ground;
   31. when it is sown in ^{g} the earth,
   — the seeds that be in ^{g} the earth:
   38. was in ^{d} the hinder part of the ship, asleep
      on ^{a} a pillow:
  5:21. much people gathered unto ^{a} him:
   33. knowing what was done in ^{d} her,
  6:25. give me by and by in ^{d} a charger
   28. And brought his head in ^{d} a charger,
   34. moved with compassion toward ^{d} them,
   39. by companies upon ^{g} the green grass.
   47. he alone on ^{g} the land.
   48. walking upon ^{g} the sea,
   49. saw him walking upon ^{g} the sea,
   52. not (the miracle) of (lit. upon ^{d}) the
   53. they came into ^{a} the land of Gennesaret,
   55. began to carry about in ^{d} beds
  7:30. her daughter laid upon ^{g} the bed.
  8: 2. I have compassion on ^{a} the multitude,
   4. with bread here in ^{g} the wilderness?
   6. to sit down on ^{g} the ground:
   25. put (his) hands again upon ^{a} his eyes,
  9: 3. so as no fuller on ^{g} earth can
   12. how it is written of ^{a} the Son of man,

Mar. 9:13. as it is written of ^{a} him.
   20. he fell on ^{g} the ground, and wallowed
   22. have compassion on ^{a} us, and help us.
   37. one of such children in ^{d} my name
   39. shall do a miracle in ^{d} my name,
  10:11. committeth adultery against ^{a} her
   16. put (his) hands upon ^{a} them,
   22. he was sad at ^{d} that saying,
   24. were astonished at ^{d} his words.
   — for them that trust in ^{d} riches
  11: 2. whereon ^{a} never man sat;
   4. in a place (lit. at ^{g}) where two ways met;
   7. he sat upon ^{d} him.
   13. when he came to ^{a} it,
   18. was astonished at ^{d} his doctrine.
  12:14. teachest the way of God in ^{g} truth:
   17. they marvelled at ^{d} him.
   26. how in ^{g} the bush God spake
   32. Master, thou hast said)(^{g} the truth:
  13: 2. left one stone upon ^{d} another,
   6. many shall come in ^{d} my name,
   8. nation shall rise against ^{a} nation, and
      kingdom against ^{a} kingdom:
   9. brought before ^{g} rulers and kings
   12. shall rise up against ^{a} (their) parents,
   15. him that is on ^{g} the housetop
   29. it is nigh, (even) at ^{d} the doors.
  14:35. fell on ^{g} the ground, and prayed
   46. they laid their hands on ^{a} him,
   48. Are ye come out, as against ^{a} a thief,
   51. a linen cloth cast about ^{g} (his) naked
  15: 1. straightway in ^{a} the morning
   22. unto ^{a} the place Golgotha,
   24. casting lots upon ^{a} them,
   33. darkness over ^{a} the whole land
   46. unto ^{a} the door of the sepulchre.
  16: 2. they came unto ^{a} the sepulchre
   18. they shall lay hands on ^{a} the sick,
Lu. 1:12. troubled, and fear fell upon ^{a} him.
   14. many shall rejoice at ^{d} his birth.
   16. shall he turn to ^{a} the Lord their God.
   17. hearts of the fathers to ^{a} the children,
   29. was troubled at ^{d} his saying,
   33. reign over ^{a} the house of Jacob
   35. Holy Ghost shall come upon ^{a} thee,
   47. hath rejoiced in ^{d} God my Saviour.
   48. hath regarded)(^{a} the low estate of
   59. after ^{d} the name of his father.
   65. fear came on ^{a} all that dwelt
  2: 8. keeping watch over ^{a} their flock
   14. on ^{g} earth peace, good will toward
   20. for ^{d} all the things that they had
   25. the Holy Ghost was upon ^{a} him.
   33. marvelled at ^{d} those things which
   40. the grace of God was upon ^{a} him.
   47. astonished at ^{d} his understanding
  3: 2. Annas and Caiaphas being the high
      priests, (lit. in the time of ^{g} the high
      priests A. and C.) the word of God came
      unto ^{a} John
   20. Added yet this above ^{d} all,
   22. like a dove upon ^{a} him,
  4: 4. shall not live by ^{d} bread alone, but by ^{d}
      every word of God.
   9. set him on ^{a} a pinnacle of the
   11. in ^{g} (their) hands they shall bear
   18. Spirit of the Lord (is) upon ^{a} me,
   22. wondered at ^{d} the gracious words
   25. I tell you of ^{g} a truth,
   — was shut up)(^{a} three years and six
   — famine was throughout ^{a} all the land;
   27. in the time of ^{g} Eliseus the

Lu. 4:29. where*on*ᵍ their city was built,
32. were astonished *at*ᵈ his doctrine:
36. they were all amazed, (lit. amazement was *upon*ᵃ all)
5: 5. nevertheless *at*ᵈ thy word I will
9. *at*ᵈ the draught of the fishes
11. had brought their ships *to*ᵃ land,
12. seeing Jesus fell *on*ᵃ (his) face,
18. men brought *in*ᵍ a bed a man
19. they went *upon*ᵃ the housetop,
24. hath power *upon*ᵍ earth to
25. took up that where*on*ᵈ he lay,
27. sitting *at*ᵃ the receipt of custom.
36. a new garment *upon*ᵃ an old ;
6:17. with them, and stood *in*ᵍ the plain,
29. smiteth thee *on*ᵃ the (one) cheek
35. he is kind *unto*ᵃ the unthankful
48. laid the foundation *on*ᵃ a rock :
— it was founded *upon*ᵃ a rock.
49. built an house *upon*ᵃ the earth ;
7:13. he had compassion *on*ᵈ her,
44. gavest me no water *for*ᵃ my feet:
8: 6. some fell *upon*ᵃ a rock ;
8. other fell *on*ᵃ good ground,
13. They *on*ᵍ the rock (are they), which,
16. setteth (it) *on*ᵍ a candlestick,
27. when he went forth *to*ᵃ land,
9: 1. power and authority *over*ᵃ all devils,
5. for a testimony *against*ᵃ them.
38. I beseech thee, look *upon*ᵃ my son:
43. *at*ᵈ the mighty power of God.
— *at*ᵈ all things which Jesus did,
48. receive this child *in*ᵈ my name
49. casting out devils *in*ᵈ thy name ;
62. put his hand *to*ᵃ the plough,
10: 6. your peace shall rest *upon*ᵃ it: if not, it shall turn *to*ᵃ you again.
9. is come nigh *unto*ᵃ you.
11. is come nigh *unto*ᵃ you.
19. *over*ᵃ all the power of the enemy:
34. set him *on*ᵃ his own beast,
35. *on*ᵃ the morrow when he departed,
11: 2. be done, as in heaven, so *in*ᵍ earth.
17. Every kingdom divided *against*ᵃ itself
— a house (divided) *against*ᵃ a house
18. Satan also be divided *against*ᵃ himself,
20. kingdom of God is come *upon*ᵃ you.
22. his armour where*in*ᵈ he trusted,
33. under a bushel, but *on*ᵃ a candlestick,
12: 3. proclaimed *upon*ᵍ the housetops.
11. bring you *unto*ᵃ the synagogues,
14. a judge or a divider *over*ᵃ you ?
25. can add *to*ᵃ his stature one
42. make ruler *over*ᵍ his houshold,
44. ruler *over*ᵈ all that he hath.
52. divided, three *against*ᵈ two, and two *against*ᵈ three.
53. *against*ᵈ the son, and the son *against*ᵈ the father ; the mother *against*ᵈ the daughter, and the daughter *against*ᵈ the mother ; the mother in law *against*ᵃ her daughter in law, and the daughter in law *against*
58. thine adversary *to*ᵃ the magistrate,
13: 4, *upon*ᵃ whom the tower in Siloam fell,
17. *for*ᵈ all the glorious things that
14:31. him that cometh *against*ᵈ him
15: 4. go *after*ᵃ that which is lost,
5. he layeth (it) *on*ᵃ his shoulders,
7. *over*ᵈ one sinner that repenteth, more than *over*ᵈ ninety and nine
10. *over*ᵈ one sinner that **repenteth**.

Lu. 15:20. fell *on*ᵃ his neck, and kissed him.
16:26. *beside*ᵈ all this, between us and you
17: 4. turn again *to*ᵃ thee, saying,
16. fell down *on*ᵃ (his) face at his feet,
31. shall be *upon*ᵍ the housetop,
34. shall be two (men) *in*ᵍ one bed ;
35. shall be grinding together ; (lit. *at*ᵃ the same)
18: 4. he would not *for*ᵃ a while:
7. though he bear long *with*ᵈ them ?
8. shall he find faith *on*ᵍ the earth ?
9. which trusted *in*ᵈ themselves
19: 4. climbed up *into*ᵃ a sycomore tree
5. when Jesus came *to*ᵃ the place.
14. this (man) to reign *over*ᵃ us.
23. my money *into*ᵃ the bank,
27. that I should reign *over*ᵃ them,
30. where*on*ᵃ yet never man sat:
35. cast their garments *upon*ᵃ the colt,
41. beheld the city, and wept *over*ᵈ it,
43. the days shall come *upon*ᵃ thee,
44. in thee one stone *upon*ᵈ another;
20:18. Whosoever shall fall *upon*ᵃ that stone
— *on*ᵃ whomsoever it shall fall,
19. sought to lay hands *on*ᵃ him ;
21. teachest the way of God truly: (lit. *in*ᵍ truth)
26. they marvelled *at*ᵈ his answer,
37. even Moses shewed *at*ᵍ the bush,
21: 6. be left one stone *upon*ᵈ another,
8. many shall come *in*ᵈ my name,
10. Nation shall rise *against*ᵃ nation, and kingdom *against*ᵃ kingdom:
12. they shall lay their hands *on*ᵃ you,
— brought *before*ᵃ kings and rulers
23. great distress *in*ᵍ the land,
25. *upon*ᵍ the earth distress of nations,
34. that day come *upon*ᵃ you unawares.
35. shall it come *on*ᵃ all them that dwell *on*ᵃ the face of the whole earth.
22:21. with me *on*ᵍ the table.
30. may eat and drink *at*ᵍ my table in my kingdom, and sit *on*ᵍ thrones judging the
40. when he was *at*ᵍ the place,
44. falling down *to*ᵃ the ground.
52. which were come *to*ᵃ him, Be ye come out, as *against*ᵃ a thief
53. no hands *against*ᵃ me:
59. *Of*ᵍ a truth this (fellow) also
23: 1. led him *unto*ᵃ Pilate.
28. weep not *for*ᵃ me, but weep *for*ᵃ yourselves, and *for*ᵃ your children.
30. to the mountains, Fall *on*ᵃ us;
33. when they were come *to*ᵃ the place,
38. also was written *over*ᵈ him
44. darkness *over*ᵃ all the earth
48. came together *to*ᵃ that sight,
24: 1. they came *unto*ᵃ the sepulchre,
12. Peter, and ran *unto*ᵃ the sepulchre ;
22. were early *at*ᵃ the sepulchre ;
24. with us went *to*ᵃ the sepulchre,
25. to believe)(ᵈ all that the prophets
47. should be preached *in*ᵈ his name
49. promise of my Father *upon*ᵃ you:
Joh. 1:32. it abode *upon*ᵃ him.
33. *Upon*ᵃ whom thou shalt see the Spirit descending, and remaining *on*ᵃ him,
51(52). descending *upon*ᵃ the Son of man.
3:36. but the wrath of God abideth *on*ᵃ him.
4: 6. sat thus *on*ᵈ the well:
27. *upon*ᵈ this came his disciples,
5: 2. *by*ᵈ the sheep (market) a pool,

Joh. 6: 2. which he did on ᵍ them that were
16. went down *unto* ᵃ the sea,
19. they see Jesus walking on ᵍ the sea,
21. the ship was *at* ᵍ the land
7:30. no man laid hands on ᵃ him,
44. no man laid hands on ᵃ him.
8: 7. let him first cast a stone *at* ᵈ her.
59. took they up stones to cast *at* ᵃ him:
9: 6. he anointed)(ᵃ the eyes of the blind
15. He put clay *upon* ᵃ mine eyes,
11:38. a stone lay *upon* ᵈ it.
12:14. found a young ass, sat there*on ;* ᵃ
15. sitting on ᵃ an ass's colt.
16. these things were written *of* ᵈ him,
13:18. lifted up his heel *against* ᵃ me.
25. lying on ᵃ Jesus' breast
17: 4. I have glorified thee on ᵍ the earth:
18: 4. that should come *upon* ᵃ him,
19:13. sat down *in* ᵍ the judgment seat
19. put (it) on ᵍ the cross.
24. *for* ᵃ my vesture they did cast lots.
31. not remain *upon* ᵍ the cross
33. when they came *to* ᵃ Jesus,
20: 7. napkin, that was *about* ᵍ his head,
21: 1. *at* ᵍ the sea of Tiberias ;
11. drew the net *to* ᵍ land full
20. leaned on ᵃ his breast at supper,
Acts 1: 8. Holy Ghost is come *upon* ᵃ you:
15. the number of the names together (lit.
at ᵃ one)
21. went in and out *among* ᵃ us,
26. the lot fell *upon* ᵃ Matthias ;
2: 1. with one accord *in* ᵃ one place.
3. it sat *upon* ᵃ each of them.
17. my Spirit *upon* ᵃ all flesh:
18 And *on* ᵃ my servants and on ᵃ my handmaidens I will pour
19. signs *in* ᵍ the earth beneath ;
26. my flesh shall rest *in* ᵈ hope.
30. Christ to sit on ᵍ his throne;
38. *in* ᵈ the name of Jesus Christ
44. all that believed were together, (lit. *at* ᵃ
one place)
3: 1. Now Peter and John went up together
(lit. *at* ᵃ the same)
10. *at* ᵈ the Beautiful gate of the
— *at* ᵈ that which had happened
11. *in* ᵈ the porch that is called
12. why marvel ye *at* ᵈ this?
16. *through* ᵈ faith in his name
4: 5. it came to pass on ᵃ the morrow,
9. examined *of* ᵈ the good deed done
17. that it spread no further (lit. spread not
unto ᵃ more)
— to no man *in* ᵈ this name.
18. teach *in* ᵈ the name of Jesus.
21. glorified God *for* ᵈ that which was done.
22. *on* ᵃ whom this miracle of
26. gathered together (lit. *at* ᵃ one) against
27. For *of* ᵍ a truth *against* ᵃ thy holy child
Jesus, whom
29. Lord, behold)(ᵃ their threatenings:
33. great grace was *upon* ᵃ them all.
5: 5. great fear came on ᵃ all them
9. (are) *at* ᵈ the door, and shall carry
11. great fear came *upon* ᵃ all the church, and
upon ᵃ as many as heard these
15. laid (them) on ᵍ beds and couches,
18. laid their hands on ᵃ the apostles,
28. should not teach *in* ᵈ this name?
— this man's blood *upon* ᵃ us.
30. ye slew and hanged on ᵍ a tree.

Acts 5:35. to do *as touching* ᵈ these men.
40. not speak *in* ᵈ the name of Jesus,
6: 3. may appoint *over* ᵍ this business.
7:10. made him governor *over* ᵃ Egypt
11. a dearth *over* ᵃ all the land
23. it came *into* ᵃ his heart
27. a ruler and a judge *over* ᵃ us ?
54. gnashed on ᵃ him with (their) teeth.
57. ran *upon* ᵃ him with one accord,
8: 1. persecution *against* ᵃ the church
2. made great lamentation *over* ᵈ him.
16. was fallen *upon* ᵈ none of them:
17. laid they (their) hands on ᵃ them,
24. have spoken come *upon* ᵃ me.
26. *unto* ᵃ the way that goeth down
27. who had the charge of all her treasure
(lit. who was *over* ᵍ all her)
28. sitting *in* ᵍ his chariot
32. as a sheep *to* ᵃ the slaughter ;
36. they came *unto* ᵃ a certain water:
9: 4. he fell *to* ᵃ the earth,
11. go *into* ᵃ the street which is
17. putting his hands on ᵃ him
21. bound *unto* ᵃ the chief priests?
33. had kept his bed (lit. lain *on* ᵈ his bed)
eight years,
35. turned *to* ᵃ the Lord.
42. many believed *in* ᵃ the Lord.
10: 9. Peter went up *upon* ᵃ the housetop
10. he fell into a trance, (lit. a trance fell
upon ᵃ him)
11. vessel descending *unto* ᵃ him,
— let down *to* ᵍ the earth:
16. This was done)(ᵃ thrice:
17. stood *before* ᵃ the gate,
25. fell down *at* ᵃ his feet,
34. *Of* ᵍ a truth I perceive that
39. slew and hanged on ᵍ a tree:
44. Holy Ghost fell on ᵃ all them
45. that on ᵃ the Gentiles also was
11:10. this was done)(ᵃ three times:
11. already come *unto* ᵃ the house
15. the Holy Ghost fell on ᵃ them, as on ᵃ us
at the beginning.
17. who believed on ᵃ the Lord Jesus
19. persecution that arose *about* ᵈ Stephen
21. turned *unto* ᵃ the Lord.
28. dearth *throughout* ᵃ all the world.
— *in the days of* ᵍ Claudius Cæsar.
12:10. they came *unto* ᵃ the iron gate
12. he came *to* ᵃ the house of Mary
20. Blastus the king's chamberlain (lit. that
was *over* ᵍ the king's bedchamber)
21. sat *upon* ᵍ his throne,
13:11. hand of the Lord (is) *upon* ᵃ thee,
— there fell on ᵃ him a mist
12. *at* ᵈ the doctrine of the Lord.
31. he was seen)(ᵃ many days of them
40. lest that come *upon* ᵈ you,
50. raised persecution *against* ᵃ Paul
51. dust of their feet *against* ᵃ them,
14: 3. speaking boldly *in* ᵈ the Lord.
10. Stand upright on ᵃ thy feet.
13. oxen and garlands *unto* ᵃ the gates,
15. *unto* ᵃ the living God,
15:10. to put a yoke *upon* ᵃ the neck
14. a people *for* ᵈ his name.
17. *upon* ᵃ whom my name is called, (lit.
upon ᵃ whom my name is called *upon* ᵃ
them)
19. are turned *to* ᵃ God:
31. they rejoiced *for* ᵈ the consolation.

Acts16:18. this did she)([a] many days.
19. marketplace *unto* [a] the rulers,
31. Believe *on* [a] the Lord Jesus Christ,
17: 2.)([a] three sabbath days reasoned
6. *unto* [a] the rulers of the city,
14. to go as it were *to* [a] the sea:
19. brought him *unto* [a] Areopagus,
26. to dwell *on* [a] all the face of the
18: 6. *upon* [a] your own heads;
12. brought him *to* [a] the judgment seat,
20. desired (him) to tarry)([a] longer time
19: 6. Holy Ghost came *on* [a] them;
8. *for the space of* [a] three months,
10. *by the space of* [a] two years,
12. were brought *unto* [a] the sick
13. to call *over* [a] them which had
16. leaped *on* [a] them, and overcame
17. fear fell *on* [a] them all,
34. about *the space of* [a] two hours
20: 9. there sat *in* [g] a window
— as Paul was)([a] long preaching,
11. talked)([a] a long while, even till
13. we went before *to* [a] ship,
37. fell *on* [a] Paul's neck, and kissed him,
38. *for* [d] the words which he spake
21: 5. kneeled down *on* [a] the shore,
23. which have a vow *on* [g] them;
24. be at charges *with* [d] them,
27. laid hands *on* [a] him,
32. ran down *unto* [a] them:
35. when he came *upon* [a] the stairs,
40. Paul stood *on* [g] the stairs,
22:19. them that believed *on* [a] thee:
23:30. also to say *before* [g] thee what
24: 4. not)([a] further tedious unto thee,
8. his accusers to come *unto* [a] thee:
19. to have been here *before* [g] thee,
20. while I stood *before* [g] the council,
25: 6. sitting *on* [g] the judgment seat
9. judged of these things *before* [g] me?
10. I stand *at* [g] Cæsar's judgment seat,
12. *unto* [a] Cæsar shalt thou go.
17. I sat *on* [g] the judgment seat,
26. brought him forth *before* [g] you, and specially *before* [g] thee, O king Agrippa,
26: 2. for myself this day *before* [g] thee
6. *for* [d] the hope of the promise
16. stand *upon* [a] thy feet:
18. (from) the power of Satan *unto* [a] God,
20. should repent and turn *to* [a] God,
27:20. nor stars *in* [a] many days appeared,
43. (into the sea), and get *to* [a] land:
44. the rest, some *on* [d] boards, and some *on* [g] (broken pieces) of the ship.
— they escaped all safe *to* [a] land.
28: 3. laid (them) *on* [a] the fire,
6. after they had looked)([a] a great while,
14. were desired to tarry *with* [d] them
Ro. 1: 9(10). of you always *in* [g] my prayers;
18. *against* [a] all ungodliness
2: 2. *against* [a] them which commit
9. *upon* [a] every soul of man that
3:22. *upon* [a] all them that believe:
4: 5. believeth *on* [a] him that justifieth
9. *upon* [a] the circumcision (only), or *upon* [a] the uncircumcision also?
18. against hope believed *in* [d] hope,
24. we believe *on* [a] him that raised
5: 2. rejoice *in* [d] hope of the glory
12. *for* [d] that all have sinned:
14. even *over* [a] them that had not sinned *after* the similitude of Adam's

Ro. 6:21. where*of* [d] ye are now ashamed?
7: 1.)([a] as long as he liveth?
8:20. subjected (the same) *in* [d] hope,
9: 5. who is *over* [g] all, God blessed
23. his glory *on* [a] the vessels of mercy,
28. the Lord make *upon* [g] the earth.
33. whosoever believeth *on* [d] him
10:11. Whosoever believeth *on* [d] him
19. to jealousy *by* [d] (them that are) no people, (and) *by* [d] a foolish nation
11:13. inasmuch [a] as I am the apostle
22. *on* [a] them which fell, severity; but *toward* [a] thee, goodness,
12:20. heap coals of fire *on* [a] his head.
15: 3. that reproached thee fell *on* [a] me.
12. *in* [d] him shall the Gentiles trust.
20. build *upon* [a] another man's foundation:
16:19. therefore *on* your *behalf* [d]:
1Co. 1: 4. *for* [d] the grace of God which is
2: 9. *into* [a] the heart of man,
3:12. build *upon* [a] this foundation
6: 1. against another, go to law *before* [g] the unjust, and not *before* [g] the saints?
6. that *before* [g] the unbelievers.
7: 5. come together again (lit. *to* [a] one), that Satan
36. uncomely *toward* [a] his virgin,
39.)([a] as long as her husband liveth;
8: 5. whether in heaven or *in* [g] earth,
11. *through* [d] thy knowledge shall
9:10. should plow *in* [d] hope; and that he that thresheth *in* [d] hope
11:10. to have power *on* [g] (her) head
20. together therefore *into* [a] one place,
13: 6. Rejoiceth not *in* [d] iniquity,
14:16. *at* [d] thy giving of thanks,
23. be come together *into* [a] one place,
25. falling down *on* [a] (his) face
16:17. I am glad *of* [d] the coming of Stephanas
2Co. 1: 4. *in* [d] all our tribulation,
9. that we should not trust *in* [d] ourselves, but *in* [d] God which raiseth the dead:
23. for a record *upon* [a] my soul,
2: 3. having confidence *in* [a] you all,
3:13. put a vail *over* [a] his face,
14. *in* [d] the reading of the old testament;
15. the vail is *upon* [a] their heart.
7: 4. joyful *in* [d] all our tribulation.
7. he was comforted *in* [d] you,
13. were comforted *in* [d] your comfort:
— *for* [d] the joy of Titus,
14. which (I made) *before* [g] Titus,
9: 6. he which soweth bountifully shall reap also bountifully. (lit. he which soweth *of* [d] blessings, or in bounties, shall reap *of* [d] blessings, or bounties)
13. *for* [d] your professed subjection
14. exceeding grace of God *in* [d] you.
15. *for* [d] his unspeakable gift.
10: 2. to be bold *against* [a] some,
12: 9. power of Christ may rest *upon* [a] me.
21. not repented *of* [d] the uncleanness
13: 1. *In* [g] the mouth of two or three
Gal. 3:13. every one that hangeth *on* [g] a tree:
16. saith not, And to seeds, as *of* [g] many; but as *of* [g] one,
4: 1.)([a] as long as he is a child,
9. turn ye again *to* [a] the weak
5:13. ye have been called *unto* [d] liberty;
6:16. peace (be) *on* [a] them, and mercy, and *upon* [a] the Israel of God.
Eph. 1:10. which are *on* [g] earth; (even) in him:

Eph. 1:16. mention of you in[g] my prayers;
2: 7. in (his) kindness toward[a] us
   10. in Christ Jesus unto[d] good works,
   20. built upon[d] the foundation of
3:15. in heaven and)([g] earth is named,
4: 6. who (is) above[g] all, and through all,
   26. down upon[d] your wrath:
5: 6. wrath of God upon[a] the children of
6: 3. live long on[g] the earth.
   16. Above[d] all, taking the shield of
Phi. 1: 3. upon[d] every remembrance of you,
   5. For[d] your fellowship in the gospel
2:17. offered upon[d] the sacrifice
   27. should have sorrow upon[d] sorrow.
3: 9. which is of God by[d] faith:
   12. that for[d] which also I am apprehended
   14. for[a] the prize of the high calling
4:10. wherein[d] ye were also careful,
Col. 1:16. in heaven, and that are in[g] earth,
   20. whether (they be) things in[g] earth,
3: 2. not on things on[g] the earth.
   5. which are upon[g] the earth;
   6. cometh on[a] the children of
   14. above[d] all these things
1Th. 1: 2. mention of you in[g] our prayers;
2:16. wrath is come upon[d] them
3: 7. brethren, we were comforted over[d] you
   in[d] all our affliction
   9. for[d] all the joy wherewith we
4: 7. not called us unto[d] uncleanness,
2Th. 1:10. our testimony among[a] you
2: 1. gathering together unto[a] him,
   4. above[a] all that is called God,
3: 4. confidence in the Lord touching[a] you,
1Ti. 1:16. should hereafter believe on[d] him
   18. which went before on[a] thee,
4:10. we trust in[d] the living God,
5: 5. trusteth in[a] God, and continueth
   19. before[g] two or three witnesses.
6:13. who before[g] Pontius Pilate
   17. nor trust in[g] uncertain riches,
2Ti. 2:14. to[d] the subverting of the hearers.
   16. will increase unto[a] more ungodliness.
3: 9. they shall proceed no)([a] further:
   13. shall wax)([a] worse and worse,
4: 4. shall be turned unto[a] fables.
Tit. 1: 2. In[d] hope of eternal life,
3: 6. he shed on[a] us abundantly
Philem. 4. of thee always in[g] my prayers,
   7. consolation in[d] thy love,
Heb 1: 2(1). Hath in[g] these last days spoken
2: 7. over[g] the works of thy hands:
   13. I will put my trust in[d] him.
3: 6. as a son over[a] his own house;
6: 1. let us go on unto[a] perfection;
   — of faith toward[a] God,
   7. rain that cometh oft upon[g] it,
7:11. for under[d] it the people received
   13. For he of[a] whom these things
8: 1. Now of[d] the things which we have spoken
   4. For if he were on[g] earth,
   6. established upon[d] better promises.
   8. a new covenant with[a] the house of Israel
   and with[a] the house of Judah:
   10. write them in[g] their hearts:
9:10. (Which stood) only in[d] meats and drinks,
   15. under[d] the first testament,
   17. of force after men are dead: (lit. *upon the basis of*[d] dead ones)
   26. in[d] the end of the world
10:16. I will put my laws into[g] their hearts, and in[g] their minds will I write them;

Heb 10:21. priest over[a] the house of God;
   28. under[d] two or three witnesses:
11: 4. God testifying of[d] his gifts:
   13. strangers and pilgrims on[g] the earth.
   21. upon[a] the top of his staff.
   30. were compassed about)([a] seven days.
12:10. he for[a] (our) profit, that (we)
   25. refused him that spake on[g] earth,
Jas. 2: 3. ye have respect to[a] him that weareth
   7. by the which ye are called? (lit. which is
   called upon[a] you)
   21. offered Isaac his son upon[a] the altar?
5: 1. for[d] your miseries that shall come upon
   (you).
   5. lived in pleasure on[g] the earth,
   7. hath long patience for[d] it,
   14. let them pray over[a] him,
   17. it rained not on[g] the earth
1Pet. 1:13. hope to the end for[a] the grace that
   20. in[g] these last times for you,
2: 6. he that believeth on[d] him shall
   24. in his own body on[a] the tree,
   25. now returned unto[a] the Shepherd
3: 5. women also, who trusted in[a] God,
   12. eyes of the Lord (are) over[a] the righteous,
   — against[a] them that do evil.
4:14. of God resteth upon[a] you:
5: 7. Casting all your care upon[a] him;
2Pet. 1:13.)([a] as long as I am in this tabernacle,
2:22. turned to[a] his own vomit again;
3: 3. shall come in[g] the last days
1Joh.3: 3. that hath this hope in[d] him
3Joh. 10. and not content therewith,[d] neither doth
Rev. 1: 7. shall wail because of[a] him.
   17. laid his right hand upon[a] me,
   20. sawest in[g] my right hand,
2:17. in[a] the stone a new name written,
   24. I will put upon[a] you none
   26. will I give power over[g] the nations:
3: 3. I will come on[a] thee as a thief,
   — what hour I will come upon[a] thee.
   10. come upon[g] all the world, to try them
   that dwell upon[g] the earth.
   12. I will write upon[a] him the name
   20. Behold, I stand at[a] the door,
4: 2. (one) sat on[g] the throne.
   4. upon[a] the seats I saw four
   — on[a] their heads crowns of gold.
   9. to him that sat on[g] the throne,
   10. him that sat on[g] the throne,
5: 1. And I saw in[a] the right hand of him that
   sat on[g] the throne
   3. no man in heaven, nor in[g] earth
   7. him that sat upon[g] the throne.
   10. we shall reign on[g] the earth.
   13. such as are in[g] the sea,
   — him that sitteth upon[g] the throne,
6: 2. he that sat on[d] him had a bow;
   4. to him that sat thereon[d] to
   5. he that sat on[d] him had a pair
   8. over[a] the fourth part of the earth,
   10. them that dwell on[g] the earth?
   16. mountains and rocks, Fall on[a] us,
   — of him that sitteth on[g] the throne,
7: 1. standing on[a] the four corners of
   — wind should not blow on[g] the earth, nor
   on[g] the sea, nor on[a] any tree.
   3. servants of our God in[g] their foreheads.
   10. which sitteth upon[g] the throne,
   11. before the throne on[a] their faces,
   15. and he that sitteth on[g] the throne shall
   dwell among[a] them.

Rev. 7:16. shall the sun light on^a them,
17. unto^a living fountains of waters:
8: 3. came and stood at^a the altar,
— of all saints upon^a the golden altar
10. fell upon^a the third part of the rivers, and upon^a the fountains of waters;
13. to the inhabiters of^g the earth
9: 4. seal of God in^g their foreheads.
7. on^a their heads (were) as it were
11. they had a king over^g them,
14. are bound in^d the great river
17. them that sit on^g them, having
10: 1. a rainbow (was) upon^g his head,
2. he set his right foot upon^a the sea, and (his) left (foot) on^a the earth,
5. the angel which I saw stand upon^g the sea and upon^g the earth
8. of the angel which standeth upon^g the sea and upon^g the earth.
11. prophesy again before^d many peoples,
11: 6. have power over^g waters to turn
8. in^g the street of the great city,
10. they that dwell upon^g the earth shall rejoice over^d them,
— them that dwelt on^g the earth.
11. of life from God entered into^a them, and they stood upon^a their feet; and great fear fell upon^a them which saw them.
16. which sat before God on^a their seats, fell upon^a their faces,
12: 1. upon^g her head a crown
3. seven crowns upon^a his heads.
17. dragon was wroth with^d the woman,
13: 1(12:18). I stood upon^a the sand of the sea,
— upon^g his horns ten crowns, and upon^a his heads the name
7. given him over^a all kindreds,
8. all that dwell upon^g the earth
14. them that dwell on^g the earth
— to them that dwell on^g the earth,
16. to receive a mark in^g their right hand, or in^g their foreheads:
14: 1. stood on^a the mount Sion,
— name written in^g their foreheads.
6. them that dwell on^g the earth,
9. and receive (his) mark in^g his forehead, or in^a his hand,
14. upon^a the cloud (one) sat like
— having on^g his head a golden
15. to him that sat on^g the cloud,
16. he that sat on^a the cloud thrust in his sickle on^a the earth;
18. which had power over^g fire;
15: 2. stand on^a the sea of glass,
16: 2. poured out his vial upon^a the earth;
8. his vial upon^a the sun;
9. hath power over^a these plagues:
10. upon^a the seat of the beast;
12. upon^a the great river Euphrates;
14. unto^a the kings of the earth
18. since men were upon^g the earth,
21. there fell upon^a men a great hail
17: 1. whore that sitteth upon^g many waters:
3. sit upon^a a scarlet coloured beast,
5. upon^a her forehead (was) a name
8. they that dwell on^g the earth
— not written in^a the book of life
9. on which (lit. where on^g them) the woman sitteth.
16. which thou sawest upon^a the beast,
18. over^g the kings of the earth.
18: 9. bewail her, and lament for^d her,

Rev.18:11. shall weep and mourn over^d her;
17. all the company in^g ships,
19. they cast dust on^a their heads,
20. Rejoice over^a her, (thou) heaven,
24. that were slain upon^g the earth.
19: 4. God that sat on^g the throne,
11. he that sat upon^a him
12. on^a his head (were) many crowns;
14. followed him upon^d white horses,
16. And he hath on^a (his) vesture and on^a his thigh a name written,
18. of them that sit on^g them,
19. him that sat on^g the horse,
21. of him that sat upon^g the horse,
20: 1. a great chain in^a his hand.
4. thrones, and they sat upon^a them,
— received (his) mark upon^a their foreheads, or in^a their hands;
6. on^g such the second death
9. up on^a the breadth of the earth,
11. throne, and him that sat on^g it,
21: 5. he that sat upon^g the throne
10. to^a a great and high mountain,
12. at^d the gates twelve angels,
16. the reed,)(^g twelve thousand furlongs.
22: 4. name (shall be) in^g their foreheads.
14. may have right to^a the tree of life,
16. these things in^d the churches.
18. God shall add unto^a him

ἐπιϐαίνω, epibaino.

Mat.21: 5. meek, and sitting upon an ass,
Acts20:18. first day that I came into Asia,
21: 2. we went aboard, and set forth.
6. we took ship; and they returned
25: 1. when Festus was come into the province,
27: 2. And entering into a ship

ἐπιϐάλλω, epiballo.

Mat. 9:16. No man putteth a piece of new cloth unto
26:50. Then came they, and laid hands
Mar 4:37. and the waves beat into the ship,
11: 7. and cast their garments on him;
14:46. they laid their hands on him,
72. when he thought thereon, he wept.
Lu. 5:36. No man putteth a piece of a new garment
9:62. having put his hand to the plough,
15:12. the portion of goods that falleth (to me).
20:19. to lay hands on him;
21:12. they shall lay their hands on you,
Joh. 7:30. no man laid hands on him,
44. no man laid hands on him.
Acts 4: 3. they laid hands on them,
5:18. And laid their hands on the apostles,
12: 1. Herod the king stretched forth (his) hands to vex
21:27. and laid hands on him,
1Co. 7:35. not that I may cast a snare upon you,

ἐπιϐαρέω, epibareo.

2Co. 2: 5. that I may not overcharge you all.
1Th. 2: 9. would not be chargeable unto any
2Th. 3: 8. might not be chargeable to any

ἐπιϐιϐάζω, epibibazo.

Lu. 10:34. and *set* him *on* his own beast, *and*
   19:35. and they *set* Jesus thereon.
Acts23:24. that they may *set* Paul *on*, *and*

ἐπιϐλέπω, epiblepo.

Lu. 1:48. he *hath regarded* the low estate
   9:38. *look upon* my son:
Jas. 2: 3. And ye *have respect to* him that weareth

ἐπίϐλημα, epibleema.

Mat. 9:16. putteth a *piece* of new cloth
Mar. 2:21. seweth a *piece* of new cloth
Lu. 5:36. No man putteth a *piece* of a new garment
   — and the *piece* that was (taken) out of the

ἐπιϐοάω, epiboao.

Acts25:24. *crying* that he ought not to live

ἐπιϐουλή, epiboulee.

Acts 9:24. their *laying await* was known of Saul.
   20: 3. when the Jews *laid wait* (lit. when there
        was a *lying in wait* of the Jews)
   19. befell me by the *lying in wait* of the Jews:
   23:30. told me how that the Jews *laid wait* (lit.
        when the *lying in wait* of the Jews, was
        told me)

ἐπιγαμϐρεύω, epigambruo.

Mat.22:24. his brother *shall marry* his wife,

ἐπίγειος, epigĭos.

Joh. 3:12. If I have told you *earthly* things,
1Co.15:40. and bodies *terrestrial:* but the
   — the (glory) of the *terrestrial* (is) another.
2Co. 5: 1. if our *earthly* house of (this)
Phi. 2:10. (things) *in earth*, and (things) under the
   earth;
   3:19. who mind *earthly* things.
Jas. 3:15. but (is) *earthly*, sensual, devilish.

ἐπιγίνομαι, epiginomai.

Acts28:13. and after one day the south wind *blew*, *and*

ἐπιγινώσκω, epiginōsko.

Mat. 7:16. Ye *shall know* them by their fruits.
   20. by their fruits ye *shall know* them.
   11:27. no man *knoweth* the Son, but the Father;
      neither *knoweth* any man the Father,
   14:35. *when* the men of that place *had knowledge*
      of him,
   17:12. and they *knew* him not, but have
Mar. 2: 8. And immediately *when* Jesus *perceived*
   5:30. Jesus, immediately *knowing* in himself
   6:33. and many *knew* him, and ran afoot
   54. the ship, straightway they *knew* him,

Lu. 1: 4. That thou *mightest know* the certainty
   22. they *perceived* that he had seen a vision
   5:22. *when* Jesus *perceived* their thoughts,
   7:37. *when* she *knew* that (Jesus) sat at meat
   23: 7. And *as soon as* he *knew* that he belonged
   24:16. holden that they should not *know* him.
   31. opened, and they *knew* him ;
Acts 3:10. And they *knew* that it was he which sat for
   4:13. and they *took knowledge of* them, that they
   9:30. (Which) *when* the brethren *knew*, they
      brought
   12:14. And *when* she *knew* Peter's voice, she
   19:34. *when* they *knew* that he was a Jew,
   22:24. that he *might know* wherefore they cried
   29. *after* he *knew* that he was a Roman,
   24: 8. thyself mayest *take knowledge of* all
   25:10. as thou very well *knowest*.
   27:39. they *knew* not the land: but they
   28: 1. then they *knew* that the island
Ro. 1:32. Who *knowing* the judgment of God,
1Co.13:12. but then *shall* I *know* even as also I *am*
      known.
   14:37. *let* him *acknowledge* that the things
   16:18. therefore *acknowledge* ye them that
2Co. 1:13. than what ye read or *acknowledge;*
   — ye *shall acknowledge* even to the end ;
   14. ye *have acknowledged* us in part,
   6: 9. *unknown*, and (yet) *well known ;*
   13: 5. *Know* ye not your own selves, how
Col. 1: 6. and *knew* the grace of God in truth:
1Ti. 4: 3. which believe and *know* the truth.
2Pet.2:21. for them not *to have known* the way
   — than, *after* they *have known* (it), to turn

ἐπίγνωσις, epignōsis.

Ro. 1:28. to retain God in (their) *knowledge*,
   3:20. by the law (is) the *knowledge* of sin.
   10: 2. zeal of God, but not according to *know-*
      ledge.
Eph. 1:17. in the *knowledge* of him:
   4:13. and of the *knowledge* of the Son of God,
Phi. 1: 9. in *knowledge* and (in) all judgment ;
Col. 1: 9. with the *knowledge* of his will in all
   10. increasing in the *knowledge* of God ;
   2: 2. to the *acknowledgement* of the mystery
   3:10. renewed in *knowledge* after the image
1Ti. 2: 4. to come unto the *knowledge* of the truth.
2Ti. 2:25. repentance to the *acknowledging* of the
      truth ;
   3: 7. never able to come to the *knowledge* of
      the truth.
Tit. 1: 1. the *acknowledging* of the truth
Philem. 6. by the *acknowledging* of every
Heb 10:26. received the *knowledge* of the truth,
2Pet.1: 2. through the *knowledge* of God,
   3. through the *knowledge* of him that hath
   8. in the *knowledge* of our Lord
   2:20. the *knowledge* of the Lord and Saviour

ἐπιγραφή, epigraphee.

Mat.22:20. Whose (is) this image and *superscription?*
Mar 12:16. this image and *superscription ?*
   15:26. the *superscription* of his accusation
Lu. 20:24. Whose image and *superscription*
   23:38. a *superscription* also was written

ἐπιγράφω, epigrapho.

Mar 15:26. of his accusation was *written over*,
Acts17:23. an altar with this inscription, (lit. on which *had been inscribed*,)
Heb. 8:10. and *write* them *in* their hearts:
　　10:16. and *in* their minds *will* I *write* them ;
Rev.21:12. and names *written thereon*,

ἐπιδείκνυμι, epidīknumi.

Mat.16: 1. that he would *shew* them a sign
　　22:19. *Shew* me the tribute money.
　　24: 1. *to shew* him the buildings
Lu. 17:14. *shew* yourselves unto the priests.
　　20:24. *Shew* me a penny.
　　24:40. he *shewed* them (his) hands and (his) feet.
Acts 9:39. *shewing* the coats and garments
　　18:28. *shewing* by the scriptures that Jesus
Heb. 6:17. *to shew* unto the heirs of promise

ἐπιδέχομαι, epidekomai.

3Joh.　9. but Diotrephes,...*receiveth* us not.
　　10. neither *doth* he himself *receive* the brethren,

ἐπιδημέω, epideemeo.

Acts 2:10. and strangers of Rome, (lit. Romans *there dwelling*)
　　17:21. and strangers *which were there*

ἐπιδιατάσσομαι, epidiatassomai.

Gal. 3:15. disannulleth, or *addeth thereto*.

ἐπιδίδωμι, epididōmi.

Mat. 7: 9. *will* he *give* him a stone ?
　　10. *will* he *give* him a serpent ?
Lu. 4:17. *was delivered unto* him the book
　　11:11. *will* he *give* him a stone ?
　　— *will* he for a fish *give* him
　　12. *will* he *offer* him a scorpion ?
　　24:30. blessed (it), and brake, and *gave* to them.
　　42. they *gave* him a piece of
Joh. 13:26. to whom I *shall give* a sop,
Acts15:30. they *delivered* the epistle:
　　27:15. we let (her) drive. (lit. *giving* her up we were borne)

ἐπιδιορθόω, epidiorthoō.

Tit. 1: 5. that thou *shouldest set in order*

ἐπιδύω, epiduo.

Eph. 4:26. *let* not the sun *go down* upon your wrath:

ἐπιείκεια, epi-īkīa.

Acts24: 4. wouldest hear us of thy *clemency*
2Co.10: 1. and *gentleness* of Christ,

ἐπιεικής, epi-īkees.

Phi. 4: 5. Let your *moderation* be known
1Ti. 3: 3. but *patient*, not a brawler,
Tit. 3: 2. to be no brawlers, (but) *gentle*,
Jas. 3:17. *gentle*, (and) easy to be intreated,
1Pet.2:18. not only to the good and *gentle*,

ἐπίειμι see ἐπιοῦσα.

ἐπιζητέω, epizeeteo.

Mat. 6:32. *after* all these things *do* the Gentiles *seek:*
　　12:39. generation *seeketh after* a sign ;
　　16: 4. adulterous generation *seeketh after*
Mar. 8:12. Why *doth* this generation *seek after*
Lu. 11:29. they *seek* a sign ; and there shall no
　　12:30. *do* the nations of the world *seek after:*
Acts12:19. when Herod *had sought for* him,
　　13: 7. and *desired* to hear the word of God.
　　19:39. if ye *enquire* any thing concerning
Ro. 11: 7. not obtained that which he *seeketh for ;*
Phi. 4:17. Not because I *desire* a gift: but I *desire* fruit that may abound
Heb11:14. plainly that they *seek* a country.
　　13:14. city, but we *seek* one to come.

ἐπιθανάτιος, epithanatios.

1Co. 4: 9. as it were *appointed to death :*

ἐπίθεσις, epithesis.

Acts 8:18. through *laying on* of the apostles' hands
1Ti. 4:14. with the *laying on* of the hands
2Ti. 1: 6. by the *putting on* of my hands.
Heb. 6: 2. and of *laying on* of hands, and of

ἐπιθυμέω, epithumeo.

Mat. 5:28. looketh on a woman to *lust after* her
　　13:17. righteous (men) have *desired* to see
Lu. 15:16. he would *fain* have filled his belly
　　16:21. *desiring* to be fed with the crumbs
　　17:22. ye shall *desire* to see one of the days
　　22:15. *desire* I have *desired* to eat this passover
Acts20:33. I have *coveted* no man's silver,
Ro. 7: 7. Thou *shalt* not *covet*.
　　13: 9. Thou *shalt* not *covet ;* and if
1Co.10: 6. after evil things, as they also *lusted*.
Gal. 5:17. For the flesh *lusteth* against the Spirit,
1Ti. 3: 1. he *desireth* a good work.
Heb. 6:11. And we *desire* that every one of you
Jas. 4: 2. Ye *lust*, and have not: ye kill,
1Pet.1:12. which things the angels *desire* to look
Rev. 9: 6. and *shall desire* to die, and death

ἐπιθυμητής, epithumeetees.

1Co.10: 6. intent we should not lust after evil things, (lit. be *desirers* of evil things)

ἐπιθυμία, epithumia.

Mar. 4:19. the *lusts* of other things

Lu. 22:15. With *desire* I have desired
Joh. 8:44. the *lusts* of your father ye will do.
Ro. 1:24. through the *lusts* of their own hearts,
6:12. should obey it in the *lusts* thereof.
7: 7. for I had not known *lust*,
8. in me all manner of *concupiscence*.
13:14. to (fulfil) the *lusts* (thereof).
Gal. 5:16. shall not fulfil the *lust* of the flesh.
24. with the affections and *lusts*.
Eph. 2: 3. in the *lusts* of our flesh,
4:22. according to the deceitful *lusts*;
Phi. 1:23. having a *desire* to depart,
Col. 3: 5. evil *concupiscence*, and covetousness,
1Th. 2:17. endeavoured...with great *desire*.
4: 5. Not in the lust of *concupiscence*,
1Ti. 6: 9. (into) many foolish and hurtful *lusts*,
2Ti. 2:22. Flee also youthful *lusts*:
3: 6. led away with divers *lusts*,
4: 3. after their own *lusts* shall they heap
Tit. 2:12. denying ungodliness and worldly *lusts*,
3: 3. serving divers *lusts* and pleasures,
Jas. 1:14. when he is drawn away of his own *lust*,
15. Then when *lust* hath conceived,
1Pet.1:14. according to the former *lusts*
2:11. abstain from fleshly *lusts*, which war
4: 2. should live...to the *lusts* of men,
3. *lusts*, excess of wine, revellings,
2Pet.1: 4. that is in the world through *lust*.
2:10. in the *lust* of uncleanness,
18. allure through the *lusts* of the flesh,
3: 3. walking after their own *lusts*,
1Joh.2:16. *lust* of the flesh, and the *lust* of the eyes,
17. world passeth away, and the *lust* thereof:
Jude 16. walking after their own *lusts*;
18. after their own ungodly *lusts*.
Rev.18:14. the fruits that thy soul lusted after (lit.
of thy soul's *desire*)

ἐπικαθίζω, *epikathizo*.

Mat.21: 7. and they *set* (him) there*on*.

ἐπικαλέομαι, *epikaleomai*.

Mat.10: 3. whose surname was Thaddæus; (lit.
surnamed T.)
Lu. 22: 3. into Judas *surnamed* Iscariot,
Acts 1:23. who *was surnamed* Justus,
2:21. whosoever *shall call on* the name
4:36. *who* by the apostles *was surnamed* Barnabas,
7:59. stoned Stephen, *calling upon* (God),
9:14. all *that call on* thy name.
21. them *which called on* this name
10: 5. Simon, whose surname is (lit. who *is*
surnamed) Peter:
18. Simon, *which was surnamed* Peter,
32. whose surname is (lit. who *is surnamed*)
Peter;
11:13. Simon, whose surname is (lit. *who is*
surnamed) Peter ;
12:12. of John, whose surname was (lit. *who was*
surnamed) Mark;
25. John, whose surname was (lit. *who was*
surnamed) Mark.
15:17. upon whom my name *is called*,
22. Judas *surnamed* Barsabas,
22:16. *calling on* the name of the Lord.
25:11. I *appeal unto* Cæsar.
12. *Hast* thou *appealed unto* Cæsar?

Acts25:21. But *when* Paul *had appealed*
25. himself *hath appealed to* Augustus,
26:32. if he *had* not *appealed unto*
28:19. constrained *to appeal unto* Cæsar ;
Ro. 10:12. unto all *that call upon* him.
13. whosoever *shall call upon* the name
14. How then *shall* they *call on* him
1Co. 1: 2. with all *that* in every place *call upon* the
name
2Co. 1:23. I *call* God for a record upon my soul,
2Ti. 2:22. with them *that call on* the Lord
Heb 11:16. *to be called* their God:
Jas. 2: 7. name by the which ye are called? (lit.
called upon you)
1Pet.1:17. And if ye *call on* the Father,

ἐπικάλυμμα, *epikalumma*.

1Pet.2:16. not using (your) liberty for a *cloke* of

ἐπικαλύπτω, *epikalupto*.

Ro. 4: 7. and whose sins *are covered*.

ἐπικατάρατος, *epikataratos*.

Joh. 7:49. people who knoweth not the law are
cursed.
Gal. 3:10. *Cursed* (is) every one that continueth not
13. *Cursed* (is) every one that hangeth on

ἐπίκειμαι, *epikīmai*.

Lu. 5: 1. as the people *pressed upon* him
23:23. And they *were instant* with loud voices,
Joh.11:38. and a stone *lay* upon it.
21: 9. and fish *laid thereon*, and bread.
Acts27:20. when...no small tempest *lay on* (us),
1Co. 9:16. for necessity *is laid upon* me;
Heb. 9:10. *imposed* (on them) until the time

ἐπικουρία, *epikouria*.

Acts26:22. Having therefore obtained *help* of God,

ἐπικρίνω, *epikrino*.

Lu. 23:24. Pilate *gave sentence* that it should be.

ἐπιλαμβάνομαι, *epilambanomai*.

Mat.14:31. *caught* him, and said unto him,
Mar. 8:23. he *took* the blind man *by* the hand, *and*
Lu. 9:47. *took* a child, *and* set him by him,
14: 4. he *took* (him), *and* healed him,
20:20. that they *might take hold of* his words,
26. they could not *take hold of* his words
23:26. they *laid hold upon* one Simon,
Acts 9:27. But Barnabas *took* him, *and* brought
16:19. they *caught* Paul and Silas, *and* drew
17:19. And they *took* him, *and* brought him
18:17. Then all the Greeks *took* Sosthenes,
21:30. and they *took* Paul, *and* drew him
33. and *took* him, and commanded

Acts23:19. the chief captain *took* him *by* the hand,
1Ti. 6:12. *lay hold on* eternal life,
19. that they *may lay hold on* eternal life.
Heb. 2:16. he *took* not *on* (him the nature of) angels;
but he *took on* (him) the seed of Abraham.
8: 9. *when* I *took* them *by* the hand

ἐπιλανθάνομαι, epilanthanomai.

Mat.16: 5. they *had forgotten* to take bread.
Mar. 8:14. *had forgotten* to take bread,
Lu. 12: 6. not one of them is *forgotten*
Phi. 3:13(14). *forgetting* those things which are
Heb. 6:10. *to forget* your work and labour
13: 2. *Be* not *forgetful* to entertain
16. and to communicate *forget* not:
Jas. 1:24. *forgetteth* what manner of man

ἐπιλέγομαι, epilegomai.

Joh. 5: 2. *which is called* in the Hebrew tongue
Acts15:40. And Paul *chose* Silas, *and*

ἐπιλείπω, epilīpo.

Heb 11:32. the time *would fail* me to tell

ἐπιλησμονή, epileesmonee.

Jas. 1:25. he being not a forgetful hearer, (lit. a hearer of *forgetfulness*)

ἐπίλοιπος, epiloipos.

1Pet.4: 2. should live the rest of (his) time in the flesh (lit. the *remaining* time, &c.)

ἐπίλυσις, epilusis.

2Pet.1:20. is of any private *interpretation.*

ἐπιλύω, epiluo.

Mar. 4:34. he *expounded* all things to his disciples.
Acts19:39. it *shall be determined* in a

ἐπιμαρτυρέω, epimartureo.

1Pet.5:12. exhorting, and *testifying*

ἐπιμέλεια, epimelia.

Acts27: 3. go unto his friends to refresh himself. (lit. to have their *care*)

ἐπιμελέομαι, epimeleomai.

Lu. 10:34. to an inn, and *took care of* him.
35. *Take care of* him ; and whatsoever
1Ti. 3: 5. how *shall* he *take care of* the church

ἐπιμελῶς, epimelōs.

Lu. 15: 8. seek *diligently* till she find (it)?

ἐπιμένω, epimeno.

Joh. 8: 7. So when they *continued* asking
Acts10:48. prayed they him to *tarry* certain days.
12:16. But Peter *continued* knocking:
13:43. *to continue in* the grace of God.
15:34. it pleased Silas *to abide* there still.
21: 4. we *tarried* there seven days:
10. And as we *tarried* (there) many days,
28:12. we *tarried* (there) three days.
14. *to tarry* with them seven days:
Ro. 6: 1. *Shall* we *continue in* sin, that grace
11:22. if thou *continue in* (his) goodness:
23. if they *abide* not *in* unbelief,
1Co.16: 7. I trust *to tarry* a while with you,
8. But I *will tarry* at Ephesus
Gal. 1:18. and *abode* with him fifteen days.
Phil. 1:24. *to abide in* the flesh (is) more needful
Col. 1:23. If ye *continue in* the faith
1Ti. 4:16. *continue in* them: for in doing this

ἐπινεύω, epinūo.

Acts18:20. time with them, he *consented* not ;

ἐπίνοια, epinoia.

Acts 8:22. the *thought* of thine heart may

ἐπιορκέω, epiorkeo.

Mat. 5:33. Thou *shalt* not *forswear thyself,*

ἐπίορκος, epiorkos.

1Ti. 1:10. for liars, for *perjured persons,*

ἐπιοῦσα, epiousa.

Acts 7:26. And the *next* day he shewed himself
16:11. and the *next* (day) to Neapolis ;
20:15. came the *next* (day) over against Chios ;
21:18. And the (day) *following* Paul went in
23:11. And the night *following* the Lord

ἐπιούσιος, epiousios.

Mat. 6:11. Give us this day our *daily* bread.
Lu. 11: 3. day by day our *daily* bread.

ἐπιπίπτω, epipipto.

Mar. 3:10. insomuch that they *pressed upon* him
Lu. 1:12. and fear *fell upon* him.
15:20. and ran, and *fell on* his neck,
Joh.13:25. He then *lying on* Jesus' breast
Acts 8:16. he was *fallen upon* none of them:
10:10. made ready, he fell into a trance, (lit. a trance *fell upon* him)

Acts10:44. the Holy Ghost *fell on* all
   11:15. the Holy Ghost *fell on* them,
   13:11. there *fell on* him a mist
   19:17. and fear *fell on* them all,
   20:10. Paul went down, and *fell on* him,
      37. and *fell on* Paul's neck, *and*
Ro. 15: 3. them that reproached thee *fell on* me.

ἐπιπλήττω, *epipleetto.*

1Ti. 5: 1. *Rebuke* not an elder, but intreat

ἐπιπνίγω, *epipnigo.*

(Most copies have ἀπεπνιξαν.)
Lu. 8: 7. thorns sprang up with it, and *choked* it.

ἐπιποθέω, *epipotheo.*

Ro. 1:11. For I *long* to see you, that
2Co. 5: 2. *earnestly desiring* to be clothed upon
   9:14. *which long after* you for the
Phi. 1: 8. how *greatly* I *long after* you all
   2:26. For he *longed after* you all,
1Th. 3: 6. *desiring greatly* to see us,
2Ti. 1: 4. *Greatly desiring* to see thee,
Jas. 4: 5. spirit that dwelleth in us *lusteth* to envy?
1Pet. 2: 2. *desire* the sincere milk of the word,

ἐπιπόθησις, *epipotheesis.*

2Co. 7: 7. he told us your *earnest desire,*
     11. yea, (what) *vehement desire,*

ἐπιπόθητος, *epipotheetos.*

Phi. 4: 1. dearly beloved and *longed for,*

ἐπιποθία, *epipothia.*

Ro. 15:23. having a *great desire* these many years

ἐπιπορεύομαι, *epiporŭomai.*

Lu. 8: 4. and *were come* to him out of

ἐπιρράπτω, *epirrapto.*

Mar. 2:21. *seweth* a piece of new cloth *on*

ἐπιρρίπτω, *epirripto.*

Lu. 19:35. they *cast* their garments *upon* the colt, *and*
1Pet. 5: 7. *Casting* all your care *upon* him ;

ἐπίσημος, *episeemos.*

Mat. 27:16. a *notable* prisoner, called Barabbas.
Ro. 16: 7. who are *of note* among the apostles,

ἐπισιτισμός, *episitismos.*

Lu. 9:12. and lodge, and get *victuals :*

ἐπισκέπτομαι, *episkeptomai.*

Mat. 25:36. sick, and ye *visited* me :
     43. and ye *visited* me not.
Lu. 1:68. for he *hath visited* and redeemed
    78. dayspring from on high *hath visited* us,
   7:16. That God *hath visited* his people.
Acts 6: 3. *look* ye *out* among you seven men
   7:23. *to visit* his brethren the children
   15:14. how God at the first *did visit*
     36. Let us go again and *visit* our brethren
Heb. 2: 6. that thou *visitest* him?
Jas. 1:27. *To visit* the fatherless and widows

ἐπισκηνόω, *episkeenoō.*

2Co. 12: 9. that the power of Christ *may rest upon* me.

ἐπισκιάζω, *episkiazo.*

Mat. 17: 5. a bright cloud *overshadowed* them :
Mar. 9: 7. there was a cloud *that overshadowed* them :
Lu. 1:35. the power of the Highest *shall overshadow* thee :
   9:34. came a cloud, and *overshadowed* them :
Acts 5:15. *might overshadow* some of them.

ἐπισκοπέω, *episkopeo.*

Heb 12:15. *Looking diligently* lest any man
1Pet. 5: 2. *taking the oversight* (thereof), not by constraint,

---

ἐπισκοπή, *episkopee.*

Lu. 19:44. knewest not the time of thy *visitation*
Acts 1:20. his *bishoprick* let another take.
1Ti. 3: 1. If a man desire *the office of a bishop,*
1Pet. 2:12. glorify God in the day of *visitation.*

ἐπίσκοπος, *episkopos.*

Acts 20:28. the Holy Ghost hath made you *overseers,*
Phi. 1: 1. with the *bishops* and deacons :
1Ti. 3: 2. A *bishop* then must be blameless,
Tit. 1: 7. For a *bishop* must be blameless,
1Pet. 2:25. Shepherd and *Bishop* of your souls.

ἐπισπάομαι, *epispaomai.*

1Co. 7:18. *let* him not *become uncircumcised.*

ἐπίσταμαι, *epistamai.*

Mar 14:68. neither *understand* I what thou sayest.
Acts10:28. Ye *know* how that it is an unlawful thing
   15: 7. Men (and) brethren, ye *know*
   18:25. *knowing* only the baptism of John.
   19:15. Paul I *know ;* but who are ye?

Acts19:25. ye *know* that by this craft
   20:18. Ye *know*, from the first day
   22:19. they *know* that I imprisoned
   24:10. *as* I *know* that thou hast been
   26:26. For the king *knoweth* of these things,
1Ti. 6: 4. He is proud, *knowing* nothing,
Heb11: 8. not *knowing* whither he went.
Jas. 4:14. Whereas ye *know* not what (shall be)
Jude 10. but what they *know* naturally,

ἐπιστάτης, *epistatees.*

Lu. 5: 5. *Master*, we have toiled all the night,
   8:24. *Master, master*, we perish.
     45. *Master*, the multitude throng thee
   9:33. *Master*, it is good for us to be here:
     49. *Master*, we saw one casting out devils
  17:13. Jesus, *Master*, have mercy on us.

ἐπιστέλλω, *epistello.*

Acts15:20. But that we *write unto* them,
   21:25. we *have written* (and) concluded
Heb13:22. I *have written a letter unto* you in few words.

ἐπιστήμων, *episteemōn.*

Jas. 3:13. and *endued with knowledge* among you?

ἐπιστηρίζω, *episteerizo.*

Acts14:22. *Confirming* the souls of the disciples,
   15:32. with many words, and *confirmed* (them).
     41. *confirming* the churches.
   18:23. *strengthening* all the disciples.

ἐπιστολή, *epistolee.*

Acts 9: 2. *letters* to Damascus to the synagogues,
   15:30. they delivered the *epistle:*
   22: 5. I received *letters* unto the brethren,
   23:25. he wrote a *letter* after this manner:
     33. and delivered the *epistle* to the
Ro. 16:22. I Tertius, who wrote (this) *epistle,*
1Co. 5: 9. I wrote unto you in an *epistle*
   16: 3. ye shall approve by (your) *letters,*
2Co. 3· 1. *epistles* of commendation to you,
     2. Ye are our *epistle* written
     3. to be the *epistle* of Christ
   7: 8. I made you sorry with a *letter,*
   — I perceive that the same *epistle*
   10: 9. as if I would terrify you by *letters.*
    10. For (his) *letters*, say they, (are) weighty
    11. by *letters* when we are absent,
Col. 4:16. when this *epistle* is read among you,
1Th. 5:27. that this *epistle* be read unto all
2Th. 2: 2. nor by *letter* as from us,
    15. whether by word, or our *epistle.*
   3:14. our word by this *epistle*, note that man,
    17. the token in every *epistle:*
2Pet.3: 1. This second *epistle*, beloved, I now write
    16. As also in all (his) *epistles,*

ἐπιστομίζω, *epistomizo.*

Tit. 1 :11. Whose *mouths* must *be stopped,*

ἐπιστρέφω, *epistrepho.*

Mat. 9:22. But Jesus *turned* him *about,*
   10:13. *let* your peace *return* to you.
   12:44. I *will return* into my house
   13:15. and *should be converted,*
   24:18. Neither *let* him...*return* back
Mar 4:12. lest...they *should be converted,*
   5:30. *turned* him *about* in the press, *and*
   8:33. But *when* he *had turned about*
   13:16. *let* him...not *turn* back *again*
Lu. 1:16. of the children of Israel *shall* he *turn*
    17. *to turn* the hearts of the fathers
   2:20. the shepherds *returned,* glorifying
   8:55. And her spirit *came again,*
  17: 4. *turn again* to thee, saying,
    31. *let* him likewise not *return*
  22:32. and *when* thou *art converted,* strengthen
Joh.12:40. and *be converted,* and I should heal
  21:20. Then Peter, *turning about,*
Acts 3:19. Repent ye therefore, and *be converted,*
   9:35. and *turned* to the Lord.
    40. *turning* (him) to the body said,
  11:21. believed, and *turned* unto the Lord.
  14:15. that ye should *turn* from these vanities
  15:19. which from among the Gentiles *are turned*
      to God:
    36. Let us *go again and* visit
  16:18. Paul, being grieved, *turned and* said
  26:18. *to turn* (them) from darkness
    20. should repent and *turn* to God,
    28:27. *should be converted,* and I should heal them.
2Co. 3:16. Nevertheless when it *shall turn* to the Lord,
Gal. 4: 9. how *turn* ye again to the weak
1Th. 1: 9. how ye *turned* to God from idols
Jas. 5:19. from the truth, and one *convert* him ;
    20. he *which converteth* the sinner
1Pet. 2:25. *are* now *returned* unto the Shepherd
2Pet. 2:21. after they have known (it), *to turn*
    22. The dog (is) *turned* to his own vomit
     again;
Rev. 1:12. I *turned* to see the voice that spake with
     me. And *being turned,* I saw seven

ἐπιστροφή, *epistrophee.*

Acts15: 3. declaring the *conversion* of the Gentiles:

ἐπισυνάγω, *episunago.*

Mat.23:37. would I *have gathered* thy children to-
    gether, even as a hen *gathereth*
  24:31. they *shall gather together* his elect
Mar. 1:33. was *gathered together* at the door.
  13:27. *shall gather together* his elect
Lu. 12: 1. *when* there *were gathered together* an in-
    numerable multitude
  13:34. would I *have gathered* thy children *together,*

ἐπισυναγωγή, *episunagōgee.*

2Th. 2: 1. (by) our *gathering together* unto him,
Heb10:25. the *assembling* of ourselves *together,*

ἐπισυντρέχω, *episuntreko.*

Mar. 9:25. that the people *came running together,*

ἐπισύστασις, episustasis.

Acts24:12. neither raising up the people, (lit. making a *tumultuous assembly*)
2Co.11:28. *that which cometh upon* me daily,

ἐπισφαλής, episphalees.

Acts27: 9. when sailing was now *dangerous,*

ἐπισχύω, episkuo.

Lu. 23: 5. And they *were the more fierce*, saying,

ἐπισωρεύω, episōrūo.

2Ti. 4: 3. *shall* they *heap* to themselves

ἐπιταγή, epitagee.

Ro. 16:26. the *commandment* of the everlasting God,
1Co. 7: 6. (and) not of *commandment.*
    25. I have no *commandment* of the Lord:
2Co. 8: 8. I speak not by *commandment,*
1Ti. 1: 1. by the *commandment* of God our Saviour,
Tit. 1: 3. according to the *commandment* of God our Saviour;
    2:15. exhort, and rebuke with all *authority.*

ἐπιτάσσω, epitasso.

Mar. 1:27. *commandeth* he even the unclean spirits,
    6:27. *commanded* his head to be brought:
    39. he *commanded* them to make all sit down
    9:25. I *charge* thee, come out of him,
Lu. 4:36. he *commandeth* the unclean spirits,
    8:25. he *commandeth* even the winds
    31. that he *would* not *command* them
    14:22. it is done as thou *hast commanded,*
Acts23: 2. Ananias *commanded* them that stood by
Philem. 8. *to injoin* thee that which is convenient,

ἐπιτελέω, epiteleo.

Lu. 13:32. I *do* cures to day and to morrow,
Ro. 15:28. *When* therefore I *have performed* this, and
2Co. 7: 1. *perfecting* holiness in the fear of God.
    8: 6. so he *would* also *finish* in you the same
    11. *perform* the doing (of it);
    — so (there may be) a performance also (lit. *to perform*)
Gal. 3: 3. *are* ye now *made perfect* by the flesh?
Phi. 1: 6. *will perform* (it) until the day
Heb. 8: 5. when he was about *to make* the tabernacle:
    9: 6. *accomplishing* the service (of God).
1Pet.5: 9. *are accomplished* in your brethren

ἐπιτήδειος, epiteedīos.

Jas. 2:16. *things which are needful to* the body;

ἐπιτίθημι, epititheemi.

Mat. 9:18. *lay* thy hand *upon* her,

Mat.19:13. that he *should put* (his) hands *on* them,
    15. he *laid* (his) hands *on* them, *and*
    21: 7. and *put on* them their clothes,
    23: 4. and *lay* (them) *on* men's shoulders;
    27:29. they *put* (it) *upon* his head,
    37. And *set up* over his head his accusation
Mar. 3:16. Simon he surnamed (lit. he *added* the name of) Peter;
    17. he surnamed (lit. he, &c.) them Boanerges,
    4:21. and not to *be set on* a candlestick?
    5:23. come and *lay* thy hands *on* her,
    6: 5. he *laid* his hands *upon* a few sick folk, *and*
    7:32. beseech him to *put* his hand *upon* him.
    8:23. *and put* his hands *upon* him,
    25. he *put* (his) hands again *upon* his eyes,
    16:18. they *shall lay* hands *on* the sick,
Lu. 4:40. he *laid* his hands *on* every one of them, *and*
    8:16. but *setteth* (it) *on* a candlestick,
    10:30. and wounded (him), (lit. *having inflicted wounds*)
    13:13. he *laid* (his) hands *on* her:
    15: 5. he *layeth* (it) *on* his shoulders,
    23:26. *on* him they *laid* the cross,
Joh. 9:15. He *put* clay *upon* mine eyes,
    19: 2. and *put* (it) *on* his head,
Acts 6: 6. they *laid* (their) hands *on* them.
    8:17. *laid* they (their) hands *on* them,
    19. *on* whomsoever I *lay* hands,
    9:12. *putting* (his) hand *on* him,
    17. *putting* his hands *on* him
    13: 3. and *laid* (their) hands *on* them,
    15:10. *to put* a yoke *upon* the neck
    28. *to lay upon* you no greater burden
    16:23. *when* they *had laid* many stripes *upon* them,
    18:10. no man *shall set on* thee
    19: 6. *when* Paul *had laid* (his) hands *upon* them,
    28: 3. and *laid* (them) *on* the fire, there came
    8. and *laid* his hands *on* him, *and*
    10. they *laded* (us) with such things as
1Ti. 5:22. *Lay* hands suddenly *on* no man,
Rev. 1:17. he *laid* his right hand *upon* me,
    22:18. If any man shall *add unto* these things, God *shall add unto* him the plagues

---

ἐπιτιμάω, epitimao.

Mat. 8:26. he arose, and *rebuked* the winds
    12:16. And *charged* them that they should not
    16:22. and began *to rebuke* him,
    17:18. And Jesus *rebuked* the devil;
    19:13. the disciples *rebuked* them.
    20:31. the multitude *rebuked* them,
Mar. 1:25. Jesus *rebuked* him, saying, Hold
    3:12. And he straitly *charged* them
    4:39. he arose, and *rebuked* the wind,
    8:30. And he *charged* them that they should tell
    32. and began *to rebuke* him.
    33. he *rebuked* Peter, saying, Get thee
    9:25. he *rebuked* the foul spirit,
    10:13. (his) disciples *rebuked* those that brought (them).
    48. many *charged* him that he should hold
Lu. 4:35. Jesus *rebuked* him, saying, Hold
    39. and *rebuked* the fever; and it left her:
    41. he *rebuking* (them) suffered them not
    8:24. he arose, and *rebuked* the wind
    9:21. And he *straitly charged* them, *and*
    42. Jesus *rebuked* the unclean spirit,
    55. he turned, and *rebuked* them,
    17: 3. trespass against thee, *rebuke* him;
    18:15. disciples saw (it), they *rebuked* them.

Lu. 18:39. they which went before *rebuked* him,
    19:39. Master, *rebuke* thy disciples.
    23:40. answering *rebuked* him, saying,
2Ti. 4: 2. reprove, *rebuke*, exhort with all
Jude   9. but said, The Lord *rebuke* thee.

ἐπιτιμία, *epitimia*.

2Co. 2: 6. Sufficient to such a man (is) this *punishment*,

ἐπιτρέπω, *epitrepo*.

Mat. 8:21. *suffer* me first to go and bury
    31. *suffer* us to go away into the
    19: 8. *suffered* you to put away your wives:
Mar. 5:13. forthwith Jesus *gave* them *leave*.
    10: 4. Moses *suffered* to write a bill
Lu. 8:32. that he *would suffer* them to enter into
    them. And he *suffered* them.
    9:59. *suffer* me first to go and bury
    61. but *let* me first go bid them
Joh. 19:38. and Pilate *gave* (him) *leave*.
Acts21:39. *suffer* me to speak unto the people.
    40. And *when* he *had given* him *licence*,
    26: 1. Thou art permitted (lit. it *is permitted* thee) to speak for-thyself.
    27: 3. and *gave* (him) *liberty* to go unto his friends
    28:16. but Paul was suffered (lit. it *was permitted* Paul) to dwell
1Co.14:34. for it *is* not *permitted* unto them
    16: 7. a while with you, if the Lord *permit*.
1Ti. 2:12. I *suffer* not a woman to teach,
Heb. 6: 3. this will we do, if God *permit*.

ἐπιτροπή, *epitropee*.

Acts26:12. with authority and *commission*

ἐπίτροπος, *epitropos*.

Mat.20: 8. saith unto his *steward*,
Lu. 8: 3. wife of Chuza Herod's *steward*,
Gal. 4: 2. is under *tutors* and governors

ἐπιτυγχάνω, *epitunkano*.

Ro. 11: 7. Israel *hath* not *obtained*
    — but the election *hath obtained* it,
Heb. 6:15. he *obtained* the promise.
    11:33. *obtained* promises, stopped the mouths
Jas. 4: 2. desire to have, and cannot *obtain :*

ἐπιφαίνω, *epiphaino*.

Lu 1:79. To give *light* to them that sit in
Acts27:20. nor stars in many days *appeared*,
Tit. 2:11. bringeth salvation *hath appeared*
    3: 4. love of God our Saviour toward man *appeared*,

ἐπιφάνεια, *epiphanìa*.

2Th. 2: 8. with the *brightness* of his coming:

1Ti. 6:14. until the *appearing* of our Lord Jesus Christ:
2Ti. 1:10. by the *appearing* of our Saviour Jesus Christ,
    4: 1. at his *appearing* and his kingdom ;
    8. them also that love his *appearing*.
Tit. 2:13. the glorious *appearing* of the great God and our Saviour Jesus Christ ;

ἐπιφανής, *epiphanees*.

Acts 2:20. that great and *notable* day of

ἐπιφαύω, *epiphauo*.

Eph. 5:14. Christ *shall give* thee *light*.

ἐπιφέρω, *epiphero*.

Acts19:12. So that from his body *were brought*
    25:18. they *brought* none accusation
Ro. 3: 5. unrighteous *who taketh* vengeance ?
Phi. 1:16. *to add* affliction to my bonds:
Jude   9. durst not *bring against* him

ἐπιφωνέω, *epiphōneo*.

Lu. 23:21. But they *cried*, saying, Crucify
Acts12:22. the people *gave a shout*,
    22:24. wherefore they *cried* so *against* him.

ἐπιφώσκω, *epiphosko*.

Mat.28: 1. *as* it *began to dawn* toward the first (day)
Lu. 23:54. and the sabbath *drew on*.

ἐπιχειρέω, *epikīreo*.

Lu. 1: 1. many *have taken in hand*
Acts 9:29. they *went about* to slay him.
    19:13. *took upon* them to call over them

ἐπιχέω, *epikeo*.

Lu. 10:34. *pouring in* oil and wine,

ἐπιχορηγέω, *epikoreegeo*.

2Co. 9:10. he *that ministereth* seed to the sower
Gal. 3: 5. He therefore *that ministereth* to you
Col. 2:19. having nourishment *ministered*, and
2Pet. 1: 5. *add* to your faith virtue ;
    11. *shall be ministered unto* you

ἐπιχορηγία, *epikoreegia*.

Eph. 4:16. by that which every joint supplieth, (lit. by the *supply* of every joint)
Phi. 1:19. the *supply* of the Spirit of Jesus Christ,

ἐπιχρίω, epikrio.

Joh. 9: 6. he *anointed* the eyes of the blind man with the clay,
11. and *anointed* mine eyes, and said

ἐποικοδομέω, epoikodomeo.

Acts20:32. *to build* you *up*, and to give you
1Co. 3:10. and another *buildeth thereon*.
— take heed how he *buildeth thereupon*.
12. Now if any man *build upon* this
14. abide which he *hath built thereupon*,
Eph. 2:20. *And are built upon* the foundation
Col. 2: 7. Rooted and *built up* in him,
Jude 20. *building up* yourselves *on* your

ἐποκέλλω, epokello.

Acts27:41. they *ran* the ship *aground*;

ἐπονομάζομαι, eponomazomai.

Ro. 2:17. Behold, thou *art called* a Jew,

ἐπόπτης, epoptees.

2Pet.1:16. but were *eyewitnesses*

ἐποπτεύω, epoptuo.

1Pet.2:12. by (your) good works, which they shall behold, (lit. *beholding*)
3: 2. *While* they *behold* your chaste

ἔπος, epos.

Heb. 7: 9. And as I may so say, (lit. *to say the word*)

ἐπουράνιος, epouranios.

Mat.18:35. shall my *heavenly* Father do
Joh. 3:12. if I tell you (of) *heavenly* things?
1Co.15:40. (There are) also *celestial* bodies,
— but the glory of the *celestial* (is) one,
48. as (is) the *heavenly*, such (are) they also that are *heavenly*.
49. the image of the *heavenly*.
Eph. 1: 3. in *heavenly* (places) in Christ:
20. at his own right hand in the *heavenly* (places),
2: 6. in *heavenly* (places) in Christ Jesus:
3:10. powers in *heavenly* (places).
6:12. wickedness in *high* (places).
Phi. 2:10. of (things) *in heaven*, and (things) in earth,
2Ti. 4:18. unto his *heavenly* kingdom:
Heb. 3: 1. partakers of the *heavenly* calling,
6: 4. tasted of the *heavenly* gift,
8: 5. serve unto the example and shadow of *heavenly* things,

Heb 9:23. but the *heavenly* things themselves
11:16. a better (country), that is, an *heavenly* :
12:22. the *heavenly* Jerusalem,

ἑπτά, hepta.

Mat.12:45. *seven* other spirits more wicked
15:34. *Seven*, and a few little fishes.
36. And he took the *seven* loaves
37. that was left *seven* baskets full.
16:10. Neither the *seven* loaves of
18:22. but, Until seventy times *seven*.
22:25. there were with us *seven* brethren:
26. unto the *seventh*.
28. whose wife shall she be of the *seven* ?
Mar. 8: 5. loaves have ye? And they said, *Seven*.
6. and he took the *seven* loaves,
8. that was left *seven* baskets.
20. And when the *seven* among four
— And they said, *Seven*.
12:20. there were *seven* brethren:
22. And the *seven* had her, and left
23. for the *seven* had her to wife.
16: 9. out of whom he had cast *seven* devils.
Lu. 2:36. lived with an husband *seven* years
8: 2. out of whom went *seven* devils,
11:26. *seven* other spirits more wicked
20:29. There were therefore *seven* brethren:
31. in like manner the *seven* also:
33. for *seven* had her to wife.
Acts 6: 3. *seven* men of honest report,
13:19. destroyed *seven* nations in the land
19:14. there were *seven* sons of (one) Sceva,
20: 6. where we abode *seven* days.
21: 4. we tarried there *seven* days:
8. which was (one) of the *seven*;
27. And when the *seven* days were
28:14. to tarry with them *seven* days:
Heb 11:30. compassed about *seven* days.
Rev. 1: 4. John to the *seven* churches which
— and from the *seven* spirits
12. I saw *seven* golden candlesticks;
13. in the midst of the *seven* candlesticks
16. in his right hand *seven* stars:
20. The mystery of the *seven* stars
— *seven* golden candlesticks. The *seven* stars are the angels of the *seven* churches: and the *seven* candlesticks which thou sawest are the *seven* churches.
2: 1. he that holdeth the *seven* stars
— in the midst of the *seven* golden
3: 1. that hath the *seven* Spirits of God, and the *seven* stars;
4: 5. (there were) *seven* lamps of fire
— which are the *seven* Spirits
5: 1. sealed with *seven* seals.
5. to loose the *seven* seals thereof.
6. having *seven* horns and *seven* eyes, which are the *seven* Spirits
8: 2. I saw the *seven* angels
— to them were given *seven* trumpets.
6. the *seven* angels which had the *seven* trumpets
10: 3. *seven* thunders uttered their voices.
4. when the *seven* thunders had uttered
— which the *seven* thunders uttered,
11:13. were slain of men *seven* thousand:
12: 3. having *seven* heads and ten horns, and *seven* crowns

Rev.13: 1. having *seven* heads and ten horns,

15: 1. *seven* angels having the *seven* last plagues;
6. the *seven* angels came out of the temple, having the *seven* plagues,
7. gave unto the *seven* angels *seven* golden vials
8. till the *seven* plagues of the *seven* angels were fulfilled.

16: 1. saying to the *seven* angels,

17: 1. one of the *seven* angels which had the *seven* vials,
3. having *seven* heads and ten horns.
7. which hath the *seven* heads
9. The *seven* heads are *seven* mountains, on which
10. there are *seven* kings: five are fallen,
11. and is of the *seven*, and goeth

21: 9. came unto me one of the *seven* angels which had the *seven* vials full of the *seven* last plagues,

---

ἑπτάκις, *heptakis.*

Mat.18:21. I forgive him? till *seven times?*
22. unto thee, Until *seven times:*

Lu. 17: 4. trespass against thee *seven times* in a day, and *seven times* in a day turn

---

ἑπτακισχίλιοι, *heptakiskilioi.*

Ro. 11: 4. reserved to myself *seven thousand* men,

ἔπω, *epo.*

Mat. 2: 5. they *said* unto him, In Bethlehem
8. he sent them to Bethlehem, and *said*,
13. until I *bring* thee *word:*

3: 7. he *said* unto them, O generation of
15. *said* unto him, Suffer (it to be)

4: 3. when the tempter came to him, he *said*, If
— *command* that these stones be made
4. *said*, It is written, Man

5:11. and shall *say* all manner of evil
22. whosoever shall *say* to his brother,
— but whosoever shall *say*, Thou fool,

8: 4. See thou *tell* no man;
8. but *speak* the word only,
10. and *said* to them that followed,
13. Jesus *said* unto the centurion,
19. and *said* unto him, Master,
21. another of his disciples *said*
22. Jesus *said* unto him, Follow me;
32. he *said* unto them, Go.

9: 2. *said* unto the sick of the palsy;
3. *said* within themselves,
4. *said*, Wherefore think ye evil
5. whether is easier, *to say*, (Thy) sins
— or *to say*, Arise, and walk?
11. they *said* unto his disciples,
12. heard (that), he *said* unto them,
15. Jesus *said* unto them,
22. and when he saw her, he *said*,

10:27. (that) *speak* ye in light:

11: 3. And *said* unto him, Art thou he
4. answered and *said* unto them, Go
25. and *said*, I thank thee, O Father,

12: 2. Pharisees saw (it), they *said* unto him,

Mat.12: 3. he *said* unto them, Have ye not read
11. And he *said* unto them, What man
24. when the Pharisees heard (it), they *said*,
25. and *said* unto them, Every kingdom
32. And whosoever *speaketh* a word
— but whosoever *speaketh* against the Holy Ghost,
39. But he answered and *said* unto them,
47. Then one *said* unto him, Behold, thy mother
48. But he answered and *said* unto him that *told* him,
49. and *said*, Behold my mother

13:10. and *said* unto him, Why speakest thou
11. He answered and *said* unto them,
27. and *said* unto him, Sir, didst not thou sow
28. The servants *said* unto him,
37. He answered and *said* unto them,
52. Then *said* he unto them, Therefore
57. *said* unto them, A prophet

14: 2. And *said* unto his servants,
16. *said* unto them, They need not
18. He *said*, Bring them hither to me.
28. And Peter answered him and *said*,
29. And he *said*, Come.

15: 3. he answered and *said* unto them,
5. Whosoever shall *say* to (his) father or (his) mother,
10. and *said* unto them, Hear,
12. and *said* unto him, Knowest thou that
13. But he answered and *said*,
15. answered Peter and *said* unto him,
16. Jesus *said*, Are ye also yet
24. and *said*, I am not sent
26. and *said*, It is not meet
27. And she *said*, Truth, Lord:
28. Jesus answered and *said* unto her,
32. and *said*, I have compassion
34. And they *said*, Seven,

16: 2. He answered and *said* unto them,
6. Then Jesus *said* unto them,
8. Jesus perceived, he *said* unto them,
11. that I *spake* (it) not to you concerning bread,
12. understood they how that he *bade* (them) not
14. they *said*, Some (say that thcu art) John
16. And Simon Peter answered and *said*,
17. And Jesus answered and *said* unto him,
20. that they *should tell* no man
23. he turned, and *said* unto Peter,
24. Then *said* Jesus unto his disciples,

17: 4. and *said* unto Jesus, Lord,
7. and *said*, Arise, and be not afraid.
9. *Tell* the vision to no man,
11. Jesus answered and *said* unto them,
13. he *spake* unto them of John
17. Then Jesus answered and *said*,
19. and *said*, Why could not we cast
20. And Jesus *said* unto them,
22. Jesus *said* unto them,
24. and *said*, Doth not your master

18: 3. And *said*, Verily I say unto you,
17. *tell* (it) unto the church:
21. and *said*, Lord, how oft

19: 4. he answered and *said* unto them,
5. And *said*, For this cause
11. But he *said* unto them,
14. But Jesus *said*, Suffer
16. one came and *said* unto him,
17. And he *said* unto him, Why
18. Jesus *said*, Thou shalt do no murder,

Mat.19:23. Then *said* Jesus unto his disciples,
26. But Jesus beheld (them), and *said* unto them,
27. answered Peter and *said* unto him,
28. And Jesus *said* unto them,
20: 4. And *said* unto them ; Go
13. one of them, and *said*, Friend,
17. and *said* unto them,
21. he *said* unto her, What wilt thou ?
— *Grant* that these my two sons may sit,
22. But Jesus answered and *said*,
25. and *said*, Ye know that the princes
32. and *said*, What will ye that
21: 3. if any (man) *say* ought unto you,
5. *Tell* ye the daughter of Sion,
16. And *said* unto him, Hearest thou
21. Jesus answered and *said* unto them,
— if ye shall *say* unto this mountain,
24. And Jesus answered and *said* unto them,
— which if ye *tell* me,
25. If we shall *say*, From heaven ;
26. But if we shall *say*, Of men ;
27. and *said*, We cannot tell.
28. he came to the first, and *said*, Son,
29. He answered and *said*, I will not:
30. to the second, and *said* likewise. And he answered and *said*,
38. they *said* among themselves,
22: 1. and *spake* unto them again by parables,
4. *Tell* them which are bidden,
13. Then *said* the king to the servants,
17. *Tell* us therefore, What thinkest thou ?
18. and *said*, Why tempt ye me,
24. Moses *said*, If a man die,
29. Jesus answered and *said* unto them,
37. Jesus *said* unto him,
44. The Lord *said* unto my Lord,
23: 3. whatsoever they *bid* you observe,
39. till ye shall *say*, Blessed
24: 2. And Jesus *said* unto them,
3. *Tell* us, when shall these things be ?
4. Jesus answered and *said* unto them,
23. if any man shall *say* unto you,
26. Wherefore if they shall *say* unto you,
48. But and if that evil servant shall *say*
25: 8. the foolish *said* unto the wise,
12. But he answered and *said*,
22. and *said*, Lord, thou deliveredst
24. and *said*, Lord, I knew thee
26. His lord answered and *said* unto him,
26: 1. he *said* unto his disciples,
10. understood (it), he *said* unto them,
15. *said* (unto them), What will ye give me,
18. And he *said*, Go into the city to such a man, and *say* unto him,
21. as they did eat, he *said*,
23. And he answered and *said*,
25. and *said*, Master, is it I ? He said unto him, Thou *hast said*.
26. and *said*, Take, eat ;
33. Peter answered and *said* unto him,
35. Likewise also *said* all the disciples.
44. *saying* the same words.
49. and *said*, Hail, master ;
50. And Jesus *said* unto him,
55. *said* Jesus to the multitudes,
61. And *said*, This (fellow) said,
62. priest arose, and *said* unto him,
63. priest answered and *said* unto him,
— that thou *tell* us whether thou be
64. Thou *hast said:* nevertheless
66. They answered and *said*,

Mat.26:73. and *said* to Peter, Surely
27: 4. And they *said*, What (is that) to us ?
6. took the silver pieces, and *said*,
17. Pilate *said* unto them, Whom will ye
21. The governor answered and *said* unto them,
— They *said*, Barabbas.
25. all the people, and *said*, His blood
43. for he *said*, I am the Son of God.
63. remember that that deceiver *said*,
64. him away, and *say* unto the people,
28: 5. and *said* unto the women,
6. for he is risen, as he *said*.
7. *tell* his disciples that he is risen
— lo, I *have told* you.
13. *Say* ye, His disciples came by night,
Mar 1:17. Jesus *said* unto them,
42. And *as soon as* he *had spoken*,
44. See thou *say* nothing to any
2: 8. he *said* unto them, Why reason ye
9. *to say* to the sick of the palsy,
— or *to say*, Arise, and take up
19. Jesus *said* unto them,
3: 9. And he *spake* to his disciples,
32. and they *said* unto him, Behold, thy mother
4:39. and *said* unto the sea, Peace,
40. *said* unto them, Why are ye so fearful ?
5: 7. cried with a loud voice, and *said*,
33. and *told* him all the truth.
34. And he *said* unto her, Daughter,
43. *commanded* that something should be
6:16. Herod...*said*, It is John, whom
22. the king *said* unto the damsel,
24. and *said* unto her mother,
— And she *said*, The head of John
31. And he *said* unto them, Come
37. He answered and *said* unto them,
7: 6. He answered and *said* unto them,
10. For Moses *said*, Honour
11. If a man shall *say* to his father
27. But Jesus *said* unto her,
29. And he *said* unto her, For this saying
36. that they *should tell* no man:
8: 5. And they *said*, Seven.
7. *commanded* to set them also before (them).
20. And they *said*, Seven.
26. nor *tell* (it) to any in the town.
34. he *said* unto them, Whosoever will
9:12. he answered and *told* them,
17. and *said*, Master, I have brought
18. and I *spake* to thy disciples
21. And he *said*, Of a child.
23. Jesus *said* unto him,
29. And he *said* unto them, This
36. in his arms, he *said* unto them,
39. But Jesus *said*, Forbid him not:
10: 3. he answered and *said* unto them,
4. And they *said*, Moses
5. Jesus answered and *said* unto them,
14. and *said* unto them, Suffer
18. And Jesus *said* unto him,
20. he answered and *said* unto him,
21. *said* unto him, One thing thou lackest:
29. And Jesus answered and *said*,
36. And he *said* unto them, What would ye
37. They *said* unto him, Grant
38. But Jesus *said* unto them,
39. they *said* unto him, We can. And Jesus *said* unto them,
49. *commanded* him to be called.
51. The blind man *said* unto him,
52. And Jesus *said* unto him,

Mar11: 3. if any man *say* unto you, Why do ye this?
   say ye that the Lord
  6. And they *said* unto them
 14. Jesus answered and *said* unto it,
 23. whosoever shall *say* unto this mountain,
 — he shall have whatsoever he *saith*.
 29. Jesus answered and *said* unto them,
 31. If we shall *say*, From heaven;
 32. But if we shall *say*, Of men;
12: 7. *said* among themselves,
 12. that he *had spoken* the parable
 15. *said* unto them, Why tempt ye me?
 16. And they *said* unto him, Cæsar's.
 17. Jesus answering *said* unto them,
 24. Jesus answering *said* unto them,
 26. how in the bush God *spake* unto him,
 32. the scribe *said* unto him, Well, Master,
   thou *hast said* the truth:
 34. discreetly, he *said* unto him,
 36. For David himself *said*
 — The Lord *said* to my Lord,
13: 2. Jesus answering *said* unto him,
 4. *Tell* us, when shall these things be?
 21. if any man shall *say* to you,
14: 6. And Jesus *said*, Let her alone;
 14. *say* ye to the goodman of the house,
 16. and found as he *had said* unto them:
 18. Jesus *said*, Verily I say
 20. he answered and *said* unto them,
 22. gave to them, and *said*,
 24. And he *said* unto them,
 39. prayed, *and spake* the same words.
 48. Jesus answered and *said* unto them,
 62. And Jesus *said*, I am:
 72. that Jesus *said* unto him,
15: 2. he answering *said* unto him,
 12. *said* again unto them,
 39. he *said*, Truly this man
16: 7. go your way, *tell* his disciples
 — as he *said* unto you.
 8. neither *said* they any thing to any
 15. he *said* unto them, Go ye
Lu. 1:13. But the angel *said* unto him,
 18. Zacharias *said* unto the angel,
 19. the angel answering *said* unto him,
 28. the angel came in unto her, and *said*,
 30. And the angel *said* unto her,
 34. Then *said* Mary unto the angel,
 35. the angel answered and *said* unto her,
 39. And Mary *said*, Behold
 42. and *said*, Blessed (art) thou
 46. And Mary *said*, My soul
 60. his mother answered and *said*,
 61. And they *said* unto her,
 2:10. And the angel *said* unto them,
 15. the shepherds *said* one to another,
 28. and blessed God, and *said*,
 34. and *said* unto Mary
 48. and his mother *said* unto him,
 49. he *said* unto them, How is
 3:12. and *said* unto him,
 13. And he *said* unto them,
 14. And he *said* unto them,
 4: 3. the devil *said* unto him,
 — *command* this stone that it
 6. the devil *said* unto him,
 8. Jesus answered and *said* unto him,
 9. and *said* unto him, If thou
 12. Jesus answering *said* unto him,
 23. And he *said* unto them,
 24. And he *said*, Verily I say
 43. And he *said* unto them,

Lu. 5: 4. he *said* unto Simon, Launch
 5. Simon answering *said* unto him,
 10. Jesus *said* unto Simon,
 13. *saying*, I will: be thou clean.
 14. charged him *to tell* no man:
 20. their faith, he *said* unto him,
 22. he answering *said* unto them,
 23. Whether is easier, *to say*,
 — or *to say*, Rise up
 24. he *said* unto the sick of the palsy,
 27. and he *said* unto him,
 31. Jesus answering *said* unto them,
 33. And they *said* unto him,
 34. And he *said* unto them,
 6: 2. of the Pharisees *said* unto them,
 3. Jesus answering them *said*,
 8. and *said* to the man
 9. Then *said* Jesus unto them,
 10. he *said* unto the man,
 26. when all men shall *speak*
 39. And he *spake* a parable unto them,
 7: 7. but *say* in a word, and
 9. and *said* unto the people that followed
 13. and *said* unto her, Weep not.
 14. And he *said*, Young man,
 20. they *said*, John Baptist
 22. Jesus answering *said* unto them,
 31. And the Lord *said*,
 39. he *spake* within himself, saying,
 40. Jesus answering *said* unto him, Simon, I
   have somewhat *to say* unto thee. And
   he saith, Master, *say on*.
 42. *Tell* me therefore, which of them
 43. Simon answered and *said*,
 — And he *said* unto him,
 48. *said* unto her, Thy sins are forgiven.
 50. And he *said* to the woman,
 8: 4. he *spake* by a parable:
 10. And he *said*, Unto you it is given
 21. answered and *said* unto them,
 22. and he *said* unto them,
 25. And he *said* unto them, Where is your
   faith?
 28. with a loud voice *said*,
 30. And he *said*, Legion:
 45. And Jesus *said*, Who touched me?
 — Peter and they that were with him *said*,
 46. And Jesus *said*, Somebody hath
 48. And he *said* unto her, Daughter,
 52. but he *said*, Weep not;
 56. that they should *tell* no man what was
   done.
 9: 3. And he *said* unto them,
 9. And Herod *said*, John have I
 12. the twelve, and *said* unto him,
 13. But he *said* unto them,
 — And they *said*, We have no more
 14. And he *said* to his disciples,
 19. They answering *said*,
 20. He *said* unto them, But whom say ye that
   I am? Peter answering *said*,
 21. *to tell* no man that thing;
 22. *Saying*, The Son of man must suffer
 33. Peter *said* unto Jesus,
 41. And Jesus answering *said*,
 43. he *said* unto his disciples,
 48. And *said* unto them, Whosoever
 49. John answered and *said*,
 50. And Jesus *said* unto him,
 54. James and John saw (this), they *said*,
 — Lord, wilt thou that we *command*
 55. and *said*, Ye know not what

Lu. 9:57. a certain (man) *said* unto him,
58. And Jesus *said* unto him,
59. And he *said* unto another, Follow me.
But he *said*, Lord,
60. Jesus *said* unto him,
61. And another also *said*,
62. And Jesus *said* unto him,
10:10. into the streets of the same, and *say*,
18. And he *said* unto them, I beheld
21. and *said*, I thank thee,
23. and *said* privately, Blessed
26. He *said* unto him,
27. And he answering *said*,
28. And he *said* unto him, Thou hast answered
29. willing to justify himself, *said*
30. Jesus answering *said*, A certain
35. and *said* unto him, Take care of him;
37. And he *said*, He that shewed mercy on
him. Then *said* Jesus unto him,
40. and came to him, and *said*,
— *bid* her therefore that she help me.
41. And Jesus answered and *said* unto her,
11: 1. one of his disciples *said*
2. he *said* unto them, When ye pray,
5. And he *said* unto them,
— at midnight, and *say* unto him,
7. shall answer and *say*,
15. But some of them *said*,
17. *said* unto them, Every kingdom
27. and *said* unto him, Blessed
28. But he *said*, Yea rather, blessed
39. And the Lord *said* unto him,
46. And he *said*, Woe unto you also,
49. *said* the wisdom of God,
12: 3. whatsoever ye *have spoken* in darkness
11. or what ye shall *say :*
12. what ye ought *to say.*
13. And one of the company *said* unto him,
Master, *speak* to my brother,
14. And he *said* unto him,
15. And he *said* unto them,
16. And he *spake* a parable
18. And he *said*, This will I do:
20. But God *said* unto him,
22. And he *said* unto his disciples,
41. Then Peter *said* unto him,
42. And the Lord *said*,
45. But and if that servant *say*
13: 2. Jesus answering *said* unto them,
7. Then *said* he unto the dresser of his vineyard,
12. and *said* unto her, Woman,
15. and *said*, (Thou) hypocrite,
20. And again he *said*, Whereunto
23. Then *said* one unto him, Lord,
— And he *said* unto them,
32. And he *said* unto them, Go ye, and *tell*
that fox, Behold, I cast out
35. until (the time) come and when ye shall
say,
14: 3. *spake* unto the lawyers
5. answered them, saying, (lit. answering
them *said*)
10. he *may say* unto thee, Friend,
15. he *said* unto him, Blessed
16. Then *said* he unto him,
17. *to say* to them that were bidden,
18. The first *said* unto him,
19. And another *said*, I have
20. another *said*, I have married a wife,
21. *said* to his servant,
22. And the servant *said*, Lord,

Lu. 14:23. the lord *said* unto the servant,
25. he turned, and *said* unto them,
15: 3. And he *spake* this parable
11. And he *said*, A certain man
12. And the younger of them *said* to (his)
father,
17. he came to himself, he *said*,
21. And the son *said* unto him,
22. But the father *said* to his servants,
27. And he *said* unto him, Thy brother
29. *said* to (his) father, Lo,
31. And he *said* unto him, Son,
16: 2. he called him, and *said* unto him,
3. the steward *said* within himself,
6. And he *said*, An hundred measures of oil.
And he *said* unto him, Take
7. Then *said* he to another,
— And he *said*, An hundred
15. And he *said* unto them, Ye
24. he cried and *said*, Father
25. But Abraham *said*, Son,
27. Then he *said*, I pray thee therefore,
30. And he *said*, Nay, father
31. And he *said* unto him, If they hear not
Moses
17: 1. Then *said* he unto the disciples,
5. the apostles *said* unto the Lord,
6. And the Lord *said*, If ye had faith
14. when he saw (them), he *said* unto them,
17. And Jesus answering *said*,
19. he *said* unto him, Arise,
20. he answered them and *said*,
22. And he *said* unto the disciples,
37. he *said* unto them, Wheresoever
18: 4. he *said* within himself,
6. And the Lord *said*, Hear
9. And he *spake* this parable
16. and *said*, Suffer little children
19. And Jesus *said* unto him,
21. he *said*, All these have I kept
22. heard these things, he *said* unto him,
24. he *said*, How hardly
26. And they that heard (it) *said*,
27. he *said*, The things which are impossible
28. Then Peter *said*, Lo,
29. And he *said* unto them, Verily
31. and *said* unto them, Behold,
41. And he *said*, Lord, that I may receive
42. And Jesus *said* unto him,
19: 5. and *said* unto him,
8. and *said* unto the Lord ;
9. and Jesus *said* unto him,
11. he added and *spake* a parable,
12. He *said* therefore, A certain
13. and *said* unto them,
15. he *commanded* these servants to be
17. And he *said* unto him, Well,
19. And he *said* likewise to him,
24. he *said* unto them that stood by,
25. And they *said* unto him, Lord,
28. And when he had thus *spoken*,
30. *Saying*, Go ye into the village
32. even as he *had said* unto them.
33. the owners thereof *said*
34. And they *said*, The Lord
39. *said* unto him, Master,
40. he answered and *said* unto them,
20: 2. *spake* unto him, saying, *Tell* us, by
what authority
3. and *said* unto them,
— and *answer* me:
5. If we shall *say*, From heaven;

Lu. 20: 6. But and if we *say*, Of men ;
8. And Jesus *said* unto them,
13. Then *said* the lord of the vineyard,
16. when they heard (it), they *said*,
17. he beheld them, and *said*,
19. that he *had spoken* this parable
23. and *said* unto them,
24. They answered and *said*, Cæsar's.
25. And he *said* unto them,
34. Jesus answering *said* unto them,
39. certain of the scribes answering *said*,
    Master, thou *hast* well *said*.
41. And he *said* unto them,
42. The Lord *said* unto my Lord,
45. he *said* unto his disciples,
21: 3. And he *said*, Of a truth
5. goodly stones and gifts, he *said*,
8. And he *said*, Take heed
29. And he *spake* to them a parable ;
22: 8. *saying*, Go and prepare
9. And they *said* unto him,
10. And he *said* unto them,
15. And he *said* unto them,
17. gave thanks, and *said*,
25. And he *said* unto them,
31. And the Lord *said*, Simon,
33. And he *said* unto him,
34. And he *said*, I tell thee,
35. And he *said* unto them,
— And they *said*, Nothing.
36. Then *said* he unto them,
38. And they *said*, Lord,
— And he *said* unto them,
40. he *said* unto them, Pray
46. And *said* unto them, Why sleep ye ?
48. But Jesus *said* unto him,
49. they *said* unto him, Lord,
51. And Jesus answered and *said*,
52. Then Jesus *said* unto
56. looked upon him, and *said*,
58. And Peter *said*, Man, I am not.
60. And Peter *said*, Man, I know not
61. how he *had said* unto him, Before
67(66 & 67). *tell* us. And he *said* unto them,
    If I *tell* you,
70. Then *said* they all,
71. And they *said*, What need we
23: 4. *said* Pilate to the chief priests
14. *Said* unto them, Ye have
22. he *said* unto them the third time,
28. *said*, Daughters of Jerusalem,
43. And Jesus *said* unto him,
46. had cried with a loud voice, he *said*,
— *having said* thus, he gave up the ghost.
24: 5. they *said* unto them,
17. And he *said* unto them,
18. Cleopas, answering *said* unto him,
19. And he *said* unto them, What things?
    And they *said* unto him,
24. even so as the women *had said* :
25. Then he *said* unto them,
32. they *said* one to another,
38. And he *said* unto them, Why
40. *when* he *had* thus *spoken*, he shewed
41. and wondered, he *said* unto them,
44. he *said* unto them, These (are) the words
46. And *said* unto them,
Joh. 1:15. This was he *of* whom I *spake*,
22. Then *said* they unto him, Who art thou ?
23. as *said* the prophet Esaias.
25. and *said* unto him, Why baptizest
30. he of whom I *said*,
33. the same *said* unto me,

Joh. 1:38(39). They *said* unto him, Rabbi,
42(43). And when Jesus beheld him, he *said*,
46(47). And Nathaniel *said* unto him,
48(49). Jesus answered and *said* unto him,
50(51). Jesus answered and *said* unto him,
    Because I *said* unto thee, I saw thee
2:16. *said* unto them that sold doves,
18. Then answered the Jews and *said* unto
19. Jesus answered and *said* unto them,
20. Then *said* the Jews,
22. the word which Jesus *had said*,
3: 2. and *said* unto him, Rabbi,
3. Jesus answered and *said* unto him,
7. that I *said* unto thee, Ye must
9. Nicodemus answered and *said* unto him,
10. Jesus answered and *said* unto him,
12. If I *have told* you earthly things,
— if I *tell* you (of) heavenly things?
26. and *said* unto him, Rabbi,
27. John answered and *said*,
28. bear me witness, that I *said*,
4:10. Jesus answered and *said* unto her,
13. Jesus answered and *said* unto her,
17. The woman answered and *said*,
— Thou *hast* well *said* I have no
27. yet no man *said*, What seekest thou ?
29. a man, which *told* me all things
32. But he *said* unto them, I
39. He *told* me all that ever I did.
48. Then *said* Jesus unto him,
50. the word that Jesus *had spoken* unto him,
52. And they *said* unto him, Yesterday
53. in the which Jesus *said* unto him,
5:11. the same *said* unto me,
12. What man is that *which said* unto thee,
14. and *said* unto him, Behold,
19. and *said* unto them, Verily, verily,
6:10. And Jesus *said*, Make the men
25. they *said* unto him, Rabbi,
26. and *said*, Verily, verily,
28. Then *said* they unto him,
29. and *said* unto them, This is
30. They *said* therefore unto him, What
32. Then Jesus *said* unto them,
34. Then *said* they unto him,
35. And Jesus *said* unto them,
36. But I *said* unto you, That
41. because he *said*, I am
43. *said* unto them, Murmur not
53. Then Jesus *said* unto them,
59. These things *said* he in the synagogue,
60. disciples, when they had heard (this), *said*,
61. he *said* unto them, Doth this offend
67. Then *said* Jesus unto the twelve,
7: 3. His brethren therefore *said* unto him,
9. *When* he *had said* these words unto them,
16. Jesus answered them, and *said*, My
20. and *said*, Thou hast a devil;
21. and *said* unto them, I have done
33. Then *said* Jesus unto them,
35. Then *said* the Jews among themselves,
36. What (manner of) saying is this that he
    said,
38. as the scripture *hath said*,
39. But this *spake* he of the Spirit,
42. Hath not the scripture *said*,
45. and they *said* unto them,
52. and *said* unto him, Art thou also
8: 7. he lifted up himself, and *said*
10. he *said* unto her, Woman,
11. She *said*, No man, Lord. And Jesus
    said unto her,
13. The Pharisees therefore *said* unto him,

Joh. 8:14. and *said* unto them, Though I bear
21. Then *said* Jesus again unto them,
23. And he *said* unto them, Ye
24. I *said* therefore unto you, that
25. And Jesus *saith* unto them,
28. Then *said* Jesus unto them,
39. They answered and *said* unto him,
41. Then *said* they to him, We
42. Jesus *said* unto them,
48. *said* unto him, Say we not well
52. Then *said* the Jews unto him,
55. and if I *should say*, I know him not,
57. Then *said* the Jews unto him,
58. Jesus *said* unto them,
9: 6. *When* he *had* thus *spoken*, he spat
7. And *said* unto him, Go,
11. He answered and *said*,
— and *said* unto me, Go
12. Then *said* they unto him, Where is he?
15. He *said* unto them, He put clay
17. He *said*, He is a prophet.
20. His parents answered them and *said*,
22. These (words) *spake* his parents,
23. Therefore *said* his parents,
24. blind, and *said* unto him,
25. and *said*, Whether he be a sinner
26. Then *said* they to him again,
27. I *have told* you already,
28. Then they reviled him, and *said*,
30. The man answered and *said* unto
34. They answered and *said* unto him,
35. found him, he *said* unto him,
36. He answered and *said*,
37. And Jesus *said* unto him,
39. And Jesus *said*, For judgment
40. heard these words, and *said* unto him,
41. Jesus *said* unto them,
10: 6. *spake* Jesus unto them:
7. Then *said* Jesus unto them again,
24. be the Christ, *tell* us plainly.
25. I *told* you, and ye believed not:
26. as I *said* unto you.
34. I *said*, Ye are gods ?
35. If he *called* them gods,
36. because I *said*, I am the Son of God?
41. all things that John *spake*
11: 4. When Jesus heard (that), he *said*,
11. These things *said* he: and after
12. Then *said* his disciples,
14. *said* Jesus unto them plainly,
16. Then *said* Thomas, which is called
21. Then *said* Martha unto Jesus,
25. Jesus *said* unto her,
28. And *when* she *had* so *said*,
— *saying*, The Master is come,
34 And *said*, Where have ye laid him?
37. And some of them *said*,
40. *Said* I not unto thee, that, if
41. and *said*, Father, I thank thee
42. because of the people...I *said*
43. And *when* he thus *had spoken*,
46. and *told* them what things Jesus
49. *said* unto them, Ye know nothing
51. this *spake* he not of himself:
12: 6. This he *said*, not that he cared
7. Then *said* Jesus, Let her alone:
19. therefore *said* among themselves,
27. and what shall I *say*? Father,
30. and *said*, This voice came not because of
35. Then Jesus *said* unto them,
38. which he *spake*, Lord, who hath
39. because that Esaias *said* again,

Joh. 12:41. These things *said* Esaias,
44. Jesus cried and *said*,
49. what I *should say*, and what I should
13: 7. Jesus answered and *said* unto him,
11. therefore *said* he,
12. again, he *said* unto them,
21. *When* Jesus *had* thus *said*,
— and testified, and *said*,
28. for what intent he *spake* this
33. as I *said* unto the Jews,
14: 2. I would *have told* you.
23. Jesus answered and *said* unto him,
26. whatsoever I *have said*
28. how I *said* unto you,
— ye would rejoice, because I *said*,
15:20. the word that I *said* unto you,
16: 4. that I *told* you of them.
— I *said* not unto you at the beginning,
15. therefore *said* I, that he shall
17. Then *said* (some) of his disciples
19. and *said* unto them,
— of that I *said*, A little while,
17: 1. to heaven, and *said*,
18: 1. *When* Jesus *had spoken* these words,
4. went forth, and *said* unto them,
6. As soon then as he *had said*
7. they *said*, Jesus of Nazareth.
8. I *have told* you that I am (he):
9. saying might be fulfilled, which he *spake*,
11. Then *said* Jesus unto Peter,
16. and *spake* unto her that kept the door,
21. they know what I *said*.
22. And *when* he *had* thus *spoken*,
— with the palm of his hand, *saying*,
25. They *said* therefore unto him, Art not
— He denied (it), and *said*,
29. and *said*, What accusation
30. They answered and *said* unto him,
31. Then *said* Pilate unto them,
— The Jews therefore *said* unto him,
32. which he *spake*, signifying
33. called Jesus, and *said* unto him,
34. or did others *tell* it thee of me?
37. Pilate therefore *said* unto him,
38. And *when* he *had said* this, he went
19:21. but that he *said*,
24. They *said* therefore among themselves,
30. he *said*, It is finished:
20:14. And *when* she *had* thus *said*,
15. *tell* me where thou hast laid him,
17. and *say* unto them,
18. and (that) he *had spoken* these
20. And *when* he *had* so *said*, he shewed
21. Then *said* Jesus to them
22. *when* he *had said* this, he breathed
25. But he *said* unto them,
26. and *said*, Peace (be) unto you.
28. and *said* unto him, My Lord
21: 6. And he *said* unto them, Cast
17. because he *said* unto him the third time,
— And he *said* unto him, Lord,
19. This *spake* he, signifying
— And *when* he *had spoken* this, he saith
20. and *said*, Lord, which is he
23. yet Jesus *said* not unto him,
Acts 1: 7. And he *said* unto them,
9. And *when* he *had spoken* these things,
11. Which also *said*, Ye men of Galilee,
15. midst of the disciples, and *said*,
24. they prayed, and *said*,
2:29. let me freely *speak* unto you
34. The Lord *said* unto my Lord,

Acts 2:37. and *said* unto Peter
3: 4. *said*, Look on us.
   6. Then Peter *said*, Silver and gold
  22. *said* unto the fathers,
4: 8. filled with the Holy Ghost, *said* unto
  19. and *said* unto them,
  23. and elders *had said* unto them.
  24. and *said*, Lord, thou (art) God,
  25. *Who* by the mouth of thy servant David hast *said*,
5: 3. But Peter *said*, Ananias,
  8. *Tell* me whether ye sold the land for so much? And she *said*, Yea, for so much.
  9. Peter *said* unto her,
  19. and brought them forth, and *said*,
  29. apostles answered and *said*,
  35. And *said* unto them,
6: 2. and *said*, It is not reason
7: 1. Then *said* the high priest,
  3. And *said* unto him,
  7. will I judge, *said* God:
  26. *saying*, Sirs, ye are brethren ;
  27. thrust him away, *saying*,
  33. Then *said* the Lord to him,
  35. whom they refused, *saying*,
  37. *which said* unto the children of Israel,
  40. *Saying* unto Aaron,
  56. And *said*, Behold, I see
  60. *when* he *had said* this, he fell asleep.
8:20. But Peter *said* unto him,
  24. Then answered Simon, and *said*,
  29. Then the Spirit *said* unto Philip,
  30. and *said*, Understandest thou
  31. And he *said*, How can I,
  34. and *said*, I pray thee,
  37. And Philip *said*, If thou
  — And he answered and *said*,
9: 5. And he *said*, Who art thou, Lord? And the Lord *said*,
  6. and astonished *said*,
  10. and to him *said* the Lord
  — he *said*, Behold, I (am here), Lord.
  15. But the Lord *said* unto him,
  17. *said*, Brother Saul, the Lord,
  34. And Peter *said* unto him,
  40. to the body *said*, Tabitha, arise.
10: 3. and *saying* unto him, Cornelius.
  4. he was afraid, and *said*,
  — And he *said* unto him, Thy prayers
  14. But Peter *said*, Not so,
  19. the Spirit *said* unto him,
  21. and *said*, Behold, I am he whom
  22. And they *said*, Cornelius
  34. and *said*, Of a truth I perceive
11: 8. But I *said*, Not so, Lord:
  12. And the spirit *bade* me go
  13. which stood and *said* unto him,
12: 8. And the angel *said* unto him,
  11. was come to himself, he *said*,
  15. they *said* unto her, Thou art mad.
  17. And he *said*, Go shew
13: 2. the Holy Ghost *said*,
  10. And *said*, O full of all subtilty
  16. beckoning with (his) hand *said*, Men
  22. he gave testimony, and *said*,
  46. and *said*, It was necessary
14:10. *Said* with a loud voice,
15: 7. Peter rose up, and *said* unto them,
  36. Paul *said* unto Barnabas,
16:18. and *said* to the spirit,
  20. brought them to the magistrates, saying,
  (lit. having brought them...*said*)

Acts16:31. And they *said*, Believe
17:32. some mocked: and others *said*,
18: 6. and *said* unto them, Your blood
  9. Then *spake* the Lord to Paul
  14. Gallio *said* unto the Jews,
  21. bade them farewell, *saying*,
19: 2. He *said* unto them, Have ye received
  — And they *said* unto him,
  3. And he *said* unto them,
  — And they *said*, Unto John's baptism.
  4. Then *said* Paul, John verily
  15. the evil spirit answered and *said*,
  21. *saying*, After I have been there,
  25. and *said*, Sirs, ye know
  41. *when* he *had* thus *spoken*, he dismissed
20:10. *said*, Trouble not yourselves ;
  18. he *said* unto them, Ye know,.
  35. he *said*, It is more blessed to give
  36. *when* he *had* thus *spoken*, he kneeled
21:11. and *said*, Thus saith the Holy Ghost,
  14. *saying*, The will of the Lord
  20. and *said* unto him, Thou seest,
  37. May I *speak* unto thee ?
  39. But Paul *said*, I am a man
22: 8. And he *said* unto me, I am Jesus
  10. And I *said*, What shall I do, Lord? And the Lord *said* unto me,
  13. and stood, and *said* unto me,
  14. he *said*, The God of our fathers
  19. And I *said*, Lord,
  21. And he *said* unto me,
  24. *and bade* that he should be examined
  25. Paul *said* unto the centurion
  27. captain came, and *said* unto him,
23: 1. beholding the council, *said*,
  3. Then *said* Paul unto him,
  4. they that stood by *said*,
  11. and *said*, Be of good cheer, Paul:
  14. and *said*, We have bound ourselves
  20. And he *said*, The Jews
  23. called unto (him) two centurions, saying,
  (lit. he having called...*said*)
24:20. *let* these same (here) *say*, if they have found any
  22. *and said*, When Lysias
25: 9. answered Paul, and *said*,
  10. Then *said* Paul, I stand
26:15. And I *said*, Who art thou, Lord? And he *said*,
  29. And Paul *said*, I would to God,
  30. And *when* he *had* thus *spoken*,
27:21. in the midst of them, and *said*,
  31. Paul *said* to the centurion
  35. And *when* he *had* thus *spoken*,
28:21. And they *said* unto him,
  25. *after that* Paul *had spoken* one word,
  26. and *say*, Hearing ye shall hear,
  29. And *when* he *had said* these words,
Ro. 10: 6. *Say* not in thine heart,
1 Co. 1:15. Lest any *should say* that
10:28. But if any man *say* unto you,
11:22. What shall I *say* to you ?
  24. he brake (it), and *said*,
12: 3. no man can *say* that Jesus is the Lord,
  15. If the foot shall *say*,
  16. And if the ear shall *say*,
  21. the eye cannot *say* unto the hand,
15:27. But when he *saith*, All things
2 Co. 4: 6. For God, *who commanded* the light to shine
  6:16. as God *hath said*, I will dwell in them,
Gal. 2:14. I *said* unto Peter before (them) all,

Col. 4:17. And *say* to Archippus, Take heed to
Tit. 1:12. a prophet of their own, *said*,
Heb. 1: 5. For unto which of the angels *said* he
    3:10. that generation, and *said*, They do alway
    7: 9. And as I may so *say*,
    10: 7. Then *said* I, Lo, I come
    30. For we know him *that hath said*,
    12:21. Moses *said*, I exceedingly fear
Jas. 2: 3. and *say* unto him, Sit thou here
    — and *say* to the poor,
    11. For he *that said*, Do not commit adultery,
        said also, Do not kill.
    16. And one of you *say* unto them,
1Joh.1: 6. If we *say* that we have fellowship
    8. If we *say* that we have no sin,
    10. If we *say* that we have not sinned,
    4:20. If a man *say*, I love God,
Jude 9. but *said*, The Lord rebuke thee.
Rev. 7:14. And he *said* to me, These are they
    17: 7. And the angel *said* unto me,
    21: 5. he that sat upon the throne *said*,
    6. And he *said* unto me, It is done.
    22: 6. And he *said* unto me, These sayings
    17. And *let* him that heareth *say*,

ἐργάζομαι, ergazomai.

Mat. 7:23. ye *that work* iniquity.
    21:28. go *work* to day in my vineyard.
    25:16. went and *traded* (lit. *worked for himself*
        gain) with the same,
    26:10. for she *hath wrought* a good work
Mar 14: 6. she *hath wrought* a good work on me.
Lu. 13:14. in which men ought *to work:*
Joh. 3:21. that they are *wrought* in God.
    5:17. answered them, My Father *worketh* hitherto,
        and I *work*.
    6:27. *Labour* not *for* the meat
    28. that we *might work* the works
    30. what *dost* thou *work* ?
    9: 4. I must *work* the works
    — when no man can *work*.
Acts10:35. and *worketh* righteousness,
    13:41. I *work* a work in your days,
    18: 3. he abode with them, and *wrought:*
Ro. 2:10. to every man *that worketh* good,
    4: 4. Now to him *that worketh* is the reward
    5. But to him *that worketh* not,
    13:10. Love *worketh* no ill to his neighbour:
1Cor.4:12. *working* with our own hands:
    9: 6. power to forbear working? (lit. not *to*
        work)
    13. they *which minister about* holy things
    16:10. he *worketh* the work of the Lord,
Gal. 6:10. *let* us *do* good unto all
Eph. 4:28. *working* with (his) hands the thing which
Col. 3:23. *do* (it) heartily,
1Th. 2: 9. *labouring* night and day, because we would
        not be chargeable
    4:11. and *to work* with your own hands,
2Th. 3: 8. but *wrought* (lit. *working*) with labour
    10. if any would not *work*,
    11. *working* not at all,
    12. that with quietness they *work*, *and* eat their
Heb 11:33. *wrought* righteousness, obtained promises,
Jas. 2· 9. ye *commit* sin, and are convinced
2Joh. 8. those things which we *have wrought*, (lit.
        have gained)
3Joh. 5. whatsoever thou *doest* to the brethren,
Rev.18:17. as many as *trade by* (lit. *work for them-*
        selves gain by) sea,

ἐργασία, ergasia.

Lu. 12:58. in the way, give *diligence*
Acts16:16. brought her masters much *gain*
    19. the hope of their *gains*
    19:24. brought no small *gain*
    25. by this *craft* we have our wealth.
Eph. 4:19. to *work* (lit. to the *working* of) all un-
        cleanness

ἐργάτης, ergatees.

Mat. 9:37. but the *labourers* (are) few ;
    38. that he will send forth *labourers*
    10:10. for the *workman* is worthy
    20: 1. to hire *labourers* into his vineyard.
    2. agreed with the *labourers* for a penny
    8. Call the *labourers*, and give them
Lu. 10: 2. but the *labourers* (are) few :
    — that he would send forth *labourers*
    7. for the *labourer* is worthy of
    13:27. (ye) *workers* of iniquity.
Acts19:25. the *workmen* of like occupation,
2Co.11:13. false apostles, deceitful *workers*,
Phi. 3: 2. beware of evil *workers*,
1Ti. 5:18. The *labourer* (is) worthy of his reward.
2Ti. 2:15. a *workman* that needeth not to be
Jas. 5: 4. the hire of the *labourers*

ἔργον, ergon.

Mat. 5:16. they may see your good *works*,
    11: 2. heard in the prison the *works* of Christ,
    23: 3. but do not ye after their *works:*
    5. But all their *works* they do
    26:10. for she hath wrought a good *work*
Mar 13:34. to every man his *work*,
    14: 6. she hath wrought a good *work* on me.
Lu. 11:48. the *deeds* of your fathers:
    24:19. mighty in *deed* and word
Joh. 3:19. their *deeds* were evil.
    20. lest his *deeds* should be reproved.
    21. his *deeds* may be made manifest,
    4:34. and to finish his *work*.
    5:20. shew him greater *works* than these,
    36. for the *works* which the Father
    — the same *works* that I do,
    6:28. that we might work the *works* of God ?
    29. This is the *work* of God,
    7: 3. the *works* that thou doest.
    7. the *works* thereof are evil.
    21. I have done one *work*,
    8:39. the *works* of Abraham.
    41. the *deeds* of your father.
    9: 3. the *works* of God should be made manifest
        in him.
    4. work the *works* of him that
    10:25. the *works* that I do
    32. Many good *works* have I shewed you from
        my Father ; for which of those *works*
    33. For a good *work* we stone thee not ;
    37. If I do not the *works* of my Father,
    38. believe not me, believe the *works :*
    14:10. dwelleth in me, he doeth the *works*.
    11. believe me for the very *works*' sake.
    12. the *works* that I do
    15:24. If I had not done among them the *works*
    17: 4. I have finished the *work*
Acts 5:38. this *work* be of men, it will come to
        nought :
    7:22. mighty in words and in *deeds*.

Acts 7:41. in the *works* of their own hands.
    9:36. this woman was full of good *works*
   13: 2. for the *work* whereunto I have called
    41. I work a *work* in your days, a *work* which
       ye shall in no wise believe,
   14:26. for the *work* which they fulfilled.
   15:18. Known unto God are all his *works*
    38. and went not with them to the *work*.
   26:20. *works* meet for repentance.
Ro. 2: 6. to every man according to his *deeds :*
    7. patient continuance in well *doing*
   15. shew the *work* of the law
   3:20. by the *deeds* of the law there shall no flesh
      be justified
    27. By what law ? of *works ?*
    28. without the *deeds* of the law.
   4: 2. were justified by *works,*
    6. righteousness without *works,*
   9:11. not of *works,* but of him that calleth ;
    32. but as it were by the *works* of the law.
  11: 6. then (is it) no more of *works :*
   — But if (it be) of *works,* then is it no
      more grace: otherwise *work* is no more
      work.
  13: 3. a terror to good *works,*
   12. the *works* of darkness,
  14:20. destroy not the *work* of God.
  15:18. by word and *deed,*
1Co. 3:13. Every man's *work* shall be made manifest :
   — every man's *work* of what sort it is.
   14. If any man's *work* abide
   15. If any man's *work* shall be burned,
   5: 2. he that hath done this *deed*
   9: 1. are not ye my *work*
  15:58. abounding in the *work* of the Lord,
  16:10. for he worketh the *work* of the Lord,
2Co. 9: 8. to every good *work :*
  10:11. in *deed* when we are present.
  11:15. according to their *works.*
Gal. 2:16. by the *works* of the law, but
   — not by the *works* of the law: for by the
      works of the law shall no flesh
   3: 2. the Spirit by the *works* of the law,
   5. by the *works* of the law, or by the hearing
   10. For as many as are of the *works* of the
      law
   5:19. the *works* of the flesh
   6: 4. But let every man prove his own *work,*
Eph. 2: 9. Not of *works,* lest any man should boast.
   10. created in Christ Jesus unto good *works,*
   4:12. for the *work* of the ministry,
   5:11. with the unfruitful *works*
Phi. 1: 6. he which hath begun a good *work* in you
   22. the fruit of my *labour :*
   2:30. for the *work* of Christ
Col. 1:10. in every good *work,*
   21. enemies in (your) mind by wicked *works,*
   3:17. do in word or *deed,*
1Th. 1: 3. your *work* of faith,
   5:13. for their *work's* sake.
2Th. 1:11. the *work* of faith with power:
   2:17. good word and *work.*
1Ti. 2:10. with good *works.*
   3: 1. he desireth a good *work.*
   5:10. Well reported of for good *works ;*
   — diligently followed every good *work.*
   25. also the good *works* (of some) are mani-
      fest beforehand;
   6:18. that they be rich in good *works,*
2Ti. 1: 9. not according to our *works,*
   2:21. prepared unto every good *work.*
   3:17. throughly furnished unto all good *works.*

2Ti. 4: 5. do the *work* of an evangelist,
   14. according to his *works :*
   18. from every evil *work,*
Tit. 1:16. but in *works* they deny (him),
   — unto every good *work* reprobate.
   2: 7. a pattern of good *works :*
   14. zealous of good *works.*
   3: 1. to be ready to every good *work,*
   5. Not by *works* of righteousness
   8. to maintain good *works.*
   14. to maintain good *works*
Heb. 1:10. the *works* of thine hands:
   2: 7. over the *works* of thy hands:
   3: 9. and saw my *works* forty years.
   4: 3. although the *works* were finished from the
      foundation of the world.
   4. rest the seventh day from all his *works.*
   10. hath ceased from his own *works,*
   6: 1. of repentance from dead *works,*
   10. your *work* and labour of love,
   9:14. purge your conscience from dead *works*
  10:24. to provoke unto love and to good *works:*
  13:21. Make you perfect in every good *work*
Jas. 1: 4. let patience have (her) perfect *work,*
   25. but a doer of the *work,*
   2:14. say he hath faith, and have not *works ?*
   17. faith, if it hath not *works,* is dead,
   18. and I have *works :* shew me thy faith
      without thy *works,* and I will shew thee
      my faith by my *works.*
   20. faith without *works* is dead ?
   21. Was not Abraham our father justified by
      works,
   22. faith wrought with his *works,* and by *works*
      was faith made perfect ?
   24. that by *works* a man is justified, and not
      by faith only.
   25. was not Rahab the harlot justified by
      works,
   26. so faith without *works* is dead also.
   3:13. his *works* with meekness of wisdom.
1Pet. 1:17. according to every man's *work,*
   2:12. by (your) good *works,* which they shall
      behold,
2Pet. 2: 8. with (their) unlawful *deeds ;*
   3:10. and the *works* that are therein
1Joh.3: 8. might destroy the *works* of the devil.
   12. his own *works* were evil,
   18. but in *deed* and in truth.
2Joh. 11. is partaker of his evil *deeds.*
3Joh. 10. his *deeds* which he doeth,
Jude 15. of all their ungodly *deeds*
Rev. 2: 2. I know thy *works,* and thy labour,
   5. repent, and do the first *works ;*
   6. the *deeds* of the Nicolaitanes,
   9. I know thy *works,* and tribulation,
   13. I know thy *works,* and where
   19. I know thy *works,* and charity,
   — thy patience, and thy *works ;*
   22. they repent of their *deeds.*
   23. unto every one of you according to your
      works.
   26. keepeth my *works* unto the end,
   3: 1. I know thy *works,* that thou hast
   2. for I have not found thy *works*
   8. I know thy *works :* behold, I
   15. I know thy *works,* that thou art
   9:20. repented not of the *works* of their hands,
  14:13. and their *works* do follow them.
  15: 3. and marvellous (are) thy *works,*
  16:11. repented not of their *deeds.*
  18: 6. double according to her *works :*

Rev 20:12. according to their *works*.
　　　13. according to their *works*.
　　　22:12. according as his *work* shall be.

ἐρεθίζω, erethizo.

2Co. 9: 2. zeal *hath provoked* very many.
Col. 3:21. *provoke* not your children (*to anger*),

ἐρείδω, erīdo.

Acts27:41. the forepart *stuck fast, and* remained

ἐρεύγομαι, erŭgomai.

Mat.13:35. I *will utter* things which have been kept
　　　　　secret

ἐρευνάω, erŭnao.

Joh. 5:39. *Search* the scriptures; for in them
　　　7:52. *Search,* and look: for out of Galilee
Ro. 8:27. And he *that searcheth* the hearts
1Co. 2:10. the Spirit *searcheth* all things,
1Pet.1:11. *Searching* what, or what manner
Rev. 2:23. I am he *which searcheth* the reins

ἐρέω, ereo.

Mat. 7: 4. Or how *wilt* thou *say* to thy brother,
　　　22. Many *will say* to me
　　　13:30. I *will say* to the reapers,
　　　17:20. ye *shall say* unto this mountain,
　　　21: 3. ye *shall say*, The Lord hath need of them;
　　　24. I in like wise *will tell* you by what
　　　25. he *will say* unto us, Why
　　　25:34. Then *shall* the King *say* unto them
　　　40. the King shall answer and *say* unto them,
　　　41. Then *shall* he *say* also unto them on the
　　　26:75. of Jesus, *which said* unto him,
Mar11:29. and I *will tell* you by what authority
　　　31. he *will say*, Why then did ye not
Lu. 2:24. according to that *which is said* in the
　　　4:12. It *is said*, Thou shalt not tempt
　　　23. Ye *will* surely *say* unto me this proverb,
　　　12:10. whosoever *shall speak* a word
　　　19. And I *will say* to my soul,
　　　13:25. he shall answer and *say* unto you,
　　　27. he *shall say*, I tell you, I know you not.
　　　14: 9. come and *say* to thee, Give this man place;
　　　15:18. and *will say* unto him, Father,
　　　17: 7. *will say* unto him by and by, when he is
　　　8. And *will* not rather *say* unto him,
　　　21. Neither *shall* they say, Lo here!
　　　23. And they *shall say* to you, See
　　　19:31. thus *shall* ye *say* unto him,
　　　20: 5. he *will say*, Why then believed ye him not?
　　　22:11. And ye *shall say* unto the goodman of
　　　13. and found as he *had said* unto them:
　　　23:29. in the which they *shall say*, Blessed
Joh. 4:18. in that *saidst* thou truly.
　　　6:65. Therefore *said* I unto you,
　　　11:13. Howbeit Jesus *spake* of his death:
　　　12:50. even as the Father *said* unto me,
　　　14:29. I *have told* you before it come to pass,
　　　15:15. but I *have called* you friends;
Acts 2:16. this is that *which was spoken*
　　　8:24. of these things which ye *have spoken*
　　　13:34. he *said* on this wise, I will give
　　　40. *which is spoken of* in the prophets;

Acts17:28. certain also of your own poets *have said*,
　　　20:38. for the words which he *spake*,
　　　23: 5. Thou *shalt* not *speak* evil *of* the ruler
Ro. 3: 5. righteousness of God, what *shall* we *say* ?
　　　4: 1. What *shall* we then *say* that Abraham,
　　　18. according to that *which was spoken*,
　　　6: 1. What *shall* we *say* then? Shall we continue
　　　7: 7. What *shall* we *say* then? (Is) the law
　　　　　sin?
　　　8:31. What *shall* we then *say* to these things?
　　　9:14. What *shall* we *say* then? (Is there)
　　　19. Thou *wilt say* then unto me, Why doth he
　　　20. *Shall* the thing formed *say* to him that
　　　30. What *shall* we *say* then? That the Gentiles,
　　　11:19. Thou *wilt say* then, The branches were
1Co.14:16. how *shall* he that occupieth the room of
　　　　　the unlearned *say* Amen
　　　23. *will* they not *say* that ye are mad?
　　　15:35. But some (man) *will say*, How
2Co.12: 6. for I *will say* the truth:
　　　9. And he *said* unto me, My grace is
Phi. 4: 4. again I *say*, Rejoice.
Heb 1:13. *said* he at any time, Sit on my right hand,
　　　4: 3. as he *said*, As I have sworn
　　　4. For he *spake* in a certain place of the
　　　7. as it *is said*, To day if ye will hear his
　　　10: 9. Then *said* he, Lo, I come
　　　13: 5. for he *hath said*, I will never leave thee,
　　　　　nor forsake thee.
Jas. 2:18. Yea, a man may *say*, Thou hast faith,
Rev. 7:14. And I *said* unto him, Sir,
　　　17: 7. I *will tell* thee the mystery
　　　19: 3. And again they *said*, Alleluia.

ἐρημία, ereemia.

Mat.15:33. so much bread in the *wilderness*, as to
Mar 8: 4. with bread here in the *wilderness*?
2Co.11:26. (in) perils in the *wilderness*,
Heb11:38. they wandered in *deserts*,

ἔρημος, ή, ereemos. subst.

Mat. 3: 1. in the *wilderness* of Judæa,
　　　3. crying in the *wilderness*, Prepare ye
　　　4: 1. led up of the spirit into the *wilderness*
　　　11: 7. What went ye out into the *wilderness* to
　　　24:26. Behold, he is in the *desert;*
Mar 1: 3. voice of one crying in the *wilderness*,
　　　4. John did baptize in the *wilderness*,
　　　12. driveth him into the *wilderness*.
　　　13. he was there in the *wilderness*
Lu. 1:80. and was in the *deserts* till the day of
　　　3: 2. the son of Zacharias in the *wilderness*.
　　　4. of one crying in the *wilderness*,
　　　4: 1. by the Spirit into the *wilderness*,
　　　5:16. withdrew himself into the *wilderness*,
　　　7:24. ye out into the *wilderness* for to see?
　　　8:29. driven of the devil into the *wilderness*.
　　　15: 4. the ninety and nine in the *wilderness*,
Joh. 1:23. of one crying in the *wilderness*,
　　　3:14. lifted up the serpent in the *wilderness*,
　　　6:31. fathers did eat manna in the *desert;*
　　　49. did eat manna in the *wilderness*,
　　　11:54. unto a country near to the *wilderness*,
Acts 7:30. in the *wilderness* of mount Sina
　　　36. in the *wilderness* forty years.
　　　38. in the church in the *wilderness*
　　　42. forty years in the *wilderness*?
　　　44. of witness in the *wilderness*,
　　　13:18. their manners in the *wilderness*.

Acts21:38. leddest out into the *wilderness*
1Co.10: 5. were overthrown in the *wilderness*.
Heb 3: 8. day of temptation in the *wilderness* :
      17. carcases fell in the *wilderness* ?
Rev.12: 6. fled into the *wilderness*,
      14. that she might fly into the *wilderness*,
   17: 3. away in the spirit into the *wilderness* :

ἔρημος, *ereemos*. adj.

Mat.14:13. into a *desert* place apart:
      15. This is a *desert* place,
   23:38. your house is left unto you *desolate*.
Mar 1:35. departed into a *solitary* place,
      45. was without in *desert* places:
   6:31. apart into a *desert* place,
      32. they departed into a *desert* place
      35. This is a *desert* place,
Lu. 4:42. and went into a *desert* place:
   9:10. into a *desert* place belonging to the city
      12. here in a *desert* place.
   13:35. your house is left unto you *desolate* :
Acts 1:20. Let his habitation be *desolate*,
   8:26. Jerusalem unto Gaza, which is *desert*.
Gal. 4:27. the desolate hath many more children (lit.
      many the children of the *desolate* rather)

ἐρημόω, *ereemoō*.

Mat.12:25. kingdom...*is brought to desolation* ;
Lu. 11:17. divided against itself *is brought to deso-*
      lation ;
Rev.17:16. shall make her *desolate*
   18:17(16). For in one hour so great riches *is come*
      to nought.
      19. in one hour *is* she *made desolate*.

ἐρήμωσις, *ereemōsis*.

Mat.24:15. the abomination of *desolation*,
Mar 13:14. the abomination of *desolation*,
Lu. 21:20. the *desolation* thereof is nigh.

ἐρίζω, *erizo*.

Mat.12:19. He *shall* not *strive*, nor cry ;

ἐριθεία, *erithīa*.

Ro. 2: 8. But unto them that are contentious, (lit.
      of *contention*)
2Co.12:20. envyings, wraths, *strifes*,
Gal. 5:20. emulations, wrath, *strife*,
Phi. 1:16. The one preach Christ of *contention*,
   2: 3. (Let) nothing (be done) through *strife*
Jas. 3:14. envying and *strife* in your hearts,
      16. For where envying and *strife*

ἔριον, *erion*.

Heb 9:19. scarlet *wool*, and hyssop,
Rev. 1:14. and (his) hairs (were) white like *wool*,

ἔρις, *eris*.

Ro. 1:29. of envy, murder, *debate*,
   13:13. not in *strife* and envying.
1Co. 1:11. there are *contentions* among you.
   3: 3. *strife*, and divisions, are ye not carnal,
2Co.12:20. lest (there be) *debates*, envyings,

Gal. 5:20. *variance*, emulations, wrath,
Phi. 1:15. preach Christ even of envy and *strife* ;
1Ti. 6: 4. cometh envy, *strife*, railings,
Tit. 3: 9. genealogies, and *contentions*, and strivings
      about the law ;

ἐρίφιον, *eriphion*.

Mat.25:33. but the *goats* on the left.

ἔριφος, *eriphos*.

Mat.25:32. divideth (his) sheep from the *goats* :
Lu. 15:29. thou never gavest me a *kid*,

ἑρμηνεία, *hermeenīa*.

1Co.12:10. the *interpretation* of tongues:
   14:26. a revelation, hath an *interpretation*.

ἑρμηνεύω, *hermeenūo*.

Joh. 1:38(39). which is to say, *being interpreted*,
      42(43). which *is by interpretation*, A stone.
   9: 7. which *is by interpretation*, Sent.
Heb 7: 2. *being by interpretation* King of righteous-
      ness,

ἑρπετόν, *herpeton*.

Acts10:12. wild beasts, and *creeping things*,
      11: 6. wild beasts, and *creeping things*,
Ro. 1:23. fourfooted beasts, and *creeping things*.
Jas. 3: 7. and of *serpents*, and of things in the sea,

ἔρχομαι, *erkomai*.

Mat. 2: 2. and *are come* to worship him.
      8. I *may come and* worship him also.
      9. till it *came and* stood over where
      11. *when* they *were come* into the house,
      21. and *came* into the land of Israel,
      23. he *came and* dwelt in a city called
   3: 7. saw many of the Pharisees and Sadducees
      come to his baptism,
      11. but he *that cometh* after me is mightier
      14. and *comest* thou to me ?
      16. like a dove, and *lighting* upon him:
   4:13. he *came and* dwelt in Capernaum,
   5:17. that I *am come* to destroy,
      — I *am* not *come* to destroy,
      24. and then *come and* offer thy gift.
   6:10. Thy kingdom *come*. Thy will be done
   7:15. which *come* to you in sheep's clothing,
      25. and the floods *came*,
      27. and the floods *came*,
   8: 2. there *came* a leper *and* worshipped
      7. I will *come and* heal him
      9. and to another, *Come*, and he *cometh* ; and
      to my
      14. And *when* Jesus *was come*
      28. *when* he *was come* to the other side
      29. *art* thou *come* hither to torment us before
   9: 1. and *came* into his own city.
      10. sinners *came and* sat down with him
      13. for I *am* not *come* to call
      15. but the days *will come*,
      18. there *came* a certain ruler, *and* worshipped
      — *come and* lay thy hand upon her,
      23. And *when* Jesus *came* into the

Mat. 9:28. And *when* he *was come* into the house,

10:13. *let* your peace *come* upon it:

23. till the Son of man *be come.*

34. that I *am come* to send peace on earth: I *came* not to send peace,

35. For I *am come* to set a man at variance

11: 3. Art thou he *that should come,*

14. which was for *to come.*

18. For John *came* neither eating

19. The Son of man *came* eating

12: 9. he *went* into their synagogue:

42. for she *came* from the uttermost parts

44. and *when* he *is come,* he findeth (it) empty,

13: 4. and the fowls *came* and devoured

19. then *cometh* the wicked (one), and

25. his enemy *came* and sowed tares

32. so that the birds of the air *come*

36. and *went* into the house:

54. when he *was come* into his own country,

14:12. and *went* and told Jesus.

28. bid me *come* unto thee on the water.

29. And he said, *Come.*

— walked on the water, *to go* to Jesus.

33. *came* and worshipped him,

34. when they were gone over, they *came* into

15:25. Then *came* she and worshipped

29. *came* nigh unto the sea

39. and *came* into the coasts of Magdala.

16: 5. *when* his disciples *were come*

13. *When* Jesus *came* into the coasts

24. If any (man) will *come* after me,

27. Son of man shall *come* in the glory

28. see the Son of man *coming* in his kingdom.

17:10. Elias must first *come?*

11. Elias truly shall first *come,*

12. That Elias *is come* already,

14. *when* they *were come* to the multitude,

24. And *when* they *were come* to Capernaum,

18: 7. that offences *come;* but woe to that man by whom the offence *cometh!*

11. For the Son of man *is come*

31. and *came* and told unto their lord

19: 1. *came* into the coasts of Judæa

14. forbid them not, *to come* unto me:

20: 9. *when* they *came* that (were hired) about the eleventh hour,

10. But *when* the first *came,* they supposed

28. *came* not to be ministered unto,

21: 1. and *were come* to Bethphage,

5. *cometh* unto thee, meek,

9. Blessed (is) he *that cometh* in the name of the Lord :

19. he *came* to it, and found nothing thereon,

23. when he *was come* into the temple,

32. For John *came* unto you

40. When the lord therefore of the vineyard *cometh,*

22: 3. they would not *come.*

23:35. That upon you *may come*

39. Blessed (is) he *that cometh* in the name of the Lord.

24: 5. For many *shall come* in my name,

30. and they shall see the Son of man *coming* in the clouds of heaven

39. until the flood *came,*

42. your Lord *doth come.*

43. the thief would *come,*

44. the Son of man *cometh.*

46. whom his lord *when* he *cometh*

48. My lord delayeth his *coming;* (lit. *to come)*

25: 6. Behold, the bridegroom *cometh;*

Mat.25:10. went to buy, the bridegroom *came;*

11. Afterward *came* also the other

13. the Son of man *cometh.*

19. the lord of those servants *cometh,*

27. at my *coming* I should have received

31. When the Son of man *shall come*

36. and ye *came* unto me.

39. in prison, and *came* unto thee ?

26:36. Then *cometh* Jesus with them

40. And he *cometh* unto the disciples,

43. he *came* and found them

45. Then *cometh* he to his disciples,

47. one of the twelve, *came,*

64. and *coming* in the clouds of heaven.

27:33. *when* they *were come* unto a place called

49. whether Elias *will come* to save him.

57. there *came* a rich man

64. lest his disciples *come* by night, and

28: 1. *came* Mary Magdalene

11. *came* into the city, *and* shewed

13. *came* by night, *and* stole him (away)

Mar 1: 7. There *cometh* one mightier than I

9. Jesus *came* from Nazareth

14. Jesus *came* into Galilee,

24. *art* thou *come* to destroy us ?

29. they *entered* into the house of Simon

40. there *came* a leper to him,

45. they *came* to him from every quarter.

2: 3. And they *come* unto him,

13. the multitude *resorted* unto him,

17. I *came* not to call the righteous,

18. they *come* and say

20. But the days *will come,*

3: 8. what great things he did, *came* unto him.

19. and they *went* into an house.

31. There *came* then his brethren

4: 4. and the fowls of the air *came*

15. Satan *cometh* immediately,

21. *Is* a candle *brought* to be put

22. that it *should come* abroad.

5: 1. they *came* over unto the other side

15. they *come* to Jesus,

22. there *cometh* one of the rulers of the

23. (I pray thee), *come* and lay thy hands on her,

26. nothing bettered, but rather *grew* worse,

27. *came* in the press behind, *and* touched

33. *came* and fell down before him,

35. there *came* from the ruler of the

38. he *cometh* to the house of the ruler

6: 1. and *came* into his own country;

29. when his disciples heard (of it), they *came*

31. for there were many *coming*

48. he *cometh* unto them,

53. when they had passed over, they *came*

7: 1. certain of the scribes, *which came*

25. *came* and fell at his feet:

31. he *came* unto the sea

8:10. *came* into the parts of Dalmanutha.

22. he *cometh* to Bethsaida ;

34. Whosoever will *come* after me,.

38. when he *cometh* in the glory

9: 1. have seen the kingdom of God *come* with power.

7. a voice *came* out of the cloud,

11. Elias must first *come?*

12. Elias verily *cometh* first, *and*

13. That Elias *is* indeed *come,*

14. *when* he *came* to (his) disciples,

33. And he *came* to Capernaum:

10: 1. and *cometh* into the coasts

14. Suffer the little children *to come* unto me,

Mar 10:30. in the world *to come*
45. *came* not to be ministered unto,
46. they *came* to Jericho:
50. rose, and *came* to Jesus.
11: 9. he *that cometh* in the name of the Lord:
10. the kingdom of our father David, *that cometh*
13. he *came*, if haply he might find any thing thereon: and *when* he *came* to it,
15. And they *come* to Jerusalem:
27. they *come* again to Jerusalem:
— there *come* to him the chief priests,
12: 9. he *will come* and destroy
14. And *when* they *were come*, they say
18. Then *come* unto him the Sadducees,
42. there *came* a certain poor widow, *and*
13: 6. For many *shall come* in my name,
26. see the Son of man *coming* in the clouds
35. the master of the house *cometh*,
36. Lest *coming* suddenly he find
14: 3. there *came* a woman having an alabaster box
16. and *came* into the city,
17. he *cometh* with the twelve.
32. And they *came* to a place
37. he *cometh*, and findeth them
41. And he *cometh* the third time,
— it is enough, the hour *is come* ;
45. And *as soon as* he *was come*, he goeth straightway
62. *coming* in the clouds of heaven.
66. there *cometh* one of the maids
15:21. *coming* out of the country,
36. whether Elias *will come*
43. also waited for the kingdom of God, *came*,
16: 1. that they might *come and* anoint him.
2. they *came* unto the sepulchre
Lu. 1:43. that the mother of my Lord *should come*
59. they *came* to circumcise the child ;
2:16. And they *came* with haste,
27. he *came* by the Spirit into
44. in the company, *went* a day's journey ;
51. and *came* to Nazareth,
3: 3. he *came* into all the country
12. Then *came* also publicans to be baptized,
16. but one mightier than I *cometh*,
4:16. he *came* to Nazareth,
34. *art* thou *come* to destroy us ?
42. and *came* unto him,
5: 7. that they should *come and* help them. And they *came*, and filled
17. which were *come* out of every town
32. I *came* not to call the righteous,
35. But the days *will come*,
6:17. which *came* to hear him,
47. *Whosoever cometh* to me,
7: 3. that he would *come and* heal his servant.
7. thought I myself worthy *to come* unto thee:
8. and to another, *Come*, and he *cometh* ; and to my
| 9. Art thou he *that should come* ?
20. Art thou he *that should come* ?
33. For John the Baptist *came* neither
34. The Son of man *is come* eating and
8:12. then *cometh* the devil,
17. not be known and *come* abroad.
35. and *came* to Jesus,
41. behold, there *came* a man
47. that she was not hid, she *came* trembling,
49. there *cometh* one from the ruler
9:23. If any (man) will *come* after me,
26. when he shall *come* in his own glory,

Lu. 9:56. *is* not *come* to destroy men's lives,
10: 1. he himself would *come*.
32. *came* and looked (on him), *and* passed by
33. as he journeyed, *came* where he was:
11: 2. Thy kingdom *come*. Thy will be done
25. And *when* he *cometh*, he findeth (it) swept
31. she *came* from the utmost parts
12:36. *when* he *cometh* and knocketh,
37. whom the lord *when* he *cometh* shall find
38. And if he shall *come* in the second watch, or *come* in the third watch,
39. the thief would *come*,
40. the Son of man *cometh*
43. whom his lord *when* he *cometh*
45. My lord delayeth his coming; (lit. *to come*)
49. I *am come* to send fire on the earth ;
54. There *cometh* a shower ;
13: 6. he *came* and sought fruit
7. I *come* seeking fruit
14. in them therefore *come and* be healed,
35. Blessed (is) he *that cometh* in the name of the Lord.
14: 1. as he *went* into the house
9. he that bade thee and him *come and* say
10. when he that bade thee *cometh*,
17. *Come* ; for all things are now ready.
20. and therefore I cannot *come*.
26. If any (man) *come* to me,
27. doth not bear his cross, and *come* after me,
31. meet him *that cometh* against him
15: 6. And *when* he *cometh* home, he calleth
17. And *when* he *came* to himself,
20. and *came* to his father.
25. as he *came and* drew nigh
30. But as soon as this thy son *was come*,
16:21. the dogs *came and* licked his sores.
28. lest they also *come* into this place of torment.
17: 1. but that offences will *come:* but woe (unto him), through whom they *come !*
20. when the kingdom of God should *come*,
— The kingdom of God *cometh* not with observation:
22. The days *will come*, when ye shall desire
27. the flood *came*, and destroyed them all.
18: 3. she *came* unto him, saying, Avenge
5. by her continual *coming* she weary me.
8. *when* the Son of man *cometh*, shall he
16. little children *to come* unto me,
30. in the world *to come* life everlasting.
19: 5. when Jesus *came* to the place,
10. For the Son of man *is come*
13. Occupy till I *come*.
18. And the second *came*,
20. And another *came*, saying,
23. at my *coming* I might have required mine
38. Blessed (be) the King *that cometh* in the name of the Lord:
20:16. He *shall come* and destroy
21: 6. the days *will come*, in the which
8. for many *shall come* in my name,
27. then shall they see the Son of man *coming* in a cloud with power
22: 7. Then *came* the day of unleavened bread,
18. until the kingdom of God shall *come*.
45. *and was come* to his disciples,
23:26. laid hold upon one Simon, a Cyrenian, *coming* out of the country,
29. behold, the days *are coming*,
42. when thou *comest* into thy kingdom.
24: 1. very early in the morning, they *came*

Lu. 24:23. found not his body, they *came*, saying,
Joh. 1: 7. The same *came* for a witness,
    9. *that cometh* into the world.
    11. He *came* unto his own,
    15. He *that cometh* after me
    27. who *coming* after me
    29. John seeth Jesus *coming* unto him,
    30. After me *cometh* a man
    31. *am* I *come* baptizing with water.
    39(40). He saith unto them, *Come* and see.
         They *came* and saw
    46(47). Philip saith unto him, *Come* and see.
    47(48). Jesus saw Nathanael *coming* to him,
  3: 2. The same *came* to Jesus by night,
    — thou art a teacher *come* from God: (lit.
         that thou *art come* a teacher from God)
    8. canst not tell whence it *cometh*,
    19. light *is come* into the world,
    20. neither *cometh* to the light,
    21. he that doeth truth *cometh* to the light,
    22. After these things *came* Jesus
    26. they *came* unto John,
    — all (men) *come* to him.
    31. He *that cometh* from above is above all:
    — he *that cometh* from heaven
  4: 5. Then *cometh* he to a city of Samaria,
    7. There *cometh* a woman of Samaria
    15. that I thirst not, neither *come* hither to
         draw.
    16. call thy husband, and *come* hither.
    21. the hour *cometh*, when
    23. But the hour *cometh*, and now is,
    25. I know that Messias *cometh*, which is called
         Christ: when he *is come*,
    27. upon this *came* his disciples,
    30. and *came* unto him.
    35. and (then) *cometh* harvest?
    40. So when the Samaritans *were come* unto
         him,
    45. Then when he *was come* into Galilee,
    — for they also *went* unto the feast.
    46. So Jesus *came* again
    54. *when* he *was come* out of Judæa
  5: 7. but while I *am coming*,
    24. and shall not *come* into condemnation ;
    25. The hour *is coming*, and now is,
    28. for the hour *is coming*,
    40. ye will not *come* to me,
    43. I *am come* in my Father's name,
    — if another shall *come* in his own name,
  6: 5. a great company *come* unto him,
    14. of a truth that prophet *that should come*
         into the world.
    15. they would *come* and take him
    17. and *went* over the sea
    — Jesus *was* not *come* to them.
    23. Howbeit there *came* other boats
    24. and *came* to Capernaum,
    35. he *that cometh* to me shall never hunger ;
    37. him *that cometh* to me I will in no wise
         cast out.
    44. No man can *come* to me, except
    45. learned of the Father, *cometh* unto me.
    65. no man can *come* unto me, except
  7:27. when Christ *cometh*, no man
    28. I *am* not *come* of myself,
    30. his hour *was* not yet *come*.
    31. When Christ *cometh*, will he do
    34. where I am, (thither) ye cannot *come*.
    36. ye cannot *come* ?
    37. *let* him *come* unto me, and
    41. Shall Christ *come* out of Galilee?

Joh. 7:42. Christ *cometh* of the seed of David,
    45. Then *came* the officers
    50. he *that came* to Jesus by night,
  8: 2. the people *came* unto him ;
    14. for I know whence I *came*,
    — ye cannot tell whence I *come*,
    20. his hour was not yet *come*.
    21. whither I go, ye cannot *come*.
    22. Whither I go, ye cannot *come*.
    42. *came* I of myself, but he sent me.
  9: 4. the night *cometh*, when no man
    7. washed, and *came* seeing.
    39. I *am come* into this world,
  10: 8. All that ever *came* before me
    10. The thief *cometh* not, but for
    — I *am come* that they might have life,
    12. seeth the wolf *coming*,
    41. many *resorted* unto him,
  11:17. Then *when* Jesus *came*, he found
    19. And many of the Jews *came*
    20. as soon as she heard that Jesus was *coming*,
         (lit. *cometh*)
    27. *which should come* into the world.
    29. she arose quickly, and *came* unto him.
    30. Now Jesus *was* not yet *come*
    32. when Mary *was come* where Jesus was,
    34. Lord, *come* and see.
    38. groaning in himself *cometh* to the grave.
    45. many of the Jews *which came* to Mary,
    48. the Romans *shall come*
    56. that he will not *come* to the feast ?
  12: 1. before the passover *came* to Bethany,
    9. and they *came* not for Jesus' sake
    12. much people *that were come* to the feast,
    — that Jesus *was coming* (lit. *cometh*)
    13. *that cometh* in the name of the Lord.
    15. behold, thy King *cometh*, sitting on
    22. Philip *cometh* and telleth Andrew:
    23. The hour *is come*, that the Son of man
    27. *came* I unto this hour.
    28. Then *came* there a voice from heaven,
    46. I *am come* a light into the world,
    47. for I *came* not to judge
  13: 1. when Jesus knew that his hour *was come*
    6. Then *cometh* he to Simon Peter:
    33. Whither I go, ye cannot *come ;*
  14: 3. I will *come* again, and receive you
    6. no man *cometh* unto the Father,
    18. I will *come* to you.
    23. we *will come* unto him, and make our abode
    28. and *come* (again) unto you.
    30. for the prince of this world *cometh*,
  15:22. If I *had* not *come* and spoken
    26. But when the Comforter *is come*,
  16: 2. the time *cometh*, that whosoever killeth
    4. when the time shall *come*,
    7. the Comforter *will* not *come*
    8. And *when* he *is come*, he will reprove
    13. Howbeit when he, the Spirit of truth, *is*
         come,
    — he will shew you things *to come*.
    21. because her hour *is come :*
    25. but the time *cometh*, when I shall no more
    28. and *am come* into the world:
    32. Behold, the hour *cometh*, yea, *is* now *come*,
         that ye shall
  17: 1. Father, the hour *is come ;* glorify
    11. these are in the world, and I *come* to thee.
    13. And now *come* I to thee ;
  18: 3. *cometh* thither with lanterns
    4. all things *that should come* upon him,
    37. for this cause *came* I into the world,

Joh.19:32. Then *came* the soldiers,
33. But when they *came* to Jesus,
38. He *came* therefore, and took the body
39. And there *came* also Nicodemus, *which* at the first *came* to Jesus by night,
20: 1. *cometh* Mary Magdalene early,
2. she runneth, and *cometh* to Simon Peter,
3. and *came* to the sepulchre.
4. and *came* first to the sepulchre.
6. Then *cometh* Simon Peter
8. that other disciple, *which came* first to the
18. Mary Magdalene *came*
19. *came* Jesus and stood
24. Didymus, was not with them when Jesus *came.*
26. *came* Jesus, the doors being shut,
21: 3. We also *go* with thee.
8. the other disciples *came* in a little ship;
13. Jesus then *cometh,* and taketh bread,
22. that he tarry till I *come,*
23. he tarry till I *come,* what (is that) to thee?
Acts 1:11. *shall* so *come* in like manner as
2:20. before that great and notable day of the Lord *come:*
3:19. the times of refreshing shall *come*
4:23. they *went* to their own company,
5:15. the shadow of Peter *passing by*
7:11. Now there *came* a dearth over
8:27. and *had come* to Jerusalem for to worship,
36. they *came* unto a certain water:
40. till he *came* to Cæsarea.
9:17. in the way as thou *camest,*
21. and *came* hither for that intent, that he
10:29. Therefore *came* I (unto you) without gainsaying,
11: 5. by four corners; and it *came* even to me:
12. Moreover these six brethren accompanied (lit. *went* with) me,
12:10. they *came* unto the iron gate
12. he *came* to the house of Mary the mother
13:13. they *came* to Perga in Pamphylia:
25. there *cometh* one after me,
44. the *next* (lit. *following*) sabbath day
51. and *came* unto Iconium.
14:24. they *came* to Pamphylia.
15:30. they *came* to Antioch:
16: 7. *After* they *were come* to Mysia,
37. but let them *come* themselves *and* fetch us
39. they *came and* besought them,
17: 1. they *came* to Thessalonica,
13. they *came* thither also, and stirred up
15. for to *come* to him with all speed,
18: 1. from Athens, and *came* to Corinth;
2. lately *come* from Italy, with his wife
7. and *entered* into a certain (man's) house,
21. keep this feast that *cometh*
19: 1. having passed through the upper coasts *came* to Ephesus:
4. on him *which should come* after him,
6. the Holy Ghost *came* on them;
18. And many that believed *came,*
27. our craft is in danger to be set at nought; (lit. *to come* into censure)
20: 2. he *came* into Greece,
6. and *came* unto them to Troas
14. we took him in, and *came* to Mitylene.
15. we *came* to Miletus.
21: 1. we *came* with a straight course unto Coos,
8. departed, and *came* unto Cæsarea:
11. And *when* he *was come* unto us, he took
22. they will hear that thou *art come.*
22:11. I *came* into Damascus.

Acts22:13. *Came* unto me, and stood, *and*
30. commanded the chief priests and all their council *to appear,*
24: 8. Commanding his accusers *to come* unto
25:23. *when* Agrippa *was come,*
27: 8. And, hardly passing it, *came* unto a place
28:13. we *came* the next day to Puteoli:
14. we *went* toward Rome.
16. we *came* to Rome,
Ro. 1:10. by the will of God *to come* unto you.
13. oftentimes I purposed *to come* unto you,
3: 8. evil, that good *may come?*
7: 9. but *when* the commandment *came,*
9: 9. At this time *will* I *come,*
15:22. much hindered from *coming* to you.
23. desire these many years *to come* unto you;
24. my journey into Spain, I *will come* to
29. *when* I *come* unto you, I *shall come* in the fulness of the blessing of the gospel
32. That I *may come* unto you with joy
1Co. 2: 1. And I, brethren, *when* I *came* to you, *came* not with excellency of speech
4: 5. until the Lord *come,* who both will bring
18. as though I would not *come*
19. But I *will come* to you shortly,
21. shall I *come* unto you with a rod,
11:26. shew the Lord's death till he *come.*
34. the rest will I set in order when I *come.*
13:10. But when that which is perfect *is come,*
14: 6. if I *come* unto you speaking with tongues,
15:35. and with what body *do* they *come?*
16: 2. that there be no gatherings when I *come.*
5. Now I *will come* unto you, when I
10. Now if Timotheus *come,* see that
11. conduct him forth in peace, that he *may come* unto me:
12. I greatly desired him *to come* unto you
— but his will was not at all *to come* at this time; but he *will come* when he
2Co. 1:15. I was minded *to come* unto you before,
16. *to come* again out of Macedonia
23. I *came* not as yet unto Corinth.
2: 1. that I would not *come* again to you in
3. lest, *when* I *came,* I should have sorrow
12. Furthermore, *when* I *came* to Troas
7: 5. *when* we *were come* into Macedonia,
9: 4. Lest haply if they of Macedonia *come*
11: 4. For if he *that cometh* preacheth
9. the brethren *which came* from Macedonia
12: 1. I *will come* to visions
14. I am ready *to come* to you;
20. lest, *when* I *come,* I shall not find you such
21. lest, *when* I *come* again, my God will
13: 1. This (is) the third (time) I *am coming* to
2. if I *come* again, I will not spare:
Gal. 1:21. Afterwards I *came* into the regions
2:11. But when Peter *was come*
12. For before that certain *came*
— but when they *were come,*
3:19. till the seed *should come*
23. But before faith *came,*
25. But *after that* faith *is come,*
4: 4. But when the fulness of the time *was come,*
Eph. 2:17. And *came and* preached peace
5: 6. for because of these things *cometh* the
Phi. 1:12. *have fallen out* rather unto the furtherance of the gospel;
27. that whether I *come* (lit. *coming*)
2:24. that I also myself *shall come* shortly.
Col. 3: 6. the wrath of God *cometh* on the
4:10. if he *come* unto you, receive

1Th. 1:10. delivered us from the wrath *to come*.	
2:18. we would *have come* unto you,	
3: 6. But now *when* Timotheus *came*	
5: 2. the day of the Lord so *cometh* as a thief	
2Th. 1:10. When he shall *come* to be glorified	
2: 3. except there *come* a falling away	
1Ti. 1:15. Christ Jesus *came* into the world	
2: 4. *to come* unto the knowledge of the truth.	
3:14. hoping *to come* unto thee shortly:	
4:13. Till I *come*, give attendance to reading,	
2Ti. 3: 7. never able *to come* to the knowledge of	
4: 9. Do thy diligence *to come* shortly unto me:	
13. *when* thou *comest*, bring (with thee),	
21. thy diligence *to come* before winter.	
Tit. 3:12. be diligent *to come* unto me	
Heb. 6: 7. drinketh in the rain *that cometh* oft	
8: 8. Behold, the days *come*,	
10:37. and he *that* shall *come* will come,	
11: 8. not knowing whither he *went*.	
13:23. with whom, if he *come* shortly,	
2Pet.3: 3. there *shall come* in the last days	
1Joh.2:18. have heard that antichrist shall *come*,	
4: 2. *that* Jesus Christ *is come* in the flesh	
3. *that...is come* in the flesh	
— ye have heard that it should *come;* (lit. *cometh*)	
5: 6. This is he that *came* by water and blood,	
2Joh. 7. *that* Jesus Christ *is come* in the flesh.	
10. If there *come* any unto you,	
12. I trust *to come* unto you,	
3Joh. 3. *when* the brethren *came*	
10. Wherefore, if I *come*, I will remember	
Jude 14. the Lord *cometh* with ten thousands of his	
Rev. 1: 4. which is, and which was, and *which is to come;*	
7. he *cometh* with clouds ;	
8. which is, and which was, and *which is to come,*	
2: 5. or else I will *come* unto thee	
16. I will *come* unto thee quickly,	
3:10. hour of temptation, which shall *come*	
11. Behold, I *come* quickly:	
4: 8. which was, and is, and *is to come*.	
5: 7. And he *came* and took	
6: 1. one of the four beasts saying, *Come* and	
3. I heard the second beast say, *Come* and	
5. the third beast say, *Come* and see.	
7. the fourth beast say, *Come* and see.	
17. For the great day of his wrath *is come ;*	
7:13. in white robes ? and whence *came* they?	
14. These are they *which came* out of great	
8: 3. another angel *came* and stood	
9:12. there *come* two woes more	
11:14. the third woe *cometh*	
17. which art, and wast, and *art to come ;*	
18. thy wrath *is come*,	
14: 7. the hour of his judgment *is come:*	
15. the time *is come* for thee to reap ;	
16:15. I *come* as a thief.	
17: 1. And there *came* one of the séven	
10. the other *is* not yet *come ;* and when he *cometh*, he must continue a short space.	
18:10. for in one hour *is* thy judgment *come*.	
19: 7. the marriage of the Lamb *is come*,	
21: 9. And there *came* unto me one of the seven	
22: 7. Behold, I *come* quickly:	
12. behold, I *come* quickly ;	
17. the Spirit and the bride say, *Come*. And let him that heareth say, *Come*. And let him that is athirst *come*.	
20. Surely I *come* quickly; Amen. Even so, *come*, Lord Jesus.	

ἐρωτάω, erōtao.

Mat.15:23. his disciples came and *besought* him,	
16:13. he *asked* his disciples, saying, Whom do	
21:24. I also *will ask* you one thing,	
Mar. 4:10. they that were about him with the twelve *asked of* him	
7:26. and she *besought* him that he would cast	
Lu. 4:38. they *besought* him for her.	
5: 3. *prayed* him that he would thrust	
7: 3. *beseeching* him that he would come	
36. And one of the Pharisees *desired* him	
8:37. *besought* him to depart from them ;	
9:45. they feared *to ask* him of that saying.	
11:37. a certain Pharisee *besought* him	
14:18. I *pray* thee have me excused.	
19. I *pray* thee have me excused.	
32. and *desireth* conditions of peace.	
16:27. I *pray* thee therefore, father,	
19:31. if any man *ask* you,	
20: 3. I *will* also *ask* you	
22:68. And if I also *ask* (you),	
Joh. 1:19. from Jerusalem to *ask* him, Who art thou?	
21. And they *asked* him, What then?	
25. they *asked* him, and said	
4:31. his disciples *prayed* him,	
40. they *besought* him that he would tarry	
47. *besought* him that he would come down,	
5:12. Then *asked* they him, What man is that	
8: 7. So when they continued *asking* him, he	
9: 2. his disciples *asked* him,	
15. the Pharisees also *asked* him	
19. they *asked* them, saying, Is this your son,	
21. he is of age; *ask* him: he shall speak	
23. said his parents, He is of age ; *ask* him.	
12:21. *desired* him, saying, Sir, we would see	
14:16. I *will pray* the Father,	
16: 5. none of you *asketh* me,	
19. they were desirous *to ask* him,	
23. ye *shall ask* me nothing.	
26. that I *will pray* the Father for you:	
30. that any man *should ask* thee:	
17: 9. I *pray* for them: I *pray* not for the world,	
15. I *pray* not that thou shouldest take	
20. Neither *pray* I for these alone,	
18:19. The high priest then *asked* Jesus of his	
19:31. *besought* Pilate that their legs	
38. *besought* Pilate that he might take	
Acts 3: 3. about to go into the temple *asked* an alms.	
10:48. *prayed* they him to tarry	
16:39. brought (them) out, and *desired* (them)	
18:20. *When* they *desired* (him) to tarry	
23:18. called me unto (him), and *prayed* me	
20. The Jews have agreed *to desire* thee	
Phi. 4: 3. I *intreat* thee also, true yokefellow,	
1Th. 4: 1. we *beseech* you, brethren, and exhort	
5:12. And we *beseech* you, brethren, to know	
2Th. 2: 1. Now we *beseech* you, brethren, by the coming of our Lord	
1Joh.5:16. I do not say that he *shall pray* for it.	
2Joh. 5. now I *beseech* thee, lady,	

ἔσεσθαι, esesthai.

From εἰμί.

Acts11:28. that there should *be* great dearth throughout all	
23:30. that the Jews laid wait (lit. that there was about *to be* a lying in wait of the Jews)	
24:15. that there shall *be* a resurrection	

Acts 24:25. and judgment to come, (lit. about *to be*)
27:10. I perceive that this voyage will *be*

ἐσθής, *esthees.*

Lu. 23:11. and arrayed him in a gorgeous *robe,*
Acts 1:10. two men stood by them in white *apparel;*
10:30. stood before me in bright *clothing,*
12:21. Herod, arrayed in royal *apparel,*
Jas. 2: 2. gold ring, in goodly *apparel,* and there come in also a poor man in vile *raiment;*
3. to him that weareth the gay *clothing,*

ἔσθησις, *estheesis.*

Lu. 24: 4. stood by them in shining *garments:*

ἐσθίω, *esthio.*

Mat. 9:11. Why *eateth* your Master with publicans
11:18. John came neither *eating* nor drinking,
19. The Son of man came *eating* and drinking,
12: 1. began to pluck the ears of corn, and *to eat.*
14:21. And they *that had eaten* were about
15: 2. wash not their hands when they *eat* bread.
27. the dogs *eat* of the crumbs
38. And they *that did eat* were four
24:49. and *to eat* and drink with the drunken;
26:21. *as they did eat,* he said, Verily
26. And *as they were eating,* Jesus took
Mar. 1: 6. he did eat (lit. *eating*) locusts and
2:16. saw him *eat* with publicans and
— How is it that he *eateth* and drinketh
7: 2. saw some of his disciples *eat* bread
3. *eat* not, holding the tradition
4. except they wash, they *eat* not.
5. but *eat* bread with unwashen hands?
28. yet the dogs under the table *eat* of the
14:18. as they sat and *did eat,* Jesus said, Verily I say unto you, One of you *which eateth*
22. *as they did eat,* Jesus took
Lu. 5:30. Why *do* ye *eat* and drink with
33. but thine *eat* and drink?
6: 1. and *did eat,* rubbing (them) in
7:33. the Baptist came neither *eating* bread
34. The Son of man is come *eating* and
10: 7. remain, *eating* and drinking such
8. *eat* such things as are set before you:
12:45. and *to eat* and drink, and to be
15:16. that the swine *did eat:*
17:27. They *did eat,* they drank, they married
28. they *did eat,* they drank, they bought,
22:30. That ye *may eat* and drink at my table
Acts 27:35. when he had broken (it), he began *to eat.*
Ro. 14: 2. another, who is weak, *eateth* herbs.
3. Let not him *that eateth* despise him *that eateth* not; and let not him *which eateth* not judge him *that eateth:*
6. He *that eateth, eateth* to the Lord, for he giveth God thanks; and he *that eateth* not, to the Lord he *eateth* not,
20. (it is) evil for that man *who eateth* with offence.
1Co. 8: 7. *eat* (it) as a thing offered unto an idol;
10. *to eat* those things which are offered to
9. 7. and *eateth* not of the fruit thereof?
— and *eateth* not of the milk of the flock?

1Co. 9:13. *live* (of the things) of the temple?
10:18. they *which eat* of the sacrifices
25. Whatsoever is sold in the shambles, (that) *eat,*
27. whatsoever is set before you, *eat,*
28. *eat* not for his sake that shewed
31. Whether therefore ye *eat,* or drink,
11:22. have ye not houses *to eat* and to drink in?
26. as often as ye *eat* this bread,
27. whosoever shall *eat* this bread,
28. *let* him *eat* of (that) bread,
29. For he *that eateth* and drinketh unworthily, *eateth* and drinketh
34. *let* him *eat* at home;
2Th. 3:10. neither should he *eat.*
12. that with quietness they work, and *eat* their own bread.
Heb 10:27. which shall *devour* the adversaries.

ἐσμέν, *esmen.*

From εἰμί.

Mar. 5: 9. Legion: for we *are* many.
Lu. 9:12. we *are* here in a desert place.
17:10. We *are* unprofitable servants:
Joh. 8:33. We *be* Abraham's seed,
9:28. we *are* Moses' disciples.
40. *Are* we blind also?
10:30. I and (my) Father *are* one.
17:22. even as we *are* one:
Acts 2:32. whereof we all *are* witnesses.
3:15. whereof we *are* witnesses.
5:32. we *are* his witnesses
10:39. And we *are* witnesses of all things
14:15. We also *are* men of like passions with you,
16:28. for we *are* all here.
17:28. live, and move, and *have our being;*
— For we *are* also his offspring.
23:15. *are* ready to kill him.
Ro. 6:15. we *are* not under the law,
8:12. brethren, we *are* debtors,
16. that we *are* the children of God:
12: 5. *are* one body in Christ,
14: 8. we *are* the Lord's.
1Co. 3: 9. For we *are* labourers together with God:
10:17. we (being) many *are* one bread, (and) one body:
22. *are* we stronger than he?
15:19. we have hope (lit. we *are* hoping) in Christ, we *are* of all men most
2Co. 1:14. we *are* your rejoicing,
24. but *are* helpers of your joy:
2:15. we *are* unto God a sweet savour of Christ,
17. For we *are* not as many,
3: 5. Not that we *are* sufficient
10:11. that, such as we *are* in word
13: 6. we *are* not reprobates.
Gal. 3:25. we *are* no longer under a schoolmaster.
4:28. we, brethren, as Isaac was, *are* the children of promise.
31. we *are* not children of the bondwoman,
Eph. 2:10. For we *are* his workmanship,
4:25. we *are* members one of another.
5:30. we *are* members of his body,
Phi. 3: 3. we *are* the circumcision,
1Th. 5: 5. we *are* not of the night, nor
Heb. 3: 6. whose house *are* we,
4: 2. For unto us was the gospel preached, (lit. we *are* evangelized)
10:10. we *are* sanctified through

Heb 10:39. we *are* not of them who draw back unto
1Joh.2: 5. that we *are* in him.
    3: 2. now *are* we the sons of God,
      19. that we *are* of the truth,
    4: 6. We *are* of God: he that knoweth
      17. as he is, so *are* we in this world.
    5:19. we know that we *are* of God,
      20. and we *are* in him that is true,

ἔσομαι, ἔση, ἔσται, ἐσόμεθα, ἔσεσθε, ἔσονται,
esomai, &c.

From εἰμί.

Mat. 5:21. *shall be* in danger of the judgment:
      22. *shall be* in danger of the judgment:
      — *shall be* in danger of the council:
      — *shall be* in danger of hell fire.
      48. *Be* ye therefore perfect,
    6: 5. thou *shalt* not *be* as the hypocrites (are):
      21. there *will* your heart *be* also.
      22. thy whole body *shall be* full of light.
      23. thy whole body *shall be* full of darkness.
    8:12. there *shall be* weeping
   10:15. It *shall be* more tolerable for the land of Sodom
      22. ye *shall be* hated of all
   11:22. It *shall be* more tolerable for Tyre and
      24. it *shall be* more tolerable for the land of
   12:11. What man *shall* there *be* among you,
      27. they *shall be* your judges.
      40. so *shall* the Son of man *be* three days
      45. so *shall* it *be* also unto this wicked
   13:40. so *shall* it *be* in the end
      42. there *shall be* wailing
      49. So *shall* it *be* at the end
      50. there *shall be* wailing
   16:19. *shall be* bound in heaven:
      — *shall be* loosed in heaven.
      22. this *shall* not *be* unto thee.
   17:17. how long *shall* I *be* with you?
   18:18. *shall be* bound in heaven:
      — *shall be* loosed in heaven.
   19: 5. they twain *shall be* one flesh?
      27. what shall we have therefore? (lit. what *shall be* to us therefore)
      30. But many (that are) first *shall be* last ;
   20:16. So the last *shall be* first,
      26. But it *shall* not *be* so among you:
   22:13. there *shall be* weeping
      28. whose wife *shall* she *be* of the seven?
   23:11. among you *shall be* your servant.
   24: 3. when *shall* these things *be?*
      7. there *shall be* famines, and pestilences,
      9. ye *shall be* hated of all nations for
      21. For then *shall be* great tribulation,
      27. so *shall* also the coming of the Son of man *be.*
      37. *shall* also the coming of the Son of man *be.*
      39. so *shall* also the coming of the Son of man *be.*
      40. Then *shall* two *be* in the field ;
      51. there *shall be* weeping
   25:30. there *shall be* weeping
   27:64. so the last error *shall be* worse
Mar. 6:11. It *shall be* more tolerable for Sodom
    9:19. *shall* I *be* with you?
      35. (the same) *shall be* last of all,
   10: 8. they twain *shall be* one flesh:

Mar.10:31. But many (that are) first *shall be* last ;
      43. But so *shall* it not *be* among you:
      — *shall be* your minister:
      44. *shall be* servant of all.
   11:23. he shall have (lit. it *shall be* to him) whatsoever he saith.
      24. that ye receive (them), and ye shall have (them). (lit. they *shall be* to you)*
   12: 7. the inheritance *shall be* our's.
      23. whose wife *shall* she *be* of them?
   13: 4. when *shall* these things *be?*
      8. there *shall be* earthquakes in divers places, and there *shall be* famines and troubles:
      13. ye *shall be* hated of all
      19. For (in) those days *shall be* affliction,
      25. the stars of heaven shall fall, (lit. *shall be* falling)
   14: 2. lest there *be* an uproar
Lu. 1:14. And thou shalt have joy (lit. joy *shall be* to thee)
      15. For he *shall be* great in the sight
      20. And, behold, thou *shalt be* dumb,
      32. He *shall be* great, and shall
      33. of his kingdom there *shall be* no end.
      34. How *shall* this *be*, seeing I know not
      45. there *shall be* a performance
      66. What manner of child *shall* this *be!*
   2:10. which *shall be* to all people.
    3: 5. the crooked *shall be* made straight,
    4: 7. wilt worship me, all *shall be* thine.
    5:10. thou shalt catch men. (lit. thou *shalt be* catching men)
    6:35. your reward *shall be* great, and ye *shall be* the children of the Highest:
      40. every one that is perfect *shall be* as
    9:41. how long *shall* I *be* with you,
      48. the same *shall be* great.
   10:12. it *shall be* more tolerable in that day
      14. it *shall be* more tolerable for Tyre
   11:19. *shall* they *be* your judges.
      30. so *shall* also the Son of man *be* to this
      36. the whole *shall be* full of light,
   12:20. then whose *shall* those things *be*,
      34. there *will* your heart *be* also.
      52. For from henceforth there *shall be*
      55. There *will be* heat ; and
   13:28. There *shall be* weeping
      30. there are last which *shall be* first, and there are first which *shall be* last.
   14:10. then shalt thou have (lit. *shall be* to thee)
      14. And thou *shalt be* blessed ;
   15: 7. likewise joy *shall be* in heaven
   17:24. so *shall* also the Son of man *be* in his
      26. so *shall* it *be* also in the days of the Son
      30. Even thus *shall* it *be* in the day
      31. he which *shall be* upon the housetop,
      34. there *shall be* two (men) in one bed ;
      35. Two (women) *shall be* grinding
      36. Two (men) *shall be* in the field ;
   21: 7. but when *shall* these things *be?*
      11. And great earthquakes *shall be* in divers
      — great signs *shall* there *be* from heaven.
      17. ye *shall be* hated of all
      23. for there *shall be* great distress
      24. Jerusalem *shall be* trodden down of
      25. there *shall be* signs in the sun,
   22:69. Hereafter shall the Son of man sit (lit. *shall be* sitting)
   23:43. *shalt* thou *be* with me in paradise.
Joh. 6:45. they *shall be* all taught of God.
    8:36. ye *shall be* free indeed.
      55. I *shall be* a liar like unto you:

Joh. 12:26. *shall* also my servant *be :*
    14:17. and *shall be* in you.
    19:24. but cast lots for it, whose it *shall be :*
Acts 1: 8. ye *shall be* witnesses unto me
    2:17. it *shall come to pass* in the last days,
    21. it *shall come to pass,* (that) whosoever
    3:23. And it *shall come to pass,* (that) every
    7: 6. That his seed should sojourn (lit. *shall be* sojourning)
    13:11. and thou *shalt be* blind,
    22:15. thou *shalt be* his witness
    27:22. there *shall be* no loss of (any man's) life
    25. that it *shall be* even as it was told me.
Ro. 4:18. So *shall* thy seed *be.*
    6: 5. likeness of his death, we *shall be* also
    9: 9. Sarah *shall have* a son.
    26. it *shall come to pass,* (that) in the place
    15:12. There *shall be* a root of Jesse,
1Co. 6:16. for two, saith he, *shall be* one flesh.
    11:27. *shall be* guilty of the body
    14: 9. for ye shall speak (lit. *shall be* speaking)
    11. I *shall be* unto him that speaketh
2Co. 3: 8. How *shall* not the ministration of the spirit be rather glorious?
    6:16. I *will be* their God, and they *shall be* my
    18. And *will be* a Father unto you, and ye *shall be* my sons and daughters,
    11:15. whose end *shall be* according to their
    12: 6. I *shall not be* a fool ;
    13:11. God of love and peace *shall be* with you.
Eph. 5:31. and they two *shall be* one flesh.
    6: 3. and thou mayest live long (lit. thou *shalt be* long lived)
Phi. 4: 9. the God of peace *shall be* with you.
Col. 2: 8. lest any man spoil you (lit. *shall be* making spoil of you)
1Th. 4:17. *shall* we ever *be* with the Lord.
1Ti. 4: 6. thou *shalt be* a good minister
2Ti. 2: 2. who *shall be* able to teach others also.
    21. he *shall be* a vessel unto honour,
    3: 2. For men *shall be* lovers of their own
    9. their folly *shall be* manifest unto all
    4: 3. For the time *will come* when
Heb. 1: 5. I *will be* to him a Father, and he *shall be*
    2:13. I will put my trust (lit. I *will be* trusting)
    3:12. lest there *be* in any of you
    8:10. I *will be* to them a God, and they *shall be* to me a people:
    12. I *will be* merciful to their unrighteousness,
Jas. 1:25. *shall be* blessed in his deed.
    5: 3. *shall be* a witness against you,
2Pet.2: 1. there *shall be* false teachers
1Joh.3: 2. it doth not yet appear what we *shall be* — we *shall be* like him ;
2Joh. 2. and *shall be* with us for ever.
    3. Grace *be* with you,
Jude 18. they told you there should *be* mockers
Rev.10: 6. there should *be* time no longer:
    9. it *shall be* in thy mouth sweet as honey.
    20: 6. they *shall be* priests of God and of Christ,
    21: 3. they *shall be* his people, and God himself *shall be* with them, (and be) their God.
    4. there *shall be* no more death,
    — neither *shall* there *be* any more pain:
    7. and I *will be* his God, and he *shall be* my
    25. for there *shall be* no night there.
    22: 3. *shall be* no more curse: but the throne of God and of the Lamb *shall be* in it;
    5. And there *shall be* no night there ;
    12. according as his work *shall be.*
    14. that they *may have* right to the tree (lit. that right to the t. of l. *shall be* theirs)

ἐσόμενος, *esomenos.*

Lu. 22:49. When they which were about him saw *what would follow,*

ἔσοπτρον, *esoptron.*

1Co.13:12. now we see through a *glass,* darkly ;
Jas. 1:23. beholding his natural face in a *glass :*

ἑσπέρα, *hespera.*

Lu. 24:29. it is toward *evening,*
Acts 4: 3. for it was now *eventide.*
    28:23. from morning till *evening.*

ἐστέ, *este.*

From εἰμί.

Mat. 5:11. Blessed *are* ye, when (men) shall revile
    13. Ye *are* the salt of the earth: but if
    14. Ye *are* the light of the world.
    8:26. Why *are* ye fearful, O ye of little faith?
    10:20. For it is not ye (lit. ye *are* not) that speak,
    15:16. *Are* ye also yet without understanding?
    23: 8. and all ye *are* brethren.
    28. but within ye *are* full of hypocrisy
    31. ye *are* the children of them which killed
Mar. 4:40. Why *are* ye so fearful?
    7:18. *Are* ye so without understanding also?
    9:41. because ye *belong* to Christ,
    13:11. for it is not ye (lit. ye *are* not) that speak,
Lu. 6:22. Blessed *are* ye, when men shall hate you,
    9:55. what manner of spirit ye *are* of.
    11:44. for ye *are* as graves
    13:25. I know you not whence ye *are :*
    27. I know you not whence ye *are;*
    16:15. Ye *are* they which justify yourselves
    22:28. Ye *are* they which have continued
    24:17. as ye walk, and *are* sad?
    38. Why *are* ye troubled?
    48. And ye *are* witnesses of these things.
Joh. 8:23. Ye *are* from beneath ; I am from above: ye *are* of this world ;
    31. (then) *are* ye my disciples indeed ;
    37. ye *are* Abraham's seed ;
    44. Ye *are* of (your) father the devil,
    47. ye *are* not of God.
    10:26. because ye *are* not of my sheep,
    34. I said, Ye *are* gods?
    13:10. ye *are* clean, but not all.
    11. Ye *are* not all clean.
    17. happy *are* ye if ye do them.
    35. that ye *are* my disciples,
    15: 3. Now ye *are* clean
    14. Ye *are* my friends,
    19. ye *are* not of the world,
    27. ye *have been* with me from the beginning.
Acts 3:25. Ye *are* the children of the prophets,
    7:26. Sirs, ye *are* brethren ; why do ye wrong
    19:15. Paul I know ; but who *are* ye?
    22: 3. zealous toward God, as ye all *are* this day.
Ro. 1: 6. Among whom *are* ye also
    6:14. for ye *are* not under the law,
    16. his servants ye *are* to whom ye obey ;
    8: 9. But ye *are* not in the flesh,
    15:14. ye also *are* full of goodness,
1Co. 1:30. But of him *are* ye in Christ Jesus,
    3: 3. For ye *are* yet carnal:

1Co. 3: 3. *are* ye not carnal,
     4. *are* ye not carnal?
     9. (ye *are*) God's building.
    16. that ye *are* the temple of God,
    17. which (temple) ye *are*.
   4: 8. Now ye *are* full, now ye
   5: 2. ye *are* puffed up, and have not
     7. as ye *are* unleavened.
   6: 2. *are* ye unworthy to judge the smallest
    19. and ye *are* not your own?
   9: 1. *are* not ye my work in the Lord?
     2. of mine apostleship *are* ye in the Lord.
12:27. Now ye *are* the body of Christ,
14:12. ye *are* zealous of spiritual (gifts),
15:17. ye *are* yet in your sins.
2Co. 1: 7. as ye *are* partakers of the sufferings,
   2: 9. whether ye *be* obedient in all things.
   3: 2. Ye *are* our epistle written in
     3. declared *to be* the epistle of Christ
   6:16. ye *are* the temple of the living God;
   7: 3. ye *are* in our hearts
  13: 5. whether ye *be* in the faith;
    — except ye *be* reprobates?
Gal. 3: 3. *Are* ye so foolish?
    26. ye *are* all the children of God by faith
    28. for ye *are* all one
    29. *are* ye Abraham's seed,
   4: 6. And because ye *are* sons,
   5:18. ye *are* not under the law.
Eph. 2: 5. by grace ye *are* saved;
     8. For by grace *are* ye saved
    19. Now therefore ye *are* no more strangers
   5: 5. For this ye know, (lit. ye *are* aware of)
Col. 2:10. And ye *are* complete in him,
1Th. 2:20. For ye *are* our glory
   4: 9. ye yourselves *are* taught of God
   5: 4. ye, brethren, *are* not in darkness,
     5. Ye *are* all the children of light,
Heb 12: 8. But if ye *be* without chastisement,
    — *are* ye bastards, and not sons.
1Joh 2:14. because ye *are* strong,
   4: 4. Ye *are* of God, little children,

ἐστί, *esti.*

From εἰμί.

Mat. 1:20. conceived in her *is* of the Holy Ghost.
    23. which being interpreted *is*,
   2: 2. Saying, Where *is* he
   3: 3. For this *is* he that was spoken of
    11. cometh after me *is* mightier than I,
    15. for thus it becometh us (lit. *is* becoming
      for us) to fulfil
    17. This *is* my beloved Son,
   5: 3. for their's *is* the kingdom of heaven.
    10. for their's *is* the kingdom of heaven.
    34. by heaven ; for it *is* God's throne;
    35. earth ; for it *is* his footstool: neither by
      Jerusalem; for it *is* the city of
    37. whatsoever is more than these *cometh* of
    48. Father which is in heaven *is* perfect.
   6:13. For thine *is* the kingdom,
    21. For where your treasure *is*,
    22. The light of the body *is* the eye:
    23. the light that is in thee *be* darkness,
    25. *Is* not the life more than meat,
   7: 9. Or what man *is* there of you,
    12. for this *is* the law and the prophets.
   8:27. What manner of man *is* this,
   9: 5. For whether *is* easier,

Mat. 9:13. learn what (that) *meaneth*, I will have
    15. the bridegroom *is* with them?
  10: 2. names of the twelve apostles *are* these;
    10. the workman *is* worthy of his meat.
    11. who in it *is* worthy;
    24. The disciple *is* not above (his) master,
    26. for there *is* nothing covered,
    37. more than me *is* not worthy of me:
    — *is* not worthy of me.
    38. followeth after me, *is* not worthy of me.
  11: 6. And blessed *is* (he), whosoever shall
    10. For this *is* (he), of whom it is
    11. he that is least in the kingdom of heaven *is*
    14. receive (it), this *is* Elias,
    16. It *is* like unto children sitting in
    30. and my burden *is* light.
  12: 6. in this place *is* (one) greater
    7. But if ye had known what (this) *meaneth*,
    8. For the Son of man *is* Lord even of the
      sabbath day.
    23. *Is* not this the son of David?
    30. He that is not with me *is* against me;
    48. Who *is* my mother?
    50. the same *is* my brother, and sister, and
      mother.
  13:19. This *is* he which received seed by
    20. the same *is* he that heareth the word,
    21. but dureth for a while: (lit. *is* temporary)
    22. *is* he that heareth the word; and the care
    23. *is* he that heareth the word, and
    31. The kingdom of heaven *is* like to a grain
    32. Which indeed *is* the least of all seeds: but
      when it is grown, it *is*
    33. The kingdom of heaven *is* like unto
    37. that soweth the good seed *is* the Son of
    38. The field *is* the world;
    39. The enemy that sowed them *is* the devil;
      the harvest *is* the end of the world;
    44. Again, the kingdom of heaven *is* like
      unto treasure
    45. of heaven *is* like unto a merchant man,
    47. kingdom of heaven *is* like unto a net,
    52. *is* like unto a man (that is) an
    55. *Is* not this the carpenter's son?
    57. A prophet *is* not without honour,
  14: 2. This *is* John the Baptist;
    15. This *is* a desert place,
    26. were troubled, saying, It *is* a spirit;
  15:20. These *are* (the things) which defile
    26. It *is* not meet to take the children's
  16:20. that he *was* Jesus the Christ.
  17: 4. Lord, it *is* good for us to be here:
    5. This *is* my beloved Son, in whom I
  18: 1. Who *is* the greatest in the kingdom
    4. as this little child, the same *is* greatest
    7. for it must needs be (lit. it *is* a necessity)
      that offences come;
    8. it *is* better for thee to enter into
    9. it *is* better for thee to enter into life with
    14. Even so it *is* not the will
  19:10. If the case of the man *be* só
    14. of such *is* the kingdom
    24. It *is* easier for a camel to go through
    26. this *is* impossible; but with God all
      things *are* possible.
  20: 1. kingdom of heaven *is* like unto a man
    15. *Is* thine eye evil,
    23. *is* not mine to give,
  21:10. was moved, saying, Who *is* this?
    11. This *is* Jesus the prophet of Nazareth
    38. This *is* the heir;
    42. and it *is* marvellous in our eyes?

Mat. 22: 8. The wedding *is* ready,
   32. God *is* not the God of the dead,
   38. This *is* the first and great commandment.
   42. whose son *is* he?
   45. how *is* he his son?
23: 8. for one *is* your Master, (even) Christ; and all ye are brethren.
   9. for one *is* your Father,
   10. for one *is* your Master, (even) Christ.
   16. swear by the temple, it *is* nothing;
   17. for whether *is* greater,
   18. swear by the altar, it *is* nothing;
24: 6. but the end *is* not yet.
   26. he *is* in the desert;
   33. it *is* near, (even) at the doors.
   45. Who then *is* a faithful and wise servant,
26: 18. My time *is* at hand;
   26. Take, eat; this *is* my body.
   28. For this *is* my blood of the new
   38. My soul *is* exceeding sorrowful,
   39. if it *be* possible, let this cup
   48. I shall kiss, that same *is* he:
   66. He *is* guilty of death.
   68. Who *is* he that smote thee?
27: 6. it *is* the price of blood.
   33. that *is* to say, a place of a skull,
   37. THIS *IS* JESUS THE KING OF THE JEWS.
   42. If he *be* the King of Israel,
   62. Now the next day, that followed (lit. which *is* after) the day of the
28: 6. He *is* not here: for he is risen,
Mar. 1: 27. saying, What thing *is* this?
2: 1. that he *was* in the house.
   9. Whether *is* it easier to say
   19. while the bridegroom *is* with them?
   28. Therefore the Son of man *is* Lord
3: 17. Boanerges, which *is*, The sons of thunder:
   29. but *is* in danger of eternal damnation:
   33. Who *is* my mother, or my brethren?
   35. *is* my brother, and my sister, and mother.
4: 22. For there *is* nothing hid,
   26. So *is* the kingdom of God, as if a man
   31. *is* less than all the seeds
   41. What manner of man *is* this,
5: 14. to see what it *was* that was done.
   41. which *is*, being interpreted, Damsel, I
6: 3. *Is* not this the carpenter,
   4. A prophet *is* not without honour,
   15. Others said, That it *is* Elias. And others said, That it *is* a prophet, or
   16. he said, It *is* John, whom I beheaded:
   35. This *is* a desert place,
   55. where they heard he *was*.
7: 4. And many other things there *be*,
   11. Corban, that *is* to say, a gift,
   15. There *is* nothing from without a man,
   — those *are* they that defile
   27. for it *is* not meet to take the children's
   34. that *is*, Be opened.
9: 5. it *is* good for us to be here:
   7. This *is* my beloved Son:
   10. what the rising from the dead should mean.
   21. How long *is* it ago since this
   39. for there *is* no man which shall do
   40. For he that *is* not against us *is* on our
   42. it *is* better for him that a millstone
   43. it *is* better for thee to enter into
   45. it *is* better for thee to enter
   47. it *is* better for thee to enter
10: 14. of such *is* the kingdom of God.

Mar. 10: 24. how hard *is* it for them that
   25. It *is* easier for a camel
   27. with God all things *are* possible.
   29. There *is* no man that hath left
   40. *is* not mine to give;
   47. it *was* Jesus of Nazareth,
12: 7. This *is* the heir;
   11. and it *is* marvellous in our eyes?
   27. He *is* not the God of the dead,
   28. Which *is* the first commandment of all?
   29. The Lord our God *is* one Lord:
   31. There *is* none other commandment
   32. for there *is* one God; and there *is* none other but he:
   33. *is* more than all whole burnt offerings
   35. that Christ *is* the son of David?
   37. whence *is* he (then) his son?
   42. two mites, which *make* a farthing.
13: 28. ye know that summer *is* near:
   29. it *is* nigh, (even) at the doors.
   33. for ye know not when the time *is*.
14: 14. Where *is* the guestchamber,
   22. Take, eat: this *is* my body.
   24. This *is* my blood of the new
   34. My soul *is* exceeding sorrowful
   35. that, if it *were* possible, the hour might
   44. Whomsoever I shall kiss, that same *is* he;
   69. This *is* (one) of them.
15: 16. into the hall, *called* Prætorium;
   22. which *is*, being interpreted, The place
   34. which *is*, being interpreted, My God,
   42. that *is*, the day before the sabbath,
16: 6. he is risen; he *is* not here:
Lu. 1: 36. this *is* the sixth month with her,
   61. There *is* none of thy kindred
   63. His name *is* John.
2: 11. which *is* Christ the Lord.
4: 22. *Is* not this Joseph's son?
   24. No prophet *is* accepted
5: 21. Who *is* this which speaketh blasphemies?
   23. Whether *is* easier, to say,
   34. while the bridegroom *is* with them?
   39. The old *is* better.
6: 5. the Son of man *is* Lord also
   20. your's *is* the kingdom of God.
   32. what thank *have* ye? (lit. *is* to you)
   33. what thank *have* ye?
   34. what thank *have* ye? (lit. *is* to you)
   35. he *is* kind unto the unthankful and
   36. as your Father also *is* merciful.
   40. The disciple *is* not above his master:
   43. For a good tree bringeth not forth (lit. *is* not bringing forth) corrupt fruit;
   47. I will shew you to whom he *is* like:
   48. He *is* like a man which built an house,
   49. *is* like a man that without a foundation
7: 4. he *was* worthy for whom he should do
   23. blessed *is* (he), whosoever shall not be
   27. This *is* (he), of whom it is written,
   28. there *is* not a greater prophet than John
   — *is* greater than he.
   39. for she *is* a sinner.
   49. Who *is* this that forgiveth sins also?
8: 11. Now the parable *is* this: The seed *is* the
   17. For nothing *is* secret,
   25. Where *is* your faith?
   — What manner of man *is* this!
   26. which *is* over against Galilee.
   30. What *is* thy name?
9: 9. but who *is* this, of whom I hear such
   33. it *is* good for us to be here:
   35. This *is* my beloved Son:

Lu. 9:38. for he *is* mine only child.
    50. Forbid (him) not: for he that *is* not against us *is* for us.
    62. *is* fit for the kingdom of God.
10: 7. for the labourer *is* worthy of his hire.
    22. knoweth who the Son *is*, but the Father; and who the Father *is*, but the Son, and (he) to
    29. And who *is* my neighbour?
    42. But one thing *is* needful:
11:21. his goods *are* in peace:
    23. not with me *is* against me:
    29. This *is* an evil generation:
    34. The light of the body *is* the eye:
    — thy whole body also *is* full of light;
    35. light which is in thee *be* not darkness.
    41. all things *are* clean unto you.
12: 1. which *is* hypocrisy.
    2. there *is* nothing covered,
    6. not one of them *is* forgotten
    15. a man's life *consisteth* not
    23. The life *is* more than meat,
    24. which neither *have* storehouse
    34. For where your treasure *is*,
    42. Who then *is* that faithful and wise
13:18. Unto what *is* the kingdom of God like?
    19. It *is* like a grain of mustard seed,
    21. It *is* like leaven,
14:17. all things *are* now ready.
    22. and yet there *is* room.
    31. whether he *be* able with ten thousand
    35. It *is* neither fit for the land, nor yet for the dunghill;
15:31. all that I have *is* thine.
16:10. *is* faithful also in much:
    — *is* unjust also in much.
    15. *is* abomination in the sight of God.
    17. And it *is* easier for heaven and
17: 1. It *is* impossible but that offences
    21. the kingdom of God *is* within you.
18:16. of such *is* the kingdom of God.
    25. For it *is* easier for a camel
    27. *are* possible with God.
    29. There *is* no man that hath left
19: 3. to see Jesus who he *was;*
    9. *is* a son of Abraham.
    46. *is* the house of prayer:
20: 2. who *is* he that gave thee
    6. for they *be* persuaded
    14. This *is* the heir:
    17. What *is* this then that is written,
    38. he *is* not a God of the dead, but
    44. how *is* he then his son?
21:30. summer *is* now nigh at hand.
    31. the kingdom of God *is* nigh at hand.
22:11. Where *is* the guestchamber,
    19. This *is* my body which is given
    38. he said unto them, It *is* enough.
    53. but this *is* your hour, and the power
    59. for he *is* a Galilæan.
    64. who *is* it that smote thee?
23: 6. whether the man *were* a Galilæan.
    7. he *belonged* unto Herod's jurisdiction,
    15. nothing worthy of death *is* done unto
    35. let him save himself, if he *be* Christ,
    38. THIS *IS* THE KING OF THE JEWS.
24: 6. He *is* not here, but is risen:
    21. that it *had been* he which should have
    29. it *is* toward evening,
Joh. 1:19. this *is* the record of John,
    27. He it *is*, who coming after
    30. This *is* he of whom I said,

Joh. 1:33. the same *is* he which baptizeth
    34. this *is* the Son of God.
    42. which *is* by interpretation,
    47(48). in whom *is* no guile!
2: 9. and knew not whence it *was :*
    17. remembered that it *was* written,
3: 6. born of the flesh *is* flesh; and that which is born of the Spirit *is* spirit.
    8. so *is* every one that is born of the Spirit.
    19. And this *is* the condemnation,
    21. they *are* wrought in God.
    29. that hath the bride *is* the bridegroom:
    31. that cometh from above *is* above all: he that is of the earth *is* earthly,
    — that cometh from heaven *is* above all.
    33. hath set to his seal that God *is* true.
4:10. who it *is* that saith to thee,
    11. the well *is* deep:
    18. *is* not thy husband:
    20. in Jerusalem *is* the place
    22. salvation *is* of the Jews.
    23. the hour cometh, and now *is*,
    29. *is* not this the Christ?
    34. My meat *is* to do the will of him that
    35. There *are* yet four months,
    37. herein *is* that saying true, One soweth, and another reapeth. (lit. one *is* the sower, and another the reaper)
    42. this *is* indeed the Christ, the Saviour of the world.
5: 2. Now there *is* at Jerusalem
    10. It *is* the sabbath day: it is not lawful
    12. What man *is* that which said
    13. wist not who it *was:*
    15. that it *was* Jesus, which had made
    25. The hour is coming, and now *is*,
    27. because he *is* the Son of man.
    30. my judgment *is* just;
    31. of myself, my witness *is* not true.
    32. There is another that beareth witness
    — that the witness which he witnesseth of me *is* true.
    45. there *is* (one) that accuseth you,
6: 9. There *is* a lad here,
    — what *are* they among so many?
    14. This *is* of a truth that prophet
    24. that Jesus *was* not there,
    29. This *is* the work of God,
    31. as it *is* written, He gave them bread from
    33. the bread of God *is* he which cometh
    39. And this *is* the Father's will
    40. And this *is* the will
    42. *Is* not this Jesus, the son
    45. It *is* written in the prophets,
    50. This *is* the bread which
    51. the bread that I will give *is* my flesh,
    55. For my flesh *is* meat indeed, and my blood *is* drink indeed.
    58. This *is* that bread which came down
    60. This *is* an hard saying;
    63. It *is* the spirit that quickeneth;
    — words that I speak unto you, (they) *are* spirit, and (they) *are* life.
    64. and who should betray (lit. who it *was* that should betray) him.
    70. one of you *is* a devil?
7: 6. but your time *is* alway ready.
    7. the works thereof *are* evil.
    11. and said, Where *is* he?
    12. some said, He *is* a good man:
    16. My doctrine *is* not mine,
    17. whether it *be* of God,

Joh. 7: 18. the same *is* true, and no unrighteousness *is* in him.
22. not because it *is* of Moses,
25. *Is* not this he, whom they seek
26. that this *is* the very Christ?
27. we know this man whence he *is*:
— no man knoweth whence he *is*.
28. but he that sent me *is* true,
36. What (manner of) saying *is* this
40. Of a truth this *is* the prophet.
41. This *is* the Christ.

8: 13. thy record *is* not true.
14. (yet) my record *is* true:
16. my judgment *is* true:
17. the testimony of two men *is* true.
19. Where *is* thy Father?
26. he that sent me *is* true;
29. And he that sent me *is* with me:
34. *is* the servant of sin.
39. Abraham *is* our father.
44. there *is* no truth in him.
— for he *is* a liar,
50. there *is* one that seeketh and judgeth.
54. If I honour myself, my honour *is* nothing: it *is* my Father that honoureth me; of whom ye say, that he *is* your God:

9: 4. the works of him that sent me, while it *is*
8. *Is* not this he that sat
9. Some said, This *is* he: others (said), He *is* like him:
12. Where *is* he? He said,
16. This man *is* not of God, because he
17. He *is* a prophet.
19. *Is* this your son,
20. this *is* our son,
24. this man *is* a sinner.
25. Whether he *be* a sinner (or no),
29. we know not from whence he *is*.
30. herein *is* a marvellous thing, that ye know not from whence he *is*,
36. Who *is* he, Lord, that I might believe
37. it *is* he that talketh with thee.

10: 1. *is* a thief and a robber.
2. *is* the shepherd of the sheep.
13. because he *is* an hireling,
16. which *are* not of this fold:
21. *are* not the words of him that hath a devil.
29. My Father, which gave (them) me, *is* greater than all;
34. *Is* it not written in your law,

11: 4. This sickness *is* not unto death,
10. there *is* no light in him.
39. for he hath been (dead) four days. (lit. *is* of the fourth day)
57. if any man knew where he *were*,

12: 9. of the Jews therefore knew that he *was*
14. sat thereon; as it *is* written,
31. Now *is* the judgment of this world:
34. who *is* this Son of man?
35. Yet a little while *is* the light with you.
50. that his commandment *is* life everlasting:

13: 10. but *is* clean every whit:
16. The servant *is* not greater
25. saith unto him, Lord, who *is* it?
26. He it *is*, to whom I shall give a sop,

14: 10. and the Father in me? (lit. *is* in me)
21. he it *is* that loveth me:
24. the word which ye hear *is* not mine, but
28. *is* greater than I.

15: 1. my Father *is* the husbandman.
12. This *is* my commandment,
20. The servant *is* not greater

Joh. 16: 15. All things that the Father hath *are* mine:
17. What *is* this that he saith unto us,
18. What *is* this that he saith, A little while?
32. the Father *is* with me.

17: 3. And this *is* life eternal,
7. whatsoever thou hast given me *are* of
10. all mine *are* thine,
17. thy word *is* truth.

18: 36. My kingdom *is* not of this world: — but now *is* my kingdom not from hence.
38. Pilate saith unto him, What *is* truth?
39. But ye *have* a custom,

19: 35. his record *is* true:
40. as the manner of the Jews *is*

20: 14. knew not that it *was* Jesus.
15. She, supposing him to *be* the gardener,
30. which *are* not written in this book:
31. might believe that Jesus *is* the Christ,

21: 4. knew not that it *was* Jesus.
7. It *is* the Lord. Now when Simon Peter heard that it *was* the Lord,
12. knowing that it *was* the Lord.
20. said, Lord, which *is* he that betrayeth
24. This *is* the disciple which testifieth — know that his testimony *is* true.
25. And there *are* also many other things

Acts 1: 7. It *is* not for you to know
12. which *is* from Jerusalem a sabbath day's

2: 15. seeing it *is* (but) the third hour
16. this *is* that which was spoken
25. he *is* on my right hand,
29. his sepulchre *is* with us
39. For the promise *is* unto you,

4: 11. This *is* the stone which was set at nought
12. Neither *is* there salvation in any other: for there *is* none other name
19. Whether it *be* right in the sight
36. which *is*, being interpreted, The son of

5: 39. But if it *be* of God,

6: 2. It *is* not reason that we

7: 33. the place where thou standest *is* holy
37. This *is* that Moses, which said
38. This *is* he, that was in the church in

8: 10. This man *is* the great power of God.
21. Thou *hast* neither part nor lot in this matter: for thy heart *is* not right in the sight of God.
26. Jerusalem unto Gaza, which *is* desert.

9: 15. he *is* a chosen vessel unto me,
20. that he *is* the Son of God.
21. *Is* not this he that destroyed
22. that this *is* very Christ.
26. that he *was* a disciple.
38. that Peter *was* there,

10: 4. What *is* it, Lord?
6. whose house *is* by the sea side:
28. it *is* an unlawful thing for a man that is a
34. that God *is* no respecter of persons:
35. *is* accepted with him.
36. he *is* Lord of all:
42. it *is* he which was ordained

12: 3. it pleased (lit. *was* pleasing to) the Jews,
9. that it *was* true which was done
15. It *is* his angel.

13: 15. if ye *have* any word of exhortation for the people, say on.

15: 18. Known unto God *are* all his works from the beginning of the world.

16: 12. which *is* the chief city of that part

17: 3. Jesus, whom I preach unto you, *is* Christ.

18: 10. I *have* much people
15. But if it *be* a question

Acts19: 2. whether there *be* any Holy Ghost.
25. we *have* our wealth.
34. that he *was* a Jew,
35. what man *is* there that knoweth not
36. ye ought (lit. it *is* fit for you) to be quiet,
20:10. his life *is* in him.
35. It *is* more blessed to give
21:11. that owneth this girdle, (lit. whose this girdle *is*)
22. What *is* it therefore? the multitude
24. informed concerning thee, *are* nothing;
28. This *is* the man, that teacheth all
33. and what he had done. (lit. he *were* the doer of)
22:26. thou doest: for this man *is* a Roman.
29. after he knew that he *was* a Roman,
23: 5. that he *was* the high priest:
6. that the one part *were* Sadducees,
19. What *is* that thou hast to tell
27. having understood that he *was* a Roman.
34. of what province he *was*.
25: 5. if there *be* any wickedness in him.
11. but if there *be* none of these things
14. There *is* a certain man left
16. It *is* not the manner of the Romans
26:26. for this thing *was* not done in a corner.
28: 4 No doubt this man *is* a murderer,
22. we know that (lit. it *is* known to us)
Ro. 1: 9. For God *is* my witness,
12. That *is*, that I may be comforted
16. for it *is* the power of God
19. that which may be known of God *is* manifest in them;
25. who *is* blessed for ever.
2: 2. the judgment of. God *is* according to
11. For there *is* no respect of persons
28. he *is* not a Jew, which is one outwardly;
3: 8. whose damnation *is* just.
10. There *is* none righteous, no, not one:
11. There *is* none that understandeth, there *is* none that seeketh after God.
12. there *is* none that doeth good, no, not one. (lit. there *is* not even one)
18. There *is* no fear of God
22. for there *is* no difference:
4:15. for where no law *is*,
16. who *is* the father of us all,
21. he *was* able also to perform.
5:14. who *is* the figure of him that was to come.
7: 3. she *is* free from that law;
14. the law *is* spiritual:
8: 9. he *is* none of his.
24. but hope that is seen *is* not hope:
34. who *is* even at the right hand
9: 2. I *have* great heaviness
10: 1. prayer to God for Israel *is*, that they
8. The word *is* nigh thee,
12. For there *is* no difference
11: 6. then *is* it no more grace: otherwise work *is* no more work.
23. for God *is* able to graff them in again.
13: 1. For there *is* no power but of God:
4. For he *is* the minister of God to thee
— for he *is* the minister of God, a revenger
14: 4. for God *is* able to make him stand.
17. For the kingdom of God *is* not
23. whatsoever (is) not of faith *is* sin.
16: 5. who *is* the firstfruits of Achaia
1Co. 1:18. *is* to them that perish foolishness;
— it *is* the power of God.
25. the foolishness of God *is* wiser than men; and the weakness of God *is* stronger

1 Co. 2:14. for they *are* foolishness unto him:
3: 5. Who then *is* Paul,
7. neither *is* he that planteth any thing,
11. than that is laid, which *is* Jesus Christ.
13. every man's work of what sort it *is*.
17. the temple of God *is* holy,
19. wisdom of this world *is* foolishness
21. For all things *are* your's;
22. present, or things to come; all *are* your's:
4: 3. But with me it *is* a very small thing
4. he that judgeth me *is* the Lord.
17. who *is* my beloved son,
6: 5. that there *is* not a wise man among you?
7. there *is* utterly a fault among you,
15. *are* the members of Christ?
16. joined to an harlot *is* one body?
17. joined unto the Lord *is* one spirit.
18. a man doeth *is* without the body;
19. your body *is* the temple of the Holy Ghost
20. in your body, and in your spirit, which *are* God's.
7: 8. *is* good for them if they abide even as I.
9. for it *is* better to marry
14. else *were* your children unclean; but now *are* they holy.
19. Circumcision *is* nothing, and uncircumcision *is* nothing,
22. *is* the Lord's freeman:
— *is* Christ's servant.
29. it remaineth (lit. what remains *is*), that both they that have wives
39. she *is* at liberty to be married to whom
40. But she *is* happier if she so abide, after my judgment:
9: 3. Mine answer to them that do examine me *is* this,
16. I *have* nothing to glory of:
— yea, woe *is* unto me,
18. What *is* my reward then?
10:16. *is* it not the communion of the blood of Christ?
— *is* it not the communion of the body of Christ?
19. that the idol *is* any thing, or that which is offered in sacrifice to idols *is* any thing?
28. This *is* offered in sacrifice unto idols,
11: 3. the head of every man *is* Christ;
5. for that *is* even all one as if she were
7. but the woman *is* the glory of the man.
8. For the man *is* not of the woman;
13. *is* it comely that a woman
14. it *is* a shame unto him?
15. it *is* a glory to her:
20. (this) *is* not to eat the Lord's supper
24. Take, eat: this *is* my body,
25. This cup *is* the new testament in my
12: 6. but it *is* the same God which worketh
12. For as the body *is* one, and hath
— being many, *are* one body:
14. *is* not one member, but
15. *is* it therefore not of the body?
16. *is* it therefore not of the body?
22. seem to be more feeble, *are* necessary:
14:10. There *are*, it may be, so many kinds of
14. my understanding *is* unfruitful.
15. What *is* it then? I will pray
25. God *is* in you of a truth.
26. How *is* it then, brethren?
33. For God *is* not (the author) of confusion,
35. for it *is* a shame for women to speak in the church.

1Co.15:12. that there *is* no resurrection of
13. there *be* no resurrection of the dead,
44. There *is* a natural body, and there *is* a spiritual body.
58. *is* not in vain in the Lord.
16:15. that it *is* the firstfruits of Achaia,
2Co. 1:12. our rejoicing *is* this,
2: 2. who *is* he then that maketh me glad,
3. my joy *is* (the joy) of you all.
3:17. Now the Lord *is* that Spirit:
4: 3. But if our gospel *be* hid, it *is* hid to them that are lost:
4. who *is* the image of God,
7:15. *is* more abundant toward you,
9: 1. it *is* superfluous for me to write
12. not only supplieth (lit. *is* supplying)
10:18. For not he that commendeth himself *is* approved,
11:10. As the truth of Christ *is* in me,
12:13. For what *is* it wherein you were
13: 5. how that Jesus Christ *is* in you, except
Gal. 1: 7. Which *is* not another; but
11. preached of me *is* not after man.
3:12. And the law *is* not of faith:
16. And to thy seed, which *is* Christ.
20. a mediator *is* not (a mediator) of one, but God *is* one.
4: 1. the heir, as long as he *is* a child,
2. But *is* under tutors and
24. Which things *are* an allegory:
— which *is* Agar.
25. *is* mount Sinai in Arabia,
26. But Jerusalem which is above *is* free, which *is* the mother of us all.
5: 3. he *is* a debtor to do the whole
19. Now the works of the flesh *are* manifest, which *are* (these);
22. the fruit of the Spirit *is* love, joy,
23. against such there *is* no law.
Eph. 1:14. Which *is* the earnest of our inheritance
18. that ye may know what *is* the hope
23. Which *is* his body,
2:14. For he *is* our peace,
3:13. for you, which *is* your glory.
4: 9. Now that he ascended, what *is* it but
10. *is* the same also that ascended up
15. which *is* the head, (even) Christ:
21. as the truth *is* in Jesus:
5: 5. who *is* an idolater, hath any
10. what *is* acceptable unto the Lord.
12. For it *is* a shame even to speak of
13. whatsoever doth make manifest *is* light.
18. wherein *is* excess;
23. the husband *is* the head of the wife,
— he *is* the saviour of the body.
32. This *is* a great mystery:
6: 1. in the Lord: for this *is* right.
2. which *is* the first commandment
9. your Master also *is* in heaven; neither *is* there respect of persons with him.
12. we wrestle not against (lit. The wrestling *is* not to us against)
17. which *is* the word of God:
Phi. 1: 7. Even as it *is* meet for me to
8. For God *is* my record,
28. which *is* to them an evident token
2:13. For it *is* God which worketh in you both
4: 8. whatsoever things *are* true, whatsoever
Col. 1: 6. and bringeth forth fruit, (lit. *is* fruit-bearing)
7. who *is* for you a faithful minister
15. Who *is* the image of the invisible God,

Col. 1: 17. he *is* before all things,
18. he *is* the head of the body, the church: who *is* the beginning, the firstborn
24. for his body's sake, which *is* the church:
27. which *is* Christ in you,
2:10. which *is* the head of all
17. Which *are* a shadow of things to come;
22. Which all *are* to perish
23. Which things have indeed a shew (lit. which *are* holding some account of wisdom)
3: 1. where Christ sitteth (lit. *is* sitting) on the right hand of God.
5. and covetousness, which *is* idolatry:
14. which *is* the bond of perfectness.
20. for this *is* well pleasing
25. there *is* no respect of persons.
4: 9. who *is* (one) of you.
1Th. 2:13. as it *is* in truth,
4: 3. For this *is* the will of God,
2Th. 1: 3. as it *is* meet, because that
2: 4. himself that he *is* God.
9. whose coming *is* after the working of Satan
3: 3. But the Lord *is* faithful,
17. which *is* the token in every epistle:
1Ti. 1: 5. the end of the commandment *is* charity
20. Of whom *is* Hymenæus
3:15. in the house of God, which *is* the church
16. great *is* the mystery of godliness:
4: 8. profiteth (lit. *is* pr. for) little: but godliness *is* profitable unto all things,
10. who *is* the saviour of all men,
5: 4. parents: for that *is* good and
8. and *is* worse than an infidel.
25. the good works (of some) *are* manifest beforehand;
6: 6. with contentment *is* great gain.
10. the love of money *is* the root of all evil:
2Ti. 1: 6. which *is* in thee by the putting on
12. he *is* able to keep that which I
15. of whom *are* Phygellus
2:17. of whom *is* Hymenæus and Philetus;
20. there *are* not only vessels
4:11. Only Luke *is* with me.
— for he *is* profitable to me
Tit. 1: 6. If any *be* blameless, the husband of one
13. This witness *is* true. Wherefore
3: 8. These things *are* good and profitable
Heb. 2: 6. What *is* man, that thou art mindful
4:13. Neither *is* there any creature that
5:13. for he *is* a babe.
14. But strong meat *belongeth to* them that
7: 2. which *is*, King of peace;
15. it *is* yet far more evident: for that
8: 6. he *is* the mediator of a better covenant,
9: 5. of which we cannot now speak (lit. it *is* not now to speak)
15. he *is* the mediator of the new testament,
11: 1. Now faith *is* the substance of things hoped for,
6. cometh to God must believe that he *is*,
12: 7. for what son *is* he whom the father
Jas. 1:13. cannot be tempted (lit. *is* not to be tempted) with evil,
17. perfect gift *is* from above, and
23. if any *be* a hearer of the word, and not
27. before God and the Father *is* this,
2:17. hath not works, *is* dead, being alone.
19. Thou believest that there *is* one God;
20. faith without works *is* dead?
26. the body without the spirit *is* dead, so faith without works *is* dead also.

Jas. 3: 5. the tongue *is* a little member,

15. This wisdom descendeth not (lit. this *is* not the wisdom that descendeth)

17. wisdom that is from above *is* first pure,

4: 4. the friendship of the world *is* enmity with God?

12. There *is* one lawgiver, who is able

14. It *is* even a vapour, that

16. all such rejoicing *is* evil.

17. to him it *is* sin.

5:11. the Lord *is* very pitiful, and of tender mercy.

1Pet.1: 6. if need *be*, ye are in heaviness

25. And this *is* the word which

2:15. so *is* the will of God,

3: 4. which *is* in the sight of God

22. *is* on the right hand of God ;

4:11. to whom *be* praise and dominion

2Pet.1: 9. *is* blind, and cannot see afar off,

14. shortly I must put off (this) my tabernacle, (lit. the putting off my tabernacle *is* at hand)

17. This *is* my beloved Son,

3: 4. Where *is* the promise of his coming?

16. in which *are* some things hard to be understood,

1Joh.1: 5. This then *is* the message

— God *is* light, and in him *is* no darkness at all.

7. as he *is* in the light,

8. and the truth *is* not in us.

9. he *is* faithful and just

10. his word *is* not in us.

2: 2. And he *is* the propitiation for our sins:

4. and keepeth not his commandments, *is* a liar, and the truth *is* not in him.

7. The old commandment *is* the word

8. which thing *is* true in him and in you:

9. hateth his brother, *is* in darkness

10. there *is* none occasion of stumbling in

11. he that hateth his brother *is* in darkness,

15. the love of the Father *is* not in him.

16. and the pride of life, *is* not of the Father, but *is* of the world.

18. children, it *is* the last time:

— whereby we know that it *is* the last time.

21. and that no lie *is* of the truth.

22. Who *is* a liar but he that denieth that Jesus *is* the Christ? He *is* antichrist, that denieth

25. And this *is* the promise that he

27. teacheth you of all things, and *is* truth, and *is* no lie,

29. If ye know that he *is* righteous,

3: 2. we shall see him as he *is*.

3. purifieth himself, even as he *is* pure.

4. sin *is* the transgression of

5. in him *is* no sin.

7. he that doeth righteousness *is* righteous, even as he *is* righteous.

8. He that committeth sin *is* of the devil ;

10. the children of God *are* manifest,

— doeth not righteousness *is* not of God,

11. For this *is* the message that ye heard

15. hateth his brother *is* a murderer:

20. God *is* greater than our heart,

23. this *is* his commandment,

4: 1. whether they *are* of God:

2. come in the flesh *is* of God:

3. *is* not of God: and this *is* that (spirit) of antichrist,

— even now already *is* it in the world.

4. greater is he that *is* in you,

1Joh. 4: 6. he that *is* not of God

7. let us love one another: for love *is* of God ;

8. for God *is* love.

10. Herein *is* love, not that we loved God,

12. and his love *is* perfected in us.

15. confess that Jesus *is* the Son of God,

16. God *is* love ; and he that dwelleth in

17. because as he *is*, so are we in this world.

18. There *is* no fear in love ;

20. and hateth his brother, he *is* a liar: for

5: 1. that Jesus *is* the Christ is born

3. For this *is* the love of God, that we

4. this *is* the victory that overcometh

5. Who *is* he that overcometh the world, but he that believeth that Jesus *is* the Son of God?

6. This *is* he that came by water and

— it *is* the Spirit that beareth witness, because the Spirit *is* truth.

9. the witness of God *is* greater: for this *is* the witness of God

11. *is* the record, that God hath given to us eternal life, and this life *is* in his Son.

14. this *is* the confidence that we have

16. There *is* a sin unto death:

17. All unrighteousness *is* sin: and there *is* a sin not unto death.

20. This *is* the true God, and eternal life.

2Joh. 6. this *is* love, that we walk after his commandments. This *is* the commandment,

7. This *is* a deceiver and

3Joh. 11. He that doeth good *is* of God:

12. ye know that our record *is* true.

Rev. 1: 4. which *are* before his throne ;

2: 7. which *is* in the midst of the paradise

5: 2. Who *is* worthy to open the book, and

12. Worthy *is* the Lamb that was slain to

13. every creature which *is* in heaven,

— such as *are* in the sea, and all

13:10. Here *is* the patience and the faith of the

18. Here *is* wisdom. Let him that

— for it *is* the number of a man ;

14:12. Here *is* the patience of the saints:

16:21. plague thereof *was* exceeding great.

17: 8. beast that thou sawest was, and *is* not ;

— behold the beast that was, and *is* not, and yet *is*.

10. one *is*, (and) the other is not yet come ;

11. the beast that was, and *is* not, even he *is* the eighth, and *is* of the seven,

14. he *is* Lord of lords, and King of kings:

18. thou sawest *is* that great city, which

19: 8. *is* the righteousness of saints.

10. the testimony of Jesus *is* the spirit of

20: 2. serpent, which *is* the devil, and Satan,

12. which *is* (the book) of life:

14. This *is* the second death.

21: 1. there *was* no more sea.

8. which *is* the second death.

12. which *are* (the names) of the twelve tribes

16. the length *is* as large as the breadth:

— and the height of it *are* equal.

17. measure of a man, that *is*, of the angel.

22. the Lord God Almighty and the Lamb *are* the temple of it.

22:10. for the time *is* at hand.

See also *τουτέστι*.

ἔστω, ἔστωσαν, esto, estōsan.

Mat. 5:37. But *let* your communication *be*, Yea, yea ;

Mat. 18:17. *let* him *be* unto thee as an heathen man
  20:26. *let* him *be* your minister;
  27. chief among you, *let* him *be* your servant:
Lu. 12:35. *Let* your loins *be* girded about, and
Acts 1:20. let no man dwell therein: (lit. *let* there
    not *be* one dwelling in it)
  2:14. *be* this known unto you, and hearken
  4:10. *Be* it known unto you all,
  13:38. *Be* it known unto you therefore,
  28:28. *Be* it known therefore unto you,
2Co.12:16. But *be* it so, I did not burden
Gal. 1: 8. *let* him *be* accursed.
  9. than that ye have received, *let* him *be*
    accursed.
1Ti. 3:12. *Let* the deacons *be* the husbands of one
Jas. 1:19. *Let* every man *be* swift to hear, slow
1Pet.3: 3. *let* it not *be* that outward (adorning)

ἔσχατος, *eskatos.*

Mat. 5:26. till thou hast paid the *uttermost* farthing.
  12:45. the *last* (state) of that man is worse than
  19:30. many (that are) first shall be *last; and*
    the *last* (shall be) first.
  20: 8. beginning from the *last* unto the first.
  12. These *last* have wrought (but) one hour,
  14. I will give unto this *last*, even as
  16. So the *last* shall be first, and the first *last*:
    for many be
  27:64. the *last* error shall be worse than
Mar. 9:35. (the same) shall be *last* of all,
  10:31. But many (that are) first shall be *last;*
    and the *last* first.
  12: 6. he sent him also *last* unto them,
  22. *last* of all the woman died
Lu. 11:26. the *last* (state) of that man is worse
  12:59. till thou hast paid the very *last* mite.
  13:30. there are *last* which shall be first, and
    there are first which shall be *last.*
  14: 9. with shame to take the *lowest* room.
  10. go and sit down in the *lowest* room;
Joh. 6:39. raise it up again at the *last* day.
  40. I will raise him up at the *last* day.
  44. I will raise him up at the *last* day.
  54. and I will raise him up at the *last* day.
  7:37. In the *last* day, that great (day)
  8: 9. at the eldest, (even) unto the *last:*
  11:24. in the resurrection at the *last* day.
  12:48. the same shall judge him in the *last* day.
Acts 1: 8. unto the *uttermost* (part) of the earth.
  2:17. shall come to pass in the *last* days,
  13:47. unto the ends of the earth. (lit. unto the
    uttermost part of the earth)
1Co. 4: 9. hath set forth us the apostles *last*, as it
    were appointed to death:
  15: 8. And *last* of all he was seen of me
  26. The *last* enemy (that) shall be destroyed
  45. the *last* Adam (was made) a quickening
  52. at the *last* trump:
2Ti. 3: 1. in the *last* days perilous times
Heb 1: 2(1). Hath in these *last* days spoken
Jas. 5: 3. treasure together for the *last* days.
1Pet.1: 5. ready to be revealed in the *last* time.
  20. was manifest in these *last* times
2Pet.2:20. the *latter* end is worse with them than
  3: 3. shall come in the *last* days scoffers,
1Joh.2:18. children, it is the *last* time:
  — whereby we know that it is the *last* time.
Jude 18. should be mockers in the *last* time,

Rev. 1:11. I am Alpha and Omega, the first and the
    last :
  17. Fear not; I am the first and the *last:*
  2: 8. saith the first and the *last,*
  19. the *last* (to be) more than the first.
  15: 1. having the seven *last* plagues;
  21: 9. vials full of the seven *last* plagues,
  22:13. the first and the *last.*

ἐσχάτως, *eskatōs.*

Mar. 5:23. lieth at the point of death: (lit. is *in the*
    last state)

ἔσω, *eso.*

Mat.26:58. went *in*, and sat with the servants,·
Mar.14:54. even into (lit. even *within* into) the palace
  15:16. led him away *into* the hall,
Joh.20:26. his disciples were *within*, and Thomas
Acts 5:23. opened, we found no man *within.*
Ro. 7:22. I delight in the law of God after the *in-*
    ward man:
1Co. 5:12. do not ye judge them that are *within ?*
Eph. 3:16. to be strengthened with might by his
    Spirit in the *inner* man;

ἔσωθεν, *esōthen.*

Mat. 7:15. but *inwardly* they are ravening wolves.
  23:25. but *within* they are full of extortion
  27. but are *within* full of dead
  28. but *within* ye are full of hypocrisy
Mar. 7:21. For *from within*, out of the heart
  23. come *from within*, and defile the man.
Lu. 11: 7. And he *from within* shall answer
  39. your *inward* part is full of ravening
  40. make that which is *within* also?
2Co. 4:16. yet the *inward* (man) is renewed
  7: 5. without (were) fightings, *within* (were)
Rev. 4: 8. (they were) full of eyes *within:*
  5: 1. a book written *within* and on the
  11: 2. But the court which is *without* the temple
    (in some copies ἔξωθεν)

ἐσώτερος, *esōteros.*

Acts16:24. thrust them into the *inner* prison,
Heb. 6:19. into that *within* the veil;

ἑταῖρος, *hetairos.*

Mat.11:16. and calling unto their *fellows,*
  20:13. *Friend*, I do thee no wrong:
  22:12. *Friend*, how camest thou in
  26:50. *Friend*, wherefore art thou come ?

ἑτερόγλωσσος, *heteroglōssos.*

1Co.14:21. With (men of) *other* tongues

ἑτεροδιδασκαλέω, *heterodidaskaleo.*

1Ti. 1: 3. that they *teach* no *other* doctrine,
  6: 3. If any man *teach otherwise,*

ἑτεροζυγέω, heterozugeo.

2Co. 6:14. *unequally yoked together with* unbelievers:

ἕτερος, heteros.

Mat. 6:24. for either he will hate the one, and love
the *other;* or else he will hold to the
one, and despise the *other.*
8:21. And *another* of his disciples said
11: 3. or do we look for *another?*
12:45. taketh with himself seven *other* spirits
more wicked
15:30. dumb, maimed, and many *others,*
16:14. and *others,* Jeremias,
Mar16:12. he appeared in *another* form
Lu. 3:18. And many *other* things in his exhortation
preached he
4:43. to *other* cities also:
5: 7. which were in the *other* ship,
6: 6. also on *another* sabbath,
7:41. and the *other* fifty.
8: 3. and many *others,* which ministered
6. And *some* fell upon a rock;
7. And *some* fell among thorns;
8. And *other* fell on good ground,
9:29. the fashion of his countenance was *altered,*
(lit. became *other*)
56. And they went to *another* village.
59. And he said unto *another,*
61. And *another* also said,
10: 1. appointed *other* seventy also,
11:16. And *others,* tempting (him),
26. seven *other* spirits
14:19. *another* said, I have bought
20. And *another* said,
31. to make war against *another* king.
16: 7. said he to *another,* And how much
13. and love the *other;* or else he will hold
to the one, and despise the *other.*
18. and marrieth *another,*
17:34. and the *other* shall be left.
35. be taken, and the *other* left.
18:10. and the *other* a publican.
19:20. And *another* came, saying,
20:11. he sent *another* servant:
22:58. *another* saw him, and said,
65. many *other* things blasphemously
23:32. there were also two *other,* malefactors,
led with him
40. But the *other* answering
Joh.19:37. again *another* scripture saith,
Acts 1:20. let *another* take.
2: 4. to speak with *other* tongues,
13. *Others* mocking said, These men
40. And with many *other* words
4:12. there is none *other* name under
7:18. *another* king arose, which
8:34. or of some *other* man?
12:17. and went into *another* place.
13:35. Wherefore he saith also in *another* (psalm),
15:35. with many *others* also.
17: 7. that there is *another* king, (one) Jesus.
21. spent their time in nothing *else,* but
34. and *others* with them.
19:39. But if ye enquire any thing concerning
other matters,
20:15. and the *next* (day) we arrived
23: 6. the one part were Sadducees, and the
other Pharisees,
27: 1. and certain *other* prisoners
3. And the *next* (day) we touched

Ro. 2: 1. thou judgest *another,*
21. Thou therefore which teachest *another,*
7: 3. she be married to *another* man,
— though she be married to *another* man.
4. that ye should be married to *another,*
23. *another* law in my members,
8:39. nor any *other* creature,
13: 8. he that loveth *another* hath fulfilled
9. if (there be) any *other* commandment,
1Co. 3: 4. and *another,* I (am) of Apollos;
4: 6. be puffed up for one against *another.*
6: 1. having a matter against *another,*
8: 4. (there is) none *other* God
10:24. but every man *another's* (wealth).
29. not thine own, but of the *other:*
12: 9. To *another* faith by the same Spirit;
10. to *another* (divers) kinds of tongues;
14:17. but the *other* is not edified.
21. and *other* lips will I speak unto this
15:40. the glory of the celestial (is) *one,* and the
(glory) of the terrestrial (is) *another.*
2Co. 8: 8. by occasion of the forwardness of *others,*
11: 4. or (if) ye receive *another* spirit,
— or *another* gospel, which ye have not
Gal. 1: 6. unto *another* gospel:
19. But *other* of the apostles
6: 4. in himself alone, and not in *another.*
Eph. 3: 5. Which in *other* ages was not made known
Phi. 2: 4. every man also on the things of *others.*
1Ti. 1:10. and if there be any *other* thing
2Ti. 2: 2. who shall be able to teach *others* also.
Heb. 5: 6. As he saith also in *another* (place),
7:11. that *another* priest should rise
13. pertaineth to *another* tribe,
15. there ariseth *another* priest,
11:36. And *others* had trial of (cruel) mockings
Jas. 2:25. and had sent (them) out *another* way?
4:12. who art thou that judgest *another?*
Jude 7. and going after *strange* flesh,

ἑτέρως, heterōs.

Phi. 3:15. if in any thing ye be *otherwise* minded,

ἔτι, eti.

Mat. 5:13. it is *thenceforth* good for nothing,
12:46. While he *yet* talked to the people,
17: 5. While he *yet* spake, behold, a bright
18:16. (then) take with thee one or two *more,*
19:20. what lack I *yet?*
26:47. And while he *yet* spake,
65. what *further* need have we
27:63. said, while he was *yet* alive,
Mar. 5:35. While he *yet* spake, there came from
— troublest thou the Master any *further?*
8:17. have ye your heart *yet* hardened?
12: 6. Having *yet* therefore one son,
14:43. immediately, while he *yet* spake,
63. What need we any *further* witnesses?
Lu. 1:15. *even* from his mother's womb.
8:49. While he *yet* spake, there cometh
9:42. And as he was *yet* a coming,
14:22. and *yet* there is room.
26. yea, and his own life *also,*
32. while the other is *yet* a great way off,
15:20. But when he was *yet* a great way off,
16: 2. for thou mayest be no *longer* steward.
18:22. *Yet* lackest thou one thing:

Lu. 20:36. can they die *any more:*
    40. And *after that* they durst not ask
   22:37. that this that is written must *yet* be accomplished in me,
    47. And while he *yet* spake,
    60. while he *yet* spake, the cock crew.
    71. What need we *any further* witness?
   24: 6. when he was *yet* in Galilee,
    41. And while they *yet* believed not
    44. while I was *yet* with you,
Joh. 4:35. There are *yet* four months,
   7:33. *Yet* a little while am I with you,
  11:54. no *more* openly among the Jews;
  12:35. *Yet* a little while is the light
  13:33. *yet* a little while I am with you.
  14:19. *Yet* a little while, and the world seeth me
    no *more;*
    30. *Hereafter* I will not talk much
  16:10. ye see me no *more;*
    12. I have *yet* many things to say
    21. she remembereth no *more* the anguish,
    25. no *more* speak unto you in proverbs,
  17:11. I am no *more* in the world,
  20: 1. when it was *yet* dark,
   21: 6. *now* they were not able to draw it
Acts 2:26. *moreover* also my flesh shall rest in hope:
   9: 1. *yet* breathing out threatenings
  10:44. While Peter *yet* spake
  18:18. Paul (after this) tarried (there) *yet* a
    good while,
  21:28. and *further* brought Greeks also
Ro. 3: 7. why *yet* am I also judged as a sinner?
   5: 6. For when we were *yet* without strength,
    8. while we were *yet* sinners,
   6: 2. dead to sin, live *any longer* therein?
    9. raised from the dead dieth no *more;* death
    hath no *more* dominion over him.
   7:17. then it is no *more* I that do it, but sin
    20. I would not, it is no *more* I that do it,
   9:19. Why doth he *yet* find fault?
  11: 6. then (is it) no *more* of works: otherwise
    grace is no *more* grace. But if (it be)
    of works, then is it no *more* grace:
    otherwise work is no *more* work.
  14:15. now walkest thou not charitably.
1Co. 3: 2. neither *yet* now are ye able.
    3. For ye are *yet* carnal:
  12:31. and *yet* shew I unto you a more excellent
  15:17. ye are *yet* in your sins.
2Co. 1:10. that he will *yet* deliver (us);
   5:16. *yet* now *henceforth* know we (him) no
    more. (lit. we know him no *more hence-
    forth*)
Gal. 1:10. for if I *yet* pleased men,
   2:20. nevertheless I live; *yet* not I, (lit. live no
    more I,) but Christ liveth in me:
   3:18. (it is) no *more* of promise:
    25. we are no *longer* under a schoolmaster.
   4: 7. thou art no *more* a servant,
   5:11. if I *yet* preach circumcision, why do I *yet*
    suffer persecution?
Phi. 1: 9. your love may abound *yet* more and more
2Th. 2: 5. when I was *yet* with you,
Heb 7:10. he was *yet* in the loins of his father,
    11. what *further* need (was there)
    15. it is *yet* far more evident:
   8:12. will I remember no *more.*
   9: 8. the first tabernacle was *yet* standing:
  10: 2. should have had no *more* conscience
    17. will I remember no *more.*
    18. (there is) no *more* offering for sin,
    26. remaineth no *more* sacrifice for sins,

Heb 10:37. For *yet* a little while, and he that
  11: 4. he being dead *yet* speaketh.
    32. And what shall I *more* say?
    36. yea, *moreover* of bonds and
  12:26. saying, *Yet* once *more* I shake
    27. And this (word), *Yet* once *more,*
Rev. 3:12. he shall go no *more* out:
   6:11. they should rest *yet* for a little
   7:16. They shall hunger no *more,* neither thirst
    any more;
   9:12. there come two woes *more*
  10: 6. there should be time no *longer :*
  12: 8. their place found *any more* in heaven.
  18:21. shall be found no *more* at all.
    22. shall be heard no *more* at all in thee;
   — shall be found *any more* in thee;
   — shall be heard no *more* at all in thee;
    23. shall shine no *more* at all in thee;
   — shall be heard no *more* at all
  20: 3. should deceive the nations no *more,*
  21: 1. there was no *more* sea.
    4. there shall be no *more* death,
   — shall there be *any more* pain:
  22: 3. there shall be no *more* curse:
    11. him be unjust *still:* and he which is filthy,
    let him be filthy *still:* and he that is
    righteous, let him be righteous *still:*
    and he that is holy, let him be holy
    still.

       See also οὐκέτι.

ἑτοιμάζω, hetoimazo.

Mat. 3: 3. *Prepare* ye the way of the Lord,
  20:23. for whom it is *prepared* of my Father.
  22: 4. I have *prepared* my dinner:
  25:34. inherit the kingdom *prepared* for you
    41. *prepared* for the devil
  26:17. that we *prepare* for thee to eat
    19. they *made ready* the passover.
Mar. 1: 3. *Prepare* ye the way of the Lord,
  10:40. for whom it is *prepared.*
  14:12. Where wilt thou that we go and *prepare*
    15. there *make ready* for us.
    16. and they *made ready* the passover.
Lu. 1:17. *to make ready* a people prepared for the
    Lord.
    76. face of the Lord *to prepare* his ways;
   2:31. Which thou *hast prepared* before the face
    of all people;
   3: 4. *Prepare* ye the way of the Lord,
   9:52. to *make ready* for him.
  12:20. which thou *hast provided?*
    47. which knew his lord's will, and *prepared*
    not (himself),
  17: 8. *Make ready* wherewith I may sup,
  22: 8. Go and *prepare* us the passover,
    9. Where wilt thou that we *prepare?*
    12. there *make ready.*
    13. they *made ready* the passover.
  23:56. *prepared* spices and ointments;
  24: 1. the spices which they *had prepared,*
Joh. 14: 2. I go *to prepare* a place for you.
    3. if I go and *prepare* a place for you,
Acts 23:23. *Make ready* two hundred soldiers
1Co. 2: 9. the things which God *hath prepared* for
    them that love him.
2Ti. 2:21. *prepared* unto every good work.
Philem 22. *prepare* me also a lodging:
Heb 11:16. for he *hath prepared* for them a city.
Rev. 8: 6. *prepared* themselves to sound.

Rev. 9: 7. like unto horses *prepared* unto battle ;
  15. *which were prepared* for an hour,
 12: 6. a place *prepared* of God,
 16:12. that the way of the kings of the east *might be prepared.*
 19: 7. and his wife *hath made* herself *ready.*
 21: 2. out of heaven, *prepared* as a bride adorned for her husband.

ἑτοιμασία, hetoimasia.

Eph. 6:15. with the *preparation* of the gospel

ἕτοιμος, hetoimos.

Mat.22: 4. and all things (are) *ready:*
  8. The wedding is *ready,* but they
 24:44. be ye also *ready:* for in such an hour as
 25:10. they that were *ready* went in with him
Mar.14:15. upper room furnished (and) *prepared:*
Lu. 12:40. Be ye therefore *ready* also: for the Son
 14:17. all things are now *ready.*
 22:33. Lord, I am *ready* to go with thee,
Joh. 7: 6. but your time is alway *ready.*
Acts23:15. ever he come near, are *ready* to kill him.
  21. and now are they *ready,* looking for
2Co. 9: 5. that the same might be *ready,*
 10: 6. And having in a *readiness* to revenge
  16. of things *made ready* to our hand.
Tit. 3: 1. to be *ready* to every good work,
1Pet.1: 5. unto salvation *ready* to be revealed
 3:15. and (be) *ready* always to (give) an answer ...with meekness and fear:

ἑτοίμως, hetoimōs.

Acts21:13. I am *ready* (lit. hold myself *preparedly*)
2Co.12:14. the third time I am *ready* (lit. hold, &c.)
1Pet.4: 5. to him that is *ready* (lit. hold, &c.)

ἔτος, etos.

Mat. 9:20. which was diseased with an issue of blood twelve *years,*
Mar 5:25. an issue of blood twelve *years,*
  42. for she was (of the age) of twelve *years.*
Lu. 2:36. had lived with an husband seven *years*
  37. of about fourscore and four *years,*
  41. parents went to Jerusalem every *year*
  42. when he was twelve *years* old,
 3: 1. Now in the fifteenth *year* of the reign
  23. began to be about thirty *years* of age,
 4:25. three *years* and six months,
 8:42. about twelve *years* of age,
  43. having an issue of blood twelve *years,*
 12:19. laid up for many *years* ;
 13: 7. these three *years* I come
  8. Lord, let it alone this *year* also,
  11. a spirit of infirmity eighteen *years,*
  16. Satan hath bound, lo, these eighteen *years,*
 15:29. these many *years* do I serve thee,
Joh. 2:20. Forty and six *years* was this temple in
 5: 5. an infirmity thirty and eight *years.*
 8:57. Thou art not yet fifty *years* old,
Acts 4:22. the man was above forty *years* old,
 7: 6. entreat (them) evil four hundred *years,*
  30. when forty *years* were expired,

Acts 7:36. and in the wilderness forty *years.*
  42. forty *years* in the wilderness ?
 9:33. had kept his bed eight *years,*
 13:20. four hundred and fifty *years,*
  21. by the space of forty *years.*
 19:10. continued by the space of two *years ;*
 24:10. thou hast been of many *years*
  17. Now after many *years* I came
Ro. 15:23. a great desire these many *years* to
2Co.12: 2. about fourteen *years* ago,
Gal. 1:18. Then after three *years* I went up
 2: 1. Then fourteen *years* after I went
 3:17. four hundred and thirty *years* after,
1Ti. 5: 9. into the number under threescore *years* old,
Heb 1:12. thy *years* shall not fail.
 3: 9. my works forty *years.*
  17. was he grieved forty *years?*
2Pet.3: 8. one day (is) with the Lord as a thousand *years,* and a thousand *years* as one day.
Rev.20: 2. bound him a thousand *years,*
  3. the thousand *years* should be fulfilled:
  4. lived and reigned with Christ a thousand *years.*
  5. until the thousand *years* were finished.
  6. shall reign with him a thousand *years.*
  7. when the thousand *years* are expired,

εὖ, ū.

Mat.25:21. *Well done,* (thou) good and faithful servant:
  23. *Well done,* good and faithful servant;
Mar 14: 7. whensoever ye will ye may do them *good:*
Lu. 19:17. *Well,* thou good servant:
Acts15:29. ye shall do *well.* Fare ye well.
Eph 6: 3. That it may be *well* with thee,

εὐαγγελίζω, -ομαι, ūangelizo, -omai.

Mat.11: 5. the poor have the gospel *preached* to them.
Lu. 1:19. to shew thee these *glad tidings.*
 2:10. I bring you *good tidings* of great joy,
 3:18. *preached* he unto the people.
 4:18. *to preach the gospel* to the poor ;
  43. I must *preach* the kingdom of God to
 7:22. to the poor *the gospel is preached.*
 8: 1. *preaching* and *shewing the glad tidings*
 9: 6. *preaching the gospel,* and healing
 16:16. the kingdom of God *is preached,*
 20: 1. in the temple, and *preached the gospel,*
Acts 5:42. to teach and *preach* Jesus Christ.
 8: 4. went every where *preaching* the word.
  12. *preaching* the things concerning
  25. *preached the gospel* in many villages
  35. and *preached* unto him Jesus.
  40. he *preached* in all the cities,
 10:36. *preaching* peace by Jesus Christ:
 11:20. *preaching* the Lord Jesus.
 13:32. we *declare* unto you *glad tidings,*
 14: 7. And there they preached the gospel. (lit. were *preaching the gospel*)
  15. and *preach* unto you that ye should turn
  21. And when they *had preached the gospel*
 15:35. and *preaching* the word of the Lord,
 16:10. *to preach the gospel* unto them.
 17:18. he *preached* unto them
Ro. 1:15. *to preach the gospel* to you that are at Rome
 10:15. of them *that preach the gospel* of peace, and *bring glad tidings* of good things !

Ro. 15:20. have I strived *to preach the gospel*,
1Co. 1:17. but *to preach the gospel :*
    9:16. For though I *preach the gospel*,
    — if I *preach* not *the gospel!*
    18. *when* I *preach the gospel*, I may make the
    15: 1. which I *preached* unto you,
      2. in memory what I *preached* unto you,
2Co.10:16. *To preach the gospel* in the (regions) be-
    yond you,
    11: 7. I *have preached* to you the gospel
Gal. 1: 8. *preach* any other *gospel* unto you than that
    which we *have preached* unto you,
    9. if any (man) *preach* any other *gospel*
    11. the gospel *which was preached* of me
    16. that I *might preach* him
    23. now *preacheth* the faith
    4:13. I *preached the gospel* unto you
Eph. 2:17. And came and *preached*
    3: 8. that I should *preach* among the Gentiles
1Th. 3: 6. and *brought* us *good tidings* of your
Heb. 4: 2. unto us *was the gospel preached*, (lit. we
    are *addressed with the gospel*)
    6. they to whom it was first preached (lit.
    those first *addressed with the gospel*)
    entered not
1Pet. 1:12. by them *that have preached the gospel*
    25. the word *which by the gospel is preached*
    unto you.
    4: 6. *was the gospel preached* also to them that
    are dead,
Rev.10: 7. as he *hath declared* to his servants the
    prophets.
    14: 6. *to preach* unto them that dwell on the
    earth, and to every nation, and

εὐαγγέλιον, *ūangelion.*

Mat. 4:23. preaching the *gospel* of the kingdom,
    9:35. and preaching the *gospel*
    24:14. this *gospel* of the kingdom
    26:13. Wheresoever this *gospel* shall be preached
Mar. 1: 1. The beginning of the *gospel* of Jesus
    Christ,
    14. the *gospel* of the kingdom of God,
    15. repent ye, and believe the *gospel*.
    8:35. for my sake and the *gospel's*,
    10:29. for my sake, and the *gospel's*,
    13:10. the *gospel* must first be published
    14: 9. this *gospel* shall be preached
    16:15. preach the *gospel* to every creature.
Acts15: 7. should hear the word of the *gospel*,
    20:24. to testify the *gospel* of the grace of God.
Ro. 1: 1. separated unto the *gospel*
    9. in the *gospel* of his Son,
    16. For I am not ashamed of the *gospel*
    2:16. according to my *gospel*.
    10:16. they have not all obeyed the *gospel*.
    11:28. As concerning the *gospel*,
    15:16. ministering the *gospel* of God, that
    19. I have fully preached the *gospel*
    29. of the blessing of the *gospel*
    16:25. according to my *gospel*,
1Co. 4:15. I have begotten you through the *gospel*.
    9:12. lest we should hinder the *gospel* of Christ.
    14. that they which preach the *gospel* should
    live of the *gospel*.
    18. I may make the *gospel* of Christ without
    charge, that I abuse not my power in
    the *gospel*.
    23. I do for the *gospel's* sake,
    15: 1. the *gospel* which I preached

2Co. 2:12. to (preach) Christ's *gospel*,
    4: 3. if our *gospel* be hid, it is hid to
    4. the light of the glorious *gospel*
    8:18. whose praise (is) in the *gospel*
    9:13. unto the *gospel* of Christ,
    10:14. in (preaching) the *gospel* of Christ:
    11: 4. or another *gospel*, which ye have not
    accepted,
    7. I have preached to you the *gospel* of God
    freely?
Gal. 1: 6. unto another *gospel :*
    7. would pervert the *gospel* of Christ.
    11. that the *gospel* which was preached
    2: 2. communicated unto them that *gospel*
    5. that the truth of the *gospel* might
    7. the *gospel* of the uncircumcision
    14. according to the truth of the *gospel*,
Eph. 1:13. the *gospel* of your salvation :
    3: 6. in Christ by the *gospel :*
    6:15. with the preparation of the *gospel*
    19. the mystery of the *gospel*,
Phi. 1: 5. For your fellowship in the *gospel*
    7. and confirmation of the *gospel*, ye all
    12. unto the furtherance of the *gospel ;*
    17. for the defence of the *gospel*.
    27. your conversation be as it becometh the
    gospel of Christ:
    — striving together for the faith of the
    gospel ;
    2:22. he hath served with me in the *gospel*.
    4: 3. laboured with me in the *gospel*,
    15. in the beginning of the *gospel*,
Col. 1: 5. in the word of the truth of the *gospel ;*
    23. from the hope of the *gospel*,
1Th. 1: 5. For our *gospel* came not unto you
    2: 2. to speak unto you the *gospel* of God
    4. to be put in trust with the *gospel*,
    8. not the *gospel* of God only,
    9. we preached unto you the *gospel* of God.
    3: 2. fellowlabourer in the *gospel* of Christ,
2Th. 1: 8. and that obey not the *gospel* of our
    2:14. he called you by our *gospel*, to the
1Ti. 1:11. According to the glorious *gospel*
2Ti. 1: 8. be thou partaker of the afflictions of the
    gospel
    10. immortality to light through the *gospel:*
    2: 8. according to my *gospel :*
Philem 13. in the bonds of the *gospel:*
1Pet. 4:17. of them that obey not the *gospel* of God?
Rev.14: 6. having the everlasting *gospel*

εὐαγγελιστής, *ūangelistees.*

Acts21: 8. the house of Philip the *evangelist*,
Eph. 4:11. and some, *evangelists ;* and some,
2Ti. 4: 5. do the work of an *evangelist*,

εὐαρεστέω, *ūaresteo.*

Heb11: 5. had this testimony, that he *pleased* God.
    6. (it is) impossible *to please* (him):
    13:16. for with such sacrifices God *is well pleased*.

εὐάρεστος, *ūarestos.*

Ro. 12: 1. a living sacrifice, holy, *acceptable* (lit.
    well-pleasing) unto God,
    2. that good, and *acceptable*, and
    14:18. *acceptable* to God, and approved of men.
2Co. 5: 9. we may be *accepted* of him. (lit. to be
    well-pleasing unto him)
Eph. 5:10. what is *acceptable* unto the Lord.

Phi. 4:18. *wellpleasing* to God.
Col. 3:20. for this is *wellpleasing* unto the Lord.
Tit. 2: 9. (and) to please (them) well (lit. to be *well-pleasing*) in all (things);
Heb 13:21. working in you that which is *wellpleasing* in his sight, through Jesus Christ;

εὐαρέστως, *ūarestōs.*

Heb 12:28. we may serve God *acceptably*

εὐγενὴς, *ūgenees.*

Lu. 19:12. A certain *noble*man went into a far
Acts17:11. These were *more noble* than
1Cor. 1:26. not many *noble*, (are called):

εὐδία, *ūdia.*

Mat.16: 2. ye say, (It will be) *fair weather:*

εὐδοκέω, *ūdokeo.*

Mat. 3:17. in whom I *am well pleased.*
12:18. in whom my soul *is well pleased:*
17: 5. in whom I *am well pleased;*
Mar. 1:11. in whom I *am well pleased.*
Lu. 3:22. in thee I *am well pleased.*
12:32. it is your Father's *good pleasure* (lit. your Father *is well pleased*) to give
Ro. 15:26. it *hath pleased* them of Macedonia and Achaia (lit. Macedonia and Achaia *have been pleased*)
27. It *hath pleased* them verily; and
1Co. 1:21. it *pleased* God (lit. God *has been pleased*) by the foolishness of preaching
10: 5. with many of them God *was not well pleased:*
2Co. 5: 8. We are confident, (I say), and *willing*
12:10. Therefore I *take pleasure* in infirmities,
Gal. 1:15. But when it *pleased* God,
Col. 1:19. it *pleased* (the Father) that in him should all fulness dwell;
1Th. 2: 8. we *were willing* to have imparted
3: 1. we *thought* it *good* to be left
2Th. 2:12. but *had pleasure* in unrighteousness.
Heb 10: 6. thou *hast had* no *pleasure.*
8. neither *hadst pleasure* (therein);
38. my soul shall *have* no *pleasure* in him.
2Pet. 1:17. in whom I *am well pleased.*

εὐδοκία, *ūdokia.*

Mat.11:26. for so it seemed good (lit. it was *well-seeming*) in thy sight.
Lu. 2:14. *good will* toward men.
10:21. for so it seemed *good* (lit. was, &c.) in thy sight.
Ro. 10: 1. Brethren, my heart's *desire*
Eph. 1: 5. according to the *good pleasure* of his will,
9. according to his *good pleasure*
Phi. 1:15. and some also of *good will:*
2.13. to will and to do of (his) *good pleasure.*
2Th. 1:11. all the *good pleasure* of (his) goodness,

εὐεργεσία, *ūergesia.*

Acts 4: 9. of the *good deed done* to the impotent man,
1Ti. 6: 2. are faithful and beloved, partakers of the *benefit.*

εὐεργετέω, *ūergeteo.*

Acts10:38. who went about *doing good,*

εὐεργέτης, *ūergetees.*

Lu. 22:25. they that exercise authority upon them are called *benefactors.*

εὔθετος, *ūthetos.*

Lu. 9:62. looking back, is *fit* for the kingdom of God.
14:35. It is neither *fit* for the land, nor yet for the dunghill;
Heb. 6: 7. bringeth forth herbs *meet* for them by whom it is dressed,

---

εὐθέως, *ūtheōs.*

Mat. 4:20. *straightway* left (their) nets,
22. *immediately* left the ship
8: 3. *immediately* his leprosy was cleansed.
13: 5. *forthwith* they sprung up,
14:22. *straightway* Jesus constrained
27. But *straightway* Jesus spake
31. And *immediately* Jesus stretched forth
20:34. *immediately* their eyes received sight,
21: 2. *straightway* ye shall find an ass
3. and *straightway* he will send them.
24:29. *Immediately* after the tribulation
25:15. and *straightway* took his journey.
26:49. And *forthwith* he came to Jesus,
74. *immediately* the cock crew.
27:48. *straightway* one of them ran,
Mar. 1:10. *straightway* coming up out of the water,
18. *straightway* they forsook their nets,
20. And *straightway* he called them:
21. and *straightway* on the sabbath day
29. *forthwith,* when they were come out of the synagogue,
30. *anon* they tell him of her.
31. *immediately* the fever left her,
42. *immediately* the leprosy departed from him,
43. *forthwith* sent him away;
2: 2. *straightway* many were gathered
8. *immediately* when Jesus perceived
12. And *immediately* he arose,
3: 6. *straightway* took counsel with the Herodians
4: 5. and *immediately* it sprang up,
15. Satan cometh *immediately,*
16. *immediately* receive it with gladness;
17. *immediately* they are offended.
29. *immediately* he putteth in the sickle,
5: 2. *immediately* there met him
13. *forthwith* Jesus gave them leave.
29. *straightway* the fountain of her blood
30. Jesus, *immediately* knowing in himself
36. As soon as Jesus heard the word
42. *straightway* the damsel arose,
6:25. she came in *straightway* with haste
27. *immediately* the king sent
45. *straightway* he constrained his
50. *immediately* he talked with them,
54. *straightway* they knew him,
7:35. *straightway* his ears were opened,
8:10. *straightway* he entered into a ship
9:15. *straightway* all the people, when they beheld

Mar 9:20. *straightway* the spirit tare
    24. *straightway* the father of the child
  10:52. And *immediately* he received his sight,
  11: 2. *as soon as* ye be entered into it,
    3. *straightway* he will send him
  14:43. *immediately*, while he yet spake,
    45. he goeth *straightway* to him, and saith,
  15: 1. *straightway* in the morning
Lu. 5:13. *immediately* the leprosy departed
    39. *straightway* desireth new:
  6:49. and *immediately* it fell ;
  12:36. they may open unto him *immediately*.
    54. *straightway* ye say, There cometh a shower ;
  14: 5. will not *straightway* pull him out
  17: 7. will say unto him *by and by*,
  21: 9. but the end (is) not *by and by*.
Joh. 5: 9. *immediately* the man was made whole,
  6:21. *immediately* the ship was at the
  13:30. received the sop went *immediately* out:
  18:27. *immediately* the cock crew.
Acts 9:18. *immediately* there fell from his eyes
    20. And *straightway* he preached Christ
    34. And he arose *immediately*.
  12:10. *forthwith* the angel departed
  16:10. *immediately* we endeavoured to go
  17:10. the brethren *immediately* sent away
    14. And then *immediately* the brethren
  21:30. *forthwith* the doors were shut.
  22:29. Then *straightway* they departed
Gal. 1:16. *immediately* I conferred not
Jas. 1:24. *straightway* forgetteth what manner
3Joh. 14. But I trust I shall *shortly* see thee,
Rev. 4: 2. *immediately* I was in the spirit:

εὐθυδρομέω, *ūthudromeo.*

Acts 16:11. we *came with a straight course* to Samo-
    thracia,
  21: 1. we came *with a straight course* (lit. *having
    run with &c.* we came)

εὐθυμέω, *ūthumeo.*

Acts 27:22. I exhort you *to be of good cheer :*
    25. Wherefore, sirs, *be of good cheer :*
Jas. 5:13. *Is any merry?* let him sing psalms.

εὔθυμος, *ūthumos.*

Acts 27:36. Then were they all *of good cheer,*

εὐθυμότερον, *ūthumoteron.*

Acts 24:10. the *more cheerfully* answer for myself:

εὐθύνω, *ūthuno.*

Joh. 1:23. *Make straight* the way of the Lord,
Jas. 3: 4. whithersoever the governor listeth. (lit.
    wh. the purpose of the *helmsman* willeth)

εὐθύς, *ūthus.*

Mat. 3: 3. make his paths *straight.*
Mar 1: 3. make his paths *straight.*
Lu. 3: 4. make his paths *straight.*
    5. the crooked shall be made *straight,*

Acts 8:21. thy heart is not *right* in the sight of God.
  9:11. into the street which is called *Straight,*
  13:10. cease to pervert the *right* ways of the
    Lord ?
2Pet. 2:15. which have forsaken the *right* way,

εὐθύς, *ūthus.* adv.

Mat. 3:16. went up *straightway* out of the water:
  13:20. and *anon* with joy receiveth it ;
    21. *by and by* he is offended.
Mar 1:12. *immediately* the spirit driveth him
    28. *immediately* his fame spread abroad
Joh. 13:32. shall *straightway* glorify him.
  19:34. *forthwith* came thereout blood
  21: 3. entered into a ship *immediately ;*

εὐθύτης, *ūthutees.*

Heb 1: 8. a sceptre of *righteousness* (is) the sceptre

εὐκαιρέω, *ūkaireo.*

Mar 6:31. they *had* no *leisure* so much as to eat.
Acts 17:21. *spent* their *time* in nothing else,
1Co. 16:12. when he *shall have convenient time.*

εὐκαιρία, *ūkairia.*

Mat. 26:16. he sought *opportunity* to betray
Lu. 22: 6. sought *opportunity* to betray him

εὔκαιρος, *ūkairos.*

Mar 6:21. when a *convenient* day was come,
Heb 4:16. find grace to help in time of need. (lit.
    for *seasonable* assistance)

εὐκαίρως, *ūkairōs.*

Mar 14:11. how he might *conveniently* betray him.
2Ti. 4: 2. be instant *in season,* out of season ;

εὐκοπώτερος, *ūkopōteros.*

Mat. 9: 5. For whether is *easier,* to say,
  19:24. It is *easier* for a camel
Mar 2: 9. Whether is it *easier*
  10:25. It is *easier* for a camel
Lu. 5:23. Whether is *easier,* to say, Thy sins
  16:17. And it is *easier* for heaven and earth
  18:25. For it is *easier* for a camel to go

εὐλάβεια, *ūlabia.*

Heb 5: 7. was heard in that he feared ; (lit. for his
    fearing)
  12:28. with reverence and *godly fear :*

εὐλαβέομαι, *ūlabeomai.*

Acts 23:10. the chief captain, *fearing* lest Paul
Heb 11: 7. *moved with fear,* prepared an ark

εὐλαβής, *ūlabees.*

Lu.   2:25. the same man (was) just and *devout,*
Acts 2: 5. Jews, *devout* men, out of every nation
     8: 2. And *devout* men carried Stephen

εὐλογέω, *ūlogeo.*

Mat. 5:44. *bless* them that curse you,
     14:19. to heaven, he *blessed,* and brake,
     21: 9. *Blessed* (is) he that cometh in the name
     23:39. *Blessed* (is) he that cometh
     25:34. ye *blessed* of my Father,
     26:26. *blessed* (it), *and* brake (it),
Mar 6:41. to heaven, and *blessed,*
     8: 7. and he *blessed, and* commanded
     10:16. hands upon them, and *blessed* them.
     11: 9. *Blessed* (is) he that cometh
        10. *Blessed* (be) the kingdom of our father
     14:22. and *blessed, and* brake (it),
Lu.   1:28. *blessed* (art) thou among women.
     42. *Blessed* (art) thou among women, and
        blessed (is) the fruit of thy womb.
     64. and he spake, *and praised* God.
     2:28. him up in his arms, and *blessed* God,
     34. And Simeon *blessed* them, and said
     6:28. *Bless* them that curse you,
     9:16. he *blessed* them, and brake, and gave
     13:35. *Blessed* (is) he that cometh
     19:38. *Blessed* (be) the King that cometh
     24:30. he took bread, and *blessed* (it),
     50. he lifted up his hands, and *blessed* them.
     51. while he blessed (lit. in his *blessing*) them,
     53. praising and *blessing* God.
Joh. 12:13. *Blessed* (is) the King of Israel that
Acts 3:26. sent him to *bless* you, in turning
Ro. 12:14. *Bless* them which persecute you: *bless,*
     and curse not.
1Co. 4:12. being reviled, we *bless;*
     10:16. The cup of blessing which we *bless,*
     14:16. Else when thou *shalt bless* with the spirit,
Gal. 3: 9. *are blessed* with faithful Abraham.
Eph. 1: 3. Father of our Lord Jesus Christ, *who hath*
     blessed us with all
Heb 6:14. Saying, Surely *blessing* I *will bless* thee,
     and multiplying
     7: 1. and *blessed* him;
     6. *blessed* him that had the promises.
     7. the less *is blessed* of the better.
     11:20. Isaac *blessed* Jacob and Esau
     21. *blessed* both the sons of Joseph;
Jas. 3: 9. Therewith *bless* we God, even the
1Pet.3: 9. but contrariwise *blessing;*

εὐλογητός, *ūlogeetos.*

Mar 14:61. the Son of the *Blessed?*
Lu.   1:68. *Blessed* (be) the Lord God
Ro.   1:25. the Creator, who is *blessed* for ever.
     9: 5. Christ (came), who is over all, God *blessed*
     for ever.
2Co. 1: 3. *Blessed* (be) God, even the Father of
     11:31. which is *blessed* for evermore,
Eph. 1: 3. *Blessed* (be) the God and Father of
1Pet.1: 3. *Blessed* (be) the God and Father of our
     Lord Jesus Christ,

εὐλογία, *ūlogia.*

Ro. 15:29. in the fulness of the *blessing*
     16:18. by good words and *fair speeches* deceive

1Co.10:16. The cup of *blessing* which we
2Co. 9: 5. your *bounty,* whereof ye had notice before,
     — as (*a matter of*) *bounty,*
     6. he which soweth *bounti*fully shall reap
     also *bountifully.*
Gal. 3:14. That the *blessing* of Abraham might come
     on the Gentiles through Jesus
Eph. 1: 3. with all spiritual *blessings*
Heb 6: 7. receiveth *blessing* from God:
     12:17. would have inherited the *blessing,*
Jas. 3:10. proceedeth *blessing* and cursing.
1Pet.3: 9. that ye should inherit a *blessing.*
Rev. 5:12. and glory, and *blessing.*
     13. *Blessing,* and honour, and glory,
     7:12. *Blessing,* and glory, and wisdom,

εὐμετάδοτος, *ūmetadotos.*

1Ti. 6:18. *ready to distribute,* willing to communi-
     cate ;

εὐνόεω, *ūnoeo.*

Mat. 5:25. Agree (lit. be thou *agreeing*) with thine
     adversary quickly,

εὔνοια, *ūnoia.*

1Co. 7: 3. unto the wife due *benevolence:*
Eph. 6: 7. With *good will* doing service,

εὐνουχίζω, *ūnoukizo.*

Mat.19:12. *were made eunuchs* of men:
     — *have made* themselves *eunuchs* for the
     kingdom of heaven's sake.

εὐνοῦχος, *ūnoukos.*

Mat.19:12. For there are some *eunuchs,* which
     — and there are some *eunuchs,* which were
     — and there be *eunuchs,* which have
Acts 8:27. an *eunuch* of great authority under Can-
     dace
     34. And the *eunuch* answered Philip,
     36. the *eunuch* said, See, (here is) water;
     38. into the water, both Philip and the
     eunuch;
     39. the *eunuch* saw him no more:

εὐοδούμαι, *ūodoumai*

Ro.   1:10. now at length I might *have a prosperous*
     journey
1Co.16: 2. lay by him in store, as (God) hath pros-
     pered him, (lit. whatever he *be pros-*
     pered in)
3Joh.   2. that thou mayest *prosper* and be in health,
     even as thy soul *prospereth.*

εὐπειθής, *ūpīthees.*

Jas. 3:17. *easy to be intreated,* full of mercy

εὐπερίστατος, *ūperistatos.*

Heb 12: 1. the sin *which doth so easily beset* (us),

εὐποιΐα, ūpoiya.

Heb 13:16. But *to do good* and to communicate forget not: (lit. forget not the *doing-good*, &c.)

εὐπορέομαι, ūporeomai.

Acts11:29. every man according to his ability, (lit. as he *abounded*)

εὐπορία, ūporia.

Acts19:25. by this craft we have our *wealth*.

εὐπρέπεια, ūprepīa.

Jas. 1:11. the *grace* of the fashion of it perisheth:

εὐπρόσδεκτος, ūprosdektos.

Ro. 15:16. the offering up of the Gentiles might be *acceptable*,
31. may be *accepted* of the saints ;
2Co. 6: 2. behold, now (is) the *accepted* time;
8:12. (it is) *accepted* according to that a man
1Pet. 2: 5. *acceptable* to God by Jesus Christ.

εὐπρόσεδρος, ūprosedros.

1Co. 7:35. that ye may attend upon the Lord (lit. with a view to *assiduous*ness unto the Lord)

εὐπροσωπέω, uprosōpeo.

Gal. 6:12. *to make a fair shew* in the flesh,

εὑρίσκω, hurisko.

Mat. 1:18. she *was found* with child of the Holy Ghost.
2: 8. and when ye *have found* (him),
11. they *saw* the young child
7: 7. seek, and ye *shall find ;*
8. he that seeketh *findeth ;*
14. and few there be *that find* it.
8:10. I *have* not *found* so great faith,
10:39. He *that findeth* his life shall
— loseth his life for my sake *shall find* it.
11:29. ye *shall find* rest unto your souls.
12:43. seeking rest, and *findeth* none.
44. he *findeth* (it) empty,
13:44. the which *when* a man *hath found*,
46. Who, *when* he *had found* one pearl of great price,
16:25. lose his life for my sake *shall find* it.
17:27. thou *shalt find* a piece of money:
18:13. if so be that he *find* it,
28. *found* one of his fellowservants,
20: 6. and *found* others standing
21: 2. ye *shall find* an ass tied,
19. *found* nothing thereon,
22: 9. as many as ye shall *find*,
10. all as many as they *found*,

Mat.24:46. when he cometh *shall find* so doing.
26:40. *findeth* them asleep,
43. and *found* them asleep again:
60. But *found* none: yea, though many false witnesses came, (yet) *found* they none.
27:32. they *found* a man of Cyrene,
Mar. 1:37. And *when* they *had found* him,
7:30. she *found* the devil gone out,
11: 2. ye shall *find* a colt tied,
4. and *found* the colt tied
13. if haply he might *find* any thing thereon:
— he *found* nothing but leaves;
13:36. he *find* you sleeping.
14:16. *found* as he had said unto them:
37. and *findeth* them sleeping,
40. he *found* them asleep again,
55. to put him to death; and *found* none.
Lu. 1:30. for thou *hast found* favour with God.
2:12. Ye *shall find* the babe wrapped in swaddling clothes,
45. And *when* they *found* him not,
46. they *found* him in the temple,
4:17. he *found* the place where it was written,
5:19. *when* they could not *find* by what (way)
6: 7. that they *might find* an accusation against him.
7: 9. I *have* not *found* so great faith,
10. *found* the servant whole that had been
8:35. and *found* the man, out of whom
9:12. and lodge, and *get* victuals:
36. Jesus *was found* alone.
11: 9. seek, and ye *shall find ;*
10. and he that seeketh *findeth ;*
24. and *finding* none, he saith, I will
25. he *findeth* (it) swept
12:37. when he cometh *shall find* watching:
38. and *find* (them) so, blessed are those
43. *shall find* so doing.
13: 6. sought fruit thereon, and *found* none.
7. on this fig tree, and *find* none:
15: 4. until he *find* it?
5. *when* he *hath found* (it), he layeth (it)
6. I *have found* my sheep
8. till she *find* (it)?
9. *when* she *hath found* (it), she calleth
— for I *have found* the piece
24. he was lost, and *is found*.
32. was lost, and *is found*.
17:18. There *are* not *found* that returned
18: 8. *shall* he *find* faith on the earth ?
19:30. ye *shall find* a colt tied,
32. and *found* even as he had said
48. *could* not *find* what they might do:
22:13. and *found* as he had said
45. he *found* them sleeping
23: 2. We *found* this (fellow) perverting
4. I *find* no fault in this man.
14. *have found* no fault in this man
22. I *have found* no cause of death in him:
24: 2. And they *found* the stone rolled away
3. and *found* not the body of the Lord
23. And *when* they *found* not his body, they came,
24. and *found* (it) even so as the women
33. *found* the eleven gathered together,
Joh. 1:41(42). He first *findeth* his own brother Simon, and saith unto him, We *have found*
43(44). and *findeth* Philip, and saith unto him,
45(46). Philip *findeth* Nathanael, and saith unto him, We *have found*

Joh. 2:14. And *found* in the temple those

  5:14. Afterward Jesus *findeth* him in the temple,

  6:25. *when* they *had found* him on the other side

  7:34. and *shall* not *find* (me):

  35. we *shall* not *find* him?

  36. and *shall* not *find* (me):

  9:35. and *when* he *had found* him, he said

  10: 9. shall go in and out, and *find* pasture.

  11:17. he *found* that he had (lain) in the grave four days already.

  12:14. And Jesus, *when* he *had found* a young ass,

  18:38. I *find* in him no fault (at all).

  19: 4. may know that I *find* no fault in him.

  6. I *find* no fault in him.

  21: 6. right side of the ship, and ye *shall find*.

Acts 4:21. *finding* nothing how they might punish

  5:10. came in, and *found* her dead,

  22. *found* them not in the prison,

  23. The prison truly *found* we shut

  — we *found* no man within.

  39. ye *be found* even to fight against God.

  7:11. and our fathers *found* no sustenance.

  46. Who *found* favour before God, and desired *to find* a tabernacle for the God

  8:40. But Philip *was found* at Azotus:

  9: 2. if he *found* any of this way,

  33. And there he *found* a certain man

  10:27. *found* many that were come together.

  11:26. *when* he *had found* him, he brought him

  12:19. and *found* him not, he examined

  13: 6. they *found* a certain sorcerer, a false prophet,

  22. I *have found* David the (son) of Jesse,

  28. And *though* they *found* no cause of death

  17: 6. And *when* they *found* them not,

  23. I *found* an altar with this inscription,

  27. they might feel after him, and *find* him,

  18: 2. And *found* a certain Jew named

  19: 1. and *finding* certain disciples,

  19. and *found* (it) fifty thousand (pieces) of silver.

  21: 2. And *finding* a ship sailing over

  23: 9. We *find* no evil in this man:

  29. Whom I *perceived* to be accused

  24: 5. For we *have found* this man

  12. they neither *found* me in the temple

  18. Jews from Asia *found* me purified

  20. if they *have found* any evil doing in me,

  27: 6. And there the centurion *found* a ship

  28. and *found* (it) twenty fathoms:

  — and *found* (it) fifteen fathoms.

  28:14. Where we *found* brethren, *and* were

Ro. 4: 1. as pertaining to the flesh, *hath found?*

  7:10. the commandment,...I found (lit. *was found* to me)

  18. but (how) to perform that which is good I *find* not.

  21. I *find* then a law, that, when I

  10:20. I *was found* of them that sought me not ;

1Co. 4: 2. that a man *be found* faithful.

  15:15. Yea, and we *are found* false witnesses

2Co. 2:13. because I *found* not Titus

  5: 3. we *shall* not *be found* naked.

  9: 4. come with me, and *find* you unprepared,

  11:12. they *may be found* even as we.

  12:20. lest,...I shall not *find* you such as I would, and (that) I shall *be found* unto you such

Gal. 2:17. we ourselves also *are found*

Phi. 2: 8. *being found* in fashion as

  3: 9. And *be found* in him, not having mine

2Ti. 1:17. very diligently, and *found* (me).

  18. that he may *find* mercy of the Lord in

Heb 4:16. that we may obtain mercy, and *find* grace

  9:12. *having obtained* eternal redemption (for us).

  11: 5. and *was* not *found*, because God

  12:17. for he *found* no place of repentance,

1Pet.1: 7. *might be found* unto praise

  2:22. neither *was* guile *found*

2Pet.3:14. that ye may *be found* of him in peace,

2Joh. 4. I *found* of thy children walking in truth,

Rev. 2: 2. and *hast found* them liars:

  3: 2. for I *have* not *found* thy works perfect

  5: 4. no man *was found* worthy to open

  9: 6. seek death, and *shall* not *find* it ;

  12: 8. neither *was* their place *found*

  14: 5. in their mouth *was found* no guile:

  16:20. the mountains *were* not *found*.

  18:14. thou *shalt find* them no more at all.

  21. and *shall be found* no more at all.

  22. *shall be found* any more in thee ;

  24. *was found* the blood of prophets, and of saints,

  20:11. there *was found* no place for them.

  15. And whosoever *was* not *found*

εὐρύχωρος, *urukōros.*

Mat. 7:13. *broad* (is) the way,

εὐσέβεια, *ūsebīa.*

Acts 3:12. as though by our own power or *holiness*

1Ti. 2: 2. in all *godliness* and honesty.

  3:16. the mystery of *godliness :*

  4: 7. and exercise thyself (rather) unto *godliness.*

  8. but *godliness* is profitable unto all things,

  6: 3. to the doctrine which is according to *godliness ;*

  5. that gain is *godliness :*

  6. *godliness* with contentment

  11. *godliness*, faith, love, patience,

2Ti. 3: 5. Having a form of *godliness,*

Tit. 1: 1. of the truth which is after *godliness ;*

2Pet.1: 3. unto life and *godliness,*

  6. and to patience *godliness ;*

  7. And to *godliness* brotherly kindness ;

  3:11. in (all) holy conversation and *godliness,*

εὐσεβέω, *ūsebeo.*

Acts17:23. Whom therefore ye ignorantly *worship,*

1Ti. 5: 4. let them learn first *to shew* piety at home, (lit. to care *piously for* their own house)

εὐσεβής, *ūsebees.*

Acts10: 2. (A) *devout* (man), and one that feared God

  7. and a *devout* soldier of them that waited on him

  22:12. a *devout* man according to the law,

2Pet.2: 9. The Lord knoweth how to deliver the *godly*

εὐσεβῶς, *ūsebōs.*

2Ti. 3:12. all that will live *godly* in Christ
Tit. 2:12. we should live *soberly*, righteously, and *godly,*

εὔσημος, *ūseemos.*

1Co.14: 9. except ye utter...words *easy to be understood,* (lit. *well-significant*)

εὔσπλαγχνος, *ūsplanknos.*

Eph. 4:32. *tenderhearted,* forgiving one another,
1Pet.3: 8. love as brethren, (be) *pitiful,*

εὐσχημόνως, *ūskeemonōs.*

Ro. 13:13. Let us walk *honestly,*
1Co.14:40. be done *decently* and in order.
1Th. 4:12. That ye may walk *honestly* toward them that are without,

---

εὐσχημοσύνη, *ūskeemosunee.*

1Co.12:23. have more abundant *comeliness.*

εὐσχήμων, *uskeemōn.*

Mar 15:43. of Arimathæa, an *honourable* counsellor,
Acts13:50. the devout and *honourable* women,
17:12. also of *honourable* women which
1Co. 7:35. but for that which is *comely,*
12:24. For our *comely* (parts) have no need:

εὐτόνως, *ūtonōs.*

Lu. 23:10. and *vehemently* accused him.
Acts18:28. For he *mightily* convinced the Jews,

εὐτραπελία, *ūtrapelia.*

Eph. 5: 4. foolish talking, nor *jesting,*

εὐφημία, *ūpheemia.*

2Co. 6: 8. by evil report and *good report:*

εὔφημος, *ūpheemos.*

Phi. 4: 8. whatsoever things (are) *of good report;*

εὐφορέω, *ūphoreo.*

Lu. 12:16. The ground of a certain rich man *brought forth plentifully:*

εὐφραίνω -ομαι, *ūphraino -omai.*

Lu. 12:19. eat, drink, (and) *be merry.*
15:23. let us eat, and *be merry:*
24. they began *to be merry.*

Lu. 15:29. I *might make merry* with my friends:
32. that we should *make merry,* and be glad:
16:19. *and fared* sumptuously every day:
Acts 2:26. Therefore *did* my heart *rejoice,*
7:41. unto the idol, and *rejoiced* in the works of their own hands.
Ro. 15:10. *Rejoice,* ye Gentiles, with his people.
2Co. 2: 2. who is he then *that maketh* me *glad,*
Gal. 4:27. *Rejoice,* (thou) barren that bearest not;
Rev.11:10. shall rejoice over them, and *make merry,*
12:12. Therefore *rejoice,* (ye) heavens, and ye
18:20. *Rejoice* over her, (thou) heaven, and (ye) holy apostles and

---

εὐφροσύνη, *ūphrosunee.*

Acts 2:28. thou shalt make me full of *joy*
14:17. with food and *gladness.*

εὐχαριστέω, *ūkaristeo.*

Mat.15:36. and *gave thanks,* and brake (them),
26:27. the cup, and *gave thanks,* and gave
Mar. 8: 6. and *gave thanks,* and brake,
14:23. and when he *had given thanks,* he gave
Lu. 17:16. *giving* him *thanks:*
18:11. God, I *thank* thee, that I am not as
22:17. and *gave thanks,* and said,
19. and *gave thanks,* and brake (it),
Joh. 6:11. when he *had given thanks,* he distributed to the
23. did eat bread, *after that* the Lord *had given thanks:*
11:41. Father, I *thank* thee that thou hast heard me.
Acts27:35. *gave thanks* to God in presence of them all:
28:15. he *thanked* God, *and* took courage.
Ro. 1: 8. I *thank* my God through Jesus Christ
21. they glorified (him) not as God, neither *were thankful;*
7:25. I *thank* God through Jesus Christ
14: 6. for he *giveth* God *thanks;*
— eateth not, and *giveth* God *thanks.*
16: 4. not only I *give thanks,* but also all
1Co. 1: 4. I *thank* my God always on your behalf,
14. I *thank* God that I baptizēd none
10:30. for that for which I *give thanks?*
11:24. when he *had given thanks,* he brake (it),
14:17. thou verily *givest thanks* well,
18. I *thank* my God, I speak with tongues
2Co. 1:11. *thanks may be given* by many on our behalf.
Eph. 1:16. Cease not to *give thanks* for you,
5. 20. *Giving thanks* always for all things
Phi. 1: 3. I *thank* my God upon every remembrance
Col. 1: 3. We *give thanks* to God and the
12. *Giving thanks* unto the Father,
3:17. *giving thanks* to God and thé Father
1Th. 1: 2. We *give thanks* to God always for you
2:13. For this cause also *thank* we God
5:18. In every thing *give thanks:*
2Th. 1: 3. We are bound *to thank* God always
2:13. are bound *to give thanks* alway
Philem. 4. I *thank* my God, making mention
Rev 11:17. We *give* thee *thanks,* O Lord God Almighty,

εὐχαριστία, *ūkaristia.*

Acts24: 3. most noble Felix, with all *thankfulness.*
1Co.14:16. say Amen at thy *giving of thanks,*

2Co. 4:15. might through the *thanksgiving* of many redound

9:11. causeth through us *thanksgiving* to

12. by many *thanksgivings* unto God;

Eph. 5: 4. but rather *giving of thanks.*

Phi. 4: 6. prayer and supplication with *thanksgiving*

Col. 2: 7. abounding therein with *thanksgiving.*

4: 2. watch in the same with *thanksgiving;*

1Th. 3: 9. For what *thanks* can we render to God again for you,

1Ti. 2: 1. intercessions, (and) *giving of thanks*, be made for all men;

4: 3. to be received with *thanksgiving*

4. if it be received with *thanksgiving:*

Rev. 4: 9. and *thanks* to him that sat on the throne,

7:12. and *thanksgiving*, and honour,

εὐχάριστος, *ūkaristos.*

Col. 3:15. and be ye *thankful.*

ευχή, *ūkee.*

Acts18:18. head in Cenchrea: for he had a *vow.*

21:23. which have a *vow* on them;

Jas. 5:15. And the *prayer* of faith shall save

εὔχομαι, *ūkomai.*

Acts26:29. I *would* to God, that not only thou,

27:29. and *wished* for the day.

Ro. 9: 3. For I could wish (lit *used to wish*) that myself

2Co.13: 7. Now I *pray* to God that

9. this also we *wish*, (even) your perfection.

Jas. 5:16. *pray* one for another, that ye may be healed.

3Joh. 2. I *wish* above all things that thou mayest prosper

εὔχρηστος, *ūkreestos.*

2Ti. 2:21. *meet for* the master's use,

4:11. *profitable* to me for the ministry.

Philem 11. *profitable* to thee and to me:

εὐψυχέω, *ūpsukeo.*

Phi. 2:19. that I also *may be of good comfort*,

εὐωδία, *ūōdia.*

2Co. 2:15. we are...a *sweet savour* of Christ,

Eph. 5: 2. for a *sweetsmelling* savour.

Phi. 4:18. odour of a *sweet smell*, a sacrifice

εὐώνυμος, *ūōnumos.*

Mat.20:21. and the other on the *left*,

23. to sit on my right hand, and on my *left*,

25:33. but the goats on the *left.*

41. say also unto them on the *left* hand,

27:38. and another on the *left.*

Mar.10:37. and the other on thy *left* hand,

40. and on my *left* hand is not mine

Mar15:27. and the other on his *left.*

Acts21: 3. we left it *on the left* hand,

Rev.10: 2. and (his) *left* (foot) on the earth,

ἐφάλλομαι, *ephallomai.*

Acts19:16. *leaped on* them,...and prevailed against

ἐφάπαξ, *ephapax.*

Ro. 6:10. he died unto sin *once:*

1Co.15: 6. five hundred brethren *at once;*

Heb 7:27. for this he did *once*, when he offered up himself.

9:12. he entered in *once* into the holy place,

10:10. through the offering of the body of Jesus Christ *once* (*for all*).

ἐφευρετής, *ephūretees.*

Ro. 1:30. *inventors* of evil things,

ἐφημερία, *epheemeria.*

Lu. 1: 5. Zacharias, of the *course* of Abia:

8. before God in the order of his *course*,

ἐφήμερος, *epheemeros.*

Jas. 2:15. be naked, and destitute of *daily* food,

ἐφικνέομαι, *ephikneomai.*

2Co.10:13. *to reach* even unto you.

14. as *though* we *reached* not unto you:

ἐφίστημι, *ephisteemi.*

Lu. 2: 9. the angel of the Lord *came upon* them,

38. And she *coming in* that instant

4:39. he *stood over* her, and rebuked

10:40. and *came to* him, *and* said, Lord,

20: 1. the chief priests and the scribes *came upon* (him)

21:34. that day *come upon* you unawares.

24: 4. two men *stood by* them in shining garments:

Acts 4: 1. and the Sadducees, *came upon* them,

6:12. *came upon* (him), *and* caught him,

10:17. and *stood before* the gate,

11:11. there *were* three men already *come unto* the house

12: 7. the angel of the Lord *came upon* (him),

17: 5. *assaulted* the house of Jason, *and* sought

22:13. Came unto me, and *stood*, and said

20. I also was *standing by*, and consenting

23:11. the Lord *stood by* him, *and* said, Be of good

27. then *came* I with an army, *and* rescued

28: 2. because of the *present* rain,

1Th. 5: 3. destruction *cometh upon* them,

2Ti. 4: 2. *be instant* in season, out of season,

6. the time of my departure *is at hand.*

ἐφοράω, ephorao.

Lu. 1:25. wherein he *looked on* (me),
Acts 4:29. Lord, *behold* their threatenings:

ἐφφαθά, ephphatha.

Mar. 7:34. *Ephphatha,* that is, Be opened.

ἔχθρα, ekthra.

Lu. 23:12. they were at *enmity* between themselves.
Ro. 8: 7. the carnal mind (is) *enmity* against God:
Gal. 5:20. witchcraft, *hatred,* variance,
Eph. 2:15. abolished in his flesh the *enmity,*
      16. having slain the *enmity* thereby:
Jas. 4: 4. the friendship of the world is *enmity* with

ἐχθρός, ekthros.

Mat. 5:43. and hate thine *enemy.*
      44. Love your *enemies,* bless
      10:36. And a man's *foes* (shall be) they of his
      13:25. his *enemy* came and sowed tares
      28. An *enemy* hath done this.
      39. The *enemy* that sowed them is the devil;
      2?:44. till I make thine *enemies* thy
Mar 12:36. thine *enemies* thy footstool.
Lu. 1:71. That we should be saved from our *enemies,*
      74. out of the hand of our *enemies*
      6:27. Love your *enemies,* do good to
      35. love ye your *enemies,*
      10:19. and over all the power of the *enemy :*
      19:27. But those mine *enemies,* which
      43. that thine *enemies* shall cast a trench about
      20:43. Till I make thine *enemies* thy footstool.
Acts 2:35. thy *foes* thy footstool.
      13:10. (thou) *enemy* of all righteousness,
Ro. 5:10. For if, when we were *enemies,*
      11:28. (they are) *enemies* for your sakes:
      12:20. if thine *enemy* hunger, feed him ;
1Co.15:25. till he hath put all *enemies*
      26. The last *enemy* (that) shall be destroyed
Gal. 4:16. Am I therefore become your *enemy,*
Phi. 3:18. (that they are) the *enemies* of the cross
Col. 1:21. and *enemies* in (your) mind
2Th. 3:15. count (him) not as an *enemy,*
Heb 1:13. I make thine *enemies* thy footstool ?
10:13. till his *enemies* be made
Jas. 4: 4. will be a friend of the world is the *enemy*
      of God.
Rev.11: 5. and devoureth their *enemies :*
      12. and their *enemies* beheld them.

ἔχιδνα, echidna.

Mat. 3: 7. O generation of *vipers,* who hath
      12:34. O generation of *vipers,* how can ye,
      23:33. (ye) generation of *vipers,* how
Lu. 3: 7. O generation of *vipers,*
Acts28: 3. a *viper* out of the heat,

ἔχω, eko.

Mat. 1:18. she was found with child (lit. *having* in
      the womb)
      23. a virgin shall be with child, (lit. *shall
      have,* &c.)

Mat. 3: 4. *had* his raiment of camel's hair,
      9. We *have* Abraham to (our) father:
      14. I *have* need to be baptized of thee,
      4:24. sick people (lit. *that had* themselves
      sickly)
      5:23. *hath* ought against thee ;
      46. what reward *have* ye ?
      6: 1. otherwise ye *have* no reward
      8. what things ye *have* need of,
      7:29. as (one) *having* authority,
      8: 9. *having* soldiers under me:
      16. all that were sick: (lit. *that had* them-
      selves sickly)
      20. The foxes *have* holes, and the birds of the
      air (have) nests ; but the Son of man
      hath not where to lay (his) head.
      9: 6. the Son of man *hath* power
      12. They that be whole need not (lit. *have*
      not need of) a physician, but they *that
      are* sick.
      36. as sheep *having* no shepherd.
      11:15. He *that hath* ears to hear, let him hear.
      18. and they say, He *hath* a devil.
      12:10. *which had* (his) hand withered.
      11. that *shall have* one sheep,
      13: 5. they *had* not much earth:
      — because they *had* no deepness
      6. because they *had* no root,
      9. *Who hath* ears to hear, let
      12. For whosoever *hath,* to him shall
      — but whosoever *hath* not, from him shall
      be taken away even that he *hath.*
      21. Yet *hath* he not root in himself,
      27. from whence then *hath* it tares ?
      43. *Who hath* ears to hear, let him hear.
      44. selleth all that he *hath,* and
      46. sold all that he *had,* and bought it.
      14: 4. It is not lawful for thee *to have* her.
      5. they *counted* him as a prophet.
      16. They need not depart ; (lit. *have* not need
      to depart)
      17. We *have* here but five loaves, and
      35. all that were diseased ; (lit. *that had*
      themselves sickly)
      15:30. came unto him, *having* with them
      32. three days, and *have* nothing to eat:
      34. How many loaves *have* ye ?
      17:20. If ye *have* faith as a grain of
      18: 8. rather than *having* two hands or two feet
      9. rather than *having* two eyes to be cast
      25. But *forasmuch as* he *had* not
      — and all that he *had,* and payment
      19:16. that I *may have* eternal life ?
      21. thou *shalt have* treasure in heaven:
      22. for he *had* great possessions. (lit. was
      having)
      21: 3. The Lord *hath* need of them ;
      21. If ye *have* faith, and doubt not,
      26. for all *hold* John as a prophet.
      28. A (certain) man *had* two sons ;
      46. they *took* him *for* a prophet.
      22:12. not *having* a wedding garment ?
      24. If a man die, *having* no children,
      25. *having* no issue, left his wife unto
      28. for they all *had* her.
      24:19. unto them that are with child, (lit. *that
      have* in the womb)
      25:25. lo, (there) thou *hast* (that is) thine.
      28. unto him *which hath* ten talents.
      29. For unto every one *that hath* shall
      — but from him *that hath* not shall be taken
      away even that which he *hath.*

Mat.26: 7. *having* an alabaster box of very
11. ye *have* the poor always with you ; but me ye *have* not always.
65. what further need *have* we of
27:16. And they *had* then a notable prisoner,
65. Pilate said unto them, Ye *have* a watch:
Mar 1:22. as one *that had* authority,
32. that were diseased, (lit. *that had* themselves sickly)
34. many that were sick (lit. *that had*, &c.)
38. into the next towns, (lit. towns *holding nigh*)
2:10. the Son of man *hath* power
17. They that are whole *have* no need
— but they *that are* sick:
19. as long as they *have* the bridegroom
25. what David did, when he *had* need,
3: 1. a man there *which had* a withered hand.
3. unto the man *which had* the
10. as many as *had* plagues.
15. And *to have* power to heal
22. He *hath* Beelzebub, and by
26. he cannot stand, but *hath* an end.
29. *hath* never forgiveness,
30. He *hath* an unclean spirit.
4: 5. it *had* not much earth ;
— because it *had* no depth
6. because it *had* no root,
9. He *that hath* ears to hear,
17. *have* no root in themselves,
23. If any man *have* ears to hear,
25. For he that *hath*, to him shall be given: and he that *hath* not, from him shall be taken even that which he *hath*.
40. how is it that ye *have* no faith ?
5: 3. Who *had* (his) dwelling among
15. *and had* the legion,
23. lieth (lit. *hath* herself) at the point of
6:18. *to have* thy brother's wife.
34. were as sheep not *having* a shepherd:
36. for they *have* nothing to eat.
38. How many loaves *have* ye ?
55. to carry about...those *that were* sick,
7:16. If any man *have* ears to hear,
25. daughter *had* an unclean spirit,
8: 1. and *having* nothing to eat,
2. *have* nothing to eat:
5. How many loaves *have* ye ?
7. they *had* a few small fishes:
14. neither *had* they in the ship with them
16. (It is) because we *have* no bread.
17. because ye *have* no bread ?
— *have* ye your heart yet hardened ?
18. *Having* eyes, see ye not ? and *having* ears,
9:17. my son, *which hath* a dumb spirit,
43. than *having* two hands to go
45. than *having* two feet to be cast
47. with one eye, than *having* two eyes
50. *Have* salt in yourselves,
10:21. sell whatsoever thou *hast*, and give to the poor, and thou *shalt have* treasure in
22. for he *had* great possessions.
23. shall they *that have* riches enter
11: 3. that the Lord *hath* need of him ;
13. seeing a fig tree afar off *having* leaves,
22. *Have* faith in God.
25. if ye *have* ought against any:
32. *counted* John, that he was a prophet
12: 6. *Having* yet therefore one son, his
23. for the seven *had* her to wife.
44. did cast in all that she *had*,
13:17. them that are with child, (lit. *that have*, &c.)

Mar 14: 3. *having* an alabaster box of ointment
7. ye *have* the poor with you always,
-- but me ye *have* not always.
8. She hath done what she could: (lit. what she *had* in her power, &c.)
63. What need we any further witnesses? (lit. What further *have* we need of witnesses)
16: 8. for they trembled (lit. trembling *took* them)
18. and they shall recover. (lit. *shall have* themselves well)
Lu. 3: 8. We *have* Abraham to (our) father:
11. He *that hath* two coats, let him impart to him *that hath* none ; and he *that hath*
4:33. a man, *which had* a spirit of an unclean
40. all they that *had* any sick
5:24. the Son of man *hath* power
31. They that are whole need not (lit. *have* not need of) a physician ; but they *that are* sick.
6: 8. to the man *which had* the withered
7: 2. centurion's servant,...*was* sick, *and*
8. *having* under me soldiers,
33. and ye say, He *hath* a devil.
40. I *have* somewhat to say unto thee.
42. And *when* they *had* nothing
8: 6. because it lacked (lit. *had* not) moisture.
8. He *that hath* ears to hear,
13. and these *have* no root, which for a
18. *hath*, to him shall be given ; and whosoever *hath* not, from him shall be taken even that which he seemeth *to have*.
27. man, which *had* devils long time,
9: 3. neither *have* two coats apiece.
11. healed them *that had* need of healing.
58. Foxes *have* holes, and birds of the air (*have*) nests; but the Son of man *hath* not where to lay (his) head.
11: 5. Which of you *shall have* a friend,
6. I *have* nothing to set before him?
36. full of light, *having* no part dark,
12: 4. and after that *have* no more that they
5. Fear him, *which* after he hath killed *hath* power to cast into hell ;
17. I *have* no room where to bestow
19. Soul, thou *hast* much goods
50. But I *have* a baptism to be baptized with ;
13: 6. A certain (man) *had* a fig tree
11. a woman *which had* a spirit of infirmity
33. to morrow, and the (day) *following:*
14:14. they cannot recompense thee: (lit. they *have* not to recompense thee)
18. I must needs go (lit. I *have* need to go) and see it: I pray thee *have* me excused.
19. I go to prove them: I pray thee *have* me
28. whether he *have* (sufficient) to finish (it) ?
35. He *that hath* ears to hear,
15: 4. *having* an hundred sheep,
7. need no repentance. (lit. *have* no need of)
8. *having* ten pieces of silver,
11. A certain man *had* two sons:
16: 1. rich man, which *had* a steward ;
28. For I *have* five brethren ;
29. They *have* Moses and the prophets;
17: 6. If ye *had* faith as a grain
7. which of you, *having* a servant plowing
9. Doth he thank that servant (lit. *hath* he favour, or thanks, to)
18:22. sell all that thou *hast*, and distribute unto the poor, and thou *shalt have* treasure in heaven:
24. How hardly shall they *that have* riches

Lu. 19.17. have thou (lit. be thou *having*) authority
over
20. thy pound, which I *have kept* laid up
24. give (it) to him *that hath* ten pounds.
25. Lord, he *hath* ten pounds.
26. unto every one *which hath* shall be given;
and from him *that hath* not, even that
he *hath* shall be taken
31. the Lord *hath* need of him.
34. The Lord *hath* need of him.
20:24. Whose image and superscription *hath* it?
28. any man's brother die, *having* a wife,
33. for seven *had* her to wife.
21: 4. hath cast in all the living that she *had*.
23. unto them that are with child, (lit. *that
have* in the womb)
22:36. he *that hath* a purse,
— he *that hath* no sword, let him sell
37. the things concerning me *have* an end.
71. What need we any further witness? (lit.
what further *have* we need of witnessing)
23:17. For of necessity he must release (lit. he
had necessity to release)
24:39. for a spirit *hath* not flesh and bones, as ye
see me *have*.
41. *Have* ye here any meat?
Joh 2: 3. They *have* no wine.
25. needed not (lit. *had* not need) that any
should testify of man:
3:15. should not perish, but *have* eternal
16. should not perish, but *have* everlasting
life.
29. He *that hath* the bride is the
36. on the Son *hath* everlasting life:
4:11. thou *hast* nothing to draw with, and the
well is deep: from whence then *hast*
thou
17. and said, I *have* no husband.
— Thou hast well said, I *have* no husband:
18. For thou *hast had* five husbands; and he
whom thou now *hast* is not
32. I *have* meat to eat that ye know not of.
44. *hath* no honour in his own country.
52. when he began to amend. (lit. he *had*
himself better)
5: 2. Bethesda, *having* five porches.
5. *which had* an infirmity thirty and
6. he *had been* now a long time
7. I *have* no man, when the water is troubled,
24. *hath* everlasting life, and shall
26. Father *hath* life in himself; so hath he
given to the Son *to have* life in himself;
36. I *have* greater witness
38. ye *have* not his word
39. ye *have* eternal life:
40. that ye *might have* life.
42. ye *have* not the love of God
6: 9. which *hath* five barley loaves,
40. *may have* everlasting life:
47. on me *hath* everlasting life.
53. ye *have* no life in you.
54. my blood, *hath* eternal life;
68. thou *hast* the words of eternal life.
7:20. Thou *hast* a devil:
8: 6. that they *might have* to accuse him.
12. but *shall have* the light of life.
26. I *have* many things to say and to judge of
you:
41. we *have* one Father, (even) God.
48. and *hast* a devil?
49. I *have* not a devil;

Joh. 8:52. that thou *hast* a devil.
57. Thou art not yet fifty years old, (lit. *hast*
not yet fifty years)
9:21. he is of age; (lit. he *hath* due age)
23. He is of age; (lit: *hath* &c.)
41. ye should *have* no sin:
10:10. that they *might have* life, and that they
might have (it) more abundantly.
16. And other sheep I *have*,
18. I *have* power to lay it down, and I *have*
power to take it again.
20. He *hath* a devil, and is mad;
11:17. he found that he *had* (lain) in the grave
four days
12: 6. *had* the bag, and bare what was put
8. ye *have* with you; but me ye *have* not
always.
35. while ye *have* the light,
36. While ye *have* light,
48. *hath* one that judgeth him:
13: 8. thou *hast* no part with me.
10. needeth not (lit. *hath* not need) save to
wash (his) feet,
29. because Judas *had* the bag, that Jesus
— that we *have* need of against the feast;
35. if ye *have* love one to another.
14:21. He *that hath* my commandments,
30. cometh, and *hath* nothing in me.
15:13. Greater love *hath* no man than this,
22. they *had not had* sin: but now they *have* no
24. they *had not had* sin:
16:12. I *have* yet many things to say unto you,
15. All things that the Father *hath* are mine:
21. *hath* sorrow, because her hour is come:
22. ye now therefore *have* sorrow:
30. and needest not (lit. *hast* not need)
33. ye *might have* peace. In the world ye
shall have tribulation:
17: 5. which I *had* with thee before the world
13. that they *might have* my joy
18:10. Simon Peter *having* a sword
19: 7. We *have* a law, and by our law
10. knowest thou not that I *have* power to
crucify thee, and *have* power to
11. Thou couldest have (lit. *hadst*) no power
— *hath* the greater sin.
15. We *have* no king but Cæsar.
20:31. believing ye *might have* life
21: 5. Children, *have* ye any meat?
Acts 1:12. which is from Jerusalem a sabbath day's
journey. (lit. which is near Jerusalem,
having a sabbath day's journey).
2:44. were together, and *had* all things common;
45. as every man *had* need.
47. *having* favour with all the people.
3: 6. but such as I *have* give I thee:
4:14. they could say nothing (lit. *had* nothing to
say) against it.
35. according as he *had* need.
7: 1. *Are* these things so?
8: 7. came out of many that were possessed
(with them): (lit. *that had* them)
9:14. he *hath* authority from the chief priests
31. Then *had* the churches rest
11: 3. to men uncircumcised, (lit. men *having*
uncircumcision)
12:15. constantly affirmed that it *was* even so.
13: 5. and they *had* also John
14: 9. that he *had* faith to be healed,
15:21. *hath* in every city them that preach him,
36. where we have preached the word of the
Lord, (and see) how they *do*.

Acts16:16. *possessed with* a spirit of divination
17:11. whether those things *were* so.
18:18. for he *had* a vow.
19:13. over them *which had* evil spirits
38. *have* a matter against any man,
20:15. and the *next* (day) we came
24. neither *count* I my life dear
21:13. I *am* ready not to be bound only,
23. men *which have* a vow on them;
26. and the *next* day purifying himself
23:17. for he *hath* a certain thing to tell
18. *who hath* something to say unto thee.
19. that thou *hast* to tell me?
29. to *have* nothing laid to his charge worthy
24: 9. that these things *were* so.
15. And *have* hope toward God,
16. *to have* always a conscience void of offence
19. if they *had* ought against me.
23. and to let (him) *have* liberty,
25. Go thy way for this time; (lit. for the time *that* now *is*)
25:16. *have* the accusers face to face,
19. But *had* certain questions against him
26. I *have* no certain thing to write unto my
— I *might have* somewhat to write.
27:39. a certain creek with a shore, (lit. *having* a shore)
28: 9. others also, *which had* diseases
19. not that I *had* ought to accuse
29. *and had* great reasoning among themselves.
Ro. 1:13. that I *might have* some fruit
28. *to retain* God in (their) knowledge,
2:14. the Gentiles, *which have* not the law,
— these, *having* not the law, are a law
20. *which hast* the form of knowledge
4: 2. he *hath* (whereof) to glory; but not before
5: 1. we *have* peace with God through
2. By whom also we *have* access by faith
6:21. What fruit *had* ye then in those things
22. ye *have* your fruit *unto* holiness,
8: 9. if any man *have* not the Spirit of Christ,
23. ourselves also, *which have* the firstfruits of the Spirit,
9:10. Rebecca also had conceived by one, (lit. *having* conception)
21. *Hath* not the potter power over the clay,
10: 2. they *have* a zeal of God,
12: 4. we *have* many members in one body, and all members *have* not the same office:
6. *Having* then gifts differing
13: 3. thou *shalt have* praise of the same:
14:22. *Hast* thou faith? *have* (it) to thyself before God.
15: 4. that we...*might have* hope.
17. I *have* therefore whereof I may glory
23. *having* no more place in these parts, and *having* a great desire
1Co. 2:16. we *have* the mind of Christ.
4: 7. and what *hast* thou that thou didst not
15. For though ye *have* ten thousand instructers in Christ,
5: 1. that one should *have* his father's wife.
6: 1. *having* a matter against another,
4. If then ye *have* judgments of things
7. ye go to law (lit. ye *have* law suits) one with another.
19. Holy Ghost (which is) in you, which ye *have* of God,
7: 2. *let* every man *have* his own wife, and *let* every woman *have* her own husband.
7. every man *hath* his proper gift
12. If any brother *hath* a wife

1Co. 7:13. which *hath* an husband that believeth not,
25. I *have* no commandment of the Lord:
28. Nevertheless such *shall have* trouble in the
29. that both they *that have* wives be as though they *had* none;
37. *having* no necessity, but *hath* power over his own will,
40. that I *have* the Spirit of God.
8: 1. we all *have* knowledge.
10. any man see thee *which hast* knowledge
9: 4. *Have* we not power to eat and
5. *Have* we not power to lead
6. *have* not we power to forbear
17. willingly, I *have* a reward:
11: 4. *having* (his) head covered,
10. *to have* power on (her) head
16. we *have* no such custom,
22. *have* ye not houses
— and shame them *that have* not?
12:12. is one, and *hath* many members,
21. I *have* no need of thee:
— I *have* no need of you.
23. *have* more abundant comeliness.
24. our comely (parts) *have* no need:
30. *Have* all the gifts of healing?
13: 1. and *have* not charity, I am become
2. though I *have* (the gift of) prophecy,
— though I *have* all faith,
— and *have* not charity,
3. to be burned, and *have* not charity,
14:26. every one of you *hath* a psalm, *hath* a doctrine, *hath* a tongue, *hath* a revelation, *hath* an interpretation.
15:31. which I *have* in Christ Jesus
34. for some *have* not the knowledge of God:
2Co. 1: 9. we *had* the sentence of death
15. that ye *might have* a second benefit;
2: 3. lest, when I came, I should *have* sorrow
4. which I *have* more abundantly unto you.
13. I *had* no rest in my spirit,
3: 4. And such trust *have* we
12. *Seeing* then *that* we *have* such hope,
4: 1. *seeing* we *have* this ministry,
7. But we *have* this treasure in
13. We *having* the same spirit
5: 1. we *have* a building of God,
12. that ye *may have* somewhat to (answer) them which
6:10. as *having* nothing, and (yet)
7: 1. *Having* therefore these promises,
5. our flesh *had* no rest, but we were
8:11. out of that which ye *have*.
12. according to that a man *hath*, (and) not according to that he *hath* not.
9: 8. that ye, always *having* all sufficiency
10: 6. And *having* in a readiness
15. but *having* hope, when your faith
12:14. I *am* ready to come to you;
Gal. 2: 4. which we *have* in Christ Jesus,
4:22. that Abraham *had* two sons,
27. than she *which hath* an husband.
6: 4. *shall* he *have* rejoicing
10. As we *have* therefore opportunity,
Eph. 1: 7. In whom we *have* redemption
2:12. *having* no hope, and without God
18. we both *have* access by one Spirit unto the Father.
3:12. In whom we *have* boldness
4:28. that he *may have* to give to him that needeth. (lit. *that hath* need)
5: 5. *hath* any inheritance in the
27. a glorious church, not *having* spot,

Phi. 1: 7. because I *have* you in my heart;
   23. *having* a desire to depart,
   30. *Having* the same conflict
  2: 2. *having* the same love,
   20. For I *have* no man likeminded,
   27. lest I *should have* sorrow upon sorrow.
   29. *hold* such in reputation:
  3: 4. I might also *have* confidence
   9. not *having* mine own righteousness,
   17. as ye *have* us for an ensample.
Col. 1: 14. In whom we *have* redemption
  2: 1. what great conflict I *have* for you,
   23. Which things *have* indeed a shew of wisdom
  3: 13. if any man *have* a quarrel against any:
  4: 1. ye also *have* a Master in heaven.
   13. he *hath* a great zeal for you,
1Th. 1: 8. that we need not (lit. *have* not need)
   9. of entering in we *had* unto you,
  3: 6. that ye *have* good remembrance of us
  4: 1. ye need not (lit. *have* not need) that I write
   12. ye *may have* lack of nothing.
   13. as others *which have* no hope.
  5: 1. ye *have* no need that I write unto you.
   3. upon a woman with child; (lit. *having* in the womb)
2Th. 3: 9. Not because we *have* not power,
1Ti. 1: 12. And I thank (lit. *have* thanks to) Christ
   19. *Holding* faith, and a good conscience;
  3: 4. *having* his children in subjection
   7. he must *have* a good report
   9. *Holding* the mystery of the faith
  4: 8. *having* promise of the life
  5: 4. But if any widow *have* children or
   12. *Having* damnation, because they
   16. If any man or woman that believeth *have* widows,
   20. that others also may fear. (lit. *may have* fear)
   25. and they *that are* otherwise
  6: 2. they *that have* believing masters,
   8. And *having* food and raiment let us
   16. *Who* only *hath* immortality,
2Ti. 1: 3. I thank God, (lit. I *have* thanks to)
  — without ceasing I *have* remembrance of
   13. *Hold* fast the form of sound words,
  2: 17. will eat (lit. *will have* corrosion) as doth a canker:
   19. standeth sure, *having* this seal,
  3: 5. *Having* a form of godliness,
Tit. 1: 6. *having* faithful children,
  2: 8. *having* no evil thing to say of you.
Philem. 5. faith, which thou *hast* toward the Lord
  7. For we *have* great joy and
  8. though I might be much bold (lit. *having* much boldness) in Christ
  17. If thou *count* me therefore a partner,
Heb. 2: 14. might destroy him *that had* the power of death, that is, the devil;
  3: 3. *hath* more honour than
  4: 14. *Seeing* then *that* we *have* a great high priest,
   15. we *have* not an high priest which
  5: 12. ye *have* need that one teach you again
  — are become *such as have* need of milk,
   14. those *who* by reason of use *have* their senses exercised
  6: 9. things *that accompany* salvation,
   13. he could swear by no greater, (lit. he *had* by no greater to swear)
   18. we *might have* a strong consolation,
   19. we *have* as an anchor of the soul,
  7: 3. *having* neither beginning of days,
   5. *have* a commandment to take tithes

Heb. 7: 6. blessed him *that had* the promises.
   24. *hath* an unchangeable priesthood.
   27. Who needeth not daily, (lit. *hath* not need, &c.)
   28. high priests *which have* infirmity;
  8: 1. We *have* such an high priest,
   3. that this man *have* somewhat also
  9: 1. Then verily the first (covenant) *had* also
   4. *Which had* the golden censer,
  — the golden pot *that had* manna,
   8. was yet standing: (lit. yet *had* standing)
  10: 1. For the law *having* a shadow
   2. because that the worshippers...should have had (lit. through the worshippers... *having*) no more conscience
   19. *Having* therefore, brethren, boldness
   34. knowing in yourselves that ye *have*
   35. which *hath* great recompence of reward.
  36 For ye *have* need of patience,
  11: 10. a city *which hath* foundations,
   15. they might have *had* opportunity to have returned.
   25. than to enjoy the pleasures of sin for a season; (lit. *to have* temporary enjoyment of sin)
  12: 1. seeing we also are compassed about with so great a cloud (lit. *having* so great a cloud of w. encompassing us)
   9. we *have had* fathers of our flesh
   28. *let* us *have* grace, whereby we may
  13: 10. We *have* an altar, whereof they *have* no right to eat
   14. For here *have* we no continuing city,
   18. we *have* a good conscience,
Jas. 1: 4. *let* patience *have* (her) perfect work,
  2: 1. *have* not the faith of our Lord
   14. though a man say he *hath* faith, and *have* not works?
   17. faith, if it *hath* not works, is dead,
   18. a man may say, Thou *hast* faith, and I *have* works:
  3: 14. if ye *have* bitter envying and strife
  4: 2. Ye lust, and *have* not:
  — yet ye *have* not, because ye ask not.
1Pet. 2: 12. *Having* your conversation honest
   16. *using* (your) liberty for a cloke
  3: 16. *Having* a good conscience;
  4: 5. give account to him *that is* ready
   8. *And* above all things *have* fervent
2Pet. 1: 15. that ye may *be able* after my decease
   19. We *have* also a more sure word
  2: 14. *Having* eyes full of adultery,
  — an heart they *have* exercised with
   16. But was rebuked (lit. *had* rebuke) for his iniquity:
1Joh. 1: 3. that ye also *may have* fellowship
   6. we *have* fellowship with him,
   7. we *have* fellowship one with another,
   8. If we say that we *have* no sin.
  2: 1. we *have* an advocate with
   7. which ye *had* from the beginning.
   20. ye *have* an unction from
   23. the same *hath* not the Father:
   27. and ye need not (lit. *have* not need)
   28. we *may have* confidence,
  3: 3. And every man *that hath* this hope
   15. murderer *hath* eternal life abiding
   17. But whoso *hath* this world's good, and seeth his brother *have* need,
   21. (then) *have* we confidence toward God.
  4: 16. the love that God *hath* to us.
   17. perfect, that we *may have* boldness

1 Joh. 4:18. because fear *hath* torment.
21. this commandment *have* we from him,
5:10. *hath* the witness in himself:
12. He *that hath* the Son *hath* life ; (and) he *that hath* not the Son of God *hath* not life.
13. may know that ye *have* eternal life,
14. the confidence that we *have* in him,
15. we know that we *have* the petitions
2 Joh. 5. that which we *had* from the beginning,
9. *hath* not God. He that abideth in the doctrine of Christ, he *hath* both
12. *Having* many things to write unto you,
3 Joh. 4. I *have* no greater joy than to hear
13. I *had* many things to write,
Jude 3. it was needful for me to write (lit. I *had* need)
19. sensual, *having* not the Spirit.
Rev. 1:16. he *had* in his right hand
18. and *have* the keys of hell and
2: 3. And hast borne, and *hast* patience,
4. Nevertheless I *have* (somewhat) against
6. But this thou *hast*, that thou
7. He *that hath* an ear, let him hear
10. and ye *shall have* tribulation ten days:
11. He *that hath* an ear, let him hear
12. he *which hath* the sharp sword
14. I *have* a few things against thee, because thou *hast* there them that hold
15. So *hast* thou also them that
17. He *that hath* an ear, let him hear
18. the Son of God, *who hath* his eyes like
20. I *have* a few things against thee,
24. as many as *have* not this doctrine,
25. that which ye *have* (already) hold fast
29. He *that hath* an ear, let him hear
3: 1. he *that hath* the seven Spirits
— thou *hast* a name that thou livest,
4. Thou *hast* a few names even
6. He *that hath* an ear, let him hear
7. he *that hath* the key of David,
8. thou *hast* a little strength,
11. hold that fast which thou *hast*,
13. He *that hath* an ear, let him hear
17. and *have* need of nothing ;
22. He *that hath* an ear, let him hear
4: 4. they *had* on their heads crowns
7. the third beast *had* a face
8. beasts *had* each of them six wings
— and they rest not (lit. *have* not rest)
5: 6. *having* seven horns and seven eyes,
8. *having* every one of them harps,
6: 2. he that sat on him *had* a bow ;
5. *had* a pair of balances in his hand.
9. the testimony which they *held:*
7: 2. *having* the seal of the living God:
8: 3. *having* a golden censer ;
6. angels *which had* the seven trumpets
9. which were in the sea, *and had* life,
9: 3. as the scorpions of the earth *have* power.
4. which *have* not the seal of God
8. they *had* hair as the hair of women,
9. And they *had* breastplates,
10. they *had* tails like unto
11. they *had* a king over them,
— *hath* (his) name Apollyon.
14. which *had* the trumpet,
17. *having* breastplates of fire,
19. and *had* heads, and with them
10: 2. he *had* in his hand a little book
11: 6. These *have* power to shut heaven,
— and *have* power over waters to turn

Rev. 12: 2. And she being with child (lit. *having* in the womb)
3. red dragon, *having* seven heads
6. where she *hath* a place prepared
12. *having* great wrath, because he knoweth that he *hath* but a short time.
17. and *have* the testimony of Jesus Christ.
13: 1. *having* seven heads and ten horns,
9. If any man *have* an ear, let him hear.
11. he *had* two horns like a lamb,
14. which *had* the wound by a sword,
17. no man might buy or sell, save he *that had* the mark,
18. Let him *that hath* understanding count
14: 1. thousand, *having* his Father's name
6. *having* the everlasting gospel
11. they *have* no rest
14. *having* on his head a golden crown,
17. he also *having* a sharp sickle.
18. *which had* power over fire ;
— to him *that had* the sharp sickle,
15: 1. angels *having* the seven last plagues;
2. *having* the harps of God.
6. *having* the seven plagues,
16: 2. upon the men *which had* the mark of
9. of God, *which hath* power over
17: 1. one of the seven angels *which had* the
3. *having* seven heads and ten horns.
4. *having* a golden cup in her hand
7. *which hath* the seven heads
9. the mind *which hath* wisdom.
13. These *have* one mind, and shall give
18. which reigneth over (lit. *which hath* reign over)
18: 1. from heaven, *having* great power ;
19. all *that had* ships in the sea
19:10. brethren *that have* the testimony of Jesus:
12. *and he had* a name written,
16. he *hath* on (his) vesture
20: 1. *having* the key of the bottomless
6. Blessed and holy (is) he *that hath* part in the first resurrection: on such the second death *hath* no power,
21: 9. of the seven angels *which had* the
11. *Having* the glory of God:
12. And *had* a wall great and high, (and) *had*
14. wall of the city *had* twelve foundations,
15. *had* a golden reed to measure
23. the city *had* no need of the sun,
22: 5. they need no candle, (lit. they *have* not need)

ἕως, heōs.

Mat. 1:17. from Abraham *to* David (are) fourteen generations ; and from David *until* the
— *unto* Christ (are) fourteen generations.
25. *till* she had brought forth her firstborn
2: 9. *till* it came and stood
13. *until* I bring thee word:
15. *until* the death of Herod:
5:18. *Till* heaven and earth pass,
— *till* all be fulfilled.
25. *whiles* thou art in the way
26. *till* thou hast paid the uttermost
10:11. and there abide *till* ye go thence.
23. *till* the Son of man be come.
11:12. And from the days of John the Baptist *until* now
13. and the law prophesied *until* John.

Mat.11:23. art exalted *unto* heaven, shalt be brought
    down *to* hell :
  12:20. *till* he send forth judgment unto victory.
  13:33. *till* the whole was leavened.
  14:22. *while* he sent the multitudes away.
  16:28. *till* they see the Son of man
  17: 9. *until* the Son of man be risen again
    17. how long (lit. *until* when) shall I be with
    you ? *how long* shall I suffer you.?
  18:21. *till* seven times ?
    22. I say not unto thee, *Until* seven times: but,
    Until seventy times seven.
    30. *till* he should pay the debt.
    34. *till* he should pay all that was due
  20: 8. beginning from the last *unto* the first.
  22:26. also, and the third, *unto* the seventh.
    44. *till* I make thine enemies
  23:35. *unto* the blood of Zacharias
    39. henceforth, *till* ye shall say,
  24:21. beginning of the world *to* this time,
    27. shineth even *unto* the west ;
    31. one end of heaven *to* the other.
    34. *till* all these things be fulfilled.
    39. *until* the flood came,
  26:29. of this fruit of the vine, *until* that day
    36. *while* I go and pray yonder.
    38. My soul is exceeding sorrowful, *even unto*
    death:
    58. *unto* the high priest's palace,
  27: 8. field of blood, *unto* this day.
    45. over all the land *unto* the ninth hour.
    51. from the top *to* the bottom;
    64. be made sure *until* the third day,
  28:20. (even) *unto* the end of the world.
Mar. 6:10. there abide *till* ye depart from that place.
    23. *unto* the half of my kingdom.
    45. *while* he sent away the people.
  9: 1. *till* they have seen the kingdom
    19. *how long* (lit. *until* when) shall I be with
    you ? *how long* shall I suffer you?
  12:36. *till* I make thine enemies
  13:19. which God created *unto* this time,
    27. *to* the uttermost part of heaven.
  14:25. *until* that day that I drink it
    32. here, *while* I shall pray.
    34. My soul is exceeding sorrowful *unto* death:
    54. *even* into the palace of the
  15:33. the whole land *until* the ninth hour.
    38. from the top *to* the bottom.
Lu. 1:80. *till* the day of his shewing
  2:15. Let us now go even *unto* Bethlehem,
  4:29. and led him *unto* the brow of the hill
    42. sought him, and came *unto* him,
  9:27. *till* they see the kingdom
    41. *how long* (lit. *until* when) shall I be with
  10:15. art exalted *to* heaven, shalt be thrust down
    to hell.
  11:51. *unto* the blood of Zacharias,
  12:50. *till* it be accomplished !
    59. *till* thou hast paid the very last
  13: 8. *till* I shall dig about it,
    21. *till* the whole was leavened.
    35. *until* (the time) come when ye shall say,
  15: 4. *until* he find it ?
    8. and seek diligently *till* she find (it) ?
  16:16. prophets (were) *until* John:
  17: 8. *till* I have eaten and drunken ;
  19:13. Occupy *till* I come.
  20:43. *Till* I make thine enemies
  21:32. *till* all be fulfilled.
  22:16. *until* it be fulfilled in the kingdom
    18. *until* the kingdom of God

Lu. 22:51. Suffer ye thus *far.*
    23: 5. beginning from Galilee *to* this place.
    44. *until* the ninth hour.
  24:49. *until* ye be endued with power
    50. *as far as* to Bethany,
Joh. 2: 7. they filled them *up to* the brim.
    10. hast kept the good wine *until* now.
  5:17. My Father worketh hitherto, (lit. *until*
    now)
  8: 9. (even) *unto* the last:
  9: 4. *while* it is day:
    18. *until* they called the parents
  10:24. How long (lit. *till* when) dost thou make
  12:35. *while* ye have the light,
    36. *While* ye have light, believe
  13:38. *till* thou hast denied me thrice.
  16:24. Hither*to* have ye asked nothing
  21:22. If I will that he tarry *till* I come,
    23. tarry *till* I come, what (is that) to thee ?
Acts 1: 8. *unto* the uttermost part of the earth.
    22. *unto* that same day that
  2:35. *Until* I make thy foes
  7:45. *unto* the days of David;
  8:10. from the least *to* the greatest,
    40. *till* he came to Cæsarea.
  9:38. he would not delay to come *to* them.
  11:19. travelled *as far as* Phenice,
    22. that he should go *as far as* Antioch.
  13:20. *until* Samuel the prophet.
    47. *unto* the ends of the earth.
  17:15. brought him *unto* Athens:
  21: 5. *till* (we were) out of the city:
    26. *until* that an offering should be offered
  23:12. *till* they had killed Paul.
    14. eat nothing *until* we have slain Paul.
    21. *till* they have killed him:
    23. soldiers to go *to* Cæsarea,
  25:21. *till* I might send him
  26:11. even *unto* strange cities.
  28:23. from morning *till* evening.
Ro. 3:12. no, not one. (lit. there is not *even* one)
  11: 8. should not hear ; *unto* this day.
1Co. 1: 8. shall also confirm you *unto* the end,
  4: 5. *until* the Lord come,
    13. the offscouring of all things *unto* this day.
  8: 7. *unto* this hour eat (it) as a thing offered
    unto an idol;
  15: 6. the greater part remain *unto* this present,
  16: 8. will tarry at Ephesus *until* Pentecost.
2Co. 1:13. ye shall acknowledge even *to* the end ;
  3:15. But *even unto* this day,
  12: 2. caught up *to* the third heaven.
2Th. 2: 7. *until* he be taken out of the way.
1Ti. 4:13. *Till* I come, give attendance
Heb. 1:13. *until* I make thine enemies
  8:11. know me, from the least *to* the greatest.
  10:13. *till* his enemies be made
Jas. 5: 7. *unto* the coming of the Lord.
  — *until* he receive the early and latter rain.
2Pet.1:19. *until* the day dawn,
1Joh.2: 9. is in darkness *even until* now.
Rev. 6:10. How long (lit. *till* when) O Lord, holy
    11. *until* their fellowservants also and
  20: 5. *until* the thousand years were finished.

ζάω, zao.

Mat. 4: 4. Man *shall* not *live* by bread alone,
  9:18. upon her, and she *shall live.*

Mat.16:16. the Son of the *living* God.
    22:32. of the dead, but of the *living.*
    26:63. I adjure thee by the *living* God,
    27:63. said, *while* he *was* yet *alive,*
Mar. 5:23. that she may be healed; and she *shall live.*
    12:27. but the God of the *living:*
    16:11. when they had heard that he *was alive,*
Lu. 2:36. *and had lived* with an husband seven years
    4: 4. man *shall* not *live* by bread alone,
    10:28. this do, and thou *shalt live.*
    15:13. with riotous *living.* (lit *living* riotously)
    20:38. of the dead, but of the *living:* for all *live* unto him.
    24: 5. the *living* among the dead?
    23. which said that he *was alive.*
Joh. 4:10. he would have given thee *living* water.
    11. hast thou that *living* water?
    50. Go thy way; thy son *liveth.*
    51. and told (him), saying, Thy son *liveth.*
    53. said unto him, Thy son *liveth:*
    5:25. they that hear *shall live.*
    6:51. I am the *living* bread which came down
    — he *shall live* for ever:
    57. As the *living* Father hath sent me, and I *live* by the Father:
    — even he *shall live* by me.
    58. eateth of this bread *shall live* for ever.
    69. the Son of the *living* God.
    7:38. shall flow rivers of *living* water.
    11:25. though he were dead, yet *shall* he *live:*
    26. *whosoever liveth* and believeth
    14:19. I *live,* ye *shall live* also.
Acts 1: 3. he shewed himself *alive*
    7:38. the *lively* oracles to give unto us:
    9:41. saints and widows, presented her *alive.*
    10:42. (to be) the Judge of *quick* and dead.
    14:15. unto the *living* God,
    17:28. For in him we *live,*
    20:12. they brought the young man *alive,*
    22:22. for it is not fit that he should *live.*
    25:19. whom Paul affirmed *to be alive.*
    24. that he ought not *to live* any longer.
    26: 5. I *lived* a Pharisee.
    28: 4. yet vengeance suffereth not *to live.*
Ro. 1:17. *shall live* by faith.
    6: 2. How *shall we,...live* any longer therein?
    10. to be but in that he *liveth,* he *liveth* unto God.
    11. dead indeed unto sin, but *alive* unto God
    13. as *those that are alive* from the dead,
    7: 1. as long as he *liveth?*
    2. is bound by the law to (her) husband *so long as he liveth;*
    3. So then if, *while* (her) husband *liveth,*
    9. I *was alive* without the law once:
    8:12. *to live* after the flesh.
    13. For if ye *live* after the flesh,
    — deeds of the body, ye *shall live.*
    9:26. the children of the *living* God.
    10: 5. which doeth those things *shall live* by
    12: 1. present your bodies a *living* sacrifice,
    14: 7. For none of us *liveth* to himself,
    8. For whether we *live,* we *live* unto the
    — whether we *live* therefore, or die,
    9. he might be Lord both of the dead and *living.*
    11. (As) I *live,* saith the Lord,
1Co. 7:39. as long as her husband *liveth;*
    9:14. should *live* of the gospel.
    15:45. The first man Adam was made a *living*
2Co. 1: 8. we despaired even of *life:* (lit. *to live*)

2Co. 3: 3. with the Spirit of the *living* God;
    4:11. For we *which live* are alway delivered
    5:15. that they *which live should* not henceforth *live* unto themselves,
    6: 9. as dying, and, behold, we *live;*
    16. ye are the temple of the *living* God;
    13: 4. yet he *liveth* by the power of God.
    — we *shall live* with him by the power of
Gal. 2:14. *livest* after the manner of Gentiles,
    19. that I *might live* unto God.
    20. nevertheless I live; yet not I (lit. and *live* no more I), but Christ *liveth* in me: and the life which I now *live* in the flesh I *live* by the faith of the Son of God,
    3:11. The just *shall live* by faith.
    12. man that doeth them *shall live* in them.
    5:25. If we *live* in the Spirit,
Phi. 1:21. For to me *to live* (is) Christ,
    22. But if I *live* in the flesh,
Col. 2:20. why, as though *living* in the world,
    3: 7. also walked some time, when ye *lived* in them.
1Th 1: 9. to serve the *living* and true God;
    3: 8. For now we *live,* if ye stand fast
    4:15. we *which are alive* (and) remain
    17. we *which are alive* (and) remain
    5:10. we *should live* together with him.
1Ti. 3:15. the church of the *living* God,
    4:10. we trust in the *living* God,
    5: 6. is dead *while* she *liveth.*
    6:17. but in the *living* God,
2Ti. 3:12. and all that will *live* godly in Christ
    4: 1. who shall judge the *quick* and the dead
Tit. 2:12. we *should live* soberly, righteously,
Heb 2:15. were all their *life*time subject to bondage.
    3:12. in departing from the *living* God.
    4:12. the word of God (is) *quick,* and powerful,
    7: 8. of whom it is witnessed that he *liveth.*
    25. *seeing* he ever *liveth* to make intercession
    9:14. to serve the *living* God?
    17. while the testator *liveth.*
    10:20. By a new and *living* way,
    31. into the hands of the *living* God.
    38. Now the just *shall live* by faith:
    12: 9. unto the Father of spirits, and *live?*
    22. unto the city of the *living* God,
Jas. 4:15. If the Lord will, we *shall live,* and do this, or that.
1Pet.1: 3. begotten us again unto a *lively* hope
    23. by the word of God, *which liveth* and
    2: 4. To whom coming, (as unto) a *living*
    5. as *lively* stones, are built up
    24. *should live* unto righteousness:
    4: 5. to judge the *quick* and the dead.
    6. but *live* according to God in the spirit.
1Joh.4: 9. that we *might live* through him.
Rev. 1:18. (I am) he *that liveth,* and was dead; and, behold, I am *alive*
    2: 8. which was dead, and *is alive;*
    3: 1. that thou *livest,* and art dead.
    4: 9. *who liveth* for ever and ever,
    10. worship him *that liveth* for ever and
    5:14. worshipped him *that liveth* for ever
    7: 2. the seal of the *living* God:
    17. unto *living* fountains of waters:
    10: 6. sware by him *that liveth* for ever
    13:14. had the wound by a sword, and *did live.*
    15: 7. of the wrath of God, *who liveth* for ever
    16: 3. every *living* soul died in the sea.
    19:20. both were cast *alive* into a lake of fire
    20: 4. they *lived* and reigned with Christ a

ζεστός, zestos.

Rev. 3:15. thou art neither cold nor *hot :* I would thou wert cold or *hot.*
    16. lukewarm, and neither cold nor *hot,*

ζεῦγος, zūgos.

Lu. 2:24. A *pair* of turtledoves,
  14:19. I have bought five *yoke* of oxen,

ζευκτηρία, zūkteeria.

Acts27:40. and loosed the rudder *bands,*

ζέω, zeo.

Acts18:25. *being fervent* in the spirit,
Ro. 12:11. *fervent* in spirit ; serving the Lord ;

ζῆλος, zeelos.

Joh. 2:17. The *zeal* of thine house hath eaten me up.
Acts 5:17. were filled with *indignation,*
  13:45. they were filled with *envy,*
Ro. 10: 2. they have a *zeal* of God,
  13:13. not in strife and *envying.*
1Co. 3: 3. *envying,* and strife, and divisions,
2Co. 7: 7. your *fervent mind* toward me ;
    11. yea, (what) *zeal,* yea, (what) revenge !
   9: 2. your *zeal* hath provoked very many.
  11: 2. For I am jealous over you with godly *jealousy:*
  12:20. *envyings,* wraths, strifes,
Gal. 5:20. variance, *emulations,* wrath, strife,
Phi. 3: 6. Concerning *zeal,* persecuting the
Col. 4:13. he hath a great *zeal* for you,
Heb 10:27. fiery *indignation,* which shall devour
Jas. 3:14. But if ye have bitter *envying*
    16. For where *envying* and strife (is),

ζηλόω, zeeloō.

Acts 7: 9. the patriarchs, *moved with envy,*
  17: 5. But the Jews which believed not, *moved with envy,* took
1Co.12:31. But *covet earnestly* the best gifts:
  13: 4. charity *envieth* not ;
  14: 1. and *desire* spiritual (gifts),
    39. *covet* to prophesy, and forbid not
2Co.11: 2. For I *am jealous over* you with godly
Gal. 4:17. They *zealously affect* you, (but) not well ;
    — that ye *might affect* them.
    18. good *to be zealously affected* always in (a) good (thing),
Jas. 4: 2. ye kill, and *desire to have,*
Rev. 3:19. *be zealous* therefore, and repent.

ζηλωτής, zeelōtees.

Acts21:20. and they are all *zealous* of the law:
  22: 3. and was *zealous* toward God,
1Co.14:12. as ye are *zealous* of spiritual (gifts),
Gal. 1:14. *zealous* of the traditions of my fathers.
Tit. 2:14. a peculiar people, *zealous* of good works.

ζημία, zeemia.

Acts27:10. will be with hurt and much *damage,*
    21. to have gained this harm and *loss.*
Phi. 3: 7. I counted *loss* for Christ.
   8. I count all things (but) *loss*

ζημιόω, zeemioō.

Mat.16:26. if he shall gain the whole world, and *lose* his own soul?
Mar. 8:36. and *lose* his own soul?
Lu. 9:25. and lose himself, or *be cast away?*
1Co. 3:15. he *shall suffer loss :* but he himself
2Co. 7: 9. ye *might receive damage* by us in nothing.
Phi. 3: 8. I *have suffered the loss* of all things,

ζητέω, zeeteo.

Mat. 2:13. for Herod will *seek* the young child
    20. they are dead *which sought* the young child's life.
  6:33. But *seek* ye first the kingdom
  7: 7. *seek,* and ye shall find ;
   8. he *that seeketh* findeth ;
  12:43. *seeking* rest, and findeth none.
    46. *desiring* to speak with him.
    47. *desiring* to speak with thee.
  13:45. unto a merchant man, *seeking* goodly
  18:12. and *seeketh* that which is gone astray?
  21:46. *when* they sought to lay hands on him,
  26:16. he *sought* opportunity to betray him.
    59. and all the council, *sought* false witness
  28: 5. ye *seek* Jesus, which was crucified.
Mar. 1:37. All (men) *seek for* thee.
  3:32. without *seek for* thee.
  8:11. *seeking* of him a sign from heaven,
  11:18. *sought* how they might destroy him:
  12:12. they *sought* to lay hold on him,
  14: 1. the chief priests and the scribes *sought*
    11. he *sought* how he might conveniently
    55. *sought for* witness against Jesus
  16: 6. Ye *seek* Jesus of Nazareth,
Lu. 2:45. back again to Jerusalem, *seeking* him.
    48. *have sought* thee sorrowing.
    49. How is it that ye *sought* me?
  4:42. and the people *sought* him,
  5:18. they *sought* (means) to bring him in,
  6:19. multitude *sought* to touch him: for
  9: 9. he *desired* to see him.
  11: 9. *seek,* and ye shall find ;
    10. he *that seeketh* findeth ;
    16. *sought* of him a sign from heaven.
    24. through dry places, *seeking* rest;
    54. *seeking* to catch something
  12:29. *seek* not ye what ye shall eat, or
    31. *seek* ye the kingdom of God ;
    48. of him *shall be* much *required :*
  13: 6. *and sought* fruit thereon,
   7. these three years I come *seeking* fruit
    24. many, I say unto you, *will seek* to enter
  15: 8. and *seek* diligently till she find
  17:33. Whosoever *shall seek* to save his life
  19: 3. he *sought* to see Jesus
    10. is come *to seek* and to save that which was
    47. *sought* to destroy him,
  20:19. scribes the same hour *sought* to lay
  22: 2. the chief priests and scribes *sought*
   6. he promised, and *sought* opportunity
  24: 5. Why *seek* ye the living among

Joh. 1:38(39). and saith unto them, What *seek* ye?
4:23. the Father *seeketh* such to worship
27. said, What *seekest* thou?
5:16. and *sought* to slay him,
18. the Jews *sought* the more to kill him,
30. I *seek* not minè own will,
44. and *seek* not the honour that
6:24. came to Capernaum, *seeking for* Jesus.
26. Ye *seek* me, not because ye saw
7: 1. because the Jews *sought* to kill him.
4. he himself *seeketh* to be known openly.
11. *sought* him at the feast,
18. *seeketh* his own glory: but he *that seeketh*
his glory that sent him,
19. Why *go* ye *about* to kill me?
20. who *goeth about* to kill thee?
25. whom they *seek* to kill?
30. Then they *sought* to take him:
34. Ye *shall seek* me, and shall not find
36. Ye *shall seek* me, and shall not find (me):
8:21. ye *shall seek* me, and shall die in your
37. but ye *seek* to kill me,
40. But now ye *seek* to kill me,
50. I *seek* not mine own glory: there is one
that seeketh and judgeth.
10:39. Therefore they *sought* again to take him
11: 8. the Jews of late *sought* to stone thee;
56. Then *sought* they for Jesus,
13:33. Ye *shall seek* me: and as
16:19. *Do* ye *enquire* among yourselves
18: 4. said unto them, Whom *seek* ye?
7. asked he them again, Whom *seek* ye?
8. if therefore ye *seek* me,
19:12. thenceforth Pilate *sought* to release
20:15. why weepest thou? whom *seekest* thou?
Acts 9:11. *enquire* in the house of Judas *for* (one)
called Saul,
10:19. Behold, three men *seek* thee.
21. I am he whom ye *seek:*
13: 8. *seeking* to turn away the deputy
11. *seeking* some to lead him by the hand.
16:10. we *endeavoured* to go into Macedonia,
17: 5. and *sought* to bring them out
27. That they should *seek* the Lord,
21:31. And *as* they *went about* to kill him,
27:30. And *as* the shipmen *were about* to flee
Ro. 2: 7. To them *who* by patient continuance in
well doing *seek for* glory and
10: 3. and *going about* to establish their own
righteousness,
20. I was found of them *that sought* me not;
11: 3. am left alone, and they *seek* my life.
1Co. 1:22. and the Greeks *seek after* wisdom:
4: 2 it *is required* in stewards,
7:27. *seek* not to be loosed. Art thou loosed
from a wife? *seek* not a wife.
10:24. *Let* no man *seek* his own,
33. not *seeking* mine own profit, but
13: 5. *seeketh* not her own, is not easily
14:12. *seek* that ye may excel
2Co.12:14. for I *seek* not your's, but you:
13: 3. ye *seek* a proof of Christ speaking in me,
Gal. 1:10. or do I *seek* to please men?
2:17. But if, *while* we *seek* to be justified
Phi. 2:21. all *seek* their own, not the things
Col. 3: 1. *seek* those things which are above,
1Th. 2: 6. Nor of men *sought* we glory,
2Ti. 1:17. he *sought* me out very diligently,
Heb 8: 7. then should no place *have been sought* for
1Pet.3:11. *let* him *seek* peace, and ensue it.
5: 8. *seeking* whom he may devour:
Rev. 9: 6. in those days *shall* men *seek* death,

ζήτημα, zeeteema.

Acts15: 2. apostles and elders about this *question.*
18:15. But if it be a *question* of words and
23:29. accused of *questions* of their law,
25:19. But had certain *questions* against him
26: 3. expert in all customs and *questions*

ζήτησις, zeeteesis.

Joh. 3:25. Then there arose a *question* between
Acts25:20. I doubted of such manner of questions,
(lit. I was at a loss about *inquiry* into
this)
1Ti. 1: 4. genealogies, which minister *questions,*
6: 4. about *questions* and strifes of words,
2Ti. 2:23. foolish and unlearned *questions* avoid,
Tit. 3: 9. But avoid foolish *questions,* and

ζιζάνια, zizania.

Mat.13:25. his enemy came and sowed *tares*
26. then appeared the *tares* also.
27. from whence then hath it *tares?*
29. while ye gather up the *tares,*
30. Gather ye together first the *tares,*
36. the parable of the *tares* of the field.
38. but the *tares* are the children of the wicked
40. As therefore the *tares* are gathered and

ζόφος, zophos.

2Pet. 2: 4. delivered (them) into chains of *darkness,*
17. to whom the *mist* of darkness is reserved
Jude 6. he hath reserved in everlasting chains
under *darkness*
13. to whom is reserved the *blackness* of darkness for ever.

ζυγός, zugos.

Mat.11:29. Take my *yoke* upon you, and
30. For my *yoke* (is) easy,
Acts15:10. to put a *yoke* upon the neck of the
Gal. 5: 1. entangled again with the *yoke* of bondage.
1Ti. 6: 1. servants as are under the *yoke*
Rev. 6: 5. had a *pair of balances* in his hand.

ζύμη, zumee.

Mat.13:33. unto *leaven,* which a woman took,
16: 6. beware of the *leaven* of the Pharisees
11. beware of the *leaven* of the Pharisees
12. not beware of the *leaven* of bread,
Mar. 8:15. of the *leaven* of the Pharisees, and (of)
the *leaven* of Herod.
Lu. 12: 1. of the *leaven* of the Pharisees,
13:21. It is like *leaven,*
1Co. 5: 6. a little *leaven* leaveneth the whole lump?
7. Purge out therefore the old *leaven,*
8. let us keep the feast, not with old *leaven,*
neither with the *leaven* of malice
Gal. 5: 9. A little *leaven* leaveneth the whole lump.

ζυμόω, zumoō.

Mat.13:33. till the whole *was leavened.*

Lu. 13:21. till the whole *was leavened*.
1Co. 5: 6. a little leaven *leaveneth* the whole lump?
Gal. 5: 9. *leaveneth* the whole lump.

ζωγρέω, *zōgreo*.

Lu. 5:10. henceforth thou shalt *catch* men.
2Ti. 2:26. *who are taken captive* by him at his will.

ζωή, *zōee*.

Mat. 7:14. the way, which leadeth unto *life*,
18: 8. is better for thee to enter into *life*
9. to enter into *life* with one eye,
19:16. that I may have eternal *life*?
17. but if thou wilt enter into *life*,
29. shall inherit everlasting *life*.
25:46. the righteous into *life* eternal.
Mar. 9:43. for thee to enter into *life* maimed,
45. to enter halt into *life*,
10.17. that I may inherit eternal *life*?
30. and in the world to come eternal *life*.
Lu. 1:75. before him, all the days of our *life*.
10:25. to inherit eternal *life*?
12:15. a man's *life* consisteth not in
16:25. thou in thy *lifetime* receivedst
18:18. to inherit eternal *life*?
30. in the world to come *life* everlasting.
Joh. 1: 4. In him was *life*; and the *life* was the light of men.
3:15. but have eternal *life*.
16. but have everlasting *life*.
36. He that believeth on the Son hath everlasting *life*:
— shall not see *life*;
4:14. into everlasting *life*.
36. fruit unto *life* eternal:
5:24. hath everlasting *life*,
— is passed from death unto *life*.
26. Father hath *life* in himself; so hath he given to the Son to have *life* in himself;
29. unto the resurrection of *life*;
39. in them ye think ye have eternal *life*:
40. that ye might have *life*.
6:27. endureth unto everlasting *life*,
33. giveth *life* unto the world.
35. I am the bread of *life*:
40. may have everlasting *life*:
47. He that believeth on me hath everlasting *life*.
48. I am that bread of *life*.
51. for the *life* of the world.
53. ye have no *life* in you.
54. hath eternal *life*;
63. (they) are spirit, and (they) are *life*.
68. thou hast the words of eternal *life*.
8:12. shall have the light of *life*.
10:10. am come that they might have *life*,
28. give unto them eternal *life*;
11:25. the resurrection, and the *life*:
12:25. shall keep it unto *life* eternal.
50. his commandment is *life* everlasting:
14: 6. am the way, the truth, and the *life*:
17: 2. he should give eternal *life* to
3. And this is *life* eternal,
20:31. believing ye might have *life*
Acts 2:28. made known to me the ways of *life*;
3:15. And killed the Prince of *life*,
5:20. all the words of this *life*.
8:33. his *life* is taken from the earth.

Acts11:18. granted repentance unto *life*.
13:46. unworthy of everlasting *life*,
48. ordained to eternal *life*
17:25. he giveth to all *life*,
Ro. 2: 7. To them who by patient...eternal *life*:
5:10. we shall be saved by his *life*.
17. shall reign in *life* by one,
18. unto justification of *life*.
21. through righteousness unto eternal *life*
6: 4. we also should walk in newness of *life*.
22. and the end everlasting *life*.
23. (is) eternal *life* through Jesus Christ
7:10. the commandment, which (was ordained) to *life*,
8: 2. the law of the Spirit of *life*
6. to be spiritually minded (is) *life* and
10. (is) *life* because of righteousness.
38. that neither death, nor *life*,
11:15. but *life* from the dead?
1Co. 3:22. or *life*, or death, or things present,
15:19. If in this *life* only we have hope in Christ,
2Co. 2:16. and to the other the savour of *life* unto *life*.
4:10. that the *life* also of Jesus might be
11. the *life* also of Jesus might be made manifest in our mortal flesh.
12. death worketh in us, but *life* in you.
5: 4. mortality might be swallowed up of *life*.
Gal. 6: 8. shall of the Spirit reap *life* everlasting.
Eph. 4:18. alienated from the *life* of God
Phi. 1:20. whether (it be) by *life*, or by death.
2:16. Holding forth the word of *life*;
4: 3. names (are) in the book of *life*.
Col. 3: 3. and your *life* is hid with Christ in God.
4. When Christ, (who is) our *life*,
1Ti. 1:16. believe on him to *life* everlasting.
4: 8. having promise of the *life* that now is,
6:12. lay hold on eternal *life*,
19. may lay hold on eternal *life*.
2Ti. 1: 1. of *life* which is in Christ Jesus,
10. brought *life* and immortality to light
Tit. 1: 2. In hope of eternal *life*,
3: 7. according to the hope of eternal *life*.
Heb. 7: 3. having neither beginning of days, nor end of *life*;
16. after the power of an endless *life*.
Jas. 1:12. he shall receive the crown of *life*,
4:14. For what (is) your *life*?
1Pet.3: 7. heirs together of the grace of *life*;
10. For he that will love *life*,
2Pet.1: 3. that (pertain) unto *life* and godliness,
1Joh.1: 1. of the Word of *life*;
2. the *life* was manifested,
— and shew unto you that eternal *life*,
2:25. hath promised us, (even) eternal *life*.
3:14. we have passed from death unto *life*,
15. hath eternal *life* abiding in him.
5:11. that God hath given to us eternal *life*, and this *life* is in his Son.
12. He that hath the Son hath *life*; (and) he that hath not the Son of God hath not *life*.
13. that ye have eternal *life*,
16. and he shall give him *life*
20. This is the true God, and eternal *life*.
Jude 21. of our Lord Jesus Christ unto eternal *life*.
Rev. 2: 7. will I give to eat of the tree of *life*,
10. I will give thee a crown of *life*.
3: 5. out of the book of *life*,
11:11. the Spirit of *life* from God
13: 8. in the book of *life* of the Lamb
17: 8. in the book of *life*

Rev.20:12. which is (the book) of *life* :
15. written in the book of *life*
21: 6. of the water of *life* freely.
27. the Lamb's book of *life.*
22: 1. river of water of *life,*
2. (was there) the tree of *life,*
14. they may have right to the tree of *life,*
17. whosoever will, let him take the water of *life* freely.
19. his part out of the book of *life,*

ζώνη, *zōnee.*

Mat. 3: 4. a leathern *girdle* about his loins;
10: 9. silver, nor brass in your *purses,*
Mar. 1: 6. a *girdle* of a skin about his loins;
6: 8. no money in (their) *purse:*
Acts21:11. he took Paul's *girdle,*
— bind the man that owneth this *girdle,*
Rev. 1:13. about the paps with a golden *girdle.*
15: 6. girded with golden *girdles.*

ζωννύω, *zōnnuo.*

Joh.21:18. When thou wast young, thou *girdedst*
— and another *shall gird* thee,

ζωογονέω, *zōogoneo.*

Lu. 17:33. lose his life *shall preserve* it.
Acts 7:19. to the end they might not *live.*

ζῶον, *zōon.*

Heb 13:11. of those *beasts,* whose blood is brought
2Pet. 2:12. as natural brute *beasts,*
Jude 10. know naturally, as brute *beasts,*
Rev. 4: 6. (were) four *beasts* full
7. the first *beast* (was) like a lion, and the second *beast* like a calf, and the third *beast* had a face as a man, and the fourth *beast*
8. And the four *beasts* had each of them
9. when those *beasts* give glory
5: 6. and of the four *beasts,*
8. the four *beasts* and
11. round about the throne and the *beasts*
14. And the four *beasts* said, Amen.
6: 1. I heard,...one of the four *beasts* saying,
3. I heard the second *beast* say,
5. I heard the third *beast* say,
6. in the midst of the four *beasts*
7. the voice of the fourth *beast*
7:11. (about) the elders and the four *beasts,*
14: 3. before the four *beasts,*
15: 7. one of the four *beasts* gave
19: 4. elders and the four *beasts* fell down

ζωοποιέω, *zōopoieo.*

Joh. 5:21. raiseth up the dead, and *quickeneth* (them); even so the Son *quickeneth* whom he
6:63. It is the spirit *that quickeneth ;*
Ro. 4:17. God, *who quickeneth* the dead,
8:11. *shall* also *quicken* your mortal bodies
1Co.15:22. *shall* all *be made alive.*

1Co.15:36. that which thou sowest *is* not *quickened,*
45. (was made) a *quickening* spirit.
2Co. 3: 6. but the spirit *giveth life.*
Gal. 3:21. which could *have given life,*
1Ti. 6:13. of God, *who quickeneth* all things,
1Pet.3:18. but *quickened* by the Spirit:

ἤ, *ee.*

Mat. 1:18. before)(they came together,
5:17. to destroy the law, *or* the prophets:
18. one jot *or* one tittle shall in no wise
36. not make one hair white *or* black.
6:24. for *either* he will hate the one,...*or else* he will hold to the one,
31. *or,* What shall we drink? *or,* Wherewithal shall we be clothed?
7: 4. *Or* how wilt thou say to thy brother,
9. *Or* what man is there of you,
16. grapes of thorns, *or* figs of thistles?
9: 5. *or* to say, Arise, and walk?
10:11. And into whatsoever city *or* town
14. depart out of that house *or* city,
15. *than* for that city.
19. how *or* what ye shall speak:
37. He that loveth father *or* mother
— he that loveth son *or* daughter
11: 3. *or* do we look for another?
22. at the day of judgment, *than* for you.
24. in the day of judgment, *than* for thee.
12: 5. *Or* have ye not read in the law,
25. and every city *or* house divided
29. *Or else* how can one enter into
33. *Either* make the tree good,
— *or else* make the tree corrupt,
13:21. *or* persecution ariseth because of the
15: 4. He that curseth father *or* mother,
5. say to (his) father *or* (his) mother,
6(5). honour not his father *or* his mother,
16:14. *or* one of the prophets.
26. *or* what shall a man give
17:25. custom *or* tribute? of their own children, *or* of strangers?
18: 8. if thy hand *or* thy foot
— halt *or* maimed, rather *than* having two hands *or* two feet
9. rather *than* having two eyes
13. *than* of the ninety and nine
16. take with thee one *or* two more, that in the mouth of two *or* three witnesses
20. For where two *or* three are gathered
19:24. *than* for a rich man to enter into the
29. that hath forsaken houses, *or* brethren, *or* sisters, *or* father, *or* mother, *or* wife, *or* children, *or* lands, for my name's sake,
20:15.)(Is it not lawful for me
—)(Is thine eye evil,
21:25. from heaven, *or* of men?
22:17. tribute unto Cæsar, *or* not?
23:17. whether is greater, the gold, *or* the temple
19. greater, the gift, *or* the altar
24:23. here (is) Christ, *or* there;
25:37. *or* thirsty, and gave (thee) drink?
38. *or* naked, and clothed (thee)?
39. sick, *or* in prison,
44. when saw we thee an hungred, *or* athirst, *or* a stranger, *or* naked, *or* sick, *or* in

Mat.26:53.)(Thinkest thou that I cannot
   — more *than* twelve legions of angels?
27:17. Barabbas, *or* Jesus which is called
Mar. 2: 9. (Thy) sins be forgiven thee ; *or* to say,
   3: 4. to do good on the sabbath days, *or* to do
     evil? to save life, *or* to kill?
   33. my mother, *or* my brethren?
   4:21. under a bushel, *or* under a bed?
   30. *or* with what comparison
   6:11. for Sodom *and* Gomorrha in the day of
     judgment, *than* for that city.
   15. it is a prophet, *or* as one of the prophets.
   56. *or* cities, *or* country,
   7:10. Whoso curseth father *or* mother,
   11. say to his father *or* mother,
   12. for his father *or* his mother;
   8:37. *Or* what shall a man give
   9:43. *than* having two hands
   45. *than* having two feet
   47. *than* having two eyes
   10:25. *than* for a rich man to enter into the
   29. hath left house, *or* brethren, *or* sisters, *or*
     father, *or* mother, *or* wife, *or* children,
     or lands,
   11:30. was (it) from heaven, *or* of men?
   12:14. to give tribute to Cæsar, *or* not?
   15(14). Shall we give, *or* shall we not give?
   13:21. here (is) Christ; *or*, lo, (he is) there ;
   35. at even, *or* at midnight, *or* at the cock-
     crowing, *or* in the morning:
   14:30. before)(the cock crow twice,
Lu. 2:24. *or* two young pigeons.
   26. before)(he had seen the Lord's Christ.
   5:23. *or* to say, Rise up
   6: 9. to do good, *or* to do evil? to save life, *or*
     to destroy (it)?
   42. *Either* how canst thou say
   7:19. *or* look we for another?
   20. *or* look we for another?
   8:16. *or* putteth (it) under a bed ;
   9:13. We have no more *but* five loaves
   25. lose himself, *or* be cast away?
   10:12. more tolerable in that day for Sodom, *than*
     for that city.
   14. at the judgment, *than* for you.
   11·12. *Or* if he shall ask an egg,
   12:11. how *or* what thing ye shall answer, *or*
     what ye shall say:
   14. who made me a judge *or* a divider
   29. what ye shall eat, *or* what ye shall drink,
   41. unto us, *or* even to all?
   51. I tell you, Nay; but *rather* division:
   13: 4. *Or* those eighteen, upon whom
   15. loose his ox *or* (his) ass from the stall,
   14: 5. an ass *or* an ox fallen into a pit,
   12. thou makest a dinner *or* a supper,
   31. *Or* what king, going to make war
   15: 7. more *than* over ninety and nine
   8. *Either* what woman having ten pieces of
   16:13. for *either* he will hate the one,
   — *or else* he will hold to the one,
   17. *than* one tittle of the law
   17: 2. *than* that he should offend
   7. a servant plowing *or* feeding cattle,
   21. Lo here! *or*, lo there !
   23. See here ; *or*, see there:
   18:11. *or* even as this publican.
   14. to his house justified (rather) *than* the
   25. *than* for a rich man to enter into the
   29. *or* parents, *or* brethren, *or* wife, *or*
   20: 2. *or* who is he that gave thee this
   4. was it from heaven, *or* of men?

Lu. 20:22. to give tribute unto Cæsar, *or* no?
   22:27. he that sitteth at meat, *or* he that serveth?
   34. before *that* thou shalt thrice deny
   68. ye will not answer me, *nor* let (me) go.
Joh. 2: 6. two *or* three firkins
   3:19. loved darkness rather *than* light,
   4: 1. baptized more disciples *than* John,
   27. What seekest thou? *or*, Why talkest thou
   6:19. five and twenty *or* thirty furlongs,
   7:17. be of God, *or* (whether) I speak of
   48. any of the rulers *or* of the Pharisees
   9: 2. this man, *or* his parents,
   21. *or* who hath opened his eyes,
   13:10. needeth not *save* to wash (his) feet,
   29. *or*, that he should give something to the
   18:34. *or* did others tell it thee of me?
Acts 1: 7. the times *or* the seasons, which
   2:20. before)(that great and notable day of the
     Lord come:
   3:12. *or* why look ye so earnestly on us, as
     though by our own power *or* holiness
   4: 7. *or* by what name, have ye done this?
   19. hearken unto you more *than* unto God,
   34. possessors of lands *or* houses
   5:29. We ought to obey God rather *than* men.
   38. if this counsel *or* this work be of men,
   7: 2. before)(he dwelt in Charran,
   49. *or* what (is) the place of my rest?
   8:34. of himself, *or* of some other
   10:14. any thing that is common *or* unclean.
   28. *or* come unto one of another nation;
   — not call any man common *or* unclean.
   11: 8. nothing common *or* unclean
   17:21. *but either* to tell, or to hear some new
   29. unto gold, *or* silver, *or* stone,
   18:14. a matter of wrong *or* wicked lewdness,
   19:12. unto the sick handkerchiefs *or* aprons,
   20:33. no man's silver, *or* gold, *or* apparel.
   35. more blessed to give *than* to receive.
   23: 9. if a spirit *or* an angel hath spoken to him,
   29. worthy of death *or* of bonds.
   24:11. there are yet but (lit. not more *than*)
     twelve days
   12. *neither* raising up the people,
   20. *Or else* let these same (here) say,
   21. *Except it be* for this one voice,
   23. to minister *or* come unto him.
   25: 6. among them more *than* ten days,
   16. before *that* he which is accused
   26:31. nothing worthy of death *or* of bonds.
   27:11. more *than* those things which
   28: 6. *or* fallen down dead suddenly:
   17. *or* customs of our fathers,
   21. *or* spake any harm of thee.
Ro. 1:21. they glorified (him) not as God, *neither*
     were thankful;
   2: 4. *Or* despisest thou the riches of his
   15. accusing *or* else excusing one another ;
   3: 1. *or* what profit (is there)
   29.)((Is he) the God of the Jews only?
   4: 9. *or* upon the uncircumcision also?
   10. *or* in uncircumcision?
   13. to Abraham, *or* to his seed,
   6: 3.)(Know ye not, that so many
   16. *or* of obedience unto righteousness?
   7: 1.)(Know ye not, brethren,
   8:35. *or* distress, *or* persecution, *or* famine, *or*
     nakedness, *or* peril, *or* sword?
   9:11. having done any good *or* evil,
   21.)(Hath not the potter power
   10: 7. *Or*, Who shall descend
   11: 2.)(Wot ye not what the scripture saith of

Ro. 11:34. *or* who hath been his counsellor?
35. *Or* who hath first given to him,
13:11. *than* when we believed.
14: 4. to his own master he standeth *or* falleth.
10. *or* why dost thou set at nought
13. *or* an occasion to fall
21. *or* is offended, *or* is made weak.
1Co. 1:13. *or* were ye baptized in the name of Paul?
2: 1. excellency of speech *or* of wisdom,
3: 5. but ministers by whom (lit. but *rather*, &c.)
4: 3. *or* of man's judgment:
21. *or* in love, and (in) the spirit
5:10. *or* with the covetous, *or* extortioners, *or*
11.)(a fornicator, *or* covetous, *or* an idolater,
or a railer, *or* a drunkard, *or* an
6: 9.)(Know ye not that the unrighteous
16. *What?* know ye not that he which is
19. *What?* know ye not that your body
7: 9. it is better to marry *than* to burn.
11. *or* be reconciled to (her) husband:
15. A brother *or* a sister is not under
16. *or* how knowest thou, O man, whether
9: 6. *Or* I only and Barnabas,
7. *or* who feedeth a flock,
8. *or* saith not the law the same also?
10. *Or* saith he (it) altogether for our sakes?
15. *than* that any man should make my
10:19. *or* that which is offered in sacrifice to idols
is any thing?
22.)(Do we provoke the Lord to jealousy?
11: 4. Every man praying *or* prophesying,
5. that prayeth *or* prophesieth
6. for a woman to be shorn *or* shaven,
14.)(Doth not even nature itself
22. *or* despise ye the church of God,
27. *and* drink (this) cup of the Lord,
12:21. *nor* again the head to the feet,
13: 1. *or* a tinkling cymbal.
14: 5. *than* he that speaketh with tongues,
6. *either* by revelation, *or* by knowledge, *or*
by prophesying, *or* by doctrine?
7. be known what is piped *or* harped?
19. *than* ten thousand words in an (unknown)
23. unlearned, *or* unbelievers,
24. that believeth not, *or* (one) unlearned,
27. (let it be) by two, *or* at the most
29. the prophets speak two *or* three,
36. *What?* came the word of God out from
you? *or* came it unto you only?
37. to be a prophet, *or* spiritual,
15:37. *or* of some other (grain):
16: 6. *yea*, and winter with you,
2Co. 1:13. *than* what ye read *or* acknowledge;
17. *or* the things that I purpose,
3: 1. to you, *or* (letters) of commendation from
6:15. *or* what part hath he that believeth with
9: 7. not grudgingly, *or* of necessity:
10:12. *or* compare ourselves with some
11: 4. *or* (if) ye receive another spirit,
— *or* another gospel, which ye have not
7.)(Have I committed an offence
12: 6. *or* (that) he heareth of me.
13: 5.)(Know ye not your own selves,
Gal. 1: 8. *or* an angel from heaven,
10. do I now persuade men, *or* God? *or* do I
seek to please men?
2: 2. I should run, *or* had run, in vain.
3: 2. *or* by the hearing of faith?
5. *or* by the hearing of faith?
15. disannulleth, *or* addeth thereto.
4:27. more children *than* she which hath
Eph. 3:20. above all that we ask *or* think,

Eph. 5: 3. *or* covetousness, let it not be once named
4. foolish talking, *nor* jesting.
5. *nor* unclean person, *nor* covetous man,
27. *or* wrinkle, *or* any such thing;
Phi. 2: 3. through strife *or* vainglory;
3:12. *either* were already perfect:
Col. 2:16. *or* in drink, *or* in respect of an holyday,
or of the new moon, *or* of the sabbath
(days):
3:17. And whatsoever ye do in word *or* deed,
1Th. 2:19. our hope, *or* joy, *or* crown of rejoicing?
)((Are) not even ye
2Th. 2: 4. is called God, *or* that is worshipped;
1Ti. 1: 4. rather *than* godly edifying
2: 9. *or* gold, *or* pearls, *or* costly array;
5: 4. have children *or* nephews,
16. any man *or* woman that believeth have
19. before two *or* three witnesses.
2Ti. 3: 4. lovers of pleasures more *than* lovers of
Tit. 1: 6. not accused of riot, *or* unruly.
3:12. unto thee, *or* Tychicus,
Philem.18. he hath wronged thee, *or* oweth
Heb. 2: 6. *or* the son of man, that
10:28. under two *or* three witnesses:
11:25. *than* to enjoy the pleasures of sin for a
12:16. *or* profane person, as Esau,
20. *or* thrust through with a dart:
Jas. 1:17. *neither* shadow of turning.
2: 3. *or* sit here under my footstool:
15. a brother *or* sister be naked,
3:12. *either* a vine, figs?
4: 5.)(Do ye think that the scripture saith in
15. we shall live, and do this, *or* that.
1Pet.1:11. *or* what manner of time the Spirit of Christ
which was in them did signify,
18. (as) silver *and* gold, from your vain
3: 3. *or* of putting on of apparel;
9. *or* railing for railing:
17. *than* for evil doing.
4:15. *or* (as) a thief, *or* (as) an evildoer, *or* as a
busybody in other men's matters.
2Pet. 2:21. *than*, after they have known (it), to turn
1Joh.4: 4. *than* he that is in the world.
Rev. 3:15. thou wert cold *or* hot.
13:16. *or* in their foreheads:
17. buy *or* sell, save he that had the mark, *or*
the name of the beast, *or* the number of
his name.
14: 9. in his forehead, *or* in his hand,

ἦ μήν, ee meen.

Heb. 6:14. *Surely* blessing I will bless

ἤπερ, eeper.

Joh. 12:43. more *than* the praise of God.

ἤτοι, eetoi.

Ro. 6:16. *whether* of sin unto death, *or*

ἡγεμονία, heegemonia.

Lu. 3: 1. of the *reign* of Tiberius Cæsar,

ἡγεμονεύω, heegemonūo.

Lu. 2: 2. *when* Cyrenius *was* governor of Syria.
3: 1. Pontius Pilate *being governor* of Judæa,

ἡγεμών, heegemōn.

Mat. 2: 6. art not the least among the *princes* of
10:18. ye shall be brought before *governors*
27: 2. him to Pontius Pilate the *governor*.
11. Jesus stood before the *governor:* and the *governor* asked him,
14. the *governor* marvelled greatly.
15. the *governor* was wont to release
21. The *governor* answered and said unto
23. And the *governor* said, Why, what evil
27. Then the soldiers of the *governor*
28:14. if this come to the *governor's* ears,
Mar13: 9. ye shall be brought before *rulers*
Lu. 20:20. the power and authority of the *governor.*
21:12. before kings and *rulers*
Acts23:24. unto Felix the *governor*.
26. unto the most excellent *governor* Felix (sendeth) greeting.
33. delivered the epistle to the *governor*,
34. And when the *governor* had read
24: 1. who informed the *governor* against Paul.
10. after that the *governor* had beckoned unto
26:30. the king rose up, and the *governor*,
1Pet.2:14. Or unto *governors*, as unto them that are sent by him

---

ἡγέομαι, heegeomai.

Mat. 2: 6. shall come a *Governor*,
Lu. 22:26. he *that is chief*, as he that doth serve.
Acts 7:10. he made him *governor* over Egypt
14:12. the *chief* speaker. (lit. *leading* in speech)
15.22. *chief* men among the brethren:
26: 2. I *think* myself happy, king Agrippa,
2Co. 9: 5. Therefore I *thought* it necessary
Phi. 2: 3. *let* each *esteem* other better than themselves.
6. *thought* it not robbery to be equal
25. Yet I *supposed* it necessary
3: 7. those I *counted* loss
8. I *count* all things (but) loss
— do *count* them (but) dung,
1Th. 5:13. And *to esteem* them very highly in love
2Th. 3:15. *count* (him) not as an enemy,
1Ti. 1:12. for that he *counted* me faithful,
6: 1. *Let* as many servants...*count* their own masters worthy
Heb 10:29. and *hath counted* the blood of the covenant,
11:11. she *judged* him faithful who had promised.
26. *Esteeming* the reproach of Christ greater
13: 7. Remember them *which have the rule over*
17. Obey them *that have the rule over* you,
24. Salute all them *that have the rule over* you,
Jas. 1: 2. *count* it all joy when ye fall into
2Pet.1:13. Yea, I *think* it meet, as long as
2:13. (as) they *that count* it pleasure to riot
3: 9. as some men *count* slackness;
15. And *account* (that) the longsuffering of our Lord (is) salvation;

ἡδέως, ἥδιστα, heedeōs, heedista.

Mar. 6:20. and heard him *gladly*.
12:37. the common people heard him *gladly*.
2Co.11:19. For ye suffer fools *gladly*,
12: 9. *Most gladly* therefore will I rather
15. I will *very gladly* spend and be spent for

ἤδη, eedee.

Mat. 3:10. And *now* also the ax is laid

Mat. 5:28. hath committed adultery with her *already*
14:15. the time is *now* past;
24. was *now* in the midst of the sea,
15:32. they continue with me *now* three days,
17:12. Elias is come *already*,
24:32. When his branch is *yet* tender,
Mar. 4:37. into the ship, so that it was *now* full.
6:35. when the day was *now* far spent,
— and *now* the time (is) far passed:
8: 2. they have *now* been with me three days,
11:11. and *now* the eventide was come,
13:28. When her branch is *yet* tender,
15:42. And *now* when the even was come,
44. if he were *already* dead:
Lu. 3: 9. And *now* also the axe
7: 6. And when he was *now* not far
11: 7. the door is *now* shut,
12:49. if it be *already* kindled?
14:17. for all things are *now* ready.
19:37. when he was come nigh, *even now* at the
21:30. When they *now* shoot forth,
— that summer is *now* nigh at hand.
Joh. 3:18. believeth not is condemned *already*,
4:35. they are white *already* to harvest.
51. And as he was *now* going down,
5: 6. that he had been *now* a long time
6:17. it was *now* dark,
7:14. *Now* about the midst of the feast
9:22. for the Jews had agreed *already*,
27. I have told you *already*,
11:17. that he had (lain) in the grave four days *already*.
39. Lord, *by this time* he stinketh:
13: 2. the devil having *now* put
15: 3. *Now* ye are clean through the word
19:28. all things were *now* accomplished,
33. that he was dead *already*,
21: 4. But when the morning was *now* come,
14. This is *now* the third time
Acts 4: 3. for it was *now* eventide.
27: 9. when sailing was *now* dangerous, because the fast was *now already* past,
Ro. 1:10. if by any means *now* at length I might have a prosperous journey
4:19. considered not his own body *now* dead,
13:11. *now* (it is) high time to awake out of
1Co. 4: 8. *Now* ye are full, *now* ye are rich,
5: 3. have judged *already*, as though I were
6: 7. *Now* therefore there is utterly
Phi. 3:12. Not as though I had *already* attained, either were *already* perfect:
4:10. that *now* at the last your care of me hath flourished again;
2Th. 2: 7. the mystery of iniquity doth *already* work:
1Ti. 5:15. For some are *already* turned aside
2Ti. 2:18. that the resurrection is past *already*;
4: 6. For I am *now* ready to be offered,
2Pet.3: 1. This second epistle, beloved, I *now*
1Joh.2: 8. the true light *now* shineth,
4: 3. *already* is it in the world.

ἥδιστα see ἡδέως.

ἡδονή, heedonee.

Lu. 8:14. and riches and *pleasures* of (this) life,
Tit. 3: 3. serving divers lusts and *pleasures*,
Jas. 4: 1. (come they) not hence, (even) of your *lusts*

Jas. 4: 3. ye may consume (it) upon your *lusts*.
2Pet.2:13.(as) they that count it *pleasure* to riot

ἡδύοσμον, *heeduosmon*.

Mat.23:23. ye pay tithe of *mint*
Lu. 11:42. tithe *mint* and rue and all manner

ἦθος, *eethos*.

1Co.15:33. communications corrupt good *manners*.

ἥκω, *heeko*.

Mat. 8:11. *shall come* from the east and west,
23:36. All these things *shall come* upon
24:14. then *shall* the end *come*.
50. The lord of that servant *shall come*
Mar 8: 3. for divers of them *came* from far.
Lu. 12:46. The lord of that servant *will come*
13:29. they *shall come* from the east,
35. until (the time) *come* when ye shall say,
15:27. Thy brother *is come* ;
19:43. the days *shall come* upon thee,
Joh. 2: 4. mine hour *is* not yet *come*.
4:47. When he heard that Jesus *was come*
6:37. *shall come* to me ;
8:42. I proceeded forth and *came* from God ;
Acts28:23. there *came* many to him
Ro. 11:26. There *shall come* out of Sion the Deliverer,
Heb 10: 7. Then said I, Lo, I *come*
9. Lo, I *come* to do thy will, O God.
37. and he that shall come *will come*,
2Pet.3:10. But the day of the Lord *will come* as a
1Joh.5:20. that the Son of God *is come*,
Rev. 2:25. hold fast till I *come*.
3: 3. I *will come* on thee as a thief, and thou shalt not know what hour I *will come* upon thee.
9. I will make them to *come* and worship
15: 4. all nations *shall come* and worship before
18: 8. *shall* her plagues *come* in one day,

Ἠλί, *Eli*.

Mat.27:46. *Eli, Eli,* lama sabachthani ? that is to say, My God, My God, why hast thou forsaken me?

ἡλικία, *heelikia*.

Mat. 6:27. can add one cubit unto his *stature* ?
Lu. 2:52. in wisdom and *stature*,
12:25. to his *stature* one cubit?
19: 3. he was little of *stature*.
Joh. 9:21. we know not: he is of *age* ; ask him:
23. said his parents, He is of *age* ; ask him.
Eph. 4:13. unto the measure of the *stature* of the fulness of Christ:
Heb11:11. when she was past *age*,

ἡλίκος, *heelikos*.

Col. 2: 1. that ye knew *what great* conflict I have
Jas. 3: 5. *how great* a matter a little fire kindleth !

ἥλιος, *heelios*.

Mat. 5:45. he maketh his *sun* to rise
13: 6. And when the *sun* was up,
43. Then shall the righteous shine forth as the *sun*
17: 2. his face did shine as the *sun*,
24:29. shall the *sun* be darkened,
Mar 1:32. when the *sun* did set,
4: 6. But when the *sun* was up,
13:24. the *sun* shall be darkened,
16: 2. at the rising of the *sun*.
Lu. 4:40. Now when the *sun* was setting,
21:25. there shall be signs in the *sun*,
23:45. the *sun* was darkened,
Acts 2:20. The *sun* shall be turned into darkness,
13:11. thou shalt be blind, not seeing the *sun*
26:13. the brightness of the *sun*,
27:20. And when neither *sun* nor stars
1Co.15:41. (There is) one glory of the *sun*,
Eph. 4:26. let not the *sun* go down upon your wrath:
Jas. 1:11. For the *sun* is no sooner risen
Rev. 1:16. as the *sun* shineth in his strength.
6:12. the *sun* became black as sackcloth of
7: 2. from the east, (lit. from the rising of the *sun*)
16. shall the *sun* light on them,
8:12. the third part of the *sun* was smitten,
9: 2. the *sun* and the air were darkened
10: 1. his face (was) as it were the *sun*,
12: 1. clothed with the *sun*,
16: 8. poured out his vial upon the *sun*:
12. kings of the east (lit. kings from the rising of the *sun*)
19:17. an angel standing in the *sun* ;
21:23. had no need of the *sun*,
22: 5. neither light of the *sun* ; for the Lord God giveth them light:

ἧλος, *heelos*.

Joh.20:25. the print of the *nails*, and put my finger into the print of the *nails*,

---

ἡμᾶς, *heemas*, from ἐγώ.

Mat. 6:13. lead *us* not into temptation, but deliver *us* from
8:25. Lord, save *us* : we perish.
29. to torment *us* before the time?
31. If thou cast *us* out, suffer
9:27. (Thou) son of David, have mercy on *us*.
13:56. are they not all with *us* ?
17: 4. it is good for *us* to be here:
20: 7. no man hath hired *us*.
30. Have mercy on *us*, O Lord,
31. Have mercy on *us*, O Lord,
27: 4. What (is that) to *us* ?
25. His blood (be) on *us*,
Mar. 1:24. art thou come to destroy *us* ?
5:12. Send *us* into the swine,
6: 3. are not his sisters here with *us* ?
9: 5. it is good for *us* to be here:
22. have compassion on *us*,
Lu. 1:71. from the hand of all that hate *us* ;
78. from on high hath visited *us*,
4:34. art thou come to destroy *us* ?
7:20. hath sent *us* unto thee,
9:33. for *us* to be here:
11: 1. Lord, teach *us* to pray, as John also

Lu. 11: 4. lead us not into temptation ; but deliver
    us from evil.
    45. thou reproachest us also.
12:41. this parable unto us,
16:26. can they pass to us,
17:13. have mercy on us.
19:14. will not have this (man) to reign over us.
20: 6. all the people will stone us :
23:30. say to the mountains, Fall on us ; and to
    the hills, Cover us.
    39. save thyself and us.
24:22. of our company made us astonished,
Joh. 1:22. to them that sent us.
9:34. and dost thou teach us ?
Acts 1:21. went in and out among us,
3: 4. said, Look on us.
4:12. whereby we must be saved.
5:28. to bring this man's blood upon us.
6: 2. It is not reason that we should leave
7:27. a ruler and a judge over us ?
    40. which brought us out of the land of
11:15. fell on them, as on us at the beginning.
14:11. are come down to us
    22. we must through much tribulation enter
16:10. the Lord had called us
    15. And she constrained us.
    37. They have beaten us openly
    — do they thrust us out privily ?
    — come themselves and fetch us out.
20: 5. tarried for us at Troas.
21: 1. after we were gotten from them, and had
    launched,
    5. when we had accomplished those days,
    — and they all brought us on our way,
    11. when he was come unto us,
    17. the brethren received us
27: 1. that we should sail into Italy,
    6. and he put us therein.
    7. the wind not suffering us,
    20. that we should be saved
    26. we must be cast upon a certain island.
28: 2. and received us every one,
    7. who received us, and lodged us
    10. Who also honoured us
Ro. 3: 8. as some affirm that we say,
4:24. But for us also, to whom it shall be
5: 8. commendeth his love toward us,
6: 6. henceforth we should not serve
7: 6. we should serve in newness
8:18. the glory which shall be revealed in us.
    35. Who shall separate us from
    37. through him that loved us.
    39. shall be able to separate us
9:24. Even us, whom he hath called,
13:11. now (it is) high time)(to awake out of
15: 7. as Christ also received us
16: 6. bestowed much labour on us.
1Co. 4: 1. Let a man so account of us,
    9. that God hath set forth us the apostles
6:14. and will also raise up us
7:15. God hath called us
8: 8. But meat commendeth us not
9:10. Or saith he (it) altogether for our sakes ?
    For our sakes, no doubt, (this) is
10: 6. to the intent we should not lust after
2Co. 1: 4. Who comforteth us in all our tribulation,
    that we may be able to
    5. the sufferings of Christ abound in us,
    8. that we despaired even of life:
    10. Who delivered us from so great a death,
    11. the gift (bestowed) upon us
    14. ye have acknowledged us in part,

2Co. 1:21. Now he which stablisheth us with you in
    Christ, and hath anointed us, (is) God ;
    22. Who hath also sealed us,
2:14. which always causeth us to triumph in
3: 6. hath made us able ministers
4:14. shall raise up us also by Jesus,
5: 5. Now he that hath wrought us
    10. For we must all appear before
    14. the love of Christ constraineth us ;
    18. hath reconciled us to himself
7: 2. Receive us ; we have wronged no man,
    6. comforted us by the coming of Titus ;
8: 4. that we would receive the gift,
    6. Insomuch that we desired
    20. that no man should blame us
10: 2. which think of us as if we walked
Gal. 1: 4. that he might deliver us
    23. he which persecuted us in times past
2: 4. that they might bring us into bondage:
3:13. Christ hath redeemed us
5: 1. wherewith Christ hath made us free,
Eph. 1: 3. who hath blessed us with all
    4. According as he hath chosen us
    — that we should be holy and
    5. Having predestinated us unto the adoption
    6. wherein he hath made us accepted
    8. Wherein he hath abounded toward us
    12. That we should be to the praise
    19. to us-ward who believe,
2: 4. wherewith he loved us.
    5. when we were dead in sins,
    7. in (his) kindness toward us
5: 2. Christ also hath loved us,
Phi. 3:17. as ye have us for an ensample.
Col. 1:12. which hath made us meet
    13. Who hath delivered us
1Th. 1: 8. so that we need not
    10. Jesus, which delivered us from the wrath
    to come.
2:15. and have persecuted us ;
    16. Forbidding us to speak to the Gentiles
    18. Satan hindered us.
3: 6. when Timotheus came from you unto us,
    — desiring greatly to see us,
4: 7. For God hath not called us
    8. given unto us his holy Spirit.
5: 9. God hath not appointed us to
2Th. 1: 4. So that we ourselves glory in you
2:16. which hath loved us,
3: 7. how ye ought to follow us:
    9. an ensample unto you to follow us.
2Ti. 1: 9. Who hath saved us, and called
2:12. if we deny (him), he also will deny us:
Tit. 2:12. Teaching us that, denying ungodliness
    14. that he might redeem us
3: 5. he saved us, by the washing
    6. Which he shed on us abundantly
    15. that love us in the faith.
Heb. 2: 1. we ought to give the more earnest heed
    3. unto us by them that heard (him) ;
13: 6. So that we may boldly say,
Jas. 1:18. Of his own will begat he us with the word
    of truth, that we should be
1Pet.1: 3. hath begotten us again unto
3:18. that he might bring us
    21. The like figure whereunto (even) baptism
    doth also now save us
5:10. who hath called us
2Pet.1: 3. of him that hath called us
3: 9. is longsuffering to us-ward,
1Joh.1: 7. cleanseth us from all sin.
    9. and to cleanse us from all

1Joh.3: 1. the world knoweth *us* not,
4:10. but that he loved *us*,
11. if God so loved *us*, we ought also
19. because he first loved *us*.
3Joh. 9. among them, receiveth *us* not.
10. prating against *us* with malicious
Rev. 1: 5. Unto him that loved *us*, and washed *us* from our sins in his own blood,
6. And hath made *us* kings and priests
5: 9. hast redeemed *us* to God
10. And hast made *us* unto our God kings and priests:
6:16. Fall on *us*, and hide *us* from the face of him that sitteth on the throne,

---

ἡμεῖς, heemîs.

From ἐγώ.

Mat. 6:12. as *we* forgive our debtors.
9:14. Why do *we* and the Pharisees fast oft,
17:19. Why could not *we* cast him out?
19:27. Behold, *we* have forsaken all,
28:14. *we* will persuade him,
Mar. 9:28. Why could not *we* cast him out?
10:28. Lo, *we* have left all, and have
14:58. *We* heard him say, I will destroy
Lu. 3:14. And what shall *we* do?
9:13. except *we* should go and buy meat
18:28. *we* have left all,
23:41. And *we* indeed justly ;
24:21. But *we* trusted that it had been he which
Joh. 1:16. of his fulness have all *we* received,
4:22. we know what *we* worship:
6:42. whose father and mother *we* know?
69. And *we* believe and are sure that thou art that Christ,
7:35. that *we* shall not find him ?
8:41. *We* be not born of fornication ;
48. Say *we* not well that thou art
9:21. who hath opened his eyes, *we* know not:
24. *we* know that this man
28. but *we* are Moses' disciples.
29. *We* know that God spake unto Moses:
40. Are *we* blind also?
11:16. Let *us* also go, that we may die
12:34. *We* have heard out of the law
17:11. that they may be one, as *we* (are).
22. even as *we* are one:
19: 7. *We* have a law,
21: 3. *We* also go with thee.
Acts 2: 8. how hear *we* every man
32. whereof *we* all are witnesses.
3:15. whereof *we* are witnesses.
4: 9. If *we* this day be examined
20. For *we* cannot but speak the things
5:32. And *we* are his witnesses
6: 4. But *we* will give ourselves continually to
10:33. *we* all here present before God,
39. And *we* are witnesses of all things
47. received the Holy Ghost as well as *we* ?
13:32. And *we* declare unto you glad tidings,
14:15. *We* also are men of like passions
15:10. nor *we* were able to bear?
20: 6. And *we* sailed away
13. And *we* went before
21: 7. And when *we* had finished (our) course
12. both *we*, and they of that place,
25. *we* have written (and) concluded
23:15. and *we*, or ever he come near,
24: 8. whereof *we* accuse him.

Acts28:21. *We* neither received letters
Ro. 6: 4. even so *we* also should walk in newness of life.
8:23. even *we* ourselves groan within ourselves,
15: 1. *We* then that are strong ought
1Co. 1:23. But *we* preach Christ crucified,
2:12. Now *we* have received, not the spirit of the world, but
16. But *we* have the mind of Christ.
4: 8. that *we* also might reign with you.
10. *We* (are) fools for Christ's sake,
— *we* (are) weak, but ye
— but *we* (are) despised.
8: 6. of whom (are) all things, and *we* in him ;
— by whom (are) all things, and *we* by him.
9:11. If *we* have sown unto you spiritual things, (is it) a great thing if *we* shall reap your carnal
12. (are) not *we* rather?
25. but *we* an incorruptible.
11:16. *we* have no such custom,
12:13. are *we* all baptized into one body,
15:30. And why stand *we* in jeopardy
52. and *we* shall be changed.
2Co. 1: 6. which *we* also suffer:
3:18. But *we* all, with open face
4:11. For *we* which live are alway
13. *we* also believe, and therefore speak ;
5:16. henceforth know *we* no man
21. that *we* might be made the righteousness
9: 4. *we* that we say not, ye should be
10: 7. even so (are) *we* Christ's.
13. But *we* will not boast of things
11:12. they may be found even as *we*.
21. as though *we* had been weak.
13: 4. For *we* also are weak in
6. that *we* are not reprobates.
7. not that *we* should appear approved,
— though *we* be as reprobates.
9. when *we* are weak,
Gal. 1: 8. But though *we*, or an angel
2: 9. that *we* (should go) unto the heathen,
15. *We* (who are) Jews by nature,
16. even *we* have believed in Jesus Christ,
4: 3. Even so *we*, when we were
28. Now *we*, brethren, as Isaac
5: 5. For *we* through the Spirit
Eph. 2: 3(2). Among whom also *we* all
Phi. 3: 3. For *we* are the circumcision,
Col. 1: 9. For this cause *we* also, since
28. Whom *we* preach, warning every man,
1Th. 2:13. For this cause also thank *we* God
17. But *we*, brethren, being taken from you
3: 6. as *we* also (to see) you:
12. even as *we* (do) toward you:
4:15. that *we* which are alive (and) remain
17. Then *we* which are alive
5: 8. But let *us*, who are of the day,
2Th. 2:13. But *we* are bound to give thanks
Tit. 3: 3. For *we ourselves* also were sometimes
5. Not by works of righteousness which *we* have done,
Heb. 2: 3. How shall *we* escape,
3: 6. whose house are *we*,
10:39. But *we* are not of them who draw back
12: 1. Wherefore seeing we also are compassed about...let *us*
25. much more (shall not) *we* (escape),
2Pet.1:18. this voice which came from heaven *we* heard, when
1Joh.3:14. *We* know that *we* have passed
16. and *we* ought to lay down (our) lives

1Joh.4: 6. *We* are of God:
10. not that *we* loved God, but that he
11. *we* ought also to love one another.
14. And *we* have seen and do testify
16. And *we* have known and believed
17. so are *we* in this world.
19. *We* love him, because he first loved us.
3Joh. 8. *We* therefore ought to receive such,
12. yea, and *we* (also) bear record;

ἡμέρα, *heemera.*

Mat. 2: 1. in the *days* of Herod the king,
3: 1. In those *days* came John
4: 2. when he had fasted forty *days*
6:34. Sufficient unto the *day* (is) the evil
7:22. Many will say to me in that *day*,
9:15. but the *days* will come,
10:15. in the *day* of judgment,
11:12. And from the *days* of John
22. at the *day* of judgment,
24. in the *day* of judgment,
12:36. account thereof in the *day* of judgment.
40. Jonas was three *days* and three nights
— three *days* and three nights in the heart of the earth.
13: 1. The same *day* went Jesus out
15:32. they continue with me now three *days*,
16:21. be raised again the third *day*.
17: 1. And after six *days* Jesus taketh
23. the third *day* he shall be raised again.
20: 2. for a penny a *day*,
6. all the *day* idle?
12. borne the burden and heat of the *day*.
19. the third *day* he shall rise again.
22:23. The same *day* came to him
46. from that *day* forth
23:30. If we had been in the *days* of our fathers,
24:19. to them that give suck in those *days!*
22. except those *days* should be shortened,
— those *days* shall be shortened.
29. after the tribulation of those *days*
36. But of that *day* and hour
37. But as the *days* of Noe (were),
38. For as in the *days* that were before the
— until the *day* that Noe entered
50. in a *day* when he looketh not for (him),
25:13. ye know neither the *day* nor
26: 2. after two *days* is (the feast of) the passover,
29. until that *day* when I drink it new with you
55. *daily* with you teaching
61. to build it in three *days*.
27:40. and buildest (it) in three *days*,
63. After three *days* I will rise again.
64. until the third *day*,
28:20. I am with you alway, (lit. all the *days*)
Mar. 1: 9. in those *days*, that Jesus came
13. there in the wilderness forty *days*,
2: 1. into Capernaum after (some) *days;*
20. But the *days* will come, when
— then shall they fast in those *days*.
4:27. sleep, and rise night and *day*,
35. the same *day*, when the even
5: 5. And always, night and *day*, he was
6:11. in the *day* of judgment,
21. when a convenient *day* was come,
8: 1. In those *days* the multitude being
2. they have now been with me three *days*,
31. after three *days* rise again.
9: 2. after six *days* Jesus taketh
31. he shall rise the third *day*.

Mar 10:34. the third *day* he shall rise again.
13:17. to them that give suck in those *days!*
19. For (in) those *days* shall be
20. had shortened those *days*,
— he hath shortened the *days*.
24. But in those *days*, after that tribulation,
32. But of that *day* and (that) hour
14: 1. After two *days* was (the feast of)
12. the first *day* of unleavened bread,
25. until that *day* that I drink it new
49. I was *daily* with you in the temple
58. within three *days* I will build another made without hands.
15:29. and buildest (it) in three *days*,
Lu. 1: 5. There was in the *days* of Herod,
7. were (now) well stricken in *years*.
18. my wife well stricken in *years*.
20. not able to speak, until the *day* that
23. that, as soon as the *days* of his ministration were accomplished,
24. And after those *days* his wife
25. in the *days* wherein he looked on (me),
39. Mary arose in those *days*, and went
59. that on the eighth *day*
75. all the *days* of our life.
80. was in the deserts till the *day* of his
2: 1. in those *days*, that there went out a decree
6. the *days* were accomplished that she
21. eight *days* were accomplished
22. when the *days* of her purification
36. she was of a great *age*,
37. with fastings and prayers night and *day*.
43. when they had fulfilled the *days*,
44. went a *day's* journey;
46. that after three *days* they found
4: 2. forty *days* tempted of the devil. And in those *days* he did eat nothing:
16. into the synagogue on the sabbath *day*,
25. were in Israel in the *days* of Elias,
42. And when it was *day*,
5:35. on a certain *day*, as he was teaching,
35. But the *days* will come, when
— then shall they fast in those *days*.
6:12. it came to pass in those *days*,
13. when it was *day*,
23. Rejoice ye in that *day*,
8:22. it came to pass on a certain *day*,
9:12. And when the *day* began to wear away,
22. be raised the third *day*.
23. and take up his cross *daily*,
28. about an eight *days*
36. told no man in those *days*
37. that on the next *day*,
51. when the *time* was come that he should be received up,
10:12. shall be more tolerable in that *day*
11: 3. Give us day by *day* (καθ' ἡμέραν)
12:46. in a *day* when he looketh not for (him),
13:14. There are six *days* in which
— and not on the sabbath *day*.
16. on the sabbath *day*?
31. The same *day* there came
14: 5. on the sabbath *day*?
15:13. not many *days* after
16:19. fared sumptuously every *day:*
17: 4. seven times in a *day*, and seven times in a *day* turn again to thee,
22. The *days* will come, when ye shall desire to see one of the *days*
24. so shall also the Son of man be in his *day*.
26. as it was in the *days* of Noe, so shall it be also in the *days* of the Son of man.

Lu. 17:27. until the *day* that Noe entered
28. in the *days* of Lot;
29. But the same *day* that Lot went out
30. in the *day* when the Son of man
31. In that *day*. he which shall be upon
18: 7. which cry *day* and night unto him,
33. the third *day* he shall rise again.
19:42. at least in this thy *day*,
43. For the *days* shall come upon thee,
47. he taught *daily* in the temple.
20: 1. (that) on one of those *days*,
21: 6. the *days* will come, in the which
22. For these be the *days* of vengeance,
23. that give suck, in those *days*!
34. and (so) that *day* come upon you
37. And in the *day time* he was teaching in the temple;
22: 7. the *day* of unleavened bread,
53. When I was *daily* with you in the temple,
66. as soon as it was *day*,
23: 7. was at Jerusalem at that *time*.
12. the same *day* Pilate and Herod
29. behold, the *days* are coming,
54. that *day* was the preparation,
24: 7. the third *day* rise again.
13. went that same *day* to a village
18. come to pass there in these *days*?
21. to day is the third *day*
29. the *day* is far spent.
46. from the dead the third *day*:
Joh. 1:39(40). abode with him that *day*:
2: 1. And the third *day* there was a marriage
12. they continued there not many *days*.
19. in three *days* I will raise it up.
20. wilt thou rear it up in three *days*?
4:40. and he abode there two *days*.
43. Now after two *days*
5: 9. on the same *day*
6:39. raise it up again at the last *day*.
40. I will raise him up at the last *day*.
44. him up at the last *day*.
54. him up at the last *day*.
7:37. In the last *day*, that great
8:56. Abraham rejoiced to see my *day*:
9: 4. while it is *day*:
11: 6. two *days* still in the same place where he
9. Are there not twelve hours in the *day*? If any man walk in the *day*,
17. he had (lain) in the grave four *days*
24. in the resurrection at the last *day*.
53. Then from that *day* forth
12: 1. six *days* before the passover
7. against the *day* of my burying
48. the same shall judge him in the last *day*.
14:20. At that *day* ye shall know that I
16:23. in that *day* ye shall ask me nothing.
26. At that *day* ye shall ask in my name:
19:31. for that sabbath *day* was an high *day*,
20:19. the same *day* at evening,
26. And after eight *days* again his
Acts 1: 2. Until the *day* in which he was taken up,
3. being seen of them forty *days*,
5. not many *days* hence.
15. And in those *days* Peter stood up
unto that same *day* that he was
2: 1. the *day* of Pentecost
15. the third hour of the *day*.
17. it shall come to pass in the last *days*,
18. I will pour out in those *days* of my Spirit;
20. before that great and notable *day* of the Lord come:
29. his sepulchre is with us unto this *day*.

Acts 2:41. the same *day* there were added
46. And they, continuing *daily*
47. the Lord added to the church *daily*
3: 2. whom they laid *daily* at the gate
24. have likewise foretold of these *days*.
5:36. For before these *days* rose up Theudas,
37. in the *days* of the taxing,
42. And *daily* in the temple,
6: 1. And in those *days*,
7: 8. circumcised him the eighth *day*;
26. And the next *day* he shewed himself
41. they made a calf in those *days*,
45. unto the *days* of David;
8: 1. at that *time* there was a great persecution
9: 9. three *days* without sight,
19. Then was Saul certain *days* with
23. many *days* were fulfilled,
24. watched the gates *day* and night
37. to pass in those *days*, that she
43. he tarried many *days* in Joppa
10: 3. the ninth hour of the *day*
30. Four *days* ago I was fasting
40. raised up the third *day*,
48. to tarry certain *days*.
11:27. And in these *days* came prophets
12: 3. Then were the *days* of unleavened bread.
18. Now as soon as it was *day*,
21. And upon a set *day* Herod,
13:14. on the sabbath *day*
31. he was seen many *days* of them
41. I work a work in your *days*,
15: 7. a good *while* ago God made choice
36. And some *days* after
16: 5. increased in number *daily*.
12. abiding certain *days*.
13. And on the sabbath)(we went
18. did she many *days*.
35. And when it was *day*,
17:11. and searched the scriptures *daily*,
17. and in the market *daily* with them that met with him.
31. Because he hath appointed a *day*,
18:18. tarried (there) yet a good *while*,
19: 9. disputing *daily* in the school of
20: 6. from Philippi after the *days* of unleavened bread, and came unto them to Troas in five *days*; where we abode seven *days*.
16. the *day* of Pentecost.
18. from the first *day*
26. I take you to record this *day*,
31. I ceased not to warn every one night and *day* with tears.
21: 4. we tarried there seven *days*:
5. we had accomplished those *days*,
7. with them one *day*.
10. And as we tarried (there) many *days*,
15. And after those *days*
26. and the next *day* purifying
— the accomplishment of the *days* of
27. the seven *days* were almost ended,
38. that Egyptian. which before these *days*
23: 1. before God until this *day*.
12. And when it was *day*,
24: 1. And after five *days*
11. there are yet but twelve *days*
24. And after certain *days*,
25: 1. after three *days* he ascended
6. more than ten *days*,
13. And after certain *days*
14. they had been there many *days*,
26: 7. serving (God) *day* and night,
13. At mid*day*, O king, I saw

Acts26:22. I continue unto this *day*,
27: 7. And when we had sailed slowly many *days*, and scarce were come
20. neither sun nor stars in many *days*
29. and wished for the *day*.
33. while the *day* was coming on,
— the fourteenth *day* that ye have tarried
39. And when it was *day*,
28: 7. lodged us three *days* courteously.
12. we tarried (there) three *days*.
13. after one *day* the south wind blew,
14. to tarry with them seven *days*:
17. that after three *days*
23. And when they had appointed him a *day*,
Ro. 2: 5. wrath against the *day* of wrath
16. In the *day* when God shall judge
8:36. we are killed all the *day* long;
10:21. All *day* long I have stretched forth
11: 8. unto this *day*.
13:12. the *day* is at hand:
13. honestly, as in the *day*;
14: 5. esteemeth one *day* above another)(: another esteemeth every *day* (alike).
6. He that regardeth the *day*,
— and he that regardeth not the *day*,
1Co. 1: 8. in the *day* of our Lord
3:13. for the *day* shall declare it,
4: 3. that I should be judged of you, or of man's *judgment:* (lit. man's *day*)
5: 5. in the *day* of the Lord Jesus.
10: 8. and fell in one *day*
15: 4. he rose again the third *day*
31. Jesus our Lord, I die *daily*.
2Co. 1:14. in the *day* of the Lord Jesus.
4:16. the inward (man) is renewed *day* by *day*.
6: 2. in the *day* of salvation have I succoured
— behold, now (is) the *day* of salvation.
11:28. that which cometh upon me *daily*,
Gal. 1:18. abode with him fifteen *days*.
4:10. Ye observe *days*,
Eph. 4:30. unto the *day* of redemption.
5:16. the *days* are evil.
6:13. to withstand in the evil *day*,
Phi. 1: 5. from the first *day* until now ;
6. until the *day* of Jesus Christ:
10. without offence till the *day* of Christ ;
2:16. in the *day* of Christ,
Col. 1: 6. since the *day* ye heard (of it),
9. since the *day* we heard (it),
1Th. 2: 9. for labouring night and *day*,
3:10. Night and *day* praying exceedingly
5: 2. the *day* of the Lord so cometh as a thief
4. that that *day* should overtake you as a
5. and the children of the *day*:
8. But let us, who are of the *day*,
2Th. 1:10. among you was believed in that *day*.
2: 2. the *day* of Christ is at hand.
3: 8. wrought with labour and travail night and *day*,
1Ti. 5: 5. continueth in supplications and prayers night and *day*.
2Ti. 1: 3. in my prayers night and *day*;
12. committed unto him against that *day*.
18. may find mercy of the Lord in that *day*:
3: 1. that in the last *days*
4: 8. shall give me at that *day*:
Heb. 1: 2(1). Hath in these last *days* spoken
3: 8. in the *day* of temptation
13. But exhort one another *daily*,
4: 4. And God did rest the seventh *day*
7. Again, he limiteth a certain *day*,
8. have spoken of another *day*.

Heb. 5: 7. in the *days* of his flesh,
7: 3. neither beginning of *days*,
27. needeth not *daily*, as those
8: 8. Behold, the *days* come, saith the Lord,
9. in the *day* when I took them
10. that I will make with the house of Israel after those *days*,
10:11. And every priest standeth *daily*
16. that I will make with them after those *days*,
25. as ye see the *day* approaching.
32. call to remembrance the former *days*,
11:30. were compassed about seven *days*.
12:10. For they verily for a few *days*
Jas. 5: 3. Ye have heaped treasure together for the last *days*.
5. as in a *day* of slaughter.
1Pet.2:12. in the *day* of visitation.
3:10. he that will love life, and see good *days*,
20. in the *days* of Noah,
2Pet.1:19. in a dark place, until the *day* dawn,
2: 8. (his) righteous soul from *day* to *day*
9. unto the *day* of judgment
13. to riot in the *day* time.
3: 3. that there shall come in the last *days*
7. against the *day* of judgment
8. one *day* (is) with the Lord as a thousand years, and a thousand years as one *day*.
10. But the *day* of the Lord will come
12. unto the coming of the *day* of God,
18. To him (be) glory both now and for ever. (εἰς ἡμέραν αἰῶνος)
1Joh.4:17. in the *day* of judgment:
Jude 6. unto the judgment of the great *day*.
Rev. 1:10. I was in the Spirit on the Lord's *day*,
2:10. ye shall have tribulation ten *days*:
13. in those *days* wherein Antipas
4: 8. and they rest not *day* and night,
6:17. the great *day* of his wrath is come;
7:15. and serve him *day* and night
8:12. the *day* shone not for a third part
9: 6. And in those *days* shall men seek
15. a *day*, and a month, and
10: 7. But in the *days* of the voice
11: 3. a thousand two hundred (and) threescore *days*.
6. in the *days* of their prophecy:
9. three *days* and an half,
11. after three *days* and an half
12: 6. a thousand two hundred (and) threescore *days*.
10. before our God *day* and night.
14:11. and they have no rest *day* nor night,
16:14. of that great *day* of God Almighty.
18: 8. shall her plagues come in one *day*,
20:10. *day* and night for ever and ever.
21:25. shall not be shut at all by *day*:

ἡμέτερος, *heemeteros.*

Acts 2:11. we do hear them speak in *our* tongues
24: 6. according to *our* law.
26: 5. sect of *our* religion
Ro. 15: 4. were written for *our* learning,
1Co.15:31. I protest by your rejoicing (some read. *our* rejoicing)
2Ti. 4:15. he hath greatly withstood *our* words.
Tit. 3:14. And let *our's* also learn

1Joh.1: 3. and truly *our* fellowship (is) with the
Father, and with his Son Jesus Christ.
2: 2. and not for *our's* only, but also

ἢ μήν see after ἤ.

ἤμην, *eemeen.*
From εἰμί.

Mat.25:35. I *was* a stranger, and ye took me in:
36. I *was* in prison, and ye came unto me.
43. I *was* a stranger, and ye took me not in:
Mar 14:49. I *was* daily with you in the temple
Joh.11:15. that I *was* not there,
16: 4. because I *was* with you.
17:12. While I *was* with them
Acts10:30. I *was* fasting until this hour;
11: 5. I *was* in the city of Joppa praying:
11. the house where I *was,*
17. what *was* I, that I could withstand God?
22:19. that I imprisoned (lit. *was* imprisoning)
20. I also *was* standing by,
1Co.13:11. When I *was* a child,
Gal. 1:10. I should not *be* the servant of Christ.
22. And *was* unknown by face

ἡμιθανής, *heemithanees.*

Lu. 10:30. leaving (him) *half dead.*

ἡμῖν, *heemin.*
From ἐγώ.

Mat. 3:15. it becometh *us* to fulfil
6:11. Give *us* this day
12. forgive *us* our debts,
8:29. What have *we* to do with thee, Jesus,
31. suffer *us* to go away
13:36. Declare unto *us* the parable
15:15. Declare unto *us* this parable.
33. Whence should *we* have so much
19:27. what shall *we* have therefore?
20:12. thou hast made them equal unto *us,*
21:25. he will say unto *us,* Why
22:17. Tell *us* therefore, What thinkest thou?
25. Now there were with *us* seven
24: 3. Tell *us,* when shall these things
25: 8. Give *us* of your oil;
9. there be not enough for *us* and you:
11. Lord, Lord, open to *us.*
26:63. that thou tell *us* whether thou be
68. Prophesy unto *us,* thou Christ,
Mar. 1:24. what have *we* to do with thee, thou Jesus
9:22. compassion on us, and help *us.*
38. and he followeth not *us:* and we forbad
him, because he followeth not *us.*
10:35. thou shouldest do for *us*
37. Grant unto *us* that we may sit, one on
12:19. Moses wrote unto *us,*
13: 4. Tell *us,* when shall these things
14:15. there make ready for *us.*
16: 3. Who shall roll *us* away the stone
Lu. 1: 1. are most surely believed among *us,*
2. Even as they delivered them unto *us,*
69. an horn of salvation *for us*
74(73). That he would grant unto *us,*
2:15. which the Lord hath made known unto *us.*

Lu. 2:48. why hast thou thus dealt with *us?*
4:34. what have *we* to do with thee, (thou) Jesus
7: 5. he hath built *us* a synagogue.
16. is risen up among *us;*
9:13. *We* have no more but five loaves
10:11. dust of your city, which cleaveth on *us,*
17. even the devils are subject unto *us*
11: 3. Give *us* day by day
4. forgive *us* our sins; for we also forgive
every one that is indebted to *us.*
13:25. Lord, Lord, open unto *us;*
17: 5. Increase our (lit. to *us*) faith.
20: 2. Tell *us,* by what authority
22. Is it lawful for *us* to give tribute unto
Cæsar,
28. Moses wrote unto *us,*
22: 8. and prepare *us* the passover,
67(66). Art thou the Christ? tell *us.*
23:18. and release unto *us* Barabbas:
24:24. certain of them which were with *us*
32. Did not our heart burn within *us,* while he
talked with *us* by the way, and while he
opened to *us* the scriptures?
Joh. 1:14. and dwelt among *us,*
2:18. What sign shewest thou unto *us,*
4:12. which gave *us* the well,
25. he will tell *us* all things.
6:34. evermore give *us* this bread.
52. give *us* (his) flesh to eat?
8: 5. Moses in the law commanded *us,*
10:24. be the Christ, tell *us* plainly.
11:50. that it is expedient for *us,* that
14: 8. shew *us* the Father, and it sufficeth *us.*
9. Shew *us* the Father?
22. that thou wilt manifest thyself unto *us,*
16:17. What is this that he saith unto *us,*
17:21. they also may be one in *us:*
18:31. It is not lawful for *us* to put any man to
Acts 1:17. he was numbered with *us,*
21. which have companied with *us.*
22. be ordained to be a witness with *us*
2:29. is with *us* unto this day.
3:12. or why look ye so earnestly on *us,*
6:14. which Moses delivered *us.*
7:38. the lively oracles to give unto *us:*
40. Make *us* gods to go before us:
10:41. (even) to *us,* who did eat and drink
42. And he commanded *us*
11:13. And he shewed *us*
17. as (he did) unto *us,* who believed
13:33(32). unto *us* their children,
47. hath the Lord commanded *us,*
14:17. gave *us* rain from heaven,
15: 7. God made choice among *us,*
8. even as (he did) unto *us;*
25. It seemed good unto *us,* being
28. to the Holy Ghost, and to *us,*
16: 9. Come over into Macedonia, and help *us.*
16. possessed with a spirit of divination met *us,*
17. The same followed Paul and *us,*
— shew unto *us* the way
21. which are not lawful for *us* to receive,
19:27. this *our* craft is in danger
20:14. And when he met with *us*
21:16. with *us* also (certain)
18. with *us* unto James;
23. *We* have four men which have a vow
25:24. men which are here present with *us,*
27: 2. (one) Aristarchus...being with *us.*
28: 2. shewed *us* no little kindness:
15. they came to meet *us*
22. for as concerning this sect, *we* know

Ro. 5: 5. which is given unto *us*.
8: 4. might be fulfilled in *us*,
32. freely give *us* all things?
9:29. had left *us* a seed,
12: 6. the grace that is given to *us*,
Co. 1:18. unto *us* which are saved it is the power
30. who of God is made unto *us* wisdom,
2:10. But God hath revealed (them) unto *us*
12. that are freely given to *us*
4: 6. that ye might learn in *us*
8: 6. But to *us* (there is but) one God, the
15:57. which giveth *us* the victory
2Co. 1: 8. which came to *us* in Asia,
4:12. So then death worketh in *us*,
17. worketh for *us* a far more exceeding
5: 5. hath given unto *us* the earnest
18. hath given to *us* the ministry
19. hath committed unto *us*
6:12. Ye are not straitened in *us*,
7: 7. when he told *us* your earnest desire,
8: 5. and unto *us* by the will of God.
7. (in) your love to *us*,
10: 8. hath given *us* for edification,
13. which God hath distributed to *us*,
Eph. 1: 9. Having made known unto *us* the mystery
3:20. that worketh in *us*,
6:12. *we* wrestle not against flesh
Col. 1: 8. Who also declared unto *us*
2:14. which was contrary to *us*,
4: 3. would open unto *us* a door of utterance,
1Th. 2: 8. ye were dear unto *us*.
3: 6. brought *us* good tidings of
1Ti. 6:17. giveth *us* richly all things to enjoy;
2Ti. 1: 7. For God hath not given *us*
9. which was given *us* in
14. which dwelleth in *us*.
Heb. 1: 2(1). spoken unto *us* by (his) Son,
4:13. with whom *we* have to do.
5:11. Of whom *we* have many things to say,
7:26. For such an high priest became *us*,
10:15. also is a witness to *us*:
20. way, which he hath consecrated for *us*,
12: 1. *we* also are compassed about with
— the race that is set before *us*,
Jas. 3: 3. that they may obey *us*;
4: 5. that dwelleth in *us*
5:17. subject to like passions as *we* are,
1Pet. 1:12. but unto *us* they did minister the things,
2:21. leaving *us* an example,
4: 3. time past of (our) life may suffice *us*
2Pet. 1: 1. that have obtained like precious faith
with *us*
3. given unto *us* all things
4. Whereby are given unto *us* exceeding
1Joh. 1: 2. and was manifested unto *us*;
8. the truth is not in *us*.
9. to forgive *us* (our) sins,
10. his word is not in *us*.
2:25. he hath promised *us*,
3: 1. the Father hath bestowed upon *us*,
23. as he gave *us* commandment.
24. that he abideth in *us*, by the Spirit which
he hath given *us*.
4: 9. the love of God toward *us*,
12. God dwelleth in *us*, and his love is perfected in *us*.
13. that we dwell in him, and he in *us*, because he hath given *us* of his Spirit.
16. that God hath to *us*.
5:11. God hath given to *us*
20. hath given *us* an understanding,
2Joh. 2. the truth's sake, which dwelleth in *us*,

ἥμισυ, *heemisu.*

Mar. 6:23. unto the *half* of my kingdom.
Lu. 19: 8. the *half* of my goods I give to the poor;
Rev. 11: 9. three days and an *half*,
11. three days and an *half*
12:14. for a time, and times, and *half* a time,

ἡμιώριον, *heemiōrion.*

Rev. 8: 1. about the space of *half* an hour.

ἡμῶν, *heemōn.*
From ἐγώ.

Mat. 1:23. being interpreted is, God with *us*.
6: 9. *Our* Father which art in heaven,
11. Give us this day *our* daily bread.
12. forgive us *our* debts, as we forgive *our*
debtors.
8:17. Himself took *our* infirmities,
15:23. she crieth after *us*.
20:33. *our* eyes may be opened.
21:42. marvellous in *our* eyes?
23:30. the days of *our* fathers,
25: 8. *our* lamps are gone out.
27:25. and on *our* children.
28:13. and stole him (away) while *we* slept.
Mar. 9:40. For he that is not against *us* is on *our*
11:10. of *our* father David,
12: 7. and the inheritance shall be *our's*.
11. marvellous in *our* eyes?
29. The Lord *our* God is one Lord:
Lu. 1:55. As he spake to *our* fathers,
71. That we should be saved from *our*
72. (promised) to *our* fathers,
73. to *our* father Abraham,
74. out of the hand of *our* enemies
75. the days of *our* life.
78. Through the tender mercy of *our* God;
79. to guide *our* feet into the way
7: 5. For he loveth *our* nation,
9:49. he followeth not with *us*.
50. Forbid (him) not: for he that is not
against *us* is for *us*.
11: 2. *Our* Father which art in heaven,
3. Give us day by day *our* daily bread.
4. And forgive us *our* sins;
13:26. thou hast taught in *our* streets.
16:26. between *us* and you there is
20:14. that the inheritance may be *our's*.
24:20. and *our* rulers delivered him
22. certain women also of *our company* (lit.
of *us*)
29. saying, Abide with *us*:
32. Did not *our* heart burn
Joh. 3:11. ye receive not *our* witness.
4:12. than *our* father Jacob,
20. *Our* fathers worshipped in this
6:31. *Our* fathers did eat manna
7:51. Doth *our* law judge
8:39. Abraham is *our* father.
53. than *our* father Abraham,
9:20. We know that this is *our* son,
10:24. dost thou make us (lit. *our* soul) to
11:11. *Our* friend Lazarus sleepeth;
48. take away both *our* place
12:38. hath believed *our* report?
19: 7. by *our* law he ought
Acts 1:22. that he was taken up from *us*,

Acts 2: 8. in *our* own tongue,
    39. the Lord *our* God
  3:13. the God of *our* fathers,
    25. which God made with *our* fathers,
  5:30. The God of *our* fathers
  7: 2. unto *our* father Abraham,
    11. *our* fathers found no sustenance.
    12. he sent out *our* fathers first.
    15. he, and *our* fathers,
    19. dealt subtilly with *our* kindred, and evil
       entreated *our* fathers,
    38. and (with) *our* fathers:
    39. *our* fathers would not obey,
    40. Make us gods to go before *us:*
    44. *Our* fathers had the tabernacle
    45. *our* fathers that came after
    — before the face of *our* fathers,
 13:17. chose *our* fathers, and exalted
 14:17. *our* hearts with food and gladness.
 15: 9. between *us* and them,
    10. neither *our* fathers nor we
    24. which went out from *us*
    25. with *our* beloved Barnabas and Paul,
    26. of *our* Lord Jesus Christ.
    36. and visit *our* brethren
 16:16. as *we* went to prayer,
    20. do exceedingly trouble *our* city,
 17:20. strange things to *our* ears:
    27. from every one of *us:*
 19:25. we have *our* wealth.
 20:21. toward *our* Lord Jesus Christ.
 21:10. And as *we* tarried (there)
    17. And when *we* were come
 22:14. The God of *our* fathers
 24: 4. that thou wouldest hear *us*
    7. took (him) away out of *our* hands,
 26: 7. *our* twelve tribes,
    14. when *we* were all fallen to the earth,
 27:10. but also of *our* lives.
    18. *we* being exceedingly tossed
    27. as *we* were driven up and down in
 28:15. when the brethren heard of *us,*
    25. Esaias the prophet unto *our* fathers,
Ro. 1: 3(4). Jesus Christ *our* Lord,
    7. from God *our* Father,
  3: 5. But if *our* unrighteousness
  4: 1. that Abraham, *our* father
    12. of *our* father Abraham,
    16. who is the father of *us* all,
    24. Jesus *our* Lord from the dead ;
    25. for *our* offences, and was raised again for
       our justification.
  5: 1. through *our* Lord Jesus Christ:
    5. is shed abroad in *our* hearts
    6. when *we* were yet without strength,
    8. in that, while *we* were yet sinners, Christ
       died for *us.*
    11. through *our* Lord Jesus
    21. by Jesus Christ *our* Lord.
  6: 6. that *our* old man is crucified with
    11. through Jesus Christ *our* Lord.
    23. through Jesus Christ *our* Lord.
  7: 5. did work in *our* members
    25. through Jesus Christ *our* Lord.
  8:16. beareth witness with *our* spirit,
    23. the redemption of *our* body.
    26. helpeth *our* infirmities:
    — maketh intercession for *us*
    31. If God (be) for *us,* who (can be) against
       us ?
    32. but delivered him up for *us* all,
    34. maketh intercession for *us.*

Ro. 8:39. in Christ Jesus *our* Lord.
  9:10. (even) by *our* father Isaac;
 10:16. who hath believed *our* report?
 13:11. (is) *our* salvation nearer
 14: 7. For none of *us* liveth to himself,
    12. So then every one of *us*
 15: 2. Let every one of *us* please
    6. the Father of *our* Lord Jesus
    30. for the (lit. *our*) Lord Jesus Christ's sake,
 16: 1. I commend unto you Phebe *our* sister,
    9. *our* helper in Christ,
    18. *our* Lord Jesus Christ,
    20. The grace of *our* Lord Jesus
    24. The grace of *our* Lord Jesus
1Co. 1: 2. the name of Jesus Christ *our* Lord, both
       theirs and *our's:*
    3. from God *our* Father,
    7. the coming of *our* Lord
    8. the day of *our* Lord Jesus Christ.
    9. Jesus Christ *our* Lord.
    10. the name of *our* Lord
  2: 7. before the world unto *our* glory :
  4: 8. ye have reigned as kings without *us:*
  5: 4. name of *our* Lord Jesus
    — the power of *our* Lord Jesus Christ,
    7. Christ *our* passover is sacrificed for *us :*
  6:11. by the Spirit of *our* God.
  9: 1. have I not seen Jesus Christ *our* Lord?
 10: 1. all *our* fathers were under the cloud,
    6. were *our* examples, to the intent
    11. they are written for *our* admonition,
 12:23. and *our* uncomely (parts)
    24. For *our* comely (parts)
 15: 3. that Christ died for *our* sins
    14. then (is) *our* preaching vain,
    31. in Christ Jesus *our* Lord,
    57. through *our* Lord Jesus Christ.
2Co. 1: 2. from God *our* Father,
    3. of *our* Lord Jesus Christ,
    4. in all *our* tribulation,
    5. *our* consolation also aboundeth
  7(6). And *our* hope of you
    8. have you ignorant of *our* trouble
    11. helping together by prayer for *us,*
    — thanks may be given by many on *our* behalf.
    12. *our* rejoicing is this, the testimony of *our*
       conscience,
    14. even as ye also (are) *our's*
    18. *our* word toward you was not
    19. who was preached among you by *us,*
    20. unto the glory of God by *us.*
    22. given the earnest of the Spirit in *our* hearts.
 2·14. the savour of his knowledge by *us*
  3: 2. Ye are *our* epistle written in *our* hearts,
    3. the epistle of Christ ministered by *us,*
    5. *our* sufficiency (is) of God ;
  4: 3. But if *our* gospel be hid,
    6. hath shined in *our* hearts,
    7. may be of God, and not of *us.*
    10. might be made manifest in *our* body.
    11. be made manifest in *our* mortal flesh.
    16. though *our* outward man perish,
    17. *our* light affliction, which is but
    18. While *we* look not at the things
  5: 1. we know that if *our* earthly house
    2. with *our* house which is from heaven:
    12. to glory on *our* behalf,
    20. did beseech (you) by *us :*
    21. he hath made him (to be) sin for *us,*
  6:11. *our* mouth is open unto you, *our* heart is
       enlarged.
  7: 3. that ye are in *our* hearts

2Co. 7: 4. in all *our* tribulation.
    5. For, when *we* were come into Macedonia, *our* flesh had no rest,
    9. ye might receive damage by *us*
    12. that *our* care for you (many copies read " your care for *us*")
    14. *our* boasting, which (I made) before
  8: 4. Praying *us* with much intreaty
    9. the grace of *our* Lord Jesus Christ,
    19. to travel with *us* with this grace, which is administered by *us*
    20. which is administered by *us* :
    22. with them *our* brother,
    23. or *our* brethren (be enquired of),
    24. and of *our* boasting
  9: 3. *our* boasting of you
    11. causeth through *us* thanksgiving
  10: 4. the weapons of *our* warfare
    8. boast somewhat more of *our* authority,
    15. according to *our* rule
  11:31. Father of *our* Lord Jesus
Gal. 1: 3. the Father, and (from) *our* Lord Jesus
    4. Who gave himself for *our* sins,
    — the will of God and *our* Father:
  2: 4. to spy out *our* liberty
  3:13. being made a curse for *us* :
    24. the law was *our* schoolmaster
  4:26. the mother of *us* all.
  6:14. the cross of *our* Lord Jesus
    18. the grace of *our* Lord Jesus Christ
Eph. 1: 2. from God *our* Father,
    3. Father of *our* Lord Jesus Christ,
    14. the earnest of *our* inheritance
    17. the God of *our* Lord Jesus Christ,
  2: 3. the lusts of *our* flesh,
    14. For he is *our* peace,
  3:11. in Christ Jesus *our* Lord:
    14. the Father of *our* Lord Jesus Christ,
  4: 7. But unto every one of *us*
  5: 2. hath given himself for *us* an offering
    20. in the name of *our* Lord Jesus
  6:22. that ye might know *our* affairs,
    24. *our* Lord Jesus Christ
Phi. 1: 2. from God *our* Father,
  3:20. For *our* conversation is in heaven ;
    21. Who shall change *our* vile body,
  4:20. unto God and *our* Father (be) glory
    23. The grace of *our* Lord Jesus Christ
Col. 1: 2. from God *our* Father
    3. the Father of *our* Lord Jesus
    7. *our* dear fellowservant,
  2:14. that was against *us*,
  3: 4. Christ, (who is) *our* life, shall appear,
  4: 3. Withal praying also for *us*,
1Th. 1: 1. from God *our* Father,
    2. making mention of you in *our* prayers ;
    3. of hope in *our* Lord Jesus Christ, in the sight of God and *our* Father ;
    5. *our* gospel came not unto you in word
    6. And ye became followers of *us*,
    9. themselves shew of *us* what manner
  2: 1. *our* entrance in unto you,
    2. we were bold in *our* God to speak unto you
    3. For *our* exhortation (was) not of
    4. but God, which trieth *our* hearts.
    9. ye remember, brethren, *our* labour and
    13. the word of God which ye heard of *us*,
    19. For what (is) *our* hope,
    — in the presence of *our* Lord Jesus Christ
    20. For ye are *our* glory and joy.
  3: 2. *our* brother, and minister of God, and *our* fellowlabourer in

1Th. 3: 5. *our* labour be in vain.
    6. that ye have good remembrance of *us*
    7. *our* affliction and distress
    9. we joy for your sakes before *our* God ;
    11. God himself and *our* Father, and *our* Lord Jesus Christ, direct *our* way unto you.
    13. even *our* Father, at the coming of *our*
  4: 1. ye have received of *us*
  5: 9. by *our* Lord Jesus
    10. Who died for *us*,
    23. of *our* Lord Jesus Christ.
    25. Brethren, pray for *us*.
    28. The grace of *our* Lord Jesus Christ
2Th. 1: 1. in God *our* Father
    2. from God *our* Father
    7. to you who are troubled rest with *us*,
    8. of *our* Lord Jesus Christ:
    10. *our* testimony among you
    11. *our* God would count you worthy of (this) calling,
    12. the name of *our* Lord Jesus Christ
    — according to the grace of *our* God
  2: 1. by the coming of *our* Lord Jesus Christ, and (by) *our* gathering together unto
    2. by letter as from *us*,
    14. by *our* gospel, to the obtaining of the glory of *our* Lord Jesus Christ.
    15. whether by word, or *our* epistle.
    16. *our* Lord Jesus Christ himself, and God, even *our* Father,
  3: 1. pray for *us*, that the word
    6. in the name of *our* Lord Jesus
    — the tradition which he received of *us*.
    12. by *our* Lord Jesus Christ,
    14. And if any man obey not *our* word
    18. The grace of *our* Lord Jesus
1Ti. 1: 1. of God *our* Saviour, and Lord Jesus Christ, (which is) *our* hope ;
    2. from God *our* Father and Jesus Christ *our*
    12. And I thank Christ Jesus *our* Lord,
    14. the grace of *our* Lord was exceeding
  2: 3. in the sight of God *our* Saviour ;
  6: 3. the words of *our* Lord Jesus Christ,
    14. the appearing of *our* Lord Jesus Christ:
2Ti. 1: 2. Christ Jesus *our* Lord.
    8. the testimony of *our* Lord,
    9. not according to *our* works,
    10. of *our* Saviour Jesus Christ,
Tit. 1: 3. the commandment of God *our* Saviour ;
    4. Jesus Christ *our* Saviour.
  2:10. the doctrine of God *our* Saviour
    13. and *our* Saviour Jesus Christ ;
    14. Who gave himself for *us*,
  3: 4. love of God *our* Saviour
    6. through Jesus Christ *our* Saviour ;
Philem. 1. *our* dearly beloved, and fellowlabourer,
    2. and Archippus *our* fellowsoldier,
    3. from God *our* Father
    25. The grace of *our* Lord Jesus
Heb 1: 3. when he had by himself purged *our* sins,
  3: 1. and high priest of *our* profession,
  4:15. with the feeling of *our* infirmities ;
  6:20. the forerunner is for *us* entered,
  7:14. *our* Lord sprang out of Juda ;
  9:24. in the presence of God for *us* :
  10:26. if *we* sin wilfully after that we have
  11:40. some better thing for *us*, that they without *us* should not
  12: 9. we have had fathers of *our* flesh
    29. *our* God (is) a consuming fire.
  13:18. Pray for *us* : for we trust
    20. again from the dead *our* Lord Jesus,

Jas. 2: 1. the faith of *our* Lord Jesus Christ,
    21. Was not Abraham *our* father justified
    3: 6. so is the tongue among *our* members,
1Pet.1: 3. Father of *our* Lord Jesus
    2:21. because Christ also suffered for *us,*
    24. Who his own self bare *our* sins
    4: 1. hath suffered for *us*
    17. and if (it) first (begin) at *us,*
2Pet.1: 1. of God and *our* Saviour
    2. and of Jesus *our* Lord,
    8. the knowledge of *our* Lord Jesus Christ.
    11. of *our* Lord and Saviour Jesus
    14. *our* Lord Jesus Christ hath shewed
    16. the power and coming of *our* Lord
    3: 2. of the commandment of *us* the apostles
    15. the longsuffering of *our* Lord (is) salva-
       tion: even as *our* beloved brother Paul
    18. of *our* Lord and Saviour Jesus
1Joh.1: 1. with *our* eyes, which we have looked upon,
       and *our* hands have handled,
    3. may have fellowship with *us :*
    9. If we confess *our* sins, he is faithful
    2: 2. he is the propitiation for *our* sins:
    19. They went out from *us,* but they were not
       of *us ;* for if they had been of *us,* they
       would(no doubt)have continued with *us:*
    — they were not all of *us.*
    3: 5. to take away *our* sins ;
    16. because he laid down his life for *us :*
    19. and shall assure *our* hearts
    20. if our heart condemn *us,* God is greater
       than *our* heart, and
    21. Beloved, if *our* heart condemn *us* not,
    4: 6. heareth *us ;* he that is not of God heareth
       not *us.*
    10. (to be) the propitiation for *our* sins.
    17. Herein is *our* love (lit. love with *us*) made
       perfect,
    5: 4. (even) *our* faith.
    14. according to his will, he heareth *us :*
    15. And if we know that he hear *us,*
2Joh.   2. and shall be with *us* for ever.
    12. that *our* joy may be full.
3Joh.   12. ye know that *our* record is true.
Jude   4. turning the grace of *our* God into
    — and *our* Lord Jesus Christ.
    17. the apostles of *our* Lord Jesus Christ ;
    21. the mercy of *our* Lord Jesus Christ
    25. To the only wise God *our* Saviour, (be)
Rev. 1: 5. washed us from *our* sins in his own blood,
    5:10. And hast made us unto *our* God kings and
    6:10. avenge *our* blood on them that dwell
    7: 3. the servants of *our* God
    10. Salvation to *our* God (τῷ θεῷ ἡμῶν most
       copies omit this)
    — Salvation to *our* God which sitteth upon
       the throne, (lit. to him which sitteth
       upon the throne of *our* God)
    12. power, and might, (be) unto *our* God
  11: 8. where also *our* Lord was crucified.
    15. (the kingdoms) of *our* Lord, and of
  12:10. and the kingdom of *our* God,
    — the accuser of *our* brethren is cast down,
       which accused them before *our* God
  19: 1. and power, unto the Lord *our* God:
    5. Praise *our* God, all ye his servants,
  22:21. The grace of *our* Lord Jesus Christ

ἦν, ἦς, ἦσθα, &c., *een, ees, eestha,* &c.

From εἰμί.

Mat. 1:18. the birth of Jesus Christ *was* on this wise:

Mat. 2: 9. where the young child *was.*
    15. And *was* there until
    3: 4. and his meat *was* locusts and
    4:18. for they *were* fishers.
    7:27. great *was* the fall of it.
    29. For he taught (lit. *was* teaching) them
    8:30. there *was* a good way off from them an
    9:36. because they fainted, (lit. *were* fainting)
  12: 4. which *was* not lawful for him to eat,
    10. there *was* a man which had (his) hand
    40. For as Jonas *was* three days
  14:21. *were* about five thousand men,
    23. he *was* there alone.
    24. *was* now in the midst of the sea, tossed
       with waves: for the wind *was* contrary.
  15:38. *were* four thousand men,
  19:22. for he had (lit. *was* having) great
  21:25. The baptism of John, whence *was* it ?
    33. There *was* a certain housholder,
  22: 8. they which were bidden *were* not worthy.
    25. Now there *were* with us
  23:30. If we *had been* in the days of our fathers,
       we would not *have been* partakers
  24:38. before the flood they *were* eating and
  25: 2. And five of them *were* wise,
    21. thou *hast been* faithful over a few things,
    23. thou *hast been* faithful over a few things,
  26:24. it *had been* good for that man if
    43. for their eyes *were* heavy.
    69. Thou also *wast* with Jesus
    71. This (fellow) *was* also with Jesus
  27:54. this *was* the Son of God.
    55. And many women *were* there,
    56. Among which *was* Mary Magdalene,
    61. And there *was* Mary Magdalene,
  28: 3. His countenance *was* like lightning,
Mar. 1: 6. And John *was* clothed with camel's hair,
    13. And he *was* there in the wilderness
    — and *was* with the wild beasts ;
    16. for they *were* fishers.
    22. for he taught (lit. *was* teaching) them
    23. And there *was* in their synagogue
    33. all the city *was* gathered together
    39. And he preached (lit. *was* preaching) in
    45. *was* without in desert places:
  2: 4. the roof where he *was:*
    6. But there *were* certain of the scribes
    15. for there *were* many,
    18. the disciples of John and of the Pharisees
       used to fast: (lit. *were* fasting)
  3: 1. and there *was* a man there
  4: 1. multitude *was* by the sea on the land.
    36. even as he *was* in the ship. And there
       were also with him other little ships.
    38. And he *was* in the hinder part of the
  5: 5. he *was* in the mountains, and in the **tombs**
    11. Now there *was* there nigh unto the
    13. they *were* about two thousand ;
    21. and he *was* nigh unto the sea.
    40. where the damsel *was* lying.
    42. for she *was* (of the age) of twelve years.
  6:31. for there *were* many coming
    34. they *were* as sheep not
    44. that did eat of the loaves *were* about
    47. the ship *was* in the midst of the sea,
    48. for the wind *was* contrary
    52. for their heart *was* hardened.
  7:26. The woman *was* a Greek,
  8: 9. And they that had eaten *were* about
  9: 4. and they *were* talking with
    6. for they *were* sore afraid.
  10:22. for he had (lit. *was* having) great

Mar 10:32. they *were* in the way going up to Jerusalem; and Jesus went before them: (lit. *was* going before)

11:13. for the time of figs *was* not (yet).

30. *was* (it) from heaven, or of men?

32. that he *was* a prophet indeed.

12:20. Now there *were* seven brethren:

14: 1. *was* (the feast of) the passover,

4. And there *were* some that had indignation

21. good *were* it for that man if he had

40. for their eyes *were* heavy,

54. and he sat (lit. *was* sitting) with the servants,

56. their witness agreed not together. (lit. *were* not commensurate)

59. neither so did their witness agree together. (lit. *was* not commensurate)

67. And thou also *wast* with

15: 7. And there *was* (one) named Barabbas,

25. And it *was* the third hour,

26. the superscription of his accusation *was*

39. *was* the Son of God.

40. There *were* also women looking on afar off: among whom *was* Mary

41. when he *was* in Galilee,

42. because it *was* the preparation,

43. which also waited for (lit. who also himself *was* waiting for) the kingdom of God,

46. which *was* hewn out of a rock,

16: 4. for it *was* very great.

Lu. 1: 6. And they *were* both righteous

7. And they had no child (lit. there *was* not a child to them), because that Elisabeth *was* barren, and they both *were*

10. *were* praying without

21. And the people waited for (lit. *was* waiting for)

22. he beckoned (lit. *was* beckoning) unto them,

66. the hand of the Lord *was* with him.

80. and *was* in the deserts

2: 7. because there *was* no room for them

8. there *were* in the same country shepherds

25. there *was* a man in Jerusalem,

— the Holy Ghost *was* upon him.

26. it *was* revealed unto him

33. And Joseph and his mother marvelled (lit. *were* marvelling)

36. And there *was* one Anna, a prophetess,

40. the grace of God *was* upon him.

51. *was* subject unto them:

3:23. Jesus himself began to be (lit. *was*) about

4:16. where he *had been* brought up:

17. where it *was* written,

20. *were* fastened on him.

25. many widows *were* in Israel in the

27. And many lepers *were* in Israel

31. and taught them (lit. *was* teaching)

32. his word *was* with power.

33. in the synagogue there *was* a man,

38. *was* taken with a great fever;

44. And he preached (lit. *was* preaching) in the synagogues

5: 1. he stood (lit. *was* standing) by the lake of Gennesaret,

3. of the ships, which *was* Simon's,

10. which *were* partners with Simon.

16. And he withdrew (lit. *was* withdrawing) himself

17. as he *was* teaching, that there *were* Pharisees and doctors of the law sitting by, which *were* come out of

Lu. 5:17. the power of the Lord *was* (present) to heal them.

18. which *was* taken with a palsy:

29. and there *was* a great company of publicans and of others that sat down (lit. *were* sitting down) with them.

6: 6. and there *was* a man whose right hand *was* withered.

12. and continued all night (lit *was* cont.)

7: 2. who *was* dear unto him,

12. a widow: and much people of the city *was* with her.

37. which *was* a sinner,

39. This man, if he *were* a prophet,

41. There was a certain creditor which *had* two

8: 2. which *had been* healed

32. And there *was* there an herd of many

40. for they all waited (lit. *were* waiting)

42. he *had* one only daughter,

9:14. For they *were* about five thousand men.

30. which *were* Moses and Elias:

32. *were* heavy with sleep:

45. and it *was* hid from them,

53. his face *was* as though he would go to

10:39. And she *had* a sister

11:14. And he *was* casting out a devil, and it *was* dumb.

13:10. And he *was* teaching in one

11. *was* a woman which had a spirit of infirmity eighteen years, and *was* bowed

14: 1. they watched him. (lit. *were* watching)

2. there *was* a certain man before him which had the dropsy.

15: 1. Then drew near (lit. *were* &c.) unto him

24. this my son *was* dead, and is alive again; he *was* lost, and is found.

25. Now his elder son *was* in the field:

32. this thy brother *was* dead, and is alive again; and *was* lost, and is found.

16: 1. There *was* a certain rich man,

19. There *was* a certain rich man,

20. there *was* a certain beggar named Lazarus,

17:16. and he *was* a Samaritan.

18: 2. There *was* in a city a judge,

3. And there *was* a widow in that city;

23. for he *was* very rich.

34. and this saying *was* hid

19: 2. which *was* the chief among the publicans, and he *was* rich.

3. he *was* little of stature.

47. And he taught (lit. *was* teaching) daily

20: 4. *was* it from heaven, or of men?

29. There *were* therefore seven brethren:

21:37. And in the day time he *was* teaching in the temple;

22:56. This man *was* also with him.

59. this (fellow) also *was* with him:

23: 8. for he *was* desirous to see him of a long (season),

19. and for murder, *was* cast into prison.

38. And a superscription also *was* written

44. And it *was* about the sixth hour,

47. Certainly this *was* a righteous man.

51. The same had not consented (lit. *was* not consenting)

53. wherein never man before *was* laid.

54. And that day *was* the preparation,

55. the women also, which came (lit. *were* come) with him

24:10. It *was* Mary Magdalene, and Joanna,

13. behold, two of them went (lit. *were* going) that same day

Lu. 24:32. Did not our heart burn within us, (lit. *was* not...burning)

53. And *were* continually in the temple,

Joh. 1: 1. In the beginning *was* the Word, and the Word *was* with God, and the Word *was*

2. The same *was* in the beginning with

4. In him *was* life; and the life *was* the light

8. He *was* not that Light,

9. (That) *was* the true Light,

10. He *was* in the world,

15. This *was* he of whom I spake,

— he *was* before me.

24. *were* of the Pharisees.

28. where John *was* baptizing.

30. for he *was* before me.

39(40). for it *was* about the tenth hour.·

40(41). *was* Andrew, Simon Peter's brother.

44(45). Now Philip *was* of Bethsaida,

2: 1. and the mother of Jesus *was*

6. And there *were* set there six waterpots

13. And the Jews' passover *was* at hand,

23. Now when he *was* in Jerusalem

25. for he knew what *was* in man.

3: 1. There *was* a man of the Pharisees,

19. because their deeds *were* evil.

23. John also *was* baptizing in Ænon near to Salim, because there *was* much water

24. For John *was* not yet cast

26. he that *was* with thee beyond

4: 6. Now Jacob's well *was* there.

— (and) it *was* about the sixth hour.

46. And there *was* a certain nobleman,

5: 1. After this there *was* a feast

5. And a certain man *was* there,

9. and on the same day *was* the sabbath.

35. He *was* a burning and a shining light:

6: 4. And the passover, a feast of the Jews, *was*

10. Now there *was* much grass

22. there *was* none other boat there,

62. where he *was* before?

7: 2. Now the Jews' feast of tabernacles *was* at

12. there *was* much murmuring

39. for the Holy Ghost *was* not yet (given);

42. town of Bethlehem, where David *was* ?

8:39. If ye *were* Abraham's children,

42. If God *were* your Father,

44. He *was* a murderer from

9: 8. before had seen him that he *was* blind,

14. And it *was* the sabbath day when

16. And there *was* a division among them.

18. that he *had been* blind,

24. the man that *was* blind,

33. If this man *were* not of God,

41. If ye *were* blind, ye should

10: 6. what things they *were* which he spake unto them.

22. and it *was* winter.

40. where John at first baptized; (lit. *was* baptizing)

41. that John spake of this man *were* true.

11: 1. a certain (man) *was* sick, (named) Lazarus,

2. It *was* (that) Mary which anointed

6. he abode two days still in the same place where he *was*.

15. that I *was* not there,

18. Now Bethany *was* nigh

21. if thou *hadst been* here, my brother

30. but *was* in that place where

32. when Mary was come where Jesus *was*,

— if thou *hadst been* here,

38. It *was* a cave, and a stone lay upon it.

41. where the dead *was* laid.

Joh. 11:55. And the Jews' passover *was* nigh at hand:

12: 1. where Lazarus *was* which had been dead,

2. *was* one of them that sat at the table with

6. but because he *was* a thief,

16. that these things *were* written of him,

20. And there *were* certain Greeks

13: 5. wherewith he *was* girded.

23. Now there *was* leaning

30. and it *was* night.

15:19. If ye *were* of the world,

17: 6. thine they *were*, and thou gavest them me;

18: 1. the brook Cedron, where *was* a garden,

10. The servant's name *was* Malchus.

13. for he *was* father in law to Caiaphas, which *was* the high priest

14. Now Caiaphas *was* he, which gave counsel

15. *was* known unto the high priest,

16. which *was* known unto the high priest,

18. for it *was* cold.

— and Peter stood (lit. *was* standing) with

25. And Simon Peter stood (lit. *was* &c.)

28. and it *was* early;

30. If he *were* not a malefactor,

36. if my kingdom *were* of this world,

40. Now Barabbas *was* a robber.

19:11. except it *were* given thee from above:

14. And it *was* the preparation of the passover,

19. And the writing *was*,

20. *was* nigh to the city: and it *was* written in Hebrew,

23. now the coat *was* without seam,

31. because it *was* the preparation,

— for that sabbath day *was* an high day,

41. Now in the place where he was crucified there *was* a garden;

42. the sepulchre *was* nigh at hand.

20: 7. the napkin, that *was* about his head,

19. where the disciples *were* assembled

24. *was* not with them

26. again his disciples *were* within,

21: 2. There *were* together Simon Peter, and

7. for he *was* naked,

8. for they *were* not far from land,

18. When thou *wast* young, thou girdedst

Acts 1:10. while they looked stedfastly (lit. *were* looking st.)

13. where abode (lit. *were* abiding) both Peter and James, and

14. These all continued (lit. *were* continuing) with one accord in prayer and

15. the number of the names together *were* about an hundred and twenty,

17. For he *was* numbered with us,

2: 1. they *were* all with one accord in one

2. where they *were* sitting.

5. And there *were* dwelling at Jerusalem

24. because it *was* not possible that he

42. And they continued (lit. *were* c.) stedfastly in

44. all that believed *were* together,

3:10. that it *was* he which sat for alms

4: 3. for it *was* now eventide.

6. as many as *were* of the kindred of the high priest,

13. that they *had been* with Jesus.

22. For the man *was* above forty years old,

31. where they *were* assembled together;

32. *were* of one heart and of one soul:

— they had (lit. to them *were*) all things common.

33. and great grace *was* upon them all.

5:12. and they *were* all with one accord

Acts 7: 9. but God *was* with him,
20. and *was* exceeding fair,
22. and *was* mighty in words and in deeds.
44. Our fathers *had* the tabernacle
8: 1. *was* consenting unto his death.
13. he continued (lit. *was* c.) with Philip
16. For as yet he *was* fallen upon none
27. who had the charge of (lit. who *was* over) all her treasure,
28. *Was* returning, and sitting in his
32. the scripture which he read *was* this,
9: 9. And he *was* three days
10. And there *was* a certain disciple
28. he *was* with them coming in
33. and *was* sick of the palsy.
36. there *was* at Joppa a certain disciple
— this woman *was* full of good works
10: 1. There *was* a certain man in Cæsarea
24. Cornelius waited for them, (lit. *was* w.)
38. God *was* with him.
11:20. And some of them *were* men of
21. And the hand of the Lord *was* with them:
24. For he *was* a good man,
12: 3. Then *were* the days of unleavened bread.
5. but prayer *was* made without ceasing
6. Peter *was* sleeping
12. where many *were* gathered together
18. there *was* no small stir
20. And Herod *was* highly displeased
13: 1. Now there *were* in the church that was at Antioch certain
7. Which *was* with the deputy of the country,
46. It *was* necessary that the word of God
48. as many as *were* ordained
14: 4. part *held* with the Jews,
7. And there they preached (lit. *were* preaching) the gospel.
12. he *was* the chief speaker.
26. from whence they *had been* recommended
16: 1. a certain disciple *was* there,
9. There stood (lit. *was* standing) a man of Macedonia,
12. and we *were* in that city
17: 1. where *was* a synagogue
11. These *were* more noble
18: 3. they *were* tentmakers.
7. joined hard (lit. *was* adjacent) to the synagogue.
14. If it *were* a matter of wrong
25. This man *was* instructed
19: 7. And all the men *were* about twelve.
14. And there *were* seven sons
16. in whom the evil spirit *was*
32. for the assembly *was* confused;
20: 8. there *were* many lights in the upper chamber, where they *were* gathered
13. for so had (lit. *was*) he appointed,
16. if it *were* possible for him,
21: 3. for there the ship *was* to unlade
9. And the same man *had* four daughters,
29. For they had seen before (lit. *were* having seen before)
22:29. because he had bound him. (lit. *was* having bound)
23:13. And they *were* more than forty
27: 8. nigh whereunto *was* the city (of) Lasea.
37. And we *were* in all in the ship
Ro. 5:13. sin *was* in the world:
6:17. that ye *were* the servants
20. For when ye *were* the servants of sin, ye *were* free from
7: 5. For when we *were* in the flesh,

1Co. 6:11. And such *were* some of you:
10: 1. *were* under the cloud,
4. and that Rock *was* Christ.
12: 2. Ye know that ye *were* Gentiles,
19. And if they *were* all one member.
16:12. but his will *was* not at all
2Co. 5:19. that God *was* in Christ,
Gal. 1:23. But they had heard (lit. *were* hearing)
2: 6. whatsoever they *were*,
11. because he *was* to be blamed.
3:21. righteousness should *have been* by the law.
4: 3. Even so we, when we *were* children, *were* in bondage
15. Where *is* then the blessedness
Eph. 2: 3. and *were* by nature the children of wrath,
12. That at that time ye *were*
5: 8. For ye *were* sometimes darkness,
Phi. 2:26. he longed after (lit. *was* longing after) you all,
3: 7. what things *were* gain to me,
Col. 2:14. that *was* against us,
1Th. 3: 4. when we *were* with you,
2Th. 3:10. when we *were* with you,
Tit. 3: 3. For we ourselves also *were* sometimes
Heb 2:15. *were* all their lifetime subject to bondage.
7:10. he *was* yet in the loins of his father,
11. If therefore perfection *were* by the
8: 4. For if he *were* on earth, he should not *be* a priest,
7. if that first (covenant) *had been* faultless,
11:38. Of whom the world *was* not worthy:
12:21. And so terrible *was* the sight,
Jas. 1:24. forgetteth what manner of man he *was*.
5:17. *was* a man subject to like passions as we
1Pet. 2:25. For ye *were* as sheep going astray;
2Pet. 2:21. For it *had been* better for them
3: 5. the heavens *were* of old,
1Joh. 1: 1. That which *was* from the beginning,
2. which *was* with the Father,
2:19. but they *were* not of us; for if they *had been* of us,
3:12. (who) *was* of that wicked one,
— Because his own works *were* evil,
Rev. 1: 4. which is, and which *was*, and which is to
8. the Lord, which is, and which *was*, and
4: 3. *was* to look upon like a
8. which *was*, and is, and is to come.
9: 8. *were* as (the teeth) of lions.
10. there *were* stings in their tails:
10:10. and it *was* in my mouth
11:17. which art, and *wast*, and art to come;
13: 2. *was* like unto a leopard,
16: 5. O Lord, which art, and *wast*, and shalt be,
17: 8. The beast that thou sawest *was*, and is
— the beast that *was*, and is not, and yet is.
11. the beast that *was*, and is not,
18:23. *were* the great men of the earth;
21:18. And the building of the wall of it *was* (of)
21. every several gate *was* of one pearl:

ἡνίκα, *heenika.*

2Co. 3:15. *when* Moses is read,
16. Nevertheless *when* it shall turn to the

ἤπερ see after ἤ.

ἤπιος, *eepios.*

1Th. 2: 7. But we were *gentle* among you,
2Ti. 2:24. must not strive; but be *gentle* unto all

ἤρεμος, *eeremos.*

1Ti. 2: 2. that we may lead a *quiet* and peaceable

ἡσυχάζω, *heesukazo.*

Lu. 14: 4(3). And they *held* their *peace.*
23:56. and *rested* the sabbath day according
Acts11:18. they *held* their *peace,* and glorified God,
21:14. not be persuaded, we *ceased,* saying,
1Th. 4:11. that ye study *to be quiet,*

ἡσυχία, *heesukia.*

Acts22: 2. they kept the more *silence :*
2Th. 3:12. that with *quietness* they work,
1Ti. 2:11. Let the woman learn in *silence*
12. but to be in *silence.*

ἡσύχιος, *heesukios.*

1Ti. 2: 2. we may lead a quiet and *peaceable* life
1Pet.3: 4. of a meek and *quiet* spirit,

ἤτοι see after ἤ.

ἡττάομαι, *heetaomai.*

2Co.12:13. For what is it wherein you *were inferior*
2Pet.2:19. for of whom a man *is overcome,*
20. they are again entangled therein, and *overcome,*

ἥττημα, *heeteema.*

Ro. 11:12. and the *diminishing* of them
1Co. 6: 7. there is utterly a *fault* among you,

ἥττον, *heeton.*

1Co.11:17. ye come together not for the better, but for the *worse.*
2Co.12:15. the *less* I be loved.

ἤτω, *eeto.*

From εἰμί.

1Co.16:22. *let* him *be* Anathema Maran-atha.
Jas. 5:12. but *let* your yea *be* yea ;

ἠχέω, *eckeo.*

Lu. 21:25. the sea and the waves *roaring ;*
1Co.13: 1. I am become (as) *sounding* brass,

ἦχος, *eekos.*

Lu. 4:37. the *fame* of him went out
Acts 2: 2. a *sound* from heaven
Heb12:19. And the *sound* of a trumpet,

Ξάλασσα, *thalassa.*

Mat. 4:15. (by) the way of the *sea,* beyond
18. by the *sea* of Galilee,
— a net into the *sea :*

Mat. 8:24. there arose a great tempest.in the *sea,*
26. rebuked the winds and the *sea ;*
27. the winds and the *sea* obey him !
32. down a steep place into the *sea,*
13: 1. and sat by the *sea* side.
47. that was cast into the *sea,*
14:24. was now in the midst of the *sea,*
25, 26. walking on the *sea.*
15:29. nigh unto the *sea* of Galilee ;
17:27. go thou to the *sea,*
18: 6. in the depth of the *sea.*
21:21. be thou cast into the *sea ;*
23:15. for ye compass *sea* and land
Mar 1:16. by the *sea* of Galilee,
— a net into the *sea :*
2:13. he went forth again by the *sea* side ;
3: 7. with his disciples to the *sea :*
4: 1. to teach by the *sea* side:
— sat in the *sea ;* and the whole multitude was by the *sea*
39. and said unto the *sea,*
41. the wind and the *sea* obey
5: 1. over unto the other side of the *sea,*
13. down a steep place into the *sea,*
— were choked in the *sea.*
21. and he was nigh unto the *sea.*
6:47. in the midst of the *sea,*
48. walking upon the *sea,*
49. walking upon the *sea,*
7:31. unto the *sea* of Galilee,
9:42. he were cast into the *sea.*
11:23. be thou cast into the *sea ;*
Lu. 17: 2. about his neck, and he cast into the *sea,*
6. be thou planted in the *sea ;*
21:25. the *sea* and the waves roaring ;
Joh. 6: 1. Jesus went over the *sea* of Galilee,
16. his disciples went down unto the *sea,*
17. and went over the *sea*
18. And the *sea* arose by reason of a great wind
19. walking on the *sea,*
22. which stood on the other side of the *sea*
25. found him on the other side of the *sea,*
21: 1. at the *sea* of Tiberias;
7. did cast himself into the *sea.*
Acts 4:24. hast made heaven, and earth, and the *sea,*
7:36. in the Red *sea,* and in the wilderness
10: 6. house is by the *sea* side:
32. a tanner by the *sea* side:
14:15. made heaven, and earth, and the *sea,*
17:14. as it were to the *sea :*
27:30. the boat into the *sea,*
38. the wheat into the *sea.*
40. they committed (themselves) unto the *sea,*
28: 4. though he hath escaped the *sea,*
Ro. 9:27. as the sand of the *sea,*
1Co.10: 1. passed through the *sea ;*
2. in the cloud and in the *sea ;*
2Co.11:26. (in) perils in the *sea,*
Heb11:12. by the *sea* shore innumerable.
29. they passed through the Red *sea*
Jas. 1: 6. that wavereth is like a wave of the *sea*
Jude 13. Raging waves of the *sea,*
Rev. 4: 6. a *sea* of glass like unto crystal:
5:13. and such as are in the *sea,*
7: 1. not blow on the earth, nor on the *sea,*
2. the earth and the *sea,*
3. neither the *sea,* nor the trees,
8: 8. was cast into the *sea :* and the third part of the *sea* became blood ;
9. which were in the *sea,*
10: 2. right foot upon the *sea,*

Rev 10: 5. upon the *sea* and
6. and the *sea*, and the things which are
8. standeth upon the *sea*
12:12. the earth and of the *sea!*
13: 1. (12:18). upon the sand of the *sea*, and saw a beast rise up out of the *sea*,
14: 7. and earth, and the *sea*,
15: 2. as it were a *sea* of glass
— stand on the *sea* of glass,
16: 3. his vial upon the *sea;*
— every living soul died in the *sea*.
18:17. as many as trade by *sea*,
19. that had ships in the *sea*
21. and cast (it) into the *sea*,
20: 8. as the sand of the *sea*.
13. And the *sea* gave up
21: 1. and there was no more *sea*.

Θάλπω, *thalpo.*

Eph. 5:29. but nourisheth and *cherisheth* it,
1Th. 2: 7. even as a nurse *cherisheth* her children:

Θαμβέομαι, *thambeomai.*

Mar 1:27. And they *were* all *amazed*,
10:24. *were astonished* at his words.
32. and they *were amazed;*
Acts 9: 6. And he trembling and *astonished*

Θάμβος, *thambos.*

Lu. 4:36. And they were all amazed, (lit. *amazement* was upon all)
5: 9. For he was astonished, (lit. *astonishment* came upon him)
Acts 3:10. they were filled with *wonder* and

Θανάσιμος, *thanasimos.*

Mar 16:18. and if they drink any *deadly* thing,

Θανατηφόρος, *thanateephoros.*

Jas. 3: 8. full of *deadly* poison.

Θάνατος, *thanatos.*

Mat. 4:16. in the region and shadow of *death*
10:21. brother shall deliver up the brother to *death*,
15: 4. let him die the *death*.
16:28. shall not taste of *death*,
20:18. they shall condemn him to *death*,
26:38. exceeding sorrowful, even unto *death :*
66. He is guilty of *death*.
Mar 7:10. let him die the *death :*
9: 1. shall not taste of *death*,
10:33. shall condemn him to *death*,
13:12. brother shall betray the brother to *death*,
14:34. soul is exceeding sorrowful unto *death :*
64. condemned him to be guilty of *death*.
Lu. 1:79. and in) the shadow of *death*,

Lu. 2:26. that he should not see *death*, before
9:27. which shall not taste of *death*,
22:33. with thee, both into prison, and to *death*.
23:15. nothing worthy of *death*
22. no cause of *death* in him:
24:20. to be condemned to *death*,
Joh. 5:24. from *death* unto life.
8:51. he shall never see *death*.
52. he shall never taste of *death*,
11: 4. This sickness is not unto *death*,
13. Jesus spake of his *death :*
12:33. what *death* he should die.
18:32. what *death* he should die.
21:19. by what *death* he should glorify God.
Acts 2:24. having loosed the pains of *death :*
13:28. though they found no cause of *death* (in him),
22: 4. I persecuted this way unto the *death*,
23:29. worthy of *death* or of bonds.
25:11. have committed any thing worthy of *death*,
25. nothing worthy of *death*,
26:31. worthy of *death* or of bonds.
28:18. no cause of *death* in me.
Ro. 1:32. commit such things are worthy of *death*,
5:10. by the *death* of his Son,
12. and *death* by sin; and so *death* passed.
14. *death* reigned from Adam
17. *death* reigned by one;
21. sin hath reigned unto *death*,
6: 3. were baptized into his *death?*
4. by baptism into *death :*
5. in the likeness of his *death*,
9. *death* hath no more dominion over him.
16. whether of sin unto *death*,
21. the end of those things (is) *death*.
23. the wages of sin (is) *death;*
7: 5. to bring forth fruit unto *death*.
10. I found (to be) unto *death*,
13. which is good made *death* unto me?
— sin, working *death* in me
24. from the body of this *death?*
8: 2. the law of sin and *death*.
6. to be carnally minded (is) *death;*
38. neither *death*, nor life,
1Co. 3:22. or life, or *death*,
11:26. ye do shew the Lord's *death*
15:21. by man (came) *death*,
26. (that) shall be destroyed (is) *death*.
54. *Death* is swallowed up in victory.
55. O *death*, where (is) thy sting?
56. The sting of *death* (is) sin;
2Co. 1: 9. we had the sentence of *death* in ourselves,
10. Who delivered us from so great a *death*,
2:16. To the one (we are) the savour of *death* unto *death ;*
3: 7. the ministration of *death*,
4:11. are alway delivered unto *death*
12. then *death* worketh in us,
7:10. the sorrow of the world worketh *death*.
11:23. in prisons more frequent, in *deaths* oft.
Phi. 1:20. whether (it be) by life, or by *death*.
2: 8. and became obedient unto *death*, even the *death* of the cross.
27. he was sick nigh unto *death :*
30. he was nigh unto *death*,
3:10. being made conformable unto his *death ;*
Col. 1:22. In the body of his flesh through *death*,
2Ti. 1:10. who hath abolished *death*,
Heb. 2: 9. for the suffering of *death*,
— should taste *death* for every man.
14. through *death* he might destroy him that had the power of *death*,

Heb. 2:15. through fear of *death*
　　5: 7. to save him from *death*,
　　7:23. they were not suffered to continue by
　　　　　reason of *death* :
　　9:15. by means of *death*, for the redemption
　　16. there must also of necessity be the *death*
　11: 5. that he should not see *death* ;
Jas. 1:15. sin, when it is finished, bringeth forth
　　　　　death.
　　5:20. shall save a soul from *death*,
1Joh.3:14. we have passed from *death* unto life,
　　— brother abideth in *death*.
　　5:16. a sin (which is) not unto *death*,
　　— that sin not unto *death*. There is a sin
　　　　unto *death*:
　　17. there is a sin not unto *death*.
Rev. 1:18. the keys of hell and of *death*.
　　2:10. be thou faithful unto *death*,
　　11. shall not be hurt of the second *death*.
　　23. I will kill her children with *death* ;
　　6: 8. his name that sat on him was *Death*,
　　— with hunger, and with *death*,
　　9: 6. men seek *death*, and shall not
　　— *death* shall flee from them.
　12:11. their lives unto the *death*.
　13: 3. as it were wounded to *death* ; and his deadly
　　　　　wound (lit. w. of *death*) was healed:
　　12. whose deadly wound (lit. w. of *death*)
　　　　was healed.
　18: 8. *death*, and mourning, and famine ;
　20: 6. the second *death* hath no power,
　　13. *death* and hell delivered up the dead
　　14. *death* and hell were cast into the lake of
　　　　fire. This is the second *death*.
　21: 4. there shall be no more *death*,
　　8. which is the second *death*.

Θανατόω, *thănatoō*.

Mat.10:21. and *cause* them *to be put to death*.
　26:59. against Jesus, to *put* him *to death* ;
　27: 1. against Jesus *to put* him *to death* :
Mar 13:12. and *shall cause* them *to be put to death*.
　14:55. against Jesus *to put* him *to death* ;
Lu. 21:16. (some) of you *shall* they *cause to be put to
　　　　　death*.
Ro. 7: 4. ye also *are become dead* to the law
　　8:13. if ye through the Spirit *do mortify* the
　　　　　deeds of the body,
　　36. For thy sake we *are killed*
2Co. 6: 9. as chastened, and not *killed* ;
1Pet. 3:18. *being put to death* in the flesh,

Θάπτω, *thapto*.

Mat. 8:21. first to go and *bury* my father.
　　22. let the dead *bury* their dead.
　14:12. and *buried* it, and went and told Jesus.
Lu. 9:59. and *bury* my father.
　　60. Let the dead *bury* their dead:
　16:22. rich man also died, and *was buried* ;
Acts 2:29. he is both dead and *buried*,
　　5: 6. carried (him) out, and *buried* (him).
　　9. the feet of them *which have buried* thy
　　　　husband
　　10. *buried* (her) by her husband.
1Co.15: 4. And that he *was buried*,

Θαῤῥέω, *tharreo*.

2Co. 5: 6. Therefore (we are) always *confident*,
　　8. We *are confident*, (I say), and willing
　　7:16. I *have confidence* in you in all (things).
　　10: 1. but being absent *am bold* toward you:
　　2. that I may not *be bold* when I
Heb 13: 6. So that we may *boldly* (lit. *being confident*)
　　　　say,

Θαρσέω, *tharseo*.

Mat. 9: 2. Son, *be of good cheer* ;
　　22. Daughter, *be of good comfort* ; thy faith
　14:27. *Be of good cheer* ; it is I;
Mar. 6:50. *Be of good cheer* : it is I;
　10:49. *Be of good comfort*, rise ; he calleth thee.
Lu. 8:48. Daughter, *be of good comfort* :
Joh.16:33. but *be of good cheer* ; I have overcome the
Acts23:11. *Be of good cheer*, Paul: for as

Θάρσος, *tharsos*.

Acts28:15. he thanked God, and took *courage*.

Θαῦμα, *thauma*.

Rev.17: 6. and when I saw her, I wondered with
　　　　great *admiration*.

Θαυμάζω, *thaumazo*.

Mat. 8:10. Jesus heard (it), he *marvelled*, and said
　　27. the men *marvelled*, saying,
　　9: 8. the multitudes saw (it), they *marvelled*,
　　33. the multitudes *marvelled*, saying,
　15:31. that the multitude *wondered*,
　21:20. they *marvelled*, saying, How soon
　22:22. When they had heard (these words), they
　　　　　marvelled,
　27:14. insomuch that the governor *marvelled*
Mar 5:20. and all (men) *did marvel*.
　　6: 6. he *marvelled* because of their unbelief.
　　51. amazed in themselves beyond measure,
　　　　and *wondered*.
　12:17. they *marvelled* at him.
　15: 5. so that Pilate *marvelled*.
　　44. Pilate *marvelled* if he were already dead:
Lu. 1:21. and *marvelled* that he tarried
　　63. And they *marvelled* all.
　　2:18. they that heard (it) *wondered*
　　33. Joseph and his mother marvelled (lit.
　　　　were *marvelling*)
　　4:22. and *wondered* at the gracious words
　　7: 9. he *marvelled* at him, and turned him about,
　　8:25. And they being afraid *wondered*,
　　9:43. But while they *wondered* every one
　11:14. and the people *wondered*.
　　38. when the Pharisee saw (it), he *marvelled*
　20:26. they *marvelled* at his answer, *and* held
　24:12. *wondering* in himself at that
　　41. believed not for joy, and *wondered*,
Joh. 3: 7. *Marvel* not that I said unto thee,
　　4:27. *marvelled* that he talked with the woman:
　　5:20. greater works than these, that ye *may
　　　　marvel*.
　　28. *Marvel* not at this:
　　7:15. And the Jews *marvelled*,
　　21. and ye all *marvel*.

Acts 2: 7. and *marvelled*, saying one to another,
  3:12. why *marvel* ye at this?
  4:13. they *marvelled;* and they took knowledge
  7:31. he *wondered* at the sight:
  13:41. ye despisers, and *wonder*, and perish:
Gal. 1: 6. I *marvel* that ye are so soon
2Th 1:10. and *to be admired* in all them that
1 Joh.3:13. *Marvel* not, my brethren,
Jude 16. *having* men's persons *in admiration*
Rev 13: 3. the world wondered (lit. it *was wondered*
      in all the world) after the beast.
  17: 6. when I saw her, I *wondered*
      7. Wherefore *didst* thou *marvel?*
      8. they that dwell on the earth *shall wonder*,

Θαυμάσιος, *thaumasios.*

Mat 21:15. the *wonderful* things that he did,

Θαυμαστός, *thaumastos.*

Mat 21:42. it is *marvellous* in our eyes?
Mar 12:11. it is *marvellous* in our eyes?
Joh. 9:30. Why herein is a *marvellous* thing,
2Co.11:14. And no *marvel;* for Satan himself
1Pet. 2: 9. out of darkness into his *marvellous* light:
Rev 15: 1. sign in heaven, great and *marvellous*,
      3. and *marvellous* (are) thy works,

Θεά, *thea.*

Acts 19:27. of the great *goddess* Diana
  35. of the great *goddess* Diana,
  37. nor yet blasphemers of your *goddess.*

Θεάομαι, *theaomai.*

Mat 6: 1. *to be seen* of them:
  11: 7. *to see?* A reed shaken with the wind?
  22:11. the king came in *to see* the guests,
  23: 5. for *to be seen* of men:
Mar 16:11. and *had been seen* of her,
  14. they believed not them *which had seen* him
Lu. 5:27. and *saw* a publican, named Levi,
  7:24. into the wilderness for *to see?*
  23:55. and *beheld* the sepulchre, and how his
Joh. 1:14. we *beheld* his glory, the glory
  32. I *saw* the Spirit descending
  38. *saw* them following, *and* saith
  4:35. and *look* on the fields;
  6: 5. *saw* a great company come unto him,
  8:10. and *saw* none but the woman,
  11:45. and *had seen* the things which Jesus did,
Acts 1:11. in like manner as ye *have seen* him
  8:18. And *when* Simon *saw* that
  21:27. *when* they *saw* him in the temple,
  22: 9. that were with me *saw* indeed the light,
Ro. 15:24. *to see* you in my journey,
1Joh.1: 1. which we *have looked upon*, and our hands
  4:12(11). No man *hath seen* God at any time.
  14. And we *have seen* and do testify

Θεατρίζομαι, *theatrizomai.*

Heb 10:33. *whilst* ye *were made a gazingstock* both by
      reproaches and afflictions;

Θέατρον, *theatron.*

Acts 19:29. with one accord into the *theatre.*
  31. that he would not adventure himself into
      the *theatre.*
1Co. 4: 9. for we are made a *spectacle*

Θεῖον, *thion.*

Lu. 17:29. fire and *brimstone* from heaven,
Rev 9:17. issued fire and smoke and *brimstone.*
  18. the smoke, and by the *brimstone,*
  14:10. with fire and *brimstone*
  19:20. lake of fire burning with *brimstone.*
  20:10. the lake of fire and *brimstone,*
  21: 8. burneth with fire and *brimstone:*

Θεῖος, *thios.* adj.

Acts 17:29. that the Godhead (lit. the *Divine*) is like
2Pet 1: 3. According as his *divine* power
  4. might be partakers of the *divine* nature,

Θειότης, *thiotees.*

Ro. 1:20. his eternal power and *Godhead;*

Θειώδης, *thiodees.*

Rev 9:17. of fire, and of jacinth, and *brimstone:*

Θέλημα, *theleema.*

Mat. 6:10. Thy *will* be done in earth,
  7:21. but he that doeth the *will*
  12:50. For whosoever shall do the *will*
  18:14. it is not the *will* of your Father
  21:31. of them twain did the *will* of (his) father?
  26:42. except I drink it, thy *will* be done.
Mar. 3:35. shall do the *will* of God,
Lu. 11: 2. Thy *will* be done, as in heaven,
  12:47. which knew his lord's *will*,
  — did according to his *will*,
  22:42. nevertheless not my *will*,
  23:25. he delivered Jesus to their *will.*
Joh. 1:13. nor of the *will* of the flesh, nor of the
      will of man,
  4:34. the *will* of him that sent me,
  5:30. I seek not mine own *will*, but the *will* of
      the Father which hath sent me.
  6:38. not to do mine own *will*, but the *will* of
      him that sent me.
  39. the Father's *will* which hath sent me,
  40. the *will* of him that sent me,
  7:17. do his *will*, he shall know of the doctrine,
  9:31. doeth his *will*, him he heareth.
Acts 13:22. shall fulfil all my *will.* (lit. *desires*)
  21:14. The *will* of the Lord be done.
  22:14. that thou shouldest know his *will*,
Ro. 1:10. by the *will* of God
  2:18. knowest (his) *will*, and approvest
  12: 2. that good, and acceptable, and perfect, *will*
      of God.
  15:32. by the *will* of God,
1Co. 1: 1. through the *will* of God,
  7:37. over his own *will*,
  16:12. his *will* was not at all to come at this time;

2Co. 1: 1. an apostle of Jesus Christ by the *will* of
8: 5. by the *will* of God.
Gal. 1: 4. according to the *will* of God
Eph. 1: 1. by the *will* of God,
5. the good pleasure of his *will*,
9. the mystery of his *will*,
11. the counsel of his own *will :*
2: 3. fulfilling the *desires* of the flesh
5:17. what the *will* of the Lord (is).
6: 6. doing the *will* of God
Col. 1: 1. by the *will* of God,
9. the knowledge of his *will*
4:12. in all the *will* of God.
1Th. 4: 3. this is the *will* of God, (even) your sanctification,
5:18. for this is the *will* of God in Christ
2Ti. 1: 1. by the *will* of God,
2:26. taken captive by him at his *will*.
Heb 10: 7. to do thy *will*, O God.
9. I come to do thy *will*, O God.
10. By the which *will* we are sanctified
36. after ye have done the *will* of God,
13:21. every good work to do his *will*,
1Pet.2:15. so is the *will* of God, that with well doing
3:17. if the *will* of God be so,
4: 2. but to the *will* of God.
3. the *will* of the Gentiles,
19. according to the *will* of God
2Pet.1:21. prophecy came not in old time by the *will*
of man:
1Joh.2:17. that doeth the *will* of God
5:14. according to his *will*,
Rev. 4:11. for thy *pleasure* they are

Θέλησις, theleesis.

Heb. 2: 4. gifts of the Holy Ghost, according to his
own *will ?*

Θέλω, thelo.

Mat. 1:19. not *willing* to make her a publick example,
2:18. and *would* not be comforted, because
5:40. *if* any man *will* sue thee at the law,
42. him *that would* borrow of thee
7:12. whatsoever ye *would* that men should do
8: 2. if thou *wilt*, thou canst
3. I *will ;* be thou clean.
9:13. I *will have* mercy, and not sacrifice:
11:14. if ye *will* receive (it),
12: 7. I *will have* mercy, and not sacrifice,
38. we *would* see a sign from thee.
13:28. *Wilt* thou then that we go
14: 5. *when* he *would* have put him to death,
15:28. be it unto thee even as thou *wilt*.
32. I *will* not send them away fasting,
16:24. If any (man) *will* come after me,
25. For whosoever *will* save his life
17: 4. if thou *wilt*, let us make
12. unto him whatsoever they *listed*.
18:23. which *would* take account
30. And he *would* not: but went and cast him
19:17. but if thou *wilt* enter
21. If thou *wilt* be perfect,
20:14. I *will* give unto this last,
15. to do what I *will* with mine own?
21. said unto her, What *wilt* thou?
26. whosoever *will* be great among you,
27. whosoever *will* be chief among you,
32. What *will* ye that I shall do unto you?

Mat.21:29. and said, I *will* not:
22: 3. and they *would* not come.
23: 4. *will* not move them with one of their
37. how often *would* I have gathered
— and ye *would* not !
26:15. What *will* ye give me,
17. Where *wilt* thou that we prepare
39. nevertheless not as I *will*,
27:15. a prisoner, whom they *would*.
17. Whom *will* ye that I release
21. Whether of the twain *will* ye that I release
34. tasted (thereof), he *would* not drink.
43. deliver him now, if he *will* have him:
Mar. 1:40. If thou *wilt*, thou canst
41. I *will ;* be thou clean.
3:13. calleth (unto him) whom he *would :*
6:19. *would* have killed him ;
22. Ask of me whatsoever thou *wilt*,
25. I *will* that thou give me
26. he *would* not reject her.
48. *would* have passed by them.
7:24. and *would* have no man know (it):
8:34. Whosoever *will* come after me,
35. For whosoever *will* save his life
9:13. unto him whatsoever they *listed*,
30. he *would* not that any man should know
(it).
35. If any man *desire* to be first,
10:35. we *would* that thou shouldest do for us
whatsoever we shall desire.
36. What *would* ye that I should do for you ?
43. whosoever *will* be great among you,
44. whosoever of you *will* be the chiefest,
51. What *wilt* thou that I should do unto thee ?
12:38. which *love* to go in long clothing,
14: 7. and whensoever ye *will* ye may
12. Where *wilt* thou that we go
36. not what I *will*, but what thou
15: 9. *Will* ye that I release unto you
12. What *will* ye then that I shall do (unto
him) whom
Lu. 1:62. how he *would* have him called.
4: 6. to whomsoever I *will* I give it.
5:12. if thou *wilt*, thou canst make me clean.
13. I *will :* be thou clean.
39. straightway *desireth* new:
6:31. And as ye *would* that men
8:20. *desiring* to see thee.
9:23. if any (man) *will* come after me,
24. For whosoever *will* save his life
54. Lord, *wilt* thou that we command
10:24. prophets and kings *have desired* to see those
things which ye see,
29. *willing* to justify himself,
12:49. what *will* I, if it be already kindled ?
13:31. for Herod *will* kill thee.
34. how often *would* I have gathered
— and ye *would* not !
14:28. *intending* to build a tower,
15:28. he was angry, and *would* not go in:
16:26. they *which would* pass from hence
18: 4. And he *would* not for a while:
13. *would* not lift up so much as (his) eyes
41. What *wilt* thou that I shall do unto thee ?
19:14. We *will* not have this (man) to reign over
27. mine enemies, *which would* not that I
20:46. the scribes, *which desire* to walk in long
22: 9. Where *wilt* thou that we prepare ?
23: 8. for he was *desirous* to see him of a long
20. *willing* to release Jesus,
Joh. 1:43(44). Jesus *would* go forth
3: 8. bloweth where it *listeth*,

Joh. 5: 6. *Wilt* thou be made whole?
21. quickeneth whom he *will*.
35. ye *were willing* for a season to rejoice
40. ye *will* not come to me,
6:11. of the fishes as much as they *would*.
21. Then they willingly received (lit. they *willed* to receive) him into the ship:
67. *Will* ye also go away?
7: 1. for he *would* not walk in Jewry,
17. If any man *will* do his will,
44. And some of them *would* have taken him;
8:44. the lusts of your father ye *will* do.
9:27. wherefore *would* ye hear (it) again? *will* ye also be his disciples?
12:21. we *would* see Jesus.
15: 7. ye shall ask what ye *will*,
16:19. they *were desirous* to ask him,
17:24. I *will* that they also, whom thou hast given me, be with me where I am;
21:18. walkedst whither thou *wouldest*:
— carry (thee) whither thou *wouldest* not.
22. If I *will* that he tarry till I come,
23. If I *will* that he tarry
Acts 2:12. one to another, What *meaneth* this?
7:28. *Wilt* thou kill me,
39. To whom our fathers *would* not obey,
9: 6. what *wilt* thou *have* me to do?
10:10. and *would* have eaten:
14:13. and *would* have done sacrifice
16: 3. Him *would* Paul *have* to go
17:18. What *will* this babbler say?
20. what these things *mean*.
18:21. return again unto you, *if* God *will*.
19:33. and *would* have made his defence
24: 6. and *would* have judged according to our
27. *willing* to shew the Jews a pleasure,
25: 9. *willing* to do the Jews a pleasure,
— *Wilt* thou go up to Jerusalem,
26: 5. if they *would* testify,
Ro. 1:13. Now I *would* not *have* you ignorant,
7:15. for what I *would*, that do I not;
16. If then I do that which I *would* not,
18. for *to will* is present with me;
19. For the good that I *would* I do not: but the evil which I *would* not,
20. I do that I *would* not,
21. *when* I *would* do good, evil is
9:16. So then (it is) not of him *that willeth*,
18. hath he mercy on whom he *will* (have mercy), and whom he *will* he hardeneth.
22. (What) if God, *willing* to shew
11:25. For I *would* not, brethren, that ye should be ignorant of
13: 3. *Wilt* thou then not be afraid
16:19. but yet I *would* have you wise
1Co. 4:19. come to you shortly, if the Lord *will*,
21. What *will* ye?...with a rod,
7: 7. For I *would* that all men
32. But I *would* have you without carefulness.
36. let him do what he *will*,
39. to be married to whom she *will;*
10: 1. Moreover, brethren, I *would* not that ye should be ignorant,
20. and I *would* not that ye should have
27. and ye *be disposed* to go;
11: 3. But I *would* have you know,
12: 1. I *would* not *have* you ignorant.
18. as it *hath pleased* him. (lit. he *hath willed*)
14: 5. I *would* that ye all spake with tongues,
19. I *had rather* speak five words
35. And if they *will* learn any thing,
15:38. as it *hath pleased* him, (lit. he *hath*, &c.)

1Co.16: 7. For I *will* not see you now
2Co. 1: 8. For we *would* not, brethren, have you
5: 4. not for that we *would* be unclothed,
8:10. have begun before,...*to be forward* a year
11. a readiness *to will*,
11:12. from them *which desire* occasion;
32. *desirous* to apprehend me:
12: 6. For though I *would desire* to glory,
20. I shall not find you such as I *would*,
— such as ye *would* not:
Gal. 1: 7. that trouble you, and *would* pervert the gospel of Christ.
3: 2. This only *would* I learn of you,
4: 9. ye *desire* again to be in bondage?
17. they *would* exclude you,
20. I *desire* to be present with you
21. Tell me, ye that *desire* to be under the law,
5:17. ye cannot do the things that ye *would*.
6:12. As many as *desire* to make a fair shew
13. *desire* to have you circumcised,
Phi. 2:13. worketh in you both *to will* and to do of (his) good pleasure.
Col. 1:27. To whom God *would* make known
2: 1. For I *would* that ye knew
18. Let no man beguile you of your reward in a voluntary humility (lit. beguile you *willing*, or at his will)
1Th. 2:18. we *would* have come unto you,
4:13. But I *would* not *have* you to be ignorant,
2Th 3:10. if any *would* not work,
1Ti. 1: 7. *Desiring* to be teachers of the law;
2: 4. Who *will have* all men to be saved,
5:11. wanton against Christ, they *will* marry;
2Ti. 3:12. all *that will* live godly in Christ
Philem.14. *would* I do nothing;
Heb 10: 5. offering thou *wouldest* not,
8. thou *wouldest* not, neither hadst pleasure
12:17. *when* he *would* have inherited
13:18. in all things *willing* to live honestly.
Jas. 2:20. But *wilt* thou know,
4:15. If the Lord *will*, we shall live,
1Pet.3:10. For he *that will* love life,
2Pet.3: 5. For this they *willingly* are ignorant of,
3Joh. 13 but I *will* not with ink
Rev.11: 5. (*bis*) if any man *will* hurt them,
6. as often as they *will*.
22:17. And whosoever *will*, let him take the

- ρν, Θεμέλιος, *themelios.*

Acts 16:26 it is Θεμέλια, i. e. neut. pl.

Lu. 6:48. laid the *foundation* on a rock:
49. without a *foundation* built
14:29. after he hath laid the *foundation*,
Acts16:26. the *foundations* of the prison were shaken:
Ro. 15:20. upon another man's *foundation:*
1Co. 3:10. I have laid the *foundation*,
11. For other *foundation* can no man
12. upon this *foundation* gold,
Eph 2:20. upon the *foundation* of the apostles
1Ti. 6:19. for themselves a good *foundation* against
2Ti. 2:19. the *foundation* of God standeth sure,
Heb 6: 1. laying again the *foundation*
11:10. a city which hath *foundations*,
Rev 21:14. wall of the city had twelve *foundations*,
19. the *foundations* of the wall of the city
— The first *foundation* (was) jasper;

Θεμελιόω, *themelioō.*

Mat 7:25. for it *was founded* upon a rock.

Lu.　6:48. for it *was founded* upon a rock.
Eph　3:17(18). being rooted and *grounded* in love,
Col.　1:23. continue in the faith *grounded* and
Heb　1:10. *hast laid the foundation* of the earth ;
1Pet 5:10. stablish, strengthen, *settle* (you).

Θεοδίδακτος, *theodidaktos.*

1Th　4: 9. ye yourselves are *taught of God* to love
　　　　one another.

Θεομαχέω, *theomakeo.*

Acts23: 9. *let* us not *fight against God.*

Θεομάχος, *theomakos,* adj.

Acts 5:39. ye be found even *to fight against God.*

Θεύπνευστος, *theopnŭstos.*

2Ti.　3:16. scripture (is) *given by inspiration of God,*

Θεός, *Theos.*

Mat. 1:23. being interpreted is, *God* with us.
　　3: 9. *God* is able of these stones
　　　16. he saw the Spirit of *God*
　　4: 3. If thou be the Son of *God,*
　　　4. out of the mouth of *God.*
　　　6. If thou be the Son of *God,* cast
　　　7. shalt not tempt the Lord thy *God.*
　　　10. Thou shalt worship the Lord thy *God,*
　　5: 8. for they shall see *God.*
　　　9. they shall be called the children of *God.*
　　　34. for it is *God's* throne :
　　6:24. serve *God* and mammon.
　　　30. *God* so clothe the grass of the field,
　　　33. first the kingdom of *God,*
　　8:29. Jesus, thou Son of *God?*
　　9: 8. and glorified *God,* which had
　　12: 4. into the house of *God,*
　　　28. cast out devils by the Spirit of *God,* then
　　　　the kingdom of *God*
　　14:33. Of a truth thou art the Son of *God.*
　　15: 3. the commandment of *God*
　　　4. For *God* commanded, saying,
　　　6. the commandment of *God*
　　　31. they glorified the *God* of Israel.
　　16:16. the Son of the living *God.*
　　　23. savourest not the things that be of *God,*
　　19: 6. What therefore *God* hath joined together,
　　　17. but one, (that is), *God :*
　　　24. into the kingdom of *God.*
　　　26. but with *God* all things
　　21:12. into the temple of *God,*
　　　31. into the kingdom of *God*
　　　43. The kingdom of *God* shall be taken
　　22:16. and teachest the way of *God*
　　　21. and unto *God* the things that are *God's.*
　　　29. nor the power of *God*
　　　30. but are as the angels of *God*
　　　31. which was spoken unto you by *God,*
　　　32. the *God* of Abraham, and the *God* of
　　　　Isaac, and the *God* of Jacob?　*God* is
　　　　not the *God* of the dead,
　　　37. Thou shalt love the Lord thy *God*

Mat 23:22. sweareth by the throne of *God,*
　　26:61. to destroy the temple of *God,*
　　　63. I adjure thee by the living *God,*
　　　-- the Christ, the Son of *God.*
　　27:40. If thou be the Son of *God,* come down
　　　43. He trusted in *God ;*
　　　— I am the Son of *God.*
　　　46. My *God,* my *God,* why hast thou forsaken
　　　54. Truly this was the Son of *God.*
Mar 1: 1. of Jesus Christ, the Son of *God ;*
　　　14. the gospel of the kingdom of *God,*
　　　15. the kingdom of *God* is at hand :
　　　24. who thou art, the Holy One of *God.*
　　2: 7. can forgive sins but *God* only?
　　　12. and glorified *God,* saying,
　　　26. into the house of *God*
　　3:11. Thou art the Son of *God.*
　　　35. shall do the will of *God,*
　　4:11. the mystery of the kingdom of *God :*
　　　26. So is the kingdom of *God,*
　　　30. shall we liken the kingdom of *God?*
　　5: 7. (thou) Son of the most high *God?* I
　　　　adjure thee by *God,*
　　7: 8. laying aside the commandment of *God,*
　　　9. ye reject the commandment of *God,*
　　13. Making the word of *God* of none effect
　　8:33. thou savourest not the things that be of
　　　　God, but
　　9: 1. they have seen the kingdom of *God*
　　　47. to enter into the kingdom of *God*
　　10: 6. *God* made them male
　　　9. What therefore *God* hath joined together,
　　　14. of such is the kingdom of *God.*
　　　15. Whosoever shall not receive the kingdom
　　　　of *God*
　　　18. none good but one, (that is), *God.*
　　　23. enter into the kingdom of *God !*
　　　24. to enter into the kingdom of *God !*
　　　25. to enter into the kingdom of *God.*
　　　27. but not with *God :* for with *God* all things
　　11:22. Have faith in *God.*
　　12:14. teachest the way of *God*
　　　17. and to *God* the things that are *God's.*
　　　24. neither the power of *God?*
　　　26. *God* spake unto him, saying, I (am) the
　　　　God of Abraham, and the *God* of Isaac,
　　　　and the *God* of Jacob?
　　　27. He is not the *God* of the dead, but the
　　　　God of the living :
　　　29. The Lord our *God* is one Lord :
　　　30. thou shalt love the Lord thy *God*
　　　32. for there is one *God ;* and
　　　34. from the kingdom of *God.*
　　13:19. which *God* created unto this time,
　　14:25. new in the kingdom of *God.*
　　15:34. My *God,* my *God,* why hast
　　　39. this man was the Son of *God,*
　　　43. waited for the kingdom of *God,*
　　16:19. on the right hand of *God.*
Lu.　1: 6. they were both righteous before *God,*
　　　8. before *God* in the order of his course,
　　16. to the Lord their *God.*
　　　19. that stand in the presence of *God ;*
　　　26. Gabriel was sent from *God*
　　　30. hast found favour with *God.*
　　　32. the Lord *God* shall give unto him
　　　35. shall be called the Son of *God.*
　　　37. with *God* nothing shall be impossible.
　　　47. in *God* my Saviour.
　　　64. he spake, and praised *God.*
　　　68. Blessed (be) the Lord *God* of Israel ;
　　　78. the tender mercy of our *God ;*

Lu. 2:13. praising *God*, and saying,
14. Glory to *God* in the highest,
20. and praising *God*
28. and blessed *God*, and said,
40. the grace of *God* was upon him.
52. with *God* and man.
3: 2. the word of *God* came unto John
6. the salvation of *God*.
8. *God* is able of these stones
38. of Adam, which was (the son) of *God*.
4: 3. If thou be the Son of *God*, command
4. by every word of *God*.
8. Thou shalt worship the Lord thy *God*,
9. If thou be the Son of *God*, cast
12. Thou shalt not tempt the Lord thy *God*.
34. the Holy One of *God*.
41. Thou art Christ the Son of *God*.
43. the kingdom of *God* to other cities also:
5: 1. to hear the word of *God*,
21. Who can forgive sins, but *God* alone?
25. to his own house, glorifying *God*.
26. and they glorified *God*,
6: 4. into the house of *God*,
12. in prayer to *God*.
20. your's is the kingdom of *God*.
7:16. and they glorified *God*,
— *God* hath visited his people.
28. in the kingdom of *God*
29. justified *God*, being baptized
30. the counsel of *God* against
8: 1. shewing the glad tidings of the kingdom
of *God*:
10. the mysteries of the kingdom of *God*:
11. The seed is the word of *God*.
21. which hear the word of *God*,
28. (thou) Son of *God* most high?
39. how great things *God* hath done unto
9: 2. to preach the kingdom of *God*,
11. of the kingdom of *God*,
20. The Christ of *God*.
27. see the kingdom of *God*.
43. at the mighty power of *God*.
60. preach the kingdom of *God*.
62. is fit for the kingdom of *God*.
10: 9. The kingdom of *God* is come nigh unto
11. the kingdom of *God* is come nigh unto
27. Thou shalt love the Lord thy *God*
11:20. But if I with the finger of *God* cast out
devils, no doubt the kingdom of *God* is
28. they that hear the word of *God*,
42. and the love of *God*:
49. said the wisdom of *God*,
12: 6. not one of them is forgotten before *God*?
8. before the angels of *God*:
9. before the angels of *God*.
20. But *God* said unto him,
21. and is not rich toward *God*.
24. *God* feedeth them: how much more
28. *God* so clothe the grass.
31. But rather seek ye the kingdom of *God*;
13:13. she was made straight, and glorified *God*.
18. is the kingdom of *God* like?
20. shall I liken the kingdom of *God*?
28. the prophets, in the kingdom of *God*,
29. shall sit down in the kingdom of *God*.
14:15. bread in the kingdom of *God*.
15:10. in the presence of the angels of *God*
16:10. serve *God* and mammon.
15. but *God* knoweth your hearts:
— abomination in the sight of *God*.
16. the kingdom of *God* is preached,
17:15. with a loud voice glorified *God*,

Lu. 17:18. to give glory to *God*,
20. when the kingdom of *God* should come,
— The kingdom of *God* cometh not
21. the kingdom of *God* is within you.
18: 2. which feared not *God*,
4. Though I fear not *God*,
7. And shall not *God* avenge
11. *God*, I thank thee, that I am not
13. *God* be merciful to me a sinner.
16. for of such is the kingdom of *God*.
17. shall not receive the kingdom of *God*
19. save one, (that is), *God*.
24. enter into the kingdom of *God*!
25. to enter into the kingdom of *God*.
27. are possible with *God*.
29. for the kingdom of *God's* sake,
43. followed him, glorifying *God*:
— gave praise unto *God*.
19:11. the kingdom of *God* should immediately
37. and praise *God* with a loud voice
20:21. teachest the way of *God* truly:
25. and unto *God* the things which be *God's*.
36. and are the children of *God*,
37. he calleth the Lord the *God* of Abraham,
and the *God* of Isaac, and the *God* of
Jacob.
38. For he is not a *God* of the dead,
21: 4. unto the offerings of *God*:
31. the kingdom of *God* is nigh at hand.
22:16. in the kingdom of *God*.
18. the kingdom of *God* shall come.
69. of the power of *God*.
70. Art thou then the Son of *God*?
23:35. if he be Christ, the chosen of *God*.
40. Dost not thou fear *God*,
47. he glorified *God*, saying,
51. also himself waited for the kingdom of
God.
24:19. before *God* and all the people:
53. praising and blessing *God*.
Joh. 1: 1. the Word was with *God*, and the Word
was *God*.
2. was in the beginning with *God*.
6. sent from *God*, whose name (was) John.
12. to become the sons of *God*,
13. Which were born, not...but of *God*.
18. No man hath seen *God*
29. Behold the Lamb of *God*,
34. this is the Son of *God*.
36. Behold the Lamb of *God*!
49(50). thou art the Son of *God*;
51(52). the angels of *God* ascending
3: 2. thou art a teacher come from *God*:
— except *God* be *with* him.
3. see the kingdom of *God*.
5. into the kingdom of *God*.
16. *God* so loved the world,
17. For *God* sent not
18. of the only begotten Son of *God*.
21. that they are wrought in *God*.
33. that *God* is true.
34. For he whom *God* hath sent speaketh the
words of *God*: for *God* giveth not the
36. the wrath of *God* abideth on him.
4:10. If thou knewest the gift of *God*,
24. *God* (is) a Spirit: and they that
5:18. said also that *God* was his Father, making
himself equal with *God*.
25. the voice of the Son of *God*:
42. ye have not the love of *God*
44. the honour that (cometh) from *God* only?
6:27. hath *God* the Father sealed.

Joh. 6:28. we might work the works of *God*?
29. This is the work of *God*,
33. For the bread of *God* is he which
45. they shall be all taught of *God*.
46. save he which is of *God*,
69. the Son of the living *God*.
7:17. whether it be of *God*,
8:40. which I have heard of *God*:
41. we have one Father, (even) *God*.
42. If *God* were your Father,
— proceeded forth and came from *God*;
47. He that is of *God* heareth *God*'s words:
— because ye are not of *God*.
54. that he is your *God*:
9: 3. the works of *God*...in him.
16. This man is not of *God*,
24. Give *God* the praise:
29. *God* spake unto Moses:
31. *God* heareth not sinners:
33. If this man were not of *God*,
35. on the Son of *God*?
10:33. being a man, makest thyself *God*.
34. I said, Ye are *gods*?
35. he called them *gods*, unto whom the word of *God* came,
36. I am the Son of *God*?
11: 4. for the glory of *God*, that the Son of *God* might be glorified
22. whatsoever thou wilt ask of *God*, *God* will give (it) thee.
27. the Christ, the Son of *God*,
40. thou shouldest see the glory of *God*?
52. the children of *God* that were scattered abroad.
12:43. more than the praise of *God*.
13: 3. he was come from *God*, and went to *God*;
31. and *God* is glorified in him.
32. *God* be glorified in him, *God* shall also glorify him
14: 1. ye believe in *God*,
16: 2. that he doeth *God* service.
27. came out from *God*.
30. that thou camest forth from *God*.
17: 3. the only true *God*,
19: 7. he made himself the Son of *God*.
20:17. (to) my *God*, and your *God*.
28. My Lord and my *God*.
31. the Christ, the Son of *God*;
21:19. death he should glorify *God*.
Acts 1: 3. the things pertaining to the kingdom of *God*:
2:11. the wonderful works of *God*.
17. saith *God*, I will pour out
22. approved of *God* among you
— *God* did by him in the midst
23. delivered by...and foreknowledge of *God*,
24. Whom *God* hath raised up,
30. *God* had sworn with an oath to him,
32. Jesus hath *God* raised up,
33. Therefore being by the right hand of *God*
36. *God* hath made that same...both Lord and Christ.
39. the Lord our *God* shall call.
47. Praising *God*, and having favour
3: 8. leaping, and praising *God*.
9. walking and praising *God*:
13. The *God* of Abraham, and of Isaac, and of Jacob, the *God* of our fathers,
15. whom *God* hath raised from the dead;
18. But those things, which *God* before had
21. which *God* hath spoken
22. the Lord your *God*

Acts 3:25. covenant which *God* made
26. *God*, having raised up his Son
4:10. whom *God* raised from the dead,
19. right in the sight of *God* to hearken unto you more than unto *God*,
21. all (men) glorified *God*
24. they lifted up their voice to *God*
— *God*, which hast made heaven,
31. they spake the word of *God*
5: 4. not lied unto men, but unto *God*.
29. We ought to obey *God* rather than men.
30. The *God* of our fathers
31. Him hath *God* exalted...a Prince and a Saviour,
32. whom *God* hath given to them that obey
39. But if it be of *God*,
6: 2. should leave the word of *God*,
7. the word of *God* increased;
11. against Moses, and (against) *God*.
7: 2. The *God* of glory appeared
6. And *God* spake on this wise,
7. will I judge, said *God*:
9. but *God* was with him,
17. which *God* had sworn to Abraham,
20. and was exceeding (lit. to *God*) fair,
25. how that *God* by his hand
32. (Saying,) I (am) the *God* of thy fathers, the *God* of Abraham, and the *God* of Isaac, and the *God* of Jacob.
35. the same did *God* send (to be) a ruler and
37. the Lord your *God* raise
40. Make us *gods* to go before us:
42. Then *God* turned, and gave
43. the star of your *god* Remphan,
45. whom *God* drave out
46. favour before *God*, and desired to find a tabernacle for the *God* of Jacob.
55. saw the glory of *God*, and Jesus standing on the right hand of *God*,
56. standing on the right hand of *God*.
8:10. the great power of *God*.
12. things concerning the kingdom of *God*,
14. Samaria had received the word of *God*,
20. thou hast thought that the gift of *God*
21. right in the sight of *God*.
22. and pray *God*, if perhaps
37. that Jesus Christ is the Son of *God*.
9:20. he is the Son of *God*.
10: 2. one that feared *God*
— prayed to *God* alway.
3. an angel of *God* coming in
4. for a memorial before *God*.
15. What *God* hath cleansed,
22. and one that feareth *God*,
28. but *God* hath shewed me
31. had in remembrance in the sight of *God*.
33. are we all here present before *God*,
— that are commanded thee of *God*.
34. *God* is no respecter of persons:
38. How *God* anointed Jesus
— *God* was with him.
40. Him *God* raised up
41. chosen before of *God*,
42. was ordained of *God*
46. speak with tongues, and magnify *God*.
11: 1. received the word of *God*.
9. What *God* hath cleansed,
17. *God* gave them the like gift
— that I could withstand *God*?
18. glorified *God*, saying, Then hath *God* also to the Gentiles granted repentance
23. had seen the grace of *God*,

Acts12: 5. church unto *God* for him.
22. (It is) the voice of a *god*, and not of a
23. he gave not *God* the glory:
24. the word of *God* grew
13: 5. they preached the word of *God*
7. to hear the word of *God*.
16. ye that fear *God*,
17. The *God* of this people
21. *God* gave unto them Saul
23. Of this man's seed hath *God*
26. whosoever among you feareth *God*,
30. But *God* raised him
33(32). *God* hath fulfilled the same
36. by the will of *God*, fell on sleep,
37. But he, whom *God* raised again,
43. to continue in the grace of *God*.
44. to hear the word of *God*.
46. the word of *God* should first have been
14:11. The *gods* are come down to us in the
15. unto the living *God*,
22. into the kingdom of *God*.
26. to the grace of *God*
27. all that *God* had done with
15: 4. all things that *God* had done with them.
7. *God* made choice among us,
8. And *God*, which knoweth the hearts,
10. why tempt ye *God*,
12. miracles and wonders *God* had wrought
among the Gentiles by them.
14. how *God* at the first did visit
18. Known unto *God* are all his works from
the beginning of the world.
19. Gentiles are turned to *God*:
40. by the brethren unto the grace of *God*.
16:14. which worshipped *God*, heard (us):
17. the servants of the most high *God*,
25. and sang praises unto *God*:
34. believing in *God* with all his house.
17:13. the word of *God* was preached of Paul
23. TO THE UNKNOWN *GOD*.
24. *God* that made the world
29. Forasmuch then as we are the offspring of
God,
30. *God* winked at; but now
18: 7. (one) that worshipped *God*,
11. the word of *God* among them.
13. to worship *God* contrary to the law.
21. return again unto you, if *God* will.
26. the way of *God* more perfectly.
19: 8. things concerning the kingdom of *God*.
11. *God* wrought special miracles by the hands
of Paul:
26. they be no *gods*, which are made with
20:21. repentance toward *God*, and faith toward
24. the gospel of the grace of *God*.
25. preaching the kingdom of *God*,
27. all the counsel of *God*.
28. to feed the church of *God*,
32. to *God*, and to the word of his grace,
21:19. what things *God* had wrought among
22: 3. and was zealous toward *God*,
14. The *God* of our fathers hath chosen
23: 1. have lived in all good conscience before
God
3. *God* shall smite thee,
4. Revilest thou *God's* high priest?
24:14. worship I the *God* of my fathers,
15. And have hope toward *God*,
16. to have always a conscience void of offence
toward *God*,
26: 6. the promise made of *God*
8. that *God* should raise the dead?

Acts26:18. of Satan unto *God*,
20. repent and turn to *God*,
22. Having therefore obtained help of *God*,
29. I would to *God*, that not only
27:23. the angel of *God*, whose I am,
24. *God* hath given thee all them
25. for I believe *God*,
35. and gave thanks to *God*
28: 6. and said that he was a *god*.
15. he thanked *God*, and took courage.
23. and testified the kingdom of *God*,
28. the salvation of *God*
31. Preaching the kingdom of *God*,
Ro. 1: 1. unto the gospel of *God*,
4. And declared (to be) the Son of *God*
7. be in Rome, beloved of *God*,
— from *God* our Father,
8. I thank my *God* through Jesus
9. For *God* is my witness,
10. by the will of *God* to come
16. for it is the power of *God*
17. For therein is the righteousness of *God*
18. the wrath of *God*...from heaven
19. that which may be known of *God*
— *God* hath shewed (it) unto them.
21. when they knew *God*, they glorified (him)
not as *God*,
23. the glory of the uncorruptible *God*
24. *God* also gave them up
25. the truth of *God*
26. *God* gave them up
28. to retain *God* in (their) knowledge, *God*
gave them over to
32. Who knowing the judgment of *God*,
2: 2. that the judgment of *God* is
3. thou shalt escape the judgment of *God*?
4. the goodness of *God*
5. of the righteous judgment of *God*;
11. respect of persons with *God*.
13. (are) just before *God*,
16. when *God* shall judge the secrets
17. and makest thy boast of *God*,
23. breaking the law dishonourest thou *God*?
24. For the name of *God*
29. not of men, but of *God*.
3: 2. the oracles of *God*.
3. make the faith of *God* without effect?
4. yea, let *God* be true,
5. commend the righteousness of *God*,
— (Is) *God* unrighteous who taketh vengeance?
6. how shall *God* judge the world?
7. the truth of *God* hath more
11. that seeketh after *God*.
18. There is no fear of *God*
19. may become guilty before *God*.
21. the righteousness of *God*...is manifested,
22. Even the righteousness of *God* (which is)
by faith
23. come short of the glory of *God*;
25. Whom *God* hath set forth (to be) a
—(26). through the forbearance of *God*;
29. (Is he) the *God* of the Jews only?
30. Seeing (it is) one *God*,
4: 2. but not before *God*.
3. Abraham believed *God*,
6. unto whom *God* imputeth righteousness
17. (even) *God*, who quickeneth
20. the promise of *God*
— giving glory to *God*;
5: 1. we have peace with *God*
2. in hope of the glory of *God*.

Ro. 5: 5. the love of *God* is shed abroad
    8. *God* commendeth his love toward us,
   10. we were reconciled to *God*
   11. we also joy in *God*
   15. the grace of *God*, and the gift
  6:10. but in that he liveth, he liveth unto *God*.
   11. but alive unto *God* through Jesus
   13. yield yourselves unto *God*,
   — instruments of righteousness unto *God*.
   17. But *God* be thanked,
   22. and become servants to *God*,
   23. but the gift of *God*
  7: 4. we should bring forth fruit unto *God*.
   22. For I delight in the law of *God*
   25. I thank *God* through Jesus Christ
   — serve the law of *God* ;
  8: 3. *God* sending his own Son
   7. (is) enmity against *God* : for it is not
     subject to the law of *God*,
   8. in the flesh cannot please *God*.
   9. if so be that the Spirit of *God* dwell
   14. are led by the Spirit of *God*, they are the
     sons of *God*.
   16. that we are the children of *God* :
   17. heirs of *God*, and joint-heirs
   19. the manifestation of the sons of *God*.
   21. of the children of *God*.
   27. he maketh intercession...according to (the
     will of) *God*.
   28. to them that love *God*,
   31. If *God* (be) for us,
   33. of *God's* elect? (It is) *God* that justifieth.
   34. at the right hand of *God*,
   39. from the love of *God*,
  9: 5. who is over all, *God*
   6. the word of *God* hath taken
   8. these (are) not the children of *God* :
   11. the purpose of *God* according to election
   14. (Is there) unrighteousness with *God* ?
   16. but of *God* that sheweth mercy.
   20. that repliest against *God* ?
   22. (What) if *God*, willing to shew
   26. shall they be called the children of the
     living *God*.
  10: 1. and prayer to *God*
   2. they have a zeal of *God*,
   3. being ignorant of *God's* righteousness,
   — unto the righteousness of *God*.
   9. that *God* hath raised him
   17. hearing by the word of *God*.
  11: 1. Hath *God* cast away his people?
   2. *God* hath not cast away his people
   — how he maketh intercession to *God*
   8. *God* hath given them the spirit
   21. For if *God* spared not the natural
   22. and severity of *God* :
   23. for *God* is able
   29. and calling of *God*
   30. have not believed *God*,
   32. For *God* hath concluded them
   33. and knowledge of *God* !
  12: 1. by the mercies of *God*,
   — acceptable unto *God*,
   2. what (is) that...will of *God*.
   3. according as *God* hath dealt
  13: 1. power but of *God* : the powers that be are
     ordained of *God*.
   2. resisteth the ordinance of *God* :
   4. For he is the minister of *God*
   — for he is the minister of *God*,
   6. for they are *God's* ministers,
 14: 3. for *God* hath received him.

Ro. 14: 4. *God* is able to make him stand.
   6. for he giveth *God* thanks ;
   — and giveth *God* thanks.
   11. shall confess to *God*.
   12. shall give account of himself to *God*.
   17. For the kingdom of *God* is not
   18. (is) acceptable to *God*,
   20. destroy not the work of *God*.
   22. have (it) to thyself before *God*.
  15: 5. Now the *God* of patience
   6. *God*, even the Father of our Lord
   7. us to the glory of *God*.
   8. for the truth of *God*,
   9. the Gentiles might glorify *God* for
   13. Now the *God* of hope
   15. that is given to me of *God*,
   16. the gospel of *God*,
   17. through Jesus Christ in those things which
     pertain to *God*.
   19. by the power of the Spirit of *God* ;
   30. prayers to *God* for me ;
   32. by the will of *God*,
   33. Now the *God* of peace
  16:20. And the *God* of peace
   26. the commandment of the everlasting *God*,
   27. To *God* only wise,
1Co. 1: 1. through the will of *God*,
   2. Unto the church of *God*
   3. peace, from *God* our Father,
   4. I thank my *God* always on your behalf,
     for the grace of *God*
   9. *God* (is) faithful, by whom ye were
   14. I thank *God* that I baptized
   18. it is the power of *God*.
   20. hath not *God* made foolish the wisdom
   21. the wisdom of *God* the world by wisdom
     knew not *God*, it pleased *God* by the
     foolishness
   24. power of *God*, and the wisdom of *God*.
   25. the foolishness of *God* is wiser than men ;
     and the weakness of *God*
   27. *God* hath chosen the foolish
   — *God* hath chosen the weak
   28. which are despised, hath *God* chosen,
   30. of *God* is made unto us wisdom,
  2: 1. the testimony of *God*.
   5. but in the power of *God*.
   7. the wisdom of *God* in a mystery,
   — which *God* ordained before
   9. which *God* hath prepared for them
   10. But *God* hath revealed (them)
   — yea, the deep things of *God*.
   11. the things of *God* knoweth no man, but
     the Spirit of *God*.
   12. the spirit which is of *God* ;
   — the things that are freely given to us of
     God.
   14. the things of the Spirit of *God* :
  3: 6. but *God* gave the increase.
   7. but *God* that giveth the increase.
   9. For we are labourers together with *God* :
     ye are *God's* husbandry, (ye are) *God's*
     building.
   10. According to the grace of *God*
   16. that ye are the temple of *God*, and (that)
     the Spirit of *God* dwelleth
   17. If any man defile the temple of *God*, him
     shall *God* destroy ; for the temple of
     God is holy,
   19. is foolishness with *God*.
   23. and Christ (is) *God's*.
  4: 1. stewards of the mysteries of *God*.

1Co. 4: 5. shall every man have praise of *God*.
    9. *God* hath set forth us the apostles
   20. For the kingdom of *God* (is) not in word,
  5:13. But them that are without *God* judgeth.
  6: 9. shall not inherit the kingdom of *God?*
   10. nor extortioners, shall inherit the kingdom of *God*.
   11. by the Spirit of our *God*.
   13. but *God* shall destroy both it
   14. And *God* hath both raised up the Lord,
   19. which ye have of *God*,
   20. therefore glorify *God* in your body, and in your spirit, which are *God's*.
  7: 7. hath his proper gift of *God*,
   15. *God* hath called us to peace.
   17. as *God* hath distributed
   19. keeping of the commandments of *God*.
   24. therein abide with *God*.
   40. that I have the Spirit of *God*.
  8: 3. But if any man love *God*,
   4. (there is) none other *God*
   5. that are called *gods*,
   — as there be *gods* many,
   6. (there is but) one *God*, the Father,
   8. commendeth us not to *God:*
  9: 9. Doth *God* take care for oxen?
   21. being not without law to *God*,
 10: 5. *God* was not well pleased:
   13. but *God* (is) faithful, who will not suffer
   20. they sacrifice to devils, and not to *God:*
   31. do all to the glory of *God*.
   32. nor to the church of *God:*
 11: 3. and the head of Christ (is) *God*.
   7. forasmuch as he is the image and glory of *God:*
   12. but all things of *God*.
   13. pray unto *God* uncovered?
   16. neither the churches of *God*.
   22. or despise ye the church of *God*,
 12: 3. speaking by the Spirit of *God*
   6. but it is the same *God* which worketh
   18. But now hath *God* set the members
   24. but *God* hath tempered the body together,
   28. *God* hath set some in the church,
 14: 2. speaketh not unto men, but unto *God:*
   18. I thank my *God*,
   25. he will worship *God*, and report that *God* is in you of a truth.
   28. let him speak to himself, and to *God*.
   33. *God* is not (the author) of confusion, but
   36. came the word of *God* out from you?
 15: 9. because I persecuted the church of *God*.
   10. But by the grace of *God* I am what I am:
   — but the grace of *God*
   15. false witnesses of *God;* because we have testified of *God* that he raised up
   24. the kingdom to *God*, even the Father;
   28. that *God* may be all
   34. for some have not the knowledge of *God:*
   38. But *God* giveth it a body
   50. inherit the kingdom of *God;*
   57. But thanks (be) to *God*, which giveth
2Co. 1: 1. by the will of *God*,
   — unto the church of *God*
   2. from *God* our Father,
   3. Blessed (be) *God*, even the Father
   — and the *God* of all comfort;
   4. we ourselves are comforted of *God*.
   9. in *God* which raiseth the dead:
   12. simplicity and *god*ly sincerity,
   — but by the grace of *God*,
   18. But (as) *God* (is) true, our word

2Co. 1:19. For the Son of *God*, Jesus Christ,
   20. For all the promises of *God*
   — unto the glory of *God*
   21. and hath anointed us, (is) *God;*
   23. I call *God* for a record
  2:14. Now thanks (be) unto *God*,
   15. we are unto *God* a sweet savour
   17. the word of *God:*
   — but as of *God*, in the sight of *God*
  3: 3. with the Spirit of the living *God;*
   4. through Christ to *God*-ward:
   5. our sufficiency (is) of *God;*
  4: 2. handling the word of *God* deceitfully;
   — in the sight of *God*.
   4. the *god* of this world
   — who is the image of *God*,
   6. For *God*, who commanded
   — of the knowledge of the glory of *God*
   7. of the power may be of *God*,
   15. to the glory of *God*.
  5: 1. we have a building of *God*,
   5. for the selfsame thing (is) *God*,
   11. but we are made manifest unto *God;*
   13. For whether we be beside ourselves, (it is) to *God:*
   18. And all things (are) of *God*,
   19. To wit, that *God* was in Christ,
   20. as though *God* did beseech (you)
   — be ye reconciled to *God*.
   21. the righteousness of *God* in him.
  6: 1. that ye receive not the grace of *God*
   4. as the ministers of *God*,
   7. by the power of *God*,
   16. the temple of *God* with idols? for ye are the temple of the living *God;* as *God* hath said,
   — I will be their *God*,
  7: 1. in the fear of *God*.
   6. *God*,...comforted us
   9. for ye were made sorry after a *god*ly manner,
   10. For *god*ly sorrow worketh
   11. that ye sorrowed after a *god*ly sort,
   12. for you in the sight of *God*
  8: 1. the grace of *God* bestowed
   5. by the will of *God*.
   16. But thanks (be) to *God*,
  9: 7. *God* loveth a cheerful giver.
   8. And *God* (is) able to make
   11. through us thanksgiving to *God*.
   12. many thanksgivings unto *God;*
   13. they glorify *God* for your
   14. grace of *God* in you.
   15. Thanks (be) unto *God* for
 10: 4. but mighty through *God*
   5. against the knowledge of *God*,
   13. *God* hath distributed to us,
 11: 2. For I am jealous over you with *god*ly jealousy:
   7. the gospel of *God*
   11. love you not? *God* knoweth.
   31. The *God* and Father of our Lord
 12: 2. I cannot tell: *God* knoweth;
   3. I cannot tell: *God* knoweth;
   19. before *God* in Christ:
   21. my *God* will humble me
 13: 4. he liveth by the power of *God*.
   — by the power of *God* toward you.
   7. Now I pray to *God*
   11. and the *God* of love
   14(13). and the love of *God*,
Gal. 1: 1. and *God* the Father,

Gal. 1: 3. from *God* the Father,
    4. according to the will of *God*
    10. do I now persuade men, or *God*?
    13. persecuted the church of *God*,
    15. But when it pleased *God*,
    20. behold, before *God*, I lie not.
    24. they glorified *God* in me.
  2: 6. *God* accepteth no man's person:
    19. that I might live unto *God*.
    20. of the Son of *God*,
    21. I do not frustrate the grace of *God* :
  3: 6. Even as Abraham believed *God*,
    8. *God* would justify the heathen
    11. is justified...in the sight of *God*,
    17. that was confirmed before of *God*
    18. *God* gave (it) to Abraham
    20. but *God* is one.
    21. against the promises of *God*?
    26. For ye are all the children of *God*
  4: 4. *God* sent forth his Son,
    6. *God* hath sent forth the Spirit
    7. then an heir of *God*
    8. when ye knew not *God*,
    — by nature are no *gods*.
    9. But now, after that ye have known *God*, or rather are known of *God*,
    14. but received me as an angel of *God*,
  5:21. shall not inherit the kingdom of *God*.
  6: 7. *God* is not mocked:
    16. upon the Israel of *God*.
Eph. 1: 1. by the will of *God*,
    2. from *God* our Father,
    3. Blessed be the *God* and Father
    17. the *God* of our Lord
  2: 4. But *God*, who is rich in
    8. (it is) the gift of *God* :
    10. which *God* hath before ordained
    16. unto *God* in one body by the cross,
    19. and of the houshold of *God* ;
    22. for an habitation of *God*
  3: 2. of the grace of *God* which
    7. the gift of the grace of *God*
    9. the beginning of the world...in *God*,
    10. the manifold wisdom of *God*,
    19. with all the fulness of *God*.
  4: 6. One *God* and Father of all,
    13. of the knowledge of the Son of *God*,
    18. the life of *God* through the ignorance
    24. which after *God* is created
    30. the holy Spirit of *God*,
    32. even as *God* for Christ's sake
  5: 1. followers of *God*, as dear children ;
    2. and a sacrifice to *God*
    5. in the kingdom of Christ and of *God*.
    6. cometh the wrath of *God*
    20. unto *God* and the Father
    21. in the fear of *God*.
  6: 6. the will of *God*
    11. the whole armour of *God*,
    13. the whole armour of *God*,
    17. which is the word of *God* :
    23. from *God* the Father
Phi. 1: 2. from *God* our Father,
    3. I thank my *God* upon every
    8. For *God* is my record,
    11. unto the glory and praise of *God*.
    28. and that of *God*.
  2: 6. being in the form of *God*,
    — to be equal with *God* :
    9. *God* also hath highly exalted him,
    11. to the glory of *God* the Father.
    13. For it is *God* which worketh

Phi. 2:15. the sons of *God*, without rebuke,
    27. but *God* had mercy on him ;
  3: 3. which worship *God* in the spirit,
    9. the righteousness which is of *God*
    14. of the high calling of *God*
    15. *God* shall reveal even this unto you.
    19. whose *God* (is their) belly,
  4: 6. let your requests be made known unto *God*.
    7. And the peace of *God*,
    9. and the *God* of peace
    18. acceptable, wellpleasing to *God*.
    19. But my *God* shall supply
    20. Now unto *God* and our Father (be) glory
Col. 1: 1. by the will of *God*,
    2. from *God* our Father
    3. We give thanks to *God*
    6. the grace of *God* in truth:
    10. in the knowledge of *God* ;
    15. Who is the image of the invisible *God*,
    25. the dispensation of *God*
    — to fulfil the word of *God* ;
    27. *God* would make known
  2: 2. of the mystery of *God*,
    12. of *God*, who hath raised him
    19. the increase of *God*.
  3: 1. on the right hand of *God*.
    3. your life is hid with Christ in *God*.
    6. the wrath of *God* cometh
    12. as the elect of *God*,
    15. And let the peace of *God*
    17. giving thanks to *God*
    22. in singleness of heart, fearing *God* :
  4: 3. that *God* would open unto us
    11. unto the kingdom of *God*,
    12. in all the will of *God*.
1 Th. 1: 1. (which is) in *God* the Father and (in) the Lord
    — from *God* our Father,
    2. We give thanks to *God*
    3. in the sight of *God*
    4. your election of *God*.
    8. to *God*-ward is spread abroad ;
    9. ye turned to *God* from idols to serve the living and true *God* ;
  2: 2. in our *God* to speak unto you the gospel of *God*
    4. we were allowed of *God*
    — not as pleasing men, but *God*, which trieth our hearts.
    5. *God* (is) witness:
    8. the gospel of *God*
    9. the gospel of *God*.
    10. Ye (are) witnesses, and *God* (also),
    12. ye would walk worthy of *God*,
    13. thank we *God* without ceasing,
    — of *God* which ye heard of us,
    — as it is in truth, the word of *God*, which
    14. of the churches of *God*
    15. they please not *God*,
  3: 2. and minister of *God*,
    9. render to *God* again for you,
    — for your sakes before our *God* ;
    11. Now *God* himself and our Father,
    13. before *God*, even our Father,
  4: 1. and to please *God*,
    3. For this is the will of *God*,
    5. which know not *God* :
    7. For *God* hath not called us
    8. *God*, who hath also given
    14. even so them also which sleep...will *God*
    16. and with the trump of *God* :

1Th.5: 9. *God* hath not appointed us to wrath,
18. for this is the will of *God*
23. And the very *God* of peace
2Th.1: 1. in *God* our Father
2. from *God* our Father
3. We are bound to thank *God* always
4. in the churches of *God*
5. of the righteous judgment of *God*,
— of the kingdom of *God*,
6. Seeing (it is) a righteous thing with *God*
8. on them that know not *God*,
11. our *God* would count you worthy of (this)
12. according to the grace of our *God*
2: 4. that is called *God*, or that is worshipped ;
so that he as *God* sitteth in the temple
of *God*, shewing himself that he is *God*.
11. *God* shall send them
13. to give thanks alway to *God*
— *God* hath from the beginning chosen you
16. *God*, even our Father,
3: 5. into the love of *God*,
1Ti. 1: 1. by the commandment of *God* our Saviour,
2. from *God* our Father
4. *god*ly edifying which is in faith:
11. of the blessed *God*,
17. the only wise *God*,
2: 3. in the sight of *God* our Saviour ;
5. For (there is) one *God*, and one mediator
between *God* and men,
3: 5. shall he take care of the church of *God* ?
15. in the house of *God*, which is the church
of the living *God*,
16. *God* was manifest in the flesh,
4: 3. which *God* hath created
4. every creature of *God* (is) good,
5. by the word of *God* and prayer.
10. we trust in the living *God*,
5: 4. good and acceptable before *God*.
5. trusteth in *God*, and continueth
21. I charge (thee) before *God*,
6: 1. that the name of *God*
11. But thou, O man of *God*,
13. thee charge in the sight of *God*,
17. but in the living *God*,
2Ti. 1: 1. by the will of *God*,
2. from *God* the Father
3. I thank *God*, whom I serve
6. the gift of *God*,
7. For *God* hath not given us
8. according to the power of *God* ;
2: 9. the word of *God* is not bound.
15. to shew thyself approved unto *God*,
19. the foundation of *God* standeth
25. *God* peradventure will give them
3:17. That the man of *God* may be perfect,
4: 1. before *God*, and the Lord
Tit. 1: 1. Paul, a servant of *God*,
— according to the faith of *God's* elect,
2. *God*, that cannot lie,
3. of *God* our Saviour;
4. from *God* the Father
7. as the steward of *God* ;
16. They profess that they know *God* ;
2: 5. the word of *God* be not blasphemed.
10. of *God* our Saviour
11. the grace of *God* that bringeth salvation
13. glorious appearing of the great *God* and
our Saviour Jesus Christ;
3: 4. of *God* our Saviour
8. they which have believed in *God*
Philem. 3. from *God* our Father
4. I thank my *God*,

Heb. 1: 1. *God*, who...spake in time past unto the
fathers by the prophets,
6(7). all the angels of *God*
8. Thy throne, O *God*,
9. *God*, (even) thy *God*, hath anointed thee
2: 4. *God* also bearing (them) witness, both
with signs
9. that he by the grace of *God*
13. which *God* hath given me.
17. in things (pertaining) to *God*,
3: 4. that built all things (is) *God*.
12. departing from the living *God*.
4: 4. *God* did rest the seventh day
9. a rest to the people of *God*.
10. *God* (did) from his.
12. For the word of *God* (is) quick,
14. Jesus the Son of *God*,
5: 1. in things (pertaining) to *God*,
4. is called of *God*,
10. of *God* an high priest
12. of the oracles of *God* ;
6: 1. and of faith toward *God*,
3. will we do, if *God* permit.
5. have tasted the good word of *God*,
6. to themselves the Son of *God*
7. receiveth blessing from *God* :
10. For *God* (is) not unrighteous
13. when *God* made promise
17. *God*, willing more abundantly
18. (it was) impossible for *God* to lie,
7: 1. priest of the most high *God*,
3. unto the Son of *God* ;
19. by the which we draw nigh unto *God*.
25. unto *God* by him,
8:10. I will be to them a *God*,
9:14. without spot to *God*,
— to serve the living *God* ?
20. *God* hath injoined unto you.
24. in the presence of *God*
10: 7. to do thy will, O *God*.
9. to do thy will, O *God*.
12. on the right hand of *God* ;
21. over the house of *God* ;
29. hath trodden under foot the Son of *God*,
31. into the hands of the living *God*.
36. after ye have done the will of *God*,
11: 3. worlds were framed by the word of *God*,
4. Abel offered unto *God*
— *God* testifying of his gifts:
5. *God* had translated him:
— that he pleased *God*.
6. he that cometh to *God*
10. and maker (is) *God*.
16. *God* is not ashamed to be called their *God* :
19. *God* (was) able to raise (him) up,
25. the people of *God*,
40. *God* having provided some better thing for
12: 2. of the throne of *God*.
7. *God* dealeth with you
15. of the grace of *God* ;
22. and unto the city of the living *God*,
23. to *God* the Judge of all,
28. *God* acceptably with reverence
29. For our *God* (is) a consuming fire.
13: 4. and adulterers *God* will judge.
7. unto you the word of *God* :
15. sacrifice of praise to *God* continually,
16. *God* is well pleased.
20. Now the *God* of peace,
Jas. 1: 1. a servant of *God* and of the Lord Jesus
Christ,
5. of *God*, that giveth

Jas. 1:13. I am tempted of *God* : for *God* cannot be tempted with evil,
20. worketh not the righteousness of *God*.
27. before *God* and the Father
2: 5. Hath not *God* chosen
19. Thou believest that there is one *God* ;
23. Abraham believed *God*,
— he was called the Friend of *God*.
3: 9. bless we *God*, even
— after the similitude of *God*.
4: 4. is enmity with *God* ?
— is the enemy of *God*.
6. *God* resisteth the proud,
7. Submit yourselves therefore to *God*.
8. Draw nigh to *God*,

1 Pet 1: 2. according to the foreknowledge of *God*
3. Blessed (be) the *God* and Father
5. Who are kept by the power of *God*
21. do believe in *God*,
— hope might be in *God*.
23. by the word of *God*, which liveth
2: 2. but chosen of *God*,
5. acceptable to *God* by Jesus
10. but (are) now the people of *God* :
12. they may...glorify *God* in the day
15. the will of *God*,
16. but as the servants of *God*.
17. Fear *God*. Honour the king.
19. if a man for conscience toward *God*
20. this (is) acceptable with *God*.
3: 4. in the sight of *God* of great price.
5. trusted in *God*, adorned themselves,
15. But sanctify the Lord *God*
17. if the will of *God* be so,
18. might bring us to *God*,
20. the longsuffering of *God*
21. the answer...toward *God*,
22. on the right hand of *God* ;
4: 2. but to the will of *God*.
6. but live according to *God* in the spirit.
10. of the manifold grace of *God*.
11. as the oracles of *God* ;
— the ability which *God* giveth : that *God* in all things may be glorified
14. the spirit of glory and of *God*
16. but let him glorify *God*
17. at the house of *God* :
— the gospel of *God* ?
19. according to the will of *God*
5: 2. the flock of *God*
5. *God* resisteth the proud,
6. the mighty hand of *God*,
10. But the *God* of all grace,
12. the true grace of *God*

2 Pet 1: 1. through the righteousness of *God*
2. through the knowledge of *God*,
17. from *God* the Father
21. holy men of *God*
2: 4. For if *God* spared not the angels that
3: 5. that by the word of *God*
12. the coming of the day of *God*,

1 Joh. 1: 5. that *God* is light,
2: 5. is the love of *God* perfected :
14. the word of *God* abideth in you,
17. doeth the will of *God*
3: 1. we should be called the sons of *God* :
2. now are we the sons of *God*,
8. the Son of *God* was manifested,
9. is born of *God*
— he is born of *God*.
10. the children of *God* are manifest,
— is not of *God*,

1 Joh. 3: 17. how dwelleth the love of *God*
20. *God* is greater than our heart,
21. (then) have we confidence toward *God*.
4: 1. whether they are of *God* :
2. know ye the Spirit of *God* :
— in the flesh is of *God* :
3. is not of *God* :
4. Ye are of *God*, little children,
6. We are of *God* : he that knoweth *God* heareth us ; he that is not of *God*
7. love is of *God* ;
— is born of *God*, and knoweth *God*.
8. knoweth not *God* ; for *God* is love.
9. the love of *God* toward us,
— *God* sent his only begotten Son into
10. not that we loved *God*,
11. if *God* so loved us,
12. No man hath seen *God* at any time.
— *God* dwelleth in us,
15. the Son of *God*, *God* dwelleth in him, and he in *God*.
16. that *God* hath to us. *God* is love ;
— dwelleth in *God*, and *God* in him.
20. I love *God*, and hateth his brother,
— *God* whom he hath not seen ?
21. That he who loveth *God*
5: 1. is born of *God* :
2. we love the children of *God*, when we love *God*,
3. the love of *God*,
4. is born of *God*
5. Jesus is the Son of *God* ?
9. the witness of *God* is greater : for this is the witness of *God*
10. that believeth on the Son of *God*
— he that believeth not *God*
— that *God* gave of his Son.
11. *God* hath given to us eternal life,
12. hath not the Son of *God*
13. on the name of the Son of *God* ;
— on the name of the Son of *God*.
18. is born of *God* sinneth not ; but he that is begotten of *God*
19. that we are of *God*,
20. that the Son of *God* is come,
— This is the true *God*,

2 Joh. 3. (and) peace, from *God* the Father,
9. of Christ, hath not *God*.

3 Joh. 6. if thou bring forward on their journey after a *god*ly sort,
11. He that doeth good is of *God* :
— hath not seen *God*.

Jude 1. are sanctified by *God* the Father,
4. the grace of our *God*
— the only Lord *God*,
21. Keep yourselves in the love of *God*,
25. To the only wise *God* our Saviour,

Rev. 1: 1. which *God* gave unto him,
2. the word of *God*, and
6. priests unto *God* and his Father ;
9. for the word of *God*,
2: 7. of the paradise of *God*.
18. These things saith the Son of *God*,
3: 1. that hath the seven Spirits of *God*,
2. found thy works perfect before *God*.
12. in the temple of my *God*,
— the name of my *God*, and the name of the city of my *God*,
— out of heaven from my *God* :
14. the beginning of the creation of *God* ;
4: 5. the seven Spirits of *God*.
8. Lord *God* Almighty, which was,

Rev. 5: 6. the seven Spirits of *God*
    9. hast redeemed us to *God*
   10. unto our *God* kings
  6: 9. were slain for the word of *God*,
  7: 2. the seal of the living *God* :
    3. the servants of our *God*
   10. Salvation to our *God* which
   11. on their faces, and worshipped *God*,
   12. and might, (be) unto our *God*
   15. before the throne of *God*,
   17. *God* shall wipe away all tears
  8: 2. which stood before *God* ;
    4. before *God* out of the angel's hand.
  9: 4. have not the seal of *God*
   13. which is before *God*,
 10: 7. the mystery of *God* should be finished,
 11: 1. measure the temple of *God*,
    4. before the *God* of the earth.
   11. the Spirit of life from *God*
   13. glory to the *God* of heaven.
   16. which sat before *God*
   — upon their faces, and worshipped *God*,
   17. O Lord *God* Almighty,
   19. the temple of *God* was opened
 12: 5. unto *God*, and (to) his throne.
    6. she hath a place prepared of *God*,
   10. the kingdom of our *God*,
   — before our *God* day and night.
   17. keep the commandments of *God*,
 13: 6. in blasphemy against *God*,
 14: 4. unto *God* and to the Lamb.
    5. before the throne of *God*.
    7. Fear *God*, and give glory to him ;
   10. the wine of the wrath of *God*,
   12. the commandments of *God*,
   19. winepress of the wrath of *God*.
 15: 1. is filled up the wrath of *God*.
    2. the harps of *God*.
    3. on the song of Moses the servant of *God*,
   — thy works, Lord *God* Almighty ;
    7. full of the wrath of *God*,
    8. from the glory of *God*,
 16: 1. the vials of the wrath of *God*
    7. Even so, Lord *God* Almighty,
    9. blasphemed the name of *God*,
   11. blasphemed the *God* of heaven.
   14. great day of *God* Almighty.
   19. came in remembrance before *God*,
   21. men blasphemed *God* because of the
 17:17. For *God* hath put in their hearts
   — the words of *God* shall be fulfilled.
 18: 5. *God* hath remembered her iniquities.
    8. *God* who judgeth her.
   20. for *God* hath avenged you
 19: 1. unto the Lord our *God* :
    4. worshipped *God* that sat on the throne,
    5. Praise our *God*, all ye his servants,
    6. the Lord *God* omnipotent
    9. are the true sayings of *God*.
   10. worship *God* : for the testimony
   13. The Word of *God*.
   15. and wrath of Almighty *God*.
   17. the supper of the great *God* ;
 20: 4. and for the word of *God*,
    6. they shall be priests of *God*
    9. fire came down from *God* out
   12. small and great, stand before *God* ;
 21: 2. coming down from *God*
    3. Behold, the tabernacle of *God*
   — and *God* himself shall be with them, (and
      be) their *God*.
    4. *God* shall wipe away all tears

Rev. 21: 7. I will be his *God*,
   10. out of heaven from *God*,
   11. Having the glory of *God* :
   22. for the Lord *God* Almighty
   23. for the glory of *God* did lighten
 22: 1. the throne of *God* and of the Lamb.
    3. the throne of *God* and of the Lamb
    5. for the Lord *God* giveth them light:
    6. and the Lord *God* of the holy prophets
    9. sayings of this book: worship *God*.
   18. *God* shall add unto him
   19. *God* shall take away his part

Θεοσέβεια, *theosebia*.

1Ti. 2:10. which becometh women professing *godliness*

Θεοσεβής, *theosebees*.

Joh. 9:31. if any man be *a worshipper of God*,

Θεοστυγης, *theostugees*.

Ro. 1:30. *haters of God*, despiteful, proud,

Θεότης, *theotees*.

Col. 2: 9. in him dwelleth all the fulness of the *Godhead* bodily.

Θεραπεία, *therapia*.

Mat. 24:45. hath made ruler over his *houshold*,
Lu. 9:11. them that had need of *healing*.
  12:42. shall make ruler over his *houshold*,
Rev. 22: 2. (were) for the *healing* of the nations.

Θεραπεύω, *therapuo*.

Mat. 4:23. *healing* all manner of sickness
   24. and he *healed* them.
  8: 7. I *will* come and *heal* him.
   16. and *healed* all that were sick:
  9:35. *healing* every sickness and every
 10: 1. and *to heal* all manner of sickness
    8. *Heal* the sick, cleanse the lepers,
 12:10. Is it lawful *to heal* on the sabbath days?
   15. he *healed* them all ;
   22. and he *healed* him,
 14:14. he *healed* their sick.
 15:30. and he *healed* them:
 17:16. and they could not *cure* him.
   18. the child *was cured*
 19: 2. he *healed* them there.
 21:14. and he *healed* them.
Mar 1:34. he *healed* many that were sick
  3: 2. whether he would *heal* him on the sabbath day ;
   10. For he *had healed* many ;
   15. *to heal* sicknesses, and to cast
  6: 5. his hands upon a few sick folk, and *healed*
   13. that were sick, and *healed* (them).

Lu. 4:23. this proverb, Physician, *heal* thyself:
40. every one of them, and *healed* them.
5:15. to hear, and *to be healed* by him
6: 7. whether he would *heal* on the sabbath day ;
18. and they *were healed.*
7:21. he *cured* many of (their) infirmities
8: 2. women, which had been *healed* of evil
43. neither could *be healed* of any,
9: 1. and *to cure* diseases.
6. and *healing* every where.
10: 9. *heal* the sick that are therein,
13:14. because that Jesus *had healed* on the sabbath day,
— in them therefore come and *be healed,*
14: 3. Is it lawful *to heal* on the sabbath day ?
Joh. 5:10. therefore said unto him *that was cured,*
Acts 4:14. beholding the man *which was healed*
5:16. and they *were healed* every one.
8: 7. and that were lame, *were healed.*
17:25. Neither *is worshipped* with men's hands,
28: 9. came, and *were healed :*
Rev.13: 3. his deadly wound *was healed :*
12. whose deadly wound *was healed.*

Θεράπων, *therapōn.*

Heb 3: 5. faithful in all his house, as a *servant,* for a testimony of those things which

Θερίζω, *therizo.*

Mat. 6:26. neither do they *reap,*
25:24. *reaping* where thou hast not sown,
26. I *reap* where I sowed not,
Lu. 12:24. for they neither sow nor *reap ;*
19:21. *reapest* that thou didst not sow.
22. *reaping* that I did not sow:
Joh. 4:36. he *that reapeth* receiveth wages,
— and he *that reapeth* may rejoice
37. One soweth, and another *reapeth.*
38. I sent you *to reap*
1Co. 9:11. if we *shall reap* your carnal things ?
2Co. 9: 6. *shall reap* also sparingly ;
— *shall reap* also bountifully.
Gal. 6: 7. that *shall* he also *reap.*
8. *shall* of the flesh *reap* corruption ;
— *shall* of the Spirit *reap* life everlasting.
9. for in due season we *shall reap,*
Jas. 5: 4. the cries of them *which have reaped*
Rev.14:15. *reap :* for the time is come for thee *to reap ;*
16. and the earth *was reaped.*

Θερισμός, *therismos.*

Mat. 9:37. The *harvest* truly (is) plenteous,
38. the Lord of the *harvest,*
— labourers into his *harvest.*
13:30. the *harvest :* and in the time of *harvest*
39. the *harvest* is the end of the world ;
Mar 4:29. the *harvest* is come.
Lu. 10: 2. The *harvest* truly (is) great,
— pray ye therefore the Lord of the *harvest,*
— labourers into his *harvest.*
Joh. 4:35. and (then) cometh *harvest ?*
— they are white already to *harvest.*
Rev.14:15. the *harvest* of the earth is ripe.

Θεριστής, *theristees.*

Mat.13:30. I will say to the *reapers,*
39. and the *reapers* are the angels.

Θερμαίνομαι, *thermainomai.*

Mar 14:54. *warmed* him*self* at the fire.
67. saw Peter *warming* him*self,*
Joh.18:18. it was cold: and they *warmed* themselves *:* and Peter stood with them, and *warmed* him*self.*
25. Simon Peter stood and *warmed* him*self.*
Jas. 2:16. *be* (ye) *warmed* and filled ;

Θέρμη, *thermee.*

Acts28: 3. there came a viper out of the *heat,*

Θέρος, *theros.*

Mat.24:32. ye know that *summer* (is) nigh:
Mar 13:28. that *summer* is near:
Lu. 21:30. that *summer* is now nigh at hand.

Θεωρέω, *theōreo.*

Mat 27:55. women were there *beholding* afar off,
28: 1. *to see* the sepulchre.
Mar 3:11. unclean spirits, when they *saw* him,
5:15. and *see* him that was possessed with the devil,
38. and *seeth* the tumult,
12:41. and *beheld* how the people
15:40. women *looking on* afar off:
47. *beheld* where he was laid.
16: 4. when they looked, they *saw*
Lu. 10:18. I *beheld* Satan as lightning
14:29. all *that behold* (it) begin to mock him,
21: 6. (As for) these things which ye *behold,*
23:35. the people stood *beholding.*
48. *beholding* the things which were done,
24:37. and supposed that they had *seen* a spirit.
39. as ye *see* me have.
Joh. 2:23. *when* they *saw* the miracles
4:19. I *perceive* that thou art a prophet.
6:19. they *see* Jesus walking on the sea,
40. every one *which seeth* the Son,
62. (What) and if ye shall *see* the Son
7: 3. that thy disciples also *may see* the works
8:51. he *shall* never *see* death.
9: 8. they *which* before *had seen* him that he was blind,
10:12. *seeth* the wolf coming,
12:19. *Perceive* ye how ye prevail nothing ?
45. And he *that seeth* me *seeth* him that sent
14:17. because it *seeth* him not,
19. a little while, and the world *seeth* me no more; but ye *see* me:
16:10. and ye *see* me no more;
16. A little while, and ye shall not *see* me:
17. A little while, and ye shall not *see* me:
19. A little while, and ye shall not *see* me:
17:24. that they *may behold* my glory,
20: 6. *seeth* the linen clothes lie,
12. *seeth* two angels in white
14. *saw* Jesus standing, and
Acts 3:16. this man strong, whom ye *see* and know:
4:13. Now *when* they *saw* the boldness of Peter

Acts 7:56. I *see* the heavens opened,
    8:13. *beholding* the miracles and signs
    9: 7. hearing a voice, but *seeing* no man.
    10:11. And *saw* heaven opened, and a certain
    17:16. *when* he *saw* the city wholly given to
    22. I *perceive...*ye are too superstitious.
    19:26. ye *see* and hear,
    20:38. that they should *see* his face no more.
    21:20. Thou *seest*, brother, how many
    25:24. ye *see* this man, about whom
    27:10. I *perceive* that this voyage will be with
    28: 6. and *saw* no harm come to him,
Heb 7: 4. Now *consider* how great this
1Joh 3:17. whoso hath this world's good, and *seeth*
    his brother have need,
Rev 11:11. fear fell upon them *which saw* them.
    12. their enemies *beheld* them.

Θεωρία, theōria.

Lu. 23:48. came together to that *sight*, beholding the

Θήκη, theekee.

Joh 18:11. Put up thy sword into the *sheath :*

Θηλάζω, theelazo.

Mat 21:16. Out of the mouth of babes and *sucklings*
    24:19. woe...and to them *that give suck* in those
    days !
Mar 13:17. and to them *that give suck*
Lu. 11:27. the paps which thou *hast sucked.*
    21:23. and to them *that give suck,*
    23:29. the paps which never *gave suck.*

-λυς,-λυ, Θήλεια, theeʾia.

Ro. 1:26. for even their *women*
    27. leaving the natural use of the *woman,*

Θῆλυ, theelu.

Mat 19: 4. made them male and *female,*
Mar 10: 6. God made them male and *female.*
Gal. 3:28. there is neither male nor *female :*

Θήρα, theera.

Ro. 11: 9. Let their table be made a snare, and a
    trap, and a stumblingblock,

Θηρεύω, theerūo.

Lu. 11:54. seeking *to catch* something out of his

Θηριομαχέω, theeriomakeo.

1Co.15:32. I *have fought with beasts* at Ephesus,

Θηρίον, theerion.

Mar. 1:13. was with the *wild beasts ;*

Acts 10:12. *wild beasts,* and creeping things,
    11: 6. *wild beasts,* and creeping things,
    28: 4. *the* (venomous) *beast* hang
    5. shook off the *beast*
Tit. 1:12. evil *beasts,* slow bellies.
Heb 12:20. And if so much as a *beast* touch the
Jas. 3: 7. of *beasts,* and of birds,
Rev. 6: 8. with the *beasts* of the earth.
    11: 7. the *beast* that ascendeth
    13: 1. a *beast* rise up out of the sea,
    2. the *beast* which I saw
    3. the world wondered after the *beast.*
    4. power unto the *beast :* and they worshipped
    the *beast,* saying, Who (is) like unto the
    beast ?
    11. I beheld another *beast*
    12. all the power of the first *beast*
    — to worship the first *beast,*
    14. to do in the sight of the *beast ;*
    — that they should make an image to the
    beast,
    15. unto the image of the *beast,* that the image
    of the *beast* should both speak,
    — worship the image of the *beast*
    17. or the name of the *beast,*
    18. count the number of the *beast :*
    14: 9. If any man worship the *beast*
    11. who worship the *beast*
    15: 2. over the *beast,* and over
    16: 2. the mark of the *beast,*
    10. upon the seat of the *beast ;*
    13. out of the mouth of the *beast,*
    17: 3. upon a scarlet coloured *beast,*
    7. of the *beast* that carrieth her,
    8. The *beast* that thou sawest
    — the *beast* that was, and is not,
    11. And the *beast* that was,
    12. received power as kings one hour with the
    beast.
    13. shall give their power and strength unto
    the *beast.*
    16. which thou sawest upon the *beast,*
    17. their kingdom unto the *beast,*
    19:19. And I saw the *beast,*
    20. the *beast* was taken,
    — the mark of the *beast,*
    20: 4. had not worshipped the *beast,*
    10. where the *beast* and the false prophet (are),

Θησαυρίζω, theesaurizo.

Mat. 6:19. *Lay* not *up* for yourselves treasures upon
    earth,
    20. But *lay up* for yourselves treasures in
    heaven,
Lu. 12:21. he *that layeth up treasure* for himself,
Ro. 2: 5. *treasurest up* unto thyself wrath
1Co.16: 2. let every one...lay by him in store, as
    (God) hath prospered him, (lit. lay by
    him *treasuring* what he be prospered in)
2Co.12:14. ought not *to lay up* for the parents,
Jas. 5: 3. Ye *have heaped treasure together* for the
    last days.
2Pet.3: 7. are *kept in store,* reserved unto fire

Θησαυρός, theesauros.

Mat. 2:11. when they had opened their *treasures,*
    6:19. yourselves *treasures* upon earth,
    20. *treasures* in heaven, where

Mat. 6:21. For where your *treasure* is,
    12:35. out of the good *treasure* of the heart
        — out of the evil *treasure* bringeth forth
    13:44. is like unto *treasure* hid in a field ;
    52. out of his *treasure* (things) new and
    19:21. thou shalt have *treasure* in heaven:
Mar 10:21. thou shalt have *treasure* in heaven:
Lu. 6:45. out of the good *treasure* of his heart
        — out of the evil *treasure* of his heart
    12:33. a *treasure* in the heavens that faileth not,
    34. For where your *treasure* is,
    18:22. thou shalt have *treasure* in heaven:
2Co. 4: 7. But we have this *treasure*
Col. 2: 3. all the *treasures* of wisdom and knowledge.
Heb 11:26. than the *treasures* in Egypt:

Θίγω, *thigo.*

Col. 2:21. taste not ; *handle* not ;
Heb 11:28. lest he that destroyed the firstborn *should touch* them.
    12:20. And if so much as a beast *touch* the

Θλίβω, *thlibo.*

Mat. 7:14. and *narrow* (is) the way,
Mar. 3: 9. lest they *should throng* him.
2Co. 1: 6. And whether we be *afflicted,*
    4: 8. (We are) *troubled* on every side,
    7: 5. but we were *troubled* on every side ;
1Th. 3: 4. that we should *suffer tribulation* ;
2Th. 1: 6. tribulation to them *that trouble* you ;
    7. And to you *who are troubled* rest
1Ti. 5:10. if she have relieved the *afflicted,*
Heb 11:37. being destitute, *afflicted,* tormented ;

Θλίψις, *thlipsis.*

Mat. 13:21. for when *tribulation* or persecution ariseth
    24: 9. shall they deliver you up to be *afflicted,*
    21. For then shall be great *tribulation,*
    29. after the *tribulation* of those days
Mar 4:17. afterward, when *affliction* or persecution ariseth
    13:19. (in) those days shall be *affliction,*
    24. after that *tribulation,* the sun
Joh. 16:21. she remembereth no more the *anguish,*
    33. In the world ye shall have *tribulation* :
Acts 7:10. out of all his *afflictions,*
    11. and Chanaan, and great *affliction* :
    11:19. upon the *persecution* that arose
    14:22. we must through much *tribulation*
    20:23. and *afflictions* abide me.
Ro. 2: 9. *Tribulation* and anguish, upon every
    5: 3. we glory in *tribulations* also: knowing that *tribulation*
    8:35. (shall) *tribulation,* or distress, or
    12:12. patient in *tribulation* ; continuing
1Co. 7:28. shall have *trouble* in the flesh:
2Co. 1: 4. in all our *tribulation,*
        — them which are in any *trouble*
    8. of our *trouble* which came
    2: 4. For out of much *affliction*
    4:17. our light *affliction,* which is
    6: 4. in *afflictions,* in necessities,
    7: 4. in all our *tribulation.*
    8: 2. in a great trial of *affliction*̄
    13. and ye burdened:(lit. *burden* to you)

Eph. 3:13. at my *tribulations* for you,
Phil. 1:16. to add *affliction* to my bonds:
    4:14. that ye did communicate with my *affliction.*
Col. 1:24. that which is behind of the *afflictions* of Christ
1Th. 1: 6. the word in much *affliction,*
    3: 3. should be moved by these *afflictions* :
    7. in all our *affliction*
2Th. 1: 4. *tribulations* that ye endure:
    6. *tribulation* to them that trouble you ;
Heb 10:33. whilst ye were made a gazingstock both by reproaches and *afflictions* ;
Jas. 1:27. and widows in their *affliction,*
Rev. 1: 9. brother, and companion in *tribulation,*
    2: 9. and *tribulation,* and poverty,
    10. ye shall have *tribulation* ten days:
    22. with her into great *tribulation,*
    7:14. out of great *tribulation,*

Θνήσκω, *thneesko.*

Mat. 2:20. for they *are dead* which sought
Mar 15:44. if he *were* already *dead* :
Lu. 7:12. there was a *dead* man carried out,
    8:49. Thy daughter *is dead* ;
Joh. 11:21. my brother *had* not *died.*
    39. the sister of him *that was dead,*
    41. where the *dead* was laid.
    44. And he *that was dead* came forth,
    12: 1. Lazarus was *which had been dead,*
    19:33. that he was *dead* already,
Acts 14:19. supposing he had *been dead.*
    25:19. of one Jesus, *which was dead,* whom Paul affirmed to be alive.
1Ti. 5: 6. *is dead* while she liveth.

Θνητός, *thneetos.*

Ro. 6:12. in your *mortal* body,
    8:11. also quicken your *mortal* bodies
1Co. 15:53. and this *mortal* (must) put on
    54. this *mortal* shall have put on
2Co. 4:11. in our *mortal* flesh.
    5: 4. mortality (lit. the *mortal*) might be swallowed up of life.

Θορυβέομαι, *thorubeomai.*

Mat. 9:23. the people *making a noise,*
Mar 5:39. Why *make* ye this *ado,* and weep ?
Acts 17: 5. and *set* all the city *on an uproar,*
    20:10. *Trouble* not your*selves* ; for his life

Θόρυβος, *thorubos.*

Mat. 26: 5. lest there be an *uproar*
    27:24. (that) rather a *tumult* was made,
Mar 5:38. and seeth the *tumult,*
    14: 2. lest there be an *uproar*
Acts 20: 1. And after the *uproar* was ceased,
    21:34. the certainty for the *tumult,*
    24:18. multitude, nor with *tumult.*

Θραύω, *thrauo.*

Lu. 4:18. to set at liberty them *that are bruised,*

Ͽρέμμα, thremma.

Joh. 4:12. his children, and his *cattle?*

Ͽρηνέω, threeneo.

Mat.11:17. we *have mourned* unto you, and
Lu. 7:32. we *have mourned* to you, and
   23:27. bewailed and *lamented* him.
Joh.16:20. ye shall weep and *lament,*

Ͽρῆνος, threenos.

Mat. 2:18. In Rama was there a voice heard, *lamentation,* and weeping,

---

Ͽρησκεία, threeskĭa.

Acts26: 5. straitest sect of our *religion*
Col. 2:18. and *worshipping* of angels,
Jas. 1:26. this man's *religion* (is) vain.
     27. Pure *religion* and undefiled

Ͽρῆσκος, threeskos.

Jas. 1:26. any man among you seem to be *religious,*

Ͽριαμϐεύω, thriambuo.

2Co. 2:14. which...*causeth* us *to triumph* in Christ,
Col. 2:15. *triumphing over* them in it.

Ͽρίξ, τριχὸς, thrix, trikos.

Mat. 3: 4. had his raiment of camel's *hair,*
    5:36. one *hair* white or black.
  10:30. the very *hairs* of your head
Mar 1: 6. John was clothed with camel's *hair,*
Lu. 7:38. with the *hairs* of her head,
    44. and wiped (them) with the *hairs* of her
  12: 7. the very *hairs* of your head
  21:18. But there shall not an *hair* of your head
Joh.11: 2. and wiped his feet with her *hair,*
  12: 3. wiped his feet with her *hair:*
Acts27:34. an *hair* fall from the head
1Pet 3: 3. of plaiting the *hair,*
Rev 1:14. and (his) *hairs* (were) white
  9: 8. And they had *hair* as the *hair* of women,

Ͽροέομαι, throeomai.

Mat 24: 6. see that ye *be* not *troubled:*
Mar13: 7. rumours of wars, *be* ye not *troubled:* for
2Th. 2: 2. or *be troubled,* neither by spirit,

Ͽρόμϐος, thrombos.

Lu. 22:44. as it were *great drops* of blood

Ͽρόνος, thronos.

Mat 5:34. for it is God's *throne:*
  19:28. in the *throne* of his glory, ye also shall sit upon twelve *thrones,*

Mat 23:22. sweareth by the *throne* of God,
  25:31. upon the *throne* of his glory:
Lu. 1:32. the *throne* of his father David:
    52. the mighty from (their) *seats,*
  22:30. sit on *thrones* judging the twelve
Acts 2:30. to sit on his *throne;*
  7:49. Heaven (is) my *throne,*
Col. 1:16. whether (they be) *thrones,* or dominions,
Heb 1: 8. Thy *throne,* O God,
 4.16. unto the *throne* of grace,
 8. 1. on the right hand of the *throne* of the Majesty
12: 2. at the right hand of the *throne* of God.
Rev 1: 4. seven spirits which are before his *throne;*
  2:13. (even) where Satan's *seat* (is):
  3:21. with me in my *throne,*
   — with my Father in his *throne.*
  4: 2. a *throne* was set in heaven, and (one) sat on the *throne.*
    3. (there was) a rainbow round about the *throne,*
    4. round about the *throne* (were) four and twenty *seats:* and upon the *seats* I saw
    5. out of the *throne* proceeded
   — burning before the *throne,*
    6. before the *throne* (there was) a sea
   — and in the midst of the *throne,* and round about the *throne,*
    9. that sat on the *throne,*
   10. that sat on the *throne,*
   — cast their crowns before the *throne,*
 5: 1. that sat on the *throne*
    6. lo, in the midst of the *throne*
    7. that sat upon the *throne,*
   11. round about the *throne* and
   13. unto him that sitteth upon the *throne,*
 6:16. of him that sitteth on the *throne,*
 7: 9. stood before the *throne,*
   10. our God which sitteth upon the *throne,*
   11. round about the *throne,*
   — fell before the *throne*
   15. before the *throne* of God,
   — he that sitteth on the *throne*
   17. which is in the midst of the *throne*
 8: 3. which was before the *throne.*
 11:16. sat before God on their *seats,*
 12: 5. God, and (to) his *throne.*
 13: 2. and his *seat,* and great authority.
 14: 3. a new song before the *throne,*
    5. before the *throne* of God.
 16:10. upon the *seat* of the beast;
   17. from the *throne,* saying, It is done.
 19: 4. sat on the *throne,*
    5. a voice came out of the *throne,*
 20: 4. And I saw *thrones,*
   11. a great white *throne,*
 21: 5. he that sat upon the *throne*
 22: 1. out of the *throne* of God and
    3. the *throne* of God and of the Lamb shall be in it;

Ͽυγάτηρ, thugateer.

Mat. 9:18. My *daughter* is even now dead:
    22. *Daughter,* be of good comfort; thy faith
  10:35. and the *daughter* against her mother,
   37. loveth son or *daughter* more than me
 14: 6. the *daughter* of Herodias danced
 15:22. my *daughter* is grievously vexed with a devil.
   28. And her *daughter* was made whole from

Mat.21: 5. Tell ye the *daughter* of Sion,
Mar 5:34. *Daughter*, thy faith hath made
　　　35. Thy *daughter* is dead:
　　　6:22. when the *daughter* of the said
　　　7:26. the devil out of her *daughter*.
　　　29. out of thy *daughter*.
　　　30. and her *daughter* laid upon the bed.
Lu.　1: 5. of the *daughters* of Aaron,
　　　2:36. the *daughter* of Phanuel, of
　　　8:42. he had one only *daughter*,
　　　48. *Daughter*, be of good comfort: thy faith
　　　49. Thy *daughter* is dead ;
　　12:53. against the *daughter*, and the *daughter*
　　　　　against the mother ;
　　13:16. being a *daughter* of Abraham,
　　23:28. *Daughters* of Jerusalem, weep not
Joh. 12:15. Fear not, *daughter* of Sion:
Acts 2:17. and your *daughters* shall prophesy,
　　　7:21. Pharaoh's *daughter* took him up,
　　21: 9. four *daughters*, virgins, which
2Co. 6:18. ye shall be my sons and *daughters*, saith
　　　　　the Lord Almighty.
Heb 11:24. the son of Pharaoh's *daughter* ;

Θυγάτριον, *thugatrion.*

Mar 5:23. My *little daughter* lieth at the point of
　　　7:25. whose *young daughter* had an unclean

Θύελλα, *thuella.*

Heb 12:18. and darkness, and *tempest*,

Θύϊνος, *thuinos.*

Rev.18:12. *thyine* wood, and all manner vessels

Θυμίαμα, *thumiama.*

Lu.　1:10. at the time of *incense.*
　　　11. of the altar of *incense.*
Rev. 5: 8. full of *odours*, which are the prayers
　　　8: 3. there was given unto him much *incense*,
　　　4. the smoke of the *incense*,...ascended up
　　18:13. cinnamon, and *odours*, and ointments,

Θυμιατήριον, *thumiateerion.*

Heb 9: 4. Which had the golden *censer*,

Θυμιάω, *thumiao.*

Lu.　1: 9. his lot was *to burn incense*

Θυμομαχέω, *thumomakeo.*

Acts12:20. Herod was *highly displeased* with them of
　　　　　Tyre and

Θυμόομαι, *thumo-omai.*

Mat. 2:16. *was* exceeding *wroth*, and sent forth,

Θυμός, *thumos.*

Lu.　4:28. were filled with *wrath*,
Acts19:28. they were full of *wrath*,
Ro.　2: 8. but obey unrighteousness, *indignation* and
2Co.12:20. debates, envyings, *wraths*, strifes,
Gal. 5:20. hatred, variance, emulations, *wrath*,
Eph. 4:31. Let all bitterness, and *wrath*, and anger,
Col. 3: 8. anger, *wrath*, malice, blasphemy,
Heb 11:27. the *wrath* of the king:
Rev.12:12. having great *wrath*, because
　　14: 8. drink of the wine of the *wrath* of her
　　　10. of the wine of the *wrath* of God,
　　　19. winepress of the *wrath* of God.
　　15: 1. is filled up the *wrath* of God.
　　　7. full of the *wrath* of God,
　　16: 1. the vials of the *wrath* of God
　　　19. of the wine of the *fierceness* of his wrath.
　　18: 3. of the wine of the *wrath* of her fornication,
　　19:15. of the *fierceness* and wrath of Almighty
　　　　　God.

Θύρα, *thura.*

Mat. 6: 6. when thou hast shut thy *door*,
　　24:33. it is near, (even) at the *doors*.
　　25:10. the *door* was shut.
　　27:60. to the *door* of the sepulchre,
　　28: 2. the stone from the *door*,
Mar 1:33. was gathered together at the *door*.
　　　2: 2. no, not so much as about the *door :*
　　11: 4. by the *door* without in
　　13:29. it is nigh, (even) at the *doors*.
　　15:46. unto the *door* of the sepulchre,
　　16: 3. from the *door* of the sepulchre ?
Lu.　11: 7. the *door* is now shut,
　　13:25. hath shut to the *door*,
　　　　— to knock at the *door*,
Joh.10: 1. by the *door* into the sheepfold,
　　　2. by the *door* is the shepherd
　　　7. the *door* of the sheep.
　　　9. I am the *door :*
　　18:16. at the *door* without.
　　20:19. when the *doors* were shut
　　　26. the *doors* being shut,
Acts 3: 2. at the *gate* of the temple
　　　5: 9. (are) at the *door*, and shall carry
　　　19. opened the prison *doors*,
　　　23. standing without before the *doors :*
　　12: 6. before the *door* kept the prison.
　　　13. the *door* of the gate,
　　14:27. the *door* of faith unto the Gentiles.
　　16:26. immediately all the *doors*
　　　27. seeing the prison *doors* open,
　　21:30. the *doors* were shut.
1Co.16: 9. For a great *door* and effectual is opened
2Co. 2:12. and a *door* was opened unto me
Col. 4: 3. would open unto us a *door* of utterance,
Jas.　5: 9. standeth before the *door*.
Rev. 3: 8. set before thee an open *door*,
　　　20. I stand at the *door*, and knock: if any
　　　　　man hear my voice, and open the *door*,
　　　4: 1. a *door* (was) opened in heaven:

Θυρεός, *thureos.*

Eph. 6:16. taking the *shield* of faith, wherewith ye
　　　　　shall be able

Θυρίς, *thuris.*

Acts20: 9. there sat in a *window* a certain young man
2Co.11:33. And through a *window* in a basket

Θυρωρός, thurōros.

Mar 13:34. and commanded the *porter* to watch.
Joh. 10: 3. To him the *porter* openeth;
18:16. and spake unto her *that kept the door*,
17. the damsel *that kept the door*

Θυσία, thusia.

Mat. 9:13. I will have mercy, and not *sacrifice:*
12: 7. I will have mercy, and not *sacrifice*,
Mar. 9:49. and every *sacrifice* shall be
12:33. whole burnt offerings and *sacrifices*.
Lu. 2:24. And to offer a *sacrifice*
13: 1. mingled with their *sacrifices*.
Acts 7:41. offered *sacrifice* unto the idol,
42. have ye offered to me slain beasts and
sacrifices
Ro. 12: 1. a living *sacrifice*, holy,
1Co.10:18. they which eat of the *sacrifices*
Eph. 5: 2. an offering and a *sacrifice* to God
Phi. 2:17. upon the *sacrifice* and service of your faith,
4:18. a *sacrifice* acceptable, wellpleasing
Heb. 5: 1. gifts and *sacrifices* for sins;
7:27. to offer up *sacrifice*, first for
8: 3. to offer gifts and *sacrifices:*
9: 9. were offered both gifts and *sacrifices*,
23. with better *sacrifices* than these.
26. by the *sacrifice* of himself.
10: 1. with those *sacrifices* which
5. *Sacrifice* and offering thou
8. *Sacrifice* and offering and
11. offering oftentimes the same *sacrifices*,
12. after he had offered one *sacrifice*
26. there remaineth no more *sacrifice*
11: 4. By faith...a more excellent *sacrifice* than
Cain,
13:15. let us offer the *sacrifice* of praise
16. for with such *sacrifices*
1Pet. 2: 5. to offer up spiritual *sacrifices*,

Θυσιαστήριον, thusiasteerion.

Mat. 5:23. bring thy gift to the *altar*,
24. thy gift before the *altar*,
23:18. shall swear by the *altar*,
19. the gift, or the *altar*
20. shall swear by the *altar*,
35. the temple and the *altar*.
Lu. 1:11. of the *altar* of incense.
11:51. between the *altar* and the temple:
Ro. 11: 3. and digged down thine *altars;*
1Co. 9:13. and they which wait at the *altar* are partakers with the *altar?*
10:18. partakers of the *altar?*
Heb. 7:13. no man gave attendance at the *altar*.
13:10. We have an *altar*, whereof
Jas. 2:21. offered Isaac his son upon the *altar?*
Rev. 6: 9. under the *altar* the souls
8: 3. stood at the *altar*,
— upon the golden *altar*
5. with fire of the *altar*,
9:13. horns of the golden *altar*
11: 1. the temple of God, and the *altar*,
14:18. came out from the *altar*,
16: 7. I heard another out of the *altar* say,

Θύω, thuo.

Mat. 22: 4. and (my) fatlings (are) *killed*,

Mar 14:12. when they *killed* the passover,
Lu. 15:23. the fatted calf, and *kill* (it);
27. thy father *hath killed* the fatted calf,
30. thou *hast killed* for him the fatted calf.
22: 7. when the passover must *be killed*.
Joh. 10:10. but for to steal, and to *kill*,
Acts 10:13. Rise, Peter; *kill*, and eat.
11: 7. Arise, Peter; *slay* and eat.
14:13. would *have done sacrifice*
18. the people, that they *had* not *done sacrifice*
1Co. 5: 7. Christ our passover *is sacrificed* for us:
10:20. the things which the Gentiles *sacrifice*,
they *sacrifice* to devils,

Θώραξ, thorax.

Eph. 6:14. having on the *breastplate* of righteousness;
1Th. 5: 8. putting on the *breastplate* of faith
Rev. 9: 9. *breastplates*, as it were *breastplates* of iron;
17. *breastplates* of fire, and of jacinth, and
brimstone:

ἴαμα, iama.

1Co.12: 9. to another the gifts of *healing*
28. miracles, then gifts of *healings*,
30. Have all the gifts of *healing?*

ἰάομαι, iaomai.

Mat. 8: 8. and my servant *shall be healed*.
13. And his servant *was healed*
13:15. and I *should heal* them.
15:28. And her daughter *was made whole*
Mar 5:29. that she was *healed* of that plague.
Lu. 4:18. he hath sent me *to heal* the brokenhearted,
5:17. the Lord was (present) *to heal* them.
6:17. *to be healed* of their diseases;
19. and *healed* (them) all.
7: 7. and my servant *shall be healed*.
8:47. and how she *was healed* immediately.
9: 2. and *to heal* the sick.
11. and *healed* them that had need of healing.
42. and *healed* the child,
14: 4. and *healed* him, and let him go;
17:15. when he saw that he *was healed*,
22:51. touched his ear, and *healed* him.
Joh. 4:47. that he would come down, and *heal* his son:
5:13. And he *that was healed* wist not who it
12:40. and I *should heal* them.
Acts 3:11. the lame man *which was healed*
9:34. Jesus Christ *maketh* thee *whole:*
10:38. and *healing* all that were oppressed
28: 8. and *healed* him.
27. and I *should heal* them.
Heb 12:13. but let it rather *be healed*.
Jas. 5:16. that ye *may be healed*.
1Pet. 2:24. by whose stripes ye *were healed*.

ἴασις, iasis.

Lu. 13:32. and I do *cures* to day and to morrow,
Acts 4:22. on whom this miracle of *healing* was
30. By stretching forth thine hand *to heal;*

ἴασπις, iaspis.

Rev. 4: 3. a *jasper* and a sardine stone:
21:11. even like a *jasper* stone,
18. of the wall of it was (of) *jasper :*
19. The first foundation (was) *jasper ;*

ἰατρός, iatros.

Mat. 9:12. They that be whole need not a *physician*,
Mar 2:17. They that are whole have no need of the *physician*,
5:26. of many *physicians*,
Lu. 4:23. *Physician*, heal thyself:
5:31. They that are whole need not a *physician ;*
8:43. had spent all her living upon *physicians*,
Col. 4:14. Luke, the beloved *physician*,

ἴδε, ide.

Mat.25:20. *behold*, I have gained beside them five
22. *behold*, I have gained two other talents
25. *lo*, (there) thou hast (that is) thine.
26:65. *behold*, now ye have heard
Mar 2:24. *Behold*, why do they on the sabbath day
3:34. *Behold* my mother and
11:21. *behold*, the fig tree which thou cursedst
13: 1. *see* what manner of stones
15: 4. *behold* how many things they witness against thee.
16: 6. *behold* the place where they laid him.
Joh. 1:29. *Behold* the Lamb of God,
36. *Behold* the Lamb of God !
47(48). *Behold* an Israelite indeed,
3:26. *behold*, the same baptizeth,
5:14. *Behold*, thou art made whole:
7:26. But, *lo*, he speaketh boldly,
11: 3. *behold*, he whom thou lovest is sick.
36. *Behold* how he loved him !
12:19. *behold*, the world is gone after him.
16:29. *Lo*, now speakest thou plainly,
18:21. *behold*, they know what I said.
19: 4. *Behold*, I bring him forth to you,
5. (Pilate) saith unto them, *Behold* the man !
14. unto the Jews, *Behold* your King !
Ro. 2:17. *Behold*, thou art called a Jew,
Gal. 5: 2. *Behold*, I Paul say

ἰδέα, idea.

Mat.28: 3. His *countenance* was like lightning,

ἴδιος, idios.

Those marked [1] are κατ᾽ ἰδίαν ; [2] the neuter plural.

Mat. 9: 1. and came into *his own* city.
14:13. into a desert place *apart :*[1]
23. into a mountain *apart* [1]
17: 1. into an high mountain *apart*,[1]
19. the disciples to Jesus *apart*,[1]
20:17. took the twelve disciples *apart* [1] in the way,
22: 5. one to *his* farm, another to
24: 3. the disciples came unto him *privately*,[1]
25:14. (who) called *his own* servants,
15. according to *his several* ability ;

Mar 4:34. and *when they were alone*,[1] he expounded all things to his disciples.
6:31. *apart* [1] into a desert place,
32. desert place by ship *privately*. [1]
7:33. *aside* [1] from the multitude,
9: 2. high mountain *apart* [1] by themselves:
28. asked him *privately*,[1] Why could
13: 3. Andrew asked him *privately*,[1]
15:20. and put *his own* clothes on him,
Lu. 2: 3. into *his own* city.
6:41. that is in *thine own* eye?
44. is known by *his own* fruit.
9:10. and went **aside** *privately*[1]
10:23. and said *privately*,[1] Blessed
34. and set him on *his own* beast,
Joh. 1:11. He came unto *his own*,[2] and his *own* (masc. plur.) received him not.
41(42). findeth *his own* brother Simon,
4:44. honour in *his own* country.
5:18. said also that God was *his* Father,
43. in *his own* name,
7:18. seeketh *his own* glory:
8:44. he speaketh of *his own :*
10: 3. he calleth *his own* sheep
4. when he putteth forth *his own* sheep,
12. whose *own* the sheep are not,
13: 1. having loved *his own*
15:19. the world would love *his own :*
16:32. shall be scattered, every man to *his own*,[2]
19:27. that disciple took her unto his *own* (home).[2]
Acts 1: 7. the Father hath put in *his own* power.
19. in their *proper* tongue,
25. that he might go to *his own* place.
2: 6. speak in his *own* language.
8. in our *own* tongue,
3:12. as though by *our own* power or
4:23. they went to *their own* (company),
32. said...ought of the things which he possessed was *his own ;*
13:36. after he had served *his own* generation
20:28. which he hath purchased with *his own*
21: 6. and they returned *home* [2] again.
23:19. went (with him) aside *privately*,[1]
24:23. he should forbid none of *his acquaintance*
25:19. of *their own* superstition,
28:30. in *his own* hired house,
Ro. 8:32. spared not *his own* Son,
10: 3. going about to establish *their own*
11:24. be graffed into *their own* olive tree?
14: 4. to *his own* master he standeth or falleth.
5. be fully persuaded in *his own* mind.
1Co. 3: 8. every man shall receive *his own* reward according to *his own* labour.
4:12. working with *our own* hands:
6:18. sinneth against *his own* body.
7: 2. have *her own* husband.
4. hath not power of *her own* body,
— hath not power of *his own* body,
7. every man hath *his proper* gift
37. over *his own* will,
9: 7. Who goeth a warfare any time at *his own* charges ?
11:21. every one taketh before (other) *his own* supper:
12:11. dividing to every man *severally* (lit. in *his own* way, or, *his own*)
14:35. let them ask *their* husbands
15:23. in *his own* order:
38. to every seed *his own* body.
Gal. 2: 2. but *privately* [1] to them which were of
6: 5. shall bear *his own* burden.
9. for in *due* season we shall reap,

Eph 5:22. yourselves unto *your own* husbands,
    24. to *their own* husbands in every thing.
Col. 3:18. submit yourselves unto *your own*
1Th 2:14. have suffered like things of *your own*
        countrymen,
    15. and *their own* prophets,
  4:11. to do *your own business*,[2] and to work with
        your own hands,
1Ti. 2: 6. to be testified in *due* time.
  3: 4. One that ruleth well *his own* house,
    5. man know not how to rule *his own* house,
  12. and *their own* houses well.
  4: 2. having *their* conscience seared with
  5: 4. shew piety at home, (lit. at *his own* home)
    8. But if any provide not for *his own*,
  6: 1. count *their own* masters worthy
  15. Which in *his* times he shall shew, (who is)
    the blessed
2Ti. 1: 9. according to *his own* purpose
  4: 3. after *their own* lusts
Tit. 1: 3. But hath in *due* times manifested
  12. (even) a prophet of *their own*,
  2: 5. obedient to *their own* husbands,
  9. to be obedient unto *their own* masters,
Heb 4:10. his own works, as God (did) from *his*.
  7:27. first for *his own* sins, and then for the
  9:12. but by *his own* blood
  13:12. that he might sanctify the people with *his*
    own blood,
Jas. 1:14. drawn away of *his own* lust, and enticed.
1Pet.3: 1. (be) in subjection to *your own* husbands;
    5. in subjection unto *their own* husbands:
2Pet.1:20. is of any *private* interpretation.
  2:16. But was rebuked for *his* iniquity:
  22. turned to *his own* vomit again;
  3: 3. walking after their *own* lusts,
  16. unto their *own* destruction.
  17. fall from *your own* stedfastness.
Jude 6. but left *their own* habitation,

ἰδιώτης, *idiōtees*.

Acts 4:13. and perceived that they were unlearned
    and *ignorant* men,
1Co.14:16. occupieth the room of the *unlearned*
  23. (those that are) *unlearned*, or
  24. there come in one that believeth not, or
    (one) *unlearned*,
2Co.11: 6. though (I be) *rude* in speech, yet not in

ἰδού, *idou*.

Mat 1:20. *behold*, the angel of the Lord
  23. *Behold*, a virgin shall be with child,
  2: 1. *behold*, there came wise men from the
    east
  9. and, *lo*, the star, which they saw
  13. *behold*, the angel of the Lord
  19. *behold*, an angel of the Lord
  3:16. *lo*, the heavens were opened unto him,
  17. And *lo* a voice from heaven,
  4:11. and, *behold*, angels came
  7: 4. and, *behold*, a beam (is) in
  8: 2. And, *behold*, there came a leper
  24. And, *behold*, there arose a great tempest
  29. And, *behold*, they cried out,
  32. *behold*, the whole herd of swine ran
  34. And, *behold*, the whole city
  9: 2. And, *behold*, they brought to him
  3. And, *behold*, certain of the scribes

Mat 9:10. *behold*, many publicans and sinners
  18. *behold*, there came a certain ruler,
  20. And, *behold*, a woman, which was diseased
    with an issue of blood
  32. *behold*, they brought to him
  10:16. *Behold*, I send you forth
  11: 8. *behold*, they that wear soft (clothing)
  10. *Behold*, I send my messenger
  19. *Behold* a man gluttonous,
  12: 2. *Behold*, thy disciples do
  10. And, *behold*, there was a man
  18. *Behold* my servant, whom I have chosen;
  41. and, *behold*, a greater than Jonas
  42. and, *behold*, a greater than Solomon
  46. *behold*, (his) mother and his brethren
  47. *Behold*, thy mother and thy brethren
  49. *Behold* my mother and my brethren!
  13: 3. *Behold*, a sower went forth
  15:22. *behold*, a woman of Canaan
  17: 3. And, *behold*, there appeared unto them
  5. *behold*, a bright cloud overshadowed them:
    and *behold* a voice out of the cloud,
  19:16. And, *behold*, one came
  27. *behold*, we have forsaken all,
  20:18. *Behold*, we go up to Jerusalem;
  30. And, *behold*, two blind men
  21: 5. *Behold*, thy King cometh
  22: 4. *Behold*, I have prepared my dinner:
  23:34. Wherefore, *behold*, I send
  38. *Behold*, your house is left unto you
  24:23. *Lo*, here (is) Christ,
  25. *Behold*, I have told you before.
  26. *Behold*, he is in the desert;
  — *behold*, (he is) in the secret chambers:
  25: 6. *Behold*, the bridegroom cometh;
  26:45. *behold*, the hour is at hand,
  46. *behold*, he is at hand that doth betray me.
  47. *lo*, Judas, one of the twelve,
  51. And, *behold*, one of them which were
  27:51. And, *behold*, the veil of the temple
  28: 2. And, *behold*, there was a great
  7. and, *behold*, he goeth before you
  — *lo*, I have told you.
  9. *behold*, Jesus met them,
  11. *behold*, some of the watch
  20. and, *lo*, I am with you
Mar. 1: 2. *Behold*, I send my messenger
  3:32. *Behold*, thy mother and thy brethren
  4: 3. *Behold*, there went out a sower
  5:22. And, *behold*, there cometh one of
  10·28. *Lo*, we have left all,
  33. *Behold*, we go up to Jerusalem;
  13:21. *Lo*, here (is) Christ; or, *lo*, (he is) there;
  23. *behold*, I have foretold you all things.
  14:41. *behold*, the Son of man is betrayed
  42. *lo*, he that betrayeth me
  15:35. *Behold*, he calleth Elias.
Lu. 1:20. And, *behold*, thou shalt be dumb,
  31. And, *behold*, thou shalt conceive in thy
  36. And, *behold*, thy cousin Elisabeth,
  38. *Behold* the handmaid of the Lord;
  44. For, *lo*, as soon as the voice of thy saluta-
    tion sounded
  48. for, *behold*, from henceforth
  2: 9. And, *lo*, the angel of the Lord
  10. for, *behold*, I bring you good tidings
  25. And, *behold*, there was a man
  34. *Behold*, this (child) is set for the fall
  48. *behold*, thy father and I
  5:12. *behold* a man full of leprosy:
  18. And, *behold*, men brought
  6:23. for, *behold*, your reward

Lu. 7:12. *behold,* there was a dead man carried out,
25. *Behold,* they which are gorgeously
27. *Behold,* I send my messenger
34. *Behold* a gluttonous man,
37. And, *behold,* a woman in the city,
8:41. And, *behold,* there came a man
9:30. And, *behold,* there talked with him two
38. And, *behold,* a man of the company
39. And, *lo,* a spirit taketh him,
10: 3. *behold,* I send you forth
19. *Behold,* I give unto you power
25. And, *behold,* a certain lawyer
11:31. and, *behold,* a greater than Solomon
32. and, *behold,* a greater than Jonas
41. and, *behold,* all things are clean
13: 7. *Behold,* these three years I come
11. And, *behold,* there was a woman
16. *lo,* these eighteen years,
30. And, *behold,* there are last
32. *Behold,* I cast out devils,
35. *Behold,* your house is left unto you
14: 2. And, *behold,* there was a certain man
15:29. *Lo,* these many years do I serve thee,
17:21. *Lo* here ! or, *lo* there ! for, *behold,* the
kingdom of God
23. *See* here ; or, *see* there:
18:28. *Lo,* we have left all,
31. *Behold,* we go up to
19: 2. And, *behold,* (there was) a man named
8. *Behold,* Lord, the half of my goods
20. *behold,* (here is) thy pound, which I have
22:10. *Behold,* when ye are entered
21. *behold,* the hand of him that betrayeth
31. *behold,* Satan hath desired (to have)
38. *behold,* here (are) two swords.
47. *behold* a multitude, and he that was called
23:14. and, *behold,* I, having examined (him)
before you,
15. and, *lo,* nothing worthy of death
29. For, *behold,* the days are coming,
50. And, *behold,* (there was) a man named
24: 4. *behold,* two men stood by them
13. And, *behold,* two of them
49. And, *behold,* I send
Joh. 4:35. *behold,* I say unto you,
12:15. *behold,* thy King cometh,
16:32. *Behold,* the hour cometh,
19:26. Woman, *behold* thy son !
27. *Behold* thy mother ! And from
Acts 1:10. *behold,* two men stood by them
2: 7. *Behold,* are not all these
5: 9. *behold,* the feet of them which have buried
25. *Behold,* the men whom
28. and, *behold,* ye have filled
7:56. *Behold,* I see the heavens opened,
8:27. and, *behold,* a man of Ethiopia,
36. *See,* (here is) water ; what doth hinder
9:10. *Behold,* I (am here), Lord.
11. for, *behold,* he prayeth,
10:17. *behold,* the men which
19. *Behold,* three men seek
21. *Behold,* I am he whom ye seek:
30. and, *behold,* a man stood before
11:11. And, *behold,* immediately there were three
12: 7. And, *behold,* the angel of the Lord
13:11. And now, *behold,* the hand of the Lord
25. But, *behold,* there cometh one after me,
46. *lo,* we turn to the Gentiles.
16: 1. and, *behold,* a certain disciple
20:22. And now, *behold,* I go bound
25. *behold,* I know that
27:24. and, *lo,* God hath given thee

Ro. 9:33. *Behold,* I lay in Sion
1Co.15:51. *Behold,* I shew you a mystery ;
2Co. 5:17. *behold,* all things are become new
6: 2. *behold,* now (is) the accepted time ; *behold,*
now (is) the day of salvation.
9. and, *behold,* we live ;
7:11. For *behold* this selfsame thing,
12:14. *Behold,* the third time I am ready
Gal. 1:20. *behold,* before God, I lie not.
Heb. 2:13. *Behold* I and the children
8: 8. *Behold,* the days come,
10: 7. *Lo,* I come, in the volume
9. *Lo,* I come to do thy will,
Jas. 3: 3. *Behold,* we put bits in the horses' mouths,
4. *Behold* also the ships,
5. *Behold,* how great a matter a little fire
5: 4. *Behold,* the hire of the labourers
7. *Behold,* the husbandman waiteth
9. *behold,* the judge standeth before the door.
11. *Behold,* we count them
1Pet. 2: 6. *Behold,* I lay in Sion
Jude 14. *Behold,* the Lord cometh with
Rev. 1: 7. *Behold,* he cometh with clouds ;
18. and, *behold,* I am alive
2:10. *behold,* the devil shall cast (some) of you
22. *Behold,* I will cast her
3: 8. *behold,* I have set before thee
9. *behold,* I will make them of the synagogue
— *behold,* I will make them
11. *Behold,* I come quickly:
20. *Behold,* I stand at the door,
4: 1. and, *behold,* a door (was) opened
2. and, *behold,* a throne was set
5: 5. *behold,* the Lion of the tribe of Juda,...
hath prevailed
6. and, *lo,* in the midst of the throne
6: 2. and *behold* a white horse:
5. and *lo* a black horse ;
8. and *behold* a pale horse:
12. and, *lo,* there was a great earthquake ;
7: 9. and, *lo,* a great multitude,
9:12. (and), *behold,* there come two woes more
11:14. (and), *behold,* the third woe
12: 3. and *behold* a great red dragon,
14: 1. And I looked and, and, *lo,* a Lamb
14. and *behold* a white cloud,
15: 5. and, *behold,* the temple of the
16:15. *Behold,* I come as a thief.
19:11. and *behold* a white horse ;
21: 3. *Behold,* the tabernacle of God
5. *Behold,* I make all things new.
22: 7. *Behold,* I come quickly:
12. And, *behold,* I come quickly ;

ἱδρώς, *hidrōs.*

Lu. 22:44. and his *sweat* was as it were great drops
of blood

ἱερατεία, *hieratīa.*

Lu. 1: 9. According to the custom of the *priest's
office,*
Heb. 7: 5. receive the *office of the priesthood,*

ἱεράτευμα, *hieratūma.*

1Pet. 2: 5. an holy *priesthood,* to offer
9. a royal *priesthood,* an holy nation,

ἱερατεύω, hieratŭo.

Lu. 1: 8. that while he *executed the priest's office*

ἱερεύς, hierŭs.

Mat. 8: 4. shew thyself to the *priest*,
12: 4. but only for the *priests?*
5. on the sabbath days the *priests*
Mar 1:44. shew thyself to the *priest*,
2:26. but for the *priests*,
Lu. 1: 5. a certain *priest* named Zacharias,
5:14. and shew thyself to the *priest*,
6: 4. but for the *priests* alone?
10:31. there came down a certain *priest* that way:
17:14. yourselves unto the *priests.*
Joh. 1:19. *priests* and Levites from Jerusalem
Acts 4: 1. *priests*, and the captain of the temple
5:24. the *high priest* and the captain
6: 7. a great company of the *priests* were obedient to the faith.
14:13. Then the *priest* of Jupiter,
Heb. 5: 6. Thou (art) a *priest* for ever
7: 1. *priest* of the most high God,
3. abideth a *priest* continually.
11. another *priest* should rise after the order
of Melchisedec,
15. after the similitude of Melchisedec there
ariseth another *priest*,
17. Thou (art) a *priest* for ever
21(20). those *priests* were made without an
oath;
— Thou (art) a *priest* for ever
23. they truly were many *priests*,
8: 4. he should not be a *priest*, seeing that there
are *priests*
9: 6. the *priests* went always
10:11. And every *priest* standeth daily ministering
21. And (having) an high *priest* over the house
of God;
Rev. 1: 6. kings and *priests* unto God
5:10. made us unto our God kings and *priests:*
20: 6. they shall be *priests* of God and of Christ,

ἱερόν, hieron.

Mat. 4: 5. on a pinnacle of the *temple*,
12: 5. in the *temple* profane the sabbath,
6. in this place is (one) greater than the
temple.
21:12. into the *temple* of God,
— bought in the *temple*,
14. and the lame came to him in the *temple;*
15. crying in the *temple*,
23. when he was come into the *temple*,
24: 1. and departed from the *temple:*
— the buildings of the *temple.*
26:55. teaching in the *temple*,
Mar 11:11. and into the *temple:*
15. Jesus went into the *temple*,
— and bought in the *temple*,
16. (any) vessel through the *temple.*
27. as he was walking in the *temple*,
12:35. while he taught in the *temple*,
13: 1. as he went out of the *temple*,
3. over against the *temple*,
14:49. in the *temple* teaching,
Lu. 2:27. by the Spirit into the *temple:*
37. departed not from the *temple*,
46. they found him in the *temple*,

Lu. 4: 9. on a pinnacle of the *temple*,
18:10. went up into the *temple*
19:45. he went into the *temple*,
47. daily in the *temple.*
20: 1. the people in the *temple*,
21: 5. spake of the *temple*,
37. teaching in the *temple;*
38. in the *temple*, for to hear him.
22:52. and captains of the *temple*,
53. with you in the *temple*,
24:53. were continually in the *temple*,
Joh. 2:14. found in the *temple* those that sold
15. he drove them all out of the *temple*,
5:14. Jesus findeth him in the *temple*,
7:14. Jesus went up into the *temple*,
28. Jesus in the *temple* as he taught,
8: 2. he came again into the *temple*,
20. as he taught in the *temple:*
59. went out of the *temple*,
10:23. Jesus walked in the *temple*
11:56. as they stood in the *temple*,
18:20. and in the *temple*, whither
Acts 2:46. with one accord in the *temple*,
3: 1. went up together into the *temple*
2. at the gate of the *temple*
— that entered into the *temple;*
3. to go into the *temple*
8. with them into the *temple*,
10. the Beautiful gate of the *temple:*
4: 1. the captain of the *temple*, and
5:20. and speak in the *temple* to the people
21. into the *temple* early in the morning,
24. and the captain of the *temple*
25. are standing in the *temple*,
42. And daily in the *temple*,
19:27. the *temple* of the great goddess Diana
21:26. entered into the *temple*, to signify
27. when they saw him in the *temple*,
28. brought Greeks also into the *temple*,
29. had brought into the *temple.*
30. him out of the *temple:*
22:17. while I prayed in the *temple*,
24: 6. hath gone about to profane the *temple:*
12. they neither found me in the *temple*
18. purified in the *temple*,
25: 8. neither against the *temple*, nor
26:21. caught me in the *temple*,
1Co. 9:13. live (of the things) of the *temple?*

ἱεροπρεπής, hieroprepees.

Tit. 2: 3. that (they be) in behaviour *as becometh holiness*,

---

ἱερός, hieros.

1Co. 9:13. they which minister about *holy* things
2Ti. 3:15. thou hast known the *holy* scriptures,

ἱεροσυλέω, hierosuleo.

Ro. 2:22. thou that abhorrest idols, dost thou *commit sacrilege?*

ἱερόσυλος, hierosulos.

Acts19:37. which are neither *robbers of churches*, nor

ἱερουργέω, hierourgeo.

Ro. 15:16. *ministering* the gospel of God,

ἱερωσύνη, hierōsunee.

Heb 7:11. perfection were by the Levitical *priesthood*,
12. For the *priesthood* being changed, there is
14. of which tribe Moses spake nothing concerning *priesthood*.
24. hath an unchangeable *priesthood*.

ἱκανός, hikanos.

Mat. 3:11. whose shoes I am not *worthy* to bear:
8: 8. I am not *worthy* that thou shouldest
28:12. gave *large* money unto the soldiers,
Mar 1: 7. shoes I am not *worthy* to stoop down
10:46. his disciples and a *great* number of people,
15:15. Pilate, willing to content (lit. to do what
was *enough for*) the people,
Lu. 3:16. shoes I am not *worthy* to unloose:
7: 6. I am not *worthy* that thou shouldest
11. *many* of his disciples went with him,
12. a widow: and *much* people of the city
8:27. a certain man, which had devils *long* time,
32. an herd of *many* swine feeding
20: 9. into a far country for a *long* time.
22:38. he said unto them, It is *enough*.
23: 8. desirous to see him of a *long* (season),
9. he questioned with him in *many* words;
Acts 5:37. drew away *much* people after him:
8:11. of *long* time he had bewitched them
9:23. after that *many* days were fulfilled,
43. he tarried *many* days in Joppa
11:24. *much* people was added unto the Lord.
26. and taught *much* people.
12:12. *many* were gathered together praying.
14: 3. *Long* time therefore abode they
21. and had taught *many*, they returned
17: 9. when they had taken *security* of Jason,
18:18. tarried (there) yet a *good* while,
19:19. *Many* of them also which used curious
26. persuaded and turned away *much* people,
20: 8. *many* lights in the upper chamber,
11. talked a *long while*, even till break
37. they all wept *sore*, and fell on Paul's
22: 6. from heaven a *great* light round about
27: 7. we had sailed slowly *many* days,
9. when *much* time was spent,
1Co.11:30. sickly among you, and *many* sleep.
15: 9. not *meet* to be called an apostle,
2Co. 2: 6. *Sufficient* to such a man (is) this
16. who (is) *sufficient* for these things?
3: 5. Not that we are *sufficient* of ourselves
2Ti. 2: 2. shall be *able* to teach others also.

ἱκανότης, hikanotees.

2Co. 3: 5. but our *sufficiency* (is) of God;

ἱκανόω, hikanoō.

2Co. 3: 6. Who also *hath made* us *able* ministers
Col. 1:12. unto the Father, *which hath made* us *meet*
to be partakers of

ἱκετηρία, hiketeeria.

Heb 5: 7. offered up prayers and *supplications*

ἱκμάς, ikmas.

Lu. 8: 6. because it lacked *moisture*.

ἱλαρός, hilaros.

2Co. 9: 7. God loveth a *cheerful* giver.

ἱλαρότης, hilarotees.

Ro. 12: 8. he that sheweth mercy, with *cheerfulness*.

ἱλάσκομαι, hilaskomai.

Lu. 18:13. God *be merciful* to me a sinner.
Heb 2:17. to *make reconciliation for* the sins

ἱλασμός, hilasmos.

1Joh.2: 2. he is the *propitiation* for our sins:
4:10. sent his Son (to be) the *propitiation* for
our sins.

–ος ἱλαστήριον, hilasteerion.

Ro. 3:25. a *propitiation* through faith in his blood,
Heb 9: 5. shadowing the *mercyseat;* of which

ἵλεως, hileōs.

Mat.16:22. saying, *Be it far* from thee, Lord:
Heb 8:12. For I will be *merciful* to their

ἱμάς, himas.

Mar 1: 7. the *latchet* of whose shoes I am not
Lu. 3:16. the *latchet* of whose shoes I am not
Joh. 1:27. whose shoe's *latchet* I am not worthy
Acts22:25. as they bound him with *thongs*,

ἱματίζομαι, himatizomai.

Mar 5:15. sitting, and *clothed*, and in his right mind:
Lu. 8:35. at the feet of Jesus, *clothed*,

ἱμάτιον, himation.

Mat 5:40. let him have (thy) *cloke* also.
9:16. new cloth unto an old *garment*,
— to fill it up taketh from the *garment*,
20. touched the hem of his *garment:*
21. If I may but touch his *garment*,
11: 8. A man clothed in soft *raiment?*
14:36. only touch the hem of his *garment:*
17: 2. his *raiment* was white as the light.
21: 7. put on them their *clothes*, and they set
8. spread their *garments* in the way;
23: 5. enlarge the borders of their *garments*,
24:18. return back to take his *clothes*.
26:65. Then the high priest rent his *clothes*,
27:31. and put his own *raiment* on him.
35. and parted his *garments*, casting lots:
— They parted my *garments* among them,

Mar 2:21. piece of new cloth on an old *garment* :
5:27. press behind, and touched his *garment*.
28. If I may touch but his *clothes*,
30. and said, Who touched my *clothes* ?
6:56. it were but the border of his *garment* :
9: 3. And his *raiment* became shining,
10:50. And he, casting away his *garment*,
11: 7. and cast their *garments* on him ;
8. And many spread their *garments*
13:16. not turn back again for to take up his *garment*.
15:20. and put his own *clothes* on him,
24. they parted his *garments*, casting lots
Lu. 5:36. a piece of a new *garment* upon an old)(;
6:29. him that taketh away thy *cloke*
7:25. A man clothed in soft *raiment* ?
8:27. and ware no *clothes*, neither abode
44. touched the border of his *garment* :
19:35. they cast their *garments* upon the colt,
36. they spread their *clothes* in the way.
22:36. let him sell his *garment*, and buy one.
23:34. And they parted his *raiment*, and cast lots.
Joh.13: 4. and laid aside his *garments* ;
12. and had taken his *garments*,
19: 2. they put on him a purple *robe*,
5. wearing the crown of thorns, and the purple *robe*.
23. took his *garments*, and made four parts,
24. They parted my *raiment* among them,
Acts 7:58. the witnesses laid down their *clothes*
9:39. shewing the coats and *garments* which
12: 8. Cast thy *garment* about thee,
14:14. they rent their *clothes*, and ran in
16:22. the magistrates rent off their *clothes*,
18: 6. he shook (his) *raiment*, and said
22:20. and kept the *raiment* of them that
23. and cast off (their) *clothes*, and threw dust
Heb 1:11. all shall wax old as doth a *garment* ;
Jas. 5: 2. your *garments* are motheaten.
1Pet.3: 3. or of putting on of *apparel* ;
Rev 3: 4. which have not defiled their *garments* ;
5. shall be clothed in white *raiment* ;
18. white *raiment*, that thou mayest be
4: 4. sitting, clothed in white *raiment* ;
16:15. that watcheth, and keepeth his *garments*,
19:13. clothed with a *vesture* dipped in blood:
16. And he hath on (his) *vesture* and on his

ἱματισμός, himatismos.

Mat 27:35. upon my *vesture* did they cast lots.
Lu. 7:25. they which are gorgeously *apparel*led,
9:29. his *raiment* (was) white (and) glistering.
Joh 19:24. for my *vesture* they did cast lots.
Acts20:33. no man's silver, or gold, or *apparel*.
1Ti. 2: 9. or gold, or pearls, or costly *array* ;

ἱμείρομαι, himīromai.

1Th. 2: 8. So *being affectionately desirous* of you, we were willing to

---

ἵνα, hina.

The mark ² shews that 'lest' is put for ἵνα μή ;
³ shews that ' to', or ' for to', is put for ' that'
with a subjunctive.

Mat. 1:22. this was done, *that* it might be fulfilled

Mat. 2:15. *that* it might be fulfilled which was
4: 3. command *that* these stones be made
14. *That* it might be fulfilled which
5:29. *that* one of thy members should perish,
30. *that* one of thy members should perish,
7: 1. Judge not, *that* ye be not judged.
12. ye would *that* men should do to you,
8: 8. *that* thou shouldest come under my roof:
9: 6. But *that* ye may know that the Son
10:25. the disciple *that* he be as his master,
12:10. *that* they might accuse him.
16. *that* they should not make him known:
14:15. *that* they may go into the villages,
36. besought him *that* they might only touch
16:20. *that* they should tell no man that he
17:27, *lest* ² we should offend them,
18: 6. better for him *that* a millstone
14. *that* one of these little ones should perish.
16. *that* in the mouth of two or three
19:13. *that* he should put (his) hands on them,
16. *that* I may have eternal life ?
20:21. Grant *that* these my two sons may sit,
31. *because* they should hold their peace:
33. Lord, *that* our eyes may be opened.
21: 4. *that* it might be fulfilled which was
23:26. *that* the outside of them may be clean
24:20. pray ye *that* your flight be not in
26: 4. consulted *that* they might take Jesus
5. *lest* ² there be an uproar
16. opportunity *to* ³ betray him.
41. *that* ye enter not into temptation:
56. *that* the scriptures of the prophets might
63. *that* thou tell us whether thou be
27:20. *that* they should ask Barabbas,
26. delivered (him) *to* ³ be crucified.
32. compelled *to* ³ bear his cross.
35. *that* it might be fulfilled
28:10. *that* they go into Galilee,
Mar 1:38. *that* I may preach there also:
2:10. But *that* ye may know that the Son
3: 2. *that* they might accuse him.
9. *that* a small ship should wait on him
— *lest* ² they should throng him.
10. pressed upon him *for* ³ to touch him,
12. *that* they should not make him known.
14. ordained twelve, *that* they should be with him, and *that* he might send them
4:12. *That* seeing they may see,
21. *to* ³ be put under a
— *to* ³ be set on a candlestick ?
22. but *that* it should come abroad.
5:10. *that* he would not send them away
12. the swine, *that* we may enter into them.
18. prayed him *that* he might be with him.
23. (I pray thee),)(come and lay thy hands on her,
43. *that* no man should know it ;
6: 8. *that* they should take nothing
12. preached *that* men should repent.
25. I will *that* thou give me by and by
36. *that* they may go into the country
41. to his disciples *to* ³ set before them ;
56. *that* they might touch if it were
7: 9. *that* ye may keep your own tradition.
26. *that* he would cast forth the devil
32. beseech him *to* ³ put his hand upon him.
36. *that* they should tell no man:
8: 6. gave to his disciples *to* ³ set before
22. and besought him *to* ³ touch him.
30. *that* they should tell no man
9: 9. *that* they should tell no man
12. *that* he must suffer many things,

Mar 9:18. *that* they should cast him out ;
22. and into the waters, *to*³ destroy him:
30. *that* any man should know (it).
10:13. *that* he should touch them:
17. *that* I may inherit eternal life ?
35. we would *that* thou shouldest do for us
37. Grant unto us *that* we may sit,
48. *that* he should hold his peace:
51. *that* I might receive my sight.
11:16. not suffer *that* any man should carry
25. *that* your Father also which is in heaven
28. gave thee this authority *to*³ do these things?
12: 2. *that* he might receive from the
13. *to*³ catch him in (his) words.
15. a penny, *that* I may see (it).
19. *that* his brother should take his wife,
13:18. *that* your flight be not in the winter.
34. and commanded the porter *to*³ watch.
14:10. went unto the chief priests, *to*³ betray
12. *that* thou mayest eat the passover ?
35. prayed *that*, if it were possible, the hour might pass from him.
38. Watch ye and pray, *lest*² ye enter into
49. but the scriptures must be fulfilled. (lit. but *that* the scriptures be fulfilled)
15:11. *that* he should rather release Barabbas
15. *to*³ be crucified.
20. led him out *to*³ crucify him.
21. *to*³ bear his cross.
32. *that* we may see and believe.
16: 1. *that* they might come and anoint him.
Lu. 1: 4. *That* thou mightest know the certainty
43. *that* the mother of my Lord should
4: 3. this stone *that* it be made bread.
5:24. But *that* ye may know that the Son
6: 7. *that* they might find an accusation
31. as ye would *that* men should do
34. lend to sinners, *to*³ receive as much again.
7: 6. not worthy *that* thou shouldest enter
36. *that* he would eat with him.
8:10. *that* seeing they might not see,
12. *lest*² they should believe and be saved.
16. *that* they which enter in may see
31. *that* he would not command them
32. *that* he would suffer them to enter
9:12. *that* they may go into the towns
40. I besought thy disciples *to*³ cast him out;
45. *that* they perceived it not:
10:40. bid her therefore *that* she help me.
11:33. *that* they which come in may see
50. *That* the blood of all the prophets,
54. *that* they might accuse him.
12:36. *that* when he cometh and knocketh,
14:10. *that* when he that bade thee cometh,
23. *that* my house may be filled.
29. *Lest*² haply,...all that behold (it) begin to mock him,
15:29. *that* I might make merry with
16: 4. *that*, when I am put out of the
9. *that*, when ye fail, they may receive
24. *that* he may dip the tip of his finger
27. *that* thou wouldest send him to my
28. *lest*² they also come into this place of torment.
17: 2. *that* he should offend one of these
18: 5. *lest*² by her continual coming she weary
15. infants, *that* he would touch them:
39. *that* he should hold his peace:
41. *that* I may receive my sight.
19: 4. into a sycomore tree *to*³ see him:
15. *that* he might know how much every
20:10. *that* they should give him of the fruit

Lu. 20:14. *that* the inheritance may be our's.
20. *that* they might take hold of his words,
28. *that* his brother should take his wife,
21:36. *that* ye may be accounted worthy
22: 8. *that* we may eat.
30. *That* ye may eat and drink at my table
32. *that* thy faith fail not:
46. *lest*² ye enter into temptation.
Joh. 1: 7. *to*³ bear witness of the Light, *that* all (men) through him might believe.
8. *to*³ bear witness of that Light.
19. from Jerusalem *to*³ ask him,
22. *that* we may give an answer to them
27. I am not worthy *to*³ unloose.
31. but *that* he should be made manifest
2:25. needed not *that* any should testify
3:15. *That* whosoever believeth in him
16. *that* whosoever believeth in him
17. into the world *to*³ condemn the world; but *that* the world through him might be
20. *lest*² his deeds should be reproved.
21. *that* his deeds may be made manifest,
4: 8. unto the city *to*³ buy meat.
15. *that* I thirst not, neither come hither
34. My meat is *to*³ do the will of him that sent me,
36. *that* both he that soweth and he that reapeth may rejoice together.
47. *that* he would come down, and heal
5: 7. *to*³ put me into the pool:
14. *lest*² a worse thing come unto thee.
20. *that* ye may marvel.
23. *That* all (men) should honour the Son,
34. I say, *that* ye might be saved.
36. given me *to*³ finish,
40. *that* ye might have life.
6: 5. buy bread, *that* these may eat ?
7. *that* every one of them may take a little.
12. that remain, *that* nothing be lost.
15. *to*³ make him a king,
28. *that* we might work the works of God ?
29. *that* ye believe on him whom he
30. *that* we may see, and believe thee ?
38. not *to*³ do mine own will, but the will of him that sent me.
39. *that* of all which he hath given me
40. *that* every one which seeth the Son,
50. *that* a man may eat thereof,
7: 3. *that* thy disciples also may see the works
23. *that* the law of Moses should not be
32. priests sent officers *to*³ take him.
8: 6. *that* they might have to accuse him.
56. rejoiced *to*³ see my day:
59. took they up stones *to*³ cast at him:
9: 2. *that* he was born blind ?
3. *that* the works of God should be made
22. *that* if any man did confess that he was Christ,
36. *that* I might believe on him ?.
39. *that* they which see not might see ;
10:10. but for *to*³ steal,
— I am come *that* they might have life,
17. *that* I might take it again.
31. again *to*³ stone him.
38. *that* ye may know, and believe,
11: 4. *that* the Son of God might be glorified
11. *that* I may awake him out of sleep.
15. *to the intent* ye may believe ;
16. Let us also go, *that* we may die
19. *to*³ comfort them concerning their brother.
31. unto the grave *to*³ weep
37. *that* even this man should not have died ?

Joh. 11:42. I said (it), *that* they may believe
50. *that* one man should die for
52. *that* also he should gather together
53. for *to*³ put him to death.
55. to³ purify themselves.
57. *that*, if any man knew where he were,
12: 9. *that* they might see Lazarus also,
10. *that* they might put Lazarus also to death;
20. among them that came up *to*³ worship at the feast:
23. *that* the Son of man should be glorified.
35. *lest*² darkness come upon you:
36. *that* ye may be the children of light.
38. *That* the saying of Esaias the prophet
40. *that* they should not see with (their) eyes,
42. *lest*² they should be put out of the
46. *that* whosoever believeth on me
47. for I came not *to*³ judge the world, but *to*³ save the world.
13: 1. *that* he should depart out of this world
2. *to*³ betray him;
15. *that* ye should do as I have done
18. *that* the scripture may be fulfilled,
19. *that*, when it is come to pass,
29. *that* he should give something to
34. *That* ye love one another;
— *that* ye also love one another.
14: 3. *that* where I am, (there) ye may be
13. *that* the Father may be glorified
16. *that* he may abide with you for ever;
29. *that*, when it is come to pass,
31. *that* the world may know that I
15: 2. *that* it may bring forth more fruit.
8. *that* ye bear much fruit;
11. *that* my joy might remain in you,
12. *That* ye love one another,
13. *that* a man lay down his life
16. *that* ye should go and bring forth fruit,
— *that* whatsoever ye shall ask
17. *that* ye love one another.
25. *that* the word might be fulfilled
16: 1. *that* ye should not be offended.
2. *that* whosoever killeth you
4. *that* when the time shall come,
7. expedient for you *that* I go away:
24. *that* your joy may be full.
30. *that* any man should ask thee:
32. *that* ye shall be scattered,
33. *that* in me ye might have peace.
17: 1. *that* thy Son also may glorify thee:
2. *that* he should give eternal life
3. *that* they might know thee the only
4. thou gavest me *to*³ do.
11. *that* they may be one, as we (are).
12. *that* the scripture might be fulfilled.
13. *that* they might have my joy fulfilled
15. *that* thou shouldest take them out
— *that* thou shouldest keep them
19. *that* they also might be sanctified
21. *That* they all may be one;
— *that* they also may be one in us: *that* the world may believe
22. *that* they may be one, even as we
23. *that* they may be made perfect
— *that* the world may know that thou
24. *that* they also, whom thou hast given
— *that* they may behold my glory,
26. *that* the love wherewith thou hast
18: 9. *That* the saying might be fulfilled,
28. *lest*² they should be defiled; but *that* they might eat the passover.
32. *That* the saying of Jesus might

Joh. 18:36. *that* I should not be delivered
37. *that* I should bear witness unto
39. *that* I should release unto you one
19: 4. *that* ye may know that I find
16. unto them *to*³ be crucified.
24. *that* the scripture might be fulfilled,
28. *that* the scripture might be fulfilled,
31. *that* the bodies should not remain
— *that* their legs might be broken,
35. *that* ye might believe.
36. *that* the scripture should be fulfilled,
38. *that* he might take away the body
20:31. *that* ye might believe that Jesus
— *that* believing ye might have life
Acts 2:25. *that* I should not be moved:
4:17. *that* it spread no further
5:15. *that* at the least the shadow of Peter
26. *lest*² they should have been stoned.
8:19. *that* on whomsoever I lay hands,
9:21. *that* he might bring them bound
16:30. Sirs, what must I do *to*³ be saved?
36. magistrates have sent *to*³ let you go:
17:15. for *to*³ come to him with all speed,
19: 4. *that* they should believe on him
21:24. *that* they may shave (their) heads:
22: 5. unto Jerusalem, *for to*³ be punished.
24. *that* he might know wherefore
23:24. *that* they may set Paul on,
24: 4. *that* I be not further tedious
27:42. counsel was *to*³ kill the prisoners,
Ro. 1:11. *that* I may impart unto you some
13. *that* I might have some fruit
3: 8. do evil, *that* good may come?
19. *that* every mouth may be stopped,
4:16. *that* (it might be) by grace;
5:20. *that* the offence might abound.
21. *That* as sin hath reigned unto death,
6: 1. continue in sin, *that* grace may abound?
4. *that* like as Christ was raised up
6. *that* the body of sin might be destroyed,
7: 4. *that* we should bring forth fruit unto God.
13. But sin, *that* it might appear sin,
— *that* sin by the commandment might
8: 4. *That* the righteousness of the law
17. *that* we may be also glorified
9:11. *that* the purpose of God according to
23. *that* he might make known
11:11. stumbled *that* they should fall?
19. *that* I might be graffed in.
25. *lest*² ye should be wise in your own
31. *that* through your mercy they also
32. *that* he might have mercy upon all.
14: 9. *that* he might be Lord both of the dead
15: 4. *that* we through patience and comfort
6. *That* ye may with one mind
16. *that* the offering up of the Gentiles
20. *lest*² I should build
31. *That* I may be delivered from them
— *that* my service which
32. *That* I may come unto you with joy
16: 2. *That* ye receive her in the Lord,
1Co. 1:10. *that* ye all speak the same thing,
15. *Lest*² any should say that I had baptized in mine own name.
17. *lest*² the cross of Christ should be made
27. *to*³ confound the wise;
— *to*³ confound the things which are
28. *to*³ bring to nought things that are:
31. *That*, according as it is written, He that glorieth, let him
2: 5. *That* your faith should not stand

1Co. 2:12. *that* we might know the things
    3:18. become a fool, *that* he may be wise.
    4: 2. *that* a man be found faithful.
       3. *that* I should be judged of you,
       6. *that* ye might learn in us
     — *that* no one of you be puffed up
       8. *that* we also might reign with you.
    5: 2. *that* he that hath done this deed might be
          taken away
       5. *that* the spirit may be saved
       7. *that* ye may be a new lump,
    7: 5. *that* ye may give yourselves to fasting
     — *that* Satan tempt you not for your
     29. *that* both they that have wives be
     34. *that* she may be holy both in body
     35. not *that* I may cast a snare upon you,
    8:13. lest [2] I make my brother to offend.
    9:12. lest [2] we should hinder the gospel of Christ.
     15. *that* it should be so done unto me:
     — *that* any man should make my glorying
     18. *that*, when I preach the gospel,
     19. *that* I might gain the more.
     20. *that* I might gain the Jews;
     — *that* I might gain them that are
     21. *that* I might gain them that are
     22. *that* I might gain the weak:
     — *that* I might by all means save some.
     23. *that* I might be partaker thereof
     24. So run, *that* ye may obtain.
     25. they (do it) to [3] obtain a corruptible crown;
   10:33. *that* they may be saved.
   11:19. *that* they which are approved may be
         made manifest
     32. *that* we should not be condemned
     34. *that* ye come not together unto
   12:25. *That* there should be no schism
   13: 3. though I give my body to [3] be burned,
   14: 1. rather *that* ye may prophesy.
     5. but rather *that* ye prophesied.
     — *that* the church may receive edifying
     12. *that* ye may excel to the edifying
     13. pray *that* he may interpret.
     19. *that* (by my voice) I might teach
     31. *that* all may learn, and all
   15:28. *that* God may be all in all.
   16: 2. *that* there be no gatherings when I come.
     6. *that* ye may bring me on
     10. see *that* he may be with you
     11. *that* he may come unto me:
     12. I greatly desired him to [3] come unto you
     — his will was not at all to [3] come at this
     16. *That* ye submit yourselves unto such,
2Co. 1: 9. *that* we should not trust in ourselves,
     11. *that* for the gift (bestowed) upon us
     15. *that* ye might have a second benefit;
     17. *that* with me there should be yea
    2: 3. lest,[2] when I came, I should have sorrow
     4. not *that* ye should be grieved, but *that* ye
        might know the love
     5. *that* I may not overcharge you all.
     9. *that* I might know the proof of you,
     11. Lest [2] Satan should get an advantage of us:
    4: 7. *that* the excellency of the power
     10. *that* the life also of Jesus might be
     11. *that* the life also of Jesus might be
     15. *that* the abundant grace might
    5: 4. *that* mortality might be swallowed
     10. *that* every one may receive the things
     12. *that* ye may have somewhat to (answer)
     15. *that* they which live should not
     21. *that* we might be made
    6: 3. *that* the ministry be not blamed:

2Co. 7: 9. *that* ye might receive damage by us
    8: 6. *that* as he had begun, so he would
     7. *that* ye abound in this grace also.
     9. *that* ye through his poverty might
     13. not *that* other men be eased,
     14. *that* their abundance also may be
    9: 3. lest [2] our boasting of you should be in vain
     — *that*, as I said, ye may be ready:
     4. we *that* we say not, ye
     5. *that* they would go before unto you,
     8. *that* ye, always having all sufficiency
   10: 9. *That* I may not seem as if I would
   11: 7. *that* ye might be exalted,
     12. *that* I may cut off occasion
     — *that* wherein they glory, they may
     16. *that* I may boast myself a little.
   12: 7. lest [2] I should be exalted
     — the messenger of Satan to [3] buffet me, lest [2]
        I should be exalted above measure.
     8. *that* it might depart from me.
     9. *that* the power of Christ may rest
   13: 7. not *that* we should appear approved, but
       that ye should do that which is
     10. lest [2] being present I should use sharpness,
Gal. 1:16. *that* I might preach him among
    2: 4. *that* they might bring us into bondage:
     5. *that* the truth of the gospel might
     9. *that* we (should go) unto the heathen,
     10. *that* we should remember the poor;
     16. *that* we might be justified by
     19. *that* I might live unto God.
    3:14. *That* the blessing of Abraham
     — *that* we might receive the promise
     22. *that* the promise by faith of Jesus
     24. *that* we might be justified by faith.
    4: 5. To [3] redeem them that were under the
       law, *that* we might receive the adoption
       of sons.
     17. *that* ye might affect them.
    5:17. so *that* ye cannot do the things
    6:12. lest [2] they should suffer persecution
     13. *that* they may glory in your flesh.
Eph. 1:17. *That* the God of our Lord Jesus Christ,
    2: 7. *That* in the ages to come he might
     9. lest [2] any man should boast.
     10. *that* we should walk in them.
     15. for to [3] make in himself of twain one new
       man,
    3:10. *To the intent that* now unto the
     16. *That* he would grant you, according
     17(18). *that* ye, being rooted and grounded in
       love,
     19. *that* ye might be filled with all
    4:10. *that* he might fill all things.
     14. *That* we (henceforth) be no more children,
     28. *that* he may have to give to him
     29. *that* it may minister grace
    5:26. *That* he might sanctify and cleanse it
     27. *That* he might present it to himself
     — *that* it should be holy and without blemish.
     33. *that* she reverence (her) husband.
    6: 3. *That* it may be well with thee,
     13. *that* ye may be able to withstand
     19. *that* utterance may be given unto me,
     20. *that* therein I may speak boldly,
     21. *that* ye also may know my affairs,
     22. *that* ye might know our affairs,
Phi. 1: 9. *that* your love may abound yet more
     10. *that* ye may be sincere and without offence
     26. *That* your rejoicing may be more
     27. *that* whether I come and see you,
    2: 2. *that* ye be likeminded,

Phi. 2:10. *That* at the name of Jesus every knee
    15. *That* ye may be blameless and harmless,
    19. *that* I also may be of good comfort,
    27. *lest*[2] I should have sorrow upon sorrow.
    28. *that*, when ye see him again,
    30. *to*[3] supply your lack of service
  3: 8. *that* I may win Christ,
Col. 1: 9. *that* ye might be filled with
    18. *that* in all (things) he might have
    28. *that* we may present every man
  2: 2. *That* their hearts might be comforted,
    4. *lest*[2] any man should beguile you
  3:21. *lest*[2] they be discouraged.
  4: 3. *that* God would open unto us a door
    4. *That* I may make it manifest,
    8. *that* he might know your estate,
    12. *that* ye may stand perfect and complete
    16. cause *that* it be read also in the church
    — *that* ye likewise read the (epistle)
    17. Take heed to the ministry... *that* thou
      fulfil it.
1Th. 2:16. the Gentiles *that* they might be saved,
  4: 1. *that*...(so) ye would abound more and
    12. *That* ye may walk honestly toward
    13. *that* ye sorrow not, even as others
  5: 4. *that* that day should overtake you
    10. *that*, whether we wake or sleep, we should
      live together with him.
2Th. 1:11. *that* our God would count you worthy
  2:12. *That* they all might be damned
  3: 1. *that* the word of the Lord may have
    2. *that* we may be delivered from
    9. but *to*[3] make ourselves an ensample
    12. *that* with quietness they work,
    14. *that* he may be ashamed.
1Ti. 1: 3. *that* thou mightest charge some that they
      teach no other doctrine,
    16. *that* in me first Jesus Christ might
    18. *that* thou by them mightest war a good
    20. *that* they may learn not to blaspheme.
  2: 2. *that* we may lead a quiet and peaceable
  3: 6. *lest*[2] being lifted up with pride he fall
    7. *lest*[2] he fall into reproach
    15. *that* thou mayest know how
  4:15. *that* thy profiting may appear
  5: 7. *that* they may be blameless.
    16. *that* it may relieve them that are
    20. *that* others also may fear.
    21. *that* thou observe these things
  6: 1. *that* the name of God and (his) doctrine
      be not blasphemed.
    19. *that* they may lay hold on eternal life.
2Ti. 1: 4. *that* I may be filled with joy ;
  2: 4. *that* he may please him who hath
    10. *that* they may also obtain the salvation
  3:17. *That* the man of God may be perfect,
  4:17. *that* by me the preaching might be fully
Tit. 1: 5. *that* thou shouldest set in order
    9. *that* he may be able by sound doctrine
    13. *that* he may be sound in the faith ;
  2: 4. *That* they may teach the young women
    5. *that* the word of God be not blasphemed.
    8. *that* he that is of the contrary part may be
      ashamed,
    10. *that* they may adorn the doctrine
    12. *that*, denying ungodliness and worldly
      lusts, we should live
    14. *that* he might redeem us from all
  3: 7. *That* being justified by his grace, we
      should be made heirs
    8. *that* they which have believed in God
    13. *that* nothing be wanting unto them.

Tit. 3:14. *that* they be not unfruitful.
Philem.13. *that* in thy stead he might
    14. *that* thy benefit should not be
    15. *that* thou shouldest receive him
    19. *albeit* I do not say to thee
Heb 2:14. *that* through death he might destroy
    17. *that* he might be a merciful
  3:13. *lest*[2] any of you be hardened
  4:11. *lest*[2] any man fall after
    16. *that* we may obtain mercy,
  5: 1. *that* he may offer both gifts
  6:12. *That* ye be not slothful,
    18. *That* by two immutable things,
  9:25. *that* he should offer himself often,
  10: 9, *that* he may establish the second.
    36. *that*, after ye have done the will of God,
      ye might receive the promise.
  11:28. *lest*[2] he that destroyed the firstborn should
      touch them.
    35. *that* they might obtain a better
    40. *that* they without us should not be made
  12: 3. *lest*[2] ye be wearied
    13. *lest*[2] that which is lame be turned out of
    27. *that* those things which cannot be shaken
  13:12. *that* he might sanctify the people
    17. *that* they may do it with joy,
    19. *that* I may be restored to you
Jas. 1: 4. *that* ye may be perfect and entire,
  4: 3. *that* ye may consume (it) upon your
  5: 9. *lest*[2] ye be condemned:
    12. *lest*[2] ye fall into condemnation.
1Pet. 1: 7. *That* the trial of your faith,
  2: 2. *that* ye may grow thereby:
    12. *that*, whereas they speak against you
    21. *that* ye should follow his steps:
    24. *that* we, being dead to sins,
  3: 1. *that*, if any obey not the word,
    9. *that* ye should inherit a blessing.
    16. *that*, whereas they speak evil of you,
    18. *that* he might bring us to God,
  4: 6. *that* they might be judged according
    11. *that* God in all things may be glorified
    13. *that*, when his glory shall be revealed,
  5: 6. *that* he may exalt you in due time:
2Pet. 1: 4. *that* by these ye might be partakers
  3:17. *lest*[2] ye also, being led away
1Joh. 1: 3. *that* ye also may have fellowship
    4. *that* your joy may be full.
    9. faithful and just *to*[3] forgive us (our) sins,
  2: 1. *that* ye sin not.
    19. *that* they might be made manifest
    27. *that* any man teach you:
    28. *that*, when he shall appear,
  3: 1. *that* we should be called
    5. was manifested *to*[3] take away our sins;
    8. *that* he might destroy the works
    11. *that* we should love one another.
    23. *That* we should believe on the name
  4: 9. *that* we might live through him.
    17. *that* we may have boldness
    21. *That* he who loveth God loveth his
  5: 3. *that* we keep his commandments:
    13. *that* ye may know that ye have
    — *that* ye may believe on the name
    16. I do not say *that* he shall pray for it.
    20. *that* we may know him that is true,
2Joh. 5. *that* we love one another.
    6. *that* we walk after his commandments.
    — *That*,...ye should walk in it.
    8. *that* we lose not those things
    12. *that* our joy may be full.
3Joh. 4. than *to*[3] hear that my children walk

3Joh.   8. *that* we might be fellowhelpers
Rev. 2:10. *that* ye may be tried ;
       21. space *to*[3] repent
    3: 9. I will make them *to*[3] come and worship
       11. *that* no man take thy crown.
       18. *that* thou mayest be rich ;
       — *that* thou mayest be clothed,
       — *that* thou mayest see.
    6: 2. conquering, and *to*[3] conquer.
       4. *that* they should kill one another:
      11. *that* they should rest yet for a little
    7: 1. *that* the wind should not blow
    8: 3. *that* he should offer (it) with the prayers
       6. prepared themselves *to*[3] sound.
      12. *so as* the third part of them was
    9: 4. *that* they should not hurt the grass
       5. *that* they should not kill them, but *that*
          they should be tormented
      15. *for to*[3] slay the third part of men.
      20. *that* they should not worship devils,
   11: 6. *that* it rain not in the days of
   12: 4. *for to*[3] devour her child as soon
       6. *that* they should feed her there
      14. *that* she might fly into the wilderness,
      15. *that* he might cause her to be carried
   13:12. *to*[3] worship the first beast,
      13. *so that* he maketh fire come down
      15. *that* the image of the beast should
      — *that* as many as would not worship
      16. *to*[3] receive (lit. *that* he should give them)
          a mark
      17. *that* no man might buy or sell,
   14:13. *that* they may rest from their labours ;
   16:12. *that* the way of the kings of the east
      15. *lest*[2] he walk naked,
   18: 4. *that* ye be not partakers of her sins, and
          that ye receive not of her plagues.
   19: 8. *that* she should be arrayed
      15. *that* with it he should smite
      18. *That* ye may eat the flesh of kings,
   20: 3. *that* he should deceive the nations
   21:15. *to*[3] measure the city,
      23. no need of the sun, neither of the moon,
          to[3] shine in it:
   22:14. *that* they may have right to the tree of

ἱνατί or ἵνα τί, hinati, hina ti.

Mat. 9: 4. *Wherefore* think ye evil in your hearts?
      27:46. *why* hast thou forsaken me?
Lu. 13: 7. *why* cumbereth it the ground?
Acts 4:25. *Why* did the heathen rage,
      7:26. *why* do ye wrong one to another?
1Co.10:29. *why* is my liberty judged of another
          (man's) conscience?

ἰός, ios.

Ro. 3:13. the *poison* of asps (is) under their lips:
Jas. 3: 8. an unruly evil, full of deadly *poison*.
    5: 3. the *rust* of them shall be a witness against

ἰουδαΐζω, ioudaizo.

Gal. 2:14. why compellest thou the Gentiles *to live as*
          do the Jews?

ἰουδαϊσμός, ioudaismos.

Gal. 1:13. my conversation in time past in the *Jews'*
          religion,
      14. And profited in the *Jews' religion*

ἱππεύς, hippūs.

Act 23:23. and *horsemen* threescore and ten,
       32. left the *horsemen* to go with him,

ἱππικόν, hippikon.

Rev. 9:16. number of the army of the *horse*men

ἵππος, hippos.

Jas. 3: 3. we put bits in the *horses'* mouths,
Rev. 6: 2. I saw, and behold a white *horse :*
       4. there went out another *horse*
       5. I beheld, and lo a black *horse ;*
       8. I looked, and behold a pale *horse :*
    9: 7. the locusts (were) like unto *horses*
       9. chariots of many *horses* running
      17. thus I saw the *horses* in the vision,
       — and the heads of the *horses* (were)
   14:20. even unto the *horse* bridles,
   18:13. and *horses*, and chariots, and slaves,
   19:11. heaven opened, and behold a white *horse ;*
      14. followed him upon white *horses*,
      18. and the flesh of *horses*,
      19. against him that sat on the *horse*,
      21. him that sat upon the *horse*,

ἶρις, iris.

Rev. 4: 3. a *rainbow* round about the throne,
    10: 1. and a *rainbow* (was) upon his head,

ἰσάγγελος, isangelos.

Lu. 20:36. for they are *equal unto the angels ;*

ἴσημι, iseemi.

Acts 26: 4. My manner of life...*know* all the Jews ;
Heb 12:17. For ye *know* how that afterward, when he
          would have

ἴσθι, isthi.

From εἰμί.

Mat. 2:13. *be* thou there until I bring thee word:
    5:25. Agree (lit. *be* agreeing) with thine
Mar. 5:34. go in peace, and *be* whole of thy plague.
Lu. 19:17. have thou (lit. *be* thou having) authority
1Ti. 4:15. give thyself wholly to (lit. *be* thou in)
          them ;

ἴσος or ἴσος, isos.

Mat.20:12. thou hast made them *equal* unto us,
Mar 14:56. their witness agreed not (lit. *was not*
          competent)

Mar 14:59. neither so did their witness agree (lit. was
　　not equal or competent)
Lu.　6:34. to receive as much again.
Joh.　5:18. making himself equal with God.
Acts11:17. God gave them the like gift as (he did)
　　unto us,
Phil. 2: 6. not robbery to be equal with God:
Rev.21:16. length and the breadth and the height of
　　it are equal.

ἰσότης, isotees.

2Co. 8:14(13). But by an equality, (that) now
　　14. that there may be equality:
Col. 4: 1. give unto (your) servants that which is
　　just and equal; (lit. equity)

ἰσότιμος, isotimos.

2Pet.1: 1. have obtained like precious faith with us

ἰσόψυχος, isopsukos.

Phil. 2:20. For I have no man likeminded, who will

ἵστημι, histeemi.

Mat. 2: 9. came and stood over where the young child
　　4: 5. and setteth him on a pinnacle of the temple,
　　6: 5. they love to pray standing in the
　　12:25. house divided against itself shall not stand:
　　26. how shall then his kingdom stand?
　　46. (his) mother and his brethren stood
　　47. thy mother and thy brethren stand without,
　　13: 2. multitude stood on the shore.
　　16:28. There be some standing here, which shall
　　　not taste
　　18: 2. Jesus called a little child unto him, and
　　　set him in the midst
　　16. three witnesses every word may be esta-
　　　blished.
　　20: 3. and saw others standing idle in the
　　6. and found others standing idle,
　　— Why stand ye here all the day idle?
　　32. And Jesus stood still, and called them,
　　24:15. the abomination of desolation, spoken of
　　　by Daniel the prophet, stand in the
　　　holy place,
　　25:33. he shall set the sheep on his right hand,
　　26:15. they covenanted with him for thirty pieces
　　73. came unto (him) they that stood by,
　　27:11. Jesus stood before the governor:
　　47. Some of them that stood there, when they
　　　heard (that),
Mar. 3:24. that kingdom cannot stand.
　　25. that house cannot stand.
　　26. and be divided, he cannot stand,
　　31. and, standing without, sent unto him,
　　9: 1. there be some of them that stand here,
　　36. he took a child, and set him in the midst
　　10:49. Jesus stood still, and commanded him
　　11: 5. certain of them that stood there said
　　13: 9. ye shall be brought before rulers and
　　14. standing where it ought not,
Lu.　1:11. an angel of the Lord standing on the right
　　4: 9. and set him on a pinnacle of the temple,
　　5: 1. he stood (lit. was standing) by the lake of
　　　Gennesaret,

Lu.　5: 2. saw two ships standing by the lake:
　　6: 8. Rise up, and stand forth in the midst.
　　　And he arose and stood forth.
　　17. and stood in the plain,
　　7:14. they that bare (him) stood still.
　　38. stood at his feet behind (him) weeping,
　　　and began to wash
　　8:20. Thy mother and thy brethren stand without,
　　44. immediately her issue of blood stanched.
　　9:27. there be some standing here,
　　47. took a child, and set him by him,
　　11:18. how shall his kingdom stand?
　　13:25. ye begin to stand without, and to knock
　　17:12. lepers, which stood afar off:
　　18:11. The Pharisee stood and prayed thus
　　13. the publican, standing afar off,
　　40. Jesus stood, and commanded him
　　19: 8. Zacchæus stood, and said unto the Lord;
　　21:36. to stand before the Son of man.
　　23:10. priests and scribes stood and
　　35. the people stood beholding.
　　49. stood afar off, beholding these things.
　　24:36. Jesus himself stood in the midst
Joh. 1:26. but there standeth one among you,
　　35. the next day after John stood, and two
　　3:29. which standeth and heareth him, rejoiceth
　　6:22. the people which stood on the other side
　　7:37. Jesus stood and cried, saying,
　　8: 3. when they had set her in the midst,
　　9. the woman standing in the midst.
　　44. and abode not in the truth,
　　11:56. spake among themselves, as they stood in
　　　the temple,
　　12:29. The people therefore, that stood by,
　　18: 5. which betrayed him, stood with them.
　　16. Peter stood at the door without.
　　18. the servants and officers stood there,
　　— and Peter stood with them,
　　25. Simon Peter stood and warmed himself.
　　19:25. Now there stood by the cross of Jesus
　　20:11. Mary stood without at the sepulchre
　　14. saw Jesus standing, and knew not
　　19. came Jesus and stood in the midst,
　　26. and stood in the midst, and said,
　　21: 4. Jesus stood on the shore:
Acts 1:11. why stand ye gazing up into heaven?
　　23. they appointed two, Joseph called Barsabas,
　　2:14. Peter, standing up with the eleven,
　　3: 8. he leaping up stood, and walked,
　　4: 7. when they had set them in the midst,
　　14. beholding the man which was healed stand-
　　　ing with them,
　　5:20. Go, stand and speak in the temple
　　23. and the keepers standing without before
　　25. the men whom ye put in prison are stand-
　　　ing in the temple,
　　27. they set (them) before the council:
　　6: 6. Whom they set before the apostles:
　　13. And set up false witnesses, which said,
　　7:33. the place where thou standest is holy
　　55. and Jesus standing on the right hand
　　56. the Son of man standing on the right
　　60. lay not this sin to their charge.
　　8:38. commanded the chariot to stand still:
　　9: 7. journeyed with him stood speechless,
　　10:30. a man stood before me in bright clothing,
　　11:13. which stood and said unto him, Send men
　　　to Joppa,
　　12:14. told how Peter stood before the gate.
　　16: 9. There stood a man of Macedonia,
　　17:22. Paul stood in the midst of Mars' hill, and
　　31. Because he hath appointed a day,

Acts 21:40. Paul *stood* on the stairs, *and* beckoned
22:25. Paul said unto the centurion *that stood by,*
30. brought Paul down, and *set* him before
24:20. *while* I *stood* before the council,
21. that I cried *standing* among them,
25:10. I *stand* at Cæsar's judgment seat,
18. *when* the accusers *stood up,*
26: 6. now I *stand* and am judged for the hope
16. rise, and *stand* upon thy feet:
22. I *continue* unto this day, witnessing
27:21. Paul *stood forth* in the midst of them, and
Ro. 3:31. yea, we *establish* the law.
5: 2. into this grace wherein we *stand,*
10: 3. *to establish* their own righteousness,
11:20. and thou *standest* by faith.
14: 4. Yea, he *shall be holden up :* for God is able
to *make* him *stand.*
1Co. 7:37. he that *standeth* stedfast in his heart,
10:12. let him that thinketh he *standeth*
15: 1. and wherein ye *stand ;*
2Co. 1:24. for by faith ye *stand.*
13: 1. *shall* every word *be established.*
Eph. 6:11. that ye may be able *to stand* against
13. and having done all, *to stand.*
14. *Stand* therefore, having your loins girt
Col. 4:12. that ye *may stand* perfect and complete
2Ti. 2:19. the foundation of God *standeth* sure,
Heb 10: 9. that he *may establish* the second.
11. And every priest *standeth* daily
Jas. 2: 3. say to the poor, *Stand* thou there,
5: 9. the judge *standeth* before the door.
1Pet. 5:12. grace of God wherein ye *stand.*
Jude 24. *to present* (you) faultless before the
Rev. 3:20. Behold, I *stand* at the door,
5: 6. stood a Lamb (lit. a Lamb *standing*) as it
had been slain,
6:17. and who shall be able *to stand ?*
7: 1. I saw four angels *standing* on the four
9. a great multitude,...*stood* (lit. *standing*)
before the throne,
11. the angels *stood* round about the throne,
8: 2. seven angels which *stood* before God ;
3. another angel came and *stood* at the altar,
10: 5. angel which I saw *stand* upon the sea
8. the angel *which standeth* upon the sea
11: 4. two candlesticks *standing* before the God
11. and they *stood* upon their feet ;
12: 4. the dragon *stood* before the woman
13: 1 (12:18). I *stood* upon the sand of the sea,
14: 1. lo, a Lamb *stood* on the mount Sion,
15: 2. *stand* on the sea of glass,
18:10. *Standing* afar off for the fear of her
15. *shall stand* afar off for the fear
17. as trade by sea, *stood* afar off,
19:17. I saw an angel *standing* in the sun ;
20:12. I saw the dead, small and great, *stand*
before God ;

See also στήκω.

ἱστορέω, *historeo.*

Gal. 1:18. I went up to Jerusalem *to see* Peter, (lit.
to hold inquiry of Peter)

ἰσχυρός, *iskuros.*

Mat. 3:11. he that cometh after me is *mightier*
12:29. enter into a *strong man's* house,
— except he first bind the *strong man ?*
14:30. when he saw the wind *boisterous,*
Mar. 1: 7. There cometh one *mightier* than I

Mar. 3:27. can enter into a *strong man's* house,
— he will first bind the *strong man ;*
Lu. 3:16. but one *mightier* than I cometh,
11:21. a *strong man* armed keepeth his palace,
22. when a *stronger* than he shall come
15:14. there arose a *mighty* famine
1Co. 1:25. the weakness of God is *stronger* than men.
27. to confound the things which are *mighty ;*
4:10. we (are) weak, but ye (are) *strong ;*
10:22. are we *stronger* than he ?
2Co.10:10. (his) letters,...(are) weighty and *powerful ;*
Heb 5: 7. with *strong* crying and tears
6:18. we might have a *strong* consolation,
11:34. waxed *valiant* in fight,
1Joh.2:14. young men, because ye are *strong,*
Rev. 5: 2. I saw a *strong* angel proclaiming
10: 1. I saw another *mighty* angel
18: 8. *strong* (is) the Lord God who judgeth her.
10. Babylon, that *mighty* city !
21. a *mighty* angel took up a stone
19: 6. as the voice of *mighty* thunderings,
18. and the flesh of *mighty* men,

ἰσχύς, *iskus.*

Mar 12:30. and with all thy *strength :*
33. and with all the *strength,*
Lu. 10:27. and with all thy *strength,*
Eph. 1:19. according to the working of his *mighty*
power,
6:10. and in the power of his *might.*
2Th. 1: 9. and from the glory of his *power ;*
1Pet. 4:11. as of the *ability* which God giveth:
2Pet. 2:11. which are greater in *power* and might,
Rev. 5:12. to receive power, and riches, and wisdom,
and *strength,*
7:12. power, and *might,* (be) unto our God
18: 2. And he cried *might*ily with a strong voice,

ἰσχύω, *iskuo.*

Mat. 5:13. it *is* thenceforth *good* for nothing,
8:28. no man *might* pass by that way.
9:12. They *that be whole* need not a physician,
26:40. *could* ye not watch with me one hour ?
Mar. 2:17. They *that are whole* have no need
5: 4. neither *could* any (man) tame him.
9:18. cast him out ; and they *could* not.
14:37. *couldest* not thou watch one hour ?
Lu. 6:48. upon that house, and *could* not shake it:
8:43. neither *could* be healed of any,
13:24. will seek to enter in, and *shall* not *be able.*
14: 6. they *could* not answer him again
29. and *is* not *able* to finish (it),
30. and *was* not *able* to finish.
16: 3. I *cannot* dig ; to beg I am ashamed.
20:26. they *could* not take hold of his words
Joh.21: 6. and now they *were* not *able* to draw it
Acts 6:10. they *were* not *able* to resist the wisdom
15:10. neither our fathers nor we *were able* to
bear ?
19:16. *prevailed* against them, so that they fled
20. mightily grew the word of God and
prevailed.
25: 7. which they *could* not prove.
27:16. we had much work to come by (lit. *were*
able with difficulty, to become masters
of) the boat:
Gal. 5: 6. neither circumcision *availeth* any thing,
6:15. neither circumcision *availeth* any thing,

Phi. 4:13. I *can do* all things through Christ
Heb 9:17. otherwise it *is of* no *strength* at all while
Jas. 5:16. prayer of a righteous man *availeth* much.
Rev.12: 8. And *prevailed* not; neither was their place

ἴσως, isōs. adv.

Lu. 20:13. *it may be* they will reverence (him)

ἰχθύδιον, ikthudion.

Mat.15:34. Seven, and a few *little fishes.*
Mar. 8: 7. And they had a few *small fishes :*

ἰχθύς, ikthus.

Mat. 7:10. Or if he ask a *fish*, will he give him
14:17. but five loaves, and two *fishes.*
19. took the five loaves, and the two *fishes,*
15:36. took the seven loaves and the *fishes,*
17:27. take up the *fish* that first cometh up ;
Mar. 6:38. they say, Five, and two *fishes.*
41. taken the five loaves and the two *fishes,*
— the two *fishes* divided he among them
43. full of the fragments, and of the *fishes.*
Lu. 5: 6. inclosed a great multitude of *fishes :*
9. at the draught of the *fishes* which
9:13. but five loaves and two *fishes ;*
16. took the five loaves and the two *fishes,*
11:11. or if (he ask) a *fish*, will he for a *fish* give
him a serpent ?
24:42. gave him a piece of a broiled *fish,*
Joh.21: 6. to draw it for the multitude of *fishes.*
8. dragging the net with *fishes.*
11. drew the net to land full of great *fishes,*
1Co.15:39. another of *fishes,* (and) another of birds.

ἴχνος, iknōs.

Ro. 4:12. but who also walk in the *steps* of that
faith
2Co.12:18. (walked we) not in the same *steps ?*
1Pet.2:21. leaving us an example, that ye should
follow his *steps :*

ἰῶτα, iōta.

Mat. 5:18. one *jot* or one tittle shall in no wise pass
from the law, till all be fulfilled.

κἀγώ, κἀμοί, κἀμέ, kago, kamoi, kamè.

Mat. 2: 8. that *I* may come and worship him *also.*
10:32. him will *I* confess *also* before my Father
33. him will *I also* deny before my Father
11:28. *and I* will give you rest.
16:18. And *I* say *also* unto thee,
21:24. *I also* will ask you one thing,
— *I in like wise* will tell you
26:15. *and I* will deliver him unto you ?
Mar 11:29. *I* will *also* ask of you one question
Lu. 1: 3. It seemed good to *me also,*
2:48. thy father *and I* have sought thee

Lu. 11: 9. *And I* say unto you, Ask,
16: 9. *And I* say unto you, Make to yourselves
friends
20: 3. *I* will *also* ask you one thing ;
22:29. *And I* appoint unto you a kingdom,
Joh. 1:31. *And I* knew him not :
33. *And I* knew him not : but he that
34. *And I* saw, and bare record
5:17. My Father worketh hitherto, *and I* work.
6:56. dwelleth in me, *and I* in him.
57. *and I* live by the Father :
7:28. Ye *both* know *me,* and ye know whence
I am :
8:26. *and I* speak to the world those things
10:15. *even so* know *I* the Father :
27. *and I* know them, and they follow me :
28. *And I* give unto them eternal life ;
38. the Father (is) in me, *and I* in him.
12:32. *And I,* if I be lifted up from the earth,
14:20. and ye in me, *and I* in you.
15: 4. Abide in me, *and I* in you.
5. He that abideth in me, *and I* in him,
9. *so* have *I* loved you :
17:18. *even so* have *I also* sent them
21. as thou, Father, (art) in me, *and I* in
26. *and I* in them.
20:15. *and I* will take him away.
21. *even so* send *I* you.
Acts 8:19. Give *me also* this power,
10:26. *I* myself *also* am a man.
22:13. *And* the same hour *I* looked up upon him.
19. *And I* said, Lord, they know that I
26:29. and altogether such as)(*I* am,
Ro. 3: 7. why yet am *I also* judged as a sinner ?
11: 3. *and I* am left alone,
1Co. 2: 1. *And I,* brethren, when I came to you,
7: 8. It is good for them if they abide *even as I.*
40. and I think *also* that *I* have the Spirit
10:33. *Even as I* please all (men) in all (things),
11: 1. *even as I also* (am) of Christ.
15: 8. he was seen of *me also,*
16: 4. And if it be meet that *I* go *also,*
2Co. 6:17. *and I* will receive you,
11:16. that)(*I* may boast myself a little.
18. *I* will glory *also.*
21. *I* am bold *also.*
22. Are they Hebrews ? *so* (am) *I.* Are they
Israelites ? *so* (am) *I.* Are they the
seed of Abraham ? *so* (am) *I.*
12:20. *and* (that) *I* shall be found unto you
Gal. 4:12. be as I (am) ; for)(*I* (am) as ye (are):
6:14. *and I* unto the world.
Eph. 1:15. Wherefore *I also,* after I heard of your
faith
Phi. 2:19. that *I also* may be of good comfort,
28. *and* that *I* may be the less sorrowful.
1Th. 3: 5. For this cause, when)(*I* could no longer
forbear,
Heb 8: 9. *and I* regarded them not, saith the Lord.
Jas. 2:18. *and I* have works :
— *and I* will shew thee my faith by my
Rev. 2: 6. which *I also* hate.
27. *even as I* received
3:10. *I also* will keep thee
21. *even as I also* overcame, and am set down

καθά, katha.

Mat.27:10. for the potter's field, *as* the Lord appointed me.

καθαίρεσις, kathairesis.

2Co.10: 4. to the *pulling down* of strong holds;
8. and not for your *destruction*,
13:10. to edification, and not to *destruction*.

καθαιρέω, kathaireo.

Mar 15:36. whether Elias will come *to take* him *down*.
46. and *took* him *down, and* wrapped
Lu. 1:52. He hath *put down* the mighty
12:18. I *will pull down* my barns,
23:53. And he *took* it *down, and* wrapped it
Acts13:19. And *when* he *had destroyed* seven nations
29. they *took* (him) *down* from the tree, *and* laid
19:27. and her magnificence should *be destroyed,*
2Co.10: 5. *Casting down* imaginations, and

καθαίρω, kathairo.

Joh.15: 2. he *purgeth* it, that it may bring
Heb10: 2. because that the worshippers once *purged*

καθάπερ, kathaper.

Ro. 4: 6. *Even as* David also describeth
12: 4. For *as* we have many members
1Co.12:12. For *as* the body is one,
2Co. 1:14. *even as* ye also (are) our's in the day of
3:13. And not *as* Moses, (which) put a vail
18. (*even*) *as* by the Spirit of the Lord.
8:11. that *as* (there was) a readiness
1Th. 2:11. *As* ye know how we exhorted
3: 6. *as* we also (to see) you:
12. *even as* we (do) toward you:
4: 5. *even as* the Gentiles which know not
Heb 4: 2. *as well as* unto them:
5: 4. called of God, *as* (was) Aaron.

καθάπτω, kathapto.

Acts28: 3. and *fastened on* his hand.

καθαρίζω, katharizo.

Mat. 8: 2. if thou wilt, thou canst *make* me *clean.*
3. I will; *be* thou *clean.* And immediately his leprosy *was cleansed.*
10: 8. *cleanse* the lepers, raise the dead,
11: 5. the lepers *are cleansed,*
23:25. for ye *make clean* the outside of the cup
26. *cleanse* first that (which is) within
Mar 1:40. If thou wilt, thou canst *make* me *clean.*
41. I will; *be* thou *clean.*
42. and he *was cleansed.*
7:19. into the draught, *purging* all meats?
Lu. 4:27. and none of them *was cleansed,* saving
5:12. if thou wilt, thou canst *make* me *clean.*
13. I will: *be* thou *clean.*
7:22. the lepers *are cleansed,*
11:39. ye Pharisees *make clean* the outside
17:14. as they went, they *were cleansed.*
17. *Were* there not ten *cleansed?*
Acts10:15. What God *hath cleansed,* (that) call not thou common.
11: 9. What God *hath cleansed,* (that) call not
15: 9. *purifying* their hearts by faith.

2Co. 7: 1. *let* us *cleanse* ourselves from all
Eph. 5:26. That he might sanctify *and cleanse* it
Tit. 2:14. and *purify* unto himself a peculiar
Heb 9:14. *shall* the blood of Christ,...*purge* your conscience from dead works to serve
22. almost all things *are* by the law *purged* with blood;
23. should *be purified* with these; but
Jas. 4: 8. *Cleanse* (your) hands, (ye) sinners;
1Joh.1: 7. the blood of Jesus Christ his Son *cleanseth* us from all sin.
9. and to *cleanse* us from all unrighteousness.

καθαρισμός, katharismos.

Mar 1:44. and offer for thy *cleansing* those things
Lu. 2:22. when the days of her *purification*
5:14. and offer for thy *cleansing,*
Joh. 2: 6. after the manner of the *purifying*
3:25. and the Jews about *purifying.*
Heb 1: 3. when he had by himself *purged* our sins, (lit. having made through himself a *cleansing* of)
2Pet.1: 9. hath forgotten that he was purged from (lit. the *cleansing* of) his old sins.

κάθαρμα, katharma.

1Co. 4:13. we are made as the *filth* of the world,

καθαρός, katharos.

Mat 5: 8. Blessed (are) the *pure* in heart:
23:26. the outside of them may be *clean* also.
27:59. he wrapped it in a *clean* linen cloth,
Lu. 11:41. all things are *clean* unto you.
Joh.13:10. but is *clean* every whit: and ye are *clean,* but not all.
11. Ye are not all *clean.*
15: 3. Now ye are *clean* through the word
Acts18: 6. upon your own heads; I (am) *clean:*
20:26. I (am) *pure* from the blood of all (men).
Ro. 14:20. All things indeed (are) *pure;* but
1Ti. 1: 5. is charity out of a *pure* heart,
3: 9. of the faith in a *pure* conscience.
2Ti. 1: 3. with *pure* conscience,
2:22. out of a *pure* heart.
Tit. 1:15. Unto the *pure* all things (are) *pure:* but unto them that are defiled and unbelieving (is) nothing *pure;*
Heb10:22(23). washed with *pure* water.
Jas. 1:27. *Pure* religion and undefiled
1Pet.1:22. with a *pure* heart fervently:
Rev 15: 6. clothed in *pure* and white linen,
19: 8. fine linen, *clean* and white:
14. clothed in fine linen, white and *clean.*
21:18. and the city (was) *pure* gold, like unto *clear* glass.
21. the street of the city (was) *pure* gold,
22: 1. And he shewed me a *pure* river

καθαρότης, katharotees.

Heb 9:13. to the *purifying* of the flesh:

καθέδρα, kathedra.

Mat 21:12. and the *seats* of them that sold doves,

Mat 23: 2. sit in Moses' *seat:*
Mar 11:15. the *seats* of them that sold doves;

καθέζομαι, *kathezomai.*

Mat 26:55. I *sat* daily with you teaching in the
Lu.　2:46. *sitting* in the midst of the doctors,
Joh.　4: 6. *sat* thus on the well:
　　11:20. but Mary *sat* (still) in the house.
　　20:12. And seeth two angels in white *sitting,*
Acts 6:15. And all *that sat* in the council,

καθείς or κᾱθ' εἷς, *kathīs or kath' hīs.*

Ro. 12: 5. and *every one* members one of another.

καθεξῆς, *kathexees.*

Lu.　1: 3. to write unto thee *in order,*
　　8: 1. And it came to pass *afterward,*
Acts 3:24. and those that follow *after,*
　　11: 4. and expounded (it) *by order* unto them,
　　18:23. country of Galatia and Phrygia *in order,*

καθεύδω, *kathŭdo.*

Mat　8:24. but he *was asleep.*
　　9:24. the maid is not dead, but *sleepeth.*
　　13:25. But while men *slept,*
　　25: 5. they all slumbered and *slept.*
　　26:40. and findeth them *asleep,*
　　　43. came and found them *asleep* again:
　　　45. *Sleep* on now, and take (your) *rest:*
Mar　4:27. And *should sleep,* and rise night
　　　38. *asleep* on a pillow:
　　5:39. the damsel is not dead, but *sleepeth.*
　　13:36. he find you *sleeping.*
　　14:37. and findeth them *sleeping,* and saith unto
　　　　　Peter, Simon, *sleepest* thou?
　　　40. he found them *asleep* again,
　　　41. *Sleep* on now, and take (your) *rest:*
Lu.　8:52. she is not dead, but *sleepeth.*
　　22:46. Why *sleep* ye? rise and pray,
Eph 5:14. Awake thou *that sleepest,*
1Th. 5: 6. let us not *sleep,*
　　　7. For they *that sleep sleep* in the night;
　　　10. whether we wake or *sleep,*

καθηγητής, *katheegeetees.*

Mat 23: 8. for one is your *Master,*
　　10. Neither be ye called *masters:* for one is
　　　　your *Master,*

καθῆκον, *katheekon.*

Acts 22:22. it is not *fit* that he should live.
Ro.　1:28. those things which are not *convenient;*

κάθημαι, *katheemai.*

Mat 4:16. The people *which sat* in darkness
　　— to them *which sat* in the region and
　9: 9. he saw a man, named Matthew, *sitting* at
　　　the receipt of

Mat 11:16. like unto children *sitting* in
　　13: 1. and *sat* by the sea side.
　　　2. so that he went into a ship, and *sat;*
　　15:29. a mountain, and *sat down* there.
　　20:30. *sitting* by the way side,
　　22:44. *Sit* thou on my right hand,
　　23:22. and by him *that sitteth* thereon.
　　24: 3. *as* he *sat* upon the mount of Olives,
　　26:58. and *sat* with the servants,
　　　64. see the Son of man *sitting* on the right
　　　69. Peter *sat* without in the palace:
　　27:19. *When* he was *set down* on the judgment
　　　　seat,
　　　36. And *sitting down* they watched him
　　　61. *sitting* over against the sepulchre.
　　28: 2. and *sat* upon it.
Mar 2: 6. certain of the scribes *sitting* there,
　　14. *sitting* at the receipt of custom,
　　3:32. the multitude *sat* about him,
　　34. on them *which sat* about him,
　　4: 1. into a ship, and *sat* in the sea;
　　5:15. had the legion, *sitting,* and clothed,
　　10:46. *sat* by the highway side begging.
　　12:36. *Sit* thou on my right hand,
　　13: 3. And *as* he *sat* upon the mount of Olives
　　14:62. ye shall see the Son of man *sitting*
　　16: 5. they saw a young man *sitting*
Lu.　1:79. to them *that sit* in darkness
　　5:17. doctors of the law *sitting by,*
　　27. *sitting* at the receipt of custom:
　　7:32. like unto children *sitting* in the
　　8:35. *sitting* at the feet of Jesus,
　　10:13. repented, *sitting* in sackcloth and
　　18:35. blind man *sat* by the way side
　　20:42. *Sit* thou on my right hand,
　　21:35. on all them *that dwell* on the face of
　　22:55. Peter *sat down* among them.
　　56. maid beheld him *as* he *sat*
　　69. shall the Son of man *sit* on the right
Joh. 2.14. the changers of money *sitting:*
　　6: 3. and there he *sat* with his disciples.
　　9: 8. Is not this he *that sat* and begged?
　　12:15. *sitting* on an ass's colt.
Acts 2: 2. where they were *sitting.*
　　34. *Sit* thou on my right hand,
　　3:10. he *which sat* for alms
　　8:28. and *sitting* in his chariot read
　　14: 8. there *sat* a certain man at Lystra,
　　20: 9. And there *sat* in a window
　　23: 3. for *sittest* thou to judge me
1Co.14:30. to another *that sitteth by,*
Col.　3: 1. where Christ *sitteth* on the right
Heb 1:13. *Sit* on my right hand,
Jas.　2: 3. *Sit* thou here in a good place;
　　— *sit* here under my footstool:
Rev. 4: 2. and (one) *sat* on the throne.
　　3. And he *that sat* was to look upon
　　4. four and twenty elders *sitting,*
　　9. and thanks to him *that sat* on
　　10. fall down before him *that sat*
　　5: 1. in the right hand of him *that sat*
　　7. out of the right hand of him *that sat*
　　13. unto him *that sitteth* upon the throne,
　　6: 2. he *that sat* on him had a bow;
　　4. to him *that sat* thereon
　　5. he *that sat* on him had
　　8. his name *that sat* on him was Death,
　　16. of him *that sitteth* on the throne,
　　7:10. *which sitteth* upon the throne,
　　15. he *that sitteth* on the throne
　　9:17. and them *that sat* on them,
　　11:16. elders, *which sat* before God

Rev.14:14. (one) *sat* like unto the Son
15. to him *that sat* on the cloud,
16. he *that sat* on the cloud
17: 1. *that sitteth* upon many waters:
3. a woman *sit* upon a scarlet
9. on which the woman *sitteth*.
15. where the whore *sitteth*.
18: 7. I *sit* a queen, and am no widow,
19: 4. worshipped God *that sat* on the
11. he *that sat* upon him (was) called
18. and of them *that sit* on them,
19. against him *that sat* on the horse,
21. with the sword of him *that sat*
20:11. white throne, and him *that sat* on it,
21: 5. *that sat* upon the throne

καθ' ἡμέραν, *kath' heemeran.*

Mat.26:55. I sat *daily* with you teaching
Mar 14:49. I was *daily* with you in the temple
Lu. 11: 3. *day by day* our daily bread.
16:19. fared sumptuously *every day*.
19:47. he taught *daily* in the temple.
22:53. I was *daily* with you in the temple,
Acts 2:46. continuing *daily* with one accord
47. the Lord added to the church *daily*
3: 2. whom they laid *daily* at the gate
16: 5. increased in number *daily*.
17:11. searched the scriptures *daily*,
17. in the market *daily* with them that
19: 9. disputing *daily* in the school
1Co.15:31. I die *daily*.
2Co.11:28. that which cometh upon me *daily*,
Heb 3:13. exhort one another *daily*,
7:27. Who needeth not *daily*,
10:11. every priest standeth *daily* ministering

καθημερινός, *katheemerinos.*

Acts 6: 1. in the *daily* ministration.

καθίζω, *kathizo.*

Mat. 5: 1. and *when he was set*, his disciples
13:48. they drew to shore, and *sat down, and*
19:28. when the Son of man *shall sit* in the throne of his glory, ye also *shall sit*
20:21. my two sons *may sit*, the one on
23. but *to sit* on my right hand, and on
23: 2. the Pharisees *sit* in Moses' seat:
25:31. then *shall* he *sit* upon the throne
26:36. *Sit* ye here, while I go and pray
Mar. 9:35. And he *sat down, and* called the twelve,
10:37. Grant unto us that we *may sit*,
40. But *to sit* on my right hand and on
11: 2. whereon never man *sat ;*
7. and he *sat* upon him.
12:41. Jesus *sat* over against the treasury, *and*
14:32. *Sit* ye here, while I shall pray.
16:19. and *sat* on the right hand of God.
Lu. 4:20. to the minister, and *sat down.*
5: 3. And he *sat down, and* taught
14:28. *sitteth* not *down* first, *and* counteth
31. *sitteth* not *down* first, *and* consulteth
16: 6. *sit down* quickly, *and* write
19:30. whereon yet never man *sat :*
22:30. and *sit* on thrones judging
24:49. but *tarry* ye in the city of Jerusalem,
Joh. 8: 2. and he *sat down, and* taught them.

Joh.12:14. found a young ass, *sat* thereon ;
19:13. and *sat down* in the judgment
Acts 2: 3. and it *sat* upon each of them.
30. Christ *to sit* on his throne ;
8:31. he would come up and *sit* with him.
12:21. *sat* upon his throne, *and* made
13:14. the sabbath day, and *sat down.*
16:13. we *sat down, and* spake unto
18:11. And he *continued* (there) a year
25: 6. *sitting* on the judgment seat
17. I *sat* on the judgment seat, *and*
1Co. 6: 4. *set* them to judge who are least
10: 7. The people *sat down* to eat and drink.
Eph. 1:20. and *set* (him) at his own right hand
2Th. 2: 4. *sitteth* in the temple of God,
Heb 1: 3. *sat down* on the right hand
8: 1. who *is set* on the right hand
10:12. *sat down* on the right hand
12: 2. *is set down* at the right hand
Rev. 3:21. will I grant *to sit* with me
— and *am set down* with my Father
20: 4. and they *sat* upon them,

καθίημι, *kathieemi.*

Lu. 5:19. and *let* him *down* through the tiling
Acts 9:25. and *let* (him) *down* by the wall
10:11. and *let down* to the earth:
11: 5. a great sheet, *let down* from heaven

καθίστημι, *kathisteemi.*

Mat.24:45. whom his lord *hath made ruler*
47. he *shall make* him *ruler* over all his
25:21. I *will make* thee *ruler* over many things:
23. I *will make* thee *ruler* over many things:
Lu. 12:14. who *made* me a judge or a divider
42. whom (his) lord *shall make ruler* over
44. that he *will make* him *ruler* over
Acts 6: 3. whom we may *appoint* over this
7:10. he *made* him governor over Egypt
27. Who *made* thee a ruler and a judge over us?
· 35. Who *made* thee a ruler and a judge ?
17:15. And they *that conducted* Paul
Ro. 5:19. many *were made* sinners,
— *shall* many *be made* righteous.
Tit. 1: 5. and *ordain* elders in every city,
Heb 2: 7. *didst set* him over the works of
5: 1. high priest...*is ordained* for men in things
7:28. the law *maketh* men high priests
8: 3. every high priest *is ordained* to offer
Jas. 3: 6. so *is* the tongue among our members,
4: 4. *is* the enemy of God.
2Pet.1: 8. they *make* (you that ye shall) neither (be) barren

---

κcθό, *katho.*

Ro. 8:26. not what we should pray for *as* we ought:
2Co. 8:12. *according to that* a man hath, (and) not *according to that* he hath not.
1Pet.4:13. But rejoice, *inasmuch as* ye are partakers

καθόλου, *katholou.*

Acts 4:18. not to speak *at all* nor teach in the name of Jesus.

καθοπλίζομαι, kathoplizomai.

Lu. 11:21. When a strong man *armed* keepeth

καθοράω, kathorao.

Ro. 1:20. *are clearly seen*, being understood by

καθότι, kathoti.

Lu. 1: 7. *because that* Elisabeth was barren,
　　19: 9. *forsomuch as* he also is a son
Acts 2:24. *because* it was not possible
　　　45. *as* every man had need.
　　4:35. unto every man *according as* he had need.

καθώς, kathōs.

Mat.21: 6. and did *as* Jesus commanded
　26:24. *as* it is written of him:
　　28: 6. he is risen, *as* he said.
Mar. 4:33. *as* they were able to hear
　　9.13. *as* it is written of him.
　11: 6. *even as* Jesus had commanded:
　14:16. found *as* he had said
　　21: 4. *as* it is written of him:
　15: 8. *as* he had even done unto them.
　16: 7. *as* he said unto you.
Lu. 1: 2. *Even as* they delivered them
　　55. *As* he spake to our fathers,
　　70. *As* he spake by the mouth of
　2:20. *as* it was told unto them.
　　23. *As* it is written in the law
　5:14. *as* Moses commanded,
　6:31. *as* ye would that men should
　　36. *as* your Father also is merciful.
　11: 1. *as* John also taught his disciples.
　　30. For *as* Jonas was a sign
　17:26. And *as* it was in the days of Noe,
　19:32. *even as* he had said unto them.
　22:13. found *as* he had said unto them:
　　29. *as* my Father hath appointed unto me ;
　24:24. *even so as* the women had said:
　　39. *as* ye see me have.
Joh. 1:23. *as* said the prophet Esaias.
　3:14. And *as* Moses lifted up the serpent
　5:23. *even as* they honour the Father.
　　30. *as* I hear, I judge:
　6:31. *as* it is written,
　　57. *As* the living Father hath sent me,
　　58. not *as* your fathers did eat manna,
　7:38. *as* the scripture hath said,
　8:28. but *as* my Father hath taught me,
　10:15. *As* the Father knoweth me,
　　26. not of my sheep, *as* I said unto you.
　12:14. *as* it is written,
　　50. *even as* the Father said unto me,
　13:15. do *as* I have done to you.
　　33. and *as* I said unto the Jews,
　　34. *as* I have loved you,
　14:27. not *as* the world giveth,
　　31. *as* the Father gave me commandment,
　15: 4. *As* the branch cannot bear fruit
　　9. *As* the Father hath loved me,
　　10. *even as* I have kept my Father's
　　12. *as* I have loved you.
　17: 2. *As* thou hast given him power over
　　11. that they may be one, *as* we (are).
　　14. *even as* I am not of the world.

Joh.17:16. *even as* I am not of the world.
　　18. *As* thou hast sent me into the world,
　　21. *as* thou, Father, (art) in me,
　　22. *even as* we are one:
　　23. *as* thou hast loved me.
　19:40. *as* the manner of the Jews is to bury.
　20:21. *as* (my) Father hath sent me,
Acts 2: 4. *as* the Spirit gave them utterance.
　　22. *as* ye yourselves also know:
　7:17. But *when* the time of the promise
　　42. *as* it is written
　　44. *as* he had appointed,
　　48. *as* saith the prophet,
　10:47. received the Holy Ghost *as* well as we?
　11:29. every man *according to* his ability,
　15: 8. even *as* (he did) unto us ;
　　14. *how* God at the first did visit
　　15. *as* it is written,
　22: 3. *as* ye all are this day.
Ro. 1:13. even *as* among other Gentiles.
　　17. *as* it is written,
　　28. And *even as* they did not like
　2:24. *as* it is written.
　3: 4. *as* it is written,
　　8. *as* we be slanderously reported, and *as*
　　　　some affirm that we say,
　　10. *As* it is written,
　4:17. *As* it is written,
　8:36. *As* it is written, For thy sake
　9:13. *As* it is written, Jacob
　　29. And *as* Esaias said before,
　　33. *As* it is written,
　10:15. *as* it is written, How
　11: 8. *According as* it is written,
　　26. *as* it is written,
　15: 3. *as* it is written, The reproaches
　　7. *as* Christ also received us
　　9. *as* it is written, For this cause
　　21. *as* it is written, To whom
1Co. 1: 6. *Even as* the testimony of Christ
　　31. *according* as it is written,
　2: 9. *as* it is written, Eye hath
　4:17. *as* I teach every where in every
　5: 7. *as* ye are unleavened.
　8: 2. nothing yet *as* he ought to know.
　10: 6. *as* they also lusted.
　　7. *as* (were) some of them ;
　　8. *as* some of them committed,
　　9. *as* some of them also tempted,
　　10. *as* some of them also murmured,
　　33. *Even as* I please all (men)
　11: 1. *even as* I also (am) of Christ.
　　2. *as* I delivered (them) to you.
　12·11. to every man severally *as* he will.
　　18. *as* it hath pleased him.
　13:12. *even as* also I am known.
　14:34. *as* also saith the law.
　15:38. a body *as* it hath pleased him,
　　49. And *as* we have borne the image
2Co. 1: 5. For *as* the sufferings of Christ
　　14. *As* also ye have acknowledged us
　4: 1. *as* we have received mercy,
　6:16. *as* God hath said,
　8: 5. And (this they did), not *as* we hoped,
　　6. that *as* he had begun,
　　15. *As* it is written, He that
　9: 3. that, *as* I said, ye may be ready:
　　7. *according as* he purposeth
　　9. *As* it is written, He hath dispersed
　10: 7. *as* he (is) Christ's, even so (are) we
　11:12. they may be found even *as* we.
Gal. 2: 7. *as* (the gospel) of the circumcision

Gal. 3: 6. *Even as* Abraham believed God,
　　5:21. *as* I have also told (you)
Eph. 1: 4. *According as* he hath chosen us
　　3: 3. *as* I wrote afore in few words,
　　4: 4. even *as* ye are called in one hope
　　　17. walk not *as* other Gentiles
　　　21. *as* the truth is in Jesus:
　　　32. even *as* God for Christ's sake hath
　　5: 2. *as* Christ also hath loved us,
　　　3. *as* becometh saints;
　　　25. even *as* Christ also loved the church,
　　　29. even *as* the Lord the church:
Phil. 1: 7. *Even as* it is meet for me
　　2:12. *as* ye have always obeyed,
　　3:17. *as* ye have us for an ensample.
Col. 1: 6. *as* (it is) in all the world;
　　' — *as* (it doth) also in you,
　　　7. *As* ye also learned of Epaphras
　　2: 7. *as* ye have been taught,
　　3:13. even *as* Christ forgave you,
1Th. 1: 5. *as* ye know what manner of men
　　2: 2. *as* ye know, at Philippi,
　　　4. But *as* we were allowed of God
　　　5. *as* ye know, nor a cloke of covetousness;
　　　13. *as* it is in truth, the word of God,
　　　14. even *as* they (have) of the Jews:
　　3: 4. even *as* it came to pass, and ye
　　4: 1. that *as* ye have received of us
　　　6. *as* we also have forewarned
　　　11. *as* we commanded you ;
　　　13. even *as* others which have no hope.
　　5:11. *even as* also ye do.
2Th. 1: 3. *as* it is meet,
　　3: 1. even *as* (it is) with you:
1Ti. 1: 3. *As* I besought thee to abide
Heb 3: 7. *as* the Holy Ghost saith,
　　4: 3. *as* he said, As I have sworn
　　　7. *as* it is said, To day
　　5: 3. *as* for the people, so also
　　　6. *As* he saith also in another
　　8: 5. *as* Moses was admonished
　　10:25. *as* the manner of some (is);
　　11:12. *as* the stars of the sky in multitude,
1Pet.4:10. *As* every man hath received
2Pet.1:14. even *as* our Lord Jesus Christ
　　3:15. even *as* our beloved brother Paul
1Joh.2: 6. *even as* he walked.
　　　18. *as* ye have heard that antichrist
　　　27. *even as* it hath taught you,
　　3: 2. for we shall see him *as* he is.
　　　3. *even as* he is pure.
　　　7. *even as* he is righteous.
　　　12. Not *as* Cain, (who) was of that
　　　23. *as* he gave us commandment.
　　4:17. because *as* he is, so are we
2Joh. 4. *as* we have received a commandment
　　　6. *as* ye have heard from the
3Joh. 2. *even as* thy soul prospereth.
　　　3. *even as* thou walkest in the truth.

καί.

(See in appendix.)

καινός, *kainos.*

Mat. 9:17. they put new wine into *new* bottles,
　13:52. treasure (things) *new* and old.
　26:28. my blood of the *new* testament,
　　29. until that day when I drink it *new*

Mat.27:60. in his own *new* tomb,
Mar 1:27. what *new* doctrine (is) this?
　2:21. else the *new* piece that filled it
　　22. must be put into *new* bottles.
　14:24. This is my blood of the *new* testament,
　　25. until that day that I drink it *new*
　16:17. speak with *new* tongues ;
Lu. 5:36. No man putteth a piece of a *new* garment
　　— both the *new* maketh a rent,
　　— out of the *new* agreeth not with
　　38. must be put into *new* bottles ;
　22:20. the *new* testament in my blood,
Joh.13:34. A *new* commandment I give
　19:41. in the garden a *new* sepulchre,
Acts17:19. what this *new* doctrine,
　　21. or to hear some *new* (lit. *newer*) thing.
1Co.11:25. This cup is the *new* testament
2Co. 3: 6. able ministers of the *new* testament ;
　5:17. (he is) a *new* creature:
　　— all things are become *new*.
Gal. 6:15. but a *new* creature.
Eph. 2:15. of twain one *new* man,
　4:24. put on the *new* man,
Heb. 8: 8. I will make a *new* covenant
　　13. In that he saith, A *new*
　9:15. the mediator of the *new* testament,
2Pet.3:13. look for *new* heavens and a *new* earth,
1Joh.2: 7. I write no *new* commandment
　　8. Again, a *new* commandment
2Joh. 5. as though I wrote a *new* commandment
Rev. 2:17. and in the stone a *new* name
　3:12. *new* Jerusalem, which cometh
　　— my *new* name.
　5: 9. And they sung a *new* song,
　14: 3. they sung as it were a *new* song
　21: 1. And I saw a *new* heaven and a *new* earth:
　　2. I John saw the holy city, *new* Jerusalem,
　　5. I make all things *new*.

καινότης, *kainotees.*

Ro. 6: 4. should walk in *newness* of life.
　7: 6. we should serve in *newness* of spirit,

καίπερ, *kaiper.*

Phi. 3: 4. *Though* I might also have confidence
Heb.5: 8. *Though* he were a Son, yet
　7: 5. *though* they come out of the loins of
　12:17. *though* he sought it carefully
2Pet.1:12. *though* ye know (them),
Rev.17: 8. that was, and is not, *and yet* is.

καιρός, *kairos.*

Mat. 8:29. to torment us before the *time* ?
　11:25. At that *time* Jesus answered
　12: 1. At that *time* Jesus went on the
　13:30. and in the *time* of harvest
　14: 1. At that *time* Herod the tetrarch
　16: 3. the signs of the *times* ?
　21:34. when the *time* of the fruit
　　41. the fruits in their *seasons*.
　24:45. meat in due *season* ?
　26:18. My *time* is at hand ;
Mar 1:15. The *time* is fulfilled,
　10:30. now in this *time*, houses,
　11:13. for the *time* of figs was not

Mar 12: 2. And at the *season* he sent
13:33. ye know not when the *time* is.
Lu. 1:20. shall be fulfilled in their *season*.
4:13. he departed from him for a *season*.
8:13. which for a *while* believe, and in *time* of temptation fall away.
12:42. portion of meat in *due season ?*
56. that ye do not discern this *time ?*
13: 1. were present at that *season*
18:30. manifold more in this present *time*,
19:44. the *time* of thy visitation.
20:10. And at the *season* he sent
21: 8. and the *time* draweth near:
24. until the *times* of the Gentiles be
36. and pray always, (lit. in every *time*)
Joh. 5: 4. at a certain *season* into the pool,
7: 6. My *time* is not yet come: but your *time* is alway ready.
8. my *time* is not yet full come.
Acts 1: 7. to know the times or the *seasons*,
3:19. when the *times* of refreshing
7:20. In which *time* Moses was born,
12: 1. about that *time* Herod
13:11. not seeing the sun for a *season*.
14:17. and fruitful *seasons*,
17:26. hath determined the *times*
19:23. And the same *time* there arose
24:25. when I have a *convenient season*,
Ro. 3:26. To declare, (I say), at this *time*
5: 6. in *due time* Christ died for
8:18. that the sufferings of this present *time*
9: 9. At this *time* will I come,
11: 5. at this present *time* also
12:11. serving the Lord ; (most copies read observant of the *time*)
13:11. And that, knowing the *time*,
1 Co. 4: 5. judge nothing before the *time*,
7: 5. with consent for a *time*,
29. the *time* (is) short:
2 Co. 6: 2. heard thee in a *time* accepted,
— now (is) the accepted *time ;*
8:14(13). now at this *time* your
Gal. 4:10. and *times*, and years.
6: 9. for in due *season* we shall reap,
10. have therefore *opportunity*,
Eph 1:10. the dispensation of the fulness of *times*
2:12. at that *time* ye were without Christ,
5:16. Redeeming the *time*, because the
6:18. Praying always (lit. in all *time*) with all prayer
Col. 4: 5. that are without, redeeming the *time*.
1 Th. 2:17. from you for a short *time*
5: 1. But of the times and the *seasons*,
2 Th. 2: 6. be revealed in his *time*.
1 Ti. 2: 6. to be testified in due *time*.
4: 1. that in the latter *times* some shall
6:15. Which in his *times* he shall
2 Ti. 3: 1. perilous *times* shall come.
4: 3. For the *time* will come when
6. the *time* of my departure is at hand.
Tit. 1: 3. But hath in due *times* manifested
Heb 9: 9. a figure for the *time* then present,
10. until the *time* of reformation.
11:11. when she was past age, (lit. the *time* of age)
15. have had *opportunity* to have returned.
1 Pet. 1: 5. to be revealed in the last *time*.
11. or what manner of *time* the Spirit
4:17. For the *time* (is come) that judgment
5: 6. he may exalt you in *due time :*
Rev 1: 3. for the *time* (is) at hand.
11:18. is come, and the *time* of the dead,

Rev 12:12. that he hath but a short *time*.
14. nourished for a *time*, and *times*, and half a *time*,
22:10. for the *time* is at hand.

καίτοι, καί-τοιγε, *kaitoi, kai-toige.*

Joh. 4: 2. *Though* Jesus himself baptized not,
Acts 14:17. *Nevertheless* he left not himself
17:27. *though* he be not far from every one
Heb 4: 3. *although* the works were finished

καίω, *kaio.*

Mat 5:15. Neither do men *light* a candle,
Lu. 12:35. and (your) lights *burning ;*
24:32. Did not our heart *burn*
Joh. 5:35. He was a *burning* and a shining
15: 6. and they are *burned*.
1 Co. 13: 3. I give my body to be *burned*,
Heb 12:18. and *that burned* with fire,
Rev 4: 5. seven lamps of fire *burning*
8: 8. a great mountain *burning* with fire
10. *burning* as it were a lamp,
19:20. lake of fire *burning* with brimstone.
21: 8. in the lake *which burneth* with fire and

κᾀκεῖ, *kakī.*

Mat 5:23. *and there* rememberest that thy brother
10:11. *and there* abide till ye go
28:10. *and there* shall they see me.
Mar 1:35. a solitary place, *and there* prayed.
38. that I may preach *there also :*
Joh. 11:54. *and there* continued with his
Acts 14: 7. *And there* they preached
17:13. they came *thither also*,
22:10. *and there* it shall be told thee
25:20. *and there* be judged of these
27: 6. *And there* the centurion found

κᾀκεῖθεν, *kakīthen.*

Mar 10: 1. *And* he arose *from thence*,
Acts 7: 4. *and from thence*, when his father was
13:21. *And afterward* they desired a king:
14:26. *And thence* sailed to Antioch,
20:15. *And* we sailed *thence*,
21: 1. *and from thence* unto Patara:
27: 4. *And* when we had launched *from thence*,
12. advised to depart *thence also*,
28:15. *And from thence*, when the brethren

κᾀκεῖνος, *kakīnos.*

Mat. 15:18. *and they* defile the man.
20: 4. *And* said unto *them ;*
23:23. *and* not to leave the *other* undone.
Mar 12: 4. *and at him* they cast stones,
5. *and him* they killed,
16:11. *And they*, when they had heard
13. *And they* went and told (it)
Lu. 11: 7. *And he* from within shall answer
42. *and* not to leave the *other* undone.
20:11. and they beat *him also*,
22:12. *And he* shall shew you a large
Joh. 6:57. *even he* shall live by me.

Joh. 7:29. *and he* hath sent me.
   10:16. *them also* I must bring,
   14:12. the works that I do shall *he* do *also;*
   17:24. I will that *they also,*
   19:35. *and he* knoweth that he saith true,
Acts 5:37. *he also* perished ; and all,
   15:11. we shall be saved, even as)(*they.*
   18:19. *and left them* there:
1Co.10: 6. as *they also* lusted.
2Ti. 2:12. *he also* will deny us:
Heb. 4: 2. as well as unto *them*)(*:*

κακία, *kakia.*

Mat. 6:34. Sufficient unto the day(is) the *evil* thereof.
Acts 8:22. of this thy *wickedness,*
Ro. 1:29. *maliciousness;* full of envy,
1Co. 5: 8. leaven of *malice* and wickedness;
   14:20. howbeit in *malice* be ye children,
Eph. 4:31. away from you, with all *malice:*
Col. 3: 8. anger, wrath, *malice,* blasphemy,
Tit. 3: 3. living in *malice* and envy,
Jas. 1:21. and superfluity of *naughtiness,*
1Pet.2: 1. laying aside all *malice,*
   16. for a cloke of *maliciousness,*

κακοήθεια, *kakoeethia.*

Ro. 1:29. debate, deceit, *malignity;* (lit. *depravity*)

κακολογέω, *kakologeo.*

Mat.15: 4. He *that curseth* father or mother,
Mar. 7:10. *Whoso curseth* father or mother,
   9:39. that can lightly *speak evil* of me.
Acts19: 9. but *spake evil* of that way

κακοπάθεια, *kakopathia.*

Jas. 5:10. an example of *suffering affliction,*

κακοπαθέω, *kakopatheo.*

2Ti. 2: 3. therefore *endure hardness,*
   9. Wherein I *suffer trouble,* as an
   4: 5. *endure afflictions,* do the work of
Jas. 5:13. *Is* any among you *afflicted?*

κακοποιέω, *kakopoyeo.*

Mar. 3: 4. or *to do evil?*
Lu. 6: 9. to do good, or *to do evil?*
1Pet. 3:17. for well doing, than for *evil doing.*
3Joh. 11. he *that doeth evil* hath not seen God.

κακοποιός, *kakopoyos.*

Joh.18:30. If he were not a *malefactor,*
1Pet. 2:12. speak against you as *evildoers,*
   14. for the punishment of *evildoers,*
   3:16. speak evil of you, as of *evildoers,*
   4:15. or (as) an *evildoer,*

κακὸς, & τὸ κακὸν, *kakos,* & *to kakon.*

Mat 21:41. miserably destroy those *wicked* men,

Mat 24:48. if that *evil* servant shall say
   27:23. Why, what *evil* hath he done?
Mar 7:21. *evil* thoughts, adulteries,
   15:14. Why, what *evil* hath he done?
Lu. 16:25. likewise Lazarus *evil* things:
   23:22. Why, what *evil* hath he done?
Joh.18:23. bear witness of the *evil:*
Acts 9:13. of this man. how much *evil* he
   16:28. Do thyself no *harm:*
   23: 9. We find no *evil* in this man:
   28: 5. and felt no *harm.*
Ro. 1:30. inventors of *evil* things,
   2: 9. upon every soul of man that doeth *evil,*
   3: 8. that we say, Let us do *evil,*
   7:19. but the *evil* which I would not,
   21. *evil* is present with me.
   9:11. done any good or *evil,*
   12:17. Recompense to no man *evil* for *evil.*
   21. Be not overcome of *evil,* but overcome
    evil with good.
   13: 3. not a terror to good works, but to the *evil.*
   4. But if thou do that which is *evil,*
   — wrath upon him that doeth *evil.*
   10. Love worketh no *ill*
   14:20. but (it is) *evil* for that man
   16:19. and simple concerning *evil.*
1Co.10: 6. should not lust after *evil* things,
   13: 5. is not easily provoked, thinketh no *evil;*
   15:33. *evil* communications corrupt
2Co. 5:10. whether (it be) good or *bad.*
   13: 7. that ye do no *evil;*
Phi. 3: 2. beware of *evil* workers,
Col. 3: 5. *evil* concupiscence, and covetousness,
1Th 5:15. See that none render *evil* for *evil*
1Ti. 6:10. love of money is the root of all *evil:*
2Ti. 4:14. did me much *evil:*
Tit. 1:12. *evil* beasts, slow bellies.
Heb 5:14. to discern both good and *evil.*
Jas. 1:13. God cannot be tempted with *evil,*
   3: 8. an unruly *evil,* full of deadly poison.
1Pet.3: 9. Not rendering *evil* for *evil,*
   10. refrain his tongue from *evil,*
   11. Let him eschew *evil,*
   12. (is) against them that do *evil.*
3Joh. 11. follow not that which is *evil,*
Rev 2: 2. not bear them which are *evil:*
   16: 2. there fell a *noisome* and grievous sore

κακοῦργος, *kakourgos.*

Lu. 23:32. two other, *malefactors,* led with him
   33. crucified him, and the *malefactors,*
   39. one of the *malefactors*
2Ti. 2: 9. as an *evil doer,* (even) unto bonds;

κακουχούμενος, *kakoukoumenos.*

Heb 11:37. destitute, afflicted, *tormented;*
   13: 3. (and) them *which suffer adversity,*

κακόω, *kakoō.*

Acts 7: 6. and *entreat* (them) *evil* four hundred
   years.
   19. and *evil entreated* our fathers,
   12: 1. *to vex* certain of the church.
   14: 2. and *made* their minds *evil affected*
   18:10. no man shall set on thee *to hurt* thee:
1Pet.3:13. who (is) he *that will harm* you,

κακῶς, kakōs. adv.

Mat. 4:24. unto him all *sick* people (lit. those having
themselves *sickly*)
8:16. and healed all that were *sick :* (lit. those,
&c.)
9:12. but they that are *sick*. (lit. those, &c.)
14:35. all that were *diseased ;* (lit. those, &c.)
15:22. is *grievously* vexed with a devil.
17:15. and *sore* vexed: for ofttimes
21:41. *miserably* destroy those wicked
Mar 1:32. all that were *diseased*, (lit. those, &c.)
34. he healed many that were *sick*
2:17. but they that are *sick :*
6:55. in beds those that were *sick*,
Lu. 5:31. but they that are *sick*.
7: 2. was *sick*, and ready to die.
Joh.18:23. If I have spoken *evil*,
Acts23: 5. Thou shalt not speak *evil* of the
Jas. 4: 3. receive not, because ye ask *amiss*,

κάκωσις, kakōsis.

Acts 7:34. I have seen the *affliction* of my people

κάλαμη, kalamee.

1Co. 3:12. gold, silver, precious stones, wood, hay,
stubble ;

κάλαμος, kalamos.

Mat.11: 7. A *reed* shaken with the wind?
12:20. A bruised *reed* shall he not break,
27:29. and a *reed* in his right hand:
30. and took the *reed*, and smote him
48. and put (it) on a *reed*,
Mar 15:19. smote him on the head with a *reed*,
36. and put (it) on a *reed*,
Lu. 7:24. A *reed* shaken with the wind?
3Joh. 13. not with ink and *pen* write unto thee:
Rev.11: 1. given me a *reed* like unto a rod:
21:15. had a golden *reed* to measure
16. he measured the city with the *reed*,

καλέω, kaleo.

Mat. 1:21. and thou *shalt call* his name JESUS:
23. they *shall call* his name Emmanuel,
25. and he *called* his name JESUS.
2: 7. privily *called* the wise men,
15. Out of Egypt *have I called* my son.
23. He *shall be called* a Nazarene.
4:21. and he *called* them.
5: 9. they *shall be called* the children of God.
19. he *shall be called* the least in the kingdom
— the same *shall be called* great in
9:13. I am not come *to call* the righteous,
10:25. If they *have called* the master
20: 8. *Call* the labourers, and give them
21:13. My house *shall be called*
22: 3. sent forth his servants *to call* them *that
were bidden*
4. Tell them *which are bidden*,
8. they *which were bidden* were not worthy.
9. *bid* to the marriage.
43. *doth* David in spirit *call* him Lord,
45. If David then *call* him Lord,
23: 7. and *to be called* of men, Rabbi,
8, *be* not ye *called* Rabbi:
9. And *call* no (man) your father

Mat.23:10. Neither *be* ye *called* masters:
25:14. *called* his own servants,
27: 8. that field *was called*,
Mar 1:20. straightway he *called* them:
2:17. came not *to call* the righteous,
11:17. My house *shall be called* of all
Lu. 1:13. thou *shalt call* his name John.
31. and *shalt call* his name JESUS.
32. and *shall be called* the Son of the
35. *shall be called* the Son of God.
36. with her, *who was called* barren.
59. and they *called* him Zacharias,
60. but he *shall be called* John.
61. kindred that *is called* by this
62. how he would have him *called*.
76. *shalt be called* the prophet
2: 4. which *is called* Bethlehem;
21. his name *was called* JESUS, *which was so
named* of the angel
23. *shall be called* holy to the Lord;
5:32. I came not *to call* the righteous,
6:15. and Simon *called* Zelotes,
46. And why *call* ye me, Lord, Lord,
7:11. he went into a city *called* Nain;
39. the Pharisee *which had bidden* him
8: 2. Mary *called* Magdalene, out of
9:10. belonging to the city *called* Bethsaida.
10:39. she had a sister *called* Mary,
14: 7. a parable to those *which were bidden*,
8. When thou *art bidden* of any (man)
— than thou be *bidden* of him;
9. And he *that bade* thee and him come
10. when thou *art bidden*, go and sit
— when he *that bade* thee cometh,
12. Then said he also to him *that bade* him,
13. when thou makest a feast, *call* the poor,
16, a great supper, and *bade* many:
17. to say to them *that were bidden*,
24. none of those men *which were bidden*
15:19. no more worthy *to be called* thy son:
21. no more worthy *to be called* thy son.
19: 2. a man *named* (lit. *called*).
13. And he *called* his ten servants, *and*
29. at the mount *called* (the mount) of Olives,
20:44. David therefore *calleth* him Lord,
21:37. *that is called* (the mount) of Olives.
22:25. upon them *are called* benefactors.
23:33. *which is called* Calvary,
Joh. 1:42(43). thou *shalt be called* Cephas,
2: 2. Jesus *was called*, and his disciples,
10: 3. and he *calleth* his own sheep by
Acts 1:12. from the mount *called* Olivet,
19. insomuch as that field *is called*
23. Joseph *called* Barsabas, who
3:11. the porch *that is called* Solomon's,
4:18. And they *called* them, and commanded
7:58. at a young man's feet, *whose name was*
(lit. *called*) Saul.
9:11. the street *which is called* Straight,
10: 1. *called* the Italian (band),
13: 1. and Simeon *that was called* Niger,
14:12. they *called* Barnabas, Jupiter ;
15:37. John, *whose surname was* (lit. *who was
called*) Mark.
24: 2. And *when* he *was called forth*,
27: 8. a place *which is called* The fair havens;
14. wind, *called* Euroclydon.
16. island *which is called* Clauda,
28: 1. the island *was called* Melita.
Ro. 4:17. and *calleth* those things which be not
8:30. them he also *called :* and whom he *called*,
them he also justified:

P   7. In Isaac *shall* thy seed *be called.*

   l. but of him *that calleth ;*

   l. Even us, whom he *hath called,*

   ‒.i. I *will call* them my people,

   26. there *shall* they *be called* the

1Co. 1: 9. by whom ye *were called* unto

   7:15. but God *hath called* us to peace.

   17. as the Lord *hath called* every

   18. *Is* any man *called* being circumcised?

   — *Is* any *called* in uncircumcision?

   20. Let every man abide in the same calling

     wherein he *was called.*

   21. *Art* thou *called* (being) a servant?

   22. For he *that is called* in the Lord, (being) a

     servant,

   — he *that is called,* (being) free,

   24. wherein he *is called,*

   10:27. If any of them that believe not *bid* you

   15: 9. am not meet *to be called* an apostle,

Gal. 1: 6. from him *that called* you into

   15. and *called* (me) by his grace,

   5: 8. not of him *that calleth* you.

   13. ye *have been called* unto liberty ;

Eph. 4: 1. wherewith ye *are called,*

   4. even as ye *are called* in one hope of your

Col. 3:15. to the which also ye *are called*

1Th. 2:12. worthy of God, *who hath called* you

   4: 7. God *hath* not *called* us unto uncleanness,

   5:24. Faithful (is) he *that calleth* you,

2Th. 2:14. he *called* you by our gospel,

1Ti. 6:12. whereunto thou *art* also *called,*

2Ti. 1: 9. and *called* (us) with an holy calling,

Heb 2:11. not ashamed *to call* them brethren,

   3:13. while it *is called* To day ;

   5: 4. but he *that is called* of God,

   9:15. they *which are called* might receive

   11: 8. Abraham, *when* he *was called*

   18. in Isaac *shall* thy seed *be called :*

Jas. 2:23. he *was called* the Friend of God.

1Pet.1:15. as he *which hath called* you is holy,

   2: 9. of him *who hath called* you out of

   21. hereunto *were* ye *called :*

   3: 6. Sara obeyed Abraham, *calling* him lord:

   9. that ye *are* thereunto *called,*

   5:10. the God of all grace, *who hath called* us

2Pet.1: 3. of him *that hath called* us to glory

1Joh.3: 1. that we *should be called* the sons of God:

Rev. 1: 9. the isle *that is called* Patmos,

   11: 8. which spiritually *is called* Sodom

   12: 9. that old serpent, *called* the Devil,

   16:16. *called* in the Hebrew tongue Armageddon.

   19: 9. (are) they *which are called* unto

   11. (was) *called* Faithful and True,

   13. his name *is called* The Word of God.

καλλιέλαιος, *kallielaios.*

Ro. 11:24. into a *good* olive tree :

κάλλιον see καλῶς.

καλοδιδάσκαλος, *kalodidaskalos.*

Tit. 2: 3. not given to much wine, *teachers of good*
     things ;

καλοποιῶν, *kalopoiōn.*

2Th. 3:13. be not weary in *well doing.*

καλός, *kalos.*

Mat. 3:10. bringeth not forth *good* fruit

   5:16. that they may see your *good* works,

   7:17. bringeth forth *good* fruit ;

   18. a corrupt tree bring forth *good* fruit.

   19. that bringeth not forth *good* fruit

   12:33. Either make the tree *good,* and his fruit
     good ;

   13: 8. other fell into *good* ground,

   23. seed into the *good* ground

   24. a man which sowed *good* seed

   27. Sir, didst not thou sow *good* seed

   37. He that soweth the *good* seed

   38. the *good* seed are the children

   45. merchant man, seeking *goodly* pearls:

   48. gathered the *good* into vessels,

   15:26. It is not *meet* to take the children's

   17: 4. Lord, it is *good* for us to be here:

   18: 8. it is *better* for thee to enter into

   9. it is *better* for thee to enter into life

   26:10. she hath wrought a *good* work upon

   24. it had been *good* for that man

Mar. 4: 8. And other fell on *good* ground,

   20. which are sown on *good* ground ;

   7:27. it is not *meet* to take the children's

   9: 5. it is *good* for us to be here:

   42. it is *better* for him that a

   43. it is *better* for thee to enter into

   45. it is *better* for thee to enter halt

   47. it is *better* for thee to enter into

   50. Salt (is) *good :* but if the salt

   14: 6. she hath wrought a *good* work

   21. *good* were it for that man

Lu. 3: 9. not forth *good* fruit is hewn

   6:38. *good* measure, pressed down,

   43. For a *good* tree bringeth not forth

   — bring forth *good* fruit.

   8:15. But that on the *good* ground are they,
     which in an *honest* and good heart,

   9:33. it is *good* for us to be here:

   14:34. Salt (is) *good :* but if the salt

   21:5. adorned with *goodly* stones

Joh. 2:10. doth set forth *good* wine ;

   — thou hast kept the *good* wine

   10:11. I am the *good* shepherd: the *good* shepherd
     giveth his life

   14. I am the *good* shepherd,

   32. Many *good* works have I shewed

   33. For a *good* work we stone thee not ;

Acts27: 8. which is called The *fair* havens;

Ro. 7:16. I consent unto the law that (it is) *good.*

   18. to perform that which is *good*

   21. when I would do *good,*

   12:17. Provide things *honest* in the

   14:21. (It is) *good* neither to eat

1Co. 5: 6. Your glorying (is) not *good.*

   7: 1. (It is) *good* for a man not to

   8. It is *good* for them if they

   26. that this is *good* for the present

   — (it is) *good* for a man so to be.

   9:15. (it were) better for me to die (lit. *good*
     for me rather to die), than

2Co. 8:21. Providing for *honest* things,

   13: 7. ye should do that which is *honest,*

Gal. 4:18. But (it is) *good* to be zealously affected
     always in (a) *good* (thing),

   6: 9. let us not be weary in *well* doing :

1Th. 5:21. hold fast that which is *good.*

1Ti. 1: 8. we know that the law (is) *good,*

   18. mightest war a *good* warfare ;

   2: 3. For this (is) *good* and acceptable

1 Ti. 3: 1. he desireth a *good* work.
     7. must have a *good* report of them
   13. to themselves a *good* degree,
   4: 4. For every creature of God (is) *good*,
     6. thou shalt be a *good* minister
     — of faith and of *good* doctrine,
   5: 4. for that is *good* and acceptable
   10. Well reported of for *good* works ;
   25. also the *good* works (of some)
   6: 12. Fight the *good* fight of faith,
     — professed a *good* profession
   13. witnessed a *good* confession ;
   18. that they be rich in *good* works,
   19. a *good* foundation against the time
2 Ti. 1: 14. That *good* thing which was committed
   2: 3. as a *good* soldier of Jesus Christ.
   4: 7. I have fought a *good* fight,
Tit. 2: 7. a pattern of *good* works:
   14. zealous of *good* works.
   3: 8. to maintain *good* works. These things are
     good and profitable
   14. to maintain *good* works
Heb 5: 14. to discern both *good* and evil.
   6: 5. have tasted the *good* word
   10: 24. provoke unto love and to *good* works:
   13: 9. a *good* thing that the heart be
   18. we trust we have a *good* conscience,
Jas. 2: 7. that *worthy* name by the which
   3: 13. out of a *good* conversation
   4: 17. to him that knoweth to do *good*,
1 Pet. 2: 12. conversation *honest* among the
     — they may by (your) *good* works,
   4: 10. as *good* stewards of the manifold grace of

κάλυμμα, *kalumma.*

2 Co. 3: 13. (which) put a *vail* over his face,
   14. the same *vail* untaken away
   15. the *vail* is upon their heart.
   16. the *vail* shall be taken away.

καλύπτω, *kalupto.*

Mat. 8: 24. the ship was *covered* with the waves:
   10: 26. there is nothing *covered*, that shall
Lu. 8: 16. *covereth* it with a vessel,
   23: 30. and to the hills, *Cover* us.
2 Co. 4: 3. But if our gospel be *hid*, it is *hid* to them
     that are lost:
Jas. 5: 20. and *shall hide* a multitude of
1 Pet. 4: 8. *shall cover* the multitude of sins.

καλῶς & κάλλιον, *kalōs* & *kallion.*

Mat. 5: 44. do *good* to them that hate you,
   12: 12. it is lawful to do *well* on the
   15: 7. *well* did Esaias prophesy of
Mar 7: 6. *Well* hath Esaias prophesied of
   9. *Full well* ye reject the commandment
   37. He hath done all things *well:*
   12: 28. that he had answered them *well*,
   32. *Well*, Master, thou hast said
   16: 18. and they shall recover. (lit. shall be *well*)
Lu. 6: 26. when all men shall speak *well*
   27. do *good* to them which hate you,
   20: 39. Master, thou hast *well* said.
Joh. 4: 17. Thou hast *well* said,
   8: 48. Say we not *well* that thou art
   13: 13. ye say *well*; for (so) I am.
   18: 23. but if *well*, why smitest thou
Acts 10: 33. thou hast *well* done that thou

Acts 25: 10. as thou *very well* knowest.
   28: 25. *Well* spake the Holy Ghost
Ro. 11: 20. *Well*; because of unbelief
1 Co. 7: 37. will keep his virgin, doeth *well*.
   38. in marriage doeth *well;*
   14: 17. thou verily givest thanks *well*,
2 Co. 11: 4. ye might *well* bear with (him).
Gal. 4: 17. affect you, (but) not *well;*
   5: 7. Ye did run *well;*
Phi. 4: 14. ye have *well* done,
1 Ti. 3: 4. One that ruleth *well* his own
   12. and their own houses *well*.
   13. used the office of a deacon *well*
   5: 17. Let the elders that rule *well*
Heb 13: 18. willing to live *honestly.*
Jas. 2: 3. Sit thou here *in a good place ;*
   8. love thy neighbour as thyself, ye do *well:*
   19. one God; thou doest *well:*
2 Pet. 1: 19. ye do *well* that ye take heed,
3 Joh. 6. thou shalt do *well:*

κἀμέ see in κἀγώ.

κάμηλος, *kameelos.*

Mat. 3: 4. his raiment of *camel's* hair,
   19: 24. easier for a *camel* to go through
   23: 24. and swallow a *camel*.
Mar. 1: 6. clothed with *camel's* hair,
   10: 25. easier for a *camel* to go through
Lu. 18: 25. easier for a *camel* to go through

κάμινος, *kaminos.*

Mat. 13: 42. into a *furnace* of fire:
   50. into the *furnace* of fire:
Rev. 1: 15. as if they burned in a *furnace;*
   9: 2. as the smoke of a great *furnace;*

καμμύω, *kammuo.*

Mat. 13: 15. their eyes they *have closed;*
Acts 28: 27. their eyes have they *closed;*

κάμνω, *kamno.*

Heb 12: 3. lest ye *be wearied* and faint
Jas. 5: 15. shall save the *sick*,
Rev. 2: 3. hast laboured, and *hast* not *fainted*.

κἀμοί see in κἀγώ.

κάμπτω, *kampto.*

Ro. 11: 4. who *have* not *bowed* the knee to
   14: 11. every knee *shall bow* to me,
Eph 3: 14. For this cause I *bow* my knees
Phi. 2: 10. of Jesus every knee *should bow*,

κἄν, *kan.*

Mat. 21: 21. but *also if* ye shall say unto
   26: 35. *Though* I should die with thee,

Mar 5:28. *If* I may touch *but* his clothes,
　　6:56. *if* it were *but* the border of
　　16:18. *and if* they drink any deadly
Lu. 13: 9. *And if* it bear fruit, (well):
Joh. 8:14. *Though* I bear record of myself,
　　10:38. *though* ye believe not me,
　　11:25. *though* he were dead,
Acts 5:15. that *at the least* the shadow
2Co.11:16. if otherwise, *yet* as a fool
Heb 12:20. *And if so much as* a beast touch
Jas. 5:15. *and if* he have committed sins,

κανών, kanōn.

2Co.10.13. but according to the measure of the *rule*
　　　　which God
　　15. according to our *rule* abundantly,
　　16. in another man's *line* of things
Gal. 6:16. as walk according to this *rule,*
Phi. 3:16. let us walk by the same *rule,*

καπηλεύω, kapeeluō.

2Co. 2:17. not as many, *which corrupt* the word of

καπνός, kapnos.

Acts 2:19. blood, and fire, and vapour of *smoke:*
Rev 8: 4. And the *smoke* of the incense,
　　9: 2. there arose a *smoke* out of the pit, as the
　　　　smoke of a great furnace;
　　— by reason of the *smoke* of the pit.
　　3. there came out of the *smoke* locusts
　　17. issued fire and *smoke* and brimstone,
　　18. men killed, by the fire, and by the *smoke,*
　　14:11. And the *smoke* of their torment
　　15: 8. was filled with *smoke*
　　18: 9. shall see the *smoke* of her burning,
　　18. when they saw the *smoke* of her
　　19: 3. And her *smoke* rose up for ever and ever.

καρδία, kardia.

Mat. 5: 8. Blessed (are) the pure in *heart:*
　　28. adultery with her already in his *heart.*
　　6:21. there will your *heart* be also.
　　9: 4. Wherefore think ye evil in your *hearts?*
　　11:29. I am meek and lowly in *heart:*
　　12:34. of the *heart* the mouth speaketh.
　　35. out of the good treasure of the *heart*
　　40. in the *heart* of the earth.
　　13:15. this people's *heart* is waxed gross,
　　— understand with (their) *heart,*
　　19. away that which was sown in his *heart.*
　　15: 8. but their *heart* is far from me.
　　18. come forth from the *heart;*
　　19. out of the *heart* proceed evil
　　18:35. if ye from your *hearts* forgive not
　　22:37. the Lord thy God with all thy *heart,*
　　24:48. if that evil servant shall say in his *heart,*
Mar. 2: 6. and reasoning in their *hearts,*
　　8. Why reason ye these things in your *hearts?*
　　3: 5. grieved for the hardness of their *hearts,*
　　4:15. that was sown in their *hearts.*
　　6:52. for their *heart* was hardened.
　　7: 6. but their *heart* is far from me.
　　19. it entereth not into his *heart,*
　　21. out of the *heart* of men,
　　8:17. have ye your *heart* yet hardened?

Mar 11:23. and shall not doubt in his *heart,*
　　12:30. love the Lord thy God with all thy *heart,*
　　33. And to love him with all the *heart,*
Lu. 1:17. to turn the *hearts* of the fathers
　　51. the imagination of their *hearts.*
　　66. laid (them) up in their *hearts,*
　　2:19. and pondered (them) in her *heart.*
　　35. the thoughts of many *hearts* may be
　　51. kept all these sayings in her *heart.*
　　3:15. all men mused in their *hearts*
　　4:18. to heal the broken*hearted,*
　　5:22. What reason ye in your *hearts?*
　　6:45. out of the good treasure of his *heart*
　　— out of the evil treasure of his *heart*
　　— of the *heart* his mouth speaketh.
　　8:12. away the word out of their *hearts,*
　　15. in an honest and good *heart,*
　　9:47. perceiving the thought of their *heart,*
　　10:27. love the Lord thy God with all thy *heart,*
　　12:34. there will your *heart* be also.
　　45. if that servant say in his *heart,*
　　16:15. God knoweth your *hearts:*
　　21:14. Settle (it) therefore in your *hearts,*
　　34. lest at any time your *hearts* be
　　24:25. slow of *heart* to believe all
　　32. Did not our *heart* burn
　　38. why do thoughts arise in your *hearts?*
Joh. 12:40. and hardened their *heart;*
　　— nor understand with (their) *heart,*
　　13: 2. now put into the *heart* of Judas
　　14: 1. Let not your *heart* be troubled:
　　27. Let not your *heart* be troubled,
　　16: 6. sorrow hath filled your *heart.*
　　22. and your *heart* shall rejoice,
Acts 2:26. Therefore did my *heart* rejoice,
　　37. they were pricked in their *heart,*
　　46. and singleness of *heart,*
　　4:32. were of one *heart* and of one soul:
　　5: 3. why hath Satan filled thine *heart* to lie
　　4. conceived this thing in thine *heart?*
　　7:23. it came into his *heart* to visit
　　39. in their *hearts* turned back
　　51. and uncircumcised in *heart*
　　54. they were cut to the *heart,*
　　8:21. thy *heart* is not right in the
　　22. the thought of thine *heart* may
　　37. If thou believest with all thine *heart,*
　　11:23. that with purpose of *heart*
　　13:22. a man after mine own *heart,*
　　14:17. filling our *hearts* with food and
　　15: 9. purifying their *hearts* by faith.
　　16:14. whose *heart* the Lord opened,
　　21:13. to weep and to break mine *heart?*
　　28:27. For the *heart* of this people
　　— and understand with (their) *heart,*
Ro. 1:21. and their foolish *heart* was darkened.
　　24. through the lusts of their own *hearts,*
　　2: 5. thy hardness and impenitent *heart*
　　15. the law written in their *hearts,*
　　29. circumcision (is that) of the *heart,*
　　5: 5. shed abroad in our *hearts* by
　　6:17. have obeyed from the *heart*
　　8:27. he that searcheth the *hearts*
　　9: 2. and continual sorrow in my *heart.*
　　10: 1. my *heart's* desire and prayer
　　6. Say not in thine *heart,*
　　8. in thy mouth, and in thy *heart:*
　　9. and shalt believe in thine *heart*
　　10. For with the *heart* man believeth
　　16:18. deceive the *hearts* of the simple.
1Co. 2: 9. neither have entered into the *heart* of
　　4: 5. the counsels of the *hearts:*

1Co. 7:37. he that standeth stedfast in his *heart,*
   — and hath so decreed in his *heart*
  14:25. are the secrets of his *heart*
2Co. 1:22. the earnest of the Spirit in our *hearts.*
  2: 4. and anguish of *heart* I wrote
  3: 2. written in our *hearts,*
   3. but in fleshy tables of the *heart.*
  15. the vail is upon their *heart.*
  4: 6. hath shined in our *hearts,*
  5:12. in appearance, and not in *heart.*
  6:11. our *heart* is enlarged.
  7: 3. ye are in our *hearts* to die and
  8:16. care into the *heart* of Titus for you.
  9: 7. as he purposeth in his *heart,*
Gal. 4: 6. the Spirit of his Son into your *hearts,*
Eph. 3:17. That Christ may dwell in your *hearts*
  4:18. of the blindness of their *heart :*
  5:19. making melody in your *heart*
  6: 5. in singleness of your *heart,*
  22. he might comfort your *hearts.*
Phi. 1: 7. I have you in my *heart ;*
  4: 7. shall keep your *hearts* and minds
Col. 2: 2. That their *hearts* might be comforted,
  3:15. let the peace of God rule in your *hearts*
  16. singing with grace in your *hearts*
  22. but in singleness of *heart,*
  4: 8. and comfort your *hearts ;*
1Th. 2: 4. but God, which trieth our *hearts.*
  17. in presence, not in *heart,*
  3:13. he may stablish your *hearts*
2Th. 2:17. Comfort your *hearts,* and stablish
  3: 5. the Lord direct your *hearts*
1Ti. 1: 5. is charity out of a pure *heart,*
2Ti. 2:22. on the Lord out of a pure *heart.*
Heb. 3: 8. Harden not your *hearts,*
  10. They do alway err in (their) *heart ;*
  12. an evil *heart* of unbelief,
  15. harden not your *hearts,*
  4: 7. harden not your *hearts.*
  12. thoughts and intents of the *heart.*
  8:10. and write them in their *hearts :*
  10:16. I will put my laws into their *hearts,*
  22. Let us draw near with a true *heart*
  — having our *hearts* sprinkled
  13: 9. a good thing that the *heart* be
Jas. 1:26. but deceiveth his own *heart,*
  3:14. and strife in your *hearts,*
  4: 8. and purify (your) *hearts,*
  5: 5. ye have nourished your *hearts,*
  8. stablish your *hearts :* for
1Pet.1:22. love one another with a pure *heart*
  3: 4. the hidden man of the *heart,*
  15. sanctify the Lord God in your *hearts :*
2Pet.1:19. the day star arise in your *hearts :*
  2:14. an *heart* they have exercised with covetous
1Joh.3:19. shall assure our *hearts* before him.
  20. For if our *heart* condemn us, God is greater
   than our *heart,*
  21. if our *heart* condemn us not,
Rev. 2:23. he which searcheth the reins and *hearts :*
  17:17. For God hath put in their *hearts*
  18: 7. saith in her *heart,* I sit a queen, and am
   no widow,

καρδιογνώστης, *kardiognōstees.*

Acts 1:24. Thou, Lord, *which knowest the hearts*
  15: 8. And God, *which knoweth the hearts,*

καρπός, *karpos.*

Mat. 3: 8. Bring forth therefore *fruits* meet

Mat. 3:10. which bringeth not forth good *fruit*
  7:16. Ye shall know them by their *fruits.*
  17. good tree bringeth forth good *fruit ;* but
   a corrupt tree bringeth forth evil *fruit.*
  18. bring forth evil *fruit,*
  — bring forth good *fruit.*
  19. that bringeth not forth good *fruit*
  20. by their *fruits* ye shall know them.
  12:33. tree good, and his *fruit* good ;
  — tree corrupt, and his *fruit* corrupt: for the
   tree is known by (his) *fruit.*
  13: 8. and brought forth *fruit,*
  26. blade was sprung up, and brought forth
   fruit,
  21:19. Let no *fruit* grow on thee
  34. when the time of the *fruit* drew near,
  — might receive the *fruits* of it.
  41. render him the *fruits* in their seasons.
  43. bringing forth the *fruits* thereof.
Mar 4: 7. and it yielded no *fruit.*
  8. and did yield *fruit*
  29. when the *fruit* is brought forth,
  11:14. No man eat *fruit* of thee hereafter
  12: 2. from the husbandmen of the *fruit* of
Lu. 1:42. blessed (is) the *fruit* of thy womb.
  3: 8. Bring forth therefore *fruits* worthy
  9. bringeth not forth good *fruit* is hewn
  6:43. bringeth not forth corrupt *fruit ;* neither
   doth a corrupt tree...good *fruit.*
  44. every tree is known by his own *fruit.*
  8: 8. sprang up, and bare *fruit* an hundredfold.
  12:17. no room where to bestow my *fruits ;*
  13: 6. he came and sought *fruit* thereon,
  7. these three years I come seeking *fruit*
  9. And if it bear *fruit,* (well):
  20:10. that they should give him of the *fruit*
Joh. 4:36. and gathereth *fruit* unto life eternal:
  12:24. if it die, it bringeth forth much *fruit.*
  15: 2. that beareth not *fruit* he taketh away:
  — that beareth *fruit,* he purgeth it, that it
   may bring forth more *fruit.*
  4. As the branch cannot bear *fruit* of itself,
  5. the same bringeth forth much *fruit :*
  8. my Father glorified, that ye bear much
   fruit ;
  16. that ye should go and bring forth *fruit,*
   and (that) your *fruit* should remain:
Acts 2:30. that of the *fruit* of his loins,
Ro. 1:13. that I might have some *fruit* among you
  6:21. What *fruit* had ye then in those things
  22. ye have your *fruit* unto holiness,
  15:28. and have sealed to them this *fruit,*
1Co. 9: 7. and eateth not of the *fruit* thereof?
Gal. 5:22. But the *fruit* of the Spirit is love,
Eph. 5: 9. For the *fruit* of the Spirit (is) in all
Phi. 1:11. Being filled with the *fruits* of
  22. this (is) the *fruit* of my labour:
  4:17. but I desire *fruit* that may abound
2Ti. 2: 6. must be first partaker of the *fruits.*
Heb 12:11. it yieldeth the peaceable *fruit* of
  13:15. the *fruit* of (our) lips giving thanks
Jas. 3:17. full of mercy and good *fruits,*
  18. And the *fruit* of righteousness is sown in
  5: 7. waiteth for the precious *fruit* of the earth,
  18. the earth brought forth her *fruit.*
Rev.22: 2. which bare twelve (manner of) *fruits,*
  (and) yielded her *fruit* every month:

καρποφορέω, *karpophoreo.*

Mat.13:23. which also *beareth fruit,*

Mar. 4:20. and *bring forth fruit*, some thirtyfold,
  28. the earth *bringeth forth fruit* of herself ;
Lu.   8:15. keep (it), and *bring forth fruit* with
Ro.   7: 4. that we *should bring forth fruit* unto God.
      5. *to bring forth fruit* unto death.
Col. 1: 6. and *bringeth forth fruit*, as (it doth)
      10. *being fruitful* in every good work,

καρποφόρος, *karpophoros.*

Acts14:17. and *fruitful* seasons, filling

καρτερέω, *kartereo.*

Heb 11:27. he *endured*, as seeing him who is invisible.

κάρφος, *karphos.*

Mat. 7: 3. the *mote* that is in thy brother's eye,
      4. Let me pull out the *mote*
      5. to cast out the *mote* out of
Lu.   6:41. the *mote* that is in thy brother's eye,
      42. let me pull out the *mote*
      — to pull out the *mote* that is in

κατά, *kata.* prep.

Mat. 1:20. appeared unto him *in*ᵃ a dream,
      2:12. warned of God *in*ᵃ a dream
      13. appeareth to Joseph *in*ᵃa dream,
      16. *according to*ᵃ the time which
      19. appeareth *in*ᵃ a dream to Joseph
      22. being warned of God *in*ᵃ a dream,
      5:11. say all manner of evil *against*ᵍ you
      23. that thy brother hath ought *against*ᵍ thee ;
      8:32. ran violently *down*ᵍ a steep place
      9:29. *According to*ᵃ your faith be it unto you.
      10:35. to set a man at variance *against*ᵍ his father,
        and the daughter *against*ᵍ her mother,
      — *against*ᵍ her mother in law.
      12:14. held a council *against*ᵍ him,
      25. kingdom divided *against*ᵍ itself
      — city or house divided *against*ᵍ itself
      30. He that is not with me is *against*ᵍ me ;
      32. speaketh a word *against*ᵍ the Son of man,
      — but whosoever speaketh *against*ᵍ the Holy
        Ghost,
      14:13. into a desert place *apart :*ᵃ (κατ' ἰδιαν)
      23. a mountain *apart*ᵃ to pray: (κατ' ἰδιαν)
      16:27. reward every man *according to*ᵃ his works.
      17: 1. bringeth them up into an high mountain
        *apart,*ᵃ
      19. came the disciples to Jesus *apart,*ᵃ
      19: 3. to put away his wife *for*ᵃ every cause ?
      20:11. murmured *against*ᵍ the goodman of
      17. took the twelve disciples *apart*ᵃ
      23: 3. but do not ye *after*ᵃ their works:
      24: 3. disciples came unto him private*ly,*ᵃ
      7. earthquakes, *in divers* (lit. *throughout*ᵃ)
        places.
      25:15. to every man *according to*ᵃ his several
      26:55. I sat dai*ly*ᵃ with you
      59. false witness *against*ᵍ Jesus,
      63. I adjure thee *by*ᵍ the living God,
      27: 1. took counsel *against*ᵍ Jesus
      15. Now *at*ᵃ (that) feast the governor
      19. I have suffered many things this day *in*ᵃ a
        dream because of him.

Mar. 1:27. for *with*ᵃ authority commandeth he
      3: 6. counsel with the Herodians *against*ᵍ him,
      4:34. when they were *alone,*ᵃ (κατ' ἰδιαν) he
      5:13. ran violently *down*ᵍ a steep place
      6:31. Come ye yourselves *apart*ᵃ
      32. into a desert place by ship private*ly.*ᵃ
      7: 5. Why walk not thy disciples *according to*ᵃ
        the tradition
      33. he took him *aside*ᵃ from the
      9: 2. mountain *apart*ᵃ by themselves:
      28. disciples asked him private*ly,*ᵃ
      40. he that is not *against*ᵍ us is on
      11:25. if ye have ought *against*ᵍ any:
      13: 3. Andrew asked him private*ly,*ᵃ
      8. be earthquakes *in divers*ᵃ places,
      14: 3. and poured (it) *on*ᵍ his head.
      49. I was dai*ly*ᵃ with you in the
      55. for witness *against*ᵍ Jesus
      56. bare false witness *against*ᵍ him,
      57. and bare false witness *against*ᵍ him,
      15: 6 Now *at*ᵃ (that) feast he released
Lu.   1: 9. *According to*ᵃ the custom of the priest's
        office,
      18. Whereby*ᵃ shall I know this?
      38. be it unto me *according to*ᵃ thy word.
      2:22. *according to*ᵃ the law of Moses
      24. *according to*ᵃ that which is said
      27. *after*ᵃ the custom of the law,
      29. *according to*ᵃ thy word:
      31. *before*ᵃ the face of all people ;
      39. *according to*ᵃ the law of the Lord,
      41. every year (lit. *by*ᵃ year) at the feast
      42. *after*ᵃ the custom of the feast.
      4:14. *through*ᵍ all the region
      16. *as* his custom was, (lit. *according to*ᵃ his
        custom)
      6:23. *in*ᵃ the like manner did their
      26. so (lit. *according to*ᵃ these things) did
        their fathers to the false
      8: 1. that he went throughout *every*ᵃ city
      4. were come to him out of every city, (lit.
        *throughout*ᵃ the cities)
      33. the herd ran violently *down*ᵍ a steep place
      39. published *throughout*ᵃ the whole city
      9: 6. and went *through*ᵃ the towns,
      10. and went aside private*ly*ᵃ
      23. and take up his cross dai*ly,*ᵃ
      50. he that is not *against*ᵍ us
      10: 4. and salute no man *by*ᵃ the way.
      23. and said private*ly,*ᵃ Blessed
      31. And *by*ᵃ chance there came down a
      32. when he was *at*ᵃ the place,
      33. came where he was: (lit. *at*ᵃ it or *by*ᵃ
        him)
      11: 3. Give us day *by*ᵃ day our daily bread.
      23. is not with me is *against*ᵍ me:
      13:22. And he went *through*ᵃ the cities
      15:14. a mighty famine *in*ᵃ that land ;
      16:19. and fared sumptuously *every*ᵃ day:
      17:30. Even thus (lit. *according to*ᵃ these things)
        shall it be in the day
      19:47. And he taught dai*ly*ᵃ in the
      21:11. earthquakes shall be *in divers*ᵃ places,
      22:22. *as* it was determined: (lit. *according to*ᵃ
        that which was determined)
      39. *as*ᵃ he was wont, to the mount
      53. When I was dai*ly*ᵃ with you in
      23: 5. teaching *throughout*ᵍ all Jewry,
      14. whereof ye accuse him: (lit. *against*ᵍ him)
      17. release one unto them *at*ᵃ the feast.
      56. *according to*ᵃ the commandment.
Joh. 2: 6. *after*ᵃ the manner of the purifying

Joh. 5: 4. For an angel went down *at*ᵃ a certain

7:24. Judge not *according to*ᵃ the appearance,

8:15. Ye judge *after*ᵃ the flesh ;

10: 3. he calleth his own sheep *by*ᵃ name,

18:29. bring ye *against*ᵍ this man ?

31. judge him *according to*ᵃ your law .

19: 7. and *by*ᵃ our law he ought to die,

11. no power (at all) *against*ᵍ me,

21:25. if they should be written *every* one, (lit. *by*ᵃ one)

Acts 2:10. of Lybia *about*ᵃ Cyrene,

30. *according to*ᵃ the flesh, he would raise

46. continuing dai*ly*ᵃ with one accord

— breaking bread from house to house, (lit. *by*ᵃ house)

47. the Lord added to the church dai*ly*ᵃ

3: 2. whom they laid dai*ly*ᵃ at the gate

13. and denied him *in*ᵃ the presence of Pilate,

17. I wot that *through*ᵃ ignorance

22. in all things whatsoever (lit. *according to*ᵃ all things whatsoever) he shall say unto

4:26. gathered together *against*ᵍ the Lord, and *against*ᵍ his Christ.

5:15. the sick into the streets, (lit. *along*ᵃ the streets)

42. and *in every* house, (lit. *by*ᵃ house)

6:13. *against*ᵍ this holy place,

7:44. should make it *according to*ᵃ the fashion that he had seen.

8: 1. *throughout*ᵃ the regions of Judæa

3. entering into *every*ᵃ house,

26. Arise, and go *toward*ᵃ the south

36. as they went *on*ᵃ (their) way,

9:31. rest *throughout*ᵍ all Judæa

42. it was known *throughout*ᵍ all Joppa ;

10:37. was published *throughout*ᵍ all Judæa,

11: 1. and brethren that were *in*ᵃ Judæa

12: 1. Now *about*ᵃ that time Herod

13: 1. Now there were *in*ᵃ the church that

22. a man *after*ᵃ mine own heart,

23. *according to*ᵃ (his) promise

27. which are read)(ᵃ every sabbath

14: 1. that they went both *together* (lit. *at*ᵃ the same) into

2. evil affected *against*ᵍ the brethren.

23. had ordained them elders *in every*ᵃ church,

15:11. we shall be saved, *even as* they. (lit. *by*ᵃ the same way)

21. *in every*ᵃ city them that

— in the synagogues *every*ᵃ sabbath

23. *in*ᵃ Antioch and Syria and Cilicia:

36. *in every*ᵃ city where we have

16: 5. and increased in number dai*ly*.ᵃ

7. After they were come *to*ᵃ Mysia, they assayed to go *into*ᵃ Bithynia:

22. rose up together *against*ᵍ them :

25. And *at*ᵃ midnight Paul

17: 2. And Paul, *as* his manner was, (lit. *according to*ᵃ his manner)

11. searched the scriptures dai*ly*,ᵃ

17. in the market dai*ly*ᵃ with them

22. I perceive that *in*ᵃ all things

25. and breath, *and*ᵃ all things;

28. as certain also of your own poets (lit. of the poets *among*ᵃ you) have said,

18: 4. in the synagogue)(ᵃ every sabbath,

14. reason would (lit. *according to*ᵃ reason) that I should bear

15. and (*of*) your law, (lit. of the law *among*ᵃ you)

19: 9. disputing dai*ly*ᵃ in the school

16. and prevailed *against*ᵍ them,

Acts19:20. So mightily (lit. *with*ᵃ might) grew the word of God

23. And)(ᵃ the same time there arose

20:20. and *from* house *to* house, (lit. *by*ᵃ houses)

23. the Holy Ghost witnesseth *in every*ᵃ city,

21:19. he declared particularly (lit. *according to*ᵃ each one)

21. all the Jews which are *among*ᵃ the Gentiles

28. every where *against*ᵍ the people,

22: 3. taught *according to*ᵃ the perfect

12. a devout man *according to*ᵃ the law,

19. beat *in every*ᵃ synagogue

23: 3. to judge me *after*ᵃ the law,

19. and went (with him) aside privat*ely*,ᵃ

31. as it was commanded them, (lit. *according to*ᵃ the command)

24: 1. who informed the governor *against*ᵍ Paul.

5. among all the Jews *throughout*ᵃ the world,

6. would have judged *according to*ᵃ our law.

12. nor *in*ᵃ the city :

14. that *after*ᵃ the way which they call

— which are written *in*ᵃ the law

22. the uttermost of your matter. (lit. the things *among*ᵃ you)

25: 2. informed him *against*ᵍ Paul,

3. desired favour *against*ᵍ him,

— laying wait *in*ᵃ the way to kill him.

7. grievous complaints *against*ᵍ Paul,

14. Paul's cause unto the king, (lit. the things *about*ᵃ Paul)

15. (to have) judgment *against*ᵍ him.

16. face *to*ᵃ face, and have licence

23. with the chief captains, and principal men of the city, (lit. those *of*ᵃ eminence)

27. the crimes (laid) *against*ᵍ him.

26: 3. which are *among*ᵃ the Jews:

5. that *after*ᵃ the most straitest

11. oft *in*ᵃ every synagogue,

13. I saw *in*ᵃ the way

27: 2. meaning to sail *by* (lit. *along*ᵃ) the coasts of Asia ;

5. sailed over the sea *of* (lit. *near*ᵃ) Cilicia

7. come *over against*ᵃ Cnidus,

— Crete, *over against*ᵃ Salmone ;

12. *toward*ᵃ the south west and)(ᵃ north west.

14. there arose *against*ᵍ it a tempestuous

25. that it shall be *even as*ᵃ it was told me.

27. *about*ᵃ midnight the shipmen

28:16. to dwell *by*ᵃ himself

Ro. 1: 3. *according to*ᵃ the flesh ;

4. *according to*ᵃ the spirit

15. as much as *in*ᵃ me is,

2: 2. the judgment of God is *according to*ᵃ truth

5. But *after*ᵃ thy hardness and impenitent

6. *according to*ᵃ his deeds:

7. *by*ᵃ patient continuance

16. *according to*ᵃ my gospel.

3: 2. Much every way: (lit. *by*ᵃ every way)

5. I speak *as*ᵃ a man

4: 1. *as pertaining to*ᵃ the flesh,

4. is the reward not reckoned *of*ᵃ grace, but *of*ᵃ debt.

16. that (it might be) *by*ᵃ grace ;

18. *according to*ᵃ that which was

5: 6. yet without strength, *in*ᵃ due time

7:13. might become exceeding sinful. (lit. *according to*ᵃ excess)

22. *after*ᵃ the inward man:

8: 1. who walk not *after*ᵃ the flesh, but *after*ᵃ

4. who walk not *after*ᵃ the flesh, but *after*ᵃ

5. that are *after*ᵃ the flesh

— they that are *after*ᵃ the Spirit

Ro. 8:12. to live *after* ᵃ the flesh.
13. if ye live *after* ᵃ the flesh,
27. *according to* ᵃ (the will of) God.
28. *according to* ᵃ (his) purpose.
31. who (can be) *against* ᵍ us?
33 Who shall lay any thing to the charge *of* God's elect?
9: 3. *according to* ᵃ the flesh:
5. *as concerning* ᵃ the flesh
9. *At* ᵃ this time will I come,
11. *according to* ᵃ election might
10: 2. but not *according to* ᵃ knowledge.
11: 2. to God *against* ᵍ Israel, saying,
5. *according to* ᵃ the election of
21. spared not the natural branches, (lit branches *according to* ᵃ nature)
24. which is wild *by* ᵃ nature,
— which be the natural ᵃ (branches),
28. *As concerning* ᵃ the gospel,
— but *as touching* ᵃ the election,
12: 6. differing *according to* ᵃ the grace
— *according to* ᵃ the proportion of
14:15. now walkest thou not charitabl*y* ᵃ.
22. have (it) *to* ᵃ thyself before God.
15: 5. *according to* ᵃ Christ Jesus:
16: 5. that is *in* ᵃ their house.
25. *according to* ᵃ my gospel,
— *according to* ᵃ the revelation
26. *according to* ᵃ the commandment
1Co. 1:26. wise men *after* ᵃ the flesh,
2: 1. came not *with* ᵃ excellency of
3: 3. and walk *as* ᵃ men?
8. *according to* ᵃ his own labour.
10. *According to* ᵃ the grace of God
4: 6. for one *against* ᵍ another.
7: 6. I speak this *by* ᵃ permission, (and) not *of* ᵃ commandment.
40. so abide, *after* ᵃ my judgment:
9: 8. Say I these things *as* ᵃ a man?
10:18. Behold Israel *after* ᵃ the flesh:
11: 4. having (his) head covered, (lit. *over* ᵍ his head)
12: 8. *by* ᵃ the same Spirit;
31. shew I unto you a more excellent way. (lit. *according to* ᵃ excellence)
14:27. (let it be) *by* ᵃ two,
31. may all prophesy one *by* ᵃ one,
40. be done decently and *in* ᵃ order.
15: 3. died for our sins *according to* ᵃ the scriptures;
4. *according to* ᵃ the scriptures:
15. we have testified *of* ᵍ God
31. I die dail*y* ᵃ.
32. If *after the manner of* ᵃ men
16: 2. *Upon* ᵃ the first (day) of the
19. the church that is *in* ᵃ their house.
2Co 1: 8. we were pressed)(ᵃ out of measure,
17. do I purpose *according to* ᵃ the flesh,
4:13. *according as* ᵃ it is written,
17. a far more exceeding (and) (lit. *as to* ᵃ excess unto excess)
5:16. know we no man *after* ᵃ the flesh: yea, though we have known Christ *after* ᵃ the flesh,
7: 9. were made sorry *after* ᵃ a godly manner,
10. For godl*y* ᵃ sorrow worketh
11. ye sorrowed *after* ᵃ a godly sort,
8: 2. their deep poverty (lit. *according to* ᵃ depth) abounded
3. For *to* ᵃ (their) power,
8. I speak not *by* ᵃ commandment,
10: 1. who *in* ᵃ presence (am) base —
2. as if we walked *according to* ᵃ the flesh.

2Co.10: 3. we do not war *after* ᵃ the flesh:
5. exalteth itself *against* ᵍ the knowledge
7. *after* ᵃ the outward appearance?
13. but *according to* ᵃ the measure
15. *according to* ᵃ our rule
11:15. *according to* ᵃ their works.
17. I speak (it) not *after* ᵃ the Lord,
18. that many glory *after* ᵃ the flesh,
21. speak *as concerning* ᵃ reproach,
28. that which cometh upon me dail*y* ᵃ,
13: 8. we can do nothing *against* ᵍ the truth,
10. *according to* ᵃ the power which
Gal. 1: 4. *according to* ᵃ the will of God
11. preached of me is not *after* ᵃ man.
13. how that beyond measure I (lit. *according to* ᵃ excess)
2: 2. I went up *by* ᵃ revelation,
— but privatel*y* ᵃ to them which
11. I withstood him *to* ᵃ the face,
3: 1. *before* ᵃ whose eyes Jesus Christ
15. I speak *after the manner of* ᵃ men;
21. (Is) the law then *against* ᵍ the promises
29. heirs *according to* ᵃ the promise.
4:23. was born *after* ᵃ the flesh;
28. Now we, brethren, *as* ᵃ Isaac was,
29. he that was born *after* ᵃ the flesh persecuted him (that was born) *after* ᵃ
5:17. the flesh lusteth *against* ᵍ the Spirit, and the Spirit *against* ᵍ the flesh:
23. *against* ᵍ such there is no law.
Eph. 1: 5. *according to* ᵃ the good pleasure
7. *according to* ᵃ the riches of his grace;
9. *according to* ᵃ his good pleasure
11. *according to* ᵃ the purpose of him who worketh all things *after* ᵃ the
15. after I heard of your faith (lit. *among* ᵃ you)
19. *according to* ᵃ the working of his
2: 2. *according to* ᵃ the course of this world, *according to* ᵃ the prince of the power
3: 3. How that *by* ᵍ revelation he
7. *according to* ᵃ the gift of the grace of God given unto me *by* ᵃ the effectual
11. *According to* ᵃ the eternal purpose
16. *according to* ᵃ the riches of his glory,
20. *according to* ᵃ the power that
4: 7. grace *according to* ᵃ the measure
16. *according to* ᵃ the effectual
22. *concerning* ᵃ the former conversation
— *according to* ᵃ the deceitful lusts;
24. which *after* ᵃ God is created
5:33. let every one of you in (lit. *by* ᵃ one)
6: 5. *according to* ᵃ the flesh,
6. Not *with* ᵃ eyeservice, as menpleasers;
21. that ye also may know my affairs, (lit. the things *with* ᵃ me)
Phi. 1:12. the things (which happened) *unto* ᵃ me
20. *According to* ᵃ my earnest expectation
2: 3. (Let) nothing (be done) *through* ᵃ strife
3: 5. *as touching* ᵃ the law, a Pharisee;
6. *Concerning* ᵃ zeal, persecuting the church; *touching* ᵃ the righteousness which
14. I press *toward* ᵃ the mark
21. *according to* ᵃ the working whereby
4:11. Not that I speak *in respect of* ᵃ want:
19. *according to* ᵃ his riches in glory
Col. 1:11. *according to* ᵃ his glorious power,
25. *according to* ᵃ the dispensation
29. striving *according to* ᵃ his working,
2: 8. *after* ᵃ the tradition of men, *after* ᵃ the rudiments of the world, and not *after* ᵃ Christ.

Col. 2:14. of ordinances that was *against*ᵍ us,
22. *after*ᵃ the commandments and
3:10. *after*ᵃ the image of him that
20. obey (your) parents *in*ᵃ all things:
22. Servants, obey *in*ᵃ all things (your) masters *according to*ᵃ the flesh;
4: 7. All my state shall Tychicus (lit. all the things *concerning*ᵃ me)
15. the church which is *in*ᵃ his house.
2Th. 1:12. *according to*ᵃ the grace of our God
2: 3. Let no man deceive you *by*ᵃ any means:
9. is *after*ᵃ the working of Satan
3: 6. and not *after*ᵃ the tradition
1Ti. 1: 1. *by*ᵃ the commandment of God
11. *According to*ᵃ the glorious gospel
18. *according to*ᵃ the prophecies
5:19. *Against*ᵍ an elder receive not
21. doing nothing *by*ᵃ partiality.
6: 3. which is *according to*ᵃ godliness;
2Ti. 1: 1. *according to*ᵃ the promise of
8. *according to*ᵃ the power of God;
9. not *according to*ᵃ our works, but *according to*ᵃ his own purpose
2: 8. *according to*ᵃ my gospel:
4: 1. and the dead *at*ᵃ his appearing and
3. but *after*ᵃ their own lusts
14. *according to*ᵃ his works:
Tit. 1: 1. *according to*ᵃ the faith of God's
— the truth which is *after*ᵃ godliness;
3. *according to*ᵃ the commandment
4. own son *after*ᵃ the common faith:
5. ordain elders *in every*ᵃ city,
9. *as*ᵃ he hath been taught,
3: 5. but *according to*ᵃ his mercy
7. *according to*ᵃ the hope of
Philem. 2. and to the church *in*ᵃ thy house:
14. be as it were *of*ᵃ necessity, but willing*ly*.ᵃ
Heb 1:10. And, Thou, Lord, *in*ᵃ the beginning
2: 4. *according to*ᵃ his own will?
17. Wherefore *in*ᵃ all things it
3: 3. ᵃ*in*asmuch as he who hath
8. *in*ᵃ the day of temptation in
13. exhort one another dai*ly*,ᵃ
4:15. but was *in*ᵃ all points tempted *like as*ᵃ
5: 6. *after*ᵃ the order of Melchisedec.
10. an high priest *after*ᵃ the order of
6:13. because he could swear *by*ᵍ no greater, he sware *by*ᵍ himself,
16. men verily swear *by*ᵍ the greater:
20. *after*ᵃ the order of Melchisedec.
7: 5. *according to*ᵃ the law,
11. rise *after*ᵃ the order of Melchisedec, and not be called *after*ᵃ the order of Aaron?
15. *after*ᵃ the similitude of Melchisedec
16. not *after*ᵃ the law of a carnal commandment, but *after*ᵃ the power of an
17. *after*ᵃ the order of Melchisedec.
20. And *in*asmuch*ᵃ* as not without
21. *after*ᵃ the order of Melchisedec:
22. *By*ᵃ so much was Jesus made
27. Who needeth not dai*ly*,ᵃ
8: 4. gifts *according to*ᵃ the law:
5. *according to*ᵃ the pattern
9. Not *according to*ᵃ the covenant
9: 5. cannot now speak particular*ly*.ᵃ
9. *in*ᵃ which were offered
— *as pertaining to*ᵃ the conscience;
19. *according to*ᵃ the law,
22. almost all things are *by*ᵃ the law
25. as the high priest entereth...*every* year (lit. *by*ᵃ year)
27. And as (lit. And *in*asmuch ᵃ as) it is

Heb 10: 1. offered year *by*ᵃ year
3. (made) of sins *every*ᵃ year.
8. offered *by*ᵃ the law
11. every priest standeth dai*ly*ᵃ
11: 7. which is *by*ᵃ faith.
13. These all died *in*ᵃ faith,
12:10. chastened (us) *after*ᵃ their own
Jas. 2: 8. *according to*ᵃ the scripture,
17. is dead, being alone. (lit. *by*ᵃ itself)
3: 9. *after*ᵃ the similitude of God.
14. and lie not *against*ᵍ the truth.
5: 9. Grudge not one *against*ᵍ another,
1Pet. 1: 2. Elect *according to*ᵃ the foreknowledge
3. *according to*ᵃ his abundant mercy
15. But *as*ᵃ he which hath called
17. judgeth *according to*ᵃ every man's
2:11. which war *against*ᵍ the soul;
3: 7. *according to*ᵃ knowledge, giving
4: 6. judged *according to*ᵃ men in the flesh, but live *according to*ᵃ God
14. *on* their *part*ᵃ he is evil spoken of, but *on* your *part*ᵃ he is glorified.
19. that suffer *according to*ᵃ the will
2Pet. 2:11. accusation *against*ᵍ them
3: 3. walking *after*ᵃ their own lusts,
13. we, *according to*ᵃ his promise,
15. *according to*ᵃ the wisdom
1Joh.5:14. any thing *according to*ᵃ his will,
2Joh. 6. we walk *after*ᵃ his commandments.
3Joh. 14. Greet the friends *by*ᵃ name.
Jude 15. To execute judgment *upon*ᵍ all,
— ungodly sinners have spoken *against*ᵍ
16. walking *after*ᵃ their own lusts;
18. who should walk *after*ᵃ their own
Rev. 2: 4. I have (somewhat) *against*ᵍ thee,
14. I have a few things *against*ᵍ thee,
20. I have a few things *against*ᵍ thee,
23. *according to*ᵃ your works.
4: 8. the four beasts had each of them (lit. each *by*ᵃ itself)
12: 7. fought *against*ᵍ the dragon;
18: 6. *according to*ᵃ her works:
20:12. *according to*ᵃ their works.
13. *according to*ᵃ their works.
22: 2. yielded her fruit *every*ᵃ month:
See also καθ᾽ εἷς and καθ᾽ ἡμέραν.

καταϐαίνω, katabaino.

Mat. 3:16. *descending* like a dove,
7:25. And the rain *descended*,
27. the rain *descended*, and the floods
8: 1. *When* he *was come down* from the
14:29. And *when* Peter *was come down* out
17: 9. *as* they *came down* from the mountain,
24:17. *Let* him which is on the housetop not *come down* to
27:40. *come down* from the cross.
42. *let* him now *come down* from the
28: 2. for the angel of the Lord *descended*
Mar 1:10. the Spirit like a dove *descending*
3:22. the scribes *which came down* from
9: 9. *as* they *came down* from the
13:15. *let* him that is on the housetop not *go down* into the house,
15:30. *come down* from the cross.
32. Let Christ the King of Israel *descend* now
Lu. 2:51. And he *went down* with them,
3:22. the Holy Ghost *descended* in a
6:17. And he *came down* with them, *and*
8:23. and there *came down* a storm

Lu. 9:54. wilt thou that we command fire *to come down*
10:30. (man) *went down* from Jerusalem
31. by chance there *came down* a
17:31. *let* him not *come down* to take it
18:14. this man *went down* to his house
19: 5. make haste, and *come down ;* for to day
6. he made haste, and *came down,*
22:44. great drops of blood *falling down*
Joh. 1:32. I saw the Spirit *descending*
33. thou shalt see the Spirit *descending,*
51(52). ascending and *descending* upon the
2:12. he *went down* to Capernaum,
3:13. but he *that came down* from
4:47. that he *would come down,*
49. *come down* ere my child die.
51. And *as* he was now *going down,*
5: 4. an angel *went down* at a
7. another *steppeth down* before me.
6:16. his disciples *went down* unto
33. is he *which cometh down* from
38. For I *came down* from heaven,
41. the bread *which came down* from heaven.
42. I *came down* from heaven?
50. the bread *which cometh down* from
51. the living bread *which came down* from
58. This is that bread *which came down*
Acts 7:15. So Jacob *went down* into Egypt,
34. and *am come down* to deliver
8:15. *when* they *were come down,*
26. unto the way *that goeth down* from
38. they *went down* both into the
10:11. a certain vessel *descending*
20. *get* thee *down,* and go with them,
21. Then Peter *went down*
11: 5. A certain vessel *descend,*
14:11. The gods *are come down*
25. they *went down* into Attalia:
16: 8. *came down* to Troas.
18:22. he *went down* to Antioch.
20:10. And Paul *went down,* and fell on him,
23:10. commanded the soldiers to *go down, and*
24: 1. Ananias the high priest *descended*
22. the chief captain shall *come down,*
25: 6. he *went down* unto Cæsarea ;
7. the Jews *which came down*
Ro. 10: 7. Or, Who *shall descend* into
Eph. 4: 9. but that he also *descended* first
10. He *that descended* is the same
1Th. 4:16. For the Lord himself *shall descend*
Jas. 1:17. and *cometh down* from the Father
Rev. 3:12. new Jerusalem, which *cometh down* out of heaven
10: 1. I saw another mighty angel *come down*
12:12. the devil *is come down* unto you,
13:13. he maketh fire *come down*
16:21. there *fell* upon men a great hail
18: 1. I saw another angel *come down*
20: 1. I saw an angel *come down*
9. and fire *came down* from God
21: 2. the holy city, new Jerusalem, *coming down*
10. the holy Jerusalem, *descending* out of heaven from God,

καταβάλλω, kataballo.

2Co. 4: 9. *cast down,* but not destroyed ;
Heb. 6: 1. not *laying* again the foundation
Rev.12:10. the accuser of our brethren *is cast down,*

καταβαρέω, katabareo.

2Co.12:16. I *did* not *burden* you:

κατάβασις, katabasis.

Lu. 19:37. at the *descent* of the mount of Olives,

καταβιβάζομαι, katabibazomai.

Mat.11:23. *shalt* be *brought down* to hell:
Lu. 10:15. *shalt* be *thrust down* to hell.

καταβολή, katabolee.

Mat.13:35. secret from the *foundation* of the
25:34. from the *foundation* of the world:
Lu. 11:50. which was shed from the *foundation*
Joh.17:24. thou lovedst me before the *foundation*
Eph. 1: 4. chosen us in him before the *foundation*
Heb. 4: 3. works were finished from the *foundation*
9:26. often have suffered since the *foundation*
11:11. received strength to *conceive* seed,
1Pet. 1:20. foreordained before the *foundation*
Rev.13: 8. the Lamb slain from the *foundation*
17: 8. book of life from the *foundation* of the

καταβραβεύω, katabrabŭo.

Col. 2:18. *Let* no man *beguile* you *of* your *reward*

καταγγελεύς, katangelūs.

Acts17:18. He seemeth to be a *setter forth* of strange gods:

καταγγέλλω, katangello.

Acts 4: 2. *preached* through Jesus the resurrection
13: 5. they *preached* the word of God
38. through this man *is preached* unto you the forgiveness of sins:
15:36. where we *have preached* the word
16:17. which *shew* unto us the way of
21. And *teach* customs, which are
17: 3. Jesus, whom I *preach* unto you, is
13. the word of God *was preached* of Paul
23. him *declare* I unto you.
26:23. and should *shew* light unto
Ro. 1: 8. your faith *is spoken of* throughout
1Co. 2: 1. *declaring* unto you the testimony
9:14. they which *preach* the gospel
11:26. ye do *shew* the Lord's death
Phi. 1:16. The one *preach* Christ of contention,
18. or in truth, Christ *is preached ;*
Col. 1:28. Whom we *preach,* warning

καταγελάω, katagelao.

Mat. 9:24. they *laughed* him *to scorn.*
Mar. 5:40. they *laughed* him *to scorn.*
Lu. 8:53. they *laughed* him *to scorn,*

καταγινώσκω, *kataginōsko*.

Gal. 2:11. because he was *to be blamed.*
1Joh.3:20. For if our heart *condemn* us,
    21. if our heart *condemn* us not,

κατάγνυμι, *katagnumi*.

Mat.12:20. A bruised reed *shall* he not *break,*
Joh.19:31. that their legs *might be broken,*
    32. and *brake* the legs of the first,
    33. they *brake* not his legs:

κατάγω, *katago*.

Lu. 5:11. *when* they *had brought* their ships to land,
Acts 9:30. they *brought* him *down* to Cæsarea,
    21: 3. into Syria, and *landed* at Tyre:
    22:30. *brought* Paul *down, and* set
    23:15. that he *bring* him *down* unto you
    20. that thou *wouldest bring down* Paul
    28. I *brought* him *forth* into their
    27: 3. the next (day) we *touched* at Sidon.
    28:12. And *landing* at Syracuse, we
Ro. 10: 6. that is, *to bring* Christ *down*

καταγωνίζομαι, *katagōnizomai*.

Heb 11:33. Who through faith *subdued* kingdoms,

καταδέω, *katadeo*.

Lu. 10:34. and *bound up* his wounds,

κατάδηλος, *katadeelos*.

Heb. 7:15. it is yet far more *evident :*

καταδικάζω, *katadikazo*.

Mat.12: 7. ye would not *have condemned* the guiltless.
    37. by thy words thou *shalt be condemned.*
Lu. 6:37. *condemn* not, and ye *shall* not *be condemned:*
Jas. 5: 6. Ye *have condemned* (and) killed the just;

καταδιώκω, *katadiōko*.

Mar. 1:36. Simon and they that were with him *followed after* him.

καταδουλόω, *katadouloō*.

2Co.11:20. if a man *bring* you *into bondage,*
Gal. 2: 4. that they *might bring* us *into bondage :*

καταδρέμω see κατατρέχω.

καταδυναστεύω, *katadunastūo*.

Acts10:38. healing all *that were oppressed* of the devil ;
Jas. 2: 6. *Do* not rich men *oppress* you,

καταισχύνω, *kataiskuno*.

Lu. 13:17. all his adversaries *were ashamed :*
Ro. 5: 5. hope *maketh* not *ashamed ;*
    9:33. believeth on him *shall* not *be ashamed.*
    10:11. on him *shall* not *be ashamed.*
1Co. 1:27. to *confound* the wise;
    — to *confound* the things which
    11: 4. head covered, *dishonoureth* his head.
    5. uncovered *dishonoureth* her head:
    22. and *shame* them that have not?
2Co. 7:14. I *am* not *ashamed ;*
    9: 4. we...*should be ashamed* in this
1Pet.2: 6. *shall* not *be confounded.*
    3:16. they *may be ashamed* that

κατακαίω, *katakaio*.

Mat 3:12. but he *will burn up* the chaff
    13:30. bind them in bundles *to burn*
    40. the tares are gathered and *burned*
Lu. 3:17. but the chaff he *will burn* with
Acts19:19. and *burned* them before all
1Co. 3:15. If any man's work *shall be burned,*
Heb 13:11. *are burned* without the camp.
2Pet.3:10. and the works that are therein *shall be burned up.*
Rev. 8: 7. the third part of trees *was burnt up,* and all green grass *was burnt up.*
    17:16. and *burn* her with fire.
    18: 8. she *shall be utterly burned* with fire:

κατακαλύπτομαι, *katakaluptomai*.

1Co.11: 6. For if the woman *be* not *covered,*
    — let her *be covered.*
    7. ought not *to cover* (his) head,

κατακαυχάομαι, *katakaukaomai*.

Ro. 11:18. *Boast* not *against* the branches. But if thou *boast,* thou bearest not
Jas. 2:13. and mercy *rejoiceth against*
    3:14. *glory* not, and lie not against the truth.

κατάκειμαι, *katakīmai*.

Mar 1:30. Simon's wife's mother *lay* sick
    2: 4. wherein the sick of the palsy *lay.*
    15. as Jesus *sat at meat* in his
    14: 3. *as* he *sat at meat,* there came a woman
Lu. 5:25. took up that whereon he *lay,*
    29. and of others *that sat down* with them.
Joh. 5: 3. In these *lay* a great multitude
    6. When Jesus saw him *lie,*
Acts 9:33. Æneas, *which had kept* his bed eight
    28: 8. that the father of Publius *lay* sick
1Co. 8:10. *sit at meat* in the idol's temple,

κατακλάω or κατακλάζω, *kataklao* or *kataklazo*.

Mar 6:41. and *brake* the loaves,
Lu. 9:16. he blessed them, and *brake,*

κατακλείω, kataklio.

Lu. 3:20. that he *shut up* John in prison.
Acts26:10. saints *did* I *shut up* in prison,

κατακληροδοτέω, katakleerodoteo.

Acts13:19. he *divided* their land to them *by lot*.

κατακλίνω, kataklino.

Lu. 9:14. *Make* them *sit down* by fifties
14: 8. *sit* not *down* in the highest
24:30. as he *sat at meat* with them,

κατακλύζομαι, katakluzomai.

2Pet.3: 6. *being overflowed* with water,

κατακλυσμός, kataklusmos.

Mat 24:38. before the *flood* they were eating
39: until the *flood* came,
Lu. 17:27. and the *flood* came, and destroyed
2Pet.2: 5. bringing in the *flood* upon the world

κατακολουθέω, katakoloutheo.

Lu. 23:55. the women also, which... *followed after*, and
beheld the sepulchre,
Acts16:17. The same *followed* Paul and us, *and* cried,

κατακόπτω, katakopto.

Mar 5: 5. *cutting* himself with stones.

κατακρημνίζω, katakreemnizo.

Lu. 4:29. that they might *cast* him *down headlong*.

κατάκριμα, katakrima.

Ro. 5:16. judgment (was) by one to *condemnation*,
18. upon all men to *condemnation;*
8: 1. now no *condemnation* to them which are
in Christ Jesus,

κατακρίνω, katakrino.

Mat 12:41. and *shall condemn* it:
42. and *shall condemn* it:
20:18. they *shall condemn* him to death,
27: 3. when he saw that he *was condemned,*
Mar 10:33. they *shall condemn* him to death,
14:64. they all *condemned* him to be
16:16. believeth not *shall be damned.*
Lu. 11:31. this generation, and *condemn* them:
32. and *shall condemn* it:
Joh. 8:10. *hath* no man *condemned* thee?
11. Neither *do* I *condemn* thee:
Ro. 2: 1. another, thou *condemnest* thyself;
8: 3. *condemned* sin in the flesh:
34. Who (is) he *that condemneth?*

Ro. 14:23. he that doubteth *is damned* if
1Co.11:32. that we *should* not *be condemned* with the
Heb 11: 7. by the which he *condemned* the world,
Jas. 5: 9. lest ye *be condemned :*
2Pet.2: 6. *condemned* (them) with an overthrow,

κατάκρισις, katakrisis.

2Co. 3: 9. ministration of *condemnation* (be) glory,
7: 3. I speak not (this) to *condemn* (you):

κατακυριεύω, katakuriuo.

Mat 20:25. princes of the Gentiles *exercise dominion
over* them,
Mar 10:42. *exercise lordship over* them ;
Acts19:16. *overcame* them, *and* prevailed against
1Pet.5: 3. Neither as *being lords over* (God's)

καταλαλέω, katalaleo.

Jas. 4:11. *Speak* not *evil* one *of* another, brethren.
He that *speaketh evil of* (his)
— *speaketh evil of* the law,
1Pet.2:12. they *speak against* you as evildoers,
3:16. whereas they *speak evil of* you,

καταλαλιά, katalalia.

2Co.12:20. strifes, *backbitings*, whisperings,
1Pet.2: 1. envies, and all *evil speakings,*

κατάλαλος, katalalos.

Ro. 1:30. *Backbiters*, haters of God,

καταλαμβάνω, katalambano.

Mar 9:18. wheresoever he *taketh* him,
Joh. 1: 5. the darkness *comprehended* it not.
8: 3. a woman *taken* in adultery ;
4. this woman *was taken* in adultery,
12:35. lest darkness *come upon* you:
Acts 4:13. and *perceived* that they were unlearned
10:34. I *perceive* that God is no respecter
25:25. But *when* I *found* that he had
Ro. 9:30. *have attained* to righteousness,
1Co. 9:24. So run, that ye *may obtain.*
Eph. 3:18. able *to comprehend* with all saints
Phi. 3:12. if that I *may apprehend* that for which also
I *am apprehended*
13. I count not myself *to have apprehended :*
1Th. 5: 4. *should overtake* you as a thief.

καταλέγομαι, katalegomai.

1Ti. 5: 9. *Let* not a widow *be taken into the number*

κατάλειμμα, kataleimma.

Ro. 9:27. a *remnant* shall be saved:

καταλείπω, *katalīpo.*

Mat. 4:13. And *leaving* Nazareth, he came
16: 4. And he *left* them, *and* departed.
19: 5. For this cause *shall* a man *leave*
21:17. he *left* them, *and* went out of the city
Mar 10: 7. For this cause *shall* a man *leave*
12:19. If a man's brother die, and *leave* (his)
14:52. And he *left* the linen cloth, *and* fled
Lu. 5:28. And he *left* all, rose up, *and*
10:40. that my sister *hath left* me to serve
15: 4. *doth* not *leave* the ninety and nine
20:31. and they *left* no children,
Joh. 8: 9. and Jesus *was left* alone,
Acts 2:31. that his soul *was* not *left* in hell,
6: 2. that we should *leave* the word of God, *and*
serve tables.
18:19. and *left* them there:
21: 3. we *left* it on the left hand, *and*
24:27. Jews a pleasure, *left* Paul bound.
25:14. a certain man *left* in bonds
Ro. 11: 4. I *have reserved* to myself
Eph. 5:31. *shall* a man *leave* his father
1Th. 3: 1. we thought it good *to be left* at Athens
Tit. 1: 5. For this cause *left* I thee in
Heb 4: 1. lest, a promise *being left* (us)
11:27. By faith he *forsook* Egypt,
2Pet.2:15. *Which have forsaken* the right way, *and are*
gone astray,

καταλιθάζω, *katalithazo.*

Lu. 20: 6. all the people *will stone* us:

καταλλαγή, *katallagee.*

Ro. 5:11. by whom we have now received the *atone-*
ment. (lit. *reconciliation*)
11:15. the *reconciling* of the world,
2Co. 5:18. the ministry of *reconciliation ;*
19. the word of *reconciliation.*

καταλλάσσω, *katallasso.*

Ro. 5:10. we *were reconciled* to God
— *being reconciled*, we shall
1Co. 7:11. let her remain unmarried, or *be reconciled*
to (her) husband:
2Co. 5:18. of God, *who hath reconciled* us to himself
by Jesus Christ,
19. *reconciling* the world unto himself,
20. *be ye reconciled* to God.

κατάλοιπος, *kataloipos.*

Acts15:17. That the *residue* of men might seek after

κατάλυμα, *kataluma.*

Mar 14:14. Where is the *guestchamber,*
Lu. 2: 7. no room for them in the *inn.*
22:11. Where is the *guestchamber,*

καταλύω, *kataluo.*

Mat. 5:17. Think not that I am come *to destroy* the

Mat. 5:17. I am not come *to destroy*, but to fulfil.
24: 2. that *shall* not *be thrown down.*
26:61. I am able *to destroy* the temple
27:40. Thou *that destroyest* the temple,
Mar 13: 2. that *shall* not *be thrown down.*
14:58. I *will destroy* this temple
15:29. Ah, thou *that destroyest* the temple,
Lu. 9:12. and *lodge,* and get victuals:
19: 7. gone *to be guest* with a man that is a
21: 6. that *shall* not *be thrown down.*
Acts 5:38. be of men, it *will come to nought :*
39. if it be of God, ye cannot *overthrow* it ;
6:14. Jesus of Nazareth *shall destroy* this
Ro. 14:20. For meat *destroy* not the work
2Co. 5: 1. of (this) tabernacle *were dissolved,*
Gal. 2:18. the things which I *destroyed,*

καταμανθάνω, *katamanthano.*

Mat. 6:28. *Consider* the lilies of the field,

καταμαρτυρέω, *katamartureo.*

Mat.26:62. what (is it which) these *witness against*
thee?
27:13. how many things they *witness against*
Mar 14:60. (which) these *witness against* thee?
15: 4. they *witness against* thee.

καταμένω, *katameno.*

Acts 1:13. where abode both Peter, and James, (lit.
were *abiding*)

καταμόνας, *katamonas.*

Mar 4:10. And when he was *alone,*
Lu. 9:18. as he was *alone* praying,

κατανάθεμα, *katanathema.*

Rev.22: 3. there shall be no more *curse :*

καταναθεματίζω, *katanathematizo.*

Mat.26:74. Then began he *to curse* and to swear,

καταναλίσκω, *katanalisko.*

Heb 12:29. For our God (is) a *consuming* fire.

καταναρκέω, *katanarkeo.*

2Co.11: 9(8). I *was chargeable* to no man:
12:13. that I myself *was* not *burdensome* to you ?
14. I *will* not *be burdensome* to you:

κατανεύω, *katanuo.*

Lu. 5: 7. they *beckoned* unto (their) partners,

κατανοέω, katanoeo.

Mat. 7: 3. but *considerest* not the beam
Lu. 6:41. but *perceivest* not the beam
 12:24. *Consider* the ravens: for they
 27. *Consider* the lilies how they grow:
 20:23. he *perceived* their craftiness, and said
Acts 7:31. and as he drew near *to behold* (it),
 32. and durst not *behold*.
 11: 6. I *considered*, and saw fourfooted
 27:39. they *discovered* a certain creek
Ro. 4:19. he *considered* not his own body
Heb 3: 1. *consider* the apostle and high priest
 10:24. *let us consider* one another
Jas. 1:23. like unto a man *beholding* his natural face
 24. For he *beholdeth* himself, and goeth

κατανταω, katantao.

Acts16: 1. Then *came* he to Derbe and Lystra:
 18:19. And he *came* to Ephesus,
 24. mighty in the scriptures, *came* to Ephesus.
 20:15. *came* the next (day) over against Chios;
 21: 7. we *came* to Ptolemais,
 25:13. Agrippa and Bernice *came* unto Cæsarea
 26: 7. serving (God) day and night, hope *to come*.
 27:12. by any means they might *attain* to Phenice,
 (*and*)
 28:13. and *came* to Rhegium:
1Co.10:11. upon whom the ends of the world *are come*.
 14:36. *came* it unto you only?
Eph. 4:13. Till we all *come* in the unity
Phi. 3:11. If by any means I *might attain* unto

κατάνυξις, katanuxis.

Ro. 11: 8. God hath given them the spirit of *slumber*,

κατανύσσω, katanusso.

Acts 2:37. they *were pricked* in their heart,

καταξιόομαι, kataxio-omai.

Lu. 20:35. which shall be *accounted worthy* to obtain
 21:36. that ye *may be accounted worthy* to escape
Acts 5:41. that they *were counted worthy* to suffer
2Th. 1: 5. that ye may *be counted worthy* of

καταπατέω, katapateo.

Mat. 5:13. and *to be trodden under foot* of men.
 7: 6. lest they *trample* them under their feet,
Lu. 8: 5. and it *was trodden down*,
 12: 1. that they *trode* one upon another,
Heb 10:29. who hath *trodden under foot* the Son of God,

κατάπαυσις, katapausis.

Acts 7:49. what (is) the place of my *rest?*
Heb. 3:11. They shall not enter into my *rest*.
 18. they should not enter into his *rest*,
 4: 1. of entering into his *rest*,
 3. do enter into *rest*,
 — if they shall enter into my *rest*:

Heb. 4:5. If they shall enter into my *rest*.
 10. he that is entered into his *rest*,
 11. to enter into that *rest*,

καταπαύω, katapauo.

Acts14:18. scarce *restrained* they the people,
Heb. 4: 4. And God *did rest* the seventh day
 8. if Jesus *had given* them *rest*,
 10. he also *hath ceased* from his own works,

καταπέτασμα, katapetasma.

Mat.27:51. behold, the *veil* of the temple was rent
Mar 15:38. And the *veil* of the temple was rent
Lu. 23:45. and the *veil* of the temple was rent
Heb. 6:19. into that within the *veil*;
 9: 3. And after the second *veil*,
 10:20. through the *veil*, that is to say, his flesh;

καταπίνω, katapino.

Mat.23:24. and *swallow* a camel.
1Co.15:54. Death is *swallowed up* in victory.
2Co. 2: 7. should be *swallowed up* with overmuch
 5: 4. might be *swallowed up* of life.
Heb 11:29. assaying to do *were drowned*.
1Pet. 5: 8. seeking whom he *may devour*:
Rev.12:16. and *swallowed up* the flood which

καταπίπτω, katapipto.

Acts26:14. when we were all *fallen* to the earth,
 28: 6. or *fallen down* dead suddenly:

καταπλέω, katapleo.

Lu. 8:26. And they *arrived* at the country

καταπονέομαι, kataponeomai.

Acts 7:24. avenged him *that was oppressed*,
2Pet.2: 7. *vexed* with the filthy conversation

καταποντίζομαι, katapontizomai.

Mat.14:30. and beginning *to sink*,
 18: 6. and (that) he *were drowned* in the

κατάρα, katara.

Gal. 3:10. are under the *curse*:
 13. hath redeemed us from the *curse* of the
 law, being made a *curse* for us:
Heb. 6: 8. nigh unto *cursing*; whose end
Jas. 3:10. proceedeth blessing and *cursing*.
2Pet.2:14. *cursed* children: (lit. children of *curse*)

καταράομαι, kataraomai.

Mat. 5:44. bless them *that curse* you,
 25:41. Depart from me, ye *cursed*,

Mar 11:21. the fig tree which thou *cursedst*
Lu. 6:28. Bless them *that curse* you,
Ro. 12:14. bless, and *curse* not.
Jas. 3: 9. and therewith *curse* we men,

καταργέω, *katargeo.*

Lu. 13: 7. why *cumbereth* it the ground?
Ro. 3: 3. *shall* their unbelief *make* the faith of God
      without effect?
    31. *Do* we then *make void* the law
    4:14. and the promise *made of none effect:*
    6: 6. the body of sin *might be destroyed,*
    7: 2. she *is loosed* from the law of
    6. now we *are delivered* from the law,
1Co. 1:28. to *bring to nought* things that are:
    2: 6. of the princes of this world, *that come to*
    nought:
    6:13. God *shall destroy* both it and them.
    13: 8. prophecies, they *shall fail;*
    — knowledge, it *shall vanish away.*
    10. is in part *shall be done away.*
    11. I *put away* childish things.
    15:24. when he *shall have put down*
    26. The last enemy (that) *shall be destroyed*
2Co. 3: 7. which (glory) *was to be done away:*
    11. if that *which is done away*
    13. to the end of that *which is abolished:*
    14. which (vail) *is done away* in Christ.
Gal. 3:17. that it should *make* the promise *of none*
    effect.
    5: 4. Christ is *become of no effect* unto you, (lit.
    ye *are ceased* from Christ)
    11. then *is* the offence of the cross *ceased.*
Eph. 2:15. *Having abolished* in his flesh
2Th. 2: 8. and *shall destroy* with the brightness of his
    coming:
2Ti. 1:10. Christ, *who hath abolished* death,
Heb. 2:14. that through death he *might destroy* him

καταριθμέομαι, *katarithmeomai.*

Acts 1:17. he was *numbered with* us,

καταρτίζω, *katartizo.*

Mat. 4:21. *mending* their nets;
    21:16. thou *hast perfected* praise?
Mar 1:19. in the ship *mending* their nets.
Lu. 6:40. every one *that is perfect* shall be
Ro. 9:22. vessels of wrath *fitted* to destruction:
1Co. 1:10. but (that) ye be *perfectly joined together*
2Co.13:11. *Be perfect,* be of good comfort,
Gal. 6: 1. *restore* such an one in the spirit of
1Th. 3:10. and might *perfect* that which is
Heb 10: 5. a body *hast thou prepared* me:
    11: 3. the worlds *were framed* by the word
    13:21. *Make* you *perfect* in every good work
1Pet.5:10. *make* you *perfect,* stablish,

κατάρτισις, *katartisis.*

2Co.13: 9. we wish, (even) your *perfection.*

καταρτισμός, *katartismos.*

Eph. 4:12. For the *perfecting* of the saints,

κατασείω, *katasio.*

Acts 12:17. *beckoning* unto them with the hand
    13:16. and *beckoning* with (his) hand
    19:33. Alexander *beckoned* with the hand, *and*
    21:40. and *beckoned* with the hand

κατασκάπτω, *kataskapto.*

Acts 15:16. I will build again the *ruins* thereof,
Ro. 11: 3. they have...and *digged down* thine altars;

κατασκευάζω, *kataskuazo.*

Mat 11:10. which *shall prepare* thy way
Mar 1: 2. which *shall prepare* thy way
Lu. 1:17. a people *prepared* for the Lord.
    7:27. which *shall prepare* thy way
Heb 3: 3. as he *who hath builded* the house
    4. every house *is builded* by some (man);
    but he *that built* all things (is) God.
    9: 2. there was a tabernacle *made;*
    6. when these things *were* thus *ordained,*
    11: 7. *prepared* an ark to the saving
1Pet.3:20. while the ark *was a preparing,*

κατασκηνόω, *kataskeenoo.*

Mat 13:32. come and *lodge* in the branches
Mar 4:32. so that the fowls of the air may *lodge*
Lu. 13:19. the fowls of the air *lodged* in the
Acts 2:26. my flesh *shall rest* in hope:

κατασκήνωσις, *kataskeenosis.*

Mat. 8:20. the birds of the air (have) *nests;*
Lu. 9:58. and birds of the air (have) *nests;*

κατασκιάζω, *kataskiazo.*

Heb 9: 5. glory *shadowing* the mercyseat;

κατασκοπέω, *kataskopeo.*

Gal. 2: 4. privily *to spy out* our liberty

κατάσκοπος, *kataskopos.*

Heb 11:31. when she had received the *spies*

κατασοφίζομαι, *katasophizomai.*

Acts 7:19. The same *dealt subtilly with* our

καταστέλλω, *katastello.*

Acts 19:35. when the townclerk *had appeased*
    36. ye ought to be *quiet,*

κατάστημα, *katasteema.*

Tit. 2: 3. that (they be) in *behaviour* as becometh

καταστολή, *katastolee.*

1Ti. 2: 9. adorn themselves in modest *apparel,*

καταστρέφω, *katastrepho.*

Mat 21:12. and *overthrew* the tables
Mar 11:15. and *overthrew* the tables

καταστρηνιάζω, *katastreeniazo.*

1Ti. 5:11. *have begun to wax wanton against* Christ,

καταστροφή, *katastrophee.*

2Ti. 2:14. to the *subverting* of the hearers.
2Pet.2: 6. condemned (them) with an *overthrow,*

καταστρώννυμι, *katastrōnnumi.*

1Co.10: 5. they *were overthrown* in the wilderness.

κατασύρω, *katasuro.*

Lu. 12:58. lest he *hale* thee to the judge,

κατασφάττω, *katasphatto.*

Lu. 19:27. and *slay* (them) before me.

κατασφραγίζομαι, *katasphragizomai.*

Rev 5: 1. *sealed* with seven seals.

κατάσχεσις, *kataskesis.*

Acts 7: 5. give it to him for a *possession,*
45. into the *possession* of the Gentiles,

κατατίθημι, *katatitheemi.*

Mar 15:46. and *laid* him in a sepulchre
Acts 24:27. willing *to shew* the Jews a pleasure,
25: 9. willing *to do* the Jews a pleasure,

κατατομή, *katatomee.*

Phi. 3: 2. beware of the *concision.*

κατατοξεύομαι, *katatoxŭomai.*

Heb 12:20. it shall be stoned, or *thrust through* with a dart:

κατατρέχω, *katatreko.*

Acts 21:32. and *ran down* unto them:

καταφάγω, *kataphago.*

Mat 13: 4. the fowls came and *devoured* them *up :*

Mar 4: 4. came and *devoured* it *up.*
Lu. 8: 5. the fowls of the air *devoured* it.
15:30. which *hath devoured* thy living
Joh. 2:17. The zeal of thine house *hath eaten* me *up.*
Rev 10: 9. Take (it), and *eat* it *up;*
10. I took the little book...and *ate* it *up;*
12: 4. for to *devour* her child as soon
20: 9. out of heaven, and *devoured* them.

καταφέρω, *kataphero.*

Acts 20: 9. *being fallen* into a deep sleep:
— he *sunk down* with sleep, *and*
26:10. I *gave* my voice against (them).

καταφεύγω, *kataphŭgo.*

Acts 14: 6. and *fled* unto Lystra and Derbe,
Heb 6:18. *who have fled* for refuge to lay hold

καταφθείρω, *kataphthīro.*

2Ti. 3: 8. men of *corrupt* minds, (lit. *corrupt* (as to) mind)
2Pet.2:12. and *shall utterly perish* in their own

καταφιλέω, *kataphileo.*

Mat 26:49. Hail, master; and *kissed* him.
Mar 14:45. Master, master; and *kissed* him.
Lu. 7:38. and *kissed* his feet,.
45. hath not ceased to *kiss* my feet.
15:20. fell on his neck, and *kissed* him.
Acts 20:37. fell on Paul's neck, and *kissed* him,

καταφρονέω, *kataphroneo.*

Mat. 6:24. will hold to the one, and *despise* the other.
18:10. that ye *despise* not one of these
Lu. 16:13. and *despise* the other.
Ro. 2: 4. Or *despisest* thou the riches of
1Co.11:22. or *despise* ye the church of
1Ti. 4:12. *Let* no man *despise* thy youth;
6: 2. *let* them not *despise* (them),
Heb 12: 2. *despising* the shame, and is
2Pet.2:10. and *despise* government.

καταφρονητής, *kataphroneetees.*

Acts 13:41. Behold, ye *despisers,* and wonder,

καταχέω, *katakeo.*

Mat. 26: 7. and *poured* it on his head,
Mar 14: 3. and *poured* (it) on his head.

καταχθόνιος, *katakthonios.*

Phi. 2:10. and (things) *under the earth;*

καταχράομαι, *katakraomai.*

1Co. 7:31. that use this world, as not *abusing* (it):
9:18. that I *abuse* not my power in

καταψύχω, katapsuko.

Lu. 16:24. in water, and *cool* my tongue;

κατείδωλος, katidolos.

Acts17:16. the city *wholly given to idolatry.*

κατέναντι, katenanti.

Mar 11: 2. into the village *over against* you:
12:41. Jesus sat *over against* the treasury,
13: 3. *over against* the temple,
Lu. 19:30. Go ye into the village *over against*
Ro. 4:17. *before* him whom he believed,

κατενώπιον, katenōpion.

2Co. 2:17. *in the sight* of God speak we
12:19. we speak *before* God in Christ:
Eph. 1: 4. and without blame *before* him
Col. 1:22. unreprovable *in his sight:*
Jude 24. faultless *before the presence* of his glory

κατεξουσιάζω, katexousiazo.

Mat.20:25. *exercise authority* upon them.
Mar 10:42. *exercise authority* upon them.

κατεργάζομαι, katergazomai.

Ro. 1:27. *working* that which is unseemly,
2: 9. upon every soul of man *that doeth* evil,
4:15. the law *worketh* wrath:
5: 3. tribulation *worketh* patience;
7: 8. *wrought* in me all manner of
13. *working* death in me by that
15. For that which I *do* I allow not:
17. it is no more I that *do* it,
18. but (how) to *perform* that which is good
20. it is no more I that *do* it,
15:18. which Christ *hath* not *wrought* by me,
1Co. 5: 3. him *that hath* so *done* this *deed,*
2Co. 4:17. *worketh* for us a far more
5: 5. he *that hath wrought* us for
7:10. godly sorrow *worketh* repentance
— sorrow of the world *worketh* death.
11. what carefulness it *wrought* in you,
9:11. which *causeth* through us thanksgiving
12:12. the signs of an apostle *were wrought.*
Eph. 6:13. and *having done* all, to stand
Phi. 2:12. *work out* your own salvation
Jas. 1: 3. trying of your faith *worketh* patience.
20. the wrath of man *worketh* not the righteousness of God.
1Pet.4: 3. suffice us *to have wrought* the

κατέρχομαι, katerkomai.

Lu. 4:31. And *came down* to Capernaum,
9:37. *when* they *were come down* from
Acts 8: 5. Philip *went down* to the city of
9:32. he *came down* also to the saints
11:27. *came* prophets from Jerusalem
12:19. he *went down* from Judæa

Acts13: 4. *departed* unto Seleucia;
15: 1. certain men *which came down* from
18: 5. and Timotheus *were come* from
22. And *when* he *had landed* at
21:10. there *came down* from Judæa
27: 5. we *came* to Myra,
Jas. 3:15. This wisdom *descendeth* not from above,

κατεσθίω, katesthio.

Mat.23:14(13). ye *devour* widows' houses,
Mar 12:40. *Which devour* widows' houses,
Lu. 20:47. Which *devour* widows' houses,
2Co.11:20. if a man *devour* (you),
Gal. 5:15. if ye bite and *devour* one another,
Rev.11: 5. and *devoureth* their enemies:

κατευθύνω, katuthuno.

Lu. 1:79. *to guide* our feet into the way
1Th. 3:11. *direct* our way unto you.
2Th. 3: 5. the Lord *direct* your hearts into the love
of God,

κατεφίστημι, katephisteemi.

Acts18:12. the Jews *made insurrection* with one accord
against Paul,

κατέχω, kateko.

Mat.21:38. *let* us *seize on* his inheritance.
Lu. 4:42. and *stayed* him, that he should not
8:15. having heard the word, *keep* (it),
14: 9. with shame *to take* the lowest
Joh. 5: 4. of whatsoever disease he had. (lit. he *was
held*)
Acts27:40. and *made toward* shore.
Ro. 1:18. *who hold* the truth in unrighteousness;
7: 6. being dead wherein we *were held;*
1Co. 7:30. as though they *possessed* not;
11: 2. and *keep* the ordinances, as I
15: 2. if ye *keep in memory* what I preached
2Co. 6:10. and (yet) *possessing* all things.
1Th. 5:21. *hold fast* that which is good.
2Th. 2: 6. ye know *what withholdeth*
7. only he *who* now *letteth* (will let),
Philem.13. I would have *retained* with me,
Heb 3: 6. if we *hold fast* the confidence
14. if we *hold* the beginning of
10:23. *Let* us *hold fast* the profession

κατηγορέω, kateegoreo.

Mat.12:10. that they *might accuse* him.
27:12. when he *was accused* of the
Mar 3: 2. that they *might accuse* him.
15: 3. the chief priests *accused* him of
Lu. 11:54. that they *might accuse* him.
23: 2. they began *to accuse* him,
10. *and* vehemently *accused* him.
14. whereof ye *accuse* him:
Joh. 5:45. Do not think that I *will accuse*
— there is (one) *that accuseth* you,
8: 6. that they might have *to accuse* him.
Acts22:30. wherefore he *was accused* of the Jews,

Acts24: 2. Tertullus began *to accuse* (him),
    8. whereof we *accuse* him.
   13. whereof they now *accuse* me.
   19. and *object*, if they had ought
25: 5. and *accuse* this man,
   11. whereof these *accuse* me,
   16. before that he *which is accused*
28:19. *to accuse* my nation of.
Ro. 2:15. (their) thoughts the mean while *accusing*
Rev 12:10. *which accused* them before our God

κατηγορία, *kateegoria.*

Lu. 6: 7. an *accusation* against him.
Joh, 18:29. What *accusation* bring ye against
1Ti. 5:19. receive not an *accusation,*
Tit. 1: 6. not accused (lit. not under *accusation*) of riot,

---

κατήγορος, *kateegoros.*

Joh. 8:10. where are those thine *accusers ?*
Acts23:30. gave commandment to his *accusers*
   35. when thine *accusers* are also come.
24: 8. Commanding his *accusers* to come
25:16. have the *accusers* face to face,
   18. when the *accusers* stood up,
Rev 12:10. for the *accuser* of our brethren is cast

κατήφεια, *kateephīa.*

Jas. 4: 9. and (your) joy to *heaviness.*

κατηχέω, *kateekeo.*

Lu. 1: 4. wherein thou *hast been instructed.*
Acts18:25. This man was *instructed* in the way of
21:21. they *are informed* of thee,
   24. they *were informed* concerning thee,
Ro. 2:18. *being instructed* out of the law ;
1Co.14:19. I *might teach* others also,
Gal. 6: 6. Let him *that is taught* in the word communicate unto him *that teacheth*

κατ᾽ ἰδίαν see in κατά & ἴδιος.

κατιόομαι, *katio-omai.*

Jas. 5: 3. Your gold and silver *is cankered ;*

κατισχύω, *katiskuo.*

Mat 16:18. of hell *shall* not *prevail against*
Lu. 23:23. and of the chief priests *prevailed.*

κατοικέω, *katoikeo.*

Mat. 2:23. and *dwelt* in a city called Nazareth :
4:13. he came and *dwelt* in Capernaum,
12:45. they enter in and *dwell* there:
23:21. and by him *that dwelleth* therein.
Lu. 11:26. they enter in, and *dwell* there:
13: 4. above all men *that dwelt* in Jerusalem ?

Acts 1:19. was known unto all the *dwellers* at
   20. and let no man *dwell* therein:
2: 5. there were *dwelling* at Jerusalem
   9. and the *dwellers* in Mesopotamia,
   14. and all (ye) *that dwell* at Jerusalem,
4:16. to all them *that dwell* in Jerusalem ;
7: 2. before he *dwelt* in Charran,
   4. and *dwelt* in Charran:
  — wherein ye now *dwell.*
   48. the most High *dwelleth* not in temples
9:22. the Jews *which dwelt* at Damascus,
   32. to the saints *which dwelt* at Lydda.
   35. all *that dwelt* at Lydda and Saron
11:29. unto the brethren *which dwelt* in Judæa:
13:27. For they *that dwell* at Jerusalem,
17:24. *dwelleth* not in temples made
   26. for *to dwell* on all the face of
19:10. all they *which dwelt* in Asia heard
   17. Greeks also *dwelling* at Ephesus ;
22:12. of all the Jews *which dwelt* (there),
Eph 3:17. That Christ may *dwell* in your hearts
Col. 1:19. that in him should all fulness *dwell ;*
2: 9. in him *dwelleth* all the fulness
Heb 11: 9. *dwelling* in tabernacles with Isaac
Jas. 4: 5. The spirit that *dwelleth* in us
2Pet.3:13. wherein *dwelleth* righteousness.
Rev 2:13. and where thou *dwellest,*
  — slain among you, where Satan *dwelleth.*
3:10. to try them *that dwell* upon the
6:10. on them *that dwell* on the earth ?
8:13. Woe, woe, woe, to the *inhabiters* of
11:10. they *that dwell* upon the earth
  — them *that dwelt* on the earth.
12:12. Woe to the *inhabiters* of the earth
13: 8. all *that dwell* upon the earth
   12. and them *which dwell* therein.
   14. deceiveth them *that dwell* on
  — saying to them *that dwell* on the
14: 6. to preach unto them *that dwell* on
17: 2. and the *inhabitants* of the earth
   8. and they *that dwell* on the earth

κατοίκησις, *katoikeesis.*

Mar 5: 3. Who had (his) *dwelling* among the tombs ;

κατοικητήριον, *katoikeeteerion.*

Eph 2:22. for an *habitation* of God through the
Rev 18: 2. is become the *habitation* of devils,

κατοικία, *katoikia.*

Acts17:26. the bounds of their *habitation ;*

κατοπτρίζομαι, *katoptrizomai.*

2Co. 3:18. *beholding as in a glass* the glory of the Lord,

κατόρθωμα, *katorthōma.*

Acts24: 2. and that *very worthy deeds* are done unto

κάτω, κατωτέρω, *kato, katotero.*

Mat. 2:16. from two years old and *under,*

Mat. 4: 6. cast thyself *down :* for it is
27:51. from the top to the *bottom ;*
Mar 14:66. as Peter was *beneath* in the palace,
15:38. from the top to the *bottom.*
Lu. 4: 9. cast thyself *down* from hence:
Joh. 8: 6. But Jesus stooped *down,*
8. again he stooped *down,* and wrote
23. Ye are from *beneath ;* I am from
Acts 2:19. and signs in the earth *beneath ;*
20: 9. and fell *down* from the third

κατώτερος, *katōteros.*

Eph 4: 9. but that he also descended first into the
lower parts

καῦμα, *kauma.*

Rev. 7:16. light on them, nor any *heat.*
16: 9. were scorched with great *heat,*

καυματίζω, *kaumatizo.*

Mat.13: 6. sun was up, they *were scorched ;*
Mar 4: 6. it *was scorched ;* and because it had
Rev.16: 8. *to scorch* men with fire.
9. And men *were scorched* with great

καῦσις, *kausis.*

Heb. 6: 8. whose end (is) to *be burned.* (lit: unto
burning)

καυσόω, *kausoō.*

2Pet.3:10. shall melt *with fervent heat,* (lit. *being set
on fire*)
12. shall melt *with fervent heat ?* (lit.*being, &c.*)

καύσων, *kausōn.*

Mat.20:12. borne the burden and *heat* of the day.
Lu. 12:55. ye say, There will be *heat ;*
Jas. 1:11. is·no sooner risen with a *burning heat,*

καυτηριάζομαι, *kauteeriazomai.*

1Ti. 4: 2. conscience *seared with a hot iron ;*

καυχάομαι, *kaukaomai.*

Ro. 2:17. and *makest* thy *boast* of God,
23. Thou that *makest* thy *boast* of the
5: 2. *rejoice* in hope of the glory of God.
3. but we *glory* in tribulations
11. we also *joy* in God through our Lord
1Co. 1:29. That no flesh *should glory*
31. He *that glorieth,* let him *glory* in the Lord.
3:21. *let* no man *glory* in men.
4: 7. why *dost* thou *glory,*
2Co. 5:12. them *which glory* in appearance,
7:14. if I *have boasted* any thing
9: 2. for which I *boast* of you

2Co.10: 8. though I *should boast* somewhat
13. we *will* not *boast* of things
15. Not *boasting* of things without
16. not *to boast* in another man's line
17. But he *that glorieth, let* him *glory* in the
11:12. that wherein they *glory,*
16. that I *may boast* myself a little.
18. Seeing that many *glory* after the flesh, I
will glory also.
30. If I must needs *glory,* I *will glory* of the
things which concern
12: 1. not expedient for me doubtless *to glory.*
5. Of such an one *will* I *glory :* yet of myself
I *will* not *glory,*
6. though I would desire to *glory,*
9. *will* I rather *glory* in my infirmities,
11. I am become a fool in *glorying ;*
Gal. 6:13. that they *may glory* in your flesh.
14. God forbid that I should *glory,*
Eph. 2: 9. lest any man *should boast.*
Phi. 3: 3. and *rejoice* in Christ Jesus,
2Th. 1: 4. So that we ourselves *glory* in you
Jas. 1: 9. *Let* the brother of low degree *rejoice* in
that he is exalted:
4:16. now ye *rejoice* in your boastings:

καύχημα, *kaukeema.*

Ro. 4: 2. he hath (*whereof*) *to glory ;* but not
1Co. 5: 6. Your *glorying* (is) not good.
9:15. man should make my *glorying* void.
16. I have nothing *to glory of :*
2Co. 1:14. that we are your *rejoicing,*
5:12. give you occasion *to glory* on our
9: 3. lest our *boasting* of you should be in
Gal. 6: 4. shall he have *rejoicing* in himself
Phi. 1:26. That your *rejoicing* may be more
2:16. that I may *rejoice* in the day of
Heb. 3: 6. the *rejoicing* of the hope firm

καύχησις, *kaukeesis.*

Ro. 3:27. Where (is) *boasting* then?
15:17. I have therefore *whereof I may glory*
1Co.15:31. I protest by your *rejoicing*
2Co. 1:12. For our *rejoicing* is this,
7: 4. great (is) my *glorying* of you:
14. even so our *boasting,* which (I made)
8:24. and of our *boasting* on your behalf.
9: 4. in this same confident *boasting.*
11:10. no man shall stop me of this *boasting*
17. in this confidence of *boasting.*
1Th. 2:19. or crown of *rejoicing ?* (Are) not even ye
Jas. 4:16. all such *rejoicing* is evil.

κεῖμαι, *kīmai.*

Mat. 3:10. the ax *is laid* unto the root
5:14. A city *that is set* on an hill
28: 6. Come, see the place where the Lord *lay.*
Lu. 2:12. *lying* in a manger.
16. and the babe *lying* in a manger.
34. Behold, this (child) *is set* for the
3: 9. the axe *is laid* unto the root
12:19. thou hast much goods *laid up*
23:53. never man before was *laid.*
24:12. the linen clothes *laid* by themselves,
Joh. 2: 6. And there were *set* there six waterpots
11:41. where the dead was *laid.*

Joh. 19:29. Now there *was set* a vessel full of vinegar:
   20: 5. saw the linen clothes *lying ;*
      6. and seeth the linen clothes *lie,*
      7. not *lying* with the linen clothes,
     12. where the body of Jesus *had lain.*
   21: 9. a fire of coals)(there,
1Co. 3:11. other foundation can no man lay than *that is laid,*
2Co. 3:15. the vail *is* upon their heart.
Phi. 1:17. I *am set* for the defence of the
1Th. 3: 3. we *are appointed* thereunto.
1Ti. 1: 9. the law *is* not *made* for a righteous
1Joh. 5:19. the whole world *lieth* in wickedness.
Rev. 4: 2. a throne *was set* in heaven,
   21:16. the city *lieth* foursquare,

κειρίαι, *kīriai.*

Joh. 11:44. bound hand and foot with *graveclothes :*

κείρω, *kīro.*

Acts 8:32. a lamb dumb before his *shearer,*
   18:18. *having shorn* (his) head
1Co. 11: 6. *let* her also *be shorn :* but if it be a shame for a woman *to be shorn*

κέλευσμα, *kelūsma.*

1Th. 4:16. shall descend from heaven with a *shout,*

κελεύω, *kelūo.*

Mat. 8:18. he *gave commandment* to depart
   14: 9. he *commanded* (it) to be given (her).
     19. he *commanded* the multitude to sit
     28. *bid* me come unto thee on the
   15:35. he *commanded* the multitude to
   18:25. his lord *commanded* him to be sold,
   27:58. Pilate *commanded* the body to be
     64. *Command* therefore that the
Lu. 18:40. and *commanded* him to be brought
Acts 4:15. *when* they *had commanded* them
   5:34. *commanded* to put the apostles forth
   8:38. he *commanded* the chariot to stand
   12:19. *commanded* that (they) should be
   16:22. and *commanded* to beat (them).
   21:33. and *commanded* (him) to be bound
     34. he *commanded* him to be carried into
   22:24. The chief captain *commanded* him
     30. *commanded* the chief priests and all
   23: 3. and *commandest* me to be smitten
     10. *commanded* the soldiers to go down,
     35. he *commanded* him to be kept in Herod's
   24: 8. *Commanding* his accusers to come
   25: 6. *commanded* Paul to be brought.
     17. *commanded* the man to be brought
   21. I *commanded* him to be kept till
   23. *at* Festus' *commandment* Paul was
   27:43. *commanded* that they which could swim

κενοδοξία, *kenodoxia.*

Phi. 2: 3. through strife or *vainglory :*

κενόδοξος, *kenodoxos.*

Gal. 5:26. Let us not be *desirous of vain glory,*

κενός, *kenos.*

Mar 12: 3. and sent (him) away *empty.*
Lu. 1:53. the rich he hath sent *empty* away.
   20:10. and sent (him) away *empty.*
     11. and sent (him) away *empty.*
Acts 4:25. and the people imagine *vain* things?
1Co. 15:10. upon me was not in *vain ;*
     14. then (is) our preaching *vain,* and your faith (is) also *vain.*
     58. your labour is not in *vain* in the
2Co. 6: 1. receive not the grace of God in *vain.*
Gal. 2: 2. or had run, in *vain.*
Eph. 5: 6. Let no man deceive you with *vain* words:
Phi. 2:16. I have not run in *vain,* neither laboured in *vain.*
Col. 2: 8. through philosophy and *vain* deceit,
1Th. 2: 1. that it was not in *vain :*
   3: 5. and our labour be in *vain.*
Jas. 2:20. O *vain* man, that faith without

κενοφωνία, *kenophōnia.*

1Ti. 6:20. avoiding profane (and) *vain babblings,*
2Ti. 2:16. shun profane (and) *vain babblings :*

κενόω, *kenoō.*

Ro. 4:14. of the law (be) heirs, faith *is made void,*
1Co. 1:17. lest the cross of Christ *should be made of none effect.*
   9:15. *should make* my glórying *void.*
2Co. 9: 3. lest our boasting of you *should be in vain*
Phi. 2: 7. But *made* himself *of no reputation,*

κέντρον, *kentron.*

Acts 9: 5. hard for thee to kick against the *pricks.*
   26:14. hard for thee to kick against the *pricks.*
1Co. 15:55. O death, where (is) thy *sting?*
     56. The *sting* of death (is) sin ;
Rev. 9:10. there were *stings* in their tails:

κεντυρίων, *kenturiōn.*

Mar 15:39. when the *centurion,* which stood
     44. and calling (unto him) the *centurion,*
     45. when he knew (it) of the *centurion,*

κενῶς, *kenōs.*

Jas. 4: 5. Do ye think that the scripture saith *in vain,*

κεραία, *keraia.*

Mat. 5:18. one jot or one *tittle* shall in no wise
Lu. 16:17. than one *tittle* of the law to fail.

κεραμεύς, *keramūs.*

Mat. 27: 7. bought with them the *potter's* field,

Mat.27:10. gave them for the *potter's* field,
Ro. 9:21. Hath not the *potter* power over the clay,

κεραμικός, *keramikos.*

Rev. 2:27. as the vessels *of a potter* shall

κεράμιον, *keramion.*

Mar 14:13. bearing a *pitcher* of water:
Lu. 22:10. bearing a *pitcher* of water;

κέραμος, *keramos.*

Lu. 5:19. let him down through the *tiling*

κεράννυμι, κεράω, *kerannumi, kerao.*

Rev.14:10. of the wine of the wrath of God, *which is poured out* without mixture
18: 6. the cup which she hath *filled fill* to her double.

κέρας, *keras.*

Lu. 1:69. hath raised up an *horn* of salvation
Rev. 5: 6. having seven *horns* and seven eyes,
9:13. a voice from the four *horns* of the golden
12: 3. having seven heads and ten *horns*,
13: 1. having seven heads and ten *horns*, and upon his *horns* ten crowns,
11. he had two *horns* like a lamb,
17: 3. having seven heads and ten *horns*.
7. which hath the seven heads and ten *horns*.
12. the ten *horns* which thou sawest
16. the ten *horns* which thou sawest

κεράτιον, *keration.*

Lu. 15:16. have filled his belly with the *husks*

κερδαίνω, *kerdaino.*

Mat.16:26. if he *shall gain* the whole world,
18:15. thou *hast gained* thy brother.
25:17. he also *gained* other two.
20. I *have gained* beside them five
22. I *have gained* two other talents
Mar 8:36. if he *shall gain* the whole world,
Lu. 9:25. *if he gain* the whole world,
Acts27:21. and *to have gained* this harm and loss.
1Co. 9:19. that I *might gain* the more.
20. that I *might gain* the Jews;
— that I *might gain* them that are under
21. *might gain* them that are without law.
22. that I *might gain* the weak;
Phi. 3: 8. that I *may win* Christ,
Jas. 4:13. and buy and sell, and *get gain:*
1Pet.3: 1. they also *may...be won* by the conversation of the wives;

κέρδος, *kerdos.*

Phi. 1:21. and to die (is) *gain.*

Phi. 3: 7. But what things were *gain* to me,
Tit. 1:11. for filthy *lucre's* sake.

κέρμα, *kerma.*

Joh. 2:15. and poured out the changers' *money,*

κερματιστής, *kermatistees.*

Joh. 2:14. and the *changers of money* sitting:

κεφάλαιον, *kephalaion.*

Acts22:28. With a great *sum* obtained I
Heb 8: 1. which we have spoken (this is) the *sum:*

κεφαλαιόω, *kephalaioō.*

Mar 12: 4. and *wounded* (him) *in the head,*

κεφαλή, *kephalee.*

Mat. 5:36. Neither shalt thou swear by thy *head,*
6:17. when thou fastest anoint thine *head,*
8:20. hath not where to lay (his) *head.*
10:30. hairs of your *head* are all numbered
14: 8. Give me here John Baptist's *head*
11. And his *head* was brought
21:42. the same is become the *head* of the corner.
26: 7. and poured it on his *head,*
27:29. they put (it) upon his *head,*
30. and smote him on the *head.*
37. And set up over his *head*
39. reviled him, wagging their *heads,*
Mar. 6:24. The *head* of John the Baptist.
25. in a charger the *head* of John
27. commanded his *head* to be brought:
28. brought his *head* in a charger,
12:10. is become the *head* of the corner:
14: 3. and poured (it) on his *head.*
15:19. they smote him on the *head*
29. wagging their *heads,* and saying,
Lu. 7:38. did wipe (them) with the hairs of her *head,*
44. wiped (them) with the hairs of her *head.*
46. My *head* with oil thou didst not
9:58. hath not where to lay (his) *head.*
12: 7. hairs of your *head* are all numbered.
20:17. is become the *head* of the corner?
21:18. there shall not an hair of your *head* perish.
28. lift up your *heads;* for
Joh.13: 9. but also (my) hands and (my) *head.*
19: 2. and put (it) on his *head,*
30. and he bowed his *head,* and gave up
20: 7. the napkin, that was about his *head,*
12. the one at the *head,* and the other
Acts 4:11. is become the *head* of the corner.
18: 6. Your blood (be) upon your own *heads;*
18. having shorn (his) *head*
21:24. that they may shave (their) *heads:*
27:34. shall not an hair fall from the *head* of
Ro. 12:20. shalt heap coals of fire on his *head.*
1Co.11: 3. the *head* of every man is Christ; and the *head* of the woman (is) the man; and the *head* of Christ (is) God.
4. or prophesying, having (his) *head* covered, dishonoureth his *head.*

1Co.11: 5. or prophesieth with (her) *head* uncovered
dishonoureth her *head :*
7. a man indeed ought not to cover (his) *head,*
10. ought the woman to have power on (her) *head*
12:21. nor again the *head* to the feet, I have no
Eph. 1:22. gave him (to be) *head* over all (things)
4:15. which is the *head,* (even) Christ:
5:23. the husband is the *head* of the wife, even
as Christ is the *head* of the church:
Col. 1:18. he is the *head* of the body, the church:
2:10. the *head* of all principality and power:
19. And not holding the *Head,*
1Pet.2: 7. is made the *head* of the corner,
Rev. 1:14. His *head* and (his) hairs (were) white
4: 4. they had on their *heads* crowns of gold.
9: 7. on their *heads* (were) as it were crowns
17. the *heads* of the horses (were) as the *heads* of lions ;
19. and had *heads,* and with them they do hurt.
10: 1. a rainbow (was) upon his *head,*
12: 1. and upon her *head* a crown of
3. having seven *heads* and ten horns, and
seven crowns upon his *heads.*
13: 1. having seven *heads* and ten horns,
— upon his *heads* the name of blasphemy.
3. And I saw one of his *heads* as it were
14:14. having on his *head* a golden crown,
17: 3. having seven *heads* and ten horns.
7. which hath the seven *heads* and ten horns.
9. The seven *heads* are seven mountains,
18:19. they cast dust on their *heads,*
19:12. on his *head* (were) many crowns ;

κεφαλίς, *kephalis.*

Heb 10: 7. in the *volume* of the book it is

κῆνσος, *keensos.*

Mat.17:25. take custom or *tribute?*
22:17. Is it lawful to give *tribute* unto
19. Shew me the *tribute* money.
Mar 12:14. Is it lawful to give *tribute* to

κῆπος, *keepos.*

Lu. 13:19. and cast into his *garden ;*
Joh.18: 1. where was a *garden,*
26. Did not I see thee in the *garden*
19:41. there was a *garden ;* and in the *garden* a
new sepulchre,

κηπουρός, *keepouros.*

Joh.20:15. supposing him to be the *gardener,*

κηρίον, *keerion.*

Lu. 24:42. and of an honey*comb.*

κήρυγμα, *keerugma.*

Mat.12:41. at the *preaching* of Jonas ;

Lu. 11:32. at the *preaching* of Jonas ;
Ro. 16:25. and the *preaching* of Jesus Christ,
1Co. 1:21. by the foolishness of *preaching* to save
2: 4. my *preaching* (was) not with enticing
15:14. then (is) our *preaching* vain,
2Ti. 4:17. by me the *preaching* might be fully known,
Tit. 1: 3. manifested his word through *preaching,*

κῆρυξ, *keerux.*

1Ti. 2: 7. I am ordained a *preacher,*
2Ti. 1:11. I am appointed a *preacher,*
2Pet.2: 5. a *preacher* of righteousness,

κηρύσσω, *keerusso.*

Mat. 3: 1. *preaching* in the wilderness
4:17. Jesus began *to preach,*
23. *preaching* the gospel of the kingdom,
9:35. *preaching* the gospel of the kingdom,
10: 7. as ye go, *preach,*
27. (that) *preach* ye upon the housetops.
11: 1. and *to preach* in their cities.
24:14. *shall be preached* in all the world
26:13. Wheresoever this gospel *shall be preached*
Mar. 1: 4. and *preach* the baptism of repentance
7. And *preached,* saying, There cometh
14. *preaching* the gospel of the
38. that I may *preach* there also:
39. he preached (lit. was *preaching*) in their
synagogues
45. began *to publish* (it) much,
3:14. might send them forth *to preach,*
5:20. and began *to publish* in Decapolis
6:12. and *preached* that men should repent.
7:36. the more a great deal they *published* (it);
13:10. must first *be published* among
14: 9. Wheresoever this gospel *shall be preached*
16:15. *preach* the gospel to every
20. and *preached* every where,
Lu. 3: 3. *preaching* the baptism of repentance
4:18(19). *to preach* deliverance to the captives,
19. *To preach* the acceptable year
44. And he preached (lit. was *preaching*) in
the synagogues
8: 1. *preaching* and shewing the glad
39. *and published* throughout the whole
9: 2. he sent them *to preach*
12: 3. *shall be proclaimed* upon the housetops.
24:47. should *be preached* in his
Acts 8: 5. and *preached* Christ unto them.
9:20. he *preached* Christ in the
10:37. the baptism which John *preached ;*
42. he commanded us *to preach* unto the
15:21. hath in every city them *that preach* him,
19:13. by Jesus whom Paul *preacheth.*
20:25. among whom I have gone *preaching*
28:31. *Preaching* the kingdom of God,
Ro. 2:21. thou *that preachest* a man
10: 8. the word of faith, which we *preach ;*
14. how shall they hear without a *preacher?*
15. how *shall* they *preach,* except they be
1Co. 1:23. But we *preach* Christ crucified,
9:27. *when* I have *preached* to others,
15:11. so we *preach,* and so ye believed.
12. if Christ *be preached* that he
2Co. 1:19. Jesus Christ, *who was preached* among
you by us,
4: 5. we *preach* not ourselves,

2Co.11: 4. if he that cometh *preacheth* another Jesus,
whom we *have* not *preached,*
Gal. 2: 2. that gospel which I *preach*
5:11. if I yet *preach* circumcision,
Phi. 1:15. Some indeed *preach* Christ even of envy
Col. 1:23. which was *preached* to every creature
1Th 2: 9. we *preached* unto you the gospel
1Ti. 3:16. *preached* unto the Gentiles,
2Ti. 4: 2. *Preach* the word; be instant
1Pet.3:19. and *preached* unto the spirits
Rev. 5: 2. I saw a strong angel *proclaiming*

κῆτος, *keetos.*

Mat.12:40. and three nights in the *whale's* belly;

κιϐωτός, *kibōtos.*

Mat 24:38. the day that Noe entered into the *ark,*
Lu. 17:27. Noe entered into the *ark,* and the
Heb 9: 4. the *ark* of the covenant
11: 7. prepared an *ark* to the saving
1Pet.3:20. while the *ark* was a preparing,
Rev 11:19. there was seen in his temple the *ark* of

κιθάρα, *kithara.*

1Co.14: 7. giving sound, whether pipe or *harp,*
Rev. 5: 8. having every one of them *harps,*
14: 2. harping with their *harps :*
15: 2. having the *harps* of God.

κιθαρίζω, *kitharizo.*

1Co.14: 7. be known what is piped or *harped?*
Rev.14: 2. of harpers *harping* with their harps:

κιθαρῳδός, *kitharōdos.*

Rev.14: 2. I heard the voice of *harpers*
18:22. And the voice of *harpers,*

κινάμωμον, *kinamōmon.*

Rev.18:13. And *cinnamon,* and odours,

κινδυνεύω, *kindunūo.*

Lu. 8:23. were filled (with water), and *were in jeopardy.*
Acts19:27. not only this our craft *is in danger*
40. we *are in danger* to be called in question
1Co.15:30. why *stand* we *in jeopardy* every hour?

κίνδυνος, *kindunos.*

Ro. 8:35. or nakedness, or *peril,* or sword?
2Co.11:26. (in) *perils* of waters, (in) *perils* of robbers,
(in) *perils* by (mine own) countrymen,
(in) *perils* by the heathen, (in) *perils* in
the city, (in) *perils* in the wilderness,
(in) *perils* in the sea, (in) *perils* among
false brethren;

κινέω, *kineo.*

Mat 23: 4. will not *move* them with one of
27:39. reviled him, *wagging* their heads,
Mar 15:29. railed on him, *wagging* their heads,
Acts17:28. in him we live, and *move,*
21:30. all the city *was moved,*
24: 5. a mover of (lit. *moving*) sedition
Rev. 2: 5. and *will remove* thy candlestick
6:14. every mountain and island *were moved* out
of their places.

κίνησις, *kineesis.*

Joh. 5: 3. waiting for the *moving* of the water.

κλάδος, *klados.*

Mat.13:32. lodge in the *branches* thereof.
21: 8. others cut down *branches* from the
24:32. When his *branch* is yet tender,
Mar 4:32. shooteth out great *branches;*
13:28. When her *branch* is yet tender,
Lu. 13:19. lodged in the *branches* of it.
Ro. 11:16. the root (be) holy, so (are) the *branches.*
17. if some of the *branches* be broken off,
18. Boast not against the *branches.*
19. The *branches* were broken off, that
21. if God spared not the natural *branches,*

κλάζω, κλάω, *klazo, klao.*

Mat 14:19. he blessed, and *brake, and* gave
15:36. and gave thanks, and *brake* (them),
26:26. Jesus took bread, and blessed (it), and
brake
Mar 8: 6. and gave thanks, and *brake,*
19. When I *brake* the five loaves
14:22. Jesus took bread, and blessed, and *brake*
Lu. 22:19. and gave thanks, and *brake* (it),
24:30. took bread, and blessed (it), and *brake, and*
Acts 2:46. and *breaking* bread from house
20: 7. came together *to break* bread,
11. and *had broken* bread, and eaten,
27:35. *when* he *had broken* (it), he began to eat.
1Co.10:16. The bread which we *break,*
11:24. he *brake* (it), and said, Take, eat: this is
my body, *which is broken* for you:

κλαίω, *klaio.*

Mat. 2:18. Rachel *weeping* (for) her children,
26:75. he went out, and *wept* bitterly.
Mar 5:38. and them *that wept* and wailed
39. Why make ye this ado, and *weep?*
14:72. And when he thought thereon, he *wept.*
16:10. as they mourned and *wept.*
Lu. 6:21. Blessed (are ye) *that weep* now:
25. for ye shall mourn and *weep.*
7:13. and said unto her, *Weep* not.
32. and ye *have* not *wept.*
38. at his feet behind (him) *weeping,*
8:52. And all *wept,* and bewailed her: but he
said, *Weep* not;
19:41. he beheld the city, and *wept* over it,
22:62. Peter went out, and *wept* bitterly.
23:28. *weep* not for me, but *weep* for yourselves,

Joh. 11:31. She goeth unto the grave to *weep*
33. When Jesus therefore saw her *weeping*, and the Jews also *weeping*
16:20. ye shall *weep* and lament,
20:11. Mary stood without at the sepulchre *weeping*: and as she *wept*,
13. Woman, why *weepest* thou ? She
15. Woman, why *weepest* thou ? whom
Acts 9:39. all the widows stood by him *weeping*,
21:13. What mean ye to *weep* and to break
Ro. 12:15. and *weep* with them *that weep*.
1Co. 7:30. And they *that weep*, as though they *wept* not ;
Phi. 3:18. and now tell you even *weeping*,
Jas. 4: 9. Be afflicted, and mourn, and *weep* :
5: 1. (ye) rich men, *weep* and howl for your
Rev. 5: 4. And I *wept* much, because no
5. *Weep* not: behold, the Lion of the
18: 9. *shall bewail* her, and lament
11. shall *weep* and mourn over her ;
15. of her torment, *weeping* and wailing,
19. cried, *weeping* and wailing, saying,

κλάσις, *klasis.*

Lu. 24:35. was known of them in *breaking* of bread.
Acts 2:42. and in *breaking* of bread, and in prayers.

κλάσμα, *klasma.*

Mat. 14:20. they took up of the *fragments*
15:37. they took up of the *broken* (meat)
Mar 6:43. twelve baskets full of the *fragments*,
8: 8. they took up of the *broken* (meat)
19. how many baskets full of *fragments*
20. how many baskets full of *fragments*
Lu. 9:17. there was taken up of *fragments*
Joh. 6:12. Gather up the *fragments* that remain,
13. filled twelve baskets with the *fragments*

κλαυθμός, *klauthmos.*

Mat. 2:18. lamentation, and *weeping*, and great
8:12. there shall be *weeping* and gnashing
13:42. there shall be *wailing* and gnashing
50. there shall be *wailing* and gnashing
22:13. there shall be *weeping* and gnashing
24:51. there shall be *weeping* and gnashing
25:30. there shall be *weeping* and gnashing
Lu. 13:28. There shall be *weeping* and gnashing
Acts 20:37. And they all wept sore, (lit. there was great *weeping* of all)

κλάω see κλάζω.

κλείς, *klis.*

Mat. 16:19. I will give unto thee the *keys* of the
Lu. 11:52. ye have taken away the *key* of knowledge:
Rev. 1:18. and have the *keys* of hell and of
3: 7. he that hath the *key* of David,
9: 1. to him was given the *key* of the
20: 1. having the *key* of the bottomless

κλείω, *klio.*

Mat. 6: 6. *when* thou *hast shut* thy door,
23:13(14). ye *shut up* the kingdom of heaven
25:10. and the door *was shut*.
Lu. 4:25. when the heaven *was shut up*
11: 7. the door *is* now *shut*,
Joh. 20:19. *when* the doors *were shut*
26. the doors *being shut*,
Acts 5:23. The prison truly found we *shut*
21:30. forthwith the doors *were shut*.
1Joh. 3:17. and *shutteth up* his bowels
Rev. 3: 7. he that openeth, and no man *shutteth* ; and *shutteth*, and no man openeth ;
8. and no man can *shut* it:
11: 6. These have power *to shut* heaven,
20: 3. into the bottomless pit, and *shut* him *up*,
21:25. the gates of it *shall* not *be shut*

κλέμμα, *klemma.*

Rev. 9:21. Neither repented they of...nor of their *thefts*.

κλέος, *kleos.*

1Pet. 2:20. For what *glory* (is it), if, when

κλέπτης, *kleptees.*

Mat. 6:19. where *thieves* break through and steal :
20. where *thieves* do not break through
24:43. in what watch the *thief* would come,
Lu. 12:33. where no *thief* approacheth,
39. what hour the *thief* would come,
Joh. 10: 1. the same is a *thief* and a robber.
8. All that ever came before me are *thieves* and robbers:
10. The *thief* cometh not, but for
12: 6. but because he was a *thief*,
1Co. 6:10. Nor *thieves*, nor covetous,
1Th. 5: 2. Lord so cometh as a *thief* in the
4. that day should overtake you as a *thief*.
1Pet. 4:15. or (as) a *thief*, or (as) an evildoer,
2Pet. 3:10. the Lord will come as a *thief*
Rev. 3: 3. I will come on thee as a *thief*,
16:15. Behold, I come as a *thief*.

κλέπτω, *klepto.*

Mat. 6:19. where thieves break through and *steal* :
20. do not break through nor *steal* :
19:18. Thou *shalt* not *steal*,
27:64. lest his disciples...and *steal* him away,
28:13. and *stole* him (away) while we slept.
Mar 10:19. *Do* not *steal*, Do not bear false
Lu. 18:20. *Do* not *steal*, Do not bear false
Joh. 10:10. but for to *steal*, and to kill,
Ro. 2:21. that preachest a man should not *steal, dost* thou *steal?*
13: 9. Thou *shalt* not *steal*,
Eph. 4:28. *Let* him *that stole steal* no more:

κλῆμα, *kleema.*

Joh. 15: 2. Every *branch* in me that beareth not
4. As the *branch* cannot bear fruit of
5. I am the vine, ye (are) the *branches* :
6. he is cast forth as a *branch*,

κληρονομέω, kleeronomeo.

Mat. 5: 5. for they *shall inherit* the earth.
   19:29. and *shall inherit* everlasting life.
   25:34. *inherit* the kingdom prepared
Mar 10:17. that I *may inherit* eternal life?
Lu. 10:25. what shall I do *to inherit* eternal
   18:18. what shall I do *to inherit* eternal
1Co. 6: 9. the unrighteous *shall not inherit*
   10. *shall inherit* the kingdom
   15:50. flesh and blood cannot *inherit* the kingdom
    of God ; neither *doth* corruption *inherit*
Gal. 4:30. *shall not be heir* with the son
   5:21. *shall* not *inherit* the kingdom
Heb 1: 4. he *hath by inheritance obtained*
   14. who shall *be heirs of* salvation ?
   6:12. of them *who* through faith and patience
    inherit the promises.
   12:17. when he would have *inherited*
1Pet.3: 9. that ye *should inherit* a blessing.
Rev.21: 7. He that overcometh *shall inherit* all

κληρονομία, kleeronomia.

Mat.21:38. let us seize on his *inheritance.*
Mar 12: 7. and the *inheritance* shall be our's.
Lu. 12:13. that he divide the *inheritance*
   20:14. that the *inheritance* may be our's.
Acts 7: 5. gave him none *inheritance* in
   20:32. and to give you an *inheritance*
Gal. 3:18. if the *inheritance* (be) of the law,
Eph. 1:14. the earnest of our *inheritance*
   18. the riches of the glory of his *inheritance* in
    the saints,
   5: 5. hath any *inheritance* in the
Col. 3:24. the reward of the *inheritance :*
Heb 9:15. the promise of eternal *inheritance.*
   11: 8. after receive for an *inheritance,*
1Pet.1: 4. To an *inheritance* incorruptible,

κληρονόμος, kleeronomos.

Mat.21:38. This is the *heir;* come, let us kill him,
Mar 12: 7. This is the *heir;* come, let us
Lu. 20:14. This is the *heir :* come, let us
Ro. 4:13. that he should be the *heir* of the world,
   14. if they which are of the law (be) *heirs,*
   8:17. And if children, then *heirs; heirs* of God,
    and joint-heirs with Christ ;
Gal. 3:29. and *heirs* according to the promise.
   4: 1. Now I say, (That) the *heir,* as long
   7. then an *heir* of God through Christ.
Tit. 3: 7. we should be made *heirs* according
Heb 1: 2. appointed *heir* of all things,
   6:17. to shew unto the *heirs* of promise
   11: 7. and became *heir* of the righteousness
Jas. 2: 5. rich in faith, and *heirs* of the kingdom

κληρόομαι, kleero-omai.

Eph. 1:11. In whom also we *have obtained an inheritance,* (lit. *have been taken as an inheritance*)

κλῆρος, kleeros.

Mat.27:35. and parted his garments, casting *lots :*
   — upon my vesture did they cast *lots.*
Mar 15:24. casting *lots* upon them,

Lu. 23:34. they parted his raiment, and cast *lots.*
Joh.19:24. for my vesture they did cast *lots.*
Acts 1:17. had obtained *part* of this ministry.
   25. That he may take *part* of this ministry
    and apostleship,
   26. And they gave forth their *lots;* and the
    lot fell upon Matthias;
   8:21. Thou hast neither part nor *lot*
   26:18. and *inheritance* among them which are
Col. 1:12. to be partakers of the *inheritance* of the
    saints in light:
1Pet.5: 3. as being lords over (God's) *heritage,*

κλῆσις, kleesis.

Ro. 11:29. the gifts and *calling* of God (are)
1Co. 1:26. For ye see your *calling,* brethren,
   7:20. abide in the same *calling* wherein
Eph. 1:18. what is the hope of his *calling,*
   4: 1. walk worthy of the *vocation*
   4. in one hope of your *calling;*
Phi. 3:14. for the prize of the high *calling*
2Th. 1:11. count you worthy of (this) *calling,*
2Ti. 1: 9. called (us) with an holy *calling,*
Heb 3: 1. partakers of the heavenly *calling,*
2Pet.1:10. give diligence to make your *calling*

κλητός, kleetos.

Mat.20:16. many be *called,* but few chosen.
   22:14. many are *called,* but few (are) chosen.
Ro. 1: 1. *called* (to be) an apostle,
   6. are ye also the *called* of Jesus
   7. *called* (to be) saints:
   8:28. to them who are the *called*
1Co. 1: 1. Paul, *called* (to be) an apostle
   2. sanctified in Christ Jesus, *called* (to be)
    saints,
   24. But unto them which are *called,*
Jude 1. preserved in Jesus Christ, (and) *called :*
Rev.17:14. they that are with him (are) *called,* and
    chosen. and faithful.

κλίβανος, klibanos.

Mat. 6:30. and to morrow is cast into the *oven,*
Lu. 12:28. and to morrow is cast into the *oven;*

κλίμα, klima.

Ro. 15:23. having no more place in these *parts,*
2Co.11:10. in the *regions* of Achaia.
Gal. 1:21. I came into the *regions* of Syria

κλίνη, klinee.

Mat. 9: 2. sick of the palsy, lying on a *bed :*
   6. take up thy *bed,* and go unto thine house.
Mar 4:21. or under a *bed ?*
   7: 4. brasen vessels, and of *tables.*
   30. and her daughter laid upon the *bed.*
Lu. 5:18. men brought in a *bed* a man
   8:16. or putteth (it) under a *bed ;* but
   17:34. there shall be two (men) in one *bed ;*
Acts 5:15. and laid (them) on *beds* and couches,
Rev. 2:22. I will cast her into a *bed,*

κλινίδιον, klinidion.

Lu. 5:19. through the tiling with (his) ccuch
24. take up thy couch, and go unto thine

κλίνω, klino.

Mat. 8:20. not where to lay (his) head.
Lu. 9:12. when the day began to wear away,
58. hath not where to lay (his) head.
24: 5. as they were afraid, and bowed down (their) faces
29. and the day is far spent.
Joh. 19:30. and he bowed his head, and gave up
Heb 11:34. turned to flight the armies of the aliens.

κλισία, klisia.

Lu. 9:14. them sit down by fifties in a company.

κλοπή, klopee.

Mat. 15:19. fornications, thefts, false witness,
Mar 7:22. Thefts, covetousness, wickedness,

κλύδων, kludōn.

Lu. 8:24. rebuked the wind and the raging of the water:
Jas. 1: 6. is like a wave of the sea

κλυδωνίζομαι, kludōnizomai.

Eph 4:14. tossed to and fro, and carried about

κνήθω, kneetho.

2Ti. 4: 3. having itching ears; (lit. itching as to hearing)

κοδράντης, kodrantees.

Mat. 5:26. till thou hast paid the uttermost farthing.
Mar 12:42. two mites, which make a farthing.

κοιλία, koilia.

Mat 12:40. and three nights in the whale's belly;
15:17. in at the mouth goeth into the belly,
19:12. so born from (their) mother's womb:
Mar 7:19. but into the belly,
Lu. 1:15. even from his mother's womb.
41. the babe leaped in her womb;
42. blessed (is) the fruit of thy womb.
44. the babe leaped in my womb for joy.
2:21. before he was conceived in the womb.
11:27. Blessed (is) the womb that bare thee,
15:16. he would fain have filled his belly
23:29. and the wombs that never bare,
Joh. 3: 4. second time into his mother's womb,
7:38. out of his belly shall flow rivers
Acts 3: 2. lame from his mother's womb
14: 8. a cripple from his mother's womb,
Ro. 16:18. serve not our Lord Jesus Christ, but their own belly;

1Co. 6:13. Meats for the belly, and the belly for
Gal. 1:15. separated me from my mother's womb,
Phi. 3:19. whose God (is their) belly,
Rev 10: 9. it shall make thy belly bitter,
10. my belly was bitter.

κοιμάομαι, koimaomai.

Mat 27:52. many bodies of the saints which slept
28:13. and stole him (away) while we slept.
Lu. 22:45. he found them sleeping for sorrow,
Joh. 11:11. Our friend Lazarus sleepeth;
12. Lord, if he sleep, he shall do well.
Acts 7:60. when he had said this, he fell asleep.
12: 6. Peter was sleeping between two
13:36. fell on sleep, and was laid unto his
1Co. 7:39. but if her husband be dead,
11:30. sickly among you, and many sleep.
15: 6. but some are fallen asleep.
18. Then they also which are fallen asleep
20. the firstfruits of them that slept.
51. We shall not all sleep,
1Th. 4:13. concerning them which are asleep,
14. them also which sleep in Jesus
15. shall not prevent them which are asleep.
2Pet. 3: 4. since the fathers fell asleep,

κοίμησις, koimeesis.

Joh. 11:13. had spoken of taking of rest in sleep.

κοινός, koinos.

Mar 7: 2. eat bread with defiled, that is to say, with unwashen, hands,
Acts 2:44. and had all things common;
4:32. but they had all things common.
10:14. eaten any thing that is common or
28. should not call any man common or
11: 8. for nothing common or unclean
Ro. 14:14. that (there is) nothing unclean of itself:
— esteemeth any thing to be unclean, to him (it is) unclean.
Tit. 1: 4. (mine) own son after the common faith:
Heb 10:29. an unholy thing, and hath done despite
Jude 3. to write unto you of the common salvation,

κοινόω, koinoō.

Mat 15:11. into the mouth defileth a man;
— this defileth a man.
18. and they defile the man.
20. These are (the things) which defile a man:
— unwashen hands defileth not a man.
Mar 7:15. entering into him can defile him:
— those are they that defile the man.
18. (it) cannot defile him;
20. that defileth the man.
23. come from within, and defile the man.
Acts 10:15. (that) call not thou common.
11: 9. (that) call not thou common.
21:28. and hath polluted this holy place.
Heb 9:13. ashes of an heifer sprinkling the unclean,
Rev 21:27. enter into it any thing that defileth,

κοινωνέω, koinōneo.

Ro. 12:13. Distributing to the necessity of saints;

Ro. 15:27. Gentiles *have been partakers* of their
Gal. 6: 6. *Let* him that is taught...*communicate* unto
him that teacheth
Phi. 4:15. no church *communicated* with me
1Ti. 5:22. neither *be partaker* of other men's sins:
Heb 2:14. as the children *are partakers* of
1Pet.4:13. as ye *are partakers* of Christ's
2Jo. 11. *is partaker* of his evil deeds.

κοινωνία, koinōnia.

Acts 2:42. and *fellowship*, and in breaking of bread,
Ro. 15:26. to make a certain *contribution*
1Co. 1: 9. called unto the *fellowship* of his Son
10:16. is it not the *communion* of the blood
— is it not the *communion* of the body
2Co. 6:14. what *communion* hath light
8: 4. and (take upon us) the *fellowship*
9:13. for (your) liberal *distribution*
13:14(13). the *communion* of the Holy Ghost,
Gal. 2: 9. the right hands of *fellowship*;
Eph 3: 9. what (is) the *fellowship* of the mystery,
Phi. 1: 5. For your *fellowship* in the gospel
2: 1. if any *fellowship* of the Spirit,
3:10. and the *fellowship* of his sufferings,
Philem 6. That the *communication* of thy faith
Heb 13:16. and to *communicate* forget not:
1Joh.1: 3. may have *fellowship* with us: and truly
our *fellowship* (is) with
6. If we say that we have *fellowship*
7. we have *fellowship* one with another,

κοινωνικός, koinōnikos.

1Ti. 6:18. ready to distribute, *willing to communicate*;

κοινωνός, koinōnos.

Mat 23:30. we would not have been *partakers*
Lu. 5:10. which were *partners* with Simon.
1Co.10:18. *partakers* of the altar?
20. ye should have *fellowship* with
2Co. 1: 7. as ye are *partakers* of the sufferings,
8:23. (he is) my *partner* and fellowhelper
Philem 17. If thou count me therefore a *partner*,
Heb 10:33. ye became *companions* of them
1Pet.5: 1. and also a *partaker* of the glory
2Pet.1: 4. be *partakers* of the divine nature, having
escaped

κοίτη, hoitee.

Lu. 11: 7. my children are with me in *bed*;
Ro. 9:10. when Rebecca also had *conceived* (κοιτην
ἐχουσα)
13:13. not in *chambering* and wantonness,
Heb 13: 4. and the *bed* undefiled:

κοιτών, hoitōn.

Acts 12:20. Blastus the king's chamberlain (lit. that
was over the king's *bedchamber*)

κόκκινος & τὸ κόκκινον, kokkinos & to kokkinon.

Mat.27:28. and put on him a *scarlet* robe.

Heb. 9:19. with water, and *scarlet* wool,
Rev.17: 3. upon a *scarlet coloured* beast,
4. in purple and *scarlet colour*,
18:12. purple, and silk, and *scarlet*,
16. and purple, and *scarlet*,

κόκκος, kokkos.

Mat.13:31. like to a *grain* of mustard seed,
17:20. faith as a *grain* of mustard seed,
Mar. 4:31. (It is) like a *grain* of mustard seed,
Lu. 13:19. a *grain* of mustard seed,
17: 6. faith as a *grain* of mustard seed,
Joh.12:24. Except a *corn* of wheat fall
1Co.15:37. bare *grain*, it may chance of wheat,

κολάζομαι, kolazomai.

Acts 4:21. nothing how they *might punish* them,
2Pet.2: 9. unto the day of judgment *to be punished*:

κολακεία, kolakīa.

1Th. 2: 5. used we *flattering* words, (lit. of *flattery*)

κόλασις, kolasis.

Mat.25:46. into everlasting *punishment*:
1Joh.4:18. because fear hath *torment*.

κολαφίζω, kolaphizo.

Mat.26:67. spit in his face, and *buffeted* him;
Mar 14:65. to cover his face, and *to buffet* him,
1Co. 4:11. and *are buffeted*, and have no certain
2Co.12: 7. the messenger of Satan *to buffet* me,
1Pet.2:20. when ye *be buffeted* for your faults,

κολλάω, kollao.

Lu. 10:11. dust of your city, which *cleaveth* on us,
15:15. and *joined* himself to a citizen
Acts 5:13. durst no man *join* himself
8:29. Go near, and *join* thyself to this chariot.
9:26. he assayed *to join* himself to the
10:28. that is a Jew *to keep company*,
17:34. certain men *clave* unto him, *and* believed:
Ro. 12: 9. *cleave* to that which is good.
1Co. 6:16. he which *is joined* to an harlot
17. But he that *is joined* unto the Lord

κολλούριον, kollourion.

Rev. 3:18. anoint thine eyes with *eyesalve*,

κολλυβιστής, kollubistees.

Mat.21:12. tables of the *moneychangers*,
Mar 11:15. tables of the *moneychangers*,
Joh. 2:15. poured out the *changers'* money,

κολοβόω, koloboō.

Mat.24:22. those days *should be shortened*,

Mat.24:22. those days *shall be shortened*,
Mar 13:20. except that the Lord *had shortened* those
— he *hath shortened* the days.

κόλπος, *kolpos.*

Lu. 6:38. shall men give into your *bosom.*
16:22. by the angels into Abraham's *bosom :*
23. and Lazarus in his *bosom.*
Joh. 1:18. which is in the *bosom* of the Father,
13:23. leaning on Jesus' *bosom*
Acts27:39. a certain *creek* with a shore,

κολυμβάω, *kolumbao.*

Acts27:43. that they which could *swim*

κολυμβήθρα, *kolumbeethra.*

Joh. 5: 2. by the sheep (market) a *pool*,
4. at a certain season into the *pool*,
7. to put me into the *pool :*
9: 7. wash in the *pool* of Siloam,
11. Go to the *pool* of Siloam,

κολώνια, *kolonia.*

Acts16:12. that part of Macedonia, (and) a *colony :*

κομάω, *komao.*

1Co.11:14. if a man *have long hair*,
15. But if a woman *have long hair*,

κόμη, *komee.*

1Co.11:15. for (her) *hair* is given her for a covering.

κομίζω, *komizo.*

Mat.25:27. I should *have received* mine own
Lu. 7:37. *brought* an alabaster box
2Co. 5:10. every one *may receive* the things
Eph. 6: 8. the same *shall he receive* of the
Col. 3:25. *shall receive* for the wrong
Heb10:36. ye *might receive* the promise.
11:19. from whence also he *received* him in a
39. *received* not the promise:
1Pet.1: 9. *Receiving* the end of your faith,
5: 4. ye *shall receive* a crown of glory
2Pet.2:13. *And shall receive* the reward of

κομψότερον, *kompsoteron.*

Joh. 4:52. when he began to amend. (lit. had himself
better)

κονιάω, *koniao.*

Mat.23:27. like unto *whited* sepulchres,
Acts23: 3. smite thee, (thou) *whited* wall:

κονιορτός, *koniortos.*

Mat.10:14. shake off the *dust* of your feet.
Lu. 9: 5. shake off the very *dust* from
10:11. the very *dust* of your city, which
Acts13:51. But they shook off the *dust*
22:23. and threw *dust* into the air,

κοπάζω, *kopazo.*

Mat.14:32. were come into the ship, the wind *ceased.*
Mar. 4:39. the wind *ceased*, and there was a
6:51. the wind *ceased :* and they were sore
amazed

κοπετός, *kopetos.*

Acts 8: 2. and made great *lamentation*

κοπή, *kopee.*

Heb 7: 1. from the *slaughter* of the kings,

κοπιάω, *kopiao.*

Mat. 6:28. they *toil* not, neither do they spin:
11:28. Come unto me, all (ye) *that labour*
Lu. 5: 5. we *have toiled* all the night, *and* have
12:27. they *toil* not, they spin not;
Joh. 4: 6. Jesus therefore, *being wearied* with (his)
journey,
38. whereon ye *bestowed* no *labour :* other men
laboured, and ye are
Acts20:35. that so *labouring* ye ought to
Ro. 16: 6. who *bestowed* much *labour* on us.
12. and Tryphosa, *who labour* in the Lord.
— which *laboured* much in the Lord.
1Co. 4:12. And *labour*, working with our
15:10. I *laboured* more abundantly
16:16. that helpeth with (us), and *laboureth.*
Gal. 4:11. lest I *have bestowed* upon you *labour* in
vain.
Eph. 4:28. but rather *let* him *labour*,
Phi. 2:16. neither *laboured* in vain.
Col. 1:29. Whereunto I also *labour*,
1Th. 5:12. to know them *which labour* among you,
1Ti. 4:10. we both *labour* and suffer reproach,
5:17. they *who labour* in the word
2Ti. 2: 6. husbandman *that laboureth* must
Rev. 2: 3. for my name's sake *hast laboured*,

κόπος, *kopos.*

Mat.26:10. Why trouble ye (lit. give ye *trouble* to)
the woman?
Mar.14: 6. why trouble ye her? (lit. give *trouble* to)
Lu. 11: 7. Trouble me not: (lit. give, &c.)
18: 5. this widow troubleth me, (lit. giveth, &c.)
Joh. 4:38. and ye are entered into their *labours.*
1Co. 3: 8. according to his own *labour.*
15:58. that your *labour* is not in vain
2Co. 6: 5. in *labours*, in watchings,
10:15. of other men's *labours ;*
11:23. in *labours* more abundant,
27. In *weariness* and painfulness,
Gal. 6:17. let no man *trouble* me: (lit. give, &c.)

1Th. 1: 3. your work of faith, and *labour* of love,
　　2: 9. our *labour* and travail:
　　3: 5. and our *labour* be in vain.
2Th. 3: 8. but wrought with *labour* and travail
Heb 6:10. your work and *labour* of love,
Rev. 2: 2. I know thy works, and thy *labour*,
　14:13. they may rest from their *labours*;

κοπρία, kopria.

Lu. 13: 8. till I shall dig about it, and dung (it):
　　　　(lit. throw *dung*)
　14:35. nor yet for the *dunghill*;

κόπτω, kopto.

Mat.11:17. and ye *have* not *lamented*.
　21: 8. others *cut down* branches
　24:30. shall all the tribes of the earth *mourn*,
Mar 11: 8. others *cut down* branches
Lu. 8:52. And all wept, and *bewailed* her:
　23:27. which also *bewailed* and lamented
Rev. 1: 7. *shall wail* because of him.
　18: 9. shall bewail her, and *lament* for her,

κόραξ, korax.

Lu. 12:24. Consider the *ravens*: for they

κοράσιον, korasion.

Mat. 9:24. the *maid* is not dead,
　25. and the *maid* arose.
　14:11. in a charger, and given to the *damsel*:
Mar. 5:41. *Damsel*, I say unto thee,
　42. the *damsel* arose, and walked;
　6:22. the king said unto the *damsel*,
　28. and gave it to the *damsel*: and the *damsel*
　　　　gave it to her mother.

κορβᾶν, κορβανᾶν, korban, korbanan.

Mat.27: 6. to put them into the *treasury*,
Mar. 7:11. (It is) *Corban*, that is to say, a gift,

κορέννυμι, korennumi.

Acts27:38. *when* they *had eaten enough*, they lightened
　　　　the ship,
1Co. 4: 8. Now ye are *full*, now ye are rich,

κόρος, koros.

Lu. 16: 7. An hundred *measures* of wheat.

κοσμέω, kosmeo.

Mat.12:44. findeth (it) empty, swept, and *garnished*.
　23:29. and *garnish* the sepulchres of the
　25: 7. arose, and *trimmed* their lamps.
Lu. 11:25. he findeth (it) swept and *garnished*.
　21: 5. how it *was adorned* with goodly stones
1Ti. 2: 9. that women *adorn* themselves in
Tit. 2:10. that they *may adorn* the doctrine

1Pet.3: 5. *adorned* themselves, being in subjection
Rev.21: 2. as a bride *adorned* for her
　19. of the wall of the city (were) *garnished*

κοσμικός, kosmikos.

Tit. 2:12. denying ungodliness and *worldly* lusts,
Heb 9: 1. and a *worldly* sanctuary.

κόσμιος, kosmios.

1Ti. 2: 9. adorn themselves in *modest* apparel,
　3: 2. vigilant, sober, *of good behaviour*,

κοσμοκράτωρ, kosmokratōr.

Eph. 6:12. against the *rulers* of the darkness of this
　　　　world, (lit. the *world-rulers* of the dark-
　　　　ness of this age)

κόσμος, kosmos.

Mat. 4: 8. him all the kingdoms of the *world*,
　5:14. Ye are the light of the *world*.
　13:35. from the foundation of the *world*.
　38. The field is the *world*;
　16:26. if he shall gain the whole *world*,
　18: 7. Woe unto the *world* because of
　24:21. not since the beginning of the *world*
　25:34. from the foundation of the *world*:
　26:13. preached in the whole *world*,
Mar. 8:36. shall gain the whole *world*,
　14: 9. throughout the whole *world*,
　16:15. Go ye into all the *world*,
Lu. 9:25. if he gain the whole *world*,
　11:50. from the foundation of the *world*,
　12:30. do the nations of the *world* seek
Joh. 1: 9. every man that cometh into the *world*.
　10. He was in the *world*, and the *world* was
　　　　made by him, and the *world* knew him
　　　　not.
　29. taketh away the sin of the *world*.
　3:16. For God so loved the *world*,
　17. God sent not his Son into the *world* to
　　　　condemn the *world*; but that the *world*
　　　　through him might
　19. light is come into the *world*,
　4:42. the Saviour of the *world*.
　6:14. that should come into the *world*.
　33. and giveth life unto the *world*.
　51. give for the life of the *world*.
　7: 4. shew thyself to the *world*.
　7. The *world* cannot hate you;
　8:12. I am the light of the *world*:
　23. ye are of this *world*; I am not of this
　　　　world.
　26. I speak to the *world* those things
　9: 5. As long as I am in the *world*, I am the
　　　　light of the *world*.
　39. I am come into this *world*, that
　10:36. sanctified, and sent into the *world*,
　11: 9. he seeth the light of this *world*.
　27. which should come into the *world*.
　12:19. behold, the *world* is gone after him.
　25. that hateth his life in this *world*
　31. Now is the judgment of this *world*: now
　　　　shall the prince of this *world* be cast out.

Joh.12:46. I am come a light into the *world*,
47. I came not to judge the *world*, but to save the *world*.
13: 1. he should depart out of this *world*
— his own which were in the *world*,
14:17. whom the *world* cannot receive,
19. and the *world* seeth me no more;
22. and not unto the *world* ?
27. not as the *world* giveth,
30. the prince of this *world* cometh,
31. But that the *world* may know
15:18. If the *world* hate you,
19. If ye were of the *world*, the *world* would love his own: but because ye are not of the *world*, but I have chosen you out of the *world*, therefore the *world* hateth you.
16: 8. he will reprove the *world* of sin,
11. the prince of this *world* is judged.
20. but the *world* shall rejoice:
21. that a man is born into the *world*.
28. and am come into the *world* : again, I leave the *world*, and go
33. In the *world* ye shall have
— I have overcome the *world*.
17: 5. which I had with thee before the *world*
6. which thou gavest me out of the *world* :
9. I pray not for the *world*,
11. I am no more in the *world*, but these are in the *world*,
12. I was with them in the *world*,
13. and these things I speak in the *world*,
14. and the *world* hath hated them, because they are not of the *world*, even as I am not of the *world*.
15. I pray not...take them out of the *world*,
16. They are not of the *world*, even as I am not of the *world*.
18. As thou hast sent me into the *world*, even so have I also sent them into the *world*.
21. that the *world* may believe that thou
23. that the *world* may know that thou
24. before the foundation of the *world*.
25. the *world* hath not known thee:
18:20. I spake openly to the *world* ;
36. My kingdom is not of this *world* : if my kingdom were of this *world*,
37. for this cause came I into the *world*,
21:25. I suppose that even the *world* itself
Acts17:24. God that made the *world* and all things
Ro. 1: 8. spoken of throughout the whole *world*.
20. from the creation of the *world*
3: 6. how shall God judge the *world* ?
19. all the *world* may become guilty
4:13. that he should be the heir of the *world*,
5:12. sin entered into the *world*,
13. until the law sin was in the *world* :
11:12. (be) the riches of the *world*,
15. (be) the reconciling of the *world*,
1Co. 1:20. made foolish the wisdom of this *world* ?
21. the *world* by wisdom knew not God,
27. the foolish things of the *world*
— the weak things of the *world*
28. And base things of the *world*,
2:12. not the spirit of the *world*,
3:19. For the wisdom of this *world*
22. or the *world*, or life, or death,
4: 9. a spectacle unto the *world*,
13. as the filth of the *world*,
5:10. with the fornicators of this *world*,
— must ye needs go out of the *world*.
6: 2. the saints shall judge the *world* ? and if the *world* shall be judged by you,

1Co. 7:31. And they that use this *world*,
— for the fashion of this *world* passeth
33. careth for the things that are of the *world*, how he may please (his) wife.
34. careth for the things of the *world*, how she may please (her) husband.
8: 4. that an idol (is) nothing in the *world*,
11:32. not be condemned with the *world*.
14:10. many kinds of voices in the *world*,
2Co. 1:12. our conversation in the *world*,
5:19. reconciling the *world* unto himself,
7:10. but the sorrow of the *world* worketh death.
Gal. 4: 3. under the elements of the *world* :
6:14. by whom the *world* is crucified unto me, and I unto the *world*.
Eph. 1: 4. before the foundation of the *world*,
2: 2. according to the course of this *world*,
12. without God in the *world* :
Phi. 2:15. ye shine as lights in the *world* ;
Col. 1: 6. as (it is) in all the *world* ;
2: 8. after the rudiments of the *world*,
20. from the rudiments of the *world*, why, as though living in the *world*,
1Ti. 1:15. came into the *world* to save sinners ;
3:16. believed on in the *world*,
6: 7. brought nothing into (this) *world*,
Heb. 4: 3. from the foundation of the *world*.
9:26. since the foundation of the *world* :
10: 5. when he cometh into the *world*,
11: 7. by the which he condemned the *world*,
38. Of whom the *world* was not worthy:
Jas. 1:27. to keep himself unspotted from the *world*.
2: 5. the poor of this *world* rich in faith, and heirs of
3: 6. a fire, a *world* of iniquity:
4: 4. the friendship of the *world* is enmity
— will be a friend of the *world* is the enemy of God.
1Pet. 1:20. before the foundation of the *world*,
3: 3. Whose *adorning* let it not be
5: 9. your brethren that are in the *world*.
2Pet. 1: 4. the corruption that is in the *world*
2: 5. And spared not the old *world*,
— flood upon the *world* of the ungodly ;
20. escaped the pollutions of the *world*
3: 6. Whereby the *world* that then was,
1Joh.2: 2. for (the sins of) the whole *world*.
15. Love not the *world*, neither the things (that are) in the *world*. If any man love the *world*, the love
16. For all that (is) in the *world*, the lust
— is not of the Father, but is of the *world*.
17. And the *world* passeth away,
3: 1. therefore the *world* knoweth
13. if the *world* hate you.
17. whoso hath this *world's* good,
4: 1. are gone out into the *world*.
3. now already is it in the *world*.
4. than he that is in the *world*.
5. They are of the *world* : therefore speak they of the *world*, and the *world* heareth
9. only begotten Son into the *world*,
14. the Saviour of the *world*.
17. so are we in this *world*.
5: 4. overcometh the *world* : and this is the victory that overcometh the *world*,
5. that overcometh the *world*,
19. and the whole *world* lieth
2Joh. 7. are entered into the *world*,
Rev.11:15. The kingdoms of this *world*
13: 8. from the foundation of the *world*.
17: 8. from the foundation of the *world*,

κοῦμι, koumi.

Mar 5:41. said unto her, Talitha cumi ; which is,...
      Damsel, I say unto thee, arise.

κουστωδία, koustōdia.

Mat.27:65. Ye have a watch : go your way,
      66. sealing the stone, and setting a watch.
      28:11. some of the watch came into the city,

κουφίζω, kouphizo.

Acts27:38. they lightened the ship,

κόφινος, kophinos.

Mat.14:20. that remained twelve baskets full.
      16: 9. and how many baskets ye took up?
Mar 6:43. twelve baskets full of the fragments,
      8:19. how many baskets full
Lu. 9:17. remained to them twelve baskets.
Joh. 6:13. and filled twelve baskets

κράββατος, krabbatos.

Mar 2: 4. they 'let down the bed wherein
      9. Arise, and take up thy bed, and walk ?
      11. Arise, and take up thy bed, and go
      12. he arose, took up the bed,
      6:55. and began to carry about in beds
Joh. 5: 8. Rise, take up thy bed,
      9. and took up his bed,
      10. for thee to carry (thy) bed.
      11. Take up thy bed, and walk.
      12. Take up thy bed, and walk ?
Acts 5:15. and laid (them) on beds and couches,
      9:33. Æneas, which had kept his bed

κράζω, krazo.

Mat. 8:29. behold, they cried out, saying,
      9:27. crying, and saying, (Thou) son of David,
      14:26. they cried out for fear.
      30. he cried, saying, Lord, save me.
      15:23. for she crieth after us.
      20:30. cried out, saying, Have mercy
      31. but they cried the more,
      21: 9. cried, saying, Hosanna
      15. and the children crying in the temple,
      27:23. But they cried out the more,
      50. when he had cried again with a loud
Mar 1:26. and cried with a loud voice,
      3:11. cried, saying, Thou art the Son of God.
      5: 5. and in the tombs, crying, and
      7. And cried with a loud voice,
      9:24. cried out, and said with tears,
      26. And (the spirit) cried, and rent him
      10:47. he began to cry out, and say, Jesus,
      48. but he cried the more
      11: 9. that followed, cried, saying,
      15:13. And they cried out again,
      14. And they cried out the more
      39. saw that he so cried out, and gave up
Lu. 4:41. came out of many, crying out, and saying,
      9:39. and he suddenly crieth out ;
      18:39. but he cried so much the more,

Lu. 19:40. stones would immediately cry out.
Joh. 1:15. and cried, saying, This was he
      7:28. Then cried Jesus in the temple as he
      37. Jesus stood and cried, saying, If any
      12:13. to meet him, and cried, Hosanna:
      44. Jesus cried and said, He that
      19:12. the Jews cried out, saying, If thou let
Acts 7:57. they cried out with a loud voice, and
      60. and cried with a loud voice,
      14:14. ran in among the people, crying out,
      16:17. and cried, saying, These men
      19:28. and cried out, saying, Great (is)
      32. Some therefore cried one thing, and
      34. cried out, Great (is) Diana
      21:28. Crying out, Men of Israel, help:
      36. crying, Away with him.
      23: 6. he cried out in the council,
      24:21. I cried standing among them,
Ro. 8:15. whereby we cry, Abba, Father.
      9:27. Esaias also crieth concerning
Gal. 4: 6. into your hearts, crying, Abba, Father.
Jas. 5: 4. of you kept back by fraud, crieth :
Rev. 6:10. they cried with a loud voice,
      7: 2. and he cried with a loud voice
      10. And cried with a loud voice,
      10: 3. And cried with a loud voice,
      — when he had cried, seven thunders
      12: 2. And she being with child cried,
      14:15. crying with a loud voice to him
      18: 2. And he cried mightily with a
      18. And cried when they saw the smoke
      19. and cried, weeping and wailing,
      19:17. and he cried with a loud voice,

κραιπάλη, kraipalee.

Lu. 21:34. lest at any time your hearts be overcharged
      with surfeiting,

κρανίον, kranion.

Mat.27:33. a place of a skull,
Mar 15:22. The place of a skull.
Lu. 23:33. which is called Calvary, (lit. skull)
Joh.19:17. into a place called (the place) of a skull,

κράσπεδον, kraspedon.

Mat. 9:20. and touched the hem of his garment:
      14:36. might only touch the hem of his
      23. 5. enlarge the borders of their garments,
Mar 6:56. if it were but the border of his
Lu. 8:44. and touched the border of his

κραταιός, krataios.

1Pet.5: 6. under the mighty hand of God,

κραταιόω, krataioō.

Lu. 1:80. and waxed strong in spirit, and was
      2:40. waxed strong in spirit, filled with
1Co.16:13. quit you like men, be strong.
Eph. 3:16. to be strengthened with might

κρατέω, krateo.

Mat. 9:25. and took her by the hand,

Mat.12:11. *will* he not *lay hold on* it,
14: 3. For Herod *had laid hold on* John, *and*
18:28. and he *laid hands on* him, *and*
21:46. when they sought *to lay hands on* him,
22: 6. the remnant *took* his servants, *and*
26: 4. consulted that they *might take* Jesus
48. that same is he: *hold* him *fast.*
50. laid hands on Jesus, and *took* him.
55. and ye *laid* no *hold on* me.
57. they *that had laid hold on* Jesus
28: 9. and *held* him *by* the feet, and
Mar 1:31. and *took* her *by* the hand,
3:21. they went out *to lay hold on* him:
5:41. he *took* the damsel *by* the hand,
6:17. and *laid hold upon* John,
7: 3. *holding* the tradition of the elders.
4. which they have received *to hold,*
8. ye *hold* the tradition of men,
9:10. they *kept* that saying with themselves,
27. Jesus *took* him *by* the hand, *and*
12:12. they sought *to lay hold on* him,
14: 1. sought how they might *take* him by craft, *and*
44. *take* him, and lead (him) away
46. their hands on him, and *took* him.
49. and ye *took* me not:
51. the young men *laid hold on* him:
Lu. 8:54. and *took* her *by* the hand, *and*
24:16. But their eyes *were holden*
Joh.20:23. whose soever (sins) ye *retain,* they are *retained.*
Acts 2:24. that he should *be holden* of it.
3:11. *as* the lame man which was healed *held*
24: 6. whom we *took,* and would have judged
27:13. supposing that they *had obtained*
Col. 2:19. And not *holding* the Head,
2Th. 2:15. stand fast, and *hold* the traditions
Heb 4:14. *let* us *hold fast* (our) profession.
6:18. *to lay hold upon* the hope
Rev. 2: 1. saith he *that holdeth* the
13. and thou *holdest fast* my name,
14. them *that hold* the doctrine of Balaam,
15. them *that hold* the doctrine of the
25. that which ye have (already) *hold fast* till I come.
3:11. *hold* that *fast* which thou hast,
7: 1. *holding* the four winds of the earth,
20: 2. And he *laid hold on* the dragon,

κράτιστος, *kratistos.*

Lu. 1: 3. *most excellent* Theophilus,
Acts23:26. unto the *most excellent* governor
24: 3. *most noble* Felix, with all thankfulness.
26:25. I am not mad, *most noble* Festus ;

κράτος, *kratos.*

Lu. 1:51. He hath shewed *strength* with
Acts19:20. So *mightily* grew the word of God
Eph 1:19. the working of his mighty *power,*
6:10. and in the *power* of his might.
Col. 1:11. according to his glorious *power,*
1Ti. 6:16. to whom (be) honour and *power*
Heb 2:14. that had the *power* of death,
1Pet.4:11. and *dominion* for ever and ever.
5:11. To him (be) glory and *dominion*
Jude 25. *dominion* and power, both now
Rev. 1: 6. to him (be) glory and *dominion* for
5:13. and glory, and *power,* (be) unto

κραυγάζω, *kraugazo.*

Mat 12:19. He shall not strive, nor *cry ;*
15:22. and *cried* unto him, saying,
Joh.11:43. he *cried* with a loud voice,
18:40. Then *cried* they all again,
19: 6. they *cried out,* saying, Crucify
15. they *cried out,* Away with (him),
Acts22:23. And *as* they *cried out,* and cast off

κραυγή, *kraugee.*

Mat 25: 6. at midnight there was a *cry* made,
Acts23: 9. And there arose a great *cry :*
Eph 4:31. and anger, and *clamour,*
Heb 5: 7. with strong *crying* and tears
Rev.14:18. and cried with a loud *cry*
21: 4. neither sorrow, nor *crying,* neither shall there be any more pain:

κρέας, *kreas.*

Ro. 14:21. (It is) good neither to eat *flesh,*
1Co. 8:13. I will eat no *flesh* while

κρεῖσσον, *krisson.* adv.

1Co. 7:38. he that giveth (her) not in marriage doeth *better.*

κρείσσων, κρείττων, *krisson, kritton.*

1Co. 7: 9. it is *better* to marry than to burn.
11:17. not for the *better,* but for the
12:31. covet earnestly the *best* gifts:
Phi. 1:23. with Christ; which is far *better:*
Heb 1: 4. Being made so much *better* than
6: 9. we are persuaded *better* things of you,
7: 7. the less is blessed of the *better.*
19. the bringing in of a *better* hope
22. a surety of a *better* testament.
8: 6. the mediator of a *better* covenant, which was established upon *better* promises.
9:23. with *better* sacrifices than these.
10:34. ye have in heaven a *better* and an
11:16. But now they desire a *better* (country),
35. might obtain a *better* resurrection:
40. some *better* thing for us,
12:24. *better* things than (that of) Abel.
1Pet.3:17. For (it is) *better,* if the will of God be so,
2Pet.2:21. For it had been *better* for them

κρέμαμαι, κρεμάω, *kremamai, kremao.*

Mat 18: 6. that a millstone *were hanged* about his
22:40. *hang* all the law and the prophets.
Lu. 23:39. one of the malefactors *which were hanged* railed on him,
Acts 5:30. whom ye slew *and hanged* on a tree.
10:39. whom they slew *and hanged* on a tree:
28: 4. (venomous) beast *hang* on his hand,
Gal. 3:13. Cursed (is) every one *that hangeth* on a

κρημνός, *kreemnos.*

Mat 8:32. ran violently down a *steep place*
Mar 5:13. down a *steep place* into the sea,
Lu. 8:33. herd ran violently down a *steep place*

κριθή, krithee.

Rev. 6: 6. three measures of *barley* for a penny ;

κρίθινος, krithinos.

Joh. 6: 9. which hath five *barley* loaves,
      13. fragments of the five *barley* loaves,

κρίμα, krima.

Mat. 7: 2. For with what *judgment* ye judge,
   23:14(13). ye shall receive the greater *damnation*.
Mar 12:40. these shall receive greater *damnation*.
Lu. 20:47. shall receive greater *damnation*.
   23:40. thou art in the same *condemnation?*
   24:20. delivered him to be *condemned* to death,
Joh. 9:39. For *judgment* I am come into
Acts24:25. and *judgment* to come, Felix
Ro. 2: 2. we are sure that the *judgment* of God
     3. thou shalt escape the *judgment* of God ?
   3: 8. whose *damnation* is just.
   5:16. for the *judgment* (was) by one
  11:33. unsearchable (are) his *judgments*,
  13: 2. shall receive to themselves *damnation*.
1Co. 6: 7. because ye go to law (lit. ye have *judg-ments*) one with another.
  11:29. eateth and drinketh *damnation* to himself,
   34. come not together unto *condemnation*.
Gal. 5:10. shall bear his *judgment*,
1Ti. 3: 6. he fall into the *condemnation*
  5:12. Having *damnation*, because they
Heb 6: 2. and of eternal *judgment*.
Jas. 3: 1. the greater *condemnation*.
1Pet.4:17. for the time (is come) that *judgment*
2Pet.2: 3. whose *judgment* now of a long time
Jude   4. ordained to this *condemnation*,
Rev.17: 1. I will shew unto thee the *judgment* of
  18:20. for God hath avenged you (lit. avenged your *judgment*) on her.
  20: 4. and *judgment* was given unto them:

κρίνον, krinon.

Mat. 6:28. Consider the *lilies* of the field,
Lu. 12:27. Consider the *lilies* how they grow :

κρίνω, krino.

Mat. 5:40. if any man will *sue* thee *at the law,*
  7: 1. *Judge* not, that ye *be* not *judged.*
     2. For with what judgment ye *judge,* ye *shall be judged :*
  19:28. *judging* the twelve tribes of Israel.
Lu. 6:37. *Judge* not, and ye *shall* not *be judged :*
  7:43. Thou *hast* rightly *judged.*
  12:57. *judge* ye not what is right?
  19:22. Out of thine own mouth *will* I *judge* thee,
  22:30. *judging* the twelve tribes of Israel.
Joh. 3:17. into the world to *condemn* the world ;
   18. believeth on him *is* not *condemned :* but he that believeth not *is condemned* already,
  5:22. the Father *judgeth* no man,
   30. as I hear, I *judge :*
  7:24. *Judge* not according to the appearance, but *judge* righteous judgment.
   51. *Doth* our law *judge* (any) man,

Joh. 8:15. Ye *judge* after the flesh ; I *judge* no man.
   16. And yet if I *judge,* my judgment is true:
   26. things to say and to *judge* of you:
   50. there is one that seeketh and *judgeth.*
  12:47. I *judge* him not: for I came not to *judge* the world,
   48. hath one *that judgeth* him :
   — the same *shall judge* him in the last day.
  16:11. the prince of this world *is judged.*
  18:31. Take ye him, and *judge* him
Acts 3:13. when he *was determined* to let (him) go.
  4:19. more than unto God, *judge* ye.
  7: 7. *will* I *judge,* said God:
  13:27. fulfilled (them) in *condemning* (him).
   46. and *judge* yourselves unworthy
  15:19. Wherefore my *sentence is,* that we
  16: 4. decrees for to keep, *that were ordained* of the apostles and elders
   15. If ye *have judged* me to be faithful
  17:31. will *judge* the world in righteousness
  20:16. Paul *had determined* to sail
  21:25. we have written (and) *concluded* that
  23: 3. for sittest thou to *judge* me after the
     6. of the hope and resurrection of the dead I *am called in question.*
  24: 6. and would have *judged* according
   21. I *am called in question* by you this day.
  25: 9. and there *be judged* of these things
   10. where I ought *to be judged :*
   20. and there *be judged* of these
   25. I *have determined* to send him.
  26: 6. And now I stand *and am judged*
     8. Why should it *be thought* a thing
  27: 1. when it *was determined* that we
Ro. 2: 1. whosoever thou art *that judgest :* for wherein thou *judgest* another, thou con-demnest thyself; for thou that *judgest* doest the same
     3. O man, *that judgest* them which do
   12. *shall be judged* by the law ;
   16. when God *shall judge* the secrets
   27. *shall* not uncircumcision...*judge* thee,
  3: 4. overcome when thou art *judged.*
     6. how *shall* God *judge* the world ?
     7. why yet *am* I also *judged* as a sinner ?
  14: 3. *let* not him which eateth not *judge* him
     4. Who art thou *that judgest* another man's
     5. One man *esteemeth* one day above another: another *esteemeth* every day (alike).
   10. why *dost* thou *judge* thy brother?
   13. *Let* us not therefore *judge* one another any more: but *judge* this
   22. Happy (is) he *that condemneth* not himself
1Co. 2: 2. For I *determined* not to know any thing
  4: 5. *judge* nothing before the time,
  5: 3. *have judged* already, as though I
   12. what have I to do *to judge* them also that are without ? *do* not ye *judge* them that
   13. them that are without God *judgeth.*
  6: 1. Dare any...*go to law* before the unjust,
     2. the saints *shall judge* the world ? and if the world *shall be judged* by you,
     3. that we *shall judge* angels ?
     6. But brother *goeth to law* with brother,
     7. *hath* so *decreed* in his heart
  10:15. *judge* ye what I say.
   29. why *is* my liberty *judged* of another
  11:13. *Judge* in yourselves: is it comely
   31. we should not *be judged.*
   32. But *when* we are *judged,* we are
2Co. 2: 1. But I *determined* this with myself,
  5:14. *because* we thus *judge,* that if one died for

Col. 2:16. *Let* no man therefore *judge* you in meat,
2Th. 2:12. That they all *might be damned*
2Ti. 4: 1. who shall *judge* the quick and
Tit. 3:12. I *have determined* there to
Heb 10: 30. The Lord *shall judge* his people.
　　13: 4. and adulterers God *will judge.*
Jas. 2:12. as they that shall *be judged*
　　4:11. and *judgeth* his brother, speaketh evil of
　　　　the law, and *judgeth* the law: but if
　　　　thou *judge* the law,
　　12. who art thou that *judgest*
1Pet. 1:17. *who* without respect of persons *judgeth*
　　　　according to every
　　2:23. to him *that judgeth* righteously:
　　4: 5. that is ready *to judge* the quick and
　　6. that they *might be judged* according to
Rev. 6:10. *dost* thou not *judge* and avenge
　　11:18. of the dead, that they should *be judged,*
　　16: 5. because thou *hast judged* thus.
　　18: 8. (is) the Lord God *who judgeth* her.
　　20. for God *hath avenged* you on her.
　　19: 2. for he *hath judged* the great whore,
　　11. in righteousness he *doth judge* and
　　20:12. the dead *were judged* out of
　　13. and they *were judged* every man according
　　　　to their works.

κρίσις, *krisis.*

Mat. 5:21. kill shall be in danger of the *judgment:*
　　22. without a cause shall be in danger of the
　　　　judgment :
　　10:15. in the day of *judgment*, than for that city.
　　11:22. at the day of *judgment*, than for you.
　　24. in the day of *judgment*, than for thee.
　　12:18. he shall shew *judgment* to the Gentiles.
　　20. till he send forth *judgment* unto victory.
　　36. account thereof in the day of *judgment*.
　　41. Nineveh shall rise in *judgment*
　　42. of the south shall rise up in the *judgment*
　　23:23. *judgment*, mercy, and faith:
　　33. how can ye escape the *damnation* of hell?
Mar 3:29. but is in danger of eternal *damnation* :
　　6:11. in the day of *judgment*, than
Lu. 10:14. at the *judgment*, than for you.
　　11:31. shall rise up in the *judgment*
　　32. Nineve shall rise up in the *judgment*
　　42. pass over *judgment* and the love of God:
Joh. 3:19. And this is the *condemnation,*
　　5:22. hath committed all *judgment* unto the
　　24. shall not come into *condemnation ;*
　　27. to execute *judgment* also,
　　29. the resurrection of *damnation.*
　　30. and my *judgment* is just ;
　　7:24. but judge righteous *judgment.*
　　8:16. my *judgment* is true:
　　12:31. Now is the *judgment* of this world:
　　16: 8. of righteousness, and of *judgment* :
　　11. Of *judgment*, because the prince of this
Acts 8:33. his *judgment* was taken away:
2Th. 1: 5. token of the righteous *judgment* of God,
1Ti. 5:24. going before to *judgment ;*
Heb 9:27. but after this the *judgment* :
　　10:27. fearful looking for of *judgment*
Jas. 2:13. he shall have *judgment* without mercy,
　　— and mercy rejoiceth against *judgment.*
2Pet. 2: 4. to be reserved unto *judgment ;*
　　9. unto the day of *judgment*
　　11. bring not railing *accusation*
　　3: 7. against the day of *judgment*
1Joh. 4:17. boldness in the day of *judgment* :

Jude 6. unto the *judgment* of the great day.
　　9. a railing *accusation*, but said,
　　15. To execute *judgment* upon all.
Rev. 14: 7. the hour of his *judgment* is come:
　　16: 7. and righteous (are) thy *judgments.*
　　18:10. in one hour is thy *judgment* come.
　　19: 2. true and righteous (are) his *judgments* :

κριτήριον, *kriteerion.*

1Co. 6: 2. are ye unworthy *to judge* the smallest
　　4. If then ye have *judgments* of things per-
　　　　taining to this life,
Jas. 2: 6. before the *judgment seats* ?

κριτής, *kritees.*

Mat. 5:25. deliver thee to the *judge*, and the *judge*
　　　　deliver thee to the
　　12:27. they shall be your *judges.*
Lu. 11:19. therefore shall they be your *judges.*
　　12:58. lest he hale thee to the *judge*, and the
　　　　judge deliver thee to the
　　18: 2. There was in a city a *judge,*
　　6. Hear what the unjust *judge* saith.
Acts 10:42. the *Judge* of quick and dead.
　　13:20. And after that he gave (unto them) *judges*
　　18:15. I will be no *judge* of such (matters).
　　24:10. thou hast been of many years a *judge*
2Ti. 4: 8. the Lord, the righteous *judge,*
Heb 12:23. to God the *Judge* of all,
Jas. 2: 4. are become *judges* of evil thoughts?
　　4:11. not a doer of the law, but a *judge.*
　　5: 9. the *judge* standeth before the door.

κριτικός, *kritikos*, adj.

Heb 4:12. and (is) *a discerner* of the thoughts

κρούω, *krouo.*

Mat. 7: 7. *knock*, and it shall be opened unto you:
　　8. to him *that knocketh* it shall be opened.
Lu. 11: 9. *knock*, and it shall be opened unto you.
　　10. to him *that knocketh* it shall be opened.
　　12:36. that when he cometh and *knocketh,*
　　13:25. and to *knock* at the door, saying,
Acts 12:13. And *as* Peter *knocked* at the door
　　16. But Peter continued *knocking* :
Rev. 3:20. I stand at the door, and *knock* :

κρυπτός, *kruptos.*

Mat. 6: 4. That thine alms may be in *secret* : and thy
　　　　Father which seeth in *secret*
　　6. to thy Father which is in *secret ;* and thy
　　　　Father which seeth in *secret*
　　18. but unto thy Father which is in *secret* :
　　　　and thy Father, which seeth in *secret,*
　　10:26. and *hid*, that shall not be known.
Mar 4:22. For there is nothing *hid*, which shall
Lu. 8:17. For nothing is *secret*, that shall not
　　11:33. putteth (it) in a *secret* place,
　　12: 2. neither *hid*, that shall not be known.
Joh. 7: 4. (that) doeth any thing in *secret,*
　　10. but as it were in *secret.*
　　18:20. and in *secret* have I said nothing.

Ro. 2:16. when God shall judge the *secrets* of men
         29. he (is) a Jew, which is one *inwardly* ;
1Co. 4: 5. bring to light the *hidden* things of
     14:25. the *secrets* of his heart made manifest ;
2Co. 4: 2. renounced the *hidden* things
1Pet.3: 4. the *hidden* man of the heart,

κρύπτω, *krupto.*

Mat. 5:14. on an hill cannot *be hid.*
    13:35. I will utter things *which have been kept secret*
        44. unto treasure *hid* in a field; the which when a man hath found, he *hideth,*
    25:25. and *hid* thy talent in the earth:
Lu. 18:34. this saying was *hid* from them,
    19:42. now they *are hid* from thine eyes.
Joh. 8:59. but Jesus *hid* him*self,*
   12:36. and *did hide* himself from them,
   19:38. but *secretly* for fear of the Jews,
Col. 3: 3. your life *is hid* with Christ in God.
1Ti. 5:25. they that are otherwise cannot *be hid.*
Heb 11:23. *was hid* three months of his parents,
Rev. 2:17. give to eat of the *hidden* manna,
    6:15. *hid* themselves in the dens
    16. *hide* us from the face of him

κρυφῆ, *kruphee.*

Eph. 5:12. which are done of them *in secret.*

κρυσταλλίζω, *krustallizo.*

Rev.21:11. a jasper stone, *clear as crystal;*

κρύσταλλος, *krustallos.*

Rev. 4: 6. a sea of glass like unto *crystal:*
    22: 1. river of water of life, clear as *crystal,*

κτάομαι, *ktaomai.*

Mat.10: 9. *Provide* neither gold, nor silver,
Lu. 18:12. of all that I *possess.*
    21:19. In your patience *possess* ye your souls.
Acts 1:18. *purchased* a field with the reward of
    8:20. that the gift of God may be *purchased*
    22:28. With a great sum *obtained* I
1Th. 4: 4. how *to possess* his vessel in sanctification

κτῆμα, *kteema.*

Mat.19:22. for he had great *possessions.*
Mar 10:22. for he had great *possessions.*
Acts 2:45. And sold their *possessions* and goods,
    5: 1. with Sapphira his wife, sold a *possession,*

κτῆνος, *kteenos.*

Lu. 10:34. and set him on his own *beast,*
Acts23:24. And provide (them) *beasts,* that they
1Co.15:39. another flesh of *beasts,*
Rev.18:13. and *beasts,* and sheep, and horses,

κτήτωρ, *kteetor.*

Acts 4:34. as many as were *possessors* of lands or houses sold them,

---

κτίζω, *ktizo.*

Mar 13:19. which God *created* unto this time,
Ro. 1:25. more than the *Creator,* who is
1Co.11: 9. Neither *was* the man *created* for the
Eph. 2:10. *created* in Christ Jesus unto good works,
    15. for to *make* in himself of twain one new man,
    3: 9. hid in God, *who created* all things by Jesus
    4:24. the new man, *which* after God *is created* in righteousness
Col. 1:16. by him *were* all things *created,*
    — all things *were created* by him, and for
    3:10. after the image of him *that created* him:
1Ti. 4: 3. which God *hath created* to be received
Rev. 4:11. for thou *hast created* all things, and for thy pleasure they are and *were created.*
    10: 6. who *created* heaven, and the things

κτίσις, *ktisis.*

Mar 10: 6. But from the beginning of the *creation* God made them
    13:19. from the beginning of the *creation* which God created
    16:15. and preach the gospel to every *creature.*
Ro. 1:20. from the *creation* of the world are clearly
    25. and served the *creature* more than the
    8:19. expectation of the *creature* waiteth
    20. For the *creature* was made subject
    21. the *creature* itself also shall be
    22. the whole *creation* groaneth and
    39. nor any other *creature,* shall be able
2Co. 5:17. (be) in Christ, (he is) a new *creature :*
Gal. 6:15. but a new *creature.*
Col. 1:15. the firstborn of every *creature :*
    23. was preached to every *creature*
Heb 4:13. Neither is there any *creature* that is
    9:11. tabernacle, not made with hands, that is to say, not of this *building ;*
1Pet.2:13. to every *ordinance* of man for the Lord's
2Pet.3: 4. continue as (they were) from the beginning of the *creation.*
Rev. 3:14. the beginning of the *creation* of God ;

κτίσμα, *ktisma.*

1Ti. 4: 4. For every *creature* of God (is) good,
Jas. 1:18. a kind of firstfruits of his *creatures.*
Rev. 5:13. And every *creature* which is in heaven,
    8: 9. third part of the *creatures* which were in the sea,

---

κτίστης, *ktistees.*

1Pet.4:19. as unto a faithful *Creator.*

κυβεία, *kubia.*

Eph. 4:14. by the *sleight* of men, (and) cunning craftiness,

κυβέρνησις, kuberneesis.

1Co.12:28. helps, *governments*, diversities of tongues.

κυβερνήτης, kuberneetees.

Acts27:11. believed the *master* and the owner of the
Rev.18:17. And every *shipmaster*, and all the company in ships,

---

κυκλόθεν, kuklothen.

Rev. 4: 3. a rainbow *round about* the throne,
4. And *round about* the throne
8. six wings *about* (him);
5:11. angels *round about* the throne

κυκλόω, kukloō.

Lu. 21:20. see Jerusalem *compassed* with armies,
Joh.10:24. Then came the Jews *round about* him,
Acts14:20. as the disciples stood *round about* him,
Heb 11:30. after they were *compassed about* seven
Rev.20: 9. and *compassed* the camp of the saints *about,*

(-λος) κύκλῳ, kuklo.

Dat. used for adv.

Mar 3:34. he looked *round about* (lit. in a *circle*) on them which sat about him,
6: 6. he went *round* about the villages.
36. into the country *round about,*
Lu. 9:12. and country *round about,* and lodge,
Ro. 15:19. from Jerusalem, and *round about* unto
Rev. 4: 6. and *round about* the throne,
7:11. all the angels stood *round about* the

κυλίομαι, kuliomai.

Mar 9:20. and *wallowed* foaming.

κύλισμα, kulisma.

2Pet.2:22. to her *wallowing* in the mire.

κυλλός, kullos.

Mat.15:30. dumb, *maimed,* and many others,
31. the *maimed* to be whole,
18: 8. to enter into life halt or *maimed,* rather
Mar 9:43. cut it off: it is better for thee to enter into life *maimed,*

κῦμα, kuma.

Mat. 8:24. the ship was covered with the *waves :*
14:24. tossed with *waves :* for the wind
Mar 4:37. the *waves* beat into the ship,
Acts27:41. broken with the violence of the *waves.*
Jude 13. Raging *waves* of the sea, foaming out

κύμβαλον, kumbalon.

1Co.13: 1. sounding brass, or a tinkling *cymbal.*

κύμινον, kuminon.

Mat 23:23. tithe of mint and anise and *cummin,*

κυνάριον, kunarion.

Mat.15:26. children's bread, and to cast (it) to *dogs.*
27. yet the *dogs* eat of the crumbs
Mar 7:27. and to cast (it) unto the *dogs.*
28. yet the *dogs* under the table eat of the

κύπτω, kupto.

Mar 1: 7. I am not worthy to *stoop down* and
Joh. 8: 6. But Jesus *stooped* down, *and* with
8. And again he *stooped* down, *and* wrote on

κυρία, kuria.

2Joh. 1. The elder unto the elect *lady* and her
5. I beseech thee, *lady,* not as though I

κυριακός, kuriakos.

1Co.11:20. (this) is not to eat the *Lord's* supper.
Rev. 1:10. in the Spirit on the *Lord's* day,

κυριεύω, kuriūo.

Lu. 22:25. The kings of the Gentiles *exercise lordship over* them ;
Ro. 6: 9. hath no more *dominion over* him.
14. sin shall not have *dominion over* you:
7: 1. the law hath *dominion over* a man
14: 9. that he might be *Lord* both of the dead
2Co. 1:24. that we have *dominion over* your faith,
1Ti. 6:15. King of kings, and *Lord* of *lords ;*

κύριος, kurios.

Mat. 1:20. behold, the angel of the *Lord* appeared
22. spoken of the *Lord* by the prophet,
24. did as the angel of the *Lord* had bidden
2:13. the angel of the *Lord* appeareth
15. was spoken of the *Lord* by the prophet,
19. an angel of the *Lord* appeareth in a
3: 3. Prepare ye the way of the *Lord,*
4: 7. shalt not tempt the *Lord* thy God.
10. shalt worship the *Lord* thy God,
5:33. shalt perform unto the *Lord*
6:24. No man can serve two *masters :*
7:21. that saith unto me, *Lord, Lord,*
22. *Lord, Lord,* have we not prophesied
8: 2. saying, *Lord,* if thou wilt, thou canst
6. *Lord,* my servant lieth at home
8. *Lord,* I am not worthy that thou
21. *Lord,* suffer me first to go
25. *Lord,* save us: we perish.
9:28. said unto him, Yea, *Lord.*
38. Pray ye therefore the *Lord* of the harvest,
10:24. nor the servant above his *lord.*
25. and the servant as his *lord.*
11:25. O Father, *Lord* of heaven and earth,
12: 8. is *Lord* even of the sabbath day.
13:27. *Sir,* didst not thou sow good seed in
51. They say unto him, Yea, *Lord.*

Mat.14:28. *Lord*, if it be thou, bid me
　　30. saying, *Lord*, save me.
　15:22. O *Lord*, (thou) son of David;
　　25. saying, *Lord*, help me.
　　27. Truth, *Lord:* yet the dogs
　　— from their *masters'* table.
　16:22. Be it far from thee, *Lord:*
　17: 4. *Lord*, it is good for us to be here:
　　15. *Lord*, have mercy on my son:
　18:21. *Lord*, how oft shall my brother
　　25. his *lord* commanded him to be sold,
　　26. saying, *Lord*, have patience with me,
　　27. Then the *lord* of that servant
　　31. told unto their *lord* all that was done.
　　32. Then his *lord*, after that he
　　34. And his *lord* was wroth,
　20: 8. the *lord* of the vineyard saith
　　30. O *Lord*, (thou) son of David.
　　31. O *Lord*, (thou) son of David.
　　33. *Lord*, that our eyes may be opened.
　21: 3. The *Lord* hath need of them;
　　9. that cometh in the name of the *Lord;*
　　30. I (go), *sir:* and went not.
　　40. When the *lord* therefore of the vineyard
　　42. this is the *Lord's* doing, and it is
　22:37. Thou shalt love the *Lord* thy God
　　43. doth David in spirit call him *Lord*,
　　44. The *Lord* said unto my *Lord*,
　　45. If David then call him *Lord*,
　23:39. (is) he that cometh in the name of the
　　Lord.
　24:42. what hour your *Lord* doth come.
　　45. whom his *lord* hath made ruler
　　46. whom his *lord* when he cometh
　　48. My *lord* delayeth his coming;
　　50. The *lord* of that servant shall come
　25:11. *Lord*, *Lord*, open to us.
　　18. and hid his *lord's* money.
　　19. After a long time the *lord* of those
　　20. *Lord*, thou deliveredst unto me
　　21. His *lord* said unto him,
　　— enter thou into the joy of thy *lord*.
　　22. *Lord*, thou deliveredst unto me
　　23. His *lord* said unto him,
　　— into the joy of thy *lord*.
　　24. *Lord*, I knew thee that thou art
　　26. His *lord* answered and said
　　37. *Lord*, when saw we thee
　　44. *Lord*, when saw we thee
　26:22. *Lord*, is it I?
　27:10. as the *Lord* appointed me.
　　63. *Sir*, we remember that
　28: 2. the angel of the *Lord*
　　6. the place where the *Lord* lay.
Mar 1: 3. Prepare ye the way of the *Lord*,
　2:28. is *Lord* also of the sabbath.
　5:19. how great things the *Lord* hath done
　7:28. Yes, *Lord:* yet the dogs
　9:24. *Lord*, I believe; help thou
　11: 3. that the *Lord* hath need of him;
　　9. cometh in the name of the *Lord:*
　　10. in the name of the *Lord:*
　12: 9. the *lord* of the vineyard do?
　　11. This was the *Lord's* doing,
　　29. The *Lord* our God is one *Lord:*
　　30. thou shalt love the *Lord* thy God
　　36. The *Lord* said to my *Lord*,
　　37. David therefore himself calleth him *Lord;*
　13:20. except that the *Lord* had shortened
　　35. when the *master* of the house
　16:19. So then after the *Lord* had spoken
　　20. the *Lord* working with (them),

Lu. 1: 6. ordinances of the *Lord* blameless.
　　9. into the temple of the *Lord*.
　　11. an angel of the *Lord* standing on the
　　15. great in the sight of the *Lord*,
　　16. shall he turn to the *Lord* their God.
　　17. a people prepared for the *Lord*.
　　25. Thus hath the *Lord* dealt with me
　　28. the *Lord* (is) with thee: blessed
　　32. and the *Lord* God shall give
　　38. Behold the handmaid of the *Lord;*
　　43. the mother of my *Lord* should come
　　45. which were told her from the *Lord*.
　　46. My soul doth magnify the *Lord*,
　　58. how the *Lord* had shewed great
　　66. the hand of the *Lord* was with him.
　　68. Blessed (be) the *Lord* God of Israel;
　　76. go before the face of the *Lord*
　2: 9. the angel of the *Lord* came upon them,
　　　and the glory of the *Lord* shone
　　11. which is Christ the *Lord*.
　　15. which the *Lord* hath made known
　　22. to present (him) to the *Lord;*
　　23. in the law of the *Lord*,
　　— shall be called holy to the *Lord;*
　　24. in the law of the *Lord*,
　　26. before he had seen the *Lord's* Christ.
　　38. gave thanks likewise unto the *Lord*,
　　39. to the law of the *Lord*,
　3: 4. Prepare ye the way of the *Lord*,
　4: 8. Thou shalt worship the *Lord* thy God,
　　12. Thou shalt not tempt the *Lord*
　　18. The Spirit of the *Lord* (is) upon me,
　　19. the acceptable year of the *Lord*.
　5: 8. I am a sinful man, O *Lord*.
　　12. *Lord*, if thou wilt, thou canst
　　17. the power of the *Lord* was (present)
　6: 5. the Son of man is *Lord* also of the
　　46. why call ye me, *Lord*, *Lord*,
　7: 6. *Lord*, trouble not thyself:
　　13. when the *Lord* saw her, he had
　　31. And the *Lord* said, Whereunto then
　9:54. *Lord*, wilt thou that we command
　　57. *Lord*, I will follow thee
　　59. *Lord*, suffer me first to go and
　　61. *Lord*, I will follow thee;
　10: 1. the *Lord* appointed other seventy
　　2. pray ye therefore the *Lord* of the
　　17. *Lord*, even the devils are subject
　　21. O Father, *Lord* of heaven and earth,
　　27. Thou shalt love the *Lord* thy God
　　40. *Lord*, dost thou not care that my sister
　11: 1. *Lord*, teach us to pray,
　　39. the *Lord* said unto him, Now do ye
　12:36. that wait for their *lord*,
　　37. whom the *lord* when he cometh shall find
　　41. *Lord*, speakest thou this parable unto us,
　　42. the *Lord* said, Who then is that faithful
　　　and wise steward, whom (his) *lord*
　　43. whom his *lord* when he cometh
　　45. My *lord* delayeth his coming;
　　46. The *lord* of that servant will
　　47. which knew his *lord's* will,
　13: 8. *Lord*, let it alone this year also,
　　15. The *Lord* then answered him, and
　　23. *Lord*, are there few that be saved?
　　25. *Lord*, *Lord*, open unto us;
　　35. cometh in the name of the *Lord*.
　14:21. Then the *master* of the house
　　22. *Lord*, it is done as thou hast
　　23. the *lord* said unto the servant,
　16: 3. my *lord* taketh away from me the
　　5. called every one of his *lord's* debtors

Lu. 16: 5. How much owest thou unto my *lord?*
    8. the *lord* commended the unjust
    13. No servant can serve two *masters:*
  17: 5. said unto the *Lord,* Increase our faith.
    6. And the *Lord* said, If ye had faith as
    37. Where, *Lord?* And he said unto them, Wheresoever
  18: 6. And the *Lord* said, Hear what
    41. *Lord,* that I may receive my sight.
  19: 8. and said unto the *Lord;* Behold, *Lord,* the half of my goods I give
    16. *Lord,* thy pound hath gained ten pounds.
    18. *Lord,* thy pound hath gained five pounds.
    20. *Lord,* behold, (here is) thy pound,
    25. *Lord,* he hath ten pounds.
    31. the *Lord* hath need of him.
    33. the *owners* thereof said unto them,
    34. The *Lord* hath need of him.
    38. cometh in the name of the *Lord:*
  20:13. Then said the *lord* of the vineyard,
    15. shall the *lord* of the vineyard do
    37. when he calleth the *Lord* the God
    42. The *Lord* said unto my *Lord,*
    44. David therefore calleth him *Lord,*
  22:31. And the *Lord* said, Simon, Simon,
    33. *Lord,* I am ready to go with thee,
    38. *Lord,* behold, here (are) two swords.
    49. *Lord,* shall we smite with the
    61. the *Lord* turned, and looked upon
    — Peter remembered the word of the *Lord,*
  23:42. *Lord,* remember me when thou comest
  24: 3. found not the body of the *Lord* Jesus.
    34. The *Lord* is risen indeed,
Joh. 1:23. Make straight the way of the *Lord,*
  4: 1. When therefore the *Lord* knew
    11. *Sir,* thou hast nothing to draw with,
    15. *Sir,* give me this water,
    19. *Sir,* I perceive that thou art a
    49. *Sir,* come down ere my child die.
  5: 7. *Sir,* I have no man, when
  6:23. after that the *Lord* had given thanks:
    34. *Lord,* evermore give us this bread.
    68. *Lord,* to whom shall we go?
  8:11. She said, No man, *Lord,*
  9:36. Who is he, *Lord,* that I might
    38. *Lord,* I believe. And he worshipped him.
  11: 2. which anointed the *Lord*
    3. *Lord,* behold, he whom thou lovest
    12. *Lord,* if he sleep, he shall do well.
    21. *Lord,* if thou hadst been here,
    27. Yea, *Lord:* I believe that thou
    32. *Lord,* if thou hadst been here,
    34(35). *Lord,* come and see.
    39. *Lord,* by this time he stinketh:
  12:13. cometh in the name of the *Lord.*
    21. *Sir,* we would see Jesus.
    38. *Lord,* who hath believed our report? and to whom hath the arm of the *Lord* been
  13: 6. *Lord,* dost thou wash my feet?
    9. *Lord,* not my feet only,
    13. Ye call me Master and *Lord:*
    14. If I then, (your) *Lord* and Master,
    16. is not greater than his *lord;*
    25. *Lord,* who is it?
    36. *Lord,* whither goest thou?
    37. *Lord,* why cannot I follow thee
  14: 5. *Lord,* we know not whither thou
    8. *Lord,* shew us the Father, and
    22. *Lord,* how is it that thou wilt
  15:15. knoweth not what his *lord*
    20. not greater than his *lord.*

Joh.20: 2. They have taken away the *Lord*
    13. Because they have taken away my *Lord,*
    15. *Sir,* if thou have borne him hence,
    18. that she had seen the *Lord,*
    20. glad, when they saw the *Lord.*
    25. We have seen the *Lord.*
    28. My *Lord* and my God.
  21: 7. It is the *Lord.* Now when Simon Peter heard that it was the *Lord,*
    12. knowing that it was the *Lord.*
    15. Yea, *Lord;* thou knowest that I
    16. Yea, *Lord;* thou knowest that I love
    17. *Lord,* thou knowest all things;
    20. and said, *Lord,* which is he that
    21. *Lord,* and what (shall) this man (do)?
Acts 1: 6. *Lord,* wilt thou at this time restore
    21. all the time that the *Lord* Jesus
    24. Thou, *Lord,* which knowest the
  2:20. notable day of the *Lord* come:
    21. on the name of the *Lord* shall be
    25. I foresaw the *Lord* always
    34. The *Lord* said unto my *Lord,*
    36. hath made that same Jesus,...both *Lord* and Christ.
    39. as many as the *Lord* our God
    47. And the *Lord* added to the church
  3:19. from the presence of the *Lord;*
    22. A prophet shall the *Lord* your God
  4:26. against the *Lord,* and against his Christ.
    29. *Lord,* behold their threatenings:
    33. of the resurrection of the *Lord*
  5: 9. to tempt the Spirit of the *Lord?*
    14. believers were the more added to the *Lord,*
    19. the angel of the *Lord* by night
  7:30. an angel of the *Lord* in a flame
    31. the voice of the *Lord* came unto him,
    33. Then said the *Lord* to him,
    37. A prophet shall the *Lord* your God
    49. will ye build me? saith the *Lord:*
    59. *Lord* Jesus, receive my spirit.
    60. *Lord,* lay not this sin to their
  8:16. in the name of the *Lord* Jesus.
    24. Pray ye to the *Lord* for me,
    25. preached the word of the *Lord,*
    26. the angel of the *Lord* spake unto
    39. the Spirit of the *Lord* caught away
  9: 1. against the disciples of the *Lord,*
    5. Who art thou, *Lord?* And the *Lord* said, I am Jesus
    6. *Lord,* what wilt thou have me to do? And the *Lord* (said) unto him,
    10. said the *Lord* in a vision, Ananias. And he said, Behold, I (am here), *Lord.*
    11. And the *Lord* (said) unto him, Arise,
    13. *Lord,* I have heard by many
    15. But the *Lord* said unto him,
    17. the *Lord,* (even) Jesus, that appeared
    27. how he had seen the *Lord* in the way,
    29(28). in the name of the *Lord* Jesus,
    31. and walking in the fear of the *Lord,*
    35. and turned to the *Lord.*
    42. and many believed in the *Lord.*
  10: 4. What is it, *Lord?*
    14. Not so, *Lord;* for I have never
    36. by Jesus Christ: he is *Lord* of all:
    48. baptized in the name of the *Lord.*
  11: 8. Not so, *Lord:* for nothing
    16. the word of the *Lord,* how that he said,
    17. who believed on the *Lord* Jesus
    20. preaching the *Lord* Jesus.
    21. the hand of the *Lord* was with them:

Acts11:21. and turned unto the *Lord*.
23. they would cleave unto the *Lord*.
24. people was added unto the *Lord*.
12: 7. the angel of the *Lord* came upon (him),
11. I know of a surety, that the *Lord* hath sent his angel,
17. how the *Lord* had brought him out of the
23. the angel of the *Lord* smote him,
13: 2. As they ministered to the *Lord*, and
10. to pervert the right ways of the *Lord*?
11. the hand of the *Lord* (is) upon thee,
12. astonished at the doctrine of the *Lord*.
47. so hath the *Lord* commanded us,
48. glorified the word of the *Lord* :
49. the word of the *Lord* was published
14: 3. speaking boldly in the *Lord*,
23. commended them to the *Lord*,
15:11. through the grace of the *Lord* Jesus
17. might seek after the *Lord*,
— saith the *Lord*, who doeth all these
26. lives for the name of our *Lord* Jesus
35. preaching the word of the *Lord*,
36. preached the word of the *Lord*,
16:10. gathering that the *Lord* had called us
14. whose heart the *Lord* opened,
15. me to be faithful to the *Lord*,
16. brought her *masters* much gain
19. when her *masters* saw that
30. *Sirs*, what must I do to be saved?
31. Believe on the *Lord* Jesus Christ,
32. unto him the word of the *Lord*,
17:24. seeing that he is *Lord* of heaven and earth,
27. That they should seek the *Lord*,
18: 8. believed on the *Lord* with all
9. Then spake the *Lord* to Paul
25. was instructed in the way of the *Lord* ;
— taught diligently the things of the *Lord*,
19: 5. baptized in the name of the *Lord*
10. heard the word of the *Lord*
13. the name of the *Lord* Jesus,
17. the name of the *Lord* Jesus was
20. mightily grew the word of *God* and
20:19. Serving the *Lord* with all
21. faith toward our *Lord* Jesus
24. which I have received of the *Lord*
35. remember the words of the *Lord* Jesus,
21:13. for the name of the *Lord* Jesus.
14. The will of the *Lord* be done.
20. they glorified the *Lord*,
22: 8. Who art thou, *Lord*?
10. What shall I do, *Lord*? And the *Lord* said unto me, Arise,
16. calling on the name of the *Lord*.
19. *Lord*, they know that I imprisoned
23:11. the *Lord* stood by him,
25:26. to write unto my *lord*.
26:15. Who art thou, *Lord*?
28:31. which concern the *Lord* Jesus
Ro. 1: 3(4). his Son Jesus Christ our *Lord*,
7. and the *Lord* Jesus Christ.
4: 8. to whom the *Lord* will not impute sin.
24. raised up Jesus our *Lord* from
5: 1. peace with God through our *Lord* Jesus
11. joy in God through our *Lord* Jesus
21. eternal life by Jesus Christ our *Lord*.
6:11. alive unto God through Jesus Christ our *Lord*.
23. eternal life through Jesus Christ our *Lord*.
7:25. I thank God through Jesus Christ our *Lord*.
8:39. which is in Christ Jesus our *Lord*.
9:28. a short work will the *Lord*
29. Except the *Lord* of Sabaoth

Ro. 10: 9. with thy mouth the *Lord* Jesus,
12. the same *Lord* over all is rich
13. call upon the name of the *Lord*
16. *Lord*, who hath believed our
11: 3. *Lord*, they have killed thy
34. known the mind of the *Lord* ?
12:19. I will repay, saith the *Lord*.
13:14. put ye on the *Lord* Jesus Christ,
14: 4. to his own *master* he standeth
6. regardeth (it) unto the *Lord* ;
— to the *Lord* he doth not regard (it).
— eateth to the *Lord*, for he giveth
— to the *Lord* he eateth not,
8. we live unto the *Lord* ;
— we die unto the *Lord* :
— or die, we are the *Lord's*.
11. (As) I live, saith the *Lord*,
14. persuaded by the *Lord* Jesus,
15: 6. Father of our *Lord* Jesus Christ.
11. Praise the *Lord*, all ye Gentiles ;
30. for the *Lord* Jesus Christ's sake,
16: 2. That ye receive her in the *Lord*,
8. Amplias my beloved in the *Lord*.
11. of Narcissus, which are in the *Lord*.
12. and Tryphosa, who labour in the *Lord*.
— Persis, which laboured much in the *Lord*.
13. Rufus chosen in the *Lord*,
18. such serve not our *Lord* Jesus
20. The grace of our *Lord* Jesus Christ
22. salute you in the *Lord*.
24. The grace of our *Lord* Jesus Christ
1Co. 1: 2. the name of Jesus Christ our *Lord*,
3. and (from) the *Lord* Jesus Christ.
7. waiting for the coming of our *Lord*
8. in the day of our *Lord* Jesus Christ.
9. his Son Jesus Christ our *Lord*.
10. by the name of our *Lord* Jesus
31. let him glory in the *Lord*.
2: 8. crucified the *Lord* of glory.
16. who hath known the mind of the *Lord*,
3: 5. even as the *Lord* gave to every
20. The *Lord* knoweth the thoughts
4: 4. he that judgeth me is the *Lord*.
5. until the *Lord* come,
17. and faithful in the *Lord*,
19. if the *Lord* will,
5: 4. In the name of our *Lord* Jesus
— with the power of our *Lord* Jesus Christ,
5. saved in the day of the *Lord*
6:11. in the name of the *Lord* Jesus,
13. but for the *Lord* ; and the *Lord* for the body.
14. God hath both raised up the *Lord*,
17. he that is joined unto the *Lord*
7:10. (yet) not I, but the *Lord*,
12. speak I, not the *Lord* :
17. as the *Lord* hath called every one,
22. that is called in the *Lord*, (being) a servant, is the *Lord's* freeman :
25. no commandment of the *Lord* :
— obtained mercy of the *Lord* to
32. that belong to the *Lord*, how he may please the *Lord* :
34. careth for the things of the *Lord*, that
35. that ye may attend upon the *Lord*
39. to whom she will ; only in the *Lord*.
8: 5. as there be gods many, and *lords* many,
6. and one *Lord* Jesus Christ,
9: 1. have I not seen Jesus Christ our *Lord* ? are not ye my work in the *Lord* ?
2. the seal of mine apostleship are ye in the *Lord*.

1Co. 9: 5. and (as) the brethren of the *Lord*, and
 14. Even so hath the *Lord* ordained
 10:21. cannot drink the cup of the *Lord*, and the
 — of the *Lord's* table, and of the table
 22. Do we provoke the *Lord* to jealousy?
 26. the earth (is) the *Lord's*, and the
 28. the *Lord's*, and the fulness thereof:
 11:11. without the man, in the *Lord*.
 23. I have received of the *Lord*
 — That the *Lord* Jesus the (same)
 26. ye do shew the *Lord's* death till
 27. drink (this) cup of the *Lord*, unworthily,
 — guilty of the body and blood of the *Lord*.
 29. not discerning the *Lord's* body.
 32. we are chastened of the *Lord*,
 12: 3. can say that Jesus is the *Lord*, but
 5. of administrations, but the same *Lord*.
 14:21. will they not hear me, saith the *Lord*.
 37. are the commandments of the *Lord*.
 15:31. I have in Christ Jesus our *Lord*,
 47. the second man (is) the *Lord* from heaven.
 57. the victory through our *Lord* Jesus
 58. abounding in the work of the *Lord*,
 — labour is not in vain in the *Lord*.
 16: 7. if the *Lord* permit.
 10. he worketh the work of the *Lord*,
 19. salute you much in the *Lord*,
 22. If any man love not the *Lord*
 23. The grace of our *Lord* Jesus
2Co. 1: 2. and (from) the *Lord* Jesus Christ.
 3. Father of our *Lord* Jesus Christ,
 14. in the day of the *Lord* Jesus.
 2:12. was opened unto me of the *Lord*,
 3:16. when it shall turn to the *Lord*,
 17. Now the *Lord* is that Spirit: and where
 the Spirit of the *Lord* (is),
 18. beholding as in a glass the glory of the
 Lord,
 — (even) as by the Spirit of the *Lord*.
 4: 5. but Christ Jesus the *Lord*;
 10. the dying of the *Lord* Jesus,   —
 14. he which raised up the *Lord*
 5: 6. we are absent from the *Lord*:
 8. to be present with the *Lord*.
 11. Knowing therefore the terror of the *Lord*,
 6:17. be ye separate, saith the *Lord*,
 18. ye shall be my sons and daughters, saith
 the *Lord* Almighty.
 8: 5. gave their own selves to the *Lord*,
 9. ye know the grace of our *Lord* Jesus
 19. to the glory of the same *Lord*,
 21. not only in the sight of the *Lord*,
 10: 8. which the *Lord* hath given us
 17. let him glory in the *Lord*.
 18. but whom the *Lord* commendeth.
 11:17. I speak (it) not after the *Lord*,
 31. Father of our *Lord* Jesus Christ,
 12: 1. and revelations of the *Lord*.
 8. I besought the *Lord* thrice,   —
 13:10. power which the *Lord* hath given me
 14(13). The grace of the *Lord* Jesus
Gal. 1: 3. and (from) our *Lord* Jesus
 19. save James the *Lord's* brother.
 4: 1. though he be *lord* of all;   —
 5:10. confidence in you through the *Lord*,
 6:14. save in the cross of our *Lord*
 17. the marks of the *Lord* Jesus.
 18. the grace of our *Lord* Jesus   —
Eph. 1: 2. and (from) the *Lord* Jesus
 3. Father of our *Lord* Jesus   —
 15. heard of your faith in the *Lord* Jesus,
 17. the God of our *Lord* Jesus

Eph. 2:21. an holy temple in the *Lord*:
 3:11. in Christ Jesus our *Lord*:
 14. Father of our *Lord* Jesus
 4: 1. the prisoner of the *Lord*,
 5. One *Lord*, one faith,
 17. and testify in the *Lord*,
 5: 8. now (are ye) light in the *Lord*:
 10. Proving what is acceptable unto the *Lord*.
 17. what the will of the *Lord* (is).
 19. melody in your heart to the *Lord*;
 20. in the name of our *Lord* Jesus
 22. own husbands, as unto the *Lord*.
 29. even as the *Lord* the church:
 6: 1. obey your parents in the *Lord*:
 4. the nurture and admonition of the *Lord*.
 5. to them that are (your) *masters*
 7. doing service, as to the *Lord*,
 8. shall he receive of the *Lord*,
 9. And, ye *masters*, do the same things
 — your *Master* also is in heaven;
 10. be strong in the *Lord*,
 21. and faithful minister in the *Lord*,
 23. and the *Lord* Jesus Christ.
 24. that love our *Lord* Jesus
Phi. 1: 2. and (from) the *Lord* Jesus
 14. brethren in the *Lord*, waxing confident
 2:11. confess that Jesus Christ (is) *Lord*,
 19. I trust in the *Lord* Jesus to
 24. I trust in the *Lord* that I
 29. Receive him therefore in the *Lord*
 3: 1. rejoice in the *Lord*.
 8. of Christ Jesus my *Lord*:
 20. the Saviour, the *Lord* Jesus Christ:
 4: 1. so stand fast in the *Lord*,
 2. be of the same mind in the *Lord*.
 4. Rejoice in the *Lord* alway:
 5. The *Lord* (is) at hand.
 10. I rejoiced in the *Lord* greatly,
 23(24). The grace of our *Lord* Jesus
Col. 1: 2. and the *Lord* Jesus Christ.
 3. Father of our *Lord* Jesus
 10. walk worthy of the *Lord* unto
 2: 6. received Christ Jesus the *Lord*, (so)
 3:16. grace in your hearts to the *Lord*.
 17. (do) all in the name of the *Lord* Jesus,
 18. as it is fit in the *Lord*.
 20. this is well pleasing unto the *Lord*.
 22. obey in all things (your) *masters*
 23. as to the *Lord*, and not unto men;
 24. Knowing that of the *Lord* ye shall
 — for ye serve the *Lord* Christ.
 4: 1. *Masters*, give unto (your) servants
 — ye also have a *Master* in heaven.
 7. fellowservant in the *Lord*:
 17. which thou hast received in the *Lord*,
1Th. 1: 1. and (in) the *Lord* Jesus Christ:
 — from God our Father, and the *Lord* Jesus
 3. patience of hope in our *Lord* Jesus Christ,
 6. followers of us, and of the *Lord*,
 8. sounded out the word of the *Lord*
 2:15. Who both killed the *Lord* Jesus,
 19. in the presence of our *Lord* Jesus
 3: 8. if ye stand fast in the *Lord*.
 11. and our *Lord* Jesus Christ,
 12. the *Lord* make you to increase
 13. at the coming of our *Lord* Jesus
 4: 1. exhort (you) by the *Lord* Jesus,
 2. we gave you by the *Lord* Jesus.
 6. because that the *Lord* (is) the avenger
 15. unto you by the word of the *Lord*,
 — remain unto the coming of the *Lord*
 16. the *Lord* himself shall descend

1Th. 4:17. to meet the *Lord* in the air: and so shall
      we ever be with the *Lord*.
  5: 2. the day of the *Lord* so cometh
    9. salvation by our *Lord* Jesus
   12. and are over you in the *Lord*,
   23. unto the coming of our *Lord*
   27. I charge you by the *Lord* that this
   28. The grace of our *Lord* Jesus
2Th. 1: 1. in God our Father and the *Lord* Jesus
    2. Father and the *Lord* Jesus Christ.
    7. when the *Lord* Jesus shall be revealed
    8. obey not the gospel of our *Lord* Jesus
    9. from the presence of the *Lord*,
   12. That the name of our *Lord* Jesus Christ
 — to the grace of our God and the *Lord*
  2: 1. by the coming of our *Lord* Jesus
    8. whom the *Lord* shall consume
   13. brethren beloved of the *Lord*,
   14. of the glory of our *Lord* Jesus
   16. Now our *Lord* Jesus Christ himself,
  3: 1. that the word of the *Lord* may have
    3. the *Lord* is faithful, who
    4. confidence in the *Lord* touching you,
    5. the *Lord* direct your hearts
    6. in the name of our *Lord* Jesus
   12. exhort by our *Lord* Jesus
   16. Now the *Lord* of peace himself
 — The *Lord* (be) with you all.
   18. The grace of our *Lord* Jesus
1Ti. 1: 1. and *Lord* Jesus Christ,
    2. and Jesus Christ our *Lord*.
   12. I thank Christ Jesus our *Lord*,
   14. the grace of our *Lord* was exceeding
  5:21. I charge (thee) before God, and the *Lord*
    Jesus Christ,
  6: 3. the words of our *Lord* Jesus
   14. until the appearing of our *Lord*
   15. the King of kings, and *Lord* of lords;
2Ti. 1: 2. and Christ Jesus our *Lord*.
    8. ashamed of the testimony of our *Lord*,
   16. The *Lord* give mercy unto the house
   18. The *Lord* grant unto him that he may find
    mercy of the *Lord* in that day:
  2: 7. the *Lord* give thee understanding
   14. charging (them) before the *Lord*
   19. The *Lord* knoweth them that are his.
   22. with them that call on the *Lord*
   24. the servant of the *Lord* must not strive;
  3:11. out of (them) all the *Lord* delivered me.
  4: 1. before God, and the *Lord* Jesus
    8. which the *Lord*, the righteous judge,
   14. the *Lord* reward him according
   17. the *Lord* stood with me,
   18. the *Lord* shall deliver me
   22. The *Lord* Jesus Christ (be) with
Tit. 1: 4. and the *Lord* Jesus Christ our Saviour.
Philem 3. and the *Lord* Jesus Christ.
    5. which thou hast toward the *Lord* Jesus,
   16. both in the flesh, and in the *Lord*?
   20. me have joy of thee in the *Lord*: refresh
    my bowels in the *Lord*.
   25. The grace of our *Lord* Jesus Christ
Heb 1:10. And, Thou, *Lord*, in the beginning
  2: 3. began to be spoken by the *Lord*,
  7:14. that our *Lord* sprang out of
   21. The *Lord* sware and will not
  8: 2. tabernacle, which the *Lord* pitched,
    8. the days come, saith the *Lord*,
    9. I regarded them not, saith the *Lord*.
   10. after those days, saith the *Lord*;
   11. saying, Know the *Lord*:
 10:16. after those days, saith the *Lord*,

Heb 10:30. I will recompense, saith the *Lord*. And
    again, The *Lord* shall judge his people.
 12: 5. despise not thou the chastening of the
    Lord,
    6. whom the *Lord* loveth he chasteneth,
   14. without which no man shall see the *Lord*:
 13: 6. The *Lord* (is) my helper,
   20. from the dead our *Lord* Jesus,
Jas. 1: 1. and of the *Lord* Jesus Christ,
    7. receive any thing of the *Lord*.
   12. which the *Lord* hath promised
  2: 1. the faith of our *Lord* Jesus
  4:10. in the sight of the *Lord*, and he
   15. (ought) to say, If the *Lord* will, we
  5: 4. into the ears of the *Lord* of sabaoth.
    7. unto the coming of the *Lord*.
    8. the coming of the *Lord* draweth nigh.
   10. have spoken in the name of the *Lord*,
   11. have seen the end of the *Lord*; that the
    Lord is very pitiful,
   14. with oil in the name of the *Lord*:
   15. the *Lord* shall raise him up;
1Pet.1: 3. Father of our *Lord* Jesus
   25. the word of the *Lord* endureth
  2: 3. that the *Lord* (is) gracious.
   13. to every ordinance of man for the *Lord's*
    sake:
  3: 6. obeyed Abraham, calling him *lord*:
   12. the eyes of the *Lord* (are) over
 — the face of the *Lord* is against
   15. sanctify the *Lord* God in
2Pet.1: 2. and of Jesus our *Lord*,
    8. knowledge of our *Lord* Jesus
   11. into the everlasting kingdom of our *Lord*
    and Saviour
   14. as our *Lord* Jesus Christ hath shewed me.
   16. and coming of our *Lord*
  2: 9. The *Lord* knoweth how to deliver
   11. against them before the *Lord*.
   20. through the knowledge of the *Lord* and
  3: 2. the apostles of the *Lord* and Saviour:
    8. one day (is) with the *Lord* as
    9. The *Lord* is not slack concerning
   10. the day of the *Lord* will come
   15. the longsuffering of our *Lord* (is)
   18. and (in) the knowledge of our *Lord* and
2Joh. 3. and from the *Lord* Jesus
Jude 4. God, and our *Lord* Jesus Christ.
    5. how that the *Lord*, having saved the
    9. The *Lord* rebuke thee.
   14. the *Lord* cometh with ten thousands of his
   17. of the apostles of our *Lord* Jesus
   21. looking for the mercy of our *Lord* Jesus
Rev. 1: 8. and the ending, saith the *Lord*,
  4: 8. Holy, holy, holy, *Lord* God Almighty,
   11. Thou art worthy, O *Lord*, to receive
  7:14. *Sir*, thou knowest.
 11: 8. where also our *Lord* was crucified.
   15. are become (the kingdoms) of our *Lord*,
    and of his Christ;
   17. give thee thanks, O *Lord* God Almighty,
 14:13. the dead which die in the *Lord* from
 15: 3. thy works, *Lord* God Almighty;
    4. Who shall not fear thee, O *Lord*,
 16: 5. Thou art righteous, O *Lord*,
    7. Even so, *Lord* God Almighty,
 17:14. for he is *Lord* of *lords*,
 18: 8. for strong (is) the *Lord* God
 19: 1. unto the *Lord* our God:
    6. for the *Lord* God omnipotent
   16. KING OF KINGS, AND *LORD* OF
    LORDS.

Rev.21:22. for the *Lord* God Almighty and the Lamb
  22: 5. for the *Lord* God giveth them light:
    6. the *Lord* God of the holy prophets
  20. Even so, come, *Lord* Jesus.
  21. The grace of our *Lord* Jesus Christ (be)
    with you all. Amen.

κυριότης, *kuriotees.*

Eph 1:21. and *dominion*, and every name
Col. 1:16. or *dominions*, or principalities, or
2Pet.2:10. and despise *government.*
Jude 8. despise *dominion*, and speak evil of

κυρόω, *kuroō.*

2Co. 2: 8. that ye would *confirm* (your) love toward
Gal. 3:15. a man's covenant, yet (if it be) *confirmed*,
    no man disannulleth,

κύων, *kuōn.*

Mat. 7: 6. Give not that which is holy unto the *dogs*,
Lu. 16:21. the *dogs* came and licked his sores.
Phi. 3: 2. Beware of *dogs*, beware of evil workers,
2Pet.2:22. The *dog* (is) turned to his own vomit
Rev.22:15. For without (are) *dogs*, and sorcerers,

κῶλον, *kōlon.*

Heb 3:17. that had sinned, whose *carcases* fell in the
    wilderness?

κωλύω, *kōluo.*

Mat.19:14. and *forbid* them not,
Mar 9:38. and we *forbad* him,
  39. But Jesus said, *Forbid* him not:
 10:14. Suffer the little children to come unto me,
    and *forbid* them not:
Lu. 6:29. *forbid* not (to take thy) coat also.
 9:49. and we *forbad* him,
  50. *Forbid* (him) not:
 11:52. that were entering in ye *hindered.*
 18:16. and *forbid* them not:
  23: 2. *forbidding* to give tribute to Cæsar,
Acts 8:36. what *doth hinder* me to be baptized?
 10:47. Can any man *forbid* water,
 11:17. that I could *withstand* God?
 16: 6. and were *forbidden* of the Holy Ghost to
 24:23. and that he should *forbid* none of his
 27:43. *kept* them from (their) purpose;
Ro. 1:13. but *was let* hitherto,
1Co.14:39. and *forbid* not to speak with tongues.
1Th. 2:16. *Forbidding* us to speak to the Gentiles
1Ti. 4: 3. *Forbidding* to marry,
Heb 7:23. because they *were not suffered* to
2Pet.2:16. *forbad* the madness of the prophet.
3Joh. 10. and *forbiddeth* them that would,

κώμη, *kōmee.*

Mat. 9:35. about all the cities and *villages*,
 10:11. city or *town* ye shall enter,
 14:15. that they may go into the *villages*,
 21: 2. Go into the *village* over against

Mar 6: 6. he went round about the *villages*,
  36. and into the *villages*,
  56. into *villages*, or cities, or
 8:23. and led him out of the *town*;
  26. Neither go into the *town*, nor tell (it) to
    any in the *town*.
  27. into the *towns* of Cæsarea Philippi:
 11: 2. Go your way into the *village*
Lu. 5:17. were come out of every *town* of
 8: 1. every city and *village*,
 9: 6. went through the *towns*,
  12. that they may go into the *towns* and
  52. and entered into a *village* of the
  56. they went to another *village*.
 10:38. he entered into a certain *village*:
 13:22. the cities and *villages*, teaching,
 17:12. into a certain *village*,
 19:30. Go ye into the *village* over
 24:13. that same day to a *village* called Emmaus,
  28. they drew nigh unto the *village*,
Joh. 7:42. out of the *town* of Bethlehem,
 11: 1. Bethany, the *town* of Mary and her sister
  30. Jesus was not yet come into the *town*,
Acts 8:25. the gospel in many *villages* of the

κωμόπολις, *kōmopolis.*

Mar. 1:38. Let us go into the next *towns*,

κῶμος, *kōmos.*

Ro. 13:13. not in *rioting* and drunkenness,
Gal. 5:21. *revellings*, and such like:
1Pet.4: 3. *revellings*, banquetings, and abominable

κώνωψ, *kōnōps.*

Mat.23:24. which strain at a *gnat*,

κωφός, *kōphos.*

Mat. 9:32. brought to him a *dumb* man possessed
  33. when the devil was cast out, the *dumb*
 11: 5. and the *deaf* hear,
 12:22. with a devil, blind, and *dumb*:
  — that the blind and *dumb* both spake and
 15:30. blind, *dumb*, maimed, and many others,
  31. when they saw the *dumb* to speak,
Mar. 7:32. one that was *deaf*, and had an impediment
    in his speech;
  37. he maketh both the *deaf* to hear, and
 9:25. (Thou) dumb and *deaf* spirit, I charge
Lu. 1:22. and remained *speechless.*
 7:22. the *deaf* hear, the dead are raised,
 11:14. was casting out a devil, and it was *dumb.*
  — when the devil was gone out, the *dumb*

λαγχάνω, *lankano.*

Lu. 1: 9. *his lot was* to burn incense
Joh.19:24. Let us not rend it, but *cast lots* for it,
Acts 1:17. had *obtained* part of this ministry.
2Pet.1: 1. to them *that have obtained* like precious

λάθρα, lathra.

Mat. 1:19. was minded to put her away *privily*.
2: 7. when he had *privily* called the wise men,
Joh.11:28. called Mary her sister *secretly*,
Acts16:37. now do they thrust us out *privily?*

λαῖλαψ, lailaps.

Mar 4:37. there arose a great *storm* of wind,
Lu. 8:23. there came down a *storm* of wind
2Pet.2:17. that are carried with a *tempest;*

λακέω, lakeo.

Acts 1:18. he *burst asunder* in the midst,

λακτίζω, laktizo.

Acts 9: 5. (it is) hard for thee *to kick* against
26:14. for thee *to kick* against the pricks.

λαλέω, laleo.

Mat. 9:18. *While* he *spake* these things
33. the devil was cast out, the dumb *spake:*
10:19. or what ye *shall speak:*
— in that same hour what ye *shall speak.*
20. it is not ye *that speak*, but the Spirit of
your Father *which speaketh* in
12:22. that the blind and dumb both *spake* and
34. how can ye, being evil, *speak* good
— of the heart the mouth *speaketh.*
36. every idle word that men *shall speak*,
46. *While* he yet *talked* to the people,
— desiring *to speak* with him.
47. desiring *to speak* with thee.
13: 3. And he *spake* many things unto them in
parables,
10. Why *speakest* thou unto them in
13. Therefore *speak* I to them
33. Another parable *spake* he
34. All these things *spake* Jesus
— without a parable *spake* he not
14:27. Jesus *spake* unto them,
15:31. when they saw the dumb *to speak*,
17: 5. *While* he yet *spake*, behold,
23: 1. Then *spake* Jesus to the multitude,
26:13. *shall* also this,...*be told* for a memorial of
47. *while* he yet *spake*, lo, Judas,
28:18. Jesus came and *spake* unto them,
Mar. 1:34. suffered not the devils *to speak*,
2: 2. and he *preached* the word
7. Why *doth* this (man) thus *speak* blasphemies?
4:33. many such parables *spake* he the word
34. without a parable *spake* he not
5:35. *While* he yet *spake*, there came
36. heard the word *that was spoken*,
6:50. immediately he *talked* with them,
7:35. and he *spake* plain.
37. and the dumb *to speak.*
8:32. he *spake* that saying openly.
9: 6. For he wist not what to *say;*
13:11. beforehand what ye *shall speak*,
— that *speak* ye: for it is not ye *that speak*,
14: 9. *shall be spoken of* for a memorial
43. *while* he yet *spake*, cometh Judas,

Mar 16:17. they *shall speak* with new tongues;
19. after the Lord *had spoken*
Lu. 1:19. and am sent *to speak* unto thee,
20. and not able *to speak*,
22. he could not *speak*
45. *which were told* her from the Lord.
55. As he *spake* to our fathers,
64. and he *spake*, and praised God.
70. As he *spake* by the mouth of
2:17. the saying *which was told* them concerning
18. at those things *which were told* them by
20. as it *was told* unto them.
33. *which were spoken* of him.
38. and *spake* of him to all them
50. which he *spake* unto them.
4:41. suffered them not *to speak:*
5: 4. when he had left *speaking*,
21. Who is this which *speaketh* blasphemies?
6:45. of the heart his mouth *speaketh.*
7:15. and began *to speak.*
8:49. *While* he yet *spake*, there cometh one
9:11. *spake* unto them of the kingdom of God,
11:14. devil was gone out, the dumb *spake;*
37. as he *spake*, a certain Pharisee
12: 3. ye *have spoken* in the ear in
22:47. *while* he yet *spake*, behold a multitude,
60. *while* he yet *spake*, the cock crew.
24: 6. remember how he *spake* unto you
25. all that the prophets *have spoken:*
32. while he *talked* with us by the way,
36. And *as* they thus *spake*, Jesus
44. These (are) the words which I *spake*
Joh. 1:37. the two disciples heard him *speak*,
3:11. We *speak* that we do know,
31. and *speaketh* of the earth:
34. *speaketh* the words of God:
4:26. I *that speak* unto thee am (he).
27. marvelled that he *talked* with
— Why *talkest* thou with her?
6:63. the words that I *speak* unto you,
7:13. no man *spake* openly of him
17. or (whether) I *speak* of myself.
18. He *that speaketh* of himself
26. lo, he *speaketh* boldly,
46. Never man *spake* like this man.
8:12. Then *spake* Jesus again unto
20. These words *spake* Jesus in the
25. Even (the same) that I *said* unto you
26. I have many things *to say* and
28. hath taught me, I *speak* these things.
30. *As* he *spake* these words, many believed
38. I *speak* that which I have seen
40. a man that *hath told* you the truth,
44. When he *speaketh* a lie, he *speaketh* of his
9:21. he *shall speak* for himself.
29. We know that God *spake* unto Moses:
37. it is he *that talketh* with thee.
10: 6. which he *spake* unto them.
12:29. An angel *spake* to him.
36. These things *spake* Jesus,
41. he saw his glory, and *spake* of him.
48. the word that I *have spoken*,
49. I *have* not *spoken* of myself;
— and what I *should speak.*
50. whatsoever I *speak* therefore, even as the
Father said unto me, so I *speak.*
14:10. the words that I *speak* unto you I *speak*
not of myself:
25. These things *have* I *spoken*
30. I *will* not *talk* much with you:
15: 3. which I *have spoken* unto you.
11. These things *have* I *spoken* unto you,

Joh. 15:22. If I had not come and *spoken* unto them,
16: 1. These things *have* I *spoken*
    4. these things *have* I *told* you,
    6. because I *have said* these things
   13. he *shall* not *speak* of himself; but what-
    soever he shall hear, (that) *shall* he
    speak :
   18. we cannot tell what he *saith.*
   25. *have* I *spoken* unto you in proverbs:
   — when I *shall* no more *speak* unto you in
   29. now *speakest* thou plainly,
   33. These things I *have spoken* unto you,
17: 1. These words *spake* Jesus,
   13. these things I *speak* in the world,
18:20. I *spake* openly to the world ;
   — in secret *have* I *said* nothing.
   21. what I *have said* unto them:
   23. If I *have spoken* evil,
19:10. *Speakest* thou not unto me ?
Acts 2: 4. began *to speak* with other
    6. heard them *speak* in his own language.
    7. are not all these *which speak*
   11. we do hear them *speak* in our
   31. *spake* of the resurrection of
3:21. God *hath spoken* by the mouth
   22. whatsoever he *shall say* unto
   24. as many as *have spoken,* have likewise
4: 1. And *as* they *spake* unto the people,
   17. that they *speak* henceforth
   20. For we cannot but *speak*
   29. all boldness they may *speak*
   31. they *spake* the word of God
5:20. Go, stand and *speak* in the temple
   40. that they should not *speak* in the name
6:10. and the spirit by which he *spake.*
   11. We have heard him *speak* blasphemous
   13. This man ceaseth not *to speak*
7: 6. God *spake* on this wise,
   38. with the angel *which spake* to him
   44. *speaking* unto Moses,
8:25. and *preached* the word of the Lord,
   26. the angel of the Lord *spake* unto Philip,
9: 6. it *shall be told* thee what thou
   27. and that he *had spoken* to him,
   29. he *spake* boldly in the name
10: 6. he *shall tell* thee what thou
   7. the angel *which spake* unto Cornelius
   32. *shall speak* unto thee.
   44. *While* Peter yet *spake* these words, the
    Holy Ghost fell on all
   46. For they heard them *speak* with
11:14. Who *shall tell* thee words,
   15. as I began *to speak,* the Holy Ghost
   19. *preaching* the word to none but
   20. *spake* unto the Grecians, preaching
13:42. might *be preached* to them
   46. should first *have been spoken*
14: 1. and so *spake,* that a great
   9. The same heard Paul *speak :*
   25. *when* they *had preached* the word in
16: 6. *to preach* the word in Asia,
   13. and *spake* unto the women
   14. the things *which were spoken* of Paul.
   32. they *spake* unto him the word
17:19. doctrine, whereof thou speakest, (lit.
   spoken by thee)
18: 9. but *speak,* and hold not thy peace:
   25. he *spake* and taught diligently
19: 6. they *spake* with tongues, and
20:30. *speaking* perverse things,
21:39. suffer me *to speak* unto the people.
22: 9. the voice of him *that spake* to me.

Acts22:10. there it *shall be told* thee of
23: 7. And *when* he *had so said,* there arose
   9. or an angel *hath spoken* to
   18. hath something *to say* unto thee.
26:14. I heard a voice *speaking* unto me,
   22. and Moses *did say* should come:
   26. before whom also I *speak* freely:
   31. they *talked* between themselves,
27:25. it shall be even as it *was told* me.
28:21. or *spake* any harm of thee.
   25. Well *spake* the Holy Ghost by
Ro. 3:19. it *saith* to them who are under
7: 1. I *speak* to them that know the law,
15:18. I will not dare *to speak* of any
1Co. 2: 6. we *speak* wisdom among them
   7. we *speak* the wisdom of God in
   13. Which things also we *speak,*
3: 1. I, brethren, could not *speak* unto you as
9: 8. *Say* I these things as a man ?
12: 3. no man *speaking* by the Spirit
   30. *do* all *speak* with tongues?
13: 1. Though I *speak* with the tongues
   11. When I was a child, I *spake* as
14: 2. he *that speaketh* in an (unknown) tongue
   speaketh not unto men,
   — in the spirit he *speaketh* mysteries.
   3. prophesieth *speaketh* unto men
   4. He *that speaketh* in an (unknown)
   5. I would that ye all *spake* with
   — than he *that speaketh* with tongues,
   6. if I come unto you *speaking* with tongues,
   what shall I profit you, except I *shall*
   speak
   9. how shall it be known *what is spoken?* for
   ye shall *speak* into the air.
   11. I shall be unto him *that speaketh* a barbarian, and he *that speaketh*
   13. let him *that speaketh* in an
   18. I *speak* with tongues more
   19. I had rather *speak* five words
   21. *will* I *speak* unto this people ;
   23. and all *speak* with tongues,
   27. If any man *speak* in an
   28. *let* him *speak* to himself,
   29. *Let* the prophets *speak* two or
   34. not permitted unto them *to speak ;*
   35. a shame for women *to speak* in the
   39. and forbid not *to speak* with
2Co. 2:17. *speak* we in Christ.
4:13. and therefore *have* I *spoken ;*
   — and therefore *speak ;*
7:14. as we *spake* all things to you in
11:17. That which I *speak,* I *speak* (it)
   23. I *speak* as a fool I (am) more ;
12: 4. not lawful for a man *to utter.*
   19. we *speak* before God in Christ:
13: 3. a proof of Christ *speaking* in me,
Eph. 4:25. *speak* every man truth
5:19. *Speaking* to yourselves in psalms
6:20. as I ought *to speak.*
Phi. 1:14. more bold *to speak* the word
Col. 4: 3. *to speak* the mystery of Christ,
   4. make it manifest, as I ought *to speak.*
1Th. 1: 8. we need not *to speak* any thing.
2: 2. bold in our God *to speak* unto you
   4. even so we *speak ;*
   16. Forbidding us *to speak* to the
1Ti. 5:13. *speaking* things which they ought not.
Tit. 2: 1. But *speak* thou the things
   15. These things *speak,* and exhort,
Heb 1: 1. God, *who...spake* in time past unto the
2(1). *Hath* in these last days *spóken* unto us

Heb 2: 2. if the word *spoken* by angels
3. began *to be spoken* by the Lord,
5. the world to come, whereof we *speak*.
3: 5. for a testimony of those things *which were to be spoken after ;*
4: 8. would he not afterward *have spoken* of
5: 5. but he *that said* unto him,
6: 9. though we thus *speak*.
7: 14. of which tribe Moses *spake* nothing
9: 19. when Moses had spoken every precept (lit. every pr. *having been spoken*)
11: 4. being dead yet *speaketh*.
18. Of whom it *was said*, That in Isaac
12: 24. *that speaketh* better things than
25. refuse not him *that speaketh*.
13: 7. who *have spoken* unto you
Jas. 1: 19. slow *to speak*, slow to wrath:
2: 12. So *speak* ye, and so do,
5: 10. who *have spoken* in the name
1Pet. 3: 10. that they *speak* no guile:
4: 11. If any man *speak*, (let him speak) as
2Pet. 1: 21. *spake* (as they were) moved
3: 16. *speaking* in them of these things ;
1Joh. 4: 5. therefore *speak* they of the world,
2Joh. 12. and *speak* face to face,
3Joh. 14. and we *shall speak* face to
Jude 15. which ungodly sinners *have spoken* against
16. mouth *speaketh* great swelling (words),
Rev. 1: 12. to see the voice that *spake*
4: 1. of a trumpet *talking* with me ;
10: 3. seven thunders *uttered* their voices.
4. thunders *had uttered* their voices,
— which the seven thunders *uttered*,
8. *spake* unto me again,
13: 5. a mouth *speaking* great things
11. he *spake* as a dragon.
15. the image of the beast *should* both *speak*,
17: 1. and *talked* with me,
21: 9. and *talked* with me, saying, Come
15. And he *that talked* with me had

λαλιά, *lalia.*

Mat. 26: 73. thy *speech* bewrayeth thee.
Mar 14: 70. thy *speech* agreeth (thereto).
Joh. 4: 42. not because of thy *saying :*
8: 43. Why do ye not understand my *speech ?*

λαμά or λαμμᾶ, *lama or lamma.*

Mat. 27: 46. Eli, Eli, *lama* sabachthani ?
Mar 15: 34. Eloi, Eloi, *lama* sabachthani ?

λαμβάνω, *lambano.*

Mat. 5: 40. and *take away* thy coat,
7: 8. every one that asketh *receiveth ;*
8: 17. Himself *took* our infirmities,
10: 8. freely ye *have received,*
38. And he that *taketh* not his cross,
41. *shall receive* a prophet's reward ;
— *shall receive* a righteous man's reward.
12: 14. and *held* a council against him,
13: 20. anon with joy *receiveth* it ;
31. which a man *took, and* sowed
33. which a woman *took, and* hid
14: 19. and *took* the five loaves,
15: 26. It is not meet *to take* the children's bread,
36. And he *took* the seven loaves

Mat. 16: 5. had forgotten *to take* bread.
7. because we *have taken* no bread.
8. ye *have brought* no bread ?
9. how many baskets ye *took up ?*
10. and how many baskets ye *took up ?*
17: 24. they *that received* tribute (money) came
25. of whom *do* the kings of the earth *take* custom or tribute ?
27. that *take, and* give unto them
19: 29. *shall receive* an hundredfold,
20: 7. whatsoever is right, (that) *shall ye receive.*
9. they *received* every man a penny.
10. they should have *received* more ; and they likewise *received*
11. *when* they *had received* (it), they murmured
21: 22. whatsoever ye shall ask in prayer believing, ye *shall receive.*
34. that they might *receive* the fruits
35. husbandmen *took* his servants, *and*
39. And they *caught* him, *and* cast
22: 15. and *took* counsel how they
23: 14(13). ye *shall receive* the greater damnation.
25: 1. which *took* their lamps, *and* went forth
3. foolish *took* their lamps, *and took* no oil
4. But the wise *took* oil
16. Then he *that had received* the five
18. But he *that had received* one
20. so he *that had received* five
22. He also *that had received* two
24. Then he *which had received* the one
26: 26. Jesus *took* bread, and blessed (it), *and*
— *Take*, eat ; this is my body.
27. And he *took* the cup, and
52. all they *that take* the sword shall
27: 1. elders of the people *took* counsel
6. chief priests *took* the silver pieces, *and*
7. And they *took* counsel, *and* bought
9. And they *took* the thirty pieces
24. he *took* water, *and* washed (his) hands
30. and *took* the reed, and smote
48. and *took* a spunge, *and*
59. *when* Joseph *had taken* the body,
28: 12. and had *taken* counsel, they gave
15. So they *took* the money, and did as
Mar 4: 16. immediately *receive* it with gladness ;
6: 41. And *when* he *had taken* the five loaves
7: 27. not meet *to take* the children's bread,
8: 6. and he *took* the seven loaves, *and*
14. had forgotten *to take* bread,
9: 36. And he *took* a child, *and* set him in
10: 30. But he shall *receive* an hundredfold
11: 24. believe that ye *receive* (them),
12: 2. that he *might receive* from the husbandmen
3. And they *caught* (him), *and* beat
8. And they *took* him, *and* killed
19. his brother *should take* his wife,
20. the first *took* a wife,
21. And the second *took* her,
22. And the seven *had* her, and left no seed:
40. these *shall receive* greater damnation.
14: 22. Jesus *took* bread, *and* blessed,
— *Take*, eat: this is my body.
23. And he *took* the cup, *and* when
15: 23. but he *received* (it) not.
Lu. 5: 5. and *have taken* nothing:
26. And they were all amazed, (lit. amazement *took* all)
6: 4. *did take* and eat the shewbread,
7: 16. And there *came* a fear *on* all:
9: 16. Then he *took* the five loaves
39. And, lo, a spirit *taketh* him,
11: 10. every one that asketh *receiveth ;*

Lu. 13:19. which a man *took, and* cast into his garden;
21. which a woman *took and* hid
19:12. *to receive* for himself a kingdom,
15. was returned, *having received* the kingdom,
20:21. neither *acceptest* thou the person (of any),
28. that his brother *should take* his wife,
29. the first *took* a wife, *and* died without children.
30. And the second *took* her to wife,
31. And the third *took* her;
47. the same *shall receive* greater damnation.
22:17. and said, *Take* this,
19. And he *took* bread, *and* gave thanks,
24:30. he *took* bread, *and* blessed (it),
43. And he *took* (it), *and* did eat before them.
Joh. 1:12. as many as *received* him,
16. have all we *received*,
3:11. and ye *receive* not our witness.
27. A man can *receive* nothing,
32. no man *receiveth* his testimony.
33. He *that hath received* his testimony
4:36. that reapeth *receiveth* wages,
5:34. I *receive* not testimony from man:
41. I *receive* not honour from men.
43. and ye *receive* me not:
— him ye *will receive*.
44. *which receive* honour one of another,
6: 7. that every one of them *may take*
11. And Jesus *took* the loaves;
21. Then they willingly *received* him
7:23. If a man on the sabbath day *receive* circumcision,
39. they that believe on him should *receive:*
10:17. that I *might take* it again.
18. I have power *to take* it again. This commandment *have* I *received*
12: 3. Then *took* Mary a pound of ointment
13. *Took* branches of palm trees,
48. and *receiveth* not my words,
13: 4. and *took* a towel, *and* girded himself.
12. and *had taken* his garments,
20. He *that receiveth* whomsoever I send *receiveth* me; and he *that receiveth* me *receiveth* him that sent me.
30. He then *having received* the sop
14:17. whom the world cannot *receive*,
15. he *shall take* of mine,
24. ask, and ye *shall receive*,
17: 8. and they *have received* (them),
18: 3. Judas then, *having received* a band
31. *Take* ye him, and judge him
19: 1. Pilate therefore *took* Jesus, and scourged
6. *Take* ye him, and crucify
23. *took* his garments, and made
27. that disciple *took* her unto
30. When Jesus therefore *had received*
40. Then *took* they the body of Jesus,
20:22. *Receive* ye the Holy Ghost:
21:13. and *taketh* bread, and giveth
Acts 1: 8. But ye *shall receive* power,
20. bishoprick let another *take*.
25. That he may *take* part
2:23. ye have *taken, and* by wicked hands
33. and *having received* of the Father
38. ye *shall receive* the gift
3: 3. asked)(an alms.
5. expecting *to receive* something
7:53. Who *have received* the law
8:15. that they *might receive* the Holy Ghost:
17. and they *received* the Holy Ghost.
19. he *may receive* the Holy Ghost.

Acts 9:19. And *when* he *had received* meat,
25. the disciples *took* him by night, *and*
10:43. shall *receive* remission of sins.
47. which *have received* the Holy Ghost
15:14. *to take* out of them a people
16: 3. and *took and* circumcised
24. Who, *having received* such a charge,
17: 9. And *when* they *had taken* security
15. and *receiving* a commandment
19: 2. *Have* ye *received* the Holy Ghost
20:24. which I *have received* of the Lord Jesus,
35. more blessed to give than *to receive*.
24:27. Porcius Festus came into Felix' room: (lit. Felix *received* Porcius Festus as his successor)
25:16. and *have* licence to answer
26:10. *having received* authority
18. that they may *receive* forgiveness of sins,
27:35. he *took* bread, *and* gave thanks to God
28:15. thanked God, and *took* courage.
Ro. 1: 5. By whom we *have received* grace and
4:11. And he *received* the sign
5:11. by whom we *have* now *received*
17. much more they *which receive* abundance
7: 8. sin, *taking* occasion by the commandment,
11. For sin, *taking* occasion by
8:15. For ye *have* not *received* the spirit of
— but ye *have received* the Spirit of adoption,
13: 2. *shall receive* to themselves
1Co. 2:12. Now we *have received*, not the spirit of the
3: 8. *shall receive* his own reward
14. he *shall receive* a reward.
4: 7. that thou *didst* not *receive?* now if thou *didst receive* (it), why dost thou glory, as *if* thou *hadst* not *received* (it)?
9:24. but one *receiveth* the prize?
25. to *obtain* a corruptible crown;
10:13. There *hath* no temptation *taken* you
11:23. in which he was betrayed *took* bread:
24. *Take*, eat: this is my body,
14: 5. that the church *may receive* edifying.
2Co.11: 4. (if) ye *receive* another spirit, which ye *have* not *received*,
8. *taking* wages (of them),
20. if a man *take* (of you),
24. five times *received* I forty
12:16. I *caught* you with guile.
Gal. 2: 6. God *accepteth* no man's person:
3: 2. *Received* ye the Spirit by the works
14. that we *might receive* the promise of the
Phi. 2: 7. *and took* (upon him) the form of a servant,
3:12. Not as though I *had* already *attained*,
Col. 4:10. whom ye *received* commandments:
1Ti. 4: 4. *if* it *be received* with thanksgiving:
2Ti. 1: 5. When I call to remembrance the (lit. *taking* remembrance)
Heb 2: 2. *received* a just recompence
3. which at the first began to be spoken (lit. *taking* commencement to be spoken) by the Lord,
4:16. that we *may obtain* mercy,
5: 1. every high priest *taken* from among men
4. no man *taketh* this honour
7: 5. *who receive* the office of the priesthood,
8. men that die *receive* tithes;
9. Levi also, *who receiveth* tithes.
9:15. *might receive* the promise
19. he *took* the blood of calves
10:26. after that we *have received*
11: 8. which he should after *receive* for
11. Sara herself *received* strength
13. not *having received* the promises,

Heb 11:29. which the Egyptians assaying to do (lit. *taking* attempt)
35. Women *received* their dead
36. And others *had* trial of (cruel) mockings
Jas. 1: 7. that he *shall receive* any thing
12. he *shall receive* the crown of
3: 1. we *shall receive* the greater condemnation.
4: 3. Ye ask, and *receive* not,
5: 7. until he *receive* the early and latter rain.
10. *Take*, my brethren, the prophets,
1Pet.4:10. As every man *hath received* the gift,
2Pet.1: 9. hath forgotten (lit. *having taken* forgetfulness) that he was purged
17. For he *received* from God the Father
1Joh.2:27. the anointing which ye *have received* of
3:22. whatsoever we ask, we *receive* of him,
5: 9. If we *receive* the witness of men,
2Joh. 4. as we *have received* a commandment
10. *receive* him not into (your) house,
3Joh. 4. *taking* nothing of the Gentiles.
Rev. 2:17. saving he *that receiveth* (it).
27. even as I *received* of my Father.
3: 3. how thou *hast received* and heard,
11. that no man *take* thy crown.
4:11. *to receive* glory and honour and
5: 7. he came and *took* the book
8. when he *had taken* the book,
9. Thou art worthy *to take* the
12. *to receive* power, and riches, and
6: 4. *to take* peace from the earth,
8: 5. the angel *took* the censer,
10: 8. Go (and) *take* the little book
9. *Take* (it), and eat it up ;
10. I *took* the little book
11:17. because thou *hast taken to* thee
14: 9. and *receive* (his) mark in
11. *receiveth* the mark of his name.
17:12. which *have received* no kingdom as yet; but *receive* power as kings one hour
18: 4. that ye *receive* not of her plagues.
19:20. them *that had received* the mark
20: 4. neither *had received* (his) mark
22:17. And whosoever will, *let* him *take* the water of life freely.

λαμμᾶ see λαμά.

λαμπάς, *lampas.*

Mat.25: 1. which took their *lamps,*
3. that (were) foolish took their *lamps,*
4. the wise took oil in their vessels with their *lamps.*
7. and trimmed their *lamps.*
8. for our *lamps* are gone out.
Joh.18: 3. with lanterns and *torches* and
Acts20: 8. And there were many *lights*
Rev. 4: 5. and (there were) seven *lamps* of fire
8:10. star from heaven, burning as it were a *lamp,*

λαμπρός, *lampros.*

Lu. 23:11. arrayed him in a *gorgeous* robe,
Acts10:30. stood before me in *bright* clothing,
Jas. 2: 2. if there come...in *goodly* apparel,
3. that weareth the *gay* clothing,
Rev.15: 6. clothed in pure and *white* linen,

Rev.18:14. all things which were dainty and *goodly* are departed
19: 8. in fine linen, clean and *white :*
22: 1. river of water of life, *clear* as crystal,
16. the *bright* and morning star.

λαμπρότης, *lamprotees.*

Acts26:13. light from heaven, above the *brightness* of the sun,

---

λαμπρῶς, *lamprōs.*

Lu. 16:19. and fared *sumptuously* every day:

λάμπω, *lampo.*

Mat. 5:15. and it giveth *light* unto all that are
16. *Let* your light so *shine* before men,
17: 2. and his face *did shine* as the sun,
Lu. 17:24. *shineth* unto the other (part)
Acts12: 7. a light *shined* in the prison:
2Co. 4: 6. God, who commanded the light *to shine* out of darkness, *hath shined* in our

---

λανθάνω, *lanthano.*

Mar 7:24. but he could not *be hid.*
Lu. 8:47. saw that she was not *hid,*
Acts26:26. that none of these things *are hidden*
Heb13: 2. some *have* entertained angels *unawares.*
2Pet.3: 5. this they willingly are ignorant of, (lit. this *escapes* them willing)
8. be not ignorant of this one thing, (lit. *let* not this one thing *escape* you)

λαξευτός, *laxūtos.*

Lu. 23:53. in a sepulchre that was *hewn in stone,*

λαός, *laos.*

[2] Denotes where the word is used in the plural: *peoples.*

Mat. 1:21. shall save his *people* from their sins.
2: 4. and scribes of the *people* together,
6. shall rule my *people* Israel.
4:16. The *people* which sat in darkness
23. of disease among the *people.*
9:35. every disease among the *people.*
13:15. For this *people's* heart is waxed
15: 8. This *people* draweth nigh unto me
21:23. and the elders of the *people* came
26: 3. and the elders of the *people,*
5. be an uproar among the *people.*
47. the chief priests and elders of the *people.*
27: 1. and elders of the *people* took counsel
25. Then answered all the *people,*
64. steal him away, and say unto the *people,*
Mar 7: 6. This *people* honoureth me with (their)
11:32. they feared the *people :*
14: 2. be an uproar of the *people.*
Lu. 1:10. And the whole multitude of the *people*
17. to make ready a *people* prepared
21. And the *people* waited for Zacharias,

Lu. 1:68. visited and redeemed his *people,*
      77. of salvation unto his *people*
  2:10. which shall be to all *people.*
      31. before the face of all *people;*[2]
      32. the glory of thy *people* Israel.
  3:15. And as the *people* were in expectation,
      18. preached he unto the *people.*
      21. when all the *people* were baptized,
  6:17. a great multitude of *people*
  7: 1. in the audience of the *people,*
      16. God hath visited his *people.*
      29. And all the *people* that heard
  8:47. before all the *people*
  9:13. and buy meat for all this *people.*
 18:43. and all the *people,* when they saw
 19:47. the chief of the *people* sought to
      48. all the *people* were very attentive
 20: 1. as he taught the *people* in the
      6. all the *people* will stone us:
      9. speak to the *people* this
      19. they feared the *people:*
      26. of his words before the *people:*
      45. in the audience of all the *people*
 21:23. and wrath upon this *people.*
      38. all the *people* came early
 22: 2. for they feared the *people.*
      66. the elders of the *people* and
 23: 5. He stirreth up the *people,*
      13. and the rulers and the *people,*
      14. as one that perverteth the *people:*
      27. a great company of *people,*
      35. And the *people* stood beholding.
 24:19. before God and all the *people:*
Joh. 8: 2. and all the *people* came unto him;
 11:50. that one man should die for the *people,*
 18:14. that one man should die for the *people.*
Acts 2:47. favour with all the *people.*
  3: 9. all the *people* saw him walking
      11. all the *people* ran together
      12. he answered unto the *people,*
      23. destroyed from among the *people.*
  4: 1. as they spake unto the *people,*
      2. grieved that they taught the *people,*
      8. Ye rulers of the *people,*
      10. and to all the *people* of Israel,
      17. spread no further among the *people,*
      21. because of the *people:*
      25. and the *people*[2] imagine vain
      27. and the *people*[2] of Israel,
  5:12. wonders wrought among the *people;*
      13. but the *people* magnified them.
      20. speak in the temple to the *people*
      25. and teaching the *people.*
      26. for they feared the *people,*
      34. in reputation among all the *people,*
      37. and drew away much *people*
  6: 8. and miracles among the *people.*
      12. And they stirred up the *people,*
  7:17. the *people* grew and multiplied
      34. the affliction of my *people*
 10: 2. gave much alms to the *people,*
      41. Not to all the *people,* but
      42. to preach unto the *people,*
 12: 4. to bring him forth to the *people.*
      11. the expectation of the *people* of
 13:15. exhortation for the *people,*
      17. The God of this *people* of Israel
      — and exalted the *people*
      24. repentance to all the *people* of
      31. his witnesses unto the *people.*
 15:14. out of them a *people* for his
 18:10. I have much *people* in this city.

Acts 19: 4. saying unto the *people,*
 21:28. against the *people,* and the law,
      30. the *people* ran together:
      36. the multitude of the *people*
      39. suffer me to speak unto the *people.*
      40. with the hand unto the *people.*
 23: 5. evil of the ruler of thy *people.*
 26:17. Delivering thee from the *people,*
      23. should shew light unto the *people,*
 28:17. nothing against the *people,*
      26. Go unto this *people,* and say,
      27. For the heart of this *people*
Ro. 9:25. I will call them my *people,* which were not
        my *people;*
      26. Ye (are) not my *people;* there shall they
        be called the children of
 10:21. and gainsaying *people.*
 11: 1. Hath God cast away his *people?*
      2. God hath not cast away his *people*
 15:10. Rejoice, ye Gentiles, with his *people.*
      11. and laud him, all ye *people*[2].
1Co.10: 7. The *people* sat down to eat and
 14:21. will I speak unto this *people;*
2Co. 6:16. and they shall be my *people.*
Tit. 2:14. a peculiar *people,* zealous
Heb. 2:17. for the sins of the *people.*
  4: 9. a rest to the *people* of God.
  5: 3. as for the *people,* so also
  7: 5. to take tithes of the *people*
      11. under it the *people* received
      27. and then for the *people's:*
  8:10. and they shall be to me a *people:*
  9: 7. and (for) the errors of the *people:*
      19. every precept to all the *people*
      — the book, and all the *people*
 10:30. The Lord shall judge his *people.*
 11:25. affliction with the *people* of God,
 13:12. might sanctify the *people*
1Pet.2: 9. an holy nation, a peculiar *people;*
      10. (were) not a *people,* but (are) now the
        people of God:
2Pet.2: 1. false prophets also among the *people,*
Jude   5. having saved the *people*
Rev. 5: 9. and *people,* and nation;
  7: 9. and *people*[2], and tongues,
 10:11. prophesy again before many *peoples*[2]
 11: 9. And they of the *people*[2] and kindreds
 14: 6. and tongue, and *people,*
 17:15. the whore sitteth, are *peoples*[2],
 18: 4. Come out of her, my *people,*
 21: 3. they shall be his *people*[2], and God himself
      shall be with them,

λάρυγξ, *larunx.*

Ro. 3:13. Their *throat* (is) an open sepulchre;

λατομέω, *latomeo.*

Mat.27:60. in his own new tomb, which he *had hewn*
      out in the rock:
Mar 15:46. sepulchre *which was hewn* out of a rock,

λατρεία, *latria.*

Joh. 16: 2. will think that he doeth God *service.*
Ro. 9: 4. and the *service* (of God), and the promises;
  12: 1. (which is) your reasonable *service.*

Heb. 9: 1. ordinances of *divine service*,
6. accomplishing the *service* (of God).

λατρεύω, *latrŭo*.

Mat. 4:10. and him only *shalt* thou *serve*.
Lu. 1:74. might *serve* him without fear,
2:37. *but served* (God) with fastings
4: 8. and him only *shalt* thou *serve*.
Acts 7: 7. shall they come forth, and *serve* me in this
42. gave them up *to worship* the host of heaven;
24:14. so *worship* I the God of my fathers,
26: 7. instantly *serving* (God) day and night,
27:23. and whom I *serve*,
Ro. 1: 9. whom I *serve* with my spirit
25. and *served* the creature more
Phi. 3: 3. *which worship* God in the spirit,
2Ti. 1: 3. I thank God, whom I *serve* from
Heb. 8: 5. Who *serve* unto the example
9: 9. not make him *that did the service* perfect,
14. *to serve* the living God?
10: 2. the *worshippers* once purged
12:28. we *may serve* God acceptably
13:10. *which serve* the tabernacle.
Rev. 7:15. and *serve* him day and night
22: 3. and his servants *shall serve* him:

λάχανον, *lakanon*.

Mat.13:32. the greatest among *herbs*,
Mar. 4:32. greater than all *herbs*,
Lu. 11:42. mint and rue and all manner of *herbs*,
Ro. 14: 2. another, who is weak, eateth *herbs*.

λεγεών, *legeōn*.

Mat.26:53. give me more than twelve *legions* of
Mar 5: 9. My name (is) *Legion:* for we are many.
15. and had the *legion*, sitting,
Lu. 8:30. And he said, *Legion:* because many

λέγω, *lego*.

Mat. 1:16. Jesus, *who is called* Christ.
20. in a dream, *saying*, Joseph,
22. by the prophet, *saying*,
2: 2. *Saying*, Where is he that is born
13. in a dream, *saying*, Arise, and
15. *saying*, Out of Egypt have I
17. by Jeremy the prophet, *saying*,
20. *Saying*, Arise, and take the young
23. dwelt in a city *called* Nazareth:
3: 2. And *saying*, Repent ye:
3. *saying*, The voice of one crying
9. think not *to say* within yourselves,
— for I *say* unto you, that God is able
14. John forbad him, *saying*,
17. a voice from heaven, *saying*,
4: 6. And *saith* unto him, If thou be
9. *saith* unto him, All these things will I
10. Then *saith* Jesus unto him,
14. by Esaias the prophet, *saying*,
17. and *to say*, Repent: for the
18. Simon *called* Peter, and Andrew
19. And he *saith* unto them,
5: 2. and taught them, *saying*,
18. verily I *say* unto you,

Mat. 5:20. For I *say* unto you,
22. But I *say* unto you,
26. Verily I *say* unto thee,
28. But I *say* unto you, That whosoever
32. But I *say* unto you, That whosoever shall
34. But I *say* unto you, Swear not at all;
39. But I *say* unto you, That ye resist not
44. But I *say* unto you, Love your enemies,
6: 2. Verily I *say* unto you, They have
5. Verily I *say* unto you, They have their
16. I *say* unto you, They have their reward.
25. Therefore I *say* unto you,
29. And yet I *say* unto you,
31. take no thought, *saying*,
7:21. Not every one *that saith* unto me,
8: 2. and worshipped him, *saying*,
3. and touched him, *saying*, I will;
4. And Jesus *saith* unto him,
6. And *saying*, Lord, my servant
7. Jesus *saith* unto him,
9. I *say* to this (man), Go, and he goeth;
10. Verily I *say* unto you,
11. And I *say* unto you,
17. *saying*, Himself took our
20. Jesus *saith* unto him,
25. *saying*, Lord, save us:
26. And he *saith* unto them,
27. *saying*, What manner of man is this,
29. they cried out, *saying*,
31. devils besought him, *saying*,
9: 6. then *saith* he to the sick of
9. a man, *named* Matthew, sitting at the
receipt of custom: and he *saith* unto
14. the disciples of John, *saying*,
18. and worshipped him, *saying*,
21. For she *said* within herself,
24(23). He *said* unto them,
27. and *saying*, (Thou) son of David,
28. and Jesus *saith* unto them,
— They *said* unto him, Yea, Lord.
29. Then touched he their eyes, *saying*,
30. *saying*, See (that) no man know (it).
33. multitudes marvelled, *saying*,
34. But the Pharisees *said*,
37. Then *saith* he unto his disciples,
10: 2. Simon, *who is called* Peter,
5. and commanded them, *saying*,
7. And as ye go, preach, *saying*,
15. Verily I *say* unto you,
23. for verily I *say* unto you,
27. What I *tell* you in darkness,
42. verily I *say* unto you,
11: 7. Jesus began *to say*
9. yea, I *say* unto you,
11. Verily I *say* unto you,
17. And *saying*, We have piped
18. and they *say*, He hath a devil.
19. and they *say*, Behold a man
22. But I *say* unto you, It shall be more tolerable for Tyre
24. But I *say* unto you, That it shall be
12: 6. But I *say* unto you, That in this place is
10. And they asked him, *saying*,
13. Then *saith* he to the man,
17. by Esaias the prophet, *saying*,
23. and *said*, Is not this the son
31. Wherefore I *say* unto you,
36. But I *say* unto you,
38. *saying*, Master, we would see
44. Then he *saith*, I will return
13: 3. *saying*, Behold, a sower
14. the prophecy of Esaias, *which saith*,

Mat.13:17. For verily I *say* unto you,
24. *saying*, The kingdom of heaven
31. put he forth unto them, *saying*, The
35. by the prophet, *saying*,
36. came unto him, *saying*,
51. Jesus *saith* unto them,
— They *say* unto him, Yea,
54. that they were astonished, and *said*,
55. *is* not his mother *called* Mary?
14: 4. For John *said* unto him,
15. came to him, *saying*,
17. And they *say* unto him,
26. *saying*, It is a spirit ;
27. *saying*, Be of good cheer ;
30. *saying*, Lord, save me.
31. and *said* unto him,
33. worshipped him, *saying*,
15: 1. which were of Jerusalem, *saying*,
4. God commanded, *saying*,
5. But ye *say*, Whosoever shall
7. well did Esaias prophesy of you, *saying*,
22. *saying*, Have mercy on me,
23. *saying*, Send her away ;
25. *saying*, Lord, help me.
33. And his disciples *say* unto him,
34. And Jesus *saith* unto them,
16: 2. When it is evening, ye *say*,
7. *saying*, (It is) because we have
13. asked his disciples, *saying*,
— Whom do men *say* that I
15. He *saith* unto them, But whom *say* ye
that I am?
18. And I *say* also unto thee,
22. began to rebuke him, *saying*,
28. Verily I *say* unto you,
17: 5. a voice out of the cloud, *which said*, This
is my beloved
9. Jesus charged them, *saying*,
10. his disciples asked him, *saying*, Why then
say the scribes
12. But I *say* unto you,
14. kneeling down to him, and *saying*,
20. verily I *say* unto you,
25. He *saith*, Yes.
— Jesus prevented him, *saying*,
26. Peter *saith* unto him, Of strangers.
18: 1. *saying*, Who is the greatest
3. Verily I *say* unto you,
10. for I *say* unto you,
13. verily I *say* unto you, he rejoiceth more
18. Verily I *say* unto you, Whatsoever ye
19. Again I *say* unto you, That if two
22. Jesus *saith* unto him, I *say* not unto thee,
26. *saying*, Lord, have patience
28. *saying*, Pay me that thou owest.
29. *saying*, Have patience with
32. *said* unto him, O thou wicked servant,
19: 3. and *saying* unto him,
7. They *say* unto him,
8. He *saith* unto them,
9. And I *say* unto you,
10. His disciples *say* unto him,
17. Why *callest* thou me good?
18. He *saith* unto him,
20. The young man *saith* unto him,
23. Verily I *say* unto you,
24. And again I *say* unto you,
25. *saying*, Who then can be saved?
28. Verily I *say* unto you,
20: 6. and *saith* unto them,
7. They *say* unto him, Because no man hath
hired us. He *saith* unto them,

Mat.20: 8. *saith* unto his steward,
12. *Saying*, These last have wrought
21. She *saith* unto him,
22. They *say* unto him, We are able.
23. And he *saith* unto them,
30. *saying*, Have mercy on us,
31. but they cried the more, *saying*, Have
mercy on us,
33. They *say* unto him, Lord,
21: 2. *Saying* unto them, Go into
4. by the prophet, *saying*,
9. *saying*, Hosanna to the son
10. the city was moved, *saying*, Who is this?
11. the multitude *said*, This is Jesus
13. And *said* unto them, It is written,
15. and *saying*, Hosanna to the son
16. Hearest thou what these *say*? And Jesus
saith unto them, Yea ;
19. and *said* unto it, Let no fruit
20. they marvelled, *saying*, How soon
21. Verily I *say* unto you,
23. *and said*, By what authority
25. *saying*, If we shall say,
27. Neither *tell* I you by what
31. They *say* unto him, The first. Jesus *saith*
unto them, Verily I *say* unto you, That
the publicans
37. *saying*, They will reverence my son.
41. They *say* unto him,
42. Jesus *saith* unto them,
43. Therefore *say* I unto you,
45. that he *spake* of them.
22: 1. again by parables, *and said*,
4. *saying*, Tell them which are
8. Then *saith* he to his servants,
12. And he *saith* unto him,
16. *saying*, Master, we know that
20. And he *saith* unto them,
21. They *say* unto him, Cæsar's. Then *saith*
he unto them,
23. *which say* that there is no resurrection,
24. *Saying*, Master, Moses said,
31. spoken unto you by God, *saying*,
35. tempting him, and *saying*,
42(41). *Saying*, What think ye of Christ?
whose son is he? They *say* unto him,
(The son) of David.
43. He *saith* unto them, How then doth David
in spirit call him Lord, *saying*,
23: 2. *Saying*, The scribes and the Pharisees sit
3. for they *say*, and do not.
16. (ye) blind guides, *which say*,
30. And *say*, If we had been
36. Verily I *say* unto you, All these
39. For I *say* unto you, Ye shall not see me
24: 2. verily I *say* unto you, There shall not
3. *saying*, Tell us, when shall
5. *saying*, I am Christ ;
34. Verily I *say* unto you, This generation
47. Verily I *say* unto you, That he shall make
25: 9. the wise answered, *saying*,
11. *saying*, Lord, Lord, open to us.
12. Verily I *say* unto you,
20. *saying*, Lord, thou deliveredst
37. answer him, *saying*, Lord,
40. Verily I *say* unto you,
44. *saying*, Lord, when saw we
45. *saying*, Verily I *say* unto you, Inasmuch
26: 3. high priest, *who was called* Caiaphas,
5. But they *said*, Not on the
8. *saying*, To what purpose (is)
13. Verily I *say* unto you,

Mat.26:14. Then one of the twelve, *called* Judas
17. *saying* unto him, Where wilt
18. The Master *saith*, My time is
21. Verily I *say* unto you,
22. every one of them *to say* unto him,
25. He *said* unto him, Thou hast said.
27. *saying*, Drink ye all of it;
29. But I *say* unto you,
31. Then *saith* Jesus unto them,
34. Verily I *say* unto thee,
35. Peter *said* unto him,
36. unto a place *called* Gethsemane, and *saith* unto the disciples,
38. Then *saith* he unto them,
39. and prayed, *saying*, O my Father,
40. and *saith* unto Peter, What,
42. and prayed, *saying*, O my Father,
45. and *saith* unto them, Sleep on now,
48. *saying*, Whomsoever I shall kiss,
52. Then *said* Jesus unto him,
64. Jesus *saith* unto him, Thou hast said: nevertheless I *say* unto you,
65. *saying*, He hath spoken blasphemy;
68. *Saying*, Prophesy unto us,
69. *saying*, Thou also wast with Jesus
70. *saying*, I know not what thou *sayest.*
71. another (maid) saw him, and *said*
27: 4. *Saying*, I have sinned
9. Jeremy the prophet, *saying*,
11. *saying*, Art thou the King of the Jews? And Jesus said unto him, Thou *sayest.*
13. Then *said* Pilate unto him,
16. prisoner, *called* Barabbas.
17. or Jesus *which is called* Christ?
19. his wife sent unto him, *saying*,
22. Pilate *saith* unto them, What shall I do then with Jesus *which is called* Christ? (They) all *say* unto him, Let
23. *saying*, Let him be crucified.
24. *saying*, I am innocent of the blood
29. *saying*, Hail, king of the Jews!
33. unto a place *called* Golgotha, that is to *say*, a place of a skull,
40. And *saying*, Thou that destroyest
41. with the scribes and elders, *said*,
46. *saying*, Eli, Eli, lama sabachthani?
47. when they heard (that), *said*,
49. The rest *said*, Let be,
54. *saying*, Truly this was the Son of God.
63. *Saying*, Sir, we remember that
28: 9. behold, Jesus met them, *saying*,
10. Then *said* Jesus unto them,
13. *saying*, Say ye, His disciples
18. *saying*, All power is given unto me
Mar 1: 7. And preached, *saying*, There cometh
15. And *saying*, The time is fulfilled,
24. *Saying*, Let (us) alone;
25. Jesus rebuked him, *saying*,
27. *saying*, What thing is this?
30. and anon they *tell* him of her.
37. they *said* unto him,
38. And he *said* unto them,
40. and *saying* unto him, If thou wilt,
41. and *saith* unto him, I will;
44. And *saith* unto him,
2: 5. he *said* unto the sick of the
10. he *saith* to the sick
11. I *say* unto thee, Arise,
12. *saying*, We never saw it on this
14. and *said* unto him, Follow me.
16. they *said* unto his disciples,
17. he *saith* unto them,

Mar 2:18. they come and *say* unto him,
24. the Pharisees *said* unto him,
25. And he *said* unto them,
27. And he *said* unto them,
3: 3. he *saith* unto the man which
4. And he *saith* unto them,
5. he *saith* unto the man,
11. *saying*, Thou art the Son of God.
21. they *said*, He is beside himself.
22. *said*, He hath Beelzebub,
23. and *said* unto them in parables,
28. Verily I *say* unto you,
30. Because they *said*, He hath an
33. he answered them, *saying*, Who is my
34. and *said*, Behold my mother and
4: 2. and *said* unto them in his doctrine,
9. And he *said* unto them, He that
11. he *said* unto them, Unto you it is given
13. he *said* unto them, Know ye not this
21. he *said* unto them, Is a candle
24. And he *said* unto them,
26. And he *said*, So is the kingdom
30. And he *said*, Whereunto shall
35. he *saith* unto them, Let us pass over
38. and *say* unto him, Master,
41. and *said* one to another,
5: 8. For he *said* unto him, Come out
9. *saying*, My name (is) Legion:
12. *saying*, Send us into the swine,
19. but *saith* unto him, Go home
23. *saying*, My little daughter
28. For she *said*, If I may touch
30. and *said*, Who touched my
31. disciples *said* unto him,
— and *sayest* thou, Who touched me?
35. *which said*, Thy daughter is dead:
36. he *saith* unto the ruler
39. he *saith* unto them,
41. and *said* unto her,
— Damsel, I *say* unto thee, arise.
6: 2. *saying*, From whence hath this (man)
4. But Jesus *said* unto them,
10. And he *said* unto them,
11. Verily I *say* unto you,
14. and he *said*, That John the Baptist
15. Others *said*, That it is Elias. And others *said*, That it is a prophet, or
18. For John *had said* unto Herod,
25. *saying*, I will that thou give me
35. and *said*, This is a desert place,
37. And they *say* unto him,
38. He *saith* unto them, How many
— they *say*, Five, and two fishes.
50. and *saith* unto them,
7: 9. he *said* unto them, Full well ye reject
11. But ye *say*, If a man shall say
14. he *said* unto them, Hearken
18. And he *saith* unto them,
20. And he *said*, That which cometh out of the man,
28. she answered and *said* unto him
34. and *saith* unto him, Ephphatha,
37. *saying*, He hath done all things well:
8: 1. and *saith* unto them,
12. and *saith*, Why doth this generation seek after a sign? verily I *say*
15. he charged them, *saying*,
16. *saying*, (It is) because we have no
17. he *saith* unto them,
19. They *say* unto him, Twelve.
21. And he *said* unto them,
24. and *said*, I see men as trees.

Mar 8:26. *saying*, Neither go into the town,
  27. *saying* unto them, Whom do men *say* that
    I am?
  29. And he *saith* unto them, But whom *say* ye
    that I am? And Peter answereth and
    saith unto him,
  30. that they *should tell* no man
  33. he rebuked Peter, *saying*,
9: 1. And he *said* unto them, Verily I *say* unto
    you, That there be some
  5. and *said* to Jesus, Master, it is good
  7. *saying*, This is my beloved Son:
  11. *saying*, Why *say* the scribes that Elias
    must first come?
  13. But I *say* unto you, That Elias is
  19. and *saith*, O faithless generation,
  24. and *said* with tears, Lord, I believe; help
    thou mine unbelief.
  25. *saying* unto him, (Thou) dumb and
  26. that many *said*, He is dead.
  31. and *said* unto them,
  35. and *saith* unto them,
  38. John answered him, *saying*,
  41. verily I *say* unto you,
10:11. And he *saith* unto them,
  15. Verily I *say* unto you,
  18. Why *callest* thou me good?
  23. and *saith* unto his disciples,
  24. and *saith* unto them,
  26. *saying* among themselves,
  27. Jesus looking upon them *saith*,
  28. Peter began *to say* unto him,
  29. Verily I *say* unto you,
  32. and began *to tell* them
  35. *saying*, Master, we would
  42. and *saith* unto them,
  47. and *say*, Jesus, (thou) son of David,
  49. *saying* unto him, Be of good comfort,
    rise; he calleth thee.
  51. Jesus answered and *said* unto him,
11: 2. And *saith* unto them, Go your way
  5. of them that stood there *said*
  9. that followed, cried, *saying*, Hosanna:
  17. he taught, *saying* unto them,
  21. *saith* unto him, Master,
  22. *saith* unto him, Have faith
  23. verily I *say* unto you,
  — those things which he *saith* shall come
  24. Therefore I *say* unto you,
  28. And *say* unto him, By what
  31. *saying*, If we shall say,
  33. and *said* unto Jesus,
  — *saith* unto them, Neither do I *tell* you by
    what authority I
12: 1. And he began *to speak* unto them
  6. *saying*, They will reverence my son.
  14. they *say* unto him, Master,
  16. And he *saith* unto them,
  18. which *say* there is no resurrection; and
    they asked him, *saying*,
  26. *saying*, I (am) the God of Abraham,
  35. Jesus answered and *said*,
  — How *say* the scribes that
  37. David therefore himself *calleth* him Lord;
  38. And he *said* unto them
  43. and *saith* unto them, Verily I *say* unto you,
    That this poor widow
13: 1. one of his disciples *saith* unto him,
  5. began *to say*, Take heed lest
  6. *saying*, I am (Christ);
  30. Verily I *say* unto you,
  37. what I *say* unto you I *say* unto all,

Mar 14: 2. But they *said*, Not on the feast (day),
  4. and *said*, Why was this waste
  9. Verily I *say* unto you,
  12. his disciples *said* unto him,
  13. and *saith* unto them,
  14. The master *saith*, Where is the
  18. Verily I *say* unto you,
  19. and *to say* unto him one by one.
  25. Verily I *say* unto you,
  27. And Jesus *saith* unto them,
  30. And Jesus *saith* unto him, Verily I *say*
    unto thee, That this day,
  31. But he *spake* the more
  — Likewise also *said* they all.
  32. and he *saith* to his disciples,
  34. And *saith* unto them, My soul
  36. And he *said*, Abba, Father,
  37. and *saith* unto Peter,
  41. and *saith* unto them,
  44. *saying*, Whomsoever I shall kiss,
  45. and *saith*, Master, master;
  57. false witness against him, *saying*,
  58. We heard him *say*,
  60. *saying*, Answerest thou nothing?
  61. and *said* unto him,
  63. and *saith*, What need we
  65. and *to say* unto him,
  67. she looked upon him, and *said*,
  68. But he denied, *saying*, I know not, neither
    understand I what thou *sayest*.
  69. and began *to say* to them
  70. they that stood by *said* again
  71. I know not this man of whom ye *speak*.
15: 2. *said* unto him, Thou *sayest* (it).
  4. *saying*, Answerest thou nothing?
  7. there was (one) *named* Barabbas,
  9. Pilate answered them, *saying*,
  12. whom ye *call* the King of the Jews?
  14. Pilate *said* unto them,
  28. scripture was fulfilled, *which saith*,
  29. and *saying*, Ah, thou that
  31. *said* among themselves with the scribes,
  34. *saying*, Eloi, Eloi, lama sabachthani?
  35. *said*, Behold, he calleth Elias.
  36. *saying*, Let alone; let us see
16: 3. And they *said* among themselves,
  6. And he *saith* unto them,
Lu. 1:24. and hid herself five months, *saying*,
  63. *saying*, His name is John.
  66. *saying*, What manner of child
  67. and prophesied, *saying*,
2:13. praising God, and *saying*,
3: 4. *saying*, The voice of one crying
  7. Then *said* he to the multitude
  8. begin not *to say* within yourselves,
  — for I *say* unto you,
  10. *saying*, What shall we do then?
  11. and *saith* unto them,
  14. *saying*, And what shall we do?
  16. *saying* unto (them) all,
  22. a voice came from heaven, *which said*,
4: 4. Jesus answered him, *saying*,
  21. he began *to say* unto them,
  22. And they *said*, Is not this
  24. Verily I *say* unto you,
  25. But I *tell* you of a truth,
  34. *Saying*, Let (us) alone;
  35. rebuked him, *saying*,
  36. *saying*, What a word (is) this!
  41. crying out, and *saying*,
5: 8. *saying*, Depart from me;
  12. besought him, *saying*, Lord,

Lu. 5:21. *saying*, Who is this which	Lu. 12:16. *saying*, The ground of a certain
24. I *say* unto thee, Arise,	17. *saying*, What shall I do,
26. *saying*, We have seen strange	22. Therefore I *say* unto you,
30. *saying*, Why do ye eat and drink	27. yet I *say* unto you, that Solomon
36. And he *spake* also a parable	37. verily I *say* unto you, that he shall gird
39. for he *saith*, The old is better.	himself, and
6: 5. And he *said* unto them,	41. *speakest* thou this parable
20. and *said*, Blessed (be ye) poor:	44. Of a truth I *say* unto you,
27. But I *say* unto you which hear,	51. I *tell* you, Nay; but rather division:
42. how canst thou *say* to thy	54. And he *said* also to the people,
46. and do not the things which I *say?*	— straightway ye *say*, There cometh
7: 4. *saying*, That he was worthy	55. ye *say*, There will be heat;
6. *saying* unto him, Lord,	59. I *tell* thee, thou shalt not depart thence,
8. and I *say* unto one, Go, and he goeth;	13: 3. I *tell* you, Nay: but, except ye repent,
9. I *say* unto you, I have not found	5. I *tell* you, Nay: but, except ye
14. I *say* unto thee, Arise.	6. He *spake* also this parable;
16. *saying*, That a great prophet	8. answering *said* unto him,
19. *saying*, Art thou he that should	14. and *said* unto the people,
20. hath sent us unto thee, *saying*, Art thou	17. *when* he *had said* these things,
24. he began *to speak* unto the people	18. Then *said* he, Unto what is the
26. Yea, I *say* unto you,	24. for many, I *say* unto you,
28. For I *say* unto you,	25. *saying*, Lord, Lord, open unto us;
32. *saying*, We have piped unto you,	26. Then shall ye begin *to say*,
33. and ye *say*, He hath a devil.	27. But he shall say, I *tell* you,
34. and ye *say*, Behold a gluttonous	31. *saying* unto him, Get thee out,
39. *saying*, This man, if he were	35. verily I *say* unto you,
47. Wherefore I *say* unto thee,	14: 3. *saying*, Is it lawful to heal
49. began *to say* within themselves,	7. And he *put forth* a parable
8: 8. *when* he *had said* these things,	— chief rooms; *saying* unto them,
9. *saying*, What might this parable be?	12. Then *said* he also to him
20. And it was told him (by certain) *which said*,	24. For I *say* unto you, That none of those men which were
24. *saying*, Master, master, we perish.	30. *Saying*, This man began to
25. *saying* one to another,	15: 2. *saying*, This man receiveth
30. Jesus asked him, *saying*,	3. this parable unto them, *saying*,
38. but Jesus sent him away, *saying*,	6. *saying* unto them, Rejoice with me;
45. and *sayest* thou, Who touched me?	7. I *say* unto you, that likewise joy shall be in heaven over
49. *saying* to him, Thy daughter is dead;	9. *saying*, Rejoice with me;
50. *saying*, Fear not: believe only,	10. Likewise, I *say* unto you, there is joy
54. and called, *saying*, Maid, arise.	16: 1. And he *said* also unto his disciples,
9: 7. because that it *was said* of some,	5. and *said* unto the first,
18. *saying*, Whom *say* the people	7. And he *said* unto him,
20. But whom *say* ye that I am?	9. And I *say* unto you, Make to yourselves
23. And he *said* to (them) all,	29. Abraham *saith* unto him, They have
27. But I *tell* you of a truth,	17: 4. turn again to thee, *saying*, I repent;
31. and *spake* of his decease	6. ye might *say* unto this sycamine
33. not knowing what he *said*.	10. *say*, We are unprofitable
34. *While* he thus *spake*,	13. *and said*, Jesus, Master,
35. *saying*, This is my beloved Son:	34. I *tell* you, in that night
38. *saying*, Master, I beseech thee,	37. they answered and *said* unto him,
10: 2. Therefore *said* he unto them,	18: 1. he *spake* a parable
5. first *say*, Peace (be) to this house.	2. *Saying*, There was in a city
9. and *say* unto them,	3. *saying*, Avenge me of mine adversary.
12. But I *say* unto you,	6. the unjust judge *saith*.
17. *saying*, Lord, even the devils	8. I *tell* you that he will avenge
24. For I *tell* you, that many prophets	13. *saying*, God be merciful to me
25. *saying*, Master, what shall I do	14. I *tell* you, this man went down
11: 2. When ye pray, *say*, Our Father	17. Verily I *say* unto you,
8. I *say* unto you, Though he will not	18. *saying*, Good Master, what shall I do
9. I *say* unto you, Ask, and it	19. Why *callest* thou me good?
18. because ye *say* that I cast out	29. Verily I *say* unto you,
24. he *saith*, I will return	34. knew they the things *which were spoken*.
27. as he *spake* these things,	38. And he cried, *saying*, Jesus,
29. he began *to say*, This is an evil	41. *Saying*, What wilt thou
45. and *said* unto him, Master, thus *saying* thou reproachest us also.	19: 7. they all murmured, *saying*,
51. verily I *say* unto you,	14. *saying*, We will not have this (man)
53. And *as* he *said* these things	16. *saying*, Lord, thy pound hath
12: 1. he began *to say* unto his	18. the second came, *saying*, Lord, thy pound
4. I *say* unto you my friends,	20. *saying*, Lord, behold, (here is) thy
5. yea, I *say* unto you, Fear him.	22. And he *saith* unto him,
8. Also I *say* unto you, Whosoever shall	26. For I *say* unto you, That unto every

Lu. 19:38. *Saying*, Blessed (be) the King
40. and said unto them, I *tell* you
42. *Saying*, If thou hadst known,
46. *Saying* unto them, It is written,
20: 2. *saying*, Tell us, by what authority
5. *saying*, If we shall say,
8. Neither *tell* I you by what
9. Then began he *to speak* to the
14. *saying*, This is the heir:
21. *saying*, Master, we know that thou *sayest*
    and teachest rightly,
28. *Saying*, Master, Moses wrote
37. when he *calleth* the Lord the God of
41. How *say* they that Christ is
42. David himself *saith* in the
21: 3. Of a truth I *say* unto you,
5. *as* some *spake* of the temple,
7. they asked him, *saying*,
8. *saying*, I am (Christ);
10. Then *said* he unto them,
32. Verily I *say* unto you,
22: 1. *which is called* the passover.
11. The Master *saith* unto thee,
16. For I *say* unto you, I will not any more
    eat thereof,
18. For I *say* unto you, I will not drink
19. *saying*, This is my body
20. *saying*, This cup (is) the new
34. And he said, I *tell* thee, Peter,
37. For I *say* unto you, that this that is
42. *Saying*, Father, if thou be willing,
47. he *that was called* Judas, one of the
57. *saying*, Woman, I know him not.
59. *saying*, Of a truth this (fellow)
60. I know not what thou *sayest*.
64. *saying*, Prophesy, who is it that
65. blasphemously *spake* they against
66. led him into their council, *saying*,
70. Ye *say* that I am.
23: 2. began to accuse him, *saying*,
— *saying* that he himself is Christ
3. *saying*, Art thou the King of the
— and said, Thou *sayest* (it).
5. *saying*, He stirreth up the people,
18. *saying*, Away with this (man),
21. *saying*, Crucify (him), crucify him.
30. Then shall they begin *to say* to
34. Then *said* Jesus, Father, forgive them;
35. *saying*, He saved others;
37. *saying*, If thou be the king
39. *saying*, If thou be Christ,
40. *saying*, Dost not thou fear God,
42. And he *said* unto Jesus, Lord,
43. Verily I *say* unto thee, To day
47. *saying*, Certainly this was a righteous
24: 7. *Saying*, The Son of man must be
10. which *told* these things unto
23. *saying*, that they had also seen a vision of
    angels, which *said*
29. *saying*, Abide with us:
34. *Saying*, The Lord is risen indeed,
36. and *saith* unto them,
Joh. 1:15. *saying*, This was he of whom I spake,
21. And he *saith*, I am not.
22. What *sayest* thou of thyself?
26. *saying*, I baptize with water:
29. and *saith*, Behold the Lamb of God,
32. And John bare record, *saying*,
36. he *saith*, Behold the Lamb of God!
38. and *saith* unto them,
—(39). Rabbi, which *is to say*,
39(40). He *saith* unto them, Come and see.

Joh. 1:41(42). and *saith* unto him, We have found
43(44). and *saith* unto him, Follow me.
45(46). and *saith* unto him, We have found
46(47). Philip *saith* unto him, Come and see.
47(48). and *saith* of him, Behold an Israelite
48(49). Nathanael *saith* unto him,
49(50). Nathanael answered and *saith*
51(52). And he *saith* unto him, Verily, verily,
    I *say* unto you, Hereafter
2: 3. the mother of Jesus *saith* unto him,
4. Jesus *saith* unto her, Woman,
5. His mother *saith* unto the servants, What-
    soever he *saith* unto
7. Jesus *saith* unto them, Fill
8. And he *saith* unto them,
10. And *saith* unto him,
21. But he *spake* of the temple of
22. that he *had said* this unto them;
3: 3. Verily, verily, I *say* unto thee,
4. Nicodemus *saith* unto him,
5. Verily, verily, I *say* unto thee,
11. I *say* unto thee, We speak that we do
4: 5. to a city of Samaria, *which is called* Sychar,
7. Jesus *saith* unto her, Give me
9. Then *saith* the woman
10. and who it is *that saith* to thee,
11. The woman *saith* unto him, Sir,
15. woman *saith* unto him, Sir, give me
16. Jesus *saith* unto her, Go, call
17. Jesus *said* unto her, Thou hast
19. The woman *saith* unto him,
20. and ye *say*, that in Jerusalem
21. Jesus *saith* unto her, Woman,
25. The woman *saith* unto him,
— Messias cometh, *which is called* Christ:
26. Jesus *saith* unto her, I that speak unto
    thee am (he).
28. and *saith* to the men,
31. *saying*, Master, eat.
33. Therefore *said* the disciples
34. Jesus *saith* unto them,
35. *Say* not ye, There are yet four months,
— behold, I *say* unto you,
42. And *said* unto the woman,
49. The nobleman *saith* unto him,
50. Jesus *saith* unto him,
51. *saying*, Thy son liveth.
5: 6. he *saith* unto him, Wilt thou be
8. Jesus *saith* unto him, Rise,
10. The Jews therefore *said* unto him
18. but *said* also that God was his
19. Verily, verily, I *say* unto you,
24. verily, I *say* unto you, He that heareth
25. verily, I *say* unto you, The hour is
34. but these things I *say*, that
6: 5. he *saith* unto Philip,
6. this he *said* to prove him:
8. Simon Peter's brother, *saith* unto him,
12. he *said* unto his disciples,
14. *said*, This is of a truth that
20. But he *saith* unto them, It is I;
26. Verily, verily, I *say* unto you,
32. verily, I *say* unto you, Moses gave you
42. And they *said*, Is not this Jesus,
— how is it then that he *saith*,
47. Verily, verily, I *say* unto you,
52. *saying*, How can this man give
53. Verily, verily, I *say* unto you,
65. And he *said*, Therefore said I
71. He *spake* of Judas Iscariot
7: 6. Then Jesus *said* unto them,
11. and *said*, Where is he?

Joh. 7:12. some *said*, He is a good man: others *said*,
   Nay;
15. *saying*, How knoweth this man
25. Then *said* some of them
26. and they *say* nothing unto him.
28. *saying*, Ye both know me, and
31. and *said*, When Christ cometh,
37. *saying*, If any man thirst,
40. *said*, Of a truth this is the prophet.
41. Others *said*, This is the Christ. But some
   said, Shall Christ
50. Nicodemus *saith* unto them,
8: 4. They *say* unto him, Master,
 5. but what *sayest* thou?
 6. This they *said*, tempting him,
12. *saying*, I am the light of the world:
19. Then *said* they unto him,
22. *said* the Jews, Will he kill himself?
   because he *saith*,
25. Then *said* they unto him,
26. I *speak* to the world those things which
27. that he *spake* to them of the Father.
31. Then *said* Jesus to those Jews
33. how *sayest* thou, Ye shall be made free?
34. Verily, verily, I *say* unto you,
39. Jesus *saith* unto them,
45. because I *tell* (you) the truth,
46. And if I *say* the truth,
48. *Say* we not well that thou art
51. Verily, verily, I *say* unto you,
52. and thou *sayest*, If a man keep
54. of whom ye *say*, that he is your God:
58. Verily, verily, I *say* unto you,
9: 2. *saying*, Master, who did sin,
 8. *said*, Is not this he that sat
 9. Some *said*, This is he:
 — he *said*, I am (he).
10. Therefore *said* they unto him,
11. A man *that is called* Jesus
12. He *said*, I know not.
16. Therefore *said* some of the Pharisees,
 — Others *said*, How can a man
17. They *say* unto the blind man again, What
   sayest thou of him,
19. *saying*, Is this your son, who ye *say* was
41. but now ye *say*, We see;
10: 1. Verily, verily, I *say* unto you,
 7. verily, I *say* unto you, I am the door
20. And many of them *said*, He hath
21. Others *said*, These are not the words
24. and *said* unto him, How long dost thou
33. Jews answered him, *saying*,
36. *Say* ye of him, whom the Father
41. and *said*, John did no miracle:
11: 3. *saying*, Lord, behold, he whom
 7. Then after that *saith* he to
 8. (His) disciples *say* unto him,
11. after that he *saith* unto them,
13. they thought that he had *spoken*
16. Thomas, *which is called* Didymus,
23. Jesus *saith* unto her,
24. Martha *saith* unto him,
27. She *saith* unto him, Yea, Lord:
31. *saying*, She goeth unto the grave
32. *saying* unto him, Lord, if thou
34(35). They *said* unto him, Lord, come and
36. Then *said* the Jews, Behold how he loved
39. Jesus *said*, Take ye away the stone.
 — *saith* unto him, Lord, by this time
40. Jesus *saith* unto her, Said I not
44. Jesus *saith* unto them, Loose
47. and *said*, What do we?

Joh. 11:54. into a city *called* Ephraim,
56. and *spake* among themselves,
12: 4. Then *saith* one of his disciples,
21. *saying*, Sir, we would see Jesus.
22. Philip cometh and *telleth* Andrew: and
   again Andrew and Philip *tell* Jesus.
23. *saying*, The hour is come,
24. Verily, verily, I *say* unto you,
29. *said* that it thundered: others *said*, An
   angel spake
33. This he *said*, signifying
34. and how *sayest* thou,
13: 6. and Peter *saith* unto him,
 8. Peter *saith* unto him,
 9. Simon Peter *saith* unto him,
10. Jesus *saith* to him,
13. and ye *say* well; for (so) I am.
16. Verily, verily, I *say* unto you,
18. I *speak* not of you all:
19. Now I *tell* you before it come,
20. Verily, verily, I *say* unto you, He that
21. verily, I *say* unto you, that one of you
22. doubting of whom he *spake*.
24. ask who it should be of whom he *spake*.
25. *saith* unto him, Lord, who is it?
27. Then *said* Jesus unto him,
29. that Jesus had *said* unto him,
31. Jesus *said*, Now is the Son of man
33. so now I *say* to you.
36. Simon Peter *said* unto him,
37. Peter *said* unto him,
38. Verily, verily, I *say* unto thee,
14: 5. Thomas *saith* unto him, Lord,
 6. Jesus *saith* unto him, I am the way,
 8. Philip *saith* unto him, Lord, shew
 9. Jesus *saith* unto him, Have I been
 — how *sayest* thou (then), Shew us
12. Verily, verily, I *say* unto you,
22. Judas *saith* unto him,
15:15. Henceforth I *call* you not servants;
16: 7. Nevertheless I *tell* you the truth;
12. many things *to say* unto you,
17. What is this that he *saith*
18. They *said* therefore, What is this that he
   saith,
20. Verily, verily, I *say* unto you, That ye
23. Verily, verily, I *say* unto you, Whatsoever
26. and I *say* not unto you, that I
29. His disciples *said* unto him, Lo, now
   speakest thou plainly, and *speakest* no
18: 5. Jesus *saith* unto them, I am (he).
17. Then *saith* the damsel
 — He *saith*, I am not.
26. *saith*, Did not I see thee in the
34. *Sayest* thou this thing of thyself,
37. Thou *sayest* that I am a king.
38. Pilate *saith* unto him, What is truth?
 — and *saith* unto them, I find in him no fault
40. *saying*, Not this man, but
19: 3. And *said*, Hail, King of the Jews!
 4. and *saith* unto them,
 5. *saith* unto them, Behold the man!
 6. *saying*, Crucify (him), crucify (him).
   Pilate *saith* unto them,
 9. and *saith* unto Jesus, Whence art thou?
10. Then *saith* Pilate unto him,
12. *saying*, If thou let this man go,
13. in a place *that is called* the Pavement,
14. he *saith* unto the Jews, Behold
15. Pilate *saith* unto them, Shall I
17. a place *called* (the place) of a skull, which
   is called in the Hebrew Golgotha:

Joh. 19:21. Then *said* the chief priests
 24. *which saith*, They parted my
 26. he *saith* unto his mother,
 27. Then *saith* he to the disciple, Behold thy
 28. scripture might be fulfilled, *saith*, I thirst.
 35. he knoweth that he *saith* true,
 37. *saith*, They shall look on him
20: 2. and *saith* unto them,
 13. they *say* unto her, Woman, why weepest thou ? She *saith* unto them,
 15. Jesus *saith* unto her, Woman,
 — *saith* unto him, Sir, if thou
 16. Jesus *saith* unto her, Mary. She turned herself, and *saith* unto him, Rabboni ; which *is to say*, Master.
 17. Jesus *saith* unto her, Touch me not ;
 19. and *saith* unto them, Peace
 22. and *saith* unto them, Receive ye
 24. *called* Didymus, was not with them
 25. disciples therefore *said* unto him,
 27. Then *saith* he to Thomas,
 29. Jesus *saith* unto him,
21: 2. and Thomas *called* Didymus,
 3. Simon Peter *saith* unto them, I go a fishing. They *say* unto him, We also
 5. Then Jesus *saith* unto them,
 7. *saith* unto Peter, It is the Lord.
 10. Jesus *saith* unto them, Bring of the fish
 12. Jesus *saith* unto them, Come (and) dine.
 15. Jesus *saith* to Simon Peter,
 — He *saith* unto him, Yea, Lord ;
 — He *saith* unto him, Feed my lambs.
 16. He *saith* to him again the second time,
 — He *saith* unto him, Yea, Lord ;
 — He *saith* unto him, Feed my sheep.
 17. He *saith* unto him the third time,
 — Jesus *saith* unto him, Feed
 18. Verily, verily, I *say* unto thee,
 19. he *saith* unto him, Follow me.
 21. *saith* to Jesus, Lord, and what
 22. Jesus *saith* unto him, If
Acts 1: 3. *speaking* of the things pertaining to
 6. *saying*, Lord, wilt thou at this time
2: 7. marvelled, *saying* one to another,
 12. were in doubt, *saying* one to another,
 13. Others mocking *said*, These men
 17. in the last days, *saith* God,
 25. For David *speaketh* concerning
 34. but he *saith* himself, The Lord said
 40. *saying*, Save yourselves from
3: 2. the gate of the temple *which is called* Beautiful,
 25. *saying* unto Abraham, And in thy seed
4:16. *Saying*, What shall we do to
 32. neither *said* any (of them)
5:23. *Saying*, The prison truly found
 25. *saying*, Behold, the men whom
 28. *Saying*, Did not we straitly
 36. *boasting* himself to be somebody ;
 38. And now I *say* unto you, Refrain
6: 9. certain of the synagogue, *which is called*
 11. they suborned men, *which said*,
 13. set up false witnesses, *which said*,
 14. For we have heard him *say*,
7:48. as *saith* the prophet,
 49. will ye build me ? *saith* the Lord:
 59. and *saying*, Lord Jesus, receive
8: 6. those things which Philip spake, (lit. *the things spoken* by)
 9. *giving out* that himself was some great one.
 10. *saying*, This man is the great power of God.
 19. *Saying*, Give me also this power,

Acts 8:26. *saying*, Arise, and go toward
 34. of whom *speaketh* the prophet
9: 4. a voice *saying* unto him,
 21. were amazed, and *said* ;
 36. by interpretation *is called* Dorcas:
10:26. Peter took him up, *saying*,
 28. that I should not *call* any man
11: 3. *Saying*, Thou wentest in to men
 4. expounded (it) by order unto them, *saying*,
 7. I heard a voice *saying* unto me,
 16. how that he *said*, John indeed
 18. and glorified God, *saying*,
12: 7. and raised him up, *saying*,
 8. And he *saith* unto him, Cast thy
 15. Then *said* they, It is his angel.
13:15. *saying*, (Ye) men (and) brethren, if ye have any word of exhortation for the people, *say on.*
 25. he *said*, Whom think ye that I am ?
 35. he *saith* also in another (psalm),
 45. against those things *which were spoken* by Paul,
14:11. *saying* in the speech of Lycaonia,
 15. And *saying*, Sirs, why do ye
 18. And with these sayings (lit. *saying* these things)
15: 5. *saying*, That it was needful
 13. James answered, *saying*,
 17. *saith* the Lord, who doeth all these
 24. *saying*, (Ye must) be circumcised,
16: 9. *saying*, Come over into Macedonia,
 15. she besought (us), *saying*,
 17. *saying*, These men are the servants
 28. *saying*, Do thyself no harm:
 35. *saying*, Let those men go.
17: 7. *saying* that there is another king,
 18. And some *said*, What will this babbler *say?*
 19. *saying*, May we know what this new
 21. either *to tell*, or to hear some
18:13. *Saying*, This (fellow) persuadeth
19: 4. *saying* unto the people,
 13. *saying*, We adjure you by Jesus
 26. *saying* that they be no gods, which are made with hands:
 28. *saying*, Great (is) Diana
20:23. *saying* that bonds and afflictions
21: 4. who *said* to Paul through the
 11. Thus *saith* the Holy Ghost,
 21. *saying* that they ought not to
 23. this that we *say* to thee:
 37. he *said* unto the chief captain,
 40. in the Hebrew tongue, *saying*,
22: 7. and heard a voice *saying*
 18 And saw him *saying* unto me,
 22. *and said*, Away with such a
 26. *saying*, Take heed what thou doest:
 27. *Tell* me, art thou a Roman ?
23: 8. the Sadducees *say* that there is
 9. *saying*, We find no evil in this
 12. *saying* that they would neither
 30. *to say* before thee what (they had)
24: 2. began to accuse (him), *saying*,
 10. beckoned unto him *to speak*,
 14. which they *call* heresy,
25:14. Paul's cause unto the king, *saying*,
 20. I *asked* (him) whether he would
26: 1. Thou art permitted *to speak*
 14. and *saying* in the Hebrew tongue,
 22. *saying* none other things than
 31. *saying*, This man doeth nothing
27:10. *And said* unto them, Sirs, I perceive
 11. than those things *which were spoken* by Paul.

Acts 27:24. *Saying*, Fear not, Paul ;
    33. *saying*, This day is the fourteenth
  28: 4. they *said* among themselves,
    6. and *said* that he was a god.
    17. he *said* unto them, Men (and)
    24. believed the things *which were spoken,*
    26. *Saying,* Go unto this people,
Ro. 2:22. Thou *that sayest* a man should not
  3: 5. I *speak* as a man
    8. as some affirm that we *say,*
    19. what things soever the law *saith,* it saith
  4: 3. For what *saith* the scripture ?
    6. as David also *describeth*
    9. for we *say* that faith
  6:19. I *speak* after the manner of men
  7: 7. except the law *had said,*
  9: 1. I *say* the truth in Christ,
    15. For he *saith* to Moses, I will have
    17. the scripture *saith* unto Pharaoh,
    25. As he *saith* also in Osee, I will
  10: 6. of faith *speaketh* on this wise,
    8. But what *saith* it ? The word is nigh
    11. For the scripture *saith,* Whosoever
    16. For Esaias *saith,* Lord, who hath
    18. But I *say,* Have they not heard ?
    19. But I *say,* Did not Israel know ? First
        Moses *saith,*
    20. But Esaias is very bold, and *saith,*
    21. But to Israel he *saith,* All day long
  11: 1. I *say* then, Hath God cast away
    2. what the scripture *saith* of Elias ?
    — to God against Israel, *saying,*
    4. what *saith* the answer of God
    9. And David *saith,* Let their table
    11. I *say* then, Have they stumbled that
    13. For I *speak* to you Gentiles,
  12: 3. For I *say,* through the grace
    19. I will repay, *saith* the Lord.
  14:11. (As) I live, *saith* the Lord,
  15: 8. Now I *say* that Jesus Christ
    10. And again he *saith,* Rejoice, ye
    12. And again, Esaias *saith,* There shall be
1Co. 1:10. that ye all *speak* the same
    12. Now this I *say,* that every one of you
        saith, I am of Paul ;
  3: 4. For while one *saith,* I am of Paul ;
  6: 5. I *speak* to your shame.
  7: 6. But I *speak* this by permission,
    8. I *say* therefore to the unmarried
    12. But to the rest *speak* I,
    35. And this I *speak* for your
  8: 5. there be *that are called* gods,
  9: 8. or *saith* not the law the same
    10. Or *saith* he (it) altogether for
  10:15. I *speak* as to wise men ;
    29. Conscience, I *say,* not thine own,
  11:25. *saying,* This cup is the new testament
  12: 3. *calleth* Jesus accursed:
  14:16. not what thou *sayest ?*
    21. will they not hear me, *saith* the Lord.
    34. to be under obedience, as also *saith* the
  15:12. how *say* some among you
    34. I *speak* (this) to your shame.
    51. I *shew* you a mystery;
2Co. 6: 2. For he *saith,* I have heard thee
    13. I *speak* as unto (my) children,
    17. be ye separate, *saith* the Lord,
    18. *saith* the Lord Almighty.
  7: 3. I *speak* not (this) to condemn
  8: 8. I *speak* not by commandment,
  9: 3. that, as I *said,* ye may be ready:
    4. that we *say* not, ye

2Co.11:16. I *say* again, Let no man think me
    21. I *speak* as concerning reproach,
    — I *speak* foolishly, I am bold
Gal. 1: 9. so *say* I now again,
  3:15. I *speak* after the manner of men ;
    16. He *saith* not, And to seeds,
    17. And this I *say,* (that) the covenant,
  4: 1. Now I *say,* (That) the heir,
    21. *Tell* me, ye that desire
    30. what *saith* the scripture ?
  5: 2. I Paul *say* unto you,
    16. I *say* then, Walk in the Spirit,
Eph 2:11. *who are called* Uncircumcision by that
        which is called the Circumcision
  4: 8. Wherefore he *saith,* When he ascended
    17. This I *say* therefore, and testify
  5:12. even *to speak* of those things
    14. Wherefore he *saith,* Awake thou
    32. but I *speak* concerning Christ
Phi. 3:18. of whom I *have told* you often, and now
        tell you even weeping,
  4:11. Not that I *speak* in respect of
Col. 2: 4. And this I *say,* lest any man should
  4:11. Jesus, *which is called* Justus,
1Th. 4:15. For this we *say* unto you by
  5: 3. For when they shall *say,* Peace
2Th. 2: 4. above all *that is called* God,
    5. I *told* you these things ?
1Ti. 1: 7. neither what they *say,* nor
  2: 7. I *speak* the truth in Christ,
  4: 1. the Spirit *speaketh* expressly,
  5:18. For the scripture *saith,* Thou shalt not
2Ti. 2: 7. Consider what I *say ;* and the Lord
    18. *saying* that the resurrection
Tit. 2: 8. having no evil thing *to say* of you.
Philem.19. albeit I *do* not *say* to thee
    21. thou wilt also do more than I *say.*
Heb 1: 6. firstbegotten into the world, he *saith,*
    7. of the angels he *saith,*
  2: 6. *saying,* What is man,
    12. *Saying,* I will declare thy name
  3: 7. as the Holy Ghost *saith,*
    15. While it *is said,* To day
  4: 7. *saying* in David, To day,
  5: 6. As he *saith* also in another (place),
    11. many things *to say,*
  6:14. *Saying,* Surely blessing I will bless
  7:11. and not *be called* after the order
    13. of whom these things *are spoken*
    21. by him *that said* unto him,
  8: 1. Now of the *things* which we have *spoken*
    8. finding fault with them, he *saith,* Behold,
        the days come, *saith* the Lord,
    9. I regarded them not, *saith* the Lord.
    10. of Israel after those days, *saith* the Lord ;
    11. *saying,* Know the Lord:
    13. In that he *saith,* A new (covenant),
  9: 2. which *is called* the sanctuary.
    3. the tabernacle *which is called* the Holiest
    5. we cannot now *speak* particularly.
    20. *Saying,* This (is) the blood of
  10: 5. he *saith,* Sacrifice and offering
    8. Above *when* he *said,* Sacrifice and
    16. *saith* the Lord, I will put my laws
    30. I will recompense, *saith* the Lord.
  11:14. For they *that say* such things
    24. refused *to be called* the son
    32. what shall I more *say ?*
  12:26. *saying,* Yet once more
  13: 6. So that we may boldly *say,*
Jas. 1:13. *Let* no man *say* when he is
  2:14. though a man *say* he hath faith,

Jas. 2:23. was fulfilled *which saith*,
4: 5. that the scripture *saith* in vain,
6. Wherefore he *saith*, God resisteth the
13. Go to now, ye *that say*,
15. For that ye (ought) *to say*,

2Pet.3: 4. And *saying*, Where is the promise
1Joh.2: 4. He *that saith*, I know him,
6. He *that saith* he abideth in him
9. He *that saith* he is in the light,
5:16. I *do* not *say* that he shall pray for it.

2Joh. 10. neither *bid* him God speed:
11. For he *that biddeth* him God

Jude 14. *saying*, Behold, the Lord cometh
18. How that they *told* you

Rev. 1: 8. *saith* the Lord, which is, and which was,
11. *Saying*, I am Alpha and Omega,
17. *saying* unto me, Fear not;
2: 1. These things *saith* he that holdeth
7. let him hear what the Spirit *saith*
8. These things *saith* the first and the last,
9. *which say* they are Jews,
11. let him hear what the Spirit *saith*
12. These things *saith* he which
17. let him hear what the Spirit *saith*
18. These things *saith* the Son of God,
20. *which calleth* herself a prophetess,
24. But unto you I *say*, and unto the
— depths of Satan, as they *speak;*
29. let him hear what the Spirit *saith*
3: 1. These things *saith* he that
6. let him hear what the Spirit *saith*
7. These things *saith* he that is holy,
9. *which say* they are Jews,
13. let him hear what the Spirit *saith*
14. These things *saith* the Amen,
17. Because thou *sayest*, I am rich,
22. let him hear what the Spirit *saith*
4: 1. *which said*, Come up hither,
8. *saying*, Holy, holy, holy,
10. before the throne, *saying*,
5: 5. one of the elders *saith* unto me,
9. they sung a new song, *saying*,
12. *Saying* with a loud voice,
13. heard I *saying*, Blessing, and
14. And the four beasts *said*, Amen.
6: 1. *saying*, Come and see.
3. the second beast *say*, Come and see.
5. the third beast *say*, Come and see.
6. in the midst of the four beasts *say*,
7. the fourth beast *say*, Come and see.
10. *saying*, How long, O Lord, holy and
16. And *said* to the mountains and
7: 3. *Saying*, Hurt not the earth,
10. *saying*, Salvation to our God
12. *Saying*, Amen: Blessing, and
13. one of the elders answered, *saying*
8:11. the star *is called* Wormwood:
13. *saying* with a loud voice,
9:14. *Saying* to the sixth angel
10: 4. I heard a voice from heaven *saying*
8. and *said*, Go (and) take the
9. *and said* unto him, Give me the little
book. And he *said* unto me, Take
11. And he *said* unto me, Thou must
11: 1. *saying*, Rise, and measure the
12. *saying* unto them, Come up hither.
15. *saying*, The kingdoms of this
17. *Saying*, We give thee thanks,
12:10. I heard a loud voice *saying* in
13: 4. *saying*, Who (is) like unto the beast?
14. *saying* to them that dwell on
14: 7. *Saying* with a loud voice,

Rev.14: 8. *saying*, Babylon is fallen,
9. *saying* with a loud voice,
13. *saying* unto me, Write,
— Yea, *saith* the Spirit,
18. *saying*, Thrust in thy sharp
15: 3. the song of the Lamb, *saying*,
16: 1. *saying* to the seven angels,
5. I heard the angel of the waters *say*,
7. I heard another out of the altar *say*,
17. *saying*, It is done.
17: 1. *saying* unto me, Come hither;
15. And he *saith* unto me,
18: 2. *saying*, Babylon the great is
4. *saying*, Come out of her, my
7. for she *saith* in her heart,
10. *saying*, Alas, alas that great city
16. *saying*, Alas, alas that great city,
18. *saying*, What (city is) like
19. *saying*, Alas, alas that great city,
21. and cast (it) into the sea, *saying*,
19: 1. *saying*, Alleluia; Salvation,
4. *saying*, Amen; Alleluia.
5. *saying*, Praise our God,
6. *saying*, Alleluia: for the Lord
9. And he *saith* unto me, Write, Blessed
— And he *saith* unto me, These are the
10. And he *said* unto me, See
17. with a loud voice, *saying* to all the fowls
21: 3. *saying*, Behold, the tabernacle of God
5. And he *said* unto me, Write:
9. *saying*, Come hither, I will shew
22: 9. Then *saith* he unto me, See
10. And he *saith* unto me, Seal not
17. the Spirit and the bride *say*, Come.
20. *saith*, Surely I come quickly;

λεῖμμα, *limma.*

Ro. 11: 5. there is a *remnant* according to the

λεῖος, *lios.*

Lu. 3: 5. the rough ways (shall be) made *smooth;*

λείπω, *lipo.*

Lu. 18:22. Yet lackest thou one thing:(lit.one thing
is *lacking* to thee)
Tit. 1: 5. the things *that are wanting*,
3:13. that nothing *be wanting* unto them.
Jas. 1: 4. that ye may be perfect and entire, *wanting*
nothing.
5. If any of you *lack* wisdom,
2:15. and *destitute* of daily food,

λειτουργέω, *litourgeo.*

Acts13: 2. *As* they *ministered* to the Lord,
Ro. 15:27. their duty is also *to minister* unto them
in carnal things.
Heb 10:11. every priest standeth daily *ministering*

λειτουργία, *litourgia.*

Lu. 1:23. as the days of his *ministration* were
2Co. 9:12. For the administration of this *service*
Phi. 2:17. upon the sacrifice and *service* of your

Phi. 2:30. to supply your lack of *service* toward me.
Heb 8: 6. he obtained a more excellent *ministry*,
9:21. sprinkled with blood...and all the vessels
of the *ministry*.

λειτουργικός, *litourgikos*.

Heb 1:14. Are they not all *ministering* spirits,

λειτουργός, *litourgos*.

Ro. 13: 6. they are God's *ministers*, attending
15:16. That I should be the *minister* of
Phi. 2:25. and *he that ministered* to my wants.
Heb 1: 7. and his *ministers* a flame of fire.
8: 2. A *minister* of the sanctuary, and of the
true tabernacle,

λέντιον, *lention*.

Joh.13: 4. and took a *towel*, and girded himself.
5. to wipe (them) with the *towel* wherewith
he was girded.

λεπίς, *lepis*.

Acts 9:18. fell from his eyes as it had been *scales:*

λέπρα, *lepra*.

Mat. 8: 3. his *leprosy* was cleansed.
Mar 1:42. immediately the *leprosy* departed
Lu. 5:12. a man full of *leprosy:*
13. immediately the *leprosy* departed

λεπρός, *lepros*.

Mat. 8: 2. And, behold, there came a *leper*
10: 8. cleanse the *lepers*, raise the dead,
11: 5. the *lepers* are cleansed,
26: 6. in the house of Simon the *leper*,
Mar 1:40. there came a *leper* to him,
14: 3. in the house of Simon the *leper*,
Lu. 4:27. many *lepers* were in Israel
7:22. the *lepers* are cleansed,
17:12. ten men that were *lepers*,

λεπτόν, *lepton*.

Mar12:42. she threw in two *mites*,
Lu. 12:59. till thou hast paid the very last *mite*.
21: 2. casting in thither two *mites*.

λευκαίνω, *lūkaino*.

Mar 9: 3. as no fuller on earth can *white* them.
Rev. 7:14. have washed their robes, and *made* them
white in the blood of the Lamb.

λευκός, *lūkos*.

Mat. 5:36. canst not make one hair *white* or black.
17: 2. his raiment was *white* as the light.
28: 3. and his raiment *white* as snow:
Mar 9: 3. exceeding *white* as snow;

Mar16: 5. clothed in a long *white* garment;
Lu. 9:29. his raiment (was) *white* (and) glistering.
Joh. 4:35. they are *white* already to harvest.
20:12. And seeth two angels in *white*
Acts 1:10. two men stood by them in *white* apparel;
Rev. 1:14. His head and (his) hairs (were) *white* like
wool, as *white* as snow;
2:17. will give him a *white* stone,
3: 4. they shall walk with me in *white:*
5. shall be clothed in *white* raiment;
18. and *white* raiment, that thou mayest be
4: 4. elders sitting, clothed in *white* raiment;
6: 2. behold a *white* horse:
11. And *white* robes were given
7: 9. clothed with *white* robes,
13. which are arrayed in *white* robes?
14:14. and behold a *white* cloud
19:11. and behold a *white* horse;
14. followed him upon *white* horses, clothed
in fine linen, *white* and clean.
20:11. I saw a great *white* throne,

λέων, *leōn*.

2Ti. 4:17. out of the mouth of the *lion*.
Heb11:33. stopped the mouths of *lions*,
1Pet.5: 8. as a roaring *lion*, walketh
Rev. 4: 7. the first beast (was) like a *lion*,
5: 5. the *Lion* of the tribe of Juda,
9: 8. were as (the teeth) of *lions*.
17. as the heads of *lions;*
10: 3. as (when) a *lion* roareth:
13: 2. and his mouth as the mouth of a *lion:*

λήθη, *leethee*.

2Pet.1: 9. and hath forgotten (lit. having taken
forgetfulness) that he was purged from

ληκέω see λακέω.

ληνός, *leenos*.

Mat.21:33. and digged a *winepress* in it,
Rev.14:19. cast (it) into the great *winepress*
20. And the *winepress* was trodden without
the city, and blood came out of the
winepress,
19:15. he treadeth the *winepress* of the fierceness

λῆρος, *leeros*.

Lu. 24:11. seemed to them as *idle tales*,

λῃστής, *leestees*.

Mat.21:13. ye have made it a den of *thieves*.
26:55. Are ye come out as against a *thief*
27:38. two *thieves* crucified with him,
44. The *thieves* also, which were crucified
Mar11:17. ye have made it a den of *thieves*.
14:48. Are ye come out, as against a *thief*,
15:27. with him they crucify two *thieves;*
Lu. 10:30. and fell among *thieves*,
36. that fell among the *thieves?*
19:46. ye have made it a den of *thieves*.
22:52. Be ye come out, as against a *thief*,

Joh. 10: 1. the same is a thief and a *robber*.
8. before me are thieves and *robbers:*
18:40. Now Barabbas was a *robber*.
2Co.11:26. (in) perils of *robbers*, (in) perils by

λῆψις, *leepsis*.

Phi. 4:15. communicated with me as concerning giving and *receiving*,

---

λίαν, *lian*.

Mat. 2:16. mocked of the wise men, was *exceeding*
4: 8. an *exceeding* high mountain,
8:28. out of the tombs, *exceeding* fierce,
27:14. the governor marvelled *greatly*.
Mar. 1:35. rising up a *great* while before day,
6:51. they were *sore* amazed
9: 3. *exceeding* white as snow;
16: 2. And *very* early in the morning
Lu. 23: 8. he was *exceeding* glad:
2Co.11: 5. the *very* chiefest apostles.
12:11. behind the *very* chiefest apostles,
2Ti. 4:15. he hath *greatly* withstood our words.
2Joh. 4. I rejoiced *greatly* that I found
3Joh. 3. I rejoiced *greatly*, when the brethren

λίϐανος, *libanos*.

Mat. 2:11. gold, and *frankincense*, and myrrh.
Rev.18:13. *frankincense*, and wine, and oil,

−τος, λιϐανωτόν, *libanōton*.

Rev. 8: 3. at the altar, having a golden *censer;*
5. the angel took the *censer*, and filled it

λιθάζω, *lithazo*.

Joh.10:31. Jews took up stones again to *stone* him.
32. of those works *do* ye *stone* me?
33. For a good work we *stone* thee not;
11: 8. of late sought *to stone* thee;
Acts 5:26. lest they *should have been stoned.*
14:19. *having stoned* Paul, drew (him) out
2Co.11:25. once *was* I *stoned*,
Heb11:37. They *were stoned*, they were sawn asunder,

λίθινος, *lithinos*.

Joh. 2: 6. six waterpots *of stone*,
2Co. 3: 3. not in tables *of stone*, but in fleshy
Rev. 9:20. *of* gold, and silver, and brass, and *stone*,.

λιθοϐολέω, *lithoboleo*.

Mat.21:35. killed another, and *stoned* another.
23:37. and *stonest* them which are sent
Mar12: 4. at him they *cast stones, and*
Lu. 13:34. and *stonest* them that are
Joh. 8: 5. that such should *be stoned:*
Acts 7:58. cast (him) out of the city, and *stoned* (him):
59. And they *stoned* Stephen.

Acts14: 5. to use (them) despitefully, and *to stone*
Heb12:20. touch the mountain, it *shall be stoned*,

λίθος, *lithos*.

Mat. 3: 9. God is able of these *stones* to
4: 3. command that these *stones* be
6. thou dash thy foot against a *stone.*
7: 9. will he give him a *stone?*
21:42. The *stone* which the builders
44. fall on this *stone* shall be
24: 2. not be left here one *stone* upon another.
(lit. *stone* upon *stone*)
27:60. rolled a great *stone* to the
66. sealing the *stone*, and setting a watch.
28: 2. and rolled back the *stone*
Mar. 5: 5. cutting himself with *stones.*
9:42. that a mill*stone* were hanged
12:10. The *stone* which the builders
13: 1. what manner of *stones*
2. shall not be left one *stone* upon another,
(lit. *stone* upon *stone*)
15:46. and rolled a *stone*
16: 3. Who shall roll us away the *stone*
4. they saw that the *stone* was
Lu. 3: 8. God is able of these *stones*
4: 3. command this *stone* that it
11. thou dash thy foot against a *stone.*
11:11. will he give him a *stone?*
19:40. the *stones* would immediately cry out.
44. one *stone* upon another; (lit. *stone* upon *stone*)
20:17. The *stone* which the builders
18. shall fall upon that *stone*
21: 5. adorned with goodly *stones*
6. not be left one *stone* upon another, (lit. *stone* upon *stone*)
22:41. about a *stone's* cast,
24: 2. they found the *stone* rolled away
Joh. 8: 7. let him first cast a *stone*
59. Then took they up *stones*
10:31. Jews took up *stones* again
11:38. and a *stone* lay upon it.
39. Take ye away the *stone.*
41. they took away the *stone*
20: 1. and seeth the *stone* taken
Acts 4:11. This is the *stone* which was
17:29. unto gold, or silver, or *stone*,
Ro. 9:32. at that stumbling*stone;*
33. in Sion a stumbling*stone*
1Co. 3:12. gold, silver, precious *stones*,
2Co. 3: 7. engraven in *stones*, was glorious,
1Pet.2: 4. (as unto) a living *stone*,
5. Ye also, as lively *stones*,
6. I lay in Sion a chief corner *stone*,
7. the *stone* which the builders disallowed,
8(7). And a *stone* of stumbling,
Rev. 4: 3. like a jasper and a sardine *stone:*
17: 4. decked with gold and precious *stones*
18:12. and silver, and precious *stones*,
16. gold, and precious *stones*,
21. angel took up a *stone* like
21:11. like unto a *stone* most precious, even like a jasper *stone*, clear as crystal;
19. with all manner of precious *stones.*

λικμάω, *likmao*.

Mat.21:44. it *will grind* him *to powder*.
Lu. 20:18. it *will grind* him *to powder*.

λιμήν, limeen.

Acts27: 8. a place which is called The fair *havens;*
12. because the *haven* was not commodious
— (which is) an *haven* of Crete, and lieth

λίμνη, limnee.

Lu. 5: 1. he stood by the *lake* of Gennesaret,◦
2. two ships standing by the *lake:*
8:22. the other side of the *lake.*
23. a storm of wind on the *lake;*
33. steep place into the *lake,*
Rev.19:20. cast alive into a *lake* of fire
20:10. was cast into the *lake* of fire
14. were cast into the *lake* of fire.
15. was cast into the *lake* of fire.
21: 8. their part in the *lake* which burneth

λιμός, limos.

Mat.24: 7. there shall be *famines,* and
Mar 13: 8. and there shall be *famines* and troubles:
Lu. 4:25. when great *famine* was
15:14. arose a mighty *famine*
17. I perish with *hunger!*
21:11. and *famines,* and pestilences;
Acts 7:11. there came a *dearth* over all the land
11:28. there should be great *dearth*
Ro. 8:35. or *famine,* or nakedness,
2Co.11:27. in *hunger* and thirst,
Rev. 6: 8. to kill with sword, and with *hunger,*
18: 8. death, and mourning, and *famine;*

λίνον, linon.

Mat.12:20. and smoking *flax* shall he not quench,
Rev.15: 6. clothed in pure and white *linen,*

λιπαρός, liparos.

Rev.18:14. all things which were *dainty* and goodly
are departed from thee,

λίτρα, litra.

Joh.12: 3. Then took Mary a *pound* of ointment of
19:39. about an hundred *pound* (weight).

λίψ, lips.

Acts27:12. toward the *south west*

λογία, logia.

1Co.16: 1. Now concerning the *collection* for the
2. that there be no *gatherings* when I come.

λογίζομαι, logizomai.

Mar 11:31. they *reasoned* with themselves,
15:28. he *was numbered* with the
Lu. 22:37. he *was reckoned* among the
Acts19:27. Diana should be despised, (lit. should *be counted* for nothing)

Ro. 2: 3. And *thinkest* thou this, O man,
26. *shall* not his uncircumcision *be counted* for circumcision?
3:28. Therefore we *conclude* that
4: 3. it *was counted* unto him for righteousness.
4. *is* the reward not *reckoned* of grace, but
5. his faith *is counted* for righteousness.
6. unto whom God *imputeth*
8. the Lord *will* not *impute*
9. faith *was reckoned* to Abraham
10. How *was* it then *reckoned?*
11. that righteousness might *be imputed* unto
22. it *was imputed* to him for
23. that it *was imputed* to him;
24. to whom it shall *be imputed,*
6:11. *reckon* ye also yourselves to be dead
8:18. For I *reckon* that the sufferings
36. we *are accounted* as sheep for
9: 8. *are counted* for the seed.
14:14. but to him *that esteemeth* any thing
1Co. 4: 1. *Let* a man so *account of* us,
13: 5. not easily provoked, *thinketh* no evil;
11. I *thought* as a child:
2Co. 3: 5. *to think* any thing as of ourselves;
5:19. not *imputing* their trespasses unto them;
10: 2. I *think* to be bold against some, *which think of* us as if we walked
7. *let* him of himself *think* this again,
11. *Let* such an one *think* this, that, such
11: 5. For I *suppose* I was not a whit
12: 6. lest any man *should think* of me above
Gal. 3: 6. it *was accounted* to him for
Phi. 3:13. I *count* not myself to have
4: 8. *think* on these things.
2Ti. 4:16. it *may* not *be laid to* their charge.
Heb 11:19. *Accounting* that God (was) able to raise
Jas. 2:23. it *was imputed* unto him for
1Pet.5:12. faithful brother unto you, as I *suppose,*

λογικός, logikos.

Ro. 12: 1. your *reasonable* service.
1Pet. 2: 2. the sincere milk *of the word,*

λόγιον, logion.

Acts 7:38. who received the lively *oracles* to give
Ro. 3: 2. were committed the *oracles* of God.
Heb 5:12. first principles of the *oracles* of God;
1Pet.4:11. (let him speak) as the *oracles* of God;

λόγιος, logios.

Acts18:24. an *eloquent* man, (and) mighty in the

λογισμός, logismos.

Ro. 2:15. also bearing witness, and (their) *thoughts*
2Co.10: 5(4). Casting down *imaginations,*

λογομαχέω, logomakeo.

2Ti. 2:14. that they *strive* not *about words*

λογομαχία, logomakia.

1Ti. 6: 4. about questions and *strifes of words,*

λόγος, logos.

Mat. 5:32.	saving for the *cause* of fornication,
37.	let your *communication* be, Yea, yea;
7:24.	heareth these *sayings* of mine, and doeth
26.	that heareth these *sayings* of mine, and
28.	Jesus had ended these *sayings*,
8: 8.	but speak the *word* only,
16.	cast out the spirits with (his) *word*,
10:14.	nor hear your *words*,
12:32.	speaketh a *word* against the Son of man,
36.	they shall give *account* thereof
37.	For by thy *words* thou shalt be justified, and by thy *words*
13:19.	heareth the *word* of the kingdom,
20.	is he that heareth the *word*,
21.	ariseth because of the *word*,
22.	he that heareth the *word* ; and the care
—	riches, choke the *word*,
23.	heareth the *word*, and understandeth
15:12.	after they heard this *saying?*
23.	answered her not a *word*.
18:23.	take *account* of his servants.
19: 1.	Jesus had finished these *sayings*,
11.	All (men) cannot receive this *saying*,
22.	the young man heard that *saying*,
21:24.	I also will ask you one *thing*,
22:15.	might entangle him in (his) *talk*.
46.	to answer him a *word*,
24:35.	my *words* shall not pass away.
25:19.	and reckoneth (lit. taketh *account*) with them.
26: 1.	finished all these *sayings*,
44.	saying the same *words*.
28:15.	this *saying* is commonly reported
Mar 1:45.	and to blaze abroad the *matter*,
2: 2.	preached the *word* unto them.
4:14.	The sower soweth the *word*.
15.	where the *word* is sown;
—	taketh away the *word*
16.	have heard the *word*,
17.	for the *word's* sake,
18.	such as hear the *word*,
19.	entering in, choke the *word*,
20.	such as hear the *word*,
33.	spake he the *word* unto them,
5:36.	As soon as Jesus heard the *word*
7:13.	Making the *word* of God of none effect
29.	For this *saying* go thy way ;
8:32.	And he spake that *saying*
38.	and of my *words*
9:10.	they kept that *saying*
10:22.	he was sad at that *saying*,
24.	astonished at his *words*.
11:29.	ask of you one *question*,
12:13.	to catch him in (his) *words*.
13:31.	but my *words* shall not pass
14:39.	and spake the same *words*.
16:20.	confirming the *word* with
Lu. 1: 2.	and ministers of the *word* ;
4.	the certainty of those *things*,
20.	thou believest not my *words*,
29.	she was troubled at his *saying*,
3: 2.	the book of the *words* of Esaias
4:22.	wondered at the gracious *words*
32.	for his *word* was with power.
36.	What a *word* (is) this !
5: 1.	to hear the *word* of God,
15.	went there a *fame* abroad
6:47.	and heareth my *sayings*,
7: 7.	but say in a *word*,
17.	this *rumour* of him went forth

Lu. 8:11.	The seed is the *word* of God.
12.	taketh away the *word* out of
13.	receive the *word* with joy ;
15.	having heard the *word*,
21.	are these which hear the *word* of God, and do it.
9:26.	of me and of my *words*,
28.	eight days after these *sayings*,
44.	Let these *sayings* sink down
10:39.	sat at Jesus' feet, and heard his *word*.
11:28.	that hear the *word* of God, and keep it.
12:10.	shall speak a *word* against the Son
16: 2.	give an *account* of thy stewardship ;
20: 3.	I will also ask you one *thing* ;
20.	might take hold of his *words*,
21:33.	but my *words* shall not pass
22:61.	Peter remembered the *word*
23: 9.	questioned with him in many *words* ;
24:17.	What manner of *communications* (are)
19.	mighty in deed and *word*
44.	These (are) the *words* which I
Joh. 1: 1.	In the beginning was the *Word*, and the *Word* was with God, and the *Word* was God.
14.	And the *Word* was made flesh,
2:22.	and the *word* which Jesus
4:37.	herein is that *saying* true,
39.	for the *saying* of the woman,
41.	because of his own *word* ;
50.	the man believed the *word*
5:24.	He that heareth my *word*,
38.	ye have not his *word*
6:60.	This is an hard *saying* ;
7:36.	What (manner of) *saying* is
40.	when they heard this *saying*,
8:31.	If ye continue in my *word*,
37.	my *word* hath no place in you.
43.	ye cannot hear my *word*.
51.	If a man keep my *saying*,
52.	thou sayest, If a man keep my *saying*,
55.	and keep his *saying*.
10:19.	among the Jews for these *sayings*.
35.	unto whom the *word* of God came,
12:38.	That the *saying* of Esaias the prophet
48.	the *word* that I have spoken,
14:23.	he will keep my *words* :
24.	keepeth not my *sayings* : and the *word* which ye hear
15: 3.	are clean through the *word*
20.	Remember the *word* that I said
—	if they have kept my *saying*,
25.	that the *word* might be fulfilled
17: 6.	and they have kept thy *word*.
14.	I have given them thy *word* ;
17.	thy *word* is truth.
20.	shall believe on me through their *word* ;
18: 9.	That the *saying* might be fulfilled,
32.	That the *saying* of Jesus might
19: 8.	When Pilate therefore heard that *saying*,
13.	heard that *saying*, he brought Jesus forth,
21:23.	Then went this *saying* abroad
Acts 1: 1.	The former *treatise* have I made,
2:22.	men of Israel, hear these *words* ;
40.	And with many other *words*
41.	they that gladly received his *word*
4: 4.	which heard the *word* believed ;
29.	they may speak thy *word*,
31.	and they spake the *word* of God
5: 5.	Ananias hearing these *words*
24.	priests heard these *things*,
6: 2.	should leave the *word* of God,
4.	the ministry of the *word*.

Acts 6: 5. the *saying* pleased the whole
7. the *word* of God increased;
7:22. mighty in *words* and in deeds.
29. Then fled Moses at this *saying,*
8: 4. preaching the *word.*
14. had received the *word* of God,
21. neither part nor lot in this *matter:*
25. and preached the *word* of the Lord,
10:29. for what *intent* ye have sent for me?
36. The *word* which (God) sent
44. which heard the *word.*
11: 1. had also received the *word* of God.
19. preaching the *word* to none but
22. Then *tidings* of these things
12:24. But the *word* of God grew
13: 5. they preached the *word* of God
7. desired to hear the *word* of God.
15. if ye have any *word* of exhortation
26. to you is the *word* of this salvation sent.
44. to hear the *word* of God.
46. It was necessary that the *word*
48. glorified the *word* of the Lord:
49. the *word* of the Lord was published
14: 3. gave testimony unto the *word* of his grace,
12. he was the chief speaker. (lit. of *speech*)
25. had preached the *word*
15: 6. to consider of this *matter.*
7. should hear the *word* of the gospel,
15. to this agree the *words* of the prophets;
24. troubled you with *words,*
27. the same things by *mouth.*
32. exhorted the brethren with many *words,*
35. preaching the *word* of the Lord,
36. preached the *word* of the Lord,
16: 6. to preach the *word* in Asia,
32. spake unto him the *word* of the Lord,
36. told this *saying* to Paul,
17:11. received the *word* with all readiness
13. had knowledge that the *word* of God
18:11. teaching the *word* of God
14. reason would that (lit. with *reason*) I
should bear with you:
15. if it be a question of *words*
19:10. heard the *word* of the Lord
20. So mightily grew the *word* of God
38. have a *matter* against any
40. may give an *account* of this concourse.
20: 2. had given them much exhortation, (lit.
had exhorted them in many *words*)
7. continued his *speech* until midnight.
24. none of these *things* move me,
32. and to the *word* of his grace,
35. and to remember the *words*
38. for the *words* which he spake,
22:22. audience unto this *word,*
Ro. 3: 4. justified in thy *sayings,*
9: 6. Not as though the *word* of God
9. For this (is) the *word* of promise,
28. For he will finish the *work,* (lit. *reckoning*)
— a short *work* will the Lord make
13: 9. comprehended in this *saying,* namely,
14:12. every one of us shall give *account*
15:18. by *word* and deed,
1Co. 1: 5. enriched by him, in all *utterance,* and (in)
17. not with wisdom of *words,*
18. For the *preaching* of the cross
2: 1. not with excellency of *speech*
4. And my *speech* and my preaching (was)
not with enticing *words*
13. not in the *words* which man's wisdom
4:19. not the *speech* of them which are
20. not in *word,* but in power.

1Co.12: 8. the *word* of wisdom; to another the *word*
of knowledge
14: 9. *words* easy to be understood,
19. I had rather speak five *words*
— than ten thousand *words* in an
36. came the *word* of God out from you?
15: 2. keep in memory what)(I preached
54. to pass the *saying* that is written,
2Co. 1:18. our *word* toward you was not
2:17. which corrupt the *word* of God:
4: 2. nor handling the *word* of God
5:19. the *word* of reconciliation.
6: 7. By the *word* of truth,
8: 7. (in) faith, and *utterance,* and knowledge,
10:10. and (his) *speech* contemptible.
11. such as we are in *word* by letters
11: 6. But though (I be) rude in *speech,*
Gal. 5:14. the law is fulfilled in one *word,*
6: 6. Let him that is taught in the *word*
Eph. 1:13. after that ye heard the *word* of truth,
4:29. Let no corrupt *communication*
5: 6. deceive you with vain *words:*
6:19. that *utterance* may be given unto me,
Phi. 1:14. to speak the *word* without fear.
2:16. Holding forth the *word* of life;
4:15. as concerning giving and receiving, (lit.
as to the *matter* of g. and r.)
17. may abound to your *account.*
Col. 1: 5. in the *word* of the truth
25. to fulfil the *word* of God;
2:23. have indeed a *shew* of wisdom
3:16. Let the *word* of Christ dwell
17. whatsoever ye do in *word* or deed,
4: 3. unto us a door of *utterance,*
6. Let your *speech* (be) alway
1Th. 1: 5. came not unto you in *word* only,
6. having received the *word* in much
8. sounded out the *word* of the Lord
2: 5. used we flattering *words,*
13. the *word* of God which ye heard of us, ye
received (it) not (as) the *word* of men,
but as it is in truth, the *word* of God,
4:15. unto you by the *word* of the Lord,
18. comfort one another with these *words.*
2Th. 2: 2. neither by spirit, nor by *word,*
15. whether by *word,* or our epistle.
17. in every good *word* and work.
3: 1. the *word* of the Lord may have (free)
14. if any man obey not our *word*
1Ti. 1:15. This (is) a faithful *saying,* and worthy
3: 1. This (is) a true *saying,*
4: 5. sanctified by the *word* of God and prayer.
6. nourished up in the *words* of faith
9. This (is) a faithful *saying*
12. in *word,* in conversation, in charity,
5:17. they who labour in the *word*
6: 3. to wholesome *words,* (even) the words of
our Lord
2Ti. 1:13. Hold fast the form of sound *words,*
2: 9. the *word* of God is not bound.
11. (It is) a faithful *saying:*
15. rightly dividing the *word* of truth.
17. And their *word* will eat as doth
4: 2. Preach the *word;* be instant
15. greatly withstood our *words.*
Tit. 1: 3. manifested his *word* through preaching,
9. Holding fast the faithful *word*
2: 5. that the *word* of God be not blasphemed.
8. Sound *speech,* that cannot be condemned;
3: 8. (This is) a faithful *saying,*
Heb. 2: 2. (For if the *word* spoken by angels
4: 2. but the *word* preached did not profit

Heb. 4:12. For the *word* of God (is) quick, and
13. with whom we have to do. (lit. *account*)
5:11. Of whom we have many *things* to say,
13. unskilful in the *word* of righteousness:
6: 1. leaving the principles of the doctrine (lit. leaving the *word* of the beginning)
7:28. but the *word* of the oath,
12:19. the *word* should not be spoken to them
13: 7. have spoken unto you the *word* of God:
17. as they that must give *account*,
22. suffer the *word* of exhortation:
Jas. 1:18. begat he us with the *word* of truth,
21. with meekness the engrafted *word*,
22. be ye doers of the *word*,
23. if any be a hearer of the *word*,
3: 2. If any man offend not in *word*,
1Pet.1:23. of incorruptible, by the *word* of God,
2: 8. which stumble at the *word*,
3: 1. if any obey not the *word*, they also may without the *word* be won by
15. a *reason* of the hope that is in you
4: 5. Who shall give *account* to him
2Pet.1:19. We have also a more sure *word*
2: 3. with feigned *words* make merchandise
3: 5. by the *word* of God the heavens
7. by the same *word* are kept in store,
1Joh.1: 1. have handled, of the *Word* of life;
10. and his *word* is not in us.
2: 5. But whoso keepeth his *word*,
7. The old commandment is the *word*
14. the *word* of God abideth in you,
3:18. let us not love in *word*,
5: 7. the Father, the *Word*, and the HolyGhost:
3Joh. 10. against us with malicious *words*:
Rev. 1: 2. bare record of the *word* of God,
3. that hear the *words* of this prophecy,
9. for the *word* of God, and for the
3: 8. and hast kept my *word*,
10. hast kept the *word* of my patience,
6: 9. were slain for the *word* of God,
12:11. and by the *word* of their testimony;
19: 9. These are the true *sayings* of God.
13. is called The *Word* of God.
20: 4. and for the *word* of God,
21: 5. for these *words* are true and faithful.
22: 6. These *sayings* (are) faithful and true:
7. blessed (is) he that keepeth the *sayings*
9. of them which keep the *sayings*
10. Seal not the *sayings* of the prophecy
18. the *words* of the prophecy of this book,
19. take away from the *words* of the book of this prophecy, God

λόγχη, *lonkee*.

Joh.19:34. with a *spear* pierced his side,

λοιδορέω, *loidoreo*.

Joh. 9:28. Then they *reviled* him, and said,
Acts23: 4. *Revilest* thou God's high priest?
1Co. 4:12. being *reviled*, we bless;
1Pet.2:23. Who, *when he was reviled*, reviled not

λοιδορία, *loidoria*.

1Ti. 5:14. to the adversary to speak *reproachfully*.
1Pet.3: 9. or *railing* for railing:

λοίδορος, *loidoros*.

1Co. 5:11. or a *railer*, or a drunkard,
6:10. nor *revilers*, nor extortioners,

λοιμός, *loimos*.

Mat.24: 7. famines, and *pestilences*,
Lu. 21:11. and famines, and *pestilences*;
Acts24: 5. found this man (a) *pestilent* (*fellow*),

το λοιπόν, ὁ λοιπόν, & λοιπον,
to loipon, ho loipon, & loipon.

(The neut. of the adj. used as an adv.)

Mat.26:45. Sleep on *now*, and take (your) rest:
Mar14:41. Sleep on *now*, and take (your) rest:
Acts27:20. all hope that we should be saved was *then* taken away.
1Co. 1:16. *besides*, I know not whether I baptized any other.
4: 2. *Moreover* it is required in stewards,
7:29. it remaineth, (lit. as *for the rest* it is) that both they that
2Co.13:11. *Finally*, brethren, farewell.
Eph. 6:10. *Finally*, my brethren, be strong
Phi. 3: 1. *Finally*, my brethren, rejoice in the Lord.
4: 8. *Finally*, brethren, whatsoever things
1Th. 4: 1. *Furthermore* then we beseech you,
2Th. 3: 1. *Finally*, brethren, pray for us,
2Ti. 4: 8. *Henceforth* there is laid up for me
Heb10:13. *From henceforth* expecting till his enemies be made his footstool.

λοιπός, *loipos*.

Mat.22: 6. And the *remnant* took his servants,
25:11. Afterward came also the *other* virgins,
27:49. The *rest* said, Let be,
Mar 4:19. and the lusts of *other* things
16:13. and told (it) unto the *residue*:
Lu. 8:10. but to *others* in parables; that seeing
12:26. why take ye thought for the *rest*?
18: 9. and despised *others*:
11. that I am not as *other* men
24: 9. unto the eleven, and to all the *rest*.
10. and *other* (women that were) with them,
Acts 2:37. unto Peter and to the *rest* of the apostles,
5:13. And of the *rest* durst no man join
17: 9. security of Jason, and of the *other*,
27:44. And the *rest*, some on boards,
28: 9. *others* also, which had diseases
Ro. 1:13. even as among *other* Gentiles.
11: 7. and the *rest* were blinded
1Co. 7:12. But to the *rest* speak I,
9: 5. as well as *other* apostles,
11:34. And the *rest* will I set in order
15:37. of wheat, or of some *other* (grain):
2Co.12:13. were inferior to *other* churches,
13: 2. I write to them which heretofore have sinned, and to all *other*, that,
Gal. 2:13. And the *other* Jews dissembled
Eph 2: 3. children of wrath, even as *others*.
4:17. walk not as *other* Gentiles.
Phi. 1:13. and in all *other* (places),
4: 3. and (with) *other* my fellowlabourers,
1Th. 4:13. even as *others* which have no hope.
5: 6. let us not sleep, as (do) *others*;
1Ti. 5:20. that *others* also may fear.

2Pet. 3:16. as (they do)also the *other* scriptures,
Rev. 2:24. and unto the *rest* in Thyatira,
　　3: 2. and strengthen the things *which remain*,
　　8:13. by reason of the *other* voices
　　9:20. the *rest* of the men which were not
　11:13. and the *remnant* were affrighted,
　12:17. to make war with the *remnant* of her
　19:21. And the *remnant* were slain
　20: 5. But the *rest* of the dead lived not again
　　　　until

τοῦ λοιποῦ, *tou loipou.*

Gen. of the adj.

Gal. 6:17. *From henceforth* let no man

λουτρόν, *loutron.*

Eph 5:26. and cleanse it with the *washing* of water
Tit. 3: 5. by the *washing* of regeneration,

λούω, *louo.*

Joh. 13:10. He *that is washed* needeth not
Acts 9:37. whom *when they had washed*, they laid
　16:33. and *washed* (their) stripes ;
Heb 10:22(23). and our bodies *washed* (lit. *washed* as
　　　　to the body) with pure water.
2Pet. 2:22. the sow *that was washed* to her
Rev. 1: 5. Unto him that loved us, and *washed* us
　　　　from our sins in his own blood,

λύκος, *lukos.*

Mat. 7:15. inwardly they are ravening *wolves.*
　10:16. as sheep in the midst of *wolves :*
Lu. 10: 3. as lambs among *wolves.*
Joh. 10:12. seeth the *wolf* coming, and leaveth
　　　　— and the *wolf* catcheth them,
Acts 20:29. shall grievous *wolves* enter in among you,

λυμαίνομαι, *lumainomai.*

Acts 8: 3. As for Saul, he *made havock* of the church,

λυπέω, *lupeo.*

Mat. 14: 9. the king *was sorry :* nevertheless
　17:23. And they *were exceeding sorry.*
　18:31. what was done, they *were very sorry,*
　19:22. he went away *sorrowful :*
　26:22. they *were exceeding sorrowful, and*
　　37. began *to be sorrowful* and very heavy.
Mar 10:22. and went away *grieved :*
　14:19. they began *to be sorrowful,*
Joh. 16:20. and ye *shall be sorrowful,*
　21:17. Peter *was grieved* because he said
Ro. 14:15. if thy brother *be grieved* with (thy) meat,
2Co. 2: 2. For if I *make you sorry,*
　　　　— *which is made sorry* by me?
　　4. not that ye *should be grieved,*
　　5. if any *have caused grief,* he *hath* not *grieved*
　　　　me, but in part :
　6:10. As *sorrowful,* yet alway rejoicing ;

2Co. 7: 8. though I *made* you *sorry* with a letter,
　　　　— epistle *hath made* you *sorry,*
　　9. not that ye *were made sorry,* but that ye
　　　　sorrowed to repentance : for ye *were
　　　　made sorry*
　11. that ye *sorrowed* after a godly
Eph 4:30. And *grieve* not the holy Spirit
1Th. 4:13. that ye *sorrow* not, even as
1Pet. 1: 6. *though* now...ye *are in heaviness* through

λύπη, *lupee.*

Lu. 22:45. he found them sleeping for *sorrow,*
Joh. 16: 6. *sorrow* hath filled your heart.
　20. but your *sorrow* shall be turned into joy.
　21. in travail hath *sorrow,*
　22. ye now therefore have *sorrow :*
Ro. 9: 2. I have great *heaviness* and
2Co. 2: 1. not come again to you in *heaviness.*
　　3. I should have *sorrow* from
　　7. swallowed up with overmuch *sorrow.*
　7:10. For godly *sorrow* worketh repentance
　　　　— the *sorrow* of the world worketh death.
　9: 7. not grudgingly (lit. of *sorrow*), or of
Phi. 2:27. lest I should have *sorrow* upon *sorrow.*
Heb 12:11. but grievous : (lit. of *grief*)
1Pet. 2:19. a man for conscience toward God endure
　　　　grief,

λύσις, *lusis.*

1Co. 7:27. seek not *to be loosed.*

λυσιτελεῖ, *lusitelī.*

Lu. 17: 2. It *were better* for him that a millstone

λύτρον, *lutron.*

Mat. 20:28. to give his life a *ransom* for many.
Mar 10:45. to give his life a *ransom* for many.

λυτρόω, *lutroō.*

Lu. 24:21. which should have *redeemed* Israel :
Tit. 2:14. that he *might redeem* us from
1Pet. 1:18. ye *were* not *redeemed* with corruptible

λύτρωσις, *lutrōsis.*

Lu. 1:68. and redeemed (lit. wrought *redemption*
　　　　for) his people,
　2:38. that looked for *redemption*
Heb 9:12. having obtained eternal *redemption* (for
　　　　us).

λυτρωτής, *lutrōtees.*

Acts 7:35. God send (to be) a ruler and a *deliverer*
　　　　by the hand of the angel

λυχνία, *luknia.*

Mat. 5:15. but on a *candlestick ;* and it giveth

Mar 4:21. to be set on a *candlestick?*
Lu.　8:16. but setteth (it) on a *candlestick,*
　　11:33. but on a *candlestick,* that they
Heb 9: 2. wherein (was) the *candlestick,* and the
Rev. 1:12. I saw seven golden *candlesticks;*
　　　13. in the midst of the seven *candlesticks*
　　　20. the seven golden *candlesticks.*
　　　— and the seven *candlesticks* which
　　2: 1. of the seven golden *candlesticks;*
　　　5. remove thy *candlestick* out of his place,
　　11: 4. and the two *candlesticks* standing before
　　　　the God of the earth.

λύχνος, *luknos.*

Mat. 5:15. Neither do men light a *candle,*
　　6:22. The *light* of the body is the eye:
Mar 4:21. Is a *candle* brought to be put
Lu.　8:16. when he hath lighted a *candle,* covereth
　　11:33. when he hath lighted a *candle,* putteth
　　　34. The *light* of the body is the eye:
　　　36. the bright shining of a *candle*
　　12:35. and (your) *lights* burning;
　　15: 8. doth not light a *candle,*
Joh. 5:35. He was a burning and a shining *light:*
2Pet.1:19. as unto a *light* that shineth
Rev.18:23. And the light of a *candle* shall shine no
　　21:23. and the Lamb (is) the *light* thereof.
　　22: 5. they need no· *candle,* neither light of the
　　　　sun;

λύω, *luo.*

Mat. 5:19. *shall break* one of these least
　　16:19. whatsoever thou *shalt loose* on earth shall
　　　　be *loosed* in heaven.
　　18:18. whatsoever ye *shall loose* on earth shall be
　　　　loosed in heaven.
　　21: 2. *loose* (them), *and* bring (them) unto me.
Mar 1: 7. not worthy to stoop down and *unloose.*
　　7:35. the string of his tongue *was loosed,*
　　11: 2. *loose* him, *and* bring (him).
　　　4. and they *loose* him.
　　　5. What do ye, *loosing* the colt?
Lu.　3:16. I am not worthy *to unloose:*
　　13:15. *doth* not each one of you on the sabbath
　　　　loose his ox
　　　16. *be loosed* from this bond
　　19:30. *loose* him, *and* bring (him hither).
　　　31. Why *do* ye *loose* (him)?
　　　33. *as* they *were loosing* the
　　　— Why *loose* ye the colt?
Joh. 1:27. I am not worthy *to unloose.*
　　2:19. *Destroy* this temple, and in three days I
　　　　will raise it up.
　　5:18. he not only *had broken* the sabbath,
　　7:23. that the law of Moses should not *be broken;*
　　10:35. the scripture cannot *be broken;*
　　11:44. *Loose* him, and let him go.
Acts 2:24. *having loosed* the pains of death:
　　7:33. *Put off* thy shoes from thy feet:
　　13:25. I am not worthy *to loose.*
　　　43. Now *when* the congregation *was broken up,*
　　22:30. he *loosed* him from (his) bands,
　　24:26. that he *might loose* him:
　　27:41. the hinder part *was broken*
1Co. 7:27. *Art* thou *loosed* from a wife?
Eph. 2:14. and *hath broken down* the middle wall
2Pet.3:10. *shall melt* with fervent heat,

2Pet.3:11. (Seeing) then (that) all these things shall
　　　　be *dissolved,*
　　12. heavens being on fire *shall be dissolved,*
1Joh.3: 8. that he *might destroy* the works of the
Rev. 5: 2. and *to loose* the seals thereof?
　　　5. and *to loose* the seven seals
　　9:14. *Loose* the four angels which
　　　15. the four angels *were loosed,*
　　20: 3. he must *be loosed* a little season.
　　　7. Satan *shall be loosed* out of his prison,

μαγεία, *magia.*

Acts 8:11. bewitched them with *sorceries.*

μαγεύω, *maguo.*

Acts 8: 9. *used sorcery,* and bewitched the people of
　　　　Samaria,

μάγος, *magos.*

Mat. 2: 1. there came *wise men* from the east
　　　7. had privily called the *wise men,*
　　　16. that he was mocked of the *wise men,*
　　　— enquired of the *wise men.*
Acts13: 6. they found a certain *sorcerer,* a false
　　　8. But Elymas the *sorcerer*

μαθητεύω, *matheetuo.*

Mat.13:52. every scribe (which is) *instructed*
　　27:57. who also himself *was* Jesus' *disciple:*
　　28:19. and *teach* (lit. *disciple*) all nations,
Acts14:21. and *had taught* many, they returned

μαθητής, *matheetees.*

Mat. 5: 1. his *disciples* came unto him:
　　8:21. another of his *disciples* said
　　　23. his *disciples* followed him.
　　　25. his *disciples* came to (him),
　　9:10. with him and his *disciples.*
　　　11. they said unto his *disciples,*
　　　14. came to him the *disciples* of John, saying,
　　　— but thy *disciples* fast not?
　　　19. and (so did) his *disciples.*
　　　37. saith he unto his *disciples,*
　　10: 1. had called unto (him) his twelve *disciples,*
　　　24. The *disciple* is not above
　　　25. It is enough for the *disciple*
　　　42. only in the name of a *disciple,*
　　11: 1. of commanding his twelve *disciples,*
　　　2. he sent two of his *disciples,*
　　12: 1. *disciples* were an hungred,
　　　2. Behold, thy *disciples* do that
　　　49. forth his hand toward his *disciples,*
　　13:10. And the *disciples* came, and said
　　　36. into the house: and his *disciples* came
　　14:12. his *disciples* came, and took up the body,
　　　15. his *disciples* came to him,
　　　19. loaves to (his) *disciples,* and the *disciples*
　　　　to the multitude.

Mat.14:22. constrained his *disciples* to get
26. when the *disciples* saw him
15: 2. Why do thy *disciples* transgress the tradition of the elders?
12. Then came his *disciples*,
23. And his *disciples* came and besought
32. Jesus called his *disciples*
33. his *disciples* say unto him,
36. and gave to his *disciples*, and the *disciples* to the multitude.
16: 5. when his *disciples* were come
13. he asked his *disciples*, saying, Whom do
20. Then charged he his *disciples*
21. to shew unto his *disciples*,
24. Then said Jesus unto his *disciples*,
17: 6. when the *disciples* heard (it),
10. his *disciples* asked him, saying, Why then
13. Then the *disciples* understood
16. I brought him to thy *disciples*,
19. Then came the *disciples*
18: 1. came the *disciples* unto Jesus,
19:10. His *disciples* say unto him,
13. and the *disciples* rebuked them.
23. Then said Jesus unto his *disciples*,
25. When his *disciples* heard (it),
20:17. took the twelve *disciples*
21: 1. then sent Jesus two *disciples*,
6. And the *disciples* went, and did as
20. when the *disciples* saw (it),
22:16. sent out unto him their *disciples*
23: 1. to the multitude, and to his *disciples*,
24: 1. and his *disciples* came to (him) for to shew him
3. the *disciples* came unto him
26: 1. he said unto his *disciples*,
8. But when his *disciples* saw (it),
17. the *disciples* came to Jesus,
18. at thy house with my *disciples*.
19. And the *disciples* did as Jesus
26. and gave (it) to the *disciples*,
35. Likewise also said all the *disciples*.
36. and saith unto the *disciples*,
40. he cometh unto his *disciples*,
45. cometh he to his *disciples*,
56. Then all the *disciples* forsook him,
27:64. lest his *disciples* come by night,
28: 7. and tell his *disciples* that he is risen from the dead;
8. did run to bring his *disciples* word.
9. as they went to tell his *disciples*,
13. Say ye, His *disciples* came
16. Then the eleven *disciples* went.
Mar. 2:15. with Jesus and his *disciples*:
16. they said unto his *disciples*,
18. the *disciples* of John and of the
— Why do the *disciples* of John...fast, but thy *disciples* fast not?
23. his *disciples* began, as they went, to pluck
3: 7. with his *disciples* to the sea:
9. And he spake to his *disciples*,
4:34. expounded all things to his *disciples*.
5:31. his *disciples* said unto him,
6: 1. his *disciples* follow him.
29. when his *disciples* heard
35. his *disciples* came unto him,
41. and gave (them) to his *disciples*
45. he constrained his *disciples* to
7: 2. when they saw some of his *disciples*
5. Why walk not thy *disciples*
17. his *disciples* asked him
8: 1. Jesus called his *disciples*
4. his *disciples* answered him,

Mar. 8: 6. gave to his *disciples* to set
10. entered into a ship with his *disciples*,
27. and his *disciples*, into the towns
— he asked his *disciples*,
33. and looked on his *disciples*,
34. with his *disciples* also,
9:14. when he came to (his) *disciples*,
18. I spake to thy *disciples*
28. his *disciples* asked him
31. For he taught his *disciples*,
10:10. in the house his *disciples*
13. and (his) *disciples* rebuked
23. and saith unto his *disciples*,
24. And the *disciples* were astonished
46. went out of Jericho with his *disciples*
11: 1. sendeth forth two of his *disciples*,
14. And his *disciples* heard (it).
12:43. he called (unto him) his *disciples*,
13: 1. one of his *disciples* saith unto him,
14:12. his *disciples* said unto him,
13. two of his *disciples*,
14. eat the passover with my *disciples*?
16. And his *disciples* went forth,
32. and he saith to his *disciples*,
16: 7. tell his *disciples* and Peter
Lu. 5:30. murmured against his *disciples*,
33. Why do the *disciples* of John
6: 1. his *disciples* plucked the ears
13. he called (unto him) his *disciples*:
17. company of his *disciples*,
20. lifted up his eyes on his *disciples*,
40. The *disciple* is not above his
7:11. many of his *disciples* went with him,
18. the *disciples* of John shewed
19(18). two of his *disciples*
8: 9. his *disciples* asked him,
22. into a ship with his *disciples*:
9: 1. he called his twelve *disciples*
14. And he said to his *disciples*,
16. and gave to the *disciples* to
18. his *disciples* were with him:
40. thy *disciples* to cast him out;
43. he said unto his *disciples*,
54. And when his *disciples* James and John
10:23. he turned him unto (his) *disciples*,
11: 1. one of his *disciples* said unto him,
— as John also taught his *disciples*.
12: 1. he began to say unto his *disciples*
22. he said unto his *disciples*,
14:26. he cannot be my *disciple*.
27. cannot be my *disciple*.
33. he cannot be my *disciple*.
16: 1. he said also unto his *disciples*,
17: 1. Then said he unto the *disciples*,
22. he said unto the *disciples*,
18:15. when (his) *disciples* saw (it),
19:29. he sent two of his *disciples*,
37. the *disciples* began to rejoice
39. Master, rebuke thy *disciples*.
20:45. he said unto his *disciples*,
22:11. eat the passover with my *disciples*?
39. his *disciples* also followed him.
45. and was come to his *disciples*,
Joh. 1:35. and two of his *disciples*;
37. the two *disciples* heard him
2: 2. and his *disciples*, to the marriage.
11. his *disciples* believed on him.
12. his brethren, and his *disciples*:
17. his *disciples* remembered that it was
22. his *disciples* remembered that he had
3:22. came Jesus and his *disciples*
25. between (some) of John's *disciples*

Joh. 4: 1. more *disciples* than John,
    2. baptized not, but his *disciples*,
    8. For his *disciples* were gone
   27. upon this came his *disciples*,
   31. his *disciples* prayed him,
   33. Therefore said the *disciples*
  6: 3. there he sat with his *disciples*.
    8. One of his *disciples*, Andrew,
   11. distributed to the *disciples*, and the *disciples* to them
   12. he said unto his *disciples*,
   16. his *disciples* went down
   22. his *disciples* were entered, and that Jesus went not with his *disciples*
   — his *disciples* were gone away
   24. neither his *disciples*, they also
   60. Many therefore of his *disciples*,
   61. that his *disciples* murmured
   66. many of his *disciples* went back,
  7: 3. that thy *disciples* also may see
  8:31. (then) are ye my *disciples* indeed;
  9: 2. his *disciples* asked him,
   27. will ye also be his *disciples*?
   28. Thou art his *disciple*; but we are Moses' *disciples*.
 11: 7. saith he to (his) *disciples*,
   8. (His) *disciples* say unto him,
   12. Then said his *disciples*,
   54. there continued with his *disciples*.
 12: 4. Then saith one of his *disciples*,
   16. understood not his *disciples*
 13: 5. to wash the *disciples*' feet,
   22. Then the *disciples* looked
   23. one of his *disciples*, whom Jesus loved.
   35. know that ye are my *disciples*,
 15: 8. so shall ye be my *disciples*.
 16:17. Then said (some) of his *disciples*
   29. His *disciples* said unto him,
 18: 1. went forth with his *disciples*
   — into the which he entered, and his *disciples*.
   2 resorted thither with his *disciples*.
   15. and (so did) another *disciple*: that *disciple* was known
   16. Then went out that other *disciple*,
   17. (one) of this man's *disciples*?
   19. asked Jesus of his *disciples*,
   25. (one) of his *disciples*?
 19:26. and the *disciple* standing by,
   27. Then saith he to the *disciple*,
   — from that hour that *disciple*
   38. being a *disciple* of Jesus,
 20: 2. to the other *disciple*, whom Jesus loved,
   3. went forth, and that other *disciple*,
   4. and the other *disciple*
   8. Then went in also that other *disciple*,
   10. Then the *disciples* went away
   18. Mary Magdalene came and told the *disciples*
   19. where the *disciples* were assembled
   20. Then were the *disciples* glad,
   25. The other *disciples* therefore
   26. his *disciples* were within,
   30. in the presence of his *disciples*,
 21: 1. again to the *disciples*
   2. and two other of his *disciples*.
   4. but the *disciples* knew not
   7. Therefore that *disciple* whom Jesus
   8. And the other *disciples* came in a
   12. none of the *disciples* durst ask him,
   14. shewed himself to his *disciples*,
   20. seeth the *disciple* whom Jesus loved
   23. that that *disciple* should not
   24. This is the *disciple* which testifieth of these

Acts 1:15. in the midst of the *disciples*,
  6: 1. when the number of the *disciples*
   2. multitude of the *disciples*
   7. the number of the *disciples*
  9: 1. against the *disciples* of the Lord,
   10. a certain *disciple* at Damascus,
   19. certain days with the *disciples*
   25. Then the *disciples* took him
   26. to join himself to the *disciples*:
   — believed not that he was a *disciple*.
   38. and the *disciples* had heard
 11:26. And the *disciples* were called
   29. Then the *disciples*, every man
 13:52. And the *disciples* were filled
 14:20. Howbeit, as the *disciples*
   22. Confirming the souls of the *disciples*,
   28. abode long time with the *disciples*.
 15:10. upon the neck of the *disciples*,
 16: 1. a certain *disciple* was there,
 18:23. strengthening all the *disciples*.
   27. exhorting the *disciples* to
 19: 1. and finding certain *disciples*,
   9. and separated the *disciples*,
   30. the *disciples* suffered him not.
 20: 1. Paul called unto (him) the *disciples*,
   7. when the *disciples* came together
   30. to araw away *disciples* after them.
 21: 4. And finding *disciples*, we tarried
   16. of the *disciples* of Cæsarea,
   — an old *disciple*, with whom we should

μαθήτρια, *matheetria*.

Acts 9:36. a certain *disciple* named Tabitha,

μαίνομαι, *mainomai*.

Joh. 10:20. He hath a devil, and *is mad*;
Acts 12:15. they said unto her, Thou *art mad*.
 26:24. Paul, thou *art beside thyself*;
   25. I *am* not *mad*, most noble Festus;
1 Co. 14:23. will they not say that ye *are mad*?

μακαρίζω, *makarizo*.

Lu. 1:48. all generations *shall call* me *blessed*.
Jas. 5:11. we *count* them *happy* which endure.

μακάριος, *makarios*.

Mat. 5: 3. *Blessed* (are) the poor in spirit:
   4. *Blessed* (are) they that mourn:
   5. *Blessed* (are) the meek:
   6. *Blessed* (are) they which do hunger
   7. *Blessed* (are) the merciful:
   8. *Blessed* (are) the pure in heart:
   9. *Blessed* (are) the peacemakers:
   10. *Blessed* (are) they which are persecuted
   11. *Blessed* are ye, when (men)
 11: 6. And *blessed* is (he), whosoever
 13:16. But *blessed* (are) your eyes,
 16:17. *Blessed* art thou, Simon
 24:46. *Blessed* (is) that servant,
Lu. 1:45. *blessed* (is) she that believed:
 6:20. *Blessed* (be ye) poor:
   21. *Blessed* (are ye) that hunger now:
   — *Blessed* (are ye) that weep now:

Lu. 6:22. *Blessed* are ye, when men shall hate you, and when they
7:23. And *blessed* is (he), whosoever shall not
10:23. *Blessed* (are) the eyes which see
11:27. *Blessed* (is) the womb that
28. Yea rather, *blessed* (are) they
12:37. *Blessed* (are) those servants,
38. *blessed* are those servants.
43. *Blessed* (is) that servant, whom his lord
14:14. And thou shalt be *blessed*;
15. *Blessed* (is) he that shall eat
23:29. they shall say, *Blessed* (are) the barren,
Joh.13:17. *happy* are ye if ye do them.
20:29. *blessed* (are) they that have not seen,
Acts20:35. It is more *blessed* to give
26: 2. I think myself *happy*,
Ro. 4: 7. *Blessed* (are) they whose iniquities are
8. *Blessed* (is) the man to whom
14:22. *Happy* (is) he that condemneth not
1Co. 7:40. But she is *happier* if she
1Ti. 1:11. the glorious gospel of the *blessed* God,
6:15. the *blessed* and only Potentate,
Tit. 2:13. Looking for that *blessed* hope,
Jas. 1:12. *Blessed* (is) the man that endureth
25. this man shall be *blessed*
1Pet.3:14. for righteousness' sake, *happy* (are ye):
4:14. for the name of Christ, *happy* (are ye);
Rev. 1: 3. *Blessed* (is) he that readeth,
14:13. Write, *Blessed* (are) the dead
16:15. *Blessed* (is) he that watcheth,
19: 9. Write, *Blessed* (are) they which
20: 6. *Blessed* and holy (is) he that hath
22: 7. *blessed* (is) he that keepeth the sayings
14. *Blessed* (are) they that do his

μακαρισμός, *makarismos.*

Ro. 4: 6. describeth the *blessedness* of the man,
9. (Cometh) this *blessedness* then upon
Gal. 4:15. Where is then the *blessedness*

μάκελλον, *makellon.*

1Co.10:25. Whatsoever is sold in the *shambles*,

μακράν, *makran.*

(Acc of the adj.—ὁδὸν being understood.)

Mat. 8:30. there was a *good way off* from them
Mar 12:34. Thou art not *far* from the kingdom of
Lu. 7: 6. when he was now not *far* from the
15:20. when he was yet a *great way off*,
Joh.21: 8. they were not *far* from land,
Acts 2:39. and to all that are *afar off*,
17:27. though he be not *far* from every one
22:21. I will send thee *far* hence
Eph 2:13. ye who sometimes were *far off*
17. to you which were *afar off*,

μακρόθεν, *makrothen.*

Mat.26:58. Peter followed him *afar off*
27:55. women were there beholding *afar off*,
Mar 5: 6. when he saw Jesus *afar off*,
8: 3. divers of them came *from far*.
11:13. seeing a fig tree *afar off*
14:54. Peter followed him *afar off*,

Mar 15:40. women looking on *afar off*:
Lu. 16:23. and seeth Abraham *afar off*,
18:13. the publican, standing *afar off*,
22:54. Peter followed *afar off*.
23:49. stood *afar off*, beholding these things.
Rev.18:10. Standing *afar off* for the fear
15. shall stand *afar off* for the fear of
17. and as many as trade by sea, stood *afar off*,

μακροθυμέω, *makrothumeo.*

Mat.18:26. Lord, *have patience* with me,
29. *Have patience* with me, and I will
Lu. 18: 7. though he *bear long* with them?
1Co.13: 4. Charity *suffereth long*, (and) is kind;
1Th. 5:14. *be patient* toward all (men).
Heb 6:15. *after* he *had patiently endured*, he
Jas. 5: 7. *Be patient* therefore,
— and *hath long patience* for it,
8. *Be ye* also *patient*;
2Pet.3. 9. but *is longsuffering* to us-ward,

μακροθυμία, *makrothumia.*

Ro. 2: 4. and forbearance and *longsuffering*;
9:22. endured with much *longsuffering*
2Co. 6: 6. by *longsuffering*, by kindness,
Gal. 5:22. is love, joy, peace, *longsuffering*,
Eph 4: 2. with *longsuffering*, forbearing
Col. 1:11. and *longsuffering* with joyfulness;
3:12. humbleness of mind, meekness, *long-suffering*;
1Ti. 1:16. might shew forth all *longsuffering*,
2Ti. 3:10. faith, *longsuffering*, charity,
4: 2. with all *longsuffering* and doctrine.
Heb 6:12. through faith and *patience* inherit
Jas. 5:10. of suffering affliction, and of *patience*.
1Pet.3:20. when once the *longsuffering* of God
2Pet.3:15. account (that) the *longsuffering* of our

μακροθύμως, *makrothumōs.*

Acts26: 3. I beseech thee to hear me *patiently*.

μακρός, *makros.*

Mat.23:14(13). for a pretence make *long* prayer:
Mar 12:40. for a pretence make *long* prayers:
Lu. 15:13. his journey into a *far* country,
19:12. went into a *far* country to receive
20:47. for a shew make *long* prayers:

μακροχρόνιος, *makrokronios.*

Eph 6: 3. mayest *live long* on the earth.

μαλακία, *malakia.*

Mat. 4:23. all manner of *disease* among the people.
9:35. every sickness and every *disease*
10: 1. of sickness and all manner of *disease*.

μαλακός, *malakos.*

Mat.11: 8. A man clothed in *soft* raiment?

Mat.11: 8. they that wear *soft* (clothing)
Lu. 7:25. A man clothed in *soft* raiment?
1Co. 6: 9. nor adulterers, nor *effeminate*,

μάλιστα, *malista*.

Acts20:38. Sorrowing *most of all* for the words
25:26. and *specially* before thee, O king
26: 3. *Especially* (because I know) thee to be
Gal. 6:10. *especially* unto them who are
Phi. 4:22. *chiefly* they that are of Cæsar's
1Ti. 4:10. *specially* of those that believe.
5: 8. and *specially* for those of his own house,
17. *especially* they who labour in
2Ti. 4:13. (but) *especially* the parchments.
Tit. 1:10. *specially* they of the circumcision:
Philem.16. a brother beloved, *specially* to me,
2Pet.2:10. But *chiefly* them that walk after the flesh

μᾶλλον, *mallon*.

Mat. 6:26. Are ye not *much* better than they?
30. (shall he) not much *more* (clothe) you,
7:11. how much *more* shall your Father
10: 6. But go *rather* to the lost sheep of
25. how much *more* (shall they call)
28. but *rather* fear him which is able
18:13. he rejoiceth *more* of that (sheep),
25: 9. but go ye *rather* to them that sell,
27:24. but (that) *rather* a tumult was made,
Mar 5:26. nothing bettered, but *rather* grew worse,
7:36. so much *the more* a great deal
9:42. it is better for him (lit. it is good for him *rather*)
10:48. but he cried *the more* a great deal,
14:31. But he spake *the more* vehemently,
15:11. that he should *rather* release Barabbas
Lu. 5:15. But *so much the more* went there
10:20. but *rather* rejoice, because your
11:13. how much *more* shall (your) heavenly
12:24. how much *more* are ye better
28. how much *more* (will he clothe) you,
18:39. but he cried so much *the more*,
Joh. 3:19. men loved darkness *rather* than light,
5:18. Therefore the Jews sought *the more*
12:43. the praise of men *more* than the praise
19: 8. he was *the more* afraid ;
Acts 4:19. to hearken unto you *more* than unto God,
5:14. believers were *the more* added to the Lord,
29. to obey God *rather* than men.
9:22. Saul increased *the more* in strength,
20:35. *more* blessed to give than to receive.
22: 2. they kept *the more* silence:
27:11. *more* than those things which were spoken
Ro. 5: 9. Much *more* then, being now justified
10. much *more*, being reconciled,
15. much *more* the grace of God, and the gift
17. much *more* they which receive
8:34. yea *rather*, that is risen again,
11:12. how much *more* their fulness?
24. how much *more* shall these,
14:13. but judge this *rather*, that no man
1Co. 5: 2. and have not *rather* mourned,
6: 7. Why do ye not *rather* take wrong? why do ye not *rather* (suffer yourselves)
7:21. thou mayest be made free, use (it) *rather*.
9:12. of (this) power over you, (are) not we *rather* ?
15. better for me to die, than that (lit. it were good for me to die, *rather* than)

1Co.12:22. Nay, much *more* those members
14: 1. but *rather* that ye may prophesy.
5. but *rather* that ye prophesied:
18. with tongues *more* than ye all:
2Co. 2: 7. ye (ought) *rather* to forgive (him),
3: 8. of the spirit be *rather* glorious?
9. much *more* doth the ministration
11. much *more* that which remaineth
5: 8. willing *rather* to be absent from the body,
7: 7. so that I rejoiced *the more*.
13. and exceedingly *the more* joyed we
12: 9. gladly therefore will I *rather* glory
Gal. 4: 9. have known God, or *rather* are known of
27. hath many *more* children than she (lit. many are the children of the desolate *rather* than of her)
Eph. 4:28. but *rather* let him labour,
5: 4. but *rather* giving of thanks.
11. of darkness, but *rather* reprove (them).
Phi. 1: 9. your love may abound yet *more and more*
12. fallen out *rather* unto the furtherance
23. and to be with Christ; which is far better: (lit. which is much *rather* better)
2:12. but now much *more* in my absence,
3: 4. he might trust in the flesh, I *more* :
1Th. 4: 1. (so) ye would abound *more and more*.
10. that ye increase *more and more* ;
1Ti. 1: 4. *rather* than godly edifying
6: 2. but *rather* do (them) service,
2Ti. 3: 4. of pleasures *more* than lovers of God ;
Philem. 9. for love's sake I *rather* beseech
16. but how much *more* unto thee,
Heb. 9:14. How much *more* shall the blood of Christ,
10:25. and so much *the more*, as ye see
11:25. Choosing *rather* to suffer affliction
12: 9. shall we not much *rather* be in
13. but let it *rather* be healed.
25. much *more* (shall not) we (escape), if
2Pet.1:10. Wherefore *the rather*, brethren, give

μάμμη, *mammee*.

2Ti. 1: 5. dwelt first in thy *grandmother* Lois,

μαμμωνᾶς & μαμωνᾶς, *mammōnas* & *mamōnas*.

Mat. 6:24. Ye cannot serve God and *mammon*.
Lu. 16: 9. friends of the *mammon* of unrighteousness;
11. faithful in the unrighteous *mammon*,
13. Ye cannot serve God and *mammon*.

μανθάνω, *manthano*.

Mat. 9:13. But go ye and *learn* what (that) meaneth,
11:29. Take my yoke upon you, and *learn* of me;
24:32. Now *learn* a parable of the fig tree ;
Mar 13:28. Now *learn* a parable of the fig tree ;
Joh. 6:45. that hath heard, and *hath learned* of the
7:15. this man letters, *having* never *learned* ?
Acts23:27. *having understood* that he was a Roman.
Ro. 16:17. to the doctrine which ye *have learned* ;
1Co. 4: 6. that ye *might learn* in us not to think
14:31. that all *may learn*, and all may be
35. And if they will *learn* any thing,
Gal. 3: 2. This only would I *learn* of you,
Eph 4:20. But ye *have* not so *learned* Christ;
Phi. 4: 9. which ye *have* both *learned*,
11. for I *have learned*, in whatsoever

Col. 1: 7. As ye also *learned* of Epaphras
1Ti. 2:11. *Let* the woman *learn* in silence
    5: 4. let them *learn* first to shew piety
   13. withal they *learn* (to be) idle,
2Ti. 3: 7. Ever *learning*, and never able to come
   14. in the things which thou *hast learned*
    — knowing of whom thou *hast learned*
Tit. 3:14. And *let* our's also *learn* to
Heb 5: 8. yet *learned* he obedience by
Rev.14: 3. no man could *learn* that song but

μανία, *mania.*

Acts26:24. much learning doth make thee mad. (lit.
    turn thee unto *madness*)

μάννα, *manna.*

Joh. 6:31. Our fathers did eat *manna*
   49. Your fathers did eat *manna*
   58. not as your fathers did eat *manna,*
Heb 9: 4. the golden pot that had *manna,*
Rev. 2:17. to eat of the hidden *manna,*

μαντεύομαι, *mantuomai.*

Acts16:16. much gain *by soothsaying*

μαραίνομαι, *marainomai.*

Jas. 1:11. so also *shall* the rich man *fade away*

μαρὰν ἀθά, *maran atha.*

1Co.16:22. let him be Anathema *Maran-atha.*

μαργαρίτης, *margaritees.*

Mat. 7: 6. neither cast ye your *pearls* before
13:45. a merchant man, seeking goodly *pearls :*
   46. found one *pearl* of great price,
1Ti. 2: 9. or *pearls*, or costly array ;
Rev.17: 4. and precious stones and *pearls,*
18:12. and precious stones, and of *pearls,*
   16. and precious stones, and *pearls !*
21:21. the twelve gates (were) twelve *pearls;*
    every several gate was of one *pearl :*

μάρμαρον, *marmaron.*

Rev.18.12. of brass, and iron, and *marble,*

μάρτυρ & μάρτυς, *martur & martus.*

Mat 18:16. in the mouth of two or three *witnesses*
26:65. what further need have we of *witnesses ?*
Mar 14:63. What need we any further *witnesses ?*
Lu. 24:48. And ye are *witnesses* of these things.
Acts 1: 8. and ye shall be *witnesses* unto me
22. to be a *witness* with us of his resurrection.
2:32. whereof we all are *witnesses.*
3:15. whereof we are *witnesses.*
5:32. we are his *witnesses* of these things;

Acts 6:13. And set up false *witnesses,*
  7:58. the *witnesses* laid down their clothes
10:39. we are *witnesses* of all things
   41. unto *witnesses* chosen before of God,
13:31. who are his *witnesses* unto the people.
22:15. thou shalt be his *witness*
  20. when the blood of thy *martyr*
26:16. and a *witness* both of these things
Ro. 1: 9. For God is my *witness,*
2Co. 1:23. call God for a *record*
13: 1. In the mouth of two or three *witnesses*
Phi. 1: 8. For God is my *record*, how greatly
1Th. 2: 5. God (is) *witness:*
  10. Ye (are) *witnesses*, and God (also),
1Ti. 5:19. but before two or three *witnesses.*
  6:12. profession before many *witnesses.*
2Ti. 2: 2. of me among many *witnesses,*
Heb 10:28. under two or three *witnesses:*
12: 1. so great a cloud of *witnesses,*
1Pet.5: 1. a *witness* of the sufferings of Christ,
Rev. 1: 5. Christ, (who is) the faithful *witness,*
2:13. Antipas (was) my faithful *martyr,*
3:14. the faithful and true *witness,*
11: 3. give (power) unto my two *witnesses,*
17: 6. with the blood of the *martyrs*

μαρτυρέω -έομαι, *martureo -eomai.*

Mat 23:31. ye be witnesses unto yourselves,
Lu. 4:22. all *bare* him *witness*, and wondered
11:48. Truly ye *bear witness* that ye allow
Joh. 1: 7. to *bear witness* of the Light,
  8. to *bear witness* of that Light.
  15. John *bare witness* of him,
  32. And John *bare record,*
  34. I saw, and *bare record*
2:25. that any *should testify* of man:
3:11. and *testify* that we have seen ;
  26. to whom thou *barest witness,*
  28. yourselves *bear* me *witness,*
  32. seen and heard, that he *testifieth ;*
4:39. of the woman, *which testified,* He
  44. For Jesus himself *testified,*
5:31. If I *bear witness* of myself,
  32. another *that' beareth witness* of me ;
   — which he *witnesseth* of me
  33. and he *bare witness* unto the truth.
  36. works that I do, *bear witness* of me,
  37. *hath borne witness* of me.
  39. are they *which testify* of me.
7: 7. because I *testify* of it,
8:13. Thou *bearest record* of thyself ;
  14. Though I *bear record* of myself.
  18. I am one *that bear witness*
   — *beareth witness* of me.
10:25. they *bear witness* of me.
12:17. from the dead, *bare record.*
13:21. and *testified,* and said,
15:26. he *shall testify* of me:
  27. ye also shall *bear witness,*
18:23. *bear witness* of the evil:
  37. I *should bear witness* unto the truth.
19:35. he that saw (it) *bare record,*
21:24. *which testifieth* of these things,
Acts 6: 3. seven men *of honest report,*
10:22. and *of good report* among
  43. *give* all the prophets *witness,*
13:22. to whom also he *gave testimony, and* said,
14: 3. in the Lord, *which gave testimony* unto
15: 8. *bare* them *witness*, giving them the Holy
    Ghost,

MAP (472) ΜΑΣ

Acts16: 2. Which *was well reported of*
22: 5. *doth bear* me *witness*, and all
12. *having* a *good report* of all
23:11. so must thou *bear witness* also
26: 5. if they would *testify*, that after
22. *witnessing* both to small and
Ro. 3:21. *being witnessed* by the law and
10: 2. For I *bear* them *record* that they
1Co.15:15. we *have testified* of God
2Co. 8: 3. I *bear record*, yea, and beyond
Gal. 4:15. for I *bear* you *record*, that, if
Col. 4:13. For I *bear* him *record*, that he
1Th. 2:11. and *charged* every one of you,
1Ti. 5:10. *Well reported of* for good works;
6:13. *who* before Pontius Pilate *witnessed* a good confession;
Heb 7: 8. whom it is *witnessed* (lit. *being witnessed*) that
17. For he *testifieth*, Thou (art) a priest
10:15. the Holy Ghost also *is* a *witness*
11: 2. elders *obtained* a *good report*.
4. he *obtained witness* that he was righteous, God *testifying* of his gifts:
5. he *had* this *testimony*, that he
39. *having obtained* a *good report* through
1Joh.1: 2. and *bear witness*, and shew unto
4:14. and *do testify* that the Father
5: 6. it is the Spirit *that beareth witness*,
7. three *that bear record* in heaven,
8. three *that bear witness* in earth,
9. he *hath testified* of his Son.
10. the *record* that God *gave* (lit. *testified*) of his Son.
3Joh. 3. and *testified* of the truth that
6. Which *have borne witness* of thy
12. *hath good report* of all (men),
— yea, and we (also) *bear record*;
Rev. 1: 2. Who *bare record* of the word
22:16. sent mine angel *to testify* unto you
20. He *which testifieth* these things saith, Surely I come quickly;

μαρτυρία, marturia.

Mar 14:55. sought for *witness* against Jesus
56. but their *witness* agreed not
59. neither so did their *witness* agree
Lu. 22:71. What need we any further *witness?*
Joh. 1: 7. The same came for a *witness*,
19. this is the *record* of John,
3:11. and ye receive not our *witness*.
32. and no man receiveth his *testimony*.
33. that hath received his *testimony*
5:31. my *witness* is not true.
32. and I know that the *witness*
34. I receive not *testimony* from man:
36. I have greater *witness* than
8:13. thy *record* is not true.
14. my *record* is true:
17. that the *testimony* of two men is true.
19:35. and his *record* is true:
21:24. we know that his *testimony* is true.
Acts22:18. they will not receive thy *testimony*
1Ti. 3: 7. have a good *report* of them which
Tit. 1:13. This *witness* is true. Wherefore
1Joh.5: 9. If we receive the *witness* of men, the *witness* of God is greater: for this is the *witness* of God
10. hath the *witness* in himself:
— believeth not the *record* that God
11. And this is the *record*,

3Joh. 12. ye know that our *record* is true.
Rev. 1: 2. and of the *testimony* of Jesus Christ,
9. for the *testimony* of Jesus Christ.
6: 9. and for the *testimony* which they held:
11: 7. they shall have finished their *testimony*,
12:11. and by the word of their *testimony*;
17. and have the *testimony* of Jesus Christ.
19:10. and of thy brethren that have the *testimony* of Jesus:
— for the *testimony* of Jesus is
20: 4. beheaded for the *witness* of Jesus, and

μαρτύριον, marturion.

Mat. 8: 4. for a *testimony* unto them.
10:18. for a *testimony* against them
24:14. for a *witness* unto all nations;
Mar 1:44. for a *testimony* unto them.
6:11. for a *testimony* against them.
13: 9. for a *testimony* against them.
Lu. 5:14. for a *testimony* unto them.
9: 5. for a *testimony* against them.
21:13. shall turn to you for a *testimony*.
Acts 4:33. gave the apostles *witness* of the
7:44. had the tabernacle of *witness* in
1Co. 1: 6. Even as the *testimony* of Christ was
2: 1. unto you the *testimony* of God.
2Co. 1:12. the *testimony* of our conscience,
2Th. 1:10. because our *testimony* among you
1Ti. 2: 6. *to be testified* in due time.
2Ti. 1: 8. ashamed of the *testimony* of our Lord,
Heb 3: 5. for a *testimony* of those things
Jas. 5: 3. the rust of them shall be a *witness* against you,
Rev.15: 5. the temple of the tabernacle of the *testimony* in heaven

μαρτύρομαι, marturomai.

Acts20:26. I *take* you *to record* this day,
Gal. 5: 3. For I *testify* again to every man
Eph 4:17. and *testify* in the Lord,

μάρτυς see μάρτυρ.

μασσάομαι, massaomai.

Rev.16:10. they *gnawed* their tongues for pain,

μαστιγόω, mastigoō.

Mat 10:17. and they *will scourge* you
20:19. to mock, and *to scourge*,
23:34. and (some) of them *shall* ye *scourge*
Mar 10:34. and *shall scourge* him,
Lu. 18:33. And they *shall scourge* (him), and
Joh.19: 1. took Jesus, and *scourged* (him).
Heb 12: 6. and *scourgeth* every son whom

μαστίζω, mastizo.

Acts22:25. Is it lawful for you *to scourge*

μάστιξ, mastix.

Mar 3:10. as many as had *plagues*.

Mar. 5:29. that she was healed of that *plague*.
 34. and be whole of thy *plague*.
Lu. 7:21. of (their) infirmities and *plagues*,
Acts22:24. be examined by *scourging*;
Heb11:36. of (cruel) mockings and *scourgings*,

μαστός, mastos.

Lu. 11:27. and the *paps* which thou hast sucked.
 23:29. the *paps* which never gave suck.
Rev. 1:13. girt about the *paps* with a golden girdle.

ματαιολογία, mataiologia.

1Ti. 1: 6. turned aside unto *vain jangling*;

ματαιολόγος, mataiologos.

Tit. 1:10. unruly and *vain talkers*

ματαιόομαι, mataiöomai.

Ro. 1:21. but *became vain* in their imaginations,

μάταιος, mataios.

Acts14:15. turn from these *vanities* unto
1Co. 3:20. thoughts of the wise, that they are *vain*.
 15:17. your faith (is) *vain*;
Tit. 3: 9. for they are unprofitable and *vain*.
Jas. 1:26. this man's religion (is) *vain*.
1Pet.1:18. from your *vain* conversation

ματαιότης, mataiotees.

Ro. 8:20. was made subject to *vanity*,
Eph 4:17. in the *vanity* of their mind,
2Pet.2:18. swelling (words) of *vanity*,

μάτην, mateen.

Mat.15: 9. But *in vain* they do worship me,
Mar. 7: 7. Howbeit *in vain* do they

μάχαιρα, makaira.

Mat.10:34. not to send peace, but a *sword*.
 26:47. with *swords* and staves
 51. and drew his *sword*, and struck
 52. Put up again thy *sword* into his place: for
  all they that take the *sword* shall perish
  with the *sword*.
 55. with *swords* and staves for to take me?
Mar14:43. with *swords* and staves,
 47. drew a *sword*, and smote
 48. with *swords* and (with) staves
Lu. 21:24. shall fall by the edge of the *sword*,
 22:36. he that hath no *sword*,
 38. behold, here (are) two *swords*.
 49. shall we smite with the *sword*?
 52. with *swords* and staves?
Joh.18:10. Peter having a *sword* drew it,
 11. Put up thy *sword* into the sheath:

Acts12: 2. the brother of John with the *sword*.
 16:27. he drew out his *sword*,
Ro. 8:35. or peril, or *sword*?
 13: 4. beareth not the *sword* in vain:
Eph. 6:17. *sword* of the Spirit, which is the word
Heb 4:12. sharper than any twoedged *sword*,
 11:34. escaped the edge of the *sword*,
 37. were slain with the *sword*:
Rev. 6: 4. given unto him a great *sword*.
 13:10. he that killeth with the *sword* must be
  killed with the *sword*.
 14. which had the wound by a *sword*,

μάχη, makee.

2Co. 7: 5. without (were) *fightings*,
2Ti. 2:23. they do gender *strifes*.
Tit. 3: 9. and *strivings* about the law;
Jas. 4: 1. and *fightings* among you?

μάχομαι, makomai.

Joh. 6:52. The Jews therefore *strove* among themselves,
Acts 7:26. himself unto them as they *strove*,
2Ti. 2:24. servant of the Lord must not *strive*;
Jas. 4: 2. ye *fight* and war, yet ye have not,

μέ, me.
From ἐγώ.

Mat. 3:14. and comest thou to *me*?
 8: 2. thou canst make *me* clean.
 10:33. whosoever shall deny *me* before men,
 40. receiveth him that sent *me*.
 11:28. Come unto *me*, all (ye) that labour
 14:28. bid *me* come unto thee on the
 30. he cried, saying, Lord, save *me*.
 15: 8. and honoureth *me* with (their) lips;
 9. in vain they do worship *me*,
 22. Have mercy on *me*, O Lord,
 16:13. Whom do men say that *I*
 15. But whom say ye that *I* am?
 18:32. because thou desiredst *me*:
 19:14. forbid them not, to come unto *me*:
 17. Why callest thou *me* good?
 22:18. Why tempt ye *me*, (ye) hypocrites?
 23:39. Ye shall not see *me* henceforth,
 25:35. and ye gave *me* drink: I was a stranger,
  and ye took *me* in:
 36. Naked, and ye clothed *me*: I was sick,
  and ye visited *me*: I was in prison, and
  ye came unto *me*.
 42. and ye gave *me* no drink:
 43. a stranger, and ye took *me* not in: naked,
  and ye clothed *me* not: sick, and in
  prison, and ye visited *me* not.
 26:12. she did (it) for my burial. (lit. for the
  burying *me*)
 21. one of you shall betray *me*.
 23. the same shall betray *me*.
 32. But after *I* am risen again,
 34. thou shalt deny *me* thrice.
 35. Though *I* should die with thee,
 46. he is at hand that doth betray *me*.
 55. and staves for to take *me*?
 — and ye laid no hold on *me*.
 75. thou shalt deny *me* thrice.
 27:46. why hast thou forsaken *me*?

Mat.28:10. there shall they see *me*.
Mar. 1:40. thou canst make *me* clean.
　　5: 7. that thou torment *me* not.
　　6:22. Ask of *me* whatsoever thou wilt,
　　　 23. Whatsoever thou shalt ask of *me*,
　　7: 6. This people honoureth *me* with
　　　 7. in vain do they worship *me*,
　　8:27. Whom do men say that *I* am?
　　　 29. But whom say ye that *I* am?
　　　 38. shall be ashamed of *me*
　　9:19. bring him unto *me*.
　　　 37. but him that sent *me*.
　　　 39. lightly speak evil of *me*.
　 10:14. Suffer the little children to come unto *me*,
　　　 18. Why callest thou *me* good?
　　　 36. that *I* should do for you?
　　　 47. have mercy on *me*.
　　　 48. son of David, have mercy on *me*.
　 12:15. Why tempt ye *me*?
　 14:18. which eateth with me shall betray *me*.
　　　 28. But after that *I* am risen,
　　　 30. thou shalt deny *me* thrice.
　　　 31. If *I* should die with thee,
　　　 42. lo, he that betrayeth *me* is at hand.
　　　 48. and (with) staves to take *me*?
　　　 49. and ye took *me* not:
　　　 72. thou shalt deny *me* thrice.
　 15:34. why hast thou forsaken *me*?
Lu. 1:43. mother of my Lord should come to *me*?
　　　 48. shall call *me* blessed.
　　2:49. How is it that ye sought *me*? wist ye not
　　　　　that *I* must be about my
　　4:18. anointed *me* to preach the gospel to the
　　　　　poor; he hath sent *me* to heal
　　　 43. *I* must preach the kingdom
　　5:12. thou canst make *me* clean.
　　6:46. And why call ye *me*, Lord, Lord,
　　　 47. Whosoever cometh to *me*,
　　8:28. I beseech thee, torment *me* not.
　　9:18. Whom say the people that *I* am?
　　　 20. But whom say ye that *I* am?
　　　 26. whosoever shall be ashamed of *me*
　　　 48. receiveth him that sent *me* :
　 10:16. despiseth him that sent *me*.
　　　 35. when *I* come again, I will repay
　　　 40. that my sister hath left *me* to serve
　 11: 6. in his journey is come to *me*,
　　　 18. because ye say that *I* cast out
　 12: 9. he that denieth *me* before men
　　　 14. Man, who made *me* a judge or
　 13:33. *I* must walk to day,
　　　 35. Ye shall not see *me*, until
　 14:18. I pray thee have *me* excused.
　　　 19. I pray thee have *me* excused.
　　　 26. If any (man) come to *me*,
　 15:19. make *me* as one of thy hired
　 16: 4. they may receive *me* into their
　　　 24. Father Abraham, have mercy on *me*,
　 18: 3. Avenge *me* of mine adversary.
　　　 5. by her continual coming she weary *me*.
　　　 16. little children to come unto *me*,
　　　 19. Why callest thou *me* good?
　　　 38. son of David, have mercy on *me*.
　　　 39. son of David, have mercy on *me*.
　 19: 5. for to day *I* must abide at thy house.
　　　 27. which would not that *I* should reign
　 20:23. Why tempt ye *me*?
　 22:15. with you before *I* suffer:
　　　 21. the hand of him that betrayeth *me*
　　　 34. thrice deny that thou knowest *me*.
　　　 61. thou shalt deny *me* thrice.
　 24:39. handle *me*, and see ;

Joh. 1:33. but he that sent *me* to baptize
　　　 48(49). Whence knowest thou *me*?
　　2:17. hath eaten *me* up.
　　4:34. is to do the will of him that sent *me*,
　　5: 7. to put *me* into the pool:
　　　 11. He that made *me* whole,
　　　 24. and believeth on him that sent *me*,
　　　 30. the Father which hath sent *me*.
　　　 36. that the Father hath sent *me*.
　　　 37. which hath sent *me*,
　　　 40. ye will not come to *me*,
　　　 43. and ye receive *me* not:
　　6:26. Ye seek *me*, not because ye
　　　 35. he that cometh to *me*
　　　 36. ye also have seen *me*, and
　　　 37. and him that cometh to *me*
　　　 38. but the will of him that sent *me*.
　　　 39. Father's will which hath sent *me*,
　　　 40. the will of him that sent *me*,
　　　 44. No man can come to *me*, except the Father
　　　　　which hath sent *me*
　　　 45. of the Father, cometh unto *me*.
　　　 57. As the living Father hath sent *me*,
　　　 — so he that eateth *me*, even he
　　　 65. no man can come unto *me*, except
　　7:16. but his that sent *me*.
　　　 19. Why go ye about to kill *me*?
　　　 28. he that sent *me* is true,
　　　 29. and he hath sent *me*.
　　　 33. (then) I go unto him that sent *me*.
　　　 34. Ye shall seek *me*, and shall not find
　　　 36. this that he said, Ye shall seek *me*,
　　　 37. let him come unto *me*, and drink.
　　8:16. but I and the Father that sent *me*.
　　　 18. the Father that sent *me*
　　　 21. and ye shall seek *me*,
　　　 26. but he that sent *me* is true;
　　　 28. but as my Father hath taught *me*,
　　　 29. And he that sent *me* is with me: the Father
　　　　　hath not left *me* alone;
　　　 37. but ye seek to kill *me*,
　　　 40. But now ye seek to kill *me*,
　　　 42. but he sent *me*
　　　 46. Which of you convinceth *me* of sin?
　　　 49. and ye do dishonour *me*.
　　　 54. it is my Father that honoureth *me*;
　　9: 4. the works of him that sent *me*,
　 10:15. As the Father knoweth *me*,
　　　 16. them also *I* must bring,
　　　 17. Therefore doth my Father love *me*,
　　　 32. of those works do ye stone *me*?
　 11:42. that thou hast sent *me*.
　 12:27. shall I say? Father, save *me* from this
　　　　　hour:
　　　 44. but on him that sent *me*.
　　　 45. he that seeth me seeth him that sent *me*.
　　　 49. but the Father which sent *me*,
　 13:13. Ye call *me* Master and Lord:
　　　 20. receiveth him that sent *me*.
　　　 21. one of you shall betray *me*.
　　　 33. Ye shall seek *me* :
　　　 38. till thou hast denied *me* thrice.
　 14: 7. If ye had known *me*,
　　　 9. yet hast thou not known *me*,
　　　 15. If ye love *me*, keep my
　　　 19. and the world seeth *me* no more; but ye
　　　　　see *me* :
　　　 21. he it is that loveth *me* : and he that loveth
　　　　　me
　　　 23. If a man love *me*,
　　　 24. He that loveth *me* not
　　　 — but the Father's which sent *me*.

Joh.14:28. If ye loved *me*, ye would rejoice,
15: 9. As the Father hath loved *me*,
16. Ye have not chosen *me*,
21. they know not him that sent *me*.
25. They hated *me* without a cause.
16: 5. to him that sent *me*; and none of you asketh *me*,
10. and ye see *me* no more;
16. and ye shall not see *me*: and again, a little while, and ye shall see *me*,
17. not see *me*: and again, a little while, and ye shall see *me*:
19. not see *me*: and again, a little while, and ye shall see *me*?
17: 5. O Father, glorify thou *me*
8. believed that thou didst send *me*.
21. may believe that thou hast sent *me*.
23. may know that thou hast sent *me*,
24. for thou lovedst *me* before the
25. have known that thou hast sent *me*.
26. wherewith thou hast loved *me*
18:21. Why askest thou *me*?
23. why smitest thou *me*?
19:11. he that delivered *me* unto thee
20:21. as (my) Father hath sent *me*,
29. Thomas, because thou hast seen *me*,
21:15. lovest thou *me* more than these?
16. (son) of Jonas, lovest thou *me*?
17. (son) of Jonas, lovest thou *me*?
— the third time, Lovest thou *me*?
Acts 2:28. thou shalt make *me* full of joy
7:28. Wilt thou kill *me*?
8:31. except some man should guide *me*?
36. what doth hinder *me* to be
9: 4. why persecutest thou *me*?
6. what wilt thou have *me* to do?
17. hath sent *me*, that thou mightest
10:29. for what intent ye have sent for *me*?
11:11. sent from Cæsarea unto *me*.
15. And as *I* began to speak,
12:11. and hath delivered *me*
13:25. Whom think ye that *I* am?
16:15. If ye have judged *me* to be
30. what must *I* do to be saved?
18:21. *I* must by all means keep
19:21. After *I* have been there, *I* must also see Rome.
20:23. that bonds and afflictions abide *me*.
22: 7. Saul, Saul, why persecutest thou *me*?
8. And he said unto *me*, I am Jesus
10. And the Lord said unto *me*,
13. Came unto *me*, and stood, and said
17. *I* was in a trance;
21. And he said unto *me*, Depart:
23: 3. sittest thou to judge *me* after the law, and commandest *me* to be
18. Paul the prisoner called *me*
22. hast shewed these things to *me*.
24:12. they neither found *me* in the
13. Neither can they prove (lit. establish against *me*)
18. found *me* purified in the
19. if they had ought against *me*.
25:10. where *I* ought to be judged:
11. no man may deliver *me* unto them.
26: 5. Which knew *me* from the beginning,
13. shining round about *me* and them
14. I heard a voice speaking unto *me*,
— why persecutest thou *me*?
21. the Jews caught *me* in the temple,
28. Almost thou persuadest *me* to be
28:18. when they had examined *me*,

Ro. 7:11. by the commandment, deceived *me*;
23. and bringing *me* into captivity
24. who shall deliver *me*
8: 2. hath made *me* free from
9:20. Why hast thou made *me* thus?
15:16. That *I* should be the minister of
19. *I* have fully preached the gospel
1Co. 1:17. Christ sent *me* not to baptize,
4: 4. but he that judgeth *me* is the Lord.
16: 6. ye may bring *me* on my journey
11. that he may come unto *me*:
2Co. 2: 2. who is he then that maketh *me* glad,
3. of whom *I* ought to rejoice;
13. because *I* found not Titus
7: 7. so that *I* rejoiced the more.
11:16. Let no man think *me* a fool;
— yet as a fool receive *me*,
32. desirous to apprehend *me*:
12: 6. above that which he seeth *me* (to be),
7. of Satan to buffet *me*,
11. ye have compelled *me*:
21. lest, when I come again, my God will humble *me*
Gal. 1:15. who separated *me* from my
2:20. the Son of God, who loved *me*,
4:12. ye have not injured *me* at all.
14. but received *me* as an angel of God,
18. not only when *I* am present
Eph. 6:20. as *I* ought to speak.
Phi. 1: 7. because *I* have you in my heart;
2:30. your lack of service toward *me*.
4:13. Christ which strengtheneth *me*.
Col. 4: 4. as *I* ought to speak.
1Ti. 1:12. Jesus our Lord, who hath enabled *me*, for that he counted *me* faithful,
2Ti. 1:15. in Asia be turned away from *me*;
16. for he oft refreshed *me*,
17. he sought *me* out very diligently,
3:11. out of (them) all the Lord delivered *me*.
4: 9. to come shortly unto *me*:
16. but all (men) forsook *me*:
17. stood with me, and strengthened *me*;
18. the Lord shall deliver *me*
Tit. 3:12. be diligent to come unto *me* to
Heb. 3: 9. When your fathers tempted *me*; proved *me*,
8:11. for all shall know *me*,
11:32. the time would fail *me* to tell
Rev.17: 3. So he carried *me* away in the
21: 9. And there came unto *me* one of
10. he carried *me* away in the spirit

μεγαλαυχέω, *megalaukeo*.

Jas. 3: 5. and *boasteth great things*.

μεγαλεῖα, *megalïa*.

Lu. 1:49. hath done to me *great things*;
Acts 2:11. the *wonderful works* of God.

μεγαλειότης, *megaliotees*.

Lu. 9:43. amazed at the *mighty power* of God.
Acts19:27. her *magnificence* should be destroyed,
2Pet. 1:16. were eyewitnesses of his *majesty*.

μεγαλοπρεπής, megaloprepees.

2Pet. 1:17. a voice to him from the *excellent* glory,

μεγαλύνω, megaluno.

Mat.23: 5. and *enlarge* the borders of their
Lu.   1:46. My soul *doth magnify* the Lord,
      58. *had shewed great* mercy upon her ;
Acts 5:13. but the people *magnified* them.
     10:46. speak with tongues, and *magnify* God.
     19:17. name of the Lord Jesus *was magnified*.
2Co.10:15. that we shall *be enlarged* by you
Phi. 1:20. now also Christ *shall be magnified* in my

μεγάλως, megalōs.

Phi. 4:10. I rejoiced in the Lord *greatly*,

μεγαλωσύνη, megalōsunee.

Heb. 1: 3. on the right hand of the *Majesty* on high;
     8: 1. throne of the *Majesty* in the heavens ;
Jude   25. (be) glory and *majesty*, dominion

μέγας, megas.

Mat. 2:10. with exceeding *great* joy.
     4:16. which sat in darkness saw *great* light ;
     5:19. shall be called *great* in the kingdom
     35. it is the city of the *great* King.
     7:27. and *great* was the fall of it.
     8:24. there arose a *great* tempest
     26. and there was a *great* calm.
    15:28. O woman, *great* (is) thy faith:
    20:25. and they that are *great* exercise
     26. whosoever will be *great* among you,
    22:36. which (is) the *great* commandment
     38. the first and *great* commandment.
    24:21. then shall be *great* tribulation,
     24. and shall shew *great* signs
     31. with a *great* sound of a trumpet,
    27:46. Jesus cried with a *loud* voice,
     50. had cried again with a *loud* voice,
     60. he rolled a *great* stone to the door
    28: 2. there was a *great* earthquake:
     8. with fear and *great* joy ;
Mar. 1:26. and cried with a *loud* voice,
     4:32. and shooteth out *great* branches ;
     37. there arose a *great* storm
     39. and there was a *great* calm.
     41. And they feared exceedingly, (lit. a *great* fear)
     5: 7. And cried with a *loud* voice,
     11. a *great* herd of swine feeding.
     42. with a *great* astonishment.
    10:42. and their *great* ones exercise
     43. whosoever will be *great* among
    13: 2. Seest thou these *great* buildings?
    14:15. a *large* upper room furnished
    15:34. Jesus cried with a *loud* voice, saying,
     37. cried with a *loud* voice, and gave up
    16: 4. for it was very *great*.
Lu. 1:15. For he shall be *great* in the
     32. He shall be *great*, and shall be
     42. she spake out with a *loud* voice,
     2: 9. and they were sore afraid. (lit. feared a *great* fear)

Lu. 2:10. I bring you good tidings of *great* joy,
     4:25. when *great* famine was
     33. and cried out with a *loud* voice,
     38. was taken with a *great* fever ;
     5:29. Levi made him a *great* feast
     6:49. the ruin of that house was *great*.
     7:16. That a *great* prophet is risen up
     8:28. and with a *loud* voice said,
     37. they were taken with *great* fear:
     9:48. the same shall be *great*.
    13:19. and waxed a *great* tree ;
    14:16. A certain man made a *great* supper,
    16:26. there is a *great* gulf fixed:
    17:15. and with a *loud* voice glorified God,
    19:37. and praise God with a *loud* voice
    21:11. And *great* earthquakes shall be
     — and *great* signs shall there be
     23. there shall be *great* distress
    22:12. he shall shew you a *large* upper room
    23:23. were instant with *loud* voices,
     46. Jesus had cried with a *loud* voice,
    24:52. to Jerusalem with *great* joy:
Joh. 6:18. by reason of a *great* wind
     7:37. that *great* (day) of the feast,
    11:43. he cried with a *loud* voice,
    19:31. for that sabbath day was an *high* day,
    21:11. the net to land full of *great* fishes,
Acts 2:20. before that *great* and notable day
     4:33. And with *great* power gave the
     — and *great* grace was upon them
     5: 5. and *great* fear came on all
     11. And *great* fear came upon all
     6: 8. did *great* wonders and miracles
     7:11. and Chanaan, and *great* affliction:
     57. they cried out with a *loud* voice,
     60. and cried with a *loud* voice,
     8: 1. there was a *great* persecution
     2. and made *great* lamentation
     7. crying with *loud* voice,
     8. there was *great* joy in that city.
     9. that himself was some *great* one:
     10. from the least to the *greatest*, saying, This man is the *great* power of God.
     13. beholding the miracles and signs (lit. signs and *great* miracles)
    10:11. as it had been a *great* sheet
    11: 5. as it had been a *great* sheet,
     28. that there should be *great* dearth
    14:10. Said with a *loud* voice,
    15: 3. they caused *great* joy unto all the
    16:26. there was a *great* earthquake,
     28. Paul cried with a *loud* voice,
    19:27. of the *great* goddess Diana
     28. *Great* (is) Diana of the Ephesians.
     34. *Great* (is) Diana of the Ephesians.
     35. of the *great* goddess Diana,
    23: 9. And there arose a *great* cry:
    26:22. witnessing both to small and *great*,
     24. Festus said with a *loud* voice,
Ro. 9: 2. That I have *great* heaviness
1Co. 9:11. (is it) a *great* thing if we
    16: 9. For a *great* door and effectual
2Co.11:15. (it is) no *great* thing if his ministers
Eph. 5:32. This is a *great* mystery:
1Ti. 3:16. *great* is the mystery of
     6: 6. with contentment is *great* gain.
2Ti. 2:20. But in a *great* house there are
Tit. 2:13. glorious appearing of the *great* God
Heb. 4:14. that we have a *great* high priest,
     8:11. from the least to the *greatest*,
    10:21. And (having) an *high* priest over
     35. which hath *great* recompence

Heb11:24. Moses, when he was come *to years,*
13:20. that *great* Shepherd of the sheep,
Jude　6. unto the judgment of the *great* day.
Rev. 1:10. and heard behind me a *great* voice,
2·22. into *great* tribulation,
5: 2. proclaiming with a *loud* voice,
12. Saying with a *loud* voice,
6: 4. there was given unto him a *great* sword.
10. with a *loud* voice, saying,
12. there was a *great* earthquake ;.
13. is shaken of a *mighty* wind.
17. the *great* day of his wrath is come ;
7: 2. he cried with a *loud* voice to
10. And cried with a *loud* voice,
14. which came out of *great* tribulation,
8: 8. as it were a *great* mountain
10. there fell a *great* star from
13. saying with a *loud* voice,
9: 2. as the smoke of a *great* furnace ;
14. bound in the *great* river Euphrates.
10: 3. cried with a *loud* voice,
11: 8. in the street of the *great* city,
11. and *great* fear fell upon them
12. they heard a *great* voice
13. there a *great* earthquake,
15. there were *great* voices in heaven,
17. hast taken to thee thy *great* power,
18. that fear thy name, small and *great ;*
19. an earthquake, and *great* hail.
12: 1. a *great* wonder in heaven ;
3. a *great* red dragon,
9. the *great* dragon was cast out,
10. I heard a *loud* voice
12. having *great* wrath, because he knoweth
14. two wings of a *great* eagle,
13: 2. and his seat, and *great* authority.
5. a mouth speaking *great* things
13. he doeth *great* wonders,
16. he caused all, both small and *great,*
14: 2. as the voice of a *great* thunder:
7. Saying with a *loud* voice,
8. that *great* city, because the
9. saying with a *loud* voice,
15. crying with a *loud* voice to
18. cried with a *loud* cry to
19. into the *great* winepress of the
15: 1. *great* and marvellous, seven angels
3. *Great* and marvellous (are) thy works,
16: 1. I heard a *great* voice out of
9. scorched with *great* heat,
12. his vial upon the *great* river
14. of that *great* day of God Almighty.
17. a *great* voice out of the temple
18. there was a *great* earthquake,
— so mighty an earthquake, (and) so *great.*
19. the *great* city was divided
— *great* Babylon came in remembrance
21. upon men a *great* hail out of
— plague thereof was exceeding *great.*
17: 1. judgment of the *great* whore,
5. MYSTERY, BABYLON THE *GREAT,*
6. I wondered with *great* admiration.
18. is that *great* city,
18: 1. having *great* power ;
2. cried mightily with a *strong* voice, saying,
Babylon the *great* is fallen,
10. Alas, alas that *great* city Babylon,
16. Alas, alas that *great* city,
18. What (city is) like unto this *great*
19. Alas, alas that *great* city,
21. a stone like a *great* millstone,
— shall that *great* city Babylon

Rev.19: 1. I heard a *great* voice of much
2. hath judged the *great* whore,
5. that fear him, both small and *great.*
17. he cried with a *loud* voice,
— unto the supper of the *great* God ;
18. both small and *great.*
20: 1. and a *great* chain in his hand.
11. I saw a *great* white throne,
. 12. I saw the dead, small and *great,*
21: 3. I heard a *great* voice out of
10. to a *great* and high mountain, and shewed
me that *great* city,
12. had a wall *great* and high,

　　See also μείζων and μέγιστος.

μέγεθος, *megethos.*

Eph. 1:19. And what (is) the exceeding *greatness* of
his power to us-ward

μεγιστᾶνες, *megistanes.*

Mar 6:21. made a supper to his *lords,*
Rev. 6:15. and the *great* men, and the rich
18:23. thy merchants were the *great men* of the
earth ;

μέγιστος, *megistos.*

2Pet.1: 4. *exceeding great* and precious promises:

μεθερμηνεύομαι, *methermeenŭomai.*

Mat. 1:23. *being interpreted* is, God with us.
Mar 5:41. which is, *being interpreted,* Damsel,
15:22. *being interpreted,* The place of a skull.
34. which is, *being internreted.* Mv God,
Joh. 1: 41(42). *being interpreted* the Christ.
Acts 4:36. which is, *being interpreted,* The son of
13: 8. for so *is* his name *by interpretation*

μέθη, *methee.*

Lu. 21:34. and *drunkenness,* and cares of this life,
Ro. 13:13. not in rioting and *drunkenness,*
Gal. 5:21. murders, *drunkenness,* revellings,

μεθιστάνω, μεθίστημι, *methistano,*
methisteemi.

Lu. 16: 4. when I *am put out of* the stewardship,
Acts13:22. *when* he *had removed* him,
19:26. and *turned away* much people,
1Co.13: 2. so that I could *remove* mountains,
Col. 1:13. and *hath translated* (us) into

μεθοδεία, *methodia.*

Eph. 4:14. whereby they lie in wait to deceive ; (lit.
unto *circumvention* of deceit)
6:11. to stand against the *wiles* of the devil.

μεθόρια, methoria.

Mar. 7:24. went into the *borders* of Tyre and

μεθύσκομαι, methuskomai.

Lu. 12:45. eat and drink, and *to be drunken;*
Eph. 5:18. And *be* not *drunk* with wine,
1Th. 5: 7. they *that be drunken* are drunken in

μέθυσος, methusos.

1Co. 5:11. or a *drunkard,* or an extortioner;
6:10. nor *drunkards,* nor revilers, nor

μεθύω, methuo.

Mat.24:49. and drink with the *drunken;*
Joh. 2:10. when men *have well drunk,*
Acts 2:15. these *are* not *drunken,* as
1Co.11:21. and another *is drunken.*
1Th. 5: 7. *are drunken* in the night.
Rev.17: 2. *have been made drunk* with the wine
6. *drunken* with the blood of the saints,

μεῖζον, mīzon. adv.

Mat.20:31. but they cried *the more,*

μειζότερος, mīzoteros.

3Joh. 4. I have no *greater* joy than to hear

μείζων, μεῖζον, mīzōn, mīzon.

Mat.11:11. hath not risen a *greater* than John
— is *greater* than he.
12: 6. is (one) *greater* than the temple.
13:32. is the *greatest* among herbs, (lit. *greater*
than herbs)
18: 1. Who is the *greatest* (lit. *greater*) in the
kingdom
4. the same is *greatest* in the kingdom
23:11. But he that is *greatest* among you
17. for whether is *greater,* the gold,
19. whether (is) *greater,* the gift, or the
Mar. 4:32. becometh *greater* than all herbs,
9:34. who (should be) the *greatest.*
12:31. commandment *greater* than these.
Lu. 7:28. there is not a *greater* prophet than
— is *greater* than he.
9:46. which of them should be *greatest.*
12:18. pull down my barns, and build *greater;*
22:24. should be accounted the *greatest.*
26. but he that is *greatest* among you,
27. For whether (is) *greater,* he that sitteth
Joh. 1:50(51). thou shalt see *greater* things than
4:12. Art thou *greater* than
5:20. *greater* works than these,
36. But I have *greater* witness
8:53. Art thou *greater* than our father
10:29. is *greater* than all;
13:16. The servant is not *greater* than his lord;
neither he that is sent *greater*
14:12. and *greater* (works) than these
28. for my Father is *greater* than I.

Joh.15:13. *Greater* love hath no man than this,
20. The servant is not *greater* than
19:11. hath the *greater* sin.
Ro. 9:12. The *elder* shall serve the younger.
1Co.13:13. but the *greatest* of these (is) charity.
14: 5. for *greater* (is) he that prophesieth
Heb 6:13. could swear by no *greater,*
16. men verily swear by the *greater:*
9:11. by a *greater* and more perfect
11:26. the reproach of Christ *greater* riches
Jas. 3: 1. receive the *greater* condemnation.
4: 6. But he giveth *more* grace.
2Pet. 2:11. which are *greater* in power and might,
1Joh.3:20. God is *greater* than our heart,
4: 4. *greater* is he that is in you,
5: 9. the witness of God is *greater:*

μέλαν, melan. subs.

2Co. 3: 3. written not with *ink,*
2Joh. 12. I would not (write) with paper and *ink:*
3Joh. 13. I will not with *ink* and pen write

μέλας, melas.

Mat. 5:36. one hair white or *black.*
Rev. 6: 5. and lo a *black* horse;
12. sun became *black* as sackcloth of hair,

μέλει, melī. impers. verb.

Mat.22:16. neither *carest* thou for any
Mar. 4:38. Master, *carest* thou not that we
12:14. and *carest* for no man:
Lu. 10:40. Lord, *dost* thou not *care* that
Joh.10:13. and *careth* not for the sheep.
12: 6. not that he *cared* for the poor;
Acts18:17. And Gallio *cared* for none of
1Co. 7:21. *care* not for it:
9: 9. *Doth* God *take care* for oxen?
1Pet.5: 7. for he *careth* for you.

μελετάω, meletao.

Mar13:11. neither *do ye premeditate:*
Acts 4:25. Why did the heathen rage, and the people
imagine vain things?
1Ti. 4:15. *Meditate* upon these things;

μέλι, meli.

Mat. 3: 4. his meat was locusts and wild *honey.*
Mar 1: 6. and he did eat locusts and wild *honey;*
Rev.10: 9. in thy mouth sweet as *honey.*
10. in my mouth sweet as *honey:*

μελίσσιος, melissios.

Lu. 24:42. and of an *honeycomb.*

μέλλω, mello.

Mat. 2:13. Herod *will* seek the young child
3: 7. to flee from the wrath *to come?*

Mat.11:14. *which was for* to come.
  12:32. neither in the (world) *to come.*
  16:27. the Son of man *shall* come in
  17:12. Likewise *shall* also the Son of
    22. The Son of man *shall* be betrayed
  20:22. that I *shall* drink of,
  24: 6. And ye *shall* hear of wars
Mar 10:32. *what things should* happen unto him,
  13: 4. when all these things *shall* be fulfilled?
Lu. 3: 7. from the wrath *to come?*
    7: 2. was sick, and *ready* to die.
    9:31. which he *should* accomplish
     44. the Son of man *shall* be delivered
  10: 1 whither he himself *would* come.
  13: 9. *after that* thou shalt cut it down.
  19: 4. he *was* to pass that (way).
    11. of God *should* immediately appear.
  21: 7. when these things *shall* come to pass?
    36. *that shall* come to pass,
  22:23. *that should* do this thing.
  24:21. he *which should* have redeemed
Joh. 4:47. for he *was at the point* of death.
    6: 6. he himself knew what he *would* do.
    15. that they *would* come and take him
    71. he it was that *should* betray him,
   7:35. Whither *will* he go, that we shall not find
      him? *will* he go unto
    39. that believe on him *should* receive:
  11:51. that Jesus *should* die for
  12: 4. *which should* betray him,
    33. what death he *should* die.
  14:22. that thou *wilt* manifest thyself
  18:32. what death he *should* die.
Acts 3: 3. seeing Peter and John *about to* go
   5:35. what ye *intend* to do as touching
  11:28. that there *should* be great dearth
  12: 6. when Herod *would* have brought
  13:34. no more to return (lit. *being* no more
      about to return) to corruption,
  16:27. and *would* have killed himself,
  17:31. in the which he *will* judge the world
  18:14. *when* Paul *was* now *about to* open
  19:27. magnificence *should* be destroyed,
  20: 3. for him, *as* he *was about* to sail into
    7. *ready* to depart on the morrow;
    13. there *intending* to take in Paul:
   — *minding* himself to go afoot.
    38. that they *should* see his face no more.
  21:27. the seven days *were almost* ended,
    37. *as* Paul *was* to be led into the
  22:16. And now why *tarriest* thou?
    26. Take heed what thou doest: (lit. *art about*
      to do)
    29. *which should* have examined him:
  23: 3. God *shall* smite thee,
    15. as *though* ye *would* enquire something
    20. as *though* they *would* enquire somewhat
    27. and *should have* been killed
    30. told me how that the Jews laid wait (lit.
      the lying wait being told me as *about to*
      be)
  24:15. that there *shall* be a resurrection
    25. and judgment *to come,*
  25: 4. he himself *would* depart shortly
  26: 2. *because* I *shall* answer for myself
    22. did say *should* come:
    23. and *should* shew light unto the
  27: 2. *meaning* to sail by the coasts of Asia;
    10. *will* be with hurt and much damage,
    30. as *though* they *would have* cast
    33. while the day *was coming* on,
  28: 6. they looked when he *should have* swollen,

Ro. 4:24. to whom it *shall* be imputed,
    5:14. figure of him *that was to come.*
    8:13. after the flesh, ye *shall* die:
     18. glory *which shall* be revealed in us.
     38. nor *things to come,*
1Co. 3:22. or *things to come;* all are your's;
Gal. 3:23. *which should afterwards* be revealed.
Eph 1:21. but also in *that which is to come:*
Col. 2:17. a shadow of *things to come;*
1Th. 3: 4. that we *should* suffer tribulation;
1Ti. 1:16. *which should hereafter* believe
    4: 8. and of *that which is to come.*
    6:19. against the *time to come,*
2Ti. 4: 1. *who shall* judge the quick and
Heb. 1:14. *who shall* be heirs of salvation?
    2: 5. put in subjection the world *to come,*
    6: 5. the powers of the world *to come,*
    8: 5. *when* he *was about* to make the
    9:11. an high priest of good things *to come,*
   10: 1. a shadow of good things *to come,*
    27. which *shall* devour the adversaries.
  11: 8. which he *should after* receive
    20. concerning *things to come.*
  13:14. but we seek one *to come.*
Jas. 2:12. as they *that shall* be judged
1Pet.5: 1. glory *that shall* be revealed:
2Pet.2: 6. *that after should* live ungodly;
Rev. 1:19. the things which *shall* be hereafter;
   2:10. which thou *shalt* suffer: behold, the devil
     shall cast (some) of you
    3: 2. that *are ready* to die:
    10. *which shall* come upon all the
    16. I *will* spue thee out of my mouth.
   6:11. *that should* be killed as they (were),
   8:13. angels, *which are yet* to sound!
  10: 4. I *was about* to write:
    7. when he *shall begin* to sound,
  12: 4. *which was ready* to be delivered,
    5. who was (lit. *is about*) to rule all nations
  17: 8. and *shall* ascend out of the

μέλος, *melos.*

Mat. 5:29. that one of thy *members* should
    30. that one of thy *members* should perish,
Ro. 6:13. Neither yield ye your *members*
   — and your *members* (as) instruments
    19. for as ye have yielded your *members*
   — now yield your *members* servants
   7: 5. did work in our *members*
    23. another law in my *members,*
   — law of sin which is in my *members.*
  12: 4. as we have many *members* in one body,
    and all *members* have not
    5. every one *members* one of another.
1Co. 6:15. your bodies are the *members* of Christ?
    shall I then take the *members* of Christ,
    and make (them) the *members* of
  12:12. and hath many *members,* and all the mem-
    bers of that
    14. the body is not one *member,*
    18. now hath God set the *members*
    19. if they were all one *member,*
    20. now (are they) many *members,* yet
    22. those *members* of the body, which
    25. but (that) the *members* should have
    26. And whether one *member* suffer, all the
    members suffer with it; or one *member*
    be honoured, all the *members* rejoice
    27. and *members* in particular.
Eph. 4:25. we are *members* one of another.

Eph. 5:30. we are *members* of his body,
Col. 3: 5. Mortify therefore your *members*
Jas. 3: 5. the tongue is a little *member*,
6. so is the tongue among our *members*,
4: 1. lusts that war in your *members?*

μεμβράνα, *membrana*.

2Ti. 4:13. and the books, (but) especially the *parchments*.

μέμφομαι, *memphomai*.

Mar. 7: 2. with unwashen, hands, they *found fault*.
Ro. 9:19. Why *doth* he yet *find fault?*
Heb. 8: 8. For *finding fault* with them,

μεμψίμοιρος, *mempsimoiros*.

Jude 16. These are murmurers, *complainers*,

μέν, *men*.

Found mostly with the first of two words or clauses that are in contrast, the second having δε; but sometimes combined with οὐν, which is denoted by [2]

Mat. 3:11. I *indeed* baptize you with water
9:37. The harvest *truly* (is) plenteous,
10:13. And if)(the house be worthy,
13: 4. some (seeds))(fell by the way side,
8. some)(an hundredfold, some
23. some)(an hundredfold, some sixty,
32. Which *indeed* is the least of all seeds:
16: 3. ye can discern the face)(of the sky;
14. Some)((say that thou art) John the
17:11. Elias *truly* shall first come,
20:23. Ye shall drink *indeed* of my cup,
21:35. and beat one)(, and killed another,
22: 5. one)(to his farm, another to his
8. The wedding)(is ready,
23:27. which *indeed* appear beautiful
28. Even so ye also outwardly)(appear
25:15. And unto one)(he gave five talents,
33. And he shall set the sheep)(on his
26:24. The Son of man)(goeth as it is written
41. the spirit *indeed* (is) willing,
Mar 1: 8. I *indeed* have baptized you with
4: 4. some)(fell by the way side,
9:12. Elias *verily* cometh first, and restoreth
10:39. Ye shall *indeed* drink of the cup
12: 5. beating some)(, and killing some.
14:21. The Son of man *indeed* goeth,
38. The spirit *truly* (is) ready, but the flesh
16:19. *So* [2] then after the Lord had spoken
Lu. 3:16. I *indeed* baptize you with
18. And many other things)(? in his
8: 5. some)(fell by the way side;
10: 2. The harvest *truly* (is) great,
6. And if)(the son of peace be there,
11:48. for they *indeed* killed them, and ye
13: 9. And if)(it bear fruit, (well):
22:22. And *truly* the Son of man goeth, as
23:33. one)(on the right hand, and the other
41. And we *indeed* justly; for we receive
56. and rested)(the sabbath day
Joh. 7:12. for some)(said, He is a good man: others
10:41. and said, John)(did no miracle:

Joh. 11: 6. he abode)(two days still in the same
16: 9. Of sin)(, because they believe not
22. And ye)([2] now therefore have sorrow:
19:24. These things)([2] therefore the soldiers did.
32. and brake the legs of the first)(,
20:30. many other signs *truly* [2] did Jesus
Acts 1: 1. The former treatise)(have I made,
5. For John *truly* baptized with
6. When they)([2] therefore were come
18. Now)([2] this man purchased a field
2:41. Then)([2] they that gladly received his
3:21. Whom the heaven)(must receive until
22. For Moses *truly* said unto the fathers,
4:16. for that *indeed* a notable miracle
5:23. The prison *truly* found we shut
41. And they)([2] departed from the presence
8: 4. Therefore)([2] they that were scattered
25. And)([2] they, when they had testified
9: 7. hearing)(a voice, but seeing no man.
31. Then)([2] had the churches rest
11:16. John *indeed* baptized with water;
19. Now)([2] they which were scattered abroad
12: 5. Peter)([2] therefore was kept in prison:
13: 4. So)([2] they, being sent forth by
36. For David)(, after he had served
14: 3. Long time therefore)([2] abode they
4. and part)(held with the Jews,
12. And they called Barnabas)(, Jupiter;
15: 3. And)([2] being brought on their way by
30. So)([2] when they were dismissed,
16: 5. And)([2] so were the churches established
17:12. Therefore)([2] many of them believed;
17. Therefore)([2] disputed he in the
30. And)([2] the times of this ignorance
32. of the dead, some)(mocked: and others
18:14. If)([2] it were a matter of wrong
19: 4. John *verily* baptized with the
32. Some therefore)([2] cried one thing,
38. Wherefore)([2] if Demetrius, and the
21:39. I am)(a man (which am) a Jew of
22: 3. I am *verily* a man (which am) a Jew,
9. they that were with me saw *indeed*
23: 8. For the Sadducees)(say that there is no
18. So)([2] he took him, and brought
22. So)([2] the chief captain (then) let the
31. Then)([2] the soldiers, as it was
25: 4. But)([2] Festus answered, that Paul
11. For if)(I be an offender, or have
26: 4. My manner of life)([2] from my youth,
9. I *verily* [2] thought with myself,
27:21. Sirs, ye should)(have hearkened unto
41. and the forepart)(stuck fast,
44. and some)(on (broken pieces) of the
28: 5. And)([2] he shook off the beast into
22. for as concerning)(this sect,
24. And some)(believed the things
Ro. 1: 8. First,)(I thank my God through Jesus
2: 7. To them)(who by patient continuance
8. and do not obey)(the truth,
25. circumcision *verily* profiteth, if
3: 2. chiefly)(, because that unto them were
5:16. for the judgment)((was) by one
6:11. to be dead *indeed* unto sin,
7:12. Wherefore the law)((is) holy,
25. So then with the mind)(I myself
8:10. the body)((is) dead because of sin;
17. heirs)(of God, and joint-heirs with
9:21. to make one vessel)(unto honour,
10: 1. my heart's desire)(and prayer to God
11:13. inasmuch as)(I am the apostle of the
22. on them which fell)(, severity;
28. As concerning)(the gospel, (they are)

Ro. 14: 2. For one)(believeth that he may eat
     5. One man)(esteemeth one day
   20. All things *indeed* (are) pure; but
  16:19. wise)(unto that which is good, and
1Co. 1:12. every one of you saith, I)(am of Paul;
   18. is to them)(that perish foolishness;
   23. unto the Jews)(a stumblingblock,
  2:15. he that is spiritual judgeth)(all things,
  3: 4. For while one saith, I)(am of Paul;
  5: 3. For I *verily*, as absent in body,
  6: 4. If)(² then ye have judgments of things
   7. Now)(² therefore there is utterly a fault
  7: 7. one)(after this manner, and another
  9:24. they which run in a race run all)(,
   25.)(² Now they (do it) to obtain
  11: 7. For a man *indeed* ought not to
   14. that, if a man)(have long hair,
   18. For first)(of all, when ye come
   21. and one)(is hungry, and another is
  12: 8. For to one)(is given by the Spirit
   20. many)(members, yet but one body.
   28. And God hath set some)(in the church,
  14:17. For thou *verily* givest thanks well,
  15:39. but (there is) one)((kind of) flesh of
   40. the glory of the celestial (is) one)(,
   51. We shall not all)(sleep,
2Co. 2:16. To the one)((we are) the savour of
  4:12. So then death)(worketh in us,
  8:17. For *indeed* he accepted the exhortation;
  9: 1. For as touching)(the ministering
  10: 1. who in presence)((am) base among you,
   10. For (his) letters)(, say they, (are)
  11: 4. For if)(he that cometh preacheth
  12:12. *Truly* the signs of an apostle
Gal. 4: 8. Howbeit then)(, when ye knew not God,
   23. But he)((who was) of the bondwoman,
   24. the one)(from the mount Sinai,
Eph. 4:11. he gave *some*)(, apostles; and some,
Phi. 1:15. Some *indeed* preach Christ even of
   16. The one)(preach Christ of contention,
   28. which is to them)(an evident token
  2:23. Him)(² therefore I hope to send
  3: 1. to me *indeed* (is) not grievous,
  13(14). forgetting those things)(which are
Col. 2:23. Which things have *indeed* a shew
1Th. 2:18. *even* I Paul, once and again;
2Ti. 1:10. who hath abolished)(death,
  2:19. Nevertheless (lit. but *indeed*) the foundation of God
   20. and some)(to honour, and some to
  4: 4. shall turn away (their) ears from the
   truth)(,
Tit. 1:15. Unto the pure all things)((are) pure:
Heb. 1: 7. And of the angels)(he saith,
  3: 5. And Moses *verily* (was) faithful
  6:16. For men *verily* swear by the
  7: 2. first)(being by interpretation
   5. And *verily* they that are of the sons
   8. And here)(men that die receive tithes;
   11. If)(² therefore perfection were by the
   18. For there is *verily* a disannulling
  21(20). For those priests)(were made without an oath;
   23. And they *truly* were many priests,
  8: 4. For if)(he were on earth,
  9: 1. Then *verily*² the first (covenant)
   6. the priests went always into the first)(
   tabernacle,
   23. necessary that the patterns)(of things
  10:11. And every priest)(standeth daily
   33. Partly)(, whilst ye were made a
  11:15. And *truly*, if they had been mindful

Heb 12: 9. Furthermore we have had fathers)(of our
  12:10. For they *verily* for a few days
   11. Now no chastening for the present)(
Jas. 3:17. wisdom that is from above is first)(pure,
1Pet. 1:20. Who *verily* was foreordained
  2: 4. disallowed *indeed* of men,
   14. for the punishment)(of evildoers,
  3:18. being put to death)(in the flesh,
  4: 6. might be judged)(according to men in
   the flesh,
   14. on their part)(he is evil spoken of,
Jude   8. defile the flesh)(, despise dominion,
   10. speak evil of those things)(which they
   know not:
   22. And of some)(have compassion,

See also μενοῦν γε and μέντοι.

μενοῦνγε, *menounge.*

Lu. 11:28. *Yea rather*, blessed (are) they that
Ro. 9:20. *Nay but*, O man, who art thou that
  10:18. *Yes verily*, their sound went into all
Phi. 3: 8. *Yea doubtless*, and I count all things

μέντοι, *mentoi.*

Joh. 4:27. *yet* no man said, What seekest thou?
  7:13. *Howbeit* no man spake openly
  12:42. *Nevertheless* (ομως μ.) among the chief
  20: 5. *yet* went he not in.
  21: 4. *but* the disciples knew not that it
2Ti. 2:19. *nevertheless* the foundation of God
Jas. 2: 8. If)(ye fulfil the royal law
Jude   8. *Likewise* (ομοιως μ.) also these (filthy)

μένω, *meno.*

Mat.10:11. and there *abide* till ye go thence.
  11:23. it would *have remained* until this
  26:38. *tarry* ye here, and watch with me.
Mar. 6:10. there *abide* till ye depart from
  14:34. *tarry* ye here, and watch.
Lu. 1:56. Mary *abode* with her about three
  8:27. neither *abode* in (any) house,
  9: 4. there *abide*, and thence depart.
  10: 7. And in the same house *remain*,
  19: 5. for to day I must *abide* at thy house.
  24:29. constrained him, saying, *Abide* with us:
   — And he went in *to tarry* with them.
Joh. 1:32. and it *abode* upon him.
   33. and *remaining* on him,
   38(39). Master, where *dwellest* thou?
   39(40). They came and saw where he *dwelt*,
   and *abode* with him that day:
  2:12. they *continued* there not many days.
  3:36. the wrath of God *abideth* on him.
  4:40. that he would *tarry* with them: and he
   abode there two days.
  5:38. ye have not his word *abiding* in you:
  6:27. for that meat *which endureth* unto
   56. *dwelleth* in me, and I in him.
  7: 9. he *abode* (still) in Galilee.
  8:31. If ye *continue* in my word,
   35. the servant *abideth* not in the house for
   ever: (but) the Son *abideth* ever.
  9:41. therefore your sin *remaineth*.
  10:40. and there he *abode*.
  11: 6. he *abode* two days still in the
  12:24. ground and die, it *abideth* alone:
   34. that Christ *abideth* for ever:

Joh. 12:46. *should* not *abide* in darkness.
14:10. the Father *that dwelleth* in me,
16. that he *may abide* with you for ever ;
17. for he *dwelleth* with you,
25. *being* (yet) *present* with you.
15: 4. *Abide* in me, and I in you.
— except it *abide* in the vine ; no more can ye, except ye *abide* in me.
5. He *that abideth* in me,
6. If a man *abide* not in me,
7. If ye *abide* in me, and my words *abide* in
9. *continue* ye in my love.
10. ye *shall abide* in my love ;
— and *abide* in his love.
11. that my joy *might remain*
16. (that) your fruit *should remain:*
19:31. that the bodies *should* not *remain* upon
21:22. If I will that he *tarry* till I come,
23. If I will that he *tarry* till I come,
Acts 5: 4. *Whiles* it *remained*, was it not thine own?
(lit. *did* it not *remain* to thee)
9:43. that he *tarried* many days in Joppa
16:15. come into my house, and *abide*
18: 3. he *abode* with them, and wrought:
20. When they desired (him) *to tarry*
20: 5. These going before *tarried for* us at
15. and *tarried* at Trogyllium; *and*
23. and afflictions *abide* me.
21: 7. *abode* with them one day.
8. and *abode* with him.
27:31. Except these *abide* in the ship,
41. stuck fast, and *remained* unmoveable,
28:16. Paul was suffered *to dwell* by himself
30. Paul *dwelt* two whole years in
Ro. 9:11. the purpose of God according to election *might stand,*
1Co. 3:14. If any man's work *abide*
7: 8. if they *abide* even as I.
11. *let* her *remain* unmarried,
20. *Let* every man *abide* in the same
24. *let* every man,...therein *abide* with God.
40. she is happier if she so *abide*,
13:13. now *abideth* faith, hope, charity,
15: 6. the greater part *remain* unto this
2Co. 3:11. much more that *which remaineth*
14. *remaineth* the same vail
9: 9. his righteousness *remaineth* for ever.
Phi. 1:25. I know that I *shall abide* and
1Ti. 2:15. if they *continue* in faith and
2Ti. 2:13. he *abideth* faithful: he cannot deny
3:14. *continue* thou in the things
4:20. Erastus *abode* at Corinth:
Heb 7: 3. *abideth* a priest continually.
24. because he *continueth* ever,
10:34. and an *enduring* substance.
12:27. cannot be shaken *may remain.*
13: 1. *Let* brotherly love *continue.*
14. here have we no *continuing* city,
1Pet. 1:23. which liveth and *abideth* for ever.
25. the word of the Lord *endureth* for ever.
1Joh. 2: 6. He that saith he *abideth* in him
10. *abideth* in the light,
14. the word of God *abideth* in you,
17. doeth the will of God *abideth* for ever.
19. they would (no doubt) *have continued* with us:
24. *Let* that therefore *abide* in you,
— shall *remain* in you ye also *shall continue*
27. received of him *abideth* in you,
— ye *shall abide* in him.
28. little children, *abide* in him ;
3: 6. *Whosoever abideth* in him

1Joh. 3: 9. his seed *remaineth* in him:
14. He that loveth not (his) brother *abideth* in death.
15. no murderer hath eternal life *abiding* in
17. how *dwelleth* the love of God in him?
24. *dwelleth* in him, and he in him. And hereby we know that he *abideth* in us,
4:12. God *dwelleth* in us,
13. that we *dwell* in him,
15. God *dwelleth* in him,
16. he *that dwelleth* in love *dwelleth* in God, and God in him.
2Joh. 2. For the truth's sake, *which dwelleth* in us,
9. and *abideth* not in the doctrine
— He *that abideth* in the doctrine
Rev. 17:10. he must *continue* a short space.

μέριμνα, merimna.

Mat. 13:22. the *care* of this world,
Mar. 4:19. the *cares* of this world,
Lu. 8:14. are choked with *cares* and riches
21:34. and *cares* of this life,
2Co. 11:28. the *care* of all the churches.
1Pet. 5: 7. Casting all your *care* upon him ;

μεριμνάω, merimnao.

Mat. 6:25. *Take* no *thought* for your life,
27. Which of you *by taking thought* can
28. why *take* ye *thought* for raiment ?
31. Therefore *take* no *thought,*
34. *Take* therefore no *thought* for the morrow: for the morrow *shall take thought*
10:19. *take* no *thought* how or what ye shall
Lu. 10:41. thou *art careful* and troubled
12:11. *take* ye no *thought* how or what thing
22. *Take* no *thought* for your life,
25. which of you *with taking thought*
26. why *take* ye *thought* for the rest?
1Co. 7:32. He that is unmarried *careth* for
33. he that is married *careth* for the
34. *careth* for the things of the Lord,
— *careth* for the things of the world,
12:25. *should* have the same *care* one for
Phi. 2:20. who *will* naturally *care* for your state.
4: 6. *Be careful* for nothing ;

μερίζω, merizo.

Mat. 12:25. Every kingdom *divided* against itself
— city or house *divided* against itself
26. he *is divided* against himself;
Mar. 3:24. if a kingdom *be divided* against
25. if a house *be divided* against itself,
26. and *be divided*, he cannot stand,
6:41. the two fishes *divided* he among them all.
Lu. 12:13. that he *divide* the inheritance with me.
Ro. 12: 3. as God *hath dealt* to every man
1Co. 1:13. *Is* Christ *divided* ?
7:17. as God *hath distributed* to every man,
34. There *is difference* (also) *between*
2Co. 10:13. which God *hath distributed* to us,
Heb 7: 2. Abraham *gave* a tenth *part* of all ;

μερίς, meris.

Lu. 10:42. Mary hath chosen that good *part,*
Acts 8:21. Thou hast neither *part* nor lot

Acts16:12. the chief city of that *part* of Macedonia,
2Co. 6:15. what *part* hath he that believeth
Col. 1:12. us meet to be partakers of the inheritance
(lit. unto the *share* of the inheritance)

μερισμός, *merismos.*

Heb 2: 4. and *gifts* of the Holy Ghost,
4:12. even to the *dividing asunder* of soul and
spirit,

μεριστής, *meristees.*

Lu. 12:14. made me a judge or a *divider* over you?

μέρος, *meros.*

Mat. 2:22. into the *parts* of Galilee:
15:21. departed into the *coasts* of Tyre and
16:13. Jesus came into the *coasts* of Cæsarea
24:51. and appoint (him) his *portion* with
Mar. 8:10. came into the *parts* of Dalmanutha.
Lu. 11:36. full of light, having no *part* dark,
12:46. will appoint him his *portion* with
15:12. give me the *portion* of goods that
24:42. they gave him a *piece* of a broiled fish,
Joh.13: 8. If I wash thee not, thou hast no *part* with
19:23. and made four *parts*, to every soldier a
part ;
21: 6. Cast the net on the right *side*
Acts 2:10. and in the *parts* of Libya
5: 2. brought a certain *part*, and laid
19: 1. passed through the upper *coasts*
27. not only this our *craft* is in danger
20: 2. when he had gone over those *parts*,
23: 6. one *part* were Sadducees, and
9. of the Pharisees' *part* arose, and
Ro. 11:25. blindness in *part* is happened to Israel,
15:15. boldly unto you in *some sort*,
24. be *somewhat* filled with your
1Co.11:18. and I partly believe it. (lit. I believe some
part)
12:27. and members in *particular*.
13: 9. For we know in *part*, and we prophesy in
part.
10. then that which is in *part* shall
12. now I know in *part ;*
14:27. and (that) by *course ;* and let one
2Co. 1:14. acknowledged us in *part*,
2: 5. he hath not grieved me, but in *part :*
3:10. had no glory in this *respect*,
9: 3. should be in vain in this *behalf ;*
Eph. 4: 9. into the lower *parts* of the earth?
16. in the measure of every *part*,
Col. 2:16. or in *respect* of an holyday,
Heb. 9: 5. we cannot now speak particularly. (lit.
according to *part*)
1Pet. 4:16. let him glorify God on this *behalf*.
Rev.16:19. was divided into three *parts*,
20: 6. hath *part* in the first resurrection :
21: 8. shall have their *part* in the lake
22:19. God shall take away his *part* out of the
book of life,

μεσημβρία, *mescembria.*

Acts 8:26. Arise, and go toward the *south*
22: 6. nigh unto Damascus about *noon,*

μεσιτεύω, *mesituo.*

Heb. 6:17. *confirmed* (it) by an oath :

μεσίτης, *mesitees.*

Gal. 3:19. in the hand of a *mediator*.
20. Now a *mediator* is not (a mediator) of one,
1Ti. 2: 5. one *mediator* between God and men,
Heb. 8: 6. is the *mediator* of a better covenant,
9:15. he is the *mediator* of the new testament,
12:24. And to Jesus the *mediator* of the new

μεσονύκτιον, *mesonuktion.*

Mar 13:35. or at *midnight*, or at the
Lu. 11: 5. and shall go unto him at *midnight*,
Acts16:25. at *midnight* Paul and Silas prayed,
20: 7. continued his speech until *midnight*.

μέσος, *mesos.*

Mat.10:16. as sheep in the *midst* of wolves :
13:25. sowed tares *among* the wheat,
49. sever the wicked from *among* the just,
14: 6. Herodias danced before them, (lit. in the
midst)
24. ship was now in the *midst* of the sea,
18: 2. and set him in the *midst* of them,
20. there am I in the *midst* of them.
25: 6. And at *midnight* there was a cry
Mar. 3: 3. had the withered hand, Stand forth. (lit.
into the *midst*)
6:47. the ship was in the *midst* of the sea,
7:31. through the *midst* of the coasts of
9:36. and set him in the *midst* of them :
14:60. high priest stood up in the *midst*,
Lu. 2:46. sitting in the *midst* of the doctors,
4:30. passing through the *midst* of them
35. the devil had thrown him in the *midst*
5:19. into the *midst* before Jesus.
6: 8. and stand forth in the *midst*.
8: 7. And some fell *among* thorns ;
10: 3. as lambs *among* wolves.
17:11. he passed through the *midst* of Samaria
21:21. in the *midst* of it depart out ;
22:27. I am *among* you as he that serveth.
55. a fire in the *midst* of the hall,
— Peter sat down *among* them.
23:45. was rent in the *midst*.
24:36. Jesus himself stood in the *midst*
Joh. 1:26. there standeth one *among* you,
8: 3. when they had set her in the *midst*,
9. and the woman standing in the *midst*.
59. through the *midst* of them,
19:18. and Jesus in the *midst*.
20:19. and stood in the *midst*, and saith
26. stood in the *midst*, and said, Peace
Acts 1:15. Peter stood up in the *midst*
18. he burst asunder in the *midst*,
2:22. God did by him in the *midst* of you,
4: 7. had set them in the *midst*,
17:22. Paul stood in the *midst* of Mars' hill,
33. Paul departed from *among* them.
23:10. by force from *among* them,
26:13. At *midday*, O king, I saw
27:21. Paul stood forth in the *midst* of them,
27. about *midnight* the shipmen
1Co. 5: 2. be taken away from *among* you.

1Co. 6: 5.able to judge *between* his brethren?
2Co. 6:17.come out from *among* them,
Phi. 2:15.in the *midst* of a crooked and
Col. 2:14.and took it out of the *way*,
1Th. 2: 7.But we were gentle *among* you,
2Th. 2: 7.until he be taken out of the *way*.
Heb. 2:12.in the *midst* of the church will I
Rev. 1:13.in the *midst* of the seven candlesticks
　　 2: 1.walketh in the *midst* of the seven
　　　 7.which is in the *midst* of the paradise
　　 4: 6.in the *midst* of the throne, and round
　　 5: 6.in the *midst* of the throne and of the four
　　　　　 beasts, and in the *midst* of the elders,
　　 6: 6.in the *midst* of the four beasts
　　 7:17.in the *midst* of the throne
　　22: 2.In the *midst* of the street of it,

μεσότοιχον, *mesotoikon*.

Eph. 2:14.hath broken down the *middle wall* of

μεσουράνημα, *mesouraneema*.

Rev. 8:13.flying through the *midst of heaven*,
　　14: 6.angel fly in the *midst of heaven*,
　　19:17.that fly in the *midst of heaven*,

μεσόω, *mesoō*.

Joh. 7:14.*about* the *midst* of the feast

μεστός, *mestos*.

Mat.23:28.within ye are *full* of hypocrisy
Joh.19:29.was set a vessel *full* of vinegar:
　　21:11.*full* of great fishes,
Ro. 1:29.*full* of envy, murder, debate,
　　15:14.that ye also are *full* of goodness,
Jas. 3: 8.unruly evil, *full* of deadly poison.
　　　17.*full* of mercy and good fruits,
2Pet. 2:14.Having eyes *full* of adultery,

μεστόω, *mestoō*.

Acts 2:13.These men are *full* of new wine.

μετά, *meta*.

[a] marks where it is followed by an accusative, and
　　 not a genitive case.

Mat. 1:12.*after*[a] they were brought to Babylon,
　　　23.being interpreted is, God *with* us.
　　 2: 3.and all Jerusalem *with* him.
　　　11.the young child *with* Mary his mother,
　　 4:21.in a ship *with* Zebedee their
　　 5:25.thou art in the way *with* him;
　　　41.go *with* him twain.
　　 8:11.and shall sit down *with* Abraham,
　　 9:11.Why eateth your Master *with* publicans
　　　15.as the bridegroom is *with* them?
　　12: 3.and they that were *with* him;
　　　 4.neither for them which were *with* him,
　　　30.He that is not *with* me is against me;
　　　　 and he that gathereth not *with* me
　　　41.in judgment *with* this generation,
　　　42.in the judgment *with* this generation,

Mat.12:45.and taketh *with* himself seven
　　13:20.*with* joy receiveth it;
　　14: 7.promised *with* an oath to give
　　15:30.having *with* them (those that were)
　　16:27.in the glory of his Father *with* his angels;
　　17: 1.And *after*[a] six days Jesus taketh
　　　 3.Moses and Elias talking *with* him.
　　　17.how long shall I be *with* you?
　　18:16.take *with* thee one or two more,
　　　23.which would take account *of* his servants.
　　19:10.If the case of the man be so *with* (his)
　　20: 2.when he had agreed *with* the labourers
　　　20.*with* her sons, worshipping
　　21: 2.and a colt *with* her:
　　22:16.their disciples *with* the Herodians,
　　24:29.Immediately *after*[a] the tribulation
　　　30.*with* power and great glory.
　　　31.shall send his angels *with* a great sound
　　　49.to eat and drink *with* the drunken ·
　　　51.his portion *with* the hypocrites:
　　25: 3.and took no oil *with* them:
　　　 4.oil in their vessels *with* their lamps.
　　　10.they that were ready went in *with* him
　　　19.*After*[a] a long time the lord of those ser-
　　　　 vants cometh, and reckoneth *with* them.
　　　31.all the holy angels *with* him,
　　26: 2.Ye know that *after*[a] two days is
　　　11.the poor always *with* you;
　　　18.at thy house *with* my disciples.
　　　20.he sat down *with* the twelve.
　　　23.dippeth (his) hand *with* me in the
　　　29.when I drink it new *with* you in
　　　32.But *after*[a] I am risen again,
　　　36.Then cometh Jesus *with* them unto
　　　38.and watch *with* me.
　　　40.could ye not watch *with* me one
　　　47.and *with* him a great multitude *with*
　　　　 swords and staves,
　　　51.one of them which were *with* Jesus
　　　55.*with* swords and staves for to
　　　58.and sat *with* the servants,
　　　69.Thou also wast *with* Jesus
　　　71.This (fellow) was also *with* Jesus
　　　72.again he denied *with* an oath,
　　　73.And *after*[a] a while came unto (him)
　　27:34.vinegar to drink mingled *with* gall:
　　　41.*with* the scribes and elders, said,
　　　53.out of the graves *after*[a] his resurrection,
　　　54.and they that were *with* him,
　　　62.that followed (lit. is *after*[a]) the day of the
　　　63.*After*[a] three days I will rise again.
　　　66.and setting a watch. (lit. *with* the watch)
　　28: 8.*with* fear and great joy;
　　　12.were assembled *with* the elders.
　　　20.I am *with* you alway,
Mar 1:13.and was *with* the wild beasts;
　　　14.Now *after*[a] that John was put in prison,
　　　20.in the ship *with* the hired servants,
　　　29.*with* James and John.
　　　36.Simon and they that were *with* him
　　 2:16.saw him eat *with* publicans and
　　　— and drinketh *with* publicans and
　　　19.while the bridegroom is *with* them? as
　　　　 long as they have the bridegroom *with*
　　　　 them,
　　　25.and they that were *with* him?
　　 3: 5.round about on them *with* anger,
　　　 6.took counsel *with* the Herodians
　　　 7.*with* his disciples to the sea:
　　　14.that they should be *with* him,
　　 4:16.receive it *with* gladness;
　　　36.were also *with* him other little ships.

Mar 5:18. prayed him that he might be *with* him.
    24. And (Jesus) went *with* him;
    40. and them that were *with* him,
  6:25. *with* haste unto the king,
    50. he talked *with* them,
  8:10. into a ship *with* his disciples,
    14. in the ship *with* them more than
    31. and *after*ᵃ three days rise again.
    38. *with* the holy angels.
  9: 2. And *after*ᵃ six days Jesus taketh
     8. save Jesus only *with* themselves.
    24. and said *with* tears,
 10:30. *with* persecutions; and in the
 11:11. unto Bethany *with* the twelve.
 13:24. *after*ᵃ that tribulation, the sun shall be
    26. *with* great power and glory.
 14: 1. *After*ᵃ two days was (the feast of)
     7. the poor *with* you always,
    14. passover *with* my disciples?
    17. he cometh *with* the twelve.
    18. which eateth *with* me shall betray me.
    20. that dippeth *with* me in the dish.
    28. But *after*ᵃ that I am risen,
    33. And he taketh *with* him Peter and
    43. *with* him a great multitude *with* swords
       and staves,
    48. *with* swords and (with) staves to take
    54. and he sat *with* the servants,
    62. and coming *in* the clouds of heaven.
    67. thou also wast *with* Jesus of Nazareth.
    70. And a little *after*,ᵃ they that stood by
 15: 1. *with* the elders and scribes
     7. bound *with* them that had made
    28. he was numbered *with* the transgressors.
    31. among themselves *with* the scribes,
 16:10. told them that had been *with* him,
    12. *After*ᵃ that he appeared in another form
    19. *after*ᵃ the Lord had spoken unto

Lu. 1:24. And *after*ᵃ those days his wife
    28. the Lord (is) *with* thee:
    39. into the hill country *with* haste,
    58. had shewed great mercy *upon* her;
    66. the hand of the Lord was *with* him.
    72. To perform the mercy (promised) *to* our
       fathers,
  2:36. had lived *with* an husband seven years
    46. *after*ᵃ three days they found him
    51. And he went down *with* them,
  5:27. *after*ᵃ these things he went forth,
    29. that sat down *with* them.
    30. Why do ye eat and drink *with* publicans
    34. while the bridegroom is *with* them?
  6: 3. and they which were *with* him;
     4. to them that were *with* him;
    17. And he came down *with* them,
  7:36. that he would eat *with* him.
  8:13. receive the word *with* joy;
    45. Peter and they that were *with* him said,
  9:28. an eight days *after*ᵃ these sayings,
    39. and it teareth him that he foameth again,
       (lit. *with* foam)
    49. because he followeth not *with* us.
 10: 1. *After*ᵃ these things the Lord appointed
    17. *with* joy, saying, Lord, even the devils
    37. He that shewed mercy *on* him.
 11: 7. my children are *with* me in bed;
    23. He that is not *with* me is against me:
       and he that gathereth not *with* me
    31. judgment *with* the men of this
    32. *with* this generation, and shall condemn
 12: 4. and *after*ᵃ that have no more that they
     5. which *after*ᵃ he hath killed

Lu. 12:13. he divide the inheritance *with* me.
    46. his portion *with* the unbelievers.
    58. When thou goest *with* thine adversary
 13: 1. had mingled *with* their sacrifices.
 14: 9. thou begin *with* shame to take
    31. against him *with* twenty thousand?
 15:13. And not many days *after*ᵃ
    29. might make merry *with* my friends:
    30. devoured thy living *with* harlots,
    31. Son, thou art ever *with* me,
 17: 8. and *afterward*ᵃ thou shalt eat and
    15. and *with* a loud voice glorified God,
    20. cometh not *with* observation:
 18: 4. but *afterward*ᵃ he said within himself,
 21:27. *with* power and great glory.
 22:11. passover *with* my disciples?
    15. passover *with* you before I suffer:
    20. also the cup *after*ᵃ supper,
    21. (is) *with* me on the table.
    28. continued *with* me in my temptations.
    33. Lord, I am ready to go *with* thee,
    37. reckoned *among* the transgressors:
    52. *with* swords and staves?
    53. I was daily *with* you in the
    58. And *after*ᵃ a little while another
    59. this (fellow) also was *with* him:
 23:12. were made friends together: (lit. *with* one
       another)
    43. be *with* me in paradise.
 24: 5. the living *among* the dead?
    29. Abide *with* us: for it is toward
    30. as he sat at meat *with* them,
    52. to Jerusalem *with* great joy:

Joh. 2:12. *After*ᵃ this he went down to Capernaum,
  3: 2. except God be *with* him.
    22. *After*ᵃ these things came Jesus
    — there he tarried *with* them,
    25. *and* (lit. *with*) the Jews about purifying.
    26. he that was *with* thee beyond
  4:27. talked *with* the woman:
    — Why talkest thou *with* her?
    43. Now *after*ᵃ two days he departed
  5: 1. *After*ᵃ this there was a feast of the Jews;
     4. first *after*ᵃ the troubling of the water
    14. *Afterward*ᵃ Jesus findeth him
  6: 1. *After*ᵃ these things Jesus went
     3. and there he sat *with* his disciples.
    43. Murmur not *among* yourselves.
    66. walked no more *with* him.
  7: 1. *After*ᵃ these things Jesus walked
    33. a little while am I *with* you,
  8:29. he that sent me is *with* me:
  9:37. it is he that talketh *with* thee.
    40. which were *with* him heard
 11: 7. Then *after*ᵃ that saith he
    11. and *after*ᵃ that he saith unto them,
    16. that we may die *with* him.
    31. which were *with* her in the house,
    54. continued *with* his disciples.
    56. and spake *among* themselves,
 12: 8. the poor always ye have *with* you;
    17. that was *with* him when he
    35. a little while is the light *with* you.
 13: 7. but thou shalt know here*after*.ᵃ
     8. thou hast no part *with* me.
    18. He that eateth bread *with* me
    27. *after*ᵃ the sop Satan entered into him.
    33. yet a little while I am *with* you.
 14: 9. Have I been so long time *with* you,
    16. that he may abide *with* you for ever;
    30. Hereafter I will not talk much *with* you:
 15:27. ye have been *with* me from the

Joh. 16: 4. because I was *with* you.

 19. Do ye enquire *among* yourselves

 32. because the Father is *with* me.

17: 12. While I was *with* them in the world,

 24. be *with* me where I am;

18: 2. resorted thither *with* his disciples.

 3. cometh thither *with* lanterns and

 5. which betrayed him, stood *with* them.

 18. and Peter stood *with* them,

 26. in the garden *with* him?

19: 18. and two other *with* him,

 28. *After* [a] this, Jesus knowing that

 38. *after* [a] this Joseph of Arimathæa,

 40. in linen clothes *with* the spices,

20: 7. not lying *with* the linen clothes,

 24. was not *with* them when Jesus came.

 26. *after* [a] eight days again his disciples were within, and Thomas *with* them:

21: 1. *After* [a] these things Jesus shewed himself

Acts 1: 3. *after* [a] his passion by many infallible

 5. not many days *hence.* [a]

 26. numbered *with* the eleven

2: 28. full of joy *with* thy countenance.

 29. let me freely (lit. *with* boldness) speak

4: 29. that *with* all boldness they may speak

 31. spake the word of God *with* boldness.

5: 26. brought them *without* violence.

 37. *After* [a] this man rose up Judas

7: 4. *when* [a] his father was dead,

 5. and to his seed *after* [a] him,

 7. and *after* [a] that shall they come forth,

 9. but God was *with* him,

 38. *with* the angel which spake to him

 45. brought in *with* Jesus into the

9: 19. *with* the disciples which were

 28. And he was *with* them coming in

 39. Dorcas made, while she was *with* them.

10: 37. *after* [a] the baptism which John

 38. for God was *with* him.

 41. *after* [a] he rose from the dead.

11: 21. the hand of the Lord was *with* them:

12· 4. intending *after* [a] Easter to bring him

13· 15. And *after* [a] the reading of the law

 17. and *with* an high arm brought he

 20. And *after* [a] that he gave (unto them)

 25. there cometh one *after* [a] me,

14: 23. had prayed *with* fasting,

 27. all that God had done *with* them,

15: 4. that God had done *with* them.

 13. And *after* [a] they had held their peace,

 16. *After* [a] this I will return,

 33. they were let go *in* peace from

 35. *with* many others also.

 36. And some days *after* [a] Paul said

17: 11. *with* all readiness of mind,

18: 1. *After* [a] these things Paul departed

 10. For I am *with* thee,

19: 4. which should come *after* [a] him,

 21. *After* [a] I have been there,

20: 1. And *after* [a] the uproar was ceased,

 6. *after* [a] the days of unleavened bread,

 18. I have been *with* you

 19. *with* all humility of mind,

 24. I might finish my course *with* joy,

 29. that *after* [a] my departing shall

 31. night and day *with* tears.

 34. and to them that were *with* me.

21: 15. And *after* [a] those days we took up

24: 1. And *after* [a] five days Ananias the high priest descended *with* the elders,

 3. *with* all thankfulness.

 7. and *with* great violence took

Acts 24: 18. neither *with* multitude, nor *with* tumult.

 24. And *after* [a] certain days,

25: 1. *after* [a] three days he ascended from

 12. conferred *with* the council,

 23. *with* great pomp, and was entered

26: 12. *with* authority and commission

27: 10. this voyage will be *with* hurt

 14. not long *after* [a] there arose

 24. all them that sail *with* thee.

28: 11. And *after* [a] three months

 13. and *after* [a] one day the south wind blew,

 17. that *after* [a] three days Paul called

 31. *with* all confidence, no man forbidding

Ro. 12: 15. Rejoice *with* them that do rejoice, and weep *with* them that weep.

 18. live peaceably *with* all men.

15: 10. Rejoice, ye Gentiles, *with* his people.

 33. God of peace (be) *with* you all.

16: 20. of our Lord Jesus Christ (be) *with* you.

 24. (be) *with* you all.

1Co. 6: 6. brother goeth to law *with* brother,

 7. ye go to law one *with* another.

7: 12. and she be pleased to dwell *with* him,

 13. if he be pleased to dwell *with* her,

11: 25. (he took) the cup, when he had supped, (lit. *after* [a] supping)

16: 11. look for him *with* the brethren.

 12. unto you *with* the brethren:

 23. of our Lord Jesus Christ (be) *with* you.

 24. My love (be) *with* you all in Christ

2Co. 6: 15. hath he that believeth *with* an infidel?

 16. the temple of God *with* idols?

7: 15. *with* fear and trembling ye received

8: 4. Praying us *with* much intreaty

 18. we have sent *with* him the brother,

13: 11. and peace shall be *with* you.

 14(13). of the Holy Ghost, (be) *with* you

Gal. 1: 18. Then *after* [a] three years I went up

2: 1. to Jerusalem *with* Barnabas,

 12. he did eat *with* the Gentiles:

 3: 17. and thirty years *after,* [a] cannot disannul,

4: 25. is in bondage *with* her children.

 30. *with* the son of the freewoman.

6: 18. Jesus Christ (be) *with* your spirit.

Eph. 4: 2. *With* all lowliness and meekness, *with* longsuffering,

 25. every man truth *with* his neighbour:

6: 5. *with* fear and trembling,

 7. *With* good will doing service,

 23. and love *with* faith,

 24. Grace (be) *with* all them that love

Phi. 1: 4. making request *with* joy,

2: 12. *with* fear and trembling.

 29. in the Lord *with* all gladness;

4: 3. *with* Clement also,

 6. and supplication *with* thanksgiving

 9. the God of peace shall be *with* you.

 23. Jesus Christ (be) *with* you all.

Col. 1: 11. longsuffering *with* joyfulness;

4: 18. Grace (be) *with* you.

1Th. 1: 6. *with* joy of the Holy Ghost:

3: 13. Jesus Christ *with* all his saints.

5: 28. our Lord Jesus Christ (be) *with* you.

2Th. 1: 7. rest *with* us, when the Lord Jesus shall be revealed from heaven *with* his

3: 12. that *with* quietness they work,

 16. The Lord (be) *with* you all.

 18. our Lord Jesus Christ (be) *with* you all.

1Ti. 1: 14. abundant *with* faith and love

2: 9. *with* shamefacedness and sobriety;

 15. and holiness *with* sobriety.

3: 4. in subjection *with* all gravity;

1Ti. 4: 3. to be received *with* thanksgiving
4. if it be received *with* thanksgiving:
14. *with* the laying on of the hands
6: 6. godliness *with* contentment is
21. Grace (be) *with* thee.

2Ti. 2:10. in Christ Jesus *with* eternal glory.
22. *with* them that call on the Lord
4:11. Only Luke is *with* me. Take Mark, and
bring him *with* thee:
22. The Lord Jesus Christ (be) *with* thy
spirit. Grace (be) *with* you.

Tit. 2:15. and rebuke *with* all authority.
3:10. *after* [a] the first and second admonition
15. All that are *with* me salute thee.
— Grace (be) *with* you all.

Philem.25(24) our Lord Jesus Christ (be) *with* your

Heb. 4: 7. *after* [a] so long a time;
8. then would he not *after*ward [a] have
16. Let us therefore come boldly (lit. *with*
boldness)
5: 7. *with* strong crying and tears
7:21. but this *with* an oath
28. which was *since* [a] the law,
8:10. *after* [a] those days, saith the Lord;
9: 3. And *after* [a] the second veil,
19. *with* water, and scarlet wool,
27. but *after* [a] this the judgment:
10:15. for *after* [a] that he had said before,
16. *after* [a] those days, saith the Lord,
22. Let us draw near *with* a true heart
26. *after* [a] that we have received the
34. took joyfully (lit. *with* joy) the spoiling
11: 9. *with* Isaac and Jacob,
31. when she had received the spies *with*
12:14. Follow peace *with* all (men),
17. he sought it carefully *with* tears.
28. *with* reverence and godly fear:
13:17. that they may do it *with* joy,
23. *with* whom, if he come shortly,
25. Grace (be) *with* you all.

1Pet. 1:11. glory that should follow. (lit. *after* [a] these)
3:15. *with* meekness and fear:

2Pet. 1:15. that ye may be able *after* [a] my decease

1Joh. 1: 3. may have fellowship *with* us: and truly
our fellowship (is) *with* the Father,
and *with* his Son
6. that we have fellowship *with* him,
7. we have fellowship one *with* another,
2:19. have continued *with* us:
4:17. Herein is our love (lit. love *with* us)
made perfect,

2Joh. 2. and shall be *with* us for ever.
3. Grace be *with* you,

Rev. 1: 7. Behold, he cometh *with* clouds;
12. to see the voice that spake *with* me.
19. the things which shall be here*after;* [a]
2:16. will fight *against* them with the sword of
22. that commit adultery *with* her
3: 4. they shall walk *with* me in white:
20. and will sup *with* him, and he *with* me.
21. to sit *with* me in my throne,
— and am set down *with* my Father
4: 1. *After* [a] this I looked, and, behold,
— of a trumpet talking *with* me;
— things which must be here*after.* [a]
6: 8. and Hell followed *with* him.
7: 1. And *after* [a] these things I saw
9. *After* [a] this I beheld, and, lo,
9:12. two woes more here*after.* [a]
10: 8. spake *unto* me again,
11: 7. shall make war *against* them,
11. And *after* [a] three days and an half

Rev.12: 9. his angels were cast out *with* him.
17. to make war *with* the remnant
13: 4. who is able to make war *with* him?
7. to make war *with* the saints,
14: 1. and *with* him an hundred forty
4. not defiled *with* women;
13. their works do follow)(them.
15: 5. And *after* [a] that I looked,
17: 1. and talked *with* me,
2. *With* whom the kings of the earth
12. one hour *with* the beast.
14. shall make war *with* the Lamb,
— they that are *with* him (are) called,
18: 1. *after* [a] these things I saw
3. fornication *with* her,
9. lived deliciously *with* her,
19: 1. *after* [a] these things I heard a great
19. war *against* him that sat on the horse,
and *against* his army.
20. and *with* him the false prophet
20: 3. *after* [a] that he must be loosed
4. they lived and reigned *with* Christ
6. shall reign *with* him a thousand years.
21: 3. the tabernacle of God (is) *with* men, and
he will dwell *with* them,
— God himself shall be *with* them,
9. and talked *with* me,
15. he that talked *with* me had
22:12. my reward (is) *with* me,
21. our Lord Jesus Christ (be) *with* you all.

μεταβαίνω, *metabaino.*

Mat. 8:34. that he *would depart* out of their
11: 1. he *departed* thence to teach and
12: 9. *when* he *was departed* thence,
15:29. Jesus *departed* from thence, *and*
17:20. *Remove* hence to yonder place; and it
shall remove;
Lu. 10: 7. *Go* not from house to house.
Joh. 5:24. *is passed* from death unto life.
7: 3. *Depart* hence, and go into Judæa,
13: 1. that he *should depart* out of this
Acts18: 7. he *departed* thence, *and* entered
1Joh.3:14. we *have passed* from death unto life,

μεταβάλλομαι, *metaballomai.*

Acts28: 6. they *changed their minds, and* said

μετάγω, *metago.*

Jas. 3: 3. and we *turn about* their whole body.
4. yet *are* they *turned about* with a very small

μεταδίδωμι, *metadidomi.*

Lu. 3:11. *let* him *impart* to him †that hath none;
Ro. 1:11. that I *may impart* unto you some
12: 8. he *that giveth,* (let him do it) with
Eph. 4:28. that he may have *to give* to him that
1Th. 2: 8. willing *to have imparted* unto you,

μετάθεσις, *metathesis.*

Heb. 7:12. of necessity a *change* also of the law.
11: 5. for before his *translation*
12:27. the *removing* of those things that are

μεταίρω, *metairo.*

Mat.13:53. finished these parables, he *departed* thence.
19: 1. he *departed* from Galilee,

μετακαλέομαι, *metakaleomai.*

Acts 7:14. and *called* his father Jacob *to* (him),
10:32. and *call hither* Simon,
20:17. and *called* the elders of the church.
24:25. I *will call for* thee.

μετακινέω, *metakineo.*

Col. 1:23. and (be) not *moved away* from the hope of
the gospel,

μεταλαμβάνω, *metalambano.*

Acts 2:46. *did eat* their meat with gladness
24:25. *when* I *have* a convenient season,
27:33. Paul besought (them) all *to take* meat,
2Ti. 2: 6. must *be* first *partaker* of the fruits.
Heb 6: 7. *receiveth* blessing from God:
12:10. that (we) might *be partakers* of his

μετάληψις, *metaleepsis.*

1Ti. 4: 3. which God hath created to be received
(lit. for *reception*)

μεταλλάττω, *metallatto.*

Ro. 1:25. Who *changed* the truth of God
26. even their women *did change* the

μεταμέλομαι, *metamelomai.*

Mat.21:29. afterward he *repented, and* went.
32. *repented* not afterward, that ye
27: 3. *repented himself,* and brought
2Co. 7: 8. I *do* not *repent,* though I *did repent:*
Heb 7:21. The Lord sware and *will* not *repent,*

μεταμορφόομαι, *metamorphöomai.*

Mat.17: 2. And *was transfigured* before them:
Mar 9: 2. he *was transfigured* before them.
Ro. 12: 2. *be ye transformed* by the renewing
2Co. 3:18. we all,...*are changed* into the same image

μετανοέω, *metanöeo.*

Mat. 3: 2. And saying, *Repent* ye: for the kingdom
4:17. and to say, *Repent:* for the kingdom
11:20. because they *repented* not:
21. they would *have repented* long ago
12:41. because they *repented* at the preaching
Mar 1:15. *repent* ye, and believe the gospel.
6:12. and preached that men *should repent.*
Lu. 10:13. they *had* a great while ago *repented,*
11:32. for they *repented* at the preaching
13: 3. but, except ye *repent,* ye shall all
5. except ye *repent,* ye shall all

Lu. 15: 7. over one sinner *that repenteth,*
10. over one sinner *that repenteth.*
16:30. from the dead, they *will repent.*
17: 3. and if he *repent,* forgive him.
4. saying, I *repent;* thou shalt forgive
Acts 2:38. *Repent,* and be baptized every one
3:19. *Repent* ye therefore, and be converted.
8:22. *Repent* therefore of this thy
17:30. all men every where *to repent:*
26:20. that they should *repent* and turn to God,
2Co.12:21. and *have* not *repented*
Rev. 2: 5. *repent,* and do the first works;
— except thou *repent.*
16. *Repent;* or else I will come
21. I gave her space to *repent* of her fornication; and she *repented* not.
22. except they *repent* of their deeds.
3: 3. and hold fast, and *repent.*
19. be zealous therefore, and *repent.*
9:20. *repented* not of the works
21. Neither *repented* they of their
16: 9. they *repented* not to give him glory.
11. and *repented* not of their deeds.

μετάνοια, *metanoya.*

Mat. 3: 8. fruits meet for *repentance:*
11. baptize you with water unto *repentance:*
9:13. but sinners to *repentance.*
Mar. 1: 4. and preach the baptism of *repentance*
2:17. but sinners to *repentance.*
Lu. 3: 3. preaching the baptism of *repentance*
8. fruits worthy of *repentance,*
5:32. but sinners to *repentance.*
15: 7. which need no *repentance.*
24:47. And that *repentance* and remission
Acts 5:31. for to give *repentance* to Israel,
11:18. granted *repentance* unto life.
13:24. the baptism of *repentance* to all the people
of Israel.
19: 4. baptized with the baptism of *repentance,*
20:21. *repentance* toward God, and faith
26:20. do works meet for *repentance.*
Ro. 2: 4. of God leadeth thee to *repentance?*
2Co. 7: 9. ye sorrowed to *repentance:*
10. worketh *repentance* to salvation
2Ti. 2:25. will give them *repentance*
Heb. 6: 1. of *repentance* from dead works,
6. to renew them again unto *repentance;*
12:17. found no place of *repentance,*
2Pet.3: 9. all should come to *repentance.*

μεταξύ, *metaxu.*

Mat.18:15. tell him his fault *between* thee and him
alone:
23:35. *between* the temple and the altar.
Lu. 11:51. *between* the altar and the temple:
16:26. *between* us and you there is a great gulf
Joh. 4:31. In the *mean while* his disciples
Acts12: 6. sleeping *between* two soldiers,
13:42. be preached to them the *next* sabbath.
15: 9. no difference *between* us and them,
Ro. 2:15. (their) thoughts the *mean while* accusing

μεταπέμπω, *metapempo.*

Acts10: 5. and *call for* (one) Simon,

Acts10:22. *to send for* thee into his house,
    29. *as soon as* I *was sent for :* I ask therefore
        for what intent ye *have sent for* me ?
  11:13. and *call for* Simon,
  24:24. he *sent for* Paul, and heard him
    26. he *sent for* him the oftener, *and*
  25: 3. that he *would send for* him to Jerusalem,

μεταστρέφω, metastrepho.

Acts 2:20. The sun *shall be turned* into darkness,
Gal. 1: 7. and would *pervert* the gospel of Christ.
Jas. 4: 9. *let* your laughter *be turned* to mourning,

μετασχηματίζω, metaskeematizo.

1Co. 4: 6. I *have in a figure transferred* to myself
2Co.11:13. *transforming themselves* into the apostles
    14. for Satan himself *is transformed* into an
        angel of light.
    15. if his ministers also *be transformed* as the
        ministers of righteousness ;
Phi. 3:21. Who *shall change* our vile body,

μετατίθημι, metatitheemi.

Acts 7:16. And *were carried over* into Sychem,
Gal. 1: 6. that ye *are* so soon *removed* from him
Heb 7:12. the priesthood *being changed*,
  11: 5. By faith Enoch *was translated*
    — because God *had translated* him:
Jude   4. *turning* the grace of our God into

μετέπειτα, metepīta.

Heb12:17. For ye know how that *afterward*, when he

μετέχω, meteko.

1Co. 9:10. should *be partaker* of his hope.
    12. If others *be partakers* of (this) power
  10:17. we *are* all *partakers* of that one bread.
    21. ye cannot *be partakers* of the Lord's
    30. if I by grace *be a partaker,*
Heb. 2:14. likewise *took part* of the same ;
  5:13. For every one *that useth* milk
  7:13. *pertaineth* to another tribe, of which

μετεωρίζομαι, meteōrizomai.

Lu. 12:29. neither *be ye of doubtful mind.*

μετοικεσία, metoikesia.

Mat. 1:11. about the time they werẹ carried away to
        (lit. of the *carrying away to*) Babylon :
    12. after they were brought (lit. the *bringing*)
        to Babylon,
    17. from David until the *carrying away into*
    — and from the *carrying away into* Babylon

μετοικίζω, metoikizo.

Acts 7: 4. he *removed* him *into* this land,
    43. I *will carry* you *away* beyond Babylon.

μετοχή, metokee.

2Co. 6:14. what *fellowship* hath righteousness with
    unrighteousness ?

μέτοχος, metokos.

Lu. 5: 7. they beckoned unto (their) *partners,*
Heb 1: 9. oil of gladness above thy *fellows.*
  3: 1. *partakers* of the heavenly calling,
    14. we are made *partakers* of Christ,
  6: 4. were made *partakers* of the Holy Ghost,
  12: 8. whereof all are *partakers,*

μετρέω, metreo.

Mat. 7: 2. with what measure ye *mete,* it shall
Mar. 4:24. with what measure ye *mete,* it *shall be
    measured* to you:
Lu. 6:38. with the same measure that ye *mete*
2Co.10:12. they *measuring* themselves by themselves,
Rev.11: 1. Rise, and *measure* the temple of God,
    2. leave out, and *measure* it not ;
  21:15. a golden reed to *measure* the city,
    16. he *measured* the city with the reed,
    17. he *measured* the wall thereof,

μετρητής, metreetees.

Joh. 2: 6. two or three *firkins* apiece.

μετριοπαθέω, metriopatheo.

Heb. 5: 2. Who can *have compassion on* the ignorant,

μετρίως, metriōs.

Acts20:12. were not *a little* comforted.

μέτρον, metron.

Mat. 7: 2. and with what *measure* ye mete,
  23:32. Fill ye up then the *measure* of your
Mar. 4:24. with what *measure* ye mete,
Lu. 6:38. good *measure,* pressed down,
    — with *the* same *measure* that ye mete
Joh. 3:34. God giveth not the Spirit by *measure*
Ro. 12: 3. to every man the *measure* of faith.
2Co.10:13. according to the *measure* of the rule
    — a *measure* to reach even unto you.
Eph. 4: 7. according to the *measure* of the gift of
    13. unto the *measure* of the stature
    16. in the *measure* of every part,
Rev.21:17. the *measure* of a man, that is, of the angel.

μέτωπον, metōpon.

Rev. 7: 3. servants of our God in their *foreheads.*
  9: 4. have not the seal of God in their *foreheads.*
  13:16. or in their *foreheads :*
  14: 1. Father's name written in their *foreheads.*
    9. and receive (his) mark in his *forehead,*
  17: 5. And upon her *forehead* (was) a name
  20: 4. (his) mark upon their *foreheads,*
  22: 4. his name (shall be) in their *foreheads.*

μέχρι & μέχρις, *mekri & mckris.*

Mat.11:23. would have remained *until* this day.
13:30. grow together *until* the harvest:
28:15. reported among the Jews *until* this day.
Mar 13:30. *till* all these things be done.
Acts10:30. I was fasting *until* this hour;
20: 7. continued his speech *until* midnight.
Ro. 5:14. death reigned from Adam *to* Moses,
15:19. and round about *unto* Illyricum,
Eph. 4:13. *Till* we all come in the unity of
Phi. 2: 8. became obedient *unto* death,
30. he was nigh *unto* death,
1Ti. 6:14. *until* the appearing of our Lord
2Ti. 2: 9. I suffer trouble, as an evil doer, (even)
unto bonds;
Heb. 3: 6. rejoicing of the hope firm *unto* the end.
14. stedfast *unto* the end;
9:10. *until* the time of reformation.
12: 4. Ye have not yet resisted *unto* blood,

μή, *mee.*

? shews where it is used interrogatively; ‖ denotes
where the double negative of the Greek is omitted; [2] marks passages where it is connected,
though not closely, with *ἵνα*.

Mat. 1:19. *not* willing to make her a publick
20. fear *not* to take unto thee Mary
2:12. that they should *not* return to Herod,
3: 9. And think *not* to say within
10. which bringeth *not* forth good fruit
5:17. Think *not* that I am come to destroy
29. and *not*[2] (that) thy whole body should be
30. and *not* (that) thy whole body should be
34. Swear *not* at all;
39. That ye resist *not* evil:
42. turn *not* thou away.
6: 1. Take heed that ye do *not* your alms before
2. do *not* sound a trumpet before thee,
3. let *not* thy left hand know what
7. use *not* vain repetitions,
8. Be *not* ye therefore like unto them:
13. lead us *not* into temptation,
16. be *not*, as the hypocrites, of a sad
18. That thou appear *not* unto men to fast,
19. Lay *not* up for yourselves
25. Take *no* thought for your life,
31. take *no* thought, saying, What shall
34. Take therefore *no* thought for
7: 1. Judge *not*, that ye be not judged.
6. Give *not* that which is holy unto
9. ? will he give him a stone?
10. ? will he give him a serpent?
19. Every tree that bringeth *not* forth
26. and doeth them *not*,
8:28. so that *no* man might pass by
9:15. ? Can the children of the bridechamber
36. as sheep having *no* shepherd.
10: 5. Go *not* into the way of the Gentiles,
— city of the Samaritans enter ye *not*:
9. Provide *neither* gold, nor silver,
10. *Nor* scrip for (your) journey,
19. take *no* thought how or what ye
26. Fear them *not* therefore:
28. And fear *not* them which kill the body,
but are *not* able to kill
31. Fear ye *not* therefore,
34. Think *not* that I am come to
12:30. He that is *not* with me is against me; and
he that gathereth *not* with me

Mat.13: 5. they had *no* deepness of earth:
6. because they had *no* root,
19. and understandeth (it) *not*,
14:27. it is I; be *not* afraid.
17: 7. Arise, and be *not* afraid.
18:10. Take heed that ye despise *not* one of
13. which went *not* astray.
25. forasmuch as he had *not* to pay,
19: 6. let *not* man put asunder.
14. and forbid them *not*,
21:21. If ye have faith, and doubt *not*,
22:12. *not* having a wedding garment?
23. that there is *no* resurrection,
24. If a man die, having *no* children,
25. and, having *no* issue,
29. Ye do err, *not* knowing the scriptures,
23: 3. but do *not* ye after their works:
8. be *not* ye called Rabbi:
9. call *no* (man) your father
23. and *not* to leave the other undone.
24: 4. Take heed that *no* man deceive you.
6. see that ye be *not* troubled:
17. *not* come down to take any
18. *Neither* let him which is in the field
23. or there; believe (it) *not*.
26. go *not* forth: behold, (he is) in the secret
chambers; believe (it) *not*.
25:29. but from him that hath *not*
26: 5. *Not* on the feast (day),
28: 5. said unto the women, Fear *not* ye:
10. Be *not* afraid: go tell my brethren
Mar 2: 4. they could *not* come nigh unto him
19. ? Can the children of the bridechamber
3:20. they could *not* so much as eat bread.
4: 5. because it had *no* depth of earth:
6. because it had *no* root,
12. may see, and *not* perceive; and hearing
they may hear, and *not* understand;
5: 7. that thou torment me *not*.
36. Be *not* afraid, only believe.
6: 8. *no* scrip, *no* bread, *no* money in (their)
9. and *not* put on two coats.
11. whosoever shall *not* receive you,
34. as sheep *not* having a shepherd:
50. it is I; be *not* afraid.
8: 1. and having *nothing* to eat,
9:39. But Jesus said, Forbid him *not*:
10: 9. let *not* man put asunder.
14. and forbid them *not*:
19. Do *not* commit adultery, Do *not* kill, Do
not steal, Do *not* bear false witness,
Defraud *not*,
11:23. and shall *not* doubt in his heart,
12:15(14). or shall we *not* give?
18. which say there is *no* resurrection;
19. and leave *no* children,
24. ye know *not* the scriptures,
13: 5. Take heed *lest* any (man) deceive you:
7. be ye *not* troubled:
11. take *no* thought beforehand
15. let him that is on the housetop *not* go
down into the house,
16. let him...*not* turn back again
21. (he is) there; believe (him) *not*:
36. *Lest* coming suddenly he find you
14: 2. *Not* on the feast (day),
16: 6. Be *not* affrighted: Ye seek Jesus
Lu. 1:13. Fear *not*, Zacharias:
20. and *not* able to speak,
30. Fear *not*, Mary: for thou hast found
2:10. Fear *not*: for, behold, I bring you
26. that he should *not* see death,

Lu. 2:45. when they found him *not*,
  3: 8. and begin *not* to say
    9. which bringeth *not* forth good fruit
    11. impart to him that hath *none* ;
  4:42. that he should *not* depart from them.
  5:10. Fear *not* ; from henceforth thou
    19. when they could *not* find by what
    34. ? Can ye make the children of the
  6:29. forbid *not* (to take thy) coat also.
    30. ask (them) *not* again.
    37. Judge *not*, and ye shall not be judged:
      condemn *not*, and ye
    49. he that heareth, and doeth *not*,
  7: 6. Lord, trouble *not* thyself:
    13. and said unto her, Weep *not*.
    30. being *not* baptized of him.
    42. when they had *nothing* to pay,
  8: 6. because it lacked (lit. had *not*) moisture.
    10. seeing they might *not*[2] see, and hearing
      they might *not* understand.
    18. and whosoever hath *not*,
    28. I beseech thee, torment me *not*.
    49. trouble *not* the Master.
    50. Fear *not*: believe only,
    52. Weep *not* ; she is not dead,
  9: 5. whosoever will *not* receive you,
    33. *not* knowing what he said.
    50. Forbid (him) *not*:
  10: 4. Carry *neither* purse, *nor* scrip,
    7. Go *not* from house to house.
    10. and they receive you *not*,
    20. in this rejoice *not*,
  11: 4. And lead us *not* into temptation ;
    7. Trouble me *not*: the door is now shut,
    11. ? will he give him a stone?
    — ? will he for a fish give him a serpent?
    12. ? will he offer him a scorpion?
    23. He that is *not* with me is against me: and
      he that gathereth *not* with me
    24. and finding *none*, he saith,
    35. which is in thee be *not* darkness.
    36. having *no* part dark,
    42. and *not* to leave the other undone.
  12: 4. Be *not* afraid of them that kill
    — have *no* more that they can do.
    7. Fear *not* therefore:
    11. take ye *no* thought how or what thing
    21. and is *not* rich toward God.
    22. Take *no* thought for your life,
    29. And seek *not* ye what ye shall eat,
    — *neither* be ye of doubtful mind.
    32. Fear *not*, little flock ;
    33. bags which wax *not* old,
    47. knew his lord's will, and prepared *not*
    48. But he that knew *not*, and
  13:11. could in *no* wise lift up (herself).
    14. and *not* on the sabbath day.
  14: 8. sit *not* down in the highest room ;
    12. call *not* thy friends,
    29. and is *not* able to finish (it),
  16:26. from hence to you can*not* ;
  17: 1. It is impossible but that offences will
      come: (lit. for offences *not* to come)
    9. ? Doth he thank that servant
    23. go *not* after (them),
    31. let him *not* come down
    — let him likewise *not* return back.
  18: 1. and *not* to faint ;
    2. a judge, which feared *not* God, *neither*
    16. and forbid them *not*:
    20. Do *not* commit adultery, Do *not* kill, Do
      not steal, Do *not* bear false witness,

Lu. 19:26. from him that hath *not*,
    27. which would *not* that I should reign
  20: 7. that they could *not* tell
    16. said, God forbid. (lit. may it *not* be)
    27. deny that there is *any* ‖ resurrection ;
  21: 8. Take heed *that* ye be *not* deceived:
    — go ye *not* therefore after them.
    9. and commotions, be *not* terrified:
    14. *not* to meditate before
    21. and let *not* them that are in the
  22:34. deny that thou)(‖ knowest me.
    35. ? lacked ye any thing ?
    36. and he that hath *no* sword,
    40. Pray that ye enter *not* into
    42. *not* my will, but thine, be done.
  23:28. weep *not* for me, but weep for yourselves,
  24:16. that they should *not* know him.
    23. And when they found *not* his body,
Joh. 2:16. make *not* my Father's house
  3: 4. ? can he enter the second time into
    7. Marvel *not* that I said unto thee,
    16. should *not*[2] perish, but have everlasting
    18. he that believeth *not* is condemned already,
      because he hath *not* believed
  4:12. ? Art thou greater than our father Jacob,
  5:23. He that honoureth *not* the Son
    28. Marvel *not* at this:
    45. Do *not* think that I will accuse you
  6:20. It is I ; be *not* afraid.
    27. Labour *not* for the meat which
    39. I should lose *nothing*,[2]
    43. Murmur *not* among yourselves.
    64. who they were that believed *not*,
    67. ? Will ye also go away?
  7:15. this man letters, having *never* learned ?
    24. Judge *not* according to the
    35. ? will he go unto the dispersed
    41. ? Shall Christ come out of Galilee ?
    47. ? Are ye also deceived ?
    49. who knoweth *not* the law
    51. ? Doth our law judge (any) man,
    52. ? Art thou also of Galilee ?
  8:53. ? Art thou greater than our father
  9:27. ? will ye also be his disciples ?
    39. that they which see *not* might see ;
    40. ? Are we blind also ?
  10: 1. He that entereth *not* by the door
    21. ? Can a devil open the eyes
    37. of my Father, believe me *not*.
    38. though ye believe *not* me,
  11:37. this man should *not*[2] have died ?
    50. that the whole nation perish *not*.[2]
  12:15. Fear *not*, daughter of Sion:
    47. hear my words, and believe *not*,
    48. and receiveth *not* my words,
  13: 9. Lord, *not* my feet only,
  14: 1. Let *not* your heart be troubled:
    24. He that loveth me *not* keepeth not
    27. Let *not* your heart be troubled,
  15: 2. that beareth *not* fruit
  18:17. Art *not* thou also (one) of this
    25. Art *not* thou also (one) of his
    40. *Not* this man, but Barabbas.
  19:21. Write *not*, The King of the Jews ;
    24. Let us *not* rend it,
  20:17. Touch me *not* ; for I am not
    27. and be *not* faithless,
    29. blessed (are) they that have *not* seen,
Acts 1: 4. that they should *not* depart
    20. and let *no* man dwell therein:
  3:23. which will *not* hear that prophet,
  4:18. commanded them *not* to speak at all

Acts 4:20. For we cannot *but* speak
   5: 7. *not* knowing what was done,
    28. that ye should *not* teach in this name?
    40. that they should *not* speak in the name
   7:19. to the end they might *not* live.
    28. *?* Wilt thou kill me, as thou diddest
    42. *?* O ye house of Israel, have ye offered
    60. Lord, lay *not* this sin to their
   9: 9. he was three days *without* sight,
    26. believed *not* that he was a disciple.
    38. that he would *not* delay to come
  10:15. (that) call *not* thou common.
    47. that these should *not* be baptized,
  11: 9. (that) call *not* thou common.
  12:19. and found him *not*,
  13:11. *not* seeing the sun for a season.
    40. *lest* that come upon you,
  14:18. that they had *not* done sacrifice
  15:19. that we trouble *not* them,
    38. Paul thought *not* good to take him
    — and went *not* with them to the work.
  17: 6. And when they found them *not*,
  18: 9. Be *not* afraid, but speak, and hold *not* thy
  19:31. that he would *not* adventure himself
  20:10. Trouble *not* yourselves; for his life
    16. he would *not* spend the time in Asia:
    20. I kept back nothing...but have shewed
      you, (lit. from *not* shewing to you)
    22. *not* knowing the things that shall
    27. For I have not shunned to declare (lit. as
      not to declare)
    29. *not* sparing the flock.
  21: 4. that he should *not* go up to Jerusalem.
    12. besought him *not* to go up to Jerusalem.
    14. when he would *not* be persuaded,
    21. that they ought *not* to circumcise
    34. when he could *not* know the certainty
  23: 8. say that there is *no* resurrection,
    9. let us *not* fight against God.
    10. fearing *lest* Paul should have been
    21. But do *not* thou yield unto them:
  25:24. that he ought *not* to live any longer.
    27. and *not* withal to signify the crimes
  27: 7. the wind *not* suffering us,
    15. and could *not* bear up into the wind,
    17. and, fearing *lest* they should fall into
    21. and *not* have loosed from Crete,
    24. Fear *not*, Paul; thou must be brought
    42. *lest* any of them should swim out,
Ro. 1:28. those things which are *not* convenient;
  2:14. which have *not* the law,
    — these, having *not* the law,
    21. preachest a man should *not* steal,
    22. a man should *not* commit adultery,
  3: 3. *?* shall their unbelief make the
    4. God forbid: (lit. may it *not* be)
    5. *?* (Is) God unrighteous who taketh
    6. God forbid: (lit. may it *not* be)
    8. And *not* (rather), as we be slanderously
    31. God forbid: (lit. may it *not* be)
  4: 5. But to him that worketh *not*,
    17. things which be *not* as though they were.
    19. And being *not* weak in faith,
  5:13. sin is not imputed when there is *no* law.
    14. even over them that had *not* sinned
  6: 2. God forbid. (lit. may it *not* be)
    12. Let *not* sin therefore reign in your
    15. God forbid. (lit. may it *not* be)
  7: 3. so that she is *no* adulteress,
    7. God forbid. (lit. may it *not* be)
    13. God forbid. (lit. may it *not* be)
  8: 1. who walk *not* after the flesh,

Ro. 8: 4. who walk *not* after the flesh,
  9:14. *?* (Is there) unrighteousness with God?
    God forbid. (lit. may it *not* be)
    20. *?* Shall the thing formed say to him
    30. which followed *not* after righteousness,
  10: 6. Say *not* in thine heart, Who shall
    20. I was found of them that sought me *not*;
    — unto them that asked *not* after me.
  11: 1. *?* Hath God cast away his people? God
    forbid. (lit. may it *not* be)
    8. eyes that they should *not* see, and ears that
    they should *not* hear;
    10. that they may *not* see,
    11. *?* Have they stumbled that they should
    fall? God forbid: (lit. may it *not* be)
    18. Boast *not* against the branches.
    20. Be *not* highminded, but fear:
  12: 2. And be *not* conformed to this world:
    3. *not* to think (of himself) more highly
    11. *Not* slothful in business;
    14. bless, and curse *not*.
    16. Mind *not* high things,
    — Be *not* wise in your own conceits.
    19. avenge *not* yourselves,
    21. Be *not* overcome of evil,
  13: 3. Wilt thou then *not* be afraid of the power?
    13. *not* in rioting and drunkenness, *not* in
    chambering and wantonness, *not* in strife
    14. make *not* provision for the flesh,
  14: 1. *not* to doubtful disputations.
    3. Let *not* him that eateth despise him that
    eateth *not*; and let *not* him which eateth
    not judge him that eateth:
    6. he that regardeth *not* the day,
    — and he that eateth *not*, to the Lord
    13. that *no* man put a stumblingblock
    15. Destroy *not* him with thy meat,
    16. Let *not* then your good be evil spoken of:
    20. For meat destroy *not* the work of God.
    21. (It is) good *neither* to eat flesh,
    22. Happy (is) he that condemneth *not* himself
  15: 1. and *not* to please ourselves.
1Co. 1: 7. ye come)(‖ behind in no gift;
    10. (that) there be *no* divisions among you;
    13. *?* was Paul crucified for you?
    28. and things which are *not*,
    29. That *no* flesh should glory
  2: 5. That your faith should *not*[2] stand in
  4: 5. judge *nothing* before the time,
    6. that *no* one of you be puffed up
    7. as if thou hadst *not* received (it)?
    18. as though I would *not* come to you.
  5: 8. *not* with old leaven,
    9. *not* to company with fornicators:
    11. *not* to keep company, if any man that is
  6: 9. Be *not* deceived: neither fornicators,
    15. God forbid. (lit. may it *not* be)
  7: 1. good for a man *not* to touch a woman.
    5. Defraud ye *not* one the other,
    10. Let *not* the wife depart from (her)
    11. and let *not* the husband put away (his)
    12. let him *not* put her away.
    13. let her *not* leave him.
    18. let him *not* become uncircumcised.
    — let him *not* be circumcised.
    21. (being) a servant? care *not* for it:
    23. be *not* ye the servants of men.
    27. bound unto a wife? seek *not* to be loosed.
    — loosed from a wife? seek *not* a wife.
    29. have wives be as though they had *none*;
    30. as though they wept *not*;
    — as though they rejoiced *not*;

1Co. 7:30. as though they possessed *not*;
 31. as *not* abusing (it):
 37. stedfast in his heart, having *no* necessity,
 38. but he that giveth (her) *not* in marriage
9: 6. power to forbear working? (lit.*not* to work)
 8. ? Say I these things as a man?
 9. ? Doth God take care for oxen?
 18. that I abuse *not* my power in the gospel.
 21. being *not* without law to God,
10: 6. to the intent we should *not* lust after evil
 12. take heed *lest* he fall.
 22. ? are we stronger than he?
 28. eat *not* for his sake that shewed it,
 33. *not* seeking mine own profit,
11:22. and shame them that have *not*?
 29. *not* discerning the Lord's body.
12:29. ? (Are) all apostles? ?(are) all prophets?
 ? (are) all teachers? ? (are) all workers
 of miracles?
 30. ? Have all the gifts of healing? ? do all
 speak with tongues? ? do all interpret?
13: 1. and have *not* charity, I am become
 2. and have *not* charity, I am nothing.
 3. have *not* charity, it profiteth me nothing.
14:20. be *not* children in understanding:
 39. and forbid *not* to speak with tongues.
15:33. Be *not* deceived: evil
 34. Awake to righteousness, and sin *not*;
16:11. Let *no* man therefore despise him:
2Co. 2: 1. that I would *not* come again to you
 13. because I found *not* Titus my brother:
3: 7. could *not* stedfastly behold the face of
 13. could *not* stedfastly look to the end
 14. the same vail *untaken* away
4: 2. *not* walking in craftiness,
 4. *lest* the light of the glorious gospel
 7. and *not* of us.
 18. we look *not* at the things which are seen,
 but at the things which are *not* seen:
 — things which are *not* seen (are) eternal.
5:19. *not* imputing their trespasses
 21. who knew *no* sin;
6: 1. that ye receive *not* the grace of God in
 9. as chastened, and *not* killed;
 14. Be ye *not* unequally yoked together
 17. touch *not* the unclean (thing);
8:20. that *no* man should blame us
9: 5. and *not* as (of) covetousness.
 7. *not* grudgingly, or of necessity:
10: 2. that I may *not* be bold when I am
 14. as though we reached *not* unto you:
11:16. Let *no* man think me a fool;
12: 6. *lest* any man should think of me above
 17. ? Did I make a gain of you by any of them
 21. *lest*, when I come again, my God
 — and have *not* repented
13: 7. pray to God)(tnat ye do no evil,
 '10. *lest*² being present I should use
Gal. 2:17. God forbid. (lit. may it *not* be)
3: 1. that ye should *not* obey the truth,
 21. God forbid: (lit. may it *not* be)
4: 8. which by nature are *no* gods.
 18. and *not* only when I am present
5: 1. and be *not* entangled again
 7. that ye should *not* obey the truth?
 13. only (use) *not* liberty for an occasion
 15. take heed *that* ye be *not* consumed
 26. Let us *not* be desirous of vain glory,
6: 1. *lest* thou also be tempted.
 7. Be *not* deceived; God is not mocked:
 9. let us *not* be weary in well doing:
 — we shall reap, if we faint *not*.

Gal. 6:14. God forbid that I should glory, (lit. be it
 not to me to glory)
Eph. 2:12. having *no* hope, and without God
3:13. I desire that ye faint *not* at my
4:26. Be ye angry, and sin *not*: let *not* the sun
 go down upon your wrath:
 29. Let *no* corrupt communication proceed
 30. And grieve *not* the holy Spirit
5: 7. Be *not* ye therefore partakers with them.
 11. And have *no* fellowship with the
 15. *not* as fools, but as wise,
 17. Wherefore be ye *not* unwise,
 18. And be *not* drunk with wine,
 27. *not* having spot, or wrinkle,
6: 4. provoke *not* your children to wrath:
 6. *Not* with eyeservice, as menpleasers;
Phi. 1:28. And in nothing)(‖ terrified by your
2: 4. Look *not* every man on his own things,
 12. *not* as in my presence only,
3: 9. *not* having mine own righteousness,
Col. 1:23. and (be) *not* moved away from the hope
2: 8. Beware *lest* any man spoil you
 16. Let *no* man therefore judge you
 18. into those things which he hath *not* seen,
 21. Touch *not*; taste not;
3: 2. *not* on things on the earth.
 9. Lie *not* one to another,
 19. and be *not* bitter against them.
 21. provoke *not* your children (to anger),
 22. *not* with eyeservice, as menpleasers;
1Th. 1: 8. so that we need *not* to speak
2: 9. because we would *not* be chargeable
 15. and they please *not* God,
4: 5. *Not* in the lust of concupiscence, even as
 the Gentiles which know *not* God:
 6. That *no* (man) go beyond and defraud
 13. even as others which have *no* hope.
5: 6. let us *not* sleep, as (do) others;
 15. See that *none* render evil for
 19. Quench *not* the Spirit.
 20. Despise *not* prophesyings.
2Th. 1: 8. vengeance on them that know *not* God,
 and that obey *not* the gospel of
2: 2. That ye be *not* soon shaken
 3. Let *no* man deceive you
 12. be damned who believed *not* the truth,
3: 6. and *not* after the tradition which he
 8. that we might *not* be chargeable
 13. be *not* weary in well doing.
 14. and have *no* company with him,
 15. Yet count (him) *not* as an enemy,
1Ti. 1: 3. that they teach *no* other doctrine,
 7.)(understanding neither what they say,
 20. that they may learn *not* to blaspheme.
2: 9. *not* with broidered hair,
3: 3. *Not* given to wine, *no* striker, *not* greedy
 of filthy lucre;
 6. *Not* a novice, lest being lifted up
 8. *not* doubletongued, *not* given to much
 wine, *not* greedy of filthy lucre;
 11. wives (be) grave, *not* slanderers,
4:14. Neglect *not* the gift that is in thee,
5: 1. Rebuke *not* an elder,
 9. Let *not* a widow be taken into the number
 13. speaking things which they ought *not*.
 16. and let *not* the church be charged;
 19. Against an elder receive *not* an accusation, but before
6: 2. let them *not* despise (them),
 3. and consent *not* to wholesome words,
 17. that they be *not* highminded,
2Ti. 1: 8. Be *not* thou therefore ashamed of

2Ti. 2:14. that they strive *not* about words
4:16. *that* it may *not* be laid to their charge.
Tit. 1: 6. *not* accused of riot, or unruly.
7. *not* selfwilled, *not* soon angry, *not* given to wine, no striker, *not* given to filthy
11. teaching things which they ought *not*,
14. *Not* giving heed to Jewish fables,
2: 3. *not* false accusers, *not* given to much
9. *not* answering again ;
10. *Not* purloining, but shewing all good
Heb 3: 8. Harden *not* your hearts, as in
15. harden *not* your hearts, as in
18. that they should *not* enter
4: 2. *not* being mixed with faith in them
7. harden *not* your hearts.
15. an high priest which can*not* be touched
6: 1. *not* laying again the foundation
7: 6. whose descent is *not* counted
9: 9. that could *not* make him that did
10:25. *Not* forsaking the assembling of
35. Cast *not* away therefore your
11: 3. were *not* made of things which do
5. that he should *not* see death;
8. *not* knowing whither he went.
13. *not* having received the promises,
27. *not* fearing the wrath of the king:
12: 5. despise *not* thou the chastening
15. *lest* any man fail of the grace of God ;
lest any root of bitterness
16. *Lest* there (be) any fornicator,
19. should *not* be spoken to them
25. See that ye refuse *not* him that
27. that those things which can*not* be
13: 2. Be *not* forgetful to entertain strangers:
9. Be *not* carried about with divers
16. and to communicate forget *not*:
17. and *not* with grief:
Jas. 1: 5. liberally, and upbraideth *not ;*
7. For let *not* that man think that he
16. Do *not* err, my beloved brethren.
22. and *not* hearers only,
26. and bridleth *not* his tongue,
2: 1. have *not* the faith...with respect of persons.
11. Do *not* commit adultery, said also, Do no*t*
13. that hath shewed *no* mercy ;
14. and have *not* works ? ? can faith save him ?
16. ye give them *not* those things which
3: 1. be *not* many masters,
12. ? Can the fig tree, my brethren,
14. glory *not*, and lie not against the truth.
4: 2. because ye ask *not*.
11. Speak *not* evil one of another,
17. and doeth (it) *not*, to him it is sin.
5: 9. Grudge *not* one against another,
12. above all things, my brethren, swear *not*,
17. that it might *not* rain:
]Pet. 1: 8. though now ye see (him) *not*,
14. *not* fashioning yourselves according
2:16. and *not* using (your) liberty for
3: 6. and are *not* afraid with any amazement.
7. that your prayers be *not* hindered.
9. *Not* rendering evil for evil,
10. his lips that they speak *no* guile:
14. be *not* afraid of their terror,
4: 4. think it strange that ye run *not* with
12. think it *not* strange concerning
15. let none (lit. *not* any) of you suffer as
16. let him *not* be ashamed ;
5: 2. *not* by constraint, but willingly;
2Pet. 1: 9. he that lacketh these things (lit. to whom these are *not*) is blind,
2:21. *not* to have known the way of

2Pet. 3: 8. be *not* ignorant of this one thing,
9. *not* willing that any should perish,
1Joh. 2: 4. and keepeth *not* his commandments,
15. Love *not* the world, neither the things
28. and *not* be ashamed before him
3:10. whosoever doeth *not* righteousness
— neither he that loveth *not* his brother.
13. Marvel *not*, my brethren,
14. He that loveth *not* (his) brother
18. let us *not* love in word,
21. if our heart condemn us *not*,
4: 1. believe *not* every spirit,
3. every spirit that confesseth *not*
8. He that loveth *not* knoweth not God ;
20. for he that loveth *not* his brother
5:10. he that believeth *not* God hath
12. he that hath *not* the Son of God
16. sin a sin (which is) *not* unto death,
— for them that sin *not* unto death.
2Joh. 7. who confess *not* that Jesus Christ is
9. and abideth *not* in the doctrine
10. receive him *not* into (your) house, *neither* bid him God speed:
3Joh. 10. and *not* content therewith,
11. follow *not* that which is evil,
Jude 5. destroyed them that believed *not*.
6. the angels which kept *not* their first
19. having *not* the Spirit.
Rev. 1:17. Fear *not ;* I am the first and the last:
3:18. that the shame of thy nakedness do *not*
5: 5. Weep *not :* behold, the Lion of the
6: 6. (see) thou hurt *not* the oil and the wine.
7: 3. Hurt *not* the earth,
16. neither)(|| shall the sun light on them,
8:12. the day shone *not*² for a third part
10: 4. and write them *not*.
11: 2. and measure it *not ;*
13:15. that as many as would *not* worship
19:10. See (thou do it) *not :* I am thy
22: 9. See (thou do it) *not :* for I am thy
10. Seal *not* the sayings of the prophecy of this

See also the following compounds: ἐὰν μή, ἵνα μή, μήγε, μηδαμῶς, μηδέ, μηδείς, μηδέποτε, μηδέπω, μηκέτι, μὴ οὐκ ; μήποτε, μήπω, μήπως, μήτε, μήτι, μήτις : interrogative οὐ μή ; and refer back to εἰ μή, εἰ δὲ μή, εἰ δὲ μήγε, εἰ μή τι.

ἐὰν μή, ean mee.

Mat. 5:20. *except* your righteousness shall exceed
6:15. But *if* ye forgive *not* men
10:13. but *if* it be *not* worthy,
14. whoso*ever* shall *not* receive you,
11: 6. whoso*ever* shall *not* be offended in me.
12:29. *except* he first bind the strong man ?
18: 3. *Except* ye be converted,
16. But *if* he will *not* hear (thee),
35. *if* ye from your hearts forgive *not*
26:42. *except* I drink it, thy will be done.
Mar 3:27. *except* he will first bind the
4:22. which shall *not* be manifested ;
7: 3. *except* they wash (their) hands oft,
4. *except* they wash, they eat not.
10:15. Whoso*ever* shall *not* receive the kingdom
30. *But* he shall receive an hundredfold
Lu. 7:23. whoso*ever* shall *not* be offended in me.
13: 3. but, *except* ye repent, ye shall all
5. but, *except* ye repent, ye shall all
18:17. Whoso*ever* shall *not* receive

Joh. 3: 2. *except* God be with him.
3. *Except* a man be born again,.
5. *Except* a man be born of water
27. *except* it be given him from heaven.
4:48. *Except* ye see signs and wonders,
5:19. *but* what he seeth the Father do:
6:44. *except* the Father which hath sent me
53. *Except* ye eat the flesh of the Son
65. *except* it were given unto him of
7:51. before it hear (lit. *except* it first have heard) him,
8:24. *if* ye believe *not* that I am (he),
12:24. *Except* a corn of wheat fall into
47. *if* any man hear my words, and believe *not*,
13: 8. *If* I wash thee *not*,
15: 4. *except* it abide in the vine; no more can ye, *except* ye abide in me.
6. *If* a man abide *not* in me,
16: 7. for *if* I go *not* away,
20:25. *Except* I shall see in his hands
Acts 8:31. How can I, *except* some man should
15: 1. *Except* ye be circumcised
27:31. *Except* these abide in the ship,
Ro. 10:15. *except* they be sent?
11:23. *if* they abide *not* in unbelief,
1Co. 8: 8. neither, *if* we eat *not*, are we the worse.
9:16. *if* I preach *not* the gospel!
14: 6. *except* I shall speak to you either
7. *except* they give a distinction in
9. *except* ye utter by the tongue
11. *if* I know *not* the meaning of the
28. But *if* there be *no* interpreter,
15:36. is not quickened, *except* it die:
Gal. 2:16. *but* by the faith of Jesus Christ,
2Th. 2: 3. *except* there come a falling away
2Ti. 2: 5. *except* he strive lawfully.
Jas. 2:17. faith, *if* it hath *not* works, is dead,
1Joh.3:21. *if* our heart condemn us *not*,
Rev. 2: 5. out of his place, *except* thou repent.
22. *except* they repent of their deeds.
3: 3. *If* therefore thou shalt *not* watch,

ἵνα μή, hina mee.

Mat. 7: 1. Judge not, *that* ye be *not* judged.
12:16. *that* they should *not* make him known:
17:27. Notwithstanding, *lest* we should offend
24:20. pray ye *that* your flight be *not* in
26: 5. *lest* there be an uproar
41. *that* ye enter *not* into temptation:
Mar. 3: 9. *lest* they should throng him.
12. *that* they should *not* make him known.
5:10. *that* he would *not* send them away
13:18. pray ye *that* your flight be *not* in
14:38. *lest* ye enter into temptation.
Lu. 8:12. *lest* they should believe and be saved.
31. *that* he would *not* command them
9:45. *that* they perceived it *not:*
16:28. *lest* they also come into this place
18: 5. *lest* by her continual coming she weary
22:32. *that* thy faith fail *not:*
46. *lest* ye enter into temptation.
Joh. 3:15. *That* whosoever believeth in him should *not* perish,
20. *lest* his deeds should be reproved.
4:15. give me this water, *that* I thirst *not,*
5:14. *lest* a worse thing come unto thee.
6:12. *that* *no*thing be lost.
50. *that* a man may eat thereof, and *not* die.
7:23. *that* the law of Moses should *not* be

Joh.12:35. *lest* darkness come upon you:
40. *that* they should *not* see with (their)
42. *lest* they should be put out of the
46. *that* whosoever believeth on me' should *not* abide in darkness.
16: 1. *that* ye should *not* be offended.
18:28. *lest* they should be defiled;
36. *that* I should *not* be delivered to
19:31. *that* the bodies should *not* remain
Acts 2:25. *that* I should *not* be moved:
4:17. But *that* it spread *no* further
5:26. *that* they should have been stoned.
24: 4. *that* I be *not* further tedious unto thee,
Ro. 11:25. *lest* ye should be wise in your own
15:20. *lest* I should build upon another
1Co. 1:15. *Lest* any should say that I had
17. *lest* the cross of Christ should be
4: 6. *that* *no* one of you be puffed up
7: 5. *that* Satan tempt you *not* for your
8:13. *lest* I make my brother to offend.
9:12. *lest* we should hinder the gospel
11:32. *that* we should *not* be condemned
34. *that* ye come *not* together unto
12:25. *That* there should be *no* schism in the
16: 2. *that* there be *no* gatherings when I come.
2Co. 1: 9. *that* we should *not* trust in ourselves,
2: 3. *lest*, when I came, I should have sorrow
5. *that* I may *not* overcharge you all.
11. *Lest* Satan should get an advantage of us:
6: 3. *that* the ministry be *not* blamed:
9: 3. *lest* our boasting of you should be
4. *that* we say *not,* ye
10: 9. *That* I may *not* seem as if
12: 7. And *lest* I should be exalted above
— *lest* I should be exalted
Gal. 5:17. so *that* ye cannot do the things
6:12. only *lest* they should suffer
Eph. 2: 9. *lest* any man should boast.
Phi. 2:27. *lest* I should have sorrow upon
Col. 2: 4. *lest* any man should beguile you
3:21. *lest* they be discouraged.
1Th. 4:13. *that* ye sorrow *not,* even as others
1Ti. 3: 6. *lest* being lifted up with pride
7. *lest* he fall into reproach
6: 1. *that* the name of God and (his) doctrine be *not*
Tit. 2: 5. *that* the word of God be *not* blasphemed.
3:14. *that* they be *not* unfruitful.
Philem.14. *that* thy benefit should *not* be as it were
19. *albeit* I do *not* say to thee how
Heb 3:13. *lest* any of you be hardened
4:11. *lest* any man fall after the same
6:12. *That* ye be *not* slothful,
11:28. *lest* he that destroyed the firstborn
40. *that* they without us should *not* be
12: 3. *lest* ye be wearied and faint
13. *lest* that which is lame be
Jas. 5: 9. *lest* ye be condemned:
12. *lest* ye fall into condemnation.
2Pet.3:17. beware *lest* ye also, being led away
1Joh.2: 1. *that* ye sin *not.*
2Joh. 8. *that* we lose *not* those things
Rev. 7: 1. *that* the wind should *not* blow
9: 4. *that* they should *not* hurt the grass
5. *that* they should *not* kill them,
20. *that* they should *not* worship devils,
11: 6. *that* it rain *not* in the days of
13:17. *that* *no* man might buy or sell,
16:15. *lest* he walk naked,
18: 4. *that* ye be *not* partakers of her sins, and *that* ye receive *not* of her plagues.
20: 3. *that* he should deceive the nations *no* more,

μήγε see εἰ δὲ μήγε.

μηδαμῶς, meedamōs.

Acts10:14. Peter said, *Not so*, Lord; for I
　11: 8. But I said, *Not so*, Lord: for nothing

μηδέ, meede.

Mat. 6:25. *nor yet* for your body, what ye shall put
　　7: 6. *neither* cast ye your pearls before
　10: 9. *nor* silver, *nor* brass in your purses,
　　10. *neither* two coats, *neither* shoes, *nor* yet
　　　　staves; for the workman
　　14. receive you, *nor* hear your words,
　22:29. the scriptures, *nor* the power of God.
　23:10. *Neither* be ye called masters:
　24:20. *neither* on the sabbath day:
Mar. 2: 2. *not so much as* about the door:
　　6:11. *nor* hear you, when ye depart thence,
　　8:26. *Neither* go into the town, *nor* tell (it) to
　　　　any in the town.
　12:24. *neither* the power of God?
　13:11. *neither* do ye premeditate:
　　15. *neither* enter (therein), to take any thing
Lu. 3:14. *neither* accuse (any) falsely;
　10: 4. Carry neither purse, nor scrip, *nor* shoes:
　12:22. *neither* for the body, what ye shall
　　47. *neither* did according to his will,
　14:12. *nor* thy brethren, *neither* thy kinsmen, *nor*
　　　　(thy) rich neighbours;
　16:26. *neither* can they pass to us,
　17:23. go not after (them), *nor* follow (them).
Joh. 4:15. *neither* come hither to draw.
　14:27. *neither* let it be afraid.
Acts 4:18. *nor* teach in the name of Jesus.
　21:21. *neither* to walk after the customs.
　23: 8. *neither* angel, nor spirit:
Ro. 6:13. *Neither* yield ye your members
　　9:11. *neither* having done any good or
　14:21. *nor* to drink wine, *nor* (any thing) whereby
　　　　thy brother
1Co. 5: 8. *neither* with the leaven of
　　11. with such an one *no not* to eat.
　10: 7. *Neither* be ye idolaters, as
　　8. *Neither* let us commit fornication,
　　9. *Neither* let us tempt Christ,
　　10. *Neither* murmur ye, as some
2Co. 4: 2. *nor* handling the word of God deceitfully;
Eph. 5: 3. let it *not* be *once* named among you,
Col. 2:21. Touch *not*; taste *not*; handle *not*;
2Th. 3:10. would not work, *neither* should he eat.
1Ti. 1: 4. *Neither* give heed to fables
　　5:22. *neither* be partaker of other men's
　　6:17. *nor* trust in uncertain riches,
2Ti. 1: 8. *nor* of me his prisoner:
Heb 12: 5. *nor* faint when thou art rebuked
1Pet.3:14. of their terror, *neither* be troubled;
　　5: 2. *not* for filthy lucre, but of a ready mind;
　　3. *Neither* as being lords over (God's)
1Joh.2:15. *neither* the things (that are) in
　　3:18. *neither* in tongue; but in deed

μηδείς, μηδεμία, μηδέν, meedīs, mœedemia, meeden.

‖ denotes where the double negative of the Greek
is omitted.

Mat. 8: 4. See thou tell *no man*;
　　9:30. See (that) *no man* know (it).

Mat.16:20. that they should tell *no man* that
　17: 9. Tell the vision to *no man*, until
　27:19. Have thou *nothing* to do with that
Mar. 1:44. See thou say *nothing* to ‖ *any man*.
　　5:26. and was *nothing* bettered,
　　43. that *no man* should know it;
　　6: 8. should take *nothing* for (their) journey,
　　7:36. that they should tell *no man*:
　　8:30. that they should tell *no man* of him.
　　9: 9. that they should tell *no man* what
　11:14. *No man* eat fruit of thee hereafter
Lu. 3:13. Exact *no* more than that which is
　　14. Do violence to *no man*,
　　4:35. he came out of him, and hurt him *not*.
　　5:14. he charged him to tell *no man*:
　　6:35. hoping for *nothing* again;
　　8:56. that they should tell *no man*
　　9: 3. Take *nothing* for (your) journey,
　　21. to tell *no man* that thing;
　10: 4. and salute *no man* by the way.
Joh. 8:10. and saw *none* but the woman,
Acts 4:17. to *no man* in this name.
　　21. finding *nothing* how they might
　　8:24. that *none* of these things which
　　9: 7. but seeing *no man*.
　10:20. doubting *nothing*: for I have sent them.
　　28. that I should *not* call *any* man common
　11:12. go with them, *nothing* doubting.
　　19. the word to *none* but unto the Jews
　13:28. though they found *no* cause of death
　15:28. to lay upon you *no* greater burden
　16:28. Do thyself *no* harm:
　19:36. and to do *nothing* rashly.
　　40. there being *no* cause whereby
　21:25. that they observe *no* such thing,
　23:14. that we will eat *nothing* until
　　22. (See thou) tell *no man* that thou
　　29. but to have *nothing* laid to his charge
　24:23. that he should forbid *none* of his
　25:17. without any delay (lit. making *no* delay)
　　　　on the morrow
　　25. *nothing* worthy of death,
　27:33. continued fasting, having taken *nothing*.
　28: 6. and saw *no* harm come to him,
　　18. there was *no* cause of death in me.
Ro. 12:17. Recompense to *no man* evil
　13: 8. Owe *no man* ‖ *any thing*,
1Co. 1: 7. So that ye come behind in *no* gift;
　　3:18. Let *no man* deceive himself.
　　21. let *no man* glory in men.
　10:24. Let *no man* seek his own,
　　25. asking *no* question for conscience sake:
　　27. asking *no* question for conscience sake.
2Co. 6: 3. Giving *no* offence in ‖ *any thing*,
　　10. as having *nothing*, and
　　7: 9. receive damage by us in *nothing*.
　11: 5. I was *not a whit* behind the
　13: 7. I pray to God that ye do *no* evil;
Gal. 6: 3. to be something, when he is *nothing*,
　　17. let *no man* trouble me:
Eph. 5: 6. Let *no man* deceive you
Phi. 1:28. in *nothing* terrified by your
　　2: 3. (Let) *nothing* (be done) through strife
　　4: 6. Be careful for *nothing*;
Col. 2:18. Let *no man* beguile you
1Th. 3: 3. That *no man* should be moved
　　4:12. (that) ye may have lack of *nothing*.
2Th. 2: 3. Let no man deceive you by ‖ *any* means:
　　3:11. working *not at all*,
1Ti. 4:12. Let *no man* despise thy youth;
　　5:14. give *none* occasion to the adversary
　　21. doing *nothing* by partiality.

1 Ti. 5:22. Lay hands suddenly on *no man*,
    6: 4. He is proud, knowing *nothing*,
Tit. 2: 8. having *no* evil *thing* to say of you.
    15. Let *no man* despise thee.
    3: 2. To speak evil of *no man*,
    13. that *nothing* be wanting unto them.
Heb 10: 2. should have had *no* more conscience
Jas. 1: 4. perfect and entire, wanting *nothing*.
    6. let him ask in faith, *nothing* wavering.
    13. Let *no man* say when he is tempted,
1 Pet. 3: 6. and are not afraid with)(*any* amazement.
1 Joh. 3: 7. let *no man* deceive you:
3 Joh. 7. taking *nothing* of the Gentiles.
Rev. 2:10. Fear *none* of those things which
    3:11. that *no man* take thy crown.

μηδέποτε, *meedepote*.

2 Ti. 3: 7. and *never* able to come to the knowledge
    of the truth.

μηδέπω, *meedepo*.

Heb 11: 7. being warned of God of things *not* seen
    as *yet*,

μηκέτι, *meeketi*.

|| denotes where the double negative of the Greek
    is omitted.

Mat. 21:19. Let *no* fruit grow on thee *henceforward*
Mar 1:45. Jesus could *no more* openly enter
    2: 2. that there was *no* room to receive
    9:25. and enter *no more* into him.
    11:14. No man eat fruit of thee || *hereafter*
Joh. 5:14. sin *no more*, lest a worse thing
    8:11. go, and sin *no more*.
Acts 4:17. speak || *henceforth* to no man in
    13:34. *no more* to return to corruption,
    25:24. he ought not to live || *any longer*.
Ro. 6: 6. that *henceforth* we should *not*
    14:13. Let us *not* therefore judge one another
    any more :
    15:23. But now having *no more* place
2 Co. 5:15. should *not henceforth* live unto
Eph. 4:14. That we (henceforth) be *no more* children,
    17. that ye *henceforth* walk *not* as
    28. Let him that stole steal *no more* :
1 Th. 3: 1. when we could *no longer* forbear,
    5. when I could *no longer* forbear,
1 Ti. 5:23. Drink *no longer* water,
1 Pet. 4: 2. That he *no longer* should live the rest of

μὴ οὐκ & οὐ μη, *mee ouk* & *ou mee*.

An interrogation put negatively.

Joh. 18:11. shall I *not* drink it?
Ro. 10:18. But I say, Have they *not* heard?
    19. Did *not* Israel know?
1 Co. 9: 4. Have we *not* power to eat and
    5. Have we *not* power to lead about a sister,
    11:22. have ye *not* houses to eat and to drink in?

μήποτε or μή ποτε, *meepotee* or *mee potee*.

Mat. 4: 6. *lest at any time* thou dash thy
    5:25. *lest at any time* the adversary

Mat. 7: 6. *lest* they trample them under
    13:15. *lest at any time* they should see
    29. Nay ; *lest* while ye gather up
    15:32. *lest* they faint in the way.
    25: 9. *lest* there be not enough
    27:64. *lest* his disciples come by night,
Mar 4:12. *lest at any time* they should be converted,
    14: 2. *lest* there be an uproar
Lu. 3:15. *whether* he were the Christ, *or not* ;
    4:11. *lest at any time* thou dash
    12:58. *lest* he hale thee to the judge,
    14: 8. *lest* a more honourable man
    12. *lest* they also bid thee again,
    29. *Lest haply*, after he hath laid
    21:34. *lest at any time* your hearts
Joh. 7:26.)(Do the rulers know indeed that this is
Acts 5:39. *lest haply* ye be found even to fight
    28:27. *lest* they should see with
2 Ti. 2:25. *if* God *peradventure* will give them
Heb 2: 1. *lest at any time* we should let (them) slip.
    3:12. *lest* there be in any of you an evil heart of
    4: 1. Let us therefore fear, *lest*, a promise
    9:17. it is of *no* strength *at all* while

μήπω, *meepo*.

Ro. 9:11. (the children) being *not yet* born,
Heb 9: 8. was *not yet* made manifest,

μήπως or μή πως, *meepōs* or *mee pōs*.

Acts 27:29. fearing *lest* we (lit. they) should have
    fallen upon rocks,
Ro. 11:21. *lest* he also spare not thee.
1 Co. 8: 9. take heed *lest by any means* this
    9:27. *lest that by any means*, when I have
2 Co. 2: 7. *lest perhaps* such a one should be
    9: 4. *Lest haply* if they of Macedonia come
    11: 3. But I fear, *lest by any means*, as the
    12:20. For I fear, *lest*, when I come, I
    — *lest* (there be) debates, envyings,
Gal. 2: 2. *lest by any means* I should run,
    4:11. *lest* I have bestowed upon you
1 Th. 3: 5. *lest by some means* the tempter have

μήτε, *meete*.

|| marks the omission of a double negative of the
    Greek.

Mat. 5:34. *neither* by heaven ; for it is God's
    35. *Nor* by the earth ; for it is his footstool:
    neither by Jerusalem ;
    36. *Neither* shalt thou swear by thy head,
    11:18. For John came *neither* eating *nor* drinking,
Mar 3:20. they could not || *so much as* eat
Lu. 7:33. John the Baptist came *neither* eating bread
    nor drinking wine ;
    9: 3. *neither* staves, *nor* scrip, *neither* bread,
    neither money ; *neither* have two coats
Acts 23: 8. neither angel, *nor* spirit:
    12. they would *neither* eat *nor* drink
    21. they will *neither* eat *nor* drink
    27:20. when *neither* sun *nor* stars
Eph. 4:27. *Neither* give place to the devil.
2 Th. 2: 2. or be troubled, *neither* by spirit, *nor* by
    word, *nor* by letter as from us,
1 Ti. 1: 7. understanding *neither* what they say, *nor*
    whereof they affirm.

Heb 7: 3. having *neither* beginning of days, *nor* end of life;

Jas. 5:12. swear not, *neither* by heaven, *neither* by the earth, *neither* by any other oath:

Rev. 7: 1. should not blow on the earth, *nor* on the sea, *nor* on any tree.

3. Hurt not the earth, *neither* the sea, *nor* the trees, till we have sealed

---

μήτι, *meeti.* adv. interrog.

Mat. 7:16.)(Do men gather grapes of thorns, or figs of thistles?

12:23. Is *not* this the son of David?

26:22. Lord,)(is it I?

25. Master,)(is it I?

Mar 4:21.)(Is a candle brought to be put under a

14:19.)((Is) it I? and another (said),)((Is) it

Lu. 6:39.)(Can the blind lead the blind?

Joh. 4:29. is *not* this the Christ?

7:31. When Christ cometh,)(will he do

8:22.)(Will he kill himself?

18:35.)(Am I a Jew?

Acts10:47.)(Can any man forbid water,

1Co. 6: 3. *how much more* things that pertain to this

2Co. 1:17.)(did I use lightness?

Jas. 3:11.)(Doth a fountain send forth

μήτις or μή τις, *meetis* or *mee tis.* interrog.

Joh. 4:33. Hath *any man* brought him (ought) to

7:48. Have *any* of the rulers or

21: 5. Children, have ye *any* meat?

2Co.12:18.)(Did Titus make a gain of you?

Though μήτις occurs in one word as an indefinite pron. it is better read as μή τις.

οὐ μή, *ou mee.* double negative.

Mat. 5:18. one jot or one tittle shall *in no wise*

20. ye shall *in no case* enter into

26. Thou shalt *by no means* come out

10:23. Ye shall *not* have gone over the

42. he shall *in no wise* lose his reward.

13:14. and shall *not* understand;

— and shall *not* perceive:

15: 6(5). And honour *not* his father or

16:22. this shall *not* be unto thee.

28. which shall *not* taste of death,

18: 3. ye shall *not* enter into the

23:39. Ye shall *not* see me henceforth,

24: 2. There shall *not* be left here one stone upon another, that shall *not* be thrown down.

21. no, *nor ever* shall be.

34. This generation shall *not* pass,

35. but my words shall *not* pass away.

26:29. I will *not* drink henceforth of

35. yet will I *not* deny thee.

Mar 9: 1. which shall *not* taste of death,

41. he shall *not* lose his reward.

10:15. he shall *not* enter therein.

13: 2. there shall *not* be left one stone upon another, that shall *not* be thrown down.

19. unto this time, *neither* shall be.

30. this generation shall *not* pass,

Mar13:31. but my words shall *not* pass away.

14:25. I will)(drink no more of the

31. I will *not* deny thee *in any wise.*

16:18. it shall *not* hurt them;

Lu. 1:15. shall drink neither wine nor strong drink; (lit. *not* drink wine or &c.);

6:37. and ye shall *not* be judged: condemn not, and ye shall *not* be condemned:

9:27. which shall *not* taste of death, till

10:19. nothing shall *by any means* hurt you.

12:59. thou shalt *not* depart thence, till

13:35. Ye shall *not* see me, until

18: 7. And shall *not* God avenge his own

17. shall *in no wise* enter therein.

30. Who shall *not* receive manifold

21:18. there shall *not* an hair of your head

32. This generation shall *not* pass

33. but my words shall *not* pass away.

22:16. I will *not* any more eat thereof,

18. I will *not* drink of the fruit

34. the cock shall *not* crow this day,

67. ye will *not* believe:

68. ye will *not* answer me, nor let (me) go.

Joh. 4:14. shall never (lit. *not* ever) thirst;

48. and wonders, ye will *not* believe.

6:35. he that cometh to me shall never (lit. *not*) hunger; and he that believeth on me shall never (lit. *not* ever) thirst.

37. I will *in no wise* cast out.

8:12. shall *not* walk in darkness,

51. he shall never (lit. *not* for ever) see death.

52. he shall never (lit. *not* for ever) taste of

10: 5. a stranger will they *not* follow,

28. and they shall never (lit. *not* for ever) perish,

11:26. and believeth in me shall never (lit. *not,* &c.) die.

56. that he will *not* come to the feast?

13: 8. Thou shalt never (lit. *not,* &c.) wash my

38. The cock shall *not* crow, till

20:25. I will *not* believe.

Acts13:41. which ye shall *in no wise* believe,

28:26. and shall *not* understand; and seeing ye shall see, and *not* perceive:

Ro. 4: 8. to whom the Lord will *not* impute sin.

1Co. 8:13. I will eat *no* flesh while the

Gal. 4:30. shall *not* be heir with the son

5:16. and ye shall *not* fulfil the lust

1Th. 4:15. shall *not* prevent them which

5: 3. and they shall *not* escape.

Heb 8:11. they shall *not* teach every man

12. will I remember *no* more.

10:17. will I remember *no* more.

13: 5. I will *never* leave thee, nor)(forsake thee.

1Pet.2: 6. shall *not* be confounded.

2Pet.1:10. if ye do these things, ye shall *never* (lit. *not* ever) fall:

Rev. 2:11. shall *not* be hurt of the second death.

3: 3. thou shalt *not* know what hour I will come

5. I will *not* blot out his name

12. and he shall go *no* more out:

15: 4. Who shall *not* fear thee, O Lord,

18: 7. and shall see *no* sorrow.

14. thou shalt find them no more)(*at all.*

21. and shall be found *no* more *at all.*

22. shall be heard *no* more *at all* in thee;

— and *no* craftsman

— shall be heard *no* more *at all* in thee;

23. shall shine *no* more *at all* in thee;

— shall be heard *no* more *at all* in thee:

21:25. shall *not* be shut *at all* by day:

27. there shall *in no wise* enter into it

μηκέτι see after μή.

μῆκος, meekos.

Eph. 3:18. and *length*, and depth, and height ;
Rev.21:16. the *length* is as large as the breadth:
— The *length* and the breadth and the height
    of it are equal.

μηκύνομαι, meekunomai.

Mar 4:27. and the seed should spring and *grow up*,

μηλωτή, meelotee.

Heb 11:37. they wandered about in *sheepskins*

μήν, meen.

Lu. 1:24. and hid herself five *months*,
      26. And in the sixth *month* the angel
      36. this is the sixth *month* with her,
      56. Mary abode with her about three *months*,
    4:25. was shut up three years and six *months*,
Acts 7:20. in his father's house three *months* :
    18:11. a year and six *months*,
    19: 8. for the space of three *months*,
    20: 3. And (there) abode three *months*.
    28:11. And after three *months* we departed
Gal. 4:10. Ye observe days, and *months*, and times,
Jas. 5:17. by the space of three years and six *months*.
Rev. 9: 5. should be tormented five *months* :
      10. to hurt men five *months*.
      15. and a day, and a *month*, and a year,
    11: 2. tread under foot forty (and) two *months*.
    13: 5. to continue forty (and) two *months*.
    22: 2. yielded her fruit every *month* :

μηνύω, meenuo.

Lu. 20:37. even Moses *shewed* at the bush,
Joh. 11:57. he *should shew* (it), that they might take
Acts 23:30. And *when it was told* me how that
1 Co.10:28. eat not for his sake *that shewed* it,

μὴ οὐκ, μήποτε, μήπω, μήπως,
see after μή.

μηρός, meeros.

Rev.19:16. and on his *thigh* a name written,

μήτε see after μή.

μήτηρ, meeteer.

Mat. 1:18. When as his *mother* Mary was espoused
    2:11. the young child with Mary his *mother*,
      13. take the young child and his *mother*,
      14. he took the young child and his *mother*
      20. take the young child and his *mother*,
      21. and took the young child and his *mother*,
    10:35. the daughter against her *mother*,
      37. He that loveth father or *mother* more
    12:46. behold, (his) *mother* and his brethren
      47. Behold, thy *mother* and thy brethren
      48. Who is my *mother* ? and who
      49. Behold my *mother* and my brethren !
      50. the same is my brother, and sister, and
          mother.
    13:55. is not his *mother* called Mary?
    14: 8. being before instructed of her *mother*,
      11. and she brought (it) to her *mother*.
    15: 4. Honour thy father and *mother* : and, He
          that curseth father or *mother*,
       5. shall say to (his) father or (his) *mother*,
     6(5). And honour not his father or his
          mother,
    19: 5. leave father and *mother*, and shall
      12. so born from (their) *mother's* womb:
      19. Honour thy father and (thy) *mother* :
      29. or *mother*, or wife, or children,
    20:20. Then came to him the *mother* of
    27:56. and Mary the *mother* of James and Joses,
          and the *mother* of Zebedee's
Mar 3:31. his brethren and his *mother*,
      32. Behold, thy *mother* and thy
      33. Who is my *mother*, or my
      34. Behold my *mother* and my brethren !
      35. and my sister, and *mother*.
    5:40. he taketh the father and the *mother*
    6:24. and said unto her *mother*,
      28. the damsel gave it to her *mother*.
    7:10. Honour thy father and thy *mother* ; and,
          Whoso curseth father or *mother*,
      11. say to his father or *mother*,
      12. for his father or his *mother* ;
    10: 7. leave his father and *mother*, and cleave
      19. Honour thy father and *mother*.
      29. or sisters, or father, or *mother*,
      30. and sisters, and *mothers*, and
    15:40. and Mary the *mother* of James
Lu. 1:15. even from his *mother's* womb.
      43. that the *mother* of my Lord should
      60. And his *mother* answered and said,
    2:33. And Joseph and his *mother*
      34. and said unto Mary his *mother*,
      43. and Joseph and his *mother* knew not
      48. and his *mother* said unto him,
      51. but his *mother* kept all these
    7:12. the only son of his *mother*,
      15. he delivered him to his *mother*.
    8:19. Then came to him (his) *mother*
      20. Thy *mother* and thy brethren
      21. My *mother* and my brethren are these
      51. and the *mother* of the maiden.
    12:53. the *mother* against the daughter, and the
          daughter against the *mother* ;
    14:26. hate not his father, and *mother*,
    18:20. Honour thy father and thy *mother*.
Joh. 2: 1. and the *mother* of Jesus was there:
       3. the *mother* of Jesus saith unto him,
       5. His *mother* saith unto the servants,
      12. he, and his *mother*, and his brethren;
    3: 4. the second time into his *mother's* womb,
    6:42. whose father and *mother* we know?

Joh.19:25. stood by the cross of Jesus his *mother*, and
        his *mother's* sister,
    26. When Jesus therefore saw his *mother*,
      — he saith unto his *mother*,
    27. Behold thy *mother* !
Acts 1:14. and Mary the *mother* of Jesus,
    3: 2. lame from his *mother's* womb
   12:12. to the house of Mary the *mother*
   14: 8. a cripple from his *mother's* womb,
Ro. 16:13. and his *mother* and mine.
Gal. 1:15. separated me from my *mother's* womb,
   4:26. which is the *mother* of us all.
Eph 5:31. leave his father and *mother*,
   6: 2. Honour thy father and *mother* ;
1Ti. 5: 2. The elder women as *mothers* ;
2Ti. 1: 5. and thy *mother* Eunice ;
Rev.17: 5. THE *MOTHER* OF HARLOTS AND

μήτι. adv., μήτις. interrog., see after
μή.

μήτρα, *meetra.*

Lu. 2:23. Every male that openeth the *womb*
Ro. 4:19. neither yet the deadness of Sarah's *womb:*

μητραλῴης, *meetraloees.*

1Ti. 1: 9. and *murderers of mothers*, for

μία, *mia.* fem. to εἷς.

Mat. 5:18. one jot or *one* tittle shall in no wise
    19. shall break *one* of these least
    36. thou canst not make *one* hair
   17: 4. *one* for thee, and *one* for Moses, and *one*
       for Elias.
   19: 5. and they twain shall be *one* flesh?
    6. they are no more twain, but *one* flesh.
   20:12. These last have wrought (but) *one* hour,
   21:19. And when he saw *a* fig tree in the way,
   24:41. the *one* shall be taken, and the other (lit.
      one) left.
   26:40. could ye not watch with me *one* hour?
    69. and *a* damsel came unto him,
   28: 1. toward the *first* (day) of the week,
Mar 9: 5. *one* for thee, and *one* for Moses, and *one*
       for Elias.
   10: 8. twain shall be *one* flesh: so then they are
      no more twain, but *one* flesh.
   12:42. there came *a certain* poor widow,
   14:37. couldest not thou watch *one* hour?
    66. there cometh *one* of the maids of
   16: 2. the *first* (day) of the week,
Lu. 5:12. when he was in *a certain* city,
    17. it came to pass on *a certain* day,
   8:22. it came to pass on *a certain* day,
   9:33. *one* for thee, and *one* for Moses, and *one*
       for Elias.
   13:10. he was teaching in *one* of the synagogues
   14:18. they all with *one* (consent) began
   15: 8. if she lose *one* piece,
   16:17. than *one* tittle of the law to fail.
   17:22. shall desire to see *one* of the days of
    34. there shall be two (men) in *one* bed;
    35. the *one* shall be taken, and the other

Lu. 20: 1. on *one* of those days,
   22:59. about the space of *one* hour after
   24: 1. Now upon the *first* (day) of the week,
Joh.10:16. and there shall be *one* fold,
   20: 1. The *first* (day) of the week cometh
    19. being the *first* (day) of the week,
Acts 4:32. were of one heart and of *one* soul :
   12:10. and passed on through *one* street ;
   19:34. all with *one* voice about the space
   20: 7. And upon the *first* (day) of the week,
   21: 7. and abode with them *one* day.
   24:21. Except it be for this *one* voice,
   28:13. and after *one* day the south wind
1Co. 6:16. for two, saith he, shall be *one* flesh.
   10: 8. fell in *one* day three and twenty thousand.
   16: 2. Upon the *first* (day) of the week
2Co.11:24. received I forty (stripes) save *one*.
Gal. 4:24. the *one* from the mount Sinai,
Eph. 4: 4. ye are called in *one* hope of
    5. One Lord, *one* faith, one baptism,
   5:31. and they two shall be *one* flesh.
Phi. 1:27. with *one* mind striving together
1Ti. 3: 2. the husband of *one* wife,
    12. be the husbands of *one* wife,
Tit. 1: 6. the husband of *one* wife,
   3:10. after the *first* and second admonition
Heb 10:12. after he had offered *one* sacrifice
    14. For by *one* offering he hath
   12:16. who for *one* morsel of meat
2Pet. 3: 8. that *one* day (is) with the Lord
    — and a thousand years as *one* day.
Rev. 6: 1. when the Lamb opened *one* of the seals,
   9:12. *One* woe is past ;
   13. I heard *a* voice from the four horns
   13: 3. I saw *one* of his heads
   17:12. as kings *one* hour with the beast.
    13. These have *one* mind,
    17. and to agree (lit. to form *one* mind), and
       give their kingdom
   18: 8. shall her plagues come in *one* day,
    10. for in *one* hour is thy judgment come.
   17(16). For in *one* hour so great riches
    19. for in *one* hour is she made desolate.

μιαίνω, *miaino.*

Joh.18:28. lest they *should be defiled* ;
Tit. 1:15. but unto them *that are defiled*
    — their mind and conscience *is defiled.*
Heb 12:15. and thereby many *be defiled* ;
Jude 8. these (filthy) dreamers *defile* the flesh,

μίασμα, *miasma.*

2Pet. 2:20. have escaped the *pollutions* of the world

μιασμός, *miasmos.*

2Pet. 2:10. in the lust of *uncleanness*,

μίγμα, *migma.*

Joh.19:39. brought a *mixture* of myrrh and aloes,

μίγνυμι, *mignumi.*

Mat.27:34. vinegar to drink *mingled* with gall :
Lu. 13: 1. whose blood Pilate *had mingled*
Rev. 8: 7. hail and fire *mingled* with blood,
   15: 2. a sea of glass *mingled* with fire:

-ός, μικρόν, mikron. adv.

Mat.26:39. And he went *a little* farther, and
　　73. And after *a while* came unto (him)
Mar 14:35. And he went forward *a little*, and
　　70. And *a little* after, they that stood by
Joh. 13:33. Little children, yet *a little while* I am
　　14:19. Yet *a little while*, and the world
　　16:16. *A little while*, and ye shall not see me: and
　　　　again, *a little while*, and ye
　　17. *A little while*, and ye shall not see me: and
　　　　again, *a little while*, and ye
　　18. What is this that he saith, *A little while?*
　　19. *A little while*, and ye shall not see me : and
　　　　again, *a little while*, and ye

μικρ-ός, -ότερος, mikros, -oteros.

Mat.10:42. unto one of these *little* ones a cup of
　　11:11. he that is *least* in the kingdom
　　13:32. is the *least* of all seeds:
　　18: 6. shall offend one of these *little* ones
　　10. despise not one of these *little* ones ;
　　14. one of these *little* ones should perish.
Mar 4:31. is *less* than all the seeds
　　9:42. shall offend one of (these) *little* ones
　　15:40. Mary the mother of James the *less*
Lu. 7:28. he that is *least* in the kingdom
　　9:48. he that is *least* among you all,
　　12:32. Fear not, *little* flock ;
　　17: 2. should offend one of these *little* ones.
　　19: 3. because he was *little* of stature.
Joh. 7:33. Yet a *little* while am I with you,
　　12:35. Yet a *little* while is the light
Acts 8:10. from the *least* to the greatest,
　　26:22. witnessing both to *small* and great,
1Co. 5: 6. Know ye not that a *little* leaven
2Co.11: 1. bear with me a *little* in (my) folly:
　　16. that I may boast myself a *little*.
Gal. 5: 9. A *little* leaven leaveneth the whole
Heb 8:11. from the *least* to the greatest.
　　10:37. For yet a *little* while, and he that
Jas. 3: 5. the tongue is a *little* member,
Rev. 3: 8. for thou hast a *little* strength,
　　6:11. they should rest yet for a *little* season,
　　11:18. that fear thy name, *small* and great ;
　　13:16. caused all, both *small* and great,
　　19: 5. that fear him, both *small* and great.
　　18. both *small* and great.
　　20: 3. must be loosed a *little* season.
　　12. I saw the dead, *small* and great,

μίλιον, milion.

Mat. 5:41. shall compel thee to go a *mile*,

μιμέομαι, mimeomai.

2Th. 3: 7. how ye ought *to follow* us:
　　9. an ensample unto you *to follow* us.
Heb 13: 7. whose faith *follow*, considering
3Joh. 11. *follow* not that which is evil,

μιμητής, mimeetees.

1Co. 4:16. be ye *followers* of me.
　　11: 1. Be ye *followers* of me, even as
Eph. 5: 1. Be ye therefore *followers* of God,

1Th. 1: 6. And ye became *followers* of us,
　　2:14. ye, brethren, became *followers* of the
Heb 6:12. but *followers* of them who through
1Pet. 3:13. if ye be *followers* of that which is good ?

μιμνήσκομαι, mimneeskomai.

Heb 2: 6. that thou *art mindful* of him ?
　　13: 3. *Remember* them that are in bonds,

μισέω, miseo.

Mat. 5:43. shalt love thy neighbour, and *hate*
　　44. do good to them that *hate* you,
　　6:24. for either he *will hate* the one,
　　10:22. ye shall be *hated* of all (men)
　　24: 9. and ye shall be *hated* of all
　　10. and *shall hate* one another.
Mar.13:13. And ye shall be *hated* of all (men)
Lu. 1:71. from the hand of all *that hate* us ;
　　6:22. when men *shall hate* you,
　　27. do good to them *which hate* you,
　　14:26. and *hate* not his father, and mother,
　　16:13. either he *will hate* the one,
　　19:14. But his citizens *hated* him,
　　21:17. ye shall be *hated* of all (men)
Joh. 3:20. *hateth* the light, neither cometh
　　7: 7. cannot *hate* you ; but me it *hateth*,
　　12:25. he *that hateth* his life in this world
　　15:18. If the world *hate* you, ye know that it
　　　　hated me before (it hated) you.
　　19. therefore the world *hateth* you.
　　23. He *that hateth* me *hateth* my Father also.
　　24. they both seen and *hated*
　　25. They *hated* me without a cause.
　　17:14. the world *hath hated* them,
Ro. 7:15. what I *hate*, that do I.
　　9:13. Esau *have* I *hated*.
Eph. 5:29. no man ever yet *hated* his own flesh ;
Tit. 3: 3. hateful, (and) *hating* one another.
Heb 1: 9. and *hated* iniquity ;
1Joh. 2: 9. that saith he is in the light, and *hateth* his
　　　　brother,
　　11. But he *that hateth* his brother is in
　　3:13. if the world *hate* you.
　　15. *Whosoever hateth* his brother
　　4:20. and *hateth* his brother,
Jude 23. *hating* even the garment spotted
Rev. 2: 6. that thou *hatest* the deeds of the Nico-
　　　　laitanes, which I also *hate*.
　　15. which thing I *hate*.
　　17:16. these *shall hate* the whore,
　　18: 2. of every unclean and *hateful* bird.

μισθαποδοσία, misthapodosia.

Heb 2: 2. received a just *recompence of reward ;*
　　10:35. great *recompence of reward*.
　　11:26. unto the *recompence of the reward*.

μισθαποδότης, misthapodotees.

Heb 11: 6. he is a *rewarder* of them that

μίσθιος, misthios.

Lu. 15:17. How many *hired servants* of my father's
　　19. as one of thy *hired servants*.

μισθόομαι, mistho-omai.

Mat.20: 1. *to hire* labourers into his vineyard.
    7. Because no man *hath hired* us.

μισθός, misthos.

Mat. 5:12. for great (is) your *reward* in heaven:
    46. what *reward* have ye?
  6: 1. ye have no *reward* of your Father
    2. They have their *reward.*
    5. They have their *reward.*
    16. They have their *reward.*
  10:41. shall receive a prophet's *reward;*
    — shall receive a righteous man's *reward*
    42. shall in no wise lose his *reward.*
  20: 8. give them (their) *hire,*
Mar 9:41. he shall not lose his *reward.*
Lu. 6:23. your *reward* (is) great in heaven:
    35. your *reward* shall be great,
  10: 7. the labourer is worthy of his *hire.*
Joh. 4:36. receiveth *wages,* and gathereth
Acts 1:18. a field with the *reward* of iniquity;
Ro. 4: 4. that worketh is the *reward* not
1Co. 3: 8. shall receive his own *reward*
    14. he shall receive a *reward.*
  9:17. willingly, I have a *reward:*
    18. What is my *reward* then?
1Ti. 5:18. The labourer (is) worthy of his *reward.*
Jas. 5: 4. Behold, the *hire* of the labourers
2Pet.2:13. receive the *reward* of unrighteousness,
    15. who loved the *wages* of unrighteousness;
2Joh. 8. but that we receive a full *reward.*
Jude 11. after the error of Balaam for *reward,*
Rev.11:18. that thou shouldest give *reward*
  22:12. and my *reward* (is) with me,

μίσθωμα, misthōma.

Acts 28:30. two whole years in his own *hired house,*

μισθωτός, misthōtos.

Mar 1:20. in the ship with the *hired servants,*
Joh.10:12. But he that is an *hireling,*
    13. The *hireling* fleeth, because he is an
    hireling, and careth not

μνᾶ, mna.

Lu. 19:13. and delivered them ten *pounds,*
    16. saying, Lord, thy *pound* hath gained ten
    pounds.
    18. Lord, thy *pound* hath gained five *pounds.*
    20. (here is) thy *pound,*
    24. Take from him the *pound,* and give (it) to
    him that hath ten *pounds.*
    25. Lord, he hath ten *pounds.*

μνάομαι, mnaomai.

Mat. 5:23. and there *rememberest* that thy brother
  26:75. And Peter *remembered* the word
  27:63. Sir, we *remember* that that deceiver
Lu. 1:54. in remembrance of (lit. to *remember*) (his)
    mercy;
    72. and *to remember* his holy covenant;

Lu. 16:25. *remember* that thou in thy lifetime
  23:42. Lord, *remember* me when thou
  24: 6. *remember* how he spake unto you
    8. they *remembered* his words,
Joh. 2:17. And his disciples *remembered* that it
    22. his disciples *remembered* that he
  12:16. then *remembered* they that these
Acts10:31. thine alms *are had in remembrance*
  11:16. Then *remembered* I the word of
1Co.11: 2. that ye *remember* me in all things,
2Ti. 1: 4. *being mindful* of thy tears,
Heb 8:12. their iniquities *will* I *remember* no more.
  10:17. and iniquities *will* I *remember* no more.
2Pet.3: 2. That ye may *be mindful* of the words
Jude 17. *remember* ye the words which
Rev.16:19. Babylon *came in remembrance* before God,

μνεία, mnīa.

Ro. 1: 9. I make *mention* of you always in my
Eph. 1:16. making *mention* of you in my prayers;
Phi. 1: 3. upon every *remembrance* of you,
1Th. 1: 2. making *mention* of you in our prayers;
  3: 6. that ye have good *remembrance* of us
2Ti. 1: 3. *remembrance* of thee in my prayers
Philem. 4. making *mention* of thee always

μνῆμα, mneema.

Mar 5: 5. and in the *tombs,* crying, and
Lu. 8:27. abode in (any) house, but in the *tombs.*
  23:53. laid it in a *sepulchre* that was hewn
  24: 1. they came unto the *sepulchre,*
Acts 2:29. his *sepulchre* is with us
  7:16. laid in the *sepulchre* that Abraham
Rev.11: 9. their dead bodies to be put in *graves.*

μνημεῖον, mneemīon.

Mat. 8:28. coming out of the *tombs,*
  23:29. and garnish the *sepulchres* of
  27:52. And the *graves* were opened;
    53. And came out of the *graves*
    60. laid it in his own new *tomb,*
    — great stone to the door of the *sepulchre,*
  28: 8. departed quickly from the *sepulchre*
Mar 5: 2. there met him out of the *tombs*
    3. had (his) dwelling among the *tombs;*
  6:29. and laid it in a *tomb.*
  15:46. and laid him in a *sepulchre*
    — a stone unto the door of the *sepulchre.*
  16: 2. they came unto the *sepulchre* at the
    3. from the door of the *sepulchre?*
    5. And entering into the *sepulchre,*
    8. and fled from the *sepulchre;*
Lu. 11:44. for ye are as *graves* which appear not,
    47. for ye build the *sepulchres* of the
    48. and ye build their *sepulchres.*
  23:55. beheld the *sepulchre,* and how
  24: 2. rolled away from the *sepulchre.*
    9. returned from the *sepulchre,*
    12. and ran unto the *sepulchre;*
    22. which were early at the *sepulchre;*
    24. were with us went to the *sepulchre,*
Joh. 5:28. all that are in the *graves* shall
  11:17. he had (lain) in the *grave* four days
    31. She goeth unto the *grave* to weep
    38. cometh to the *grave.*

Joh. 12:17. when he called Lazarus out of his *grave*,
　 19:41. and in the garden a new *sepulchre*,
　　　 42. for the *sepulchre* was nigh at hand.
　 20: 1. unto the *sepulchre*, and seeth the stone
　　　　　taken away from the *sepulchre*.
　　　 2. taken away the Lord out of the *sepulchre*,
　　　 3. and came to the *sepulchre*.
　　　 4. and came first to the *sepulchre*.
　　　 6. and went into the *sepulchre*,
　　　 8. which came first to the *sepulchre*,
　　 11. Mary stood without at the *sepulchre*
　　 — (and looked) into the *sepulchre*,
Acts13:29. and laid (him) in a *sepulchre*.

μνήμη, *mneemee*.

2Pet. 1:15. these things always in *remembrance*.

μνημονεύω, *mneemonūo*.

Mat.16: 9. neither *remember* the five loaves of
Mar 8:18. and *do* ye not *remember?*
Lu. 17:32. *Remember* Lot's wife.
Joh.15:20. *Remember* the word that I said
　 16: 4. ye *may remember* that I told you of them.
　　 21. she *remembereth* no more the anguish,
Acts20:31. *and remember*, that by the space
　　 35. and *to remember* the words of the Lord
Gal. 2:10. that we *should remember* the poor ;
Eph. 2:11. Wherefore *remember*, that ye
Col. 4:18. *Remember* my bonds.
1Th. 1: 3. *Remembering* without ceasing your work
　 2: 9. For ye *remember*, brethren, our labour
2Th. 2: 5. *Remember* ye not, that,
2Ti. 2: 8. *Remember* that Jesus Christ
Heb11:15. if they *had been mindful* of that (country)
　　 22. Joseph, when he died, *made mention* of
　 13: 7. *Remember* them which have the rule
Rev. 2: 5. *Remember* therefore from whence
　 3: 3. *Remember* therefore how thou hast
　 18: 5. God *hath remembered* her iniquities.

μνημόσυνον, *mneemosunon*.

Mat.26:13. be told for a *memorial* of her.
Mar 14: 9. shall be spoken of for a *memorial* of her.
Acts10: 4. thine alms are come up for a *memorial*

μνηστεύομαι, *mneestūomai*.

Mat. 1:18. *When* as his mother Mary *was espoused* to
Lu. 1:27. To a virgin *espoused* to a man whose
　 2: 5. To be taxed with Mary his *espoused* wife,

μογιλάλος, *mogilalos*.

Mar 7:32. that was deaf, and *had an impediment in
his speech ;*

μόγις, *mogis*.

Lu. 9:39. *hardly* departeth from him.

μόδιος, *modios*.

Mat. 5:15. a candle, and put it under a *bushel*,

Mar 4:21. to be put under a *bushel*,
Lu. 11:33. neither under a *bushel*,

μοί, *moi*.

From ἐγώ.

Mat. 2: 8. bring *me* word again,
　 4: 9. if thou wilt fall down and worship *me*.
　 7:21. Not every one that saith unto *me*,
　　 22. Many will say to *me* in that day,
　 8:21. Lord, suffer *me* first to go and bury
　　 22. Follow *me ;* and let the dead
　 9: 9. Follow *me*. And he arose,
　 11:27. All things are delivered unto *me*
　 14: 8. Give *me* here John Baptist's head
　　 18. Bring them hither to *me*.
　 15: 8. draweth nigh unto *me* with their
　　 25. Lord, help *me*.
　　 32. they continue with *me* now three days,
　 16:24. and take up his cross, and follow *me*.
　 17:17. bring him hither to *me*.
　 18:28. Pay *me* that thou owest.
　 19:21. and come (and) follow *me*.
　　 28. ye which have followed *me*,
　 20:13. didst not thou agree with *me* for
　　 15. Is it not lawful for *me* to do
　 21: 2. bring (them) unto *me*.
　　 24. which if ye tell *me*,
　 22:19. Shew *me* the tribute money.
　 25:20. Lord, thou deliveredst unto *me* five
　　 22. Lord, thou deliveredst unto *me* two
　　 35. and ye gave *me* meat:
　　 42. and ye gave *me* no meat:
　 26:15. What will ye give *me*,
　　 53. and he shall presently give *me* more
　 27:10. as the Lord appointed *me*.
　 28:18. All power is given unto *me* in heaven and
　　　　in earth.
Mar 2:14. Follow *me*. And he arose
　 5: 9. *My* name (is) Legion:
　 6:25. I will that thou give *me* by and by
　 8: 2. now been with *me* three days,
　　 34. take up his cross, and follow *me*.
　 10:21. take up the cross, and follow *me*.
　 11:29. one question, and answer *me*,
　　 30. or of men? answer *me*.
　 12:15. bring *me* a penny,
Lu. 1:25. Thus hath the Lord dealt with *me*
　　 38. be it unto *me* according to thy word.
　　 43. And whence (is) this to *me*,
　　 49. hath done to *me* great things ;
　 4:23. Ye will surely say unto *me*
　 5:27. said unto him, Follow *me*.
　 7:45. Thou gavest *me* no kiss:
　 9:23. his cross daily, and follow *me*.
　　 38. for he is *mine* (lit. to *me* an) only child.
　　 59. Follow *me*. But he said, Lord, suffer *me*
　　　 first to go
　　 61. but let *me* first go bid
　 10:22. All things are delivered to *me*
　　 40. bid her therefore that she help *me*.
　 11: 5. lend *me* three loaves ;
　　 7. Trouble *me* not: the door is
　 15: 6. Rejoice with *me ;* for I have found
　　 9. Rejoice with *me ;* for I have found
　　 12. give *me* the portion of goods
　 17: 8. gird thyself ; and serve *me*,
　 18: 5. this widow troubleth *me*,
　　 13. God be merciful to *me* a sinner.

Lu. 18:22. and come, follow *me*.
    20: 3. ask you one thing; and answer *me:*
      24. Shew *me* a penny. Whose
    22:29. as my Father hath appointed unto *me;*
      68. ye will not answer *me*,
    23:14. Ye have brought this man unto *me*,
Joh. 1:33. the same said unto *me*,
    43(44). saith unto him, Follow *me*.
    3:28. Ye yourselves bear *me* witness,
    4: 7. Jesus saith unto her, Give *me* to drink.
    10. that saith to thee, Give *me* to drink;
    15. give *me* this water,
    21. Woman, believe *me*, the hour
    29. which told *me* all things
    39. He told *me* all that ever I did.
    5:11. the same said unto *me*,
    36. which the Father hath given *me*
    6:37. All that the Father giveth *me*
    39. of all which he hath given *me*
    8:45. ye believe *me* not.
    46. why do ye not believe *me?*
    9:11. and said unto *me*, Go
    10:27. and they follow *me:*
    29. which gave (them) *me*, is greater than
    37. works of my Father, believe *me* not.
    12:49. he gave *me* a commandment,
    50. as the Father said unto *me*,
    13:36. canst not follow *me* now; but thou shalt follow *me* afterwards.
    14:11. Believe *me* that I (am) in the Father,
    — or else believe *me* for the very
    31. as the Father gave *me* commandment,
    17: 4. which thou gavest *me* to do.
    6. which thou gavest *me* out of the world:
    7. whatsoever thou hast given *me*
    8. the words which thou gavest *me ;*
    9. but for them which thou hast given *me ;*
    11. those whom thou hast given *me*,
    12. those that thou gavest *me*
    22. the glory which thou gavest *me*
    24. whom thou hast given *me*, be with
    — my glory, which thou hast given *me:*
    18: 9. Of them which thou gavest *me* have I
    11. the cup which my Father hath given *me*,
    20:15. tell *me* where thou hast laid him,
    21:19. he saith unto him, Follow *me*.
    22. what (is that) to thee? follow thou *me*.
Acts 1: 8. ye shall be witnesses unto *me*
    2:28. Thou hast made known to *me* the ways
    3: 6. Silver and gold have I none; (lit. is not to *me*)
    5: 8. Tell *me* whether ye sold the land
    7: 7. and serve *me* in this place.
    42. have ye offered to *me* slain beasts
    49. Heaven (is) *my* throne, (lit. to *me*)
    — what house will ye build *me ?*
    9:15. he is a chosen vessel unto *me*,
    11: 7. a voice saying unto *me*,
    9. the voice answered *me* again
    12. And the spirit bade *me* go
    12: 8. garment about thee, and follow *me*.
    13: 2. Separate *me* Barnabas and Saul
    18:10. *I* have much people (lit. much people is to *me*)
    20:19. which befell *me* by the lying in wait
    22. that shall befall *me* there:
    21:37. May I (lit. is it allowed to *me* to)
    39. suffer *me* to speak unto the people.
    22: 5. doth bear *me* witness,
    6. it came to pass, that, as *I* made my journey, (lit. to *me* journeying)
    7. and heard a voice saying unto *me*,

Acts22: 9. the voice of him that spake to *me*.
    11. by the hand of them that were with *me*,
    13. and stood, and said unto *me*,
    17. it came to pass, that, when *I* was come again (lit. to *me* having returned)
    18. saw him saying unto *me*,
    27. Tell *me*, art thou a Roman?
    23:19. What is that thou hast to tell *me?*
    30. And when it was told *me*
    24:11. there are yet but twelve days since *I* went (lit. there are not to *me* more days than)
    25:24. have dealt with *me*, both at Jerusalem,
    27. it seemeth to *me* unreasonable
    27:21. ye should have hearkened unto *me*,
    23. stood by *me* this night
    25. even as it was told *me*.
Ro. 7:10. *I* found (to be) (lit. has been found to *me*)
    13. working death in *me* by that which is good;
    18. for to will is present with *me ;*
    9: 1. my conscience also bearing *me* witness
    2. *I* have great heaviness
    19. Thou wilt say then unto *me*,
    12: 3. the grace given unto *me*,
    15:15. because of the grace that is given to *me*
    30. ye strive together with *me*
1Co. 1:11. For it hath been declared unto *me*
    3:10. which is given unto *me*,
    5:12. For what have *I* to do to judge them
    6:12. All things are lawful unto *me*,
    — all things are lawful for *me*,
    7: 1. whereof ye wrote unto *me:*
    9:15. for (it were) better for *me* to die,
    16. *I* have nothing to glory of: for necessity is laid upon *me:* yea, woe is unto *me*, if I preach not
    18. What is *my* reward then?
    10:23. All things are lawful for *me*,
    — all things are lawful for *me*,
    15:32. what advantageth it *me*,
    16: 9. and effectual is opened unto *me*,
2Co. 2:12. a door was opened unto *me*
    6:16. shall be *my* people. (lit. a people to *me*)
    18. ye shall be *my* sons
    7: 4. Great (is) *my* boldness of speech toward you, great (is) *my* glorying
    9: 1. it is superfluous for *me* to write
    12: 1. It is not expedient for *me*
    7. there was given to *me* a thorn
    9. And he said unto *me*, My grace
    13. forgive *me* this wrong.
    13:10. which the Lord hath given *me*
Gal. 2: 6. it maketh no matter to *me:*
    9. the grace that was given unto *me*,
    4:15. and have given them to *me*,
    21. Tell *me*, ye that desire to be under
    6:17. let no man trouble *me:*
Eph 3: 2. which is given *me* to you-ward:
    3. made known unto *me* the mystery;
    7. given unto *me* by the effectual
    6:19. utterance may be given unto *me*,
Phi. 1:19. this shall turn to *my* salvation
    22. this (is) the fruit of my labour: (lit. this is to *me* fruit of labour)
    2:18. and rejoice with *me*.
    3: 7. what things were gain to *me*,
    4: 3. laboured with *me* in the gospel,
    15. no church communicated with *me*
    16. once and again unto *my* necessity.
Col. 1:25. which is given to *me* for you,
    4:11. which have been a comfort unto *me*.

2Ti. 3:11. which came unto *me* at Antioch,
4: 8. Henceforth there is laid up for *me*
— the righteous judge, shall give *me*
11. he is profitable to *me* for the ministry.
14. did *me* much evil:
16. no man stood with *me*,
17. the Lord stood with *me*,
Philem. 13. he might have ministered unto *me*
19. owest unto *me* even thine own self
22. prepare *me* also a lodging:
Heb 1: 5. he shall be to *me* a Son?
2:13. which God hath given *me*.
8:10. they shall be to *me* a people:
10: 5. a body hast thou prepared *me* :
13: 6. what man shall do unto *me*.
Jas. 2:18. shew *me* thy faith
2Pet. 1:14. Christ hath shewed *me*.
Rev. 1:17. saying unto *me*, Fear not;
5: 5. saith unto *me*, Weep not:
7:13. saying unto *me*, What are these
14. And he said to *me*,
10: 4. saying unto *me*, Seal up
9. Give *me* the little book. And he said
unto *me*,
11. And he said unto *me*, Thou must
11: 1. And there was given *me* a reed
14:13. saying unto *me*, Write, Blessed
17: 1. saying unto *me*, Come hither;
7. And the angel said unto *me*,
15. And he saith unto *me*, The waters
19: 9. And he saith unto *me*, Write,
— And he saith unto *me*, These are
10. And he said unto *me*, See
21: 5. And he said unto *me*, Write:
6. And he said unto *me*, It is done.
7. and he shall be *my* son.
10. and shewed *me* that great city,
22: 1. And he shewed *me* a pure river
6. And he said unto *me*, These sayings
8. which shewed *me* these things.
9. Then saith he unto *me*, See
10. And he saith unto *me*, Seal not

μοιχαλίς, *moikalis*.

Mat. 12:39. An evil and *adulterous* generation
16: 4. A wicked and *adulterous* generation
Mar 8:38. in this *adulterous* and sinful generation;
Ro. 7: 3. she shall be called an *adulteress*:
— so that she is no *adulteress*,
Jas. 4: 4. Ye adulterers and *adulteresses*,
2Pet. 2:14. Having eyes full of *adultery*,

μοιχάομαι, *moikaomai*.

Mat. 5:32. causeth her *to commit adultery*:
— her that is divorced *committeth adultery*.
19: 9. marry another, *committeth adultery*:
— is put away *doth commit adultery*.
Mar 10:11. *committeth adultery* against her.
12. to another, she *committeth adultery*.

μοιχεία, *moikīa*.

Mat. 15:19. murders, *adulteries*, fornications,
Mar 7:21. evil thoughts, *adulteries*, fornications,
Joh. 8: 3. unto him a woman taken in *adultery*;
Gal. 5:19. *Adultery*, fornication, uncleanness,

μοιχεύω, *moikūo*.

Mat. 5:27. Thou *shalt* not *commit adultery*:
28. *hath committed adultery* with her
19:18. Thou *shalt* not *commit adultery*,
Mar 10:19. *Do* not *commit adultery*,
Lu. 16:18. marrieth another, *committeth adultery*:
— from (her) husband *committeth adultery*.
18:20. *Do* not *commit adultery*,
Joh. 8: 4. was taken *in adultery*,
Ro. 2:22. a man should not *commit adultery*, *dost*
thou *commit adultery?*
13: 9. Thou *shalt* not *commit adultery*,
Jas. 2:11. *Do* not *commit adultery*,
— Now if thou *commit* no *adultery*,
Rev. 2:22. and them *that commit adultery* with her

μοιχός, *moikos*.

Lu. 18:11. extortioners, unjust, *adulterers*,
1Co. 6: 9. nor idolaters, nor *adulterers*,
Heb 13: 4. whoremongers and *adulterers* God will
Jas. 4: 4. Ye *adulterers* and adulteresses,

μόλις, *molis*.

Acts 14:18. *scarce* restrained they the people,
27: 7. and *scarce* were come over against
8. And, *hardly* passing it, came unto
16. we had much work to come by (lit. we
were able *with difficulty* to get) the boat:
Ro. 5: 7. *scarcely* for a righteous man will one die:
1Pet. 4:18. if the righteous *scarcely* be saved,

μολύνω, *moluno*.

1Co. 8: 7. their conscience being weak *is defiled*.
Rev. 3: 4. which *have* not *defiled* their garments;
14: 4. which *were* not *defiled* with women;

μολυσμός, *molusmos*.

2Co. 7: 1. from all *filthiness* of the flesh

μομφή, *momphee*.

Col. 3:13. if any man have a *quarrel* against any:

μονή, *monee*.

Joh. 14: 2. In my Father's house are many *mansions:*
23. and make our *abode* with him.

μονογενής, *monogenees*.

Lu. 7:12. the *only* son of his mother,
8:42. For he had one *only* daughter,
9:38. for he is mine *only* child.
Joh. 1:14. as of the *only* begotten of the Father,
18. the *only* begotten Son, which is
3:16. his *only* begotten Son, that whosoever
18. of the *only* begotten Son of God.
Heb 11:17. offered up his *only* begotten (son),
1Joh. 4: 9. God sent his *only* begotten Son

μόνον, monon.

Mat. 5:47. if ye salute your brethren *only*,
8: 8. but speak the word *only*,
9:21. If I may *but* touch his garment,
10:42. a cup of cold (water) *only*
14:36. that they might *only* touch the
21:19. nothing thereon, but leaves *only*,
21. not *only* do this (which is done) to the
Mar 5:36. Be not afraid, *only* believe.
6: 8. for (their) journey, save a staff *only*;
Lu. 8:50. Fear not: believe *only*,
Joh. 5:18. not *only* had broken the sabbath,
11:52. not for that nation *only*, but that also
12: 9. not for Jesus' sake *only*, but
13: 9. not my feet *only*, but also
17:20. pray I for these *alone*, but for them
Acts 8:16. *only* they were baptized in the
11:19. but unto the Jews *only*.
18:25. knowing *only* the baptism of John.
19:26. not *alone* at Ephesus, but almost
27. So that not *only* this our craft
21:13. not to be bound *only*, but also to die
26:29. not *only* thou, but also all that
27:10. not *only* of the lading and ship,
Ro. 1:32. not *only* do the same, but have pleasure
3:29. the God of the Jews *only*?
4:12. not of the circumcision *only*, but who also
16. not to that *only* which is of the law,
23. for his sake *alone*,
5: 3. And not *only* (so), but we glory in
11. And not *only* (so), but we also joy
8:23. And not *only* (they), but ourselves
9:10. And not *only* (this); but when
24. not of the Jews *only*, but also
13: 5. not *only* for wrath, but also for
1Co. 7:39. to whom she will; *only* in the Lord.
15:19. If in this life *only* we have hope
2Co. 7: 7. And not by his coming *only*, but by
8:10. not *only* to do, but also to be forward
19. And not (that) *only*, but who was also
21. not *only* in the sight of the Lord,
9:12. not *only* supplieth the want of
Gal. 1:23. But they had heard *only*,
2:10. *Only* (they would) that we should
3: 2. This *only* would I learn of you,
4:18. not *only* when I am present with you.
5:13. *only* (use) not liberty for an occasion
6:12. *only* lest they should suffer persecution
Eph. 1:21. not *only* in this world, but also
Phi. 1:27. *Only* let your conversation be
29. not *only* to believe on him, but also
2:12. not as in my presence *only*, but
27. and not on him *only*, but on me also,
1Th. 1: 5. not unto you in word *only*, but also in
8. not *only* in Macedonia and Achaia, but
2: 8. not the gospel of God *only*, but also
2Th. 2: 7. *only* he who now letteth (will let),
1Ti. 5:13. not *only* idle, but tattlers also
2Ti. 2:20. there are not *only* vessels of gold
4: 8. and not to me *only*, but unto all them
Heb 9:10. *only* in meats and drinks, and divers
12:26. I shake not the earth *only*, but also
Jas. 1:22. and not hearers *only*, deceiving
2:24. and not by faith *only*.
1Pet. 2:18. not *only* to the good and gentle,
1Joh. 2: 2. and not for our's *only*, but also for
5: 6. not by water *only*, but by water and blood.

μονόομαι, monŏomai.

1Ti. 5: 5. that is a widow indeed, and *desolate*.

μόνος, monos.

Mat. 4: 4. shall not live by bread *alone*,
10. and him *only* shalt thou serve.
12: 4. but *only* for the priests?
14:23. he was there *alone*.
17: 8. saw no man, save Jesus *only*.
18:15. between thee and him *alone*:
24:36. but my Father *only*.
Mar 6:47. and he *alone* on the land.
9: 2. high mountain apart *by themselves*:
8. save Jesus *only* with themselves.
Lu. 4: 4. not live by bread *alone*, but
8. him *only* shalt thou serve.
5:21. can forgive sins, but God *alone*?
6: 4. but for the priests *alone*?
9:36. Jesus was found *alone*.
10:40. hath left me to serve *alone*?
24:12. the linen clothes laid *by themselves*,
18. Art thou *only* a stranger in Jerusalem,
Joh. 5:44. that (cometh) from God *only*?
6:15. into a mountain himself *alone*.
22. his disciples were gone away *alone*;
8: 9. and Jesus was left *alone*,
16. for I am not *alone*,
29. the Father hath not left me *alone*;
12:24. and die, it abideth *alone*:
16:32. and shall leave me *alone*: and yet I am
not *alone*,
17: 3. the *only* true God, and Jesus
Ro. 11: 3. and I am left *alone*, and they seek
16: 4. unto whom not *only* I give thanks, but
27. To God *only* wise,
1Co. 9: 6. Or I *only* and Barnabas,
14:36. or came it unto you *only*?
Gal. 6: 4. have rejoicing in himself *alone*,
Phi. 4:15. giving and receiving, but ye *only*.
Col. 4:11. These *only* (are my) fellowworkers
1Th. 3: 1. to be left at Athens *alone*;
1Ti. 1:17. the *only* wise God,
6:15. the blessed and *only* Potentate,
16. Who *only* hath immortality,
2Ti. 4:11. *Only* Luke is with me.
Heb 9: 7. (went) the high priest *alone*
2Joh. 1. and not I *only*, but also all they
Jude 4. and denying the *only* Lord God,
25. To the *only* wise God our Saviour,
Rev. 9: 4. but *only* those men which have not
15: 4. for (thou) *only* (art) holy:

μονόφθαλμος, monophthalmos.

Mat.18: 9. to enter into life *with one eye*,
Mar 9:47. into the kingdom of God *with one eye*,

μορφή, morphee.

Mar 16:12. he appeared in another *form*
Phi. 2: 6. Who, being in the *form* of God,
7. took upon him the *form* of a servant,

μορφόομαι, morphŏomai.

Gal. 4:19. until Christ *be formed* in you,

μόρφωσις, morphōsis.

Ro. 2:20. which hast the *form* of knowledge
2Ti. 3: 5. Having a *form* of godliness, but

μοσχοποίεω, moskopoyeo.

Acts 7:41. And they *made a calf* in those days,

μόσχος, moskos.

Lu. 15:23. And bring hither the fatted *calf*,
27. thy father hath killed the fatted *calf*,
30. hast killed for him the fatted *calf*.
Heb 9:12. Neither by the blood of goats and *calves*,
19. the blood of *calves* and of goats,
Rev. 4: 7. the second beast like a *calf*,

μόχθος, mokthos.

2Co.11:27. In weariness and *painfulness*,
1Th. 2: 9. our labour and *travail* :
2Th. 3: 8. wrought with labour and *travail*

μοῦ, mou.
From ἐγώ.

Mat. 2: 6. that shall rule *my* people Israel.
15. Out of Egypt have I called *my* son.
3:11. he that cometh after *me* is mightier than *I*,
17. This is *my* beloved Son,
4:19. saith unto them, Follow *me*,
7:21. the will of *my* Father which is in
24. heareth these sayings of mine, (lit. of *me*)
26. these sayings of mine, (lit. of *me*)
8: 6. *my* servant lieth at home
8. shouldest come under *my* roof:
— and *my* servant shall be healed.
9. and to *my* servant, Do this,
21. to go and bury *my* father.
9:18. *My* daughter is even now dead:
10:22. for *my* name's sake:
32. before *my* Father which is
33. *my* Father which is in heaven.
37. is not worthy of *me* :
— is not worthy of *me*.
38. after *me*, is not worthy of *me*.
11:10. I send *my* messenger before
27. unto me of *my* Father:
29. Take *my* yoke upon you,
30. For *my* yoke (is) easy, and *my* burden is
12:18. Behold *my* servant, whom I have chosen ; *my* beloved, in whom *my* soul is well pleased: I will put *my* spirit upon him,
44. into *my* house from whence
48. Who is *my* mother? and who are *my* brethren ?
49. Behold *my* mother and *my* brethren !
50. shall do the will of *my* Father
— the same is *my* brother, and sister,
13:30. but gather the wheat into *my* barn.
35. I will open *my* mouth in parables;
15:13. Every plant, which *my* heavenly Father
22. *my* daughter is grievously vexed
16:17. but *my* Father which is in heaven.
18. upon this rock I will build *my* church;
23. Get thee behind *me*, Satan: thou art an offence unto *me* :
24. If any (man) will come after *me*,
17: 5. This is *my* beloved Son,
15. Lord, have mercy on *my* son:
18: 5. little child in *my* name
10. the face of *my* Father which is in

Mat.18:19. of *my* Father which is in heaven.
21. how oft shall *my* brother sin against
35. So likewise shall *my* heavenly Father
19:20. have I kept from *my* youth up:
29. or lands, for *my* name's sake,
20:21. Grant that these *my* two sons may sit,
23. Ye shall drink indeed of *my* cup,
— but to sit on *my* right hand, and on *my* left, is not mine to give, but
— for whom it is prepared of *my* Father.
21:13. *My* house shall be called the house
28. go work to day in *my* vineyard.
37. They will reverence *my* son.
22: 4. I have prepared *my* dinner: *my* oxen and (my) fatlings
44. The Lord said unto *my* Lord, Sit thou on *my* right hand,
24: 5. For many shall come in *my* name,
9. hated of all nations for *my* name's sake.
35. but *my* words shall not pass away.
36. but *my* Father only.
48. *My* Lord delayeth his coming;
25:27. to have put *my* money to
34. Come, ye blessed of *my* Father,
40. of the least of these *my* brethren,
26:12. poured this ointment on *my* body,
18. *My* time is at hand;
— at thy house with *my* disciples.
26. Take, eat; this is *my* body.
28. For this is *my* blood of the new
29. in *my* Father's kingdom.
38. *My* soul is exceeding sorrowful,
39. O *my* Father, if it be possible,
42. O *my* Father, if this cup may not
53. that I cannot now pray to *my* Father,
27:35. They parted *my* garments among them, and upon *my* vesture did they cast lots.
46. *My* God, *my* God, why hast thou
28:10. go tell *my* brethren
Mar 1: 2. Behold, I send *my* messenger
7. There cometh one mightier than *I* after *me*,
11. Thou art *my* beloved Son,
17. Come ye after *me*,
3:33. Who is *my* mother, or *my* brethren?
34. Behold *my* mother and *my* brethren !
35. the same is *my* brother, and *my* sister, and mother.
5:23. *My* little daughter lieth at the
30. Who touched *my* clothes?
31. and sayest thou, Who touched *me*?
6:23. unto the half of *my* kingdom.
7:14. Hearken unto *me* every one
8:33. Get thee behind *me*, Satan:
34. Whosoever will come after *me*,
9: 7. This is *my* beloved Son:
17. I have brought unto thee *my* son,
24. help thou *mine* unbelief.
37. one of such children in *my* name,
39. shall do a miracle in *my* name,
41. of water to drink in *my* name,
10:20. have I observed from *my* youth.
40. But to sit on *my* right hand and on *my* left
11:17. *My* house shall be called
12: 6. They will reverence *my* son.
36. The Lord said to *my* Lord, Sit thou on *my* right hand,
13: 6. many shall come in *my* name,
13. hated of all (men) for *my* name's sake:
31. but *my* words shall not pass
14: 8. to anoint *my* body to the burying.
14. the passover with *my* disciples?

Mar 14:22. Take, eat: this is *my* body.
24. This is *my* blood of the new
34. *My* soul is exceeding sorrowful
15:34. *My* God, *my* God, why hast thou
16:17. In *my* name shall they cast out
Lu. 1:18. and *my* wife well stricken in years.
20. because thou believest not *my* words,
25. to take away *my* reproach
43. that the mother of *my* Lord should
44. salutation sounded in *mine* ears, the babe
    leaped in *my* womb
46. *My* soul doth magnify the Lord,
47. And *my* spirit hath rejoiced in God *my*
2:30. For *mine* eyes have seen thy
49. must be about *my* Father's business?
3:16. one mightier than *I* cometh,
22. Thou art *my* beloved Son ;
4: 7. wilt worship *me*, all shall be
8. Get thee behind *me*, Satan:
6:47. and heareth *my* sayings, and
7: 6. shouldest enter under *my* roof :
7. and *my* servant shall be healed.
8. and to *my* servant, Do this,
27. Behold, I send *my* messenger before
44. thou gavest me no water for *my* feet: but
    she hath washed *my* feet with tears,
45. hath not ceased to kiss *my* feet.
46. *My* head with oil thou didst not
— hath anointed *my* feet with ointment.
8:21. *My* mother and *my* brethren are these
45. Who touched *me* ?
— sayest thou, Who touched *me* ?
46. Somebody hath touched *me* :
9:23. If any (man) will come after *me*,
35. This is *my* beloved Son: hear him.
38. I beseech thee, look upon *my* son:
48. shall receive this child in *my* name
59. to go and bury *my* father.
61. which are at home at *my* house.
10:22. are delivered to me of *my* Father:
29. And who is *my* neighbour ?
40. dost thou not care that *my* sister
11: 6. For a friend of mine (lit. of *me*)
7. and *my* children are with me
24. I will return unto *my* house
12: 4. I say unto you *my* friends,
13. Master, speak to *my* brother,
17. where to bestow *my* fruits ?
18. I will pull down *my* barns, and
— and there will I bestow all *my* fruits and
    my goods.
19. And I will say to *my* soul,
45. *My* lord delayeth his coming ;
14:23. that *my* house may be filled.
24. shall taste of *my* supper.
26. he cannot be *my* disciple.
27. and come after *me*, cannot be *my* disciple.
33. he cannot be *my* disciple.
15: 6. I have found *my* sheep which
17. How many hired servants of *my* father's
18. I will arise and go to *my* father,
24. this *my* son was dead,
29. might make merry with *my* friends:
16: 3. *my* lord taketh away from me
5. How much owest thou unto *my* lord ?
24. and cool *my* tongue ;
27. send him to *my* father's house:
18: 3. Avenge me of *mine* adversary.
21. have I kept from *my* youth up.
19: 8. Lord, the half of *my* goods
23. gavest not thou *my* money
27. But those *mine* enemies,

Lu. 19:27. and slay (them) before *me*.
46. *My* house is the house of prayer:
20:13. I will send *my* beloved son:
42. The Lord said unto *my* Lord, Sit thou on
    my right hand,
21: 8. for many shall come in *my* name,
12. and rulers for *my* name's sake.
17. hated of all (men) for *my* name's sake.
33. but *my* words shall not pass away.
22:11. eat the passover with *my* disciples ?
19. This is *my* body which is given
20. the new testament in *my* blood,
28. continued with me in *my* temptations.
29. as *my* Father hath appointed unto me ;
30. and drink at *my* table in *my* kingdom,
42. not *my* will, but thine, be done.
53. When *I* was daily with you in
23:42. Lord, remember *me* when thou comest
46. into thy hands I commend *my* spirit:
24:39. Behold *my* hands and *my* feet,
49. I send the promise of *my* Father
Joh. 1:15. He that cometh after *me* is preferred before
    me : for he was before *me.*
27. He it is, who coming after *me* is preferred
    before *me,*
30. After *me* cometh a man which is preferred
    before *me :* for he was before *me.*
2: 4. *mine* hour is not yet come.
16. make not *my* Father's house an
4:49. Sir, come down ere *my* child die.
5:17. *My* Father worketh hitherto, and I
24. He that heareth *my* word,
31. of myself, *my* witness is not true.
43. I am come in *my* Father's name,
6:32. but *my* Father giveth you the
51. the bread that I will give is *my* flesh,
54. Whoso eateth *my* flesh, and drinketh *my*
    blood, hath
55. For *my* flesh is meat indeed, and *my* blood
56. He that eateth *my* flesh, and drinketh *my*
    blood, dwelleth in me,
65. given unto him of *my* Father.
8:14. *my* record is true:
19. Ye neither know me, nor *my* Father:
— should have known *my* Father also.
28. but as *my* Father hath taught me,
31. (then) are ye *my* disciples indeed ;
38. that which I have seen with *my* Father:
49. but I honour *my* Father,
50. I seek not *mine own* glory:
52. If a man keep *my* saying,
54. If I honour myself, *my* honour is nothing:
    it is *my* Father that
9:11. and anointed *mine* eyes,
15. He put clay upon *mine* eyes,
30. (yet) he hath opened *mine* eyes.
10:15. I lay down *my* life for the sheep.
16. and they shall hear *my* voice ;
17. because I lay down *my* life,
18. have I received of *my* Father.
25. the works that I do in *my* Father's name,
27. *My* sheep hear *my* voice,
28. pluck them out of *my* hand.
29. *My* Father, which gave (them) me,
— to pluck (them) out of *my* Father's hand.
32. have I shewed you from *my* Father ;
37. If I do not the works of *my* Father,
11:21. *my* brother had not died.
32. *my* brother had not died.
41. I thank thee that thou hast heard *me*.
42. I knew that thou hearest *me* always:
12: 7. against the day of *my* burying

Joh. 12:27. Now is *my* soul troubled ;
47. if any man hear *my* words,
48. and receiveth not *my* words,
13: 6. Lord, dost thou wash *my* feet?
8. Thou shalt never wash *my* feet.
9. Lord, not *my* feet only,
37. I will lay down *my* life for thy sake.
14: 2. In *my* Father's house are many mansions:
7. ye should have known *my* Father
12. because I go unto *my* Father.
13. whatsoever ye shall ask in *my* name,
14. ask any thing in *my* name,
20. ye shall know that I (am) in *my* Father,
21. He that hath *my* commandments,
— loveth me shall be loved of *my* Father,
23. If a man love me, he will keep *my* words:
and *my* Father will love him,
24. loveth me not keepeth not *my* sayings:
26. the Father will send in *my* name,
28. for *my* Father is greater than *I.*
15: 1. and *my* Father is the husbandman.
7. and *my* words abide in you,
8. Herein is *my* Father glorified,
10. If ye keep *my* commandments, ye shall
abide in *my* love ; even as I have kept
my Father's
14. Ye are *my* friends, if ye do
15. all things that I have heard of *my* Father
16. ye shall ask of the Father in *my* name,
20. if they have kept *my* saying,
21. they do unto you for *my* name's sake,
23. He that hateth me hateth *my* Father
24. and hated both me and *my* Father.
16:10. because I go to *my* Father,
23. ye shall ask the Father in *my* name,
24. have ye asked nothing in *my* name:
26. At that day ye shall ask in *my* name:
18:37. heareth *my* voice.
19:24. They parted *my* raiment among them,
and for *my* vesture they did
20:13. Because they have taken away *my* Lord,
17. Touch *me* not ; for I am not yet ascended
to *my* Father: but go to *my* brethren,
and say unto them, I ascend unto *my*
Father, and your Father ; and (to) *my*
God, and your God.
25. put *my* finger into the print of the nails,
and thrust *my* hand
27. thy finger, and behold *my* hands ; and
reach hither thy hand, and thrust (it)
into *my* side:
28. *My* Lord and *my* God.
21:15. saith unto him, Feed *my* lambs.
16. saith unto him, Feed *my* sheep.
17. Feed *my* sheep.
Acts 1: 4. which, (saith he), ye have heard of *me.*
2:14. and hearken to *my* words:
17. I will pour out of *my* Spirit upon
18. And on *my* servants and on *my* handmaidens I will pour out in those days
of *my* Spirit ;
25. the Lord always before *my* face, for he is
on *my* right hand,
26. did *my* heart rejoice, and *my* tongue was
glad ; moreover also *my* flesh
27. thou wilt not leave *my* soul in hell,
34. The Lord said unto *my* Lord, Sit thou on
my right hand,
7:34. I have seen the affliction of *my* people
49. Heaven (is) my throne, and earth (is) *my*
— or what (is) the place of *my* rest ?
50. Hath not *my* hand made all

Acts 7:59. Lord Jesus, receive *my* spirit.
9:15. to bear *my* name before the Gentiles,
16. he must suffer for *my* name's sake.
10:30. at the ninth hour I prayed in *my* house,
and, behold, a man stood before *me* in
11: 8. at any time entered into *my* mouth.
13:22. a man after *mine own* heart, which shall
fulfil all *my* will.
33. Thou art *my* Son, this day have I
15: 7. that the Gentiles by *my* mouth should
13. brethren, hearken unto *me :*
17. upon whom *my* name is called,
16:15. come into *my* house, and abide
20:24. neither count I *my* life dear unto myself,
so that I might finish *my* course with
25. shall see *my* face no more.
29. after *my* departing shall grievous
34. have ministered unto *my* necessities,
21:13. to weep and to break *mine* heart ?
22: 1. hear ye *my* defence
17. even while *I* prayed in the temple,
24:13. whereof they now accuse *me.*
17. I came to bring alms to *my* nation,
20. while *I* stood before the council,
25:11. whereof these accuse *me,*
15. when *I* was at Jerusalem,
26: 3. I beseech thee to hear *me* patiently.
4. *My* manner of life from my youth,
— at the first among *mine own* nation
29. but also all that hear *me* this day,
28:19. I had ought to accuse *my* nation of.
Ro. 1: 8. I thank *my* God through Jesus
9. For God is *my* witness, whom I serve with
my spirit in the gospel
—(10). mention of you always in *my* prayers ;
2:16. according to *my* gospel.
7: 4. Wherefore, *my* brethren, ye also
18. that is, in *my* flesh,
23. another law in *my* members, warring
against the law of *my* mind,
— the law of sin which is in *my* members.
9: 1. I lie not, *my* conscience also bearing me
2. and continual sorrow in *my* heart.
3. for *my* brethren, *my* kinsmen according
to the flesh:
17. that I might shew *my* power in thee, and
that *my* name might be declared
25. I will call them *my* people, which were
not *my* people ;
26. Ye (are) not *my* people ;
10:21. I have stretched forth *my* hands
11: 3. and they seek *my* life.
13. I magnify *mine* office:
14. to emulation (them which are) *my* flesh,
15:14. persuaded of you, *my* brethren,
31. that *my* service which (I have)
16: 3. *my* helpers in Christ Jesus:
4. Who have for *my* life laid down
5. Salute *my* wellbeloved Epenetus,
7. Andronicus and Junia, *my* kinsmen, and
my fellowprisoners,
8. Greet Amplias *my* beloved
9. and Stachys *my* beloved.
11. Salute Herodion *my* kinsman.
21. Timotheus *my* workfellow,
— Jason, and Sosipater, *my* kinsmen,
23. Gaius *mine* host, and of the whole church,
25. according to *my* gospel,
1Co. 1: 4. I thank *my* God always on your
11. declared unto me of you, *my* brethren,
2: 4. And *my* speech and *my* preaching (was)
not with enticing words

1Co. 4:14. but as *my* beloved sons I warn
 16. be ye followers of *me*.
 17. Timotheus, who is *my* beloved son,
 — into remembrance of *my* ways
 18. as though *I* would not come to you.
 8:13. if meat make *my* brother to offend,
 — lest I make *my* brother to offend,
 9: 1. are not ye *my* work in the Lord?
 15. should make *my* glorying void.
 18. that I abuse not *my* power in the
 27. I keep under *my* body,
 10:14. *my* dearly beloved, flee from idolatry.
 29. why is *my* liberty judged of another
 11: 1. Be ye followers of *me*,
 2. that ye remember *me* in all things,
 24. Take, eat: this is *my* body,
 33. Wherefore, *my* brethren, when ye
 13: 3. though I bestow all *my* goods
 — though I give *my* body to be burned,
 14:14. *my* spirit prayeth, but *my* understanding
  is unfruitful.
 18. I thank *my* God, I speak with
 19. five words with *my* understanding,
 21. will they not hear *me*, saith the Lord.
 15:58. *my* beloved brethren, be ye stedfast,
 16:24. *My* love (be) with you all in Christ
2Co. 2:13. I had no rest in *my* spirit, because I found
  not Titus *my* brother:
 11: 1. bear with *me* a little in (my) folly: and
  indeed bear with *me*.
 9. that which was lacking to *me*
 28. that which cometh upon *me* daily,
 30. which concern *mine* infirmities.
 12: 5. but in *mine* infirmities.
 9. *My* grace is sufficient for thee: for *my*
  strength is made perfect
 — will I rather glory in *my* infirmities,
 21. *my* God will humble me among you,
Gal. 1:14. my equals in *mine own* nation,
 — of the traditions of *my* fathers.
 15. separated me from *my* mother's womb,
 4:14. And *my* temptation which was in *my* flesh
 19. *My* little children, of whom I
 20. and to change *my* voice;
 6:17. I bear in *my* body the marks
Eph 1:16. making mention of you in *my* prayers;
 3: 4. ye may understand *my* knowledge
 13. at *my* tribulations for you,
 14. For this cause I bow *my* knees
 6:10. *my* brethren, be strong in the Lord,
 19. that I may open *my* mouth boldly,
Phi. 1: 3. I thank *my* God upon every remembrance
 4. in every prayer of *mine* for you
 7. inasmuch as both in *my* bonds,
 — ye all are partakers of *my* grace.
 8. For God is *my* record,
 13. So that *my* bonds in Christ
 14. waxing confident by *my* bonds,
 16. to add affliction to *my* bonds:
 20. According to *my* earnest expectation
 — Christ shall be magnified in *my* body,
 2: 2. Fulfil ye *my* joy,
 12. Wherefore, *my* beloved, as ye have
 — not as in *my* presence only, but now much
  more in *my* absence.
 25. *my* brother, and companion in labour,
 — and he that ministered to *my* wants.
 3: 1. Finally, *my* brethren, rejoice in
 8. the knowledge of Christ Jesus *my* Lord:
 17. be followers together of *me*,
 4: 1. *my* brethren dearly beloved and longed
  for, *my* joy and crown,

Phi. 4: 3. (with) other *my* fellowlabourers,
 14. did communicate with *my* affliction.
 19. But *my* God shall supply all your need
Col. 1:24. Who now rejoice in *my* sufferings for you,
 — in *my* flesh for his body's sake,
 2: 1. as have not seen *my* face in the flesh;
 4:10. Aristarchus *my* fellowprisoner
 18. Remember *my* bonds.
2Ti. 1: 3. in *my* prayers night and day;
 6. by the putting on of *my* hands.
 12. that which *I* have committed unto him
 16. and was not ashamed of *my* chain:
 2: 1. *my* son, be strong in the grace
 8. according to *my* gospel:
 3:10. thou hast fully known *my* doctrine,
 4:16. At *my* first answer no man
Philem 4. I thank *my* God, making mention of
  thee always in *my* prayers,
 10. whom I have begotten in *my* bonds:
 20. refresh *my* bowels in the Lord.
 23. Epaphras, *my* fellowprisoner
 24. Demas, Lucas, *my* fellowlabourers.
Heb 1: 5. Thou art *my* Son, this day have I
 13. Sit on *my* right hand,
 2:12. declare thy name unto *my* brethren,
 3: 9. saw *my* works forty years.
 10. have not known *my* ways.
 11. So I sware in *my* wrath, They shall not
  enter into *my* rest.
 4: 3. As I have sworn in *my* wrath, if they shall
  enter into *my* rest:
 5. If they shall enter into *my* rest.
 5: 5. Thou art *my* Son,
 8: 9. when *I* took them by the hand
 — they continued not in *my* covenant,
 10. I will put *my* laws into their mind,
 10:16. put *my* laws into their hearts,
 34. compassion of me in *my* bonds,
 38. *my* soul shall have no pleasure
 12: 5. *My* son, despise not thou the
Jas. 1: 2. *My* brethren, count it all joy
 16. Do not err, *my* beloved brethren.
 19. Wherefore, *my* beloved brethren, let
 2: 1. *My* brethren, have not the faith
 3. or sit here under *my* footstool:
 5. Hearken, *my* beloved brethren,
 14. What (doth it) profit, *my* brethren,
 18. I will shew thee *my* faith by *my* works.
 3: 1. *My* brethren, be not many masters,
 10. *My* brethren. these things ought not
 12. Can the fig tree, *my* brethren,
 5:10. Take, *my* brethren, the prophets,
 12. above all things, *my* brethren,
1Pet. 5:13. and (so doth) Marcus *my* son.
2Pet. 1:14. I must put off (this) *my* tabernacle,
 17. This is *my* beloved Son, in whom I am
  well pleased.
1Joh. 2: 1. *My* little children, these things
 3:13. Marvel not, *my* brethren, if the world
 18. *My* little children, let us
Rev. 1:10. and heard behind *me* a great voice,
 20. which thou sawest in *my* right hand,
 2: 3. for *my* name's sake hast laboured,
 13. thou holdest fast *my* name, and hast not
  denied *my* faith,
 — Antipas (was) *my* faithful martyr,
 16. with the sword of *my* mouth.
 26. and keepeth *my* works unto the end,
 27. even as I received of *my* Father.
 3: 5. I will confess his name before *my* Father,
 8. and hast kept *my* word, and hast not
  denied *my* name.

Rev. 3:10. hast kept the word of *my* patience,
　　　12. a pillar in the temple of *my* God,
　　　— I will write upon him the name of *my* God,
　　　　　and the name of the city of *my* God,
　　　— out of heaven from *my* God: and (I will
　　　　　write upon him) *my* new name.
　　　16. I will spue thee out of *my* mouth.
　　　20. if any man hear *my* voice,
　　　21. to sit with me in *my* throne,
　　　— with *my* Father in his throne.
　10:10. in *my* mouth sweet as honey:
　　　— *my* belly was bitter.
　11: 3. I will give (power) unto *my* two witnesses,
　18: 4. Come out of her, *my* people,
　22:12. and *my* reward (is) with me,
　　　16. I Jesus have sent *mine* angel to

μουσικός, *mousikos.*

Rev.18:22. and *musicians,* and of pipers,

μυελός, *muelos.*

Heb 4:12. and of the joints and *marrow,*

μυέομαι, *mueomai.*

Phil. 4:12. and in all things I *am instructed* both to be

μῦθος, *muthos.*

1Ti. 1: 4. Neither give heed to *fables* and
　　4: 7. refuse profane and old wives' *fables,*
2Ti. 4: 4. and shall be turned unto *fables.*
Tit. 1:14. Not giving heed to Jewish *fables,*
2Pet.1:16. followed cunningly devised *fables,*

μυκάομαι, *mukaomai.*

Rev.10: 3. as (when) a lion *roareth:*

μυκτηρίζομαι, *mukteerizomai.*

Gal. 6: 7. God *is* not *mocked:*

μυλικός, *mulikos.*

Mar 9:42. that a *millstone* were hanged about

μύλος, *mulos.*

Mat.18: 6. that a *millstone* were hanged about
Lu. 17: 2. that a *millstone* were hanged about
Rev.18:21. took up a stone like a great *millstone,*
　　　22. the sound of a *millstone* shall

μύλων, *mulon.*

Mat.24:41. grinding at the *mill;* the one shall

μυριάς, *murias.*

Lu. 12: 1. an *innumerable multitude* of people,

Acts19:19. fifty thousand (lit. five *ten-thousands*)
　　　(pieces) of silver.
　21:20. how many thousands (lit. *myriads*) of Jews
　　　there are
Heb 12:22. to an *innumerable company* of angels,
Jude 14. the Lord cometh with *ten thousands* of his
　　　saints, (lit. with holy *myriads*)
Rev. 5:11. *ten thousand* times *ten thousand* (Elz.)
　9:16. two hundred thousand thousand

μυρίζω, *murizo.*

Mar14: 8. *to anoint* my body to the burying.

μύριοι, *murioi.*

Mat.18:24. which owed him *ten thousand* talents.
1Co. 4:15. though ye have *ten thousand* instructers
　14:19. than *ten thousand* words in an (unknown)
　　　tongue.

μύρον, *muron.*

Mat.26: 7. of very precious *ointment,*
　　　9. For this *ointment* might have
　　　12. hath poured this *ointment* on my body,
Mar14: 3. an alabaster box of *ointment*
　　　4. this waste of the *ointment* made?
Lu. 7:37. an alabaster box of *ointment,*
　　38. anointed (them) with the *ointment.*
　　46. anointed my feet with *ointment.*
　23:56. and prepared spices and *ointments;*
Joh.11: 2. anointed the Lord with *ointment,*
　12: 3. took Mary a pound of *ointment*
　　　— filled with the odour of the *ointment.*
　　　5. Why was not this *ointment* sold
Rev.18:13. and odours, and *ointments,*

μυστήριον, *musteerion.*

Mat.13:11. to know the *mysteries* of the kingdom of
Mar 4:11. the *mystery* of the kingdom of God:
Lu. 8:10. the *mysteries* of the kingdom of God:
Ro. 11:25. should be ignorant of this *mystery,*
　16:25. of the *mystery,* which was kept secret
1Co. 2: 7. the wisdom of God in a *mystery,*
　　4: 1. stewards of the *mysteries* of God.
　13: 2. and understand all *mysteries,*
　14: 2. in the spirit he speaketh *mysteries.*
　15:51. Behold, I shew you a *mystery;* We
Eph. 1: 9. unto us the *mystery* of his will,
　　3: 3. made known unto me the *mystery;*
　　　4. knowledge in the *mystery* of Christ
　　　9. the fellowship of the *mystery,*
　　5:32. This is a great *mystery:* but I speak
　　6:19. to make known the *mystery* of the gospel,
Col. 1:26. the *mystery* which hath been hid
　　27. this *mystery* among the Gentiles;
　　2: 2. *mystery* of God, and of the Father,
　　4: 3. to speak the *mystery* of Christ,
2Th. 2: 7. For the *mystery* of iniquity doth already
1Ti. 3: 9. Holding the *mystery* of the faith
　　16. great is the *mystery* of godliness:
Rev. 1:20. The *mystery* of the seven stars
　10: 7. the *mystery* of God should be finished,
　17: 5. *MYSTERY,* BABYLON THE GREAT,
　　7. the *mystery* of the woman,

μυωπάζω, muōpazo.

2Pet. 1: 9. is blind, *and cannot see afar off,*

μώλωψ, mōlōps.

1Pet. 2:24. by whose *stripes* ye were healed.

μωμέομαι, mōmeomai.

2Co. 6: 3. that the ministry *be not blamed:*
8:20. that no man *should blame* us

μῶμος, mōmos.

2Pet. 2:13. Spots (they are) and *blemishes,*

μωραίνω, mōraino.

Mat. 5:13. but if the salt *have lost* his *savour,*
Lu. 14:34. but if the salt *have lost* his *savour,*
Ro. 1:22. to be wise, they *became fools,*
1Co. 1:20. hath not God *made foolish* the wisdom

μωρία, mōria.

1Co. 1:18. to them that perish *foolishness;*
21. by the *foolishness* of preaching
23. unto the Greeks *foolishness;*
2:14. for they are *foolishness* unto him:
3:19. the wisdom of this world is *foolishness*
with God.

μωρολογία, mōrologia.

Eph. 5: 4. nor *foolish talking,* nor jesting,

μωρός, mōros.

Mat. 5:22. whosoever shall say, Thou *fool,*
7:26. shall be likened unto a *foolish* man,
23:17. (Ye) *fools* and blind: for whether
19. (Ye) *fools* and blind:
25: 2. and five (were) *foolish.*
3. They that (were) *foolish* took
8. the *foolish* said unto the wise,
1Co. 1:25. the *foolishness* of God is wiser than men;
27. God hath chosen the *foolish* things
3:18. let him become a *fool,* that he may
4:10. We (are) *fools* for Christ's sake,
2Ti. 2:23. *foolish* and unlearned questions avoid,
Tit. 3: 9. But avoid *foolish* questions,

ναί, nai.

Mat. 5:37. let your communication be, *Yea, yea;*
9:28. They said unto him, *Yea,* Lord.
11: 9. A prophet? *yea,* I say unto you
26. *Even so,* Father: for so it seemed good
13:51. They say unto him, *Yea,* Lord.
15:27. And she said, *Truth,* Lord: yet
17:25. He saith, *Yes.*

Mat. 21:16. *Yea;* have ye never read, Out of
Mar 7:28. *Yes,* Lord: yet the dogs
Lu. 7:26. A prophet? *Yea,* I say unto you,
10:21. *even so,* Father; for so it seemed good
11:51. *verily* I say unto you, It shall be
12: 5. *yea,* I say unto you, Fear him.
Joh. 11:27. *Yea,* Lord: I believe that thou
21:15. He saith unto him, *Yea,* Lord;
16. *Yea,* Lord; thou knowest that I
Acts 5: 8. And she said, *Yea,* for so much.
22:27. art thou a Roman? He said, *Yea.*
Ro. 3:29. *Yes,* of the Gentiles also:
2Co. 1:17. should be *yea yea,* and nay nay?
18. was not *yea* and nay.
19. was not *yea* and nay, but in him was *yea.*
20. all the promises of God in him (are) *yea,*
Philem. 20. *Yea,* brother, let me have joy of thee
Jas. 5:12. but let your *yea* be *yea;* and
Rev. 1: 7. *Even so,* Amen.
14:13. *Yea,* saith the Spirit,
16: 7. *Even so,* Lord God Almighty,
22:20. *Surely* I come quickly; Amen. *Even so,*
come, Lord Jesus.

ναός, naos.

Mat. 23:16. shall swear by the *temple,*
— shall swear by the gold of the *temple,*
17. or the *temple* that sanctifieth
21. whoso shall swear by the *temple,*
35. between the *temple* and the altar.
26:61. to destroy the *temple* of God, and to
27: 5. the pieces of silver in the *temple,*
40. Thou that destroyest the *temple,*
51. the veil of the *temple* was rent
Mar 14:58. I will destroy this *temple*
15:29. Ah, thou that destroyest the *temple,*
38. the veil of the *temple* was rent
Lu. 1: 9. when he went into the *temple*
21. that he tarried so long in the *temple.*
22. had seen a vision in the *temple:*
23:45. the veil of the *temple* was rent
Joh. 2:19. Destroy this *temple,* and in three days
20. Forty and six years was this *temple*
21. But he spake of the *temple* of his body.
Acts 7:48. the most High dwelleth not in *temples*
made with hands;
17:24. dwelleth not in *temples* made
19:24. which made silver *shrines* for Diana,
1Co. 3:16. that ye are the *temple* of God,
17. If any man defile the *temple* of God,
— for the *temple* of God is holy,
6:19. your body is the *temple* of the Holy Ghost
2Co. 6:16. hath the *temple* of God with idols? for ye
are the *temple* of the living God;
Eph. 2:21. groweth unto an holy *temple* in the Lord:
2Th. 2: 4. sitteth in the *temple* of God,
Rev. 3:12. make a pillar in the *temple* of my God,
7:15. serve him day and night in his *temple:*
11: 1. and measure the *temple* of God,
2. which is without the *temple*
19. the *temple* of God was opened in heaven,
and there was seen in his *temple* the ark
14:15. angel came out of the *temple,*
17. another angel came out of the *temple,*
15: 5. the *temple* of the tabernacle of
6. seven angels came out of the *temple,*
8. And the *temple* was filled with smoke
— was able to enter into the *temple,*
16: 1. a great voice out of the *temple*
17. voice out of the *temple* of heaven,

Rev.21:22. And I saw no *temple* therein:
— and the Lamb are the *temple* of it.

νάρδος, *nardos.*

Mar 14: 3. of ointment of spike*nard*
Joh. 12: 3. a pound of ointment of spike*nard,*

ναυαγέω, *nauageo.*

2Co.11:25. thrice I *suffered shipwreck,*
1Ti. 1:19. concerning faith *have made shipwreck:*

ναύκληρος, *naukleeros.*

Acts27:11. and the *owner of the ship,* more than

ναῦς, *naus.*

Acts27:41. they ran the *ship* aground ;

ναύτης, *nautees.*

Acts27:27. the *shipmen* deemed that they drew near
30. as the *shipmen* were about to flee out
Rev.18:17. *sailors,* and as many as trade by sea,

νεανίας, *neanias.*

Acts 7:58. their clothes at a *young man's* feet,
20: 9. a certain *young man* named Eutychus,
23:17. Bring this *young man* unto the
18. to bring this *young man* unto thee,
22. captain (then) let the *young man* depart,

νεανίσκος, *neaniskos.*

Mat.19:20. The *young man* saith unto him,
22. when the *young man* heard that
Mar 14:51. followed him a certain *young man,*
— the *young men* laid hold on him:
16: 5. they saw a *young man* sitting
Lu. 7:14. *Young man,* I say unto thee, Arise.
Acts 2:17. your *young men* shall see visions,
5:10. the *young men* came in, and found
1Joh.2:13. I write unto you, *young men,*
14. I have written unto you, *young men,*

νεκρός, *nekros.*

Mat. 8:22. Follow me; and let the *dead* bury their
dead.
10: 8. raise the *dead,* cast out devils:
11: 5. the *dead* are raised up,
14: 2. he is risen from the *dead;*
17: 9. be risen again from the *dead.*
22:31. touching the resurrection of the *dead,*
32. God is not the God of the *dead,*
23:27. within full of *dead* (men's) bones,
27:64. He is risen from the *dead:*
28: 4. and became as *dead* (men).
7. he is risen from the *dead;*
Mar 6:14. the Baptist was risen from the *dead,*
16. he is risen from the *dead.*

Mar 9: 9. Son of man were risen from the *dead.*
10. the rising from the *dead* should mean.
26. out of him: and he was as one *dead;*
12:25. when they shall rise from the *dead,*
26. as touching the *dead,* that they rise:
27. He is not the God of the *dead,*
Lu. 7:15. And he that was *dead* sat up,
22. the deaf hear, the *dead* are raised,
9: 7. that John was risen from the *dead;*
60. Jesus said unto him, Let the *dead* bury
their *dead:*
15:24. For this my son was *dead,* and is alive
32. for this thy brother was *dead,* and is
16:30. if one went unto them from the *dead,*
31. though one rose from the *dead.*
20:35. and the resurrection from the *dead,*
37. Now that the *dead* are raised,
38. For he is not a God of the *dead,*
24: 5. Why seek ye the living among the *dead?*
46. to rise from the *dead* the third day:
Joh. 2:22. he was risen from the *dead,*
5:21. as the Father raiseth up the *dead,*
25. when the *dead* shall hear the voice
12: 1. whom he raised from the *dead.*
9. whom he had raised from the *dead.*
17. and raised him from the *dead,*
20: 9. that he must rise again from the *dead.*
21:14. after that he was risen from the *dead.*
Acts 3:15. whom God hath raised from the *dead;*
4: 2 the resurrection from the *dead.*
10. whom God raised from the *dead,*
5:10. and found her *dead,*
10:41. after he rose from the *dead.*
42. the Judge of quick and *dead.*
13:30. God raised him from the *dead:*
34. he raised him up from the *dead,*
17: 3. and risen again from the *dead;*
31. he hath raised him from the *dead.*
32. the resurrection of the *dead,*
20: 9. and was taken up *dead.*
23: 6. hope and resurrection of the *dead*
24:15. there shall be a resurrection of the *dead,*
21. Touching the resurrection of the *dead*
26: 8. that God should raise the *dead?*
23. that should rise from the *dead,* and
28: 6. or fallen down *dead* suddenly:
Ro. 1: 4. by the resurrection from the *dead:*
4:17. who quickeneth the *dead,*
24. Jesus our Lord from the *dead;*
6: 4. was raised up from the *dead*
9. Christ being raised from the *dead*
11. to be *dead* indeed unto sin,
13. as those that are alive from the *dead,*
7: 4. be married to another, (even) to him who
is raised from the *dead,*
8. without the law sin (was) *dead.*
8:10. the body (is) *dead* because of sin;
11. raised up Jesus from the *dead* dwell in
you, he that raised up Christ from the
dead
10: 7. to bring up Christ again from the *dead.*
9. hath raised him from the *dead,*
11:15. but life from the *dead?*
14: 9. be Lord both of the *dead* and living.
1Co.15:12. that he rose from the *dead,*
— is no resurrection of the *dead?*
13. if there be no resurrection of the *dead,*
15. if so be that the *dead* rise not.
16. For if the *dead* rise not,
20. now is Christ risen from the *dead,*
21. by man (came) also the resurrection of
the *dead.*

1Co.15:29. which are baptized for the *dead*, if the
dead rise not at all? why are they then
baptized for the *dead?*
32. if the *dead* rise not?
35. How are the *dead* raised up?
42. So also (is) the resurrection of the *dead.*
52. the *dead* shall be raised incorruptible,
2Co. 1: 9. but in God which raiseth the *dead :*
Gal. 1: 1. who raised him from the *dead ;*
Eph. 1:20. when he raised him from the *dead,*
2: 1. who were *dead* in trespasses and
5. when we were *dead* in sins,
5:14. and arise from the *dead,*
Phi. 3:11. unto the resurrection of the *dead.*
Col. 1:18. the firstborn from the *dead ;*
2:12. who hath raised him from the *dead.*
13. And you, being *dead* in your sins
1Th. 1:10. whom he raised from the *dead,*
4:16. the *dead* in Christ shall rise first:
2Ti. 2: 8. was raised from the *dead*
4: 1. shall judge the quick and the *dead* at
Heb 6: 1. repentance from *dead* works,
2. resurrection of the *dead,*
9:14. your conscience from *dead* works
17. of force after men are dead: (lit. force
upon the basis of *dead ones*)
11:19. to raise (him) up, even from the *dead;*
35. received their *dead* raised to life
13:20. brought again from the *dead* our Lord
Jas. 2:17. hath not works, is *dead,* being alone.
20. faith without works is *dead?*
26. the body without the spirit is *dead,* so faith
without works is *dead*
1Pet.1: 3. of Jesus Christ from the *dead,*
21. that raised him up from the *dead,*
4: 5. judge the quick and the *dead.*
6. preached also to them that are *dead,*
Rev. 1: 5. the first begotten of the *dead,*
17. I fell at his feet as *dead.*
18. he that liveth, and was *dead ;*
2: 8. which was *dead,* and is alive ;
3: 1. a name that thou livest, and art *dead.*
11:18. the time of the *dead,* that they
14:13. Blessed (are) the *dead* which die in
16: 3. became as the blood of a *dead* (man):
20: 5. the rest of the *dead* lived not again
12. And I saw the *dead,* small and great,
— and the *dead* were judged out of
13. sea gave up the *dead* which were in it;
and death and hell delivered up the *dead*

νεκρόω, nekroō.

Ro. 4:19. considered not his own body now *dead,*
Col. 3: 5. *Mortify* therefore your members
Heb 11:12. even of one, and him as good as *dead,*

νέκρωσις, nekrōsis.

Ro. 4:19. neither yet the *deadness* of Sarah's womb:
2Co. 4:10. bearing about in the body the *dying* of the
Lord Jesus,

νέος, νεώτερος, neos, neōteros.

Mat. 9:17. Neither do men put *new* wine
— but they put *new* wine into new
Mar 2:22. no man putteth *new* wine into old bottles:
else the *new* wine doth burst

Mar 2:22. but *new* wine must be put into new
Lu. 5:37. no man putteth *new* wine into old bottles;
else the *new* wine will burst
38. But *new* wine must be put into
39. drunk old (wine) straightway desireth *new :*
15:12. the *younger* of them said to (his) father,
13. the *younger* son gathered all
22:26. let him be as the *younger ;*
Joh.21:18. When thou wast *young,* thou girdedst
Acts 5: 6. And the *young men* arose, wound
1Co. 5: 7. that ye may be a *new* lump,
Col. 3:10. And have put on the *new* (man),
1Ti. 5: 1. the *younger men* as brethren ;
2. the *younger* as sisters, with all purity.
11. But the *younger* widows refuse.
14. that the *younger women* marry,
Tit. 2: 4. teach the *young women* to be sober,
6. *Young men* likewise exhort to be
Heb 12:24. mediator of the *new* covenant,
1Pet.5: 5. Likewise, ye *younger,* submit

νεοσσός, neossos.

Lu. 2:24. or two *young* pigeons.

νεότης, neotees.

Mat.19:20. have I kept from my *youth* up:
Mar 10:20. have I observed from my *youth.*
Lu. 18:21. have I kept from my *youth* up.
Acts26: 4. My manner of life from my *youth,*
1Ti. 4:12. Let no man despise thy *youth ;*

νεόφυτος, neophutos.

1Ti. 3: 6. Not a *novice,* lest being lifted up

νεύω, nūo.

Joh.13:24. Peter therefore *beckoned* to him,
Acts24:10. *after that* the governor *had beckoned* unto

νεφέλη, nephelee.

Mat.17: 5. a bright *cloud* overshadowed them : and
behold a voice out of the *cloud,*
24:30. coming in the *clouds* of heaven.
26:64. and coming in the *clouds* of heaven.
Mar 9: 7. a *cloud* that overshadowed them: and a
voice came out of the *cloud,*
13:26. the Son of man coming in the *clouds*
14:62. and coming in the *clouds* of heaven.
Lu. 9:34. there came a *cloud,* and overshadowed
— as they entered into the *cloud.*
35. came a voice out of the *cloud,*
12:54. When ye see a *cloud* rise out of the west,
21:27. coming in a *cloud* with power
Acts 1: 9. a *cloud* received him out of their sight.
1Co.10. 1. all our fathers were under the *cloud,*
2. unto Moses in the *cloud* and in the sea ;
1Th. 4.17. together with them in the *clouds,*
2Pet.2.17. *clouds* that are carried with a tempest ;
Jude 12. *clouds* (they are) without water,
Rev. 1: 7. Behold, he cometh with *clouds ,*
10: 1. clothed with a *cloud .*
11:12. ascended up to heaven in a *cloud*
14:14. a white *cloud,* and upon the *cloud* (one)
sat like unto the Son of man,

Rev.14:15. to him that sat on the *cloud*,
16. And he that sat on the *cloud* thrust

νέφος, *nephos.*

Heb12: 1. with so great a *cloud* of witnesses,

νεφρός, *nephros.*

Rev. 2:23. I am he which searcheth the *reins* and hearts:

νεωκόρος, *neōkoros.*

Acts19:35. is a *worshipper* (lit. *temple-keeper*) of the great goddess

---

νεωτερικός, *neōterikos.*

2Ti. 2:22. Flee also *youthful* lusts:

νεώτερος see νέος.

νή, *nee.*

1Co.15:31. *I protest by* your rejoicing which

νήθω, *neetho.*

Mat. 6:28. neither do they *spin:*
Lu. 12:27. they toil not, they *spin* not;

νηπιάζω, *neepiazo.*

1Co.14:20. howbeit in malice be ye *children*,

νήπιος, *neepios.*

Mat.11:25. hast revealed them unto *babes*.
21:16. Out of the mouth of *babes*
Lu. 10:21. hast revealed them unto *babes:*
Ro. 2:20. a teacher of *babes*,
1Co. 3: 1. as unto *babes* in Christ.
13:11. When I was a *child*, I spake as a *child*,
I understood as a *child*, I thought as a *child:*
— I put away childish things. (lit. of a *child*)
Gal. 4: 1. the heir, as long as he is a *child*,
3. when we were *children*, were in
Eph. 4:14. be no more *children*, tossed to and fro,
Heb 5:13. for he is a *babe*.

νησίον, *neesion.*

Acts27:16. And running under a certain *island*

νῆσος, *neesos.*

Acts13: 6. had gone through the *isle* unto Paphos,
27:26. be cast upon a certain *island*.
28: 1. that the *island* was called Melita.

Acts28: 7. the chief man of the *island*,
9. in the *island*, came, and were healed:
11. which had wintered in the *isle*,
Rev. 1: 9. was in the *isle* that is called Patmos,
6:14. every mountain and *island* were moved
16:20. And every *island* fled away,

νηστεία, *neestia.*

Mat.17:21. not out but by prayer and *fasting*.
Mar 9:29. by nothing, but by prayer and *fasting*.
Lu. 2:37. with *fastings* and prayers night and day.
Acts14:23. and had prayed with *fasting*,
27: 9. because the *fast* was now already past,
1Co. 7: 5. give yourselves to *fasting* and prayer;
2Co. 6: 5. in watchings, in *fastings;*
11:27. in *fastings* often, in cold

νηστεύω, *neestūo.*

Mat. 4: 2. *when* he *had fasted* forty days
6:16. Moreover when ye *fast*, be not,
— may appear unto men to *fast*.
17. *when* thou *fastest*, anoint thine head,
18. appear not unto men to *fast*,
9:14. Why *do* we and the Pharisees *fast* oft, but thy disciples *fast* not?
15. and then *shall* they *fast*.
Mar 2:18. the Pharisees used to *fast:*
— Why *do* the disciples of John and of the Pharisees *fast*, but thy disciples *fast* not?
19. children of the bridechamber *fast*,
— bridegroom with them, they cannot *fast*.
20. and then *shall* they *fast* in those days.
Lu. 5:33. Why *do* the disciples of John *fast* often,
34. of the bridechamber *fast*, while the
35. and then *shall* they *fast* in those days.
18:12. I *fast* twice in the week,
Acts10:30. Four days ago I was *fasting* until
13: 2. As they ministered to the Lord, and *fasted*,
3. *when* they *had fasted* and prayed,

νῆστις, *neestis.*

Mat.15:32. I will not send them away *fasting*,
Mar 8: 3. And if I send them away *fasting*

νηφάλεος, & νεφάλιος, *neephaleos*, & *nephalios.*

1Ti. 3: 2. *vigilant*, sober, of good behaviour,
11. *sober*, faithful in all things.
Tit. 2: 2. That the aged men be *sober*, grave,

νήφω, *neepho.*

1Th. 5: 6. but let us watch and be *sober*.
8. *let* us, who are of the day, be *sober*,
2Ti. 4: 5. But *watch* thou in all things,
1Pet.1:13. be *sober*, and hope to the end
4: 7. be ye therefore sober, and *watch* unto
5: 8. Be *sober*, be vigilant;

νικάω, *nikao.*

Lu. 11:22. shall come upon him and *overcome* him,
Joh. 16:33. I *have overcome* the world.

Ro. 3: 4. *mightest overcome* when thou art judged.
12:21. *Be* not *overcome* of evil, but *overcome* evil
with good.
1Joh.2:13. ye *have overcome* the wicked one.
14. and ye *have overcome* the wicked one.
4: 4. and *have overcome* them:
5: 4. born of God *overcometh* the world:
— the victory *that overcometh* the world,
5. Who is he *that overcometh* the world,
Rev. 2: 7. To him *that overcometh* will I give
11. He *that overcometh* shall not be hurt
17. To him *that overcometh* will I
26. And he *that overcometh*, and keepeth
3: 5. He *that overcometh*, the same
12. Him *that overcometh* will I make
21. To him *that overcometh* will I grant
— even as I also *overcame*, and am set
5: 5. *hath prevailed* to open the book,
6: 2. went forth *conquering*, and to *conquer*.
11: 7. and *shall overcome* them,
12:11. And they *overcame* him by the blood
13: 7. and *to overcome* them:
15: 2. and them *that had gotten the victory* over
the beast,
17:14. and the Lamb *shall overcome* them:
21: 7. He *that overcometh* shall inherit all things;

νίκη, *nikee.*

1Joh.5: 4. this is the *victory* that overcometh the
world, (even) our faith.

νῖκος, *nikos.*

Mat.12:20. send forth judgment unto *victory.*
1Co.15:54. Death is swallowed up in *victory.*
55. O grave, where (is) thy *victory?*
57. which giveth us the *victory* through our
Lord Jesus Christ.

νιπτήρ, *nipteer.*

Joh.13: 5. he poureth water into a *bason,*

νίπτω, *nipto.*

Mat. 6:17. and *wash* thy face ;
15: 2. for they *wash* not their hands when
Mar 7: 3. except they *wash* (their) hands oft,
Joh. 9: 7. Go, *wash* in the pool of Siloam,
— and *washed*, and came seeing.
11. Go to the pool of Siloam, and *wash* : and
I went and *washed, and* I received sight.
15. and I *washed*, and do see.
13: 5. and began *to wash* the disciples' feet,
6. Lord, *dost* thou *wash* my feet ?
8. Thou *shalt* never *wash* my feet.
— If I *wash* thee not, thou hast no
10. needeth not save *to wash* (his) feet,
12. So after he *had washed* their feet,
14. and Master, *have washed* your feet ; ye
also ought *to wash* one another's feet.
1Ti. 5:10. if she *have washed* the saints' feet,

νοέω, *noeo.*

Mat.15:17. *Do* not ye yet *understand*, that
16: 9. *Do* ye not yet *understand*, neither

Mat.16:11. How is it that ye *do* not *understand*
24:15. whoso readeth, *let* him *understand :*
Mar 7:18. *Do* ye not *perceive*, that whatsoever
8:17. *perceive* ye not yet, neither understand ?
13:14. *let* him that readeth *understand,*
Joh.12:40. nor *understand* with (their) heart,
Ro. 1:20. *being understood* by the things that
Eph. 3: 4. ye may *understand* my knowledge in
20. above all that we ask or *think,*
1Ti. 1: 7. *understanding* neither what they say,
2Ti. 2: 7. *Consider* what I say ; and the Lord
Heb11: 3. Through faith we *understand* that

νόημα, *noeema.*

2Co. 2:11. we are not ignorant of his *devices.*
3:14. But their *minds* were blinded:
4: 4. hath blinded the *minds* of them
10: 5. bringing into captivity every *thought*
11: 3. so your *minds* should be corrupted
Phi. 4: 7. shall keep your hearts and *minds* through
Christ Jesus.

νόθος, *nothos.*

Heb12: 8. then are ye *bastards*, and not sons.

νομή, *nomee.*

Joh.10: 9. go in and out, and find *pasture.*
2Ti. 2:17. their word will eat (lit. will have *pasture*)
as doth a canker:

νομίζω, *nomizo.*

Mat. 5:17. *Think* not that I am come to destroy
10:34. *Think* not that I am come to send peace
20:10. they *supposed* that they should
Lu. 2:44. *supposing* him to have been in the
3:23. being as *was supposed* the son of
Acts 7:25. For he *supposed* his brethren would have
8:20. because thou *hast thought* that the gift
14:19. *supposing* he had been dead.
16:13. where prayer *was wont* to be made ;
27. *supposing* that the prisoners had been fled.
17:29. we ought not *to think* that the Godhead
21:29. whom they *supposed* that Paul had
1Co. 7:26. I *suppose* therefore that this is good
36. if any man *think* that he behaveth
1Ti. 6: 5. *supposing* that gain is godliness:

νομικός, *nomikos.*

Mat.22:35. one of them, (which was) a *lawyer*, asked
Lu. 7:30. the Pharisees and *lawyers* rejected
10:25. a certain *lawyer* stood up, and
11:45. Then answered one of the *lawyers,*
46. Woe unto you also, (ye) *lawyers !*
52. Woe unto you, *lawyers !* for ye have
14: 3. spake unto the *lawyers* and Pharisees,
Tit. 3: 9. and strivings *about the law ;*
13. Bring Zenas the *lawyer* and Apollos

νομίμως, *nomimōs.*

1Ti. 1: 8. if a man use it *lawfully ;*
2Ti. 2: 5. except he strive *lawfully.*

νόμισμα, nomisma.

Mat.22:19. Shew me the tribute *money*.

νομοδιδάσκαλος, nomodidaskalos.

Lu. 5:17. and *doctors of the law* sitting by,
Acts 5:34. Gamaliel, a *doctor of the law,*
1Ti. 1: 7. Desiring to be *teachers of the law ;*

νομοθεσία, nomothesia.

Ro. 9: 4. and the *giving of the law*, and ·

νομοθετέω, nomotheteo.

Heb 7:11. for under it the people *received the law,*
8: 6. which *was established* upon better

νομοθέτης, nomothetees.

Jas. 4:12. There is one *lawgiver,* who is able to save
and to destroy:

νόμος, nomos.

[1] denotes that the article is not in the Greek,
though inserted in the English.

Mat. 5:17. that I am come to destroy the *law,*
18. shall in no wise pass from the *law,*
7:12. for this is the *law* and the prophets.
11:13. and the *law* prophesied until John.
12: 5. have ye not read in the *law,*
22:36. the great commandment in the *law ?*
40. hang all the *law* and the prophets.
23:23. the weightier (matters) of the *law,*
Lu. 2:22. according to the *law* of Moses
23. As it is written in[1] the *law* of the Lord,
24. said in[1] the *law* of the Lord,
27. after the custom of the *law,*
39. according to the *law* of the Lord,
10:26. What is written in the *law ?*
16:16. The *law* and the prophets (were) until
17. than one tittle of the *law* to fail.
24:44. written in the *law* of Moses,
Joh. 1:17. For the *law* was given by Moses,
45(46). of whom Moses in the *law,* and
7:19. Did not Moses give you the *law,* and (yet)
none of you keepeth the *law ?*
23. that the *law* of Moses should not
49. who knoweth not the *law* are cursed.
51. Doth our *law* judge (any) man, before
8: 5. Now Moses in the *law* commanded
17. It is also written in your *law,*
10:34. Is it not written in your *law,*
12:34. We have heard out of the *law* that
15:25. that is written in their *law,*
18:31. judge him according to your *law.*
19: 7. We have a *law,* and by our *law* he ought
Acts 6:13. against this holy place, and the *law :*
7:53. Who have received the *law* by
13:15. after the reading of the *law*
39. could not be justified by the *law*
15: 5. to keep the *law* of Moses.
24. be circumcised, and keep the *law :*
18:13. to worship God contrary to the *law.*
15. and (of) your *law,* look ye (to it);

Acts 21:20. are all zealous of the *law :*
24. and keepest the *law.*
28. against the people, and the *law,*
22: 3. to the perfect manner of the *law*
12. a devout man according to the *law,*
23: 3. to judge me after the *law,*
29. accused of questions of their *law,*
24: 6. have judged according to our *law.*
14. in the *law* and in the prophets:
25: 8. Neither against the *law* of the Jews,
28:23. both out of the *law* of Moses,
Ro. 2:12. as many as have sinned in[1] the *law* shall
be judged by the[1] *law ;*
13. For not the hearers of the *law* (are) just
before God, but the doers of the *law*
14. the Gentiles, which have not[1] the *law,* do
by nature the things contained in the
law, these, having not[1] the *law,* are a
law unto themselves:
15. the work of the *law* written in their
17. and restest in the *law,*
18. being instructed out of the *law ;*
20. and of the truth in the *law.*
23. Thou that makest thy boast of[1] the *law,*
through breaking the *law* dishonourest
thou God?
25. if thou keep[1] the *law :* but if thou be a
breaker of[1] the *law,* thy
26. keep the righteousness of the *law,*
27. if it fulfil the *law,*
— dost transgress[1] the *law ?*
3:19. soever the *law* saith, it saith to them who
are under the *law :*
20. Therefore by the deeds of[1] the *law*
— for by[1] the *law* (is) the knowledge of sin.
21. of God without[1] the *law* is manifested,
being witnessed by the *law* and
27. By what *law ?* of works? Nay: but by[1]
the *law* of faith.
28. by faith without the deeds[1] of the *law.*
31. make void[1] the *law* through faith? God
forbid: yea, we establish[1] the *law.*
4:13. or to his seed, through[1] the *law,*
14. For if they which are of[1] the *law*
15. Because the *law* worketh wrath: for where
no *law* is, (there is) no
16. which is of the *law,* but
5:13. until[1] the *law* sin was in the world :
— not imputed when there is no *law.*
20. Moreover[1] the *law* entered, that
6:14. for ye are not under[1] the *law,* but
15. because we are not under[1] the *law,*
7: 1. for I speak to them that know[1] the *law,*
how that the *law* hath dominion over
2. is bound by[1] the *law* to (her) husband
— is loosed from the *law* of (her) husband.
3. she is free from that *law ;*
4. become dead to the *law* by the body of
5. which were by the *law,*
6. now we are delivered from the *law,*
7. (Is) the *law* sin? God forbid. Nay, I
had not known sin, but by[1] the *law :*
— except the *law* had said,
8. For without[1] the *law* sin (was) dead.
9. I was alive without[1] the *law* once:
12. Wherefore the *law* (is) holy,
14. we know that the *law* is spiritual:
16. I consent unto the *law* that (it is) good.
21. I find then a (lit. the) *law,* that, when I
22. I delight in the *law* of God
23. But I see another *law* in my members,
warring against the *law* of my mind,

Ro. 7:23. into captivity to the *law* of sin
25. with the mind I myself serve [1] the *law* of
God ; but with the flesh [1] the *law* of sin.
8: 2. For the *law* of the Spirit of life
— free from the *law* of sin and death.
3. For what the *law* could not do,
4. the righteousness of the *law*
7. it is not subject to the *law* of God,
9:31. after [1] the *law* of righteousness, hath not
attained to [1] the *law* of righteousness.
32. by the works of [1] the *law*.
10: 4. Christ (is) the end of [1] the *law*
5. the righteousness which is of the *law*,
13: 8. hath fulfilled [1] the *law*.
10. love (is) the fulfilling of [1] the *law*.
1Co. 7:39. The wife is bound by [1] the *law*
9: 8. saith not the *law* the same also?
9. it is written in the *law* of Moses,
20. to them that are under [1] the *law*, as under [1]
the *law*, that I might gain them that are
under [1] the *law*;
14:21. In the *law* it is written, With
34. under obedience, as also saith the *law*.
15:56. the strength of sin (is) the *law*.
Gal. 2:16. not justified by the works of [1] the *law*,
— and not by the works of [1] the *law:* for by
the works of [1] the *law* shall no flesh
19. I through [1] the *law* am dead to [1] the *law*,
21. if righteousness (come) by [1] the *law*,
3: 2. the Spirit by the works of [1] the *law*, or
5. by the works of [1] the *law*, or by the hearing
10. as many as are of the works of [1] the *law*
— in the book of the *law* to do them.
11. no man is justified by [1] the *law*
12. And the *law* is not of faith:
13. from the curse of the *law*,
17. the *law*, which was four hundred and
18. if the inheritance (be) of [1] the *law*,
19. Wherefore then (serveth) the *law?*
21. (Is) the *law* then against the promises
— for if there had been a *law* given
— righteousness should have been by [1] the
law.
23. we were kept under [1] the *law*,
24. Wherefore the *law* was our schoolmaster
4: 4. made under [1] the *law*,
5. To redeem them that were under [1] the *law*,
21. Tell me, ye that desire to be under [1] the
law, do ye not hear the *law?*
5: 3. is a debtor to do the whole *law*.
4. of you are justified by [1] the *law;*
14. For all the *law* is fulfilled in one
18. ye are not under [1] the *law*.
23. against such there is no *law*.
6: 2. and so fulfil the *law* of Christ.
13. who are circumcised keep [1] the *law;*
Eph. 2:15. enmity, (even) the *law* of commandments
Phi. 3: 5. as touching [1] the *law*, a Pharisee;
6. which is in [1] the *law*, blameless.
9. righteousness, which is of [1] the *law*.
1Ti. 1: 8. we know that the *law* (is) good,
9. that [1] the *law* is not made for a righteous
Heb 7: 5. tithes of the people according to the *law*,
12. a change also of [1] the *law*.
16. after [1] the *law* of a carnal commandment,
19. the *law* made nothing perfect,
28. the *law* maketh men high priests which
— which was since the *law*, (maketh) the
8: 4. that offer gifts according to the *law :*
10. I will put my *laws* into their mind,
9:19. every precept to all the people according
to [1] the *law*,

Heb 9:22. things are by the *law* purged with blood ;
10: 1. For the *law* having a shadow of
8. which are offered by the *law ;*
16. I will put my *laws* into their hearts,
28. He that despised Moses' *law* died
Jas. 1:25. into [1] the perfect *law* of liberty,
2: 8. If ye fulfil [1] the royal *law*
9. and are convinced of the *law*
10. whosoever shall keep the whole *law*,
11. a transgressor of [1] the *law*.
12. be judged by [1] the *law* of liberty.
4:11. speaketh evil of [1] the *law*, and judgeth [1] the
law: but if thou judge [1] the *law*, thou
art not a doer of [1] the *law*, but a judge.

νοσέω, noseo.

1Ti. 6: 4. but *doting* about questions and strifes of

νόσημα, noseema.

Joh. 5. 4. was made whole of whatsoever *disease*

νόσος, nosos.

Mat. 4:23. healing all manner of *sickness*
24. that were taken with divers *diseases*
8:17. and bare (our) *sicknesses*.
9:35. and healing every *sickness* and
10: 1. to heal all manner of *sickness* and
Mar 1:34. many that were sick of divers *diseases*,
3:15. power to heal *sicknesses*,
Lu. 4:40. sick with divers *diseases*
6:17. and to be healed of their *diseases ;*
7:21. cured many of (their) *infirmities*
9: 1. over all devils, and to cure *diseases*.
Acts19:12. and the *diseases* departed from them,

νοσσιά, nossia.

Lu. 13:34. as a hen (doth gather) her *brood*

νοσσίον, nossion.

Mat.23:37. as a hen gathereth her *chickens*

νοσφίζομαι, nosphizomai.

Acts 5: 2. *kept back* (part) of the price,
3. to *keep back* (part) of the price
Tit. 2:10. Not *purloining*, but shewing

νότος, notos.

Mat.12:42. The queen of the *south* shall rise up
Lu. 11:31. The queen of the *south* shall rise up
12:55. when (ye see) the *south wind* blow,
13:29. and (from) the *south*, and shall sit down
Acts27:13. And when the *south wind* blew softly,
28:13. the *south wind* blew, and we came
Rev.21:13. on the *south* three gates ;

νουθεσία, nouthesia.

1Co.10:11. they are written for our *admonition*,

Eph. 6: 4. and *admonition* of the Lord.
Tit. 3:10. after the first and second *admonition* reject;

νουθετέω, *noutheteo*.

Acts20:31. I ceased not to *warn* every one night and
Ro. 15:14. able also *to admonish* one another.
1Co. 4:14. but as my beloved sons I *warn* (you)
Col. 1:28. *warning* every man, and teaching
    3:16. and *admonishing* one another in psalms
1Th. 5:12. over you in the Lord, and *admonish* you;
    14. *warn* them that are unruly,
2Th. 3:15. but *admonish* (him) as a brother.

νουμηνία, *noumeenia*.

Col. 2:16. or of the *new moon*, or of the sabbath

νουνεχῶς, *nounekōs*.

Mar 12:34. saw that he answered *discreetly*,

νοῦς, *nous*.

Lu. 24:45. Then opened he their *understanding*,
Ro. 1:28. God gave them over to a reprobate *mind*,
    7:23. warring against the law of my *mind*,
    25. with the *mind* I myself serve
    11:34. who hath known the *mind* of the Lord?
    12: 2. by the renewing of your *mind*,
    14: 5. be fully persuaded in his own *mind*.
1Co. 1:10. joined together in the same *mind*
    2:16. who hath known the *mind* of the Lord,
    — But we have the *mind* of Christ.
    14:14. but my *understanding* is unfruitful.
    15. I will pray with the *understanding* also:
    — I will sing with the *understanding* also.
    19. five words with my *understanding*,
Eph. 4:17. in the vanity of their *mind*,
    23. be renewed in the spirit of your *mind*;
Phi. 4: 7. which passeth all *understanding*,
Col. 2:18. puffed up by his fleshly *mind*,
2Th. 2: 2. be not soon shaken in *mind*,
1Ti. 6: 5. disputings of men of corrupt *minds*,
2Ti. 3: 8. men of corrupt *minds*, (lit. men corrupt
    in *mind*)
Tit. 1:15. even their *mind* and conscience is defiled.
Rev.13:18. Let him that hath *understanding*
    17: 9. And here (is) the *mind* which hath wisdom.

νύμφη, *numphee*.

Mat.10:35. and the *daughter in law* against
Lu. 12:53. against her *daughter in law*, and the
    daughter in law against her
Joh. 3:29. He that hath the *bride* is the
Rev.18:23. and of the *bride* shall be heard
    21: 2. prepared as a *bride* adorned for
    9. shew thee the *bride*, the Lamb's wife.
    22:17. the Spirit and the *bride* say, Come.

νυμφίος, *numphios*.

Mat. 9:15. as long as the *bridegroom* is with them?
    — when the *bridegroom* shall be taken
    25: 1. went forth to meet the *bridegroom*.

Mat.25: 5. While the *bridegroom* tarried,
    6. Behold, the *bridegroom* cometh;
    10. went to buy, the *bridegroom* came;
Mar 2:19. while the *bridegroom* is with them? as
    long as they have the *bridegroom*
    20. when the *bridegroom* shall be taken
Lu. 5:34. while the *bridegroom* is with them?
    35. when the *bridegroom* shall be taken
Joh. 2: 9. of the feast called the *bridegroom*,
    3:29. that hath the bride is the *bridegroom*: but
    the friend of the *bridegroom*,
    — because of the *bridegroom's* voice:
Rev.18:23. and the voice of the *bridegroom* and

νυμφών, *numphōn*.

Mat. 9:15. Can the children of the *bridechamber*
Mar 2:19. Can the children of the *bridechamber*
Lu. 5:34. the children of the *bridechamber* fast,

νῦν, *nun*.

Mat.24:21. since the beginning of the world to *this
    time*,
    26:65. *now* ye have heard his blasphemy.
    27:42. let him *now* come down from the cross,
    43. let him deliver him *now*, if he will
Mar 10:30. an hundredfold *now* in this time,
    13:19. unto *this time*, neither shall be.
    15:32. descend *now* from the cross, that we may
Lu. 1:48. from *henceforth* all generations
    2:29. Lord, *now* lettest thou thy servant
    5:10. from *henceforth* thou shalt catch men.
    6:21. Blessed (are ye) that hunger *now*:
    — Blessed (are ye) that weep *now*:
    25. Woe unto you that laugh *now*!
    11:39. *Now* do ye Pharisees make clean
    12:52. from *henceforth* there shall be five
    16:25. but *now* he is comforted,
    19:42. but *now* they are hid from thine eyes.
    22:36. But *now*, he that hath a purse,
    69. Hereafter shall the Son of man sit (lit.
    from *now* shall the Son of man be
    sitting)
Joh. 2: 8. Draw out *now*, and bear unto the governor
    4:18. he whom thou *now* hast is not thy
    23. But the hour cometh, and *now* is,
    5:25. The hour is coming, and *now* is,
    8:40. But *now* ye seek to kill me,
    52. *Now* we know that thou hast a devil.
    9:21. But by what means he *now* seeth,
    41. but *now* ye say, We see;
    11: 8. Master, the Jews *of late* sought to stone
    22. I know, that even *now*, whatsoever
    12:27. *Now* is my soul troubled;
    31. *Now* is the judgment of this world: *now*
    shall the prince of this world be cast
    13:31. *Now* is the Son of man glorified,
    36. thou canst not follow me *now*;
    14:29. And *now* I have told you before it
    15:22. but *now* they have no cloke for their sin.
    24. but *now* have they both seen and
    16: 5. But *now* I go my way to him
    22. And ye *now* therefore have sorrow:
    29. Lo, *now* speakest thou plainly,
    30. *Now* are we sure that thou knowest
    32. the hour cometh, yea, is *now* come,
    17: 5. And *now*, O Father, glorify thou me
    7. *Now* they have known that all things

Joh. 17:13. And *now* come I to thee;
18:36. but *now* is my kingdom not from hence.
21:10. fish which ye have *now* caught.
Acts 2:33. this, which ye *now* see and hear.
3:17. And *now*, brethren, I wot that
7: 4. wherein ye *now* dwell.
34. And *now* come, I will send thee
52. of whom ye have been *now* the betrayers
10: 5. And *now* send men to Joppa,
33. *Now* therefore are we all here
12:11. *Now* I know of a surety, that the Lord
13:11. And *now*, behold, the hand of the Lord
15:10. *Now* therefore why tempt ye God,
16:36. *now* therefore depart, and go in
37. and *now* do they thrust us out privily?
18: 6. from *henceforth* I will go unto the
20:22. And *now*, behold, I go bound in the
25. And *now*, behold, I know that ye all,
22: 1. my defence (which I make) *now*
16. And *now* why tarriest thou?
23:15. *Now* therefore ye with the council
21. and *now* are they ready, looking
24:13. things whereof they *now* accuse me.
25. Go thy way for *this time*;
26: 6. And *now* I stand and am judged
17. unto whom *now* I send thee,
Ro. 3:21. But *now* the righteousness of God
26. To declare, (I say), at this time (lit. in the *now* time)
5: 9. being *now* justified by his blood,
11. by whom we have *now* received the
6:19. even so *now* yield your members
21. whereof ye are *now* ashamed?
8: 1. *now* no condemnation to them
18. the sufferings of this *present* time
22. in pain together until *now*.
11: 5. Even so then at this *present* time
30. yet have *now* obtained mercy
31. so have these also *now* not believed,
13:11. for *now* (is) our salvation nearer
16:26. But *now* is made manifest,
1Co. 3: 2. neither yet *now* are ye able.
7:14. but *now* are they holy.
12:20. But *now* (are they) many members,
16:12. was not at all to come *at this time*;
2Co. 5:16. *henceforth* know we no man after
— yet *now* henceforth know we (him) no
6: 2. behold, *now* (is) the accepted time; behold, *now* (is) the day of salvation.
7: 9. *Now* I rejoice, not that ye were
8:14(13). now at this time (lit. in the *now* time) your abundance
13: 2. and being absent *now* I write
Gal. 1:23. *now* preacheth the faith
2:20. life which I *now* live in the flesh
3: 3. are ye *now* made perfect by the flesh?
4: 9. But *now*, after that ye have known
25. to Jerusalem which *now* is,
29. even so (it is) *now*.
Eph. 2: 2. the spirit that *now* worketh in
3: 5. as it is *now* revealed unto his holy
10. To the intent that *now* unto the
5: 8. but *now* (are ye) light in the Lord:
Phi. 1: 5. from the first day until *now*;
20. as always, (so) *now* also Christ
30. (and) *now* hear (to be) in me.
2:12. but *now* much more in my absence,
3:18. and *now* tell you even weeping,
Col. 1:24. Who *now* rejoice in my sufferings
1Th. 3: 8. For *now* we live, if ye stand fast
2Th. 2: 6. And *now* ye know what withholdeth
1Ti. 4: 8. promise of the life that *now* is, and

1Ti. 6:17. Charge them that are rich in *this* world,
2Ti. 1:10. But is *now* made manifest
4:10. having loved this *present* world,
Tit. 2:12. godly, in this *present* world;
Heb 2: 8. But *now* we see not yet all things
9: 5. of which we cannot *now* speak
24. *now* to appear in the presence of God
26. but *now* once in the end of the world
12:26. but *now* he hath promised,
Jas. 4:13. Go to *now*, ye that say,
16. But *now* ye rejoice in your boastings:
5: 1. Go to *now*, (ye) rich men,
1Pet.1:12. which are *now* reported unto you
2:10. but (are) *now* the people of God:
— but *now* have obtained mercy
25. but are *now* returned unto the
3:21. baptism doth also *now* save us not the
2Pet.3: 7. and the earth, which are *now*,
18. To him (be) glory both *now* and for ever.
1Joh.2:18. even *now* are there many antichrists,
28. And *now*, little children, abide in him;
3: 2. *now* are we the sons of God,
4: 3. even *now* already is it in the world.
2Joh. 5. And *now* I beseech thee, lady,
Jude 25. and power, both *now* and ever. Amen.
See also τὰ νῦν and νυνί.

τὰ νῦν or τανῦν, *ta nun* or *tanun*.

Acts 4:29. And *now*, Lord, behold their threatenings:
5:38. And *now* I say unto you, Refrain
17:30. *but now* commandeth all men
20:32. And *now*, brethren, I commend you
27:22. And *now* I exhort you to be of good

νυνί, *nuni.*

Ro. 6:22. But *now* being made free from sin,
7: 6. But *now* we are delivered from the law,
17. *Now* then it is no more I that do it,
15:23. But *now* having no more place
25. But *now* I go unto Jerusalem
1Co. 5:11. But *now* I have written unto you
12:18. But *now* hath God set the members
13:13. And *now* abideth faith, hope, charity,
14: 6. *Now*, brethren, if I come unto you
15:20. But *now* is Christ risen from the dead,
2Co. 8:11. *Now* therefore perform the doing
22. but *now* much more diligent,
Eph 2:13. But *now* in Christ Jesus ye who
Col. 1:21. yet *now* hath he reconciled
26. but *now* is made manifest to his
3: 8. But *now* ye also put off all these;
Philem 9. and *now* also a prisoner of Jesus
11. but *now* profitable to thee and to me:
Heb 8: 6. But *now* hath he obtained a more
11:16. But *now* they desire a better (country), that is, an heavenly:

νύξ, *nux.*

Mat. 2:14. child and his mother by *night*, and
4: 2. forty days and forty *nights*,
12:40. Jonas was three days and three *nights*
— and three *nights* in the heart of the earth.
14:25. in the fourth watch of the *night*
25: 6. And at mid*night* there was a cry
26:31. be offended because of me this *night*:
34. That this *night*, before the cock crow,
27:64. lest his disciples come by *night*,

Mat.28:13. Say ye, His disciples came by *night*,
Mar 4:27. and rise *night* and day, and the seed
    5: 5. And always, *night* and day,
    6:48. the fourth watch of the *night*
  14:27. offended because of me this *night:*
    30. That this day, (even) in this *night*,
Lu. 2: 8. over their flock by *night*.
    37. fastings and prayers *night* and day.
    5: 5. Master, we have toiled all the *night*,
  12:20. this *night* thy soul shall be required
  17:34. in that *night* there shall be two
  18: 7. which cry day and *night* unto him,
  21:37. and at *night* he went out, and abode in
    the mount
Joh. 3: 2. The same came to Jesus by *night*,
  7:50. he that came to Jesus by *night*,
  9: 4. the *night* cometh, when no man
  11:10. if a man walk in the *night*,
  13:30. and it was *night*.
  19:39. at the first came to Jesus by *night*,
  21: 3. and that *night* they caught nothing.
Acts 5:19. But the angel of the Lord by *night*
  9:24. day and *night* to kill him.
    25. Then the disciples took him by *night*,
  12: 6. the same *night* Peter was sleeping
  16: 9. appeared to Paul in the *night;*
    33. the same hour of the *night*,
  17:10. sent away Paul and Silas by *night*
  18: 9. the Lord to Paul in the *night* by a vision,
  20:31. to warn every one *night* and day with
  23:11. And the *night* following the Lord
    23. at the third hour of the *night;*
    31. by *night* to Antipatris.
  26: 7. serving (God) day and *night*,
  27:23. For there stood by me this *night*
    27. But when the fourteenth *night* was
    — about mid*night* the shipmen
Ro. 13:12. The *night* is far spent,
1Co.11:23. the (same) *night* in which he was
1Th. 2: 9. for labouring *night* and day, because
  3:10. *Night* and day praying exceedingly
  5: 2. so cometh as a thief in the *night*.
    5. we are not of the *night*, nor of darkness.
    7. they that sleep sleep in the *night;*
    — are drunken in the *night*.
2Th. 3: 8. with labour and travail *night* and day,
1Ti. 5: 5. and prayers *night* and day.
2Ti. 1: 3. in my prayers *night* and day;
2Pet.3:10. will come as a thief in the *night;*
Rev. 4: 8. they rest not day and *night*, saying,
  7:15. serve him day and *night* in his temple:
  8:12. and the *night* likewise.
  12:10. accused them before our God day and
    night.
  14:11. they have no rest day nor *night*,
  20:10. tormented day and *night* for ever and
  21:25. for there shall be no *night* there.
  22: 5. And there shall be no *night* there;

νυστάζω, *nustazo.*

Mat.25: 5. they all *slumbered* and slept.
2Pet. 2: 3. their damnation *slumbereth* not.

νύττω, *nutto.*

Joh.19:34. with a spear *pierced* his side,

νυχθήμερον, *nuktheemeron.*

2Co.11:25. *a night and a day* I have been in the deep;

νωθρός, *nōthros.*

Heb 5:11. seeing ye are *dull* of hearing,
  6:12. That ye be not *slothful*, but

νῶτος, *nōtos.*

Ro. 11:10. and bow down their *back* alway.

ξενία, *xenia.*

Acts28:23. came many to him unto (his) *lodging;*
Philem 22. prepare me also a *lodging:*

ξενίζω, *xenizo.*

Acts10: 6. He *lodgeth* with one Simon a tanner,
    18. whether Simon, which was surnamed
    Peter, *were lodged* there.
    23. called he them in, and *lodged* (them).
    32. he *is lodged* in the house of (one) Simon
  17:20. thou bringest certain *strange* things
  21:16. with whom we *should lodge.*
  28: 7. and *lodged* us three days courteously.
Heb 13: 2. some *have entertained* angels unawares.
1Pet.4: 4. they *think it strange* that ye run not
    12. Beloved, *think it* not *strange* concerning
    the fiery trial

ξενοδοχέω, *xenodokeo.*

1Ti. 5:10. if she *have lodged strangers*,

ξένος, *xenos.*

Mat.25:35. was a *stranger*, and ye took me in:
    38. When saw we thee a *stranger*,
    43. I was a *stranger*, and ye took me not in:
    44. or a *stranger*, or naked, or sick,
  27: 7. the potter's field, to bury *strangers* in.
Acts17:18. a setter forth of *strange* gods:
    21. the Athenians and *strangers* which were
Ro. 16:23. Gaius mine *host*, and of the whole church,
Eph. 2:12. and *strangers* from the covenants
    19. ye are no more *strangers* and foreigners,
Heb 11:13. confessed that they were *strangers* and
  13: 9. with divers and *strange* doctrines.
1Pet.4:12. as though some *strange* thing happened
3Joh. 5. to the brethren, and to *strangers;*

ξέστης, *xestees.*

Mar 7: 4. the washing of cups, and *pots*,
    8. the washing of *pots* and cups:

ξηραίνω, *xeeraino.*

Mat.13: 6. had no root, they *withered away.*
  21:19. presently the fig tree *withered away.*
    20. How soon *is* the fig tree *withered away!*
Mar 3: 1. which had a *withered* hand.
    3. which had the *withered* hand,

Mar 4: 6. had no root, it *withered away*.
  5:29. the fountain of her blood *was dried up*;
  9:18. gnasheth with his teeth, and *pineth away*:
  11:20. saw the fig tree *dried up* from the roots.
  21. which thou cursedst *is withered away*.
Lu. 8: 6. it *withered away*, because it lacked
Joh. 15: 6. as a branch, and *is withered*;
Jas. 1:11. but it *withereth* the grass, and the
1Pet. 1:24. The grass *withereth*, and the flower
Rev. 14:15. for the harvest of the earth *is ripe*.
  16:12. and the water thereof *was dried up*,

ξηρός, *xeeros*.

Mat. 12:10. which had (his) hand *withered*.
  23:15. for ye compass sea and *land* to make
Lu. 6: 6. whose right hand was *withered*.
  8. which had the *withered* hand,
  23:31. what shall be done in the *dry?*
Joh. 5: 3. of blind, halt, *withered*, waiting
Heb 11:29. through the Red sea as by *dry* (land):

ξύλινος, *xulinos*.

2Ti. 2:20. but also *of wood* and of earth;
Rev. 9:20. and *of wood:* which neither can see,

ξύλον, *xulon*.

Mat. 26:47. with swords and *staves*,
  55. with swords and *staves* for to take me?
Mar 14:43. with swords and *staves*,
  48. with swords and (with) *staves* to take me?
Lu. 22:52. as against a thief, with swords and *staves?*
  23:31. if they do these things in a green *tree*,
Acts 5:30. whom ye slew and hanged on a *tree*.
  10:39. whom they slew and hanged on a *tree:*
  13:29. they took (him) down from the *tree*,
  16:24. and made their feet fast in *the stocks*.
1Co. 3:12. precious stones, *wood*, hay, stubble;
Gal. 3:13. Cursed (is) every one that hangeth on a
  tree:
1Pet. 2:24. bare our sins in his own body on the *tree*,
Rev. 2: 7. will I give to eat of the *tree* of life,
  18:12. and all thyine *wood*,
  — vessels of most precious *wood*,
  22: 2. (was there) the *tree* of life,
  — and the leaves of the *tree*
  14. may have right to the *tree* of life,

ξυράω, *xurao*.

Acts 21:24. that they *may shave* (their) heads:
1Co. 11: 5. is even all one as *if* she were *shaven*.
  6. for a woman to be shorn or *shaven*,

ὁ, ἡ, τό.

(See in appendix.)

ὅδε, ἥδε, τόδε, *hode, heede, tode*.

Lu. 10:39. And *she* had a sister called Mary,

Lu. 16:25. but now *he* is comforted, and thou
Acts 15:23. they wrote (letters) by them after this
  manner; (lit. wrote *these* things)
  21:11. *Thus* saith the Holy Ghost,
Jas. 4:13. we will go into *such* a city,
Rev. 2: 1. *These* things saith he that holdeth
  8. *These* things saith the first and the
  12. *These* things saith he which hath
  18. *These* things saith the Son of God,
  3: 1. *These* things saith he that hath
  7. *These* things saith he that is holy,
  14. *These* things saith the Amen,

ὅ ἐστι, *ho esti*.

(As used in interpretation or specification, like *i. e.*
The passages in which the relative pronoun,
with ἐστι, forms a clause of a sentence, are
classed with ἐστι; and the passages in which it
is given at full length with μεθερμηνεύομαι, may
be seen under that verb.)

Mar 3:17. Boanerges, *which is*, The sons of thunder:
  7:11. Corban, *that is to say*, a gift,
  34. Ephphatha, *that is*, Be opened.
  12:42. two mites, *which make* a farthing.
  15:16. into the hall, *called* Prætorium;
  42. *that is*, the day before the sabbath,
Eph. 6:17. the sword of the Spirit, *which is* the word
  of God:
Col. 1·24. for his body's sake, *which is* the church:
Heb 7: 2. King of Salem, *which is*, King of peace;
Rev. 21: 8. *which is* the second death.
  17. the measure of a man, *that is*, of the angel.

ὁ ὢν καὶ ὁ ἦν καὶ ὁ ἐρχόμενος, *ho ōn kai ho een kai ho erkomenos*.

(Used as a descriptive title of God.)

Rev. 1: 4. *which is, and which was, and which is to*
  come;
  8. *which is, and which was, and which is to*
  come,
  4: 8. *which was, and is, and is to come*.
  11:17. *which art, and wast, and art to come;*
  16: 5. *which art, and wast, and shalt be,*
Note. The reading of this last in the most approved
  modern editions, is ὁ ὢν καὶ ὁ ἦν καὶ ὁ ὅσιος.

ὀγδοήκοντα, *ogdoeekonta*.

Lu. 2:37. a widow of about *fourscore* and four
  16: 7. Take thy bill, and write *fourscore*.

ὄγδοος, *ogdoos*.

Lu. 1:59. the *eighth* day they came to circumcise
Acts 7: 8. and circumcised him the *eighth* day;
2Pet. 2: 5. but saved Noah the *eighth* (person),
Rev. 17:11. even he is the *eighth*,
  21:20. the *eighth*, beryl;

ὄγκος, *onkos*.

Heb 12: 1. let us lay aside every *weight*,

ὁδεύω, hodŭo.

Lu. 10:33. a certain Samaritan, *as* he *journeyed*,

ὁδηγέω, hodeegeo.

Mat.15:14. if the blind *lead* the blind,
Lu. 6:39. Can the blind *lead* the blind?
Joh.16:13. he *will guide* you into all truth:
Acts 8:31. except some man *should guide* me?
Rev. 7:17. and *shall lead* them unto living

ὁδηγός, hodeegos.

Mat.15:14. they be blind *leaders* of the blind.
23:16. Woe unto you, (ye) blind *guides*,
24. (Ye) blind *guides*, which strain
Acts 1:16. which was *guide* to them that took Jesus.
Ro. 2:19. art a *guide* of the blind, a light

ὁδοιπορέω, hodoiporeo.

Acts10: 9. *as* they *went on* their *journey*,

ὁδοιπορία, hodoiporia.

Joh. 4: 6. being wearied with (his) *journey*,
2Co.11:26. (In) *journeyings* often, (in) perils

ὁδός, hodos.

Mat. 2:12. into their own country another *way*.
3: 3. Prepare ye the *way* of the Lord,
4:15. (by) the *way* of the sea, beyond Jordan,
5:25. whiles thou art in the *way* with him;
7:13. and broad (is) the *way*,
14. and narrow (is) the *way*,
8:28. so that no man might pass by that *way*.
10: 5. Go not into the *way* of the Gentiles,
10. Nor scrip for (your) *journey*,
11:10. which shall prepare thy *way*
13: 4. some (seeds) fell by the *way* side,
19. received seed by the *way* side.
15:32. lest they faint in the *way*.
20:17. disciples apart in the *way*,
30. sitting by the *way* side,
21: 8. spread their garments in the *way*;
— strawed (them) in the *way*.
19. he saw a fig tree in the *way*,
32. came unto you in the *way* of righteousness,
22: 9. Go ye therefore into the *highways*,
10. servants went out into the *highways*
16. and teachest the *way* of God in truth,
Mar 1: 2. which shall prepare thy *way*
3. Prepare ye the *way* of the Lord,
2:23. began, as they went, to pluck (lit. to make *way* plucking) the
4: 4. some fell by the *way* side,
15. these are they by the *way* side,
6: 8. take nothing for (their) *journey*,
8: 3. they will faint by the *way*:
27. by the *way* he asked his disciples,
9:33. disputed among yourselves by the *way*?
34. for by the *way* they had disputed
10:17. when he was gone forth into the *way*,
32. they were in the *way* going up to
46. sat by the *highway* side begging,
52. and followed Jesus in the *way*.

Mar11: 8. spread their garments in the *way*:
— and strawed (them) in the *way*.
12:14. teachest the *way* of God in truth:
Lu. 1:76. to prepare his *ways*;
79. to guide our feet into the *way* of peace.
2:44. went a day's *journey*;
3: 4. Prepare ye the *way* of the Lord,
5. the rough *ways* (shall be) made smooth;
7:27. which shall prepare thy *way* before
8: 5. some fell by the *way* side;
12. Those by the *way* side are they
9: 3. nothing for (your) *journey*,
57. as they went in the *way*,
10: 4. and salute no man by the *way*.
31. a certain priest that *way*:
11: 6. in his *journey* is come to me,
12:58. (as thou art) in the *way*, give diligence
14:23. Go out into the *highways*
18:35. sat by the *way* side begging:
19:36. they spread their clothes in the *way*.
20:21. but teachest the *way* of God truly:
24:32. while he talked with us by the *way*,
35. told what things (were done) in the *way*,
Joh. 1:23. Make straight the *way* of the Lord,
14: 4. and the *way* ye know.
5. and how can we know the *way*?
6. I am the *way*, the truth, and the life:
Acts 1:12. a sabbath day's *journey*.
2:28. hast made known to me the *ways* of life;
8:26. unto the *way* that goeth down from
36. And as they went on (their) *way*,
39. he went on his *way* rejoicing.
9: 2. that if he found any of this *way*,
17. that appeared unto thee in the *way*
27. had seen the Lord in the *way*,
13:10. cease to pervert the right *ways*
14:16. to walk in their own *ways*.
16:17. shew unto us the *way* of salvation.
18:25. in the *way* of the Lord;
26. the *way* of God more perfectly.
19: 9. but spake evil of that *way*
23. no small stir about that *way*.
22: 4. And I persecuted this *way* unto
24:14. that after the *way* which they call
22. perfect knowledge of (that) *way*,
25: 3. laying wait in the *way* to kill him.
26:13. I saw in the *way* a light from heaven,
Ro. 3:16. and misery (are) in their *ways*:
17. the *way* of peace have they not known:
11:33. and his *ways* past finding out!
1Co. 4:17. of my *ways* which be in Christ,
12:31. a more excellent *way*.
1Th. 3:11. direct our *way* unto you.
Heb 3:10. they have not known my *ways*.
9: 8. the *way* into the holiest of all
10:20. By a new and living *way*,
Jas. 1: 8. (is) unstable in all his *ways*.
2:25. and had sent (them) out another *way*?
5:20. from the error of his *way*
2Pet. 2: 2. the *way* of truth shall be evil spoken of.
15. Which have forsaken the right *way*,
— following the *way* of Balaam
21. not to have known the *way* of
Jude 11. they have gone in the *way* of Cain,
Rev.15: 3. just and true (are) thy *ways*,
16:12. that the *way* of the kings of the east might be prepared.

ὁδούς, odous.

Mat. 5:38. and a *tooth* for a *tooth*:

Mat. 8:12. shall be weeping and gnashing of *teeth.*
13:42. shall be wailing and gnashing of *teeth.*
50. shall be wailing and gnashing of *teeth.*
22:13. shall be weeping and gnashing of *teeth.*
24:51. shall be weeping and gnashing of *teeth.*
25:30. shall be weeping and gnashing of *teeth,*
Mar 9:18. and gnasheth with his *teeth,*
Lu. 13:28. shall be weeping and gnashing of *teeth.*
Acts 7:54. they gnashed on him with (their) *teeth.*
Rev. 9: 8. their *teeth* were as (the teeth) of lions.

ὀδυνάομαι, *odunaomai.*

Lu. 2:48. and I have sought thee *sorrowing.*
16:24. for I *am tormented* in this flame.
25. and thou *art tormented.*
Acts 20:38. *Sorrowing* most of all for the words

ὀδυνή, *odunee.*

Ro. 9: 2. and continual *sorrow* in my heart.
1Ti. 6:10. themselves through with many *sorrows.*

ὀδυρμός, *odurmos.*

Mat. 2:18. and great *mourning,* Rachel weeping
2Co. 7: 7. your *mourning,* your fervent mind toward

ὄζω, *ozo.*

Joh. 11:39. by this time he *stinketh:*

ὅθεν, *hothen.*

Mat 12:44. *from whence* I came out;
14: 7. *Whereupon* he promised with an oath
25:24. and gathering *where* thou hast not
26. and gather *where* I have not strawed:
Lu. 11:24. unto my house *whence* I came out.
Acts 14:26. *from whence* they had been recommended
26:19. *Whereupon,* O king Agrippa, I was
28:13. And *from thence* we fetched a compass,
Heb 2:17. *Wherefore* in all things it behoved
3: 1. *Wherefore,* holy brethren,
7:25. *Wherefore* he is able also to save
8: 3. *wherefore* (it is) of necessity that
9:18. *Whereupon* neither the first (testament)
11:19. *from whence* also he received him
1Joh. 2:18. *whereby* we know that it is the last time.

ὀθόνη, *othonee.*

Acts 10:11. as it had been a great *sheet*
11: 5. as it had been a great *sheet,*

ὀθόνιον, *othonion.*

Lu. 24:12. beheld the *linen clothes* laid by
Joh. 19:40. and wound it in *linen clothes*
20: 5. saw the *linen clothes* lying;
6. and seeth the *linen clothes* lie,
7. not lying with the *linen clothes,*

οἶδα see εἰδέω.

οἰκεῖος, *oikīos.*

Gal. 6:10. who are *of the houshold* (lit. the *domestics*)
of faith.
Eph. 2:19. and *of the houshold* of God;
1Ti. 5: 8. specially for *those of his own house,*

οἰκέτης, *oiketees.*

Lu. 16:13. No *servant* can serve two masters:
Acts 10: 7. he called two of his *houshold servants,*
Ro. 14: 4. that judgest another man's *servant?*
1Pet. 2:18. *Servants,* (be) subject to (your) masters

οἰκέω, *oikeo.*

Ro. 7:17. but sin *that dwelleth* in me.
18. *dwelleth* no good thing:
20. but sin *that dwelleth* in me.
8: 9. if so be that the Spirit of God *dwell* (lit.
dwells) in you.
11. if the Spirit of him that raised up Jesus
from the dead *dwell* (lit. *dwells*) in you,
1Co. 3:16. the Spirit of God *dwelleth* in you?
7:12. and she be pleased *to dwell* with him,
13. if he be pleased *to dwell* with her,
1Ti. 6:16. *dwelling* in the light which no man

οἴκημα, *oikeema.*

Acts 12: 7. a light shined in the *prison:*

οἰκητήριον, *oikeeteerion.*

2Co. 5: 2. to be clothed upon with our *house* which
is from heaven:
Jude 6. but left their own *habitation,*

οἰκία, *oikia.*

Mat. 2:11. were come into the *house,*
5:15. light unto all that are in the *house.*
7:24. which built his *house* upon a rock:
25. and beat upon that *house;*
26. which built his *house* upon the sand:
27. and beat upon that *house;*
8: 6. my servant lieth at *home* sick
14. when Jesus was come into Peter's *house,*
9:10. as Jesus sat at meat in the *house,*
23. Jesus came into the ruler's *house,*
28. when he was come into the *house,*
10:12. come into an *house,* salute it.
13. And if the *house* be worthy,
14. when ye depart out of that *house*
12:25. every city or *house* divided
29. enter into a strong man's *house,*
— and then he will spoil his *house.*
13: 1. went Jesus out of the *house,*
36. and went into the *house:*
57. and in his own *house.*
17:25. when he was come into the *house,*
19:29. that hath forsaken *houses,*
23:14(13). ye devour widows' *houses,*
24:17. to take any thing out of his *house:*
43. not have suffered his *house*
26: 6. in the *house* of Simon the leper,
Mar 1:29. they entered into the *house* of
2:15. as Jesus sat at meat in his *house,*

Mar 3:25. if a *house* be divided against itself, that *house* cannot stand.
27. into a strong man's *house*,
— and then he will spoil his *house*.
6: 4. and in his own *house*.
10. ye enter into an *house*,
7:24. and entered into an *house*,
9:33. and being in the *house* he asked
10:10. And in the *house* his disciples asked
29. no man that hath left *house*,
30. *houses*, and brethren, and sisters,
12:40. Which devour widows' *houses*,
13:15. not go down into the *house*,
— to take any thing out of his *house* :
34. who left his *house*, and gave authority
35. when the master of the *house* cometh,
14: 3. in the *house* of Simon the leper,
Lu. 4:38. and entered into Simon's *house*.
5:29. a great feast in his own *house* :
6:48. like a man which built an *house*,
— vehemently upon that *house*,
49. built an *house* upon the earth;
— the ruin of that *house* was great.
7: 6. he was now not far from the *house*,
36. he went into the Pharisee's *house*,
37. sat at meat in the Pharisee's *house*,
44. I entered into thine *house*,
8:27. neither abode in (any) *house*,
51. when he came into the *house*,
9: 4. whatsoever *house* ye enter into,
10: 5. into whatsoever *house* ye enter,
7. in the same *house* remain,
— Go not from *house* to *house*.
15: 8. and sweep the *house*, and seek
25. and drew nigh to the *house*,
17:31. and his stuff in the *house*,
18:29. no man that hath left *house*,
20:47. Which devour widows' *houses*,
22:10. follow him into the *house*
11. say unto the goodman of the *house*,
Joh. 4:53. believed, and his whole *house*.
8:35. servant abideth not in the *house* for ever:
11:31. with her in the *house*,
12: 3. and the *house* was filled with the odour
14: 2. In my Father's *house* are many
Acts 4:34. possessors of lands or *houses* sold them,
9:11. and enquire in the *house* of Judas
17. and entered into the *house* ;
10: 6. whose *house* is by the sea side:
17. made enquiry for Simon's *house*,
32. in the *house* of (one) Simon
11:11. come unto the *house* where I was,
12:12. he came to the *house* of Mary
16:32. to all that were in his *house*.
17: 5. and assaulted the *house* of Jason,
18: 7. into a certain (man's) *house*,
— whose *house* joined hard to the
1Co.11:22. have ye not *houses* to eat and to
16:15. ye know the *house* of Stephanas,
2Co. 5: 1. For we know that if our earthly *house*
— a building of God, an *house* not made
Phi. 4:22. they that are of Cæsar's *houshold*.
1Ti. 5:13. wandering about from house to house;
(lit. going the round of the *houses*)
2Ti. 2:20. But in a great *house* there are
3: 6. are they which creep into *houses*,
2Joh. 10. receive him not into (your) *house*,

(shall be) *they of* his own *houshold*.

οἰκοδεσποτέω, *oikodespoteo.*

1Ti. 5:14. *guide the house,* give none occasion

οἰκοδεσπότης, *oikodespotees.*

Mat.10:25. have called the *master of the house*
13:27. servants of the *housholder* came
52. unto a man (that is) an *housholder*,
20: 1. unto a man (that is) an *housholder*,
11. against the *goodman of the house*,
21:33. There was a certain *housholder*,
24:43. if the *goodman of the house* had
Mar 14:14. say ye to the *goodman of the house*,
Lu. 12:39. if the *goodman of the house* had
13:25. When once the *master of the house* is
14:21. Then the *master of the house* being
22:11. shall say unto the *goodman* (lit. *housholder*)
of the house,

οἰκοδομέω, *oikodomeo.*

Mat. 7:24. which *built* his house upon a rock:
26. which *built* his house upon the sand:
16:18. upon this rock I *will build* my church;
21:33. a winepress in it, and *built* a tower,
42. The stone which the *builders* rejected,
23:29. because ye *build* the tombs of the
26:61. and *to build* it in three days.
27:40. and *buildest* (it) in three days,
Mar 12: 1. and *built* a tower, and let it out
10. The stone which the *builders* rejected
14:58. within three days I *will build* another
15:29. and *buildest* (it) in three days,
Lu. 4:29. whereon their city *was built*,
6:48. like a man *which built* an house,
49. like a man *that...built* an house upon the earth;
7: 5. and he *hath built* us a synagogue.
11:47. for ye *build* the sepulchres of
48. and ye *build* their sepulchres.
12:18. I will pull down my barns, and *build*
14:28. intending *to build* a tower,
30. This man began *to build*,
17:28. they planted, they *builded*;
20:17. The stone which the *builders* rejected,
Joh. 2:20. *was* this temple *in building*,
Acts 4:11. was set at nought of you *builders*,
7:47. But Solomon *built* him an house.
49. what house *will* ye *build* me?
9:31. had the churches rest...*and were edified*;
Ro. 15:20. lest I *should build* upon another
1Co. 8: 1. Knowledge puffeth up, but charity *edifieth*.
10. *shall* not the conscience...*be emboldened* to eat those things
10:23. but all things *edify* not.
14: 4. in an (unknown) tongue *edifieth* himself; but he that prophesieth *edifieth* the
17. but the other *is* not *edified*.
Gal. 2:18. if I *build* again the things which
1Th. 5:11. and *edify* one another,
1Pet.2: 5. Ye also, as lively stones, *are built up*
7. the stone which the *builders* disallowed,

οἰκιακός, *oikiakos.*

Mat.10:25. (shall they call) *them of* his *houshold?*

οἰκοδομή, *oikodomee.*

Mat.24: 1. to shew him the *buildings* of the temple.

Mar 13: 1. and what *buildings* (are here)!
2. Seest thou these great *buildings* ?
Ro. 14:19. and things wherewith one may edify (lit. of *edifying*)
15: 2. for (his) good to *edification*.
1Co. 3: 9. (ye are) God's *building*.
14: 3. speaketh unto men (to) *edification*,
5. that the church may receive *edifying*.
12. to the *edifying* of the church.
26. Let all things be done unto *edifying*.
2Co. 5: 1. we have a *building* of God,
10: 8. the Lord hath given us for *edification*,
12:19. beloved, for your *edifying*.
13:10. hath given me to *edification*,
Eph 2:21. In whom all the *building*
4:12. for the *edifying* of the body
16. unto the *edifying* of itself in love.
29. which is good to the use of *edifying*,

οἰκονομέω, *oikonomeo*.

Lu. 16: 2. thou mayest *be* no longer *steward*.

οἰκονομία, *oikonomia*.

Lu. 16: 2. give an account of thy *stewardship;*
3. taketh away from me the *stewardship:*
4. when I am put out of the *stewardship*,
1Co. 9:17. a *dispensation* (of the gospel) is
Eph 1:10. That in the *dispensation* of the fulness
3: 2. If ye have heard of the *dispensation* of the grace of God
Col. 1:25. according to the *dispensation* of God
1Ti. 1: 4. rather than godly *edifying* which is in faith:
Note. The Translators appear to have read οἰκοδομήν in this last passage.

οἰκονόμος, *oikonomos*.

Lu. 12:42. that faithful and wise *steward*,
16: 1. rich man, which had a *steward;*
3. the *steward* said within himself,
8. commended the unjust *steward*,
Ro. 16:23. Erastus the *chamberlain* of the city
1Co. 4: 1. and *stewards* of the mysteries of God.
2. it is required in *stewards*, that
Gal. 4: 2. But is under tutors and *governors*
Tit. 1: 7. blameless, as the *steward* of God;
1Pet. 4:10. as good *stewards* of the manifold grace of God.

οἶκος, *oikos*.

Mat. 9: 6. and go unto thine *house*.
7. and departed to his *house*.
10: 6. to the lost sheep of the *house* of Israel.
11: 8. wear soft (clothing) are in kings' *houses*.
12: 4. entered into the *house* of God,
44. I will return into my *house*
15:24. lost sheep of the *house* of Israel.
21:13. My *house* shall be called the *house* of
23:38. your *house* is left unto you desolate.
Mar 2: 1. it was noised that he was in the *house*.
11. go thy way into thine *house*.
26. How he went into the *house* of God
3:19(20). they went into an *house*.

Mar 5:19. Go *home* to thy friends, and tell them
38. he cometh to the *house* of the ruler
7:17. when he was entered into the *house*
30. when she was come to her *house*,
8: 3. fasting to their own *houses*,
26. he sent him away to his *house*,
9:28. when he was come into the *house*,
11:17. My *house* shall be called of all nations the *house* of prayer?
Lu. 1:23. he departed to his own *house*.
27. Joseph, of the *house* of David;
33. reign over the *house* of Jacob for ever;
40. entered into the *house* of Zacharias,
56. and returned to her own *house*.
69. in the *house* of his servant David;
2: 4. he was of the *house* and lineage
5:24. and go unto thine *house*.
25. departed to his own *house*,
6: 4. How he went into the *house* of God,
7:10. returning to the *house*, found the
8:39. Return to thine own *house*,
41. that he would come into his *house:*
9:61. which are at home at my *house*.
10: 5. Peace (be) to this *house*.
38. received him into her *house*.
11:17. a *house* (divided) against a *house* falleth.
24. I will return unto my *house*
51. the altar and the *temple:*
12:39. not have suffered his *house* to be
52. five in one *house* divided,
13:35. Behold, your *house* is left unto you
14: 1. as he went into the *house* of one
23. that my *house* may be filled.
15: 6. when he cometh *home*, he calleth
16: 4. may receive me into their *houses*.
27. send him to my father's *house:*
18:14. this man went down to his *house*
19: 5. I must abide at thy *house*.
9. This day is salvation come to this *house*,
46. My *house* is the *house* of prayer:
22:54. into the high priest's *house*.
Joh. 2:16. make not my Father's *house* an *house* of merchandise.
17. The zeal of thine *house* hath eaten me up.
7:53. every man went unto his own *house*.
11:20. but Mary sat (still) in the *house*.
Acts 2: 2. it filled all the *house* where
36. let all the *house* of Israel know
46. breaking bread from house to *house*,
5:42. and in every *house*, they ceased not
7:10. over Egypt and all his *house*.
20. in his father's *house* three months:
42. O ye *house* of Israel, have ye
47. Solomon built him an *house*.
49. what *house* will ye build me?
8: 3. entering into every *house*, and
10: 2. feared God with all his *house*,
22. to send for thee into his *house*,
30. I prayed in my *house*, and, behold,
11:12. we entered into the man's *house:*
13. he had seen an angel in his *house:*
14. whereby thou and all thy *house* shall
16:15. was baptized, and her *houshold*,
come into my *house*, and abide
31. thou shalt be saved, and thy *house*.
34. brought them into his *house*,
18: 8. believed on the Lord with all his *house;*
19:16. they fled out of that *house* naked
20:20. publickly, and from house to *house*,
21: 8. entered into the *house* of Philip
Ro. 16: 5. the church that is in their *house*.
1Co. 1:16. I baptized also the *houshold* of

1Co.11:34. let him eat at *home;*
　14:35. ask their husbands at *home:*
　16:19. church that is in their *house.*
Col. 4:15. church which is in his *house.*
1Ti. 3: 4. ruleth well his own *house,*
　　5. know not how to rule his own *house,*
　12. and their own *houses* well.
　15. to behave thyself in the *house* of God,
　5: 4. first to shew piety at *home,*
2Ti. 1:16. The Lord give mercy unto the *house* of
　4:19. and the *houshold* of Onesiphorus.
Tit. 1:11. who subvert whole *houses,*
Philem 2. and to the church in thy *house:*
Heb 3: 2. Moses (was faithful) in all his *house.*
　3. hath more honour than the *house.*
　4. every *house* is builded by some
　5. (was) faithful in all his *house,*
　6. Christ as a son over his own *house;* whose
　　house are we,
　8: 8. with the *house* of Israel and with the *house*
　　of Judah:
　10. I will make with the *house* of Israel
　10:21. an high priest over the *house* of God;
　11: 7. to the saving of his *house;*
1Pet.2: 5. are built up a spiritual *house,*
　4:17. must begin at the *house* of God:

οἰκουμένη, *oikoumenee.*

Mat.24:14. shall be preached in all the *world*
Lu. 2: 1. that all the *world* should be taxed.
　4: 5. unto him all the kingdoms of the *world*
　21:26. which are coming on the *earth:*
Acts11:28. dearth throughout all the *world:*
　17: 6. have turned the *world* upside down
　31. in the which he will judge the *world*
　19:27. whom all Asia and the *world* worshippeth.
　24: 5. amogn all the Jews throughout the *world,*
Ro. 10:18. their words unto the ends of the *world.*
Heb 1: 6. the firstbegotten into the *world,*
　2: 5. not put in subjection the *world* to come,
Rev. 3:10. which shall come upon all the *world,*
　12: 9. which deceiveth the whole *world:*
　16:14. kings of the earth and of the whole *world,*

οἰκουρός, *oikouros.*

Tit. 2: 5. *keepers at home,* good, obedient

οἰκτείρω, οἰκτειρέω, *oiktīro, oiktīreo.*

Ro. 9:15. I *will have compassion on* whom I will *have
　　compassion.*

οἰκτιρμός, *oiktirmos.*

Ro. 12: 1. by the *mercies* of God, that ye
2Co. 1: 3. the Father of *mercies,*
Phi. 2: 1. if any bowels and *mercies,*
Col. 3:12. bowels of *mercies,* kindness,
Heb10:28. despised Moses' law died without *mercy*

οἰκτίρμων, *oiktirmōn.*

Lu. 6:36. Be ye therefore *merciful,* as your Father
　　also is *merciful.*
Jas. 5:11. is very pitiful, and *of tender mercy.*

οἶμαι, *oimai.*

Joh.21:25. I *suppose* that even the world

οἰνοπότης, *oinopotees.*

Mat.11:19. and a *winebibber,*
Lu. 7:34. a gluttonous man, and a *winebibber,*

οἶνος, *oinos.*

Mat. 9:17. Neither do men put new *wine*
　— and the *wine* runneth out,
　— but they put new *wine* into new
Mar 2:22. no man putteth new *wine* into old bottles,
　　else the new *wine* doth burst the bottles,
　　and the *wine* is
　— but new *wine* must be put into new
　15:23. they gave him to drink *wine*
Lu. 1:15. shall drink neither *wine* nor strong
　5:37. no man putteth new *wine* into
　— else the new *wine* will burst the
　38. But new *wine* must be put into new
　7:33. neither eating bread nor drinking *wine;*
　10:34. pouring in oil and *wine,*
Joh. 2: 3. And when they wanted *wine,*
　— They have no *wine.*
　9. tasted the water that was made *wine,*
　10. doth set forth good *wine;*
　— hast kept the good *wine* until now.
　4:46. where he made the water *wine.*
Ro. 14:21. nor to drink *wine,*
Eph. 5:18. be not drunk with *wine,*
1Ti. 3: 8. not given to much *wine,*
　5:23. but use a little *wine* for thy
Tit. 2: 3. not given to much *wine,*
Rev. 6: 6. hurt not the oil and the *wine.*
　14: 8. drink of the *wine* of the wrath
　10. shall drink of the *wine* of the wrath
　16:19. unto her the cup of the *wine* of
　17: 2. drunk with the *wine* of her
　18: 3. have drunk of the *wine* of the wrath
　13. and *wine,* and oil,
　19:15. he treadeth the *winepress* of

οἰνοφλυγία, *oinophlugia.*

1Pet.4: 3. *excess of wine,* revellings,

οἴομαι, *oiomai.*

Phi. 1:16. *supposing* to add affliction
Jas. 1: 7. *let* not that man *think* that he

οἷος, *hoios.*

Mat.24:21. tribulation, *such as* was not since
Mar 9: 3. *so as* no fuller on earth can white them.
　13:19. affliction, *such as* was not from the
Lu. 9:55. Ye know not *what manner of* spirit
Ro. 9: 6. Not *as* though the word of God
1Co.15:48. *As* (is) the earthy, *such* (are) they
　— *as* (is) the heavenly, *such* (are) they
2Co.10:11. *such as* we are in word by letters
　12:20. I shall not find you *such as* I would,
　— unto you *such as* ye would not:
Phi. 1:30. Having the same conflict *which* ye saw
1Th. 1: 5. ye know *what manner of* men we were

2Ti. 3:11. afflictions, *which* came unto me at
　　　— *what* persecutions I endured:
Rev.16:18. *such as* was not since men were

οἴσει & οἴσουσι see φερω.

ὀκνέω, *okneo.*

Acts 9:38. that he would not *delay* to come

ὀκνηρός, *okneeros.*

Mat.25:26. (Thou) wicked and *slothful* servant,
Ro. 12:11. Not *slothful* in business ; fervent
Phi. 3: 1. to me indeed (is) not *grievous,*

ὀκταήμερος, *oktaeemeros.*

Phi. 3: 5. Circumcised *the eighth day,*

ὀκτώ, *okto.*

Lu. 2:21. when *eight* days were accomplished
　　9:28. about an *eight* days after
　　13: 4. Or those *eight*een, upon whom
　　11. a spirit of infirmity *eight*een years,
　　16. lo, these *eight*een years,
Joh. 5: 5. an infirmity thirty and *eight* years.
　　20:26. after *eight* days again his disciples
Acts 9:33. which had kept his bed *eight* years,
1Pet.3:20. *eight* souls were saved by water.

ὄλεθρος, *olethros.*

1Co. 5: 5. for the *destruction* of the flesh,
1Th. 5: 3. then sudden *destruction* cometh
2Th. 1: 9. with everlasting *destruction* from
1Ti. 6: 9. which drown men in *destruction* and

ὀλιγόπιστος, *oligopistos.*

Mat. 6:30 O ye *of little faith?*
　　8:26. Why are ye fearful, O ye *of little faith?*
　　14:31. O thou *of little faith,* wherefore didst
　　16: 8. O ye *of little faith,* why reason ye
Lu. 12:28. (will he clothe) you, O ye *of little faith?*

ὀλίγος, *oligos.*

Mat. 7:14. and *few* there be that find it.
　　9:37. but the labourers (are) *few ;*
　　15:34. and a *few* little fishes.
　　20:16. for many be called, but *few* chosen.
　　22:14. but *few* (are) chosen.
　　25:21. hast been faithful over a *few* things,
　　23. hast been faithful over a *few* things,
Mar 1:19. when he had gone a *little* farther
　　6: 5. he laid his hands upon a *few* sick
　　31. and rest a *while :*
　　8: 7. And they had a *few* small fishes:
Lu. 5: 3. thrust out a *little* from the land.
　　7:47. to whom *little* is forgiven, (the same)
　　　loveth *little.*
　　10: 2. but the labourers (are) *few :*

Lu. 12:48. shall be beaten with *few* (stripes).
　　13:23. Lord, are there *few* that be saved ?
Acts12:18. there was no *small* stir among the
　　14:28. there they abode long (lit. not a *little*)
　　　time with
　　15: 2. no *small* dissension and disputation
　　17: 4. and of the chief women not a *few.*
　　12. and of men, not a *few.*
　　19:23. there arose no *small* stir
　　24. no *small* gain unto the craftsmen ;
　　26:28. Almost (lit. in a *little*) thou persuadest me
　　29. were both almost, and altogether (lit. in
　　　a *little,* and in much)
　　27:20. and no *small* tempest lay on (us),
2Co. 8:15. he that (had gathered) *little* had no lack.
Eph. 3: 3. as I wrote afore in *few* words,
1Ti. 4: 8. bodily exercise profiteth *little :*
　　5:23. but use a *little* wine
Heb12:10. for a *few* days chastened (us)
Jas. 3: 5. how great a matter a *little* fire
　　4:14. appeareth for a *little* time,
1Pet.1: 6. though now for a *season,*
　　3:20. wherein *few,* that is, eight souls
　　5:10. after that ye have suffered a *while,*
　　12. I have written *briefly,*
Rev. 2:14. I have a *few* things against thee,
　　20. I have a *few* things against thee,
　　3: 4. Thou hast a *few* names even in Sardis
　　12:12. that he hath but a *short* time.
　　17:10. he must continue a *short* space.

ὀλιγόψυχος, *oligopsukos.*

1Th. 5:14. comfort the *feebleminded,*

ὀλιγωρέω, *oligōreo.*

Heb12: 5. *despise* not thou the chastening of the
　　　Lord, nor faint

ὀλοθρευτής, *olothrūtees.*

1Co.10:10. were destroyed of the *destroyer.*

ὀλοθρεύω, *olothrūo.*

Heb11:28. lest he *that destroyed* the firstborn

ὁλοκαύτωμα, *holokautōma.*

Mar12:33. is more than all *whole burnt offerings*
Heb10: 6. In *burnt offerings* and (sacrifices) for sin
　　8. and *burnt offerings* and (offering) for sin
　　　thou wouldest not,

ὁλοκληρία, *holokleeria.*

Acts 3:16. hath given him this *perfect soundness*

ὁλόκληρος, *holokleeros.*

1Th. 5:23. (I pray God) your *whole* spirit and
Jas. 1: 4. that ye may be perfect and *entire,*

ὀλολύζω, ololuzo.

Jas. 5: 1. weep *and howl* for your miseries

ὅλος, holos.

Mat. 1:22. Now *all* this was done, that
4:23. Jesus went about *all* Galilee,
24. his fame went throughout *all* Syria:
5:29. and not (that) thy *whole* body should
30. and not (that) thy *whole* body should
6:22. thy *whole* body shall be full of light.
23. thy *whole* body shall be full of darkness.
9:26. fame hereof went abroad into *all* that land.
31. his fame in *all* that country.
13:33. till the *whole* was leavened.
14:35. they sent out into *all* that country
16:26. if he shall gain the *whole* world,
20: 6. Why stand ye here *all* the day idle?
21: 4. *All* this was done, that
22:37. love the Lord thy God with *all* thy heart,
and with *all* thy soul, and with *all* thy
40. hang *all* the law and the prophets.
24:14. in *all* the world for a witness
26:13. be preached in the *whole* world,
56. But *all* this was done, that
59. and *all* the council, sought false
27:27. gathered unto him the *whole* band
Mar 1:28. throughout *all* the region round about
Galilee.
33. *all* the city was gathered
39. synagogues throughout *all* Galilee,
6:55. ran through that *whole* region
8:36. if he shall gain the *whole* world,
12:30. love the Lord thy God with *all* thy heart,
and with *all* thy soul, and with *all* thy
mind, and with *all* thy strength:
33. to love him with *all* the heart, and with
all the understanding, and with *all* the
soul, and with *all* the strength,
44. (even) *all* her living.
14: 9. throughout the *whole* world,
55. and *all* the council sought
15: 1. and the *whole* council,
16. they call together the *whole* band.
33. darkness over the *whole* land
Lu. 1:65. throughout *all* the hill country of
4:14. a fame of him through *all* the region
5: 5. we have toiled *all* the night,
7:17. went forth throughout *all* Judæa,
8:39. published throughout the *whole* city
43. had spent *all* her living upon
9:25. if he gain the *whole* world,
10:27. love the Lord thy God with *all* thy heart,
and with *all* thy soul, and with *all* thy
strength, and with *all* thy mind ;
11:34. thy *whole* body also is full of
36. If thy *whole* body therefore (be)
— the *whole* shall be full of light,
13:21. till the *whole* was leavened.
23: 5. teaching throughout *all* Jewry,
44. darkness over *all* the earth until
Joh. 4:53. believed, and his *whole* house.
7:23. I have made a man *every whit* whole on
the sabbath
9:34. Thou wast *altogether* born in sins,
11:50. that the *whole* nation perish not.
13:10. but is clean *every whit* :
19:23. woven from the top through*out*.
Acts 2: 2. and it filled *all* the house
47. favour with *all* the people.

Acts 5:11. great fear came upon *all* the church,
7:10. governor over Egypt and *all* his house.
11. a dearth over *all* the land of Egypt
8:37. If thou believest with *all* thine heart,
9:31. churches rest throughout *all* Judæa
42. it was known throughout *all* Joppa ;
10:22. among *all* the nation of the Jews,
37. was published throughout *all* Judæa,
11:26. that a *whole* year they assembled
28. throughout *all* the world:
13:49. throughout *all* the region.
15:22. and elders, with the *whole* church,
18: 8. believed on the Lord with *all* his house ;
19:27. whom *all* Asia and the world
29. the *whole* city was filled with
21:30. And *all* the city was moved,
31. that *all* Jerusalem was in an uproar.
22:30. And *all* their council to appear,
28:30. Paul dwelt two *whole* years in
Ro. 1: 8. spoken of throughout the *whole* world.
8:36. we are killed *all* the day long ;
10:21. *All* day long I have stretched forth
16:23. mine host, and of the *whole* church,
1Co. 5: 6. leaveneth the *whole* lump ?
12:17. If the *whole* body (were) an eye,
— If the *whole* (were) hearing,
14:23. If therefore the *whole* church
2Co. 1: 1. which are in *all* Achaia:
Gal. 5: 3. he is a debtor to do the *whole* law.
9. leaveneth the *whole* lump.
Phi. 1:13. are manifest in *all* the palace,
1Th. 4:10. which are in *all* Macedonia:
Tit. 1:11. who subvert *whole* houses,
Heb 3: 2. Moses (was faithful) in *all* his house.
5. verily (was) faithful in *all* his house,
Jas. 2:10. whosoever shall keep the *whole* law,
3: 2. (and) able also to bridle the *whole* body.
3. and we turn about their *whole* body.
6. that it defileth the *whole* body,
1Joh. 2: 2. but also for (the sins of) the *whole* world.
5:19. the *whole* world lieth in wickedness.
Rev. 3:10. which shall come upon *all* the world,
12: 9. which deceiveth the *whole* world:
13: 3. *all* the world wondered after the beast.
16:14. and of the *whole* world, to gather them

ὁλοτελής, holotelees.

1Th. 5:23. very God of peace sanctify you *wholly* ;

ὄλυνθος, olunthos.

Rev. 6:13. as a fig tree casteth her *untimely figs*,

ὅλως, holos.

Mat. 5:34. Swear not *at all* ;
1Co. 5: 1. It is reported *commonly* (that there is)
6: 7. there is *utterly* a fault among you,
15:29. if the dead rise not *at all* ?

ὄμβρος, ombros.

Lu. 12:54. ye say, There cometh a *shower* ;

ὁμιλέω, homileo.

Lu. 24:14. they *talked* together of all these

Lu. 24.15. that, while they *communed* (together)
Acts20:11. and *talked* a long while,
    24:26. and *communed* with him.

ὁμιλία, *homilia.*

1Co.15:33. evil *communications* corrupt

ὅμιλος, *homilos.*

Rev.18:17. and all the *company* in ships,

ὄμμα, *omma.*

Mar 8:23. and when he had spit on his *eyes,*

ὄμνυμι, ὀμνύω, *omnumi, omnuo.*

With the tenses from ὀμόω.

Mat. 5:34. *Swear* not at all ; neither by heaven ;
    36. Neither *shalt* thou *swear* by thy head,
23:16. Whosoever *shall swear* by the temple, it is
        nothing ; but whosoever *shall swear* by
        the gold of the temple, he is a debtor !
    18. Whosoever *shall swear* by the altar,
    — but whosoever *sweareth* by the gift
    20. *Whoso* therefore shall *swear* by the altar,
        sweareth by it, and by all
    21. And *whoso* shall *swear* by the temple,
        sweareth by it, and by him that
    22. he *that* shall *swear* by heaven, *sweareth* by
26:74. Then began he to curse and *to swear,*
Mar 6:23. And he *sware* unto her, Whatsoever
14:71. began to curse and *to swear,* (saying),
Lu. 1:73. which he *sware* to our father Abraham,
Acts 2:30. that God *had sworn* with an oath
    7:17. which God *had sworn* to Abraham,
Heb 3:11. So I *sware* in my wrath, They shall not
    18. to whom *sware* he that they
    4: 3. As I *have sworn* in my wrath,
    6:13. because he could *swear* by no greater, he
        sware by himself,
    16. For men verily *swear* by the greater:
    7:21. The Lord *sware* and will not repent,
Jas. 5:12. above all things, my brethren, *swear* not,
Rev.10: 6. And *sware* by him that liveth for ever

ὁμοθυμαδόν, *homothumadon.*

Acts 1:14. continued *with one accord* in prayer and
    2: 1. were all *with one accord* in one place.
    46. daily *with one accord* in the temple,
    4:24. their voice to God *with one accord,*
    5:12. they were all *with one accord*
    7:57. and run upon him *with one accord,*
    8: 6. the people *with one accord* gave heed
12:20. but they came *with one accord* to him,
15:25. being assembled *with one accord,*
18:12. made insurrection *with one accord*
19:29. rushed *with one accord* into the theatre.
Ro. 15: 6. That ye may *with one mind* (and) one

ὁμοιάζω, *homoiazo.*

Mar 14:70. and thy speech *agreeth* (thereto).

ὁμοιοπαθής, *homoiopathees.*

Acts14:15. We also are men *of like passions* with you,
Jas. 5:17. a man *subject to like passions* as we are,

ὅμοιος, *homoios.*

Mat.11:16. It is *like* unto children sitting
    13:31. The kingdom of heaven is *like* to a grain
    33. of heaven is *like* unto leaven,
    44. is *like* unto treasure hid in a field ;
    45. is *like* unto a merchant man,
    47. kingdom of heaven is *like* unto a net,
    52. *like* unto a man (that is) an housholder,
    20: 1. is *like* unto a man (that is) an housholder,
    22:39. And the second (is) *like* unto it,
Mar 12:31. And the second (is) *like,* (namely)
Lu. 6:47. I will shew you to whom he is *like :*
    48. He is *like* a man which built
    49. *like* a man that without a foundation
    7:31. to what are they *like ?*
    32. They are *like* unto children sitting
    12:36. *like* unto men that wait for their
    13:18. Unto what is the kingdom of God *like ?*
    19. It is *like* a grain of mustard seed,
    21. It is *like* leaven, which a woman
Joh. 8:55. I shall be a liar *like* unto you:
    9: 9. others (said), He is *like* him:
Acts17:29. that the Godhead is *like* unto gold,
Gal. 5:21. revellings, and such *like :*
1Joh.3: 2. when he shall appear, we shall be *like*
        him ;
Jude 7. in *like* manner, giving themselves
Rev. 1:13. (one) *like* unto the Son of man,
    15. his feet *like* unto fine brass,
    2:18. feet (are) *like* fine brass ;
    4: 3. was to look upon *like* a jasper and
    — in sight *like* unto an emerald.
    6. a sea of glass *like* unto crystal:
    7. the first beast (was) *like* a lion, and the
        second beast *like* a calf, and
    — the fourth beast (was) *like* a flying eagle.
    9: 7. (were) *like* unto horses prepared
    — as it were crowns *like* gold,
    10. they had tails *like* unto scorpions,
    19. their tails (were) *like* unto serpents,
    11: 1. a reed *like* unto a rod:
    13: 2. was *like* unto a leopard,
    4. Who (is) *like* unto the beast ?
    11. he had two horns *like* a lamb,
    14:14. (one) sat *like* unto the Son of man,
    16:13. three unclean spirits *like* frogs
    18:18. What (city is) *like* unto this great city !
    21:11. her light (was) *like* unto a stone most
    18. pure gold, *like* unto clear glass.

ὁμοιότης, *homoiotees.*

Heb 4:15. in all points tempted *like as* (we are), (lit.
        according to *likeness*)
    7:15. after the *similitude* of Melchisedec

ὁμοιόω, *homoioō.*

Mat. 6: 8. *Be* not ye therefore *like* unto them:
    7:24. I *will liken* him unto a wise man,
    26. *shall be likened* unto a foolish man,
    11:16. whereunto *shall I liken* this generation ?
    13:24. is *likened* unto a man which sowed

Mat.18:23. Therefore *is* the kingdom of heaven *likened* unto a certain king,

22: 2. *is like* unto a certain king, which made a

25: 1. Then *shall...be likened* unto ten virgins,

Mar 4:30. Whereunto *shall* we *liken* the kingdom

Lu. 7:31. *shall* I *liken* the men of this generation?

13:18. whereunto *shall* I *resemble* it?

20. Whereunto *shall* I *liken* the kingdom

Acts 14:11. *in the likeness* of men.

Ro. 9:29. and *been made like* unto Gomorrha.

Heb 2:17. *to be made like* unto (his) brethren,

ὁμοίωμα, homoiōma.

Ro. 1:23. into an image made like to (lit. in the *similitude* of an image of)

5:14. after the *similitude* of Adam's

6: 5. in the *likeness* of his death,

8: 3. in the *likeness* of sinful flesh,

Phi. 2: 7. was made in the *likeness* of men:

Rev. 9: 7. And the *shapes* of the locusts (were)

ὁμοίως, homoiōs.

Mat.22:26. *Likewise* the second also,

26:35. *Likewise* also said all the disciples.

27:41. *Likewise* also the chief priests

Mar 4:16. these are they *likewise* which are

15:31. *Likewise* also the chief priests

Lu. 3:11. let him do *likewise*.

5:10. And *so* (was) also James, and John,

33. and *likewise* (the disciples) of the

6:31. do ye also to them *likewise*.

10:32. And *likewise* a Levite,

37. Go, and do thou *likewise*.

13: 5. ye shall all *likewise* perish.

16:25. *likewise* Lazarus evil things:

17:28. *Likewise* also as it was in the days

31. let him *likewise* not return back.

22:36. and *likewise* (his) scrip:

Joh. 5:19. these also doeth the Son *likewise*.

6:11. and *likewise* of the fishes as much

21:13. and giveth them, and fish *likewise*.

Ro. 1:27. *likewise* also the men,

1Co. 7: 3. *likewise* also the wife unto the

4. *likewise* also the husband hath

22. *likewise* also he that is called,

Heb 9:21. he sprinkled (lit. he sprinkled *likewise*) with blood

Jas. 2:25. *Likewise* also was not Rahab

1Pet.3: 1. *Likewise*, ye wives, (be) in

7. *Likewise*, ye husbands, dwell with

5: 5. *Likewise*, ye younger, submit

Jude 8. *Likewise* also these (filthy)

Rev. 8:12. and the night *likewise*.

ὁμοίωσις, homoiōsis.

Jas. 3: 9. are made after the *similitude* of God.

ὁμολογέω, homologeo.

Mat. 7:23. then *will* I *profess* unto them,

10:32. *shall confess* me before men, him *will* I *confess* also before my Father

14: 7. he *promised* with an oath

Lu. 12: 8. *shall confess* me before men, him *shall* the Son of man also *confess*

Joh. 1:20. he *confessed*, and denied not; but *confessed*, I am not the Christ.

9:22. that if any man did *confess* that he was Christ,

12:42. because of the Pharisees they *did* not *confess* (him),

Acts23: 8. but the Pharisees *confess* both.

24:14. But this I *confess* unto thee,

Ro. 10: 9. if thou *shalt confess* with thy mouth

10. with the mouth *confession is* made

1Ti. 6:12. and *hast professed* a good profession

Tit. 1:16. They *profess* that they know God;

Heb 11:13. and *confessed* that they were strangers

13:15. of (our) lips *giving thanks* to his name.

1Joh.1: 9. If we *confess* our sins,

4: 2. Every spirit that *confesseth*

3. every spirit that *confesseth* not

15. Whosoever *shall confess* that Jesus is

2Joh. 7. *who confess* not that Jesus Christ

ὁμολογία, homologia.

2Co. 9:13. for your *professed* subjection

1Ti. 6:12. hast professed a good *profession*

13. witnessed a good *confession;*

Heb 3: 1. and high priest of our *profession*,

4:14. let us hold fast (our) *profession*.

10:23. Let us hold fast the *profession* of

ὁμολογουμένως, homologoumenōs.

1Ti. 3:16. And *without controversy* great is

ὁμότεχνος, homoteknos.

Acts 18: 3. because he was *of the same craft*,

ὁμοῦ, homou.

Joh. 4:36. that reapeth may rejoice *together*.

20: 4. So they ran both *together*.

21: 2. There were *together* Simon Peter, and

ὁμόφρων, homophrōn.

1Pet. 3: 8. Finally, (be ye) all *of one mind*,

ὁμόω see ὄμνυμι.

ὅμως, homōs.

Joh. 12:42. *Nevertheless* among the (ο. μεντοι)

1Co.14: 7. *And even* things without life

Gal. 3:15. *Though* (it be) *but* a man's covenant,

ὄναρ, onar.

Mat. 1:20. appeared unto him in a *dream*,

2:12. being warned of God in a *dream*

13. appeareth to Joseph in a *dream*,

19. appeareth in a *dream* to Joseph

22. being warned of God in a *dream*,

27:19. this day in a *dream* because of him.

ὀνάριον, onarion.

Joh. 12:14. when he had found a *young ass,*

ὀνειδίζω, onīdizo.

Mat. 5:11. when (men) *shall revile* you,
   11:20. Then began he *to upbraid* the cities
   27:44. *cast* the same *in his teeth.*
Mar 15:32. were crucified with him *reviled* him.
   16:14. and *upbraided* them with their
Lu. 6:22. and *shall reproach* (you),
Ro. 15: 3. of them *that reproached* thee fell on me.
1Ti. 4:10. we both labour and *suffer reproach,*
Jas. 1: 5. and *upbraideth* not ;
1Pet. 4:14. If ye *be reproached* for the name

ὀνειδισμός, onīdismos.

Ro. 15: 3. The *reproaches* of them that
1Ti. 3: 7. lest he fall into *reproach*
Heb 10:33. both by *reproaches* and afflictions ;
   11:26. Esteeming the *reproach* of Christ
   13:13. bearing his *reproach.*

ὄνειδος, onīdos.

Lu. 1:25. to take away my *reproach* among men.

ὄνημι, oneemi.

Philem. 20. let me *have joy* of thee in the Lord:

ὀνικός, onikos.

Mat 18: 6. that a millstone (lit. a mill turned *by an
      ass*) were hanged
Lu. 17: 2. that a millstone (lit. a mill turned *&c.*)
      were

ὄνομα, onoma.

Mat. 1:21. thou shalt call his *name* JESUS:
   23. they shall call his *name* Emmanuel,
   25. and he called his *name* JESUS.
   6: 9. Hallowed be thy *name.*
   7:22. have we not prophesied in thy *name?* and
      in thy *name* have cast out devils? and
      in thy *name* done
  10: 2. Now the *names* of the twelve
   22. hated of all (men) for my *name's* sake:
   41. in the *name* of a prophet
    — in the *name* of a righteous man
   42. in the *name* of a disciple,
   12:21. And in his *name* shall the Gentiles trust.
   18: 5. one such little child in my *name*
   20. are gathered together in my *name,*
   19:29. for my *name's* sake, shall receive
   21: 9. that cometh in the *name* of the Lord ;
   23:39. he that cometh in the *name* of the Lord.
   24: 5. many shall come in my *name,*
    9. of all nations for my *name's* sake.
   27:32. a man of Cyrene, Simon by *name:*
   57. rich man of Arimathæa, *named* Joseph,
   28:19. in the *name* of the Father, and
Mar 3:16. Simon he surnamed (lit. added the *name*)
      Peter ;

Mar 3:17. he surnamed (lit. added the *name* to) them
      Boanerges,
   5: 9. What (is) thy *name?*
    — My *name* (is) Legion:
   22. rulers of the synagogue, Jairus by *name;*
   6:14. for his *name* was spread abroad:
   9:37. one of such children in my *name,*
   38. casting out devils in thy *name,*
   39. which shall do a miracle in my *name,*
   41. water to drink in my *name,*
  11: 9. that cometh in the *name* of the Lord:
   10. that cometh in the *name* of the Lord:
   13: 6. many shall come in my *name,*
   13. for my *name's* sake,
   14:32. which was named (lit. of which the *name*
      was) Gethsemane:
   16:17. In my *name* shall they cast out devils ;
Lu. 1: 5. a certain priest *named* Zacharias,
    — and her *name* (was) Elisabeth.
   13. thou shalt call his *name* John.
   26. a city of Galilee, *named* Nazareth,
   27. to a man whose *name* was Joseph,
    — the virgin's *name* (was) Mary.
   31. and shalt call his *name* JESUS.
   49. and holy (is) his *name.*
   59. after the *name* of his father.
   61. that is called by this *name.*
   63. His *name* is John.
   2:21. his *name* was called JESUS,
   25. whose *name* (was) Simeon ;
   5:27. saw a publican, *named* Levi,
   6:22. and cast out your *name* as evil,
   8:30. What is thy *name?*
   41. there came a man *named* Jairus,
   9:48. this child in my *name*
   49. casting out devils in thy *name ;*
  10:17. are subject unto us through thy *name.*
   20. because your *names* are written in
   38. *named* (lit. by *name*) Martha
  11: 2. Hallowed be thy *name.*
   13:35. that cometh in the *name* of the Lord.
   16:20. a certain beggar *named* Lazarus,
   19: 2. *named* (lit. by *name* called) Zacchæus,
   38. that cometh in the *name* of the Lord:
   21: 8. many shall come in my *name,*
   12. for my *name's* sake.
   17. hated of all (men) for my *name's* sake.
   23:50. a man *named* Joseph,
   24:13. to a village *called* Emmaus,
   18. whose *name* was Cleopas,
   47. should be preached in his *name*
Joh. 1: 6. whose *name* (was) John.
   12. to them that believe on his *name :*
   2:23. many believed in his *name,*
   3: 1. *named* Nicodemus, (lit. N. his *name*)
   18. hath not believed in the *name* of
   5:43. I am come in my Father's *name,*
    — if another shall come in his own *name,*
  10: 3. he calleth his own sheep by *name,*
   25. that I do in my Father's *name,*
   12:13. that cometh in the *name* of the Lord.
   28. Father, glorify thy *name.*
   14:13. whatsoever ye shall ask in my *name,*
   14. shall ask any thing in my *name,*
   26. the Father will send in my *name,*
   15:16. shall ask of the Father in my *name,*
   21. do unto you for my *name's* sake,
   16:23. ye shall ask the Father in my *name,*
   24. have ye asked nothing in my *name :*
   26. ye shall ask in my *name :*
   17: 6. I have manifested thy *name* unto
   11. keep through thine own *name*

Joh. 17:12. I kept them in thy *name:*
    26. I have declared unto them thy *name,*
  18:10. The servant's *name* was Malchus.
  20:31. might have life through his *name.*
Acts 1:15. the number of the *names* together
  2:21. shall call on the *name* of the Lord
    38. in the *name* of Jesus Christ for
  3: 6. In the *name* of Jesus Christ of
    16. And his *name* through faith in his *name* hath made this man strong,
  4: 7. or by what *name*, have ye done this?
    10. that by the *name* of Jesus Christ
    12. there is none other *name* under
    17. to no man in this *name.*
    18. nor teach in the *name* of Jesus.
    30. by the *name* of thy holy child Jesus.
  5: 1. a certain man *named* Ananias,
    28. that ye should not teach in this *name?*
    34. a Pharisee, *named* Gamaliel,
    40. should not speak in the *name* of Jesus,
    41. worthy to suffer shame for his *name.*
  8: 9. there was a certain man, *called* Simon,
    12. and the *name* of Jesus Christ,
    16. baptized in the *name* of the Lord Jesus.
  9:10. *named* (lit. by *name*) Ananias;
    11. for (one) *called* Saul, (lit. by *name* Saul)
    12. a man *named* Ananias coming in,
    14. to bind all that call on thy *name.*
    15. to bear my *name* before the Gentiles,
    16. he must suffer for my *name's* sake.
    21. which called on this *name* in Jerusalem,
    27. at Damascus in the *name* of Jesus.
  29(28) spake boldly in the *name* of the Lord
    33. a certain man *named* Æneas,
    36. a certain disciple *named* Tabitha,
  10: 1. *called* (lit. by *name*) Cornelius,
    43. that through his *name* whosoever
    48. to be baptized in the *name* of the Lord.
  11:28. one of them *named* Agabus,
  12:13. came to hearken, *named* Rhoda.
  13: 6. a Jew, whose *name* (was) Bar-jesus:
    8. for so is his *name* by interpretation
  15:14. out of them a people for his *name.*
    17. upon whom my *name* is called,
    26. for the *name* of our Lord Jesus
  16: 1. disciple was there, *named* Timotheus,
    14. *named* Lydia, a seller of purple,
    18. in the *name* of Jesus Christ
  17:34. and a woman *named* Damaris,
  18: 2. *named* Aquila, born in Pontus,
    7. *named* Justus, (one) that worshipped God,
    15. if it be a question of words and *names,*
    24. *named* Apollos, born at Alexandria,
  19: 5. baptized in the *name* of the Lord Jesus.
    13. which had evil spirits the *name* of
    17. and the *name* of the Lord Jesus was
    24. *named* Demetrius, a silversmith,
  20: 9. *named* Eutychus, being fallen into a deep
  21:10. a certain prophet, *named* Agabus.
    13. for the *name* of the Lord Jesus.
  22:16. calling on the *name* of the Lord.
  26: 9. contrary to the *name* of Jesus of
  27: 1. *named* Julius, a centurion
  28: 7. whose *name* was Publius;
Ro. 1: 5. among all nations, for his *name:*
  2:24. For the *name* of God is blasphemed
  9:17. that my *name* might be declared
  10:13. shall call upon the *name* of the Lord
  15: 9. and sing unto thy *name.*
1Co. 1: 2. in every place call upon the *name* of
    10. by the *name* of our Lord Jesus
    13. were ye baptized in the *name* of Paul?

1Co. 1:15. I had baptized in mine own *name.*
  5: 4. In the *name* of our Lord Jesus
  6:11. in the *name* of the Lord Jesus,
Eph. 1:21. and every *name* that is named,
  5:20. in the *name* of our Lord Jesus
Phi. 2: 9. a *name* which is above every *name:*
    10. That at the *name* of Jesus every knee
  4: 3. whose *names* (are) in the book of life.
Col. 3:17. (do) all in the *name* of the Lord
2Th. 1:12. That the *name* of our Lord Jesus
  3: 6. in the *name* of our Lord Jesus
1Ti. 6: 1. that the *name* of God and (his) doctrine
2Ti. 2:19. that nameth the *name* of Christ
Heb 1: 4. a more excellent *name* than they.
  2:12. I will declare thy *name* unto
  6:10. ye have shewed toward his *name,*
  13:15. giving thanks to his *name.*
Jas. 2: 7. that worthy *name* by the which
  5:10. who have spoken in the *name* of the Lord,
    14. with oil in the *name* of the Lord:
1Pet. 4:14. If ye be reproached for the *name* of Christ,
1Joh. 2:12. forgiven you for his *name's* sake.
  3:23. That we should believe on the *name* of
  5:13. believe on the *name* of the Son of God;
  — may believe on the *name* of the Son of
3Joh.   7. for his *name's* sake they went forth,
  14(15). Greet the friends by *name.*
Rev. 2: 3. for my *name's* sake hast laboured,
    13. thou holdest fast my *name,*
    17. and in the stone a new *name*
  3: 1. thou hast a *name* that thou livest,
    4. Thou hast a few *names* even in Sardis
    5. I will not blot out his *name*
    — but I will confess his *name* before
    8. and hast not denied my *name.*
    12. the *name* of my God, and the *name* of the city of my God,
    — my new *name.*
  6: 8. his *name* that sat on him was Death,
  8:11. the *name* of the star is called
  9:11. whose *name* in the Hebrew tongue
    — hath (his) *name* Apollyon.
  11:13. were slain)(of men seven thousand:
    18. and them that fear thy *name,*
  13: 1. upon his heads, the *name* of blasphemy.
    6. to blaspheme his *name,* and his
    8. whose *names* are not written in
    17. or the *name* of the beast, or the number of his *name.*
  14: 1. having his Father's *name* written in
    11. receiveth the mark of his *name.*
  15: 2. (and) over the number of his *name,*
    4. O Lord, and glorify thy *name?*
  16: 9. and blasphemed the *name* of God,
  17: 3. full of *names* of blasphemy,
    5. upon her forehead (was) a *name*
    8. whose *names* were not written in
  19:12. he had a *name* written, that no
    13. his *name* is called The Word of God.
    16. and on his thigh a *name* written,
  21:12. and *names* written thereon,
    14. in them the *names* of the twelve apostles
  22: 4. his *name* (shall be) in their foreheads.

ὀνομάζω, *onomazo.*

Lu. 6:13. whom also he *named* apostles;
    14. Simon, whom he also *named* Peter,
Acts 19:13. to *call* over them which had evil spirits
Ro. 15:20. not where Christ *was named*, lest

1Co. 5: 1. as *is* not so much as *named* among
    11. if any man *that is called* a brother be
Eph 1:21. and every name *that is named,*
    3:15. family in heaven and earth *is named,*
    5: 3. *let* it not *be* once *named* among you,
2Ti. 2:19. Let every one *that nameth* the name

ὄνος, *onos.*

Mat.21: 2. ye shall find an *ass* tied,
    5. meek, and sitting upon an *ass,*
    7. And brought the *ass,*
Lu. 13:15. loose his ox or (his) *ass* from the stall,
    14: 5. Which of you shall have an *ass* or
Joh.12:15. sitting on an *ass's* colt.

ὄντα, ὄντας, &c. see under ὤν.

ὄντως, *ontōs.*

Mar 11:32. that he was a prophet *indeed.*
Lu. 23:47. *Certainly* this was a righteous man.
    24:34. The Lord is risen *indeed,*
Joh. 8:36. ye shall be free *indeed.*
1Co.14:25. that God is in you *of a truth.*
Gal. 3:21. *verily* righteousness should have
1Ti. 5: 3. Honour widows that are widows *indeed.*
    5. Now she that is a widow *indeed,*
    16. relieve them that are widows *indeed.*
2Pet. 2:18. those that were *clean* escaped

ὄξος, *oxos.*

Mat.27:34. gave him *vinegar* to drink mingled
    48. and filled (it) with *vinegar,*
Mar 15:36. and filled a spunge full of *vinegar,*
Lu. 23:36. and offering him *vinegar,*
Joh.19:29. a vessel full of *vinegar:* and they filled a
    spunge with *vinegar,*
    30. had received the *vinegar,* he said,

ὀξύς, *oxus.*

Ro. 3:15. Their feet (are) *swift* to shed blood:
Rev. 1:16. went a *sharp* twoedged sword:
    2:12. which hath the *sharp* sword
    14:14. and in his hand a *sharp* sickle.
    17. he also having a *sharp* sickle.
    18. to him that had the *sharp* sickle, saying,
    Thrust in thy *sharp* sickle,
    19:15. out of his mouth goeth a *sharp* sword,

ὀπή, *opee.*

Heb 11:38. and (in) dens and *caves* of the earth.
Jas 3:11. at the same *place* sweet (water) and

ὄπισθεν, *opisthen.*

Mat. 9:20. came *behind* (him), and touched
    15:23. for she crieth *after* us.
Mar 5:27. came in the press *behind,* and touched

Lu. 8:44. Came *behind* (him), and touched
    23:26. that he might bear (it) *after* Jesus.
Rev. 4: 6. full of eyes before and *behind.*
    5: 1. written within and on the *backside,*

ὀπίσω, *opiso.*

Mat. 3:11. but he that cometh *after* me
    4:19. Follow me, (lit. come *after* me)
    10:38. and followeth *after* me,
    16:23. Get thee *behind* me, Satan:
    24. If any (man) will come *after* me,
    24:18. return *back* to take his clothes.
Mar 1: 7. cometh one mightier than I *after* me,
    17. Come ye *after* me,
    20. and went *after* him.
    8:33. Get thee *behind* me, Satan:
    34. Whosoever will come *after* me.
    13:16. that is in the field not turn *back*
Lu. 4: 8. Get thee *behind* me, Satan:
    7:38. And stood at his feet *behind* (him)
    9:23. If any (man) will come *after* me.
    62. and looking *back,* is fit for the
    14:27. and come *after* me, cannot be
    17:31. let him likewise not return *back.*
    19:14. and sent a message *after* him,
    21: 8. go ye not therefore *after* them.
Joh. 1:15. He that cometh *after* me is
    27. He it is, who coming *after* me is
    30. *After* me cometh a man which is
    6:66. many of his disciples went *back,*
    12:19. the world is gone *after* him.
    18: 6. they went *backward,* and fell to the
    20:14. she turned herself *back,*
Acts 5:37. drew away much people *after* him:
    20:30. to draw away disciples *after* them.
Phi. 3:13(14). forgetting those things which are
    behind,
1Ti. 5:15. are already turned aside *after* Satan.
2Pet. 2:10. that walk *after* the flesh in
Jude 7. and going *after* strange flesh,
Rev. 1:10. and heard *behind* me a great voice,
    12:15. as a flood *after* the woman,
    13: 3. all the world wondered *after* the beast.

ὅπλα, *hopla.*

Joh.18: 3. and torches and *weapons.*
Ro. 6:13. (as) *instruments* of unrighteousness
    — (as) *instruments* of righteousness
    13:12. let us put on the *armour* of light.
2Co. 6: 7. by the *armour* of righteousness
    10: 4. For the *weapons* of our warfare

ὁπλίζομαι, *hoplizomai.*

1Pet.4: 1. *arm yourselves* likewise with the same

ὁποῖος, *hopoios.*

Acts26:29. and altogether *such as* I am,
1Co. 3:13. every man's work *of what sort* it is.
Gal. 2: 6. *whatsoever* they were, it maketh no
1Th. 1: 9. *what manner of* entering in we had
Jas. 1:24. forgetteth *what manner of* man he was.

ὁπότε, *hopote.*

Lu. 6: 3. *when* himself was an hungred,

ὅπου, hopou.

Mat. 6:19. *where* moth and rust doth corrupt, and
　　　 where thieves break through and steal:
　　20. *where* neither moth nor rust doth corrupt,
　　　 and *where* thieves do not break
　　21. For *where* your treasure is, there
　　8:19. I will follow thee *whither*soever thou
　　13: 5. *where* they had not much earth:
　　24:28. *where*soever the carcase is, there
　　25:24. reaping *where* thou hast not sown,
　　26. that I reap *where* I sowed not,
　　26:13. *Where*soever this gospel shall be
　　57. *where* the scribes and the elders were
　　28: 6. Come, see the place *where* the Lord lay.
Mar 2: 4. uncovered the roof *where* he was:
　　4: 5. *where* it had not much earth;
　　15. *where* the word is sown;
　　5:40. entereth in *where* the damsel was
　　6:10. *In what place* soever ye enter
　　55. *where* they heard he was.
　　56. And *whither*soever he entered,
　　9:18. *where*soever he taketh him,
　　44. *Where* their worm dieth not,
　　46. *Where* their worm dieth not,
　　48. *Where* their worm dieth not,
　　13:14. standing *where* it ought not,
　　14: 9. *Where*soever this gospel shall be
　　14. *where*soever he shall go in,
　　— *where* I shall eat the passover
　　16: 6. behold the place *where* they laid him.
Lu. 9:57. *whither*soever thou goest.
　　12:33. *where* no thief approacheth,
　　34. For *where* your treasure is,
　　17:37. *Where*soever the body (is), thither
　　22:11. *where* I shall eat the passover
Joh. 1:28. *where* John was baptizing.
　　3: 8. The wind bloweth *where* it listeth,
　　4:20. *where* men ought to worship.
　　46. *where* he made the water wine.
　　6:23. unto the place *where* they did eat bread,
　　62. ascend up *where* he was before?
　　7:34. *where* I am, (thither) ye cannot come.
　　36. and *where* I am, (thither) ye cannot
　　42. of Bethlehem, *where* David was?
　　8:21. *whither* I go, ye cannot come.
　　22. *Whither* I go, ye cannot come.
　　10:40. *where* John at first baptized;
　　11:30. was in that place *where* Martha met him.
　　32. when Mary was come *where* Jesus
　　12: 1. *where* Lazarus was which had been
　　26. *where* I am, there shall also my
　　13:33. *Whither* I go, ye cannot come;
　　36. *Whither* I go, thou canst not
　　14: 3. that *where* I am, (there) ye may be
　　4. And *whither* I go ye know,
　　17:24. be with me *where* I am ;
　　18: 1. *where* was a garden,
　　20. *whither* the Jews always resort;
　　19:18. *Where* they crucified him, and
　　20. for the place *where* Jesus was
　　41. in the place *where* he was
　　20:12. *where* the body of Jesus had lain.
　　19. *where* the disciples were assembled
　　21:18. and walkedst *whither* thou wouldest:
　　— and carry (thee) *whither* thou wouldest
　　　 not.
Acts17: 1. *where* was a synagogue of the Jews:
Ro. 15:20. not *where* Christ was named, lest
1Co. 3: 3. for *whereas* (there is) among you
Col. 3:11. *Where* there is neither Greek nor
Heb 6:20. *Whither* the forerunner is for us

Heb 9:16. For *where* a testament (is), there
　　10:18. Now *where* remission of these (is),
Jas. 3: 4. *whither*soever the governor listeth.
　　16. For *where* envying and strife (is),
2Pet.2:11. *Whereas* angels, which are greater
Rev. 2:13. *where* Satan's seat (is):
　　— *where* Satan dwelleth.
　　11: 8. *where* also our Lord was crucified.
　　12: 6. *where* she hath a place prepared
　　14. *where* she is nourished for a time, and
　　14: 4. follow the Lamb *whither*soever he goeth.
　　17: 9. on which the woman sitteth. (lit. *where*
　　　 the woman sitteth on them)
　　20:10. *where* the beast and the false prophet

ὀπτάνομαι, optanomai.

Acts 1: 3. *being seen* of them forty days,

ὀπτασία, optasia.

Lu. 1:22. that he had seen a *vision* in the temple:
　　24:23. they had also seen a *vision* of angels,
Acts26:19. disobedient unto the heavenly *vision:*
2Co.12: 1. I will come to *visions* and revelations

ὄπτομαι, optomai.

Mat. 5: 8. for they *shall see* God.
　　17: 3. there *appeared* unto them Moses and
　　24:30. they *shall see* the Son of man
　　26:64. Hereafter *shall* ye *see* the Son of man
　　27: 4. *see* thou (to that).
　　24. of this just person: *see* ye (to it).
　　28: 7. there *shall* ye *see* him:
　　10. and there *shall* they *see* me.
Mar 9: 4. there *appeared* unto them Elias with
　　13:26. then *shall* they *see* the Son of man
　　14:62. ye *shall see* the Son of man sitting on
　　16: 7. there *shall* ye *see* him,
Lu. 1:11. there *appeared* unto him an angel
　　3: 6. all flesh *shall see* the salvation
　　9:31. Who *appeared* in glory, *and* spake
　　13:28. when ye *shall see* Abraham,
　　17:22. and ye *shall* not *see* (it).
　　21:27. then *shall* they *see* the Son of man
　　22:43. And there *appeared* an angel
　　24:34. and *hath appeared* to Simon.
Joh. 1:50(51). thou *shalt see* greater things than
　　51(52). Hereafter ye *shall see* heaven open,
　　3:36. believeth not the Son *shall* not *see* life ;
　　11:40. thou shouldest *see* the glory of God?
　　16:16. and ye *shall see* me,
　　17. a little while, and ye *shall see* me:
　　19. a little while, and ye *shall see* me?
　　22. but I *will see* you again,
　　19:37. They *shall look* on him whom they
Acts 2: 3. there *appeared* unto them cloven tongues
　　17. your young men *shall see* visions,
　　7: 2. The God of glory *appeared* unto our
　　26. he shewed *himself* unto them as
　　30. there *appeared* to him in the
　　35. of the angel which *appeared* to him in the
　　　 bush.
　　9:17. Jesus, *that appeared* unto thee
　　13:31. he *was seen* many days of them

Acts16: 9.a vision *appeared* to Paul
18:15. *look* ye (to it); for I will be no
20:25. *shall see* my face no more.
26:16. I *have appeared* unto thee for this
— in the which I *will appear* unto thee;
Ro. 15:21. not spoken of, they *shall see:*
1Co.15: 5. And that he *was seen* of Cephas,
6. After that, he *was seen* of above
7. After that, he *was seen* of James;
8. And last of all he *was seen* of me
1Ti. 3:16. *seen* of angels, preached unto the
Heb 9:28. unto them that look for him *shall he appear*
12:14. without which no man *shall see* the Lord:
13:23. with whom, if he come shortly, I *will see* you.
1Joh.3: 2. for we *shall see* him as he is.
Rev. 1: 7. and every eye *shall see* him,
11:19. there *was seen* in his temple the ark
12: 1. And there *appeared* a great wonder in
3. there *appeared* another wonder
22: 4. And they *shall see* his face ;

ὀπτός, *optos.*

Lu. 24:42. they gave him a piece of a *broiled* fish,

ὀπώρα, *opōra.*

Rev.18:14. And the *fruits* that thy soul lusted after

ὅπως, *hopōs.*

Mat. 2: 8. *that* I may come and worship him
23. *that* it might be fulfilled which
5:16. *that* they may see your good works,
45. *That* ye may be the children of your
6: 2. *that* they may have glory of men.
4. *That* thine alms may be in secret:
5. *that* they may be seen of men.
16. *that* they may appear unto men to fast.
18. *That* thou appear not unto men to
8:17. *That* it might be fulfilled which
34. *that* he would depart out of their
9:38. *that* he will send forth labourers
12:14. *how* they might destroy him.
17. *That* it might be fulfilled which
13:35. *That* it might be fulfilled which
22:15. *how* they might entangle him
23:35. *That* upon you may come all the
26:59. *to* put him to death; (lit. *that* they might &c.)
Mar 3: 6. *how* they might destroy him.
5:23. *that* she may be healed;
Lu. 2:35. *that* the thoughts of many hearts may
7: 3. *that* he would come and heal his
10: 2. *that* he would send forth labourers
11:37. besought him *to* dine with him:
16:26. so *that* he which would pass
28. *that* he may testify unto them,
24:20. And *how* the chief priests and
Joh.11:57. *that* they might take him.
Acts 3:19. *when* the times of refreshing shall come (lit. *that* the times...may come)
8:15. *that* they might receive the Holy Ghost:
24. *that* none of these things which ye
9: 2. *that* if he found any of this way,

Acts 9:12. *that* he might receive his sight.
17. *that* thou mightest receive thy sight,
24. day and night *to* kill him.
15:17. *That* the residue of men might
20:16. *because* he would not spend the time
23:15. *that* he bring him down unto you
20. *that* thou wouldest bring down Paul
23. *to* go to Cæsarea,
24:26. *that* he might loose him:
25: 3. *that* he would send for him to
26. *that*, after examination had, I might
Ro. 3: 4. *That* thou mightest be justified
9:17. *that* I might shew my power in thee, and *that* my name might be
1Co. 1:29. *That* no flesh should glory in his
2Co. 8:11. *that* as (there was) a readiness
14. *that* there may be equality:
Gal. 1: 4. *that* he might deliver us from
2Th. 1:12. *That* the name of our Lord Jesus
Philem. 6. *That* the communication of thy faith
Heb 2: 9. *that* he by the grace of God should
9:15. *that* by means of death, for the
Jas. 5:16. *that* ye may be healed.
1Pet.2: 9. *that* ye should shew forth the

ὅραμα, *horama.*

Mat.17: 9. Tell the *vision* to no man,
Acts 7:31. he wondered at the *sight :*
9:10. to him said the Lord in a *vision*,
12. And hath seen in a *vision* a man
10: 3. He saw in a *vision* evidently
17. what this *vision* which he had
19. While Peter thought on the *vision*,
11: 5. and in a trance I saw a *vision*,
12: 9. but thought he saw a *vision*.
16: 9. a *vision* appeared to Paul in the night;
10. And after he had seen the *vision*,
18: 9. to Paul in the night by a *vision*,

ὅρασις, *horasis.*

Acts 2:17. your young men shall see *visions*,
Rev. 4: 3. was *to look upon* like a jasper and
— *in sight* like unto an emerald.
9:17. I saw the horses in the *vision*,

ὁρατός, *horatos.*

Col. 1:16. *visible* and invisible, whether

ὁράω, *horao.*

Mat. 8: 4. *See* thou tell no man ;
9:30. *See* (that) no man know (it).
16: 6. *Take heed* and beware of the leaven
18:10. *Take heed* that ye despise not one
24: 6. *see* that ye be not troubled:
Mar 1:44. *See* thou say nothing to any man:
8:15. *Take heed,* beware of the leaven
24. I *see* men as)(trees, walking.
Lu. 1:22. perceived that he *had seen* a vision
9:36. those things which they *had seen.*
12:15. *Take heed,* and beware of covetousness:
16:23. and *seeth* Abraham afar off,

Lu. 23:49. stood afar off, *beholding* these things.
24:23. saying, that they *had* also *seen* a vision
Joh. 1:18. No man *hath seen* God at any time;
34. And I *saw*, and bare record that
3:11. and testify that we *have seen*;
32. what he *hath seen* and heard,
4:45. *having seen* all the things that he did
5:37. nor *seen* his shape.
6: 2. because they *saw* his miracles
36. ye also *have seen* me, and believe not.
46. Not that any man *hath seen* the Father,
— he *hath seen* the Father.
8:38. I speak that which I *have seen*
— ye do that which ye *have seen*
57. and *hast* thou *seen* Abraham?
9:37. Thou *hast* both *seen* him, and it is he
14: 7. ye know him, and *have seen* him.
9. he that *hath seen* me *hath seen* the Father;
15:24. now *have* they both *seen* and hated
19:35. And he *that saw* (it) bare record,
20:18. that she *had seen* the Lord,
25. We *have seen* the Lord.
29. because thou *hast seen* me,
Acts 7:44. to the fashion that he *had seen*.
8:23. I *perceive* that thou art in the
22:15. of what thou *hast seen* and heard.
26. *Take heed* what thou doest:
1Co. 9: 1. *have* I not *seen* Jesus Christ our Lord?
Col. 2: 1. as many as *have* not *seen* my face
18. things which he *hath* not *seen*,
1Th. 5:15. *See* that none render evil for evil
Heb 2: 8. But now we *see* not yet all things put
8: 5. *See*, saith he, (that) thou make
11:27. as *seeing* him who is invisible.
Jas. 2:24. Ye *see* then how that by works
1Pet.1: 8. *though* now ye *see* (him) not,
1Joh.1: 1. which we *have seen* with our eyes,
2. we *have seen* (it), and bear witness,
3. That which we *have seen* and heard
3: 6. *hath* not *seen* him, neither known him.
4:20. his brother whom he *hath seen*, how can
he love God whom he *hath* not *seen*?
3Joh. 11. he that doeth evil *hath* not *seen* God.
Rev.18:18. *when* they *saw* the smoke of her
19:10. *See* (thou do it) not: I am thy
22: 9. saith he unto me, *See* (thou do it) not:

ὀργή, orgee.

Mat. 3: 7. to flee from the *wrath* to come?
Mar 3: 5. round about on them with *anger*,
Lu. 3: 7. to flee from the *wrath* to come?
21:23. and *wrath* upon this people.
Joh. 3:36. but the *wrath* of God abideth on him.
Ro. 1:18. For the *wrath* of God is revealed
2: 5. *treasurest* up unto thyself *wrath* against
the day of *wrath*
8. unrighteousness, indignation and *wrath*,
3: 5. God unrighteous who taketh *vengeance*?
4:15. the law worketh *wrath*:
5: 9. be saved from *wrath* through him.
9:22. if God, willing to shew (his) *wrath*,
— the vessels of *wrath* fitted to destruction:
12:19. but (rather) give place unto *wrath*:
13: 4. to (execute) *wrath* upon him that doeth
evil.
5. not only for *wrath*, but also
Eph 2: 3. by nature the children of *wrath*,
4:31. and wrath, and *anger*, and clamour,
5: 6. because of these things cometh the *wrath*
Col. 3: 6. For which things' sake the *wrath* of God

Col. 3: 8. put off all these; *anger*, wrath,
1Th. 1:10. which delivered us from the *wrath*
2:16. for the *wrath* is come upon them
5: 9. God hath not appointed us to *wrath*,
1Ti. 2: 8. without *wrath* and doubting.
Heb 3:11. So I sware in my *wrath*,
4: 3. As I have sworn in my *wrath*,
Jas. 1:19. slow to speak, slow to *wrath*:
20. For the *wrath* of man worketh not
Rev. 6:16. and from the *wrath* of the Lamb:
17. For the great day of his *wrath* is come;
11:18. and thy *wrath* is come,
14:10. into the cup of his *indignation*;
16:19. the wine of the fierceness of his *wrath*.
19:15. and *wrath* of Almighty God.

ὀργίζομαι, orgizomai.

Mat. 5:22. *whoso*ever *is angry* with his brother
18:34. his lord *was wroth*, *and* delivered
22: 7. he *was wroth*: and he sent forth
Lu. 14:21. the master of the house *being angry*
15:28. he *was angry*, and would not go in:
Eph. 4:26. *Be* ye *angry*, and sin not:
Rev.11:18. the nations *were angry*,
12:17. the dragon *was wroth* with the woman,

ὀργίλος, orgilos.

Tit. 1: 7. not *soon angry*, not given to wine,

ὀργυια, orguya.

Acts27:28. and found (it) twenty *fathoms*:
— and found (it) fifteen *fathoms*.

ὀρέγομαι, oregomai.

1Ti. 3: 1. If a man *desire* the office of a bishop,
6:10. which *while* some *coveted* after, they
Heb 11:16. But now they *desire* a better

ὀρεινός, orinos.

Lu. 1:39. and went into the *hill* country
65. throughout all the *hill* country

ὄρεξις, orexis.

Ro. 1:27. burned in their *lust* one toward

ὀρθοποδέω, orthopodeo.

Gal. 2:14. that they *walked* not *uprightly*

ὀρθός, orthos.

Acts14:10. Stand *upright* on thy feet.
Heb 12:13. make *straight* paths for your feet,

ὀρθοτομέω, orthotomeo.

2Ti. 2:15. *rightly dividing* the word of truth.

ὀρθρίζω, orthrizo.

Lu. 21:38. all the people *came early in the morning*

ὀρθρινός, orthrinos.

Rev 22:16. the bright and *morning* star.

ὄρθριος, orthrios.

Lu. 24:22. which were *early* at the sepulchre;

ὄρθρος, orthros.

Lu. 24: 1. very *early in the morning*, they came
Joh. 8: 2. *early in the morning* he came again
Acts 5:21. into the temple *early in the morning*,

ὀρθῶς, orthōs.

Mar 7:35. and he spake *plain*.
Lu. 7:43. Thou hast *rightly* judged.
10:28. Thou hast answered *right:*
20:21. thou sayest and teachest *rightly*,

ὅρια, horia.

Mat. 2:16. and in all the *coasts* thereof,
4:13. in the *borders* of Zabulon and
8:34. would depart out of their *coasts*.
15:22. out of the same *coasts*, and cried
39. came into the *coasts* of Magdala.
19: 1. and came into the *coasts* of Judæa
Mar 5:17. to depart out of their *coasts*.
7:31. from the *coasts* of Tyre and Sidon,
— the midst of the *coasts* of Decapolis.
10: 1. and cometh into the *coasts* of Judæa
Acts 13:50. expelled them out of their *coasts*.

ὁρίζω, horizo.

Lu. 22:22. as it *was determined:*
Acts 2:23. by the *determinate* counsel and
10:42. *which was ordained* of God (to be) the Judge
11:29. *determined* to send relief unto
17:26. *and hath determined* the times
31. by (that) man whom he *hath ordained;*
Ro. 1: 4. And *declared* (to be) the Son of God with power,
Heb 4: 7. he *limiteth* a certain day,

ὁρκίζω, horkizo.

Mar 5: 7. I *adjure* thee by God, that thou torment me not.
Acts 19:13. We *adjure* you by Jesus whom Paul
1Th. 5:27. I *charge* you by the Lord that this epistle be read

---

ὅρκος, horkos.

Mat. 5:33. shalt perform unto the Lord thine *oaths:*
14: 7. promised with an *oath* to give her

Mat. 14: 9. for the *oath's* sake,
26:72. again he denied with an *oath*,
Mar 6:26. (yet) for his *oath's* sake,
Lu. 1:73. The *oath* which he sware to our
Acts 2:30. God had sworn with an *oath* to him,
Heb 6:16. an *oath* for confirmation (is)
17. confirmed (it) by an *oath :*
Jas. 5:12. neither by any other *oath:*

ὁρκωμοσία, horkōmosia.

Heb 7:20. inasmuch as not without an *oath*
21(20). For those priests were made without an *oath;* but this with an *oath* by him
28. but the word of the *oath*, which was since the law,

ὁρμάω, hormao.

Mat. 8:32. *ran violently* down a steep place
Mar 5:13. herd *ran violently* down a steep place
Lu. 8:33. herd *ran violently* down a steep place
Acts 7:57. and *ran* upon him with one accord,
19:29. they *rushed* with one accord into

ὁρμή, hormee.

Acts 14: 5. when there was an *assault* made
Jas. 3: 4. whithersoever the governor (lit. the *impulse* of the governor) listeth.

ὅρμημα, hormeema.

Rev. 18:21. Thus with *violence* shall that great city

ὄρνεον, orneon.

Rev 18: 2. a cage of every unclean and hateful *bird.*
19:17. saying to all the *fowls* that fly
21. all the *fowls* were filled with their flesh.

ὄρνις, ornis.

Mat 23:37. as a *hen* gathereth her chickens
Lu. 13:34. as a *hen* (doth gather) her brood

ὁροθεσία, horothesia.

Acts 17:26. and the *bounds* of their habitation ;

ὄρος, oros.

Mat. 4: 8. into an exceeding high *mountain*,
5: 1. he went up into a *mountain:*
14. A city that is set on an *hill* cannot be hid.
8: 1. was come down from the *mountain*,
14:23. he went up into a *mountain* apart
15:29. and went up into a *mountain*,
17: 1. into an high *mountain* apart
9. as they came down from the *mountain*,
20. ye shall say unto this *mountain*,
18:12. and goeth into the *mountains*,
21: 1. unto the *mount* of Olives, then sent
21. if ye shall say unto this *mountain*,

Mat.24: 3. as he sat upon the *mount* of Olives,
    16. which be in Judæa flee into the *mountains:*
    26:30. they went out into the *mount* of Olives.
    28:16. into a *mountain* where Jesus had
Mar 3:13. And he goeth up into a *mountain*,
    5: 5. he was in the *mountains*, and in
    11. nigh unto the *mountains* a great herd
    6:46. he departed into a *mountain* to pray.
    9: 2. into an high *mountain* apart
    9. as they came down from the *mountain*,
    11: 1. at the *mount* of Olives,
    23. shall say unto this *mountain*,
    13: 3. as he sat upon the *mount* of Olives,
    14. that be in Judæa flee to the *mountains :*
    14:26. they went out into the *mount* of Olives.
Lu. 3: 5. every *mountain* and hill shall be
    4: 5. taking him up into an high *mountain*,
    29. unto the brow of the *hill*
    6:12. he went out into a *mountain* to pray,
    8:32. feeding on the *mountain :*
    9:28. and went up into a *mountain* to pray.
    37. were come down from the *hill*,
    19:29. at the *mount* called (the mount) of Olives,
    37. at the descent of the *mount* of Olives,
    21:21. are in Judæa flee to the *mountains ;*
    37. and abode in the *mount*
    22:39. to the *mount* of Olives ;
    23:30. to say to the *mountains*, Fall on us ;
Joh. 4:20. worshipped in this *mountain ;*
    21. neither in this *mountain*, nor
    6: 3. Jesus went up into a *mountain*,
    15. into a *mountain* himself alone.
    8: 1. Jesus went unto the *mount* of Olives.
Acts 1:12. from the *mount* called Olivet,
    7:30. in the wilderness of *mount* Sina
    38. spake to him in the *mount* Sina,
1Co.13: 2. so that I could remove *mountains*,
Gal. 4:24. the one from the *mount* Sinai,
    25. For this Agar is *mount* Sinai
Heb 8: 5. shewed to thee in the *mount*.
    11:38. and (in) *mountains*, and (in) dens
    12:18. unto the *mount* that might be touched,
    20. as a beast touch the *mountain*,
    22. ye are come unto *mount* Sion,
2Pet.1:18. with him in the holy *mount*.
Rev. 6:14. every *mountain* and island were moved
    15. in the rocks of the *mountains ;*
    16. said to the *mountains* and rocks,
    8: 8. as it were a great *mountain*
    14: 1. a Lamb stood on the *mount* Sion,
    16:20. and the *mountains* were not found.
    17: 9. seven heads are seven *mountains*,
    21:10. to a great and high *mountain*,

ὀρύσσω, *orusso.*

Mat.21:33. and *digged* a winepress in it,
    25:18. and *digged* in the earth, and hid
Mar 12: 1. and *digged* (a place for) the winefat,

ὀρφανός, *orphanos.*

Joh.14:18. I will not leave you *comfortless :*
Jas. 1:27. To visit the *fatherless* and widows

ὀρχέομαι, *orkeomai.*

Mat.11:17. and ye *have* not *danced ;*
    14: 6. the daughter of Herodias *danced*

Mar 6:22. came in, and *danced*,
Lu. 7:32. and ye *have* not *danced ;*

ὅς, ἥ, ὅ, see Appendix.

ὁσάκις, *hosakis.*

1Co.11:25. as oft as ye drink (it), in remembrance
    26. For *as often as* ye eat this bread,
Rev.11: 6. with all plagues, *as often as* they will.

ὅσιος, *hosios.*

Acts 2:27. thine *Holy* One to see corruption.
    13:34. I will give you the sure *mercies* of David.
    35. Thou shalt not suffer thine *Holy* One to
1Ti. 2: 8. lifting up *holy* hands, without wrath
Tit. 1: 8. sober, just, *holy*, temperate ;
Heb 7:26. (who is) *holy*, harmless, undefiled,
Rev.15: 4. for (thou) only (art) *holy :*
    16: 5. which art, and wast, and *shalt be*,

    Note.—The reading in Rev. 16:5, appears to
    have been in some copies ὁ ἐσόμενος.

ὁσιότης, *hosiotees.*

Lu. 1:75. In *holiness* and righteousness before
Eph. 4:24. in righteousness and true *holiness*.

ὁσίως, *hosiōs.*

1Th. 2:10. how *holily* and justly and

ὀσμή, *osmee.*

Joh.12: 3. filled with the *odour* of the ointment
2Co. 2:14. the *savour* of his knowledge by us
    16. To the one (we are) the *savour* of death
    — to the other the *savour* of life unto
Eph. 5: 2. for a sweetsmelling *savour*.
Phi. 4:18. an *odour* of a sweet smell,

ὅσος, *hosos.*

    [2] denotes that it is coupled with ἄν.

Mat. 7:12. all things *whatsoever*[2] ye would that
    9:15. *as long as* the bridegroom is with them ?
    13:44. goeth and selleth all *that* he hath,
    46. went and sold all *that* he had,
    14:36. *as many as* touched were made perfectly
    17:12. done unto him *whatsoever* they listed.
    18:18. *Whatsoever* (ὅσα ἐὰν) ye shall bind on
    — *whatsoever* (ὅσα ἐὰν) ye shall loose on
    25. and all *that* he had, and payment
    21:22. *whatsoever*[2] ye shall ask in prayer
    22: 9. *as many as*[2] ye shall find, bid
    10. *as many as* they found, both bad and
    23: 3. *whatsoever*[2] they bid you observe,
    25:40. Inasmuch *as* ye have done (it) unto
    45. Inasmuch *as* ye did (it) not to one
    28:20. *whatsoever* I have commanded you:
Mar 2:19. *as long as* they have the bridegroom
    3: 8. when they had heard *what great* things
    10. *as many as* had plagues.

Mar 3:28. *wherewith soever* [2] they shall blaspheme:
5:19. tell them *how great* things the Lord
20. *how great* things Jesus had done for
6:11. And *whosoever* [2] shall not receive you,
30. both *what* they had done, and *what* they
56. *as many as* [2] touched him were
7:36. but *the more* he charged them,
9:13. done unto him *whatsoever* they listed,
10:21. sell *whatsoever* thou hast,
11:24. *What* things soever [2] ye desire,
12:44. did cast in all *that* she had,
Lu. 4:23. *whatsoever* we have heard done
40. all they *that* had any sick
8:39. shew *how great* things God hath done
— *how great* things Jesus had done
9: 5. And *whosoever* [2] will not receive you,
10. told him *all that* they had done.
11: 8. *as many as* he needeth.
12: 3. *whatsoever* ye have spoken in darkness
18:12. I give tithes of all *that* I possess.
22. sell all *that* thou hast, and
Joh. 1:12. But *as many as* received him,
4:29. which told me all things *that* ever
39. He told me all *that* ever I did.
6:11. of the fishes *as much as* they would.
10: 8. All *that* ever came before me are
41. but all things *that* John spake of
11:22. *whatsoever* [2] thou wilt ask of God,
15:14. if ye do *whatsoever* I command you.
16:13. *whatsoever* [2] he shall hear, (that)
15. All things *that* the Father hath are mine:
23. *Whatsoever* [2] ye shall ask the Father
17: 7. that all things *whatsoever* thou hast given
21:25. also many other things *which* Jesus did,
Acts 2:39. *as many as* [2] the Lord our God shall call
3:22. in all things *whatsoever* [2] he shall
24. *as many as* have spoken,
4: 6. *as many as* were of the kindred of
23. and reported *all that* the chief priests
28. For to do *whatsoever* thy hand
34. for *as many as* were possessors of
5:36. and all, *as many as* obeyed him,
37. *as many as* obeyed him,
9:13. *how much* evil he hath done
16. *how great* things he must suffer
39. garments *which* Dorcas made,
10:45. *as many as* came with Peter,
13:48. and *as many as* were ordained to
14:27. *all that* God had done with them,
15: 4. declared *all things that* God had done
12. declaring *what* miracles and wonders
Ro. 2:12. *as many as* have sinned without
— and *as many as* have sinned in
3:19. that *what* things soever the law saith,
6: 3. *so many* of us *as* were baptized into
7: 1. *as long as* he liveth?
8:14 For *as many as* are led
11:13. in*asmuch as* I am the apostle
15: 4. For *whatsoever* things were written
1Co. 7:39. *as long as* her husband liveth;
2Co. 1:20. For *all* the promises of God in him
Gal. 3:10. For *as many as* are of the works of
27. For *as many of* you *as* have been
4: 1. the heir, *as long as* he is a child,
6:12. *As many as* desire to make
16. *as many as* walk according to
Phi. 3:15. *as many as* be perfect,
4: 8. *whatsoever* things are true, *whatsoever*
— *whatsoever* things (are) just, *whatsoever*
— *whatsoever* things (are) lovely, *whatsoever*
Col. 2: 1. and (for) *as many as* have not seen
1Ti. 6: 1. Let *as many* servants *as* are under

2Ti. 1:18. and in *how many* things he ministered
Heb 1: 4. *as* he hath by inheritance obtained
2:15. deliver them *who* through fear of death
3: 3. in*asmuch as* he who hath builded
7:20. And in*asmuch as* not without an oath
8: 6. by *how much* also he is the mediator
9:27. And *as* it is appointed unto men
10:25. so much the more, *as* ye see the day
37. For yet a little while, (lit. *how* little *how!*)
2Pet.1:13. *as long as* I am in this tabernacle,
Jude 10. of *those things* which they know not: but
what they know naturally.
Rev. 1: 2. and of *all things that* he saw.
2:24. *as many as* have not this doctrine,
3:19. *As many as* (ὅσους ἐὰν) I love, I rebuke
and chasten:
13:15. that *as many as* [2] would not worship
18: 7. *How much* she hath glorified herself,
17. *as many as* trade by sea,
21:16. the length is as large *as* the breadth:

ὀστέον, osteon.

Mat.23:27. full of dead (men's) *bones*,
Lu. 24:39. hath not flesh and *bones*, as ye see me
Joh.19:36. A *bone* of him shall not be broken.
Eph. 5:30. of his flesh, and of his *bones*.
Heb 11:22. commandment concerning his *bones*.

ὅστις, hostis.

[2] denotes that it is coupled with ἄν, [3] that it is
coupled with both πᾶς and ἄν,

Mat. 2: 6. a Governor, *that* shall rule my people
5:39. but *whosoever* shall smite thee
41. And *whosoever* shall compel thee
7:15. *which* come to you in sheep's clothing,
24. *whosoever* heareth these sayings
— *which* built his house upon a rock:
26. *which* built his house upon the sand:
10:32. *Whosoever* therefore shall confess me
33. *whosoever* [2] shall deny me
12:50. *whosoever* [2] shall do the will of
13:12. *whosoever* hath, to him shall be
— but *whosoever* hath not, from him
52. *which* bringeth forth out of his
16:28. *which* shall not taste of death,
18: 4. *Whosoever* therefore shall humble
28. Pay me *that* thou owest.
19:12. *which* were so born
— *which* were made eunuchs of men:
— *which* have made themselves eunuchs
20: 1. *which* went out early in the morning
21:33. *which* planted a vineyard,
41. *which* shall render him the fruits
22: 2. *which* made a marriage for his son,
23:12. *whosoever* shall exalt himself
— and *he that* shall humble himself
27. *which* indeed appear beautiful
25: 1. *which* took their lamps, and
3. *They that* (were) foolish took
27:55. *which* followed Jesus from Galilee,
62. *that* followed the day of the
Mar 4:20. such *as* hear the word, and
8:34. *Whosoever* will come after me,
9: 1. *which* shall not taste of death,
12:18. *which* say there is no resurrection;
15: 7. *who* had committed murder
Lu. 1:20. *which* shall be fulfilled in
2: 4. *which* is called Bethlehem;

Lu. 2:10. *which* shall be to all people.
7:37. *which* was a sinner,
39. woman (this is) *that* toucheth him:
8: 3. *which* ministered unto him
15. *which* in an honest and good heart,
26. *which* is over against Galilee.
43. *which* had spent all her living
9:30. *which* were Moses and Elias:
10:35. and *whatsoever* [2] thou spendest more,
42. *which* shall not be taken away
12: 1. leaven of the Pharisees, *which* is
14:27. *whosoever* doth not bear his cross,
15: 7. *which* need no repentance.
23:19. *Who* for a certain sedition made in
55. *which* came with him from Galilee,
Joh. 2: 5. *Whatsoever* [2] he saith unto you, do
8:25. even (the same) *that* I said unto you
53. Abraham, *which* is dead?
14:13. *whatsoever* [2] ye shall ask in my name,
15:16. that *whatsoever* [2] ye shall ask of the
21:25. *the which*, if they should be written
Acts 3:23. every soul, *which* [3] will not hear that
5:16. *and they* were healed every one.
7:53. *Who* have received the law by the
8:15. *Who*, when they were come down,
9:35. and (lit. *who*) turned to the Lord.
10:41. to us, *who* did eat and drink with him
47. *which* have received the Holy Ghost
11:20. *which*, when they were come to Antioch,
28. *which* came to pass in the days of
12:10. *which* opened to them of his own
13:31. *who* are his witnesses unto the people.
43. *who*, speaking to them, persuaded
16:12. *which* is the chief city of that
16. *which* brought her masters much
17. *which* shew unto us the way of
17:10. *who* coming (thither) went into
11. *in that they* received the word
21: 4. *who* said to Paul through the Spirit,
23:14. *And they* came to the chief priests
21. *which* have bound themselves
33. *Who*, when they came to Cæsarea,
24: 1. *who* informed the governor against
28:18. *Who*, when they had examined me,
Ro. 1:25. *Who* changed the truth of God into
32. *Who* knowing the judgment of God,
2:15. *Which* shew the work of the law
6: 2. How shall we, *that* are dead to sin,
9: 4. *Who* are Israelites; to whom
11: 4. *who* have not bowed the knee to
16: 4. *Who* have for my life laid down
6. *who* bestowed much labour on us.
7. *who* are of note among the apostles,
12. *which* laboured much in the Lord.
1Co. 3:17. *which* (temple) ye are.
5: 1. *such* fornication *as* is not so much as
6:20. in your spirit, *which* are God's.
7:13. woman *which* hath an husband that
16: 2. *as* [2] (God) hath prospered him,
2Co. 3:14. *which* (vail) is done away in Christ.
8:10. *who* have begun before, not only to
9:11. *which* causeth through us thanksgiving
Gal. 2: 4. *who* came in privily to spy out
4:24. *Which* things are an allegory:
— gendereth to bondage, *which* is Agar.
26. is free, *which* is the mother of us all.
5: 4. *whosoever* of you are justified by
10. bear his judgment, *whosoever* [2] he be.
19. *which* are (these); Adultery,
Eph. 1:23. *Which* is his body, the fulness of
3:13. *which* is your glory.
4:19. *Who* being past feeling

Eph. 6: 2. *which* is the first commandment with
Phi. 1:28. *which* is to them an evident token
2:20. *who* will naturally care for
3: 7. But *what* things were gain to me,
4: 3. women *which* laboured with me in
Col. 2:23. *Which* things have indeed a shew
3: 5. and covetousness, *which* is idolatry:
14. *which* is the bond of perfectness.
17. And *whatsoever* [3] ye do in word
23. *whatsoever* [3] ye do, do (it) heartily, as
4:11. *which* have been a comfort unto me.
2Th. 1: 9. *Who* shall be punished with
1Ti. 1: 4. *which* minister questions, rather than
3:15. *which* is the church of the living God,
6: 9. *which* drown men in destruction
2Ti. 1: 5. *which* dwelt first in thy grandmother
2: 2. *who* shall be able to teach others
18. *Who* concerning the truth have erred,
Tit. 1:11. *who* subvert whole houses,
Heb 2: 3. *which* at the first began to be spoken
8: 5. *Who* serve unto the example and
6. *which* was established upon better
9: 2. *which* is called the sanctuary.
9. *Which* (was) a figure for the time
10: 8. *which* are offered by the law;
11. *which* can never take away sins:
35. *which* hath great recompence of
12: 5. *which* speaketh unto you as unto
13: 7. *who* have spoken unto you the word
Jas. 2:10. For *whosoever* shall keep the whole law,
4:14. *Whereas ye* know not what (shall be)
1Pet.2:11. *which* war against the soul;
2Pet.2: 1. *who* privily shall bring in damnable
1Joh.1: 2. *which* was with the Father,
Rev. 1: 7. and *they* (also) *which* pierced him:
12. to see the voice *that* spake with me.
2:24. and *which* have not known the
9: 4. *which* have not the seal of God
11: 8. *which* spiritually is called Sodom
12:13. *which* brought forth the man (child).
17: 8. the beast *that* was, and is not, and yet is.
12. *which* have received no kingdom as yet;
19: 2. *which* did corrupt the earth
20: 4. and *which* had not worshipped the beast,

See also ὅτου.

ὀστράκινος, *ostrakinos.*

2Co. 4: 7. this treasure in *earthen* vessels,
2Ti. 2:20. but also of wood and of *earth;*

ὄσφρησις, *osphreesis.*

1Co.12:17. where (were) the *smelling?*

ὀσφύς, *osphus.*

Mat. 3: 4. a leathern girdle about his *loins;*
Mar 1: 6. girdle of a skin about his *loins;*
Lu. 12:35. Let your *loins* be girded about,
Acts 2:30. that of the fruit of his *loins,*
Eph. 6:14. having your *loins* girt about
Heb 7: 5. come out of the *loins* of Abraham:
10. he was yet in the *loins* of his father,
1Pet.1:13. gird up the *loins* of your mind,

ὅταν, *hotan.*

Mat. 5:11. *when* (men) shall revile you,

Mat. 6: 2. *when* thou doest (thine) alms,
    5. And *when* thou prayest,
    6. But thou, *when* thou prayest,
    16. *when* ye fast, be not, as the
    9:15. *when* the bridegroom shall be taken
    10:19. But *when* they deliver you up,
    23. But *when* they persecute you
    12:43. *When* the unclean spirit is gone
    13:32. *when* it is grown, it is the greatest
    15: 2. *when* they eat bread.
    19:28. *when* the Son of man shall sit
    21:40. *When* the lord therefore of the
    23:15. *when* he is made, ye make him twofold
    24:15. *When* ye therefore shall see the
    32. *When* his branch is yet tender,
    33. *when* ye shall see all these things,
    25:31. *When* the Son of man shall come
    26:29. until that day *when* I drink it
Mar 2:20. *when* the bridegroom shall be taken
    3:11. unclean spirits, *when* they saw him,
    4:15. but *when* they have heard, Satan
    16. *when* they have heard the word,
    29. *when* the fruit is brought forth,
    31. *when* it is sown in the earth,
    32. But *when* it is sown, it groweth up,
    8:38. *when* he cometh in the glory of his
    9: 9. till (lit. except *when*) the Son of man
    11:25. *when* ye stand praying, forgive,
    12:23. *when* they shall rise,
    25. For *when* they shall rise from the
    13: 4. *when* all these things shall be
    7. *when* ye shall hear of wars and
    11. But *when* they shall lead (you), and
    14. But *when* ye shall see the abomination
    28. *When* her branch is yet tender,
    29. *when* ye shall see these things
    14: 7. *whensoever* ye will ye may do them good:
    25. until that day *that* I drink it new
Lu. 5:35. *when* the bridegroom shall be taken
    6:22. *when* men shall hate you, and *when* they
      shall separate you (from their company),
    26. Woe unto you, *when* all men shall
    8:13. which, *when* they hear, receive the word
    9:26. *when* he shall come in his own
    11: 2. *When* we pray, say, Our Father
    21. *When* a strong man armed keepeth
    24. *When* the unclean spirit is gone
    34. *when* thine eye is single,
    36. as *when* the bright shining of a
    12:11. *when* they bring you unto the synagogues,
    54. *When* ye see a cloud rise out of the
    55. *when* (ye see) the south wind blow,
    13:28. *when* ye shall see Abraham,
    14: 8. *When* thou art bidden of any (man)
    10. But *when* thou art bidden,
    — that *when* he that bade thee cometh,
    12. *When* thou makest a dinner or a
    13. But *when* thou makest a feast,
    16: 4. *when* I am put out of the stewardship,
    9. that, *when* ye fail, they may
    17:10. *when* ye shall have done all those
    21: 7. *when* these things shall come to pass?
    9. But *when* ye shall hear of wars and
    20. And *when* ye shall see Jerusalem
    30. *When* they now shoot forth,
    31. *when* ye see these things come to pass,
    23:42. *when* thou comest into thy kingdom.
Joh. 2:10. and *when* men have well drunk,
    4:25. *when* he is come, he will tell us all
    5: 7. I have no man, *when* the water is troubled,
    7:27. but *when* Christ cometh,

Joh. 7:31. *When* Christ cometh, will he do more
    8:28. *When* ye have lifted up the Son
    44. *When* he speaketh a lie,
    9: 5. *As long as* I am in the world,
    10: 4. And *when* he putteth forth his own
    13:19. that, *when* it is come to pass,
    14:29. that, *when* it is come to pass,
    15:26. But *when* the Comforter is come,
    16: 4. that *when* the time shall come,
    13. *when* he, the Spirit of truth, is come.
    21. A woman *when* she is in travail
    — but *as soon as* she is delivered
    21:18. but *when* thou shalt be old,
Acts23:35. *when* thine accusers are also come
    24:22. *When* Lysias the chief captain
Ro. 2:14. For *when* the Gentiles,
    11:27. *when* I shall take away their sins.
1Co. 3: 4. For *while* one saith, I am of Paul;
    13:10. But *when* that which is perfect is come,
    14:26. *when* ye come together,
    15:24. *when* he shall have delivered up
    — *when* he shall have put down
    27. But *when* he saith, All things are
    28. And *when* all things shall be subdued
    54. So *when* this corruptible shall have
    16: 2. that there be no gatherings *when* I come.
    3. And *when* I come, whomsoever ye
    5. *when* I shall pass through Macedonia:
    12. *when* he shall have convenient time.
2Co.10: 6. *when* your obedience is fulfilled.
    12:10. for *when* I am weak, then am I strong.
    13: 9. we are glad, *when* we are weak,
Col. 3: 4. *When* Christ, (who is) our life, shall
    4:16. And *when* this epistle is read
1Th. 5: 3. For *when* they shall say, Peace and safety;
2Th. 1:10. *When* he shall come to be glorified
1Ti. 5:11. for *when* they have begun to wax
Tit. 3:12. *When* I shall send Artemas
Heb 1: 6. *when* he bringeth in the firstbegotten
Jas. 1: 2. *when* ye fall into divers temptations;
1Joh.2:28. that, *when* he shall appear, we may
    5: 2. *when* we love God, and keep his
Rev 4: 9. And *when* those beasts give glory
    9: 5. of a scorpion, *when* he striketh a man.
    10: 7. *when* he shall begin to sound,
    11: 7. *when* they shall have finished their
    12: 4. to devour her child *as soon as* it was born.
    17:10. and *when* he cometh, he must
    18: 9. *when* they shall see the smoke
    20: 7. *when* the thousand years are expired,

ὅτε, hote.

Mat. 7:28. *when* Jesus had ended these sayings,
    9:25. But *when* the people were put forth,
    11: 1. *when* Jesus had made an end of
    12: 3. what David did, *when* he was an hungred,
    13:26. But *when* the blade was sprung up,
    48. Which, *when* it was full, they drew
    53. *when* Jesus had finished these parables,
    17:25. And *when* he was come into the house,
    19: 1. *when* Jesus had finished these sayings,
    21: 1. And *when* they drew nigh unto Jerusalem,
    34. And *when* the time of the fruit drew near,
    26: 1. *when* Jesus had finished all these
    27:31. And *after that* they had mocked him,
Mar 1:32. *when* the sun did set,
    2:25. *when* he had need, and was an hungred,
    4:10. And *when* he was alone,
    ●:21. day was come, *that* Herod on his
    7:17. And *when* he was entered into the house

Mar 8:19. *When* I brake the five loaves
20. And *when* the seven among
11: 1. And *when* they came nigh to
19. And *when* even was come,
14:12. *when* they killed the passover,
15:20. And *when* they had mocked him,
41. *when* he was in Galilee,
Lu. 2:21. And *when* eight days were accomplished
22. And *when* the days of her purification
42. And *when* he was twelve years old,
4:25. *when* the heaven was shut up
6:13. And *when* it was day, he called
13:35. come *when* ye shall say, Blessed
15:30. But *as soon as* this thy son was come.
17:22. *when* ye shall desire to see one of
22:14. And *when* the hour was come,
35. *When* I sent you without purse, and
23:33. And *when* they were come to the place,
Joh. 1:19. *when* the Jews sent priests and
2:22. *When* therefore he was risen from
4:21. *when* ye shall neither in this
23. *when* the true worshippers shall
45. Then *when* he was come into Galilee,
5:25. *when* the dead shall hear the voice
6:24. *When* the people therefore saw
9: 4. the night cometh, *when* no man can work.
14. *when* Jesus made the clay,
12:16. but *when* Jesus was glorified,
17. *when* he called Lazarus out of his
41. *when* he saw his glory, and
13:12. So *after* he had washed their feet,
31(30). *when* he was gone out,
16:25. the time cometh, *when* I shall
17:12. *While* I was with them in the world,
19: 6. *When* the chief priests therefore
8. *When* Pilate therefore heard that
23. *when* they had crucified Jesus,
30. *When* Jesus therefore had received
20:24. was not with them *when* Jesus came.
21:15. So *when* they had dined,
18. *When* thou wast young,
Acts 1:13. And *when* they were come in,
8:12. But *when* they believed Philip
39. And *when* they were come up out of
11: 2. And *when* Peter was come up to
12: 6. And *when* Herod would have brought
21: 5. And *when* we had accomplished those
35. And *when* he came upon the stairs,
22:20. And *when* the blood of thy martyr
27:39. And *when* it was day, they knew not
28:16. And *when* we came to Rome,
Ro. 2:16. In the day *when* God shall judge
6:20. For *when* ye were the servants of sin,
7: 5. For *when* we were in the flesh,
13:11. nearer than *when* we believed.
1Co.13:11. *When* I was a child,
— but *when* I became a man,
Gal. 1:15. But *when* it pleased God, who
2:11. But *when* Peter was come to Antioch,
12. *when* they were come, he withdrew
14. But *when* I saw that they walked not
4: 3. *when* we were children, were in
4. But *when* the fulness of the time was
Phi. 4:15. *when* I departed from Macedonia,
Col. 3: 7. *when* ye lived in them.
1Th. 3: 4. *when* we were with you,
2Th. 3:10. For even *when* we were with you,
2Ti. 4: 3. *when* they will not endure sound
Tit. 3: 4. But *after that* the kindness and love
Heb 7:10. *when* Melchisedec met him.
9:17. *while* the testator liveth.
1Pet. 3:20. *when* once the longsuffering of God

Jude 9. *when* contending with the devil
Rev 1:17. And *when* I saw him, I fell at his feet
5: 8. And *when* he had taken the book,
6: 1. And I saw *when* the Lamb opened one
3. And *when* he had opened the second
5. And *when* he had opened the third
7. And *when* he had opened the fourth
9. And *when* he had opened the fifth
12. I beheld *when* he had opened the sixth
8: 1. And *when* he had opened the seventh
10: 3. and *when* he had cried, seven
4. And *when* the seven thunders had
10. and *as soon as* I had eaten it,
12:13. And *when* the dragon saw that he
22: 8. And *when* I had heard and seen, I fell

ὅτι, hoti.

Mat. 2:16. when he saw *that* he was mocked
18. *because* they are not.
22. But when he heard *that* Archelaus
23.)(He shall be called a Nazarene.
3: 9. I say unto you, *that* God is able of
4: 6.)(He shall give his angels charge
12. Now when Jesus had heard *that* John
5: 3. *for* their's is the kingdom of heaven.
4. *for* they shall be comforted.
5. *for* they shall inherit the earth.
6. *for* they shall be filled.
7. *for* they shall obtain mercy.
8. *for* they shall see God.
9. *for* they shall be called the children of
10. *for* their's is the kingdom of heaven.
12. *for* great (is) your reward in heaven:
17. Think not *that* I am come to destroy
20. *That* except your righteousness shall
21. Ye have heard *that* it was said by
22. *That* whosoever is angry with his
23. *that* thy brother hath ought against thee ;
27. *that* it was said by them of old time,
28. *That* whosoever looketh on a woman
31. It hath been said,)(Whosoever shall put
32. But I say unto you, *That* whosoever shall
33. ye have heard *that* it hath been said
34. *for* it is God's throne:
35. *for* it is his footstool: neither by Jerusalem; *for* it is the city of the great King.
36. *because* thou canst not make one hair
38. Ye have heard *that* it hath been said,
43. Ye have heard *that* it hath been said,
45. *for* he maketh his sun to rise on
6: 5. *for* they love to pray standing in the
—)(They have their reward.
7. *for* they think that they shall be heard
13. *For* thine is the kingdom,
16.)(They have their reward.
26. *for* they sow not,
29. And yet I say unto you, *That* even
32. knoweth *that* ye have need of all these
7:13. *for* wide (is) the gate,
14. *Because* strait (is) the gate,
23.)(I never knew you:
8:11. *That* many shall come from the east and
27. *that* even the winds and the sea
9: 6. But that ye may know *that* the Son
18.)(My daughter is even now dead:
28. Believe ye *that* I am able to do this?
33.)(It was never so seen in Israel.
36. *because* they fainted, and were scattered
10: 7.)(The kingdom of heaven is at hand.
34. Think not *that* I am come to send

Mat.11:20. *because* they repented not:

21. *for* if the mighty works, which were

23. *for* if the mighty works, which have

24. *That* it shall be more tolerable for

25. *because* thou hast hid these things

26. *for* so it seemed good in thy sight.

29. *for* I am meek and lowly in heart:

12: 5. *how that* on the sabbath days

6. *That* in this place is (one) greater than

36. *That* every idle word that men shall

41. *because* they repented at the

42. *for* she came from the uttermost

13:11. *Because* it is given unto you to know

13. *because* they seeing see not ;

16. *for* they see: and your ears, *for* they hear.

17. *That* many prophets and righteous

14: 5. *because* they counted him as a prophet.

26. were troubled, saying,)(It is a spirit;

15:12. Knowest thou *that* the Pharisees

17. *that* whatsoever entereth in at the

23. *for* she crieth after us.

32. *because* they continue with me

16: 7. (It is) *because* we have taken no bread.

8. *because* ye have brought no bread ?

11. that ye do not understand *that* I spake

12. Then understood they how *that* he bade (them) not

17. *for* flesh and blood hath not revealed (it)

18. *That* thou art Peter,

20. tell no man *that* he was Jesus

21. *how that* he must go unto Jerusalem,

23. *for* thou savourest not the things

17:10. *that* Elias must first come ?

12. *That* Elias is come already,

13. *that* he spake unto them of John

15. *for* he is lunatick, and sore vexed:

18:10. *That* in heaven their angels do

13. I say unto you,)(he rejoiceth more

19. *That* if two of you shall agree

19: 4. *that* he which made (them) at the

8.)(Moses because of the hardness of your

9. I say unto you,)(Whosoever shall

23. *That* a rich man shall hardly

28. *That* ye which have followed me,

20: 7. *Because* no man hath hired us.

10. they supposed *that* they should have received more ;

12. Saying,)(These last have wrought

15. *because* I am good ?

25. Ye know *that* the princes of the

30. when they heard *that* Jesus

21: 3. ye shall say,)(The Lord hath need of

16. have ye never read,)(Out of the mouth

31. *That* the publicans and the harlots

43. say I unto you,)(The kingdom of God

45. heard his parables, they perceived *that* he

22:16. Master, we know *that* thou art true,

34. Pharisees had heard *that* he had put

23:13(14). *for* ye shut up the kingdom of heaven

14(13). *for* ye devour widows' houses,

15. *for* ye compass sea and land to make

23. *for* ye pay tithe of mint and

25. *for* ye make clean the outside

27. *for* ye are like unto whited

29. *because* ye build the tombs of

31. *that* ye are the children of them

24:32. ye know *that* summer (is) nigh:

33. know *that* it is near, (even) at the doors.

42. *for* ye know not what hour your

43. *that* if the goodman of the house

44. *for* in such an hour as ye think not

47. *That* he shall make him ruler over

Mat.25: 8. *for* our lamps are gone out.

13. *for* ye know neither the day nor

24. Lord, I knew thee *that* thou art an

26. thou knewest *that* I reap where I

26: 2. Ye know *that* after two days is

21. *that* one of you shall betray me.

29. But I say unto you,)(I will not drink

34. *That* this night, before the cock crow,

53. Thinkest thou *that* I cannot now pray

54. *that* thus it must be ?

65. saying,)(He hath spoken blasphemy;

72. with an oath,)(I do not know the man.

74. (saying),)(I know not the man.

75. said unto him,)(Before the cock crow,

27: 3. when he saw *that* he was condemned,

18. For he knew *that* for envy they had

24. saw *that* he could prevail nothing,

43. he said,)(I am the Son of God.

47. said,)(This (man) calleth for Elias.

63. Sir, we remember *that* that deceiver

28: 5. *for* I know *that* ye seek Jesus,

7. *that* he is risen from the dead ;

13. Say ye,)(His disciples came by night,

Mar 1:15. And saying,)(The time is fulfilled,

27. *for* with authority commandeth he

34. *because* they knew him.

37.)(All (men) seek for thee.

40.)(If thou wilt, thou canst make me

2: 1. it was noised *that* he was in the house.

8. *that* they so reasoned within themselves,

10. *that* the Son of man hath power

12.)(We never saw it on this fashion.

16. How is it *that* he eateth and drinketh

3:11.)(Thou art the Son of God.

21.)(He is beside himself.

22.)(He hath Beelzebub, and)(by the prince of the devils casteth he

28.)(All sins shall be forgiven

30. *Because* they said, He hath an

4:29. *because* the harvest is come.

38. carest thou not *that* we perish ?

41. *that* even the wind and the sea

5: 9. *for* we are many.

23.)(My little daughter lieth

28.)(If I may touch but his clothes,

29. *that* she was healed of that plague.

35.)(Thy daughter is dead: why troublest

6: 2. *that* even such mighty works

4.)(A prophet is not without honour,

14. *That* John the Baptist was risen

15. Others said, *That* it is Elias. And others said, *That* it is a prophet,

16.)(It is John, whom I beheaded: he is risen

17. *for* he had married her.

18.)(It is not lawful for thee to

23.)(Whatsoever thou shalt ask of me,

34. *because* they were as sheep not

35.)(This is a desert place, and now

55. where they heard)(he was.

7: 6.)(Well hath Esaias prophesied

18. Do ye not perceive, *that* whatsoever

19. *Because* it entereth not into

20.)(That which cometh out of the man,

8: 2. *because* they have now been with

16. (It is) *because* we have no bread.

17. reason ye, *because* ye have no bread ?

24. said)(I see men as trees, walking.

31. to teach them, *that* the Son of man

33. *for* thou savourest not the things

9: 1. *That* there be some of them that stand

11. *Why* say the scribes *that* Elias must first

Mar 9:13. I say unto you, *That* Elias is indeed come,
    25. saw *that* the people came running
    26. many said,)(He is dead.
    28. *Why* could not we cast him out?
    31.)(The Son of man is delivered into
    38. *because* he followeth not us.
    41. *because* ye belong to Christ,
  10:33.)(Behold, we go up to Jerusalem;
    42. Ye know *that* they which are accounted
         to rule
    47. And when he heard *that* it was Jesus
  11: 3. say ye *that* the Lord hath need of him;
    17. written,)(My house shall be called of all
    18. *because* all the people was astonished
    23. I say unto you, *That* whosoever
    — believe *that* those things which he saith
    24. believe *that* ye receive (them),
    32. counted John, *that* he was a prophet
  12: 6.)(They will reverence my son.
    7.)(This is the heir; come, let us
    12. *that* he had spoken the parable against
    14. we know *that* thou art true,
    19.)(If a man's brother die,
    26. the dead, *that* they rise:
    28. perceiving *that* he had answered them
    29.)(The first of all the commandments
    32. *for* there is one God; and there is
    34. saw *that* he answered discreetly,
    35. say the scribes *that* Christ is the son
    43. say unto you, *That* this poor widow hath
  13: 6. saying,)(I am (Christ); and shall
    28. ye know *that* summer is near:
    29. *that* it is nigh, (even) at the doors.
    30. *that* this generation shall not pass,
  14:14.)(The master saith, Where is the
    18. I say unto you,)(One of you which
    25.)(I will drink no more of the fruit
    27.)(All ye shall be offended because of me
         this night: *for* it is written, I will smite
    30. *That* this day, (even) in this night,
    58.)(We heard him say,)(I will destroy
         this temple
    69.)(This is (one) of them.
    71.)(I know not this man of whom ye
    72.)(Before the cock crow twice,
  15:10. *that* the chief priests had delivered
    39. saw *that* he so cried out, and gave
  16: 4. they saw *that* the stone was rolled
    7. *that* he goeth before you into
    11. heard *that* he was alive,
    14. *because* they believed not them
Lu. 1:22. perceived *that* he had seen a vision
    25.)(Thus hath the Lord dealt with me
    37. *For* with God nothing shall be impossible.
    45. *for* there shall be a performance
    48. *For* he hath regarded the low
    49. *For* he that is mighty hath done
    58. *how* the Lord had shewed great
    61.)(There is none of thy kindred
    68. *for* he hath visited and redeemed
  2:11. *For* unto you is born this day
    23.)(Every male that openeth
    30. *For* mine eyes have seen
    49. How is it *that* ye sought me? wist ye not
         that I must be
  3: 8. for I say unto you, *That* God is able
  4: 4. written, *That* man shall not live by
    6. *for* that is delivered unto me;
    10.)(He shall give his angels charge
    11. And)(in (their) hands they shall
    12.)(It is said, Thou shalt not tempt
    21.)(This day is this scripture fulfilled

Lu. 4:24.)(No prophet is accepted in his own
    32. *for* his word was with power.
    36. *for* with authority and power he
    41.)(Thou art Christ the Son of God.
    — *for* they knew that he was Christ.
    43.)(I must preach the kingdom of God
    — *for* therefore am I sent.
  5: 8. *for* I am a sinful man, O Lord.
    24. ye may know *that* the Son of man hath
    26.)(We have seen strange things
    36.)(No man putteth a piece of
  6: 5. *That* the Son of man is Lord also
    19. *for* there went virtue out of him,
    20. *for* your's is the kingdom of God.
    21. *for* ye shall be filled.
    — *for* ye shall laugh.
    24. *for* ye have received your consolation.
    25. *for* ye shall hunger.
    — *for* ye shall mourn.
    35. *for* he is kind unto the unthankful
  7: 4. *That* he was worthy for whom he
    16. *That* a great prophet is risen up among
         us; and, *That* God hath visited his
         people.
    22. *how that* the blind see, the lame
    37. knew *that* (Jesus) sat at meat
    39. *for* she is a sinner.
    43. I suppose *that* (he), to whom he forgave
    47. *for* she loved much:
  8:25. *for* he commandeth even the winds
    30. *because* many devils were entered into
    37. *for* they were taken with great fear:
    42. *For* he had one only daughter,
    47. saw *that* she was not hid,
    49.)(Thy daughter is dead; trouble not
    53. knowing *that* she was dead.
  9: 7. *that* John was risen from the dead;
    8. *that* Elias had appeared; and of others,
         that one of the old prophets
    12. *for* we are here in a desert place.
    19. others (say), *that* one of the old prophets
    22.)(The Son of man must suffer
    38. *for* he is mine only child.
    49. *because* he followeth not with us.
    53. *because* his face was as though
  10:11. *that* the kingdom of God is come nigh
    12. *that* it shall be more tolerable
    13. *for* if the mighty works had been
    20. *that* the spirits are subject unto you;
    — *because* your names are written
    21. *that* thou hast hid these things
    — *for* so it seemed good in thy sight.
    24. I tell you, *that* many prophets
    40. *that* my sister hath left me to serve
  11:18. *because* ye say that I cast out
    31. *for* she came from the utmost parts
    32. *for* they repented at the preaching
    38. he marvelled *that* he had not first
    42. *for* ye tithe the mint and rue and all
    43. *for* ye love the uppermost seats
    44. *for* ye are as graves which
    46. *for* ye lade men with burdens
    47. *for* ye build the sepulchres of
    48. *for* they indeed killed them,
    52. *for* ye have taken away the key of
  12:15. *for* a man's life consisteth not
    17. *because* I have no room where to
    24. *for* they neither sow nor reap;
    30. your Father knoweth *that* ye have
    32. *for* it is your Father's good pleasure
    37. *that* he shall gird himself, and
    39. And this know, *that* if the goodman

Lu. 12:40. *for* the Son of man cometh at an hour
44. *that* he will make him ruler over all
51. Suppose ye *that* I am come to give
55. ye say,)(There will be heat ;
13: 2. Suppose ye *that* these Galilæans
— *because* they suffered such things ?
4. think ye *that* they were sinners
14. *because* that Jesus had healed on
24. *for* many, I say unto you, will seek
31. *for* Herod will kill thee.
33. *for* it cannot be that a prophet
35.)(Ye shall not see me, until
14:11. *For* whosoever exalteth himself shall
14. *for* they cannot recompense thee:
17. Come ; *for* all things are now ready.
24. *That* none of those men which
30.)(This man began to build,
15: 2.)(This man receiveth sinners, and
6. *for* I have found my sheep which
7. *that* likewise joy shall be in heaven
9. *for* I have found the piece which I
24. *For* this my son was dead,
27. he said unto him,)(Thy brother is come ;
— *because* he hath received him safe
32. *for* this thy brother was dead,
16: 3. *for* my lord taketh away from me
8. *because* he had done wisely: *for* the children of this world are
15. *for* that which is highly esteemed
24. *for* I am tormented in this flame.
25. remember *that* thou in thy lifetime
17: 9. *because* he did the things that were
10.)(We are unprofitable servants:)(we have done that which was our
15. when he saw *that* he was healed,
18: 8. I tell you *that* he will avenge them
9. trusted in themselves *that* they
11. I thank thee, *that* I am not as other
14. *for* every one that exalteth himself
29.)(There is no man that hath left house,
37. And they told him, *that* Jesus of
19: 3. *because* he was little of stature.
4. *for* he was to pass that (way).
7. *That* he was gone to be guest with
9.)(This day is salvation come to this
11. *because* they thought that the kingdom
17. *because* thou hast been faithful
21. *because* thou art an austere man:
22. Thou knewest *that* I was an austere man,
26. *That* unto every one which hath
31. *Because* the Lord hath need of him.
40. *that*, if these should hold their peace,
42.)(If thou hadst known, even thou,
43. *For* the days shall come upon thee,
20: 5.)(If we shall say, From heaven ;
19. for they perceived *that* he had spoken
21. we know *that* thou sayest and
37. Now *that* the dead are raised,
21: 3. *that* this poor widow hath cast
5. *how* it was adorned with goodly
8. saying,)(I am (Christ) ;
20. then know *that* the desolation
22. *For* these be the days of vengeance,
30. *that* summer is now nigh at hand.
31. know ye *that* the kingdom of God
32.)(This generation shall not pass away,
22:16.)(I will not any more eat thereof,
18.)(I will not drink of the fruit of the vine,
37. *that* this that is written must yet
61.)(Before the cock crow, thou shalt
70. Ye say *that* I am.
23: 5.)(He stirreth up the people,

Lu. 23: 7. as soon as he knew *that* he belonged
29. *For*, behold, the days are coming,
31. *For* if they do these things in a
40. seeing)(thou art in the same
24: 7.)(The Son of man must be delivered
21. But we trusted *that* it had been
29. *for* it is toward evening,
34.)(The Lord is risen indeed,
39. *that* it is I myself:
— *for* a spirit hath not flesh and
44. *that* all things must be fulfilled,
46.)(Thus it is written, and thus it
Joh. 1:15. *for* he was before me.
17. *For* the law was given by Moses,
20.)(I am not the Christ.
30. *for* he was before me.
32.)(I saw the Spirit descending
34. *that* this is the Son of God.
50(51). *Because* I said unto thee,
2:17. remembered *that* it was written,
18. seeing *that* thou doest these things ?
22. remembered *that* he had said
25. and)(needed not that any
3: 2. we know *that* thou art a teacher
7. Marvel not *that* I said unto thee,
11. I say unto thee,)(We speak that
18. *because* he hath not believed in
19. *that* light is come into the world,
21. *that* they are wrought in God.
23. *because* there was much water
28. *that* I said, I am not the Christ, but *that* I am sent before him.
33. hath set to his seal *that* God is true.
4: 1. When therefore the Lord knew *how* the Pharisees had heard *that* Jesus
17. Thou hast well said,)(I have no husband:
19. Sir, I perceive *that* thou art a prophet.
20. and ye say, *that* in Jerusalem
21. believe me,)(the hour cometh,
22. *for* salvation is of the Jews.
25. I know *that* Messias cometh,
27. and marvelled *that* he talked with
35. Say not ye,)(There are yet four months,
— *for* they are white already to harvest.
37.)(One soweth, and another reapeth.
39.)(He told me all that ever I did.
42.)(Now we believe, not because of
— and know *that* this is indeed
44. *that* a prophet hath no honour
47. When he heard *that* Jesus was come
51.)(Thy son liveth.
52.)(Yesterday at the seventh hour the fever
53. So the father knew *that* (it was)
—)(Thy son liveth: and himself believed,
5: 6. and knew *that* he had been now
15. and told the Jews *that* it was Jesus,
16. *because* he had done these things
18. *because* he not only had broken the
24.)(He that heareth my word,
25.)(The hour is coming, and now is,
27. *because* he is the Son of man.
28. *for* the hour is coming,
30. *because* I seek not mine own will,
32. and I know *that* the witness
36. *that* the Father hath sent me.
38. *for* whom he hath sent,
39. *for* in them ye think ye have
42. But I know you, *that* ye have not
45. Do not think *that* I will accuse
6: 2. *because* they saw his miracles
5. and saw)(a great company come
14.)(This is of a truth that prophet

Joh. 6:15. perceived *that* they would come
22. saw *that* there was none other boat
— and *that* Jesus went not with his
24. saw *that* Jesus was not there,
26. not *because* ye saw the miracles, but *because* ye did eat of the loaves,
36. unto you, *That* ye also have seen
38. *For* I came down from heaven,
41. *because* he said, I am the bread which
42.)(I came down from heaven?
46. Not *that* any man hath seen the Father,
61. knew in himself *that* his disciples
65. *that* no man can come unto me,
69. *that* thou art that Christ,
7: 1. *because* the Jews sought to kill him.
7. but me it hateth, *because* I testify of it, *that* the works thereof are evil.
8. *for* my time is not yet full come.
12. for some said,)(He is a good man:
22. not *because* it is of Moses,
23. are ye angry at me, *because* I have
26. Do the rulers know indeed *that* this
29. But I know him: *for* I am from him,
30. *because* his hour was not yet come.
31.)(When Christ cometh, will he do
35. Whither will he go, *that* we shall not
39. *because* that Jesus was not yet
42. *That* Christ cometh of the seed of
52. Search, and look: *for* out of Galilee
8:14. *for* I know whence I came,
16. *for* I am not alone,
17. *that* the testimony of two men is true.
20. *for* his hour was not yet come.
22. *because* he saith, Whither I go,
24. *that* ye shall die in your sins: for if ye believe not *that* I am (he),
27. They understood not *that* he spake
28. then shall ye know *that* I am (he),
29. *for* I do always those things that
33. how sayest thou,)(Ye shall be made free?
34.)(Whosoever committeth sin is the
37. I know *that* ye are Abraham's seed;
— *because* my word hath no place in you.
43. *because* ye cannot hear my word.
44. *because* there is no truth in him.
— *for* he is a liar, and the father of it.
45. And *because* I tell (you) the truth,
47. *because* ye are not of God.
48. Say we not well *that* thou art a
52. Now we know *that* thou hast a devil.
54. *that* he is your God:
55. and if I should say,)(I know him not,
9: 8. had seen him *that* he was blind,
9. Some said,)(This is he: others (said),)(He is like him: (but) he said,)(I am (he).
16. *because* he keepeth not the sabbath
17. *that* he hath opened thine eyes? He said,)(He is a prophet.
18. *that* he had been blind,
19. who ye say)(was born blind?
20. We know *that* this is our son, and *that* he was born blind:
22. *because* they feared the Jews:
23.)(He is of age; ask him.
24. we know *that* this man is a sinner.
25. *that*, whereas I was blind, now I see.
29. We know *that* God spake unto Moses:
30. *that* ye know not from whence he is,
31. Now we know *that* God heareth not
32. *that* any man opened the eyes of
35. Jesus heard *that* they had cast him out:

Joh. 9:41. but now ye say,)(We see;
10: 4. *for* they know his voice.
5. *for* they know not the voice of
7.)(I am the door of the sheep.
13. fleeth, *because* he is an hireling,
17. *because* I lay down my life,
33. and *because* that thou, being a man,
36.)(Thou blasphemest; *because* I said, I am the Son of God?
38. *that* the Father (is) in me,
41.)(John did no miracle:
11: 6. had heard therefore *that* he was sick,
9. *because* he seeth the light of this world.
10. *because* there is no light in him.
13. they thought *that* he had spoken of
15. for your sakes *that* I was not there,
20. as soon as she heard *that* Jesus
22. But I know, *that* even now,
24. I know *that* he shall rise again
27. I believe *that* thou art the Christ,
31. *that* she rose up hastily and
—)(She goeth unto the grave to weep
40. Said I not unto thee, *that*, if thou
41. I thank thee *that* thou hast heard me.
42. I knew *that* thou hearest me always:
— may believe *that* thou hast sent me.
47. *for* this man doeth many miracles.
50. Nor consider *that* it is expedient
51. he prophesied *that* Jesus should die
56. *that* he will not come to the feast?
12: 6. not *that* he cared for the poor; but *because* he was a thief,
9. knew *that* he was there:
11. *Because* that by reason of him
12. when they heard *that* Jesus was coming
16. remembered they *that* these things
18. *for that* they heard that he had
19. Perceive ye *how* ye prevail nothing?
34. *that* Christ abideth for ever: and how sayest thou,)(The Son of man
39. *because* that Esaias said again,
49. *For* I have not spoken of myself;
50. I know *that* his commandment is
13: 1. when Jesus knew *that* his hour was
3. Jesus knowing *that* the Father
— and *that* he was come from God,
19. ye may believe *that* I am (he).
21. *that* one of you shall betray me.
29. *that* Jesus had said unto him, Buy
33.)(Whither I go, ye cannot come;
35. *that* ye are my disciples.
14:10. Believest thou not *that* I am in
11. Believe me *that* I (am) in the Father,
12. *because* I go unto my Father.
17. *because* it seeth him not,
— *for* he dwelleth with you, and
19. *because* I live, ye shall live also.
20. *that* I (am) in my Father,
22. how is it *that* thou wilt manifest
28. Ye have heard *how* I said unto you,
— *because* I said, I go unto the Father: *for* my Father is greater than I.
31. may know *that* I love the Father;
15: 5. *for* without me ye can do nothing.
15. *for* the servant knoweth not what
— *for* all things that I have heard
18. ye know *that* it hated me before
19. but *because* ye are not of the world,
21. *because* they know not him that sent me.
25.)(They hated me without a cause.
27. *because* ye have been with me from
16: 3. *because* they have not known the Father,

Joh.16: 4. remember *that* I told you of them.
— *because* I was with you.
6. But *because* I have said these things
9. *because* they believe not on me;
10. *because* I go to my Father,
11 *because* the prince of this world is judged.
14. *for* he shall receive of mine,
15. *that* he shall take of mine,
16. *because* I go to the Father.
17. *Because* I go to the Father?
19. Jesus knew *that* they were desirous
— enquire among yourselves of that)(I said,
20. *That* ye shall weep and lament,
21. *because* her hour is come:
— for joy *that* a man is born
23.)(Whatsoever ye shall ask the Father in
26. *that* I will pray the Father for you:
27. *because* ye have loved me, and have
believed *that* I came out from God.
30. Now are we sure *that* thou knowest
— by this we believe *that* thou camest
32. *because* the Father is with me.
17: 7. Now they have known *that* all things
8. *For* I have given unto them the words
which
— *that* I came out from thee, and they have
believed *that* thou didst send me.
9. *for* they are thine.
14. *because* they are not of the world,
21. that the world may believe *that* thou
23. may know *that* thou hast sent me,
24. *for* thou lovedst me before the foundation
25. and these have known *that* thou hast
18: 2. *for* Jesus ofttimes resorted thither
6. had said unto them,)(I am (he),
8. I have told you *that* I am (he):
9.)(Of them which thou gavest me
14. *that* it was expedient that one man
18. *for* it was cold:
37. Thou sayest *that* I am a king.
19: 4. that ye may know *that* I find no fault
7. *because* he made himself the Son of God.
10. *that* I have power to crucify thee,
20. *for* the place where Jesus was crucified
21. but *that* he said, I am King of the Jews.
28. Jesus knowing *that* all things were now
35. he knoweth *that* he saith true,
42. *for* the sepulchre was nigh
20: 9. *that* he must rise again
13. *Because* they have taken away my Lord,
14. and knew not *that* it was Jesus.
15. She, supposing)(him to be the gardener,
18. *that* she had seen the Lord,
29. Thomas, *because* thou hast seen me,
31. that ye might believe *that* Jesus
21: 4. the disciples knew not *that* it was Jesus.
7. Peter heard *that* it was the Lord,
12. knowing *that* it was the Lord.
15. thou knowest *that* I love thee.
16. thou knowest *that* I love thee.
17. Peter was grieved *because* he said
— thou knowest *that* I love thee.
23. *that* that disciple should not die: yet Jesus
said unto him,)(He shall not die;
24. we know *that* his testimony is true.
Acts 1: 5. *For* John truly baptized with water;
17. *For* he was numbered with us,
2: 6. *because* that every man heard them
13. said,)(These men are full of new wine.
25. *for* he is on my right hand, that
27. *Because* thou wilt not leave my soul
29. *that* he is both dead and buried,

Acts 2:30. and knowing *that* God had sworn
31. *that* his soul was not left in hell,
36. *that* God hath made that same Jesus,
3:10. they knew *that* it was he which
17. I wot *that* through ignorance ye did (it),
22.)(A prophet shall the Lord your God
4:10. *that* by the name of Jesus Christ
13. perceived *that* they were unlearned
— *that* they had been with Jesus.
16. for *that* indeed a notable miracle
21. *for* all (men) glorified God for
5: 4. why)(hast thou conceived this thing
9. How is it *that* ye have agreed
23.)(The prison truly found we shut
25.)(Behold, the men whom ye put in
38. *for* if this counsel or this work
41. rejoicing *that* they were counted worthy
6: 1. *because* their widows were neglected
11.)(We have heard him speak blasphemous
14. *that* this Jesus of Nazareth shall
7: 6. *That* his seed should sojourn in
25. *how that* God by his hand would
8:14. heard *that* Samaria had received .
18. when Simon saw *that* through laying on
20. *because* thou hast thought that the
33. *for* his life is taken from the earth.
9:15. *for* he is a chosen vessel unto me,
20. *that* he is the Son of God.
22. proving *that* this is very Christ.
26. and believed not *that* he was a disciple.
27. and *that* he had spoken to him,
38. had heard *that* Peter was there,
10:14. *for* I have never eaten any thing that is
34. I perceive *that* God is no respecter
38. *for* God was with him.
42. and to testify *that* it is he
45. *because that* on the Gentiles also
11: 1. heard *that* the Gentiles had also
3.)(Thou wentest in to men uncircumcised,
8. *for* nothing common or unclean
24. *For* he was a good man,
12: 3. And because he saw)(it pleased the Jews,
9. and wist not *that* it was true
11. *that* the Lord hath sent his angel,
13:32. glad tidings, *how that* the promise
34. And *as concerning that* he raised
—)(I will give you the sure mercies of
David.
38. *that* through this man is preached
41. *for* I work a work in your days,
14: 9. perceiving *that* he had faith to be
22. and *that* we must through much
27. and *how* he had opened the door of faith
15: 1.)(Except ye be circumcised
5. *That* it was needful to circumcise
7. ye know *how that* a good while ago
24. *that* certain which went out from us
16: 3. for they knew all *that* his father
10. assuredly gathering *that* the Lord
19. when her masters saw *that* the hope
36.)(The magistrates have sent to let
38. when they heard *that* they were Romans.
17: 3. *that* Christ must needs have suffered,
— and *that* this Jesus, whom I preach
6.)(These that have turned the world
13. had knowledge *that* the word of God
18. *because* he preached unto them Jesus,
18:13.)(This (fellow) persuadeth men to
19:21.)(After I have been there, I must
25. ye know *that* by this craft we have our
26. *that* not alone at Ephesus, but
— saying *that* they be no gods,

Acts19:34. But when they knew *that* he was a Jew,
20:23. Save *that* the Holy Ghost witnesseth in every city, saying *that* bonds
25. I know *that* ye all, among whom
26. to record this day, *that* I (am) pure from
29. For I know this, *that* after my
31. remember, *that* by the space of three
34. *that* these hands have ministered
35. *how that* so labouring ye ought
— *how* he said, It is more blessed
38. *that* they should see his face no more.
21:21. *that* thou teachest all the Jews
22. for they will hear *that* thou art come.
24. *that* those things, whereof they
29. whom they supposed *that* Paul had
31. *that* all Jerusalem was in an uproar.
22: 2. when they heard *that* he spake in
15. *For* thou shalt be his witness
19. Lord, they know *that* I imprisoned
21. Depart: *for* I will send thee far hence
29. after he knew *that* he was a Roman, and *because* he had bound him.
23: 5. I wist not, brethren, *that* he was
6. when Paul perceived *that* the one part
20.)(The Jews have agreed to desire thee
22. tell no man *that* thou hast shewed
27. having understood *that* he was a Roman.
34. understood *that* (he was) of Cilicia ;
24:11. understand, *that* there are yet
14. *that* after the way which they
21.)(Touching the resurrection
26. He hoped also *that* money should
25: 8.)(Neither against the law of the Jews,
16.)(It is not the manner of the Romans
26: 5. *that* after the most straitest sect
27. I know *that* thou believest.
31.)(This man doeth nothing worthy of death
27:10. I perceive *that* this voyage will
25. *that* it shall be even as
28: 1. then they knew *that* the island
22. *that* every where it is spoken against.
25.)(Well spake the Holy Ghost
28. *that* the salvation of God is sent
Ro. 1: 8. *that* your faith is spoken of
13. *that* oftentimes I purposed to
32. *that* they which commit such
2: 2. we are sure *that* the judgment
3. *that* thou shalt escape the judgment
4. not knowing *that* the goodness of God
3: 2. because *that* unto them were
8.)(Let us do evil,
10.)(There is none righteous, no, not one:
19. *that* what things soever the law saith,
4: 9. for we say *that* faith was reckoned
17.)(I have made thee a father of many
21. being fully persuaded *that*, what
23. *that* it was imputed to him ;
5: 3. knowing *that* tribulation worketh
5. *because* the love of God is shed
8. *in that*, while we were yet sinners,
6: 3. Know ye not, *that* so many of us
6. Knowing this, *that* our old man
8. believe *that* we shall also live
9. Knowing *that* Christ being raised
15. *because* we are not under the law,
16. Know ye not, *that* to whom ye yield
17. But God be thanked, *that* ye were
7: 1. *how that* the law hath dominion
14. For we know *that* the law is spiritual:
16. I consent unto the law *that* (it is) good.
18. For I know *that* in me

Ro. 7:21. *that*, when I would do good, evil is
8:16. *that* we are the children of God:
18. For I reckon *that* the sufferings
21. *Because* the creature itself also
22. For we know *that* the whole creation
27. *because* he maketh intercession
28. we know *that* all things work
29. *For* whom he did foreknow,
36. *For* thy sake we are killed
38. For I am persuaded, *that* neither
9: 2. *That* I have great heaviness and
6. Not as *though* the word of God
7. Neither, *because* they are the seed
12.)(The elder shall serve the younger.
17.)(Even for this same purpose have I
28. *because* a short work will the Lord
30. *That* the Gentiles, which followed not
32. *Because* (they sought it) not by faith,
10: 2. *that* they have a zeal of God,
5. *That* the man which doeth those things
9. *That* if thou shalt confess with thy
— *that* God hath raised him from the
11:25. *that* blindness in part is happened
36. *For* of him, and through him, and to him,
13:11. *that* now (it is) high time to awake
14:11.)(every knee shall bow to me,
14. *that* (there is) nothing unclean of:
23. *because* (he eateth) not of faith:
15:14. *that* ye also are full of goodness,
29. And I am sure *that*, when I come
1Co. 1: 5. *That* in every thing ye are enriched
11. *that* there are contentions among you.
12. *that* every one of you saith,
14. *that* I baptized none of you, but
15. Lest any should say *that* I had
25. *Because* the foolishness of God is wiser
26. *how that* not many wise men
2:14. *because* they are spiritually
3:13. *because* it shall be revealed by fire ;
16. Know ye not *that* ye are the temple
20. thoughts of the wise, *that* they are vain.
4: 9. For I think *that* God hath set forth
— *for* we are made a spectacle unto
5: 6. Know ye not *that* a little leaven
6: 2. Do ye not know *that* the saints
3. Know ye not *that* we shall judge
7. *because* ye go to law one with another.
9. Know ye not *that* the unrighteous
15. Know ye not *that* your bodies
16. know ye not *that* he which is joined
19. know ye not *that* your body is
7:26. *that* (it is) good for a man so to be.
8: 1. we know *that* we all have knowledge.
4. we know *that* an idol (is) nothing
— *that* (there is) none other God but one.
9:10. *that* he that ploweth should
13. Do ye not know *that* they which
24. Know ye not *that* they which run
10: 1. be ignorant, *how that* all our fathers
17. *For* we (being) many are one bread,
19. What say I then ? *that* the idol is any thing, or)(that which is offered
20. But (I say), *that* the things which the
11: 2. *that* ye remember me in all things,
3. *that* the head of every man is Christ ;
14. *that*, if a man have long hair,
15. *for* (her) hair is given her for a
17. I praise (you) not, *that* ye come together
23. *That* the Lord Jesus the (same) night
12: 2. Ye know *that* ye were Gentiles,
3. *that* no man speaking by the Spirit
15. *Because* I am not the hand,

1 Co. 12:16. *Because* I am not the eye,
14:21.)(With (men of) other tongues
23. will they not say *that* ye are mad?
25. and report *that* God is in you
37. *that* the things that I write
15: 3. *how that* Christ died for our sins
4. And *that* he was buried, and *that* he rose again the third day
5. And *that* he was seen of Cephas,
12. Now if Christ be preached *that* he rose
— *that* there is no resurrection
15. *because* we have testified of God *that* he raised up Christ:
27. But when he saith,)(All things are put under (him, it is) manifest *that* he is
50. *that* flesh and blood cannot inherit
58. ye know *that* your labour is not
16:15. *that* it is the firstfruits of Achaia,
17. *for* that which was lacking
2 Co. 1: 5. *For* as the sufferings of Christ
7. knowing, *that* as ye are partakers
8. *that* we were pressed out of measure,
10. in whom we trust *that* he will yet
12. *that* in simplicity and godly sincerity,
13. and I trust)(ye shall acknowledge
14. *that* we are your rejoicing,
18. But (as) God (is) true,)(our word toward you
23. *that* to spare you I came not as yet
24. Not *for that* we have dominion over
2: 3. *that* my joy is (the joy) of you all.
15. *For* we are unto God a sweet savour
3: 3. manifestly declared)(to be the epistle
5. Not *that* we are sufficient of ourselves
4: 6. *For* God, who commanded the light
14. Knowing *that* he which raised up
5: 1. *For* we know *that* if our earthly
6. knowing *that*, whilst we are
14(15). because we thus judge, *that* if one died
19. To wit, *that* God was in Christ,
6:16. as God hath said,)(I will dwell in them,
7: 3. *that* ye are in our hearts to die
8. *For* though I made you sorry with
— for I perceive *that* the same epistle
9. not *that* ye were made sorry, but *that* ye sorrowed to repentance:
13. *because* his spirit was refreshed
14. *For* if I have boasted any thing
16. *that* I have confidence in you in all
8: 2. *How that* in a great trial of affliction
3. *For* to (their) power, I bear record,
9. *that*, though he was rich, yet for
17. *For* indeed he accepted the
9: 2. *that* Achaia was ready a year ago;
12. *For* the administration of this
10: 7. *that*, as he (is) Christ's, even so
10. *For* (his) letters, say they, (are) weighty
11. *that*, such as we are in word by
11: 7. *because* I have preached to you
10.)(no man shall stop me of this
11. Wherefore? *because* I love you not?
21. as *though* we had been weak.
31. knoweth *that* I lie not.
12: 4. *How that* he was caught up into
13. *that* I myself was not burdensome
19. think ye *that* we excuse ourselves
13: 2. *that*, if I come again, I will not spare:
5. *how that* Jesus Christ is in you,
6. But I trust *that* ye shall know *that* we are not reprobates.
Gal. 1: 6. I marvel *that* ye are so soon
11. *that* the gospel which was preached

Gal. 1:13. *how that* beyond measure I persecuted
20. behold, before God,)(I lie not.
23. *That* he which persecuted us
2: 7. when they saw *that* the gospel of the
11. *because* he was to be blamed.
14. But when I saw *that* they walked not
16. Knowing *that* a man is not justified
3: 7. *that* they which are of faith,
8. foreseeing *that* God would justify
—)(In thee shall all nations be blessed.
11. But *that* no man is justified by
— *for*, The just shall live by faith.
4: 6. And *because* ye are sons,
12. *for* I (am) as ye
13. Ye know *how* through infirmity
15. for I bear you record, *that*, if
20. *for* I stand in doubt of you.
22. *that* Abraham had two sons,
27. *for* the desolate hath many more
5: 2. *that* if ye be circumcised,
3. *that* he is a debtor to do
10. *that* ye will be none otherwise minded:
21. *that* they which do such things
6: 8. *For* he that soweth to his flesh
Eph. 2:11. *that* ye (being) in time past Gentiles
12. *That* at that time ye were without Christ
18. *For* through him we both have access
3: 3. *How that* by revelation
4: 9. what is it but *that* he also descended
25. *for* we are members one of another.
5: 5. *that* no whoremonger, nor unclean person,
16. *because* the days are evil.
23. *For* the husband is the head of
30. *For* we are members of his body,
6: 8. Knowing *that* whatsoever good
9. knowing *that* your Master also
12. *For* we wrestle not against flesh
Phi. 1: 6. *that* he which hath begun a good work
12. *that* the things (which happened)
17. knowing *that* I am set for the
19. For I know *that* this shall turn
20. *that* in nothing I shall be ashamed,
25. know *that* I shall abide
27. *that* ye stand fast in one spirit,
29. *For* unto you it is given
2:11. *that* Jesus Christ (is) Lord,
16. *that* I have not run in vain,
22. *that*, as a son with the father,
24. *that* I also myself shall come shortly.
26. ye had heard *that* he had been sick.
30. *Because* for the work of Christ
3:12. Not *as though* I had already attained,
4:10. *that* now at the last your care of me
11. Not *that* I speak in respect of want:
15. *that* in the beginning of the gospel,
16. *For* even in Thessalonica ye sent
17. Not *because* I desire a gift:
Col. 1:16. *For* by him were all things created,
19. *For* it pleased (the Father) that
2: 9. *For* in him dwelleth all the fulness
3:24. Knowing *that* of the Lord ye shall
4: 1. knowing *that* ye also have a Master
13. *that* he hath a great zeal for you,
1 Th. 1: 5. *For* our gospel came not unto you
2: 1. *that* it was not in vain:
13. *because*, when ye received the word
14. *for* ye also have suffered like things
3: 3. know *that* we are appointed thereunto.
4. *that* we should suffer tribulation;
6. and *that* ye have good remembrance
8. *For* now we live, if ye stand fast
4:14. For if we believe *that* Jesus died

1 Th. 4:15. *that* we which are alive (and) remain
16. *For* the Lord himself shall descend
5: 2. *that* the day of the Lord so cometh
9. *For* God hath not appointed us to wrath,
2 Th. 1: 3. *because that* your faith groweth
10. *because* our testimony among you
2: 2. as *that* the day of Christ is at hand.
3. *for* (that day shall not come), except
4. shewing himself *that* he is God.
5. *that*, when I was yet with you,
13. *because* God hath from the beginning
3: 4. *that* ye both do and will do
7. *for* we behaved not ourselves
9. Not *because* we have not power,
10. *that* if any would not work,
1 Ti. 1: 8. But we know *that* the law (is) good,
9. *that* the law is not made for
12. *for that* he counted me faithful,
13. *because* I did (it) ignorantly
15. *that* Christ Jesus came into
4: 1. *that* in the latter times some
4. *For* every creature of God (is) good,
10. *because* we trust in the living God,
5:12. *because* they have cast off their
6: 2. *because* they are brethren ;
— *because* they are faithful
7. (it is) certain)(we can carry nothing out.
2 Ti. 1: 5. I am persuaded *that* in thee also.
12. persuaded *that* he is able to keep
15. *that* all they which are in Asia
16. *for* he oft refreshed me,
2:23. knowing *that* they do gender strifes.
3: 1. *that* in the last days perilous
15. And *that* from a child
Tit. 3:11. Knowing *that* he that is such
Philem. 7. *because* the bowels of the saints
19. I do not say to thee *how* thou owest
21. knowing *that* thou wilt also do
22. for I trust *that* through your prayers
Heb 2: 6. What is man, *that* thou art mindful
— *that* thou visitest him ?
3:19. we see *that* they could not enter
7: 8. of whom it is witnessed *that* he liveth.
14. For (it is) evident *that* our Lord
17.)(Thou (art) a priest for ever
8: 9. *because* they continued not in my
10. *For* this (is) the covenant that I will
11. *for* all shall know me,
12. *For* I will be merciful to their
10: 8.)(Sacrifice and offering and
11: 6. must believe *that* he is,
13. confessed *that* they were strangers
14. declare plainly *that* they seek a
18. *That* in Isaac shall thy seed be called:
19. Accounting *that* God (was) able
12:17. For ye know *how that* afterward,
13:18. for we trust)(we have a good conscience,
Jas. 1: 3. *that* the trying of your faith
7. let not that man think *that* he
10. *because* as the flower of the grass
12. *for* when he is tried,
13.)(I am tempted of God :
23. *For* if any be a hearer of the word,
2:19. Thou believest *that* there is one God ;
20. *that* faith without works is dead?
22. Seest thou *how* faith wrought
24. Ye see then *how that* by works
3: 1. knowing *that* we shall receive
4: 4. *that* the friendship of the world
5. Do ye think *that* the scripture
5: 8. *for* the coming of the Lord draweth nigh.
11. *that* the Lord is very pitiful, and of tender

Jas. 5:20. *that* he which converteth the sinner
1 Pet. 1:12. *that* not unto themselves, but
16. Be ye holy ; *for* I am holy.
18. *that* ye were not redeemed with
2: 3. tasted *that* the Lord (is) gracious.
15. *For* so is the will of God,
21. *because* Christ also suffered
3: 9. knowing *that* ye are thereunto called,
12. *For* the eyes of the Lord (are) over
18. *For* Christ also hath once suffered
4: 1. *for* he that hath suffered in the
8. *for* charity shall cover the
14. *for* the spirit of glory and of God
17. *For* the time (is come) that judgment
5: 5. *for* God resisteth the proud,
7. *for* he careth for you.
8. *because* your adversary the devil,
2 Pet. 1:14. Knowing *that* shortly I must put off
20. *that* no prophecy of the scripture
3: 3. *that* there shall come in the last days
5. *that* by the word of God
8. *that* one day (is) with the Lord as
1 Joh. 1: 5. *that* God is light,
6. If we say *that* we have fellowship
8. If we say *that* we have no sin,
10. If we say *that* we have not sinned,
2: 3. hereby we do know *that* we know him,
5. hereby know we *that* we are in him.
8. *because* the darkness is past,
11. *because that* darkness hath blinded
12. *because* your sins are forgiven
13. *because* ye have known him
— *because* ye have overcome
— *because* ye have known the Father.
14. *because* ye have known him
— *because* ye are strong,
16. *For* all that (is) in the world,
18. as ye have heard *that* antichrist
— we know *that* it is the last time.
19. *that* they were not all of us.
21. *because* ye know not the truth, but *because*
ye know it, and *that* no lie is
22. that denieth *that* Jesus is the Christ?
29. If ye know *that* he is righteous, ye know
that every one that
3: 1. *because* it knew him not.
2. we know *that*, when he shall appear,
— *for* we shall see him as he is.
5. And ye know *that* he was manifested
8. *for* the devil sinneth from the
9. *for* his seed remaineth in him:
— *because* he is born of God.
11. *For* this is the message that
12. *Because* his own works were evil,
14. We know *that* we have passed from death
unto life, *because* we love the
15. and ye know *that* no murderer
16. *because* he laid down his life
19. we know *that* we are of the truth,
20. *For* if our heart condemn us,)(God is
greater than
22. *because* we keep his commandments,
24. we know *that* he abideth in us,
4: 1. *because* many false prophets
3. ye have heard *that* it should come ;
4. *because* greater is he that is in you,
7. *for* love is of God ;
8. *for* God is love.
9. *because that* God sent his only
10. not *that* we loved God, but *that* he loved
us,
13. know we *that* we dwell in him,

1Joh.4:13. *because* he hath given us of his Spirit.
14. *that* the Father sent the Son
15. shall confess *that* Jesus is the Son
17. *because* as he is, so are we in
18. *because* fear hath torment.
19. *because* he first loved us.
20. If a man say,)(I love God,
5: 1. Whosoever believeth *that* Jesus
2. By this we know *that* we love
4. *For* whatsoever is born of God
5. but he that believeth *that* Jesus
6. *because* the Spirit is truth.
7. *For* there are three that bear record
9. *for* this is the witness of God
10. *because* he believeth not the
11. *that* God hath given to us eternal life,
13. may know *that* ye have eternal
14. *that*, if we ask any thing according
15. if we know *that* he hear us,
— we know *that* we have the petitions
18. We know *that* whosoever is born of
19. we know *that* we are of God,
20. we know *that* the Son of God is come,
2Joh.　　4. *that* I found of thy children
7. *For* many deceivers are entered
3Joh.　12. and ye know *that* our record is true.
Jude　　5. *how that* the Lord, having saved
11. *for* they have gone in the way of Cajn,
18. *How that* they told you)(there should be mockers in the
Rev. 2: 2. and *how* thou canst not bear
4. *because* thou hast left thy first love.
6. *that* thou hatest the deeds of
14. *because* thou hast there them
20. *because* thou sufferest that woman
23. the churches shall know *that* I am he
3: 1. *that* thou hast a name *that* thou livest, and art dead.
4. *for* they are worthy.
8. *for* thou hast a little strength,
9. and to know *that* I have loved thee.
10. *Because* thou hast kept the word
15. *that* thou art neither cold nor hot:
16. So then *because* thou art lukewarm,
17. *Because* thou sayest,)(I am rich,
— knowest not *that* thou art wretched,
4:11. *for* thou hast created all things,
5: 4. *because* no man was found worthy
9. *for* thou wast slain,
6:17. *For* the great day of his wrath is
7:17. *For* the Lamb which is in the
8:11. *because* they were made bitter.
10: 6. *that* there should be time no longer:
11: 2. *for* it is given unto the Gentiles:
10. *because* these two prophets
17. *because* thou hast taken to thee
12:10. *for* the accuser of our brethren is cast
12. *for* the devil is come down
— knoweth *that* he hath but a short time.
13. when the dragon saw *that* he was cast
14: 7. *for* the hour of his judgment is come:
8. *because* she made all nations drink
15. *for* the time is come for thee to reap ; *for* the harvest of the earth is ripe.
18. *for* her grapes are fully ripe.
15: 1. *for* in them is filled up the wrath of God:
4. *for* (thou) only (art) holy: *for* all nations shall come and worship before thee ; *for* thy judgments are made
16: 5. *because* thou hast judged thus.
6. *For* they have shed the blood of saints
21. *for* the plague thereof was exceeding

Rev.17.14. *for* he is Lord of lords, and
18: 3. *For* all nations have drunk
5. *For* her sins have reached unto
7. *for* she saith in her heart,
8. *for* strong (is) the Lord God who
10. *for* in one hour is thy judgment
11. *for* no man buyeth their merchandise
17(16). *For* in one hour so great riches
19. *for* in one hour is she made
20. *for* God hath avenged you on her.
23. *for* thy merchants were the great
— *for* by thy sorceries were all
19: 2. *For* true and righteous (are) his judgments: *for* he hath judged the great
6. *for* the Lord God omnipotent reigneth.
7. *for* the marriage of the Lamb is come,
21: 4. *for* the former things are passed away.
5. *for* these words are true and
22: 5. *for* the Lord God giveth them light:
10. *for* the time is at hand.

ὅτου, *hotou*, for οὗτινος, gen. of ὅστις.

It is combined with ἕως, and has χρόνον understood.

Mat. 5:25. *whiles* thou art in the way with
Lu. 13: 8. till)(I shall dig about it, and dung
15: 8. seek diligently till)(she find (it) ?
22:16. until)(it be fulfilled in thee
18. until)(the kingdom of God shall come.
Joh. 9:18. until)(they called the parents

οὗ, *hou*. adv. of place.

Mat. 2: 9. and stood over *where* the young child
18:20. For *where* two or three are gathered
28:16. *where* Jesus had appointed them.
Lu. 4:16. *where* he had been brought up:
17. found the place *where* it was written,
10: 1. *whither* he himself would come.
22:10. into the house *where* he entereth in.
23:53. *wherein* never man before was laid.
24:28. unto the village, *whither* they went:
Joh.11:41. *where* the dead was laid.
Acts 1:13. *where* abode both Peter, and James,
2: 2. it filled all the house *where* they were sitting.
7:29. *where* he begat two sons.
12:12. *where* many were gathered
16:13. *where* prayer was wont to be made;
20: 6. *where* we abode seven days.
8. *where* they were gathered together.
25:10. *where* I ought to be judged:
28:14. *Where* we found brethren, and
Ro. 4:15. for *where* no law is, (there is) no
5:20. But *where* sin abounded, grace did
9:26. in the place *where* it was said
1Co.16: 6. on my journey *whithersoever* I go.
2Co. 3:17. and *where* the Spirit of the Lord (is),
Col. 3: 1. *where* Christ sitteth on the right hand
Heb 3: 9. When (lit. *where*) your fathers tempted
Rev 17:15. *where* the whore sitteth,

οὐ, οὐκ, οὐχ, *ou, ouk, ouk.*

Those passages in which it is combined with μή, as a strong double negation, will be found above in the series οὐ μή ; and for those in which it is closely combined with ἔτι, see οὐκέτι. ‖ shews that it is combined with another negative in the Greek.

Mat. 1:25. And knew her *not* till she had
2:18. and would *not* be comforted, because they are *not*.
3:11. whose shoes I am *not* worthy to bear:
4: 4. Man shall *not* live by bread alone,
   7. Thou shalt *not* tempt the Lord
5:14. A city that is set on an hill can*not* be hid.
  17. I am *not* come to destroy, but
  21. Thou shalt *not* kill;
  27. Thou shalt *not* commit adultery:
  33. Thou shalt *not* forswear thyself,
  36. because thou canst *not* make one hair
  37. Yea, yea; *Nay, nay:*
6: 1. otherwise ye have *no* reward of
  5. thou shalt *not* be as the hypocrites
  20. where thieves do *not* break through
  24. Ye can*not* serve God and
  26. for they sow *not*, neither do
  — Are ye *not* much better than they?
  28. they toil *not*, neither do they spin:
  30. (shall he) *not* much more (clothe)
7: 3. considerest *not* the beam
  18. A good tree can*not* bring forth
  21. *Not* every one that saith unto me,
  22. have we *not* prophesied in thy name?
  25. and it fell *not:*
  29. and *not* as the scribes.
8: 8. I am *not* worthy that thou
  20. the Son of man hath *not* where to
9:12. need *not* a physician,
  13. and *not* sacrifice: for I am *not* come to
  14. but thy disciples fast *not?*
  24. for the maid is *not* dead, but sleepeth.
10:20. For it is *not* ye that speak,
  24. The disciple is *not* above (his)
  26. nothing covered, that shall *not* be revealed; and hid, that shall *not* be known.
  29. and one of them shall *not* fall
  34. I came *not* to send peace, but
  37. is *not* worthy of me:
  — is *not* worthy of me.
  38. he that taketh *not* his cross,
  — is *not* worthy of me.
11:11. there hath *not* risen a greater
  17. and ye have *not* danced;
  — and ye have *not* lamented.
  20. because they repented *not :*
12. 2. do that which is *not* lawful
  3. Have ye *not* read what David did,
  4. which was *not* lawful for him
  5. Or have ye *not* read in the law,
  7. I will have mercy, and *not* sacrifice, ye would *not* have condemned
  19. He shall *not* strive, nor cry;
  20. shall he *not* break, and smoking flax shall he *not* quench,
  24. doth *not* cast out devils, but by
  25. against itself shall *not* stand:
  31. shall *not* be forgiven unto men.
  32. it shall *not* be forgiven him,
  39. and there shall *no* sign be given
  43. seeking rest, and findeth *none.*
13: 5. where they had *not* much earth:
  11. but to them it is *not* given.
  12. but whosoever hath *not*,
  13. because they seeing see *not ;* and hearing they hear *not*,
  17. and have *not* seen (them);

Mat.13:17. and have *not* heard (them).
  21. Yet hath he *not* root in himself,
  29. But he said, *Nay;* lest while
  34. without a parable spake he *not* unto them:
  55. Is *not* this the carpenter's son?
  57. A prophet is *not* without honour,
  58. And he did *not* many mighty works
14: 4. It is *not* lawful for thee to have her.
  16. They need *not* depart;
  17. We have here but (lit. we have *not* here except) five loaves,
15: 2. for they wash *not* their hands when
  11. *Not* that which goeth into the mouth
  13. hath *not* planted, shall be rooted up.
  20. defileth *not* a man.
  23. he answered her *not* a word.
  24. I am *not* sent but unto the lost
  26. It is *not* meet to take the children's
  32. and have *nothing* to eat (lit. *not* any-thing): and I will *not* send them away fasting,
16: 3. but can ye *not* (discern) the signs
  4. there shall *no* sign be given unto it,
  7. because we have taken *no* bread.
  8. because ye have brought *no* bread?
  11. How is it that ye do *not* understand that I spake (it) *not* to you
  12. how that he bade (them) *not* beware
  17. flesh and blood hath *not* revealed
  18. and the gates of hell shall *not* prevail
  23. for thou savourest *not* the things
17:12. and they knew him *not*,
  16. and they could *not* cure him.
  19. Why could *not* we cast him out?
  21. this kind goeth *not* out but by
  24. Doth *not* your master pay tribute?
18:14. it is *not* the will of your Father
  22. I say *not* unto thee, Until seven times:
  30. And he would *not:*
  33. Shouldest *not* thou also have had
19: 4. Have ye *not* read, that he which
  8. from the beginning it was *not* so.
  10. it is *not* good to marry.
  11. All (men) can*not* receive this
  18. thou shalt do *no* murder, Thou shalt *not* commit adultery, Thou shalt *not* steal, Thou shalt *not* bear false witness,
20:13. I do thee *no* wrong:
  15. Is it *not* lawful for me to do
  22. Ye know *not* what ye ask.
  23. is *not* mine to give,
  26. But it shall *not* be so among you:
  28. the Son of man came *not* to be
21:21. ye shall *not* only do this
  25. Why did ye *not* then believe him?
  27. We can*not* tell.
  29. and said, I will *not:* but
  30. I (go), sir: and went *not.*
  32. and ye believed him *not:*
  — repented *not* afterward, that ye
22: 3. and they would *not* come.
  8. which were bidden were *not* worthy.
  11. which had *not* on a wedding
  16. *neither* ‖ carest thou for any (man): for thou regardest *not* the person of men.
  17. to give tribute unto Cæsar, or *not?*
  31. have ye *not* read that which was spoken
  32. God is *not* the God of the dead,
23: 3. for they say, and do *not.*
  4. will *not* move them with one
  13(14). for ye *neither* go in (yourselves),
  30. we would *not* have been partakers

Mat.23:37. and ye would *not!*
24: 2. See ye *not* all these things?
21. such as was *not* since the beginning
22. there should *no* flesh be saved:
29. the moon shall *not* give her light,
39. And knew *not* until the flood came,
42. for ye know *not* what hour your Lord
43. would *not* have suffered his house
44. in such an hour as ye think *not*
50. in a day when he looketh *not* for (him),
and in an hour that he is *not* aware of,
25: 3. and took *no* oil with them:
9. lest there be *not* enough for us
12. I know you *not.*
13. for ye know *neither* the day
24. reaping where thou hast *not* sown, and
gathering where thou hast *not* strawed:
26. that I reap where I sowed *not,* and gather
where I have *not* strawed:
42. and ye gave me *no* meat: I was thirsty,
and ye gave me *no* drink:
43. and ye took me *not* in: naked, and ye
clothed me *not:* sick, and in prison,
and ye visited me *not.*
44. and did *not* minister unto thee?
45. as ye did (it) *not* to one of the least
26:11. but me ye have *not* always.
24. if he had *not* been born.
39. nevertheless *not* as I will,
40. What, could ye *not* watch with me
42. if this cup may *not* pass away
53. Thinkest thou that I can*not* now
55. and ye laid *no* hold on me.
60. But found *none:*
— (yet) found they *none.*
70. I know *not* what thou sayest.
72. I do *not* know the man.
74. I know *not* the man.
27: 6. It is *not* lawful for to put them into
13. Hearest thou *not* how many things
14. he answered)(‖ him to never a word ;
34. he would *not* drink.
42. himself he can*not* save.
28: 6. He is *not* here:
Mar 1: 7. I am *not* worthy to stoop down
22. and *not* as the scribes.
34. and suffered *not* the devils to speak,
2:17. They that are whole have *no* need
— I came *not* to call the righteous,
18. but thy disciples fast *not?*
19. bridegroom with them, they can*not* fast.
24. that which is *not* lawful?
26. which is *not* lawful to eat
27. and *not* man for the sabbath.
3:24. that kingdom can*not* stand.
25. that house can*not* stand.
26. he can*not* stand, but hath an end.
27. No man can)(‖ enter into a strong
29. hath *never* forgiveness, but is in danger
4: 5. where it had *not* much earth ;
7. and it yielded *no* fruit.
13. Know ye *not* this parable?
17. have *no* root in themselves,
21. and *not* to be set on a candlestick?
22. For there is *nothing* hid, which
25. and he that hath *not,* from him shall
27. he knoweth *not* how.
34. without a parable spake he *not* unto them:
38. Master, carest thou *not* that we
40. how is it that ye have *no* faith?
5:19. Jesus suffered him *not,*
37. he suffered)(‖ no man to follow him,

Mar 5:39. the damsel is *not* dead, but
6: 3. Is *not* this the carpenter,
— and are *not* his sisters here
4. A prophet is *not* without honour,
5. he could there)(‖ do no mighty work,
18. It is *not* lawful for thee to have
19. but she could *not :*
26. he would *not* reject her.
36. for they have *nothing* to eat.
52. they considered *not* (the miracle)
7: 3. except they wash (their) hands oft, eat
not,
4. except they wash, they eat *not.*
5. Why walk *not* thy disciples according
18. Do ye *not* perceive,
— (it) can*not* defile him ;
19. Because it entereth *not* into
24. but he could *not* be hid.
27. for it is *not* meet to take the
8: 2. and have *nothing* to eat:
14. *neither* had they (lit. and they had *not*) in
the ship
16. because we have *no* bread.
17. because ye have *no* bread?
18. Having eyes, see ye *not?* and having ears,
hear ye *not?* and do ye *not* remember?
21. How is it that ye do *not* understand?
33. thou savourest *not* the things
9: 3. so as *no* fuller on earth can
6. For he wist *not* what to say ;
18. and they could *not.*
28. Why could *not* we cast him out?
30. and he would *not* that any man
37. receiveth *not* me, but him that
38. and he followeth *not* us:
— because he followeth *not* us.
40. For he that is *not* against us
44. Where their worm dieth *not,* and the fire
is *not* quenched.
46. Where their worm dieth *not,* and the fire
is *not* quenched.
48. Where their worm dieth *not,* and the fire
is *not* quenched.
10:27. impossible, but *not* with God:
38. Ye know *not* what ye ask:
40. is *not* mine to give ;
43. so shall it *not* be among you:
45. the Son of man came *not* to be
11:13. for the time of figs was *not* (yet).
16. would *not* suffer that any man
17. Is it *not* written, My house
26. if ye do *not* forgive,
31. Why then did ye *not* believe him?
33. We can*not* tell.
12:14. and carest)(‖ for no man: for thou regardest *not* the person of men,
— to give tribute to Cæsar, or *not?*
20. and dying left *no* seed.
22. And the seven had her, and left *no* seed:
24. Do ye *not* therefore err,
26. have ye *not* read in the book of
27. He is *not* the God of the dead,
31. There is *none* other commandment greater
32. and there is *none* other but he:
34. Thou art *not* far from the kingdom
13:11. for it is *not* ye that speak,
14. standing where it ought *not,*
19. such as was *not* from the beginning
20. *no* flesh should be saved:
24. the moon shall *not* give her light,
33. for ye know *not* when the time is.
35. for ye know *not* when the master

Mar 14: 7. but me ye have *not* always.
21. if he had *never* been born.
29. be offended, yet (will) *not* I.
36. nevertheless *not* what I will,
37. couldest *not* thou watch one hour?
40. *neither* wist they what to answer
49. and ye took me *not:*
55. to put him to death; and found *none.*
56. but their witness agreed *not*
60. Answerest)(‖ thou nothing?
68. I know *not*, neither understand
71. I know *not* this man of whom
15: 4. Answerest)(‖ thou nothing?
23. but he received (it) *not.*
31. himself he can*not* save.
16: 6. he is risen; he is *not* here:
14. because they believed *not*

Lu. 1: 7. And they had *no* child,
20. because thou believest *not* my words,
22. he could *not* speak unto them:
33. of his kingdom there shall be *no* end.
34. seeing I know *not* a man?
37. with God *nothing* shall be impossible.
2: 7. there was *no* room for them in the inn.
37. which departed *not* from the temple,
43. Joseph and his mother knew *not* (of it).
49. wist ye *not* that I must be
50. they understood *not* the saying
3:16. I am *not* worthy to unloose:
4: 2. in those days he did)(‖ eat nothing:
4. shall *not* live by bread alone,
12. Thou shalt *not* tempt the Lord
22. Is *not* this Joseph's son?
41. suffered them *not* to speak:
5:31. need *not* a physician;
32. I came *not* to call the righteous,
36. agreeth *not* with the old.
6: 2. that which is *not* lawful to do on
4. which it is *not* lawful to eat
40. The disciple is *not* above his master:
41. but perceivest *not* the beam that is
42. when thou thyself beholdest *not*
43. good tree bringeth *not* forth
44. of thorns men do *not* gather figs,
46. and do *not* the things which I say?
48. and could *not* shake it:
7: 6. he was now *not* far from the house,
— for I am *not* worthy that thou
32. and ye have *not* danced;
— and ye have *not* wept.
44. thou gavest me *no* water for my feet:
45. Thou gavest me *no* kiss:
— hath *not* ceased to kiss my feet.
46. thou didst *not* anoint:
8:13. and these have *no* root,
14. and bring *no* fruit to perfection.
17. For *nothing* is secret, that shall *not* be made manifest;
— that shall *not* be known
19. and could *not* come at him
27. and ware *no* clothes, *neither* abode in (any) house,
43. *neither* ‖ could be healed of any,
47. that she was *not* hid,
51. he suffered)(‖ *no* man to go in,
52. she is *not* dead, but sleepeth.
9:13. We have *no* more but five ˄ves
40. and they could *not.*
49. because he followeth *not* with us.
50. he that is *not* against us
53. And they did *not* receive him,
55. Ye know *not* what manner of spirit

Lu. 9:56. is *not* come to destroy men's lives,
58. hath *not* where to lay (his) head.
10:24. and have *not* seen (them);
— and have *not* heard (them).
40. dost thou *not* care that my sister
42. which shall *not* be taken away
11: 6. and I have *nothing* to set before him?
7. I can*not* rise and give thee.
8. Though he will *not* rise and give him,
29. there shall *no* sign be given
38. marvelled that he had *not* first washed
40. did *not* he that made that which
44. are *not* aware (of them).
46. yourselves touch *not* the burdens
52. ye entered *not* in yourselves,
12: 2. that shall *not* be revealed; neither hid, that shall *not* be known.
6. and *not* one of them is forgotten
10. it shall *not* be forgiven
15. consisteth *not* in the abundance
17. because I have *no* room where
24. for they *neither* sow nor reap; which *neither* have storehouse
27. they toil *not*, they spin not;
33. where *no* thief approacheth,
39. and *not* have suffered his house
40. at an hour when ye think *not.*
46. when he looketh *not* for (him), and at an hour when he is *not* aware,
56. how is it that ye do *not* discern
57. judge ye *not* what is right?
13: 6. sought fruit thereon, and found *none.*
7. on this fig tree, and find *none:*
15. doth *not* each one of you on the
16. And ought *not* this woman,
24. and shall *not* be able.
25. I know you *not* whence ye are:
27. I know you *not* whence ye are;
33. for it can*not* be that
34. and ye would *not!*
14: 5. and will *not* straightway pull
6. And they could *not* answer
14. for they can*not* recompense
20. and therefore I can*not* come.
26. and hate *not* his father, and
— he can*not* be my disciple.
27. whosoever doth *not* bear his
— can*not* be my disciple.
30. and was *not* able to finish.
33. that forsaketh *not* all that he hath, he can*not* be my disciple.
15: 4. doth *not*, leave the ninety and nine
7. which need *no* repentance.
13. And *not* many days after
28. and would *not* go in:
16: 2. for thou mayest be *no* longer steward.
3. I can*not* dig; to beg I am ashamed.
11. ye have *not* been faithful
12. if ye have *not* been faithful in that
13. Ye can*not* serve God and mammon.
31. If they hear *not* Moses and the
17: 9. that were commanded him? I trow *not.*
18. There are *not* found that returned
20. The kingdom of God cometh *not* with
22. and ye shall *not* see (it).
18: 4. And he would *not* for a while:
— Though I fear *not* God, *nor* regard man;
11. that I am *not* as other men
13. would *not* ‖ lift up so much
˙˙ *neither* knew they the things which
19: ˦. and could *not* for the press,
14. We will *not* have this (man) to reign

Lu. 19:21. that thou layedst *not* down, and reapest
  that thou didst *not* sow.
 22. that I laid *not* down, and reaping that I
  did *not* sow:
 23. Wherefore then gavest *not* thou
 44. they shall *not* leave in thee one
 — thou knewest *not* the time of thy
 48. And could *not* find what they
20: 5. Why then believed ye him *not*?
 21. *neither* acceptest thou the person
 22. to give tribute unto Cæsar, or *no*?
 26. And they could *not* take hold
 31. and they left *no* children,
 38. For he is *not* a God of the dead,
21: 6. shall *not* be left one stone upon another,
  that shall *not* be thrown down.
 9. but the end (is) *not* by and by.
 15. shall *not* be able to gainsay
22:26. But ye (shall) *not* (be) so:
 53. ye stretched forth *no* hands
 57. Woman, I know him *not*.
 58. And Peter said, Man, I am *not*.
 60. Man, I know *not* what thou sayest.
23:29. and the wombs that *never* bare, and the
  paps which *never* gave suck.
 34. for they know *not* what they do.
 51. The same had *not* consented to the
 53. wherein)(‖ *never* man before was laid.
24: 3. and found *not* the body of the Lord
 6. He is *not* here, but is risen:
 18. and hast *not* known the things
 24. but him they saw *not*.
 39. for a spirit hath *not* flesh and bones,
Joh. 1: 5. the darkness comprehended it *not*.
 8. He was *not* that Light,
 10. and the world knew him *not*.
 11. and his own received him *not*.
 13. Which were born, *not* of blood,
 20. he confessed, and denied *not* ; but confessed, I am *not* the Christ.
 21. I am *not*. Art thou that prophet ? And
  he answered, *No*.
 25. if thou be *not* that Christ,
 26. whom ye know *not*;
 27. I am *not* worthy to unloose.
 31. And I knew him *not*:
 33. And I knew him *not*:
 47(48). in whom is *no* guile !
2: 3. They have *no* wine.
 9. and knew *not* whence it was:
 12. they continued there *not* many days.
 24. Jesus did *not* commit himself
 25. And needed *not* that any should
3: 3. he can*not* see the kingdom of God.
 5. he can*not* enter into the kingdom
 8. but canst *not* tell whence it cometh,
 10. and knowest *not* these things?
 11. and ye receive *not* our witness.
 12. and ye believe *not*,
 17. For God sent *not* his Son into the
 18. is *not* condemned:
 20. *neither* cometh to the light,
 27. A man can)(‖ receive nothing, except it
  be given him
 28. that I said, I am *not* the Christ,
 34. God giveth *not* the Spirit by measure
 36. shall *not* see life ;
4: 2. Jesus himself baptized *not*, but
 9. for the Jews have *no* dealings with
 17. I have *no* husband.
 — Thou hast well said, I have *no* husband:
 18. is *not* thy husband:

Joh. 4:22. Ye worship ye know *not* what:
 32. I have meat to eat that ye know *not* of.
 35. Say *not* ye, There are yet four months,
 38. whereon ye bestowed *no* labour:
 44. that a prophet hath *no* honour in
5: 7. Sir, I have *no* man, when the
 10. it is *not* lawful for thee to
 13. he that was healed wist *not* who
 18. because he *not* only had broken the
 19. The Son can)(‖ do nothing of himself,
  but what he
 23. honoureth *not* the Father
 24. and shall *not* come into condemnation ;
 30. I can)(‖ of mine own self do nothing:
 — I seek *not* mine own will,
 31. of myself, my witness is *not* true.
 34. I receive *not* testimony from man:
 38. ye have *not* his word abiding
 — him ye believe *not*.
 40. And ye will *not* come to me,
 41. I receive *not* honour from men.
 42. ye have *not* the love of God in you.
 43. and ye receive me *not*:
 44. and seek *not* the honour that
 47. But if ye believe *not* his writings,
6: 7. of bread is *not* sufficient for them,
 17. and Jesus was *not* come to them.
 22. that there was *none* other boat
 — and that Jesus went *not* with
 24. saw that Jesus was *not* there,
 26. *not* because ye saw the miracles,
 32. Moses gave you *not* that bread
 36. have seen me, and believe *not*.
 38. *not* to do mine own will,
 42. Is *not* this Jesus, the son of
 46. *Not* that any man hath seen
 53. ye have *no* life in you.
 58. *not* as your fathers did eat
 63. the flesh)(‖ profiteth nothing:
 64. some of you that believe *not*.
 70. Have *not* I chosen you twelve,
7: 1. for he would *not* walk in Jewry,
 7. The world can*not* hate you ; but
 10. *not* openly, but as it were in secret.
 12. *Nay* ; but he deceiveth the people.
 16. My doctrine is *not* mine,
 18. and *no* unrighteousness is in him.
 19. Did *not* Moses give you the law,
 22. *not* because it is of Moses,
 25. Is *not* this he, whom they seek
 28. I am *not* come of myself,
 — whom ye know *not*.
 34. and shall *not* find (me): and where I am,
  (thither) ye can*not* come.
 35. that we shall *not* find him ?
 36. and shall *not* find (me): and where I am,
  (thither) ye can*not* come ?
 45. Why have ye *not* brought him ?
 52. out of Galilee ariseth *no* prophet.
8:13. thy record is *not* true.
 14. but ye can*not* tell whence I come,
 15. I judge)(‖ *no* man.
 16. for I am *not* alone,
 21. whither I go, ye can*not* come.
 22. Whither I go, ye can*not* come.
 23. I am *not* of this world.
 27. They understood *not* that he spake
 29. hath *not* left me alone ;
 35. abideth *not* in the house for ever:
 37. hath *no* place in you.
 40. this did *not* Abraham.
 41. We be *not* born of fornication ;

Joh. 8:43. Why do ye *not* understand my speech?
(even) because ye can*not* hear my word.

44. and abode *not* in the truth, because there is *no* truth in him.

45. ye believe me *not*.

46. why do ye *not* believe me?

47. ye therefore hear (them) *not*, because ye are *not* of God.

48. Say we *not* well that thou art

49. I have *not* a devil;

50. I seek *not* mine own glory:

55. Yet ye have *not* known him;
— if I should say, I know him *not*,

9: 8. Is *not* this he that sat and begged?

12. He said, I know *not*.

16. This man is *not* of God, because he keepeth *not* the sabbath

18. But the Jews did *not* believe

21. we know *not*; or who hath opened his eyes, we know *not*:

25. I know *not*: one thing I know,

27. and ye did *not* hear:

29. we know *not* from whence he is.

30. that ye know *not* from whence he is,

31. God heareth *not* sinners:

32. Since the world began was it *not* heard

33. he could)(|| do nothing.

41. ye should have *no* sin:

10: 5. they know *not* the voice of strangers.

6. they understood *not* what things

8. but the sheep did *not* hear them.

10. The thief cometh *not*, but for

12. and *not* the shepherd, whose own the sheep are *not*,

13. and careth *not* for the sheep.

16. which are *not* of this fold:

21. These are *not* the words of him that

25. I told you, and ye believed *not*:

26. But ye believe *not*, because ye are *not* of my sheep,

28. *neither* shall any (man) pluck them

33. For a good work we stone thee *not*;

34. Is it *not* written in your law,

35. and the scripture can*not* be broken;

37. If I do *not* the works of my Father,

11: 4. This sickness is *not* unto death,

9. he stumbleth *not*,

10. because there is *no* light in him.

15. that I was *not* there,

21. my brother had *not* died.

32. my brother had *not* died.

37. Could *not* this man, which opened

40. Said I *not* unto thee,

49. Ye know)(|| nothing at all,

51. this spake he *not* of himself:

52. And *not* for that nation only,

12: 5. Why was *not* this ointment sold

6. *not* that he cared for the poor;

8. but me ye have *not* always.

9. came *not* for Jesus' sake only,

16. These things understood *not* his

19. Perceive ye how ye prevail)(|| nothing?

30. This voice came *not* because

35. knoweth *not* whither he goeth.

37. yet they believed *not* on him:

39. Therefore they could *not* believe,

42. they did *not* confess (him),

44. believeth *not* on me, but on him

47. I judge him *not*: for I came *not* to judge the world,

49. For I have *not* spoken of myself;

13: 7. What I do thou knowest *not* now;

Joh. 13. 8. thou hast *no* part with me.

10. He that is washed needeth *not*

16. The servant is *not* greater than

18. I speak *not* of you all:

33. Whither I go, ye can*not* come;

36. thou canst *not* follow me now;

37. why can*not* I follow thee now?

14: 5. Lord, we know *not* whither thou

9. and yet hast thou *not* known me,

10. Believest thou *not* that I am in
— I speak *not* of myself: but

17. whom the world can*not* receive, because it seeth him *not*,

18. I will *not* leave you comfortless:

22. Judas saith unto him, *not* Iscariot,

24. keepeth *not* my sayings: and the word which ye hear is *not* mine,

27. *not* as the world giveth, give I

30. and hath)(|| nothing in me.

15: 4. As the branch can*not* bear fruit

5. for without me ye can)(|| do nothing.

15. for the servant knoweth *not* what

16. Ye have *not* chosen me, but

19. but because ye are *not* of the world,

20. The servant is *not* greater than

21. because they know *not* him that

22. they had *not* had sin: but now they have *no* cloke for their sin.

24. they had *not* had sin:

16: 3. because they have *not* known the Father,

4. these things I said *not* unto you at

7. the Comforter will *not* come unto you;

9. because they believe *not* on me;

12. but ye can*not* bear them now.

13. for he shall *not* speak of himself;

16. and ye shall *not* see me:

17. A little while, and ye shall *not* see me:

18. we can*not* tell what he saith.

19. and ye shall *not* see me:

23. in that day ye shall)(|| ask me nothing.

24. Hitherto have ye)(|| asked nothing in

26. and I say *not* unto you,

30. and needest *not* that any man

32. and yet I am *not* alone,

17: 9. I pray *not* for the world,

14. they are *not* of the world, even as I am *not* of the world.

15. I pray *not* that thou shouldest

16. They are *not* of the world, even as I am *not* of the world.

20. *Neither* pray I for these alone,

25. the world hath *not* known thee:

18: 9. which thou gavest me have I)(|| lost none.

17. He saith, I am *not*.

25. He denied (it), and said, I am *not*.

26. Did *not* I see thee in the garden with

28. went *not* into the judgment hall,

30. we would *not* have delivered him up

31. It is *not* lawful for us to put any

36. My kingdom is *not* of this world:
— but now is my kingdom *not* from hence.

19: 6. for I find *no* fault in him.

9. But Jesus gave him *no* answer.

10. Speakest thou *not* unto me? knowest thou *not* that I

11. Thou couldest)(|| have no power (at all)

12. thou art *not* Cæsar's friend:

15. We have *no* king but Cæsar.

33. they brake *not* his legs:

36. A bone of him shall *not* be broken.

20: 2. and we know *not* where they have

5. yet went he *not* in.

Joh.20: 7. *not* lying with the linen clothes,
    13. and I know *not* where they have laid him.
    14. and knew *not* that it was Jesus.
    24. was *not* with them when Jesus came.
    30. which are *not* written in this book:
    21: 4. but the disciples knew *not* that it
     5. They answered him, *No.*
     8. for they were *not* far from land,
    11. yet was *not* the net broken.
    18. carry (thee) whither thou wouldest *not.*
    23. that that disciple should *not* die: yet Jesus
       said *not* unto him, He shall *not* die ;
Acts 1: 5. *not* many days hence.
     7. It is *not* for you to know
   2: 7. Behold, are *not* all these which
    15. For these are *not* drunken, as
    24. because it was *not* possible
    27. Because thou wilt *not* leave
    31. his soul was *not* left in hell,
    34. For David is *not* ascended
   3: 6. Silver and gold have I *none ;*
   4:12. *Neither* is there salvation in any other:
    16. and we can*not* deny (it).
    20. For we can*not* but speak the things
   5: 4. thou hast *not* lied unto men,
    22. and found them *not* in the prison,
    26. without violence: (lit. *not* with violence)
    28. Did *not* we straitly command
    39. ye can*not* overthrow it ;
    42. they ceased *not* to teach
   6: 2. It is *not* reason that we should
    10. And they were *not* able to resist
    13. This man ceaseth *not* to speak
   7: 5. And he gave him *none* inheritance
    — when (as yet) he had *no* child.
    11. and our fathers found *no* sustenance.
    18. which knew *not* Joseph.
    25. but they understood *not.*
    32. and durst *not* behold.
    39. our fathers would *not* obey,
    40. we wot *not* what is become of him.
    48. dwelleth *not* in temples made
    52. have *not* your fathers persecuted ?
    53. and have *not* kept (it).
   8:21. Thou hast *neither* part nor lot
    — is *not* right in the sight of God.
    32. so opened he *not* his mouth:
    39. that the eunuch saw)(‖ him no more:
   9: 9. and *neither* did eat nor drink.
    21. Is *not* this he that destroyed
  10:34. that God is *no* respecter of persons:
    41. *Not* to all the people,
  12: 9. and wist *not* that it was true
    14. she opened *not* the gate
    18. there was *no* small stir
    22. the voice of a god, and *not* of a man.
    23. because he gave *not* God the glory:
  13:10. wilt thou *not* cease to pervert
    25. I am *not* (he). But, behold,
    — I am *not* worthy to loose.
    35. Thou shalt *not* suffer thine Holy One
    37. whom God raised again, saw *no* corruption.
    39. from which ye could *not* be justified
    46. and judge yourselves *unworthy*
  14:17. he left *not* himself without witness,
    28. they abode long time (lit. *no* small time)
  15: 1. ye can*not* be saved.
    2. had *no* small dissension
    24. whom we gave *no* (such) commandment:
  16: 7. but the Spirit suffered them *not.*
    21. which are *not* lawful for us to
    37. *nay* verily ; but let them come

Acts17: 4. and of the chief women *not* a few.
    12. and of men, *not* a few.
    24. dwelleth *not* in temples made with hands;
    27. though he be *not* far from every one
    29. we ought *not* to think that the
  18:15. I will be *no* judge of such (matters).
    20. with them, he consented *not ;*
  19:11. God wrought special miracles (lit. *no*
       common miracles)
    23. there arose *no* small stir
    24. *no* small gain unto the craftsmen ;
    26. that *not* alone at Ephesus, but
    — that they be *no* gods, which are made
    27. *not* only this our craft
    30. the disciples suffered him *not.*
    32. the more part knew *not* wherefore
    35. that knoweth *not* how that the city
  20:12. and were *not* a little comforted.
    27. I have *not* shunned to declare
    31. I ceased *not* to warn every one
  21:13. I am ready *not* to be bound only,
    38. Art *not* thou that Egyptian,
    39. a citizen of *no* mean city:
  22: 9. but they heard *not* the voice
    11. And when I could *not* see for
    18. for they will *not* receive thy
    22. for it is *not* fit that he should live.
  23: 5. I wist *not,* brethren, that he
    — Thou shalt *not* speak evil of
  24:11. that there are yet but (lit. *not* more than)
       twelve days
    18. *neither* with multitude, nor
  25: 7. which they could *not* prove.
    11. I refuse *not* to die:
    16. It is *not* the manner of the Romans
    26. I have *no* certain thing to write
  26:19. I was *not* disobedient
    25. I am *not* mad,
    26. I am)(‖ persuaded that none of these
    — was *not* done in a corner.
    29. that *not* only thou, but also all
  27:10. *not* only of the lading and ship,
    14. But *not* long after there arose
    20. and *no* small tempest lay
    31. ye can*not* be saved.
    39. they knew *not* the land:
  28: 2. shewed us *no* little kindness:
    4. vengeance suffereth *not* to live.
    19. *not* that I had ought to accuse
Ro. 1:13. I would *not* have you ignorant,
    16. For I am *not* ashamed
    21. glorified (him) *not* as God,
    28. even as they did *not* like
    32. *not* only do the same, but
   2:11. For there is *no* respect of persons
    13. For *not* the hearers of the law
    21. teachest thou *not* thyself?
    28. For he is *not* a Jew which is
    29. in the spirit, (and) *not* in the letter; whose
       praise (is) *not* of men,
   3: 9. *No,* in no wise: for we have before
    10. There is *none* righteous,
    11. There is *none* that understandeth, there is
       none that seeketh after God.
    12. there is *none* that doeth good, *no,* not one.
    17. the way of peace have they *not* known:
    18. There is *no* fear of God before
    20. there shall *no* flesh be justified
    22. for there is *no* difference:
   4: 2. but *not* before God.
    4. is the reward *not* reckoned of grace,
    10. *Not* in circumcision, but in

Ro. 4:12. to them who are *not* of the circumcision
13. (was) *not* to Abraham, or to his seed, through the law,
15. for where *no* law is,
16. *not* to that only which is of the law,
19. he considered *not* his own body
20. He staggered *not* at the promise
23. it was *not* written for his sake
5: 3. *not* only (so), but we glory
5. hope maketh *not* ashamed;
11. *not* only (so), but we also joy
13. is *not* imputed when there is no
15. But *not* as the offence, so also (is)
16. And *not* as (it was) by one that
6:14. For sin shall *not* have dominion over you: for ye are *not* under the law,
15. because we are *not* under the law,
16. Know ye *not*, that to whom ye
7: 6. and *not* (in) the oldness of the letter.
7. Nay, I had *not* known sin, but by the law: for I had *not* known lust, except the law had said, Thou shalt *not* covet.
15. For that which I do I allow *not:* for what I would, that do I *not;*
16. If then I do that which I would *not*,
18. dwelleth *no* good thing:
— to perform that which is good I find *not*.
19. the good that I would I do *not:* but the evil which I would *not*,
20. if I do that I would *not*,
8: 7. for it is *not* subject to the law of God,
8. they that are in the flesh can*not* please God.
9. But ye are *not* in the flesh,
— if any man have *not* the Spirit of Christ, he is *none* of his.
12. we are debtors, *not* to the flesh,
15. ye have *not* received the spirit of
18. (are) *not* worthy (to be compared)
20. *not* willingly, but by reason of
23. And *not* only (they), but
24. hope that is seen is *not* hope:
25. if we hope for that we see *not*,
26. we know *not* what we should
32. He that spared *not* his own Son,
9: 1. I say the truth in Christ, I lie *not*,
6. *Not* as though the word of God
— For they (are) *not* all Israel, which
8. these (are) *not* the children of God:
10. And *not* only (this); but when
11. *not* of works, but of him that calleth;
16. *not* of him that willeth,
21. Hath *not* the potter power over
24. *not* of the Jews only,
25. *not* my people; and her beloved, which was *not* beloved.
26. Ye (are) *not* my people;
31. hath *not* attained to the law of
32. (they sought it) *not* by faith,
33. believeth on him shall *not* be ashamed.
10: 2. *not* according to knowledge.
3. have *not* submitted themselves
11. shall *not* be ashamed.
12. For there is *no* difference
14. in whom they have *not* believed?
— of whom they have *not* heard?
16. they have *not* all obeyed
19. (them that are) *no* people,
11: 2. God hath *not* cast away his people
— Wot ye *not* what the scripture
4. who have *not* bowed the knee
7. Israel hath *not* obtained that which
18. thou bearest *not* the root,

Ro. 11:21. if God spared *not* the natural branches,
25. I would *not*, brethren, that ye
12: 4. all members have *not* the same
13: 1. there is *no* power but of God:
3. rulers are *not* a terror to good
4. for he beareth *not* the sword in vain:
5. *not* only for wrath, but
9. Thou shalt *not* commit adultery, Thou shalt *not* kill, Thou shalt *not* steal, Thou shalt *not* bear false witness, Thou shalt *not* covet;
10. Love worketh *no* ill
14: 6. to the Lord he doth *not* regard (it).
— to the Lord he eateth *not*,
17. the kingdom of God is *not* meat and
23. (he eateth) *not* of faith: for whatsoever (is) *not* of faith is sin.
15: 3. even Christ pleased *not* himself;
18. I will *not* dare to speak of any
— which Christ hath *not* wrought by me,
20. *not* where Christ was named,
21. To whom he was *not* spoken of, they
— they that have *not* heard shall
16: 4. unto whom *not* only I give thanks,
18. serve *not* our Lord Jesus Christ,
1Co. 1:16. I know *not* whether I baptized
17. Christ sent me *not* to baptize,
— *not* with wisdom of words,
21. the world by wisdom knew *not* God,
26. *not* many wise men after the flesh, *not* many mighty, *not* many noble, (are called):
2: 1. *not* with excellency of speech
2. *not* to know any thing among you,
4. *not* with enticing words of man's
6. *not* the wisdom of this world,
8. they would *not* have crucified
9. Eye hath *not* seen, *nor* ear heard, *neither* have entered into the heart of man,
12. *not* the spirit of the world,
13. *not* in the words which man's wisdom
14. the natural man receiveth *not*
— *neither* can he know (them),
3: 1. could *not* speak unto you as
2. with milk, and *not* with meat:
16. Know ye *not* that ye are the temple
4: 4. yet am I *not* hereby justified:
7. that thou didst *not* receive?
14. I write *not* these things to shame
15. yet (have ye) *not* many fathers:
19. *not* the speech of them which are
20. the kingdom of God (is) *not* in word,
5: 6. Your glorying (is) *not* good. Know ye *not* that a little leaven
10. Yet *not* altogether with the
6: 2. Do ye *not* know that the saints
3. Know ye *not* that we shall judge
5. that there is *not* a wise man among
9. Know ye *not* that the unrighteous shall *not* inherit the kingdom of God?
10. *nor* revilers, *nor* extortioners, shall)(‖ inherit the kingdom of God.
12. but all things are *not* expedient:
— but I will *not* be brought under
13. Now the body (is) *not* for fornication,
15. Know ye *not* that your bodies
16. know ye *not* that he which is
19. know ye *not* that your body is
— and ye are *not* your own?
7: 4. The wife hath *not* power of her own body,
— husband hath *not* power of his own body,
6. (and) *not* of commandment.

1Co. 7: 9. But if they can*not* contain,
  10. (yet) *not* I, but the Lord,
  12. But to the rest speak I, *not* the Lord:
  15. or a sister is *not* under bondage
  25. I have *no* commandment of the Lord:
  28. thou hast *not* sinned ; and if a virgin
    marry, she hath *not* sinned.
  35. *not* that I may cast a snare upon you,
  36. he sinneth *not :* let them marry.
  8: 7. *not* in every man that knowledge:
   8. meat commendeth us *not* to God:
  9: 1. Am I *not* an apostle? am I *not* free?
   — are *not* ye my work in the Lord?
   2. If I be *not* an apostle unto others,
   6. have *not* we power to forbear working?
   7. and eateth *not* of the fruit thereof?
   — eateth *not* of the milk of the flock?
   9. Thou shalt *not* muzzle the mouth
  12. (are) *not* we rather? Nevertheless we
    have *not* used this power;
  13. Do ye *not* know that they which
  15. *neither* have I written these things,
  16. I have *nothing* to glory of:
  24. Know ye *not* that they which run
  26. *not* as uncertainly ; so fight I, *not* as one
    that beateth the air:
 10: 1. I would *not* that ye should be
   5. God was *not* well pleased:
  13. There hath *no* temptation taken you
  — who will *not* suffer you to be tempted
  20. and *not* to God: and I would *not* that ye
    should have
  21. Ye can*not* drink the cup of the Lord, and
  — ye can*not* be partakers of the
  23. but all things are *not* expedient:
  — all things edify *not*.
 11: 6. if the woman be *not* covered,
   7. ought *not* to cover (his) head,
   8. the man is *not* of the woman ;
   9. *Neither* was the man created for
  16. we have *no* such custom,
  17. I praise (you) *not*, that ye come together
    not for the better, but
  20. (this) is *not* to eat the Lord's supper.
  22. I praise (you) *not*.
  31. we should *not* be judged.
 12: 1. I would *not* have you ignorant.
  14. the body is *not* one member,
  15. Because I am *not* the hand, I am *not* of
    the body ; is it therefore *not* of the
  16. Because I am *not* the eye, I am *not* of the
    body ; is it therefore *not* of the body?
  21. the eye can*not* say unto the hand, I have
    no need of thee:
  — I have *no* need of you.
  24. For our comely (parts) have *no* need:
 13: 4. charity envieth *not ;* charity vaunteth *not*
    itself, is *not* puffed up,
   5. Doth *not* behave itself unseemly, seeketh
    not her own, is *not* easily provoked,
    thinketh *no* evil ;
   6. Rejoiceth *not* in iniquity,
 14: 2. speaketh *not* unto men, but
  16. seeing he understandeth *not* what
  17. the other is *not* edified.
  22. *not* to them that believe, but
  — *not* for them that believe not, but
  23. will they *not* say that ye are mad?
  33. God is *not* (the author) of confusion,
  34. it is *not* permitted unto them
 15: 9. that am *not* meet to be called
  10. was *not* in vain ;

1Co.15: 10. yet *not* I, but the grace of God
  12. that there is *no* resurrection of the dead?
  13. if there be *no* resurrection of the dead,
  14. And if Christ be *not* risen,
  15. whom he raised *not* up, if so be that the
    dead rise *not*.
  16. For if the dead rise *not*,
  17. And if Christ be *not* raised,
  29. if the dead rise *not* at all?
  32. if the dead rise *not ?*
  36. is *not* quickened, except
  37. thou sowest *not* that body that shall be,
  39. All flesh (is) *not* the same flesh:
  46. that (was) *not* first which is spiritual,
  50. can*not* inherit the kingdom
  51. We shall *not* all sleep,
  58. is *not* in vain in the Lord.
 16: 7. I will *not* see you now by the way ;
  12. but his will was *not* at all to come
  22. If any man love *not* the Lord Jesus Christ,
2Co. 1: 8. For we would *not*, brethren, have you
  12. *not* with fleshly wisdom,
  13. For we write *none* other things
  17. be yea yea, and *nay nay ?*
  18. was *not* yea and *nay*.
  19. was *not* yea and *nay*,
  24. *Not* for that we have dominion
  2: 4. *not* that ye should be grieved,
   5. he hath *not* grieved me,
  11. we are *not* ignorant of his
  13. I had *no* rest in my spirit,
  17. For we are *not* as many,
  3: 3. written *not* with ink,
  — *not* in tables of stone, but in fleshy
   5. *Not* that we are sufficient of
   6. *not* of the letter, but of the spirit:
  13. And *not* as Moses, (which) put a vail
  4: 1. received mercy, we faint *not ;*
   5. For we preach *not* ourselves,
   8. yet *not* distressed ; (we are) perplexed,
    but *not* in despair ;
   9. Persecuted, but *not* forsaken ; cast down,
    but *not* destroyed ;
  16. For which cause we faint *not ;*
  5: 3. we shall *not* be found naked.
   4. *not* for that we would be unclothed,
   7. we walk by faith, *not* by sight:
  12. we commend *not* ourselves
  — in appearance, and *not* in heart.
  6: 12. Ye are *not* straitened in us,
  7: 3. I speak *not* (this) to condemn (you):
   7. And *not* by his coming only,
   8. I do *not* repent,
   9. *not* that ye were made sorry,
  12. *not* for his cause that had done
  14. I am *not* ashamed ;
  8: 5. *not* as we hoped,
   8. I speak *not* by commandment,
  10. *not* only to do, but also
  12. *not* according to that he hath *not*.
  13. *not* that other men be eased,
  15. much had *nothing* over ; and he that (had
    gathered) little had *no* lack.
  19. And *not* (that) only, but who was
  21. *not* only in the sight of the Lord,
  9: 12. *not* only supplieth the want of
 10: 3. we do *not* war after the flesh:
   4. of our warfare (are) *not* carnal,
   8. and *not* for your destruction, I should *not*
    be ashamed:
  12. For we dare *not* make ourselves of the
  — among themselves, are *not* wise.

2Co.10:14. For we stretch *not* ourselves
    15. *Not* boasting of things without
    16. *not* to boast in another man's
    18. For *not* he that commendeth himself
  11: 4. whom we have *not* preached,
    — which ye have *not* received, or another
      gospel, which ye have *not* accepted,
    6. yet *not* in knowledge ;
    9(8). I was)(‖ chargeable to no man:
    10. no man shall stop me of this boasting (lit.
      this boasting shall *not* be stopped to me)
    11. because I love you *not ?*
    14. And *no* marvel ; for Satan himself
    15. Therefore (it is) *no* great thing if
    17. I speak (it) *not* after the Lord,
    29. am *not* weak? who is offended, and I burn
      not ?
    31. knoweth that I lie *not.*
  12: 1. It is *not* expedient for me
    2. I can*not* tell ; or whether out of the body,
      I can*not* tell:
    3. or out of the body, I can*not* tell:
    4. which it is *not* lawful for a man
    5. yet of myself I will *not* glory,
    6. I shall *not* be a fool ;
    13. that I myself was *not* burdensome
    14. I will *not* be burdensome to you: for I
      seek *not* your's, but you: for the chil-
      dren ought *not* to lay up
    16. I did *not* burden you:
    18. walked we *not* in the same spirit? (walked
      we) *not* in the same steps?
    20. I shall *not* find you such as I would,
    — such as ye would *not :*
  13: 2. if I come again, I will *not* spare:
    3. which to you-ward is *not* weak,
    5. Know ye *not* your own selves,
    6. that we are *not* reprobates.
    7. *not* that we should appear approved,
    8. For we can do *nothing* against
    10. and *not* to destruction.
Gal. 1: 1. Paul, an apostle, *not* of men,
    7. Which is *not* another ;
    10. I should *not* be the servant of Christ.
    11. is *not* after man.
    16. I conferred *not* with flesh and blood:
    19. other of the apostles saw I *none*, save
    20. behold, before God, I lie *not.*
  2: 6. God accepteth *no* man's person:
    14. I saw that they walked *not* uprightly
    — and *not* as do the Jews,
    15. and *not* sinners of the Gentiles,
    16. a man is *not* justified by the
    — and *not* by the works of the law: for by
      the works of the law shall *no* flesh
    21. I do *not* frustrate the grace of God:
  3:10. that continueth *not* in all things
    12. the law is *not* of faith:
    16. He saith *not*, And to seeds,
    17. can*not* disannul, that it should
    20. Now a mediator is *not* (a mediator)
    28. There is *neither* Jew nor Greek, there is
      neither bond nor free, there is *neither*
  4: 8. when ye knew *not* God,
    14. in my flesh ye despised *not*,
    17. affect you, (but) *not* well ;
    21. do ye *not* hear the law?
    27. barren that bearest *not;*
    — thou that travailest *not:*
    31. we are *not* children of the
  5: 8. This persuasion (cometh) *not* of him that
    18. ye are *not* under the law.

Gal. 5:21. shall *not* inherit the kingdom
    23. against such there is *no* law.
  6: 4. and *not* in another.
    7. God is *not* mocked:
Eph 1:16. Cease *not* to give thanks for you,
    21. *not* only in this world, but also
  2: 8. and that *not* of yourselves:
    9. *Not* of works, lest any
  3: 5. was *not* made known unto the sons
  4:20. But ye have *not* so learned Christ;
  5: 4. which are *not* convenient:
    5. that *no* whoremonger, nor...hath any
  6: 7. as to the Lord, and *not* to men:
    9. *neither* is there respect of persons
    12. For we wrestle *not* against flesh
Phi. 1:16. *not* sincerely, supposing to add
    22. what I shall choose I wot *not.*
    29. *not* only to believe on him,
  2: 6. thought it *not* robbery to be
    16. that I have *not* run in vain,
    21. *not* the things which are Jesus Christ's.
    27. and *not* on him only,
  3: 1. to me indeed (is) *not* grievous,
    3. and have *no* confidence in the
    12. *Not* as though I had already
    13. I count *not* myself to have
  4:11. *Not* that I speak in respect of
    17. *Not* because I desire a gift:
Col. 1: 9. do *not* cease to pray for you,
  2: 1. as have *not* seen my face in
    8. and *not* after Christ.
    19. And *not* holding the Head,
    23. *not* in any honour to the
  3:11. Where there is *neither* Greek
  •23. and *not* unto men ;
    25. and there is *no* respect of persons.
1Th. 1: 5. our gospel came *not* unto you in
    8. *not* only in Macedonia and
  2: 1. that it was *not* in vain:
    3. (was) *not* of deceit,
    4. *not* as pleasing men,
    8. *not* the gospel of God only,
    13. ye received (it) *not* (as) the word of
    17. in presence, *not* in heart,
  4: 7. God hath *not* called us unto
    8. despiseth *not* man, but God,
    9. ye need *not* that I write unto you:
    13. I would *not* have you to be
  5: 1. ye have *no* need that I write
    4. are *not* in darkness,
    5. we are *not* of the night,
    9. God hath *not* appointed us to wrath,
2Th. 2: 5. Remember ye *not*, that, when I
    10. received *not* the love of the truth,
  3: 2. for all (men) have *not* faith.
    7. we behaved *not* ourselves disorderly
    9. *Not* because we have *not* power,
    10. if any would *not* work,
    14. if any man obey *not* our word
1Ti. 1: 9. the law is *not* made for a
  2: 7. truth in Christ, (and) lie *not ;*
    12. I suffer *not* a woman to teach,
    14. Adam was *not* deceived,
  3: 5. if a man know *not* how to rule
  5: 8. if any provide *not* for his own,
    13. and *not* only idle,
    18. Thou shalt *not* muzzle the ox that
    25. that are otherwise can*not* be hid.
2Ti. 1: 7. For God hath *not* given us the
    9. *not* according to our works,
    12. I am *not* ashamed:
    16. was *not* ashamed of my chain:

2Ti. 2: 5. (yet) is he *not* crowned, except
     9. the word of God is *not* bound.
   13. he can*not* deny himself.
   20. there are *not* only vessels of gold
   24. the servant of the Lord must *not* strive;
  3: 9. they shall proceed *no* further:
  4: 3. will *not* endure sound doctrine;
    8. and *not* to me only,
Tit. 3: 5. *Not* by works of righteousness
Heb 1:12. and thy years shall *not* fail.
  2: 5. hath he *not* put in subjection
   11. he is *not* ashamed to call them
   16. he took *not* on (him the nature of)
  3:10. they have *not* known my ways.
   16. *not* all that came out of Egypt
   19. they could *not* enter in because
  4: 2. the word preached did *not* profit
   6. entered *not* in because of
   8. then would he *not* afterward
   13. *Neither* is there (lit. and there is *not*) any
     creature that
   15. For we have *not* an high priest
  5: 4. *no* man taketh this honour unto
   5. Christ glorified *not* himself
   12. and *not* of strong meat.
  6:10. God (is) *not* unrighteous to forget
  7:11. and *not* be called after the order
   16. *not* after the law of a carnal
   20. as *not* without an oath
   21. and will *not* repent,
   27. Who needeth *not* daily, as
  8: 2. which the Lord pitched, and *not* man.
   7. then should *no* place have been
   9. *Not* according to the covenant
   — because they continued *not* in
  9: 5. of which we can*not* now speak
   7. once every year, *not* without blood,
   11. *not* made with hands, that is to say, *not* of
     this building;
   22. without shedding of blood is *no* remission.
   24. Christ is *not* entered into the holy
  10: 1. *not* the very image of the things,
   2. would they *not* have ceased to be
   5. and offering thou wouldest *not*,
   6. thou hast had *no* pleasure.
   8 for sin thou wouldest *not*,
   37. and will *not* tarry.
   38. my soul shall have *no* pleasure
   39. we are *not* of them who draw back
  11: 1. the evidence of things *not* seen.
   5. and was *not* found,
   16. God is *not* ashamed to be called their
   23. they were *not* afraid of the kings
   31. Rahab perished *not* with them
   35. were tortured, *not* accepting deliverance;
   38. Of whom the world was *not* worthy:
   39. received *not* the promise:
  12: 7. whom the father chasteneth *not* ?
   8. are ye bastards, and *not* sons.
   9. shall we *not* much rather be
   11. *no* chastening for the present
   17. he found *no* place of repentance,
   18. For ye are *not* come unto the mount
   20. they could *not* endure that which
   25. if they escaped *not* who
   26. I shake *not* the earth only, but
  13: 6. I will *not* fear what man
   9. *not* with meats, which have *not* profited
   10. they have *no* right to eat which
   14. here have we *no* continuing city,
Jas. 1:17. with whom is *no* variableness,
   20. the wrath of man worketh *not* the

Jas. 1:23. and *not* a doer,
   25. being *not* a forgetful hearer,
  2: 4. Are ye *not* then partial in
   5. Hath *not* God chosen the poor
   6. Do *not* rich men oppress you,
   7. Do *not* they blaspheme that worthy
   11. Now if thou commit *no* adultery,
   21. Was *not* Abraham our father justified
   24. and *not* by faith only.
   25. was *not* Rahab the harlot justified
  3: 2. If any man offend *not* in word,
   10. these things ought *not* so to be.
   15. descendeth *not* from above,
  4: 1. (come they) *not* hence,
   2. Ye lust, and have *not* :
   — and can*not* obtain: ye fight and war, yet ye
     have *not*,
   3. Ye ask, and receive *not*, because
   4. know ye *not* that the friendship
   11. thou art *not* a doer of the law,
   14. ye know *not* what (shall be) on
  5: 6. (and) he doth *not* resist you.
   12. and (your) nay, nay;
   17. and it rained *not* on the earth
1Pet. 1: 8. Whom having *not* seen, ye love;
   12. that *not* unto themselves,
   18. *not* redeemed with corruptible
   23. *not* of corruptible seed, but
  2:10. in time past (were) *not* a people,
   — had *not* obtained mercy, but
   18. *not* only to the good and gentle,
   22. Who did *no* sin,
   23. reviled *not* again; when he suffered, he
     threatened *not*;
  3: 3. let it *not* be that outward
   21. *not* the putting away of the filth of
2Pet. 1: 8. *neither* (be) barren nor unfruitful
   12. I will *not* be negligent to put
   16. we have *not* followed cunningly
   20. *no* prophecy of the scripture is of
   21. came *not* in old time by the will of
  2: 3. now of a long time lingereth *not* and their
     damnation slumbereth *not*.
   4. if God spared *not* the angels
   5. And spared *not* the old world,
   10. *not* afraid to speak evil of
   11. bring *not* railing accusation
  3: 9. The Lord is *not* slack
1Joh.1: 5. and in him is)(‖ *no* darkness
   6. and do *not* the truth:
   8. If we say that we have *no* sin,
   — and the truth is *not* in us.
   10. If we say that we have *not* sinned,
   — and his word is *not* in us.
  2: 2. and *not* for our's only,
   4. the truth is *not* in him.
   7. I write *no* new commandment
   10. there is *none* occasion of stumbling
   11. knoweth *not* whither he goeth,
   15. the love of the Father is *not* in him.
   16. is *not* of the Father, but
   19. but they were *not* of us;
   — that they were *not* all of us.
   21. I have *not* written unto you because ye
     know *not* the truth,
   — and that *no* lie is of the truth.
   22. but he that denieth that Jesus is)(the
     Christ ?
   27. and ye need *not* that any man
   — and is *no* lie,
  3: 1. the world knoweth us *not*, because it knew
     him *not*.

1Joh.3: 5. and in him is *no* sin.
    6. abideth in him sinneth *not:* whosoever sinneth hath *not* seen him,
    9. doth *not* commit sin;
    — and he can*not* sin,
    10. doeth not righteousness is *not* of God,
    12. *Not* as Cain, (who) was of that
    15. that *no* murderer hath eternal life
  4: 3. is *not* of God:
    6. he that is *not* of God heareth *not* us.
    8. knoweth *not* God; for God is love.
    10. *not* that we loved God,
    18. There is *no* fear in love;
    — is *not* made perfect in love.
    20. whom he hath *not* seen?
  5: 3. his commandments are *not* grievous.
    6. *not* by water only,
    10. because he believeth *not* the record
    12. not the Son of God hath *not* life.
    16. I do *not* say that he shall pray for it.
    17. there is a sin *not* unto death.
    18. is born of God sinneth *not;*
    — that wicked one toucheth him *not.*
2Joh. 1. and *not* I only,
    5. *not* as though I wrote a new
    9. doctrine of Christ, hath *not* God.
    10. and bring *not* this doctrine,
    12. I would *not* (write) with paper and
3Joh. 4. I have *no* greater joy than
    9. preeminence among them, receiveth us *not.*
    11. he that doeth evil hath *not* seen God.
    13. but I will *not* with ink and pen
Jude 9. durst *not* bring against him
    10. of those things which they know *not:*
Rev. 2: 2. how thou canst *not* bear them
    — say they are apostles, and are *not,*
    3. and hast *not* fainted.
    9. say they are Jews, and are *not,*
    13. and hast *not* denied my faith,
    21. and she repented *not.*
    24. as many as have *not* this doctrine, and which have *not* known the depths
    — I will put upon you *none* other
  3: 2. I have *not* found thy works
    4. which have *not* defiled their
    8. and hast *not* denied my name.
    9. say they are Jews, and are *not,*
    17. and knowest *not* that thou art
  4: 8. they rest *not* day and night, saying,
  6:10. dost thou *not* judge and avenge
  7:16. They shall hunger *no* more,
  9: 4. which have *not* the seal of God
    6. and shall *not* find it;
    20. which were *not* killed by these
    21. *Neither* repented (lit. and they repented *not*) they of their
  10: 6. that there should be time *no* longer:
  11: 9. shall *not* suffer their dead bodies
  12: 8. And prevailed *not;*
    11. they loved *not* their lives
  13: 8. whose names are *not* written
  14: 4. which were *not* defiled with
    5. And in their mouth was found *no* guile:
    11. and they have *no* rest day nor
  16: 9. and they repented *not*
    11. and repented *not* of their deeds.
    18. such as was *not* since men
    20. and the mountains were *not* found.
  17: 8. that thou sawest was, and is *not;*
    — were *not* written in the book of
    — that was, and is *not,* and yet is.

Rev.17:11. the beast that was, and is *not,*
    18: 7. I sit a queen, and am *no* widow,
    20: 4. had *not* worshipped the beast,
    — *neither* had received (his) mark
    5. the rest of the dead lived *not* again until
    6. the second death hath *no* power,
    11. there was found *no* place for them.
    15. was *not* found written in
    21: 1. and there was *no* more sea.
    4. there shall be *no* more death,
    — neither shall there)(‖ be any more pain:
    22. I saw *no* temple therein:
    23. the city had *no* need of the sun,
    25. for there shall be *no* night there.
    22: 3. And there shall be *no* more curse:
    5. And there shall be *no* night there; and they need *no* candle, neither

See also *ov* and *ovκ* in the compounds μὴ οὐκ, οὐ μὴ, and οὐκέτι.

οὐά or οὐαί, *oua* or *ouai.*

Mar 15:29. *Ah,* thou that destroyest the

οὐαί, *ouai.*

Mat.11:21. *Woe* unto thee, Chorazin! *woe* unto thee,
    18: 7. *Woe* unto the world
    — but *woe* to that man by whom
  23:13(14). *woe* unto you, scribes and
    14(13). *Woe* unto you, scribes and
    15. *Woe* unto you, scribes and Pharisees,
    16. *Woe* unto you, (ye) blind guides,
    23. *Woe* unto you, scribes and
    25. *Woe* unto you, scribes and
    27. *Woe* unto you, scribes and
    29. *Woe* unto you, scribes and
  24:19. *woe* unto them that are with child,
  26:24. but *woe* unto that man by
Mar 13:17. *woe* to them that are with child,
  14:21. *woe* to that man by whom
Lu. 6:24. *woe* unto you that are rich!
    25. *Woe* unto you that are full!
    — *Woe* unto you that laugh now!
    26. *Woe* unto you, when all men
  10:13. *Woe* unto thee, Chorazin! *woe* unto thee,
  11:42. *woe* unto you, Pharisees!
    43. *Woe* unto you, Pharisees!
    44. *Woe* unto you, scribes and
    46. *Woe* unto you also, (ye) lawyers!
    47. *Woe* unto you! for ye build
    52. *Woe* unto you, lawyers!
  17: 1. *woe* (unto him), through whom they
  21:23. But *woe* unto them that are
  22:22. *woe* unto that man by whom
1Co. 9:16. *woe* is unto me, if I preach not
Jude 11. *Woe* unto them! for they have
Rev. 8:13. *Woe, woe, woe,* to the inhabiters
  9:12. One *woe* is past; (and), behold, there come two *woes* more
  11:14. The second *woe* is past; (and), behold, the third *woe* cometh
  12:12. *Woe* to the inhabiters of the
  18:10. *Alas, alas* that great city Babylon,
    16. *Alas, alas* that great city, that
    19. *Alas, alas* that great city, wherein

οὐδαμῶς, *oudamōs.*

Mat. 2: 6. art *not* the least among the

οὐδέ, oude.

‖ is placed where the Greek has two or more
negatives.

Mat. 5:15. *Neither* do men light a candle, and
    6:15. *neither* will your Father forgive
      20. do not break through *nor* steal:
      26. they sow *not*, *neither* do they reap, *nor*
         gather into barns ;
      28. *neither* do they spin :
      29. That *even* Solomon in all his glory was
         not arrayed
    7:18. *neither* (can) a corrupt tree
    8:10. so great faith, *no*, *not* in Israel.
    9:17. *Neither* do men put new wine
   10:24. *nor* the servant above his lord.
   11:27. *neither* knoweth any man the Father,
   12: 4. *neither* for them which were with him,
      19. He shall not strive, *nor* cry ; *neither* shall
         any man hear his
   13:13. *neither* do they understand.
   16: 9. *neither* remember the five loaves
      10. *Neither* the seven loaves
   21:27. *Neither* tell I you by what authority ·
   22:46. *neither* durst any (man) from that day
   23:13(14). *neither* suffer ye them that
   24:21. no, *nor* ‖ ever shall be.
      36. no, *not* the angels of heaven,
   25:13. *nor* the hour wherein the Son of man
      45. ye did (it) *not* to me.
   27:14. he answered him to ‖ *never* a word ;
Mar 4:22. *neither* was any thing kept secret,
   6:31. they had *no* leisure *so much as* to eat.
   8:17. perceive ye not yet, *neither* understand ?
   11:26. *neither* will your Father which
      33. *Neither* do I tell you by what
   12:10. have ye *not* read this scripture ;
      21. *neither* left he any seed :
   13:32. no, *not* the angels which are in heaven,
         neither the Son,
   14:59. *neither* so did their witness
      68. *neither* understand I what thou sayest.
   16:13. *neither* believed they them.
Lu.   6: 3. Have ye *not* read *so much as* this,
      43. *neither* doth a corrupt tree
      44. *nor* of a bramble bush gather
   7: 7. *neither* thought I myself worthy
      9. so great faith, *no*, *not* in Israel.
   8:17. *neither* (any thing) hid, that shall
   11:33. *neither* under a bushel,
   12:24. they neither sow *nor* reap ; which neither
         have storehouse *nor* barn ;
      27. they toil not, they spin *not ;*
      — that Solomon in all his glory was *not*
      33. *neither* moth corrupteth,
   16:31. *neither* will they be persuaded,
   17:21. *Neither* shall they say, Lo here !
   18:13. would not lift up ‖ *so much as* (his) eyes
         unto heaven,
   20: 8. *Neither* tell I you by what
   21:15. not be able to gainsay *nor* resist.
   23:15. *No*, *nor* yet Herod: for I sent you
      40. Dost *not* thou fear God,
Joh. 1: 3. without him was *not* any thing made
      13. *nor* of the will of the flesh, *nor* of the will
         of man,
   5:22. For)(‖ the Father judgeth no man,
   6:24. *neither* his disciples,
   7: 5. *neither* did his brethren believe
   8:11. *Neither* do I condemn thee:
      42. *neither* came I of myself,
   11:50. *Nor* consider that it is expedient

Joh.13:16. *neither* he that is sent greater
   14:17. seeth him not, *neither* knoweth him :
   15: 4. *no more* (lit. so *neither*) can ye, except ye
   16: 3. not known the Father, *nor* me.
   21:25. *even* the world itself could *not*
Acts 2:27. *neither* wilt thou suffer thine
      31. *neither* his flesh did see corruption.
   4:32. *neither* said any (of them) that
      34. *Neither* was there any among
   7: 5. *no*, *not* (so much as) to set his
   8:21. Thou hast neither part *nor* lot
   9: 9. and neither did eat *nor* drink.
   16:21. *neither* to observe, being Romans.
   17:25. *Neither* is worshipped with
   19: 2. We have *not so much as* (αλλ' o.)
   20:24. *neither* count I my life dear
   24:18. with multitude, *nor* with tumult.
Ro.   2:28. *neither* (is that) circumcision,
   3:10. There is none righteous, *no*, *not* one:
   4:15. (there is) *no* transgression.
   8: 7. *neither* indeed can be.
   9: 7. *Neither*, because they are the seed
   16. *nor* of him that runneth,
   11:21. lest he *also* spare *not* thee.
1Co. 2: 6. *nor* of the princes of this world,
      4. 3. yea, I judge *not* mine own self.
   5: 1. as is *not so much as* named
   6: 5. *no*, *not* one that shall be able
   11:14. Doth *not even* nature itself
      16. *neither* the churches of God.
   14:21. yet for all that will they *not* hear me,
   15:13. *then* is Christ *not* risen:
      16. *then* is *not* Christ raised:
      50. *neither* doth corruption inherit
2Co. 3:10. even that which was made glorious had *no*
   7:12. *nor* for his cause that suffered
Gal. 1: 1. not of men, *neither* by man,
      12. For I *neither* received it of man,
      17. *Neither* went I up to Jerusalem
   2: 3. But *neither* Titus, who was with me,
      5. *no*, *not* for an hour;
   3:28. There is neither Jew *nor* Greek, there is
         neither bond *nor* free,
   4:14. ye despised not, *nor* rejected ;
   6:13. For *neither* they themselves who
Phi. 2:16. *neither* laboured in vain.
1Th. 2: 3. *nor* of uncleanness, nor in guile:
   5: 5. we are not of the night, *nor* of darkness.
2Th. 3: 8. *Neither* did we eat any man's
1Ti. 2:12. *nor* to usurp authority over
   6: 7. (and it is) certain we can carry nothing
         out. (lit. certain that *neither* can we carry
         any thing out)
      16. no man hath seen, *nor* can see:
Heb 8: 4. he should *not* be a priest,
   9:12. *Neither* by the blood of goats and
      18. *neither* the first (testament) was
      25. *Nor yet* that he should offer himself
   10: 8. *neither* hadst pleasure (therein);
   13: 5. I will never leave thee, *nor* ‖ forsake
1Pet. 2:22. *neither* was guile found in his
2Pet. 1: 8. *nor* unfruitful in the knowledge
1Joh.2:23. the same hath *not* the Father:
   3: 6. not seen him, *neither* known him.
Rev 5: 3. no man in heaven, *nor* in earth, *neither*
         under the earth, was able
      — *neither* to look thereon.
   7:16. *neither* thirst any more; *neither* ‖ shall the
         sun light on them, *nor* any heat.
   9: 4. *neither* any green thing, *neither* any
         tree;
   21:23. *neither* of the moon, to shine in it:

οὐδέποτε, oudepote.

Mat. 7:23. I *never* knew you:
    9:33. It was *never* so seen in Israel.
    21:16. have ye *never* read, Out of the
    42. Did ye *never* read in the scriptures,
    26:33. (yet) will I *never* be offended.
Mar 2:12. We *never* saw it on this fashion.
    25. Have ye *never* read what David
Lu. 15:29. *neither* transgressed I *at any time*
    — and yet thou *never* gavest me a kid,
Joh. 7:46. *Never* man spake like this man.
Acts10:14. I have *never* eaten any thing that is
    11: 8. *nothing* common or unclean hath *at any time*
    14: 8. who *never* had walked:
1Co.13: 8. Charity *never* faileth:
Heb 10: 1. can *never* with those sacrifices
    11. which can *never* take away sins:

οὐδέπω, oudepo.

|| denotes where there is a double negative in the Greek.

Lu. 23:53. wherein *never* || man *before* was laid.
Joh. 7:39. Jesus was *not yet* glorified.
    19:41. wherein was *never* || man *yet* laid.
    20: 9. For *as yet* they knew *not* the
1Co. 8: 2. he knoweth nothing || *yet* as he ought

οὐδείς, oudis.

|| denotes where there is a double negative in the Greek.
' *No one*,' is the literal rendering of the passages translated ' *no man.*'

Mat. 5:13. it is thenceforth good for *nothing*,
    6:24. *No man* can serve two masters:
    9:16. *No man* putteth a piece of new
    10:26. for there is *nothing* covered, that
    11:27. and *no man* knoweth the Son,
    17: 8. they saw *no man*, save Jesus
    20. and *nothing* shall be impossible
    19:17. (there is) *none* good but one,
    20: 7. Because *no man* hath hired us.
    21:19. and found *nothing* thereon,
    22:16. neither carest thou for || *any* (man):
    46. *no man* was able to answer him
    23:16. swear by the temple, it is *nothing;*
    18. swear by the altar, it is *nothing;*
    24:36. and hour knoweth *no* (man),
    26:62. Answerest thou *nothing?*
    27:12. he answered *nothing.*
    24. saw that he could prevail *nothing*,
Mar 2:21. *No man* also seweth a piece
    22. *no man* putteth new wine
    3:27. *No man* can enter into a strong
    5: 3. *no man* could bind him,
    4. neither could any (man) tame him. (lit. and *no one* could, &c.)
    37. he suffered || *no man* to follow him,
    6: 5. he could there do || *no* mighty work,
    7:12. ye suffer him no more to do || *ought* for
    15. There is *nothing* from without
    24. would have *no man* know (it):
    9: 8. they saw || *no man* any more, save
    29. can come forth by *nothing*, but
    39. for there is *no man* which shall
    10:18. (there is) *none* good but one,
    29. There is *no man* that hath left
    11: 2. whereon *never* man sat; (lit. *no one of* men)
    13. he found *nothing* but leaves;

Mar 12:14. and carest || for *no man:*
    34. And *no man* || after that durst
    13:32. and (that) hour knoweth *no man*,
    14:60. Answerest || thou *nothing?*
    61. held his peace, and answered *nothing.*
    15: 4. Answerest thou *nothing?*
    5. Jesus yet answered || *nothing;*
    16: 8. *neither* said they *any thing* to || *any*
Lu. 1:61. There is *none* of thy kindred
    4: 2. in those days he did eat || *nothing :*
    24. *No* prophet is accepted in his own
    26. But unto *none* of them was Elias
    27. and *none* of them was cleansed, saving
    5: 5. and have taken *nothing:*
    36. *No man* putteth a piece of a new
    37. *no man* putteth new wine
    39. *No man* also having drunk old
    7:28. there is *not a* greater prophet
    8:16. *No man*, when he hath lighted a
    43. neither could be healed of || *any*,
    51. he suffered || *no man* to go in, save
    9:36. and told *no man* in those days|| *any* of
    62. *No man*, having put his hand to
    10:19. and *nothing* || shall by any means
    22. *no man* knoweth who the Son is,
    11:33. *No man*, when he hath lighted
    12: 2. For there is *nothing* covered,
    14:24. That *none* of those men which
    15:16. *no man* gave unto him.
    16:13. *No* servant can serve two
    18:19. *none* (is) good, save one,
    29. There is *no man* that hath left
    34. they understood *none* of these
    19:30. whereon yet never man sat: (lit. *no man* ever sat)
    20:40. they durst not ask him || *any*
    22:35. And they said, *Nothing*.
    23: 4. I find *no* fault in this man.
    9. but he answered him *nothing.*
    14. have found *no* fault in this man
    15. *nothing* worthy of death is done
    22. I have found *no* cause of death in him:
    41. this man hath done *nothing* amiss.
    53. wherein never || *man* before was laid.
Joh. 1:18. *No man* hath seen God at any time ;
    3: 2. for *no man* can do these miracles
    13. And *no man* hath ascended up to
    27. A man can receive *nothing*, except
    32. and *no man* receiveth his
    4:27. yet *no man* said, What seekest
    5:19. The Son can do || *nothing* of himself,
    22. For the Father judgeth *no man*,
    30. I can of mine own self do *nothing :*
    6:44. *No man* can come to me, except
    63. the flesh profiteth || *nothing :*
    65. *no man* can come unto me,
    7: 4. *no man* (that) doeth any thing in
    13. *no man* spake openly of him
    19. and (yet) *none* of you keepeth the law?
    26. and they say *nothing* unto him.
    27. *no man* knoweth whence he is.
    30. *no man* laid hands on him,
    44. but *no man* laid hands on him.
    8:10. hath *no man* condemned thee?
    11. She said, *No man*, Lord.
    15. I judge || *no man.*
    20. *no man* laid hands on him ;
    28. and (that) I do *nothing* of myself ;
    33. and were never in bondage to any man: (lit. were in bondage to *none* ever)
    54. my honour is *nothing :*
    9: 4. when *no man* can work.

Joh. 9:33. he could do ‖ *nothing.*
  10:18. *No man* taketh it from me,
    29. and *no* (man) is able to pluck
    41. John did *no* miracle:
  11:49. Ye know ‖ *nothing* at all,
  12:19. how ye prevail ‖ *nothing ?*
  13:28. Now *no man* at the table knew
  14: 6. *no man* cometh unto the Father, but
    30. and hath ‖ *nothing* in me.
  15: 5. without me ye can do ‖ *nothing.*
    13. Greater love hath *no man* than this,
    24. which *none* other man did,
  16: 5. and *none* of you asketh me,
    22. your joy *no man* taketh from you.
    23. in that day ye shall ask me ‖ *nothing.*
    24. Hitherto have ye asked ‖ *nothing* in
    29. and speakest *no* proverb.
  17:12. and *none* of them is lost, but
  18: 9. have I lost ‖ *none.*
    20. and in secret have I said *nothing.*
    31. It is not lawful for us to put ‖ *any man*
    38. I find in him *no* fault (at all).
  19: 4. that I find *no* fault in him.
    11. Thou couldest have *no* power (at all)
    41. wherein was never ‖ *man* yet laid.
  21: 3. that night they caught *nothing.*
    12. And *none* of the disciples durst
Acts 4:12. Neither is there salvation in ‖ *any* other:
    14. they could say *nothing* against it.
  5:13. of the rest durst *no man* join himself
    23. we found *no man* within.
    36. and brought to *nought.*
  8:16. he was fallen upon *none* of them:
  9: 8. he saw *no* man:
  15: 9. And put *no* difference between us
  17:21. spent their time in *nothing* else,
  18:10. *no man* shall set on thee to hurt
    17. Gallio cared for *none* of those things.
  19:27. Diana should be despised, (lit. be counted
      for *nothing*)
  20:20. how I kept back *nothing* that
    24. But *none* of these things move me,
    33. I have coveted *no man's* silver,
  21:24. concerning thee, are *nothing*,
  23: 9. We find *no* evil in this man:
  25:10. to the Jews have I done *no* wrong,
    11. but if there be *none* of these things
    — *no man* may deliver me unto them.
    18. they brought *none* accusation
  26:22. saying *none* other things than
    26. that *none* of these things are
    31. This man doeth *nothing* worthy
  27.22. *no* loss of (any man's) life
    34. there shall *not* an hair fall from the head
      of *any* of you.
  28: 5. and felt *no* harm.
    17. I have committed *nothing* against
Ro. 8: 1. now *no* condemnation to them
  14: 7. For *none* of us liveth to himself, and *no*
      man dieth to himself.
    14. that (there is) *nothing* unclean of
1Co. 1:14. that I baptized *none* of you, but
  2: 8. Which *none* of the princes of
    11. the things of God knoweth *no man,*
    15. he himself is judged of *no man.*
  3:11. can *no man* lay than that is laid,
  4: 4. I know *nothing* by myself ;
  7:19. Circumcision is *nothing*, and uncircumci-
      sion is *nothing*,
  8: 2. he knoweth *nothing* ‖ yet as he ought
    4. an idol (is) *nothing* in the world, and that
      (there is) *none* other

1Co. 9:15. I have used *none* of these things:
  12: 3. that *no man* speaking by the Spirit
    — *no man* can say that Jesus is
  13: 2. and have not charity, I am *nothing.*
    3. it profiteth me *nothing.*
  14: 2. for *no man* understandeth (him) ;
    10. *none* of them (is) without signification.
2Co. 5:16. know we *no man* after the flesh:
  7: 2. have wronged *no man,* we have corrupted
      no man, we have defrauded *no man.*
    5. our flesh had *no* rest,
  11: 9. I was chargeable ‖ to *no man :*
  12:11. for in *nothing* am I behind the
    — though I be *nothing.*
Gal. 2: 6. it maketh *no* matter to me:
    — in conference added *nothing* to me:
  3:11. But that *no man* is justified by
    15. *no man* disannulleth, or
  4: 1. differeth *nothing* from a servant,
    12. ye have *not* injured me *at all.*
  5: 2. Christ shall profit you *nothing.*
    10. that ye will be *none* otherwise minded:
Eph. 5:29. For *no man* ever yet hated his own
Phi. 1:20. that in *nothing* I shall be ashamed,
  2:20. I have *no man* likeminded,
  4:15. *no* church communicated with me
1Ti. 4: 4. and *nothing* to be refused,
  6: 7. For we brought *nothing* into (this)
    16. whom *no man* hath seen,
2Ti. 2: 4. *No man* that warreth
    14. about words to *no* profit,
  4:16. *no man* stood with me,
Tit. 1:15. unbelieving (is) *nothing* pure ;
Philem.14. would I do *nothing ;*
Heb 2: 8. he left *nothing* (that is) not put
  6:13. because he could swear by *no* greater,
  7:13. of which *no man* gave attendance
    14. Moses spake *nothing* concerning
    19. the law made *nothing* perfect,
  12:14. without which *no man* shall see
Jas. 1:13. *neither* tempteth he *any* man:
  3: 8. the tongue can *no* man tame ;
    12. so (can) *no* fountain both yield
1Joh.1: 5. and in him is ‖ *no* darkness at all.
  4:12. *No man* hath seen God at any time.
Rev. 2:17. which *no man* knoweth saving
  3: 7. and *no man* shutteth; and shutteth, and
      no man openeth ;
    8. and *no man* can shut it:
    17. and have need of *nothing ;*
  5: 3. And *no man* in heaven, nor
    4. because *no man* was found worthy
  7: 9. which *no man* could number,
  14: 3. and *no man* could learn that song
  15: 8. and *no man* was able to enter
  18:11. for *no man* ‖ buyeth their merchandise
  19:12. that *no man* knew, but he himself.

οὐθέν, see under οὐδείς.
1 Cor. 13:2. in some copies.

οὐκέτι or οὐκ ἔτι, *ouketi* or *ouk eti.*

[2] is placed where the words are printed apart, οὐκ
ἔτι ; and ‖ shews where either form is combined
with an additional negative in the Greek.

Mat.19: 6. they are *no more* twain,
  22:46. from that day forth ask him ‖ *any more*
Mar 7:12. *no more* to do ‖ ought for his father
  9: 8. they saw no man ‖ *any more,*

Mar 10: 8. they are *no more* twain,
   12:34. no man ‖ *after that* durst ask him
   14:25. I will ‖ drink *no more* of the fruit
   15: 5. Jesus ‖ *yet* answered nothing;
Lu. 15:19. And am *no more* worthy to be called
   21. and am *no more* worthy to be called
   20:40. *after that*[2] they durst *not* ‖ ask him any
   22:16. I will *not any more* ‖ eat thereof,
Joh. 4:42. *Now* we believe, *not* because of thy
   6:66. and walked *no more* with him.
   11:54. Jesus therefore walked *no more*[2] openly
   14:19. and the world seeth me *no more*;[2]
   30. *Hereafter* I will *not*[2] talk much
   15:15. *Henceforth* I call you *not* servants;
   16:10. and ye see me *no more*;[2]
   21. she remembereth *no more*[2] the
   25. when I shall *no more*[2] speak unto
   17:11. And *now* I am *no more*[2] in the world,
   21: 6. and *now* they were *not*[2] able to draw it
Acts 8:39. the eunuch saw him ‖ *no more:*
   20:25. shall see my face *no more.*
   38. they should see his face *no more.*
Ro. 6: 9. dieth *no more*;[2] death hath *no more*[2] dominion over him.
   7:17. Now then it is *no more*[2] I that do it,
   20. it is *no more*[2] I that do it, but
   11: 6. then (is it) *no more*[2] of works: otherwise grace is *no more*[2] grace. But if (it be) of works, then is it *no more*[2] grace: otherwise work is *no more*[2] work.
   14:15. *now* walkest thou *not*[2] charitably.
2Co. 1:23. I came *not as yet* unto Corinth.
   5:16. now henceforth know we (him) *no more.*[2]
Gal. 2:20. *yet not*[2] I, but Christ liveth in me:
   3:18. (it is) *no more*[2] of promise:
   25. we are *no longer*[2] under a schoolmaster.
   4: 7. thou art *no more*[2] a servant, but
Eph 2:19. ye are *no more* strangers and
Philem 16. *Not now* as a servant, but above
Heb 10:18. (there is) *no more*[2] offering for sin.
   26. *no more*[2] sacrifice for sins,
Rev. 18:11. for no man buyeth their merchandise ‖ *any more:*
   14. shalt find them *no more* ‖ at all.

Those passages in which ἔτι is combined with ου, ουκ, ουδε, ουτε, but with the intervention of words between them, will be found under ἔτι.

οὐκοῦν, *oukoun.*

Joh. 18:37. *?* Art thou a king *then?*

οὐ μή see after μή.

οὖν, *oun.*

[1] is affixed to those passages where it is combined with μέν.

Mat. 1:17. *So* all the generations from Abraham
   3: 8. Bring forth *therefore* fruits meet
   10. *therefore* every tree which
   5:19. Whosoever *therefore* shall break one
   23. *Therefore* if thou bring thy gift
   48. Be ye *therefore* perfect,
   6: 2. *Therefore* when thou doest (thine) alms,
   8. Be not ye *therefore* like unto them:
   9. After this manner *therefore* pray ye:
   22. if *therefore* thine eye be single,
   23. If *therefore* the light that is in thee
   31. *Therefore* take no thought,

Mat. 6:34. Take *therefore* no thought for
   7:11. If *ye then*, being evil, know
   12. *Therefore* all things whatsoever
   24. *Therefore* whosoever heareth these
   9:38. Pray ye *therefore* the Lord of the
   10:16. be ye *therefore* wise as serpents,
   26. Fear them not *therefore:*
   31. Fear ye not *therefore*,
   32. Whosoever *therefore* shall confess
   12:12. How much *then* is a man better
   26. how shall *then* his kingdom
   13:18. Hear ye *therefore* the parable
   27. from whence *then* hath it tares?
   28. Wilt thou *then* that we go and
   40. As *therefore* the tares are gathered
   56. Whence *then* hath this (man) all
   17:10. Why *then* say the scribes
   18: 4. Whosoever *therefore* shall humble
   26. The servant *therefore* fell down,
   29. *And* his fellowservant fell down
   19: 6. What *therefore* God hath joined
   7. Why did Moses *then* command
   21:25. Why did ye not *then* believe
   40. When the lord *therefore* of the
   22: 9. Go ye *therefore* into the highways,
   17. Tell us *therefore*, What thinkest thou?
   21. Render *therefore* unto Cæsar
   28. *Therefore* in the resurrection
   43. How *then* doth David in spirit call
   45. If David *then* call him Lord,
   23: 3. All *therefore* whatsoever they bid
   20. Whoso *therefore* shall swear
   24:15. When ye *therefore* shall see the
   26. *Wherefore* if they shall say unto you,
   42. Watch *therefore:* for ye know not what
   25:13. Watch *therefore*, for ye know neither
   27. Thou oughtest *therefore* to have
   28. Take *therefore* the talent from
   26:54. But how *then* shall the scriptures
   27:17. *Therefore* when they were gathered
   22. What shall I do *then* with Jesus
   64. Command *therefore* that the sepulchre
   28:19. Go ye *therefore*, and teach all
Mar 3:31. There came *then* his brethren and
   10: 9. What *therefore* God hath joined
   11:31. Why *then* did ye not believe him?
   12: 6. Having yet *therefore* one son,
   9. What shall *therefore* the lord of
   23. In the resurrection *therefore*,
   27. ye *therefore* do greatly err.
   37. David *therefore* himself calleth him
   13:35. Watch ye *therefore:* for ye know not
   15:12. What will ye *then* that I shall do
   16:19. *So then*[1] after the Lord had spoken
Lu. 3: 7. *Then* said he to the multitude
   8. Bring forth *therefore* fruits
   9. every tree *therefore* which
   10. What shall we do *then?*
   18. *And*[1] many other things in his
   4: 7. If thou *therefore* wilt worship me,
   6: 9. *Then* said Jesus unto them,
   36. Be ye *therefore* merciful, as your
   7:31. Whereunto *then* shall I liken
   42. Tell me *therefore*, which of them
   8:18. Take heed *therefore* how ye hear:
   10: 2. *Therefore* said he unto them,
   — pray ye *therefore* the Lord of the
   36. Which *now* of these three,
   37. *Then* said Jesus unto him, Go, and do
   40. bid her *therefore* that she help me.
   11:13. If ye *then*, being evil, know how
   34. *therefore* when thine eye is single,

Lu. 11:35. Take heed *therefore* that the light
36. If thy whole body *therefore*
12: 7. Fear not *therefore :* ye are of more value
26. If ye *then* be not able to do that
40. Be ye *therefore* ready also:
13:14. in them *therefore* come and be
15. The Lord *then* answered him,
14:33. So *likewise*, whosoever he be
15:28. *therefore* came his father out,
16:11. If *therefore* ye have not been
27. I pray thee *therefore*, father,
19:12. He said *therefore*, A certain
20: 5. Why *then* believed ye him not?
15. What *therefore* shall the lord
17. What is this *then* that is written,
29. There were *therefore* seven
33. *Therefore* in the resurrection
44. David *therefore* calleth him Lord,
21: 7. *but* when shall these things be?
8. go ye not *therefore* after them.
14. Settle (it) *therefore* in your hearts,
36. Watch ye *therefore*, and pray always,
22:36. *Then* said he unto them,
70. Art thou *then* the Son of God?
23:16. I will *therefore* chastise him, and
20. Pilate *therefore*, willing to
22. I will *therefore* chastise him, and let
Joh. 1:21. What *then ?* Art thou Elias?
22. *Then* said they unto him,
25. Why baptizest thou *then*,
2:18. *Then* answered the Jews
20. *Then* said the Jews, Forty and six
22. When *therefore* he was risen
3:25. *Then* there arose a question
29. this my joy *therefore* is fulfilled.
4: 1. When *therefore* the Lord knew
5. *Then* cometh he to a city of
6. Jesus *therefore*, being wearied with
9. *Then* saith the woman of Samaria
11. from whence *then* hast thou that
28. The woman *then* left her waterpot, –
30. *Then* they went out of the city,
33. *Therefore* said the disciples
40. *So* when the Samaritans were
45. *Then* when he was come into Galilee,
46. *So* Jesus came again into Cana
48. *Then* said Jesus unto him,
52. *Then* enquired he of them the hour
53. *So* the father knew that (it was)
5: 4. whosoever *then* first after the
10. The Jews *therefore* said unto him
12. *Then* asked they him, What man
18. Therefore)(the Jews sought the more
19. *Then* answered Jesus and said
6: 5. When Jesus *then* lifted up (his) eyes,
10. *So* the men sat down,
13. *Therefore* they gathered (them) together,
14. *Then* those men, when they had seen
15. When Jesus *therefore* perceived
19. *So* when they had rowed about
21. *Then* they willingly received him
24. When the people *therefore* saw
28. *Then* said they unto him,
30. They said *therefore* unto him, What sign shewest thou *then*,
32. *Then* Jesus said unto them,
34. *Then* said they unto him, Lord,
41. The Jews *then* murmured at him,
42. how is it *then* that he saith,
43. Jesus *therefore* answered and said
45. Every man *therefore* that hath heard,
52. The Jews *therefore* strove among

Joh. 6:53. *Then* Jesus said unto them,
60. Many *therefore* of his disciples,
62. (What) and if)(ye shall see the Son
67. *Then* said Jesus unto the twelve,
68. *Then* Simon Peter answered him,
7: 3. His brethren *therefore* said unto him,
6. *Then* Jesus said unto them,
11. *Then* the Jews sought him
25. *Then* said some of them
28. *Then* cried Jesus in the temple
30. *Then* they sought to take him:
33. *Then* said Jesus unto them,
35. *Then* said the Jews among themselves,
40. Many of the people *therefore*,
43. *So* there was a division among
45. *Then* came the officers
47. *Then* answered them the Pharisees,
8: 5. *but* what sayest thou ?
12. *Then* spake Jesus again unto them,
13. The Pharisees *therefore* said unto
19. *Then* said they unto him,
21. *Then* said Jesus again unto
22. *Then* said the Jews, Will he kill
24. I said *therefore* unto you,
25. *Then* said they unto him,
28. *Then* said Jesus unto them,
31. *Then* said Jesus to those
36. If the Son *therefore* shall make
38. and ye)(do that which ye have seen
41. *Then* said they to him, We be not
42. Jesus)(said unto them, If God
48. *Then* answered the Jews, and
52. *Then* said the Jews unto him,
57. *Then* said the Jews unto him,
59. *Then* took they up stones
9: 7. He went his way *therefore*, and washed,
8. The neighbours *therefore*, and they
10. *Therefore* said they unto him,
12. *Then* said they unto him,
15. *Then* again the Pharisees also
16. *Therefore* said some of the Pharisees,
18. *But* the Jews did not believe
19. how *then* doth he now see ?
24. *Then* again called they the man
25. He)(answered and said, Whether he
28. *Then* they reviled him,
41. *therefore* your sin remaineth.
10: 7. *Then* said Jesus unto them
19. There was a division *therefore* again
24. *Then* came the Jews round about him,
31. *Then* the Jews took up stones again
39. *Therefore* they sought again to take him:
11: 3. *Therefore* his sisters sent unto him,
6. When he had heard *therefore* that he
12. *Then* said his disciples, Lord, if he
14. *Then* said Jesus unto them plainly,
16. *Then* said Thomas, which is called
17. *Then* when Jesus came, he found
20. *Then* Martha, as soon as she heard
21. *Then* said Martha unto Jesus,
31. The Jews *then* which were with her
32. *Then* when Mary was come
33. When Jesus *therefore* saw her weeping,
36. *Then* said the Jews, Behold how
38. Jesus *therefore* again groaning
41. *Then* they took away the stone
45. *Then* many of the Jews which came
47. *Then* gathered the chief priests and
53. *Then* from that day forth
54. Jesus *therefore* walked no more
56. *Then* sought they for Jesus,
12: 1. *Then* Jesus six days before the

Joh.12: 2. There)(they made him a supper ;
3. *Then* took Mary a pound of ointment
4. *Then* saith one of his disciples,
7. *Then* said Jesus, Let her alone:
9. Much people of the Jews *therefore* knew
17. The people *therefore* that was with
19. The Pharisees *therefore* said
21. The same came *therefore* to Philip,
28. *Then* came there a voice from
29. The people *therefore*, that stood by,
35. *Then* Jesus said unto them,
50. whatsoever I speak *therefore*,
13: 6. *Then* cometh he to Simon Peter:
12. *So* after he had washed their feet,
14. If I *then*, (your) Lord and Master,
22. *Then* the disciples looked one on
24. Simon Peter *therefore* beckoned
27. *Then* said Jesus unto him,
30. He *then* having received the sop
31(30). *Therefore*, when he was gone out,.
16:17. *Then* said (some) of his disciples
18. They said *therefore*, What is this
19. *Now* Jesus knew that they were desirous
to ask him,
22. And ye now *therefore* have sorrow:
18: 3. Judas *then*, having received a band
4. Jesus *therefore*, knowing all things
6. As soon *then* as he had said
7. *Then* asked he them again, Whom
8. if *therefore* ye seek me, let these
10. *Then* Simon Peter having a sword
11. *Then* said Jesus unto Peter,
12. *Then* the band and the captain
16. *Then* went out that other disciple,
17. *Then* saith the damsel that kept
19. The high priest *then* asked Jesus
25. They said *therefore* unto him,
27. Peter *then* denied again:
28. *Then* led they Jesus from Caiaphas
29. Pilate *then* went out unto them,
31. *Then* said Pilate unto them,
— The Jews *therefore* said unto him,
33. *Then* Pilate entered into the judgment
37. Pilate *therefore* said unto him,
39. will ye *therefore* that I release
40. *Then* cried they all again,
19: 1. Then Pilate *therefore* took Jesus,
4. Pilate *therefore* went forth again,
5. *Then* came Jesus forth, wearing
6. When the chief priests *therefore*
8. When Pilate *therefore* heard that
10. *Then* saith Pilate unto him,
13. When Pilate *therefore* heard that
16. Then delivered he him *therefore*
20. This title *then* read many of the
21. *Then* said the chief priests
23. *Then* the soldiers, when they had
24. They said *therefore* among themselves,
— These things *therefore*[1] the soldiers
26. When Jesus *therefore* saw his mother,
29. *Now* there was set a vessel full of
30. When Jesus *therefore* had received
31. The Jews *therefore*, because it was
32. *Then* came the soldiers, and brake the
38. He came *therefore*, and took the body
40. *Then* took they the body of Jesus,
42. There laid they Jesus *therefore*
20: 2. *Then* she runneth, and cometh to
3. Peter *therefore* went forth,
6. *Then* cometh Simon Peter
8. Then)(went in also that other
10. *Then* the disciples went away

Joh.20:11. *and* as she wept, she stooped
19. *Then* the same day at evening,
20. *Then* were the disciples glad, when
21. *Then* said Jesus to them again,
25. The other disciples *therefore* said
30. *And*[1] many other signs *truly* did Jesus
21: 5. *Then* Jesus saith unto them,
6. They cast *therefore*, and now they
7. *Therefore* that disciple whom
— *Now* when Simon Peter heard
9. As soon *then* as they were come
13. Jesus *then* cometh, and taketh
15. *So* when they had dined,
23. *Then* went this saying abroad
Acts 1: 6. When they *therefore*[1] were come
18. *Now*[1] this man purchased a field
21. *Wherefore* of these men which
2:30. *Therefore* being a prophet,
33. *Therefore* being by the right hand
36. *Therefore* let all the house of
41. *Then*[1] they that gladly received
3:19. Repent ye *therefore*, and be
5:41. *And*[1] they departed from the
6: 3. *Wherefore*, brethren, look ye out
8: 4. *Therefore*[1] they that were scattered
22. Repent *therefore* of this thy
25. *And*[1] they, when they had testified and
9:31. *Then*[1] had the churches rest
10:23. *Then* called he them in,
29. I ask *therefore* for what
32. Send *therefore* to Joppa,
33. Immediately *therefore* I sent to
— Now *therefore* are we all here
11:17. Forasmuch *then* as God gave them
19. *Now*[1] they which were scattered
12: 5. Peter *therefore*[1] was kept in prison:
13: 4. *So*[1] they, being sent forth by the
38. Be it known unto you *therefore*,
40. Beware *therefore*, lest that come
14: 3. Long time *therefore*[1] abode they
15: 2. When *therefore* Paul and Barnabas had
3. *And*[1] being brought on their way
10. Now *therefore* why tempt ye God,
27. We ha:e sent *therefore* Judas and
30. *So*[1] when they were dismissed,
39. *And* the contention was so sharp
16: 5. *And so*[1] were the churches established
11. *Therefore* loosing from Troas,
36. *therefore* depart, and go in peace.
17:12. *Therefore*[1] many of them believed ;
17. *Therefore*[1] disputed he in the
20. we would know *therefore* what
23. Whom *therefore* ye ignorantly
29. Forasmuch *then* as we are
30. *And*[1] the times of this ignorance
18:14. If)([1] it were a matter of wrong or
19: 3. Unto what *then* were ye baptized ?
32. Some *therefore*[1] cried one thing,
36. Seeing *then* that these things
38. *Wherefore*[1] if Demetrius, and
20:28. Take heed *therefore* unto yourselves,
21:22. What is it *therefore* ?
23. Do *therefore* this that we say
22:29. *Then* straightway they departed
23:15. Now *therefore* ye with the
18. *So*[1] he took him, and brought
21. *But* do not thou yield unto them:
22. *So*[1] the chief captain (then)
31. *Then*[1] the soldiers, as it was
25: 1. *Now* when Festus was come
4. *But*[1] Festus answered, that Paul
5. Let them *therefore*, said he,

Acts25:17. *Therefore*, when they were come
23. *And* on the morrow, when Agrippa
26: 4. My)(¹ *manner* of life from my youth,
9. I *verily*¹ thought with myself,
22. Having *therefore* obtained help
28: 5. *And*¹ he shook off the beast into
9. *So* when this was done,
20. For this cause *therefore* have I
28. Be it known *therefore* unto you,
Ro. 2:21. Thou *therefore* which teachest
26. *Therefore* if the uncircumcision
3: 1. What advantage *then* hath the Jew?
9. What *then?* are we better (than)
27. Where (is) boasting *then?*
28. *Therefore* we conclude that
31. Do we *then* make void the law
4: 1. What shall we *then* say
9. (Cometh) this blessedness *then*
10. How was it *then* reckoned?
5: 1. *Therefore* being justified by faith,
9. Much more *then*, being now
18. *Therefore* (ἀρα οὖν) as by the offence of
6: 1. What shall we say *then?*
4. *Therefore* we are buried with him
12. Let not sin *therefore* reign in
15. What *then?* shall we sin,
21. What fruit had ye *then* in
7: 3. *So then* if, while (her) husband
7. What shall we say *then?*
13. Was *then* that which is good
25. *So then* (ἀρα οὖν) with the mind I myself
8:12. *Therefore* (ἀρα οὖν), brethren, we are
31. What shall we *then* say to these
9:14. What shall we say *then?*
16. *So* then (it is) not of him that
18. *Therefore* (ἀρα οὖν) hath he mercy on
19. Thou wilt say *then* unto me,
30. What shall we say *then?*
10:14. How *then* shall they call on
11: 1. I say *then*, Hath God cast away
5. Even so *then* at this present
7. What *then?* Israel hath not
11. I say *then*, Have they stumbled
19. Thou wilt say *then*,
22. Behold *therefore* the goodness
12: 1. I beseech you *therefore*, brethren,
20. *Therefore* if thine enemy hunger,
13: 7. Render *therefore* to all their dues:
10. *therefore* love (is) the fulfilling
12. let us *therefore* cast off the
14: 8. whether we live *therefore*, or
12. *So* then every one of us shall
13. Let us not *therefore* judge
16. Let not *then* your good be evil
19. Let us *therefore* (ἀρα οὖν) follow after
15:17. I have *therefore* whereof I may glory
28. When *therefore* I have performed
16:19. I am glad *therefore* on your
1Co. 3: 5. Who *then* is Paul, and who
4:16. *Wherefore* I beseech you,
5: 7. Purge out *therefore* the old leaven,
6: 4. If *then*¹ ye have judgments of things
7. Now *therefore*¹ there is utterly
15. shall I *then* take the members of Christ,
7:26. I suppose *therefore* that this is
8: 4. As concerning *therefore* the eating
9:18. What is my reward *then?*
25. *Now*¹ they (do it) to obtain a corruptible
10:19. What say I *then?*
31. Whether *therefore* ye eat, or drink,
11:20. When ye come together *therefore*
14:11. *Therefore* if I know not the meaning

1Co.14:15. What is it *then?*
23. If *therefore* the whole church
26. How is it *then*, brethren?
15:11. *Therefore* whether (it were) I
16:11. Let no man *therefore* despise him:
18. *therefore* acknowledge ye them that
2Co. 1:17. When I *therefore* was thus minded,
3:12. Seeing *then* that we have such hope,
5: 6. *Therefore* (we are) always confident,
11. Knowing *therefore* the terror of
20. *Now then* we are ambassadors
7: 1. Having *therefore* these promises,
8:24. *Wherefore* shew ye to them, and
9: 5. *Therefore* I thought it necessary
11:15. *Therefore* (it is) no great thing
12: 9. Most gladly *therefore* will I
Gal. 3: 5. He *therefore* that ministereth
19. *Wherefore then* (serveth) the law?
21. (Is) the law *then* against the promises
4:15. Where is *then* the blessedness
5: 1. Stand fast *therefore* in the liberty
6:10. we have *therefore* (ἀρα οὖν) opportunity,
Eph. 2:19. *Now* therefore ye are no more
4: 1. I *therefore*, the prisoner of the Lord,
17. This I say *therefore*, and testify
5: 1. Be ye *therefore* followers of God,
7. Be not ye *therefore* partakers
15. See *then* that ye walk circumspectly,
6:14. Stand *therefore*, having your loins
Phi. 2: 1. If (there be) *therefore* any consolation
23. Him *therefore*¹ I hope to send
28. I sent him *therefore* the more
29. Receive him *therefore* in the Lord
3:15. Let us *therefore*, as many as be
Col. 2: 6. As ye have *therefore* received Christ
16. Let no man *therefore* judge you
20. *Wherefore* if ye be dead with Christ
3: 1. If ye *then* be risen with Christ,
5. Mortify *therefore* your members
12. Put on *therefore*, as the elect
1Th. 4: 1. Furthermore *then* we beseech you,
5: 6. *Therefore* (ἀρα οὖν) let us not sleep, as
2Th. 2:15. *Therefore* (ἀρα οὖν), brethren, stand fast,
1Ti. 2: 1. I exhort *therefore*, that, first
8. I will *therefore* that men pray
3: 2. A bishop *then* must be blameless,
5:14. I will *therefore* that the younger
2Ti. 1: 8. Be not thou *therefore* ashamed
2: 1. Thou *therefore*, my son, be strong
3. Thou *therefore* endure hardness,
21. If a man *therefore* purge himself
4: 1. I charge (thee) *therefore* before God,
Philem 17. If thou count me *therefore* a
Heb 2:14. Forasmuch *then* as the children
4: 1. Let us *therefore* fear, lest,
6. Seeing *therefore* it remaineth
11. Let us labour *therefore* to enter
14. Seeing *then* that we have a great
16. Let us *therefore* come boldly
7:11. If *therefore*¹ perfection were by
9: 1. *Then*¹ verily the first (covenant)
23. (It was) *therefore* necessary
10:19. Having *therefore*, brethren, boldness
35. Cast not away *therefore* your
13:15. By him *therefore* let us offer
Jas. 4: 4. whosoever *therefore* will be a friend
7. Submit yourselves *therefore* to God.
17. *Therefore* to him that knoweth
5: 7. Be patient *therefore*, brethren,
1Pet.2: 1. *Wherefore* laying aside all malice,
7. Unto you *therefore* which believe (he is)
13. Submit yourselves)(to every ordinance

1Pet. 4: 1. Forasmuch *then* as Christ hath
    7. be ye *therefore* sober,
    5: 6. Humble yourselves *therefore*
2Pet. 3:11. (Seeing) *then* (that) all these things
    17. Ye *therefore*, beloved, seeing ye
1Joh. 2:24. Let that *therefore* abide in you, which
3Joh.   8. We *therefore* ought to receive such,
Rev. 2: 5. Remember *therefore* from whence
    3: 3. Remember *therefore* how thou hast
    — If *therefore* thou shalt not watch,
    19. be zealous *therefore*, and repent.

οὔπω, oupo.

Mat.15:17. Do *not* ye *yet* understand,
   16: 9. Do ye *not yet* understand,
   24: 6. but the end is *not yet*.
Mar 8:17. perceive ye *not yet*,
   13: 7. but the end (shall) *not* (be) *yet*.
Joh. 2: 4. mine hour is *not yet* come.
   3:24. John was *not yet* cast into prison.
   7: 6. My time is *not yet* come:
    8. I go *not* up *yet* unto this feast; for my
     time is *not yet* full come.
   30. his hour was *not yet* come.
   39. the Holy Ghost was *not yet* (given);
   8:20. his hour was *not yet* come.
   57. Thou art *not yet* fifty years old,
   11:30. Jesus was *not yet* come into the
   20:17. for I am *not yet* ascended to my
Acts 8:16. For ‖ *as yet* he was fallen upon none
1Co. 3: 2. for *hitherto* ye were *not* able
Heb 2: 8. now we see *not yet* all things put
   12: 4. Ye have *not yet* resisted unto
1Joh.3: 2. it doth *not yet* appear what we
Rev.17:10. the other is *not yet* come;
   12. have received *no* kingdom *as yet;*

οὐρά, oura.

Rev. 9:10. And they had *tails* like unto scorpions,
    and there were stings in their *tails:*
   19. for their *tails* (were) like unto serpents,
   12: 4. And his *tail* drew the third part

οὐράνιος, ouranios.

Mat. 6:14. your *heavenly* Father will also forgive
   26. yet your *heavenly* Father feedeth
   32. for your *heavenly* Father knoweth
   15:13. my *heavenly* Father hath not planted,
Lu. 2:13. a multitude of the *heavenly* host
Acts26:19. I was not disobedient unto the *heavenly*
    vision:

οὐρανόθεν, ouranothen.

Acts14:17. gave us rain *from heaven,*
   26:13. in the way a light *from heaven,*

οὐρανός, ouranos.

[2] denotes the word in Greek to be plural.

Mat. 3: 2. the kingdom of *heaven* [2] is at hand.
   16. and, lo, the *heavens* [2] were opened
   17. And lo a voice from *heaven,* [2]
   4:17. the kingdom of *heaven* [2] is at hand.

Mat. 5: 3. for their's is the kingdom of *heaven.* [2]
   10. for their's is the kingdom of *heaven.* [2]
   12. great (is) your reward in *heaven:* [2]
   16. your Father which is in *heaven.* [2]
   18. Till *heaven* and earth pass,
   19. least in the kingdom of *heaven:* [2]
   — great in the kingdom of *heaven.* [2]
   20. into the kingdom of *heaven.* [2]
   34. neither by *heaven;* for it is God's
   45. of your Father which is in *heaven:* [2]
   48. even as your Father which is in *heaven* [2]
   6: 1. of your Father which is in *heaven.* [2]
   9. Our Father which art in *heaven,* [2]
   10. as (it is) in *heaven.*
   20. treasures in *heaven,*
   26. Behold the fowls of the *air:*
   7:11. your Father which is in *heaven* [2]
   21. the kingdom of *heaven;* [2]
   — which is in *heaven.* [2]
   8:11. and Jacob, in the kingdom of *heaven.* [2]
   20. the birds of the *air* (have) nests;
   10: 7. The kingdom of *heaven* [2] is at hand.
   32. my Father which is in *heaven.* [2]
   33. before my Father which is in *heaven.* [2]
   11:11. that is least in the kingdom of *heaven* [2]
   12. the kingdom of *heaven* [2] suffereth
   23. art exalted unto *heaven,*
   25. Lord of *heaven* and earth,
   12:50. my Father which is in *heaven,* [2]
   13:11. mysteries of the kingdom of *heaven,* [2]
   24. The kingdom of *heaven* [2] is likened unto
   31. The kingdom of *heaven* [2] is like to
   32. the birds of the *air* come and lodge
   33. The kingdom of *heaven* [2] is like unto
   44. Again, the kingdom of *heaven* [2] is like
   45. the kingdom of *heaven* [2] is like
   47. the kingdom of *heaven* [2] is like unto a net,
   52. instructed unto the kingdom of *heaven* [2]
   14:19. looking up to *heaven,*
   16: 1. a sign from *heaven.*
   2. for the *sky* is red.
   3. for the *sky* is red and lowring.
   — ye can discern the face of the *sky;*
   17. my Father which is in *heaven.* [2]
   19. the keys of the kingdom of *heaven:* [2]
   — shall be bound in *heaven:* [2]
   — shall be loosed in *heaven.* [2]
   18: 1. the greatest in the kingdom of *heaven?* [2]
   3. not enter into the kingdom of *heaven.* [2]
   4. is greatest in the kingdom of *heaven.* [2]
   10. That in *heaven* [2] their angels
   — my Father which is in *heaven.* [2]
   14. your Father which is in *heaven,* [2]
   18. shall I bound in *heaven:*
   — shall be loosed in *heaven,*
   19. my Father which is in *heaven.* [2]
   23. the kingdom of *heaven* [2]
   19:12. the kingdom of *heaven's* [2] sake.
   14. of such is the kingdom of *heaven.* [2]
   21. shalt have treasure in *heaven:*
   23. enter into the kingdom of *heaven.* [2]
   20: 1. For the kingdom of *heaven* [2] is like
   21:25. from *heaven,* or of men?
   — From *heaven;* he will say unto us,
   22: 2. The kingdom of *heaven* [2] is like
   30. as the angels of God in *heaven.*
   23: 9. which is in *heaven.* [2]
   13(14). shut up the kingdom of *heaven* [2]
   22. that shall swear by *heaven,*
   24:29. the stars shall fall from *heaven,* and the
    powers of the *heavens* [2] shall
   30. sign of the Son of man in *heaven:*

Mat.24:30. coming in the clouds of *heaven*
    31. from one end of *heaven*[2] to
    35. *Heaven* and earth shall pass
    36. not the angels of *heaven*,[2]
  25: 1. the kingdom of *heaven*[2]
  26:64. coming in the clouds of *heaven*.
  28: 2. descended from *heaven*, and came
    18. is given unto me in *heaven* and in earth.
Mar 1:10. he saw the *heavens*[2] opened,
    11. there came a voice from *heaven*,[2]
  4: 4. the fowls of the *air* came and
    32. the fowls of the *air* may lodge
  6:41. he looked up to *heaven*,
  7:34. And looking up to *heaven*,
  8:11. seeking of him a sign from *heaven*,
  10:21. thou shalt have treasure in *heaven* :
  11:25. your Father also which is in *heaven*[2]
    26. your Father which is in *heaven*[2]
    30. from *heaven*, or of men ?
    31. If we shall say, From *heaven* ;
  12:25. as the angels which are in *heaven*.[2]
  13:25. the stars of *heaven* shall fall, and the
    powers that are in *heaven*[2]
    27. to the uttermost part of *heaven*.
    31. *Heaven* and earth shall pass away:
    32. not the angels which are in *heaven*,
  14:62. and coming in the clouds of *heaven*.
  16:19. he was received up into *heaven*,
Lu. 2:15. gone away from them into *heaven*,
  3:21. the *heaven* was opened,
    22. and a voice came from *heaven*,
  4:25. when the *heaven* was shut up
  6:23. your reward (is) great in *heaven* :
  8: 5. the fowls of the *air* devoured it.
  9:16. and looking up to *heaven*,
    54. fire to come down from *heaven*,
    58. and birds of the *air* (have) nests ;
  10:15. which art exalted to *heaven*,
    18. Satan as lightning fall from *heaven*.
    20. your names are written in *heaven*.[2]
    21. Lord of *heaven* and earth,
  11: 2. Our Father which art in *heaven*,[2]
    — as in *heaven*, so in earth.
    13. shall (your) *heavenly* Father give
    16. sought of him a sign from *heaven*.
  12:33. a treasure in the *heavens*[2]
    56. ye can discern the face of the *sky*
  13:19. the fowls of the *air* lodged in the
  15: 7. joy shall be in *heaven* over one
    18. I have sinned against *heaven*,
    21. Father, I have sinned against *heaven*,
  16:17. it is easier for *heaven* and earth to
  17:24. out of the one (part) under *heaven*, shineth
    unto the other (part) under *heaven* ;
    29. and brimstone from *heaven*,
  18:13. so much as (his) eyes unto *heaven*,
    22. thou shalt have treasure in *heaven* :
  19:38. peace in *heaven*, and glory in
  20: 4. was it from *heaven*, or of men ?
    5. If we shall say, From *heaven* ;
  21:11. great signs shall there be from *heaven*.
    26. the powers of *heaven*[2] shall be shaken.
    33. *Heaven* and earth shall pass away:
  22:43. an angel unto him from *heaven*,
  24:51. and carried up into *heaven*.
Joh. 1:32. from *heaven* like a dove,
  51(52). ye shall see *heaven* open,
  3:13. no man hath ascended up to *heaven*, but
    he that came down from *heaven*, (even)
    the Son of man which is in *heaven*.
    27. except it be given him from *heaven*.
    31. he that cometh from *heaven* is

Joh. 6:31. He gave them bread from *heaven*
    32. not that bread from *heaven* ;
    — the true bread from *heaven*.
    33. is he which cometh down from *heaven*,
    38. I came down from *heaven*,
    41. which came down from *heaven*.
    42. I came down from *heaven* ?
    50. which cometh down from *heaven*,
    51. which came down from *heaven* :
    58. that bread which came down from *heaven* :
  12:28. Then came there a voice from *heaven*,
  17: 1. lifted up his eyes to *heaven*,
Acts 1:10. looked stedfastly toward *heaven*
    11. gazing up into *heaven* ?
    — taken up from you into *heaven*,
    — as ye have seen him go into *heaven*.
  2: 2. there came a sound from *heaven*
    5. of every nation under *heaven*.
    19. shew wonders in *heaven*
    34. not ascended into the *heavens* :[2]
  3:21. Whom the *heaven* must receive
  4:12. none other name under *heaven*
    24. which hast made *heaven*, and
  7:42. to worship the host of *heaven* ;
    49. *Heaven* (is) my throne,
    55. looked up stedfastly into *heaven*,
    56. Behold, I see the *heavens*[2] opened,
  9: 3. a light from *heaven* :
  10:11. And saw *heaven* opened,
    12. and fowls of the *air*.
    16. received up again into *heaven*.
  11: 5. let down from *heaven*
    6. and fowls of the *air*.
    9. answered me again from *heaven*,
    10. drawn up again into *heaven*.
  14:15. which made *heaven*, and earth,
  17:24. Lord of *heaven* and earth,
  22: 6. there shone from *heaven* a great
Ro. 1:18. is revealed from *heaven*
  10: 6. Who shall ascend into *heaven* ?
1Co. 8: 5. whether in *heaven* or in earth,
  15:47. (is) the Lord from *heaven*.
2Co. 5: 1. eternal in the *heavens*.[2]
    2. our house which is from *heaven* :
  12: 2. caught up to the third *heaven*.
Gal. 1: 8. or an angel from *heaven*,
Eph. 1:10. both which are in *heaven*,[2]
  3:15. in *heaven*[2] and earth is named,
  4:10. far above all *heavens*,[2]
  6: 9. your Master also is in *heaven* ;[2]
Phi. 3:20. our conversation is in *heaven* ;[2]
Col. 1: 5. laid up for you in *heaven*,[2]
    16. that are in *heaven*,[2] and that are
    20. or things in *heaven*.[2]
    23. which is under *heaven* ;
  4: 1. ye also have a Master in *heaven*.[2]
1Th. 1:10. to wait for his Son from *heaven*,[2]
  4:16. shall descend from *heaven*
2Th. 1: 7. be revealed from *heaven*
Heb 1:10. and the *heavens*[2] are the works of
  4:14. that is passed into the *heavens*,[2]
  7:26. made higher than the *heavens* ;[2]
  8: 1. the Majesty in the *heavens* ;[2]
  9:23. patterns of things in the *heavens*[2]
    24. but into *heaven* itself,
  10:34. that ye have in *heaven*[2] a better
  11:12. as the stars of the *sky*
  12:23. written in *heaven*,[2]
    25. that (speaketh) from *heaven* :[2]
    26. not the earth only, but also *heaven*.
Jas. 5:12. neither by *heaven*,
    18. and the *heaven* gave rain,

1Pet.1: 4. reserved in *heaven*² for you,
  12. Holy Ghost sent down from *heaven ;*
  3:22. Who is gone into *heaven,*
2Pet.1:18. this voice which came from *heaven*
  3: 5. the *heavens*² were of old,
   7. But the *heavens*² and the earth,
  10. the *heavens*² shall pass away
  12. the *heavens*² being on fire
  13. for new *heavens*² and a new earth,
1Joh.5: 7. three that bear record in *heaven,*
Rev. 3:12. out of *heaven* from my God:
  4: 1. a door (was) opened in *heaven :*
   2. a throne was set in *heaven,*
  5: 3. no man in *heaven,* nor in earth,
  13. every creature which is in *heaven,*
  6:13. And the stars of *heaven* fell
  14. And the *heaven* departed
  8: 1. there was silence in *heaven*
  10. there fell a great star from *heaven,*
  9: 1. I saw a star fall from *heaven*
  10: 1. angel come down from *heaven,*
   4. I heard a voice from *heaven*
   5. lifted up his hand to *heaven,*
   6. who created *heaven,* and the things
   8. which I heard from *heaven*
  11: 6. have power to shut *heaven,*
  12. a great voice from *heaven*
  — they ascended up to *heaven*
  13. gave glory to the God of *heaven.*
  15. great voices in *heaven,*
  19. was opened in *heaven,*
  12: 1. a great wonder in *heaven ;*
   3. another wonder in *heaven ;*
   4. third part of the stars of *heaven,*
   7. And there was war in *heaven :*
   8. found any more in *heaven.*
  10. a loud voice saying in *heaven,*
  12. Therefore rejoice, (ye) *heavens,*²
  13: 6. them that dwell in *heaven.*
  13. fire come down from *heaven*
  14: 2. I heard a voice from *heaven,*
   7. that made *heaven,* and earth,
  13. I heard a voice from *heaven*
  17. the temple which is in *heaven,*
  15: 1. I saw another sign in *heaven,*
   5. the tabernacle of the testimony in *heaven*
    was opened:
  16:11. blasphemed the God of *heaven*
  17. out of the temple of *heaven,*
  21. a great hail out of *heaven,*
  18: 1. down from *heaven,* having
   4. another voice from *heaven,*
   5. have reached unto *heaven,*
  20. Rejoice over her, (thou) *heaven,*
  19: 1. of much people in *heaven,*
  11. And I saw *heaven* opened,
  14. (which were) in *heaven* followed him
  20: 1. down from *heaven,* having
   9. from God out of *heaven,*
  11. the earth and the *heaven* fled away;
  21: 1. I saw a new *heaven* and a new earth: for
    the first *heaven* and
   2. from God out of *heaven,*
   3. a great voice out of *heaven*
  10. descending out of *heaven* from God,

οὖς, *ous.*

Mat.10:27. what ye hear in the *ear,*
 11:15. He that hath *ears* to hear,
 13: 9. Who hath *ears* to hear,

Mat.13:15. and (their) *ears* are dull of
  — and hear with (their) *ears,*
  16. and your *ears,* for they hear.
  43. Who hath *ears* to hear,
Mar 4: 9. He that hath *ears* to hear,
  23. If any man have *ears* to hear,
  7:16. If any man have *ears* to hear,
  33. and put his fingers into his *ears,*
  8:18. and having *ears,* hear ye not?
Lu. 1:44. thy salutation sounded in mine *ears,*
  4:21. fulfilled in your *ears.*
  8: 8. He that hath *ears* to hear,
  9:44. sink down into your *ears :*
  12: 3. which ye have spoken in the *ear*
  14:35. He that hath *ears* to hear,
  22:50. and cut off his right *ear.*
Acts 7:51. uncircumcised in heart and *ears,*
  57. and stopped their *ears,* and
  11:22. came unto the *ears* of the church
  28:27. and their *ears* are dull of hearing,
  — and hear with (their) *ears,*
Ro. 11: 8. and *ears* that they should not hear ;
1Co. 2: 9. nor *ear* heard, neither have entered
  12:16. And if the *ear* shall say,
Jas. 5: 4. are entered into the *ears* of the Lord
1Pet.3:12. and his *ears* (are open) unto their
Rev. 2: 7. He that hath an *ear,* let him hear
  11. He that hath an *ear,* let him hear
  17. He that hath an *ear,* let him hear
  29. He that hath an *ear,* let him hear
  3: 6. He that hath an *ear,* let him hear
  13. He that hath an *ear,* let him hear
  22. He that hath an *ear,* let him hear
  13: 9. If any man have an *ear,*

οὖσα, οὖση, &c., see ὤν.

οὐσία, *ousia.*

Lu. 15:12. give me the portion of *goods*
  13. wasted his *substance* with

οὔτε, *oute.*

Mat. 6:20. where *neither* moth *nor* rust doth
  12:32. *neither* in this world, *neither* in the (world)
   to come.
  22:30. they *neither* marry, *nor* are given
Mar 5: 3. ‖ *no, not* with chains:
  12:25. *neither* marry, *nor* are given in
Lu. 12:26. If ye then be *not* able to do that thing
   which is least,
  14:35. It is *neither* fit for the land, *nor yet*
  20:35. *neither* marry, *nor* are given in
  36. *Neither* can they die any more:
Joh. 1:25. *nor* Elias, *neither* that prophet ?
  4:11. thou hast *nothing* to draw with,
  21. *neither* in this mountain, *nor yet* at
  5:37. Ye have *neither* heard his voice at any
   time, *nor* seen his shape.
  8:19. Ye *neither* know me, *nor* my Father:
  9: 3. *Neither* hath this man sinned, *nor* his
   parents:
Acts 4:12. for there is *none* other name
  15:10. which *neither* our fathers *nor* we were
  19:37. *neither* robbers of churches, *nor yet*
  24:12. they *neither* found me in the temple
  — *neither* in the synagogues, *nor* in the city:
  13. *Neither* can they prove the things

Acts 25: 8. *Neither* against the law of the Jews, *neither* against the temple, *nor yet* against

28:21. We *neither* received letters
— *neither* any of the brethren

Ro. 8:38. For I am persuaded, that *neither* death, *nor* life, *nor* angels, *nor* principalities, *nor* powers, *nor* things present, *nor* things to come,

39. *Nor* height, *nor* depth, *nor* any other

1 Co. 3: 2. *neither* yet now are ye able.

7. *neither* is he that planteth any thing, *neither* he that watereth;

6: 9. *neither* fornicators, *nor* idolaters, *nor* adulterers, *nor* effeminate, *nor* abusers of themselves with

10. *Nor* thieves, *nor* covetous, *nor* drunkards,

8: 8. for *neither*, if we eat, are we the better; *neither*, if we eat not, are

11:11. *neither* is the man without the woman, *neither* the woman without the

Gal. 1:12. *neither* was I taught (it),

5: 6. Jesus Christ *neither* circumcision availeth any thing, *nor* uncircumcision;

6:15. *neither* circumcision availeth any thing, *nor*

1 Th. 2: 3. nor of uncleanness, *nor* in guile:

5. For *neither* at any time used we
— *nor* a cloke of covetousness;

6. *Nor* of men sought we glory, *neither* of you, *nor* (yet) of others,

3 Joh. 10. *neither* doth he himself receive

Rev. 3:15. that thou art *neither* cold *nor* hot:

16. and *neither* cold *nor* hot,

5: 4. *neither* to look thereon.

9:20. yet repented *not* of the works
— which *neither* can see, *nor* hear, *nor* walk:

21. *nor* of their sorceries, *nor* of their fornication, *nor* of their thefts.

12: 8. *neither* was their place found

20: 4. worshipped the beast, *neither* his image,

21: 4. *neither* sorrow, *nor* crying, *neither* shall there be any more pain:

οὗτος, *houtos.*

Mat. 3: 3. For *this* is he that was spoken of

17. *This* is my beloved Son,

5:19. *the same* shall be called great

7:12. for *this* is the law and the prophets.

8:27. What manner of man is *this,*

9: 3. *This* (man) blasphemeth.

10:22. endureth to the end)(shall be saved.

11:10. For *this* is (he), of whom it is written,

12:23. Is not *this* the son of David?

24. *This* (fellow) doth not cast out

13:19. *This* is he which received seed by

20. *the same* is he that heareth

22. is *he* that heareth the word;

23. is *he* that heareth the word,

55. Is not *this* the carpenter's son?

14: 2. *This* is John the Baptist;

15: 8. *This* people draweth nigh unto me

17: 5. *This* is my beloved Son,

18: 4. *the same* is greatest in the kingdom

21:10. city was moved, saying, Who is *this?*

11. *This* is Jesus the prophet

38. *This* is the heir; come, let us kill him,

42. *the same* is become the head of the

24:13. *the same* shall be saved.

26:23. *the same* shall betray me.

61. *This* (fellow) said, I am able

71. *This* (fellow) was also with Jesus

Mat. 27:37. *THIS* IS JESUS THE KING OF THE JEWS.

47. *This* (man) calleth for Elias.

54. Truly *this* was the Son of God.

58. *He* went to Pilate, and begged the body

28:15. *this* saying is commonly reported

Mar 2: 7. Why doth *this* (man) thus speak

3:35. *the same* is my brother,

4:41. What manner of man is *this,* that

6: 3. Is not *this* the carpenter?

16. *It* (lit. *this*) is John, whom I beheaded:

7: 6. *This* people honoureth me with (their)

8:35. *the same* shall save it.

9: 7. *This* is my beloved Son: hear him.

12: 7. *This* is the heir; come, let us

10. which the builders rejected)(is become

13:13. *the same* shall be saved.

14:69. *This* is (one) of them.

15:39. Truly *this* man was the Son of God.

Lu. 1:29. what manner of salutation *this* should be.

32. *He* shall be great, and

36. *this* is the sixth month with her,

2:25. *the same* man (was) just and

34. *this* (child) is set for the fall and

4:22. Is not *this* Joseph's son?

36. What a word (is) *this!*

5:21. Who is *this* which speaketh

7:17. *this* rumour of him went forth

27. *This* is (he), of whom it is written,

39. *This man,* if he were a prophet,

49. Who is *this* that forgiveth sins

8:25. What manner of man is *this!*

9:24. *the same* shall save it.

35. *This* is my beloved Son: hear him.

48. *the same* shall be great.

14:30. *This* man began to build,

15: 2. *This man* receiveth sinners,

24. For *this* my son was dead,

30. But as soon as *this* thy son

32. for *this* thy brother was dead,

16: 1. *the same* was accused unto him

17:18. glory to God, save *this* stranger.

18:11. or even as *this* publican.

14. *this* man went down to his house

19: 2. and *he* was rich.

20:14. *This* is the heir: come, let us kill him,

17. *the same* is become the head

28. and *he* die without children,

30. and *he* died childless.

22:56. *This* man was also with him.

59. Of a truth *this* (fellow) also

23:22. Why, what evil hath *he* done?

35. if *he* be Christ, the chosen of God.

38. *THIS* IS THE KING OF THE JEWS.

41. *this* man hath done nothing amiss.

47. Certainly *this* was a righteous man.

51. *The same* had not consented to

52. *This* (man) went unto Pilate, and

Joh. 1: 2. *The same* was in the beginning

7. *The same* came for a witness,

15. *This* was he of whom I spake,

30. *This* is he of whom I said,

33. *the same* is he which baptizeth

34. that *this* is the Son of God.

41(42). *He* first findeth his own brother

2:20. Forty and six years was this temple in

3: 2. *The same* came to Jesus by night,

26. behold, *the same* baptizeth,

4:29. is not *this* the Christ?

42. *this* is indeed the Christ, the

47. When *he* heard that Jesus

6:14. *This* is of a truth that prophet

Joh. 6:42. Is not *this* Jesus,
— how is it then that *he* saith,
46. *he* hath seen the Father.
50. *This* is the bread which cometh down
52. How can *this man* give us (his) flesh
58. *This* is that bread which came
60. *This* is aɪ. hard saying;
71. for *he it was that* should betray
7:15. How knoweth *this man* letters,
18. *the same* is true,
25. Is not *this* he, whom they seek,
26. that *this* is the very Christ?
31. which *this* (man) hath done?
35. Whither will *he* go,
36. What (manner of) saying is *this*
40. Of a truth *this* is the prophet.
41. *This* is the Christ.
46. Never man spake like *this* man.
49. But *this* people who knoweth not
9: 2. who did sin, *this man*, or his
3. Neither hath *this man* sinned,
8. Is not *this* he that sat and begged?
9. Some said, *This* is he:
16. *This* man is not of God,
19. Is *this* your son,
20. We know that *this* is our son,
24. we know that *this* man is a sinner.
33. If *this man* were not of God,
11:37. Could not *this man*, which
— that even *this man* should not
47. for *this* man doeth many miracles.
12:34. who is *this* Son of man?
15: 5. *the same* bringeth forth much fruit:
18:30. If *he* were not a malefactor,
21:21. what (shall) *this man* (do)?
23. Then went *this* saying abroad
24. *This* is the disciple which
Acts 1:11. *this same* Jesus, which is taken up
18. Now *this man* purchased a field
3:10. they knew that it was *he* which sat
4: 9. by what means *he* is made whole;
10. (even) by him doth *this man* stand
11. *This* is the stone which was set
6:13. *This* man ceaseth not to speak
14. that *this* Jesus of Nazareth shall
7:19. *The same* dealt subtilly with our
36. *He* brought them out, after
37. *This* is that Moses, which said
38. *This* is he, that was in the church
40. for (as for) *this* Moses, which brought us
8:10. *This man* is the great power of God.
9:15. for *he* is a chosen vessel unto me,
20. that *he* is the Son of God.
21. Is not *this* he that destroyed them
22. proving that *this* is very Christ.
10: 6. *He* lodgeth with one Simon a tanner,
— *he* shall tell thee what thou
32. *he* is lodged in the house of (one)
36. *he* is Lord of all:
13: 7. *who* called for Barnabas and Saul,
14: 9. *The same* heard Paul speak:
17: 3. and that *this* Jesus, whom I preach
18. What will *this* babbler say?
24. seeing that *he* is Lord of heaven
18:13. *This* (fellow) persuadeth men to
25. *This man* was instructed in the
26. And *he* began to speak boldly
19:26. *this* Paul hath persuaded and
21:28. *This* is the man, that teacheth
22:26. for *this* man is a Roman.
26:31. *This* man doeth nothing worthy of death
32. *This* man might have been set

Acts28: 4. No doubt *this* man is a murderer,
Ro. 4: 9. (Cometh) *this* blessedness then
8: 9. *he* is none of his.
9: 9. For *this* (is) the word of promise,
1Co. 8: 3. *the same* is known of him.
Heb 3: 3. For *this* (man) was counted worthy
7: 1. For *this* Melchisedec, king of Salem,
4. consider how great *this man* (was),
Jas. 1:23. *he* is like unto a man beholding
25. *he* being not a forgetful hearer,
— *this man* shall be blessed
3: 2. *the same* (is) a perfect man,
1Pet.2: 7. *the same* is made the head of the
2Pet.1:17. *This* is my beloved Son,
1Joh.2:22. *He* is antichrist, that denieth
5: 6. *This* is he that came by water and
20. *This* is the true God,
2Joh. 7. *This* is a deceiver and an antichrist.
9. *he* hath both the Father and the Son.
Rev. 3: 5. *the same* shall be clothed in white
20:14. *This* is the second death.

οὗτοι, *houtoi.* from οὗτος.

[2] denotes it to be compounded with αὐτός.

Mat. 4: 3. command that *these* stones be made
13:38. the good seed)(are the children of the
20:12. *These* last have wrought (but)
21. Grant that *these* my two sons
21:16. Hearest thou what *these* say?
25:46. And *these* shall go away into
26:62. what (is it which) *these* witness
Mar 4:15. And *these* are they by the way side,
16. And *these* are they likewise
18. And *these* are they which are
— *such as* hear the word,
20. And *these* are they which are sown
12:40. *these* shall receive greater damnation.
14:60. what (is it which) *these* witness
Lu. 8:13. and *these* have no root,
14. are *they*, which, when they have heard,
15. are *they*, which in an honest and
21. are *these* which hear the word
9: 9. but who is *this*, of whom I hear
13: 2. Suppose ye that *these* Galilæans
4. think ye that *they* were sinners above
19:40. I tell you that, if *these* should hold
20:47. *the same* shall receive greater damnation.
21: 4. For all *these* have of their abundance
24:17. communications (are) *these* that ye
44. *These* (are) the words which I
Joh. 6: 5. that *these* may eat?
12:21. *The same* came therefore to Philip,
17:11. but *these* are in the world,
25. and *these* have known that thou
18:21. *they* know what I said.
Acts 1:14. *These* all continued with one accord
2: 7. are not all *these* which speak Galilæans?
15. For *these* are not drunken,
11:12. *these* six brethren accompanied me,
13: 4. So *they*, being sent forth by the Holy
16:17. *These* men are the servants of
20. *These* men, being Jews,
17: 6. *These* that have turned the world upside
7. and *these* all do contrary to
11. *These* were more noble than those
20: 5. *These* going before tarried for us
24:15. which *they* [2] themselves also allow,
20. Or else let *these* [2] same (here) say,
25:11. whereof *these* accuse me,

Acts 27:31. Except *these* abide in the ship,
Ro. 2:14. *these*, having not the law,
   8:14. *they* are the sons of God.
   9: 6. For *they* (are) not all Israel, which
  11:24. how much more shall *these*, which be the
     31. Even so have *these* also now
1 Co.16:17. on your part *they* have supplied.
Gal. 3: 7. *the same* are the children of
   6:12. *they* constrain you to be circumcised ;
Col. 4:11. *These* only (are my) fellowworkers
1 Ti. 3:10. let *these* also first be proved ;
2 Ti. 3: 8. so do *these* also resist
Heb 11:13. *These* all died in faith,
    39. And *these* all, having obtained a
2 Pet. 2:12. But *these*, as natural brute
    17. *These* are wells without water,
1 Joh.5: 7. and *these* three are one.
Jude 8. Likewise also *these* (filthy) dreamers
   10. But *these* speak evil of those things
   12. *These* are spots in your feasts
   16. *These* are murmurers, complainers,
   19. *These* be they who separate
Rev. 7:13. What are *these* which are arrayed
    14. *These* are they which came out
  11: 4. *These* are the two olive trees,
    6. *These* have power to shut heaven,
    10. because *these* two prophets
  14: 4. *These* are they which were not defiled
   — *These* are they which follow
   — *These* were redeemed from
  17:13. *These* have one mind,
    14. *These* shall make war with
    16. *these* shall hate the whore,
  19: 9. *These* are the true sayings of God.
  21: 5. *these* words are true and faithful.
  22: 6. *These* sayings (are) faithful and true:

αὕτη, hautee. fem. sing. of οὗτος.

Mat. 9:26. the fame *hereof* went abroad
  13:54. Whence hath this (man) *this* wisdom,
  21:42. *this* is the Lord's doing, and it is
  22:20. unto them, Whose (is) *this* image
    38. *This* is the first and great commandment.
  24:34. *This* generation shall not pass,
  26: 8. To what purpose (is) *this* waste ?
    12. in that *she* hath poured this ointment on
    13. that *this woman* hath done, be
Mar 1:27. what new doctrine (is) *this* ?
  8:12. Why doth *this* generation seek
  12:11. *This* was the Lord's doing, and it is
    16. Whose (is) *this* image and superscription ?
    30. *this* (is) the first commandment.
    31. second (is) like, (namely) *this*,
    43. *this* poor widow hath cast more
    44. *she* of her want did cast in
  13:30. *this* generation shall not pass,
  14: 4. Why was *this* waste of the ointment
    8. She hath done what *she* could:
    9. that *she* hath done shall be
Lu. 2: 2. *this* taxing was first made
    36. *she* was of a great age, and had
    37. *she* (was) a widow of about
    38. *she* coming in that instant
  4:21. *this* scripture fulfilled in your ears.
  7:44. *she* hath washed my feet with tears,
    45. *this woman* since the time
    46. *this woman* hath anointed my
  8: 9. What might *this* parable be ?
    11. Now the parable is *this* :
    42. of age, and *she* lay a dying.

Lu. 11:29. *This* is an evil generation: they
  21: 3. that *this* poor widow hath cast
    4. *she* of her penury hath cast in
    32. *This* generation shall not pass
  22:53. *this* is your hour, and the power
Joh. 1:19. *this* is the record of John, when
  3:19. And *this* is the condemnation,
    29. *this* my joy therefore is fulfilled.
  8: 4. *this* woman was taken in
  11: 4. *This* sickness is not unto death,
  12:30. *This* voice came not because of me,
  15:12. *This* is my commandment, That
  17: 3. *this* is life eternal, that they might
Acts 5:38. for if *this* counsel or this work
  8:26. Jerusalem unto Gaza, *which* is desert.
    32. scripture which he read was *this*,
  9:36. *this* woman was full of good works
  16:17. *The same* followed Paul and us,
  17:19. we know what *this* new doctrine,
  21:11. the man that owneth *this* girdle,
Ro. 7:10. the commandment,...I found)((to be)
     unto death.
  11:27. For *this* (is) my covenant unto them,
  16: 2. for *she* hath been a succourer of many,
1 Co. 8: 9. by any means *this* liberty of your's
  9: 3. Mine answer to them that do examine me
     is *this*,
2 Co. 1:12. For our rejoicing is *this*, the
  2: 6. to such a man (is) *this* punishment.
  11:10. shall stop me of *this* boasting
Eph. 3: 8. is *this* grace given, that I should
Tit. 1:13. *This* witness is true. Wherefore
Heb 8:10. For *this* (is) the covenant that I
  10:16. *This* (is) the covenant that I will
Jas. 1:27. before God and the Father is *this*, To visit
  3:15. *This* wisdom descendeth not from
1 Joh.1: 5. *This* then is the message which
  2:25. *this* is the promise that he
  3:11. For *this* is the message that ye
    23. *this* is his commandment,
  5: 3. For *this* is the love of God, that
    4. *this* is the victory that overcometh
    9. for *this* is the witness of God
    11. *this* is the record, that God
   — *this* life is in his Son.
    14. *this* is the confidence that we
2 Joh. 6. *this* is love, that we walk after
   — *This* is the commandment,
Rev.20: 5. *This* (is) the first resurrection.

αὗται, hautai. fem. plur. of οὗτος.

Lu. 21:22. For *these* be the days of vengeance,
Acts 20:34. that *these* hands have ministered
Gal. 4:24. for *these* are the two covenants ;

The other cases of this pronoun, viz: ταῦτα, ταύτη, τοῦτο, τούτων, &c., will be found severally in their alphabetical places.

οὕτω, οὕτως, houto, houtōs.

[2] denotes where the force of καί is blended into that of οὕτω.

Mat. 1:18. the birth of Jesus Christ was *on this wise*:
  2: 5. for *thus* it is written by the prophet,
  3:15. for *thus* it becometh us to fulfil
  5:12. for *so* persecuted they the prophets
    16. Let your light *so* shine before men,
    19. and shall teach men *so*,
    47. do not even the publicans *so* ?
  6: 9. *After this manner* therefore pray ye:

Mat. 6:30. if God *so* clothe the grass
7:12. do ye *even so* [2] to them:
17. *Even so* every good tree
9:33. It was never *so* seen in Israel.
11:26. for *so* it seemed good in thy sight.
12:40. *so* shall the Son of man be three days
45. *Even so* shall it be also unto this
13:40. *so* shall it be in the end of this
49. *So* shall it be at the end of the
17:12. *Likewise* shall also the Son of man
18:14. *Even so* it is not the will of your
35. *So* likewise shall my heavenly
19: 8. but from the beginning it was not *so.*
10. If the case of the man be *so* with
12. which were *so* born from (their)
20:16. *So* the last shall be first,
26. But it shall not be *so* among you:
23:28. *Even so* ye also outwardly
24:27. *so* shall also the coming of the
33. *So* likewise ye, when ye shall see
37. *so* shall also the coming of
39. *so* shall also the coming of the Son of
46. shall find *so* doing.
26:40. *What,* could ye not watch with me
54. that *thus* it must be?
Mar 2: 7. Why doth this (man) *thus* speak
8. that they *so* reasoned within
12. We never saw it *on this fashion.*
4:26. *So* is the kingdom of God
40. Why are ye *so* fearful?
7:18. Are ye *so* without understanding also?
10:43. But *so* shall it not be among you:
13:29. *So* ye *in like manner,* [2] when ye
14:59. But neither *so* did their witness
15:39. saw that he *so* cried out,
Lu. 1:25. *Thus* hath the Lord dealt with me
2:48. why hast thou *thus* dealt with us?
6:10. And he did *so:* and his hand
9:15. And they did *so,* and made them
10:21. for *so* it seemed good in thy sight.
11:30. *so* shall also the Son of man
12:21. *So* (is) he that layeth up treasure
28. If then God *so* clothe the grass,
38. and find (them) *so,* blessed are
43. shall find *so* doing.
54. and *so* it is.
14:33. *So* likewise, whosoever he be of you
15: 7. that *likewise* joy shall be in
10. *Likewise,* I say unto you, there is joy
17:10. *So* likewise ye, when ye shall
24. *so* shall also the Son of man be
26. *so* shall it be also in the days
19:31. *thus* shall ye say unto him,
21:31. *So* likewise ye, when ye see
22:26. But ye (shall) not (be) *so:*
24:24. and found (it) even *so* as the women
46. *Thus* it is written, and *thus* it behoved Christ to suffer,
Joh. 3: 8. *so* is every one that is born of the Spirit.
14. *even so* must the Son of man be
16. For God *so* loved the world,
4: 6. sat *thus* on the well:
5:21. *even so* [2] the Son quickeneth whom
26. *so* hath he given to the Son to
7:46. Never man spake *like* (lit. *so* spake as) this man.
8:59. and *so* passed by.
11:48. If we let him *thus* alone,
12:50. said unto me, *so* I speak.
14:31. gave me commandment, *even so* I do.
15: 4. *no more* (lit. *so* neither) can ye,
18:22. Answerest thou the high priest *so?*

Joh.21: 1. and *on this wise* shewed he (himself).
Acts 1:11. shall *so* come in like manner as
3:18. he hath *so* fulfilled.
7: 1. Are these things *so?*
6. And God spake *on this wise,*
8. and *so* (Abraham) begat Isaac,
8:32. *so* opened he not his mouth:
12: 8. And *so* he did.
15. affirmed that it was *even so.*
13: 8. for *so* is his name by interpretation
34. he said *on this wise,* I will give
47. For *so* hath the Lord commanded
14: 1. and *so* spake, that a great multitude
17:11. whether those things were *so.*
33. *So* Paul departed from among them.
19:20. *So* mightily grew the word of God
20:11. till break of day, *so* he departed.
13. for *so* had he appointed,
35. how that *so* labouring ye ought
21:11. *So* shall the Jews at Jerusalem bind
22:24. wherefore they cried *so* against him.
23:11. *so* must thou bear witness also at Rome.
24: 9. saying that these things were *so.*
14. *so* worship I the God of my fathers,
27:17. and *so* were driven.
25. it shall be *even* as it was told me.
44. And *so* it came to pass, that
28:14. and *so* we went toward Rome.
Ro. 1:15. *So,* as much as in me is, I am ready
4:18. *So* shall thy seed be.
5:12. and *so* death passed upon all
15. *so* also (is) the free gift.
18. *even so* [2] by the righteousness of one
19. *so* [2] by the obedience of one
21. *even so* [2] might grace reign
6: 4. *even so* we also should walk
11. *Likewise* reckon ye also yourselves
19. *even so* now yield your members
9:20. Why hast thou made me *thus?*
10: 6. speaketh *on this wise,* Say not
11: 5. *Even so* [2] then at this present
26. And *so* all Israel shall be saved:
31. *Even so* have these also now not
12: 5. *So* we, (being) many, are one
15:20. Yea, *so* have I strived to preach
1Co. 2:11. *even so* [2] the things of God
3:15. yet *so* as by fire.
4: 1. Let a man *so* account of us,
5: 3. that hath *so* done this deed,
6: 5. Is it *so,* that there is not a
7: 7. one *after this manner,* and another *after that.*
17. *so* let him walk. And *so* ordain I in all churches.
26. good for a man *so* to be.
36. and need *so* require,
40. But she is happier if she *so* abide,
8:12. when ye sin *so* against the brethren,
9:14. *Even so* [2] hath the Lord ordained
15. that it should be *so* done unto me:
24. *So* run, that ye may obtain.
26. I therefore *so* run, not as uncertainly; *so* fight I, not as
11:12. *even so* (is) the man also by the
28. and *so* let him eat of (that)
12:12. *so* also (is) Christ.
14: 9. *So* likewise ye, except ye utter
12. *Even so* [2] ye, forasmuch as ye are
21. and yet *for all that* (lit. and neither *thus*) will they not hear me,
25. And *thus* are the secrets of his heart made manifest; and *so* falling down

1Co.15:11. *so* we preach, and *so* ye believed.
      22. *even so* ² in Christ shall all
      42. *So* also (is) the resurrection of
      45. And *so* it is written,
    16: 1. *even so* ² do ye.
2Co. 1: 5. *so* our consolation also aboundeth
      7. *so* (shall ye be) also of the consolation.
    7:14. *even so* ² our boasting,
    8: 6. *so* he would also finish
     11. *so* (there may be) a performance also
    9: 5. might be ready, as (a matter of) bounty,
        (lit. ready *thus*, as, &c.)
    10: 7. *even so* ² (are) we Christ's.
    11: 3. *so* your minds should be corrupted
Gal. 1: 6. I marvel that ye are *so* soon removed
    3: 3. Are ye *so* foolish?
    4: 3. *Even so* ² we, when we were children,
     29. *even so* ² (it is) now.
    6: 2. and *so* fulfil the law of Christ.
Eph 4:20. But ye have not *so* learned Christ;
    5:24. *so* ² (let) the wives (be) to their own
     28. *So* ought men to love their wives
     33. *so* love his wife even as himself;
Phi. 3:17. and mark them which walk *so*
    4: 1. *so* stand fast in the Lord.
Col. 3:13. *so* also (do) ye.
1Th. 2: 4. *even so* we speak ;
     8. *So* being affectionately desirous
    4:14. *even so* them also which sleep
     17. and *so* shall we ever be with the Lord.
    5: 2. the day of the Lord *so* cometh
2Th. 3:17. token in every epistle: *so* I write.
2Ti. 3: 8. *so* do these also resist the truth:
Heb 4: 4. of the seventh (day) *on this wise*,
    5: 3. *so* also for himself,
     5. *So* also Christ glorified not himself
    6: 9. though we *thus* speak.
     15. And *so*, after he had patiently
    9: 6. when these things were *thus* ordained,
     28. *So* Christ was once offered
   10:33. companions of them that were *so* used.
   12:21. And *so* terrible was the sight,
Jas. 1:11. *so* also shall the rich man fade
    2:12. *So* speak ye, and *so* do,
     17. *Even so* ² faith, if it hath not works,
     26. *so* faith without works is dead also.
    3: 5. *Even so* ² the tongue is a little
     6. *so* is the tongue among our
     10. these things ought not *so* to be.
     12. *so* (can) no fountain both yield
1Pet.2:15. For *so* is the will of God,
    3: 5. For *after this manner* in the old time the
       holy women also,
2Pet.1:11. For *so* an entrance shall be
    3: 4. all things continue *as* (they were)
1Joh.2: 6. ought himself also *so* to walk, even as he
    4:11. Beloved, if God *so* loved us,
Rev. 2:15. *So* hast thou also them that
    3:16. *So* then because thou art lukewarm,
    9:17. And *thus* I saw the horses in the
   11: 5. he must *in this manner* be killed.
   16:18. so mighty an earthquake, (and) *so* great.
   18:21. *Thus* with violence shall that great city

οὐχ see οὐ.

οὐχί, *ouhi.*

Mat. 5:46. do *not* even the publicans the same?
     47. do *not* even the publicans so?

Mat. 6:25. Is *not* the life more than meat,
  10:29. Are *not* two sparrows sold for
  12:11. will he *not* lay hold on it, and
  13:27. Sir, didst *not* thou sow good seed
    55. is *not* his mother called Mary?
    56. are they *not* all with us?
  18:12. doth he *not* leave the ninety and
  20:13. didst *not* thou agree with me
Lu. 1:60. *Not* (so); but he shall be called John.
  6:39. shall they *not* both fall into
  12: 6. Are *not* five sparrows sold for
    51. I tell you, *Nay;* but rather division:
  13: 3. I tell you, *Nay:* but, except ye
    5. *Nay:* but, except ye repent, ye
  14:28. sitteth *not* down first, and counteth
    31. sitteth *not* down first, and consulteth
  15: 8. doth *not* light a candle, and
  16:30. And he said, *Nay*, father Abraham:
  17: 8. And will *not* rather say unto him,
    17. Were there *not* ten cleansed?
  22:27. (is) *not* he that sitteth at meat?
  24:26. Ought *not* Christ to have suffered
    32. Did *not* our heart burn within us,
Joh. 7:42. Hath *not* the scripture said,
  11: 9. Are there *not* twelve hours in
  13:10. and ye are clean, but *not* all.
    11. Ye are *not* all clean.
  14:22. and *not* unto the world?
Acts 5: 4. was it *not* thine own?
  7:50. Hath *not* my hand made all
Ro. 2:26. shall *not* his uncircumcision
  3:27. *Nay:* but by the law of faith.
    29. (is he) *not* also of the Gentiles?
  8:32. how shall he *not* with him also
1Co. 1:20. hath *not* God made foolish the
  3: 3. are ye *not* carnal, and walk as men?
    4. are ye *not* carnal?
  5: 2. and have *not* rather mourned,
    12. do *not* ye judge them that are
  6: 1. and *not* before the saints?
    7. Why do ye *not* rather take wrong? why do
      ye *not* rather (suffer)
  8:10. shall *not* the conscience of him
  9: 1. have I *not* seen Jesus Christ
    8. or saith *not* the law the same
  10:16. is it *not* the communion of the blood
  — is it *not* the communion of the body
    18. are *not* they which eat of the
    29. Conscience, I say, *not* thine own,
2Co. 3: 8. How shall *not* the ministration
  10:13. we will *not* boast of things without
1Th. 2:19. (Are) *not* even ye in the presence
Heb 1:14. Are they *not* all ministering
  3:17. (was it) *not* with them that had sinned,

ὀφειλέτης, *ophīletees.*

Mat. 6:12. as we forgive our *debtors*.
  18:24. *which owed* him ten thousand
Lu. 13: 4. think ye that they were *sinners* above
Ro. 1:14. I am *debtor* both to the Greeks, and
  8:12. we are *debtors*, not to the flesh,
  15:27. and their *debtors* they are.
Gal. 5: 3. he is a *debtor* to do the whole law.

ὀφειλή, *ophilee.*

Mat.18:32. I forgave thee all that *debt*,
Ro. 13: 7. Render therefore to all their *dues:*

ὀφείλημα, ophīleema.

Mat. 6:12. And forgive us our *debts*,
Ro. 4: 4. not reckoned of grace, but of *debt*.

ὀφείλω, ophīlo.

Mat.18:28. which *owed* him an hundred pence:
— Pay me that thou *owest*.
30. till he should pay the *debt*.
31. till he should pay all *that was due*
23:16. he *is a debtor!* (lit. *oweth*, or *is bound*)
18. he is *guilty* (lit. *oweth*, or *is bound*)
Lu. 7:41. the one *owed* five hundred pence,
11: 4. every one *that is indebted* to us.
16: 5. How much *owest* thou unto my lord?
7. And how much *owest* thou ?
17:10. we have done that which *was* our *duty* to
Joh.13:14. ye also *ought* to wash one another's feet.
19: 7. by our law he *ought* to die,
Acts17:29. we *ought* not to think that
Ro. 13: 8. *Owe* no man any thing,
15: 1. that are strong *ought* to bear the
27. their *duty is* also to minister unto
1Co. 5:10. then *must* ye *needs* go out of the
7: 3. unto the wife *due* benevolence:
36. and *need* so require, (lit. it *needs* so to be)
9:10. he that ploweth *should* plow (lit. *ought* to
plough) in hope;
11: 7. a man indeed *ought* not to cover
10. For this cause *ought* the woman
2Co.12:11. for I *ought* to have been commended
14. the children *ought* not to lay up for
Eph 5:28. So *ought* men to love their wives
2Th. 1: 3. We *are bound* to thank God
2:13. we *are bound* to give thanks
Philem 18. or *oweth* (thee) ought,
Heb 2:17. in all things it *behoved* him
5: 3. by reason hereof he *ought*, as for
12. *when* for the time ye *ought* to be
1Joh.2: 6. *ought* himself also so to walk,
3:16. we *ought* to lay down (our) lives
4:11. we *ought* also to love one another.
3Joh. 8. We therefore *ought* to receive such,

ὄφελον, ophelon.

1Co. 4: 8. and I *would to God* (lit. I *would*) ye did
reign,
2Co.11: 1. *Would to God* (lit. , *&c.*) ye could bear
Gal. 5:12. I *would* they were even cut off
Rev. 3:15. I *would* thou wert cold or hot.

ὄφελος, ophelos.

1Co.15:32. what *advantageth* it me, (lit. what the
profit to me)
Jas. 2:14. What (doth it) *profit*, my brethren,
16. what (doth it) *profit* ?

ὀφθαλμοδουλεία, ophthalmodoulīa.

Eph 6: 6. Not with *eyeservice*, as menpleasers;
Col. 3:22. not with *eyeservice*, as menpleasers ;

ὀφθαλμός, ophthalmos.

Mat. 5:29. if thy right *eye* offend thee,
38. An *eye* for an *eye*,

Mat. 6:22. The light of the body is the *eye:* if therefore thine *eye* be single,
23. But if thine *eye* be evil,
7: 3. that is in thy brother's *eye*,
— that is in thine own *eye* ?
4. the mote out of thine *eye ;* and, behold, a
beam (is) in thine own *eye* ?
5. out of thine own *eye ;*
— out of thy brother's *eye*.
9:29. Then touched he their *eyes*,
30. And their *eyes* were opened;
13:15. their *eyes* they have closed;
— they should see with (their) *eyes*,
16. But blessed (are) your *eyes*,
17: 8. when they had lifted up their *eyes*,
18: 9. And if thine *eye* offend thee,
— rather than having two *eyes*
20:15. Is thine *eye* evil, because
33. Lord, that our *eyes* may be opened.
34. and touched their *eyes:*
— their *eyes* received sight,
21:42. and it is marvellous in our *eyes* ?
26:43. for their *eyes* were heavy.
Mar 7:22. an evil *eye*, blasphemy, pride,
8:18. Having *eyes*, see ye not ?
25. hands again upon his *eyes*,
9:47. And if thine *eye* offend thee,
— than having two *eyes*
12:11. it is marvellous in our *eyes* ?
14:40. for their *eyes* were heavy,
Lu. 2:30. For mine *eyes* have seen thy
4:20. And the *eyes* of all them that were
6:20. lifted up his *eyes* on his disciples,
41. that is in thy brother's *eye*,
— that is in thine own *eye* ?
42. the mote that is in thine *eye*,
— the beam that is in thine own *eye* ?
— the beam out of thine own *eye*,
— the mote that is in thy brother's *eye*.
10:23. Blessed (are) the *eyes* which see the
11:34. The light of the body is the *eye:* therefore
when thine *eye* is single,
16:23. in hell he lift up his *eyes*,
18:13. so much as (his) *eyes* unto heaven,
19:42. they are hid from thine *eyes*.
24:16. But their *eyes* were holden
31. And their *eyes* were opened,
Joh. 4:35. Lift up your *eyes*, and look on the
6: 5. Jesus then lifted up (his) *eyes*,
9: 6. he anointed the *eyes* of the blind
10. How were thine *eyes* opened ?
11. and anointed mine *eyes*,
14. and opened his *eyes*.
15. He put clay upon mine *eyes*,
17. that he hath opened thine *eyes* ?
21. who hath opened his *eyes*,
26. how opened he thine *eyes* ?
30. he hath opened mine *eyes*.
32. that any man opened the *eyes*
10:21. Can a devil open the *eyes* of the
11:37. which opened the *eyes* of the blind,
41. Jesus lifted up (his) *eyes*,
12:40. He hath blinded their *eyes*,
— should not see with (their) *eyes*,
17: 1. and lifted up his *eyes*
Acts 1: 9. received him out of their *sight*.
9: 8. when his *eyes* were opened,
18. there fell from his *eyes*
40. And she opened her *eyes:*
26:18. To open their *eyes*, (and) to turn
28:27. their *eyes* have they closed ; lest they
should see with (their) *eyes*,

Ro. 3:18. no fear of God before their *eyes*.
    11: 8. *eyes* that they should not see,
      10. Let their *eyes* be darkened,
1Co. 2: 9. *Eye* hath not seen, nor ear
   12:16. Because I am not the *eye*,
      17. If the whole body (were) an *eye*,
      21. And the *eye* cannot say unto
   15:52. in the twinkling of an *eye*,
Gal. 3: 1. before whose *eyes* Jesus Christ
   4:15. have plucked out your own *eyes*,
Eph. 1:18. The *eyes* of your understanding
Heb 4:13. opened unto the *eyes* of him
1Pet.3:12. For the *eyes* of the Lord (are) over
2Pet.2:14. Having *eyes* full of adultery,
1Joh.1: 1. which we have seen with our *eyes*,
   2:11. darkness hath blinded his *eyes*.
    16. and the lust of the *eyes*,
Rev. 1: 7. and every *eye* shall see him,
    14. his *eyes* (were) as a flame of fire;
   2:18. who hath his *eyes* like unto
   3:18. anoint thine *eyes* with eyesalve,
   4: 6. four beasts full of *eyes*
    8. and (they were) full of *eyes* within:
   5: 6. and seven *eyes*, which are the
   7:17. wipe away all tears from their *eyes*.
  19:12. His *eyes* (were) as a flame of fire,
  21: 4. wipe away all tears from their *eyes*;

ὄφις, *ophis.*

Mat. 7:10. will he give him a *serpent?*
   10:16. be ye therefore wise as *serpents*,
   23:33. (Ye) *serpents*, (ye) generation of vipers,
Mar 16:18. They shall take up *serpents;*
Lu. 10:19. power to tread on *serpents*
   11:11. will he for a fish give him a *serpent?*
Joh. 3:14. And as Moses lifted up the *serpent* in
1Co.10: 9. and were destroyed of *serpents*.
2Co.11: 3. as the *serpent* beguiled Eve
Rev. 9:19. their tails (were) like unto *serpents*,
  12: 9. that old *serpent*, called the Devil,
    14. from the face of the *serpent*.
    15. And the *serpent* cast out of his
  20: 2. that old *serpent*, which is the devil,

ὀφρύς, *ophrus.*

Lu. 4:29. and led him unto the *brow* of the hill

ὀχλέομαι, *okleomai.*

Lu. 6:18. And they *that were vexed* with
Acts 5:16. and them *which were vexed* with unclean
      spirits:

ὀχλοποιέω, *oklopoyeo.*

Acts17: 5. *gathered a company, and* set all the city on
     an uproar,

ὄχλος, *oklos.*

Mat. 4:25. there followed him great *multitudes*
   5: 1. And seeing the *multitudes*,
   7:28. the *people* were astonished at his
   8: 1. great *multitudes* followed him.
    18. when Jesus saw great *multitudes*

Mat. 9: 8. But when the *multitudes* saw (it),
    23. and the *people* making a noise,
    25. But when the *people* were put forth,
    33. and the *multitudes* marvelled,
    36. when he saw the *multitudes*,
  11: 7. began to say unto the *multitudes*
  12:15. and great *multitudes* followed him,
    23. And all the *people* were amazed,
    46. While he yet talked to the *people*,
  13: 2. And great *multitudes* were gathered
   — and the whole *multitude* stood on
    34. spake Jesus unto the *multitude*
    36. Then Jesus sent the *multitude*
  14: 5. he feared the *multitude*,
    13. and when the *people* had heard
    14. and saw a great *multitude*,
    15. send the *multitude* away,
    19. he commanded the *multitude*
   — and the disciples to the *multitude*.
    22. while he sent the *multitudes*
    23. sent the *multitudes* away,
  15:10. he called the *multitude*,
    30. And great *multitudes* came
    31. Insomuch that the *multitude*
    32. compassion on the *multitude*,
    33. as to fill so great a *multitude?*
    35. he commanded the *multitude*
    36. and the disciples to the *multitude*.
    39. And he sent away the *multitude*,
  17:14. were come to the *multitude*,
  19: 2. And great *multitudes* followed
  20:29. a great *multitude* followed him.
    31. And the *multitude* rebuked
  21: 8. And a very great *multitude*
    9. And the *multitudes* that went before,
    11. And the *multitude* said, This is
    26. we fear the *people*
    46. they feared the *multitude*,
  22:33. And when the *multitude* heard
  23: 1. Then spake Jesus to the *multitude*,
  26:47. with him a great *multitude*
    55. said Jesus to the *multitudes*,
  27:15. to release unto the *people* a
    20. persuaded the *multitude* that they
    24. hands before the *multitude*,
Mar 2: 4. nigh unto him for the *press*,
    13. and all the *multitude* resorted
  3: 9. because of the *multitude*, lest
    20. And the *multitude* cometh
    32. And the *multitude* sat about him,
  4: 1. unto him a great *multitude*,
   — and the whole *multitude* was by
    36. sent away the *multitude*,
  5:21. much *people* gathered unto him:
    24. much *people* followed him,
    27. came in the *press* behind,
    30. turned him about in the *press*,
    31. Thou seest the *multitude* thronging
  6:33. And the *people* saw them
    34. saw much *people*, and was moved
    45. while he sent away the *people*.
  7:14. when he had called all the *people*
    17. into the house from the *people*,
    33. aside from the *multitude*,
  8: 1. the *multitude* being very great,
    2. compassion on the *multitude*,
    6. he commanded the *people* to
   — set (them) before the *people*.
    34. when he had called the *people*
  9:14. he saw a great *multitude*
    15. straightway all the *people*, when
    17. And one of the *multitude* answered

Mar 9:25. When Jesus saw that the *people* came
10: 1. and the *people* resort unto him again
46. and a great *number of people*,
11:18. because all the *people* was astonished
12:12. but feared the *people* :
37. the common *people* heard him gladly.
41. and beheld how the *people* cast
14:43. with him a great *multitude* with
15: 8. And the *multitude* crying aloud
11. the chief priests moved the *people*,
15. willing to content the *people*,
Lu. 3: 7. Then said he to the *multitude*
10. And the *people* asked him,
4:42. and the *people* sought him,
5: 1. as the *people* pressed upon him
3. and taught the *people*
15. and great *multitudes* came
19. because of the *multitude*,
29. a great *company* of publicans and
6:17. and the *company* of his disciples,
19. And the whole *multitude* sought
7: 9. and said unto the *people* that followed
11. went with him, and much *people*.
12. much *people* of the city was with her.
24. he began to speak unto the *people*
8: 4. And when much *people* were
19. could not come at him for the *press*.
40. the *people* (gladly) received him:
42. the *people* thronged him.
45. the *multitude* throng thee
9:11. And the *people*, when they knew
12. Send the *multitude* away,
16. to set before the *multitude*.
18. Whom say the *people* that I am ?
37. much *people* met him.
38. a man of the *company* cried out,
11:14. and the *people* wondered.
27. a certain woman of the *company*
29. And when the *people* were gathered
12: 1. innumerable multitude of *people*,
13. one of the *company* said unto him,
54. And he said also to the *people*,
13:14. and said unto the *people*,
17. and all the *people* rejoiced
14:25. there went great *multitudes* with him:
18:36. hearing the *multitude* pass by,
19: 3. and could not for the *press*,
39. from among the *multitude*
22: 6. in the absence of the *multitude*.
47. yet spake, behold a *multitude*,
23: 4. to the chief priests and (to) the *people*,
48. And all the *people* that came together
Joh. 5:13. a *multitude* being in (that) place.
6: 2. And a great *multitude* followed him,
5. saw a great *company* come
22. when the *people* which stood
24. When the *people* therefore saw
7:12. among the *people* concerning him:
— he deceiveth the *people*.
20. The *people* answered and said,
31. And many of the *people* believed
32. heard that the *people* murmured such
40. Many of the *people* therefore,
43. was a division among the *people*
49. But this *people* who knoweth not
11:42. because of the *people* which
12: 9. Much *people* of the Jews therefore
12. On the next day much *people*
17. The *people* therefore that was
18. For this cause the *people* also met him,
29. The *people* therefore, that stood by,
34. The *people* answered him,

Acts 1:15. the *number* of the names together
6: 7. and a great *company* of the priests
8: 6. And the *people* with one accord
11:24. and much *people* was added unto
26. and taught much *people*.
13:45. when the Jews saw the *multitudes*,
14:11. when the *people* saw what Paul
13. would have done sacrifice with the *people*.
14. and ran in among the *people*,
18. restrained they the *people*,
19. who persuaded the *people*,
16:22. And the *multitude* rose up together
17: 8. And they troubled the *people* and the
13. and stirred up the *people*.
19:26. and turned away much *people*,
33. drew Alexander out of the *multitude*,
35. had appeased the *people*,
21:27. stirred up all the *people*,
34. some another, among the *multitude* :
35. for the violence of the *people*.
24:12. neither raising up the *people*,
18. neither with *multitude*, nor with tumult.
Rev. 7: 9. and, lo, a great *multitude*,
17:15. peoples, and *multitudes*, and nations,
19: 1. a great voice of much *people*
6. the voice of a great *multitude*,

ὀχύρωμα, okurōma.

2Co.10: 4. the pulling down of *strong holds* ;

ὀψάριον, opsarion.

Joh. 6: 9. loaves, and two *small fishes* :
11. and likewise of the *fishes*
21: 9. and *fish* laid thereon,
10. Bring of the *fish* which ye have now
13. giveth them, and *fish* likewise.

ὀψέ, opse.

Mat.28: 1. *In the end* of the sabbath,
Mar 11:19. And when *even* was come,
13:35. *at even*, or at midnight,

ὀψία, opsia.

Mat. 8:16. When the *even* was come,
14:15. And when it was *evening*,
23. and when the *evening* was come,
16: 2. When it is *evening*, ye say,
20: 8. So when *even* was come, the lord of
26:20. Now when the *even* was come,
27:57. When the *even* was come, there came
Mar 1:32. And at *even*, when the sun did set,
4:35. when the *even* was come, he saith
6:47. And when *even* was come, the ship
11:11. and now the *eventide* was come,
14:17. in the *evening* he cometh with the twelve.
15:42. And now when the *even* was come,
Joh. 6:16. And when *even* was (now) come,
20:19. the same day at *evening*, being the

ὄψιμος, opsimos.

Jas. 5: 7. the early and *latter* rain.

ὄψις, opsis.

Joh. 7:24. Judge not according to the *appearance*,
　　11:44. and his *face* was bound about with a
Rev. 1:16. his *countenance* (was) as the sun

ὀψώνιον, opsōnion

Lu. 3:14. and be content with your *wages*.
Ro. 6:23. For the *wages* of sin (is) death ;
1Co. 9: 7. warfare any time at his own *charges*?
2Co.11: 8. taking *wages* (of them), to do you service.

παγιδεύω, pagidūo.

Mat.22:15. how they *might entangle* him in (his) talk.

παγίς, pagis.

Lu. 21:35. as a *snare* shall it come
Ro. 11: 9. Let their table be made a *snare*,
1Ti. 3: 7. and the *snare* of the devil,
　　6: 9. fall into temptation and a *snare*,
2Ti. 2:26. out of the *snare* of the devil,

πάθημα, pathēema.

Ro. 7: 5. the *motions* of sins, which were by
　　8:18. I reckon that the *sufferings* of this
2Co. 1: 5. For as the *sufferings* of Christ abound
　　　6. in the enduring of the same *sufferings*
　　　7. as ye are partakers of the *sufferings*, so
Gal. 5:24. have crucified the flesh with the *affections*
Phi. 3:10. the fellowship of his *sufferings*,
Col. 1:24. Who now rejoice in my *sufferings*
2Ti. 3:11. Persecutions, *afflictions*, which came
Heb 2: 9. for the *suffering* of death, crowned
　　10. perfect through *sufferings*.
　　10:32. endured a great fight of *afflictions*;
1Pet. 1:11. the *sufferings* of Christ, and the
　　4:13. ye are partakers of Christ's *sufferings*;
　　5: 1. a witness of the *sufferings* of Christ,
　　　9. the same *afflictions* are accomplished

παθητός, pathēctos.

Acts26:23. That Christ should *suffer*,

πάθος, pathos.

Ro. 1:26. gave them up unto vile *affections*:
Col. 3: 5. uncleanness, *inordinate affection*,
1Th. 4: 5. Not in the *lust* of concupiscence,

παιδαγωγός, paidagōgos.

1Co. 4:15. ten thousand *instructers* in Christ, yet
Gal. 3:24. the law was our *schoolmaster*
　　25. no longer under a *schoolmaster*.

παιδάριον, paidarion.

Mat.11:16. It is like unto *children* sitting in the
Joh. 6: 9. There is a *lad* here,

παιδεία, paidīa.

Eph 6: 4. in the *nurture* and admonition
2Ti. 3:16. for *instruction* in righteousness:
Heb 12: 5. despise not thou the *chastening* of
　　　7. If ye endure *chastening*, God
　　　8. But if ye be without *chastisement*,
　　11. Now no *chastening* for the present

παιδευτής, paidūtees.

Ro. 2:20. An *instructor* of the foolish,
Heb.12: 9. fathers of our flesh *which corrected* (us),

παιδεύω, paidūo.

Lu. 23:16. I will therefore *chastise* him, *and*
　　22: I will therefore *chastise* him, *and*
Acts 7:22. And Moses *was learned* in all
　　22: 3. *taught* according to the perfect manner
1Co.11:32. we *are chastened* of the Lord,
2Co. 6: 9. as *chastened*, and not killed ;
1Ti. 1:20. that they *may learn* not to blaspheme.
2Ti. 2:25. In meekness *instructing* those that
Tit. 2:12. *Teaching* us that, denying ungodliness
Heb 12: 6. whom the Lord loveth he *chasteneth*,
　　　7. whom the father *chasteneth* not ?
　　10. for a few days *chastened* (us)
Rev. 3:19. As many as I love, I rebuke and *chasten*:

παιδιόθεν, paidiothen.

Mar 9:21. And he said, *Of a child*.

παιδίον, paidion.

Mat. 2: 8. search diligently for the *young child*;
　　　9. over where the *young child* was.
　　11. they saw the *young child* with Mary
　　13. Arise, and take the *young child* and his
　　― Herod will seek the *young child* to
　　14. he took the *young child* and his mother
　　20. Arise, and take the *young child* and his
　　― which sought the *young child's* life.
　　21. and took the *young child* and his mother,
　　14:21. beside women and *children*.
　　15:38. beside women and *children*.
　　18: 2. And Jesus called a *little child* unto
　　　3. and become as *little children*,
　　　4. humble himself as this *little child*,
　　　5. receive one such *little child* in
　　19:13. brought unto him *little children*,
　　14. Jesus said, Suffer *little children*,
Mar 5:39. the *damsel* is not dead, but sleepeth.
　　40. father and the mother of the *damsel*,
　　― and entereth in where the *damsel* was
　　41. he took the *damsel* by the hand,
　　7:28. eat of the *children's* crumbs.
　　9:24. And straightway the father of the *child*
　　36. And he took a *child*, and set him
　　37. receive one of such *children* in my
　　10:13. brought *young children* to him,
　　14. Suffer the *little children* to come
　　15. kingdom of God as a *little child*,
Lu. 1:59. to circumcise the *child*;
　　66. What manner of *child* shall this be !
　　76. And thou, *child*, shalt be called
　　80. And the *child* grew, and waxed strong
　　2:17. was told them concerning this *child*.

Lu. 2:21. for the circumcising of the *child*,
    27. the parents brought in the *child* Jesus,
    40. And the *child* grew, and waxed strong in
  7:32. unto *children* sitting in the marketplace,
  9:47. took a *child*, and set him by him,
    48. Whosoever shall receive this *child* in my
 11: 7. my *children* are with me in bed ;
 18:16. Suffer *little children* to come unto me,
    17. receive the kingdom of God as a *little child*
Joh. 4:49. Sir, come down ere my *child* die.
 16:21. as soon as she is delivered of the *child*,
 21: 5. *Children*, have ye any meat ?
1Co.14:20. be not *children* in understanding :
Heb 2:13. Behold I and the *children* which
    14. Forasmuch then as the *children* are
 11:23. they saw (he was) a proper *child ;*
1Joh.2:13. I write unto you, *little children*,
    18. *Little children*, it is the last time :

παιδίσκη, *paidiskee.*

Mat.26:69. and a *damsel* came unto him,
Mar14:66. there cometh one of the *maids* of the
    69. And a *maid* saw him again,
Lu. 12:45. to beat the menservants and *maidens,*
 22:56. But a certain *maid* beheld him as
Joh.18:17. Then saith the *damsel* that kept the door
Acts12:13. a *damsel* came to hearken, named Rhoda.
 16:16. a certain *damsel* possessed with a spirit
Gal. 4:22. two sons, the one by a *bondmaid,*
    23. But he (who was) of the *bondwoman*
    30. Cast out the *bondwoman* and her son : for
        the son of the *bondwoman* shall not
    31. we are not children of the *bondwoman,*

παίζω, *paizo.*

1Co.10: 7. and rose up *to play.*

παῖς, *pais.*

Mat. 2:16. and slew all the *children* that were
  8: 6. Lord, my *servant* lieth at home
    8. and my *servant* shall be healed.
    13. And his *servant* was healed
 12:18. Behold my *servant*, whom I have
 14: 2. And said unto his *servants*, This is
 17:18. and the *child* was cured from
 21:15. and the *children* crying in the temple,
Lu. 1:54. He hath holpen his *servant* Israel,
    69. in the house of his *servant* David ;
  2:43. the *child* Jesus tarried behind in
  7: 7. and my *servant* shall be healed.
  8:51. and the mother of the *maiden.*
    54. and called, saying, *Maid,* arise.
  9:42. and healed the *child,* and delivered
 12:45. to beat the *menservants* and
 15:26. and he called one of the *servants,*
Joh. 4:51. Thy *son* liveth.
Acts 3:13. hath glorified his *Son* Jesus ;
    26. God, having raised up his *Son* Jesus,
  4:25. Who by the mouth of thy *servant* David
    27. against thy holy *child* Jesus, whom
    30. name of thy holy *child* Jesus.
 20:12. And they brought the *young man* alive,

παίω, *paio.*

Mat.26:68. Who is he *that smote* thee :

Mar 14:47. and *smote* a servant of the high priest,
Lu. 22:64. who is it *that smote* thee ?
Joh.18:10. and *smote* the high priest's servant,
Rev. 9: 5. a scorpion, when he *striketh* a man.

πάλαι, *palai.*

Mat.11:21. they would have repented *long ago* in
Mar 15:44. whether he had been *any while* dead.
Lu. 10:13. they had *a great while ago* repented,
Heb 1: 1. spake *in time past* unto the fathers by
2Pet.1: 9. purged from his *old* sins.
Jude   4. were before *of old* ordained to this

παλαιός, *palaios.*

Mat. 9:16. new cloth unto an *old* garment.
    17. new wine into *old* bottles:
 13:52. out of his treasure (things) new and *old.*
Mar 2:21. a piece of new cloth on an *old* garment:
    — taketh away from the *old,*
    22. putteth new wine into *old* bottles:
Lu. 5:36. of a new garment upon an *old ;*
    — agreeth not with the *old.*
    37. putteth new wine into *old* bottles:
    39. No man also having drunk *old* (wine)
    — for he saith, The *old* is better.
Ro. 6: 6. our *old* man is crucified with
1Co. 5: 7. Purge out therefore the *old* leaven,
    8. not with *old* leaven,
2Co. 3:14. in the reading of the *old* testament ;
Eph. 4:22. the *old* man, which is corrupt
Col. 3: 9. ye have put off the *old* man with
1Joh.2: 7. but an *old* commandment which ye
    — The *old* commandment is the word which

παλαιότης, *palaiotees.*

Ro. 7: 6. and not (in) the *oldness* of the letter.

παλαιόω, *palaioō.*

Lu. 12:33. bags *which wax* not *old,*
Heb 1:11. they all *shall wax old* as doth a
  8:13. he *hath made* the first *old.* Now that
    which decayeth

πάλη, *palee.*

Eph. 6:12. we wrestle not against flesh and blood,
    (lit. the *wrestling* is not to us &c.)

παλίγγενεσία, *palingenesia.*

Mat.19:28. in the *regeneration* when the Son of man
Tit. 3: 5. by the washing of *regeneration,*

πάλιν, *palin.*

Mat. 4: 7. It is written *again,* Thou shalt not
    8. *Again,* the devil taketh him up
  5:33. *Again,* ye have heard that it hath
 13:44. *Again,* the kingdom of heaven is like
    45. *Again,* the kingdom of heaven is
    47. *Again,* the kingdom of heaven is

Mat.18:19. *Again* I say unto you, That if two
19:24. And *again* I say unto you, It is easier
20: 5. *Again* he went out about the sixth
21:36. *Again*, he sent other servants more
22: 1. and spake unto them *again* by parables,
4. *Again*, he sent forth other servants,
26:42. He went away *again* the second time,
43. came and found them asleep *again :*
44. and went away *again*, and prayed
72. And *again* he denied with an oath,
27:50. Jesus, when he had cried *again*
Mar 2: 1. And *again* he entered into Capernaum
13. And he went forth *again* by the sea
3: 1. And he entered *again* into the synagogue;
20. the multitude cometh together *again*,
4: 1. And he began *again* to teach by the
5:21. when Jesus was passed over *again* by ship
7:31. and *again*, departing from the coasts
8:13. and entering into the ship *again*
25. he put (his) hands *again* upon his eyes,
10: 1. resort unto him *again ;* and, as he was
wont, he taught them *again*.
10. his disciples asked him *again* of the
24. But Jesus answereth *again*, and saith
32. And he took *again* the twelve, and
11:27. And they come *again* to Jerusalem :
12: 4. And *again* he sent unto them another
5. And *again* he sent another ; and him
14:39. And *again* he went away, and prayed,
40. he found them asleep *again*,
61. *Again* the high priest asked him,
69. And a maid saw him *again*,
70. he denied it *again*. And a little after,
they that stood by said *again* to Peter,
15: 4. And Pilate asked him *again*, saying,
12. Pilate answered and said *again* unto
13. And they cried out *again*, Crucify him.
Lu. 13:20. And *again* he said, Whereunto shall
23:20. willing to release Jesus, spake *again*
Joh. 1:35. *Again* the next day after John stood, and
4: 3. and departed *again* into Galilee.
13. of this water shall thirst *again* .
46. So Jesus came *again* into Cana of Galilee,
54. This (is) *again* the second miracle
6:15. he departed *again* into a mountain
8: 2. he came *again* into the temple,
8. And *again* he stooped down, and
12. Then spake Jesus *again* unto them,
21. Then said Jesus *again* unto them,
9:15. Then *again* the Pharisees also asked
17. They say unto the blind man *again*,
26. Then said they to him *again*,
27. wherefore would ye hear (it) *again ?*
10: 7. Then said Jesus unto them *again*,
17. my life, that I might take it *again*.
18. and I have power to take it *again*.
19. There was a division therefore *again*
31. the Jews took up stones *again* to
39. Therefore they sought *again* to take
40. And went away *again* beyond Jordan
11: 7. Let us go into Judæa *again*.
8. and goest thou thither *again ?*
38. *again* groaning in himself
12:22. and *again* Andrew and Philip
28. and will glorify (it) *again*.
39. because that Esaias said *again*,
13:12. and was set down *again*, he said
14: 3. I will come *again*, and receive you
16:16. and *again*, a little while, and ye
17. and *again*, a little while, and
19. and *again*, a little while, and
22. but I will see you *again*,

Joh. 16:28. *again*, I leave the world, and go to
18: 7. Then asked he them *again*, Whom seek
27. Peter then denied *again :*
33. into the judgment hall *again*,
38. he went out *again* unto the Jews,
40. Then cried they all *again*, saying,
19: 4. Pilate therefore went forth *again*,
9. And went *again* into the judgment hall,
37. And *again* another scripture saith,
20:10. the disciples went away *again*
21. said Jesus to them *again*,
26. And after eight days *again* his disciples
21: 1. Jesus shewed himself *again* to the
16. He saith to him *again* the second time,
Acts10:15. the voice (spake) unto him *again*
16. the vessel was received up *again*
11:10. all were drawn up *again* into heaven.
17:32. We will hear thee *again* of this
18:21. I will return *again* unto you,
27:28. they sounded *again*, and found
Ro. 8:15. the spirit of bondage *again* to fear;
11:23. is able to graff them in *again*.
15:10. And *again* he saith, Rejoice, ye Gentiles,
11. And *again*, Praise the Lord, all ye
12. And *again*, Esaias saith,
1Co. 3:20. And *again*, The Lord knoweth the
7: 5. and come together *again*, that Satan
12:21. nor *again* the head to the feet, I have
2Co. 1:16. and to come *again* out of Macedonia
2: 1. not come *again* to you in heaviness.
3: 1. begin *again* to commend ourselves ?
5:12. we commend not ourselves *again* unto
10: 7. let him of himself think this *again*,
11:16. I say *again*, Let no man think me
12:19. *Again*, think ye that we excuse
21. (And) lest, when I come *again*,
13: 2. that, if I come *again*, I will not spare:
Gal. 1: 9. so say I now *again*,
17. returned *again* unto Damascus.
2: 1. I went up *again* to Jerusalem
18. For if I build *again* the things
4: 9. how turn ye *again* to the weak
— ye desire *again* (πάλιν ἄνωθεν lit. *again*,
anew) to be in bondage ?
19. of whom I travail in birth *again*
5: 1. be not entangled *again* with the yoke
3. For I testify *again* to every man
Phi. 1:26. by my coming to you *again*.
2:28. that, when ye see him *again*, ye may
4: 4. (and) *again* I say, Rejoice.
Heb 1: 5. And *again*, I will be to him a Father,
6. And *again*, when (lit. and when *again*)
he bringeth in the firstbegotten
2:13. And *again*, I will put my trust in him.
And *again*, Behold I and the
4: 5. And in this (place) *again*, If they shall
7. *Again*, he limiteth a certain day,
5:12. ye have need that one teach you *again*
(lit. ye have need *again*, &c.)
6: 1. not laying *again* the foundation of
6. to renew them *again* unto repentance ;
10:30. And *again*, The Lord shall judge his
Jas. 5:18. And he prayed *again*, and the heaven
2Pet. 2:20. they are *again* entangled therein,
1Joh.2: 8. *Again*, a new commandment I write
Rev.10: 8. from heaven spake unto me *again*,
11. Thou must prophesy *again* before

παμπληθεί, *pampleethi.*

Lu. 23:18. they cried out *all at once*, saying,

πάμπολυς, *pampolus*.

Mar 8: 1. the multitude being *very great,*

πανδοχεῖον, *pandokīon*.

Lu. 10:34. brought him to an *inn,*

πανδοχεύς, *pandokūs*.

Lu. 10:35. two pence, and gave (them) to the *host,*

πανήγυρις, *paneeguris*.

Heb 12:23. To the *general assembly* and church of

πανοικί, *panoiki*.

Acts16:34. believing in God *with all* his *house.*

πανοπλία, *panoplīa*.

Lu. 11:22. taketh from him *all* his *armour*
Eph. 6:11. Put on the *whole armour* of God, ,
13. take unto you the *whole armour* of God,

πανουργία, *panourgia*.

Lu. 20:23. perceived their *craftiness,* and said
1Co. 3:19. the wise in their own *craftiness.*
2Co. 4: 2. not walking in *craftiness,*
11: 3. beguiled Eve through his *subtilty,*
Eph. 4:14. sleight of men, (and) *cunning craftiness,*

πανοῦργος, *panourgos*.

2Co.12:16. nevertheless, being *crafty,* I caught you

πανταχόθεν, *pantakothen*.

Mar 1:45. they came to him *from every quarter.*

πανταχοῦ, *pantakou*.

Mar 16:20. went forth, and preached *every where,*
Lu. 9: 6. and healing *every where.*
Acts17:30. commandeth all men *every where*
21:28. that teacheth all (men) *every where*
24: 3. always, and *in all places,* most noble Felix,
28:22. that *every where* it is spoken against.
1Co. 4:17. as I teach *every where* in every church.

παντελές, *panteles*.

(εἰς τὸ παντελές).

Lu. 13:11. could in no wise (lit. not *altogether*) lift
up (herself).
Heb 7:25. to save them to the *uttermost*

πάντη, *pantee*.

Acts24: 3. We accept (it) *always,* and in

πάντοθεν, *pantothen*.

Lu. 19:43. and keep thee in *on every side,*
Heb 9: 4. overlaid *round about* with gold,

παντοκράτωρ, *pantokratōr*.

2Co. 6:18. saith the Lord *Almighty.*
Rev. 1: 8. and which is to come, the *Almighty.*
4: 8. Holy, holy, holy, Lord God *Almighty,*
11:17. O Lord God *Almighty,* which
15: 3. thy works, Lord God *Almighty;*
16: 7. Lord God *Almighty,* true and
14. that great day of God *Almighty.*
19: 6. the Lord God *omnipotent* reigneth.
15. and wrath of *Almighty* God.
21:22. the Lord God *Almighty* and the Lamb

πάντοτε, *pantote*.

Mat.26:11. ye have the poor *always* with you ; but
me ye have not *always.*
Mar 14: 7. ye have the poor with you *always,*
— but me ye have not *always.*
Lu. 15:31. Son, thou art *ever* with me,
18: 1. that men ought *always* (to) pray,
Joh. 6:34. Lord, *evermore* give us this bread.
7: 6. but your time is *alway* ready.
8:29. for I do *always* those things that
11:42. I knew that thou hearest me *always:*
12: 8. the poor *always* ye have with you ; but
· me ye have not *always.*
18:20. I *ever* taught in the synagogue,
— whither the Jews *always* resort ;·
Ro. 1: 9(10). *always* in my prayers,
1Co. 1: 4. thank my God *always* on your behalf,
15:58. *always* abounding in the work of the
2Co. 2:14. which *always* causeth us to triumph
4:10. *Always* bearing about in the body
5: 6. Therefore (we are) *always* confident,
9: 8. that ye, *always* having all sufficiency
Gal. 4:18. good to be zealously affected *always* in
Eph 5:20. Giving thanks *always* for all things
Phi. 1: 4. *Always* in every prayer of mine
20. with all boldness, as *always,* (so) now
2:12. my beloved, as ye have *always* obeyed,
4: 4. Rejoice in the Lord *alway* :
Col. 1: 3. praying *always* for you,
4: 6. Let your speech (be) *alway* with grace,
12. *always* labouring fervently for you
1Th. 1: 2. We give thanks to God *always* for you all,
2:16. to fill up their sins *alway:*
3: 6. ye have good remembrance of us *always,*
4:17. and so shall we *ever* be with the Lord.
5:15. *ever* follow that which is good,
16. Rejoice *evermore.*
2Th. 1: 3. We are bound to thank God *always* for
11. Wherefore also we pray *always* for you,
2:13. bound to give thanks *alway* to God
2Ti. 3: 7. *Ever* learning, and never able
Philem. 4. mention of thee *always* in my prayers,
Heb 7:25. he *ever* liveth to make intercession

πάντως, *pantōs*.

Lu. 4:23. Ye will *surely* say unto me this
Acts18:21. I must *by all means* keep this feast
21:22. the multitude must *needs* (lit. *by all means*
must) come together:
28: 4. *No doubt* this man is a murderer,

Ro. 3: 9. No, *in no wise:* (lit. not *at all*)
1Co. 5:10. Yet not *altogether* with the
      9:10. Or saith he (it) *altogether* for our
      22. that I might *by all means* save some.
     16:12. his will was not *at all* to come

παρά, *para.*

The cases governed are respectively marked by
                g, d, a.

Mat. 2: 4. demanded *of*ᵍ them where Christ
      7. enquired *of*ᵍ them diligently
     16. enquired *of*ᵍ the wise men.
   4:18. walking *by*ᵃ the sea of Galilee,
   6: 1. no reward *of*ᵈ your Father which
  13: 1. and sat *by*ᵃ the sea side.
      4. fell *by*ᵃ the way side,
     19. received seed *by*ᵃ the way side.
  15:29. and came *nigh unto*ᵃ the sea of
     30. and cast them down *at*ᵃ Jesus' feet ;
  18:19. it shall be done for them *of*ᵍ my Father
  19:26. *With*ᵈ men this is impossible ; but *with*ᵈ
          God all things are possible.
  20:20. a certain thing *of*ᵍ him.
     30. sitting *by*ᵃ the way side,
  21:25. reasoned *with*ᵈ themselves,
     42. this is the Lord's doing, (lit. *from*ᵍ the
          Lord)
  22:25. there were *with*ᵈ us seven brethren:
  28:15. reported *among*ᵈ the Jews until
Mar 1:16. as he walked *by*ᵃ the sea of
   2:13. went forth again *by*ᵃ the sea side ;
   3:21. when *his* friends (lit. they *of*ᵍ him) heard
          (of it),
   4: 1. to teach *by*ᵃ the sea side:
      4. some fell *by*ᵃ the way side,
     15. these are they *by*ᵃ the way side,
   5:21. he was *nigh unto*ᵃ the sea.
     26. spent all that she had, (lit. *all* things *of*ᵍ
          herself)
   8:11. seeking *of*ᵍ him a sign
  10:27. *With*ᵈ men (it is) impossible, but not
          *with*ᵈ God: for *with*ᵈ God all things are
          possible.
     46. sat *by*ᵃ the highway side
  12: 2. might receive *from*ᵍ the husbandmen
     11. This was the Lord's doing, (lit. *from*ᵍ the
          Lord)
  14:43. *from*ᵍ the chief priests and
Lu. 1:30. thou hast found favour *with*ᵈ God.
     37. For *with*ᵈ God nothing shall be
     45. which were told her *from*ᵍ the Lord.
   2: 1. there went out a decree *from*ᵍ Cæsar
     52. and in favour *with*ᵈ God and man.
   3:13. no more *than*ᵃ that which is appointed
   5: 1. he stood *by*ᵃ the lake of Gennesaret,
      2. two ships standing *by*ᵃ the lake:
   6:19. there went virtue out *of*ᵍ him,
     34. ye lend (to them) *of*ᵍ whom ye hope to
   7:38. And stood *at*ᵃ his feet behind (him)
   8: 5. some fell *by*ᵃ the way side ;
     12. Those *by*ᵃ the way side are they
     35. sitting *at*ᵃ the feet of Jesus,
     41. and he fell down *at*ᵃ Jesus' feet,
     49. *from*ᵍ the ruler of the synagogue's (house),
   9:47. and set him *by*ᵈ him,
  10: 7. such things as they give: (lit. the things
          *of*ᵍ them)
     39. which also sat *at*ᵃ Jesus' feet,
  11:16. sought *of*ᵍ him a sign

Lu. 11:37. besought him to dine *with*ᵈ him:
  12:48. *of*ᵍ him shall be much required:
  13: 2. sinners *above*ᵃ all the Galilæans,
      4. that they were sinners *above*ᵃ all
  17:16. fell down on (his) face *at*ᵃ his feet,
  18:27. things which are impossible *with*ᵈ men
          are possible *with*ᵈ God.
     35. blind man sat *by*ᵃ the way side
  19: 7. guest *with*ᵈ a man that is a sinner.
Joh. 1: 6. a man sent *from*ᵍ God,
     14. the only begotten *of*ᵍ the Father,
     39(40). and abode *with*ᵈ him that day:
     40(41). One of the two which heard John
          (speak), (lit. heard *of*ᵍ John)
   4: 9. askest drink *of*ᵍ me,
     40. that he would tarry *with*ᵈ them:
     52. Then enquired he *of*ᵍ them the hour
   5:34. I receive not testimony *from*ᵍ man:
     41. I receive not honour *from*ᵍ men.
     44. which receive honour one *of*ᵍ another,
      — not the honour that (cometh) *from*ᵍ God
   6:45. and hath learned *of*ᵍ the Father,
     46. save he which is *of*ᵍ God,
   7:29. I am *from*ᵍ him,
     51. before it hear) (ᵍ him,
   8:26. which I have heard *of*ᵍ him.
     38. which I have seen *with*ᵈ my Father:
      — which ye have seen *with*ᵈ your father.
     40. which I have heard *of*ᵍ God:
   9:16. This man is not *of*ᵍ God,
     33. If this man were not *of*ᵍ God,
  10:18. have I received *of*ᵍ my Father.
  14:17. for he dwelleth *with*ᵈ you,
     23. and make our abode *with*ᵈ him.
     25. being (yet) present *with*ᵈ you.
  15:15. that I have heard *of*ᵍ my Father
     26. send unto you *from*ᵍ the Father,
      — which proceedeth *from*ᵍ the Father,
  16:27. that I came out *from*ᵍ God.
     28. I came forth *from*ᵍ the Father,
  17: 5. *with*ᵈ thine own self with the glory which
          I had *with*ᵈ thee.
      7. thou hast given me are *of*ᵍ thee.
      8. that I came out *from*ᵍ thee,
  19:25. Now there stood *by*ᵈ the cross
Acts 2:33. having received *of*ᵍ the Father
   3: 2. to ask alms *of*ᵍ them that
      . 5. to receive something *of*ᵍ them.
   4:35. laid (them) down *at*ᵃ the apostles' feet:
     37. and laid (it) *at*ᵃ the apostles' feet.
   5: 2. and laid (it) *at*ᵃ the apostles' feet.
     10. *at*ᵃ his feet, and yielded up the
   7:16. money *of*ᵍ the sons of Emmor
     58. *at*ᵃ a young man's feet,
   9: 2. And desired *of*ᵍ him letters
     14. authority *from*ᵍ the chief priests
     43. *with*ᵈ one Simon a tanner.
  10: 6. *with*ᵈ one Simon a tanner, whose house
          is *by*ᵃ the sea side:
     22. to hear words *of*ᵍ thee.
     32. (one) Simon a tanner *by*ᵃ the sea side:
  16:13. we went out of the city *by*ᵃ a river side,
  17: 9. they had taken security *of*ᵍ Jason,
  18: 3. he abode *with*ᵈ them,
     13. *contrary to*ᵃ the law.
     20. to tarry longer time *with*ᵈ them,
  20:24. I have received *of*ᵍ the Lord Jesus,
  21: 7. and abode *with*ᵈ them one day.
      8. and abode *with*ᵈ him.
     16. *with*ᵈ whom we should lodge.
  22: 3. *at*ᵃ the feet of Gamaliel,
      5. *from*ᵍ whom also I received letters

Acts22:30. he was accused *of* ᵍ the Jews,
24: 8. by examining of whom thyself (lit. *of* ᵍ
whom thyself examining) mayest take
knowledge
26: 8. a thing incredible *with* ᵈ you,
10. authority *from* ᵍ the chief priests ;
12. commission *from* ᵍ the chief priests,
22. obtained help *of* ᵍ God,
28:22. we desire to hear *of* ᵍ thee what thou
Ro. 1:25. the creature *more than* ᵃ the Creator,
26. which is *against* ᵃ nature:
2:11. no respect of persons *with* ᵈ God.
13. (are) just *before* ᵈ God, but
4:18. Who *against* ᵃ hope believed
9:14. (Is there) unrighteousness *with* ᵈ God ?
11:24. graffed *contrary to* ᵃ nature
25. be wise *in* ᵈ your own conceits;
27. this (is) my covenant (lit. the covenant
from ᵍ me) unto them,
12: 3. more highly *than* ᵃ he ought
16. Be not wise *in* ᵈ your own conceits.
14: 5. one day *above* ᵃ another:
16:17. *contrary to* ᵃ the doctrine which
1Co. 3:11. *than* ᵃ that is laid,
19. is foolishness *with* ᵈ God.
7:24. therein abide *with* ᵈ God.
12:15. is it *therefore* ᵃ (lit. *notwithstanding* this)
not of the body ?
16. is it *therefore* ᵃ (lit. *&c.*) not of the body ?
16: 2. every one of you lay *by* ᵈ him in store,
2Co. 1:17. that *with* ᵈ me there should be yea
11:24. forty (stripes) *save* ᵃ one.
Gal. 1: 8. *than* ᵃ that which we have preached
9. *than* ᵃ that ye have received,
12. I neither received it *of* ᵍ man,
3:11. by the law *in the sight of* ᵈ God,
Eph 6: 8. the same shall he receive *of* ᵍ the Lord,
9. respect of persons *with* ᵈ him.
Phi. 4:18. received *of* ᵍ Epaphroditus the things
(which were sent) *from* ᵍ you,
Col. 4:16. when this epistle is read *among* ᵈ you,
1Th. 2:13. which ye heard *of* ᵍ us,
4: 1. as ye have received *of* ᵍ us,
2Th. 1: 6. a righteous thing *with* ᵈ God
3: 6. which he received *of* ᵍ us.
8. any man's bread for nought ; (lit. bread
of ᵍ any)
2Ti. 1:13. which thou hast heard *of* ᵍ me,
18. may find mercy *of* ᵍ the Lord
2: 2. that thou hast heard *of* ᵍ me
3:14. knowing *of* ᵍ whom thou hast learned
4:13. that I left at Troas *with* ᵈ Carpus,
Heb 1: 4. a more excellent name *than* ᵃ they.
9. *above* ᵃ thy fellows.
2: 7. a little lower *than* ᵃ the angels ;
9. made a little lower *than* ᵃ the angels
3: 3. worthy of more glory *than* ᵃ Moses,
9:23. with better sacrifices *than* ᵃ these.
11: 4. a more excellent sacrifice *than* ᵃ Cain,
11. when she was *past* ᵃ age,
12. which is *by* ᵃ the sea shore
12:24. better things *than* ᵃ (that of) Abel.
Jas. 1: 5. let him ask *of* ᵍ God,
7. receive any thing *of* ᵍ the Lord.
17. *with* ᵈ whom is no variableness,
27. *before* ᵈ God and the Father
1Pet. 2: 4. chosen *of* ᵈ God, (lit. *before* or *with* God)
20. this (is) acceptable *with* ᵈ God.
2Pet. 1:17. he received *from* ᵍ God the Father
2:11. against them *before* ᵈ the Lord.
3: 8. one day (is) *with* ᵈ the Lord
1Joh. 3:22. we ask, we receive *of* ᵍ him,

1Joh.5:15. that we desired *of* ᵍ him.
2Joh. 3. *from* ᵍ God the Father. and *from* ᵍ the Lord
Jesus Christ,
4. commandment *from* ᵍ the Father,
Rev. 2:13. who was slain *among* ᵈ you,
27. as I received *of* ᵍ my Father.
3:18. to buy *of* ᵍ me gold tried in the fire,

παραβαίνω, *parabaino.*

Mat.15: 2. Why *do* thy disciples *transgress* the
3. Why *do* ye also *transgress* the
Acts 1:25. from which Judas *by transgression fell,*
2Joh. 9. *Whosoever transgresseth,* and abideth

παραβάλλω, *paraballo.*

Mar 4:30. with what comparison shall we *compare*
Acts20:15. and the next (day) we *arrived* at Samos,

παράβασις, *parabasis.*

Ro. 2:23. through *breaking* the law dishonourest
4:15. where no law is, (there is) no *transgression.*
5:14. not sinned after the similitude of Adam's
transgression,
Gal. 3:19. It was added because of *transgressions,*
1Ti. 2:14. was in the *transgression.*
Heb 2: 2. and every *transgression* and disobedience
9:15. for the redemption of the *transgressions*
(that)

παραβάτης, *parabatees.*

Ro. 2:25. but if thou be a *breaker* of the law,
27. judge thee, *who...dost transgress* the law ?
Gal. 2:18. I make myself a *transgressor.*
Jas. 2: 9. are convinced of the law as *transgressors.*
11. art become a *trangressor* of the law.

παραβιάζομαι, *parabiazomai.*

Lu. 24:29. But they *constrained* him, saying,
Acts16:15. And she *constrained* us.

παραβολή, *parabolee.*

Mat.13: 3. many things unto them in *parables,*
10. Why speakest thou unto them in *parables?*
13. Therefore speak I to them in *parables.*
18. Hear ye therefore the *parable* of the
24. Another *parable* put he forth
31. Another *parable* put he forth unto
33. Another *parable* spake he unto them ;
34. spake Jesus unto the multitude in *parables;*
and without a *parable* spake he not
35. I will open my mouth in *parables ;*
36. Declare unto us the *parable* of the tares
53. when Jesus had finished these *parables,*
15:15. Declare unto us this *parable.*
21:33. Hear another *parable :* There was
45. and Pharisees had heard his *parables,*
22: 1. spake unto them again by *parables,*
24:32. Now learn a *parable* of the fig tree ;
Mar 3:23. and said unto them in *parables,*
4: 2. taught them many things by *parables,*
10. the twelve asked of him the *parable.*

Mar 4:11. all (these) things are done in *parables*:
13. Know ye not this *parable?* and how then will ye know all *parables?*
30. or with what *comparison* shall we compare
33. And with many such *parables* spake
34. But without a *parable* spake he not
7:17. asked him concerning the *parable.*
12: 1. began to speak unto them by *parables.*
12. had spoken the *parable* against them:
13:28. Now learn a *parable* of the fig tree;
Lu. 4:23. say unto me this *proverb*, Physician,
5:36. And he spake also a *parable* unto them;
6:39. And he spake a *parable* unto them,
8: 4. he spake by a *parable*:
9. What might this *parable* be?
10. but to others in *parables*; that
11. Now the *parable* is this: The seed is
12:16. And he spake a *parable* unto them,
41. Lord, speakest thou this *parable* unto us,
13: 6. He spake also this *parable*;
14: 7. And he put forth a *parable* to those
15: 3. And he spake this *parable* unto them,
18: 1. And he spake a *parable* unto them
9. And he spake this *parable* unto
19:11. he added and spake a *parable*,
20: 9. to speak to the people this *parable*;
19. had spoken this *parable* against them.
21:29. And he spake to them a *parable*;
Heb 9: 9. Which (was) a *figure* for the time then
11:19. whence also he received him in a *figure*.

παραβουλεύομαι, *paraboulŭomai.*

Phi. 2:30. *not regarding* his life, to supply your

παραγγελία, *parangelia.*

Acts 5:28. Did not we straitly command you (lit. with *commandment* command)
16:24. Who, having received such a *charge*, thrust
1Th. 4: 2. ye know what *commandments* we gave
1Ti. 1: 5. Now the end of the *commandment* is
18. This *charge* I commit unto thee, son

παραγγέλλω, *parangello.*

Mat.10: 5. *and commanded* them, saying, Go not
Mar 6: 8. And *commanded* them that they should
8: 6. And he *commanded* the people to sit down
Lu. 5:14. And he *charged* him to tell no man:
8:29. For he had *commanded* the unclean spirit
56. but he *charged* them that they should
9:21. he straitly *charged* them, and *commanded*
Acts 1: 4. *commanded* them that they should not
4:18. and *commanded* them not to speak at all
5:28. *Did* not we straitly *command* you that ye
40. they *commanded* that they should not
10:42. he *commanded* us to preach unto
15: 5. and *to command* (them) to keep the law
16:18. I *command* thee in the name of Jesus Christ
23. *charging* the jailor to keep them safely:
17:30. but now *commandeth* all men every
23:22. *and charged* (him, See thou) tell no man
30. and *gave commandment* to his accusers
1Co. 7:10. unto the married I *command*,
11:17. in this that I *declare* (unto you) (lit. *declaring* this) I praise (you) not,
1Th. 4:11. as we *commanded* you;

2Th. 3: 4. do the things which we *command*
6. Now we *command* you, brethren,
10. this we *commanded* you, that if
12. that are such we *command*
1Ti. 1: 3. that thou *mightest charge* some that
4:11. These things *command* and teach.
5: 7. And these things *give in charge*,
6:13. I *give* thee *charge* in the sight of
17. *Charge* them that are rich

παραγίνομαι, *paraginomai.*

Mat. 2: 1. behold, there *came* wise men from
3: 1. In those days *came* John the Baptist,
13. Then *cometh* Jesus from Galilee
Mar 14:43. while he yet spake, *cometh* Judas,
Lu. 7: 4. And when they *came* to Jesus,
20. When the men *were come* unto him,
8:19. Then *came* to him (his) mother and
11: 6. in his journey *is come* to me, and
12:51. Suppose ye that I *am come* to give
14:21. So that servant *came*, and shewed
19:16. Then *came* the first, saying, Lord,
22:52. and the elders, which *were come* to him,
Joh. 3:23. and they *came*, and were baptized.
8: 2. in the morning he *came* again into
Acts 5:21. But the high priest *came*, and they that
22. But when the officers *came*, and
25. Then *came* one and told them,
9:26. And when Saul *was come* to Jerusalem,
39. When he *was come*, they brought him
10:32. who, when he *cometh*, shall speak
33. well done that thou *art come*.
11:23. Who, when he *came*, and had seen
13:14. they *came* to Antioch in Pisidia,
14:27. And when they *were come*, and
15: 4. And when they *were come* to Jerusalem,
17:10. who *coming* (thither) went into the
18:27. who, when he *was come*, helped them
20:18. And when they *were come* to him, he said
21:18. and all the elders *were present*.
23:16. he *went* and entered into the castle,
35. when thine accusers *are* also *come*.
24:17. I *came* to bring alms to my nation,
24. when Felix *came* with his wife
25: 7. And when he *was come*, the Jews which
28:21. neither any of the brethren that *came*
1Co.16: 3. And when I *come*, whomsoever
Heb 9:11. But Christ *being come* an high priest

παράγω, *parago.*

Mat. 9: 9. And as Jesus *passed forth* from thence,
27. And when Jesus *departed* thence, two
20:30. when they heard that Jesus *passed by*, cried
Mar 2:14. And as he *passed by*, he saw Levi
15:21. Simon a Cyrenian, who *passed by*,
Joh. 8:59. midst of them, and so *passed by*.
9: 1. And as (Jesus) *passed by*, he saw
1Co. 7:31. the fashion of this world *passeth away*.
1Joh.2: 8. because the darkness *is past*, and
17. And the world *passeth away*,

παραδειγματίζω, *paradigmatizo.*

Mat. 1:19. *to make* her a *publick example*, was
Heb 6: 6. and *put* (him) *to an open shame*.

παράδεισος, paradisos.

Lu. 23:43. shalt thou be with me in *paradise.*
2Co.12: 4. he was caught up into *paradise,*
Rev. 2: 7. in the midst of the *paradise* of God.

παραδέχομαι, paradekomai.

Mar 4:20. such as hear the word, and *receive* (it),
Acts16:21. which are not lawful for us *to receive,*
22:18. for they *will* not *receive* thy testimony
1Ti. 5:19. Against an elder *receive* not an
Heb12: 6. scourgeth every son whom he *receiveth.*

παραδιατριϐή, paradiatribee.

1Ti. 6: 5. *Perverse disputings* of men of

παραδίδωμι, paradidōmi.

Mat. 4:12. heard that John *was cast into prison,*
5:25. adversary *deliver* thee to the judge, and
the judge *deliver* thee
10: 4. Iscariot, *who* also *betrayed* him.
17. will *deliver* you *up* to the councils,
19. But when they *deliver* you *up,*
21. the brother *shall deliver up* the
11:27. All things *are delivered* unto me of
17:22. The Son of man shall *be betrayed*
18:34. and *delivered* him to the tormentors,
20:18. the Son of man *shall be betrayed*
19. And *shall deliver* him to the Gentiles
24: 9. Then *shall* they *deliver* you *up* to be
10. and *shall betray* one another,
25:14. and *delivered* unto them his goods.
20. Lord, thou *deliveredst* unto me five
22. Lord, thou *deliveredst* unto me two talents:
26: 2. Son of man *is betrayed* to be crucified.
15. and I *will deliver* him unto you?
16. he sought opportunity to *betray* him.
21. one of you *shall betray* me.
23. dish, the same *shall betray* me.
24. by whom the Son of man *is betrayed!*
25. Then Judas, *which betrayed* him,
45. *is betrayed* into the hands of sinners.
46. he is at hand *that doth betray* me.
48. Now he *that betrayed* him gave
27: 2. and *delivered* him to Pontius Pilate.
3. Then Judas, *which had betrayed* him,
4. have sinned *in that* I have *betrayed*
18. for envy they *had delivered* him.
26. he *delivered* (him) to be crucified.
Mar 1:14. after that John *was put in prison,*
3:19. Judas Iscariot, which also *betrayed* him:
4:29. when the fruit *is brought forth,*
7:13. your tradition, which ye *have delivered:*
9:31. *is delivered* into the hands of men,
10:33. the Son of man *shall be delivered*
— and *shall deliver* him to the Gentiles:
13: 9. they *shall deliver* you *up* to
11. *and deliver* you *up,* take no thought
12. the brother *shall betray* the brother
14:10. priests, to *betray* him unto them.
11. how he *might* conveniently *betray* him.
18. eateth with me *shall betray* me.
21. by whom the Son of man *is betrayed!*
41. the Son of man *is betrayed* into the
42. he *that betrayeth* me is at hand.
44. And he *that betrayed* him had given

Mar 15: 1. and *delivered* (him) to Pilate.
10. priests *had delivered* him for envy.
15. and *delivered* Jesus, when he had
Lu. 1: 2. Even as they *delivered* them unto us,
4: 6. the glory of them: for that *is delivered*
unto me;
9:44. the Son of man shall *be delivered* into
10:22. All things *are delivered* to me of
12:58. and the judge *deliver* thee to
18:32. For he *shall be delivered* unto the
20:20. that so they might *deliver* him unto
21:12. *delivering* (you) up to the synagogues,
16. And ye *shall be betrayed* both by
22: 4. how he *might betray* him unto
6. sought opportunity *to betray* him
21. the hand of him *that betrayeth* me
22. unto that man by whom he *is betrayed!*
48. Judas, *betrayest* thou the Son of man
23:25. but he *delivered* Jesus to their will.
24: 7. must *be delivered* into the hands of
20. and our rulers *delivered* him to be
Joh. 6:64. and who should *betray* him.
71. he it was that should *betray* him,
12: 4. Simon's (son), which should *betray* him,
13: 2. Simon's (son), to *betray* him;
11. For he knew *who* should *betray* him;
21. that one of you *shall betray* me.
18: 2. And Judas also, *which betrayed* him,
5. *which betrayed* him, stood with them.
30. we would not *have delivered* him
35. the chief priests *have delivered* thee
36. that I *should* not *be delivered* to the
19:11. therefore he *that delivered* me unto
16. Then *delivered* he him therefore
30. and *gave up* the ghost.
21:20. Lord, which is he *that betrayeth* thee?
Acts 3:13. whom ye *delivered up,* and
6:14. the customs which Moses *delivered* us.
7:42. and *gave* them *up* to worship the
8: 3. men and women *committed* (them) to
12: 4. *and delivered* (him) to four.quaternions
14:26. they had been *recommended* to the grace
15:26. Men *that have hazarded* their lives
40. *being recommended* by the brethren
16: 4. they *delivered* them the decrees for
21:11. and *shall deliver* (him) into the hands
22: 4. and *delivering* into prisons both men
27: 1. they *delivered* Paul and certain
28:16. the centurion *delivered* the prisoners
17. yet *was* I *delivered* prisoner from
Ro. 1:24. Wherefore God also *gave* them *up* to
26. God *gave* them *up* unto vile affections:
28. God *gave* them *over* to a reprobate
4:25. Who *was delivered* for our offences,
6:17. form of doctrine which was delivered
you. (lit. into which ye *were delivered*)
8:32. but *delivered* him *up* for us all,
1Co. 5: 5. *To deliver* such an one unto Satan
11: 2. ordinances, as I *delivered* (them) to you.
23. which also I *delivered* unto you,
— night in which he *was betrayed* took bread:
13: 3. though I *give* my body to be burned,
15: 3. For I *delivered* unto you first of
24. when he shall *have delivered up*
2Co. 4:11. *are* alway *delivered* unto death for
Gal. 2:20. who loved me, and *gave* himself for me.
Eph 4:19. past feeling *have given* themselves *over*
5: 2. and *hath given* himself for us
25. the church, and *gave* himself for it;
1Ti. 1:20. whom I *have delivered* unto Satan,
1Pet.2:23. but *committed* (himself) to him
2Pet. 2: 4. and *delivered* (them) into chains

2Pet. 2:21. holy commandment *delivered* unto
Jude   3. the faith *which was* once *delivered* unto the

παραδόξος, *paradoxos.*

Lu.   5:26. We have seen *strange* things to day.

παράδοσις, *paradosis.*

Mat.15: 2. transgress the *tradition* of the elders?
       3. commandment of God by your *tradition* ?
       6. of none effect by your *tradition.*
Mar 7: 3. not, holding the *tradition* of the elders.
      5. according to the *tradition* of the elders,
      8. ye hold the *tradition* of men,
      9. that ye may keep your own *tradition.*
     13. of none effect through your *tradition,*
1Co.11: 2. and keep the *ordinances,* as I delivered
Gal. 1:14. zealous of the *traditions* of my fathers.
Col. 2: 8. after the *tradition* of men, after
2Th. 2:15. stand fast, and hold the *traditions* which
    3: 6. and not after the *tradition* which he

παραζηλόω, *parazeeloō.*

Ro. 10:19. I *will provoke* you *to jealousy*
    11:11. for *to provoke* them *to jealousy.*
      14. I *may provoke to emulation*
1Co.10:22. *Do* we *provoke* the Lord *to jealousy* ?

παραθαλάσσιος, *parathalassios.*

Mat. 4:13. in Capernaum, *which is upon the sea coast,*

παραθεωρέω, *paratheōreo.*

Acts 6: 1. their widows *were neglected* in

παραθήκη, *paratheekee.*

2Ti. 1:12. is able to keep *that which* I have *committed*
        unto him

παραινέω, *paraineo.*

Acts27: 9. Paul *admonished* (them),
      22. And now I *exhort* you to be of

παραιτέομαι, *paraiteomai.*

Lu. 14:18. with one (consent) began *to make excuse.*
       — I *pray* thee have me *excused.*
      19. I *pray* thee have me *excused.*
Acts25:11. I *refuse* not to die:
1Ti. 4: 7. *refuse* profane and old wives' fables,
    5:11. But the younger widows *refuse:*
2Ti. 2:23. foolish and unlearned questions *avoid,*
Tit. 3:10. and second admonition *reject ;*
Heb 12:19. *intreated* that the word should not
      25. See that ye *refuse* not him that
      — who *refused* him that spake on earth,

παρακαθίζω, *parakathizo.*

Lu. 10:39. which also *sat* at Jesus' feet, *and*

παρακαλέω, *parakaleo.*

Mat. 2:18. would not *be comforted,* because
    5: 4. for they *shall be comforted.*
    8: 5. a centurion, *beseeching* him,
     31. the devils *besought* him, saying,
     34. they *besought* (him) that he would
   14:36. And *besought* him that they
   18:29. and *besought* him, saying,
     32. because thou *desiredst* me:
   26:53. I cannot now *pray* to my
Mar 1:40. a leper to him, *beseeching* him,
    5:10. And he *besought* him much
     12. And all the devils *besought* him,
     17. And they began *to pray* him to
     18. *prayed* him that he might be
     23. And *besought* him greatly,
    6:56. and *besought* him that they
    7:32. and they *beseech* him to put his
    8:22. and *besought* him to touch him.
Lu.   3:18. *in* his *exhortation* preached he
    7: 4. they *besought* him instantly,
    8:31. And they *besought* him that
     32. and they *besought* him that
     41. and *besought* him that he would
   15:28. his father out, and *intreated* him.
   16:25. but now he *is comforted,* and thou
Acts 2:40. did he testify and *exhort,* saying,
    8:31. And he *desired* Philip that
    9:38. *desiring* (him) that he would not
   11:23. and *exhorted* them all, that with
   13:42. the Gentiles *besought* that these words
   14:22. *exhorting* them to continue in
   15:32. *exhorted* the brethren with many
   16: 9. *and prayed* him, saying, Come
     15. she *besought* (us), saying, If ye
     39. And they came and *besought* them,
     40. the brethren, they *comforted* them,
   19:31. *desiring* (him) that he would not
   20: 2. and *had given* them much *exhortation,*
     12. and *were* not a little *comforted.*
   21:12. *besought* him not to go up to Jerusalem.
   24: 4. I *pray* thee that thou wouldest
   25: 2. against Paul, and *besought* him,
   27:33. Paul *besought* (them) all to take
     34. I *pray* you to take (some) meat:
   28:14. and *were desired* to tarry with them
     20. have I *called for* you, to see (you),
Ro. 12: 1. I *beseech* you therefore, brethren,
     8. Or he *that exhorteth,* on exhortation:
   15:30. Now I *beseech* you, brethren, for
   16:17. Now I *beseech* you, brethren, mark
1Co. 1:10. Now I *beseech* you, brethren, by
    4:13. Being defamed, we *intreat :*
     16. Wherefore I *beseech* you, be ye
   14:31. and all *may be comforted.*
   16:12. Apollos, I greatly *desired* him to come
     15. I *beseech* you, brethren,
2Co. 1: 4. *Who comforteth* us in all our tribulation,
       that we may be able *to comfort*
       — wherewith we ourselves *are comforted* of
     6. or whether we *be comforted,*
   2: 7. to forgive (him), and *comfort* (him),
     8. Wherefore I *beseech* you that
   5:20. as *though* God *did beseech* (you)
   6: 1. *beseech* (you) also that ye receive
   7: 6. God, *that comforteth* those that are cast
       down, *comforted* us by
     7. wherewith he *was comforted* in you,
     13. we *were comforted* in your comfort:
   8: 6. Insomuch that we *desired* Titus.
   9: 5. I thought it necessary *to exhort* the

2Co.10: 1. I Paul myself *beseech* you by
12: 8. I *besought* the Lord thrice,
18. I *desired* Titus, and with
13:11. Be perfect, *be of good comfort,*
Eph. 4: 1. *beseech* you that ye walk
6:22. and (that) he *might comfort* your
Phi. 4: 2. I *beseech* Euodias, and *beseech* Syntyche,
Col. 2: 2. That their hearts *might be comforted,*
4: 8. and *comfort* your hearts;
1Th. 2:11. ye know how we *exhorted*
3: 2. and *to comfort* you concerning
7. we *were comforted* over you
4: 1. and *exhort* (you) by the Lord
10. but we *beseech* you, brethren,
18. Wherefore *comfort* one another
5:11. Wherefore *comfort* yourselves together,
14. Now we *exhort* you, brethren,
2Th. 2:17. *Comfort* your hearts, and stablish
3:12. and *exhort* by our Lord Jesus,
1Ti. 1: 3. As I *besought* thee to abide
2: 1. I *exhort* therefore, that, first
5: 1. but *intreat* (him) as a father;
6: 2. These things teach and *exhort.*
2Ti. 4: 2. rebuke, *exhort* with all
Tit. 1: 9. both *to exhort* and to convince the
2: 6. *exhort* to be sober minded.
15. speak, and *exhort,* and rebuke
Philem 9. Yet for love's sake I rather *beseech*
10. I *beseech* thee for my son Onesimus,
Heb 3:13. But *exhort* one another daily,
10:25. but *exhorting* (one another): and
13:19. But I *beseech* (you) the rather
22. I *beseech* you, brethren, suffer
1Pet. 2:11. Dearly beloved, I *beseech* (you) as
5: 1. I *exhort,* who am also an elder,
12. I have written briefly, *exhorting,* and
Jude 3. for me to write unto you, *and exhort*

παρακαλύπτω, *parakalupto.*

Lu. 9:45. and it was *hid* from them, that they

παρακαταθήκη, *parakatatheekee.*

1Ti. 6:20. keep *that which is committed to* thy *trust,*
2Ti. 1:14. *That* good *thing which was committed unto*
thee keep

παράκειμαι, *parakimai.*

Ro. 7:18. for to will *is present* with me;
21. evil *is present* with me.

παράκλησις, *parakleesis.*

Lu. 2:25. waiting for the *consolation* of Israel:
6:24. ye have received your *consolation.*
Acts 4:36. The son of *consolation,*
9:31. and in the *comfort* of the Holy Ghost,
13:15. any word of *exhortation* for the people,
15:31. they rejoiced for the *consolation.*
Ro. 12: 8. Or he that exhorteth, on *exhortation:*
15: 4. and *comfort* of the scriptures
5. the God of patience and *consolation*
1Co.14: 3. and *exhortation,* and comfort.
2Co. 1: 3. and the God of all *comfort;*
4. by the *comfort,* wherewith we
5. so our *consolation* also aboundeth

2Co. 1: 6. (it is) for your *consolation* and
— for your *consolation* and salvation.
7. also of the *consolation.*
7: 4. I am filled with *comfort,*
7. but by the *consolation* wherewith
13. we were comforted in your *comfort:*
8: 4. Praying us with much *intreaty* that
17. he accepted the *exhortation;*
Phi. 2: 1. any *consolation* in Christ, if
1Th. 2: 3. For our *exhortation* (was) not
2Th. 2:16. given (us) everlasting *consolation*
1Ti. 4:13. to *exhortation,* to doctrine.
Philem. 7. joy and *consolation* in thy love,
Heb 6:18. we might have a strong *consolation,*
12: 5. forgotten the *exhortation* which
13:22. suffer the word of *exhortation:*

παράκλητος, *parakleetos.*

Joh.14:16. give you another *Comforter,*
26. the *Comforter,* (which is) the Holy Ghost,
15:26. But when the *Comforter* is come,
16: 7. the *Comforter* will not come unto
1Joh.2: 1. an *advocate* with the Father, Jesus

παρακοή, *parakoee.*

Ro. 5:19. by one man's *disobedience*
2Co.10: 6. to revenge all *disobedience,*
Heb 2: 2. every transgression and *disobedience*

παρακολουθέω, *parakoloutheo.*

Mar 16:17. And these signs *shall follow*
Lu. 1: 3. *having had* perfect *understanding* of all
1Ti. 4: 6. whereunto thou *hast attained.*
2Ti. 3:10. But thou *hast fully known* my doctrine,

παρακούω, *parakouo.*

Mat.18:17. And if he *shall neglect to hear* them,
— but if he *neglect to hear* the church,

παρακύπτω, *parakupto.*

Lu. 24:12. and *stooping down,* he beheld the
Joh.20: 5. And he *stooping down,*
11. she *stooped down,* (and looked) into
Jas. 1:25. But whoso *looketh* into the
1Pet.1:12. angels desire *to look into.*

παραλαμβάνω, *paralambano.*

Mat. 1:20. fear not *to take unto* thee Mary
24. and *took unto* him his wife:
2:13. Arise, and *take* the young child
14. When he arose, he *took* the
20. Saying, Arise, and *take* the
21. And he arose, and *took*
4: 5. Then the devil *taketh* him *up*
8. Again, the devil *taketh* him *up*
12:45. Then goeth he, and *taketh* with himself
17: 1. Jesus *taketh* Peter, James, and
18.16. *take* with thee one or two
20:17. *took* the twelve disciples apart
24:40. the one shall *be taken,* and

Mat.24:41. the one shall *be taken*, and the

26:37. And he *took with* him Peter and

27:27. *took* Jesus into the common hall, *and*

Mar 4:36. they *took* him even as he was

5:40. he *taketh* the father and the mother

7: 4. which they *have received* to hold,

9: 2. Jesus *taketh* (with him) Peter,

10:32. he *took* again the twelve, *and*

14:33. And he *taketh* with him Peter

Lu. 9:10. And he *took* them, *and* went aside

28. he *took* Peter and John and James, *and*

11:26. and *taketh* (to him) seven other

17:34. the one *shall be taken*, and

35. the one *shall be taken*, and (& 36, Elz.)

18:31. he *took* (unto him) the twelve, *and*

Joh. 1:11. his own *received* him not.

14: 3. I will come again, and *receive* you unto myself;

19:16. And they *took* Jesus, and led

Acts15:39. so Barnabas *took* Mark, *and*

16:33. And he *took* them the same hour

21:24. Them *take*, *and* purify thyself

26. Then Paul *took* the men, *and*

32. Who immediately *took* soldiers

23:18. So he *took* him, *and* brought

1Co.11:23. For I *have received* of the Lord

15: 1. which also ye *have received*,

3. that which I also *received*,

Gal. 1: 9. than that ye *have received*,

12. For I neither *received* it of man,

Phi. 4: 9. ye have both learned, and *received*,

Col. 2: 6. As ye *have* therefore *received* Christ Jesus

4:17. ministry which thou *hast received* in the

1Th. 2:13. *when* ye *received* the word of God

4: 1. that as ye *have received* of us

2Th. 3: 6. which he *received* of us.

Heb 12:28. Wherefore we *receiving* a kingdom

παραλέγομαι, *paralegomai.*

Acts27: 8. And, hardly *passing* it, came

13. they *sailed* close *by* Crete.

παράλιος, *paralios.*

Lu. 6:17. from the *sea coast* of Tyre (lit. *maritime* Tyre) and Sidon,

---

παραλλαγή, *parallagee.*

Jas. 1:17. with whom is no *variableness*, neither

παραλογίζομαι, *paralogizomai.*

Col. 2: 4. lest any man *should beguile* you

Jas. 1:22. *deceiving* your own selves.

παραλύομαι, *paraluomai.*

Lu. 5:18. a man which was taken with a palsy: (lit. *palsied*)

24. he said unto the *sick of the palsy*,

Acts 8: 7. and many *taken with palsies*,

9:33. and was *sick of the palsy*.

Heb 12:12. which hang down, and the *feeble* knees ;

παραλυτικός, *paralutikos.*

Mat. 4:24. and those *that had the palsy;*

Mat. 8: 6. lieth at home *sick of the palsy*,

9: 2. brought to him a man *sick of the palsy*,

— said unto the *sick of the palsy* ; Son,

6. then saith he to the *sick of the palsy*,

Mar 2: 3. bringing one *sick of the palsy*, which

4. bed wherein the *sick of the palsy* lay.

5. he said unto the *sick of the palsy*, Son,

9. easier to say to the *sick of the palsy*,

10. he saith to the *sick of the palsy*,

παραμένω, *parameno.*

1Co.16: 6. And it may be that I *will abide*, yea,

Heb 7:23. they were not suffered *to continue*

Jas. 1:25. law of liberty. and *continueth* (therein),

παραμυθέομαι, *paramutheomai.*

Joh.11:19. came to Martha and Mary, to *comfort* them

31. in the house, and *comforted* her,

1Th. 2:11. ye know how we exhorted and *comforted*

5:14. *comfort* the feebleminded,

παραμυθία, *paramuthia.*

1Co.14: 3. and exhortation, and *comfort*.

παραμύθιον, *paramuthion.*

Phi. 2: 1. if any *comfort* of love,

παρανομέω, *paranomeo.*

Acts23: 3. commandest me to be smitten *contrary to the law ?* (lit. *transgressing law*)

παρανομία, *paranomia.*

2Pet. 2:16. But was rebuked for his *iniquity :*

παραπικραίνω, *parapikraino.*

Heb 3:16. when they had heard, *did provoke :*

παραπικρασμός, *parapikrasmos.*

Heb 3: 8. your hearts, as in the *provocation,*

15. not your hearts, as in the *provocation.*

παραπίπτω, *parapipto.*

Heb 6: .6. *If* they shall *fall away*, to renew

παραπλέω, *parapleo.*

Acts20:16. Paul had determined *to sail by* Ephesus,

παραπλήσιον, *parapleesion.*

Phi. 2:27. he was sick *nigh unto* death:

παραπλησίως, *parapleesiōs*.

Heb 2:14. he also himself *likewise* took part

παραπορεύομαι, *paraporūomai*.

Mat. 27:39. And they *that passed by* reviled
Mar 2:23. came to pass, that he *went* through the
    9:30. and *passed* through Galilee ;
   11:20. *as they passed by*, they saw the fig tree
   15:29. And they *that passed by* railed on him,

παράπτωμα, *paraptōma*.

Mat. 6:14. if ye forgive men their *trespasses*,
     15. not men their *trespasses*, neither will your
         Father forgive your *trespasses*.
   18:35. every one his brother their *trespasses*.
Mar 11:25. may forgive you your *trespasses*.
     26. in heaven forgive your *trespasses*.
Ro. 4:25. Who was delivered for our *offences*,
   5:15. But not as the *offence*, so also (is) the
    — For if through the *offence* of one
    16. free gift (is) of many *offences* unto
    17. For if by one man's *offence* death
    18. Therefore as by the *offence* of one
    20. the law entered, that the *offence* might
  11:11. through their *fall* salvation (is come)
    12. Now if the *fall* of them (be) the
2Co. 5:19. not imputing their *trespasses*
Gal. 6: 1. if a man be overtaken in a *fault*,
Eph. 1: 7. the forgiveness of *sins*,
  2: 1. dead in *trespasses* and sins ;
    5. when we were dead in *sins*,
Col. 2:13. you, being dead in your *sins*
    — having forgiven you all *trespasses*,
Jas. 5:16. Confess (your) *faults* one to another,

παραρρύέω, *pararrueo*.

Heb 2: 1. lest at any time we *should let* (them) *slip*.

παράσημος, *paraseemos*.

Acts 28:11. *whose sign was* Castor and Pollux.

παρασκευάζω, *paraskūazo*.

Acts 10:10. but *while* they *made ready*, he fell
1Co. 14: 8. who *shall prepare* himself to the battle ?
2Co. 9: 2. Achaia *was ready* a year ago ;
    3. ye may be *ready :*

παρασκευή, *paraskūee*.

Mat. 27:62. followed the day of the *preparation*,
Mar 15:42. because it was the *preparation*,
Lu. 23:54. that day was the *preparation*,
Joh. 19:14. it was the *preparation* of the passover,
   31. because it was the *preparation*,
   42. because of the Jews' *preparation* (day);

παρατείνω, *paratīno*.

Acts 20: 7. and *continued* his speech until midnight.

παρατηρέω, *parateereo*.

Mar 3: 2. And they *watched* him,
Lu. 6: 7. *watched* him, whether he would heal
   14: 1. that they *watched* him.
  20:20. And they *watched* (him), *and*
Acts 9:24. And they *watched* the gates day and
Gal. 4:10. Ye *observe* days, and months, and

παρατήρησις, *parateereesis*.

Lu. 17:20. The kingdom of God cometh not with
    observation :

παρατίθημι, *paratitheemi*.

Mat. 13:24. Another parable *put* he *forth* unto
    31. Another parable *put* he *forth* unto
Mar 6:41. to his disciples to *set before* them ;
  8: 6. to his disciples to *set before* (them); and
    they *did set* (them) *before* the people.
    7. to *set* them also *before* (them).
Lu. 9:16. to *set before* the multitude.
  10: 8. eat such things *as are set before* you:
  11: 6. I have nothing to *set before* him?
  12:48. to whom men *have committed* much,
  23:46. into thy hands I *commend* my spirit:
Acts 14:23. they *commended* them to the Lord,
  16:34. he *set* meat *before* them,
  17: 3. Opening and *alledging*, that Christ
  20:32. brethren, I *commend* you to God,
1Co. 10:27. *whats*oever is *set before* you,
1Ti. 1:18. This charge I *commit* unto thee,
2Ti. 2: 2. the same *commit* thou to faithful
1Pet. 4:19. *let* them that...*commit the keeping of* their
    souls

παρατυγχάνω, *paratunkano*.

Acts 17:17. daily with them *that met with* him.

παραυτίκα, *parautika*.

2Co. 4:17. *affliction, which is but for a moment,*

παραφέρω, *paraphero*.

Mar 14:36. *take away* this cup from me:
Lu. 22:42. *remove* this cup from me:

παραφρονέω, *paraphroneo*.

2Co. 11:23. I speak *as a fool*

παραφρονία, *paraphronia*.

2Pet. 2:16. forbad the *madness* of the prophet.

παραχειμάζω, *parakīmazo*.

Acts 27:12. to Phenice, (and there) *to winter ;*
  28:11. *which had wintered* in the isle,
1Co. 16: 6. yea, and *winter* with you, that
Tit. 3:12. I have determined there *to winter*.

παραχειμασία, parakīmasia.

Acts27:12. haven was not commodious *to winter in,*

παραχρῆμα, parakreema.

Mat.21:19. And *presently* the fig tree withered
20. How *soon* is the fig tree withered
Lu. 1:64. mouth was opened *immediately,*
4:39. and *immediately* she arose and
5:25. And *immediately* he rose up
8:44. and *immediately* her issue of blood
47. how she was healed *immediately.*
55. and she arose *straightway :*
13:13. and *immediately* she was made straight,
18:43. And *immediately* he received his sight,
19:11. of God should *immediately* appear.
22:60. And *immediately,* while he yet spake,
Acts 3: 7. and *immediately* his feet and ancle
5:10. Then fell she down *straightway* at
9:18. and he received sight *forthwith,*
12:23. And *immediately* the angel of the
13:11. And *immediately* there fell on
16:26. and *immediately* all the doors were
33. he and all his, *straightway.*

πάρδαλις, pardalis.

Rev.13: 2. which I saw was like unto a *leopard,*

πάρειμι, parīmi.

Mat.26:50. Friend, wherefore *art thou come ?*
Lu. 13: 1. There were *present* at that season
Joh. 7: 6. My time *is* not yet *come :*
11:28. The Master *is come,* and
Acts10:21. the cause wherefore ye *are come?*
33. Now therefore *are* we all *here present*
12:20. they *came* with one accord to him,
17: 6. *are come* hither also ;
24:19. ought *to have been here* before thee,
1Co. 5: 3. but *present* in spirit, have judged already,
as *though* I *were present,*
2Co.10: 2. may not be bold *when* I *am present*
11. also in deed *when* we *are present.*
11: 9(8). And *when* I *was present* with you,
13: 2. as *if* I *were present,*
10. lest *being present* I should use
Gal. 4:18. when I *am present* with you.
20. I desire *to be present* with you
Col. 1: 6. *Which is come* unto you,
Heb12:11. no chastening for the *present*
13: 5. content with such things as ye have : (lit.
things *that are present*)
2Pet.1: 9. But he that lacketh (lit. to whom *are* not
present) these things is blind,
12. established in the *present* truth.

παρεισάγω, parīsago.

2Pet.2: 1. who *privily shall bring in* damnable

παρείσακτος, parīsaktos.

Gal. 2: 4. because of false brethren *unawares brought in,*

παρεισδύνω, parīsduno.

Jude 4. For there *are* certain men *crept in* una-
wares,

παρεισέρχομαι, parīserkomai.

Ro. 5:20. Moreover the law *entered,* that the
Gal. 2: 4. who *came in privily* to spy out our

παρεισφέρω, parīsphero.

2Pet.1: 5. *giving* all diligence, add to

παρεκτός, parektos.

Mat. 5:32. *saving* for the cause of fornication,
Acts26:29. such as I am, *except* these bonds.
2Co.11:28. Beside those things that are *without,*

παρεμβολή, parembolee.

Acts21:34. to be carried into the *castle.*
37. Paul was to be led into the *castle,*
22:24. to be brought into the *castle,*
23:10. to bring (him) into the *castle.*
16. entered into the *castle,* and told Paul.
32. and returned to the *castle .*
Heb 11:34. turned to flight the *armies* of the aliens.
13:11. are burned without the *camp.*
13. unto him without the *camp,*
Rev.20: 9. and compassed the *camp* of the saints

παρενοχλέω, parenokleo.

Acts15:19. that we *trouble* not them, which

παρεπίδημος, parepideemos.

Heb 11:13. confessed that they were strangers and
pilgrims
1Pet.1: 1. to the *strangers* scattered throughout
2:11. as strangers and *pilgrims,* abstain

παρέρχομαι, parerkomai.

Mat. 5:18. Till heaven and earth *pass,*
— one tittle shall in no wise *pass* from
8:28. that no man might *pass* by that way.
14:15. and the time *is* now *past ;*
24:34. This generation shall not *pass,* till
35. Heaven and earth *shall pass away,* but my
words shall not *pass away.*
26:39. *let* this cup *pass* from me:
42. if this cup may not *pass away*
Mar 6:48. and would have *passed by* them.
13:30. this generation shall not *pass,* till
31. Heaven and earth *shall pass away .* but
my words shall not *pass away.*
14:35. the hour *might pass* from him.
Lu. 11:42. and *pass over* judgment and
12:37. and will *come forth and* serve them.
15:29. neither *transgressed* I at any time
16:17. it is easier for heaven and earth *to pass,*
17: 7. *Go and* sit down to meat ?
18:37. that Jesus of Nazareth *passeth by.*

Lu. 21:32. This generation shall not *pass away*,
  33. Heaven and earth *shall pass away*: but my
      words shall not *pass away*.
Acts16: 8. And they *passing by* Mysia
  24: 7. the chief captain Lysias *came* (upon us),
          and
  27: 9. because the fast *was* now already *past*,
2Co. 5:17. old things *are passed away*;
Jas. 1:10. of the grass he *shall pass away*.
1Pet.4: 3. For the time *past* of (our) life
2Pet.3:10. the heavens *shall pass away*
Rev.21: 1. first earth *were passed away*;

πάρεσις, *paresis*.

Ro. 3:25. for the *remission* of sins that are past,

παρέχω, *pareko*.

Mat.26:10. Why trouble ye (lit. *give* ye trouble to)
            the woman?
Mar14: 6. why trouble ye her? (lit. *give* &c.)
Lu. 6:29. (one) cheek *offer* also the other;
  7: 4. worthy for whom he should *do* this:
  11: 7. Trouble me not: (lit. *give* me not &c.)
  18: 5. because this widow troubleth me, (lit.
          giveth &c.)
Acts16:16. which *brought* her masters much
  17:31. (whereof) he hath *given* assurance
  19:24. *brought* no small gain unto the
  22: 2. they *kept* the more silence:
  28: 2. *shewed* us no little kindness:
Gal. 6:17. let no man trouble me: (lit. *let* none
          give &c.)
Col. 4: 1. *give* unto (your) servants that
1Ti. 1: 4. which *minister* questions,
  6:17. who *giveth* us richly all things to
Tit. 2: 7. *shewing* thyself a pattern of good works:

παρηγορία, *pareegoria*.

Col. 4:11. which have been a *comfort* unto me.

παρθενία, *parthenia*.

Lu. 2:36. seven years from her *virginity*;

παρθένος, *parthenos*.

Mat. 1:23. Behold, a *virgin* shall be with child,
  25: 1. ten *virgins*, which took their
  7. Then all those *virgins* arose,
  11. came also the other *virgins*,
Lu. 1:27. To a *virgin* espoused to a
  — and the *virgin's* name (was) Mary.
Acts21: 9. had four daughters, *virgins*,
1Co. 7:25. Now concerning *virgins* I have no
  28. and if a *virgin* marry,
  34. between a wife and a *virgin*.
  36. uncomely toward his *virgin*,
  37. keep his *virgin*, doeth well.
2Co.11: 2. a chaste *virgin* to Christ.
Rev.14: 4. for they are *virgins*.

παριστάνω, *paristano*.

Ro. 6:13. Neither *yield* ye your members
  16. that to whom ye *yield* yourselves

παρίστημι, *paristeemi*.

Mat.26:53. and he *shall presently give* me more
Mar 4:29. because the harvest *is come*.
  14:47. one of them *that stood by* drew
  69. began to say to them *that stood by*,
  70. they *that stood by* said again
  15:35. some of them *that stood by*, when
  39. centurion, *which stood* over against him,
Lu. 1:19. Gabriel, *that stand* in the presence
  2:22. *to present* (him) to the Lord;
  19:24. he said unto them *that stood by*,
Joh.18:22. one of the officers *which stood by*
  19:26. and the disciple *standing by*,
Acts 1: 3. To whom also he *shewed* himself
  10. two men *stood by* them in white
  4:10. *doth* this man *stand here* before you
  26. The kings of the earth *stood up*,
  9:39. and all the widows *stood by* him weeping,
  41. *presented* her alive.
  23: 2. them *that stood by* him to smite
  4. they *that stood by* said,
  24. And *provide* (them) beasts,
  33. *presented* Paul also before him.
  24:13. Neither can they *prove* the things
  27:23. For there *stood by* me this night
  24. thou must *be brought before* (lit. *stand
      before*) Cæsar:
Ro. 6:13. but *yield* yourselves unto God,
  19. as ye *have yielded* your members
  — so now *yield* your members
  12: 1. that ye *present* your bodies a
  14:10. we *shall* all *stand before* the
  16: 2. and that ye *assist* her in whatsoever
1Co. 8: 8. But meat *commendeth* us not to God:
2Co. 4:14. and *shall present* (us) with you.
  11: 2. that I may *present* (you as) a chaste
Eph. 5:27. That he might *present* it to himself
Col. 1:22. *to present* you holy and unblameable
  28. that we *may present* every man
2Ti. 2:15. Study *to shew* thyself approved
  4:17. the Lord *stood with* me, and

παρίεμαι, *pariemai*.

Heb12:12. lift up the hands *which hang down*,

πάροδος, *parodos*.

1Co.16: 7. For I will not see you now by the *way*;
            (lit. en *passant*) but

παροικέω, *paroikeo*.

Lu. 24:18. *Art* thou only a *stranger* in Jerusalem,
Heb11: 9. he *sojourned in* the land of promise, as
            (in) a strange country,

παροικία, *paroikia*.

Acts13:17. when they dwelt as strangers (lit. in the
            sojourning)
1Pet. 1:17. pass the time of your *sojourning* (here)

πάροικος, *paroikos*.

Acts 7: 6. his seed should *sojourn* in a strange land;
  29. and was a *stranger* in the land of
Eph. 2:19. no more strangers and *foreigners*,
1Pet. 2:11. as *strangers* and pilgrims,

παροιμία, *paroimia.*

Joh.10: 6. This *parable* spake Jesus
16:25. have I spoken unto you in *proverbs :*
— no more speak unto you in *proverbs,*
29. and speakest no *proverb.*
2Pet. 2:22. according to the true *proverb,*

παρομοιάζω, *paromoiazo.*

Mat.23:27. for ye *are like unto* whited sepulchres,

παρόμοιος, *paromoios.*

Mar 7: 8. and many other such *like* things ye
13. and many such *like* things do ye.

πάροινος, *paroinos.*

1Ti. 3: 3. Not *given to wine*, no striker,
Tit. 1: 7. not soon angry, not *given to wine,*

παροίχομαι, *paroikomai.*

Acts14:16. Who in times *past* suffered all

παροξύνομαι, *paroxunomai.*

Acts17:16. his spirit *was stirred* in him,
1Co.13: 5. *is* not *easily provoked,*

παροξυσμός, *paroxusmos.*

Acts15:39. And the *contention* was *so sharp*
Heb10:24. *to provoke* unto love and to

παροργίζω, *parorgizo.*

Ro. 10:19. by a foolish nation I *will anger* you.
Eph 6: 4. ye fathers, *provoke* not your children *to wrath:*

παροργισμός, *parorgismos.*

Eph 4:26. let not the sun go down upon your *wrath:*

παροτρύνω, *parotruno.*

Acts13:50. But the Jews *stirred up* the devout

παρουσία, *parousia.*

Mat.24: 3. what (shall be) the sign of thy *coming,*
27. so shall also the *coming* of the Son of
37. so shall also the *coming* of the Son
39. so shall also the *coming* of the Son
1Co.15:23. they that are Christ's at his *coming.*
16:17. glad of the *coming* of Stephanas
2Co. 7: 6. by the *coming* of Titus;
7. And not by his *coming* only,
10:10. but (his) bodily *presence* (is) weak,
Phi. 1:26. by my *coming* to you again.

Phi. 2:12. not as in my *presence* only,
1Th. 2:19. Christ at his *coming ?*
3:13. at the *coming* of our Lord Jesus
4:15. (and) remain unto the *coming* of
5:23. unto the *coming* of our Lord
2Th. 2: 1. by the *coming* of our Lord
8. the brightness of his *coming :*
9. (Even him), whose *coming* is after
Jas. 5: 7. unto the *coming* of the Lord.
8. for the *coming* of the Lord draweth nigh.
2Pet. 1:16. the power and *coming* of our Lord
3: 4. Where is the promise of his *coming ?*
12. and hasting unto the *coming* of the day
1Joh. 2:28. before him at his *coming.*

παροψίς, *paropsis.*

Mat.23:25. the outside of the cup and of the *platter,*
26. that (which is) within the cup and *platter,*

παῤῥησία, *parreesia.*

Note.—The dative case is used adverbially

Mar 8:32. And he spake that saying *openly.*
Joh. 7: 4. seeketh to be known *openly.*
13. no man spake *openly* of him
26. But, lo, he speaketh *boldly,*
10:24. If thou be the Christ, tell us *plainly.*
11:14. Then said Jesus unto them *plainly.*
54. walked no more *openly*
16:25. but I shall shew you *plainly*
29. Lo, now speakest thou *plainly,*
18:20. I spake *openly* to the world ;
Acts 2:29. let me *freely* speak unto you
4:13. when they saw the *boldness* of
29. with all *boldness* they may speak
31. and they spake the word of God with *boldness.*
28:31. with all *confidence*, no man forbidding
2Co. 3:12. we use great *plainness* of speech:
7: 4. Great (is) my *boldness of speech*
Eph 3:12. In whom we have *boldness*
6:19. may open my mouth *boldly,*
Phi. 1:20. but (that) with all *boldness,*
Col. 2:15. he made a shew of them *openly,*
1Ti. 3:13. and great *boldness* in the faith
Philem. 8. though I might be much *bold* in
Heb 3: 6. if we hold fast the *confidence*
4:16. Let us therefore come *boldly*
10:19. *boldness* to enter into the holiest
35. your *confidence*, which hath
1Joh. 2:28. we may have *confidence,*
3:21. (then) have we *confidence* toward
4:17. that we may have *boldness* in
5:14. this is the *confidence* that

παῤῥησιάζομαι, *parreesiazomai.*

Acts 9:27. how he had *preached boldly* at Damascus
29(28). And he spake *boldly* (lit. *having bold-ness*) in the name
13:46. Paul and Barnabas *waxed bold, and*
14: 3. *speaking boldly* in the Lord,
18:26. he began *to speak boldly* in the
19: 8. and *spake boldly* for the space of
26:26. before whom also I speak *freely:*
Eph 6:20. I *may speak boldly*, as I ought
1Th. 2: 2. we *were bold* in our God to speak

πᾶς, πᾶσα, πᾶν, pas, pasa, pan.

[2] denotes it to be used with ὅστις: [3] with ὅσος: and one of the two words is frequently omitted in the rendering.

Mat. 1:17. So *all* the generations from Abraham
   2: 3. and *all* Jerusalem with him.
     4. had gathered *all* the chief priests
    16. and slew *all* the children that
    — and in *all* the coasts thereof,
   3: 5. and *all* Judæa, and *all* the region round
       about Jordan,
    10. therefore *every* tree which
    15. us to fulfil *all* righteousness.
   4: 4. but by *every* word that proceedeth
    8. and sheweth him *all* the kingdoms
    9. *All* these things will I give thee,
    23. healing *all manner of* sickness and *all manner of* disease among the
    24. brought unto him *all* sick people
   5:11. and shall say *all manner of* evil
    15. giveth light unto *all* that are in
    18. till *all* be fulfilled.
    22. That *whosoever* is angry with his brother
    28. *whosoever* looketh on a woman
   6:29. Solomon in *all* his glory was not
    32. For after *all* these things do the
    33. and *all* these things shall be added
   7: 8. For *every* one that asketh receiveth ;
    12. Therefore *all*[3] things whatsoever
    17. Even so *every* good tree bringeth
    19. *Every* tree that bringeth not forth
    21. Not *every* one that saith unto me,
    24. Therefore *whosoever*[2] heareth
    26. And *every* one that heareth
   8:16. and healed *all* that were sick:
    32. and, behold, the *whole* herd of swine
    33. and told *every* thing,
    34. *the whole* city came out to meet
   9:35. Jesus went about *all* the cities
    — healing *every* sickness and *every* disease among the people.
   10: 1. and to heal *all manner of* sickness and *all manner of* disease.
    22. ye shall be hated of *all* (men) for
    30. hairs of your head are *all* numbered.
    32. *Whosoever*[2] therefore shall confess
   11:13. For *all* the prophets and the law
    27. *All* things are delivered unto me
    28. Come unto me, *all* (ye) that labour
   12:15. and he healed them *all ;*
    23. And *all* the people were amazed,
    25. *Every* kingdom divided against
    — and *every* city or house divided
    31. *All manner of* sin and blasphemy
    36. That *every* idle word that men
   13: 2. and *the whole* multitude stood
    19. When *any* one heareth the word
    32. is the least of *all* seeds:
    34. *All* these things spake Jesus
    41. out of his kingdom *all* things that
    44. and selleth *all*[3] that he hath,
    46. went and sold *all*[3] that he had,
    47. and gathered of *every* kind:
    51. Have ye understood *all* these things?
    52. Therefore *every* scribe (which is)
    56. sisters, are they not *all* with us?
    — this (man) *all* these things?
   14:20. And they did *all* eat, and
    35. and brought unto him *all* that were

Mat.15:13. *Every* plant, which my heavenly
    17. *whatsoever* entereth in at the mouth
    37. And they did *all* eat, and were filled:
   17:11. first come, and restore *all* things.
   18:10. angels do *always* (διὰ παντὸς) behold
    16. *every* word may be established.
    19. as touching *any* thing that they
    25. and *all*[3] that he had,
    26. and I will pay thee *all.*
    29. and I will pay thee *all.*
    31. told unto their lord *all* that was done.
    32. I forgave thee *all* that debt,
    34. till he should pay *all* that was due
   19: 3. put away his wife for *every* cause ?
    11. *All* (men) cannot receive this saying,
    20. *All* these things have I kept from
    26. with God *all* things are possible.
    27. we have forsaken *all*, and followed thee ;
    29. And *every* one that hath forsaken
   21:10. *all* the city was moved, saying, Who
    12. and cast out *all* them that sold
    22. *all*[3] things, whatsoever ye shall ask
    26. for *all* hold John as a prophet.
   22: 4. and *all* things (are) ready: come
    10. and gathered together *all*[3] as many
    27. And last of *all* the woman died also.
    28. for they *all* had her.
   23: 3. *All*[3] therefore whatsoever they bid
    5. But *all* their works they do for
    8. and *all* ye are brethren.
    20. and by *all* things thereon.
    27. bones, and of *all* uncleanness.
    35. may come *all* the righteous blood
    36. *All* these things shall come
   24: 2. See ye not *all* these things ?
    6. for *all* (these things) must come to pass,
    8. *All* these (are) the beginning of sorrows.
    9. ye shall be hated of *all* nations for
    14. for a witness unto *all* nations ;
    22. there should no (lit. not *any*) flesh be saved:
    30. then shall *all* the tribes of the earth
    33. when ye shall see *all* these things,
    34. till *all* these things be fulfilled.
    47. ruler over *all* his goods.
   25: 5. they *all* slumbered and slept.
    7. Then *all* those virgins arose,
    29. For unto *every* one that hath
    31. and *all* the holy angels with
    32. before him shall be gathered *all* nations:
   26: 1. when Jesus had finished *all* these sayings,
    27. saying, Drink ye *all* of it ;
    31. *All* ye shall be offended because
    33. Though *all* (men) shall be offended
    35. Likewise also said *all* the disciples.
    52. for *all* they that take the sword
    56. Then *all* the disciples forsook him,
    70. But he denied before (them) *all*, saying,
   27: 1. morning was come, *all* the chief priests
    22. (They) *all* say unto him, Let him
    25. Then answered *all* the people,
    45. there was darkness over *all* the land
   28:18. *All* power is given unto me in
    19. and teach *all* nations,
    20. to observe *all*[3] things whatsoever
    — lo, I am with you *alway*, (πάσας τὰς ἡμέρας)
Mar 1: 5. went out unto him *all* the land of
    — and were *all* baptized of him in
    27. And they were *all* amazed,
    32. brought unto him *all* that were diseased,
    37. *All* (men) seek for thee.

Mar 2:12. went forth before them *all*; insomuch
that they were *all* amazed,
 13. and *all* the multitude resorted
3:28. *All* sins shall be forgiven
4: 1. and the *whole* multitude was
 11. *all* (these) things are done in parables:
 13. how then will ye know *all* parables?
 31. is less than *all* the seeds that be
 32. becometh greater than *all* herbs,
 34. he expounded *all* things to his disciples.
5:12. And *all* the devils besought
 20. and *all* (men) did marvel.
 26. and had spent *all* that she had,
 33. and told him *all* the truth.
6:30. and told him *all* things, both
 33. ran afoot thither out of *all* cities,
 39. to make *all* sit down by
 41. fishes divided he among them *all*.
 42. And they did *all* eat,
 50. For they *all* saw him, and were troubled.
7: 3. and *all* the Jews, except they wash
 14. when he had called *all* the people
 — Hearken unto me *every one* (of you),
 18. that *whatsoever* thing from without
 19. purging *all* meats?
 23. *All* these evil things come from
 37. He hath done *all* things well:
9:12. and restoreth *all* things;
 15. And straightway *all* the people,
 23. *all* things (are) possible to him that
 35. (the same) shall be last of *all*, and servant
of *all*.
 49. *every one* shall be salted with fire, and
every sacrifice
10:20. *all* these have I observed from
 27. with God *all* things are possible.
 28. Lo, we have left *all*, and have
 44. chiefest, shall be servant of *all*.
11:11. looked round about upon *all* things,
 17. called of *all* nations the house of prayer?
 18. *all* the people was astonished at
 24. *What* things *soever* [3] ye desire, when ye
12:22. last of *all* the woman died also.
 28. Which is the first commandment of *all*?
 29. The first of *all* the commandments (is),
 33. is more than *all* whole burnt offerings
 43. hath cast more in, than *all* they
 44. For *all* (they) did cast in of their
 — did cast in *all* [3] that she had,
13: 4. when *all* these things shall be
 10. be published among *all* nations.
 13. hated of *all* (men) for my name's
 20. no (lit. not *any*) flesh should be saved:
 23. behold, I have foretold you *all* things.
 30. till *all* these things be done.
 37. I say unto *all*, Watch.
14:23. and they *all* drank of it.
 27. *All* ye shall be offended because
 29. Although *all* shall be offended,
 31. Likewise also said they *all*.
 36. *all* things (are) possible unto thee;
 50. And they *all* forsook him, and fled.
 53. were assembled *all* the chief priests
 64. And they *all* condemned him to
16:15. and preach the gospel to *every* creature.
Lu. 1: 3. perfect understanding of *all* things
 6. walking in *all* the commandments
 10. And the *whole* multitude of the
 37. with God nothing (lit. not *any* thing)
shall be impossible.
 48. from henceforth *all* generations shall
 63. And they marvelled *all*.

Lu. 1:65. And fear came on *all* that dwelt
 — and *all* these sayings were noised
 66. And *all* they that heard (them)
 71. and from the hand of *all* that hate us;
 75. before him, *all* the days of our life.
2: 1. that *all* the world should be taxed.
 3. And *all* went to be taxed, every
 10. which shall be to *all* people.
 18. And *all* they that heard (it) wondered
 19. But Mary kept *all* these things,
 20. praising God for *all* the things
 23. *Every* male that openeth the
 31. before the face of *all* people;
 38. and spake of him to *all* them that
 47. And *all* that heard him were astonished
 51. his mother kept *all* these sayings
3: 3. he came into *all* the country about
 5. *Every* valley shall be filled, and *every*
mountain and hill
 6. And *all* flesh shall see the
 9. *every* tree therefore which
 15. and *all* men mused in their hearts
 19. and for *all* the evils which Herod
 20. Added yet this above *all*, that he
4: 4. but by *every* word of God.
 5. shewed unto him *all* the kingdoms
 7. worship me, *all* shall be thine.
 13. the devil had ended *all* the temptation,
 15. being glorified of *all*.
 20. And the eyes of *all* them that
 22. And *all* bare him witness,
 25. famine was throughout *all* the land;
 28. And *all* they in the synagogue,
 36. And they were *all* amazed,
 37. of him went out into *every* place
 40. *all* [3] they that had any sick
5: 9. and *all* that were with him,
 17. out of *every* town of Galilee,
6:10. round about upon them *all*,
 17. people out of *all* Judæa and
 19. And the *whole* multitude sought
 — and healed (them) *all*.
 26. when *all* men shall speak well
 30. Give to *every* man that asketh
 40. but *every one* that is perfect
 47. *Whosoever* cometh to me, and
7: 1. when he had ended *all* his sayings
 17. throughout *all* the region round about.
 18. shewed him of *all* these things.
 29. And *all* the people that heard (him),
 35. wisdom is justified of *all* her children.
8:40. for they were *all* waiting for him.
 45. When *all* denied, Peter and they that
 47. declared unto him before *all* the people
 52. And *all* wept, and bewailed
 54. And he put them *all* out, and took
9: 1. and authority over *all* devils, and to
 7. heard of *all* that was done by him:
 13. buy meat for *all* this people.
 17. and were *all* filled:
 23. he said to (them) *all*, If any (man) will
 43. And they were *all* amazed at the
 — while they wondered *every one* at *all* things
which Jesus did,
 48. that is least among you *all*, the same
10: 1. into *every* city and place, whither he
 19. and over *all* the power of the enemy:
 22. *All* things are delivered to me of
11: 4. for we also forgive *every one* that
 10. For *every one* that asketh receiveth;
 17. *Every* kingdom divided against
 41. and, behold, *all* things are clean

Lu. 11:42. rue and *all manner of* herbs,
 50. That the blood of *all* the prophets,
12: 7. hairs of your head are *all* numbered.
 8. *Whosoever* shall confess me before
 10. And *whosoever* shall speak a word
 18. there will I bestow *all* my fruits
 27. Solomon in *all* his glory was not
 30. For *all* these things do the nations
 31. and *all* these things shall be added
 41. this parable unto us, or even to *all?*
 44. make him ruler over *all* that he hath.
 48. For unto *whomsoever* much is
13: 2. were sinners above *all* the Galilæans,
 3. ye shall *all* likewise perish.
 4. sinners above *all* men that
 5. ye shall *all* likewise perish.
 17. *all* his adversaries were ashamed: and *all*
  the people rejoiced for *all* the glorious
 27. depart from me, *all* (ye) workers
 28. and *all* the prophets, in the kingdom
14:11. For *whosoever* exalteth himself
 17. Come ; for *all* things are now ready.
 18. And they *all* with one (consent)
 29. *all* that behold (it) begin to
 33. *whosoever* he be of you that forsaketh not
  all that he hath,
15: 1. *all* the publicans and sinners
 14. And when he had spent *all*,
 31. and *all* that I have is thine.
16:14. covetous, heard *all* these things:
 16. and *every* man presseth into it.
 18. *Whosoever* putteth away his wife,
 — and *whosoever* marrieth her
 26. And beside *all* this, between us
17:10. when ye shall have done *all*
18:12. I give tithes of *all*[3] that I possess.
 14. *every one* that exalteth himself
 21. *All* these have I kept from
 22. sell *all*[3] that thou hast, and
 28. Lo, we have left *all*, and followed
 31. and *all* things that are written
 43. and *all* the people, when they saw
19:26. That unto *every one* which hath
 37. with a loud voice for *all* the mighty
20: 6. *all* the people will stone us:
 18. *Whosoever* shall fall upon that
 32. Last of *all* the woman died also.
 38. for *all* live unto him.
 45. Then in the audience of *all* the people
21: 3. cast in more than they *all:*
 15. which *all* your adversaries
 17. be hated of *all* (men) for my
 22. that *all* things which are written
 24. captive into *all* nations.
 29. Behold the fig tree, and *all* the trees ;
 32. shall not pass away, till *all* be fulfilled.
 35. shall it come on *all* them that dwell on the
  face of the *whole* earth.
 36. and pray *always*, (ἐν παντὶ καιρῷ)
 — to escape *all* these things
 38. And *all* the people came early
22:70. Then said they *all*, Art thou then
23:48. And *all* the people that came
 49. And *all* his acquaintance,
24: 9. told *all* these things unto the eleven, and
  to *all* the rest.
 14. talked together of *all* these things
 19. before God and *all* the people:
 21. and beside *all* this, to day is
 25. slow of heart to believe *all* that
 27. at Moses and *all* the prophets, he expounded unto them in *all* the scriptures

Lu. 24:44. that *all* things must be fulfilled,
 47. among *all* nations, beginning at
Joh. 1: 3. *All* things were made by him ;
 7. that *all* (men) through him
 9. which lighteth *every* man that
 16. fulness have *all* we received,
2:10. *Every* man at the beginning
 15. he drove them *all* out of the temple,
 24. because he knew *all* (men),
3: 8. so is *every one* that is born of
 15. That *whosoever* believeth in him
 16. that *whosoever* believeth in him
 20. For *every one* that doeth evil
 26. and *all* (men) come to him.
 31. that cometh from above is above *all:*
 — that cometh from heaven is above *all.*
 35. given *all* things into his hand.
4:13. *Whosoever* drinketh of this water
 25. he will tell us *all* things.
 29. which told me *all*[3] things that
 39. He told me *all*[3] that ever I did.
 45. having seen *all* the things that he
5:20. and sheweth him *all* things
 22. hath committed *all* judgment unto
 23. That *all* (men) should honour the
 28. *all* that are in the graves shall
6:37. *All* that the Father giveth me
 39. of *all* which he hath given me
 40. *every one* which seeth the Son,
 45. they shall be *all* taught of God.
 — *Every* man therefore that
7:21. I have done one work, and ye *all* marvel.
8: 2. and *all* the people came unto
 34. *Whosoever* committeth sin is
10: 8. *All*[3] that ever came before me
 29. gave (them) me, is greater than *all ;*
 41. but *all*[3] things that John spake
11:26. And *whosoever* liveth and believeth
 48. *all* (men) will believe on him:
12:32. will draw *all* (men) unto me.
 46. that *whosoever* believeth on me
13: 3. Father had given *all* things
 10. ye are clean, but not *all.*
 11. Ye are not *all* clean.
 18. I speak not of you *all :*
 35. By this shall *all* (men) know
14:26. he shall teach you *all* things, and bring *all*
  things to your remembrance, whatsoever
15: 2. *Every* branch in me that
 — and *every* (branch) that beareth
 15. for *all* things that I have heard
 21. But *all* these things will they
16: 2. that *whosoever* killeth you will
 13. he will guide you into *all* truth:
 15. *All*[3] things that the Father hath
 30. that thou knowest *all* things, and
17: 2. given him power over *all* flesh,
 — eternal life to *as many as* (πᾶν ὅ) thou
  hast given him.
 7. known that *all*[3] things whatsoever
 10. And *all* mine are thine,
 21. That they *all* may be one ;
18: 4. knowing *all* things that should come upon
 37. *Every one* that is of the truth
 40. Then cried they *all* again, saying,
19:12. *whosoever* maketh himself a king
 28. that *all* things were now accomplished,
21:17. Lord, thou knowest *all* things ;
Acts 1: 1. of *all* that Jesus began both to do
 8. and in *all* Judæa, and in Samaria,
 14. These *all* continued with one accord
 18. and *all* his bowels gushed out.

Acts 1:19. it was known unto *all* the dwellers
21. companied with us *all* the time that
24. which knowest the hearts of *all* (men),
2: 5. out of *every* nation under heaven.
7. And they were *all* amazed and
— are not *all* these which speak
12. And they were *all* amazed,
17. out of my Spirit upon *all* flesh:
21. *whosoever* shall call on the name
25. I foresaw the Lord *always* (διὰ παντὸς)
32. whereof we *all* are witnesses.
36. Therefore let *all* the house of Israel
39. and to *all* that are afar off,
43. And fear came upon *every* soul:
44. *all* that believed were together,
45. and parted them to *all* (men), as
3: 9. And *all* the people saw him walking
11. *all* the people ran together
16. in the presence of you *all*.
18. by the mouth of *all* his prophets,
21. of restitution of *all* things, which
— by the mouth of *all* his holy prophets
22. hear in *all*[3] things whatsoever
23. come to pass, (that) *every*[2] soul, which
24. Yea, and *all* the prophets from
25. in thy seed shall *all* the kindreds
4:10. Be it known unto you *all*, and to *all* the people of Israel,
16. (is) manifest to *all* them that dwell
21. for *all* (men) glorified God for
24. sea, and *all* that in them is:
29. that with *all* boldness they
33. and great grace was upon them *all*.
5: 5. and great fear came on *all*
11. upon *as many as* heard
17. and *all* they that were-with him,
20. *all* the words of this life.
21. and *all* the senate of the
23. found we shut with *all* safety,
34. in reputation among *all* the people,
36. and *all*,[3] as many as obeyed him,
37. and *all*,[3] (even) as many as obeyed
42. And daily (lit. *every* day) in the temple,
6: 5. pleased the *whole* multitude:
7:10. And delivered him out of *all* his afflictions,
14. and *all* his kindred, threescore and
22. learned in *all* the wisdom of the
50. my hand made *all* these things?
8: 1. and they were *all* scattered abroad
10. To whom they *all* gave heed,
27. the charge of *all* her treasure,
40. he preached in *all* the cities,
9:14. to bind *all* that call on thy name.
21. But *all* that heard (him)
26. but they were *all* afraid of him,
32. throughout *all* (quarters),
35. And *all* that dwelt at Lydda
39. and *all* the widows stood by
40. But Peter put them *all* forth, and
10: 2. feared God with *all* his house,
12. Wherein were *all manner of* fourfooted
14. I have never eaten *any* thing that is
33. Now therefore are we *all* here
— to hear *all* things that
35. But in *every* nation he that
36. he is Lord of *all* :
38. healing *all* that were oppressed of
39. we are witnesses of *all* things which
41. Not to *all* the people, but unto
43. To him give *all* the prophets witness,
— *whosoever* believeth in him
44. the Holy Ghost fell on *all* them

Acts11: 8. for nothing (lit. not *any* thing) common
14. whereby thou and *all* thy house
23. and exhorted them *all*, that with
12:11. and (from) *all* the expectation of
13:10. O full of *all* subtilty and *all* mischief,
— (thou) enemy of *all* righteousness,
22. which shall fulfil *all* my will. [plural]
24. repentance to *all* the people of Israel.
27. which are read *every* sabbath day,
39. And by him *all* that believe are justified from *all* things, from
44. came almost the *whole* city
14:15. and *all* things that are therein:
16. in times past suffered *all* nations
15: 3. caused great joy unto *all* the brethren.
12. Then *all* the multitude kept silence,
17. and *all* the Gentiles, upon whom
— who doeth *all* these things.
18. Known unto God are *all* his works
21. read in the synagogues *every* sabbath day.
36. visit our brethren in *every* city
16:26. immediately *all* the doors were opened, and *every one's* bands
32. to *all* that were in his house.
33. and was baptized, he and *all* his,
17: 7. and these *all* do contrary to
11. received the word with *all* readiness
17. in the market daily (lit. on *every* day)
21. For *all* the Athenians and
22. I perceive that in *all* things ye
24. made the world and *all* things
25. he giveth to *all* life, and breath, and *all* things;
26. made of one blood *all* nations of men for to dwell on *all* the face of
30. now commandeth *all* men every where
31. hath given assurance unto *all*
18: 2. Claudius had commanded *all* Jews
4. reasoned in the synagogue *every* sabbath,
17. Then *all* the Greeks took Sosthenes,
23. strengthening *all* the disciples.
19: 7. And *all* the men were about twelve.
10. so that *all* they which dwelt in Asia
17. this was known to *all* the Jews
— and fear fell on them *all*,
19. and burned them before *all* (men):
26. almost throughout *all* Asia, this Paul
34. *all* with one voice about the
20:18. been with you at *all* seasons,
19. with *all* humility of mind,
25. I know that ye *all*, among whom
26. pure from the blood of *all*
27. *all* the counsel of God.
28. and to *all* the flock, over the which
32. among *all* them which are sanctified.
35. I have shewed you *all* things,
36. and prayed with them *all*.
37. And they *all* wept sore, and
21: 5. and they *all* brought us on our way,
18. and *all* the elders were present.
20. and they are *all* zealous of the law:
21. that thou teachest *all* the Jews which
24. and *all* may know that those things,
27. stirred up *all* the people, and laid
28. that teacheth *all* (men) every where
22: 3. as ye *all* are this day.
5. and *all* the estate of the elders:
10. it shall be told thee of *all* things
12. having a good report of *all* the Jews
15. shalt be his witness unto *all* men of
23: 1. I have lived in *all* good conscience
24: 3. most noble Felix, with *all* thankfulness.

Acts24: 5. a mover of sedition among *all* the Jews
    8. mayest take knowledge of *all* these things,
   14. believing *all* things which are written
25:24. King Agrippa, and *all* men which
   — about whom *all* the multitude of
26: 2. touching *all* the things whereof
   3. to be expert in *all* customs and
   4. know *all* the Jews ;
   11. I punished them oft in *every* synagogue,
   14. when we were *all* fallen to the earth,
   20. and throughout *all* the coasts of Judæa,
   29. but also *all* that hear me this day,
27:20. *all* hope that we should be saved
   24. God hath given thee *all* them
   35. in presence of them *all :*
   36. Then were they *all* of good cheer,
   37. we were in *all* in the ship (lit. *all* the souls)
   44. they escaped *all* safe to land.
28: 2. and received us *every* one, because
   30. and received *all* that came in unto him,
   31. with *all* confidence, no man
Ro. 1: 5. faith among *all* nations, for
   7. To *all* that be in Rome,
   8. through Jesus Christ for you *all*,
   16. salvation to *every* one that believeth ;
   18. against *all* ungodliness and
   29. Being filled with *all* unrighteousness,
2: 1. O man, *whosoever* thou art that
   9. upon *every* soul of man that
   10. to *every* man that worketh good,
3: 2. Much *every* way: chiefly, because
   4. but *every* man a liar ; as it is
   9. that they are *all* under sin ;
   12. They are *all* gone out of the way,
   19. that *every* mouth may be stopped, and *all*
     the world may
   20. there shall no (lit. *not any*) flesh be
   22. unto *all* and upon *all* them that believe:
   23. For *all* have sinned, and come
4:11. might be the father of *all* them that
   16. might be sure to *all* the seed ;
   — who is the father of us *all*,
5:12. and so death passed upon *all* men, for that
     all have sinned:
   18. upon *all* men to condemnation ;
   — upon *all* men unto justification ;
7: 8. in me *all manner of* concupiscence.
8:22. the *whole* creation groaneth
   28. *all* things work together for
   32. delivered him up for us *all*,
   — also freely give us *all* things?
   37. Nay, in *all* these things we
9: 5. who is over *all*, God blessed for ever.
   6. For they (are) not *all* Israel,
   7. Neither,...(are they) *all* children:
   17. declared throughout *all* the earth.
   33. *whosoever* believeth on him
10: 4. for righteousness to *every* one that
   11. *Whosoever* believeth on him
   12. the same Lord over *all* is rich unto *all* that
     call upon him.
   13. For *whosoever* shall call upon
   16. But they have not *all* obeyed
   18. their sound went into *all* the earth,
11:26. And so *all* Israel shall be
   32. concluded them *all* in unbelief, that he
     might have mercy upon *all*.
   36. and to him, (are) *all* things:
12: 3. God hath dealt to *every* man
   4. and *all* members have not the
   17. honest in the sight of *all* men.
   18. live peaceably with *all* men.

Ro. 13: 1. Let *every* soul be subject unto
   7. Render therefore to *all* their dues:
14: 2. that he may eat *all* things:
   5. another esteemeth *every* day
   10. for we shall *all* stand before
   11. *every* knee shall bow to me, and *every*
     tongue shall confess to God.
   20. *All* things indeed (are) pure ; but
   23. *whatsoever* (is) not of faith is sin.
15:11. Praise the Lord, *all* ye Gentiles ; and laud
     him, *all* ye people.
   13. fill you with *all* joy and peace
   14. filled with *all* knowledge,
   33. the God of peace (be) with you *all*.
16: 4. but also *all* the churches of
   15. and *all* the saints which are
   19. is come abroad unto *all* (men).
   24. (be) with you *all*. Amen.
   26. made known to *all* nations
1Co. 1: 2. with *all* that in *every* place
   5. That in *every* thing ye are enriched by
     him, in *all* utterance, and (in) *all*
     knowledge ;
   10. that ye *all* speak the same thing,
   29. That no (lit. *not any*) flesh should glory
2:10. the Spirit searcheth *all* things,
   15. is spiritual judgeth *all* things,
3:21. For *all* things are your's ;
   22. or things to come ; *all* are your's ;
4:13. the offscouring of *all* things
   17. I teach every where in *every* church.
6:12. *All* things are lawful unto me, but *all*
     things are not expedient: *all* things are
     lawful for me,
   18. *Every* sin that a man doeth is
7: 7. For I would that *all* men were
   17. And so ordain I in *all* churches.
8: 1. we know that we *all* have knowledge.
   6. of whom (are) *all* things, and we in him ;
   — by whom (are) *all* things, and we by him.
   7. Howbeit (there is) not in *every* man
9:12. but suffer *all* things, lest we should
   19. though I be free from *all* (men), yet have
     I made myself servant unto *all*,
   22. I am made *all* things to *all* (men), that I
   24. run in a race run *all*, but one
   25. And *every* man that striveth for the
     mastery is temperate in *all* things.
10: 1. how that *all* our fathers were
   — and *all* passed through the sea ;
   2. And were *all* baptized unto Moses
   3. And did *all* eat the same
   4. And did *all* drink the same
   11. Now *all* these things happened
   17. for we are *all* partakers of that
   23. *All* things are lawful for me, but *all* things
     are not expedient: *all* things are lawful
     for me, but *all* things edify not.
   25. *Whatsoever* is sold in the
   27. *whatsoever* is set before you,
   31. do *all* to the glory of God.
   33. I please *all* (men) in *all* (things),
11: 2. that ye remember me in *all* things,
   3. the head of *every* man is Christ ;
   4. *Every* man praying or
   5. But *every* woman that
   12. but *all* things of God.
12: 6. same God which worketh *all* in *all*.
   11. But *all* these worketh that one
   12. and *all* the members of that one
   13. are we *all* baptized into one
   — and have been *all* made to drink

1Co.12:19. And if they were *all* one member,
26. *all* the members suffer with it;
— *all* the members rejoice with it.
29. (Are) *all* apostles? (are) *all* prophets?
(are) *all* teachers? (are) *all* workers
of miracles?
30. Have *all* the gifts of healing? do *all* speak
with tongues? do *all* interpret?
13: 2. and understand *all* mysteries, and *all* knowledge; and though I have *all* faith,
3. though I bestow *all* my goods to feed
7. Beareth *all* things, believeth *all* things,
hopeth *all* things, endureth *all* things.
14: 5. I would that ye *all* spake with
18. with tongues more than ye *all:*
23. and *all* speak with tongues, and
24. But if *all* prophesy, and there come
— he is convinced of *all*, he is judged of *all:*
26. Let *all* things be done unto
31. For ye may *all* prophesy one by one, that
all may learn, and *all* may be
33. as in *all* churches of the saints.
40. Let *all* things be done decently and
15: 7. then of *all* the apostles.
8. And last of *all* he was seen of
10. more abundantly than they *all:*
19. we are of *all* men most miserable.
22. For as in Adam *all* die, even so in Christ
shall *all* be made alive.
24. when he shall have put down *all* rule and
all authority
25. till he hath put *all* enemies
27. hath put *all* things under his feet. But
when he saith, *All* things
— which did put *all* things under him.
28. And when *all* things shall be
— unto him that put *all* things under him,
that God may be *all* in *all*.
30. why stand we in jeopardy *every* hour?
39. *All* flesh (is) not the same flesh:
51. We shall not *all* sleep, but we shall *all* be
changed,
16:14. Let *all* your things be done with charity.
16. and to *every* one that helpeth with
20. *All* the brethren greet you.
24. My love (be) with you *all* in
2Co. 1: 1. with *all* the saints which are in
3. the God of *all* comfort;
4. in *all* our tribulation,
— them which are in *any* trouble
2: 3. having confidence in you *all*, that my joy
is (the joy) of you *all*.
5. I may not overcharge you *all*.
9. whether ye be obedient in *all* things.
14. his knowledge by us in *every* place.
3: 2. known and read of *all* men:
18. But we *all*, with open face
4. 2. to *every* man's conscience (lit. to *all* conscience of men)
8. (We are) troubled on *every* side, (lit. in *all*.)
15. For *all* things (are) for your sakes,
5:10. For we must *all* appear before
14(15). if one died for *all*, then were *all* dead:
15. And (that) he died for *all*, that
17. behold, *all* things are become new.
18. And *all* things (are) of God,
6: 4. But in *all* (things) approving
10. and (yet) possessing *all* things.
7: 1. from *all* filthiness of the
4. joyful in *all* our tribulation.
5. we were troubled on *every* side; (lit. in *all*.)
11. In *all* (things) ye have approved

2Co. 7:13. was refreshed by you *all*.
14. but as we spake *all* things to you in
15. remembereth the obedience of you *all*,
16. I have confidence in you in *all* (things).
8: 7. as ye abound in *every* (thing),
— and (in) *all* diligence,
18. throughout *all* the churches;
9: 8. God (is) able to make *all* grace
— having *all* sufficiency in *all* (things), may
abound to *every* good work:
11. in *every* thing to *all* bountifulness,
13. unto them, and unto *all* (men);
10: 5. and *every* high thing that exalteth
— into captivity *every* thought
6. a readiness to revenge *all* disobedience,
11: 6. have been *throughly* made manifest among
you in *all* things.
9. and in *all* (things) I have kept
28. daily, the care of *all* the churches.
12:12. wrought among you in *all* patience,
19. but (we do) *all* things, dearly beloved,
13: 1. three witnesses shall *every* word be
2. and to *all* other, that, if I come again,
13(12). *All* the saints salute you.
14(13). (be) with you *all*.   Amen.
Gal. 1: 2. And *all* the brethren which are
2:14. I said unto Peter before (them) *all*,
16. shall no (lit. not *any*) flesh be justified.
3: 8. In thee shall *all* nations be blessed.
10. *every* one that continueth not in *all* things
which
13. Cursed (is) *every* one that hangeth
22. hath concluded *all* under sin,
26. For ye are *all* the children of God
28. for ye are *all* one in Christ Jesus.
4: 1. though he be lord of *all;*
26. which is the mother of us *all*.
5: 3. For I testify again to *every* man that
14. For *all* the law is fulfilled in
6: 6. him that teacheth in *all* good things.
10. let us do good unto *all* (men),
Eph 1: 3. hath blessed us with *all* spiritual
8. abounded toward us in *all* wisdom
10. gather together in one *all* things
11. who worketh *all* things
15. and love unto *all* the saints,
21. Far above *all* principality,
— and *every* name that is named,
22. put *all* (things) under his feet, and gave
him (to be) the head over *all* (things)
23. of him that filleth *all* in *all*.
2: 3. Among whom also we *all* had our
21. In whom *all* the building
3: 8. less than the least of *all* saints,
9. And to make *all* (men) see
— who created *all* things by Jesus
15. Of whom the *whole* family in
18. to comprehend with *all* saints
19. with *all* the fulness of God.
20. above *all* that we ask or
21. throughout *all* ages, world
4: 2. With *all* lowliness and
6. One God and Father of *all*, who (is) above
all, and through *all*, and in you *all*.
10. up far above *all* heavens, that he might
fill *all* things.
13. Till we *all* come in the
14. and carried about with *every* wind
15. grow up into him in *all* things,
16. From whom the *whole* body fitly
— by that which *every* joint supplieth,
19. to work *all* uncleanness with

Eph 4:29. no (lit. not *any*) corrupt communication
  31. Let *all* bitterness, and wrath,
   — with *all* malice:
 5: 3. and *all* uncleanness,
  5. that no (lit. not *any*) whoremonger.
  9. (is) in *all* goodness
  13. *all* things that are reproved
   — for *whatsoever* doth make
  20. thanks always for *all* things unto God
  24. to their own husbands in *every* thing.
 6:16. Above *all*, taking the shield
   — to quench *all* the fiery darts
  18. Praying *always* (ἐν. π. κ.) with *all* prayer
   — thereunto with *all* perseverance and
      supplication for *all* saints;
  21. make known to you *all* things:
  24. Grace (be) with *all* them that love
Phi. 1: 1. to *all* the saints in Christ
  3. upon *every* remembrance of you,
  4. in *every* prayer of mine for you *all* making
      request with joy,
  7. to think this of you *all*,
   — ye *all* are partakers of my grace.
  8. I long after you *all* in
  9. and (in) *all* judgment;
  13. in all the palace, and in *all* other (places);
  18. notwithstanding, *every* way, whether
  20. with *all* boldness, as always,
  25. with you *all* for your furtherance
 2: 9. a name which is above *every* name:
  10. *every* knee should bow,
  11. And (that) *every* tongue should
  14. Do *all* things without murmurings
  17. and rejoice with you *all*.
  21. For *all* seek their own,
  26. longed after you *all*,
  29. with *all* gladness; and hold such
 3: 8. I count *all* things (but) loss
   — suffered the loss of *all* things,
  21. to subdue *all* things unto himself.
 4: 5. be known unto *all* men.
  6. but in *every* thing by prayer
  7. passeth *all* understanding,
  12. *every* where and in *all* things I am
  13. I can do *all* things through
  18. But I have *all*, and abound:
  19. shall supply *all* your need
  21. Salute *every* saint in Christ Jesus.
  22. *All* the saints salute you,
  23. (be) with you *all*.   Amen.
Col. 1: 4. to *all* the saints,
  6. in *all* the world;
  9. of his will in *all* wisdom
  10. unto *all* pleasing, being fruitful in *every*
      good work,
  11. Strengthened with *all* might,
   — unto *all* patience
  15. the firstborn of *every* creature:
  16. were *all* things created,
   — *all* things were created by him,
  17. he is before *all* things, and by him *all*
      things consist.
  18. that in *all* (things) he might
  19. should *all* fulness dwell,
  20. to reconcile *all* things unto himself;
  23. to *every* creature which is under
  28. warning *every* man, and teaching *every*
      man in *all* wisdom; that we may present
      every man
 2: 2. and unto *all* riches of the
  3. are hid *all* the treasures of
  9. dwelleth *all* the fulness of

Col. 2:10. the head of *all* principality
  13. forgiven you *all* trespasses;
  19. from which *all* the body
  22. Which *all* are to perish
 3: 8. put off *all* these; anger. wrath,
  11. but Christ (is) *all*, and in *all*.
  14. And above *all* these things
  16. richly in *all* wisdom;
  17. *whatsoever* [2] ye do in word
   — (do) *all* in the name of
  20. in *all* things: for this is
  22. obey in *all* things (your)
  23. And *whatsoever* [2] ye do,
 4: 7. *All* my state shall Tychicus
  9. make known unto you *all* things
  12. complete in *all* the will of God.
1Th. 1: 2. to God always for you *all*,
  7. ensamples to *all* that believe
  8. in *every* place your faith
 2:15. and are contrary to *all* men:
 3: 7. in *all* our affliction
  9. for *all* the joy wherewith we
  12. and toward *all* (men),
  13. Jesus Christ with *all* his saints.
 4: 6. the avenger of *all* such,
  10. toward *all* the brethren which are
 5: 5. Ye are *all* the children of light,
  14. be patient toward *all* (men).
  15. among yourselves, and to *all* (men).
  18. In *every* thing give thanks:
  21. Prove *all* things; hold fast that
  22. Abstain from *all* appearance
  26. Greet *all* the brethren
  27. be read unto *all* the holy brethren.
2Th. 1: 3. charity of every one of you *all*
  4. in *all* your persecutions
  10. admired in *all* them that
  11. and fulfil *all* the good pleasure
 2: 4. above *all* that is called God,
  9. with *all* power and signs
  10. And with *all* deceivableness
  12. That they *all* might be damned
  17. in *every* good word and work.
 3: 2. for *all* (men) have not faith.
  6. from *every* brother that
  16. peace *always* (διὰ παντὸς) by *all* means.
      The Lord (be) with you *all*.
  17. the token in *every* epistle:
  18. (be) with you *all*.   Amen.
1Ti. 1:15. worthy of *all* acceptation,
  16. shew forth *all* longsuffering,
 2: 1. that, first of *all*, supplications,
   — be made for *all* men;
  2. (for) *all* that are in authority;
   — peaceable life in *all* godliness
  4. Who will have *all* men to be
  6. a ransom for *all*,
  8. that men pray *every* where,
  11. learn in silence with *all* subjection.
 3: 4. in subjection with *all* gravity;
  11. faithful in *all* things.
 4: 4. For *every* creature of God (is)
  8. profitable unto *all* things,
  9. worthy of *all* acceptation.
  10. the saviour of *all* men, specially
  15. may appear to *all*.
 5: 2. younger as sisters, with *all* purity.
  10. followed *every* good work.
  20. rebuke before *all*, that others
 6: 1. worthy of *all* honour,
  10. the root of *all* evil:
  13. who quickeneth *all* things,

1Ti. 6:17. richly *all* things to enjoy;

2Ti. 1:15. *all* they which are in Asia be turned

2: 7. give thee understanding in *all* things.

10. I endure *all* things for the

19. Let *every one* that nameth

21. prepared unto *every* good work.

24. gentle unto *all* (men),

3: 9. shall be manifest unto *all*

11. out of (them) *all* the Lord delivered

12. Yea, and *all* that will live

16. *All* scripture (is) given

17. unto *all* good works.

4: 2. exhort with *all* longsuffering

5. watch thou in *all* things,

8. but unto *all* them also that love

16. but *all* (men) forsook me:

17. and (that) *all* the Gentiles

18. from *every* evil work,

21. and *all* the brethren.

Tit. 1:15. Unto the pure *all* things (are)

16. unto *every* good work reprobate.

2: 7. In *all* things shewing thyself

9. to please (them) well in *all* (things);

10. shewing *all* good fidelity;

— of God our Saviour in *all* things.

11. hath appeared to *all* men,

14. might redeem us from *all* iniquity,

15. rebuke with *all* authority

3: 1. to *every* good work,

2. shewing *all* meekness unto *all* men.

15. *All* that are with me

— Grace (be) with you *all*.

Philem. 5. and toward *all* saints;

6. acknowledging of *every* good thing

Heb 1: 2. appointed heir of *all* things,

3. upholding *all* things by the word

6. And let *all* the angels of God

11. and they *all* shall wax old

14. Are they not *all* ministering

2: 2. and *every* transgression

8. Thou hast put *all* things in

— in that he put *all* in subjection under

— we see not yet *all* things put under him.

9. should taste death for *every* man.

10. for whom (are) *all* things, and by whom (are) *all* things,

11. (are) *all* of one:

15. were *all* their lifetime subject

17. Wherefore in *all* things

3: 4. For *every* house is builded by some (man); but he that built *all* things (is) God.

16. not *all* that came out of Egypt

4: 4. the seventh day from *all* his works.

12. sharper than *any* twoedged sword,

13. but *all* things (are) naked

15. was in *all* points tempted

5: 1. For *every* high priest

9. unto *all* them that obey him;

13. For *every one* that useth milk

6:16. an end of *all* strife.

7: 2. gave a tenth part of *all;*

7. And without *all* contradiction

8: 3. For *every* high priest

5. make *all* things according to

11. for *all* shall know me,

9:19. spoken *every* precept to *all* the people

— both the book, and *all* the people,

21. and *all* the vessels of the ministry.

22. And almost *all* things are by

10:11. And *every* priest standeth

11:13. These *all* died in faith, not having

39. And these *all*, having obtained a

Heb 12: 1. let us lay aside *every* weight,

6. and scourgeth *every* son whom

8. whereof *all* are partakers,

11. Now no (lit. not *any*) chastening

14. Follow peace with *all* (men),

23. to God the Judge of *all*,

13: 4. honourable in *all*,

18. in *all* things willing to live

21. in *every* good work to do his will,

24. Salute *all* them that have

— and *all* the saints.

25. Grace (be) with you *all*. Amen.

Jas. 1: 2. count it *all* joy when ye fall

5. that giveth to *all* (men) liberally,

8. in *all* his ways.

17. *Every* good gift and *every* perfect gift

19. let *every* man be swift to hear,

21. lay apart *all* filthiness

2:10. he is guilty of *all*.

3: 7. For *every* kind of beasts,

16. and *every* evil work.

4:16. *all* such rejoicing is evil.

5:12. above *all* things, my brethren,

1Pet. 1:15. holy in *all manner of* conversation;

24. For *all* flesh (is) as grass, and *all* the glory of man

2: 1. laying aside *all* malice, and *all* guile,

— and *all* evil speakings,

13. to *every* ordinance of·man

17. Honour *all* (men). Love the brotherhood.

18. masters with *all* fear;

3: 8. (be ye) *all* of one mind,

15. an answer to *every* man that

4: 7. the end of *all* things is at hand:

8. And above *all* things have

11. that God in *all* things may be

5: 5. Yea, *all* (of you) be subject one to

7. Casting *all* your care upon

10. But the God of *all* grace,

14. Peace (be) with you *all* that are in

2Pet. 1: 3. given unto us *all* things that

5. giving *all* diligence, add to your

20. that no (lit. not *any*) prophecy of the

3: 4. *all* things continue as

9. but that *all* should come to

11. (that) *all* these things shall be dissolved,

16. As also in *all* (his) epistles,

1Joh. 1: 7. cleanseth us from *all* sin.

9. cleanse us from *all* unrighteousness.

2:16. For *all* that (is) in the world,

19. that they were not *all* of us.

20. and ye know *all* things.

21. that no (lit. not *any*) lie is of the truth.

23. *Whosoever* denieth the Son,

27. teacheth you of *all* things,

29. *every one* that doeth righteousness

3: 3. And *every* man that hath this

4. *Whosoever* committeth sin

6. *Whosoever* abideth in him

— *whosoever* sinneth hath not seen

9. *Whosoever* is born of God

10. *whosoever* doeth not righteousness

15. *Whosoever* hateth his brother

— that no (lit. not *any*) murderer hath

20. and knoweth *all* things.

4: 1. believe not *every* spirit,

2. *Every* spirit that confesseth

3. And *every* spirit that

7. and *every* one that loveth

5: 1. *Whosoever* believeth that Jesus

— and *every* one that loveth

4. For *whatsoever* is born of

1Joh.5:17. *All* unrighteousness is sin:
    18. *whosoever* is born of God
2Joh. 1. but also *all* they that have known
    9. *Whosoever* transgresseth, and
3Joh. 2. I wish above *all* things
    12. hath good report of *all*
Jude 3. when I gave *all* diligence
    15. judgment upon *all*, and to convince *all*
    — of *all* their ungodly deeds...and of *all* their hard (speeches) which
    25. both now and ever. (lit. to *all* ages)
Rev. 1: 7. and *every* eye shall see him,
    — and *all* kindreds of the earth shall
  2:23. and *all* the churches shall know
  4:11. for thou hast created *all* things,
  5: 6. sent forth into *all* the earth.
    9. out of *every* kindred, and tongue,
    13. And *every* creature which is
    — sea, and *all* that are in them,
  6:14. *every* mountain and island were
    15. *every* bondman, and *every* free man,
  7: 1. nor on *any* tree.
    4. of *all* the tribes of the children of
    9. of *all* nations, and kindreds,
    11. And *all* the angels stood round
    16. sun light on them, nor *any* heat.
    17. wipe away *all* tears from their eyes.
  8: 3. with the prayers of *all* saints
    7. and *all* green grass was burnt
  9: 4. neither *any* green thing, neither *any* tree;
  11: 6. to smite the earth with *all* plagues,
  12: 5. who was to rule *all* nations with
  13: 7. over *all* kindreds, and tongues,
    8. And *all* that dwell upon the
    12. And he exerciseth *all* the power of
    16. And he caused *all*, both small
  14: 6. and to *every* nation, and kindred,
    8. because she made *all* nations drink
  15: 4. for *all* nations shall come and
  16: 3. and *every* living soul died in the
    20. And *every* island fled away,
  18: 2. the hold of *every* foul spirit, and a cage of *every* unclean
    3. For *all* nations have drunk
    12. and *all* thyine wood,
    — and *all* *manner* vessels of ivory, and *all* *manner* vessels of most
    14. and *all* things which were dainty
    17. And *every* shipmaster, and *all* the company
    19. were made rich *all* that had ships
    22. and. no (lit. not *any*) craftsman, of *whatsoever* craft (he be),
    23. were *all* nations deceived.
    24. and of *all* that were slain upon
  19: 5. Praise our God, *all* ye his servants,
    17. saying to *all* the fowls that fly in
    18. and the flesh of *all* (men, both) free
    21. and *all* the fowls were filled with
  21: 4. God shall wipe away *all* tears from
    5. Behold, I make *all* things new.
    7. shall inherit *all* things;
    8. and *all* liars, shall have their part
    19. with *all* *manner* *of* precious stones.
    27. into it *any* thing that defileth,
  22: 3. And there shall be no more)(curse:
    15. and *whosoever* loveth and maketh
    18. I testify unto *every* man that heareth
    21. (be) with you *all*. Amen.

πάσχα, *paska.*

Mat.26: 2. two days is (the feast of) the *passover*,

Mat.26:17. prepare for thee to eat the *passover* ?
    18. I will keep the *passover* at thy house
    19. and they made ready the *passover*.
Mar 14: 1. was (the feast of) the *passover*,
    12. when they killed the *passover*,
    — that thou mayest eat the *passover* ?
    14. where I shall eat the *passover* with
    16. and they made ready the *passover*.
Lu. 2:41. every year at the feast of the *passover*.
  22: 1. which is called the *passover*.
    7. when the *passover* must be killed.
    8. Go and prepare us the *passover*,
    11. where I shall eat the *passover*
    13. and they made ready the *passover*.
    15. desired to eat this *passover* with you
Joh. 2:13. And the Jews' *passover* was at hand,
    23. when he was in Jerusalem at the *passover*, in the feast
  6: 4. And the *passover*, a feast of the Jews,
  11:55. And the Jews' *passover* was nigh at
    — before the *passover*, to purify themselves.
  12: 1. Jesus six days before the *passover*
  13: 1. Now before the feast of the *passover*,
  18:28. but that they might eat the *passover*.
    39. release unto you one at the *passover* :
  19:14. it was the preparation of the *passover*,
Acts12: 4. intending after *Easter* to bring him forth
1Co. 5: 7. Christ our *passover* is sacrificed for us:
Heb 11:28. Through faith he kept the *passover*,

πάσχω, *pasko.*

Mat.16:21. and *suffer* many things of the elders
  17:12. shall also the Son of man *suffer* of them.
    15. he is lunatick, and sore *vexed* .
  27:19. for I *have suffered* many things this
Mar 5:26. And *had suffered* many things of
  8:31. the Son of man must *suffer* many
  9:12. that he *must suffer* many things,
Lu. 9:22. The Son of man must *suffer* many
  13: 2. because they *suffered* such things ?
  17:25. But first must he *suffer* many
  22:15. this passover with you before I *suffer* :
  24:26. Ought not Christ *to have suffered*
    46. it behoved Christ *to suffer*, and to
Acts 1; 3. he shewed himself alive after his *passion*
  3:18. that Christ should *suffer*, he hath so
  9:16. how great things he must *suffer* for
  17: 3. Christ must needs *have suffered*,
  28: 5. beast into the fire, and *felt* no harm.
1Co.12:26. one member *suffer*, all the members
2Co. 1: 6. same sufferings which we also *suffer* :
Gal. 3: 4. *Have* ye *suffered* so many things in vain?
Phi. 1:29. but also *to suffer* for his sake ;
1Th. 2:14. for ye also *have suffered* like things
2Th. 1: 5. for which ye also *suffer* :
2Ti. 1:12. For the which cause I also *suffer* these things:
Heb 2:18. he himself *hath suffered* being tempted,
  5: 8. by the things which he *suffered* ;
  9:26. For then must he often *have suffered*
  13:12. *suffered* without the gate.
1Pet. 2:19. endure grief, *suffering* wrongfully.
    20. when ye do well, and *suffer* (for it),
    21. Christ also *suffered* for us, leaving
    23. *when* he *suffered*, he threatened not ;
  3:14. But and if ye *suffer* for righteousness'
    17. that ye *suffer* for well doing,
    18. Christ also *hath* once *suffered* for
  4: 1. *Forasmuch* then as Christ *hath suffered* for us

1Pet.4: 1. for he *that hath suffered* in the flesh
15. But *let* none of you *suffer* as a
19. Wherefore let them *that suffer*
5:10. *after that* ye *have suffered* a while,
Rev. 2:10. of those things which thou shalt *suffer:*

πατάσσω, *patasso.*

Mat.26:31. I *will smite* the shepherd, and
51. *struck* a servant of the high priest's, *and*
Mar 14:27. I *will smite* the shepherd,
Lu. 22:49. Lord, *shall* we *smite* with the sword?
50. *smote* the servant of the high priest,
Acts 7:24. *and smote* the Egyptian:
12: 7. he *smote* Peter on the side, *and*
23. the angel of the Lord *smote* him,
Rev.11: 6. and *to smite* the earth with
19:15. that with it he *should smite* the nations:

πατέω, *pateo.*

Lu. 10:19. power *to tread* on serpents
21:24. Jerusalem shall be *trodden down*
Rev.11: 2. holy city *shall* they *tread under foot*
14:20. And the winepress *was trodden*
19:15. and he *treadeth* the winepress of

πατήρ, *pateer.*

Mat. 2:22. in the room of his *father* Herod,
3: 9. We have Abraham to (our) *father :*
4:21. in a ship with Zebedee their *father,*
22. left the ship and their *father,*
5:16. and glorify your *Father* which is
45. That ye may be the children of your *Father*
48. perfect, even as your *Father* which is
6: 1. of your *Father* which is in heaven.
4. and thy *Father* which seeth in secret
6. pray to thy *Father* which is in secret; and
thy *Father* which seeth in
8. your *Father* knoweth what things
9. Our *Father* which art in heaven,
14. your heavenly *Father* will also
15. neither will your *Father* forgive
18. but unto thy *Father* which is in secret:
and thy *Father,* which seeth
26. yet your heavenly *Father* feedeth
32. for your heavenly *Father* knoweth
7:11. how much more shall your *Father*
21. he that doeth the will of my *Father*
8:21. first to go and bury my *father.*
10:20. but the Spirit of your *Father* which
21. and the *father* the child:
29. fall on the ground without your *Father.*
32. before my *Father* which is in heaven.
33. before my *Father* which is in heaven.
35. a man at variance against his *father,*
37. He that loveth *father* or mother
11:25. I thank thee, O *Father,* Lord of
26. Even so, *Father :* for so it seemed good
27. delivered unto me of my *Father:* and no
man knoweth the Son, but the *Father ;*
neither knoweth any man the *Father,*
12:50. shall do the will of my *Father*
13:43. in the kingdom of their *Father.*
15: 4. Honour thy *father* and mother: and, He
that curseth *father* or mother,
5. Whosoever shall say to (his) *father*

Mat.15: 6(5). And honour not his *father* or his
13. which my heavenly *Father* hath not
16:17. but my *Father* which is in heaven.
27. come in the glory of his *Father*
18:10. always behold the face of my *Father*
14. it is not the will of your *Father* which
19. be done for them of my *Father* which
35. shall my heavenly *Father* do also
19: 5. shall a man leave *father* and mother,
19. Honour thy *father* and (thy) mother:
29. or brethren, or sisters, or *father,* or
20:23. for whom it is prepared of my *Father.*
21:31. twain did the will of (his) *father?*
23: 9. And call no (man) your *father*
— for one is your *Father,* which is
30. If we had been in the days of our *fathers,*
32. the measure of your *fathers.*
24:36. but my *Father* only.
25:34. Come, ye blessed of my *Father,*
26:29. with you in my *Father's* kingdom.
39. O my *Father,* if it be possible,
42. O my *Father,* if this cup may not
53. that I cannot now pray to my *Father,*
28:19. in the name of the *Father,* and of
Mar 1:20. they left their *father* Zebedee in
5:40. he taketh the *father* and the
7:10. Honour thy *father* and thy mother ; and,
Whoso curseth *father* or mother,
11. If a man shall say to his *father*
12. no more to do ought for his *father*
8:38. the glory of his *Father* with the
9:21. And he asked his *father,* How long
24. And straightway the *father* of the
10: 7. shall a man leave his *father*
19. Honour thy *father* and mother.
29. or brethren, or sisters, or *father,* or
11:10. the kingdom of our *father* David,
25. that your *Father* also which is
26. neither will your *Father* which
13:12. and the *father* the son;
32. neither the Son, but the *Father.*
14:36. And he said, Abba, *Father,* all
15:21. the *father* of Alexander and Rufus,
Lu. 1:17. to turn the hearts of the *fathers*
32. the throne of his *father* David:
55. As he spake to our *fathers,*
59. Zacharias, after the name of his *father.*
62. made signs to his *father,* how
67. And his *father* Zacharias was
72. the mercy (promised) to our *fathers,*
73. sware to our *father* Abraham,
2:48. behold, thy *father* and I have sought
49. must be about my *Father's* business?
3: 8. We have Abraham to (our) *father :*
6:23. did their *fathers* unto the prophets.
26. did their *fathers* to the false prophets.
36. as your *Father* also is merciful.
8:51. and the *father* and the mother of
9:26. and (in his) *Father's,* and of the holy
42. and delivered him again to his *father.*
59. to go and bury my *father.*
10:21. I thank thee, O *Father,* Lord of
— even so, *Father ;* for so it
22. delivered to me of my *Father:*
— but the *Father ;* and who the *Father :*
11: 2. Our *Father* which art in
11. of any of you that is a *father,*
13. much more shall (your) heavenly *Father*
47. and your *fathers* killed them.
48. allow the deeds of your *fathers:*
12:30. and your *Father* knoweth
32. it is your *Father's* good pleasure

Lu. 12:53. The *father* shall be divided against the
son, and the son against the *father;*
14:26. and hate not his *father,* and
15:12. said to (his) *father, Father,* give me
17. servants of my *father's* have
18. arise and go to my *father,* and will say
unto him, *Father,* I have sinned
20. he arose, and came to his *father.*
— his *father* saw him, and had compassion,
21. *Father,* I have sinned against
22. But the *father* said to his servants,
27. and thy *father* hath killed the fatted
28. therefore came his *father* out,
29. said to (his) *father,* Lo, these many years
16:24. *Father* Abraham, have mercy on me,
27. I pray thee therefore, *father,* that thou
wouldest send him to my *father's* house:
30. And he said, Nay, *father* Abraham:
18:20. Honour thy *father* and thy
22:29. as my *Father* hath appointed unto me;
42. Saying, *Father,* if thou be willing,
23:34. *Father,* forgive them;
46. *Father,* into thy hands I commend
24:49. I send the promise of my *Father* upon
Joh. 1:14. as of the only begotten of the *Father,*
18. in the bosom of the *Father,* he
2:16. make not my *Father's* house an
3:35. The *Father* loveth the Son, and
4:12. greater than our *father* Jacob,
20. Our *fathers* worshipped in this
21. nor yet at Jerusalem, worship the *Father.*
23. shall worship the *Father* in spirit and in
truth: for the *Father* seeketh such
53. So the *father* knew that
5:17. My *Father* worketh hitherto,
18. said also that God was his *Father,*
19. but what he seeth the *Father* do:
20. For the *Father* loveth the Son,
21. For as the *Father* raiseth up
22. For the *Father* judgeth no man,
23. as they honour the *Father.*
— honoureth not the *Father*
26. For as the *Father* hath life
30. but the will of the *Father* which
36. which the *Father* hath given me
— that the *Father* hath sent me.
37. And the *Father* himself, which
43. I am come in my *Father's* name,
45. that I will accuse you to the *Father:*
6:27. for him hath God the *Father* sealed.
31. Our *fathers* did eat manna in
32. but my *Father* giveth you
37. All that the *Father* giveth
39. And this is the *Father's* will
42. whose *father* and mother we
44. except the *Father* which
45. hath learned of the *Father,*
46. that any man hath seen the *Father,*
— he hath seen the *Father.*
49. Your *fathers* did eat manna
57. the living *Father* . . . . by the *Father:*
58. not as your *fathers* did eat
65. given unto him of my *Father.*
7:22. of Moses, but of the *fathers;*
8:16. the *Father* that sent me.
18. the *Father* that sent me
19. Where is thy *Father?*
— know me, nor my *Father .*
— ye should have known my *Father* also.
27. he spake to them of the *Father.*
28. as my *Father* hath taught me,
29. the *Father* hath not left me alone;

Joh. 8:38. I have seen with my *Father:*
— which ye have seen with your *father.*
39. Abraham is our *father.*
41. Ye do the deeds of your *father.*
— we have one *Father,* (even) God.
42. If God were your *Father,*
44. Ye are of (your) *father* the devil, and the
lusts of your *father* ye will do.
— for he is a liar, and the *father* of it.
49. but I honour my *Father,*
53. greater than our *father* Abraham,
54. it is my *Father* that honoureth
56. Your *father* Abraham rejoiced
10:15. As the *Father* knoweth me, even so know
I the *Father:*
17. Therefore doth my *Father* love me,
18. have I received of my *Father.*
25. that I do in my *Father's* name, they
29. My *Father,* which gave (them) me,
— out of my *Father's* hand.
30. I and (my) *Father* are one.
32. I shewed you from my *Father;*
36. whom the *Father* hath sanctified,
37. the works of my *Father,* believe me not.
38. that the *Father* (is) in me, and I in him.
11:41. *Father,* I thank thee that thou hast
12:26. him will (my) *Father* honour.
27. *Father,* save me from this hour:
28. *Father,* glorify thy name.
49. but the *Father* which sent me,
50. even as the *Father* said unto me,
13: 1. this world unto the *Father,*
3. that the *Father* had given all things into
14: 2. In my *Father's* house are many
6. unto the *Father,* but by me.
7. have known my *Father* also:
8. Lord, shew us the *Father,* and it
9. hath seen the *Father;* and how sayest
thou (then), Shew us the *Father?*
10. that I am in the *Father,* and the *Father*
in me?
— but the *Father* that dwelleth in me,
11. that I (am) in the *Father,* and the *Father*
in me:
12. because I go unto my *Father.*
13. that the *Father* may be glorified
16. And I will pray the *Father,*
20. I (am) in my *Father,*
21. shall be loved of my *Father,*
23. and my *Father* will love him,
24. but the *Father's* which sent me.
26. whom the *Father* will send in my
28. because I said, I go unto the *Father:* for
my *Father* is greater than I.
31. that I love the *Father;* and as the *Father*
gave me commandment,
15: 1. and my *Father* is the husbandman.
8. Herein is my *Father* glorified,
9. As the *Father* hath loved me,
10. I have kept my *Father's*
15. that I have heard of my *Father*
16. ask of the *Father* in my
23. hateth my *Father* also.
24. hated both me and my *Father.*
26. send unto you from the *Father,*
— which proceedeth from the *Father,*
16: 3. not known the *Father,* nor me.
10. because I go to my *Father,*
15. All things that the *Father* hath
16. because I go to the *Father.*
17. Because I go to the *Father?*
23. ye shall ask the *Father* in my

Joh. 16:25. shew you plainly of the *Father*.
26. will pray the *Father* for you:
27. For the *Father* himself loveth
28. I came forth from the *Father*,
— and go to the *Father*.
32. because the *Father* is with me.
17: 1. *Father*, the hour is come ;
5. And now, O *Father*, glorify thou
11. Holy *Father*, keep through
21. as thou, *Father*, (art) in me,
24. *Father*, I will that they also,
25. O righteous *Father*, the world
18:11. the cup which my *Father* hath
20:17. not yet ascended to my *Father :*
— I ascend unto my *Father*, and your *Father ;*
21. as (my) *Father* hath sent me,
Acts 1: 4. the promise of the *Father*,
7. which the *Father* hath put in his
2:33. having received of the *Father*
3:13. the God of our *fathers*, hath glorified
22. Moses truly said unto the *fathers*,
25. which God made with our *fathers*,
5:30. The God of our *fathers* raised up
7: 2. Men, brethren, and *fathers*, hearken ;
— appeared unto our *father* Abraham,
4. when his *father* was dead,
11. and our *fathers* found no sustenance.
12. sent out our *fathers* first.
14. and called his *father* Jacob to (him),
15. he, and our *fathers*,
19. and evil entreated our *fathers*,
20. nourished up in his *father's* house
32. I (am) the God of thy *fathers*,
38. and (with) our *fathers :*
39. To whom our *fathers* would not
44. Our *fathers* had the tabernacle
45. Which also our *fathers* that came after
— before the face of our *fathers*,
51. as your *fathers* (did), so (do) ye.
52. have not your *fathers* persecuted ?
13:17. chose our *fathers*, and exalted the people
32. promise which was made unto the *fathers*,
36. and was laid unto his *fathers*,
15:10. which neither our *fathers* nor we
16: 1. but his *father* (was) a Greek:
3. that his *father* was a Greek.
22: 1. Men, brethren, and *fathers*, hear ye
14. The God of our *fathers* hath chosen
26: 6. made of God unto our *fathers:*
28: 8. that the *father* of Publius lay sick
25. the prophet unto our *fathers*,
Ro. 1: 7. from God our *Father*,
4: 1. our *father* as pertaining to the flesh,
11. the *father* of all them that believe,
12. And the *father* of circumcision
— faith of our *father* Abraham,
16. who is the *father* of us all,
17. I have made thee a *father* of many
18. become the *father* of many nations,
6: 4. by the glory of the *Father*,
8:15. we cry, Abba, *Father*.
9: 5. Whose (are) the *fathers*, and of whom
10. (even) by our *father* Isaac ;
11:28. beloved for the *fathers'* sakes.
15: 6. God, even the *Father* of our Lord
8. promises (made) unto the *fathers :*
1Co. 1: 3. and peace, from God our *Father*,
4:15. yet (have ye) not many *fathers :*
5: 1. one should have his *father's* wife.
8: 6. one God, the *Father*, of whom (are)
10: 1. all our *fathers* were under the cloud,
15:24. the kingdom to God, even the *Father ;*

2Co. 1: 2. from God our *Father*, and (from)
3. even the *Father* of our Lord
— the *Father* of mercies, and the God of
6:18. And will be a *Father* unto you,
11:31. The God and *Father* of our Lord Jesus Christ,
Gal. 1: 1. and God the *Father*, who raised
3. peace from God the *Father*, and (from)
4. the will of God and our *Father:*
4: 2. the time appointed of the *father*.
6. your hearts, crying, Abba, *Father*.
Eph. 1: 2. from God our *Father*,
3. the God and *Father* of our Lord
17. the *Father* of glory, may give
2:18. by one Spirit unto the *Father*.
3:14. my knees unto the *Father* of our Lord
4: 6. One God and *Father* of all,
5:20. unto God and the *Father*
31. leave his *father* and mother,
6: 2. Honour thy *father* and mother ;
4. And, ye *fathers*, provoke not
23. from God the *Father* and the Lord
Phi. 1: 2. from God our *Father*, and (from) the
2:11. to the glory of God the *Father*.
22. as a son with the *father*, he hath served
4:20. unto God and our *Father* (be) glory
Col. 1: 2. from God our *Father*
3. to God and the *Father* of our Lord Jesus
12. Giving thanks unto the *Father*,
2: 2. and of the *Father*, and of Christ ;
3:17. to God and the *Father* by him.
21. *Fathers*, provoke not your children
1Th. 1: 1. in God the *Father* and (in) the Lord
— from God our *Father*, and the Lord Jesus Christ.
3. in the sight of God and our *Father ;*
2:11. as a *father* (doth) his children,
3:11. Now God himself and our *Father*,
13. before God, even our *Father*,
2Th. 1: 1. in God our *Father* and the Lord
2. from God our *Father* and the Lord
2:16. and God, even our *Father*, which
1Ti. 1: 2. from God our *Father* and Jesus Christ
5: 1. but intreat (him) as a *father ;*
2Ti. 1: 2. from God the *Father* and Christ Jesus our Lord.
Tit. 1: 4. from God the *Father* and the Lord Jesus
Philem. 3. from God our *Father* and the Lord Jesus
Heb 1: 1. spake in time past unto the *fathers*
5. I will be to him a *Father*,
3: 9. When your *fathers* tempted me,
7:10. in the loins of his *father*,
8: 9. that I made with their *fathers* in the day
11:23. was hid three months of his *parents*,
12: 7. what son is he whom the *father*
9. Furthermore we have had *fathers*
— unto the *Father* of spirits, and live ?
Jas. 1:17. from the *Father* of lights,
27. before God and the *Father*
2:21. Was not Abraham our *father* justified
3: 9. bless we God, even the *Father ;*
1Pet. 1: 2. the foreknowledge of God the *Father*,
3. Blessed (be) the God and *Father* of our
17. And if ye call on the *Father*,
2Pet. 1:17. For he received from God the *Father*
3: 4. since the *fathers* fell asleep, all things
1Joh. 1: 2. life, which was with the *Father*,
3. with the *Father*, and with his Son Jesus
2: 1. an advocate with the *Father*, Jesus
13. I write unto you, *fathers*,
— ye have known the *Father*.
14. I have written unto you, *fathers*,

1Joh. 2:15. the love of the *Father* is not in him.
    16. is not of the *Father*, but is of the world.
    22. that denieth the *Father* and the Son.
    23. the same hath not the *Father:*
    24. continue in the Son, and in the *Father.*
    3: 1. love the *Father* hath bestowed
    4:14. that the *Father* sent the Son
    5: 7. the *Father*, the Word, and the Holy
        Ghost:
2Joh. 3. from God the *Father*, and from the Lord
    — the Son of the *Father*, in truth and love.
    4. received a commandment from the *Father.*
    9. hath both the *Father* and the Son.
Jude 1. sanctified by God the *Father*,
Rev. 1: 6. priests unto God and his *Father;*
    2:27. as I received of my *Father.*
    3: 5. before my *Father*, and before his angels.
    21. set down with my *Father* in his throne.
    14: 1. having his *Father's* name written

πατραλώψης, *patraloees.*

1Ti. 1: 9. for *murderers of fathers* and

πατριά, *patria.*

Lu. 2: 4. of the house and *lineage* of David:
Acts 3:25. in thy seed shall all the *kindreds* of the
Eph. 3:15. Of whom the whole *family* in heaven and

πατριάρχης, *patriarkees.*

Acts 2:29. speak unto you of the *patriarch* David,
    7: 8. Jacob (begat) the twelve *patriarchs.*
    9. the *patriarchs*, moved with envy, sold
Heb 7: 4. the *patriarch* Abraham gave

πατρικός, *patrikos.*

Gal. 1:14. zealous of the traditions *of my fathers.*

πατρίς, *patris.*

Mat.13:54. he was come into his *own country*,
    57. save in his *own country*,
Mar 6: 1. and came into his *own country;*
    4. without honour, but in his *own country*,
Lu. 4:23. do also here in thy *country.*
    24. accepted in his *own country.*
Joh. 4:44. hath no honour in his own *country.*
Heb 11:14. that they seek a *country.*

πατροπαράδοτος, *patroparadotos.*

1Pet. 1:18. conversation (received) by *tradition from
    your fathers;*

πατρῷος, *patroos.*

Acts 22: 3. manner of the law *of the fathers*,
    24:14. so worship I the God *of my fathers*,
    28:17. against the people, or customs *of our
    fathers*,

παύομαι, *pauomai.*

Lu. 5: 4. Now when he *had left* speaking,
    8:24. and they *ceased*, and there was a calm.
    11: 1. when he *ceased*, one of his disciples said
Acts 5:42. they *ceased* not to teach and preach
    6:13. This man *ceaseth* not to speak blasphemous
    13:10. *wilt* thou not *cease* to pervert
    20: 1. And after the uproar *was ceased*,
    31. I *ceased* not to warn every one
    21:32. they *left* beating of Paul.
1Co.13: 8. whether (there be) tongues, they *shall
    cease;*
Eph. 1:16. *Cease* not to give thanks for you,
Col. 1: 9. *do* not *cease* to pray for you,
Heb 10: 2. would they not *have ceased* to be offered ?
1Pet. 3:10. *let* him *refrain* his tongue from evil,
    4: 1. suffered in the flesh *hath ceased* from sin ;

παχύνομαι, *pakunomai.*

Mat.13:15. For this people's heart *is waxed gross*,
Acts 28:27. For the heart of this people *is waxed gross*,

πέδη, *pedee.*

Mar 5: 4. often bound with *fetters* and chains,
    — and the *fetters* broken in pieces:
Lu. 8:29. bound with chains and in *fetters;*

πεδινός, *pedinos.*

Lu. 6:17. and stood in the *plain*,

πεζεύω, *pezuo.*

Acts 20:13. minding himself *to go afoot.*

πεζῇ, *pezee.*

Mat.14:13. followed him *on foot* out of the cities.
Mar 6:33. and ran *afoot* thither out of all

πειθαρχέω, *pitharkeo.*

Acts 5:29. We ought *to obey* God rather than
    32. hath given to them *that obey* him.
    27:21. ye should *have hearkened* unto me, *and*
Tit. 3: 1. *to obey magistrates*, to be ready to

πειθός, *pithos.*

1Co. 2: 4. not with *enticing* words of man's wisdom,

πείθω πέποιθα, *pitho, pepoitha.*

Mat.27:20. priests and elders *persuaded* the multitude
    43. He *trusted* in God ; let him deliver
    28:14. we *will persuade* him, and secure you.
Mar 10:24. for them *that trust* in riches to
Lu. 11:22. his armour wherein he *trusted*,
    16:31. neither *will* they *be persuaded*,
    18: 9. certain *which trusted* in themselves
    20: 6. for they *be persuaded* that John

Acts 5:36. and all, as many as *obeyed* him,
     37. and all, (even) as many as *obeyed* him,
     40. And to him they *agreed :*
  12:20. and, *having made* Blastus...their *friend,*
  13:43. *persuaded* them to continue
  14:19. who *persuaded* the people, and, having
  17: 4. And some of them *believed,*
  18: 4. and *persuaded* the Jews and the
  19: 8. and *persuading* the things concerning
     26. this Paul *hath persuaded and* turned
  21:14. And *when* he *would* not *be persuaded,*
  23:21. *do* not thou *yield* unto them:
  26:26. for I *am persuaded* that none
     28. Almost thou *persuadest* me to be
  27:11. the centurion *believed* the master
  28:23. *persuading* them concerning Jesus,
     24. And some *believed* the things which
Ro. 2: 8. but *obey* unrighteousness,
     19. And *art confident* that thou thyself
  8:38. For I *am persuaded,* that neither
  14:14. and *am persuaded* by the Lord Jesus,
  15:14. also *am persuaded* of you, my brethren,
2Co. 1: 9. that we should not *trust* in ourselves,
  2: 3. *having confidence* in you all,
  5:11. we *persuade* men ; but we are made
  10: 7. If any man *trust* to himself that
Gal. 1:10. For *do* I now *persuade* men, or God?
  3: 1. that ye should not *obey* the truth,
  5: 7. that ye should not *obey* the truth?
  10. I *have confidence* in you through the Lord,
Phi. 1: 6. *Being confident* of this very thing,
  14. *waxing confident* by my bonds,
  25. And *having* this *confidence,* I know
  2:24. But I *trust* in the Lord that I
  3: 3. and *have* no *confidence* in the flesh.
  4. thinketh that he hath whereof he might
     trust (lit. thinketh *to trust*)
2Th. 3: 4. we *have confidence* in the Lord
2Ti. 1: 5. and I *am persuaded* that in thee also.
  12. and *am persuaded* that he is able
Philem 21. *Having confidence* in thy obedience
Heb 2:13. I will put my trust (lit. I will be *having
    trusted*) in him.
  6: 9. we *are persuaded* better things of you,
  11:13. and *were persuaded* of (them), and
  13:17. *Obey* them that have the rule over you,
  18. for we *trust* we have a good conscience,
Jas. 3: 3. that they may *obey* us ;
1Joh.3:19. and *shall assure* our hearts before him.

πεινάω, *pīnao.*

Mat. 4: 2. he *was* afterward *an hungred.*
  5: 6. Blessed (are) they *which do hunger,*
  12: 1. his disciples *were an hungred,*
  3. when he *was an hungred,*
  21:18. into the city, he *hungered.*
  25:35. I *was an hungred,* and ye gave me
  37. when saw we thee *an hungred,*
  42. For I *was an hungred,* and ye
  44. when saw we thee *an hungred,*
Mar 2:25. he had need, and *was an hungred,*
  11:12. come from Bethany, he *was hungry:*
Lu. 1:53. He hath filled the *hungry* with
  4: 2. he afterward *hungered.*
  6: 3. when himself *was an hungred,*
  21. Blessed (are ye) *that hunger* now:
  25. that are full! for ye *shall hunger.*
Joh. 6:35. *shall* never *hunger ;* and he that
Ro. 12:20. Therefore if thine enemy *hunger,*
1Co. 4:11. we both *hunger,* and thirst, and

1Co.11:21. one *is hungry,* and another
  34. And if any man *hunger,*
Phi. 4:12. to be full and *to be hungry,*
Rev. 7:16. They *shall hunger* no more,

πεῖρα, *pīra.*

Heb 11:29. which the Egyptians *assaying* to do (lit.
    of which the Egyptians taking the *trial*)
  36. had *trial* of (cruel) mockings and

πειράζω, *pīrazo.*

Mat. 4: 1. wilderness *to be tempted* of the devil.
  3. And when the *tempter* came to him,
  16: 1. and *tempting* desired him that he
  19: 3. came unto him, *tempting* him,
  22:18. Why *tempt* ye me, (ye) hypocrites?
  35. *tempting* him, and saying,
Mar 1:13. forty days, *tempted* of Satan ;
  8:11. a sign from heaven, *tempting* him.
  10: 2. to put away (his) wife? *tempting* him.
  12:15. Why *tempt* ye me? bring me
Lu. 4: 2. *Being* forty days *tempted* of the devil.
  11:16. And others, *tempting* (him), sought of
  20:23. said unto them, Why *tempt* ye me?
Joh. 6: 6. And this he said to *prove* him:
  8: 6. This they said, *tempting* him,
Acts 5: 9. agreed together *to tempt* the Spirit of
  15:10. Now therefore why *tempt* ye God,
  16: 7. they *assayed* to go into Bithynia:
  24: 6. † Who also *hath gone about* to profane
1Co. 7: 5. that Satan *tempt* you not for
  10: 9. † as some of them also *tempted,*
  13. will not suffer you *to be tempted* above
2Co.13: 5. *Examine* yourselves, whether ye be in
Gal. 6: 1. lest thou also *be tempted.*
1Th. 3: 5. † lest by some means the *tempter have
    tempted* you,
Heb 2:18. hath suffered *being tempted,* he is able to
    succour them *that are tempted.*
  3: 9. † When your fathers *tempted* me,
  4:15. but *was* in all points *tempted* like as
  11:17. *when* he *was tried,* offered up Isaac:
  37. sawn asunder, *were tempted,*
Jas. 1:13. say *when* he *is tempted,* I *am tempted* of
    God:
  — neither *tempteth* he any man:
  14. But every man *is tempted,* when
Rev. 2: 2. † and thou *hast tried* them which say
  10. into prison, that ye *may be tried ;*
  3:10. *to try* them that dwell upon the earth.

Note.—" Those marked † may be formed also from
  πειράω."—*Schmid.*

πειρασμός, *pīrasmos.*

Mat. 6:13. And lead us not into *temptation,*
  26:41. that ye enter not into *temptation :*
Mar 14:38. lest ye enter into *temptation.*
Lu. 4:13. the devil had ended all the *temptation,*
  8:13. and in time of *temptation* fall away.
  11: 4. lead us not into *temptation ;*
  22:28. continued with me in my *temptations.*
  40. that ye enter not into *temptation.*
  46. lest ye enter into *temptation.*
Acts 20:19. and *temptations,* which befell me by
1Co.10:13. There hath no *temptation* taken you

1Co.10:13. will with the *temptation* also make
Gal. 4:14. And my *temptation* which was in my
1Ti. 6: 9. fall into *temptation* and a snare,
Heb 3: 8. in the day of *temptation* in the wilderness:
Jas. 1: 2. when ye fall into divers *temptations;*
    12. Blessed (is) the man that endureth *temptation:*
1Pet.1: 6. heaviness through manifold *temptations:*
  4:12. the fiery trial which is to try you, (lit. the fiery proof for *trial* to you)
2Pet.2: 9. deliver the godly out of *temptations,* [sing.]
Rev. 3:10. from the hour of *temptation,* which

πειράω, *pīrao.*

Acts 9:26. he *assayed* to join himself to the
  26:21. and *went about* to kill (me).

See also those in πειράζω which have the mark †
  affixed.

πεισμονή, *pīsmonee.*

Gal. 5: 8. This *persuasion* (cometh) not of him

πέλαγος, *pelagos.*

Mat.18: 6. drowned in the *depth* of the sea.
Acts27: 5. sailed over the *sea* of Cilicia

πελεκίζομαι, *pelekizomai.*

Rev.20: 4. the souls of them *that were beheaded*

πέμπτος, *pemptos.*

Rev. 6: 9. when he had opened the *fifth* seal,
  9: 1. And the *fifth* angel sounded,
  16:10. the *fifth* angel poured out his vial
  21:20. The *fifth,* sardonyx;

πέμπω, *pempo.*

Mat. 2: 8. And he *sent* them to Bethlehem, *and*
  11: 2. he *sent* two of his disciples,
  14:10. he *sent, and* beheaded John
  22: 7. he *sent* forth his armies, *and* destroyed
Mar 5:12. *Send* us into the swine,
Lu. 4:26. *was* Elias *sent,* save unto Sarepta,
  7: 6. the centurion *sent* friends to him,
  10. And they *that were sent,* returning
  19. *sent* (them) to Jesus, saying,
  15:15. and he *sent* him into his fields
  16:24. and *send* Lazarus, that he may
  27. that thou *wouldest send* him to
  20:11. again he sent (lit. added *to send*) another servant:
  12. And again he sent (lit. he added *to send*) a third:
  13. I *will send* my beloved son:
Joh. 1:22. give an answer to them *that sent* us.
  33. but he *that sent* me to baptize
  4:34. the will of him *that sent* me,
  5:23. the Father *which hath sent* him.
  24. on him *that sent* me,
  30. of the Father *which hath sent* me.
  37. the Father himself, *which hath sent* me,
  6:38. the will of him *that sent* me.

Joh. 6:39. the Father's will *which hath sent* me,
  40. the will of him *that sent* me,
  44. the Father *which hath sent* me
  7:16. but his *that sent* me.
  18. his glory *that sent* him,
  28. but he *that sent* me is true,
  33. I go unto him *that sent* me.
  8:16. but I and the Father *that sent* me.
  18. and the Father *that sent* me beareth
  26. but he *that sent* me is true;
  29. And he *that sent* me is with me:
  9: 4. the works of him *that sent* me,
  12:44. on him *that sent* me.
  45. seeth him *that sent* me.
  49. but the Father *which sent* me,
  13:16. greater than he *that sent* him.
  20. whomsoever I *send* receiveth me;
  — receiveth him *that sent* me.
  14:24. but the Father's *which sent* me.
  26. whom the Father *will send* in my name,
  15:21. they know not him *that sent* me.
  26. whom I *will send* unto you from
  16: 5. I go my way to him *that sent* me;
  7. I *will send* him unto you.
  20:21. even so *send* I you.
Acts10: 5. now *send* men to Joppa,
  32. *Send* therefore to Joppa, and
  33. therefore I *sent* to thee;
  11:29. determined *to send* relief unto
  15:22. *to send* chosen men of their own
  25. *to send* chosen men unto you
  19:31. *sent* unto him, desiring (him)
  20:17. he *sent* to Ephesus, *and* called
  23:30. I *sent* straightway to thee,
  25:21. till I *might send* him to Cæsar.
  25. I have determined *to send* him.
  27. *to send* a prisoner, *and* not withal
Ro. 8: 3. God *sending* his own Son
1Co. 4:17. *have I sent* unto you Timotheus,
  16: 3. them *will I send* to bring your
2Co. 9: 3. Yet *have I sent* the brethren, lest
Eph. 6:22. Whom I *have sent* unto you
Phi. 2:19. *to send* Timotheus shortly
  23. I hope *to send* presently,
  25. necessary *to send* to you Epaphroditus,
  28. I *sent* him therefore
  4:16. ye *sent* once and again
Col. 4: 8. Whom I *have sent* unto you
1Th. 3: 2. And *sent* Timotheus, our brother,
  5. I *sent* to know your faith,
2Th. 2:11. God *shall send* them strong delusion,
Tit. 3:12. When I *shall send* Artemas
1Pet.2:14. as unto them *that are sent* by him
Rev. 1:11. and *send* (it) unto the seven churches
  11:10. and *shall send* gifts one to another;
  14:15. *Thrust in* thy sickle, and reap:
  18. *Thrust in* thy sharp sickle,
  22:16. I Jesus *have sent* mine angel

πένης, *penees.*

2Co. 9: 9. he hath given to the *poor:*

πενθερά, *penthera.*

Mat. 8:14. he saw his *wife's mother* laid, and
  10:35. against her *mother in law.*
Mar 1:30. Simon's *wife's mother* lay sick
Lu. 4:38. And Simon's *wife's mother* was taken with
  12:53. the *mother in law* against her
  — against her *mother in law.*

πενθερός, pentheros.

Joh. 18:13. for he was *father in law* to Caiaphas,

πενθέω, pentheo.

Mat. 5: 4. Blessed (are) they *that mourn:*
9:15. Can the children of the bridechamber *mourn,*
Mar 16:10. *as* they *mourned* and wept.
Lu. 6:25. for ye *shall mourn* and weep.
1Co. 5: 2. and *have* not rather *mourned,*
2Co.12:21. and (that) I *shall bewail* many
Jas. 4: 9. and *mourn,* and weep; let
Rev.18:11. shall weep and *mourn* over her;
15. weeping and *wailing,*
19. and cried, weeping and *wailing,*

πένθος, penthos.

Jas. 4: 9. laughter be turned to *mourning,*
Rev.18: 7. so much torment and *sorrow* give her:
— and shall see no *sorrow.*
8. death, and *mourning,* and famine;
21: 4. neither *sorrow,* nor crying,

πενιχρός, penikros.

Lu. 21: 2. a certain *poor* widow casting in

πεντάκις, pentakis.

2Co.11:24. *five times* received I forty (stripes) save one.

πεντακισχίλιοι, pentakiskilioi.

Mat.14:21. were about *five thousand* men,
16: 9. the five loaves of the *five thousand,*
Mar 6:44. were about *five thousand* men.
8:19. the five loaves among *five thousand,*
Lu. 9:14. they were about *five thousand* men.
Joh. 6:10. in number about *five thousand.*

πεντακόσιοι, pentakosioi.

Lu. 7:41. the one owed *five hundred* pence,
1Co.15: 6. seen of above *five hundred* brethren

πέντε, pente.

Mat.14:17. but *five* loaves, and two fishes.
19. and took the *five* loaves,
16: 9. neither remember the *five* loaves
25: 2. And *five* of them were wise, and *five* (were) foolish.
15. unto one he gave *five* talents,
16. he that had received *five* talents
— and made (them) other *five* talents.
20. And so he that had received *five* talents came and brought other *five*
— thou deliveredst unto me *five* talents:
— beside them *five* talents more.
Mar 6:38. they say, *Five,* and two fishes.
41. when he had taken the *five* loaves
8:19. When I brake the *five* loaves

Lu. 1:24. and hid herself *five* months,
9:13. no more but *five* loaves
16. he took the *five* loaves
12: 6. Are not *five* sparrows sold
52. there shall be *five* in one house
14:19. I have bought *five* yoke of oxen,
16:28. For I have *five* brethren;
19:18. thy pound hath gained *five* pounds.
19. Be thou also over *five* cities.
Joh. 4:18. For thou hast had *five* husbands;
5: 2. Bethesda, having *five* porches.
6: 9. which hath *five* barley loaves,
13. of the *five* barley loaves,
19. had rowed about *five* and twenty
Acts 4: 4. of the men was about *five* thousand.
7:14. his kindred, threescore and fifteen (lit. seventy *five*) souls
19:19. and found (it) fifty thousand (pieces) (lit. *five* ten thousands) of silver.
20: 6. came unto them to Troas in *five* days;
24: 1. And after *five* days
1Co.14:19. I had rather speak *five* words
Rev. 9: 5. be tormented *five* months:
10. to hurt men *five* months.
17:10. *five* are fallen, and one is,

πεντεκαιδέκατος, pentekaidekatos.

Lu. 3: 1. Now in the *fifteenth* year

πεντήκοντα, penteekonta.

Mar 6:40. by hundreds, and by *fifties.*
Lu. 7:41. and the other *fifty.*
9:14. by *fifties* in a company.
16: 6. quickly, and write *fifty.*
Joh. 8:57. Thou art not yet *fifty* years old,
21:11. an hundred and *fifty* and three:
Acts13:20. four hundred and *fifty* years,

πεντηκοστή, penteekostee.

Acts 2: 1. And when the day of *Pentecost*
20:16. at Jerusalem the day of *Pentecost.*
1Co.16: 8. at Ephesus until *Pentecost.*

πέποιθα see πείθω.

πεποίθησις, pepoitheesis.

2Co. 1:15. And in this *confidence* I was minded
3: 4. And such *trust* have we
8:22. the great *confidence* which (I have) in
10: 2. with that *confidence,* wherewith
Eph. 3:12. access with *confidence* by the faith
Phi. 3: 4. might also have *confidence* in the flesh.

πέρ, per.

Mar15: 6. whomsoever they desired.
Heb 3: 6. if)(we hold fast the confidence
14. if)(we hold the beginning of our
6: 3. if)(God permit.

See the compound forms of this word in εἴπερ, ἔπειπερ, ἐπειδήπερ, ἤπερ, καθάπερ, καίπερ, ὥσπερ. Its force is perhaps limitation, e. g. ἐάνπερ, that is to say if.

πέραν, peran.

Mat. 4:15. the way of the sea, *beyond* Jordan,
25. and (from) *beyond* Jordan.
8:18. commandment to depart unto the *other side.*
28. when he was come to the *other side*
14:22. before him unto the *other side,*
16: 5. disciples were come to the *other side,*
19: 1. coasts of Judæa *beyond* Jordan;
Mar 3: 8. and (from) *beyond* Jordan;
4:35. pass over unto the *other side.*
5: 1. unto the *other side* of the sea,
21. by ship unto the *other side,*
6:45. to go to the *other side* before
8:13. departed to the *other side.*
10: 1. by the *farther side* of Jordan:
Lu. 8:22. unto the *other side* of the lake.
Joh. 1:28. in Bethabara *beyond* Jordan,
3:26. he that was with thee *beyond* Jordan,
6: 1. went *over* the sea of Galilee,
17. went *over* the sea toward Capernaum.
22. stood *on the other side* of the sea
25. found him *on the other side* of the sea,
10:40. went away again *beyond* Jordan
18: 1. *over* the brook Cedron,

πέρας, peras.

Mat.12:42. from the *uttermost parts* of the earth
Lu. 11:31. from the *utmost parts* of the earth
Ro. 10:18. their words unto the *ends* of the world.
Heb 6:16. (is) to them an *end* of all strife.

περί, peri.

Governs a genitive and an accusative. ᵃ denotes the latter.

Mat. 2: 8. search diligently *for* the young child;
3: 4. girdle *about*ᵃ his loins;
4: 6. his angels charge *concerning* thee:
6:28. why take ye thought *for* raiment?
8:18. great multitudes *about*ᵃ him,
9:36. moved with compassion *on* them,
11: 7. unto the multitudes *concerning* John,
10. is (he), *of* whom it is written,
12:36. shall give account there*of*
15: 7. did Esaias prophesy *of* you,
16:11. spake (it) not to you *concerning* bread,
17:13. spake unto them *of* John the
18:19. agree on earth *as touching* any thing
20: 3. went out *about*ᵃ the third hour,
5. *about*ᵃ the sixth and ninth hour,
6. And *about*ᵃ the eleventh hour
9. (hired) *about*ᵃ the eleventh hour,
24. indignation *against* the two brethren.
21:45. perceived that he spake *of* them.
22:16. neither carest thou *for* any (man):
31. But *as touching* the resurrection of
42. What think ye *of* Christ?
24:36. But *of* that day and hour knoweth
26:24. as it is written *of* him:
28. which is shed *for* many
27:46. And *about*ᵃ the ninth hour
Mar 1: 6. girdle of a skin *about*ᵃ his loins;
30. they tell him *of* her.
44. offer *for* thy cleansing
3: 8. and they *about*ᵃ Tyre and Sidon,
32. And the multitude sat *about*ᵃ him,

Mar 3:34. on them which sat *about*ᵃ him,
4:10. they that were *about*ᵃ him
19. and the lusts *of*ᵃ other things
5:16. and (also) *concerning* the swine.
27. When she had heard *of* Jesus,
6:48. and *about*ᵃ the fourth watch of the night
7: 6. prophesied *of* you hypocrites,
17. asked him *concerning* the parable.
25. heard *of* him, and came and fell
8:30. tell no man *of* him.
9:14. a great multitude *about*ᵃ them,
42. were hanged *about*ᵃ his neck,
10:10. asked him again *of* the same (matter).
41. much displeased *with* James and John.
12:14. and carest *for* no man:
26. And *as touching* the dead, that they
13:32. But *of* that day and (that) hour knoweth
14:21. as it is written *of* him:
24. which is shed *for* many.
Lu. 1: 1. a declaration *of* those things which are
4. where*in* thou hast been instructed.
2:17. they made known abroad)(the saying
— told them *concerning* this child.
18. wondered *at* those things which were
27. to do *for* him after the custom
33. things which were spoken *of* him.
38. spake *of* him to all them
3:15. mused in their hearts *of* John,
19. reproved by him *for* Herodias
— and *for* all the evils which Herod
4:10. angels charge *over* thee,
14. fame *of* him through all the region
37. the fame *of* him went out into every
38. besought him *for* her.
5:14. offer *for* thy cleansing,
15. a fame abroad *of* him:
7: 3. when he heard *of* Jesus, he sent
17. And this rumour *of* him went forth
18. shewed him *of* all these things.
24. unto the people *concerning* John,
27. *of* whom it is written,
9: 9. *of* whom I hear such things?
11. spake unto them *of* the kingdom of God,
45. to ask him *of* that saying.
10:40. was cumbered *about*ᵃ much serving,
41. and troubled *about*ᵃ many things:
11:53. provoke him to speak *of* many things:
12:26. why take ye thought *for* the rest?
13: 1. told him *of* the Galilæans,
8. till I shall dig *about*ᵃ it,
16: 2. How is it that I hear this *of* thee?
17: 2. hanged *about*ᵃ his neck,
19:37. *for* all the mighty works that
21: 5. And as some spake *of* the temple,
22:32. I have prayed *for* thee,
37. the things *concerning* me have an end.
49. When they which were *about*ᵃ him
23: 8. he had heard many things *of* him;
24: 4. as they were much perplexed there*about,*
14. talked together *of* all these things
19. *Concerning* Jesus of Nazareth,
27. the things *concerning* himself.
44. and (in) the psalms, *concerning* me.
Joh. 1: 7. to bear witness *of* the Light,
8. to bear witness *of* that Light.
15. bare witness *of* him,
22. What sayest thou *of* thyself?
30. This is he *of* whom I said,
47(48). and saith *of* him, Behold an Israelite
2:21. he spake *of* the temple of his body.
25. should testify *of* man: for he knew
3:25. and the Jews *about* purifying.

Joh. 5:31. If I bear witness *of* myself,
32. another that beareth witness *of* me ;
— which he witnesseth *of* me
36. bear witness *of* me,
37. hath borne witness *of* me.
39. which testify *of* me.
46. for he wrote *of* me.
6:41. The Jews then murmured *at* him,
61. disciples murmured *at* it,
7: 7. I testify *of* it, that the works
12. murmuring among the people *concerning* him:
13. no man spake openly *of* him
17. he shall know *of* the doctrine,
32. murmured such things *concerning* him;
39. this spake he *of* the Spirit,
8:13. Thou bearest record *of* thyself ;
14. Though I bear record *of* myself,
18. I am one that bear witness *of* myself,
— that sent me beareth witness *of* me.
26. to say and to judge *of* you:
46. convinceth me *of* sin?
9:17. What sayest thou *of* him,
18. believe *concerning* him, that he had
21. he shall speak *for* (lit. *about*) himself.
10:13. and careth not *for* the sheep.
25. they bear witness *of* me.
33. *For* a good work we stone thee not; but *for* blasphemy ;
41. that John spake *of* this man
11:13. Jesus spake *of* his death:
— spoken *of* taking of rest in sleep.
19. came to Martha and Mary, (lit. to those *around*ᵃ Martha and Mary)
— *concerning* their brother.
12: 6. not that he cared *for* the poor ;
41. and spake *of* him.
13:18. I speak not *of* you all:
22. doubting *of* whom he spake.
24. who it should be *of* whom he spake.
15:22. no cloke *for* their sin.
26. he shall testify *of* me:
16: 8. he will reprove the world *of* sin, and *of* righteousness, and *of* judgment:
9. *Of* sin, because they believe not
10. *Of* righteousness, because I go
11. *Of* judgment, because the prince
19. enquire among yourselves *of* that I said,
25. I shall shew you plainly *of* the Father.
26. pray the Father *for* you:
17: 9. I pray *for* them: I pray not *for* the world, but *for* them which thou hast given me ;
20. Neither pray I *for* these alone, but *for* them also which shall
18:19. asked Jesus *of* his disciples, and *of* his doctrine.
23. bear witness *of* the evil:
34. did others tell it thee *of* me ?
19:24. but cast lots *for* it, whose
21:24. which testifieth *of* these things,
Acts 1: 1. have I made, O Theophilus, *of* all that
3. the things *pertaining to* the kingdom
16. *concerning* Judas, which was guide
2:29. unto you *of* the patriarch David,
31. spake *of* the resurrection of Christ,
5:24. they doubted *of* them
7:52. shewed before *of* the coming of the
8:12. things *concerning* the kingdom of God,
15. prayed *for* them, that they
34. *of* whom speaketh the prophet this? *of* himself, or *of* some other
9:13. heard by many *of* this man, how

Acts 10: 9. *about*ᵃ the sixth hour:
19. thought *on* the vision,
11:22. Then tidings *of* these things came
13:13. when Paul and his company (lit. when they *about*ᵃ Paul)
29. all that was written *of* him,
15: 2. apostles and elders *about* this question.
6. to consider *of* this matter.
17:32. hear thee again *of* this (matter).
18:15. a question *of* words and names,
25. diligently the things *of* the Lord,
19: 8. the things *concerning* the kingdom
23. no small stir *about* that way.
25. the workmen of like occupation, (lit. the workmen *about*ᵃ such things)
39. enquire any thing *concerning* other
40. *for* this day's uproar, there being no cause where*by* we may give
21: 8. we that were of Paul's company (lit. those *about*ᵃ Paul)
21. And they are informed *of* thee,
24. informed *concerning* thee,
25. *As touching* the Gentiles which believe,
22: 6. *about*ᵃ noon, suddenly there shone
— light round *about*ᵃ me.
10. told thee *of* all things which are
18. thy testimony *concerning* me.
23: 6. *of* the hope and resurrection of the dead
11. as thou hast testified *of* me in Jerusalem,
15. more perfectly *concerning* him:
20. enquire somewhat *of* him more
29. accused *of* questions of their law,
24: 8. take knowledge *of* all these things,
10. cheerfully answer *for* myself:
13. the things where*of* they now accuse
21. Except it be *for* this one voice,
— *Touching* the resurrection of the dead
22. having more perfect knowledge *of* (that) way,
24. *concerning* the faith in Christ.
25. reasoned *of* righteousness, temperance,
25: 9. and there be judged *of* these things
15. *About* whom, when I was at
16. *concerning* the crime laid against him.
18. *Against* whom when the accusers
19. questions against him *of* their own superstition, and *of* one Jesus,
20. I doubted *of* such manner of questions, (lit. as to the question *about* this)
— and there be judged *of* these matters.
24. *about* whom all the multitude
26. *Of* whom I have no certain thing to
26: 2. *touching* all the things whereof
7. *For* which hope's *sake*, king Agrippa,
26. knoweth *of* these things,
28: 7. In the same quarters were (lit. in the (quarters) *about*ᵃ the place)
15. the brethren heard *of* us, they came
21. letters out of Judæa *concerning* thee,
— or spake any harm *of* thee.
22. *as concerning* this sect, we know
23. persuading them *concerning* Jesus,
31. those things *which concern* the Lord Jesus
Ro. 1: 3. *Concerning* his Son Jesus Christ
8: 3. likeness of sinful flesh, and *for* sin,
*14:12. shall give account *of* himself to God.
15:14. am persuaded *of* you, my brethren,
21. To whom he was not spoken of, (lit. to whom it was not announced *concerning* him)
1 Co. 1: 4. I thank my God always *on* your *behalf,*
11. declared unto me *of* you,

1Co. 7: 1. where *of* ye wrote unto me:
25. Now *concerning* virgins I have
37. but hath power *over* his own will,
8: 1. *as touching* things offered unto idols,
4. *As concerning* therefore the eating
12: 1. Now *concerning* spiritual (gifts),
16: 1. *concerning* the collection for the saints,
12. *As touching* (our) brother Apollos,
2Co. 9: 1. *as touching* the ministering
10: 8. boast somewhat more *of* our authority,
Eph. 6:18. and supplication *for* all saints ;
22. ye might know our affairs, (lit. the things *concerning* us)
Phi. 1:27. I may hear of your affairs, (lit. the things *concerning* you)
2:19. when I know your state. (lit. the things *concerning* you)
20. care for your state. (lit. the things *concerning* you)
23. I shall see how it will go with me. (lit. the things *about*ᵃ me)
Col. 1: 3. praying always *for* you,
2: 1. great conflict I have *for* you,
4: 3. praying also *for* us,
8. he might know your estate, (lit. the things *concerning* you)
10. *touching* whom ye received
1Th. 1: 2. to God always *for* you all,
9. themselves shew *of* us
3: 2. comfort you *concerning* your faith:
9. render to God again *for* you,
4: 6. the avenger *of* all such,
9. *as touching* brotherly love
13. *concerning* them which are asleep,
5: 1. But *of* the times and the seasons,
25. Brethren, pray *for* us.
2Th. 1: 3. thank God always *for* you,
11. pray always *for* you,
2:13. thanks alway to God *for* you,
3: 1. Finally, brethren, pray *for* us,
1Ti. 1: 7. nor where*of* they affirm.
19. *concerning*ᵃ faith have made shipwreck:
6: 4. but doting *about*ᵃ questions
21. have erred *concerning*ᵃ the faith.
2Ti. 1: 3. I have remembrance *of* thee
2:18. *concerning*ᵃ the truth have erred,
3: 8. reprobate *concerning*ᵃ the faith.
Tit. 2: 7. *In*ᵃ all things shewing thyself
8. having no evil thing to say *of* you.
3: 8.)(these things I will that thou affirm
Philem.10. I beseech thee *for* my son Onesimus,
Heb 2: 5. the world to come, where*of* we speak.
4: 4. spake in a certain place *of* the seventh (day)
8. have spoken *of* another day.
5: 3. he ought, as *for* the people, so also *for* himself, to offer for sins.
11. *Of* whom we have many things to say,
6: 9. persuaded better things *of* you,
7:14. spake nothing *concerning* priesthood.
9: 5. *of* which we cannot now speak
10: 6. In burnt offerings and (sacrifices) *for* sin
7. it is written *of* me,
8. and (offering) *for* sin thou wouldest not,
18. no more offering *for* sin.
26. no more sacrifice *for* sins,
11: 7. warned of God *of* things not seen as yet,
20. *concerning* things to come.
22. mention *of* the departing of the children
— commandment *concerning* his bones.
32. would fail me to tell *of* Gedeon,
40. some better thing *for* us,

Heb 13:11. by the high priest *for* sin,
18. Pray *for* us: for we trust we
1Pet. 1:10. *Of* which salvation the prophets
— prophesied *of* the grace (that should)
3:15. a reason *of* the hope that is in you
18. hath once suffered *for* sins,
5: 7. for he careth *for* you.
2Pet. 1:12. in remembrance *of* these things,
3:16. speaking in them *of* these things ;
1Joh.1: 1. have handled, *of* the Word of life ;
2: 2. the propitiation *for* our sins: and not *for* our's only, but also *for* (the sins of) the
26. *concerning* them that seduce you.
27. teacheth you *of* all things,
4:10. the propitiation *for* our sins.
5: 9. he hath testified *of* his Son.
10. that God gave *of* his Son.
16. say that he shall pray *for* it.
3Joh. 2. I wish *above* all things that
Jude 3. to write unto you *of* the common
7. and the cities *about*ᵃ them
9. disputed *about* the body of Moses,
15. *of* all their ungodly deeds
— and *of* all their hard (speeches)
Rev.15: 6. having their breasts girded with golden (lit. girded *about*ᵃ their breasts with)

περιάγω, *periago.*

Mat. 4:23. And Jesus *went about* all Galilee,
9:35. And Jesus *went about* all the cities
23:15. for ye *compass* sea and land
Mar 6: 6. And he *went* round *about* the villages,
Acts13:11. and he *went about* seeking some
1Co. 9: 5. power *to lead about* a sister, a wife,

περιαιρέω, *periaireo.*

Acts27:20. all hope that we should be saved *was* then *taken away.*
40. And *when* they *had taken up* the anchors, they committed (themselves) unto the sea, (lit. *having unfastened* the anchors they let go into the sea)
2Co. 3:16. the vail shall *be taken away.*
Heb 10:11. which can never *take away* sins:

περιαστράπτω, *periastrapto.*

Acts 9: 3. there *shined round about* him
22: 6. there *shone* from heaven a great light *round* about me.

περιϐάλλω, *periballo.*

Mat. 6:29. *was* not *arrayed* like one of these.
31. Wherewithal shall we *be clothed?*
25:36. Naked, and ye *clothed* me:
38. or naked, and *clothed* (thee) ?
43. naked, and ye *clothed* me not:
Mar 14:51. having a linen cloth cast about (lit. *clothed about* with a linen)
16: 5. *clothed* in a long white garment ;
Lu. 12:27. *was* not *arrayed* like one of these.
19:43. thine enemies *shall cast* a trench *about* thee,
23:11. *arrayed* him in a gorgeous robe, *and*
Joh.19: 2. and they *put on* him a purple robe,
Acts12: 8. *Cast* thy garment *about* thee,
Rev. 3: 5. the same *shall be clothed* in white raiment;

Rev. 3:18. raiment, that thou *mayest be clothed*,
 4: 4. *clothed* in white raiment ;
 7: 9. *clothed* with white robes,
 13. these *which are arrayed* in white robes?
10: 1. from heaven, *clothed* with a cloud:
11: 3. *clothed* in sackcloth.
12: 1. a woman *clothed* with the sun,
17: 4. And the woman was *arrayed* in purple
18:16. city, *that was clothed* in fine linen,
19: 8. that she *should be arrayed* in fine linen,
 13. And he (was) *clothed* with a vesture

περιβλέπω, *periblepo.*

Mar 3: 5. And *when he had looked round about on*
 34. he *looked* round *about on* them
 5:32. And he *looked round about* to see
 9: 8. *when they had looked round about,*
10:23. Jesus *looked round about,* and
11:11. and *when he had looked round about upon* all
Lu. 6:10. And *looking round about upon* them

περιβόλαιον, *peribolaion.*

1Co.11:15. hair is given her for a *covering.*
Heb 1:12. And as a *vesture* shalt thou fold

περιδέομαι, *perideomai.*

Joh.11:44. his face *was bound about* with a napkin.

περιδρέμω see περιτρέχω.

περιελών see περιαιρέω.

περιεργάζομαι, *periergazomai.*

2Th. 3:11. working not at all, but *are busybodies.*

περίεργος, *periergos.*

Acts19:19. which used *curious* arts
1Ti. 5:13. but tattlers also and *busybodies,*

περιέρχομαι, *perierkomai.*

Acts19:13. certain of the *vagabond* Jews,
 28:13. thence we *fetched a compass, and* came
1Ti. 5:13. *wandering about* from house to house ;
Heb11:37. they *wandered about* in sheepskins

περιέχω, *perieko.*

Lu. 5: 9. For he was astonished, and all (lit. asto-nishment *involved* him and all)
Acts23:25. a letter after this manner: (lit. *having* this form)
1Pet. 2: 6. also it *is contained* in the scripture,

περιζώννυμι, *perizonnumi.*

Lu. 12:35. Let your loins be *girded about,*
 37. that he *shall gird* him*self,*

Lu. 17: 8. and *gird* thy*self, and* serve me,
Acts12: 8. *Gird* thy*self,* and bind on thy sandals.
Eph. 6:14. having your loins *girt* about with (lit. *girt about* your loins with)
Rev. 1:13. *girt* about the paps with a golden
 15: 6. having their breasts *girded* (lit. *girded* about the breasts) with golden girdles.

περίθεσις, *perithesis.*

1Pet. 3: 3. of plaiting the hair, and of *wearing* of gold,

περιΐστημι, *periisteemi.*

Joh.11:42. because of the people *which stand by*
Acts25: 7. from Jerusalem *stood round about,*
2Ti. 2:16. *shun* profane (and) vain babblings:
Tit. 3: 9. But *avoid* foolish questions,

περικάθαρμα, *perikatharma.*

1Co. 4:13. we are made as the *filth* of the world,

περικαλύπτω, *perikalupto.*

Mar14:65. to spit on him, and *to cover* his face,
Lu. 22:64. And *when* they *had blindfolded* him,
Heb 9: 4. *over'laid* round about with gold,

περίκειμαι, *perikīmai.*

Mar 9:42. that a millstone were *hanged about*
Lu. 17: 2. were *hanged about*
Acts28:20. of Israel I *am bound with* this chain.
Heb 5: 2. himself also *is compassed with* infirmity.
 12: 1. we also are *compassed about with* so great a cloud (lit. having so great... *encompassing* us)

περικεφαλαία, *perikephalaia.*

Eph. 6:17. And take the *helmet* of salvation,
1Th. 5: 8. and for an *helmet,* the hope of

περικρατής, *perikratees.*

Acts27:16. we had much work *to come by* the boat: (lit. to become *masters* of the boat)

περικρύπτω, *perikrupto.*

Lu. 1:24. and *hid* herself five months,

περικυκλόω, *perikukloō.*

Lu. 19:43. shall cast a trench about thee, and *compass* thee *round,*

περιλάμπω, *perilampo.*

Lu. 2: 9. glory of the Lord *shone round about* them ;
Acts26:13. *shining round about* me and them

περιλείπομαι, perilīpomai.

1Th. 4:15. (and) remain unto the coming of the Lord
17. which are alive (and) remain shall be

περίλυπος, perilupos.

Mat.26:38. My soul is exceeding sorrowful,
Mar 6:26. And the king was exceeding sorry ;
14:34. My soul is exceeding sorrowful
Lu. 18:23. heard this, he was very sorrowful :
24. Jesus saw that he was very sorrowful,

περιμένω, perimeno.

Acts 1: 4. but wait for the promise of the Father,

πέριξ, perix.

Acts 5:16. (out) of the cities round about

περιοικέω, perioikeo.

Lu. 1:65. on all that dwelt round about them:

περίοικος, perioikos.

Lu. 1:58. And her neighbours and her cousins

περιούσιος, periousios.

Tit. 2:14. unto himself a peculiar people,

περιοχή, periokee.

Acts 8:32. The place (lit. the period or context) of the
scripture which he read

περιπατέω, peripateo.

Mat. 4:18. walking by the sea of Galilee,
9: 5. or to say, Arise, and walk?
11: 5. and the lame walk,
14:25. walking on the sea.
26. disciples saw him walking on the sea,
29. he walked on the water, to go to
15:31. the lame to walk,
Mar 1:16. Now as he walked by the sea
2: 9. take up thy bed, and walk?
5:42. the damsel arose, and walked;
6:48. walking upon the sea,
49. But when they saw him walking
7: 5. Why walk not thy disciples
8:24. I see men as trees, walking.
11:27. and as he was walking in the temple,
12:38. which love to go in long clothing,
16:12. unto two of them, as they walked,
Lu. 5:23. or to say, Rise up and walk?
7:22. the blind see, the lame walk,
11:44. the men that walk over (them)
20:46. which desire to walk in long robes,
24:17. as ye walk, and are sad?
Joh. 1:36. looking upon Jesus as he walked,
5: 8. Rise, take up thy bed, and walk.
9. took up his bed, and walked:
11. Take up thy bed, and walk.

Joh. 5:12. Take up thy bed, and walk?
6:19. they see Jesus walking on the sea,
66. and walked no more with him.
7: 1. Jesus walked in Galilee: for he would not
walk in Jewry,
8:12. shall not walk in darkness,
10:23. Jesus walked in the temple in
11: 9. If any man walk in the day,
10. But if a man walk in the night,
54. walked no more openly among
12:35. Walk while ye have the light,
— for he that walketh in darkness
21:18. and walkedst whither thou wouldest:
Acts 3: 6. rise up and walk.
8. he leaping up stood, and walked,
— into the temple, walking, and leaping,
9. saw him walking and praising God:
12. we had made this man to walk?
14: 8. who never had walked :
10. And he leaped and walked.
21:21. neither to walk after the customs.
Ro. 6: 4. we also should walk in newness of life.
8: 1. who walk not after the flesh,
4. in us, who walk not after the flesh,
13:13. Let us walk honestly, as in
14:15. now walkest thou not charitably.
1Co. 3: 3. are ye not carnal, and walk as men?
7:17. so let him walk.
2Co. 4: 2. not walking in craftiness,
5: 7. we walk by faith, not by sight:
10: 2. as if we walked (lit. as walking) according
to the flesh,
3. For though we walk in the flesh,
12:18. walked we not in the same spirit?
Gal. 5:16. Walk in the Spirit,
Eph. 2: 2. in time past ye walked
10. that we should walk in them.
4: 1. that ye walk worthy of the vocation
17. that ye henceforth walk not as other
Gentiles walk,
5: 2. And walk in love,
8. walk as children of light:
15. See then that ye walk circumspectly,
Phi. 3:17. mark them which walk so as
18. For many walk, of whom I
Col. 1:10. That ye might walk worthy of the Lord
2: 6. (so) walk ye in him:
3: 7. In the which ye also walked
4: 5. Walk in wisdom toward them :
1Th. 2:12. That ye would walk worthy of God,
4: 1. how ye ought to walk
12. That ye may walk honestly toward
2Th. 3: 6. from every brother that walketh disorderly,
11. some which walk among you disorderly,
Heb 13: 9. profited them that have been occupied
therein.
1Pet.5: 8. walketh about, seeking whom
1Joh.1: 6. and walk in darkness, we lie,
7. But if we walk in the light,
2: 6. ought himself also so to walk, even as he
walked.
11. and walketh in darkness,
2Joh. 4. I found of thy children walking in truth,
6. that we walk after his commandments.
— ye should walk in it.
3Joh. 3. thou walkest in the truth.
4. that my children walk in truth.
Rev. 2: 1. who walketh in the midst of the
3: 4. they shall walk with me in white:
9:20. neither can see, nor hear, nor walk:
16:15. lest he walk naked,
21:24. shall walk in the light of it:

περιπείρω, peripīro.

1Ti. 6:10. and *pierced* themselves *through* with

περιπίπτω, peripipto.

Lu. 10:30. and *fell among* thieves,
Acts27:41. And *falling into* a place where two seas
Jas. 1: 2. when ye *fall into* divers temptations ;

περιποιέομαι, peripoyeomai.

Acts20:28. he *hath purchased* with his own blocd.
1Ti. 3:13. *purchase* to themselves a good degree,

περιποίησις, peripoyeesis.

Eph 1:14. the redemption of the *purchased possession,*
1Th. 5: 9. but *to obtain* salvation
2Th. 2:14. to the *obtaining* of the glory of our Lord
Heb 10:39. to the *saving* of the soul.
1Pet. 2: 9. a *peculiar* people; (lit. a people of *acquirement* to himself)

περιρρήγνυμι, perirreegnumi.

Acts16:22. the magistrates *rent off* their clothes, *and*

περισπάομαι, perispaomai.

Lu. 10:40. Martha *was cumbered* about much

περισσεία, perissīa.

Ro. 5:17. they which receive *abundance* of grace
2Co. 8: 2. the *abundance* of their joy
10:15. according to our rule *abundant*ly,
Jas. 1:21. and *superfluity* of naughtiness,

περίσσευμα, perissūma.

Mat.12:34. out of the *abundance* of the heart
Mar 8: 8. took up of the broken (meat) *that was left* (lit. the *remnants over and above*)
Lu. 6:45. for of the *abundance* of the heart
2Co. 8:14(13). your *abundance* (may be a supply)
— that their *abundance* also may be

περισσεύω, perissūo.

Mat. 5:20. except your righteousness *shall exceed*
13:12. and he *shall have more abundance:*
14:20. of the fragments *that remained* (lit. that which was over of the fragments)
15:37. of the broken (meat) *that was left*
25:29. and he *shall have abundance :*
Mar 12:44. did cast in of their *abundance ;*
Lu. 9:17. of fragments *that remained* to them
12:15. consisteth not in the *abundance* of the
15:17. *have* bread *enough and to spare,*
21: 4. these have of their *abundance* cast in
Joh. 6:12. Gather up the fragments *that remain,*
13. which *remained over and above* unto them

Acts16: 5. and *increased* in number daily.
Ro. 3: 7. hath *more abounded* through my lie
5:15. *hath abounded* unto many.
15:13. that ye may *abound* in hope,
1Co. 8: 8. neither, if we eat, *are* we *the better ;*
14:12. that ye *may excel* to the edifying
15:58. always *abounding* in the work
2Co. 1: 5. sufferings of Christ *abound* in us, so our consolation also *aboundeth* by Christ.
3: 9. of righteousness *exceed* in glory.
4:15. abundant grace might...*redound* to
8: 2. *abounded* unto the riches of their
7. as ye *abound* in every (thing, in) faith,
— that ye *abound* in this grace also.
9: 8. *to make* all grace *abound* toward you ;
— may *abound* to every good work:
12. is *abundant* also by many thanksgivings
Eph 1: 8. Wherein he *hath abounded* toward us
Phi. 1: 9. that your love *may abound* yet more
26. rejoicing *may be more abundant* in
4:12. and I know how *to abound :*
— both *to abound* and to suffer need.
18. I have all, and *abound :*
Col. 2: 7. *abounding* therein with thanksgiving.
1Th. 3:12. make you to increase and *abound*
4: 1. (so) ye *would abound* more and more.
10. that ye *increase* more and more ;

περισσός & περισσότερος, perissos & perissoteros.

Mat. 5:37. for whatsoever is *more* than these
47. what do ye *more* (than others)?
11: 9. and *more* than a prophet.
23:14. ye shall receive the *greater* damnation.
Mar 6:51. sore amazed in themselves *beyond measure,*
12:40. shall receive *greater* damnation.
14:31. spake the more *vehemently,*
Lu. 7:26. and *much more* than a prophet.
12: 4. have no *more* that they can do.
48. of him they will ask the *more.*
20:47. shall receive *greater* damnation.
Joh.10:10. might have (it) *more abundantly.*
Ro. 3: 1. What *advantage* then hath the Jew?
1Co.12:23. we bestow *more abundant* honour ;
— have *more abundant* comeliness.
24. given *more abundant* honour.
2Co. 2: 7. swallowed up with *overmuch* sorrow.
9: 1. it is *superfluous* for me to write to you:
10: 8. I should boast somewhat *more* of
Eph 3:20. able to do *exceeding abundantly* above
1Th. 3:10. Night and day praying *exceedingly*
5:13. And to esteem them *very highly*

Note.—These three last passages are the rendering of the compound form, ὑπὲρ ἐκ περισσοῦ.

περισσότερον, perissoteron. adv.

Mar 7:36. so much the more *a great deal*
1Co.15:10. I laboured *more abundantly* than they all:
Heb 6:17. willing *more abundantly* to shew (lit. *extremely* desirous to shew)
7:15. it is yet *far more* evident:

περισσοτέρως, perissoterōs.

Mar 15:14. they cried out the *more exceedingly,*
2Co. 1:12. and *more abundantly* to you-ward.
2: 4. I have *more abundantly* unto you.

2Co. 7:13. *exceedingly* the more joyed we
    15. his inward affection is *more abundant* toward you,
    11:23. in labours *more abundant*,
    — in prisons *more frequent*,
    12:15. *the more abundantly* I love you,
Gal. 1:14. being *more exceedingly* zealous
Phi. 1:14. are *much more* bold to speak
1Th. 2:17. endeavoured *the more abundantly*
Heb 2: 1. we ought to give the more earnest heed
    (lit. we ought *much more* to attend)
    13:19. I beseech (you) *the rather* to do this, that

περισσῶς, *perissōs*.

Mat.27:23. they cried out *the more*, saying,
Mar10:26. they were astonished *out of measure*,
Acts26:11. being *exceedingly* mad against them,

περιστερά, *peristera*.

Mat. 3:16. descending like a *dove*,
    10:16. and harmless as *doves*,
    21:12. the seats of them that sold *doves*,
Mar 1:10. and the Spirit like a *dove* descending
    11:15. the seats of them that sold *doves*;
Lu. 2:24. A pair of turtledoves, or two young *pigeons*.
    3:22. in a bodily shape like a *dove*
Joh. 1:32. descending from heaven like a *dove*,
    2:14. that sold oxen and sheep and *doves*,
    16. said unto them that sold *doves*,

περιτέμνω, *peritemno*.

Lu. 1:59. they came *to circumcise* the child;
    2:21. accomplished for the *circumcising* of the child,
Joh. 7:22. ye on the sabbath day *circumcise* a man.
Acts 7: 8. and *circumcised* him the eighth day;
    15: 1. Except ye *be circumcised*
    5. That it was needful *to circumcise* them,
    24. saying, (Ye must) *be circumcised*,
    16: 3. and took and *circumcised* him
    21:21. saying that they ought not *to circumcise*
1Co. 7:18. Is any man called *being circumcised?*
    — let him not *be circumcised.*
Gal. 2: 3. was compelled *to be circumcised:*
    5: 2. that if ye *be circumcised*,
    3. to every man *that is circumcised*,
    6:12. they constrain you *to be circumcised*;
    13. they themselves *who are circumcised*
    — desire *to have* you *circumcised*, (lit. you *to be circumcised*)
Col. 2:11. In whom also ye *are circumcised* with the

περιτίθημι, *perititheemi*.

Mat.21:33. and hedged it round about, (lit. *placed about* it a hedge)
    27:28. and *put on* him a scarlet robe.
    48. *put* (it) *on* a reed, *and* gave
Mar12: 1. *set* an hedge *about* (it),
    15:17. *put it about* his (head),
    36. and *put* (it) *on* a reed, *and* gave
Joh.19:29. and *put* (it) *upon* hyssop, *and*
1Co.12:23. *upon* these we *bestow* more abundant

περιτομή, *peritomee*.

Joh. 7:22. gave unto you *circumcision;*
    23. on the sabbath day receive *circumcision*,
Acts 7: 8. gave him the covenant of *circumcision:*
    10:45. they of the *circumcision*
    11: 2. they that were of the *circumcision*
Ro. 2:25. For *circumcision* verily profiteth, if
    — thy *circumcision* is made
    26. be counted for *circumcision?*
    27. by the letter and *circumcision*
    28. (is that) *circumcision*, which is outward
    29. and *circumcision* (is that) of the heart,
    3: 1. what profit (is there) of *circumcision?*
    30. shall justify the *circumcision* by
    4: 9. upon the *circumcision* (only),
    10. when he was in *circumcision*,
    — Not in *circumcision*, but
    11. received the sign of *circumcision*,
    12. the father of *circumcision* to them who are not of the *circumcision* only,
    15: 8. was a minister of the *circumcision*
1Co. 7:19. *Circumcision* is nothing, and
Gal. 2: 7. (the gospel) of the *circumcision* (was)
    8. to the apostleship of the *circumcision*,
    9. and they unto the *circumcision*.
    12. them which were of the *circumcision*.
    5: 6. neither *circumcision* availeth any thing,
    11. if I yet preach *circumcision*,
    6:15. neither *circumcision* availeth any thing,
Eph. 2:11. called the *Circumcision* in the flesh
Phi. 3: 3. For we are the *circumcision*,
    5. Circumcised the eighth day, (lit. of the eighth day in *circumcision*) [The best copies read π. in the dative.]
Col. 2:11. with the *circumcision* made without hands,
    — by the *circumcision* of Christ:
    3:11. *circumcision* nor uncircumcision,
    4:11. who are of the *circumcision*.
Tit. 1:10. specially they of the *circumcision:*

περιτρέπω, *peritrepo*.

Acts26:24. much learning doth make thee mad. (lit. *perverts* thee to madness)

περιτρέχω, *peritreko*.

Mar 6:55. *And ran through* that whole region

περιφέρω, *periphero*.

Mar 6:55. *to carry about* in beds those that were sick,
2Co. 4:10. Always *bearing about* in the body
Eph. 4:14. and *carried about* with every wind
Heb13: 9. *Be* not *carried about* with divers
Jude 12. *carried about* of winds;

περιφρονέω, *periphroneo*.

Tit. 2:15. *Let* no man *despise* thee.

περίχωρος, *perikōros*.

Mat. 3: 5. all the *region round about* Jordan,
    14:35. all that *country round about*,
Mar 1:28. all the *region round about* Galilee.
    6:55. through that whole *region round about*,

Lu. 3: 3. into all the *country about* Jordan,
   4:14. through all the *region round about.*
     37. every place of the *country round about.*
   7:17. throughout all the *region round about.*
   8:37. of *the country* of the Gadarenes *round about*
Acts14: 6. and unto *the region that lieth round about :*

περίψημα, *peripseema.*

1Co. 4:13. the *offscouring* of all things unto this day.

περπερεύομαι, *perperūomai.*

1Co.13: 4. charity *vaunteth* not *itself,*

πέρυσι, *perusi.*

2Co. 8:10. to be forward *a year ago.*
   9: 2. was ready *a year ago ;*

πετάομαι, *petaomai.*

Rev. 4: 7. (was) like a *flying* eagle.
   8:13. an angel *flying* through the midst
  14: 6. saw another angel *fly*
 19:17. saying to all the fowls *that fly* in

πετεινόν, *petinon.*

Mat. 6:26. Behold the *fowls* of the air:
   8:20. and the *birds* of the air (have) nests ;
  13: 4. the *fowls* came and devoured
    32. the *birds* of the air come and lodge
Mar 4: 4. and the *fowls* of the air came
    32. the *fowls* of the air may lodge
Lu. 8: 5. the *fowls* of the air devoured it.
  9:58. *birds* of the air (have) nests ;
 12:24. are ye better than the *fowls ?*
 13:19. the *fowls* of the air lodged in
Acts10:12. and *fowls* of the air.
  11: 6. and *fowls* of the air.
Ro. 1:23. to corruptible man, and to *birds,*
Jas. 3: 7. every kind of beasts, and of *birds,*

πέτομαι, *petomai.*

Rev.12:14. that she *might fly* into the wilderness,

πέτρα, *petra.*

Mat. 7:24. built his house upon a *rock :*
    25. for it was founded upon a *rock.*
 16:18. upon this *rock* I will build
 27:51. and the *rocks* rent ;
    60. which he had hewn out in the *rock :*
Mar 15:46. which was hewn out of a *rock,*
Lu. 6:48. laid the foundation on a *rock :*
   — for it was founded upon a *rock.*
 8: 6. And some fell upon a *rock ;*
 13. They on the *rock* (are they), which,
Ro. 9:33. a stumblingstone and *rock* of offence
1Co.10: 4. drank of that spiritual *Rock* that followed
    them: and that *Rock* was Christ.
1Pet. 2: 8(7). and a *rock* of offence,

Rev. 6:15. in the dens and in the *rocks* of the
   16. And said to the mountains and *rocks,*

πέτρος, *petros.*

Joh. 1:42(43). by interpretation, A *stone.*

πετρώδης, *petrōdees.*

Mat.13: 5. Some fell upon *stony* places,
   20. received the seed into *stony* places,
Mar 4: 5. And some fell on *stony* ground,
  16. which are sown on *stony* ground ;

πήγανον, *peeganon.*

Lu. 11:42. for ye tithe mint and *rue*

πηγή, *peegee.*

Mar 5:29. the *fountain* of her blood was dried up ;
Joh. 4: 6. Now Jacob's *well* was there.
   — sat thus on the *well :*
  14. shall be in him a *well* of water
Jas. 3:11. Doth a *fountain* send forth
  12. so (can) no *fountain* both yield
2Pet. 2:17. These are *wells* without water,
Rev. 7:17. unto living *fountains* of waters:
  8:10. and upon the *fountains* of waters ;
 14: 7. and the *fountains* of waters.
 16: 4. upon the rivers and *fountains*
 21: 6. of the *fountain* of the water of life

πήγνυμι, *peegnumi.*

Heb 8: 2. which the Lord *pitched,* and not man.

πηδάλιον, *peedalion.*

Acts27:40. and loosed the *rudder* bands,
Jas. 3: 4. turned about with a very small *helm,*

πηλίκος, *peelikos.*

Gal. 6:11. Ye see *how large* a letter I have written
    (lit. in *how large* letters)
Heb 7: 4. Now consider *how great* this man (was),

πηλός, *peelos.*

Joh. 9::6. and made *clay* of the spittle, and he
    anointed the eyes of the blind man with
    the *clay,*
  11. A man that is called Jesus made *clay,*
  14. when Jesus made the *clay,*
  15. He put *clay* upon mine eyes,
Ro. 9:21. Hath not the potter power over the *clay,*

πήρα, *peera.*

Mat.10:10. Nor *scrip* for (your) journey,
Mar 6: 8. no *scrip,* no bread, no money
Lu. 9: 3. neither staves, nor *scrip,*
  10: 4. Carry neither purse, nor *scrip,*

Lu. 22:35. and *scrip*, and shoes, lacked ye
36. let him take (it), and likewise (his) *scrip :*

πῆχυς, *peekus.*

Mat. 6:27. one *cubit* unto his stature ?
Lu. 12:25. can add to his stature one *cubit?*
Joh. 21: 8. as it were two hundred *cubits,*
Rev. 21:17. an hundred (and) forty (and) four *cubits,*

πιάζω, *piazo.*

Joh. 7:30. Then they sought *to take* him:
32. sent officers *to take* him.
44. some of them would *have taken* him ;
8:20. and no man *laid hands on* him ;
10:39. they sought again *to take* him:
11:57. that they *might take* him.
21: 3. that night they *caught* nothing.
10. which ye *have* now *caught.*
Acts 3: 7. he *took* him by the right hand, *and*
12: 4. *when* he *had apprehended* him,
2Co. 11:32. desirous *to apprehend* me:
Rev. 19:20. And the beast *was taken,*

πιέζω, *piezo.*

Lu. 6:38. good measure, *pressed down*, and shaken
together,

πιθανολογία, *pithanologia.*

Col. 2: 4. beguile you with *enticing words.*

πικραίνω, *pikraino.*

Col. 3:19. and *be* not *bitter* against them.
Rev. 8:11. because they *were made bitter.*
10: 9. it *shall make* thy belly *bitter,*
10. my belly *was bitter.*

πικρία, *pikria.*

Acts 8:23. thou art in the gall of *bitterness,*
Ro. 3:14. full of cursing and *bitterness :*
Eph. 4:31. Let all *bitterness,* and wrath,
Heb 12:15. lest any root of *bitterness*

πικρός, *pikros.*

Jas. 3:11. sweet (water) and *bitter ?*
14. if ye have *bitter* envying

πικρῶς, *pikrōs.*

Mat. 26:75. And he went out, and wept *bitterly.*
Lu. 22:62. Peter went out, and wept *bitterly.*

πίμπραμαι, *pimpramai.*

Acts 28: 6. when he should have *swollen,*

πινακίδιον, *pinakidion.*

Lu. 1:63. he asked for a *writing table*, (lit. *tablet*)

πίναξ, *pinax.*

Mat. 14: 8. John Baptist's head in a *charger.*
11. was brought in a *charger,*
Mar 6:25. by and by in a *charger,*
28. brought his head in a *charger,*
Lu. 11:39. outside of the cup and the *platter ;*

πίνω, πίω, πίομαι, *pino, pio, piomai.*

Mat. 6:25. or what ye shall *drink ;*
31. What shall we *drink ?*
11:18. came neither eating nor *drinking,*
19. came eating and *drinking,*
20:22. Are ye able *to drink* of the cup that I shall
drink of,
23. Ye *shall drink* indeed of my cup,
24:38. they were eating and *drinking,*
49. to eat and *drink* with the drunken ;
26:27. *Drink* ye all of it ;
29. I will not *drink* henceforth
— when I *drink* it new with you
42. except I *drink* it,
27:34. They gave him vinegar *to drink*
— he would not *drink.*
Mar 2:16. eateth and *drinketh* with publicans
10:38. can ye *drink* of the cup that I *drink* of ?
39. Ye *shall* indeed *drink* of the cup that I
drink of;
14:23. and they all *drank* of it.
25. I will *drink* no more of the fruit of the
vine, until that day that I *drink* it
15:23. they gave him *to drink* wine
16:18. and if they *drink* any deadly
Lu. 1:15. and shall *drink* neither wine
5:30. Why do ye eat and *drink* with
33. but thine eat and *drink ?*
39. No man also *having drunk* old (wine)
7:33. nor *drinking* wine ;
34. is come eating and *drinking ;*
10: 7. eating and *drinking* such things
12:19. take thine ease, eat, *drink,* (and) be
29. or what ye shall *drink,*
45. to eat and *drink,* and to be drunken ;
13:26. We have eaten and *drunk* in thy
17: 8. till I have eaten and *drunken;* and afterward thou shalt eat and *drink?*
27. They did eat, they *drank,* they
28. they did eat, they *drank,* they bought,
22:18. I will not *drink* of the fruit of
30. That ye may eat and *drink* at my
Joh. 4: 7. Give me *to drink.*
9. askest *drink* of me, which am a woman
10. Give me *to drink ;*
12. and *drank* thereof himself,
13. *Whosoever drinketh* of this water
14. But whosoever *drinketh* of the
6:53. and *drink* his blood,
54. and *drinketh* my blood,
56. He that eateth my flesh, and *drinketh*
7:37. let him come unto me, and *drink.*
18:11. shall I not *drink* it ?
Acts 9: 9. and neither did eat nor *drink.*
23:12. they would neither eat nor *drink*
21. they will neither eat nor *drink*
Ro. 14:21. nor *to drink* wine, nor
1Co. 9: 4. power to eat and *to drink ?*
10: 4. *did* all *drink* the same spiritual drink: for
they *drank* of that spiritual
7. sat down to eat and *drink,*
21. Ye cannot *drink* the cup of the Lord,

1Co.10:31. Whether therefore ye eat, or *drink*,
  11:22. houses to eat and *to drink* in?
  25. as oft as ye *drink* (it),
  26. as ye eat this bread, and *drink*
  27. and *drink* (this) cup of the Lord,
  28. let him eat of (that) bread, and *drink*
  29. For he that eateth and *drinketh* unworthily, eateth and *drinketh*
  15:32. let us eat and *drink;*
Heb 6: 7. the earth *which drinketh* in the rain
Rev.14:10. The same *shall drink* of the wine
  16: 6. thou hast given them blood *to drink;*
  18: 3. all nations *have drunk* of the wine

πιότης, *piotees.*

Ro. 11:17. and *fatness* of the olive tree;

πιπράσκω, *piprasko.*

Mat.13:46. went and *sold* all that he had, and
  18:25. his lord commanded him *to be sold,*
  26: 9. might *have been sold* for much,
Mar 14: 5. might *have been sold* for more
Joh.12: 5. Why *was* not this ointment *sold*
Acts 2:45. And *sold* their possessions and goods,
  4:34. prices of the things *that were sold,*
  5: 4. and *after* it *was sold,* was it not
Ro. 7:14. but I am carnal, *sold* under sin.

πίπτω, ἔπεσον, *pipto, epeson.*

Mat. 2:11. and *fell down,* and worshipped him:
  4: 9. if thou wilt *fall down and* worship me.
  7:25. and it *fell* not: for it was founded
  27. and it *fell:* and great was the fall of it.
  10:29. *shall* not *fall* on the ground
  13: 4. some (seeds) *fell* by the way side,
  5. Some *fell* upon stony places,
  7. And some *fell* among thorns;
  8. other *fell* into good ground,
  15:14. both *shall fall* into the ditch.
  27. crumbs *which fall* from their masters'
  17: 6. they *fell* on their face,
  15. ofttimes he *falleth* into the fire,
  18:26. *fell down,* and worshipped him,
  29. *fell down* at his feet, *and*
  21:44. *whosoever shall fall* on this stone
  — on whomsoever it shall *fall,*
  24:29. the stars *shall fall* from heaven,
  26:39. and *fell* on his face, and prayed,
Mar 4: 4. some *fell* by the way side,
  5. some *fell* on stony ground,
  7. some *fell* among thorns,
  8. other *fell* on good ground,
  5:22. when he saw him, he *fell* at his feet,
  9:20. he *fell* on the ground, *and* wallowed
  14:35. and *fell* on the ground, and prayed
Lu. 5:12. *fell* on (his) face, *and* besought
  6:39. *shall* they not both *fall* into the
  49. and immediately it *fell;*
  8: 5. some *fell* by the way side;
  6. And some *fell* upon a rock;
  7. some *fell* among thorns;
  8. other *fell* on good ground,
  14. that *which fell* among thorns
  41. he *fell down* at Jesus' feet, *and*

Lu. 10:18. Satan as lightning *fall* from heaven.
  11:17. a house (divided) against a house *falleth*
  13: 4. upon whom the tower in Siloam *fell,*
  16:17. than one tittle of the law *to fail.*
  21. with the crumbs *which fell* from the
  17:16. And *fell down* on (his) face
  20:18. *Whosoever shall fall* upon that stone shall be broken; but on whomsoever it shall *fall,*
  21:24. And they *shall fall* by the edge of
  23:30. *Fall* on us; and to the hills, Cover us.
Joh.11:32. she *fell down* at his feet,
  12:24. *fall* into the ground *and* die,
  18: 6. and *fell* to the ground.
Acts 1:26. and the lot *fell* upon Matthias;
  5: 5. *fell down,* and gave up the ghost:
  10. Then *fell* she *down* straightway
  9: 4. he *fell* to the earth, and heard
  10:25. and *fell down* at his feet, *and*
  15:16. tabernacle of David, *which is fallen down;*
  20: 9. and *fell down* from the third loft,
  22: 7. And I *fell* unto the ground,
  27:34. there *shall* not an hair *fall* from the head
Ro. 11:11. Have they stumbled that they *should fall?*
  22. on them *which fell,* severity;
  14: 4. to his own master he standeth or *falleth.*
1Co.10: 8. and *fell* in one day
  12. thinketh he standeth take heed lest he *fall.*
  14:25. and so *falling down* on (his) face
Heb 3:17. whose carcases *fell* in the wilderness?
  4:11. lest any man *fall* after the same
  11:30. the walls of Jericho *fell down,*
Jas. 5:12. lest ye *fall* into condemnation.
Rev. 1:17. I *fell* at his feet as dead.
  4:10. elders *fall down* (lit. *shall f. d.*) before him
  5: 8. *fell down* before the Lamb,
  14. *fell down* and worshipped him
  6:13. the stars of heaven *fell* unto the earth,
  16. and rocks, *Fall* on us,
  7:11. and *fell* before the throne on their
  16. neither shall the sun *light* on them,
  8:10. and there *fell* a great star from
  — and it *fell* upon the third part
  9: 1. and I saw a star *fall* from heaven
  11:11. and great fear *fell* upon them
  13. and the tenth part of the city *fell,*
  16. *fell* upon their faces, and worshipped God,
  14: 8. Babylon *is fallen, is fallen,*
  16:19. and the cities of the nations *fell:*
  17:10. five *are fallen,* and one is,
  18: 2. Babylon the great *is fallen, is fallen,*
  19: 4. and the four beasts *fell down* and
  10. And I *fell* at his feet to worship
  22: 8. I *fell down* to worship before

πιστεύω, *pistŭo.*

Mat. 8:13. and as thou *hast believed,*
  9:28. *Believe* ye that I am able to do
  18: 6. little ones *which believe* in me,
  21:22. ye shall ask in prayer *believing,*
  25. Why *did* ye not then *believe* him?
  32. and ye *believed* him not: but the publicans and the harlots *believed* him: — that ye might *believe* him.
  24:23. *believe* (it) not.
  26. *believe* (it) not.
  27:42. and we *will believe* him.
Mar 1:15. and *believe* the gospel.
  5:36. Be not afraid, only *believe.*

Mar 9:23. If thou canst *believe*, all things (are) possible to him *that believeth*.
    24. Lord, I *believe ;* help thou mine unbelief.
    42. little ones *that believe* in me,
  11:23. but *shall believe* that those things
    24. *believe* that ye receive (them),
    31. Why then *did* ye not *believe* him ?
  13:21. *believe* (him) not:
  15:32. that we may see and *believe*.
  16:13. neither *believed* they them.
    14. because they *believed* not them
    16. He *that believeth* and is baptized
    17. these signs shall follow them *that believe ;*
Lu. 1:20. because thou *believest* not my words,
    45. blessed (is) she *that believed :*
  8:12. lest they should *believe and* be saved.
    13. which for a while *believe*,
    50. *believe* only, and she shall be made whole.
  16:11. who *will commit* to your *trust*
  20: 5. Why then *believed* ye him not ?
  22:67. ye will not *believe :*
  24:25. O fools, and slow of heart *to believe*
Joh. 1: 7. all (men) through him *might believe*.
    12. to them *that believe* on his name:
  50(51). Because I said unto thee,...*believest* thou ?
  2:11. his disciples *believed* on him.
    22. and they *believed* the scripture.
    23. many *believed* in his name,
    24. Jesus *did* not *commit* himself unto them,
  3:12. and ye *believe* not, how *shall* ye *believe*, if I tell you (of) heavenly things ?
    15. *whosoever believeth* in him should not
    16. *whosoever believeth* in him should not
    18. He *that believeth* on him is not condemned: but he *that believeth* not is condemned already, because he *hath* not *believed*
    36. He *that believeth* on the Son hath
  4:21. Woman, *believe* me, the hour cometh,
    39. of the Samaritans of that city *believed*
    41. many more *believed* because of his
    42. Now we *believe*, not because
    48. ye will not *believe*.
    50. the man *believed* the word
    53. himself *believed*, and his whole house.
  5:24. and *believeth* on him that sent me,
    38. him ye *believe* not.
    44. How can ye *believe*,
    46. For *had* ye *believed* Moses, ye would *have believed* me:
    47. But if ye *believe* not his writings, how *shall* ye *believe* my words ?
  6:29. that ye *believe* on him whom he hath
    30. that we may see, and *believe* thee ?
    35. he *that believeth* on me shall never thirst.
    36. ye also have seen me, and *believe* not.
    40. and *believeth* on him, may have
    47. He *that believeth* on me hath
    64. some of you that *believe* not.
    — who they were *that believed* not,
    69. And we *believe* and are sure that thou art
  7: 5. neither *did* his brethren *believe* in him.
    31. many of the people *believed* on him,
    38. He *that believeth* on me, as the
    39. which they *that believe* on him should
    48. or of the Pharisees *believed* on him ?
  8:24. if ye *believe* not that I am (he),
    30. many *believed* on him.
    31. to those Jews *which believed* on him,
    45. ye *believe* me not.
    46. why *do* ye not *believe* me?
  9:18. the Jews *did* not *believe*

Joh. 9:35. *Dost* thou *believe* on the Son of God ?
    36. that I *might believe* on him ?
    38. Lord, I *believe*.
  10:25. and ye *believed* not:
    26. But ye *believe* not,
    37. *believe* me not.
    38. though ye *believe* not me, *believe* the works: that ye may know, and *believe*, that the Father
    42. many *believed* on him there.
  11:15. to the intent ye *may believe ;*
    25. he *that believeth* in me,
    26. and *believeth* in me shall never die. *Believest* thou this?
    27. I *believe* that thou art the Christ,
    40. if thou *wouldest believe*,
    42. that they *may believe* that
    45. *believed* on him.
    48. all (men) *will believe* on him:
  12:11. and *believed* on Jesus.
    36. *believe* in the light,
    37. yet they *believed* not on him:
    38. who *hath believed* our report?
    39. Therefore they could not *believe*,
    42. many *believed* on him ;
    44. He *that believeth* on me, *believeth* not on
    46. that *whosoever believeth* on me
    47. and *believe* not,
  13:19. ye *may believe* that I am (he).
  14: 1. ye *believe* in God, *believe* also in me.
    10. *Believest* thou not that I am in
    11. *Believe* me that I (am) in the Father,
    — or else *believe* me for the very works'
    12. He *that believeth* on me, the works
    29. when it is come to pass, ye *might believe*.
  16: 9. because they *believe* not on me ;
    27. and *have believed* that I came out
    30. by this we *believe* that thou camest
    31. *Do* ye now *believe ?*
  17: 8. and they *have believed* that thou didst
    20. for them also *which shall believe*
    21. that the world *may believe* that thou
  19:35. he saith true, that ye *might believe*.
  20: 8. and he saw, and *believed*.
    25. I *will* not *believe*.
    29. thou *hast believed :*
    — and (yet) *have believed*.
    31. that ye *might believe* that Jesus
    — and that *believing* ye might have life
Acts 2:44. And all *that believed* were together,
  4: 4. which heard the word *believed ;*
    32. of them *that believed* were of one heart
  5:14. And *believers* were the more added
  8:12. But when they *believed* Philip
    13. Then Simon himself *believed* also:
    37. If thou *believest* with all thine heart,
    — I *believe* that Jesus Christ is the Son of
  9:26. *and believed* not that he was a disciple.
    42. and many *believed* in the Lord.
  10:43. *whosoever believeth* in him shall
  11:17. *who believed* on the Lord Jesus Christ ;
    21. a great number *believed, and* turned
  13:12. when he saw what was done, *believed*,
    39. by him all *that believe* are justified
    41. which ye shall in no wise *believe*,
    48. were ordained to eternal life *believed*.
  14: 1. and also of the Greeks *believed*.
    23. on whom they *believed*.
  15: 5. certain...of the Pharisees *which believed*,
    7. hear the word of the gospel, and *believe*.
    11. But we *believe* that through the grace
  16:31. *Believe* on the Lord Jesus Christ,

Acts16:34. *believing* in God with all his house.
17:12. Therefore many of them *believed;*
34. clave unto him, and *believed:*
18: 8. *believed* on the Lord with all his house ;
— many of the Corinthians hearing *believed,*
27. helped them much *which had believed*
19: 2. received the Holy Ghost *since ye believed?*
4. that they *should believe* on him
18. And many *that believed* came,
21:20. of Jews there are *which believe ;*
25. touching the Gentiles *which believe,*
22:19. them *that believed* on thee:
24:14. *believing* all things which are
26:27. King Agrippa, *believest* thou the prophets ?
I know that thou *believest.*
27:25. for I *believe* God, that it shall
Ro. 1:16. to every one *that believeth ;*
3: 2. unto them *were committed* (lit. they *were intrusted with*) the oracles of God.
22. unto all and upon all them *that believe :*
4: 3. Abraham *believed* God, and it was
5. but *believeth* on him that
11. the father of all them *that believe,*
17. before him whom he *believed,*
18. against hope *believed* in hope,
24. *if* we *believe* on him that raised
6: 8. we *believe* that we shall also (live)
9:33. whosoever *believeth* on him
10: 4. to every one *that believeth.*
9. and shalt *believe* in thine heart
10. with the heart man believeth (lit. *is it believed*)
11. *Whosoever believeth* on him
14. in whom they *have* not *believed ?* and how *shall* they *believe*
16. who *hath believed* our report?
13:11. nearer than when we *believed.*
14: 2. For one *believeth* that he may
15:13. with all joy and peace in *believing,*
1Co. 1:21. to save them *that believe.*
3: 5. ministers by whom ye *believed,*
9:17. a dispensation (of the gospel) *is committed* unto me. (lit. I *am intrusted* with a dispensation)
11:18. and I partly *believe* it.
13: 7. *believeth* all things, hopeth all
14:22. not to them *that believe,* but
— but for them *which believe.*
15: 2. unless ye *have believed* in vain.
11. so we preach, and so ye *believed.*
2Co. 4:13. I *believed,* and therefore have I spoken ; we also *believe,* and therefore speak ;
Gal. 2: 7. *was committed* unto me, (lit. I *was intrusted with* the gospel)
16. even we *have believed* in Jesus Christ,
3: 6. as Abraham *believed* God,
22. might be given to them *that believe.*
Eph. 1:13. in whom also *after that* ye *believed,*
19. to us-ward *who believe,*
Phi. 1:29. not only *to believe* on him,
1Th. 1: 7. ensamples to all *that believe*
2: 4. *to be put in trust with* the gospel,
10. among you *that believe :*
13. also in you *that believe.*
4:14. For if we *believe* that Jesus died and
2Th. 1:10. admired in all them *that believe*
— our testimony among you *was believed*
2:11. that they should *believe* a lie:
12. *who believed* not the truth,
1Ti. 1:11. which *was committed* to my trust. (lit. *with* which I *was intrusted*)
16. should hereafter *believe* on him

1Ti. 3:16. *believed on* in the world,
2Ti. 1:12. I know whom I *have believed,*
Tit. 1: 3. which *is committed* unto me (lit. *with* which I *have been intrusted*)
3: 8. that they *which have believed*
Heb 4: 3. we *which have believed* do enter
11: 6. must *believe* that he is, and
Jas. 2:19. Thou *believest* that there is one God ;
— the devils also *believe,* and tremble.
23. Abraham *believed* God,
1Pet.1: 8. yet *believing,* ye rejoice
21. *Who* by him *do believe* in God,
2: 6. and he *that believeth* on him
7. Unto you therefore *which believe*
1Joh.3:23. That we *should believe* on the
4: 1. Beloved, *believe* not every spirit,
16. we have known and *believed*
5: 1. *Whosoever believeth* that Jesus
5. he *that believeth* that Jesus is
10. He *that believeth* on the Son
— he *that believeth* not God
— because he *believeth* not the
13. unto you *that believe* on the name
— that ye *may believe* on the name
Jude 5. destroyed them *that believed* not.

πιστικός, *pistikos.*

Mar14: 3. of *spike*nard very precious ;
Joh.12: 3. of ointment of *spike*nard, very costly,

πίστις, *pistis.*

[1] indicates that there is no article before π. in the Greek, though one is inserted in the English ; [2] that there is an article in the Greek, though omitted in the English. When a pronoun, pers. or poss., or an adj. accompanies πίστις, the article is mostly blended with it in the rendering.

Mat. 8:10. I have not found so great *faith,*
9: 2. Jesus seeing their *faith*
22. thy *faith* hath made thee whole.
29. According to your *faith* be it
15:28. O woman, great (is) thy *faith :*
17:20. If ye have *faith* as a grain of
21:21. If ye have *faith,* and doubt not,
23:23. judgment, mercy, and [2]*faith :*
Mar 2: 5. When Jesus saw their *faith,*
4:40. how is it that ye have no *faith ?*
5:34. Daughter, thy *faith* hath made
10:52. thy *faith* hath made thee whole.
11:22. Have *faith* in God.
Lu. 5:20. when he saw their *faith,*
7: 9. I have not found so great *faith,*
50. Thy *faith* hath saved thee ;
8:25. Where is your *faith ?*
48. thy *faith* hath made thee whole ;
17: 5. Increase our *faith.*
6. If ye had *faith* as a grain of
19. thy *faith* hath made thee whole.
18: 8. shall he find [2]*faith* on the earth ?
42. thy *faith* hath saved thee.
22:32. that thy *faith* fail not:
Acts 3:16. through [2]*faith* in his name
— yea, the *faith* which is by him
6: 5. a man full of *faith*
7. of the priests were obedient to the *faith.*
8. Stephen, full of *faith* and power,
11:24. full of the Holy Ghost and of *faith :*
13: 8. to turn away the deputy from the *faith.*
14: 9. that he had *faith* to be healed,

Acts14:22. to continue in the *faith*,

27. how he had opened the door of *faith*

15: 9. purifying their hearts by ²*faith*.

16: 5. established in the *faith*,

17:31. he hath given *assurance* unto all

20:21. and *faith* toward our Lord Jesus

24:24. concerning the *faith* in Christ.

26:18. sanctified by *faith* that is in me.

Ro. 1: 5. for obedience to the ¹*faith* (lit. of *faith*)

8. that your *faith* is spoken of

12. by the mutual *faith* both of you and

17. revealed from *faith* to *faith* :

— The just shall live by *faith*.

3: 3. make the *faith* of God without effect ?

22. (which is) by *faith* of Jesus Christ

25. a propitiation through ²*faith*

26. of him which believeth (lit. of *faith*) in Jesus.

27. but by the law of *faith*.

28. a man is justified by *faith*

30. justify the circumcision by *faith*, and uncircumcision through ²*faith*.

31. make void the law through ²*faith* ?

4: 5. his *faith* is counted for righteousness.

9. for we say that ²*faith* was reckoned

11. a seal of the righteousness of the *faith*

12. walk in the steps of that *faith* of our

13. through the righteousness of *faith*.

14. ²*faith* is made void, and the promise

16. Therefore (it is) of *faith*,

— which is of the ¹*faith* of Abraham ;

19. being not weak in ²*faith*,

20. but was strong in ²*faith*,

5: 1. being justified by *faith*,

2. we have access by ²*faith* into

9:30. righteousness which is of *faith*.

32. Because (they sought it) not by *faith*,

10: 6. righteousness which is of *faith*

8. that is, the word of ²*faith*,

17. So then ²*faith* (cometh) by hearing,

11:20. and thou standest by ²*faith*.

12: 3. to every man the measure of *faith*.

6. the proportion of ²*faith* ;

14: 1. Him that is weak in the *faith*

22. Hast thou *faith*?

23. because (he eateth) not of *faith* : for whatsoever (is) not of *faith* is

16:26. to all nations for the obedience of *faith* :

1Co. 2: 5. That your *faith* should not stand in

12: 9. To another *faith* by the same

13: 2. though I have all *faith*,

13. And now abideth *faith*, hope,

15:14. and your *faith* (is) also vain.

17. your *faith* (is) vain ;

16:13. stand fast in the *faith*,

2Co. 1:24. have dominion over your *faith*,

— for by ²*faith* ye stand.

4:13. having the same spirit of ²*faith*,

5: 7. For we walk by *faith*,

8: 7. (in) *faith*, and utterance, and knowledge,

10:15. when your *faith* is increased,

13: 5. whether ye be in the *faith* ;

Gal. 1:23. now preacheth the *faith* which

2:16. but by the ¹*faith* of Jesus Christ,

— justified by the ¹*faith* of Christ,

20. I live by the ¹*faith* of the Son

3: 2. or by the hearing of *faith*?

5. or by the hearing of *faith* ?

7. they which are of *faith*,

8. justify the heathen through *faith*,

9. they which be of *faith* are blessed

11. The just shall live by *faith*.

Gal. 3:12. the law is not of *faith* :

14. promise of the Spirit through ²*faith*.

22. the promise by *faith* of Jesus Christ

23. But before ²*faith* came,

— shut up unto the *faith*

24. that we might be justified by *faith*.

25. But after that ²*faith* is come,

26. children of God by ²*faith* in Christ

5: 5. the hope of righteousness by *faith*.

6. but *faith* which worketh by love.

22. gentleness, goodness, *faith*,

6:10. who are of the houshold of ²*faith*.

Eph 1:15. after I heard of your *faith* in the Lord

2: 8. are ye saved through ²*faith* ;

3:12. with confidence by the *faith* of him.

17. dwell in your hearts by ²*faith* ;

4: 5. One Lord, one *faith*, one baptism,

13. in the unity of the *faith*,

6:16. taking the shield of ²*faith*,

23. and love with *faith*,

Phi. 1:25. your furtherance and joy of ²*faith* ;

27. for the *faith* (τῇ πίστει) of the gospel ;

2:17. sacrifice and service of your *faith*,

3: 9. which is through the ¹*faith* of Christ,

— which is of God by ²*faith* :

Col. 1: 4. Since we heard of your *faith* in Christ

23. If ye continue in the *faith* grounded

2: 5. and the stedfastness of your *faith* in

7. and stablished in the *faith*,

12. through the *faith* of the operation of God,

1Th. 1: 3. your work of *faith*, and labour of love,

8. your *faith* to God-ward is spread abroad ;

3: 2. to comfort you concerning your *faith* :

5. I sent to know your *faith*,

6. good tidings of your *faith* and charity,

7. our affliction and distress by your *faith* :

10. which is lacking in your *faith*?

5: 8. the breastplate of *faith* and love ;

2Th. 1: 3. your *faith* groweth exceedingly,

4. for your patience and *faith* in all

11. and the work of *faith* with power :

2:13. and *belief* of the truth :

3: 2. for all (men) have not ²*faith*.

1Ti. 1: 2. (my) own son in the ¹*faith* :

4. godly edifying which is in *faith* :

5. and (of) *faith* unfeigned :

14. with *faith* and love which is in

19. Holding *faith*, and a good conscience ;

— concerning ²*faith* have made shipwreck :

2: 7. of the Gentiles in *faith* and verity.

15. if they continue in *faith*

3: 9. Holding the mystery of the *faith* in a

13. great boldness in the ¹*faith* which is

4: 1. some shall depart from the *faith*,

6. in the words of ²*faith* and of good

12. in spirit, in *faith*, in purity.

5: 8. he hath denied the *faith*, and is

12. they have cast off their first *faith*.

6:10. they have erred from the *faith*,

11. godliness, *faith*, love, patience,

12. Fight the good fight of *faith*,

21. have erred concerning the *faith*.

2Ti. 1: 5. the unfeigned *faith* that is in thee,

13. in *faith* and love which is in Christ

2:18. and overthrow the *faith* of some.

22. follow righteousness, *faith*,

3: 8. reprobate concerning the *faith*.

10. ²*faith*, longsuffering, charity,

15. through *faith* which is in Christ

4: 7. I have kept the *faith* :

Tit. 1: 1. according to the ¹*faith* of God's elect,

4. (mine) own son after the common *faith* :

Tit. 1:13. may be sound in the *faith;*
2: 2. sound in ²*faith,* in charity, in patience.
10. but shewing all good *fidelity;*
3:15. that love us in the ¹*faith.*
Philem. 5. of thy love and *faith,*
6. the communication of thy *faith*
Heb 4: 2. not being mixed with ²*faith* in them
6: 1. and of *faith* toward God,
12. who through *faith* and patience
10:22. in full assurance of *faith,*
38. the just shall live by *faith:*
39. but of them that believe (lit. of *faith*) to the saving of
11: 1. Now *faith* is the substance of things
3. Through *faith* we understand that
4. By *faith* Abel offered unto God a more excellent
5. By *faith* Enoch was translated
6. But without *faith* (it is) impossible to
7. By *faith* Noah, being warned of God
— righteousness which is by *faith.*
8. By *faith* Abraham, when he was
9. By *faith* he sojourned in the land
11. Through *faith* also Sara herself
13. These all died in *faith,* not having
17. By *faith* Abraham, when he was tried,
20. By *faith* Isaac blessed Jacob and Esau
21. By *faith* Jacob, when he was a dying,
22. By *faith* Joseph, when he died,
23. By *faith* Moses, when he was born,
24. By *faith* Moses, when he was come to
27. By *faith* he forsook Egypt,
28. Through *faith* he kept the passover,
29. By *faith* they passed through the Red sea
30. By *faith* the walls of Jericho fell
31. By *faith* the harlot Rahab
33. Who through *faith* subdued kingdoms,
39. a good report through ²*faith,*
12: 2. and finisher of (our) *faith;*
13: 7. whose *faith* follow,
Jas. 1: 3. the trying of your *faith* worketh
6. But let him ask in *faith,*
2: 1. brethren, have not the *faith* of our Lord
5. rich in *faith,* and heirs of the kingdom
14. though a man say he hath *faith,* and have not works? can ²*faith* save him?
17. Even so ²*faith,* if it hath not works,
18. Thou hast *faith,* and I have works: shew me thy *faith* without thy works, and I will shew thee my *faith* by my works.
20. that ²*faith* without works is dead?
22. Seest thou how ²*faith* wrought, with his works, and by works was ²*faith*
24. and not by *faith* only.
26. so ²*faith* without works is dead
5:15. the prayer of ²*faith* shall save
1Pet.1: 5. through *faith* unto salvation
7. That the trial of your *faith,*
9. Receiving the end of your *faith,*
21. that your *faith* and hope might
5: 9. stedfast in the *faith,*
2Pet.1: 1. obtained like precious *faith* with us
5. add to your *faith* virtue;
1Joh.5: 4. that overcometh the world, (even) our *faith.*
Jude 3. contend for the *faith* which was once
20. on your most holy *faith,*
Rev. 2:13. and hast not denied my *faith,*
19. thy works, and charity, and service, and *faith,*
13:10. the patience and the *faith* of the saints.
14:12. and the *faith* of Jesus

πιστός, *pistos.*

Mat.24:45. Who then is a *faithful* and wise servant,
25:21. Well done, (thou) good and *faithful* servant: thou hast been *faithful* over a few
23. Well done, good and *faithful* servant; thou hast been *faithful* over a few
Lu. 12:42. Who then is that *faithful* and wise steward,
16:10. He that is *faithful* in that which is least is *faithful* also in much:
11. ye have not been *faithful* in the
12. And if ye have not been *faithful*
19:17. thou hast been *faithful* in
Joh. 20:27. be not faithless, but *believing.*
Acts10:45. they of the circumcision *which believed* were astonished,
13:34. the *sure* mercies of David.
16: 1. which was a Jewess, *and believed;* (lit. a *believing* Jewess)
15. If ye have judged me to be *faithful* to the Lord,
1Co. 1: 9. God (is) *faithful,* by whom ye were
4: 2. that a man be found *faithful.*
17. and *faithful* in the Lord,
7:25. mercy of the Lord to be *faithful.*
10:13. but God (is) *faithful,* who will not
2Co. 1:18. But (as) God (is) *true,* our word
6:15. he *that believeth* with an infidel?
Gal. 3: 9. are blessed with *faithful* Abraham.
Eph. 1: 1. and to the *faithful* in Christ Jesus:
6:21. and *faithful* minister in the Lord,
Col. 1: 2. To the saints and *faithful* brethren
7. a *faithful* minister of Christ;
4: 7. and a *faithful* minister
9. a *faithful* and beloved brother,
1Th. 5:24. *Faithful* (is) he that calleth you,
2Th. 3: 3. But the Lord is *faithful,*
1Ti. 1:12. that he counted me *faithful,*
15. This (is) a *faithful* saying, and worthy
3: 1. This (is) a *true* saying, If a man
11. *faithful* in all things.
4: 3. them *which believe* and know the truth.
9. This (is) a *faithful* saying and
10. specially of those *that believe.*
12. be thou an example of the *believers,*
5:16. If any man or woman *that believeth* (lit. if any *believing* (man) or *believing* (woman))
6: 2. they that have *believing* masters,
— because they are *faithful*
2Ti. 2: 2. commit thou to *faithful* men,
11. (It is) a *faithful* saying: For if we
13. he abideth *faithful:*
Tit. 1: 6. having *faithful* children,
9. Holding fast the *faithful* word
3: 8. (This is) a *faithful* saying, and these
Heb 2:17. a merciful and *faithful* high priest
3: 2. Who was *faithful* to him that
5. Moses verily (was) *faithful* in all his
10:23. he (is) *faithful* that promised;
11:11. she judged him *faithful* who had
1Pet.4:19. as unto a *faithful* Creator.
5:12. By Silvanus, a *faithful* brother
1Joh.1: 9. he is *faithful* and just to forgive
3Joh. 5. thou doest *faithfully* whatsoever
Rev. 1: 5. (who is) the *faithful* witness,
2:10. be thou *faithful* unto death,
13. Antipas (was) my *faithful* martyr,
3:14. the *faithful* and true witness,
17:14. called, and chosen, and *faithful.*
19:11. (was) called *Faithful* and True,

Rev.21: 5. these words are true and *faithful*.
22: 6. These sayings (are) *faithful* and true:

πιστόω, *pistoō*.

2Ti. 3:14. and *hast been assured of*,

πλανάω, *planao*.

Mat.18:12. and one of them *be gone astray*,
— and seeketh that *which is gone astray?*
13. which *went* not *astray*.
22:29. Ye *do err*, not knowing
24: 4. Take heed that no man *deceive* you.
5. and *shall deceive* many.
11. and *shall deceive* many.
24. they shall *deceive* the very elect.
Mar 12:24. *Do* ye not therefore *err*,
27. ye therefore *do* greatly *err*.
13: 5. Take heed lest any (man) *deceive* you:
6. and *shall deceive* many.
Lu. 21: 8. Take heed that ye *be not deceived*:
Joh. 7:12. Nay; but he *deceiveth* the people.
47. *Are* ye also *deceived?*
1Co. 6: 9. *Be* not *deceived*: neither fornicators,
15:33. *Be* not *deceived*: evil communications
Gal. 6: 7. *Be* not *deceived*; God is not mocked:
2Ti. 3:13. *deceiving*, and *being deceived*.
Tit. 3: 3. *deceived*, serving divers lusts
Heb 3:10. They *do* alway *err* in (their) heart;
5: 2. and on them *that are out of the way*;
11:38. they *wandered* in deserts,
Jas. 1:16. *Do* not *err*, my beloved brethren.
5:19. Brethren, if any of you *do err* from
1Pet.2:25. ye were as sheep *going astray*;
2Pet.2:15. and *are gone astray*, following
1Joh.1: 8. we *deceive* ourselves, and the
2:26. concerning them *that seduce* you.
3: 7. *let* no man *deceive* you:
Rev. 2:20. to teach and *to seduce* my servants
12: 9. and Satan, *which deceiveth* the whole
13:14. And *deceiveth* them that dwell on
18:23. *were* all nations *deceived*.
19:20. with which he *deceived* them
20: 3. that he *should deceive* the nations no more,
8. go out *to deceive* the nations
10. the devil *that deceived* them

πλάνη, *planee*.

Mat.27:64. so the last *error* shall be worse than
Ro. 1:27. that recompence of their *error* which
Eph. 4:14. whereby they lie in wait *to deceive*; (lit.
unto circumvention of *deception*)
1Th. 2: 3. our exhortation (was) not of *deceit*,
2Th. 2:11. God shall send them strong *delusion*,
Jas. 5:20. from the *error* of his way
2Pet.2:18. from them who live in *error*.
3:17. being led away with the *error* of the
1Joh.4: 6. and the spirit of *error*.
Jude 11. ran greedily after the *error* of Balaam

πλανήτης, *planeetees*.

Jude 13. *wandering* stars, to whom is reserved

πλάνος, *planos*.

Mat.27:63. we remember that that *deceiver* said,
2Co. 6: 8. as *deceivers*, and (yet) true;

1Ti. 4: 1. giving heed to *seducing* spirits,
2Joh. 7. For many *deceivers* are entered
— This is a *deceiver* and an antichrist.

πλάξ, *plax*.

2Co. 3: 3. not in *tables* of stone, but in fleshy *tables*
of the heart.
Heb 9: 4. and the *tables* of the covenant;

πλάσμα, *plasma*.

Ro. 9:20. Shall the *thing formed* say to him

πλάσσω, *plasso*.

Ro. 9:20. say to him *that formed* (it),
1Ti. 2:13. For Adam *was* first *formed*,

πλαστός, *plastos*.

2Pet.2: 3. with *feigned* words make merchandise

πλατεῖα, *platia*.

Mat. 6: 5. and in the corners of the *streets*,
12:19. hear his voice in the *streets*.
Lu. 10:10. out into the *streets* of the same,
13:26. and thou hast taught in our *streets*.
14:21. Go out quickly into the *streets* and
Acts 5:15. the sick into the *streets*, and
Rev.11: 8. their dead bodies (shall lie) in the *street*
21:21. and the *street* of the city (was)
22: 2. In the midst of the *street* of it,

πλάτος, *platos*.

Eph. 3:18. what (is) the *breadth*, and length,
Rev.20: 9. they went up on the *breadth* of the earth,
21:16. the length is as large as the *breadth*:
— and the *breadth* and the height of it

πλατύνω, *platuno*.

Mat.23: 5. they *make broad* their phylacteries,
2Co. 6:11. our heart *is enlarged*.
13. *be* ye also *enlarged*.

πλατύς, *platus*.

Mat. 7:13. for *wide* (is) the gate, and broad (is) the

πλέγμα. *plegma*.

1Ti. 2: 9. not with *broidered* hair,

πλείων, πλεῖον or πλέον, πλεῖστος, *plīōn, plīon or pleon, pĩistos*.

Mat. 5:20. shall exceed (the righteousness) of the
scribes (lit. shall abound *more* than, &c.)

Mat. 6:25. Is not the life *more* than meat,
　11:20. wherein *most* of his mighty works
　12:41. a *greater* than Jonas (is) here.
　　42. a *greater* than Solomon (is) here.
　20:10. that they should have received *more;*
　21: 8. And a *very great* multitude spread
　　36. other servants *more* than the first:
　26:53. *more* than twelve legions of angels?
Mar 12:33. is *more* than all whole burnt offerings
　43. hath cast *more* in, than all they
Lu. 3:13. Exact no *more* than that which is
　7:42. which of them will love him *most?*
　　43. that (he), to whom he forgave *most.*
　9:13. We have no *more* but five loaves and
　11:31. a *greater* than Solomon (is) here.
　　32. a *greater* than Jonas (is) here.
　　53. to speak of *many* things:
　12:23. The life is *more* than meat,
　21: 3. hath cast in *more* than they all:
Joh. 4: 1. baptized *more* disciples than John,
　　41. And many *more* believed
　7:31. will he do *more* miracles than
　15: 2. may bring forth *more* fruit.
　21:15. lovest thou me *more* than these?
Acts 2:40. And with *many* other words
　4:17. that it spread no *further* among
　　22. For the man was *above* (lit. of *more* than)
　　　forty years
　13:31. he was seen *many* days of them
　15:28. to lay upon you no *greater* burden
　18:20. to tarry *longer* time with them,
　19:32. and the *more part* knew not
　20: 9. and as Paul was *long* preaching,
　21:10. as we tarried (there) *many* days,
　23:13. they were *more* than forty
　　21. *more* than forty men, which have
　24: 4. that I be not *further* tedious
　　11. there are yet but twelve days (lit. not
　　　more than, &c.)
　　17. Now after *many* years I came
　25: 6. among them *more* than ten days,
　　14. when they had been there *many* days,
　27:12. the *more part* advised to depart
　　20. nor stars in *many* days appeared,
　28:23. there came *many* to him into
1Co. 9:19. that I might gain the *more.*
　10: 5. But with *many* of them God was
　14:27. by two, or at the *most* (by) three,
　15: 6. the *greater part* remain unto
2Co. 2: 6. which (was inflicted) of *many.*
　4:15. through the thanksgiving of *many*
　9: 2. your zeal hath provoked *very many.*
Phi. 1:14. And *many* of the brethren in the Lord,
2Ti. 2:16. they will increase unto *more* ungodliness.
　3: 9. they shall proceed no *further :*
Heb 3: 3. counted worthy of *more* glory
　　— hath *more* honour than the house.
　7:23. they truly were *many* priests,
　11: 4. a *more excellent* sacrifice than
Rev. 2:19. and the last (to be) *more* than the first.

πλέκω, *pleko.*

Mat.27:29. *when* they *had platted* a crown of thorns,
Mar 15:17. and *platted* a crown of thorns, *and*
Joh.19: 2. the soldiers *platted* a crown of thorns, *and*

πλεονάζω, *pleonazo.*

Ro. 5:20. that the offence *might abound.* But where
　　sin *abounded,*

Ro. 6: 1. that grace *may abound?*
2Co. 4:15. that the *abundant* grace might
　8:15. (gathered) much *had* nothing *over;*
Phi. 4:17. that may abound (lit. *abounding*) to your
　　　account.
1Th. 3:12. the Lord *make* you *to increase* and abound
2Th. 1: 3. toward each other *aboundeth;*
2Pet.1: 8. these things be in you, and *abound,*

πλεονεκτέω, *pleonekteo.*

2Co. 2:11. Lest Satan *should get an advantage of* us:
　　　(lit. lest we *should be overreached* by
　　　Satan)
　7: 2. we *have defrauded* no man.
　12:17. *Did* I make a *gain of* you
　　18. *Did* Titus make a *gain of* you?
1Th. 4: 6. and *defraud* his brother in (any) matter:

πλεονέκτης, *pleonektees.*

1Co. 5:10. or with the *covetous,*
　　11. or *covetous,* or an idolater,
　6:10. nor *covetous,* nor drunkards,
Eph. 5: 5. nor *covetous* man, who is an idolater,

πλεονεξία, *pleonexia.*

Mar 7:22. *covetousness* [plural], wickedness,
Lu. 12:15. and beware of *covetousness :*
Ro. 1:29. wickedness, *covetousness,* maliciousness;
2Co. 9: 5. and not as (of) *covetousness.*
Eph 4:19. to work all uncleanness with *greediness.*
　5: 3. all uncleanness, or *covetousness,*
Col. 3: 5. and *covetousness,* which is idolatry:
1Th. 2: 5. nor a cloke of *covetousness;*
2Pet.2: 3. through *covetousness* shall they
　　14. exercised with *covetous practices;*

πλευρά, *plūra.*

Joh.19:34. with a spear pierced his *side,*
　20:20. (his) hands and his *side.*
　　25. and thrust my hand into his *side,*
　　27. and thrust (it) into my *side:*
Acts12: 7. and he smote Peter on the *side,*

πλέω, *pleo.*

Lu. 8:23. But *as* they *sailed* he fell asleep:
Acts21: 3. we left it on the left hand, and *sailed*
　27: 2. meaning *to sail* by the coasts
　　6. a ship of Alexandria *sailing* into Italy;
　　24. all them *that sail* with thee.

πληγή, *pleegee.*

Lu. 10:30. *wounded* (him), *and* departed, (lit. having
　　　laid on *wounds*)
　12:48. things worthy of *stripes,*
Acts16:23. when they had laid many *stripes* upon
　　33. and washed (their) *stripes;*
2Co. 6: 5. In *stripes,* in imprisonments,
　11:23. in *stripes* above measure,
Rev. 9:20. were not killed by these *plagues*
　11: 6. and to smite the earth with all *plagues,*

Rev.13: 3. and his deadly *wound* was healed:
    12. whose deadly *wound* was healed.
    14. which had the *wound* by a sword,
  15: 1. having the seven last *plagues;*
    6. having the seven *plagues,*
    8. till the seven *plagues* of the seven
  16: 9. hath power over these *plagues:*
    21. because of the *plague* of the hail; for the
        plague thereof was exceeding great.
  18: 4. that ye receive not of her *plagues.*
    8. shall her *plagues* come in one day,
  21: 9. full of the seven last *plagues,*
  22:18. God shall add unto him the *plagues* that

πλῆθος, *pleethos.*

Mar 3: 7. and a great *multitude* from Galilee
    8, a great *multitude,* when they had heard
Lu. 1:10. And the whole *multitude* of the people
  2:13. a *multitude* of the heavenly host
  5: 6. a great *multitude* of fishes:
  6:17. and a great *multitude* of people
  8:37. Then the whole *multitude* of the country
  19:37. the whole *multitude* of the disciples
  23: 1. the whole *multitude* of them arose,
    27. a great *company* of people,
Joh. 5: 3. In these lay a great *multitude*
  21: 6. for the *multitude* of fishes.
Acts 2: 6. the *multitude* came together,
  4:32. And the *multitude* of them that
  5:14. *multitudes* both of men and women.
    16. There came also a *multitude* (out)
  6: 2. the twelve called the *multitude* of the
      disciples
    5. pleased the whole *multitude:*
  14: 1. a great *multitude* both of the Jews
    4. But the *multitude* of the city was
  15:12. Then all the *multitude* kept silence,
    30. gathered the *multitude* together,
  17: 4. devout Greeks a great *multitude,*
  19: 9. evil of that way before the *multitude,*
  21:22. the *multitude* must needs come
    36. the *multitude* of the people followed
  23: 7. and the *multitude* was divided.
  25:24. all the *multitude* of the Jews
  28: 3. gathered a *bundle* of sticks,
Heb 11:12. the stars of the sky in *multitude,*
Jas. 5:20. shall hide a *multitude* of sins.
1Pet.4: 8. shall cover the *multitude* of sins.

πληθύνω, *pleethuno.*

Mat.24:12. because iniquity shall *abound,*
Acts 6: 1. *when* the number of the disciples *was*
    multiplied,
    7. the number of the disciples *multiplied*
  7:17. people grew and *multiplied*
  9:31. in the comfort of the Holy Ghost, *were*
    multiplied.
  12:24. the word of God grew and *multiplied.*
2Co. 9:10. and *multiply* your seed sown,
Heb 6:14. and *multiplying* I *will multiply* thee.
1Pet.1: 2. and peace, *be multiplied.*
2Pet.1: 2. Grace and peace *be multiplied* unto
Jude   2. and love, *be multiplied.*

πλήθω, *pleetho.*

Mat.22:10. the wedding *was furnished* with guests

Mat.27:48. and *filled* (it) with vinegar,
Lu. 1:15. he *shall be filled* with the Holy Ghost,
    23. the days of...*were accomplished,*
    41. *was filled* with the Holy Ghost:
    57. Elisabeth's *full* time *came*
    67. Zacharias *was filled* with the
  2: 6. the days *were accomplished* that
    21. eight days *were accomplished*
    22. when the days...*were accomplished,*
  4:28. heard these things, *were filled* with wrath,
  5: 7. and *filled* both the ships,
    26. and *were filled* with fear,
  6:11. they *were filled* with madness;
Joh.19:29. and they *filled* a spunge with vinegar,
Acts 2: 4. they *were* all *filled* with the Holy Ghost.
  3:10. and they *were filled* with wonder and
  4: 8. Then Peter, *filled* with the Holy Ghost,
    31. they *were* all *filled* with the Holy Ghost,
  5:17. and *were filled* with indignation,
  9:17. and *be filled* with the Holy Ghost.
  13: 9. Paul, *filled* with the Holy Ghost,
    45. they *were filled* with envy,
  19:29. the whole city *was filled* with confusion:

πλήκτης, *pleektees.*

1Ti. 3: 3. Not given to wine, no *striker,*
Tit. 1: 7. no *striker,* not given to filthy lucre;

πλημμύρα, *pleemmura.*

Lu. 6:48. and when the *flood* arose,

πλήν, *pleen.*

Mat.11:22. *But* I say unto you, It shall be
    24. *But* I say unto you, That it shall
  18: 7. *but* woe to that man by whom
  26:39. *nevertheless* not as I will, but
    64. *nevertheless* I say unto you,
Mar 12:32. and there is none other *but* he:
Lu. 6:24. *But* woe unto you that are rich!
    35. *But* love ye your enemies,
  10:11. *notwithstanding* be ye sure of this,
    14. *But* it shall be more tolerable for
    20. *Notwithstanding* in this rejoice not,
  11:41. *But rather* give alms of such things
  12:31. *But rather* seek ye the kingdom
  13:33. *Nevertheless* I must walk to day,
  18: 8. *Nevertheless* when the Son of man
  19:27. *But* those mine enemies, which
  22:21. *But,* behold, the hand of him that
    22. *but* woe unto that man by
    42. *nevertheless* not my will, but
  23:28. *but* weep for yourselves, and
Joh. 8:10. and saw none *but* the woman,
Acts 8: 1. *except* the apostles.
  15:28. *than* these necessary things;
  20:23. *Save* that the Holy Ghost witnesseth
  27:22. life among you, *but* of the ship.
1Co.11:11. *Nevertheless* neither is the man
Eph. 5:33. *Nevertheless* let every one of
Phi. 1:18. What then? *notwithstanding,* every
  3:16. *Nevertheless,* whereto we have
  4:14. *Notwithstanding* ye have well
Rev. 2:25. *But* that which ye have (already)

πλήρης, *pleerees.*

Mat.14:20. that remained twelve baskets *full.*

Mat.15:37. left seven baskets *full*.

Mar 4:28. the *full* corn in the ear.

6:43. twelve baskets *full* of the fragments,

8:19. how many baskets *full* of

Lu. 4: 1. Jesus being *full* of the Holy Ghost

5:12. behold a man *full* of leprosy:

Joh. 1:14. *full* of grace and truth.

Acts 6: 3. *full* of the Holy Ghost

5. a man *full* of faith and of

8. Stephen, *full* of faith and power,

7:55. he, being *full* of the Holy Ghost,

9:36. this woman was *full* of good works

11:24. and *full* of the Holy Ghost

13:10. O *full* of all subtilty

19:28. they were *full* of wrath,

2Joh. 8. that we receive a *full* reward.

πληροφορέω, *pleerophoreo.*

Lu. 1: 1. of those things *which are most surely believed* among us, (lit. *which have full course*)

Ro. 4:21. And *being fully persuaded* that,

14: 5. *Let* every man *be fully persuaded*

2Ti. 4: 5. *make full* proof of thy ministry.

17. the preaching *might be fully known*,

πληροφορία, *pleerophoria.*

Col. 2: 2. of the *full assurance* of understanding,

1Th. 1: 5. and in much *assurance;*

Heb 6:11. to the *full assurance* of hope

10:22. in *full assurance*(lit. in *full bearing*)of faith,

πληρόω, *pleeroō.*

Mat. 1:22. that it *might be fulfilled*

2:15. that it *might be fulfilled* which was

17. Then *was fulfilled* that which was

23. that it *might be fulfilled*

3:15. *to fulfil* all righteousness.

4:14. That *it might be fulfilled*

5:17. not come to destroy, but *to fulfil*

8:17. That it *might be fulfilled*

12:17. That it *might be fulfilled* which

13:35. That it *might be fulfilled* which

48. Which, when it *was full*, they drew

21: 4. that it *might be fulfilled*

23:32. *Fill* ye *up* then the measure of

26:54. shall the scriptures *be fulfilled,*

56. that the scriptures of the prophets *might be fulfilled.*

27: 9. Then *was fulfilled* that which

35. that it *might be fulfilled* which

Mar 1:15. The time is *fulfilled*, and the kingdom

14:49. but the scriptures must be fulfilled. (lit. but that the scriptures *be fulfilled*)

15:28. And the scripture *was fulfilled,*

Lu. 1:20. which *shall be fulfilled* in their season.

2:40. strong in spirit, *filled* with wisdom:

3: 5. Every valley *shall be filled,*

4:21. This day is this scripture *fulfilled*

7: 1. when he *had ended* all his sayings

9:31. which he should *accomplish* at

21:22. are written may *be fulfilled.*

24. until the times of the Gentiles *be fulfilled.*

22:16. until it *be fulfilled* in the kingdom

24:44. that all things must *be fulfilled,*

Joh. 3:29. this my joy therefore is *fulfilled.*

Joh. 7: 8. my time is not yet *full come.*

12: 3. the house *was filled* with the

38. *might be fulfilled,* which he spake,

13:18. that the scripture *may be fulfilled,*

15:11. (that) your joy *might be full.*

25. that the word *might be fulfilled*

16: 6. sorrow *hath filled* your heart.

24. that your joy may be *full.*

17:12. the scripture *might be fulfilled.*

13. might have my joy *fulfilled*

18: 9. the saying *might be fulfilled,*

32. saying of Jesus *might be fulfilled,*

19:24. the scripture *might be fulfilled,*

36. the scripture *should be fulfilled,*

Acts 1:16. must needs *have been fulfilled,*

2: 2. and it *filled* all the house

28. thou *shalt make* me *full* of joy

3:18. he hath so *fulfilled.*

5: 3. why *hath* Satan *filled* thine heart

28. and, behold, ye *have filled* Jerusalem

7:23. when he was full forty years old, (lit. when the space of...*was fulfilled*)

30. *when* forty years *were expired,*

9:23. after that many days *were fulfilled,*

12:25. *when* they *had fulfilled* (their) ministry,

13:25. as John *fulfilled* his course,

27. they *have fulfilled* (them) in condemning

52. the disciples *were filled* with joy,

14:26. for the work which they *fulfilled.*

19:21. After these things *were ended,*

24:27. But *after* two years (lit. two years *having been fulfilled*)

Ro. 1:29. *Being filled* with all unrighteousness,

8: 4. the law *might be fulfilled* in us,

13: 8. *hath fulfilled* the law.

15:13. *fill* you with all joy and peace in

14. *filled* with all knowledge,

19. I *have fully preached* the gospel of

2Co. 7: 4. I *am filled* with comfort,

10: 6. when your obedience is *fulfilled.*

Gal. 5:14. all the law is *fulfilled* in one word,

Eph. 1:23. of him *that filleth* (lit. that *is filled*) all in all.

3:19. *might be filled* with all the fulness of God.

4:10. that he *might fill* all things.

5:18. but *be filled* with the Spirit,

Phi. 1:11. *Being filled* with the fruits of

2: 2. *Fulfil* ye my joy, that ye be

4:18. I *am full,* having received

19. my God *shall supply* all your need

Col. 1: 9. that ye *might be filled* with the

25. *to fulfil* the word of God;

2:10. And ye are *complete* in him,

4:12. perfect and *complete* in all the will

17. that thou *fulfil* it.

2Th. 1:11. and *fulfil* all the good pleasure

2Ti. 1: 4. that I *may be filled* with joy;

Jas. 2:23. the scripture *was fulfilled*

1Joh.1: 4. that your joy may be *full.*

2Joh. 12. that our joy may be *full.*

Rev. 3: 2. I have not found thy works *perfect*

6:11. their brethren, that should be killed as they (were), should *be fulfilled.*

πλήρωμα, *pleerōma.*

Mat. 9:16. that *which is put in to fill* it *up* taketh

Mar 2:21. the new *piece that filled* it *up*

8:20. how many baskets *full* of fragments

Joh. 1:16. of his *fulness* have all we received,

Ro. 11:12. how much more their *fulness?*
25. until the *fulness* of the Gentiles
13:10. love (is) the *fulfilling* of the law.
15:29. come in the *fulness* of the blessing
1Co.10:26. (is) the Lord's, and the *fulness* thereof.
28. the Lord's, and the *fulness* thereof:
Gal. 4: 4. when the *fulness* of the time was come,
Eph. 1:10. dispensation of the *fulness* of times
23. the *fulness* of him that filleth
3:19. with all the *fulness* of God.
4:13. stature of the *fulness* of Christ:
Col. 1:19. in him should all *fulness* dwell;
2: 9. all the *fulness* of the Godhead bodily.

πλησίον, *pleesion.* adv.

Joh. 4: 5. *near* to the parcel of ground

ὁ πλησίον, *ho pleesion.*

The adv. used as an adj.

Mat. 5:43. shalt love thy *neighbour*, (lit. the one *near*)
19:19. Thou shalt love thy *neighbour* as thyself.
22:39. Thou shalt love thy *neighbour* as
Mar 12:31. Thou shalt love thy *neighbour* as
33. and to love (his) *neighbour* as himself,
Lu. 10:27. and thy *neighbour* as thyself.
29. And who is my *neighbour?*
36. was *neighbour* unto him that
Acts 7:27. But he that did his *neighbour* wrong
Ro. 13: 9. Thou shalt love thy *neighbour* as
10. Love worketh no ill to his *neighbour:*
15: 2. please (his) *neighbour* for (his) good
Gal. 5:14. Thou shalt love thy *neighbour* as
Eph. 4:25. truth with his *neighbour:*
Heb 8:11. not teach every man his *neighbour,*
Jas. 2: 8. Thou shalt love thy *neighbour* as

πλησμονή, *pleesmonee.*

Col. 2:23. to the *satisfying* of the flesh.

πλήσσω, *pleesso.*

Rev. 8:12. part of the sun *was smitten,*

πλοιάριον, *ploiarion.*

Mar 3: 9. that a *small ship* should wait on him
4:36. also with him other *little ships.*
Joh. 6:22. there was none other *boat* there,
— went not with his disciples into the *boat,*
23. there came other *boats* from Tiberias
21: 8. the other disciples came in a *little ship;*

πλοῖον, *ploion.*

Mat. 4:21. in a *ship* with Zebedee their father,
22. they immediately left the *ship* and
8:23. when he was entered into a *ship,*
24. insomuch that the *ship* was covered
9: 1. And he entered into a *ship,*
13: 2. so that he went into a *ship,*
14:13. he departed thence by *ship*
22. constrained his disciples to get into a *ship,*

Mat.14:24. But the *ship* was now in the midst of
29. when Peter was come down out of the *ship,*
32. when they were come into the *ship,*
33. Then they that were in the *ship* came
15:39. and took *ship,* and came into
Mar 1:19. in the *ship* mending their nets.
20. left their father Zebedee in the *ship*
4: 1. so that he entered into a *ship,*
36. even as he was in the *ship.*
37. the waves beat into the *ship,*
5: 2. when he was come out of the *ship,*
18. when he was come into the *ship,*
21. by *ship* unto the other side,
6:32. into a desert place by *ship* privately.
45. to get into the *ship,* and to go
47. the *ship* was in the midst of the sea,
51. he went up unto them into the *ship;*
54. when they were come out of the *ship,*
8:10. straightway he entered into a *ship*
13. and entering into the *ship* again
14. neither had they in the *ship*
Lu. 5: 2. And saw two *ships* standing by
3. he entered into one of the *ships,*
— taught the people out of the *ship.*
7. which were in the other *ship,*
— they came, and filled both the *ships,*
11. when they had brought their *ships* to
8:22. that he went into a *ship* with
37. he went up into the *ship,*
Joh. 6:17. And entered into a *ship,*
19. and drawing nigh unto the *ship:*
21. received him into the *ship:*
— and immediately the *ship* was
24. they also took *shipping,* (lit. entered into *ships*)
21: 3. and entered into a *ship*
6. Cast the net on the right side of the *ship,*
Acts20:13. And we went before to *ship,*
38. they accompanied him unto the *ship.*
21: 2. And finding a *ship* sailing
3. for there the *ship* was to unlade
6. we took *ship;* and they
27: 2. And entering into a *ship* of
6. there the centurion found a *ship* of
10. not only of the lading and *ship,*
15. And when the *ship* was caught,
17. undergirding the *ship;*
19. the tackling of the *ship.*
22. but of the *ship.*
30. about to flee out of the *ship,*
31. Except these abide in the *ship,*
37. we were in all in the *ship*
38. they lightened the *ship,*
39. to thrust in the *ship.*
44. some on (broken pieces) of the *ship.*
28:11. we departed in a *ship* of
Jas. 3: 4. Behold also the *ships,*
Rev. 8: 9. the third part of the *ships* were
18:17. all the company in *ships,*
19. all that had *ships* in the sea

πλόος, *plous.*

Acts21: 7. finished (our) *course* from Tyre,
27: 9. when *sailing* was now dangerous,
10. I perceive that this *voyage* will be

πλούσιος, *plousios.*

Mat.19:23. That a *rich* man shall hardly enter

Mat.19:24. than for a *rich* man to enter
    27:57. there came a *rich* man of Arimathæa,
Mar 10:25. than for a *rich* man to enter into the
    12:41. and many that were *rich* cast in
Lu. 6:24. woe unto you that are *rich !*
    12:16. The ground of a certain *rich* man
    14:12. nor (thy) *rich* neighbours;
    16: 1. There was a certain *rich* man,
       19. There was a certain *rich* man,
       21. which fell from the *rich* man's table:
       22. the *rich* man also died,
    18:23. for he was very *rich.*
       25. than for a *rich* man to enter into
    19: 2. and he was *rich.*
       21: 1. and saw the *rich* men casting their
2Co. 8: 9. though he was *rich,* yet for your
Eph. 2: 4. God, who is *rich* in mercy,
1Ti. 6:17. Charge them that are *rich* in this world,
Jas. 1:10. But the *rich,* in that he is made low:
       11. so also shall the *rich* man fade away
    2: 5. *rich* in faith, and heirs of
      6. Do not *rich* men oppress you,
    5: 1. Go to now, (ye) *rich* men,
Rev. 2: 9. but thou art *rich*
    3:17. Because thou sayest, I am *rich,*
    6:15. and the *rich* men, and the chief
    13:16. *rich* and poor, free and bond,

πλουσίως, *plousiōs.*

Col. 3:16. word of Christ dwell in you *richly*
1Ti. 6:17. who giveth us *richly* all things
Tit. 3: 6. Which he shed on us *abundantly*
2Pet.1:11. shall be ministered unto you *abundantly*

πλουτέω, *plouteo.*

Lu. 1:53. the *rich* he hath sent empty away.
    12:21. and *is not rich* toward God.
Ro. 10:12. *is rich* unto all that call
1Co. 4: 8. now ye *are rich,*
2Co. 8: 9. ye through his poverty *might be rich.*
1Ti. 6: 9. they that will *be rich* fall
      18. that they *be rich* in good works,
Rev. 3:17. I am *rich,* and *increased with goods,*
    18. that thou *mayest be rich ;*
    18: 3. *are waxed rich* through the abundance
      15. *which were made rich* by her, shall
      19. wherein *were made rich* all that

πλουτίζω, *ploutizo.*

1Co. 1: 5. ye *are enriched* by him,
2Co. 6:10. as poor, yet *making* many *rich ;*
    9:11. *Being enriched* in every thing

πλοῦτος, *ploutos.*

Mat.13:22. the deceitfulness of *riches,*
Mar 4:19. and the deceitfulness of *riches,*
Lu. 8:14. choked with cares and *riches*
Ro. 2: 4. Or despisest thou the *riches* of his
    9:23. make known the *riches* of his glory
    11:12. if the fall of them (be) the *riches* of the
       world, and the diminishing of them the
       riches of the Gentiles;
      33. O the depth of the *riches* both of

2Co. 8: 2. unto the *riches* of their liberality.
Eph 1: 7. according to the *riches* of his grace;
      18. what the *riches* of the glory of
    2: 7. the exceeding *riches* of his grace
    3: 8. the unsearchable *riches* of Christ;
      16. according to the *riches* of his glory,
Phi. 4:19. according to his *riches* in glory
Col. 1:27. what (is) the *riches* of the glory
    2: 2. unto all *riches* of the full assurance of
1Ti. 6:17. nor trust in uncertain *riches,*
Heb 11:26. greater *riches* than the treasures in
Jas. 5: 2. Your *riches* are corrupted,
Rev. 5:12. to receive power, and *riches,* and wisdom,
    18:17(16). so great *riches* is come to nought.

πλύνω, *pluno.*

Rev. 7:14. and *have washed* their robes, and

πνεῦμα, *pnūma.*

Note. — [1]. πνεῦμα.   [2]. τὸ πνεῦμα.   [3]. πνεῦμα ἅγιον.   [4]. τὸ ἅγιον πνεῦμα.   [5]. τὸ πνεῦμα τὸ ἅγιον. The passages not marked are defined by some genitive or other adjunct.

Mat. 1:18. she was found with child of the Holy
       Ghost.[3]
      20. is of the Holy *Ghost.*[3]
    3:11. with the Holy *Ghost,*[3] and (with) fire:
      16. he saw the *Spirit* of God descending
    4: 1. led up of the *spirit*[2] into the wilderness
    5: 3. Blessed (are) the poor in *spirit:*[2]
    8:16. he cast out the *spirits* with (his) word,
    10: 1. power (against) unclean *spirits,*
      20. but the *Spirit* of your Father
    12:18. I will put my *spirit* upon him,
      28. if I cast out devils by the *Spirit* of God,
      31. blasphemy (against) the (Holy) *Ghost*[2]
      32. speaketh against the Holy *Ghost,*[5].
      43. When the unclean *spirit* is gone out
      45. seven other *spirits* more wicked
    22:43. How then doth David in *spirit*[1] call
    26:41. the *spirit*[2] indeed (is) willing,
    27:50. yielded up the *ghost.*[2]
    28:19. and of the Son, and of the Holy *Ghost :*[4]
Mar 1: 8. shall baptize you with the Holy *Ghost.*[3]
      10. and the *Spirit*[2] like a dove
      12. immediately the *spirit*[2] driveth him
      23. a man with an unclean *spirit ;*
      26. when the unclean *spirit* had torn
      27. even the unclean *spirits,*
    2: 8. perceived in his *spirit* that they
    3:11. And unclean *spirits,* when they saw
      29. blaspheme against the Holy *Ghost*[5]
      30. they said, He hath an unclean *spirit.*
    5: 2. a man with an unclean *spirit,*
      8. out of the man, (thou) unclean *spirit.*
      13. And the unclean *spirits* went out,
    6: 7. power over unclean *spirits ;*
    7:25. had an unclean *spirit,*
    8:12. he sighed deeply in his *spirit,*
    9:17. which hath a dumb *spirit ;*
      20. the *spirit*[2] tare him;
      25. he rebuked the foul *spirit,*
      — (Thou) dumb and deaf *spirit,*
    12:36. David himself said by the Holy *Ghost,*[5]
    13:11. not ye that speak, but the Holy *Ghost.*[5]
    14:38. The *spirit*[2] truly (is) ready,
Lu. 1:15. shall be filled with the Holy *Ghost,*[3]
      17. in the *spirit* and power of Elias,

Lu. 1:35. The Holy *Ghost* [3] shall come upon thee,
    41. was filled with the Holy *Ghost* : [3]
    47. my *spirit* hath rejoiced in God
    67. was filled with the Holy *Ghost*, [3]
    80. and waxed strong in *spirit*, [1]
  2:25. and the Holy *Ghost* [3] was upon him.
    26. unto him by the Holy *Ghost*, [5]
    27. he came by the *Spirit* [2] into
    40. and waxed strong in *spirit*, [1]
  3:16. baptize you with the Holy *Ghost* [3] and
    22. And the Holy *Ghost* [5] descended
  4: 1. being full of the Holy *Ghost* [3]
    — was led by the *Spirit* [2] into
    14. in the power of the *Spirit* [2]
    18. The *Spirit* of the Lord (is) upon me,
    33. which had a *spirit* of an unclean devil,
    36. he commandeth the unclean *spirits*,
  6:18. vexed with unclean *spirits* :
  7:21. and of evil *spirits* ;
  8: 2. had been healed of evil *spirits*
    29. commanded the unclean *spirit* to
    55. And her *spirit* came again,
  9:39. lo, a *spirit* [1] taketh him,
    42. Jesus rebuked the unclean *spirit*,
    55. what manner of *spirit* ye are of.
 10:20. that the *spirits* are subject unto you;
    21. Jesus rejoiced in *spirit*, [2]
 11:13. give the Holy *Spirit* [3] to them that ask
    him ?
    24. When the unclean *spirit* is gone out
    26. seven other *spirits* more wicked than
 12:10. against the Holy *Ghost* [4]
    12. For the Holy *Ghost* [4] shall teach you
 13:11. which had a *spirit* of infirmity
 23:46. into thy hands I commend my *spirit* :
 24:37. that they had seen a *spirit*. [1]
    39. a *spirit* [1] hath not flesh and bones,
Joh. 1:32. I saw the *Spirit* [2] descending from heaven
    like a dove,
    33. thou shalt see the *Spirit* [2] descending,
    — baptizeth with the Holy *Ghost*. [3]
  3: 5. of water and (of) the *Spirit*, [1]
    6. that which is born of the *Spirit* [2] is *spirit*. [1]
    8. The *wind* [2] bloweth where it listeth,
    — so is every one that is born of the *Spirit*. [2]
    34. for God giveth not the *Spirit* [2] by measure
  4:23. worship the Father in *spirit* [1] and
    24. God (is) a *Spirit* : [1] and they that worship
    him must worship (him) in *spirit* [1] and
  6:63. It is the *spirit* [2] that quickeneth;
    — (they) are *spirit*, [1] and (they) are life.
  7:39. this spake he of the *Spirit*, [2]
    — for the Holy *Ghost* [3] was not yet (given);
 11:33. he groaned in the *spirit*, [2]
 13:21. he was troubled in *spirit*, [2]
 14:17. the *Spirit* of truth; whom the world
    26. the Holy *Ghost*, [5] whom the Father
 15:26. the *Spirit* of truth, which
 16:13. when he, the *Spirit* of truth, is come,
 19:30. and gave up the *ghost*. [2]
 20:22. Receive ye the Holy *Ghost* : [3]
Acts 1: 2. he through the Holy *Ghost* [3] had given
    5. be baptized with the Holy *Ghost* [3]
    8. after that the Holy *Ghost* [4] is come
    16. which the Holy *Ghost* [5] by the mouth of
  2: 4. all filled with the Holy *Ghost*, [3]
    — as the *Spirit* [2] gave them utterance,
    17. I will pour out of my *Spirit* upon
    18. pour out in those days of my *Spirit* ;
    33. the promise of the Holy *Ghost*, [4]
    38. receive the gift of the Holy *Ghost*. [4]
  4: 8. Peter, filled with the Holy *Ghost*, [3]

Acts 4:31. filled with the Holy *Ghost*, [3]
  5: 3. to lie to the Holy *Ghost*, [5]
    9. to tempt the *Spirit* of the Lord ?
    16. vexed with unclean *spirits* :
    32. and (so is) also the Holy *Ghost*, [5]
  6: 3. full of the Holy *Ghost* [3] and
    5. full of faith and of the Holy *Ghost*, [3]
    10. the wisdom and the *spirit* [2] by which
  7:51. ye do always resist the Holy *Ghost* : [5]
    55. being full of the Holy *Ghost*, [3]
    59. Lord Jesus, receive my *spirit*.
  8: 7. For unclean *spirits*, crying
    15. might receive the Holy *Ghost* : [3]
    17. they received the Holy *Ghost*. [3]
    18. the Holy *Ghost* [5] was given,
    19. he may receive the Holy *Ghost*. [3]
    29. Then the *Spirit* [2] said unto Philip,
    39. the *Spirit* of the Lord caught away
  9:17. and be filled with the Holy *Ghost*. [3]
    31. and in the comfort of the Holy *Ghost*, [4]
 10:19. the *Spirit* [2] said unto him,
    38. with the Holy *Ghost* [3] and with power:
    44. the Holy *Ghost* [5] fell on all them
    45. the gift of the Holy *Ghost*. [4]
    47. have received the Holy *Ghost* [5] as well
 11:12. And the *spirit* [2] bade me go
    15. the Holy *Ghost* [5] fell on them,
    16. be baptized with the Holy *Ghost*. [3]
    24. and full of the Holy *Ghost* [3]
    28. signified by the *spirit* [2] that
 13: 2. the Holy *Ghost* [5] said, Separate me
    4. being sent forth by the Holy *Ghost*, [5]
    9. Paul, filled with the Holy *Ghost*, [3]
    52. and with the Holy *Ghost*. [3]
 15: 8. giving them the Holy *Ghost*, [5]
    28. it seemed good to the Holy *Ghost*, [4]
 16: 6. were forbidden of the Holy *Ghost* [4]
    7. but the *Spirit* [2] suffered them not.
    16. possessed with a *spirit* of divination (lit.
    spirit of Python)
    18. turned and said to the *spirit*, [2]
 17:16. his *spirit* was stirred in him,
 18: 5. Paul was pressed in the *spirit*, [2]
    25. being fervent in the *spirit*, [2]
 19: 2. Have ye received the Holy *Ghost* [3]
    — whether there be any Holy *Ghost*. [3]
    6. the Holy *Ghost* [5] came on them ;
    12. the evil *spirits* went out of them.
    13. which had evil *spirits*
    15. And the evil *spirit* answered
    16. the man in whom the evil *spirit* was
    21. Paul purposed in the *spirit*, [2]
 20:22. I go bound in the *spirit* [2] unto Jerusalem,
    23. Save that the Holy *Ghost* [5] witnesseth
    28. the Holy *Ghost* [5] made you overseers,
 21: 4. who said to Paul through the *Spirit*, [2]
    11. Thus saith the Holy *Ghost*, [5]
 23: 8. neither angel, nor *spirit* : [1]
    9. but if a *spirit* [1] or an angel
 28:25. Well spake the Holy *Ghost* [5] by
Ro. 1: 4. according to the *spirit* of holiness,
    9. whom I serve with my *spirit*
  2:29. in the *spirit*, [1] (and) not in the letter ;
  5: 5. by the Holy *Ghost* [3] which is given
  7: 6. in newness of *spirit*, [1] and not
  8: 1. not after the flesh, but after the *Spirit*. [1]
    2. For the law of the *Spirit* of life
    4. not after the flesh, but after the *Spirit*. [1]
    5. but they that are after the *Spirit* [1] the
    things of the *Spirit*. [2]
    6. but to be *spiritually* minded (lit. the mind
    of the *Spirit* [2]) (is) life and peace:

Ro. 8: 9. but in the *Spirit*,[1] if so be that the *Spirit* of God dwell in you.
— have not the *Spirit* of Christ,
10. but the *Spirit*[2] (is) life because
11. But if the *Spirit* of him that
— by his *Spirit* that dwelleth in you.
13. if ye through the *Spirit*[1] do mortify
14. as are led by the *Spirit* of God,
15. received the *spirit* of bondage
— received the *Spirit* of adoption,
16. The *Spirit*[2] itself beareth witness with our *spirit*,
23. the firstfruits of the *Spirit*,[2]
26. Likewise the *Spirit*[2] also helpeth
— but the *Spirit* itself maketh
27. what (is) the mind of the *Spirit*,[2]
9: 1. bearing me witness in the Holy *Ghost*,[3]
11: 8. hath given them the *spirit* of slumber,
12:11. fervent in *spirit*;[2] serving the Lord;
14:17. and joy in the Holy *Ghost*.[3]
15:13. the power of the Holy *Ghost*.[3]
16. sanctified by the Holy *Ghost*.[3]
19. by the power of the *Spirit* of God; (πνεύματος Θεοῦ)
30. for the love of the *Spirit*,[2]
1Co. 2: 4. in demonstration of the *Spirit*[1]
10. unto us by his *Spirit*: for the *Spirit*[2] searcheth all things,
11. save the *spirit* of man which
— but the *Spirit* of God.
12. Now we have received, not the *spirit* of the world, but the *spirit* which is of God;
13. but which the Holy *Ghost*[3] teacheth;
14. the things of the *Spirit* of God:
3:16. and (that) the *Spirit* of God dwelleth
4:21. and (in) the *spirit* of meekness?
5: 3. but present in *spirit*,[2]
4. and my *spirit*, with the power of
5. that the *spirit*[2] may be saved
6:11. and by the *Spirit* of our God.
17. he that is joined unto the Lord is one *spirit*.
19. the temple of the Holy *Ghost*[4] (which is) in you,
20. and in your *spirit*, which are God's.
7:34. both in body and in *spirit*:[1]
40. also that I have the *Spirit* of God.
12: 3. no man speaking by the *Spirit* of God
— but by the Holy *Ghost*.[3]
4. but the same *Spirit*.
7. the manifestation of the *Spirit*[2]
8. to one is given by the *Spirit*[2]
— knowledge by the same *Spirit*;
9. faith by the same *Spirit*;
— of healing by the same *Spirit*;
10. to another discerning of *spirits*;
11. that one and the selfsame *Spirit*,
13. For by one *Spirit* are we all baptized
— all made to drink into one *Spirit*.
14: 2. howbeit in the *spirit*[1] he speaketh
12. zealous of *spiritual* (gifts), (lit. of *spirits*)
14. my *spirit* prayeth,
15. I will pray with the *spirit*,[2]
— I will sing with the *spirit*,[2]
16. when thou shalt bless with the *spirit*,[2]
32. the *spirits* of the prophets are
15:45. a quickening *spirit*.
16:18. they have refreshed my *spirit*
2Co. 1:22. given the earnest of the *Spirit*[2]
2:13. I had no rest in my *spirit*,
3: 3. but with the *Spirit* of the living God;
6. not of the letter, but of the *spirit*:[1]
— but the *spirit*[2] giveth life.

2Co. 3: 8. the ministration of the *spirit*[2]
17. Now the Lord is that *Spirit*:[2] and where the *Spirit* of the Lord (is),
18. as by the *Spirit* of the Lord. (ἀπὸ Κυρίου πνεύματος)
4:13. We having the same *spirit* of faith,
5: 5. the earnest of the *Spirit*.[2]
6: 6. by the Holy *Ghost*,[3] by love
7: 1. filthiness of the flesh and *spirit*,[1]
13. because his *spirit* was refreshed
11: 4. or (if) ye receive another *spirit*,
12:18. walked we not in the same *spirit*?
13:14(13). the communion of the Holy *Ghost*,[4]
Gal. 3: 2. Received ye the *Spirit*[2] by the works
3. having begun in the *Spirit*,[1]
5. that ministereth to you the *Spirit*,[2]
14. the promise of the *Spirit*[2]
4: 6. sent forth the *Spirit* of his Son
29. (that was born) after the *Spirit*,[1]
5: 5. For we through the *Spirit*[1] wait
16. Walk in the *Spirit*,[1]
17. For the flesh lusteth against the *Spirit*,[2] and the *Spirit*[2] against the flesh:
18. if ye be led of the *Spirit*,[1]
22. the fruit of the *Spirit*[2] is love,
25. If we live in the *Spirit*,[1] let us also walk in the *Spirit*.[1]
6: 1. restore such an one in the *spirit* of meekness;
8. he that soweth to the *Spirit*[2] shall of the *Spirit*[2] reap life
18. (be) with your *spirit*.
Eph. 1:13. sealed with that holy *Spirit*[5] of promise,
17. give unto you the *spirit* of wisdom
2: 2. the *spirit* that now worketh
18. access by one *Spirit* unto the Father.
22. habitation of God through the *Spirit*.[1]
3: 5. and prophets by the *Spirit*;[1]
16. by his *Spirit* in the inner man;
4: 3. the unity of the *Spirit*[2] in the
4. one body, and one *Spirit*, even
23. be renewed in the *spirit* of your mind;
30. grieve not the Holy *Spirit*[5] of God,
5: 9. For the fruit of the *Spirit*[2] (is)
18. be filled with the *Spirit*;[1]
6:17. the sword of the *Spirit*,[2]
18. prayer and supplication in the *Spirit*,[1]
Phi. 1:19. supply of the *Spirit* of Jesus Christ,
27. that ye stand fast in one *spirit*,
2: 1. if any fellowship of the *Spirit*,[1]
3: 3. which worship God in the *spirit*,[1]
Col. 1: 8. your love in the *Spirit*.[1]
2: 5. yet am I with you in the *spirit*,[2]
1Th. 1: 5. in power, and in the Holy *Ghost*,[3]
6. with joy of the Holy *Ghost*:[3]
4: 8. also given unto us his holy *Spirit*.[5]
5:19. Quench not the *Spirit*.[2]
23. your whole *spirit* and soul and body
2Th. 2: 2. neither by *spirit*,[1] nor by word,
8. with the *spirit* of his mouth,
13. through sanctification of the *Spirit*[1]
1Ti. 3:16. justified in the *Spirit*,[1]
4: 1. Now the *Spirit*[2] speaketh expressly,
— giving heed to seducing *spirits*,
12. in charity, in *spirit*,[1] in faith,
2Ti. 1: 7. God hath not given us the *spirit* of fear;
14. keep by the Holy *Ghost*[3] which dwelleth in us.
4:22. (be) with thy *spirit*.
Tit. 3: 5. and renewing of the Holy *Ghost*;[3]
Philem 25. (be) with your *spirit*.
Heb 1: 7. Who maketh his angels *spirits*,

Heb 1:14. Are they not all ministering *spirits*,
2: 4. and gifts of the Holy *Ghost*,[3]
3: 7. as the Holy *Ghost*[5] saith,
4:12. dividing asunder of soul and *spirit*,[1]
6: 4. made partakers of the Holy *Ghost*,[3]
9: 8. The Holy *Ghost*[5] this signifying,
14. who through the eternal *Spirit*
10:15. the Holy *Ghost*[5] also is a witness to us:
29. despite unto the *Spirit* of grace ?
12: 9. unto the Father of *spirits*,
23. and to the *spirits* of just men
Jas. 2:26. as the body without the *spirit*[1] is dead,
4: 5. The *spirit* that dwelleth in us
1Pet. 1: 2. through sanctification of the *Spirit*,[1]
11. the *Spirit* of Christ which was in them
12. with the Holy *Ghost*[3] sent down
22. obeying the truth through the *Spirit*[1] unto
3: 4. of a meek and quiet *spirit*,
18. quickened by the *Spirit*:[2]
19. preached unto the *spirits* in prison ;
4: 6. according to God in the *spirit*.[1]
14. for the *spirit* of glory and of God
2Pet. 1:21. moved by the Holy *Ghost*.[3]
1Joh. 3:24. by the *Spirit*[2] which he hath given us.
4: 1. believe not every *spirit*, but try the *spirits*
whether
2. Hereby know ye the *Spirit* of God: Every
spirit that confesseth
3. every *spirit* that confesseth not
6. the *spirit* of truth, and the *spirit* of error.
13. he hath given us of his *Spirit*.
5: 6. it is the *Spirit*[2] that beareth witness,
because the *Spirit*[2] is truth.
7. and the Holy *Ghost* :[4] and these three
8. the *spirit*,[2] and the water, and the blood:
Jude 19. having not the *Spirit*.[1]
20. praying in the Holy *Ghost*,[3]
Rev. 1: 4. from the seven *spirits* which are
10. I was in the *Spirit*[1] on the Lord's
2: 7. let him hear what the *Spirit*[2] saith
11. let him hear what the *Spirit*[2] saith
17. let him hear what the *Spirit*[2] saith
29. let him hear what the *Spirit*[2] saith
3: 1. that hath the seven *Spirits* of God,
6. let him hear what the *Spirit*[2] saith
13. let him hear what the *Spirit*[2] saith
22. let him hear what the *Spirit*[2] saith
4: 2. immediately I was in the *spirit* :[1]
5. which are the seven *Spirits* of God.
5: 6. which are the seven *Spirits* of God
11:11. the *Spirit* of life from God entered into
13:15. he had power to give *life*[1] unto the image
14:13. Yea, saith the *Spirit*,[2] that they may rest
16:13. I saw three unclean *spirits* like frogs
14. For they are the *spirits* of devils,
17: 3. So he carried me away in the *spirit*[1]
18: 2. and the hold of every foul *spirit*,
19:10. of Jesus is the *spirit* of prophecy.
21:10. he carried me away in the *spirit*[1] to
22:17. And the *Spirit*[2] and the bride say, Come.

πνευματικός, *pnūmatikos.*

Ro. 1:11. unto you some *spiritual* gift, to the end
7:14. that the law is *spiritual* :
15:27. partakers of their *spiritual* things,
1Co. 2:13. comparing *spiritual* things with *spiritual*.
15. But he that is *spiritual* judgeth all
3: 1. as unto *spiritual*, but as unto carnal,
9:11. have sown unto you *spiritual* things,
10: 3. did all eat the same *spiritual* meat ;

1Co.10: 4. the same *spiritual* drink: for they drank
of that *spiritual* Rock
12: 1. Now concerning *spiritual* (gifts),
14: 1. and desire *spiritual* (gifts),
37. to be a prophet, or *spiritual*,
15:44. it is raised a *spiritual* body.
— and there is a *spiritual* body.
46. not first which is *spiritual*,
— afterward that which is *spiritual*.
Gal. 6: 1. ye which are *spiritual*, restore
Eph. 1: 3. with all *spiritual* blessings
5:19. and hymns and *spiritual* songs,
6:12. against *spiritual* wickedness in
Col. 1: 9. wisdom and *spiritual* understanding ;
3:16. psalms and hymns and *spiritual* songs,
1Pet.2: 5. are built up a *spiritual* house, an holy
priesthood, to offer up *spiritual* sacrifices,

πνευματικῶς, *pnūmatikōs.*

1Co. 2:14. because they are *spiritually* discerned.
Rev.11: 8. which *spiritually* is called Sodom and

πνέω, *pneo.*

Mat. 7:25. and the winds *blew*,
27. the winds *blew*, and beat upon that house;
Lu. 12:55. when (ye see) the south wind *blow*,
Joh. 3: 8. The wind *bloweth* where it listeth,
6:18. by reason of a great wind *that blew*.
Acts27:40. the mainsail to the *wind*,
Rev. 7: 1. that the wind *should* not *blow*

πνίγω, *pnigo.*

Mat.18:28. and *took* (him) *by the throat*, saying,
Mar 5:13. and *were choked* in the sea.

πνικτός, *pniktos.*

Acts15:20. and (from) things *strangled*,
29. from things *strangled*, and from
21:25. from blood, and from *strangled*,

πνοή, *pnoee.*

Acts 2: 2. as of a rushing mighty *wind*,
17:25. he giveth to all life, and *breath*,

ποδήρης, *podeerees.*

Rev. 1:13. clothed with a *garment down to the foot*,

πόθεν, *pothen.*

Mat.13:27. *from whence* then hath it tares?
54. *Whence* hath this (man) this wisdom,
56. *Whence* then hath this (man) all these
things?
15:33. *Whence* should we have so much bread in
21:25. *whence* was it? from heaven, or of men?
Mar 6: 2. *From whence* hath this (man) these
8: 4. *From whence* can a man satisfy these
12:37. and *whence* is he (then) his son?
Lu. 1:43. And *whence* (is) this to me,
13:25. I know you not *whence* ye are:
27. I know you not *whence* ye are;

Lu. 20: 7. that they could not tell *whence* (it was).
Joh. 1:48(49). *Whence* knowest thou me?
   2: 9. knew not *whence* it was:
   3: 8. but canst not tell *whence* it cometh,
   4:11. *from whence* then hast thou that living
       water?
   6: 5. *Whence* shall we buy bread, that
   7:27. we know this man *whence* he is:
    — no man knoweth *whence* he is.
   28. and ye know *whence* I am:
   8:14. for I know *whence* I came, and whither I
       go; but ye cannot tell *whence* I come,
   9:29. we know not *from whence* he is.
   30. that ye know not *from whence* he is,
 19: 9. *Whence* art thou? But Jesus
Jas. 4: 1. *From whence* (come) wars and
Rev. 2: 5. *from whence* thou art fallen,
   7:13. and *whence* came they?

ποιέω, poyeo.

Mat. 1:24. *did* as the angel of the Lord had bidden
   3: 3. *make* his paths straight.
   8. *Bring forth* therefore fruits meet for
   10. every tree *which bringeth* not *forth* good
   4:19. and I *will make* you fishers of men.
   5:19. but whosoever *shall do* and teach (them),
   32. *causeth* her to commit adultery:
   36. thou canst not *make* one hair
   44. *do* good to them that hate you,
   46. *do* not even the publicans the same?
   47. what *do* ye more (than others)? *do* not
      even the publicans so?
   6: 1. Take heed that ye *do* not your
   2. when thou *doest* (thine) alms,
   — as the hypocrites *do* in the synagogues
   3. But *when* thou *doest* alms,
   — what thy right hand *doeth :*
   7:12. that men *should do* to you, *do* ye even so
   17. good tree *bringeth forth* good fruit; but
      a corrupt tree *bringeth forth* evil
   18. A good tree cannot *bring forth* evil
   — a corrupt tree *bring forth* good
   19. Every tree *that bringeth* not *forth*
   21. but he *that doeth* the will of
   22. and in thy name *done* many wonderful
   24. heareth these sayings of mine, and *doeth*
      them,
   26. and *doeth* them not,
   8: 9. *Do* this, and he *doeth* (it).
   9:28. Believe ye that I am able *to do* this?
 12: 2. thy disciples *do* that which is not lawful
      to do upon
   3. Have ye not read what David *did*,
   12. it is lawful *to do* well on the
   16. that they *should* not *make* him known:
   33. Either *make* the tree good,
   — or else *make* the tree corrupt,
   50. whosoever shall *do* the will of my
 13:23. and *bringeth forth,* some an
   26. and *brought forth* fruit,
   28. An enemy *hath done* this.
   41. and them *which do* iniquity;
   58. And he *did* not many mighty works
 17: 4. *let* us *make* here three tabernacles;
   12. but *have done* unto him
 18:35. *shall* my heavenly Father *do* also
 19: 4. that he *which made* (them) at
   — *made* them male and female,
   16. what good thing *shall* I *do*, that
 20: 5. ninth hour, and *did* likewise.

Mat.20:12. These last *have wrought* (but) one hour,
      and thou *hast made* them equal unto us,
   15. Is it not lawful for me *to do* what I will
   32. that I *shall do* unto you?
 21: 6. and *did* as Jesus commanded them,
   13. but ye *have made* it a den of thieves.
   15. the wonderful things that he *did*,
   21. ye *shall* not only *do* this
   23. By what authority *doest* thou these
   24. by what authority I *do* these things.
   27. by what authority I *do* these things.
   31. Whether of them twain *did* the will of
   36. and they *did* unto them likewise.
   40. what *will* he *do* unto those husbandmen?
   43. and given to a nation *bringing forth* the
      fruits thereof.
 22: 2. which *made* a marriage for his son,
 23: 3. Observe and *do ;* but *do* not ye after their
      works: for they say, and *do* not.
   5. they *do* for to be seen of men:
   15. compass sea and land *to make* one
   — ye *make* him twofold more the child
   23. these ought ye *to have done*,
 24:46. when he cometh shall find so *doing.*
 25:16. and *made* (them) other five talents.
   40. Inasmuch as ye *have done* (it) unto one
   — ye *have done* (it) unto me.
   45. Inasmuch as ye *did* (it) not to one
   — ye *did* (it) not to me.
 26:12. she *did* (it) for my burial.
   13. that this woman *hath done*,
   18. I will *keep* the passover at thy house
   19. the disciples *did* as Jesus had
   73. for thy speech bewrayeth thee. (lit. *maketh*
      thee manifest)
 27:22. What *shall* I *do* then with Jesus
   23. Why, what evil *hath* he *done ?*
 28:14. and secure you. (lit. *make* you without
      care)
   15. and *did* as they were taught:
Mar 1: 3. *make* his paths straight.
   17. I *will make* you to become fishers of
 2:23. began, as they went, to pluck (lit. *to make*
      their way plucking)
   24. why *do* they on the sabbath day
   25. Have ye never read what David *did*,
 3: 6. *took* counsel with the Herodians against
      him,
   8. they had heard what great things he *did*,
   12. they *should* not *make* him known.
   14. And he *ordained* twelve, that they
   35. whosoever shall *do* the will of God,
 4:32. and *shooteth out* great branches ;
 5:19. how great things the Lord *hath done* for
      thee,
   20. how great things Jesus *had done* for him:
   32. to see her *that had done* this thing.
 6: 5. he could there *do* no mighty work,
   20. he *did* many things, and heard
   21. *made* a supper to his lords,
   30. both what they *had done*,
 7: 8. other such like things ye *do.*
   12. ye suffer him no more *to do* ought
   13. many such like things *do* ye.
   37. He *hath done* all things well: he *maketh*
      both the deaf to hear,
 8:25. upon his eyes, and *made* him look up:
 9: 5. *let* us *make* three tabernacles ;
   13. they *have done* unto him whatsoever
   39. no man which *shall do* a miracle
 10: 6. God *made* them male and female.
   17. what *shall* I *do* that I may

Mar 10:35. that thou *shouldest do* for us
36. What would ye that I should *do* for you ?
51. What wilt thou that I *should do*
11: 3. Why *do* ye this ?
5. What *do* ye, loosing the colt ?
17. ye *have made* it a den of thieves.
28. By what authority *doest* thou
— authority to *do* these things ?
29. by what authority I *do* these things.
33. by what authority I *do* these things.
12: 9. What *shall* therefore the lord of the vine-yard *do ?*
14: 7. whensoever ye will ye may *do* them good:
8. She *hath done* what she could:
9. (this) also that she *hath done*
15: 1. the chief priests *held* a consultation
7. who *had committed* murder in the
8. as he *had* ever *done* unto them.
12. What will ye then that I *shall do* (unto him)
14. Why, what evil *hath* he *done ?*
15. willing to content the people, (lit. *to do* that which suited)
Lu. 1:25. Thus *hath* the Lord *dealt* with me
49. *hath done* to me great things ;
51. He *hath shewed* strength with his arm ;
68. for he hath visited and redeemed his people, (lit. *made* redemption for his people)
72. To *perform* the mercy (promised) to
2:27. *to do* for him after the custom of
48. why *hast* thou thus *dealt* with us ?
3: 4. *make* his paths straight.
8. *Bring forth* therefore fruits worthy of
9. *which bringeth* not *forth* good fruit
10. What *shall* we *do* then ?
11. he that hath meat, *let* him *do* likewise.
12. Master, what *shall* we *do ?*
14. And what *shall* we *do ?*
19. all the evils which Herod *had done,*
4:23. *do* also here in thy country.
5: 6. *when* they *had* this *done,*
29. Levi *made* him a great feast
33. fast often, and *make* prayers,
34. Can ye *make* the children of the
6: 2. Why *do* ye that which is not lawful *to do* on the sabbath days ?
3. what David *did,* when himself was an
10. And he *did* so: and his hand
11. what they *might do* to Jesus.
23. in the like manner *did* their fathers unto
26. for so *did* their fathers to the false
27. *do* good to them which hate you,
31. as ye would that men *should do* to you, *do* ye also to them likewise.
33. for sinners also *do* even the same.
43. *bringeth* not *forth* (lit. is not *bringing forth*) corrupt fruit; neither *doth* a corrupt tree *bring forth* good fruit.
46. and *do* not the things which I say ?
47. and heareth my sayings, and *doeth* them,
49. But he that heareth, and *doeth* not,
7: 8. *Do* this, and he *doeth* (it).
8: 8. and *bare* fruit an hundredfold.
21. hear the word of God, and *do* it.
39. great things God *hath done* unto thee.
— Jesus *had done* unto him.
9:10. told him all that they *had done.*
15. And they *did* so, and made them
33. *let* us *make* three tabernacles;
43. at all things which Jesus *did,*
54. even as Elias *did ?*

Lu. 10:25. what shall I *do* to inherit (lit. *having done* what shall I inherit)
28. this *do,* and thou shalt live.
37. He *that shewed* mercy on him.
— Go, and *do* thou likewise.
11:40. *did* not he *that made* that which is without *make* that which is within also ?
42. these ought ye *to have done,*
12: 4. no more that they can *do.*
17. What *shall* I *do,* because I have no
18. And he said, This *will* I *do :*
33. *provide* yourselves bags which
43. when he cometh shall find so *doing.*
47. neither *did* according to his will,
48. and *did commit* things worthy of stripes,
13: 9. And if it *bear* fruit, (well):
22. and journeying (lit. *making* a journey) toward Jerusalem.
14:12. When thou *makest* a dinner or a
13. when thou *makest* a feast,
16. A certain man *made* a great supper,
15:19. *make* me as one of thy hired servants.
16: 3. What *shall* I *do ?* for my lord
4. I am resolved what to *do,* that, when
8. because he *had done* wisely:
9. *Make* to yourselves friends of the
17: 9. because he *did* the things that were
10. when ye *shall have done* all those
— we *have done* that which was our duty *to do.*
18: 7. shall not God avenge his own elect, (lit. *shall* not God *make* the avenging of)
8. that he will avenge them speedily. (lit. he *will make* the avenging of them)
18. what shall I *do* to inherit eternal life ? (lit. *having done* what shall I inherit, &c.)
41. that I *shall do* unto thee ?
19:18. thy pound *hath gained* five pounds.
46. but ye *have made* it a den of thieves.
48. could not find what they *might do :*
20: 2. by what authority *doest* thou these things ?
8. by what authority I *do* these things.
13. What *shall* I *do ?* I will send
15. *shall* the lord of the vineyard *do* unto them ?
22:19. this *do* in remembrance of me.
23:22. Why, what evil *hath* he *done ?*
31. if they *do* these things in a green tree,
34. for they know not what they *do.*
Joh. 2: 5. Whatsoever he saith unto you, *do*
11. This beginning of miracles *did* Jesus
15. *when* he *had made* a scourge
16. *make* not my Father's house an
18. seeing that thou *doest* these things ?
23. the miracles which he *did.*
3: 2. can *do* these miracles that thou *doest,*
21. But he *that doeth* truth cometh to the
4: 1. that Jesus *made* and baptized more
29. told me all things that ever I *did:*
34. My meat is to *do* the will of him that
39. He told me all that ever I *did.*
45. all the things that he *did* at
46. where he *made* the water wine.
54. the second miracle (that) Jesus *did,*
5:11. He *that made* me whole,
15. *which had made* him whole.
16. because he *had done* these things on
18. *making* himself equal with God.
19. The Son can *do* nothing of himself, but what he seeth the Father *do :* for what things soever he *doeth,* these also *doeth* the Son likewise.

Joh. 5:20. all things that himself *doeth :*
27. authority *to execute* judgment also,
29. they *that have done* good,
30. I can of mine own self *do* nothing:
36. the same works that I *do,*
6: 2. which he *did* on them that were
6. he himself knew what he would *do.*
10. *Make* the men sit down.
14. the miracle that Jesus *did,*
15. take him by force to *make* him a king,
28. What shall we *do,* that we
30. What sign *shewest* thou then,
38. not to *do* mine own will,
7: 3. see the works that thou *doest.*
4. (that) *doeth* any thing in secret,
— If thou *do* these things, shew
17. If any man will *do* his will,
19. (yet) none of you *keepeth* the law?
21. I *have done* one work,
23. because I *have made* a man every
31. When Christ cometh, *will he do*
— which this (man) *hath done?*
51. and know what he *doeth?*
8:28. I *do* nothing of myself;
29. for I *do* always those things
34. *Whosoever committeth* sin is
38. ye *do* that which ye have seen
39. ye would *do* the works of
40. this *did* not Abraham.
41. Ye *do* the deeds of your father.
44. the lusts of your father ye will *do.*
53. whom *makest* thou thyself?
9: 6. and *made* clay of the spittle,
11. A man that is called Jesus *made* clay,
14. when Jesus *made* the clay,
16. How can a man that is a sinner *do* such
26. What *did* he to thee?
31. and *doeth* his will, him he heareth.
33. he could *do* nothing.
10:25. the works that I *do* in my Father's name,
33. being a man, *makest* thyself God.
37. If I *do* not the works of my Father,
38. But if I *do,* though ye believe
41. John *did* no miracle: but
11:37. *have caused* that even this man
45. had seen the things which Jesus *did,*
46. what things Jesus *had done.*
47. What *do* we? for this man *doeth* many miracles.
12: 2. There they *made* him a supper;
16. (that) they *had done* these things
18. that he *had done* this miracle.
37. *though* he *had done* so many miracles
13: 7. What I *do* thou knowest not now;
12. Know ye what I *have done* to you?
15. that ye *should do* as I *have done* to you.
17. happy are ye if ye *do* them.
27. That thou *doest, do* quickly.
14:10. he *doeth* the works.
12. the works that I *do* shall he *do* also; and greater (works) than these *shall* he *do;* because
13. that *will* I *do,* that the Father may
14. I *will do* (it).
23. will come unto him, and *make* our abode
31. even so I *do.*
15: 5. without me ye can *do* nothing.
14. if ye *do* whatsoever I command
15. knoweth not what his lord *doeth:*
21. all these things *will* they *do* unto you
24. If I *had* not *done* among them the works which none other man *did,*

Joh. 16: 2. They shall put you out of the synagogues: (lit. they *shall make* you put out &c.)
3. these things *will* they *do* unto you,
17: 4. which thou gavest me to *do.*
18:18. *who had made* a fire of coals ;
35. what *hast* thou *done?*
19: 7. because he *made* himself the Son
12. *whosoever maketh* himself a king
23. and *made* four parts,
24. These things therefore the soldiers *did.*
20:30. many other signs truly *did* Jesus
21:25. many other things which Jesus *did,*
Acts 1: 1. The former treatise *have* I *made,*...of all that Jesus began both *to do* and teach,
2:22. which God *did* by him in the midst
36. God *hath made* that same Jesus,
37. what *shall* we *do?*
3:12. we *had made* this man to walk?
4: 7. by what name, *have* ye *done* this?
16. What *shall* we *do* to these men?
24. *which hast made* heaven, and earth,
28. For *to do* whatsoever thy hand
5:34. *to put* the apostles forth a little
6: 8. *did* great wonders and miracles
7:19. so that they *cast out* (lit. *made* cast out) their young
24. and avenged (lit. *made* avenging of) him that was
36. *after* that he *had shewed* wonders
40. *Make* us gods to go before us:
43. which ye *made* to worship them:
44. that he should *make* it
50. *Hath* not my hand *made* all these
8: 2. and *made* great lamentation
6. seeing the miracles which he *did.*
9: 6. what wilt thou have me *to do?*
— be told thee what thou must *do.*
13. how much evil he *hath done*
36. and almsdeeds which she *did.*
39. garments which Dorcas *made,*
10: 2. *which gave* much alms
6. tell thee what thou oughtest *to do.*
33. thou *hast* well *done* that thou art
39. which he *did* both in the land of
11:30. Which also they *did,* and sent it
12: 8. bind on thy sandals. And so he *did.*
13:22. which *shall fulfil* all my will.
14:11. saw what Paul *had done,*
15. why *do* ye these things?
— the living God, which *made* heaven, and earth,
27. all that God *had done* with them,
15: 3. they *caused* great joy unto all the
4. all things that God *had done* with
12. God *had wrought* among the Gentiles
17. the Lord, *who doeth* all these things.
33. *after* they *had tarried* (there) a space,
16:18. And this *did* she many days.
21. neither to *observe,* being Romans.
30. Sirs, what must I *do* to be saved?
17:24. God *that made* the world
26. And *hath made* of one blood
18:21. I must by all means *keep* this feast
23. *after* he *had spent* some time (there),
19:11. God *wrought* special miracles by
14. seven sons of...*which did* so.
24. *which made* silver shrines for Diana,
20: 3. And (there) *abode* three months.
24. But none of these things move me, (lit. 1 *make* account of none)
21:13. What mean ye to weep and to break (lit. What *do* ye weeping &c.)

Acts21:19. God *had wrought* among the Gentiles	Gal. 6: 9. let us not be weary in well *doing*:
23. *Do* therefore this that we say to thee:	Eph 1:16. *making* mention of you in my prayers;
33. who he was, and what he *had done*.	2: 3. *fulfilling* the desires of the flesh
22:10. What *shall* I *do*, Lord?	14. *who hath made* both one,
— which are appointed for thee *to do*.	15. one new man, (so) *making* peace;
26. Take heed what thou *doest*: (lit. art about *to do*)	3:11. purpose which he *purposed* (lit. *made*) in Christ Jesus
23:12. certain of the Jews banded together, (lit. *having made* a confederation)	20. that is able *to do* exceeding
13. *which had made* this conspiracy.	4:16. *maketh* increase of the body unto
24:12. neither raising up the people, (lit. *making* an insurrection)	6: 6. *doing* the will of God from the heart;
17. I came to *bring* alms to my nation,	8. whatsoever good thing any man *doeth*,
25: 3. laying wait in the way to kill him. (lit. *making* a lying in wait)	9. *do* the same things unto them,
17. without any delay (lit. *having made* no delay) on the morrow I sat	Phi. 1: 4. *making* request with joy,
26:10. Which thing I also *did* in Jerusalem:	2:14. *Do* all things without murmurings
27:18. the next (day) they lightened the ship; (lit. they *made* a casting out)	4:14. ye *have* well *done*, that ye did
28:17. *though* I *have committed* nothing against	Col. 3:17. whatsoever ye *do* in word or
Ro. 1: 9. I *make* mention of you always in	23. whatsoever ye *do*, do (it) heartily,
28. *to do* those things which are not	4:16. *cause* that it be read also in
32. not only *do* the same, but have	1Th. 1: 2. *making* mention of you in our prayers;
2: 3. and *doest* the same,	4:10. And indeed ye *do* it toward all the
14. *do* by nature the things contained	5:11. even as also ye *do*.
3: 8. *Let* us *do* evil, that good may come?	24. who also *will do* (it).
12. there is none *that doeth* good,	2Th. 3: 4. that ye both *do* and *will do* the things
4:21. he was able also *to perform*.	1Ti. 1:13. I *did* (it) ignorantly in unbelief.
7:15. but what I hate, that *do* I.	2: 1. giving of thanks, *be made* for all men;
16. If then I *do* that which I would not,	4:16. for in *doing* this thou shalt
19. the good that I would I *do* not:	5:21. *doing* nothing by partiality.
20. Now if I *do* that I would not,	2Ti. 4: 5. *do* the work of an evangelist,
21. that, when I would *do* good,	Tit. 3: 5. Not by works of righteousness which we *have done*,
9:20. Why *hast* thou *made* me thus?	Philem. 4. *making* mention of thee always
21. *to make* one vessel unto honour,	14. would I *do* nothing;
28. a short work *will* the Lord *make*	21. that thou *wilt* also *do* more than
10: 5. the man *which doeth* those things	Heb 1: 2. by whom also he *made* the worlds;
12:20. for in so *doing* thou shalt heap	3. when he had by himself purged (lit. *having made* purgation of, &c.)
13: 3. *do* that which is good, and	7. *Who maketh* his angels spirits,
4. But if thou *do* that which is evil,	3: 2. faithful to him *that appointed* him,
14. and *make* not provision for the flesh,	6: 3. And this *will* we *do*, if God permit.
15:26. *to make* a certain contribution	7:27. for this he *did* once, when he
16:17. mark them *which cause* divisions	8: 5. See,...thou *make* all things according
1Co. 5: 2. he *that hath done* this deed	9. that I *made* with their fathers
6:15. and *make* (them) the members	10: 7. I come...*to do* thy will, O God.
18. Every sin that a man *doeth* is	9. Lo, I come *to do* thy will, O God.
7:36. *let* him *do* what he will,	36. *after* ye *have done* the will of God,
37. will keep his virgin, *doeth* well.	11:28. Through faith he *kept* the passover,
38. that giveth (her) in marriage *doeth* well;	12:13. *make* straight paths for your feet,
— not in marriage *doeth* better.	27. as of things *that are made*,
9:23. And this I *do* for the gospel's sake,	13: 6. what man *shall do* unto me.
10:13. *will* with the temptation also *make* a way	17. that they *may do* it with joy,
31. or whatsoever ye *do*, *do* all to the glory of God.	19. I beseech (you) the rather *to do* this,
11:24. this *do* in remembrance of me.	21. *to do* his will, *working* in you that which
25. this *do* ye, as oft as ye drink (it),	Jas. 2: 8. ye *do* well:
15:29. Else what *shall* they *do* which are	12. So speak ye, and so *do*, as they
16: 1. even so *do* ye.	13. *that hath shewed* no mercy;
2Co. 5:21. he *hath made* him (to be) sin for us,	19. thou *doest* well:
8:10. not only *to do*, but also	3:12. Can the fig tree,...*bear* olive berries?
11. Now therefore perform the *doing*	— no fountain both *yield* salt
11: 7. *Have* I *committed* an offence in	18. of them *that make* peace.
12. But what I *do*, that I *will do*,	4:13. and *continue* there a year,
25. a night and a day I *have been* in the deep;	15. and *do* this, or that.
13: 7. I pray to God that ye *do* no evil;	17. to him that knoweth *to do* good, and *doeth* (it) not,
— but that ye *should do* that which is	5:15. if he *have committed* sins,
Gal. 2:10. which I also was forward *to do*.	1Pet. 2:22. Who *did* no sin, neither was guile
3:10. the book of the law *to do* them.	3:11. Let him eschew evil, and *do* good;
12. The man *that doeth* them shall live	12. (is) against them *that do* evil.
5: 3. a debtor *to do* the whole law.	2Pet.1:10. *to make* your calling and election sure: for if ye *do* these things,
17. so that ye *cannot do* the things	15. *to have* these things always in remembrance.
	19. ye *do* well that ye take heed,

1Joh.1: 6. we lie, and *do* not the truth:
     10. we *make* him a liar,
    2:17. but he *that doeth* the will of God
     29. that every one *that doeth* righteousness
    3: 4. Whosoever *committeth* sin transgresseth
       also the law: (lit. *doeth* also lawlessness)
      7. he *that doeth* righteousness is
      8. He *that committeth* sin is of the devil ;
      9. *doth* not *commit* sin ;
     10. whosoever *doeth* not righteousness
     22. and *do* those things that are
    5:10. *hath made* him a liar;
3Joh.   5. thou *doest* faithfully whatsoever
      6. thou *shalt do* well:
     10. his deeds which he *doeth*,
Jude   3. when I *gave* all diligence to write
     15. To *execute* judgment upon all,
Rev. 1: 6. And *hath made* us kings and priests
    2: 5. and *do* the first works ;
    3: 9. I *will make* them to come and worship
     12. Him that overcometh *will I make* a
    5:10. And *hast made* us unto our God kings
   11: 7. *shall make* war against them,
   12:15. that he *might cause* her to be carried
     17. and went *to make* war with the
   13: 5. *to continue* forty (and) two months.
      7. *to make* war with the saints,
     12. he *exerciseth* all the power of the first
       beast before him, and *causeth* the earth
     13. And he *doeth* great wonders, so that he
       maketh fire come down from
     14. which he had power *to do* in the sight
     — that they should *make* an image
     15. and *cause* that as many as
     16. And he *causeth* all, both small
   14: 7. worship him *that made* heaven,
   16:14. spirits of devils, *working* miracles,
   17:16. and *shall make* her desolate and
     17. to *fulfil* his will, and to agree, (lit. *to make*
       one mind)
   19:19. *to make* war against him that
     20. false prophet *that wrought* miracles
   21: 5. Behold, I *make* all things new.
     27. (whatsoever) *worketh* abomination,
   22: 2. *which bare* twelve (manner of)
     14. Blessed (are) they *that do* his
     15. whosoever loveth and *maketh* a lie.

ποίημα, *poyeema.*

Ro. 1:20. by the *things that are made*,
Eph. 2:10. For we are his *workmanship*,

ποίησις, *poyeesis.*

Jas.   1:25. shall be blessed in his *deed*. (lit. *doing*)

ποιητής, *poyeetees.*

Acts17:28. of your own *poets* have said,
Ro.   2:13. but the *doers* of the law
Jas.   1:22. be ye *doers* of the word,
     23. and not a *doer*,
     25. but a *doer* of the work,
    4:11. art not a *doer* of the law, but a judge.

ποικίλος, *poikilos.*

Mat. 4:24. with *divers* diseases and

Mar 1:34. sick of *divers* diseases,
Lu. 4:40. sick with *divers* diseases
2Ti. 3: 6. led away with *divers* lusts,
Tit. 3: 3. serving *divers* lusts and pleasures,
Heb 2: 4. and with *divers* miracles, and gifts
    13: 9. with *divers* and strange doctrines.
Jas. 1: 2. when ye fall into *divers* temptations ;
1Pet.1: 6. through *manifold* temptations:
    4:10. stewards of the *manifold* grace of God.

ποιμαίνω, *poimaino.*

Mat. 2: 6. *shall rule* (lit. *shall tend*) my people Israel.
Lu. 17: 7. a servant plowing or *feeding cattle*,
Joh.21:16. He saith unto him, *Feed* my sheep.
Acts20:28. to *feed* the church of God,
1Co. 9: 7. who *feedeth* a flock, and eateth not
1Pet.5: 2. *Feed* the flock of God which is
Jude   12. *feeding* themselves without fear:
Rev. 2:27. he *shall rule* them with a rod of iron ;
    7:17. midst of the throne *shall feed* them,
   12: 5. who was *to rule* all nations with
   19:15. he *shall rule* them with a rod of iron:

ποιμήν, *poimeen.*

Mat. 9:36. as sheep having no *shepherd.*
   25:32. as a *shepherd* divideth (his) sheep
   26:31. I will smite the *shepherd,*
Mar 6:34. as sheep not having a *shepherd:*
   14:27. I will smite the *shepherd,*
Lu. 2: 8. *shepherds* abiding in the field,
     15. the *shepherds* said one to another,
     18. told them by the *shepherds.*
     20. And the *shepherds* returned,
Joh.10: 2. is the *shepherd* of the sheep.
     11. I am the good *shepherd:* the good *shepherd*
       giveth his life
     12. and not the *shepherd,*
     14. I am the good *shepherd,*
     16. one fold, (and) one *shepherd.*
Eph. 4:11. and some, *pastors* and teachers ;
Heb 13:20. that great *Shepherd* of the sheep,
1Pet.2:25. returned unto the *Shepherd* and Bishop of
       your souls.

ποίμνη, *poimnee.*

Mat.26:31. and the sheep of the *flock* shall
Lu. 2: 8. over their *flock* by night.
Joh.10:16. one *fold*, (and) one shepherd.
1Co. 9: 7. who feedeth a *flock*, and eateth not of the
       milk of the *flock* ?

ποιμνίον, *poimnion.*

Lu. 12:32. Fear not, little *flock ;*
Acts20:28. and to all the *flock,*
     29. not sparing the *flock.*
1Pet.5: 2. Feed the *flock* of God which
      3. being ensamples to the *flock.*

ποῖος, *poios.*

Mat.19:18. He saith unto him, *Which ?*
   21:23. By *what* authority doest thou
     24. by *what* authority I do these things.
     27. by *what* authority I do these things.

Mat.22:36. *which* (is) the great commandment
24:42. for ye know not *what* hour
43. known in *what* watch the thief
Mar 4:30. or with *what* comparison shall we
11:28. By *what* authority doest thou these things?
29. by *what* authority I do these things.
33. by *what* authority I do these things.
12:28. *Which* is the first commandment of all?
Lu. 5:19. by *what* (way) they might bring
6:32. *what* thank have ye? for sinners
33. *what* thank have ye? for sinners
34. *what* thank have ye? for sinners
12:39. *what* hour the thief would come,
20: 2. by *what* authority doest thou these things?
8. Neither tell I you by *what* authority
24:19. he said unto them, *What* things?
Joh.10:32. for *which* of those works do ye
12:33. signifying *what* death he should die.
18:32. signifying *what* death he should die.
21:19. by *what* death he should glorify
Acts 4: 7. they asked, By *what* power, or by *what* name,
7:49. *what* house will ye build me?
23:34. he asked of *what* province he was.
Ro. 3:27. By *what* law? of works? Nay:
1Co.15:35. and with *what* body do they come?
Jas. 4:14. For *what* (is) your life?
1Pet.1:11. Searching what, or *what manner of* time
2.20. For *what* glory (is it),
Rev. 3: 3. thou shalt not know *what* hour

πολεμέω, polemeo.

Jas. 4: 2. ye fight and *war*, yet ye have not,
Rev. 2:16. and *will fight* against them with
12: 7. Michael and his angels *fought* against the dragon; and the dragon *fought* and his angels,
13: 4. who is able *to make war* with him?
17:14. These *shall make war* with the Lamb,
19:11. he doth judge and *make war*.

πόλεμος, polemos.

Mat.24: 6. shall hear of *wars* and rumours of *wars*:
Mar 13: 7. of *wars* and rumours of *wars*, be ye not
Lu. 14:31. going to make *war* against another
21: 9. shall hear of *wars* and commotions,
1Co.14: 8. prepare himself to the *battle?*
Heb 11:34. waxed valiant in *fight*,
Jas. 4: 1. From whence (come) *wars* and fightings
Rev. 9: 7. horses prepared unto *battle*;
9. many horses running to *battle*.
11: 7. shall make *war* against them,
12: 7. And there was *war* in heaven:
17. and went to make *war* with the remnant
13: 7. to make *war* with the saints,
16:14. to the *battle* of that great day of
19:19. to make *war* against him that sat on the horse,
20: 8. to gather them together to *battle*:

πόλις, polis.

Mat. 2:23. and dwelt in a *city* called Nazareth:
4: 5. taketh him up into the holy *city*,
5:14. A *city* that is set on an hill cannot
35. for it is the *city* of the great King.
8:33. and went their ways into the *city*,

Mat. 8:34. behold, the whole *city* came out to
9: 1. and came into his own *city*.
35. went about all the *cities* and villages,
10: 5. and into (any) *city* of the Samaritans
11. into whatsoever *city* or town ye shall enter,
14. when ye depart out of that house or *city*,
15. in the day of judgment, than for that *city*.
23. when they persecute you in this *city*,
— over the *cities* of Israel, till
11: 1. to teach and to preach in their *cities*.
20. Then began he to upbraid the *cities*
12:25. and every *city* or house divided
14:13. they followed him on foot out of the *cities*.
21:10. all the *city* was moved, saying,
17. and went out of the *city* into
18. as he returned into the *city*,
22: 7. and burned up their *city*.
23:34. persecute (them) from *city* to *city*:
26:18. Go into the *city* to such a man,
27:53. and went into the holy *city*,
28:11. some of the watch came into the *city*,
Mar 1:33. And all the *city* was gathered together
45. openly enter into the *city*,
5:14. and told (it) in the *city*,
6:11. day of judgment, than for that *city*.
33. ran afoot thither out of all *cities*,
56. into villages, or *cities*, or country,
11:19. he went out of the *city*.
14:13. Go ye into the *city*,
16. and came into the *city*,
Lu. 1:26. unto a *city* of Galilee,
39. with haste, into a *city* of Juda;
2: 3. every one into his own *city*.
4. out of the *city* of Nazareth, into Judæa, unto the *city* of David,
11. in the *city* of David a Saviour,
39. to their own *city* Nazareth.
4:29. and thrust him out of the *city*,
— the hill whereon their *city* was built,
31. Capernaum, a *city* of Galilee,
43. the kingdom of God to other *cities* also:
5:12. when he was in a certain *city*,
7:11. he went into a *city* called Nain;
12. he came nigh to the gate of the *city*,
— much people of the *city* was with her.
37. And, behold, a woman in the *city*,
8: 1. throughout every *city* and village,
4. were come to him out of every *city*,
27. there met him out of the *city*
34. went and told (it) in the *city*
39. published throughout the whole *city*
9: 5. when ye go out of that *city*,
10. belonging to the *city* called Bethsaida.
10: 1. into every *city* and place,
8. into whatsoever *city* ye enter,
10. into whatsoever *city* ye enter,
11. Even the very dust of your *city*,
12. for Sodom, than for that *city*.
13:22. he went through the *cities* and villages,
14:21. into the streets and lanes of the *city*,
18: 2. There was in a *city* a judge,
3. there was a widow in that *city*;
19:17. have thou authority over ten *cities*.
19. Be thou also over five *cities*.
41. he beheld the *city*, and wept over it,
22:10. when ye are entered into the *city*,
23:19. for a certain sedition made in the *city*,
51. of Arimathæa, a *city* of the Jews:
24:49. tarry ye in the *city* of Jerusalem,
Joh. 1:44(45). Bethsaida, the *city* of Andrew and Peter.

Joh. 4: 5. Then cometh he to a *city* of Samaria,
　　　 8. unto the *city* to buy meat.
　　　28. and went her way into the *city*,
　　　30. Then they went out of the *city*,
　　　39. the Samaritans of that *city* believed
11:54. into a *city* called Ephraim,
19:20. was nigh to the *city* :
Acts 5:16. (out) of the *cities* round about
　 7:58. And cast (him) out of the *city*,
　 8: 5. went down to the *city* of Samaria,
　　　 8. there was great joy in that *city*.
　　　 9. in the same *city* used sorcery,
　　　40. he preached in all the *cities*,
　 9: 6. Arise, and go into the *city*,
10: 9. and drew nigh unto the *city*,
11: 5. I was in the *city* of Joppa praying:
12:10. that leadeth unto the *city*;
13:44. came almost the whole *city* together
　　　50. and the chief men of the *city*,
14: 4. But the multitude of the *city* was
　　　 6. Lystra and Derbe, *cities* of Lycaonia,
　　　13. which was before their *city*,
　　　19. drew (him) out of the *city*,
　　　20. he rose up, and came into the *city* :
　　　21. preached the gospel to that *city*,
15:21. in every *city* them that preach him,
　　　36. visit our brethren in every *city*
16: 4. they went through the *cities*,
　　　12. the chief *city* of that part of
　　　 — we were in that *city* abiding
　　　13. we went out of the *city* by a river
　　　14. of the *city* of Thyatira,
　　　20. exceedingly trouble our *city*,
　　　39. depart out of the *city*.
17: 5. set all the *city* on an uproar,
　　　16. when he saw the *city* wholly given
18:10. I have much people in this *city*.
19:29. And the whole *city* was filled
　　　35. how that the *city* of the Ephesians
20:23. witnesseth in every *city*,
21: 5. till (we were) out of the *city* :
　　　29. with him in the *city* Trophimus an Ephe-
　　　　　sian,
　　　30. And all the *city* was moved,
　　　39. a citizen of no mean *city* :
22: 3. brought up in this *city*
24:12. neither in the synagogues, nor in the *city* :
25:23. principal men of the *city*,
26:11. persecuted(them)even unto strange *cities*.
27: 8. whereunto was the *city* (of) Lasea.
Ro. 16:23. Erastus the chamberlain of the *city*
2Co.11:26. (in) perils in the *city*,
　　　32. kept the *city* of the Damascenes
Tit. 1: 5. ordain elders in every *city*,
Heb11:10. For he looked for a *city* which
　　　16. he hath prepared for them a *city*.
12:22. unto the *city* of the living God,
13:14. here have we no continuing *city*,
Jas. 4:13. we will go into such a *city*,
2Pet. 2: 6. turning the *cities* of Sodom and
Jude 　 7. and the *cities* about them
Rev. 3:12. the name of the *city* of my God,
11: 2. and the holy *city* shall they tread
　　　 8. the street of the great *city*,
　　　13. and the tenth part of the *city* fell,
14: 8. is fallen, that great *city*,
　　　20. trodden without the *city*,
16:19. And the great *city* was divided into three
　　　　　parts, and the *cities* of the nations fell:
17:18. is that great *city*, which reigneth
18:10. Alas, alas that great *city* Babylon, that
　　　　　mighty *city* !

Rev.18:16. Alas, alas that great *city*,
　　　18. What (city is) like unto this great *city*!
　　　19. Alas, alas that great *city*,
　　　21. that great *city* Babylon be thrown down,
20: 9. and the beloved *city* :
21: 2. I John saw the holy *city*,
　　　10. and shewed me that great *city*,
　　　14. And the wall of the *city*
　　　15. had a golden reed to measure the *city*,
　　　16. And the *city* lieth foursquare,　　．
　　　 — he measured the *city* with the reed,
　　　18. the *city* (was) pure gold,
　　　19. the foundations of the wall of the *city*
　　　21. and the street of the *city* (was) pure gold,
　　　23. the *city* had no need of the sun,
22:14. through the gates into the *city*.
　　　19. and out of the holy *city*,

πολιτάρχης, *politarkees*.

Acts17: 6. unto the *rulers of the city*,
　　　 8. and the *rulers of the city*, when

πολιτεία, *politīa*.

Acts22:28. With a great sum obtained I this *freedom*.
　　　　　(lit. *citizenship*)
Eph 2:12. aliens from the *commonwealth* (lit. *polity*)
　　　　　of Israel,

πολίτευμα, *politūma*.

Phi. 3:20. For our *conversation* (lit. *enfranchisement*
　　　　　or *community*) is in heaven ;

πολιτεύομαι, *politūomai*.

Acts23: 1. I *have lived* in all good conscience before
　　　　　God
Phi. 1:27. *let* your *conversation be* (lit. *be regulated*)
　　　　　as it becometh

πολίτης, *politees*.

Lu. 15:15. joined himself to a *citizen* of that
19:14. But his *citizens* hated him,
Acts21:39. a *citizen* of no mean city:

πολλά see πολύς.

πολλάκις, *pollakis*.

Mat.17:15. for *ofttimes* he falleth into the fire, and
　　　　　oft into the water.
Mar 5: 4. had been *often* bound with fetters
　　 9:22. And *ofttimes* it hath cast him
Joh.18: 2. for Jesus *ofttimes* resorted thither
Acts26:11. I punished them *oft* in every synagogue,
Ro. 1:13. that *oftentimes* I purposed to come
2Co. 8:22. whom we have *oftentimes* proved
　　11:23. in prisons more frequent, in deaths *oft*.
　　　26. (In) journeyings *often*,
　　　27. in watchings *often*,
　　　 — in fastings *often*,
Phi. 3:18. of whom I have told you *often*,
2Ti. 1:16. for he *oft* refreshed me,
Heb 6: 7. the rain that cometh *oft* upon it,
　 9:25. that he should offer himself *often*,

Heb 9:26. For then must he *often* have suffered
   10:11. offering *oftentimes* the same

πολλαπλασίων, *pollaplasiōn.*

Lu. 18:30. shall not receive *manifold more* in this

πολυλογία, *polulogia.*

Mat. 6: 7. be heard for their *much speaking.*

πολυμερῶς, *polumerōs.*

Heb 1: 1. God, who *at sundry times* (lit. *by many
   portions*) and in divers manners

πολυποίκιλος, *polupoikilos.*

Eph 3:10. the *manifold* wisdom of God,

πολύς, *polus.*

[1] indicates the use of the neut. sing. πολύ, as
an adv. [2] the same use of the neut. plur. πολλά.
† denotes the article to be combined with the plural.

Mat. 2:18. and *great* mourning, Rachel weeping
   3: 7. when he saw *many* of the Pharisees
   4:25. *great* multitudes of people from
   5:12. for *great* (is) your reward
   6:30. (shall he) not *much* more (clothe) you,
   7:13. and *many* there be which go in thereat:
     22. *Many* will say to me in that day,
     — done *many* wonderful works?
   8: 1. *great* multitudes followed him.
     11. *many* shall come from the east
     16. unto him *many* that were possessed
     18. when Jesus saw *great* multitudes
     30. an herd of *many* swine feeding.
   9:10. *many* publicans and sinners came
     14. Why do we and the Pharisees fast *oft,*[2]
     37. The harvest truly (is) *plenteous,*
   10:31. of more value than *many* sparrows.
   12:15. and *great* multitudes followed
   13: 2. And *great* multitudes were
     3. he spake *many* things unto them
     5. where they had not *much* earth:
     17. That *many* prophets and righteous
     58. did not *many* mighty works there
   14:14. and saw a *great* multitude,
   15:30. And *great* multitudes came unto
     — dumb, maimed, and *many* others,
   16:21. and suffer *many* things of the
   19: 2. And *great* multitudes followed him;
     22. for he had *great* possessions.
     30. But *many* (that are) first
   20:16. for *many* be called, but few chosen.
     28. and to give his life a ransom for *many.*
     29. a *great* multitude followed him.
   22:14. For *many* are called, but few (are) chosen.
   24: 5. For *many* shall come in my name,
     — and shall deceive *many.*
     10. And then shall *many* be offended,
     11. And *many* false prophets shall rise, and
     shall deceive *many.*
     12. the love of † *many* shall wax cold.
     30. with power and *great* glory.

Mat.25:19. After a *long* time the lord
     21. make thee ruler over *many* things:
     23. make thee ruler over *many* things:
   26: 9. might have been sold for *much,*
     28. which is shed for *many* for the remission
     47. and with him a *great* multitude
     60. though *many* false witnesses came,
   27:19. for I have suffered *many* things this day
     52. and *many* bodies of the saints
     53. and appeared unto *many.*
     55. And *many* women were there
Mar 1:34. healed *many* that were sick of divers
     diseases, and cast out *many* devils;
     45. and began to publish (it) *much,*[2]
   2: 2. *many* were gathered together,
     15. *many* publicans and sinners sat
     — for there were *many,* and they
   3: 7. a *great* multitude from Galilee
     8. a *great* multitude, when they had heard
     10. For he had healed *many*;
     12. And he *straitly*[2] charged them
   4: 1. gathered unto him a *great* multitude,
     2. he taught them *many* things
     5. where it had not *much* earth;
     33. And with *many* such parables
   5: 9. My name (is) Legion: for we are *many.*
     10. And he besought him *much*[2]
     21. *much* people gathered unto him:
     23. And besought him *greatly,*[2]
     24. and *much* people followed him,
     26. And had suffered *many* things of *many*
     physicians,
     38. that wept and wailed *greatly.*
     43. he charged them *straitly*[2] that
   6: 2. and *many* hearing (him) were astonished,
     13. they cast out *many* devils, and anointed
     with oil *many* that were sick,
     20. he did *many* things, and heard him gladly.
     31. there were *many* coming and going,
     33. and *many* knew him, and ran afoot
     34. saw *much* people, and was moved
     — he began to teach them *many* things.
     35. when the day was now *far spent,*
     — now the time (is) *far passed:*
   7: 4. And *many* other things there be,
     8. *many* other such like things ye do.
     13. *many* such like things do ye.
   8:31. Son of man must suffer *many* things,
   9:12. he must suffer *many* things,
     14. he saw a *great* multitude
     26. (the spirit) cried, and rent him *sore,*[2]
     — that *many* said, He is dead.
   10:22. for he had *great* possessions.
     31. But *many* (that are) first shall be
     45. and to give his life a ranson for *many.*
     48. *many* charged him that he
     — he cried the more a *great deal,*
   11: 8. And *many* spread their garments
   12: 5. and him they killed, and *many* others;
     27. ye therefore do *greatly*[1] err.
     37. And the *common* people heard him gladly.
     41. and *many* that were rich cast in *much*[1]
   13: 6. For *many* shall come in my name,
     — and shall deceive *many.*
     26. with *great* power and glory.
   14:24. which is shed for *many.*
     43. and with him a *great* multitude
     56. For *many* bare false witness
   15: 3. the chief priests accused him of *many*
     things:
     41. and *many* other women
Lu. 1: 1. Forasmuch as *many* have taken in hand

Lu. 1:14. and *many* shall rejoice at his birth.
16. And *many* of the children of Israel
2:34. and rising again of *many* in Israel ;
35. that the thoughts of *many* hearts
36. she was of a *great* age, and had lived
3:18. And *many* other things in his exhortation
4:25. *many* widows were in Israel
27. And *many* lepers were in Israel
41. And devils also came out of *many*,
5: 6. they inclosed a *great* multitude of fishes:
15. and *great* multitudes came together
29. and there was a *great* company
6:17. and a *great* multitude of people
23. your reward (is) *great* in heaven,
35. and your reward shall be *great*,
7:11. went with him, and *much* people.
21. he cured *many* of (their) infirmities
— and unto *many* (that were) blind
47. Her sins, which are † *many*, are forgiven ;
for she loved *much :*[1]
8: 3. Susanna, and *many* others, which ministered
4. *much* people were gathered together,
29. For *oftentimes* it had caught him:
30. because *many* devils were entered
9:22. The Son of man must suffer *many* things,
37. *much* people met him.
10: 2. The harvest truly (is) *great*,
24. that *many* prophets and kings
40. cumbered about *much* serving,
41. troubled about *many* things:
12: 7. more value than *many* sparrows.
19. thou hast *much* goods laid up for *many* years ;
47. shall be beaten with *many* (stripes).
48. unto whomsoever *much* is given, of him shall be *much* required: and to whom men have committed *much*,
13:24. for *many*, I say unto you, will seek
14:16. made a great supper, and bade *many:*
25. there went *great* multitudes
15:13. And not *many* days after
16:10. is faithful also in *much :*
— is unjust also in *much*.
17:25. first must he suffer *many* things,
18:39. but he cried *so much* the more,
21: 8. for *many* shall come in my name,
27. with power and *great* glory.
22:65. *many* other things blasphemously
23: 8. he had heard *many* things of him ;
27. a *great* company of people,
Joh. 2:12. continued there not *many* days.
23. *many* believed in his name,
3:23. because there was *much* water there:
4:39. And *many* of the Samaritans
41. And *many* more believed because
5: 3. a *great* multitude of impotent folk,
6. he had been now a *long* time
6: 2. And a *great* multitude followed him,
5. and saw a *great* company come unto him,
10. Now there was *much* grass in the place.
60. *Many* therefore of his disciples,
66. *many* of his disciples went back,
7:12. there was *much* murmuring among
31. And *many* of the people believed
40. *Many* of the people therefore,
8:26. I have *many* things to say
30. *many* believed on him.
10:20. And *many* of them said, He hath
32. *Many* good works have I shewed
41. And *many* resorted unto him,
42. And *many* believed on him there.

Joh.11:19. And *many* of the Jews came to
45. Then *many* of the Jews which
47. this man doeth *many* miracles.
55. and *many* went out of the country
12: 9. *Much* people of the Jews therefore
11. *many* of the Jews went away,
12. *much* people that were come
24. it bringeth forth *much* fruit.
42. also *many* believed on him ;
14: 2. In my Father's house are *many* mansions:
30. I will not talk *much*[2] with you:
15: 5. the same bringeth forth *much* fruit:
8. that ye bear *much* fruit ;
16:12. I have yet *many* things to say
19:20. This title then read *many* of the Jews:
20:30. And *many* other signs truly did Jesus
21:25. there are also *many* other things
Acts 1: 3. by *many* infallible proofs,
5. the Holy Ghost not *many* days hence.
2:43. and *many* wonders and signs were done
4: 4. *many* of them which heard the word
5:12. were *many* signs and wonders wrought
6: 7. a *great* company of the priests
8: 7. came out of *many* that were possessed (with them): and *many* taken with palsies,
25. in *many* villages of the Samaritans.
9:13. I have heard by *many* of this man,
42. and *many* believed in the Lord.
10: 2. which gave *much* alms to the people,
27. and found *many* that were come
11:21. and a *great* number believed,
13:43. *many* of the Jews and religious proselytes
14: 1. that a *great* multitude both
22. we must through *much* tribulation
15: 7. when there had been *much* disputing,
32. exhorted the brethren with *many* words,
35. with *many* others also.
16:16. brought her masters *much* gain
18. And this did she *many* days.
23. when they had laid *many* stripes
17: 4. devout Greeks a *great* multitude,
12. Therefore *many* of them believed ;
18: 8. and *many* of the Corinthians hearing
10. I have *much* people in this city.
27. helped them *much*[1] which had
19:18. And *many* that believed came,
20: 2. had given them *much* exhortation,
19. and with *many* tears, and temptations,
21:40. there was made a *great* silence,
22:28. With a *great* sum obtained I this
23:10. there arose a *great* dissension,
24: 2. by thee we enjoy *great* quietness,
7. with *great* violence took (him)
10. thou hast been of *many* years a judge
25: 7. laid *many* and grievous complaints
23. and Bernice, with *great* pomp,
26: 9. I ought to do *many* things contrary
10. and *many* of the saints did I shut up
24. † *much* learning doth make thee mad.
29. were both almost, and *altogether* (lit. both in little and in *much*) such as I am,
27:10. will be with hurt and *much* damage,
14. But not *long* after there arose
21. But after *long* abstinence
28: 6. after they had looked a *great while*,
10. honoured us with *many* honours ;
29. and had *great* reasoning among themselves.
Ro. 3: 2. *Much* every way: chiefly, because
4:17. a father of *many* nations,
18. the father of *many* nations,
5: 9. *Much* more then, being now justified

Ro. 5:10. *much* more, being reconciled,
15. the offence of one † *many* be dead, *much* more the grace of God,
— hath abounded unto † *many*.
16. of *many* offences unto justification.
17. *much* more they which receive
19. † *many* were made sinners,
— shall † *many* be made righteous.
8:29. the firstborn among *many* brethren.
9:22. with *much* longsuffering
12: 4. as we have *many* members in one body,
5. So we, (being) † *many*, are one body
15:22. I have been † *much*[2] hindered
23. these *many* years to come unto you ;
16: 2. she hath been a succourer of *many*,
6. who bestowed *much*[2] labour on us.
12. which laboured *much*[2] in the Lord.
1Co. 1:26. how that not *many* wise men after the flesh, not *many* mighty, not *many* noble, (are called):
2: 3. and in fear, and in *much* trembling.
4:15. yet (have ye) not *many* fathers:
8: 5. as there be gods *many*, and lords *many*,
10:17. For we (being) † *many* are one bread,
33. but the (profit) of † *many*,
11:30. For this cause *many* (are) weak
12:12. and hath *many* members,
— being *many*, are one body:
14. the body is not one member, but *many*.
20. But now (are they) *many* members,
22. Nay, *much* more those members
16: 9. and (there are) *many* adversaries.
12. I *greatly*[2] desired him to come unto you
19. salute you *much*[2] in the Lord,
2Co. 1:11. by the means of *many* persons thanks may be given by *many*
2: 4. For out of *much* affliction and anguish
— I wrote unto you with *many* tears ;
17. For we are not as † *many*,
3: 9. *much* more doth the ministration
11. *much* more that which remaineth
12. we use *great* plainness of speech:
6: 4. in *much* patience, in afflictions,
10. as poor, yet making *many* rich ;
7: 4. *Great* (is) my boldness of speech toward you, *great* (is) my glorying of you:
8: 2. How that in a *great* trial of affliction
4. Praying us with *much* intreaty
15. He that (had gathered) *much*
22. proved diligent in *many* things, but now *much*[1] more diligent, upon the *great* confidence which
9:12. by *many* thanksgivings unto God ;
11:18. Seeing that *many* glory after the flesh,
12:21. I shall bewail *many* which have
Gal. 1:14. above *many* my equals
3:16. And to seeds, as of *many* ;
4:27. hath many more children than (lit. *many* children rather than)
Eph. 2: 4. for his *great* love wherewith he
Phi. 1:23. which is *far* better: (lit. by *much* more better)
2:12. but now *much* more in my absence,
3:18. For *many* walk, of whom I have told
Col. 4:13. that he hath a *great* zeal for you,
1Th. 1: 5. in the Holy Ghost, and in *much* assurance;
6. received the word in *much* affliction,
2: 2. with *much* contention.
17. to see your face with *great* desire.
1Ti. 3: 8. not given to *much* wine,
13. and *great* boldness in the faith
6: 9. *many* foolish and hurtful lusts,

1Ti. 6:10. pierced themselves through with *many* sorrows.
12. a good profession before *many* witnesses.
2Ti. 2: 2. among *many* witnesses,
4:14. the coppersmith did me *much* evil:
Tit. 1:10. For there are *many* unruly and vain
2: 3. not given to *much* wine,
Philem. 7. For we have *great* joy and consolation
8. I might be *much* bold in Christ
Heb 2:10. in bringing *many* sons unto glory,
5:11. we have *many* things to say,
9:28. once offered to bear the sins of *many?*
10:32. ye endured a *great* fight of afflictions ;
12: 9. shall we not *much* rather be in subjection
15. thereby *many* be defiled;
25. *much* more (shall not) we (escape),
Jas. 3: 1. My brethren, be not *many* masters,
2. For in *many*[2] things we offend all.
5:16. of a righteous man availeth *much*.[1]
1Pet.1: 3. according to his *abundant* mercy
7. being *much*[1] more precious than
2Pet.2: 2. And *many* shall follow their
1Joh.2.18. even now are there *many* antichrists ;
4: 1. because *many* false prophets are
2Joh. 7. For *many* deceivers are entered
12. Having *many* things to write
3Joh. 13. I had *many* things to write,
Rev. 1:15. as the sound of *many* waters.
5: 4. And I wept *much*,[2] because no man
11. I heard the voice of *many* angels
7: 9. and, lo, a *great* multitude,
8: 3. *much* incense, that he should offer
11. and *many* men died of the waters,
9: 9. of *many* horses running to battle.
10:11. before *many* peoples, and nations,
14: 2. as the voice of *many* waters,
17: 1. that sitteth upon *many* waters:
19: 1. I heard a great voice of *much* people
6. the voice of a *great* multitude, and as the voice of *many* waters,
12. and on his head (were) *many* crowns ;

πολύσπλαγχνος, *poluspla꞉nos.*

Jas. 5:11. that the Lord is *very pitiful,*

πολυτελής, *polutelees.*

Mar14: 3. of spikenard *very precious;*
1Ti. 2: 9. or pearls, or *costly* array ;
1Pet.3: 4. in the sight of God *of great price.*

πολύτιμος, *polutimos.*

Mat.13:46. found one pearl *of great price,*
Joh.12: 3. ointment of spikenard, *very costly,*

πολυτρόπως, *polutropōs.*

Heb 1: 1. God, who at sundry times and *in divers manners*

πόμα, *poma.*

1Co.10: 4. did all drink the same spiritual *drink:*
Heb 9:10. (Which stood) only in meats and *drinks,*

πονηρία, *poneeria.*

Mat.22:18. Jesus perceived their *wickedness,*

Mar 7:22.covetousness, *wickedness*, [plural]
Lu. 11:39.full of ravening and *wickedness*.
Acts 3:26.every one of you from his *iniquities*.
Ro. 1:29.*wickedness*, covetousness,
1Co. 5: 8.leaven of malice and *wickedness;*
Eph 6:12.against spiritual *wickedness*

πονηρός, *poneeros*.

Mat. 5:11.shall say all manner of *evil* against
 37.whatsoever is more than these cometh of
  evil.
 39.That ye resist not *evil:*
 45.he maketh his sun to rise on the *evil*
6:13.but deliver us from *evil:*
 23.But if thine eye be *evil*,
7:11.If ye then, being *evil*, know
 17.a corrupt tree bringeth forth *evil* fruit.
 18.cannot bring forth *evil* fruit,
9: 4.Wherefore think ye *evil* in your hearts?
12:34.how can ye, being *evil*, speak good
 35.an *evil* man out of the *evil* treasure
  bringeth forth *evil* things.
 39.An *evil* and adulterous generation
 45.spirits *more wicked* than himself,
 — unto this *wicked* generation.
13:19.then cometh the *wicked* (one),
 38.tares are the children of the *wicked* (one);
 49.and sever the *wicked* from among
15:19.out of the heart proceed *evil* thoughts,
16: 4.A *wicked* and adulterous generation
18:32.O thou *wicked* servant, I forgave
20:15.Is thine eye *evil*, because I am good?
22:10.as many as they found, both *bad* and good:
25:26.(Thou) *wicked* and slothful servant,
Mar 7:22.lasciviousness, an *evil* eye, blasphemy,
 23.All these *evil* things come from within,
Lu. 3:19.for all the *evils* which Herod had done,
6:22.cast out your name as *evil*,
 35.unto the unthankful and (to) the *evil*.
 45.and an *evil* man out of the *evil* treasure of
  his heart bringeth forth that which is
  evil:
7:21.and plagues, and of *evil* spirits;
8: 2.healed of *evil* spirits and infirmities,
11: 4.but deliver us from *evil*.
 13.If ye then, being *evil*, know how
 26.spirits *more wicked* than himself;
 29.This is an *evil* generation:
 34.but when (thine eye) is *evil*,
19:22.will I judge thee, (thou) *wicked* servant.
Joh. 3:19.because their deeds were *evil*.
7: 7.that the works thereof are *evil*.
17:15.shouldest keep them from the *evil*.
Acts17: 5.*lewd* fellows of the baser sort,
18:14.of wrong or *wicked* lewdness,
19:12.and the *evil* spirits went out of them.
 13.call over them which had *evil* spirits the
 15.And the *evil* spirit answered
 16.the man in whom the *evil* spirit
28:21.or spake any *harm* of thee.
Ro. 12: 9.Abhor that which is *evil;*
1Co. 5:13.put away...that *wicked* person.
Gal. 1: 4.deliver us from this present *evil* world,
Eph 5:16.because the days are *evil*.
6:13.to withstand in the *evil* day,
 16.the fiery darts of the *wicked*.
Col. 1:21.in (your) mind by *wicked* works,
1Th. 5:22.Abstain from all appearance of *evil*.
2Th 3: 2.from unreasonable and *wicked* men:
 3.and keep (you) from *evil*.

1Ti. 6: 4.railings, *evil* surmisings,
2Ti. 3:13.But *evil* men and seducers shall
4:18.from every *evil* work,
Heb 3:12.an *evil* heart of unbelief,
10:22.sprinkled from an *evil* conscience,
Jas. 2: 4.are become judges of *evil* thoughts?
4:16.all such rejoicing is *evil*.
1Joh.2:13.ye have overcome the *wicked* one.
 14.ye have overcome the *wicked* one.
3:12.(who) was of that *wicked* one,
 — Because his own works were *evil*,
5:18.and that *wicked* one toucheth him not.
 19.the whole world lieth in wickedness. (lit.
  in the *wicked*)
2Joh. 11.is partaker of his *evil* deeds.
3Joh. 10.prating against us with *malicious* words:
Rev.16: 2.a noisome and *grievous* sore upon

πόνος, *ponos*.

Rev.16:10.they gnawed their tongues for *pain*,
 11.because of their *pains* and their sores,
21: 4.neither shall there be any more *pain:*

πορεία, *poria*.

Lu. 13:22.and *journey*ing toward Jerusalem.
Jas. 1:11.shall the rich man fade away in his *ways*.

πορεύομαι, *poruomai*.

Mat. 2: 8.*Go and* search diligently for the
 9.they *departed;* and, lo, the star,
 20.and *go* into the land of Israel:
8: 9.I say to this (man), *Go*, and he *goeth;*
9:13.But *go ye and* learn what (that)
10: 6.But *go* rather to the lost sheep
 7.And *as ye go*, preach, saying,
11: 4.*Go and* shew John again those things
 7.And *as they departed*, Jesus began
12: 1.At that time Jesus *went* on the sabbath
 45.Then *goeth* he, and taketh with
17:27.*go* thou to the sea, *and* cast
18:12.*goeth* into the mountains, *and*
19:15.and *departed* thence.
21: 2.*Go* into the village over against
 6.And the disciples *went*,
22: 9.*Go* ye therefore into the highways,
 15.Then *went* the Pharisees, *and*
24: 1.and *departed* from the temple:
25: 9.but *go* ye rather to them that sell,
 16.*went and* traded with the same,
 41.*Depart* from me, ye cursed,
26:14.*went* unto the chief priests,
27:66.So they *went, and* made the sepulchre
28: 7.And *go* quickly, *and* tell his disciples
 9.And as they *went* to tell his disciples,
 11.Now *when* they *were going*,
 16.the eleven disciples *went away* into
 19.*Go* ye therefore, *and* teach all nations,
Mar 16:10.she *went and* told them that had been
 12.as they walked, and *went* into the country.
 15.*Go* ye into all the world, *and*
Lu. 1: 6.*walking* in all the commandments
 39.and *went* into the hill country
2: 3.And all *went* to be taxed,
 41.Now his parents *went* to Jerusalem
4:30.through the midst of them *went* his *way*,
 42.he departed and *went* into a desert
 — that he should not *depart* from them.

Lu. 5:24. and *go* unto thine house.
  7: 6. Then Jesus *went* with them.
   8. I say unto one, *Go*, and he *goeth;*
   11. that he *went* into a city called Nain;
   22. *Go* your *way, and* tell John
   50. Thy faith hath saved thee; *go* in peace.
  8:14. *go forth, and* are choked with cares
   48. thy faith hath made thee whole; *go* in peace.
  9:13. except we should *go and* buy meat
   51. set his face *to go* to Jerusalem,
   52. and *they went, and* entered into a
   53. *as though* he *would go* to Jerusalem.
   56. And they *went* to another village.
   57. *as* they *went* in the way,
  10:37. *Go*, and do thou likewise.
   38. as they *went*, that he entered
  11: 5. and *shall go* unto him at midnight,
   26. Then *goeth* he, and taketh (to him)
  13:31. Get thee out, and *depart* hence: for
   32. *Go* ye, *and* tell that fox,
   33. I must *walk* to day, and
  14:10. *go and* sit down in the lowest room;
   19. and I *go* to prove them:
   31 *going* to make war against
  15: 4. and *go* after that which is lost,
   15. And he *went and* joined himself to
   18. I will arise and *go* to my father,
  16:30. but if one *went* unto them from the
  17:11. as he *went* to Jerusalem,
   14. *Go* shew yourselves unto the priests.
   19. Arise, *go* thy *way:*
  19:12. *went* into a far country
   28. he *went* before, ascending up to
   36. And *as* he *went*, they spread
  21: 8. *go* ye not therefore after them.
  22: 8. *Go and* prepare us the passover,
   22. the Son of man *goeth*, as it
   33. I am ready *to go* with thee, both into
   39. and *went*, as he was wont,
  24:13. two of them went (lit. were *going*) that same day
   28. unto the village, whither they *went:* and he made as though he would have gone (lit. *to go*) further.
Joh. 4:50. *Go* thy *way;* thy son liveth.
   — and he *went* his *way*.
  7:35. Whither will he *go*,
   — will he *go* unto the dispersed
   53. every man *went* unto his own house.
  8: 1. Jesus *went* unto the mount of Olives.
   11. *go*, and sin no more.
  10: 4. he *goeth* before them,
  11:11. but I *go*, that I may awake him
  14: 2. I *go* to prepare a place for you.
   3. if I *go* and prepare a place for you,
   12. because I *go* unto my Father.
   28. I *go* unto the Father:
  16: 7. but if I *depart*, I will send him
   28. I leave the world, and *go* to the Father.
  20:17. but *go* to my brethren,
Acts 1:10. *as* he *went up*, behold, two men
   11. as ye have seen him *go* into heaven.
   25. that he might *go* to his own place.
  5:20. *Go*, stand and speak in the temple
   41. And they *departed* from the presence
  8:26. Arise, and *go* toward the south
   27. And he arose and *went:*
   36. And as they *went* on (their) way,
   39. and he *went* on his way rejoicing.
  9: 3. And as he *journeyed*, he came near
   11. Arise, and *go* into the street which is

Acts 9:15. *Go* thy *way:* for he is a chosen
   31. and *walking* in the fear of the Lord,
  10:20. get thee down, and *go* with them,
  12:17. and *went* into another place.
  14:16. suffered all nations *to walk* in their
  16: 7. they assayed *to go* into Bithynia:
   16. *as* we *went* to prayer, a certain damsel
   36. depart, and *go* in peace.
  17:14. *to go* as it were to the sea:
  18: 6. I *will go* unto the Gentiles.
  19:21. *to go* to Jerusalem, saying,
  20: 1. departed for *to go* into Macedonia.
   22. behold, I *go* bound in the spirit
  21: 5. we departed and *went* our *way;*
  22: 5. and *went* to Damascus, to bring
   6. that, *as* I *made* my *journey*,
   10. Arise, and *go* into Damascus;
   21. *Depart:* for I will send thee far
  23:23. two hundred soldiers to *go* to Cæsarea,
   32. left the horsemen *to go* with him,
  24:25. *Go* thy *way* for this time;
  25:12. unto Cæsar *shalt* thou *go*.
   20. whether he would *go* to Jerusalem,
  26:12. *as* I *went* to Damascus
   13. them *which journeyed* with me.
   27. 3. gave (him) liberty *to go* unto his friends
  28:26. *Go* unto this people, and say,
Ro. 15:24. Whensoever I *take* my *journey* into Spain,
   25. now I *go* unto Jerusalem
1Co.10:27. and ye be disposed *to go;*
  16: 4. if it be meet that I *go* also, they *shall go* with me.
   6. on my journey whithersoever I *go*.
1Ti. 1: 3. *when* I *went* into Macedonia,
2Ti. 4:10. and *is departed* unto Thessalonica;
Jas. 4:13. we will *go* into such a city,
1Pet.3:19. By which also he *went and* preached
   22. Who *is gone* into heaven, *and* is on
  4: 3. *when* we *walked* in lasciviousness,
2Pet. 2:10. them *that walk* after the flesh
  3: 3. *walking* after their own lusts,
Jude 11. they *have gone* in the way of Cain,
   16. *walking* after their own lusts;
   18. *who should walk* (lit. *walking*) after their own

πορθέω, *portheo*.

Acts 9:21. Is not this he *that destroyed* them
Gal. 1:13. the church of God, and *wasted* it:
   23. the faith which once he *destroyed*.

πορισμός, *porismos*.

1Ti. 6: 5. supposing that *gain* is godliness: (lit. that godliness is *gain*)
   6. godliness with contentment is great *gain*.

πορνεία, *pórnīa*.

Mat. 5:32. saving for the cause of *fornication*,
  15:19. adulteries, *fornications*, thefts,
  19: 9. except (it be) for *fornication*,
Mar 7:21. adulteries, *fornications*, murders,
Joh. 8:41. We be not born of *fornication;*
Acts15:20. and (from) *fornication*, and
   29. and from *fornication:*
  21:25. from strangled, and from *fornication*.
Ro. 1:29. *fornication*, wickedness, covetousness,

1Co. 5: 1.(that there is) *fornication* among you, and
such *fornication* as is not
6:13.Now the body (is) not for *fornication*,
18.Flee *fornication*.
7: 2.(to avoid) *fornication*, let every
2Co.12:21.and *fornication* and lasciviousness
Gal. 5:19.Adultery, *fornication*, uncleanness,
Eph. 5: 3.But *fornication*, and all uncleanness,
Col. 3: 5.*fornication*, uncleanness,
1Th. 4: 3.ye should abstain from *fornication :*
Rev. 2:21.to repent of her *fornication ;*
9:21.nor of their *fornication*,
14: 8.the wine of the wrath of her *fornication.*
17: 2.with the wine of her *fornication.*
4.filthiness of her *fornication :*
18: 3.wine of the wrath of her *fornication*,
19: 2.corrupt the earth with her *fornication*,

πορνεύω, *pornŭo.*

1Co. 6:18.but he *that committeth fornication*
10: 8.Neither *let* us *commit fornication*, as some
of them *committed*,
Rev. 2:14.unto idols, and *to commit fornication.*
20.to commit fornication, and to eat
17: 2.the kings of the earth *have committed for-*
nication,
18: 3.*have committed fornication* with her,
9.*who have committed fornication* and

πόρνη, *pornee.*

Mat.21:31.and the *harlots* go into the kingdom
32.and the *harlots* believed him:
Lu. 15:30.devoured thy living with *harlots*,
1Co. 6:15.the members of an *harlot ?*
16.is joined to an *harlot* is one body ?
Heb 11:31.By faith the *harlot* Rahab perished not
Jas. 2:25.was not Rahab the *harlot* justified by
Rev.17: 1.the judgment of the great *whore*
5.THE MOTHER OF *HARLOTS*
15.where the *whore* sitteth,
16.these shall hate the *whore*,
19: 2.he hath judged the great *whore*,

πόρνος, *pornos.*

1Co. 5: 9.not to company with *fornicators :*
10.with the *fornicators* of this world,
11.is called a brother be a *fornicator*,
6: 9.neither *fornicators*, nor idolaters,
Eph. 5: 5.that no *whoremonger*, nor unclean
1Ti. 1:10.For *whoremongers*, for them that defile
Heb 12:16.Lest there (be) any *fornicator*, or profane
13: 4.but *whoremongers* and adulterers God
Rev.21: 8.and *whoremongers*, and sorcerers,
22:15.*whoremongers*, and murderers,

πόῤῥω, πόῤῥωτέρω, *porro, porrŏtero.*

Mat.15: 8.but their heart is *far* from me.
Mar 7: 6.but their heart is *far* from me.
Lu. 14:32.while the other is yet *a great way off*,
24:28.as though he would have gone *further*.

πόῤῥωθεν, *porrŏthen.*

Lu. 17:12.which stood *afar off :*

Heb 11:13.but having seen them *afar off*,

πορφύρα, *porphura.*

Mar 15:17.And they clothed him with *purple*,
20.they took off the *purple* from him,
Lu. 16:19.which was clothed in *purple* and
Rev.17: 4.was arrayed in *purple* and scarlet
18:12.and *purple*, and silk, and scarlet,

πορφύρεος, πορφυροῦς, *porphureos, porphurous.*

Joh.19: 2.and they put on him a *purple* robe,
5.crown of thorns, and the *purple* robe.
Rev.18:16.in fine linen, and *purple*, and scarlet,

πορφυρόπωλις, *porphuropōlis.*

Acts16:14.Lydia, a *seller of purple*,

ποσάκις, *posakis.*

Mat.18:21.*how oft* shall my brother sin
23:37.*how often* would I have gathered
Lu. 13:34.*how often* would I have gathered

πόσις, *posis.*

Joh. 6:55.and my blood is *drink* indeed.
Ro. 14:17.the kingdom of God is not meat and
drink ;
Col. 2:16.judge you in meat, or in *drink*,

πόσος, *posos.*

Mat. 6:23.*how great* (is) that darkness!
7:11.*how much* more shall your Father
10:25.*how much* more (shall they call)
12:12.*How much* then is a man better than
15:34.*How many* loaves have ye?
16: 9.and *how many* baskets ye took up?
10.and *how many* baskets ye took up?
27:13.Hearest thou not *how many* things
Mar 6:38.*How many* loaves have ye?
8: 5.*How many* loaves have ye?
19.*how many* baskets full of
20.*how many* baskets full of fragments
9:21.*How long* is it ago since this came
15: 4.*how many* things they witness
Lu. 11:13.*how much* more shall (your)
12:24.*how much* more are ye better than
28.*how much* more (will he clothe) you,
15:17.*How many* hired servants of my
16: 5.*How much* owest thou unto
7.And *how much* owest thou?
Acts21:20.*how many* thousands of Jews
Ro. 11:12.*how much* more their fulness?
24.*how much* more shall these, which be
2Co. 7:11.*what* carefulness it wrought in you,
Philem 16.but *how much* more unto thee,
Heb 9:14.*How much* more shall the blood
10:29.Of *how much* sorer punishment,

ποταμός, potamos.

Mat. 7:25. and the *floods* came,
　　　27. rain descended, and the *floods* came,
Mar 1: 5. baptized of him in the *river* of Jordan,
Lu. 6:48. when the flood arose, the *stream* beat
　　　49. against which the *stream* did beat
Joh. 7:38. shall flow *rivers* of living water.
Acts 16:13. we went out of the city by a *river*
2 Co. 11:26. (in) perils of *waters*, (in) perils of robbers,
Rev. 8:10. upon the third part of the *rivers*,
　　9:14. bound in the great *river* Euphrates.
　　12:15. cast out of his mouth water as a *flood*
　　　16. and swallowed up the *flood*
　　16: 4. poured out his vial upon the *rivers*
　　　12. upon the great *river* Euphrates;
　　22: 1. a pure *river* of water of life,
　　　2. and on either side of the *river*,

ποταμοφόρητος, potamophoreetos.

Rev. 12:15. cause her to be *carried away of the flood.*

ποταπός, potapos.

Mat. 8:27. *What manner of* man is this,
Mar 13: 1. Master, see *what manner of* stones and *what* buildings (are here)!
Lu. 1:29. *what manner of* salutation this should be.
　　7:39. and *what manner of* woman
2 Pet. 3:11. *what manner* (of persons) ought ye to be
1 Joh. 3· 1. Behold, *what manner of* love the

ποτέ, pote. indefinitely.

Lu. 22:32. and *when* thou art converted,
Joh. 9:13. him that *aforetime* was blind.
Acts 28:27. lest)(they should see with (their) eyes,
Ro. 1:10. now *at length* I might have a
　　7: 9. I was alive without the law *once:*
　　11:30. For as ye *in times past* have not
1 Co. 9: 7. Who goeth a warfare *any time* at his
Gal. 1:13. of my conversation *in time past*
　　　23. which persecuted us *in times past* now preacheth the faith which *once* he
　　2: 6. whatsoever)(they were, it maketh no matter
Eph. 2: 2. Wherein *in time past* ye walked
　　　3. *in times past* in the lusts of our flesh,
　　　11. that ye (being) *in time past* Gentiles
　　　13. ye who *sometimes* were far off
　　5: 8. For ye were *sometimes* darkness,
　　　29. no man *ever* yet hated his own flesh;
Phi. 4:10. that now *at the last* your care of me
Col. 1:21. that were *sometime* alienated
　　3: 7. ye also walked *some time*, when ye
1 Th. 2: 5. neither *at any time* used we
Tit. 3: 3. ourselves also were *sometimes* foolish,
Philem 11. Which *in time past* was to thee
Heb 1: 5. unto which of the angels said he *at any time*,
　　　13. to which of the angels said he *at any time*,
　　2: 1. lest *at any time* we should let
　　4: 1. Let us therefore fear, lest,)(a promise
1 Pet. 2:10. Which *in time past* (were) not a
　　3: 5. after this manner *in the old time*
　　　20. Which *sometime* were disobedient,
2 Pet. 1:10. if ye do these things, ye shall never (lit. not *ever*) fall:
　　　21. prophecy came not *in old time* by the

πότε, pote. interrog., or definitely.

Mat. 17:17. how long (lit. until *when*) shall I be with you? how long (lit. &c.) shall I suffer you?
　　24: 3. *when* shall these things be?
　　25:37. *when* saw we thee an hungred, and fed (thee)?
　　　38. *When* saw we thee a stranger,
　　　39. Or *when* saw we thee sick,
　　　44. *when* saw we thee an hungred,
Mar 9:19. how long (lit. until *when*) shall I be with you? how long (lit. &c.) shall I suffer you?
　　13: 4. *when* shall these things be?
　　　33. for ye know not *when* the time is.
　　　35. for ye know not *when* the master
Lu. 9:41. how long (lit. until *when*) shall I be with you,
　　12:36. *when* he will return from the wedding;
　　17:20. *when* the kingdom of God should come,
　　21: 7. but *when* shall these things be?
Joh. 6:25. Rabbi, *when* camest thou hither?
　　10:24. How long (lit. &c.) dost thou make us to doubt?
Rev. 6:10. How long (lit. &c.), O Lord, holy

πότερον, poteron.

Joh. 7:17. *whether* it be of God, or (whether)

ποτήριον, poteerion.

Mat. 10:42. a *cup* of cold (water) only in the
　　20:22. Are ye able to drink of the *cup*
　　　23. Ye shall drink indeed of my *cup*,
　　23:25. ye make clean the outside of the *cup*
　　　26. cleanse first that (which is) within the *cup*
　　26:27. And he took the *cup*, and gave thanks,
　　　39. let this *cup* pass from me:
　　　42. if this *cup* may not pass away
Mar 7: 4. (as) the washing of *cups*, and pots,
　　　8. (as) the washing of pots and *cups*:
　　9:41. a *cup* of water to drink
　　10:38. can ye drink of the *cup* that I
　　　39. Ye shall indeed drink of the *cup*
　　14:23. And he took the *cup*, and when
　　　36. take away this *cup* from me:
Lu. 11:39. make clean the outside of the *cup* and
　　22:17. And he took the *cup*, and gave thanks,
　　　20. Likewise also the *cup* after supper, saying, This *cup* (is) the new testament
　　　42. if thou be willing, remove this *cup*
Joh. 18:11. the *cup* which my Father hath given
1 Co. 10:16. The *cup* of blessing which we bless,
　　　21. Ye cannot drink the *cup* of the Lord, and the *cup* of devils.
　　11:25. After the same manner also (he took) the *cup*,
　　— This *cup* is the new testament
　　　26. and drink this *cup*, ye do shew
　　　27. and drink (this) *cup* of the Lord,
　　　28. and drink of (that) *cup*.
Rev. 14:10. into the *cup* of his indignation;
　　16:19. the *cup* of the wine of the fierceness
　　17: 4. having a golden *cup* in her hand
　　18: 6. in the *cup* which she hath filled

ποτίζω, potizo.

Mat. 10:42. whosoever shall *give to drink*

Mat.25:35. and ye *gave* me *drink :*
　37. and *gave* (thee) *drink ?*
　42. and ye *gave* me no *drink :*
　27:48. and *gave* him *to drink.*
Mar 9:41. shall *give* you a cup of water *to drink*
　15:36. and *gave* him *to drink,* saying,
Lu. 13:15. and lead (him) away to *watering ?*
Ro. 12:20. if he thirst, *give* him *drink :*
1Co. 3: 2. I have *fed* you with milk,
　6. I have planted, Apollos *watered ;*
　7. neither he *that watereth ;*
　8. and he *that watereth* are one:
　12:13. and *have been* all *made to drink* into
Rev.14: 8. because she *made* all nations *drink*

πότος, potos.

1Pet.4: 3. *banquetings,* (lit. *drinkings*) and abominable idolatries:

που, pou. indefinitely.

Ro. 4:19. when he was *about* an hundred
Heb 2: 6. But one *in a certain place* testified,
　4: 4. spake *in a certain place* of the seventh

ποῦ, pou. interrog., or definitely.

Mat. 2: 2. *Where* is he that is born King of
　4. *where* Christ should be born.
　8:20. the Son of man hath not *where* to lay
　26:17. *Where* wilt thou that we prepare
Mar 14:12. *Where* wilt thou that we go and
　14. *Where* is the guestchamber,
　15:47. beheld *where* he was laid.
Lu. 8:25. *Where* is your faith?
　9:58. the Son of man hath not *where* to lay
　12:17. *where* to bestow my fruits?
　17:17. but *where* (are) the nine?
　37. *Where,* Lord? And he said
　22: 9. *Where* wilt thou that we prepare?
　11. *Where* is the guestchamber,
Joh. 1:38(39). *where* dwellest thou?
　39(40). They came and saw *where* he dwelt,
　3: 8. and *whither* it goeth:
　7:11. at the feast, and said, *Where* is he?
　35. *Whither* will he go, that we shall not
　8:10. *where* are those thine accusers?
　14. whence I came, and *whither* I go ;
　— whence I come, and *whither* I go.
　19. *Where* is thy Father?
　9:12. *Where* is he? He said, I know not.
　11:34. *Where* have ye laid him?
　57. if any man knew *where* he were,
　12:35. knoweth not *whither* he goeth.
　13:36. Lord, *whither* goest thou?
　14: 5. we know not *whither* thou goest ;
　16: 5. *Whither* goest thou?
　20: 2. we know not *where* they have laid
　13. I know not *where* they have laid
　15. tell me *where* thou hast laid him,
Ro. 3:27. *Where* (is) boasting then?
1Co. 1:20. *Where* (is) the wise? *where* (is) the scribe? *where* is the disputer of this world?
　12:17. *where* (were) the hearing?
　— *where* (were) the smelling?
　19. *where* (were) the body?

1Co.15:55. O death, *where* (is) thy sting? O grave, *where* (is) thy victory?
Heb 11: 8. not knowing *whither* he went.
1Pet. 4:18. *where* shall the ungodly and
2Pet. 3: 4. *Where* is the promise of his coming?
1Joh. 2:11. and knoweth not *whither* he goeth,
Rev. 2:13. and *where* thou dwellest,

πούς, pous.

Mat. 4: 6. lest at any time thou dash thy *foot*
　5:35. for it is his *footstool :* (lit. the footstool of his *feet*)
　7: 6. lest they trample them under their *feet,*
　10:14. shake off the dust of your *feet.*
　15:30. cast them down at Jesus' *feet ;*
　18: 8. if thy hand or thy *foot* offend thee,
　— than having two hands or two *feet*
　29. fellowservant fell down at his *feet,*
　22:13. Bind him hand and *foot,*
　44. till I make thine enemies thy *footstool?* (lit. &c.)
　28: 9. and held him by the *feet,*
Mar 5:22. he fell at his *feet,*
　6:11. the dust under your *feet* for a testimony
　7:25. and came and fell at his *feet :*
　9:45. if thy *foot* offend thee, cut it off:
　— than having two *feet* to be cast
　12:36. make thine enemies thy *footstool.* (lit. &c.)
Lu. 1:79. to guide our *feet* into the way of peace.
　4:11. thou dash thy *foot* against a stone.
　7:38. stood at his *feet* behind (him) weeping, and began to wash his *feet* with tears,
　— and kissed his *feet,*
　44. thou gavest me no water for my *feet :* but she hath washed my *feet* with
　45. hath not ceased to kiss my *feet,*
　46. anointed my *feet* with ointment.
　8:35. sitting at the *feet* of Jesus, clothed,
　41. he fell down at Jesus' *feet,*
　9: 5. the very dust from your *feet*
　10:39. which also sat at Jesus' *feet,*
　15:22. and shoes on (his) *feet :*
　17:16. fell down on (his) face at his *feet,*
　20:43. thine enemies thy *footstool.* (lit. &c.)
　24:39. Behold my hands and my *feet,*
　40. shewed them (his) hands and (his) *feet.*
Joh. 11: 2. and wiped his *feet* with her hair,
　32. she fell down at his *feet,*
　44. bound hand and *foot* with graveclothes:
　12: 3. and anointed the *feet* of Jesus, and wiped his *feet* with her hair:
　13: 5. to wash the disciples' *feet,*
　6. dost thou wash my *feet ?*
　8. Thou shalt never wash my *feet.*
　9. Lord, not my *feet* only, but also
　10. save to wash (his) *feet,*
　12. after he had washed their *feet,*
　14. and Master, have washed your *feet ;* ye also ought to wash one anothers' *feet.*
　20:12. and the other at the *feet,*
Acts 2:35. Until I make thy foes thy *footstool.* (lit. &c.)
　4:35. laid (them) down at the apostles' *feet :*
　37. and laid (it) at the apostles' *feet.*
　5: 2. and laid (it) at the apostles' *feet.*
　9. behold, the *feet* of them which have
　10. fell she down straightway at his *feet,*
　7: 5. no, not (so much as) to set his *foot* on:
　33. Put off thy shoes from thy *feet :*
　49. and earth (is) my *footstool :* (lit. &c.)
　58. at a young man's *feet,*
　10:25. and fell down at his *feet,*

Acts13:25. whose shoes of (his) *feet* I am not
    51. shook off the dust of their *feet*
14: 8. impotent in his *feet*,
    10. Stand upright on thy *feet*.
16:24. made their *feet* fast in the stocks.
21:11. bound his own hands and *feet*,
22: 3. at the *feet* of Gamaliel,
26:16. rise, and stand upon thy *feet* :
Ro. 3:15. Their *feet* (are) swift to shed blood:
    10:15. How beautiful are the *feet* of them
    16:20. shall bruise Satan under your *feet* shortly.
1Co.12:15. If the *foot* shall say, Because
    21. nor again the head to the *feet*,
    15:25. hath put all enemies under his *feet*.
    27. he hath put all things under his *feet*.
Eph. 1:22. hath put all (things) under his *feet*,
    6:15. And your *feet* shod with the
1Ti. 5:10. if she have washed the saints' *feet*,
Heb 1:13. thine enemies thy *footstool*?
    2: 8. in subjection under his *feet*.
    10:13. till his enemies be made his *footstool*.
    12:13. make straight paths for your *feet*,
Rev. 1:15. And his *feet* like unto fine brass,
    17. I fell at his *feet* as dead.
    2:18. and his *feet* (are) like fine brass ;
    3: 9. and worship before thy *feet*,
    10: 1. and his *feet* as pillars of fire:
    2. and he set his right *foot* upon the sea,
    11:11. and they stood upon their *feet* ;
    12: 1. and the moon under her *feet*,
    13: 2. and his *feet* were as (the feet) of
    19:10. I fell at his *feet* to worship him.
    22: 8. before the *feet* of the angel which

πρᾶγμα, *pragma*.

Mat.18:19. touching any *thing* that they shall ask,
Lu. 1: 1. a declaration of those *things*
Acts 5: 4. why hast thou conceived this *thing*
Ro. 16: 2. in whatsoever *business* she hath need
1Co. 6: 1. having a *matter* against another,
2Co. 7:11. to be clear in this *matter*.
1Th. 4: 6. defraud his brother in (any) *matter* :
Heb 6:18. That by two immutable *things*,
    10: 1. not the very image of the *things*,
    11: 1. is the substance of *things* hoped for,
Jas. 3:16. confusion and every evil *work*.

πραγματεία, *pragmatia*.

2Ti. 2: 4. entangleth himself with the *affairs* (lit. *negotiations*) of (this) life ;

πραγματεύομαι, *pragmatūomai*.

Lu. 19:13. *Occupy* (lit. *trade*) till I come.

πραιτώριον, *praitōrion*.

Mat.27:27. took Jesus into the *common hall*,
Mar 15:16. into the hall, called *Prætorium*,
Joh.18:28. unto the *hall of judgment* :
    — went not into the *judgment hall*,
    33. Pilate entered into the *judgment hall*
    19: 9. went again into the *judgment hall*,
Acts23:35. to be kept in Herod's *judgment hall*.
Phi. 1:13. are manifest in all the *palace*,

πράκτωρ, *practor*.

Lu. 12:58. the judge deliver thee to the *officer*, and the *officer* cast thee

---

πρᾶξις, *praxis*.

Mat.16:27. according to his *works*. (lit. *acting*)
Lu. 23:51. to the counsel and *deed* of them ;
Acts19:18. confessed, and shewed their *deeds*.
Ro. 8:13. do mortify the *deeds* of the body,
    12: 4. all members have not the same *office* :
Col. 3: 9. the old man with his *deeds* ;

πρᾷος, *praos*.

Mat.11:29. for I am *meek* and lowly in heart:

πρᾳότης, *praotees*.

1Co. 4:21. and (in) the spirit of *meekness* ?
2Co.10: 1. by the *meekness* and gentleness of Christ,
Gal. 5:23. *Meekness*, temperance:
    6: 1. in the spirit of *meekness* ;
Eph. 4: 2. With all lowliness and *meekness*,
Col. 3:12. *meekness*, longsuffering ;
1Ti. 6:11. patience, *meekness*.
2Ti. 2:25. In *meekness* instructing those
Tit. 3: 2. shewing all *meekness* unto all

πρασιά, *prasia*.

Mar 6:40. And they sat down in *ranks*, (lit. *range by range*)

πράσσω, πράττω, *prasso*, *pratto*.

Lu. 3:13. *Exact* no more than that which is appointed you.
    19:23. I might *have required* mine own
    22:23. that should *do* this thing.
    23:15. nothing worthy of death is *done* unto him.
    41. we receive the due reward of our *deeds* :
    but this man *hath done* nothing amiss.
Joh. 3:20. every one *that doeth* evil hateth
    5:29. and they *that have done* evil,
Acts 3:17. through ignorance ye *did* (it),
    5:35. what ye intend *to do* as touching
    15:29. ye *shall do* well.
    16:28. *Do* thyself no harm:
    17: 7. these all *do* contrary to the decrees
    19:19. of them also *which used* curious *arts*
    36. and *to do* nothing rashly.
    25:11. or *have committed* any thing worthy
    25. that he *had committed* nothing
    26: 9. that I ought *to do* many things
    20. *and do* works meet for repentance.
    26. this thing was not *done* in a corner.
    31. This man *doeth* nothing worthy of
Ro. 1:32. that they *which commit* such
    — have pleasure in them *that do* them.
    2: 1. *doest* the same things.
    2. against them *which commit* such things.
    3. judgest them *which do* such things,
    25. if thou *keep* the law:
    7:15. what I would, that *do* I not;
    19. which I would not, that I *do*.
    9:11. neither *having done* any good or evil,

Ro. 13: 4. upon him *that doeth* evil.
1Co. 9:17. For if I *do* this thing willingly,
2Co. 5:10. according to that he *hath done*,
    12:21. which they *have committed*.
Gal. 5:21. that they *which do* such things
Eph. 6:21. (and) how I *do*, Tychicus,
Phi. 4: 9. and seen in me, *do :*
1Th. 4:11. and *to do* your own business,

πραΰς, *praüs.*

Mat. 5: 5. Blessed (are) the *meek :* for
    21: 5. thy King cometh unto thee, *meek*, and
1Pet.3: 4. of a *meek* and quiet spirit,

πραΰτης, *praütees.*

Jas. 1:21. receive with *meekness* the engrafted
    3:13. his works with *meekness* of wisdom.
1Pet.3:15. with *meekness* and fear:

πράω see πιπράσκω.

πρέπει, *prepi.*

Mat. 3:15. for thus it *becometh* (lit. is *becoming* for)
    us to fulfil all
1Co.11:13. is it *comely* that a woman
Eph. 5: 3. as *becometh* saints ;
1Ti. 2:10. which *becometh* women professing
Tit. 2: 1. which *become* sound doctrine:
Heb 2:10. For it *became* him, for whom
    7:26. such an high priest *became* us,

πρεσβεία, *presbia.*

Lu. 14:32. he sendeth an *ambassage*,
    19:14. and sent a *message* after him,

πρεσβεύω, *presbūo.*

2Co. 5:20. we *are ambassadors* for Christ,
Eph. 6:20. I *am* an *ambassador* in bonds:

πρεσβυτέριον, *presbuterion.*

Lu. 22:66. the *elders* of the people and
Acts22: 5. and all the *estate of* the *elders :*
1Ti. 4:14. of the hands of the *presbytery.*

πρεσβύτερος, -τέρα, *presbuteros, -tera.*

Mat.15: 2. the tradition of the *elders?*
    16:21. suffer many things of the *elders*
    21:23. and the *elders* of the people
    26: 3. and the *elders* of the people,
    47. and *elders* of the people.
    57. and the *elders* were assembled.
    59. the chief priests, and *elders*,
    27: 1. and *elders* of the people
    3. to the chief priests and *elders,*
    12. accused of the chief priests and *elders,*
    20. the chief priests and *elders* persuaded
    41. with the scribes and *elders,*
    28:12. were assembled with the *elders,*

Mar 7: 3. holding the tradition of the *elders.*
    5. according to the tradition of the *elders,*
    8:31. and be rejected of the *elders,*
    11:27. and the scribes, and the *elders,*
    14:43. priests and the scribes and the *elders.*
    53. and the *elders* and the scribes.
    15: 1. with the *elders* and scribes
Lu. 7: 3. he sent unto him the *elders* of the Jews,
    9:22. and be rejected of the *elders*
    15:25. Now his *elder* son was in the field:
    20: 1. came upon (him) with the *elders,*
    22:52. and captains of the temple, and the *elders,*
Joh. 8: 9. beginning at the *eldest*, [plural]
Acts 2:17. and your *old men* shall dream dreams:
    4: 5. that their rulers, and *elders,*
    8. Ye rulers of the people, and *elders* of
    Israel,
    23. and *elders* had said unto them.
    6:12. and the *elders*, and the scribes,
    11:30. and sent it to the *elders* by
    14:23. ordained them *elders* in every church,
    15: 2. unto the apostles and *elders* about this
    4. and (of) the apostles and *elders,*
    6. And the apostles and *elders*
    22. pleased it the apostles and *elders,*
    23. The apostles and *elders* and brethren
    16: 4. that were ordained of the apostles and
    elders
    20:17. and called the *elders* of the church.
    21:18. and all the *elders* were present.
    23:14. the chief priests and *elders,*
    24: 1. high priest descended with the *elders,*
    25:15. the chief priests and the *elders* of the Jews
1Ti. 5: 1. Rebuke not an *elder*, but intreat
    2. The *elder women* as mothers ;
    17. Let the *elders* that rule well
    19. Against an *elder* receive not an accusation,
    but before two
Tit. 1: 5. ordain *elders* in every city,
Heb11: 2. For by it the *elders* obtained a good report.
Jas. 5:14. let him call for the *elders* of the church ;
1Pet.5: 1. The *elders* which are among you
    5. submit yourselves unto the *elder.* [plural]
2Joh. 1. The *elder* unto the elect lady
3Joh. 1. The *elder* unto the wellbeloved Gaius,
Rev. 4: 4. I saw four and twenty *elders* sitting,
    10. The four and twenty *elders*
    5: 5. And one of the *elders* saith unto me,
    6. and in the midst of the *elders,*
    8. four (and) twenty *elders* fell down
    11. and the beasts and the *elders :*
    14. the four (and) twenty *elders* fell down
    7:11. and (about) the *elders* and the four
    13. And one of the *elders* answered,
    11:16. the four and twenty *elders*, which sat
    14: 3. before the four beasts, and the *elders :*
    19: 4. the four and twenty *elders* and the four

πρεσβύτης, *presbutees.*

Lu. 1:18. for I am an *old man*, and my wife
Tit. 2: 2. That the *aged men* be sober,
Philem. 9. being such an one as Paul the *aged,*

πρεσβῦτις, *presbutis.*

Tit. 2: 3. The *aged women* likewise,

πρηνής, *preenees.*

Acts 1:18. and falling *headlong*, he burst

πρίζω, prizo.

Heb 11:37. they *were sawn asunder,*

πρίν,; πρὶν ἤ, prin, & prin ee.

Mat. 1:18. *before* they came together,
   26:34. *before* the cock crow,
     75. *Before* the cock crow, thou shalt
Mar 14:30. *before* the cock crow twice,
     72. *Before* the cock crow twice,
Lu. 2:26. *before* he had seen the Lord's Christ.
  22:34. *before that* thou shalt thrice deny
     61. *Before* the cock crow,
Joh. 4:49. Sir, come down *ere* my child die.
   8:58. *Before* Abraham was, I am.
  14:29. I have told you *before* it come to pass,
Acts 2:20. *before* that great and notable day
   7: 2. *before* he dwelt in Charran,
  25:16. *before that* he which is accused

πρίω see πρίζω.

πρό, pro.

Note.—It governs the genitive.

Mat. 5:12. the prophets which were *before* you.
   6: 8. ye have need of, *before* ye ask him.
   8:29. to torment us *before* the time?
  11:10. I send my messenger *before* thy face,
  24:38. in the days that were *before* the flood
Mar 1: 2. I send my messenger *before* thy face,
Lu. 1:76. thou shalt go *before* the face of the Lord
   2:21. *before* he was conceived in the womb.
   7:27. I send my messenger *before* thy face,
   9:52. And sent messengers *before* his face:
  10: 1. two and two *before* his face into every
  11:38. he had not first washed *before* dinner.
  21:12. But *before* all these, they shall
  22:15. this passover with you *before* I suffer:
Joh. 1:48(49). *Before* that Philip called thee,
   5: 7. another stepeth down *before* me.
  10: 8. All that ever came *before* me are thieves
  11:55. up to Jerusalem *before* the passover,
  12: 1. Then Jesus six days *before* the passover
     (πρὸ ἐξ ἡμερῶν τοῦ πάσχα)
  13: 1. Now *before* the feast of the passover,
    19. Now I tell you *before* it come,
  17: 5. which I had with thee *before* the world
    24. *before* the foundation of the world.
Acts 5:23. standing without *before* the doors:
    36. For *before* these days rose up Theudas,
  12: 6. and the keepers *before* the door kept
    14. told how Peter stood *before* the gate.
  13:24. *before* (lit. *before* the face of) his coming
  14:13. which was *before* their city,
  21:38. which *before* these days madest
  23:15. and we, *or ever* he come near, are ready
Ro. 16: 7. who also were in Christ *before* me.
1Co. 2: 7. God ordained *before* the world
   4: 5. judge nothing *before* the time,
2Co.12: 2. about fourteen years *ago,*
Gal. 1:17. which were apostles *before* me ;
   2:12. For *before* that certain came from James,
   3:23. But *before* faith came,
Eph. 1: 4. *before* the foundation of the world,
Col. 1:17. And he is *before* all things, and
2Ti. 1: 9. *before* the world began ;
   4:21. Do thy diligence to come *before* winter.

Tit. 1: 2. promised *before* the world began ;
Heb 11: 5. for *before* his translation he had
Jas. 5: 9. the judge standeth *before* the door.
    12. But *above* all things, my brethren,
1Pet. 1:20. foreordained *before* the foundation of
   4: 8. *above* all things have fervent charity

προάγω, proago.

Mat. 2: 9. went *before* them, till it came and
  14:22. *to go before* him unto the other side,
  21: 9. the multitudes *that went before,*
    31. *go* into the kingdom of God *before* you.
  26:32. I *will go before* you into Galilee.
  28: 7. he *goeth before* you into Galilee ;
Mar 6:45. *to go* to the other side *before* unto
  10:32. and Jesus *went before* them:
  11: 9. And they *that went before,*
  14:28. I *will go before* you into Galilee.
  16: 7. that he *goeth before* you into Galilee:
Lu. 18:39. they *which went before* rebuked him,
Acts 12: 6. when Herod would have *brought* him *forth,*
  16:30. And *brought* them **out,** *and* **said,**
  25:26. I have *brought* him *forth* before you,
1Ti. 1:18. according to the prophecies *which went before* on thee,
   5:24. *going before* to judgment;
Heb 7:18. of the commandment *going before*

προαιρέομαι, proaireomai.

2Co. 9: 7. according as he *purposeth* in his heart,

προαιτιάομαι, proaitiaomai.

Ro. 3: 9. for we *have before* proved both Jews and Gentiles,

---

προακούω, proakouo.

Col. 1: 5. whereof ye *heard before* in the word

προαμαρτάνω, proamartano.

2Co.12:21. bewail many *which have sinned already,*
  13: 2. write to them *which heretofore have sinned,*

προαύλιον, proaulion.

Mar 14:68. And he went out into the *porch ;*

προβαίνω, probaino.

Mat. 4:21. And *going on* from thence,
Mar 1:19. *when* he *had gone* a little *farther* thence,
Lu. 1: 7. both were (now) *well stricken* in years.
    18. and my wife *well stricken* in years.
   2:36. she was of a great age, (lit. *advanced* in days)

προβάλλω, proballo.

Lu. 21:30. When they now *shoot forth.*
Acts 19:33. the Jews *putting* him *forward.*

προβατικός, probatikos.

Joh. 5: 2. by the *sheep* (market) a pool,

πρόβατον, probaton.

Mat. 7:15. come to you in *sheep's* clothing,
    9:36. as *sheep* having no shepherd.
    10: 6. go rather to the lost *sheep* of the
      16. I send you forth as *sheep* in the
    12:11. that shall have one *sheep*,
      12. is a man better than a *sheep* ?
    15:24. but unto the lost *sheep* of the
    18:12. have an hundred *sheep*,
    25:32. divideth (his) *sheep* from the goats:
      33. he shall set the *sheep* on his
    26:31. the *sheep* of the flock shall be scattered
Mar 6:34. they were as *sheep* not having a
    14:27. and the *sheep* shall be scattered.
Lu. 15: 4. having an hundred *sheep*,
     6. for I have found my *sheep* which
Joh. 2:14. that sold oxen and *sheep* and doves,
    15. and the *sheep*, and the oxen;
    10: 1. by the door into the *sheep*fold,
    2. is the shepherd of the *sheep*.
    3. and the *sheep* hear his voice: and he
       calleth his own *sheep* by name,
    4. he putteth forth his own *sheep*, he goeth
       before them, and the *sheep* follow him:
    7. I am the door of the *sheep*.
    8. but the *sheep* did not hear them.
    11. giveth his life for the *sheep* .
    12. whose own the *sheep* are not,
    — leaveth the *sheep*, and fleeth:
    — and scattereth the *sheep*.
    13. and careth not for the *sheep*.
    15. I lay down my life for the *sheep*.
    16. And other *sheep* I have,
    26. ye are not of my *sheep*,
    27. My *sheep* hear my voice,
    21:16. He saith unto him, Feed my *sheep*.
    17. Jesus saith unto him, Feed my *sheep*.
Acts 8:32. He was led as a *sheep* to the slaughter;
Ro. 8:36. accounted as *sheep* for the slaughter.
Heb 13:20. that great Shepherd of the *sheep*,
1Pet.2:25. For ye were as *sheep* going astray ;
Rev.18:13. beasts, and *sheep*, and horses,

προβιβάζω, probibazo.

Mat.14: 8. *being before instructed* of her mother,
Acts19:33. they *drew* Alexander out of the multitude,

προβλέπω, problepo.

Heb 11:40. God *having provided* some better thing
    for us,

προγίνομαι, proginomai.

Ro. 3:25. for the remission of sins *that are past*,

προγινώσκω, proginōsko.

Acts26: 5. *Which knew* me from the beginning,
Ro. 8:29. For whom he *did foreknow*,
    11: 2. his people which he *foreknew*.
1Pet.1:20. *Who* verily *was foreordained* before
2Pet.3:17. *seeing* ye *know* (these things) *before*,

πρόγνωσις, prognōsis.

Acts 2:23. and *foreknowledge* of God,
1Pet.1: 2. according to the *foreknowledge* of

πρόγονοι, progonoi.

1Ti. 5: 4. and to requite their *parents :*
2Ti. 1: 3. whom I serve from (my) *forefathers*

προγράφω, prographo.

Ro. 15: 4. whatsoever things *were written aforetime*
       were written for our learning,
Gal. 3: 1. Jesus Christ *hath been evidently set forth,*
Eph. 3: 3. as I *wrote afore* in few words,
Jude 4. *who were before* of old *ordained* to this

πρόδηλος, pródeelos.

1Ti. 5:24. Some men's sins are *open beforehand,*
    25. the good works (of some) are *manifest*
      beforehand ;
Heb 7:14. For (it is) *evident* that our Lord

προδίδωμι, prodidōmi.

Ro. 11:35. Or who *hath first given* to him,

προδότης, prodotees.

Lu. 6:16. which also was the *traitor.*
Acts 7:52. ye have been now the *betrayers* and
2Ti. 3: 4. *Traitors,* heady, highminded,

προδρέμω see προτρέχω.

πρόδρομος, prodromos.

Heb 6:20. Whither the *forerunner* is for us

προειδέω, proideo.

Acts 2:31. He *seeing* this *before* spake of
Gal. 3: 8. And the scripture, *foreseeing* that

προελπίζω, proelpizo.

Eph. 1:12. who *first trusted* in Christ.

προέπω, proëpo.

Acts 1:16. the Holy Ghost by the mouth of David
    spake before concerning Judas,
Gal. 5:21. as I *have* also *told* (you) *in time past,*
1Th. 4: 6. as we also *have forewarned* you

προενάρχομαι, proenarkomai.

2Co. 8: 6. that as he *had begun,* so he would also
    finish in you
    10. who *have begun before,* not only to do,

προεπαγγέλλομαι, *proepangellomai.*

Ro. 1: 2. Which he *had promised afore* by his

προερέω, *proereo.*

Mat 24:25. I *have told* you *before.*
Mar 13:23. I *have foretold* you all things.
Ro. 9:29. as Esaias *said before,* Except
2Co. 7: 3. I *have said before,* that ye are
13: 2. I *told* you *before,* and foretell
Gal. 1: 9. As we *said before,* so say I now
Heb 10:15. after that he *had said before,*
2Pet.3: 2. of the words *which were spoken before*
Jude 17. the words *which were spoken before*

προέρχομαι, *proerkomai.*

Mat 26:39. he *went* a little *farther,* and
Mar 6:33. out of all cities, and *outwent* them,
14:35. And he *went forward* a little, *and*
Lu. 1:17. he *shall go before* him in the
22:47. one of the twelve, *went before* them,
Acts 12:10. and *passed on* through one street ;
20: 5. These *going before* tarried for us
13. And we *went before* to ship, *and*
2Co. 9: 5. that they *would go before* unto you,

προετοιμάζω, *proetoimazo.*

Ro. 9:23. which he *had afore prepared*
Eph. 2:10. which God *hath before ordained* that

προευαγγελίζομαι, *proūangelizomai.*

Gal. 3: 8. *preached before the gospel* unto Abraham,

προέχομαι, *proëkomai.*

Ro. 3: 9. What then? *are we better* (than they)?

προηγέομαι, *proeegeomai.*

Ro. 12:10. in honour *preferring* one another ;

πρόθεσις, *prothesis.*

Mat 12: 4. and did eat the *shew*bread, (lit. the bread of *setting before*)
Mar 2:26. did eat the *shew*bread, (lit. the bread &c.)
Lu. 6: 4. did take and eat the *shew*bread, (lit. &c.)
Acts 11:23. that with *purpose* of heart
27:13. that they had obtained (their) *purpose,*
Ro. 8:28. the called according to (his) *purpose.*
9:11. that the *purpose* of God according to election
Eph. 1:11. according to the *purpose* of him
3:11. According to the eternal *purpose*
2Ti. 1: 9. according to his own *purpose*
3:10. manner of life, *purpose,* faith,
Heb 9: 2. and the *shew*bread ; (lit. the *setting before* of bread)

προθεσμία, *prothesmia.*

Gal. 4: 2. until the *time appointed* of the father.

προθυμία, *prothumia.*

Acts 17:11. with all *readiness of mind,*
2Co. 8:11. as (there was) a *readiness* to will,
12. if there be first a *willing mind,*
19. and (declaration of) your *ready mind :*
9: 2. I know the *forwardness* of your *mind,*

πρόθυμος, *prothumos.*

Mat.26:41. the spirit indeed (is) *willing,*
Mar 14:38. The spirit truly (is) *ready,*
Ro. 1:15. So, as much as in me is, I am *ready* to preach the gospel to

---

προθύμως, *prothumōs.*

1Pet.5: 2. but *of a ready mind*

προΐστημι, *proïsteemi.*

Ro. 12: 8. he *that ruleth,* with diligence ;
1Th. 5:12. and *are over* you in the Lord,
1Ti. 3: 4. One *that ruleth* well his own house,
5. if a man know not how *to rule* his
12. *ruling* their children and their own
5:17. Let the elders *that rule* well be
Tit. 3: 8. be careful *to maintain* good works.
14. learn *to maintain* good works

προκαλέομαι, *prokaleomai.*

Gal. 5:26. *provoking* one another, envying

προκαταγγέλλω, *prokatangello.*

Acts 3:18. which God *before had shewed* by
24. have likewise *foretold* of these days.
7:52. slain them *which shewed before* of
2Co. 9: 5. your bounty, whereof ye *had notice before,* (lit. your *previously notified* bounty)

προκαταρτίζω, *prokatartizo.*

2Co. 9: 5. and *make up beforehand* your bounty,

πρόκειμαι, *prokīmai.*

2Co. 8:12. if there be *first* a willing mind,
Heb. 6:18. to lay hold upon the hope *set before* us:
12: 1. the race *that is set before* us,
2. for the joy *that was set before* him
Jude 7. *are set forth* for an example,

προκηρύσσω, *prokeerusso.*

Acts 3:20. Jesus Christ, *which before was preached* unto you:
13:24. When John *had first preached* before his coming the baptism of

---

προκοπή, *prokopee.*

Phi. 1:12. unto the *furtherance* of the gospel ;

Phi. 1:25. for your *furtherance* and joy of faith ;
1Ti. 4:15. that thy *profiting* may appear to all.

προκόπτω, *prokopto.*

Lu. 2:52. Jesus *increased* in wisdom and
Ro. 13:12. The night *is far spent,*
Gal. 1:14. And *profited* in the Jews' religion
2Ti. 2:16. for they *will increase* unto more
    3: 9. But they *shall proceed* no further:
      13. *shall wax* worse and worse, deceiving,

πρόκριμα, *prokrima.*

1Ti. 5:21. without *preferring one before another,*

προκυρόομαι, *prokuroömai.*

Gal. 3:17. the covenant, *that was confirmed before* of
     God in Christ,

προλαμβάνω, *prolambano.*

Mar14: 8. she *is come aforehand* (lit. *hath anticipated*)
     to anoint
1Co.11:21. every one *taketh before* (other) his
Gal. 6: 1. if a man *be overtaken* in a fault,

προλέγω, *prolego.*

2Co.13: 2. and *foretell* (you), as if I were present,
Gal. 5:21. of the which I *tell* you *before,*
1Th. 3: 4. we *told* you *before* that we should

προμαρτύρομαι, *promarturomai.*

1Pet.1:11. *when it testified beforehand* the sufferings
     of Christ, and the glory

προμελετάω, *promeletao.*

Lu. 21:14. not *to meditate before* what ye shall

προμεριμνάω, *promerimnao.*

Mar13:11. *take* no *thought beforehand* what

προνοέω, *pronoeo.*

Ro. 12:17. *Provide* things honest in the sight
2Co. 8:21. *Providing for* honest things,
1Ti. 5: 8. But if any *provide* not *for* his own,

πρόνοια, *pronoya.*

Acts24: 2. unto this nation by thy *providence,*
Ro. 13:14. and make not *provision for* the

προοράω, *proörao.*

Acts 2:25. I *foresaw* the Lord always before my face,
    21:29. For they had *seen before* with him

προορίζω, *proörizo.*

Acts 4:28. *determined before* to be done.
Ro. 8:29. *did predestinate* (to be) conformed
     30. whom he *did predestinate,* them he also
1Co. 2: 7. which God *ordained* (lit. *pre-ordained*)
     before the world
Eph 1: 5. *Having predestinated* us unto the adoption
     11. *being predestinated* according to the pur-
     pose of him

προπάσχω, *propasko.*

1Th. 2: 2. *after that* we had *suffered before,*

προπέμπω, *propempo.*

Acts15: 3. And *being brought on* their *way* by the
     church,
    20:38. And they *accompanied* him unto the ship.
    21: 5. *and* they all *brought* us *on* our *way,*
Ro. 15:24. and *to be brought on* my *way* thitherward
1Co.16: 6. that ye *may bring* me *on* my *journey*
     11. but *conduct* him *forth* in peace,
2Co. 1:16. of you *to be brought on* my *way*
Tit. 3:13. *Bring* Zenas the lawyer and Apollos *on*
     their *journey* diligently,
3Joh. 6. *if* thou *bring forward on* their *journey*

προπετής, *propetees.*

Acts19:36. and to do nothing *rashly.*
2Ti. 3: 4. Traitors, *heady,* highminded,

προπορεύομαι, *proporuomai.*

Lu. 1:76. thou *shalt go before* the face of the Lord
Acts 7:40. Make us gods to *go before* us:

πρός, *pros.*

Note.—It governs the accusative case with these
few exceptions: In five places it is found with
a dative, marked [d]; in one passage, Acts. 27:34,
it has a genitive, marked [g].

Mat. 2:12. they should not return *to* Herod,
    3: 5. Then went out *to* him Jerusalem,
     10. the ax is laid *unto* the root
     13. to Jordan *unto* John,
     14. and comest thou *to* me?
     15. Jesus answering said *unto* him,
    4: 6. thou dash thy foot *against* a stone.
    5:28. on a woman *to* lust after her
    6: 1. *to* be seen of them:
    7:15. which come *to* you in sheep's
   10: 6. But go rather *to* the lost sheep of
     13. let your peace return *to* you.
   11:28. Come *unto* me, all (ye) that labour
   13: 2. were gathered together *unto* him,
     30. bind them in bundles *to* burn them:
     56. are they not all *with* us ?
   14:25. Jesus went *unto* them,
     28. bid me come *unto* thee on the water.
     29. on the water, to go *to* Jesus.
   17:14. when they were come *to* the multitude,
   19: 8. *because of* the hardness of your hearts
     14. and forbid them not, to come *unto* me.

Mat.21: 1. *unto* the mount of Olives,
32. For John came *unto* you
34. sent his servants *to* the husbandmen,
37. he sent *unto* them his son,
23: 5. *for* to be seen of men:
34. I send *unto* you prophets,
37. which are sent *unto* thee,
25: 9. but go ye rather *to* them that sell,
36. and ye came *unto* me.
39. and came *unto* thee?
26:12. she did (it) *for* my burial.
14. went *unto* the chief priests,
18. Go into the city *to* such a man,
— keep the passover *at* thy house (πρὸς σὲ)
40. he cometh *unto* the disciples,
45. Then cometh he *to* his disciples,
55. I sat daily *with* you teaching
57. led (him) away *to* Caiaphas
27: 4. What (is that) *to* us?
14. he answered him *to* never a word;
19. his wife sent *unto* him,
62. Pharisees came together *unto* Pilate,
Mar 1: 5. And there went out *unto* him all
27. they questioned *among* themselves,
32. they brought *unto* him all that
33. was gathered together *at* the door.
40. And there came a leper *to* him,
45. and they came *to* him from
2: 2. not so much as *about* the door:
3. And they come *unto* him,
13. the multitude resorted *unto* him,
3: 7. with his disciples *to* the sea:
8. came *unto* him.
13. and they came *unto* him.
31. sent *unto* him, calling him.
4: 1. there was gathered *unto* him
— was *by* the sea on the land.
41. and said one *to* another,
5:11. *nigh unto* the mountains
15. And they come *to* Jesus,
19. Go home *to* thy friends,
22. he fell *at* his feet,
6: 3. are not his sisters here *with* us?
25. with haste *unto* the king,
30. themselves together *unto* Jesus,
33. and came together *unto* him.
45. *unto* Bethsaida, while' he
48. he cometh *unto* them,
51. he went up *unto* them into the ship;
7: 1. Then came together *unto* him
25. and came and fell *at* his feet:
31. he came *unto* the sea of Galilee,
8:16. they reasoned *among* themselves,
9:10. they kept that saying *with* themselves,
14. And when he came *to* (his) disciples,
16. What question ye *with* them?
17. I have brought *unto* thee my son,
19. how long shall I be *with* you?
— bring him *unto* me.
20. And they brought him *unto* him:
33. that ye disputed *among* yourselves,
34. they had disputed *among* themselves,
10: 1. the people resort *unto* him again;
5. *For* the hardness of your heart he wrote
7. and cleave *to* his wife;
14. the little children to come *unto* me,
26. saying *among* themselves,
50. and came *to* Jesus.
11: 1. *at* the mount of Olives,
4. and found the colt tied *by* the door
7. And they brought the colt *to* Jesus,
27. there come *to* him the chief priests,

Mar 11:31. they reasoned *with* themselves,
12: 2. he sent *to* the husbandmen
4. he sent *unto* them another
6. he sent him also last *unto* them,
7. said *among* themselves,
12. had spoken the parable *against* them:
13. And they send *unto* him
18. Then come *unto* him the Sadducees,
13:22. *to* seduce, if (it were) possible,
14: 4. that had indignation *within* themselves,
10. went *unto* the chief priests,
49. I was daily *with* you in the temple
53. they led Jesus away *to* the high priest:
54. and warmed himself *at* the fire.
15:31. said *among* themselves
43. went in boldly *unto* Pilate,
16: 3. they said *among* themselves,
Lu. 1:13. But the angel said *unto* him,
18. Zacharias said *unto* the angel,
19. and am sent to speak *unto* thee,
27. *To* a virgin espoused to a man
28. the angel came in *unto* her,
34. Then said Mary *unto* the angel,
43. of my Lord should come *to* me?
55. As he spake *to* our fathers,
61. And they said *unto* her,
73. which he sware *to* our father
80. till the day of his shewing *unto* Israel.
2:15. the shepherds said one *to* another,
18. which were told)(them by the shepherds.
20. as it was told *unto* them.
34. and said *unto* Mary his mother,
48. and his mother said *unto* him,
49. And he said *unto* them,
3: 9. the axe is laid *unto* the root
12. and said *unto* him, Master,
13. And he said *unto* them, Exact no
14. And he said *unto* them, Do
4: 4. And Jesus answered)(him, saying,
11. thou dash thy foot *against* a stone.
21. And he began to say *unto* them,
23. And he said *unto* them, Ye will
26. But *unto* none of them was Elias
— *unto* a woman (that was) a widow.
36. and spake *among* themselves,
40. brought them *unto* him;
43. And he said *unto* them, I must
5: 4. he said *unto* Simon, Launch
10. And Jesus said *unto* Simon, Fear not;
22. he answering said *unto* them;
30. murmured *against* his disciples,
31. Jesus answering said *unto* them,
33. And they said *unto* him, Why do
34. And he said *unto* them, Can ye
36. spake also a parable *unto* them;
6: 3. Jesus answering)(them said,
9. Then said Jesus *unto* them,
11. and communed one *with* another
47. Whosoever cometh *to* me,
7: 3. he sent *unto* him the elders
4. And when they came *to* Jesus,
6. the centurion sent friends *to* him,
7. worthy to come *unto* thee:
19. sent (them) *to* Jesus, saying,
20. When the men were come *unto* him,
— John Baptist hath sent us *unto* thee,
24. he began to speak *unto* the people
40. said *unto* him, Simon,
44. he turned *to* the woman,
50. And he said *to* the woman,
8: 4. and were come *to* him out of
13. which *for* a while believe,

Lu. 8:19. Then came *to* him (his) mother
21. and said *unto* them, My mother
22. and he said *unto* them, Let us go
25. saying one *to* another,
35. and came *to* Jesus,

9: 3. And he said *unto* them, Take nothing
13. But he said *unto* them, Give ye
14. he said *to* his disciples,
23. And he said *to* (them) all, If any
33. Peter said *unto* Jesus,
41. how long shall I be *with* you,
43. he said *unto* his disciples,
50. And Jesus said *unto* him, Forbid (him)
57. a certain (man) said *unto* him,
59. And he said *unto* another, Follow
62. And Jesus said *unto* him,

10: 2. Therefore said he *unto* them,
23. he turned him *unto* (his) disciples,
26. He said *unto* him, What is written
29. said *unto* Jesus, And who is

11: 1. one of his disciples said *unto* him,
5. And he said *unto* them, Which of you
shall have a friend, and shall go *unto* him
6. in his journey is come *to* me,
39. And the Lord said *unto* him,
53. as he said these things *unto* them,

12: 1. he began to say *unto* his disciples
3. which ye have spoken *in* the ear
15. And he said *unto* them, Take heed,
16. he spake a parable *unto* them, saying,
22. And he said *unto* his disciples,
41. speakest thou this parable *unto* us, or
even *to* all?
47. neither did *according to* his will,
58. lest he hale thee *to* the judge,

13: 7. Then said he *unto* the dresser of
23. And he said *unto* them,
34. stonest them that are sent *unto* thee ;

14: 3. spake *unto* the lawyers and Pharisees,
5. And answered)(them, saying,
6. could not answer him again *to* these things.
7. a parable *to* those which were bidden,
— saying *unto* them,
23. the lord said *unto* the servant,
25. he turned, and said *unto* them,
26. If any (man) come *to* me, and hate not
28. whether he have (sufficient) *to* finish
(it)? (lit. the things *unto* completion)
32. and desireth conditions of peace. (lit. the
things *unto* peace)

15: 3. he spake this parable *unto* them,
18. I will arise and go *to* my father,
20. and came *to* his father.
22. But the father said *to* his servants,

16: 1. And he said also *unto* his disciples,
20. which was laid *at* his gate,
26. which would pass from hence *to* you
cannot ; neither can they pass *to* us,
30. but if one went *unto* them from the

17: 1. Then said he *unto* the disciples,
22. And he said *unto* the disciples,

18: 1. a parable unto them (*to this end*), *that*
men ought always
3. and she came *unto* him, saying,
7. which cry day and night *unto* him,
9. he spake this parable *unto* certain
11. and prayed thus *with* himself,
16. Suffer little children to come *unto* me,
31. and said *unto* them, Behold, we go
40. to be brought *unto* him:

19: 5. and said *unto* him, Zacchæus,
8. and said *unto* the Lord ; Behold,

Lu. 19: 9. Jesus said *unto* him, This day
13. and said *unto* them, Occupy till I come.
29. *at* the mount called (the mount) of Olives,
33. the owners thereof said *unto* them,
35. And they brought him *to* Jesus:
37. *at* [d] the descent of the mount of Olives,
39. the multitude said *unto* him,
42. the things (which belong) *unto* thy peace !

20: 2. And spake *unto* him, saying,
3. and said *unto* them, I will also
5. they reasoned *with* themselves,
9. Then began he to speak *to* the people
10. he sent a servant *to* the husbandmen,
14. they reasoned *among* themselves,
19. he had spoken this parable *against* them.
23. and said *unto* them, Why tempt ye me?
41. And he said *unto* them, How say

21:38. came early in the morning *to* him

22:15. And he said *unto* them,
23. began to enquire *among* themselves,
45. and was come *to* his disciples,
52. Then Jesus said *unto* the chief priests,
56. as he sat *by* the fire,
70. And he said *unto* them,

23: 4. Then said Pilate *to* the chief priests
7. he sent him *to* Herod,
12. they were at enmity *between* themselves.
14. Said *unto* them, Ye have brought
15. for I sent you *to* him ;
22. And he said *unto* them
28. But Jesus turning *unto* them

24: 5. they said *unto* them,
10. told these things *unto* the apostles.
12. wondering *in* himself at that
14. And they talked together (lit. one *to*
another) of all
17. And he said *unto* them,
— that ye have one *to* another,
18. answering said *unto* him,
25. Then he said *unto* them,
29. for it is *toward* evening,
32. And they said one *to* another,
44. which I spake *unto* you,

Joh. 1: 1. and the Word was *with* God,
2. The same was in the beginning *with* God.
29. John seeth Jesus coming *unto* him,
42(43). And he brought him *to* Jesus.
47(48). saw Nathanael coming *to* him,

2: 3. the mother of Jesus saith *unto* him,

3: 2. The same came *to* Jesus by night,
4. Nicodemus saith *unto* him,
20. neither cometh *to* the light,
21. doeth truth cometh *to* the light,
26. And they came *unto* John,
— and all (men) come *to* him.

4:15. The woman saith *unto* him,
30. and came *unto* him.
33. the disciples one *to* another,
35. are white already *to* harvest.
40. were come *unto* him,
47. he went *unto* him,
48. Then said Jesus *unto* him,
49. The nobleman saith *unto* him,

5:33. Ye sent *unto* John,
35. ye were willing *for* a season
40. And ye will not come *to* me,
45. that I will accuse you *to* the Father:

6: 5. a great company come *unto* him, he saith
unto Philip,
17. Jesus was not come *to* them.
28. Then said they *unto* him, What
34. Then said they *unto* him, Lord,

Joh. 6:35. he that cometh *to* me shall never	Acts 1: 7. And he said *unto* them,
37. shall come *to* me; and him that cometh *to* me I will	2: 7. saying one *to* another, Behold,
44. No man can come *to* me, except	12. saying one *to* another, What
45. cometh *unto* me.	29. let me freely speak *unto* you of the
52. strove *among* themselves,	37. and said *unto* Peter
65. no man can come *unto* me, except	38. Then Peter said *unto* them,
68. *to* whom shall we go?	47. having favour *with* all the people.
7: 3. said *unto* him, Depart hence,	3: 2. daily *at* the gate of the temple
33. I go *unto* him that sent me.	10. which sat *for* alms at the Beautiful
35. Then said the Jews *among* themselves,	11. the people ran together *unto* them
37. let him come *unto* me, and drink.	12. he answered *unto* the people,
45. Then came the officers *to* the chief	22. Moses truly said *unto* the fathers,
50. Nicodemus saith *unto* them, he that came *to* Jesus by night,	— whatsoever he shall say *unto* you.
8: 2. all the people came *unto* him ;	25. which God made *with* our fathers, saying *unto* Abraham,
3. brought *unto* him a woman taken	4: 1. And as they spake *unto* the people,
7. and said *unto* them,	8. said *unto* them, Ye rulers of
31. Then said Jesus *to* those Jews which	15. they conferred *among* themselves,
57. Then said the Jews *unto* him,	19. and said *unto* them,
9:13. They brought *to* the Pharisees him	23. they went *to* their own company,
10:35. *unto* whom the word of God came,	— priests and elders had said *unto* them.
41. many resorted *unto* him,	24. lifted up their voice *to* God
11: 3. his sisters sent *unto* him,	5: 9. Then Peter said *unto* her,
4. This sickness is not *unto* death,	10. buried (her) *by* her husband.
15. let us go *unto* him.	35. And said *unto* them,
19. many of the Jews came *to* Martha and	6: 1. of the Grecians *against* the Hebrews,
21. Then said Martha *unto* Jesus,	7: 3. And said *unto* him, Get thee
29. and came *unto* him.	31. the voice of the Lord came *unto* him,
45. which came *to* Mary,	8:14. sent *unto* them Peter and John:
46. went their ways *to* the Pharisees,	20. But Peter said *unto* him,
12:19. said *among* themselves,	24. Pray ye *to* the Lord for me,
32. will draw all (men) *unto* me.	26. spake *unto* Philip, saying,
13: 1. out of this world *unto* the Father,	9: 2. letters to Damascus *to* the synagogues,
3. and went *to* God ;	5. to kick *against* the pricks.
6. Then cometh he *to* Simon Peter:	6. And the Lord (said) *unto* him,
28. *for* what *intent* he spake this unto him.	10. *to* him said the Lord in a vision,
14: 3. and receive you *unto* myself ;	11. And the Lord (said) *unto* him,
6. no man cometh *unto* the Father, but	15. But the Lord said *unto* him,
12. because I go *unto* my Father.	27. and brought (him) *to* the apostles,
18. I will come *to* you.	29. and disputed *against* the Grecians:
23. we will come *unto* him,	32. he came down also *to* the saints which
28. and come (again) *unto* you.	38. they sent *unto* him two men,
— I go *unto* the Father:	40. and turning (him) *to* the body
16: 5. I go my way *to* him that sent me ;	10: 3. coming in *to* him,
7. the Comforter will not come *unto* you ;	13. And there came a voice *to* him,
— I will send him *unto* you.	15. the voice (spake) *unto* him again
10. because I go *to* my Father,	21. Peter went down *to* the men which were sent *unto* him from Cornelius ;
16. because I go *to* the Father.	28. And he said *unto* them,
17. of his disciples *among* themselves,	33. therefore I sent *to* thee ;
— Because I go *to* the Father ?	11: 2. contended *with* him,
28. and go *to* the Father.	3. Thou wentest in *to* men uncircumcised,
17:11. and I come *to* thee.	11. sent from Cæsarea *unto* me.
13. And now come I *to* thee ;	14. Who shall tell)(thee words,
18:13. And led him away *to* Annas first ;	20. spake *unto* the Grecians,
16. But Peter stood *at*[d] the door	30. and sent it *to* the elders
24. had sent him bound *unto* Caiaphas	12: 5. prayer was made...*unto* God for him.
29. Pilate then went out *unto* them,	8. And the angel said *unto* him,
38. he went out again *unto* the Jews,	15. And they said *unto* her,
19:24. said therefore *among* themselves,	20. they came with one accord *to* him,
39. at the first came *to* Jesus by night,	21. and made an oration *unto* them.
20: 2. and cometh *to* Simon Peter, and *to* the other disciple,	13:15. sent *unto* them, saying,
10. *unto* their own home. (πρὸς ἑαυτοὺς)	— of exhortation *for* the people,
11. without *at* the sepulchre	31. his witnesses *unto* the people.
12. the one *at*[d] the head, and the other *at*[d] the feet,	32. which was made *unto* the fathers,
17. I am not yet ascended *to* my Father: but go *to* my brethren, and say unto them, I ascend *unto* my Father, and	36. and was laid *unto* his fathers,
21:22. what (is that) *to* thee? follow thou me.	14:11. The gods are come down *to* us
23. what (is that) *to* thee ?	15: 2. and disputation *with* them,
	— *unto* the apostles and elders
	7. and said *unto* them,
	25. to send chosen men *unto* you
	33. from the brethren *unto* the apostles.

Acts15:36. Paul said *unto* Barnabas,
　16:36. told this saying *to* Paul,
　　37. But Paul said *unto* them,
　17: 2. went in *unto* them,
　　15. a commandment *unto* Silas and Timotheus
　　　　for to come *to* him
　　17. *with* them that met with him.
　18: 6. and said *unto* them,
　　14. Gallio said *unto* the Jews,
　　21. I will return again *unto* you, if
　19: 2. He said *unto* them,
　　— And they said *unto* him,
　　3. And he said *unto* them,
　　31. his friends, sent *unto* him,
　　38. have a matter *against* any man,
　20: 6. came *unto* them to Troas
　　18. when they were come *to* him,
　21:11. when he was come *unto* us,
　　18. Paul went in with us *unto* James;
　　37. May I speak *unto* thee?
　　39. suffer me to speak *unto* the people.
　22:•1. (which I make) now *unto* you.
　　5. I received letters *unto* the brethren,
　　8 And he said *unto* me,
　　10. And the Lord said *unto* me,
　　13. Came *unto* me, and stood, and said
　　15. thou shalt be his witness *unto* all
　　21. And he said *unto* me, Depart:
　　25. Paul said *unto* the centurion
　23: 3. Then said Paul *unto* him,
　　15. that he bring him down *unto* you
　　17. Bring this young man *unto* the chief
　　18. and brought (him) *to* the chief captain,
　　— to bring this young man *unto* thee,
　　22. thou hast shewed these things *to* me.
　　24. bring (him) safe *unto* Felix
　　30. I sent straightway *to* thee,
　　— what (they had) *against* him.
　24:12. disputing *with* any man,
　　16. void of offence *toward* God, and
　　19. if they had ought *against* me.
　25:16. *To* whom I answered,
　　19. certain questions *against* him of
　　21. till I might send him *to* Cæsar.
　　22. Then Agrippa said *unto* Festus,
　26: 1. Then Agrippa said *unto* Paul,
　　6. made of God *unto* our fathers:
　　9. contrary *to* the name of Jesus
　　14. I heard a voice speaking *unto* me,
　　— for thee to kick *against* the pricks.
　　26. *before* whom also I speak freely:
　　28. Then Agrippa said *unto* Paul,
　　31. they talked *between* themselves,
　27: 3. liberty to go *unto* his friends
　　12. was not commodious *to* winter in,
　　34. for this is *for* your health:
　28: 4. they said *among* themselves,
　　8. *to* whom Paul entered in,
　　10. with such things as were necessary. (lit.
　　　　for need)
　　17. he said *unto* them,
　　21. And they said *unto* him,
　　23. there came many *to* him
　　25. when they agreed not *among* themselves,
　　— the prophet *unto* our fathers,
　　26. Go *unto* this people, and say,
　　30. and received all that came in *unto* him,
Ro. 1:10. by the will of God to come *unto* you.
　　13. I purposed to come *unto* you,
　3:26. *To* declare, (I say), at this time
　4: 2. but not *before* God.
　5: 1. we have peace *with* God through

Ro. 8:18. not worthy (to be compared) *with* the
　　　　glory
　　31. What shall we then say *to* these things?
　10: 1. and prayer *to* God for Israel is,
　　21. But *to* Israel he saith,
　　— *unto* a disobedient and gainsaying people.
　15: 2. for (his) good *to* edification.
　　17. in those things *which pertain to* God.
　　22. hindered from coming *to* you.
　　23. these many years to come *unto* you;
　　24. I will come *to* you:
　　29. I am sure that, when I come *unto* you,
　　30. in (your) prayers *to* God for me;
　　32. That I may come *unto* you with joy
1Co. 2: 1. when I came *to* you,
　　3. And I was *with* you in weakness,
　4:18. as though I would not come *to* you.
　　19. But I will come *to* you shortly, if
　　21. shall I come *unto* you with a rod,
　6: 1. having a matter *against* another,
　　5. I speak *to* your shame.
　7: 5. except (it be) with consent *for* a time,
　　35. this I speak *for* your own profit;
　　— but *for* that which is comely,
　10:11. they are written *for* our admonition,
　12: 2. carried away *unto* these dumb idols,
　　7. to every man *to* profit withal.
　13:12. but then face *to* face:
　14: 6. if I come *unto* you speaking with
　　12. *to* the edifying of the church.
　　26. Let all things be done *unto* edifying.
　15:34. I speak (this) *to* your shame.
　16: 5. Now I will come *unto* you,
　　6. I will abide, yea, and winter *with* you,
　　7. I trust to tarry a while *with* you,
　　10. that he may be *with* you without fear:
　　11. that he may come *unto* me:
　　12. to come *unto* you with the brethren:
2Co. 1:12. and more abundantly *to* you-*ward.*
　　15. I was minded to come *unto* you before,
　　16. out of Macedonia *unto* you,
　　18. our word *toward* you was not yea and nay.
　　20. *unto* the glory of God by us.
　2: 1. not come again *to* you in heaviness.
　　16. who (is) sufficient *for* these things?
　3: 1. epistles of commendation *to* you,
　　4. have we through Christ *to* God-*ward:*
　　13. *that* the children of Israel could not
　　16. when it shall turn *to* the Lord,
　4: 2. commending ourselves *to* every man's
　　　　conscience
　　6. *to* (give) the light of the knowledge
　5: 8. and to be present *with* the Lord.
　　10. *according to* that he hath done,
　　12. somewhat *to* (answer) them which glory in
　6:11. our mouth is open *unto* you,
　　14. hath light *with* darkness?
　　15. what concord hath Christ *with* Belial?
　7: 3. I speak not (this) *to* condemn (you):
　　4. my boldness of speech *toward* you,
　　8. though (it were) but *for* a season.
　　12. might appear *unto* you.
　8:17. of his own accord he went *unto* you.
　　19. administered by us *to* the glory of the
　10: 4. mighty through God *to* the pulling down
　11: 8. *to* do you service.
　　9(8). And when I was present *with* you,
　12:14. I am ready to come *unto* you;
　　17. whom I sent *unto* you?
　　21. my God will humble me *among* you,
　13: 1. I am coming *to* you.
　　7. Now I pray *to* God that ye do no evil;

Gal. 1:17. *to* them which were apostles
18. and abode *with* him fifteen days.
2: 5. no, not *for* an hour;
— might continue *with* you.
14. *according to* the truth of the gospel,
4:18. not only when I am present *with* you.
20. I desire to be present *with* you now,
6:10. let us do good *unto* all (men), especially *unto* them who are of

Eph 2:18. by one Spirit *unto* the Father.
3: 4. Where*by*, when ye read,
14. I bow my knees *unto* the Father
4:12. *For* the perfecting of the saints,
14. whereby they lie in wait to deceive; (lit. *unto* circumvention of deception)
29. good *to* the use of edifying,
5:31. shall be joined *unto* his wife,
6: 9. do the same things *unto* them,
11. *that* ye may be able to stand *against* the wiles of the devil.
12. we wrestle not *against* flesh and blood, but *against* principalities, *against* powers, *against* the rulers of the darkness of this world, *against* spiritual wickedness in high (places).
22. Whom I have sent *unto* you

Phi. 1:26. by my coming *to* you again.
2:25. supposed it necessary to send *to* you
30. your lack of service *toward* me.
4: 6. let your requests be made known *unto*

Col. 2:23. *to* the satisfying of the flesh.
3:13. if any man have a quarrel *against* any:
19. be not bitter *against* them.
4: 5. Walk in wisdom *toward* them that
8. Whom I have sent *unto* you,
10. if he come *unto* you,

1Th. 1: 8. your faith *to* God-*ward*
9. entering in we had *unto* you, and how ye turned *to* God from idols
2: 1. our entrance in *unto* you,
2. to speak *unto* you the gospel
9. because we would not (lit. *in order* not to) be chargeable unto any of you,
17. *for* a short time
18. we would have come *unto* you,
3: 4. when we were *with* you,
6. came from you *unto* us,
11. direct our way *unto* you.
4:12. *toward* them that are without,
5:14. be patient *toward* all (men).

2Th. 2: 5. when I was yet *with* you,
3: 1. even as (it is) *with* you:
8. *that* we might (lit. *in order*) not be chargeable to any of you:
10. For even when we were *with* you,

1Ti. 1:16. *for* a pattern to them which should
3:14. hoping to come *unto* thee shortly:
4: 7. exercise thyself (rather) *unto* godliness.
8. bodily exercise profiteth)(little: but godliness is profitable *unto* all things,

2Ti. 2:24. but be gentle *unto* all
3:16. and (is) profitable *for* doctrine, *for* reproof, *for* correction, *for* instruction in righteousness:
17. furnished *unto* all good works.
4: 9. to come shortly *unto* me:

Tit. 1:16. and *unto* every good work reprobate,
3: 1. to be ready *to* every good work,
2. all meekness *unto* all men.
12. When I shall send Artemas *unto* thee,
— be diligent to come *unto* me

Philem. 5. *toward* the Lord Jesus,

Philem. 13. I would have retained *with* me,
15. he therefore departed *for* a season,

Heb 1: 7. And *of* the angels he saith,
8. But *unto* the Son (he saith),
13. But *to* which of the angels said he
2:17. in things (pertaining) *to* God,
4:13. *with* whom we have to do.
5: 1. in things (pertaining) *to* God,
5. but he that said *unto* him,
7. *unto* him that was able to save him
14. exercised *to* discern both good and evil.
6:11. the same diligence *to* the full assurance of hope
7:21. by him that said *unto* him,
9:13. sanctifieth *to* the purifying of the flesh:
20. which God hath injoined *unto* you.
10:16. that I will make *with* them
11:18. *Of* whom it was said, That in Isaac
12: 4. striving *against* sin.
10. they verily *for* a few days
11. no chastening *for* the present
13:13. Let us go forth therefore *unto* him without the camp,

Jas. 3: 3. *that* they may obey us ;
4: 5. lusteth *to* envy ?
14. that appeareth *for* a little time,

1Pet. 2: 4. *To* whom coming,
3:15. ready always *to* (give) an answer
4:12. which is to try you, (lit. *for* trial to you)

2Pet. 1: 3. all things that (pertain) *unto* life and godliness,
3:16. *unto* their own destruction.

1Joh. 1: 2. which was *with* the Father,
2: 1. we have an advocate *with* the Father,
3:21. have we confidence *toward* God.
5:14. the confidence that we have *in* him,
16. a sin (which is) not *unto* death,
— for them that sin not *unto* death. There is a sin *unto* death:
17. and there is a sin not *unto* death.

2Joh. 10. If there come any *unto* you,
12. but I trust to come *unto* you, and speak face *to* face,

3Joh. 14. we shall speak face *to* face.

Rev. 1:13. girt *about*ᵈ the paps with
17. I fell *at* his feet as dead.
3:20. I will come in *to* him, and
10: 9. And I went *unto* the angel,
12: 5. her child was caught up *unto* God,
12. the devil is come down *unto* you,
13: 6. in blasphemy *against* God,
21: 9. And there came *unto* me
22:18. If any man shall add *unto* these

προσάββατον, *prosabbaton.*

Mar 15:42. that is, *the day before the sabbath,*

προσαγορεύομαι, *prosagoruomai.*

Heb 5:10. *Called* of God an high priest

προσάγω, *prosago.*

Lu. 9:41. *Bring* thy son hither.
Acts 16:20. And *brought* them to the magistrates,
27:27. that they *drew near* to some country; (lit. some country *drew near* them)
1Pet. 3:18. that he *might bring* us to God,

προσαγωγή, prosagōgee.

Ro. 5: 2. we have *access* by faith into this
Eph. 2:18. we both have *access* by one Spirit
　　 3:12. and *access* with confidence by the faith of him.

προσαιτέω, prosaiteo.

Mar 10:46. sat by the highway side *begging*.
Lu. 18:35. sat by the way side *begging* :
Joh. 9: 8. Is not this he that sat and *begged*?

προσαναβαίνω, prosanabaino.

Lu. 14:10. Friend, *go up* higher:

προσαναλίσκω, prosanalisko.

Lu. 8:43. which *had spent* all her living upon

προσαναπληρόω, prosanapleeroō.

2Co. 9:12. not only *supplieth* the want of the saints,
　　 11: 9. the brethren which came from Macedonia *supplied* :

προσανατίθημι, prosanatitheemi.

Gal. 1:16. I *conferred* not with flesh and blood:
　　 2: 6. in conference *added* nothing to me:

προσαπειλέομαι, prosapileomai.

Acts 4:21. when they *had further threatened*

προσδαπανάω, prosdapanao.

Lu. 10:35. whatsoever thou *spendest more,*

προσδέομαι, prosdeomai.

Acts17:25. as though he *needed* any thing,

προσδέχομαι, prosdekomai.

Mar 15:43. which also *waited for* the kingdom
Lu. 2:25. *waiting for* the consolation of Israel:
　　 38. to all them that *looked for* redemption
　　 12:36. like unto men that *wait for* their lord,
　　 15: 2. This man *receiveth* sinners, and
　　 23:51. *waited for* the kingdom of God.
Acts23:21. *looking for* a promise from thee.
　　 24:15. which they themselves also *allow,*
Ro. 16: 2. That ye *receive* her in the Lord,
Phi. 2:29. *Receive* him therefore in the Lord
Tit. 2:13. *Looking for* that blessed hope,
Heb 10:34. and *took* joyfully the spoiling of
　　 11:35. not *accepting* deliverance ; that
Jude　 21. *looking for* the mercy of our Lord

προσδοκάω, prosdokao.

Mat.11: 3. or do we *look for* another ?
　　 24:50. when he *looketh* not *for* (him),
Lu. 1:21. the people *waited for* Zacharias,
　　 3:15. as the people *were in expectation,*
　　 7:19. or *look* we *for* another ?
　　 20. or *look* we *for* another ?
　　 8:40. for they were all *waiting for* him.
　　 12:46. when he *looketh* not *for* (him),
Acts 3: 5. *expecting* to receive something
　　 10:24. And Cornelius *waited for* them,
　　 27:33. the fourteenth day that ye have *tarried* and continued
　　 28: 6. they *looked* when he should have
　　　 — but after they *had looked* a great while,
2Pet. 3:12. *Looking for* and hasting unto the
　　 13. *look for* new heavens and a new earth,
　　 14. seeing that ye *look for* such things,

προσδοκία, prosdokia.

Lu. 21:26. and for *looking after* those things
Acts12:11. and (from) all the *expectation* of the people of the Jews.

προσδρέμω see προστρέχω.

προσεάω, proseao.

Acts27: 7. the wind not *suffering* us,

προσεγγίζω, prosengizo.

Mar 2: 4. they could not *come nigh unto* him

προσεδρεύω, prosedrūo.

1Co. 9:13. and they *which wait at* the altar are

προσεργάζομαι, prosergazomai.

Lu. 19:16. thy pound *hath gained* ten pounds.

προσέρχομαι, proserkomai.

Mat. 4: 3. when the tempter *came to* him,
　　 11. angels *came* and ministered unto him.
　　 5: 1. his disciples *came unto* him:
　　 8: 5. there *came unto* him a centurion,
　　 19. And a certain scribe *came,* and
　　 25. And his disciples *came to* (him), and
　　 9:14. Then *came to* him the disciples of
　　 20. *came* behind (him), and touched
　　 28. the blind men *came to* him:
　　 13:10. And the disciples *came,* and said
　　 27. *came* and said unto him, Sir,
　　 36. and his disciples *came unto* him,
　　 14:12. And his disciples *came, and* took up
　　 15. his disciples *came to* him,
　　 15: 1. Then *came to* Jesus scribes and
　　 12. Then *came* his disciples, *and*
　　 23. And his disciples *came and*
　　 30. And great multitudes *came unto* him,

Mat.16: 1. with the Sadducees *came, and* tempting
17: 7. Jesus *came and* touched them,
14. there *came to* him a (certain) man,
19. *came* the disciples *to* Jesus apart, *and*
24. *came to* Peter, and said, Doth not
18: 1. *came* the disciples *unto* Jesus,
21. Then *came* Peter *to* him, *and* said,
19: 3. The Pharisees also *came unto* him,
16. And, behold, one *came and* said
20:20. Then *came to* him the mother of
21:14. the blind and the lame *came to* him
23. the elders of the people *came unto* him
28. and he *came to* the first, *and* said,
30. And he *came to* the second, *and* said
22:23. The same day *came to* him the Sadducees,
24: 1. and his disciples *came to* (him)
3. the disciples *came unto* him
25:20. *came and* brought other five talents,
22. *came and* said, Lord, thou
24. *came and* said, Lord, I knew thee
26: 7. There *came unto* him a woman
17. the disciples *came to* Jesus,
49. he *came to* Jesus, *and* said, Hail, master;
50. Then *came* they, *and* laid hands on Jesus,
60. *though* many false witnesses *came,*
— At the last *came* two false witnesses,
69. a damsel *came unto* him,
73. *came unto* (him) they that stood by, *and*
27:58. He *went to* Pilate, *and* begged the body
28: 2. and *came and* rolled back the stone
9. they *came and* held him by the feet,
18. And Jesus *came and* spake unto them,
Mar 1:31. And he *came* and took her by the hand,
6:35. his disciples *came unto* him, *and*
10: 2. the Pharisees *came to* him, *and*
12:28. And one of the scribes *came, and*
14:45. he *goeth* straightway *to* him,
Lu. 7:14. And he *came and* touched the bier:
8:24. And they *came to* him, and awoke
44. *Came* behind (him), *and* touched
9:12. then *came* the twelve, *and* said
42. And *as* he was yet *a coming,*
10:34. And *went to* (him), *and* bound up
13:31. The same day there *came* certain of
20:27. Then *came to* (him) certain of the
23:36. *coming to* him, and offering him
52. This (man) *went unto* Pilate, *and*
Joh.12:21. The same *came* therefore to Philip,
Acts 7:31. and *as* he *drew near* to behold (it),
8:29. *Go near*, and join thyself to this
9: 1. *went unto* the high priest,
10:28. or *come unto* one of another nation ;
12:13. a damsel *came* to hearken,
18: 2. and *came unto* them.
22:26. he *went and* told the chief captain,
27. Then the chief captain *came, and*
23:14. And they *came to* the chief priests
24:23. to minister or *come unto* him.
28: 9. *came*, and were healed:
1Ti. 6: 3. and *consent* not to wholesome words,
Heb 4:16. *Let* us therefore *come* boldly *unto*
7:25. *that* come unto God by him,
10: 1. the *comers thereunto* perfect.
22. *Let* us *draw near* with a true
11: 6. for he *that cometh to* God
12:18. For ye *are* not *come unto* the mount
22. But ye *are come unto* mount Sion,
1Pet.2: 4. To whom *coming*, (as unto) a living stone,

προσευχή, *prosŭkee.*

Mat.17:21. but by *prayer* and fasting.

Mat.21:13. shall be called the house of *prayer ;*
22. whatsoever ye shall ask in *prayer*
Mar 9:29. but by *prayer* and fasting.
11:17. called of all nations the house of *prayer ?*
Lu. 6:12. continued all night in *prayer* to God.
19:46. My house is the house of *prayer :*
22:45. when he rose up from *prayer,*
Acts 1:14. continued with one accord in *prayer* and
supplication,
2:42. in breaking of bread, and in *prayers.*
3: 1. at the hour of *prayer*, (being) the ninth
(hour).
6: 4. continually to *prayer*, and to the ministry
of the word.
10: 4. Thy *prayers* and thine alms are come up
31. Cornelius, thy *prayer* is heard, and
12: 5. but *prayer* was made without ceasing
16:13. where *prayer* was wont to be made ;
16. as we went to *prayer*, a certain damsel
Ro. 1: 9(10). mention of you always in my *prayers ;*
12:12. continuing instant in *prayer ;*
15:30. in (your) *prayers* to God for me ;
1Co. 7: 5. give yourselves to fasting and *prayer ;*
Eph. 1:16. making mention of you in my *prayers ;*
6:18. Praying always with all *prayer* and supplication in
Phi. 4: 6. but in every thing by *prayer* and supplication with
Col. 4: 2. Continue in *prayer*, and watch
12. fervently for you in *prayers,*
1Th. 1: 2. making mention of you in our *prayers ;*
1Ti. 2: 1. supplications, *prayers*, intercessions,
5: 5. in supplications and *prayers* night and day.
Philem. 4. mention of thee always in my *prayers,*
22. I trust that through your *prayers*
Jas. 5:17. and he prayed earnestly (lit. prayed with
prayer)
1Pet.3: 7. that your *prayers* be not hindered.
4: 7. and watch unto *prayer.*
Rev. 5: 8. which are the *prayers* of saints.
8: 3. with the *prayers* of all saints upon the
4. with the *prayers* of the saints,

προσεύχομαι, *prosŭkomai.*

Mat. 5:44. *pray* for them which despitefully
6: 5. And when thou *prayest*, thou shalt not
— for they love *to pray* standing in
6. when thou *prayest*, enter into
— *pray* to thy Father which is in secret ;
7. But *when ye pray*, use not vain
9. After this manner therefore *pray* ye:
14:23. into a mountain apart *to pray :*
19:13. put (his) hands on them, and *pray :*
23:14(13). for a pretence *make* long *prayer:*
24:20. But *pray* ye that your flight
26:36. while I go and *pray* yonder.
39. and fell on his face, *and prayed,*
41. Watch and *pray*, that ye enter not into
42. and *prayed*, saying, O my Father,
44. and *prayed* the third time,
Mar 1:35. solitary place, and there *prayed.*
6:46. into a mountain *to pray.*
11:24. ye desire, *when ye pray*, believe
25. And when ye stand *praying,*
12:40. for a pretence *make* long *prayers :*
13:18. And *pray* ye that your flight
33. watch and *pray :* for ye know not
14:32. Sit ye here, while I shall *pray.*
35. and *prayed* that, if it were
38. Watch ye and *pray*, lest ye enter

Mar 14:39. and *prayed*, and spake the same
Lu. 1:10. the people were *praying* without
3:21. Jesus also being baptized, and *praying*,
5:16. into the wilderness, and *prayed*.
6:12. went out into a mountain *to pray*,
28. and *pray* for them which
9:18. as he was alone *praying*,
28. into a mountain *to pray*.
29. And as he *prayed*,
11: 1. as he was *praying* in a certain
— Lord, teach us *to pray*,
2. When ye *pray*, say, Our Father
18: 1. men ought always *to pray*,
10. into the temple *to pray ;*
11. and *prayed* thus with himself,
20:47. *make* long *prayers :*
22:40. *Pray* that ye enter not into
41. and kneeled down, and *prayed*,
44. he *prayed* more earnestly.
46. rise and *pray*, lest ye enter into
Acts 1:24. And they *prayed, and* said,
6: 6. and *when* they *had prayed*, they
8:15. *prayed* for them, that they
9:11. for, behold, he *prayeth*,
40. and kneeled down, and *prayed ;*
10: 9. upon the housetop *to pray*
30. I *prayed* in my house,
11: 5. I was in the city of Joppa *praying:*
12:12. many were gathered together *praying*.
13: 3. when they had fasted and *prayed*,
14:23. *and had prayed* with fasting,
16:25. Paul and Silas *prayed, and* sang praises
20:36. and *prayed* with them all.
21: 5. we kneeled down on the shore, and *prayed*.
22:17. *while* I *prayed* in the temple,
28: 8. and *prayed, and* laid his hands on him,
Ro. 8:26. what we *should pray for* as we
1Co.11: 4. Every man *praying* or prophesying,
5. But every woman *that prayeth*
13. is it comely that a woman *pray*
14:13. *let* him...*pray* that he may interpret.
14. For if I *pray* in an (unknown) tongue,
my spirit *prayeth*, but
15. I *will pray* with the spirit, and I *will pray*
with the understanding
Eph. 6:18. *Praying* always with all prayer
Phi. 1: 9. And this I *pray*, that your love
Col. 1: 3. *praying* always for you,
9. do not cease to *pray* for you,
4: 3. Withal *praying* also for us,
1Th. 5:17. *Pray* without ceasing.
25. Brethren, *pray* for us.
2Th. 1:11. we *pray* always for you,
3: 1. Finally, brethren, *pray* for us,
1Ti. 2: 8. that men *pray* every where,
Heb 13:18. *Pray* for us: for we trust
Jas. 5:13. afflicted? *let* him *pray*.
14. *let* them *pray* over him,
17. and he *prayed* earnestly that it
18. And he *prayed* again, and the heaven
Jude 20. *praying* in the Holy Ghost,

προσέχω, *proscho*.

Mat 6: 1. *Take heed* that ye do not your alms
7:15. *Beware* of false prophets,
10:17. But *beware* of men:
16: 6. Take heed and *beware* of the leaven
11. that ye should *beware* of the leaven
12. not *beware* of the leaven of bread, but
Lu. 12: 1. *Beware* ye of the leaven of the

Lu. 17: 3. *Take heed to* yourselves:
20:46. *Beware* of the scribes,
21:34. *take heed to* yourselves, lest
Acts 5:35. *take heed to* yourselves what ye intend
8: 6. *gave heed unto* those things
10. *To* whom they all *gave heed*,
11. And *to* him they *had regard*,
16:14. that she *attended unto* the things
20:28. *Take heed* therefore *unto* yourselves,
1Ti. 1: 4. Neither *give heed to* fables and
3: 8. not *given to* much wine,
4: 1. *giving heed to* seducing spirits,
13. *give attendance to* reading,
Tit. 1:14. Not *giving heed to* Jewish fables,
Heb 2: 1. *to give* the more earnest *heed to* the
7:13. no man *gave attendance at* the altar.
2Pet. 1:19. where*unto* ye do well *that ye take heed*,

προσηλόω, *proseeloō*.

Col. 2:14. *nailing* it *to* his cross;

προσήλυτος, *proseelutos*.

Mat.23:15. to make one *proselyte*,
Acts 2:10. Jews and *proselytes*,
6: 5. Nicolas a *proselyte* of Antioch:
13:43. many of the Jews and religious *proselytes*
followed Paul

πρόσκαιρος, *proskairos*.

Mat.13:21. but *dureth for a while :* (lit. is *temporary*)
Mar 4:17. and so *endure but for a time :*
2Co. 4:18. the things which are seen (are) *temporal;*
Heb 11:25. to enjoy the pleasures of sin *for a season ;*
(lit. to have *temporary* enjoyment of sin)

προσκαλέομαι, *proskaleomai*.

Mat.10: 1. And *when* he *had called unto* (him) his
15:10. And he *called* the multitude, *and*
32. Then Jesus *called* his disciples (*unto* him),
and
18: 2. And Jesus *called* a little child *unto* ·him,
and
32. *after that* he *had called* him,
20:25. But Jesus *called* them (*unto* him), *and*
Mar 3:13. and *calleth* (*unto* him) whom he
23. And he *called* them (*unto* him), *and*
6: 7. And he *called* (*unto* him) the twelve,
7:14. *when* he *had called* all the people (*unto*)
8: 1. Jesus *called* his disciples (*unto* him), *and*
34. *when* he *had called* the people (*unto* him)
10:42. But Jesus *called* them (*to* him), *and*
12:43. he *called* (*unto* him) his disciples, *and*
15:44. and *calling* (*unto* him) the centurion,
Lu. 7:19(18) And John *calling* (*unto* him) two
15:26. he *called* one of the servants, *and*
16: 5. So he *called* every one of his lord's debtors
(*unto* him), *and*
18:16. But Jesus *called* them (*unto* him), *and*
Acts 2:39. as the Lord our God shall *call*.
5:40. *when* they *had called* the apostles,
6: 2. Then the twelve *called* the...(*unto* them),
and
13: 2. where*unto* I *have called* them.
7. who *called for* Barnabas and Saul, *and*
16:10. that the Lord *had called* us

Acts 20: 1. Paul *called unto* (him) the disciples, and
23:17. *called* one of the centurions *unto* (him),
and
18. Paul the prisoner *called* me *unto* (him),
and
23. And he *called unto* (him) two
Jas. 5:14. *let* him *call for* the elders

προσκαρτερέω, *proskartereo.*

Mar 3: 9. a small ship *should wait on* him
Acts 1:14. These all *continued* with one accord
2:42. And they *continued stedfastly* in
46. And they, *continuing* daily with one accord
6: 4. we *will give* ourselves *continually to* prayer,
and to
8:13. he *continued with* Philip,
10: 7. of them *that waited on* him *continually ;*
Ro. 12:12. *continuing instant in* prayer,
13: 6. *attending continually upon* this very thing.
Col. 4: 2. *Continue in* prayer,

προσκαρτέρησις, *proskartereesis.*

Eph. 6:18. with all *perseverance* and supplication

προσκεφάλαιον, *proskephalaion.*

Mar 4:38. asleep on a *pillow :*

προσκληρόομαι, *proskleeroömai.*

Acts 17: 4. and *consorted with* Paul and Silas ;

πρόσκλισις, *prosklisis.*

1Ti. 5:21. doing nothing by *partiality.*

προσκολλάομαι, *proskollaomai.*

Mat 19: 5. and *shall cleave to* his wife:
Mar 10: 7. and *cleave to* his wife ;
Acts 5:36. about four hundred, *joined* them*selves :*
Eph. 5:31. and *shall be joined* unto his wife,

πρόσκομμα, *proskomma.*

Ro. 9:32. they stumbled at that *stumbling*stone ;
33. I lay in Sion a *stumbling*stone and rock
14:13. that no man put a *stumbling*block
20. for that man who eateth with *offence.*
1Co. 8: 9. become a *stumbling*block to them that
1Pet. 2: 8(7). And a stone of *stumbling,*

προσκοπή, *proskopee.*

2Co. 6: 3. Giving no *offence* in any thing,

προσκόπτω, *proskopto.*

Mat 4: 6. lest at any time thou *dash* thy foot against
a stone.
7:27. and *beat upon* that house ;
Lu. 4:11. lest at any time thou *dash* thy foot against
a stone.

Joh. 11: 9. walk in the day, he *stumbleth* not,
10. walk in the night, he *stumbleth,*
Ro. 9:32. they *stumbled at* that stumblingstone ;
14:21. whereby thy brother *stumbleth,*
1Pet. 2: 8. which *stumble at* the word,

προσκυλίω, *proskulio.*

Mat 27:60. and he *rolled* a great stone *to* the door
Mar 15:46. and *rolled* a stone unto the

προσκυνέω, *proskuneo.*

Mat. 2: 2. and are come *to worship* him.
8. that I may come and *worship* him
11. fell down, and *worshipped* him:
4: 9. if thou wilt fall down and *worship* me.
10. Thou *shalt worship* the Lord
8: 2. a leper and *worshipped* him,
9:18. came a certain ruler, and *worshipped* him,
14:33. came and *worshipped* him,
15:25. came she and *worshipped* him, saying,
18:26. fell down, and *worshipped* him,
20:20. with her sons, *worshipping* (him),
28: 9. by the feet, and *worshipped* him.
17. they *worshipped* him: but some doubted.
Mar 5: 6. he ran and *worshipped* him,
15:19. bowing (their) knees *worshipped* him.
Lu. 4: 7. If thou therefore wilt *worship* me,
8. Thou *shalt worship* the Lord
24:52. And they *worshipped* him, *and*
Joh. 4:20. Our fathers *worshipped* in this mountain ;
— where men ought *to worship.*
21. when ye *shall* neither in this...*worship* the
Father.
22. Ye *worship* ye know not what: we know
what we *worship :*
23. *shall worship* the Father in spirit
— seeketh such *to worship* him.
24. they *that worship* him must *worship* (him)
in spirit and in
9:38. I believe. And he *worshipped* him.
12:20. that came up *to worship* at the feast:
Acts 7:43. which ye made *to worship* them:
8:27. to Jerusalem for to *worship,*
10:25. at his feet, and *worshipped* (him).
24:11. to Jerusalem for to *worship.*
1Co. 14:25. falling down on (his) face he *will worship*
God,
Heb 1: 6(7). *let* all the angels of God *worship* him.
11:21. and *worshipped,* (leaning) upon
Rev. 3: 9. to come and *worship* before thy feet,
4:10. and *worship* him that liveth
5:14. and *worshipped* him that liveth
7:11. on their faces, and *worshipped* God,
9:20. that they *should* not *worship* devils,
11: 1. and them *that worship* therein.
16. upon their faces, and *worshipped* God,
13: 4. they *worshipped* the dragon
— and they *worshipped* the beast,
8. *shall worship* him, whose names
12. to *worship* the first beast,
15. as many as *would* not *worship*
14: 7. *worship* him that made heaven, and
9. If any man *worship* the beast
11. *who worship* the beast and his image,
15: 4. shall come and *worship* before thee ;
16: 2. them *which worshipped* his image.
19: 4. fell down and *worshipped* God
10. I fell at his feet *to worship* him.

Rev.19:10. *worship* God:
    20. and them *that worshipped* his image.
  20: 4. which *had* not *worshipped* the beast,
  22: 8. fell down *to worship* before the feet
     9. *worship* God.

προσκυνητής, *proskuneetees.*

Joh. 4:23. when the true *worshippers* shall

προσλαλέω, *proslaleo.*

Acts13:43. who, *speaking to* them, persuaded
  28:20. to see (you), and *to speak with* (you):

προσλαμβάνω, *proslambano.*

Mat.16:22. Then Peter *took* him, *and* began
Mar 8:32. Peter *took* him, *and* began to rebuke him.
Acts17: 5. *took unto* them certain lewd fellows
  18:26. they *took* him *unto* (them),
  27:33. fasting, *having taken* nothing.
    34. I pray you *to take* (some) meat:
    36. and they also *took* (some) meat.
  28: 2. and *received* us every one,
Ro. 14: 1. weak in the faith *receive* ye,
    3. for God *hath received* him.
  15: 7. *receive* ye one another, as Christ also
     received us
Philem 12. thou therefore *receive* him, that is,
    17. *receive* him as myself.

πρόσληψις, *prosleepsis.*

Ro. 11:15. what (shall) the *receiving* (of them be),

προσμένω, *prosmeno.*

Mat.15:32. because they *continue with* me
Mar 8: 2. they *have* now *been with* me
Acts11:23. they would *cleave unto* the Lord.
  18:18. Paul (after this) *tarried* (there) yet
1Ti. 1: 3. *to abide still* at Ephesus,
  5: 5. *continueth in* supplications and prayers

προσορμίζομαι, *prosormizomai.*

Mar 6:53. and *drew to the shore.*

προσοφείλω, *prosophilo.*

Philem.19. thou *owest* unto me even thine own self
    besides.

προσοχθίζω, *prosokthizo.*

Heb 3:10. I *was grieved with* that generation,
    17. *with* whom *was* he *grieved* forty years?

πρόσπεινος, *prospinos.*

Acts10:10. And he became *very hungry,*

προσπήγνυμι, *prospeegnumi.*

Acts 2:23. by wicked hands have *crucified and* slain:

προσπίπτω, *prospipto.*

Mat. 7:25. and *beat upon* that house ;
Mar 3:11. when they saw him, *fell down before* him,
  5:33. came and *fell down before* him,
  7:25. and came and *fell at* his feet:
Lu. 5: 8. he *fell down* at Jesus' knees,
  8:28. and *fell down before* him,
  47. and *falling down before* him, she
Acts16:29. and *fell down before* Paul and

προσποιέομαι, *prospoyeomai.*

Lu. 24:28. he *made as though* he would have gone
    further.

προσπορεύομαι, *prosporuomai.*

Mar 10:35. the sons of Zebedee, *come unto* him,

προσρήγνυμι, *prosreegnumi.*

Lu. 6:48. stream *beat vehemently upon* that
  49. *against* which the stream *did beat vehemently,*

προστάσσω, *prostasso.*

Mat. 1:24. as the angel of the Lord *had bidden* him,
  8: 4. offer the gift that Moses *commanded,*
  21: 6. and did as Jesus *commanded* them,
Mar 1:44. those things which Moses *commanded,*
Lu. 5:14. according as Moses *commanded,*
Acts10:33. *that are commanded* thee of God.
  48. he *commanded* them to be baptized

προστάτις, *prostatis.*

Ro. 16: 2. she hath been a *succourer* of many,

προστίθημι, *prostitheemi.*

Mat. 6:27. can *add* one cubit unto his stature ?
  33. all these things *shall be added* unto you.
Mar 4:24. *unto* you that hear *shall more be given.*
Lu. 3:20. *Added* yet this above all,
  12:25. can *add* to his stature one cubit ?
  31. all these things *shall be added* unto you.
  17: 5. Lord, *Increase* our faith.
  19:11. he *added and* spake a parable,
  20:11. And again he sent (lit. he *added* to send)
    another servant:
  12. again he sent (lit. he *added &c.*) a third:
Acts 2:41. there *were added* (unto them)
  47. And the Lord *added* to the church daily
  5:14. believers *were* the more *added* to the Lord,
  11:24. and much people was *added* unto the Lord.
  12: 3. he *proceeded further* to take Peter
  13:36. *was laid* unto his fathers, and saw
Gal. 3:19. It *was added* because of transgressions,
Heb 12:19. that the word should not *be spoken to* them
    any more :

προστρέχω, prostreko.

Mar 9:15. and *running to* (him) saluted him.
　　10:17. there came one *running*, and
Acts 8:30. Philip *ran thither to* (him), *and* heard

προσφάγιον, prosphagion.

Joh.21: 5. Children, have ye any *meat ?*

πρόσφατος, prosphatos.

Heb 10:20. By a *new* and living way,

προσφάτως, prosphatōs.

Acts18: 2. *lately* come from Italy,

προσφέρω, προσήνεγκα, prosphero, proseenenka.

Mat. 2:11. they *presented unto* him gifts ;
　　4:24. they *brought unto* him all sick
　　5:23. if thou *bring* thy gift to the altar,
　　24. then come and *offer* thy gift.
　　8: 4. and *offer* the gift that Moses
　　16. they *brought unto* him many that
　　9: 2. they *brought to* him a man
　　32. they *brought to* him a dumb
　　12:22. Then *was brought unto* him one
　　14:35. and *brought unto* him all that
　　17:16. And I *brought* him *to* thy
　　18:24. one *was brought unto* him,
　　19:13. Then *were* there *brought unto* him
　　22:19. they *brought unto* him a penny.
　　25:20. came and *brought* other five talents,
Mar 1:44. and *offer* for thy cleansing
　　10:13. they *brought* young children *to* him,
　　— disciples rebuked those *that brought*
Lu. 5:14. and *offer* for thy cleansing,
　　12:11. when they *bring* you *unto* the
　　18:15. And they *brought unto* him also
　　23:14. Ye *have brought* this man *unto* me,
　　36. and *offering* him vinegar,
Joh.16: 2. will think that he *doeth* God service.
　　19:29. and *put* (it) *to* his mouth.
Acts 7:42. *have* ye *offered to* me slain beasts
　　8:18. he *offered* them money,
　　21:26. until that an offering should be *offered*
Heb 5: 1. that he *may offer* both gifts and
　　3. so also for himself, *to offer* for sins.
　　7. *when* he *had offered up* prayers
　　8: 3. *to offer* gifts and sacrifices:
　　— that this man have somewhat also to *offer*.
　　4. priests *that offer* gifts according to
　　9: 7. which he *offered* for himself,
　　9. in which were *offered* both gifts and
　　14. *offered* himself without spot
　　25. Nor yet that he *should offer* himself
　　28. So Christ was once *offered* to bear the
　　10: 1. which they *offered* year by year
　　2. would they not have ceased to be *offered ?*
　　8. which *are offered* by the law ;
　　11. and *offering* oftentimes the same
　　12. *after* he *had offered* one sacrifice for sins,
　　11: 4. By faith Abel *offered unto* God
　　17. when he was tried, *offered up* Isaac:
　　— *offered up* his only begotten (son),
　　12: 7. God *dealeth with* you as with sons ;

προσφιλής, prosphilees.

Phi. 4: 8. whatsoever things (are) *lovely,*

προσφορά, prosphora.

Acts21:26. until that an *offering* should be
　　24:17. alms to my nation, and *offerings.*
Ro. 15:16. that the *offering up* of the Gentiles
Eph. 5: 2. an *offering* and a sacrifice to God
Heb 10: 5. Sacrifice and *offering* thou wouldest not,
　　8. Sacrifice and *offering* and burnt offerings
　　10. through the *offering* of the body
　　14. For by one *offering* he hath
　　18. (there is) no more *offering* for sin.

προσφωνέω, prosphōneo.

Mat.11:16. and *calling unto* their fellows,
Lu. 6:13. he *called* (*unto* him) his disciples:
　　7:32. *calling* one *to* another, and saying,
　　13:12. he *called* (her *to* him),
　　23:20. to release Jesus, *spake* again *to* them.
Acts21:40. he *spake unto* (them) in the Hebrew
　　22: 2. he *spake* in the Hebrew tongue *to* them,

πρόσχυσις, proskusis.

Heb 11:28. the passover, and the *sprinkling* of blood,

προσψαύω, prospsauo.

Lu. 11:46. ye yourselves *touch* not the burdens

προσωποληπτέω, prosōpoleepteo.

Jas. 2: 9. But if ye *have respect to persons,*

προσωπολήπτης, prosōpoleeptees.

Acts10.34. God is no *respecter of persons :*

προσωποληψία, prosōpoleepsia.

Ro. 2:11. there is no *respect of persons* with God.
Eph. 6: 9. neither is there *respect of persons*
Col. 3:25. and there is no *respect of persons.*
Jas. 2: 1. have not the faith...with *respect of persons.*

πρόσωπον, prosōpon.

Mat. 6:16. for they disfigure their *faces,*
　　17. anoint thine head, and wash thy *face ;*
　　11:10. I send my messenger before thy *face,*
　　16: 3. ye can discern the *face* of the sky ;
　　17: 2. and his *face* did shine as the sun,
　　6. they fell on their *face,* and were
　　18:10. do always behold the *face* of my Father
　　22:16. thou regardest not the *person* of men.
　　26:39. and fell on his *face,* and prayed,
　　67. Then did they spit in his *face,*
Mar 1: 2. I send my messenger before thy *face,*
　　12:14. thou regardest not the *person* of men,
　　14:65. and to cover his *face,* and to buffet him,

Lu. 1:76. thou shalt go before the *face* of the Lord
2:31. prepared before the *face* of all people;
5:12. who seeing Jesus fell on (his) *face*,
7:27. I send my messenger before thy *face*,
9:29. the fashion of his *countenance* was
51. he stedfastly set his *face* to go to
52. And sent messengers before his *face :*
53. because his *face* was as though he
10: 1. and sent them two and two before his *face*
12:56. ye can discern the *face* of the sky
17:16. And fell down on (his) *face* at his feet,
20:21. neither acceptest thou the *person* (of any),
21:35. on the *face* of the whole earth,
22:64. they struck him on the *face*,
24: 5. bowed down (their) *faces* to the earth,
Acts 2:28. full of joy with thy *countenance*.
3:13. and denied him in the *presence* of Pilate,
19. shall come from the *presence* of the Lord;
5:41. from the *presence* of the council,
6:15. looking stedfastly on him, saw his *face* as it had been the *face* of an angel.
7:45. before the *face* of our fathers,
13:24. had first preached *before* his coming (πρὸ προσώπου τῆς εἰσόδου)
17:26. to dwell on all the *face* of the earth,
20:25. shall see my *face* no more.
38. should see his *face* no more.
25:16. have the accusers face to face,
1Co.13:12. but then *face* to *face* :
14:25. and so falling down on (his) *face*
2Co. 1:11. by the means of many *persons*
2:10. (forgave I it) in the *person* of Christ;
3: 7. Israel could not stedfastly behold the *face* of Moses for the glory of his *countenance;*
13. (which) put a vail over his *face*,
18. with open *face* beholding as in
4: 6. glory of God in the *face* of Jesus Christ.
5:12. which glory in *appearance*,
8:24. and before (εἰς πρόσωπον) the churches,
10: 1. who in *presence* (am) base among you,
7. after the *outward appearance ?*
11:20. if a man smite you on the *face*.
Gal. 1:22. And was unknown by *face*
2: 6. God accepteth no man's *person :*
11. I withstood him to the *face*,
Col. 2: 1. as have not seen my *face*
1Th. 2:17. for a short time in *presence*,
— to see your *face* with great
3:10. that we might see your *face*,
2Th. 1: 9. from the *presence* of the Lord,
Heb 9:24. in the *presence* of God for us:
Jas. 1:11. the grace of the *fashion* of it
23. beholding his natural *face* in
1Pet. 3:12. the *face* of the Lord (is) against
Jude 16. having *men's persons* in admiration
Rev. 4: 7. third beast had a *face* as a man,
6:16. hide us from the *face* of him that
7:11. fell before the throne on their *faces*,
9: 7. and their *faces* (were) as the *faces* of men.
10: 1. and his *face* (was) as it were the sun,
11:16. fell upon their *faces*, and worshipped God,
12:14. from the *face* of the serpent.
20:11. from whose *face* the earth and the
22: 4. And they shall see his *face ;*

προτάσσομαι, *protassomai.*

Acts17:26. determined the times *before appointed,*

προτείνω, *protĭno.*

Acts22:25. And as they *bound* him (lit. as he *bound* him)

πρότερον, τὸ πρότερον, *proteron*, & *to proteron.*

Joh. 6:62. ascend up where he was *before ?*
7:51. judge (any) man, *before* (lit. unless *previously*) it hear him,
9: 8. they which *before* had seen him
2Co. 1:15. minded to come unto you *before*,
Gal. 4:13. I preached the gospel unto you *at the first.*
1Ti. 1:13. Who was *before* a blasphemer,
Heb 4: 6. to whom it was *first* preached
7:27. *first* for his own sins,
10:32. call to remembrance the *former* days,
1Pet. 1:14. according to the *former* lusts

πρότερος, *proteros.*

Eph. 4:22. concerning the *former* conversation

προτίθημι, *protitheemi.*

Ro. 1:13. I *purposed* to come unto you,
3:25. Whom God *hath set forth* (to be)
Eph. 1: 9. which he *hath purposed* in himself:

προτρέπομαι, *protrepomai.*

Acts18:27. the brethren wrote, *exhorting* the disciples to receive him:

προτρέχω, *protreko.*

Lu. 19: 4. And he *ran before, and* climbed
Joh.20: 4. the other disciple *did outrun* (lit. *ran before* more quickly than) Peter,

---

προϋπάρχω, *proüparko.*

Lu. 23:12. for *before* they *were* at enmity
Acts 8: 9. there *was* a certain man...which *beforetime* in the same city

---

πρόφασις, *prophasis.*

Mat.23:14. for a *pretence* make long prayer:
Mar 12:40. for a *pretence* make long prayers:
Lu. 20:47. and for a *shew* make long prayers:
Joh.15:22. they have no *cloke* for their sin.
Acts27:30. under *colour* as though they would
Phi. 1:18. whether in *pretence*, or in truth,
1Th. 2: 5. nor a *cloke* of covetousness ;

προφέρω, *prophero.*

Lu. 6:45. *bringeth forth* that which is good ;
— *bringeth forth* that which is evil:

προφητεία, *propheetĭa.*

Mat.13:14. is fulfilled the *prophecy* of Esaias,
Ro. 12: 6. whether *prophecy*, (let us prophesy)

1 Co. 12:10. to another *prophecy* ;
13: 2. And though I have (the gift of) *prophecy*,
    8. whether (there be) *prophecies*, they shall
14: 6. or by *prophesying*, or by doctrine?
  22. but *prophesying* (serveth) not for
1 Th. 5:20. Despise not *prophesyings*.
1 Ti. 1:18. according to the *prophecies* which went
    before on thee,
  4:14. which was given thee by *prophecy*, with
2 Pet. 1:20. that no *prophecy* of the scripture
  21. For the *prophecy* came not in old
Rev. 1: 3. that hear the words of this *prophecy*,
  11: 6. in the days of their *prophecy* :
  19:10. of Jesus is the spirit of *prophecy*.
  22: 7. the sayings of the *prophecy* of this
  10. Seal not the sayings of the *prophecy* of
  18. heareth the words of the *prophecy* of
  19. of the book of this *prophecy*,

προφητεύω, *propheetuo.*

Mat. 7:22. *have* we not *prophesied* in thy name ?
11:13. prophets and the law *prophesied* until John.
15: 7. well *did* Esaias *prophesy* of you,
26:68. Saying, *Prophesy* unto us,
Mar 7: 6. Well *hath* Esaias *prophesied* of you
14:65. buffet him, and to say unto him, *Prophesy:*
Lu. 1:67. and *prophesied*, saying,
22:64. saying, *Prophesy*, who is it that smote
Joh. 11:51. he *prophesied* that Jesus should die
Acts 2:17. your daughters *shall prophesy*,
  18. of my Spirit; and they *shall prophesy* :
  19: 6. they spake with tongues, and *prophesied*.
  21: 9. virgins, *which did prophesy.*
1 Co. 11: 4. Every man praying or *prophesying*,
  5. that prayeth or *prophesieth* with (her)
13: 9. know in part, and we *prophesy* in part.
14: 1. but rather that ye *may prophesy*.
  3. But he *that prophesieth* speaketh
  4. he *that prophesieth* edifieth the church.
  5. but rather that ye *prophesied* : for greater
    (is) he *that prophesieth*
  24. But if all *prophesy*, and there come
  31. For ye may all *prophesy* one by one,
  39. covet *to prophesy*, and forbid not to
1 Pet. 1:10. who *prophesied* of the grace
Jude 14. *prophesied* of these, saying, Behold,
Rev. 10:11. Thou must *prophesy* again before
  11: 3. two witnesses, and they *shall prophesy*

προφήτης, *propheetees.*

Mat. 1:22. spoken of the Lord by the *prophet*,
2: 5. thus it is written by the *prophet*,
  15. spoken of the Lord by the *prophet*,
  17. by Jeremy the *prophet*,
  23. which was spoken by the *prophets*,
3: 3. spoken of by the *prophet* Esaias,
4:14. spoken by Esaias the *prophet*, saying,
5:12. so persecuted they the *prophets*
  17. to destroy the law, or the *prophets* :
7:12. this is the law and the *prophets*.
8:17. spoken by Esaias the *prophet*,
10:41. He that receiveth a *prophet* in the name
    of a *prophet* shall receive a *prophet's*
    reward;
11: 9. A *prophet* ? yea, I say unto you, and more
    than a *prophet*.
  13. For all the *prophets* and the law
12:17. spoken by Esaias the *prophet*,

Mat. 12:39. the sign of the *prophet* Jonas:
13:17. That many *prophets* and righteous
  35. spoken by the *prophet*, saying, I will
  57. A *prophet* is not without honour,
14: 5. they counted him as a *prophet*.
16: 4. the sign of the *prophet* Jonas.
  14. Jeremias, or one of the *prophets*.
21: 4. spoken by the *prophet*, saying,
  11. This is Jesus the *prophet* of Nazareth
  26. for all hold John as a *prophet*.
  46. because they took him for a *prophet*.
22:40. hang all the law and the *prophets*.
23:29. ye build the tombs of the *prophets*,
  30. in the blood of the *prophets*.
  31. of them which killed the *prophets*.
  34. I send unto you *prophets*, and wise
  37. (thou) that killest the *prophets*,
24:15. spoken of by Daniel the *prophet*,
  26:56. that the scriptures of the *prophets* might
27: 9. was spoken by Jeremy the *prophet*,
  35. which was spoken by the *prophet*,
Mar 1: 2. As it is written in the *prophets*,
6: 4. A *prophet* is not without honour,
  15. others said, That it is a *prophet*, or as one
    of the *prophets*.
8:28. and others, One of the *prophets*.
11:32. that he was a *prophet* indeed.
13:14. spoken of by Daniel the *prophet*,
Lu. 1:70. by the mouth of his holy *prophets*,
  76. be called the *prophet* of the Highest:
3: 4. the words of Esaias the *prophet*,
4:17. the book of the *prophet* Esaias.
  24. No *prophet* is accepted in his own
  27. in the time of Eliseus the *prophet* ;
6:23. did their fathers unto the *prophets*.
7:16. That a great *prophet* is risen up
  26. A *prophet* ? Yea, I say unto you, and
    much more than a *prophet*.
  28. there is not a greater *prophet* than John
  39. This man, if he were a *prophet*,
9: 8. that one of the old *prophets* was risen
  19. that one of the old *prophets* is risen
10:24. that many *prophets* and kings
11:29. but the sign of Jonas the *prophet*.
  47. ye build the sepulchres of the *prophets*,
  49. I will send them *prophets* and apostles,
  50. That the blood of all the *prophets*,
13:28. and all the *prophets*, in the kingdom
  33. that a *prophet* perish out of Jerusalem.
  34. Jerusalem, which killest the *prophets*,
16:16. The law and the *prophets* (were) until
    John:
  29. They have Moses and the *prophets* ;
  31. If they hear not Moses and the *prophets*,
18:31. that are written by the *prophets*
20: 6. persuaded that John was a *prophet*.
24:19. which was a *prophet* mighty in deed
  25. all that the *prophets* have spoken:
  27. at Moses and all the *prophets*,
  44. in the law of Moses, and (in) the *prophets*,
    and (in) the psalms,
Joh. 1:21. Art thou that *prophet* ?
  23. as said the *prophet* Esaias.
  25. nor Elias, neither that *prophet* ?
  45(46). and the *prophets*, did write
4:19. I perceive that thou art a *prophet*.
  44. that a *prophet* hath no honour in
6:14. that *prophet* that should come
  45. It is written in the *prophets*,
7:40. said, Of a truth this is the *prophet*.
  52. for out of Galilee ariseth no *prophet*.
8:52. Abraham is dead, and the *prophets* :

Joh. 8:53. and the *prophets* are dead:
  9:17. He said, He is a *prophet.*
  12:38. That the saying of Esaias the *prophet*
Acts 2:16. spoken by the *prophet* Joel;
  30. Therefore being a *prophet,* and
  3:18. by the mouth of all his *prophets,*
  21. the mouth of all his holy *prophets*
  22. A *prophet* shall the Lord your
  23. which will not hear that *prophet,*
  24. Yea, and all the *prophets* from
  25. the children of the *prophets,*
  7:37. A *prophet* shall the Lord your God
  42. written in the book of the *prophets,*
  48. made with hands; as saith the *prophet,*
  52. Which of the *prophets* have not
  8:28. in his chariot read Esaias the *prophet.*
  30. heard him read the *prophet* Esaias,
  34. of whom speaketh the *prophet* this?
  10:43. To him give all the *prophets* witness,
  11:27. came *prophets* from Jerusalem
  13: 1. certain *prophets* and teachers;
  15. after the reading of the law and the *prophets*
  20. until Samuel the *prophet.*
  27. because they knew him not, nor yet the voices of the *prophets* which
  40. spoken of in the *prophets;*
  15:15. agree the words of the *prophets;*
  32. being *prophets* also themselves,
  21:10. a certain *prophet,* named Agabus.
  24:14. written in the law and in the *prophets:*
  26:22. which the *prophets* and Moses did say
  27. believest thou the *prophets?*
  28:23. and (out of) the *prophets,* from morning till evening.
  25. the Holy Ghost by Esaias the *prophet*
Ro. 1: 2. by his *prophets* in the holy scriptures,
  3:21. witnessed by the law and the *prophets;*
  11: 3. Lord, they have killed thy *prophets,*
1Co.12:28. first apostles, secondarily *prophets,*
  29. (are) all *prophets?* (are) all teachers?
  14:29. Let the *prophets* speak two or three,
  32. And the spirits of the *prophets* are subject to the *prophets.*
  37. think himself to be a *prophet,*
Eph 2:20. of the apostles and *prophets,*
  3: 5: unto his holy apostles and *prophets*
  4:11. some, *prophets;* and some, evangelists;
1Th. 2:15. both killed the Lord Jesus, and their own *prophets,*
Tit. 1:12. (even) a *prophet* of their own, said, The Cretians
Heb 1: 1. unto the fathers by the *prophets,*
  11:32. and Samuel, and (of) the *prophets:*
Jas. 5:10. the *prophets,* who have spoken in the name of the Lord,
1Pet. 1:10. Of which salvation the *prophets*
2Pet. 2:16. forbad the madness of the *prophet.*
  3: 2. before by the holy *prophets,*
Rev.10: 7. hath declared to his servants the *prophets.*
  11:10. because these two *prophets* tormented
  18. unto thy servants the *prophets,*
  16: 6. the blood of saints and *prophets,*
  18:20. (ye) holy apostles and *prophets;* for God
  24. the blood of *prophets,* and of saints,
  22: 6. the Lord God of the holy *prophets*
  9. and of thy brethren the *prophets,*

προφητικός, *propheetikos.*

Ro. 16:26. by the scriptures *of the prophets,*

2Pet. 1:19. a more sure word *of prophecy;*

προφῆτις, *propheetis.*

Lu. 2:36. Anna, a *prophetess,* the daughter of
Rev. 2:20. which calleth herself a *prophetess,*

προφθάνω, *prophthano.*

Mat.17:25. Jesus *prevented* (lit. *forestalled*) him,

προχειρίζομαι, *prokīrizomai.*

Acts22:14. *hath chosen* thee, that thou shouldest
  26:16. *to make* thee a minister and a witness

προχειροτονέομαι, *prokīrotoneomai.*

Acts10:41. unto witnesses *chosen before* of God,

πρύμνα, *prumna.*

Mar 4:38. he was in the *hinder part of the ship,*
Acts27:29. they cast four anchors out of the *stern,*
  41. but the *hinder part* was broken

πρωΐ, *prōï.*

Mat.16: 3. And *in the morning,* (It will be) foul
  20: 1. went out *early in the morning*
Mar 1:35. *in the morning,* rising up a great while
  11:20. And *in the morning,* as they passed
  13:35. at the cockcrowing, or *in the morning:*
  15: 1. And straightway *in the morning*
  16: 2. And very *early in the morning*
  9. was risen *early* the first (day) of
Joh.20: 1. cometh Mary Magdalene *early,*
Acts28:23. from *morning* till evening.

πρωΐα, *prōïa.*

Mat.21:18. Now in the *morning* as he returned
  27: 1. When the *morning* was come, all the
Joh.18:28. and it was *early;* and they themselves
  21: 4. But when the *morning* was now come,

πρώϊμος, *prōïmos.*

Jas. 5: 7. he receive the *early* and latter rain.

πρωϊνός, *prōïnos.*

Rev. 2:28. I will give him the *morning* star.

πρώρα, *prōra.*

Acts27:30. cast anchors out of the *foreship,*
  41. and the *forepart* stuck fast,

πρωτεύω, *prōtūo.*

Col. 1:18. he might *have the* preeminence.

πρωτοκαθεδρία, prōtokathedria.

Mat.23: 6. the *chief seats* in the synagogues,
Mar 12:39. the *chief seats* in the synagogues,
Lu.11:43. love the *uppermost seats* in the synagogues,
   20:46. and the *highest seats* in the synagogues,

πρωτοκλισία, prōtoklisia.

Mat.23: 6. love the *uppermost rooms* (lit. the *first place*) at feasts,
Mar 12:39. the *uppermost rooms* (lit. *first places*) at
Lu 14: 7. how they chose out the *chief rooms ;*
     8. sit not down in the *highest room ;*
   20:46. and the *chief rooms* at feasts ;

πρῶτον & τὸ πρῶτον. prōton & to prōton.

Mat. 5:24. *first* be reconciled to thy brother,
   6.33. But seek ye *first* the kingdom of God,
   7: 5. *first* cast out the beam out of
   8:21. suffer me *first* to go and bury my
  12:29. except he *first* bind the strong
  13:30. Gather ye together *first* the tares,
  17:10. that Elias must *first* come ?
    11. Elias truly shall *first* come,
  23:26. cleanse *first* that (which is) within
Mar. 3:27. he will *first* bind the strong man ;
   4:28. *first* the blade, then the ear,
   7:27. Let the children *first* be filled:
   9:11. that Elias must *first* come ?
    12. Elias verily cometh *first*,
  13:10. the gospel must *first* be published
  16: 9. he appeared *first* to Mary
Lu. 6:42. cast out *first* the beam
   9:59. suffer me *first* to go and bury my
    61. let me *first* go bid them farewell,
  10: 5. *first* say, Peace (be) to this house.
  11:38. that he had not *first* washed
  12: 1. to say unto his disciples *first of all*,
  14:28. sitteth not down *first*, and counteth
    31. sitteth not down *first*, and consulteth
  17:25. But *first* must he suffer
  21: 9. these things must *first* come
Joh. 2:10. Every man *at the beginning*
  10:40. where John *at first* baptized ;
  12:16. understood not his disciples *at the first :*
  15:18. *before* (it hated) you.
  18:13. to Annas *first ;* for he was
  19:39. which *at the first* came to Jesus by
Acts 3:26. Unto you *first* God, having raised up
   7:12. he sent out our fathers *first*.
  11:26. called Christians *first* in Antioch.
  13:46. should *first* have been spoken to you:
  15:14. how God *at the first* did visit
  26:20. But shewed *first* unto them of Damascus,
Ro. 1: 8. *First*, I thank my God through
    16. to the Jew *first*, and also to the Greek.
   2: 9. of the Jew *first*, and also of the Gentile ;
    10. to the Jew *first*, and also to the Gentile:
   3: 2. *chiefly*, because that unto them
  15:24. if *first* I be somewhat filled
1Co.11:18. For *first of all*, when ye come
  12:28. *first* apostles, secondarily prophets,
  15:46. that (was) not *first* which is spiritual,
2Co. 8: 5. but *first* gave their own selves
Eph. 4: 9. he also descended *first* into the lower
1Th. 4:16. the dead in Christ shall rise *first:*
2Th. 2: 3. except there come a falling away *first*,

1Ti. 2: 1. that, *first* of all, supplications,
   3:10. let these also *first* be proved ;
   5: 4. let them learn *first* to shew piety
2Ti. 1: 5. which dwelt *first* in thy grandmother
Heb. 7: 2. *first* being by interpretation
Jas. 3:17. is *first* pure, then peaceable,
1Pet.4:17. if (it) *first* (begin) at us,
2Pet.1:20. Knowing this *first*, that
   3: 3. Knowing this *first*, that there shall

πρῶτος, prōtos.

Mat.10: 2. The *first*, Simon, who is called Peter,
  12:45. of that man is worse than the *first*.
  17:27. the fish that *first* cometh up ;
  19:30. many (that are) *first* shall be last ; and the last (shall be) *first*.
  20: 8. beginning from the last unto the *first*.
    10. But when the *first* came,
    16. So the last shall be *first*, and the *first* last:
    27. whosoever will be *chief* among you,
  21:28. and he came to the *first*,
    31. They say unto him, The *first*.
    36. servants more than the *first :*
  22:25. and the *first*, when he had married
    38. This is the *first* and great commandment.
  26:17. Now the *first* (day) of the (feast of)
  27:64. last error shall be worse than the *first*.
Mar 6:21. and *chief* (estates) of Galilee;
   9:35. If any man desire to be *first*,
  10:31. But many (that are) *first* shall be last; and the last *first*.
    44. will be the *chiefest*, shall be
  12:20. and the *first* took a wife,
    28. Which is the *first* commandment
    29. The *first* of all the commandments
    30. this (is) the *first* commandment.
  14:12. And the *first* day of unleavened
  16: 9. early the *first* (day) of the week,
Lu. 2: 2. this taxing was *first* made
  11:26. worse than the *first*.
  13:30. shall be *first*, and there are *first*
  14:18. The *first* said unto him,
  15:22. Bring forth the *best* robe,
  16: 5. and said unto the *first*, How much
  19:16. Then came the *first*, saying, Lord,
    47. and the *chief* of the people
  20:29. and the *first* took a wife,
Joh. 1:15. for he was *before* me.
    30. for he was *before* me.
    41(42). He *first* findeth his own brother
   5: 4. whosoever then *first* after the
   8: 7. let him *first* cast a stone at her.
  19:32. and brake the legs of the *first*,
  20: 4. and came *first* to the sepulchre.
    8. which came *first* to the sepulchre.
Acts 1: 1. The *former* treatise have I made,
  12:10. When they were past the *first* and the second ward,
  13:50. and the *chief* men of the city,
  16:12. which is the *chief* city of that part of
  17: 4. and of the *chief* women not a few.
  20:18. Ye know, from the *first* day
  25: 2. and the *chief* of the Jews
  26:23. he should be the *first* that should rise
  27:43. should cast (themselves) *first* (into the sea),
  28: 7. of the *chief* man of the island,
    17. Paul called the *chief* of the Jews
Ro. 10:19. *First* Moses saith, I will provoke
1Co.14:30. let the *first* hold his peace.

1Co.15: 3. I delivered unto you *first of all*
     45. The *first* man Adam was made a
     47. The *first* man (is) of the earth,
Eph 6: 2. which is the *first* commandment with
Phi. 1: 5. from the *first* day until now;
1Ti. 1:15. of whom I am *chief*.
     16. that in me *first* Jesus Christ might
   2:13. For Adam was *first* formed,
   5:12. cast off their *first* faith.
2Ti. 2: 6. must be *first* partaker of the fruits.
   4:16. At my *first* answer no man
Heb 8: 7. For if that *first* (covenant)
    13. he hath made the *first* old.
   9: 1. Then verily the *first* (covenant)
     2. the *first,* wherein (was) the candlestick,
     6. went always into the *first* tabernacle,
     8. while as the *first* tabernacle was yet
    15. under the *first* testament,
    18. neither the *first* (testament) was
  10: 9. He taketh away the *first,* that he may
2Pet.2:20. is worse with them than the *beginning.*
1Joh. 4:19. because he *first* loved us.
Rev. 1:11. I am Alpha and Omega, the *first* and the
       last:
    17. I am the *first* and the last:
  2: 4. thou hast left thy *first* love.
    5. and do the *first* works; or else
    8. the *first* and the last, which was
    19. the last (to be) more than the *first.*
  4: 1. and the *first* voice which I heard
    7. And the *first* beast (was) like
  8: 7. The *first* angel sounded,
 13.12. all the power of the *first* beast
    — to worship the *first* beast,
 16: 2. And the *first* went, and poured out
 20: 5. This (is) the *first* resurrection.
    6. part in the *first* resurrection:
 21: 1. the *first* heaven and the *first* earth were
     passed away ;
    4. the *former* things are passed away.
    19. The *first* foundation (was) jasper ;
 22:13. the *first* and the last.

πρωτοστάτης, *prōtostatees.*

Acts24: 5. a *ringleader* of the sect of the

πρωτοτόκια, *prōtotokia.*

(substantive plural.)
Heb12:16. for one morsel of meat sold his *birthright.*

πρωτότοκος, *prōtotokos.*

Mat. 1:25. had brought forth her *firstborn* son:
Lu. 2: 7. she brought forth her *firstborn* son,
Ro. 8:29. the *firstborn* among many brethren.
Col. 1:15. the *firstborn* of every creature: (or it may
    be,—*born before* all creation)
    18. the *firstborn* from the dead ;
Heb 1: 6. bringeth in the *firstbegotten* into the world,
  11:28. he that destroyed the *firstborn* [neut. plur.]
  12:23. and church of the *firstborn,* [plur.]
Rev. 1: 5. the *first begotten* of the dead,

πταίω, *ptaio.*

Ro. 11:11. *Have* they *stumbled* that they should fall ?
Jas. 2:10. shall keep the whole law, and yet *offend*
    in one (point),

Jas. 3: 2. For in many things we *offend* all.   If any
    man *offend* not in word,
2Pet.1:10. if ye do these things, ye shall never *fall:*

πτέρνα, *pterna.*

Joh.13:18. hath lifted up his *heel* against me.

πτερύγιον, *pterugion.*

Mat. 4: 5. on a *pinnacle* of the temple,
Lu. 4: 9. set him on a *pinnacle* of the temple,

πτέρυξ, *pterux.*

Mat.23:37. her chickens under (her) *wings,*
Lu. 13:34. her brood under (her) *wings,*
Rev. 4: 8. four beasts had each of them six *wings*
  9: 9. the sound of their *wings* (was) as
 12:14. two *wings* of a great eagle,

πτηνόν, *pteenon.*

1Co.15:39. (and) another of *birds.*

πτοέομαι, *ptoĕomai.*

Lu. 21: 9. *be* not *terrified :* for these things
  24:37. But they were *terrified* and

πτόησις, *ptoeesis.*

1Pet.3: 6. and are not afraid with any *amazement.*

πτύον, *ptuon.*

Mat. 3:12. Whose *fan* (is) in his hand, and
Lu. 3:17. Whose *fan* (is) in his hand, and he

πτύρομαι, *pturomai.*

Phi. 1:28. in nothing *terrified* by your adversaries:

πτύσμα, *ptusma.*

Joh. 9: 6. and made clay of the *spittle,*

πτύσσω, *ptusso.*

Lu. 4:20. And he *closed* the book, and

πτύω, *ptuo.*

Mar. 7:33. and he *spit, and* touched his tongue;
  8:23. *when* he *had spit* on his eyes,
Joh. 9: 6. he *spat* on the ground,

πτῶμα, *ptōma.*

Mat.24:28. For wheresoever the *carcase* is,
Mar. 6:29. they came and took up his *corpse,*

Rev.11: 8.And their *dead bodies* (shall lie) in the
       9. shall see their *dead bodies* three days
       — shall not suffer their *dead bodies* to

πτῶσις, *ptōsis.*

Mat. 7:27. and great was the *fall* of it.
Lu. 2:34. this (child) is set for the *fall* and rising
           again of many in Israel ;

πτωχεία, *ptōkīa.*

2Co. 8: 2. their deep *poverty* abounded
       9. ye through his *poverty* might be rich.
Rev. 2: 9. works, and tribulation, and *poverty,*

πτωχεύω, *ptōkūo.*

2Co. 8: 9. yet for your sakes he *became poor,*

πτωχός, *ptōkos.*

Mat. 5: 3. Blessed (are) the *poor* in spirit:
      11: 5. the *poor* have the gospel
      19:21. sell that thou hast, and give to the *poor,*
      26: 9. and given to the *poor.*
          11. For ye have the *poor* always
Mar.10:21. sell whatsoever thou hast, and give to the
           poor,
      12:42. a certain *poor* widow,
          43. That this *poor* widow hath
      14: 5. and have been given to the *poor.*
           7. ye have the *poor* with you always,
Lu. 4:18. preach the gospel to the *poor ;*
      6:20. Blessed (be ye) *poor:* for your's is
      7:22. to the *poor* the gospel is preached.
     14:13. when thou makest a feast, call the *poor,*
          21. bring in hither the *poor*, and the maimed,
     16:20. there was a certain *beggar*
          22. that the *beggar* died,
     18:22. and distribute unto the *poor,*
      19: 8. half of my goods I give to the *poor ;*
      21: 3. that this *poor* widow hath cast in more
Joh.12: 5. and given to the *poor ?*
          6. not that he cared for the *poor ;*
          8. For the *poor* always ye have with you ;
     13:29. should give something to the *poor.*
Ro. 15:26. contribution for the *poor* saints
2Co. 6:10. as *poor*, yet making many rich ;
Gal. 2:10. should remember the *poor ;*
      4: 9. and *beggarly* elements,
Jas. 2: 2. there come in also a *poor* man
          3. and say to the *poor*, Stand thou
          5. Hath not God chosen the *poor* of this
          6. But ye have despised the *poor.*
Rev. 3:17. and *poor*, and blind, and naked:
     13:16. rich and *poor*, free and bond,

πυγμῇ, *pugmee.*

Mar 7: 3. except they wash (their) hands *oft* (lit.
           to the *wrist*, or, the *fist*)

πυκνός, *puknos.*

Note.—The neut. of this, as of many other adjectives, is used adverbially.

Lu. 5:33. the disciples of John fast *often,*

Acts24:26. he sent for him *the oftener,*
1Ti. 5:23. and thine *often* infirmities.

πυκτεύω, *puktūo.*

1Co. 9:26. so *fight* I, not as one that beateth

πύλη, *pulee.*

Mat. 7:13. Enter ye in at the strait *gate ;* for wide
           (is) the *gate,*
          14. Because strait (is) the *gate,*
     16:18. the *gates* of hell shall not prevail
Lu. 7:12. when he came nigh to the *gate* of
     13:24. Strive to enter in at the strait *gate ;*
Acts 3:10. at the Beautiful *gate* of the temple:
      9:24. And they watched the *gates* day and
     12:10. they came unto the iron *gate*
Heb13:12. suffered without the *gate.*

πυλών, *pulōn.*

Mat.26:71. out into the *porch*, another (maid)
Lu. 16:20. which was laid at his *gate,*
Acts10:17. and stood before the *gate,*
     12:13. knocked at the door of the *gate,*
          14. she opened not the *gate* for gladness,
          — told how Peter stood before the *gate.*
     14:13. oxen and garlands unto the *gates,*
Rev.21:12. (and) had twelve *gates*, and at the *gates*
           twelve angels,
          13. On the east three *gates ;* on the north
           three *gates ;* on the south three *gates ;*
           and on the west three *gates.*
          15. and the *gates* thereof, and the wall
          21. And the twelve *gates* (were) twelve pearls ;
           every several *gate* was
          25. And the *gates* of it shall not be shut
     22:14. enter in through the *gates* into the city.

πυνθάνομαι, *punthanomai.*

Mat. 2: 4. he *demanded* of them where Christ
Lu. 15:26. and *asked* what these things meant.
     18:36. pass by, he *asked* what it meant.
Joh. 4:52. Then *enquired* he of them the hour
     13:24. that he should *ask* who it should be
Acts 4: 7. they *asked*, By what power, or by what
     10:18. and *asked* whether Simon,
          29. I *ask* therefore for what intent
     21:33. and *demanded* who he was, and what
     23:19. aside privately, and *asked* (him), What
          20. as though they would *enquire*
          34. And *when* he *understood* that (he was) of

πῦρ, *pur.*

Mat. 3:10. hewn down, and cast into the *fire.*
          11. with the Holy Ghost, and (with) *fire ;*
          12. the chaff with unquenchable *fire.*
      5:22. shall be in danger of hell *fire.* (lit. gehenna
           of *fire*)
      7:19. hewn down, and cast into the *fire.*
     13:40. are gathered and burned in the *fire ;*
          42. into a furnace of *fire ;* there shall be
          50. shall cast them into the furnace of *fire ;*

Mat.17:15. ofttimes he falleth into the *fire*,
　18: 8. to be cast into everlasting *fire*.
　　　9. to be cast into hell *fire*. (lit. gehenna of
　　　　　fire)
　25:41. ye cursed, into everlasting *fire*, prepared
Mar 9:22. it hath cast him into the *fire*,
　　43. into the *fire* that never shall be
　　44. and the *fire* is not quenched.
　　45. into the *fire* that never shall be
　　46. and the *fire* is not quenched.
　　47. to be cast into hell *fire*: (lit. gehenna of
　　　　fire)
　　48. and the *fire* is not quenched.
　　49. every one shall be salted with *fire*,
Lu. 3: 9. is hewn down, and cast into the *fire*.
　　16. with the Holy Ghost and with *fire*:
　　17. he will burn with *fire* unquenchable.
　9:54. that we command *fire* to come
　12:49. I am come to send *fire* on the earth ;
　17:29. it rained *fire* and brimstone
　22:55. when they had kindled a *fire*
Joh. 15: 6. and cast (them) into the *fire*,
Acts 2: 3. cloven tongues like as of *fire*,
　　19. blood, and *fire*, and vapour of smoke:
　7:30. in a flame of *fire* in a bush.
　28: 5. he shook off the beast into the *fire*,
Ro. 12:20. heap coals of *fire* on his head.
1Co. 3:13. it shall be revealed by *fire*; and the *fire*
　　　　shall try every
　　15. shall be saved ; yet so as by *fire*.
2Th. 1: 8. In flaming *fire* taking vengeance on
Heb 1: 7. his ministers a flame of *fire*.
　10:27. and *fiery* indignation,
　11:34. Quenched the violence of *fire*,
　12:18. and that burned with *fire*,
　　29. our God (is) a consuming *fire*.
Jas. 3: 5. a little *fire* kindleth !
　　6. And the tongue (is) a *fire*,
　5: 3. shall eat your flesh as it were *fire*.
1Pet. 1: 7. though it be tried with *fire*,
2Pet. 3: 7. reserved unto *fire* against
Jude　7. the vengeance of eternal *fire*.
　　23. pulling (them) out of the *fire* ;
Rev. 1:14. his eyes (were) as a flame of *fire* ;
　2:18. his eyes like unto a flame of *fire*,
　3:18. gold tried in the *fire*,
　4: 5. seven lamps of *fire* burning
　8: 5. and filled it with *fire* of the altar,
　　7. hail and *fire* mingled with blood,
　　8. mountain burning with *fire*
　9:17. out of their mouths issued *fire* and
　　18. by the *fire*, and by the smoke,
　10: 1. his feet as pillars of *fire* :
　11: 5. *fire* proceedeth out of their mouth,
　13:13. he maketh *fire* come down from
　14:10. with *fire* and brimstone
　　18. which had power over *fire* ;
　15: 2. a sea of glass mingled with *fire* :
　16: 8. to scorch men with *fire*.
　17:16. and burn her with *fire*.
　18: 8. she shall be utterly burned with *fire* :
　19:12. His eyes (were) as a flame of *fire*,
　　20. into a lake of *fire* burning with
　20: 9. and *fire* came down from God
　　10. into the lake of *fire* and brimstone,
　　14. cast into the lake of *fire*.
　　15. was cast into the lake of *fire*.
　21: 8. which burneth with *fire* and brimstone:

πυρά, *pura*.

Acts28: 2. they kindled a *fire*, and received us

Acts28: 3. of sticks, and laid (them) on the *fire*,

πύργος, *purgos*.

Mat.21:33. a winepress in it, and built a *tower*,
Mar 12: 1. winefat, and built a *tower*,
Lu. 13: 4. upon whom the *tower* in Siloam fell,
　14:28. intending to build a *tower*, sitteth not

πυρέσσω, *puresso*.

Mat. 8:14. and *sick of a fever*.
Mar 1:30. wife's mother lay *sick of a fever*,

πυρετός, *puretos*.

Mat. 8:15. and the *fever* left her:
Mar 1:31. and immediately the *fever* left her,
Lu. 4:38. was taken with a great *fever* ;
　　39. rebuked the *fever* ; and it left her:
Joh. 4:52. at the seventh hour the *fever* left him.
Acts28: 8. lay sick of a *fever* and of a

πυρινός, *purinos*.

Rev. 9:17. having breastplates *of fire*,

πυρόομαι, *puroŏmai*.

1Co. 7: 9. better to marry than *to burn*.
2Co.11:29. and I *burn* not ?
Eph 6:16. all the *fiery* darts of the wicked.
2Pet. 3:12. the heavens *being on fire* shall
Rev. 1:15. as if they *burned* in a furnace ;
　3:18. gold *tried* in the fire,

πυῤῥάζω, *purrazo*.

Mat.16: 2. for the sky *is red*.
　　3. for the sky *is red* and lowring.

πυῤῥός, *purros*.

Rev. 6: 4. another horse (that was) *red* :
　12: 3. a great *red* dragon,

πύρωσις, *purōsis*.

1Pet. 4:12. concerning the *fiery* trial
Rev.18: 9. the smoke of her *burning*,
　　18. saw the smoke of her *burning*,

πω see μήπω, μηδέπω, οὔπω, & οὐδέπω.

πωλέω, *pōleo*.

Mat.10:29. *Are* not two sparrows *sold* for a
　13:44. and *selleth* all that he hath,
　19:21. go (and) *sell* that thou hast,
　21:12. cast out all them *that sold* and
　— and the seats of them *that sold* doves,

Mat.25: 9. go ye rather to them *that sell*,
Mar 10:21. *sell* whatsoever thou hast,
   11:15. to cast out them *that sold* and
   — the seats of them *that sold* doves;
Lu. 12: 6. *Are* not five sparrows *sold* for
   33. Sell that ye have, and give alms;
   17:28. they bought, they *sold*, they planted,
   18·22. *sell* all that thou hast, and distribute
   19:45. to cast out them *that sold* therein,
   22:36. *let* him *sell* his garment, and buy one.
Joh. 2:14. those *that sold* oxen and sheep
   16. said unto them *that sold* doves,
Acts 4:34. *sold* them, *and* brought the prices
   37. Having land, *sold* (it), *and* brought
   5: 1. *sold* a possession,
1Co.10:25. *Whatsoever is sold* in the shambles,
Rev.13:17. that no man might buy or *sell*,

πῶλος, *pōlos*.

Mat.21: 2. and a *colt* with her:
   5. and a *colt* the foal of an ass.
   7. and the *colt*, and put on them their
Mar 11: 2. ye shall find a *colt* tied,
   4. and found the *colt* tied by the door
   5. What do ye, loosing the *colt* ?
   7. they brought the *colt* to Jesus,
Lu. 19:30. ye shall find a *colt* tied,
   33. as they were loosing the *colt*,
   — Why loose ye the *colt* ?
   35. cast their garments upon the *colt*,
Joh.12:15. sitting on an ass's *colt*.

πώποτε, *pōpote*.

Lu. 19:30. whereon yet never man sat: (lit. none
   ever)
Joh. 1:18. No man hath seen God *at any time;*
   5:37. neither heard his voice *at any time*,
   6:35. shall never (lit. not *ever*) thirst.
   8:33. were never (lit. to none *ever*) in bondage
   to any man:
1Joh.4:12. No man hath seen God *at any time.*

πωρόω, *pōroō*.

Mar 6:52. for their heart was *hardened*.
   8:17. have ye your heart yet *hardened* ?
Joh.12:40. He hath blinded their eyes, and *hardened*
   their heart;
Ro. 11: 7. and the rest *were blinded*
2Co. 3:14. But their minds *were blinded :*

πώρωσις, *pōrōsis*.

Mar 3: 5. for the *hardness* of their hearts,
Ro. 11:25. that *blindness* in part is happened to
Eph 4:18. because of the *blindness* of their heart:

πώς, *pōs.* indefinitely.

Acts27:12. if *by any means* they might
   29. Then fearing lest)(we should have
Ro. 1:10. if *by any means* now at length
   11:14. If *by any means* I may provoke
   21. lest)(he also spare not thee.
1Co. 8: 9. lest *by any means* this liberty

1Co. 9:27. lest that *by any means*, when I have
2Co. 2: 7. lest *perhaps* such a one should
   9: 4. Lest *haply* if they of Macedonia
   11: 3. lest *by any means*, as the serpent
   12:20. For I fear, lest,)(when I come,
   — lest)((there be) debates,
Gal. 2: 2. lest *by any means* I should run,
   4:11. lest)(I have bestowed upon you
Phi. 3:11. If *by any means* I might attain
1Th. 3: 5. lest *by some means* the tempter

πῶς, *pōs*. interrog. or definitely.

Mat. 6:28. *how* they grow; they toil not,
   7: 4. Or *how* wilt thou say to thy brother,
   10:19. *how* or what ye shall speak:
   12: 4. *How* he entered into the house of God,
   26. *how* shall then his kingdom stand?
   29. *how* can one enter into a strong man's
   34. *how* can ye, being evil, speak good
   16:11. *How* is it that ye do not understand
   21:20. *How* soon is the fig tree withered
   22:12. *how* camest thou in hither
   43. *How* then doth David in spirit call
   45. *how* is he his son?
   23:33. *how* can ye escape the damnation of hell?
   26:54. *how* then shall the scriptures be fulfilled,
Mar 2:26. *How* he went into the house of God
   3:23. *How* can Satan cast out Satan?
   4:13. *how* then will ye know all parables?
   40. *how* is it that ye have no faith?
   5:16. told them *how* it befell to him that was
   8:21. *How* is it that ye do not understand?
   9:12. and *how* it is written of the Son of man,
   10:23. *How* hardly shall they that have riches
   24. *how* hard is it for them that trust in
   11:18. sought *how* they might destroy him:
   12:35. *How* say the scribes that Christ is the
   41. beheld *how* the people cast money into
   14: 1. sought *how* they might take him
   11. sought *how* he might conveniently betray
Lu. 1:34. *How* shall this be, seeing
   6:42. *how* canst thou say to thy brother,
   8:18. Take heed therefore *how* ye hear:
   36. told them *by what means* he that was
   10:26. *how* readest thou ?
   11:18. *how* shall his kingdom stand ?
   12:11. take ye no thought *how* or what
   27. Consider the lilies *how* they grow:
   50. and *how* am I straitened till it
   56. *how* is it that ye do not discern
   14: 7. *how* they chose out the chief rooms ;
   18:24. *How* hardly shall they that have
   20:41. *How* say they that Christ is
   44. *how* is he then his son?
   22: 2. sought *how* they might kill him ;
   4. *how* he might betray him
Joh. 3: 4. *How* can a man be born when he is
   9. *How* can these things be ?
   12. *how* shall ye believe, if I tell you
   4: 9. *How* is it that thou, being a Jew,
   5:44. *How* can ye believe, which
   47. *how* shall ye believe my words?
   6:42. *how* is it then that he saith, I came
   52. *How* can this man give us (his)
   7:15. *How* knoweth this man letters,
   8:33. *how* sayest thou, Ye shall be
   9:10. *How* were thine eyes opened ?
   15. *how* he had received his sight.
   16. *How* can a man that is a sinner
   19. *how* then doth he now see ?

Joh. 9:21. But *by what means* he now seeth,
26. *how* opened he thine eyes?
11:36. Behold *how* he loved him!
12:34. and *how* sayest thou,
14: 5. *how* can we know the way?
9. *how* sayest thou (then), Shew us
Acts 2: 8. And *how* hear we every man in
4:21. *how* they might punish them,
8:31. *How* can I, except some man
9:27. *how* he had seen the Lord in the way,
— and *how* he had preached boldly at
11:13. *how* he had seen an angel
12:17. *how* the Lord had brought him out
15:36. (and see) *how* they do.
20:18. *after what manner* I have been with
Ro. 3: 6. for then *how* shall God judge the world?
4:10. *How* was it then reckoned?
6: 2. *How* shall we, that are dead to sin,
8:32. *how* shall he not with him also freely
10:14. *How* then shall they call on him
— and *how* shall they believe in him
— and *how* shall they hear without a
15. And *how* shall they preach, except
1Co. 3:10. take heed *how* he buildeth thereupon.
7:32. *how* he may please the Lord:
33. *how* he may please (his) wife.
34. *how* she may please (her) husband.
14: 7. *how* shall it be known what is piped
9. *how* shall it be known what
16. *how* shall he that occupieth the room of
15:12. *how* say some among you that
35. *How* are the dead raised up?
2Co. 3: 8. *How* shall not the ministration of the
Gal. 4: 9. *how* turn ye again to the weak and
Eph. 5:15. See then *that* ye walk circumspectly,
Col. 4: 6. *how* ye ought to answer every man.
1Th. 1: 9. *how* ye turned to God from idols
4: 1. *how* ye ought to walk and
2Th. 3: 7. *how* ye ought to follow us:
1Ti. 3: 5. *how* shall he take care of the church
15. *how* thou oughtest to behave thyself
Heb 2: 3. *How* shall we escape, if we neglect
1Joh.3:17. *how* dwelleth the love of God in him?
4:20. *how* can he love God whom he hath not seen?
Rev. 3: 3. Remember therefore *how* thou hast received and heard,

---

ῥαββί, *rabbi.*

Mat.23: 7. to be called of men, *Rabbi, Rabbi.*
8. But be not ye called *Rabbi :*
26:25. *Master*, is it I?
49. Hail, *master ;* and kissed him.
Mar 9: 5. *Master*, it is good for us to be here:
11:21. *Master*, behold, the fig·tree
14:45. *Master, master ;* and kissed him.
Joh. 1:38(39). They said unto him, *Rabbi*,
49(50). *Rabbi*, thou art the Son of God ;
3: 2. *Rabbi*, we know that thou art a
26. *Rabbi*, he that was with thee
4:31. saying, *Master*, eat.
6:25. *Rabbi*, when camest thou hither?
9: 2. *Master*, who did sin, this man, or
11: 8. *Master*, the Jews of late sought to

ῥαββονί, ῥαββουνί, *rabboni, rabbouni.*

Mar 10.51. *Lord*, that I might receive my sight.
Joh.20:16. *Rabboni ;* which is to say, Master.

ῥαβδίζω, *rabdizo.*

Acts16:22. and commanded *to beat* (them).
2Co.11:25. Thrice *was I beaten with rods,*

ῥάβδος, *rabdos.*

Mat.10:10. nor yet *staves :*
Mar 6: 8. save a *staff* only ;
Lu. 9: 3. neither *staves*, nor scrip,
1Co. 4:21. shall I come unto you with a *rod*,
Heb. 1: 8. a *sceptre* of righteousness (is) the *sceptre* of thy kingdom.
9: 4. and Aaron's *rod* that budded,
11:21. (leaning) upon the top of his *staff.*
Rev. 2:27. rule them with a *rod* of iron ;
11: 1. a reed like unto a *rod :*
12: 5. to rule all nations with a *rod* of iron:
19:15. shall rule them with a *rod* of iron:

ῥαβδοῦχος, *rabdoukos.*

Acts16:35. the magistrates sent the *serjeants,*
38. And the *serjeants* told these words

ῥαδιούργημα, *radiourgeema.*

Acts18:14. matter of wrong or wicked *lewdness,*

ῥαδιουργία, *radiourgia.*

Acts13:10. full of all subtilty and all *mischief,*

ῥακά, *raka.*

Mat. 5:22. shall say to his brother, *Raca,*

ῥάκος, *rakos.*

Mat. 9:16. a piece of new *cloth* unto an old garment,
Mar 2:21. a piece of new *cloth* on an old garment:

ῥαντίζω, *rantizo.*

Heb 9:13. *sprinkling* the unclean,
19. and *sprinkled* both the book,
21. Moreover he *sprinkled* with blood
10:22. having our hearts *sprinkled* from an evil conscience,

---

ῥαντισμός, *rantismos.*

Heb12:24. to the blood of *sprinkling,*
1Pet.1: 2. unto obedience and *sprinkling* of the blood of Jesus Christ:

ῥαπίζω, *rapizo.*

Mat. 5:39. whosoever *shall* smite thee on thy right cheek,
26:67. others *smote* (him) *with the palms of their hands,*

ῥάπισμα, rapisma.

Mar 14:65. did strike him with the *palms of* their *hands.*
Joh. 18:22. *struck* Jesus *with the palm of* his *hand,* (lit. gave a *slap* to Jesus)
　　19: 3. they smote him with their hand　(lit. they gave him *smitings*)

ῥαφίς, raphis.

Mat.19:24. to go through the eye of a *needle,*
Mar 10:25. to go through the eye of a *needle,*
Lu. 18:25. to go through a *needle's* eye,

ῥέδα, reda.,

Rev.18:13. and horses, and *chariots,*

ῥέω, reo.

Joh. 7:38. out of his belly *shall flow* rivers of living water.

ῥέω, reo.

Note.—It is only used in the passive: Some trace to this root several of the words given in the series ἐρέω.

Mat. 1:22. *which was spoken* of the Lord by
　　2:15. *which was spoken* of the Lord by
　　　17. *which was spoken* by Jeremy
　　　23. *which was spoken* by the prophets,
　　3: 3. is he *that was spoken of* by the prophet
　　4:14. *which was spoken* by Esaias
　　5:21. it *was said* by them of old time,
　　　27. it *was said* by them of old time,
　　　31. It *hath been said,* Whosoever
　　　33. it *hath been said* by them of old time,
　　　38. that it *hath been said,* An eye
　　　43. it *hath been said,* Thou shalt
　　8:17. *which was spoken* by Esaias
　12:17. *which was spoken* by Esaias
　13:35. *which was spoken* by the prophet,
　21: 4. *which was spoken* by the prophet,
　22:31. *which was spoken* unto you by God,
　24:15. *spoken of* by Daniel the prophet,
　27: 9. *which was spoken* by Jeremy
　　35. *which was spoken* by the prophet,
Mar 13:14. *spoken of* by Daniel the prophet,
Ro. 9:12. It *was said* unto her, The elder
　　26. where it *was said* unto them,
Gal. 3:16. *were* the promises *made.*
Rev. 6:11. and it *was said* unto them,
　9: 4. And it *was commanded* them that

ῥῆγμα, reegma.

Lu. 6:49. and the *ruin* of that house was great.

ῥήγνυμι, ῥήσσω, reegnumi, & reesso.

Mat. 7: 6. lest they...and turn again and *rend* you.
　9:17. else the bottles *break,*
Mar 2:22. *doth burst* the bottles,
　9:18. he *teareth* him :
Lu. 5:37. new wine *will burst* the bottles.
　9:42. the devil *threw* him *down,* and tare (him).
Gal. 4:27. *break forth* and cry, thou that

ῥῆμα, reema.

Mat. 4: 4. but by every *word* that proceedeth
　5:11. shall say all manner of evil (lit. every evil *word*) against you falsely,
　12:36. That every idle *word* that men
　18:16. every *word* may be established.
　26:75. Peter remembered the *word* of Jesus,
　27:14. answered him to never a *word ;*
Mar 9:32. understood not that *saying,*
　14:72. the *word* that Jesus said unto him,
Lu. 1:37. with God no*thing* shall be impossible.
　　38. be it unto me according to thy *word.*
　　65. and all these *sayings* were noised
　2:15. and see this *thing* which is come
　　17. made known abroad the *saying*
　　19. But Mary kept all these *things,*
　　29. depart in peace, according to thy *word :*
　　50. understood not the *saying* which
　　51. his mother kept all these *sayings* in her heart.
　3: 2. the *word* of God came unto John
　4: 4. but by every *word* of God.
　5: 5. at thy *word* I will let down the net.
　7: 1. when he had ended all his *sayings*
　9:45. they understood not this *saying,*
　　— they feared to ask him of that *saying.*
　18:34. and this *saying* was hid from them,
　20:26. they could not take hold of his *words*
　24: 8. And they remembered his *words,*
　　11. their *words* seemed to them as idle
Joh. 3:34. speaketh the *words* of God:
　5:47. how shall ye believe my *words ?*
　6:63. the *words* that I speak unto you,
　　68. thou hast the *words* of eternal life.
　8:20. These *words* spake Jesus in the
　　47. He that is of God heareth God's *words:*
　10:21. These are not the *words* of him that
　12:47. if any man hear my *words,*
　　48. and receiveth not my *words,*
　14:10. the *words* that I speak unto you
　15: 7. and my *words* abide in you,
　17: 8. I have given unto them the *words* which
Acts 2:14. and hearken to my *words :*
　5:20. all the *words* of this life.
　　32. we are his witnesses of these *things ;*
　6:11. blasphemous *words* against Moses,
　　13. blasphemous *words* against this holy
　10:22. and to hear *words* of thee.
　　37. That *word,* (I say,) ye know; which
　　44. While Peter yet spake these *words,*.
　11:14. Who shall tell thee *words,*
　　16. remembered I the *word* of the Lord,
　13:42. besought that these *words* might
　16:38. the serjeants told these *words*
　26:25. but speak forth the *words* of truth and
　28:25. after that Paul had spoken one *word,*
Ro. 10: 8. The *word* is nigh thee,
　　— the *word* of faith, which we preach;
　　17. and hearing by the *word* of God.
　　18. and their *words* unto the ends of
2Co.12: 4. and heard unspeakable *words,*
　13: 1. shall every *word* be established.
Eph 5:26. the washing of water by the *word,*
　6:17. the sword of the Spirit, which is the *word* of God:
Heb 1: 3. all things by the *word* of his power,
　6: 5. have tasted the good *word* of God,
　11: 3. were framed by the *word* of God,
　12:19. and the voice of *words ;*
1Pet. 1:25. But the *word* of the Lord endureth for ever. And this is the *word* which by

2Pet.3: 2. That ye may be mindful of the *words*
Jude 17. remember ye the *words* which were spoken
before of the apostles
Rev.17:17. until the *words* of God shall be fulfilled.

ῥήσσω see ῥήγνυμι.

ῥήτωρ, *reetor.*

Acts24: 1.(with) a certain *orator* (named)

ῥητῶς, *reetos.*

1Ti. 4: 1. the Spirit speaketh *expressly,*

ῥίζα, *riza.*

Mat. 3:10. the ax is laid unto the *root* of the
13: 6. because they had no *root,*
21. Yet hath he not *root* in himself,
Mar 4: 6. because it had no *root,*
17. And have no *root* in themselves,
11:20. dried up from the *roots.*
Lu. 3: 9. the axe is laid unto the *root* of the
8:13. and these have no *root,*
Ro. 11:16. and if the *root* (be) holy, so (are)
17. partakest of the *root* and fatness of
18. thou bearest not the *root,* but the *root* thee
15:12. There shall be a *root* of Jesse,
1Ti. 6:10. the love of money is the *root* of all evil:
Heb12:15. lest any *root* of bitterness springing up
Rev. 5: 5. the *Root* of David, hath prevailed
22:16. I am the *root* and the offspring of David,

ῥιζόομαι, *rizoümai.*

Eph. 3:17(18). *being rooted* and grounded in love,
Col. 2: 7. *Rooted* and built up in him,

ῥιπή, *ripee.*

1Co.15:52. in the *twinkling* of an eye,

ῥιπίζομαι, *ripizomai.*

Jas. 1: 6. driven with the wind and *tossed.*

ῥίπτω, *ripto.*

Mat. 9:36. and were *scattered abroad,* as sheep
15:30. and *cast* them *down* at Jesus' feet ;
27: 5. And he *cast down* the pieces of silver
Lu. 4:35. *when* the devil *had thrown* him
17: 2. and he *cast* into the sea,
Acts22:23. And as they cried out, and *cast off* (their)
clothes,
27:19. we *cast out* with our own hands
29. they *cast* four anchors out of the stern,
and

ῥοιζηδόν, *roizeedon.*

2Pet.3:10. shall pass away *with a great noise,*

ῥομφαία, *romphaia.*

Lu. 2:35. Yea, a *sword* shall pierce through
Rev. 1:16. a sharp twoedged *sword :*
2:12. which hath the sharp *sword*
16. with the *sword* of my mouth.
6: 8. to kill with *sword,*
19:15. out of his mouth goeth a sharp *sword,*
21. slain with the *sword* of him that sat

ῥύμη, *rumee.*

Mat. 6: 2. and in the *streets,* that they may
Lu. 14:21. into the streets and *lanes* of the city,
Acts 9:11. Arise, and go into the *street* which is
called Straight,
12:10. passed on through one *street ;*

ῥυπαρία, *ruparia.*

Jas. 1:21. lay apart all *filthiness* and superfluity of

ῥυπαρός, *ruparos.*

Jas. 2: 2. a poor man in *vile* raiment ;

ῥύπος, *rupos.*

1Pet. 3:21. the putting away of the *filth* of the flesh,

ῥυπόω, *rupoö.*

Rev.22:11. he *which is filthy, let* him *be filthy* still:

ῥύσις, *rusis.*

Mar 5:25. which had an *issue* of blood
Lu. 8:43. having an *issue* of blood
44. her *issue* of blood stanched.

ῥυτίς, *rutis.*

Eph 5:27. or *wrinkle,* or any such thing ;

ῥύομαι, *ruomai.*

Mat. 6:13. but *deliver* us from evil:
27:43. *let* him *deliver* him now,
Lu. 1:74. that we *being delivered* out of
11: 4. but *deliver* us from evil.
Ro. 7:24. who *shall deliver* me from the body of this
death?
11:26. out of Sion the *Deliverer,*
15:31. That I *may be delivered* from
2Co. 1:10. Who *delivered* us from so great a death,
and *doth deliver :* in whom we trust that
he *will* yet *deliver* (us);
Col. 1:13. *hath delivered* us from the power
1Th. 1:10. Jesus, *which delivered* us from the wrath
2Th. 3: 2. that we *may be delivered* from
2Ti. 3:11. the Lord *delivered* me.
4:17. and I *was delivered* out of the mouth of
the lion.
18. the Lord *shall deliver* me
2Pet. 2: 7. And *delivered* just Lot,
9. The Lord knoweth how *to deliver*

ῥώννυμαι, rōnnumai.

Acts15:29. Fare ye *well*.
23:30. to say before thee what (they had) against him. *Farewell*.

'σαϐαχθανί, saḅakthani.

Mat.27:46. Eli, Eli, lama *sabacthani*? that is to say, My God, my God, why hast thou forsaken me?
Mar15:34. Eloi, Eloi, lama *sabacthani*? which is,... why hast thou forsaken me?

σαϐαώθ, sabaōth.

Ro. 9:29. Except the Lord of *Sabaoth* had left
Jas. 5: 4. are entered into the ears of the Lord of *sabaoth* (i. e. of *hosts*)

σαϐϐατισμός, sabbatismos.

Heb 4: 9. There remaineth therefore a *rest* to the

σάϐϐατον, σάϐϐατα, sabbaton, & sabbata.

Note.—Those which are the cases of σάϐϐατον, a noun of the second declension, and in the singular, have the figure ². Those which are of the third declension, and are neut. plur., are marked ³.

Mat.12: 1. Jesus went on the *sabbath day* ³ through
2. lawful to do upon the *sabbath day*. ²
5. on the *sabbath days* ³ the priests in the temple profane the *sabbath*, ²
8. is Lord even of the *sabbath day*. ²
10. lawful to heal on the *sabbath days*? ³
11. if it fall into a pit on the *sabbath day*, ³
12. is lawful to do well on the *sabbath days*. ³
24:20. neither on the *sabbath day* : ²
28: 1. In the end of the *sabbath*, ³ as it began to dawn toward the first (day) of the *week*, ³
Mar 1:21. on the *sabbath day* ³ he entered into
2:23. the corn fields on the *sabbath day* ; ³
24. why do they on the *sabbath day* ³
27. The *sabbath* ² was made for man, and not man for the *sabbath* : ²
28. is Lord also of the *sabbath*. ²
3: 2. heal him on the *sabbath day* ; ³
4. to do good on the *sabbath days*, ³
6. 2. And when the *sabbath day* ² was come,
16: 1. And when the *sabbath* ² was past,
2. in the morning the first (day) of the *week*, ³
9. risen early the first (day) of the *week*, ²
Lu. 4:16. the synagogue on the *sabbath* ³ day,
31. taught them on the *sabbath days*. ³
6: 1. on the second *sabbath* ² after the first,
2. lawful to do on the *sabbath days* ? ³
5. Lord also of the *sabbath*. ²
6. to pass also on another *sabbath*, ²
7. whether he would heal on the *sabbath day* ; ²
9. lawful on the *sabbath days* ³ to do good,
13:10. in one of the synagogues on the *sabbath*. ³
14. had healed on the *sabbath day*, ²
— and not on the *sabbath* ² day.
15. doth not each one of you on the *sabbath* ²
16. be loosed from this bond on the *sabbath* ² day?

Lu..14: 1. to eat bread on the *sabbath day*, ²
3. Is it lawful to heal on the *sabbath day* ? ²
5. pull him out on the *sabbath* ² day?
18:12. I fast twice in the *week*, ²
23:54. and the *sabbath* ² drew on.
56. and rested the *sabbath day* ²
24: 1. upon the first (day) of the *week*, ³
Joh. 5: 9. the same day was the *sabbath*. ²
10. It is the *sabbath day* : ²
16. done these things on the *sabbath day*. ²
18. he not only had broken the *sabbath*, ²
7:22. ye on the *sabbath day* ² circumcise
23. If a man on the *sabbath day* ²
— whole on the *sabbath day* ? ²
9:14. And it was the *sabbath day* ² when
16. he keepeth not the *sabbath day*. ²
19:31. upon the cross on the *sabbath day*, ² for that *sabbath* ² *day* was an high day,
20: 1. The first (day) of the *week* ³
19. the first (day) of the *week*, ³
Acts 1:12. a *sabbath day's* ² journey.
13:14. into the synagogue on the *sabbath* ³ day,
27. which are read every *sabbath day*, ²
42. preached to them the next *sabbath*. ²
44. And the next *sabbath* ² *day* came
15:21. read in the synagogues every *sabbath day*. ²
16:13. And on the *sabbath* ³ (lit. the day of the *sabbath*) we went out
17: 2. three *sabbath days* ³ reasoned
18: 4. in the synagogue every *sabbath*, ²
20: 7. the first (day) of the *week*, ³
1Co.16: 2. Upon the first (day) of the *week* ³ let·
Col. 2:16. new moon, or of the *sabbath* ³ (days):

σαγήνη, sageenee.

Mat.13:47. kingdom of heaven is like unto a *net*,

σαίνω, saino.

1Th. 3: 3. That no man should *be moved* by these

σάκκος, sakkos.

Mat.11:21. long ago in *sackcloth* and ashes.
Lu. 10:13. sitting in *sackcloth* and ashes.
Rev. 6:12. black as *sackcloth* of hair,
11: 3. clothed in *sackcloth*.

σαλεύω, saluo.

Mat.11: 7. A reed *shaken* with the wind?
24:29. the powers of the heavens *shall be shaken*:
Mar13:25. powers that are in heaven *shall be shaken*.
Lu. 6:38. pressed down, and *shaken together*,
48. and could not *shake* it:
7:24. A reed *shaken* with the wind?
21:26. the powers of heaven *shall be shaken*.
Acts 2:25. that I *should* not *be moved*:
4:31. the place *was shaken* where they
16:26. foundations of the prison *were shaken*:
17:13. *and stirred up* the people.
2Th. 2: 2. That ye *be* not soon *shaken* in mind,
Heb 12:26. Whose voice then *shook* the earth:
27. of those things *that are shaken*,
— that those things *which cannot be shaken* (lit. the things not *shaken*) may remain.

σάλον, salon.

Lu. 21:25. the sea and the *waves* roaring;

σάλπιγξ, salpinx.

Mat.24:31. with a great sound of a *trumpet*,
1Co.14: 8. if the *trumpet* give an uncertain
15:52. at the last *trump* :
1Th. 4:16. and with the *trump* of God:
Heb 12:19. And the sound of a *trumpet*, and
Rev. 1:10. a great voice, as of a *trumpet*,
4: 1. as it were of a *trumpet*
8: 2. to them were given seven *trumpets*.
6. which had the seven *trumpets*
13. the other voices of the *trumpet*
9:14. the sixth angel which had the *trumpet*,

σαλπίζω, salpizo.

Mat. 6: 2. do not *sound a trumpet* before thee,
1Co.15:52. for the *trumpet shall sound*,
Rev. 8: 6. prepared themselves to *sound*.
7. The first angel *sounded*,
8. the second angel *sounded*,
10. And the third angel *sounded*,
12. And the fourth angel *sounded*,
13. angels, which are yet *to sound* !
9: 1. And the fifth angel *sounded*,
13. And the sixth angel *sounded*,
10: 7. when he shall begin *to sound*,
11:15. And the seventh angel *sounded* ;

σαλπιστής, salpistees.

Rev.18:22. and of pipers, and *trumpeters*,

σανδάλιον, sandalion.

Mar 6: 9. But (be) shod with *sandals* ;
Acts12: 8. and bind on thy *sandals*.

σανίς, sanis.

Acts27:44. And the rest, some on *boards*, and some

σαπρός, sapros.

Mat. 7:17. but a *corrupt* tree bringeth forth
18. neither (can) a *corrupt* tree
12:33. or else make the tree *corrupt*, and his
fruit *corrupt* :
13:48. but cast the *bad* away.
Lu. 6:43. a good tree bringeth not forth *corrupt*
fruit ; neither doth a *corrupt* tree bring
Eph. 4:29. Let no *corrupt* communication

σάπφειρος, sapphiros.

Rev.21:19. the second, *sapphire* ;

σαργάνη, sarganee.

2Co.11:33. in a *basket* was I let down

σάρδινος, sardinos

Rev. 4: 3. like a jasper and a *sardine* stone .

σάρδιος, sardios.

Rev.21:20. the sixth, *sardius* ;

σαρδόνυξ, sardonux.

Rev.21:20. The fifth, *sardonyx* ;

σαρκικός, sarkikos.

Ro. 7:14. but I am *carnal*, sold under sin.
15:27. to minister unto them in *carnal* things.
1Co. 3: 1. but as unto *carnal*,
3. For ye are yet *carnal* :
— are ye not *carnal*, and walk as men ?
4. are ye not *carnal* ?
9:11. if we shall reap your *carnal* things ?
2Co. 1:12. not with *fleshly* wisdom, but
10: 4. the weapons of our warfare (are) not
carnal,
Heb 7:16. not after the law of a *carnal* commandment,
1Pet. 2:11. abstain from *fleshly* lusts.

σάρκινος, sarkinos.

2Co. 3: 3. but in *fleshy* tables of the heart.

σάρξ, sarx.

Mat.16:17. *flesh* and blood hath not revealed (it)
19: 5. and they twain shall be one *flesh* ?
6. are no more twain, but one *flesh*.
24:22. there should no *flesh* be saved.
26:41. willing, but the *flesh* (is) weak.
Mar 10: 8. shall be one *flesh* : so then they are no
more twain, but one *flesh*.
13:20. no *flesh* should be saved:
14:38. but the *flesh* (is) weak.
Lu. 3: 6. And all *flesh* shall see the salvation .
24:39. a spirit hath not *flesh* and bones,
Joh. 1:13. nor of the will of the *flesh*,
14. And the Word was made *flesh*,
3: 6. That which is born of the *flesh* is *flesh* ;
6:51. and the bread that I will give is my *flesh*,
52. give us (his) *flesh* to eat?
53. Except ye eat the *flesh* of the Son
54. Whoso eateth my *flesh*,
55. For my *flesh* is meat indeed,
56. He that eateth my *flesh*,
63. the *flesh* profiteth nothing:
8:15. Ye judge after the *flesh* ;
17: 2. given him power over all *flesh*,
Acts 2:17. pour out of my Spirit upon all *flesh* :
26. also my *flesh* shall rest in hope :
30. of his loins, according to the *flesh*, he
31. neither his *flesh* did see corruption.
Ro. 1: 3. the seed of David according to the *flesh* ;
2:28. which is outward in the *flesh* :
3:20. there shall no *flesh* be justified
4: 1. our father as pertaining to the *flesh*, hath
found ?
6:19. because of the infirmity of your *flesh* :
7: 5. For when we were in the *flesh*,
18. in me, that is, in my *flesh*,
25. but with the *flesh* the law of sin.
8: 1. who walk not after the *flesh*,
3. it was weak through the *flesh*,

Ro. 8: 3. in the likeness of sinful *flesh*, and for sin, condemned sin in the *flesh* :

4. who walk not after the *flesh*,

5. they that are after the *flesh* do mind the things of the *flesh* ;

6. to be *carnally* minded (is) death ; (lit. the minding of the *flesh*)

7. the *carnal* mind (is) (lit. the minding of the *flesh*) enmity against God:

8. they that are in the *flesh* cannot

9. ye are not in the *flesh*, but in the

12. we are debtors, not to the *flesh*, to live after the *flesh*.

13. For if ye live after the *flesh*, ye

9: 3. my kinsmen according to the *flesh* :

5. of whom as concerning the *flesh* Christ

8. They which are the children of the *flesh*,

11:14. emulation (them which are) my *flesh*,

13:14. make not provision for the *flesh*, to

1Co. 1:26. not many wise men after the *flesh*,

29. That no *flesh* should glory

5: 5. unto Satan for the destruction of the *flesh*,

6:16. two, saith he, shall be one *flesh*.

7:28. such shall have trouble in the *flesh* :

10:18. Behold Israel after the *flesh* :

15:39. All *flesh* (is) not the same *flesh* : but (there is) one (kind of) *flesh* of men, another *flesh* of beasts,

50. *flesh* and blood cannot inherit the

2Co. 1:17. do I purpose according to the *flesh*,

4:11. be made manifest in our mortal *flesh*.

5:16. no man after the *flesh* : yea, though we have known Christ after the *flesh*,

7: 1. from all filthiness of the *flesh* and spirit,

5. our *flesh* had no rest, but we were

10: 2. as if we walked according to the *flesh*.

3. in the *flesh*, we do not war after the *flesh* :

11:18. that many glory after the *flesh*,

12: 7. a thorn in the *flesh*, the messenger of

Gal. 1:16. I conferred not with *flesh* and blood:

2:16. shall no *flesh* be justified.

20. the life which I now live in the *flesh*

3: 3. are ye now made perfect by the *flesh* ?

4:13. through infirmity of the *flesh* I

14. temptation which was in my *flesh*

23. was born after the *flesh* ;

29. he that was born after the *flesh*

5:13. liberty for an occasion to the *flesh*, but

16. ye shall not fulfil the lust of the *flesh*.

17. the *flesh* lusteth against the Spirit, and the Spirit against the *flesh* :

19. the works of the *flesh* are manifest,

24. have crucified the *flesh* with the

6: 8. he that soweth to his *flesh* shall of the *flesh* reap corruption ;

12. to make a fair shew in the *flesh*,

13. that they may glory in your *flesh*.

Eph. 2: 3. in the lusts of our *flesh*, fulfilling the desires of the *flesh* and of the mind ;

11. in time past Gentiles in the *flesh*,

— called the Circumcision in the *flesh*

15. Having abolished in his *flesh* the enmity,

5:29. no man ever yet hated his own *flesh* ;

30. of his *flesh*, and of his bones.

31. they two shall be one *flesh*.

6: 5. masters according to the *flesh*,

12. we wrestle not against *flesh* and blood,

Phi. 1:22. But if I live in the *flesh*, this

24. Nevertheless to abide in the *flesh*

3: 3. and have no confidence in the *flesh*.

4. might also have confidence in the *flesh*.

— whereof he might trust in the *flesh*,

Col. 1:22. In the body of his *flesh* through death,

24. in my *flesh* for his body's sake,

2: 1. as have not seen my face in the *flesh* ;

5. absent in the *flesh*, yet am I

11. putting off the body of the sins of the *flesh*

13. the uncircumcision of your *flesh*,

18. puffed up by his *fleshly* mind,

23. to the satisfying of the *flesh*.

3:22. masters according to the *flesh* ;

1Ti. 3:16. God was manifest in the *flesh*,

Philem.16. both in the *flesh*, and in the Lord ?

Heb. 2:14. children are partakers of *flesh* and blood,

5: 7. Who in the days of his *flesh*,

9:10. and *carnal* ordinances,

13. to the purifying of the *flesh* :

10:20. through the veil, that is to say, his *flesh* ;

12: 9. we have had fathers of our *flesh*

Jas. 5: 3. shall eat your *flesh* as it were fire.

1Pet. 1:24. For all *flesh* (is) as grass,

3:18. put to death in the *flesh*, but

21. putting away of the filth of the *flesh*,

4: 1. hath suffered for us in the *flesh*,

— he that hath suffered in the *flesh*

2. live the rest of (his) time in the *flesh*

6. judged according to men in the *flesh*,

2Pet. 2:10. that walk after the *flesh* in the lust

18. they allure through the lusts of the *flesh*,

1Joh. 2:16. the lust of the *flesh*, and the lust

4: 2. Jesus Christ is come in the *flesh*

3. Jesus Christ is come in the *flesh*

2Joh. 7. Jesus Christ is come in the *flesh*.

Jude 7. going after strange *flesh*,

8. dreamers defile the *flesh*, despise

23. even the garment spotted by the *flesh*.

Rev.17:16. and shall eat her *flesh*, and burn her

19:18. *flesh* of kings, and the *flesh* of captains, and the *flesh* of mighty men, and the *flesh*,

— and the *flesh* of all (men, both)

21. fowls were filled with their *flesh*.

σαρόω, saroō.

Mat.12:44. *swept*, and garnished.

Lu. 11:25. he findeth (it) *swept* and garnished.

15: 8. doth not light a candle, and *sweep* the

σαυτοῦ, ῷ, όν see σεαυτοῦ.

σάτον, saton.

Mat.13:33. hid in three *measures* of meal,

Lu. 13:21. hid in three *measures* of meal,

σϐέννυμι, sbennumi.

Mat.12:20. smoking flax *shall* he not *quench*,

25: 8. for our lamps *are gone out*.

Mar 9:44. and the fire *is* not *quenched*.

46. and the fire *is* not *quenched*.

48. and the fire *is* not *quenched*.

Eph. 6:16. able *to* quench all the fiery darts

1Th. 5:19. *Quench* not the Spirit.

Heb 11:34. *Quenched* the violence of fire,

σέ, se.

From σύ.

Mat. 4: 6. they shall bear *thee* up,

Mat. 5:25. deliver *thee* to the judge, and the judge deliver *thee*

29. thy right eye offend *thee*,
30. thy right hand offend *thee*,
39. whosoever shall smite *thee*
41. shall compel *thee* to go a mile,
42. Give to him that asketh *thee*,

9:22. thy faith hath made *thee* whole.

14:28. bid me come unto *thee*

18: 8. if thy hand or thy foot offend *thee*,
9. And if thine eye offend *thee*,
15. thy brother shall trespass against *thee*,
33. Shouldest not *thou* also have had
— even as I had pity on *thee?*

20:13. I do *thee* no wrong:

25:21. I will make *thee* ruler
23. I will make *thee* ruler
24. I knew *thee* that thou art
27. *Thou* oughtest (lit. it behoved *thee*)
37. when saw we *thee* an hungred,
38. When saw we *thee* a stranger,
39. Or when saw we *thee* sick, or in prison, and came unto *thee?*
44. when saw we *thee* an hungred,

26:18. keep the passover at *thy house* (πρός σε)
35. yet will I not deny *thee*.
63. I adjure *thee* by the living God,
68. Who is he that smote *thee?*
73. thy speech bewrayeth *thee*.

Mar 1:24. I know *thee* who thou art,
3:32. thy brethren without seek for *thee*.
5: 7. I adjure *thee* by God,
19. hath had compassion on *thee*.
31. the multitude thronging *thee*,
34. thy faith hath made *thee* whole ;
9:17. I have brought unto *thee* my son,
43. And if thy hand offend *thee*,
45. And if thy foot offend *thee*,
47. And if thine eye offend *thee*,
10:49. rise ; he calleth *thee*.
52. thy faith hath made *thee* whole.
14:31. I will not deny *thee*

Lu. 1:19. and am sent to speak unto *thee*,
35. The Holy Ghost shall come upon *thee*,
2:48. have sought *thee* sorrowing.
4:10. charge over thee, to keep *thee :*
11. they shall bear *thee* up,
34. I know *thee* who thou art ;
6:29. And unto him that smiteth *thee*
30. Give to every man that asketh of *thee ;*
7: 7. myself worthy to come unto *thee :*
20. John Baptist hath sent us unto *thee*,
50. Thy faith hath saved *thee ;*
8:20. desiring to see *thee*.
45. the multitude throng *thee* and press
48. thy faith hath made *thee* whole ;
11:27. Blessed (is) the womb that bare *thee*,
36. shining of a candle doth give *thee* light.
12:58. lest he hale *thee* to the judge, and the judge deliver *thee* to the officer, and the officer cast *thee* into prison.
13:31. for Herod will kill *thee*.
14: 9. And he that bade *thee* and him
10. he that bade *thee* cometh,
12. lest they also bid *thee* again,
18. I pray *thee* have me excused.
19. I pray *thee* have me excused.
16:27. I pray *thee* therefore, father,
17: 3. thy brother trespass against *thee*,
4. against *thee* seven times in a day, and seven times in a day turn again to *thee*,
19. thy faith hath made *thee* whole.

Lu. 18:42. thy faith hath saved *thee*.
19:21. For I feared *thee*,
22. Out of thine own mouth will I judge *thee*,
43. For the days shall come upon *thee*,
— and compass *thee* round, and keep *thee* in on every side,
44. And shall lay *thee* even with the ground,
22:64. Prophesy, who is it that smote *thee?*

Joh. 1:48(49). Before that Philip called *thee*, when thou wast under the fig tree, I saw *thee*.
50(51). I saw *thee* under the fig tree,
7:20. who goeth about to kill *thee?*
8:10. hath no man condemned *thee?*
11. Neither do I condemn *thee :*
10:33. For a good work we stone *thee* not ;
11: 8. Jews of late sought to stone *thee ;*
28. and calleth for *thee*.
13: 8. If I wash *thee* not,
16:30. that any man should ask *thee :*
17: 1. that thy Son also may glorify *thee :*
3. that they might know *thee*
4. I have glorified *thee* on the earth:
11. and I come to *thee*.
13. And now come I to *thee ;*
25. the world hath not known *thee :* but I have known *thee*,
18:26. Did not I see *thee* in the garden with him?
35. priests have delivered *thee* unto me:
19:10. to crucify *thee*, and have power to release *thee ?*
21:15. Lord ; thou knowest that I love *thee*.
16. thou knowest that I love *thee*.
17. thou knowest that I love *thee*.
18. another shall gird *thee*,
20. which is he that betrayeth *thee?*
22. what (is that) to *thee?*
23. what (is that) to *thee?*

Acts 4:30. By)(stretching forth thine hand to heal ;
5: 3. filled thine heart)(to lie to the Holy
9. and shall carry *thee* out.
7:27. Who made *thee* a ruler and a
34. I will send *thee* into Egypt.
35. saying, Who made *thee* a ruler
8:23. I perceive that *thou* art in the gall of
9: 6. it shall be told thee what *thou* must do.
34. Jesus Christ maketh *thee* whole:
10: 6. shall tell thee what *thou* oughtest to do.
19. Behold, three men seek *thee*.
22. to send for *thee* into his house,
33. therefore I sent to *thee ;*
11:14. Who shall tell *thee* words,
13:11. the hand of the Lord (is) upon *thee*,
33. this day have I begotten *thee*.
47. I have set *thee* to be a light of the Gentiles, that *thou* shouldest be for
18:10. no man shall set on thee to hurt *thee :*
21:37. May I speak unto *thee?*
22:14. hath chosen *thee*, that thou shouldest know (lit. hath chosen *thee* to know)
19. them that believed on *thee :*
21. I will send *thee* far hence unto
23: 3. God shall smite *thee*,
11. so must *thou* bear witness also at Rome.
18. to bring this young man unto *thee*,
20. have agreed to desire *thee* that
30. I sent straightway to *thee*,
24: 4. that I be not further tedious unto *thee*, I pray thee that *thou* wouldest hear us
8. accusers to come unto *thee :*
10. that *thou* hast been of many years
25. I will call for *thee*.
26: 3. *thee* to be expert in all customs

Acts26:16. to make *thee* a minister and a witness
17. Delivering *thee* from the people,
— unto whom now I send *thee*,
24. much learning doth make *thee* mad.
29. that not only *thou*, but also all
27:24. *thou* must be brought before Cæsar:
Ro. 2: 4. goodness of God leadeth *thee* to
27. judge *thee*, who by the letter
3: 4. overcome when *thou* art judged.
4:17. I have made *thee* a father of many
9:17. have I raised *thee* up,
11:18. bearest not the root, but the root *thee*.
22. but toward *thee*, goodness,
15: 3. of them that reproached *thee*
1Co. 4: 7. For who maketh *thee* to differ
8:10. For if any man see *thee*
Phi. 4: 3. And I intreat *thee* also,
1Ti. 1: 3. As I besought *thee* to abide still
18. prophecies which went before on *thee*,
3:14. hoping to come unto *thee* shortly:
6:14. That *thou* keep (this) commandment
2Ti. 1: 4. Greatly desiring to see *thee*,
6. Wherefore I put *thee* in remembrance
3:15. which are able to make *thee* wise unto
4:21. Eubulus greeteth *thee*,
Tit. 1: 5. For this cause left I *thee* in Crete,
3: 8. I will that *thou* affirm constantly,
12. I shall send Artemas unto *thee*,
15. All that are with me salute *thee*.
Philem.10. I beseech *thee* for my son
18. If he hath wronged *thee*,
23. There salute *thee* Epaphras,
Heb. 1: 5. this day have I begotten *thee* ?
9. thy God, hath anointed *thee*
2:12. will I sing praise unto *thee*.
5: 5. to day have I begotten *thee*.
6:14. blessing I will bless *thee*, and multiplying
I will multiply *thee*.
13: 5. I will never leave *thee*, nor forsake *thee*.
2Joh.   5. And now I beseech *thee*, lady,
13. The children of thy elect sister greet *thee*.
3Joh.   2. that *thou* mayest prosper
14. I shall shortly see *thee*,
— (Our) friends salute *thee*.
Rev. 3: 3. I will come on *thee* as a thief,
— what hour I will come upon *thee*.
9. and to know that I have loved *thee*.
10. I also will keep *thee* from the hour
16. I will spue *thee* out of my mouth.
10:11. *Thou* must prophesy again before
15: 4. Who shall not fear *thee*, O Lord,

σεαυτοῦ, τῷ, τόν, *seautou, to, ton,* also
σαυτοῦ, τῷ, τόν.

Mat. 4: 6. cast *thyself* down:
8: 4. shew *thyself* to the priest,
19:19. love thy neighbour as *thyself*.
22:39. love thy neighbour as *thyself*.
27:40. save *thyself*.
Mar 1:44. shew *thyself* to the priest,
12:31. love thy neighbour as *thyself*.
15:30. Save *thyself*, and come down
Lu. 4: 9. cast *thyself* down from hence:
23. Physician, heal *thyself* :
5:14. shew *thyself* to the priest,
10:27. and thy neighbour as *thyself*.
23:37. the king of the Jews, save *thyself*.
39. save *thyself* and us.
Joh. 1:22. What sayest thou of *thyself* ?
7: 4. shew *thyself* to the world.

Joh. 8:13. Thou bearest record of *thyself* ;
53. whom makest thou *thyself* ?
10:33. makest *thyself* God.
14:22. manifest *thyself* unto us,
17: 5. glorify thou me with *thine own self* with
21:18. thou girdedst *thyself*,
Acts 9:34. make *thy* bed. (lit. for *thyself*)
16:28. Do *thyself* no harm:
26: 1. permitted to speak for *thyself*.
Ro. 2: 1. thou condemnest *thyself* ;
5. treasurest up unto *thyself*
19. that *thou thyself* art a guide
21. teachest thou not *thyself* ?
14:22. have (it) to *thyself*
Gal. 6: 1. considering *thyself*, lest thou also
1Ti. 4: 7. exercise *thyself* (rather) unto godliness.
16. Take heed unto *thyself*,
— thou shalt both save *thyself*, and
5:22. keep *thyself* pure.
2Ti. 2:15. Study to shew *thyself* approved
4:11. bring him with *thee* :
Tit. 2: 7. In all things shewing *thyself* a pattern
Philem.19. owest unto me even *thine own self*
Jas. 2: 8. thy neighbour as *thyself*,

σεβάζομαι, *sebazomai.*

Ro. 1:25. and *worshipped* and served the creature

σέβασμα, *sebasma.*

Acts17:23. and beheld your *devotions*,
2Th. 2: 4. that is called God, or *that is worshipped* ;

σεβαστός, *sebastos,* adj.

Acts27: 1. a centurion of *Augustus'* band. (or it may
be rendered, of the *imperial* guard)

σέβομαι, *sebomai.*

Mat.15: 9. in vain they *do worship* me,
Mar 7: 7. in vain *do* they *worship* me,
Acts13:43. many of the Jews and *religious* proselytes
50. the *devout* and honourable women,
16:14. *which worshipped* God, heard (us) ;
17: 4. of the *devout* Greeks a great multitude,
17. and with the *devout* persons,
18: 7. Justus, (one) *that worshipped* God,
13. persuadeth men *to worship* God contrary
19:27. Asia and the world *worshippeth*.

σειρά, *sira.*

2Pet. 2: 4. into *chains* of darkness,

σεισμός, *sismos.*

Mat. 8:24. there arose a great *tempest* in the sea,
24: 7. and *earthquakes*, in divers places.
27:54. saw the *earthquake*, and those things
28: 2. behold, there was a great *earthquake* :
Mar 13: 8. there shall be *earthquakes* in divers
Lu. 21:11. great *earthquakes* shall be in
Acts16:26. there was a great *earthquake*, so that
Rev. 6:12. lo, there was a great *earthquake* ;
8: 5. lightnings, and an *earthquake*.
11:13. was there a great *earthquake*,

Rev.11:13. and in the *earthquake* were slain
    19. and an *earthquake*, and great hail.
16:18. and there was a great *earthquake*,
    — so mighty an *earthquake*,

σείω, *sīo*.

Mat.21:10. all the city *was moved*, saying,
    27:51. and the earth *did quake*, and the rocks
    28: 4. the keepers *did shake*, and became as dead
Heb12:26. I *shake* not the earth only,
Rev. 6:13. *when* she *is shaken* of a mighty wind.

σελήνη, *seleenee*.

Mat.24:29. the *moon* shall not give her light,
Mar13:24. the *moon* shall not give her light,
Lu. 21:25. signs in the sun, and in the *moon*,
Acts 2:20. and the *moon* into blood,
1Co.15:41. and another glory of the *moon*,
Rev. 6:12. and the *moon* became as blood;
    8:12. and the third part of the *moon*,
    12: 1. and the *moon* under her feet,
    21:23. no need of the sun, neither of the *moon*,

σεληνιάζομαι, *seleeniazomai*.

Mat. 4:24. and those *which were lunatick*,
    17:15. for he *is lunatick*,

σεμίδαλις, *semidalis*.

Rev.18:13. and *fine flour*, and wheat,

σεμνός, *semnos*.

Phi. 4: 8. whatsoever things (are) *honest*,
1Ti. 3: 8. Likewise (must) the deacons (be) *grave*,
    11. Even so (must their) wives (be) *grave*,
Tit. 2: 2. the aged men be sober, *grave*,

σεμνότης, *semnotees*.

1Ti. 2: 2. in all godliness and *honesty*.
    3: 4. children in subjection with all *gravity*;
Tit. 2: 7. uncorruptness, *gravity*, sincerity,

σημαίνω, *seemaino*.

Joh.12:33. *signifying* what death he should die.
    18:32. *signifying* what death he
    21:19. *signifying* by what death he should
Acts11:28. and *signified* by the spirit that
    25:27. *to signify* the crimes (laid) against him.
Rev. 1: 1. and *signified* (it) by his angel unto

σημεῖον, *seemion*.

Mat.12:38. we would see a *sign* from thee.
    39. seeketh after a *sign*; and there shall no
    sign be given to it, but the *sign* of the
    prophet Jonas:
16. 1. would shew them a *sign*
    3. (discern) the *signs* of the times?
    4. seeketh after a *sign*; and there shall no
    sign be given unto it. but the *sign* of
    the prophet Jonas.

Mat.24: 3. and what (shall be) the *sign* of thy
    24. and shall shew great *signs*
    30. shall appear the *sign* of the Son of man
    26:48. gave them a *sign*, saying,
Mar 8:11. seeking of him a *sign* from heaven,
    12. this generation seek after a *sign*?
    — no *sign* be given unto this generation.
    13: 4. and what (shall be) the *sign* when all
    22. and shall shew *signs* and wonders,
    16:17. And these *signs* shall follow them
    20. confirming the word with *signs* following.
Lu. 2:12. And this (shall be) a *sign* unto you;
    34. and for a *sign* which shall be spoken
    11:16. sought of him a *sign* from heaven.
    29. they seek a *sign*; and there shall no *sign*
    be given it, but the *sign* of Jonas the
    prophet.
    30. For as Jonas was a *sign* unto the
    21: 7. what *sign* (will there be) when
    11. and great *signs* shall there be
    25. And there shall be *signs* in the sun,
    23: 8. to have seen some *miracle*
Joh. 2:11. This beginning of *miracles*
    18. What *sign* shewest thou unto us,
    23. saw the *miracles* which he did.
    3: 2. can do these *miracles*
    4:48. Except ye see *signs* and wonders,
    54. This (is) again the second *miracle*
    6: 2. because they saw his *miracles*
    14. they had seen the *miracle* that
    26. not because ye saw the *miracles*,
    30. What *sign* shewest thou then,
    7:31. will he do more *miracles*
    9:16. that is a sinner do such *miracles*?
    10:41. John did no *miracle*:
    11:47. this man doeth many *miracles*.
    12:18. he had done this *miracle*.
    37. he had done so many *miracles*
    20:30. And many other *signs* truly did Jesus
Acts 2:19. and *signs* in the earth beneath;
    22. by miracles and wonders and *signs*,
    43. many wonders and *signs* were done
    4:16. a notable *miracle* hath been done
    22. on whom this *miracle* of healing
    30. that *signs* and wonders may be done
    5:12. were many *signs* and wonders wrought
    6: 8. did great wonders and *miracles*
    7:36. had shewed wonders and *signs* in the
    8: 6. seeing the *miracles* which he did.
    13. beholding the miracles and *signs* which
    14: 3. and granted *signs* and wonders to be done
    15:12. declaring what *miracles* and wonders
Ro. 4:11. And he received the *sign* of circumcision,
    15:19. Through mighty *signs* and wonders,
1Co. 1:22. For the Jews require a *sign*, and the
    14:22. Wherefore tongues are for a *sign*, not
2Co.12:12. Truly the *signs* of an apostle were
    — in *signs*, and wonders, and mighty deeds
2Th. 2: 9. all power and *signs* and lying wonders,
    3:17. which is the *token* in every epistle:
Heb 2: 4. witness, both with *signs* and wonders,
Rev.12: 1. appeared a great *wonder* in heaven;
    3. appeared another *wonder* in heaven;
    13:13. And he doeth great *wonders*,
    14. those *miracles* which he had power to do
    15: 1. And I saw another *sign* in heaven,
    16:14. the spirits of devils, working *miracles*,
    19:20. the false prophet that wrought *miracles*

Note.—In Acts 8:13 some copies read δυνάμεις και σημεῖα μεγάλα γινόμενα, with which the order of words in the English Translation agrees.

σημειόομαι, seemiŏŏmai.

2Th. 3:14. *note* that man, and have no company

σήμερον, seemeron.

Mat. 6:11. Give us *this day* our daily bread.
    30. which *to day* is, and to morrow
    11:23. it would have remained until *this day*.
    16: 3. (It will be) foul weather *to day* :
    21:28. go work *to day* in my vineyard.
    27: 8. called, The field of blood, unto *this day*.
    19. suffered many things *this day* in a dream
    28:15. reported among the Jews until *this day*.
Mar 14:30. That *this day*, (even) in this night,
Lu. 2:11. For unto you is born *this day*
    4:21. *This day* is this scripture fulfilled
    5:26. We have seen strange things *to day*.
    12:28. which is *to day* in the field,
    13:32. and I do cures *to day* and to morrow,
    33. I must walk *to day*, and to morrow,
    19: 5. for *to day* I must abide at thy house.
    9. *This day* is salvation come
    22:34. the cock shall not crow *this day*,
    23:43. *To day* shalt thou be with me
    24:21. *to day* is the third day since
Acts 4: 9. If we *this day* be examined
    13:33. *this day* have I begotten thee.
    19:40. called in question for *this day*'s uproar,
    20.26. I take you to record *this day*,
    22: 3. as ye all are *this day*.
    24:21. I am called in question by you *this day*.
    26: 2. I shall answer for myself *this day*
    29. but also all that hear me *this day*,
    27:33. *This day* is the fourteenth day
Ro. 11: 8. unto this day. (lit. unto the *to day* day)
2Co. 3:14. for until *this day* remaineth
    15. But even unto *this day*, when Moses
Heb 1: 5. *this day* have I begotten thee ?
    3: 7. *To day* if ye will hear his voice,
    13. while it is called *To day* ;
    15. *To day* if ye will hear his voice,
    4: 7. *To day*, after so long a time ;
    — *To day* if ye will hear his voice,
    5: 5. *to day* have I begotten thee.
    13: 8. the same yesterday, and *to day*, and for
       ever.
Jas. 4:13. *To day* or to morrow we will go

σήπω, seepo.

Jas. 5: 2. Your riches *are corrupted*,

σηρικόν, seerihon.

Rev.18:12. and purple, and *silk*, and scarlet,

σής, sees.

Mat. 6:19. where *moth* and rust doth corrupt,
    20. where neither *moth* nor rust
Lu. 12:33. neither *moth* corrupteth.

σητοβρωτος, seetobrōtos.

Jas. 5: 2. and your garments are *motheaten*.

σθενόω, sthenoō.

1Pet.5:10. stablish, *strengthen*, settle (you).

σιαγών, siagon.

Mat. 5:39. smite thee on thy right *cheek*,
Lu. 6:29. smiteth thee on the (one) *cheek*

σιγάω, sigao.

Lu. 9:36. And they *kept* (it) *close*,
    20:26. and *held* their *peace*.
Acts12:17 beckoning unto...*to hold* their *peace*,
    15:12. Then all the multitude *kept silence*,
    13. after they *had held* their *peace*,
Ro. 16:25. of the mystery, *which was kept secret*
1Co.14:28. let him *keep silence* in the church ;
    30. let the first *hold* his *peace*.
    34. Let your women *keep silence* in the

σιγή, sigee.

Acts21:40. And when there was made a great *silence*,
Rev. 8: 1. there was *silence* in heaven

σιδήρεος, sideereos.

Acts12:10. they came unto the *iron* gate
Rev. 2:27. And he shall rule them with a rod *of iron* ;
    9: 9. as it were breastplates *of iron* ;
    12: 5. to rule all nations with a rod *of iron* :
    19:15. he shall rule them with a rod *of iron* :

σίδηρος, sideeroъ.

Rev.18:12. and of brass, and *iron*, and marble,

σικάριος, sikarios.

Acts21:38. men that were *murderers* ?

σίκερα, sikera.

Lu. 1:15. neither wine nor *strong drink* ;

σιμικίνθιον, simikinthion.

Acts19:12. handkerchiefs or *aprons*, and the

σίναπι, sinapi.

Mat.13:31. is like to a grain of *mustard seed*,
    17:20. faith as a grain of *mustard seed*,
Mar 4:31. (It is) like a grain of *mustard seed*,
Lu. 13:19. It is like a grain of *mustard seed*,
    17: 6. faith as a grain of *mustard seed*,

σινδών, sindon.

Mat.27:59. wrapped it in a clean *linen cloth*,
Mar 14:51. having a *linen cloth* cast about
    52. And he left the *linen cloth*,
    15:46. And he bought *fine linen*,
    — and wrapped him in the *linen*,
Lu. 23:53. and wrapped it in *linen*, and laid

σινιάζω, siniazo.

Lu. 22:31. that he may *sift* (you) as wheat:

σιτευτός, sitūtos.

Lu. 15:23. And bring hither the *fatted* calf,
27. hath killed the *fatted* calf,
30. killed for him the *fatted* calf.

σιτιστός, sitistos.

Mat.22: 4. and (my) *fatlings* (are) killed,

σιτομέτριον, sitometrion.

Lu. 12:42. to give (them their) *portion of meat* in due season?

σῖτος, sitos.

Mat. 3:12. and gather his *wheat* into the garner;
13:25. and sowed tares among the *wheat,*
29. ye root up also the *wheat* with them.
30. but gather the *wheat* into my barn.
Mar 4:28. after that the full *corn* in the ear.
Lu. 3:17. will gather the *wheat* into his garner;
16: 7. An hundred measures of *wheat.*
22:31. that he may sift (you) as *wheat :*
Joh.12:24. Except a corn of *wheat* fall into
Acts 7:12. heard that there was *corn* in Egypt,
27:38. and cast out the *wheat* into the sea.
1Co.15:37. it may chance of *wheat,*
Rev. 6: 6. A measure of *wheat* for a penny,
18:13. and fine flour, and *wheat,*

σιωπάω, siōpao.

Mat.20:31. because they *should hold* their *peace :*
26:63. But Jesus *held* his *peace.*
Mar 3: 4. But they *held* their *peace.*
4:39. *Peace,* be still.
9:34. But they *held* their *peace :*
10:48. that he *should hold* his *peace :*
14:61. But he *held* his *peace,*
Lu. 1:20. *dumb,* and not able to speak,
18:39. rebuked him, that he *should hold* his *peace :*
19:40. if these *should hold* their *peace,*
Acts18: 9. speak, and *hold* not thy *peace :*

σκανδαλίζω, scandalizo.

Mat. 5:29. if thy right eye *offend* thee,
30. if thy right hand *offend* thee,
11: 6. whosoever shall not *be offended* in me.
13:21. by and by he *is offended.*
57. And they *were offended* in him.
15:12. that the Pharisees *were offended,* after
17:27. lest we *should offend* them, go thou
18: 6. whoso shall *offend* one of these little
8. if thy hand or thy foot *offend* thee,
9. And if thine eye *offend* thee,
24:10. And then *shall* many *be offended,*
26:31. All ye *shall be offended* because of me
33. Though all (men) *shall be offended* because of thee, (yet) *will* I never *be offended.*
Mar 4:17. immediately they *are offended.*
6: 3. And they *were offended* at him.
9:42. whosoever shall *offend* one of (these)
43. And if thy hand *offend* thee,
45. And if thy foot *offend* thee,
47. And if thine eye *offend* thee,

Mar 14:27. All ye *shall be offended* because of me
29. Although all *shall be offended,*
Lu. 7:23. whosoever *shall* not *be offended* in me.
17: 2. than that he *should offend* one of these
Joh. 6:61. *Doth* this *offend* you?
16: 1. that ye *should* not *be offended.*
Ro. 14:21. stumbleth, or *is offended,*
1Co. 8:13. if meat *make* my brother *to offend,*
— lest I *make* my brother *to offend.*
2Co.11:29. who *is offended,* and I burn not?

σκάνδαλον, scandalon.

Mat.13:41. all *things that offend,*
16:23. thou art an *offence* unto me:
18: 7. Woe unto the world because of *offences !*
for it must needs be that *offences* come;
— by whom the *offence* cometh !
Lu. 17: 1. but that *offences* will come:
Ro. 9:33. and rock of *offence :*
11: 9. a *stumblingblock,* and a recompence
14:13. or an *occasion to fail* in (his) brother's way.
16:17. which cause divisions and *offences*
1Co. 1:23. unto the Jews a *stumblingblock,* and unto
Gal. 5:11. then is the *offence* of the cross ceased.
1Pet.2: 8(7). a stone of stumbling, and a rock of *offence,*
1Joh.2:10. there is none *occasion of stumbling* in him.
Rev. 2:14. to cast a *stumblingblock* before the

σκάπτω, skapto.

Lu. 6:48. and *digged* deep, (lit. who *digged* and deepened)
13: 8. till I *shall dig* about it,
16: 3. I cannot *dig ;* to beg

σκάφη, skaphee.

Acts27:16. much work to come by the *boat :*
30. when they had let down the *boat*
32. cut off the ropes of the *boat,* and let

σκέλος, skelos.

Joh.19:31. that their *legs* might be broken,
32. brake the *legs* of the first, and of
33. they brake not his *legs :*

σκέπασμα, skepasma.

1Ti. 6: 8. having food and *raiment* (lit. *coverings*)

σκευή, skūee.

Acts27:19. we cast out...the *tackling* of the ship.

σκεῦος, skūos.

Mat.12:29. and spoil his *goods,* except
Mar 3:27. and spoil his *goods,* except
11:16. carry (any) *vessel* through the temple.
Lu. 8:16. a candle, covereth it with a *vessel,*
17:31. and his *stuff* in the house.

Joh.19:29. there was set a *vessel* full of vinegar:
Acts 9:15. he is a chosen *vessel* unto me,
    10:11. and a certain *vessel* descending
      16. and the *vessel* was received up again
    11: 5. A certain *vessel* descend,
    27:17. strake *sail*, and so were driven.
Ro. 9:21. to make one *vessel* unto honour,
      22. the *vessels* of wrath fitted to
      23. on the *vessels* of mercy, which he
2Co. 4: 7. have this treasure in earthen *vessels*,
1Th. 4: 4. possess his *vessel* in sanctification
2Ti. 2:20. not only *vessels* of gold and of silver,
      21. he shall be a *vessel* unto honour,
Heb 9:21. and all the *vessels* of the ministry.
1Pet.3: 7. as unto the weaker *vessel*,
Rev. 2:27. as the *vessels* of a potter shall they
   18:12. all manner *vessels* of ivory, and all manner *vessels* of most precious wood,

σκηνή, *skeenee.*

Mat.17: 4. make here three *tabernacles;*
Mar 9: 5. make three *tabernacles;* one for thee,
Lu. 9:33. let us make three *tabernacles;* one
    16: 9. receive you into everlasting *habitations.*
Acts 7:43. took up the *tabernacle* of Moloch,
      44. Our fathers had the *tabernacle* of witness in the wilderness,
   15:16. build again the *tabernacle* of David,
Heb 8: 2. of the true *tabernacle*, which the Lord
     '5. when he was about to make the *tabernacle:*
    9: 1. Then verily the first (covenant) had (some copies read ἡ πρώτη σκηνή)
      2. there was a *tabernacle* made; the first,
      3. after the second veil, the *tabernacle* which is called the Holiest of all;
      6. went always into the first *tabernacle*,
      8. as the first *tabernacle* was yet standing:
     11. by a greater and more perfect *tabernacle*,
     21. with blood both the *tabernacle*, and
    11: 9. dwelling in *tabernacles* with Isaac
   13:10. which serve the *tabernacle.*
Rev.13: 6. blaspheme his name, and his *tabernacle*,
    15: 5. the temple of the *tabernacle* of the testimony in heaven
    21: 3. the *tabernacle* of God (is) with men,

σκηνοπηγία, *skeenopeegia.*

Joh. 7: 2. the Jews' feast of *tabernacles* (lit. the *tabernacle-fixing*)

σκηνοποιός, *skeenopoyos.*

Acts18: 3. they were *tentmakers.*

σκῆνος, *skeenos.*

2Co. 5: 1. our earthly house of (this) *tabernacle*
      4. we that are in (this) *tabernacle* do groan,

σκηνόω, *skeenoō.*

Joh. 1:14. and *dwelt* among us, (lit. *tabernacled*)
Rev. 7:15. *shall dwell* among them. (lit. *shall tab.*)
   12.12. heavens, and ye *that dwell* in them.
    13: 6. and them *that dwell* in heaven.
    21: 3. and he *will dwell* with them,

σκήνωμα, *skeenōma.*

Acts 7:46. to find a *tabernacle* for the God of Jacob.
2Pet. 1:13. as long as I am in this *tabernacle*,
     14. I must put off (this) my *tabernacle*,

σκιά, *skia.*

Mat. 4:16. sat in the region and *shadow* of death
Mar 4:32. may lodge under the *shadow* of it.
Lu. 1:79. and (in) the *shadow* of death,
Acts 5:15. the *shadow* of Peter passing by
Col. 2:17. Which are a *shadow* of things to come;
Heb 8: 5. the example and *shadow* of heavenly things,
   10: 1. the law having a *shadow* of good things to come,

σκιρτάω, *skirtao.*

Lu. 1:41. the babe *leaped* in her womb;
     44. the babe *leaped* in my womb for joy.
   6:23. *leap for joy:* for, behold, your reward

σκληροκαρδία, *skleerokardia.*

Mat.19: 8. because of the *hardness of* your *hearts*
Mar 10: 5. For the *hardness of* your *heart*
   16:14. their unbelief and *hardness of heart*,

σκληρός, *skleeros.*

Mat.25:24. that thou art an *hard* man,
Joh. 6:60. This is an *hard* saying; who
Acts 9: 5. *hard* for thee to kick against
   26:14. *hard* for thee to kick against
Jas. 3: 4. driven of *fierce* winds,
Jude   15. and of all their *hard* (speeches) which

σκληρότης, *skleerotees.*

Ro. 2: 5. thy *hardness* and impenitent heart

σκληροτράχηλος, *skleerotrakeelos.*

Acts 7:51. Ye *stiffnecked* and uncircumcised

σκληρύνω, *skleeruno.*

Acts19: 9. But when divers *were hardened*,
Ro. 9:18. and whom he will he *hardeneth.*
Heb 3: 8. *Harden* not your hearts, as in
     13. lest any of you be *hardened*
     15. *harden* not your hearts, as in
    4: 7. *harden* not your hearts.

σκολιός, *skolios.*

Lu. 3: 5. and the *crooked* shall be made straight.
Acts 2:40. from this *untoward* generation.
Phi. 2:15. in the midst of a *crooked* and perverse nation,
1Pet 2:18. but also to the *froward.*

σκόλοψ, skolops.

2Co.12: 7. was given to me a *thorn* in the flesh,

σκοπέω, skopeo.

Lu. 11:35. *Take heed* therefore that the light
Ro. 16:17. *mark* them which cause divisions
2Co. 4:18. *While* we *look* not at the things which
Gal. 6: 1. *considering* thyself, lest thou also
Phi. 2: 4. *Look* not every man *on* his own
    3:17. *mark* them which walk so as

σκοπός, skopos.

Phi. 3:14. I press toward the *mark*

σκορπίζω, skorpizo.

Mat.12:30. gathereth not with me *scattereth abroad*.
Lu. 11:23. he that gathereth not with me *scattereth*.
Joh.10:12. the wolf catcheth them, and *scattereth*
   16:32. is now come, that ye shall *be scattered*,
2Co. 9: 9. He *hath dispersed abroad* ; he hath

σκορπίος, skorpios.

Lu. 10:19. to tread on serpents and *scorpions*,
   11:12. will he offer him a *scorpion* ?
Rev. 9: 3. as the *scorpions* of the earth have power.
   5. as the torment of a *scorpion*,
   10. tails like unto *scorpions*,

σκοτεινός, skotinos.

Mat. 6:23. body shall be *full of darkness*.
Lu. 11:34. thy body also (is) *full of darkness*.
   36. having no part *dark*,

σκοτία, skotia.

Mat.10:27. What I tell you in *darkness*,
Lu. 12: 3. whatsoever ye have spoken in *darkness*
Joh. 1: 5. the light shineth in *darkness* ; and the
    darkness comprehended it not.
   6:17. And it was now *dark*,
   8:12. shall not walk in *darkness*,
   12:35. lest *darkness* come upon you: for he that
    walketh in *darkness*
   46. should not abide in *darkness*.
   20: 1. when it was yet *dark*,
1Joh.1: 5. in him is no *darkness* at all.
   2: 8. because the *darkness* is past,
   9. is in *darkness* even until now.
   11. is in *darkness*, and walketh in *darkness*,
   — because that *darkness* hath blinded

σκοτίζομαι, skotizomai.

Mat.24:29. *shall* the sun *be darkened*,
Mar.13:24. the sun *shall be darkened*, and the
Lu. 23:45. the sun *was darkened*, and the veil
Ro. 1:21. their foolish heart *was darkened*.
   11:10. *Let* their eyes *be darkened*,
Eph 4:18. Having the understanding *darkened*,

Rev. 8:12. so as the third part of them *was darkened*,
   9: 2. the sun and the air *were darkened*

σκοτόομαι, skotoōmai.

Rev.16:10. his kingdom was *full of darkness* ; (lit.
   darkened)

σκότος, skotos.

Mat. 4:16. The people which sat in *darkness*
   6:23. be *darkness*, how great (is) that *darkness* !
   8:12. be cast out into outer *darkness* :
   22:13. cast (him) into outer *darkness* ;
   25:30. unprofitable servant into outer *darkness* :
   27:45. there was *darkness* over all the land
Mar 15:33. there was *darkness* over the whole land
Lu. 1:79. light to them that sit in *darkness*
   ·11:35. the light which is in thee be not *darkness*.
   22:53. your hour, and the power of *darkness*.
   23:44. there was a *darkness* over all the earth
Joh. 3:19. men loved *darkness* rather than light,
Acts 2:20. The sun shall be turned into *darkness*,
   13:11. fell on him a mist and a *darkness*,
   26:18. to turn (them) from *darkness* to light,
Ro. 2:19. a light of them which are in *darkness*,
   13:12. cast off the works of *darkness*,
1Co. 4: 5. the hidden things of *darkness*,
2Co. 4: 6. the light to shine out of *darkness*,
   6:14. what communion hath light with *dark-
    ness* ?
Eph 5: 8. ye were sometimes *darkness*,
   11. the unfruitful works of *darkness*,
   6:12. the rulers of the *darkness* of this world,
Col. 1:13. delivered us from the power of *darkness*,
1Th. 5: 4. ye, brethren, are not in *darkness*,
   5. we are not of the night, nor of *darkness*.
Heb 12:18. nor unto blackness, and *darkness*, and
1Pet.2: 9. called you out of *darkness* into his
2Pet.2:17. mist of *darkness* is reserved for ever.
1Joh.1: 6. and walk in *darkness*, we lie,
Jude 13. the blackness of *darkness* for ever.

Note.—It occurs in Heb. 12:18 as the dat. sing. of
   the second declension.

σκύβαλον, skubalon.

Phi. 3: 8. and do count them (but) *dung*,

σκυθρωπός, skuthrōpos.

Mat. 6:16. as the hypocrites, *of a sad countenance* :
Lu. 24:17. as ye walk, and are *sad* ?

σκύλλω, skullo.

Mar 5:35. why *troublest* thou the Master
Lu. 7: 6. Lord, *trouble* not thyself : for I
   8:49. *trouble* not the Master.

σκῦλον, skulon.

Lu. 11:22. and divideth his *spoils*.

σκωληκόϐρωτος, skōleekobrōtos.

Acts 12:23. and he was *eaten of worms*,

σκώληξ, skōleex.

Mar 9:44. Where their *worm* dieth not,
46. Where their *worm* dieth not,
48. Where their *worm* dieth not,

σμαράγδινος, smaragdinos.

Rev. 4: 3. in sight like unto an *emerald*.

σμάραγδος, smaragdos.

Rev. 21:19. the fourth, an *emerald* ;

σμύρνα, smurna.

Mat. 2:11. gold, and frankincense, and *myrrh*.
Joh. 19:39. a mixture of *myrrh* and aloes,

σμυρνίζομαι, smurnizomai.

Mar 15:23. wine *mingled with myrrh* : but he

σόι, soi.
From σύ.

Mat. 2:13. until I bring *thee* word:
4: 9. All these things will I give *thee*,
5:26. Verily I say unto *thee*,
29. for it is profitable for *thee*
30. for it is profitable for *thee*
40. if any man will sue *thee* at the law,
6: 4. himself shall reward *thee* openly.
6. shall reward *thee* openly.
18. shall reward *thee* openly.
23. the light that is in *thee* be darkness,
8:13. (so) be it done unto *thee*.
19. Master, I will follow *thee*
29. What have we to do with *thee*, Jesus,
9: 2. thy sins be forgiven *thee*.
5. (Thy) sins be forgiven *thee* ;
11:21. woe unto *thee*, Chorazin! woe unto *thee*, Bethsaida!
23. works, which have been done in *thee*,
24. in the day of judgment, than for *thee*.
25. I thank *thee*, O Father, Lord of heaven
12:47. desiring to speak with *thee*.
14: 4. It is not lawful for *thee* to have
15:28. be it unto *thee* even as thou wilt.
16:17. hath not revealed (it) unto *thee*,
18. And I say also unto *thee*, That thou art
19. And I will give unto *thee* the keys
22. Be it far from *thee*, Lord: this shall not be unto *thee*.
17: 4. three tabernacles; one for *thee*,
25. What thinkest *thou*, Simon?
18: 8 it is better for *thee* to enter into life
9. it is better for *thee* to enter into life
17. let him be unto *thee* as an heathen man
22. I say not unto *thee*, Until seven times:
26. and I will pay *thee* all.
29. and I will pay *thee* all.

Mat. 18:32. I forgave *thee* all that debt,
19:27. have forsaken all, and followed *thee* ;
20:14. unto this last, even as unto *thee*.
21: 5. thy King cometh unto *thee*,
23. and who gave *thee* this authority?
22:16. neither carest *thou* for any (man):
17. What thinkest *thou* ?
25:44. and did not minister unto *thee* ?
26:17. that we prepare for *thee* to eat
33. shall be offended because of *thee*,
34. Verily I say unto *thee*,
35. Though I should die with *thee*,
27:19. Have *thou* nothing to do with that just man:
Mar 1:24. what have we to do with *thee*,
2: 5. thy sins be forgiven *thee*.
9. (Thy) sins be forgiven *thee* ;
11. I say unto *thee*, Arise,
4:38. Master, carest *thou* not that we
5: 7. What have I to do with *thee*, Jesus,
9. What (is) *thy* name?
19. how great things the Lord hath done for *thee*,
41. Damsel, I say unto *thee*, arise.
6:18. It is not lawful for *thee*
22. and I will give (it) *thee*.
23. I will give (it) *thee*,
9: 5. three tabernacles; one for *thee*,
25. (Thou) dumb and deaf spirit, I charge *thee*,
43. better for *thee* to enter into life maimed,
45. better for *thee* to enter halt into life,
47. better for *thee* to enter into the kingdom
10:21. One thing *thou* lackest:
28. and have followed *thee*.
51. that I should do unto *thee* ?
11:28. and who gave *thee* this authority
12:14. and)(carest for no man:
14:30. Verily I say unto *thee*,
31. If I should die with *thee*,
36. all things (are) possible unto *thee* ;
Lu. 1: 3. to write unto *thee* in order,
13. Elisabeth shall bear *thee* a son,
14. And *thou* shalt have joy and gladness;
19. and to shew *thee* these glad tidings.
35. the power of the Highest shall overshadow *thee*:
3:22. in *thee* I am well pleased.
4: 6. All this power will I give *thee*,
34. what have we to do with *thee*,
5:20. thy sins are forgiven *thee*.
23. Thy sins be forgiven *thee* ;
24. I say unto *thee*, Arise,
7:14. Young man, I say unto *thee*, Arise.
40. I have somewhat to say unto *thee*.
47. Wherefore I say unto *thee*,
8:28. What have I to do with *thee*, Jesus,
30. saying, What is *thy* name?
39. how great things God hath done unto *thee*.
9:33. three tabernacles; one for *thee*,
57. I will follow *thee* whithersoever thou
61. Lord, I will follow *thee* ;
10:13. Woe unto *thee*, Chorazin! woe unto *thee*, Bethsaida!
21. I thank *thee*, O Father, Lord of heaven
35. when I come again, I will repay *thee*.
36. Which now of these three, thinkest *thou*,
40. Lord, dost *thou* not care that my sister
11: 7. I cannot rise and give *thee*.
35. that the light which is in *thee* be not
12:59. I tell *thee*, thou shalt not depart thence,
14: 9. and say to *thee*, Give this man place ;

Lu. 14:10. say unto *thee*, Friend, go up higher: then
shalt *thou* have worship in the presence
of them that sit at meat with *thee*.
12. and a recompence be made *thee*.
14. for they cannot recompense *thee: for thou*
shalt be recompensed at
15:29. these many years do I serve *thee*,
18:11. God, I thank *thee*, that I am not as other
men
22. Yet lackest *thou* one thing:
28. we have left all, and followed *thee*.
41. What wilt thou that I shall do unto *thee?*
19:43. shall cast a trench about *thee*,
44. and thy children within *thee;*
— leave in *thee* one stone upon another ;
20: 2. who is he that gave *thee* this authority?
22:11. The Master saith unto *thee*,
34. And he said, I tell *thee*, Peter,
23:43. Verily I say unto *thee*,
Joh. 1:50. Because I said unto *thee*, I saw thee
2: 4. what have I to do with *thee?*
3: 3. Verily, verily, I say unto *thee*,
5. Verily, verily, I say unto *thee*,
7. Marvel not that I said unto *thee*,
11. Verily, verily, I say unto *thee*
4:10. who it is that saith to *thee*,
— he would have given *thee* living water.
26. I that speak unto *thee* am (he).
5:10. it is not lawful for *thee* to carry (thy) bed.
I2. What man is that which said unto *thee*,
14. lest a worse thing come unto *thee*.
6:30. that we may see, and believe *thee?*
9:26. What did he to *thee?*
11:22. God will give (it) *thee*.
40. Said I not unto *thee*, that, if thou
41. Father, I thank *thee* that thou hast heard
13:37. Lord, why cannot I follow *thee* now?
38. Verily, verily, I say unto *thee*,
17: 5. which I had with *thee* before the world
21. as thou, Father, (art) in me, and I in
thee,
18:30. have delivered him up unto *thee*.
34. or did others tell it *thee* of me?
19:11. except it were given *thee* from above:
therefore he that delivered me unto *thee*
21: 3. We also go with *thee*.
18. Verily, verily, I say unto *thee*,
Acts 3: 6. but such as I have give I *thee :*
5: 4. Whiles it remained, was it not *thine own?*
7: 3. into the land which I shall shew *thee*.
8:20. Thy money perish with *thee*,
21. *Thou* hast neither part nor lot
22. thought of thine heart may be forgiven
thee.
9: 5. hard for *thee* to kick against the pricks.
6. and it shall be told *thee*
17. Jesus, that appeared unto *thee*
10: 6. he shall tell *thee* what thou oughtest to do.
32. when he cometh, shall speak unto *thee*.
33. all things that are commanded *thee*
16:18. I command *thee* in the name of
18:10. and no man shall set on *thee*
21:23. this that we say to *thee :*
22:10. there it shall be told *thee* of all things
which are appointed for *thee* to do.
23:18. who hath something to say unto *thee*.
24:14. But this I confess unto *thee*,
26: 1. *Thou* art permitted to speak for thyself.
14. hard for *thee* to kick against the pricks.
16. I have appeared unto *thee* for this purpose,
— in the which I will appear unto *thee ;*
27:24. lo, God hath given *thee* all them

Ro. 9: 7. In Isaac shall *thy* seed be called.
17. that I might shew my power in *thee*,
13: 4. the minister of God to *thee* for good.
15: 9. I will confess to *thee* among the Gentiles,
1Co. 7:21. care)(not for it:
2Co. 6: 2. have I succoured *thee :*
12: 9. My grace is sufficient for *thee :*
Gal. 3: 8. In *thee* shall all nations be blessed.
Eph. 5:14. and Christ shall give *thee* light.
6: 3. That it may be well with *thee*,
1Ti. 1:18. This charge I commit unto *thee*,
3:14. These things write I unto *thee*,
4:14. Neglect not the gift that is in *thee*, which
was given *thee*
6:13. I give *thee* charge in the sight of
2Ti. 1: 5. the unfeigned faith that is in *thee*,
— and I am persuaded that in *thee* also.
6. the gift of God, which is in *thee*
2: 7. and the Lord give *thee* understanding
Tit. 1: 5. in every city, as I had appointed *thee :*
Philem 8. to injoin *thee* that which is convenient,
11. was to *thee* unprofitable, but now profitable to *thee* and to me ;
16. but how much more unto *thee*,
19. albeit I do not say to *thee* how thou
21. I wrote unto *thee*, knowing that
Heb. 8: 5. the pattern shewed to *thee* in the mount.
11:18. in Isaac shall *thy* seed be called:
Jas. 2:18. I will shew *thee* my faith by my works.
2Joh. 5. I wrote a new commandment unto *thee*,.
3Joh. 13. with ink and pen write unto *thee :*
14. Peace (be) to *thee*.
Jude 9. but said, The Lord rebuke *thee*.
Rev. 2: 5. I will come unto *thee* quickly,
10. and I will give *thee* a crown of life.
16. I will come unto *thee* quickly,
3:18. I counsel *thee* to buy of me
4: 1. and I will shew *thee* things
11:17. We give *thee* thanks, O Lord
14:15. for the time is come for *thee* to reap ;
17: 1. I will shew unto *thee* the judgment
7. I will tell *thee* the mystery
18:22. shall be heard no more at all in *thee ;*
— shall be found any more in *thee ;*
— shall be heard no more at all in *thee ;*
23. shall shine no more at all in *thee ;*
— shall be heard no more at all in *thee :*
21: 9. Come hither, I will shew *thee* the bride,

σορός, *soros.*

Lu. 7:14. And he came and touched the *bier :*

σός, *sos.*

Mat. 7: 3. the beam that is in *thine own* eye?
22. prophesied in *thy* name? and in *thy* name
have cast out devils? and in *thy* name
13:27. sow good seed in *thy* field?
20:14. Take (that) *thine* (is), and go thy way:
24: 3. and what (shall be) the sign of *thy* coming,
25:25. lo, (there) thou hast (that is) *thine*.
Mar 2:18. but *thy* disciples fast not?
5:19. Go home to *thy friends*,
Lu. 5:33. but *thine* eat and drink?
6:30. of him that taketh away *thy* goods
15:31. and all that I have is *thine*.
22:42. not my will, but *thine*, be done.
Joh. 4:42. we believe, not because of *thy* saying:

Joh.17: 6. *thine* they were, and thou gavest them me;
 9. for they are *thine*.
 10. And all mine are *thine*, and *thine* are mine;
 17. *thy* word is truth.
18:35. *Thine own* nation and the chief priests
Acts 5: 4. was it not in *thine own* power?
 24: 2. done unto this nation by *thy* providence,
 4. hear us of *thy* clemency a few words.
1Co. 8:11. And through *thy* knowledge shall the weak
 14:16. at *thy* giving of thanks,
Philem.14. But without *thy* mind would I do nothing;

σοῦ, *sou*.
From σύ.

Mat. 1:20. to take unto thee Mary *thy* wife:
 2: 6. for out of *thee* shall come a Governor,
 3:14. I have need to be baptized of *thee*,
 4: 6. give his angels charge concerning *thee :*
 — thou dash *thy* foot against a stone.
 7. Thou shalt not tempt the Lord *thy* God.
 10. Thou shalt worship the Lord *thy* God,
 5:23. bring *thy* gift to the altar, and there
 rememberest that *thy* brother hath ought
 against *thee ;*
 24. Leave there *thy* gift
 — first be reconciled to *thy* brother, and then
 come and offer *thy* gift.
 25. Agree with *thine* adversary quickly,
 29. if *thy* right eye offend thee, pluck it out,
 and cast (it) from *thee :*
 — that one of *thy* members should perish, and
 not (that) *thy* whole body
 30. And if *thy* right hand offend thee, cut it
 off, and cast (it) from *thee ·*
 — that one of *thy* members should perish,
 and not (that) *thy* whole body
 33. perform unto the Lord *thine* oaths:
 36. Neither shalt thou swear by *thy* head,
 39. smite thee on *thy* right cheek,
 40. and take away *thy* coat,
 42. that would borrow of *thee*
 43. Thou shalt love *thy* neighbour, and hate
 thine enemy.
 6: 2. do not sound a trumpet before *thee*,
 3. But when *thou* doest alms, let not *thy* left
 hand know what *thy* right hand doeth:
 4. That *thine* alms may be in secret: and *thy*
 Father which seeth in secret
 6. enter into *thy* closet, and when thou hast
 shut *thy* door, pray to *thy* Father which
 is in secret; and *thy* Father which seeth
 in secret
 9. Hallowed be *thy* name.
 10. *Thy* kingdom come. *Thy* will be done
 13. For *thine* is the kingdom,
 17. anoint *thine* head, and wash *thy* face ;
 18. but unto *thy* Father which is in secret: and
 thy Father, which
 22. if therefore *thine* eye be single, *thy* whole
 body shall be full of light.
 23. But if *thine* eye be evil, *thy* whole body
 shall be full of darkness.
 7: 3. the mote that is in *thy* brother's eye,
 4. Or how wilt thou say to *thy* brother, Let
 me pull out the mote out of *thine* eye ;
 and, behold, a beam (is) in *thine own* eye?
 5. cast out the beam out of *thine own* eye :
 — to cast out the mote out of *thy* brother's eye.
 9: 2. *thy* sins be forgiven thee.
 6. take up *thy* bed, and go unto *thine* house.

Mat. 9:14. but *thy* disciples fast not?
 18. lay *thy* hand upon her,
 22. *thy* faith hath made thee whole.
 11:10. my messenger before *thy* face, which shall
 prepare *thy* way before *thee*.
 26. so it seemed good in *thy* sight.
 12: 2. *thy* disciples do that which
 13. Stretch forth *thine* hand.
 37. by *thy* words thou shalt be justified, and
 by *thy* words thou shalt
 38. we would see a sign from *thee*.
 47. *thy* mother and *thy* brethren stand
 15: 2. Why do *thy* disciples transgress
 4. Honour *thy* father and mother:
 28. O woman, great (is) *thy* faith:
 17:16. And I brought him to *thy* disciples,
 27. and give unto them for me and *thee*.
 18: 8. if *thy* hand or *thy* foot offend thee, cut
 them off, and cast (them) from *thee :*
 9. And if *thine* eye offend thee,
 — cast (it) from *thee :*
 15. if *thy* brother shall trespass against
 — between *thee* and him alone: if he shall
 hear *thee*, thou hast gained *thy* brother.
 16. take with *thee* one or two more,
 33. have had compassion on *thy* fellowservant,
 19:19. Honour *thy* father and (thy) mother:
 — love *thy* neighbour as thyself.
 21. (and) sell that *thou* hast,
 20:15. Is *thine* eye evil, because I am good?
 21. the one on *thy* right hand,
 — in *thy* kingdom.
 21: 5. Behold, *thy* King cometh unto thee,
 19. Let no fruit grow on *thee* henceforward
 22:37. Thou shalt love the Lord *thy* God with all
 thy heart, and with all *thy* soul, and
 with all *thy* mind.
 39. love *thy* neighbour as thyself.
 44. till I make *thine* enemies *thy* footstool?
 23:37. have gathered *thy* children together,
 25:21. into the joy of *thy* lord.
 23. into the joy of *thy* lord.
 25. and hid *thy* talent in the earth:
 26:42. except I drink it, *thy* will be done.
 52. Put up again *thy* sword into
 62. (which) these witness against *thee ?*
 73. for *thy* speech bewrayeth thee.
 27:13. they witness against *thee ?*
Mar 1: 2. I send my messenger before *thy* face,
 which shall prepare *thy* way before *thee*.
 44. and offer for *thy* cleansing
 2: 5. *thy* sins be forgiven thee.
 9. take up *thy* bed, and walk?
 11. Arise, and take up *thy* bed, and go *thy*
 way into *thine* house.
 3: 5. Stretch forth *thine* hand.
 32. Behold, *thy* mother and *thy* brethren
 without seek for thee.
 5:19. Go home (lit. to *thy* house) to *thy* friends,
 34. *thy* faith hath made thee whole ;
 — and be whole of *thy* plague.
 35. *Thy* daughter is dead: why
 6:18. to have *thy* brother's wife.
 7: 5. Why walk not *thy* disciples
 10. Honour *thy* father and *thy* mother ;
 29. the devil is gone out of *thy* daughter.
 9:18. I spake to *thy* disciples
 38. casting out devils in *thy* name,
 43. And if *thy* hand offend thee,
 45. And if *thy* foot offend thee,
 47. And if *thine* eye offend thee,
 10:19. Honour *thy* father and mother.

Mar 10:37. we may sit, one on *thy* right hand, and
the other on *thy* left hand, in *thy* glory.
52. *thy* faith hath made thee whole.
11:14. eat fruit of *thee* hereafter
12:30. love the Lord *thy* God with all *thy* heart,
and with all *thy* soul, and with all *thy*
mind, and with all *thy* strength:
31. love *thy* neighbour as thyself.
36. till I make *thine* enemies *thy* footstool.
14:60. (which) these witness against *thee?*
70. and *thy* speech agreeth (thereto).
15: 4. they witness against *thee.*

Lu. 1:13. *thy* prayer is heard; and *thy* wife Elisabeth
28. the Lord (is) with *thee :*
35. which shall be born of *thee*
36. And, behold, *thy* cousin Elisabeth,
38. according to *thy* word. And
42. blessed (is) the fruit of *thy* womb.
44. the voice of *thy* salutation
61. There is none of *thy* kindred
2:29. now lettest thou *thy* servant depart in
peace, according to *thy* word:
30. have seen *thy* salvation,
32. and the glory of *thy* people Israel.
35. shall pierce through *thy* own soul
48 *thy* father and I have sought thee
4: 7. all shall be *thine.*
8. shalt worship the Lord *thy* God,
10. He shall give his angels charge over *thee,*
11. thou dash *thy* foot against a stone.
12. Thou shalt not tempt the Lord *thy* God.
23. do also here in *thy* country.
5: 5. nevertheless at *thy* word
14. and offer for *thy* cleansing,
20. *thy* sins are forgiven thee.
23. *Thy* sins be forgiven thee;
24. take up *thy* couch, and go unto *thine* house.
6:10. Stretch forth *thy* hand.
29. him that taketh away *thy* cloke
41. the mote that is in *thy* brother's eye,
42. how canst thou say to *thy* brother, Brother,
— the mote that is in *thine* eye,
— the beam that is in *thine own* eye?
— first the beam out of *thine own* eye,
— the mote that is in *thy* brother's eye.
7:27. messenger before *thy* face, which shall
prepare *thy* way before *thee.*
44. I entered into *thine* house,
48. *Thy* sins are forgiven.
50. *Thy* faith hath saved thee;
8:20. *Thy* mother and *thy* brethren
28. I beseech *thee,* torment me not.
39. Return to *thine own* house,
48. *thy* faith hath made thee whole;
49. *Thy* daughter is dead;
9:38. Master, I beseech *thee,* look upon
40. And I besought *thy* disciples to cast
41. Bring *thy* son hither.
49. casting out devils in *thy* name;
10:17. subject unto us through *thy* name.
21. it seemed good in *thy* sight.
27. Thou shalt love the Lord *thy* God with all
thy heart, and with all *thy* soul, and
with all *thy* strength, and with all *thy*
mind; and *thy* neighbour as thyself.
11: 2. Hallowed be *thy* name. *Thy* kingdom
come. *Thy* will be done,
34. when *thine* eye is single, *thy* whole body
also is full of light;
— *thy* body also (is) full of darkness.
36. If *thy* whole body therefore
12:20. *thy* soul shall be required of *thee*

Lu. 12:58. goest with *thine* adversary
13:12. thou art loosed from *thine* infirmity.
26. eaten and drunk in *thy* presence,
34. gathered *thy* children together,
14: 8. a more honourable man than *thou*
12. call not *thy* friends, nor *thy* brethren,
neither *thy* kinsmen,
15:18. sinned against heaven, and before *thee,*
19. no more worthy to be called *thy* son:
make me as one of *thy* hired servants.
21. and in *thy* sight, and am no more worthy
to be called *thy* son.
27. *Thy* brother is come; and *thy* father hath
killed
29. transgressed I at any time *thy* commandment:
30. But as soon as this *thy* son was come,
which hath devoured *thy* living
32. for this *thy* brother was dead, and is alive
16: 2. How is it that I hear this of *thee?* give an
account of *thy* stewardship;
6. Take *thy* bill, and sit down quickly,
7. Take *thy* bill, and write fourscore.
25. thou in *thy* lifetime receivedst *thy* good
17: 3. If *thy* brother trespass against thee,
19. *thy* faith hath made thee whole.
18:20. Honour *thy* father and *thy* mother.
42. *thy* faith hath saved thee.
19: 5. I must abide at *thy* house.
16. Lord, *thy* pound hath gained ten
18. Lord, *thy* pound hath gained five
20. Lord, behold, (here is) *thy* pound,
22. Out of *thine own* mouth will I judge thee,
39. Master, rebuke *thy* disciples.
42. even thou, at least in this *thy* day, the
things (which belong) unto *thy* peace !
but now they are hid from *thine* eyes.
43. *thine* enemies shall cast a trench about
44. and *thy* children within thee ;
— the time of *thy* visitation.
20:43. Till I make *thine* enemies *thy* footstool.
22:32. But I have prayed for *thee,* that *thy* faith
fail not:
— strengthen *thy* brethren.
33. I am ready to go with *thee,*
23:42. when thou comest into *thy* kingdom.
46. Father, into *thy* hands I commend
Joh. 2:17. The zeal of *thine* house hath
3:26. he that was with *thee* beyond Jordan,
4:16. Go, call *thy* husband, and come
18. whom thou now hast is not *thy* husband:
50. Go thy way ; *thy* son liveth.
51. saying, *Thy* son liveth.
53. *Thy* son liveth:
5: 8. Rise, take up *thy* bed, and walk.
11. Take up *thy* bed, and walk.
12. Take up *thy* bed, and walk ?
7: 3. that *thy* disciples also may see the works
that *thou* doest.
8:10. where are those *thine* accusers ?
13. *thy* record is not true.
19. Where is *thy* Father ?
9:10. How were *thine* eyes opened ?
17. that he hath opened *thine* eyes ?
26. how opened he *thine* eyes ?
37. it is he that talketh with *thee.*
11:23. *Thy* brother shall rise again.
12:15. behold, *thy* King cometh,
28. Father, glorify *thy* name.
13:37. I will lay down my life for *thy* sake.
38. Wilt thou lay down *thy* life for my sake ?
17: 1. glorify *thy* Son, that *thy* Son also may

Joh.17: 6. I have manifested *thy* name unto the
— and they have kept *thy* word.
7. whatsoever thou hast given me are of *thee*.
8. that I came out from *thee*,
11. keep through *thine own* name those
12. I kept them in *thy* name:
14. I have given them *thy* word ;
17. Sanctify them through *thy* truth:
26. declared unto them *thy* name,
18:11. Put up *thy* sword into the sheath:
19:26. Woman, behold *thy* son !
27. Behold *thy* mother !
20:27. Reach hither *thy* finger,
— and reach hither *thy* hand,
21:18. thou shalt stretch forth *thy* hands,
Acts 2:27. wilt thou suffer *thine* Holy One
28. full of joy with *thy* countenance.
35. Until I make *thy* foes *thy* footstool.
3:25. And in *thy* seed shall all the kindreds
4:25. by the mouth of *thy* servant David
27. against *thy* holy child Jesus,
28. whatsoever *thy* hand and *thy* counsel
29. and grant unto *thy* servants,
— they may speak *thy* word,
30. By stretching forth *thine* hand
— by the name of *thy* holy child Jesus.
5: 3. why hath Satan filled *thine* heart
4. conceived this thing in *thine* heart ?
9. them which have buried *thy* husband
7: 3. Get thee out of *thy* country, and from *thy* kindred,
32. I (am) the God of *thy* fathers,
33. Put off *thy* shoes from *thy* feet:
8:20. *Thy* money perish with thee,
21. for *thy* heart is not right
22. Repent therefore of this *thy* wickedness,
— the thought of *thine* heart may
34. I pray *thee*, of whom speaketh the prophet
9:13. he hath done to *thy* saints
14. to bind all that call on *thy* name.
10: 4. *Thy* prayers and *thine* alms are come up
22. and to hear words of *thee*.
31. *thy* prayer is heard, and *thine* alms are
11:14. whereby thou and all *thy* house
12: 8. and bind on *thy* sandals.
— Cast *thy* garment about thee,
13:35. Thou shalt not suffer *thine* Holy One
14:10. Stand upright on *thy* feet.
16:31. thou shalt be saved, and *thy* house.
17:19. new doctrine, whereof *thou* speakest,
32. We will hear *thee* again of this (matter).
18:10. For I am with *thee*,
21:21. And they are informed of *thee*,
24. whereof they were informed concerning *thee*,
39. and I beseech *thee*, suffer me to speak
22:16. and wash away *thy* sins,
18. they will not receive *thy* testimony
20. the blood of *thy* martyr Stephen
23: 5. evil of the ruler of *thy* people.
21. looking for a promise from *thee*.
30. to say before *thee* what (they had) against him.
35. I will hear *thee*, said he, when *thine* accusers are also come.
24: 2. by *thee* we enjoy great quietness,
11. Because that *thou* mayest understand,
19. Who ought to have been here before *thee*,
25:26. specially before *thee*, O king Agrippa,
26: 2. answer for myself this day before *thee*
3. I beseech *thee* to hear me patiently.
16. and stand upon *thy* feet:

Acts27:24. given thee all them that sail with *thee*.
28:21. letters out of Judæa concerning *thee*,
— spake any harm of *thee*.
22. But we desire to hear of *thee*
Ro. 2: 5. But after *thy* hardness and
25. *thy* circumcision is made
3: 4. be justified in *thy* sayings,
4:18. So shall *thy* seed be.
8:36. For *thy* sake we are killed
10: 6. Say not in *thine* heart,
8. The word is nigh *thee*, (even) in *thy* mouth, and in *thy* heart:
9. confess with *thy* mouth the Lord Jesus, and shalt believe in *thine* heart
11: 3. Lord, they have killed *thy* prophets, and digged down *thine* altars ;
21. lest he also spare not *thee*.
12:20. if *thine* enemy hunger,
13: 9. love *thy* neighbour as thyself.
14:10. why dost thou judge *thy* brother ? or why dost thou set at nought *thy* brother ?
15. But if *thy* brother be grieved
— Destroy not him with *thy* meat,
21. whereby *thy* brother stumbleth,
15: 9. and sing unto *thy* name.
1Co.12:21. I have no need of *thee* :
15:55. O death, where (is) *thy* sting ? O grave, where (is) *thy* victory ?
2Co. 6: 2. I have heard *thee* in a time accepted,
Gal. 3:16. And to *thy* seed, which is Christ.
5:14. Thou shalt love *thy* neighbour as thyself.
Eph 6: 2. Honour *thy* father and mother ;
1Ti. 4:12. Let no man despise *thy* youth ;
15. that *thy* profiting may appear to all.
16. and them that hear *thee*.
5:23. for *thy* stomach's sake and *thine* often infirmities.
6:21. Grace (be) with *thee*. Amen.
2Ti. 1: 3. I have remembrance of *thee*
4. being mindful of *thy* tears,
5. which dwelt first in *thy* grandmother Lois, and *thy* mother Eunice ;
4: 5. make full proof of *thy* ministry.
22. The Lord Jesus Christ (be) with *thy* spirit.
Tit. 2:15. Let no man despise *thee*.
Philem. 2. and to the church in *thy* house:
4. making mention of *thee* always
5. Hearing of *thy* love and faith,
6. That the communication of *thy* faith
7. consolation in *thy* love,
— the saints are refreshed by *thee*,
13. in *thy* stead he might have ministered unto me
14. that *thy* benefit should not be as it were of necessity,
20. let me have joy of *thee* in the Lord:
21. Having confidence in *thy* obedience
Heb 1: 8. *Thy* throne, O God, (is) for ever and ever:
— the sceptre of *thy* kingdom.
9. *thy* God, hath anointed thee with the oil of gladness above *thy* fellows.
10. the heavens are the works of *thine* hands:
12. and *thy* years shall not fail.
13. until I make *thine* enemies *thy* footstool ?
2: 7. over the works of *thy* hands:
12. I will declare *thy* name unto my
10: 7. to do *thy* will, O God.
9. I come to do *thy* will, O God.
Jas. 2: 8. Thou shalt love *thy* neighbour as thyself,
18. shew me *thy* faith without *thy* works,
2Joh. 4. I found of *thy* children walking in

2Joh. 13. The children of *thy* elect sister
3Joh. 2. even as *thy* soul prospereth.
    3. testified of the truth that is in *thee*,
    6. borne witness of *thy* charity
Rev. 2: 2. I know *thy* works, and *thy* labour, and *thy* patience,
    4. I have (somewhat) against *thee*, because thou hast left *thy* first love.
    5. and will remove *thy* candlestick
    9. I know *thy* works, and
    13. I know *thy* works, and where
    14. I have a few things against *thee*,
    19. I know *thy* works,
    — and *thy* patience, and *thy* works;
    20. I have a few things against *thee*,
  3: 1. I know *thy* works,
    2. I have not found *thy* works perfect
    8. I know *thy* works: behold, I have set before *thee* an open door,
    9. and worship before *thy* feet,
    11. that no man take *thy* crown.
    15. I know *thy* works,
    18. (that) the shame of *thy* nakedness
    — and anoint *thine* eyes with eyesalve,
  4:11. and for *thy* pleasure they are
  5: 9. redeemed us to God by *thy* blood
  10: 9. it shall make *thy* belly bitter, but it shall be in *thy* mouth sweet
  11:17. taken to thee *thy* great power,
    18. and *thy* wrath is come,
    — give reward unto *thy* servants the prophets,
    — and them that fear *thy* name,
  14:15. Thrust in *thy* sickle, and reap:
    18. Thrust in *thy* sharp sickle,
  15: 3. marvellous (are) *thy* works,
    — just and true (are) *thy* ways,
    4. and glorify *thy* name?
    — shall come and worship before *thee*; for *thy* judgments are made manifest.
  16: 7. righteous (are) *thy* judgments.
  18:10. in one hour is *thy* judgment come.
    14. And the fruits that *thy* soul lusted after are departed from *thee*,
    — are departed from *thee*,
    23. for *thy* merchants were the great men of the earth; for by *thy* sorceries
  19:10. I am *thy* fellowservant, and of *thy* brethren that
  22: 9. for I am *thy* fellowservant, and of *thy* brethren the prophets,

---

σουδάριον, *soudarion.*

Lu. 19:20. kept laid up in a *napkin:*
Joh.11:44. bound about with a *napkin.*
  20: 7. the *napkin*, that was about his head,
Acts19:12. brought unto the sick *handkerchiefs*

σοφία, *sophia.*

Mat.11:19. But *wisdom* is justified of her children.
  12:42. to hear the *wisdom* of Solomon;
  13:54. Whence hath this (man) this *wisdom*,
Mar 6: 2. what *wisdom* (is) this which is given unto him,
Lu. 2:40. filled with *wisdom:* and the grace of God
    52. Jesus increased in *wisdom* and stature,
  7:35. *wisdom* is justified of all her children.
  11:31. to hear the *wisdom* of Solomon;
    49. Therefore also said the *wisdom* of God,

Lu. 21:15. I will give you a mouth and *wisdom*,
Acts 6: 3. full of the Holy Ghost and *wisdom*,
    10. they were not able to resist the *wisdom*
  7:10. and gave him favour and *wisdom*
    22. in all the *wisdom* of the Egyptians,
Ro. 11:33. the depth of the riches both of the *wisdom* and knowledge of God!
1Co. 1:17. not with *wisdom* of words, lest
    19. I will destroy the *wisdom* of the wise,
    20. made foolish the *wisdom* of this world?
    21. For after that in the *wisdom* of God the world by *wisdom* knew not God,
    22. the Greeks seek after *wisdom:*
    24. the power of God, and the *wisdom* of God.
    30. who of God is made unto us *wisdom*,
  2: 1. with excellency of speech or of *wisdom*,
    4. with enticing words of man's *wisdom*,
    5. not stand in the *wisdom* of men,
    6. Howbeit we speak *wisdom* among
    — yet not the *wisdom* of this world,
    7. we speak the *wisdom* of God in a mystery,
    13. words which man's *wisdom* teacheth,
  3:19. the *wisdom* of this world is foolishness
  12: 8. by the Spirit the word of *wisdom*;
2Co. 1:12. not with fleshly *wisdom*, but by
Eph. 1: 8. abounded toward us in all *wisdom*
    17. the spirit of *wisdom* and revelation in
  3:10. the manifold *wisdom* of God,
Col. 1: 9. in all *wisdom* and spiritual understanding;
    28. teaching every man in all *wisdom*;
  2: 3. treasures of *wisdom* and knowledge.
    23. a shew of *wisdom* in will worship,
  3:16. dwell in you richly in all *wisdom*;
  4: 5. Walk in *wisdom* toward them that
Jas. 1: 5. If any of you lack *wisdom*, let him
  3:13. his works with meekness of *wisdom*.
    15. This *wisdom* descendeth not from above,
    17. But the *wisdom* that is from above
2Pet.3:15. according to the *wisdom* given unto him
Rev. 5:12. and *wisdom*, and strength, and honour,
  7:12. Blessing, and glory, and *wisdom*,
  13:18. Here is *wisdom*. Let him that hath
  17: 9. here (is) the mind which hath *wisdom*.

σοφίζω, *sophizo*

2Ti. 3:15. which are able *to make* thee *wise* unto salvation
2Pet.1:16. not followed *cunningly devised* fables,

σοφός, *sophos.*

Mat.11:25. hid these things from the *wise* and prudent,
  23:34. I send unto you prophets, and *wise* men,
Lu. 10:21. these things from the *wise* and prudent,
Ro. 1:14. both to the *wise*, and to the unwise.
    22. Professing themselves to be *wise*, they
  16:19. *wise* unto that which is good, and
    27. To God only *wise*, (be) glory
1Co. 1:19. I will destroy the wisdom of the *wise*,
    20. Where (is) the *wise*? where (is) the scribe?
    25. the foolishness of God is *wiser* than men;
    26. not many *wise* men after the flesh,
    27. of the world to confound the *wise*;
  3:10. as a *wise* masterbuilder, I have laid
    18. seemeth to be *wise* in this world, let him become a fool, that he may be *wise*.
    19. He taketh the *wise* in their own craftiness.
    20. The Lord knoweth the thoughts of the *wise*,

1Co. 6: 5. Is it so, that there is not a *wise* man among
you ?
Eph. 5:15. not as fools, but as *wise,*
1Ti. 1:17. the only *wise* God, (be) honour
Jas. 3:13. Who (is) a *wise* man and endued with
Jude 25. To the only *wise* God our Saviour,

σπαράσσω, *sparasso.*

Mar 1:26. *when* the unclean spirit *had torn* him,
9:20. straightway the spirit *tare* him ;
26. (the spirit) cried, and *rent* him sore, *and*
Lu. 9:39. it *teareth* him that he foameth again,

σπαργανόω, *sparganoō.*

Lu. 2: 7. and *wrapped* him *in swaddling clothes,*
12. the babe *wrapped in swaddling clothes,*

σπάομαι, *spaomai.*

Mar 14:47. them that stood by *drew* a sword, *and*
Acts 16:27. he *drew out* his sword, *and* would

σπαταλάω, *spatalav.*

1Ti. 5: 6. But she *that liveth in pleasure* is
Jas. 5: 5. and *been wanton ;*

σπείρα, *spīra.*

Mat. 27:27. gathered unto him the whole *band*
Mar 15:16. and they call together the whole *band.*
Joh. 18: 3. having received a *band* (of men) and
12. Then the *band* and the captain and
Acts 10: 1. a centurion of the *band* called the
21:31. unto the chief captain of the *band,*
27: 1. Julius, a centurion of Augustus' *band.*

σπείρω, *spīro.*

Mat. 6:26. Behold the fowls of the air: for they *sow*
not,
13: 3. a *sower* went forth *to sow ;*
4. And when he *sowed,* some (seeds) fell
18. Hear ye therefore the parable of the *sower.*
19. that *which was sown* in his heart. This is
he *which received seed* by the way side.
20. But he *that received* the *seed* into stony
places,
22. He also *that received seed* among the thorns
23. But he *that received seed* into the good
ground
24. is likened unto a man *which sowed* good
25. and *sowed* tares among the wheat,
27. *didst* not thou *sow* good seed in thy field?
31. a man took, and *sowed* in his field:
37. He *that soweth* the good seed is
39. The enemy *that sowed* them is the
25:24. reaping where thou *hast* not *sown,*
26. I reap where I *sowed* not,
Mar 4: 3. there went out a *sower to sow :*
4. And it came to pass, as he *sowed,*
14. The *sower soweth* the word.
15. where the word *is sown ;*
— taketh away the word *that was sown*

Mar 4:16. *which are sown* on stony ground ;
18. they *which are sown* among thorns;
20. they *which are sown* on good ground;
31. when it *is sown* in the earth,
32. But when it *is sown,* it groweth up,
Lu. 8: 5. A *sower* went out *to sow* his seed: and as
he *sowed,* some fell by
12:24. for they neither *sow* nor reap ;
19:21. and reapest that thou *didst* not *sow.*
22. and reaping that I *did* not *sow :*
Joh. 4:36. that both he *that soweth* and he that
37. One *soweth,* and another reapeth.
1Co. 9:11. If we *have sown* unto you spiritual
15:36. that which thou *sowest* is not quickened,
37. And that which thou *sowest,* thou *sowest*
not that body that shall be,
42. It *is sown* in corruption;
43. It *is sown* in dishonour;
— it *is sown* in weakness;
44. It *is sown* a natural body;
2Co. 9: 6. He *which soweth* sparingly shall reap
— and he *which soweth* bountifully shall
10. he that ministereth seed to the *sower*
Gal. 6: 7. for whatsoever a man *soweth,*
8. For he *that soweth* to his flesh
— but he *that soweth* to the Spirit
Jas. 3:18. the fruit of righteousness *is sown* in peace

σπεκουλάτωρ, *spekoulator.*

Mar 6:27. the king sent an *executioner,* and

σπένδομαι, *spendomai.*

Phi. 2:17. Yea, and if I *be offered* upon
2Ti. 4: 6. For I am now *ready to be offered,*

σπέρμα, *sperma.*

Mat. 13:24. unto a man which sowed good *seed*
27. Sir, didst not thou sow good *seed*
32. is the least of all *seeds :*
37. He that soweth the good *seed* is the
38. the good *seed* are the children of the
kingdom ;
22:24. and raise up *seed* unto his brother.
25. and, having no *issue,* left his wife
Mar 4:31. is less than all the *seeds* that be
12:19. and raise up *seed* unto his brother.
20. and dying left no *seed.*
21. neither left he any *seed :*
22. seven had her, and left no *seed :*
Lu. 1:55. to Abraham, and to his *seed* for ever.
20:28. and raise up *seed* unto his brother.
Joh. 7:42. That Christ cometh of the *seed* of David,
8:33. We be Abraham's *seed,* and were
37. I know that ye are Abraham's *seed ;*
Acts 3:25. And in thy *seed* shall all the kindreds
7: 5. and to his *seed* after him,
6. That his *seed* should sojourn in a
13:23. Of this man's *seed* hath God
Ro. 1: 3. which was made of the *seed* of David
4:13. (was) not to Abraham, or to his *seed,*
16. promise might be sure to all the *seed*
18. was spoken, So shall thy *seed* be.
9: 7. because they are the *seed* of Abraham,
— In Isaac shall thy *seed* be called.
8. are counted for the *seed.*
29. the Lord of Sabaoth had left us a *seed,*

Ro. 11: 1. an Israelite, of the *seed* of Abraham,
1Co.15:38. and to every *seed* his own body.
2Co. 9:10. Now he that ministereth *seed* to the sower
    11:22. Are they the *seed* of Abraham? so (am) I.
Gal. 3:16. Now to Abraham and his *seed* were the
        promises made. He saith not, And to
        seeds, as of many; but as of one, And
        to thy *seed*, which
    19. till the *seed* should come to whom
    29. then are ye Abraham's *seed*,
2Ti. 2: 8. Jesus Christ of the *seed* of David
Heb 2:16. but he took on (him) the *seed* of Abraham.
    11:11. received strength to conceive *seed*,
    18. That in Isaac shall thy *seed* be called:
1Joh.3: 9. for his *seed* remaineth in him:
Rev.12:17. to make war with the remnant of her *seed*,

σπερμολόγος, *spermologos*.

Acts17:18. What will this *babbler* say?

σπεύδω, *spūdo*.

Lu. 2:16. And they came *with haste*,
  19: 5. Zacchæus, *make haste, and* come down;
    6. And he *made haste, and* came down,
Acts20:16. for he *hasted*, if it were possible
  22:18. *Make haste*, and get thee quickly out
2Pet.3:12. and *hasting unto* the coming of the day

σπήλαιον, *speelaion*.

Mat.21:13. but ye have made it a *den* of thieves.
Mar 11:17. but ye have made it a *den* of thieves.
Lu. 19:46. but ye have made it a *den* of thieves.
Joh. 11:38. It was a *cave*, and a stone lay upon it.
Heb11:38. and (in) *dens* and caves of the earth.
Rev. 6:15. hid themselves in the *dens*

σπιλάς, *spilas*.

Jude 12. These are *spots* in your feasts of

σπιλόω, *spiloō*.

Jas. 3: 6. *that* it *defileth* the whole body,
Jude 23. the garment *spotted* by the flesh.

σπῖλος, *spilos*.

Eph. 5:27. not having *spot*, or wrinkle,
2Pet.2:13. *Spots* (they are) and blemishes,

σπλάγχνα, *splankna*.
(neut. plur.)

Lu. 1:78. Through the tender mercy (lit. *bowels* of
    mercy) of our God;
Acts 1:18. and all his *bowels* gushed out.
2Co. 6:12. ye are straitened in your own *bowels*.
  7:15. And his *inward affection* is more
Phi. 1: 8. how greatly I long after you all in the
    bowels of Jesus Christ.
  2: 1. if any *bowels* and mercies,
Col. 3:12. *bowels* of mercies, kindness,
Philem. 7. the *bowels* of the saints are refreshed

Philem.12. receive him, that is, mine own *bowels:*
  20. refresh my *bowels* in the Lord.
1Joh.3:17. shutteth up his *bowels* (of compassion)

σπλαγχνίζομαι, *splanknizomai*.

Mat. 9:36. he *was moved with compassion* on them,
  14:14. *was moved with compassion* toward
  15:32. I *have compassion* on the multitude,
  18:27. *was moved with compassion, and* loosed
  20:34. Jesus *had compassion* (on them), *and*
Mar 1:41. Jesus, *moved with compassion*, put forth
  6:34. *was moved with compassion* toward
  8: 2. I *have compassion* on the multitude,
  9:22. *have compassion* on us, *and* help us.
Lu. 7:13. he *had compassion* on her,
  10:33. he *had compassion* (on him),
  15:20. saw him, and *had compassion*, and ran,

σπόγγος, *spongos*.

Mat.27:48. took a *spunge*, and filled (it)
Mar 15:36. And one ran and filled a *spunge*
Joh.19:29. and they filled a *spunge* with vinegar,

σποδός, *spodos*.

Mat.11:21. repented long ago in sackcloth and *ashes*.
Lu. 10:13. sitting in sackcloth and *ashes*.
Heb 9:13. the *ashes* of an heifer sprinkling the

σπορά, *spora*.

1Pet.1:23. not of corruptible *seed*, but of

σπόριμα, *sporima*.
(neut. plur.)

Mat.12: 1. went on the sabbath day through the *corn;*
Mar 2:23. that he went through the *corn fields*
Lu. 6: 1. that he went through the *corn fields;*

σπόρος, *sporos*.

Mar 4:26. as if a man should cast *seed* into the
    ground;
  27. and the *seed* should spring and grow up,
Lu. 8: 5. A sower went out to sow his *seed:*
  11. The *seed* is the word of God.
2Co. 9:10. and multiply your *seed sown*,

σπουδάζω, *spoudazo*.

Gal. 2:10. the same which I also *was forward* to do.
Eph 4: 3. *Endeavouring* to keep the unity of the
    Spirit
1Th. 2:17. *endeavoured* the more abundantly
2Ti. 2:15. *Study* to shew thyself approved
  4: 9. *Do* thy *diligence* to come shortly unto me:
  21. *Do* thy *diligence* to come before winter.
Tit. 3:12. *be diligent* to come unto me to
Heb 4:11. *Let* us *labour* therefore to enter into
2Pet.1:10. *give diligence* to make your calling
  15. I *will endeavour* that ye may be able
  3:14. *be diligent* that ye may be found of him

σπουδαῖος, spoudaios.

2Co. 8:17. but being *more forward*,
22. proved *diligent* in many things, but now
much *more diligent*,

σπουδαιότερον, spoudaioteron.

2Ti. 1:17. he sought me out *very diligently*,

σπουδαίως, -οτέρως, spoudaios, spoudaioterōs.

Lu. 7: 4. they besought him *instantly*, saying,
Phi. 2:28. I sent him therefore *the more carefully*,
Tit. 3:13. and Apollos on their journey *diligently*,

σπουδή, spoudee.

Mar 6:25. she came in straightway with *haste*
Lu. 1:39. went into the hill country with *haste*,
Ro. 12: 8. he that ruleth, with *diligence ;*
11. Not slothful in *business ;*
2Co. 7:11. what *carefulness* it wrought in you,
12. our *care* for you in the sight of God
8: 7. and knowledge, and (in) all *diligence*,
8. by occasion of the *forwardness* of others,
16. put the same *earnest care* into the heart
Heb. 6:11. do shew the same *diligence*
2Pet. 1: 5. giving all *diligence*, add to your faith
Jude 3. when I gave all *diligence* to write

σπυρίς, spuris.

Mat.15:37. (meat) that was left seven *baskets* full.
16:10. and how many *baskets* ye took up?
Mar 8: 8. the broken (meat) that was left seven
baskets.
20. how many *baskets* full of fragments
Acts 9·25. down by the wall in a *basket.*

στάδιος, στάδιον, stadios, stadion.

Lu. 24:13. (about) threescore *furlongs.*
Joh. 6:19. five and twenty or thirty *furlongs,*
11:18. about fifteen *furlongs* off :
1Co. 9:24. they which run in a *race* run all,
Rev.14:20. a thousand (and) six hundred *furlongs.*
21:16. the reed, twelve thousand *furlongs.*

στάμνος, stamnos.

Heb. 9: 4. wherein (was) the golden *pot* that had
manna,

στάσις, stasis.

Mar 15: 7. committed murder in the *insurrection.*
Lu. 23:19. for a certain *sedition* made in the city,
25. him that for *sedition* and murder
Acts15: 2. had no small *dissension* and
19:40. called in question for this day's *uproar,*
23: 7. there arose a *dissension* between the
10. when there arose a great *dissension,*
Acts24: 5. and a mover of *sedition* among
Heb 9: 8. the first tabernacle was yet standing: (lit.
yet having a *standing*)

στατήρ, stateer.

Mat.17:27. thou shalt find a *piece of money :*

σταυρός, stauros.

Mat.10:38. And he that taketh not his *cross,*
16:24. deny himself, and take up his *cross,*
27:32. him they compelled to bear his *cross.*
40. Son of God, come down from the *cross.*
42. let him now come down from the *cross,*
Mar 8:34. deny himself, and take up his *cross,*
10:21. and come, take up the *cross,*
15:21. Rufus, to bear his *cross.*
30. and come down from the *cross.*
32. descend now from the *cross,*
Lu. 9:23. deny himself, and take up his *cross* daily,
14:27. And whosoever doth not bear his *cross,*
23:26. and on him they laid the *cross,*
Joh.19:17. And he bearing his *cross*
19. and put (it) on the *cross.*
25. Now there stood by the *cross* of Jesus
31. the bodies should not remain upon the
cross
1Co. 1:17. lest the *cross* of Christ should be made
18. For the preaching of the *cross* is to
Gal. 5:11. then is the offence of the *cross* ceased.
6:12. persecution for the *cross* of Christ.
14. save in the *cross* of our Lord Jesus
Eph. 2:16. both unto God in one body by the *cross,*
Phi. 2: 8. even the death of the *cross.*
3:18. the enemies of the *cross* of Christ.
Col. 1:20. peace through the blood of his *cross,*
2:14. nailing it to his *cross ;*
Heb 12: 2. endured the *cross,* despising the shame,

σταυρόω, stauroō.

Mat.20:19. and to scourge, and *to crucify* (him):
23:34. (some) of them ye shall kill and *crucify ;*
26: 2. Son of man is betrayed *to be crucified.*
27:22. *Let* him *be crucified.*
23. *Let* him *be crucified.*
26. he delivered (him) *to be crucified.*
31. and led him away *to crucify* (him).
35. and *crucified* him, *and* parted
38. Then *were* there two thieves *crucified*
28: 5. ye seek Jesus, *which was crucified.*
Mar 15:13. they cried out again, *Crucify* him.
14. out the more exceedingly, *Crucify* him.
15. delivered Jesus,...*to be crucified.*
20. and led him out *to crucify* him.
24. And *when* they *had crucified* him,
25. and they *crucified* him.
27. And with him they *crucify* two thieves ;
16: 6. Jesus of Nazareth, *which was crucified :*
Lu. 23:21. saying, *Crucify* (him), *crucify* him.
23. requiring that he might *be crucified.*
33. there they *crucified* him,
24: 7. and *be crucified,* and the third day
20. and *have crucified* him.
Joh.19: 6. saying, *Crucify* (him), *crucify* (him)
— Take ye him, and *crucify* (him):
10. I have power *to crucify* thee,
15. away with (him), *crucify* him.

Joh. 19:15. *Shall* I *crucify* your King?
　16. unto them to *be crucified*.
　18. Where they *crucified* him, and two other
　20. for the place where Jesus *was crucified*
　23. when they *had crucified* Jesus,
　41. Now in the place where he *was crucified*
Acts 2:36. Jesus, whom ye *have crucified*,
　4:10. of Nazareth, whom ye *crucified*,
1Co. 1:13. *was* Paul *crucified* for you?
　23. But we preach Christ *crucified*,
　2: 2. save Jesus Christ, and him *crucified*.
　8. would not *have crucified* the Lord of
2Co.13: 4. he *was crucified* through weakness,
Gal. 3: 1. set forth, *crucified* among you?
　5:24. *have crucified* the flesh with the
　6:14. by whom the world *is crucified* unto me,
Rev.11: 8. where also our Lord *was crucified*.

σταφυλή, staphulee.

Mat. 7:16. Do men gather *grapes* of thorns,
Lu. 6:44. nor of a bramble bush gather they *grapes*.
Rev.14:18. for her *grapes* are fully ripe.

στάχυς, stakus.

Mat.12: 1. and began to pluck the *ears of corn*,
Mar 2:23. to pluck the *ears of corn*.
　4:28. first the blade, then the *ear*,
　— after that the full corn in the *ear*.
Lu. 6: 1. his disciples plucked the *ears of corn*,

στέγη, stegee.

Mat. 8: 8. shouldest come under my *roof:*
Mar 2: 4. they uncovered the *roof* where he was:
Lu. 7: 6. that thou shouldest enter under my *roof:*

στέγω, stego.

1Co. 9:12. but *suffer* all things, lest we
　13: 7. *Beareth* all things, believeth all things,
1Th. 3: 1. *when* we *could* no longer *forbear*,
　5. *when* I *could* no longer *forbear*, I sent

στεῖρα, stira.

Lu. 1: 7. because that Elisabeth was *barren*,
　36. month with her, who was called *barren*.
　23:29. Blessed (are) the *barren*, and the wombs
Gal. 4:27. Rejoice, (thou) *barren* that bearest not;

στέλλομαι, stellomai.

2Co. 8:20. *Avoiding* this, that no man should
2Th. 3: 6. that ye *withdraw* yourselves from every

στέμμα, stemma.

Acts14:13. brought oxen and *garlands* unto the gates,

στεναγμός, stenagmos.

Acts 7:34. and I have heard their *groaning*,
Ro. 8:26. with *groanings* which cannot be uttered.

στενάζω, stenazo.

Mar 7:34. he *sighed*, and saith unto him,
Ro. 8:23. even we ourselves *groan* within ourselves,
2Co. 5: 2. For in this we *groan*, earnestly desiring
　4. For we that are in (this) tabernacle do *groan*,
Heb13:17. do it with joy, and not *with grief:* (lit. not *groaning*)
Jas. 5: 9. *Grudge* not one against another,

στενός, stenos.

Mat. 7:13. Enter ye in at the *strait* gate:
　14. Because *strait* (is) the gate, and narrow
Lu. 13:24. Strive to enter in at the *strait* gate:

στενοχωρέομαι, stenokōreomai.

2Co. 4: 8. troubled on every side yet not *distressed;*
　6:12. Ye *are* not *straitened* in us, but ye *are straitened* in your own bowels.

στενοχωρία, stenokōria.

Ro. 2: 9. Tribulation and *anguish*, upon every soul
　8:35. (shall) tribulation, or *distress*,
2Co. 6: 4. in necessities, in *distresses*,
　12:10. in *distresses* for Christ's sake:

στερεός, stereos.

2Ti. 2:19. the foundation of God standeth *sure*,
Heb 5:12. and not of *strong* meat. (lit. *solid* food)
　14. But *strong* meat (lit. *solid* food) belongeth to them that
1Pet.5: 9. Whom resist *stedfast* in the faith,

στερεόω, stereoō.

Acts 3: 7. his feet and ancle bones *received strength*.
　16. *hath made* this man *strong*,
　16: 5. And so *were* the churches *established* in the faith,

---

στερέωμα, stereōma.

Col. 2: 5. and the *stedfastness* of your faith in Christ.

στέφανος, stephanos.

Mat.27:29. when they had platted a *crown* of thorns,
Mar15:17. and platted a *crown* of thorns,
Joh.19: 2. the soldiers platted a *crown* of thorns,
　5. wearing the *crown* of thorns,
1Co. 9:25. to obtain a corruptible *crown ;*
Phi. 4: 1. my joy and *crown*, so stand fast
1Th. 2:19. our hope, or joy, or *crown* of rejoicing?
2Ti. 4: 8. for me a *crown* of righteousness,
Jas. 1:12. he shall receive the *crown* of life,
1Pet.5: 4. a *crown* of glory that fadeth not away.
Rev. 2:10. I will give thee a *crown* of life.
　3:11. that no man take thy *crown*.
　4: 4. on their heads *crowns* of gold.
　10. cast their *crowns* before the throne,
　6: 2. and a *crown* was given unto him:

Rev. 9: 7. as it were *crowns* like gold,
12: 1. upon her head a *crown* of twelve stars:
14:14. having on his head a golden *crown*,

στεφανόω, *stephanoō*.

2Ti. 2: 5. (yet) *is* he not *crowned*, except
Heb 2: 7. thou *crownedst* him with glory and honour,
9. *crowned* with glory and honour ;

στῆθος, *steethos*.

Lu. 18:13. but smote upon his *breast*,
23:48. smote their *breasts*, and returned.
Joh.13:25. He then lying on Jesus' *breast*
21:20. which also leaned on his *breast*
Rev.15: 6. their *breasts* girded with golden girdles.

στήκω, *steeko*.

Mar11:25. And when ye *stand* praying,
Ro. 14: 4. to his own master he *standeth* or falleth.
1Co.16:13. *stand fast* in the faith,
Gal. 5: 1. *Stand fast* therefore in the liberty
Phi. 1:27. that ye *stand fast* in one spirit,
4: 1. so *stand fast* in the Lord,
1Th. 3: 8. if ye *stand fast* in the Lord.
2Th. 2:15. brethren, *stand fast*, and hold

στηριγμός, *steerigmos*.

2Pet 3:17. fall from your own *stedfastness*.

στηρίζω, *steerizo*.

Lu. 9:51. he *stedfastly set* his face to go to Jerusalem,
16:26. there *is* a great gulf *fixed :*
22:32. when thou art converted, *strengthen* thy brethren.
Ro. 1:11. to the end ye may *be established ;*
16:25. to *stablish* you according to my gospel,
1Th. 3: 2. to *establish* you, and to comfort you
13. To the end he may *stablish* your hearts
2Th. 2:17. and *stablish* you in every good word
3: 3. who *shall stablish* you, and keep (you)
Jas. 5: 8. Be ye also patient ; *stablish* your hearts:
1Pet. 5:10. make you perfect, *stablish*,
2Pet. 1:12. and be *established* in the present truth.
Rev. 3: 2. *strengthen* the things which remain, that

στίγμα, *stigma*.

Gal. 6:17. the *marks* of the Lord Jesus.

στιγμή, *stigmee*.

Lu. 4: 5. in a *moment* of time.

στίλβω, *stilbo*.

Mar 9: 3. And his raiment became *shining*,

στόα, *stoa*.

Joh. 5: 2. having five *porches*.
10:23. walked in the temple in Solomon's *porch*.
Acts 3:11. in the *porch* that is called Solomon's,
5:12. with one accord in Solomon's *porch*.

στοιβάς, *stoibas*.

Mar 11: 8. and others cut down *branches*

στοιχεῖον, *stoikion*.

Gal. 4: 3. were in bondage under the *elements* of the world:
9. to the weak and beggarly *elements*,
Col. 2: 8. after the *rudiments* of the world, and not
20. dead with Christ from the *rudiments* of the world,
Heb 5:12. the first *principles* of the oracles of God ;
2Pet. 3:10. the *elements* shall melt with fervent
12. the *elements* shall melt with fervent

στοιχέω, *stoikeo*.

Acts21:24. *walkest orderly*, and keepest the law.
Ro. 4:12. but *who* also *walk* in the steps of that
Gal. 5:25. *let* us also *walk* in the Spirit.
6:16. as many as *walk* (lit. in rec. text. *shall walk*) according to this rule,
Phi. 3:16. let us *walk* by the same rule,

στολή, *stolee*.

Mar 12:38. which love to go in *long clothing*,
16: 5. clothed in a *long* white *garment ;*
Lu. 15:22. Bring forth the best *robe*,
20:46. which desire to walk in *long robes*,
Rev. 6:11. white *robes* were given unto every one
7: 9. clothed with white *robes*,
13. What are these which are arrayed in white *robes ?*
14. have washed their *robes*, and made them (lit. their *robes*) white in the blood of the Lamb.

στόμα, *stoma*.

Mat. 4: 4. that proceedeth out of the *mouth* of God.
5: 2. And he opened his *mouth*, and taught them,
12:34. abundance of the heart the *mouth* speaketh.
13:35. I will open my *mouth* in parables ;
15: 8. draweth nigh unto me with their *mouth*,
11. Not that which goeth into the *mouth*
— but that which cometh out of the *mouth*,
17. whatsoever entereth in at the *mouth*
18. which proceed out of the *mouth*
17:27. when thou hast opened his *mouth*,
18:16. that in the *mouth* of two or three
21:16. Out of the *mouth* of babes and sucklings
Lu. 1:64. And his *mouth* was opened immediately,
70. by the *mouth* of his holy prophets,
4:22. which proceeded out of his *mouth*.
6:45. of the abundance of the heart his *mouth* speaketh.
11:54. to catch something out of his *mouth*,

Lu. 19:22. Out of thine own *mouth* will I judge thee,
  21:15. For I will give you a *mouth* and wisdom,
  24. fall by the *edge* of the sword,
  22:71. have heard of his own *mouth*.
Joh. 19:29. and put (it) to his *mouth*.
Acts 1:16. by the *mouth* of David spake before
  3:18. had shewed by the *mouth* of all his prophets,
  21. by the *mouth* of all his holy prophets
  4:25. by the *mouth* of thy servant David
  8:32. so opened he not his *mouth* :
  35. Then Philip opened his *mouth*, and
  10:34. Then Peter opened (his) *mouth*, and
  11: 8. at any time entered into my *mouth*.
  15: 7. that the Gentiles by my *mouth*
  18:14. Paul was now about to open (his) *mouth*,
  22:14. shouldest hear the voice of his *mouth*.
  23: 2. to smite him on the *mouth*.
Ro. 3:14. Whose *mouth* (is) full of cursing and
  19. that every *mouth* may be stopped,
  10: 8. The word is nigh thee, (even) in thy *mouth*,
  9. confess with thy *mouth* the Lord Jesus,
  10. and with the *mouth* confession is made
  15: 6. with one mind (and) one *mouth*
2Co. 6:11. our *mouth* is open unto you, our
  13: 1. In the *mouth* of two or three witnesses
Eph. 4:29. proceed out of your *mouth*, but
  6:19. that I may open my *mouth* boldly,
Col. 3: 8. filthy communication out of your *mouth*.
2Th. 2: 8. consume with the spirit of his *mouth*,
2Ti. 4:17. delivered out of the *mouth* of the lion.
Heb 11:33. stopped the *mouths* of lions,
  34. escaped the *edge* of the sword,
Jas. 3: 3. we put bits in the horses' *mouths*,
  10. Out of the same *mouth* proceedeth
1Pet. 2:22. neither was guile found in his *mouth* :
2Joh. 12. and speak *face to face*,
3Joh. 14. and we shall speak *face to face*.
Jude 16. and their *mouth* speaketh great swelling
Rev. 1:16. and out of his *mouth* went a sharp
  2:16. against them with the sword of my *mouth*.
  3:16. I will spue thee out of my *mouth*.
  9:17. and out of their *mouths* issued fire
  18. which issued out of their *mouths*.
  19. For their power is in their *mouth*,
  10: 9. it shall be in thy *mouth* sweet as honey.
  10. it was in my *mouth* sweet as honey :
  11: 5. fire proceedeth out of their *mouth*,
  12:15. cast out of his *mouth* water as a
  16. and the earth opened her *mouth*,
  — which the dragon cast out of his *mouth*.
  13: 2. and his *mouth* as the *mouth* of a lion :
  5. a *mouth* speaking great things and
  6. And he opened his *mouth* in blasphemy
  14: 5. and in their *mouth* was found no guile :
  16:13. (come) out of the *mouth* of the dragon,
  and out of the *mouth* of the beast, and
  out of the *mouth* of the false prophet.
  19:15. out of his *mouth* goeth a sharp sword,
  21. which (sword) proceeded out of his *mouth* :

στόμαχος, *stomakos.*

1Ti. 5:23. a little wine for thy *stomach*'s sake

στρατεία, *stratia.*

2Co.10: 4. the weapons of our *warfare* (are) not carnal,

1Ti. 1:18. that thou by them mightest war a good *warfare* ;

στράτευμα, *stratūma.*

Mat.22: 7. and he sent forth his *armies*,
Lu. 23:11. And Herod with his *men of war*
Acts23:10. commanded the *soldiers* to go down,
  27. then came I with an *army*,
Rev. 9:16. the number of the *army* of the horsemen
  19:14. And the *armies* (which were) in heaven
  19. and their *armies*, gathered together
  — and against his *army*.

στρατεύομαι, *stratūomai.*

Lu. 3:14. the *soldiers* likewise demanded of him,
1Co. 9: 7. Who *goeth a warfare* any time at
2Co.10: 3. we *do not war* after the flesh :
1Ti. 1:18. that thou by them *mightest war* a good warfare ;
2Ti. 2: 4. No man *that warreth* entangleth himself
Jas. 4: 1. of your lusts *that war* in your members ?
1Pet.2:11. lusts, which *war* against the soul ;

στρατηγός, *strateegos.*

Lu. 22: 4. with the chief priests and *captains*,
  52. and *captains* of the temple,
Acts 4: 1. and the *captain* of the temple,
  5:24. and the *captain* of the temple
  26. Then went the *captain* with the
  16:20. And brought them to the *magistrates*,
  22. and the *magistrates* rent off their clothes,
  35. the *magistrates* sent the serjeants,
  36. The *magistrates* have sent to let you go :
  38. told these words unto the *magistrates* :

στρατία, *stratia.*

Lu. 2:13. a multitude of the heavenly *host*
Acts 7:42. to worship the *host* of heaven ;

στρατιώτης, *stratiōtees.*

Mat. 8: 9. having *soldiers* under me :
  27:27. Then the *soldiers* of the governor
  28:12. they gave large money unto the *soldiers*,
Mar 15:16. And the *soldiers* led him away
Lu. 7: 8. having under me *soldiers*,
  23:36. And the *soldiers* also mocked him,
Joh.19: 2. And the *soldiers* platted a crown
  23. Then the *soldiers*, when they had crucified Jesus,
  — to every *soldier* a part ;
  24. These things therefore the *soldiers* did.
  32. Then came the *soldiers*, and brake
  34. But one of the *soldiers* with a spear
Acts10: 7. and a devout *soldier* of them that
  12: 4. (him) to four quaternions of *soldiers*
  6. Peter was sleeping between two *soldiers*,
  18. there was no small stir among the *soldiers*
  21:32. Who immediately took *soldiers*
  — saw the chief captain and the *soldiers*,
  35. he was borne of the *soldiers*

Acts23:23. Make ready two hundred *soldiers*
    31. Then the *soldiers*, as it was commanded
  27:31. said to the centurion and to the *soldiers*,
    32. Then the *soldiers* cut off the ropes
    42. And the *soldiers'* counsel was to kill
  28:16. by himself with a *soldier* that kept him.
2Ti. 2: 3. endure hardness, as a good *soldier* of

στρατολογέω, stratologeo.

2Ti. 2: 4. that he may please him *who hath chosen
    him to be a soldier.*

στρατοπεδάρχης, stratopedarkees.

Acts28:16. delivered the prisoners to the *captain of
    the guard:*

στρατόπεδον, stratopedon.

Lu. 21:20. Jerusalem compassed with *armies,*

στρεϐλόω, strebloō.

2Pet.3:16. unlearned and unstable *wrest*, as

στρέφω, strepho.

Mat. 5:39. *turn* to him the other also.
   7: 6. and *turn again and* rend you.
  16:23. But he *turned, and* said unto Peter,
  18: 3. Except ye *be converted*, and become as
Lu. 7: 9. and *turned him about, and* said
    44. And he *turned* to the woman, *and* said
    unto Simon,
  9:55. But he *turned, and* rebuked them,
  10:23. And he *turned him* unto (his) disciples,
    and said privately,
  14:25. And he *turned, and* said unto them,
  22:61. And the Lord *turned, and* looked
  23:28. But Jesus *turning* unto them said,
Joh. 1:38. Then Jesus *turned*, and saw them
  20:14. she *turned herself* back, and saw Jesus
    16. She *turned herself, and* saith unto him,
Acts 7:39. and in their hearts *turned back again* into
    Egypt,
    42. Then God *turned*, and gave them up
  13:46. lo, we *turn* to the Gentiles.
Rev.11: 6. power over waters *to turn* them to blood,

στρηνιάω, streeniao.

Rev.18: 7. she hath glorified herself, and *lived deli-
    ciously,*
    9. and *lived deliciously* with her,

στρῆνος, streenos.

Rev.18: 3. through the abundance of her *delicacies.*

στρουθίον, strouthion.

Mat.10:29. Are not two *sparrows* sold for a farthing?

Mat.10:31. ye are of more value than many *sparrows.*
Lu. 12: 6. not five *sparrows* sold for two farthings,
    7. ye are of more value than many *sparrows.*

στρώννυμι, στρωννύω, strōnnumi, strōnnuo.

Mat.21: 8. *spread* their garments in the way;
    — from the trees, and *strawed* (them) in
Mar 11: 8. And many *spread* their garments
    — off the trees, and *strawed* (them) in
  14:15. a large upper room *furnished*
Lu. 22:12. a large upper room *furnished:*
Acts 9:34. arise, and *make thy bed.*

στυγητός, stugeetos.

Tit. 3: 3. *hateful*, (and) hating one another.

στυγνάζω, stugnazo.

Mat.16: 3. for the sky is red and *lowring.*
Mar 10:22. And he *was sad* at that saying, *and*

στύλος, stulos.

Gal. 2: 9. who seemed to be *pillars,*
1Ti. 3:15. the *pillar* and ground of the truth.
Rev. 3:12. a *pillar* in the temple of my God,
  10: 1. and his feet as *pillars* of fire:

σύ, su.

Mat. 2: 6. And *thou* Bethlehem, (in) the land of Juda,
  3:14. and comest *thou* to me?
  6: 6. But *thou*, when thou prayest,
    17. But *thou*, when thou fastest,
  11: 3. Art *thou* he that should come,
    23. And *thou*, Capernaum, which *art* exalted
  14:28. Lord, if it be *thou*, bid me come
  16:16. *Thou* art the Christ, the Son of the living
    God.
  18. I say also unto thee, That *thou* art Peter,
  26:25. He said unto him, *Thou* hast said.
    39. not as I will, but as *thou* (wilt).
    63. that thou tell us whether *thou* be the
    Christ,
    64. Jesus saith unto him, *Thou* hast said:
    69. *Thou* also wast with Jesus
    73. Surely *thou* also art (one) of them;
  27. 4. What (is that) to us? see *thou* (to that).
    11. Art *thou* the King of the Jews? And Jesus
    said unto him, *Thou* sayest.
Mar 1:11. *Thou* art my beloved Son,
  3:11. saying, *Thou* art the Son of God.
  8:29. *Thou* art the Christ.
  14:36. not what I will, but what *thou* wilt.
    61. Art *thou* the Christ, the Son of the Blessed?
    67. And *thou* also wast with Jesus
    68. neither understand I what *thou* sayest.
  15: 2. Art *thou* the King of the Jews? And he
    answering said unto him, *Thou* sayest
    (it).
Lu. 1:28. blessed (art) *thou* among women.
    42. Blessed (art) *thou* among women,
    76. And *thou*, child, shalt be called the prophet
  3:22. *Thou* art my beloved Son;

Lu. 4: 7. If *thou* therefore wilt worship me,
    41. *Thou* art Christ the Son of God.
  7:19. Art *thou* he that should come?
    20. Art *thou* he that should come?
  9:60. but go *thou* and preach the kingdom of
        God.
10:15. And *thou*, Capernaum, which art exalted
    37. Go, and do *thou* likewise.
15:31. Son, *thou* art ever with me,
16: 7. And how much owest *thou*?
    25. remember that *thou* in thy lifetime
      — and *thou* art tormented.
17: 8. afterward *thou* shalt eat and drink?
19:19. Be *thou* also over five cities.
    42. If thou hadst known, even *thou*,
22:32. and when *thou* art converted,
    58. *Thou* art also of them. And
    67. Art *thou* the Christ? tell us.
    70. Art *thou* then the Son of God?
23: 3. Art *thou* the King of the Jews? And he
      answered him and said, *Thou* sayest (it).
    37. If *thou* be the king of the Jews,
    39. If *thou* be Christ, save thyself and us.
    40. Dost not *thou* fear God,
24:18. Art *thou* only a stranger in Jerusalem,
Joh. 1:19. to ask him, Who art *thou*?
    21. What then? Art *thou* Elias?
    — Art *thou* that prophet?
    25. if *thou* be not that Christ, nor Elias,
    42(43). *Thou* art Simon the son of Jona:
       thou shalt be called Cephas,
    49(50). *thou* art the Son of God; *thou* art
       the King of Israel.
  2:10. *thou* hast kept the good wine until now.
    20. and wilt *thou* rear it up in three days?
  3: 2. can do these miracles that *thou* doest,
    10. Art *thou* a master of Israel, and
    26. to whom *thou* barest witness,
  4: 9. How is it that *thou*, being a Jew,
    10. *thou* wouldest have asked of him,
    12. Art *thou* greater than our father Jacob,
    19. I perceive that *thou* art a prophet.
  6:30. What sign shewest *thou* then, that we
    69. and are sure that *thou* art that Christ,
  7:52. Art *thou* also of Galilee?
  8: 5. should be stoned: but what sayest *thou*?
    13. *Thou* bearest record of thyself;
    25. Then said they unto him, Who art *thou*?
    33. how sayest *thou*, Ye shall be made free?
    48. Say we not well that *thou* art a Samaritan,
    52. and *thou* sayest, If a man keep my
    53. Art *thou* greater than our father
    — whom makest *thou* thyself?
  9:17. What sayest *thou* of him,
    28. and said, *Thou* art his disciple;
    34. *Thou* wast altogether born in sins, and
      dost *thou* teach us?
    35. Dost *thou* believe on the Son of God?
10:24. If *thou* be the Christ, tell us plainly.
    33. *thou*, being a man, makest thyself God.
11:27. I believe that *thou* art the Christ,
    42. they may believe that *thou* hast sent me.
12:34. and how sayest *thou*, The Son of man
      must be
13: 6. Lord, dost *thou* wash my feet?
    7. What I do *thou* knowest not now;
14: 9. and how sayest *thou* (then), Shew us
17: 5. And now, O Father, glorify *thou* me
    8. have believed that *thou* didst send me.
    21. as *thou*, Father, (art) in me, and I in thee,
    — may believe that *thou* hast sent me.
    23. I in them, and *thou* in me,

Joh.17:23. may know that *thou* hast sent me,
    25. these have known that *thou* hast sent me.
18:17. Art not *thou* also (one) of this man's
    25. Art not *thou* also (one) of his disciples?
    33. Art *thou* the King of the Jews?
    34. Sayest *thou* this thing of thyself,
    37. Art *thou* a king then? Jesus answered,
      Thou sayest that I am a king.
19: 9. and saith unto Jesus, Whence art *thou*?
20:15. Sir, if *thou* have borne him hence,
21:12. durst ask him, Who art *thou*?
    15. Yea, Lord; *thou* knowest that I love thee.
    16. Yea, Lord; *thou* knowest that I love thee.
    17. Lord, *thou* knowest all things; *thou* know-
      est that I love thee.
    22. what (is that) to thee? follow *thou* me.
Acts 1:24. *Thou*, Lord, which knewest the hearts
  4:24. Lord, *thou* (art) God, which hast made
  7:28. Wilt *thou* kill me, as thou diddest the
  9: 5. I am Jesus whom *thou* persecutest:
10:15. (that) call not *thou* common.
    33. and *thou* hast well done that thou art come.
11: 9. (that) call not *thou* common.
    14. whereby *thou* and all thy house
13:33. *Thou* art my Son, this day have I begotten
      thee.
16:31. and *thou* shalt be saved, and thy house.
21:38. Art not *thou* that Egyptian,
22: 8. Jesus of Nazareth, whom *thou* persecutest.
    27. Tell me, art *thou* a Roman?
23: 3. for sittest *thou* to judge me after the law,
    21. But do not *thou* yield unto them:
25:10. done no wrong, as *thou* very well knowest.
26:15. I am Jesus whom *thou* persecutest.
Ro. 2: 3. that *thou* shalt escape the judgment of
    17. Behold, *thou* art called a Jew,
  9:20. who art *thou* that repliest against God?
11:17. and *thou*, being a wild olive tree,
    18. *thou* bearest not the root, but the root
      thee.
    20. and *thou* standest by faith.
    22. otherwise *thou* also shalt be cut off.
    24. For if *thou* wert cut out of the olive
14: 4. Who art *thou* that judgest another man's
    10. But why dost *thou* judge thy brother? or
      why dost *thou* set at nought
    32. Hast *thou* faith? have (it) to thyself
1Co.14:17. For *thou* verily givest thanks well,
15:36. that which *thou* sowest is not quickened,
Gal. 2:14. If *thou*, being a Jew, livest after the
  6: 1. lest *thou* also be tempted.
1Ti. 6:11. But *thou*, O man of God, flee these
2Ti. 1:18. at Ephesus, *thou* knowest very well.
  2: 1. *Thou* therefore, my son, be strong in
    3. *Thou* therefore endure hardness,
  3:10. But *thou* hast fully known my
    14. But continue *thou* in the things
  4: 5. But watch *thou* in all things,
    15. Of whom be *thou* ware also;
Tit. 2: 1. But speak *thou* the things which become
      sound doctrine:
Philem 12. *thou* therefore receive him,
Heb. 1: 5. *Thou* art my Son, this day have I begotten
      thee?
    10. And, *Thou*, Lord, in the beginning
    11. They shall perish; but *thou* remainest;
    12. but *thou* art the same, and thy years
  5: 5. *Thou* art my Son, to day have I begotten
      thee.
    6. *Thou* (art) a priest for ever
  7:17. *Thou* (art) a priest for ever
    21. *Thou* (art) a priest for ever

Jas. 2: 3. Sit *thou* here in a good place ;
— Stand *thou* there, or sit here under
18. *Thou* hast faith, and I have works:
19. *Thou* believest that there is one God ;
4:12. who art *thou* that judgest another ?
3Joh. 3. even as *thou* walkest in the truth.
Rev. 2:15. So hast *thou* also them that hold the
3:17. knowest not that *thou* art wretched,
4:11. for *thou* hast created all things,
7:14. and I said unto him, Sir, *thou* knowest.

συγγένεια, *sungenīa.*

Lu. 1:61. There is none of thy *kindred* that is
Acts 7: 3. out of thy country, and from thy *kindred,*
14. and all his *kindred,* threescore and fifteen
souls.

συγγενής, *sungenees.*

Mar 6: 4. among his own *kin,* and in his own house.
Lu. 1:36. And, behold, thy *cousin* Elisabeth,
58. And her neighbours and her *cousins*
2:44. and they sought him among (their) *kinsfolk*
14:12. thy *kinsmen,* nor (thy) rich neighbours ;
21:16. brethren, and *kinsfolks,* and friends ;
Joh. 18:26. being (his) *kinsman* whose ear Peter
Acts 10:24. and had called together his *kinsmen*
Ro. 9: 3. for my brethren, my *kinsmen* according to
the flesh.
16: 7. Salute Andronicus and Junia, my *kinsmen,*
11. Salute Herodion my *kinsman.*
21. Lucius, and Jason, and Sosipater, my
kinsmen,

συγγνώμη, *sungnōmee.*

1Co. 7: 6. But I speak this by *permission,*

συγκάθημαι, *sunkatheemai.*

Mar 14:54. and he *sat with* the servants,
Acts 26:30. and Bernice, and they *that sat with* them:

συγκαθίζω, *sunkathizo.*

Lu. 22:55. and *were set down together,*
Eph. 2: 6. and *made* (us) *sit together* in heavenly
(places) in Christ Jesus:

συγκακοπαθέω, *sunkakopatheo.*

2Ti. 1: 8. but *be thou partaker of the afflictions* of the
gospel

συγκακουχέομαι, *sunkakoukeomai.*

Heb 11:25. Choosing rather *to suffer affliction with* the
people of God,

συγκαλέω, *sunkaleo.*

Mar 15·16. and they *call together* the whole band.

Lu. 9: 1. *called* his twelve disciples *together, and*
15: 6. he *calleth together* (his) friends
9. *calleth* (her) friends and (her) neighbours
together,
23:13. when he had *called together* the chief
Acts 5:21. and *called* the council *together,*
10:24. *and had called together* his kinsmen
28.17. Paul *called* the chief of the Jews *together:*

συγκαλύπτομαι, *sunkaluptomai.*

Lu. 12: 2. there is nothing *covered,* that shall not

συγκάμπτω, *sunkampto.*

Ro. 11:10. and *bow down* their back alway.

συγκαταβαίνω, *sunkatabaino.*

Acts 25: 5. *go down with* (me), *and* accuse

σνγκατατίθεμαι, *sunkatatithemai.*

Lu. 23:51. had not *consented* to the counsel and

συγκατάθεσις, *sunkatathesis.*

2Co. 6:16. what *agreement* hath the temple of God
with idols ?

συγκαταψηφίζομαι, *sunkatapseephizomai.*

Acts 1:26. and he *was numbered with* the eleven
apostles.

συγκεράννυμι, *sunkerannumi.*

1Co. 12:24. God hath *tempered* the body *together,*
Heb 4: 2. not *being mixed with* faith in them

συγκινέω, *sunkineo.*

Acts 6:12. they *stirred up* the people, and the

συγκλείω, *sunklio.*

Lu. 5: 6. they *inclosed* a great multitude of fishes:
Ro. 11:32. For God hath *concluded* them all in unbelief,
Gal. 3:22. But the scripture hath *concluded* all under
sin,
23. *shut up* unto the faith which should

συγκληρονόμος, *sunkleeronomos.*

Ro. 8:17. heirs of God, and *joint-heirs* with Christ ;
Eph. 3: 6. That the Gentiles should be *fellowheirs,*
Heb 11: 9. *the heirs with* him of the same promise:
1Pet. 3: 7. *heirs together* of the grace of life ;

συγκοινωνέω, sunkoinōneo.

Eph. 5:11. And *have* no *fellowship with* the unfruitful works of darkness,

Phi. 4:14. ye have well done, *that ye did communicate with* my affliction.

Rev. 18: 4. that ye *be* not *partakers of* her sins,

συγκοινωνός, sunkoinōnos.

Ro. 11:17. and *with* them *partakest* of the root

1Co. 9:23. I might be *partaker* thereof *with* (you).

Phi. 1: 7. ye all are *partakers* of my grace.

Rev. 1: 9. and *companion* in tribulation,

συγκομίζω, sunkomizo.

Acts 8: 2. And devout men *carried* Stephen (to his burial),

συγκρίνω, sunkrino.

1Co. 2:13. *comparing* spiritual things *with* spiritual.

2Co. 10:12. or *compare* ourselves *with* some that
— *comparing* themselves *among* themselves,

συγκύπτω, sunkupto.

Lu. 13:11. and was *bowed together*, and could in no wise

συγκυρία, sunkuria.

Lu. 10:31. by *chance* (lit. *coincidence*) there came down a certain

---

συγχαίρω, sunkairo.

Lu. 1:58. and they *rejoiced with* her.

15: 6. *Rejoice with* me; for I have found my sheep

9. *Rejoice with* me; for I have found the piece

1Co. 12:26. all the members *rejoice with* it.

13: 6. but *rejoiceth in* the truth;

Phi. 2:17. I joy, and *rejoice with* you all.

18. also do ye joy, and *rejoice with* me.

συγχέω, sunkeo.

Acts 21:27. *stirred up* all the people, and laid hands

συγχράομαι, sunkraomai.

Joh. 4: 9. for the Jews *have* no *dealings with* the Samaritans.

συγχύνω, sunkuno.

Acts 2: 6. the multitude came together, and *were confounded*, because

9:22. and *confounded* the Jews which dwelt at

19:32. for the assembly was *confused;*

21:31. that all Jerusalem *was in an uproar*.

σύγχυσις, sunkusis.

Acts 19:29. whole city was filled with *confusion :*

συζάω, suzao.

Ro. 6: 8. we believe that we *shall* also *live with* him:

2Co. 7: 3. ye are in our hearts to die and *live with* (you).

2Ti. 2:11. we *shall* also *live with* (him):

συζευγνύω, suzūgnuo.

Mat. 19: 6. What therefore God *hath joined together*,

Mar 10: 9. What therefore God *hath joined together*,

συζητέω, suzeeteo.

Mar 1:27. they *questioned* among themselves,

8:11. and began to *question with* him,

9:10. *questioning* one with another

14. and the scribes *questioning with* them.

16. What *question* ye with them?

12:28. and having heard them *reasoning together*,

Lu. 22:23. they began to *enquire* among themselves,

24:15. while they communed (together) and *reasoned*,

Acts 6: 9. and of Asia, *disputing with* Stephen.

9:29. and *disputed* against the Grecians:

συζήτησις, suzeeteesis.

Acts 15: 2. no small dissension and *disputation*

7. when there had been much *disputing*,

28:29. had great *reasoning* among themselves.

συζητητής, suzeeteetees.

1Co. 1:20. where (is) the *disputer* of this world?

σύζυγος, suzugos.

Phi. 4: 3. I intreat thee also, true *yokefellow*,

συζωοποιέω, suzōöpoyeo.

Eph 2: 5. *hath quickened* us *together with* Christ,

Col. 2:13. *hath* he *quickened together with* him,

συκάμινος, sukaminos.

Lu. 17: 6. ye might say unto this *sycamine tree*,

συκῆ, sukee.

Mat. 21:19. And when he saw a *fig tree* in the way,
— And presently the *fig tree* withered away.

20. How soon is the *fig tree* withered away!

21. not only do this (which is done) to the *fig tree*,

24:32. Now learn a parable of the *fig tree;*

Mar 11:13. And seeing a *fig tree* afar off having

20. they saw the *fig tree* dried up

21. behold, the *fig tree* which thou cursedst

Mar 13:28. Now learn a parable of the *fig tree ;*
Lu. 13: 6. A certain (man) had a *fig tree* planted
     7. I come seeking fruit on this *fig tree,*
  21:29. Behold the *fig tree,* and all the trees ;
Joh. 1:48(49). when thou wast under the *fig tree,*
    50(51). I saw thee under the *fig tree,*
Jas. 3:12. Can the *fig tree,* my brethren, bear olive
    berries ?
Rev. 6:13. as a *fig tree* casteth her untimely figs,

συκομωραία, *sukomōraia.*

Lu. 19: 4. and climbed up into a *sycomore tree*

σῦκον, *sukon.*

Mat. 7:16. grapes of thorns, or *figs* of thistles ?
Mar 11:13. the time of *figs* was not (yet).
Lu. 6:44. of thorns men do not gather *figs,*
Jas. 3:12. either a vine, *figs ?* so (can)

συκοφαντέω, *sukophanteo.*

Lu. 3:14. neither *accuse* (any) *falsely ;*
  19: 8. if I *have taken* any thing from any man *by
    false accusation,*

συλαγωγέω, *sulagōgeo.*

Col. 2: 8. Beware lest any man *spoil* you

συλάω, *sulao.*

2Co.11: 8. I *robbed* other churches, taking wages

συλλαλέω, *sullaleo.*

Mat.17: 3. Moses and Elias *talking with* him.
Mar 9: 4. and they were *talking with* Jesus.
Lu. 4:36. and *spake among* themselves,
  9:30. there *talked with* him two men,
  22: 4. and *communed with* the chief priests
Acts25:12. Then Festus, *when he had conferred with*
    the council,

συλλαμβάνω, *sullambano.*

Mat.26:55. with swords and staves for *to take* me ?
Mar 14:48. with swords and (with) staves *to take* me ?
Lu. 1:24. his wife Elisabeth *conceived,* and
    31. thou *shalt conceive* in thy womb,
    36. she *hath* also *conceived* a son
  2:21. before he *was conceived* in the womb.
  5: 7. that they should come and *help* them.
    9. at the draught of the fishes which they
    had *taken :*
  22:54. Then *took* they him, *and* led (him),
Joh. 18:12. and officers of the Jews *took* Jesus.
Acts 1:16. guide to them *that took* Jesus.
  12: 3. he proceeded further *to take* Peter
  23:27. This man was *taken* of the Jews,
  26:21. the Jews *caught* me in the temple, *and*
Phi. 4: 3. *help* those women which laboured with me
Jas. 1:15. Then *when* lust *hath conceived,*

συλλέγω, *sullego.*

Mat. 7:16. *Do* men *gather* grapes of thorns,
  13:28. that we go and *gather* them *up ?*
    29. Nay ; lest *while* ye *gather up* the tares,
    30. *Gather* ye *together* first the tares,
    40. As therefore the tares *are gathered*
    41. and they *shall gather* out of his kingdom
    48. and *gathered* the good into vessels,
Lu. 6:44. of thorns men *do not gather* figs,

συλλογίζομαι, *sullogizomai.*

Lu. 20: 5. And they *reasoned with* themselves,

συλλυπέομαι, *sullupeomai.*

Mar 3: 5. *being grieved* for the hardness of their
    hearts,

συμβαίνω, *sumbaino.*

Mar 10:32. what things should *happen unto* him,
Lu. 24:14. of all these things *which had happened.*
Acts 3:10. at that *which had happened unto* him.
  20:19. and temptations, *which befell* me by
  21:35. *so it was,* that he was borne of the soldiers
1Co.10:11. all these things *happened unto* them for
1Pet.4:12. as though some strange thing *happened
    unto* you :
2Pet.2:22. But it *is happened* unto them

συμβάλλω, *sumballo.*

Lu. 2:19. and *pondered* (them) in her heart.
  14:31. *to make* war (lit. *to encounter* in **war**)
    against another king,
Acts 4:15. they *conferred* among themselves,
  17:18. and of the Stoicks, *encountered* him.
  18:27. *helped* them much which had believed
  20:14. And when he *met with* us at Assos,

συμβασιλεύω, *sumbasiluo.*

1Co. 4: 8. that we also *might reign with* you.
2Ti. 2:12. we *shall* also *reign with* (him) :

συμβιβάζω, *sumbibazo.*

Acts 9:22. *proving* that this is very Christ.
  16:10. *assuredly gathering* that the Lord had
1Co. 2:16. mind of the Lord, that he may **instruct**
    him ?
Eph. 4:16. and *compacted* by that which every joint
Col. 2: 2. *being knit together* in love,
    19. and *knit together,* increaseth with the in-
    crease of God.

συμβουλεύω, *sumbouluo.*

Mat.26: 4. *consulted* that they might take
Joh.11:53. they *took counsel together* for to put
  18:14. Caiaphas was he, *which gave counsel to*

Acts 9:23. the Jews *took counsel* to kill him:
Rev. 3:18. I *counsel* thee to buy of me gold

συμβούλιον, *sumboulion.*

Mat 12:14. and held a *council* against him,
   22:15. and took *counsel* how they might entangle
   27: 1. and elders of the people took *counsel*
     7. And they took *counsel*, and bought
   28:12. and had taken *counsel*, they gave
Mar 3: 6. and straightway took *counsel*
   15: 1. the chief priests held a *consultation*
Acts 25:12. when he had conferred with the *council*,

σύμβουλος, *sumboulos.*

Ro. 11:34. or who hath been his *counsellor?*

συμμαθητής, *summatheetees.*

Joh. 11:16. unto his *fellowdisciples,* Let us

συμμαρτυρέω, *summartureo.*

Ro. 2:15. their conscience *also bearing witness,*
   8:16. The Spirit itself *beareth witness with*
   9: 1. my conscience also *bearing me witness*
Rev. 22:18. For I *testify unto* every man that

συμμερίζομαι, *summerizomai.*

1Co. 9:13. are *partakers with* the altar?

συμμέτοχος, *summetokos.*

Eph. 3: 6. and *partakers* (lit. *co-partakers*) of his pro-
     mise in Christ
   5: 7. Be not ye therefore *partakers* with them.

συμμιμητής, *summimeetees.*

Phi. 3:17. be *followers together* of me,

συμμορφόομαι, *summorphŏŏmai.*

Phi. 3:10. *being made conformable unto* his death;

σύμμορφος, *summorphos.*

Ro. 8:29. (to be) *conformed to* the image of his Son,
Phi. 3:21. *fashioned like unto* his glorious body,

συμπαθέω, *sumpatheo.*

Heb 4:15. which cannot *be touched with the feeling of*
     our infirmities;
   10:34. *had compassion of* me in my bonds,

συμπαθής, *sumpathees.*

1Pet. 3: 8. *having compassion one of another,*

συμπαραγίνομαι, *sumparaginomai.*

Lu. 23:48. And all the people *that came together*
2Ti. 4:16. no man *stood with* me,

συμπαρακαλέομαι, *sumparakaleomai.*

Ro. 1:12. that I may *be comforted together* with you

συμπαραλαμβάνω, *sumparalambano.*

Acts 12:25. and *took with* them John,
   15:37. determined *to take with* them John,
     38. thought not good *to take* him *with* them,
Gal. 2: 1. *and took* Titus *with* (me) also.

συμπαραμένω, *sumparameno.*

Phi. 1:25. that I shall abide and *continue with* you all

συμπάρειμι, *sumparīmi.*

Acts 25:24. and all men *which are here present with* us,

συμπάσχω, *sumpasko.*

Ro. 8:17. if so be that we *suffer with* (him),
1Co. 12:26. all the members *suffer with* it;

συμπέμπω, *sumpempo.*

2Co. 8:18. And we *have sent with* him the brother,
    22. And we *have sent with* them our brother,

συμπεριλαμβάνω, *sumperilambano.*

Acts 20:10. and fell on him, and *embracing* (him)

συμπίνω, *sumpino.*

Acts 10:41. who did eat and *drink with* him

συμπληρόω, *sumpleeroō.*

Lu. 8:23. and they *were filled* (with water),
   9:51. when the time *was come*
Acts 2: 1. the day of Pentecost *was fully come,*

συμπνίγω, *sumpnigo.*

Mat. 13:22. and the deceitfulness of riches, *choke* the
     word,
Mar 4: 7. and *choked* it, and it yielded no
   19. entering in, *choke* the word,
Lu. 8:14. go forth, and *are choked* with cares
   42. But as he went the people *thronged* him.

συμπολίτης, *sumpolitees.*

Eph 2:19. but *fellowcitizens* with the saints,

συμπορεύομαι, *sumporŭomai.*

Mar 10: 1. and the people *resort* unto him again;
Lu. 7:11. and many of his disciples *went with* him,
14:25. And there *went* great multitudes *with*
24:15. drew near, and *went with* them.

συμπόσιον, *sumposion.*

Mar 6:39. to make all sit down by *companies* (lit. *company* by *company*)

συμπρεσβύτερος, *sumpresbuteros.*

1Pet.5: 1. who am *also* an *elder*, (lit. a *co-elder*)

συμφαγεῖν see συνεσθίω.

συμφέρω, *sumphero.*

Mat. 5:29. for it *is profitable for* thee that one
30. for it *is profitable for* thee that one
18: 6. it were *better for* him that a millstone
19:10. it *is not good* to marry.
Joh. 11:50. Nor consider that it *is expedient for* us,
16: 7. It *is expedient for* you that I go away:
18:14. that it *was expedient* that one man
Acts19:19. *brought* their books *together, and*
20:20. nothing *that was profitable* (unto you),
1Co. 6:12. but all things *are not expedient:*
7:35. And this I speak for your own *profit;*
10:23. but all things *are not expedient:*
33. not seeking mine own *profit,*
12: 7. given to every man to *profit* withal.
2Co. 8:10. for this *is expedient for* you,
12: 1. It *is* not *expedient for* me doubtless to glory.
Heb12:10. but he for (our) *profit,*

Note. That the verb is used transitively in Acts 19: 19, whereas in all the other passages it is intransitive, and in most of them impersonal.

σύμφημι, *sumpheemi.*

Ro. 7:16. I *consent* unto the law that (it is) good.

συμφυλέτης, *sumphuletees.*

1Th. 2:14. suffered like things of your own *country-men,*

συμφύομαι, *sumphuŏmai.*

Lu. 8: 7. the thorns *sprang up with* it, *and*

σύμφυτος, *sumphutos.*

Ro. 6: 5. if we have been *planted together* in

συμφωνέω, *sumphōneo.*

Mat.18:19. That if two of you *shall agree* on earth
20: 2. And *when* he *had agreed* with the labourers
13. *didst* not thou *agree with* me for
Lu. 5:36. *agreeth* not *with* the old.
Acts 5: 9. ye *have agreed together* to tempt
15:15. to this *agree* the words of the prophets;

συμφώνησις, *sumphōneesis.*

2Co. 6:15. And what *concord* hath Christ with Belial?

συμφωνία, *sumphōnia.*

Lu. 15:25. he heard *musick* and dancing.

σύμφωνος, *sumphōnos.*

1Co. 7: 5. except (it be) with *consent* for a time,

συμψηφίζω, *sumpseephizo.*

Acts19:19. and they *counted* the price of them,

σύμψυχος, *sumpsukos.*

Phi. 2: 2. (being) *of one accord*, of one mind.

σύν, *sun.*

prep. governing the dative case.

Mat.25:27. have received mine own *with* usury.
26:35. Though I should die *with* thee, yet
27:38. Then were there two thieves crucified *with* him,
Mar 2:26. gave also to them which were *with* him?
4:10. they that were about him *with* the twelve
8:34. called the people (unto him) *with* his disciples
9: 4. appeared unto them Elias *with* Moses:
15:27. And *with* him they crucify two thieves;
Lu. 1:56. And Mary abode *with* her about
2: 5. To be taxed *with* Mary his espoused wife,
13. And suddenly there was *with* the angel
5: 9. and all that were *with* him,
19. *with* (his) couch into the midst
7: 6. Then Jesus went *with* them.
12. much people of the city was *with* her.
8: 1. and the twelve (were) *with* him,
38. besought him that he might be *with* him:
9:32. Peter and they that were *with* him
19:23. required mine own *with* usury?
20: 1. the scribes came upon (him) *with* the elders,
22:14. and the twelve apostles *with* him.
56. This man was also *with* him.
23:11. And Herod *with* his men of war
32. led *with* him to be put to death.
35. And the rulers also *with* them
24: 1. and certain (others) *with* them.
10. and other (women that were) *with* them,
21. and *beside* all this, to day
24. certain of them which were *with* us
29. to tarry *with* them.

Lu. 24:33. and them that were *with* them,
    44. while I was yet *with* you,
Joh. 18: 1. he went forth *with* his disciples
  21: 3. We also go *with* thee. They went
Acts 1:14. *with* the women, and Mary the mother of Jesus, and *with* his brethren.
    17. For he was numbered *with* us,
    22. ordained to be a witness *with* us
  2:14. But Peter, standing up *with* the eleven,
  3: 4. fastening his eyes upon him *with* John,
    8. and entered *with* them into the temple,
  4:13. that they had been *with* Jesus,
    14. the man which was healed standing *with*
    27. and Pontius Pilate, *with* the Gentiles,
  5: 1. Ananias, *with* Sapphira his wife,
    17. and all they that were *with* him,
    21. and they that were *with* him,
    26. Then went the captain *with* the officers,
  8:20. Thy money perish *with* thee,
    31. he would come up and sit *with* him.
  10: 2. one that feared God *with* all his house,
    20. get thee down, and go *with* them,
    23. Peter went away *with* them,
  11:12. accompanied me, (lit. came *with* me)
  13: 7. Which was *with* the deputy
  14: 4. and part held *with* the Jews, and part *with* the apostles.
    5. and also of the Jews *with* their rulers,
    13. done sacrifice *with* the people.
    20. he departed *with* Barnabas to Derbe.
    28. they abode long time *with* the disciples.
  15:22. and elders, *with* the whole church,
  — *with* Paul and Barnabas;
    25. *with* our beloved Barnabas and Paul,
  16: 3. Him would Paul have to go forth *with* him;
  17:34. Damaris, and others *with* them.
  18: 8. believed on the Lord *with* all his house;
    18. and *with* him Priscilla and Aquila;
  19:38. and the craftsmen which are *with* him,
  20:36. and prayed *with* them all.
  21: 5. *with* wives and children,
    16. There went *with* us also (certain) of the disciples
    18. Paul went in *with* us unto James;
    24. and purify thyself *with* them,
    26. purifying himself *with* them
    29. they had seen before *with* him in the city
  22: 9. And they that were *with* me saw
  23:15. Now therefore ye *with* the council
    27. then came I *with* an army,
    32. they left the horsemen to go *with* him,
  24:24. when Felix came *with* his wife
  25:23. *with* the chief captains, and
  26:13. and them which journeyed *with* me.
  27: 2. a Macedonian of Thessalonica, being *with* us.
  28:16. *with* a soldier that kept him.
Ro. 6: 8. Now if we be dead *with* Christ,
  8:32. *with* him also freely give us all things?
  16:14. and the brethren which are *with* them.
    15. all the saints which are *with* them.
1Co. 1: 2. *with* all that in every place
  5: 4. *with* the power of our Lord Jesus Christ,
  10:13. *with* the temptation also make a way
  11:32. not be condemned *with* the world.
  15:10. the grace of God which was *with* me.
  16: 4. they shall go *with* me.
    19. *with* the church that is in their house.
2Co. 1: 1. *with* all the saints which are in all
    21. he which stablisheth us *with* you
  4:14. and shall present (us) *with* you.

2Co. 8:19. to travel with us *with* this grace,
  9: 4. if they of Macedonia come *with* me,
  13: 4. but we shall live *with* him
Gal. 1: 2. And all the brethren which are *with* me,
  2: 3. neither Titus, who was *with* me,
  3: 9. are blessed *with* faithful Abraham.
  5:24. have crucified the flesh *with* the affections
Eph. 3:18. to comprehend *with* all saints
  4:31. be put away from you, *with* all malice :
Phi. 1: 1. *with* the bishops and deacons:
    23. to depart, and to be *with* Christ;
  2:22. he hath served *with* me in the gospel.
  4:21. The brethren which are *with* me
Col. 2: 5. yet am I *with* you in the spirit,
    13. hath he quickened together *with* him,
    20. Wherefore if ye be dead *with* Christ
  3: 3. your life is hid *with* Christ in God.
    4. ye also shall appear *with* him in glory.
    9. ye have put off the old man *with* his deeds;
  4: 9. *With* Onesimus, a faithful and
1Th. 4:14. will God bring *with* him.
    17. shall be caught up together *with* them
  — so shall we ever be *with* the Lord.
  5:10. we should live together *with* him.
Jas. 1:11. is no sooner risen *with* a burning heat,
2Pet. 1:18. when we were *with* him in the holy mount

συνάγω, sunago.

Mat. 2: 4. *when* he had gathered . . . . *together*
  3:12. and *gather* his wheat into the garner ;
  6:26. nor *gather* into barns ;
  12:30. and he *that gathereth* not with me
  13: 2. And great multitudes *were gathered together*
    30. but *gather* the wheat into my barn.
    47. and *gathered* of every kind:
  18:20. are *gathered together* in my name,
  22:10. and *gathered together* all
    34. they were *gathered* together.
    41. *While* the Pharisees *were gathered together*,
  24:28. there *will* the eagles *be gathered together*.
  25:24. and *gathering* where thou hast not strawed:
    26. and *gather* where I have not strawed:
    32. And before him *shall be gathered* all nations:
    35. a stranger, and ye *took* me *in :*
    38. a stranger, and *took* (thee) *in ?*
    43. a stranger, and ye *took* me not *in :*
  26: 3. Then *assembled together* the chief priests,
    57. scribes and the elders *were assembled.*
  27:17. *when* they *were gathered together,*
    27. and *gathered* unto him the whole band
    62. priests and Pharisees *came together*
  28:12. And *when* they *were assembled* with
Mar 2: 2. many *were gathered together,*
  4: 1. and there *was gathered* unto him
  5:21. much people *gathered* unto him:
  6:30. the apostles *gathered* themselves *together*
  7: 1. *came together* unto him the Pharisees,
Lu. 3:17. and *will gather* the wheat into his
  11:23. and he *that gathereth* not with me
  12:17. no room where to *bestow* my fruits ?
    18. there *will* I *bestow* all my fruits
  15:13. younger son *gathered* all *together, and*
  17:37. *will* the eagles *be gathered together.*
  22:66. priests and the scribes *came together,*
Joh. 4:36. and *gathereth* fruit unto life eternal :
  6:12. *Gather up* the fragments that remain,
    13. Therefore they *gathered* (them) *together,*
  11:47. Then *gathered* the chief priests and

Joh. 11:52. but that also he *should gather together* in one the children of God
15: 6. and men *gather* them, and cast
18: 2. for Jesus ofttimes *resorted* thither with
20:19. where the disciples were *assembled*
Acts 4: 6(5). *were gathered together* at Jerusalem.
26. and the rulers were *gathered* together
27. and the people of Israel, *were gathered together*,
31. where they were *assembled together*;
11:26. they *assembled* themselves with the church,
13:44. *came* almost the whole city *together*
14:27. and had *gathered* the church *together*,
15: 6. the apostles and elders *came together*
30. and *when* they had *gathered* the multitude *together*,
20: 7. *when* the disciples *came together*
8. where they were *gathered together*.
1Co. 5: 4. *when* ye are *gathered together*,
Rev. 13:10. He that *leadeth into* captivity
16:14. *to gather* them to the battle
16. And he *gathered* them *together*
19:17. Come and *gather* yourselves *together*
19. and their armies, *gathered together*
20: 8. *to gather* them *together* to battle:

συναγωγή, sunagōgee

Mat. 4:23. teaching in their *synagogues*,
6: 2. as the hypocrites do in the *synagogues*
5. love to pray standing in the *synagogues*
9:35. teaching in their *synagogues*,
10:17. they will scourge you in their *synagogues*;
12: 9. he went into their *synagogue*:
13:54. he taught them in their *synagogue*,
23: 6. chief seats in the *synagogues*,
34. shall ye scourge in your *synagogues*,
Mar. 1:21. he entered into the *synagogue*,
23. And there was in their *synagogue*
29. they were come out of the *synagogue*,
39. And he preached in their *synagogues*
3: 1. he entered again into the *synagogue*;
6: 2. he began to teach in the *synagogue*:
12:39. And the chief seats in the *synagogues*,
13: 9. in the *synagogues* ye shall be beaten:
Lu. 4:15. And he taught in their *synagogues*,
16. he went into the *synagogue*
20. all them that were in the *synagogue*
28. And all they in the *synagogue*,
33. in the *synagogue* there was a man,
38. And he arose out of the *synagogue*,
44. And he preached in the *synagogues*
6: 6. he entered into the *synagogue* and
7: 5. and he hath built us a *synagogue*.
8:41. he was a ruler of the *synagogue*:
11:43. the uppermost seats in the *synagogues*,
12:11. when they bring you unto the *synagogues*,
13:10. he was teaching in one of the *synagogues*
20:46. the highest seats in the *synagogues*,
21:12. delivering (you) up to the *synagogues*,
Joh. 6:59. These things said he in the *synagogue*,
18:20. I ever taught in the *synagogue*,
Acts 6: 9. certain of the *synagogue*, which is called
9: 2. letters to Damascus to the *synagogues*,
20. he preached Christ in the *synagogues*,
13: 5. preached the word of God in the *synagogues*
14. and went into the *synagogue*
42. the Jews were gone out of the *synagogue*,
43. when the *congregation* was broken up,
14: 1. went both together into the *synagogue*

Acts 15:21. being read in the *synagogues*
17: 1. where was a *synagogue* of the Jews:
10. went into the *synagogue* of the Jews.
17. disputed he in the *synagogue*
18: 4. And he reasoned in the *synagogue*
7. whose house joined hard to the *synagogue*.
19. he himself entered into the *synagogue*,
26. to speak boldly in the *synagogue*:
19: 8. And he went into the *synagogue*,
22:19. and beat in every *synagogue*
24:12. neither in the *synagogues*, nor in
26:11. punished them oft in every *synagogue*,
Jas. 2: 2. if there come unto your *assembly*
Rev. 2: 9. but (are) the *synagogue* of Satan.
3: 9. them of the *synagogue* of Satan,

συναγωνίζομαι, sunagōnizomai.

Ro. 15:30. that ye *strive together with* me

συναθλέω, sunathleo.

Phi. 1:27. *striving together for* the faith of the gospel;
4: 3. which *laboured with* me in the gospel,

συναθροίζω, sunathroizo.

Lu. 24:33. and found the eleven *gathered together*,
Acts 12:12. where many were *gathered together*
19:25. Whom he *called together* with the

συναίρω, sunairo.

Mat. 18:23. which would *take* account of his servants.
24. And when he had begun *to reckon*,
25:19. cometh, and *reckoneth* (lit. *taketh* account) with them.

συναιχμάλωτος, sunaikmalōtos.

Ro. 16: 7. my kinsmen, and my *fellowprisoners*,
Col. 4:10. Aristarchus my *fellowprisoner*
Philem 23. Epaphras, my *fellowprisoner* in Christ Jesus;

συνακολουθέω, sunakoloutheo.

Mar 5:37. And he suffered no man *to follow* him,
Lu. 23:49. and the women *that followed* him from Galilee,

συναλίζομαι, sunalizomai.

Acts 1: 4. And *being assembled together* with (them), commanded them that

---

συναναβαίνω, sunanabaino.

Mar 15:41. many other women *which came up with* him unto Jerusalem.
Acts 13:31. of them *which came up with* him

συνανάκειμαι, *sunanakīmai.*

Mat. 9:10. came and *sat down with* him and his
 14: 9. and them *which sat with* him *at meat,*
Mar 2:15. sinners *sat* also *together with* Jesus
 6:22. pleased Herod and them *that sat with* him,
 26. and for their sakes *which sat with* him,
Lu. 7:49. And they *that sat at meat with* him
 14:10. of them *that sit at meat with* thee.
 15. one of them *that sat at meat with* him
Joh.12: 2. of them *that sat at the table with* him.

συναναμίγνυμι, *sunanamignumi.*

1Co. 5: 9. not *to company with* fornicators:
 11. written unto you not *to keep company,*
2Th. 3:14. and *have* no *company with* him,

συναναπαύομαι, *sunanapauomai.*

Ro. 15:32. and may *with* you *be refreshed.*

συναντάω, *sunantao.*

Lu. 9:37. much people *met* him.
 22:10. there *shall* a man *meet* you, bearing
Acts10:25. Cornelius *met* him, and fell down at
 20:22. not knowing the things *that shall befall* me
Heb 7: 1. *who met* Abraham returning
 10. when Melchisedec *met* him.

συνάντησις, *sunanteesis.*

Mat. 8:34. the whole city came out to *meet* Jesus:

συναντιλαμβάνομαι, *sunantilambanomai.*

Lu. 10:40. bid her therefore that she *help* me.
Ro. 8:26. the Spirit also *helpeth* our infirmities:

συναπάγομαι, *sunapagomai.*

Ro. 12:16. but *condescend* to men of low estate.
Gal. 2:13. Barnabas also *was carried away with*
2Pet.3:17. *being led away with* the error of the

συναποθνήσχω, *sunapothneesko.*

Mar14:31. If I should *die with* thee, I will
2Co. 7: 3. ye are in our hearts *to die* and live *with*
 (you).
2Ti. 2:11. For if we *be dead with* (him),

συναπόλλυμαι, *sunapollumai.*

Heb 11:31. Rahab *perished* not *with* them that believed
 not,

συναποστέλλω, *sunapostello.*

2Co.12:18. and *with* (him) I *sent* a brother.

συναρμολογέομαι, *sunarmologeomai.*

Eph 2:21. In whom all the building *fitly framed*
 together
 4:16. From whom the whole body *fitly joined*
 together

συναρπάζω, *sunarpazo.*

Lu. 8:29. For oftentimes it *had caught* him:
Acts 6:12. *caught* him, and brought (him)
 19:29. and *having caught* Gaius and
 27:15. And *when* the ship *was caught,* and could
 not bear up

συναυξάνομαι, *sunauxanomai.*

Mat.13:30. Let both *grow together* until the harvest:

συνδέομαι, *sundeomai.*

Heb13: 3. that are in bonds, as *bound with* them;

σύνδεσμος, *sundesmos.*

Acts 8:23. and (in) the *bond* of iniquity.
Eph 4: 3. unity of the Spirit in the *bond* of peace.
Col. 2:19. the body by joints and *bands* having nourishment ministered,
 3:14. which is the *bond* of perfectness.

συνδοξάζομαι, *sundoxazomai.*

Ro. 8:17. that we *may* be also *glorified together.*

σύνδουλος, *sundoulos.*

Mat.18:28. and found one of his *fellowservants,*
 29. And his *fellowservant* fell down
 31. So when his *fellowservants* saw what was
 33. have had compassion on thy *fellowservant,*
 24:49. shall begin to smite (his) *fellowservants,*
Col. 1: 7. Epaphras our dear *fellowservant,*
 4: 7. and *fellowservant* in the Lord:
Rev. 6:11. until their *fellowservants* also
 19:10. I am thy *fellowservant,* and of thy
 22: 9. I am thy *fellowservant,* and of thy

συνδρομή, *sundromee.*

Acts21:30. and the people *ran together:* (lit. there
 was a *concourse* &c. of)

συνεγείρω, *sunegiro.*

Eph 2: 6. And *hath raised* (us) *up together,*
Col. 2:12. wherein also ye *are risen with* (him)
 3: 1. If ye then *be risen with* Christ,

συνέδριον, *sunedrion.*

Mat. 5:22. shall be in danger of the *council:*

Mat. 10:17. they will deliver you up to the *councils*,
26:59. and elders, and all the *council*,
Mar 13: 9. for they shall deliver you up to *councils;*
14:55. the chief priests and all the *council*
15: 1. and scribes and the whole *council*,
Lu. 22:66. and led him into their *council*, saying,
Joh. 11:47. Then gathered the chief priests and the
Pharisees a *council*,
Acts 4:15. to go aside out of the *council*,
5:21. and called the *council* together,
27. they set (them) before the *council :*
34. Then stood there up one in the *council*,
41. from the presence of the *council*,
6:12. and brought (him) to the *council*,
15. And all that sat in the *council*,
22:30. and all their *council* to appear,
23: 1. Paul, earnestly beholding the *council*,
6. he cried out in the *council*,
15. Now therefore ye with the *council*
20. bring down Paul to morrow into the
council,
28. brought him forth into their *council :*
24:20. while I stood before the *council*,

συνειδέω, *sunideo.*

Acts 5: 2. his wife also *being privy* (to it),
12:12. And *when* he *had considered* (the thing),
14: 6. They *were ware* of (it), *and* fled unto
Lystra
1Co. 4: 4. For I *know* nothing *by* myself; (lit. *am
conscious* of nought)

συνείδησις, *sunideesis.*

Joh. 8: 9. being convicted by (their own) *conscience*,
Acts 23: 1. I have lived in all good *conscience*
24:16. to have always a *conscience* void of
Ro. 2:15. their *conscience* also bearing witness,
9: 1. my *conscience* also bearing me witness
13: 5. but also for *conscience* sake.
1Co. :8 7. for some with *conscience* of the idol
— and their *conscience* being weak is defiled.
10. shall not the *conscience* of him which is
weak
12. and wound their weak *conscience*,
10:25. asking no question for *conscience* sake:
27. asking no question for *conscience* sake.
28. and for *conscience* sake: for the earth
29. *Conscience*, I say, not thine own,
— judged of another (man's) *conscience ?*
2Co. 1:12. the testimony of our *conscience*,
4: 2. commending ourselves to every man's
conscience
5:11. are made manifest in your *consciences.*
1Ti. 1: 5. and (of) a good *conscience*, and
19. Holding faith, and a good *conscience ;*
3: 9. the mystery of the faith in a pure *conscience.*
4: 2. having their *conscience* seared
2Ti. 1: 3. with pure *conscience*, that without
Tit. 1:15. their mind and *conscience* is defiled.
Heb 9: 9. perfect, as pertaining to the *conscience ;*
14. purge your *conscience* from dead works
10: 2. no more *conscience* of sins.
22. sprinkled from an evil *conscience*,
13:18. we trust we have a good *conscience*,
1Pet. 2:19. if a man for *conscience* toward God
3:16. Having a good *conscience ;*
21. but the answer of a good *conscience*

σύνειμι, *sunimi.*

Lu. 9:18. his disciples *were with* him:
Acts 22:11. led by the hand of them *that were with* me

συνεῖμι, *sunimi.*

Lu. 8: 4. when much people *were gathered together*,

συνεισέρχομαι, *suniserkomai.*

Joh. 6:22. Jesus *went* not *with* his disciples *into* the
boat,
18:15. *went in with* Jesus into the palace of

συνέκδημος, *sunekdeemos.*

Acts 19:29. Paul's *companions in travel*,
2Co. 8:19. chosen of the churches to *travel with* us

συνεκλεκτός, *suneklektos.*

1Pet. 5:13. *elected together with* (you), saluteth you;

συνελαύνω, *sunelauno.*

Acts 7:26. and would have set them at one again,
(lit. *drew* them *together* to peace)

συνεπιμαρτυρέω, *sunepimartureo.*

Heb 2: 4. God *also* bearing (them) *witness*,

συνέπομαι, *sunepomai.*

Acts 20: 4. there *accompanied* him into Asia

συνεργέω, *sunergeo.*

Mar 16:20. the Lord *working with* (them),
Ro. 8:28. all things *work together* for good to them
1Co. 16:16. and to every one *that helpeth with* (us),
2Co. 6: 1. We then, (as) *workers together* (with him),
Jas. 2:22. how faith *wrought with* his works,

συνεργός, *sunergos.*

Ro. 16: 3. Priscilla and Aquila my *helpers* in Christ
Jesus:
9. Salute Urbane, our *helper* in Christ,
21. Timotheus my *workfellow*, and
1Co. 3: 9. For we are *labourers together with* God:
2Co. 1:24. but are *helpers* of your joy:
8:23. my partner and *fellowhelper* concerning
you:
Phi. 2:25. my brother, and *companion in labour*,
4: 3. (with) other my *fellowlabourers*,
Col. 4:11. These only (are my) *fellowworkers* unto
1Th. 3: 2. our *fellowlabourer* in the gospel
Philem. 1. our dearly beloved, and *fellowlabourer*,
24. Demas, Lucas, my *fellowlabourers.*
3Joh. 8. might be *fellowhelpers* to the truth.

συνέρχομαι, sunerkomai.

Mat. 1:18. before they *came together,* she
Mar 3:20. the multitude *cometh together* again,
  6:33. and *came together* unto him.
  14:53. and *with* him *were assembled*
Lu. 5:15. great multitudes *came together* to hear,
  23:55. the women also, *which came with* him from
Joh. 11:33. the Jews also weeping *which came with* her,
  18:20. whither the Jews always *resort;* and
Acts 1: 6. *When* they therefore *were come together,*
  21. of these men *which have companied with* us
  2: 6. the multitude *came together,*
  5:16. There *came* also a multitude (out) of
  9:39. Then Peter arose and *went with* them.
  10:23. brethren from Joppa *accompanied* him.
  27. and found many *that were come together.*
  45. as many as *came with* Peter, because
  11:12. the spirit bade me *go with* them,
  15:38. and *went* not *with* them to the work.
  16:13. unto the women *which resorted* (thither).
  19:32. knew not wherefore they *were come together.*
  21:16. There *went with* us also (certain) of the
  22. the multitude must needs *come together:*
  25:17. *when* they *were come* hither,
  28:17. and *when* they *were come together,* he
1Co. 7: 5. and *come together* again,
  11:17. that ye *come together* not for the better,
  18. *when* ye *come together* in the church,
  20. *When* ye *come together* therefore
  33. *when* ye *come together* to eat,
  34. that ye *come* not *together* unto condemnation.
  14:23. the whole church *be come together*
  26. when ye *come together,* every one of you

συνεσθίω, sunesthio.

Lu. 15: 2. receiveth sinners, and *eateth with* them.
Acts 10:41. who *did eat* and drink *with* him
  11: 3. and *didst eat with* them.
1Co. 5:11. *with* such an one no not *to eat.*
Gal. 2:12. he *did eat with* the Gentiles:

σύνεσις, sunesis.

Mar 12:33. and with all the *understanding,*
Lu. 2:47. were astonished at his *understanding*
1Co. 1:19. bring to nothing the *understanding* of the prudent.
Eph. 3: 4. my *knowledge* in the mystery of Christ
Col. 1: 9. in all wisdom and spiritual *understanding;*
  2: 2. unto all riches of the full assurance of *understanding,*
2Ti. 2: 7. and the Lord give thee *understanding* in all things.

συνετός, sunetos.

Mat. 11:25. from the wise and *prudent,*
Lu. 10:21. from the wise and *prudent,*
Acts 13: 7. Sergius Paulus, a *prudent* man;
1Co. 1:19. will bring to nothing the understanding of the *prudent.*

συνευδοκέω, sunŭodokeo.

Lu. 11:48. that ye *allow* the deeds of your fathers:

Acts 8: 1. And Saul was *consenting* unto his death.
  22:20. and *consenting* unto his death,
Ro. 1:32. but *have pleasure* in them that do them.
1Co. 7:12. and she *be pleased* to dwell with him,
  13. and if he *be pleased* to dwell with her,

συνευωχέομαι, sunŭōkeomai.

2Pet. 2:13. while they *feast with* you;
Jude 12. when they *feast with* you,

συνεφίστημι, sunephisteemi.

Acts 16:22. And the multitude *rose up together* against them:

συνέχω, suneko.

Mat. 4:24. sick people *that were taken with* divers diseases
Lu. 4:38. Simon's wife's mother was *taken with* a great fever;
  8:37. for they *were taken with* great fear:
  45. Master, the multitude *throng* thee and
  12:50. how *am* I *straitened* till it be accomplished!
  19:43. and *keep* thee *in* on every side,
  22:63. the men *that held* Jesus mocked him,
Acts 7:57. *stopped* their ears, and ran upon him
  18: 5. Paul *was pressed* in the spirit,
  28: 8. the father of Publius lay *sick of* a fever and of
2Co. 5:14. the love of Christ *constraineth* us; because
Phi. 1:23. For I *am in a strait* betwixt two,

συνήδομαι, suneedomai.

Ro. 7:22. For I *delight* in the law of God

συνήθεια, suneethīa.

Joh. 18:39. But ye have a *custom,*
1Co. 11:16. we have no such *custom,*

συνηλικιώτης, suneelikiōtees.

Gal. 1:14. above many my *equals* in mine own nation,

συνθάπτομαι, sunthaptomai.

Ro. 6: 4. we *are buried with* (lit. *have been buried with*) him by baptism into death:
Col. 2:12. *Buried with* him in baptism,

συνθλάομαι, sunthlaomai.

Mat. 21:44. fall on this stone *shall be broken:*
Lu. 20:18. fall upon that stone *shall be broken;*

συνθλίβω, sunthlibo.

Mar 5:24. people followed him, and *thronged* him.
  31. Thou seest the multitude *thronging* thee,

συνθρύπτω, sunthrupto.

Acts21:13. What mean ye to weep and to *break* mine heart?

συνίημι, sunieemi.

Mat.13:13. neither *do* they *understand.*
  14. ye shall hear, and shall not *understand;*
  15. and *should understand* with (their) heart,
  19. and *understandeth* (it) not, then
  23. heareth the word, and *understandeth*
  51. *Have* ye *understood* all these things?
 15:10. Hear, and *understand:*
 16:12. Then *understood* they how that he
 17:13. Then the disciples *understood*
Mar 4:12. they may hear, and not *understand;*
 6:52. For they *considered* not
 7:14. Hearken unto me every one (of you), and *understand:*
 8:17. perceive ye not yet, neither *understand?*
 21. How is it that ye *do* not *understand?*
Lu. 2:50. And they *understood* not the saying which
 8:10. and hearing they *might* not *understand.*
 18:34. And they *understood* none of these things:
 24:45. they might *understand* the scriptures,
Acts 7:25. his brethren would have *understood*
 — but they *understood* not.
 28:26. ye shall hear, and shall not *understand;*
 27. and *understand* with (their) heart,
Ro. 3:11. There is none *that understandeth,*
 15:21. that have not heard *shall understand.*
2Co.10:12. comparing themselves among themselves, *are* not *wise.*
Eph. 5:17. but *understanding* what the will of the

συνιστάνω, sunistano.

2Co. 3: 1. Do we begin again *to commend* ourselves?
 5:12. we *commend* not ourselves again unto you,
 10:12. with some *that commend* themselves:

συνιστάω, συνίστημι, sunistao, sunisteemi.

Lu. 9:32. and the two men *that stood with* him.
Ro. 3: 5. But if our unrighteousness *commend* the
 5: 8. But God *commendeth* his love toward us,
 16: 1. I *commend* unto you Phebe our sister,
2Co. 4: 2. *commending* ourselves to every man's conscience
 6: 4. But in all (things) *approving* ourselves
 7:11. In all (things) ye *have approved* yourselves
 10:18. For not he *that commendeth* himself
 — but whom the Lord *commendeth.*
 12:11. I ought *to have been commended* of you:
Gal. 2:18. I *make* myself a transgressor.
Col. 1:17. and by him all things *consist.*
2Pet.3: 5. *standing* out of the water and in the water:

συνοδεύω, sunoduo.

Acts 9: 7. And the men *which journeyed with* him

συνοδία, sunodia.

Lu. 2:44. supposing him to have been in the *company,*

συνοικέω, sunoikeo.

1Pet. 3: 7. *dwell with* (them) according to knowledge,

συνοικοδομέομαι, sunoikodomeomai.

Eph 2:22. In whom ye also *are builded together*

συνομιλέω, sunomileo.

Acts10:27. And *as* he *talked with* him, he went

συνομορέω, sunomoreo.

Acts18: 7. whose house *joined hard* to the synagogue.

συνοχή, sunokee.

Lu. 21:25. upon the earth *distress* of nations,
2Co. 2: 4. out of much affliction and *anguish* of heart I wrote unto you

---

συντάσσω, suntasso.

Mat.26:19. And the disciples did as Jesus *had appointed* them;
 27:10. as the Lord *appointed* me.

συντέλεια, suntelia.

Mat.13:39. the harvest is the *end* of the world;
  (συντέλεια τοῦ αἰῶνός)
 40. so shall it be in the *end* of this world.
  (συντ. τ. ἀι.)
 49. So shall it be at the *end* of the world:
  (σ. τ. ἀι.)
 24: 3. and of the *end* of the world? (σ. τ. ἀι.)
 28:20. unto the *end* of the world. (σ. τ. ἀι.)
Heb 9:26. once in the *end* of the world hath he (σ. τ. ἀι.)

συντελέω, sunteleo.

Mat. 7:28. when Jesus *had ended* these sayings,
Mar13: 4. when all these things shall *be fulfilled?*
Lu. 4: 2. and *when* they *were ended,* he
 13. And *when* the devil *had ended* all the
Acts21:27. when the seven days were almost *ended,*
Ro. 9:28. he will *finish* the work, and cut (it) short
Heb 8: 8. I *will make* a new covenant with the

συντέμνω, suntemno.

Ro. 9:28. and *cut* (it) *short* in righteousness: because a *short* work will the Lord make

---

συντηρέω, sunteereo.

Mat. 9:17. and both *are preserved.*
Mar 6:20. and *observed* him; and when he heard him,

Lu.　2:19. Mary *kept* all these things, and pondered
　　5:38. and both *are preserved*.

σύντίθημι, *suntitheemi*.

Lu. 22: 5. and *covenanted* to give him money.
Joh. 9:22. for the Jews *had agreed* already, that if
Acts 23:20. The Jews *have agreed* to desire thee that
　24: 9. And the Jews also *assented*, saying

συντόμως, *suntomōs*.

Acts 24: 4. hear us of thy clemency *a few words*. (lit.
　　　　concisely)

συντρέχω, *suntreko*.

Mar. 6:33. and *ran* afoot thither out of all cities,
Acts 3:11. all the people *ran together* unto them
1 Pet. 4: 4. *that* ye *run* not *with* (them) to the same
　　　　excess

συντρίβω, *suntribo*.

Mat. 12:20. A *bruised* reed shall he not break,
Mar 5: 4. and the fetters *broken in pieces:*
　14: 3. and she *brake* the box, and poured
Lu. 4:18. he hath sent me to heal the *broken*hearted,
　9:39. *bruising* him hardly departeth from him.
Joh. 19:36. A bone of him *shall* not *be broken*
Ro. 16:20. shall *bruise* Satan under your feet
Rev. 2:27. as the vessels of a potter *shall* they *be
　　　broken to shivers*: (lit. *are broken*, &c.)

Note.—Some copies here read συντριβήσεται.

σύντριμμα, *suntrimma*.

Ro. 3:16. *Destruction* and misery (are) in their ways:

σύντροφος, *suntrophos*.

Acts 13: 1. *which had been brought up with* Herod

συντυγχάνω, *suntunkano*.

Lu. 8:19. and could not *come at* him for the press.

συνυποκρίνομαι, *sunupokrinomai*.

Gal. 2:13. And the other Jews *dissembled* likewise
　　　with him ;

συνυπουργέω, *sunupourgeo*.

2 Co. 1:11. Ye also *helping together* by prayer

συνωδίνω, *sunōdino*.

Ro. 8:22. *travaileth in pain together* until now.

συνωμοσία, *sunōmosia*.

Acts 23: 13. which had made this *conspiracy*.

σύρτις, *surtis*.

Acts 27:17. lest they should fall into the *quicksands,*

σύρω, *suro*.

Joh. 21: 8. *dragging* the net with fishes.
Acts 8: 3. and *haling* men and women
　14:19. having stoned Paul, *drew* (him) out of
　17: 6. *drew* Jason and certain brethren unto
Rev 12: 4. his tail *drew* the third part of the stars

συσπαράσσω, *susparasso*.

Lu. 9:42. the devil threw him down, and *tare* (him)

σύσσημον, *susseemon*.

Mar 14:44. had given them a *token*, saying,

σύσσωμα, *sussōma*.

Eph 3: 6. fellowheirs, and *of the same body,*

συστασιαστής, *sustasiastees*.

Mar 15: 7. bound with them *that had made insurrection
　　　with* him,

συστατικός, *sustatikos*.

2 Co. 3: 1. epistles *of commendation* to you, or (letters)
　　　of commendation from you?

συσταυρόω, *sustauroō*.

Mat. 27:44. The thieves also, *which were crucified with*
　　　him,
Mar 15:32. they *that were crucified with* him
Joh. 19:32. and of the other *which was crucified with*
　　　him.
Ro. 6: 6. our old man *is crucified with* (him), (lit.
　　　has been crucified with)
Gal. 2:20. I *am crucified with* Christ: (lit. I *have been
　　　crucified with*)

συστέλλω, *sustello*.

Acts 5: 6. And the young men arose, *wound* him *up,*
1 Co. 7:29. But this I say, brethren, the time (is)
　　　short :

συστενάζω, *sustenazo*.

Ro. 8:22. *groaneth* and travaileth in pain *together*

συστοιχέω, sustoikeo.

Gal. 4:25. and *answereth to* Jerusalem which now is,

συστρατιώτης, sustratiōtees.

Phi. 2:25. companion in labour, and *fellowsoldier,*
Philem 2. and Archippus our *fellowsoldier,*

συστρέφω, sustrepho.

Acts28: 3. And *when* Paul *had gathered* a bundle of

συστροφή, sustrophee.

Acts19:40. may give an account of this *concourse.*
   23:12. certain of the Jews banded together, (lit.
    having made a *combination*)

συσχηματίζομαι, suskeematizomai.

Ro. 12: 2. And *be* not *conformed to* this world:
1Pet. 1:14. not *fashioning* yourselves *according to* the
    former lusts

σφαγή, sphagee.

Acts 8:32. He was led as a sheep to the *slaughter;*
Ro. 8:36. accounted as sheep for the *slaughter.*
Jas. 5: 5. as in a day of *slaughter.*

σφάγιον, sphagion.

Acts 7:42. have ye offered to me *slain beasts*

σφάττω, sphatto.

1Joh.3:12. and *slew* his brother. And wherefore *slew*
    he him?
Rev. 5: 6. stood a Lamb as it *had been slain,*
    9. for thou *wast slain,* and hast redeemed us
   12. Worthy is the Lamb *that was slain.*
  6: 4. that they *should kill* one another:
    9. the souls of them *that were slain*
 13: 3. one of his heads as it were *wounded to*
    death;
    8. written in the book of life of the Lamb *slain*
    from the foundation of the world.
18:24. and of all *that were slain* upon the earth.

σφόδρα, sphodra.

Mat. 2:10. they rejoiced with *exceeding* great joy.
  17: 6. and were *sore* afraid.
    23. And they were *exceeding* sorry.
  18:31. they were *very* sorry, and came
  19:25. they were *exceedingly* amazed,
  26:22. And they were *exceeding* sorrowful,
  27:54. they feared *greatly,* saying,
Mar 16: 4. for it was *very* great.
Lu. 18:23. for he was *very* rich.
Acts 6: 7. the number of the disciples multiplied in
    Jerusalem *greatly;*
Rev.16:21. the plague thereof was *exceeding* great.

σφοδρῶς, sphodrōs.

Acts27:18. And we being *exceedingly* tossed

σφραγίζω, sphragizo.

Mat.27:66. *sealing* the stone, and setting a watch.
Joh. 3:33. *hath set to* his *seal* that God is true.
  6:27. for him *hath* God the Father *sealed.*
Ro. 15:28. and *have sealed* to them this fruit,
2Co. 1:22. *Who hath* also *sealed* us, and given
  11:10. no man shall stop me of this boasting (lit.
    this boasting *shall* not *be sealed* to me)
Eph. 1:13. ye *were sealed* with that holy Spirit
  4:30. whereby ye *are sealed* unto the day
Rev. 7: 3. till we have *sealed* the servants of our God
   4. the number of them *which were sealed:*
    (and there were) *sealed* an hundred
    (and) forty
   5. of Juda (were) *sealed* twelve thousand.
  — of Reuben (were) *sealed* twelve thousand.
  — of Gad (were) *sealed* twelve thousand.
   6. of Aser (were) *sealed* twelve thousand.
  — of Nepthalim (were) *sealed* twelve thou-
    sand.
  — of Manasses (were) *sealed* twelve thousand.
   7. of Simeon (were) *sealed* twelve thousand.
  — of Levi (were) *sealed* twelve thousand.
  — of Issachar (were) *sealed* twelve thousand.
   8. of Zabulon (were) *sealed* twelve thousand.
  — of Joseph (were) *sealed* twelve thousand.
  — of Benjamin (were) *sealed* twelve thou-
    sand.
10: 4. *Seal up* those things which the seven
20: 3. and shut him up, and *set a seal* upon him,
22:10. *Seal* not the sayings of the prophecy of
    this book:

Note.—In 2 Cor. 11:10, the received text reads
    φραγήσεται.

σφραγίς, sphragis.

Ro. 4:11. a *seal* of the righteousness of the faith
1Co. 9: 2. the *seal* of mine apostleship are ye
2Ti. 2:19. having this *seal,* The Lord knoweth...his.
Rev. 5: 1. sealed with seven *seals.*
    2. and to loose the *seals* thereof?
    5. and to loose the seven *seals* thereof.
    9. and to open the *seals* thereof:
  6: 1. the Lamb opened one of the *seals,*
    3. when he had opened the second *seal,*
    5. when he had opened the third *seal,*
    7. when he had opened the fourth *seal,*
    9. when he had opened the fifth *seal,*
   12. when he had opened the sixth *seal,*
  7: 2. having the *seal* of the living God:
  8: 1. when he had opened the seventh *seal,*
  9: 4. have not the *seal* of God in their foreheads.

σφυρόν, sphuron.

Acts 3: 7. his feet and *ancle bones* received strength.

σχεδόν, skedon.

Acts13:44. came *almost* the whole city together
  19:26. but *almost* throughout all Asia,
Heb 9:22. And *almost* all things are by the law

σχῆμα, skeema.

1Co. 7:31. for the *fashion* of this world passeth
Phi. 2: 8. And being found in *fashion* as a man,

σχίζω, skizo.

Mat.27:51. the veil of the temple *was rent* in twain
— the earth did quake, and the rocks *rent;*
Mar 1:10. he saw the heavens *opened,*
15:38. the veil of the temple *was rent* in twain
Lu. 5:36. then both the new *maketh a rent,*
23:45. veil of the temple *was rent* in the midst.
Joh.19:24. *Let* us not *rend* it, but cast lots for it,
21:11. yet *was* not the net *broken.*
Acts14: 4. the multitude of the city *was divided:*
23: 7. and the multitude *was divided.*

σχίσμα, skisma.

Mat. 9:16. and the *rent* is made worse.
Mar 2:21. and the *rent* is made worse.
Joh. 7:43. there was a *division* among the people
9:16. there was a *division* among them.
10:19. There was a *division* therefore
1Co. 1:10. (that) there be no *divisions* among you;
11:18. I hear that there be *divisions* among you;
12:25. That there should be no *schism* in the

σχοινίον, skoinion.

Joh. 2:15. made a scourge of *small cords,*
Acts27:32. soldiers cut off the *ropes* of the boat,

σχολάζω, skolazo.

Mat.12:44. he findeth (it) *empty,* swept,
1Co. 7: 5. that ye *may give yourselves to* fasting

σχολή, skolee.

Acts19: 9. daily in the *school* of one Tyrannus.

σώζω, sōzo.

Mat. 1:21. for he *shall save* his people from their sins.
8:25. saying, Lord, *save* us: we perish.
9:21. but touch his garment, I *shall be whole.*
22. thy faith *hath made* thee *whole.* And the woman *was made whole* from that hour.
10:22. he that endureth to the end *shall be saved.*
14:30. he cried, saying, Lord, *save* me.
16:25. whosoever will *save* his life shall lose it:
18:11. is come *to save* that which was lost.
19:25. saying, Who then can *be saved?*
24:13. endure unto the end, the same *shall be saved.*
22. there should no flesh *be saved:*
27:40. buildest (it) in three days, *save* thyself.
42. He *saved* others; himself he cannot *save.*
49. whether Elias will come to *save* him.
Mar 3: 4. to *save* life, or to kill?
5:23. hands on her, that she *may be healed;*
28. may touch but his clothes, I *shall be whole.*
34. thy faith *hath made* thee *whole;*

Mar 6:56. as many as touched him *were made whole.*
8:35. whosoever will *save* his life shall lose it;
— the same *shall save* it.
10:26. Who then can *be saved?*
52. thy faith *hath made* thee *whole.*
13:13. unto the end, the same *shall be saved.*
20. no flesh should *be saved:*
15:30. *Save* thyself, and come down
31. He *saved* others; himself he cannot *save.*
16:16. and is baptized *shall be saved;*
Lu. 6: 9. *to save* life, or to destroy (it)?
7:50. Thy faith *hath saved* thee; go in peace.
8:12. lest they should believe and *be saved.*
36. was possessed of the devils *was healed.*
48. thy faith *hath made* thee *whole;*
50. and she *shall be made whole.*
9:24. whosoever will *save* his life shall lose it:
— the same *shall save* it.
56. to destroy men's lives, but *to save*
13:23. Lord, are there few *that be saved?*
17:19. thy faith *hath made* thee *whole.*
33. seek *to save* his life shall lose it;
18:26. Who then can *be saved?*
42. thy faith *hath saved* thee.
19:10. and *to save* that which was lost.
23:35. He *saved* others; *let* him *save* himself,
37. If thou be the king of the Jews, *save* thyself.
39. If thou be Christ, *save* thyself and us.
Joh. 3:17. that the world through him *might be saved.*
5:34. these things I say, that ye *might be saved.*
10: 9. he *shall be saved,* and shall go in and out,
11:12. Lord, if he sleep, he *shall do well.*
12:27. Father, *save* me from this hour:
47. to judge the world, but to *save* the world.
Acts 2:21. on the name of the Lord *shall be saved.*
40. *Save* yourselves (lit. *be saved*) from this untoward generation.
47. the Lord added to the church daily such as should be saved. (lit. the *saved*)
4: 9. by what means he *is made whole;*
12. whereby we must *be saved.*
11:14. thou and all thy house *shall be saved.*
14: 9. he had faith *to be healed,*
15: 1. after the manner of Moses, ye cannot *be saved.*
11. we shall *be saved,* even as they.
16:30. what must I do to *be saved?*
31. and thou *shalt be saved,* and thy house.
27:20. all hope that we should *be saved*
31. Except these abide in the ship, ye cannot *be saved.*
Ro. 5: 9. we *shall be saved* from wrath through him.
10. we *shall be saved* by his life.
8:24. For we *are saved* by hope:
9:27. a remnant *shall be saved:*
10: 9. that God hath raised him from the dead, thou *shalt be saved.*
13. upon the name of the Lord *shall be saved.*
11:14. and might *save* some of them.
26. And so all Israel *shall be saved:*
1Co. 1:18. unto us *which are saved* it is the power of God.
21. *to save* them that believe.
3:15. but he himself *shall be saved;* yet so as by fire.
5: 5. that the spirit *may be saved* in the day
7:16. whether thou *shalt save* (thy) husband?
— whether thou *shalt save* (thy) wife?
9:22. that I might by all means *save* some.
10:33. but the (profit) of many, that they *may be saved.*

1Co.15: 2. By which also ye *are saved*,
2Co. 2:15. a sweet savour of Christ, in them *that are saved*,
Eph 2: 5. by grace ye are *saved*;
    8. For by grace are ye *saved* through faith;
1Th. 2:16. that they *might be saved*,
2Th. 2:10. the love of the truth, that they might *be saved*.
1Ti. 1:15. Christ Jesus came into the world *to save* sinners;
  2: 4. Who will have all men *to be saved*,
   15. Notwithstanding she *shall be saved* in childbearing,
  4:16. thou *shalt* both *save* thyself, and them that
2Ti. 1: 9. *Who hath saved* us, and called (us)
  4:18. and *will preserve* (me) unto his heavenly kingdom:
Tit. 3: 5. but according to his mercy he *saved* us,
Heb 5: 7. unto him that was able *to save* him
  7:25. able also *to save* them to the uttermost
Jas. 1:21. the engrafted word, which is able *to save* your souls.
  2:14. and have not works? can faith *save* him?
  4:12. who is able *to save* and to destroy:
  5:15. And the prayer of faith *shall save* the sick,
  20. *shall save* a soul from death,
1Pet. 3:21. (even) baptism *doth* also now *save* us
  4:18. And if the righteous scarcely *be saved*,
Jude 5. *having saved* the people out of the land of
  23. And others *save* with fear, pulling (them) out
Rev.21:24. And the nations of them *which are saved*

σῶμα, sōma.

Mat. 5:29. not (that) thy whole *body* should be
  30. thy whole *body* should be cast into hell.
  6:22. The light of the *body* is the eye:
  — thy whole *body* shall be full of light.
  23. thy whole *body* shall be full of darkness.
  25. for your *body*, what ye shall put on.
  — and the *body* than raiment?
  10:28. And fear not them which kill the *body*,
  — to destroy both soul and *body* in hell.
  14:12. came, and took up the *body*, and
  26:12. she hath poured this ointment on my *body*,
  26. Take, eat; this is my *body*.
  27:52. and many *bodies* of the saints which slept
  58. begged the *body* of Jesus. Then Pilate commanded the *body* to be delivered.
  59. when Joseph had taken the *body*,
Mar 5:29. and she felt in (her) *body* that she
  14: 8. to anoint my *body* to the burying.
  22. Take, eat: this is my *body*.
  15:43. and craved the *body* of Jesus.
  45. he gave the *body* to Joseph.
Lu. 11:34. The light of the *body* is the eye:
  — thy whole *body* also is full of light;
  — thy *body* also (is) full of darkness.
  36. If thy whole *body* therefore (be) full of light,
  12: 4. Be not afraid of them that kill the *body*,
  22. for the *body*, what ye shall put on.
  23. and the *body* (is more) than raiment.
  17:37. Wheresoever the *body* (is), thither will
  22:19. This is my *body* which is given for you:
  23:52. unto Pilate, and begged the *body* of Jesus.
  55. and how his *body* was laid.
  24: 3. found not the *body* of the Lord Jesus.
  23. when they found not his *body*, they came,
Joh. 2:21. he spake of the temple of his *body*.

Joh.19:31. the *bodies* should not remain upon the cross
  38. that he might take away the *body* of Jesus: — and took the *body* of Jesus.
  40. Then took they the *body* of Jesus,
  20:12. where the *body* of Jesus had lain.
Acts 9:40. and turning (him) to the *body* said,
Ro. 1:24. to dishonour their own *bodies*
  4:19. he considered not his own *body* now dead,
  6: 6. that the *body* of sin might be destroyed,
  12. reign in your mortal *body*,
  7: 4. dead to the law by the *body* of Christ;
  24. deliver me from the *body* of this death?
  8:10. the *body* (is) dead because of sin;
  11. shall also quicken your mortal *bodies*
  13. do mortify the deeds of the *body*,
  23. (to wit), the redemption of our *body*.
  12: 1. that ye present your *bodies* a living
  4. as we have many members in one *body*,
  5. we, (being) many, are one *body* in Christ,
1Co. 5: 3. For I verily, as absent in *body*,
  6:13. Now the *body* (is) not for fornication, — and the Lord for the *body*.
  15. your *bodies* are the members of Christ?
  16. joined to an harlot is one *body*?
  18. that a man doeth is without the *body*; — sinneth against his own *body*.
  19. your *body* is the temple of the Holy Ghost
  20. therefore glorify God in your *body*,
  7: 4. The wife hath not power of her own *body*, — the husband hath not power of his own *body*,
  34. she may be holy both in *body* and in spirit:
  9:27. But I keep under my *body*,
  10:16. the communion of the *body* of Christ?
  17. (being) many are one bread, (and) one *body*:
  11:24. Take, eat: this is my *body*,
  27. shall be guilty of the *body* and blood of
  29. not discerning the Lord's *body*.
  12:12. For as the *body* is one, and hath — the members of that one *body*, being many, are one *body*: so also (is) Christ.
  13. are we all baptized into one *body*,
  14. For the *body* is not one member, but
  15. I am not of the *body*; is it therefore not of the *body*?
  16. I am not of the *body*; is it therefore not of the *body*?
  17. If the whole *body* (were) an eye,
  18. every one of them in the *body*,
  19. all one member, where (were) the *body*?
  20. many members, yet but one *body*.
  22. those members of the *body*,
  23. And those (members) of the *body*,
  24. but God hath tempered the *body* together,
  25. should be no schism in the *body*;
  27. Now ye are the *body* of Christ,
  13: 3. though I give my *body* to be burned,
  15:35. and with what *body* do they come?
  37. thou sowest not that *body* that shall be,
  38. But God giveth it a *body* as it hath pleased him, and to every seed his own *body*.
  40. also celestial *bodies*, and *bodies* terrestrial:
  44. It is sown a natural *body*; it is raised a spiritual *body*. There is a natural *body*, and there is a spiritual *body*.
2Co. 4:10. bearing about in the *body* the dying of — might be made manifest in our *body*.
  5: 6. whilst we are at home in the *body*,
  8. rather to be absent from the *body*,
  10. receive the things (done) in (his) *body*,
  10:10. but (his) *bodily* presence (is) weak,

2Co.12: 2. the *body*, I cannot tell; or whether out of the *body*,
     3. in the *body*, or out of the *body*, I cannot tell:
Gal. 6:17. I bear in my *body* the marks of the Lord
Eph. 1:23. Which is his *body*, the fulness of him
     2:16. unto God in one *body* by the cross,
     4: 4. (There is) one *body*, and one Spirit,
     12. for the edifying of the *body* of Christ:
     16. From whom the whole *body* fitly joined
     — maketh increase of the *body* unto
     5:23. and he is the saviour of the *body*.
     28. to love their wives as their own *bodies*.
     30. For we are members of his *body*,
Phi. 1:20. Christ shall be magnified in my *body*,
     3:21. Who shall change our vile *body*,
     — like unto his glorious *body*,
Col. 1:18. And he is the head of the *body*,
     22. In the *body* of his flesh through death,
     24. in my flesh for his *body's* sake,
     2:11. putting off the *body* of the sins of the flesh
     17. but the *body* (is) of Christ.
     19. from which all the *body* by joints and
     23. humility, and neglecting of the *body*;
     3:15. to the which also ye are called in one *body*;
1Th. 5:23. and *body* be preserved blameless unto
Heb 10: 5. but a *body* hast thou prepared me:
     10. through the offering of the *body* of Jesus
     22. our *bodies* washed with pure water.
     13: 3. as being yourselves also in the *body*.
     11. For the *bodies* of those beasts,
Jas. 2:16. things which are needful to the *body*;
     26. as the *body* without the spirit is dead,
     3: 2. able also to bridle the whole *body*.
     3. and we turn about their whole *body*.
     6. that it defileth the whole *body*,
1Pet.2:24. bare our sins in his own *body* on the tree,
Jude   9. he disputed about the *body* of Moses,
Rev.18:13. *slaves*, (lit. *bodies*) and souls of men.

σωματικός, *sōmatikos*.

Lu. 3:22. the Holy Ghost descended in a *bodily* shape
1Ti. 4: 8. For *bodily* exercise profiteth little: but

σωματικῶς, *sōmatikōs*.

Col. 2: 9. all the fulness of the Godhead *bodily*.

σωρεύω, *sōruo*.

Ro. 12:20. thou *shalt heap* coals of fire on his head.
2Ti. 3: 6. and lead captive silly women *laden* with

σωτήρ, *soteer*.

Lu. 1:47. hath rejoiced in God my *Saviour*.
     2:11. a *Saviour*, which is Christ the Lord.
Joh. 4:42. the Christ, the *Saviour* of the world.
Acts 5:31. (to be) a Prince and a *Saviour*, for to
     13:23. raised unto Israel a *Saviour*, Jesus:
Eph 5:23. and he is the *saviour* of the body.
Phi. 3:20. we look for the *Saviour*, the Lord Jesus
1Ti. 1: 1. by the commandment of God our *Saviour*, and Lord Jesus Christ,

1Ti. 2: 3. in the sight of God our *Saviour*;
     4:10. who is the *saviour* of all men, specially
2Ti. 1:10. by the appearing of our *Saviour* Jesus
Tit. 1: 3. the commandment of God our *Saviour*;
     4. and the Lord Jesus Christ our *Saviour*.
     2:10. adorn the doctrine of God our *Saviour*
     13. of the great God and our *Saviour* Jesus
     3: 4. and love of God our *Saviour* toward
     6. through Jesus Christ our *Saviour*;
2Pet.1: 1. of God and our *Saviour* Jesus Christ:
     11. kingdom of our Lord and *Saviour* Jesus
     2:20. the knowledge of the Lord and *Saviour* Jesus Christ,
     3: 2. of us the apostles of the Lord and *Saviour*:
     18. our Lord and *Saviour* Jesus Christ.
1Joh.4:14. the Father sent the Son (to be) the *Saviour* of the world.
Jude 25. To the only wise God our *Saviour*,

σωτηρία, *soteeria*.

Lu. 1:69. hath raised up an horn of *salvation* for us
     71. *That* we *should be saved* (lit. *salvation*) from our enemies.
     77. To give knowledge of *salvation* unto his people
     19: 9. This day is *salvation* come to this house,
Joh. 4:22. for *salvation* is of the Jews.
Acts 4:12. Neither is there *salvation* in any other:
     7:25. by his hand would *deliver* them:
     13:26. to you is the word of this *salvation* sent.
     47. for *salvation* unto the ends of the earth.
     16:17. shew unto us the way of *salvation*.
     27:34. for this is for your *health*:
Ro. 1:16. is the power of God unto *salvation*
     10: 1. that they *might be saved*.
     10. confession is made unto *salvation*.
     11:11. *salvation* (is come) unto the Gentiles,
     13:11. for now (is) our *salvation* nearer than
2Co. 1: 6. (it is) for your consolation and *salvation*,
     — (it is) for your consolation and *salvation*.
     6: 2. in the day of *salvation* have I succoured
     — behold, now (is) the day of *salvation*.
     7:10. worketh repentance to *salvation*
Eph 1:13. the gospel of your *salvation*:
Phi. 1:19. this shall turn to my *salvation*
     28. but to you of *salvation*, and that of God.
     2:12. work out your own *salvation* with fear
1Th. 5: 8. for an helmet, the hope of *salvation*.
     9. to obtain *salvation* by our Lord Jesus
2Th. 2:13. chosen you to *salvation* through
2Ti. 2:10. that they may also obtain the *salvation*
     3:15. able to make thee wise unto *salvation*
Heb 1:14. who shall be heirs of *salvation*?
     2: 3. if we neglect so great *salvation*;
     10. make the captain of their *salvation* perfect
     5: 9. the author of eternal *salvation*
     6: 9. and things that accompany *salvation*,
     9:28. second time without sin unto *salvation*.
     11: 7. prepared an ark to the *saving* of his house;
1Pet.1: 5. by the power of God through faith unto *salvation*
     9. (even) the *salvation* of (your) souls.
     10. Of which *salvation* the prophets
2Pet.3:15. longsuffering of our Lord (is) *salvation*;
Jude 3. unto you of the common *salvation*,
Rev 7:10. *Salvation* to our God which sitteth upon the throne,
     12:10. Now is come *salvation*, and strength,
     19: 1. *Salvation*, and glory, and honour, and

σωτήριον, sōteerion.

Lu. 2:30. For mine eyes have seen thy *salvation*,
    3: 6. all flesh shall see the *salvation* of God.
Acts28:28. that the *salvation* of God is sent unto the Gentiles,
Eph. 6:17. And take the helmet of *salvation*,

σωτήριος, sōteerios.

Tit. 2:11. the grace of God *that bringeth salvation*

σωφρονέω, sōphroneo.

Mar 5:15. and clothed, and *in* his *right mind*:
Lu. 8:35. clothed, and *in* his *right mind*:
Ro. 12: 3. but to think *soberly*, according as God
2Co. 5:13. or whether we *be sober*,
Tit. 2: 6. likewise exhort *to be sober minded*.
1Pet.4: 7. *be* ye therefore *sober*, and watch unto

σωφρονίζω, sōphronizo.

Tit. 2: 4. That they *may teach* the young women
    to be sober,

σωφρονισμός, sōphronismos.

2Ti. 1: 7. and of love, and of a *sound mind*.

σωφρόνως, sōphronōs.

Tit. 2:12. we should live *soberly*, righteously, and godly,

σωφροσύνη, sōphrosunee.

Acts26:25. the words of truth and *soberness*.
1Ti. 2: 9. with shamefacedness and *sobriety*;
    15. and charity and holiness with *sobriety*.

σώφρων, sōphron.

1Ti. 3: 2. vigilant, *sober*, of good behaviour,
Tit. 1: 8. *sober*, just, holy, temperate ;
    2: 2. *temperate*, sound in faith,
    5. *discreet*, chaste, keepers at home,

τάγμα, tagma.

1Co.15:23. But every man in his own *order:*

τακτός, taktos.

Acts12:21. And upon a *set* day Herod, arrayed

ταλαιπωρέω, talaipōreo.

Jas. 4: 9. *Be afflicted*, and mourn, and weep:

ταλαιπωρία, talaipōria.

Ro. 3:16. Destruction and *misery* (are) in their ways:
Jas. 5: 1. weep and howl for your *miseries*

ταλαίπωρος, talaipōros.

Ro. 7:24. O *wretched* man that I am !
Rev. 3:17. and knowest not that thou art *wretched*,

ταλαντιαῖος, talantiaios.

Rev.16:21. (every stone) about *the weight of a talent* :

τάλαντον, talanton.

Mat.18:24. which owed him ten thousand *talents*.
    25:15. And unto one he gave five *talents*,
    16. he that had received the five *talents*
    — and made (them) other five *talents*.
    20. he that had received five *talents* came and brought other five *talents*,
    — thou deliveredst unto me five *talents*: behold, I have gained beside them five *talents* more.
    22. He also that had received two *talents* came and said, Lord, thou deliveredst unto me two *talents*:
    — gained two other *talents* beside them.
    24. he which had received the one *talent*
    25. and hid thy *talent* in the earth:
    28. Take therefore the *talent* from him, and give (it) unto him which hath ten *talents*.

ταλιθά, talitha.

Mar 5:41. *Talitha* cumi; which is, being interpreted, Damsel, I say unto thee, arise.

ταμεῖον, tamion.

Mat. 6: 6. when thou prayest, enter into thy *closet*,
    24:26. behold, (he is) in the *secret chambers*;
Lu. 12: 3. that which ye have spoken in the ear in *closets*
    24. which neither have *storehouse* nor barn ;

τανῦν see after νῦν.

τάξις, taxis.

Lu. 1: 8. before God in the *order* of his course,
1Co.14:40. be done decently and in *order*.
Col. 2: 5. joying and beholding your *order*,
Heb 5: 6. for ever after the *order* of Melchisedec.
    10. high priest after the *order* of Melchisedec.
    6:20. after the *order* of Melchisedec.
    7:11. after the *order* of Melchisedec, and not be called after the *order* of Aaron?
    17. for ever after the *order* of Melchisedec.
    21. after the *order* of Melchisedec:

ταπεινός, tapīnos.

Mat.11:29. for I am meek and *lowly* in heart:
Lu. 1:52. and exalted them *of low degree.*
Ro. 12:16. condescend to men *of low estate.*
2Co. 7: 6. comforteth those that are *cast down,*
10: 1. who in presence (am) *base* among you,
Jas. 1: 9. Let the brother *of low degree* rejoice
4: 6. but giveth grace unto the *humble.*
1Pet.5: 5. and giveth grace to the *humble.*

ταπεινοφροσύνη, tapīnophrosunee.

Acts20:19. Serving the Lord with all *humility of mind,*
Eph. 4: 2. With all *lowliness* and meekness,
Phi. 2: 3. but in *lowliness of mind* let each esteem
Col. 2:18. in a voluntary *humility*
23. and *humility,* and neglecting of the body;
3:12. *humbleness of mind,* meekness,
1Pet.5: 5. and be clothed with *humility :*

ταπεινόω, tapīnoō.

Mat.18: 4. Whosoever therefore *shall humble* himself
23:12. whosoever shall exalt himself *shall be abased ;* and he that *shall humble* himself
Lu. 3: 5. mountain and hill *shall be brought low ;*
14:11. whosoever exalteth himself *shall be abased;* and he *that humbleth* himself
18:14. *shall be abased ;* and he *that humbleth* himself shall
2Co.11: 7. in *abasing* myself that ye might
12:21. my God *will humble* me among you,
Phi. 2: 8. he *humbled* himself, and became obedient
4:12. I know both how *to be abased,* and
Jas. 4:10. *Humble* yourselves in the sight of the Lord,
1Pet.5: 6. *Humble* yourselves therefore under the

ταπείνωσις, tapīnōsis.

Lu. 1:48. For he hath regarded the *low estate* of his handmaiden:
Acts 8:33. In his *humiliation* his judgment was taken away:
Phi. 3:21. Who shall change our *vile* body, (lit. body of *humiliation*)
Jas. 1:10. But the rich, in *that he is made low :*

ταράσσω, tarasso.

Mat. 2: 3. he *was troubled,* and all Jerusalem
14:26. they *were troubled,* saying, It is a spirit ;
Mar 6:50. For they all saw him, and *were troubled.*
Lu. 1:12. when Zacharias saw (him), he *was troubled,*
24:38. Why are ye *troubled ?* and why do thoughts
Joh. 5: 4. into the pool, and *troubled* the water:
7. no man, when the water *is troubled,*
11:33. he groaned in the spirit, and was *troubled,*
12:27. Now is my soul *troubled ;*
13:21. he *was troubled* in spirit, and testified,
14: 1. *Let* not your heart *be troubled :*
27. *Let* not your heart *be troubled,*
Acts15:24. which went out from us *have troubled* you
17: 8. And they *troubled* the people
Gal. 1: 7. but there be some *that trouble* you,
5:10. he *that troubleth* you shall bear his judgment,
1Pet.3:14. be not afraid of their terror, neither *be troubled ;*

ταραχή, tarakee.

Mar13: 8. there shall be famines and *troubles :*
Joh. 5: 4. after the *troubling* of the water

τάραχος, tarakos.

Acts12:18. no small *stir* among the soldiers,
19:23. there arose no small *stir* about that way.

ταρταρόω, tartaroō.

2Pet. 2: 4. but *cast* (them) *down to hell,* and

τάσσω, tasso.

Mat.28:16. where Jesus had *appointed* them.
Lu. 7: 8. am a man *set* under authority,
Acts13:48. as were *ordained* to eternal life believed.
15: 2. they *determined* that Paul and Barnabas,
22:10. which are *appointed* for thee to do.
28:23. And when they had *appointed* him a day,
Ro. 13: 1. the powers that be are *ordained* of God.
1Co.16:15. they have *addicted* themselves to the ministry

ταῦρος, tauros.

Mat.22: 4. my *oxen* and (my) fatlings (are) killed,
Acts14:13. brought *oxen* and garlands unto the gates,
Heb 9:13. if the blood of *bulls* and of goats,
10: 4. not possible that the blood of *bulls* and

ταὐτά, tauta, from ὁ αὐτός.

Lu. 6:23. for in the *like manner* (κατὰ ταὐτὰ) did their fathers
26. *so* (κ. τ.) did their fathers to the false
17:30. *Even thus* (κ.τ.) shall it be in the day when
1Th. 2:14. have suffered *like* things of your own countrymen, even as they

Note.—In the three first of the above passages many copies read ταῦτα.

ταῦτα, tauta. from οὗτος.

Mat. 1:20. But while he thought on *these* things,
4: 9. All *these* things will I give thee,
6:32. after all *these* things do the Gentiles
33. and all *these* things shall be added
9:18. While he spake *these* things unto them,
10: 2. the names of the twelve apostles are *these ;*
11:25. hast hid *these* things from the wise
13:34. All *these* things spake Jesus unto
51. Have ye understood all *these* things ?
56. hath this (man) all *these* things ?
15:20. *These* are (the things) which defile
19:20. All *these* things have I kept from
21:23. By what authority doest thou *these* things ?
24. by what authority I do *these* things.
27. by what authority I do *these* things.
23:23. *these* ought ye to have done,
36. All *these* things shall come upon this
24: 2. See ye not all *these* things ?
3. Tell us, when shall *these* things be ?

Mat.24: 8. *these* (are) the beginning of sorrows.
 33. when ye shall see all *these* things,
 34. till all *these* things be fulfilled.
Mar 2: 8. Why reason ye *these* things in your hearts?
 6: 2. whence hath this (man) *these* things?
 7:23. *these* evil things come from within,
 10:20. all *these* have I observed from
 11:28. authority doest thou *these* things?
 — this authority to do *these* things?
 29. by what authority I do *these* things.
 33. by what authority I do *these* things.
 13: 4. Tell us, when shall *these* things be?
 — all *these* things shall be fulfilled?
 8(9). *these* (are) the beginnings of sorrows.
 29. shall see *these* things come to pass,
 30. shall not pass, till all *these* things be done.
 16:12. After *that* he appeared in another
 17. And *these* signs shall follow
Lu. 1:19. to shew thee *these* glad tidings.
 20. that *these* things shall be performed,
 65. all *these* sayings were noised abroad
 2:19. But Mary kept all *these* things,
 51. his mother kept all *these* sayings
 4:28. when they heard *these* things,
 5:27. And after *these* things he went forth,
 7: 9. When Jesus heard *these* things,
 8: 8. when he had said *these* things,
 9:34. While he *thus* spake, (lit. *these things*)
 10: . After *these* things the Lord appointed
 21. that thou hast hid *these* things
 11:27. as he spake *these* things,
 42. *these* ought ye to have done,
 45. *thus* saying thou reproachest us also.
 53. And as he said *these* things unto
 12: 4. and after *that* have no more
 30. For all *these* things do the nations
 31. all *these* things shall be added
 13:17. when he had said *these* things,
 14: 6. answer him again to *these* things.
 15. heard *these* things, he said unto him,
 21. and shewed his lord *these* things.
 15:26. asked what *these* things meant.
 16:14. covetous, heard all *these* things:
 17: 8. and afterward thou shalt eat and drink?
 18: 4. but afterward he said within himself,
 11. prayed *thus* with himself, (lit. *these things*)
 21. All *these* have I kept from my youth up.
 22. Now when Jesus heard *these* things
 23. when he heard *this*, (lit. *these things*)
 19:11. And as they heard *these* things,
 28. when he had *thus* spoken,
 20: 2. authority doest thou *these* things?
 8. by what authority I do *these* things.
 21: 6. (As for) *these* things which ye behold,
 7. but when shall *these* things be?
 — when *these* things shall come to pass?
 9 *these* things must first come to pass;
 31. when ye see *these* things come to pass,
 36. worthy to escape all *these* things
 23:31. if they do *these* things in a green tree,
 46. having said *thus*,
 49. stood afar off, beholding *these* things.
 24: 9. told all *these* things unto the eleven,
 10. told *these* things unto the apostles.
 21. third day since *these* things were done.
 26. Christ to have suffered *these* things,
 36. And as they *thus* spake,
Joh. 1:28. *These* things were done in Bethabara
 2:16. Take *these* things hence;
 18. that thou doest *these* things?
 3: 2. no man can do *these* miracles
 9. How can *these* things be?

Joh. 3:10. and knowest not *these* things?
 22. After *these* things came Jesus and
 5: 1. After *this* there was a feast
 14. Afterward Jesus findeth him
 16. because he had done *these* things
 19. *these* also doeth the Son likewise.
 34. *these* things I say, that ye might be saved.
 6: 1. After *these* things Jesus went over
 9. but what are *they* among so many?
 59. *These* things said he in the synagogue,
 7: 1. After *these* things Jesus walked in
 4. If thou do *these* things, shew thyself
 9. When he had said *these* words
 32. the people murmured *such* things
 8:20. *These* words spake Jesus in the treasury,
 26. *those* things which I have heard of him.
 28. hath taught me, I speak *these* things.
 30. As he spake *these* words, many believed
 9: 6. When he had *thus* spoken, he spat on
 22. *These* (words) spake his parents,
 40. heard *these* words, and said unto him,
 10:21. *These* are not the words of him that
 25. *they* (lit. *these*) bear witness of me.
 11:11. *These* things said he: and after that
 28. And when she had *so* said,
 43. And when he *thus* had spoken,
 12:16. *These* things understood not his
 — that *these* things were written of him,
 — they had done *these* things unto him.
 36. *These* things spake Jesus, and
 41. *These* things said Esaias, when he
 13: 7. but thou shalt know *hereafter*. (lit. **after** *these*)
 17. If ye know *these* things,
 21. When Jesus had *thus* said,
 14:25. *These* things have I spoken unto you,
 15:11. *These* things have I spoken unto you,
 17. *These* things I command you,
 21. But all *these* things will they do
 16: 1. *These* things have I spoken unto you,
 3. And *these* things will they do
 4. But *these* things have I told you,
 — And *these* things I said not unto you
 6. because I have said *these* things
 25. *These* things have I spoken unto you in
 33. *These* things I have spoken unto you,
 17: 1. *These* words spake Jesus, and lifted
 13. and *these* things I speak in the world,
 18: 1. When Jesus had spoken *these* words,
 22. when he had *thus* spoken,
 19:24. *These* things therefore the soldiers did.
 36. For *these* things were done, that
 38. And after *this* Joseph
 20:14. And when she had *thus* said,
 18. he had spoken *these* things unto her.
 31. *these* are written, that ye might believe
 21: 1. After *these* things Jesus shewed himself again
 24. and wrote *these* things: and we know
Acts 1: 9. And when he had spoken *these* things,
 5: 5. on all them that heard *these* things.
 11. upon as many as heard *these* things.
 7: 1. the high priest, Are *these* things so?
 7. and after *that* shall they come forth,
 50. Hath not my hand made all *these* things?
 54. When they heard *these* things,
 10:44. While Peter yet spake *these* words,
 11:18. When they heard *these* things,
 12:17. Go shew *these* things unto James,
 13:20. after *that* he gave (unto them) judges
 42. the Gentiles besought that *these* words
 14:15. Sirs, why do ye *these* things?

Acts14:18. with *these* sayings scarce restrained they
15:16. After *this* I will return,
17. the Lord, who doeth all *these* things.
16:38. And the serjeants told *these* words
17: 8. when they heard *these* things.
11. daily, whether *those* things were so.
20. therefore what *these* things mean.
18: 1. After *these* things Paul departed
19:21. After *these* things were ended,
41. And when he had *thus* spoken,
20:36. And when he had *thus* spoken,
21:12. And when we heard *these* things,
23:22. thou hast shewed *these* things to me.
24: 9. saying that *these* things were so.
22. when Felix heard *these* things,
26:24. And as he *thus* spake for himself,
30. And when he had *thus* spoken,
27:35. And when he had *thus* spoken,
28:29. And when he had said *these* words,
Ro. 8:31. What shall we then say to *these* things?
9: 8. *these* (are) not the children of God:
1Co. 4: 6. And *these* things, brethren, I have
14. I write not *these* things to shame you,
6: 8. ye do wrong, and defraud, and *that* (your) brethren.
11. And *such* were some of you:
13. God shall destroy both it and *them*.
9: 8. Say I *these* things as a man? or saith not the law *the same* also?
15. neither have I written *these* things,
10: 6. *these* things were our examples,
11. Now all *these* things happened
12:11. But all *these* worketh that one and
13:13. faith, hope, charity, *these* three; but
2Co. 2:16. who (is) sufficient for *these* things?
13:10. I write *these* things being absent,
Gal. 2:18. For if I build again the (lit. *those*) things which I
5:17. *these* are contrary the one to the other: so that ye cannot do the (lit. *those*) things
Eph 5: 6. because of *these* things cometh the wrath
Phi. 3: 7. *those* I counted loss for Christ.
4: 8. think on *these* things.
9. *Those* things, which ye have both learned,
2Th. 2: 5. yet with you, I told you *these* things?
1Ti. 3:14. *These* things write I unto thee,
4: 6. in remembrance of *these* things,
11. *These* things command and teach.
15. Meditate upon *these* things;
5: 7. And *these* things give in charge,
21. that thou observe *these* things
6: 2. *These* things teach and exhort.
11. O man of God, flee *these* things;
2Ti. 1:12. I also suffer *these* things:
2: 2. the *same* commit thou to faithful men,
14. Of *these* things put (them) in remembrance,
Tit. 2:15. *These* things speak, and exhort,
3: 8. *These* things are good and profitable
Heb 4: 8. would he not afterward have spoken of
7:13. he of whom *these* things are spoken
11:12. of one, and him as good as dead, (lit. of one, and *that*, of one dead)
Jas. 3:10. *these* things ought not so to be.
1Pet.1:11. and the glory that should follow. (lit. the glories after *these*)
2Pet.1: 8. For if *these* things be in you,
9. But he that lacketh *these* things
10. for if ye do *these* things,
3: 4. seeing that ye look for *such* things,
1Joh.1: 4. And *these* things write we unto you,
2: 1. *these* things write I unto you,

1Joh.2:26. *These* (things) have I written unto you
5:13. *These* things have I written unto you
Rev. 1:19. the things which shall be *hereafter*; (lit. after *these*)
4: 1. After *this* I looked, and, behold,
— things which must be *hereafter*. (lit. after *these*)
7: 1. after *these* things I saw four angels
9. After *this* I beheld, and, lo,
9:12. two woes more *hereafter*. (lit. after *these*)
10: 4. and write *them* not. (lit. *these*)
15: 5. And after *that* I looked, and, behold,
16: 5. because thou hast judged *thus*.
18: 1. And after *these* things I saw another
19: 1. And after *these* things I heard a
20: 3. and after *that* he must be loosed
22: 8. And I John saw *these* things,
— which shewed me *these* things.
16. to testify unto you *these* things
18. If any man shall add unto *these* things,
20. He which testifieth *these* things

ταύταις, *tautais*, from οὗτος.

Mat.22:40. On *these* two commandments hang all
Lu. 1:39. And Mary arose in *those* days,
6:12. And it came to pass in *those* days,
13:14. in *them* therefore come and be healed,
23: 7. was at Jerusalem at *that* time. (lit. in *those* days)
24:18. are come to pass there in *these* days?
Joh. 5: 3. In *these* lay a great multitude of
Acts 1:15. And in *those* days Peter stood up
6: 1. And in *those* days, when the number
11:27. And in *these* days came prophets
1Th. 3: 3. should be moved by *these* afflictions:
Rev. 9:20. which were not killed by *these* plagues

ταύτας, *tautas*, from οὗτος.

Mat.13:53. when Jesus had finished *these* parables,
Mar13: 2. Seest thou *these* great buildings?
Lu. 1:24. And after *those* days his wife Elisabeth
Acts 1: 5. with the Holy Ghost not many days *hence*.
3:24. likewise foretold of *these* days.
21:15. And after *those* days we took up our
2Co. 7: 1. Having therefore *these* promises,
Heb 9:23. with better sacrifices than *these*.
Rev.16: 9. which hath power over *these* plagues:

ταύτῃ, *tautee*, from οὗτος.

Mat.10:23. they persecute you in *this* city,
12:45. be also unto *this* wicked generation.
16:18. and upon *this* rock I will build
26:31. offended because of me *this* night:
34. That *this* night, before the cock crow,
Mar 8:12. no sign be given unto *this* generation.
38. in *this* adulterous and sinful
14:27. offended because of me *this* night:
30. That this day, (even) in *this* night,
Lu. 11:30. the Son of man be to *this* generation.
12:20. *this* night thy soul shall be required
13: 7. seeking fruit on *this* fig tree,
32. Go ye, and tell *that* fox, Behold,
16:24. I am tormented in *this* flame.
17: 6. say unto *this* sycamine tree,
34. I tell you, in *that* night there shall be
19:42. even thou, at least in *this* thy day,

Acts16:12. and we were in *that* city abiding
18:10. I have much people in *this* city.
22: 3. yet brought up in *this* city at the feet
27:23. For there stood by me *this* night
1Co. 7:20. abide in *the same* calling wherein he was
9:12. we have not used *this* power;
15:19. If in *this* life only we have hope in
2Co. 1:15. And in *this* confidence I was minded
8: 7. that ye abound in *this* grace also.
19. to travel with us with *this* grace,
20. in, *this* abundance which is administered
9: 4. ashamed in *this same* confident boasting.
11:17. in *this* confidence of boasting.
Heb 11: 2. by *it* the elders obtained a good report.

ταύτην, *tauteen*, from οὗτος.

Mat.11:16. whereunto shall I liken *this* generation?
15:15. Declare unto us *this* parable.
21:23. and who gave thee *this* authority?
23:36. shall come upon *this* generation.
Mar 4:13. Know ye not *this* parable?
10: 5. he wrote you *this* precept.
11:28. and who gave thee *this* authority
12:10. have ye not read *this* scripture;
Lu. 4: 6. All *this* power will I give thee,
23. Ye will surely say unto me *this* proverb,
7:44. unto Simon, Seest thou *this* woman?
12:41. speakest thou *this* parable unto us,
13: 6. He spake also *this* parable;
16. And ought not *this* woman, being a
15: 3. And he spake *this* parable unto them,
18: 5. Yet because *this* widow troubleth me,
9. And he spake *this* parable unto certain
20: 2. who is he that gave thee *this* authority?
9. to speak to the people *this* parable;
19. he had spoken *this* parable against them.
23:48. came together to *that* sight,
24:21. to day is *the* third day (lit. *this*)
Joh. 2:11. *This* beginning of miracles did Jesus
7: 8. Go ye up unto *this* feast: I go not up yet
unto *this* feast;
10: 6. *This* parable spake Jesus unto them:
18. *This* commandment have I received
12:27. for this cause came I unto *this* hour.
Acts 1:16. *this* scripture must needs have been fulfilled,
3:16. hath given him *this* perfect soundness
7: 4. he removed him into *this* land,
60. lay not *this* sin to their charge.
8:19. Give me also *this* power,
13:33. God hath fulfilled *the same*
22: 4. persecuted *this* way unto the death,
28. With a great sum obtained I *this* freedom.
23:13. which had made *this* conspiracy,
27:21. to have gained *this* harm and loss.
28:20. For *this* cause therefore have I
— I am bound with *this* chain.
Ro. 5: 2. into *this* grace wherein we stand,
1Co. 6:13. God shall destroy both *it* and them.
2Co. 4: 1. Therefore seeing we have *this* ministry,
8: 6. finish in you *the same* grace also.
9: 5. that *the same* might be ready,
12:13. forgive me *this* wrong.
1Ti. 1:18. *This* charge I commit unto thee,
2Ti. 2:19. standeth sure, having *this* seal,
Heb 5: 3. And by reason *hereof* (lit. *of this*) he ought,
1Pet.5:12. that *this* is the true grace of God
2Pet.1:18. *this* voice which came from heaven
3: 1. *This* second epistle, beloved,

1Joh.3: 3. every man that hath *this* hope in him
4:21. And *this* commandment have we
2Joh. 10. and bring not *this* doctrine,
Rev. 2:24. as many as have not *this* doctrine,
12:15. might cause *her* to be carried away

ταύτης, *tautees*, from οὗτος.

Mat.12:41. in judgment with *this* generation,
42. in the judgment with *this* generation,
Lu. 7:31. shall I liken the men of *this* generation?
11:31. with the men of *this* generation,
32. in the judgment with *this* generation,
50. may be required of *this* generation;
51. It shall be required of *this* generation.
17:25. and be rejected of *this* generation.
Joh.10:16. which are not of *this* fold:
12:27. Father, save me from *this* hour:
15:13. Greater love hath no man than *this*,
Acts 1:17. had obtained part of *this* ministry.
25. That he may take part of *this* ministry
2: 6. Now when *this* was noised abroad,
29. his sepulchre is with us unto *this* day.
40. Save yourselves from *this* untoward
5:20. to the people all the words of *this* life.
6: 3. we may appoint over *this* business.
8:22. Repent therefore of *this* thy wickedness,
35. began at the *same* scripture, and
10:30. I was fasting until *this* hour;
13:26. is the word of *this* salvation sent.
19:25. by *this* craft we have our wealth.
40. may give an account of *this* concourse.
23: 1. conscience before God until *this* day.
24:21. Except it be for *this* one voice,
26:22. I continue unto *this* day,
28:22. for as concerning *this* sect,
2Co. 9:12. For the administration of *this* service
13. by the experiment of *this* ministration
Heb. 9:11. that is to say, not of *this* building;
12:15. *thereby* (lit. by *this*) many be defiled;
13: 2. *thereby* (lit. *&c.*) some have entertained
Rev.22:19. words of the book of *this* prophecy,
Note.—For the other cases, see οὗτος, τοῦτο, &c.

ταφή, *taphee.*

Mat.27: 7. to bury strangers in. (lit. for the *burial*
of strangers)

τάφος, *taphos.*

Mat.23:27. ye are like unto whited *sepulchres*,
29. ye build the *tombs* of the prophets,
27:61. sitting over against the *sepulchre*.
64. that the *sepulchre* be made sure
66. went, and made the *sepulchre* sure,
28: 1. and the other Mary to see the *sepulchre*.
Ro. 3:13. Their throat (is) an open *sepulchre*;

τάχα, *taka.*

Ro. 5: 7. yet *peradventure* for a good man
Philem 15. For *perhaps* he therefore departed

ταχέως, *takeōs.*

Lu. 14:21. Go out *quickly* into the streets
16: 6. sit down *quickly*, and write fifty.

Joh. 11:31. that she rose up *hastily* and went out,
1Co. 4:19. But I will come to you *shortly*,
Gal. 1: 6. that ye are so *soon* removed from
Phi. 2:19. to send Timotheus *shortly* unto you,
    24. that I also myself shall come *shortly*.
2Th. 2: 2. That ye be not *soon* shaken in mind,
1Ti. 5:22. Lay hands *suddenly* on no man,
2Ti. 4: 9. Do thy diligence to come *shortly*

ταχινός, *takinos*.

2Pet. 1:14. that *shortly* I must put off
    2: 1. bring upon themselves *swift* destruction.

τάχιον, *takion*.

Joh. 13:27. That thou doest, do *quickly*.
    20: 4. the other disciple *outrun* Peter,
1T . 3:14. hoping to come unto thee *shortly*:
Heb 13:19. that I may be restored to you *the sooner*.
    23. with whom, if he come *shortly*,

τάχιστα, *takista*.

Acts17:15. to come to him *with all speed*, (ὡς τ.)

τάχος, *takos*.

Lu. 18: 8. he will avenge them *speedily*. (lit. with *speed*·)
Acts12: 7. saying, Arise up *quickly*. (lit. in *speed*)
    22:18. get thee *quickly* out of Jerusalem:
    25: 4. would depart *shortly* (thither).
Ro. 16:20. bruise Satan under your feet *shortly*.
Rev. 1: 1. things which must *shortly* come to pass;
    22: 6. things which must *shortly* be done.

ταχύ, *taku*.

Mat. 5:25. Agree with thine adversary *quickly*,
    28: 7. And go *quickly*, and tell his disciples
       8. And they departed *quickly* from the
Mar 9:39. that can *lightly* speak evil of me.
    16: 8. And they went out *quickly*,
Joh. 11:29. she arose *quickly*, and came unto him.
Rev. 2: 5. else I will come unto thee *quickly*,
    16. else I will come unto thee *quickly*,
    3:11. Behold, I come *quickly*:
    11:14. the third woe cometh *quickly*.
    22: 7. Behold, I come *quickly*:
    12. And, behold, I come *quickly*;
    20. Surely I come *quickly*; Amen.

ταχύς, *takus*.

Jas. 1:19. let every man be *swift* to hear,

τε, *te*.

[2] shews where the two particles τε καὶ are in corre-
lative connection, in a more forcible way than
being mere copulatives. τε is sometimes followed by καὶ twice repeated, as Heb. 11:32.

Mat.22:10. many as they found, *both*[2] bad and good:

Mat.23: 6. *And* love the uppermost rooms
    27:48. *and* filled (it) with vinegar,
    28:12. *and* had taken counsel,
Mar 15:36. full of vinegar, *and* put (it) on a reed,
Lu. 2:16. *and*[2] found Mary and Joseph,
    12:45. *and*[2] to eat and drink, and
    21:11. *And* great earthquakes shall be
    — *and* fearful sights and great signs
    22:66. *and*[2] the chief priests and the scribes
    23:12. *And* the same day)([2] Pilate and Herod
    24:20. *And* how the chief priests and
Joh. 2:15. *and*[2] the sheep, and the oxen;
    4:42. *And* said unto the woman,
    6:18. *And* the sea arose by reason of
Acts 1: 1. Jesus began *both*[2] to do and teach,
    8. *both* in Jerusalem, and in all Judæa,
    13. *both* Peter, and James, and
    15.)(the number of the names together were
    2: 3. *and* it sat upon each of them.
    9. *and* in Judæa, and Cappadocia,
    10.)(Phrygia, *and* Pamphylia, in Egypt,
    —)([2] Jews *and* proselytes,
    33. *and* having received of the Father
    37. *and* said unto Peter and to the rest
    40. *And* with many other words did he
    43. *and* many wonders and signs were done
    46. *And* they, continuing daily with one
    — *and* breaking bread from house to
    3:10. *And* they knew that it was he
    4:13. *and* they took knowledge of them,
    27. *both*[2] Herod, and Pontius Pilate,
    33. *and* great grace was upon them all.
    5:14. to the Lord, multitudes *both*[2] of men and
    19. *and* brought them forth, and said,
    24. Now when)([2] the high priest and the captain of the temple
    35. *And* said unto them, Ye men of
    42. *And* daily in the temple, and in
    6: 7. *and* a great company of the priests
    12. *And* they stirred up the people,
    13. *And* set up false witnesses, which
    7:26. *And* the next day he shewed himself
    8: 1. *and* they were all scattered abroad
    3. *and* haling men and women
    6. *And* the people with one accord gave
    12. they were baptized, *both*[2] men and
    13. *and* wondered, beholding the miracles and signs
    25. *and* preached the gospel in many
    28.)(Was returning, and sitting in his
    31. *And* he desired Philip that he would
    38. *both*[2] Philip and the eunuch;
    9: 2. *whether*[2] they were men or women,
    6. *And* he trembling and astonished said,
    15. and kings, *and* the children of Israel:
    18. *and* he received sight forthwith,
    24. *And* they watched the gates)([2] day and night to kill him.
    29. And he)([2] spake boldly in...and
    10: 2.)(which gave much alms to the people
    22. *and* of good report among all
    28. *And* he said unto them, Ye know
    33. *and* thou hast well done that thou
    39. *both*[2] in the land of the Jews, and in
    48. *And* he commanded them to be baptized
    11:13. *And* he shewed us how he had
    21. *and* a great number believed,
    26. *And* the disciples were called Christians
    12: 6. *and* the keepers before the door
    8. *And* the angel said unto him, Gird
    12. *And* when he had considered (the thing),
    13: 1. as)(Barnabas, and Simeon that was

Acts13: 1. *and* Manaen, which had been brought up
2. Separate me)(Barnabas and Saul
4. *and* from thence they sailed to Cyprus.
14: 1. *both*[2] of the Jews and also of the Greeks
5. *both*[2] of the Gentiles, and also of the Jews
12. *And* they called Barnabas, Jupiter;
21. *And* when they had preached the gospel
15: 4. *and* they declared all things that God
5. *and* to command (them) to keep the law
9. no difference between)([2] us and them,
39. *and* so Barnabas took Mark,
16:11. *and* the next (day) to Neapolis;
12. *And* from thence to Philippi,
13. *And* on the sabbath we went out
23. *And* when they had laid many stripes
26. *and* immediately all the doors
34. *And* when he had brought them into his
17: 4. *and* of the devout Greeks a great multitude, *and* of the chief women not a few.
5. *and* assaulted the house of Jason,
10. sent away)([2] Paul and Silas by night
14. but)([2] Silas and Timotheus abode
19. *And* they took him, and brought
26. *And* hath made of one blood all nations
18: 4. *and* persuaded the Jews and the Greeks.
5. when)([2] Silas and Timotheus were come
11. *And* he continued (there) a year
26. *And* he began to speak boldly in
19: 3. *And* he said unto them, Unto what
6. *and* they spake with tongues, and
10. *both*[2] Jews and Greeks.
11. *And* God wrought special miracles
12. *and* the evil spirits went out of them.
17. known)([2] to all the Jews and Greeks also
18. *And* many that believed came,
29. *and* having caught Gaius and
20: 3. *And* (there) abode three months.
7. *and* continued his speech until
11. *and* talked a long while, even
21. *both*[2] to the Jews, and also to the Greeks,
35. *and* to remember the words of the Lord
21:11. *and* bound his own hands and feet,
12. *both*[2] we, and they of that place,
18. *and* all the elders were present.
20. *and* said unto him, Thou seest, brother,
25.)(from (things) offered to idols, and
28. *and* further brought Greeks also
30. *And* all the city was moved, and
37. *And* as Paul was to be led into the
22: 4. into prisons *both*[2] men and women.
7. *And* I fell unto the ground, and
8. *And* he said unto me, I am Jesus
28. *And* the chief captain answered,
23: 5. *Then* said Paul, I wist not, (lit. *and*)
10. *and* to bring (him) into the castle.
24. *And* provide (them) beasts, that they
35. *And* he commanded him to be kept
24: 3. We accept (it))([2] always, and in all
places,
5. *and* a ringleader of the sect of the Nazarenes:
15. *both*[2] of the just and unjust.
23. *And* he commanded a centurion to keep
Paul, *and* to let (him) have liberty,
27. *and* Felix, willing to shew the Jews a
25:23. with)([2] the chief captains, and principal
24. *both*[2] at Jerusalem, and (also) here,
26: 3. expert)([2] in all customs and questions
10. *and* when they were put to death,
11. *and* being exceedingly mad against
16. a witness *both* of these things which thou
hast seen, *and* of those things in

Acts26:20. *and*[2] throughout all the coasts of Judæa,
and
22. witnessing *both*[2] to small and great,
— which)([2] the prophets and Moses did
30. *and* Bernice, and they that sat with them:
27: 1. delivered)([2] Paul and certain other
3. *And* the next (day) we touched at
5. *And* when we had sailed over the sea of
8. *And*, hardly passing it, came unto a place
17. *and*, fearing lest they should fall
20. *and* no small tempest lay on (us),
21. *and* to have gained this harm and loss.
29. *Then* fearing lest we should (lit. *and*)
43. *and* commanded that they which
28:23.)(persuading them concerning Jesus,
both[2] out of the law of Moses, and (out
of) the prophets,
Ro. 1:12. the mutual faith *both*[2] of you and me.
14. *both*[2] to the Greeks, and to the Barbarians;
both[2] to the wise, and to the unwise.
16.)([2] to the Jew first, and also to the Greek.
20. (even))([2] his eternal power and Godhead;
26. for *even* (lit. *both*) their women did change
27. *And* likewise also the men,
2: 9.)([2] of the Jew first, and also of
10.)([2] to the Jew first, and also to
19. *And* art confident that thou thyself
3: 9. *both*[2] Jews and Gentiles, that they are all
7: 7. for)(I had not known lust, except
10:12. difference between)([2] the Jew and the
14: 8. whether (lit. if *either*) we live
— *and* whether we die, we die unto
— whether (lit. if *either*) we live therefore,
or (lit. if *either*) die, we are the Lord's.
16:26. *and* by the scriptures of the prophets,
1Co. 1: 2. Jesus Christ our Lord, *both*[2] their's and
our's:
24. *both*[2] Jews and Greeks, Christ the power
of God,
30. God is made unto us)(wisdom, and
4:21. *and* (in) the spirit of meekness?
2Co.10: 8. For)(though I should boast
Eph. 1:10. *both*[2] which are in heaven, and which are
on earth;
3:19. *And* to know the love of Christ,
Phi. 1: 7. inasmuch as *both* in my bonds, and
Heb 1: 3. *and* upholding all things by the word
2: 4. *both* with signs and wonders, and with
11. For *both*[2] he that sanctifieth and they
4:12. dividing asunder)([2] of soul and spirit,
and[2] of the joints and marrow,
5: 1. that he may offer *both*[2] gifts and sacrifices
7. offered up)([2] prayers and supplications
14. to discern *both*[2] good and evil.
6: 2. *and* of laying on of hands, *and* of resurrection of the dead,
4. *and* have tasted of the heavenly gift,
5. *and* the powers of the world to come,
19. an anchor of the soul, *both*[2] sure and stedfast,
8: 3. to offer)([2] gifts and sacrifices:
9: 1. *and* a worldly sanctuary.
2.)(the candlestick, and the table,
9. were offered *both*[2] gifts and sacrifices,
19. sprinkled *both*[2] the book, and all the
10:33. *both*[2] by reproaches and afflictions;
11:32. *and* (of) Barak, and (of) Samson, and
— (of) David *also*, and Samuel, and
12: 2. *and* is set down at the right hand
Jas. 3: 7. every kind)([2] of beasts, and of birds, *and*[2]
of serpents, and of things in the sea,

Jude   6. *And* the angels which kept not
Rev. 1: 2. *and* of all things that he saw.
    21:12. *And* had a wall great and high,

τεῖχος, *tikos.*

Acts 9:25. down by the *wall* in a basket.
2Co.11:33. was I let down by the *wall*,
Heb 11:30. By faith the *walls* of Jericho fell
Rev.21:12. And had a *wall* great and high,
    14. And the *wall* of the city had twelve
    15. the gates thereof, and the *wall* thereof.
    17. And he measured the *wall* thereof,
    18. And the building of the *wall* of it
    19. And the foundations of the *wall* of

τεκμήριον, *tekmeerion.*

Acts 1: 3. by many *infallible proofs,*

τεκνίον, *teknion.*

Joh.13:33. *Little children,* yet a little while I am
Gal. 4:19. My *little children,* of whom I travail
1Joh.2: 1. My *little children,* these things write I
    12. I write unto you, *little children,*
    28. And now, *little children,* abide in him ;
    3: 7. *Little children,* let no man deceive you:
    18. My *little children,* let us not love in word,
    4: 4. Ye are of God, *little children,* and
    5:21. *Little children,* keep yourselves from idols.

τεκνογονέω, *teknogoneo.*

1Ti. 5:14. that the younger women marry, *bear
    children,*

τεκνογονία, *teknogonia.*

1Ti. 2:15. she shall be saved in *childbearing,*

τέκνον, *teknon.*

Mat. 2:18. Rachel weeping (for) her *children,*
    3: 9. to raise up *children* unto Abraham.
    7:11. to give good gifts unto your *children,*
    9: 2. *Son,* be of good cheer ; thy sins
    10:21. and the father the *child :* and the *children*
        shall rise up
    11:19. But wisdom is justified of her *children.*
    15:26. not meet to take the *children's* bread,
    18:25. to be sold, and his wife, and *children,*
    19:29. or *children,* or lands, for my name's sake,
    21:28. A (certain) man had two *sons ;*
    — *Son,* go work to day in my vineyard.
    22:24. If a man die, having no *children,*
    23:37. have gathered thy *children* together,
    27:25. His blood (be) on us, and on our *children.*
Mar 2: 5. *Son,* thy sins be forgiven thee.
    7:27. Let the *children* first be filled:
    — not meet to take the *children's* bread,
    10:24. *Children,* how hard is it for them that
    29. or *children,* or lands, for my sake,
    30. and *children,* and lands, with persecutions;
    12:19. and leave no *children,* that his brother
    13:12. to death, and the father the *son* (lit. the
        child); and *children* shall rise up against
        (their)

Lu. 1: 7. And they had no *child,* because that
    17. the hearts of the fathers to the *children,*
    2:48. *Son,* why hast thou thus dealt
    3: 8. to raise up *children* unto Abraham.
    7:35. wisdom is justified of all her *children.*
    11:13. to give good gifts unto your *children :*
    13:34. have gathered thy *children* together,
    14:26. *children,* and brethren, and sisters
    15:31. *Son,* thou art ever with me,
    16:25. *Son,* remember that thou in thy lifetime,
    18:29. or *children,* for the kingdom of God's sake,
    19:44. and thy *children* within thee ;
    20:31. and they left no *children,* and died.
    23:28. for yourselves, and for your *children.*
Joh. 1:12. power to become the *sons* of God, (lit.
        children)
    8:39. If ye were Abraham's *children,*
    11:52. in one the *children* of God that were scat-
        tered abroad.
Acts 2:39. is unto you, and to your *children,*
    7: 5. when (as yet) he had no *child.*
    13:33(32). God hath fulfilled the same unto us
        their *children,*
    21: 5. all brought us on our way, with wives and
        children,
    21. not to circumcise (their) *children,*
Ro. 8:16. that we are the *children* of God:
    17. And if *children,* then heirs ;
    21. into the glorious liberty of the *children* of
        God.
    9: 7. the seed of Abraham, (are they) all *chil-
        dren :*
    8. They which are the *children* of the flesh,
        these (are) not the *children* of God: but
        the *children* of the promise
1Co. 4:14. but as my beloved *sons* I warn (you). (lit.
        children)
    17. Timotheus, who is my beloved *son,*
    7:14. else were your *children* unclean;
2Co. 6:13. I speak as unto (my) *children,*
    12:14. the *children* ought not to lay up for the
        parents, but the parents for the *children.*
Gal. 4:25. and is in bondage with her *children.*
    27. the desolate hath many more *children*
    28. as Isaac was, are the *children* of promise.
    31. we are not *children* of the bondwoman,
Eph. 2: 3. were by nature the *children* of wrath,
    5: 1. followers of God, as dear *children ;*
    8. walk as *children* of light:
    6: 1. *Children,* obey your parents in the Lord:
    4. provoke not your *children* to wrath:
Phi. 2:15. the *sons* of God, without rebuke, (lit.
        children)
    22. that, as a *son* with the father,
Col. 3:20. *Children,* obey (your) parents in all things:
    21. Fathers, provoke not your *children*
1Th. 2: 7. even as a nurse cherisheth her *children :*
    11. as a father (doth) his *children,*
1Ti. 1: 2. Unto Timothy, (my) own *son*
    18. I commit unto thee, *son* Timothy,
    3: 4. having his *children* in subjection
    12. ruling their *children* and their own houses
    5: 4. But if any widow have *children*
2Ti. 1: 2. To Timothy, (my) dearly beloved *son :*
    2: 1. Thou therefore, my *son,* be strong
Tit. 1: 4. To Titus, (mine) own *son* after
    6. having faithful *children,* not accused
Philem 10. I beseech thee for my *son* Onesimus,
1Pet.1:14. As obedient *children,* not fashioning
    3: 6. whose *daughters* ye are, (lit. *children*)
2Pet. 2:14. exercised with covetous practises; cursed
        children :

1Joh. 3: 1. that we should be called the *sons* of God: (lit. *children*)

2. now are we the *sons* of God, (lit. *children*)

10. In this the *children* of God are manifest, and the *children* of the devil;

5: 2. we know that we love the *children* of God,

2Joh. 1. unto the elect lady and her *children,*

4. that I found of thy *children* walking in truth,

13. The *children* of thy elect sister greet

3Joh. 4. to hear that my *children* walk in truth.

Rev. 2:23. And I will kill her *children*

12: 4. to devour her *child* as soon as

5. her *child* was caught up unto God, and (to) his throne.

τεκνοτροφέω, *teknotropheo.*

1Ti. 5:10. if she *have brought up children,*

τέκτων, *tekton.*

Mat.13:55. Is not this the *carpenter's* son?

Mar 6: 3. Is not this the *carpenter,*

τέλειος, *telios.*

Mat. 5:48. Be ye therefore *perfect,* even as your Father which is in heaven is *perfect.*

19:21. If thou wilt be *perfect,* go (and)

Ro. 12: 2. and acceptable, and *perfect,* will of God.

1Co. 2: 6. wisdom among them that are *perfect :*

13:10. when that which is *perfect* is come,

14:20. but in understanding be *men.*

Eph 4:13. unto a *perfect* man, unto the measure of

Phi. 3:15. Let us therefore, as many as be *perfect,*

Col. 1:28. that we may present every man *perfect* in Christ Jesus:

4:12. that ye may stand *perfect* and complete

Heb 5:14. belongeth to them that are *of full age,*

9:11. greater and more *perfect* tabernacle,

Jas. 1: 4. let patience have (her) *perfect* work, that ye may be *perfect* and entire,

17. and every *perfect* gift is from above,

25. looketh into the *perfect* law of liberty,

3: 2. the same (is) a *perfect* man, (and)

1Joh.4:18. but *perfect* love casteth out fear:

τελειότης, *teliotees.*

Col. 3:14. which is the bond of *perfectness.*

Heb 6: 1. let us go on unto *perfection ;*

τελειόω, *telioo.*

Lu. 2:43. And *when* they *had fulfilled* the days,

13:32. the third (day) I shall be *perfected.*

Joh. 4:34. and to *finish* his work.

5:36. the Father hath given me to *finish,*

17: 4. I *have finished* the work which

23. that they may be *made perfect* in one;

19:28. that the scripture *might be fulfilled,*

Acts20:24. that I might *finish* my course with joy,

2Co.12: 9. my strength *is made perfect* in weakness.

Phi. 3:12. either *were* already *perfect :*

Heb 2:10. *to make* the captain of their salvation *perfect*

Heb 5: 9. And *being made perfect,* he became

7:19. For the law *made* nothing *perfect,*

28. the Son, *who is consecrated* for evermore.

9: 9. that could not *make* him that did the service *perfect,*

10: 1. *make* the comers thereunto *perfect.*

14. For by one offering he *hath perfected* for ever

11:40. that they without us *should* not *be made perfect.*

12:23. to the spirits of just men *made perfect,*

Jas. 2:22. by works *was* faith *made perfect ?*

1Joh.2: 5. in him verily *is* the love of God *perfected :*

4:12. and his love is *perfected* in us.

17. Herein *is* our love *made perfect,* that

18. He that feareth *is* not *made perfect* in love

τελείως, *telios.*

1Pet.1:13. and hope *to the end* (lit. trust *perfectly*) for the grace

---

τελείωσις, *teliosis.*

Lu. 1:45. there shall be a *performance* of those

Heb 7:11. If therefore *perfection* were by the Levitical priesthood,

---

τελειωτής, *teliotees.*

Heb 12: 2. Jesus the author and *finisher* of (our)

τελεσφορέω, *telesphoreo.*

Lu. 8:14. and *bring* no *fruit to perfection.*

τελευτάω, *telutao.*

Mat. 2:19. But *when* Herod *was dead,*

9:18. My daughter *is* even now *dead :*

15: 4. *let* him *die* the death.

22:25. the first, when he had married a wife, *deceased,*

Mar 7:10. *let* him *die* the death :

9:44. Where their worm *dieth* not,

46. Where their worm *dieth* not,

48. Where their worm *dieth* not,

Lu. 7: 2. was sick, and ready to *die.*

Acts 2:29. David, that he *is* both *dead* and buried,

7:15. So Jacob went down into Egypt, and *died,*

Heb 11:22. By faith Joseph, *when* he *died,* (lit. *dying*)

τελευτή, *telutee.*

Mat. 2:15. And was there until the *death* of Herod ;

τελέω, *teleo.*

Mat.10:23. Ye *shall* not *have gone over* the cities

11: 1. when Jesus *had made an end* of commanding his

13:53. when Jesus *had finished* these parables,

17:24. *Doth* not your master *pay* tribute ?

19: 1. when Jesus *had finished* these sayings,

Mat.26: 1. *had finished* all these sayings,
Lu. 2:39. when they *had performed* all things
12:50. straitened till it be *accomplished!*
18:31. concerning the Son of man *shall be accomplished.*
22:37. must yet *be accomplished* in me,
Joh.19:28. all things *were* now *accomplished,*
30. he said, It *is finished:* and he bowed
Acts13:29. when they *had fulfilled* all that
Ro. 2:27. if it *fulfil* the law, judge thee,
13: 6. for this cause *pay* ye tribute also:
Gal. 5:16. ye *shall* not *fulfil* the lust of the flesh.
2Ti. 4: 7. I *have finished* (my) course,
Jas. 2: 8. If ye *fulfil* the royal law according to
Rev.10: 7. the mystery of God *should be finished,*
11: 7. And when they *shall have finished* their
15: 1. for in them *is filled* up the wrath of God.
8. till the seven plagues of the seven angels *were fulfilled.*
17:17. until the words of God *shall be fulfilled.*
20: 3. till the thousand years *should be fulfilled:*
5. until the thousand years were (lit. *should be*) *finished.*
7. when the thousand years are (lit. *should be*) *expired*

τέλος, telos.

Mat.10:22. but he that endureth to the *end* shall be
17:25. of whom do the kings of the earth take *custom*
24: 6. but the *end* is not yet.
13. But he that shall endure unto the *end,*
14. and then shall the *end* come.
26:58. with the servants, to see the *end.*
Mar 3:26. he cannot stand, but hath an *end.*
13: 7. but the *end* (shall) not (be) yet.
13. but he that shall endure unto the *end,*
Lu. 1:33. of his kingdom there shall be no *end.*
18: 5. lest by her continual coming (lit. unto the *end*)
21: 9. but the *end* (is) not by and by.
22:37. the things concerning me have an *end.*
Joh.13: 1. he loved them unto the *end.*
Ro. 6:21. for the *end* of those things (is) death.
22. and the *end* everlasting life.
10: 4. For Christ (is) the *end* of the law
13: 7. *custom* to whom *custom;*
1Co. 1: 8. Who shall also confirm you unto the *end,*
10:11. upon whom the *ends* of the world are come.
15:24. Then (cometh) the *end,* when he shall have
2Co. 1:13. ye shall acknowledge even to the *end;*
3:13. to the *end* of that which is abolished:
11:15. whose *end* shall be according to
Phi. 3:19. Whose *end* (is) destruction,
1Th. 2:16. wrath is come upon them to the *uttermost.*
1Ti. 1: 5. Now the *end* of the commandment
Heb 3: 6. the rejoicing of the hope firm unto the *end.*
14. our confidence stedfast unto the *end;*
6: 8. whose *end* (is) to be burned.
11. assurance of hope unto the *end:*
7: 3. beginning of days, nor *end* of life;
Jas. 5:11. and have seen the *end* of the Lord;
1Pet.1: 9. Receiving the *end* of your faith,
3: 8. *Finally,* (be ye) all of one mind,
4: 7. But the *end* of all things is at hand:
17. what shall the *end* (be) of them that obey not
Rev. 1: 8. the beginning and the *ending,*
2:26. and keepeth my works unto the *end,*

Rev.21: 6. the beginning and the *end.*
22:13. Alpha and Omega, the beginning and the *end,*

τελώνης, telōnecs.

Mat. 5:46. do not even the *publicans* the same?
47. do not even the *publicans* so?
9:10. many *publicans* and sinners came
11. Why eateth your Master with *publicans*
10: 3. Thomas, and Matthew the *publican* ·
11:19. a friend of *publicans* and sinners.
18:17. as an heathen man and a *publican.*
21:31. That the *publicans* and the harlots go into
32. the *publicans* and the harlots believed him:
Mar 2:15. many *publicans* and sinners sat also
16. *publicans* ... drinketh with *publicans*
Lu. 3:12. Then came also *publicans* to be baptized,
5:27. and saw a *publican,* named Levi,
29. there was a great company of *publicans*
30. drink with *publicans* and sinners?
7:29. and the *publicans,* justified God,
34. a friend of *publicans* and sinners!
15: 1. all the *publicans* and sinners for to hear him.
18:10. the one a Pharisee, and the other a *publican.*
11. adulterers, or even as this *publican.*
13. And the *publican,* standing afar off,

τελώνιον, telōnion.

Mat. 9: 9. sitting at the *receipt of custom:*
Mar 2:14. sitting at the *receipt of custom,*
Lu. 5:27. sitting at the *receipt of custom:*

τέρας, teras.

Mat.24:24. and shall shew great signs and *wonders;*
Mar 13:22. and shall shew signs and *wonders,*
Joh. 4:48. Except ye see signs and *wonders,*
Acts 2:19. And I will shew *wonders* in heaven above,
22. by miracles and *wonders* and signs,
43. and many *wonders* and signs were done
4:30. that signs and *wonders* may be done
5:12. were many signs and *wonders* wrought
6: 8. did great *wonders* and miracles among
7:36. after that he had shewed *wonders*
14: 3. granted signs and *wonders* to be done
15:12. declaring what miracles and *wonders*
Ro. 15:19. Through mighty signs and *wonders,*
2Co.12:12. in signs, and *wonders,* and mighty deeds.
2Th. 2: 9. with all power and signs and lying *wonders,*
Heb 2: 4. both with signs and *wonders,*

τεσσαράκοντα, tessarakonta.

Mat. 4: 2. he had fasted *forty* days and *forty* nights,
Mar 1:13. was there in the wilderness *forty* days,
Lu. 4: 2. Being *forty* days tempted of the devil.
Joh. 2:20. *Forty* and six years was this temple
Acts 1: 3. being seen of them *forty* days,
4:22. the man was above *forty* years old,
7:30. And when *forty* years were expired,
36. and in the wilderness *forty* years.
42. *forty* years in the wilderness?
13:21. by the space of *forty* years.

Acts23:13. And they were more than *forty* which had made
21. of them more than *forty* men,
2Co.11:24. received I *forty* (stripes) save one.
Heb 3: 9. and saw my works *forty* years.
17. with whom was he grieved *forty* years?
Rev. 7: 4. an hundred (and) *forty* (and) four thousand
11: 2. tread under foot *forty* (and) two months.
13: 5. to continue *forty* (and) two months.
14: 1. with him an hundred *forty* (and) four thousand,
3. but the hundred (and) *forty* (and) four thousand,
21:17. an hundred (and) *forty* (and) four cubits,

τεσσαρακονταετής, *tessarakontaetees.*

Acts 7:23. when he was full *forty years old*, (lit. when the time *of forty years* was completed to him)
13:18. And about the time *of forty years*

τέσσαρες, -ρα, *tessares, -ra.*

Mat.24:31. his elect from the *four* winds,
Mar 2: 3. sick of the palsy, which was borne of *four.*
13:27. his elect from the *four* winds,
Lu. 2:37. of about fourscore and *four* years,
Joh.11:17. (lain) in the grave *four* days already.
19:23. *four* parts, to every soldier a part ;
Acts10:11. sheet knit at the *four* corners,
11: 5. let down from heaven by *four* corners ;
12: 4. and delivered (him) to *four* quaternions
21: 9. the same man had *four* daughters,
23. We have *four* men which have a vow
27:29. cast *four* anchors out of the stern,
Rev. 4: 4. (were) *four* and twenty seats :
— I saw *four* and twenty elders sitting,
6. *four* beasts full of eyes before and
8. And the *four* beasts had each of them
10. The *four* and twenty elders fall down
5: 6. of the throne and of the *four* beasts,
8. the *four* beasts and *four* (and) twenty elders fell down before the Lamb,
14. And the *four* beasts said, Amen. And the *four* (and) twenty elders fell down
6: 1. one of the *four* beasts saying, Come
6. in the midst of the *four* beasts say,
7: 1. after these things I saw *four* angels standing on the *four* corners of the earth, holding the *four* winds of the earth,
2. he cried with a loud voice to the *four* angels,
4. an hundred (and) forty (and) *four* thousand
11. (about) the elders and the *four* beasts,
9:13. I heard a voice from the *four* horns
14. Loose the *four* angels which are bound
15. And the *four* angels were loosed,
11:16. And the *four* and twenty elders, which
14: 1. an hundred forty (and) *four* thousand,
3. and before the *four* beasts,
— but the hundred (and) forty (and) *four* thousand,
15: 7. And one of the *four* beasts gave
19: 4. the *four* and twenty elders and the *four* beasts
20: 8. are in the *four* quarters of the earth,
21:17. an hundred (and) forty (and) *four* cubits,

τεσσαρεσκαιδέκατος, *tessareskaidekatos.*

Acts27:27. when the *fourteenth* night was come,
33. This day is the *fourteenth* day that ye

τεταρταῖος, *tetartaios.*

Joh.11:39. for he hath been (dead) four days. (lit. he is *of the fourth day*)

τέταρτος, *tetartos.*

Mat.14:25. And in the *fourth* watch of the night
Mar. 6:48. about the *fourth* watch of the night
Acts10:30. *Four* days ago I was fasting until
Rev. 4: 7 *fourth* beast (was) like a flying eagle.
6: 7. opened the *fourth* seal, I heard the voice of the *fourth* beast
8. over the *fourth* part of the earth,
8:12. And the *fourth* angel sounded,
16: 8. the *fourth* angel poured out his vial
21:19. the *fourth*, an emerald ;

τετράγωνος, *tetragōnos.*

Rev.21:16. And the city lieth *foursquare*,

τετράδιον, *tetradion.*

Acts12: 4. to four *quaternions* of soldiers

τετρακισχίλιοι, *tetrakiskilioi.*

Mat.15:38. *four thousand* men, beside women and
16:10. the seven loaves of the *four thousand*,
Mar 8: 9. were about *four thousand :* and he
20. And when the seven among *four thousand*,
Acts21:38. *four thousand* men that were murderers?

τετρακόσιοι, -σια, *tetrakosioi, -sia.*

Acts 5:36. a number of men, about *four hundred*,
7: 6. entreat (them) evil *four hundred* years.
13:20. space of *four hundred* and fifty years,
Gal. 3:17. *four hundred* and thirty years after,

τετράμηνον, *tetrameenon.*

Joh. 4:35. Say not ye, There are yet *four months*,

τετραπλόος, *tetraplóos.*

Lu. 19: 8. I restore (him) *fourfold.*

τετράπους, *tetrapous.*

Acts10:12. all manner of *fourfooted beasts* of the earth,
11: 6. and saw *fourfooted beasts* of the earth,
Ro. 1:23. *fourfooted beasts*, and creeping things.

τετράρχης, tetrarkees.

Mat.14: 1. At that time Herod the *tetrarch* heard
Lu.　3:19. But Herod the *tetrarch*, being reproved
　　 9: 7. Now Herod the *tetrarch* heard of all
Acts13: 1. brought up with Herod the *tetrarch*,

τετραρχέω, tetrarkeo.

Lu.　3: 1. Herod *being tetrarch* of Galilee, and his
　　　　 brother Philip *tetrarch* of Ituræa
　　 — Lysanias the *tetrarch* (lit. being *tetrarch*)
　　　　 of Abilene,

τεφρόω, tephroō.

2Pet 2: 6. *turning* the cities of Sodom and Gomorrha
　　　　 into ashes

τέχνη, teknee.

Acts17:29. stone, graven by *art* and man's device.
　　 18: 3. by their *occupation* they were tentmakers.
Rev.18:22. craftsman, of whatsoever *craft* (he be),

τεχνίτης, teknitees.

Acts19:24. no small gain unto the *craftsmen ;*
　　　 38. and the *craftsmen* which are with him,
Heb 11:10. whose *builder* and maker (is) God.
Rev.18:22. no *craftsman*, of whatsoever craft

τήκομαι, teekomai.

2Pet. 3:12. elements shall *melt* with fervent heat ?

τηλαυγῶς, teelaugōs.

Mar 8:25. and saw every man *clearly.*

τηλικοῦτος, teelikoutos.

2Co.　1:10. Who delivered us from *so great* a death,
Heb　 2: 3. if we neglect *so great* salvation;
Jas.　 3: 4. which though (they be) *so great,*
Rev.16:18. *so mighty* an earthquake, (and) so great.

τηρέω, tecreo.

Mat.19:17. *keep* the commandments.
　　 23: 3. whatsoever they bid you *observe,* (that)
　　　　 observe
　　 27:36. they *watched* him there;
　　　 54. they that were with him, *watching* Jesus,
　　 23: 4. for fear of him the *keepers* did shake,
　　　 20. Teaching them *to observe* all things
Mar　7: 9. that ye *may keep* your own tradition.
Joh.　2:10. thou *hast kept* the good wine until now.
　　 8:51. If a man *keep* my saying,
　　　 52. thou sayest, If a man *keep* my saying,
　　　 55. but I know him, and *keep* his saying.
　　 9:16. because he *keepeth* not the sabbath day.
　　 12: 7. of my burying *hath* she *kept* this.

Joh.14:15. If ye love me, *keep* my commandments.
　　　 21. and *keepeth* them, he it is that loveth me:
　　　 23. If a man love me, he *will keep* my words:
　　　 24. loveth me not *keepeth* not my sayings:
　　 15:10. If ye *keep* my commandments,
　　 — even as I *have kept* my Father's
　　　 20. if they *have kept* my saying, they *will keep*
　　　　 your's also.
　　 17: 6. and they *have kept* thy word.
　　　 11. Holy Father, *keep* through thine own
　　　 12. I *kept* them in thy name:
　　　 15. *shouldest keep* them from the evil.
Acts12: 5. Peter therefore *was kept* in prison:
　　　 6. the keepers before the door *kept* the
　　 15: 5. to command (them) *to keep* the law of
　　　 24. (Ye must) be circumcised, and *keep* the
　　　　 law:
　　 16:23. charging the jailor *to keep* them safely:
　　 21:25. that they *observe* no such thing,
　　 24:23. he commanded a centurion *to keep* Paul,
　　　　 (lit. that Paul *be kept*)
　　 25: 4. that Paul should *be kept* at Cæsarea,
　　　 21. when Paul had appealed *to be reserved*
　　 — I commanded him *to be kept* till
1Co.　7:37. that he will *keep* his virgin, doeth well.
2Co.11: 9. in all (things) I *have kept* myself from
　　 — and (so) *will* I *keep* (myself).
Eph　4: 3. Endeavouring *to keep* the unity of the
1Th.　5:23. *be preserved* blameless unto the coming
1Ti.　5:22. *keep* thyself pure.
　　 6:14. That thou *keep* (this) commandment
2Ti.　4: 7. I *have kept* the faith:
Jas.　1:27. (and) *to keep* himself unspotted from the
　　　　 world.
　　 2:10. whosoever *shall keep* the whole law,
1Pet.1: 4. *reserved* in heaven for you,
2Pet.2: 4. to be *reserved* unto judgment;
　　　 9. and *to reserve* the unjust unto the day
　　　 17. to whom the mist of darkness *is reserved*
　　　　 for ever.
　　 3: 7. *reserved* unto fire against the day of
1Joh 2: 3. if we *keep* his commandments.
　　　 4. and *keepeth* not his commandments,
　　　 5. But whoso *keepeth* his word, in him
　　 3:22. because we *keep* his commandments,
　　　 24. And he *that keepeth* his commandments
　　 5: 2. and *keep* his commandments.
　　　 3. that we *keep* his commandments:
　　　 18. begotten of God *keepeth* himself, and
Jude　1. and *preserved* in Jesus Christ,
　　　 6. And the angels *which kept* not their
　　 — he *hath reserved* in everlasting chains
　　　 13. to whom *is reserved* the blackness
　　　 21. *Keep* yourselves in the love of God,
Rev.　1: 3. and *keep* those things which are written
　　 2:26. and *keepeth* my works unto the end,
　　 3: 3. and *hold fast,* and repent.
　　　 8. and *hast kept* my word, and hast not
　　　 10. thou *hast kept* the word of my patience, I
　　　　 also *will keep* thee
　　 12:17. *which keep* the commandments of God,
　　 14:12. they *that keep* the commandments of
　　 16:15. that *watcheth,* and *keepeth* his garments,
　　 22: 7. blessed (is) he *that keepeth* the sayings
　　　 9. and of them *which keep* the sayings of this
　　　　 book:

τήρησις, tecreesis.

Acts 4: 3. and put (them) in *hold* unto the next

Acts 5:18. put them in the common *prison*.
1Co. 7:19. but the *keeping* of the commandments

τίθημι, ἔθηκα, ἐθέμην, ϑῶ, &c. *titheemi, etheeka, ethemeen, tho,* &c.

Mat. 5:15. and *put* it under a bushel,
12:18. I *will put* my spirit upon him,
14: 3. *put* (him) in prison for Herodias' sake,
22:44. till I *make* thine enemies thy footstool?
24:51. shall cut him asunder, and *appoint* (him) his portion with
27:60. And *laid* it in his own new tomb,
Mar 4:21. Is a candle brought to *be put* under a
6:29. and *laid* it in a tomb.
56. they *laid* the sick in the streets,
10:16. *put* (his) hands upon them, *and*
12:36. till I *make* thine enemies thy footstool.
15:19. *bowing* (their) knees worshipped him.
47. beheld where he was *laid*.
16: 6. behold the place where they *laid* him.
Lu. 1:66. *laid* (them) *up* in their hearts,
5:18. and *to lay* (him) before him.
6:48. and *laid* the foundation on a rock:
8:16. or *putteth* (it) under a bed;
9:44. *Let* these sayings *sink down* into your ears: (lit. *put* ye these &c.)
11:33. *putteth* (it) in a secret place,
12:46. and *will appoint* him his portion with
14:29. *after* he *hath laid* the foundation,
19:21. takest up that thou *layedst* not *down*,
22. taking up that I *laid* not *down*,
20:43. Till I *make* thine enemies thy footstool.
21:14. *Settle* (it) therefore in your hearts,
22:41. kneeled down, and (lit. *having placed* his knees) prayed,
23:53. and *laid* it in a sepulchre
55. and how his body *was laid*.
Joh. 2:10. at the beginning *doth set forth* good
10:11. the good shepherd *giveth* his life for
15. I *lay down* my life for the sheep.
17. because I *lay down* my life,
18. but I *lay* it *down* of myself. I have power *to lay* it *down*,
11:34. Where *have* ye *laid* him?
13: 4. and *laid aside* his garments;
37. I *will lay down* my life for thy sake.
38. *Wilt* thou *lay down* thy life for
15:13. that a man *lay down* his life for his
16. I have chosen you, and *ordained* you, that ye should go
19:19. wrote a title, and *put* (it) on the cross.
41. wherein *was* never man yet *laid*.
42. There *laid* they Jesus therefore
20: 2. we know not where they *have laid* him.
13. I know not where they *have laid* him.
15. tell me where thou *hast laid* him,
Acts 1: 7. which the Father *hath put* in his own power.
2:35. Until I *make* thy foes thy footstool.
3: 2. whom they *laid* daily at the gate of the
4: 3. and *put* (them) in hold unto the next day:
35. And *laid* (them) *down* at the apostles' feet:
37. and *laid* (it) at the apostles' feet.
5: 2. and *laid* (it) at the apostles' feet.
4. why *hast* thou *conceived* this thing in thine heart?
15. and *laid* (them) on beds and couches,
18. and *put* them in the common prison.

Acts 5:25. the men whom ye *put* in prison
7:16. were carried over into Sychem, and *laid* in the sepulchre that
60. And he kneeled down, and cried (lit. *having placed* his knees)
9:37. they *laid* (her) in an upper chamber.
40. kneeled down, and (lit. *having &c.*) prayed;
12: 4. he *put* (him) in prison, and
13:29. and *laid* (him) in a sepulchre.
47. I *have set* thee to be a light of the
19:21. Paul *purposed* in the spirit,
20:28. the Holy Ghost *hath made* you overseers,
36. he kneeled down, and (lit. *having &c.*) prayed
21: 5. and we kneeled down (lit. *having &c.*)
27:12. the more part advised (lit. *formed* the counsel) to depart thence also,
Ro. 4:17. I *have made* thee a father of
9:33. I *lay* in Sion a stumblingstone
14:13. that no man *put* a stumblingblock
1Co. 3:10. I *have laid* the foundation, and another
11. For other foundation can no man *lay*
9:18. I may *make* the gospel of Christ without charge,
12:18. But now *hath* God *set* the members
28. And God *hath set* some in the church,
15:25. till he *hath put* all enemies under his feet.
16: 2. *let* every one of you *lay* by him in store,
2Co. 3:13. *put* a vail over his face,
5:19. and *hath committed* unto us the word of reconciliation.
1Th. 5: 9. God *hath* not *appointed* us to wrath,
1Ti. 1:12. *putting* me into the ministry;
2: 7. Whereunto I *am ordained* a preacher,
2Ti. 1:11. Whereunto I *am appointed* a preacher,
Heb 1: 2. whom he *hath appointed* heir of all
13. until I *make* thine enemies thy footstool?
10:13. till his enemies be *made* his footstool.
1Pet.2: 6. I *lay* in Sion a chief corner stone,
8. whereunto also they *were appointed*.
2Pet.2: 6. *making* (them) an ensample unto those
1Joh.3:16. because he *laid down* his life for us:
— and we ought *to lay down* (our) lives
Rev.10: 2. he *set* his right foot upon the sea,
11: 9. and shall not suffer their dead bodies *to be put* in graves.

τίκτω, ἔτεκον, tikto, etekon.

Mat. 1:21. And she *shall bring forth* a son,
23. and *shall bring forth* a son,
25. till she *had brought forth* her firstborn son:
2: 2. Where is he *that is born* King of the Jews?
Lu. 1:31. and *bring forth* a son, and shalt call
57. time came that she should *be delivered;*
2: 6. that she should *be delivered*.
7. she *brought forth* her firstborn son,
11. For unto you *is born* this day in the
Joh.16:21. A woman when she *is in travail*
Gal. 4:27. Rejoice, (thou) barren *that bearest* not;
Heb 6: 7. and *bringeth forth* herbs meet for them
11:11. and *was delivered* of a child when
Jas. 1:15. Then when lust hath conceived, it *bringeth forth* sin:
Rev.12: 2. and pained *to be delivered*.
4. the woman which was ready *to be delivered,* for to devour her child as soon as it was *born.* (lit. when she *should have brought forth*)
5. And she *brought forth* a man child,
13. the woman which *brought forth* the man

τίλλω, tillo.

Mat.12: 1. and began *to pluck* the ears of corn,
Mar 2:23. began, as they went, to *pluck* the ears of
   corn.
Lu. 6: 1. his disciples *plucked* the ears of corn,

τιμάω, timao.

Mat.15: 4. *Honour* thy father and mother:
  6(5). And *honour* not his father or his mother,
   8. and *honoureth* me with (their) lips ;
 19:19. *Honour* thy father and (thy) mother:
  27: 9. price of him *that was valued,* whom they
    of the children of Israel *did value ;*
Mar 7: 6. This people *honoureth* me with (their) lips,
   10. *Honour* thy father and thy mother ;
 10:19. *Honour* thy father and thy mother.
Lu. 18:20. *Honour* thy father and thy mother.
Joh. 5:23. That all (men) *should honour* the Son,
   even as they *honour* the Father. He
   that honoureth not the Son *honoureth*
   not the Father which
  8:49. but I *honour* my Father, and ye
 12:26. him *will* (my) Father *honour.*
Acts28:10. Who also *honoured* us with many honours;
Eph. 6: 2. *Honour* thy father and mother ;
1Ti. 5: 3. *Honour* widows that are widows indeed.
1Pet.2:17. *Honour* all (men). Love the brotherhood.
   Fear God. *Honour* the king.

τιμή, timee.

Mat.27: 6. because it is the *price* of blood.
   9. the *price* of him that was valued,
Joh. 4:44. hath no *honour* in his own country.
Acts 4:34. and brought the *prices* of the things that
   were sold,
  5: 2. kept back (part) of the *price,* his wife also
   being privy (to it),
   3. (part) of the *price* of the land ?
  7:16. Abraham bought for a *sum* of money
 19:19. and they counted the *price* of them,
 28:10. honoured us with many *honours ;*
Ro. 2: 7. seek for glory and *honour*
   10. But glory, *honour,* and peace,
  9:21. to make one vessel unto *honour,*
 12:10. in *honour* preferring one another ;
 13: 7. *honour* to whom *honour.*
1Co. 6:20. For ye are bought with a *price:*
  7:23. Ye are bought with a *price ;*
 12:23. we bestow more abundant *honour ;*
   24. having given more abundant *honour*
Col. 2:23. not in any *honour* to the satisfying
1Th. 4: 4. vessel in sanctification and *honour ;*
1Ti. 1:17. (be) *honour* and glory for ever and ever.
  5:17. be counted worthy of double *honour,*
  6: 1. their own masters worthy of all *honour,*
  16. to whom (be) *honour* and power
2Ti. 2:20. some to *honour,* and some to dishonour.
  21. he shall be a vessel unto *honour,*
Heb 2: 7. crownédst him with glory and *honour,*
   9. crowned with glory and *honour ;*
  3: 3. hath more *honour* than the house.
  5: 4. taketh this *honour* unto himself,
1Pet.1: 7. be found unto praise and *honour*
  2: 7. Unto you therefore which believe (he is)
   precious : (lit. the *preciousness*)
  3: 7. giving *honour* unto the wife, as unto
2Pet.1:17. from God the Father *honour* and glory,

Rev. 4: 9. those beasts give glory and *honour*
  11. to receive glory and *honour* and
  5:12. and *honour,* and glory, and blessing.
  13. Blessing, and *honour,* and glory,
  7:12. and *honour,* and power, and might,
 19: 1. Salvation, and glory, and *honour,*
 21:24. bring their glory and *honour* into it.
  26. glory and *honour* of the nations into it.

τίμιος, timios.

Acts 5:34. *had in reputation* among all the people,
 20:24. neither count I my life *dear*
1Co. 3:12. *precious* stones, wood, hay, stubble ;
Heb 13: 4. Marriage (is) *honourable* in all,
Jas. 5: 7. waiteth for the *precious* fruit
1Pet.1: 7. being much *more precious* than of gold
  19. But with the *precious* blood of Christ,
2Pet.1: 4. exceeding great and *precious* promises:
Rev.17: 4. decked with gold and *precious* stones
 18:12. of gold, and silver, and *precious* stones,
  — vessels of *most precious* wood,
  16. decked with gold, and *precious* stones,
 21:11. like unto a stone *most precious,*
  19. with all manner of *precious* stones.

τιμιότης, timiotees.

Rev.18:19. by reason of her *costliness !*

τιμωρέω, timōreo.

Acts22: 5. unto Jerusalem, for to *be punished.*
 26:11. And I *punished* them oft in every synagogue, *and*

τιμωρία, timōria.

Heb 10:29. Of how much sorer *punishment,*

τις, tis. indefinite.

Note.—It is frequently rendered 'a man,' 'any man,'
 —the literal in such cases is simply 'any' or 'any
 one.'

Mat. 5:23. thy brother hath *ought* against thee ;
  8:28. that no *man* (lit. not *any*) might pass by
   that
   9: 3. *certain* of the scribes said within
 11:27. neither knoweth *any man* the Father,
 12:19. neither shall *any man* hear his voice
  29. how can *one* enter into a strong man's
  38. Then *certain* of the scribes and of the
  47. Then *one* said unto him, Behold,
 16:28. There be *some* standing here,
 18:12. if *a man* have an hundred sheep,
 20:20. and desiring a *certain thing* of him.
 21: 3. And if *any* (man) say *ought* unto you,
  33. There was a *certain* housholder,
 22:24. If a *man* die, having no children,
  46. neither durst *any* (man) from that day
 24: 4. Take heed that no *man* (lit. lest *any*)
   deceive you.
  17. to take *any thing* out of his house:
  23. Then if *any man* shall say unto you,
 27:47. *Some* of them that stood there,
 28:11. *some* of the watch came into the city,

Mar 2: 6. But there were *certain* of the scribes
　　4:22. there is nothing hid, (lit. not *any thing*)
　　5:25. a *certain* woman, which had an issue
　　7: 1. and *certain* of the scribes,
　　　　2. when they saw *some* of his disciples
　　8: 2. have nothing to eat: (lit. not *any* thing)
　　　　3. for *divers* of them came from far.
　　　　4. whence can a *man* satisfy
　　　26. nor tell (it) to *any* in the town.
　　9: 1. there be *some* of them that stand here,
　　　30. that *any man* should know (it).
　　　38. we saw *one* casting out devils in
　　11: 3. And if *any man* say unto you,
　　　　5. And *certain* of them that stood there
　　　13. he might find *any thing* thereon:
　　　16. that *any man* should carry (any) vessel
　　　25. if ye have *ought* against *any* :
　　12:13. send unto him *certain* of the Pharisees
　　　19. If a *man's* brother die,
　　13: 5. Take heed lest *any* (man) deceive
　　　15. to take *any thing* out of his house:
　　　21. And then if *any man* shall say
　　14: 4. were *some* that had indignation
　　　47. And one)(of them that stood by
　　　51. followed him a *certain* young man,
　　　57. And there arose *certain*, and bare
　　　65. And *some* began to spit on him,
　　15:21. And they compel *one* Simon
　　　35. And *some* of them that stood by,
　　16:18. and if they drink *any* deadly thing,
Lu. 1: 5. a *certain* priest named Zacharias,
　　6: 2. And *certain* of the Pharisees said
　　7: 2. And a *certain* centurion's servant,
　　19(18). calling (unto him) two)(of his
　　　36. *one* of the Pharisees desired him
　　　40. I have *somewhat* to say unto thee.
　　　41. a *certain* creditor which had
　　8: 2. *certain* women, which had been healed
　　　27. a *certain* man, which had devils
　　　46. *Somebody* hath touched me:
　　　49. there cometh *one* from the ruler
　　9: 7. because that it was said of *some*,
　　　8. And of *some*, that Elias
　　　19. *one* of the old prophets is risen
　　　23. If *any* (man) will come after me,
　　　27. there be *some* standing here,
　　　49. we saw *one* casting out devils
　　　57. a *certain* (man) said unto him,
　　10:25. a *certain* lawyer stood up, and
　　　30. A *certain* (man) went down from
　　　31. there came down a *certain* priest
　　　33. But a *certain* Samaritan,
　　　38. he entered into a *certain* village: and a
　　　　certain woman named Martha
　　11: 1. as he was praying in a *certain* place, when
　　　　he ceased, *one* of his
　　　15. But *some* of them said, He casteth
　　　27. a *certain* woman of the company
　　　36. having no (lit. not having *any*) part dark,
　　　37. a *certain* Pharisee besought
　　　45. Then answered *one* of the lawyers,
　　　54. seeking to catch *something* out of his
　　12: 4. after that have no (lit. not *any*) more
　　　13. And *one* of the company said
　　　15. a *man's* life consisteth not (lit. not in
　　　　abundance to *any* is his life)
　　　16. The ground of a *certain* rich man
　　13: 1. *some* that told him of the Galilæans,
　　　6. A *certain* (man) had a fig tree
　　　23. Then said *one* unto him, Lord,
　　　31. there came *certain* of the Pharisees,
　　14: 1. house of *one* of the chief Pharisees

Lu. 14: 2. there was a *certain* man before him
　　　8. When thou art bidden of *any* (man)
　　　15. And when *one* of them that sat at
　　　16. A *certain* man made a great supper,
　　15:11. A *certain* man had two sons:
　　16: 1. There was a *certain* rich man,
　　　19. There was a *certain* rich man,
　　　20. And there was a *certain* beggar
　　　30. if *one* went unto them from the dead,
　　　31. though *one* rose from the dead.
　　17:12. he entered into a *certain* village,
　　18: 2. There was in a)(city a)(judge,
　　　9. this parable unto *certain* which
　　　18. And a *certain* ruler asked him,
　　　35. a *certain* blind man sat by the way
　　19: 8. if I have taken *any thing* from *any man*
　　　12. A *certain* nobleman went into
　　　31. And if *any man* ask you,
　　　39. And *some* of the Pharisees
　　20: 9. A *certain* man planted a vineyard,
　　　27. *certain* of the Sadducees,
　　　28. If *any man's* brother die,
　　　39. Then *certain* of the scribes
　　21: 2. he saw also a *certain* poor widow
　　　5. And as *some* spake of the temple,
　　22:35. lacked ye *any thing* ?
　　　50. one)(of them smote the servant
　　　56. But a *certain* maid beheld him
　　　59. another)(confidently affirmed,
　　23: 8. to have seen *some* miracle done
　　　19. Who for a *certain* sedition made
　　　26. laid hold upon *one* Simon, a Cyrenian,
　　24: 1. and *certain* (others) with them.
　　　22. Yea, and *certain* women also
　　　24. And *certain* of them which were
　　　41. Have ye here *any* meat ?
Joh. 1:46(47). Can there *any* good thing come
　　2:25. that *any* should testify of man:
　　3: 3. Except a *man* be born again,
　　　5. Except a *man* be born of water
　　4:33. Hath *any man* brought him (ought)
　　　46. there was a *certain* nobleman,
　　5: 5. And a *certain* man was there,
　　　14. lest a worse *thing* (lit. *something* worse)
　　　　come unto thee.
　　　19. but *what* he seeth the Father do:
　　6: 7. every one of them may take a)(little.
　　　12. that nothing (lit. lest *ought*) be lost.
　　　46. Not that *any man* hath seen the
　　　50. that a *man* may eat thereof, and not die.
　　　51. if *any man* eat of this bread,
　　　64. But there are *some* of you that
　　7: 4. (that) doeth *any thing* in secret,
　　　17. If *any man* will do his will,
　　　25. Then said *some* of them of Jerusalem,
　　　37. If *any man* thirst, let him come unto me,
　　　44. *some* of them would have taken him ;
　　　48. Have *any* of the rulers or of the
　　8:51. If a *man* keep my saying,
　　　52. If a *man* keep my saying,
　　9:16. said *some* of the Pharisees,
　　　22. if *any man* did confess that he
　　　31. if *any man* be a worshipper of God,
　　　32. that *any man* opened the eyes
　　10: 9. by me if *any man* enter in,
　　　28. neither shall *any* (man) pluck them
　　11: 1. Now a *certain* (man) was sick,
　　　9. If *any man* walk in the day,
　　　10. But if a *man* walk in the night,
　　　37. And *some* of them said,
　　　46. *some* of them went their ways
　　　49. one)(of them, (named) Caiaphas,

Joh. 11:57. that, if *any man* knew where he were,
12:20. And there were *certain* Greeks
26. If *any man* serve me, let him
  — if *any man* serve me, him will
47. And if *any man* hear my words,
13:20. He that receiveth *whom*soever I send
29. For *some* (of them) thought, because
  — he should give *something* to the poor.
14:14. If ye shall ask *any thing* in my name,
23. If a *man* love me, he will
15: 6. If a *man* (lit. *any*) abide not in me,
13. that a *man* lay down his life
16:30. that *any man* should ask thee:
20:23. *Whose* soever sins ye remit,
  — (and) *whose* soever (sins) ye retain,
Acts 2:45. as *every man* had need.
3: 2. And a *certain* man lame from
5. to receive *something* of them.
4:32. neither said any (of them) that *ought*
34. Neither was there *any* among them
35. according as *he* (lit. *any*) had need.
5: 1. But a *certain* man named Ananias,
2. and brought a *certain* part,
15. might overshadow *some* of them.
25. Then came *one* and told them,
34. Then stood there up *one* in the council,
  — put the apostles forth a)(little space ;
36. boasting himself to be *somebody* ;
6: 9. arose *certain* of the synagogue,
7:24. seeing *one* (of them) suffer wrong,
8: 9. But there was a *certain* man,
  — that himself was *some* great one:
31. except *some man* should guide me?
34. of himself, or of *some* other man?
36. they came unto a *certain* water:
9: 2. that if he found *any* of this way,
10. And there was a *certain* disciple
19. Then was Saul *certain* days
33. And there he found a *certain* man
36. at Joppa a *certain* disciple
43. with *one* Simon a tanner.
10: 1. a *certain* man in Cæsarea
6. lodgeth with *one* Simon a tanner,
11. and a *certain* vessel descending
23. and *certain* brethren from Joppa
47. Can *any man* forbid water,
48. Then prayed they him to tarry *certain* days.
11: 5. A *certain* vessel descend, as
20. And *some* of them were men of
29. every man according to his ability, (lit.
  each of them according as *any* abounded)
12: 1. to vex *certain* of the church.
13: 1. *certain* prophets and teachers ;
6. they found a *certain* sorcerer,
41. though a *man* declare it unto you.
14: 8. there sat a *certain* man at Lystra,
15: 1. And *certain* men which came down
2. Barnabas, and *certain* other of them,
5. *certain* of the sect of the Pharisees
24. that *certain* which went out from us
36. And *some* days after Paul said
16: 1. a *certain* disciple was there, named Timotheus, the son of a *certain* woman,
9. There stood a)(man of Macedonia,
12. in that city abiding *certain* days.
14. a *certain* woman named Lydia,
16. a *certain* damsel possessed with a
17: 4. And *some* of them believed,
5. took unto them *certain* lewd fellows
6. they drew Jason and *certain* brethren
18. Then *certain* philosophers of the
  — *some* said, What will this babbler say?

Acts 17:20. thou bringest *certain* strange things
21. or to hear *some* new thing.
25. as though he needed *any thing,*
28. as *certain* also of your own poets
34. *certain* men clave unto him,
18: 2. a *certain* Jew named Aquila,
7. entered into a *certain* (man's) house,
14. If it were *a* (lit. *any*) matter of wrong
23. after he had spent *some* time (there),
24. And a *certain* Jew named Apollos,
19: 1. and finding *certain* disciples,
9. But when *divers* were hardened,
  — daily in the school of *one* Tyrannus.
13. Then *certain* of the vagabond Jews,
14. there were seven sons of (one) Sceva, (lit.
  certain sons of Sceva seven)
24. a *certain* (man) named Demetrius,
31. And *certain* of the chief of Asia,
32. Some therefore cried)(one thing,
38. have a matter against *any* man,
39. if ye enquire *any thing* concerning
20: 9. a *certain* young man named
21:10. a *certain* prophet, named Agabus.
16. with them *one* Mnason of Cyprus,
34. And some cried)(one thing,
37. May I speak)(unto thee?
22:12. *one* Ananias, a devout man
23:12. *certain* of the Jews banded together,
17. hath a *certain thing* to tell him.
18. hath *something* to say unto thee.
20. would enquire *somewhat* of him
23. unto (him))(two centurions,
24: 1. a *certain* orator (named) Tertullus,
12. in the temple disputing with *any man,*
18. Whereupon *certain* Jews from Asia
20. have found *any* evil doing in me,
24. And after *certain* days, when Felix
25: 5. if there be *any* wickedness in him.
8. have I offended *any thing* at all.
11. committed *any thing* worthy of death,
13. after *certain* days king Agrippa
14. There is a *certain* man left in bonds
16. to deliver *any* man to die,
19. had *certain* questions against him
  — of *one* Jesus, which was dead, whom
26. Of whom I have no certain *thing* to write
  — I might have *somewhat* to write.
26:26. I am persuaded that none (lit. not *any*) of
  these things are hidden from him ;
27: 1. Paul and *certain* other prisoners
8. came unto a)(place which is called
16. running under a *certain* island
26. be cast upon a *certain* island.
27. they drew near to *some* country ;
39. they discovered a *certain* creek
42. lest *any* of them should swim out,
44. on (broken pieces) of the ship. (lit. upon
  some of the things from the ship)
28:19. not that I had *ought* to accuse
21. neither *any* of the brethren that came
  shewed or spake *any* harm of thee.
Ro. 1:11. impart unto you *some* spiritual gift,
13. that I might have *some* fruit among you
3: 3. For what if *some* did not believe?
8. and as *some* affirm that we say,
5: 7. scarcely for a righteous man will *one* die:
  — *some* would even dare to die.
8: 9. if *any man* have not the Spirit of Christ,
24. for what a *man* seeth, why doth,
39. nor depth, nor *any* other creature,
9:11. having done *any* good or evil,
11:14. and might save *some* of them.

Ro. 11:17. if *some* of the branches be broken off,
14:14. esteemeth *any thing* to be unclean,
15:18. dare to speak of *any* of those things
26. to make a *certain* contribution
1 Co. 1:15. Lest *any* should say that I had baptized
2: 2. not to know *any thing* among you,
3: 4. For while *one* saith, I am of Paul ;
7. neither is he that planteth *any thing*,
12. Now if *any man* build upon this
14. If *any man's* work abide which he
17. If *any man* defile the temple of
4: 2. that a *man* be found faithful.
5. judge nothing (lit. not *ought*) before the
18. Now *some* are puffed up, as though
5: 1. that *one* should have his father's wife.
11. if *any man* that is called a brother
6: 1. Dare *any* of you, having a matter
11. And such were *some* of you:
12. be brought under the power of *any*.
7: 5. except (it be))(with consent for a time,
12. If *any* brother hath a wife that
18. Is *any man* called being circumcised ?
— Is *any* called in uncircumcision ?
36. But if *any man* think that he
8: 2. And if *any man* think that he knoweth *any thing*,
3. But if *any man* love God, the
7. for *some* with conscience of the idol
10. For if *any man* see thee which hast
9:12. lest we should hinder the gospel (lit. should give *any* hindrance to)
15. than that *any man* should make my
22. that I might by all means save *some*.
10: 7. be ye idolaters, as (were) *some* of them ;
8. as *some* of them committed,
9. as *some* of them also tempted,
10. as *some* of them also murmured,
19. that the idol is *any thing*, or that which is offered in sacrifice to idols is *any thing?*
27. If *any* of them that believe not
28. But if *any man* say unto you,
31. or *whatsoever* ye do, do all to the
11:16. But if *any man* seem to be contentious,
18. and I partly believe it. (lit. in *some* part)
34. And if *any man* hunger, let him
14:24. there come in *one* that believeth not,
27. If *any man* speak in an (unknown) tongue,
35. And if they will learn *any thing*,
38. But if *any man* be ignorant,
15: 6. but *some* are fallen asleep.
12. how say *some* among you that there is no
34. for *some* have not the knowledge of God:
35. But *some* (man) will say, How are the dead
37. chance of wheat, or of *some* other (grain):
16: 7. I trust to tarry *a* while (lit. *some* time) with you,
11. Let no man (lit. not *any*) therefore despise
22. If *any man* love not the Lord Jesus Christ,
2 Co. 2: 5. But if *any* have caused grief,
10. To whom ye forgive *any thing*, I (forgive) also: for if I forgave *any thing*,
3: 1. or need we, as *some* (others), epistles of
5. to think *any thing* as of ourselves ;
8:12. according to that a *man* hath,
20. that no man (lit. lest *any*) should blame
10: 2. against *some*, which think of us
7. If *any man* trust to himself that he
8. For though I should boast *somewhat*
12. with *some* that commend themselves:
11:16. Let no man (lit. not *any*) think me a fool ;
— that I may boast myself a little. (lit. *some* little)

2 Co. 11:20. if a *man* bring you into bondage, if a *man* devour (you), if a *man* take (of you), if a *man* exalt himself, if a *man* smite you on the face.
21. whereinsoever *any* is bold,
12: 6. lest *any man* should think of me
— or (that) he heareth)(of me.
17. by *any* of them whom I sent unto you ?
13: 5. except ye be)(reprobates ?
8. can do nothing (lit. not *any* thing) against
Gal. 1: 7. but there be *some* that trouble you,
2: 6. who seemed to be *somewhat*,
12. before that *certain* came from James,
5: 6. neither circumcision availeth *any thing*,
6: 1. if a man be overtaken in a)(fault,
3. For if a *man* think himself to be *something*,
15. neither circumcision availeth *any thing*,
Eph. 2: 9. Not of works, lest *any man* should boast.
5:27. spot, or wrinkle, or *any* such thing ;
6: 8. *whatsoever* good thing any man doeth,
Phi. 1:15. *Some* indeed preach Christ even of envy and strife ; and *some* also of good will:
2: 1. If (there be) therefore *any* consolation in Christ, if *any* comfort of love, if *any* fellowship of the Spirit, if *any* bowels and mercies,
3:15. if in *any thing* ye be otherwise minded,
4: 8. *any* virtue, and if (there be) *any* praise,
Col. 2: 4. lest *any man* should beguile you
8. Beware lest *any man* spoil you
16. Let no man (lit. not *any*) therefore judge
23. not in *any* honour to the satisfying
3:13. if *any man* have a quarrel against *any:*
1 Th. 1: 8. so that we need not to speak *any thing*.
2: 9. not be chargeable unto *any* of you,
5:15. See that none (lit. not *any*) render evil for evil unto *any*
2 Th. 2: 3. Let no man (lit. not *any*) deceive you
3: 8. did we eat *any man's* bread for nought ;
— not be chargeable to *any* of you:
11. For we hear that there are *some* which
14. And if *any man* obey not our word
1 Ti. 1: 3. that thou mightest charge *some* that
6. From which *some* having swerved
8. if a *man* use it lawfully ;
19. which *some* having put away
3: 1. If a *man* desire the office of a bishop,
5. if a *man* know not how to rule
4: 1. *some* shall depart from the faith,
5: 4. But if *any* widow have children
8. But if *any* provide not for his own,
15. For *some* are already turned aside
24. *Some* men's sins are open beforehand,
— and *some* (men) they follow after.
6: 7. we can carry nothing (lit. not *ought*) out.
10. which while *some* coveted after,
21. Which *some* professing have erred
2 Ti. 2: 5. if a *man* also strive for masteries,
18. and overthrow the faith of *some*.
21. If a *man* therefore purge himself from these,
Tit. 1:12. *One* of themselves, (even) a prophet of
Philem 18. hath wronged thee, or oweth (thee) *ought*,
Heb 2: 6. But *one* in a certain place testified,
7. Thou madest him *a* (lit. *some*) little lower than
9. who was made *a* (lit. *&c.*) little lower than
3: 4. every house is builded by *some* (*man*);
12. lest there be in *any* of you an evil heart
13. lest *any* of you be hardened
16. For *some*, when they had heard,
4: 1. *any* of you should seem to come short

Heb 4: 6. it remaineth that *some* must enter
7. Again, he limiteth a *certain* day,
11. lest *any man* fall after the same example
5: 4. no man (lit. not *any*) taketh this honour
8: 3. that this man have *somewhat* also
10:25. as the manner of *some* (is);
27. But a *certain* fearful looking for
28. He (lit. *any*) that despised Moses' law died
11:40. having provided *some* better thing for us,
12:15. lest *any man* fail of the grace of God; lest *any* root of bitterness
16. Lest there (be) *any* fornicator, or profane
13: 2. for thereby *some* have entertained angels
Jas. 1: 5. If *any* of you lack wisdom,
7. that he shall receive *any thing* of the Lord.
18. *a kind of* firstfruits of his creatures.
26. If *any man* among you seem to be religious,
2:14. though a *man* say he hath faith,
16. And *one* of you say unto them,
18. Yea, a *man* may say, Thou hast faith,
5:12. neither by *any* other oath:
13. Is *any* among you afflicted? let him pray. Is *any* merry? let
14. Is *any* sick among you? let him
19. if *any* of you do err from the truth, and *one* convert him;
1Pet.2:19. if a *man* for conscience toward
3: 1. that, if *any* obey not the word, they
4:11. If *any man* speak, (let him speak) as the
— if *any man* minister, (let him do it) as
15. But let none (lit. not *any*) of you suffer as a
2Pet.2:19. of whom a *man* is overcome,
3: 9. as *some* men count slackness;
— not willing that *any* should perish,
16. *some* things hard to be understood,
1Joh.2: 1. And if *any man* sin, we have an advocate
15. If *any man* love the world, the love of
27. and ye need not that *any man* teach you:
4:20. If a *man* say, I love God, and hateth
5:14. if we ask *any thing* according to his will,
16. If *any man* see his brother sin a sin
2Joh. 10. If there come *any* unto you,
Jude 4. For there are *certain* men crept in
Rev. 3:20. if *any man* hear my voice,
11: 5. and if *any man* will hurt them, he
13: 9. If *any man* have an ear, let him hear.
10. He that (lit. if *any*) leadeth into captivity
— he that (lit. if *any*) killeth with the sword
17. that no man (lit. that not *any*) might buy or sell,
14: 9. If *any man* worship the beast
11. and *whosoever* receiveth the mark of his
22:18. If *any man* shall add unto these things,
19. And if *any man* shall take away

see also *εἴτις, μήτις, ὅστις.*

τίς, *tis.*

Interrogative or definite.

Mat. 3: 7. *who* hath warned you to flee
5:13. *wherewith* shall it be salted?
46. *what* reward have ye? do not even
47. *what* do ye more (than others)?
6: 3. *what* thy right hand doeth:
25. *what* ye shall eat, or *what* ye shall drink; — *what* ye shall put on.
27. *Which* of you by taking thought
28. *why* take ye thought for raiment?

Mat. 6:31. *What* shall we eat? or, *What* shall we drink? or, *Where*withal shall we be clothed?
7: 3. And *why* beholdest thou the mote
9. Or *what* man is there of you,
8:26. *Why* are ye fearful, O ye of little faith?
29. *What* have we to do with thee, Jesus,
9: 5. For *whether* is easier, to say,
13. go ye and learn *what* (that) meaneth,
10:11. enquire *who* in it is worthy; and
19. take no thought how or *what* ye shall speak: — in that same hour *what* ye shall speak.
11: 7. *What* went ye out in the wilderness to see?
8. But *what* went ye out for to see?
9. But *what* went ye out for to see?
16. But *whereunto* shall I liken this
12: 3. Have ye not read *what* David did,
7. But if ye had known *what* (this) meaneth,
11. *What* man shall there be among you,
27. by *whom* do your children cast
48. *Who* is my mother? and *who* are my brethren?
14:31. O thou of little faith, *wherefore* didst thou doubt?
15:32. and have nothing (lit. not *what*) to eat:
16: 8. *why* reason ye among yourselves,
13. *Whom* do men say that I the Son of man
15. But *whom* say ye that I am?
26. For *what* is a man profited, if — or *what* shall a man give in exchange
17:10. *Why* then say the scribes that Elias
25. saying, *What* thinkest thou, Simon? of *whom* do the kings of the earth
18: 1. *Who* is the greatest in the kingdom
12. *How* think ye? if a man have
19: 7. *Why* did Moses then command to give
16. *what* good thing shall I do, that
17. *Why* callest thou me good?
20. from my youth up: *what* lack I yet?
25. *Who* then can be saved?
27. *what* shall we have therefore?
20: 6. *Why* stand ye here all the day idle?
21. And he said unto her, *What* wilt thou?
22. Ye know not *what* ye ask.
32. *What* will ye that I shall do unto you?
21:10. the city was moved, saying, *Who* is this?
16. Hearest thou *what* these say?
23. and *who* gave thee this authority?
28. But *what* think ye? A (certain)
31. *Whether* of them twain did the will
40. *what* will he do unto those husbandmen?
22:17. Tell us therefore, *What* thinkest thou?
18. *Why* tempt ye me, (ye) hypocrites?
20. *Whose* (is) this image and superscription?
28. *whose* wife shall she be of the seven?
42. *What* think ye of Christ? *whose* son is he?
23:17. for *whether* is greater, the gold,
19. for *whether* (is) greater, the gift,
24: 3. and *what* (shall be) the sign of thy
45. *Who* then is a faithful and wise servant,
26: 8. To *what* purpose (is) this waste?
10. *Why* trouble ye the woman?
15. *What* will ye give me, and I will deliver
62. *what* (is it which) these witness against thee?
65. *what* further need have we of witnesses?
66. *What* think ye? They answered and said,
68. *Who* is he that smote thee?
70. I know not *what* thou sayest.
27: 4. *What* (is that) to us? see thou (to that)
17. *Whom* will ye that I release unto you?
21. *Whether* of the twain will ye that I release
22. *What* shall I do then with Jesus

Mat.27:23. Why, *what* evil hath he done?

Mar 1:24. *what* have we to do with thee,
— I know thee *who* thou art, the Holy
27. *What* thing is this? *what* new doctrine (is) this?

2: 7. *Why* doth this (man) thus speak blasphemies? *who* can forgive sins but
8. *Why* reason ye these things in
9. *Whether* is it easier to say
16. *How* is it that he eateth and drinketh
24. *why* do they on the sabbath day that
25. Have ye never read *what* David did,

3:33. *Who* is my mother, or my brethren?

4:24. Take heed *what* ye hear:
30. *Whereunto* (lit. to *what*) shall we liken the
40. *Why* are ye so fearful? how is it that ye
41. *What* manner of man is this, that even

5: 7. *What* have I to do with thee, Jesus,
9. And he asked him, *What* (is) thy name?
14. they went out to see *what* it was that
30. and said, *Who* touched my clothes?
31. and sayest thou, *Who* touched me?
35. *why* troublest thou the Master any
39. *Why* make ye this ado, and weep?

6: 2. and *what* wisdom (is) this which is given
24. *What* shall I ask? And she said,
36. for they have nothing (lit. have not *what*) to eat.

8: 1. having nothing (lit. not having *what*) to eat,
12. *Why* doth this generation seek after
17. *Why* reason ye, because ye have no bread?
27. *Whom* do men say that I am?
29. But *whom* say ye that I am?
36. For *what* shall it profit a man,
37. Or *what* shall a man give in exchange

9: 6. For he wist not *what* to say;
10. *what* the rising from the dead should
16. *What* question ye with them?
33. *What* was it that ye disputed
34. *who* (should be) the greatest.
50. *wherewith* will ye season it?

10: 3. *What* did Moses command you?
17. *what* shall I do that I may inherit
18. *Why* callest thou me good?
26. *Who* then can be saved?
36. *What* would ye that I should do
38. Ye know not *what* ye ask:
51. *What* wilt thou that I should do

11: 3. *Why* do ye this? say ye that
5. *What* do ye, loosing the colt?
28. and *who* gave thee this authority

12: 9. *What* shall therefore the lord of the
15. *Why* tempt ye me? bring me a penny,
16. *Whose* (is) this image and superscription?
23. *whose* wife shall she be of them?

13: 4. and *what* (shall be) the sign when
11. beforehand *what* ye shall speak,

14: 4. *Why* was this waste of the ointment
6. Let her alone; *why* trouble ye her?
36. not *what* I will, but *what* thou wilt.
40. neither wist they *what* to answer him.
60. *what* (is it which) these witness against
63. *What* need we any further witnesses?
64. Ye have heard the blasphemy: *what* think ye?
68. neither understand I *what* thou sayest.

15:12. *What* will ye then that I shall do
14. Why, *what* evil hath he done?
24. *what* every man should take.
34. *why* hast thou forsaken me?

16: 3. *Who* shall roll us away the stone

Lu. 1:18. *Whereby* shall I know this?
62. *how* he would have him called.
66. *What* manner of child shall this be!

2:48. *why* hast thou thus dealt with us?
49. *How* is it that ye sought me?

3: 7. *who* hath warned you to flee
10. saying, *What* shall we do then?
12. Master, *what* shall we do?
14. And *what* shall we do?

4:34. *what* have we to do with thee,
— I know thee *who* thou art; the Holy
36. saying, *What* a word (is) this!

5:21. *Who* is this which speaketh blasphemies? *Who* can forgive sins, but
22. *What* reason ye in your hearts?
23. *Whether* is easier, to say, Thy

6: 2. *Why* do ye that which is not lawful
9. ask you one thing; Is it lawful on (lit. I will ask you: *Whether* is it lawful on, &c.)
11. *what* they might do to Jesus.
41. And *why* beholdest thou the mote
46. And *why* call ye me, Lord,
47. I will shew you to *whom* he is like:

7:24. *What* went ye out into the wilderness
25. But *what* went ye out for to see?
26. But *what* went ye out for to see?
31. *Whereunto* then shall I liken the men
— and to *what* are they like?
39. *who* and what manner of woman (this is)
42. *which* of them will love him most?
49. *Who* is this that forgiveth sins also?

8: 9. *What* might this parable be?
25. *What* manner of man is this!
28. *What* have I to do with thee, Jesus,
30. asked him, saying, *What* is thy name?
45. And Jesus said, *Who* touched me?
— and sayest thou, *Who* touched me?

9: 9. but *who* is this, of whom I hear such
18. *Whom* say the people that I am?
20. But *whom* say ye that I am?
25. For *what* is a man advantaged,
46. *which* of them should be greatest.

10:22. no man knoweth *who* the Son is, but the Father; and *who* the Father is, but the Son, and (he) to
25. *what* shall I do to inherit eternal
26. *What* is written in the law?
29. And *who* is my neighbour?
36. *Which* now of these three, thinkest thou,

11: 5. *Which* of you shall have a friend,
11. If a son shall ask bread of any of you that is a father, (lit. *Which* of you, a father, if his son ask bread, will)
19. by *whom* do your sons cast (them) out?

12: 5. I will forewarn you *whom* ye shall fear:
11. how or *what thing* ye shall answer, or *what* ye shall say:
14. Man, *who* made me a judge or
17. *What* shall I do, because I have no room
20. then *whose* shall those things be,
22. thought for your life, *what* ye shall eat; neither for the body, *what* ye shall put
25. *which* of you with taking thought
26. *why* take ye thought for the rest?
29. *what* ye shall eat, or *what* ye shall drink,
42. *Who* then is that faithful and wise
49. *what* will I, if it be already kindled?
57. Yea, and *why* even of yourselves

13:18. Unto *what* is the kingdom of God like? and *whereunto* shall I resemble it?

Lu. 13:20. *Whereunto* shall I liken the kingdom
 14: 5. *Which* of you shall have an ass
  28. For *which* of you, intending to build
  31. Or *what* king, going to make war
  34. *wherewith* shall it be seasoned?
 15: 4. *What* man of you, having an hundred
  8. Either *what* woman having ten pieces
  26. and asked *what* these things meant.
 16: 2. *How* is it that I hear this of thee?
  3. *What* shall I do? for my lord
  4. I am resolved *what* to do, that,
  11. *who* will commit to your trust the true
  12. *who* shall give you that which is your
 17: 7. But *which* of you, having a servant
  8. Make ready *wherewith* I may sup,
 18: 6. Hear *what* the unjust judge saith.
  18. *what* shall I do to inherit eternal life?
  19. *Why* callest thou me good? none
  26. *Who* then can be saved?
  36. he asked *what* it meant.
  41. *What* wilt thou that I shall do unto thee?
 19: 3. he sought to see Jesus *who* he was;
  15. that he might know *how much* every man
   had gained by trading.
  33. *Why* loose ye the colt?
  48. And could not find *what* they might do:
 20: 2. or *who* is he that gave thee this
  13. *What* shall I do? I will send my beloved
   son:
  15. *What* therefore shall the lord of the
  17. *What* is this then that is written,
  23. said unto them, *Why* tempt ye me?
  24. *Whose* image and superscription
  33. *whose* wife of them is she?
 21: 7. and *what* sign (will there be) when
 22:23. *which* of them it was that should
  24. *which* of them should be accounted
  27. For *whether* (is) greater, he that sitteth
  46. *Why* sleep ye? rise and pray,
  64. Prophesy, *who* is it that smote thee?
  71. *What* need we any further witness?
 23:22. Why, *what* evil hath he done?
  31. *what* shall be done in the dry?
  34. for they know not *what* they do.
 24: 5. *Why* seek ye the living among the dead?
  17. *What manner of* communications
  38. *Why* are ye troubled?
Joh. 1:19. to ask him, *Who* art thou?
  21. *What* then? Art thou Elias?
  22. Then said they unto him, *Who* art thou?
  — *What* sayest thou of thyself?
  25. *Why* baptizest thou then, if thou be not
  38(39). and saith unto them, *What* seek ye?
 2: 4. Woman, *what* have I to do with thee?
  18. *What* sign shewest thou unto us,
  25. for he knew *what* was in man.
 4:10. and *who* it is that saith to thee,
  27. *What* seekest thou? or, *Why* talkest thou
   with her?
 5:12. *What* man is that which said unto thee,
  13. wist not *who* it was: for Jesus had
 6: 6. he himself knew *what* he would do.
  9. but *what* are they among so many?
  28. *What* shall we do, that we might work
  30. *What* sign shewest thou then,
  — *what* dost thou work?
  60. an hard saying; *who* can hear it?
  64. *who* they were that believed not, and *who*
   should betray him.
  68. Lord, to *whom* shall we go?
 7:19. *Why* go ye about to kill me?
  20. *who* goeth about to kill thee?

Joh. 7:36. *What* (manner of) saying is this that he
  51. and know *what* he doeth?
 8: 5. but *what* sayest thou?
  25. Then said they unto him, *Who* art thou?
  46. *Which* of you convinceth me of sin?
  53. *whom* makest thou thyself?
 9: 2. *who* did sin, this man, or his parents,
  17. *What* sayest thou of him, that he hath
  21. or *who* hath opened his eyes, we know
   not:
  26. to him again, *What* did he to thee?
  27. *wherefore* would ye hear (it) again?
  36. *Who* is he, Lord, that I might believe
   on him?
 10: 6. they understood not *what* things they were
  20. and is mad; *why* hear ye him?
 11:47. *What* do we? for this man doeth
  56. *What* think ye, that he will not come
 12:27. and *what* shall I say? Father, save
  34. *who* is this Son of man?
  38. Lord *who* hath believed our report? and
   to *whom* hath the arm of the Lord
  49. *what* I should say, and *what* I should
   speak.
 13:12. Know ye *what* I have done to you?
  22. doubting of *whom* he spake.
  24. *who* it should be of whom he spake.
  25. saith unto him, Lord, *who* is it?
  28. no man at the table knew for *what* intent
 14:22. Lord, *how* is it that thou wilt manifest
 15:15. knoweth not *what* his lord doeth:
 16:17. *What* is this that he saith unto us,
  18. *What* is this that he saith, A little while?
   we cannot tell *what* he saith.
 18: 4. and said unto them, *Whom* seek ye?
  7. Then asked he them again, *Whom* seek
  21. *Why* askest thou me? ask them
  — *what* I have said unto them:
  23. but if well, *why* smitest thou me?
  29. *What* accusation bring ye against
  35. *what* hast thou done?
  38. Pilate saith unto him, *What* is truth?
 19:24. but cast lots for it, *whose* it shall be:
 20:13. Woman, *why* weepest thou?
  15. *why* weepest thou? *whom* seekest thou?
 21:12. durst ask him, *Who* art thou?
  20. Lord, *which* is he that betrayeth thee?
  21. Lord, and *what* (shall) this man (do)?
  22. *what* (is that) to thee?
  23. *what* (is that) to thee?
Acts 1:11. *why* stand ye gazing up into heaven?
 2:12. saying one to another, *What* meaneth this?
  37. Men (and) brethren, *what* shall we do?
 3:12. *why* marvel ye at this? or *why* look ye so
   earnestly on us,
 4: 9. by *what* means he is made whole;
  16. *What* shall we do to these men?
 5: 4. *why* hast thou conceived this thing
  9. *How* is it that ye have agreed
  24. *whereunto* this would grow. (lit. *what* this
   might be)
  35. *what* ye intend to do as touching
 7:27. *Who* made thee a ruler and a judge over
  35. *Who* made thee a ruler and a judge?
  40. we wot not *what* is become of him.
  49. or, *what* (is) the place of my rest?
  52. *Which* of the prophets have not your
 8:33. and *who* shall declare his generation?
  34. of *whom* speaketh the prophet this?
  36. *what* doth hinder me to be baptized?
 9: 4. Saul, Saul, *why* persecutest thou me?
  5. And he said, *Who* art thou, Lord?

Acts 9: 6. Lord, *what* wilt thou have me to do?
— it shall be told thee *what* thou must do.
10: 4. and said, *What* is it, Lord?
6. tell thee *what* thou oughtest to do.
17. *what* this vision which he had seen
21. *what* (is) the cause wherefore ye are come?
29. for *what* intent ye have sent for me?
11:17. *what* was I, that I could withstand God?
12:18. *what* was become of Peter.
13:25. *Whom* think ye that I am?
14:15. Sirs, *why* do ye these things?
15:10. Now therefore *why* tempt ye God,
16:30. Sirs, *what* must I do to be saved?
17:18. *What* will this babbler say?
19. May we know *what* this new doctrine,
20. *what* these things mean.
19: 3. Unto *what* then were ye baptized?
15. and Paul I know; but *who* are ye?
32. knew not *where*fore they were come
35. *what* man is there that knoweth not
21:13. *What* mean ye to weep and to break
22. *What* is it therefore? the multitude
33. and demanded *who* he was, and *what* he had done.
22: 7. Saul, Saul, *why* persecutest thou me?
8. And I answered, *Who* art thou, Lord?
10. And I said, *What* shall I do, Lord?
16. And now *why* tarriest thou?
26. Take heed *what* thou doest:
30. *wherefore* he was accused of the Jews,
23:19. *What* is that thou hast to tell me?
26: 8. *Why* should it be thought a thing
14. Saul, Saul, *why* persecutest thou me?
15. And I said, *Who* art thou, Lord?
Ro. 3: 1. *What* advantage then hath the Jew? or *what* profit (is there) of
3. For *what* if some did not believe?
5. *what* shall we say? (Is) God unrighteous
7. *why* yet am I also judged as a sinner?
9. *What* then? are we better (than they)?
4: 1. *What* shall we then say that Abraham,
3. For *what* saith the scripture?
6: 1. *What* shall we say then? Shall we
15. *What* then? shall we sin, because
21. *What* fruit had ye then in those
7: 7. *What* shall we say then? (Is) the law
24. *who* shall deliver me from the body
8:24. for what a man seeth, *why* doth he
26. for we know not *what* we should pray for
27. *what* (is) the mind of the Spirit,
31. *What* shall we then say to these things?
— *who* (can be) against us?
33. *Who* shall lay any thing to the charge of
34. *Who* (is) he that condemneth?
35. *Who* shall separate us from the love of
9:14. *What* shall we say then? (Is there)
19. *Why* doth he yet find fault? For *who* hath resisted his will?
20. *who* art thou that repliest against
— *Why* hast thou made me thus?
30. *What* shall we say then?
10: 6. *Who* shall ascend into heaven?
7. Or, *Who* shall descend into the deep?
8. But *what* saith it? The word is nigh thee,
16. *who* hath believed our report?
11: 2. *what* the scripture saith of Elias?
4. But *what* saith the answer of God
7. *What* then? Israel hath not obtained
15. *what* (shall) the receiving (of them be),
34. For *who* hath known the mind of the Lord? or *who* hath been his counsellor?
35. Or *who* hath first given to him,

Ro. 12: 2. that ye may prove *what* (is) that good,
14: 4. *Who* art thou that judgest another man's
10. *why* dost thou judge thy brother? or *why* dost thou set at nought thy
1Co. 2:11. For *what* man knoweth the things of a man,
16. For *who* hath known the mind of the Lord,
3: 5. *Who* then is Paul, and *who* (is) Apollos,
4: 7. For *who* maketh thee to differ
— and *what* hast thou that thou
— *why* dost thou glory, as if thou hadst
21. *What* will ye? shall I come unto you
5:12. For *what* have I to do to judge them
7:16. For *what* knowest thou, O wife,
— or *how* knowest thou, O man,
9: 7. *Who* goeth a warfare any time at
— *who* planteth a vineyard, and
— or *who* feedeth a flock, and eateth not
18. *What* is my reward then?
10:19. *What* say I then? that the idol
29. for *why* is my liberty judged
30. *why* am I evil spoken of for that
11:22. *What* shall I say to you?
14: 6. *what* shall I profit you, except
8. *who* shall prepare himself to the battle?
15. *What* is it then? I will pray with the
16. he understandeth not *what* thou sayest?
26. *How* is it then, brethren?
15: 2. saved, if ye keep in memory *what* I preached (lit. saved, with *what* word I preached, if ye, &c.)
29. Else *what* shall they do which are
— *why* are they then baptized for the dead?
30. And *why* stand we in jeopardy every
32. *what* advantageth it me, if the dead
2Co. 2: 2. *who* is he then that maketh me glad,
16. And *who* (is) sufficient for these things?
6:14. for *what* fellowship hath righteousness
— and *what* communion hath light
15. *what* concord hath Christ with Belial? or *what* part hath he that believeth
16. *what* agreement hath the temple of God
11:29. *Who* is weak, and I am not weak? *who* is offended, and I burn not?
12:13. For *what* is it wherein you were inferior
Gal. 2:14. *why* compellest thou the Gentiles to live
3: 1. *who* hath bewitched you, that ye
19. *Wherefore* then (serveth) the law?
4:15. *Where* is then the blessedness ye spake of? (lit. *what* then was your blessedness? —some copies read *ποῦ*)
30. Nevertheless *what* saith the scripture?
5: 7. *who* did hinder you that ye should not
11. *why* do I yet suffer persecution?
Eph. 1:18. *what* is the hope of his calling, and *what* the riches of the glory of
19. And *what* (is) the exceeding greatness of
3: 9. *what* (is) the fellowship of the mystery,
18. *what* (is) the breadth, and length, and
4: 9. *what* is it but that he also descended
5:10. Proving *what* is acceptable unto the Lord.
17. *what* the will of the Lord (is).
6:21. may know my affairs, (and) *how* I do,
Phi. 1:18. *What* then? notwithstanding, every way,
22. yet *what* I shall choose I wot not.
Col. 1:27. *what* (is) the riches of the glory of
2:20. *why*, as though living in the world,
1Th. 2:19. For *what* (is) our hope, or joy, or
3: 9. For *what* thanks can we render to God
4: 2. For ye know *what* commandments
1Ti. 1: 7. nor *whereof* they affirm.
2Ti. 3:14. knowing of *whom* thou hast learned (them);
Heb. 1: 5. For unto *which* of the angels said he at

Heb. 1:13. But to *which* of the angels said he at
2: 6. *What* is man, that thou art mindful
3:17. But with *whom* was he grieved
18. And to *whom* sware he that they
5:12. *which* (be) the first principles of
7:11. *what* further need (was there) that
11:32. And *what* shall I more say? for the
12: 7. for *what* son is he whom the father
13: 6. fear *what* man shall do unto me.
Jas. 2:14. *What* (doth it) profit, my brethren,
16. *what* (doth it) profit?
3:13. *Who* (is) a wise man and endued
4:12. *who* art thou that judgest another?
1Pet. 1:11. Searching *what*, or what manner of time
3:13. And *who* (is) he that will harm you,
4:17. *what* shall the end (be) of them that
5: 8. seeking *whom* he may devour:
1Joh.2:22. *Who* is a liar but he that denieth
3: 2. not yet appear *what* we shall be:
12. And *wherefore* slew he him?
5: 5. *Who* is he that overcometh the world,
Rev. 2: 7. *what* the Spirit saith unto the churches;
11. *what* the Spirit saith unto the churches;
17. *what* the Spirit saith unto the churches;
29. *what* the Spirit saith unto the churches.
3: 6. *what* the Spirit saith unto the churches.
13. *what* the Spirit saith unto the churches.
22. *what* the Spirit saith unto the churches.
5: 2. *Who* is worthy to open the book,
6:17. and *who* shall be able to stand?
7:13. *What* are these which are arrayed in white
13: 4. *Who* (is) like unto the beast? *who* is able
to make war with him?
15: 4. *Who* shall not fear thee, O Lord,
18:18. *What* (city is) like unto this great city.
See also διατί.

τίτλος, titlos.

Joh. 19:19. And Pilate wrote a *title*, and put
20. This *title* then read many of the Jews:

τίω, tio.

2Th. 1: 9. Who shall be punished with (lit. *shall suffer* (as) punishment) everlasting destruction from

---

τοι, toi.

2Ti. 2:19. Nevertheless (lit. *but* indeed) the foundation

τοιγαροῦν, toigaroun.

1Th. 4: 8. He *therefore* that despiseth,
Heb 12: 1. *Wherefore* seeing we also are compassed

τοίνυν, toinun.

Lu. 20:25. Render *therefore* unto Cæsar the
1Co. 9:26. I *therefore* so run, not as uncertainly;
Heb 13:13. Let us go forth *therefore* unto him without
the camp,
Jas. 2:24. Ye see *then* how that by works a man

τοιόσδε, toiosde.

2Pet. 1:17. when there came *such* a voice to him

τοιοῦτος, toioutos.

Mat. 9: 8. which had given *such* power unto men.
18: 5. shall receive one *such* little child
19:14. for of *such* is the kingdom of heaven.
Mar 4:33. And with many *such* parables
6: 2. that even *such* mighty works are
7: 8. and many other *such* like things ye do.
13. and many *such* like things do ye.
9:37. one of *such* children in my name,
10:14. for of *such* is the kingdom of God.
13:19. *such* as was not from the beginning
Lu. 9: 9. of whom I hear *such* things?
13: 2. because they suffered *such* things?
18:16. for of *such* is the kingdom of God.
Joh. 4:23. the Father seeketh *such* to worship him.
8: 5. that *such* should be stoned:
9:16. a man that is a sinner do *such* miracles?
Acts16:24. Who, having received *such* a charge,
19:25. the workmen of *like* occupation,
21:25. that they observe no *such* thing,
22:22. Away with *such* a (fellow) from
26:29. and altogether *such* as I am,
Ro. 1:32. they which commit *such* things
2: 2. against them which commit *such* things.
3. them which do *such* things,
16:18. For they that are *such* serve not
1Co. 5: 1. and *such* fornication as is not
5. To deliver *such* an *one* unto Satan
11. with *such* an *one* no not to eat.
7:15. is not under bondage in *such* (cases):
28. *such* shall have trouble in the flesh:
11:16. we have no *such* custom,
15:48. *such* (are) they also that are earthy:
— *such* (are) they also that are heavenly.
16:16. submit yourselves unto *such*,
18. acknowledge ye them that are *such*.
2Co. 2: 6. Sufficient to *such* a man (is) this
7. *such* a *one* should be swallowed up
3: 4. And *such* trust have we through
12. Seeing then that we have *such* hope,
10:11. Let *such* an *one* think this,
— *such* (will we be) also in deed when
11:13. For *such* (are) false apostles,
12: 2. *such* an *one* caught up to the third
3. And I knew *such* a man, whether
5. Of *such* an *one* will I glory:
Gal. 5:21. that they which do *such* things shall
23. against *such* there is no law.
6: 1. restore *such* an *one* in the spirit of
Eph 5:27. or wrinkle, or any *such* thing;
Phi. 2:29. and hold *such* in reputation:
2Th. 3:12. Now them that are *such* we command
1Ti. 6: 5. from *such* withdraw thyself.
Tit. 3:11. he that is *such* is subverted,
Philem. 9. being *such* an one as Paul the aged,
Heb 7:26. For *such* an high priest became us, (who)
8: 1. We have *such* an high priest, who is set
11:14. For they that say *such* things declare
12: 3. him that endured *such* contradiction
13:16. with *such* sacrifices God is well pleased.
Jas. 4:16. all *such* rejoicing is evil.
3Joh. 8. We therefore ought to receive *such*,

τοῖχος, toikos.

Acts23: 3. shall smite thee, (thou) whited *wall:*

τόκος, tokos.

Mat.25:27. received mine own with *usury.*
Lu. 19:23. required mine own with *usury?*

τολμάω, tolmao.

Mat.22:46. neither *durst* any (man) from
Mar 12:34. no man after that *durst* ask him
　　15:43. and went in *boldly* unto Pilate,
Lu. 20:40. they *durst* not ask him any
Joh.21:12. none of the disciples *durst* ask him,
Acts 5:13. And of the rest *durst* no man join
　　7:32. Moses trembled, and *durst* not behold.
Ro. 5: 7. some would even *dare* to die.
　　15:18. For I *will* not *dare* to speak of
1Co. 6: 1. *Dare* any of you, having a matter
2Co.10: 2. wherewith I think *to be bold* against
　　12. For we *dare* not make ourselves
　　11:21. whereinsoever any *is bold,*
　　— I *am bold* also.
Phi. 1:14. *are* much more *bold* to speak
Jude　9. *durst* not bring against him

τολμηρότερον, tolmeeroteron.

Ro. 15:15. I have written *the more boldly* unto

τολμητής, tolmeetees.

2Pet.2:10. *Presumptuous* (are they), selfwilled,

τομώτερος, tomōteros.

Heb 4:12. and *sharper* than any twoedged sword,

τόξον, toxon.

Rev. 6: 2. he that sat on him had a *bow;*

τοπάζιον, topazion.

Rev.21:20. the ninth, a *topaz;*

τόπος, topos.

Mat.12:43. he walketh through dry *places,*
　　14:13. by ship into a desert *place* apart:
　　15. saying, This is a desert *place,*
　　35. And when the men of that *place*
　　24: 7. and earthquakes, in divers *places.*
　　15. stand in the holy *place,*
　　26:52. again thy sword into his *place:*
　　27:33. unto a *place* called Golgotha, that is to
　　　　say, a *place* of a skull,
　　28: 6. see the *place* where the Lord lay.
Mar 1:35. departed into a solitary *place,*
　　45. but was without in desert *places:*
　　6:31. apart into a desert *place,* and
　　32. they departed into a desert *place* by
　　35. This is a desert *place,* and now
　　13: 8. earthquakes in divers *places,*
　　15:22. unto the *place* Golgotha, which is, being
　　　　interpreted, The *place* of a skull.
　　16: 6. behold the *place* where they laid him.
Lu. 2: 7. no *room* for them in the inn.
　　4:17. found the *place* where it was written,
　　37. went out into every *place* of the
　　42. and went into a desert *place:*
　　6:17. and stood in the plain, (lit. plain *place*)
　　9:10. privately into a desert *place*
　　12. we are here in a desert *place.*
　　10: 1. before his face into every city and *place,*

Lu. 10:32. a Levite, when he was at the *place,*
　　11: 1. as he was praying in a certain *place,*
　　24. he walketh through dry *places,*
　　14: 9. Give this man *place;* and thou begin with
　　　　shame to take the lowest *room.* (lit.
　　　　place)
　　10. sit down in the lowest *room;*
　　22. and yet there is *room.*
　　16:28. come into this *place* of torment.
　　19: 5. And when Jesus came to the *place,*
　　21:11. earthquakes shall be in divers *places,*
　　22:40. And when he was at the *place,*
　　23:33. And when they were come to the *place,*
Joh. 4:20. that in Jerusalem is the *place* where
　　5:13. a multitude being in (that) *place.*
　　6:10. there was much grass in the *place.*
　　23. nigh unto the *place* where they did eat
　　10:40. into the *place* where John at first
　　11: 6. in the same *place* where he was.
　　30. was in that *place* where Martha met him.
　　48. take away both our *place* and nation.
　　14: 2. I go to prepare a *place* for you.
　　3. And if I go and prepare a *place* for you,
　　18: 2. which betrayed him, knew the *place:*
　　19:13. in a *place* that is called the Pavement
　　17. forth into a *place* called (the place) of
　　20. for the *place* where Jesus was crucified
　　41. Now in the *place* where he was crucified
　　20: 7. but wrapped together in a *place* by itself.
Acts 1:25. that he might go to his own *place.*
　　4:31. the *place* was shaken where they were
　　6:13. against this holy *place,* and the law:
　　14. Jesus of Nazareth shall destroy this *place,*
　　7: 7. and serve me in this *place.*
　　33. for the *place* where thou standest
　　49. or what (is) the *place* of my rest?
　　12:17. and went into another *place.*
　　16: 3. of the Jews which were in those *quarters:*
　　21:28. against the people, and the law, and this
　　　　place:
　　— and hath polluted this holy *place.*
　　25:16. and have *licence* to answer for
　　27: 2. to sail by the *coasts* of Asia; (lit. the *places*
　　　　along Asia)
　　8. came unto a *place* which is called
　　29. we should have fallen upon rocks, (lit.
　　　　rough *places*)
　　41. And falling into a *place* where two
　　28: 7. In the same *quarters* were possessions (lit.
　　　　in the (parts) about that *place*)
Ro. 9:26. in the *place* where it was said
　　12:19. (rather) give *place* unto wrath:
　　15:23. having no more *place* in these parts,
1Co. 1: 2. with all that in every *place*
　　14:16. that occupieth the *room* of the unlearned
2Co. 2:14. of his knowledge by us in every *place.*
Eph. 4:27. Neither give *place* to the devil.
1Th. 1: 8. but also in every *place* your faith
1Ti. 2: 8. that men pray every *where,*
Heb. 8: 7. then should no *place* have been sought for
　　　　the second.
　　11: 8. when he was called to go out into a *place*
　　12:17. for he found no *place* of repentance,
2Pet. 1:19. that shineth in a dark *place,*
Rev. 2: 5. remove thy candlestick out of his *place,*
　　6:14. island were moved out of their *places.*
　　12: 6. where she hath a *place* prepared of
　　8. neither was their *place* found any more
　　14. into her *place,* where she is nourished for
　　16:16. together into a *place* called in the Hebrew
　　　　tongue Armageddon.
　　20:11. and there was found no *place* for them.

τοσοῦτος, tosoutos.

Mat. 8:10. I have not found *so great* faith, no, not in
  15:33. *so much* bread in the wilderness, as to fill
      so great a multitude?
Lu. 7: 9. I have not found *so great* faith, no, not
  15:29. Lo, *these many* years do I serve thee, neither
Joh. 6: 9. but what are they among *so many?*
  12:37. had done *so many* miracles before them,
  14: 9. Have I been *so long* time with you, and
  21:11. and for all there were *so many,*
Acts 5: 8. whether ye sold the land for *so much?* And
     she said, Yea, for *so much.*
1Co.14:10. *so many* kinds of voices in the world,
Gal. 3: 4. Have ye suffered *so many* things in vain?
Heb. 1: 4. made *so much* better than the angels,
  4: 7. To day, after *so long* a time; as it is said,
  7:22. By *so much* was Jesus made a surety of a
     better
  10:25. and *so much* the more, as ye see the day
  12: 1. with *so great* a cloud of witnesses,
Rev.18: 7. *so much* torment and sorrow give her:
  17. *so great* riches is come to nought.
  21:16. the length is *as large* as the breadth:

τότε, tote.

Mat. 2: 7. *Then* Herod, when he had privily
  16. *Then* Herod, when he saw that
  17. *Then* was fulfilled that which was
  3: 5. *Then* went out to him Jerusalem,
  13. *Then* cometh Jesus from Galilee
  15. *Then* he suffered him.
  4: 1. *Then* was Jesus led up of the spirit
  5. *Then* the devil taketh him up
  10. *Then* saith Jesus unto him, Get
  11. *Then* the devil leaveth him, and,
  17. From *that time* Jesus began to preach,
  5:24. and *then* come and offer thy gift.
  7: 5. and *then* shalt thou see clearly
  23. And *then* will I profess unto them,
  8:26. *Then* he arose, and rebuked the winds
  9: 6. *then* saith he to the sick of the palsy,
  14. *Then* came to him the disciples of John,
  15. and *then* shall they fast.
  29. *Then* touched he their eyes, saying,
  37. *Then* saith he unto his disciples,
  11:20. *Then* began he to upbraid the
  12:13. *Then* saith he to the man, Stretch forth
  22. *Then* was brought unto him one
  29. and *then* he will spoil his house.
  38. *Then* certain of the scribes and of
  44. *Then* he saith, I will return into my house
  45. *Then* goeth he, and taketh with himself
  13:26. *then* appeared the tares also.
  36. *Then* Jesus sent the multitude away,
  43. *Then* shall the righteous shine forth as
  15: 1. *Then* came to Jesus scribes and
  12. *Then* came his disciples, and said
  28. *Then* Jesus answered and said unto
  16:12. *Then* understood they how that he bade
  20. *Then* charged he his disciples that
  21. From *that time* forth began Jesus to
  24. *Then* said Jesus unto his disciples,
  27. and *then* he shall reward every man
  17:13. *Then* the disciples understood that
  19. *Then* came the disciples to Jesus
  18:21. *Then* came Peter to him, and said,
  32. *Then* his lord, after that he had called
  19:13. *Then* were there brought unto him
  27. *Then* answered Peter and said unto him,

Mat.20:20. *Then* came to him the mother of Zebedee's
  21: 1. *then* sent Jesus two disciples,
  22: 8. *Then* saith he to his servants,
  13. *Then* said the king to the servants,
  15. *Then* went the Pharisees, and took counsel
  21. *Then* saith he unto them,
  23: 1. *Then* spake Jesus to the multitude,
  24: 9. *Then* shall they deliver you up
  10. And *then* shall many be offended,
  14. and *then* shall the end come.
  16. *Then* let them which be in Judæa
  21. For *then* shall be great tribulation,
  23. *Then* if any man shall say unto you,
  30. And *then* shall appear the sign
  — and *then* shall all the tribes of the
  40. *Then* shall two be in the field;
  25: 1. *Then* shall the kingdom of heaven
  7. *Then* all those virgins arose, and
  31. *then* shall he sit upon the throne
  34. *Then* shall the King say unto them
  37. *Then* shall the righteous answer
  41. *Then* shall he say also unto them
  44. *Then* shall they also answer him,
  45. *Then* shall he answer them, saying,
  26: 3. *Then* assembled together the chief
  14. *Then* one of the twelve, called
  16. And from *that time* he sought
  31. *Then* saith Jesus unto them, All ye
  36. *Then* cometh Jesus with them unto
  38. *Then* saith he unto them, My soul
  45. *Then* cometh he to his disciples,
  50. *Then* came they, and laid hands
  52. *Then* said Jesus unto him, Put up
  56. *Then* all the disciples forsook him,
  65. *Then* the high priest rent his clothes,
  67. *Then* did they spit in his face,
  74. *Then* began he to curse and to swear,
  27: 3. *Then* Judas, which had betrayed him,
  9. *Then* was fulfilled that which was
  13. *Then* said Pilate unto him, Hearest
  16. And they had *then* a notable prisoner,
  26. *Then* released he Barabbas unto them:
  27. *Then* the soldiers of the governor
  38. *Then* were there two thieves crucified
  58. *Then* Pilate commanded the body to be
  28:10. *Then* said Jesus unto them, Be not
Mar 2:20. and *then* shall they fast in those days.
  3:27. and *then* he will spoil his house.
  13:14. *then* let them that be in Judæa flee
  21. And *then* if any man shall say to you,
  26. And *then* shall they see the Son of man
  27. And *then* shall he send his angels,
Lu. 5:35. *then* shall they fast in those days.
  6:42. and *then* shalt thou see clearly to
  11:26. *then* goeth he, and taketh (to him) seven
  13:26. *Then* shall ye begin to say, We have eaten
  14: 9. and)(thou begin with shame to take
  10. *then* shalt thou have worship in the
  21. *Then* the master of the house being angry
  16:16. since *that time* the kingdom of God is
  21:10. *Then* said he unto them, Nation
  20. *then* know that the desolation thereof
  21. *Then* let them which are in Judæa
  27. And *then* shall they see the Son of man
  23:30. *Then* shall they begin to say to the
  24:45. *Then* opened he their understanding,
Joh. 2:10. *then* that which is worse: (but) thou
  7:10. *then* went he also up unto the feast,
  8:28. *then* shall ye know that I am (he),
  11: 6.)(he abode two days still in the same
  14. *Then* said Jesus unto them plainly,
  12:16. *then* remembered they that these

Joh.13:27. And after the sop)(Satan entered into
19: 1. *Then* Pilate therefore took Jesus,
16. *Then* delivered he him therefore
20: 8. *Then* went in also that other disciple,
Acts 1:12. *Then* returned they unto Jerusalem
4: 8. *Then* Peter, filled with the Holy Ghost,
5:26. *Then* went the captain with the
6:11. *Then* they suborned men, which said,
7: 4. *Then* came he out of the land of
8:17. *Then* laid they (their) hands on them,
10:46. *Then* answered Peter,
48. *Then* prayed they him to tarry
13: 3. And when they had fasted (lit. *then* having fasted)
12. *Then* the deputy, when he saw
15:22. *Then* pleased it the apostles and
17:14. And *then* immediately the brethren
21:26. *Then* Paul took the men, and the next
33. *Then* the chief captain came near,
23: 3. *Then* said Paul unto him, God shall
25:12. *Then* Festus, when he had conferred
26: 1. *Then* Paul stretched forth the hand, and
27:21.)(Paul stood forth in the midst of them,
32. *Then* the soldiers cut off the ropes
28: 1. *then* they knew that the island was
Ro. 6:21. What fruit had ye *then* in those things
1Co. 4: 5. and *then* shall every man have praise
13:10. *then* that which is in part shall
12. but *then* face to face:
— but *then* shall I know even as
15:28. *then* shall the Son also himself
54. *then* shall be brought to pass the
16: 2. that there be no gatherings)(when I come.
2Co.12:10. when I am weak, *then* am I strong.
Gal. 4: 4. Howbeit *then*, when ye knew not God,
29. But as *then* he that was born after the
6: 4. *then* shall he have rejoicing in himself
Col. 3: 4. *then* shall ye also appear with him in glory.
1Th. 5: 3. *then* sudden destruction cometh
2Th. 2: 8. And *then* shall that Wicked be revealed,
Heb10: 7. *Then* said I, Lo, I come
9. *Then* said he, Lo, I come to do thy will,
12:26. Whose voice *then* shook the earth:
2Pet.3: 6. Whereby the world that *then* was,

τοῦ, *tou*, for τούτου.

Acts17:28. we are also *his* offspring.

τοῦ &c. see Appendix.

τοὐναντίον, *tounantion*.

2Co. 2: 7. So that *contrariwise* ye (ought)
Gal. 2: 7. But *contrariwise*, when they saw
1Pet.3: 9. but *contrariwise* blessing;

τοὔνομα, *tounoma*.

Mat.27:57. a rich man of Arimathæa, named Joseph, (lit. the *name* Joseph)
See also ὄνομα.

τουτέστι or τοῦτ᾽ ἔστι, *toutesti* or *tout᾽ esti*.

Mat.27:46. *that is to say*, My God, my God,
Mar 7: 2. *that is to say*, with unwashen hands,

Acts 1:19. *that is to say*, The field of blood.
19: 4. *that is*, on Christ Jesus.
Ro. 7:18. *that is*, in my flesh,
9: 8. *That is*, They which are the children
10: 6. *that is*, to bring Christ down
7. *that is*, to bring up Christ again
8. *that is*, the word of faith, which
Philem 12. receive him, *that is*, mine own bowels:
Heb 2:14. him that had the power of death, *that is*, the devil;
7: 5. *that is*, of their brethren, though they
9:11. *that is to say*, not of this building;
10:20. through the veil, *that is to say*, his flesh;
11:16. a better (country), *that is*, an heavenly:
13:15. *that is*, the fruit of (our) lips giving
1Pet.3:20. wherein few, *that is*, eight souls were saved by water.

τοῦτο, *touto*.

From οὗτος.

Obs. The words 'therefore' and 'wherefore,' when partly in italics in this series, are the rendering of διὰ τοῦτο, excepting in three cases for εἰς τοῦτο, and in two cases for παρὰ τοῦτο, which are noted. [2] denotes its being compounded with αὐτός.

Mat. 1:22. Now all *this* was done, that it
6:25. *Therefore* I say unto you,
8: 9. and to my servant, Do *this*, and he
9:28. Believe ye that I am able to do *this*?
12:11. and if *it* fall into a pit on the sabbath
27. *therefore* they shall be your judges.
31. *Wherefore* I say unto you, All manner
13:13. *Therefore* speak I to them in parables:
28. An enemy hath done *this*.
52. *Therefore* every scribe (which is)
14: 2. and *therefore* mighty works do shew
15:11. *this* defileth a man.
16:22. *this* shall not be unto thee.
17:21. Howbeit *this* kind goeth not out
18: 4. humble himself as *this* little child,
23. *Therefore* is the kingdom of heaven
19:26. With men *this* is impossible;
21: 4. All *this* was done, that it might be
43. *Therefore* say I unto you,
23:14. *therefore* ye shall receive the greater
34. *Wherefore*, behold, I send unto you
24:14. And *this* gospel of the kingdom
44. *Therefore* be ye also ready:
26: 9. For *this* ointment might have been
12. she hath poured *this* ointment
13. Wheresoever *this* gospel shall be
26. Take, eat; *this* is my body.
28. For *this* is my blood of the new
39. let *this* cup pass from me:
42. if *this* cup may not pass away
56. But all *this* was done, that the
28:14. if *this* come to the governor's ears.
Mar 1:27. saying, What thing is *this*?
38. for *therefore* (εἰς τοῦτο) came I forth.
5:32. her that had done *this* thing.
43. that no man should know *it*;
6:14. and *therefore* mighty works
9:21. since *this* came unto him?
29. *This* kind can come forth by nothing
11: 3. Why do ye *this*? say ye that
24. *Therefore* I say unto you,
12:24. Do ye not *therefore* err,
13:11. in that hour, *that* speak ye.

Mar 14: 5. For *it* might have been sold
9. Wheresoever *this* gospel shall be
22. Take, eat: *this* is my body.
24. *This* is my blood of the new testament,
36. take away *this* cup from me:

Lu. 1:18. Whereby shall I know *this?*
34. How shall *this* be, seeing I know not a man?
43. And whence (is) *this* to me,
66. What manner of child shall *this* be!
2:12. And *this* (shall be) a sign unto you;
15. and see *this* thing which is come to pass,
3:20. Added yet *this* above all,
4:43. for *therefore* (εἰς τοῦτο) am I sent.
5: 6. And when they had *this* done,
6: 3. Have ye not read so much as *this,*
7: 4. for whom he should do *this:*
8. to my servant, Do *this,* and he doeth (it).
9:21. to tell no man *that* thing;
45. But they understood not *this* saying,
48. Whosoever shall receive *this* child
10:11. notwithstanding be ye sure of *this,*
28. *this* do, and thou shalt live.
11:19. *there*fore shall they be your judges,
49. *There*fore also said the wisdom of God,
12:18. And he said, *This* will I do:
22. *There*fore I say unto you,
39. And *this* know, that if the goodman
13: 8. let it alone *this* year also,
14:20. and *there*fore I cannot come.
16: 2. How is it that I hear *this* of thee?
18:34. and *this* saying was hid from them,
36. he asked what *it* meant.
20:17. What is *this* then that is written,
22:15. I have desired to eat *this* passover
17. Take *this,* and divide (it) among yourselves:
19. *This* is my body which is given for you: *this* do in remembrance of me.
20. *This* cup (is) the new testament in my
23. that should do *this* thing.
37. that *this* that is written must
42. remove *this* cup from me:
24:40. And when he had *thus* spoken,

Joh. 1:31. *there*fore am I come baptizing
2:12. After *this* he went down to Capernaum,
22. he had said *this* unto them;
3:32. and heard, *that* he testifieth;
4:15. Sir, give me *this* water,
18. in *that* saidst thou truly.
54. *This* (is) again the second miracle
5:16. And *there*fore did the Jews persecute
18. *There*fore the Jews sought the more
28. Marvel not at *this:* for the hour
6: 6. And *this* he said to prove him.
29. *This* is the work of God, that ye
39. And *this* is the Father's will
40. And *this* is the will of him
61. he said unto them, Doth *this* offend you?
65. *There*fore said I unto you,
7:22. Moses *there*fore gave unto you circumcision;
39. But *this* spake he of the Spirit,
8: 6. *This* they said, tempting him,
40. *this* did not Abraham.
47. ye *there*fore hear (them) not,
9:23. *There*fore said his parents, He is of age;
10:17. *There*fore doth my Father love me,
11: 7. after *that* saith he to (his) disciples,
11. and after *that* he saith unto them,
26. Believest thou *this?*
51. And *this* spake he not of himself:

Joh. 12: 5. Why was not *this* ointment sold
6. *This* he said, not that he cared for
18. For *this* cause the people also met him,
— that he had done *this* miracle.
27. for *this* cause came I unto this hour.
33. *This* he said, signifying what death
39. *There*fore they could not believe,
13:11. *there*fore said he, Ye are not all clean.
28. for what intent he spake *this* unto him.
14:13. *that* will I do, that the Father may be
15:19. *there*fore the world hateth you.
16:15. *there*fore said I, that he shall take of
17. What is *this* that he saith unto us,
18. What is *this* that he saith,
18:34. Sayest thou *this* thing of thyself,
37. To *this* end was I born, and for *this* cause came I into the world,
38. And when he had said *this,* he went
19:11. *there*fore he that delivered me
28. After *this,* Jesus knowing that all
20:20. And when he had *so* said,
22. And when he had said *this,*
21:14. *This* is now the third time that
19. *This* spake he, signifying by what
— And when he had spoken *this,*

Acts 2:12. one to another, What meaneth *this?*
14. be *this* known unto you, and
16. But *this* is that which was spoken
26. *There*fore did my heart rejoice,
33. he hath shed forth *this,* which ye now
3: 6. but such as I have give)(I thee: In the name of
4: 7. by what name, have ye done *this?*
22. on whom *this* miracle of healing
5: 4. conceived *this* thing in thine heart?
24. whereunto *this* would grow.
38. or *this* work be of men,
7:60. when he had said *this,* he fell asleep.
8:34. of whom speaketh the prophet *this?*
9:21. which called on *this* name in Jerusalem, and came hither for *that* intent,
10:16. *This* was done thrice:
11:10. And *this* was done three times:
16:18. And *this* did she many days.
19:10. And *this* continued by the space of
14. seven sons of (one) Sceva,...which did *so.*
17. And *this* was known to all the Jews
27. So that not only *this* our craft is
20:29. For I know *this,* that after my
21:23. Do therefore *this* that we say to thee:
23: 7. And when he had *so* said,
24:14. But *this* I confess unto thee, that
26:16. appeared unto thee for *this* purpose,
26. for *this* thing was not done in a corner.
27:34. for *this* is for your health:

Ro. 1:12. *That* is, that I may be comforted
26. For *this* cause God gave them up unto
2: 3. And thinkest thou *this,* O man,
4:16. *There*fore (it is) of faith,
5:12. *Where*fore, as by one man sin entered
6: 6. Knowing *this,* that our old man is
7:15. for what I would, *that* do I not; but what I hate, *that* do I.
16. If then I do *that* which I would not,
19. the evil which I would not, *that* I do.
20. Now if I do *that* I would not,
9:17. Even for *this* [2] same purpose have I raised
10: 6. *that* is, to bring Christ down (from above):
7. *that* is, to bring up Christ again
8. *that* is, the word of faith, which
11:25. should be ignorant of *this* mystery,
12:20. for in *so* doing thou shalt heap

Ro. 13: 6. for *this* cause pay ye tribute also:
— continually upon *this*[2] very thing.
11. And *that*, knowing the time,
14: 9. For to *this* end Christ both died,
13. but judge *this* rather, that no man
15: 9. For *this* cause I will confess to thee
28. When therefore I have performed *this*,
1Co. 1:12. Now *this* I say, that every one of
4:17. For *this* cause have I sent unto you
5: 2. he that hath done *this* deed
3. him that hath so done *this* deed,
6: 6. and *that* before the unbelievers.
7: 6. But I speak *this* by permission,
26. that *this* is good for the present
29. But *this* I say, brethren, the time
35. And *this* I speak for your own profit ;
37. and hath so decreed in his heart
9:17. For if I do *this* thing willingly,
23. And *this* I do for the gospel's sake,
10:28. *This* is offered in sacrifice unto idols,
11:10. For *this* cause ought the woman
17. Now in *this* that I declare (unto you)
24. Take, eat: *this* is my body,
— *this* do in remembrance of me.
25. *This* cup is the new testament in my
blood: *this* do ye, as oft as
26. and drink *this* cup, ye do shew
30. For *this* cause many (are) weak
12:15. is it *therefore* (παρὰ τοῦτο) not of the
body?
16. is it *therefore* (παρὰ τοῦτο) not of the
15:50. Now *this* I say, brethren, that flesh
53. For *this* corruptible must put on
— and *this* mortal (must) put on
54. when *this* corruptible shall have
— and *this* mortal shall have put on
2Co. 1:17. When I therefore was *thus* minded,
2: 1. I determined *this* with myself,
3. And I wrote *this*[2] same unto you,
9. For to *this* end also did I write,
4: 1. *Therefore* seeing we have this ministry,
5: 5. wrought us for the *self*same[2] thing
14. because we *thus* judge,
7:11. For behold *this*[2] selfsame thing, that ye
13. *Therefore* we were comforted in your
8:10. for *this* is expedient for you,
20. Avoiding *this*, that no man should
9: 6. But *this* (I say), He which soweth
10: 7. let him of himself think *this* again,
11. Let such an one think *this*,
13: 1. *This* (is) the third (time) I am coming
9. and *this* also we wish, (even) your perfection.
10. *Therefore* I write these things being absent,
Gal. 2:10. the same)([2] which I also was forward to
3: 2. *This* only would I learn of you,
17. And *this* I say, (that) the covenant,
6: 7. man soweth, *that* shall he also reap.
Eph 1:15. *Wherefore* I also, after I heard
2: 8. and *that* not of yourselves: (it is)
4:17. *This* I say therefore, and testify
5: 5. *this* ye know, that no whoremonger,
17. *Wherefore* be ye not unwise,
32. *This* is a great mystery:
6: 1. parents in the Lord: for *this* is right.
8. *the same* shall he receive of the Lord,
13. *Wherefore* take unto you the whole
18. watching thereunto (lit. unto *this*[2] same)
with all
22. sent unto you for the (lit. for *this*[2] same)
same purpose,
Phi. 1: 6. Being confident of *this*[2] very thing,

Phi. 1: 7. meet for me to think *this* of you all,
9. And *this* I pray, that your love
19. that *this* shall turn to my salvation
22. *this* (is) the fruit of my labour:
25. And having *this* confidence,
28. to you of salvation, and *that* of God.
2: 5. Let *this* mind be in you,
3:15. as many as be perfect, be *thus* minded:
— God shall reveal even *this* unto you.
Col. 1: 9. For *this* cause we also, since the
2: 4. And *this* I say, lest any man should
3:20. *this* is well pleasing unto the Lord.
4: 8. unto you for the same (lit. for *this*[2] same)
purpose,
1Th. 2:13. For *this* cause also thank we God
3: 3. that we are appointed *thereunto*.
5. For *this* cause, when I could no longer
7. *Therefore*, brethren, we were comforted
4: 3. For *this* is the will of God,
15. For *this* we say unto you by the word
5:18. for *this* is the will of God in Christ
2Th. 2:11. And for *this* cause God shall send
3:10. *this* we commanded you, that if any
1Ti. 1: 9. Knowing *this*, that the law is not
16. for *this* cause I obtained mercy,
2: 3. For *this* (is) good and acceptable
4:10. *therefore* (εἰς τοῦτο) we both labour and
16. doing *this* thou shalt both save thyself,
5: 4. for *that* is good and acceptable
2Ti. 1:15. *This* thou knowest, that all they which
2:10. *Therefore* I endure all things for
3: 1. *This* know also, that in the last days
Philem 15. he *therefore* departed for a season,
18. put *that* on mine account ;
Heb 1: 9. *therefore* God, (even) thy God,
2: 1. *Therefore* we ought to give the more
6: 3. And *this* will we do, if God permit.
7:27. for *this* he did once, when he offered
9: 8. The Holy Ghost *this* signifying,
15. And for *this* cause he is the mediator
20. *This* (is) the blood of the testament
27. but after *this* the judgment:
10:33. *Partly*, whilst ye were made a
— and *partly*, whilst ye became
13:17. they may do *it* with joy, and not with
grief: for *that* (is) unprofitable for you.
19. the rather to do *this*, that I may
Jas. 4:15. we shall live, and do *this*, or that.
1Pet. 1:25. And *this* is the word which by
2:19. For *this* (is) thankworthy, if a man
20. *this* (is) acceptable with God.
21. For even *hereunto* were ye called:
3: 9. that ye are *thereunto* called,
4: 6. For for *this* cause was the gospel preached
2Pet. 1: 5. And beside *this*, (lit. *this*[2] same) giving
all diligence,
20. Knowing *this* first, that no prophecy
3: 3. Knowing *this* first, that there shall
5. For *this* they willingly are ignorant of,
8. be not ignorant of *this* one thing,
1Joh. 3: 1. *therefore* the world knoweth us not,
8. For *this* purpose the Son of God was
4: 3. and *this* is that (spirit) of antichrist,
5. *therefore* speak they of the world,
3Joh. 10. *Wherefore*, if I come, I will
Jude 4. ordained to *this* condemnation,
5. though ye once knew *this*,
Rev. 2: 6. But *this* thou hast, that thou
7:15. *Therefore* are they before the throne
12:12. *Therefore* rejoice, (ye) heavens,
18: 8. *Therefore* shall her plagues come in
See also τουτέστι.

τούτοις, toutois.

From οὗτος.

Lu. 16:26. And beside all *this*, between us
24:21. and beside all *this*, to day is the third
Acts 4:16. What shall we do to *these* men?
5:35. intend to do as touching *these* men.
Ro. 8:37. in all *these* things we are more
14:18. For he that in *these* things serveth
15:23. no more place in *these* parts,
1Co.12:23. upon *these* we bestow more abundant
Gal. 5:21. revellings, and *such* like: of the which
Col. 3:14. And above all *these* things (put on)
1Th. 4:18. comfort one another with *these* words.
1Ti. 4:15. give thyself wholly to *them;*
6: 8. let us be *there*with content.
Heb 9:23. should be purified with *these;*
2Pet.2:20. they are again entangled *there*in,
3Joh. 10. and not content *there*with,
Jude 7. in like manner, (lit. in like manner to *these*) giving themselves over
10. in *those* things they corrupt themselves.
14. prophesied of *these*, saying, Behold,

τοῦτον, touton.

From οὗτος.

Mat.19:11. All (men) cannot receive *this* saying,
21:44. shall fall on *this* stone shall be
27:32. *him* they compelled to bear his cross.
Mar 7:29. For *this* saying go thy way;
14:58. I will destroy *this* temple that is
71. I know not *this* man of whom ye
Lu. 9:13. and buy meat for all *this* people.
26. of *him* shall the Son of man be
12: 5. yea, I say unto you, Fear *him*.
56. that ye do not discern *this* time?
16:28. come into *this* place of torment.
19:14. not have *this* (man) to reign over us.
20:12. and they wounded *him* also,
13. reverence (him) when they see *him*.
23: 2. We found *this* (fellow) perverting
14. Ye have brought *this* man unto me,
18. Away with *this* (man), and release
Joh. 2:19. Destroy *this* temple, and in three days
5: 6. When Jesus saw *him* lie,
6:27. for *him* hath God the Father sealed.
34. Lord, evermore give us *this* bread.
58. he that eateth of *this* bread shall live
7:27. we know *this* man whence he is:
9:29. *this* (fellow), we know not from whence he is.
39. I am come into *this* world, that
18:40. Not *this* man, but Barabbas.
19: 8. When Pilate therefore heard *that* saying,
12. If thou let *this* man go, thou art not
13. Pilate therefore heard *that* saying,
20. *This* title then read many of the Jews:
21:21. Peter seeing *him* saith to Jesus,
Acts 2:23. *Him*, being delivered by the determinate
32. *This* Jesus hath God raised up,
36. *that* same Jesus, whom ye have crucified.
3:16. made *this* man strong, whom ye see
5:31. *Him* hath God exalted with his right hand
37. After *this* man rose up Judas of
6:14. shall destroy *this* place,
7:35. *This* Moses whom they refused,
— the *same* did God send (to be) a ruler
10:40. *Him* God raised up the third day,
13:27. because they knew *him* not,
|5:38. not good to take *him* with them,

Acts16: 3. *Him* would Paul have to go forth
17:23. *him* declare I unto you.
21:28. and hath polluted *this* holy place.
23:17. Bring *this* young man unto the chief
18. to bring *this* young man unto thee.
25. a letter after *this* manner:
27. *This* man was taken of the Jews,
24: 5. For we have found *this* man
25:24. ye see *this* man, about whom
28:26. Go unto *this* people, and say,
Ro. 9: 9. At *this* time will I come,
15:28. have sealed to them *this* fruit,
1Co. 2: 2. Jesus Christ, and *him* crucified.
3:12. if any man build upon *this* foundation
17. *him* shall God destroy;
11:26. as often as ye eat *this* bread,
27. whosoever shall eat *this* bread,
2Co. 4: 7. But we have *this* treasure
Phi. 2:23. *Him* therefore I hope to send
2Th. 3:14. note *that* man, and have no company
Heb 8: 3. that *this* man have somewhat also to offer

τούτου, toutou.

From οὗτος.

Note.—² denotes it to be compounded with αὐτός.

Mat.13:15. For *this* people's heart is vaxed gross,
22. and the care of *this* world,
40. in the end of *this* world.
19: 5. For *this* cause shall a man leave
26:29. henceforth of *this* fruit of the vine,
27:24. of the blood of *this* just person:
Mar 4:19. And the cares of *this* world,
10: 7. For *this* cause shall a man leave
Lu. 2:17. told them concerning *this* child.
9:45. to ask *him* of *that* saying.
13:16. be loosed from *this* bond
16: 8. for the children of *this* world
20:34. The children of *this* world marry,
22:51. Suffer ye *thus* far.
24: 4. is they were much perplexed *there*about,
Joh. 4:13. Whosoever drinketh of *this* water
6:51. if any man eat of *this* bread,
61. his disciples murmured at *it*,
66. From *that* (time) many of his disciples
8:23. ye are of *this* world; I am not of *this*
9:31. and doeth his will, *him* he heareth.
10:41. that John spake of *this* man
11: 9. he seeth the light of *this* world.
12:31. Now is the judgment of *this* world: now shall the prince of *this* world be cast out.
13: 1. he should depart out of *this* world
14:30. for the prince of *this* world cometh,
16:11. the prince of *this* world is judged.
19. among yourselves of *that* I said,
18:17. also (one) of *this* man's disciples?
29. What accusation bring ye against *this* man?
36. My kingdom is not of *this* world: if my kingdom were of *this* world,
19:12. And from *thence*forth Pilate sought
Acts 5:28. to bring *this* man's blood upon us.
6:13. words against *this* holy place,
9:13. I have heard by many of *this* man,
13:17. The God of *this* people of Israel
23. Of *this* man's seed hath God
38. through *this* man is preached unto you
15: 2. and elders about *this* question.
6. for to consider of *this* matter.
17:32. We will hear thee again of *this*
21:28. and the law, and *this* place:
22:22. *him* audience unto *this* word,

Acts25: 20. because I doubted of such manner of questions, (lit. I was at a loss about enquiry into *this*)

    25. that he himself hath appealed (lit. that *this*[2] man, himself &c.)

   28: 9. So when *this* was done, others

    27. For the heart of *this* people is waxed

Ro. 7: 24. from the body of *this* death?

   11: 7. Israel hath not obtained *that* which

1Co. 1: 20. the disputer of *this* world?

    — foolish the wisdom of *this* world?

   2: 6. not the wisdom of *this* world, nor of the princes of *this* world,

    8. none of the princes of *this* world knew:

   3: 19. For the wisdom of *this* world

   5: 10. the fornicators of *this* world,

   7: 31. the fashion of *this* world passeth

2Co. 4: 4. In whom the god of *this* world

   12: 8. For *this* thing I besought the Lord

Eph. 2: 2. according to the course of *this* world,

   3: 1. For *this* cause I Paul,

    14. For *this* cause I bow my knees

   5: 31 For *this* cause shall a man leave

   6: 12. the rulers of the darkness of *this* world,

Col. 1: 27. the riches of the glory of *this* mystery

Tit. 1: 5. For *this* cause left I thee in Crete,

Jas. 1: 26. *this* man's religion (is) vain.

   2: 5. chosen the poor of *this* world

1Joh.4: 6. *Hereby* know we the spirit of truth,

Rev.19:20. and with *him* the false prophet

   22: 7. of the prophecy of *this* book.

    9. which keep the sayings of *this* book:

    10. the sayings of the prophecy of *this* book:

    18. words of the prophecy of *this* book,

τούτους, *toutous*.

From οὗτος.

Mat. 7: 24. whosoever heareth *these* sayings of mine,

    26. that heareth *these* sayings of mine,

    28. Jesus had ended *these* sayings,

   10: 5. *These* twelve Jesus sent forth,

   19: 1. when Jesus had finished *these* sayings,

   26: 1. when Jesus had finished all *these* sayings,

Mar 8: 4. whence can a man satisfy *these* (men)

Lu. 9: 28. eight days after *these* sayings,

    44. Let *these* sayings sink down into

   19: 15. then he commanded *these* servants

   20: 16. and destroy *these* husbandmen,

Joh.10: 19. among the Jews for *these* sayings.

   18: 8. let *these* go their way:

Acts 2: 22. Ye men of Israel, hear *these* words;

   5: 5. And Ananias hearing *these* words

    24. and the chief priests heard *these* things,

   10: 47. that *these* should not be baptized,

   16: 36. told *this* saying to Paul,

   19: 37. ye have brought hither *these* men,

   21: 24. *Them* take, and purify thyself with them,

Ro. 8: 30. *them* he also called:

    — *them* he also justified:

    — *them* he also glorified.

1Co. 6: 4. set *them* to judge who are least

   16: 3. *them* will I send to bring your

2Ti. 3: 5. from *such* turn away.

Heb. 2: 15. And deliver *them* who through fear

τούτῳ, *toutō*.

From οὗτος.

Mat. 8: 9. and I say to *this* (man), Go, and he

Mat.12:32. forgiven him, neither in *this* world,

   13: 54. Whence hath *this* (man) this wisdom,

    56. Whence then hath *this* (man) all these

   17: 20. ye shall say unto *this* mountain,

   20: 14. I will give unto *this* last,

   21: 21. if ye shall say unto *this* mountain,

Mar 6: 2. whence hath *this* (man) these things?

   10: 30. an hundredfold now in *this* time,

   11: 23. shall say unto *this* mountain,

Lu. 1: 61. that is called by *this* name.

   4: 3. command *this* stone that it be made bread.

   7: 8. and I say unto *one*, Go, and he goeth;

   10: 5. first say, Peace (be) to *this* house.

    20. Notwithstanding in *this* rejoice not,

   14: 9, Give *this* man place; and thou

   18: 30. manifold more in *this* present time,

   19: 9. salvation come to *this* house,

    19. And he said likewise to *him*,

   21: 23. and wrath upon *this* people.

   23: 4. I find no fault in *this* man.

    14. have found no fault in *this* man

Joh. 4: 20. worshipped in *this* mountain;

    21. ye shall neither in *this* mountain,

    27. And upon *this* came his disciples,

    37. And *herein* is that saying true,

   5: 38. *him* ye believe not.

   9: 30. Why *herein* is a marvellous thing,

   10: 3. To *him* the porter openeth;

   12: 25. hateth his life in *this* world

   13: 24. Simon Peter therefore beckoned to *him*,

    35. By *this* shall all (men) know

   15: 8. *Herein* is my Father glorified,

   16: 30. by *this* we believe that thou camest

   20: 30. which are not written in *this* book:

Acts 1: 6. Lord, wilt thou at *this* time restore

   3: 12. why marvel ye at *this*? or why

   4: 10. by *him* doth this man stand here

    17. henceforth to no man in *this* name.

   5: 28. ye should not teach in *this* name?

   7: 7. and serve me in *this* place.

    29. Then fled Moses at *this* saying,

   8: 21. part nor lot in *this* matter:

    29. and join thyself to *this* chariot.

   10: 43. To *him* give all the prophets witness,

   13: 39. And by *him* all that believe are

   15: 15. And to *this* agree the words of

   21: 9. And *the same* man had four daughters,

   23: 9. We find no evil in *this* man:

   24: 2(3). worthy deeds are done unto *this* nation

    10. a judge unto *this* nation,

    16. And *herein* do I exercise myself,

   25: 5. if there be any wickedness in *him*.

Ro. 12: 2. And be not conformed to *this* world:

   13: 9. comprehended in *this* saying,

1Co. 3: 18. to be wise in *this* world,

   4: 4. yet am I not *hereby* justified:

   7: 24. *therein* abide with God.

    31. And they that use *this* world,

   11: 22. shall I praise you in *this*?

   14: 21. will I speak unto *this* people;

2Co. 3: 10. had no glory in *this* respect,

   5: 2. For in *this* we groan, earnestly desiring

   8: 10. And *herein* I give (my) advice:

   9: 3. should be in vain in *this* behalf;

Gal. 6: 16. as walk according to *this* rule,

Eph 1: 21. not only in *this* world, but also in that

Phi. 1: 18. and I *therein* do rejoice, yea, and will

Heb 4: 5. And in *this* (place) again, If they

1Pet.4: 16. let him glorify God on *this* behalf.

2Pet.1: 13. as long as I am in *this* tabernacle,

   2: 19. of the same (lit. to *the same*) is he brought in bondage.

1Joh.2: 3. And *hereby* we do know that we
4. and the truth is not in *him*.
5. in *him* verily is the love of God perfected: *hereby* know we that we are in him.
3:10. In *this* the children of God are manifest,
16. *Hereby* perceive we the love (of God),
19. And *hereby* we know that we are
24. And *hereby* we know that he abideth
4: 2. *Hereby* know ye the Spirit of God:
9. In *this* was manifested the love of
10. *Herein* is love, not that we loved God,
13. *Hereby* know we that we dwell in him,
17. *Herein* is our love made perfect,
— so are we in *this* world.
5: 2. By *this* we know that we love the children
Rev.22:18. plagues that are written in *this* book:
19. things which are written in *this* book.

τούτων, *touton.*
From οὗτος.

Mat. 3: 9. God is able of *these* stones to raise up
5:19. one of *these* least commandments,
37. for whatsoever is more than *these*
6:29. was not arrayed like one of *these*.
32. ye have need of all *these* things.
10:42. unto one of *these* little ones a cup
11: 7. And as *they* departed, Jesus
18: 6. shall offend one of *these* little ones
10. ye despise not one of *these* little ones;
14. that one of *these* little ones should
25:40. of the least of *these* my brethren,
45. not to one of the least of *these*,
Mar 12:31. commandment greater than *these*.
Lu. 3: 8. is able of *these* stones to raise up
7:18. shewed him of all *these* things.
10:36. Which now of *these* three,
12:27. arrayed like one of *these*.
30. that ye have need of *these* things.
17: 2. offend one of *these* little ones.
18:34. they understood none of *these* things:
21:12. But before all *these*, they shall
28. And when *these* things begin to
24:14. they talked together of all *these* things
48. And ye are witnesses of *these* things.
Joh. 1:50(51). thou shalt see greater things than *these*.
5:20. shew him greater works than *these*,
7:31. will he do more miracles than *these*
14:12. greater (works) than *these* shall he do;
17:20. Neither pray I for *these* alone, but for
21:15. lovest thou me more than *these?*
24. which testifieth of *these* things,
Acts 1:21(22). Wherefore of *these* men which...must one be ordained to be a witness
24. whether of *these* two thou hast chosen,
5:32. we are his witnesses of *these* things;
36. For before *these* days rose up Theudas,
38. Refrain from *these* men, and let them
14:15. should turn from *these* vanities
15:28. than *these* necessary things;
18:15. for I will be no judge of *such* (matters).
17. And Gallio cared for none of *those* things.
19:36. Seeing then that *these* things cannot be
21:38. that Egyptian, which before *these* days
24: 8. take knowledge of all *these* things,
25: 9. be judged of *these* things before me?
20. and there be judged of *these* matters.
26:21. For *these* causes the Jews caught me
26. the king knoweth of *these* things,
— that none of *these* things are hidden
29. such as I am, except *these* bonds.

Ro. 11:30. obtained mercy through *their* unbelief:
1Co. 9:15. But I have used none of *these* things:
13:13. but the greatest of *these* (is) charity.
1Th. 4: 6. the Lord (is) the avenger of all *such,*
2Ti. 2:21. therefore purge himself from *these,*
3: 6. For of *this sort* are they which creep
Tit. 3: 8. *these* things I will that thou affirm
Heb 1: 2(1). Hath in *these* last days spoken unto
9: 6. Now when *these* things were thus
10:18. Now where remission of *these* (is),
13:11. For the bodies of *those* beasts,
2Pet.1: 4. that by *these* ye might be partakers
12. always in remembrance of *these* things,
15. to have *these* things always in remembrance.
3:11. all *these* things shall be dissolved,
16. speaking in them of *these* things;
3Joh. 4. I have no greater joy (lit. greater than *these*)
Rev. 9:18. By *these* three was the third part of
18:15. The merchants of *these* things,
20: 6. on *such* the second death hath no power,
Note. — οὗτος, αὕτη, ταῦτα, &c. are arranged severally.

τράγος, *tragos.*

Heb. 9:12. Neither by the blood of *goats* and
13. if the blood of bulls and of *goats,*
19. the blood of calves and of *goats,*
10: 4. the blood of bulls and of *goats*

τράπεζα, *trapeza.*

Mat.15:27. which fall from their masters' *table.*
21:12. the *tables* of the moneychangers,
Mar 7:28. yet the dogs under the *table* eat of
11:15. the *tables* of the moneychangers,
Lu. 16:21. which fell from the rich man's *table:*
19:23. thou my money into the *bank,*
22:21. (is) with me on the *table.*
30. at my *table* in my kingdom,
Joh. 2:15. and overthrew the *tables;*
Acts 6: 2. leave the word of God, and serve *tables.*
16:34. he set *meat* before them,
Ro. 11: 9. Let their *table* be made a snare,
1Co.10:21. ye cannot be partakers of the Lord's *table,* and of the *table* of devils.
Heb 9: 2. and the *table,* and the shewbread;

τραπεζίτης, *trapezitees.*

Mat.25:27. to have put my money to the *exchangers,*

τραῦμα, *trauma.*

Lu. 10:34. and bound up his *wounds,*

τραυματίζω, *traumatizo.*

Lu. 20:12. they *wounded* him also, *and* cast
Acts19:16. out of that house naked and *wounded.*

τραχηλίζομαι, *trakeelizomai.*

Heb 4:13. naked and *opened* unto the eyes of him with

τράχηλος, *trakeelos.*

Mat.18: 6. were hanged about his *neck,*
Mar 9:42. were hanged about his *neck,*
Lu. 15:20. fell on his *neck,* and kissed him.
17: 2. millstone were hanged about his *neck,*
Acts15:10. a yoke upon the *neck* of the disciples,
20:37. and fell on Paul's *neck,* and kissed him,
Ro. 16: 4. laid down their own *necks:*

τραχύς, *trakus.*

Lu. 3: 5. *rough* ways (shall be) made smooth;
Acts27:29. lest we should have fallen upon rocks,
(lit. upon *rough* places)

τρεῖς, τρία, *trīs, tria.*

Mat.12:40. as Jonas was *three* days and *three* nights
— be *three* days and *three* nights in
13:33. and hid in *three* measures of meal,
15:32. with me now *three* days,
17: 4. make here *three* tabernacles ;
18:16. of two or *three* witnesses every word
20. where two or *three* are gathered
26:61. and to build it in *three* days.
27:40. and buildest (it) in *three* days,
63. After *three* days I will rise again.
Mar 8: 2. have now been with me *three* days,
31. and after *three* days rise again.
9: 5. let us make *three* tabernacles ;
14:58. and within *three* days I will build
15:29. and buildest (it) in *three* days,
Lu. 1:56. abode with her about *three* months,
2:46. after *three* days they found him
4:25. was shut up *three* years and six months,
9:33. let us make *three* tabernacles ;
10:36. Which now of these *three,*
11: 5. Friend, lend me *three* loaves ;
12:52. *three* against two, and two against *three.*
13: 7. these *three* years I come seeking fruit
21. and hid in *three* measures of meal,
Joh. 2: 6. two or *three* firkins apiece.
19. in *three* days I will raise it up.
20. thou rear it up in *three* days ?
21:11. an hundred and fifty and *three :*
Acts 5: 7. the space of *three* hours after,
7:20. in his father's house *three* months:
9: 9. And he was *three* days without sight,
10:19. Behold, *three* men seek thee.
11:11. there were *three* men already come
17: 2. and *three* sabbath days reasoned
19: 8. for the space of *three* months,
20: 3. And (there) abode *three* months.
25: 1. after *three* days he ascended from Cæsarea
28: 7. lodged us *three* days courteously.
11. And after *three* months we departed
12. we tarried (there) *three* days.
17. that after *three* days Paul called
1Co.10: 8. in one day *three* and twenty thousand.
13:13. faith, hope, charity, these *three ;*
14:27. or at the most (by) *three,*
29. Let the prophets speak two or *three,*
2Co.13: 1. In the mouth of two or *three* witnesses
Gal. 1:18. Then after *three* years I went up
1Ti. 5:19. but before two or *three* witnesses :
Heb10:28. under two or *three* witnesses:
Jas. 5:17. by the space of *three* years and six months.
1Joh.5: 7. For there are *three* that bear record in
— and these *three* are one.

1Joh.5: 8. are *three* that bear witness in earth,
— and these *three* agree in one.
Rev. 6: 6. *three* measures of barley for a penny ;
8:13. of the trumpet of the *three* angels,
9:18. By these *three* was the third part
11: 9. their dead bodies *three* days and an half,
11. And after *three* days and an half
16:13. And I saw *three* unclean spirits
19. the great city was divided into *three* parts,
21:13. On the east *three* gates ; on the north
three gates ; on the south *three* gates ;
and on the west *three* gates.

τρέμω, *tremo.*

Mar 5:33. the woman fearing and *trembling,*
Lu. 8:47. she came *trembling,* and falling down
Acts 9: 6. And he *trembling* and astonished
2Pet.2:10. they *are* not *afraid* to speak evil of

τρέφω, *trepho.*

Mat. 6:26. yet your heavenly Father *feedeth* them.
25:37. an hungred, and *fed* (thee)?
Lu. 4:16. where he had been *brought up :*
12:24. and God *feedeth* them:
Acts12:20. because their country *was nourished* by
Jas. 5: 5. ye *have nourished* your hearts, as in
Rev.12: 6. that they *should feed* her there
14. where she *is nourished* for a time,

τρέχω, *treko.*

Mat.27:48. straightway one of them *ran, and*
28: 8. *did run* to bring his disciples word.
Mar 5: 6. he *ran* and worshipped him,
15:36. And one *ran* and filled a spunge
Lu. 15:20. and *ran, and* fell on his neck,
24:12. Then arose Peter, and *ran* unto the
Joh.20: 2. Then she *runneth,* and cometh
4. So they *ran* both together:
Ro. 9:16. nor of him *that runneth,* but of
1Co. 9:24. they *which run* in a race *run* all,
— So *run,* that ye may obtain.
26. I therefore so *run,* not as
Gal. 2: 2. lest by any means I should *run,* or *had*
run, in vain.
5: 7. Ye *did run* well ; who
Phi. 2:16. that I *have* not *run* in vain,
2Th. 3: 1. that the word of the Lord *may have* (free)
course, and be glorified,
Heb12: 1. and *let* us *run* with patience the
Rev. 9: 9. of many horses *running* to battle.

τρία see τρεῖς.

τριάκοντα, *triakonta.*

Mat.13: 8. some sixtyfold, some *thirtyfold.*
23. some sixty, some *thirty.*
26:15. with him for *thirty* pieces of silver.
27: 3. brought again the *thirty* pieces of silver
9. they took the *thirty* pieces of silver,
Mar 4: 8. some *thirty,* and some sixty, and
20. some *thirtyfold,* some sixty, and
Lu. 3:23. to be about *thirty* years of age,
Joh. 5: 5. an infirmity *thirty* and eight years.

Joh. 6:19. five and twenty or *thirty* furlongs,
Gal. 3:17. four hundred and *thirty* years after,

τριακόσιοι, *triakosioi*.

Mar 14: 5. for more than *three hundred* pence,
Joh. 12: 5. sold for *three hundred* pence,

τρίϐολος, *tribolos*.

Mat. 7:16. or figs of *thistles?*
Heb 6: 8. that which beareth thorns and *briers*

τρίϐος, *tribos*.

Mat. 3: 3. make his *paths* straight.
Mar 1: 3. make his *paths* straight.
Lu. 3: 4. make his *paths* straight.

τριετία, *trietia*.

Acts 20:31. by the *space of three years* I ceased not

τρίζω, *trizo*.

Mar 9:18. and *gnasheth* with his teeth,

τρίμηνον, *trimeenon*.

Heb 11:23. was hid *three months* of his parents,

τρίς, *tris*.

Mat. 26:34. thou shalt deny me *thrice*.
75. thou shalt deny me *thrice*.
Mar 14:30. thou shalt deny me *thrice*.
72. thou shalt deny me *thrice*.
Lu. 22:34. before that thou shalt *thrice* deny
61. thou shalt deny me *thrice*.
Joh. 13:38. till thou hast denied me *thrice*.
Acts 10:16. This was done *thrice :* and the
11:10. And this was done *three times :*
2Co. 11:25. *Thrice* was I beaten with rods,
— *thrice* I suffered shipwreck,
12: 8. I besought the Lord *thrice*, that it

τρίστεγον, *tristegon*.

Acts 20: 9. and fell down from the *third loft*,

τρισχίλιοι, *triskilioi*.

Acts 2:41. about *three thousand* souls.

τρίτος, *tritos*.

Mat. 16:21. and be raised again the *third* day.
17:23. and the *third* day he shall be raised
20: 3. he went out about the *third* hour,
19. and the *third* day he shall rise again.
22:26. also, and the *third*, unto the seventh.
26:44. and prayed the *third* time,

Mat. 27:64. be made sure until the *third* day,
Mar 9:31. he shall rise the *third* day.
10:34. and the *third* day he shall rise again.
12:21. and the *third* likewise.
14:41. And he cometh the *third* time, and
15:25. And it was the *third* hour,
Lu. 9:22. and be raised the *third* day.
12:38. or come in the *third* watch,
13:32. and the *third* (day) I shall be perfected.
18:33. and the *third* day he shall rise again.
20:12. And again he sent a *third :* and they
31. And the *third* took her ;
23:22. he said unto them the *third* time,
24: 7. and the *third* day rise again.
21. to day is the *third* day
46. to rise from the dead the *third* day :
Joh. 2: 1. And the *third* day there was
21:14. This is now the *third* time that Jesus
17. He saith unto him the *third* time, Simon,
— because he said unto him the *third* time,
Acts 2:15. it is (but) the *third* hour of the day.
10:40. Him God raised up the *third* day,
23:23. at the *third* hour of the night ;
27:19. And the *third* (day) we cast out
1Co. 12:28. *third*ly teachers, after that miracles,
15: 4. he rose again the *third* day
2Co. 12: 2. caught up to the *third* heaven.
14. Behold, the *third* time I am ready to come
13: 1. This (is) the *third* (time) I am coming to you.
Rev. 4: 7. and the *third* beast had a face as
6: 5. when he had opened the *third* seal, I heard the *third* beast say,
8: 7. the *third* part of trees was burnt up,
8. the *third* part of the sea became blood,
9. the *third* part of the creatures
— and the *third* part of the ships
10. And the *third* angel sounded,
— upon the *third* part of the rivers, and
11. the *third* part of the waters became
12. the *third* part of the sun was smitten, and the *third* part of the moon, and the *third* part of the stars ; so as the *third* part of them was darkened, and the day shone not for a *third* part of it,
9:15. for to slay the *third* part of men.
18. was the *third* part of men killed,
11:14. the *third* woe cometh quickly.
12: 4. drew the *third* part of the stars of
14: 9. And the *third* angel followed them,
16: 4. And the *third* angel poured out
21:19. the *third*, a chalcedony ;

Note.—In 1 Co. 12:28, and other places, the neuter is used as an adverb.

τρίχες see θρίξ.

τρίχινος, *trikinos*.

Rev. 6:12. black as sackcloth *of hair*,

τρόμος, *tromos*.

Mar 16: 8. for they trembled and were amazed: (lit. *trembling* and amazement held them)
1Co. 2: 3. in fear, and in much *trembling*.
2Co. 7:15. how with fear and *trembling* ye received

Eph 6: 5. be obedient to...with fear and *trembling*,
Phi. 2:12. work out your own salvation with fear
and *trembling*.

τροπή, *tropee*.

Jas. 1:17. neither shadow of *turning*.

τοόπος, *tropos*.

Mat.23:37. even as (lit. what *manner*) a hen gathereth
her chickens
Lu. 13:34. as (lit. &c.) a hen (doth gather) her brood
Acts 1:11. shall so come in like *manner* as
7:28. as (lit. &c.) thou diddest the Egyptian
15:11. we shall be saved, even as (lit. &c.) they.
27:25. it shall be even as (lit. &c.) it was told me.
Ro. 3: 2. Much every *way*: chiefly, because
Phi. 1:18. every *way*, whether in pretence, or in
2Th. 2: 3. Let no man deceive you by any *means*:
3:16. give you peace always by all *means*.
2Ti. 3· 8. Now as (lit. what *manner*) Jannes and
Jambres
Heb 13: 5. (Let your) *conversation* (be) without covetousness;
Jude 7. in like *manner*, giving themselves

τροποφορέω, *tropophoreo*.

Acts 13:18. *suffered* he their *manners* in the wilderness.

τροφή, *trophee*.

Mat. 3: 4. his *meat* was locusts and wild honey.
6:25. Is not the life more than *meat*,
10:10. the workman is worthy of his *meat*.
24:45. to give them *meat* in due season?
Lu. 12:23. The life is more than *meat*,
Joh. 4: 8. unto the city to buy *meat*.
Acts 2:46. did eat their *meat* (lit. *food*) with gladness
9:19. And when he had received *meat*,
14:17. filling our hearts with *food* and
27:33. Paul besought (them) all to take *meat*,
(lit. *food*)
34. I pray you to take (some) *meat*:
36. they also took (some) *meat*. (lit. *food*)
38. when they had eaten enough, (lit. being
satisfied with *food*)
Heb 5:12. and not of strong *meat*. (lit. solid *food*)
14. But strong *meat* belongeth to them
Jas. 2:15. and destitute of daily *food*,

τροφός, *trophos*.

1 Th. 2: 7. as a *nurse* cherisheth her children:

τροχία, *trokia*.

Heb 12:13. And make straight *paths* for your feet,

τροχός, *trokos*.

Jas. 3: 6. setteth on fire the *course* of nature;

τρυβλίον *trublion*.

Mat. 26:23. (his) hand with me in the *dish*,
Mar 14:20. that dippeth with me in the *dish*.

τρυγάω, *trugao*.

Lu. 6:44. nor of a bramble bush *gather* they grapes.
Rev. 14:18. *gather* the clusters of the vine
19. and *gathered* the vine of the earth,

τρυγών, *trugōn*.

Lu. 2:24. A pair of *turtledoves*,

τρυμαλιά, *trumalia*.

Mar 10:25. to go through the *eye* of a needle,
Lu. 18:25. camel to go through a needle's *eye*,

τρύπημα, *trupeema*.

Mat. 19:24. to go through the *eye* of a needle,

τρυφάω, *truphao*.

Jas. 5: 5. Ye *have lived in pleasure* on the earth,

τρυφή, *truphee*.

Lu. 7:25. and live *delicately*, are in kings' courts.
2 Pet. 2:13. that count it pleasure *to riot* in the day
time.

τρώγω, *trōgo*.

Mat. 24:38. they were *eating* and drinking,
Joh. 6:54. *Whoso eateth* my flesh, and drinketh
56. He *that eateth* my flesh, and drinketh
57. so he *that eateth* me, even he shall live
58. he *that eateth* of this bread shall live
13:18. He *that eateth* bread with me hath lifted

τυγχάνω, *tunkano*.

Lu. 10:30. leaving (him) half dead. (lit. *being* half
dead)
20:35. worthy *to obtain* that world,
Acts 19:11. And God wrought special miracles (lit.
no *common* miracles)
24: 2(3). *Seeing that* by thee we *enjoy* great
quietness,
26:22. *Having* therefore *obtained* help of God,
27: 3. to go unto his friends to refresh himself.
(lit. to *meet with* care)
28: 2. shewed us no *little* kindness: (lit. no
common k.)
1 Co. 14:10. There are, it *may be*, so many kinds
15:37. bare grain, it *may chance* of wheat,
2 Ti. 2:10. they *may* also *obtain* the salvation
Heb 8: 6. But now *hath* he *obtained* a more excellent
11:35. that they *might obtain* a better resurrection.

See also τυχόν.

τυμπανίζομαι, tumpanizomai.

Heb 11:35. and others *were tortured,*

τύπος, tupos.

Joh. 20:25. in his hands the *print* of the nails, and put
my finger into the *print* of the nails,
Acts 7:43. *figures* which ye made to worship
44. make it according to the *fashion* that he
had seen.
23:25. he wrote a letter after this *manner:*
Ro. 5:14. who is the *figure* of him that was to come.
6:17. that *form* of doctrine which was
1Co.10: 6. Now these things were our *examples,*
11. happened unto them for *ensamples:*
Phi. 3:17. as ye have us for an *ensample.*
1Th. 1: 7. So that ye were *ensamples* to all
2Th. 3: 9. but to make ourselves an *ensample*
1Ti. 4:12. be thou an *example* of the believers,
Tit. 2: 7. shewing thyself a *pattern* of good works:
Heb 8: 5. according to the *pattern* shewed to thee
1Pet.5: 3. but being *ensamples* to the flock.

τύπτω, tupto.

Mat.24:49. And shall begin to *smite* (his)
27:30. and *smote* him on the head.
Mar 15:19. And they *smote* him on the head
Lu. 6:29. And unto him *that smiteth* thee on
12:45. and shall begin *to beat* the menservants
18:13. but *smote* upon his breast, saying,
22:64. they *struck* him on the face,
23:48. *smote* their breasts, *and* returned.
Acts18:17. and *beat* (him) before the judgment seat.
21:32. they left *beating* of Paul.
23: 2. *to smite* him on the mouth.
3. God shall *smite* thee, (thou) whited wall:
— commandest me *to be smitten* contrary
1Co. 8:12. and *wound* their weak conscience,

τυρβάζομαι, turbazomai.

Lu. 10:41. thou art careful and *troubled* about many
things:

τυφλός, tuphlos.

Mat. 9:27. two *blind* men followed him,
28. the *blind* men came to him:
11: 5. The *blind* receive their sight,
12:22. one possessed with a devil, *blind,*
— insomuch that the *blind* and dumb
15:14. they be *blind* leaders of the *blind.* And if
the *blind* lead the *blind,*
30. lame, *blind,* dumb, maimed,
31. and the *blind* to see:
20:30. And, behold, two *blind* men
21:14. And the *blind* and the lame came
23:16. Woe unto you, (ye) *blind* guides,
17. (Ye) fools and *blind:* for whether is
19. (Ye) fools and *blind:* for whether
24. (Ye) *blind* guides, which strain at a gnat,
26. (Thou) *blind* Pharisee, cleanse first that
Mar 8:22. they bring a *blind* man unto him,
23. he took the *blind* man by the hand,
10:46. *blind* Bartimæus, the son of Timæus,

Mar 10:49. And they call the *blind* man,
51. The *blind* man said unto him,
Lu. 4:18. and recovering of sight to the *blind,*
6:39. Can the *blind* lead the *blind?*
7:21. unto many (that were) *blind* he gave
sight.
22. how that the *blind* see,
14:13. the maimed, the lame, the *blind:*
21. the maimed, and the halt, and the *blind.*
18:35. a certain *blind* man sat by the way side
Joh. 5: 3. of *blind,* halt, withered, waiting for
9: 1. which was *blind* from (his) birth.
2. that he was born *blind?*
6. anointed the eyes of the *blind* man
8. had seen him that he was *blind,*
13. him that aforetime was *blind.*
17. They say unto the *blind* man again,
18. that he had been *blind,* and received
19. who ye say was born *blind?*
20. and that he was born *blind:*
24. called they the man that was *blind,*
25. whereas I was *blind,* now I see.
32. the eyes of one that was born *blind.*
39. they which see might be made *blind.*
40. Are we *blind* also?
41. If ye were *blind,* ye should have no sin:
10:21. open the eyes of the *blind?*
11:37. which opened the eyes of the *blind,*
Acts13:11. and thou shalt be *blind,*
Ro. 2:19. thyself art a guide of the *blind,*
2Pet.1: 9. he that lacketh these things is *blind,* and
Rev. 3:17. and poor, and *blind,* and naked:

τυφλόω, tuphloō.

Joh.12:40. He *hath blinded* their eyes,
2Co. 4: 4. In whom the god of this world *hath blinded* the minds
1Joh.2:11. darkness *hath blinded* his eyes.

τύφομαι, tuphomai.

Mat.12:20. and *smoking* flax shall he not quench,

τυφόομαι, tuphŏŏmai.

1Ti. 3: 6. lest *being lifted up with pride* he fall
6: 4. He *is proud,* knowing nothing,
2Ti. 3: 4. *heady, highminded,* (lit. *puffed up*)

τυφωνικός, tuphōnikos.

Acts27:14. a *tempestuous* wind, called Euroclydon.

τυχόν, tukon.

1Co.16: 6. And it *may be* that I will abide,

ὑακίνθινος, huakinthinos.

Rev. 9:17. breastplates of fire, and *of jacinth,*

ὑάκινθος, huakinthos.

Rev.21:20. the eleventh, a *jacinth*;

ὑάλινος, hualinos.

Rev. 4: 6. a sea *of glass* like unto crystal:
15: 2. as it were a sea *of glass* mingled with fire:
— stand on the sea *of glass*, having the harps of God.

ὕαλος, hualos.

Rev.21:18. city (was) pure gold, like unto clear *glass*.
21. pure gold, as it were transparent *glass*.

ὑβρίζω, hubrizo.

Mat.22: 6. and *entreated* (them) *spitefully*,
Lu. 11:45. thus saying thou *reproachest* us also.
18:32. shall be mocked, and *spitefully entreated*,
Acts14: 5. to *use* (them) *despitefully*, and to stone
1Th. 2: 2. after that we had suffered before, and were *shamefully entreated*,

---

ὕβρις, hubris.

Acts27:10. will be with *hurt* and much damage,
21. to have gained this *harm* and loss.
2Co.12:10. I take pleasure in infirmities, in *reproaches*,

ὑβριστής, hubristees.

Ro. 1:30. haters of God, *despiteful*,
1Ti. 1:13. and a persecutor, and *injurious*:

ὑγιαίνω, hugiaino.

Lu. 5:31. They *that are whole* need not a physician;
7:10. found the servant *whole* that had been sick.
15:27. he hath received him *safe and sound*.
1Ti. 1:10. that is contrary to *sound* doctrine;
6: 3. and consent not to *wholesome* words,
2Ti. 1:13. Hold fast the form of *sound* words,
4: 3. when they will not endure *sound* doctrine;
Tit. 1: 9. he may be able by *sound* doctrine
13. that they *may be sound* in the faith;
2: 1. things which become *sound* doctrine:
2. *sound* (lit. *being sound*) in faith, in
3Joh. 2. mayest prosper and *be in health*,

ὑγιής, hugiees.

Mat.12:13. it was restored *whole*, like as the other.
15:31. the maimed to be *whole*,
Mar 3: 5. was restored *whole* as the other.
5:34. and be *whole* of thy plague.
Lu. 6:10. hand was restored *whole* as the other.
Joh. 5: 4. was made *whole* of whatsoever disease
6. Wilt thou be made *whole*?
9. was made *whole*, and took up his bed,
11. He that made me *whole*,
14. thou art made *whole*: sin no more,
15. it was Jesus, which had made him *whole*.

Joh. 7:23. every whit *whole* on the sabbath day?
Acts 4:10. this man stand here before you *whole*.
Tit. 2: 8. *Sound* speech, that cannot be condemned

ὑγρός, hugros.

Lu. 23:31. they do these things in a *green* tree,

ὑδρία, hudria.

Joh. 2: 6. And there were set there six *waterpots* of
7. Fill the *waterpots* with water.
4:28. The woman then left her *waterpot*,

ὑδροποτέω, hudropoteo.

1Ti. 5:23. *Drink* no longer *water*, but use a

ὑδρωπικός, hudrōpikos.

Lu. 14: 2. man before him *which had the dropsy*.

ὕδωρ, hudōr.

Mat. 3:11. I indeed baptize you with *water*
16. went up straightway out of the *water*:
8:32. and perished in the *waters*.
14:28. come unto thee on the *water*.
29. he walked on the *water*, to go to
17:15. and oft into the *water*.
27:24. he took *water*, and washed (his) hands
Mar 1: 8. I indeed have baptized you with *water*:
10. coming up out of the *water*, he saw
9:22. into the fire, and into the *waters*,
41. a cup of *water* to drink in my name,
14:13. a man bearing a pitcher of *water*:
Lu. 3:16. I indeed baptize you with *water*;
7:44. thou gavest me no *water* for my feet:
8:24. and the raging of the *water*:
16:24. he commandeth even the winds and *water*,
22:10. bearing a pitcher of *water*;
Joh. 1:26. I baptize with *water*:
31. am I come baptizing with *water*.
33. that sent me to baptize with *water*,
2: 7. Fill the waterpots with *water*.
9. tasted the *water* that was made wine,
— the servants which drew the *water* knew;
3: 5. Except a man be born of *water* and
23. there was much *water* there:
4: 7. a woman of Samaria to draw *water*:
10. he would have given thee living *water*.
11. whence then hast thou that living *water*?
13. Whosoever drinketh of this *water*
14. whosoever drinketh of the *water* that
— but the *water* that I shall give him shall be in him a well of *water*
15. Sir, give me this *water*, that I
46. where he made the *water* wine.
5: 3. waiting for the moving of the *water*.
4. and troubled the *water*: whosoever then first after the troubling of the *water*
7. when the *water* is troubled,
7:38. shall flow rivers of living *water*.
13: 5. After that he poureth *water* into a bason,
19:34. came thereout blood and *water*.
Acts 1: 5. For John truly baptized with *water*;

Acts 8:36. they came unto a certain *water :*
　　　　　— See, (here is) *water ;* what doth hinder
　　　 38. they went down both into the *water,*
　　　 39. they were come up out of the *water,*
　　 10:47. Can any man forbid *water,* that
　　 11:16. John indeed baptized with *water ;*
Eph 5:26. with the washing of *water* by the word,
Heb 9:19. with *water,* and scarlet wool, and
　　 10:22(23). our bodies washed with pure *water.*
Jas. 3:12. both yield salt *water* and fresh.
1Pet.3:20. eight souls were saved by *water.*
2Pet.3: 5. and the earth standing out of the *water*
　　　　　and in the *water :*
　　　 6. being overflowed with *water,* perished:
1Joh.5: 6. that came by *water* and blood, (even)
　　　　　Jesus Christ; not by *water* only, but by
　　　　　water and blood.
　　　 8. the spirit, and the *water,* and the blood:
Rev. 1:15. his voice as the sound of many *waters.*
　　　 7:17. unto living fountains of *waters :* and God
　　　 8:10. and upon the fountains of *waters ;*
　　　 11. and the third part of the *waters* became
　　　　　wormwood; and many men died of the
　　　　　waters,
　　　 11: 6. and have power over *waters* to turn
　　　 12:15. out of his mouth *water* as a flood
　　　 14: 2. as the voice of many *waters,*
　　　　　7. and the fountains of *waters.*
　　　 16: 4. upon the rivers and fountains of *waters ;*
　　　　　5. I heard the angel of the *waters* say,
　　　　 12. and the *water* thereof was dried up,
　　　 17: 1. whore that sitteth upon many *waters :*
　　　　 15. The *waters* which thou sawest, where
　　　 19: 6. and as the voice of many *waters,*
　　　 21: 6. of the fountain of the *water* of life freely.
　　　 22: 1. a pure river of *water* of life,, clear
　　　　 17. let him take the *water* of life freely.

νετός, *huetos.*

Acts14:17. and gave us *rain* from heaven,
　　　 28: 2. because of the present *rain,*
Heb 6: 7. the earth which drinketh in the *rain*
Jas. 5: 7. he receive the early and latter *rain.*
　　　 18. prayed again, and the heaven gave *rain,*
Rev.11: 6. to shut heaven, that it rain not (lit. that
　　　　　the *rain* wet not) in the days

υἱοθεσία, *whyothesia.*

Ro. 8:15. ye have received the Spirit of *adoption,*
　　　 23. waiting for the *adoption,* (to wit), the
　　　 9: 4. to whom (pertaineth) the *adoption,* and
Gal. 4: 5. we might receive the *adoption of sons.*
Eph 1: 5. us unto the *adoption of children* by Jesus
　　　　　Christ to himself,

υἱός, *whyos.*

Mat. 1: 1. of Jesus Christ, the *son* of David, the *son*
　　　　　of Abraham.
　　　 20. Joseph, thou *son* of David, fear not to
　　　 21. she shall bring forth a *son,* and thou
　　　 23. and shall bring forth a *son,*
　　　 25. had brought forth her firstborn *son :*
　　　 2:15. Out of Egypt have I called my *son.*
　　　 3:17. This is my beloved *Son,* in whom I am
　　　　　well pleased.
　　　 4: 3. If thou be the *Son* of God, command

Mat. 4: 6. If thou be the *Son* of God, cast
　　　 5: 9. for they shall be called the *children* of God.
　　　 45. That ye may be the *children* of your Father
　　　　　which is in heaven:
　　　 7: 9. if his *son* ask bread, will he give him
　　　 8:12. But the *children* of the kingdom shall be
　　　　　cast out
　　　 20. but the *Son* of man hath not where
　　　 29. with thee, Jesus, thou *Son* of God?
　　　 9: 6. may know that the *Son* of man hath
　　　 15. Can the *children* of the bridechamber
　　　 27. (Thou) *son* of David, have mercy on us.
　　 10:23. till the *Son* of man be come.
　　　 37. he that loveth *son* or daughter more
　　 11:19. The *Son* of man came eating and
　　　 27. and no man knoweth the *Son,* but the
　　　　　Father;
　　　　　— save the *Son,* and (he) to whomsoever the
　　　　　Son will reveal (him).
　　 12: 8. For the *Son* of man is Lord even of
　　　 23. Is not this the *son* of David ?
　　　 27. by whom do your *children* cast (them)
　　　 32. a word against the *Son* of man,
　　　 40. so shall the *Son* of man be three days
　　 13:37. He that soweth the good seed is the *Son*
　　　　　of man ;
　　　 38. the good seed are the *children* of the king-
　　　　　dom ; but the tares are the *children* of
　　　　　the wicked (one) ;
　　　 41. The *Son* of man shall send forth
　　　 55. Is not this the carpenter's *son ?*
　　 14:33. Of a truth thou art the *Son* of God.
　　 15:22. on me, O Lord, (thou) *son* of David ;
　　 16:13. that I the *Son* of man am ?
　　　 16. Thou art the Christ, the *Son* of the living
　　　　　God.
　　　 27. For the *Son* of man shall come in the
　　　　　glory of his Father
　　　 28. till they see the *Son* of man coming
　　 17: 5. This is my beloved *Son,* in whom I am
　　　　　well pleased ; hear ye him.
　　　　9. until the *Son* of man be risen
　　　 12. Likewise shall also the *Son* of man suffer
　　　 15. Lord, have mercy on my *son :*
　　　 22. The *Son* of man shall be betrayed
　　　 25. of their own *children,* or of strangers ?
　　　 26. Then are the *children* free.
　　 18:11. For the *Son* of man is come to save
　　 19:28. when the *Son* of man shall sit in the throne
　　　　　of his glory,
　　 20:18. and the *Son* of man shall be betrayed
　　　 20. came to him the mother of Zebedee's
　　　　　children with her *sons,* worshipping
　　　 21. Grant that these my two *sons* may sit,
　　　 28. Even as the *Son* of man came not to
　　　 30. on us, O Lord, (thou) *son* of David.
　　　 31. O Lord, (thou) *son* of David.
　　 21: 5. and a colt the *foal* of an ass.
　　　　9. Hosanna to the *son* of David:
　　　 15. Hosanna to the *son* of David ;
　　　 37. he sent unto them his *son,* saying, They
　　　　　will reverence my *son.*
　　　 38. when the husbandmen saw the *son,*
　　 22: 2. which made a marriage for his *son,*
　　　 42. What think ye of Christ? whose *son* is he?
　　　 45. call him Lord, how is he his *son ?*
　　 23:15. twofold more the *child* of hell than
　　　 31. that ye are the *children* of them which
　　　 35. blood of Zacharias *son* of Barachias,
　　 24:27. so shall also the coming of the *Son* of man
　　　　　be.
　　　 30. the sign of the *Son* of man in heaven:

Mat.24:30. and they shall see the *Son* of man coming
    37. so shall also the coming of the *Son* of man be.
    39. the coming of the *Son* of man be.
    44. the *Son* of man cometh.
  25:13. the hour wherein the *Son* of man cometh.
    31. When the *Son* of man shall come in his
  26: 2. and the *Son* of man is betrayed
    24. The *Son* of man goeth as it is written
    — by whom the *Son* of man is betrayed !
    37. Peter and the two *sons* of Zebedee,
    45. and the *Son* of man is betrayed
    63. whether thou be the Christ, the *Son* of God.
    64. Hereafter shall ye see the *Son* of man
  27: 9. they of the *children* of Israel did value ;
    40. If thou be the *Son* of God, come down
    43. for he said, I am the *Son* of God.
    54. Truly this was the *Son* of God.
    56. and the mother of Zebedee's *children*.
  28:19. in the name of the Father, and of the *Son*, and of the Holy Ghost:
Mar 1: 1. of Jesus Christ, the *Son* of God ;
    11. Thou art my beloved *Son*, in whom
  2:10. that the *Son* of man hath power
    19. Can the *children* of the bridechamber
    28. the *Son* of man is Lord also of the sabbath.
  3:11. Thou art the *Son* of God.
    17. Boanerges, which is, The *sons* of thunder:
    28. forgiven unto the *sons* of men,
  5: 7. Jesus, (thou) *Son* of the most high God ?
  6: 3. the carpenter, the *son* of Mary, the
  8:31. the *Son* of man must suffer many
    38. of him also shall the *Son* of man be ashamed,
  9: 7. This is my beloved *Son :* hear him.
    9. till the *Son* of man were risen
    12. it is written of the *Son* of man,
    17. I have brought unto thee my *son*,
    31. The *Son* of man is delivered into
  10:33. the *Son* of man shall be delivered unto
    35. James and John, the *sons* of Zebedee,
    45. For even the *Son* of man came not to
    46. Bartimæus, the *son* of Timæus,
    47. Jesus, (thou) *son* of David, have
    48. *son* of David, have mercy on me.
  12: 6. Having yet therefore one *son*, his wellbeloved,
    — They will reverence my *son*.
    35. that Christ is the *son* of David ?
    37. and whence is he (then) his *son ?*
  13:26. shall they see the *Son* of man coming in
    32. neither the *Son*, but the Father.
  14:21. The *Son* of man indeed goeth,
    — by whom the *Son* of man is betrayed !
    41. the *Son* of man is betrayed into
    61. Art thou the Christ, the *Son* of the Blessed?
    62. Jesus said, I am: and ye shall see the *Son* of man sitting on
  15:39. Truly this man was the *Son* of God.
Lu. 1:13. Elisabeth shall bear thee a *son*,
    16. many of the *children* of Israel shall he
    31. and bring forth a *son*, and shalt
    32. and shall be called the *Son* of the Highest:
    35. shall be called the *Son* of God.
    36. she hath also conceived a *son*
    57. and she brought forth a *son*.
  2: 7. she brought forth her firstborn *son*,
  3: 2. came unto John the *son* of Zacharias
    22. Thou art my beloved *Son ;* in thee I am
    23. being, as was supposed, the *son* of Joseph,

Lu. 4: 3. If thou be the *Son* of God, command
    9. If thou be the *Son* of God, cast
    22. Is not this Joseph's *son ?*
    41. Thou art Christ the *Son* of God.
  5:10. James, and John, the *sons* of Zebedee,
    24. that the *Son* of man hath power
    34. Can ye make the *children* of the
  6: 5. That the *Son* of man is Lord also of
    22. for the *Son* of man's sake.
    35. ye shall be the *children* of the Highest:
  7:12. the only *son* of his mother, and she
    34. The *Son* of man is come eating
  8:28. Jesus, (thou) *Son* of God most high ?
  9:22. The *Son* of man must suffer
    26. of him shall the *Son* of man be ashamed,
    35. This is my beloved *Son :* hear him.
    38. I beseech thee, look upon my *son :*
    41. Bring thy *son* hither.
    44. the *Son* of man shall be delivered
    56. For the *Son* of man is not come to
    58. but the *Son* of man hath not where
  10: 6. And if the *son* of peace be there,
    22. no man knoweth who the *Son* is, but the Father; and who the Father is, but the *Son*, and (he) to whom the *Son* will reveal (him).
  11:11. If a *son* shall ask bread of any
    19. by whom do your *sons* cast (them) out ?
    30. so shall also the *Son* of man be to this
  12: 8. him shall the *Son* of man also confess
    10. a word against the *Son* of man,
    40. for the *Son* of man cometh at an hour
    53. The father shall be divided against the *son*, and the *son* against the father ;
  15:11. A certain man had two *sons :*
    13. the younger *son* gathered all together,
    19. no more worthy to be called thy *son :*
    21. And the *son* said unto him, Father,
    — am no more worthy to be called thy *son*.
    24 For this my *son* was dead, and is alive
    25 Now his elder *son* was in the field:
    30. But as soon as this thy *son* was come,
  16: 8. for the *children* of this world are
    — wiser than the *children* of light.
  17:22. one of the days of the *Son* of man,
    24. so shall also the *Son* of man be in his day.
    26. be also in the days of the *Son* of man.
    30. in the day when the *Son* of man is revealed.
  18: 8. Nevertheless when the *Son* of man cometh,
    31. concerning the *Son* of man
    38. Jesus, (thou) *son* of David, have mercy
    39. *son* of David, have mercy on me.
  19: 9. as he also is a *son* of Abraham.
    10. For the *Son* of man is come to seek
  20:13. I will send my beloved *son :*
    34. The *children* of this world marry,
    36. and are the *children* of God, being the *children* of the resurrection.
    41. How say they that Christ is David's *son ?*
    44. how is he then his *son ?*
  21:27. shall they see the *Son* of man coming
    36. and to stand before the *Son* of man.
  22:22. And truly the *Son* of man goeth,
    48. betrayest thou the *Son* of man with a kiss ?
    69. Hereafter shall the *Son* of man sit on
    70. Art thou then the *Son* of God ?
  24: 7. The *Son* of man must be delivered
Joh. 1:18. the only begotten *Son*, which is in the bosom of the Father,
    34. that this is the *Son* of God.
    42(43). Thou art Simon the *son* of Jona:

Joh. 1:45(46). Jesus of Nazareth, the *son* of Joseph.
49(50). thou art the *Son* of God; thou art
51(52). and descending upon the *Son* of man.
3:13. the *Son* of man which is in heaven.
14. must the *Son* of man be lifted up:
16. he gave his only begotten *Son*, that
17. God sent not his *Son* into the world to
18. name of the only begotten *Son* of God.
35. The Father loveth the *Son*, and hath
36. He that believeth on the *Son* hath
— he that believeth not the *Son* shall not
4: 5. ground that Jacob gave to his *son* Joseph.
12. and his *children*, and his cattle?
46. whose *son* was sick at Capernaum.
47. come down, and heal his *son :*
50. Go thy way; thy *son* liveth.
53. Jesus said unto him, Thy *son* liveth:
5:19. The *Son* can do nothing of himself, but
— these also doeth the *Son* likewise.
20. For the Father loveth the *Son*, and
21. even so the *Son* quickeneth whom he will.
22. hath committed all judgment unto the *Son:*
23. That all men) should honour the *Son*, even
— He that honoureth not the *Son*
25. shall hear the voice of the *Son* of God:
26. hath he given to the *Son* to have life in himself;
27. because he is the *Son* of man.
6:27. which the *Son* of man shall give
40. that every one which seeth the *Son*,
42. Is not this Jesus, the *son* of Joseph,
53. ye eat the flesh of the *Son* of man,
62. if ye shall see the *Son* of man ascend
69. thou art that Christ, the *Son* of the living God.
8:28. When ye have lifted up the *Son* of man,
35. (but) the *Son* abideth ever.
36. If the *Son* therefore shall make you free,
9:19. Is this your *son*, who ye say was born blind?
20. We know that this is our *son*, and that
35. Dost thou believe on the *Son* of God?
10:36. because I said, I am the *Son* of God?
11: 4. that the *Son* of God might be glorified
27. that thou art the Christ, the *Son* of God,
12:23. that the *Son* of man should be glorified.
34. The *Son* of man must be lifted up? who is this *Son* of man?
36. that ye may be the *children* of light.
13:31. Now is the *Son* of man glorified,
14:13. the Father may be glorified in the *Son*.
17: 1. the hour is come; glorify thy *Son*, that thy *Son* also may glorify thee:
12. is lost, but the *son* of perdition;
19: 7. because he made himself the *Son* of God.
26. Woman, behold thy *son!*
20:31. that Jesus is the Christ, the *Son* of God;
Acts 2:17. your *sons* and your daughters shall
3:25. Ye are the *children* of the prophets,
4:36. interpreted, The *son* of consolation,
5:21. the senate of the *children* of Israel,
7:16. for a sum of money of the *sons* of Emmor
21. nourished him for her own son.
23. visit his brethren the *children* of Israel.
29. Madian, where he begat two *sons*.
37. which said unto the *children* of Israel,
56. heavens opened, and the *Son* of man
8:37. I believe that Jesus Christ is the *Son* of God.
9:15. and the *children* of Israel:
20. that he is the *Son* of God.

Acts 10:36. sent unto the *children* of Israel,
13:10. (thou) *child* of the devil, (thou) enemy
21. gave unto them Saul the *son* of Cis,
26. *children* of the stock of Abraham,
33. Thou art my *Son*, this day have I begotten thee.
16: 1. Timotheus, the *son* of a certain woman,
19:14. there were seven *sons* of (one) Sceva,
23: 6. I am a Pharisee, the *son* of a Pharisee:
16. And when Paul's sister's *son* heard of
Ro. 1: 3. Concerning his *Son* Jesus Christ our Lord,
4. declared (to be) the *Son* of God with
9. serve with my spirit in the gospel of his *Son*,
5:10. reconciled to God by the death of his *Son*,
8: 3. God sending his own *Son* in the likeness
14. as many as are led by the Spirit of God, they are the *sons* of God.
19. for the manifestation of the *sons* of God.
29. conformed to the image of his *Son*,
32. He that spared not his own *Son*, but
9: 9. and Sarah shall have a *son*.
26. be called the *children* of the living God.
27. Though the number of the *children* of
1Co. 1: 9. called unto the fellowship of his *Son* Jesus Christ our Lord.
15:28. then shall the *Son* also himself be subject
2Co. 1:19. For the *Son* of God, Jesus Christ, who
3: 7. so that the *children* of Israel could not
13. that the *children* of Israel could not
6:18. and ye shall be my *sons* and daughters,
Gal. 1:16. To reveal his *Son* in me, that
2:20. I live by the faith of the *Son* of God, who
3: 7. the same are the *children* of Abraham.
26. ye are all the *children* of God by faith in Christ Jesus.
4: 4. God sent forth his *Son*,
6. because ye are *sons*, God hath sent forth the Spirit of his *Son* into
7. no more a servant, but a *son;* and if a *son*, then an heir of God through Christ
22. that Abraham had two *sons*,
30. Cast out the bondwoman and her *son :* for the *son* of the bondwoman shall not be heir with the *son* of the freewoman.
Eph. 2: 2. worketh in the *children* of disobedience:
3: 5. not made known unto the *sons* of men,
4:13. and of the knowledge of the *Son* of God,
5: 6. upon the *children* of disobedience.
Col. 1:13. into the kingdom of his dear *Son :*
3: 6. on the *children* of disobedience:
1Th. 1:10. And to wait for his *Son* from heaven,
5: 5. Ye are all the *children* of light, and the *children* of the day:
2Th. 2: 3. that man of sin be revealed, the *son* of perdition;
Heb 1: 2(1). spoken unto us by (his) *Son*,
5. Thou art my *Son*, this day have I begotten thee?
— and he shall be to me a *Son ?*
8. But unto the *Son* (he saith), Thy throne,
2: 6. or the *son* of man, that thou visitest him?
10. in bringing many *sons* unto glory,
3: 6. But Christ as a *son* over his own house;
4:14. Jesus the *Son* of God, let us hold fast
5: 5. Thou art my *Son*, to day have I begotten thee.
8. Though he were a *Son*, yet learned he
6: 6. crucify to themselves the *Son* of God afresh,
7: 3. but made like unto the *Son* of God;
5. that are of the *sons* of Levi,

Heb 7:28. the *Son*, who is consecrated for evermore.

10:29. hath trodden under foot the *Son* of God,

11:21. blessed both the *sons* of Joseph ;

22. the departing of the *children* of Israel ;

24. to be called the *son* of Pharaoh's daughter;

12: 5. speaketh unto you as unto *children*, My *son*, despise not thou the chastening

6. scourgeth every *son* whom he receiveth.

7. God dealeth with you as with *sons ;* for what *son* is he whom the father

8. then are ye bastards, and not *sons*.

Jas. 2:21. offered Isaac his *son* upon the altar ?

1Pet.5:13. and (so doth) Marcus my *son*.

2Pet.1:17. This is my beloved *Son*, in whom I am well pleased.

1Joh.1: 3. and with his *Son* Jesus Christ.

7. the blood of Jesus Christ his *Son* cleanseth

2:22. that denieth the Father and the *Son*.

23. Whosoever denieth the *Son*, the same hath not the Father:

24. shall continue in the *Son*, and in the Father.

3: 8. For this purpose the *Son* of God was

23. That we should believe on the name of his *Son* Jesus Christ,

4: 9. God sent his only begotten *Son* into

10. sent his *Son* (to be) the propitiation

14. the Father sent the *Son* (to be) the Saviour of the world.

15. shall confess that Jesus is the *Son* of God,

5: 5. believeth that Jesus is the *Son* of God ?

9. which he hath testified of his *Son*.

10. He that believeth on the *Son* of God hath

— the record that God gave of his *Son*.

11. and this life is in his *Son*.

12. He that hath the *Son* hath life ; (and) he that hath not the *Son* of God hath not life.

13. believe on the name of the *Son* of God ;

— believe on the name of the *Son* of God.

20. we know that the *Son* of God is come,

— we are in him that is true, (even) in his *Son* Jesus Christ.

2Joh. 3. and from the Lord Jesus Christ, the *Son* of the Father,

9. he hath both the Father and the *Son*.

Rev. 1:13. like unto the *Son* of man,

2:14. before the *children* of Israel, to eat

18. These things saith the *Son* of God,

7: 4. of all the tribes of the *children* of Israel.

12: 5. she brought forth a man *child*, who was to rule all nations

14:14. like unto the *Son* of man, having on

21: 7. I will be his God, and he shall be my *son*.

12. the twelve tribes of the *children* of Israel:

ὕλη, *hulee*.

Jas. 3: 5. how great a *matter* a little fire kindleth! (lit. how much *material*)

ὑμᾶς, *humas*.

From σύ.

Mat. 3:11. I indeed baptize *you* with water

— he shall baptize *you* with the Holy Ghost,

4:19. and I will make *you* fishers of men.

5:11. when (men) shall revile *you*, and

Mat. 5:44. bless them that curse *you*, do good to them that hate *you*, and pray for them which despitefully use *you*, and persecute *you ;*

46. if ye love them which love *you*,

6: 8. things ye have need of, before *ye* ask him.

30. (shall he) not much more (clothe) *you*,

7: 6. and turn again and rend *you*.

15. which come to *you* in sheep's clothing,

23. I never knew *you :* depart from me,

10:13. let your peace return to *you*.

14. And whosoever shall not receive *you*,

16. Behold, I send *you* forth as sheep in

17. they will deliver *you* up to the councils, and they will scourge *you* in

19. But when they deliver *you* up,

23. But when they persecute *you* in this

40. He that receiveth *you* receiveth me,

11:28. and I will give *you* rest.

29. Take my yoke upon *you*, and

12:28. the kingdom of God is come unto *you*.

21:24. I also will ask *you* one thing,

31. into the kingdom of God before *you*.

32. For John came unto *you* in the way of

23:34. I send unto *you* prophets,

35. That upon *you* may come all

24: 4. Take heed that no man deceive *you*.

9. Then shall they deliver *you* up to be afflicted, and shall kill *you :*

25:12. I say unto you, I know *you* not.

26:32. I will go before *you* into Galilee.

55. I sat daily with *you* teaching in

28: 7. he goeth before *you* into Galilee ;

14. persuade him, and secure *you*.

Mar 1: 8. I indeed have baptized *you* with water: but he shall baptize *you* with

17. and I will make *you* to become

6:11. whosoever shall not receive *you*,

9:19. how long shall I be with *you ?*

41. whosoever shall give *you* a cup of water

11:29. I will also ask of *you* one question,

13: 5. lest any (man) deceive *you :*

9. for they shall deliver *you* up to

11. shall lead (you), and deliver *you* up,

36. Lest coming suddenly he find *you* sleeping.

14:28. I will go before *you* into Galilee.

49. I was daily with *you* in the temple

16: 7. he goeth before *you* into Galilee:

Lu. 3:16. I indeed baptize *you* with water ;

— he shall baptize *you* with the Holy Ghost and

6: 9. I will ask *you* one thing ;

22. when men shall hate *you*, and when they shall separate *you*

26. all men shall speak well of *you !*

27. do good to them which hate *you*,

28. for them which despitefully use *you*.

32. if ye love them which love *you*,

33. to them which do good to *you*,

9: 5. whosoever will not receive *you*,

41. how long shall I be with *you*,

10: 3. I send *you* forth as lambs among

6. if not, it shall turn to *you* again.

8. ye enter, and they receive *you*,

9. The kingdom of God is come nigh unto *you*.

10. and they receive *you* not, go your ways

11. the kingdom of God is come nigh unto *you*.

16. he that despiseth *you* despiseth me ;

19. shall by any means hurt *you*.

11:20. the kingdom of God is come upon *you*.

12:11. when they bring *you* unto the synagogues,

12. For the Holy Ghost shall teach *you*

14. a judge or a divider over *you ?*

Lu. 12:28. how much more (will he clothe) *you*,
13:25. I know *you* not whence ye are:
27. I know *you* not whence ye are;
28. and *you* (yourselves) thrust out.
16: 9. receive *you* into everlasting habitations.
26. from hence to *you* cannot;
19:31. if any man ask *you*, Why do ye
20: 3. I will also ask *you* one thing;
21:12. they shall lay their hands on *you*,
34. that day come upon *you* unawares.
22:31. Satan hath desired (to have) *you*, that he
35. When I sent *you* without purse,
23:15. nor yet Herod: for I sent *you* to him;
24:44. the words which I spake unto *you*, while
49. the promise of my Father upon *you*:
Joh. 3: 7. *Ye* must be born again.
4:38. I sent *you* to reap that whereon
5:42. But I know *you*, that ye have not the love
6:61. he said unto them, Doth this offend *you*?
70. Have not I chosen *you* twelve,
7: 7. The world cannot hate *you*;
8:32. the truth shall make *you* free.
36. If the Son therefore shall make *you* free,
11:15. And I am glad for *your* sakes (lit. on account of *you*) that
12:30. but for *your* sakes.
35. lest darkness come upon *you*:
13:34. love one another; as I have loved *you*,
14: 3. and receive *you* unto myself;
18. I will not leave *you* comfortless: I will come to *you*.
26. he shall teach *you* all things, and bring all things to *your* remembrance,
28. I go away, and come (again) unto *you*.
15: 9. As the Father hath loved me, so have I loved *you*:
12. love one another, as I have loved *you*.
15. Henceforth I call *you* not servants;
— but I have called *you* friends;
16. but I have chosen *you*, and ordained *you*, that ye should
18. If the world hate *you*, ye know
19. but I have chosen *you* out of the world, therefore the world hateth *you*.
20. they will also persecute *you*;
16: 2. They shall put *you* out of the synagogues:
— that whosoever killeth *you* will think
7. the Comforter will not come unto *you*;
— I will send him unto *you*.
13. he will guide *you* into all truth:
22. but I will see *you* again, and your heart
27. For the Father himself loveth *you*,
20:21. hath sent me, even so send I *you*.
Acts 1: 8. the Holy Ghost is come upon *you*:
2:22. a man approved of God among *you*
29. speak unto *you* of the patriarch David,
3:22. whatsoever he shall say unto *you*.
26. sent him to bless *you*, in turning
7:43. I will carry *you* away beyond Babylon.
13:32. And we declare unto *you* glad tidings,
40. lest that come upon *you*, which is
14:15. preach unto you that *ye* should turn
15:24. have troubled *you* with words,
25. to send chosen men unto *you*
17:22. in all things *ye* are too superstitious.
28. as certain also of your own poets (lit. of poets among *you*)
18:15. and (of) your law, (lit. the law which is among *you*)
21. but I will return again unto *you*,
19:13. saying, We adjure *you* by Jesus
36. *ye* ought to be quiet, and to do

Acts 20:20. and have taught *you* publickly,
28. the Holy Ghost hath made *you* overseers,
29. shall grievous wolves enter in among *you*,
32. I commend *you* to God, and to the word
22: 1. defence (which I make) now unto *you*.
23:15. that he bring him down unto *you*
24:22. I will know the uttermost of *your* matter. (lit. the things among *you*)
27:22. I exhort *you* to be of good cheer:
34. Wherefore I pray *you* to take (some) meat:
28:20. have I called for *you*, to see (you),
Ro. 1:10. by the will of God to come unto *you*.
11. For I long to see *you*, that I may
— to the end *ye* may be established;
13. Now I would not have *you* ignorant,
— I purposed to come unto *you*,
2:24. blasphemed among the Gentiles through *you*,
7: 4. that *ye* should be married to another,
10:19. I will provoke *you* to jealousy by
— by a foolish nation I will anger *you*.
11:25. that *ye* should be ignorant of
28. (they are) enemies for *your* sakes:
12: 1. I beseech *you* therefore, brethren,
2. that *ye* may prove what (is) that good,
14. Bless them which persecute *you*:
15:13. Now the God of hope fill *you* with all joy
— that *ye* may abound in hope, through the
15. as putting *you* in mind, because of the grace
22. much hindered from coming to *you*.
23. these many years to come unto *you*;
24. into Spain, I will come to *you*: for I trust to see *you* in my journey,
29. that, when I come unto *you*, I shall
30. Now I beseech *you*, brethren, for the Lord
32. That I may come unto *you* with joy by
16:16. The churches of Christ salute *you*.
17. Now I beseech *you*, brethren, mark
19. but yet I would have *you* wise unto
21. and Sosipater, my kinsmen, salute *you*.
22. who wrote (this) epistle, salute *you* in the
23. saluteth *you*. Erastus the chamberlain of the city saluteth *you*,
25. that is of power to stablish *you*
1Co. 1: 7. So that *ye* come behind in no gift;
8. Who shall also confirm *you* unto
10. Now I beseech *you*, brethren, by
2: 1. brethren, when I came to *you*,
3. And I was with *you* in weakness,
3: 2. I have fed *you* with milk, and not
4: 6. to myself and (to) Apollos for *your* sakes;
14. write not these things to shame *you*,
15. in Christ Jesus I have begotten *you*
16. Wherefore I beseech *you*, be ye
17. who shall bring *you* into remembrance of my ways which be in Christ,
18. as though I would not come to *you*.
19. But I will come to *you* shortly,
21. shall I come unto *you* with a rod,
7: 5. that Satan tempt *you* not for your
32. I would have *you* without carefulness.
10: 1. I would not that *ye* should be ignorant,
13. There hath no temptation taken *you* but
— will not suffer *you* to be tempted above
— that *ye* may be able to bear (it).
20. that *ye* should have fellowship with devils.
27. If any of them that believe not bid *you*
11: 2. Now I praise *you*, brethren, that ye
3. But I would have *you* know, that
14. Doth not even nature itself teach *you*,

1Co.11:22. shall I praise *you* in this?
12: 1. I would not have *you* ignorant.
14: 5. I would that *ye* all spake with tongues,
   6. if I come unto *you* speaking with tongues, what shall I profit *you*, except
  36. or came it unto *you* only?
16: 5. Now I will come unto *you*, when
   6. that I will abide, yea, and winter with *you*,
   7. I will not see *you* now by tne way; but I trust to tarry a while with *you*,
  10. he may be with *you* without fear:
  12. him to come unto *you* with the brethren:
  15. I beseech *you*, brethren, ye know
  19. The churches of Asia salute *you*. Aquila and Priscilla salute *you* much
  20. All the brethren greet *you*.
2Co. 1: 8. have *you* ignorant of our trouble
  12. and more abundantly to *you*-ward.
  15. I was minded to come unto *you* before,
  16. to come again out of Macedonia unto *you*,
  18. our word toward *you* was not yea and nay.
2: 1. come again unto *you* in heaviness.
  2. For if I make *you* sorry, who is he then
  3. having confidence in *you* all,
  4. which I have more abundantly unto *you*.
  5. that I may not overcharge *you* all.
  7. *ye* (ought) rather to forgive (him),
  8. Wherefore I beseech *you* that ye
  10. for *your* sakes (forgave I it) in the person of Christ ;
3: 1. epistles of commendation to *you*,
4:15. For all things (are) for *your* sakes,
6: 1. that *ye* receive not the grace of God in vain.
  11. our mouth is open unto *you*,
  17. and I will receive *you*,
7: 4. Great (is) my boldness of speech toward *you*,
  8. For though I made *you* sorry with a letter,
  — the same epistle hath made *you* sorry,
  11. that *ye* sorrowed after a godly sort,
  12. in the sight of God might appear unto *you*.
  15. is more abundant toward *you*,
8: 6. he would also finish in *you* the same
  9. yet for *your* sakes he became poor,
  17. of his own accord he went unto *you*.
  22. the great confidence which (I have) in *you*.
  23. and fellowhelper concerning *you* :
9: 4. and find *you* unprepared,
  5. that they would go before unto *you*,
  8. to make all grace abound toward *you* ;
  14. which long after *you* for the exceeding
10: 1. Now I Paul myself beseech *you*
  — being absent am bold toward *you* :
  9. as if I would terrify *you* by letters.
  14. as though we reached not unto *you* :
11: 2. For I am jealous over *you* with
  — I have espoused *you* to one husband,
  6. made manifest among *you* in all things.
  9(8). And when I was present with *you*,
  11. because I love *you* not?
  20. if a man bring *you* into bondage,
  — if a man smite *you* on the face.
12:14. I am ready to come to *you* ;
  — for I seek not your's, but *you* :
  15. though the more abundantly I love *you*,
  16. But be it so, I did not burden *you* :
  — being crafty, I caught *you* with guile.
  17. Did I make a gain of *you* by any of them whom I sent unto *you* ?
  18. Did Titus make a gain of *you* ?
  20. I shall not find *you* such as I would,
  21. my God will humble me among *you*

2Co.13: 1. I am coming to *you*.
  3. which to *you*-ward is not weak,
  4. by the power of God toward *you*.
  7. I pray to God that *ye* do no evil ;
  13(12). All the saints salute *you*.
Gal. 1: 6. removed from him that called *you*
  7. there be some that trouble *you*,
  9. preach any other gospel unto *you*
2: 5. of the gospel might continue with *you*.
3: 1. who hath bewitched *you*,
4:11. I am afraid of *you*, lest I have bestowed upon *you* labour in vain.
  17. They zealously affect *you*, (but) not well ; yea, they would exclude *you*,
  18. when I am present with *you*.
  20. to be present with *you* now,
5: 2. Christ shall profit *you* nothing.
  7. who did hinder *you* that ye should not
  8. (cometh) not of him that calleth *you*.
  10. I have confidence in *you* through the Lord,
  — but he that troubleth *you* shall bear
  12. were even cut off which trouble *you*.
6:12. they constrain *you* to be circumcised ;
  13. but desire to have *you* circumcised,
Eph 1:15. after I heard of *your* faith
  18. that *ye* may know what is the hope
2: 1. And *you* (hath he quickened), who were dead
3: 2. which is given me to *you*-ward :
4: 1. beseech *you* that ye walk worthy
  17. that *ye* henceforth walk not
  22. That *ye* put off concerning the former
5: 6. Let no man deceive *you* with vain
6:11. that *ye* may be able to stand
  22. Whom I have sent unto *you*
Phi. 1: 7. because I have *you* in my heart ;
  — *ye* all are partakers of my grace.
  8. how greatly I long after *you* all
  10. That *ye* may approve things that
  12. But I would *ye* should understand,
  24. in the flesh (is) more needful for *you*.
  26. by my coming to *you* again.
  27. that whether I come and see *you*,
2:25. to send to *you* Epaphroditus,
  26. For he longed after *you* all,
4:21. which are with me greet *you*.
  22. All the saints salute *you*,
Col. 1: 6. Which is come unto *you*,...and bringeth
  10. That *ye* might walk worthy of the Lord
  21. And *you*, that were sometime alienated
  22. to present *you* holy and unblameable,
  25. which is given to me for *you*, to fulfil
2: 1. For I would that *ye* knew what
  4. beguile *you* with enticing words.
  8. Beware lest any man spoil *you*
  13. And *you*, being dead in your sins
  16. Let no man therefore judge *you*
  18. Let no man beguile *you* of your reward
4: 6. how *ye* ought to answer every man.
  8. Whom I have sent unto *you*
  10. my fellowprisoner saluteth *you*,
  — if he come unto *you*, receive him ;
  12. a servant of Christ, saluteth *you*,
  14. the beloved physician, and Demas, greet *you*.
1Th. 1: 5. came not unto *you* in word only,
  — we were among you for *your* sake.
  7. So that *ye* were ensamples
  9. manner of entering in we had unto *you*,
2: 1. know our entrance in unto *you*,
  2. to speak unto *you* tne gospel of God
  9. we preached unto *you* the gospel

1Th. 2:11. and charged every one of *you*,
12. That *ye* would walk worthy of God, who hath called *you* unto his kingdom
18. we would have come unto *you*,
3: 2. to establish *you*, and to comfort *you* concerning your faith:
4. verily, when we were with *you*,
5. the tempter have tempted *you*,
6. as we also (to see) *you*:
9. wherewith we joy for *your* sakes
11. direct our way unto *you*.
12. the Lord make *you* to increase and
— even as we (do) toward *you*:
4: 1. we beseech *you*, brethren, and exhort
— how *ye* ought to walk
3. that *ye* should abstain from
10. but we beseech *you*, brethren, that *ye*
13. I would not have *you* to be ignorant,
5: 4. should overtake *you* as a thief.
12. And we beseech *you*, brethren, to know
— over you in the Lord, and admonish *you*;
14. Now we exhort *you*, brethren, warn
18. will of God in Christ Jesus concerning *you*.
23. God of peace sanctify *you* wholly;
24. Faithful (is) he that calleth *you*,
27. I charge *you* by the Lord that this
2Th. 1: 5. that *ye* may be counted worthy
6. to them that trouble *you*;
10. because our testimony among *you* was
11. that our God would count *you* worthy
2: 1. Now we beseech *you*, brethren, by the
2. That *ye* be not soon shaken in mind,
3. Let no man deceive *you*
5. when I was yet with *you*, I told
13. God hath from the beginning chosen *you*
14. Whereunto he called *you* by our gospel,
17. and stablish *you* in every good word
3: 1. and be glorified, even as (it is) with *you*:
3. is faithful, who shall stablish *you*,
4. have confidence in the Lord touching *you*,
6. that *ye* withdraw yourselves from every
10. For even when we were with *you*,
Heb 5:12. ye have need that one teach *you* again
9:20. which God hath injoined unto *you*.
13:21. Make *you* perfect in every good work
22. And I beseech *you*, brethren, suffer
23. if he come shortly, I will see *you*.
24. They of Italy salute *you*.
Jas. 2: 6. and draw *you* before the judgment seats?
7. by the which *ye* are called?
4: 2. ye have not, because *ye* ask not.
10. and he shall lift *you* up.
15. For that *ye* (ought) to say,
1Pet.1: 4. reserved in heaven for *you*,
10. of the grace (that should come) unto *you*:
12. that have preached the gospel unto *you*
15. as he which hath called *you* is holy,
20. manifest in these last times for *you*,
25. by the gospel is preached unto *you*.
2: 9. who hath called *you* out of darkness
3:13. who (is) he that will harm *you*,
15. to every man that asketh *you*
4:14. of glory and of God resteth upon *you*:
— but on *your* part he is glorified.
5: 6. that he may exalt *you* in due time:
10. make *you* perfect, stablish, strengthen,
13. elected together with (you), saluteth *you*;
2Pet.1:12. to put *you* always in remembrance
13. to stir *you* up by putting (you)
15. I will endeavour that *ye* may be able
2: 3. make merchandise of *you*:

2Pet.3: 8. But, beloved, be not)(ignorant of
11. what manner (of persons) ought *ye* to be
1Joh.2:26. concerning them that seduce *you*.
27. ye need not that any man teach *you*: but as the same anointing teacheth *you*
— and even as it hath taught *you*,
3: 7. Little children, let no man deceive *you*:
13. if the world hate *you*.
2Joh. 10. If there come any unto *you*,
12. but I trust to come unto *you*,
Jude 5. I will therefore put *you* in remembrance, though *ye* once knew. this,
24. able to keep *you* from falling,
Rev. 2:24. I will put upon *you* none other burden.
12:12. the devil is come down unto *you*, having great wrath, because

Note.—Some editions have given ἥμας as in Gal. 4:17, 1 Pet. 1:4, &c. Some copies read αὐτούς.

ὑμεῖς, humīs.
From σύ.

Mat. 5:13. *Ye* are the salt of the earth:
14. *Ye* are the light of the world.
48. Be *ye* therefore perfect,
6: 9. After this manner therefore pray *ye*:
26. Are *ye* not much better than they?
7:11. If *ye* then, being evil, know how
12. do *ye* even so to them:
9: 4. Wherefore think *ye* evil in your hearts?
10:20. For it is not *ye* that speak,
31. *ye* are of more value than many
13:18. Hear *ye* therefore the parable
14:16. They need not depart; give *ye* them to eat.
15: 3. do *ye* also transgress the commandment
5. But *ye* say, Whosoever shall say to
16. Are *ye* also yet without understanding?
16:15. But whom say *ye* that I am?
19:28. That *ye* which have followed me,
— *ye* also shall sit upon twelve thrones,
20: 4. Go *ye* also into the vineyard, and
7. Go *ye* also into the vineyard; and
21:13. but *ye* have made it a den of thieves.
32. and *ye*, when ye had seen (it),
23: 8. But be not *ye* called Rabbi: for one
— and all *ye* are brethren.
13. for *ye* neither go in (yourselves),
28. Even so *ye* also outwardly appear
32. Fill *ye* up then the measure of your
24:33. So likewise *ye*, when ye shall see all
44. Therefore be *ye* also ready:
26:31. All *ye* shall be offended because of me
27:24. of this just person: see *ye* (to it).
28: 5. Fear not *ye*: for I know that ye seek
Mar 6:31. Come *ye* yourselves apart into a
37. and said unto them, Give *ye* them to eat.
7:11. But *ye* say, If a man shall say to
18. Are *ye* so without understanding also?
8:29. But whom say *ye* that I am?
11:17. but *ye* have made it a den of thieves.
26. But if *ye* do not forgive, neither
12:27. *ye* therefore do greatly err.
13: 9. But take)(heed to yourselves:
11. for it is not *ye* that speak,
23. But take *ye* heed: behold, I have
29. So *ye* in like manner, when ye
Lu. 6:31. do to you, do *ye* also to them likewise.
9:13. said unto them, Give *ye* them to eat.
20. But whom say *ye* that I am?

Lu. 9:44. Let these sayings sink down (lit. put ye these sayings) into your ears:

55. what manner of spirit ye are of.

10:23. which see the things that ye see:

24. to see those things which ye see,

11:13. If ye then, being evil, know how to

39. Now ᴜo ye Pharisees make clean

48. and ye build their sepulchres.

12:24. much more are ye better than the fowls?

29. And seek not ye what ye shall eat,

36. And ye yourselves like unto men

40. Be ye therefore ready also:

16:15. Ye are they which justify yourselves

17:10. So likewise ye, when ye shall have done

19:46. but ye have made it a den of thieves.

21:31. So likewise ye, when ye see these

22:26. But ye (shall) not (be) so: but he that

28. Ye are they which have continued

70. Ye say that I am.

24:48. And ye are witnesses of these things.

49. but tarry ye in the city of Jerusalem,

Joh. 1:26. one among you, whom ye know not;

3:28. Ye yourselves bear me witness,

4:20. and ye say, that in Jerusalem

22. Ye worship ye know not what:

32. meat to eat that ye know not of.

35. Say not ye, There are yet four months,

38. whereon ye bestowed no labour:

— and ye are entered into their labours.

5:20. than these, that ye may marvel.

33. Ye sent unto John, and he bare

34. that ye might be saved.

35. and ye were willing for a season

38. him ye believe not.

39. for in them ye think ye have eternal life:

44. How can ye believe, which receive

45. Moses, in whom ye trust.

6:67. Will ye also go away?

7: 8. Go ye up unto this feast:

28. is true, whom ye know not.

34. where I am, (thither) ye cannot come.

36. where I am, (thither) ye cannot come?

47. Are ye also deceived?

8:14. but ye cannot tell whence I come,

15. Ye judge after the flesh; I judge

21. whither I go, ye cannot come.

22. Whither I go, ye cannot come.

23. Ye are from beneath; I am from

— ye are of this world; I am not of this

31. If ye continue in my word,

38. and ye do that which ye have seen

41. Ye do the deeds of your father.

44. Ye are of (your) father the devil,

46. why do ye not believe me?

47. ye therefore hear (them) not,

49. and ye do dishonour me.

54. of whom ye say, that he is your God:

9:19. who ye say was born blind?

27. will ye also be his disciples?

30. that ye know not from whence he is,

10:26. But ye believe not, because ye are not

36. Say ye of him, whom the Father

11:49. Ye know nothing at all,

13:10. and ye are clean, but not all.

13. Ye call me Master and Lord:

14. ye also ought to wash one another's

15. that ye should do as I have done

33. Whither I go, ye cannot come;

34. that ye also love one another.

14: 3. where I am, (there) ye may be also.

17. but ye know him; for he dwelleth

19. but ye see me: because I live, ye shall

Joh. 14:20. At that day ye shall know that I (am) in my Father, and ye in me, and I in you.

15: 3. Now ye are clean through the word

4. no more can ye, except ye abide in me.

5. I am the vine, ye (are) the branches:

14. Ye are my friends, if ye do whatsoever

16. Ye have not chosen me, but I have

— that ye should go and bring forth fruit,

27. And ye also shall bear witness,

16:20. That ye shall weep and lament, but

— and ye shall be sorrowful, but

22. And ye now therefore have sorrow:

27. because ye have loved me, and have

18:31. Take ye him, and judge him

19: 6. Take ye him, and crucify (him):

35. he saith true, that ye might believe.

Acts 1: 5. but ye shall be baptized with the

2:15. not drunken, as ye suppose, seeing it is

33. which ye now see and hear.

36. that same Jesus, whom ye have crucified,

3:13. whom ye delivered up, and denied

14. But ye denied the Holy One

25. Ye are the children of the prophets,

4: 7. by what name, have ye done this?

10. whom ye crucified, whom God raised

5:30. whom ye slew and hanged on a

7: 4. into this land, wherein ye now dwell.

26. Sirs, ye are brethren; why do

51. ye do always resist the Holy Ghost: as your fathers (did), so (do) ye.

52. of whom ye have been now the betrayers

8:24. Pray ye to the Lord for me,

10:28. Ye know how that it is an unlawful

37. That word, (I say), ye know, which was

11:16. but ye shall be baptized with the Holy

15: 7. ye know how that a good while ago

19:15. and Paul I know; but who are ye?

20:18. Ye know, from the first day that I came

25. I know that ye all, among whom I

22: 3. zealous toward God, as ye all are this day.

23:15. Now therefore ye with the council

27:31. abide in the ship, ye cannot be saved.

Ro. 1: 6. Among whom are ye also the called of

6:11. Likewise reckon ye also yourselves to

7: 4. ye also are become dead to the law

8: 9. But ye are not in the flesh,

9:26. Ye (are) not my people;

11:30. For as ye in times past have not

16:17. the doctrine which ye have learned;

1Co. 1:30. But of him are ye in Christ Jesus,

3:17. the temple of God is holy, which (temple) ye are.

23. And ye are Christ's; and Christ (is)

4:10. but ye (are) wise in Christ; we (are) weak, but ye (are) strong; ye (are) honourable, but we (are) despised.

5: 2. And ye are puffed up, and have not

12. do not ye judge them that are within?

6: 8. Nay, ye do wrong, and defraud,

9: 1. are not ye my work in the Lord?

2. the seal of mine apostleship are ye

10:15. judge ye what I say.

12:27. Now ye are the body of Christ, and

14: 9. So likewise ye, except ye utter by

12. Even so ye, forasmuch as ye are zealous

16: 1. to the churches of Galatia, even so do ye.

6. that ye may bring me on my journey

16. That ye submit yourselves unto such,

2Co. 1:14. even as ye also (are) our's in the day

3: 2. Ye are our epistle written in our hearts,

6:13. be ye also enlarged.

16. for ye are the temple of the living God;

2Co. 6:18. and *ye* shall be my sons and daughters,
  8: 9. that *ye* through his poverty
  9: 4. that we say not, *ye*
  11: 7. abasing myself that *ye* might be exalted,
  12:11. *ye* have compelled me:
  13: 7. but that *ye* should do that which
   9. when we are weak, and *ye* are strong:
Gal. 3:28. for *ye* are all one in Christ Jesus.
  29. And if *ye* (be) Christ's, then are ye
  4:12. be as I (am); for I (am) as *ye* (are):
  5:13. *ye* have been called unto liberty ;
  6: 1. *ye* which are spiritual, restore such
Eph. 1:13. In whom *ye* also (trusted), after that
  2:11. that *ye* (being) in time past Gentiles
  13. *ye* who sometimes were far off
  22. In whom *ye* also are builded together
  4:20. But *ye* have not so learned Christ ;
  5:33. let every one of *you* in particular
  6:21. But that *ye* also may know my
Phi. 2:18. For the same cause also do *ye* joy,
  4:15. Now *ye* Philippians know also,
  — concerning giving and receiving, but *ye* only.
Col. 3: 4. then shall *ye* also appear with him
  7. In the which *ye* also walked some time,
  8. But now *ye* also put off all these ;
  13. as Christ forgave you, so also (do) *ye*.
  4: 1. knowing that *ye* also have a Master
  16. and that *ye* likewise read the (epistle)
1Th. 1: 6. And *ye* became followers of us,
  2:10. *Ye* (are) witnesses, and God (also),
  14. For *ye*, brethren, became followers
  — for *ye* also have suffered like things
  19. (Are) not even *ye* in the presence of our
  20. For *ye* are our glory and joy.
  3: 8. if *ye* stand fast in the Lord.
  4: 9. for *ye* yourselves are taught of God
  5: 4. But *ye*, brethren, are not in darkness,
  5. *Ye* are all the children of light,
2Th. 1:12. be glorified in you, and *ye* in him,
  3:13. But *ye*, brethren, be not weary
Jas. 2: 6. But *ye* have despised the poor.
  5: 8. Be *ye* also patient; stablish your hearts:
1Pet.2: 9. But *ye* (are) a chosen generation,
  4: 1. arm)(yourselves likewise with the same mind:
2Pet.3:17. *Ye* therefore, beloved, seeing ye know
1Joh.1: 3. that *ye* also may have fellowship with us:
  2:20. But *ye* have an unction from the Holy One,
  24. Let that therefore abide in you, (lit. *ye* therefore let abide in you that which)
  — *ye* also shall continue in the Son,
  27. But the anointing which ye have received (lit. And *ye*, the anointing which, &c.)
  4: 4. *Ye* are of God, little children, and
Jude   17. beloved, remember *ye* the words which
  20. But *ye*, beloved, building up yourselves

ὑμέτερος, *humeteros.*

Lu. 6:20. for *your's* is the kingdom of God.
  16:12. who shall give you that which is *your own* ?
Joh. 7: 6. but *your* time is alway ready.
  8:17. It is also written in *your* law,
  15:20. kept my saying, they will keep *your's* also.
Acts27:34. meat: for this is for *your* health:
Ro. 11:31. not believed, that through *your* mercy they also (lit. have not believed *your* mercy, i. e. the mercy *to* you,)
1Co.15:31. I protest by *your* rejoicing which

2Co. 8: 8. to prove the sincerity of *your* love.
Gal. 6:13. that they may glory in *your* flesh.

ὑμῖν, *humin.*

From σύ.

Mat. 3: 7. who hath warned *you* to flee
  9. for I say unto *you*, that God is able
  5:18. For verily I say unto *you*, Till heaven
  20. For I say unto *you*, That except your
  22. But I say unto *you*, That whosoever
  28. But I say unto *you*, That whosoever
  32. But I say unto *you*, That whosoever
  34. But I say unto *you*, Swear not
  39. But I say unto *you*, That ye
  44. But I say unto *you*, Love your
  6: 2. Verily I say unto *you*, They have their
  5. Verily I say unto *you*, They have their
  14. your heavenly Father will also forgive *you*:
  16. Verily I say unto *you*, They have their
  19. Lay not up for *yourselves* treasures
  20. But lay up for *yourselves* treasures in
  25. Therefore I say unto *you*, Take no thought
  29. And yet I say unto *you*, That even
  33. all these things shall be added unto *you*.
  7: 2. it shall be measured to *you* again.
  7. Ask, and it shall be given *you*; seek,
  — knock, and it shall be opened unto *you:*
  12. ye would that men should do to *you*,
  8:10. Verily I say unto *you*, I have not found
  11. And I say unto *you*, That many shall come
  9:29. According to your faith be it unto *you*.
  10:15. Verily I say unto *you*, It shall be
  19. for it shall be given *you* in that same
  20. of your Father which speaketh in *you*.
  23. for verily I say unto *you*,
  27. What I tell *you* in darkness,
  42. verily I say unto *you*,
  11: 9. I say unto *you*, and more than a prophet.
  11. Verily I say unto *you*,
  17. We have piped unto *you*,
  — we have mourned unto *you*,
  21. which were done in *you*, had been
  22. But I say unto *you*, It shall be
  — at the day of judgment, than for *you*.
  24. But I say unto *you*, That it shall be
  12: 6. But I say unto *you*, That in this place
  31. Wherefore I say unto *you*,
  36. But I say unto *you*, That every
  13:11. Because it is given unto *you* to know
  17. For verily I say unto *you*,
  16:11. I spake (it) not to *you* concerning bread,
  28. Verily I say unto *you*, There be some
  17:12. But I say unto *you*, That Elias is
  20. for verily I say unto *you*,
  — nothing shall be impossible unto *you*.
  18: 3. And said, Verily I say unto *you*,
  10. for I say unto *you*, That in heaven
  12. How think *ye* ? if a man have an hundred
  13. verily I say unto *you*, he rejoiceth
  18. Verily I say unto *you*, Whatsoever
  19. Again I say unto *you*, That if two
  35. my heavenly Father do also unto *you*,
  19: 8. suffered *you* to put away your wives:
  9. And I say unto *you*, Whosoever shall
  23. Verily I say unto *you*, That a rich man
  24. And again I say unto *you*, It is easier
  28. Verily I say unto *you*, That ye which
  20: 4. whatsoever is right I will give *you*.
  26. it shall not be so among *you:* but whosoever will be great among *you*,

Mat.20:27. whosoever will be chief among *you*,
 32. What will ye that I shall do unto *you?*
21: 3. And if any (man) say ought unto *you*,
 21. Verily I say unto *you*, If ye have faith,
 24. I in like wise will tell *you*
 27. Neither tell I *you* by what authority
 28. But what think *ye?* A (certain) man
 31. Verily I say unto *you*, That the publicans
 43. Therefore say I unto *you*, The kingdom
22:31. which was spoken unto *you* by God,
 42. What think *ye* of Christ?
23: 3. whatsoever they bid *you* observe,
 13. But woe unto *you*, scribes and Pharisees,
 14. Woe unto *you*, scribes and Pharisees,
 15. Woe unto *you*, scribes and Pharisees,
 16. Woe unto *you*, (ye) blind guides,
 23. Woe unto *you*, scribes and
 25. Woe unto *you*, scribes and
 27. Woe unto *you*, scribes and
 29. Woe unto *you*, scribes and
 36. Verily I say unto *you*, All these things
 38. your house is left unto *you* desolate.
 39. For I say unto *you*, Ye shall not see
24: 2. verily I say unto *you*, There shall
 23. if any man shall say unto *you*,
 25. Behold, I have told *you* before.
 26. if they shall say unto *you*,
 34. Verily I say unto *you*, This generation
 47. Verily I say unto *you*, That he shall
25: 9. there be not enough for us and *you*:
 12. Verily I say unto *you*, I know you not.
 34. inherit the kingdom prepared for *you*
 40. Verily I say unto *you*, Inasmuch as
 45. Verily I say unto *you*, Inasmuch as
26:13. Verily I say unto *you*, Wheresoever
 15. and I will deliver him unto *you?*
 21. Verily I say unto *you*, that one of you
 29. But I say unto *you*, I will not drink
 64. nevertheless I say unto *you*,
 66. What think *ye?* They answered and
27:17. Whom will ye that I release unto *you?*
 21. will ye that I release unto *you?*
28: 7. there shall ye see him: lo, I have told *you.*
 20. whatsoever I have commanded *you*:
Mar 3:28. Verily I say unto *you*, All sins shall be
4:11. Unto *you* it is given to know the mystery
 24. it shall be measured to *you*: and unto *you*
  that hear shall more be given.
6:11. Verily I say unto *you*, It shall be
8:12. verily I say unto *you*, There shall no
9: 1. Verily I say unto *you*, That there
 13. But I say unto *you*, That Elias is indeed
 41. verily I say unto *you*, he shall not lose
10: 3. What did Moses command *you?*
 5. he wrote *you* this precept.
 15. Verily I say unto *you*, Whosoever
 29. Verily I say unto *you*, There is no man
 36. What would ye that I should do for *you?*
 43. But so shall it not be among *you*: but
  whosoever will be great among *you*,
11: 3. And if any man say unto *you*,
 23. For verily I say unto *you*, That
 24. Therefore I say unto *you*, What things
 — receive (them), and *ye* shall have (them).
 25. may forgive *you* your trespasses.
 29. and I will tell *you* by what authority
 33. Neither do I tell *you* by what authority
12:43. Verily I say unto *you*, That this poor
  widow
13:11. whatsoever shall be given *you* in that hour,
 21. if any man shall say to *you*, Lo,
 23. I have foretold *you* all things.

Mar 13:30. Verily I say unto *you*, that this generation
 37. And what I say unto *you* I say unto all,
14: 9. Verily I say unto *you*, Wheresoever
 13. and there shall meet *you* a man
 15. And he will shew *you* a large upper room
 18. Verily I say unto *you*, One of you
 25. Verily I say unto *you*, I will drink
 64. have heard the blasphemy: what think *ye?*
15: 9. Will ye that I release unto *you*
16: 7. there shall ye see him, as he said unto *you.*
Lu. 2:10. I bring *you* good tidings of great joy,
 11. For unto *you* is born this day in
 12. And this (shall be) a sign unto *you;*
3: 7. who hath warned *you* to flee from the
 8. for I say unto *you*, That God is able
 13. than that which is appointed *you.*
4:24. Verily I say unto *you*, No prophet
 25. But I tell *you* of a truth, many
6:24. But woe unto *you* that are rich!
 25. Woe unto *you* that are full!
 — Woe unto *you* that laugh now!
 26. Woe unto *you*, when all men shall
 27. But I say unto *you* which hear,
 28. Bless them that curse *you*,
 31. that men should do to *you*,
 32. what thank have *ye?*
 33. what thank have *ye?*
 34. what thank have *ye?*
 38. and it shall be given unto *you;*
 — it shall be measured to *you* again.
 47. I will shew *you* to whom he is like:
7: 9. I say unto *you*, I have not found
 26. Yea, I say unto *you*, and much more
 28. For I say unto *you*, Among those that
 32. We have piped unto *you*,
 — we have mourned to *you*,
8:10. Unto *you* it is given to know the mysteries
9:27. But I tell *you* of a truth,
 48. for he that is least among *you* all,
10: 8. eat such things as are set before *you*:
 11. we do wipe off against *you*:
 12. But I say unto *you*, that it shall be
 13. which have been done in *you*,
 14. at the judgment, than for *you.*
 19. Behold, I give unto *you* power
 20. that the spirits are subject unto *you;*
 24. For I tell *you*, that many prophets
11: 8. I say unto *you*, Though he will not rise
 9. And I say unto *you*, Ask, and it shall be
  given *you;*
 — knock, and it shall be opened unto *you.*
 41. all things are clean unto *you.*
 42. But woe unto *you*, Pharisees!
 43. Woe unto *you*, Pharisees! for ye
 44. Woe unto *you*, scribes and Pharisees,
 46. Woe unto *you* also, (ye) lawyers!
 47. Woe unto *you!* for ye build the sepulchres
 51. verily I say unto *you*, It shall be required
 52. Woe unto *you*, lawyers! for ye have taken
  away
12: 4. And I say unto *you* my friends,
 5. But I will forewarn *you* whom ye shall
  fear:
 — yea, I say unto *you*, Fear him.
 8. Also I say unto *you*, Whosoever
 22. Therefore I say unto *you*, Take no thought
 27. and yet I say unto *you*, that Solomon
 31. these things shall be added unto *you.*
 32. pleasure to give *you* the kingdom.
 37. verily I say unto *you*, that he shall gird
 44. Of a truth I say unto *you*,
 51. I tell *you*, Nay; but rather division:

Lu. 13: 3. I tell *you*, Nay: but, except
     5. I tell *you*, Nay: but, except
   24. for many, I say unto *you*, will seek
   25. he shall answer and say unto *you*,
   27. I tell *you*, I know you not whence ye are ;
   35. your house is left unto *you* desolate: and
       verily I say unto *you*,
14:24. For I say unto *you*, That none of those
       men
15: 7. I say unto *you*, that likewise joy shall be
   10. Likewise, I say unto *you*, there is joy
16: 9. And I say unto *you*, Make to yourselves
   11. who will commit to *your* trust the true
   12. who shall give *you* that which is your
       own ?
17: 6. and it should obey *you*.
   10. those things which are commanded *you*,
   23. And they shall say to *you*, See here ;
   34. I tell *you*, in that night there shall be
18: 8. I tell *you* that he will avenge them
   14. I tell *you*, this man went down to his
   17. Verily I say unto *you*, Whosoever
   29. Verily I say unto *you*, There is no man
19:26. For I say unto *you*, That unto every one
   40. I tell *you* that, if these should hold
20: 8. Neither tell I *you* by what authority
21: 3. Of a truth I say unto *you*, that this poor
       widow hath cast in more
   13. And it shall turn to *you* for a testimony.
   15. For I will give *you* a mouth and wisdom,
       which all *your* adversaries shall not
   32. Verily I say unto *you*, This generation
22:10. there shall a man meet *you*,
   12. And he shall shew *you* a large upper room
   16. For I say unto *you*, I will not any more
   18. For I say unto *you*, I will not drink
   26. but he that is greatest among *you*,
   29. And I appoint unto *you* a kingdom,
   37. I say unto *you*, that this that is written
   67. If I tell *you*, ye will not believe:
24: 6. remember how he spake unto *you*
   36. saith unto them, Peace (be) unto *you*.
   44. while I was yet with *you*,
Joh. 1:51(52). Verily, verily, I say unto *you*,
 2: 5. Whatsoever he saith unto *you*, do (it).
 3:12. If I have told *you* earthly things,
   — if I tell *you* (of) heavenly things?
 4:35. behold, I say unto *you*, Lift up
 5:19. Verily, verily, I say unto *you*,
   24. Verily, verily, I say unto *you*,
   25. Verily, verily, I say unto *you*,
   38. ye have not his word abiding in *you*:
 6:26. Verily, verily, I say unto *you*,
   27. which the Son of man shall give unto *you*:
   32. Verily, verily, I say unto *you*, Moses gave
     you not that bread from heaven ; but
     my Father giveth *you* the true bread
   36. But I said unto *you*, That ye also
   47. Verily, verily, I say unto *you*,
   53. Verily, verily, I say unto *you*,
   63. the words that I speak unto *you*,
   65. Therefore said I unto *you*,
 7:19. Did not Moses give *you* the law,
   22. Moses therefore gave unto *you* circum-
     cision ;
 8:24. I said therefore unto *you*,
   25. that I said unto *you* from the beginning.
   34. Verily, verily, I say unto *you*,
   37. because my word hath no place in *you*.
   40. a man that hath told *you* the truth,
   51. Verily, verily, I say unto *you*,
   58. Verily, verily, I say unto *you*,

Joh. 9:27. I have told *you* already,
10: 1. Verily, verily, I say unto *you*,
   7. Verily, verily, I say unto *you*,
   25. I told *you*, and ye believed not:
   26. ye are not of my sheep, as I said unto *you*.
   32. works have I shewed *you* from my Father
11:56. What think *ye*, that he will not come
12:24. Verily, verily, I say unto *you*,
13:12. Know ye what I have done to *you* ?
   15. For I have given *you* an example, that ye
      should do as I have done to *you*.
   16. Verily, verily, I say unto *you*,
   19. Now I tell *you* before it come,
   20. Verily, verily, I say unto *you*,
   21. Verily, verily, I say unto *you*,
   33. so now I say to *you*.
   34. A new commandment I give unto *you*,
14: 2. if (it were) not (so), I would have told
     you. I go to prepare a place for *you*.
   3. and prepare a place for *you*,
   10. the words that I speak unto *you*
   12. Verily, verily, I say unto *you*,
   16. and he shall give *you* another Comforter,
   17. for he dwelleth with *you*, and shall be in
     you.
   20. and ye in me, and I in *you*.
   25. spoken unto *you*, being (yet) present with
     you.
   26. whatsoever I have said unto *you*.
   27. Peace I leave with *you*, my peace I give
     unto *you*: not as the world giveth, give
     I unto *you*.
   28. Ye have heard how I said unto *you*,
   29. And now I have told *you* before
15: 3. which I have spoken unto *you*.
   4. Abide in me, and I in *you*.
   7. and my words abide in *you*,
   — and it shall be done unto *you*.
   11. These things have I spoken unto *you*, that
     my joy might remain in *you*, (lit. that
     my joy in *you* might remain)
   14. whatsoever I command *you*.
   15. I have made known unto *you*.
   16. the Father in my name, he may give it *you*.
   17. These things I command *you*,
   20. the word that I said unto *you*,
   21. But all these things will they do unto *you*
   26. whom I will send unto *you* from
16: 1. These things have I spoken unto *you*,
   3. these things will they do unto *you*,
   4. But these things have I told *you*,
   — ye may remember that I told *you* of them.
     And these things I said not unto *you* at
   6. because I have said these things unto *you*,
   7. Nevertheless I tell *you* the truth ; It is
     expedient for *you* that I go away:
   12. I have yet many things to say unto *you*,
   13. he will shew *you* things to come.
   14. and shall shew (it) unto *you*.
   15. and shall shew (it) unto *you*.
   20. Verily, verily, I say unto *you*,
   23. verily, I say unto *you*, Whatsoever ye shall
     ask the Father in my name, he will give
     (it) *you*.
   25. have I spoken unto *you* in proverbs:
   — no more speak unto *you* in proverbs, but I
     shall shew *you* plainly of the Father.
   26. and I say not unto *you*, that I
   33. These things I have spoken unto *you*,
18: 8. I have told *you* that I am (he):
   39. But *ye* have a custom, that I should release
     unto *you* one

Joh. 18:39. that I release unto *you*
  19: 4. Behold, I bring him forth to *you*,
  20:19. Peace (be) unto *you*.
  21. Peace (be) unto *you:*
  26. Peace (be) unto *you*.
Acts 2:14. be this known unto *you*,
  39. For the promise is unto *you*,
  3:14. a murderer to be granted unto *you ;*
  20. which before was preached unto *you:*
  22. the Lord your God raise up unto *you*
  26. Unto *you* first God, having raised up
  4:10. Be it known unto *you* all, and to
  5: 9. that ye have agreed together (lit. that it hath been agreed together by *you*)
  28. Did not we straitly command *you*
  38. And now I say unto *you*,
  7:37. the Lord your God raise up unto *you*
  13:15. if *ye* have any word of exhortation
  26. whosoever among *you* feareth God, to *you* is the word of this salvation sent.
  34. I will give *you* the sure mercies
  38. Be it known unto *you* therefore,
  — that through this man is preached unto *you*
  41. though a man declare it unto *you*.
  46. first have been spoken to *you :*
  14:15. men of like passions with *you*,
  15:28. to lay upon *you* no greater burden
  17: 3. whom I preach unto *you*, is Christ.
  23. him declare I unto *you*.
  20:20. but have shewed *you*, and have taught
  26. Wherefore I take *you* to record
  27. I have not shunned to declare unto *you*
  32. and to give *you* an inheritance
  35. I have shewed *you* all things,
  22:25. Is it lawful for *you* to scourge a man
  25: 5. which among *you* are able,
  26: 8. be thought a thing incredible with *you*
  28:28. Be it known therefore unto *you*,
Ro. 1: 7. Grace to *you* and peace from God
  11. that I may impart unto *you* some
  12. be comforted together with *you* by
  13. I might have some fruit among *you* also,
  15. am ready to preach the gospel to *you*
  8: 9. that the Spirit of God dwell in *you*.
  10. And if Christ (be) in *you*,
  11. if the Spirit of him that raised up Jesus from the dead dwell in *you*,
  — by his Spirit that dwelleth in *you*.
  11:13. For I speak to *you* Gentiles, inasmuch
  12: 3. to every man that is among *you*,
  15: 5. grant *you* to be likeminded
  15. I have written the more boldly unto *you*
  32. and may with *you* be refreshed.
  16: 1. I commend unto *you* Phebe our sister,
  19. I am glad therefore on *your* behalf:
1Co. 1: 3. Grace (be) unto *you,* and peace,
  4. which is given *you* by Jesus Christ ;
  6. the testimony of Christ was confirmed in *you :*
  10. and (that) there be no divisions among *you ;*
  11. that there are contentions among *you*.
  2: 1. declaring unto *you* the testimony of God.
  2. to know any thing among *you*,
  3: 1. speak unto *you* as unto spiritual,
  3. for whereas (there is) among *you* envying,
  16. the Spirit of God dwelleth in *you ?*
  18. If any man among *you* seemeth to be
  4: 8. that we also might reign with *you*.
  17. have I sent unto *you* Timotheus,
  5: 1. (that there is) fornication among *you*,

1Co. 5: 9. I wrote unto *you* in an epistle
  11. But now I have written unto *you*
  6: 2. and if the world shall be judged by *you*,
  5. I speak to *your* shame. Is it so, that there is not a wise man among *you ?*
  7. there is utterly a fault among *you*,
  19. temple of the Holy Ghost (which is) in *you*,
  7:35. may cast a snare upon *you*,
  9: 2. yet doubtless I am to *you :*
  11. If we have sown unto *you* spiritual
  10:27. whatsoever is set before *you*,
  28. But if any man say unto *you*,
  11: 2. as I delivered (them) to *you*.
  13. Judge in *yourselves*: Is it comely
  18. there be divisions among *you ;*
  19. there must be also heresies among *you*,
  — be made manifest among *you*.
  22. What shall I say to *you ?*
  23. which also I delivered unto *you*,
  30. many (are) weak and sickly among *you*,
  12: 3. Wherefore I give *you* to understand,
  31. and yet shew I unto *you*
  14: 6. except I shall speak to *you* either by
  25. that God is in *you* of a truth.
  37. the things that I write unto *you*
  15: 1. I declare unto *you* the gospel which I preached unto *you*,
  2. what I preached unto *you*,
  3. For I delivered unto *you* first of all
  12. how say some among *you* that
  34. I speak (this) to *your* shame.
  51. Behold, I shew *you* a mystery ;
2Co. 1: 2. Grace (be) to *you* and peace
  13. we write none other things unto *you*,
  19. who was preached among *you* by us,
  21. which stablisheth us with *you* in Christ,
  2: 3. And I wrote this same unto *you*,
  4. I wrote unto *you* with many tears ;
  4:12. death worketh in us, but life in *you*.
  14. and shall present (us) with *you*.
  5:12. we commend not ourselves again unto *you*, but give *you* occasion to glory on our behalf,
  13. whether we be sober, (it is) for *your* cause.
  6:18. And will be a Father unto *you*,
  7: 7. wherewith he was comforted in *you*,
  11. what carefulness it wrought in *you*,
  12. Wherefore, though I wrote unto *you*,
  14. we spake all things to *you* in truth,
  16. that I have confidence in *you* in all (things).
  8: 1. we do *you* to wit of the grace of God
  10. for this is expedient for *you*,
  13. other men be eased, and ye burdened: (lit. burden to *you*)
  9: 1. superfluous for me to write to *you:*
  14. the exceeding grace of God in *you*.
  10: 1. in presence (am) base among *you*,
  15. that we shall be enlarged by *you* (lit. magnified in *you*)
  11: 7. because I have preached to *you* the
  9. from being burdensome unto *you*,
  12:12. wrought among *you* in all patience,
  19. that we excuse ourselves unto *you ?*
  20. I shall be found unto *you* such
  13: 3. but is mighty in *you*.
  5. how that Jesus Christ is in *you*,
Gal. 1: 3. Grace (be) to *you* and peace from
  8. preach any other gospel unto *you* than that which we have preached unto *you*,
  11. But I certify *you*, brethren,

Gal. 1:20. the things which I write unto *you*,
3: 1. evidently set forth, crucified among *you*?
5. that ministereth to *you* the Spirit, and worketh miracles among *you*,
4:13. I preached the gospel unto *you*
15. for I bear *you* record, that, if
16. because I tell *you* the truth?
19. again until Christ be formed in *you*,
20. for I stand in doubt of *you*.
5: 2. Behold, I Paul say unto *you*,
21. of the which I tell *you* before,
6:11. I have written unto *you* with mine own hand.
Eph 1: 2. Grace (be) to *you*, and peace, from
17. may give unto *you* the spirit of wisdom
2:17. and preached peace to *you* which were
3:16. That he would grant *you*, according
4: 6. and through all, and in *you* all.
32. for Christ's sake hath forgiven *you*.
5: 3. not be once named among *you*,
6:21. shall make known to *you* all things:
Phi. 1: 2. Grace (be) unto *you*, and peace,
6. hath begun a good work in *you*
25. and continue with *you* all
28. but to *you* of salvation, and that of God.
29. For unto *you* it is given in the behalf
2: 5. Let this mind be in *you*, which was also
13. which worketh in *you* both to will
17. I joy, and rejoice with *you* all.
19. to send Timotheus shortly unto *you*,
3: 1. To write the same things to *you*, to me indeed (is) not grievous, but for *you* (it is) safe.
15. God shall reveal even this unto *you*.
18. of whom I have told *you* often,
Col. 1: 2. Grace (be) unto *you*, and peace, from
5. For the hope which is laid up for *you*
6. as (it doth) also in *you*, since the day
27. which is Christ in *you*, the hope of glory:
2: 5. yet am I with *you* in the spirit,
13. having forgiven *you* all trespasses;
3:13. even as Christ forgave *you*, so also (do)
16. dwell in *you* richly in all wisdom;
4: 7. shall Tychicus declare unto *you*,
9. They shall make known to *you*
16. And when this epistle is read among *you*,
1Th. 1: 1. Grace (be) unto *you*, and peace,
5. we were among *you* for your sake.
2: 8. willing to have imparted unto *you*,
10. we behaved ourselves among *you* that
13. worketh also in *you* that believe.
3: 4. we told *you* before that we should
7. we were comforted over *you* in all
4: 2. what commandments we gave *you*
6. as we also have forewarned *you*
9. ye need not that I write unto *you*:
11. as we commanded *you*;
15. For this we say unto *you* by the word
5: 1. ye have no need that I write unto *you*.
12. them which labour among *you*,
2Th. 1: 2. Grace unto *you*, and peace,
4. So that we ourselves glory in *you*
7. And to *you* who are troubled rest with us,
12. may be glorified in *you*,
2: 5. I told *you* these things?
3: 4. the things which we command *you*.
6. Now we command *you*, brethren,
7. ourselves disorderly among *you*;
9. an ensample unto *you* to follow us.
10. this we commanded *you*, that if any
11. which walk among *you* disorderly,
16. give *you* peace always by all means.

Philem. 3. Grace to *you*, and peace, from God
6. which is in *you* in Christ Jesus.
22. I shall be given unto *you*.
Heb 12: 5. which speaketh unto *you* as unto children,
7. God dealeth with *you* as with sons;
13: 7. who have spoken unto *you* the word of God:
17. for that (is) unprofitable for *you*.
19. that I may be restored to *you* the sooner.
21. working in *you* that which is wellpleasing
22. written a letter unto *you* in few words.
Jas. 1:26. If any man among *you* seem to be
3:13. and endued with knowledge among *you*?
4: 1. wars and fightings among *you*?
8. and he will draw nigh to *you*.
5: 3. shall be a witness against *you*,
6. (and) he doth not resist *you*.
13. Is any among *you* afflicted?
14. Is any sick among *you*?
19. if any of *you* do err from the truth,
1Pet.1: 2. Grace unto *you*, and peace,
12. which are now reported unto *you* by
13. the grace that is to be brought unto *you*
2: 7. Unto *you* therefore which believe (he is)
3:15. a reason of the hope that is in *you*
4:12. think it not strange concerning the fiery trial which is to try *you* (lit. among *you* for trial to *you*), as though some strange thing happened unto *you*:
5: 1. The elders which are among *you*
2. the flock of God which is among *you*,
12. By Sylvanus, a faithful brother unto *you*,
14. Peace (be) with *you* all that are in Christ Jesus.
2Pet. 1: 2. Grace and peace be multiplied unto *you*
8. For if these things be in *you*,
11. an entrance shall be ministered unto *you* abundantly into
16. when we made known unto *you*
2: 1. there shall be false teachers among *you*,
13. while they feast with *you*;
3: 1. beloved, I now write unto *you*;
15. hath written unto *you*;
1Joh.1: 2. and shew unto *you* that eternal life,
3. and heard declare we unto *you*,
4. And these things write we unto *you*,
5. and declare unto *you*, that God is light,
2: 1. these things write I unto *you*,
7. I write no new commandment unto *you*,
8. a new commandment I write unto *you*, which thing is true in him and in *you*:
12. I write unto *you*, little children, because your sins are forgiven *you*.
13. I write unto *you*, fathers, because
— I write unto *you*, young men, because
— I write unto *you*, little children,
14. I have written unto *you*, fathers,
— I have written unto *you*, young men,
— and the word of God abideth in *you*,
21. I have not written unto *you* because
— from the beginning shall remain in *you*,
26. These (things) have I written unto *you*
27. received of him abideth in *you*,
4: 4. greater is he that is in *you*, than he that is in
5:13. These things have I written unto *you*
2Joh. 12. Having many things to write unto *you*,
Jude 2. Mercy unto *you*, and peace, and love,
3. diligence to write unto *you* of the common salvation, it was needful for me to write unto *you*,

Jude 18. How that they told *you* there should be
Rev. 1: 4. Grace (be) unto *you*, and peace,
2:13. martyr, who was slain among *you*,
23. and I will give unto every one of *you*
24. But unto *you* I say, and unto the rest in
18: 6. Reward her even as she rewarded *you*,
22:16. I Jesus have sent mine angel to testify
unto *you* these things

ὑμνέω, *humneo.*

Mat 26:30. And *when they had sung an hymn,*
Mar 14:26. And *when they had sung an hymn,*
Acts 16:25. and *sang praises unto* God:
Heb 2:12. *will* I *sing praise unto* thee.

ὕμνος, *humnos.*

Eph. 5:19. in psalms and *hymns* and spiritual
Col. 3:16. in psalms and *hymns* and spiritual

ὑμῶν, *humōn.*

From σύ.

Note.—"Of you" is the literal rendering of this
word, instead of "your," and is frequently
more strict to the point.

Mat. 5:11. say all manner of evil against *you*
12. for great (is) *your* reward in heaven:
— the prophets which were before *you*.
16. Let *your* light so shine before men, that
they may see *your* good works, and glorify *your* Father which is
20. That except *your* righteousness
37. But let *your* communication be,
44. Love *your* enemies, bless them
45. be the children of *your* Father
47. And if ye salute *your* brethren only,
48. even as *your* Father which is in heaven
6: 1. ye do not *your* alms before men,
— otherwise ye have no reward of *your* Father
8. for *your* Father knoweth what things
14. *your* heavenly Father will also forgive
you:
15. neither will *your* Father forgive *your* trespasses.
21. For where *your* treasure is, there will *your*
heart be also.
25. Take no thought for *your* life,
— nor yet for *your* body,
26. yet *your* heavenly Father feedeth them.
27. Which of *you* by taking thought
32. for *your* heavenly Father knoweth
7: 6. neither cast ye *your* pearls before swine,
9. Or what man is there of *you*, whom if his
11. to give good gifts unto *your* children,
— how much more shall *your* Father
9: 4. Wherefore think ye evil in *your* hearts?
11. Why eateth *your* Master with publicans
29. According to *your* faith be it unto you.
10: 9. nor silver, nor brass in *your* purses,
13. let *your* peace come upon it:
— let *your* peace return to you.
14. receive you, nor hear *your* words,
— shake off the dust of *your* feet.
20. but the Spirit of *your* Father which
speaketh

Mat.10:29. fall on the ground without *your* Father.
30. But the very hairs of *your* head are
11:29. and ye shall find rest unto *your* souls.
12:11. What man shall there be among *you*,
27. by whom do *your* children cast
— therefore they shall be *your* judges.
13:16. But blessed (are) *your* eyes, for they see:
and *your* ears, for they hear.
15: 3. the commandment of God by *your* tradition?
6. of none effect by *your* tradition.
7. well did Esaias prophesy of *you*,
17:17. how long shall I be with *you?* how long
shall I suffer *you?*
20. Because of *your* unbelief:
24. Doth not *your* master pay tribute?
18:14. it is not the will of *your* Father
19. That if two of *you* shall agree
35. if ye from *your* hearts forgive not
19: 8. because of the hardness of *your* hearts
suffered you to put away *your* wives:
20:26. let him be *your* minister;
27. let him be *your* servant:
21: 2. into the village over against *you*,
43. shall be taken from *you*,
23: 8. for one is *your* Master, (even) Christ;
9. And call no (man) *your* father upon the
earth: for one is *your* Father,
10. for one is *your* Master, (even) Christ.
11. But he that is greatest among *you* shall
be *your* servant.
15. more the child of hell than *yourselves*.
32. Fill ye up then the measure of *your* fathers.
34. shall ye scourge in *your* synagogues,
38. *your* house is left unto you desolate.
24:20. But pray ye that *your* flight be not
42. what hour *your* Lord doth come.
25: 8. Give us of *your* oil; for our lamps
26:21. that one of *you* shall betray me.
29. when I drink it new with *you* in
28:20. and, lo, I am with *you* alway,
Mar 2: 8. Why reason ye these things in *your* hearts?
6:11. shall not receive you, nor hear *you*,
— shake off the dust under *your* feet for
7: 6. Esaias prophesied of *you* hypocrites,
9. that ye may keep *your own* tradition.
13. of none effect through *your* tradition,
8:17. have ye *your* heart yet hardened?
9:19. how long shall I suffer *you?*
10: 5. For the hardness of *your* heart he wrote
43. shall be *your* minister:
44. And whosoever of *you* will be the chiefest,
11: 2. into the village over against *you:*
25. that *your* Father also which is in heaven
may forgive you *your* trespasses.
26. neither will *your* Father which is in heaven
forgive *your* trespasses.
13:18. And pray ye that *your* flight be not
14:18. One of *you* which eateth with me
Lu. 3:14. and be content with *your* wages.
4:21. is this scripture fulfilled in *your* ears.
5: 4. and let down *your* nets for a draught.
22. What reason ye in *your* hearts?
6:22. and cast out *your* name as evil,
23. *your* reward (is) great in heaven:
24. ye have received *your* consolation.
27. Love *your* enemies, do good to them
35. But love ye *your* enemies,
— and *your* reward shall be great,
36. as *your* Father also is merciful.
38. shall men give into *your* bosom.
8:25. Where is *your* faith? And they

Lu. 9: 5. shake off the very dust from *your* feet
41. shall I be with you, and suffer *you?*
44. Let these sayings sink down into *your* ears:
10: 6. *your* peace shall rest upon it:
11. Even the very dust of *your* city, which
16. He that heareth *you* heareth me ;
20. because *your* names are written in heaven.
11: 5. Which of *you* shall have a friend,
11. of any of *you* that is a father,
13. to give good gifts unto *your* children:
19. by whom do *your* sons cast (them) out ?
— therefore shall they be *your* judges.
39. but *your* inward part is full of ravening
46. the burdens with one of *your* fingers.
47. and *your* fathers killed them.
48. that ye allow the deeds of *your* fathers:
12: 7. hairs of *your* head are all numbered.
22. Take no thought for *your* life,
25. And which of *you* with taking thought
30. and *your* Father knoweth that ye have need
32. for it is *your* Father's good pleasure
33. Sell that *ye* have, and give alms ;
34. For where *your* treasure is, there will *your* heart be also.
35. Let *your* loins be girded about,
13:15. doth not each one of *you* on the sabbath
35. *your* house is left unto you desolate:
14: 5. Which of *you* shall have an ass
28. For which of *you*, intending to build
33. whosoever he be of *you* that forsaketh not
15: 4. What man of *you*, having an hundred
16:15. but God knoweth *your* hearts:
26. between us and *you* there is a great gulf
17: 7. But which of *you*, having a servant
21. the kingdom of God is within *you*.
21:14. Settle (it) therefore in *your* hearts,
16. and (some) of *you* shall they cause
18. there shall not an hair of *your* head perish.
19. In *your* patience possess ye *your* souls.
28. lift up *your* heads; for *your* redemption draweth nigh.
34. *your* hearts be overcharged with surfeiting,
22:10. when *ye* are entered into the city,
15. to eat this passover with *you* before
19. my body which is given for *you:*
20. in my blood, which is shed for you.
27. I am among *you* as he that serveth.
53. When I was daily with *you* in the temple,
— but this is *your* hour, and the power
23:14. I, having examined (him) before *you*,
28. for yourselves, and for *your* children.
24:38. why do thoughts arise in *your* hearts?
Joh. 1:26. there standeth one among *you*,
4:35. Lift up *your* eyes, and look on
5:45. that I will accuse *you* to the Father: there is (one) that accuseth *you*,
6:49. *Your* fathers did eat manna
58. not as *your* fathers did eat manna,
64. there are some of *you* that believe not.
70. and one of *you* is a devil ?
7:19. and (yet) none of *you* keepeth the law ?
33. Yet a little while am I with *you*,
8: 7. He that is without sin among *you*,
21. and shall die in *your* sins:
24. that ye shall die in *your* sins:
— ye shall die in *your* sins.
26. many things to say, and to judge of *you:*
38. which ye have seen with *your* father.
41. Ye do the deeds of *your* father.
42. If God were *your* Father, ye would love me:

Joh. 8:44. and the lusts of *your* father ye will do.
46. Which of *you* convinceth me of sin?
54. of whom ye say, that he is *your* God:
55. I shall be a liar like unto *you:*
56. *Your* Father Abraham rejoiced to see
9:19. Is this *your* son, who ye say was
41. therefore *your* sin remaineth.
10:34. Is it not written in *your* law,
12:35. little while is the light with *you*.
13:14. have washed *your* feet; ye also ought
18. I speak not of *you* all: I know whom
21. that one of *you* shall betray me.
33. yet a little while I am with *you*.
14: 1. Let not *your* heart be troubled:
9. Have I been so long time with *you*,
16. that he may abide with *you* for ever;
27. Let not *your* heart be troubled,
30. I will not talk much with *you:*
15:11. and (that) *your* joy might be full.
16. and (that) *your* fruit should remain:
18. it hated me before (it hated) *you*.
16: 4. because I was with *you*.
5. and none of *you* asketh me,
6. sorrow hath filled *your* heart.
20. but *your* sorrow shall be turned into joy.
22. and *your* heart shall rejoice, and *your* joy no man taketh from *you*.
24. that *your* joy may be full.
26. that I will pray the Father for *you:*
18:31. and judge him according to *your* law.
19:14. he saith unto the Jews, Behold *your* King !
15. Shall I crucify *your* King?
20:17. I ascend unto my Father, and *your* Father; and (to) my God, and *your* God.
Acts 1: 7. It is not for *you* to know the times
11. which is taken up from *you* into
2:17. and *your* sons and *your* daughters shall prophesy, and *your* young men shall see visions, and *your* old men shall
22. God did by him in the midst of *you*,
38. and be baptized every one of *you*
39. is unto you, and to *your* children,
3:16. in the presence of *you* all.
17. ye did (it), as (did) also *your* rulers.
19. that *your* sins may be blotted out,
22. A prophet shall the Lord *your* God raise up unto you of *your* brethren,
26. in turning away every one of you from his iniquities. (lit. from *your* iniquities)
4:10. stand here before *you* whole.
11. set at nought of *you* builders,
19. to hearken unto *you* more than
5:28. filled Jerusalem with *your* doctrine,
6: 3. among *you* seven men of honest report,
7:37. shall the Lord *your* God raise up unto you of *your* brethren,
43. and the star of *your* god Remphan,
51. as *your* fathers (did), so (do) ye.
52. have not *your* fathers persecuted?
13:41. for I work a work in *your* days,
15:24. subverting *your* souls, saying,
17:23. and beheld *your* devotions,
18: 6. *Your* blood (be) upon *your* own heads ;
14. that I should bear with *you:*
19:37. nor yet blasphemers of *your* goddess.
20:18. I have been with *you* at all seasons,
30. Also of *your* own selves shall men arise,
24:21. I am called in question by *you* this day.
25:26. I have brought him forth before *you*,
27:22. no loss of (any man's) life among *you*,
34. fall from the head of any of *you*.

Ro. 1: 8. through Jesus Christ for *you* all, that *your* faith is spoken of throughout
9. without ceasing I make mention of *you*
12. the mutual faith both of *you* and me.
6:12. reign in *your* mortal body,
13. Neither yield ye *your* members
— and *your* members (as) instruments
14. For sin shall not have dominion over *you:*
19. because of the infirmity of *your* flesh: for as ye have yielded *your* members
— even so now yield *your* members
22. ye have *your* fruit unto holiness,
8:11. shall also quicken *your* mortal bodies
12: 1. that ye present *your* bodies a living sacrifice,
— (which is) *your* reasonable service.
2. by the renewing of *your* mind,
18. as much as lieth in *you,*
14:16. Let not then *your* good be evil spoken of:
15:14. I myself also am persuaded of *you,*
24. brought on my way thitherward by *you,* if first I be somewhat filled with *your* (company).
28. I will come by *you* into Spain.
33. Now the God of peace (be) with *you* all.
16: 2. in whatsoever business she hath need of *you:*
19. For *your* obedience is come abroad
20. bruise Satan under *your* feet shortly. The grace of our Lord Jesus Christ (be) with *you.*
24. The grace of our Lord Jesus Christ (be) with *you* all.
1Co. 1: 4. I thank my God always on *your* behalf,
11. it hath been declared unto me of *you,*
12. that every one of *you* saith, I am of
13. was Paul crucified for *you?*
14. I baptized none of *you,* but Crispus and
26. For ye see *your* calling, brethren,
2: 5. That *your* faith should not stand
3:21. For all things are *your's;*
22. or things to come; all are *your's;*
4: 3. that I should be judged of *you,*
5: 2. might be taken away from among *you.*
4. when *ye* are gathered together,
6. *Your* glorying (is) not good.
13. Therefore put away from among *yourselves*
6: 1. Dare any of *you,* having a matter
15. that *your* bodies are the members of Christ?
19. that *your* body is the temple of the
20. therefore glorify God in *your* body, and in *your* spirit, which are God's.
7: 5. tempt you not for *your* incontinency.
14. else were *your* children unclean;
28. but I spare *you.*
35. And this I speak for *your* own profit;
8: 9. liberty of *your's* become a stumblingblock
9:11. if we shall reap *your* carnal things?
12. be partakers of (this) power over *you,*
11:18. when *ye* come together in the church,
20. When *ye* come together therefore
24. my body, which is broken for *you:*
12:21. to the feet, I have no need of *you.*
14:18. I speak with tongues more than *ye* all:
26. every one of *you* hath a psalm,
34. Let *your* women keep silence in the
36. came the word of God out from *you?*
15:14. and *your* faith (is) also vain.
17. *your* faith (is) vain; ye are yet in *your* sins.

1Co.15:58. that *your* labour is not in vain in the Lord.
16: 2. let every one of *you* lay by him in store,
3. them will I send to bring *your* liberality
14. Let all *your* things be done with charity.
17. for that which was lacking on *your* part
18. they have refreshed my spirit and *your's:*
23. The grace of our Lord Jesus Christ (be) with *you.*
24. My love (be) with *you* all in Christ Jesus.
2Co. 1: 6. (it is) for *your* consolation and salvation,
— (it is) for *your* consolation and
7(6). And our hope of *you* (is) stedfast,
11. *Ye* also helping toge her by prayer
14. that we are *your* rejoicing, even as ye
16. And to pass by *you* into Macedonia,
— and of *you* to be brought on my way
23. that to spare *you* I came not as yet
24. that we have dominion over *your* faith, but are helpers of *your* joy:
2: 3. that my joy is (the joy) of *you* all.
9. that I might know the proof of *you,*
3: 1. or (letters) of commendation from *you?*
4: 5. ourselves *your* servants for Jesus' sake.
5:11. are made manifest in *your* consciences.
6:12. but ye are straitened in *your* own bowels.
7: 4. great (is) my glorying of *you:*
7. *your* earnest desire, *your* mourning, *your* fervent mind toward me;
12. but that our care for *you* [many copies read, " *your* care for us"]
13. we were comforted in *your* comfort:
— his spirit was refreshed by. *you* all.
14. if I have boasted any thing to him of *you,*
15. he remembereth the obedience of *you* all,
8: 7. and (in) *your* love to us, (see) that
14(13). now at this time *your* abundance
— may be (a supply) for *your* want:
16. care into the heart of Titus for *you.*
19. and (declaration of) *your* ready mind:
24. the proof of *your* love, and of our boasting on *your* behalf.
9: 2. For I know the forwardness of *your* mind, for which I boast of *you* to them of
— and *your* zeal hath provoked very many.
3. lest our boasting of *you* should be in vain
5. and make up beforehand *your* bounty,
10. and multiply *your* seed sown, and increase the fruits of *your* righteousness;
13. for *your* professed subjection unto
14. And by their prayer for *you,*
10: 6. when *your* obedience is fulfilled.
8. and not for *your* destruction,
13. a measure to reach even unto *you.*
14. for we are come as far as to *you* also
15. when *your* faith is increased,
16. the gospel in the (regions) beyond *you,*
11: 3. so *your* minds should be corrupted
8. taking wages (of them), to do *you* service.
12:11. for I ought to have been commended of *you:*
13. was not burdensome to *you?*
14. and I will not be burdensome to *you:* for I seek not *your's,* but you:
15. gladly spend and be spent for *you;* (lit. for *your* souls)
19. dearly beloved, for *your* edifying.
13: 9. this also we wish, (even) *your* perfection.
11. the God of love and peace shall be with *you.*
14(13). (be) with *you* all. Amen.
Gal. 3: 2. This only would I learn of *you,*
4: 6. the Spirit of his Son into *your* hearts,

Gal. 4:12. Brethren, I beseech *you*, be as I (am);
15. Where is then the blessedness *ye* spake of?
(lit. *your* blessedness)
— would have plucked out *your* own eyes,
16. Am I therefore become *your* enemy,
6:18. (be) with *your* spirit. Amen.
Eph. 1:13. the gospel of *your* salvation:
16. Cease not to give thanks for *you*, making mention of *you* in my prayers;
18. The eyes of *your* understanding being
2: 8. and that not of *yourselves* : (it is) the gift
3: 1. the prisoner of Jesus Christ for *you* Gentiles,
13. faint not at my tribulations for *you*, which is *your* glory.
17. That Christ may dwell in *your* hearts
4: 4. ye are called in one hope of *your* calling;
23. And be renewed in the spirit of *your* mind;
26. sun go down upon *your* wrath:
29. proceed out of *your* mouth,
31. be put away from *you*, with all malice:
5:19. and making melody in *your* heart to
6: 1. Children, obey *your* parents in the Lord:
4. provoke not *your* children to wrath:
5. in singleness of *your* heart, as unto Christ;
9. knowing that *your* Master also is in heaven;
14. having *your* loins girt about with truth,
22. and (that) he might comfort *your* hearts.
Phi. 1: 3. upon every remembrance of *you*,
4. in every prayer of mine for *you* all
5. For *your* fellowship in the gospel
7. meet for me to think this of *you* all,
9. that *your* love may abound yet more
19. to my salvation through *your* prayer,
25. for *your* furtherance and joy of faith;
26. That *your* rejoicing may be more abundant
27. I may hear of *your* affairs,
2:17. and service of *your* faith,
19. of good comfort, when I know *your* state.
20. who will naturally care for *your* state.
25. and fellowsoldier, but *your* messenger,
30. to supply *your* lack of service toward me.
4: 5. Let . *your* moderation be known unto all men.
6. let *your* requests be made known unto God.
7. shall keep *your* hearts and minds through Christ Jesus.
9. and the God of peace shall be with *you*.
17. fruit that may abound to *your* account.
18. the things (which were sent) from *you*,
19. my God shall supply all *your* need
23. The grace of our Lord Jesus Christ (be) with *you* all.
Col. 1: 3. praying always for *you*,
4. Since we heard of *your* faith
7. who is for *you* a faithful minister
8. unto us *your* love in the Spirit.
9. do not cease to pray for *you*,
24. Who now rejoice in my sufferings for *you*,
2: 1. what great conflict I have for *you*,
5. joying and beholding *your* order, and the stedfastness of *your* faith
13. and the uncircumcision of *your* flesh,
3: 3. and *your* life is hid with Christ in God.
5. Mortify therefore *your* members
8. filthy communication out of *your* mouth.
15. let the peace of God rule in *your* hearts,
16. singing with grace in *your* hearts
21. Fathers, provoke not *your* children
4: 6. Let *your* speech (be) alway with grace,
8. that he might know *your* estate, and comfort *your* hearts;

Col. 4: 9. and beloved brother, who is (one) of *you*.
12. Epaphras, who is (one) of *you*, a servant of
— always labouring fervently for *you* in
13. that he hath a great zeal for *you*,
18. Grace (be) with *you*. Amen.
1Th. 1: 2. We give thanks to God always for *you* all, making mention of *you* in our prayers;
3. *your* work of faith, and labour of love,
4. Knowing, brethren beloved, *your* election
8. For from *you* sounded out the word
— *your* faith to God-ward is spread abroad;
2: 6. glory, neither of *you*, nor (yet) of others,
7. But we were gentle among *you*,
8. So being affectionately desirous of *you*,
9. be chargeable unto any of *you*,
11. and charged every one of *you*,
17. being taken from *you* for a short time
— to see *your* face with great desire.
3: 2. to comfort you concerning *your* faith:
5. I sent to know *your* faith,
6. when Timotheus came from *you* unto us, and brought us good tidings of *your* faith and charity,
7. in all our affliction and distress by *your* faith:
9. can we render to God again for *you*,
10. that we might see *your* face,
— that which is lacking in *your* faith?
13. he may stablish *your* hearts unblameable
4: 3. is the will of God, (even) *your* sanctification,
4. That every one of *you* should know how
11. and to work with *your* own hands,
5:12. and are over *you* in the Lord,
23. the very God of peace sanctify *you* wholly;
28. The grace of our Lord Jesus Christ (be) with *you*.
2Th. 1: 3. to thank God always for *you*,
— that *your* faith groweth exceedingly, and the charity of every one of *you* all
4. for *your* patience and faith in all *your* persecutions and tribulations
11. also we pray always for *you*,
2:13. to give thanks alway to God for *you*,
17. Comfort *your* hearts, and stablish
3: 5. And the Lord direct *your* hearts
8. not be chargeable to any of *you* :
16. The Lord (be) with *you* all.
18. The grace of our Lord Jesus Christ (be) with *you* all.
2Ti. 4:22. Grace (be) with *you*. Amen.
Tit. 2: 8. having no evil thing to say of *you*.
3:15. Grace (be) with *you* all. Amen.
Philem 22. I trust that through *your* prayers
25. (be) with *your* spirit. Amen.
Heb 3: 8. Harden not *your* hearts, as in
9. When *your* fathers tempted me,
12. lest there be in any of *you*
13. lest any of *you* be hardened
15. harden not *your* hearts, as in
4: 1. any of *you* should seem to come short of it.
7. harden not *your* hearts.
6: 9. persuaded better things of *you*,
10. unrighteous to forget *your* work
11. we desire that every one of *you* do shew
9:14. purge *your* conscience from dead works
10:34. the spoiling of *your* goods,
35. Cast not away therefore *your* confidence,
12: 3. and faint in *your* minds.
13. And make straight paths for *your* feet,
13: 7. which have the rule over *you*,

Heb 13:17. Obey them that have the rule over *you*,
— for they watch for *your* souls,
24. all them that have the rule over *you*,
25. Grace (be) with *you* all. Amen.

Jas. 1: 3. that the trying of *your* faith worketh
5. If any of *you* lack wisdom,
21. which is able to save *your* souls.
2: 2. if there come unto *your* assembly
6. Do not rich men oppress *you*, and
16. And one of *you* say unto them,
3:14. envying and strife in *your* hearts,
4: 1. of *your* lusts that war in *your* members?
3. ye may consume (it) upon *your* lusts.
7. and he will flee from *you*.
9. let *your* laughter be turned to mourning,
14. For what (is) *your* life? It is even a vapour,
16. now ye rejoice in *your* boastings:
5: 1. for *your* miseries that shall come
2. *Your* riches are corrupted, and *your* garments are motheaten.
3. *Your* gold and silver is cankered;
— and shall eat *your* flesh as it were fire.
4. who have reaped down *your* fields, which is of *you* kept back by fraud,
5. ye have nourished *your* hearts, as in
8. stablish *your* hearts: for the coming
12. but let *your* yea be yea;

1Pet.1: 7. That the trial of *your* faith,
9. Receiving the end of *your* faith,
13. gird up the loins of *your* mind,
14. to the former lusts in *your* ignorance:
17. pass the time of *your* sojourning (here)
18. from *your* vain conversation
21. that *your* faith and hope might be in God.
22. Seeing ye have purified *your* souls
2:12. Having *your* conversation honest among
— whereas they speak against *you*
25. unto the Shepherd and Bishop of *your*
3: 2. While they behold *your* chaste conversation
7. that *your* prayers be not hindered.
15. sanctify the Lord God in *your* hearts:
16. whereas they speak evil of *you*,
— *your* good conversation in Christ.
4: 4. that *ye* run not with (them) to
15. But let none of *you* suffer as
5: 7. Casting all *your* care upon him; for he careth for *you*.
8. because *your* adversary the devil,
9. are accomplished in *your* brethren

2Pet.1: 5. add to *your* faith virtue;
10. to make *your* calling and election
19. the day star arise in *your* hearts:
3: 1. I stir up *your* pure minds by way of

1Joh.1: 4. that *your* joy may be full. [some copies, "*our* joy"]

2Joh. 3. Grace be with *you*, [some copies "with *us*"]

Jude 12. These are spots in *your* feasts of charity,
20. building up yourselves on *your* most holy faith,

Rev. 1: 9. I John, who also am *your* brother,
2:10. shall cast (some) of *you* into prison,
23. unto every one of you according to *your* works.
18:20. for God hath avenged *you* (lit. judged *your* judgment)
22:21. The grace of our Lord Jesus Christ (be) with *you* all.

ὑπάγω, *hupago*.

Mat. 4:10. *Get* thee *hence*, Satan: for it is written,

Mat. 5:24. thy gift before the altar, and *go* thy *way*;
41. to go a mile, *go* with him twain.
8: 4. but *go* thy *way*, shew thyself to the priest,
13. *Go* thy *way*; and as thou hast believed,
32. And he said unto them, *Go*. And
9: 6. thy bed, and *go* unto thine house.
13:44. and for joy thereof *goeth* and selleth
16:23. unto Peter, *Get* thee behind me, Satan:
18:15. *go* and tell him his fault between thee
19:21. *go* (and) sell that thou hast, and give
20: 4. *Go* ye also into the vineyard,
7. *Go* ye also into the vineyard;
14. Take (that) thine (is), and *go* thy *way*:
21:28. Son, *go* work to day in my vineyard.
26:18. *Go* into the city to such a man,
24. The Son of man *goeth* as it is written
27:65. Ye have a watch: *go* your *way*,
28:10. Be not afraid: *go* tell my brethren
Mar 1:44. but *go* thy *way*, shew thyself to the priest,
2:11. and *go* thy *way* into thine house.
5:19. *Go* home to thy friends, and tell them
34. *go* in peace, and be whole of thy plague.
6:31. there were many coming and *going*,
33. And the people saw them *departing*,
38. How many loaves have ye? *go* and see.
7:29. For this saying *go* thy *way*; the devil
8:33. *Get* thee behind me, Satan: for thou
10:21. *go* thy *way*, sell whatsoever thou hast,
52. *Go* thy *way*; thy faith hath made thee whole.
11: 2. *Go* your *way* into the village over
14:13. *Go* ye into the city, and there shall meet
21. The Son of man indeed *goeth*,
16: 7. But *go* your *way*, tell his disciples
Lu. 4: 8. *Get* thee behind me, Satan: for it is written,
8:42. But as he *went* the people thronged him.
10: 3. *Go* your *ways*: behold, I send you
12:58. When thou *goest* with thine adversary
17:14. as they *went*, they were cleansed.
19:30. *Go* ye into the village over against (you);
Joh. 3: 8. tell whence it cometh, and whither it *goeth*:
4:16. *Go*, call thy husband, and come hither.
6:21. was at the land whither they *went*.
67. Will ye also *go away*?
7: 3. Depart hence, and *go* into Judæa,
33. and (then) I *go* unto him that sent me.
8:14. whence I came, and whither I *go*;
— whence I come, and whither I *go*.
21. I *go* my *way*, and ye shall seek me,
— whither I *go*, ye cannot come.
22. Whither I *go*, ye cannot come.
9: 7. *Go*, wash in the pool of Siloam,
11. *Go* to the pool of Siloam, and wash.
11: 8. and *goest* thou thither again?
31. She *goeth* unto the grave to weep there.
44. Loose him, and let him *go*.
12:11. by reason of him many of the Jews *went* away, and believed on Jesus.
35. knoweth not whither he *goeth*.
13: 3. that he was come from God, and *went* to God;
33. Whither I *go*, ye cannot come;
36. Lord, whither *goest* thou?
— Whither I *go*, thou canst not follow me now;
14: 4. And whither I *go* ye know, and the way
5. Lord, we know not whither thou *goest*;
28. I *go away*, and come (again) unto you.
15:16. that ye should *go* and bring forth fruit,

Joh.16: 5. I *go* my *way* to him that sent me; and
none of you asketh me, Whither *goest*
thou?
10. because I *go* to my Father,
16. because I *go* to the Father.
17. and, Because I *go* to the Father?
18: 8. if therefore ye seek me, let these *go* their
way:
21: 3. Simon Peter saith unto them, I *go* a
fishing.
Jas. 2:16. say unto them, *Depart* in peace,
1Joh.2:11. and knoweth not whither he *goeth*
Rev.10: 8. *Go* (and) take the little book which
13:10. into captivity shall *go* into captivity:
14: 4. follow the Lamb whithersoever he *goeth*.
16: 1. *Go* your *ways*, and pour out the vials
17: 8. shall ascend out of the bottomless pit, and
go into perdition:
11. and *goeth* into perdition.

ὑπακοή, *hupakoee.*

Ro. 1: 5. for *obedience* to the faith among all nations,
5:19. so by the *obedience* of one shall many
6:16. ye yield yourselves servants to *obey*,
— or of *obedience* unto righteousness?
15:18. to make the Gentiles obedient, (lit. for
obedience of the Gentiles)
16:19. For your *obedience* is come abroad
26. to all nations for the *obedience* of faith:
2Co. 7:15. whilst he remembereth the *obedience* of
you all, how with fear
10: 5. every thought to the *obedience* of Christ;
6. to revenge all disobedience, when your
obedience is fulfilled.
Philem 21. Having confidence in thy *obedience*
Heb. 5: 8. yet learned he *obedience* by the things
which
1Pet. 1: 2. unto *obedience* and sprinkling of the blood
of Jesus Christ:
14. As *obedient* children, not fashioning
22. Seeing ye have purified your souls in *obeying* the truth (lit. through *obedience* of
the truth)

ὑπακούω, *hupakouo.*

Mat. 8:27. the winds and the sea *obey* him!
Mar 1:27. and they do *obey* him.
4:41. the wind and the sea *obey* him?
Lu. 8:25. and water, and they *obey* him.
17: 6. planted in the sea; and it should *obey* you.
Acts 6: 7. a great company of the priests were *obedient* to the faith.
12:13. a damsel came *to hearken*, (lit. *to answer*)
Ro. 6:12. that ye should *obey* it in the lusts
16. his servants ye are to whom ye *obey*;
17. but ye have *obeyed* from the heart that
form of doctrine
10:16. But they *have* not all *obeyed* the gospel.
Eph. 6: 1. Children, *obey* your parents in the Lord:
5. Servants, *be obedient to* them that are
Phi. 2:12. my beloved, as ye *have* always *obeyed*,
Col. 3:20. Children, *obey* (your) parents in all things:
22. Servants, *obey* in all things (your) masters
2Th. 1: 8. on them that know not God, and *that
obey* not the gospel of
3:14. And if any man *obey* not our word
Heb. 5: 9. salvation unto all them *that obey* him;
11: 8. *obeyed*; and he went out, not knowing

1Pet. 3: 6. Even as Sara *obeyed* Abraham, calling him
lord:

ὕπανδρος, *hupandros.*

Ro. 7: 2. For the woman *which hath an husband*

ὑπαντάω, *hupantao.*

Mat. 8:28. there *met* him two possessed with
Lu. 8:27. there *met* him out of the city a
Joh.11:20. *went and met* him: but Mary sat (still)
30′ was in that place where Martha *met* him.
12:18. For this cause the people also *met* him,

ὑπάντησις, *hupanteesis.*

Joh.12:13. and went forth to *meet* him,

ὕπαρξις, *huparxis.*

Acts 2:45. sold their possessions and *goods*, and parted
them to all
Heb 10:34. ye have in heaven a better and an enduring
substance.

ὑπάρχοντα, *huparkonta.*

The participle used as a substantive.

Mat.19:21. go (and) sell *that* thou *hast*,
24:47. make him ruler over all his *goods.*
25:14. and delivered unto them his *goods.*
Lu. 8: 3. ministered unto him of their *substance.*
11:21. his *goods* are in peace:
12:15. in the abundance of the *things which* he
possesseth.
33. Sell *that* ye *have*, and give alms;
44. make him ruler over all *that* he *hath.*
14:33. that forsaketh not all *that* he *hath,*
16: 1. that he had wasted his *goods.*
19: 8. Lord, the half of my *goods* I give to the
poor;
Acts 4:32. that ought of the *things* which he *possessed*
1Co.13: 3. though I bestow all my *goods* to feed
Heb 10:34. took joyfully the spoiling of your *goods,*

ὑπάρχω, *huparko.*

Lu. 7:25. and *live* delicately, are in kings' courts.
8:41. and he *was* a ruler of the synagogue:
9:48. for he *that is* least among you all,
11:13. If ye then, *being* evil, know how to give
16:14. the Pharisees also, *who were* covetous,
23. he lift up his eyes, *being* in torments,
23:50. a man named Joseph,)(a counsellor;
Acts 2:30. Therefore *being* a prophet, and knowing
3: 2. And a certain man)(lame from his
6. Silver and gold *have* I none; (lit. *is* not
to me)
4:34. Neither *was* there any among them that
lacked: for as many as *were* possessors
of lands
37. *Having* land (lit. land *being* to him),
sold (it),
5: 4. *was* it not in thine own power?
7:55. But he, *being* full of the Holy Ghost,

Acts 8:16. only they *were* baptized in the name of
   10:12. Wherein *were* all manner of fourfooted
   14: 8. *being* a cripple from his mother's womb,
   16: 3. that his father *was* a Greek.
     20. These men, *being* Jews, do exceedingly
       trouble
     37. us openly uncondemned, *being* Romans,
   17:24. *seeing that* he *is* Lord of heaven and
     27. though he *be* not far from every one of us:
     29. *Forasmuch* then *as* we *are* the offspring
       of God, we ought not
   19:36. ye ought *to be* quiet, and to do nothing
     40. there *being* no cause whereby we may give
   21:20. and they *are* all zealous of the law:
   22: 3. *and was* zealous toward God, as ye
   27:12. And *because* the haven *was* not commodious
     21. But after (lit. but there *being*) long absti-
       nence
     34. for this *is* for your health:
   28: 7. In the same quarters *were* possessions
     18. because there *was* no cause of death in me.
Ro. 4:19. when he *was* about an hundred years old,
1Co. 7:26. that this *is* good for the present distress,
   11: 7. *forasmuch as* he *is* the image and
     18. I hear that there *be* divisions among you;
   12:22. which seem *to be* more feeble,
2Co. 8:17. but *being* more forward, of his own accord
   12:16. *being* crafty, I caught you with guile.
Gal. 1:14. *being* more exceedingly zealous
   2:14. If thou, *being* a Jew, livest after the
Phi. 2: 6. Who, *being* in the form of God,
   3:20. For our conversation *is* in heaven;
Jas. 2:15. If a brother or sister *be* naked,
2Pet 1: 8. For *if* these things *be* in you, and abound,
   2:19. themselves *are* the servants of corruption:
   3:11. what manner (of persons) ought ye *to be*

     See also ὑπάρχοντα.

ὑπείκω, hupīko.

Heb 13:17. and *submit* your*selves :* for they watch

ὑπεναντίος, hupenantios.

Col. 2:14. which was *contrary* to us,
Heb 10:27. which shall devour the *adversaries.*

ὑπέρ, huper.

Governing a genitive case, except where ª is placed
to mark the accusative: and six elliptical passages, marked †.

Mat. 5:44. and pray *for* them which despitefully
   10:24. The disciple is not *above*ª (his) master,
       nor the servant *above*ª his lord.
     37. loveth father or mother *more than*ª me
   — loveth son or daughter *more than*ª me
Mar 9:40. that is not against us is *on our part.*
Lu. 6:28. and pray *for* them which despitefully
     40. The disciple is not *above*ª his master:
   9:50. that is not against us is *for* us.
   16: 8. wiser *than*ª the children of light.
   22:19. my body which is given *for* you:
     20. my blood, which is shed *for* you.
Joh. 6:51. I will give *for* the life of the world.
   10:11. giveth his life *for* the sheep.
     15. I lay down my life *for* the sheep.
   11: 4. but *for* the glory of God, that the Son
     50. that one man should die *for* the people,
     51. that Jesus should die *for* that nation;

Joh. 11:52. And not *for* that nation only, but that
   13:37. I will lay down my life *for* thy *sake.*
     38. thou lay down thy life *for* my *sake ?*
   15:13. lay down his life *for* his friends.
   17:19. And *for* their *sakes* I sanctify myself,
   18:14. one man should die *for* the people.
Acts 5:41. worthy to suffer shame *for* his name.
   8:24. Pray ye to the Lord *for* me,
   9:16. he must suffer *for* my name's *sake.*
   12: 5. of the church unto God *for* him.
   15:26. *for* the name of our Lord Jesus Christ.
   21:13. *for* the name of the Lord Jesus.
     26. should be offered *for* every one of them.
   26: 1. Thou art permitted to speak *for* thyself.
     13. *above*ª the brightness of the sun,
Ro. 1: 5. among all nations, *for* his name.
     8. through Jesus Christ *for* you all,
   5: 6. Christ died *for* the ungodly.
     7. For scarcely *for* a righteous man will one
       die: yet peradventure *for* a good man
       some
     8. we were yet sinners, Christ died *for* us.
   8:26. the Spirit itself maketh intercession *for*
     27. he maketh intercession *for* the saints
     31. If God (be) *for* us, who (can be) against
       us?
     32. but delivered him up *for* us all,
     34. who also maketh intercession *for* us.
   9: 3. accursed from Christ *for* my brethren,
     27. Esaias also crieth *concerning* Israel,
   10: 1. and prayer to God *for* Israel is,
   14:15. with thy meat, *for* whom Christ died.
   15: 8. of the circumcision *for* the truth of God,
     9. the Gentiles might glorify God *for* (his)
       mercy;
     30. in (your) prayers to God *for* me;
   16: 4. Who have *for* my life laid down their
1Co. 1:13. was Paul crucified *for* you?
   4: 6. not to think (of men) *above*ª that which is
       written,
   — be puffed up *for* one against another.
   5: 7. Christ our passover is sacrificed *for* us:
   10:13. to be tempted *above*ª that ye are able;
     30. *for* which I give thanks?
   11:24. my body, which is broken *for* you:
   12:25. have the same care one *for* another.
   15: 3. how that Christ died *for* our sins
     29. which are baptized *for* the dead,
   — why are they then baptized *for* the dead?
2Co. 1: 6. *for* your consolation and
   — *for* your consolation and
     7(6). And our hope *of* you (is) stedfast,
     8. have you ignorant *of* our trouble
   — pressed out of measure, *above*ª strength,
     11. helping together by prayer *for* us,
   — may be given by many *on* our *behalf.*
   5:12. occasion to glory *on* our *behalf,*
     14(15). that if one died *for* all, then were all
       dead:
     15. And (that) he died *for* all, that they
   — but unto him which died *for* them,
     20. we are ambassadors *for* Christ, as
   — we pray (you) *in* Christ's *stead,* be ye
     21. made him (to be) sin *for* us, who knew
       no sin;
   7: 4. great (is) my glorying *of* you:
     7. your fervent mind *toward* me;
     12. but that our care *for* you [many copies
       read, "your care *for* us"]
     14. boasted any thing to him *of* you,
   8: 3. yea, and *beyond*ª (their) power
     16. care into the heart of Titus *for* you.

2Co. 8:23. Whether (any do enquire) of Titus,
24. and of our boasting on your behalf.
9: 2. for which I boast of you to them
3. lest our boasting of you should be in vain
14. And by their prayer for you,
11: 5. a whit behind the very chiefest apostles.
(lit. those above† very apostles)
23. I speak as a fool I (am) more;†
12: 5. Of such an one will I glory: yet of myself
I will not glory, but in
6. above a that which he seeth me (to be),
8. For this thing I besought the Lord thrice,
10. in distresses for Christ's sake:
11. behind the very chiefest apostles, (lit.
those above,† &c.)
13. you were inferior to a other churches,
15. gladly spend and be spent for you; (lit.
for the souls of you)
19. all things, dearly beloved, for your edifying.
13: 8. against the truth, but for the truth.
Gal. 1: 4. Who gave himself for our sins,
14. above a many my equals in mine own nation,
2:20. and gave himself for me.
3:13. being made a curse for us:
Eph 1:16. Cease not to give thanks for you,
22. the head over a all (things) to the church,
3: 1. prisoner of Jesus Christ for you Gentiles,
13. at my tribulations for you,
20. to do exceeding† abundantly above a all
that we ask or think,
5: 2. and hath given himself for us
20. thanks always for all things unto God
25. loved the church, and gave himself for it;
6 19. And for me, that utterance may be given
20. For which I am an ambassador in bonds:
Phi. 1: 4. in every prayer of mine for you all
7. to think this of you all,
29. it is given in the behalf of Christ,
— but also to suffer for his sake;
2: 9. a name which is above a every name:
13. and to do of (his) good pleasure.
4:10. your care of me hath flourished again;
Col. 1: 7. who is for you a faithful minister
9. do not cease to pray for you,
24. rejoice in my sufferings for you,
— in my flesh for his body's sake,
4:12. labouring fervently for you in prayers,
13. that he hath a great zeal for you,
1Th. 3:10. Night and day praying exceedingly†(ὑπὲρ
ἐκπερισσοῦ)
5:10. Who died for us, that, whether we wake
13. esteem them very† highly in love
2Th. 1: 4. for your patience and faith in all
5. kingdom of God, for which ye also suffer:
2: 1. we beseech you, brethren, by the coming
of our Lord
1Ti. 2: 1. be made for all men;
2. For kings, and (for) all that are in
6. Who gave himself a ransom for all,
Tit. 2:14. Who gave himself for us, that he
Philem.13. that in thy stead he might have ministered
16. Not now as a servant, but above a a servant,
21. thou wilt also do more than a I say.
Heb 2: 9. should taste death for every man.
4:12. and sharper than any twoedged sword,
5: 1. is ordained for men in things (pertaining)
to God, that he may offer both gifts and
sacrifices for sins:
3. so also for himself, to offer for sins.
6:20. the forerunner is for us entered,
7:25. liveth to make intercession for them.

Heb 7:27. first for his own sins, and then
9: 7. which he offered for himself, and (for) the
errors
24. to appear in the presence of God for us:
10:12. after he had offered one sacrifice for sins,
13:17. for they watch for your souls,
Jas. 5:16. and pray one for another,
1Pet. 2:21. because Christ also suffered for us,
3:18. the just for the unjust, that he might bring
4: 1. as Christ hath suffered for us in the flesh,
1Joh. 3:16. because he laid down his life for us:
— to lay down (our) lives for the brethren.
3Joh. 7. Because that for his name's sake they went
forth,

ὑπεραίρομαι, huperairomai.

2Co.12: 7. lest I should be exalted above measure
— lest I should be exalted above measure.
2Th. 2: 4. Who opposeth and exalteth himself above all

ὑπέρακμος, huperakmos.

1Co. 7:36. if she pass the flower of (her) age, (lit.
be past prime)

ὑπεράνω, huperano.

Eph. 1:21. Far above all principality, and
4:10. that ascended up far above all heavens,
Heb 9: 5. And over it the cherubims of glory

ὑπεραυξάνω, huperauxano.

2Th. 1: 3. that your faith groweth exceedingly,

ὑπερϐαίνω, huperbaino.

1Th. 4: 6. That no (man) go beyond and defraud

ὑπερϐαλλόντως, huperballontōs.

2Co.11:23. in stripes above measure,

ὑπερϐάλλω, huperballo.

2Co. 3:10. by reason of the glory that excelleth.
9:14. for the exceeding grace of God in you.
Eph. 1:19. And what (is) the exceeding greatness of
his power to us-ward
2: 7. shew the exceeding riches of his grace
3:19. the love of Christ, which passeth knowledge,

ὑπερϐολή, huperbolee.

Ro. 7:13. might become exceeding (καθ᾽ ὑπ. lit. of
excess) sinful.
1Co.12:31. shew I unto you a more excellent way. (κ.ὑ.)
2Co. 1: 8. we were pressed out of measure, (κ. ὑ.)
4: 7. that the excellency of the power may be
17. worketh for us a far more exceeding (κ. ὑ.
εἰς ὑ.)
12: 7. through the abundance of the revelations,
Gal. 1:13. beyond measure (κ. ὑ.) I persecuted the
church

ὑπερείδω, *huperido.*

Acts17:30. the times of this ignorance God *winked at;* but

ὑπερέκεινα, *huperekīna.*

2Co.10:16. the gospel in the (regions) *beyond* you,

ὑπερεκτείνω, *huperektīno.*

2Co.10:14. For we *stretch* not ourselves *beyond* (our measure),

---

ὑπερεκχύνομαι, *huperekkunomai.*

Lu. 6:38 and *running over,* shall men give

ὑπερεντυγχάνω, *huperentunkano.*

Ro. 8:26. the Spirit itself *maketh intercession for* us with groanings which

---

ὑπερέχω, *hupereko.*

Ro. 13: 1. be subject unto the *higher* powers.
Phi. 2: 3. each esteem other *better* than themselves.
3: 8. for the *excellency* of the knowledge of Christ Jesus my Lord:
4: 7. the peace of God, *which passeth* all understanding,
1Pet.2:13. whether it be to the king, as *supreme;*

ὑπερηφανία, *hupereephania.*

Mar 7:22. blasphemy, *pride,* foolishness:

ὑπερήφανος, *hupereephanos.*

Lu. 1:51. scattered the *proud* in the imagination of their hearts.
Ro. 1:30. *proud,* boasters, inventors of evil things,
2Ti. 3: 2. boasters, *proud,* blasphemers,
Jas. 4: 6. he saith, God resisteth the *proud,* but
1Pet.5: 5. for God resisteth the *proud,* and giveth

ὑπερνικάω, *hupernikao.*

Ro. 8:37. we *are more than conquerors* through him

ὑπέρογκος, *huperonkos.*

2Pet.2:18. they speak *great swelling* (words) of vanity,
Jude 16. mouth speaketh *great swelling* (words),

ὑπεροχή, *huperokee.*

1Co. 2: 1. came not with *excellency* of speech
1Ti. 2: 2. and (for) all that are in *authority;*

ὑπερπερισσεύω, *huperperissuo.*

Ro. 5:20. grace *did much more abound :*
2Co. 7: 4. I *am exceeding* joyful in all our

ὑπερπερισσῶς, *huperperissōs.*

Mar 7:37. And were *beyond measure* astonished,

ὑπερπλεονάζω, *huperpleonazo.*

1Ti. 1:14. And the grace of our Lord *was exceeding abundant* with faith and

---

ὑπερυψόω, *huperupsoō.*

Phi. 2: 9. God also *hath highly exalted* him,

ὑπερφρονέω, *huperphroneo.*

Ro. 12: 3. not *to think* (of himself) *more highly*

ὑπερῷον, *huperōon.*

Acts 1:13. went up into an *upper room,* where abode
9:37. they laid (her) in an *upper chamber.*
39. they brought him into the *upper chamber:*
20: 8. there were many lights in the *upper chamber,*

ὑπέχω, *hupeko.*

Jude 7. *suffering* the vengeance of eternal fire.

ὑπήκοος, *hupeekoös.*

Acts 7:39. To whom our fathers would not obey, (lit. be *obedient*)
2Co. 2: 9. whether ye be *obedient* in all things.
Phi. 2: 8. and became *obedient* unto death,

ὑπηρετέω, *hupeereteo.*

Acts13:36. David, *after* he *had served* his own generation
20:34. these hands *have ministered unto* my
24:23. *to minister* or come unto him.

ὑπηρέτης, *hupeeretees.*

Mat. 5:25. the judge deliver thee to the *officer,*
26:58. and sat with the *servants,* (lit. (court) *officers*) to see the end.
Mar 14:54. and he sat with the *servants,*
65. and the *servants* did strike him
Lu. 1: 2. eyewitnesses, and *ministers* of the word ;
4:20. and he gave (it) again to the *minister,*
Joh. 7:32. and the chief priests sent *officers*
45. Then came the *officers* to the chief priests
46. The *officers* answered, Never man spake
18: 3. received a band (of men) and *officers* from the chief priests and Pharisees,
12. the band and the captain and *officers* of the Jews took Jesus,
18. And the servants and *officers* stood there,
22. one of the *officers* which stood by struck
36. then would my *servants* fight,
19: 6. chief priests therefore and *officers* saw him, they cried out,
Acts 5:22. But when the *officers* came, and found them not

Acts 5:26. Then went the captain with the *officers*,
  13: 5. and they had also John to (their) *minister*.
  26:16. to make thee a *minister* and a witness
1Co. 4: 1. Let a man so account of us, as of the *ministers* of Christ,

---

ὕπνος, *hupnos.*

Mat. 1:24. Joseph being raised from *sleep*
Lu. 9:32. that were with him were heavy with *sleep:*
Joh. 11:13. he had spoken of taking of rest in *sleep.*
Acts 20: 9. Eutychus, being fallen into a deep *sleep:*
  — he sunk down with *sleep*, and fell
Ro. 13:11. high time to awake out of *sleep:*

ὑπό, *hupo.*

Governing a genitive case, with the exception of the passages marked [a]

Mat. 1:22. spoken *of* the Lord by the prophet,
  2:15. spoken *of* the Lord by the prophet,
  16. that he was mocked *of* the wise men,
  17. spoken *by* Jeremy the prophet,
  3: 3. that was spoken of *by* the prophet Esaias,
  6. And were baptized *of* him in Jordan,
  13. unto John, to be baptized *of* him.
  14. I have need to be baptized *of* thee,
  4: 1. led up *of* the spirit into the wilderness to be tempted *of* the devil.
  5:13. and to be trodden under foot *of* men.
  15. and put it *under*[a] a bushel,
  6: 2. that they may have glory *of* men.
  8: 8. that thou shouldest come *under*[a] my roof:
  9. a man *under*[a] authority, having soldiers *under*[a] me:
  24. that the ship was covered *with* the waves:
  10:22. And ye shall be hated *of* all (men)
  11: 7. A reed shaken *with* the wind?
  27. are delivered unto me *of* my Father:
  14: 8. being before instructed *of* her mother,
  24. in the midst of the sea, tossed *with* waves:
  17:12. shall also the Son of man suffer *of* them.
  19:12. which were made eunuchs *of* men:
  20:23. for whom it is prepared *of* my Father.
  22:31. that which was spoken unto you *by* God,
  23: 7. and to be called *of* men, Rabbi, Rabbi.
  37. as a hen gathereth her chickens *under*[a] (her) wings,
  24: 9. and ye shall be hated *of* all nations for
  27:12. And when he was accused *of* the chief priests
  35. which was spoken *by* the prophet,
Mar 1: 5. baptized *of* him in the river of Jordan,
  9. and was baptized *of* John in Jordan.
  13. forty days, tempted *of* Satan;
  2: 3. which was borne *of* four.
  4:21. Is a candle brought to be put *under*[a] a bushel, or *under*[a] a bed?
  32. may lodge *under* the shadow of it.
  5: 4. chains had been plucked asunder *by* him,
  26. suffered many things *of* many physicians,
  13:13. And ye shall be hated *of* all (men)
  14. spoken of *by* Daniel the prophet,
  16:11. and had been seen *of* her, believed not.
Lu. 1:26. the angel Gabriel was sent *from* God
  2:18. which were told them *by* the shepherds.
  21. which was so named *of* the angel
  26. revealed unto him *by* the Holy Ghost,
  3: 7. that came forth to be baptized *of* him,
  19. being reproved *by* him for Herodias

Lu. 4: 2. forty days tempted *of* the devil.
  15. in their synagogues, being glorified *of* all
  5:15. to be healed *by* him of their infirmities.
  6:18. they that were vexed *with* unclean spirits
  7: 6. thou shouldest enter *under*[a] my roof:
  8. I also am a man set *under*[a] authority, having *under*[a] me soldiers,
  24. A reed shaken *with* the wind?
  30. being not baptized *of* him.
  8:14. are choked *with* cares and riches
  29. and was driven *of* the devil into the wilderness.
  43. neither could be healed *of* any,
  9: 7. heard *of* all that was done *by* him:
  — it was said *of* some, that John was
  8. And *of* some, that Elias had appeared;
  10:22. are delivered to me *of* my Father:
  11:33. neither *under*[a] a bushel,
  13:17. the glorious things that were done *by* him.
  34. (doth gather) her brood *under*[a] (her)
  14: 8. art bidden *of* any (man) to a wedding,
  — than thou be bidden *of* him;
  16:22. carried *by* the angels into Abraham's bosom:
  17:20. when he was demanded *of* the Pharisees,
  24. out of the one (part) *under*[a] heaven, shineth unto the other (part) *under*[a] heaven;
  21:16. ye shall be betrayed both *by* parents,
  17. And ye shall be hated *of* all (men)
  20. Jerusalem compassed *with* armies,
  24. be trodden down *of* the Gentiles,
  23: 8. to have seen some miracle done *by* him.
Joh. 1:48(49). when thou wast *under*[a] the fig tree,
  8: 9. being convicted *by* (their own) conscience,
  10:14. and am known *of* mine.
  14:21. shall be loved *of* my Father,
Acts 2: 5. devout men, out of every nation *under*[a] heaven.
  24. not possible that he should be holden *of* it.
  4:11. which was set at nought *of* you builders,
  12. none other name *under*[a] heaven given
  36. who *by* the apostles was surnamed Barnabas,
  5:16. vexed *with* unclean spirits:
  21. into the temple early *in* the morning, (lit. *on*[a] the dawn)
  8: 6. those things which Philip spake, (lit. spoken *by* Philip)
  10:22. of good report *among* all the nation of the Jews, was warned from God *by* an holy angel
  33. all things that are commanded thee *of* God.
  38. all that were oppressed *of* the devil;
  41. unto witnesses chosen before *of* God,
  42. that it is he which was ordained *of* God (to be) the Judge of quick and dead.
  12: 5. without ceasing *of* the church unto God
  13: 4. being sent forth *by* the Holy Ghost,
  45. those things which were spoken *by* Paul,
  15: 3. brought on their way *by* the church,
  4. they were received *of* the church,
  40. being recommended *by* the brethren
  16: 2. well reported *of* *by* the brethren
  4. that were ordained *of* the apostles and elders
  6. and were forbidden *of* the Holy Ghost
  14. unto the things which were spoken *of* Paul.
  17:13. the word of God was preached *of* Paul
  19. this new doctrine, whereof thou speakest, (lit. spoken *by* thee)

Acts17:25. Neither is worshipped *with* men's hands,

20: 3. when the Jews laid wait for him, (lit. there being a design against him *by* the Jews)

21:35. that he was borne *of* the soldiers

22:11. led by the hand *of* them that were with me,

12. having a good report *of* all the Jews

23:10. Paul should have been pulled in pieces *of*

27. This man was taken *of* the Jews,

— and should have been killed *of* them:

30. how that the Jews laid wait for the man, (lit. an enterprise against him *by* the Jews)

24:21. I am called in question *by* you this day.

26. money should have been given him *of* Paul,

25:14. There is a certain man left in bonds *by* Felix.

26: 2. whereof I am accused *of* the Jews:

6. of the promise made *of* God unto our fathers:

7. king Agrippa, I am accused *of* the Jews.

27:11. than those things which were spoken *by* Paul.

41. broken *with* the violence of the waves.

Ro. 3: 9. that they are all *under* a sin ;

13. the poison of asps (is) *under* a their lips:

21. witnessed *by* the law and the prophets ;

6:14. ye are not *under* a the law, but *under* a grace.

15. we are not *under* a the law, but *under* a grace?

7:14. but I am carnal, sold *under* a sin.

12:21. Be not overcome *of* evil, but overcome

13: 1. the powers that be are ordained *of* God.

15:15. the grace that is given to me *of* God,

24. to be brought on my way thitherward *by* you,

16:20. shall bruise Satan *under* a your feet shortly.

1Co. 1:11. *by* them (which are of the house) of Chloe,

2:12. that are freely given to us *of* God.

15. yet he himself is judged *of* no man.

4: 3. that I should be judged *of* you, or *of* man's judgment:

6:12. not be brought under the power *of* any.

7:25. as one that hath obtained mercy *of* the Lord

8: 3. the same is known *of* him.

9:20. to them that are *under* a the law, as *under* a the law, that I might gain them that are *under* a the law ;

10: 1. all our fathers were *under* a the cloud,

9. and were destroyed *of* serpents.

10. and were destroyed *of* the destroyer.

29. judged *of* another (man's) conscience ?

11:32. we are chastened *of* the Lord,

14:24. he is convinced *of* all, he is judged *of* all:

15:25. he hath put all enemies *under* a his feet.

27. he hath put all things *under* a his feet.

2Co. 1: 4. we ourselves are comforted *of* God.

16. and *of* you to be brought on my way

2: 6. which (was inflicted) *of* many.

11. Lest Satan should get an advantage of us: (lit. lest we should be taken advantage *of by* Satan)

3: 2. known and read *of* all men:

3. ministered *by* us, written not with

5: 4. might be swallowed up *of* life.

8:19. who was also chosen *of* the churches

— grace, which is administered *by* us

20. abundance which is administered *by* us:

11:24. *Of* the Jews five times received I

2Co.12:11. to have been commended *of* you:

Gal. 1:11. the gospel which was preached *of* me

3:10. are *under* a the curse: for it is written,

17. confirmed before *of* God in Christ,

22. hath concluded all *under* a sin,

23. we were kept *under* a the law,

25. no longer *under* a a schoolmaster.

4: 2. But is *under* a tutors and governors

3. *under* a the elements of the world:

4. of a woman, made *under* a the law,

5. them that were *under* a the law,

9. or rather are known *of* God,

21. that desire to be *under* a the law,

5:15. that ye be not consumed one *of* another.

18. ye are not *under* a the law.

Eph. 1:22. And hath put all (things) *under* a his feet,

2:11. *by* that which is called the Circumcision

5:12. which are done *of* them in secret.

13. are made manifest *by* the light:

Phi. 1:28. in nothing terrified *by* your adversaries:

3:12. I am apprehended *of* Christ Jesus.

Col. 1:23. to every creature which is *under* a heaven ;

2:18. vainly puffed up *by* his fleshly mind,

1Th. 1: 4. Knowing, brethren beloved, your election *of* God. [or, beloved *by* God, your election]

2: 4. But as we were allowed *of* God

14. like things *of* your own countrymen, even as they (have) *of* the Jews:

2Th. 2:13. brethren beloved *of* the Lord,

1Ti. 6: 1. servants as are *under* a the yoke

2Ti. 2:26. who are taken captive *by* him at

Heb 2: 3. confirmed unto us *by* them that heard (him);

3: 4. For every house is builded *by* some (man);

5: 4. but he that is called *of* God,

10. Called *of* God an high priest

7: 7. the less is blessed *of* the better.

9:19. when Moses had spoken every precept (lit. every precept having been spoken *by* Moses)

11:23. hid three months *of* his parents,

12: 3. endured such contradiction *of* sinners

5. when thou art rebuked *of* him:

Jas. 1:14. he is drawn away *of* his own lust,

2: 3. or sit here *under* a my footstool:

9. and are convinced *of* the law

3: 4. and (are) driven *of* fierce winds,

— turned about *with* a very small helm,

6. and it is set on fire *of* hell.

1Pet.2: 4. disallowed indeed *of* men,

5: 6. *under* a the mighty hand of God,

2Pet.1:17. to him *from* the excellent glory,

21. spake (as they were) moved *by* the Holy Ghost.

2: 7. vexed *with* the filthy conversation of the wicked:

17. clouds that are carried *with* a tempest ;

3: 2. were spoken before *by* the holy prophets,

3Joh. 12. Demetrius hath good report *of* all (men), and *of* the truth itself:

Jude 6. in everlasting chains *under* a darkness unto

12. carried about *of* winds ;

17. which were spoken before *of* the apostles

Rev. 6: 8. with death, and *with* the beasts of the

13. when she is shaken *of* a mighty wind.

9:18. *By* these three was the third part of men

ὑποϐάλλω, *hupoballo.*

Acts 6:11. Then they *suborned* men, which said,

ὑπογραμμός, hupogrammos.

1Pet.2:21. leaving us an *example*, that ye should

ὑπόδειγμα, hupodigma.

Joh.13:15. For I have given you an *example*, that ye
Heb 4:11. after the same *example* of unbelief.
    8: 5. Who serve unto the *example* and shadow
    9:23. that the *patterns* of things in the heavens
Jas. 5:10. for an *example* of suffering affliction,
2Pet.2: 6. making (them) an *ensample* unto those
    that after should live ungodly ;

ὑποδείκνυμι, hupodiknumi.

Mat. 3: 7. who *hath warned* you to flee
Lu. 3: 7. who *hath warned* you to flee
    6:47. I *will shew* you to whom he is like:
   12: 5. But I *will forewarn* you whom
Acts 9:16. For I *will shew* him how great things
  20:35. I *have shewed* you all things,

ὑποδέομαι, hupodeomai.

Mar 6: 9. But (be) *shod* with sandals ;
Acts12: 8. Gird thyself, and *bind on* thy sandals.
Eph. 6:15. your feet *shod* with the preparation

ὑποδέχομαι, hupodekomai.

Lu. 10:38. Martha *received* him into her house.
  19: 6. and *received* him joyfully.
Acts17: 7. Whom Jason *hath received* :
Jas. 2:25. *when* she *had received* the messengers,

ὑπόδημα, hupodeema.

Mat. 3:11. whose *shoes* I am not worthy to bear:
  10:10. neither two coats, neither *shoes*,
Mar 1: 7. the latchet of whose *shoes* I am not worthy
Lu. 3:16. the latchet of whose *shoes* I am not worthy
  10: 4. neither purse, nor scrip, nor *shoes :*
  15:22. and put a ring on his hand, and *shoes* on
    (his) feet:
  22:35. without purse, and scrip, and *shoes*,
Joh. 1:27. whose *shoe's* latchet I am not worthy
Acts 7:33. Put off thy *shoes* from thy feet:
  18:25. whose *shoes* of (his) feet I am not

ὑπόδικος, hupodikos.

Ro. 3:19. all the world may become *guilty* before
    God.

ὑποζύγιον, hupozugion.

Mat.21: 5. and a colt the foal of an *ass.*
2Pet. 2:16. the dumb *ass* speaking with man's voice

ὑποζώννυμι, hupozonnumi.

Acts27:17. they used helps, *undergirding* the ship ;

ὑποκάτω, hupokato.

Mar 6:11. shake off the dust *under* your feet
  7:28. yet the dogs *under* the table eat of
Lu. 8:16. or putteth (it) *under* a bed ;
Joh. 1:50(51). I saw thee *under* the fig tree,
Heb 2: 8. all things in subjection *under* his feet.
Rev. 5: 3. nor in earth, neither *under* the earth,
  13. and on the earth, and *under* the earth,
  6: 9. I saw *under* the altar the souls
  12: 1. and the moon *under* her feet,

ὑποκρίνομαι, hupokrinomai.

Lu. 20:20. sent forth spies, *which should feign* (lit.
    feigning) themselves just men,

ὑπόκρισις, hupokrisis.

Mat.23:28. within ye are full of *hypocrisy*
Mar12:15. But he, knowing their *hypocrisy*,
Lu. 12: 1. the leaven of the Pharisees, which is
    hypocrisy.
Gal. 2:13. was carried away with their *dissimulation.*
1Ti. 4: 2. Speaking lies in *hypocrisy ;*
Jas. 5:12. lest ye fall into *condemnation.*
1Pet.2: 1. and all guile, and *hypocrisies*,
Note.—The rendering of Jas.5:12 has arisen from
    a different reading, ὑπὸ κρίσιν.

ὑποκριτής, hupokritees.

Mat. 6: 2. as the *hypocrites* do in the synagogues
  5. thou shalt not be as the *hypocrites*
  16. when ye fast, be not, as the *hypocrites*, of
  7: 5. Thou *hypocrite*, first cast out the beam
  15: 7. (Ye) *hypocrites*, well did Esaias prophesy.
  16: 3. O (ye) *hypocrites*, ye can discern
  22:18. Why tempt ye me, (ye) *hypocrites ?*
  23:13. scribes and Pharisees, *hypocrites !*
  14. scribes and Pharisees, *hypocrites !*
  15. scribes and Pharisees, *hypocrites !*
  23. scribes and Pharisees, *hypocrites !*
  25. scribes and Pharisees, *hypocrites !*
  27. scribes and Pharisees, *hypocrites !*
  29. scribes and Pharisees, *hypocrites !*
  24:51. and appoint (him) his portion with the
    hypocrites :
Mar 7: 6. Esaias prophesied of you *hypocrites*,
Lu. 6:42. Thou *hypocrite*, cast out first the beam
  11:44. scribes and Pharisees, *hypocrites !* for ye
    are
  12:56. (Ye) *hypocrites*, ye can discern the face
  13:15. (Thou) *hypocrite*, doth not each one of

ὑπολαμβάνω, hupolambano.

Lu. 7:43. I *suppose* that (he), to whom he forgave
    most.
  10:30. And Jesus *answering* said, A certain
Acts 1: 9. a cloud *received* him out of their sight.
  2:15. these are not drunken, as ye *suppose*,

ὑπολείπομαι, hupoleipomai.

Ro. 11: 3. and I *am left* alone, and they seek

ὑπολήνιον, *hupoleenion.*

Mar 12: 1. and digged (a place for) the *winefat,*

ὑπολιμπάνω, *hupolimpano.*

1Pet. 2: 21. suffered for us, *leaving* us an example,

ὑπομένω, *hupomeno.*

Mat. 10: 22. but he *that endureth* to the end
 24: 13. But he *that shall endure* unto the end,
Mar 13: 13. but he *that shall endure* unto the end,
Lu. 2: 43. the child Jesus *tarried behind* in
Acts 17: 14. Silas and Timotheus *abode* there still.
Ro. 12: 12. *patient* in tribulation ;
1Co. 13: 7. hopeth all things, *endureth* all things.
2Ti. 2: 10. Therefore I *endure* all things for the
 12. If we *suffer,* we shall also reign wjth
  (him):
Heb 10: 32. ye *endured* a great fight of afflictions ;
 12: 2. *endured* the cross, despising the shame,
 3. him *that endured* such contradiction
 7. If ye *endure* chastening, God dealeth
Jas. 1: 12. Blessed (is) the man that *endureth* temptation:
 5: 11. we count them happy *which endure.*
1Pet. 2: 20. for your faults, ye shall *take* it *patiently ?*
 — ye *take* it *patiently,* this (is) acceptable

ὑπομιμνήσκω, *hupomimneesko.*

Lu. 22: 61. Peter *remembered* the word of the Lord,
Joh. 14: 26. shall teach you all things, and *bring* all
  things *to* your *remembrance,*
2Ti. 2: 14. Of these things *put* (them) *in remem-*
  brance,
Tit. 3: 1. *Put* them *in mind* to be subject
2Pet. 1: 12. to *put* you always *in remembrance*
3Joh. 10. I *will remember* his deeds which he doeth,
Jude 5. I will therefore *put* you *in remembrance,*

ὑπόμνησις, *hupomneesis.*

2Ti. 1: 5. When I call to *remembrance* the unfeigned
2Pet. 1: 13. by *putting* (you) *in remembrance ;*
 3: 1. your pure minds by way of *remembrance :*

ὑπομονή, *hupomonee.*

Lu. 8: 15. and bring forth fruit with *patience.*
 21: 19. In your *patience* possess ye your souls.
Ro. 2: 7. by *patient continuance* in well doing
 5: 3. that tribulation worketh *patience ;*
 4. And *patience,* experience;
 8: 25. do we with *patience* wait for (it).
 15: 4. through *patience* and comfort of the
 5. Now the God of *patience* and consolation
2Co. 1: 6. which is effectual in the *enduring* of the
  same sufferings
 6: 4. in much *patience,* in afflictions,
 12: 12. wrought among you in all *patience,*
Col. 1: 11. unto all *patience* and longsuffering
1Th. 1: 3. and *patience* of hope in our Lord
2Th. 1: 4. for your *patience* and faith
 3: 5. and into the *patient waiting* for Christ.
  (lit. the *patience* of Christ)

1Ti. 6: 11. faith, love, *patience,* meekness.
2Ti. 3: 10. faith, longsuffering, charity, *patience,*
Tit. 2: 2. sound in faith, in charity, in *patience.*
Heb 10: 36. For ye have need of *patience,*
 12: 1. and let us run with *patience* the race
Jas. 1: 3. the trying of your faith worketh *patience.*
 4. But let *patience* have (her) perfect work,
 5: 11. Ye have heard of the *patience* of Job,
2Pet. 1: 6. and to temperance *patience ;* and to
  patience godliness ;
Rev. 1: 9. in the kingdom and *patience* of Jesus Christ,
 2: 2. and thy labour, and thy *patience,*
 3. And hast borne, and hast *patience,*
 19. and thy *patience,* and thy works ;
 3: 10. thou hast kept the word of my *patience,*
 13: 10. Here is the *patience* and the faith of
 14: 12. Here is the *patience* of the saints:

ὑπονοέω, *huponoeo.*

Acts 13: 25. Whom *think* ye that I am ?
 25: 18. of such things as I *supposed :*
 27: 27. the shipmen *deemed* that they drew near

ὑπόνοια, *huponoya.*

1Ti. 6: 4. strife, railings, evil *surmisings,*

ὑποπλέω, *hupopleo.*

Acts 27: 4. we *sailed under* Cyprus,
 7. we *sailed under* Crete,

ὑποπνέω, *hupopneo.*

Acts 27: 13. And *when* the south wind *blew softly,*

ὑποπόδιον, *hupopodion.*

Mat. 5: 35. by the earth ; for it is his *footstool :*
 22: 44. till I make thine enemies thy *footstool ?*
Mar 12: 36. till I make thine enemies thy *footstool.*
Lu. 20: 43. Till I make thine enemies thy *footstool.*
Acts 2: 35. Until I make thy foes thy *footstool.*
 7: 49. and earth (is) my *footstool ?*
Heb 1: 13. until I make thine enemies thy *footstool ?*
 10: 13. till his enemies be made his *footstool.*
Jas. 2: 3. or sit here under my *footstool :*

ὑπόστασις, *hupostasis.*

2Co. 9: 4. in this same *confident* boasting. (lit.
  confidence of boasting)
 11: 17. in this *confidence* of boasting.
Heb 1: 3. and the express image of his *person,*
 3: 14. if we hold the beginning of our *confidence*
 11: 1. faith is the *substance* of things hoped for,

ὑποστέλλω, *hupostello.*

Acts 20: 20. (And) how I *kept back* nothing
 27. For I *have* not *shunned* to declare
Gal. 2: 12. he *withdrew* and separated himself,
Heb 10: 38. but if (any man) *draw back,*

ὑποστολή, hupostolee.

Heb 10:39: we are not of them who *draw back* (lit. of the *drawing back*) unto perdition ;

ὑποστρέφω, hupostrepho.

Mar 14:40. And *when he returned*, he found them
Lu.　1:56. and *returned* to her own house.
　　2:39. they *returned* into Galilee,
　　43. as they *returned*, the child Jesus
　　45. they *turned back again* to Jerusalem,
　　4: 1. *returned* from Jordan, and was led
　　14. And Jesus *returned* in the power
　　7:10. *returning* to the house, found the servant
　　8:37. into the ship, and *returned back again.*
　　39. *Return* to thine own house,
　　40. that, when Jesus *was returned,*
　　9:10. the apostles, *when they were returned*, told
　　10:17. the seventy *returned again* with joy,
　　11:24. I *will return* unto my house
　　17:15. *turned back*, and with a loud voice
　　18. *that returned* to give glory to God, save
　　19:12. for himself a kingdom, and *to return.*
　　23:48. smote their breasts, and *returned.*
　　56. they *returned, and* prepared spices
　　24: 9. *returned* from the sepulchre, and told
　　33. and *returned* to Jerusalem,
　　52. *returned* to Jerusalem with great joy:
Acts 1:12. Then *returned* they unto Jerusalem
　　8:25. *returned* to Jerusalem, and
　　28. Was *returning*, and sitting in his chariot
　　12:25. Barnabas and Saul *returned* from Jerusalem,
　　13:13. John departing from them *returned* to
　　34. no more *to return* to corruption,
　　14:21. they *returned again* to Lystra,
　　20: 3. *to return* through Macedonia.
　　21: 6. and they *returned* home *again.*
　　22:17. *when I was come again* to Jerusalem,
　　23:32. and *returned* to the castle:
Gal.　1:17. and *returned* **again** unto Damascus.
Heb. 7: 1. met Abraham *returning* from the slaughter of the kings,

---

ὑποστρώννυμι, hupostrŏnnumi.

Lu. 19:36. they *spread* their clothes in the way.

ὑποταγή, hupotagee.

2 Co. 9:13. for your professed *subjection* unto the gospel
Gal. 2: 5. we gave place by *subjection*, no, not for an hour;
1 Ti. 2:11. learn in silence with all *subjection.*
　　3: 4. having his children in *subjection*

ὑποτάσσω, hupotasso.

Lu.　2:51. and was *subject unto* them:
　　10:17. even the devils *are subject unto* us
　　20. that the spirits *are subject unto* you;
Ro.　8: 7. for it *is* not *subject to* the law of God,
　　20. the creature *was made subject to* vanity,
　　— by reason of him who *hath subjected*
　　10: 3. *have* not *submitted* themselves *unto* the
　　13: 1. *Let* every soul *be subject unto* the higher

Ro. 13: 5. Wherefore (ye) must needs *be subject,*
1 Co. 14:32. *are subject to* the prophets,
　　34. *to be under obedience*, as also saith
　　15:27. For he *hath put* all things *under* his feet.
　　— All things *are put under* (him, it is)
　　— which *did' put* all things *under* him.
　　28. when all things shall *be subdued unto* him, then *shall* the Son also himself *be subject unto* him *that put* all things *under* him,
　　16:16. That ye *submit* yourselves unto such,
Eph. 1:22. And *hath put* all (things) *under* his 'feet,
　　5:21. *Submitting* yourselves one *to* another
　　22. Wives, *submit* yourselves *unto* your
　　24. as the church *is subject unto* Christ,
Phi. 3:21. *to subdue* all things *unto* himself.
Col. 3:18. Wives, *submit* yourselves *unto* your
Tit. 2: 5. *obedient to* their own husbands,
　　9. servants *to be obedient unto* their own
　　3: 1. *to be subject to* principalities and
Heb. 2: 5. *hath* he not *put in subjection* the world
　　8. Thou *hast put* all things *in subjection*
　　— For in that he *put* all *in subjection under*
　　— we see not yet all things *put under* him.
　　12: 9. *shall* we not much rather *be in subjection unto* the Father of spirits,
Jas. 4: 7. *Submit* yourselves therefore *to* God.
1 Pet. 2:13. *Submit* yourselves *to* every ordinance of man
　　18. Servants, (be) *subject to* (your) masters
　　3: 1. *in subjection to* your own husbands;
　　5. *being in subjection unto* their own husbands.
　　22. angels and authorities and powers *being made subject unto* him.
　　5: 5. ye younger, *submit* yourselves *unto* the elder. Yea, all (of you) *be subject* one *to* another, *and*

ὑποτίθημι, hupotitheemi.

Ro. 16: 4. Who *have* for my life *laid down* their own necks:
1 Ti. 4: 6. *If* thou *put* the brethren *in remembrance* of these things,

---

ὑποτρέχω, hupotreko.

Acts 27:16. And *running under* a certain island

ὑποτύπωσις, hupotupōsis.

1 Ti. 1:16. for a *pattern* to them (lit. *pattern* of them) which should hereafter believe
2 Ti. 1:13. Hold fast the *form* of sound words,

ὑποφέρω, hupophero.

1 Co. 10:13. that ye may be able *to bear* (it).
2 Ti. 3:11. what persecutions I *endured :*
1 Pet. 2:19. if a man for conscience toward God *endure* grief,

---

ὑποχωρέω, hupokōreo.

Lu.　5:16. *withdrew* himself into the wilderness,
　　9:10. and *went aside* privately into a desert place belonging to

ὑπωπιάζω, hupōpiazo.

Lu. 18: 5. lest by her continual coming she *weary* me.
1Co. 9:27. But I *keep under* my body, and bring

ὗς, hus.

2Pet. 2:22. and the *sow* that was washed to her

ὕσσωπος, hussōpos.

Joh.19:29. and put (it) upon *hyssop*, and
Heb 9:19. with water, and scarlet wool, and *hyssop*,

ὑστερέω, hustereo.

Mat.19:20. from my youth up: what *lack* I yet?
Mar 10:21. One thing thou *lackest* : go thy way,
Lu. 15:14. and he began *to be in want.*
22:35. *lacked* ye any thing ? And they said,
Joh. 2: 3 when they wanted wine, (lit. the wine *having failed*)
Ro. 3:23. and *come short* of the glory of God ;
1Co. 1: 7. So that ye *come behind* in no gift ;
8: 8. neither, if we eat not, *are* we *the worse.*
12:24. honour *to that* (part) *which lacked :*
2Co.11: 5. I suppose I *was* not a whit *behind* the very
9(8). I was present with you, and *wanted,*
12:11. for in nothing *am* I *behind* the very
Phi. 4:12. both to abound and *to suffer need.*
Heb 4: 1. should seem *to come short of* it.
11:37. *being destitute,* afflicted, tormented ;
12:15. lest any man *fail* of the grace of God ;

ὑστέρημα, hustereema.

Lu. 21: 4. but she of her *penury* hath cast in
1Co.16:17. for *that which was lacking* on your part
2Co. 8:14(13). (may be a supply) for their *want,*
— may be (a supply) for your *want :*
9:12. not only supplieth the *want* of the saints,
11: 9. for *that which was lacking* to me
Phi. 2:30. to supply your *lack* of service toward me.
Col. 1:24. and fill up *that which is behind* of the afflictions of Christ
1Th. 3:10. *that which is lacking* in your faith ?

ὑστέρησις, hustereesis.

Mar 12:44. but she of her *want* did cast in
Phi. 4:11. Not that I speak in respect of *want :*

ὕστερον, husteron. adv.

Mat. 4: 2. he was *afterward* an hungered.
21:29. but *afterward* he repented, and went.
32. when ye had seen (it), repented not *afterward,*
37. But *last of all* he sent unto them his son,
22:27. And *last* of all the woman died also.
25:11. *Afterward* came also the other virgins,
26:60. *At the last* came two false witnesses,
Mar 16:14. *Afterward* he appeared unto the eleven as
Lu. 4: 2. he *afterward* hungered.
20:32. *Last* of all the woman died also.
Joh.13:36. but thou shalt follow me *afterwards.*
Heb 12:11. *afterward* it yieldeth the peaceable fruit

ὕστερος, husteros.

1Ti. 4: 1. in the *latter* times some shall depart from the faith,

ὑφαντός, huphantos.

Joh.19:23. *woven* from the top throughout.

ὑψηλός, hupseelos.

Mat. 4: 8. him up into an exceeding *high* mountain,
17: 1. bringeth them up into an *high* mountain
Mar 9: 2. leadeth them up into an *high* mountain
Lu. 4: 5. taking him up into an *high* mountain,
16:15. for that which is *highly esteemed* among men
Acts13:17. and with an *high* arm brought he them out
Ro. 12:16. Mind not *high* things,
Heb 1: 3. the right hand of the Majesty on *high* ;
7:26. and made *higher* than the heavens ;
Rev.21:10. in the spirit to a great and *high* mountain,
12. And had a wall great and *high,*

ὑψηλοφρονέω, hupseelophroneo.

Ro. 11:20. *Be* not *highminded,* but fear:
1Ti. 6:17. that they be not *highminded,*

ὕψιστος, hupsistos.

The mark † denotes that the plural is used to supply the word "places."

Mat.21: 9. Hosanna in the *highest.*†
Mar 5: 7. Jesus, (thou) Son of the *most high* God ?
11:10. Hosanna in the *highest.*†
Lu. 1:32. be called the Son of the *Highest :*
35. and the power of the *Highest* shall overshadow thee:
76. be called the prophet of the *Highest :*
2:14. Glory to God in the *highest,*† and on earth peace,
6:35. ye shall be the children of the *Highest :*
8:28. Jesus, (thou) Son of God *most high* ?
19:38. peace in heaven, and glory in the *highest.*†
Acts 7:48. Howbeit the *most High* dwelleth not
16:17. the servants of the *most high* God,
Heb 7: 1. priest of the *most high* God, who met

ὕψος, hupsos.

Lu. 1:78. dayspring from *on high* hath visited us,
24:49. ye be endued with power from *on high.*
Eph. 3:18. and length, and depth, and *height ;*
4: 8. When he ascended up on *high,*
Jas. 1: 9. rejoice in that he is exalted: (lit. in his *exaltation*)
Rev.21:16. and the *height* of it are equal.

ὑψόω, hupsoō.

Mat.11:23. Capernaum, which art *exalted* unto
23:12. And whosoever *shall exalt* himself
— shall humble himself *shall be exalted.*
Lu. 1:52. and *exalted* them of low degree.
10:15. which art *exalted* to heaven,
14:11. For whosoever *exalteth* himself
— that humbleth himself *shall be exalted.*

Lu. 18:14. every one *that exalteth* himself
    — that humbleth himself *shall be exalted.*
Joh. 3:14. And as Moses *lifted up* the serpent
    — so must the Son of man *be lifted up :*
  8:28. When ye *have lifted up* the Son of man,
12:32. if I *be lifted up* from the earth,
    34. The Son of man must *be lifted up ?* who
Acts 2:33. *being* by the right hand of God *exalted,*
  5:31. Him *hath* God *exalted* with his right hand
13:17. and *exalted* the people when they dwelt as
2Co.11: 7. abasing myself that ye *might be exalted,*
Jas. 4:10. and he *shall lift* you *up.*
1Pet.5: 6. that he *may exalt* you in due time:

ὕψωμα, *hupsōma.*

Ro. 8:39. Nor *height,* nor depth, nor any other
2Co.10: 5. and every *high thing* that exalteth itself

φάγος, *phagos.*

Mat.11:19. Behold a man *gluttonous,* and a
Lu. 7:34. Behold a *gluttonous* man, and a

φάγω, *phago.*

Mat. 6:25. what ye shall *eat,* or what ye
    31. saying, What shall we *eat?* or,
12: 4. and *did eat* the shewbread, which was not
    lawful for him *to eat,*
14:16. give ye them *to eat.*
    20. And they *did* all *eat,* and were filled:
15:20. but *to eat* with unwashen hands
    32. three days, and have nothing to *eat :* (lit.
    what they *may eat*)
    37. And they *did* all *eat,* and were filled.
25:35. and ye gave me *meat :* (lit. *to eat*)
    42. an hungred, and ye gave me no *meat :*
26:17. that we prepare for thee *to eat* the
    26. Take, *eat ;* this is my body.
Mar 2:26. and *did eat* the shewbread, which is not
    lawful *to eat* but for the priests,
  3:20. could not so much as *eat* bread.
  5:43. something should be given her *to eat.*
  6:31. they had no leisure so much as *to eat.*
    36. for they have nothing to *eat.*
    37. Give ye them *to eat.*
    — of bread, and give them *to eat?*
    42. And they *did* all *eat,* and were filled.
    44. And they *that did eat* of the loaves
  8: 1. and having nothing to *eat,*
    2. and have nothing to *eat :*
    8. So they *did eat,* and were filled:
    9. And they *that had eaten* were
11:14. No man *eat* fruit of thee hereafter
14:12. and prepare that thou *mayest eat* the
    14. where I shall *eat* the passover with
    22. Take, *eat :* this is my body.
Lu. 4: 2. in those days he *did eat* nothing:
  6: 4. and did take and *eat* the shewbread,
    — which it is not lawful *to eat* but for
  7:36. desired him that he *would eat* with him.
  8:55. he commanded to give her *meat.*
  9:13. Give ye them *to eat.*
    17. And they *did eat,* and were all filled:
12:19. take thine ease, *eat,* drink, (and) be
    merry.
    22. for your life, what ye shall *eat ;*

Lu. 12:29. seek not ye what ye shall *eat,*
13:26. We *have eaten* and drunk in thy
14: 1. *to eat* bread on the sabbath day,
    15. Blessed (is) he that *shall eat* bread in
15:23. and let us *eat, and* be merry:
17: 8. till I *have eaten* and drunken ; and after-
    ward thou *shalt eat* and drink ?
22: 8. prepare us the passover, that we *may eat.*
    11. where I shall *eat* the passover with
    15. I have desired *to eat* this passover
    16. I will not any more *eat* thereof,
24:43. he took (it), and *did eat* before them.
Joh. 4:31. saying, Master, *eat.*
    32. I have meat *to eat* that ye
    33. Hath any man brought him (ought) *to
    eat ?*
  6: 5. that these *may eat ?*
    23. where they *did eat* bread,
    26. but because ye *did eat* of the loaves,
    31. Our fathers *did eat* manna in the
    — gave them bread from heaven *to eat.*
    49. Your fathers *did eat* manna in the
    50. that a man *may eat* thereof, and not die.
    51. if any man *eat* of this bread,
    52. this man give us (his) flesh *to eat ?*
    53. Except ye *eat* the flesh of the Son of
    58. not as your fathers *did eat* manna,
18:28. but that they *might eat* the passover.
Acts 9: 9. and neither *did eat* nor drink.
10:13. Rise, Peter ; kill, and *eat.*
    14. for I *have* never *eaten* any thing that
11: 7. Arise, Peter ; slay and *eat.*
23:12. saying that they would neither *eat* nor
    21. an oath, that they will neither *eat* nor
Ro. 14: 2. believeth that he may *eat* all things:
    21. (It is) good neither *to eat* flesh, nor
    23. that doubteth is damned if he *eat,*
1Co. 8: 8. neither, if we *eat,* are we the better;
    neither, if we *eat* not, are we the worse.
    13. I will *eat* no flesh while the world
  9: 4. Have we not power *to eat* and to drink ?
10: 3. *did* all *eat* the same spiritual meat;
    7. The people sat down *to eat* and drink,
11:20. (this) is not *to eat* the Lord's supper.
    21. For in *eating* every one taketh before
    24. Take, *eat :* this is my body,
    33. when ye come together *to eat,*
15:32. *let us eat* and drink ; for to morrow
2Th. 3: 8. Neither *did* we *eat* any man's bread
Heb 13:10. whereof they have no right *to eat* which
Jas. 5: 3. and *shall eat* your flesh as it were fire.
Rev. 2: 7. will I give *to eat* of the tree of life,
    14. *to eat* things sacrificed unto idols,
    17. will I give *to eat* of the hidden
    20. *to eat* things sacrificed unto idols.
10:10. as soon as I *had eaten* it,
17:16. and *shall eat* her flesh, and burn
19:18. That ye *may eat* the flesh of kings,

φαιλόνης, *phailonees.*

2Ti. 4:13. The *cloke* that I left at Troas

φαίνω, *phaino.*

Mat. 1:20. the angel of the Lord *appeared* unto
  2: 7. what time the star *appeared.*
    13. *appeareth* to Joseph in a dream,
    19. *appeareth* in a dream to Joseph
  6: 5. that they *may be seen* of men.
    16. that they *may appear* unto men to fast.

Mat. 6:18. That thou *appear* not unto men to fast,
   9:33. It *was* never so *seen* in Israel.
  13:26. then *appeared* the tares also.
  23:27. which indeed *appear* beautiful outward,
    28. ye also outwardly *appear* righteous
  24:27. and *shineth* even unto the west ;
    30. then *shall appear* the sign of the Son
Mar 14:64. what think ye ? (lit. *seems* to you)
  16: 9. he *appeared* first to Mary Magdalene,
Lu. 9: 8. of some, that Elias *had appeared ;*
  24:11. their words *seemed* to them as idle tales,
Joh. 1: 5: And the light *shineth* in darkness ;
   5:35. He was a burning and a *shining* light:
Ro. 7:13. But sin, that it *might appear* sin,
2Co.13: 7. not that we *should appear* approved,
Phi. 2:15. among whom ye *shine* as lights in
Heb11: 3. not made of things *which do appear*.
Jas. 4:14. a vapour, *that appeareth* for a little
1Pet.4:18. where *shall* the ungodly and the sinner
      appear ?
2Pet.1:19. as unto a light *that shineth* in a dark place,
1Joh.2: 8. and the true light now *shineth*.
Rev. 1:16. as the sun *shineth* in his strength.
   8:12. and the day *shone* not for a third
  18:23. the light of a candle shall *shine* no more
  21:23. neither of the moon, to *shine* in it:

φανερός, *phaneros.*

Mat. 6: 4. shall reward thee *openly*.
    6. shall reward thee *openly*.
   18. shall reward thee *openly*.
  12:16. they should not make him *known :*
Mar 3:12. they should not make him *known*.
  4:22. secret, but that it should come *abroad*.
  6:14. for his name was spread *abroad :*
Lu. 8:17. that shall not be made *manifest ;*
   — be known and come *abroad*.
Acts 4:16. (is) *manifest* to all them that
  7:13. Joseph's kindred was made *known* unto
Ro. 1:19. is *manifest* in them; for God
  2:28. a Jew, which is one *outwardly ;*
   — which is *outward* in the flesh:
1Co. 3:13. shall be made *manifest:* for the day
  11:19. may be made *manifest* among you.
  14:25. the secrets of his heart made *manifest ;*
Gal. 5:19. the works of the flesh are *manifest,*
Phi. 1:13. my bonds in Christ are *manifest* in all
1Ti. 4:15. that thy profiting may appear (lit. may
    be *apparent*) to all.
1Joh.3:10. In this the children of God are *manifest,*

φανερόω, *phaneroō.*

Mar 4:22. hid, which *shall* not *be manifested ;*
  16:12. After that he *appeared* in another form
    14. Afterward he *appeared* unto the eleven
Joh. 1:31. that he *should be made manifest* to
  2:11. and *manifested forth* his glory;
  3:21. that his deeds *may be made manifest,*
  7: 4. *shew* thyself to the world.
  9: 3. that the works of God *should be made*
    manifest in him.
  17: 6. I *have manifested* thy name
  21: 1. Jesus *shewed* himself again to the
   — on this wise *shewed* he (himself).
    14. third time that Jesus *shewed himself* to
Ro. 1:19. for God *hath shewed* (it) unto them.
  3:21. without the law *is manifested*, (lit. *has*
    been manifested)

Ro. 16:26. But now is *made manifest,* and
1Co. 4: 5. and *will make manifest* the counsels of
2Co. 2:14. and *maketh manifest* the savour of
  3: 3. *manifestly declared* to be the epistle of
  4:10. *might be made manifest* in our body.
   11. *might be made manifest* in our
  5:10. we must all *appear* before the judgment
   11. but we *are made manifest* unto God; and
    I trust also are *made manifest* in your
    consciences.
  7:12. might *appear* unto you.
  11: 6. but we have been throughly *made mani-*
    fest among you
Eph 5:13. are *made manifest* by the light: for *what-*
    soever *doth make manifest*
Col. 1:26. but now *is made manifest* to his saints:
  3: 4. When Christ, (who is) our life, *shall*
    appear, then *shall* ye also *appear* with
    him in glory.
  4: 4. That I *may make* it *manifest,*
1Ti. 3:16. God *was manifest* in the flesh,
2Ti. .1:10. But is now *made manifest* by the
Tit. 1: 3. *hath* in due times *manifested* his word
Heb 9: 8. that the way into the holiest of all *was*
    not yet *made manifest,*
   26. *hath* he *appeared* to put away sin by
1Pet.1:20. but *was manifest* in these last times
  5: 4. *when* the chief Shepherd *shall appear,*
1Joh.1: 2. the life *was manifested,*
   — and *was manifested* unto us ;
  2:19. that they *might be made manifest* that
   28. that, when he *shall appear,* we may
  3: 2. it *doth* not yet *appear* what we shall be:
   — when he *shall appear,* we shall be
   5. that he *was manifested* to take away
   8. the Son of God *was manifested,*
  4: 9. In this *was manifested* the love of God
Rev. 3:18. (that) the shame of thy nakedness *do* not
    appear ;
  15: 4. for thy judgments *are made manifest.*

φανερῶς, *phanerōs.*

Mar 1:45. could no more *openly* enter
Joh. 7:10. not *openly*, but as it were in secret.
Acts10: 3. He saw in a vision *evidently*

φανέρωσις, *phanerōsis.*

1Co.12: 7. the *manifestation* of the Spirit
2Co. 4: 2. but by *manifestation* of the truth

φανός, *phanos*

Joh.18: 3. thither with *lanterns* and torches

φαντάζομαι, *phantazomai.*

Heb 12:21. And so terrible was the *sight,*

φαντασία, *phantasia.*

Acts25:23. with great *pomp,* and was entered

φάντασμα, *phantasma.*

Mat.14:26. It is a *spirit ;* (lit. a *phantom*)
Mar 6:49. they supposed it had been a *spirit,*

φάραγξ, *pharanx.*

Lu. 3: 5. Every *valley* shall be filled, and

φαρμακεία, *pharmakīa.*

Gal. 5:20. Idolatry, *witchcraft*, hatred,
Rev. 9:21. nor of their *sorceries*, nor of their
18:23. for by thy *sorceries* were all nations

φαρμακεύς, *pharmakūs.*

Rev.21: 8. whoremongers, and *sorcerers*, and

φαρμακός, *pharmakos.*

Rev.22:15. For without (are) dogs, and *sorcerers,*

φάσις, *phasis.*

Acts21:31. *tidings* came unto the chief captain

φάσκω, *phasko.*

Acts24: 9. *saying* that these things were so.
25:19. whom Paul *affirmed* to be alive.
Ro. 1:22. *Professing* themselves to be wise,
Rev. 2: 2. tried them *which say* they are apostles,

φάτνη, *phatnee.*

Lu. 2: 7. and laid him in a *manger ;*
12. in swaddling clothes, lying in a *manger.*
16. and the babe lying in a *manger.*
13:15. loose his ox or (his) ass from the *stall,*

φαῦλος, *phaulos.*

Joh. 3:20. every one that doeth *evil* hateth the
5:29. and they that have done *evil*, unto the
Tit. 2: 8. having no *evil* thing to say of you.
Jas. 3:16. there (is) confusion and every *evil* work.

φέγγος, *phengos.*

Mat.24:29. the moon shall not give her *light,*
Mar13:24. moon shall not give her *light,*
Lu. 11:33. they which come in may see the *light.*

φείδομαι, *phīdomai.*

Acts20:29. among you, not *sparing* the flock.
Ro. 8:32. He that *spared* not his own Son,
11:21. if God *spared* not the natural branches,
(take heed) lest he also *spare* not thee.
1Co. 7:28. trouble in the flesh: but I *spare* you.
2Co. 1:23. to *spare* you I came not as yet
12: 6. I *forbear*, lest any man should think of me
13: 2. if I come again, I *will* not *spare :*
2Pet. 2: 4. if God *spared* not the angels that sinned,
5. And *spared* not the old world, but

φειδομένως, *phīdomenōs.*

2Co. 9: 6. He which soweth *sparingly* shall reap also
sparingly ;

φελόνης see φαιλόνης.

φέρω, οἴσω, ἤνεγκα, *phero, oiso, eenenka.*

Mat.14:11. his head *was brought* in a charger,
— and she *brought* (it) to her mother.
18. He said, *Bring* them hither to me.
17:17. *bring* him hither to me.
Mar 1:32. they *brought* unto him all that were
2: 3. *bringing* one sick of the palsy,
4: 8. and *brought forth*, some thirty,
6:27. and commanded his head *to be brought :*
28. And *brought* his head in a charger,
7:32. they *bring* unto him one that was deaf,
8:22. and they *bring* a blind man unto him,
9:17. I *have brought* unto thee my son,
19. *bring* him unto me.
20. And they *brought* him unto him:
12:15. *bring* me a penny,
16. And they *brought* (it).
15:22. they *bring* him unto the place Golgotha,
Lu. 5:18. And, behold, men *brought* in a bed
15:23. *bring* hither the fatted calf,
23:26. that he might *bear* (it) after Jesus.
24: 1. *bringing* the spices which they had prepared,
Joh. 2: 8. and *bear* unto the governor of the feast.
And they *bare* (it).
4:33. *Hath* any man *brought* him (ought) to eat?
12:24. it *bringeth forth* much fruit.
15: 2. branch in me *that beareth* not fruit
— every (branch) that *beareth* fruit, he
purgeth it, that it *may bring forth* more
fruit.
4. As the branch cannot *bear* fruit of itself,
5. the same *bringeth forth* much fruit:
8. that ye *bear* much fruit ;
16. that ye should go and *bring forth* fruit,
18:29. What accusation *bring* ye against this
man ?
19:39. *and brought* a mixture of myrrh
20:27. *Reach* hither thy finger, and behold my
hands ; and *reach* hither thy hand,
21:10. *Bring* of the fish which ye have now
18. shall gird thee, and *carry* (thee) whither
Acts 2: 2. as of a *rushing* mighty wind,
4:34. and *brought* the prices of the things
37. and *brought* the money, and laid (it) at
5: 2. and *brought* a certain part, and laid
16. unto Jerusalem, *bringing* sick folks,
12:10. the iron gate *that leadeth* unto the city;
14:13. *brought* oxen and garlands unto the gates,
25: 7. *and laid* many and grievous complaints
27:15. we let (her) drive. (lit. giving to it we
were borne along)
17. strake sail, and so *were driven.*
Ro. 9:22. *endured* with much longsuffering the
2Ti. 4:13. *bring* (with thee), and the books,
Heb 1: 3. *upholding* all things by the word of his
power,
6: 1. *let* us *go on* unto perfection; (lit. *be
brought* forward)
9:16. there must also of necessity *be the death*
of the testator.

Heb 12:20. For they could not *endure* that which was commanded,

13:13. Let us go forth...*bearing* his reproach.

1Pet. 1:13. for the grace that is to be brought (lit. *that is brought*) unto you

2Pet. 1:17. *when* there *came* such a voice to him

18. And this voice *which came* from heaven

21. For the prophecy *came* not in old time by

— spake (as they were) *moved* by the Holy Ghost.

2:11. *bring* not railing accusation against

2Joh. 10. and *bring* not this doctrine,

Rev.21:24. *do bring* their glory and honour into it.

26. *they shall bring* the glory and honour

φεύγω, *phūgo.*

Mat. 2:13. and *flee* into Egypt,

3: 7. *to flee* from the wrath to come?

8:33. And they that kept them *fled,*

10:23. *flee* ye into another:

23:33. how *can* ye *escape* the damnation of hell?

24:16. Then *let* them which be in Judæa *flee* into

26:56. Then all the disciples forsook him, and *fled.*

Mar 5:14. And they that fed the swine *fled,*

13:14. then *let* them that be in Judæa *flee* to

14:50. And they all forsook him, and *fled.*

52. and *fled* from them naked.

16: 8. and *fled* from the sepulchre;

Lu. 3: 7. *to flee* from the wrath to come?

8:34. they *fled,* and went and told

21:21. Then *let* them which are in Judæa *flee* to the mountains;

Joh. 10: 5. but *will flee* from him:

12. and leaveth the sheep, and *fleeth :*

13. The hireling *fleeth,* because he is an

Acts 7:29. Then *fled* Moses at this saying,

27:30. were about *to flee* out of the ship,

1Co. 6:18. *Flee* fornication. Every sin that a man

10.14. my dearly beloved, *flee* from idolatry.

1Ti. 6:11. O man of God, *flee* these things;

2Ti. 2:22. *Flee* also youthful lusts:

Heb 11:34. *escaped* the edge of the sword,

12:25. For if they *escaped* not who refused

Jas. 4: 7. and he *will flee* from you.

Rev. 9: 6. and death *shall flee* from them.

12: 6. the woman *fled* into the wilderness,

16:20. And every island *fled away,*

20:11. the earth and the heaven *fled away;*

φήμη, *pheemee.*

Mat. 9:26. And the *fame* hereof went abroad

Lu. 4:14. and there went out a *fame* of him

φημί, *pheemi.*

Mat. 4: 7. Jesus *said* unto him, It is written

8: 8. The centurion answered and *said,*

13.28. He *said* unto them, An enemy hath

29. But he *said,* Nay; lest while ye

14: 8. *said,* Give me here John Baptist's head

17:26. Jesus *saith* unto him, Then are the children

19:21. Jesus *said* unto him, If thou wilt be

21:27. And he *said* unto them, Neither tell I

25:21. His lord *said* unto him, Well done,

23. His lord *said* unto him, Well done,

26:34. Jesus *said* unto him, Verily I say

Mat.26:61. This (fellow) *said,* I am able to

27:11. And Jesus *said* unto him, Thou sayest.

23. the governor *said,* Why, what evil

65. Pilate *said* unto them, Ye have a watch:

Mar 14:29. But Peter *said* unto him, Although all

Lu. 7:40. And he *saith,* Master, say on.

44. *said* unto Simon, Seest thou this woman?

22:58. another saw him, and *said,* Thou art

70. And he *said* unto them, Ye say that I am.

23: 3. he answered him and *said,* Thou sayest (it).

Joh. 1:23. He *said,* I (am) the voice of one crying

9:38. And he *said,* Lord, I believe.

Acts 2:38. Peter *said* unto them, Repent, and be

7: 2. And he *said,* Men, brethren, and fathers,

8:36. and the eunuch *said,* See, (here is) water;

10:28. he *said* unto them, Ye know how that

30. And Cornelius *said,* Four days ago

31. And *said,* Cornelius, thy prayer is heard,

16:30. and *said,* Sirs, what must I do to

37. But Paul *said* unto them, They have beaten

17:22. and *said,* (Ye) men of Athens,

19:35. he *said,* (Ye) men of Ephesus,

21:37. Who *said,* Canst thou speak Greek?

22:2(3). they kept the more silence: and he *saith,*

27. art thou a Roman? He *said,* Yea.

28. And Paul *said,* But I was (free) born.

23: 5. Then *said* Paul, I wist not, brethren,

17. and *said,* Bring this young man unto

18. and *said,* Paul the prisoner called me

35. I will hear thee, *said* he, when thine

25: 5. Let them therefore, *said* he, which among

22. Then Agrippa *said* unto Festus, I would

— To morrow, *said* he, thou shalt hear him.

24. And Festus *said,* King Agrippa, and all men

26: 1. Then Agrippa *said* unto Paul, Thou

24. Festus *said* with a loud voice,

25. But he *said,* I am not mad,

28. Then Agrippa *said* unto Paul, Almost

32. Then *said* Agrippa unto Festus, This

Ro. 3: 8. and as some *affirm* that we say,

1Co. 6:16. for two, *saith* he, shall be one flesh.

7:29. But this I *say,* brethren, the time (is) short;

10:15. judge ye what I *say.*

19. What *say* I then? that the idol is any thing,

15:50. Now this I *say,* brethren, that flesh and

2Co.10:10. For (his) letters, *say* they, (lit. *saith* he) (are) weighty

Heb 8: 5. for, See, *saith* he, (that) thou make all

φθάνω, *phthano.*

Mat.12:28. then the kingdom of God *is come* unto you.

Lu. 11:20. the kingdom of God *is come* upon you.

Ro. 9:31. hath not *attained* to the law of

2Co.10:14. for we *are come* as far as to you also

Phi. 3:16. whereto we *have already attained,*

1Th. 2:16. for the wrath *is come* upon them to

4:15. *shall* not *prevent* them which are asleep.

φθαρτός, *phthartos.*

Ro. 1:23. an image made like to *corruptible* man,

1Co. 9:25. to obtain a *corruptible* crown;

15:53. this *corruptible* must put on incorruption,

54. So when this *corruptible* shall have put

1Pet.1:18. ye were not redeemed with *corruptible*

23. not of *corruptible* seed, but of

φθέγγομαι, phthengomai.

Acts 4:18. not *to speak* at all nor teach in the name
2Pet.2:16. the dumb ass *speaking* with man's voice
　　18. For *when* they *speak* great swelling

φθείρω, phthīro.

1Co. 3:17. If any man *defile* the temple of God, him
　　　　shall God *destroy;*
　15:33. evil communications *corrupt* good
2Co. 7: 2. we *have corrupted* no man,
　　11: 3. so your minds *should be corrupted* from
Eph. 4:22. the old man, *which is corrupt* according to
　　　　the deceitful lusts;
Jude　10. in those things they *corrupt* them*selves.*
Rev.19: 2. which *did corrupt* the earth with her
　　　　fornication,

φθινοπωρινός, phthinopōrinos.

Jude　12. trees *whose fruit withereth,*

φθόγγος, phthongos.

Ro. 10:18. Yes verily, their *sound* went into all
1Co.14: 7. except they give a distinction in the *sounds,*

φθονέω, phthoneo.

Gal. 5:26. *envying* one another.

φθόνος, phthonos.

Mat.27:18. that for *envy* they had delivered him.
Mar15:10. had delivered him for *envy.*
Ro.　1:29. full of *envy,* murder, debate,
Gal. 5:21. *Envyings,* murders, drunkenness,
Phi. 1:15. preach Christ even of *envy* and strife;
1Ti. 6: 4. whereof cometh *envy,* strife,
Tit. 3: 3. living in malice and *envy,*
Jas. 4: 5. The spirit that dwelleth in us lusteth to
　　　　envy?
1Pet.2: 1. guile, and hypocrisies, and *envies,*

φθορά, phthora.

Ro.　8:21. delivered from the bondage of *corruption*
1Co.15:42. It is sown in *corruption;* it is raised
　　50. neither doth *corruption* inherit incorrup-
　　　　tion.
Gal. 6: 8. shall of the flesh reap *corruption;*
Col. 2:22. Which all are to *perish* with the using;
2Pet.1: 4. having escaped the *corruption* that is
　　2:12. beasts, made to be taken and *destroyed,*
　　— shall utterly perish in their own *corruption;*
　　19. themselves are the servants of *corruption:*

φιάλη, phialee.

Rev. 5: 8. and golden *vials* full of odours,
　15: 7. unto the seven angels seven golden *vials*
　16: 1. pour out the *vials* of the wrath of God
　　2. poured out his *vial* upon the earth;
　　3. poured out his *vial* upon the sea;

Rev.16: 4. poured out his *vial* upon the rivers and
　　8. poured out his *vial* upon the sun;
　10. out his *vial* upon the seat of the beast;
　12. his *vial* upon the great river Euphrates;
　17. poured out his *vial* into the air;
17: 1. angels which had the seven *vials,*
21: 9. which had the seven *vials* full of the

φιλάγαθος, philagathos.

Tit.　1: 8. But a lover of hospitality, a *lover of good
　　　　men,*

φιλαδελφία, philadelphia.

Ro. 12:10. (Be) kindly affectioned one to another
　　　　with *brotherly love;*
1Th. 4: 9. But as touching *brotherly love*
Heb 13: 1. Let *brotherly love* continue.
1Pet.1:22. unto unfeigned *love of the brethren,*
2Pet.1: 7. And to godliness *brotherly kindness;* and
　　　　to *brotherly kindness* charity.

φιλάδελφος, philadelphos.

1Pet.3: 8. *love as brethren,* (be) pitiful,

φίλανδρος, philandros.

Tit.　2: 4. to *love their husbands,* to love their

φιλανθρωπία, philanthrōpia.

Acts28: 2. shewed us no little *kindness:*
Tit.　3: 4. after that the kindness and *love* of God
　　　　our Saviour *toward man* appeared,

φιλανθρώπως, philanthrōpōs.

Acts27: 3. Julius *courteously* entreated Paul,

φιλαργυρία, philarguria.

1Ti.　6:10. For the *love of money* is the root of all evil:

φιλάργυρος, philarguros.

Lu. 16:14. the Pharisees also, who were *covetous,*
2Ti. 3: 2. lovers of their own selves, *covetous,*

φίλαυτος, philautos.

2Ti. 3: 2. *lovers of their own selves,* covetous.

φιλέω, phileo.

Mat. 6: 5. for they *love* to pray standing in the
　10:37. He *that loveth* father or mother more
　　　　than me
　　— and he *that loveth* son or daughter more
　23: 6. And *love* the uppermost rooms at feasts,

Mat.26:48. Whomsoever I *shall kiss*, that same is he:
Mar 14:44. Whomsoever I *shall kiss*, that same is he ;
Lu. 20:46. and *love* greetings in the markets,
   22:47. and drew near unto Jesus *to kiss* him.
Joh. 5:20. For the Father *loveth* the Son,
   11: 3. he whom thou *lovest* is sick.
      36. Behold how he *loved* him !
   12:25. He *that loveth* his life shall lose it ;
   15:19. the world would *love* his own:
   16:27. For the Father himself *loveth* you, because
         ye *have loved* me,
   20: 2. to the other disciple, whom Jesus *loved,*
   21:15. thou knowest that I *love* thee.
      16. thou knowest that I *love* thee.
      17. Simon, (son) of Jonas, *lovest* thou me ?
      — *Lovest* thou me ?
      — thou knowest that I *love* thee.
1Co.16:22. If any man *love* not the Lord Jesus Christ,
Tit. 3:15. Greet them *that love* us in the faith.
Rev. 3:19. As many as I *love,* I rebuke and
   22:15. and whosoever *loveth* and maketh a lie.

φιλήδονος, phileedonos.

2Ti. 3: 4. *lovers of pleasures* more than lovers of
      God ;

φίλημα, phileema.

Lu. 7:45. Thou gavest me no *kiss :*
   22:48. betrayest thou the Son of man with a
      kiss ?
Ro. 16:16. Salute one another with an holy *kiss.*
1Co.16:20. Greet ye one another with an holy *kiss.*
2Co.13:12. Greet one another with an holy *kiss.*
1Th. 5:26. Greet all the brethren with an holy *kiss.*
1Pet 5:14. one another with a *kiss* of charity.

φιλία, philia.

Jas. 4: 4. that the *friendship* of the world is enmity
      with God ?

φιλόθεος, philotheos.

2Ti. 3: 4. lovers of pleasures more than *lovers of*
      God ;

φιλονεικία, philonīkia.

Lu. 22:24. there was also a *strife* among them, which

φιλόνεικος, philonīkos.

1Co.11:16. But if any man seem to be *contentious,*

φιλοξενία, philoxenia.

Ro. 12:13. given to *hospitality.*
Heb 13: 2. Be not forgetful to *entertain strangers :*

φιλόξενος, philoxenos.

1Ti. 3: 2. *given to hospitality,* apt to teach ;

Tit. 1: 8. But a *lover of hospitality,* a lover of
1Pet.4: 9. *Use hospitality* one to another without

φιλοπρωτεύω, philoprōtūo.

3Joh. 9. but Diotrephes, *who loveth to have the pre-*
      eminence among them,

φίλος, philos.

Mat.11:19. a *friend* of publicans and sinners.
Lu. 7: 6. the centurion sent *friends* to him,
     34. a *friend* of publicans and sinners !
   11: 5. Which of you shall have a *friend,*
      — *Friend,* lend me three loaves ;
      6. For a *friend* of mine in his journey is
      8. and give him, because he is his *friend,*
   12: 4. And I say unto you my *friends,*
   14:10. *Friend,* go up higher:
     12. call not thy *friends,* nor thy brethren,
   15: 6. he calleth together (his) *friends* and
     9. she calleth (her) *friends* and (her)
     29. that I might make merry with my *friends :*
   16: 9. Make to yourselves *friends* of the mammon
   21:16. brethren, and kinsfolks, and *friends ;*
   23:12. Pilate and Herod were made *friends*
Joh. 3:29. but the *friend* of the bridegroom,
   11:11. Our *friend* Lazarus sleepeth ;
   15:13. a man lay down his life for his *friends.*
     14. Ye are my *friends,* if ye do whatsoever
     15. but I have called you *friends ;*
   19:12. thou art not Cæsar's *friend :*
Acts10:24. his kinsmen and near *friends.*
   19:31. the chief of Asia, which were his *friends,*
   27: 3. to go unto his *friends* to refresh himself.
Jas. 2:23. and he was called the *Friend* of God.
   4: 4. whosoever therefore will be a *friend* of
      the world is the enemy of God.
3Joh. 14(15) (Our) *friends* salute thee. Greet the
      friends by name.

φιλοσοφία, philosophia.

Col. 2: 8. spoil you, through *philosophy* and vain
      deceit, after the tradition of

φιλόσοφος, philosophos.

Acts17:18. certain *philosophers* of the Epicureans,

φιλόστοργος, philostorgos.

Ro. 12:10. (Be) *kindly affectioned* one to another

φιλότεκνος, philoteknos.

Tit. 2: 4. to *love their children,*

φιλοτιμέομαι, philotimeomai.

Ro. 15:20. Yea, so *have I strived* to preach the gospel,
2Co. 5: 9. Wherefore we *labour,* that, whether
1Th. 4:11. And that ye *study* to be quiet, and to do

φιλοφρόνως, philophronōs.

Acts28: 7. and lodged us three days *courteously*.

φιλόφρων, philophrōn.

1Pet.3: 8. (be) pitiful, (be) *courteous :*

φιμόω, phimoō.

Mat.22:12. And he *was* speechless.
    34. that he *had put* the Sadducees *to silence*,
Mar 1:25. *Hold* thy *peace*, and come out of him.
  4:39. and said unto the sea, Peace, *be still*.
Lu. 4:35. *Hold* thy *peace*, and come out of him.
1Co. 9: 9. Thou *shalt* not *muzzle* the mouth of the
1Ti. 5:18. Thou *shalt* not *muzzle* the ox that treadeth
1Pet.2:15. may *put to silence* the ignorance of

φλογίζω, phlogizo.

Jas. 3: 6. and *setteth on fire* the course of nature;
    and it *is set on fire* of hell.

φλόξ, phlox.

Lu. 16:24. for I am tormented in this *flame*.
Acts 7:30. in a *flame* of fire in a bush.
2Th. 1: 8. In *flaming* fire taking vengeance
Heb 1: 7. and his ministers a *flame* of fire.
Rev. 1:14. his eyes (were) as a *flame* of fire ;
  2:18. his eyes like unto a *flame* of fire,
  19:12. His eyes (were) as a *flame* of fire,

φλυαρέω, phluareo.

3Joh. 10. *prating against* us with malicious words:

φλύαρος, phluaros.

1Ti. 5:13. but *tattlers* also and busybodies,

φοβέομαι, phobeomai.

Mat. 1:20. *fear* not to take unto thee Mary
  2:22. he *was afraid* to go thither:
  10:26. *Fear* them not therefore:
    28. and *fear* not them which kill the
    — but rather *fear* him which is able to
    31. *Fear* ye not therefore, ye are of
  14: 5. he *feared* the multitude, because they
    27. it is I ; *be not afraid*.
    30. the wind boisterous, he *was afraid ;*
  17: 6. fell on their face, and *were* sore *afraid*.
    7. Arise, and *be not afraid*.
  21:26. we *fear* the people ; for all hold John
    46. they *feared* the multitude, because they
  25:25. And I was *afraid*, and went and hid thy
  27:54. they *feared* greatly, saying, Truly this
  28: 5. *Fear* not ye : for I know that ye seek
    10. *Be not afraid :* go tell my brethren that
Mar 4:41. they *feared* exceedingly, and said
  5:15. and they *were afraid*.
    33. But the woman *fearing* and trembling,

Mar 5:36. *Be* not *afraid*, only believe.
  6:20. For Herod *feared* John, knowing
    50. it is I ; *be not afraid*.
  9:32. and *were afraid* to ask him.
  10:32. and as they followed, they *were afraid*.
  11:18. for they *feared* him, because all
    32. Of men ; they *feared* the people:
  12:12. to lay hold on him, but *feared* the people :
  16: 8. for they *were afraid*.
Lu. 1:13. *Fear* not, Zacharias : for thy prayer
    30. *Fear* not, Mary : for thou hast found
    50. And his mercy (is) on them *that fear* him
  2: 9. and they *were* sore *afraid*.
    10. *Fear* not : for, behold, I bring you
  5:10. And Jesus said unto Simon, *Fear* not ;
  8:25. And they *being afraid* wondered
    35. and they *were afraid*.
    50. *Fear* not : believe only,
  9:34. *feared* as they entered into the cloud.
    45. they *feared* to ask him of that saying.
  12: 4. *Be* not *afraid* of them that kill the
    5. whom ye *shall fear : Fear* him, which
      after he hath killed
    — I say unto you, *Fear* him.
    7. *Fear* not therefore : ye are of more value
    32. *Fear* not, little flock;
  18: 2. a judge, *which feared* not God,
    4. Though I *fear* not God,
  19:21. For I *feared* thee, because thou art
  20:19. and they *feared* the people : for they
  22: 2. for they *feared* the people.
  23:40. *Dost* not thou *fear* God, seeing thou art
Joh. 6:19. unto the ship : and they *were afraid*.
    20. It is I ; *be not afraid*.
  9:22. because they *feared* the Jews
  12:15. *Fear* not, daughter of Sion : behold,
  19: 8. he *was* the more *afraid ;*
Acts 5:26. for they *feared* the people, lest
  9:26. but they *were* all *afraid* of him,
  10: 2. and one *that feared* God with
    22. and one *that feareth* God,
    35. But in every nation he *that feareth* him,
  13:16. and ye *that fear* God, give audience.
    26. and whosoever among you *feareth* God,
  16:38. they *feared*, when they heard that they
  18: 9. *Be* not *afraid*, but speak, and hold not
  22:29. and the chief captain also *was afraid*,
  27:17. and, *fearing* lest they should fall into
    24. Saying, *Fear* not, Paul ; thou must be
    29. *fearing* lest we should have fallen
Ro. 11:20. *Be* not highminded, but *fear :*
  13: 3. Wilt thou then not *be afraid* of the power?
    4. if thou do that which is evil, *be afraid ;*
2Co.11: 3. But I *fear*, lest by any means, as the
  12:20. For I *fear*, lest, when I come, I
Gal. 2:12. *fearing* them which were of the
  4:11. I am *afraid* of you, lest I have bestowed
Eph 5:33. and the wife (see) that she *reverence* (her)
Col. 3.22. but in singleness of heart, *fearing* God:
Heb 4: 1. *Let* us therefore *fear*, lest, a promise
  11:23. and they *were* not *afraid* of the king's
    27. not *fearing* the wrath of the king:
  13: 6. I *will* not *fear* what man shall do unto
1Pet.2:17. *Fear* God. Honour the king.
  3: 6. and *are* not *afraid* with any amazement.
    14. and *be* not *afraid* of their terror,
1Joh.4:18. He *that feareth* is not made perfect in
Rev. 1:17. saying unto me, *Fear* not ; I am the
  2:10. *Fear* none of those things which thou
  11:18. to the saints, and them *that fear* thy
    name,
  14: 7. *Fear* God, and give glory to him ;

Rev.15: 4. Who *shall* not *fear* thee, O Lord, and
19: 5. and ye *that fear* him, both small and

φοβερός, *phoberos.*

Heb 10:27. *fearful* looking for of judgment
31. (It is) a *fearful* thing to fall into the
12:21. And so *terrible* was the sight,

φόβητρον, *phobeetron.*

Lu. 21:11. and *fearful sights* and great signs

φόβος, *phobos.*

Mat.14:26. and they cried out for *fear.*
28: 4. for *fear* of him the keepers did shake,
8. from the sepulchre with *fear* and great joy;
Mar 4:41. And they feared exceedingly, (lit. f. a great *fear*)
Lu. 1:12. and *fear* fell upon him.
65. And *fear* came on all that dwelt
2: 9. and they were sore afraid. (lit. feared, &c.)
5:26. and were filled with *fear,* saying, We
7:16. And there came a *fear* on all:
8:37. for they were taken with great *fear:*
21:26. for *fear,* and for looking after those
Joh. 7:13. openly of him for *fear* of the Jews.
19:38. but secretly for *fear* of the Jews,
20:19. assembled for *fear* of the Jews, came Jesus
Acts 2:43. And *fear* came upon every soul:
5: 5. great *fear* came on all them that
11. great *fear* came upon all the church,
9:31. and walking in the *fear* of the Lord,
19:17. and *fear* fell on them all,
Ro. 3:18. There is no *fear* of God before
8:15. the spirit of bondage again to *fear;*
13: 3. rulers are not a *terror* to good works,
7. *fear* to whom *fear;*
1Co. 2: 3. and in *fear,* and in much trembling.
2Co. 5:11. Knowing therefore the *terror* of the Lord,
7: 1. perfecting holiness in the *fear* of God.
5. within (were) *fears.*
11. (what) indignation, yea, (what) *fear,*
15. how with *fear* and trembling ye received
Eph. 5:21. one to another in the *fear* of God.
6: 5. with *fear* and trembling, in singleness
Phi. 2:12. your own salvation with *fear* and
1Ti. 5:20. others also may fear. (lit. may have *fear*)
Heb 2:15. who through *fear* of death were all
1Pet. 1:17. the time of your sojourning (here) in *fear:*
2:18. subject to (your) masters with all *fear;*
3: 2. your chaste conversation (coupled) with *fear.*
14. and be not afraid of their *terror,*
15. with meekness and *fear:*
1Joh.4:18. There is no *fear* in love; but perfect love casteth out *fear:* because *fear* hath torment.
Jude 23. And others save with *fear,* pulling
Rev.11:11. great *fear* fell upon them which saw them.
18:10. afar off for the *fear* of her torment,
15. stand afar off for the *fear* of her torment, weeping and wailing.

φοῖνιξ, *phoinix.*

Joh.12:13. Took branches of *palm trees,*
Rev. 7: 9. white robes, and *palms* in their hands;

φονεύς, *phonūs.*

Mat.22: 7. and destroyed those *murderers,*
Acts 3:14. desired a *murderer* to be granted unto you;
7:52. of whom ye have been now the betrayers and *murderers:*
28: 4. No doubt this man is a *murderer,*
1Pet. 4:15. let none of you suffer as a *murderer,* or
Rev.21: 8. and *murderers,* and whoremongers,
22:15. and *murderers,* and idolaters, and

φονεύω, *phonūo.*

Mat. 5:21. Thou *shalt* not·*kill;* and whosoever *shall kill*
19:18. Thou *shalt* do no *murder,*
23:31. of them *which killed* the prophets.
35. whom ye *slew* between the temple and
Mar 10:19. *Do* not *kill,*
Lu. 18:20. *Do* not *kill,*
Ro. 13: 9. Thou *shalt* not *kill,*
Jas. 2:11. said also, *Do* not *kill.*
— yet if thou *kill,* thou art become a
4: 2. ye *kill,* and desire to have,
5: 6. Ye have condemned (and) *killed* the just;

φόνος, *phonos.*

Mat.15:19. proceed evil thoughts, *murders,*
Mar 7:21. adulteries, fornications, *murders,*
15: 7. committed *murder* in the insurrection.
Lu. 23:19. in the city, and for *murder,*
25. him that for sedition and *murder* was
Acts 9: 1. breathing out threatenings and *slaughter* against the disciples
Ro. 1:29. full of envy, *murder,* debate,
Gal. 5:21. Envyings, *murders,* drunkenness,
Heb 11:37. were slain with the sword: (lit. *slaughter* of the sword)
Rev. 9:21. Neither repented they of their *murders,*

φορέω, *phoreo.*

Mat.11: 8. they *that wear* soft (clothing) are in kings' houses.
Joh.19: 5. *wearing* the crown of thorns,
Ro. 13: 4. for he *beareth* not the sword in vain:
1Co.15:49. as we *have borne* the image of the earthy, we *shall* also *bear* the image of
Jas. 2: 3. to him *that weareth* the gay clothing,

φόρος, *phoros.*

Lu. 20:22. Is it lawful for us to give *tribute* unto Cæsar, or no?
23: 2. and forbidding to give *tribute* to Cæsar,
Ro. 13: 6. For for this cause pay ye *tribute* also:
7. *tribute* to whom *tribute* (is due);

φορτίζω, *phortizo.*

Mat.11:28. Come unto me, all (ye) that labour and are *heavy laden,*
Lu. 11:46. for ye *lade* men with burdens grievous to

φορτίον, *phortion.*

Mat.11:30. and my *burden* is light.

Mat.23: 4. For they bind heavy *burdens* and
Lu. 11:46. with *burdens* grievous to be borne, and ye
　　　　　 yourselves touch not the *burdens* with
Gal. 6: 5. For every man shall bear his own *burden*.

φόρτος, *phortos.*

Acts27:10. not only of the *lading* and ship, but also

φραγέλλιον, *phragellion.*

Joh. 2:15. when he had made a *scourge* of small
　　　　 cords,

φραγελλόω, *phragelloō.*

Mat.27:26. *when* he *had scourged* Jesus,
Mar15:15. del vered Jesus, *when* he *had scourged*
　　　　 (him),

φραγμός, *phragmos.*

Mat.21:33. and *hedged* it round about,
Mar12: 1. and set an *hedge* about (it),
Lu. 14:23. Go out into the highways and *hedges*,
Eph. 2:14. and hath broken down the middle wall of
　　　　 partition (between us);

φράζω, *phrazo.*

Mat.13:36. *Declare* unto us the parable
　　15:15. *Declare* unto us this parable.

φράσσω, *phrasso.*

Ro. 3:19. that every mouth *may be stopped*,
2Co.11:10. no man shall stop me of this boasting (lit.
　　　　 this boasting *shall* not *be stopped* to me)
Heb11:33. *stopped* the mouths of lions,

φρέαρ, *phrear.*

Lu. 14: 5. have an ass or an ox fallen into a *pit*,
Joh. 4:11. and the *well* is deep:
　　 12. which gave us the *well*,
Rev. 9: 1. was given the key of the bottomless *pit*.
　　 2. And he opened the bottomless *pit*; and
　　　　 there arose a smoke out of the *pit*,
　　 — by reason of the smoke of the *pit*.

φρεναπατάω, *phrenapatao.*

Gal. 6: 3. when he is nothing, he *deceiveth* himself.

φρεναπάτης, *phrenapatees.*

Tit. 1:10. and vain talkers and *deceivers*,

φρένες, *phrenes.*

Plural from φρήν.

1Co.14:20. be not children in *understanding*:
　　 — but in *understanding* be men.

φρίσσω, *phrisso.*

Jas. 2:19. the devils also believe, and *tremble*. (lit.
　　　　 quiver)

φρονέω, *phroneo.*

Mat.16:23. *savourest* not the things that be of God,
Mar 8:33. thou *savourest* not the things that be
Acts28:22. to hear of thee what thou *thinkest*:
Ro. 8: 5. do *mind* the things of the flesh;
　　12: 3. more highly than he ought *to think*; but
　　　　 to think soberly,
　　 16. (Be) of the same mind (lit. *minding* the
　　　　 same) one toward another. *Mind* not
　　　　 high things,
　　14: 6. He *that regardeth* the day, *regardeth* (it)
　　　　 unto the Lord; and he *that regardeth*
　　　　 not the day, to the Lord he *doth* not
　　　　 regard (it).
　　15: 5. *to be* like*minded* one toward another
1Co. 4: 6. not *to think* (of men) above that which is
　　13:11. I *understood* as a child:
2Co.13:11. *be of* one *mind*, (lit. *mind* ye the same)
Gal. 5:10. that ye *will be* none otherwise *minded*:
Phi. 1: 7. meet for me *to think* this of you all,
　　 2: 2. that ye *be* like*minded*,
　　 — (being) of one accord, of one *mind*. (lit.
　　　　 minding the one thing)
　　 5. *Let* this *mind be* in you, which was
　　 3:15. *Let* us therefore, as many as be perfect,
　　　　 be thus *minded*: and if in any thing ye
　　　　 be otherwise *minded*,
　　 16. let us *mind* the same thing.
　　 19. who *mind* earthly things.
　　 4: 2. that they *be* of the same *mind* in the Lord.
　　 10. your *care* of me hath flourished again;
　　　　 wherein ye *were* also *careful*, but
Col. 3: 2. *Set* your *affection on* things above,

φρόνημα, *phroneema.*

Ro. 8: 6. *to be* carnally *minded* (is) death; but *to be*
　　　　 spiritually *minded* (is) life and peace.
　　 7. Because the carnal *mind* (is) enmity
　　 27. knoweth what (is) the *mind* of the Spirit,

φρόνησις, *phroneesis.*

Lu. 1:17. the disobedient to the *wisdom* of the just;
Eph. 1: 8. in all wisdom and *prudence*;

φρόνιμος, *phronimos.*

Mat. 7:24. I will liken him unto a *wise* man,
　　10:16. be ye therefore *wise* as serpents,
　　24:45. Who then is a faithful and *wise* servant,
　　25: 2. And five of them were *wise*,
　　 4. the *wise* took oil in their vessels with
　　 8. And the foolish said unto the *wise*,
　　 9. But the *wise* answered, saying,
Lu. 12:42. Who then is that faithful and *wise* steward,
　　16: 8. *wiser* than the children of light.
Ro. 11:25. lest ye should be *wise* in your own conceits;
　　12:16. Be not *wise* in your own conceits.
1Co. 4:10. but ye (are) *wise* in Christ;
　　10:15. I speak as to *wise* men; judge ye
2Co.11:19. seeing ye (yourselves) are *wise*.

φρονίμως, phronimōs.

Lu. 16: 8. because he had done *wisely :*

φροντίζω, phrontizo.

Tit. 3: 8. *might be careful* to maintain good works.

φρουρέω, phroureo.

2Co.11:32. *kept* the city of the Damascenes *with a garrison,*
Gal. 3:23. we *were kept* under the law, shut up unto
Phi. 4: 7. *shall keep* your hearts and minds through
1Pet.1: 5. *Who are kept* by the power of God through faith unto salvation

---

φρυάσσω, phruasso.

Acts 4:25. Why *did* the heathen *rage,* and the

φρύγανον, phruganon.

Acts28: 3. Paul had gathered a bundle of *sticks,*

φυγή, phugee.

Mat.24:20. that your *flight* be not in the winter,
Mar 13:18. that your *flight* be not in the winter.

φυλακή, phulakee.

Mat. 5:25. and thou be cast into *prison.*
14: 3. and put (him) in *prison* for Herodias' sake,
10. and beheaded John in the *prison.*
25. And in the fourth *watch* of the night
18:30. went and cast him into *prison,* till he
24:43. in what *watch* the thief would come,
25:36. I was in *prison,* and ye came unto me.
39. when saw we thee sick, or in *prison,*
43. sick, and in *prison,* and ye
44. or sick, or in *prison,* and did not
Mar 6:17. bound him in *prison* for Herodias' sake,
27(28). and beheaded him in the *prison,*
48. about the fourth *watch* of the night
Lu. 2: 8. keeping *watch* over their flock by night.
3:20. that he shut up John in *prison.*
12:38. in the second *watch,* or come in the third *watch,*
58. and the officer cast thee into *prison.*
21:12. to the synagogues, and into *prisons,*
22:33. both into *prison,* and to death.
23:19. and for murder, was cast into *prison.*
25. and murder was cast into *prison,*
Joh. 3:24. For John was not yet cast into *prison.*
Acts 5:19. by night opened the *prison* doors,
22. and found them not in the *prison,*
25. the men whom ye put in *prison*
8: 3. men and women committed (them) to *prison.*
12: 4. he put (him) in *prison,* and delivered
5. Peter therefore was kept in *prison :*
6. keepers before the door kept the *prison.*
10. were past the first and the second *ward,*
17. had brought him out of the *prison.*
16:23. they cast (them) into *prison,*

Acts16:24. thrust them into the inner *prison,*
27. and seeing the *prison* doors open,
37. and have cast (us) into *prison ;*
40. And they went out of the *prison,*
22: 4. and delivering into *prisons* both
26:10. of the saints did I shut up in *prison,*
2Co. 6: 5. In stripes, in *imprisonments,*
11:23. in *prisons* more frequent,
Heb 11:36. moreover of bonds and *imprisonment :*
1Pet. 3:19. preached unto the spirits in *prison ;*
Rev. 2:10. devil shall cast (some) of you into *prison,*
18: 2. and the *hold* of every foul spirit, and a *cage* of every unclean and hateful bird.
20: 7. Satan shall be loosed out of his *prison,*

φυλακίζω, phulakizo.

Acts22:19. that I *imprisoned* and beat in every

φυλακτήριον, phulakteerion.

Mat.23: 5. they make broad their *phylacteries,*

φύλαξ, phulax.

Acts 5:23. and the *keepers* standing without
12: 6. and the *keepers* before the door kept
19. he examined the *keepers,* and commanded

φυλάσσω, phulasso.

Mat.19:20. All these things *have I kept* from
Mar 10:20. all these *have I observed* from my youth.
Lu. 2: 8. *keeping* watch over their flock
8:29. he was *kept* bound with chains and in
11:21. When a strong man armed *keepeth* his
28. that hear the word of God, and *keep* it.
12:15. and *beware* of covetousness:
18:21. All these *have I kept* from my youth up.
Joh.12:25. *shall keep* it unto life eternal.
17:12. that thou gavest me I *have kept,*
Acts 7:53. of angels, and *have* not *kept* (it).
12: 4. to four quaternions of soldiers *to keep* him ;
16: 4. delivered them the decrees *for to keep,*
21:24. walkest orderly, and *keepest* the law.
25. only that they *keep* themselves from
22:20. *kept* the raiment of them that slew him.
23:35. *to be kept* in Herod's judgment hall.
28:16. with a soldier that *kept* him.
Ro. 2:26. *keep* the righteousness of the law,
Gal. 6:13. who are circumcised *keep* the law ;
2Th. 3: 3. shall stablish you, and *keep* (you) from evil.
1Ti. 5:21. that thou *observe* these things
6:20. *keep* that which is committed to thy trust,
2Ti. 1:12. that he is able *to keep* that which I have
14. which was committed unto thee *keep* by the Holy Ghost
4:15. Of whom be thou *ware* also ;
2Pet. 2: 5. but *saved* Noah the eighth (person),
3:17. ye know (these things) before, *beware* lest
1Joh. 5:21. *keep* yourselves from idols.
Jude 24. that is able *to keep* you from falling,

φυλή, phulee.

Mat.19:28. judging the twelve *tribes* of Israel.

Mat. 24:30. and then shall all the *tribes* of the earth
Lu. 2:36. daughter of Phanuel, of the *tribe* of Aser:
22:30. judging the twelve *tribes* of Israel.
Acts 13:21. son of Cis, a man of the *tribe* of Benjamin,
Ro. 11: 1. (of) the *tribe* of Benjamin.
Phi. 3: 5. (of) the *tribe* of Benjamin, an Hebrew of
Heb 7:13. pertaineth to another *tribe*, of which no
14. of which *tribe* Moses spake nothing
Jas. 1: 1. to the twelve *tribes* which are scattered
Rev. 1: 7. and all *kindreds* of the earth shall wail
5. 5. the Lion of the *tribe* of Juda,
9. out of every *kindred*, and tongue,
7: 4. of all the *tribes* of the children of Israel.
5. Of the *tribe* of Juda (were) sealed twelve
— Of the *tribe* of Reuben (were),
— Of the *tribe* of Gad (were)
6. Of the *tribe* of Aser (were)
— Of the *tribe* of Nepthalim (were)
— Of the *tribe* of Manasses (were)
7. Of the *tribe* of Simeon (were)
— Of the *tribe* of Levi (were)
— Of the *tribe* of Issachar (were)
8. Of the *tribe* of Zabulon (were)
— Of the *tribe* of Joseph (were)
— Of the *tribe* of Benjamin (were)
9. and *kindreds*, and people, and tongues,
11: 9. and *kindreds* and tongues and nations
13: 7. over all *kindreds*, and tongues, and
14: 6. and to every nation, and *kindred*, and
21:12. (the names) of the twelve *tribes* of the
children of Israel:

φύλλον, *phullon.*

Mat. 21:19. nothing thereon, but *leaves* only,
24:32. tender, and putteth forth *leaves*,
Mar 11:13. seeing a fig tree afar off having *leaves*,
— he found nothing but *leaves*;
13:28. and putteth forth *leaves*, ye know
Rev. 22: 2. and the *leaves* of the tree (were) for the
healing of the nations.

φῦμι see φύω.

φύραμα, *phurama.*

Ro. 9:21. of the same *lump* to make one vessel
11:16. firstfruit (be) holy, the *lump* (is) also
(holy):
1Co. 5: 6. a little leaven leaveneth the whole *lump*?
7. that ye may be a new *lump*,
Gal. 5: 9. A little leaven leaveneth the whole *lump*.

φυσικός, *phusikos.*

Ro. 1:26. their women did change the *natural* use
27. leaving the *natural* use of the woman,
2Pet. 2:12. But these, as *natural* brute beasts,

φυσικῶς, *phusikōs.*

Jude 10. but what they know *naturally*, as

φυσιόω, *phusioo.*

1Co. 4: 6. that no one of you be *puffed up* for one

1Co. 4:18. Now some *are puffed up*, as though I
19. not the speech of them *which are puffed up*,
5: 2. And ye are *puffed up*, and have not
8: 1. Knowledge *puffeth up*, but charity
13: 4. *is* not *puffed up*,
Col. 2:18. vainly *puffed up* by his fleshly mind,

φύσις, *phusis.*

Ro. 1:26. into that which is against *nature*:
2:14. do by *nature* the things contained in the law,
27. uncircumcision which is by *nature*,
11:21. For if God spared not the *natural* branches,
24. out of the olive tree which is wild by
nature, and wert graffed contrary to
nature into
— shall these, which be the *natural* (branches),
1Co. 11:14. Doth not even *nature* itself teach you,
Gal. 2:15. We (who are) Jews by *nature*,
4: 8. which by *nature* are no gods.
Eph. 2: 3. and were by *nature* the children of wrath,
Jas. 3: 7. every *kind* of beasts, and of birds, and
— hath been tamed of man*kind*:
2Pet. 1: 4. ye might be partakers of the divine *nature*,

φυσίωσις, *phusiōsis.*

2Co. 12:20. whisperings, *swellings*, tumults:

φυτεία, *phutīa.*

Mat. 15:13. Every *plant*, which my heavenly Father
hath not planted,

φυτεύω, *phutūo.*

Mat. 15:13. which my heavenly Father *hath* not *planted*,
21:33. which *planted* a vineyard,
Mar 12: 1. A (certain) man *planted* a vineyard,
Lu. 13: 6. A certain (man) had a fig tree *planted* in
17: 6. and *be* thou *planted* in the sea;
28. they *planted*, they builded;
20: 9. A certain man *planted* a vineyard,
1Co. 3: 6. I have *planted*, Apollos watered;
7. neither is he that *planteth* any thing,
8. Now he that *planteth* and he that
9: 7. who *planteth* a vineyard, and eateth not

φύω, *phuo.*

Lu. 8: 6. *as soon as* it *was sprung up*, it withered away,
8. and *sprang up, and* bare fruit
Heb 12:15. any root of bitterness *springing* up

φωλεός, *pholeos.*

Mat. 8:20. The foxes have *holes*, and the birds
Lu. 9:58. Foxes have *holes*, and birds of the air

φωνέω, *phōneo.*

Mat. 20:32. Jesus stood still, and *called* them,
26:34. That this night, before the cock *crow*,
74. And immediately the cock *crew*.

Mat.26:75. Before the cock *crow*, thou shalt deny me
  27:47. This (man) *calleth for* Elias.
Mar 3:31. standing without, sent unto him, *calling* him.
  9:35. and *called* the twelve, and saith
  10:49. and commanded him *to be called.* And *they call* the blind man,
  — rise ; he *calleth* thee.
  14:30. before the cock *crow* twice, thou shalt
  68. and the cock *crew*.
  72. And the second time the cock *crew*.
  — Before the cock *crow* twice, thou
  ˈ5:35. Behold, he *calleth* Elîas.
Lu. 8: 8. when he had said these things, he *cried*, He
  54. and *called*, saying, Maid, arise.
  14:12. *call* not thy friends,
  16: 2. And he *called* him, *and* said unto him,
  24. And he *cried and* said, Father Abraham,
  19:15. these servants *to be called* unto him,
  22:34. the cock *shall* not *crow* this day, before
  60. while he yet spake, the cock *crew*.
  61. Before the cock *crow*, thou shalt
  23:46. *when* Jesus *had cried* with a loud voice. he said, Father,
Joh. 1:48(49). Before that Philip *called* thee,
  2: 9. of the feast *called* the bridegroom,
  4:16. *call* thy husband, and come hither.
  9:18. until they *called* the parents of him that
  24. Then again *called* they the man that
  11:28. and *called* Mary her sister secretly,
  — The master is come, and *calleth for* thee.
  12:17. when he *called* Lazarus out of his grave,
  13:13. Ye *call* me Master and Lord:
  38. The cock *shall* not *crow*, till thou
  18:27. and immediately the cock *crew*.
  33. *called* Jesus, and said unto him, Art
Acts 9:41. *when* he *had called* the saints and widows,
  10: 7. he *called* two of his houshold servants,
  18. And *called, and* asked whether Simon,
  16:28. Paul *cried* with a loud voice. saying,
Rev.14:18. *cried* with a loud cry to him that had

φωνή, *phōnee.*

Mat. 2:18. In Rama was there a *voice* heard,
  3: 3. The *voice* of one crying in the wilderness,
  17. And lo a *voice* from heaven, saying,
  12:19. hear his *voice* in the streets.
  17: 5. and behold a *voice* out of the cloud,
  24:31. with a great *sound* of a trumpet,
  27:46. Jesus cried with a loud *voice*,
  50. when he had cried again with a loud *voice*,
Mar 1: 3. The *voice* of one crying in the wilderness,
  11. And there came a *voice* from heaven,
  26. and cried with a loud *voice*,
  5: 7. And cried with a loud *voice*,
  9: 7. and a *voice* came out of the cloud,
  15:34. Jesus cried with a loud *voice*,
  37. Jesus cried with a loud *voice*,
Lu. 1:42. she spake out with a loud *voice*,
  44. as soon as the *voice* of thy salutation
  3: 4. The *voice* of one crying in the wilderness,
  22. and a *voice* came from heaven,
  4:33. and cried out with a loud *voice*,
  8:28. and with a loud *voice* said,
  9:35. And there came a *voice* out of the cloud,
  36. And when the *voice* was past,
  11:27. a certain woman...lifted up her *voice*,
  17:13. And they lifted up (their) *voices*,
  15. and with a loud *voice* glorified God,
  19:37. and praise God with a loud *voice*

Lu. 23:23. And they were instant with loud *voices*,
  — And the *voices* of them and of the chief
  46. when Jesus had cried with a loud *voice*,
Joh. 1:23. I (am) the *voice* of one crying in the
  3: 8. and thou hearest the *sound* thereof,
  29. because of the bridegroom's *voice :*
  5:25. shall hear the *voice* of the Son of God:
  28. in the graves shall hear his *voice*,
  37. Ye have neither heard his *voice*
  10: 3. and the sheep hear his *voice :*
  4. for they know his *voice*.
  5. they know not the *voice* of strangers.
  16. and they shall hear my *voice ;*
  27. My sheep hear my *voice*,
  11:43. he cried with a loud *voice*, Lazarus,
  12:28. Then came there a *voice* from heaven,
  30. This *voice* came not because of me,
  18:37. that is of the truth heareth my *voice*.
Acts 2: 6. Now when this was noised (lit. the *report* of this was) abroad,
  14. lifted up his *voice*, and said
  4:24. they lifted up their *voice* to God
  7:31. the *voice* of the Lord came unto him,
  57. they cried out with a loud *voice*,
  60. and cried with a loud *voice*,
  8: 7. crying with loud *voice*, came out
  9: 4. and heard a *voice* saying unto him,
  7. hearing a *voice*, but seeing no man.
  10:13. And there came a *voice* to him,
  15. And the *voice* (spake) unto him again
  11: 7. And I heard a *voice* saying unto me,
  9. But the *voice* answered me again
  12:14. And when she knew Peter's *voice*,
  22. the *voice* of a god, and not of a man.
  13:27. nor yet the *voices* of the prophets which
  14:10. Said with a loud *voice*, Stand upright
  11. they lifted up their *voices*, saying
  16:28. Paul cried with a loud *voice*,
  19:34. all with one *voice* about the space
  22: 7. and heard a *voice* saying unto me,
  9. but they heard not the *voice* of him that
  14. and shouldest hear the *voice* of his mouth.
  22. and (then) lifted up their *voices*,
  24:21. Except it be for this one *voice*,
  26:14. I heard a *voice* speaking unto me,
  24. Festus said with a loud *voice*,
1Co.14: 7. even things without life giving *sound*,
  8. if the trumpet give an uncertain *sound*,
  10. so many kinds of *voices* in the world,
  11. if I know not the meaning of the *voice*,
Gal. 4:20. and to change my *voice ;*
1Th. 4:16. with the *voice* of the archangel,
Heb 3: 7. To day if ye will hear his *voice*,
  15. To day if ye will hear his *voice*,
  4: 7. To day if ye will hear his *voice*,
  12:19. and the *voice* of words ;
  26. Whose *voice* then shook the earth:
2Pet.1:17. when there came such a *voice* to him
  18. this *voice* which came from heaven we
  2:16. the dumb ass speaking with man's *voice*
Rev. 1:10. and heard behind me a great *voice*,
  12. And I turned to see the *voice*
  15. and his *voice* as the *sound* of many waters.
  3:20. if any man hear my *voice*, and open
  4: 1. and the first *voice* which I heard
  5. and thunderings and *voices :*
  5: 2. proclaiming with a loud *voice*,
  11. and I heard the *voice* of many angels
  12. Saying with a loud *voice*, Worthy is
  6: 1. as it were the *noise* of thunder,
  6. And I heard a *voice* in the midst of
  7. I heard the *voice* of the fourth beast

Rev. 6:10. And they cried with a loud *voice*,
7: 2. and he cried with a loud *voice*
10. And cried with a loud *voice*,
8: 5. there were *voices*, and thunderings,
13. saying with a loud *voice*, Woe,
— by reason of the other *voices* of the
9: 9. and the *sound* of their wings (was) as the *sound* of chariots
13. and I heard a *voice* from the four horns
10: 3. And cried with a loud *voice*, as
— seven thunders uttered their *voices*.
4. seven thunders had uttered their *voices*,
— and I heard *a voice* from heaven
7. But in the days of the *voice* of the seventh
8. And the *voice* which I heard from heaven
11:12. they heard a great *voice* from heaven
15. and there were great *voices* in heaven,
19. and *voices*, and thunderings,
12:10. I heard a loud *voice* saying in heaven,
14: 2. And I heard a *voice* from heaven, as the *voice* of many waters, and as the *voice* of a great thunder: and I heard the *voice* of harpers harping with their harps:
7. Saying with a loud *voice*, Fear God,
9. saying with a loud *voice*, If any
13. And I heard a *voice* from heaven
15. crying with a loud *voice* to him
16: 1. And I heard a great *voice* out of
17. came a great *voice* out of the temple
18. And there were *voices*, and thunders,
18: 2. cried mightily with a strong *voice*,
4. I heard another *voice* from
22. And the *voice* of harpers, and
— and the *sound* of a millstone shall be
23. the *voice* of the bridegroom and of the bride
19: 1. I heard a great *voice* of much people
5. And a *voice* came out of the throne,
6. as it were the *voice* of a great multitude, and as the *voice* of many waters, and as the *voice* of mighty thunderings, saying, Alleluia:
17. and he cried with a loud *voice*,
21: 3. a great *voice* out of heaven saying, Behold,

φῶς, *phōs.*

Mat. 4:16. which sat in darkness saw great *light*;
— *light* is sprung up.
5:14. Ye are the *light* of the world.
16. Let your *light* so shine before men;
6:23. If therefore the *light* that is in thee
10:27. (that) speak ye in *light*:
17: 2. his raiment was white as the *light*.
Mar 14:54. and warmed himself at the *fire*.
Lu. 2:32. A *light* to lighten the Gentiles, and
8:16. that they which enter in may see the *light*.
11:35. that the *light* which is in thee
12: 3. shall be heard in the *light*;
16: 8. wiser than the children of *light*.
22:56. beheld him as he sat by the *fire*,
Joh. 1: 4. and the life was the *light* of men.
5. And the *light* shineth in darkness;
7. to bear witness of the *Light*,
8. He was not that *Light*, but (was sent) to bear witness of that *Light*.
9. (That) was the true *Light*, which lighteth
3:19. that *light* is come into the world, and men loved darkness rather than *light*,
20. that doeth evil hateth the *light*, neither cometh to the *light*, lest

Joh. 3:21. he that doeth truth cometh to the *light*,
5:35. for a season to rejoice in his *light*.
8:12. I am the *light* of the world:
— but shall have the *light* of life.
9: 5. I am the *light* of the world.
11: 9. because he seeth the *light* of this world.
10. because there is no *light* in him.
12:35. Yet a little while is the *light* with you. Walk while ye have the *light*, lest
36. While ye have *light*, believe in the *light*, that ye may be the children of *light*.
46. I am come a *light* into the world,
Acts 9: 3. round about him a *light* from heaven:
12: 7. and a *light* shined in the prison:
13:47. I have set thee to be a *light* of the Gentiles,
16:29. he called for a *light*, and sprang in,
22: 6. a great *light* round about me.
9. saw indeed the *light*, and were afraid;
11. not see for the glory of that *light*,
26:13. I saw in the way a *light* from heaven,
18. to turn (them) from darkness to *light*,
23. should shew *light* unto the people,
Ro. 2:19. a *light* of them which are in darkness,
13:12. and let us put on the armour of *light*.
2Co. 4: 6. who commanded the *light* to shine out of darkness,
6:14. what communion hath *light* with darkness?
11:14. is transformed into an angel of *light*.
Eph. 5: 8. but now (are ye) *light* in the Lord: walk as children of *light*:
13. are made manifest by the *light*: for whatsoever doth make manifest is *light*.
Col. 1:12. of the inheritance of the saints in *light*:
1Th. 5: 5. Ye are all the children of *light*,
1Ti. 6:16. dwelling in the *light* which no man can
Jas. 1:17. cometh down from the Father of *lights*,
1Pet.2: 9. out of darkness into his marvellous *light*:
1Joh.1: 5. that God is *light*, and in him is no
7. But if we walk in the *light*, as he is in the *light*, we have fellowship
2: 8. and the true *light* now shineth.
9. He that saith he is in the *light*,
10. abideth in the *light*, and there is none
Rev.18:23. the *light* of a candle shall shine no more
21:24. shall walk in the *light* of it:
22: 5. need no candle, neither *light* of the sun;

φωστήρ, *phōsteer*

Phi. 2:15. among whom ye shine as *lights* in the world;
Rev.21:11. and her *light* (was) like unto a stone most precious,

---

φωσφόρος, *phōsphoros.*

2Pet.1:19. and the *day star* arise in your hearts:

φωτεινός, *phōtinos.*

Mat. 6:22. thy whole body shall be *full of light*.
17: 5. a *bright* cloud overshadowed them:
Lu. 11:34. thy whole body also is *full of light*;
36. If thy whole body therefore (be) *full of light*,
— the whole shall be *full of light*, as when

φωτίζω, *phōtizo.*

Lu. 11:36. as when the bright shining of a candle doth give thee *light*.

Joh. 1: 9. which *lighteth* every man that cometh
1Co. 4: 5. who both *will bring to light* the hidden
Eph. 1:18. The eyes of your understanding *being enlightened ;*
3: 9. And *to make* all (men) *see* what
2Ti. 1:10. and *hath brought* life and immortality *to light*
Heb 6: 4. for those *who were* once *enlightened,*
10:32. in which, *after* ye *were illuminated,*
Rev.18: 1. the earth *was lightened* with his glory.
21:23. for the glory of God *did lighten* it,
22: 5. for the Lord God *giveth* them *light :*

φωτισμός, *phŏtismos.*

2Co. 4: 4. lest the *light* of the glorious gospel of
6. to (give) the *light* of the knowledge of the glory of God

---

χαίρω, *kairo.*

The mark † shews where it is used as a phrase of salutation.

Mat. 2:10. they *rejoiced* with exceeding great joy.
5:12. *Rejoice,* and be exceeding glad:
18:13. he *rejoiceth* more of that (sheep),
26:49. and said, *Hail,*† master ;
27:29. *Hail,*† king of the Jews !
28: 9. Jesus met them, saying, All *hail.*†
Mar14:11. when they heard (it), they *were glad,*
15:18. *Hail,*† King of the Jews !
Lu. 1:14. and many *shall rejoice* at his birth.
28. *Hail,*† (thou that art) highly favoured,
6:23. *Rejoice* ye in that day, and leap for joy:
10:20. Notwithstanding in this *rejoice* not,
— but rather *rejoice,* because your names
13:17. and all the people *rejoiced* for all
15: 5. layeth (it) on his shoulders, *rejoicing.*
32. we should make merry, and *be glad :*
19: 6. and received him *joyfully.*
37. began to *rejoice and* praise God
22: 5. And they *were glad,* and covenanted to
23: 8. Herod saw Jesus, he *was* exceeding *glad :*
Joh. 3:29. *rejoiceth* greatly because of the
4:36. and he that reapeth *may rejoice* together.
8:56. and he saw (it), and *was glad.*
11:15. And I *am glad* for your sakes
14:28. ye *would rejoice,* because I said,
16:20. and lament, but the world *shall rejoice :*
22. and your heart *shall rejoice,*
19: 3. *Hail,*† King of the Jews !
20:20. Then *were* the disciples *glad,* when
Acts 5:41. *rejoicing* that they were counted
8:39. and he went on his way *rejoicing.*
11:23. *was glad,* and exhorted them all,
13:48. Gentiles heard this, they *were glad,*
15:23. (send) *greeting*† unto the brethren
31. they *rejoiced* for the consolation.
23:26. unto...Felix (sendeth) *greeting.*†
Ro. 12:12. *Rejoicing* in hope ; patient
15. *Rejoice* with them *that do rejoice,*
16:19. I *am glad* therefore on your behalf:
1Co. 7:30. they *that rejoice,* as though they *rejoiced* not ;
13: 6. *Rejoiceth* not in iniquity, but
16:17. I *am glad* of the coming of Stephanas
2Co. 2: 3. of whom I ought *to rejoice ;*
6:10. sorrowful, yet alway *rejoicing ;*
7: 7. so that I *rejoiced* the more.

2Co. 7: 9. Now I *rejoice,* not that ye were made
13. exceedingly the more *joyed* we for the
16. I *rejoice* therefore that I have
13: 9. For we *are glad,* when we are weak,
11. Finally, brethren, *farewell.* †
Phi. 1:18. and I therein *do rejoice,* yea, and *will rejoice.*
2:17. I *joy,* and rejoice with you all.
18. *do* ye *joy,* and rejoice with me.
28. when ye see him again, ye *may rejoice,*
3: 1. Finally, my brethren, *rejoice* in the Lord.
4: 4. *Rejoice* in the Lord alway: (and) again I say, *Rejoice.*
10. But I *rejoiced* in the Lord greatly,
Col. 1:24. Who now *rejoice* in my sufferings for you,
2: 5. *joying* and beholding your order,
1Th. 3: 9. wherewith we *joy* for your sakes
5:16. *Rejoice* evermore.
Jas. 1: 1. to the twelve tribes which are scattered abroad, *greeting.*†
1Pet.4:13. *rejoice,* inasmuch as ye are partakers
— ye may be *glad* also with exceeding joy.
2Joh. 4. I *rejoiced* greatly that I found of thy
10. neither bid him *God speed :* †
11. For he that biddeth him *God speed*†
3Joh. 3. For I *rejoiced* greatly, when the brethren
Rev.11:10. they that dwell upon the earth *shall rejoice* over them,
19: 7. *Let* us *be glad* and rejoice, and

χάλαζα, *kalaza.*

Rev. 8: 7. followed *hail* and fire mingled with
11:19. earthquake, and great *hail.*
16:21. there fell upon men a great *hail* out of
— because of the plague of the *hail ;*

χαλάω, *kalao.*

Mar 2: 4. they *let down* the bed wherein the sick
Lu. 5: 4. and *let down* your nets for a draught.
5. at thy word I *will let down* the net.
Acts 9:25. and let (him) down by the wall in a basket. (lit. *lowering* him in a basket)
27:17. *strake* sail, and so were driven.
30. *when* they *had let down* the boat into the sea,
2Co.11:33. in a basket *was* I *let down* by the wall,

χαλεπός, *kalepos.*

Mat. 8:28. exceeding *fierce,* so that no man
2Ti. 3: 1. last days *perilous* times shall come.

χαλιναγωγέω, *kalinagōgeo.*

Jas. 1:26. and *bridleth* not his tongue,
3: 2. able also *to bridle* the whole body.

χαλινός, *kalinos.*

Jas. 3: 3. we put *bits* in the horses' mouths,
Rev.14:20. even unto the horse *bridles,*

χάλκεος, *kalkeos.*

Rev. 9:20. idols of gold, and silver, and *brass,*

χαλκεύς, kalkūs.

2Ti. 4:14. Alexander the *coppersmith* did me much

χαλκηδών, kalkeedōn.

Rev.21:19. the third, a *chalcedony;*

χαλκίον, kalkion.

Mar 7: 4. the washing of cups, and pots, *brasen vessels*, and of tables.

χαλκολίβανον, kalkolibanon.

Rev. 1:15. And his feet like unto *fine brass,*
2:18. and his feet (are) like *fine brass;*

χαλκός, kalkos.

Mat.10: 9. gold, nor silver, nor *brass* in your purses,
Mar 6: 8. no bread, no *money* in (their) purse:
12:41. people cast *money* into the treasury:
1Co.13: 1. I am become (as) sounding *brass,*
Rev.18:12. and of *brass*, and iron, and marble,

χαμαί, kamai.

Joh. 9: 6. he spat *on the ground*, and made clay
18: 6. went backward, and fell *to the ground.*

χαρά, kara.

Mat. 2:10. rejoiced with exceeding great *joy.*
13:20. and anon with *joy* receiveth it;
44. and for *joy* thereof goeth and selleth
25:21. enter thou into the *joy* of thy lord.
23. enter thou into the *joy* of thy lord.
28: 8. from the sepulchre with fear and great *joy;*
Mar 4:16. immediately receive it with *gladness;*
Lu. 1:14. And thou shalt have *joy* and gladness;
2:10. bring you good tidings of great *joy,*
8:13. receive the word with *joy;*
10:17. the seventy returned again with *joy,*
15: 7. likewise *joy* shall be in heaven
10. there is *joy* in the presence of the
24:41. while they yet believed not for *joy,*
52. returned to Jerusalem with great *joy:*
Joh. 3:29. rejoiceth greatly (lit. rejoiceth with *joy)* because of the bridegroom's voice: this my *joy* therefore is fulfilled.
15:11. that my *joy* might remain in you (lit. my *joy* in you might remain), and (that) your *joy* might be full.
16:20. your sorrow shall be turned into *joy.*
21. for *joy* that a man is born into the world.
22. your *joy* no man taketh from you.
24. that your *joy* may be full.
17:13. might have my *joy* fulfilled in themselves.
Acts 8: 8. And there was great *joy* in that city.
12:14. opened not the gate for *gladness,*
13:52. the disciples were filled with *joy,*
15: 3. caused great *joy* unto all the brethren.
20:24. might finish my course with *joy,*
Ro. 14:17. and *joy* in the Holy Ghost.

Ro. 15:13. fill you with all *joy* and peace in
32. That I may come unto you with *joy*
2Co. 1:24. but are helpers of your *joy :*
2: 3. that my *joy* is (the joy) of you all
7: 4. I am exceeding *joy*ful in all our
13. the more joyed we for the *joy* of Titus,
8: 2. the abundance of their *joy* and their
Gal. 5:22. the fruit of the Spirit is love, *joy,*
Phi. 1: 4. for you all making request with *joy,*
25. for your furtherance and *joy* of faith ;
2: 2. Fulfil ye my *joy*, that ye be likeminded,
29. Receive him therefore in the Lord with all *gladness ;*
4: 1. my *joy* and crown, so stand fast
Col. 1:11. and longsuffering with *joyfulness ;*
1Th. 1: 6. with *joy* of the Holy Ghost:
2:19. For what (is) our hope, or *joy*, or
20. For ye are our glory and *joy.*
3: 9. for all the *joy* wherewith we joy for
2Ti. 1: 4. that I may be filled with *joy ;*
Heb 10:34. took *joy*fully the spoiling of your goods,
12: 2. who for the *joy* that was set before him
11. seemeth to be joyous, (lit. of *joy*)
13:17. that they may do it with *joy,*
Jas. 1: 2. My brethren, count it all *joy* when
4: 9. and (your) *joy* to heaviness.
1Pet.1: 8. ye rejoice with *joy* unspeakable and
1Joh.1: 4. that your *joy* may be full.
2Joh. 12. that our *joy* may be full.
3Joh. 4. I have no greater *joy* than to hear that

χάραγμα, karagma.

Acts17:29. or stone, *graven* by art (lit. by the *sculpture* of art) and man's device.
Rev.13:16. to receive a *mark* in their right hand,
17. save he that had the *mark,*
14: 9. and receive (his) *mark* in his forehead,
11. whosoever receiveth the *mark* of his name.
15: 2. and over his image, and over his *mark,*
16: 2. upon the men which had the *mark* of the
19:20. that had received the *mark* of the beast,
20: 4. neither had received (his) *mark* upon

χαρακτήρ, karakteer.

Heb 1: 3. and the *express image* of his person,

χάραξ, karax.

Lu. 19:43. thine enemies shall cast a *trench* about thee, and compass thee

---

χαρίζομαι, karizomai.

Lu. 7:21. unto many (that were) blind he *gave* sight.
42. he *frankly forgave* them both.
43. (he), to whom he *forgave* most.
Acts 3:14. desired a murderer *to be granted* unto you;
25:11. no man may *deliver* me unto them.
16. *to deliver* any man to die, before that
27:24. and, lo, God *hath given* thee all them that sail with thee.
Ro. 8:32. how *shall* he not with him also *freely give* us all things?
1Co. 2:12. that we might know the things that are *freely given* to us of God.

2Co. 2: 7. ye (ought) rather *to forgive* (him),
10. To whom ye *forgive* any thing,
— for if I *forgave* any thing, to whom I *forgave* (it), for
12:13. *forgive* me this wrong.
Gal. 3:18. but God *gave* (it) to Abraham by promise.
Eph 4:32. *forgiving* one another, even as God for Christ's sake *hath forgiven* you.
Phi. 1:29. you it *is given* in the behalf of Christ,
2: 9. and *given* him a name which is above
Col. 2:13. *having forgiven* you all trespasses;
3:13. and *forgiving* one another, if any
— even as Christ *forgave* you, so also (do) ye.
Philem 22. I *shall be given* unto you.

χάριν, *karin.*

Lu. 7:47. Where*fore* I say unto thee, Her sins,
Gal. 3:19. It was added *because of* transgressions,
Eph 3: 1. *For* this *cause* I Paul, the prisoner of
14. *For* this *cause* I bow my knees unto
1Ti. 5:14. give none occasion to the adversary to speak reproachfully. (lit. to the adversary *for cause of* reproach)
Tit. 1: 5. *For* this *cause* left I thee in Crete,
11. *for* filthy lucre's *sake.*
1Joh.3:12. And where*fore* slew he him?
Jude 16. having men's persons in admiration be*cause of* advantage.

χάρις, *karis.*

Lu. 1:30. for thou hast found *favour* with God.
2:40. and the *grace* of God was upon him.
52. and in *favour* with God and man.
4:22. wondered at the *gracious* words which
6:32. what *thank* have ye?
33. what *thank* have ye?
34. what *thank* have ye?
17: 9. Doth he *thank* that servant (lit. hath he favor, or *thanks,* to)
Joh. 1:14. full of *grace* and truth.
16. of his fulness have all we received, and *grace* for *grace.*
17. *grace* and truth came by Jesus Christ.
Acts 2:47. and having *favour* with all the people.
4:33. and great *grace* was upon them all.
7:10. gave him *favour* and wisdom in the sight of Pharaoh
46. Who found *favour* before God,
11:23. and had seen the *grace* of God, was glad,
13:43. to continue in the *grace* of God.
14: 3. testimony unto the word of his *grace,*
26. recommended to the *grace* of God for
15:11. through the *grace* of the Lord Jesus
40. being recommended by the brethren unto the *grace* of God.
18:27. which had believed through *grace:*
20:24. to testify the gospel of the *grace* of God.
32. you to God, and to the word of his *grace,*
24:27. willing to shew the Jews a *pleasure,*
25: 3. And desired *favour* against him,
9. willing to do the Jews a *pleasure,*
Ro. 1: 5. By whom we have received *grace* and
7. *Grace* to you and peace from
3:24. Being justified freely by his *grace*
4: 4. is the reward not reckoned of *grace,* but of debt.
16. of faith, that (it might be) by *grace;*

Ro. 5: 2. by faith into this *grace* wherein we stand,
15. much more the *grace* of God, and the gift by *grace,*
17. they which receive abundance of *grace*
20. *grace* did much more abound:
21. even so might *grace* reign through
6: 1. continue in sin, that *grace* may abound?
14. ye are not under the law, but under *grace.*
15. not under the law, but under *grace?*
17. But God be thanked, (lit. *thanks* to God) that ye were
11: 5. remnant according to the election of *grace.*
6. if by *grace,* then (is it) no more of works: otherwise *grace* is no more *grace.*
— of works, then is it no more *grace:*
12: 3. through the *grace* given unto me,
6. according to the *grace* that is given to us,
15:15. because of the *grace* that is given to me
16:20. The *grace* of our Lord Jesus Christ (be)
24. The *grace* of our Lord Jesus Christ (be)
1Co. 1: 3. *Grace* (be) unto you, and peace, from
4. for the *grace* of God which is given you
3:10. According to the *grace* of God which
10:30. For if I by *grace* be a partaker,
15:10. But by the *grace* of God I am what I am: and his *grace* which (was bestowed) upon me
— not I, but the *grace* of God which was with me.
57. But *thanks* (be) to God, which giveth us
16: 3. to bring your *liberality* unto Jerusalem.
23. The *grace* of our Lord Jesus Christ (be)
2Co. 1: 2. *Grace* (be) to you and peace from
12. but by the *grace* of God, we have had our
15. that ye might have a second *benefit;*
2:14. Now *thanks* (be) unto God, which
4:15. that the abundant *grace* might through
6: 1. ye receive not the *grace* of God in vain.
8: 1. do you to wit of the *grace* of God bestowed
4. that we would receive the *gift,* and
6. finish in you the same *grace* also.
7. (see) that ye abound in this *grace* also.
9. ye know the *grace* of our Lord Jesus
16. But *thanks* (be) to God, which put
19. to travel with us with this *grace,* which
9: 8. And God (is) able to make all *grace* abound toward you;
14. for the exceeding *grace* of God in you.
15. *Thanks* (be) unto God for his
12: 9. My *grace* is sufficient for thee:
13:14(13). The *grace* of the Lord Jesus Christ,
Gal. 1: 3. *Grace* (be) to you and peace from
6. that called you into the *grace* of Christ
15. and called (me) by his *grace,*
2: 9. perceived the *grace* that was given unto
21. I do not frustrate the *grace* of God:
5: 4. ye are fallen from *grace.*
6:18. the *grace* of our Lord Jesus Christ (be)
Eph. 1: 2. *Grace* (be) to you, and peace, from
6. To the praise of the glory of his *grace,*
7. according to the riches of his *grace;*
2: 5. by *grace* ye are saved;
7. shew the exceeding riches of his *grace*
8. For by *grace* are ye saved through faith;
3: 2. of the dispensation of the *grace* of God which is given me
7. according to the gift of the *grace* of God
8. is this *grace* given, that I should preach
4: 7. unto every one of us is given *grace*
29. it may minister *grace* unto the hearers.
6:24. *Grace* (be) with all them that love our Lord Jesus Christ

Phi. 1: 2. *Grace* (be) unto you, and peace, from
7. ye all are partakers of my *grace.*
4:23. The *grace* of our Lord Jesus Christ (be)

Col. 1: 2. *Grace* (be) unto you, and peace, from
6. and knew the *grace* of God in truth:
3:16. singing with *grace* in your hearts to
4: 6. Let your speech (be) alway with *grace,*
18. *Grace* (be) with you. Amen.

1Th. 1: 1. *Grace* (be) unto you, and peace, from
5:28. The *grace* of our Lord Jesus Christ (be)

2Th. 1: 2. *Grace* unto you, and peace, from
12. according to the *grace* of our God and
2:16. consolation and good hope through *grace,*
3:18. The *grace* of our Lord Jesus Christ (be)

1Ti. 1: 2. *Grace,* mercy, (and) peace, from
12. And I *thank* Christ Jesus our Lord,
14. And the *grace* of our Lord was exceeding
abundant
6:21. *Grace* (be) with thee. Amen.

2Ti. 1: 2. *Grace,* mercy, (and) peace, from
3. I *thank* God, whom I serve from
9. according to his own purpose and *grace,*
2: 1. be strong in the *grace* that is in Christ
4:22. *Grace* (be) with you. Amen.

Tit. 1: 4. *Grace,* mercy, (and) peace, from
2:11. For the *grace* of God that bringeth
3: 7. That being justified by his *grace,* we
15. *Grace* (be) with you all. Amen.

Philem. 3. *Grace* to you, and peace, from
7. we have great *joy* and consolation
25. The *grace* of our Lord Jesus Christ (be)

Heb 2: 9. that he by the *grace* of God should taste
4:16. come boldly unto the throne of *grace,*
— and find *grace* to help in time of need.
10:29. done despite unto the Spirit of *grace?*
12:15. lest any man fail of the *grace* of God;
28. let us have *grace,* whereby we may serve
13: 9. the heart be established with *grace;*
25. *Grace* (be) with you all. Amen.

Jas. 4: 6. But he giveth more *grace.*
— but giveth *grace* unto the humble.

1Pet.1: 2. *Grace* unto you, and peace, be multiplied.
10. who prophesied of the *grace* (that should
come) unto you:
13. for the *grace* that is to be brought
2:19. For this (is) *thankworthy,* if a man
20. this (is) *acceptable* with God.
3: 7. being heirs together of the *grace* of life;
4:10. stewards of the manifold *grace* of God.
5: 5. and giveth *grace* to the humble.
10. But the God of all *grace,* who hath
12. testifying that this is the true *grace* of God
wherein ye stand.

2Pet.1: 2. *Grace* and peace be multiplied unto you
3:18. But grow in *grace,* and (in) the knowledge

2Joh. 3. *Grace* be with you, mercy, (and) peace,

Jude 4. turning the *grace* of our God into

Rev. 1: 4. *Grace* (be) unto you, and peace, from
22:21. The *grace* of our Lord Jesus Christ (be)

χάρισμα, *karisma.*

Ro. 1:11. impart unto you some spiritual *gift,*
5:15. so also (is) the *free gift.*
16. but the *free gift* (is) of many offences
6:23. the *gift* of God (is) eternal life
11:29. For the *gifts* and calling of God (are)
12: 6. Having then *gifts* differing

1Co. 1: 7. ye come behind in no *gift;*
7: 7. every man hath his proper *gift*
12: 4. there are diversities of *gifts,* but the

1Co.12: 9. to another the *gifts* of healing by the
28. then *gifts* of healings, helps,
30. Have all the *gifts* of healing?
31. covet earnestly the best *gifts:* and yet

2Co. 1:11. for the *gift* (bestowed) upon us by the

1Ti. 4:14. Neglect not the *gift* that is in thee,

2Ti. 1: 6. stir up the *gift* of God, which is in thee

1Pet.4:10. As every man hath received the *gift,*

χαριτόω, *karitoō.*

Lu. 1:28. Hail, (thou that art) *highly favoured,*
Eph 1: 6. of his grace, wherein he hath *made us
accepted* (lit. *hath graced* us) in the
beloved.

χάρτης, *kartees.*

2Joh. 12. I would not (write) with *paper* and ink:

χάσμα, *kasma.*

Lu. 16:26. there is a great *gulf* fixed:

χεῖλος, *kilos.*

Mat.15: 8. and honoureth me with (their) *lips;*
Mar 7: 6. honoureth me with (their) *lips,*
Ro. 3:13. poison of asps (is) under their *lips:*
1Co.14:21. With (men of) other tongues and other
lips
Heb 11:12. and as the sand which is by the sea *shore*
13:15. the fruit of (our) *lips* giving thanks to
1Pet.3:10. and his *lips* that they speak no guile:

χειμάζομαι, *kimazomai.*

Acts27:18. And we *being* exceedingly *tossed with a
tempest,*

χείμαρρος, *kimarros.*

Joh.18: 1. over the *brook* Cedron,

χειμών, *kimōn.*

Mat.16: 3. (It will be) *foul weather* to day:
24:20. that your flight be not in the *winter,*
Mar 13:18. your flight be not in the *winter.*
Joh.10:22. dedication, and it was *winter.*
Acts27:20. no small *tempest* lay on (us),
2Ti. 4:21. Do thy diligence to come before *winter.*

χείρ, *kir.*

Mat. 3:12. Whose fan (is) in his *hand,*
4: 6. in (their) *hands* they shall bear thee up,
5:30. if thy right *hand* offend thee,
8: 3. Jesus put forth (his) *hand,* and touched
him,
15. he touched her *hand,* and the fever left
9:18. lay thy *hand* upon her, and she shall live.
25. took her by the *hand,* and the maid arose.

Mat.12:10. which had (his) *hand* withered.
13. Stretch forth thine *hand*.
49. he stretched forth his *hand* toward his
14:31. stretched forth (his) *hand*, and caught him,
15: 2. for they wash not their *hands* when
20. but to eat with unwashen *hands*
17:22. shall be betrayed into the *hands* of men:
18: 8. if thy *hand* or thy foot offend thee,
— rather than having two *hands* or two feet
19:13. should put (his) *hands* on them, and
15. he laid (his) *hands* on them, and departed
22:13. Bind him *hand* and foot,
26:23. He that dippeth (his) *hand* with me
45. is betrayed into the *hands* of sinners.
50. laid *hands* on Jesus, and took him.
51. stretched out (his) *hand*, and drew his sword,
27:24. washed (his) *hands* before the multitude,
Mar 1:31. and took her by the *hand*,
41. put forth (his) *hand*, and touched
3: 1. which had a withered *hand*.
3. which had the withered *hand*, Stand forth.
5. Stretch forth thine *hand*.
— and his *hand* was restored whole as
5:23. come and lay thy *hands* on her,
41. took the damsel by the *hand*,
6: 2. are wrought by his *hands* ?
5. laid his *hands* upon a few sick folk,
7: 2. with unwashen, *hands*, they found fault.
3. except they wash (their) *hands* oft,
5. eat bread with unwashen *hands* ?
32. to put his *hand* upon him.
8:23. he took the blind man by the *hand*,
— his eyes, and put his *hands* upon him,
25. he put (his) *hands* again upon his eyes,
9:27. took him by the *hand*, and lifted him up;
31. is delivered into the *hands* of men,
43. if thy *hand* offend thee, cut it
— than having two *hands* to go into hell,
10:16. in his arms, put (his) *hands* upon them, and blessed them.
14:41. is betrayed into the *hands* of sinners.
46. laid their *hands* on him, and took him.
16:18. they shall lay *hands* on the sick, and they
Lu. 1:66. And the *hand* of the Lord was with him.
71. and from the *hand* of all that hate us;
74. delivered out of the *hand* of our enemies
3:17. Whose fan (is) in his *hand*,
4:11. And in (their) *hands* they shall bear
40. laid his *hands* on every one of them,
5:13. he put forth (his) *hand*, and touched him,
6: 1. did eat, rubbing (them) in (their) *hands*.
6. whose right *hand* was withered.
8. which had the withered *hand*,
10. Stretch forth thy *hand*.
— his *hand* was restored whole
8:54. and took her by the *hand*, and called,
9:44. shall be delivered into the *hands* of men.
62. No man, having put his *hand* to the plough,
13:13. And he laid (his) *hands* on her:
15:22. and put a ring on his *hand*, and
20:19. sought to lay *hands* on him;
21:12. they shall lay their *hands* on you,
22:21. the *hand* of him that betrayeth me
53. ye stretched forth no *hands* against me:
23:46. into thy *hands* I commend my spirit:
24: 7. be delivered into the *hands* of sinful men,
39. Behold my *hands* and my feet,
40. he shewed them (his) *hands* and (his) feet.
50. he lifted up his *hands*, and blessed them.

Joh. 3:35. and hath given all things into his *hand*.
7:30. but no man laid *hands* on him, because
44. but no man laid *hands* on him.
10:28. pluck them out of my *hand*.
29. to pluck (them) out of my Father's *hand*.
39. he escaped out of their *hand*,
11:44. bound *hand* and foot with graveclothes:
13: 3. given all things into his *hands*,
9. but also (my) *hands* and (my) head.
20:20. shewed unto them (his) *hands*
25. Except I shall see in his *hands*
— and thrust my *hand* into his side,
27. Reach hither thy finger, and behold my *hands*; and reach hither thy *hand*, and thrust
21:18. thou shalt stretch forth thy *hands*,
Acts 2:23. by wicked *hands* have crucified
3: 7. took him by the right *hand*, and lifted
4: 3. they laid *hands* on them, and put
28. whatsoever thy *hand* and thy counsel
30. stretching forth thine *hand* to heal;
5:12. by the *hands* of the apostles were many
18. laid their *hands* on the apostles, and put
6: 6. prayed, they laid (their) *hands* on them.
7:25. how that God by his *hand* would
35. by the *hand* of the angel which appeared
41. rejoiced in the works of their own *hands*.
50. Hath not my *hand* made
8:17. Then laid they (their) *hands* on them, and they received
18. through laying on of the apostles' *hands*
19. that on whomsoever I lay *hands*,
9:12. coming in, and putting (his) *hand* on him,
17. and putting his *hands* on him said,
41. he gave her (his) *hand*, and lifted
11:21. And the *hand* of the Lord was with them:
30. by the *hands* of Barnabas and Saul.
12: 1. the king stretched forth (his) *hands* to vex
7. chains fell off from (his) *hands*.
11. me out of the *hand* of Herod,
17. beckoning unto them with the *hand* to
13: 3. prayed, and laid (their) *hands* on them,
11. behold, the *hand* of the Lord (is) upon thee,
16. beckoning with (his) *hand* said,
14: 3. and wonders to be done by their *hands*.
15:23. they wrote (letters) by them (lit. by the *hand* of them)
17:25. Neither is worshipped with men's *hands*,
19: 6. when Paul had laid (his) *hands* upon them,
11. special miracles by the *hands* of Paul:
26. be no gods, which are made with *hands* :
33. Alexander beckoned with the *hand*,
20:34. these *hands* have ministered unto my
21:11. bound his own *hands* and feet,
— shall deliver (him) into the *hands* of the
27. all the people, and laid *hands* on him,
40. beckoned with the *hand* unto the people.
23:19. captain took him by the *hand*, and went
24: 7. took (him) away out of our *hands*,
26: 1. Paul stretched forth the *hand*,
28: 3. and fastened on his *hand*.
4. beast hang on his *hand*,
8. laid his *hands* on him, and healed him.
17. into the *hands* of the Romans.
Ro. 10:21. I have stretched forth my *hands* unto
1Co. 4:12. labour, working with our own *hands* :
12:15. Because I am not the *hand*, I am not of
21. And the eye cannot say unto the *hand*,
16:21. salutation of (me) Paul with mine own *hand*.

2Co.11:33. and escaped his *hands*.
Gal. 3:19. by angels in the *hand* of a mediator.
6:11. written unto you with mine own *hand*.
Eph. 4:28. working with (his) *hands* the thing which
Col. 4:18. The salutation by the *hand* of me Paul.
1Th. 4:11. and to work with your own *hands*,
2Th. 3:17. of Paul with mine own *hand*,
1Ti. 2: 8. lifting up holy *hands*, without wrath
4:14. with the laying on of the *hands* of the
ᴗpresbytery.
5:22. Lay *hands* suddenly on no man,
2Ti. 1: 6. in thee by the putting on of my *hands*.
Philem 19. written (it) with mine own *hand*,
Heb 1:10. the heavens are the works of thine *hands :*
2: 7. set him over the works of thy *hands :*
6: 2. of baptisms, and of laying on of *hands*,
8: 9. when I took them by the *hand* to lead
them
10:31. to fall into the *hands* of the living God.
12:12. lift up the *hands* which hang down,
Jas. 4: 8. Cleanse (your) *hands*, (ye) sinners ;
1Pet.5: 6. under the mighty *hand* of God, that he
1Joh.1: 1. and our *hands* have handled, of the
Rev. 1:16. he had in his right *hand* seven stars :
17. he laid his right *hand* upon me,
6: 5. pair of balances in his *hand*.
7: 9. and palms in their *hands ;*
8: 4. up before God out of the angel's *hand*.
9:20. repented not of the works of their *hands*,
that they should not worship
10: 2. he had in his *hand* a little book
5. lifted up his *hand* to heaven,
8. which is open in the *hand* of the angel
10. book out of the angel's *hand*,
13:16. to receive a mark in their right *hand*, or
14: 9. mark in his forehead, or in his *hand*,
14. and in his *hand* a sharp sickle.
17: 4. having a golden cup in her *hand* full of
19: 2. and hath avenged the blood of his servants
at her *hand*.
20: 1. and a great chain in his *hand*.
4. upon their foreheads, or in their *hands ;*

χειραγωγέω, *kīragōgeo*.

Acts 9: 8. they *led* him *by the hand, and*
22:11. *being led by the hand* of them that

χειραγωγός, *kīragōgos*.

Acts13:11. seeking *some to lead* him *by the hand*.

χειρόγραφον, *kīrographon*.

Col. 2:14. Blotting out the *handwriting* of ordinances
that was against us,

χειροποίητος, *kīropoyeetos*.

Mar 14:58. this temple that is *made with hands*,
Acts 7:48. dwelleth not in temples *made with hands ;*
17:24. not in temples *made with hands ;*
Eph 2:11. Circumcision in the flesh *made by hands ;*
Heb 9:11. tabernacle, not *made with hands*,
24. into the holy places *made with hands*,

χειροτονέω, *kīrotoneo*.

Acts14:23. *when* they *had ordained* them elders in
every church,
2Co. 8:19. *who was* also *chosen* of the churches to
travel with us with this grace,

χείρων, χεῖρον, *kīrōn, kīron*.

Mat. 9:16. and the rent is made *worse*.
12:45. of that man is *worse* than the first.
27:64. last error shall be *worse* than the first.
Mar 2:21. and the rent is made *worse*.
5:26. but rather grew *worse*,
Lu. 11:26. of that man is *worse* than the first.
Joh. 5:14. lest a *worse* thing come unto thee.
1Ti. 5: 8. and is *worse* than an infidel.
2Ti. 3:13. But evil men and seducers shall wax
worse and worse,
Heb 10:29. Of how much *sorer* punishment,
2Pet.2:20. the latter end is *worse* with them than

χήρα, *keera*.

Mat.23:14. for ye devour *widows'* houses,
Mar 12:40. Which devour *widows'* houses,
42. And there came a certain poor *widow*,
43. this poor *widow* hath cast more in,
Lu. 2:37. she (was) a *widow* of about fourscore
4:25. many *widows* were in Israel in
26. unto a woman (that was) a *widow*.
7:12. only son of his mother, and she was a
widow :
18: 3. And there was a *widow* in that city ;
5. Yet because this *widow* troubleth me,
20:47. Which devour *widows'* houses,
21: 2. a certain poor *widow* casting in
3. this poor *widow* hath cast in more than
Acts 6: 1. because their *widows* were neglected in
9:39. all the *widows* stood by him weeping,
41. when he had called the saints and *widows*,
1Co. 7: 8. to the unmarried and *widows*, It is good
1Ti. 5: 3. Honour *widows* that are *widows* indeed.
4. if any *widow* have children or nephews,
5. she that is a *widow* indeed, and desolate,
trusteth in God,
9. Let not a *widow* be taken into the number
under
11. But the younger *widows* refuse :
16. If any man or woman that believeth have
widows, let them
— may relieve them that are *widows* indeed.
Jas. 1:27. To visit the fatherless and *widows* in their
affliction,
Rev.18: 7. sit a queen, and am no *widow*, and shall
see no sorrow.

χθές, *kthes*.

Joh. 4:52. *Yesterday* at the seventh hour the fever
Acts 7:28. as thou diddest the Egyptian *yesterday ?*
Heb 13: 8. Jesus Christ the same *yesterday*, and to
day, and for ever.

χιλιάδες, *kiliades*.

Lu. 14:31. able with ten *thousand* to meet him that
cometh against him with twenty *thou-
sand ?*

Acts 4: 4. of the men was about five *thousand*.
1Co.10: 8. one day three and twenty *thousand*.
Rev. 5:11. and *thousands* of *thousands;*
    7: 4. an hundred (and) forty (and) four *thou-sand* of all the tribes of the
      5. of Juda (were) sealed twelve *thousand*.
      — of Reuben (were) sealed twelve *thousand*.
      — of Gad (were) sealed twelve *thousand*.
      6. of Aser (were) sealed twelve *thousand*.
      — of Nepthalim (were) sealed twelve *thou-sand*.
      — of Manasses (were) sealed twelve *thou-sand*.
      7. of Simeon (were) sealed twelve *thousand*.
      — of Levi (were) sealed twelve *thousand*.
      — of Issachar (were) sealed twelve *thousand*.
      8. of Zabulon (were) sealed twelve *thousand*.
      — of Joseph (were) sealed twelve *thousand*.
      — of Benjamin (were) sealed twelve *thou-sand*.
  11:13. slain of men seven *thousand:*
  14: 1. an hundred forty (and) four *thousand*, having his Father's name
      3. but the hundred (and) forty (and) four *thousand*,
  21:16. twelve *thousand* furlongs.

χιλίαρχος, *kiliarkos*.

Mar 6:21. a supper to his lords, *high captains*, and
Joh.18:12. Then the band and the *captain* and
Acts21:31. tidings came unto the *chief captain*
    32 they saw the *chief captain* and the
    33. Then the *chief captain* came near,
    37. he said unto the *chief captain*,
  22:24. The *chief captain* commanded him to be brought
    26. he went and told the *chief captain*,
    27. Then the *chief captain* came, and said
    28. And the *chief captain* answered, With
    29. the *chief captain* also was afraid,
  23:10. the *chief captain*, fearing lest Paul
    15. signify to the *chief captain* that he
    17. Bring this young man unto the *chief captain:*
    18. and brought (him) to the *chief captain*,
    19. the *chief captain* took him by the hand,
    22. *chief captain* (then) let the young man
  24: 7. But the *chief captain* Lysias came
    22. When Lysias the *chief captain* shall
  25:23. with the *chief captains*, and principal men
Rev. 6:15. the rich men, and the *chief captains*,
  19:18. of kings, and the flesh of *captains*,

χίλιοι, *kilioi*.

Obs.—This word is only used for 'one thousand,' but χιλιάδες signifies 'thousands.'

2Pet.3: 8. as a *thousand* years, and a *thousand* years as one day.
Rev.11: 3. prophesy a *thousand* two hundred (and) threescore days,
  12: 6. feed her there a *thousand* two hundred (and) threescore days.
  14:20. a *thousand* (and) six hundred furlongs.
  20: 2. and bound him a *thousand* years,
    3. till the *thousand* years should be fulfilled:
    4. and they lived and reigned with Christ a *thousand* years.

Rev.20: 5. until the *thousand* years were finished.
    6. shall reign with him a *thousand* years.
    7. when the *thousand* years are expired,

χιτών, *kitōn*.

Mat. 5:40. at the law, and take away thy *coat*, let
  10:10. neither two *coats*, neither shoes, nor
Mar 6: 9. and not put on two *coats*.
  14:63. Then the high priest rent his *clothes*,
Lu. 3:11. He that hath two *coats*, let him impart to
  6:29. cloke forbid not (to take thy) *coat* also.
  9: 3. neither have two *coats* apiece.
Joh.19:23. and also (his) *coat :* now the *coat* was without seam, woven from
Acts 9:39. shewing the *coats* and garments which
Jude 23. hating even the *garment* spotted by the

χιών, *kiōn*.

Mat.28: 3. and his raiment white as *snow :*
Mar 9: 3. became shining, exceeding white as *snow ;*
Rev. 1:14. white like wool, as white as *snow ;*

χλαμύς, *klamus*.

Mat.27:28. and put on him a scarlet *robe*.
    31. they took the *robe* off from him,

χλευάζω, *klūazo*.

Acts 2:13. Others *mocking* said, These men
  17:32. resurrection of the dead, some *mocked :*

χλιαρός, *kliaros*.

Rev. 3:16. So then because thou art *lukewarm*,

χλωρός, *klōros:*

Mar 6:39. by companies upon the *green* grass.
Rev. 6: 8. I looked, and behold a *pale* horse:
  8: 7. and all *green* grass was burnt up.
  9: 4. neither any *green* thing, neither any tree;

χξϛ′ (Rev. 13:18), see respectively ἑξακόσιοι, ἑξήκοντα and ἕξ.

χοϊκός, *koïkos*.

1Co.15:47. The first man (is) of the earth, *earthy :*
    48. As (is) the *earthy*, such (are) they also that are *earthy :* and as
    49. we have borne the image of the *earthy*, we

χοῖνιξ, *koinix*.

Rev. 6: 6. A *measure* of wheat for a penny, and three *measures* of barley for a penny ;

χοῖρος, *koiros*.

Mat. 7: 6. neither cast ye your pearls before *swine*,
  8:30. an herd of many *swine* feeding.

Mat. 8:31. to go away into the herd of *swine*.
　　32. went into the herd of *swine*: and behold,
　　　　the whole herd of *swine* ran
Mar 5:11. great herd of *swine* feeding.
　　12. Send us into the *swine*, that we may
　　13. and entered into the *swine*:
　　14. they that fed the *swine* fled,
　　16. and (also) concerning the *swine*.
Lu. 8:32. an herd of many *swine* feeding
　　33. and entered into the *swine*:
　15:15. he sent him into his fields to feed *swine*.
　　16. with the husks that the *swine* did eat:

χολάω, *kolao*.

Joh. 7:23. *are* ye *angry* at me, because I

χολή, *kolee*.

Mat. 27:34. vinegar to drink mingled with *gall*:
Acts 8:23. thou art in the *gall* of bitterness,

χόος, *koòs*.

Mar 6:11. shake off the *dust* under your feet for a
Rev. 18:19. And they cast *dust* on their heads,

χορηγέω, *koreegeo*.

2Co. 9:10. both *minister* bread for (your) food,
1Pet. 4:11. as of the ability which God *giveth*:

χορός, *koros*.

Lu. 15:25. he heard musick and *dancing*.

χορτάζω, *kortazo*.

Mat. 5: 6. for they *shall be filled*.
　14:20. they did all eat, and *were filled*:
　15:33. as *to fill* so great a multitude?
　　37. they did all eat, and *were filled*:
Mar 6:42. they did all eat, and *were filled*.
　 7:27. Let the children first *be filled*:
　 8: 4. whence can a man *satisfy* these
　　 8. they did eat, and *were filled*:
Lu. 6:21. that hunger now. for ye *shall be filled*.
　 9:17. they did eat, and *were* all *filled*:
　16:21. desiring *to be fed* with the crumbs
Joh. 6:26. eat of the loaves, and *were filled*.
Phi. 4:12. both *to be full* and to be hungry,
Jas. 2:16. be (ye) warmed and *filled*;
Rev. 19:21. the fowls *were filled* with their flesh.

χόρτασμα, *kortasma*.

Acts 7:11. and our fathers found no *sustenance*.

χόρτος, *kortos*.

Mat. 6:30. if God so clothe the *grass* of the field,
　13:26. But when the *blade* was sprung up,
　14:19. to sit down on the *grass*, and took
Mar 4:28. first the *blade*, then the ear,
　 6:39. by companies upon the green *grass*.
Lu. 12:28. If then God so clothe the *grass*,
Joh. 6:10. there was much *grass* in the place.

1Co. 3:12. precious stones, wood, *hay*, stubble;
Jas. 1:10. as the flower of the *grass* he shall pass
　　11. but it withereth the *grass*, and the
1Pet. 1:24. For all flesh (is) as *grass*, and all the
　　　glory of man as the flower of *grass*.
　　　The *grass* withereth, and the flower
Rev. 8: 7. all green *grass* was burnt up.
　 9: 4. should not hurt the *grass* of the earth,

χράομαι, *kraomai*.

Acts 27: 3. Julius courteously *entreated* Paul, *and*
　　17. they *used* helps, undergirding
1Co. 7:21. if thou mayest be made free, *use* (it) rather
　　31. And they *that use* this world, as not
　 9:12. Nevertheless we *have* not *used* this power;
　　15. But I *have used* none of these things:
2Co. 1:17. thus minded, *did* I *use* lightness?
　 3:12. we *use* great plainness of speech:
　13:10. lest being present I *should use* sharpness,
1Ti. 1: 8. the law (is) good, if a man *use* it lawfully;
　 5:23. but *use* a little wine for thy

χράω, *krao*.

Lu. 11: 5. Friend, *lend* me three loaves;

χρεία, *kria*.

Mat. 3:14. I have *need* to be baptized of thee,
　 6: 8. knoweth what things ye have *need* of,
　 9:12. They that be whole *need* not a
　14:16. They *need* not depart;
　21: 3. The Lord hath *need* of them;
　26:65. what further *need* have we of witnesses?
Mar 2:17. They that are whole have no *need* of the
　　25. when he had *need*, and was an hungred,
　11: 3. the Lord hath *need* of him;
　14:63. What *need* we any further witnesses?
Lu. 5:31. They that are whole *need* not a
　 9:11. healed them that had *need* of healing.
　10:42. But one thing is *needful*: and Mary
　15: 7. just persons, which *need* no repentance.
　19:31. the Lord hath *need* of him.
　　34. The Lord hath *need* of him.
　22:71. What *need* we any further witness?
Joh. 2:25. *needed* (lit. had *need*) not that any should
　　　testify of man:
　13:10. *needeth* not save to wash (his) feet,
　　29. that we have *need* of against the feast;
　16:30. *needest* not that any man should ask thee:
Acts 2:45. to all (men), as every man had *need*.
　 4:35. unto every man according as he had *need*.
　 6: 3. whom we may appoint over this *business*.
　20:34. that these hands have ministered unto my
　　　necessities,
　28:10. with such things as were *necessary*.
Ro. 12:13. Distributing to the *necessity* of saints;
1Co. 12:21. I have no *need* of thee:
　— I have no *need* of you.
　　24. For our comely (parts) have no *need*:
Eph 4:28. to give to him that *needeth*.
　　29. but that which is good to the *use* of
　　　edifying, (lit. to the edifying of *need*)
Phi. 2:25. and he that ministered to my *wants*
　 4:16. once and again unto my *necessity*.
　　19. my God shall supply all your *need*
1Th. 1: 8. we *need* not to speak any thing.
　 4: 9. ye *need* not that I write unto you:
　　12. ye may have *lack* of nothing.

1Th. 5: 1. ye have no *need* that I write unto you.
Tit. 3:14. to maintain good works for necessary *uses*,
Heb 5:12. ye have *need* that one teach you again
— are become such as have *need* of milk,
7:11. what further *need* (was there) that another
10:36. For ye have *need* of patience, that,
1Joh.2:27. ye *need* not that any man teach you:
3:17. seeth his brother have *need*, and shutteth
Rev. 3:17. and have *need* of nothing;
21:23. the city had no *need* of the sun,
22: 5. they *need* no candle, neither light of

χρεωφειλέτης, kreōphīletees.

Lu. 7:41. a certain creditor which had two *debtors*:
16: 5. called every one of his lord's *debtors*

χρή, kree.

Jas. 3:10. these things *ought* not so to be.

χρήζω, kreezo.

Mat. 6:32. that ye *have need* of all these things.
Lu. 11: 8. and give him as many as he *needeth*.
12:30. knoweth that ye *have need* of these things.
Ro. 16: 2. assist her in whatsoever business she *hath need* of you:
2Co. 3: 1. or *need* we, as some (others), epistles of

χρῆμα, kreema.

Mar 10:23. shall they that have *riches* enter
24. is it for them that trust in *riches*
Lu. 18:24. How hardly shall they that have *riches*
Acts 4:37. and brought the *money*, and laid (it) at
8:18. he offered them *money*,
20. may be purchased with *money*.
24:26. He hoped also that *money* should

χρηματίζω, kreematizo.

Mat. 2:12. *being warned of God* in a dream that they
22. *being warned of God* in a dream, he
Lu. 2:26. it was *revealed* unto him by the Holy Ghost,
Acts 10:22. *was warned from God* by an holy angel to
11:26. the disciples *were called* (lit. *to call* the disciples) Christians first in Antioch.
Ro. 7: 3. she *shall be called* an adulteress:
Heb 8: 5. as Moses *was admonished of God* when
11: 7. Noah, *being warned of God* of things not
12:25. who refused him *that spake* on earth,

χρηματισμός, kreematismos.

Ro. 11: 4. what saith the *answer of God* unto him?

χρήσιμος, kreesimos.

2Ti. 2:14. strive not about words to no *profit*, (but)

χρῆσις, kreesis.

Ro. 1:26. did change the natural *use*
27. leaving the natural *use* of the woman,

χρηστεύομαι, kreestŭomai.

1Co.13: 4. suffereth long, (and) *is kind*;

χρηστολογία, kreestologia.

Ro. 16:18. by *good words* and fair speeches deceive

χρηστός, kreestos.

Mat.11:30. For my yoke (is) *easy*, and my burden is light.
Lu. 5:39. he saith, The old is *better*.
6:35. for he is *kind* unto the unthankful and
Ro. 2: 4. not knowing that the *goodness* of God leadeth thee to
1Co.15:33. evil communications corrupt *good*
Eph 4:32. And be ye *kind* one to another,
1Pet.2: 3. tasted that the Lord (is) *gracious*

χρηστότης, kreestotees.

Ro. 2: 4. despisest thou the riches of his *goodness*
3:12. there is none that doeth *good*,
11:22. Behold therefore the *goodness* and
— but toward thee, *goodness*, if thou continue in (his) *goodness*:
2Co. 6: 6. by longsuffering, by *kindness*, by the Holy Ghost,
Gal. 5:22. longsuffering, *gentleness*, goodness,
Eph 2: 7. in (his) *kindness* toward us through Christ
Col. 3:12. *kindness*, humbleness of mind, meekness,
Tit. 3: 4. But after that the *kindness* and love of God our Saviour

χρίω, krio.

Lu. 4:18. because he *hath anointed* me to preach
Acts 4:27. against thy holy child Jesus, whom thou *hast anointed*,
10:38. How God *anointed* Jesus of Nazareth with the Holy Ghost and
2Co. 1:21. and *hath anointed* us, (is) God;
Heb 1: 9. *hath anointed* thee with the oil of gladness

χρίσμα, krisma.

1Joh.2:20. ye have an *unction* from the Holy One,
27. But the *anointing* which ye have received of
— but as the same *anointing* teacheth you

χρονίζω, kronizo.

Mat.24:48. My lord *delayeth* his coming;
25: 5. *While* the bridegroom *tarried*, they
Lu. 1:21. marvelled that he *tarried* so long in
12:45. My lord *delayeth* his coming;
Heb 10:37. he that shall come will come, and *will* not *tarry*.

χρόνος, *kronos.*

Mat. 2: 7. enquired of them diligently what *time*
16. according to the *time* which he had
25:19. After a long *time* the lord of those
Mar 2:19. as long)(as they have the bridegroom
9:21. How long)(is it ago since this came
Lu. 1:57. Now Elisabeth's full *time* came that
4: 5. in a moment of *time.*
8:27. which had devils long *time,*
29. For often*times* it had caught him:
18: 4. And he would not for a *while:*
20: 9. into a far country for a long *time.*
Joh. 5: 6. that he had been now a long *time*
7:33. Yet a little *while* am I with you,
12:35. Yet a little *while* is the light with you.
14: 9. Have I been so long *time* with you,
Acts 1: 6. Lord, wilt thou at this *time* restore
7. to know the *times* or the seasons,
21. have companied with us all the *time*
3:21. must receive until the *times* of restitution
7:17. when the *time* of the promise drew nigh,
23. when he was full forty years old, (lit.
when the *time* of forty years was filled
to him)
8:11. of long *time* he had bewitched them
13:18. about the *time* of forty years suffered
14: 3. Long *time* therefore abode they
28. they abode long *time* with the disciples.
15:33. after they had tarried (there) a *space,*
17:30. And the *times* of this ignorance God
18:20. to tarry longer *time* with them,
23. after he had spent some *time* (there),
19:22. himself stayed in Asia for a *season.*
20:18. I have been with you at all *seasons,*
27: 9. Now when much *time* was spent,
Ro. 7: 1. as long)(as he liveth?
16:25. kept secret since the world began, (lit. in
the *times* of ages)
1Co. 7:39. as long)(as her husband liveth;
16: 7. but I trust to tarry a *while* with you,
Gal. 4: 1. as long)(as he is a child,
4. when the fulness of the *time* was come,
1Th. 5: 1. But of the *times* and the seasons,
2Ti. 1: 9. given us in Christ Jesus before the world
began; (lit. before the *times* of ages)
Tit. 1: 2. promised before the world began; (lit.
&c.)
Heb 4: 7. To day, after so long a *time ;*
5:12. when for the *time* ye ought to be teachers,
11:32. for the *time* would fail me to tell of
1Pet. 1:17. pass the *time* of your sojourning (here)
20. was manifest in these last *times* for you,
4: 2. should live the rest of (his) *time* in
3. For the *time* past of (our) life may
Jude 18. there should be mockers in the last *time,*
Rev. 2:21. And I gave her *space* to repent of
6:11. should rest yet for a little *season,*
10: 6. that there should be *time* no longer:
20: 3. he must be loosed a little *season.*

χρονοτριβέω, *kronotribeo.*

Acts20:16. he would not *spend* the *time* in Asia:

χρύσεος, *kruseos.*

2Ti. 2:20. not only vessels *of gold* and of silver,
Heb 9: 4. Which had the *golden* censer,
— the *golden* pot that had manna,

Rev. 1:12. I saw seven *golden* candlesticks ;
13. about the paps with a *golden* girdle.
20. and the seven *golden* candlesticks.
2: 1. midst of the seven *golden* candlesticks ;
4: 4. they had on their heads crowns *of gold.*
5: 8. and *golden* vials full of odours,
8: 3. having a *golden* censer ;
— upon the *golden* altar which was before
9:13. from the four horns of the *golden* altar
20. devils, and idols *of gold,* and silver,
14:14. having on his head a *golden* crown,
15: 6. breasts girded with *golden* girdles.
7. seven *golden* vials full of the wrath of God,
17: 4. having a *golden* cup in her hand full
21:15. had a *golden* reed to measure the city,

χρυσίον, *krusion.*

Acts 3: 6. Silver and *gold* have I none ;
20:33. I have coveted no man's silver, or *gold,*
Heb 9: 4. overlaid round about with *gold,*
1Pet. 1: 7. much more precious than of *gold* that
18. not redeemed with corruptible things, (as)
silver and *gold,*
3: 3. plaiting the hair, and of wearing of *gold,*
Rev. 3:18. to buy of me *gold* tried in the fire,
21:18. and the city (was) pure *gold,* like unto
clear glass.
21. the street of the city (was) pure *gold,* as
it were transparent glass.

χρυσοδακτύλιος, *krusodaktulios.*

Jas. 2: 2. a man *with a gold ring,* in

χρυσόλιθος, *krusolithos.*

Rev.21:20. the seventh, *chrysolite ;*

χρυσόπρασος, *krusoprasos.*

Rev.21:20. the tenth, a *chrysoprasus ;*

χρυσός, *krusos.*

Mat. 2:11. unto him gifts ; *gold,* and frankincense,
10: 9. Provide neither *gold,* nor silver, nor
23:16. shall swear by the *gold* of the temple,
17. whether is greater, the *gold,* or the temple
that sanctifieth the *gold?*
Acts17:29. that the Godhead is like unto *gold,* or
1Co. 3:12. upon this foundation *gold,* silver,
1Ti. 2: 9. not with broidered hair, or *gold,* or
Jas. 5: 3. Your *gold* and silver is cankered ;
Rev. 9: 7. as it were crowns like *gold,*
17: 4. decked with *gold* and precious stones
18:12. The merchandise of *gold,* and silver,
16. decked with *gold,* and precious stones,

χρυσόω, *krusoo.*

Rev.17: 4. *decked* with gold (lit. *made golden* with
gold)
18:16. *decked* with gold, (lit. *made golden,* &c.)

χρώς, krōs.

Acts19: 12. So that from his *body* were brought

χωλός, kōlos.

Mat.11 : 5. the *lame* walk, the lepers are cleansed,
　15:30. *lame*, blind, dumb, maimed,
　　　31. the *lame* to walk, and the blind to see:
　18: 8. to enter into life *halt* or
　21:14. the blind and the *lame* came to him
Mar 9:45. better for thee to enter *halt* into life,
Lu. 7:22. the *lame* walk, the lepers are
　14:13. the maimed, the *lame*, the blind:
　　　21. and the *halt*, and the blind.
Joh. 5: 3. of blind, *halt*, withered, waiting for
Acts 3: 2. man *lame* from his mother's womb
　　　11. as the *lame* man which was healed held
　8: 7. and that were *lame*, were healed.
　14: 8. impotent in his feet, being a *cripple* from
　　　his mother's womb,
Heb12:13. lest that which is *lame* be turned out of the
　　　way ;

χώρα, kōra.

Mat. 2:12. into their own *country* another way.
　4:16. to them which sat in the *region* and
　8:28. into the *country* of the Gergesenes,
Mar 1: 5. unto him all the *land* of Judæa,
　5: 1. into the *country* of the Gadarenes.
　　10. away out of the *country*.
Lu. 2: 8. were in the same *country* shepherds
　3: 1. and of the *region* of Trachonitis,
　8:26. at the *country* of the Gadarenes,
　12:16. The *ground* of a certain rich man brought
　15:13. took his journey into a far *country*,
　　14. a mighty famine in that *land*;
　　15. to a citizen of that *country*;
　19:12. went into a far *country* to receive
　21:21. let not them that are in the *countries* enter
　　　thereinto.
Joh. 4:35. look on the *fields*; for they are white
　11:54. unto a *country* near to the wilderness,
　　55. many went out of the *country* up to
Acts 8: 1. throughout the *regions* of Judæa and
　10:39. which he did both in the *land* of the Jews,
　12:20. because their *country* was nourished by
　13:49. published throughout all the *region*.
　16: 6. and the *region* of Galatia,
　18:23. went over (all) the *country* of Galatia
　26:20. and throughout all the *coasts* of Judæa,
　27:27. that they drew near to some *country*;
Jas. 5: 4. who have reaped down your *fields*,

χωρέω, kōreo.

Mat.15:17. *goeth* into the belly, and is cast
　19:11. All (men) cannot *receive* this saying,
　　12. He that is able *to receive* (it), *let* him *re-*
　　　ceive (it).
Mar 2: 2. insomuch that there *was* no *room to receive*
　　　(them), no, not
Joh. 2: 6. *containing* two or three firkins apiece.
　8:37. because my word *hath* no *place* in you.
　21:25. I suppose that even the world itself *could*
　　　not *contain* the books
2Co. 7: 2. *Receive* us; we have wronged no man,
2Pet.3: 9. but that all should *come* to repentance.

χωρίζω, kōrizo.

Mat.19: 6. *let* not man *put asunder*.
Mar 10: 9. *let* not man *put asunder*.
Acts 1: 4. that they should not *depart* from
　18: 1. Paul *departed* from Athens, *and*
　　2. commanded all Jews *to depart* from Rome:
Ro. 8:35. Who *shall separate* us from the love of
　　39. shall be able *to separate* us from the love
1Co. 7:10. Let not the wife *depart* from (her)
　　11. But and if she *depart*, let her
　　15. if the unbelieving *depart*, *let* him *depart*.
Philem 15. For perhaps he therefore *departed* for a
Heb 7:26. undefiled, *separate* (lit. *separated*) from
　　　sinners,

χωρίον, kōrion.

Mat.26:36. unto a *place* called Gethsemane,
Mar 14:32. a *place* which was named Gethsemane:
Joh. 4: 5. near to the *parcel of ground* that Jacob
Acts 1:18. purchased a *field* with the reward of
　　19. that *field* is called in their proper tongue,
　　　Aceldama, that is to say, The *field* of
　　　blood.
　4:34. as many as were possessors of *lands* or
　5: 3. (part) of the price of the *land*?
　　8. whether ye sold the *land* for so much?
　28: 7. were *possessions* of the chief man of the

χωρίς, kōris.

Mat.13:34. *without* a parable spake he not unto them:
　14:21. *beside* women and children.
　15:38. *beside* women and children.
Mar 4:34. *without* a parable spake he not unto them:
Lu. 6:49. a man that *without* a foundation
Joh. 1: 3. *without* him was not any thing made
　15: 5. *without* me ye can do nothing.
　20: 7. wrapped together in a place *by itself*.
Ro. 3:21. righteousness of God *without* the law
　　28. by faith *without* the deeds of the law.
　4: 6. imputeth righteousness *without* works,
　7: 8. For *without* the law sin (was) dead.
　　9. I was alive *without* the law once:
　10:14. how shall they hear *without* a preacher?
1Co. 4: 8. ye have reigned as kings *without* us:
　11:11. neither is the man *without* the woman,
　　　neither the woman *without* the man, in
　　　the Lord.
2Co.11:28. *Beside* those things that are without,
Eph. 2:12. at that time ye were *without* Christ,
Phi. 2:14. Do all things *without* murmurings and
1Ti. 2: 8. *without* wrath and doubting.
　5:21. *without* preferring one before another,
Philem 14. *without* thy mind would I do nothing;
Heb 4:15. tempted like as (we are, yet) *without* sin.
　7: 7. *without* all contradiction the less
　　20. inasmuch as not *without* an oath
　21(20). those priests were made *without* an
　　　oath ;
　9: 7. not *without* blood, which he offered
　　18. was dedicated *without* blood.
　　22. and *without* shedding of blood is no re-
　　　mission.
　　28. appear the second time *without* sin unto
　10:28. died *without* mercy under two or three
　11: 6. But *without* faith (it is) impossible
　　40. that they *without* us should not be
　12: 8. But if ye be *without* chastisement,
　　14. *without* which no man shall see the Lord:

Jas. 2:20. that faith *without* works is dead?
26. as the body *without* the spirit is dead, so faith *without* works

---

χῶρος, *kōros.*

Acts27:12. toward the south west and *north west.*

ψάλλω, *psallo.*

Ro. 15: 9. I will confess...and *sing* unto thy name.
1Co.14:15. I *will sing* with the spirit, and I *will sing* with the understanding
Eph. 5:19. singing and *making melody* in your heart to the Lord;
Jas. 5:13. Is any merry? *let* him *sing psalms.*

ψαλμός, *psalmos.*

Lu. 20:42. David himself saith in the book of *Psalms,*
24:44. and (in) the *psalms,* concerning me.
Acts 1:20. it is written in the book of *Psalms,* Let
13:33. it is also written in the second *psalm,*
1Co.14:26. every one of you hath a *psalm,*
Eph. 5:19. Speaking to yourselves in *psalms* and
Col. 3:16. admonishing one another in *psalms*

ψευδάδελφος, *psūdadelphos.*

2Co.11:26. (in) perils among *false brethren;*
Gal. 2: 4. And that because of *false brethren*

ψευδαπόστολος, *psūdapostolos.*

2Co.11:13. For such (are) *false apostles,*

ψευδής, *psūdees.*

Acts 6:13. And set up *false* witnesses,
Rev. 2: 2. and hast found them *liars:*
21: 8. sorcerers, and idolaters, and all *liars,*

ψευδοδιδάσκαλος, *psūdodidaskalos.*

2Pet.2: 1. there shall be *false teachers* among you,

ψευδολόγος, *psūdologos.*

1Ti. 4: 2. *Speaking lies* in hypocrisy;

ψεύδομαι, *psūdomai.*

Mat. 5:11. all manner of evil against you *falsely,*
Acts 5: 3. why hath Satan filled thine heart *to lie* to the Holy Ghost,
4. thou *hast* not *lied* unto men, but
Ro. 9: 1. I say the truth in Christ, I *lie* not,
2Co.11:31. knoweth that I *lie* not.
Gal. 1:20. behold, before God, I *lie* not.
Col. 3: 9. *Lie* not one to another, seeing that ye
1Ti. 2: 7. I speak the truth in Christ, (and) *lie* not;

Heb 6:18. in which (it was) impossible for God *to lie,*
Jas. 3:14. glory not, and *lie* not against the truth.
1Joh.1: 6. we *lie,* and do not the truth:
Rev. 3: 9. say they are Jews, and are not, but *do lie*

ψευδομάρτυρ, *psūdomartur.*

Mat.26:60. though many *false witnesses* came,
— At the last came two *false witnesses,*
1Co.15:15. we are found *false witnesses* of God;

ψευδομαρτυρέω, *psūdomartureo.*

Mat.19:18. Thou shalt not *bear false witness,*
Mar 10:19. *Do* not *bear false witness,*
14:56. For many *bare false witness* against him,
57. arose certain, and *bare false witness* against him,
Lu. 18:20. *Do* not *bear false witness,*
Ro. 13: 9. Thou *shalt* not *bear false witness,*

ψευδομαρτυρία, *psūdomarturia.*

Mat.15:19. thefts, *false witness,* blasphemies:
26:59. sought *false witness* against Jesus,

ψευδοπροφήτης, *psūdopropheetees.*

Mat. 7:15. Beware of *false prophets,*
24:11. And many *false prophets* shall rise,
24. and *false prophets,* and shall shew
Mar 13:22. For false Christs and *false prophets* shall rise,
Lu. 6:26. so did their fathers to the *false prophets.*
Acts13: 6. sorcerer, a *false prophet,* a Jew,
2Pet.2: 1. But there were *false prophets* also
1Joh.4: 1. because many *false prophets* are gone out into the world.
Rev.16:13. and out of the mouth of the *false prophet.*
19:20. and with him the *false prophet* that
20:10. where the beast and the *false prophet*

ψεῦδος, *psūdos.*

Joh. 8:44. When he speaketh a *lie,* he speaketh
Ro. 1:25. changed the truth of God into a *lie,*
Eph 4:25. Wherefore putting away *lying,*
2Th. 2: 9. all power and signs and *lying* wonders,
11. that they should believe a *lie:*
1Joh.2:21. and that no *lie* is of the truth.
27. and is truth, and is no *lie,*
Rev.21:27. worketh abomination, or (maketh) a *lie:*
22:15. whosoever loveth and maketh a *lie.*

ψευδόχριστος, *psūdokristos.*

Mat.24:24. For there shall arise *false Christs,*
Mar 13:22. For *false Christs* and false prophets shall rise,

---

ψευδώνυμος, *psūdōnumos.*

1Ti. 6:20. oppositions of science *falsely so called:*

ψεῦσμα, psūsma.

Ro. 3: 7. abounded through my *lie* unto his glory;

ψεύστης, psūstees.

Joh. 8:44. for he is a *liar*, and the father of it.
    55. I shall be a *liar* like unto you:
Ro. 3: 4. let God be true, but every man a *liar;*
1Ti. 1:10. for *liars*, for perjured persons,
Tit. 1:12. said, The Cretians (are) alway *liars*, evil beasts,
1Joh.1:10. that we have not sinned, we make him a *liar*,
    2: 4. keepeth not his commandments, is a *liar*,
    22. Who is a *liar* but he that denieth
    4:20. and hateth his brother, he is a *liar:*
    5:10. believeth not God hath made him a *liar;*

ψηλαφάω, pseelaphao.

Lu. 24:39. *handle* me, and see; for a spirit
Acts17:27. if haply they *might feel after* him,
Heb12:18. unto the mount *that might be touched*,
1Joh.1: 1. and our hands *have handled*,

ψηφίζω, pseephizo.

Lu. 14:28. and *counteth* the cost,
Rev.13:18. *Let* him that hath understanding *count* the number of the beast:

ψῆφος, pseephos.

Acts26:10. I gave my *voice* (lit. *pebble of voting*) against (them).
Rev. 2:17. will give him a white *stone*, and in the *stone* a new name written,

---

ψιθυρισμός, psithurismos.

2Co.12:20. *whisperings*, swellings, tumults:

ψιθυριστής, psithuristees.

Ro. 1:29(30). full of...deceit, malignity; *whisperers*,

ψιχίον, psikion.

Mat.15:27. eat of the *crumbs* which fall from
Mar 7:28. eat of the children's *crumbs.*
Lu. 16:21. to be fed with the *crumbs* which fell

ψυχή, psukee.

Mat. 2:20. which sought the young child's *life.*
    6:25. Take no thought for your *life*, what ye
    — Is not the *life* more than meat,
    10:28. but are not able to kill the *soul:*
    — to destroy both *soul* and body in hell.
    39. He that findeth his *life* shall lose it: and he that loseth his *life* for my sake
    11:29. and ye shall find rest unto your *souls.*
    12:18. in whom my *soul* is well pleased:

Mat.16:25. whosoever will save his *life* shall lose it: and whosoever will lose his *life* for my
    26. the whole world, and lose his own *soul?* or what shall a man give in exchange for his *soul?*
    20:28. to give his *life* a ransom for many.
    22:37. with all thy heart, and with all thy *soul,*
    26:38. My *soul* is exceeding sorrowful,
Mar 3: 4. to save *life*, or to kill?
    8:35. whosoever will save his *life* shall lose it; but whosoever shall lose his *life* for my
    36. gain the whole world, and lose his own *soul?*
    37. give in exchange for his *soul?*
    10:45. to give his *life* a ransom for many.
    12:30. with all thy heart, and with all thy *soul,*
    33. the understanding, and with all the *soul,*
    14:34. My *soul* is exceeding sorrowful
Lu. 1:46. My *soul* doth magnify the Lord,
    2:35. shall pierce through thy own *soul*
    6: 9. to save *life*, or to destroy (it)?
    9:24. whosoever will save his *life* shall
    — whosoever will lose his *life* for my
    56. is not come to destroy men's *lives*, but to
    10:27. all thy heart, and with all thy *soul,*
    12:19. And I will say to my *soul*, Soul, thou hast much goods
    20. this night thy *soul* shall be required
    22. Take no thought for your *life*, what
    23. The *life* is more than meat,
    14:26. yea, and his own *life* also, he cannot be
    17:33. Whosoever shall seek to save his *life*
    21:19. In your patience possess ye your *souls.*
Joh.10:11. the good shepherd giveth his *life* for
    15. I lay down my *life* for the sheep.
    17. because I lay down my *life,*
    24. How long dost thou make us (lit. our *soul*) to doubt?
    12:25. He that loveth his *life* shall lose it; and he that hateth his *life* in this
    27. Now is my *soul* troubled ;
    13:37. I will lay down my *life* for thy sake.
    38. Wilt thou lay down thy *life* for my sake?
    15:13. that a man lay down his *life* for his
Acts 2:27. thou wilt not leave my *soul* in hell,
    31. that his *soul* was not left in hell,
    41. about three thousand *souls.*
    43. fear came upon every *soul:*
    3:23. every *soul*, which will not hear that
    4:32. were of one heart and of one *soul:*
    7:14. his kindred, threescore and fifteen *souls.*
    14: 2. and made their *minds* evil affected
    22. Confirming the *souls* of the disciples,
    15:24. subverting your *souls*, saying,
    26. Men that have hazarded their *lives* for
    20:10. for his *life* is in him.
    24. neither count I my *life* dear unto myself,
    27:10. lading and ship, but also of our *lives.*
    22. there shall be no loss of (any man's) *life*
    37. we were in all in the ship two hundred threescore and sixteen *souls.*
Ro. 2: 9. upon every *soul* of man that doeth evil,
    11: 3. I am left alone, and they seek my *life.*
    13: 1. Let every *soul* be subject unto the
    16: 4. have for my *life* laid down their own necks:
1Co.15:45. The first man Adam was made a living *soul;*
2Co. 1:23. I call God for a record upon my *soul,*
    12:15. gladly spend and be spent for you; (lit. for your *souls*)
Eph 6: 6. doing the will of God from the *heart;*

Phi. 1:27. with one *mind* striving together for the
    2.30. not regarding his *life*, to supply
Col. 3:23. whatsoever ye do, do (it) *heartily*,
1Th. 2: 8. gospel of God only, but also our own *souls*,
    5:23. your whole spirit and *soul* and body
Heb 4:12. the dividing asunder of *soul* and spirit,
    6:19. we have as an anchor of the *soul*,
  10:38. my *soul* shall have no pleasure in him.
    39. that believe to the saving of the *soul*.
  12: 3. lest ye be wearied and faint in your *minds*.
  13:17. for they watch for your *souls*, as
Jas. 1:21. word, which is able to save your *souls*.
    5:20. shall save a *soul* from death,
1Pet.1: 9.(even) the salvation of (your) *souls*.
    22. Seeing ye have purified your *souls* in
    2:11. which war against the *soul*;
    25. unto the Shepherd and Bishop of your
      souls.
    3:20. few, that is, eight *souls* were saved
    4:19. commit the keeping of their *souls*
2Pet.2: 8. vexed (his) righteous *soul* from day to day
    14. beguiling unstable *souls* :
1Joh.3:16. he laid down his *life* for us: and we ought
    to lay down (our) *lives* for the brethren.
3Joh. 2. even as thy *soul* prospereth.
Rev. 6: 9. I saw under the altar the *souls* of them
    8: 9. which were in the sea, and had *life*, died ;
  12:11. they loved not their *lives* unto the death.
  16: 3. every living *soul* died in the sea.
  18:13. and slaves, and *souls* of men.
    14. the fruits that thy *soul* lusted after
  20: 4. the *souls* of them that were beheaded for

ψυχικός, *psukikos*.

1Co. 2:14. But the *natural* man receiveth not
  15:44. It is sown a *natural* body ; it is
   — There is a *natural* body, and there
    46. but that which is *natural*; and afterward
Jas. 3:15. but (is) earthly, *sensual*, devilish.
Jude 19. *sensual*, having not the Spirit.

ψύχομαι, *psukomai*.

Mat.24:12. the love of many *shall wax cold*.

ψύχος, *psukos*.

Joh.18:18. a fire of coals ; for it was *cold* :
Acts28: 2. present rain, and because of the *cold*.
2Co.11:27. in fastings often, in *cold* and nakedness.

ψυχρός, *psukros*.

Mat.10:42. of these little ones a cup of *cold* (water)
Rev. 3:15. that thou art neither *cold* nor hot: I
    would thou wert *cold* or hot.
    16. and neither *cold* nor hot, I will

ψωμίζω, *psomizo*.

Ro. 12:20. if thine enemy hunger, *feed* him ;
1Co.13: 3. And though I *bestow* all my goods *to feed*
    (the poor),

ψωμίον, *psomion*.

Joh.13:26. He it is, to whom I shall give a *sop*, when
   — when he had dipped the *sop*, he gave (it)
    27. after the *sop* Satan entered into him.
    30. He then having received the *sop* went

ψώχω, *psoko*.

Lu. 6: 1. did eat, *rubbing* (them) in (their) hands.

Ω, *ōmega*.

Rev. 1: 8. I am Alpha and *Omega*,
    11. Saying, I am Alpha and *Omega*,
  21: 6. I am Alpha and *Omega*,
  22:13. I am Alpha and *Omega*,

ὦ, *ō*.

Mat.15:28. *O* woman, great (is) thy faith :
  17:17. *O* faithless and perverse generation,
Mar 9:19. *O* faithless generation, how long
Lu. 9:41. *O* faithless and perverse generation,
  24:25. *O* fools, and slow of heart to believe
Acts 1: 1. treatise have I made, *O* Theophilus, of all
  13:10. *O* full of all subtilty and all mischief,
  18:14. *O* (ye) Jews, reason would that I should
    bear
  27:21.)(Sirs, ye should have hearkened
Ro. 2: 1. *O* man, whosoever thou art that judgest:
    3. And thinkest thou this, *O* man, that
  9:20. Nay but, *O* man, who art thou
  11:33. *O* the depth of the riches
Gal. 3: 1. *O* foolish Galatians, who hath
1Ti. 6:20. *O* Timothy, keep that which is
Jas. 2:20. But wilt thou know, *O* vain man,

ὦ, ἦς, ᾖ &c., *ō, ees, ee*.

From εἰμὶ.

Mat. 6: 4. That thine alms *may be* in secret:
    22. if therefore thine eye *be* single,
    23. But if thine eye *be* evil,
  10:13. And if the house *be* worthy,
   — but if it *be* not worthy, let your
  20: 4. and whatsoever *is* right I will give you.
    7. whatsoever *is* right, (that) shall ye receive.
  24:28. For wheresoever the carcase *is*, there
Mar 3:14. that they *should be* with him,
  5:18. prayed him that he *might be* with him.
Lu. 10: 6. And if the son of peace *be* there,
  11:34. therefore when thine eye *is* single,
   — but when (thine eye) *is* evil, thy
  14: 8. lest a more honourable...*be* bidden
Joh. 3: 2. except God *be* with him.
    27. except it *be* given him from heaven.
  6:65. except it *were* given unto him of my
  9: 5. As long as I *am* in the world, I am
    31. but if any man *be* a worshipper of God,
  14: 3. that where I am, (there) ye *may be* also.
  16:24. shall receive, that your joy *may be* full.
  17:11. that they *may be* one, as we (are).
    19. that they also *might be* sanctified
    21. That they all *may be* one ;
   — that they also *may be* one in us:

Joh. 17:22. that they *may be* one, even as we are one:
 23. that they *may be* made perfect in one;
 24. I will that they also, whom thou hast given me, *be* with me where I am;
 26. *may be* in them, and I in them.
Acts 5:38. if this counsel or this work *be* of men,
Ro. 2:25. but if thou *be* a breaker of the law,
 9:27. Though the number of...*be* as the sand
 11:25. lest ye *should be* wise in your own
1Co. 1:10. (that) there *be* no divisions among you; but (that) ye *be* perfectly joined
 2: 5. That your faith *should* not *stand* in the wisdom of men,
 5: 7. that ye *may be* a new lump,
 7:29. *be* as though they had none;
 34. that she *may be* holy both in body and
 36. if she pass the flower of (her) age, (lit. *be* past-prime)
 12:25. That there *should be* no schism in
 14:28. But if there *be* no interpreter,
 15:28. that God *may be* all in all.
 16: 4. And if it *be* meet that I go also,
2Co. 1: 9. that we should not trust in ourselves, (lit. *should* not *be* trusting)
 17. that with me there *should* *be* yea yea, and
 4: 7. *may be* of God, and not of us.
 9: 3. that, as I said, ye *may be* ready:
 13: 7. though we *be* as reprobates.
 9. when we are weak, and ye *are* strong:
Gal. 5:10. bear his judgment, whosoever he *be*.
Eph. 4:14. That we (henceforth) *be* no more children,
 5:27. but that it *should be* holy and without
Phi. 1:10. that ye *may be* sincere and without
 2:28. and that I *may be* the less sorrowful.
1Ti. 4:15. that thy profiting may appear (lit. *may be* apparent) to all.
 5: 7. that they *may be* blameless.
2Ti. 3:17. That the man of God *may be* perfect,
Tit. 1: 9. that he *may be* able by sound
 3:14. that they *be* not unfruitful.
Philem 14. that thy benefit *should* not *be* as
Jas. 1: 4. that ye *may be* perfect and entire,
 2:15. be naked, and)(destitute of daily food,
 5:15. and if he have committed sins, (lit. *be* having committed)
1Joh.1: 4. that your joy *may be* full.
2Joh. 12. that our joy *may be* full.

ὧδε, hōde.

Mat. 8:29. art thou come *hither* to torment us
 12: 6. *in this place* is (one) greater than the temple.
 41. a greater than Jonas (is) *here*.
 42. a greater than Solomon (is) *here*.
 14: 8. Give me *here* John Baptist's head
 17. We have *here* but five loaves,
 18. Bring them *hither* to me.
 16:28. There be some standing *here*,
 17: 4. it is good for us to be *here :*
 — let us make *here* three tabernacles;
 17. bring him *hither* to me.
 20: 6. Why stand ye *here* all the day idle?
 22:12. Friend, how camest thou in *hither*
 24: 2. There shall not be left *here* one stone
 23. say unto you, Lo, *here* (is) Christ, or *there*; believe (it) not.
 26:38. tarry ye *here*, and watch with me.
 28: 6. He is not *here :* for he is risen, as
Mar 6: 3. are not his sisters *here* with us?
 8: 4. with bread *here* in the wilderness?

Mar 9: 1. there be some of them that stand *here*,
 5. it is good for us to be *here :*
 11: 3. straightway he will send him *hither*.
 13:21. Lo, *here* (is) Christ; or, lo,
 14:32. Sit ye *here*, while I shall pray.
 34. tarry ye *here*, and watch.
 16: 6. he is not *here :* behold the place
Lu. 4:23. do also *here* in thy country.
 9:12. for we are *here* in a desert place.
 27. there be some standing *here*, which
 33. it is good for us to be *here :*
 41. Bring thy son *hither*.
 11:31. a greater than Solomon (is) *here*.
 32. a greater than Jonas (is) *here*.
 14:21. bring in *hither* the poor, and the maimed,
 17:21. Neither shall they say, Lo *here !* or,
 23. And they shall say to you, See *here ;*
 19:27. bring *hither*, and slay (them) before me.
 22:38. behold, *here* (are) two swords.
 23: 5. beginning from Galilee to *this place*.
 24: 6. He is not *here*, but is risen:
Joh. 6: 9. There is a lad *here*, which hath
 25. Rabbi, when camest thou *hither ?*
 11:21. Lord, if thou hadst been *here*,
 32. if thou hadst been *here*, my brother
 20:27. Reach *hither* thy finger, and
Acts 9:14. And *here* he hath authority from
 21. and came *hither* for that intent,
Col. 4: 9. unto you all things which (are done) *here*.
Heb 7: 8. And *here* men that die receive tithes;
 13:14. For *here* have we no continuing city,
Jas. 2: 3. Sit thou *here* in a good place;
 — or sit *here* under my footstool;
Rev. 4: 1. which said, Come up *hither*, and I
 11:12. saying unto them, Come up *hither*.
 13:10. *Here* is the patience and the faith of the saints.
 18. *Here* is wisdom. Let him that hath
 14:12. *Here* is the patience of the saints: *here* (are) they that keep the
 17: 9. And *here* (is) the mind which hath wisdom.

ᾠδή, ōdee.

Eph 5:19. hymns and spiritual *songs*,
Col. 3:16. psalms and hymns and spiritual *songs*,
Rev. 5: 9. And they sung a new *song*, saying,
 14: 3. they sung as it were a new *song*
 — no man could learn that *song*
 15: 3. they sing the *song* of Moses the servant of God, and the *song* of the Lamb,

---

ὠδίν, ōdin.

Mat.24: 8. All these (are) the beginning of *sorrows*.
Mar 13: 8. these (are) the beginnings of *sorrows*.
Acts 2:24. having loosed the *pains* of death:
1Th. 5: 3. as *travail* upon a woman with child;

ὠδίνω, ōdino.

Gal. 4:19. of whom I *travail in birth* again
 27. and cry, thou *that travailest* not:
Rev.12: 2. cried, *travailing in birth*, and

ὦμος, ōmos.

Mat.23: 4. and lay (them) on men's *shoulders ;*
Lu. 15: 5. he layeth (it) on his *shoulders*, rejoicing.

ὤν, οὖσα, ὄν, ōn, ousa, on.
From εἰμί.

Mat. 1:19. *being* a just (man),
    6:30. grass of the field, *which* to day *is,* and
    7:11. If ye then, *being* evil, know how to
  12:30. He *that is* not with me is against me ;
    34. how can ye, *being* evil, speak good things?
Mar 2:26. gave also to them *which were* with him ?
    5:25. woman, which had an issue of blood (lit.
        being in a flowing of blood) twelve
        years,
    8: 1. the multitude *being* very great,
  11:11. *and* now the eventide *was* come,
  13:16. And let him *that is* in the field
  14: 3. And *being* in Bethany in the house of
    43.)(one of the twelve,
    66. *as* Peter *was* beneath in the palace,
Lu. 2: 5. *being* great with child.
    3:23. *being* as was supposed the son of
    6: 3. and they *which were* with him ;
    8:43. a woman *having* an issue of blood
  11:23. He *that is* not with me is against me:
  12:28. the grass, *which is* to day in the field,
  13:16. *being* a daughter of Abraham,
  14:32. *while* the other *is* yet a great way off,
  20:36. *being* the children of the resurrection.
  22: 3. *being* of the number of the twelve.
    53. *When* I *was* daily with you in the temple,
  23: 7. to Herod, *who* himself also *was* at Jerusalem
    12. for before they were)(at enmity
  24: 6. *when* he *was* yet in Galilee,
    44. unto you, *while* I *was* yet with you,
Joh. 1:18. *which is* in the bosom of the Father,
  48(49). *when* thou *wast* under the fig tree,
  3: 4. How can a man be born *when* he *is* old?
    13. the Son of man *which is* in heaven.
    31. he *that is* of the earth is earthly,
  4: 9. How is it that thou, *being* a Jew, askest drink of me, *which am* a woman of
  5:13. a multitude *being* in (that) place.
  6:46. save he *which is* of God,
    71. *being* one of the twelve.
  7:50. *being* one of them,
  8:47. He *that is* of God heareth God's words:
  9:25. that, *whereas* I *was* blind, now I see.
    40. (some) of the Pharisees *which were* with him
  10:12. he that is an hireling, and not)(the shepherd,
    33. because that thou, *being* a man, makest thyself God.
  11:31. The Jews then *which were* with her
    49. *being* the high priest that same year,
    51. but *being* high priest that year,
  12:17. The people therefore *that was* with him
  18:26. *being* (his) kinsman whose ear Peter
    37. Every one *that is* of the truth
  19:38. *being* a disciple of Jesus, but secretly
  20: 1. *when* it *was* yet dark,
    19. the same day at evening, (lit. it *being* evening)
  21:11. *for all* there *were* so many,
Acts 5:17. *which is* the sect of the Sadducees,
  7: 2. *when* he *was* in Mesopotamia,
    5. when (as yet) he had no child. (lit. a child not *being* to him)
    12. Jacob heard that there *was* corn in
  8:23. I perceive that thou *art* in the gall
  9: 2. that if he found any)(of this way,
    38. *forasmuch as* Lydda *was* nigh to

Acts 9:39. Dorcas made, *while* she *was* with them.
  11: 1. and brethren *that were* in Judæa
  13: 1. in the church *that was* at Antioch
  14:13. of Jupiter, *which was* before their city,
  15:32. *being* prophets also themselves,
  16: 3. because of the Jews *which were* in those
    21. neither to observe, *being* Romans.
  17:16. when he saw the city)(wholly given to idolatry.
  18:24.)(mighty in the scriptures,
  19:31. *which were* his friends, sent unto him,
    35. city of the Ephesians *is* a worshipper
    36. Seeing then that these things cannot be spoken against, (lit. these things *being* undeniable)
  20:34. and to them *that were* with me.
  21: 8. *which was* (one) of the seven ;
  22: 5. to bring them *which were* there bound
    9. And they *that were* with me saw
  24:10. Forasmuch as I know that thou *hast been*
    24. his wife Drusilla, *which was* a Jewess,
  25:23. and principal men of the city, (lit. men *being* of eminence)
  26: 3. (because I know) thee *to be* expert
  27: 2. Aristarchus,...*being* with us.
    9. *when* sailing *was* now dangerous,
  28:17. Paul called the chief (lit. those *that were* the chief) of the Jews together:
    25. when they agreed not (lit. they *being* discordant)
Ro. 1: 7. To all *that be* in Rome, beloved of God,
  4:10. *when* he *was* in circumcision, or in
    17. calleth those things *which be* not as though they were. (lit. as *being*)
  5: 6. *when* we *were* yet without strength,
    8. in that, *while* we *were* yet sinners,
    10. For if, *when* we *were* enemies, we
    13. sin is not imputed *when* there *is* no law.
  7:23. to the law of sin *which is* in my members.
  8: 5. For they *that are* after the flesh do
    8. So then they *that are* in the flesh
    28. to them *who are* the called according
  9: 5. *who is* over all, God blessed for ever.
  11:17. and thou, *being* a wild olive tree,
  12: 3. to every man *that is* among you,
  13: 1. the powers *that be* are ordained of God.
  16: 1. Phebe our sister, *which is* a servant of
    11. of Narcissus, *which are* in the Lord.
1Co. 1: 2. Unto the church of God *which is* at Corinth,
    28. and things *which are* not, to bring to nought things *that are* ;
  8: 7. their conscience *being* weak is defiled.
    10. the conscience of him *which is* weak
  9:19. For *though* I *be* free from all
    21. *being* not without law to God, but
  12:12. *being* many, are one body:
2Co. 1: 1. unto the church of God *which is* at Corinth, with all the saints *which are* in
  5: 4. we *that are* in (this) tabernacle
  8: 9. that, *though* he *was* rich, yet for
    22. have oftentimes proved)(diligent
  11:19. *seeing* ye (yourselves) *are* wise.
    31. *which is* blessed for evermore,
Gal. 2: 3. Titus, who was with me, *being* a Greek,
  4: 1. *though* he *be* lord of all ;
    8. unto them *which* by nature *are* no gods.
  6: 3. to be something, *when* he *is* nothing,
Eph 1: 1. to the saints *which are* at Ephesus,
  2: 1. *who were* dead in trespasses and sins;
    4. But God, *who is* rich in mercy,
    5. Even *when* we *were* dead in sins,

Eph 2:13. ye *who* sometimes *were* far off
    20. Jesus Christ himself *being* the chief corner
        (stone);
  4:18. *being* alienated from the life of God
        through the ignorance *that is* in them,
Phi. 1: 1. saints in Christ Jesus *which are* at Philippi,
    7. *inasmuch as*...ye all *are* partakers of my
        grace.
Col. 1:21. you, *that were* sometime alienated
  2:13. And you, *being* dead in your sins
  4:11. *who are* of the circumcision.
1Th. 2:14. of the churches of God *which* in Judæa
      are in Christ Jesus:
    5: 8. But let us, *who are* of the day,
2Th. 2: 5. that, *when* I *was* yet with you,
1Ti. 1:13. *Who was* before a blasphemer, and
  2: 2. and (for) all *that are* in authority;
  3:10. *being* (found) blameless.
2Ti. 2:19. The Lord knoweth them *that are* his.
Tit. 1:16. *being* abominable, and disobedient,
  3:11. sinneth, *being* condemned of himself.
Philem 9. *being* such an one as Paul the aged,
Heb 1: 3. Who *being* the brightness of (his) glory,
  3: 2. *Who was* faithful to him that appointed
  5: 8. **Though** he *were* a Son, yet learned
  8: 4. *seeing that there are* priests that
  13: 3. as *being* yourselves also in the body.
Jas. 3: 4. Behold also the ships, which *though* (they
      be) so great,
2Pet.1:18. *when* we *were* with him in the holy mount.
  2:11. angels, *which are* greater in power
Rev. 5: 5. behold, the Lion)(of the tribe of Juda,

ὁ ὢν, καὶ ὁ ἦν, καὶ ὁ ἐρχόμενος, see
under O.

ὠνέομαι, *ōneomai.*

Acts 7:16. Abraham *bought* for a sum of

ᾠόν, *ōon.*

Lu. 11:12. Or if he shall ask an *egg*, will he

ὥρα, *hōra.*

Mat. 8:13. was healed in the selfsame *hour.*
  9:22. was made whole from that *hour.*
  10:19. it shall be given you in that same *hour*
  14:15. and the *time* is now past;
  15:28. And her daughter was made whole from
      that very *hour.*
  17:18. cured from that very *hour.*
  18: 1. At the same *time* came the disciples
  20: 3. he went out about the third *hour,*
    5. about the sixth and ninth *hour,*
    6. about the eleventh *hour* he went out, and
    9. that (were hired) about the eleventh *hour,*
    12. These last have wrought (but) one *hour,*
  24:36. But of that day and *hour* knoweth no
    42. ye know not what *hour* your Lord
    44. in such an *hour* as ye think not
    50. in an *hour* that he is not aware of,

Mat.25:13. ye know neither the day nor the *hour*
  26:40. could ye not watch with me one *hour* ?
    45. the *hour* is at hand, and the Son
    55. In that same *hour* said Jesus to the
  27:45. from the sixth *hour* there was darkness
      over all the land unto the ninth *hour.*
    46. about the ninth *hour* Jesus cried
Mar 6:35. And when the *day* was now far spent,
    — and now the *time* (is) far passed:
  11:11. and now the *eventide* was come,
  13:11. shall be given you in that *hour,*
    32. of that day and (that) *hour* knoweth no
  14:35. the *hour* might pass from him.
    37. couldest not thou watch one *hour* ?
    41. it is enough, the *hour* is come;
  15:25. And it was the third *hour,* and they
    33. And when the sixth *hour* was come,
    — whole land until the ninth *hour.*
    34. And at the ninth *hour* Jesus cried
Lu. 1:10. praying without at the *time* of incense.
  2:38. And she coming in that *instant*
  7:21. And in the same *hour* he cured many of
    (their) infirmities
  10:21. In that *hour* Jesus rejoiced
  12:12. shall teach you in the same *hour*
    39. had known what *hour* the thief
    40. Son of man cometh at an *hour*
    46. at an *hour* when he is not aware,
  14:17. sent his servant at supper *time*
  20:19. and the scribes the same *hour* sought
  22:14. when the *hour* was come, he sat down,
    53. but this is your *hour,* and the
    59. And about the space of one *hour* after
  23:44. it was about the sixth *hour,*
    — over all the earth until the ninth *hour.*
  24:33. they rose up the same *hour,* and returned
    to Jerusalem.
Joh. 1:39(40). for it was about the tenth *hour.*
  2: 4. mine *hour* is not yet come.
  4: 6. it was about the sixth *hour.*
    21. the *hour* cometh, when ye shall neither
    23. the *hour* cometh, and now is, when the
    true
    52. enquired he of them the *hour* when he
    — Yesterday at the seventh *hour*
    53. knew that (it was) at the same *hour,* in
  5:25. The *hour* is coming, and now is, when
    the dead
    28. the *hour* is coming, in the which all that
    35. were willing for a *season* to rejoice in
  7:30. because his *hour* was not yet come.
  8:20. for his *hour* was not yet come.
  11: 9. Are there not twelve *hours* in the day?
  12:23. The *hour* is come, that the Son of
    27. Father, save me from this *hour :* but for
    this cause came I unto this *hour.*
  13: 1. when Jesus knew that his *hour* was come
  16: 2. yea, the *time* cometh, that whosoever
    4. that when the *time* shall come, ye
    21. because her *hour* is come:
    25. the *time* cometh, when I shall no more
    32. Behold, the *hour* cometh, yea, is now
    come,
  17: 1. Father, the *hour* is come;
  19:14. of the passover, and about the sixth *hour :*
    27. from that *hour* that disciple took her
Acts 2:15. it is (but) the third *hour* of the day.
  3: 1. into the temple at the *hour* of prayer,
    (being) the ninth (hour).
  5: 7. about the space of three *hours* after,
  10: 3. about the ninth *hour* of the day
    9. to pray about the sixth *hour :*

Acts10:30. I was fasting until this *hour ;* and at the
    ninth *hour* I prayed in
  16:18. And he came out the same *hour.*
    33. he took them the same *hour* of the night,
  19:34. about the space of two *hours* cried out,
  22:13. And the same *hour* I looked up upon him.
  23:23. at the third *hour* of the night;
Ro. 13:11. that now (it is) *high time* to awake
1Co. 4:11. Even unto this present *hour* we
  15:30. why stand we in jeopardy every *hour ?*
2Co. 7: 8. sorry, though (it were) but for a *season.*
Gal. 2: 5. by subjection, no, not for an *hour ;*
1Th. 2:17. taken from you for a *short* time (lit. for
    the time of an *hour*)
Philem 15. he therefore departed for a *season,* that
1Joh.2:18. Little children, it is the last *time :*
  — whereby we know that it is the last *time.*
Rev. 3: 3. shalt not know what *hour* I will come
  10. keep thee from the *hour* of temptation,
  9:15. prepared for an *hour,* and a day, and a
  11:13. And the same *hour* was there a great
  14: 7. for the *hour* of his judgment is come:
  15. for the *time* is come for thee to reap;
  17:12. as kings one *hour* with the beast.
  18:10. for in one *hour* is thy judgment come.
  17(16). For in one *hour* so great riches
  19. for in one *hour* is she made desolate.

ὡραῖος, *hōraios.*

Mat.23:27. which indeed appear *beautiful* outward,
Acts 3: 2. which is called *Beautiful,*
  10. sat for alms at the *Beautiful* gate
Ro. 10:15. How *beautiful* are the feet of them

ὡρύομαι, *ōruomai.*

1Pet.5: 8. as a *roaring* lion, walketh about,

ὡς, *hōs.*

Mat. 1:24. did *as* the angel of the Lord had bidden
  6:10. in earth, *as* (it is) in heaven.
  12. our debts, *as* we forgive our debtors.
  29. was not arrayed *like* one of these.
  7:29. taught them *as* (one) having authority,
    and not *as* the scribes.
  8:13. *as* thou hast believed, (so) be it done
  10:16. I send you forth *as* sheep in the midst of
    wolves: be ye therefore wise *as* serpents,
    and harmless *as* doves.
  25. for the disciple that he be *as* his master,
    and the servant *as* his lord.
  12:13. it was restored whole, *like as* the other.
  13:43. shine forth *as* the sun in the kingdom of
  14: 5. they counted him *as* a prophet.
  15:28. be it unto thee *even as* thou wilt.
  17: 2. his face did shine *as* the sun, and his rai-
    ment was white *as* the light.
  20. If ye have faith *as* a grain of
  18: 3. and become *as* little children, ye
  4. shall humble himself *as* this little child,
  33. even *as* I had pity on thee?
  19:19. Thou shalt love thy neighbour *as* thyself.
  20:14. unto this last, even *as* unto thee.
  21:26. all hold John *as* a prophet.
  46. they took him *for* a prophet.

Mat.22:30. are *as* the angels of God
  39. love thy neighbour *as* thyself.
  26:19. disciples did *as* Jesus had appointed them ;
  39. nevertheless not *as* I will, but *as* thou
    (wilt).
  55. Are ye come out *as* against a thief
  27:65. make (it) as sure *as* ye can.
  28: 3. His countenance was *like* lightning,
  9. And *as* they went to tell his
  15. and did *as* they were taught:
Mar 1: 2. *As* it is written in the prophets,
  22. *as* one that had authority, and not *as* the
    scribes.
  3: 5. restored whole *as* the other.
  4:26. *as* if a man should cast seed
  27. grow up, he knoweth not *how.* (lit. *as*
    he knoweth not)
  31. (It is) *like* a grain of mustard seed,
  36. took him *even as* he was in the ship.
  5:13. they were *about* two thousand ;
  6:15. or *as* one of the prophets.
  34. *as* sheep not having a shepherd:
  7: 6. *as* it is written, This people
  8: 9. had eaten were *about* four thousand:
  24. I see men *as* trees, walking.
  9: 3. exceeding white *as* snow;
  21. How long is it ago *since* this came unto
    him?
  10: 1. and, *as* he was wont, he taught them
  15. the kingdom of God *as* a little child,
  12:25. but are *as* the angels which are in
  26. *how* in the bush God spake unto him,
  31. love thy neighbour *as* thyself.
  33. love (his) neighbour *as* himself,
  13:34. *as* a man taking a far journey, who
  14:48. Are ye come out, *as* against a thief,
Lu. 1:23. *as soon as* the days of his
  41. that, *when* Elisabeth heard the
  44. *as soon as* the voice of thy salutation
  2:15. *as* the angels were gone away
  37. a widow of *about* fourscore and
  39. And *when* they had performed all
  3: 4. *As* it is written in the book
  23. being *as* was supposed the son of Joseph,
  4:25. *when* great famine was throughout
  5: 4. Now *when* he had left speaking,
  6: 4. *How* he went into the house of God,
  10. restored whole *as* the other.
  22. cast out your name *as* evil,
  40. that is perfect shall be *as* his master.
  7:12. Now *when* he came nigh to the gate of
    the city,
  8:42. *about* twelve years of age,
  47. and *how* she was healed immediately.
  9:54. consume them, even *as* Elias did?
  10: 3. *as* lambs among wolves.
  18. I beheld Satan *as* lightning fall from
  27. and thy neighbour *as* thyself.
  11: 1. *when* he ceased, one of his
  2. Thy will be done, *as* in heaven, so in
  36. *as* when the bright shining of a candle
    doth give thee light.
  44. ye are *as* graves which appear not,
  12:27. not arrayed *like* one of these.
  58. *When* thou goest with thine
  14:22. it is done *as* thou hast commanded,
  15:19. make me *as* one of thy hired
  25. and *as* he came and drew nigh
  16: 1. accused unto him that he had wasted (lit.
    as wasting) his goods.
  17: 6. faith *as* a grain of mustard seed,
  28. also *as* it was in the days of Lot ;

Lu. 18:11. or even *as* this publican.

　　 17. the kingdom of God *as* a little child

　 19: 5. And *when* Jesus came to the place,

　　 29. *when* he was come nigh to Bethphage

　　 41. *when* he was come near, he beheld the city,

　 20:37. *when* he calleth the Lord the God of

　 21:35. For *as* a snare shall it come

　 22:26. let him be *as* the younger; and he that is chief, *as* he that doth serve.

　　 27. among you *as* he that serveth.

　　 31. he may sift (you) *as* wheat:

　　 52. Be ye come out, *as* against a thief,

　　 61. *how* he had said unto him, Before

　　 66. And *as soon as* it was day, the elders

　 23:14. *as* one that perverteth the people:

　　 26. And *as* they led him away, they

　　 55. and *how* his body was laid.

　 24: 6. remember *how* he spake

　　 32. *while* he talked with us by the way, and *while* he opened to us the

　　 35. and *how* he was known of them in

Joh. 1:14. the glory *as* of the only begotten

　 39(40). for it was *about* the tenth hour.

　 2: 9. *When* the ruler of the feast had tasted

　　 23. Now *when* he was in Jerusalem

　 4: 1. *When* therefore the Lord knew

　　 40. So *when* the Samaritans were come unto him, they

　 6:12. *When* they were filled, he

　　 16. And *when* even was (now) come,

　　 19. rowed *about* five and twenty or

　 7:10. But *when* his brethren were gone up,

　　 — but *as it were* in secret.

　　 46. Never man spake *like* this man.

　 8: 7. So *when* they continued asking

　 11: 6. *When* he had heard therefore

　　 18. *about* fifteen furlongs off:

　　 20. Then Martha, *as soon as* she heard

　　 29. *As soon as* she heard (that), she arose

　　 32. Then *when* Mary was come where

　　 33. *When* Jesus therefore saw her weeping,

　 15: 6. he is cast forth *as* a branch,

　 18: 6. *As soon* then as he had said unto them,

　 19:33. *when* they came to Jesus, and saw that he

　 20:11. and *as* she wept, she stooped down,

　 21: 8. *as it were* two hundred cubits,

　　 9. *As soon* then *as* they were come to land,

Acts 1:10. And *while* they looked stedfastly

　　 15. together were *about* an hundred and twenty,

　 2:15. are not drunken, *as* ye suppose,

　 3:12. *as* though by our own power

　　 22. *like* unto me; him shall ye hear

　 5: 7. *about* the space of three hours after,

　　 24. Now *when* the high priest

　 7:23. And *when* he was full forty years

　　 37. brethren, *like* unto me; him shall

　　 51. *as* your fathers (did), so (do) ye.

　 8:32. He was led *as* a sheep to the slaughter; and *like* a lamb dumb before

　　 36. And *as* they went on (their) way,

　 9:23. And *after that* many days were fulfilled,

　 10: 7. And *when* the angel which spake unto

　　 11. *as it had been* a great sheet knit at

　　 17. Now *while* Peter doubted in himself

　　 25. And *as* Peter was coming in,

　　 28. Ye know *how* that it is an unlawful

　　 38. *How* God anointed Jesus of

　 11: 5. *as it had been* a great sheet,

　　 16. *how* that he said, John indeed

　　 17. the like gift *as* (he did) unto us,

Acts 13:18. And *about* the time of forty years

　　 20. *about* the space of four hundred and

　　 25. And *as* John fulfilled his course,

　　 29. And *when* they had fulfilled all

　　 33. *as* it is also written in the second

　 14: 5. And *when* there was an assault

　 16: 4. And *as* they went through the cities,

　　 10. And *after* he had seen the vision,

　　 15. And *when* she was baptized,

　 17:13. But *when* the Jews of Thessalonica

　　 14. to go *as it were* to the sea:

　　 15. to come to him with all speed, (lit. *as* most quickly)

　　 22. I perceive that in all things ye are too superstitious. (lit. I see you *as* very &c.)

　　 28. *as* certain also of your own poets

　 18: 5. And *when* Silas and Timotheus were

　 19: 9. But *when* divers were hardened,

　　 21. *After* these things were ended,

　　 34. *about* the space of two hours cried

　 20:14. And *when* he met with us at Assos,

　　 18. And *when* they were come to him,

　　 20. (And) *how* I kept back nothing

　　 24. *so that* I might finish my course with

　 21: 1. it came to pass, that after we were gotten from (lit. *when* it was that we &c.)

　　 12. And *when* we heard these things,

　　 27. And *when* the seven days were

　 22: 5. *As* also the high priest doth bear me

　　 11. And *when* I could not see for

　　 25. And *as* they bound him with thongs,

　 23:11. for *as* thou hast testified of me in

　　 15. *as* though ye would enquire something

　　 20. *as* though they would enquire somewhat

　 25:10. *as* thou very well knowest.

　　 14. And *when* they had been there many days,

　 27: 1. And *when* it was determined

　　 27. But *when* the fourteenth night

　　 30. under colour *as* though they would

　 28: 4. And *when* the barbarians saw

　　 19. not *that* I had ought to accuse

Ro. 1: 9. *that* without ceasing I make mention

　　 21. they glorified (him) not *as* God,

　 3: 7. why yet am I also judged *as* a sinner?

　 4:17. things which be not *as* though they were.

　 5:15. But not *as* the offence, so also

　　 16. And not *as* (it was) by one that sinned,

　　 18. Therefore *as* by the offence of one

　 6:13. *as* those that are alive from the dead,

　 8:36. accounted *as* sheep for the slaughter.

　 9:27. Israel be *as* the sand of the sea,

　　 29. we had been *as* Sodoma, and been made like *unto* (lit *as*) Gomorrha.

　　 32. but *as it were* by the works of the law.

　 10:15. *How* beautiful are the feet of

　 11: 2. *how* he maketh intercession to God against Israel,

　　 33. *how* unsearchable (are) his judgments,

　 12: 3. *according as* God hath dealt to every

　 13: 9. love thy neighbour *as* thyself.

　　 13. Let us walk honestly, *as* in the day;

　 15:15. *as* putting you in mind,

　　 24. *Whensoever* I take my journey into Spain,

1Co. 3: 1. speak unto you *as* unto spiritual, but *as* unto carnal, (even) *as* unto babes in Christ.

　　 5. even *as* the Lord gave to every man?

　　 10. *as* a wise masterbuilder,

　　 15. shall be saved; yet so *as* by fire.

　 4: 1. *as* of the ministers of Christ,

　　 7. *as* if thou hadst not received (it)?

　　 9. *as it were* appointed to death:

1Co. 4:13. we are made *as* the filth of the world,
  14. but *as* my beloved sons I warn (you).
  18. are puffed up, *as* though I would not
   come
  5: 3. *as* absent in body, but present in spirit,
   have judged already, *as* though I were
   present,
  7: 7. all men were even *as* I myself.
  8. if they abide even *as* I.
  17. But *as* God hath distributed to every man,
   as the Lord hath called every one, so
  25. *as* one that hath obtained mercy of
  29. be *as* though they had none ;
  30. they that weep, *as* though they wept not ;
   and they that rejoice, *as* though they
   rejoiced not ; and they that buy, *as*
   though they possessed not ;
  31. they that use this world, *as* not abusing
  8: 7. eat (it) *as* a thing offered unto an idol ;
  9: 5. a wife, as well *as* other apostles,
  20. unto the Jews I became *as* a Jew,
  — that are under the law, *as* under the law,
  21. are without law, *as* without law,
  22. To the weak became I *as* weak,
  26. run, not *as* uncertainly ; so fight I, not *as*
   one that beateth the air:
  10: 7. *as* it is written, The people sat
  15. I speak *as* to wise men ;
  11:34. will I set in order *when* I come.
  12: 2. even *as* ye were led.
  13:11. a child, I spake *as* a child, I understood
   as a child, I thought *as* a child:
  14:33. *as* in all churches of the saints.
  16:10. worketh the work of the Lord, *as* I also
   (do).
2Co. 2:17. For we are not *as* many, which corrupt
   the word of God: but *as* of sincerity,
   but *as* of God, in the sight
  3: 1. or need we, *as* some (others), epistles of
  5. to think any thing *as* of ourselves ;
  5:19. *To wit*, (lit. *how*) that God was in Christ,
  20. *as* though God did beseech (you) by us:
  6: 4. ourselves *as* the ministers of God,
  8. *as* deceivers, and (yet) true ;
  9. *As* unknown, and (yet) well known ; *as*
   dying, and, behold, we live ; *as* chastened, and not killed ;
  10. *As* sorrowful, yet alway rejoicing ; *as*
   poor, yet making many rich ; *as* having
   nothing, and (yet)
  13. I speak *as* unto (my) children,
  7:14. but *as* we spake all things to you
  15. *how* with fear and trembling ye
  9: 5. *as* (a matter of) bounty, and not
  10: 2. *as* if we walked according to
  9. *as* if I would terrify you by
  14. *as* though we reached not unto you:
  11: 3. *as* the serpent beguiled Eve
  15. be transformed *as* the ministers of
  16. yet *as* a fool receive me,
  17. but *as* *it were* foolishly, in this
  21. *as* though we had been weak.
  13: 2. *as* if I were present, the second time ;
  7. though we be *as* reprobates.
Gal. 1: 9. *As* we said before, so say I now
  3:16. *as* of many ; but *as* of one,
  4:12. I beseech you, be *as* I (am) ; for I (am)
   as ye (are):
  14. received me *as* an angel of God, (even)
   as Christ Jesus.
  5:14. love thy neighbour *as* thyself.
  6:10. *As* we have therefore opportunity,

Eph 2: 3. children of wrath, even *as* others.
  3: 5. *as* it is now revealed unto
  5: 1. followers of God, *as* dear children ;
  8. walk *as* children of light:
  15. walk circumspectly, not *as* fools, but *as*
   wise,
  22. *as* unto the Lord.
  23. even *as* Christ is the head of the
  28. to love their wives *as* their own bodies.
  33. so love his wife *even as* himself ;
  6: 5. of your heart, *as* unto Christ ;
  6. Not with eyeservice, *as* menpleasers ; **but**
   as the servants of Christ,
  20. boldly, *as* I ought to speak.
Phi. 1: 8. *how* greatly I long after you all in
  20. *as* always, (so) now also Christ shall
  2: 8. And being found in fashion *as* a man,
  12. not *as* in my presence only,
  15. shine *as* lights in the world ;
  22. *as* a son with the father,
  23. *as* soon *as* I shall see how it
Col. 2: 6. *As* ye have therefore received
  20. why, *as* though living in the world,
  3:12. *as* the elect of God, holy and
  18. *as* it is fit in the Lord.
  22. not with eyeservice, *as* menpleasers ;
  23. *as* to the Lord, and not unto men ;
  4: 4. it manifest, *as* I ought to speak.
1Th. 2: 4. not *as* pleasing men, but God,
  6(7). *as* the apostles of Christ.
  7. even *as* a nurse cherisheth her
  10. *how* holily and justly and
  11. ye know *how* we exhorted and
  — *as* a father (doth) his children,
  5: 2. cometh *as* a thief in the
  4. overtake you *as* a thief.
  6. not sleep, *as* (do) others ;
2Th. 2: 2. *as* from us, *as* that the day of Christ is at
   hand.
  4. he *as* God sitteth in the temple
  3:15. Yet count (him) not *as* an enemy, but
   admonish (him) *as* a brother.
1Ti. 5: 1. but intreat (him) *as* a father ; (and) the
   younger men *as* brethren ;
  2. The elder women *as* mothers ; the younger
   as sisters, with all purity.
2Ti. 1: 3. *that* without ceasing I have
  2: 3. *as* a good soldier of Jesus Christ.
  9. *as* an evil doer, (even) unto bonds ;
  17. their word will eat *as* doth a canker:
  3: 9. *as* their's also was.
Tit. 1: 5. *as* I had appointed thee:
  7. *as* the steward of God ;
Philem 9. such an one *as* Paul the aged,
  14. should not be *as* *it were* of necessity, but
  16. Not now *as* a servant, but
  17. receive him *as* myself.
Heb 1:11. shall wax old *as* doth a garment ;
  3: 2. *as* also Moses (was faithful)
  5. *as* a servant, for a testimony of
  6. But Christ *as* a son over his own house ;
  8. your hearts, *as* in the provocation,
  11. *So* I sware in my wrath,
  15. your hearts, *as* in the provocation.
  4: 3. *As* I have sworn in my wrath,
  6:19. we have *as* an anchor of
  7: 9. And *as* I may so say, Levi
  11: 9. *as* (in) a strange country,
  27. *as* seeing him who is invisible.
  29. Red sea *as* by dry (land):
  12: 5. speaketh unto you *as* unto children,
  7. dealeth with you *as* with sons ;

Heb 12:16. or profane person, *as* Esau,
27. *as* of things that are made,
13: 3. in bonds, *as* bound with them ;
— *as* being yourselves also in the body.
17. *as* they that must give account,
Jas. 1:10. because *as* the flower of the
2: 8. love thy neighbour *as* thyself,
9. convinced of the law *as* transgressors.
12. *as* they that shall be judged by
5: 3. shall eat your flesh *as it were* fire.
5. *as* in a day of slaughter.
1Pet.1:14. *As* obedient children, not
19. *as* of a lamb without blemish
24. For all flesh (is) *as* grass,
— *as* the flower of grass.
2: 2. *As* newborn babes, desire
5. Ye also, *as* lively stones, are
11. I beseech (you) *as* strangers and
12. speak against you *as* evildoers,
13. to the king, *as* supreme ;
14. *as* unto them that are sent
16. *As* free, and not using (your) liberty *for*
(lit. *as*) a cloke of maliciousness, but
as the servants of God.
25. ye were *as* sheep going astray ;
3: 6. *Even as* Sara obeyed Abraham,
7. *as* unto the weaker vessel, and *as* being
heirs together of
16. evil of you, *as* of evildoers,
4:10. *as* good stewards of the manifold
11. (let him speak) *as* the oracles of God ;
— *as* of the ability which God giveth:
12. *as* though some strange thing
15. let none of you suffer *as* a murderer,
— or *as* a busybody in other men's matters.
16. if (any man suffer) *as* a Christian,
19. *as* unto a faithful Creator.
5: 3. Neither *as* being lords over
8. *as* a roaring lion, walketh about,
12. a faithful brother unto you, *as* I suppose,
I have written briefly,
2Pet.1: 3. *According as* his divine power
19. *as* unto a light that shineth
2: 1. even *as* there shall be false teachers
12. these, *as* natural brute beasts,
3: 8. with the Lord *as* a thousand years, and a
thousand years *as* one day.
9. *as* some men count slackness ;
10. will come *as* a thief in the
16. *As* also in all (his) epistles,
— *as* (they do) also the other scriptures,
1Joh.1: 7. in the light, *as* he is in the light,
2:27. *as* the same anointing teacheth you
2Joh. 5. not *as* though I wrote a new
Jude 7. *Even as* Sodom and Gomorrha,
10. know naturally, *as* brute beasts,
Rev. 1:10. a great voice, *as* of a trumpet,
14. white like wool, as white *as* snow ;
— eyes (were) *as* a flame of fire ;
15. *as* if they burned in a furnace ;
— *as* the sound of many waters.
16. *as* the sun shineth in his strength.
17. I fell at his feet *as* dead.
2:18. his eyes *like unto* a flame
24. the depths of Satan, *as* they speak ;
27. *as* the vessels of a potter shall they
— even *as* I received of my Father.
3: 3. will come on thee *as* a thief,
21. *as* I also overcame, and am
4: 1. *as it were* of a trumpet
7. beast had a face *as* a man,
5: 6. a Lamb, *as* it had been slain,

Rev. 6: 1. *as it were* the noise of thunder,
11. that should be killed *as* they (were),
12. black *as* sackcloth of hair,
— the moon became *as* blood ;
13. *as* a fig tree casteth her
14. departed *as* a scroll when
8: 1. *about* the space of half an hour.
8. *as it were* a great mountain
10. burning *as it were* a lamp,
9: 2. *as* the smoke of a great furnace;
3. *as* the scorpions of the earth
5. *as* the torment of a scorpion,
7. *as it were* crowns like gold, and their faces
(were) *as* the faces of men.
8. hair *as* the hair of women, and their teeth
were *as* (the teeth) of lions.
9. *as it were* breastplates of iron;
— *as* the sound of chariots of many horses
17. (were) *as* the heads of lions;
10: 1. his face (was) *as it were* the sun, and his
feet *as* pillars of fire:
7. *as* he hath declared to his
9. in thy mouth sweet *as* honey.
10. and it was in my mouth sweet *as* honey:
12:15. water *as* a flood after the woman,
13: 2. his feet were *as* (the feet) of a bear, and
his mouth *as* the mouth of a lion:
3. *as it were* wounded to death ;
11. he spake *as* a dragon.
14: 2. *as* the voice of many waters, and *as* the
voice of a great thunder:
3. they sung *as it were* a new song
15: 2. I saw *as it were* a sea of glass
16: 3. it became *as* the blood of a dead (man):
15. Behold, I come *as* a thief.
21. (every stone) *about* the weight of a talent:
17:12. receive power *as* kings one hour
18: 6. even *as* she rewarded you,
21. a stone *like* a great millstone,
19: 6. heard *as it were* the voice of a great multitude, and *as* the voice of many waters,
and *as* the voice of mighty thunderings,
12. His eyes (were) *as* a flame of fire;
20: 8. of whom (is) *as* the sand of the sea.
21: 2. prepared *as* a bride adorned for
11. *even like* a jasper stone,
21. *as it were* transparent glass.
22: 1. water of life, clear *as* crystal,
12. *according as* his work shall be.

ὡσαύτως & Ὡσαννά, see after ὥστε.

ὡσεί, *hosī.*

Mat. 3:16. descending *like* a dove,
9:36. *as* sheep having no shepherd.
14:21. were *about* five thousand men,
28: 3. his raiment white *as* snow:
4. and became *as* dead (men).
Mar 1:10. the Spirit *like* a dove descending
6:44. were *about* five thousand men.
9:26. and he was *as* one dead;
Lu. 1:56. abode with her *about* three months,
3:22. in a bodily shape *like* a dove
23. began to be *about* thirty years of age,
9:14. were *about* five thousand men.
28. *about* an eight days after these
22:41. from them *about* a stone's cast,

Lu. 22:44. was *as it were* great drops of blood
    59. *about* the space of one hour after
  23:44. And it was *about* the sixth hour,
  24:11. seemed to them *as* idle tales,
Joh. 1:32. descending from heaven *like* a dove,
  4: 6. it was *about* the sixth hour.
  6:10. in number *about* five thousand.
  19:14. and *about* the sixth hour:
    39. *about* an hundred pound (weight).
Acts 2: 3. cloven tongues *like as* of fire,
    41. (unto them) *about* three thousand souls.
  4: 4. of the men was *about* five thousand.
  5:36. men, *about* four hundred,
  6:15. *as it had been* the face of an angel.
  9:18. from his eyes *as it had been* scales:
  10: 3. *about* the ninth hour of the
  19: 7. all the men were *about* twelve.
Heb 1:12. And *as* a vesture shalt thou
  11:12. and *as* the sand which is by the sea
Rev. 1:14. white *like* wool, as white as snow;

ὥσπερ, *hōsper.*

Mat. 5:48. *even as* your Father which is in
  6: 2. *as* the hypocrites do in the
    5. thou shalt not be *as* the hypocrites
    7. use not vain repetitions, *as* the heathen
  16. be not, *as* the hypocrites, of a sad
  12:40. For *as* Jonas was three days and
  13:40. *As* therefore the tares are gathered
  18:17. let him be unto thee *as* an heathen
  20:28. *Even as* the Son of man came
  24:27. For *as* the lightning cometh
    37. But *as* the days of Noe (were),
    38. For *as* in the days that were
  25:14. For (the kingdom of heaven is) *as* a man travelling into a far
    32. *as* a shepherd divideth (his) sheep from
Lu. 17:24. For *as* the lightning, that lighteneth
  18:11. that I am not *as* other men (are),
Joh. 5:21. For *as* the Father raiseth up
    26. For *as* the Father hath life in
Acts 2: 2. *as* of a rushing mighty wind,
  3:17. *as* (did) also your rulers.
  11:15. *as* on us at the beginning.
Ro. 5:12. Wherefore, *as* by one man
    19. For *as* by one man's disobedience
    21. That *as* sin hath reigned unto
  6: 4. that *like as* Christ was raised
    19. for *as* ye have yielded your members
  11:30. For *as* ye in times past have
1Co. 8: 5. *as* there be gods many, and lords many,
  11:12. For *as* the woman (is) of the man,
  15:22. For *as* in Adam all die,
  16: 1. *as* I have given order to the
2Co. 1: 7. *as* ye are partakers of the
  8: 7. Therefore, *as* ye abound in every
  9: 5. and not *as* (of) covetousness.
Gal. 4:29. But *as* then he that was born
Eph. 5:24. Therefore *as* the church is
1Th. 5: 3. *as* travail upon a woman with
Heb 4:10. *as* God (did) from his.
  7:27. needeth not daily, *as* those high priests,
  9:25. *as* the high priest entereth
Jas. 2:26. For *as* the body without the
Rev.10: 3. *as* (when) a lion roareth:

ὡσπερεί, *hōsperī.*

1Co.15: 8. *as* of one born out of due time.

ὥστε, *hōste.*

Mat. 8:24. *insomuch that* the ship was covered
    28. *so that* no man might pass
  10: 1. (against) unclean spirits, *to* cast them out, (lit. *so as to* cast, &c.)
  12:12. *Wherefore* (lit. *so that*) it is lawful to do well on the
    22. *insomuch that* the blind and dumb
  13: 2. *so that* he went into a ship,
    32. *so that* the birds of the air
    54. *insomuch that* they were astonished,
  15:31. *Insomuch that* the multitude
    33. *as to* fill (lit. *so as to* fill) so great
  19: 6. *Wherefore* they are no more twain,
  23:31. *Wherefore* ye be witnesses unto
  24:24. *insomuch that,* if (it were) possible,
  27: 1. *against* Jesus *to* put him to death:
    14. *insomuch that* the governor
Mar 1:27. *insomuch that* they questioned
    45. *insomuch that* Jesus could no
  2: 2. *insomuch that* there was no room
    12. *insomuch that* they were all amazed,
    28. *Therefore* the Son of man is Lord
  3:10. *insomuch that* they pressed upon him
    20. *so that* they could not so much as eat
  4: 1. *so that* he entered into a ship,
    32. *so that* the fowls of the air
    37. *so that* it was now full.
  9:26. *insomuch that* many said, He is dead.
  10: 8. *so then* they are no more twain,
  15: 5. *so that* Pilate marvelled.
Lu. 5: 7. *so that* they began to sink.
  9:52. to (lit. *so as* to) make ready for him.
  12: 1. *insomuch that* they trode one
Joh. 3:16. *that* he gave his only begotten Son,
Acts 1:19. *insomuch as* that field is called
  5:15. *Insomuch that* they brought forth
  14: 1. and so spake, *that* a great multitude... believed.
  15:39. *that* (lit. *so that*) they departed asunder
  16:26. *so that* the foundations of the
  19:10. *so that* all they which dwelt
    12. *So that* from his body were
    16. *so that* they fled out of that house
Ro. 7: 4. *Wherefore,* my brethren, ye also are
    6. *that* we should serve in newness
    12. *Wherefore* the law (is) holy,
  13: 2. Whosoever *therefore* resisteth (lit. *so that* whosoever)
  15:19. *so that* from Jerusalem, and
1Co. 1: 7. *So that* ye come behind in no
  3: 7. *So then* neither is he that planteth
    21. *Therefore* let no man glory in men.
  4: 5. *Therefore* judge nothing before the
  5: 1. *that* one should have his father's wife.
    8. *Therefore* let us keep the feast,
  7:38. *So then* he that giveth (her) in
  10:12. *Wherefore* let him that thinketh
  11:27. *Wherefore* whosoever shall eat
    33. *Wherefore,* my brethren, when
  13: 2. *so that* I could remove mountains,
  14:22. *Wherefore* tongues are for a sign,
    39. *Wherefore,* brethren, covet to
  15:58. *Therefore,* my beloved brethren, be ye
2Co. 1: 8. *insomuch that* we despaired
  2: 7. *So that* contrariwise ye (ought)
  3: 7. *so that* the children of Israel could not
  4:12. *So then* death worketh in us,
  5:16. *Wherefore* henceforth know we no man
    17. *Therefore* if any man (be) in Christ,
  7: 7. *so that* I rejoiced the more.

Gal. 2:13. *insomuch that* Barnabas
3: 9. *So then* they which be of faith
24. *Wherefore* the law was our
4: 7. *Wherefore* thou art no more a servant,
16. Am I *therefore* become your enemy,
Phi. 1:13. *So that* my bonds in Christ are
2:12. *Wherefore*, my beloved, as ye have
4: 1. *Therefore*, my brethren dearly
1Th. 1: 7. *So that* ye were ensamples
8. *so that* we need not to speak
4:18. *Wherefore* comfort one another
2Th. 1: 4. *So that* we ourselves glory in you
2: 4. *so that* he as God sitteth in the
Heb 13: 6. *So that* we may boldly say,
Jas. 1:19. *Wherefore*, my beloved brethren, let
1Pet.1:21. *that* your faith and hope might be in God.
4:19. *Wherefore* let them that suffer

ὡσαύτως, *hōsautōs.*

Mat.20: 5. the ninth hour, and did *likewise.*
21:30. came to the second, and said *likewise.*
36. they did unto them *likewise.*
25:17. And *likewise* he that (had received) two,
Mar 12:21. and the third *likewise.*
14:31. *Likewise* also said they all.
Lu. 13: 3. ye shall all *likewise* perish.
20:31. and *in like manner* the seven also:
22:20. *Likewise* also the cup after
Ro. 8:26. *Likewise* the Spirit also helpeth
1Co.11:25. *After the same manner* also (he took)
1Ti. 2: 9. *In like manner* also, that women
3: 8. *Likewise* (must) the deacons
11. *Even so* (must their) wives (be) grave,
5:25. *Likewise* also the good works (of some)
Tit. 2: 3. The aged women *likewise*, that
6. Young men *likewise* exhort to

Ὡσαννά, *hosanna.*

Mat.21: 9. *Hosanna* to the son of David:
— *Hosanna* in the highest.
15. *Hosanna* to the son of David;
Mar 11: 9. *Hosanna*; Blessed (is) he that cometh in
10. *Hosanna* in the highest.
Joh.12:13. *Hosanna*: Blessed (is) the King of Israel

ὡσεί see after ὡς.

ὥσπερ, ὥστε see after ὡς.

ὠτίον, *ōtion.*

Mat.26:51. and smote off his *ear.*
Mar 14:47. and cut off his *ear.*
Lu. 22:51. he touched his *ear*, and healed him.
Joh.18:10. and cut off his right *ear.*
26. (his) kinsman whose *ear* Peter cut off,

ὠφέλεια, *ōphelīa.*

Ro. 3: 1. what *profit* (is there) of circumcision?
Jude 16. having men's persons in admiration because of *advantage.*

ὠφελέω, *ōpheleo.*

Mat.15: 5. thou *mightest be profited* by me;
16:26. For what *is* a man *profited*, if he
27:24. Pilate saw that he could *prevail* nothing,
Mar 5:26. and was nothing *bettered*, but rather
7:11. thou *mightest be profited* by me;
8:36. For what *shall* it *profit* a man,
Lu. 9:25. For what *is* a man *advantaged*,
Joh. 6:63. the flesh *profiteth* nothing:
12:19. Perceive ye how ye *prevail* nothing?
Ro. 2:25. circumcision verily *profiteth*, if
1Co.13: 3. it *profiteth* me nothing.
14: 6. what *shall* I *profit* you, except I
Gal. 5: 2. Christ *shall profit* you nothing.
Heb 4: 2. the word preached did not *profit* them,
13: 9. which have not *profited* them that (lit. by which they *have* not *been profited*)

ὠφέλιμος, *ōphelimos.*

1Ti. 4: 8. For bodily exercise *profiteth* (lit. is *profitable*) little: but godliness is *profitable* unto all things,
2Ti. 3:16. and (is) *profitable* for doctrine, for
Tit. 3: 8. These things are good and *profitable* unto men.

PROPER NAMES.

Ἀαρών, Aärōn.

Lu. 1: 5. his wife (was) of the daughters of *Aaron*,
Acts 7:40. Saying unto *Aaron*, Make us gods to go
Heb 5: 4. called of God, as (was) *Aaron*.
     7:11. and not be called after the order of *Aaron?*
     9: 4. that had manna, and *Aaron's* rod

Ἀβαδδών, Abaddōn.

Rev. 9:11. in the Hebrew tongue (is) *Abaddon*,

Ἄβελ, Abel.

Mat.23:35. from the blood of righteous *Abel*
Lu. 11:51. From the blood of *Abel* unto the blood
Heb 11: 4. By faith *Abel* offered unto God
    12:24. speaketh better things than (that of) *Abel*.

Ἀβιά, Abia.

Mat. 1: 7. begat *Abia;* and *Abia* begat Asa;
Lu. 1: 5. of the course of *Abia:*

Ἀβιάθαρ, Abiathar.

Mar 2:26. in the days of *Abiathar* the high priest,

Ἀβιληνή, Abileenee.

Lu. 3: 1. Lysanias the tetrarch of *Abilene*,

Ἀβιούδ, Abioud.

Mat. 1:13. begat *Abiud;* and *Abiud* begat Eliakim;

Ἀβραάμ, Abraäm.

Mat. 1: 1. the son of David, the son of *Abraham*.
     2. *Abraham* begat Isaac;
    17. all the generations from *Abraham*
 3: 9. We have *Abraham* to (our) father:
    — to raise up children unto *Abraham*.
 8:11. shall sit down with *Abraham*,
22:32. I am the God of *Abraham*,
Mar 12:26. I (am) the God of *Abraham*,
Lu. 1:55. As he spake to our fathers, to *Abraham*,
    73. he sware to our father *Abraham*,
 3: 8. We have *Abraham* to (our) father:
    — to raise up children unto *Abraham*.

Lu. 3:34. which was (the son) of *Abraham*,
    13:16. this woman, being a daughter of *Abraham*,
    28. when ye shall see *Abraham*,
    16:22. carried by the angels into *Abraham's* bosom:
    23. and seeth *Abraham* afar off,
    24. Father *Abraham*, have mercy on me,
    25. But *Abraham* said, Son, remember that
    29. *Abraham* saith unto him,
    30. Nay, father *Abraham*:
    19: 9. forsomuch as he also is a son of *Abraham*.
    20:37. when he calleth the Lord the God of *Abraham*,
Joh. 8:33. We be *Abraham's* seed,
    37. I know that ye are *Abraham's* seed;
    39. *Abraham* is our father.
    — If ye were *Abraham's* children, ye would do the works of *Abraham*.
    40. this did not *Abraham*.
    52. *Abraham* is dead, and the prophets;
    53. Art thou greater than our father *Abraham*,
    56. *Abraham* rejoiced to see my day:
    57. and hast thou seen *Abraham?*
    58. Before *Abraham* was, I am.
Acts 3:13. The God of *Abraham*,
    25. saying unto *Abraham*, And in thy seed
 7: 2. appeared unto our father *Abraham*,
    16. the sepulchre that *Abraham* bought
    17. which God had sworn to *Abraham*,
    32. the God of thy fathers, the God of *Abraham*,
    13:26. children of the stock of *Abraham*,
Ro. 4: 1. What shall we then say that *Abraham*,
     2. if *Abraham* were justified by works,
     3. *Abraham* believed God,
     9. faith was reckoned to *Abraham*
    12. that faith of our father *Abraham*,
    13. not to *Abraham*, or to his seed, through the law,
    16. which is of the faith of *Abraham;*
 9: 7. Neither, because they are the seed of *Abraham*,
    11: 1. of the seed of *Abraham*,
2Co.11:22. Are they the seed of *Abraham?* so am I.
Gal. 3: 6. Even as *Abraham* believed God,
     7. are the children of *Abraham*.
     8. preached before the gospel unto *Abraham*,
     9. blessed with faithful *Abraham*.
    14. the blessing of *Abraham* might come
    16. to *Abraham* and his seed were the promises
    18. God gave (it) to *Abraham* by promise.
    29. then are ye *Abraham's* seed,
 4:22. *Abraham* had two sons, the one by
Heb 2:16. but he took on (him) the seed of *Abraham*.
 6:13. when God made promise to *Abraham*,
 7: 1. met *Abraham* returning from the
     2. To whom also *Abraham* gave a tenth

Heb 7: 4. *Abraham* gave the tenth
    5. though they come out of the loins of *Abraham :*
    6. received tithes of *Abraham,*
    9. payed tithes in *Abraham.*
  11: 8. By faith *Abraham,* when he was called
    17. By faith *Abraham,* when he was tried,
Jas. 2:21. Was not *Abraham* our father justified
    23. *Abraham* believed God, and it was imputed
1Pet. 3: 6. Sara obeyed *Abraham,* calling him lord:

'Αγαϐος, *Agabos.*

Acts11:28. one of them named *Agabus,*
  21:10. a certain prophet, named *Agabus.*

"Αγαρ, *Agar.*

Gal. 4:24. gendereth to bondage, which is *Agar.*
    25. For this *Agar* is mount Sinai

'Αγρίππας, *Agrippas.*

Acts25:13. king *Agrippa* and Bernice came
    22. Then *Agrippa* said unto Festus,
    23. when *Agrippa* was come,
    24. And Festus said, King *Agrippa,*
    26. before thee, O king *Agrippa,* that,
  26: 1. Then *Agrippa* said unto Paul,
    2. I think myself happy, king *Agrippa,*
    7. For which hope's sake, king *Agrippa,*
    19. Whereupon, O king *Agrippa,*
    27. King *Agrippa,* believest thou the
    28. Then *Agrippa* said unto Paul,
    32. Then said *Agrippa* unto Festus,

'Αδάμ, *Adam.*

Lu. 3:38. which was (the son) of *Adam,*
Ro. 5:14. death reigned from *Adam* to Moses,
    — similitude of *Adam's* transgression,
1Co.15:22. For as in *Adam* all die, even so
    45. The first man *Adam* was made a
    — the last *Adam* (was made)
1Ti. 2:13. For *Adam* was first formed,
    14. And *Adam* was not deceived,
Jude 14. And Enoch also, the seventh from *Adam,*

'Αδδί, *Addi.*

Lu. 3:28. which was (the son) of *Addi,*

'Αδραμυττηνός, *Adramutteenos.*

Acts27: 2. entering into a ship of *Adramyttium,*

'Αδρίας, *Adrias.*

Acts27:27. driven up and down in *Adria,*

'Αζώρ, *Azor.*

Mat. 1:13. and Eliakim begat *Azor ;*
    14. And *Azor* begat Sadoc ;

"Αζωτος, *Azōtos.*

Acts 8:40. But Philip was found at *Azotus :*

'Αθῆναι, *Atheenai.*

Acts17:15. brought him unto *Athens :*
    16. while Paul waited for them at *Athens,*
  18: 1. Paul departed from *Athens,*
1Th. 3: 1. left at *Athens* alone ;

'Αθηναῖος, *Atheenaios.*

Acts17:21. For all the *Athenians* and strangers
    22. (Ye) men of *Athens,*

'Αιγύπτιος, *Aiguptios.*

Acts 7:22. all the wisdom of the *Egyptians,*
    24. and smote the *Egyptian :*
    28. as thou diddest the *Egyptian* yesterday?
  21:38. Art not thou that *Egyptian,*
Heb 11:29. *Egyptians* assaying to do were drowned.

Αἴγυπτος, *Aiguptos.*

Mat. 2:13. flee into *Egypt,* and be thou
    14. departed into *Egypt :*
    15. Out of *Egypt* have I called my son.
    19. to Joseph in *Egypt,*
Acts 2:10. in *Egypt,* and in the parts of Libya
  7: 9. sold Joseph into *Egypt :*
    10. Pharaoh king of *Egypt ;* and he made him governor over *Egypt*
    11. dearth over all the land of *Egypt*
    12. corn in *Egypt,* he sent out our
    15. Jacob went down into *Egypt,*
    17. grew and multiplied in *Egypt,*
    34. the affliction of my people which is in *Egypt,*
    — I will send thee into *Egypt.*
    36. wonders and signs in the land of *Egypt,*
    39. back again into *Egypt,*
    40. out of the land of *Egypt,*
  13:17. strangers in the land of *Egypt,*
Heb 3:16. came out of *Egypt* by Moses.
  8: 9. to lead them out of the land of *Egypt ;*
  11:26. than the treasures in *Egypt :*
    27. By faith he forsook *Egypt,*
Jude 5. saved the people out of the land of *Egypt,*
Rev.11: 8. spiritually is called Sodom and *Egypt,*

Αἰθίοψ, *Aithiops.*

Acts 8:27. and, behold, a man of *Ethiopia,*
    — queen of the *Ethiopians,*

Αἰνέας, *Aineas.*

Acts 9:33. a certain man named *Æneas,*
    34. And Peter said unto him, *Æneas,*

Αἰνών, *Ainōn.*

Joh. 3:23. baptizing in *Ænon* near to Salim,

Ἀκελδαμά, *Akeldama.*

Acts 1:19. *Aceldama*, that is to say, The field of blood.

Ἀκύλας, *Akulas.*

Acts18. 2. a certain Jew named *Aquila*,
18. with him Priscilla and *Aquila* ;
26. when *Aquila* and Priscilla had heard,
Ro. 16: 3. Greet Priscilla and *Aquila*
1Co.16:19. *Aquila* and Priscilla salute you
2Ti. 4:19. Salute Prisca and *Aquila*,

Ἀλεξανδρεύς, *Alexandrūs.*

Acts 6: 9. *Alexandrians*, and of them of Cilicia
18:24. Apollos, born at Alexandria (lit. an *Alexandrian* by birth),

---

Ἀλεξανδρῖνος, *Alexandrinos.*

Acts27: 6. a ship *of Alexandria*
28:11. we departed in a ship *of Alexandria*,

Ἀλέξανδρος, *Alexandros.*

Mar 15:21. the father of *Alexander* and
Acts 4: 6. John, and *Alexander*, and as many as were
19:33. they drew *Alexander* out of the multitude,
— *Alexander* beckoned with the hand,
1Ti. 1:20. Of whom is Hymenæus and *Alexander* ;
2Ti. 4:14. *Alexander* the coppersmith did

Ἀλφαῖος, *Alphaios.*

Mat.10: 3. James (the son) of *Alphæus*,
Mar 2:14. Levi the (son) of *Alphæus* sitting
3:18. James the (son) of *Alphæus*,
Lu. 6:15. James the (son) of *Alphæus*,
Acts 1:13. James (the son) of *Alphæus*,

Ἀμιναδάϐ, *Aminadab.*

Mat. 1: 4. Aram begat *Aminadab* ; and *Aminadab*
Lu. 3:33. Which was (the son) of *Aminadab*,

Ἀμπλίας, *Amplias.*

Ro. 16: 8. Greet *Amplias* my beloved

Ἀμφίπολις, *Amphipolis.*

Acts17: 1. passed through *Amphipolis*

Ἀμών, *Amōn.*

Mat. 1:10. Manasses begat *Amon* ; and *Amon* begat Josias ;

Ἀμώς, *Amōs.*

Lu. 3:25. which was (the son) of *Amos*,

Ἀνανίας, *Ananias.*

Acts 5: 1. a certain man named *Ananias*,
3. But Peter said, *Ananias*,

Acts 5: 5. And *Ananias* hearing these words
9:10. a certain disciple at Damascus, named *Ananias* ;
— said the Lord in a vision, *Ananias*.
12. in a vision a man named *Ananias*
13. Then *Ananias* answered, Lord,
17. And *Ananias* went his way,
22:12. one *Ananias*, a devout man
23: 2. the high priest *Ananias* commanded
24: 1. after five days *Ananias* the high priest

Ἀνδρέας, *Andreas.*

Mat. 4:18. Simon called Peter, and *Andrew*
10: 2. Peter, and *Andrew* his brother ;
Mar 1:16. Simon and *Andrew* his brother
29. the house of Simon and *Andrew*,
3:18. And *Andrew*, and Philip,
13: 3. John and *Andrew* asked him privately,
Lu. ' 6:14. and *Andrew* his brother,
Joh. 1:40(41). *Andrew*, Simon Peter's brother.
44(45). city of *Andrew* and Peter.
6: 8. One of his disciples, *Andrew*,
12:22. Philip cometh and telleth *Andrew* : and again *Andrew* and Philip tell Jesus.
Acts 1:13. *Andrew*, Philip, and Thomas,

Ἀνδρόνικος, *Andronikos.*

Ro. 16: 7. Salute *Andronicus* and Junia,

Ἄννα, *Anna.*

Lu. 2:36. one *Anna*, a prophetess,

Ἄννας, *Annas.*

Lu. 3: 2. *Annas* and Caiaphas being the
Joh.18:13. led him away to *Annas* first;
24. *Annas* had sent him bound unto
Acts 4: 6. *Annas* the high priest, and

Ἀντιόχεια, *Antiokīa.*

Acts11:19. Cyprus, and *Antioch*,
20. when they were come to *Antioch*,
22. go as far as *Antioch*.
26(25). brought him unto *Antioch*.
— called Christians first in *Antioch*.
27. from Jerusalem unto *Antioch*.
13: 1. in the church that was at *Antioch*
14. they came to *Antioch* in Pisidia,
14:19. (certain) Jews from *Antioch*
21. Iconium, and *Antioch*,
26. And thence sailed to *Antioch*,
15:22. chosen men of their own company to *Antioch*
23. Gentiles in *Antioch* and Syria
30. they came to *Antioch* :
35. continued in *Antioch*, teaching
18:22. he went down to *Antioch*.
Gal. 2:11. when Peter was come to *Antioch*,
2Ti. 3:11. afflictions, which came unto me at *Antioch*,

Ἀντιοχεύς, *Antiokūs.*

Acts 6: 5. a proselyte *of Antioch* :

’Αντίπας, *Antipas.*

Rev. 2:13. wherein *Antipas* (was) my faithful martyr,

’Αντιπατρίς, *Antipatris.*

Acts23:31. by night to *Antipatris.*

’Αντίχριστος, see amongst Appellatives.

’Απελλῆς, *Apellees.*

Ro. 16:10. Salute *Apelles* approved in Christ.

’Απολλύων, *Apolluōn.*

Rev. 9:11. (his) name *Apollyon.*

’Απολλωνία, *Apollōnia.*

Acts17: 1. Amphipolis and *Apollonia,*

’Απολλώς, *Apollōs.*

Acts18:24. a certain Jew named *Apollos,*
19: 1. while *Apollos* was at Corinth,
1 Co. 1:12. and I of *Apollos;*
3: 4. another, I (am) of *Apollos;*
5. and who (is) *Apollos,*
6. *Apollos* watered; but God gave the increase.
22. Whether Paul, or *Apollos,*
4: 6. and (to) *Apollos* for your sakes;
16:12. touching (our) brother *Apollos,*
Tit. 3:13. Zenas the lawyer and *Apollos*

’Αππίου φόρον, *Appiou phoron.*

Acts28:15. as far as *Appii forum,*

’Απφία, *Apphia.*

Philem. 2. to (our) beloved *Apphia,*

’Αραβία, *Arabia.*

Gal. 1:17. I went into *Arabia,*
4:25. mount Sinai in *Arabia,*

’Αράμ, *Aram.*

Mat. 1: 3. Esrom begat *Aram;*
4. *Aram* begat Aminadab;
Lu. 3:33. which was (the son) of *Aram,*

’Άραψ, *Araps.*

Acts 2:11. Cretes and *Arabians,*

’Αρέτας, *Aretas.*

2Co.11:32. *Aretas* the king kept the city

’Άρειος Πάγος, *Arios pagos.*

Acts17:19. brought him unto *Areopagus,*
22. Paul stood in the midst of *Mars' hill,*

’Αρεοπαγίτης, *Areopagitees.*

Acts17:34. Dionysius the *Areopagite,*

’Αριμαθεία, *Arimathīa.*

Mat.27:57. a rich man of *Arimathæa,*
Mar15:43. Joseph of *Arimathæa,*
Lu. 23:51. *Arimathæa,* a city of the Jews:
Joh.19:38. Joseph of *Arimathæa,*

’Αρίσταρχος, *Aristarkos.*

Acts19:29. Gaius and *Aristarchus,*
20: 4. *Aristarchus* and Secundus;
27: 2. (one) *Aristarchus,* a Macedonian
Col. 4:10. *Aristarchus* my fellowprisoner
Philem 24(23). Marcus, *Aristarchus,* Demas,

’Αριστόβουλος, *Aristoboulos.*

Ro. 16:10. which are of *Aristobulus'* (houshold).

’Αρμαγεδδών, *Armageddōn.*

Rev.16:16. in the Hebrew tongue *Armageddon.*

’Αρτεμᾶς, *Artemas.*

Tit. 3:12. send *Artemas* unto thee,

’Άρτεμις, *Artemis.*

Acts19:24. silver shrines for *Diana,*
27. temple of the great goddess *Diana*
28. Great (is) *Diana* of the Ephesians.
34. Great (is) *Diana* of the Ephesians.
35. worshipper of the great goddess *Diana,*

’Αρφαξάδ, *Arphaxad.*

Lu. 3:36. which was (the son) of *Arphaxad,*

’Αρχέλαος, *Arkelaos.*

Mat. 2:22. that *Archelaus* did reign

’Άρχιππος, *Arkippos.*

Col. 4:17. say to *Archippus,* Take heed
Philem 2. *Archippus* our fellowsoldier,

’Ασά, *Asa.*

Mat. 1: 7. and Abia begat *Asa;*
8. And *Asa* begat Josaphat;

Ἀσήρ, *Aseer.*

Lu. 2:36. of the tribe of *Aser :*
Rev. 7: 6. Of the tribe of *Aser* (were) sealed

Ἀσία, *Asia.*

Acts 2: 9. Pontus, and *Asia,*
  6: 9. them of Cilicia and of *Asia,*
  16: 6. to preach the word in *Asia,*
  19:10. all they which dwelt in *Asia*
    22. stayed in *Asia* for a season.
    26. but almost throughout all *Asia,*
    27. all *Asia* and the world worshippeth.
  20: 4. accompanied him into *Asia*
    16. would not spend the time in *Asia :*
    18. that I came into *Asia,*
  21:27. the Jews which were of *Asia,*
  24:18. certain Jews from *Asia*
  27: 2. by the coasts of *Asia ;*
1Co.16:19(18). The churches of *Asia* salute you·
2Co. 1: 8. which came to us in *Asia,*
2Ti. 1:15. all they which are in *Asia*
1Pet.1: 1. *Asia,* and Bithynia,
Rev. 1: 4. seven churches which are in *Asia :*
    11. seven churches which are in *Asia ;*

Ἀσιανός, *Asianos.*

Acts20: 4. *of Asia,* Tychicus and Trophimus.

Ἀσιάρχης, *Asiarkees.*

Acts19:31. certain of the *chief of Asia,*

Ἄσσος, *Assos.*

Acts20:13. sailed unto *Assos,* there intending
    14. he met with us at *Assos,*

N.B. Stephens considers ἆσσον, Acts 27:13, as
    a proper name.

Ἀσύγκριτος, *Asunkritos.*

Ro. 16:14. Salute *Asyncritus,* Phlegon,

Ἀττάλεια, *Attalīa.*

Acts14:25. they went down into *Attalia :*

Αὔγουστος, *Augoustos.*

Lu. 2: 1. a decree from Cæsar *Augustus,*

Ἄχαζ, *Akaz.*

Mat. 1: 9. Joatham begat *Achaz ;* and *Achaz* begat
    Ezekias ;

Ἀχαΐα, *Akaïa.*

Acts18:12. Gallio was the deputy of *Achaia,*
    27. to pass into *Achaia,*
  19:21. Macedonia and *Achaia,*

Ro. 15:26. them of Macedonia and *Achaia*
  16: 5. Epenetus, who is the firstfruits of *Achaia*
1Co.16:15. firstfruits of *Achaia,*
2Co. 1: 1. saints which are in all *Achaia :*
    9: 2. *Achaia* was ready a year ago ;
  11:10. the regions of *Achaia.*
1Th. 1: 7. to all that believe in Macedonia and
    Achaia.
    8. not only in Macedonia and *Achaia,*

Ἀχαϊκός, *Akaïkos.*

1Co.16:17. Fortunatus and *Achaicus :*

Ἀχείμ, *Akīm.*

Mat. 1:14. and Sadoc begat *Achim ;* and *Achim*

Ἄψινθος, *Apsinthos.*

Rev. 8:11. the name of the star is called *Wormwood :*

Βάαλ, *Baäl.*

Ro. 11: 4. to (the image of) *Baal.*

Βαϵυλών, *Babulōn.*

Mat. 1:11. carried away to *Babylon :*
    12. brought to *Babylon,*
    17. the carrying away into *Babylon*
    — carrying away into *Babylon*
Acts 7:43. carry you away beyond *Babylon.*
1Pet.5:13. The (church that is) at *Babylon,*
Rev.14: 8. *Babylon* is fallen,
  16:19. great *Babylon* came in remembrance
  17: 5. BABYLON THE GREAT,
  18: 2. *Babylon* the great is fallen,
    10. that great city *Babylon,*
    21. great city *Babylon* be thrown down,

Βαλαάμ, *Balaäm.*

2Pet.2:15. following the way of *Balaam*
Jude 11. the error of *Balaam*
Rev. 2:14. the doctrine of *Balaam,*

Βαλάκ, *Balak.*

Rev. 2:14. who taught *Balac* to cast

Βαπτιστής, see amongst Appellatives.

Βαραϵϵᾶς, *Barabbas.*

Mat.27:16. a notable prisoner, called *Barabbas.*
    17. *Barabbas,* or Jesus which is called Christ?
    20. that they should ask *Barabbas,*
    21. They said, *Barabbas,*
    26. Then released he *Barabbas*

Mar 15: 7. And there was (one) named *Barabbas*,
11. that he should rather release *Barabbas*
15. released *Barabbas* unto them,
Lu. 23:18. and release unto us *Barabbas:*
Joh. 18:40. Not this man, but *Barabbas*. Now *Barabbas* was a robber.

Βαράκ, *Barak.*

Heb 11:32. to tell of Gedeon, and (of) *Barak*,

Βαραχίας, *Barakias.*

Mat. 23:35. Zacharias son of *Barachias*,

Βαρθολομαῖος, *Bartholomaios.*

Mat. 10: 3. Philip, and *Bartholomew;*
Mar 3:18. and *Bartholomew*, and Matthew,
Lu. 6:14. Philip and *Bartholomew*,
Acts 1:13. Philip, and Thomas, *Bartholomew*,

Βαριησοῦς, *Barïeesous.*

Acts 13: 6. a Jew, whose name (was) *Bar-jesus:*

Βὰρ-Ἰωνᾶ, *Bar-ïōna.*

Mat. 16:17. Blessed art thou, Simon *Bar-jona:*

Βαρνάβας, *Barnabas.*

Acts 4:36. And Joses, who by the apostles was surnamed *Barnabas*,
9:27. But *Barnabas* took him,
11:22. and they sent forth *Barnabas*,
25. Then departed *Barnabas* to Tarsus,
30. and sent it to the elders by the hands of *Barnabas*
12:25. And *Barnabas* and Saul returned from Jerusalem,
13: 1. as *Barnabas*, and Simeon
2. Separate me *Barnabas* and Saul for the work
7. who called for *Barnabas* and Saul,
43. followed Paul and *Barnabas:*
46. Then Paul and *Barnabas* waxed bold,
50. and raised persecution against Paul and *Barnabas*,
14:12. And they called *Barnabas*,
14. (Which) when the apostles, *Barnabas* and Paul,
20. and the next day he departed with *Barnabas*
15: 2. When therefore Paul and *Barnabas*
— they determined that Paul and *Barnabas*,
12. and gave audience to *Barnabas* and Paul,
22. to Antioch with Paul and *Barnabas;*
25. with our beloved *Barnabas* and Paul,
35. Paul also and *Barnabas* continued in Antioch,
36. And some days after Paul said unto *Barnabas*,
37. And *Barnabas* determined to take with them
39. and so *Barnabas* took Mark,
1 Co. 9: 6. Or I only and *Barnabas*,

Gal. 2: 1. I went up again to Jerusalem with *Barnabas*,
9. they gave to me and *Barnabas*
13. insomuch that *Barnabas* also was carried away
Col. 4:10. and Marcus, sister's son to *Barnabas*,

Βαρσαβᾶς, *Barsabas.*

Acts 1:23. *Barsabas*, who was surnamed Justus,
15:22. (namely), Judas surnamed *Barsabas*,

Βαρτίμαιος, *Bartimaios.*

Mar 10:46. blind *Bartimæus*, the son of Timæus,

Βεελζεβούλ, *Beëlzeboul.*

Mat. 10:25. called the master of the house *Beelzebub*,
12:24. but by *Beelzebub* the prince of the devils.
27. And if I by *Beelzebub* cast out devils,
Mar 3:22. said, He hath *Beelzebub*,
Lu. 11:15. He casteth out devils through *Beelzebub*
18. I cast out devils through *Beelzebub*.
19. And if I by *Beelzebub* cast out devils,

Βελίαλ, *Belial.*

2 Co. 6:15. And what concord hath Christ with *Belial?*

Βενιαμίν, *Benïamin.*

Acts 13:21. a man of the tribe of *Benjamin*,
Ro. 11: 1. (of) the tribe of *Benjamin*.
Phi. 3: 5. (of) the tribe of *Benjamin*,
Rev. 7: 8. Of the tribe of *Benjamin*

Βερνίκη, *Bernikee.*

Acts 25:13. and *Bernice* came unto Cæsarea
23. and *Bernice*, with great pomp,
26:30. and *Bernice*, and they that sat with them:

Βέροια, *Beroya.*

Acts 17:10. sent away Paul and Silas by night unto *Berea:*
13. was preached of Paul at *Berea*,

Βεροιαῖος, *Beroyaios.*

Acts 20: 4. into Asia Sopater of *Berea;*

Βηθαβαρά, *Beethabara.*

Joh. 1:28. These things were done in *Bethabara*

Βηθανία, *Beethania.*

Mat. 21:17. and went out of the city into *Bethany;*
26: 6. Now when Jesus was in *Bethany*,
Mar 11: 1. unto Bethphage and *Bethany*,
11. he went out unto *Bethany* with the twelve.
12. when they were come from *Bethany*,

Mar 14: 3. And being in *Bethany* in the house of Simon
Lu. 19:29. when he was come nigh to Bethphage and *Bethany*,
24:50. And he led them out as far as to *Bethany*,
Joh. 11: 1. (named) Lazarus, of *Bethany*,
18. Now *Bethany* was nigh unto Jerusalem,
12: 1. before the passover came to *Bethany*,

Βηθεσδά, *Beethesda.*

Joh. 5: 2. in the Ηebrew tongue *Bethesda*,

Βηθλεέμ, *Beethleëm.*

Mat. 2: 1. Jesus was born in *Bethlehem*
5. In *Bethlehem* of Judæa:
6. And thou *Bethlehem*, (in) the land of Juda,
8. And he sent them to *Bethlehem*,
16. and slew all the children that were in *Bethlehem*,
Lu. 2: 4. which is called *Bethlehem ;*
15. Let us now go even unto *Bethlehem*,
Joh. 7:42. and out of the town of *Bethlehem*,

Βηθσαϊδάν, -δά, *Beethsaïdan, -da.*

Mat. 11:21. woe unto thee, *Bethsaida !*
Mar 6:45. and to go to the other side before unto *Bethsaida*,
8:22. And he cometh to *Bethsaida ;*
Lu. 9:10. belonging to the city called *Bethsaida*.
10:13. woe unto thee, *Bethsaida !*
Joh. 1:44(45). Now Philip was of *Bethsaida*,
12:21. which was of *Bethsaida*

Βηθφαγή, *Beethphagee.*

Mat. 21: 1. and were come to *Bethphage*,
Mar 11: 1. unto *Bethphage* and Bethany,
Lu. 19:29. come nigh to *Bethphage* and Bethany,

Βιθυνία, *Bithunia.*

Acts 16: 7. they assayed to go into *Bithynia:*
1 Pet. 1: 1. Cappadocia, Asia, and *Bithynia*,

Βλάστος, *Blastos.*

Acts 12:20. and, having made *Blastus*

Βοανεργές, *Boanerges.*

Mar 3:17. and he surnamed them *Boanerges*,

Βοόζ, *Boöz.*

Mat. 1: 5. And Salmon begat *Booz* of Rachab ; and *Booz* begat Obed of Ruth ;
Lu. 3:32. which was (the son) of *Booz*,

Βορρᾶς, see amongst Appellatives.

Βοσόρ, *Bosor.*

2 Pet. 2:15. Balaam (the son) of *Bosor*,

Γαββαθᾶ, *Gabbatha.*

Joh. 19:13. but in the Hebrew, *Gabbatha*.

Γαβριήλ, *Gabrieel.*

Lu. 1:19. I am *Gabriel*, that stand in the
26. And in the sixth month the angel *Gabriel*

Γάδ, *Gad.*

Rev. 7: 5. Of the tribe of *Gad*

Γαδαρηνός, *Gadareenos.*

Mar 5: 1. into the country of the *Gadarenes*.
Lu. 8:26. And they arrived at the country of the *Gadarenes*,
37. of the country of the *Gadarenes*

Γάζα, *Gaza.*

Acts 8:26. down from Jerusalem unto *Gaza*,

Γάϊος, *Gaïos.*

Acts 19:29. and having caught *Gaius*
20: 4. and *Gaius* of Derbe,
Ro. 16:23. *Gaius* mine host, and of the whole church,
1 Co. 1:14. but Crispus and *Gaius ;*
3 Joh. 1. The elder unto the wellbeloved *Gaius*,

Γαλάται, *Galatai.*

Gal. 3: 1. O foolish *Galatians*, who hath

Γαλατία, *Galatia.*

1 Co. 16: 1. to the churches of *Galatia*,
Gal. 1: 2. unto the churches of *Galatia :*
2 Ti. 4:10. Crescens to *Galatia*, Titus unto Dalmatia.
1 Pet. 1: 1. throughout Pontus, *Galatia*,

Γαλατικός, *Galatikos.*

Acts 16: 6. and the region of *Galatia*,
18:23. the country of *Galatia*

Γαλιλαία, *Galilaia.*

Mat. 2:22. into the parts of *Galilee :*
3:13. Then cometh Jesus from *Galilee*
4:12. he departed into *Galilee ;*
15. *Galilee* of the Gentiles,
18. walking by the sea of *Galilee*,
23. And Jesus went about all *Galilee*,
25. multitudes of people from *Galilee*,
15:29. unto the sea of *Galilee ;*

Mat.17:22. And while they abode in *Galilee*,
19: 1. he departed from *Galilee*,
21:11. the prophet of Nazareth of *Galilee*.
26:32. I will go before you into *Galilee*.
27:55. which followed Jesus from *Galilee*,
28: 7. he goeth before you into *Galilee*;
10. that they go into *Galilee*,
16. went away into *Galilee*,
Mar 1: 9. came from Nazareth of *Galilee*,
14. Jesus came into *Galilee*,
16. walked by the sea of *Galilee*,
28. all the region round about *Galilee*.
39. throughout all *Galilee*, and cast out
3: 7. and a great multitude from *Galilee*
6:21. and chief (estates) of *Galilee*;
7:31. he came unto the sea of *Galilee*,
9:30. and passed through *Galilee*;
14:28. I will go before you into *Galilee*.
15:41. when he was in *Galilee*,
16: 7. that he goeth before you into *Galilee*:
Lu. 1:26. unto a city of *Galilee*,
2: 4. And Joseph also went up from *Galilee*,
39. they returned into *Galilee*,
3: 1. and Herod being tetrarch of *Galilee*,
4:14. in the power of the Spirit into *Galilee*:
31. a city of *Galilee*, and taught them
44. And he preached in the synagogues of *Galilee*.
5:17. out of every town of *Galilee*,
8:26. which is over against *Galilee*.
17:11. midst of Samaria and *Galilee*.
23: 5. beginning from *Galilee* to this place.
6. When Pilate heard of *Galilee*,
49. that followed him from *Galilee*,
55. which came with him from *Galilee*,
24: 6. when he was yet in *Galilee*,
Joh. 1:43(44). would go forth into *Galilee*,
2: 1. there was a marriage in Cana of *Galilee*;
11. did Jesus in Cana of *Galilee*,
4: 3. and departed again into *Galilee*.
43. and went into *Galilee*.
45. Then when he was come into *Galilee*,
46. So Jesus came again into Cana of *Galilee*,
47. was come out of Judæa into *Galilee*,
54. when he was come out of Judæa into *Galilee*,
6: 1. went over the sea of *Galilee*,
7: 1. After these things Jesus walked in *Galilee*:
9. he abode (still) in *Galilee*.
41. Shall Christ come out of *Galilee*?
52. Art thou also of *Galilee*?
— for out of *Galilee* ariseth no prophet.
12:21. which was of Bethsaida of *Galilee*,
21: 2. and Nathanael of Cana in *Galilee*,
Acts 9:31. throughout all Judæa and *Galilee*
10:37. and began from *Galilee*,
13:31. which came up with him from *Galilee*

Γαλιλαῖος, *Galilaios*.

Mat.26:69. Thou also wast with Jesus *of Galilee*.
Mar 14:70. for thou art a *Galilæan*,
Lu. 13: 1. some that told him of the *Galilæans*,
2. Suppose ye that these *Galilæans* were sinners above all the *Galilæans*,
22:59. for he is a *Galilæan*.
23: 6. asked whether the man were a *Galilæan*.
Joh. 4:45. the *Galilæans* received him,
Acts 1:11. Ye men *of Galilee*, why stand ye
2: 7. are not all these which speak *Galilæans*?
5:37. rose up Judas *of Galilee*

Γαλλίων, *Galliōn*.

Acts18:12. And when *Gallio* was the deputy
14. *Gallio* said unto the Jews,
17. And *Gallio* cared for none of those

Γαμαλιήλ, *Gamalieel*.

Acts 5:34. a Pharisee, named *Gamaliel*,
22: 3. at the feet of *Gamaliel*,

Γεδεών, *Gedeōn*.

Heb 11:32. would fail me to tell of *Gedeon*,

Γεθσημανῆ, *Gethseemanee*.

Mat.26:36. a place called *Gethsemane*,
Mar 14:32. which was named *Gethsemane*:

Γεννησαρέτ, *Genneesaret*.

Mat.14:34. into the land of *Gennesaret*.
Mar 6:53. into the land of *Gennesaret*.
Lu. 5: 1. he stood by the lake of *Gennesaret*,

Γεργεσηνός, *Gergeseenos*.

Mat. 8:28. the country of the *Gergesenes*,

Γολγοθᾶ, *Golgotha*.

Mat.27:33. a place called *Golgotha*,
Mar 15:22. unto the place *Golgotha*,
Joh.19:17. which is called in the Hebrew *Golgotha*:

Γόμορρα, τὰ, *Gomorra*.

Mat.10:15. the land of Sodom and *Gomorrha*
Mar 6:11. for Sodom and *Gomorrha*

Γόμορρα, ἡ, *Gomorra*.

Ro. 9:29. been made like unto *Gomorrha*.
2Pet.2: 6. the cities of Sodom and *Gomorrha*
Jude 7. Even as Sodom and *Gomorrha*,

Γώγ, *Gōg*.

Rev.20: 8. *Gog* and Magog, to gather them

Δαβίδ, *Dabid*.

Mat. 1: 1. the son of *David*, the son of Abraham.
6. And Jesse begat *David* the king; and *David*
17. So all the generations from Abraham to *David*
— from *David* until the carrying away into Babylon

Mat. 1:20. Joseph, thou son of *David*, fear not to
9:27. (Thou) son of *David*, have mercy on us.
12: 3. Have ye not read what *David* did, when
23. said, Is not this the son of *David*?
15:22. O Lord, (thou) son of *David*; my daughter
20:30. on us, O Lord, (thou) son of *David*.
31. on us, O Lord, (thou) son of *David*.
21: 9. Hosanna to the son of *David*: Blessed (is)
15. Hosanna to the son of *David*; they were
22:42. They say unto him, (The son) of *David*.
43. How then doth *David* in spirit call him
45. If *David* then call him Lord, how is
Mar 2:25. Have ye never read what *David* did, when
10:47. Jesus, (thou) son of *David*, have mercy on
48. (Thou) son of *David*, have mercy on me.
11:10. of our father *David*, that cometh in the
12:35. that Christ is the son of *David*?
36. For *David* himself said by the Holy Ghost,
37. *David* therefore himself calleth him Lord;
and whence
Lu. 1:27. name was Joseph, of the house of *David*;
32. unto him the throne of his father *David*:
69. in the house of his servant *David*;
2: 4. the city of *David*, which is called Bethlehem;
— was of the house and lineage of *David*:
11. is born this day in the city of *David*
3:31. of Nathan, which was (the son) of *David*,
6: 3. what *David* did, when himself was an
hungred,
18:38. Jesus, (thou) son of *David*, have mercy on
39. (Thou) son of *David*, have mercy on me.
20:41. How say they that Christ is *David's* son?
42. And *David* himself saith in the book of
44. *David* therefore calleth him Lord, how is he
Joh. 7:42. That Christ cometh of the seed of *David*,
— out of the town of Bethlehem, where *David*
Acts 1:16. which the Holy Ghost by the mouth of
David
2:25. For *David* speaketh concerning him, I
foresaw
29. of the patriarch *David*, that he is both
34. For *David* is not ascended into the heavens:
4:25. Who by the mouth of thy servant *David*
7:45. of our fathers, unto the days of *David*;
13:22. raised up unto them *David* to be
— I have found *David* the (son) of Jesse,
34. will give you the sure mercies of *David*.
36. For *David*, after he had served his own
15:16. will build again the tabernacle of *David*,
Ro. 1: 3. which was made of the seed of *David*
4: 6. Even as *David* also describeth the blessedness
11: 9. And *David* saith, Let their table be made
2Ti. 2: 8. that Jesus Christ of the seed of *David*
Heb 4: 7. he limiteth a certain day, saying in *David*,
11:32. *David* also, and Samuel, and (of) the
prophets:
Rev. 3: 7. he that hath the key of *David*, he
5: 5. the Root of *David*, hath prevailed to open
22:16. I am the root and the offspring of *David*,

Δαλμανουθά, *Dalmanoutha*.

Mar 8:10. disciples, and came into the parts of
Dalmanutha.

Δαλματία, *Dalmatia*.

2Ti. 4:10. unto Thessalonica; Crescens to Galatia,
Titus unto *Dalmatia*.

Δάμαρις, *Damaris*.

Acts17:34. and a woman named *Damaris*, and others
with

Δαμασκηνός, *Damaskeenos*.

2Co.11:32. the king kept the city of the *Damascenes*

Δαμασκός, *Damaskos*.

Acts 9: 2. And desired of him letters to *Damascus*
3. as he journeyed, he came near *Damascus*:
8. by the hand, and brought (him) into
Damascus.
10. there was a certain disciple at *Damascus*,
19. days with the disciples which were at
Damascus.
22. and confounded the Jews which dwelt at
Damascus,
27. how he had preached boldly at *Damascus*
22: 5. and went to *Damascus*, to bring them
6. my journey, and was come nigh unto
Damascus
10. Arise, and go into *Damascus*; and there it
11. that were with me, I came into *Damascus*.
26:12. Whereupon as I went to *Damascus* with
authority
20. But shewed first unto them of *Damascus*,
and
2Co.11:32. In *Damascus* the governor under Aretas
the king
Gal. 1:17. went into Arabia, and returned again unto
Damascus.

Δανιήλ, *Danieel*.

Mat.24:15. spoken of by *Daniel* the prophet,
Mar 13:14. spoken of by *Daniel* the prophet, standing

Δεκάπολις, *Dekapolis*.

Mat. 4:25. and (from) *Decapolis*, and (from) Jerusalem, and (from)
Mar 5:20. and began to publish in *Decapolis* how
7:31. through the midst of the coasts of *Decapolis*.

Δερβαῖος, *Derbaios*.

Acts20: 4. Aristarchus and Secundus; and Gaius *of
Derbe*, and

Δέρβη, *Derbee*.

Acts14: 6. and fled unto Lystra and *Derbe*, cities of
20. next day he departed with Barnabas to
Derbe.
16: 1. Then came he to *Derbe* and Lystra: and,

Δημᾶς, *Deemas*.

Col. 4:14. Luke, the beloved physician, and *Demas*,
greet you.

2Ti. 4:10. For *Demas* hath forsaken me, having
Philem 24. Marcus, Aristarchus, *Demas*, Lucas, my
    fellowlabourers.

Δημήτριος, *Deemeetrios.*

Acts 19.24. For a certain (man) named *Demetrius*, a
    silversmith,
    38. Wherefore if *Demetrius*, and the craftsmen
    which are
3Joh. 12. *Demetrius* hath good report of all (men),

Δίδυμος, *Didumos.*

Joh. 11:16. Then said Thomas, which is called *Didy-
    mus*, unto
    20:24. Thomas, one of the twelve, called *Didy-
    mus*,
    21: 2. were together Simon Peter, and Thomas
    called *Didymus*,

Διονύσιος, *Dionusios.*

Acts 17:34. and believed: among the which (was)
    Dionysius the

Διοπετής.

The neuter of this adjective is placed among the
    Appellatives.

Διόσκουροι, *Dioskouroi.*

Acts 28:11. a ship...whose sign was *Castor and Pollux.*
    (lit. the *Dioscuri*)

Διοτρεφής, *Diotrephees.*

3Joh. 9. I wrote unto the church: but *Diotrephes*,
    who

Δορκάς, *Dorkas.*

Acts 9:36. which by interpretation is called *Dorcas:*
    this woman
    39. which *Dorcas* made, while she was with

Δρούσιλλα, *Drousilla.*

Acts 24:24. when Felix came with his wife *Drusilla*,
    which

Ἑβέρ, *Heber.*

Lu. 3:35. which was (the son) of *Heber*,

Ἑβραϊκός, *Hebraïkos.*

Lu. 23:38. letters of Greek, and Latin, and *Hebrew*,

Ἑβραῖος, *Hebraios.*

Acts 6: 1. of the Grecians against the *Hebrews*,
2Co. 11:22. Are they *Hebrews?* so (am) I,
Phi. 3: 5. an *Hebrew* of the *Hebrews;*

Ἑβραΐς, *Hebraïs.*

Acts 21:40. spake unto (them) in the *Hebrew* tongue,
    22: 2. that he spake in the *Hebrew* tongue
    26:14. saying in the *Hebrew* tongue, Saul,

Ἑβραϊστί, *Hebraïsti.*

Joh. 5: 2. called *in the Hebrew tongue* Bethesda,
    19:13. the Pavement, but *in the Hebrew*, Gab-
    batha.
    17. called *in the Hebrew* Golgotha:
    20. written *in Hebrew*, (and) Greek, (and)
    Latin.
Rev. 9:11. name *in the Hebrew tongue* (is) Abaddon.
    16:16. called *in the Hebrew tongue* Armageddon.

Ἐζεκίας, *Ezekias.*

Mat. 1: 9. and Achaz begat *Ezekias;*
    10. And *Ezekias* begat Manasses;

Ἐλαμῖται, *Elamitai.*

Acts 2: 9. Parthians, and Medes, and *Elamites*,

Ἐλεάζαρ, *Eleazar.*

Mat. 1:15. And Eliud begat *Eleazar;* and *Eleazar*
    begat Matthan;

Ἐλιακείμ, *Eliakim.*

Mat. 1:13. Abiud begat *Eliakim;* and *Eliakim* begat
    Azor;
Lu. 3:30. which was (the son) of *Eliakim*,

Ἐλιέζερ, *Eliezer.*

Lu. 3:29. which was (the son) of *Eliezer*,

Ἐλιούδ, *Elioud.*

Mat. 1:14. and Achim begat *Eliud;*
    15. And *Eliud* begat Eleazar;

Ἐλισάβετ, *Elisabet.*

Lu. 1: 5. and her name (was) *Elisabeth.*
    7. because that *Elisabeth* was barren,
    13. and thy wife *Elisabeth* shall bear
    24. his wife *Elisabeth* conceived,
    36. And, behold, thy cousin *Elisabeth*,
    40. into the house of Zacharias, and saluted
    Elisabeth.

Lu. 1:41. when *Elisabeth* heard the salutation
— and *Elisabeth* was filled with the Holy
57. Now *Elisabeth's* full time came

'Ελισσαῖος, *Elissaios*.

Lu. 4:27. in the time of *Eliseus* the prophet;

'Ελλάς, *Hellas*.

Acts20: 2. exhortation, he came into *Greece,*

"Ελλην, *Helleen*.

Joh. 7:35. the dispersed among *the Gentiles,* and
teach the *Gentiles?*
12:20. there were certain *Greeks* among
Acts14: 1. the Jews and also of the *Greeks*
16: 1. his father (was) a *Greek:*
3. knew all that his father was a *Greek.*
17: 4. the devout *Greeks* a great multitude,
18: 4. persuaded the Jews and the *Greeks.*
17. all the *Greeks* took Sosthenes,
19:10. Lord Jesus, both Jews and *Greeks.*
17. known to all the Jews and *Greeks*
20:21. to the Jews, and also to the *Greeks,*
21:28. brought *Greeks* also into the temple,
Ro. 1:14. I am debtor both to the *Greeks,*
16. the Jew first, and also to the *Greek.*
2: 9. the Jew first, and also of the *Gentile;*
10. the Jew first, and also to the *Gentile:*
3: 9. proved both Jews and *Gentiles,*
10:12. between the Jew and the *Greek:*
1Co. 1:22. the *Greeks* seek after wisdom:
23. unto the *Greeks* foolishness;
24. are called, both Jews and *Greeks,*
10:32. to the Jews, nor to the *Gentiles,*
12:13. whether (we be) Jews or *Gentiles,*
Gal. 2: 3. who was with me, being a *Greek,*
3:28. There is neither Jew nor *Greek,*
Col. 3:11. there is neither *Greek* nor Jew,

'Ελληνικός, *Helleenikos*.

Lu. 23:38. in letters *of Greek,* and Latin, and Hebrew,
Rev. 9:11. in the *Greek* tongue hath (his) name

'Ελληνίς, *Helleenis*.

Mar 7:26. The woman was a *Greek,*
Acts17:12. honourable women which were *Greeks,*

'Ελληνιστής, *Helleenistees*.

Acts 6: 1. arose a murmuring of the *Grecians*
9:29. disputed against the *Grecians :*
11:20. spake unto the *Grecians,* preaching

'Ελληνιστί, *Helleenisti*.

Joh.19:20. written in Hebrew, (and) *Greek,* (and)
Latin.
Acts21:37. Who said, Canst thou speak *Greek?*

'Ελμωδάμ, *Elmōdam*.

Lu. 3:28. which was (the son) of *Elmodam,*

'Ελύμας, *Elumas*.

Acts13: 8. But *Elymas* the sorcerer

'Εμμανουήλ, *Emmanoueel*.

Mat. 1:23. they shall call his name *Emmanuel,*

'Εμμαούς, *Emmäous*.

Lu. 24:13. to a village called *Emmaus,*

'Εμμόρ, *Emmor*.

Acts 7:16. of the sons of *Emmor* (the father) of
Sychem.

'Ενώς, *Enōs*.

Lu. 3:38. Which was (the son) of *Enos,*

'Ενώχ, *Enōk*.

Lu. 3:37. which was (the son) of *Enoch,*
Heb11: 5. By faith *Enoch* was translated
Jude 14. And *Enoch* also, the seventh from

'Επαινετός, *Epainetos*.

Ro. 16: 5. Salute my wellbeloved *Epenetus,*

'Επαφρᾶς, *Epaphras*.

Col. 1: 7. As ye also learned of *Epaphras*
4:12. *Epaphras,* who is (one) of you,
Philem 23. There salute thee *Epaphras,*

'Επαφρόδιτος, *Epaphroditos*.

Phi. 2:25. to send to you *Epaphroditus,*
4:18. having received of *Epaphroditus*

'Επικούρειος, *Epikourios*.

Acts17:18. certain philosophers of the *Epicureans,*

"Εραστος, *Erastos*.

Acts19:22. Timotheus and *Erastus;*
Ro. 16:23. *Erastus* the chamberlain of the city
2Ti. 4:20. *Erastus* abode at Corinth:

'Ερμᾶς, *Hermas*.

Ro. 16:14. Phlegon, *Hermas,* Patrobas, Hermes,

'Ερμῆς, *Hermees*.

Acts14:12. Barnabas, Jupiter; and Paul, *Mercurius,*
Ro. 16:14. *Hermes,* and the brethren which are

Ἑρμογένης, *Hermogenees.*

2Ti. 1:15. of whom are Phygellus and *Hermogenes.*

Ἐρυθρὰ Θάλασσα, *Eruthra Thalassa.*

Acts 7:36. in the land of Egypt, and in the *Red sea,*
Heb 11:29. they passed through the *Red sea*

Ἐσλί, *Esli.*

Lu. 3:25. which was (the son) of *Esli,*

Ἑσρώμ, *Esrōm.*

Mat. 1: 3. and Phares begat *Esrom;* and *Esrom* begat
Aram;
Lu. 3:33. which was (the son) of *Esrom,*

Εὖα, *Ūa.*

2Co.11: 3. as the serpent beguiled *Eve*
1Ti. 2:13. For Adam was first formed, then *Eve.*

Εὔβουλος, *Ūboulos.*

2Ti. 4:21. *Eubulus* greeteth thee, and Pudens,

Εὐνείκη, *Ūnīkee.*

2Ti. 1: 5. and thy mother *Eunice;*

Εὐοδία, *Ūodia.*

Phi. 4: 2. I beseech *Euodias,* and beseech Syntyche,

Εὐροκλύδων, *Ūroklūdōn.*

Acts27:14. a tempestuous wind, called *Euroclydon.*

Εὔτυχος, *Ūtukos.*

Acts20: 9. young man named *Eutychus,*

Εὐφράτης, *Ūphratees.*

Rev. 9:14. in the great river *Euphrates.*
16:12. upon the great river *Euphrates;*

Ἐφεσῖνος, *Ephesinos.*

Rev. 2: 1. of the church *of Ephesus* write;

Ἐφέσιος, *Ephesios.*

Acts19:28. Great (is) Diana of the *Ephesians.*
34. Great (is) Diana of the *Ephesians.*
35. (Ye) men *of Ephesus,* what man is there
Acts19:35. that the city of the *Ephesians*
21:29. in the city Trophimus an *Ephesian,*

Ἔφεσος, *Ephesos.*

Acts18:19. And he came to *Ephesus,*
21. And he sailed from *Ephesus.*
24. mighty in the scriptures, came to *Ephesus.*
19: 1. passed through the upper coasts came to
Ephesus:
17. Greeks also dwelling at *Ephesus;*
26. that not alone at *Ephesus,*
20:16. had determined to sail by *Ephesus,*
17. And from Miletus he sent to *Ephesus,*
1Co.15:32. I have fought with beasts at *Ephesus,*
16: 8. But I will tarry at *Ephesus*
Eph. 1: 1. to the saints which are at *Ephesus,*
1Ti. 1: 3. As I besought thee to abide still at *Ephesus*
2Ti. 1:18. he ministered unto me at *Ephesus,*
4:12. And Tychicus have I sent to *Ephesus.*
Rev. 1:11. unto *Ephesus,* and unto Smyrna,

Ἐφραΐμ, *Ephraïm.*

Joh.11:54. into a city called *Ephraim,*

===

Ζαβουλών, *Zaboulōn.*

Mat. 4:13. in the borders of *Zabulon*
15. The land of *Zabulon,*
Rev. 7: 8. Of the tribe of *Zabulon*

Ζακχαῖος, *Zakkaios.*

Lu. 19: 2. (there was) a man named *Zacchæus,*
5. and said unto him, *Zacchæus,*
8. And *Zacchæus* stood, and said

Ζαρά, *Zara.*

Mat. 1: 3. Judas begat Phares and *Zara*

Ζαρούχ see Σαρούχ.

Ζαχαρίας, *Zakarias.*

Mat.23:35. unto the blood of *Zacharias*
Lu. 1: 5. a certain priest named *Zacharias,*
12. And when *Zacharias* saw (him),
13. said unto him, Fear not, *Zacharias:*
18. And *Zacharias* said unto the angel,
21. And the people waited for *Zacharias,*
40. And entered into the house of *Zacharias,*
59. and they called him *Zacharias,*
67. And his father *Zacharias* was filled
3: 2. the son of *Zacharias* in the wilderness.
11:51. unto the blood of *Zacharias,*

Ζεβεδαῖος, *Zebedaios.*

Mat. 4:21. James (the son) of *Zebedee,*

Mat. 4:21. in a ship with *Zebedee* their father,
10: 2. James (the son) of *Zebedee*,
20:20. *Zebedee's* children with her sons,
26:37. and the two sons of *Zebedee*,
27:56. and the mother of *Zebedee's* children.
Mar 1:19. James the (son) of *Zebedee*,
20. and they left their father *Zebedee*
3:17. And James the (son) of *Zebedee*,
10:35. James and John, the sons of *Zebedee*,
Lu. 5:10. James, and John, the sons of *Zebedee*,
Joh. 21: 2. and the (sons) of *Zebedee*,

Ζεύς, *Zūs*.

Acts 14:12. And they called Barnabas, *Jupiter*;
13. Then the priest of *Jupiter*,

Ζηλωτής, *Zeelōtees*.

Lu. 6:15. and Simon called *Zelotes*,
Acts 1:13. and Simon *Zelotes*, and Judas

Ζηνᾶς, *Zeenas*.

Tit. 3:13. Bring *Zenas* the lawyer

Ζοροβάβελ, *Zorobabel*.

Mat. 1:12. and Salathiel begat *Zorobabel*;
13. And *Zorobabel* begat Abiud;
Lu. 3:27. which was (the son) of *Zorobabel*,

Ἡλί, *Heeli*.

Lu. 3:23. which was (the son) of *Heli*,

Ἡλίας, *Eelias*.

Mat. 11:14. this is *Elias*, which was for to come.
16:14. some, *Elias*; and others, Jeremias,
17: 3. Moses and *Elias* talking with him.
4. and one for Moses, and one for *Elias*.
10. that *Elias* must first come?
11. *Elias* truly shall first come,
12. That *Elias* is come already,
27:47. This (man) calleth for *Elias*.
49. whether *Elias* will come to save him.
Mar 6:15. Others said, That it is *Elias*.
8:28. but some (say), *Elias*; and others,
9: 4. And there appeared unto them *Elias*
5. and one for Moses, and one for *Elias*.
11. that *Elias* must first come?
12. *Elias* verily cometh first,
13. That *Elias* is indeed come,
15:35. Behold, he calleth *Elias*.
36. whether *Elias* will come to take him
Lu. 1:17. in the spirit and power of *Elias*,
4:25. were in Israel in the days of *Elias*,
26. But unto none of them was *Elias* sent,
9: 8. And of some, that *Elias* had appeared;
19. but some (say), *Elias*;
30. which were Moses and *Elias*:
33. and one for Moses, and one for *Elias*:

Lu. 9:54. and consume them, even as *Elias* did?
Joh. 1:21. What then? Art thou *Elias*?
25. nor *Elias*, neither that prophet?
Ro. 11: 2. Wot ye not what the scripture saith of *Elias*?
Jas. 5:17. *Elias* was a man subject to

Ἤρ, *Eer*.

Lu. 3:28. which was (the son) of *Er*,

Ἡρωδίων, *Heerōdiōn*.

Ro. 16:11. Salute *Herodion* my kinsman. Greet them that be

Ἡρώδης, *Heerōdees*.

Mat. 2: 1. in the days of *Herod* the king, behold, there
3. When *Herod* the king had heard (these things),
7. Then *Herod*, when he had privily called
12. that they should not return to *Herod*, they
13. for *Herod* will seek the young child to
15. And was there until the death of *Herod*:
16. Then *Herod*, when he saw that he was
19. But when *Herod* was dead, behold, an angel
22. in the room of his father *Herod*, he
14: 1. At that time *Herod* the tetrarch heard of
3. For *Herod* had laid hold on John, and
6. when *Herod's* birthday was kept, the daughter of Herodias danced before them, and pleased *Herod*.
Mar 6:14. king *Herod* heard (of him); for his name
16. But when *Herod* heard (thereof), he said,
17. For *Herod* himself had sent forth and laid
18. For John had said unto *Herod*, It is
20. For *Herod* feared John, knowing that he
21. that *Herod* on his birthday made a
22. came in, and danced, and pleased *Herod*
8:15. the Pharisees, and (of) the leaven of *Herod*.
Lu. 1: 5. There was in the days of *Herod*, the
3: 1. and *Herod* being tetrarch of Galilee, and
19. But *Herod* the tetrarch, being reproved by
— for all the evils which *Herod* had done,
8: 3. And Joanna the wife of Chuza *Herod's* steward,
9: 7. Now *Herod* the tetrarch heard of all that
9. And *Herod* said, John have I beheaded:
13:31. and depart hence: for *Herod* will kill thee.
23: 7. that he belonged unto *Herod's* jurisdiction, he sent him to *Herod*, who himself also
8. And when *Herod* saw Jesus, he was exceeding
11. And *Herod* with his men of war set
12. Pilate and *Herod* were made friends
15. No, nor yet *Herod*: for I sent you to
Acts 4:27. whom thou hast anointed, both *Herod*, and Pontius
12: 1. Now about that time *Herod* the king
6. And when *Herod* would have brought him
11. out of the hand of *Herod*, and (from)
19. And when *Herod* had sought for him,
20. And *Herod* was highly displeased with them of
21 And upon a set day *Herod*, arrayed in
13: 1. brought up with *Herod* the tetrarch, and Saul.
23:35. him to be kept in *Herod's* judgment hall.

Ἡρωδιανοί, *Heerōdianoi.*

Mat.22:16. their disciples with the *Herodians,* saying,
Mar 3: 6. took counsel with the *Herodians* against
    12:13. the Pharisees and of the *Herodians,* to catch

Ἡρωδιάς, *Heerōdias.*

Mat.14: 3. and put (him) in prison for *Herodias'* sake,
    6. daughter of *Herodias* danced before them,
Mar 6:17. for *Herodias'* sake, his brother Philip's
    wife:
    19. Therefore *Herodias* had a quarrel against
    him,
    22. when the daughter of the said *Herodias*
Lu. 3:19. being reproved by him for *Herodias* his
    brother

Ἡσαΐας, *Heesaïas.*

Mat. 3: 3. spoken of by the prophet *Esaias,* saying,
    4:14. which was spoken by *Esaias* the prophet,
    saying,
    8:17. which was spoken by *Esaias* the prophet,
    saying,
    12:17. might be fulfilled which was spoken by
    Esaias
    13:14. is fulfilled the prophecy of *Esaias,* which
    saith,
    15: 7. (Ye) hypocrites, well did *Esaias* prophesy
Mar 7: 6. Well hath *Esaias* prophesied of you hypo-
    crites,
Lu. 3: 4. in the book of the words of *Esaias* the
    4:17. unto him the book of the prophet *Esaias.*
Joh. 1:23. of the Lord, as said the prophet *Esaias.*
    12:38. That the saying of *Esaias* the prophet might
    39. could not believe, because that *Esaias* said
    41. These things said *Esaias,* when he saw his
Acts 8:28. sitting in his chariot read *Esaias* the pro-
    phet.
    30. and heard him read the prophet *Esaias,*
    28:25. Well spake the Holy Ghost by *Esaias* the
Ro. 9:27. *Esaias* also crieth concerning Israel,
    Though
    29. And as *Esaias* said before, Except the Lord
    10:16. For *Esaias* saith, Lord, who hath believed
    20. But *Esaias* is very bold, and saith, I
    15:12. And again, *Esaias* saith, There shall be a

Ἠσαῦ, *Eesau.*

Ro. 9:13. Jacob have I loved, but *Esau* have I hated.
Heb 11:20. By faith Isaac blessed Jacob and *Esau*
    12:16. (be) any fornicator, or profane person, as
    Esau,

Θαδδαῖος, *Thaddaios.*

Mat.10: 3. And Lebbæus, whose surname was *Thaddæus;*
Mar 3:18. the (son) of Alphæus, and *Thaddæus,* and
    Simon

Θάμαρ, *Thamar.*

Mat. 1: 3. And Judas begat Phares and Zara of
    Thamar;

Θάρα, *Thara.*

Lu. 3:34. which was (the son) of *Thara,* which was

Θεόφιλος, *Theophilos.*

Lu. 1: 3. most excellent *Theophilus,*
Acts 1: 1. have I made, O *Theophilus,*

Θεσσαλονικεύς, *Thessalonikūs.*

Acts20: 4. and of the *Thessalonians,* Aristarchus
    27: 2. (one) Aristarchus, a Macedonian *of Thes-
salonica,*
1Th. 1: 1. unto the church of the *Thessalonians*
2Th. 1: 1. unto the church of the *Thessalonians*

Θεσσαλονίκη, *Thessalonikee.*

Acts17: 1. they came to *Thessalonica,*
    11. more noble than those in *Thessalonica,*
    13. the Jews of *Thessalonica*
Phi. 4:16. For even in *Thessalonica*
2Ti. 4:10. is departed unto *Thessalonica;*

Θευδᾶς, *Thūdas.*

Acts 5:36. rose up *Theudas,* boasting

Θυάτειρα, τὰ, *Thuatīra.*

Acts16:14. of the city of *Thyatira,*
Rev. 1:11. and unto *Thyatira,* and unto Sardis,
    2:18. of the church in *Thyatira*
    24. unto the rest in *Thyatira,*

Θωμᾶς, *Thōmas.*

Mat.10: 3. *Thomas,* and Matthew the publican;
Mar 3:18. *Thomas,* and James the (son) of Alphæus,
Lu. 6:15. Matthew and *Thomas,* James
Joh.11:16. *Thomas,* which is called Didymus,
    14: 5. *Thomas* saith unto him,
    20:24. But *Thomas,* one of the twelve,
    26. and *Thomas* with them:
    27. Then saith he to *Thomas,*
    28. *Thomas* answered and said
    29. *Thomas,* because thou hast seen me,
    21: 2. Simon Peter, and *Thomas*
Acts 1:13. Philip, and *Thomas,* Bartholomew,

Ἰάειρος, *Ïaïros.*

Mar 5:22. of the synagogue, *Jairus* by name;
Lu. 8:41. there came a man named *Jairus,*

Ἰακώ6, Ïakōb.

Mat. 1: 2. begat *Jacob ;* and *Jacob* begat
15. and Matthan begat *Jacob ;*
16. And *Jacob* begat Joseph
8:11. and Isaac, and *Jacob,*
22:32. and the God of *Jacob ?*
Mar 12:26. and the God of *Jacob ?*
Lu. 1:33. over the house of *Jacob*
3:34. Which was (the son) of *Jacob,* which was (the son) of Isaac,
13:28. and Isaac, and *Jacob,*
20:37. and the God of *Jacob.*
Joh. 4: 5. that *Jacob* gave to his son Joseph.
6. *Jacob's* well was there.
12. than our father *Jacob,*
Acts 3:13. and of Isaac, and of *Jacob,*
7: 8. (begat) *Jacob ;* and *Jacob*
12. But when *Jacob* heard
14. his father *Jacob* to (him),
15. *Jacob* went down into Egypt,
32. and the God of *Jacob.*
46. the God of *Jacob.*
Ro. 9:13. *Jacob* have I loved,
11:26. turn away ungodliness from *Jacob :*
Heb 11: 9. with Isaac and *Jacob,*
20. Isaac blessed *Jacob* and Esau
21. By faith *Jacob,* when he was a dying,

Ἰάκω6ος, Ïakōbos.

Mat. 4:21. *James* (the son) of Zebedee,
10: 2(3). *James* (the son) of Zebedee,
3. *James* (the son) of Alphæus,
13:55. *James,* and Joses, and Simon,
17: 1. *James,* and John his brother,
27:56. Mary the mother of *James*
Mar 1:19. *James* the (son) of Zebedee,
29. with *James* and John.
3:17. *James* the (son) of Zebedee, and John the brother of *James ;*
18. and *James* the (son) of Alphæus,
5:37. *James,* and John the brother of *James.*
6: 3. the brother of *James,* and
9: 2. *James,* and John, and leadeth
10:35. *James* and John, the sons of
41. with *James* and John.
13: 3. Peter and *James*
14:33. *James* and John, and began to be
15:40. the mother of *James* the less
16: 1. Mary the (mother) of *James,*
Lu. 5:10. also *James,* and John,
6:14. *James* and John, Philip and
15. *James* the (son) of Alphæus,
16. And Judas (the brother) of *James,*
8:51. and *James,* and John,
9:28. John and *James,* and went up
54. *James* and John saw (this),
24:10. and Mary the (mother) of *James,*
Acts 1:13. Peter, and *James,* and John,
— *James* (the son) of Alphæus,
— and Judas (the brother) of *James.*
12: 2. And he killed *James* the brother
17. *James,* and to the brethren.
15:13. *James* answered, saying,
21:18. with us unto *James ;*
1Co.15: 7. After that, he was seen of *James ;*
Gal. 1:19. save *James* the Lord's brother.
2: 9. *James,* Cephas, and John,
12. that certain came from *James,*

Jas. 1: 1. *James,*...of God and of the Lord Jesus Christ,
Jude 1. and brother of *James,*

Ἰαμ6ρῆς, Ïambrees.

2Ti. 3: 8. Jannes and *Jambres* withstood Moses,

Ἰαννά, Ïanna.

Lu. 3:24. which was (the son) of *Janna,* which was (the son) of Joseph,

Ἰαννῆς, Ïannees.

2Ti. 3: 8. *Jannes* and Jambres withstood Moses,

Ἰαρέδ, Ïared.

Lu. 3:37. which was (the son) of *Jared,* which was (the son) of Maleleel,

Ἰάσων, Ïasōn.

Acts17: 5. the house of *Jason,*
6. they drew *Jason* and certain brethren
7. Whom *Jason* hath received:
9. of *Jason,* and of the other,
Ro. 16:21. Lucius, and *Jason,* and

Ἰδουμαία, Idoumaia.

Mar 3: 8. from Jerusalem, and from *Idumæa,*

Ἰεζα6ήλ, Ïezabeel.

Rev. 2:20. thou sufferest that woman *Jezebel,*

Ἰεράπολις, Hierapolis.

Col. 4:13. and them in *Hierapolis.*

Ἰερεμίας, Hieremias.

Mat. 2:17. by *Jeremy* the prophet,
16:14. and others, *Jeremias,* or one
27: 9. by *Jeremy* the prophet,

Ἰεριχώ, Hieriko.

Mat.20:29. as they departed from *Jericho,*
Mar 10:46. they came to *Jericho :* and as he went out of *Jericho*
Lu. 10:30. from Jerusalem to *Jericho,*
18:35. as he was come nigh unto *Jericho,*
19: 1. and passed through *Jericho.*
Heb 11:30. the walls of *Jericho* fell down,

Ἰεροσόλυμα, Hierosoluma.

Mat. 2: 1. there came...to *Jerusalem,*

Mat. 2: 3. all *Jerusalem* with him.
   3: 5. to him *Jerusalem*, and all Judæa,
   4:25. and (from) *Jerusalem*, and
   5:35. neither by *Jerusalem;* for it is
   15: 1. which were of *Jerusalem*,
   16:21. go unto *Jerusalem*, and suffer
   20:17. Jesus going up to *Jerusalem*
    18. we go up to *Jerusalem;*
   21: 1. when they drew nigh unto *Jerusalem*,
    10. when he was come into *Jerusalem*,
Mar 3: 8. from *Jerusalem*, and from
    22. which came down from *Jerusalem*
   7: 1. which came from *Jerusalem*.
   10:32. going up to *Jerusalem;*
    33. we go up to *Jerusalem;*
   11:11. entered into *Jerusalem*,
    15. they come to *Jerusalem:*
    27. they come again to *Jerusalem:*
   15:41. came up with him unto *Jerusalem*.
Lu. 2:22. they brought him to *Jerusalem*,
    42. they went up to *Jerusalem*
   18:31. we go up to *Jerusalem*,
   19:28. ascending up to *Jerusalem*.
   23: 7. who himself also was at *Jerusalem*
Joh. 1:19. priests and Levites from *Jerusalem*
   2:13. went up to *Jerusalem*,
    23. he was in *Jerusalem*
   4:20. that in *Jerusalem* is the place
    21. nor yet at *Jerusalem*,
    45. at *Jerusalem* at the feast:
   5: 1. Jesus went up to *Jerusalem*.
    2. Now there is at *Jerusalem*
   10:22. at *Jerusalem* the feast of the dedication,
   11:18. Bethany was nigh unto *Jerusalem*,
    55. many went...to *Jerusalem*
   12:12. Jesus was coming to *Jerusalem*,
Acts 1: 4. not depart from *Jerusalem*,
   8: 1. which was at *Jerusalem;*
    14. the apostles which were at *Jerusalem*
   11: 2. Peter was come up to *Jerusalem*,
    22. which was in *Jerusalem:*
    27. came prophets from *Jerusalem*
   13:13. departing from them returned to *Jerusalem*.
   18:21. keep this feast that cometh in *Jerusalem:*
   20:16. to be at *Jerusalem*
   21:17. we were come to *Jerusalem*,
   25: 1. he ascended from Cæsarea to *Jerusalem*.
    7. which came down from *Jerusalem*
    9. Wilt thou go up to *Jerusalem*,
    15. when I was at *Jerusalem*,
    24. at *Jerusalem*, and (also) here,
   26: 4. mine own nation at *Jerusalem*,
    10. I also did in *Jerusalem:*
    20. first...and at *Jerusalem*,
   28:17. delivered prisoner from *Jerusalem*
Gal. 1:17. Neither went I up to *Jerusalem*
    18. I went up to *Jerusalem* to see
   2: 1. I went up again to *Jerusalem*

Ἱεροσολυμῖται, *Hierosolumitai*.

Mar 1: 5. and they of *Jerusalem*,
Joh. 7:25. some of them of *Jerusalem*,

Ἱερουσαλήμ, *Hierousaleem*.

Mat.23:37. O *Jerusalem, Jerusalem*, (thou) that killest
Mar 11: 1. they came nigh to *Jerusalem*,
Lu. 2:25. there was a man in *Jerusalem*,

Lu. 2:38. looked for redemption in *Jerusalem*.
    41. to *Jerusalem* every year
    43. child Jesus tarried behind in *Jerusalem;*
    45. they turned back again to *Jerusalem*,
   4: 9. he brought him to *Jerusalem*,
   5:17. and Judæa, and *Jerusalem:*
   6:17. of all Judæa and *Jerusalem*,
   9:31. which he should accomplish at *Jerusalem*.
    51. to go to *Jerusalem*,
    53. was as though he would go to *Jerusalem*.
   10·30. from *Jerusalem* to Jericho,
   13: 4. men that dwelt in *Jerusalem?*
    22. journeying toward *Jerusalem*.
    33. a prophet perish out of *Jerusalem*.
    34. O *Jerusalem, Jerusalem*, which killest
   17:11. as he went to *Jerusalem*,
   19:11. he was nigh to *Jerusalem*,
   21:20. *Jerusalem* compassed with armies,
    24. and *Jerusalem* shall be trodden down
   23:28. Daughters of *Jerusalem*, weep not
   24:13. from *Jerusalem* (about) threescore
    18. a stranger in *Jerusalem*,
    33. and returned to *Jerusalem*,
    47. among all nations, beginning at *Jerusalem*.
    49. in the city of *Jerusalem*,
    52. and returned to *Jerusalem*
Acts 1: 8. witnesses unto me both in *Jerusalem*,
    12. returned they unto *Jerusalem*
    — from *Jerusalem* a sabbath day's journey.
    19. the dwellers at *Jerusalem;*
   2: 5. And there were dwelling at *Jerusalem*
    14. (ye) that dwell at *Jerusalem*,
   4: 6(5). were gathered together at *Jerusalem*.
    16. to all them that dwell in *Jerusalem;*
   5:16. (out) of the cities round about unto *Jerusalem*,
    28. ye have filled *Jerusalem*
   6: 7. of the disciples multiplied in *Jerusalem*
   8:25. returned to *Jerusalem*, and preached
    26. from *Jerusalem* unto Gaza,
    27. to *Jerusalem* for to worship,
   9: 2. might bring them bound unto *Jerusalem*.
    13. to thy saints at *Jerusalem:*
    21. that destroyed...in *Jerusalem*,
    26. Saul was come to *Jerusalem*,
    28. going out at *Jerusalem*.
   10:39. the land of the Jews, and in *Jerusalem;*
   12:25. And Barnabas and Saul returned from *Jerusalem*,
   13:27. For they that dwell at *Jerusalem*, and their
    31. came up with him from Galilee to *Jerusalem*,
   15: 2. other of them, should go up to *Jerusalem*
    4. And when they were come to *Jerusalem*,
   16: 4. the apostles and elders which were at *Jerusalem*.
   19:21. through Macedonia and Achaia, to go to *Jerusalem*,
   20:22. I go bound in the spirit unto *Jerusalem*,
   21: 4. that he should not go up to *Jerusalem*.
    11. So shall the Jews at *Jerusalem* bind the
    12. besought him not to go up to *Jerusalem*
    13. but also to die at *Jerusalem* for the
    15. up our carriages, and went up to *Jerusalem*.
    31. chief captain of the band, that all *Jerusalem*
   22: 5. bring them which were there bound unto *Jerusalem*,
    17. that, when I was come again to *Jerusalem*,
    18. haste, and get thee quickly out of *Jerusalem*.
   23:11. as thou hast testified of me in *Jerusalem*,
   24:11. twelve days since I went up to *Jerusalem*

Acts25: 3. that he would send for him to *Jerusalem*,
20. asked (him) whether he would go to *Jerusalem*,
Ro. 15:19. so that from *Jerusalem*, and round
25. But now I go unto *Jerusalem* to minister
26. for the poor saints which are at *Jerusalem*.
31. that my service which (I have) for *Jerusalem*
1Co.16: 3. I send to bring your liberality unto *Jerusalem*.
Gal. 4:25. mount Sinai in Arabia, and answereth to *Jerusalem*
26. But *Jerusalem* which is above is free, which
Heb 12:22. city of the living God, the heavenly *Jerusalem*,
Rev. 3:12. city of my God, (which is) new *Jerusalem*,
21: 2. I John saw the holy city, new *Jerusalem*,
10. shewed me that great city, the holy *Jerusalem*,

’Ισαβήλ see ’Ιεζαβήλ.

’Ιεσσαί, *Ïessai.*

Mat. 1: 5. begat Obed of Ruth; and Obed begat *Jesse;*
6. And *Jesse* begat David the king; and David
Lu. 3:32. Which was (the son) of *Jesse*, which was
Acts13:22. I have found David the (son) of *Jesse*,
Ro. 15:12. saith, There shall be a root of *Jesse*,

’Ιεφθάε, *Ïephthaë.*

Heb 11:32. (of) Samson, and (of) *Jephthae;* (of) David also,

---

’Ιεχονίας, *Ïekonias.*

Mat. 1:11. And Josias begat *Jechonias* and his brethren, about
12. And after they were brought to Babylon, *Jechonias*

’Ιησοῦς, *Ïeesous.*

Mat. 1: 1. The book of the generation of *Jesus* Christ,
16. whom was born *Jesus*, who is called Christ.
18. Now the birth of *Jesus* Christ was on
21. a son, and thou shalt call his name *JESUS:*
25. firstborn son: and he called his name *JESUS.*
2: 1. when *Jesus* was born in Bethlehem of Judæa
3:13. Then cometh *Jesus* from Galilee to Jordan unto
15. And *Jesus* answering said unto him, Suffer
16. And *Jesus*, when he was baptized, went up
4: 1. Then was *Jesus* led up of the spirit
7. *Jesus* said unto him, It is written again,
10. Then saith *Jesus* unto him, Get thee hence,
12. Now when *Jesus* had heard that John was
17. From that time *Jesus* began to preach, and
18. And *Jesus*, walking by the sea of Galilee,
23. And *Jesus* went about all Galilee, teaching
7:28. And it came to pass, when *Jesus* had
8: 3. And *Jesus* put forth (his) hand, and touched

Mat. 8: 4. And *Jesus* saith unto him, See thou tell
5. And when *Jesus* was entered into Capernaum, there
7. And *Jesus* saith unto him, I will come
10. When *Jesus* heard (it), he marvelled, and
13. And *Jesus* said unto the centurion, Go thy
14. And when *Jesus* was come into Peter's
18. Now when *Jesus* saw great multitudes about him,
20. And *Jesus* saith unto him, The foxes have
22. But *Jesus* said unto him, Follow me; and
29. What have we to do with thee, *Jesus*,
34. the whole city came out to meet *Jesus :*
9: 2. *Jesus* seeing their faith said unto the sick
4. And *Jesus* knowing their thoughts said, Wherefore think
9. And as *Jesus* passed forth from thence, he
10. And it came to pass, as *Jesus* sat
12. when *Jesus* heard (that), he said unto them,
15. And *Jesus* said unto them, Can the children
19. And *Jesus* arose, and followed him, and
22. But *Jesus* turned him about, and when he
23. And when *Jesus* came into the ruler's house,
27. And when *Jesus* departed thence, two blind men
28. the blind men came to him: and *Jesus*
30. And their eyes were opened ; and *Jesus*
35. *Jesus* went about all the cities and villages,
10: 5. These twelve *Jesus* sent forth, and commanded them,
11: 1. when *Jesus* had made an end of commanding
4. *Jesus* answered and said unto them, Go and
7. And as they departed, *Jesus* began to say
25. *Jesus* answered and said, I thank thee,
12: 1. At that time *Jesus* went on the sabbath
15. But when *Jesus* knew (it), he withdrew
25. And *Jesus* knew their thoughts, and said
13: 1. The same day went *Jesus* out of the
34. All these things spake *Jesus* unto the
36. Then *Jesus* sent the multitude away, and
51. *Jesus* saith unto them, Have ye understood
53. when *Jesus* had finished these parables, he
57. But *Jesus* said unto them, A prophet is
14: 1. the tetrarch heard of the fame of *Jesus*,
12. and buried it, and went and told *Jesus*.
13. When *Jesus* heard (of it), he departed
14. And *Jesus* went forth, and saw a great
16. But *Jesus* said unto them, They need not
22. And straightway *Jesus* constrained his disciples to get
25. in the fourth watch of the night *Jesus*
27. But straightway *Jesus* spake unto them,
29. walked on the water, to go to *Jesus*.
31. And immediately *Jesus* stretched forth (his) hand,
15: 1. Then came to *Jesus* scribes and Pharisees,
16. And *Jesus* said, Are ye also yet without
21. Then *Jesus* went thence, and departed into
28. *Jesus* answered and said unto her, O woman,
29. And *Jesus* departed from thence, and came nigh
30. and cast them down at *Jesus'* feet ; and
32. Then *Jesus* called his disciples (unto him),
34. And *Jesus* saith unto them, How many
16: 6. Then *Jesus* said unto them, Take heed
8. (Which) when *Jesus* perceived, he said unto them,
13. When *Jesus* came into the coasts of Cæsarea
17. And *Jesus* answered and said unto him,

Mat.16:20. should tell no man that he was *Jesus*

21. From that time forth began *Jesus* to shew

24. Then said *Jesus* unto his disciples, If any

17: 1. after six days *Jesus* taketh Peter, James,

4. Then answered Peter, and said unto *Jesus*,

7. *Jesus* came and touched them, and said,

8. their eyes, they saw no man, save *Jesus*

9. as they came down from the mountain, *Jesus*

11. And *Jesus* answered and said unto them,

17. *Jesus* answered and said, O faithless and

18. And *Jesus* rebuked the devil; and he

19. Then came the disciples to *Jesus* apart,

20. *Jesus* said unto them, Because of your

22. while they abode in Galilee, *Jesus* said

25. when he was come into the house, *Jesus*

26. Peter saith unto him, Of strangers. *Jesus*

18: 1. the same time came the disciples unto *Jesus*,

2. And *Jesus* called a little child unto him,

22. *Jesus* saith unto him, I say not unto

19: 1. when *Jesus* had finished these sayings, he

14. But *Jesus* said, Suffer little children, and

18. Which? *Jesus* said, Thou shalt do no murder,

21. *Jesus* said unto him, If thou wilt be perfect,

23. Then said *Jesus* unto his disciples, Verily I

26. But *Jesus* beheld (them), and said unto

28. And *Jesus* said unto them, Verily I say

20:17. And *Jesus* going up to Jerusalem took the

22. But *Jesus* answered and said, Ye know

25. But *Jesus* called them (unto him), and

30. when they heard that *Jesus* passed by,

32. *Jesus* stood still, and called them, and

34. So *Jesus* had compassion (on them), and

21: 1. the mount of Olives, then sent *Jesus* two

6. the disciples went, and did as *Jesus* commanded

11. This is *Jesus* the prophet of Nazareth of Galilee.

12. And *Jesus* went into the temple of God,

16. Hearest thou what these say? And *Jesus*

21. *Jesus* answered and said unto them, Verily

24. *Jesus* answered and said unto them, I

27. they answered *Jesus*, and said, We cannot

31. The first. *Jesus* saith unto them, Verily I

42. *Jesus* saith unto them, Did ye never read

22: 1. And *Jesus* answered and spake unto them

18. *Jesus* perceived their wickedness, and said,

29. *Jesus* answered and said unto them, Ye do

37. *Jesus* said unto him, Thou shalt love the

41. While the Pharisees were gathered together, *Jesus* asked

23: 1. Then spake *Jesus* to the multitude, and to

24: 1. *Jesus* went out, and departed from the

2. And *Jesus* said unto them, See ye not

4. *Jesus* answered and said unto them, Take

26: 1. And it came to pass, when *Jesus* had

4. consulted that they might take *Jesus* by

6. Now when *Jesus* was in Bethany, in the

10. When *Jesus* understood (it), he said unto

17. (of) unleavened bread the disciples came to *Jesus*,

19. the disciples did as *Jesus* had appointed

26. And as they were eating, *Jesus* took bread,

31. Then saith *Jesus* unto them, All ye shall

34. *Jesus* said unto him, Verily I say unto

36. Then cometh *Jesus* with them unto a place

49. he came to *Jesus*, and said, Hail, master;

50. *Jesus* said unto him, Friend, wherefore

— Then came they, and laid hands on *Jesus*,

51. one of them which were with *Jesus*

Mat.26:52. Then said *Jesus* unto him, Put up again

55. In that same hour said *Jesus* to the

57. And they that had laid hold on *Jesus*

59. all the council, sought false witness against *Jesus*,

63. *Jesus* held his peace. And the high priest

64. *Jesus* saith unto him, Thou hast said:

69. saying, Thou also wast with *Jesus* of Galilee.

71. This (fellow) was also with *Jesus* of Nazareth.

75. Peter remembered the word of *Jesus*, which

27: 1. took counsel against *Jesus* to put him to

11. *Jesus* stood before the governor: and the

— And *Jesus* said unto him, Thou sayest.

17. that I release unto you? Barabbas, or *Jesus*

20. that they should ask Barabbas, and destroy *Jesus*.

22. What shall I do then with *Jesus* which

26. when he had scourged *Jesus*, he delivered

27. the soldiers of the governor took *Jesus*

37. THIS IS *JESUS* THE KING OF THE JEWS.

46. about the ninth hour *Jesus* cried with

50. *Jesus*, when he had cried again with a

54. watching *Jesus*, saw the earthquake, and

55. which followed *Jesus* from Galilee, ministering unto him:

57. named Joseph, who also himself was *Jesus'* disciple:

58. went to Pilate, and begged the body of *Jesus*.

28: 5. for I know that ye seek *Jesus*, which

9. *Jesus* met them, saying, All hail. And they

10. Then said *Jesus* unto them, Be not afraid:

16. into a mountain where *Jesus* had appointed

18. *Jesus* came and spake unto them, saying,

Mar 1: 1. The beginning of the gospel of *Jesus* Christ,

9. *Jesus* came from Nazareth of Galilee, and

14. after that John was put in prison, *Jesus*

17. *Jesus* said unto them, Come ye after me,

24. thou *Jesus* of Nazareth? art thou come to

25. *Jesus* rebuked him, saying, Hold thy peace,

41. And *Jesus*, moved with compassion, put forth (his)

2: 5. When *Jesus* saw their faith, he said unto

8. And immediately when *Jesus* perceived in his spirit

15. And it came to pass, that, as *Jesus*

17. When *Jesus* heard (it), he saith unto them,

19. *Jesus* said unto them, Can the children

3: 7. *Jesus* withdrew himself with his disciples to

5: 6. when he saw *Jesus* afar off, he ran

7. What have I to do with thee, *Jesus*,

13. And forthwith *Jesus* gave them leave. And

15. And they come to *Jesus*, and see him

19. Howbeit *Jesus* suffered him not, but saith

20. how great things *Jesus* had done for him:

21. And when *Jesus* was passed over again by

27. When she had heard of *Jesus*, came in

30. *Jesus*, immediately knowing in himself that

36. As soon as *Jesus* heard the word that

6: 4. But *Jesus* said unto them, A prophet is

30. And the apostles gathered themselves together unto *Jesus*,

34. And *Jesus*, when he came out, saw much

7:27. But *Jesus* said unto her, Let the children

8: 1. and having nothing to eat, *Jesus* called his

17. And when *Jesus* knew (it), he saith unto

27. And *Jesus* went out, and his disciples, into

Mar 9: 2. after six days *Jesus* taketh (with him) Peter,
4. with Moses: and they were talking with *Jesus*.
5. Peter answered and said to *Jesus*, Master,
8. they saw no man any more, save *Jesus*
23. *Jesus* said unto him, If thou canst believe,
25. When *Jesus* saw that the people came
27. But *Jesus* took him by the hand, and
39. But *Jesus* said, Forbid him not: for there

10: 5. And *Jesus* answered and said unto them,
14. But when *Jesus* saw (it), he was much
18. *Jesus* said unto him, Why callest thou me
21. Then *Jesus* beholding him loved him, and
23. And *Jesus* looked round about, and saith
24. But *Jesus* answereth again, and saith unto
27. *Jesus* looking upon them saith, With men
29. And *Jesus* answered and said, Verily I say
32. and *Jesus* went before them: and they were
38. But *Jesus* said unto them, Ye know not
39. *Jesus* said unto them, Ye shall indeed drink
42. But *Jesus* called them (to him), and saith
47. When he heard that it was *Jesus* of Nazareth, he began to cry out, and say, *Jesus*,
49. *Jesus* stood still, and commanded him to
50. away his garment, rose, and came to *Jesus*.
51. *Jesus* answered and said unto him, What
52. And *Jesus* said unto him, Go thy way;
— he received his sight, and followed *Jesus*

11: 6. And they said unto them even as *Jesus*
7. And they brought the colt to *Jesus*, and
11. *Jesus* entered into Jerusalem, and into the
14. And *Jesus* answered and said unto it, No
15. And they come to Jerusalem: and *Jesus*
22. *Jesus* answering saith unto them, Have faith
29. And *Jesus* answered and said unto them, I
33. And they answered and said unto *Jesus*,
— *Jesus* answering saith unto them, Neither

12:17. *Jesus* answering said unto them, Render
24. And *Jesus* answering said unto them, Do
29. And *Jesus* answered him, The first of all the
34. when *Jesus* saw that he answered discreetly,
35. *Jesus* answered and said, while he taught
41. *Jesus* sat over against the treasury, and

13: 2. *Jesus* answering said unto him, Seest thou
5. *Jesus* answering them began to say, Take

14: 6. *Jesus* said, Let her alone; why trouble
18. And as they sat and did eat, *Jesus*
22. And as they did eat, *Jesus* took bread,
27. And *Jesus* saith unto them, All ye shall
30. And *Jesus* saith unto him, Verily I say
48. *Jesus* answered and said unto them, Are
53. they led *Jesus* away to the high priest:
55. all the council sought for witness against *Jesus*
60. and asked *Jesus*, saying, Answerest thou nothing?
62. And *Jesus* said, I am: and ye shall see
67. And thou also wast with *Jesus* of Nazareth.
72. Peter called to mind the word that *Jesus*

15: 1. and bound *Jesus*, and carried (him) away,
5. *Jesus* yet answered nothing; so that Pilate
15. and delivered *Jesus*, when he had scourged (him),
34. And at the ninth hour *Jesus* cried with
37. And *Jesus* cried with a loud voice,
43. unto Pilate, and craved the body of *Jesus*.

16: 6. Be not affrighted: Ye seek *Jesus* of Nazareth,

Lu. 1:31. a son, and shalt call his name *JESUS*.
2:21. his name was called *JESUS*, which was
27. when the parents brought in the child *Jesus*,

Lu. 2:43. as they returned, the child *Jesus* tarried
52. And *Jesus* increased in wisdom and stature,
3:21. it came to pass, that *Jesus* also being
23. And *Jesus* himself began to be about thirty

4: 1. And *Jesus* being full of the Holy Ghost
4. And *Jesus* answered him, saying, It is written,
8. *Jesus* answered and said unto him, Get
12. *Jesus* answering said unto him, It is said,
14. *Jesus* returned in the power of the Spirit
34. *Jesus* of Nazareth? art thou come to
35. And *Jesus* rebuked him, saying, Hold

5: 8. Peter saw (it), he fell down at *Jesus*'
10. And *Jesus* said unto Simon, Fear not;
12. a man full of leprosy: who seeing *Jesus*
19. with (his) couch into the midst before *Jesus*.
22. But when *Jesus* perceived their thoughts,
31. And *Jesus* answering said unto them,

6: 3. *Jesus* answering them said, Have ye not
9. Then said *Jesus* unto them, I will ask
11. with another what they might do to *Jesus*.

7: 3. And when he heard of *Jesus*, he sent
4. when they came to *Jesus*, they besought
6. Then *Jesus* went with them. And when
9. When *Jesus* heard these things, he
19. two of his disciples sent (them) to *Jesus*,
22. Then *Jesus* answering said unto them,
40. *Jesus* answering said unto him, Simon,

8:28. When he saw *Jesus*, he cried out, and
— What have I to do with thee, *Jesus*,
30. *Jesus* asked him, saying, What is thy
35. see what was done; and came to *Jesus*,
— sitting at the feet of *Jesus*,
38. that he might be with him: but *Jesus*
39. throughout the whole city how great things *Jesus*
40. And it came to pass, that, when *Jesus*
41. and he fell down at *Jesus*' feet, and
45. *Jesus* said, Who touched me? When all
46. And *Jesus* said, Somebody hath touched
50. But when *Jesus* heard (it), he answered

9:33. Peter said unto *Jesus*, Master, it is good
36. And when the voice was past, *Jesus* was
41. And *Jesus* answering said, O faithless
42. And *Jesus* rebuked the unclean spirit,
43. every one at all things which *Jesus* did,
47. And *Jesus*, perceiving the thought of their
50. And *Jesus* said unto him, Forbid (him)
58. And *Jesus* said unto him, Foxes have
60. *Jesus* said unto him, Let the dead bury
62. And *Jesus* said unto him, No man,

10:21. In that hour *Jesus* rejoiced in spirit, and
29. said unto *Jesus*, And who is my neighbour?
30. And *Jesus* answering said, A certain (man) went
37. Then said *Jesus* unto him, Go, and do
39. called Mary, which also sat at *Jesus*' feet,
41. *Jesus* answered and said unto her, Martha,

13: 2. And *Jesus* answering said unto them,
12. And when *Jesus* saw her, he called
14. because that *Jesus* had healed on the

14: 3. And *Jesus* answering spake unto the

17:13. they lifted up (their) voices, and said, *Jesus*,
17. *Jesus* answering said, Were there not ten

18:16. But *Jesus* called them (unto him), and
19. *Jesus* said unto him, Why callest thou
22. Now when *Jesus* heard these things, he
24. when *Jesus* saw that he was very sorrowful,
37. And they told him, that *Jesus* of Nazareth
38. he cried, saying, *Jesus*, (thou) son of

Lu. 18:40. *Jesus* stood, and commanded him to be
42. And *Jesus* said unto him, Receive thy
19: 3. And he sought to see *Jesus* who he was;
5. And when *Jesus* came to the place, he
9. *Jesus* said unto him, This day is salvation
35. And they brought him to *Jesus:* and
— upon the colt, and they set *Jesus* thereon.
20: 8. And *Jesus* said unto them, Neither tell I
34. And *Jesus* answering said unto them, The children
22:47. and drew near unto *Jesus* to kiss him.
48. But *Jesus* said unto him, Judas, betrayest thou
51. *Jesus* answered and said, Suffer ye thus
52. Then *Jesus* said to the chief priests,
63. And the men that held *Jesus* mocked him,
23: 8. And when Herod saw *Jesus*, he was
20. Pilate therefore, willing to release *Jesus*,
25. whom they had desired; but he delivered *Jesus*
26. cross, that he might bear (it) after *Jesus*.
28. But *Jesus* turning unto them said,
34. Then said *Jesus*, Father, forgive them;
42. And he said unto *Jesus*, Lord, remember
43. And *Jesus* said unto him, Verily I say
46. And when *Jesus* had cried with a loud
52. unto Pilate, and begged the body of *Jesus*.
24: 3. found not the body of the Lord *Jesus*.
15. and reasoned, *Jesus* himself drew near,
19. they said unto him, Concerning *Jesus* of
36. And as they thus spake, *Jesus* himself
Joh. 1:17. grace and truth came by *Jesus* Christ.
29. The next day John seeth *Jesus* coming
36. And looking upon *Jesus* as he walked, he
37. disciples heard him speak, and they followed *Jesus*.
38. *Jesus* turned, and saw them following,
42(43). he brought him to *Jesus*. And when *Jesus* beheld
43(44). The day following *Jesus* would go
45(46). and the prophets, did write, *Jesus* of
47(48). *Jesus* saw Nathanael coming to him,
48(49). Whence knowest thou me? *Jesus* answered and said
50(51). *Jesus* answered and said unto him,
2: 1. Cana of Galilee; and the mother of *Jesus*
2. *Jesus* was called, and his disciples, to the
3. they wanted wine, the mother of *Jesus*
4. *Jesus* saith unto her, Woman, what have
7. *Jesus* saith unto them, Fill the waterpots
11. This beginning of miracles did *Jesus* in
13. the Jews' passover was at hand, and *Jesus*
19. *Jesus* answered and said unto them,
22. believed the scripture, and the word which *Jesus*
24. But *Jesus* did not commit himself unto
3: 2. The same came to *Jesus* by night, and
3. *Jesus* answered and said unto him, Verily,
5. *Jesus* answered, Verily, verily, I say unto
10. *Jesus* answered and said unto him, Art
22. After these things came *Jesus* and his
4: 1. that *Jesus* made and baptized more disciples than
2. Though *Jesus* himself baptized not, but his
6. Jacob's well was there. *Jesus* therefore,
7. a woman of Samaria to draw water: *Jesus*
10. *Jesus* answered and said unto her, If thou
13. *Jesus* answered and said unto her,
16. *Jesus* saith unto her, Go, call thy husband,
17. I have no husband. *Jesus* said unto her,
21. *Jesus* saith unto her, Woman, believe me,
26. *Jesus* saith unto her, I that speak unto

Joh. 4:34. *Jesus* saith unto them, My meat is to
44. For *Jesus* himself testified, that a prophet
46. So *Jesus* came again into Cana of Galilee,
47. When he heard that *Jesus* was come out
48. Then said *Jesus* unto him, Except ye see
50. *Jesus* saith unto him, Go thy way;
— And the man believed the word that *Jesus*
53. which *Jesus* said unto him, Thy son liveth:
54. This (is) again the second miracle (that) *Jesus*
5: 1. was a feast of the Jews; and *Jesus*
6. When *Jesus* saw him lie, and knew that
8. *Jesus* saith unto him, Rise, take up thy
13. for *Jesus* had conveyed himself away, a multitude
14. Afterward *Jesus* findeth him in the temple,
15. and told the Jews that it was *Jesus*,
16. And therefore did the Jews persecute *Jesus*,
17. But *Jesus* answered them, My Father worketh hitherto,
19. Then answered *Jesus* and said unto them,
6: 1. *Jesus* went over the sea of Galilee, which
3. And *Jesus* went up into a mountain, and
5. When *Jesus* then lifted up (his) eyes, and
10. And *Jesus* said, Make the men sit down.
11. And *Jesus* took the loaves; and when he
14. the miracle that *Jesus* did, said, This is
15. When *Jesus* therefore perceived that they would come
17. And it was now dark, and *Jesus* was not
19. they see *Jesus* walking on the sea, and
22. and that *Jesus* went not with his disciples
24. *Jesus* was not there, neither his disciples,
— and came to Capernaum, seeking for *Jesus*,
26. *Jesus* answered them and said, Verily,
29. *Jesus* answered and said unto them,
32. Then *Jesus* said unto them, Verily, verily,
35. And *Jesus* said unto them, I am the
42. And they said, Is not this *Jesus*, the
43. *Jesus* therefore answered and said unto them, Murmur
53. Then *Jesus* said unto them, Verily, verily,
61. When *Jesus* knew in himself that his
64. For *Jesus* knew from the beginning who
67. Then said *Jesus* unto the twelve, Will ye
70. *Jesus* answered them, Have not I chosen
7: 1. After these things *Jesus* walked in Galilee:
6. Then *Jesus* said unto them, My time is
14. Now about the midst of the feast *Jesus*
16. *Jesus* answered them, and said, My doctrine is
21. *Jesus* answered and said unto them, I have
28. Then cried *Jesus* in the temple as he
33. Then said *Jesus* unto them, Yet a little
37. that great (day) of the feast, *Jesus* stood
39. not yet (given); because that *Jesus* was
8: 1. *Jesus* went unto the mount of Olives.
6. But *Jesus* stooped down, and with (his)
9. and *Jesus* was left alone, and the woman
10. When *Jesus* had lifted up himself,
11. She said, No man, Lord. And *Jesus* said
12. Then spake *Jesus* again unto them, saying,
14. *Jesus* answered and said unto them, Though
19. Where is thy Father? *Jesus* answered, Ye neither know me,
20. These words spake *Jesus* in the treasury,
21. Then said *Jesus* again unto them, I go
25. And *Jesus* saith unto them, Even (the same)
28. Then said *Jesus* unto them, When ye have
31. Then said *Jesus* to those Jews which
34. *Jesus* answered them, Verily, verily, I say
39. Abraham is our father. *Jesus* saith unto

Joh. 8:42. *Jesus* said unto them, If God were your
49. *Jesus* answered, I have not a devil; but
54. *Jesus* answered, If I honour myself, my
58. *Jesus* said unto them, Verily, verily, I say
59. but *Jesus* hid himself, and went out of
9: 3. *Jesus* answered, Neither hath this man
11. A man that is called *Jesus* made clay,
14. the sabbath day when *Jesus* made the clay,
35. *Jesus* heard that they had cast him out;
37. And *Jesus* said unto him, Thou hast both
39. And *Jesus* said, For judgment I am come
41. *Jesus* said unto them, If ye were blind,
10: 6. This parable spake *Jesus* unto them: but
7. Then said *Jesus* unto them again, Verily,
23. *Jesus* walked in the temple in Solomon's
25. *Jesus* answered them, I told you, and ye
32. *Jesus* answered them, Many good works
have I
34. *Jesus* answered them, Is it not written in
11: 4. When *Jesus* heard (that), he said, This
5. Now *Jesus* loved Martha, and her sister,
9. *Jesus* answered, Are there not twelve hours
13. Howbeit *Jesus* spake of his death: but they
14. Then said *Jesus* unto them plainly, Lazarus is dead.
17. Then when *Jesus* came, he found that he
20. Martha, as soon as she heard that *Jesus*
21. Then said Martha unto *Jesus*, Lord, if thou
23. *Jesus* saith unto her, Thy brother
25. *Jesus* said unto her, I am the resurrection,
30. Now *Jesus* was not yet come into the town,
32. Then when Mary was come where *Jesus*
33. When *Jesus* therefore saw her weeping,
35. *Jesus* wept.
38. *Jesus* therefore again groaning in himself
39. *Jesus* said, Take ye away the stone. Martha,
40. *Jesus* saith unto her, Said I not unto
41. And *Jesus* lifted up (his) eyes, and said,
44. *Jesus* saith unto them, Loose him, and let
45. and had seen the things which *Jesus* did,
46. and told them what things *Jesus* had done.
51. he prophesied that *Jesus* should die for that
54. *Jesus* therefore walked no more openly
among the
56. Then sought they for *Jesus*, and spake
12: 1. Then *Jesus* six days before the passover
3. And anointed the feet of *Jesus*, and wiped
7. Then said *Jesus*, Let her alone: against the
9. and they came not for *Jesus*' sake only,
11. the Jews went away, and believed on
Jesus.
12. when they heard that *Jesus* was coming to
14. And *Jesus*, when he had found a young
16. but when *Jesus* was glorified, then
21. desired him, saying, Sir, we would see
Jesus.
22. Andrew: and again Andrew and Philip
tell *Jesus*.
23. And *Jesus* answered them, saying, The
30. *Jesus* answered and said, This voice came
35. Then *Jesus* said unto them, Yet a little
36. These things spake *Jesus*, and departed,
44. *Jesus* cried and said, He that believeth on
13: 1. before the feast of the passover, when
Jesus
3. *Jesus* knowing that the Father had given
7. *Jesus* answered and said unto him, What I
8. Thou shalt never wash my feet. *Jesus*
10. *Jesus* saith to him, He that is washed
21. When *Jesus* had thus said, he was troubled
23. Now there was leaning on *Jesus*' bosom
one of his disciples, whom *Jesus* loved.

Joh. 13:25. He then lying on *Jesus*' breast saith unto
26. *Jesus* answered, He it is, to whom I
27. Then said *Jesus* unto him, That thou doest,
29. because Judas had the bag, that *Jesus* had
31. Therefore, when he was gone out, *Jesus*
36. *Jesus* answered him, Whither I go, thou
38. *Jesus* answered him, Wilt thou lay down
14: 6. *Jesus* saith unto him, I am the way,
9. *Jesus* saith unto him, Have I been so
23. *Jesus* answered and said unto him, If a
16:19. Now *Jesus* knew that they were desirous
31. *Jesus* answered them, Do ye now believe?
17: 1. These words spake *Jesus*, and lifted up his
3. the only true God, and *Jesus* Christ,
18: 1. When *Jesus* had spoken these words,
2. which betrayed him, knew the place: for
Jesus
4. *Jesus* therefore, knowing all things that
should come
5. They answered him, *Jesus* of Nazareth.
Jesus saith
7. Whom seek ye? And they said, *Jesus* of
8. *Jesus* answered, I have told you that I
11. Then said *Jesus* unto Peter, Put up thy
12. captain and officers of the Jews took *Jesus*,
15. And Simon Peter followed *Jesus*,
— and went in with *Jesus* into the palace
19. The high priest then asked *Jesus* of his
20. *Jesus* answered him, I spake openly to the
22. which stood by struck *Jesus* with the palm
23. *Jesus* answered him, If I have spoken evil,
28. Then led they *Jesus* from Caiaphas unto
32. That the saying of *Jesus* might be fulfilled,
33. and called *Jesus*, and said unto him, Art
34. *Jesus* answered him, Sayest thou this thing
36. *Jesus* answered, My kingdom is not of this
37. Art thou a king then? *Jesus* answered, Thou
19: 1. Then Pilate therefore took *Jesus*, and
scourged (him).
5. Then came *Jesus* forth, wearing the crown
9. and saith unto *Jesus*, Whence art thou?
But *Jesus* gave him no answer.
11. *Jesus* answered, Thou couldest have no
13. he brought *Jesus* forth, and sat down in
16. And they took *Jesus*, and led (him) away.
18. on either side one, and *Jesus* in the
19. *JESUS* OF NAZARETH THE KING
OF THE JEWS.
20. for the place where *Jesus* was crucified was
23. Then the soldiers, when they had crucified
Jesus,
25. Now there stood by the cross of *Jesus*
26. When *Jesus* therefore saw his mother, and
28. After this, *Jesus* knowing that all things
30. When *Jesus* therefore had received the
vinegar,
33. But when they came to *Jesus*, and saw
38. Joseph of Arimathæa, being a disciple of
Jesus,
— that he might take away the body of *Jesus*:
— He came therefore, and took the body of
Jesus.
39. Nicodemus, which at the first came to *Jesus*
40. Then took they the body of *Jesus*, and
42. There laid they *Jesus* therefore because of
20: 2. and to the other disciple, whom *Jesus* loved,
12. at the feet, where the body of *Jesus*
14. she turned herself back, and saw *Jesus*
standing, and knew not that it was *Jesus*.
15. *Jesus* saith unto her, Woman, why weepest
16. *Jesus* saith unto her, Mary. She turned
17. *Jesus* saith unto her, Touch me not; for

Joh. 20:19. for fear of the Jews, came *Jesus* and
21. Then said *Jesus* to them again, Peace (be)
24. Didymus, was not with them when *Jesus*
26. (then) came *Jesus*, the doors being shut,
29. *Jesus* saith unto him, Thomas, because thou hast
30. And many other signs truly did *Jesus* in
31. believe that *Jesus* is the Christ, the Son
21: 1. After these things *Jesus* shewed himself
4. was now come, *Jesus* stood on the shore: but the disciples knew not that it was *Jesus*.
5. Then *Jesus* saith unto them, Children, have
7. that disciple whom *Jesus* loved saith unto Peter,
10. *Jesus* saith unto them, Bring of the fish
12. *Jesus* saith unto them, Come (and) dine.
13. *Jesus* then cometh, and taketh bread, and
14. This is now the third time that *Jesus*
15. when they had dined, *Jesus* saith to Simon
17. I love thee. *Jesus* saith unto him, Feed
20. Peter, turning about, seeth the disciple whom *Jesus*
21. Peter seeing him saith to *Jesus*, Lord, and
22. *Jesus* saith unto him, If I will that
23. yet *Jesus* said not unto him, He shall
25. which *Jesus* did, the which, if they should
Acts 1: 1. O Theophilus, of all that *Jesus* began both
11. ye gazing up into heaven? this same *Jesus*,
14. and Mary the mother of *Jesus*, and with
16. which was guide to them that took *Jesus*.
21. all the time that the Lord *Jesus* went in
2:22. Ye men of Israel, hear these words; *Jesus*
32. This *Jesus* hath God raised up, whereof we
36. that God hath made that same *Jesus*, whom
38. in the name of *Jesus* Christ for the
3: 6. In the name of *Jesus* Christ of Nazareth
13. of our fathers, hath glorified his Son *Jesus;*
20. he shall send *Jesus* Christ, which before
26. God, having raised up his Son *Jesus*, sent
4: 2. and preached through *Jesus* the resurrection from the
10. by the name of *Jesus* Christ of Nazareth,
13. of them, that they had been with *Jesus*.
18. all nor teach in the name of *Jesus*.
27. of a truth against thy holy child *Jesus*,
30. by the name of thy holy child *Jesus*.
33. witness of the resurrection of the Lord *Jesus:*
5:30. The God of our fathers raised up *Jesus*,
40. should not speak in the name of *Jesus*,
42. ceased not to teach and preach *Jesus* Christ.
6:14. that this *Jesus* of Nazareth shall destroy this
7:55. and saw the glory of God, and *Jesus*
59. Stephen, calling upon (God), and saying, Lord *Jesus*,
8:12. and the name of *Jesus* Christ, they were
16. baptized in the name of the Lord *Jesus*.
35. the same scripture, and preached unto him *Jesus*.
37. I believe that *Jesus* Christ is the Son
9: 5. And the Lord said, I am *Jesus* whom
17. Brother Saul, the Lord, (even) *Jesus*, that
27. boldly at Damascus in the name of *Jesus*.
29(28). boldly in the name of the Lord *Jesus*,
34. Peter said unto him, Æneas, *Jesus* Christ
10:36. preaching peace by *Jesus* Christ :
38. How God anointed *Jesus* of Nazareth with
11:17. who believed on the Lord *Jesus* Christ ;
20. spake unto the Grecians, preaching the Lord *Jesus*.
13:23. promise raised unto Israel a Saviour, *Jesus:*

Acts 13:33(32). in that he hath raised up *Jesus* again;
15:11. that through the grace of the Lord *Jesus*
26. their lives for the name of our Lord *Jesus*
16:18. I command thee in the name of *Jesus*
31. Believe on the Lord *Jesus* Christ, and thou
17: 3. risen again from the dead ; and that this *Jesus*,
7. that there is another king, (one) *Jesus*.
18. he preached unto them *Jesus*, and the
18: 5. and testified to the Jews (that) *Jesus* (was) Christ.
28. shewing by the scriptures that *Jesus* was Christ.
19: 4. come after him, that is, on Christ *Jesus*.
5. baptized in the name of the Lord *Jesus*.
10. Asia heard the word of the Lord *Jesus*,
13. evil spirits the name of the Lord *Jesus*, saying, We adjure you by *Jesus* whom
15. evil spirit answered and said, *Jesus* I know,
17. and the name of the Lord *Jesus* was
20:21. and faith toward our Lord *Jesus* Christ.
24. which I have received of the Lord *Jesus*,
35. to remember the words of the Lord *Jesus*,
21:13. Jerusalem for the name of the Lord *Jesus*.
22: 8. And he said unto me, I am *Jesus*
25:19. and of one *Jesus*, which was dead, whom
26: 9. contrary to the name of *Jesus* of Nazareth.
15. And he said, I am *Jesus* whom thou
28:23. the kingdom of God, persuading them concerning *Jesus*,
31. which concern the Lord *Jesus* Christ, with all confidence,
Ro. 1: 1. Paul, a servant of *Jesus* Christ, called (to be)
3(4). his Son *Jesus* Christ our Lord,
6. are ye also the called of *Jesus* Christ:
7. God our Father, and the Lord *Jesus* Christ.
8. I thank my God through *Jesus* Christ
2:16. secrets of men by *Jesus* Christ according
3:22. (which is) by faith of *Jesus* Christ unto
24. the redemption that is in Christ *Jesus :*
26. the justifier of him which believeth in *Jesus*.
4:24. on him that raised up *Jesus* our Lord
5: 1. peace with God through our Lord *Jesus* Christ:
11. joy in God through our Lord *Jesus* Christ,
15. (which is) by one man, *Jesus* Christ, hath
17. shall reign in life by one, *Jesus* Christ.
21. righteousness unto eternal life by *Jesus* Christ
6: 3. baptized into *Jesus* Christ were baptized
11. unto God through *Jesus* Christ our Lord.
23. God (is) eternal life through *Jesus* Christ
7:25. I thank God through *Jesus* Christ our Lord.
8: 1. which are in Christ *Jesus*, who walk not
2. of the Spirit of life in Christ *Jesus*
11. the Spirit of him that raised up *Jesus*
39. love of God, which is in Christ *Jesus*
10: 9. confess with thy mouth the Lord *Jesus*,
13:14. But put ye on the Lord *Jesus* Christ,
14:14. I know, and am persuaded by the Lord *Jesus*,
15: 5. toward another according to Christ *Jesus :*
6. the Father of our Lord *Jesus* Christ.
8. Now I say that *Jesus* Christ
16. I should be the minister of *Jesus* Christ
17. I may glory through *Jesus* Christ
30. for the Lord *Jesus* Christ's sake
16: 3. my helpers in Christ *Jesus:*
18. serve not our Lord *Jesus* Christ,
20. The grace of our Lord *Jesus* Christ
24. The grace of our Lord *Jesus* Christ

Ro. 16:25. and the preaching of *Jesus* Christ,
    27. (be) glory through *Jesus* Christ
1Co. 1: 1. (to be) an apostle of *Jesus* Christ
    2. to them that are sanctifed in Christ *Jesus,*
    — call upon the name of *Jesus* Christ
    3. and (from) the Lord *Jesus* Christ.
    4. which is given you by *Jesus* Christ ;
    7. coming of our Lord *Jesus* Christ:
    8. in the day of our Lord *Jesus* Christ.
    9. of his Son *Jesus* Christ our Lord.
    10. by the name of our Lord *Jesus* Christ,
    30. But of him are ye in Christ *Jesus,*
  2: 2. save *Jesus* Christ, and him crucified.
  3:11. that is laid, which is *Jesus* Christ.
  4:15. for in Christ *Jesus* I have begotten you
  5: 4. In the name of our Lord *Jesus*
    — the power of our Lord *Jesus* Christ,
    5. in the day of the Lord *Jesus.*
  6:11. in the name of the Lord *Jesus,*
  8: 6. and one Lord *Jesus* Christ,
  9: 1. have I not seen *Jesus* Christ our Lord ?
  11:23. That the Lord *Jesus* the (same) night
  12: 3. Spirit of God calleth *Jesus* accursed: and
    (that) no man can say that *Jesus*
  15:31. I have in Christ *Jesus* our Lord,
    57. through our Lord *Jesus* Christ.
  16:22. love not the Lord *Jesus* Christ,
    23. The grace of our Lord *Jesus* Christ
    24. My love (be) with you all in Christ *Jesus.*
2Co. 1: 1. Paul, an apostle of *Jesus* Christ
    2. and (from) the Lord *Jesus* Christ.
    3. the Father of our Lord *Jesus* Christ,
    14. in the day of the Lord *Jesus.*
    19. For the Son of God, *Jesus* Christ,
  4: 5. but Christ *Jesus* the Lord ;
    — your servants for *Jesus'* sake.
    6. in the face of *Jesus* Christ.
    10. the dying of the Lord *Jesus,* that the life
    also of *Jesus*
    11. delivered unto death for *Jesus'* sake, that
    the life also of *Jesus*
    14. the Lord *Jesus* shall raise up us also
    by *Jesus,* and shall present (us) with
  5:18. reconciled us to himself by *Jesus* Christ,
  8: 9. the grace of our Lord *Jesus* Christ,
  11: 4. he that cometh preacheth another *Jesus,*
    31. and Father of our Lord *Jesus* Christ,
  13: 5. how that *Jesus* Christ is in you,
  14(13). The grace of the Lord *Jesus* Christ,
Gal. 1: 1. by *Jesus* Christ, and God the Father,
    3. and (from) our Lord *Jesus* Christ,
    12. by the revelation of *Jesus* Christ.
  2: 4. which we have in Christ *Jesus,*
    16. but by the faith of *Jesus* Christ, even we
    have believed in *Jesus* Christ,
  3: 1. before whose eyes *Jesus* Christ
    14. come on the Gentiles through *Jesus*
    Christ ;
    22. that the promise by faith of *Jesus* Christ
    26. by faith in Christ *Jesus.*
    28. for ye are all one in Christ *Jesus.*
  4:14. an angel of God, (even) as Christ *Jesus.*
  5: 6. For in *Jesus* Christ neither circumcision
  6:14. save in the cross of our Lord *Jesus* Christ,
    15. For in Christ *Jesus* neither circumcision
    17. the marks of the Lord *Jesus.*
    18. the grace of our Lord *Jesus* Christ
Eph. 1: 1. Paul, an apostle of *Jesus* Christ
    — and to the faithful in Christ *Jesus :*
    2. and (from) the Lord *Jesus* Christ.
    3. and Father of our Lord *Jesus* Christ,
    5. the adoption of children by *Jesus* Christ

Eph. 1:15. I heard of your faith in the Lord *Jesus,*
    17. the God of our Lord *Jesus* Christ,
  2: 6. in heavenly (places) in Christ *Jesus :*
    7. kindness toward us through Christ *Jesus.*
    10. created in Christ *Jesus* unto good works,
    13. But now in Christ *Jesus*
    20. *Jesus* Christ himself being the chief
  3: 1. the prisoner of *Jesus* Christ
    9. who created all things by *Jesus* Christ:
    11. purposed in Christ *Jesus* our Lord:
    14. the Father of our Lord *Jesus* Christ,
    21. by Christ *Jesus* throughout all ages,
  4:21. as the truth is in *Jesus :*
  5:20. in the name of our Lord *Jesus* Christ ;
  6:23. and the Lord *Jesus* Christ.
    24. that love our Lord *Jesus* Christ
Phi. 1: 1. the servants of *Jesus* Christ, to all the
    saints in Christ *Jesus*
    2. and (from) the Lord *Jesus* Christ.
    6. until the day of *Jesus* Christ:
    8. in the bowels of *Jesus* Christ.
    11. which are by *Jesus* Christ,
    19. of the Spirit of *Jesus* Christ,
    26. may be more abundant in *Jesus* Christ
  2: 5. which was also in Christ *Jesus :*
    10. That at the name of *Jesus*
    11. should confess that *Jesus* Christ (is) Lord,
    19. But I trust in the Lord *Jesus*
    21. not the things which are *Jesus* Christ's.
  3: 3. and rejoice in Christ *Jesus,*
    8. of the knowledge of Christ *Jesus*
    12. I am apprehended of Christ *Jesus.*
    14. the high calling of God in Christ *Jesus.*
    20. the Saviour, the Lord *Jesus* Christ:
  4: 7. hearts and minds through Christ *Jesus.*
    19. to his riches in glory by Christ *Jesus.*
    21. Salute every saint in Christ *Jesus.*
    23. The grace of our Lord *Jesus* Christ
Col. 1: 1. Paul, an apostle of *Jesus* Christ
    2. our Father and the Lord *Jesus* Christ.
    3. the Father of our Lord *Jesus* Christ,
    4. we heard of your faith in Christ *Jesus,*
    28. every man perfect in Christ *Jesus :*
  2: 6. therefore received Christ *Jesus* the Lord,
  3:17. (do) all in the name of the Lord *Jesus,*
1Th. 1: 1. and (in) the Lord *Jesus* Christ:
    — and the Lord *Jesus* Christ.
    3. patience of hope in our Lord *Jesus* Christ,
    10. whom he raised from the dead, (even)
    Jesus,
  2:14. which in Judæa are in Christ *Jesus :*
    15. Who both killed the Lord *Jesus,*
    19. in the presence of our Lord *Jesus* Christ
  3:11. and our Lord *Jesus* Christ,
    13. at the coming of our Lord *Jesus* Christ
  4: 1. exhort (you) by the Lord *Jesus,*
    2. we gave you by the Lord *Jesus.*
    14. if we believe that *Jesus* died
    — them also which sleep in *Jesus*
  5: 9. salvation by our Lord *Jesus* Christ,
    18. this is the will of God in Christ *Jesus*
    23. the coming of our Lord *Jesus* Christ.
    28. The grace of our Lord *Jesus* Christ
2Th. 1: 1. and the Lord *Jesus* Christ:
    2. and the Lord *Jesus* Christ.
    7. the Lord *Jesus* shall be revealed
    8. the gospel of our Lord *Jesus* Christ:
    12. the name of our Lord *Jesus* Christ
    — our God and the Lord *Jesus* Christ.
  2: 1. the coming of our Lord *Jesus* Christ,
    14. of the glory of our Lord *Jesus* Christ.
    16. Now our Lord *Jesus* Christ

2Th. 3: 6. in the name of our Lord *Jesus* Christ,
12. and exhort by our Lord *Jesus* Christ,
18. The grace of our Lord *Jesus* Christ.
1Ti. 1: 1. Paul, an apostle of *Jesus* Christ
— our Saviour, and Lord *Jesus* Christ,
2. our Father and *Jesus* Christ our Lord.
12. And I thank Christ *Jesus* our Lord.
14. and love which is in Christ *Jesus.*
15. that Christ *Jesus* came into the world
16. that in me first *Jesus* Christ
2: 5. the man Christ *Jesus ;*
3: 13. in the faith which is in Christ *Jesus.*
4: 6. a good minister of *Jesus* Christ,
5: 21. before God, and the Lord *Jesus* Christ,
6: 3. the words of our Lord *Jesus* Christ,
13. and (before) Christ *Jesus,*
14. appearing of our Lord *Jesus* Christ:
2Ti. 1: 1. Paul, an apostle of *Jesus* Christ
— of life which is in Christ *Jesus,*
2. the Father and Christ *Jesus* our Lord.
9. which was given us in Christ *Jesus*
10. appearing of our Saviour *Jesus* Christ,
13. and love which is in Christ *Jesus.*
2: 1. the grace that is in Christ *Jesus.*
3. as a good soldier of *Jesus* Christ.
8. Remember that *Jesus* Christ
10. the salvation which is in Christ *Jesus*
3: 12. all that will live godly in Christ *Jesus*
15. through faith which is in Christ *Jesus.*
4: 1. before God, and the Lord *Jesus* Christ,
22. The Lord *Jesus* Christ (be) with thy spirit.
Tit. 1: 1. and an apostle of *Jesus* Christ,
4. and the Lord *Jesus* Christ our Saviour.
2: 13. God and our Saviour *Jesus* Christ ;
3: 6. through *Jesus* Christ our Saviour;
Philem. 1. Paul, a prisoner of *Jesus* Christ,
3. our Father and the Lord *Jesus* Christ.
5. which thou hast toward the Lord *Jesus,*
6. which is in you in Christ *Jesus.*
9. now also a prisoner of *Jesus* Christ.
23. my fellowprisoner in Christ *Jesus ;*
25. The grace of our Lord *Jesus* Christ
Heb 2: 9. But we see *Jesus,* who was made
3: 1. of our profession, Christ *Jesus ;*
4: 14. *Jesus* the Son of God,
6: 20. (even) *Jesus,* made an high priest
7: 22. By so much was *Jesus* made
10: 10. of the body of *Jesus* Christ once (for all).
19. into the holiest by the blood of *Jesus,*
12: 2. Looking unto *Jesus* the author
24. And to *Jesus* the mediator
13: 8. *Jesus* Christ the same yesterday,
12. Wherefore *Jesus* also, that he might
20. again from the dead our Lord *Jesus,*
21. in his sight, through *Jesus* Christ;
Jas. 1: 1. and of the Lord *Jesus* Christ,
2: 1. the faith of our Lord *Jesus* Christ,
1Pet.1: 1. Peter, an apostle of *Jesus* Christ,
2. sprinkling of the blood of *Jesus* Christ:
3. and Father of our Lord *Jesus* Christ,
— by the resurrection of *Jesus* Christ
7. at the appearing of *Jesus* Christ:
13. at the revelation of *Jesus* Christ;
2: 5. acceptable to God by *Jesus* Christ.
3: 21. by the resurrection of *Jesus* Christ:
4: 11. may be glorified through *Jesus* Christ,
5: 10. unto his eternal glory by Christ *Jesus,*
14. Peace (be) with you all that are in Christ *Jesus.*
2Pet. 1: 1. and an apostle of *Jesus* Christ,
— of God and our Saviour *Jesus* Christ:
2. and of *Jesus* our Lord,

2Pet.1: 8. the knowledge of our Lord *Jesus* Christ.
11. of our Lord and Saviour *Jesus* Christ.
14. our Lord *Jesus* Christ hath shewed me.
16. and coming of our Lord *Jesus* Christ,
2: 20. of the Lord and Saviour *Jesus* Christ,
3: 18. of our Lord and Saviour *Jesus* Christ.
1Joh. 1: 3. and with his Son *Jesus* Christ.
7. the blood of *Jesus* Christ his Son
2: 1. *Jesus* Christ the righteous:
22. he that denieth that *Jesus* is the Christ ?
3: 23. on the name of his Son *Jesus* Christ,
4: 2. that *Jesus* Christ is come in the flesh
3. that *Jesus* Christ is come in the flesh
15. Whosoever shall confess that *Jesus*
5: 1. Whosoever believeth that *Jesus*
5. believeth that *Jesus* is the Son of God ?
6. by water and blood, (even) *Jesus* Christ ;
20. (even) in his Son *Jesus* Christ.
2Joh. 3. and from the Lord *Jesus* Christ,
7. that *Jesus* Christ is come in the flesh.
Jude 1. Jude, the servant of *Jesus* Christ,
— and preserved in *Jesus* Christ,
4. and our Lord *Jesus* Christ.
17. the apostles of our Lord *Jesus* Christ;
21. for the mercy of our Lord *Jesus* Christ
Rev. 1: 1. The Revelation of *Jesus* Christ,
2. and of the testimony of *Jesus* Christ,
5. And from *Jesus* Christ,
9. the kingdom and patience of *Jesus* Christ,
— the testimony of *Jesus* Christ.
12: 17. and have the testimony of *Jesus* Christ.
14: 12. of God, and the faith of *Jesus.*
17: 6. the blood of the martyrs of *Jesus :*
19: 10. that have the testimony of *Jesus :*
— for the testimony of *Jesus*
20: 4. beheaded for the witness of *Jesus,*
22: 16. I *Jesus* have sent mine angel
20. Even so, come, Lord *Jesus.*
21. The grace of our Lord *Jesus* Christ

'Ιησοῦς, *Īeesous.*
(Joshua).

Acts 7: 45. that came after brought in with *Jesus*
Heb 4: 8. For if *Jesus* had given them rest,

'Ιησοῦς, *Īeesous.*
(Justus).

Col. 4: 11. And *Jesus,* which is called Justus,

'Ικόνιον, *Ikonion.*

Acts 13: 51. and came unto *Iconium.*
14: 1. And it came to pass in *Iconium,*
19. Jews from Antioch and *Iconium,*
21. and (to) *Iconium,* and Antioch,
16: 2. that were at Lystra and *Iconium.*
2Ti. 3: 11. at Antioch, at *Iconium,* at Lystra ;

'Ιλλυρικόν, *Illurikon.*

Ro. 15: 19. and round about unto *Illyricum,*

'Ιόππη, *Īoppee.*

Acts 9: 36. Now there was at *Joppa*
38. forasmuch as Lydda was nigh to *Joppa,*
42. And it was known throughout all *Joppa ;*
43. that he tarried many days in *Joppa*

Acts 10: 5. And now send men to *Joppa*,
      8. he sent them to *Joppa*.
    23. and certain brethren from *Joppa*
    32. Send therefore to *Joppa*,
  11: 5. I was in the city of *Joppa*
    13. said unto him, Send men to *Joppa*,

Ἰορδάνης, Ĭordanees.

Mat. 3: 5. and all the region round about *Jordan*,
    6. And were baptized of him in *Jordan*,
    13. Then cometh Jesus from Galilee to *Jordan*
  4:15. (by) the way of the sea, beyond *Jordan*,
    25. and (from) beyond *Jordan*.
  19: 1. the coasts of Judæa beyond *Jordan*;
Mar 1: 5. baptized of him in the river of *Jordan*,
    9. was baptized of John in *Jordan*.
  3: 8. and (from) beyond *Jordan*;
  10: 1. by the farther side of *Jordan*:
Lu. 3: 3. into all the country about *Jordan*,
  4: 1. returned from *Jordan*, and was led
Joh. 1:28. in Bethabara beyond *Jordan*,
  3:26. he that was with thee beyond *Jordan*,
  10:40. And went away again beyond *Jordan*

Ἰουδαία, Ĭoudaia.

Mat. 2: 1. in Bethlehem of *Judæa*
    5. In Bethlehem of *Judæa*:
    22. that Archelaus did reign in *Judæa*
  3: 1. preaching in the wilderness of *Judæa*,
    5. Jerusalem, and all *Judæa*,
  4:25. and (from) Jerusalem, and (from) *Judæa*,
  19: 1. the coasts of *Judæa* beyond Jordan;
  24:16. Then let them which be in *Judæa*
Mar 1: 5. out unto him all the land of *Judæa*,
  3: 7. followed him, and from *Judæa*,
  10: 1. cometh into the coasts of *Judæa*
  13:14. then let them that be in *Judæa*
Lu. 1: 5. Herod, the king of *Judæa*,
    65. all the hill country of *Judæa*.
  2: 4. out of the city of Nazareth, into *Judæa*,
  3: 1. Pontius Pilate being governor of *Judæa*,
  5:17. out of every town of Galilee, and *Judæa*,
  6:17. multitude of people out of all *Judæa*
  7:17. went forth throughout all *Judæa*,
  21:21. Then let them which are in *Judæa*
  23: 5. teaching throughout all *Jewry*,
Joh. 3:22. and his disciples into the land of *Judæa*;
    [see Ἰουδαῖος]
  4: 3. He left *Judæa*, and departed again
    47. that Jesus was come out of *Judæa*
    54. when he was come out of *Judæa*
  7: 1. for he would not walk in *Jewry*,
    3. Depart hence, and go into *Judæa*,
  11: 7. Let us go into *Judæa* again.
Acts 1: 8. and in all *Judea*, and in Samaria,
  2: 9. dwellers in Mesopotamia, and in *Judæa*,
  8: 1. the regions of *Judæa* and Samaria,
  9:31. throughout all *Judæa* and Galilee
  10:37. was published throughout all *Judæa*,
  11: 1. brethren that were in *Judæa*
    29. the brethren which dwelt in *Judæa*:
  12:19. And he went down from *Judæa*
  15: 1. which came down from *Judæa*
  21:10. there came down from *Judæa*
  26:20. throughout all the coasts of *Judæa*,
  28:21. neither received letters out of *Judæa*
Ro. 15:31. them that do not believe in *Judæa*;
2Co. 1:16. brought on my way toward *Judæa*.
Gal. 1:22. unto the churches of *Judæa*
1Th. 2:14. which in *Judæa* are in Christ Jesus:

Ἰουδαϊκός, Ĭoudaïkos.

Tit. 1:14. Not giving heed to *Jewish* fables,

Ἰουδαϊκῶς, Ĭoudaïkōs.

Gal. 2:14. after the manner of Gentiles, and not *as do the Jews*,

Ἰουδαῖος, Ĭoudaios.

Mat. 2: 2. he that is born King of the *Jews*?
  27:11. Art thou the King of the *Jews*?
    29. saying, Hail, king of the *Jews*!
    37. THIS IS JESUS THE KING OF THE *JEWS*.
  28:15. is commonly reported among the *Jews*
Mar 1: 5. unto him all the land *of Judæa*,
  7: 3. For the Pharisees, and all the *Jews*,
  15: 2. Art thou the King of the *Jews*?
    9. release unto you the King of the *Jews*?
    12. whom ye call the King of the *Jews*?
    18. salute him, Hail, King of the *Jews*!
    26. THE KING OF THE *JEWS*.
Lu. 7: 3. he sent unto him the elders of the *Jews*,
  23: 3. Art thou the King of the *Jews*?
    37. If thou be the king of the *Jews*,
    38. THIS IS THE KING OF THE *JEWS*.
    51. (he was) of Arimathæa, a city of the *Jews*:
Joh. 1:19. when the *Jews* sent priests and Levites
  2: 6. manner of the purifying of the *Jews*,
    13. And the *Jews*' passover was at hand,
    18. Then answered the *Jews* and said
    20. Then said the *Jews*, Forty and six years
  3: 1. Nicodemus, a ruler of the *Jews*:
    22. into the land *of Judæa*;
    25. and the *Jews* about purifying.
  4: 9. How is it that thou, being a *Jew*,
    — for the *Jews* have no dealings with
    22. for salvation is of the *Jews*.
  5: 1. there was a feast of the *Jews*;
    10. The *Jews* therefore said unto him
    15. The man departed, and told the *Jews*
    16. And therefore did the *Jews* persecute Jesus,
    18. Therefore the *Jews* sought the more
  6: 4. And the passover, a feast of the *Jews*,
    41. The *Jews* then murmured at him,
    52. The *Jews* therefore strove among
  7: 1. because the *Jews* sought to kill him.
    2. Now the *Jews*' feast of tabernacles
    11. Then the *Jews* sought him at the feast,
    13. openly of him for fear of the *Jews*.
    15. And the *Jews* marvelled, saying,
    35. Then said the *Jews* among themselves,
  8:22. Then said the *Jews*, Will he kill himself?
    31. Then said Jesus to those *Jews*
    48. Then answered the *Jews*, and said
    52. Then said the *Jews* unto him,
    57. Then said the *Jews* unto him,
  9:18. But the *Jews* did not believe
    22. because they feared the *Jews*: for the *Jews* had agreed already,
  10:19. among the *Jews* for these sayings.
    24. Then came the *Jews* round about him,
    31. Then the *Jews* took up stones
    33. The *Jews* answered him, saying,
  11: 8. the *Jews* of late sought to stone thee;
    19. And many of the *Jews* came to Martha
    31. The *Jews* then which were with her
    33. and the *Jews* also weeping which came
    36. said the *Jews*, Behold how he loved him!
    45. Then many of the *Jews* which came

Joh. 11:54. walked no more openly among the *Jews ;*
   55. And the *Jews'* passover was nigh
12: 9. Much people of the *Jews* therefore
   11. many of the *Jews* went away,
13.33. and as I said unto the *Jews,*
18:12. the captain and officers of the *Jews*
   14. which gave counsel to the *Jews,*
   20. whither the *Jews* always resort;
   31. The *Jews* therefore said unto him,
   33. Art thou the King of the *Jews?*
   35. Pilate answered, Am I a *Jew?*
   36. I should not be delivered to the *Jews :*
   38. he went out again unto the *Jews,*
   39. release unto you the King of the *Jews?*
19: 3. And said, Hail, King of the *Jews !*
   7. The *Jews* answered him, We have a law,
   12. but the *Jews* cried out, saying,
   14. saith unto the *Jews,* Behold your King!
   19. JESUS OF NAZARETH THE KING OF THE *JEWS.*
   20. This title then read many of the *Jews :*
   21. Then said the chief priests of the *Jews*
   — Write not, The King of the *Jews ;* but that he said, I am King of the *Jews.*
   31. The *Jews* therefore, because it was
   38. but secretly for fear of the *Jews,*
   40. as the manner of the *Jews* is to bury.
   42. because of the *Jews'* preparation (day);
20:19. were assembled for fear of the *Jews,*
Acts 2: 5. were dwelling at Jerusalem *Jews,*
   10. strangers of Rome, *Jews* and proselytes,
   14. Ye men *of Judæa* (lit. *Jews*), and all (ye)
9:22. the *Jews* which dwelt at Damascus,
   23. the *Jews* took counsel to kill him:
10:22. among all the nation of the *Jews,*
   28. a man that is a *Jew* to keep company,
   39. in the land of the *Jews,* and in Jerusalem;
11:19. the word to none but unto the *Jews* only.
12: 3. because he saw it pleased the *Jews,*
   11. expectation of the people of the *Jews.*
13: 5. in the synagogues of the *Jews :*
   6. a *Jew,* whose name (was) Bar-jesus:
   42. And when the *Jews* were gone out
   43. many of the *Jews* and religious proselytes
   45. when the *Jews* saw the multitudes,
   50. But the *Jews* stirred up the devout
14: 1. into the synagogue of the *Jews,*
   — both of the *Jews* and also of the Greeks.
   2. unbelieving *Jews* stirred up the Gentiles,
   4. and part held with the *Jews,*
   5. and also of the *Jews* with their rulers,
   19. And there came thither (certain) *Jews*
16: 1. which was a *Jewess,* and believed;
   3. circumcised him because of the *Jews*
   20. saying, These men, being *Jews,*
17: 1. where was a synagogue of the *Jews :*
   5. But the *Jews* which believed not,
   10. went into the synagogue of the *Jews.*
   13. But when the *Jews* of Thessalonica
   17. in the synagogue with the *Jews,*
18: 2. And found a certain *Jew* named Aquila,
   — all *Jews* to depart from Rome:
   4. persuaded the *Jews* and the Greeks.
   5. to the *Jews* (that) Jesus (was) Christ.
   12. the *Jews* made insurrection with one accord
   14. Gallio said unto the *Jews,*
   — O (ye) *Jews,* reason would that I should
   19. and reasoned with the *Jews.*
   24. And a certain *Jew* named Apollos,
   28. For he mightily convinced the *Jews,*
19:10. the Lord Jesus, both *Jews* and Greeks.
   13. Then certain of the vagabond *Jews,*

Acts19:14. Sceva, a *Jew,* (and) chief of the priests,
   17. And this was known to all the *Jews*
   33. the *Jews* putting him forward.
   34. But when they knew that he was a *Jew,*
20: 3. when the *Jews* laid wait for him,
   19. by the lying in wait of the *Jews :*
   21. Testifying both to the *Jews,*
21:11. So shall the *Jews* at Jerusalem
   20. thousands of *Jews* there are which believe;
   21. that thou teachest all the *Jews*
   27. the *Jews* which were of Asia,
   39. I am a man (which am) a *Jew*
22: 3. I am verily a man (which am) a *Jew,*
   12. having a good report of all the *Jews*
   30. wherefore he was accused of the *Jews,*
23:12. certain of the *Jews* banded together,
   20. The *Jews* have agreed to desire thee
   27. This man was taken of the *Jews,*
   30. that the *Jews* laid wait for the man,
24: 5. a mover of sedition among all the *Jews*
   9. And the *Jews* also assented,
   18. Whereupon certain *Jews* from Asia
   24. his wife Drusilla, which was a *Jewess,*
   27. willing to shew the *Jews* a pleasure,
25: 2. and the chief of the *Jews* informed him
   7. the *Jews* which came down
   8. Neither against the law of the *Jews,*
   9. willing to do the *Jews* a pleasure,
   10. to the *Jews* have I done no wrong,
   15. the elders of the *Jews* informed (me),
   24. all the multitude of the *Jews*
26: 2. whereof I am accused of the *Jews :*
   3. which are among the *Jews :*
   4. at Jerusalem, know all the *Jews ;*
   7. king Agrippa, I am accused of the *Jews.*
   21. the *Jews* caught me in the temple,
28:17. Paul called the chief of the *Jews* together:
   19. But when the *Jews* spake against (it),
   29. said these words, the *Jews* departed,
Ro. 1:16. to the *Jew* first, and also to the Greek.
2: 9. of the *Jew* first, and also of the Gentile;
   10. to the *Jew* first, and also to the Gentile:
   17. Behold, thou art called a *Jew,*
   28. he is not a *Jew,* which is one outwardly;
   29. he (is) a *Jew,* which is one inwardly;
3: 1. What advantage then hath the *Jew ?*
   9. proved both *Jews* and Gentiles,
   29. (Is he) the God of the *Jews* only?
9:24. *Jews* only, but also of the Gentiles?
10:12. between the *Jew* and the Greek:
1Co. 1:22. For the *Jews* require a sign,
   23. unto the *Jews* a stumblingblock,
   24. which are called, both *Jews* and Greeks,
9:20. And unto the *Jews* I became as a *Jew,* that I might gain the *Jews ;*
10:32. neither to the *Jews,* nor to the Gentiles,
12:13. whether (we be) *Jews* or Gentiles,
2Co.11:24. Of the *Jews* five times received I
Gal. 2:13. And the other *Jews* dissembled
   14. If thou, being a *Jew,*
   15. We (who are) *Jews* by nature,
3:28. There is neither *Jew* nor Greek,
Col. 3:11. Where there is neither Greek nor *Jew*
1Th. 2:14. even as they (have) of the *Jews :*
Rev. 2: 9. them which say they are *Jews,*
3: 9. which say they are *Jews,* and are not,

Ἰούδας, *Ioudas.*

Mat. 1: 2. and Jacob begat *Judas* and
   3. And *Judas* begat Phares and Zara

Mat. 2: 6. Bethlehem, (in) the land of *Juda*, art not
     the least among the princes of *Juda :*
  10: 4. and *Judas* Iscariot, who also betrayed him.
  13:55. and Joses, and Simon, and *Judas ?*
  26:14. Then one of the twelve, called *Judas*
     Iscariot,
   25. Then *Judas*, which betrayed him,
   47. And while he yet spake, lo, *Judas*,
  27: 3. Then *Judas*, which had betrayed him,
Mar 3:19. And *Judas* Iscariot, which also betrayed
     him :
  6: 3. Joses, and of *Juda*, and Simon ?
  14:10. And *Judas* Iscariot, one of the twelve,
   43. cometh *Judas*, one of the twelve,
Lu. 1:39. with haste, into a city of *Juda ;*
  3:26. which was (the son) of *Juda*,
   30. which was (the son) of *Juda*,
   33. which was (the son) of *Juda*,
  6:16. And *Judas* (the brother) of James, and
     Judas Iscariot, which also was the traitor.
  22: 3. Then entered Satan into *Judas*
   47. and he that was called *Judas*,
   48. But Jesus said unto him, *Judas*,
Joh. 6:71. He spake of *Judas* Iscariot
  12: 4. *Judas* Iscariot, Simon's (son),
  13: 2. put into the heart of *Judas* Iscariot,
   26. to *Judas* Iscariot, (the son) of Simon.
   29. because *Judas* had the bag,
  14:22. *Judas* saith unto him, not Iscariot,
  18: 2. And *Judas* also, which betrayed him,
   3. *Judas* then, having received a band
   5. And *Judas* also, which betrayed him,
Acts 1:13. and *Judas* (the brother) of James.
   16. spake before concerning *Judas*,
   25. from which *Judas* by transgression fell,
  5:37. After this man rose up *Judas*
  9:11. and enquire in the house of *Judas*
  15:22. (namely), *Judas* surnamed Barsabas,
   27. We have sent therefore *Judas*
   32. And *Judas* and Silas, being prophets
Heb 7:14. that our Lord sprang out of *Juda ;*
  8: 8. with the house of *Judah :*
Jude 1. *Jude*, the servant of Jesus Christ,
Rev. 5: 5. Lion of the tribe of *Juda*,
  7: 5. Of the tribe of *Juda*

'Ιουλία, *Ĭoulia.*

Ro. 16:15. Salute Philologus, and *Julia*,

'Ιούλιος, *Ĭoulios.*

Acts27: 1. unto (one) named *Julius*, a centurion
  3. And *Julius* courteously entreated Paul,

'Ιουνίας, *Ĭounias.*

Ro. 16: 7. Salute Andronicus and *Junia*,

'Ιοῦστος, *Ĭoustos.*

Acts 1:23. Barsabas, who was surnamed *Justus*,
  18: 7. *Justus*, (one) that worshipped God,
Col. 4:11. And Jesus, which is called *Justus*,

'Ισαάκ, *Isaäk.*

Mat. 1: 2. Abraham begat *Isaac ;* and *Isaac* begat
     Jacob ;
  8:11. shall sit down with Abraham, and *Isaac*,
  22:32. and the God of *Isaac*,
Mar 12:26. and the God of *Isaac*,
Lu. 3:34. which was (the son) of *Isaac*,
  13:28. Abraham, and *Isaac*, and Jacob,
  20:37. and the God of *Isaac*,
Acts 3:13. God of Abraham, and of *Isaac*,
  7: 8. and so (Abraham) (begat) *Isaac*,
  — and *Isaac* (begat) Jacob ;
   32. and the God of *Isaac*,
Ro. 9: 7. In *Isaac* shall thy seed be called.
   10. (even) by our father *Isaac ;*
Gal. 4:28. Now we, brethren, as *Isaac* was,
Heb 11: 9. in tabernacles with *Isaac* and Jacob,
   17. when he was tried, offered up *Isaac :*
   18. That in *Isaac* shall thy seed be called :
   20. By faith *Isaac* blessed Jacob
Jas. 2:21. offered *Isaac* his son upon the altar ?

'Ισαχάρ, *Isakar.*

Rev. 7: 7. Of the tribe of *Issachar*

'Ισκαριώτης, *Iskariōtees.*

Mat.10: 4. *Iscariot*, who also betrayed him.
  26:14. one of the twelve, called Judas *Iscariot*,
Mar 3:19. *Iscariot*, which also betrayed him :
  14:10. *Iscariot*, one of the twelve,
Lu. 6:16. *Iscariot*, which also was the traitor.
  22: 3. into Judas surnamed *Iscariot*,
Joh. 6:71. He spake of Judas *Iscariot*
  12: 4. Judas *Iscariot*, Simon's (son),
  13: 2. *Iscariot*, Simon's (son), to betray him ;
   26. he gave (it) to Judas *Iscariot*,
  14:22. Judas saith unto him, not *Iscariot*,

'Ισραήλ, *Israeel.*

Mat. 2: 6. that shall rule my people *Israel*.
   20. and go into the land of *Israel :*
   21. and came into the land of *Israel*.
  8:10. found so great faith, no, not in *Israel*.
  9:33. It was never so seen in *Israel*.
  10: 6. the lost sheep of the house of *Israel*.
   23. have gone over the cities of *Israel*,
  15:24. the lost sheep of the house of *Israel*.
   31. and they glorified the God of *Israel*.
  19:28. judging the twelve tribes of *Israel*.
  27: 9. the children of *Israel* did value ;
   42. If he be the King of *Israel*,
Mar 12:29. commandments (is), Hear, O *Israel ;*
  15:32. Let Christ the King of *Israel*
Lu. 1:16. And many of the children of *Israel*
   54. He hath holpen his servant Israel,
   68. Blessed (be) the Lord God of *Israel ;*
   80. the day of his shewing unto *Israel*.
  2:25. waiting for the consolation of *Israel :*
   32. and the glory of thy people *Israel*.
   34. and rising again of many in *Israel ;*
  4:25. many widows were in *Israel*
   27. And many lepers were in *Israel*
  7: 9. so great faith, no, not in *Israel*.
  22:30. judging the twelve tribes of *Israel*.
  24:21. which should have redeemed *Israel :*

Joh. 1:31. should be made manifest to *Israel*,
49(50). thou art the King of *Israel*.
3:10. Art thou a master of *Israel*,
12:13. Blessed (is) the King of *Israel*
Acts 1: 6. restore again the kingdom to *Israel?*
2:36. Therefore let all the house of *Israel*
4: 8. rulers of the people, and elders of *Israel*,
10. and to all the people of *Israel*,
27. the Gentiles, and the people of *Israel*,
5:21. senate of the children of *Israel*,
31. for to give repentance to *Israel*,
7:23. his brethren the children of *Israel*.
37. said unto the children of *Israel*,
42. O ye house of *Israel*,
9:15. and kings, and the children of *Israel :*
10:36. sent unto the children of *Israel*,
13:17. The God of this people of *Israel*
23. to (his) promise raised unto *Israel*
24. repentance to all the people of *Israel*.
28:20. for the hope of *Israel* I am bound
Ro. 9: 6. For they (are) not all *Israel*, which are of
Israel :
27. Esaias also crieth concerning *Israel*,
— of *Israel* be as the sand of the sea,
31. But *Israel*, which followed after
10: 1. and prayer to God for *Israel*
19. But I say, Did not *Israel* know?
21. But to *Israel* he saith,
11: 2. intercession to God against *Israel*,
7. *Israel* hath not obtained
25. in part is happened to *Israel*,
26. And so all *Israel* shall be saved:
1 Co.10:18. Behold *Israel* after the flesh:
2Co. 3: 7. so that the children of *Israel*
13. that the children of *Israel*
Gal. 6:16. and upon the *Israel* of God.
Eph. 2:12. from the commonwealth of *Israel*,
Phi. 3: 5. the eighth day, of the stock of *Israel*,
Heb. 8: 8. covenant with the house of *Israel*
10. I will make with the house of *Israel*
11:22. departing of the children of *Israel;*
Rev. 2:14. before the children of *Israel*,
7: 4. tribes of the children of *Israel*.
21: 12. tribes of the children of *Israel :*

'Ισραηλίτης, *Israeelitees.*

Joh. 1:47(48). Behold an *Israelite* indeed,
Acts 2:22. Ye men of *Israel*, hear these words;
3:12. Ye men of *Israel*, why marvel
5:35. Ye men of *Israel*, take heed
13:16. Men of *Israel*, and ye that fear God,
21:28. Crying out, Men of *Israel*,
Ro. 9: 4. Who are *Israelites;* to whom (pertaineth)
11: 1. For I also am an *Israelite*,
2Co.11:22. Are they *Israelites?* so (am) I.

'Ιταλία, *Italia.*

Acts18: 2. lately come from *Italy*,
27: 1. that we should sail into *Italy*,
6. ship of Alexandria sailing into *Italy;*
Heb 13:24. They of *Italy* salute you.

'Ιταλικός, *Italikos.*

Acts10: 1. of the band called the *Italian* (band),

'Ιτουραία, *Itouraia.*

Lu. 3: 1. Philip tetrarch of *Ituræa*

'Ιωάθαμ, *Ïoatham.*

Mat. 1: 9. And Ozias begat *Joatham;* and *Joatham*
begat Achaz;

'Ιωάννα, *Ïoanna.*

Lu. 8: 3. And *Joanna* the wife of Chuza
24:10. It was Mary Magdalene, and *Joanna*,

'Ιωαννᾶς, *Ïoannas.*

Lu. 3:27. Which was (the son) of *Joanna*,

'Ιωάννης, *Ïoannees.*
(Apostle).

Mat. 4:21. Zebedee, and *John* his brother,
10: 2(3). Zebedee, and *John* his brother;
17: 1. Peter, James, and *John* his brother,
Mar 1:19. Zebedee, and *John* his brother,
29. and Andrew, with James and *John*.
3:17. and *John* the brother of James;
5:37. and *John* the brother of James.
9: 2. Peter, and James, and *John*,
38. And *John* answered him, saying,
10:35. And James and *John*, the sons of Zebedee,
41. much displeased with James and *John*.
13: 3. Peter and James and *John*
14:33. Peter and James and *John*,
Lu. 5:10. James, and *John*, the sons of Zebedee,
6:14. *John*, Philip and Bartholomew,
8:51. save Peter, and James, and *John*,
9:28. he took Peter and *John* and James,
49. And *John* answered and said,
54. when his disciples James and *John*
22: 8. And he sent Peter and *John*,
Acts 1:13. both Peter, and James, and *John*,
3: 1. Now Peter and *John* went up together
3. Who seeing Peter and *John*
4. with *John*, said, Look on us.
11. was healed held Peter and *John*,
4:13. saw the boldness of Peter and *John*,
19. But Peter and *John* answered
8:14. they sent unto them Peter and *John :*
12: 2. the brother of *John* with the sword.
12. of Mary the mother of *John*,
Gal. 2: 9. And when James, Cephas, and *John*,
Rev. 1: 1. unto his servant *John :*
4. *John* to the seven churches
9. I *John*, who also am your brother,
21: 2. And I *John* saw the holy city,
22: 8. And I *John* saw these things,

'Ιωάννης, *Ïoannees.*
(Baptist).

Mat. 3: 1. In those days came *John* the Baptist,
4. the same *John* had his raiment
13. unto *John*, to be baptized of him.
14. But *John* forbad him, saying,
4:12. that *John* was cast into prison,
9:14. came to him the disciples of *John*,
11: 2. Now when *John* had heard in the prison

Mat.11: 4. Go and shew *John* again those things
 7. the multitudes concerning *John*,
 11. a greater than *John* the Baptist:
 12. from the days of *John* the Baptist
 13. and the law prophesied until *John*.
 18. For *John* came neither eating
 14: 2. This is *John* the Baptist;
 3. For Herod had laid hold on *John*,
 4. For *John* said unto him,
 8. *John* Baptist's head in a charger.
 10. and beheaded *John* in the prison.
 16:14. Some (say that thou art) *John* the Baptist:
 17:13. he spake unto them of *John* the Baptist.
 21:25. The baptism of *John*, whence was it?
 26. for all hold *John* as a prophet.
 32. For *John* came unto you
Mar 1: 4. *John* did baptize in the wilderness,
 6. And *John* was clothed with camel's hair,
 9. was baptized of *John* in Jordan.
 14. Now after that *John* was put in prison,
 2:18. And the disciples of *John*
 — Why do the disciples of *John*
 6:14. That *John* the Baptist was risen
 16. It is *John*, whom I beheaded:
 17. and laid hold upon *John*,
 18. For *John* had said unto Herod,
 20. For Herod feared *John*,
 24. said, The head of *John* the Baptist.
 25. in a charger the head of *John* the Baptist.
 8:28. And they answered, *John* the Baptist:
 11:30. The baptism of *John*, was (it) from heaven,
 32. *John*, that he was a prophet indeed.
Lu. 1:13. and thou shalt call his name *John*.
 60. Not (so); but he shall be called *John*.
 63. and wrote, saying, His name is *John*.
 3: 2. came unto *John* the son of Zacharias
 15. mused in their hearts of *John*,
 16. *John* answered, saying unto (them)
 20. that he shut up *John* in prison.
 5:33. Why do the disciples of *John* fast
 7:18. And the disciples of *John* shewed him
 19. And *John* calling (unto him)
 20. they said, *John* Baptist hath sent us
 22. tell *John* what things ye have seen
 24. messengers of *John* were departed,
 — unto the people concerning *John*,
 28. a greater prophet than *John* the Baptist:
 29. baptized with the baptism of *John*.
 33. For *John* the Baptist came
 9: 7. that *John* was risen from the dead;
 9. And Herod said, *John* have I beheaded:
 19. They answering said, *John* the Baptist;
 11: 1. as *John* also taught his disciples.
 16:16. and the prophets (were) until *John*:
 20: 4. The baptism of *John*, was it from heaven,
 6. persuaded that *John* was a prophet.
Joh. 1: 6. from God, whose name (was) *John*.
 15. *John* bare witness of him,
 19. And this is the record of *John*,
 26. *John* answered them, saying,
 28. where *John* was baptizing.
 29. The next day *John* seeth Jesus
 32. And *John* bare record, saying,
 35. *John* stood, and two of his disciples;
 40(41). One of the two which heard *John*
 3:23. And *John* also was baptizing.
 24. For *John* was not yet cast into prison.
 25. between (some) of *John's* disciples
 26. And they came unto *John*, and said
 27. *John* answered and said,
 4: 1. baptized more disciples than *John*,
 5:33. Ye sent unto *John*, and he bare witness

Joh. 5:36. greater witness than (that) of *John*.
 10:40. where *John* at first baptized;
 41. and said, *John* did no miracle:
 — that *John* spake of this man were true.
Acts 1: 5. For *John* truly baptized with water;
 22. Beginning from the baptism of *John*,
 10:37. the baptism which *John* preached;
 11:16. *John* indeed baptized with water;
 13:24. When *John* had first preached
 25. And as *John* fulfilled his course,
 18:25. knowing only the baptism of *John*.
 19: 3. And they said, Unto *John's* baptism.
 4. Then said Paul, *John* verily baptised

Ἰωάννης, *Ῐōannees.*
(Chief priest).
Acts 4: 6. Caiaphas, and *John*, and Alexander.

Ἰωάννης, *Ῐōannees.*
(Mark).
Acts12:25. *John*, whose surname was Mark.
 13: 5. they had also *John* to (their) minister.
 13. and *John* departing from them
 15:37. *John*, whose surname was Mark.

Ἰώβ, *Ῐōb.*
Jas. 5:11. Ye have heard of the patience of *Job*,

Ἰωήλ, *Ῐōeel.*
Acts 2:16. which was spoken by the prophet *Joel*;

Ἰωνάν, *Ῐōnan.*
Lu. 3:30. which was (the son) of *Jonan*,

Ἰωνᾶς, *Ῐōnas.*
(Prophet).
Mat.12:39. but the sign of the prophet *Jonas*:
 40. For as *Jonas* was three days
 41. repented at the preaching of *Jonas*; and,
 behold, a greater than *Jonas* (is) here.
 16: 4. but the sign of the prophet *Jonas*.
Lu. 11:29. but the sign of *Jonas* the prophet.
 30. *Jonas* was a sign unto the Ninevites,
 32. repented at the preaching of *Jonas*;
 — a greater than *Jonas* (is) here.

Ἰωνᾶς, *Ῐōnas.*
Joh. 1:42. Thou art Simon the son of *Jona*:
 21:15. Simon Peter, Simon, (son) of *Jonas*,
 16. Simon, (son) of *Jonas*, lovest thou me?
 17. Simon, (son) of *Jonas*, lovest thou me?

Ἰωράμ, *Ῐōram.*
Mat. 1: 8. and Josaphat begat *Joram*; and *Joram*
 begat Ozias;

’Ιωρείμ, Iōrīm.

Lu. 3:29. which was (the son) of Jorim,

’Ιωσαφάτ, Iōsaphat.

Mat. 1: 8. And Asa begat Josaphat ; and Josaphat begat Joram ;

’Ιωσῆς, Iōsees.

Mat.13:55. James, and Joses, and Simon,
27:56. the mother of James and Joses,
Mar 6: 3. the brother of James, and Joses,
15:40. mother of James the less and of Joses,
47. and Mary (the mother) of Joses
Lu. 3:29. Which was (the son) of Jose,
Acts 4:36. And Joses, who by the apostles

’Ιωσήφ, Iōseeph.
(Of Arimathæa).

Mat.27:57. man of Arimathæa, named Joseph,
59. when Joseph had taken the body,
Mar 15:43. Joseph of Arimathæa,
45. he gave the body to Joseph.
Lu. 23:50. a man named Joseph, a counsellor ;
Joh.19:38. after this Joseph of Arimathæa,

’Ιωσήφ, Iōseeph.
(Barsabas).

Acts 1:23. Joseph called Barsabas,

’Ιωσήφ, Iōseeph.
(Son of Jacob).

Joh. 4: 5. that Jacob gave to his son Joseph.
Acts 7: 9. moved with envy, sold Joseph
13. Joseph was made known to his brethren ;
and Joseph's kindred was made known
14. Then sent Joseph, and called his father
18. another king arose, which knew not Joseph.
Heb 11:21. blessed both the sons of Joseph ;
22. By faith Joseph, when he died,
Rev. 7: 8. Of the tribe of Joseph

’Ιωσήφ, Iōseeph.
(Son of Judas).

Lu. 3:26. which was (the son) of Joseph,

’Ιωσήφ, Iōseeph.
(Son of Jonan).

Lu. 3:30. which was (the son) of Joseph,

’Ιωσήφ, Iōseeph.
(Husband of Mary).

Mat. 1:16. And Jacob begat Joseph
18. Mary was espoused to Joseph,
19. Then Joseph her husband,
20. Joseph, thou son of David, fear not
24. Then Joseph being raised from sleep
2:13. appeareth to Joseph in a dream,
19. appeareth in a dream to Joseph

Lu. 1:27. a man whose name was Joseph,
2: 4. Joseph also went up from Galilee,
16. and found Mary, and Joseph,
33. And Joseph and his mother marvelled
43. Joseph and his mother knew not (of it).
3:23. as was supposed the son of Joseph,
4:22. they said, Is not this Joseph's son ?
Joh. 1:45. Jesus of Nazareth, the son of Joseph.
6:42. Is not this Jesus, the son of Joseph,

’Ιωσήφ, Iōseeph.
(Son of Mattathias).

Lu. 3:24. which was (the son) of Joseph,

’Ιωσίας, Iōsias.

Mat. 1:10. and Amon begat Josias ;
11. And Josias begat Jechonias

Καϊάφας, Kaïaphas.

Mat.26: 3. who was called Caiaphas,
57. led (him) away to Caiaphas
Lu. 3: 2. and Caiaphas being the high priests,
Joh.11:49. And one of them, (named) Caiaphas,
18:13. he was father in law to Caiaphas,
14. Now Caiaphas was he,
24. unto Caiaphas the high priest.
28. Then led they Jesus from Caiaphas
Acts 4: 6. and Caiaphas, and John,

Κάϊν, Kaïn.

Heb 11: 4. a more excellent sacrifice than Cain,
1 Joh.3:12. Not as Cain, (who) was of that
Jude 11. gone in the way of Cain,

Καϊνάν, Kaïnan.

Lu. 3:36. Which was (the son) of Cainan,
37. which was (the son) of Cainan,

Καῖσαρ, Kaisar.

Mat.22:17. to give tribute unto Cæsar, or not ?
21. They say unto him, Cæsar's.
— unto Cæsar the things which are Cæsar's;
Mar 12:14. to give tribute to Cæsar, or not ?
16. And they said unto him, Cæsar's.
17. to Cæsar the things that are Cæsar's,
Lu. 2: 1. a decree from Cæsar Augustus,
3: 1. the reign of Tiberius Cæsar,
20:22. to give tribute unto Cæsar, or no ?
24. They answered and said, Cæsar's.
25. unto Cæsar the things which be Cæsar's,
23: 2. forbidding to give tribute to Cæsar,
Joh.19:12. thou art not Cæsar's friend:
— speaketh against Cæsar.
15. We have no king but Cæsar.
Acts11:28. in the days of Claudius Cæsar.
17: 7. contrary to the decrees of Cæsar,
25: 8. nor yet against Cæsar,

Acts25:10. I stand at *Cæsar's* judgment seat,
11. I appeal unto *Cæsar*.
12. Hast thou appealed unto *Cæsar?* unto
Cæsar shalt thou go.
21. till I might send him to *Cæsar*.
26:32. if he had not appealed unto *Cæsar*.
27:24. thou must be brought before *Cæsar:*
28:19. to appeal unto *Cæsar;*
Phi. 4:22. they that are of *Cæsar's* houshold.

Καισάρεια, *Kaisarīa.*
(ἡ Φιλίππου)

Mat.16:13. the coasts of *Cæsarea* Philippi,
Mar 8:27. into the towns of *Cæsarea* Philippi:

Καισάρεια, *Kaisarīa.*
(ἡ Στράτωνος)

Acts 8:40. till he came to *Cæsarea*.
9:30. they brought him down to *Cæsarea,*
10: 1. a certain man in *Cæsarea*
|24. they entered into *Cæsarea.*
11:11. sent from *Cæsarea* unto me.
12:19. from Judæa to *Cæsarea,*
18:22. he had landed at *Cæsarea,*
21: 8. and came unto *Cæsarea:*
16. of the disciples of *Cæsarea,*
23:23. soldiers to go to *Cæsarea,*
33. when they came to *Cæsarea,*
25: 1. from *Cæsarea* to Jerusalem.
4. Paul should be kept at *Cæsarea,*
6. he went down unto *Cæsarea;*
13. Bernice came unto *Cæsarea*

Καλοὶ λιμένες see among the Appellatives.

Κανᾶ, *Kana.*

Joh. 2: 1. in *Cana* of Galilee;
11. did Jesus in *Cana* of Galilee,
4:46. Jesus came again into *Cana*
21: 2. Nathanael of *Cana* in Galilee,

Καναάν see Χαναάν.

Κανανίτης, *Kananitees.*

Mat.10: 4. Simon the *Canaanite*, and Judas
Mar 3:18. and Simon the *Canaanite,*

Κανδάκη, *Kandakee.*

Acts 8:27. under *Candace* queen of the

Καπερναούμ, *Kapernaoum.*

Mat. 4:13. he came and dwelt in *Capernaum*,
8: 5. when Jesus was entered into *Capernaum,*
11:23. And thou, *Capernaum*, which art
17:24. were come to *Capernaum,*

Mar 1:21. they went into *Capernaum;*
2: 1. he entered into *Capernaum*
9:33. And he came to *Capernaum:*
Lu. 4:23. in *Capernaum*, do also here
31. And came down to *Capernaum,*
7: 1. he entered into *Capernaum.*
10:15. And thou, *Capernaum*, which
Joh. 2:12. he went down to *Capernaum,*
4:46. was sick at *Capernaum.*
6:17. over the sea toward *Capernaum.*
24. and came to *Capernaum,*
59. as he taught in *Capernaum.*

Καππαδοκία, *Kappadokia.*

Acts 2: 9. and *Cappadocia*, in Pontus,
1Pet.1: 1. Galatia, *Cappadocia*, Asia, and

Κάρπος, *Karpos.*

2Ti. 4:13. cloke that I left at Troas with *Carpus,*

Καῤῥάν see Χαῤῥάν.

Κεγχρεαί, *Kenkreai.*

Acts18:18. having shorn (his) head in *Cenchrea:*
Ro. 16: 1. the church which is at *Cenchrea:*

Κέδρος, or Κεδρών, *Kedros,* or *Kedrōn.*

Joh.18: 1. over the brook *Cedron,*
Note.—Some copies read τῶν Κέδρων, others τοῦ Κεδρών.

Κηφᾶς, *Keephas.*

Joh. 1:42(43). thou shalt be called *Cephas,*
1Co. 1:12. and I of *Cephas;*
3:22. Whether Paul, or Apollos, or *Cephas,*
9: 5. the brethren of the Lord, and *Cephas?*
15: 5. he was seen of *Cephas,*
Gal. 2: 9. And when James, *Cephas*, and John,

Κιλικία, *Kilikia.*

Acts 6: 9. and of them of *Cilicia* and of Asia,
15:23. in Antioch and Syria and *Cilicia:*
41. he went through Syria and *Cilicia,*
21:39. a Jew of Tarsus, (a city) in *Cilicia,*
22: 3. born in Tarsus, (a city) in *Cilicia,*
23:34. when he understood that (he was) of *Cilicia;*
27: 5. we had sailed over the sea of *Cilicia*
Gal. 1:21. into the regions of Syria and *Cilicia;*

Κίς, *Kis.*

Acts13:21. Saul the son of *Cis,*

Κλαύδη, *Klaudee.*

Acts27:16. a certain island which is called *Clauda,*

Κλαυδία, *Klaudia.*

2Ti. 4:21. and *Claudia*, and all the brethren.

Κλαύδιος, *Klaudios.*

Acts11:28. in the days of *Claudius* Cæsar.
   18: 2. *Claudius* had commanded all Jews
   23:26. *Claudius* Lysias unto the most

Κλεόπας, *Kleopas.*

Lu. 24:18. one of them, whose name was *Cleopas,*

Κλήμης, *Kleemees.*

Phi. 4: 3. in the gospel, with *Clement* also,

Κλωπᾶς, *Klōpas.*

Joh.19:25. Mary the (wife) of *Cleophas,*

Κνίδος, *Knidos.*

Acts27: 7. scarce were come over against *Cnidus,*

Κολασσαί, *Kolassai.*

Col. 1: 2. in Christ which are at *Colosse :*
   Note. Some copies read Κολοσσαῖς.

Κορέ, *Kore.*

Jude   11. perished in the gainsaying of *Core.*

Κορίνθιος, *Korinthios.*

Acts18: 8. many of the *Corinthians*
2Co. 6:11. O (ye) *Corinthians ;* our mouth is open

Κόρινθος, *Korinthos.*

Acts18: 1. and came to *Corinth ;*
   19: 1. while Apollos was at *Corinth,*
1Co. 1: 2. the church of God which is at *Corinth,*
2Co. 1: 1. church of God which is at *Corinth,*
   23. I came not as yet unto *Corinth.*
2Ti. 4:20. Erastus abode at *Corinth :*

Κορνήλιος, *Korneelios.*

Acts10: 1. *Cornelius*, a centurion of the band
   3. saying unto him, *Cornelius.*
   7. the angel which spake unto *Cornelius*
   17. the men which were sent from *Cornelius*
   21. were sent unto him from *Cornelius ;*
   22. they said, *Cornelius* the centurion,
   24. *Cornelius* waited for them,
   25. *Cornelius* met him, and fell down
   30. *Cornelius* said, Four days ago
   31. *Cornelius*, thy prayer is heard,

Κούαρτος, *Kouartos.*

Ro. 16:23. and *Quartus* a brother.

Κρήσκης, *Kreeskees.*

2Ti. 4:10. *Crescens* to Galatia, Titus unto

Κρής, Κρῆτες, *Krees, Kreetes.*

Acts 2:11. *Cretes* and Arabians, we do hear them
Tit. 1:12. The *Cretians* (are) alway liars,

Κρήτη, *Kreetee.*

Acts27: 7. we sailed under *Crete*, (marg *Candy*)
   12. (which is) an haven of *Crete,*
   13. they sailed close by *Crete.*
   21. and not have loosed from *Crete,*
Tit. 1: 5. For this cause left I thee in *Crete,*

Κρίσπος, *Krispos.*

Acts18: 8. And *Crispus*, the chief ruler of the
1Co. 1.14. I baptized none of you, but *Crispus*

Κύπριος, *Kuprios.*

Acts 4:36. of the country of *Cyprus*, (lit. a *Cyprian*
   by nation)
   11:20. some of them were men of *Cyprus*
   21:16. with them one Mnason of *Cyprus,*

Κύπρος, *Kupros.*

Acts11:19. and *Cyprus*, and Antioch, preaching
   13: 4. from thence they sailed to *Cyprus.*
   15:39. took Mark, and sailed unto *Cyprus ;*
   21: 3. when we had discovered *Cyprus,*
   27: 4. we sailed under *Cyprus,*

Κυρηναῖος, *Kureenaios.*

Mat.27:32. a man of *Cyrene*, Simon by name:
Mar 15:21. compel one Simon a *Cyrenian,*
Lu. 23:26. upon one Simon, a *Cyrenian,*
Acts 6: 9. of the Libertines, and *Cyrenians,*
   11:20. were men of Cyprus and *Cyrene,*
   13: 1. and Lucius of *Cyrene,*

Κυρήνη, *Kureenee.*

Acts 2:10. parts of Libya about *Cyrene,*

Κυρήνιος, *Kureenios.*

Lu. 2: 2. when *Cyrenius* was governor of Syria.

Κῶς, *Kōs.*

Acts21: 1. with a straight course unto *Coos,*

Κωσάμ, *Kōsam.*

Lu. 3:28. Addi, which was (the son) of *Cosam,*

Λάζαρος, *Lazaros.*

Lu. 16:20. a certain beggar named *Lazarus,*
    23. and *Lazarus* in his bosom.
    24. mercy on me, and send *Lazarus,*
    25. and likewise *Lazarus* evil things:
Joh. 11: 1. (named) *Lazarus,* of Bethany,
    2. whose brother *Lazarus* was sick.
    5. and her sister, and *Lazarus.*
    11. Our friend *Lazarus* sleepeth;
    14. them plainly, *Lazarus* is dead.
    43. *Lazarus,* come forth.
   12: 1. where *Lazarus* was which had been dead,
    2. but *Lazarus* was one of them
    9. but that they might see *Lazarus*
    10. might put *Lazarus* also to death;
    17. called *Lazarus* out of his grave,

Λάμεχ, *Lamek.*

Lu. 3:36. which was (the son) of *Lamech,*

Λαοδίκεια, *Laodikīa.*

Col. 2: 1. and (for) them at *Laodicea,*
   4:13. and them (that are) in *Laodicea,*
    15. the brethren which are in *Laodicea,*
    16. the (epistle) from *Laodicea.*
Rev. 1:11. and unto *Laodicea.*

Λαοδικεύς, *Laodikūs.*

Col. 4:16. in the church of the *Laodiceans;*
Rev. 3:14. church of the *Laodiceans* write;

Λασαία, *Lasaia.*

Acts 27: 8. whereunto was the city (of) *Lasea.*

Λεββαῖος, *Lebbaios.*

Mat. 10: 3. James (the son) of Alphæus, and *Lebbæus,*

Λευί, *Lūi.*
(on of Jacob.)

Heb 7: 5. that are of the sons of *Levi,*
    9. as I may so say, *Levi* also,
Rev. 7: 7. Of the tribe of *Levi* (were) séaled

Λευί, *Lūi.*
(Son of Melchi.)

Lu. 3:24. which was (the son) of *Levi,*

Λευί, *Lūi.*
(Son of Simeon.)

Lu. 3:29. which was (the son) of *Levi,*

Λευίς, *Lūis.*

Mar 2:14. as he passed by, he saw *Levi*
Lu. 5:27. saw a publican, named *Levi,*
   29. And *Levi* made him a great feast

Λευίτης, *Lūitees.*

Lu. 10:32. And likewise a *Levite,*
Joh. 1:19. when the Jews sent priests and *Levites*
Acts 4:36. The son of consolation, a *Levite*

Λευϊτικός, *Lūitikos.*

Heb 7:11. were by the *Levitical* priesthood,

Λιβερτῖνοι, *Libertinoi.*

Acts 6: 9. (the synagogue) of the *Libertines,*

Λιβύα, *Libua.*

Acts 2:10. and in the parts of *Libya*

Λιθόστρωτος, *Lithostrōtos.*

Joh. 19:13. the *Pavement,* but in the Hebrew, Gabbatha.

Λῖνος, *Linos.*

2Ti. 4:21. Pudens, and *Linus,* and Claudia,

Λίψ, see among Appellatives.

Λουκᾶς, *Loukas.*

Col. 4:14. *Luke,* the beloved physician,
2Ti. 4:11. Only *Luke* is with me.
Philem 24(23). Demas, *Lucas,* my fellowlabourers.

Λούκιος, *Loukios.*

Acts 13: 1. and *Lucius* of Cyrene, and Manaen,
Ro. 16:21. and *Lucius,* and Jason, and Sosipater,

Λύδδα, *Ludda.*

Acts 9:32. the saints which dwelt at *Lydda.*
   35. And all that dwelt at *Lydda*
   38. as *Lydda* was nigh to Joppa,

Λυδία, *Ludia.*

Acts 16:14. a certain woman named *Lydia,*
   40. entered into (the house of) *Lydia:*

Λυκαονία, *Lukaonia.*

Acts 14: 6. Lystra and Derbe, cities of *Lycaonia,*

Λυκαονιστί, *Lukaonisti.*

Acts14:11. saying in the *speech of Lycaonia,*

Λυκία, *Lukia.*

Acts27: 5. we came to Myra, (a city) of *Lycia.*

Λυσανίας, *Lusanias.*

Lu. 3: 1. *Lysanias* the tetrarch of Abilene,

Λυσίας, *Lusias.*

Acts23:26. Claudius *Lysias* unto the most
24: 7. the chief captain *Lysias* came (upon us),
22. When *Lysias* the chief captain shall come

Λύστρα (ή), *Lustra.*

Acts14: 6. and fled unto *Lystra* and Derbe,
21. they returned again to *Lystra,*
16: 1. Then came he to Derbe and *Lystra:*

Λύστρα (τά), *Lustra.*

Acts14: 8. there sat a certain man at *Lystra,*
16: 2. by the brethren that were at *Lystra*
2Ti. 3:11. at Antioch, at Iconium, at *Lystra;*

Λωΐς, *Lōis.*

2Ti. 1: 5. first in thy grandmother *Lois,*

Λώτ, *Lōt.*

Lu. 17:28. as it was in the days of *Lot;*
29. the same day that *Lot* went out of Sodom
32. Remember *Lot's* wife.
2Pet.2: 7. And delivered just *Lot,*

Μαάθ, *Maäth.*

Lu. 3:26. Which was (the son) of *Maath,*

Μαγδαλά, *Magdala.*

Mat.15:39. and came into the coasts of *Magdala.*

Μαγδαληνή, *Magdaleenee.*

Mat.27:56. Among which was Mary *Magdalene,*
61. And there was Mary *Magdalene,*
28: 1. came Mary *Magdalene* and the other
Mar15:40. among whom was Mary *Magdalene,*
47. And Mary *Magdalene* and Mary
16: 1. Mary *Magdalene,* and Mary the
9. he appeared first to Mary *Magdalene,*

Lu. 8: 2. Mary called *Magdalene,* out of whom
24:10. It was Mary *Magdalene,* and Joanna,
Joh.19:25. (wife) of Cleophas, and Mary *Magdalene.*
20: 1. cometh Mary *Magdalene* early,
18. Mary *Magdalene* came and told

Μαγώγ, *Magōg.*

Rev.20: 8. Gog and *Magog,* to gather them

Μαδιάμ, *Madiam.*

Acts 7:29. stranger in the land of *Madian,*

Μαθουσάλα, *Mathousala.*

Lu. 3:37. Which was (the son) of *Mathusala,*

Μαϊνάν, *Maïnan.*

Lu. 3:31. which was (the son) of *Menan,*

Μακεδονία, *Makedonia.*

Acts16: 9. Come over into *Macedonia,*
10. we endeavoured to go into *Macedonia,*
12. of that part of *Macedonia,*
18: 5. were come from *Macedonia,*
19:21. when he had passed through *Macedonia*
22. So he sent into *Macedonia* two of them
20: 1. departed for to go into *Macedonia.*
3. purposed to return through *Macedonia.*
Ro. 15:26. it hath pleased them of *Macedonia*
1Co.16: 5. *Macedonia:* for I do pass through *Macedonia.*
2Co. 1:16. to pass by you into *Macedonia,* and to come again out of *Macedonia*
2:13. I went from thence into *Macedonia.*
7: 5. when we were come into *Macedonia,*
8: 1. bestowed on the churches of *Macedonia;*
11: 9. brethren which came from *Macedonia*
Phi. 4:15. when I departed from *Macedonia,*
1Th. 1: 7. all that believe in *Macedonia*
8. word of the Lord not only in *Macedonia*
4:10. brethren which are in all *Macedonia:*
1Ti. 1: 3. when I went into *Macedonia,*

Μακεδών, *Makedōn.*

Acts16: 9. There stood a man of *Macedonia,*
19:29. men of *Macedonia,* Paul's companions
27: 2. a *Macedonian* of Thessalonica,
2Co. 9: 2. I boast of you to them of *Macedonia,*
4. Lest haply if they of *Macedonia*

Μαλελεήλ or Μαλαλεήλ, *Maleleeel or Malaleeel.*

Lu. 3:37. which was (the son) of *Maleleel,*

Μάλχος, *Malkos.*

Joh.18:10. The servant's name was *Malchus.*

Μαμμωνᾶς & Μαμωνᾶς, *Mammōnas* & *Mamōnas.*

Mat. 6:24. Ye cannot serve God and *mammon.*
Lu. 16: 9. friends of the *mammon* of unrighteousness;
    11. faithful in the unrighteous *mammon,*
    13. Ye cannot serve God and *mammon.*

Μαναήν, *Manaeen.*

Acts13: 1. Lucius of Cyrene, and *Manaen,*

Μανασσῆς, *Manassees.*

Mat. 1:10. And Ezekias begat *Manasses;* and *Ma-*
    nasses begat Amon;
Rev. 7: 6. Of the tribe of *Manasses* (were) sealed

Μάρθα, *Martha.*

Lu. 10:38. a certain woman named *Martha*
    40. But *Martha* was cumbered about much
    41. and said unto her, *Martha, Martha,*
Joh.11: 1. town of Mary and her sister *Martha.*
    5. Now Jesus loved *Martha,*
    19. the Jews came to *Martha* and Mary,
    20. Then *Martha,* as soon as she heard
    21. Then said *Martha* unto Jesus,
    24. *Martha* saith unto him,
    30. place where *Martha* met him.
    39. *Martha,* the sister of him that was dead,
    12: 2. made him a supper; and *Martha* served:

Μαρία, Μαριάμ, *Maria, Mariam.*

Mat. 1:16. begat Joseph the husband of *Mary,*
    18. *Mary* was espoused to Joseph,
    20. fear not to take unto thee *Mary*
    2:11. saw the young child with *Mary*
    13:55. is not his mother called *Mary?*
    27:56. Among which was *Mary* Magdalene, and
      Mary the mother of James and
    61. And there was *Mary* Magdalene, and the
      other *Mary,* sitting over
    28: 1. came *Mary* Magdalene and the other *Mary*
      to see the sepulchre.
Mar 6: 3. the carpenter, the son of *Mary,*
    15:40. among whom was *Mary* Magdalene, and
      Mary the mother of James
    47. And *Mary* Magdalene and *Mary* (the
      mother) of Joses
    16: 1. *Mary* Magdalene, and *Mary* the (mother)
      of James,
    9. appeared first to *Mary* Magdalene,
Lu. 1:27. and the virgin's name (was) *Mary.*
    30. angel said unto her, Fear not, *Mary:*
    34. Then said *Mary* unto the angel,
    38. And *Mary* said, Behold the handmaid
    39. And *Mary* arose in those days,
    41. heard the salutation of *Mary,*
    46. *Mary* said, My soul doth magnify the Lord,
    56. And *Mary* abode with her about
    2: 5. To be taxed with *Mary* his espoused
    16. and found *Mary,* and Joseph,
    19. But *Mary* kept all these things,
    34. and said unto *Mary* his mother.
    8: 2. *Mary* called Magdalene, out of

Lu. 10:39. she had a sister called *Mary,*
    42. *Mary* hath chosen that good part,
    24:10. *Mary* Magdalene, and Joanna, and *Mary*
      (the mother) of James,
Joh.11: 1. Lazarus, of Bethany, the town of *Mary*
    2. *Mary* which anointed the Lord
    19. Jews came to Martha and *Mary,*
    20. but *Mary* sat (still) in the house.
    28. called *Mary* her sister secretly,
    31. when they saw *Mary,*
    32. when *Mary* was come where Jesus
    45. the Jews which came to *Mary,*
    12: 3. took *Mary* a pound of ointment
    19:25. *Mary* the (wife) of Cleophas, and *Mary*
      Magdalene.
    20: 1. cometh *Mary* Magdalene early,
    11. But *Mary* stood without
    16. Jesus saith unto her, *Mary.*
    18. *Mary* Magdalene came and told
Acts 1:14. and *Mary* the mother of Jesus,
    12:12. he came to the house of *Mary*
Ro. 16: 6. Greet *Mary,* who bestowed much

Μάρκος, *Markos.*

Acts12:12. whose surname was *Mark;*
    25. whose surname was *Mark.*
    15:37. whose surname was *Mark.*
    39. and so Barnabas took *Mark,*
Col. 4:10. and *Marcus,* sister's son to Barnabas,
2Ti. 4:11. Take *Mark,* and bring him with thee:
Philem 24. *Marcus,* Aristarchus, Demas,
1Pet. 5:13. and (so doth) *Marcus* my son.

Ματθαῖος, *Matthaios.*

Mat. 9: 9. he saw a man, named *Matthew,*
    10: 3. Thomas, and *Matthew* the publican;
Mar 3:18. Bartholomew, and *Matthew,* and Thomas,
Lu. 6:15. *Matthew* and Thomas, James the (son)
Acts 1:13. Thomas, Bartholomew, and *Matthew,*

Ματθάν, *Matthan.*

Mat. 1:15. and Eleazar begat *Matthan;* and *Matthan*
    begat Jacob;

Ματθάτ, *Matthat.*

Lu. 3:24. Which was (the son) of *Matthat,*
    29. which was (the son) of *Matthat,*

Ματθίας, *Matthias.*

Acts 1:23. who was surnamed Justus, and *Matthias;*
    26. the lot fell upon *Matthias;*

Ματταθά, *Mattatha.*

Lu. 3:31. which was (the son) of *Mattatha,*

Ματταθίας, *Mattathias.*

Lu. 3:25. Which was (the son) of *Mattathias;*
    26. which was (the son) of *Mattathias,*

Μελεᾶς, *Meleas.*

Lu. 3:31. Which was (the son) of *Melea,*

Μελίτη, *Melitee.*

Acts28: 1. the island was called *Melita.*

Μελχί, *Melki.*

Lu. 3:24. which was (the son) of *Melchi,*
28. Which was (the son) of *Melchi,*

Μελχισεδέκ, *Melkisedek.*

Heb 5: 6. after the order of *Melchisedec.*
10. after the order of *Melchisedec.*
6:20. after the order of *Melchisedec.*
7: 1. For this *Melchisedec,* king of Salem,
10. when *Melchisedec* met him.
11. rise after the order of *Melchisedec,*
15. after the similitude of *Melchisedec*
17. after the order of *Melchisedec.*
21. after the order of *Melchisedec :*

Μεσοποταμία, *Mesopotamia.*

Acts 2: 9. and the dwellers in *Mesopotamia,*
7: 2. when he was in *Mesopotamia,*

Μεσσίας, *Messias.*

Joh. 1:41(42). We have found the *Messias,*
4:25. I know that *Messias* cometh,

Μῆδος, *Meedos.*

Acts 2: 9. Parthians, and *Medes,* and Elamites,

Μίλητος, *Mileetos.*

Acts20:15. the next (day) we came to *Miletus.*
17. from *Miletus* he sent to Ephesus,
2Ti. 4:20. Trophimus have I left at *Miletum*

Μιτυλήνη, *Mituleenee.*

Acts20:14. and came to *Mitylene.*

Μιχαήλ, *Mikaeel.*

Jude 9. Yet *Michael* the archangel,
Rev.12: 7. *Michael* and his angels fought

Μνάσων, *Mnasōn.*

Acts21:16. brought with them one *Mnason* of Cyprus,

Μολόχ, *Molok.*

Acts 7:43. took up the tabernacle of *Moloch,*

Μύρα, *Mura.*

Acts27: 5. to *Myra,* (a city) of Lycia.

Μυσία, *Musia.*

Acts16: 7. After they were come to *Mysia,*
8. passing by *Mysia* came down to Troas.

Μωσεύς, *Mōsūs.*

Mat.23: 2. Pharisees sit in *Moses'* seat:
Mar 9: 4. appeared unto them Elias with *Moses :*
5. one for thee, and one for *Moses,*
12:26. read in the book of *Moses,*
Lu. 2:22. according to the law of *Moses*
9:33. one for *Moses,* and one for Elias:
16:29. They have *Moses* and the prophets ;
31. If they hear not *Moses* and the
24:27. And beginning at *Moses* and all
44. written in the law of *Moses,*
Joh. 1:17. For the law was given by *Moses,*
7:22. not because it is of *Moses,*
23. law of *Moses* should not be broken ;
9:28. but we are *Moses'* disciples.
Acts13:39. justified by the law of *Moses.*
21:21. among the Gentiles to forsake *Moses,*
28:23. both out of the law of *Moses,*
Ro. 5:14. death reigned from Adam to *Moses,*
1Co. 9: 9. written in the law of *Moses,*
2Co. 3: 7. stedfastly behold the face of *Moses*
Heb 3:16. came out of Egypt by *Moses.*
10:28. He that despised *Moses'* law
Jude 9. disputed about the body of *Moses,*
Rev.15: 3. And they sing the song of *Moses*

See also Μωσῆς, Μωϋσεύς & Μωϋσῆς.

Μωσῆς, *Mōsees.*

Mat. 8: 4. the gift that *Moses* commanded,
17: 3. appeared unto them *Moses* and
4. one for *Moses,* and one for Elias.
19: 7. Why did *Moses* then command to
8. *Moses* because of the hardness
22:24. Saying, Master, *Moses* said,
Mar 1:44. those things which *Moses* commanded,
7:10. *Moses* said, Honour thy father
10: 3. What did *Moses* command you ?
4. And they said, *Moses* suffered to write
12:19. Master, *Moses* wrote unto us,
Lu. 5:14. according as *Moses* commanded,
9:30. which were *Moses* and Elias:
20:28. Saying, Master, *Moses* wrote
37. even *Moses* shewed at the bush,
Joh. 1:45(46). of whom *Moses* in the law,
3:14. as *Moses* lifted up the serpent
5:45. (even) *Moses,* in whom ye trust.
46. For had ye believed *Moses,*
6:32. *Moses* gave you not that bread
7:19. Did not *Moses* give you the law,
22. *Moses* therefore gave unto you
8: 5. *Moses* in the law commanded us,
9:29. We know that God spake unto *Moses :*
Acts 3:22. For *Moses* truly said unto the fathers,
6:11. blasphemous words against *Moses,*
7:20. In which time *Moses* was born,
22. *Moses* was learned in all the wisdom
29. Then fled *Moses* at this saying,

Acts 7:31. When *Moses* saw (it), he wondered
    32. Then *Moses* trembled, and durst not
    40. for (as for) this *Moses*, which brought
    44. had appointed, speaking unto *Moses*,
  15:21. For *Moses* of old time hath
  26:22. the prophets and *Moses* did say
Ro. 9:15. For he saith to *Moses*, I will
  10: 5. *Moses* describeth the righteousness
    19. First *Moses* saith, I will
1Co.10: 2. And were all baptized unto *Moses*
2Co. 3:13. not as *Moses*, (which) put a vail
    15. even unto this day, when *Moses* is read,
Heb 3: 2. as also *Moses* (was faithful) in all
    3. worthy of more glory than *Moses*,
    5. And *Moses* verily (was) faithful
  7:14. of which tribe *Moses* spake nothing
  8: 5. as *Moses* was admonished of God
 11:23. By faith *Moses*, when he was born,
    24. By faith *Moses*, when he was come
 12:21. *Moses* said, I exceedingly fear
    See also Μωϋσῆς, Μωσεύς & Μωϋσεύς.

Μωϋσεύς, *Mōŭsŭs.*

Acts15: 1. circumcised after the manner of *Moses*,
    5. to keep the law of *Moses*.
2Ti. 3: 8. as Jannes and Jambres withstood *Moses*,
Heb 9:19. when *Moses* had spoken every precept
    See also Μωσεύς, Μωσῆς & Μωϋσῆς.

Μωϋσῆς, *Mōŭsees.*

Acts 6:14. customs which *Moses* delivered us.
  7:35. This *Moses* whom they refused,
    37. This is that *Moses*, which said unto
    See also Μωσεύς, Μωσῆς & Μωϋσεύς.

═══════════

Ναασσών, *Naässōn.*

Mat. 1: 4. Aminadab begat *Naasson*; and *Naasson* begat Salmon;
Lu. 3:32. which was (the son) of *Naasson*,

Ναγγαί, *Nangai.*

Lu. 3:25. which was (the son) of *Nagge*,

Ναζαραῖος, see Ναζωραῖος.

Ναζαρέθ, -ρέτ, *Nazareth, -ret.*

Mat. 2:23. dwelt in a city called *Nazareth*:
  4:13. And leaving *Nazareth*, he came
 21:11. Jesus the prophet of *Nazareth*
Mar 1: 9. that Jesus came from *Nazareth*
Lu. 1:26. a city of Galilee, named *Nazareth*,
  2: 4. out of the city of *Nazareth*,
    39. to their own city *Nazareth*.
    51. with them, and came to *Nazareth*.
  4:16. And he came to *Nazareth*,
Joh. 1:45(46). Jesus of *Nazareth*, the son of Joseph.
   46(47). good thing come out of *Nazareth*?
Acts10:38. How God anointed Jesus of *Nazareth*

Ναζαρηνός, *Nazareenos.*

Mar 1:24. do with thee, thou Jesus of *Nazareth*?
 14:67. thou also wast with Jesus of *Nazareth*.
 16: 6. Ye seek Jesus of *Nazareth*,
Lu. 4:34. do with thee, (thou) Jesus of *Nazareth*?

Ναζωραῖος, *Nazōraios.*

Mat. 2:23. He shall be called a *Nazarene*.
 26:71. was also with Jesus of *Nazareth*,
Mar 10:47. heard that it was Jesus of *Nazareth*,
Lu. 18:37. that Jesus of *Nazareth* passeth by.
 24:19. Concerning Jesus of *Nazareth*,
Joh.18: 5. answered him, Jesus of *Nazareth*.
    7. And they said, Jesus of *Nazareth*.
 19:19. JESUS OF *NAZARETH* THE KING OF THE JEWS.
Acts 2:22. Jesus of *Nazareth*, a man approved of God
  3: 6. In the name of Jesus Christ of *Nazareth*
  4:10. name of Jesus Christ of *Nazareth*,
  6:14. that this Jesus of *Nazareth* shall destroy
 22: 8. Jesus of *Nazareth*, whom thou persecutest.
 24: 5. ringleader of the sect of the *Nazarenes*:
 26: 9. to the name of Jesus of *Nazareth*.

Ναθάν, *Nathan.*

Lu. 3:31. which was (the son) of *Nathan*,

Ναθαναήλ, *Nathanaeel.*

Joh. 1:45(46). Philip findeth *Nathanael*, and saith
  46(47). And *Nathanael* said unto him,
  47(48). Jesus saw *Nathanael* coming to him,
  48(49). *Nathanael* saith unto him, Whence
  49(50). *Nathanael* answered and saith
 21: 2. and *Nathanael* of Cana in Galilee,

Ναΐν, *Naïn.*

Lu. 7:11. he went into a city called *Nain*;

Ναούμ, *Naoum.*

Lu. 3:25. which was (the son) of *Naum*,

Νάρκισσος, *Narkissos.*

Ro. 16:11. that be of the (houshold) of *Narcissus*,

Ναχώρ, *Nakōr*

Lu. 3:34. which was (the son) of *Nachor*,

Νεάπολις, *Neapolis.*

Acts16:11. and the next (day) to *Neapolis*;

Νεεμάν, *Neëman*.

Lu. 4:27. saving *Naaman* the Syrian.

Νεφθαλείμ, *Nephthalīm*.

Mat. 4:13. borders of Zabulon and *Nephthalim :*
15. and the land of *Nephthalim*,
Rev. 7: 6. Of the tribe of *Nepthalim* (were) sealed

Νηρεύς, *Neerūs*.

Ro. 16:15. Salute Philologus, and Julia, *Nereus,*

Νηρί, *Neeri*.

Lu. 3:27. which was (the son) of *Neri,*

Νίγερ, *Niger*.

Acts 13: 1. and Simeon that was called *Niger,*

Νικάνωρ, *Nikanōr*.

Acts 6: 5. and Prochorus, and *Nicanor*, and

Νικόδημος, *Nikodeemos*.

Joh. 3: 1. named *Nicodemus*, a ruler of the Jews :
4. *Nicodemus* saith unto him,
9. *Nicodemus* answered and said unto him,
7:50. *Nicodemus* saith unto them,
19:39. And there came also *Nicodemus,*

Νικολαΐτης, *Nikolaïtees*.

Rev. 2: 6. the deeds of the *Nicolaitanes,*
15. the doctrine of the *Nicolaitanes,*

Νικόλαος, *Nikolaos*.

Acts 6: 5. *Nicolas* a proselyte of Antioch :

Νικόπολις, *Nikopolis*.

Tit. 3:12. to come unto me to *Nicopolis :*

Νινευΐ, *Ninūï*.

Lu. 11:32. The men of *Nineve* shall rise

Νινευΐτης, *Ninūïtees*.

Mat. 12:41. The men of *Nineveh* shall rise
Lu. 11:30. was a sign unto the *Ninevites,*

Νότος, see among Appellatives.

Νυμφᾶς, *Numphas*.

Col. 4:15. and *Nymphas*, and the church

Νῶε, *Noë*.

Mat. 24:37. But as the days of *Noe* (were),
38. that *Noe* entered into the ark,
Lu. 3:36. which was (the son) of *Noe,*
17:26. as it was in the days of *Noe,*
27. day that *Noe* entered into the ark,
Heb 11: 7. By faith *Noah*, being warned of God
1 Pet. 3:20. of God waited in the days of *Noah,*
2 Pet. 2: 5. but saved *Noah* the eighth (person),

'Οζίας, *Ozias*.

Mat. 1: 8. and Joram begat *Ozias :*
9. And *Ozias* begat Joatham ;

'Ολυμπᾶς, *Olumpas*.

Ro. 16:15. and *Olympas*, and all the saints

'Ονήσιμος, *Oneesimos*.

Col. 4: 9. With *Onesimus*, a faithful and
Philem 10. I beseech thee for my son *Onesimus,*

'Ονησίφορος, *Oneesiphoros*.

2 Ti. 1:16. unto the house of *Onesiphorus :*
4:19. and the houshold of *Onesiphorus.*

Οὐρβανός, *Ourbanos*.

Ro. 16: 9. Salute *Urbane*, our helper in Christ,

Οὐρίας, *Ourias*.

Mat. 1: 6. (that had been the wife) of *Urias ;*

Παμφυλία, *Pamphulia*.

Acts 2:10. Phrygia, and *Pamphylia*, in Egypt,
13:13. they came to Perga in *Pamphylia :*
14:24. Pisidia, they came to *Pamphylia.*
15:38. departed from them from *Pamphylia,*
27: 5. sea of Cilicia and *Pamphylia,*

Πάρθος, *Parthos*.

Acts 2: 9. *Parthians*, and Medes, and Elamites,

Παρμενᾶς, *Parmenas*.

Acts 6: 5. and Timon, and *Parmenas,* and

Πάσχα, see among Appellatives.

Πάταρα, *Patara.*

Acts21: 1. and from thence unto *Patara* :

Πάτμος, *Patmos.*

Rev. 1: 9. in the isle that is called *Patmos,*

Πατρόϐας, *Patrobas.*

Ro. 16:14. *Patrobas,* Hermes, and the brethren

Παῦλος, *Paulos.*

(The Deputy.)

Acts13: 7. with the deputy of the country, Sergius *Paulus,*

Παῦλος, *Paulos.*

Acts13: 9. Then Saul, who also (is called) *Paul,*
13. Now when *Paul* and his company (lit. those about *Paul*)
16. Then *Paul* stood up, and beckoning with (his) hand
43. followed *Paul* and Barnabas:
45. which were spoken by *Paul,*
46. Then *Paul* and Barnabas waxed bold,
50. persecution against *Paul* and Barnabas,
14: 9. The same heard *Paul* speak:
11. saw what *Paul* had done,
12. and *Paul,* Mercurius, because he was
14. the apostles, Barnabas and *Paul,* heard (of),
19. and, having stoned *Paul,* drew (him) out
15: 2. When therefore *Paul* and Barnabas had
— they determined that *Paul* and Barnabas,
12. gave audience to Barnabas and *Paul,*
22. to Antioch with *Paul* and Barnabas;
25. with our beloved Barnabas and *Paul,*
35. *Paul* also and Barnabas continued in
36. *Paul* said unto Barnabas,
38. But *Paul* thought not good to take him
40. And *Paul* chose Silas, and departed,
16: 3. Him would *Paul* have to go forth with him ;
9. a vision appeared to *Paul* in the night;
14. unto the things which were spoken of *Paul.*
17. The same followed *Paul* and us,
18. But *Paul,* being grieved, turned and
19. they caught *Paul* and Silas, and drew
25. And at midnight *Paul* and Silas prayed,
28. But *Paul* cried with a loud voice,
29. and fell down before *Paul* and Silas,
36. told this saying to *Pai í,*
37. But *Paul* said unto them,
17: 2. And *Paul,* as his manner was,
4. and consorted with *Paul* and Silas ;
10. sent away *Paul* and Silas by night
13. was preached of *Paul* at Berea,
14. sent away *Paul* to go as it were
15. they that conducted *Paul* brought
16. Now while *Paul* waited for them
22. Then *Paul* stood in the midst of Mars' hill,
33. So *Paul* departed from among them.
18: 1. After these things *Paul* departed
5. *Paul* was pressed in the spirit,

Acts18: 9. spake the Lord to *Paul* in the night
12. with one accord against *Paul,*
14. And when *Paul* was now about
18. And *Paul* (after this) tarried (there)
19: 1. *Paul* having passed through the
4. Then said *Paul,* John verily
6. And when *Paul* had laid (his) hands
11. miracles by the hands of *Paul :*
13. Jesus whom *Paul* preacheth.
15. Jesus I know, and *Paul* I know ;
21. *Paul* purposed in the spirit,
26. this *Paul* hath persuaded and turned
29. of Macedonia, *Paul's* companions
30. when *Paul* would have entered in
20: 1. *Paul* called unto (him) the disciples,
7. *Paul* preached unto them,
9. and as *Paul* was long preaching,
10. *Paul* went down, and fell on him,
13. there intending to take in *Paul :*
16. For *Paul* had determined to sail
37. and fell on *Paul's* neck, and kissed him,
21: 4. who said to *Paul* through the Spirit,
8. we that were of *Paul's* company
11. he took *Paul's* girdle, and bound his own hands
13. Then *Paul* answered, What mean ye
18. *Paul* went in with us unto James ;
26. Then *Paul* took the men, and the next day
29. they supposed that *Paul* had brought
30. took *Paul,* and drew him out of the temple:
32. they left beating of *Paul.*
37. And as *Paul* was to be led into the castle,
39. But *Paul* said, I am a man (which am)
40. *Paul* stood on the stairs, and beckoned
22:25. *Paul* said unto the centurion
28. And *Paul* said, But I was (free) born.
30. brought *Paul* down, and set him
23: 1. And *Paul,* earnestly beholding the council,
3. Then said *Paul* unto him,
5. said *Paul,* I wist not, brethren,
6. when *Paul* perceived that the one part
10. lest *Paul* should have been pulled in pieces
11. Be of good cheer, *Paul :*
12. till they had killed *Paul.*
14. nothing until we have slain *Paul.*
16. And when *Paul's* sister's son
— the castle, and told *Paul.*
17. *Paul* called one of the centurions
18. and said, *Paul* the prisoner called
20. bring down *Paul* to morrow
24. that they may set *Paul* on, and bring
31. took *Paul,* and brought (him)
33. presented *Paul* also before him.
24: 1. informed the governor against *Paul.*
10. Then *Paul,* after that the governor
23. a centurion to keep *Paul,*
24. he sent for *Paul,* and heard him
26. money should have been given him of *Paul,*
27. left *Paul* bound.
25: 2. informed him against *Paul,*
4. *Paul* should be kept at Cæsarea,
6. commanded *Paul* to be brought.
7. grievous complaints against *Paul,*
9. answered *Paul,* and said,
10. Then said *Paul,* I stand at Cæsar's
14. Festus declared *Paul's* cause
19. *Paul* affirmed to be alive.
21. But when *Paul* had appealed to be
23. *Paul* was brought forth.
26: 1. Agrippa said unto *Paul,*
— *Paul* stretched forth the hand,

Acts26:24. *Paul*, thou art beside thyself;
  28. Agrippa said unto *Paul*,
  29. *Paul* said, I would to God,
 27: 1. delivered *Paul* and certain other
  3. Julius courteously entreated *Paul*,
  9. *Paul* admonished (them),
  11. which were spoken by *Paul*.
  21. *Paul* stood forth in the midst of them,
  24. Saying, Fear not, *Paul*;
  31. *Paul* said to the centurion
  33. *Paul* besought (them) all to take meat,
  43. willing to save *Paul*, kept them
 28: 3. when *Paul* had gathered a bundle
  8. *Paul* entered in, and prayed,
  15. whom when *Paul* saw, he thanked God,
  16. but *Paul* was suffered to dwell
  17. *Paul* called the chief of the Jews
  25. after that *Paul* had spoken
  30. *Paul* dwelt two whole years
Ro. 1: 1. *Paul*, a servant of Jesus Christ,
1Co. 1: 1. *Paul*, called (to be) an apostle of
  12. I am of *Paul*; and I of Apollos;
  13. was *Paul* crucified for you? or were ye
   baptized in the name of *Paul*?
 3: 4. I am of *Paul*; and another, I (am) of
  5. Who then is *Paul*, and who (is) Apollos,
  22. Whether *Paul*, or Apollos, or Cephas,
 16:21. The salutation of (me) *Paul*
2Co. 1: 1. *Paul*, an apostle of Jesus Christ
 10: 1. Now I *Paul* myself beseech you
Gal. 1: 1. *Paul*, an apostle, not of men,
 5: 2. Behold, I *Paul* say unto you,
Eph. 1: 1. *Paul*, an apostle of Jesus Christ
 3: 1. For this cause I *Paul*, the prisoner
Phi. 1: 1. *Paul* and Timotheus, the servants
Col. 1: 1. *Paul*, an apostle of Jesus Christ
  23. whereof I *Paul* am made a minister;
 4:18. The salutation by the hand of me *Paul*.
1Th. 1: 1. *Paul*, and Silvanus, and Timotheus,
 2:18. even I *Paul*, once and again;
2Th. 1: 1. *Paul*, and Silvanus, and Timotheus,
 3:17. The salutation of *Paul* with mine own
   hand,
1Ti. 1: 1. *Paul*, an apostle of Jesus Christ
2Ti. 1: 1. *Paul*, an apostle of Jesus Christ
Tit. 1: 1. *Paul*, a servant of God, and an apostle of
   Jesus Christ,
Philem 1. *Paul*, a prisoner of Jesus Christ,
  9. being such an one as *Paul* the aged,
  19. I *Paul* have written (it) with mine
2Pet.3:15. as our beloved brother *Paul* also

Πάφος, *Paphos.*

Acts13: 6. gone through the isle unto *Paphos*,
  13. and his company loosed from *Paphos*,

Πέργαμος, *Pergamos.*

Rev. 1:11. unto Smyrna, and unto *Pergamos*,
 2:12. of the church in *Pergamos* write;

Πέργη, *Pergee.*

Acts13:13. they came to *Perga* in Pamphylia:
  14. when they departed from *Perga*,
 14:25. had preached the word in *Perga*,

Περσίς, *Persis.*

Ro. 16:12. Salute the beloved *Persis*,

Πέτρος, *Petros.*

Mat. 4:18. Simon called *Peter*, and Andrew
 8:14. was come into *Peter's* house,
 10: 2. The first, Simon, who is called *Peter*,
 14:28. And *Peter* answered him and said,
  29. And when *Peter* was come down out
 15:15. Then answered *Peter* and said
 16:16. And Simon *Peter* answered and said,
  18. unto thee, That thou art *Peter*,
  22. Then *Peter* took him, and began
  23. turned, and said unto *Peter*,
 17: 1. Jesus taketh *Peter*, James, and John
  4. Then answered *Peter*, and said
  24. tribute (money) came to *Peter*,
  26. *Peter* saith unto him,
 18:21. Then came *Peter* to him,
 19:27. Then answered *Peter* and said unto him,
 26:33. *Peter* answered and said
  35. *Peter* said unto him,
  37. took with him *Peter* and the two sons
  40. and saith unto *Peter*, What, could
  58. But *Peter* followed him afar off
  69. Now *Peter* sat without
  73. and said to *Peter*, Surely thou also
  75. And *Peter* remembered the word
Mar 3:16. And Simon he surnamed *Peter*;
 5:37. to follow him, save *Peter*, and James, and
   John
 8:29. And *Peter* answereth and saith
  32. And *Peter* took him, and began
  33. he rebuked *Peter*, saying,
 9: 2. taketh (with him) *Peter*, and James, and
   John,
  5. And *Peter* answered and said
 10:28. Then *Peter* began to say unto him, Lo,
 11:21. And *Peter* calling to remembrance
 13: 3. *Peter* and James and John and Andrew
   asked
 14:29. But *Peter* said unto him,
  33. taketh with him *Peter* and James and
   John,
  37. and saith unto *Peter*, Simon, sleepest
  54. And *Peter* followed him afar off,
  66. And as *Peter* was beneath in
  67. when she saw *Peter* warming
  70. said again to *Peter*, Surely thou
  72. And *Peter* called to mind
 16: 7. tell his disciples and *Peter*
Lu. 5: 8. When Simon *Peter* saw (it), he fell
 6:14. Simon, whom he also named *Peter*,
 8:45. *Peter* and they that were with
  51. to go in, save *Peter*, and James, and John,
 9:20. *Peter* answering said, The Christ of God.
  28. he took *Peter* and John and James,
  32. But *Peter* and they that were with
  33. *Peter* said unto Jesus,
 12:41. Then *Peter* said unto him,
 18:28. Then *Peter* said, Lo, we have left
 22: 8. And he sent *Peter* and John, saying,
  34. I tell thee, *Peter*, the cock
  54. And *Peter* followed afar off.
  55. *Peter* sat down among them.
  58. *Peter* said, Man, I am not.
  60. *Peter* said, Man, I know not
  61. and looked upon *Peter*. And *Peter* remembered the word

Lu. 22:62. And *Peter* went out, and wept bitterly.
24:12. Then arose *Peter*, and ran
Joh. 1:40(41). Andrew, Simon *Peter's* brother.
44(45). Bethsaida, the city of Andrew and *Peter*.
6: 8. Simon *Peter's* brother, saith unto him,
68. Simon *Peter* answered him,
13: 6. Then cometh he to Simon *Peter* :
8. *Peter* saith unto him,
9. Simon *Peter* saith unto him,
24. Simon *Peter* therefore beckoned
36. Simon *Peter* said unto him,
37. *Peter* said unto him, Lord, why
18:10. Simon *Peter* having a sword
11. said Jesus unto *Peter*, Put up
15. And Simon *Peter* followed Jesus,
16. *Peter* stood at the door without.
— and brought in *Peter*.
17. that kept the door unto *Peter*,
18. and *Peter* stood with them,
25. Simon *Peter* stood and warmed himself.
26. whose ear *Peter* cut off,
27. *Peter* then denied again:
20: 2. and cometh to Simon *Peter*,
3. *Peter* therefore went forth,
4. the other disciple did outrun *Peter*,
6. Then cometh Simon *Peter*
21: 2. together Simon *Peter*, and Thomas
3. Simon *Peter* saith unto them,
7. saith unto *Peter*, It is the Lord. Now when Simon *Peter* heard that
11. Simon *Peter* went up, and drew the net
15. Jesus saith to Simon *Peter*,
17. *Peter* was grieved because he said
20. Then *Peter*, turning about, seeth
21. *Peter* seeing him saith
Acts 1:13. abode both *Peter*, and James, and John,
15. in those days *Peter* stood up
2:14. But *Peter*, standing up with the eleven,
37. said unto *Peter* and to the rest
38. Then *Peter* said unto them,
3: 1. *Peter* and John went up together
3. Who seeing *Peter* and John
4. *Peter*, fastening his eyes
6. *Peter* said, Silver and gold have I none ;
11. held *Peter* and John,
12. when *Peter* saw (it), he answered
4: 8. *Peter*, filled with the Holy Ghost,
13. the boldness of *Peter* and John,
19. *Peter* and John answered and said
5: 3. But *Peter* said, Ananias, why
8. And *Peter* answered unto her,
9. Then *Peter* said unto her,
15. the shadow of *Peter* passing by
29. *Peter* and the (other) apostles
8:14. sent unto them *Peter* and John :
20. But *Peter* said unto him,
9:32. as *Peter* passed throughout all
34. And *Peter* said unto him,
38. heard that *Peter* was there,
39. *Peter* arose and went with them.
40. *Peter* put them all forth,
— saw *Peter*, she sat up.
10: 5. whose surname is *Peter* :
9. *Peter* went up upon the housetop
13. Rise, *Peter* ; kill, and eat.
14. *Peter* said, Not so, Lord ;
17. while *Peter* doubted in himself
18. which was surnamed *Peter*,
19. While *Peter* thought on the vision,
21. Then *Peter* went down
23. on the morrow *Peter* went away

Acts10:25. as *Peter* was coming in,
26. But *Peter* took him up,
32. Simon, whose surname is *Peter* ;
34. Then *Peter* opened (his) mouth,
44. While *Peter* yet spake
45. as many as came with *Peter*,
46. Then answered *Peter*,
11: 2. *Peter* was come up to Jerusalem,
4. *Peter* rehearsed (the matter)
7. Arise, *Peter* ; slay and eat.
13. whose surname is *Peter* ;
12: 3. proceeded further to take *Peter*
5. *Peter* therefore was kept in prison :
6. the same night *Peter* was sleeping
7. smote *Peter* on the side,
11. *Peter* was come to himself,
13. as *Peter* knocked at the door
14. she knew *Peter's* voice,
— how *Peter* stood before the gate.
16. But *Peter* continued knocking :
18. what was become of *Peter*.
15: 7. *Peter* rose up, and said unto them,
Gal. 1:18. went up to Jerusalem to see *Peter*,
2: 7. of the circumcision (was) unto *Peter* ;
8. wrought effectually in *Peter*
11. when *Peter* was come to Antioch,
14. I said unto *Peter* before (them) all,
1Pet.1: 1. *Peter*, an apostle of Jesus Christ,
2Pet.1: 1. Simon *Peter*, a servant and an apostle of Jesus Christ,

---

Πιλάτος, *Pilatos*.

Mat.27: 2. and delivered him to Pontius *Pilate*
13. Then said *Pilate* unto him,
17. gathered together, *Pilate* said unto them,
22. *Pilate* saith unto them, What
24. When *Pilate* saw that he could
58. He went to *Pilate*, and begged the body of Jesus. Then *Pilate* commanded the
62. Pharisees came together unto *Pilate*,
65. *Pilate* said unto them, Ye have
Mar15: 1. and delivered (him) to *Pilate*.
2. *Pilate* asked him, Art thou
4. And *Pilate* asked him again,
5. nothing ; so that *Pilate* marvelled.
9. But *Pilate* answered them,
12. *Pilate* answered and said again
14. Then *Pilate* said unto them,
15. And (so) *Pilate*, willing to content
43. went in boldly unto *Pilate*, and craved
44. And *Pilate* marvelled if he were
Lu. 3: 1. *Pilate* being governor of Judæa,
13: 1. whose blood *Pilate* had mingled
23: 1. and led him unto *Pilate*.
3. And *Pilate* asked him, saying,
4. Then said *Pilate* to the chief priests
6. When *Pilate* heard of Galilee,
11. and sent him again to *Pilate*.
12. *Pilate* and Herod were made friends
13. And *Pilate*, when he had called
20. *Pilate* therefore, willing to release
24. And *Pilate* gave sentence that it
52. This (man) went unto *Pilate*,
Joh.18:29. *Pilate* then went out unto them,
31. Then said *Pilate* unto them,
33. Then *Pilate* entered into the judgment hall
35. *Pilate* answered, Am I a Jew ?
37. *Pilate* therefore said unto him,
38. *Pilate* saith unto him, What is truth ?

Joh.19: 1. *Pilate* therefore took Jesus, and scourged (him).
4. *Pilate* therefore went forth again,
6. *Pilate* saith unto them, Take ye him,
8. When *Pilate* therefore heard that saying,
10. Then saith *Pilate* unto him, Speakest
12. thenceforth *Pilate* sought to release him:
13. When *Pilate* therefore heard that saying,
15. *Pilate* saith unto them, Shall I crucify
19. And *Pilate* wrote a title, and put
21. chief priests of the Jews to *Pilate*,
22. *Pilate* answered, What I have written
31. besought *Pilate* that their legs
38. besought *Pilate* that he might take away the body of Jesus: and *Pilate* gave (him) leave.
Acts 3:13. denied him in the presence of *Pilate*,
4:27. both Herod, and Pontius *Pilate*,
13:28. yet desired they *Pilate* that he should
1Ti. 6:13. who before Pontius *Pilate* witnessed

Πισιδία, *Pisidia.*

Acts13:14. they came to Antioch in *Pisidia*,
14:24. after they had passed throughout *Pisidia*,

Ποντικός, *Pontikos.*

Acts18: 2. a certain Jew named Aquila, born in *Pontus*,

Πόντιος, *Pontios.*

Mat.27: 2. and delivered him to *Pontius* Pilate
Lu. 3: 1. *Pontius* Pilate being governor of Judæa,
Acts 4:27. both Herod, and *Pontius* Pilate,
1Ti. 6:13. who before *Pontius* Pilate witnessed

Πόντος, *Pontos.*

Acts 2: 9. and Cappadocia, in *Pontus*, and Asia,
1Pet.1: 1. to the strangers scattered throughout *Pontus*,

Πόπλιος, *Poplios.*

Acts28: 7. whose name was *Publius*;
8. the father of *Publius* lay sick of a fever

Πόρκιος, *Porkios.*

Acts24:27. after two years *Porcius* Festus

Ποτίολοι, *Potioloi.*

Acts28:13. and we came the next day to *Puteoli*:

Πούδης, *Poudees.*

2Ti. 4:21. Eubulus greeteth thee, and *Pudens*,

Πρίσκα, *Priska.*

2Ti. 4:19. Salute *Prisca* and Aquila,

Πρίσκιλλα, *Priskilla.*

Acts18: 2. from Italy, with his wife *Priscilla*;
18. and with him *Priscilla* and Aquila;
26. when Aquila and *Priscilla* had heard,
Ro. 16: 3. Greet *Priscilla* and Aquila my helpers
1Co.16:19. Aquila and *Priscilla* salute you

Πρόχορος, *Prokoros.*

Acts 6: 5. and Philip, and *Prochorus*, and Nicanor,

Πτολεμαΐς, *Ptolemaïs.*

Acts21: 7. from Tyre, we came to *Ptolemais*,

Πύθων, *Puthōn.*

Acts16:16. possessed with a spirit of *divination* (lit. of *Pytho*)

Ῥαάβ, *Raäb.*

Heb 11:31. By faith the harlot *Rahab* perished not
Jas. 2:25. was not *Rahab* the harlot justified
See also Ῥαχαβ.

Ῥαγαῦ, *Ragau.*

Lu. 3:35. which was (the son) of *Ragau*,

Ῥαμά, *Rama.*

Mat. 2:18. In *Rama* was there a voice heard,

Ῥαχάβ, *Rakab.*

Mat. 1: 5. Salmon begat Booz of *Rachab*;
See also Ῥαάβ.

Ῥαχήλ, *Rakeel.*

Mat. 2:18. *Rachel* weeping (for) her children,

Ῥεβέκκα, *Rebekka.*

Ro. 9:10. but when *Rebecca* also had conceived

Ῥεμφάν, *Remphan.*

Acts 7:43. and the star of your god *Remphan*,

Ῥήγιον, *Reegion.*

Acts28:13. fetched a compass, and came to *Rhegium*:

Ῥησά, *Reesa.*

Lu. 3:27. which was (the son) of *Rhesa*,

'Ροβοάμ, *Roboam.*

Mat. 1: 7. And Solomon begat *Roboam;* and *Roboam* begat Abia;

'Ρόδη, *Rodee.*

Acts 12:13. a damsel came to hearken, named *Rhoda.*

'Ρόδος, *Rodos.*

Acts 21: 1. and the (day) following unto *Rhodes,*

'Ρουβήν, *Roubeen.*

Rev. 7: 5. Of the tribe of *Reuben* (were) sealed

'Ρούθ, *Routh.*

Mat. 1: 5. Booz begat Obed of *Ruth;*

'Ρούφος, *Rouphos.*

Mar 15:21. the father of Alexander and *Rufus,*
Ro. 16:13. Salute *Rufus* chosen in the Lord,

'Ρωμαϊκός, *Rōmaïkos.*

Lu. 23:38. letters of Greek, and *Latin,* and Hebrew,

'Ρωμαῖος, *Rōmaios.*

Joh.11:48. the *Romans* shall come and take away
Acts 2:10. and strangers of *Rome,* Jews
16:21. neither to observe, being *Romans.*
37. openly uncondemned, being *Romans,*
38. when they heard that they were *Romans.*
22:25. to scourge a man that is a *Roman,*
26. for this man is a *Roman.*
27. Tell me, art thou a *Roman?*
29. after he knew that he was a *Roman,*
23:27. understood that he was a *Roman.*
25:16. It is not the manner of the *Romans*
28:17. into the hands of the *Romans.*

'Ρωμαϊστί, *Romaïsti.*

Joh.19:20. in Hebrew, (and) Greek, (and) *Latin.*

'Ρώμη, *Rōmee.*

Acts 18: 2. all Jews to depart from *Rome:*
19:21. I must also see *Rome.*
23:11. thou bear witness also at *Rome.*
28:14. and so we went toward *Rome.*
16. And when we came to *Rome,*
Ro. 1: 7. To all that be in *Rome,*
15. gospel to you that are at *Rome* also.
2Ti. 1:17. But, when he was in *Rome,*

===

Σαδδουκαῖος, *Saddoukaios.*

Mat. 3: 7. many of the Pharisees and *Sadducees*

Mat.16: 1. The Pharisees also with the *Sadducees*
6. the leaven of the Pharisees and of the *Sadducees.*
11. leaven of the Pharisees and of the *Sadducees?*
12. doctrine of the Pharisees and of the *Sadducees.*
22:23. came to him the *Sadducees,*
34. put the *Sadducees* to silence,
Mar 12:18. Then come unto him the *Sadducees,*
Lu. 20:27. certain of the *Sadducees,*
Acts 4: 1. and the *Sadducees,* came upon them,
5:17. which is the sect of the *Sadducees,*
23: 6. the one part were *Sadducees,*
7. a dissension between the Pharisees and the *Sadducees:*
8. For the *Sadducees* say

Σαδώκ, *Sadōk.*

Mat. 1:14. Azor begat *Sadoc;* and *Sadoc* begat

Σαλά, *Sala.*

Lu. 3:35. Heber, which was (the son) of *Sala,*

Σαλαθιήλ, *Salathieel.*

Mat. 1:12. Jechonias begat *Salathiel;* and *Salathiel*
Lu. 3:27. Zorobabel, which was (the son) of *Salathiel,*

Σαλαμίς, *Salamis.*

Acts 13: 5. And when they were at *Salamis,*

Σαλείμ, *Salim.*

Joh. 3:23. in Ænon near to *Salim,*

Σαλήμ, *Saleem.*

Heb 7: 1. this Melchisedec, king of *Salem,*
2. also King of *Salem,*

Σαλμών, *Salmōn.*

Mat. 1: 4. Naasson begat *Salmon;*
5. And *Salmon* begat Booz
Lu. 3:32. Booz, which was (the son) of *Salmon,*

Σαλμώνη, *Salmōnee.*

Acts 27: 7. under Crete, over against *Salmone;*

Σαλώμη, *Salōmee.*

Mar 15:40. and of Joses, and *Salome;*
16: 1. Mary the (mother) of James, and *Salome,*

Σαμάρεια, *Samaria.*

Lu. 17:11. the midst of *Samaria* and Galilee.

Joh. 4: 4. And he must needs go through *Samaria.*
    5. to a city of *Samaria,*
    7. a woman of *Samaria* to draw water:
Acts 1: 8. and in *Samaria,* and unto the
    8: 1. the regions of Judæa and *Samaria,*
    5. Philip went down to the city of *Samaria,*
    9. and b·witched the people of *Samaria,*
    14. *Samaria* had received the word
    9:31. and Galilee and *Samaria,*
    15: 3. through Phenice and *Samaria,*

Σαμαρείτης, *Samaritees.*

Mat.10: 5. into (any) city of the *Samaritans*
Lu. 9:52. into a village of the *Samaritans,*
    10:33. But a certain *Samaritan,*
    17:16. and he was a *Samaritan.*
Joh. 4: 9. dealings with the *Samaritans.*
    39. And many of the *Samaritans* of that city
    40. So when the *Samaritans* were come
    8:48. thou art a *Samaritan,* and hast a devil?
Acts 8:25. in many villages of the *Samaritans.*

Σαμαρεῖτις, *Samaritis.*

Joh. 4. 9. Then saith the woman of *Samaria*
    — which am a woman of *Samaria?*

Σαμοθράκη, *Samothrakee.*

Acts16:11. with a straight course to *Samothracia,*

Σάμος, *Samos.*

Acts20:15. the next (day) we arrived at *Samos,*

Σαμουήλ, *Samoueel.*

Acts 3:24. Yea, and all the prophets from *Samuel*
    13:20. until *Samuel* the prophet.
Heb11:32. David also, and *Samuel,*

Σαμψών, *Sampsōn.*

Heb11:32. and (of) *Samson* and (of) Jephthae;

Σαούλ, *Säoul.*

Acts 9: 4. *Saul, Saul,* why persecutest thou me?
    17. Brother *Saul,* the Lord, (even) Jesus,
    13:21. God gave unto them *Saul* the son of Cis,
    22: 7. *Saul, Saul,* why persecutest thou me?
    13. Brother *Saul,* receive thy sight.
    26:14. *Saul, Saul,* why persecutest thou me?

Σαπφείρη, *Sapphīree.*

Acts 5: 1. Ananias, with *Sapphira* his wife,

Σάρδεις, *Sardīs.*

Rev. 1:11. unto Thyatira, and unto *Sardis,*

Rev. 3: 1. angel of the church in *Sardis* write;
    4. Thou hast a few names even in *Sardis*

Σάρεπτα, *Sarepta.*

Lu. 4:26. was Elias sent, save unto *Sarepta,*

Σαρούχ, *Sarouk.*

Lu. 3:35. Which was (the son) of *Saruch,*

Σάῤῥα, *Sarra.*

Ro. 4:19. the deadness of *Sarah's* womb:
    9: 9. and *Sarah* shall have a son.
Heb11:11. *Sara* herself received strength
1Pet.3: 6. Even as *Sara* obeyed Abraham,

Σάρων *Sarōn.*

Acts 9:35. all that dwelt at Lydda and *Saron,*

Σατᾶν, *Satan.*

2Co.12: 7. the messenger of *Satan*

Σατανᾶς, *Satanas.*

Mat. 4:10. Get thee hence, *Satan:*
    12:26. And if *Satan* cast out *Satan,*
    16:23. Get thee behind me, *Satan:*
Mar 1:13. forty days, tempted of *Satan;*
    3:23. How can *Satan* cast out *Satan?*
    26. And if *Satan* rise up against himself,
    4:15. *Satan* cometh immediately, and
    8:33. Get thee behind me, *Satan:*
Lu. 4: 8. Get thee behind me, *Satan:*
    10:18. I beheld *Satan* as lightning
    11:18. If *Satan* also be divided
    13:16. whom *Satan* hath bound,
    22: 3. Then entered *Satan* into Judas
    31. behold, *Satan* hath desired (to have) you,
Joh.13:27. *Satan* entered into him.
Acts 5: 3. Ananias, why hath *Satan*
    26:18. and (from) the power of *Satan*
Ro. 16:20. bruise *Satan* under your feet
1Co. 5: 5. unto *Satan* for the destruction
    7: 5. that *Satan* tempt you not
2Co. 2:11. Lest *Satan* should get an advantage
    11:14. for *Satan* himself is transformed
1Th. 2:18. but *Satan* hindered us.
2Th. 2: 9. after the working of *Satan*
1Ti. 1:20. whom I have delivered unto *Satan,*
    5:15. already turned aside after *Satan.*
Rev. 2: 9. but (are) the synagogue of *Satan.*
    13. where *Satan's* seat (is):
    — where *Satan* dwelleth.
    24. known the depths of *Satan,*
    3: 9. them of the synagogue of *Satan,*
    12: 9. called the Devil, and *Satan,*
    20: 2. which is the devil, and *Satan,*
    7. *Satan* shall be loosed

Σαῦλος, *Saulos.*

Acts 7:58. whose name was *Saul.*

Acts 8: 1. And *Saul* was consenting unto his death.
3. As for *Saul*, he made havock
9: 1. And *Saul*, yet breathing out threatenings
8. And *Saul* arose from the earth;
11. for (one) called *Saul*, of Tarsus:
19. Then was *Saul* certain days
22. But *Saul* increased the more in
24. their laying await was known of *Saul*.
26. And when *Saul* was come
11:25. for to seek *Saul*:
30. by the hands of Barnabas and *Saul*.
12:25. And Barnabas and *Saul* returned
13: 1. Herod the tetrarch, and *Saul*.
2. Separate me Barnabas and *Saul*
7. who called for Barnabas and *Saul*,
9. Then *Saul*, who also (is called) Paul,

Σεϐαστός, *Sebastos*.

Acts25:21. reserved unto the hearing of *Augustus*,
25. himself hath appealed to *Augustus*,

Σεκοῦνδος, *Sekoundos*.

Acts20: 4. Aristarchus and *Secundus*;

Σελεύκεια, *Selūkīa*.

Acts13: 4. departed unto *Seleucia*;

Σεμεί, *Semeï*.

Lu. 3:26. which was (the son) of *Semei*,

Σέργιος, *Sergios*.

Acts13: 7. *Sergius* Paulus, a prudent man;

Σήθ, *Seeth*.

Lu. 3:38. which was (the son) of *Seth*,

Σήμ, *Seem*.

Lu. 3:36. which was (the son) of *Sem*,

Σιδών, *Sidōn*.

Mat.11:21. had been done in Tyre and *Sidon*,
22. It shall be more tolerable for Tyre and *Sidon*
15:21. into the coasts of Tyre and *Sidon*.
Mar 3: 8. and they about Tyre and *Sidon*,
7:24. into the borders of Tyre and *Sidon*,
31. from the coasts of Tyre and *Sidon*,
Lu. 4:26. Sarepta, (a city) of *Sidon*,
6:17. the sea coast of Tyre and *Sidon*,
10:13. done in Tyre and *Sidon*,
14. more tolerable for Tyre and *Sidon*
Acts27:3. we touched at *Sidon*.

Σιδώνιος, *Sidōnios*.

Acts12:20. with them of Tyre and *Sidon*:

Σίλας, *Silas*.

Acts15:22. Barsabas, and *Silas*, chief men
27. Judas and *Silas*, who shall also
32. Judas and *Silas*, being prophets
34. it pleased *Silas* to abide there
40. And Paul chose *Silas*, and
16:19. they caught Paul and *Silas*,
25. Paul and *Silas* prayed, and sang
29. and fell down before Paul and *Silas*,
17: 4. consorted with Paul and *Silas*;
10. sent away Paul and *Silas*
14. but *Silas* and Timotheus abode there
15. receiving a commandment unto *Silas*
18: 5. when *Silas* and Timotheus were come

Σιλουανός, *Silouanos*.

2Co. 1:19. (even) by me and *Silvanus*
1Th. 1: 1. Paul, and *Silvanus*, and Timotheus,
2Th. 1: 1. Paul, and *Silvanus*, and Timotheus,
1Pet.5:12. By *Silvanus*, a faithful brother

Σιλωάμ, *Silōam*.

Lu. 13: 4. upon whom the tower in *Siloam*
Joh. 9: 7. Go, wash in the pool of *Siloam*,
11. Go to the pool of *Siloam*,

Σίμων, *Simōn*.

Mat. 4:18. *Simon* called Peter, and Andrew
10: 2. The first, *Simon*, who is called Peter,
4. *Simon* the Canaanite, and Judas
13:55. Joses, and *Simon*, and Judas?
16:16. And *Simon* Peter answered
17. Blessed art thou, *Simon* Bar-jona:
17:25. What thinkest thou, *Simon*?
26: 6. in the house of *Simon* the leper,
27:32. a man of Cyrene, *Simon* by name:
Mar 1:16. he saw *Simon* and Andrew
29. entered into the house of *Simon*
30. But *Simon's* wife's mother
36. And *Simon* and they that were
3:16. and *Simon* he surnamed Peter;
18. and *Simon* the Canaanite,
6: 3. of Juda, and *Simon*?
14: 3. the house of *Simon* the leper,
37. *Simon*, sleepest thou?
15:21. they compel one *Simon*
Lu. 4:38. and entered into *Simon's* house. And
Simon's wife's mother was taken
5: 3. of the ships, which was *Simon's*,
4. he said unto *Simon*, Launch out
5. And *Simon* answering said
8. When *Simon* Peter saw (it),
10. which were partners with *Simon*. And
Jesus said unto *Simon*, Fear not;
6:14. *Simon*, whom he also named Peter,
15. and *Simon* called Zelotes,
7:40. *Simon*, I have somewhat to say unto thee.
43. *Simon* answered and said,
44. and said unto *Simon*,
22:31. *Simon*, *Simon*, behold, Satan hath desired
23:26. they laid hold upon one *Simon*,
24:34. hath appeared to *Simon*.
Joh. 1:40(41). Andrew, *Simon* Peter's brother.
41(42). his own brother *Simon*,
42(43). Thou art *Simon* the son of Jona:

Joh. 6: 8. Andrew, *Simon* Peter's brother,
    68. *Simon* Peter answered him,
    71. Judas Iscariot (the son) of *Simon :*
12: 4. Judas Iscariot, *Simon's* (son),
13: 2. Judas Iscariot, *Simon's* (son),
    6. Then cometh he to *Simon* Peter.
    9. *Simon* Peter saith unto him,
    24. *Simon* Peter therefore beckoned to him,
    26. to Judas Iscariot, (the son) of *Simon.*
    36. *Simon* Peter said unto him, Lord,
18:10. *Simon* Peter having a sword
    15. And *Simon* Peter followed Jesus,
    25. *Simon* Peter stood and warmed himself.
20: 2. Then she runneth, and cometh to *Simon* Peter,
    6. Then cometh *Simon* Peter following him,
21: 2. There were together *Simon* Peter, and Thomas
    3. *Simon* Peter saith unto them,
    7. Now when *Simon* Peter heard
    11. *Simon* Peter went up, and drew
    15. Jesus saith to *Simon* Peter, *Simon*, (son) of Jonas, lovest thou me
    16. *Simon*, (son) of Jonas, lovest thou me?
    17. *Simon*, (son) of Jonas, lovest thou me?
Acts 1:13. and *Simon* Zelotes, and Judas
8: 9. a certain man, called *Simon*,
    13. Then *Simon* himself believed
    18. And when *Simon* saw
    24. Then answered *Simon*, and said,
9:43. with one *Simon* a tanner
10: 5. *Simon*, whose surname is Peter:
    6. He lodgeth with one *Simon*
    17. had made enquiry for *Simon's* house,
    18. *Simon*, which was surnamed Peter,
    32. and call hither *Simon*,
    — in the house of (one) *Simon* a tanner
11:13. and call for *Simon*,

Σινᾶ, *Sina*.

Acts 7:30. in the wilderness of Mount *Sina*
    38. which spake to him in the mount *Sina*,
Gal. 4:24. covenants; the one from the mount *Sinai*,
    25. For this Agar is mount *Sinai*

Σιών, *Sion*.

Mat.21: 5. Tell ye the daughter of *Sion*,
Joh.12:15. Fear not, daughter of *Sion :*
Ro. 9:33. I lay in *Sion* a stumblingstone
    11:26. There shall come out of *Sion* the Deliverer,
Heb 12:22. But ye are come unto mount *Sion*,
1Pet.2: 6. I lay in *Sion* a chief corner stone,
Rev.14: 1. a Lamb stood on the mount *Sion*,

Σκευᾶς, *Skŭas*.

Acts19:14. there were seven sons of (one) *Sceva*,

Σκύθης, *Skuthees*.

Col. 3:11. Barbarian, *Scythian*, bond (nor) free:

Σμύρνα, *Smurna*.

Rev. 1:11. and unto *Smyrna*, and unto Pergamos,

Σμυρναῖος, *Smurnaios*.

Rev. 2: 8. the angel of the church in *Smyrna*

Σόδομα, (τα), *Sodoma*.

Mat.10:15. tolerable for the land of *Sodom*
    11:23. had been done in *Sodom*,
    24. tolerable for the land of *Sodom*
Mar 6:11. more tolerable for *Sodom*
Lu. 10:12. tolerable in that day for *Sodom*,
    17:29. day that Lot went out of *Sodom*
Ro. 9:29. we had been as *Sodoma*,
2Pet.2: 6. the cities of *Sodom* and Gomorrha
Jude 7. Even as *Sodom* and Gomorrha,
Rev.11: 8. which spiritually is called *Sodom* and Egypt,

Σολομών, -ῶν, *Solomōn*.

Mat. 1: 6. and David the king begat *Solomon*
    7. And *Solomon* begat Roboam ;
6:29. even *Solomon* in all his glory
12:42. to hear the wisdom of *Solomon ;* and, behold, a greater than *Solomon* (is) here.
Lu. 11:31. to hear the wisdom of *Solomon ;* and, behold, a greater than *Solomon* (is) here.
12:27. *Solomon* in all his glory
Joh.10:23. in *Solomon's* porch.
Acts 3:11. in the porch that is called *Solomon's*,
    5:12. with one accord in *Solomon's* porch.
    7:47. But *Solomon* built him an house.

Σουσάννα, *Sousanna*.

Lu. 8: 3. Herod's steward, and *Susanna*,

Σπανία, *Spania*.

Ro. 15:24. I take my journey into *Spain*,
    28. I will come by you into *Spain*.

Στάχυς, *Stakus*.

Ro. 16: 9. and *Stachys* my beloved.

Στεφανᾶς, *Stephanas*.

1Co. 1:16. also the houshold of *Stephanas :*
    16:15. ye know the house of *Stephanas*,
    17. I am glad of the coming of *Stephanas*

Στέφανος, *Stephanos*.

Acts 6: 5. and they chose *Stephen*,
    8. And *Stephen*, full of faith and power
    9. disputing with *Stephen*.
7:59. And they stoned *Stephen*,
8: 2. And devout men carried *Stephen*
11:19. the persecution that arose about *Stephen*
22:20. the blood of thy martyr *Stephen*

Στωϊκός, *Stōïkos*.

Acts17:18. of the *Stoicks*, encountered him.

Συμεών, Sumeōn.

Lu. 2:25. whose name (was) Simeon;
      34. And Simeon blessed them,
     3:30. Which was (the son) of Simeon,
Acts13: 1. and Simeon that was called Niger,
     15:14. Simeon hath declared how God
2Pet.1: 1. Simon Peter, a servant and an apostle
Rev. 7: 7. Of the tribe of Simeon (were) sealed

Συντύχη, Suntukee.

Phi. 4: 2. I beseech Euodias, and beseech Syntyche,

Συράκουσαι, Surakousai.

Acts28:12. And landing at Syracuse,

Συρία, Suria.

Mat. 4:24. And his fame went throughout all Syria:
Lu. 2: 2. when Cyrenius was governor of Syria.
Acts15:23. of the Gentiles in Antioch and Syria
      41. And he went through Syria
     18:18. and sailed thence into Syria,
     20: 3. as he was about to sail into Syria,
     21: 3. and sailed into Syria,
Gal. 1:21. I came into the regions of Syria

Σύρος, Suros.

Lu. 4:27. saving Naaman the Syrian.

Συροφοίνισσα, Surophoinissa.

Mar 7:26. a Syrophenician by nation;

Συχάρ, Sukar.

Joh. 4: 5. of Samaria, which is called Sychar,

Συχέμ, Sukem.

Acts 7:16. And were carried over into Sychem,
          — of Emmor (the father) of Sychem.

Σώπατρος, Sōpatros.

Acts20: 4. accompanied him into Asia Sopater

Σωσθένης, Sōsthenees.

Acts18:17. the Greeks took Sosthenes, the chief ruler
1Co. 1: 1. and Sosthenes (our) brother,

Σωσίπατρος, Sōsipatros.

Ro. 16:21. and Sosipater, my kinsmen, salute you.

Ταβέρναι see Τρεῖς Ταβέρναι.

Ταβιθά, Tabitha.

Acts 9:36. certain disciple named Tabitha,
      40. to the body said, Tabitha, arise.

Ταρσεύς, Tarsūs.

Acts 9:11. for (one) called Saul, of Tarsus:
     21:39. I am a man (which am) a Jew of Tarsus,
             (a city) in Cilicia,

Ταρσός, Tarsos.

Acts 9:30. and sent him forth to Tarsus.
     11:25. Then departed Barnabas to Tarsus,
     22: 3. a man (which am) a Jew, born in Tarsus,

Τέρτιος, Tertios.

Ro. 16:22. I Tertius, who wrote (this) epistle, salute
          you

Τέρτυλλος, Tertullos.

Acts24: 1. a certain orator (named) Tertullus,
      2. Tertullus began to accuse (him), saying,

Τιβεριάς, Tiberias.

Joh. 6: 1. which is (the sea) of Tiberias.
      23. there came other boats from Tiberias nigh
          unto the place
     21: 1. to the disciples at the sea of Tiberias;

Τιβέριος, Tiberios.

Lu. 3: 1. of the reign of Tiberius Cæsar,

Τίμαιος, Timaios.

Mar10:46. blind Bartimæus, the son of Timæus,

Τιμόθεος, Timotheos.

Acts16: 1. a certain disciple was there, named Timo-
             theus,
     17:14. but Silas and Timotheus abode there still.
      15. commandment unto Silas and Timotheus
          for to come to him with all speed,
     18: 5. when Silas and Timotheus were come
     19:22. Timotheus and Erastus; but he himself
             stayed in Asia
     20: 4. and Gaius of Derbe, and Timotheus;
Ro. 16:21. Timotheus my workfellow,
1Co. 4:17. have I sent unto you Timotheus,
     16:10. Now if Timotheus come, see that he may
          be with you without fear:
2Co. 1: 1. and Timothy (our) brother, unto the
          church
      19. by me and Silvanus and Timotheus,
Phi. 1: 1. Paul and Timotheus, the servants of Jesus
          Christ,
     2:19. to send Timotheus shortly unto you,
Col. 1: 1. and Timotheus (our) brother,

1Th. 1: 1. Paul, and Silvanus, and *Timotheus*,
   3: 2. And sent *Timotheus*, our brother,
   6. But now when *Timotheus* came from you
2Th. 1: 1. Paul, and Silvanus, and *Timotheus*,
1Ti. 1: 2. Unto *Timothy*, (my) own son in the faith:
   18. This charge I commit unto thee, son *Timothy*,
   6:20. O *Timothy*, keep that which is committed
2Ti. 1: 2. To *Timothy*, (my) dearly beloved son:
Philem. 1. and *Timothy* (our) brother, unto Philemon
Heb 13:23. brother *Timothy* is set at liberty ;

Τίμων, *Timōn*.

Acts 6: 5. and *Timon*, and Parmenas,

Τίτος, *Titos*.

2Co. 2:13(12). I found not *Titus* my brother:
   7: 6. comforted us by the coming of *Titus* ;
   13. joyed we for the joy of *Titus*,
   14. which (I made) before *Titus*,
   8: 6. Insomuch that we desired *Titus*,
   16. into the heart of *Titus* for you.
   23. Whether (any do enquire) of *Titus*,
   12:18. I desired *Titus*, and with (him) I sent
   — Did *Titus* make a gain of you ?
Gal. 2: 1. and took *Titus* with (me) also.
   3. But neither *Titus*, who was with me,
2Ti. 4:10. *Titus* unto Dalmatia.
Tit. 1: 4. To *Titus*, (mine) own son after the common faith:

Τραχωνῖτις, *Trakōnitis*.

Lu. 3: 1. of the region of *Trachonitis*,

Τρεῖς Ταβέρναι, *Trīs Tabernai*.

Acts28:15. as far as Apii forum, and *The three taverns :*

Τρόφιμος, *Trophimos*.

Acts20: 4. of Asia, Tychicus and *Trophimus*.
   21:29. with him in the city *Trophimus*
2Ti. 4:20. but *Trophimus* have I left at Miletum

Τρύφαινα, *Truphaina*.

Ro. 16:12. Salute *Tryphena* and Tryphosa,

Τρυφῶσα, *Truphōsa*.

Ro. 16:12. Salute Tryphena and *Tryphosa*,

Τρωάς, *Trōas*.

Acts16: 8. came down to *Troas*.
   11. Therefore loosing from *Troas*,
   20: 5. tarried for us at *Troas*.
   6. and came unto them to *Troas*
2Co. 2:12. Furthermore, when I came to *Troas*
2Ti. 4:13. The cloke that I left at *Troas*

Τρωγύλλιον, *Trōgullion*.

Acts20:15. and tarried at *Trogyllium* ;

Τύραννος, *Turannos*.

Acts19: 9. in the school of one *Tyrannus*.

Τύριος, *Turios*.

Acts12:20. was highly displeased with them *of Tyre*

Τύρος, *Turos*.

Mat.11:21. had been done in *Tyre* and Sidon,
   22. It shall be more tolerable for *Tyre*
   15:21. departed into the coasts of *Tyre*
Mar 3: 8. and they about *Tyre* and Sidon,
   7:24. into the borders of *Tyre* and Sidon,
   31. departing from the coasts of *Tyre*
Lu. 6:17. and from the sea coast of *Tyre*
   10:13. had been done in *Tyre* and Sidon,
   14. it shall be more tolerable for *Tyre*
Acts21: 3. and landed at *Tyre* : for there
   7. we had finished (our) course from *Tyre*,

Τυχικός, *Tukikos*.

Acts20: 4. *Tychicus* and Trophimus.
Eph 6:21. *Tychicus*, a beloved brother
Col. 4: 7. All my state shall *Tychicus* declare
2Ti. 4:12. And *Tychicus* have I sent to Ephesus.
Tit. 3:12. or *Tychicus*, be diligent to come unto me

Ὑμέναιος, *Humenaios*.

1Ti. 1:20. Of whom is *Hymenæus* and Alexander ;
2Ti. 2:17. of whom is *Hymenæus* and Philetus ;

Φαλέκ, *Phalek*.

Lu. 3:35. which was (the son) of *Phalec*,

Φανουήλ, *Phanoueel*.

Lu. 2:36. the daughter of *Phanuel*,

Φαραώ, *Pharaō*.

Acts 7:10. wisdom in the sight of *Pharaoh*
   13. kindred was made known unto *Pharaoh*.
   21. *Pharaoh's* daughter took him up,
Ro. 9:17. the scripture saith unto *Pharaoh*,
Heb 11:24. called the son of *Pharaoh's* daughter ;

Φαρές, *Phares*.

Mat. 1: 3. Judas begat *Phares*...and *Phares* begat Esrom ;
Lu. 3:33. which was (the son) of *Phares*,

Φαρισαῖος, Pharisaios.

Mat. 3: 7. when he saw many of the *Pharisees*
5:20. of the scribes and *Pharisees*,
9:11. And when the *Pharisees* saw (it),
14. we and the *Pharisees* fast oft,
34. the *Pharisees* said, He casteth
12: 2. But when the *Pharisees* saw (it),
14. Then the *Pharisees* went out,
24. But when the *Pharisees* heard (it),
38. scribes and of the *Pharisees* answered,
15: 1. came to Jesus scribes and *Pharisees*,
12. that the *Pharisees* were offended,
16: 1. *Pharisees* also with the Sadducees came,
6. beware of the leaven of the *Pharisees*
11. beware of the leaven of the *Pharisees*
12. but of the doctrine of the *Pharisees*
19: 3. The *Pharisees* also came unto him,
21:45. *Pharisees* had heard his parables,
22:15. Then went the *Pharisees*, and took counsel
34. But when the *Pharisees* had heard
41. While the *Pharisees* were gathered
23: 2. The scribes and the *Pharisees* sit in
13. woe unto you, scribes and *Pharisees*,
14. Woe unto you, scribes and *Pharisees*,
15. Woe unto you, scribes and *Pharisees*,
23. Woe unto you, scribes and *Pharisees*,
25. Woe unto you, scribes and *Pharisees*,
26. (Thou) blind *Pharisee*, cleanse first
27. Woe unto you, scribes and *Pharisees*,
29. Woe unto you, scribes and *Pharisees*,
27:62. chief priests and *Pharisees* came together
Mar 2:16. when the scribes and *Pharisees* saw
18. of the *Pharisees* used to fast:
— of John and of the *Pharisees* fast,
24. And the *Pharisees* said unto him,
3: 6. And the *Pharisees* went forth,
7: 1. came together unto him the *Pharisees*,
3. For the *Pharisees*, and all the Jews,
5. the *Pharisees* and scribes asked him,
8:11. And the *Pharisees* came forth,
15. beware of the leaven of the *Pharisees*,
10: 2. And the *Pharisees* came to him,
12:13. unto him certain of the *Pharisees*
Lu. 5:17. there were *Pharisees* and doctors
21. and the *Pharisees* began to reason,
30. their scribes and *Pharisees* murmured
33. likewise (the disciples) of the *Pharisees*;
6: 2. certain of the *Pharisees* said
7. the scribes and *Pharisees* watched him,
7:30. But the *Pharisees* and lawyers
36. one of the *Pharisees* desired him
— he went into the *Pharisee's* house,
37. at meat in the *Pharisee's* house,
39. *Pharisee* which had bidden him saw
11:37. a certain *Pharisee* besought him to dine
38. And when the *Pharisee* saw (it),
39. ye *Pharisees* make clean the outside
42. But woe unto you, *Pharisees*!
43. Woe unto you, *Pharisees*!
44. Woe unto you, scribes and *Pharisees*,
53. the *Pharisees* began to urge (him)
12: 1. Beware ye of the leaven of the *Pharisees*,
13:31. came certain of the *Pharisees*,
14: 1. one of the chief *Pharisees* to eat
3. spake unto the lawyers and *Pharisees*,
15: 2. the *Pharisees* and scribes murmured,
16:14. *Pharisees* also, who were covetous,
17:20. of the *Pharisees*, when the kingdom
18:10. the one a *Pharisee*, and the other
11. The *Pharisee* stood and prayed
19:39. some of the *Pharisees* from among

Joh. 1:24. were sent were of the *Pharisees*.
3: 1. of the *Pharisees*, named Nicodemus,
4: 1. the *Pharisees* had heard that Jesus
7:32. The *Pharisees* heard that the people
— *Pharisees* and the chief priests sent officers
45. to the chief priests and *Pharisees*;
47. answered them the *Pharisees*,
48. or of the *Pharisees* believed on him?
8: 3. *Pharisees* brought unto him a woman
13. The *Pharisees* therefore said unto him,
9:13. They brought to the *Pharisees*
15. again the *Pharisees* also asked him
16. said some of the *Pharisees*, This man
40. of the *Pharisees* which were with him
11:46. went their ways to the *Pharisees*,
47. gathered the chief priests and the *Pharisees*
57. both the chief priests and the *Pharisees*
12:19. The *Pharisees* therefore said
42. *Pharisees* they did not confess (him),
18: 3. and *Pharisees*, cometh thither with lanterns
Acts 5:34. a *Pharisee*, named Gamaliel,
15: 5. sect of the *Pharisees* which believed,
23: 6. were Sadducees, and the other *Pharisees*.
— I am a *Pharisee*, the son of a *Pharisee*.
7. dissension between the *Pharisees* and
8. but the *Pharisees* confess both.
9. of the *Pharisees'* part arose,
26: 5. our religion I lived a *Pharisee*.
Phi. 3: 5. as touching the law, a *Pharisee*;

Φῆλιξ, Pheelix.

Acts 23:24. safe unto *Felix* the governor.
26. unto the most excellent governor *Felix*
24: 3. and in all places, most noble *Felix*,
22. And when *Felix* heard these things,
24. when *Felix* came with his wife
25. *Felix* trembled, and answered,
27. Porcius Festus came into *Felix'* room:
and *Felix*, willing to shew the Jews
25:14. left in bonds by *Felix*:

Φῆστος, Pheestos.

Acts 24:27. Porcius *Festus* came into Felix' room:
25: 1. Now when *Festus* was come into the province,
4. But *Festus* answered, that Paul
9. But *Festus*, willing to do the Jews
12. Then *Festus* when he had conferred
13. unto Cæsarea to salute *Festus*.
14. *Festus* declared Paul's cause unto the king,
22. Then Agrippa said unto *Festus*,
23. at *Festus'* commandment Paul was brought
24. And *Festus* said, King Agrippa,
26:24. *Festus* said with a loud voice,
25. I am not mad, most noble *Festus*;
32. Then said Agrippa unto *Festus*,

Φιλαδέλφια, Philadelphia.

Rev. 1:11. unto Sardis, and unto *Philadelphia*,
3: 7. the church in *Philadelphia* write;

Φιλήμων, Phileemōn:

Philem 1. unto *Philemon* our dearly beloved,

Φιλητός, *Phileetos.*

2Ti. 2:17. of whom is Hymenæus and *Philetus;*

Φιλιππήσιοι, *Philippeesioi.*

Phi. 4:15. Now ye *Philippians* know also,

Φίλιπποι, *Philippoi.*

Acts16:12. And from thence to *Philippi,*
  20: 6. And we sailed away from *Philippi*
Phi. 1: 1. which are at *Philippi,*
1Th. 2: 2. as ye know, at *Philippi,*

Φίλιππος, *Philippos.*

Mat.10: 3. *Philip,* and Bartholomew;
  14: 3. his brother *Philip's* wife.
  16:13. into the coasts of Cæsarea *Philippi,* (lit.
    of *Philip*)
Mar 3:18. And Andrew, and *Philip,*
  6:17. his brother *Philip's* wife:
  8:27. into the towns of Cæsarea *Philippi:* (lit.
    of *Philip*)
Lu. 3: 1. his brother *Philip* tetrarch of Ituræa
  19. his brother *Philip's* wife,
  6:14. *Philip* and Bartholomew,
Joh. 1:43(44). and findeth *Philip,* and saith
  44(45). Now *Philip* was of Bethsaida,
  45(46). *Philip* findeth Nathanael,
  46(47). *Philip* saith unto him, Come and see.
  48(49). Before that *Philip* called thee,
  6: 5. he saith unto *Philip,* Whence shall
  7. *Philip* answered him, Two hundred
  12:21. The same came therefore to *Philip,*
  22. *Philip* cometh and telleth Andrew:
  — Andrew and *Philip* tell Jesus.
  14: 8. *Philip* saith unto him, Lord, shew
  9. and yet hast thou not known me, *Philip?*
Acts 1:13. and Andrew, *Philip,* and Thomas,
  6: 5. and *Philip,* and Prochorus,
  8: 5. Then *Philip* went down to the city
  6. unto those things which *Philip* spake,
  12. But when they believed *Philip*
  13. he continued with *Philip,*
  26. And the angel of the Lord spake unto
    Philip,
  29. Then the Spirit said unto *Philip,*
  30. And *Philip* ran thither to (him),
  31. And he desired *Philip* that he would
  34. And the eunuch answered *Philip,*
  35. Then *Philip* opened his mouth,
  37. And *Philip* said, If thou believest
  38. into the water, both *Philip* and the eunuch;
  39. the Spirit of the Lord caught away *Philip,*
  40. But *Philip* was found at Azotus:
  21: 8. into the house of *Philip* the evangelist,

Φιλόλογος, *Philologos.*

Ro. 16:15. Salute *Philologus,* and Julia,

Φλέγων, *Phlegōn.*

Ro. 16:14. Salute Asyncritus, *Phlegon,*

Φοίβη, *Phoibee.*

Ro. 16: 1. I commend unto you *Phebe* our sister,

Φοινίκη, *Phoinikee.*

Acts11:19. travelled as far as *Phenice,*
  15: 3. they passed through *Phenice* and Samaria,
  21: 2. a ship sailing over unto *Phenicia,*

Φοίνιξ, *Phoinix.*

Acts27:12. they might attain to *Phenice,* (and there)
  to winter;

Φόρον Ἀππίου see Ἀππίου Φόρον.

Φορτουνάτος, *Phortounatos.*

1Co.16:17. coming of Stephanas and *Fortunatus*

Φρυγία, *Phrugia.*

Acts 2:10. *Phrygia,* and Pamphylia,
  16: 6. Now when they had gone throughout
    Phrygia
  18:23. over (all) the country of Galatia and
    Phrygia

Φύγελλος, *Phugellos.*

2Ti. 1:15. of whom are *Phygellus* and Hermogenes.

Χαλδαῖος, *Kaldaios.*

Acts 7: 4. out of the land of the *Chaldæans,*

Χαναάν, *Kanaän.*

Acts 7:11. over all the land of Egypt and *Chanaan,*
  13:19. destroyed seven nations in the land of
    Chanaan,

Χαναναῖος, *Kananaios.*

Mat.15:22. And, behold, a woman of *Canaan* came

Χαῤῥάν, *Karran.*

Acts 7: 2. before he dwelt in *Charran,*
  4. and dwelt in *Charran:*

Χερουβίμ, *Keroubim.*

Heb. 9: 5. *cherubims* of glory shadowing the mercyseat;

Χίος, Kios.

Acts20:15. came the next (day) over against *Chios ;*

Χλόη, Kloee.

1Co. 1:11. (which are of the house) of *Chloe,*

Χοραζίν, Korazin.

Mat.11:21. Woe unto thee, *Chorazin !*
Lu. 10:13. Woe unto thee, *Chorazin !*

Χουζᾶς, Kouzas.

Lu. 8: 3. Joanna the wife of *Chuza* Herod's steward,

Χριστιανός, Kristianos.

Acts11:26. disciples were called *Christians* first in
　　　　　Antioch.
　26:28. persuadest me to be a *Christian.*
1Pet.4:16. if (any man suffer) as a *Christian,*

Χριστός, Kristos.

Mat. 1: 1. generation of Jesus *Christ,*
　　16. Jesus, who is called *Christ.*
　　17. unto *Christ* (are) fourteen generations.
　　18. the birth of Jesus *Christ* was on
　 2: 4. where *Christ* should be born.
　11: 2. in the prison the works of *Christ,*
　16:16. Thou art the *Christ,* the Son of
　　20. that he was Jesus the *Christ.*
　22:42. What think ye of *Christ ?*
　23: 8. one is your Master, (even) *Christ ;*
　　10. one is your Master, (even) *Christ.*
　24: 5. my name, saying, I am *Christ ;*
　　23. Lo, here (is) *Christ,* or there ;
　26:63. whether thou be the *Christ,*
　　68. Prophesy unto us, thou *Christ,*
　27:17. Jesus which is called *Christ ?*
　　22. Jesus which is called *Christ ?*
Mar 1: 1. beginning of the gospel of Jesus *Christ,*
　 8:29. Thou art the *Christ.*
　 9:41. because ye belong to *Christ,*
　12:35. How say the scribes that *Christ* is the
　13:21. Lo, here (is) *Christ ;* or, lo, (he is) there ;
　14:61. Art thou the *Christ,* the Son of the
　　　　Blessed ?
　15:32. Let *Christ* the King of Israel descend
Lu. 2:11. a Saviour, which is *Christ* the Lord.
　　26. he had seen the Lord's *Christ.*
　 3:15. whether he were the *Christ,* or not ;
　 4:41. Thou art *Christ* the Son of God.
　　— they knew that he was *Christ.*
　 9:20. said, The *Christ* of God.
　20:41. *Christ* is David's son ?
　22:67(66). Art thou the *Christ ?*
　23: 2. saying that he himself is *Christ*
　　35. if he be *Christ,* the chosen of God.
　　39. If thou be *Christ,* save thyself
　24:26. Ought not *Christ* to have suffered
　　46. thus it behoved *Christ* to suffer,
Joh. 1:17. grace and truth came by Jesus *Christ.*
　　20. confessed, I am not the *Christ.*
　　25. if thou be not that *Christ,*

Joh. 1:41(42). being interpreted, the *Christ.*
　 3:28. said, I am not the *Christ,*
　 4:25. Messias cometh, which is called *Christ :*
　　29. is not this the *Christ ?*
　　42. this is indeed the *Christ,*
　 6:69. sure that thou art that *Christ,*
　 7:26. indeed that this is the very *Christ ?*
　　27. when *Christ* cometh, no man
　　31. When *Christ* cometh, will he do
　　41. This is the *Christ.*
　　— Shall *Christ* come out of Galilee ?
　　42. *Christ* cometh of the seed of
　 9:22. confess that he was *Christ.*
　10:24. If thou be the *Christ,* tell us
　11:27. I believe that thou art the *Christ,*
　12:34. that *Christ* abideth for ever:
　17: 3. and Jesus *Christ,* whom thou
　20:31. believe that Jesus is the *Christ,*
Acts 2:30. raise up *Christ* to sit on
　　31. spake of the resurrection of *Christ,*
　　36. crucified, both Lord and *Christ.*
　　38. in the name of Jesus *Christ*
　 3: 6. In the name of Jesus *Christ*
　　18. prophets, that *Christ* should
　　20. he shall send Jesus *Christ,*
　 4:10. by the name of Jesus *Christ*
　　26. and against his *Christ.*
　 5:42. to teach and preach Jesus *Christ.*
　 8: 5. preached *Christ* unto them.
　　12. and the name of Jesus *Christ,*
　　37. Jesus *Christ* is the Son of God.
　 9:20. preached *Christ* in the
　　22. proving that this is very *Christ.*
　　34. Jesus *Christ* maketh thee
　10:36. peace by Jesus *Christ :*
　11:17. believed on the Lord Jesus *Christ ;*
　15:11. through the grace of the Lord Jesus
　　　　Christ
　　26. name of our Lord Jesus *Christ.*
　16:18. thee in the name of Jesus *Christ*
　　31. Believe on the Lord Jesus *Christ,*
　17: 3. *Christ* must needs have
　　— preach unto you, is *Christ.*
　18: 5. (that) Jesus (was) *Christ.*
　　28. that Jesus was *Christ.*
　19: 4. that is, on *Christ* Jesus.
　20:21. faith toward our Lord Jesus *Christ.*
　24:24. concerning the faith in *Christ.*
　26:23. That *Christ* should suffer,
　28:31. which concern the Lord Jesus *Christ,*
Ro. 1: 1. Paul, a servant of Jesus *Christ,*
　　3(4). Concerning his Son Jesus *Christ*
　　6. ye also the called of Jesus *Christ :*
　　7. and the Lord Jesus *Christ.*
　　8. I thank my God through Jesus *Christ*
　　16. not ashamed of the gospel of *Christ :*
　 2:16. secrets of men by Jesus *Christ*
　 3:22. by faith of Jesus *Christ*
　　24. redemption that is in *Christ* Jesus:
　 5: 1. through our Lord Jesus *Christ :*
　　6. in due time *Christ* died
　　8. *Christ* died for us.
　　11. through our Lord Jesus *Christ,*
　　15. by one man, Jesus *Christ,*
　　17. life by one, Jesus *Christ.*
　　21. life by Jesus *Christ* our Lord.
　 6: 3. were baptized into Jesus *Christ*
　　4. that like as *Christ* was raised
　　8. if we be dead with *Christ,*
　　9. Knowing that *Christ* being raised
　　11. through Jesus *Christ* our Lord.
　　23. eternal life through Jesus *Christ*

Ro. 7: 4. law by the body of *Christ;*
25. through Jesus *Christ*
8: 1. them which are in *Christ*
2. Spirit of life in *Christ* Jesus
9. have not the Spirit of *Christ,*
10. if *Christ* (be) in you,
11. he that raised up *Christ*
17. joint-heirs with *Christ;*
34. (It is) *Christ* that died,
35. from the love of *Christ?*
39. which is in *Christ* Jesus
9: 1. say the truth in *Christ,*
3. accursed from *Christ* for my brethren,
5. *Christ* (came), who is over all,
10: 4. *Christ* (is) the end of the law
6. to bring *Christ* down
7. bring up *Christ* again
12: 5. one body in *Christ,*
13: 14. on the Lord Jesus *Christ,*
14: 9. *Christ* both died, and rose,
10. judgment seat of *Christ.*
15. for whom *Christ* died.
18. that in these things serveth *Christ*
15: 3. *Christ* pleased not himself;
5. according to *Christ* Jesus:
6. Father of our Lord Jesus *Christ.*
7. as *Christ* also received us
8. Jesus *Christ* was a minister
16. minister of Jesus *Christ*
17. I may glory through Jesus *Christ*
18. which *Christ* hath not
19. fully preached the gospel of *Christ.*
20. where *Christ* was named,
29. blessing of the gospel of *Christ.*
30. for the Lord Jesus *Christ's* sake,
16: 3. helpers in *Christ* Jesus:
5. firstfruits of Achaia unto *Christ.*
7. in *Christ* before me.
9. our helper in *Christ,*
10. Salute Apelles approved in *Christ.*
16. churches of *Christ* salute you.
18. our Lord Jesus *Christ,*
20. grace of our Lord Jesus *Christ*
24. grace of our Lord Jesus *Christ*
25. the preaching of Jesus *Christ,*
27. glory through Jesus *Christ*
1Co. 1: 1. apostle of Jesus *Christ*
2. sanctified in *Christ* Jesus,
— name of Jesus *Christ*
3. and (from) the Lord Jesus *Christ.*
4. given you by Jesus *Christ;*
6. testimony of *Christ* was confirmed
7. coming of our Lord Jesus *Christ:*
8. day of our Lord Jesus *Christ.*
9. fellowship of his Son Jesus *Christ*
10. beseech you, brethren, by the name of our Lord Jesus *Christ,*
12. and I of *Christ.*
13. Is *Christ* divided?
17. *Christ* sent me not to baptize,
— lest the cross of *Christ* should
23. But we preach *Christ* crucified,
24. *Christ* the power of God,
30. are ye in *Christ* Jesus,
2: 2. save Jesus *Christ,* and him crucified.
16. But we have the mind of *Christ.*
3: 1. as unto babes in *Christ.*
11. which is Jesus *Christ.*
23. ye are *Christ's;* and *Christ* (is) God's.
4: 1. ministers of *Christ,* and stewards
10. for *Christ's* sake, but ye (are) wise in *Christ;*

1Co. 4: 15. instructers in *Christ,* yet (have ye) not many fathers: for in *Christ* Jesus I have
17. which be in *Christ,*
5: 4. In the name of our Lord Jesus *Christ,*
— power of our Lord Jesus *Christ,*
7. *Christ* our passover is sacrificed
6: 15. members of *Christ?* shall I then take the members of *Christ,*
7: 22. (being) free, is *Christ's* servant.
8: 6. and one Lord Jesus *Christ,*
11. for whom *Christ* died?
12. ye sin against *Christ.*
9: 1. have I not seen Jesus *Christ*
12. hinder the gospel of *Christ.*
18. make the gospel of *Christ*
21. under the law to *Christ,*
10: 4. that Rock was *Christ.*
9. Neither let us tempt *Christ,*
16. the blood of *Christ?*
— of the body of *Christ?*
11: 1. even as I also (am) of *Christ.*
3. of every man is *Christ;*
— head of *Christ* (is) God.
12: 12. so also (is) *Christ.*
27. ye are the body of *Christ,*
15: 3. *Christ* died for our sins
12. if *Christ* be preached
13. then is *Christ* not risen:
14. if *Christ* be not risen,
15. he raised up *Christ:*
16. then is not *Christ* raised:
17. if *Christ* be not raised,
18. which are fallen asleep in *Christ*
19. only we have hope in *Christ,*
20. now is *Christ* risen
22. in *Christ* shall all be made alive.
23. *Christ* the firstfruits; afterward they that are *Christ's* at his coming.
31. have in *Christ* Jesus our Lord,
57. through our Lord Jesus *Christ.*
16: 22. love not the Lord Jesus *Christ,*
23. grace of our Lord Jesus *Christ*
24. all in *Christ* Jesus.
2Co. 1: 1. apostle of Jesus *Christ*
2. and (from) the Lord Jesus *Christ.*
3. Father of our Lord Jesus *Christ,*
5. sufferings of *Christ* abound in us, so our consolation also aboundeth by *Christ.*
19. Jesus *Christ,* who was preached
21. with you in *Christ,*
2: 10. in the person of *Christ;*
12. *Christ's* gospel, and a door
14. causeth us to triumph in *Christ,*
15. unto God a sweet savour of *Christ,*
17. speak we in *Christ.*
3: 3. epistle of *Christ* ministered by us,
4. we through *Christ* to God-ward:
14. which (vail) is done away in *Christ.*
4: 4. the glorious gospel of *Christ,*
5. but *Christ* Jesus the Lord;
6. face of Jesus *Christ.*
5: 10. judgment seat of *Christ;*
14. the love of *Christ* constraineth
16. known *Christ* after the flesh,
17. man (be) in *Christ,*
18. himself by Jesus *Christ,*
19. God was in *Christ,*
20. we are ambassadors for *Christ,*
— in *Christ's* stead, be ye reconciled
6: 15. hath *Christ* with Belial?
8: 9. of our Lord Jesus *Christ,*
23. the glory of *Christ.*

2Co. 9:13. unto the gospel of *Christ,*
10: 1. meekness and gentleness of *Christ,*
    5. thought to the obedience of *Christ;*
    7. trust to himself that he is *Christ's,*
    — he (is) *Christ's,* even so (are) we *Christ's.*
    14. (preaching) the gospel of *Christ:*
11: 2. chaste virgin to *Christ.*
    3. simplicity that is in *Christ.*
    10. truth of *Christ* is in me,
    13. into the apostles of *Christ.*
    23. Are they ministers of *Christ?*
    31. Father of our Lord Jesus *Christ,*
12: 2. a man in *Christ*
    9. power of *Christ* may
    10. distresses for *Christ's* sake:
    19. before God in *Christ:*
13: 3. of *Christ* speaking in me,
    5. Jesus *Christ* is in you,
    14(13). grace of the Lord Jesus *Christ,*
Gal. 1: 1. but by Jesus *Christ,*
    3. (from) our Lord Jesus *Christ,*
    6. grace of *Christ* unto another
    7. pervert the gospel of *Christ.*
    10. the servant of *Christ.*
    12. revelation of Jesus *Christ.*
    22. which were in *Christ:*
2: 4. have in *Christ* Jesus,
    16. by the faith of Jesus *Christ,*
    — believed in Jesus *Christ,*
    — justified by the faith of *Christ,*
    17. we seek to be justified by *Christ,*
    — (is) therefore *Christ* the
    20. I am crucified with *Christ:*
    — *Christ* liveth in me:
    21. *Christ* is dead in vain.
3: 1. Jesus *Christ* hath been
    13. *Christ* hath redeemed us
    14. Gentiles through Jesus *Christ;*
    16. seed, which is *Christ.*
    17. of God in *Christ,*
    22. by faith of Jesus *Christ*
    24. (bring us) unto *Christ,*
    26. faith in *Christ* Jesus.
    27. baptized into *Christ* have put on *Christ.*
    28. for ye are all one in *Christ* Jesus.
    29. if ye (be) *Christ's,* then
4: 7. heir of God through *Christ.*
    14. (even) as *Christ* Jesus.
    19. until *Christ* be formed
5: 1. in the liberty wherewith *Christ*
    2. *Christ* shall profit you nothing.
    4. *Christ* is become of no effect
    6. in Jesus *Christ* neither
    24. are *Christ's* have crucified
6: 2. fulfil the law of *Christ.*
    12. for the cross of *Christ.*
    14. cross of our Lord Jesus *Christ,*
    15. For in *Christ* Jesus
    18. grace of our Lord Jesus *Christ*
Eph. 1: 1. Paul, an apostle of Jesus *Christ*
    — faithful in *Christ* Jesus:
    2. (from) the Lord Jesus *Christ.*
    3. Father of our Lord Jesus *Christ,*
    — in heavenly (places) in *Christ:*
    5. children by Jesus *Christ*
    10. all things in *Christ,*
    12. first trusted in *Christ.*
    17. God of our Lord Jesus *Christ,*
    20. Which he wrought in *Christ,*
2: 5. quickened us together with *Christ,*
    6. (places) in *Christ* Jesus:
    7. toward us through *Christ* Jesus.

Eph. 2:10. created in *Christ* Jesus
    12. without *Christ,* being aliens
    13. now in *Christ* Jesus
    — by the blood of *Christ.*
    20. Jesus *Christ* himself
3: 1. prisoner of Jesus *Christ*
    4. in the mystery of *Christ*
    6. partakers of his promise in *Christ*
    8. unsearchable riches of *Christ;*
    9. all things by Jesus *Christ:*
    11. purposed in *Christ* Jesus
    14. Father of our Lord Jesus *Christ,*
    17. *Christ* may dwell in your hearts
    19. know the love of *Christ,*
    21. by *Christ* Jesus throughout all ages,
4: 7. measure of the gift of *Christ.*
    12. of the body of *Christ:*
    13. of the fulness of *Christ:*
    15. which is the head, (even) *Christ:*
    20. ye have not so learned *Christ;*
    32. God for *Christ's* sake
5: 2. as *Christ* also hath loved us,
    5. kingdom of *Christ* and of God.
    14. *Christ* shall give thee light.
    20. name of our Lord Jesus *Christ;*
    23. *Christ* is the head of the church:
    24. the church is subject unto *Christ,*
    25. even as *Christ* also loved the
    32. concerning *Christ* and the church.
6: 5. singleness of your heart, as unto *Christ;*
    6. but as the servants of *Christ,*
    23. and the Lord Jesus *Christ.*
    24. love our Lord Jesus *Christ*
Phi. 1: 1. the servants of Jesus *Christ,* to all the
    saints in *Christ* Jesus
    2. (from) the Lord Jesus *Christ.*
    6. until the day of Jesus *Christ:*
    8. in the bowels of Jesus *Christ.*
    10. offence till the day of *Christ;*
    11. which are by Jesus *Christ,*
    13. So that my bonds in *Christ*
    15. Some indeed preach *Christ*
    16. The one preach *Christ*
    18. in truth, *Christ* is preached;.
    19. of the Spirit of Jesus *Christ,*
    20. *Christ* shall be magnified
    21. For to me to live (is) *Christ,*
    23. and to be with *Christ ,*
    26. more abundant in Jesus *Christ*
    27. becometh the gospel of *Christ:*
    29. given in the behalf of *Christ,*
2: 1. any consolation in *Christ,*
    5. which was also in *Christ* Jesus:
    11. that Jesus *Christ* (is) Lord,
    16. rejoice in the day of *Christ,*
    21. which are Jesus *Christ's.*
    30. Because for the work of *Christ*
3: 3. and rejoice in *Christ* Jesus,
    7. I counted loss for *Christ.*
    8. knowledge of *Christ* Jesus my Lord:
    — that I may win *Christ,*
    9. which is through the faith of *Christ,*
    12. I am apprehended of *Christ* Jesus.
    14. calling of God in *Christ* Jesus.
    18. enemies of the cross of *Christ:*
    20. the Saviour, the Lord Jesus *Christ:*
4: 7. minds through *Christ* Jesus.
    13. *Christ* which strengtheneth me.
    19. riches in glory by *Christ* Jesus.
    21. Salute every saint in *Christ* Jesus.
    23. The grace of our Lord Jesus *Christ*
Col. 1: 1. an apostle of Jesus *Christ*

Col. 1: 2. saints and faithful brethren in *Christ*
— and the Lord Jesus *Christ*.
3. of our Lord Jesus *Christ*,
4. of your faith in *Christ* Jesus,
7. faithful minister of *Christ* ;
24. the afflictions of *Christ* in
27. *Christ* in you, the hope of glory:
28. perfect in *Christ* Jesus:
2: 2. of the Father, and of *Christ* ;
5. stedfastness of your faith in *Christ*.
6. *Christ* Jesus the Lord,
8. world, and not after *Christ*.
11. by the circumcision of *Christ* :
17. but the body (is) of *Christ*.
20. if ye be dead with *Christ*
3: 1. If ye then be risen with *Christ*,
— where *Christ* sitteth on the right
3. hid with *Christ* in God.
4. When *Christ*, (who is) our life,
11. *Christ* (is) all, and in all.
13. even as *Christ* forgave you,
16. Let the word of *Christ* dwell
24. ye serve the Lord *Christ*.
4: 3. to speak the mystery of *Christ*,
12. a servant of *Christ*, saluteth
1Th. 1: 1. (in) the Lord Jesus *Christ* :
— and the Lord Jesus *Christ*.
3. hope in our Lord Jesus *Christ*,
2: 6. as the apostles of *Christ*.
14. Judæa are in *Christ* Jesus:
19. presence of our Lord Jesus *Christ*
3: 2. labourer in the gospel of *Christ*,
11. and our Lord Jesus *Christ*,
13. coming of our Lord Jesus *Christ*
4:16. the dead in *Christ* shall rise
5: 9. salvation by our Lord Jesus *Christ*,
18. this is the will of God in *Christ* Jesus
23. coming of our Lord Jesus *Christ*.
28. The grace of our Lord Jesus *Christ*
2Th. 1: 1. and the Lord Jesus *Christ* :
2. and the Lord Jesus *Christ*.
8. gospel of our Lord Jesus *Christ* :
12. name of our Lord Jesus *Christ*
— and the Lord Jesus *Christ*.
2: 1. coming of our Lord Jesus *Christ*,
2. the day of *Christ* is at hand.
14. glory of our Lord Jesus *Christ*.
16. Now our Lord Jesus *Christ*
3: 5. patient waiting for *Christ*.
6. in the name of our Lord Jesus *Christ*,
12. exhort by our Lord Jesus *Christ*,
18. The grace of our Lord Jesus *Christ*
1Ti. 1: 1. an apostle of Jesus *Christ*
— Saviour, and Lord Jesus *Christ*,
2. and Jesus *Christ* our Lord.
12. I thank *Christ* Jesus our Lord,
14. which is in *Christ* Jesus.
15. that *Christ* Jesus came into
16. in me first Jesus *Christ*
2: 5. the man *Christ* Jesus ;
7. I speak the truth in *Christ*,
3:13. which is in *Christ* Jesus.
4: 6. good minister of Jesus *Christ*,
5:11. wax wanton against *Christ*,
21. and the Lord Jesus *Christ*,
6: 3. the words of our Lord Jesus *Christ*,
13. and (before) *Christ* Jesus,
14. appearing of our Lord Jesus *Christ* :
2Ti. 1: 1. an apostle of Jesus *Christ*
— which is in *Christ* Jesus,
2. and *Christ* Jesus our Lord.
9. given us in *Christ* Jesus

2Ti. 1:10. appearing of our Saviour Jesus *Christ*,
13. love which is in *Christ* Jesus.
2: 1. grace that is in *Christ* Jesus.
3. good soldier of Jesus *Christ*.
8. Remember that Jesus *Christ*
10. which is in *Christ* Jesus
19. nameth the name of *Christ*
3:12. will live godly in *Christ* Jesus
15. faith which is in *Christ* Jesus.
4: 1. and the Lord Jesus *Christ*,
22. The Lord Jesus *Christ* (be)
Tit. 1: 1. an apostle of Jesus *Christ*,
4. Lord Jesus *Christ* our Saviour.
2:13. our Saviour Jesus *Christ* ;
3: 6. through Jesus *Christ* our Saviour ;
Philem. 1. a prisoner of Jesus *Christ*,
3. and the Lord Jesus *Christ*.
6. in you in *Christ* Jesus.
8. might be much bold in *Christ*
9. a prisoner of Jesus *Christ*.
23. fellowprisoner in *Christ* Jesus ;
25. grace of our Lord Jesus *Christ*
Heb 3: 1. high priest of our profession, *Christ* Jesus ;
6. But *Christ* as a son over his
14. we are made partakers of *Christ*,
5: 5. So also *Christ* glorified not
6: 1. of the doctrine of *Christ*,
9:11. But *Christ* being come an
14. much more shall the blood of *Christ*,
24. For *Christ* is not entered
28. So *Christ* was once offered
10:10. body of Jesus *Christ* once
11:26. Esteeming the reproach of *Christ*
13: 8. Jesus *Christ* the same yesterday,
21. through Jesus *Christ* ;
Jas. 1: 1. of the Lord Jesus *Christ*,
2: 1. faith of our Lord Jesus *Christ*,
1Pet.1: 1. an apostle of Jesus *Christ*,
2. of the blood of Jesus *Christ* :
3. Father of our Lord Jesus *Christ*,
— resurrection of Jesus *Christ*
7. the appearing of Jesus *Christ* :
11 the Spirit of *Christ* which
— beforehand the sufferings of *Christ*,
13. at the revelation of Jesus *Christ* ;
19. with the precious blood of *Christ*,
2: 5. acceptable to God by Jesus *Christ*.
21. because *Christ* also suffered
3:16. your good conversation in *Christ*.
18. For *Christ* also hath once
21. the resurrection of Jesus *Christ* :
4: 1. Forasmuch then as *Christ* hath
11. glorified through Jesus *Christ*,
13. partakers of *Christ's* sufferings ;
14. for the name of *Christ*,
5: 1. of the sufferings of *Christ*,
10. eternal glory by *Christ* Jesus,
14. all that are in *Christ* Jesus.
2Pet.1: 1. an apostle of Jesus *Christ*,
— our Saviour Jesus *Christ* :
8. knowledge of our Lord Jesus *Christ*.
11. Lord and Saviour Jesus *Christ*.
14. Lord Jesus *Christ* hath shewed
16. coming of our Lord Jesus *Christ*,
2:20. Lord and Saviour Jesus *Christ*,
3:18. our Lord and Saviour Jesus *Christ*.
1Joh.1: 3. and with his Son Jesus *Christ*.
7. the blood of Jesus *Christ*
2: 1. Jesus *Christ* the righteous:
22. denieth that Jesus is the *Christ* ?
3:23. name of his Son Jesus *Christ*,
4: 2. confesseth that Jesus *Christ* is

1Joh.4: 3. confesseth not that Jesus *Christ* is
 5: 1. believeth that Jesus is the *Christ*
  6. by water and blood, (even) Jesus *Christ*;
  20. (even) in his Son Jesus *Christ*.
2Joh. 3. from the Lord Jesus *Christ*,
  7. Jesus *Christ* is come in the flesh.
  9. abideth not in the doctrine of *Christ*,
  —- abideth in the doctrine of *Christ*,
Jude 1. the servant of Jesus *Christ*,
  — preserved in Jesus *Christ*,
  4. and our Lord Jesus *Christ*.
  17. apostles of our Lord Jesus *Christ*;
  21. the mercy of our Lord Jesus *Christ*
Rev. 1: 1. The Revelation of Jesus *Christ*,
  2. the testimony of Jesus *Christ*,
  5. And from Jesus *Christ*, (who is)
  9. and patience of Jesus *Christ*,
  — and for the testimony of Jesus *Christ*.
 11:15. our Lord, and of his *Christ*;
 12:10. and the power of his *Christ*:
  17. have the testimony of Jesus *Christ*.
 20: 4. lived and reigned with *Christ*

Rev.20: 6. priests of God and of *Christ*,
 22:21. The grace of our Lord Jesus *Christ*

Χωραζίν see Χοραζίν.

Χῶρος see among Appellatives.

Ὠϐήδ, *Ōbeed.*

Mat. 1: 5. Booz begat *Obed* of Ruth; and *Obed* begat Jesse;
Lu. 3:32. which was (the son) of *Obed*,

Ὠσηέ, *Ōseeë.*

Ro. 9:25. As he saith also in *Osee*,

INDEX.

ENGLISH AND GREEK.

*_*_ *A few of the Proper Names are here given in one Alphabet with the Appellatives; those being inserted which might occasion some difficulty from their form being very different in the Greek and in the English.*

measure, put up, raise,
raise to life, remembrance,
restore, return, rise, rising,
send, set, that, turn, word.

against, εις 197
εμπροσθεν 239
εν 240
επι 275
κατα 406
μετα 484
παρα 586
περι 613
προς 656

against, εναντιος 259

against, *see* beat, boast, bring,
crime, cry, mad, murmur,
over, prate, prevail, quarrel, rejoice, rise up, say,
speak, spoken, strive, war,
will.

age, ηλικια 344
ημερα 347

age, *see* flower, great, old,
pass.

age (of full), τελειος 727
aged, πρεσβυτης 652
aged man, πρεσβυτης ..... —
aged woman, πρεσβυτις .... —
ages, αιων 19
γενεα 113
ago, απο 63
προ 653
ago, *see* year.
agony, αγωνια 11
agree, εισι 213
ευνοεω 324
{ ην 354
  ισος 390
ομοιαζω 530
πειθω 609
(Rev. 17:17) { ποιεω 636
              μια .. 500
              γνωμη 124
συμφωνεω 707
συντιθημι 714
agree with, συμφωνεω 707
agree together, συμφωνεω .. —
agreed (Mar. 14:56), ισος .. 390
agreeing (not), ασυμφωνος 89
agreement, συνκαταθεσις .. 703
aground, *see* run.
ah, ουα, or ουαι 563
air, αηρ 15
ουρανος 571
alabaster box, αλαβαστρον 26
alas, ουαι 563
albeit, ινα 385
albeit.. not, ινα μη 495
alien, αλλοτριος 31
alienate, απαλλοτριοω..... 59
aliens (be), απαλλοτριοω .. —
alive (be), ζαω 335
alive again, αναζαω 41
alive (make), ζωοποιεω 340
all, απας 60
ολος 529

all, οσος 539
πας 597

all, *see* any, at, first, house,
most, no, places, speed.

all (at), παντως 585
all at once, παμπληθει 584
all (for), *see* once.
all manner, πας 597
all night, *see* continue.
all one's, *see* armour.
all that, οσος 539
all that, *see* for.
all things, απας 60
alledge, παρατιθημι 593
allegory, αλληγορεω ...... ' 29
Alleluia, αλληλουια .... —
allow, γινωσκω 122
δοκιμαζω 160
προσδεχομαι 662
συνευδοκεω 712
allure, δελεαζω 134
Almighty, παντοκρατωρ.... 585
almost { ολιγος 528
         εν 240
σχεδον 715
almost (be), μελλω 478
alms, ελεημοσυνη 233
almsdeeds, ελεημοσυνη.... —
aloes, αλοη 32
alone, εαυτου 172
κατ' ιδιαν.......... { 380
                      406
καταμονας 413
μονον 506
μονος .... —
alone (when they { ιδιος.... 380
were)........... { κατα.... 406
alone, *see* let.
aloud, *see* cry.
Alpha, A 1
already, ηδη 343
already, *see* attain, now, sin.
also, αμα 32
δη 138
ετι 318
μεντοι 481
τε 724
also, *see* me, there.
also if, καν 403
also.. not, ουδε 564
altar, βωμος 112
θυσιαστηριον 379
altered, ετερος 318
although, ει 183
καιτοι 399
altogether, ολος 529
παντως 585
(Acts { πολυς 643
26:29) { εν ... 240
alway, διαπαντος 147
{ ημερα 347
  πας 597
παντοτε 585
always, αει 15
δια 139
διαπαντος 147
εκαστοτε 222

always, { καιρος 398
          πας 597
παντη 585
παντοτε .... —
{ πας 597
  δια 138
amazed (Lu. 4:36), θαμβος 359
amazed (be), εκπλησσω 229
{ εκστασις 230
  λαμβανω 445
εξιστημι 269
θαμβεομαι 359
amazed (be greatly), εκθαμβεω 226
amazed (be sore), εκθαμβεω —
amazement, εκστασις 230
πτοησις 672
ambassador (be an), πρεσ-
βευω 652
ambassage, πρεσβεια .... —
amen, αμην 35
amend { κομψοτερον.... 428
(began to) { εχω 329
amethyst, αμεθυστος 34
amiss, ατοπος 90
κακως 401
among, δια 142
εις 197
εκ 215
εν 240
επι 275
κατα 406
μεσος 483
μετα 484
παρα 586
προς 656
υπο.................. 776

among, *see* compare, dwell,
fall, from, in, out, speak.

anathema, αναθεμα 41
anchor, αγκυρα 8
ancle bone, σφυρον.......... 715
and, αλλα 29
αμα 32
γαρ 112
δη 133
η 340
κατα 406
(Joh. 3:25), μετα...... 484
οστις 540
ουν 567
τε 724
and afterward, κακειθεν 399
and even, ομως 531
and from thence, κακειθεν.. 399
and he, *see* he also, him also.
and his, *see* company.
and I, καγω 393
and if, καν 403
and if, *see* if.
and if so much, καν 403
and so, ουν 567
and they, οστις 540
and there, κακει 399
and.. truly, ουν 567
and [two *and* two], ανα.... 39
and yet, καιπερ 398

beg, προσαιτεω............ 662

began, *see* amend, world.

beget, αποκυεω............ 73

    γενναω 114

beget again, αναγενναω 40

beggar, πτωχος 673

beggarly, πτωχος .... —

begin, αρχομαι............ 85

    εναρχομαι............ 259

    προεναρχομαι 654

begin, *see* sink.

begin before, προεναρχομαι............ 654

begin to, *see* dawn.

beginning, αρξαμενος 82

    αρχη 84

    πρωτος.......... 671

beginning, *see* begin, rehearse from, world.

beginning (at the), πρωτον 671

beginning (from the), ανωθεν 58

begotten (only), μονογενης 505

beguile, δελεαζω 134

    εξαπαταω 266

    παραλογιζομαι 592

beguile of reward, καταβραβευω 410

behalf, μερος 483

behalf, *see* on.

behalf of (in), ὑπερ 773

behalf of (on), ὑπερ .... —

behave..self, αναστρεφω.... 45

    γινομαι 117

behave..self disorderly ατακτεω 90

behave..self uncomely, ασχημονεω 89

behave..self unseemly, ασχημονεω .... —

behaviour, καταστημα 415

behaviour (of good), κοσμιος 429

behead, αποκεφαλιζω 71

beheaded (be), πελεκιζομαι 611

behind, οπισθεν 534

    οπισω .... —

behind, *see* come, tarry.

behind (that which is), ὑστερημα 781

behold, αναθεωρεω.......... 42

    βλεπω 108

    ειδεω 188

    εμβλεπω 235

    εποπτευω 290

    εφοραω 329

    Ͽεαομαι 361

    Ͽεωρεω............ 374

    ιδε 380

    ιδου 381

    κατανοεω 414

    ὁραω 536

behold, as in a glass, κατοπτριζομαι................ 418

behold (earnestly), ατενιζω 90

behold (stedfastly), ατενιζω —

behove, δει 132

    οφειλω 579

beyond, περαν 613

being, *see* burdensome, dead.

being (have our) (Acts 17: 28), εσμεν 307

belief, πιστις............ 624

believe, πειθω 609

    πιστευω 622

    πιστις 624

    πιστος............ 626

believe not, απειθεω 60

    απιστεω 62

believed (be most surely), πληροφορεω 630

believer (1 Ti. 4:12), πιστος 626

believers (Acts 5:14), πιστευω 622

believing, πιστος 626

believing (not), απιστος.... 63

belly, γαστηρ............ 113

    κοιλια 426

belong (Mar 9:41), εστε.... 309

    εστι 310

beloved, αγαπαω 2

    αγαπητος 4

beloved (dearly), αγαπητος —

beneath, κατω 418

benefactor, ευεργετης 322

benefit, αγαθος............ 1

    ευεργεσια 322

    χαρις 797

benevolence, εννοια 324

berry, *see* olive.

beryl, βηρυλλος 106

beseech, δεομαι............ 135

    ερωταω 306

    παρακαλεω 590

besets (which easily), ευπεριστατος................ 324

beside, γε............ 113

beside, επι 275

    συν 707

    χωρις............ 805

beside..self (be), μαινομαι 468

    εξιστημι.. 269

besides, λοιπον............ 464

besides, *see* owe.

best, κρειττων 432

    πρωτος 671

bestow, διδωμι 151

    συναγω 708

bestow labour, κοπιαω...... 428

bestow to feed, ψωμιζω 808

bestow upon, περιτιθημι .. 619

betray, παραδιδωμι 589

betrayer, προδοτης.......... 654

better, καλος 402

    (1 Co. 7:38), κρεισσον 432

    κρεισσων .... —

    (Mar 9:42, ∫μαλλον 470

    1 Co. 9:15) ∖καλος.. 402

    (Phi. 2:3), ὑπερεχω 775

    χρηστος 803

better, ὠφελεω 817

better (be), διαφερω 149

    προεχομαι...... 655

better for (be), συμφερω 707

better (be the), περισσευω .. 618

better (it were) (Lu.17:2), λυσιτελει.................. 465

between, εν 240

    μεσος 483

    μεταξυ 488

    προς 656

between, *see* difference.

betwixt, εκ 215

bewail, κλαιω............ 423

    κοπτω 429

    πενθεω 612

beware, βλεπω 108

    προσεχω 664

    φυλασσω 791

bewitch, βασκαινω.......... 105

    εξιστημι 269

bewray(Mat.26:73) ∫ποιεω 636 ∖δηλος 138

beyond, εκ 215

    επεκεινα 274

    (Gal.1:13), κατα .. 406

    ὑπερ 773

    ὑπερεκεινα 775

beyond, *see* go, measure, stretch.

bid, επω **291**

    καλεω **401**

    κελευω **420**

    λεγω **449**

    προστασσω **666**

bid, *see* farewell.

bid again, αντικαλεω 56

bier, σορος 690

bill, βιβλιον 107

    γραμμα 126

bind, δεσμευω 136

    δεω 137

    προτεινω 668

bind on, ὑποδεομαι 778

bind under a, *see* curse.

bind up, καταδεω 411

bind with, *see* oath.

bird, ορνεον 538

    πετεινον 620

    πτηνον 672

birth, γενετη 114

    γεννησις 115

birth, *see* travail.

birthday, γενεσια 114

birthright, πρωτοτοκια...... 672

bishop, επισκοπος 286

bishop, *see* office.

bishoprick, επισκοπη 286

bit, χαλινος 795

bite, δακνω............ 131

bitter, πικρος 621

bitter (be), πικραινω............ —

bitter (make), πικραινω.... —

bitterly, πικρως .... —

bitterness, πικρια .... —

black, μελας 478

blackness, γνοφος 124

    ζοφος 338

blade, χορτος............ 802

blame, καταγινωσκω........ 410
    μωμεομαι 512
blame (without), αμωμος .. 37
blameless, αμεμπτος 34
    αμωμητος........ 37
    αναιτιος 42
    ανεγκλητος.... 46
    ανεπιληπτος 47
blameless, adv. αμεμπτως .. 35
blaspheme, βλασφημεω 107
blasphemer, βλασφημεω.... —
    βλασφημος.... 108
blasphemous, βλασφημος .. —
blasphemously, βλασφημεω 107
blasphemy, βλασφημια 108
blasphemy, see speak.
blaze abroad, διαφημιζω.... 149
blemish, μωμος 512
blemish (without), αμωμος 37
bless, ευλογεω 324
blessed, ευλογητος.......... —
    μακαριος 468
blessed (be), ενευλογεομαι 261
blessed (call), μακαριζω.... 468
blessedness, μακαρισμος.... 469
blessing, ευλογια............ 324
blind, τυφλος............... 752
blind, τυφλοω .... —
blinded (be), πωροω........ 675
blindfold, περικαλυπτω 616
blindness, πωρωσις 675
blood, αιμα................. 16
blood, see issue, shedding.
bloody flux, δυσεντερια 168
blot out, εξαλειφω,.......... 266
blow, επιγινομαι............. 282
    πνεω.................. 635
blow softly, υποπνεω 779
board, σανις 680
boast, κατακαυχαομαι...... 411
    καυχαομαι 419
    λεγω.................. 449
boast against, κατακαυχαο-
    μαι.................... 411
boast great things, μεγαλαυ-
    χεω.................... 475
boast (make), καυχαομαι .. 419
boaster, αλαζων 27
boasting, αλαζονεια 26
    καυχημα........... 419
    καυχησις........... —
boat, πλοιαριον 631
    σκαφη 686
bodily (2 Co. 10:10), σωμα 717
    σωματικος 718
bodily, σωματικως .... —
body, σωμα................. 717
    χρως.................. 805
body, see dead.
body (of the same), συσσωμα 714
boisterous, ισχυρος 392
bold (Philem 8), παρρησια 596
bold (be), Joh. 8:57), εχω.. 329
    θαρρεω 360
    παρρησιαζομαι.. 596
    τολμαω 741

bold (be very), αποτολμαω 78
bold (wax), παρρησιαζομαι 596
boldly (Heb. 13:6), θαρρεω 360
    παρρησια.......... 596
    (Acts 9:28), παρρη-
    σιαζομαι .... —
    (Mar.15:43),τολμαω 741
boldly, see preach, speak.
boldly (the more), τολμηρο-
    τερον...................... 741
boldness, παρρησια 596
boldness, see speech.
bond, δεσμος.............. 136
bond, δουλος.............. 163
bond, συνδεσμος........... 710
bondage, δουλεια........... 163
bondage (be in), δουλευω .. —
bondage (be under), δουλοω 164
bondage (bring into), δουλοω —
    κατα-
    δουλοω.. 411
bondmaid, παιδισκη 583
bondman, δουλος........... 163
bonds, αλυσις 32
bonds (be in), δεω........ 137
bonds (that are in), δεσμιος 136
bondwoman, παιδισκη...... 583
bone, οστεον 540
bone, see ancle.
book, βιβλιον 107
    βιβλος . ... —
book (little), βιβλαριδιον .. —
border, κρασπεδον...... 431
border, μεθορια............. 478
    ορια 538
born, γενος............... 115
born (be), γενναω 114
    τικτω.................. 731
born again (be), αναγεννaω 40
born out of due time εκτρωμα 231
born (they that are), γεννη-
    τος.................. 115
borne, see grievous.
borrow, δανειζω 132
bosom, κολπος............. 428
both, αμφοτερος 37
    δυο 167
    εκαστος 221
    τε 724
both me, καμε 393
bottles, ασκος 87
bottom, κατω............. 418
bottomless, αβυσσος 1
bottomless pit, αβυσσος .... —
bought, see buy.
bound, οροθεσια 538
bound about (be), περιδεομαι 616
bound (be), δεσμεω 136
    οφειλω 579
bound with (be), περικειμαι —
    συνδεομαι 710
bountifully, ευλογια 324
bountifulness, απλοτης 63
bounty, ευλογια 324
bow, τοξον................. 741
bow, καμπτω 403
    κλινω 426

bow, τιθημι 731
bow down, κλινω 426
    συγκαμπτω 703
bow the knee, γονυπετεω .. 126
bow together, συγκυπτω.... 704
bowels, σπλαγχνα 696
box, αλαβαστρον............ 26
box, see alabaster.
bramble bush, η βατος..... 106
branch, βαιον 100
    κλαδος.............. 423
    κλημι.............. 424
    στοιβεας 699
brasen vessel, χαλκιον...... 796
brass, χαλκεος 795
brass, χαλκος............... 796
brass (fine), χαλκολιβανον —
brawler (not a), αμαχος.... 34
bread, αρτος 83
bread, see unleavened.
breadth, πλατος 627
break, διαρρηγνυμι........ 148
    καταγνυμι 411
    κατακλαω........... —
    κλαζω.............. 423
    λυω.................. 466
    ρηγνυμι 677
    συνθρυπτω........... 713
    συντριβω 714
    σχιζω.............. 716
break forth, ρηγνυμι........ 677
break in pieces, συντριβω .. 714
break of day, αυγη........ 90
break off, εκκλαζω.......... 227
break through, διορυσσω ... 158
break to shivers, συντριβω 714
break up, εξορυττω......... 269
    λυω, break down 466
breaker, παραβατης 587
breakers, see covenant.
breaking, κλασις............ 424
    (Ro. 2:23), παρα-
    βασις.......... 587
breast, στηθος 699
breastplate, θωραξ......... 379
breath, πνοη............... 635
breathe, εμπνεω 239
breathe on, εμφυσαω 240
brethren, αδελφοτης 13
brethren, see brother.
brethren, see love as, love of
    the.
brethren (false), ψευδαδελ-
    φος.................. 806
bride, νυμφη 519
bridechamber, νυμφων.... —
bridegroom, νυμφιος........ —
bridle, χαλινος............. 795
bridle, χαλιναγωγεω ...... —
briefly, { δια 138
       { ολιγος 528
briefly, see comprehend.
brier, τριβολος............. 750
bright, λαμπρος........... 447
    φωτεινος........... 794
bright, see shine.
brightness, απαυγασμα 60

brightness, επιφανεια	......	289
λαμπροτης	......	447
brim, ανω	......	57
brimstone, θειον	......	361
θειωδης	......	—
bring, αγω	......	10
απαγω	......	59
αποφερω	......	78
επιφερω	......	289
ερχομαι	......	301
ιστημι	......	391
κομιζω	......	428
λαμβανω	......	445
παρεχω	......	595
ποιεω	......	636
προσαγω	......	661
προσφερω	......	667
φερω	......	784

bring, *see* light, word.

bring again, αποστρεφω	...	77
αναγω	......	41
bring against, επιφερω	......	289
bring before, παριστημι	......	595
bring down, καταγω	......	411
bring forth, αναγω	......	41
αποκυεω	......	73
βλαστανω	......	107
γενναω	......	114
διδωμι	......	151
εκβαλλω	......	222
εκφερω	......	231
εξαγω	......	265
καταγω	......	411
παραδιδωμι	...	589
ποιεω	......	636
προαγω	......	653
προφερω	......	668
τικτω	......	731
φερω	......	784

bring forth fruit, καρποφορεω 405

bring forth plentifully, ευφο-
ρεω...................... 327

bring forward on ... journey,
προπεμπω................ 656

bring fruit, *see* perfection.

bring in, *see* privily.

bring in.. into, εισφερω	......	214
εισαγω	......	211

bring into, *see* bondage, captivity, subjection.

bring low, ταπεινοω	......	720
bring on journey, προπεμπω		656
bring on way, προπεμπω	..	656
bring out, εξαγω	......	265
προαγω(with εζω)		653
bring safe, διασωζω	......	148

bring tidings, *see* glad, good.

bring to, προσφερω	......	667

bring to, *see* desolation, nothing, nought, remem-
brance.

bring (to land), καταγω	...	411
bring together, συμφερω	...	707

bring under, *see* power.

bring unto, προσφερω	......	667

---

bring up, ανατρεφω	......	45
αναφερω	......	46
εκτρεφω	......	231
τρεφω	......	749

bring up, *see* children.

bring up again, αναγω	......	41
bring upon, επαγω	......	272

bringing, *see* salvation.

bringing in, επεισαγωγη	...	274
broad, ευρυχωρος	......	326
broad (make), πλατυνω	...	627

broidered, *see* hair.

broiled, οπτος	......	536
broken (be), συνθλαομαι	..	712
broken (meat), κλασμα	...'	424
broken up (be), διορυσσω	..	158
brokenhearted { καρδια	...	404
(Lu. 4:18) { συντριβω	..	714
brood, νοσσια	......	518
brook, χειμαρρος	......	798
brother, αδελφος	......	11
brotherhood, αδελφοτης	...	13

brotherly, *see* kindness, love.

brought (Mat. 1:12), μετοι-		
κεσια	......	489
brought (be), γινομαι	......	117
brought down, (be), κατα-		
βιβαζομαι		410
brought forth, αγω	......	10
brought in (unawares), πα-		
ρεισακτος	......	594
brought to pass (be), γινο-		
μαι	......	117
brought up with, συντροφος		714
brow, οφρυς	...	580
bruise, θραυω	......	376
συντριβω	......	714
brute, αλογος	......	32
bud, βλαστανω	......	107
buffet, κολαφιζω	......	427
build, κατασκευαζω	......	415
οικοδομεω	......	525
build again, ανοικοδομεω	...	55
build thereon } εποικοδο-		
build thereupon } μεω	......	290
build up, εποικοδομεω	......	—
οικοδομεω	......	525
build upon, εποικοδομεω	....	290
builded together (be), συν-		
οικοδομεομαι	......	713
builder, οικοδομεω	......	525
τεχνιτης	......	730
building, ενδομησις	..	260
κτισις	......	435
οικοδομη	......	525
bull, ταυρος	......	720
bundle, δεσμη	......	136
πληθος	......	629
burden, βαρος	......	102
φορτιον	......	789
burden, καταβαρεω	......	410
burden [ship's], γομος	......	125
burdened (2 Co. 8 : 13),		
θλιψις	......	376
burdened, (be), βαρεω	......	102
burdensome βαρος	......	—

---

burdensome (be), καταναρ-		
καω	......	413
burdensome (from being),		
αβαρης	......	1
burial, ενταφιαζω	......	263
buried with (be), συνθαπ-		
τομαι	......	712
burn, εκκαιομαι	......	227
καιω	......	399
κατακαιω	......	411
πυροομαι	......	674

burn, *see* incense.

burn up, εμπρηθω	......	239
κατακαιω	......	411
burn utterly, κατακαιω	....	
burned (be), (Heb. 6 : 8)		
καυσις	......	419
burning, πυρωσις	......	674

burning, *see* heat.

burnt offering, ολοκαυτωμα		528
burnt offering (whole), ολο-		
καυτωμα	......	—
burst, ρηγνυμι	......	677
burst asunder, λακεω	......	443
bury, ενταφιαζω	......	263
θαπτω	......	360
bury (Mat. 27:7), ταφη	......	723
burying, ενταφιασμος	......	263
bush, βατος (η)	......	106

bush, *see* bramble.

bushel, μοδιος	......	503
business, πραγμα	......	651
σπουδη	......	697
χρεια	......	802

business, *see* your.

busybody, περιεργος	......	616
busybody (be a), περιεργαζ-		
ομαι	......	—
busybody in other men's mat-		
ters, αλλοτριοεπισκοπος		31
but, αλλα	......	29
γαρ	......	112
εαν	......	170
ει μη	......	186
εκτος	......	231
η	......	340
μεντοι	......	481
μη	......	490
εαν μη	......	494
μονον	......	506
ουν	......	567
πλην	......	629

but, *see* if, nay, yet.

but either, η	......	340

but for a, *see* moment.

but now, τα νυν	......	520
but rather, πλην	......	629
but that, μη	......	490

but even, *see* moreover.

buy, αγοραζω	......	9
ωνεομαι	......	811
buy and sell, εμπορευομαι	..	239
by, απο	......	63
δια	......	138
εις	......	197
εκ	......	215
εν	......	240

corrupt, καπηλευω......... 404
    καταφθειρω........ 416
    φθειρω.............. 786
corrupt..self, φθειρω....... —
corrupted (be), σηπω 685
corruptible, φθαρτος....... 785
corruption, διαφθορα 149
    φθορα 786
cost, δαπανη 132
costliness, τιμιοτης 732
costly, πολυτελης 645
costly (very), πολυτιμος.... —
couch, κλινιδιον 426
    κραββατος 431
could, δυναμαι.............. 164
    δυνατος 167
could, see can.
council, συμβουλιον 706
    συνεδριον 710
counsel, βουλη.............. 110
    συμβουλιον 706
counsel, συμβουλευω 705
counsel (give), συμβουλευω —
counsel (take), βουλευομαι 110
    συμβουλευω 705
counsel together (take), συμβουλευω .... —
counsellor, βουλευτης 110
    συμβουλος 706
count, εχω 329
    ηγεομαι............ 343
    λογιζομαι........... 461
    συμψηφιζω 707
    ψηφιζω 807
count, see descent, happy,
worthy.
countenance, ιδεα 380
    οψις 582
    προσωπον.... 667
countenance (of a sad), σκυ-
θρωπος.................... 688
country, αγρος.............. 10
    γενος.............. 115
    γη .... —
    πατρις 609
    χωρα.............. 805
country about, περιχωρος.. 619
country (go or travel into a
far), αποδημεω 68
country (own), πατρις 609
country round about, περιχωρος 619
countryman, γενος......... 115
    συμφυλετης .. 707
courage, θαρσος 360
course, δρομος 164
    εφημερια............ 328
    μερος.............. 483
    πλοος 631
    τροχος............. 751
course, see come, straight.
course (have), τρεχω 749
course [of this world], αιων 19
court, αυλη.......... 90
court, see king's.
courteous, φιλοφρων....... 788
courteously, φιλανθρωπως.. 786

courteously, φιλοφρονως.... 788
cousin, συγγενης............ 703
covenant, διαθηκη 144
covenant, ιστημι............ 391
    συντιθημι.......... 714
covenant breakers, ασυνθετος 89
cover, επικαλυπτω 284
    καλυπτω............ 403
    κατακαλυπτομαι ... 411
    περικαλυπτω 616
    συγκαλυπτομαι...... 703
covered (1 Cor. 11:4), κατα 406
covering, περιβολαιον 616
covet, επιθυμεω 283
    ζηλοω 337
covet after, ορεγομαι....... 537
covet earnestly, ζηλοω.... 337
covetous, πλεονεκτης 628
    φιλαργυρος 786
covetous practices, πλεονεξια 628
covetousness, πλεονεξια.... —
covetousness (without), αφι-
λαργυρος 98
craft, δολος............. 161
    εργασια 298
    μερος................ 483
    τεχνη 730
craft (of the same), ομοτεχ-
νος.................... 531
craftiness, πανουργια 585
craftiness, see cunning.
craftsman, τεχνιτης 730
crafty, πανουργος 585
crave, αιτεω 18
create, κτιζω 435
creation, κτισις............ —
creator (Ro. 1:25), κτιζω.. —
    κτιστης .... —
creature, κτισις............ —
    κτισμα .... —
creditor, δανειστης......... 132
creek, κολπος 428
creep, ενδυνω 260
creep in unawares, παρεισ-
δυνω 594
creeping thing, ερπετον 301
Crescens, Κρησκης......... 849
Cretes, Κρης............. —
crime, αιτια 18
crime laid against, εγκλημα 178
cripple, χωλος............ 805
crooked, σκολιος........... 687
cross, σταυρος 697
crow, φωνεω 792
crown, διαδημα 144
    στεφανος 698
crown, στεφανοω........... 699
crucify, προσπηγνυμι 666
    σταυροω........... 697
crucify afresh, ανασταυροω 45
crucify with, συσταυροω.... 714
crumb, ψιχιον 807
cry, βοη 109
    κραυγη 432
cry, αφιημι............. 97
    βοαω 109

cry, επιβοαω 282
    επιφωνεω 289
    κραζω 431
    κραυγαζω 432
    φωνεω 792
cry against, επιφωνεω 289
cry aloud, αναβοαω 40
cry out, αναβοαω ......
    ανακραζω 42
    κραζω.......... 431
    κραυγαζω........... 432
crying, κραυγη.............. 432
crystal, κρυσταλλος 435
crystal (be clear as), κρυσ-
ταλλιζω .... —
cubit, πηχυς............... 621
cumber, καταργεω......... 415
cumbered (be), περισπαομαι 618
cumi, κουμι 431
cummin, κυμινον 436
cunning craftiness, πανουργια 585
cunningly, see devised.
cup, ποτηριον 649
cure, ιασις 379
cure, θεραπευω 373
curious, περιεργος 616
curse, αναθεμα.......... 41
    καταναθεμα 413
    καταρα 414
curse, αναθεματιζω 42
    κακολογεω 400
    καταναθεματιζω.... 413
    καταραομαι 414
curse, (bind under a), αναθεματιζω............... 42
cursed, επικαταρατος 284
    καταρα.............. 414
cursing, αρα 79
    καταρα 414
custom, εθος 182
    συνηθεια 712
    τελος 728
custom, εθιζω 181
custom(receipt of), τελωνιον 728
custom was, εθω........... 182
cut, κατακοπτω 412
cut asunder, } διχοτομεω.. 159
in sunder, }
cut down, εκκοπτω.......... 228
    κοπτω.......... 429
cut off, αποκοπτω 71
    αφαιρεω 96
    εκκοπτω 228
cut out, εκκοπτω........... —
cut short, συντεμνω........ 713
cut to the heart (be), δια-
πριομαι 147
cymbal, κυμβαλον 436

daily, επιουσιος 285
    εφημερος.............. 328
    { ημερα.............. 347
    { κατα 406
    { ημερα.......... 347
    { πας 597
    καθ' ημεραν 396

doubting, διαλογισμος...... 146

doubtless, γε 113

     δη 138

doubtless, see yea.

dove, περιστερα 619

down, κατα.............. 406

down, κατω 418

down, see bow, bring, brought, cast, come, cut, driven, fall, get, go, hang, kneel, let, press, put, run, sink, sit, step, stoop, take, throw, thrust, tread.

down at, see fall.

down before, see fall.

down (let), χαλαω......... 795

down with, see go.

drag, συρω 714

dragon, δρακων 164

draught, αφεδρων 97

draught [of fishes], αγρα .. 9

draw, αντλεω 57

    αποσπαω 76

    ἑλκυω 234

    ἑλκω .... —

    (Acts 19:33), προβι-

    βαζω.............. 654

    σπαομαι 695

    συρω 714

draw away, αποσπαω 76

    αφιστημι 98

    εξελκομαι 266

draw back, ὑποστελλω ... 779

    (Heb. 10:39), } 780

    ὑποστολη .... }

draw near, εγγιζω 175

    προσαγω........ 661

    προσερχομαι.... 662

draw [nigh], γινομαι 117

draw nigh, εγγιζω 175

draw on, επιφωσκω 289

draw out, αντλεω 57

    σπαομαι............ 695

draw [to shore], αναβιβαζω 40

draw to the shore, προσορ-

    μιζομαι 666

draw up, ανασπαω......... 44

draw with (thing to), αν-

    τλημα 57

dream, ενυπνιον........... 264

    οναρ 531

dream, ενυπνιαζομαι 264

dreamer, ενυπνιαζομαι .... —

dress, γεωργεομαι 115

dresser, see vineyard.

drink, πομα 645

    ποσις 648

drink, πινω 621

drink see water.

drink (give)   }

drink (give to)   }ποτιζω .. 649

drink (make to)   }

drink (strong), σικερα..... 685

drink well, μεθυω 478

drink with, συμπινω........ 706

drive, απελαω 61

drive (let her) { επιδιδωμι.. 283

   Acts 27:15) { φερω 784

---

drive out, εκβαλλω......... 222

    εξωθω 271

driven, see wind.

driven (be), ελαυνω....... 232

    φερω 784

driven up and down (be),

    διαφερω 149

drops (great), θρομβος 377

dropsy (having the), ὑδρω-

    πικος................ 753

drown, βυθιζω., ... 111

drowned (be), καταπινω .. 414

    καταποντιζομαι —

drunk (be), μεθυσκομαι 478

drunk (make), μεθυω ..... —

drunkard, μεθυσος .... —

drunken (be), μεθυω........ —

    μεθυσκομαι.. —

drunkenness, μεθη......... 477

dry, αννδρος 57

    ξηρος 522

dry up, ξηραινω 521

due, ιδιος 380

    οφειλη.............. 578

    οφειλω.............. 579

due, see born.

due reward, αξιος 58

due season, καιρος 398

due time, καιρος .... —

dull, βαρεως 102

    νωθρος 521

dumb, αλαλος 27

    αφωνος 99

    κωφος 442

    (Lu. 1:20), σιωπαω 686

dung, σκυβαλον 688

dung { κοπρια 429

     { βαλλω 100

dunghill, κοπρια 429

dure, εισι 213

dure for a while { προσκαιρος 664

(Mat. 13:21) { εστι........ 310

durst, τολμαω 741

dust, κονιορτος............ 428

    χοος 802

duty (be), οφειλω 579

dwell, καθημαι 395

    κατοικεω 418

    μενω.............. 481

    οικεω 524

    σκηνοω 687

dwell among, εγκατοικεω .. 177

dwell in, ενοικεω 262

dwell round about, περιοικεω 617

dwell with, συνοικεω........ 713

dwellers, κατοικεω 418

dwelling, κατοικησις .... —

dwelling, see there.

dwellingplace (to have no

    certain), αστατεω 88

dying (2 Co. 4:10), νεκρωσις 514

dying (lay a), αποθνησκω.. 69

---

each, ανα.............. 39

each, see other.

each one, ἑκαστος 221

---

eagle, αετος.............. 15

ear, ους.............. 573

    ωτιον.............. 817

ear [of corn], σταχυς ... 698

early, ορθριος.............. 538

    πρωι.............. 670

    πρωια .... —

    πρωιμος .... —

early, see morning.

early (very), βαθυς 100

earnest, αρραβων........... 82

earnest, see care, desire, ex-

    pectation.

earnest (the more), (Heb.

    2:1), περισσοτερως 618

earnestly, see behold, covet, desire, look, pray.

earnestly for, see contend.

earnestly (more), εκτενεσ-

    τερον................. 230

ears (come to the), ακουω.. 22

ears [for 'hearing'], ακοη .. —

earth, γη.............. 115

    οικουμενη 527

earth (under the), καταχθο-

    νιος 416

earth (in), επιγειος 282

earth (of), οστρακινος 541

earthen, οστρακινος ...... —

earthly, γη.............. 115

    επιγειος 282

earthquake, σεισμος 683

earthy, χοικος 801

ease (take), αναπαυω 44

eased, ανεσις 47

easier, ευκοπωτερος......... 323

easily, see besets, provoked.

east, ανατολη 45

    { ηλιος 344

    { with ανατολη 45

Easter, πασχα 605

easy, χρηστος 803

easy, see intreat, understood.

eat, βρωσκω 111

    γενομαι 115

    εσθιω 306

    μεταλαμβανω 488

    (2 Ti. 2:17) { εχω 329

           { νομη.... 516

    τρωγω 751

    φαγω.............. 782

eat enough, κορεννυμι 429

eat up, καταφαγω 416

eat with, συνεσθιω 712

eaten, see worms.

eating, βρωσις 111

edge, στομα 699

edged, see two.

edges (with two), διστομος 158

edification, οικοδομη 525

edify, οικοδομεω .... —

edify (wherewith one may),

    (Ro. 14:19), οικοδομη.... —

edifying, οικοδομη .... —

    (1Ti.1:4), οικονομια 526

effect (become of none), κα-

    ταργεω..................... 415

exhortation (give), παρακαλεω 590

exorcist, εξορκιστης 269

expect, εκδεχομαι 223

   προσδοκαω.......... 662

expectation, προσδοκια .... —

expectation (be in) προσ-
δοκαω .... —

expectation (earnest), απο-
καραδοκια 70

expedient (be), } συμφερω 707
expedient for (be), }

expel, εκβαλλω............. 222

experience, δοκιμη 160

experiment, δοκιμη......... —

expert, γνωστης 125

expire, πληροω.............. 630

   τελεω............... 727

expound, διερμηνευω...... 154

   εκτιθημι 230

   επιλυω............. 285

express, see image.

expressly, ρητως 678

extortion, αρπαγη 82

extortioner, αρπαξ......... —

eye, ομμα................... 530

   οφθαλμος 579

eye [as of a needle], τρυμαλια 751

   τρυπημα —

eye (with one), μονοφθαλμος 506

eyes, see fasten, set.

eyesalve, κολλουριον...... 427

eyeservice, οφθαλμοδουλεια 579

eyewitness, αυτοπτης 91

   εποπτης 290

fable, μυθος................. 511

face, οψις................... 582

   προσωπον 667

   στομα.............. 699

face, see before.

fade away, μαραινομαι...... 471

fading not away, αμαραντι-
νος.... 32

   αμαραντος —

fail, εκλειπω 228

   εκπιπτω............... 229

   επιλειπω 285

   καταργεω............. 415

   πιπτω................ 622

   υστερεω............... 781

failing, see hearts.

failing not, ανεκλειπτος.... 46

fain [would fain], επιθυμεω 283

faint, εκκακεω 227

   εκλυω 229

   καμνω 403

fair, αστειος 88

   καλος............... 402

fair, see shew, speech.

fair weather, ευδια......... 322

faith, ελπις................. 234

   πιστις............... 624

faith (of little), ολιγοπιστος 528

faithful, πιστος 626

faithfully (3 Joh. 5), πιστος —

faithless, απιστος 63

fall, παραπτωμα............. 593

   πτωσις 673

fall, γινομαι 117

 (Mar. { εκπιπτω...... 229
 13:25) { εσομαι....... 308

   εκπιπτω............... 229

   επιβαλλω 281

   καταβαινω 409

   καταπιπτω 414

   καταφερω 416

   πιπτω................ 622

   πταιω 672

fall, see asleep, occasion,
transgression.

fall among, εμπιπτω....... 239

   περιπιπτω...... 618

fall asleep, κοιμαομαι 426

fall at, προσπιπτω.........,. 666

fall away, αφιστημι 98

   εκπιπτω.............. 229

   παραπιπτω 592

fall down, καταβαινω 409

   καταπιπτω 414

   πιπτω.............. 622

fall down at, προσπιπτω ... 666

fall down before, προσπιπτω —

fall from, αποπιπτω........ 75

fall into, εμπιπτω 239

 (Acts 10:10), επι-
πιπτω 285

   περιπιπτω 618

fall off, εκπιπτω 229

fall on, επιπιπτω 285

fall on sleep, κοιμαομαι 426

fall out, ερχομαι 301

fall upon, επιπιπτω 285

falling away, αποστασια.... 76

falling (from), απταιστος .. 79

false, ψευδης.............. 806

false, see accusation, accusers, apostle, brethren,
Christs, prophet, teacher,
witness.

falsely, ψευδομαι........... 806

falsely, see accuse.

falsely so, see called.

fame, ακοη 22

   ηχος 358

   λογος 462

   φημη 785

fame, see spread abroad.

family, πατρια 609

famine, λιμος.............. 461

fan, πτυον 672

far, εως.................... 334

   μακραν 469

   μακρος............... —

 (Phi. { μαλλον 470
 1:23) { πολυς 643

   πορρω 648

far, see be, country, from,
journey, more, spent.

far above, υπερανω........ 774

far as, see as.

far (be it), (Mat. 16:22), ιλεως 384

far more, περισσοτερον...... 618

far off, μακραν............. 469

far passed, πολυς 643

far spent, πολυς .... —

fare, ευφραινω 327

farewell, ρωννυμαι.......... 679

   χαιρω 795

farewell (bid), αποτασσομαι 78

farm, αγρος 10

farther, see go.

farther side, περαν........ 613

farthing, ασσαριον......... 88

   κοδραντης 426

fashion, ειδος.............. 192

   προσωπον 667

   σχημα.............. 716

   τυπος 752

fashion (on this), ουτω ... 576

fashion..self according to,
συσχηματιζομαι.......... 715

fashioned like unto, συμμορ-
φος.................... 706

fast, νηστεια 515

fast, νηστευω.............. —

fast, see hold, stand, stick.

fast (make), ασφαλιζω...... 89

fasten, ατενιζω............. 90

fasten..eyes, ατενιζω ...... —

fasten on, καθαπτω 394

fasting, ασιτος 87

   νηστεια 515

   νηστις .... —

father, πατηρ 606

father in law, πενθερος 612

father (of, or, belonging to a),
πατρικος 609
   πατρωος —

father (received by tradition
from), πατροπαραδοτος.. —

father (without), απατωρ .. 60

fatherless, ορφανος......... 539

fathers (murderer of), πα-
τραλψης 609

fathom, οργυια............. 537

fatling, σιτιστος 686

fatness, πιοτης............. 622

fatted, σιτευτος 686

fault, αιτια................ 18

   αιτιον 19

   ηττημα 358

   παραπτωμα 593

fault, see tell.

fault (being in), αμαρτανω 32

fault (find), μεμφομαι 480

fault (without), αμωμος.... 37

faultless, αμεμπτος......... 34

   αμωμος............. 37

favour, χαρις.............. 797

favoured (be highly), χαρι-
τοω.................... 798

fear, δειλια 133

   φοβος 789

fear, ευλαβεομαι 323

   φοβεομαι 788

 (1 Ti. { φοβος 789
 5:20) { εχω 329

fear, see godly, move.

fear exceedingly, εκφοβος ... 231

fear exceedingly, (Mar.4:41),
 φοβεομαι .. 788
 { φοβος 789
 { μεγας..... 476
fear ['in that he feared'],
 ευλαβεια 323
fear (without), αφοβως 99
fearful, δειλος 133
 φοβερος 789
fearful, see sight.
feast, δειπνον 134
 δοχη 164
 εορτη................. 271
feast, see governor, ruler.
feast (keep a), εορταζω 271
feast of, see charity.
feast of the dedication, εγ-
 καινια 177
feast with, συνευωχεομαι .. 712
feeble (Heb. 12:12), παρα-
 λυομαι................. 592
feeble (more), ασθενης 87
feebleminded, ολιγοψυχος.. 528
feed, βοσκω 109
 ποιμαινω 640
 ποτιζω 649
 τρεφω 749
 χορταζω 802
 ψωμιζω 808
feed, see bestow.
feed cattle, ποιμαινω....... 640
feel, γινωσκω.............. 122
 πασχω 605
feel after, ψηλαφαω 807
feeling, see touch.
feeling (to be past), απαλγεω 59
feign, υποκρινομαι.......... 778
feigned, πλαστος........... 627
Felix, Φηλιξ 866
fellow, ανηρ 47
 εταιρος 317
 μετοχος.............. 489
fellowcitizen, συμπολιτης .. 706
fellowdisciple, συμμαθητης —
fellowheir, συγκληρονομος.. 703
fellowhelper, συνεργος .. 711
fellowlabourer, συνεργος.... —
fellowprisoner, συναιχμαλω-
 τος 709
fellowservant, συνδουλος.... 710
fellowship, κοινωνια 427
 (1 Co. 10 : 20),
 κοινωνος ... —
 μετοχη 489
fellowship with (have), συγ-
 κοινωνεω................. 704
fellowsoldier, συστρατιωτης 715
fellowworker, συνεργος.... 711
female, θηλυ 375
fervent, εκτενης........... 230
fervent, see effectual, heat.
fervent (be), ζεω........... 337
fervent mind, ζηλος .... —
fervently, εκτενως.......... 230
fervently, see labour.
Festus, Φηστος 866
fetch a, see compass.

fetch out, εξαγω 265
fetter, πεδη 609
fever, πυρετος 674
fever (be sick of a), πυρεσσω —
few, ολιγος 528
few, see words.
few words, βραχυς.......... 110
fidelity, πιστις 624
field, αγρος 10
 χωρα 805
 χωριον .... —
field, see abide in the, corn.
fierce, ανημερος.............. 47
 σκληρος 687
 χαλεπος.............. 795
fierce (be more), επισχυω.. 288
fierceness, θυμος 378
fiery (Heb. 10:27), πυρ .. 673
 (Eph. 6:16), πυροομαι 674
fiery, see trial.
fifteen, δεκαπεντε.......... 134
fifteenth, πεντεκαιδεκατος .. 612
fifth, πεμπτος.............. 611
fifty, πεντηκοντα.......... 612
fifty, see thousand.
fig, συκον 705
fig tree, συκη 704
fig (untimely), ολυνθος 529
fight, αγων 10
 αθλησις................. 15
 πολεμος 641
fight, αγωνιζομαι.......... 11
 μαχομαι 473
 πολεμεω 641
 πυκτευω 673
fight against, see God.
fight with, see beasts.
fighting, μαχη 473
figure, αντιτυπον........... 57
 παραβολη 587
 τυπος 752
figure, see transfer.
figure unto (like), αντιτυπον 57
fill, γεμιζω.............. 113
 εμπιπλαω 239
 εμπληθω .... —
 κεραννυμι................. 421
 (Acts 2:13) μεστοω 484
 πληθω.............. 629
fill up, πληροω 630
 συμπληροω 706
 χορταζω 802
fill up, αναπληροω 44
 ανταναπληροω 55
 πληροω 630
 τελεω 727
fill up, see piece.
fill up (which is put into),
 πληρωμα 630
filth, καθαρμα.............. 394
 περικαθαρμα 616
 ρυπος 678
filthiness, αισχροτης 18
 ακαθαρτης........ 21
 μολυσμος 505
 ρυπαρια ..,....... 678

filthy, αισχρος 18
 ασελγεια 87
filthy, see lucre.
filthy (be), ρυπow 678
filthy communication, αισ-
 χρολογια................. 18
filthy lucre (for the sake of),
 αισχροκερδως .... —
filthy lucre (given to), αισ-
 χροκερδης .... —
filthy lucre (greedy of), αισ-
 χροκερδης .... —
finally, λοιπον & το λοιπον.. 464
 τελος 728
find, ανευρισκω 47
 ευρισκω 325
 καταλαμβανω......... 412
finding out, see past.
fine, see brass, flour, linen.
finger, δακτυλος 132
finish, απαρτισμος 60
finish, αποτελεω 78
 διανυω................. 147
 εκτελεω 230
 επιτελεω 288
 συντελεω 713
 τελειοω 727
 τελεω .... —
finished (be), γινομαι....... 117
finisher, τελειωτης 727
fire, πυρ 673
 πυρα 674
 φως 794
fire (be on), πυροομαι 674
fire of, see coals.
fire (set on), φλογιζω....... 788
firkin, μετρητης.......... 489
firm, βεβαιος.............. 106
first, μια.............. 500
 προτερον 668
 πρωτον 671
 πρωτος.............. —
first, see give, trust.
first (after the), see second.
first (at), το πρωτον....... 671
first (at the), αρχη 84
 το προτερον.. 668
 πρωτον & το
 πρωτον.... 671
first (be), προκειμαι....... 655
first estate, αρχη 84
first (from the very), ανωθεν 58
first of all, πρωτον....... 671
 πρωτος......... —
firstbegotten, πρωτοτοκος.. 672
firstborn, πρωτοτοκος ..... —
firstfruits, απαρχη......... 60
fish, αλιευω 29
fish, ιχθυς 393
 οψαριον 581
fish (little), ιχθυδιον 393
fish (small), ιχθυδιον ..... —
 οψαριον 581
fisher's coat, επενδυτης 274
fishers & fishermen, αλιευς.. 29
fit, ενθετος 322
fit, καθηκον 395

forgetful (Jas. 1:25), επι-
ληϲμονη 285

forgetful (be), επιλανθανο-
μαι .... —

forgive, απολυω 75

αφιημι.............. 97

forgive frankly, & forgive,
χαριζομαι 796

forgiveness, αφεϲιϲ 97

form, μορφη 506

μορφωϲιϲ.............. —

τυποϲ 752

ὑποτυπωϲιϲ 780

form, πλαϲϲω 627

formed (be), μορφοομαι 506

formed (thing), πλαϲμα.... 627

former, προτερον............ 668

προτεροϲ.............. —

πρωτοϲ............. 671

fornication, πορνεια 647

fornication (commit), πορ-
νευω 648

fornication (give self over
to), εκπορνευω............. 230

fornicator, πορνοϲ 648

forsake, αποϲταϲια.......... 76

αποταϲϲομαι 78

αφιημι.............. 97

εγκαταλειπω 177

καταλειπω.......... 413

forswear self, επιορκεω...... 285

forth, εξω................... 270

(Mar. {μεϲοϲ 483
3:3) {ειϲ............. 197

..forth, απο 63

forth, see break, bring,
brought, call, carry, cast,
come, conduct, from, go,
hold, launch, let, minister,
pass, proceed, put, reach,
send, set, setter, shed,
shew, shine, shoot, speak,
stand, stretch.

forth at, εκ 215

forth fruit, see bring.

forthwith, ευθεωϲ 322

ευθυϲ 323

παραχρημα...... 594

forty, τεϲϲαρακοντα 728

forty years (of), τεϲϲαρα-
κονταετηϲ 729

forty years old, τεϲϲαρακον-
ταετηϲ .... —

forward, see go, put.

forward (be), θελω......... 362

ϲπουδαζω...... 696

forward (more), ϲπουδαιοϲ 697

forward on journey, see
bring

forwardness, ϲπουδη........ 697

forwardness of mind, προθυμια.......................... 655

foul, ακαθαρτοϲ 21

foul, see weather.

found, θεμελιοω 363

found (be), γινομαι 117

foundation, θεμελιοϲ........ 363

καταβολη 410

foundation (lay the), θεμελιοω 363

fountain, πηγη............... 620

four, τεϲϲαρεϲ 729

τεταρτοϲ .... —

four days, τεταρταιοϲ ..... —

four hundred, τετρακοϲιοι.. —

four months, τετραμηνον .. —

four thousand, τετρακιϲχι-
λιοι .... —

fourfold, τετραπλοοϲ .... —

fourfooted beasts, τετραπουϲ —

fourscore, ογδοηκοντα..... 522

foursquare, τετραγωνοϲ 729

fourteen, δεκατεϲϲαρεϲ..... 134

fourteenth, τεϲϲαρεϲκαιδε-
κατοϲ 729

fourth, τεταρτοϲ .... —

fowl, ορνεον 538

πετεινον 620

fox, αλωπηξ 32

fragments, κλαϲμα........... 424

frame, καταρτιζω 415

framed fitly together (be),
ϲυναρμολογεομαι 710

frankincense, λιβανοϲ 460

frankly, see forgive.

fraud (kept back by), αποϲ-
τερεω...................... 77

free, ελευθεροϲ 233

free, see gift.

free (make), ελευθεροω 234

free man, ελευθεροϲ 233

freed (be), δικαιοω......... 157

freedom, πολιτεια 642

freely, δωρεαν 170

παρρηϲια............. 596

(Acts 26:26), παρρη-
ϲιαζομαι .... —

freely, see give.

freeman, απελευθεροϲ 61

freewoman, ελευθεροϲ 233

frequent (more), περιϲϲοτε-
ρωϲ.......................... 618

fresh, γλυκυϲ................. 124

friend, ἑταιροϲ 317

φιλοϲ 787

friend, see thy.

friend (make any one a),
πειθω 609

friends(his), {παρα 586
(Mar.3:21) {with αὑτου

friendship, φιλια 787

frog, βατραχοϲ............. 106

from, απο 63

δια................... 142

εγγυϲ 176

εκ..................... 215

παρα 586

ὑπο 776

from, see fall, heaven, off,
out, put, thrust, turn,
whence.

from above, see above.

from among, εκ 215

from being, see burdensome.

from far, μακροθεν......... 469

from.. forth, εκ.............. 215

from hence, εντευθεν 263

from [house] to [house],
κατα...................... 406

from that place, εκειθεν 224

from the, see beginning.

from thence, see and.

from thence, εκειθεν 224

ὁθεν 524

from up, εκ................ 215

from whence, ποθεν 635

from within, εϲωθεν 317

from without, εξωθεν 271

froward, ϲκολιοϲ 687

fruit, γεννημα 114

καρποϲ 405

οπωρα 536

fruit, see bear, bring, perfection.

fruit ..withereth (whose),
φθινοπωρινοϲ 786

fruit (without), ακαρποϲ ... 21

fruitful, καρποφοροϲ 406

fruitful (be), καρποφορεω .. 405

frustrate, αθετεω........... 15

fulfil, αναπληροω 44

εκπληροω 229

πληροω................ 630

ποιεω................. 636

ϲυντελεω 713

τελειοω 727

τελεω .... —

fulfilled (be), γινομαι 117

fulfilling, πληρωμα.......... 630

full, γεμω................... 113

μεϲτοϲ................ 484

πληρηϲ 629

(1 Joh. 1:4
2 Joh.12) } πληροω.. 630

(Mar. 8:20), πληρωμα —

full, see age, assurance, glory,
heaviness, light, make,
sores.

full (be), γεμιζω 113

γεμω .... —

εμπληθω............... 239

κορεννυμι 429

full come (be), πληροω 630

full (make), πληροω .... —

full of, see darkness.

full [time], came (Lu. 1:57),
πληθω 629

full well, καλωϲ............. 403

fuller, γναφευϲ............. 124

fulness, πληρωμα 630

fully, see come, know, known,
preach, ripe.

furlong, ϲταδιοϲ 697

furnace, καμινοϲ 403

furnish, πληθω............. 629

ϲτρωννυμι 701

furnish throughly, εξαρτιζω 266

further, πλειων 627

further, ετι 318

πορρω 648

further, see any, proceed,
threaten.

further (go), διιϲτημι 155

glorified together (be), συν-
δοξαζομαι 710
glorify, δοξαζω............ 162
glorious, δοξα 161
    ενδοξος............ 260
glorious, *see* make.
glory, δοξα 161
    καυχημα 419
    κλεος 424
glory, κατακαυχαομαι 411
    καυχαομαι........... 419
glory, *see* have, vain.
glory (desirous of vain), κε-
νοδοξος 420
glory (full of), δοξαζω 162
glory of, καυχημα 419
glory (whereof I may), καυ-
χησις .... —
glorying, καυχημα .... —
    καυχησις.......... —
gluttonous, φαγος 782
gnash, βρυχω 111
    τριζω 750
gnashing, βρυγμος 111
gnat, κωνωψ 442
gnaw, μασσαομαι 472
go, αγω..................... 10
    απειμι 61
    απερχομαι 155
    διερχομαι........... 155
    εκπορευομαι 229
    εξερχομαι........... 266
    ερχομαι............. 301
    μεταβαινω 487
    παραγινομαι 588
    παραπορευομαι 593
    παρερχομαι 594
    περιπατεω 617
    πορευομαι 646
    προσερχομαι.. 662
    υπαγω 771
    χωρεω 805
go, *see* aside, compel, country, further, law, let, warfare.
go aboard, επιβαινω 281
go about, διερχομαι 155
    επιχειρεω 289
    ζητεω 337
    πειραζω 610
    πειραω 611
    περιαγω 615
go abroad, διερχομαι....... 155
    εξερχομαι 266
go again, επιστρεφω 287
go and meet, υπανταω 772
go aside, απερχομαι 61
    υποχωρεω 780
go astray, πλαναω.......... 627
go away, απερχομαι 61
    εξερχομαι 266
    πορευομαι 646
    υπαγω 771
go back, απερχομαι 61
go before, προαγω 653
    προερχομαι 655

go before, προπορευομαι ... 656
go beyond, υπερβαινω 774
go down, επιδυω 283
go down, καταβαινω...... 409
    κατερχομαι 417
go down with, συγκατα-
βαινω 703
go every where, διερχομαι.. 155
go farther, προβαινω 653
    προερχομαι..... 655
go forth, εκπορευομαι 229
    εξερχομαι 266
    πορευομαι 646
go forward, προερχομαι 655
go in..into, εισειμι.......... 211
    εισερχομαι...... —
    εισπορευομαι .. 214
go into with, & go in with,
συνεισερχομαι 711
go (let), απολυω 75
go near, προσερχομαι 662
go on, προβαινω 653
    φερω.................. 784
go on a journey, οδοιπορεω 523
go one's way, πορευομαι... 646
go out, απερχομαι 61
    αποβαινω 68
    εκπορευομαι 229
    εξειμι 266
    εξερχομαι .... —
go out, σβεννυμι 681
go out of the way, εκκλινω. 228
go over, διαπεραω 147
    διερχομαι 155
    τελεω 727
go... about, περιαγω 615
go through, διαπορευομαι .. 147
    διερχομαι 155
    εισερχομαι 211
go throughout, διερχομαι .. 155
    διοδευω 158
go to, προσερχομαι 662
go to, αγε 6
go unto, προσερχομαι 662
go up, αναβαινω 39
    ανερχομαι 47
    πορευομαι 646
    προσαναβαινω 662
go up into, εμβαινω 235
go...way, υπαγω 771
go....ways, απερχομαι 61
go with, συμπορευομαι...... 707
    συνερχομαι 712
goat, εριφιον 301
    εριφος................. —
    τραγος 748
goat [skins], αιγειος........ 15
God, Θεος................ 364
    (Acts19:20), κυριος . 436
    δαιμονιον.............. 131
God, *see* admonished, answer,
lover, ward, would.
God (fight against), Θεο-
μαχεω 364
God forbid, {γινομαι....... 117
          {μη............. 490

God (given by inspiration
of , Θεοπνευστος.......... 364
God (hater of), Θεοστυγης.. 373
God speed, χαιρω 795
God (taught of), Θεοδιδακ-
τος..................... 364
God (to fight against) (Acts
5:39), Θεομαχος........ —
God (without), αθεος 15
God (worshipper of), Θεο-
σεβης.................... 373
goddess, Θεα 361
Godhead, Θειος ....
    Θειοτης ....
    Θεοτης........... 373
godliness, ευσεβεια 326
    Θεοσεβεια 373
godly, ευσεβης 326
    {Θεος 364
    {κατα............. 406
godly, ευσεβως 327
godly (after a), *see* sort.
godly fear, ευλαβεια 323
gold, χρυσιον 804
    χρυσος .... —
gold (of), χρυσεος .... —
gold ring (with a), χρυσο-
δακτυλος............... —
golden, χρυσεος .... —
good, βιος 107
good, χρηστοτης 803
good, αγαθος............. 1
    καλος 402
    χρηστος 803
good, ευ................. 320
    καλως 403
good, *see* behaviour, cheer,
comfort, deed, increased,
olive tree, pleasure, re-
port, seem, think, way.
good (be), ισχυω........... 392
good (be), συμφερω 707
good (do), αγαθοεργεω 1
    αγαθοποιεω ..... —
    ενεργετεω........ 322
    ευποια 325
good men, *see* lover.
good place (in a), καλως.... 403
good things, αγαθος........ 1
good things, *see* teachers.
good (think), αξιοω 58
good (those that are), *see*
despisers.
good tidings (bring), ευαγγελιζω 320
good [while], ικανος 384
good will, ευδοκια 322
    ευνοια 324
good words, χρηστολογια .. 803
goodly, καλος................ 402
    λαμπρος............. 447
goodman, οικοδεσποτης 525
goodness, αγαθωσυνη 2
    χρηστος............ 803
    χρηστοτης ...... —
goods, αγαθος 1
    ουσια 573
    σκευο 686

goods, υπαρξις.............. 772
  υπαρχοντα .... —
gorgeous, ενδοξος 260
  λαμπρος.......... 447
gospel, ευαγγελιον 321
gospel, see preach, preach
 before.
gospel preached) ευαγγε-
(unto us was the), } λιζω.. 320
(Heb. 4:2)   ) εσμιν.. 307
gotten (from), αποσπαω.... 76
government, κυβερνησις.... 436
  κυριοτης 442
governor, εθναρχης 181
  ηγεμων 343
  (Mat.2:6),ηγεομαι 343
  οικονομος 526
governor (be), ηγεμονευω.. 342
governor of the feast, αρχι-
τρικλινος 85
grace, ευπρεπεια 325
grace, χαρις 797
gracious, χαρις...
  χρηστος 803
graff in.. or into, εγκεντριζω 177
grain, κοκκος............... 427
grandmother, μαμμη....... 470
grant, διδωμι.............. 151
  επω 291
  χαριζομαι........ 796
grapes, σταφυλη 698
grass, χορτος 802
grave, αδης............... 13
  μνημα............... 502
  μνημειον .... —
grave, σεμνος............... 684
grave (Acts 17:29), χαραγμα 796
graveclothes, κειριαι 420
gravity, σεμνοτης 684
great, ικανος 384
  λιαν 460
  μεγας 476
  πολυς 643
great, see authority, deal, desire, drops, how, noise,
 price, shew, so, swelling,
 very, way, what, while.
great age (be of (προβαινω 654
a), (Lu. 2:36) { ημερα ... 347
   (πολυς ... 643
great [curse], αναθεμα 41
great deal, πολυς........... 643
great (exceeding), μεγιστος 477
great (how), ηλικος 344
great men, μεγιστανες...... 477
great (so), τηλικουτος...... 730
great things, μεγαλεια...... 475
great things, see boast.
great (very), παμπολυς 585
great (what), ηλικος 344
great while, πολυς 643
great with child, εγκυος ... 178
greater, μειζοτερος.......... 478
  μειζων...............
  περισσοτερος 618
  πλειων 627
greater part, πλειων .... —

greatest, μεγας.............. 476
  μειζων 478
greatly, λιαν 460
  μεγαλως............ 476
  πολυς 643
  σφοδρα 715
  χαρα 796
greatly, see amazed, desire,
 long, rejoice, wonder.
greatness, μεγεθος 477
Grecian, Ελληνιστης 828
Greece, Ελλας .... —
greedily, see run.
greediness, πλεονεξια 628
greedy, see filthy lucre.
Greek, Ελλην 828
Greek, Ελληνις .... —
Greek, Ελληνικος .... —
Greek, Ελληνιστι .... —
green, υγρος 753
  χλωρος 801
greet, ασπαζομαι............ 88
greeting, χαιρω 795
greetings, ασπασμος 88
grief, λυπη 465
grief (cause), λυπεω .... —
grief (with), (Heb. 13:17),
στεναζω 698
grieve, λυπεω............... 465
grieved (be), διαπονεομαι.. 147
  συλλυπεομαι 705
grieved with (be), προσοχ-
θιζω 666
grievous, βαρυς 102
  (Heb.12:11),λυπη 465
  οκνηρος 528
  πονηρος 646
grievous to be borne, δυσ-
βαστακτος 168
grievously, δεινως 133
  κακως 401
grind, αληθω............... 28
grind to powder, λικμαω.... 460
groan, εμβριμαομαι......... 235
  στεναζω 698
groan together, συστεναζω 714
groaning, στεναγμος 698
gross (wax), παχυνομαι.... 609
ground, γη 115
  εδαφος 181
  εδραιωμα .... —
  χωρα 805
ground, θεμελιοω........... 363
ground, see parcel.
ground (even with), see lay.
ground (on the), χαμαι 796
ground (piece of), αγρος.... 10
ground (to the), χαμαι...... 796
grow, αυξανω 91
  γινομαι............. 117
  ερχομαι 301
grow exceedingly, υπεραυ-
ξανω 774
grow together, συναυξανο-
μαι 710
grow up, αναβαινω 39
  μηκυνομαι........ 499

grudge, στεναζω 698
grudging, γογγυσμος....... 125
grudgingly, (λυπη 465
 (2Co. 9:7) { εκ....... 215
guard, see captain.
guest (be), καταλυω 413
guestchamber, καταλυμα .. —
guests, ανακειμαι.......... 42
guide, οδηγος................ 523
guide, κατευθυνω............ 417
  οδηγεω............ 523
guide, see house.
guile, δολος 161
guiltless, αναιτιος 42
guilty, υποδικος 778
guilty (be), οφειλω 579
guilty of, ενοχος 262
gulf, χασμα................. 798
gush out, εκχυνω.......... 231

habitation, επαυλις......... 273
  κατοικητηριον .. 418
  κατοικια .... —
  οικητηριον 524
  σκηνη 687
had (that she), (εαυτου ... 172
   { παρα 586
hail, χαιρω 795
hail, χαλαζα ....
hair, θριξ 377
  κομη 428
hair (broidered), πλεγμα.... 627
hair (have long), κομαω 428
hair (of), τριχινος 750
hale, κατασυρω............. 416
  συρω 714
half, ημισυ 351
half, see hour.
half dead, ημιθανης 350
hall, αυλη................. 90
hall, see judgment.
hall (common), πραιτωριον 651
hall of judgment, πραιτωριον
hallow, αγιαζω.............. 6
halt, χωλος 805
hand, χειρ 798
hand, see nigh, palm, smite,
 strike.
hand (at), εγγυς 176
hand (be at), εγγιζω........ 175
  ενιστημι...... 262
  εφιστημι...... 328
hand (right), δεξιος.......... 135
hand (some to lead
 him by the), } χειρα-
 (Acts 13:11) } γωγος 800
hand (take in), επιχειρεω... 289
handkerchief, σουρδαριον, .. 694
handle, θιγω 376
  ψηλαφαω............ 806
handle deceitfully, δολοω.... 161
handle, see shamefully.
handmaid,-en, δουλη 163
hand on (lay), κρατεω 431
  πιαζω 621
hand (lead by the), χειρα-
γωγεω 800

hands(made with), ⎫ χειρο-
hands (made by), ⎭ ποιητος 800
hands (made without), αχει-
ροποιητος 99
hands (with own), αυτο-
χειρ 96
handwriting, χειρογραφον .. 800
hang, κρεμαμαι............. 432
hang about, περικειμαι...... 616
hang down, παριεμαι....... 595
hang.. self, απαγχομαι...... 59
haply, αρα 79
πως 675
haply, see lest.
happen, γινομαι 117
συμβαινω 705
happier, μακαριος............ 468
happy, μακαριος .... —
happy (count), μακαριζω .. —
hard, δυσκολος 169
σκληρος 687
hard, see join, understood,
uttered.
harden, πωροω 675
σκληρυνω 687
hardly, δυσκολως............ 169
μογις 503
μολις 505
hardness, πωρωσις 675
σκληροτης 687
hardness (endure), κακοπα-
θεω 400
hardness of heart, σκληρο-
καρδια 687
harlot, πορνη............. 648
harm, ατοπος................ 90
κακος 400
(Acts 28:21), πονηρος 646
υβρις................. 753
harm, κακοω 400
harmless, ακακος............ 21
ακεραιος .... —
harp, κιθαρα 423
harp, κιθαριζω .... —
harper, κιθαρωδος .... —
harvest, θερισμος 374
haste, σπουδη 697
haste ⎫
haste unto ⎬ σπευδω 696
haste (with) ⎪
Lu. 2:16 ⎭
haste (make), σπευδω ..... —
hastily, ταχεως............. 723
hate, μισεω 501
hateful (Rev. 18:2), μισεω —
στυγητος 701
hater, see God.
hatred, εχθρα 329
have, αντιβαλλω........... 56
απεχω 62
γινομαι 117
have (Rev. 22:14), εσομαι 308
εστι 310
εχω 329
ην 354
(Joh. 5:4)κατεχω... 417
λαμβανω............. 445

have, μεταλαμβανω 488
(Heb. 13:5), παρειμι 594
ποιεω 636
υπαρχω 772
ων 810
have, see admiration, care,
company, compassion,
confidence, convenient,
conversation, course, de-
vil, dominion, enough,
hope, indignation, jour-
ney, knowledge, lack, leisure, let, need, nourish-
ment, palsy, patience,
peace, pity, place, plea-
sure, power, preemi-
nence, regard, reputation,
respect, rule over, tes-
timony, understanding,
will.
have abundance, see abun-
dance.
have against, see quarrel.
have charge of ⎧ ην 354
(Acts 8:27) ⎨ επι 275
have glory, δοξαζω 162
have in, see remembrance.
have long, see hair.
have mercy on, see mercy.
have on, ενδυω.............. 260
have our, see being.
have over, πλεοναζω 628
have respect, see persons.
have to do (Heb. ⎫ λογος 462
4:13) ⎭
have with, see fellowship.
haven, λιμην................. 461
having, see compassion,
dropsy.
havock (make), λυμαινομαι 465
hay, χορτος 802
hazard, παραδιδωμι 589
he, οδε,.................... 522
ουτος 574
τις 732
he also.. and he.. ⎫ κακεινος 399
even he ⎭
he, him & his, αυτος........ 91
εκεινος 225
he himself, εαυτου.......... 172
he it was that (Joh. 6:71),
ουτος 574
he that, ει τις 187
οστις 540
head, κεφαλη 421
head (wound in the), κεφα-
λαιοω .... —
headlong, πρηνης 652
headlong, see cast.
heady, προπετης............ 656
heal, διασωζω 148
θεραπευω 373
(Acts 4:30), ιασις..... 379
σωζω 716
healed (be), ιαομαι 379
healing, θεραπεια 373
ιαμα................ 379
ιασις............... —
health, σωτηρια 718

health (be in), υγιαινω 753
heap, επισωρευω 288
σωρευω 718
heap treasure together, θη-
σαυριζω 375
hear, ακουω 22
διακονομαι 145
εισακουω 211
επακουω 272
επακροαομαι .... —
hear, see neglect.
hear before, προακουω 653
heard [i. q. of hearing], ακοη 22
hearer, ακουω .... —
ακροατης............ 26
hearing, ακοη 22
διαγνωσις 144
hearing, see audience.
hearing (place of), ακροατη-
ριον 26
hearken, ακουω............ 22
πειθαρχεω 609
υπακουω 772
hearken to, ενωτιζομαι 265
heart, καρδια 404
ψυχη 807
heart, see cut, hardness.
hearted, καρδια............ 404
hearted, see tender.
heartily (Col. ⎧ ψυχη 807
3:23) ⎨ εκ 215
hearts failing, αποψυχω ... 78
hearts (which knoweth the),
καρδιογνωστης 405
heat, θερμη............. .. 374
καυμα 419
καυσων............ —
heat (burning), καυσων .... —
heat (fervent), καυσοω ... —
heathen, εθνος 181
εθνικος............ —
heathen man, εθνικος ...... —
heaven, ουρανος 571
heaven (from), ουρανοθεν.. —
heaven (in), επουρανιος ... 290
heaven (midst of), μεσουρα-
νημα 484
heavenly, επουρανιος 290
ουρανιος.......... 571
heavenly (Lu. ⎧ ουρανος.... —
11:13) ⎨ εκ......... 215
heaviness, κατηφεια 418
λυπη 465
heaviness (be full of), αδημονεω 13
heaviness (be in), λυπεω .. 465
heavy, βαρεω.............. 102
βαρυς............... —
heavy, see lade.
heavy (be very), αδημονεω 13
Hebrew, Εβραικος.......... 827
Hebrew, Εβραιος ....
Hebrew, Εβραις ....
Hebrew (in the), Εβραιστι —
Hebrew tongue (in the),
Εβραιστι................. —
hedge, φραγμος 790

holily, ὁσιως 539

holiness, ἁγιασμος......... 6

    ἁγιοτης 8

    ἁγιωσυνη.........

    ευσεβεια 326

    ὁσιοτης......... 539

holiness (as becometh), ἱεροπρεπης 383

holy, ἁγιος.............. 7

    ἱερος 383

    ὁσιος 539

holy (be), ἁγιαζω 6

holy (most), ἁγιος 7

holy one, ἁγιος .... —

holy place, ἁγιον.... 6

holy thing, ἁγιος.... 7

holyday, ἑορτη 271

home, ἰδιος.............. 380

    οικια 524

    οικος 526

    (Mar. 5:19), σου .. 691

home (be at), ενδημεω 260

home (keeper at), οικουρος 527

honest, καλος 402

    σεμνος 684

honest, see report.

honestly, ευσχημονως 327

    καλως 403

honesty, σεμνοτης 684

honey, μελι............. 478

honey [comb], μελισσιος .. —

honour, δοξα 161

    τιμη 732

honour, δοξαζω 162

    τιμαω 732

honour (without), ατιμος.. 90

honourable, ενδοξος 260

    ευσχημων...... 327

    τιμιος 732

honourable (less), ατιμος .. 90

honourable (more), εντιμος 263

hook, αγκιστρον 8

hope, ελπις............... 234

hope, ελπιζω............... —

hope for again, απελπιζω .. 61

hope (have), ελπιζω 234

hope (have), { ελπιζω ....
(1 Co. 15:19 { εσμεν ... 307

hoped for (things), ελπιζω 234

horn, κερας............... 421

horse, ἱππος 390

horse [man], ἱππικον.......

horseman, ἱππευς .... —

Hosanna, Ὡσαννα. 817

hospitality, φιλοξενια 787

hospitality, see lover.

hospitality (given to), φιλοξενος.................. 787

hospitality (use), (1 Pet. 4: 9), φιλοξενος.............

host, ξενος 521

    πανδοχευς 585

host, στρατια................. 700

hot, ζεστος 337

hot iron, see seared.

hour, ὡρα................. 811

hour (half an), ἡμιωριον ... 351

hour (this), αρτι...... 82

house, οικητηριον 524

    οικια .... —

    οικος 526

house, see thy.

house (goodman of the), οικοδεσποτης................ 525

house (guide the), οικοδεσποτεω .... —

house (hired), μισθωμα 502

house (master of the), οικοδεσποτης................ 525

house (those of his own), (1 Ti. 5:8), οικειος........ 524

house (with all his), πανοικι 585

housetop, δωμα 169

houshold, θεραπεια 373

    οικια 524

    οικος 526

houshold (of the), οικειος .. 524

houshold servant, οικετης .. —

houshold (them of [his]), οικιακος 525

houshold (they of [his own]), οικιακος .... —

housholder, οικοδεσποτης ..

how, καθως................. 397

    ὁπως 536

    ὁτι 543

    πως 675

    τις 736

    ὡς... 812

how, see great.

how great, ὁσος 539

    πηλικος 620

    ποσος 648

how greatly, ὡς 812

how it will go with, { περι .. 613
(Phi. 2:23,) { with τα

how large, πηλικος.... 620

how long, ἑως............... 334

    { ἑως .... —
    { ποτε 649

    ποσος 648

how many, ὁσος 539

    ποσος 648

how much, ὁσος 539

    ποσος 648

    τίς 736

how much more, μητι 498

how oft, ποσακις......... 648

how often, ποσακις .... —

how that, ὁτι 543

howbeit, αλλα 29

    μεντοι 481

howl, ολολυζω 529

humble, ταπεινος 720

humble, & humble self, ταπεινοω ....

humbleness of mind, ταπεινοφροσυνη ....

humiliation, ταπεινωσις....

humility, ταπεινοφροσυνη .

humility of mind, ταπεινοφροσυνη ....

hundred, ἑκατον 222

hundred, see five, four, six, three, two.

hundred thousand }
thousand, (Rev. } μυριας . 511
9:16),

hundred years old, ἑκατονταετης 222

hundredfold, ἑκατονταπλασιων .... —

hundreds, see by.

hunger, λιμος 461

hunger, πειναω 610

hungry (very), προσπεινος. 666

hurt, ὑβρις 753

hurt, αδικεω 14

hurt, βλαπτω 107

    κακοω............ 400

hurtful, βλαβερος 107

husband, ανηρ 47

husband, see love.

husband (having an), ὑπανδρος 772

husbandman, γεωργος 115

husbandry, γεωργιον....... —

husk, κερατιον 421

Hymenæus, Ὑμεναιος 865

hymn, ὑμνος............. 767

hymn, see sing.

hypocrisy, ὑποκρισις........ 778

hypocrisy (without), ανυποκριτος 57

hypocrite, ὑποκριτης........ 778

hyssop, ὑσσωπος....... 781

I, εγω.................. 178

    εμε 236

    εμοι .... —

    καγω.................. 393

    με 473

    μοι 503

    μου.................. 507

I, see and, even, so.

I also, καγω 393

I also, see even.

I in like wise, καγω 393

idle, αργος 80

idle tale, ληρος. 459

idol, ειδωλον 193

idol, see offered.

idol's temple, ειδωλειον 192

idolater, ειδωλολατρης...... 193

idolatry, ειδωλολατρεια 192

idolatry (wholly given to), κατειδωλος 417

if, ει 183

    ειγε 185

    ει και 186

    ειτε................. 187

if, see also, and.

if a man, ει τις.......... 187

if (and), εαν 170

if any.. man, ει τις 187

if any thing, ει τις .... —

if.. but, καν............. 403

if by any means, ει πως .. 187

if.. no, εαν μη 494

if not, ει δε μη 186

instruction, παιδεια 582

instruments, ὁπλα 534

insurrection, στασις 697

insurrection against (make),
κατεφιστημι 417

insurrection with (make),
συστασιαστης 714

intend, βουλομαι 110

Θελω 362

μελλω 478

intent, εννοια 262

λογος 462

intent, see for, to.

intercession, εντευξις 263

intercession for (make),
ὑπερεντυγχανω 775

intercession (make), εντυγ-
χανω............... 264

interpret, διερμηνευω 154

ἑρμηνευω 301

interpretation, επιλυσις 285

ἑρμηνεια 301

interpretation (be by), ἑρμηνευω 301

μεθερμηνευομαι 477

interpretation (by), διερμηνευω 154

interpreted (be), μεθερμηνευομαι 477

interpreter, διερμηνευτης .. 154

into, αχρι 99

εις 197

εν 240

επι 275

κατα 406

into, εσω 317

into, see ashes, bear, beat,
bondage, bring, captivity,
carrying, cast, come, enter,
fall, get, go, graff, lead,
look.

into with, see go.

intreat, ερωταω 306

παραιτεομαι........ 590

παρακαλεω......... —

intreated (easy to be), ευ-
πειθης................ 324

intreaty, παρακλησις 591

intrude into, εμβατευω 235

inventor, εφευρετης 328

invisible, αορατος 58

inward, εσω 317

εσωθεν............. —

inward, see affection.

inwardly, { κρυπτος 434
{ εν 240

εσωθεν............. 317

iron, σιδηρεος................ 685

iron, σιδηρος .... —

iron, see seared.

iron (of), σιδηρεος.......... 685

is to say (that), { εστι ... 310
(Mar. 7:11), { with ὁ

island, νησιον 515

νησιον .... —

isle, νησος .... —

issue ῥυσις................. 678

---

issue, σπερμα.............. 695

issue, εκπορευομαι.......... 229

issue of blood (diseased with),
αἱμορροεω 16

it, αυτος 91

εκεινος 225

(Mat. 6:16), οὑτος 574

ταυτη 722

ταυτην 723

τουτο 743

τουτου. 746

it, see becometh.

it may be, see may.

it (of), αὑτου............... 92

it were, see as, better.

Italian, Ιταλικος 845

itching [ears] (having), κνη-
θω 426

itself, αυτος 91

ἑαυτου 172

itself, see shew forth.

itself (by), χωρις........... 805

ivory (of), ελεφαντινος 234

jacinth, ὑακινθινος......... 752

jacinth, ὑακινθος........... 753

jailor, δεσμοφυλαξ 136

James, Ιακωβος 832

jangling (vain), ματαιολογια 473

jasper, ιασπις 380

jealous over (be), ζηλοω.... 337

jealousy, ζηλος............. —

jealousy, see provoke.

jeopardy (be in), κινδυνευω 423

jeopardy (stand in), κινδυνευω .... —

jesting, ευτραπελια......... 327

Jesus, Ιησους 834

Jew, Ιουδαιος 842

Jewish, Ιουδαικος .... —

Jewry, Ιουδαια .... —

Jews (as do the), Ιουδαικως —

Jews (live as the), ιουδαιζω 390

Jews' religion, ιουδαισμος .. —

John, Ιωαννης.............. 845

join, κολλαω 427

join hard, συνομορεω 713

join ... self, κολλαω 427

προσκολλαομαι . 665

join together, συζευγνυω .. 704

join together (perfectly), καταρτιζω 415

joined (be), προσκολλαομαι 665

joined fitly together (be), συ-
ναρμολογεομαι 710

joint, ἁφη 97

joint-heir, συγκληρονομος .. 703

joints, ἁρμος 81

jot, ιωτα 393

journey, ὁδοιπορια 523

ὁδος .... —

journey, ὁδευω .... —

πορευομαι....... 646

journey, see bring, go.

journey (have a prosperous),
ευοδουμαι 324

journey (in a), διαπορευομαι 147

---

journey (make a), πορευομαι 646

journey (take a) αποδημεω.. 68

πορευομαι. 646

journey (taking a far), απο-
δημος 68

journey with, συνοδευω 713

journeying, ὁδοιπορια 523

(Lu. { ποιεω . 636
13:22), { πορεια 646

joy, αγαλλιασις 2

ευφροσυνη............. 327

χαρα 796

χαρις 797

joy, καυχαομαι 419

χαιρω 795

joy, see leap.

joy (exceeding), αγαλλιασις 2

joy (have), ονη ις 532

joy (with exceeding), αγαλ-
λιαω 2

joyfully (Lu.19:6), χαιρω .. 795

(Heb. { χαρα..... 796
10:34), { μετα 484

joyfulness, χαρα 796

joyous (Heb.12:11), χαρα.. —

judge, δικαστης 157

κριτης................. 434

judge, ανακρινω 43

διακρινω 145

ἡγεομαι 343

κρινω 433

judge (to) (1 Co.6:2), κριτηριον 434

judgment, αισθησις 18

γνωμη 124

δικαιωμα 157

δικη............. —

ἡμερα........... 347

κριμα 433

κρισις........... 434

κριτηριον...... —

judgment, see righteous.

judgment hall, πραιτωριον . 651

judgment seat, βημα 106

κριτηριον .. 434

Jupiter, Ζευς 830

Jupiter (which fell down
from), διοπετες 158

jurisdiction, εξουσια 269

just, δικαιος 155

ενδικος 260

justification, δικαιωμα 157

δικαιωσις..... —

justifier, δικαιοω .... —

justify, δικαιοω .... —

justly, δικαιως .... —

keep, βοσκω 109

keep, διατηρεω 149

διαφυλαττω .... —

εχω 329

κατεχω............... 417

κρατεω 431

παρεχω 595

ποιεω............... 636

πρασσω 651

συντηρεω............. 713

law (Acts 19:38), αγοραιος   9
    νομος 517
law, see daughter, doctor,
    mother, sue, teacher,
    transgress.
law (about the), νομικος .. 516
law (contrary to the) (Acts
    23:3), παρανομεω........ 592
law (giving of the), νομο-
    θεσια...................... 517
law (go to), (1Co. ⎧κριμα.. 433
    6:7), ⎩εχω.... 329
    κρινω 433
law (receive the), νομοθετεω 517
law (transgression of the),
    ανομια.................... 55
law (without), ανομος..... —
law (without), ανομως .... —
lawful, εννομος.............. 262
lawful (be), εξεστι 268
lawfully, νομιμως 516
lawgiver, νομοθετης 517
lawless, ανομος............. 55
lawyer, νομικος............. 516
lay, ανακλινω 42
    βαλλω 100
    ιστημι 391
    κατατιθημι 416
    κειμαι 419
    κλινω 426
    τιθημι 731
    φερω 784
lay, see dying, foundation,
    hands, hold.
lay apart, αποτιθημι 78
lay [as a foundation], κατα-
    βαλλω 410
lay aside, αποτιθημι 78
    αφιημι 97
    τιθημι 731
lay down, αποτιθημι........ 78
    τιθημι 731
    υποτιθημι 780
lay even with the ground,
    εδαφιζω 181
lay hold on (and upon),
    επιλαμβανομαι 284
lay on, επιβαλλω........... 281
    επιτιθημι............. 288
lay sick of, συνεχω......... 712
lay [to charge], λογιζομαι.. 461
lay to the, see charge.
lay unto, προστιθημι........ 666
lay up, αποκειμαι 70
    θησαυριζω.......... 375
    τιθημι 731
lay up, see treasure.
lay up in store, αποθησαυ-
    ριζω 69
lay upon, επιτιθημι 288
lay wait, ενεδρα 261
    ενεδρευω ....
    (Acts ⎧ενεδρα ....   —
    25:3) ⎩ποιεω 636
laying await, επιβουλη..... 282
laying on, επιθεσις......... 283
lead, απαγω 59
    οδηγεω 523

lead, φερω 784
    αγω 10
lead, see captive, hand.
lead   διαγω 144
lead about, περιαγω 615
lead away, απαγω 59
lead into, εισφερω 214
    συναγω 708
lead out, εξαγω 265
lead up, αναγω.............. 41
    αναφερω 46
leader, οδηγος 523
leaf, φυλλον 792
lean, ανακειμαι 42
    αναπιπτω 44
leap, αλλομαι............ 30
    σκιρταω 687
leap for joy, σκιρταω.... —
leap on, εφαλλομαι........ 328
leap up, εξαλλομαι........ 266
learn, μανθανω............. 470
    παιδευω 582
learning, γραμμα.......... 126
    διδασκαλια 150
least, ελαχιστος 232
    μικρος 501
least, see at, esteemed, less.
leathern, δερματινος........ 135
leave, ανιημι 53
    απολειπω 73
    αφιημι 97
    εαω 175
    εγκαταλειπω 177
    εκβαλλω 222
    καταλειπω............ 413
    παυομαι 609
    υπολιμπανω.......... 779
leave, see take.
leave (give), επιτρεπω...... 289
leaven, ζυμη 338
leaven, ζυμοω .... —
led away with (be), συνα-
    παγομαι 710
led (be)..led away, αγω 10
led into (be), εισαγω........ 211
left, ευωνυμος 328
left (be), περισσευω 618
left (be), υπολειπομαι...... 778
left (hand), αριστερος 81
left (on the), ευωνυμος 328
left (that was), (Mar. 8:8),
    περισσευμα 618
leg, σκελος 686
legion, λεγεων 449
leisure (have), ευκαιρεω 323
lend, δανειζω 132
    χραω 802
length, μηκος 499
length (at), ποτε........... 649
leopard, παρδαλις 594
leper, λεπρος............. 459
leprosy, λεπρα .... —
less, ελασσων................ 232
    ηττ 358
    μικρος 501
less, see honourable, sorrow-
    ful.

less than the least, ελαχισ-
    τοτερος................. 232
lest, ινα 385
    μη 490
    ινα μη.................. 495
    μηποτε 497
    μηπως..., ... —
lest at any time, μηποτε ....
lest by any means, μηπως..
lest by some means, μη-
    πως .... —
lest haply, μηποτε ....
    μηπως ....
lest perhaps, μηπως .... —
let, αφιημι 97
    εαω 175
    εξεστι 268
    επιτρεπω 289
let [i. e. hinder], κατεχω.... 417
    κωλυω 442
let, see conversation, depart,
    down, drive, go, slip.
let alone, αφιημι 97
    εα 170
    εαω 175
let down, καθιημι 396
let forth, εκδιδωμι 223
let [give up], επιδιδωμι 283
let go, αφιημι............... 97
let have, αφιημι ....
let out, εκδιδωμι 223
let this, see mind.
letter, γραμμα 126
    επιστολη 287
letter, see write.
Levitical, Λευιτικος.......... 850
lewd, πονηρος 646
lewdness, ρᾳδιουργημα...... 676
liar, ψευδης................. 806
    ψευστης ....
liberal, απλοτης 63
liberality, απλοτης.......... —
    χαρις 797
liberally, απλως 63
liberty, ανεσις 47
    αφεσις 97
    ελευθερια.......... 233
    εξουσια 269
liberty, see set.
liberty (at), ελευθερος 233
liberty (give), επιτρεπω 289
liberty (set at), απολυω 75
licence, τοπος 741
licence (give), επιτρεπω 289
lick, απολειχω 74
lie, ψευδος 806
    ψευσμα ....
lie, ανακειμαι 42
    βαλλω 100
    επικειμαι................ 284
    εχω 329
    κατακειμαι 411
    κειμαι.................. 419
lie, ψευδομαι 806
lie on, επιπιπτω 285

lie on [as a tempest], επι-κειμαι	284
lie (that cannot), αψευδης	100
lie [towards the north], βλεπω	108
life, βιος	107
ζωη	339
πνευμα	632
ψυχη	807
life (2Cor.1:8), ζαω	335
life, see manner.	
life again, see raise to.	
life (give), ζωοποιεω	340
life (of this), βιωτικος	107
life (pertaining to this), βιωτικος	—
life (without), αψυχος	100
lifetime, ζωη	339
ζαω	335
lift,..lift up, εγειρω	176
lift up, αιρω	17
ανακυπτω	43
ανιστημι	53
ανορθοω	55
επαιρω	272
υψοω	781
lifted up with pride (be), τυφοομαι	752
light, ελαφρος	232
light, λαμπας	447
λυχνος	466
φεγγος	784
φως	794
φωστηρ	—
φωτισμος	795
light, απτω	79
καιω	399
φωτιζω	794
light, ερχομαι	301
light (bring to), φωτιζω	794
light (full of), φωτεινος	—
light (give), επιφαινω	289
επιφαυω	—
λαμπω	447
φωτιζω	794
light of (make), αμελεω	34
light on, πιπτω	622
lighten, αστραπτω	89
κουφιζω	431
lighten the ship, { εκβολη ..	223
(Acts27:18), { ποιεω....	636
lighten (to), αποκαλυψις ..	70
lightly, ταχυ	724
lightness, ελαφρια	232
lightning, αστραπη	89
like, ουτω	576
like, ισος	390
ομοιος	530
παρομοιος	596
like, ταυτα	720
τοιουτος	740
ως	812
ωσει	815
like, δοκιμαζω	160
like, see even, figure, manner, men, passions, precious.	

like as, κατα	406
(Heb. { ομοιοτης ..	530
4:15), { κατα.......	406
ως	812
ωσει	815
ωσπερ	816
like (be), εικω	193
like (made), αφομοιοω	99
like (make) & be like, ομοιοω	530
like (manner), ταυτα	720
like manner (in), ωσαυτως	817
like manner (so..in), ουτω	576
like to (made), (Ro. 1:23), ομοιωμα	531
like unto, see fashioned.	
like unto (be), παρομοιαζω	596
likeminded, ισοψυχος	391
likeminded (be), { φρονεω..	790
{ with αυτο	
liken, ομοιοω	530
likeness, ομοιωμα	531
likeness (in the), (Acts 14: 11), ομοιοω	530
likewise, ομοιως	531
ουτω	576
παραπλησιως	593
ωσαυτως	817
likewise, see I, so.	
lily, κρινον	433
limit, οριζω	538
line, κανων	404
lineage, πατρια	609
linen, λινον	461
σινδων	685
linen cloth, σινδων	—
linen clothes, οθονιον	524
linen (fine), βυσσινος	111
βυσσος	—
σινδων	685
linger, αργεω	80
lion, λεων	459
lip, χειλος	798
list, βουλομαι	110
list (Jas.3:4), ευθυνω	323
θελω	362
little, βραχυς	110
μικρος	501
ολιγος	528
(Acts 28:2), τυγχανω	751
little, see book, child, daughter, faith, fish, ship.	
little (a), μετριως	489
μικρον	501
little space, βραχυς	110
little (very), ελαχιστος	232
little while, βραχυς	110
little while (a), μικρον	501
live, αναστρεφω	45
βιοω	107
εσθιω	306
ζαω	335
ζωογονεω	340
πολιτευομαι	642
υπαρχω	772
live, see Jews, peace, pleasure, ungodly.	

live again, αναζαω	41
live deliciously, στρηνιαω ..	701
live long (Eph. { μακροχρο-	
6:3) { νιος	469
{ εσομαι ..	308
live peaceably, ειρηνευω	196
live ungodly, see after that.	
live with, συζαω	704
lively, ζαω	335
living, βιος	107
living, διαγω	144
lo, ιδε	380
ιδου	381
load, σωρευω	718
loaf, αρτος	83
locust, ακρις	26
lodge, αυλιζομαι	91
καταλυω	413
κατασκηνοω	415
ξενιζω	521
lodge, see strangers.	
lodging, ξενια	521
loin, οσφυς	541
long, ικανος	384
μακρος	469
{ ολιγος	528
{ ουκ	553
πλειων	627
πολυς	643
long, see bear, clothing, garment, hair, how, live, patience, robe, so, suffer, time.	
long, επιποθεω	286
long after, επιποθεω	—
long after (greatly), επιπο-θεω	—
long ago, παλαι	583
long as, see as.	
long while, ικανος	384
longed for, επιποθητος	286
longer, ετι	318
πλειων	627
longer, see any, no.	
longsuffering, μακροθυμια ..	469
longsuffering (be), μακροθυ-μεω	—
look, ατενιζω	90
αφοραω	99
βλεπω	108
ειδεω	188
θεαομαι	361
οπτομαι	535
παρακυπτω	591
προσδοκαω	662
look about on, & look about, περιβλεπω	616
look at & look on, σκοπεω..	688
look diligently, επισκοπεω..	286
look earnestly, ατενιζω	90
look for, απεκδεχομαι	61
εκδεχομαι	223
προσδεχομαι	662
προσδοκαω	—
look on, βλεπω	108
ειδεω	188

make of, *see* number.
make of no, *see* reputation.
make of none, *see* effect.
make peace, ειρηνοποιεω.... 197
make perfect, επιτελεω...... 288
make ready, ετοιμαζω 319
make to rise, ανατελλω 45
make towards, κατεχω...... 417
make up, *see* beforehand.
make [war], (Lu. 14:31),
    συμβαλλω 705
make with, *see* insurrection.
make without, *see* effect.
maker, δημιουργος......... 138
male, αρσην 82
malefactor, κακοποιος 400
    κακουργος ..... —
malice, κακια............... —
malicious, πονηρος......... 646
maliciousness, κακια 400
malignity, κακοηθεια....... —
mammon, μαμμωνας 470
man, ανηρ 47
    ανθρωπινος 49
    ανθρωπος .... —
    αρρην.............. 82
    εις................ 209
    ουδεις............... 565
    (1Co.14:20), τελειος . 727
    τις 732
man, *see* aged, another, any,
    every, forbidding, free,
    heathen, if, impotent, love
    toward; manner, never,
    no, not, old, other,
    some, such, this, wise,
    yet, young.
man (common to), ανθρω-
    πινος.................. 49
man of war, (Lu. 23:11),
    στρατευμα 700
man (strong), ισχυρος...... 392
man (young), νεανιας...... 513
    νεανισκος.... —
manger, φατνη............. 784
manifest, δηλος 138
    εκδηλος............. 223
    εμφανης 240
    φανερος 783
manifest, φανεροω .... —
    εμφανιζω.......... 240
manifest, *see* token.
manifest beforehand, προδη-
    λος.................. 654
manifest forth, φανεροω 783
manifest (make), φανεροω.. —
manifest (not), αφανης 97
manifestation, αποκαλυψις . 70
    φανερωσις .. 783
manifestly, *see* declare.
manifold, ποικιλος 640
    πολυποικιλος 643
manifold more, πολλαπλα-
    σιων .... —
man[kind], ανθρωπινος.... 49
mankind, *see* abusers, de-
    file.
manna, μαννα 471

manner,   αρα, 79 | εθος 182
    τυπος 752
manner, *see* after, all, like,
    perfect, this, what.
manner (after the), *see*
    Gentiles.
manner (after this), (Acts
    15:23), οδε 522
manner (after this), ουτω .. 576
manner (after what), πως.. 675
manner[like](Acts { τροπος 751
    1:11),   { with ος —
        (Jude { τροπος 751
        7),   { ομοιος . 530
manner of, *see* men.
manner of life, αγωγη 10
    βιωσις 107
manner of man, αρα........ 79
manner of (such), { περι .. 613
                  { τουτου 746
manner was, εθω............ 182
manners, ηθος 344
manners, *see* divers.
manners (suffer the), τρο-
    ποφορεω 751
manservant, παις 583
mansion, μονη 505
manslayer, ανδροφονος 46
many, ικανος............... 384
    πλειων 627
    πολυς 643
many, *see* how, so, these, very.
many as, *see* as.
maran-atha, μαραν αθα 471
marble, μαρμαρον .... —
mark, σκοπος............... 688
mark, στιγμα............... 699
    χαραγμα 796
mark, επεχω 275
    σκοπεω 688
market, & market-place,
    αγορα ......:....... 9
marred (be), απολλυμι ... 74
marriage, γαμος 112
marriage, *see* given.
marriage (be given in), εκ-
    γαμισκομαι 223
marriage (give in), εκγαμιζω —
married (be), γινομαι 117
marrow, μυελος 511
marry, γαμεω 112
    επιγαμβρευω 282
marry a wife, γαμεω 112
Mars' hill, Αρειος Παγος .. 821
martyr, μαρτυρ 471
marvel, θαυμαστος......... 361
marvel, θαυμαζω 360
marvellous, θαυμαστος 361
master, δεσποτης 136
    διδασκαλος 150
    επιστατης 287
    καθηγητης 395
    κυριος.............. 436
    ραββι 676
master [of a ship], κυβερνη-
    της.................. 436
master, *see* house.
masterbuilder, αρχιτεκτων.. 85

matter, λογος 462
    πραγμα 651
    υλη.................. 757
matter, *see* wrong.
matter (make), διαφερω.... 149
matters, *see* busybody.
may & might, δυναμαι...... 164
may & mayest, εξεστι....... 268
may, ισχυω.............. 392
may be (it), ισως 393
me, εγω 178
    εμαυτου 235
    εμε 236
    εμοι .... —
    εμου 238
    με 473
    μοι............ 503
    μου 507
me also, καμοι 393
me (of), εμος 237
meal, αλευρον 27
mean, ασημος 87
mean, ειην 193
    εστι 310
    θελω............ 362
    μελλω 478
    (Acts 21:13), ποιεω 636
mean while, μεταξυ 488
meaning, δυναμις 166
means, *see* by, no, seek.
means (by all), παντως 585
        { τροπος 751
    (2Th.{ εν 240
    3:16){ πας.... 597
means (by any), πως 675
        (2Th.{ τροπος 751
        2:3) { κατα .. 406
means (by some), πως...... 675
means (by what), πως...... —
means of, *see* by.
measure, βατος (ο) 106
    κορος............. 429
    μετρον 489
    σατον 681
    χοινιξ 801
measure, μετρεω 489
measure (above), υπερβαλ-
    λοντως.................. 774
measure (above), *see* exalted.
measure again, αντιμετρεω .. 57
measure (beyond), περισσος 618
        { κατα 406
        { υπερβολη 774
        υπερπερισ-
        σως 775
measure (out of), περισσως 619
    (2 Co. { κατα 406
    1:8) { υπερβολη 774
measure (without), αμετρος 35
meat, βρωμα 111
    βρωσιμος .... —
    βρωσις .... —
    προσφαγιον 667
    (Acts 16: 34), τραπε-
    ζα 748
    τροφη 751
    φαγω................ 782

meat, *see* broken, offered to idols, portion, sit.

mediator, μεσιτης 483

meditate, μελεταω 478

meditate before, προμελεταω 656

meek, πραος 651
πραυς 652

meekness, πραοτης 651
πραυτης 652

meet, αξιος................ 58
δικαιος................ 155
ευθετος 322
ικανος 384
καλος 402

meet, απανταω 59
απαντησις............. —
συνανταω 710
(Mat.8:34), συναντη-
σις .... —
ὑπανταω 772
(Joh. 12:13), ὑπαντη-
σις .... —

meet, *see* go, seas.

meet (be), δει 132

meet for use, ευχρηστος.... 328

meet (make), ικανοω........ 384

meet with, παρατυγχανω .. 593
συμβαλλω 705

meeting (two ways), αμφο-
δον........................ 37

melody (make), ψαλλω ... 806

melt, λυω.................. 466
τηκομαι 730

member, μελος 479

memorial, μνημοσυνον 503

memory, *see* keep.

men, αρσην 82

men, *see* great, mighty, ungodly.

men (manner of), ανθρωπι-
νος........................ 49

men's persons, προσωπον .. 667

men (quit like), ανδριζομαι 46

mend, καταρτιζω 415

menpleasers, ανθρωπαρεσ-
κος 49

menstealer, ανδραποδιστης 46

mention, μνεια............. 502

mention(make), μνημονευω 503

merchandise, γομος 125
εμπορια 239
εμποριον..... —

merchandise, *see* make.

merchant, εμπορος 239

mercies (Acts 13:34), ὁσιος 539

merciful, ελεημων 233
(Heb.8:12), ιλεως 384
οικτιρμων 527

merciful (be), ιλασκομαι .. 384

Mercurius, Ἑρμης 828

mercy, ελεος 233
οικτιρμος............ 527

mercy, *see* tender.

mercy (obtain), ελεεω 233

mercy (of tender), οικτιρμων 527

mercy on (have) ελεεω...... 233

mercy (receive), ελεεω...... 233

mercy (shew), ελεεω........ —

mercy (without), ανιλεως.. 53

mercyseat, ιλαστηριον...... 384

merry (be), ευθυμεω........ 323
ευφραινω 327

merry (make), ευφραινω.... —

message, αγγελια 5
επαγγελια 271
πρεσβεια 652

messenger, αγγελος 5
αποστολος... .. 77

mete, μετρεω............... 489

mid-day, { μεσος 483
{ ἡμερα 347

middle wall, μεσοτοιχον .. 484

midnight, μεσονυκτιον..... 483
{ μεσος.......... —
{ νυξ.......... 520

midst, μεσος 483

midst, *see* heaven.

midst (be about the), (Joh.
7:14), μεσοω 484

might, δυναμις............. 166
ισχυς 392

might, *see* may.

mightier, ισχυρος 392

mightily, { εν 240
{ ισχυς......... 392
(Acts { κατα 406
19:20) { κρατος .. 432
δυναμις 166
ευτονως......... 327

mighty, βιαιος 106
δυναμις 166
δυναστης 167
δυνατος .... —
ισχυρος, ισχυς.... 392
κραταιος............ 431
μεγας 476

mighty, *see* deed, power,
works.

mighty (be), δυνατεω 167
ενεργεω 261

mighty men, δυνατος 167

mighty (so), τηλικουτως.... 730

mile, μιλιον 501

milk, γαλα 112

mill, μυλων................ 511

mill, *see* stone.

millstone, μυλος 511
ονικος 532

mind, γνωμη 124
διανοια 147
εννοια 262
νοημα 516
νους 519
φρονημα............. 790
ψυχη 807

mind, μελλω 478
φρονεω 790

mind, *see* cast, change, doubtful, fervent, forwardness,
humbleness, humility, lowliness, put in, readiness,
ready, sound, willing.

mind (be in a right), σωφρονεω........................ 719

mind [be in you],
(let this), (Phi. { φρονεω 790
2:5) { τουτο 743

mind (be of one, { φρονεω.. 790
or, the same) { αυτος ... 91

mind (call to), αναμιμνησκω 43

mind (of one), ὁμοφρων.... 531
(Phi. 2:2) { φρονεω .. 790
{ εις.... 209

mind (put in), ὑπομιμνησκω 779

mind (with one), ὁμοθυμαδον 530

minded (be), βουλευομαι .. 110
βουλομαι ..... —

minded (be car- { φρονημα 790
nally), (Ro. 8:6) { σαρξ.... 680

minded (be sober), σωφρονεω 719

minded (be spiri- { φρονημα 790
tually), (Ro.8:6) { πνευμα 632

minded (high), (2 Ti. 3:4),
τυφοομαι................. 752

mindful (be), μιμνησκομαι 501
μναομαι.... 502
μνημονευω.. 503

mine, εμοι 236
εμος 237
εμου 238
μοι 503
μου 507

mine own, αυτος 91
εμαυτου.......... 235
εμος............ 237
μου............ 507

mine own self, εμαυτου 235

mingle, μιγνυμι............. 500

mingled with, *see* myrrh.

minister, διακονος 145
λειτουργος 459
ὑπηρετης......... 775

minister, διακονεω 144
διδωμι 151
επιχορηγεω 289
ιερουργεω 383
λειτουργεω........ 458
παρεχω............ 595
ὑπηρετεω.......... 775
χορηγεω.......... 802

minister about, εργαζομαι.. 298

minister [sent forth to],
διακονια 145

minister unto, διακονεω 144
επιχορηγεω .. 289
ὑπηρετεω... 775

ministered (Phi. 2:25), λειτουργος 459

ministered, *see* nourishment.

ministering, διακονια 145

ministering, λειτουργικος .. 459

ministration, διακονια 145
λειτουργια.... 458

ministry, διακονια 145
λειτουργια...... 458

minstrel, αυλητης 91

mint, ἡδυοσμον............. 344

miracle, δυναμις 166
σημειον 684

miracles (workers of), δυναμις................... 166

mire, βορβορος............. 109

possess, κτ⸍αομαι............ 435

possessed with (be), εχω.... 329

possessed with devils, δαιμο-
νιζομαι 131

possesseth (things which
one), ὑπαρχοντα 772

possession, κατασχεσις 416

κτημα 435

χωριον.......... 805

possession (purchased), πε-
ριποιησις.................. 618

possessor, κτητωρ 435

possible, δυνατος............ 167

possible (be), δυναμαι...... 164

possible (not), αδυνατος...: 15

pot, ξεστης................. 521

σταμνος................. 697

potentate, δυναστης........ 167

potter, κεραμευς 420

potter (of a), κεραμικος 421

pound, λιτρα................ 461

μνα............ 502

pour, βαλλω 100

κατεχεω 416

pour in, επιχεω 289

pour out, εκχεω 231

εκχυννω .... —

κεραννυμι........ 421

poverty, πτωχεια 673

powder, see grind.

power, αρχη 84

δυναμις.............. 166

δυνατος............. 167

εξουσια 269

ισχυς 392

κρατος 432

power (be of), δυναμαι 164

power (have), διδωμι....... 151

εξουσιαζω .. 270

power (mighty), μεγαλειο-
της.................... 475

power of (bring under the),
εξουσιαζω 270

powerful, ενεργης 261

ισχυρος 392

practices, see covetous.

prætorium, πραιτωριον 651

praise, αινεσις 16

αινος 17

αρετη 80

δοξα................. 161

επαινος 272

praise, ευλογεω............ 324

αινεω 16

επαινεω 272

praise, see sing.

prate against, φλυαρεω...... 788

pray, δεομαι 135

ερωταω 306

ευχομαι 328

παρακαλεω........... 590

προσευχομαι.......... 663

pray earnest-
ly (Jas.
5:17), { προσευχομαι —
προσευχη .. —

pray for, προσευχομαι ...... —

prayer, δεησις 132

prayer, εντευξις 263

ευχη 328

προσευχη 663

prayer (make), προσευχομαι —

preach, διαγγελλω.......... 143

διαλεγομαι 146

ευαγγελιζω.......... 320

καταγγελλω 410

κηρυσσω 422

λαλεω 443

preach before, προκηρυσσω . 655

preach before the gospel,
προευαγγελιζομαι .... —

preach boldly, παρρησιαζομαι...................... 596

preach first, προκηρυσσω ... 655

preach (fully), πληροω 630

preach the gospel, ευαγγελιζω 320

preach unto, διαλεγομαι.... 146

preached (i. q. of preaching),
ακοη 22

preached, see gospel.

preacher, κηρυξ 422

κηρυσσω .... —

preaching, κηρυγμα.......... —

λογος 462

precept, εντολη............. 263

precious, εντιμος............
(1Pet.2:7), τιμη 732

τιμιος............. —

precious (like), ισοτιμος 391

precious (very), βαρυτιμος . 103

πολυτελης . 645

predestinate, προοριζω...... 656

preeminence (have the),
πρωτευω 670

preeminence (love to have
the) φιλοπρωτευω 787

prefer, προηγεομαι.......... 655

preferred (be), γινομαι 117

preferring one before another
προκριμα... .. 656

premeditate, μελεταω....... 478

preparation, ετοιμασια 320

παρασκευη...... 593

prepare, ετοιμαζω 319

καταρτιζω............ 415

κατασκευαζω ...... —

prepare afore, προετοιμαζω 655

prepare self, παρασκευαζω... 593

prepared, ετοιμος 320

presbytery, πρεσβυτεριον .. 652

presence, παρουσια 596

προσωπον 667

presence, see before.

presence of (in), εμπροσθεν 239

presence of (in), ενωπιον .. 264

presence of (in the), απε-
ναντι 61

present, αρτι............... 82

ενιστημι 262
(Acts 28:2), εφισ-
τημι.............. 328

νυν 519
(2 Pet.1:12), παρει-
μι 594

present, ιστημι............. 391

present, παριστημι.......... 595

present, see here.

present (be), ενδημεω 260

μενω.......... 481

παραγινομαι. 588

παρακειμαι .. 591

present here with (be), συμ-
παρειμι 706

present (this), αρτι.......... 82

present unto, προσφερω 667

presently, εξαυτης 266

παραχρημα...... 594

presently, see give.

preserve, ζωογονεω 340

συντηρεω 713

σωζω 716

τηρεω 730

press, οχλος 580

press, αποθλιβω 69

βιαζομαι............. 106

συνεχω 712

press down, πιεζω 621

press διωκω 159

press upon, επικειμαι 284

επιπιπτω 285

pressed (be), βαρεω 102

presumptuous, τολμητης .. 741

pretence, προφασις 668

prevail, ισχυω 392

κατισχυω 418

νικαω 515

ωφελεω............. 817

prevail against, κατισχυω .. 418

prevent, προφθανω.......... 670

φθανω............. 785

price, τιμη 732

price (of great), πολυτελης 645

πολυτιμος —

prick, κεντρον 420

prick, καταννσσω 414

pride, αλαζονεια............. 26

ὑπερηφανια 775

pride, see lifted up.

priest, ιερευς 383

priest (chief), αρχιερευς 84

priest (high), αρχιερευς .... —

priest (of the high), αρχιερα-
τικος .... —

priesthood, ιερατευμα 382

ιερωσυνη........ 384

priesthood, see office.

priests (chief of the), αρχιερευς...................... 84

priest's office, ιερατεια...... 382

priest's office (execute the),
ιερατευω 383

prince, αρχηγος 84

αρχων 86

ηγεμων............. 343

principal, εξοχη 270

principality, αρχη 84

principle, στοιχειον 699

principles, αρχη 84

print, τυπος 752

prison, δεσμωτηριον 136

οικημα 524

τηρησις............. 730

prison, φυλακη............. 791
prison, see keeper.
prison (put in), παραδιδωμι 589
prisoner, δεσμιος............ 136
    δεσμωτης.......... —
private, ιδιος 380
privately, { ιδιος............ —
           { κατα 406
privily, λαθρα 443
privily, see come.
privily bring in, παρεισαγω 594
privy to (be), συνειδεω 711
prize, βραβειον............. 110
proceed, εξερχομαι.......... 266
proceed, προκοπτω 656
proceed forth, εξερχομαι.... 266
proceed further, προστιθημι 666
proceed—out of, εκπορευο-
    μαι..................... 229
proclaim, κηρυσσω 422
profane—profane person, βε-
    βηλος.................. 106
profane, βεβηλοω............ —
profess, επαγγελλομαι 272
    ομολογεω 531
    φασκω 784
professed (2 Co. 9:13), ομο-
    λογια................. 531
profession, ομολογια .... —
profit, οφελος............... 579
profit, συμφερω............. 707
    χρησιμος 803
    ωφελεια 817
    (1Ti.4:8), ωφελιμος .
profit, προκοπτω 656
    συμφερω 707
    ωφελεω 817
    (1Ti. { ωφελιμος .... —
    4:8), { εστι 310
profitable, ευχρηστος 328
    ωφελιμος 817
profitable (be), } συμφερω 707
profitable for(be), }
profiting, προκοπη 655
promise, επαγγελλια 271
    επαγγελμα 272
promise, εξομολογεομαι ... 269
    επαγγελλομαι 272
    ομολογεω 531
promise afore, προεπαγγελ-
    λομαι.................. 655
promise (make), επαγγελ-
    λομαι 272
proof, δοκιμη 160
    ενδειξις 260
proof (infallible), τεκμηριον 726
proper, αστειος 88
    ιδιος 380
proper (his), ιδιος .... —
prophecy, προφητεια.. 668
prophecy (of) (2 Pet. 1:19),
    προφητικος 670
prophesy, προφητευω 669
prophesying, προφητεια 668
prophet, προφητης.......... 669
prophet (false), ψευδοπρο-
    φητης 806
prophetess, προφητις 670

prophets (of the), προφη-
    τικος 670
propitiation, ιλασμος........ 384
    ιλαστηριον .... —
proportion, αναλογια 43
proselyte, προσηλυτος 664
prosper, ευοδουμαι 324
prosperous, see journey.
protest by (I), νη 515
proud, υπερηφανος.......... 775
proud (be), τυφοομαι 752
prove, αποδεικνυμι.......... 68
    δοκιμαζω 160
    παριστημι............ 595
    πειραζω.............. 610
    συμβιβαζω 705
prove before, προαιτιαομαι 653
proverb, παραβολη......... 587
    παροιμια 596
provide, ετοιμαζω 319
    κταομαι 435
    παριστημι.......... 595
    ποιεω 636
    προβλεπω 654
    προνοεω........... 656
provide for, προνοεω........ —
providence, προνοια .... —
province, επαρχια 273
provision, προνοια 656
provocation, παραπικρασ-
    μος 592
provoke, ερεθιζω 300
    παραπικραινω......592
    προκαλεομαι 655
provoke, see emulation, wrath.
provoke [to anger], ερεθιζω 300
provoke to jealousy, παρα-
    ζηλοω 590
provoke to speak, αποστο-
    ματιζω 77
provoke unto (Heb.10:24),
    παροξυσμος 596
provoked (be easily), παροξ-
    υνομαι .... —
prudence, φρονησις 790
prudent, συνετος........... 712
psalm, ψαλμος 806
psalms (sing), ψαλλω ..... —
publican, τελωνης 728
publicans (chief among the),
    αρχιτελωνης.............. 85
publick, see example.
publickly, δημοσιος.......... 138
publish, κηρυσσω.......... 422
published (be), γινομαι 117
    διαφερω 149
Pudens, Πουδης 859
puff up, φυσιοω 792
pull, αρπαζω 82
pull down, καθαιρεω 394
pull out, ανασπαω 44
    εκβαλλω 222
pulled in pieces (be), διασ-
    παω 148
pulling down, καθαιρεσις ... 394
punish, δικη 157
    κολαζομαι 427

punish, τιμωρεω 732
punished with (be), τιω 740
punishment, εκδικησις 223
    επιτιμια 289
    κολασις........... 427
    τιμωρια....... 732
purchase, κταομαι 435
    περιποιεομαι ... 618
purchase, see possession.
pure, αγνος................. 9
    ειλικρινης 193
    καθαρος 394
pureness, αγνοτης 9
purge, εκκαθαιρω........... 227
    καθαριζω 394
    καθαιρω........... —
purge out, εκκαθαιρω....... 227
purge throughly, διακαθα-
    ριζω 144
purged,(have) { καθαρισμος 394
    (Heb. 1:3) { ποιεω 636
purification, αγνισμος ... 8
    καθαρισμος 394
purify, αγνιζω 8
    καθαριζω 394
purify himself, αγνιζω...... 8
purifying, καθαρισμος 394
    καθαροτης........ —
purity, αγνεια 8
purloin, νοσφιζομαι 518
purple, πορφυρα 648
purple, πορφυρεος .... —
purple (seller of), πορφυρο-
    πωλις .... —
purpose, βουλημα 110
    προθεσις 655
purpose, βουλευομαι 110
    γνωμη 124
    ποιεω 636
    προαιρεομαι 653
    προτιθημι 668
    τιθημι.............. 731
purpose, see for.
purse, βαλαντιον 100
    ζωνη 340
put, βαλλω............... 100
    διδωμι............ 151
    επιβαλλω 281
    ποιεω 636
    τιθημι............. 731
put, see difference, prison,
    silence, trust.
put about, put on, put upon,
    περιτιθημι 619
put asunder, χωριζω 805
put away, αθετησις.......... 15
    αιρω 17
    απολυω 75
    αποτιθημι 78
    απωθομαι 79
    αφιημι 97
    εξαιρω 265
    καταργεω 415
put down, καθαιρεω 394
    καταργεω 415
put forth, εκβαλλω.......... 222
    εκτεινω 230

send out, εξαποστελλω 266
send rain, βρεχω 111
send with, συμπεμπω 706
    συναποστελλω .. 710
senses, αισθητηριον 18
sensual, ψυχικος 808
sent forth to, see minister.
sent (he that is), αποστολος 77
sentence, αποκριμα.......... 71
sentence (give), επικρινω .. 284
sentence is (Acts15:19), κρινω 433
separate, αφοριζω 99
    χωριζω.......... 805
separate ... self, αποδιοριζω . 69
sepulchre, μνημα..... 502
    μνημειον .... —
    ταφος 723
serjeant, ραβδουχος 676
serpent, ερπετον 301
    οφις 580
servant, διακονος............ 145
    δουλον.............. 163
    δουλος............ —
    θεραπων 374
    οικετης 524
    παις ...,........ 583
    υπηρετη 775
servant (hired), μισθιος 501
    μισθωτος .. 502
servants see houshold.
servants (become), δουλοω . 164
servants (make), δουλοω .. —
serve, διακονεω 144
    δουλευω 163
    λατρευω.............. 449
    υπηρετεω 775
service, διακονια 145
    λατρεια 448
    λειτουργια 458
service, see divine.
service (do), διακονια 145
    δουλευω 163
service (do the), λατρευω .. 449
serving, διακονια 145
set, διδωμι 151
    ιστημι 391
    καθιζω 396
    καθιστημι .... —
    τασσω 720
    τιθημι 731
set, δυνω 167
set, τακτος 719
set, see fire, seal, uproar,
  variance.
set .. about, περιτιθημι. 619
set at, see liberty.
set (at liberty), αποστελλω .. 76
set at nought, εξουδενοω.... 269
    εξουθενεω.... —
set at one again ⎧ συνελαυνω 711
    (Acts7:26), ⎨ εις 197
    ⎩ ειρηνη 196
set (be), (Acts19:27), ερχομαι 301
set (be), κειμαι.............. 419

set before, παρατιθημι...... 593
    προκειμαι........ 655
set eyes, ατενιζω............ 90
set [foot] on, βημα 106
set forth, αναγω 41
    αποδεικνυμι....... 68
    προκειμαι 655
    προτιθημι 668
    τιθημι 731
set forth evidently, προγραφω 654
set forth in order, ανατασ-
  σομαι...................... 45
set in order, διατασσω 148
    επιδιορθοω 283
set on, επιβιβαζω............ 282
    επικαθιζω 284
    επιτιθημι........ 288
set stedfastly, στηριζω 699
set the, see affection.
set up, ανορθοω 55
    επιτιθημι........ 288
    ιστημι 391
setter forth, καταγγελευς .. 410
setting (and), (Mat. 27:66),
  μετα 484
settle, θεμελιοω............ 363
    τιθημι.............. 731
settled, εδραιος.............. 181
seven, επτα.............. 290
seven thousand, επτακισχι-
  λιοι...................... 291
seven times, επτακις........ —
seventh, εβδομος............ 175
    επτα 290
seventy, εβδομηκοντα 175
seventy times, εβδομηκον-
  τακις..................... —
sever, αφοριζω 99
several (see his), ανα...... **39**
severally, ιδιος 380
severity, αποτομια.......... 78
sew on, επιρραπτω.......... 286
shadow, αποσκιασμα........ 76
    σκια 687
shadow, κατασκιαζω........ 415
shake, εκτινασσω............ 230
    σαλευω 679
    σειω 684
shake off, αποτινασσω...... 78
    εκτινασσω........ 230
shake together, σαλευω 679
shall, μελλω 478
shall answer ⎰ μελλω........ —
  (Acts 26:2), ⎱ απολογεομαι 74
shall ascend ⎰ μελλω........ 478
  (Rev.17:8), ⎱ αναβαινω 39
shall be (Rev. ⎰ μελλω...... 478
  1:19), ⎱ γινομαι.... 117
shall be betrayed ⎰ μελλω .. 478
  & should betray ⎨ παραδι-
  (Joh. 6:71), ⎩ δωμι .. 589
shall be delivered ⎰ μελλω ... 478
  ⎨ παραδι-
  (Lu. 9:44), ⎩ δωμι .. 589
shall be fulfilled ⎰ μελλω.... 478
  (Mar. 13:4), ⎱ συντελεω 713
shall be heirs of ⎰ μελλω.... 478
  (Heb.1:14), ⎱ κληρονομεω 425

shall be imputed ⎰ μελλω ... 478
  (Ro. 4:24), ⎱ λογιζομαι 461
shall be revealed⎫
  (Ro. 8:18, 1 Pet. ⎬ μελλω 478
  5:1), should after- ⎬ αποκα-
  wards be revealed ⎮ λυπτω 70
  (Gal. 3:23), ⎭
shall come ⎰ μελλω........ 478
  ⎱ ερχομαι........ 301
shall come to pass, ⎰ μελλω 478
  should   come ⎨ γινομαι 117
  (Acts 26:22), ⎩
shall devour (Heb. ⎰ μελλω 478
  10:27), ⎱ εσθιω.. 307
shall drink (Mat. ⎰ μελλω .. 478
  20:22), ⎱ πινω.... 621
shall hear (Mat. ⎰ μελλω.. 478
  24:6), ⎱ ακουω.... 22
shall smite (Acts ⎰ μελλω .. 478
  23:3), ⎱ τυπτω.. 752
shall suffer (Rev. ⎰ μελλω .. 478
  2:10), ⎱ πασχω.. 605
shalt be (Rev. 16:5), οσιος.. 539
shambles, μακελλον 469
shame, αισχρον 18
    αισχυνη 18
    ασχημοσυνη 89
    ατιμια 90
    εντροπη 264
    εντρεπω 264
shame, καταισχυνω 411
shame, see suffer.
shame, (put to an open),
  παραδειγματιζω 588
shamefacedness, αιδως 16
shamefully, see entreat.
shamefully (entreat), ατι-
  μαζω 90
shamefully handled, ατιμαω —
shape, ειδος................. 192
    ομοιωμα.............. 531
sharp, οξυς 534
sharper, τομωτερος.......... 741
sharply, αποτομως.......... 78
sharpness, αποτομως........ —
shave, ξυραω 522
she, αυτος 91
    εκεινος.......... 225
    οδε 522
    αυτη 576
shear, κειρω 420
shearer, κειρω...............
sheath, θηκη 375
shed, εκχεω................. 231
    εκχυνω..............
shed abroad, εκχυνω .... —
shed forth, εκχεω............ —
shedding of blood, αιματεκ-
  χυσια...................... 16
sheep, προβατον 654
sheep-fold (Joh. ⎰ προβατον
  10:1), ⎱ αυλη 90
sheep [market], προβατικος 654
sheepskin, μηλωτη 499
sheet, οθονη 524
shepherd, ποιμην........... 640
shepherd (chief), αρχιποι-
  μην........................ 85
shew, λογος 462

some, αλλος 30
  εις 209
  ετερος 318
  μεν 480
  τις 732
some, see sort.
some man, τις 732
some means, see lest.
some time, ποτε 649
somebody, τις 732
something, τις .... —
sometimes, ποτε 649
somewhat, μερος 483
  τις 732
son, παις 583
  τεκνον 726
  υιος 754
son, see bear, sister's.
song, ῳδη 809
sons (adoption of), υιοθεσια 754
soon, παραχρημα 594
soon, ταχεως 723
soon, see angry, as.
" soon as it was," γινομαι.. 117
sooner, ταχιον 724
soothsaying (Acts 16 : 16),
  μαντευομαι 471
sop, ψωμιον 808
sorcerer, μαγος 466
  φαρμακευς 784
  φαρμακος .... —
sorcery, μαγεια 466
  φαρμακεια 784
sorcery (use), μαγευω 466
sore, ικανος 384
  κακως 401
  λιαν 460
  {μεγας 476
  {with φοβος 789
  πολυς 643
  σφοδρα 715
sore, see afraid, amazed, displeased.
sorer, χειρων 800
sores, ελκος 234
sores (full of), ελκοομαι .... —
sorrow, λυπη 465
  οδυνη 524
  πενθος 612
  ωδιν 809
sorrow, λυπεω 465
  οδυναομαι 524
sorrowful (be), λυπεω 465
sorrowful (exceeding), περιλυπος 617
sorrowful (less), αλυποτερος 32
sorrowful (very), {περιλυ-
sorry (exceeding), { πος .. 617
sorry (make), λυπεω 465
sort, see baser, this, what.
sort (after a godly), αξιως.. 58
sort (some), μερος 483
soul, ψυχη 807
sound, ηχος 358
  φθογγος 786
  φωνη 793
sound, υγιης 753

sound, υγιαινω 753
sound, βολιζω 109
sound, γινομαι 117
sound, ηχεω 358
  σαλπιζω 680
sound, see safe.
sound a trumpet, σαλπιζω.. 680
sound (be), υγιαινω 753
sound mind, σωφρονισμος .. 719
sound out, εξηχεομαι 269
soundness (perfect), ολοκληρια 528
south, μεσημβρια 483
  νοτος 518
south west, λιψ 461
south wind, νοτος 518
sow, υς 781
sow, σπειρω 695
sower, σπειρω .... —
sown, see seed.
space, διαστημα 148
  χρονος 804
space, see little, three years.
space of, see by, for, the.
space of—after (the), διιστημι 155
spare, φειδομαι 784
spare, see enough.
sparingly, φειδομενως 784
sparrow, στρουθιον 701
speak, διαλεγομαι 146
  επω 291
  ερεω 300
  λαλεω 443
  λεγω 449
  ρεω 677
  φθεγγομαι 786
  χρηματιζω 803
speak, see provoke, truth.
speak against, αντιλεγω 56
  καταλαλεω .. 412
speak among, συλλαλεω 705
speak before, προεπω 654
  προερεω 655
speak blasphemy, βλασφημεω 107
speak boldly, παρρησιαζομαι 596
speak (can), γινωσκω 122
speak evil, βλασφημεω 107
  κακολογεω 400
  καταλαλεω 412
speak for self, απολογεομαι . 74
speak forth, αποφθεγγομαι.. 78
speak of, ερεω 300
  καταγγελω 410
speak out, αναφωνεω 46
speak to, } προσλαλεω .. 666
speak with, }
speak to, } προσφωνεω .. 667
speak unto, }
speak to any more, προστιθημι 666
speaker (Acts 14 :12), λογος. 462
speaking, see evil.
speaking lies, ψευδολογος .. 806
speaking (much), πολυλογια 643
speakings (evil), καταλαλια 412
spear, λογχη 464
spearman, δεξιολαβος 135

special (Acts {τυγχανω .. 751
  19:11), {ου 552
specially, μαλιστα 470
spectacle, θεατρον 361
speech, λαλια 445
  λογος 462
speech, see impediment.
speech (boldness of), παρρησια 596
speech (fair), ευλογια 324
speech of Lycaonia, Λυκαονιστι 851
speechless, εννεος 262
  κωφος 442
speechless (be), φιμοω 788
speed, see God.
speed (with all), {ταχιστα . 724
  {ως 812
speedily, ταχος 724
spend, δαπαναω 132
  ποιεω 636
  προσαναλισκω 662
spend more, προσδαπαναω . —
spend time, ευκαιρεω 323
  χρονοτριβεω .. 804
spent, see far.
spent (be), διαγινομαι 143
  εκδαπαναω 223
spent (be far), κλινω 426
  προκοπτω .. 656
spices, αρωμα 86
spices (sweet), αρωμα ......
spikenard, {ναρδος 513
  {πιστικος 624
spilled (be), εκχεω 231
  εκχυνω .... —
spin, νηθω 515
spirit, πνευμα 632
  φαντασμα 783
spiritual (1 Co. 14 : 12),
  πνευμα 632
  πνευματικος 635
spiritually (Ro. 8:6), πνευμα 632
  πνευματικως 635
spiritually, see minded.
spit, spit upon, εμπτυω 239
spit, πτυω 672
spitefully, see entreat.
spittle, πτυσμα 672
spoil, απεκδυομαι 61
  διαρπαζω 147
  συλαγωγεω 705
spoiling, αρπαγη 82
spoils, ακροθινιον 26
  σκυλον 688
spoken against (not to be),
  αναντιρρητος 43
spoken (be), αναγγελλω.... 40
sport.. selves, εντρυφαω 264
spot, σπιλας 696
  σπιλος .... —
spot, σπιλοω .... —
spot (without), αμωμος 37
  ασπιλος 88
spread, διανεμομαι 147
  στρωννυμι 701

weary (be), εκκακεω 227

weather, *see* fair.

weather (foul), χειμων...... 798

wedding, γαμος 112

week, σαββατον 679

    σαββατα............. —

weep, δακρυω 131

    κλαιω 423

weeping, κλανθμος........ 424

weight, βαρος 102

    ογκος.............. 522

weight, *see* talent.

weighty, βαρυς.............. 102

well, αγαθος 1

well, εν 320

    καλως.............. 403

well, πηγη 620

    φρεαρ................. 790

well, *see* doing, drink, full,
know, please, reported,
stricken, very.

well as, *see* as.

well (do), αγαθοποιεω 1

    σωζω 716

well doing, αγαθοποιια 1

well (doing), καλος......... 402

well done, εν 320

well pleased (be), ευδοκεω .. 322

well (them that do), αγαθο-
ποιος 1

well very, βελτιον 106

wellbeloved, αγαπητος 4

wellpleasing, ευαρεστος...... 321

wept (Acts 20:37), κλανθμος 424

west, δυσμη................. 169

west, *see* north, south.

whale, κητος.............. 423

what, η 340

what, οιος.................. 527

    οσος 539

    οστις 540

    ουτω 576

    ποιος.................. 640

    ποσος 648

    (Mar. 13:1), ποταπος 649

    τις 732

    τίς 736

what, *see* great.

what great, οσος 539

what manner, } οιος...... 527
what manner of, }

what manner of, οποιος 534

    ποιος 640

    ποταπος .. 649

    τίς 736

what place (in), οπου 535

what. soever (Mar. { οσος.. 539
11:24), { πας .. 597

what sort (of), οποιος 534

what thing, τίς.............. 736

whatsoever, οποιος......... 534

    οσος........... 539

    οστις 540

    πας 597

    τις 732

whatsoever, (Eph. { τις 732
6:8), { εαν 170

wheat, σιτος 686

when, εαν 170

    (Luke 2:27), εν 240

    επαν 273

    επει .... —

    ηνικα 357

    καθως.................. 397

    μετα.................. 484

    οποτε 534

    οπως.................. 536

    οταν 541

    οτε.................. 542

    (Heb. 3:9), ου 552

    ποτε 649

    πότε.................. —

    ως 812

when, *see* alone.

when I call, *see* call,

whence, οθεν 524

    ποθεν 635

whence, *see* from.

whence (from), οθεν....... 524

whensoever, οταν 541

    { ως............. 812
    { εαν 170

where (Acts 7:33), εν...... 240

    κατα 406

    οθεν 524

    οπου 535

    ου 552

    που 650

    τίς.................. 736

where (1 Ti. 2:8), τοπος .. 741

where, *see* every.

whereas, οπου 535

whereas ye, οστις 540

whereby, οθεν 524

whereby, { τίς 736
    { κατα 406

whereby, *see* by.

wherefore? διατι 149

wherefore, αρα............. 79

    διο 158

    διοπερ .... —

    ινα τι 390

    οθεν 524

    ουν............. 567

    τίς 736

    (Acts { τίς ..
    19:32), { ενεκεν 261

    1 Joh. { τίς .. 736
    3:12), { χαριν.. 797

    { τουτο 743
    { δια 138

    τοιγαρουν 740

    ωστε 816

wherefore, *see* cause.

wherein, ου.............. 552

wheresoever, οπου........ 535

wheresoever, { οπου ..... —
    { αν......... 37

wheresoever, { οπου 535
    { εαν 170

whereunto, τίς.............. 736

whereupon, οθεν 524

wherewith (Lu. 17:8), τίς.. 736

    { τίς .... —
    { εν 240

wherewith, *see* edify.

wherewith soever, οσος 539

wherewithal, τίς 736

whether, εαν 170

    ει 183

    ειτε 187

    ητοι 342

    ποτερον 649

    τε.................. 724

    τίς 736

whether any, ει τις......... 187

whether.. or not, μηποτε ... 497

which, αυτος 91

    οιος.................. 527

    οσος 539

    οστις 540

    (Acts 3:26), αυτη .. 576

    ποιος 640

    τίς 736

which, *see* behind, cause,
come, concern, corrected.

which art, and } ο ων και ο
wast, and art } ην και ο 522
to come, } ερχομενος

which art, and } ο ων και ο
wast, and } ην και ο ερ- —
shalt be, } χομενος

which easily, *see* besets.

which is, *see* committed.

which is, ο εστι.......... 522

which is, and } ο ων και ο
which was, } ην και ο ερ- —
and which is } χομενος
to come,

which make, ο εστι.

which was, *see* commanded.

which was, and } ο ων και ο
is, and is to } ην και ο 522
come, } ερχομενος

while, αχρι 99

    (Luke 1:8), εν 240

    εως 334

    ημερα 347

    (Heb. 10:37), οσος .. 539

    οταν.................. 541

    οτε.................. 542

    ως 812

while, *see* a while, dure, great,
little, long.

while (a), καιρος.......... 398

    μικρον 501

    ολιγος........... 528

    χρονος.......... 804

while ago (a great), παλαι. 583

while (any), παλαι......... —

whiles, εως 334

    οτου 552

whisperer, ψιθυριστης 807

whispering, ψιθυρισμος ....

whit, *see* every, not.

white, λαμπρος 447

    λευκος............ 459

white (make), λευκαινω 459

whiten, κονιαω 428

    λευκαινω 459

whither, ὁπου 535

    οὐ 552

    που 650

whithersoever, { οὐ 552

    { εαν 170

    { ὁπου 535

    { αν 37

    { ὁπου 535

    { εαν 170

who, ὁσος 539

    ὁστις 540

    ουτος 574

    τίς 736

whole, ἁπας 60

    ὁλοκληρος 528

    ὁλος 529

    πας 597

whole, ὑγιαινω 753

whole, ὑγιης .... —

whole, see armour, burnt offering.

whole (be), ισχυω 392

    σωζω 716

    ὑγιαινω 753

whole (be made perfectly), διασωζω 148

whole (make), ιαομαι 379

    σωζω 716

wholesome, ὑγιαινω 753

wholly, ὁλοτελης 529

wholly, see give.

wholly given, see idolatry.

whom, τίς 736

whom [soever], { τις 732

    { εαν 170

whore, πορνη 648

whoremonger, πορνος ..... —

whose, τις 732

    τίς 736

whosoever, ειτις 187

    ὁσος 539

    ὁστις 540

    πας 597

why, γαρ 112

    διατι 149

    ἱνατι 390

    ὁτι 543

    τίς 735

wicked, αθεσμος 15

    ανομος........... 55

    κακος 400

    πονηρος........ 646

wicked (more), πονηρος.... —

wickedness, κακια 400

    πονηρια........ 645

    (1Joh.5:19), πο-νηρος........ 646

wide, πλατυς............... 627

widow, χηρα 800

wife, γυναικειος 129

    γυνη .... —

wife, see marry.

wife's mother, πενθερα 611

wild, αγριος 10

wild, see beast, olive tree.

wilderness, ερημια 300

    ερημος (ἡ)...... —

wile, μεθοδεια 477

wilfully, ἑκουσιως 229

will, βουλη 110

    βουλημα........... —

    γνωμη 124

    θελημα 361

    θελησις 362

will, βουλομαι 110

will, γινομαι 117

    ευχομαι 328

    θελω.............. 362

will, see good.

will (against the), ακων .. . 26

will go (Joh. { μελλω 478

    7:35), { πορευομαι .. 646

will have, θελω 362

will judge, { μελλω 478

    { κρινω 433

will manifest { μελλω 478

    (Joh.14:22), { εμφανιζω.... 240

will (of his own), βουλομαι 110

will seek (Mat. { μελλω ... 478

    2:13), { ζητεω ... 337

will spue (Rev. { μελλω ... 478

    3:16), { εμεω.... 236

will-worship, εθελοθρησκεια 181

willing, προθυμος 655

willing (be), βουλομαι...... 110

    ευδοκεω 322

    θελω 362

willing mind, προθυμια 655

willing of ... selves, αυθαιρε-τος 90

willing to, see communicate.

willingly, ἑκουσιος 229

    ἑκουσιως .... —

    ἑκων 232

willingly, θελω 362

win, κερδαινω 421

wind, ανεμος 46

    πνευμα.............. 632

    (Acts27:40), πνεω 635

    πνοη.................. —

wind, see south.

wind, δεω................... 137

wind (driven with the), ανε-μιζομαι 46

wind up [for burial], συσ-τελλω 714

window, θυρις 378

wine, οινος 527

wine, see excess of.

wine (given to), παροινος .. 596

wine (new), γλευκος 124

winebibber, οινοποτης 527

winefat, ὑποληνιον 779

winepress, ληνος............ 459

    { οινος 527

    { ληνος 459

wing, πτερυξ 672

wink at, ὑπερειδω 775

winter, χειμων 798

winter, παραχειμαζω 593

winter in (Acts27:12), παρα-χειμασια 594

wipe, εκμασσω 229

wipe away, εξαλειφω........ 266

wipe off, απομασσομαι...... 75

wisdom, σοφια 694

    φρονησις 790

wise, σοφος................. 694

    φρονιμος 790

wise, see no, this.

wise (be), συνιημι 713

wise (in no), { παντελες .. 585

    (Lu.13:11), { μη 490

    παντως 585

wise (make), σοφιζω........ 694

wise man, μαγος........... 466

wise (on this), ουτω 576

wisely, φρονιμως............ 791

wish, ευχομαι 328

wist, ειδεω 188

wit, see to.

wit (do to), γνωριζω 125

witchcraft, φαρμακεια 784

with, ἁμα 32

with, απο 63

    δια 139

    εις 197

    εκ 215

    εν 240

    επι 275

    κατα 406

    μετα 484

    παρα............... 586

    περι 613

    προς 656

    συν 707

    ὑπο 776

with, see accord, affliction, agree, away, be, bear, beasts, bound, brought, buried, clothe, clothed, come, commune, communicate, company, compare, compassed, compassion, confer, consort, continue, crucify, dwellers, entangle, feast, go, indignation, labour, meet, mixed, reason, rejoice, rise, run, send, sit, sit at meat, speak, spring up, stand, suffer, take, talk, travel, work.

with child, { εν 240

    { γαστηρ 113

with fear, see move.

with one, see mind.

with rods, see beat.

withal, ἁμα................ 32

withdraw, αποσπαω 76

    ὑποστελλω 779

withdraw.. self, στελλομαι.. 698

    αναχωρεω.. 46

    αφιστημι .. 98

    ὑποχωρεω.. 780

wither, ξηραινω 521

wither away, ξηραινω ..... —

withered, ξηρος 522

withereth (whose fruit), φθινοπωρινος 786

withhold, κατεχω 417

within, δια 139

    εν 240

within, εντος.............. 264
 εσω................. 317
 εσωθεν .... —
 εσωτερος............ —
 προς 656
within, *see* from.
without, ανευ............. 47
 ατερ.............. 90
 εκ................ 215
 εκτος 231
 (Acts {μετα ... 484
 5:26), {ου.... 552
 μη................ 490
 παρεκτος 594
 χωρις 805
without, εξω............. 270
 εξωθεν 271
 (Rev.11:2), εσωθεν 317
without, *see* affection, blame, blemish, care, ceasing, charge, children, controversy, covetousness, descent, dissimulation, distraction, effect, excuse, father, fear, from, fruit, gainsaying, God, hands, honour, hypocrisy, life, measure, mercy, mixture, mother, offence, partiality, rebuke, repentance, signification, sin, strength, understanding, water, wavering, witness.
without a, *see* cause.

without any delay {αναβολη 40
 {ποιεω .. 636
(Acts 25:17), {μηδεις .. 496

without respect, *see* persons.
without seam, αρραφος 82
withstand, ανθιστημι 49
 κωλυω 442
witness, μαρτυρ 471
 μαρτυρια 472
 μαρτυριον......... —
witness, διαμαρτυρομαι ... 146
 μαρτυρεω 471
witness against, καταμαρτυρεω...................... 413
witness also (bear),
witness with (bear), } συμμαρτυρεω 706
witness also (bear), συνεπιμαρτυρεω 711
witness (be a), }
witness (bear), } μαρτυρεω 471
witness (bear false), ψευδομαρτυρεω 806
witness (false), ψευδομαρτυρ.
witness (false), ψευδομαρτυρια .... —
witness (give), } μαρτυ-
witness (obtain), } ρεω... 471
witness, (without), αμαρτυρος 34
wives' (old), γραωδης 128
woe, ουαι.................. 563
wolf, λυκος................ 465
woman, γυνη............... 129
 θηλεια 375

woman, *see* aged, every, this, elder
womb, γαστηρ 113
 κοιλια 426
 μητρα 500
women (silly), γυναικαριον 129
wonder, θαμβος 359
 σημειον 684
 τερας 728
wonder, εξιστημι........... 269
 θαυμαζω 360
wonderful, θαυμασιος 361
wonderful, *see* works.
wonderful works, μεγαλεια 475
wondering (greatly), εκθαμβος 227
wont, εθος 182
 εθω .... —
wont (be), εθω ....
 νομιζω 516
wood, ξυλον 522
wood (of), ξυλινος.......... —
wool, εριον 301
word, λογος 462
 ρημα 677
words, *see* enticing, few, good.
words (a few), συντομως .. 714
word again (bring), απαγγελλω 58
word (bring), απαγγελλω..
 επω 291
word (of the), λογικος...... 461
words (strive about), λογομαχεω 461
work (Eph. 4:19), εργασια.. 298
 εργον............. —
 λογος............. 462
 πραγμα 651
 πραξις .... —
work, ενεργεω 261
 εργαζομαι 298
 κατεργαζομαι 417
 ποιεω 636
work effectually, ενεργεω ... 261
work (much) {ισχυω 392
(Acts27:16), {μολις 505
work out, κατεργαζομαι. 417
work with, }
work together, } συνεργεω.. 711
worker, εργατης 298
workers of, *see* miracles.
workers together (2Co.6:1), συνεργεω................. 711
workfellow, συνεργος........ —
working, ενεργεια 261
 ενεργημα............
working, *see* effectual.
workman, εργατης 298
workmanship, ποιημα......640
works, *see* wonderful.
works (mighty), δυναμις .. 166
works (wonderful), δυναμις
world, αιων................. 19
 αιωνιος 20
 γη................. 115
 κοσμος 429
 οικουμενη.......... 527

world began, αιων 19
 αιωνιος 20
world (beginning of), }
world standeth, } αιων 19
world without end, }
worldly, κοσμικος 429
worm, σκωληξ 689
worms (eaten of), σκωληκοβρωτος .... —
wormwood, αψινθος 100
Wormwood, Αψινθος 822
worse, ελασσων 232
 ηττον 358
χειρων, worse and worse 800
worse (be the), υστερεω 781
worship, δοξα............. 161
worship, ευσεβεω 326
 θεραπευω 373
 λατρευω 449
 προσκυνεω 665
 σεβαζομαι......... 683
 σεβομαι .... —
worship, *see* will.
worshipped (that is), σεβασμα 683
worshipper, νεωκορος 515
 προσκυνητης.. 666
worshipper, *see* God.
worshippers (Heb. 10 : 2), λατρευω 449
worshipping, θρησκεια 377
worthy, αξιος 58
 ικανος............. 384
 καλος 402
worthy, αξιως. 58
worthy, *see* deeds.
worthy (account), καταξιοομαι 414
worthy (count), αξιοω...... 58
 καταξιοομαι 414
worthy (think), αξιοω...... 58
wot, γνωριζω 125
 ειδεω 188
would & would to God, οφελον 579
would depart {μελλω 478
(Acts 25:4), {εκπορευομαι 229
would do {μελλω.......... 478
(Joh. 6:6), {ποιεω 636
would enquire {μελλω...... 478
(Acts 23:15), {διαγινωσκω 143
 (Acts {μελλω.. 478
 23:20), {πυνθανομαι. 673
would have brought {μελλω. 478
(Acts12:6), {προαγω 653
would have cast {μελλω.... 478
(Acts27:30), {εκτεινω .. 230
would have killed {μελλω.. 478
(Acts16:27), {αναιρεω 42
wound, πληγη 628
 τραυμα 748
wound (Lu. {επιτιθημι.. 288
10:30), {πληγη 628
 σφαττω 715
 τραυματιζω.......... 748
 τυπτω 752
wound, *see* head.
woven, υφαντος 781

INDEX.

GREEK AND ENGLISH.

contention
fight
race

ἀγωνία . . . 11
agony

ἀγωνίζομαι . . 11
fight
labour fervently
strive

ἀδάπανος . . . 11
charge, without

ἀδελφή . . . 11
sister

ἀδελφός . . . 11
brother

ἀδελφότης . . . 13
brethren
brotherhood

ἄδηλος . . . 13
appear not
uncertain

ἀδηλότης . . . 13
uncertain

'δήλως . . . 13
uncertainly

ἀδημονέω . . . 13
heaviness, be full of
heavy, be very

ᾅδης . . . 13
grave
hell

ἀδιάκριτος . . . 14
partiality, without

ἀδιαλείπτος . . 14
ceasing, without
continual

ἀδιαλείπτως . . 14
ceasing, without

ἀδιαφθορία . . 14
uncorruptness

ἀδικέω . . . 14
hurt
injure
offender, be an
unjust, be
wrong
wrong, do
wrong, suffer
wrong, take

ἀδίκημα . . . 14
evil doing
iniquity
wrong, matter of

ἰδικια . . . 14
iniquity
unjust
unrighteousness
wrong

ἄδικος . . . 14
unjust
unrighteous

ἀδίκως . . . 14
wrongfully

ἀδόκιμος . . . 14
castaway, a
rejected
reprobate

ἄδολος . . . 14
sincere

ἀδρότης . . . 14
abundance

ἀδυνατέω . . 14
impossible, be

ἀδύνατος . . . 15
could not do
impossible
impotent
possible, not
weak

ᾄδω . . . 15
sing

ἀεί . . . 15
always
ever

ἀετός . . . 15
eagle

ἄζυμος . . . 15
unleavened
unleavened bread

ἀήρ . . . 15
air

ἀθανασία . . . 15
inmortality

ἀθέμιτος . . . 15
abominable
unlawful thing

ἄθεος . . . 15
God, without

ἄθεσμος . . . 15
wicked

ἀθετέω . . . 15
cast off
despise
disannul
frustrate
nothing, bring to
reject

ἀθέτησις . . . 15
disannulling
put away

ἀθλέω . . . 15
strive

ἄθλησις . . . 15
fight

ἀθυμέω . . . 15
discourage

ἀθῶος . . . 15
innocent

αἴγειος . . . 15
goat

αἰγιαλός . . . 15
shore

ἀΐδιος . . . 16
eternal
everlasting

αἰδώς . . . 16
reverence
shamefacedness

αἷμα . . . 16
blood

αἱματεκχυσία . . 16
blood, shedding of

αἱμορροέω . . 16
blood, diseased with an
issue of

αἴνεσις . . . 16
praise

αἰνέω . . . 16
praise

αἴνιγμα . . . 16
darkly

αἶνος . . . 17
praise

αἱρέομαι . . . 17
choose

αἵρεσιν . . . 17
heresy
sect

αἱρετίζω . . . 17
choose

αἱρετικός . . . 17
heretick

αἴρω . . . 17
away with
bear
bear up
carry
lift up
loose
make to doubt
put away
removed, be
take
take away
take up

αἰσθάνομαι . . 17
perceive

αισνησις . . . 18
judgment

αἰσθητήριον . . 18
senses

αἰσχροκερδής . . 18
filthy lucre, given to
filthy lucre, greedy of

αἰσχροκερδῶς . . 18
filthy lucre's sake, for

αἰσχρολογία . . 18
filthy communication

αἰσχρόν . . . 18
shame

αἰσχρός . . . 18
filthy

αἰσχρότης . . . 18
filthiness

αἰσχύνη . . . 18
dishonesty
shame

αἰσχύνομαι . . 18
ashamed, be

αἰτέω . . . 18
ask
beg
call for
crave
desire
require

αἴτημα . . . 18
petition
request
required

αἰτία . . . 19
accusation
case
cause
crime
fault
where[fore]

αἰτίαμα . . . 19
complaint

αἴτιον . . . 19
cause
fault

αἴτιος . . . 19
author

αἰφνίδιος . . . 19
sudden
unawares

αἰχμαλωσία . . 19
captivity

αἰχμαλωτεύω . . 19
captive, lead

αἰχμαλωτίζω . . 19
captive, lead away
captivity, bring into

αἰχμάλωτος . . 19
captive

αἰών . . . 19
ages
course
eternal
ever
ever (with πᾶς Jude 25)

ever, for (with ἡμέρα)
evermore
never (with ου, μη, &
world [εις]
world began
world, beginning of the
world standeth, while
the
world without end

ἀιώνιος . . . 20
eternal
ever, for
everlasting
world
world began

ἀκαθαρσία . . . 20
uncleanness

ἀκαθάρτης . . . 21
filthiness

ἀκάθαρτος . . . 21
foul
unclean

ἀκαιρέομαι . . . 21
lack opportunity

ἀκαιρως . . . 21
season, out of

ἄκικος . . . 21
harmless
simple

ἄκανθα . . . 21
thorns

ἀκάνθινος . . . 21
thorns, of

ἄκαρπος . . . 21
fruit, without
unfruitful

ακατάγνωστος . 21
condemned, cannot be

ἀκατακάλυπτος . 21
uncovered

ἀκατάκριτος . . 21
uncondemned

ἀκατάλυτος . . 21
endless

ἀκατάπαυστος . 21
cannot cease

ἀκαταστασία . . 21
commotion
confusion
tumult

ἀκατάστατος . 21
unstable

ἀκατασχετος . 21
unruly

ἀκέραιος . . 21
harmless
simple

ἀκλινής . . . 21
wavering, without

ἀκμάζω . . . 22
fully ripe, be

ἀκμήν . . . 22
yet

ἀκοή . . . 22
audience
ears
fame
heard, which ye
hearing
preached
report
rumour

ἀκολουθέω . . . 22
follow
reach

ἀκούω . . . 22
audience, give
audience of, in the
come
ears, come to the
hear
hear, shall (with μελλω,
Mat. 24:6)
hearer
hearken
noised, be
reported, be
understand

ἀκρασία . . . 26
excess
incontinency

ἀκρατής . . . 26
incontinent

ἄκρατον . . . 26
mixture, without

ἀκρίβεια . . . 26
manner, perfect

ἀκριβέστατος . . 26
straitest, most

ἀκριβέστερον . . 26
perfect, more
perfectly, more

ἀκριβόω . . . 26
enquire diligently

ἀκριβῶς . . . 26
circumspectly
diligently
perfect
perfectly

ἀκρίς . . . 26
locust

ἀκροατήριον . . 26
hearing, place of

ἀκροατής . . . 26
hearer

ἀκροβυστία . . 26
circumcised, not

---

uncircumcised (with
εχω, Acts 11: 3)
uncircumcision

ἀκρογωνιαῖος . . 26
chief corner

ἀκροθίνιον . . . 26
spoils

ἄκρον . . . 26
end...other, one
tip
top
uttermost part

ἀκυρόω . . . 26
disannul
none effect, have made
of

ἀκωλύτως . . . 26
no man forbidding him

ἄκων . . . 26
against the will

ἀλάβαστρον . . 26
alabaster box
box

ἀλαζονεία . . . 26
boasting
pride

ἀλαζών . . . 27
boaster

ἀλαλάζω . . . 27
tinkle
wail

ἀλάλητος . . . 27
(unutterable or)
uttered, which cannot
be

ἄλαλος . . . 27
dumb

ἅλας . . . 27
salt

ἀλείφω . . . 27
anoint

ἀλεκτοροφωνία . 27
cockcrowing

ἀλέκτωρ . . . 27
cock

ἄλευρον . . . 27
meal

ἀλήθεια . . . 27
true
truly
truth
verity

ἀληθεύω . . . 28
truth, speak the
truth. tell the

ἀληθής . . . 28
true
truly
truth

ἀληθινός . . . 28
true

ἀλήθω . . . 28
grind

ἀληθῶς . . . 28
indeed
surely
surety, of a
truly
truth, in
truth, of a
verily
very

ἀλιεύς 29
fisher
fisherman

ἀλιεύω . . . 29
fishing, go a

ἁλίζω . . . 29
salt

ἀλίσγημα . . 29
pollution

ἀλλά 29
and
but
howbeit
indeed
moreover, but even
nay
nevertheless
no
notwithstanding
save
therefore
yea
yet

ἀλλάττω . . . 29
change

ἀλλαχόθεν . . 29
some other way

ἀλληγορέω . . 29
allegory, be an

ἀλληλούια . . 29
alleluia

ἀλλήλων . . . 29
each other
mutual
one another
one the other
selves
themselves
together
together (with μετα, Lu.
23:12)
together (with προς,
Lu. 24:14)
together, selves
yourselves

ἀλλογενής . . . 30
stranger

ἄλλομαι . . . 30
leap
spring up

ἄλλος . . . 30
another
more
one
one another
other
otherwise
some
some another
some others

ἀλλοτριοεπίσκοπος 31
busybody in other
  men's matters

ἀλλότριος . . . 31
alien
another man's
other
other men's
strange
stranger

ἀλλόφυλος . . 32
one of another nation

ἄλλως . . . 32
otherwise

ἀλοάω . . . 32
thresh
tread out the corn

ἄλογος . . . 32
brute
unreasonable

ἀλόη 32
aloes

ἅλς 32
salt

ἁλυκός . . . 32
salt

ἀλυπότερος . . 32
sorrowful, less

ἄλυσις . . . 32
bonds
chain

ἀλυσιτελής . . 32
unprofitable

ἅλων . . . 32
floor

ἀλώπηξ . . . 32
fox

ἅλωσις . . . 32
taken, be [see lit.]

ἅμα . . . 32
also
and
together
with
withal

ἀμαθής . . . 32
unlearned

ἀμαράντινος . . 32
fadeth not away, that

ἀμάραντος . . 32
fadeth not away, that

ἁμαρτάνω . . . 32
faults, for your
offend
sin
trespass

ἁμάρτημα . . . 33
sin

ἁμαρτία . . . 33
offence
sin
sinful

ἀμάρτυρος . . . 34
witness, without

ἁμαρτωλός . . 34
sinful
sinner

ἄμαχος . . . 34
brawler, not a

ἀμάω . . . 34
reap down

ἀμέθυστος . . . 34
amethyst

ἀμελέω . . . 34
light of, make
neglect
negligent, be
regard not

ἄμεμπτος . . . 34
blameless
faultless
unblameable

ἀμέμπτως . . . 35
blameless
unblameably

ἀμέριμνος . . . 35
care, without
carefulness, without
secure, [see lit.]

ἀμετάθετος . . 35
immutability
immutable

ἀμετακίνητος . . 35
unmoveable

ἀμεταμέλητος . . 35
repentance, without
repented of, not to be

ἀμετανόητος . . 35
impenitent

ἄμετρος . . . 35
measure, things without
measure, without

ἀμήν 35
Amen
verily

ἀμήτωρ . . . 36
mother, without

ἀμίαντος . . . 36
undefiled

ἄμμος 36
sand

ἀμνός 36
Lamb

ἀμοιβή . . . 36
requite

ἄμπελος . . . 36
vine

ἀμπελουργός . . 36
dresser of his vineyard

ἀμπελών . . . 36
vineyard

ἀμύνομαι . . . 36
defend

ἀμφίβληστρον . . 36
net

ἀμφιέννυμι . . 37
clothe

ἄμφοδον . . . 37
where two ways met

ἀμφότερος . . . 37
both

ἀμώμητος . . . 37
blameless
rebuke, without

ἄμωμος . . . 37
blame, without
blemish, without
fault, without
faultless
spot, without
unblameable

ἄν . . . 37
wheresoever
whithersoever

ἀνά 39
and
apiece
by
each
several
every man

ἀνά 39
by
in
through

ἀναβαθμός . . 39
stairs

ἀναβαίνω . . . 39
arise
ascend

ascend, shall (with
  μελλω, Rev. 17: 8)
ascend up
climb up
come
come up
enter
go up
grow up
rise up
spring up

ἀναβάλλομαι . . 40
defer

ἀναβιβάζω . . 40
draw

ἀναβλέπω . . 40
look
look up
see
sight, receive

ἀνάβλεψις . . 40
sight, recovering of

ἀναβοάω . . 40
cry
cry aloud
cry out

ἀναβολή . . . 40
delay
delay, without any (with
  ποιεω, μηδεις, Acts
  25:17)

ἀναγγέλλω . . 40
declare
rehearse
report
shew
spoken, be
tell

ἀναγεννάω . . . 40
again
beget
born again, be

ἀναγινώσκω . . 40
read

ἀναγκάζω . . 40
compel
constrain

ἀναγκαῖος . . 41
more needful
near
necessary
necessity

ἀναγκαστῶς . . 41
constraint, by

ἀνάγκη . . . 41
distress
must needs
must needs (with εχω)
necessary
necessity

ἀνατάσσομαι . . 45 set forth in order	ἀνεκδιήγητος . . 46 unspeakable	ἀνήμερος . . . 47 fierce	ἄνοια . . . 54 folly madness
ἀνατέλλω . . . 45 arise rise rise, make to rising of, at the spring spring up up, be	ἀνεκλάλητος . . 46 unspeakable	ἀνήρ . . . 47 fellow husband man Sir	ἀνοίγω . . . 54 open
	ἀνέκλειπτος . . 46 faileth not, that		ἀνοικοδομέω . . 55 build again
	ἀνεκτότερος . . 46 tolerable, more	ἀνθίστημι . . . 49 resist withstand	ἄνοιξις . . . 55 open [see lit.]
ἀνατίθημι . . . 45 communicate declare	ἀνελεήμων . . 46 unmerciful	ἀνθομολογέομαι . 49 give thanks	ἀνομία . . . 55 iniquity transgress the law (with ποιεω, 1 Joh. 3 : 4) transgression of the law [see lit.] unrighteousness
ἀνατολή . . . 45 dayspring east east (with ἥλιος) rising	ἀνεμίζομαι . . 46 wind, driven with the ἄνεμος . . . 46 wind	ἄνθος . . . 49 flower ἀνθρακιά . . . 49 fire of coals	
ἀνατρέπω . . . 45 overthrow subvert	ἀνένδεκτον . . 47 impossible ἀνεξερεύνητος . 47 unsearchable	ἄνθραξ . . . 49 coals ἀνθρωπάρεσκος . 49 menpleaser	ἄνομος . . . 55 law, without lawless transgressor unlawful wicked
ἀνατρέφω . . . 45 bring up nourish nourish up	ἀνεξίκακος . . 47 patient ἀνεξιχνίαστος . 47 past finding out unsearchable	ἀνθρώπινος . . 49 human man, common to mankind mankind man's men, after the manner of	ἀνόμως . . . 55 law, without
ἀναφαίνομαι . . 45 appear appear, should (Lu. 19: discover [11]	ἀνεπαίσχυντος . 47 ashamed, that needeth not to be ἀνεπίληπτος . . 47 blameless unrebukeable	ἀνθρωποκτόνος . 49 murderer	ἀνορθόω . . . 55 lift up set up straight, make
ἀναφέρω . . . 46 bear bring up carry up lead up offer offer up	ἀνέρχομαι . . 47 go up ἄνεσις . . . 47 eased liberty rest	ἄνθρωπος . . . 49 certain man	ἀνόσιος . . . 55 unholy ἀνοχή . . . 55 forbearance
ἀναφωνέω . . . 46 speak out	ἀνετάζω . . . 47 examine examined, should have (Acts 22 : 24)	ἀνθυπατεύω . . 53 deputy, be the ἀνθύπατος . . . 53 deputy	ἀνταγωνίζομαι . 55 strive against ἀντάλλαγμα . . 55 exchange, in
ἀνάχυσις . . . 46 excess	ἄνευ . . . 47 without	ἀνίημι . . . 53 forbear leave loose loosed, be	ἀνταναπληρόω . 55 fill up
ἀναχωρέω . . . 46 depart give place go aside turn aside withdraw self	ἀνεύθετος . . . 47 commodious, not ἀνευρίσκω . . . 47 find	ἀνίλεως . . . 53 mercy, without	ἀνταποδίδωμι . . 56 recompense (r. again) render (r. again) repay
ἀνάψυξις . . . 46 refreshing	ἀνέχομαι . . . 47 bear with endure forbear suffer	ἄνιπτος . . . 53 unwashen	ἀνταπόδομα . . 56 recompense
ἀναψύχω . . . 46 refresh		ἀνίστημι . . . 53 arise lift up raise up raise up again rise rise again stand up stand upright	ἀνταπόδοσις . . 56 reward
ἀνδραποδιστής . 46 menstealers	ἀνεψιός . . . 47 sister's son		ἀνταποκρίνομαι . 56 answer again reply against
ἀνδρίζομαι . . 46 men, quit like	ἄνηθον . . . 47 anise		ἀντέπω . . . 56 gainsay say against
ἀνδροφόνος . . 46 manslayers	ἀνήκω . . . 47 convenient fit, be	ἀνόητος . . . 54 fool foolish unwise	ἀντέχομαι . . . 56 hold fast hold to support
ἀνέγκλητος . . 46 blameless unreprovable			

ἀντί 56	ἀντιτάσσομαι . 57	ἀξίως 58
for	oppose selves	becometh, as
room, in the	resist	godly sort, after a
ἀντιβάλλω . . 56	ἀντίτυπον . . . 57	worthily
have	figure	worthy
	figure whereunto, like	ἀόρατος . . . 58
ἀντιδιατιθέμενος 56	ἀντίχριστος . . 57	invisible
oppose themselves, that	antichrist	invisible things
ἀντίδικος . . 56	ἀντλέω . . . 57	ἀπαγγέλλω . . 58
adversary	draw	bring word
ἀντίθεσις . . 56	draw out	bring word again
opposition	ἄντλημα . . . 57	declare
ἀντικαθίστημι . 56	draw with, thing to	report
resist	ἀντοφθαλμέω . 57	shew
ἀντικαλέω . 56	bear up into	shew again
bid again	ἄνυδρος . . . 57	tell
ἀντίκειμαι . 56	dry	ἀπάγχομαι . . 59
adversary	water, without	hang himself
contrary, be	ἀνυπόκριτος . . 57	ἀπάγω . . . 59
oppose	dissimulation, without	bring
ἀντικρύ . . 56	hypocrisy, without	carry away
over against	unfeigned	lead
ἀντιλαμβάνομαι . 56	ἀνυπότακτος . 57	lead away
help	disobedient	put to death
partaker	put under, that is not	take away
support	unruly	ἀπαίδευτος . . 59
ἀντιλέγω . . 56	ἄνω . . . 57	unlearned
answer again	above	ἀπαίρομαι . . 59
contradict	brim	take
deny	high	take away
gainsay	up	ἀπαιτέω . . 59
gainsayers	ἀνώγεον . . . 57	ask again
speak against	upper room	require
ἀντίληψις . . . 57	ἄνωθεν . 58	ἀπαλγέω . . 59
help	above, from	past feeling, to be
ἀντιλογία . . . 57	again	ἀπαλλάσσω . . 59
contradiction	beginning, from the	deliver
gainsaying	first, from the very	depart
strife	top, the	ἀπαλλοτριόω . 59
ἀντιλοιδορέω . . 57	ἀνωτερικός . 58	alienate
revile again	upper	aliens, be
ἀντίλυτρον . 57	ἀνώτερον . . . 58	ἀπαλός . . . 59
ransom	above	tender
	higher	ἀπαντάω . . 59
ἀντιμετρέω . 57	ἀνωφελής . . 58	meet
measure again	unprofitable	ἀπάντησις . . 59
ἀντιμισθία . 57	unprofitableness	meet
recompence	ἀξίνη . . . 58	ἄπαξ . . . 59
	axe	once
ἀντιπαρέρχομαι . 57	ἄξιος . . . 58	ἀπαράβατος . 59
pass by on the other	due reward	unchangeable
side	meet	ἀπαρασκεύαστος 59
ἀντιπέραν . . 57	unworthy (with οὐκ)	unprepared
over against	worthy	ἀπαρνέομαι . 59
ἀντιπίπτω . . 57	ἀξιόω . . . 58	deny
resist	desire	ἀπάρτι . . . 60
ἀντιστρατεύομαι 57	good, think	henceforth, from
war against	worthy, count	
	worthy, think	

ἀπαρτισμός . . 60
finishing
ἀπαρχή . . . 60
first fruits
ἅπας . . . 60
all
all things
every
every one
whole
ἀπατάω . . . 60
deceive
ἀπάτη . . . 60
deceit
deceitful
deceitfulness
deceivableness
deceivings
ἀπάτωρ . . . 60
father, without
ἀπαύγασμα . . 60
brightness
ἀπειδέω, see ἀφοράω
see
ἀπείθεια . . . 60
disobedience
unbelief
ἀπειθέω . . . 60
believe not
disobedient
obey not
unbelieving
ἀπειθής . . . 61
disobedient
ἀπειλέω . . . 61
threaten
ἀπειλή . . . 61
straitly
threatening
ἄπειμι . . . 61
absent, be
ἄπειμι . . . 61
go
ἀπειπεῖν . . . 61
renounce
ἀπείραστος . . 61
tempted, not be
ἄπειρος . . . 61
unskilful
ἀπεκδέχομαι . 61
look for
wait for
ἀπεκδύομαι . . 61
put off
spoil
ἀπέκδυσις . . . 61
putting off

ἀπελάω	61	ἁπλῶς	63	ἀποδέχομαι	68	revealed, shall be (Ro. 8 : 18, 1 Pet. 5 : 1)	
drive		liberally		accept			
ἀπελεγμός	61	ἀπό	63	receive		revealed, should afterwards be(with μελλω, Gal. 3 : 23)	
nought		after		receive, gladly			
ἀπελεύθερος	61	ago		ἀποδημέω	68	ἀποκάλυψις	70
freeman		at		go into a far country		appearing	
ἀπελπίζω	61	because of		journey, take		coming	
hope for again		before		travel into a far country		lighten, to	
		by				manifestation	
ἀπέναντι	61	by the space of		ἀπόδημος	68	revealed, be	
before		for		journey, taking a far		revelation	
contrary		forth		ἀποδίδωμι	68	ἀποκαραδοκία	70
over against		...forth		deliver		earnest expectation	
presence of, in the		from		deliver again		ἀποκαταλλάττω	70
ἀπέραντος	61	hereafter (with νυν)		give		reconcile	
endless		in		give again			
ἀπερισπάστως	61	of		pay		ἀποκατάστασις	70
distraction, without		off		payment to be made		restitution	
		on		perform		ἀπόκειμαι	70
ἀπερίτμητος	61	once		recompense		appoint	
uncircumcised		out of		render		lay up	
ἀπέρχομαι	61	since		repay		ἀποκεφαλίζω	71
come		upon		requite		behead	
depart		with		restore		ἀποκλείω	71
go				reward		shut to	
go aside		ἀποβαίνω	68	sell			
go away		come, be		yield		ἀποκόπτω	71
go back		go out		ἀποδιορίζω	69	cut off	
go out		turn		separate self		ἀπόκριμα	71
go...ways		ἀποβάλλω	68	ἀποδοκιμάζω	69	sentence	
pass away		cast away		disallow			
past, be		ἀποβλέπω	68	reject		ἀποκρίνομαι	71
ἀπέχει	62	have respect		ἀποδοχή	69	answer	
enough, it is		ἀπόβλητος	68	acceptation		ἀπόκρισις	72
ἀπέχομαι	62	refused, be		ἀπόθεσις	69	answer	
abstain		ἀποβολή	68	putting away		ἀποκρύπτω	73
ἀπέχω	62	casting away		putting off		hide	
be		loss		ἀποθήκη	69	ἀπόκρυφος	73
have		ἀπογενόμενος	68	barn		hid	
receive		dead, being		garner		secret	
ἀπιστέω	62	ἀπογραφή	68	ἀποθησαυρίζω	69	ἀποκτείνω	73
believe not		taxing		lay up in store		death, put to	
ἀπιστία	63	ἀπογράφω	68	ἀποθλίβω	69	kill	
unbelief		taxed, be		press		slay	
ἄπιστος	63	written, be		ἀποθνήσκω	69	ἀποκυέω	73
believeth not, that		ἀποδείκνυμι	68	dead, be		beget	
faithless		approve		death		bring forth	
incredible, thing		prove		die		ἀποκυλίζω	73
infidel		set forth		dying, lay a		roll away	
unbelievers		shew		perish		roll back	
unbelieving		ἀπόδειξις	68	slain, be		ἀπολαμβάνω	73
ἁπλότης	63	demonstration		slain with. be (with φονος Heb. 11 : 37)		receive	
bountifulness		ἀποδεκατόω	68	ἀποκαθιστ- άω, -άνω,		take	
liberal		tithe		-ημι,	70	ἀπόλαυσις	73
liberality		tithe, give		restore		enjoy	
simplicity		tithe, pay		restore again		enjoy (with εχω, Heb. 11 : 25)	
singleness		tithe, take				enjoyment	
ἁπλοῦς	63	ἀπόδεκτος	68	ἀποκαλύπτω	70		
single		acceptable		reveal			

ἀπολείπω . . . 73	**ἀποπνίγω** . . . 75	**ἀποσυνάγωγος** . 78	**ἀπρόσκοπος** . 78
leave	choke	synagogue, put out of	offence, none
remain	**ἀπορέομαι** . 75	the	offence, void of
ἀπολείχω . . . 74	doubt	synagogues, out of the	offence, without
lıck	doubt, stand in	**ἀποτάσσομαι** . . 78	**ἀπροσωπολήπτως** . 79
ἀπόλλυμι . . . 74	perplexed	farewell, bid	respect of persons, with-
destroy	**ἀπορία** . . . 75	forsake	out
die	perplexity	leave, take	**ἄπταισ** . . . 79
lose	**ἀπορρίπτω** . . 75	send away	falling, from
lost, be	cast	**ἀποτελέω** . . 78	**ἅπτομαι** . . 79
marred, be	**ἀπορφανίζομαι** . 75	finish	touch
perish	taken, be	**ἀποτίθημι** . . . 78	**ἅπτω** . . 79
ἀπολογέομαι . . 74	**ἀποσκευάζομο** 76	cast off	kindle
answer	take up our carriages	lay apart	light
answer for self	**ἀποσκίασμα** . 76	lay aside	**ἀπωθέομαι** . . 79
answer, shall (with	shadow	lay down	put from
μελλω, Acts 26:2)	**ἀποσπάω** . . . 76	put away	**ἀπώθομαι** . . . 79
defence, make	draw	put off	cast away
excuse	draw away	**ἀποτινάσσω** . . 78	put away
excuse self	gotten from, after were	shake off	thrust away
speak for self	withdraw	**ἀποτίω** . . . 78	thrust from
ἀπολογία . . . 74	**ἀποστασία** . . . 76	repay	**ἀπώλεια** . . . 79
answer	falling away	**ἀποτολμάω** . . 78	damnable
answer for self	forsake	bold, be very	damnation
clearing of self	**ἀποστάσιον** . . 76	**ἀποτομία** . . . 78	destruction
defence	divorcement	severity	die
ἀπολούω . . . 74	divorcement, writing of	**ἀποτόμως** . . 78	perdition
wash	**ἀποστεγάζω** . . 76	sharply	perish (with ειην and
wash away	uncover	sharpness	εις, Acts 8:20)
ἀπολύτρωσις . . 74	**ἀποστέλλω** . . 76	**ἀποτρέπομαι** . . 78	pernicious ways
delıverance	put in	turn away	waste
redemption	send	**ἀπουσία** . . . 78	**ἀρά** . . . 79
ἀπολύω . . 75	send away	absence	cursing
depart	send forth	**ἀποφέρω** . . 78	**ἄρα** . . . 79
dismiss	send out	bring	haply
divorce	set [at liberty]	carry	manner of man
forgive	**ἀποστολή** . . . 77	carry away	manner
let depart	apostleship	**ἀποφεύγω** . . 78	no doubt
let go	**ἀπόστολος** . . . 77	escape	perhaps
loose	apostle	**ἀποφθέγγομαι** . 78	so be
put away	messenger	say	then
release	sent, he that is	speak forth	therefore
send away	**ἀποστερέω** . . . 77	utterance	truly
set at liberty	defraud	**ἀποφορτίζομαι** . 78	wherefore
ἀπομάσσομαι . . 75	destitute	unlade	**ἆρα** . . . 80
wipe off	fraud, kept back by	**ἀπόχρησις** . . 78	therefore
ἀπονέμω . . . 75	**ἀποστοματίζω** . . 77	using	**ἀργέω** . 80
give	provoke to speak	**ἀποχωρέω** . . 78	linger
ἀπονίπτω . . . 75	**ἀποστρέφω** . . 77	depart	**ἀργός** . . 80
wash	bring again	**ἀποχωρίζομαι** . 78	barren
ἀποπίπτω . . . 75	pervert	depart	idle
fall from	put up again	depart asunder	slow
ἀποπλανάω . . 75	turn away	**ἀποψύχω** . . 78	**ἀργύριον** . . . 80
err	turn away from	hearts failing	money
seduce	turn from	**ἀπρόσιτος** . . . 78	silver
ἀποπλέω . . . 75	**ἀποστυγέω** . . 78	approach, which no man	silver pieces
saıl	abhor	can	silver, pieces of
ἀποπλύνω . . 75			**ἀργυροκόπος** . 80
wash			silversmith

αργυρως . . . 80
silver

ἄροτρον . . . 82
plough

ἀρτύω 83
season

ἀσάλευτος . . . 86
moved, which cannot be
unmoveable

ἀργυρο῀ς . . 80
silver
silver, of

ἁρπαγή . . . 82
extortion
ravening
spoiling

ἀρχάγγελος . . 83
archangel

ἀσβεστος . . . 86
quenched. not to be
unquenchable

ἀρέσκεια . . . 80
pleasing

ἁρπαγμός . . . 82
robbery

ἀρχαῖος . . . 83
old
old time, them of

ἀσέβεια . . . 86
ungodliness
ungodly

ἄρέσκω 80
please

ἁρπάζω . . . 82
catch
catch away
caught up, be
pluck
pull
take
take by force

ἀρχή 84
beginning
corner
first
first, at the
first estate
first, the
magistrate
power
principality
principles
rule

ἀσεβέω . . . 86
ungodly, commit
ungodly, live
ungodly, that after
should live (2 Pet.
2:6)

ἀρεστός . . . 80
please
please, things that
pleasing
reason

ἀρετή 80
praise
virtue

ἄρπαξ 82
extortioner
ravening

ἀσεβής . . . 86
ungodly
ungodly men

αρήν 80
lamb

ἀρραβών . . . 82
earnest

ἀρχηγός . . . 84
author
captain
prince

ἀσέλγεια . . 87
filthy
lasciviousness
wantonness

ἀριθμέω . . . 80
number

ἄρραφος . . . 82
seam, without

ἀριθμός . . . 81
number

ἄρρην 82
man

ἀρχιερατικός . . 84
priest, of the high

ἄσημος . . . 87
mean

ἀρχιερεύς . . . 84
priest, chief
priest, high
priests, chief of the

ἀσθένεια . . . 87
disease
infirmity
sickness
weakness

ἀριστάω . . . 81
dine

ἄρρητος . . . 82
unspeakable

ἀριστερός . . . 81
left [hand]

ἄρρωστος . . . 82
sick
sick folk
sickly

ἀρχιποίμην . . 85
shepherd, chief

ἀσθενέω . . 87
diseased, be
impotent folk
impotent man
sick
sick, be
weak
weak, be
weak, be made

ἄριστον 81
dinner

ἀρκετός . . . 81
enough
suffice
sufficient

ἀρσενοκοίτης . . 82
abusers of selves with
mankind
defile selves with man-
kind, that

ἀρχισυνάγωγος . 85
synagogue, chief ruler
of the
synagogue, ruler of the

ἀρχιτέκτων . . 85
masterbuilder

ἀρκέω 81
content, be
enough, be
suffice
sufficient, be

ἄρσην 82
male
men

ἀρχιτελώνης . . 85
publicans, chief among
the

ἀσθένημα . . . 87
infirmities

ἀρτέμων . . . 82
mainsail

ἀρχιτρίκλινος . . 85
feast, governor of the
feast, ruler of the

ἀσθενής . . . 87
feeble, more
impotent
sick
strength, without
weak
weak things
weaker
weakness

ἄρκτος 81
bear

ἅρμα 81
chariot

ἄρτι 82
day, this
even now
henceforth
hereafter
hitherto
hour, this
now
present
present, this

ἄρχομαι . . . 85
begin
beginning, rehearse
from the

ἁρμός . . . 81
joints

ἄρχω 86
reign over
rule over

ἀρμόζω . . . 81
espouse

ἀσιτία . . . 87
abstinence

ἀρνέομαι . . . 81
deny
refuse

ἀρτιγέννητος . . 83
newborn

ἄρχων . . . 86
chief
chief ruler
magistrate
prince
ruler

ἄσιτος . . . 87
fasting

ἄρτιος . . . 83
perfect

ἀσκέω . . . 87
exercise

ἀρνίον . . . 81
lamb

ἄρτος . . . 83
bread
loaf
shewbread

ἀσκός . . . 87
bottle

ἀρχ᾽ ιενος . . 82
beginning

ἄρωμα . . . 86
spices
sweet spices

ασμένως . . . 88
gladly

αρ᾽ ιαω . . 82
plow

ἄσοφος . . . 88	ἀσφαλής . . . 89	ἄτιμος 90	αὐτάρκης . . . 91

ἄσοφος . . . 88
fool

ἀσπάζομαι . . 88
embrace
greet
salute
take leave

ἀσπασμος . . 88
greetings
salutations

ἄσπιλος . . . 88
spot, without
unspotted

ἀσπίς 88
asps

ἄσπονδος . . . 88
implacable
trucebreakers

ἀσσάριον . . . 88
farthing

ᾱ̓σσον . . 88
close

ἀστατέω . . . 88
dwellingplace, have no
certain

ἀστεῖος . . . 88
fair
proper

ἀστήρ . . . 89
star

ἀστήρικτος . . 89
unstable

ἄστοργος . . . 89
natural affection, with-
out

ἀστοχέω . . . 89
err
swerve

ἀστραπή . . . 89
lightning
shining, bright

ἀστράπτω . . . 89
lighten
shine

ἄστρον 89
star

ἀσύμφωνος . . 89
agree not

ἀσύνετος . . . 89
foolish
understanding, without

ἀσύνθετος . . 89
covenantbreakers

ἀσφάλεια . . . 89
certainty
safety

ἀσφαλής . . . 89
certain
certainty
safe
sure

ἀσφαλίζω . . . 89
fast, make
sure, make

ἀσφαλῶς . . . 89
assuredly
safely

ἀσχημονέω . . 89
uncomely, behave self
unseemly, behave self

ἀσχημοσύνη . . 89
shame
unseemly, that which is

ἀσχήμων . . . 89
uncomely

ἀσωτία . . . 89
excess
riot

ἀσώτως . . . 90
riotous

ἀτακτέω . . . 90
disorderly, behaved self

ἄτακτος . . . 90
unruly

ἀτάκτως . . . 90
disorderly

ἄτεκνος . . . 90
childless
children, without

ἀτενίζω . . . 90
behold, earnestly
behold, stedfastly
fasten
fasten eyes
look
look, earnestly
look, stedfastly
look up stedfastly
set eyes

ᾱ̓́τερ 90
absence of, in the
without

ἀτιμάζω . . . 90
despise
dishonour
shame, suffer
shamefully, entreat

ἀτιμαω, -όω . . 90
shamefully handle

ἀτιμία 90
dishonour
reproach
shame
vile

ἄτιμος 90
despised
honour, without
honourable, less

ἀτμίς 90
vapour

ἄτομος 90
moment

ἄτοπος 90
amiss
harm
unreasonable

αὐγάζω . . . 90
shine

αὐγή 90
break of day

αὐθάδης . . . 90
selfwilled

αὐθαίρετος . . . 90
accord, of own
willing of selves

αὐθεντέω . . . 90
authority over, usurp

αὐλέω 90
pipe

ἄτακτος . . . 90

αὐλή 90
court
fold
hall
palace
sheepfold (with προ-
βατον, Joh.10:1)

αὐλητής . . . 91
minstrel
piper

αὐλίζομαι . . . 91
abide
lodge

αὐλός 91
pipe

αὐξάνω & αὔξω . 91
grow
grow up
increase
increase, gave the

αὔξησις . . . 91
increase

αὔριον 91
morrow
next day
to morrow

αὐστηρός . . . 91
austere

αὐτάρκεια . . 91
contentment
sufficiency

αὐτάρκης . . . 91
content

αὐτοκατάκριτος 91
condemned of self

αὐτόματος . . . 91
accord, of own
self, of

αὐτόπτης . . . 91
eyewitnesses

αὐτός 91
her
him
himself
it
itself
mine own
myself
other, the
own
said
same
same mind (with
φρονεω), be of one us
the
same, the
self
selfsame
she
that
their
their's
them
themselves
thereat
thereby
therein
thereinto
thereof
thereon
therewith
these things
they
things
this
this man
those
thyself
together
very
which
yourselves

αὐτοῦ, adv. . . . 92
here
there

αὐτοῦ . . . 92
her
her own
him
him, of
himself
himself, of
his
his own

it. of
thee
their
their own
them
themselves
they

αὐτοχειρ . . . 96
hands, with own

αὐχμηρός . . . 96
dark

ἀφαιρέω . . . 96
cut off
smite off
take away

ἀφανής . . . 97
manifest, that is not

ἀφανίζω . . . 97
corrupt
disfigure
perish
vanish away

ἀφανισμός . . 97
vanish away

ἄφαντος . . . 97
vanish out of sight

ἀφεδρών . . . 97
draught

ἀφειδία . . . 97
neglecting

ἀφελότης . . . 97
singleness

ἄφεσις . . . 97
deliverance
forgiveness
liberty
remission

ἀφή 97
joint

ἀφθαρσία . . 97
immortality
incorruption
sincerity

ἄφθαρτος . . . 97
corruptible, not
immortal
incorruptible
uncorruptible

ἀφίημι . . . 97
ry
forgive
forsake
lay aside
leave
let
let alone
let be
let go

let have
omit
put away
remit
send away
suffer
yield up

ἀφικνέομαι . . 98
come abroad

ἀφιλάγαθος . . 98
despisers of those that
are good

ἀφιλάργυρος . . 98
covetousness, without
covetous, not

ἄφιξις 98
departing

ἀφίστημι . . . 98
depart
draw away
fall away
refrain
withdraw self

ἄφνω 98
suddenly

ἀφόβως . . . 99
fear, without

ἀφομοιόω . . . 99
made like

ἀφοράω . . . 99
look
see

ἀφορίζω . . . 99
divide
separate
sever

ἀφορμή . . . 99
occasion

ἀφρίζω . . . 99
foam

ἀφρός 99
[with] foaming

ἀφροσύνη . . . 99
folly
foolishly
foolishness

ἄφρων . . . 99
fool
foolish
unwise

ἀφυπνόω . . . 99
fall asleep

ἄφωνος . . . 99
dumb
signification, without

ἀχάριστος . . . 99
unthankful

ἀχειροποίητος . 99
hands, made without
hands, not made with

ἀχλύς 99
mist

ἀχρειόομαι . . 99
unprofitable, be become

ἀχρεῖος . . . 99
unprofitable

ἄχρηστος . . . 99
unprofitable

ἄχρι & ἄχρις 99
as far as
even to
for
in
into
till
to
until
unto
while

ἄχυρον . . . 100
chaff

ἀψευδής . . . 100
lie, that cannot

ἄψινθος . . . 100
wormwood

ἄψυχος . . . 100
life, without

βαθμός . . . 100
degree

βάθος . . . 100
deep
deep things
deepness
depth

βαθύνω . . . 100
deep

βαθύς . . . 100
deep
early, very

βαΐον . . . 100
branch

βαλάντιον . . 100
bag
purse

βάλλω . . . 100
arise
cast
cast out
dung
lay
lie
pour
put
put up
send

strike
throw
throw down
thrust

βαπτίζω . . 101
baptist
baptize
wash

βάπτισμα . . 102
baptism

βαπτισμός . . 102
baptism
washing

βαπτιστής . . 102
baptist

βάπτω . . . 102
dip

βάρβαρος . . 102
barbarian
barbarous

βαρέω . . . 102
burdened, be
charged, be
heavy
pressed, be

βαρέως . . . 102
dull

βάρος 102
burden
burdensome
weight

βαρύνω . . 102
overcharged, be

βαρύς 102
grievous
heavy
weightier

βαρύτιμος . . 103
precious, very

βασανίζω . . 103
pain
toil
torment
toss
vexed

βασανισμός . . 103
torment

βασανιστής . . 103
tormentor

βάσανος . . 103
torment

βασιλεία . . . 103
kingdom
reign (with εχω Rev.
17:18)

βασίλειον 104
king's courts

βασίλειος . 104
royal

βασιλεύς . 104
king

βασιλεύω . . 105
king
reign

βασιλικός . . 105
king's
nobleman
royal

βασίλισσα . 105
queen

βάσις 105
foot

βασκαίνω . . 105
bewitch

βαστάζω . 105
bear
carry
take up

ὁ βάτος . . . 106
measure

ἡ βάτος . . 106
bramble
bush

βάτραχος . . 106
frog

βαττολογέω . 106
repetitions, use vain

βδέλυγμα . . 106
abomination

βδελυκτός . . 106
abominable

βδελύσσομαι . 106
abhor
abominable

βέβαιος . . . 106
firm
force, of
stedfast
sure

βεβαιόω . . 106
confirm
establish
stablish

βεβαίωσις . 106
confirmation

βέβηλος . . . 106
profane
profane person

βεβηλόω . 106
profane

βελος . . . 106
dart

βέλτιον . . . 106
very well

βῆμα 106
judgment seat
set [foot] on
throne

βήρυλλος . . 106
beryl

βία . . . 106
violence

βιάζομαι . . . 106
press
suffer violence

βίαιος . . . 106
mighty

βιαστης . . 107
violent

βιβλαρίδιον . 107
book, little

βιβλίον . . . 107
bill
book
scroll
writing

βίβλος . . . 107
book

βίος . . . 107
good
life
living

βιόω 107
live

βίωσις . . . 107
life, manner of

βιωτικός . . . 107
life, of this
life, pertaining to this
life, things that pertain
to this

βλαβερός . . 107
hurtful

βλάπτω . . . 107
hurt

βλαστάνω . . 107
bring forth
bud
spring
spring up

βλασφημέω . 107
blaspheme
blasphemer
blasphemously
blasphemy, speak
defame
rail on
revile
slanderously report
speak evil

βλασφημία . . 108
blasphemy
evil speaking
railing

βλάσφημος . 108
blasphemer
blasphemous
railing

βλέμμα . . . 108
seeing

βλέπω . . . 108
behold
beware
lie
look
look on
look to
perceive
regard
see
sight
take heed

βλητέος . . 109
must be put

βοάω 109
cry

βοή 109
cry

βοήθεια . . 109
help

βοηθέω . . 109
help
succour

βοηθός . . 109
helper

βόθυνος . . . 109
ditch
pit

βολή 109
cast [a stone's cast]

βολίζω . . . 109
sound

βολίς . . . 109
dart

βόρβορος . . 109
mire

βορρᾶς . . . 109
north

βόσκω . . 109
feed
keep

βοτάνη . . . 109
herb

βότρυς . . . 109
clusters of the vine
vine cluster

βουλεύομαι . . 110
consult
counsel, take
determine
minded, be
purpose

βουλευτής . . 110
counsellor

βουλή . . . 110
advise (with τιθημι,
Acts 27:12)
counsel
will

βούλημα . . . 110
purpose
will

βούλομαι . . 110
disposed, be
intend
list
minded, be
will
will, of own
willing, be

βουνός . 110
hill

βοῦς 110
ox

βραβεῖον . . . 110
prize

βραβεύω . . . 110
rule

βραδύνω . . 110
slack, be
tarry

βραδυπλοέω . 110
sail slowly

βραδύς . . . 110
slow

βραδυτής . . 110
slackness

βραχίων . . . 110
arm

βραχύς . . . 110
little
little space
little while
words, few

βρέφος . . . 111
babe
child
infant
young children

βρέχω . . . 111
rain
sendeth rain
wash

βροντή . . . 111	γάμος . . . 112	γεννάω . . . 114	befall
thunder	marriage	bear	behave self
thunderings	wedding	beget	brought, be
		born, be	brought to pass, be
βροχή . . . 111	γάρ 112	bring forth	come
rain	and	conceive	come, be
	as	delivered of, be	come, should (with
βρόχοι . . . 111	because	gender	μέλλω, Acts, 26:22)
snare	because that	make	come to pass
	but	spring	continue
βρυγμός . 111	even		divided, be
gnashing	for	γέννημα . . . 114	do
	indeed	fruit	draw
βρύχω . . . 111	no doubt	generation	ended, be
gnash	seeing		fall
	then	γέννησις . . 115	finished, be
βρύω 111	therefore	birth	follow
send forth	verily		found, be
	what	γεννητός . . . 115	fulfilled, be
βρῶμα . . . 111	why	born, they that are	God forbid (with μη)
meat	yet		grow
victuals		γένος . . . 115	happen
	γαστήρ . . . 113	born	have
βρώσιμος . . 111	belly	country	kept, be
meat	child, with (with εν)	countryman	made, be
	womb	diversity	married, be
βρῶσις . . 111		generation	ordained to be, be
eating	γέ . . . 113	kind	partake (Rom. 11:17)
food	beside, and	kindred	pass, shall come to
meat	doubtless	nation	past
morsel of meat	least, at	offspring	performed, be
rust	yet	stock	preferred, be
			published, be
βρώσκω . . . 111	γέεννα . . 113	γερουσία . . . 115	require
eat	hell	senate	seem
			shewed, be
βυθίζω . . . 111	γείτων . 113	γέρων . . . 115	"soon as it was"
begin to sink	neighbour	old	sound
drown			taken, be
	γελάω . . . 113	γεύομαι . . . 115	turned, be
βυθός . . . 111	laugh	eaten	use
deep		taste	wax
	γέλως . . . 113		will
βυρσεύς . . . 111	laughter	γεωργεομαι . . 115	would
tanner		dress	wrought, be
	γεμίζω . . . 113		
βύσσινος . . 111	fill full	γεώργιον . . 115	γινώσκ-ω & -ομα. 122
fine linen	full, be	husbandry	allow
			aware, be
βύσσος . . . 111	γέμω . . . 113	γεωργός . . . 115	aware of, be
fine linen	full, be	husbandman	feel
			knew
βωμός . . . 112	γενεά . . . 113	γῆ . . . 115	knowledge, have
altar	ages	country	perceive
	generation	earth	resolved, be
γάγγραινα . 112	nation	earthly	speak, can
canker	time	ground	sure, be
		land	understand
γάζα . . 112	γενεαλογέομαι . 114	world	
treasure	descent be counted		γλεῦκος . . 124
		γῆρας . . . 117	new wine
γαζοφυλάκιον . 112	γενεαλογία . 114	old age	
treasury	genealogies		γλυκύς . . . 124
		γηράσκω . . . 117	fresh
γάλα . . . 112	γενεσια . . 114	old, be	sweet
milk	birthday	old. wax	
			γλῶσσα . . . 124
γαλήνη . . 112	γένεσις . . 114	γίνομαι . . 117	tongue
calm	generation	arise	
	natural	assembled, be	
γαμέω . . . 112	nature	be	
marry		become	
marry a wife	γενετή . . 114		
γαμίσκομαι . . 112	birth		
given in marriage, be			

γλωσσοκυμον . 124 bag	**γράμμα** . . . 126 bill learning letter scriptures writings written	**δαίμων** . . 131 devil	**δεῖνα** . . . 133 such a man
παφεύς . . . 124 fuller		**δάκνω** . . 131 bite	**δεινῶς** . . . 133 grievously vehemently
γνήσιος . . . 124 own sincerity rue	**γραμματεύς** . 126 scribe townclerk	**δάκρυ & δακρύον** . 131 tears	**δειπνέω** . . . 133 sup supper [lit. supping]
γνησίως . . . 124 naturally	**γραπτός** . . . 126 written	**δακρύω** . . . 131 weep	**δεῖπνον** . . . 134 feast supper
γνόφος . . . 124 blackness	**γραφή** . . . 126 scripture	**δακτύλιος** . . 132 ring	**δεισιδαιμονέστερος** 134 superstitious, too
γνώμη . . . 124 advice agree (with ποιεω, μια Rev. 17:17) judgment mind purpose will	**γράφω** . . . 127 describe write writing written	**δάκτυλος** . . 132 finger	**δεισιδαιμονία** . 134 superstition
		δαμάζω . . . 132 tame	**δέκα** . . . 134 eighteen (with οκτω) ten
	γραώδης . . 128 old wives'	**δάμαλις** . . 132 heifer	
		δανείζω . . . 132 borrow lend	**δεκαδύο** . . . 134 twelve
γνωρίζω . . . 125 certify declare known, make understand, give to wit, do to wot	**γρηγορέω** . . 128 vigilant, be wake watch watchful, be	**δάνειον** . . . 132 debt	**δεκαπέντε** . . 134 fifteen
		δανειστής . . 132 creditor	**δεκατέσσαρες** . 134 fourteen
	γυμνάζω . . . 129 exercise	**δαπανάω** . . 132 charges, be at consume spend	**δεκάτη** . . 134 tenth tenth part tithe
γνῶσις . . . 125 knowledge science	**γυμνασία** . . 129 exercise	**δαπάνη** . . . 132 cost	**δέκατος** . . . 134 tenth
γνώστης . . . 125 expert	**γυμνητεύομαι** . 129 naked, be	**δέησις** . . . . 132 prayer request supplication	**δεκατόω** . . . 134 tithes, pay tithes, receive
γνωστός . . . 125 acquaintance known known, which may be notable	**γυμνός** . . . 129 bare naked	**δεῖ** . . . . 132 behove meet, be must must needs need needful, be needs, must (Acts 21: 22) ought should	**δεκτός** . . . 134 acceptable accepted
γογγύζω . . . 125 murmur	**γυμνότης** . . 129 nakedness		**δελεάζω** . . . 134 allure beguile entice
γογγυσμός . . 125 grudging murmuring	**γυναικάριον** . . 129 silly women		
	γυναικεῖος . . 129 wife		**δένδρον** . . . 134 tree
γογγυστής . . 125 murmurer	**γυνή** . . . . 129 wife woman		
γόης . . . 125 seducer	**γωνια** . . . 131 corners quarter	**δεῖγμα** . . . 133 example	**δεξιολάβος** . . 135 spearman
γόμος . . . 125 burden merchandise		**δειγματίζω** . . 133 shew, make a	**δεξιός** . . . 135 right right hand right side
	δαιμονίζομαι . 131 devil, have a devil, vexed with a devils, be possessed with	**δεικνύ-ω &-υμι** . 133 shew	
νονεύς . . . 125 parent		**δειλία** . . . 133 fear	**δεομαι** . . . 135 beseech pray pray to request, make
γόνυ . . . . 126 knee kneel [see iit.]	**δαιμόνιον** . . 131 devil god	**δειλιάω** . . . 133 afraid, be	
γονυπετέω . . 126 knee, bowed the kneel down	**δαιμονιώδης** . . 131 devilish	**δειλός** . . . 133 fearful	**δέρμα** . . . 135 skin

δερμάτινος . . 135 leathern skin, of a	tie wind	though [lit. through] through throughout throughout throughout (with ὁλος Joh. 19:23)	διάδοχος . . . 144 room (lit. successor)
δέρω . . . 135 beat smite	δή . . . . 138 also and doubtless now therefore	to wherefore wherefore with within	διαζώννυμι . 144 gird
δεσμεύω . . 136 bind			διαθήκη . . 144 covenant testament
δεσμεω . . 136 bind bound, be	δῆλος . . . 138 bewray (with ποιεω Matt. 26:73) certain evident manifest	διαβαίνω . 143 come over pass pass through	διαίρεσις . . . 144 difference diversities
δέσμη . . . 136 bundle	δηλόω . . 138 declare shew signify	διαβάλλομαι . 143 accused	διαιρέω ο. . . 144 divide
δέσμιος . . 136 bonds, in prisoner	δημηγορέω . . 138 oration, make an	διαβεβαιόομαι . 143 affirm affirm constantly	διακαθαρίζω . . 144 purge, throughly
ὁ δεσμὸς & τὰ δεσμά . . . 136 bands bond chain string	δημιουργός . . 138 maker	διαβλέπω . . 143 see clearly	διακατελέγχομαι. 144 convince
	δῆμος . . . 138 people	διάβολος . . . 143 accuser, false devil slanderer	διακονέω . . 144 administered, be deacon, use the office of a minister minister unto serve
δεσμοφύλαξ . . 136 jailor prison, keeper of the	δημόσιος . . 138 common openly publickly	διαγγέλλω . . 143 declared, be preach signify	διακονία 145 administration minister ministering ministration ministry office relief service serving
δεσμωτήριον . . 136 prison	δηνάριον . . 138 pence pennyworth	διαγίνομαι . . 143 after past, be spent, be	
δεσμώτης . . 136 prisoner	δήποτε . . . 138 soever whatsoever	διαγινώσκω . . 143 enquire enquire, would. (Acts 23:15) know the uttermost	διάκονος . . . 145 deacon minister servant
δεσπότης . . 136 Lord master	δήπου . . . 138 verily	διαγνωρίζω . . 144 known, make	διακόσιοι . . . 145 two hundred
δεῦρο . . . 136 come come hither hitherto	διά . . . . 138 after always always (with πας) among at avoid, to because of because that briefly by cause, for for ...fore from in occasion of, by of reason of, by sake, for that thereby thereby therefore therefore though	διάγνωσις . . 144 hearing	διακόνομαι . . 145 hear
δεῦτε . . . 136 come follow (with οπισω)		διαγογγύζω . . 144 murmur	διακρίνω . . . 145 contend differ, maketh to difference, make difference, put discern doubt judge partial be stagger waver
δευτεραῖος . . 136 next day		διαγρηγορέω . . 144 awake, be	
δευτερόπρωτος . 136 second after the first		διάγω . . . . 144 lead living	διάκρισις . . . 145 discern discerning disputation
δεύτερος . 137 afterward again second second time secondarily		διαδέχομαι . . 144 come after	διακωλύω . . . 146 forbid
δέχομαι . 137 accept receive take		διάδημα . . 144 crown	
δέω . . . 137 bind bonds, be in knit		διαδίδωμι . . 144 distribute distribution make divide give	

bestow
bring forth
commit
deliver
deliver up
give
grant
hinder
make
minister
number
offer
power, have
put
receive
set
shew
smite
smite with the hand
  (with ῥάπισμα)
strike
strike with the palm of
  the hand (Joh. 18:22)
suffer
take
utter
yield
	διετής . . . 155
	  two years
	διετία 155
	  two years
	διηγέομαι . . 155
	  declare
	  shew
	  tell
	διήγησις . . . 155
	  declaration
	(εἰς τὸ) διηνεκής. 155
	  continually
	  ever, for
	διθάλασσος . . 155
	  where two seas meet
	διϊκνέομαι . . 155
	  pierce
	διΐστημι . . . 155
	  go further
	  parted, be
	  space of, after the
	διϊσχυρίζομαι 155
	  affirm, confidently
	  affirm, constantly
	δικαιοκρισία . . 155
	  righteous judgment
	δίκαιος . . . 155
	  just
	  meet
	  right
	  righteous
	δικαιοσύνη . . 156
	  righteousness
	δικαιόω . . . 157
	  freed, be [lit. is justified]
	  justifier
	  justify
	  righteous, be
	δικαίωμα . . 157
	  judgment
	  justification
	  ordinance
	  righteousness
	δικαίως . . 157
	  justly
	  righteously
	  righteousness, to
	δικαίωσις . . 157
	  justification
	δικαστής . . . 157
	  judge
	δίκη 157
	  judgment
	  punish
	  vengeance
	δίκτυον . . 157
	  net
		δίλογος . . . 157
		  double tongued
		διό 158
		  cause, for which
		  therefore
		  wherefore
		διοδεύω . . 158
		  go throughout
		  pass through
		διόπερ . . 158
		  wherefore
		διοπετής . . . 158
		  which fell down from
		    Jupiter
		διόρθωσις . . 158
		  reformation
		διορύσσω . . . 158
		  break through
		  broken up, be
		διότι 158
		  because
		  because that
		  for
		  therefore
		διπλοῦς . . 158
		  double
		  twofold more
		διπλόω . . . 158
		  double
		δίς 158
		  again
		  twice
		διστάζω . . . 158
		  doubt
		δίστομος . . 158
		  edges, with two
		  two-edged
		δισχίλιοι . . 159
		  two thousand
		διϋλίζω . . . 159
		  strain at
		διχάζω . . . 159
		  set at variance
		διχοστασία . . 159
		  division
		  sedition
		διχοτομέω . 159
		  cut asunder
		  cut in sunder
		διψάω . . . 159
		  athirst, be
		  thirst
		  thirsty, be
		δίψος . . . 159
		  thirst
		δίψυχος . . . 159
		  double minded
			διωγμός . . . 159
			  persecution
			διώκτης . . 159
			  persecutor
			διώκω 159
			  ensue
			  follow
			  follow after
			  given to
			  persecute
			  press
			  suffer persecution
			δόγμα . . . 159
			  decree
			  ordinance
			δογματίζομαι . 160
			  subject to ordinances,
			    be
			δοκέω 160
			  accounted, be
			  good, seem
			  please
			  pleasure, of own
			  reputation, be of
			  seem
			  suppose
			  think
			  trow
			δοκιμάζω . . . 160
			  alloweth
			  approve
			  discern
			  examine
			  like
			  prove
			  try
			δοκιμή . . 160
			  experience
			  experiment
			  proof
			  trial
			δοκίμιον . . . 160
			  trial
			  trying
			δόκιμος . . . 160
			  approved
			  tried
			δοκός . . . 160
			  beam
			δόλιος . . . 161
			  deceitful
			δολιόω . . . 161
			  use deceit
			δόλος . . . 161
			  craft
			  deceit
			  guile
			  subtilty
			δολόω 161
			  handle deceitfully

διεγείρω . . 154
  arise
  awake
  raised, be
  stir up			

διέξοδος . . . 154 highway [see lit.]			
διερμηνευτής 154 interpreter			

διερμηνεύω . . 154
  expound
  interpret
  interpretation, by			

διέρχομαι . . 155
  come
  depart
  go
  go about
  go abroad
  go every where
  go over
  go through
  go throughout
  pass
  pass by
  pass over
  pass through
  pass throughout
  pass, was, to (with
    μέλλω, Lu. 19:4)
  pierce through
  travel
  walk through			

διερωτάω . . . 155 enquiry for. make			

δόμα . . . 161
  gift

δοξα . . . 161
  dignities
  glorious
  glory
  honour
  praise
  worship

δοξάζω . . . 162
  glorify
  glorious, make
  glory, full of
  glory, have
  honour
  magnify

δόσις . . . 163
  gift
  giving

δότης 163
  giver

δουλαγωγέω . . 163
  subjection, bring into

δουλεία . . . 163
  bondage

δουλεύω . . . 163
  bondage, be in
  serve
  service, do

δούλη . . . 163
  handmaid
  handmaiden

δοῦλον . . . 163
  servant

δοῦλος . . 163
  bond
  bondman
  servant

δουλόω . . . 164
  bondage, bring into
  bondage, be under
  given
  servant, became
  servants, make

δοχή . . . 164
  feast

δράκων . . 164
  dragon

δράσσομαι . . 164
  take

δραχμή . . 164
  piece
  piece of silver

δρέπανον . . 164
  sickle

ὄρομος . . 164
  course

δύναμαι . . . 164
  able, be
  can
  can do
  cannot (with μη)
  cannot (with ου)
  could
  may
  might
  possible, be
  power, be of

δύναμις . . . 166
  ability
  abundance
  deeds, mighty
  meaning
  might
  mightily
  mighty
  miracle
  miracles, workers of
  power
  strength
  violence
  virtue
  works, mighty
  works, wonderful

δυναμόω . . . 167
  strengthen

δυνάστης . . . 167
  authority, of great
  mighty
  potentate

δυνατέω . . . 167
  mighty, be

δυνατος . . . 167
  able
  could
  mighty
  mighty men
  mighty, that is
  possible
  power
  strong

δύνω & δῦμι . . 167
  set

δύο . . . 167
  both
  twain
  two

δυσβάστακτος . 168
  grievous to be borne

δυσεντερία . . 168
  bloody flux

δυσερμήνευτος . 168
  uttered, hard to be

δύσκολος . . . 169
  hard

δυσκόλως . . 169
  hardly

δυ~μή . . . 169
  west

δυσνόητος . . 169
  understood, hard to be

δυσφημία . . . 169
  report, evil

δώδεκα . . . 169
  twelve

δωδέκατος . 169
  twelfth

δωδεκάφυλον . . 169
  twelve tribes

δῶμα . . . 169
  housetops

δωρεά . . . 169
  gift

δωρεάν . . . 170
  cause, without a
  freely
  nought, for
  vain, in

δωρέω . . . 170
  give

δώρημα . . 170
  gift

δῶρον . . . 170
  gift
  offering

ἔα . . . 170
  alone, let

ἐάν . . . 170
  and if
  before
  but
  except
  if
  if so
  so
  though
  to whom
  whatsoever (with τις
    Eph. 6 : 8.)
  when
  whensoever
  wheresoever
  whether
  whether or
  whithersoever
  whoso
  whosoever

ἑαυτ-οῦ,-ῷ,-ὸν . 172
  alone
  he himself
  her
  her own
  herself
  him
  himself

his
his own
itself
one another
one to another
our own
ourselves
that she had (with
  πασα)
their
their own
their own selves
them
them, of
themselves
they
thine own
thyself
you
your
your own
your own conceits
your own selves
yourselves

ἐάω 175
  alone, let
  commit
  leave
  let
  suffer

ἑβδομήκοντα . 175
  seventy
  threescore and ten

ἑβδομηκοντάκις . 175
  seventy times

ἕβδομος . . . 175
  seventh

ἐγγίζω . . . 175
  approach
  come near
  draw nigh
  hand, be at
  near, draw
  nigh, be
  nigh, come

ἐγγράφω . . . 176
  write
  written in

ἔγγυος . . . 176
  surety

ἐγγύς . . . 176
  from
  hand, at
  hand, nigh at
  near
  nigh
  nigh unto
  ready

ἐγγίττερον . . 176
  nearer

ἐγείρω . . . 176
  arise

awake
lift
lift up
raise
raise again
raise up
rear up
rise
rise again
rise up
stand
take up

ἔγερσις . . . 177
resurrection

ἐγκάθετος . . 177
spy

ἐγκαίνια . . . 177
feast of the dedication

ἐγκαινίζω . . 177
consecrate
dedicate

ἐγκαλέω . . . 177
accuse
call in question
implead
lay to the charge

ἐγκαταλείπω . . 177
forsake
leave

ἐγκατοικέω . . 177
dwell among

ἐγκεντρίζω . . 177
graff in, *or*, into

ἔγκλημα . . . 178
crime laid against
laid to charge

ἐγκομβόομαι . . 178
clothed with, be

ἐγκοπή . . . 178
hinder

ἐγκόπτω . . . 178
hinder
tedious unto, be

ἐγκράτεια . . 178
temperance

ἐγκρατεύομαι . . 178
cannot contain (with ουκ)
contain, can
temperate, be

ἐγκρατής . . . 178
temperate

ἐγκρίνω . . 178
number, make of the

ἐγ ρύπτω . . . 178
hide in

ἔγκυος . . . 178
great with child

ἐγχρίω . . . 178
anoint

ἐγώ . . . 178
I
me

ἐδαφίζω . . . 181
lay even with the ground

ἔδαφος . . . 181
ground

ἑδραῖος . . . 181
settled
stedfast

ἑδραίωμα . . . 181
ground

ἐθελοθρησκεία . 181
will worship

ἐθίζω . . . 181
custom

ἐθνάρχης . . . 181
governor

ἐθνικός . . . 181
heathen
heathen man

ἐθνικῶς . . 181
manner of Gentiles, after the

ἔθνος . . 181
Gentile
heathen
nation
people

ἔθος . . . 182
custom
manner
wont, be

ἔθω, εἴωθα . 182
custom, be
manner, be
wont, be

εἰ, from εἰμί . 182
art
be

εἰ . . . 183
although
forasmuch as
if
that
though
whether

εἴγε . . . 185
if
if so be that
if yet

εἰ δὲ μή & εἰ δὲ
μήγε . . . 186
else
if not
if otherwise
or else
otherwise

εἰ καί . . . 186
if
if that
though

εἰ μή . . . 186
but
except
except that
if not
more than
save
save only that
save that
saving
till
till (with ὅταν Mark 9:9)

εἰ μή τι . . . 187
except

εἴ περ . . . 187
if so be
if so be that| if that
seeing
though

εἴ πως . . . 187
if by any means

εἴτε . . . 187
if
or
whether

εἴ τις . . . 187
he that
if a man
if any ...man
if any man's
if any thing
if from any
if ought
whether any
whosoever

εἰδέω, εἴδω, οἶδα . 188
aware, be
behold
can
can (Mat. 27:65)
cannot tell (with ου)
consider
know
knowledge, have
look
look on
perceive
see
sure, be
tell

understand
wist
wot

εἶδος . . . 192
appearance
fashion
shape
sight

εἰδωλεῖον . . 192
idol's temple

εἰδωλόθυτον . . 192
idols, meats offered to
idols, offered in sacrifice to
idols, offered to
idols, sacrificed to
idols, things that are offered in sacrifice unto

εἰδωλολατρεία . 192
idolatry

εἰδωλολάτρης . 193
idolater

εἴδωλον . . . 193
idol

εἴην, εἴης, εἴη, &c. from εἰμί . . 193
mean
perish (with απωλεια, εις, Acts 8:20)
should be
was
were

εἰκῆ . . . 193
cause, without a
vain, in
vainly

εἴκοσι . . . 193
twenty

εἴκω . . . 193
place, give

εἴκω . . . 193
like, be

εἰκών . . . 193
image

εἰλικρίνεια . . 193
sincerity

εἰλικρινής . 193
pure
sincere

εἰλίσσω . . 193
roll together

εἰμί . . . 194
am
have been
it is
was

εἶναι, from εἰμί . 195
am
are

come
is
lust after (with επιθυ-
μητης, 1 Cor. 10:6)
made, to be
please ... well (with
ευαρεστος, 'Ἰ'ἑ 2:9)
there is
to be
was

ειρηνεύω . . . 196
peace, be at
peace, have
peace, live in
peaceably, live

ειρήνη . . . 196
one
peace
quietness
rest
set at one again (with
συνελαυνω, εις, Acts
7:26)

ειρηνικός . . . 197
peaceable

ειρηνοποιέω . . 197
peace, make

ειρηνοποιός . . 197
peacemaker

εἰς . . . 197
abundantly
against
among
as
at
backward
before
before (with προσωπον,
2 Cor. 8:24)
by
concerning
continual (with τελος,
Lu. 13:5)
far more exceeding
(with κατα, 2 Cor. 4:
17)
for
for intent
for purpose
...fore
forth (with μεσος, Mark
3:3)
hereunto (1 Pet. 2:21)
in
in among
in at
in unto
insomuch that
intent, to the
into
mind, of one (with
φρονεω, Phi. 2:2)

never (with ου μη,
αιων)
of
on
perish (with απωλεια,
εις, Acts 8:20)
set at one again (with
συνελαυνω, ειρηνη,
Acts 7:26)
so that
that
therefore
therefore
thereunto
throughout
till
to
to be (Acts 13:22)
to the end
toward
until
unto
upon
...ward
wherefore
with

εἰς, ἕν . 209
a
abundantly (with πε-
ρισσεια, 2 Cor. 10:15)
an
any
certain, a
man
one
one another
only
other
some

εἰς καθ' εἰς . 211
one by one

εἰσάγω . . . 211
bring in
bring into
lead into
led into, be
led into, was to be (with
μελλω, Acts 21:37)

εἰσακούω . . . 211
hear

εἰσδέχομαι . 211
receive

εἴσειμι . . 211
enter into
go into

εἰσέρχομαι . . 211
arise
come
come in
come into
enter in
enter into

go in
go through

εἰσί, from εἰμί . 213
agree
are
be
dure
is
were

εἰσκαλέω . . . 214
call in

εἴσοδος . . 214
coming
enter into
entering in

εἰσπηδάω . . . 214
run in
spring in

εἰσπορεύομαι . 214
come in
enter in
go into

εἰστρέχω . . . 214
run in

εἰσφέρω . 214
bring
bring in
lead into

εἶτα . . 214
after that
afterward
furthermore
then

ἐκ, ἐξ . . 215
after
among
are
at
because of
betwixt
beyond
by
by the means of
exceeding abundantly
above (with υπερ,
Eph. 3:20)
exceedingly (1 Th. 3:
10)
for
forth at
from
from among
from forth
from up
grudgingly (with λυπη,
2 Cor. 9:7)
heartily (with ψυχη,
Col. 3:23)
heavenly (Lu. 11:13)
hereby (1 Joh. 4:6)
highly, very (with υπερ,
1 Th. 5:13)

in
...ly
of
off
off from
on
out among
out from
out of
over
reason of, by
since
thenceforth (Joh. 19:12)
through
unto
vehemently (Mar. 14:
31)
with
without

ἕκαστος . . . 221
any
both
each
each one
every
every man
every one
every woman
particularly

ἑκάστοτε . . . 222
always

ἑκατόν . . 222
hundred (h .fold)

ἑκατονταέτης . 222
hundred years old

ἑκατονταπλασίων 222
hundredfold

ἑκατοντάρχης . 222
centurion

ἑκατόνταρχος . 222
centurion

ἐκβάλλω . . 222
bring forth
cast
cast forth
cast out
drive
drive out
expel
leave
pluck out
pull out
put forth, be
put out
send away
send forth
send out
take out| thrust
thrust out

ἔκβασις . . . 223 end way to escape	**ἐκεῖθεν** . . . 224 from that place from thence	**ἐκκομίζομαι** . 228 carried out, be
ἐκβολή . . . 223 lighten the ship (with ποιεω. Acts 27: 18)	thence there	**ἐκκόπτω** . . . 228 cut down cut off
ἐκγαμίζω . . 223 marriage, give in	**ἐκεῖνος** . . . 225 he it	cut out hew down hinder
ἐκγαμίσκομαι . 223 marriage, be given in	other, the same, the selfsame	**ἐκκρέμαμαι** . . 228 attentive, be very
ἔκγονα . . . 223 nephews	she that that same	**ἐκλαλέω** . . . 228 tell
ἐκδαπανάω . 223 spent, be	that very their them	**ἐκλάμπω** . . . 228 shine forth
ἐκδέχομαι . . 223 expect look for	they this those	**ἐκλανθάνομαι** . 228 forget
tarry for wait wait for	**ἐκεῖσε** . . . . 226 there	**ἐκλέγομαι** . . 228 choice, made choose
ἔκδηλος . . . 223 manifest	**ἐκζητέω** . . . 226 enquire required, be	choose out chosen
ἐκδημέω . . . 223 absent, be	seek after seek carefully seek, diligently	**ἐκλείπω** . . . 228 fail
ἐκδίδωμι . . . 223 let forth let out	**ἐκθαμβέω** . 226 affrighted, be amazed, be greatly	**ἐκλεκτός** . . . 228 chosen elect
ἐκδιηγέομαι . . 223 declare	amazed, be sore	**ἐκλογή** . . 228 chosen election
ἐκδικέω . . . 223 avenge revenge	**ἔκθαμβος** . . . 227 greatly wondering	**ἐκλύω** . . . 229 faint
ἐκδίκησις . . . 223 avenge punishment	**ἔκθετος** . . . 227 cast out (Acts 7:19)	**ἐκμάσσω** . . 229 wipe
revenge vengeance	**ἐκκαθαίρω** . . 227 purge purge out	**ἐκμυκτηρίζω** . . 229 deride
ἔκδικος . . . 223 avenger revenger	**ἐκκαίομαι** . . 227 burn	**ἐκνεύω** . . . 229 convey self away
ἐκδιώκω . . . 223 persecute	**ἐκκακέω** . . . 227 faint, to weary, be	**ἐκνήφω** . . . 229 awake
ἔκδοτος . . . 224 delivered	**ἐκκεντέω** . . . 227 pierce	**ἑκούσιος** . . . 229 willingly
ἐκδοχή . . . 224 looking for	**ἐκκλάζω** . . . 227 break off	**ἑκουσίως** . . . 229 wilfully willingly
ἐκδύω . . . . 224 strip take off from	**ἐκκλείω** . . . 227 exclude	**ἔκπαλαι** . . . 229 long time, of a of old
unclothe	**ἐκκλησία** . . . 227 assembly church	**ἐκπειράζω** . . 229 tempt
ἐκεῖ . . . 224 there thither	**ἐκκλίνω** . . . 228 avoid eschew	**ἐκπέμπω** . . . 229 send away send forth
thitherward yonder yonder place, to	go out of the way	
	ἐκκολυμβάω . . 228 swim out	**ἐκπετάννυμι** . . 229 stretch forth

ἐκπίπτω . . . 229 cast, be fail fall fall away fall off take none effect
ἐκπλέω . . . 229 sail sail away sail thence
ἐκπληρόω . . . 229 fulfil
ἐκπλήρωσις . . 229 accomplishment
ἐκπλήσσω . . 229 amazed, be astonished, be
ἐκπνέω . . . 229 give up the ghost
ἐκπορεύομαι . . 229 come come forth come out of depart go go forth go out issue proceed proceed out of would depart (Acts 25:4)
ἐκπορνεύω . . 230 fornication, give self over to
ἐκπτύω . . . 230 reject
ἐκριζόω . . 230 pluck up by the root root up
ἔκστασις . . . 230 amazed, be (with λαμβανω) amazement astonishment trance
ἐκστρέφομαι . . 230 subvert
ἐκταράσσω . . 230 trouble, exceedingly
ἐκτείνω . . . 230 cast cast, would have (Acts 27.30) put forth stretch forth stretch out
ἐκτελέω . . . 230 finish

ἐκτένεια . . . 230	ἐκχύνω . . . 231	rebuke	Ἐλωΐ . . . 235
instantly	gush out	reprove	Eloi
ἐκτενεστερον . . 230	pour out	ἐλεεινός . . . 233	ἐμ αυτοῦ, -τῷ, -τον 235
earnestly, more	run greedily	miserable	me
ἐκτενής . . . 230	shed	ἐλεέω 233	mine own
ceasing, without	shed abroad	compassion, have	mine own self
fervent	spilled, be	mercy, obtain	myself
ἐκτενῶς . 230	ἐκχωρέω . . . 231	mercy on, have	ἐμβαίνω . . . 235
fervently	depart out	mercy, receive	come into
ἐκτίθημι . . . 230	ἐκψύχω . . . 232	mercy, shew	enter
cast out	ghost, give up the	pity on, have	enter into
expound	ghost, yield up the	ἐλεημοσύνη . . 233	get into
ἐκτινάσσω . . 230	ἑκών 232	alms	go into
shake	willingly	almsdeeds	go up into
shake off	ἐλαία . . . 232	ἐλεήμων . . . 233	step in
ἔκτος . . . 231	olive	merciful	take ship
sixth	olive berries	ἔλεος . . . 233	ἐμβάλλω . 235
ἐκτός . . . 231	olive tree	mercy	cast into
but	ἔλαιον . . . 232	mercy, tender (with	ἐμβάπτω . 235
except	oil	σπλαγχνα, Lu.1:78)	dip
excepted	ἐλαιών . . . 232	ἐλευθερία . . . 233	ἐμβατεύω . 235
other than	Olivet	liberty	intrude into
out of	ἐλάσσων & ἐλάτ-	ἐλεύθερος . . . 233	ἐμβιβάζω . 235
outside	των . . . 232	free	put in
unless	less	free man	ἐμβλέπω . . 235
without	under	free woman	behold
ἐκτρέπομαι . . 231	worse	liberty, at	could see
avoid	younger	ἐλευθερόω . . . 234	gaze up
turn	ἐλαττονέω . 232	deliver	look upon
turn aside	lack, have	free, make	see
turn out of the way	ἐλαττόω . . . 232	ἔλευσις . . . 234	ἐμβριμάομαι . 235
ἐκτρέφω . . . 231	decrease	coming	groan
bring up	lower, make	ἐλεφάντινος . . 234	murmur against
nourish	ἐλαύνω . . . 232	ivory, of	straitly charge
ἔκτρωμα . . . 231	carry	ἐλίσσω . . . 234	ἐμέ, from ἐγώ 236
born out of due time	driven, be	fold up	I
ἐκφέρω . . . 231	row	ἑλκόομαι . . . 234	me
bear	ἐλαφρία . . 232	sores, full of	my
bring forth	lightness	ἔλκος . . . 234	myself
carry forth	ἐλαφρός . . . 232	sores	ἐμέω 236
carry out	light	ἑλκύω . . . 234	spue
ἐκφεύγω . . . 231	ἐλάχιστος . . 232	draw	spue, will (Rev. 3:16)
escape	least	ἕλκω . . . 234	ἐμμαίνομαι . . 236
flee	little, very	draw	mad against, be
ἐκφοβέω . . 231	small, very	ἐλλογέω . . . 234	ἐμμένω . . . 236
terrify	smallest	impute	continue
ἔκφοβος . . . 231	ἐλαχιστότερος . 232	put on account	ἐμοί, from ἐγώ 236
fear exceedingly	least, less than the	ἐλπίζω . . . 234	I
sore afraid	ἔλεγξις . . . 232	hope	me
ἐκφύω . . . 231	rebuke	hope for	mine
put forth	ἔλεγχος . . . 232	hope, have	my
ἐκχέω . . 231	evidence	hope, have (with εσμεν,	ἐμός . . . 237
pour out	reproof	1 Co. 15:19)	me, of
run out	ἐλέγχω . . . 232	hoped for, things	mine
shed	convicted, be	trust	mine own
shed forth	convince	ἐλπίς . . . 234	my
spilled, be	fault tell a	faith	ἐμοῦ, from ἐγω 238
		hope	me
			mine
			my

ἐμπαιγμος . . 238
mocking

ἐμπαίζω . . . 238
mock

ἐμπαικται . . 239
mockers
scoffers

ἐμπεριπατέω . 239
walk in

ἐμπιπλάω . . 239
fill

ἐμπίπτω . . . 239
fall among
fall into

ἐμπλέκω . . . 239
entangle
entangle in
entangle self with

ἐμπλήθω . . 239
fill
full, be

ἐμπλοκή . . . 239
plaiting

ἐμπνέω . . . 239
breathe

ἐμπορεύομαι . . 239
buy and sell
merchandise, make

ἐμπορία . . . 239
merchandise

ἐμπορίον . . . 239
merchandise

ἔμπορος . . . 239
merchant

ἐμπρήθω . . . 239
burn up

ἔμπροσθεν . . 239
against
at
before
of
presence of, in
sight of, in

ἐμπτύω . . . 239
spit
spit upon

ἐμφανής . . . 240
manifest
openly

ἐμφανίζω . . 240
appear
declare plainly
inform
manifest
manifest, will (Joh. 14:
22)

shew
signify

ἔμφοβος . . . 240
affrighted
afraid
tremble

ἐμφυσάω . . . 240
breathe on

ἔμφυτος . . . 240
engrafted

ἐν 240
about
after
against
almost (with ολιγος)
altogether (Acts 26:29)
among
as (Lu. 8:5)
at
because of
before
between
by
child, with (with
γαστηρ)
for
for ... sake of
give self wholly to (with
ισθι, 1 Ti. 4:15)
hereby
herein
in
into
inwardly
... ly
means, by all (with πας,
2 Th. 3:16)
mightily
of
on
openly
outwardly
over
quickly
shortly
speedily
that (Lu. 1:21)
there (Acts 9:38)
therein
thereon
through
throughout
to
toward
under
anto
upon
when (Lu. 2:27)
where (Acts 7:33)
wherewith
while (Lu. 1:8)
with
within

ἐναγκαλίζομαι . 259
take up in arms

ἐνάλιος . . . 259
sea, things in the

ἔναντι . . . 259
before

ἐναντίον . . . 259
before
sight of, in the

ἐναντίος . . . 259
against
contrary
over against [opposite]

ἐνάρχομαι . . 259
begin

ἐνδεής . . . 259
lacking

ἔνδειγμα . . . 259
manifest token

ἐνδείκνυμι . . 259
do
shew
shew forth

ἔνδειξις . . . 260
declare
evident token
proof

ἔνδεκα . . . 260
eleven

ἐνδέκατος . . 260
cleventh

ἐνδέχεται . . . 260
can be
cannot be (with ον, Lu.
13:33)

ἐνδημέω . . . 260
home, be at
present, be

ἐνδιδύσκομαι . . 260
clothed in, be
wear

ἔνδικος . . . 260
just

ἐνδόμησις . . 260
building

ἐνδοξάζομαι . . 260
glorified, be

ἔνδοξος . . . 260
glorious
gorgeously
honourable

ἔνδυμα . . . 260
clothing
garment
raiment

ἐνδυναμόω . . 260
enable
strength, increase in
strengthen
strong, be
strong, be ma -

ἐνδύνω . . . 260
creep

ἔνδυσις . . . 260
putting on

ἐνδύω 260
arrayed, be
clothe with
clothed, be
endued, be
have on
put on

ἐνέδρα & -δρον . 261
lay wait
lay wait (Acts 25:3)
lying in wait

ἐνεδρεύω . . . 261
lay wait for

ἐνειλέω . . . 261
wrap in

ἔνειμι 261
such things as have

ἔνεκα, ἔνεκεν, εἵ-
νεκεν . . 261
because
cause, for
for
...fore
reason of, by
sake, for
that
wherefore
wherefore (with τις,
Acts 19:32)

ἐνέργεια . . . 261
effectual working
operation
strong
working

ἐνεργέω . . . 261
do
effectual, be
effectual fervent
mighty in, be
shew forth self
work
work effectually in

ἐνέργημα . . . 261
operation
working

ἐνεργής . . . 261
effectual
powerful

ἐπιούσιος . . 285
daily

ἐπιπίπτω . . 285
fall into (Acts 10: 10)
fall upon
fell on
lie on
press upon

ἐπιπλήττω . . 286
rebuke

ἐπιπνίγω . . . 286
choke

ἐπιποθέω . . . 286
desire
desiring greatly
earnestly desire
long
long after
long after, greatly
lust

ἐπιπόθησις . . 286
desire, earnest
desire, vehement

ἐπιπόθητος . . 286
longed for

ἐπιποθία . . . 286
desire, great

ἐπιπορεύομαι . 286
come

ἐπιρράπτω . . 286
sew on

ἐπιρρίπτω . . 286
cast upon

ἐπίσημος . . . 286
notable
note, of

ἐπισιτισμός . . 286
victuals

ἐπισκέπτομαι . 286
look out
visit

ἐπισκηνόω . . 286
rest upon

ἐπισκιάζω . . 286
overshadow

ἐπισκοπέω . . 286
look diligently
take the oversight

ἐπισκοπή . . . 286
bishop, the office of a
bishoprick
visitation

ἐπίσκοπος . 286
bishop
overseer

ἐπισπάομαι . . 286
become uncircumcised

ἐπίσταμαι . . 286
know
understand

ἐπιστάτης . . 287
master

ἐπιστέλλω . . 287
write
write a letter unto
write unto

ἐπιστήμων . . 287
endued with knowledge

ἐπιστηρίζω . . 287
confirming
strengthening

ἐπιστολή . . . 287
epistle
letter

ἐπιστομίζω . . 287
mouths be stopped

ἐπιστρέφω . . 287
come again
convert
go again
return
turn
turn about
turn again

ἐπιστροφή . . 287
conversion

ἐπισυνάγω . . 287
gather
gather together

ἐπισυναγωγή . 287
assembling together
gathering together

ἐπισυντρέχω . . 287
come running together

ἐπισύστασις . . 288
cometh upon, that
which
raising up (with ποιεω,
Acts 24:12)

ἐπισφαλής . 288
dangerous

ἐπισχύω . . . 288
fierce, be the more

ἐπισωρεύω . 288
heap

ἐπιταγή . . 288
authority
commandment

ἐπιτάσσω . . . 288
charge
command
injoin

ἐπιτελέω . . 288
accomplish
do
finish
make
perfect
perfect, make
perform
performance (2 Cor. 8:
11)

ἐπιτήδειος . . 288
needful, things which
are

ἐπιτίθημι . . 288
add unto
lade
lay upon
put on
put upon
set on, be
set up
surname (with ονομα,
Mar. 3:16, 17)
wound (Lu. 10:30)

ἐπιτιμάω . . . 288
charge
rebuke
straitly charge

ἐπιτιμία . . . 289
punishment

ἐπιτρέπω . . . 289
leave, give
let
liberty, give
licence, give
permit
suffer

ἐπιτροπή . . . 289
commission

ἐπίτροπος . . 289
steward
tutor

ἐπιτυγχάνω . . 289
obtain

ἐπιφαίνω . . . 289
appear
light, give

ἐπιφάνεια . . 289
appearing
brightness

ἐπιφανής . . . 289
notable

ἐπιφαύω . . . 289
light, give

ἐπιφέρω . . . 289
add
bring
bring against
take

ἐπιφωνεω . . 289
cry
cry against
shout, give a

ἐπιφώσκω . . 289
begin to dawn
draw on

ἐπιχειρέω . . 289
go about
take in hand
take upon

ἐπιχέω . . . 289
pour in

ἐπιχορηγέω . . 289
add
minister
minister unto
nourishment, minister

ἐπιχορηγία . . 289
supply
supply (Eph. 4:16)

ἐπιχρίω . . 290
anoint

ἐποικοδομέω . 290
build thereon
build thereupon
build up
build upon

ἐποκέλλω . 290
run aground

ἐπονομάζομαι . 290
called, be

ἐπόπτης . . 290
eyewitness

ἐποπτεύω . . 290
behold

ἔπος 290
say (with επω, Heb. 7.
9)

ἐπουράνιος . . 290
celestial
heaven, in
heavenly
high

ἑπτά 290
seven
seventh

ἑπτάκις . 291
seven times

ἑπτακισχίλιοι . 291
seven thousand

ἔπω . . . 291
answer
bid
bring word
call
command

grant
say
say (with ετος, Heb. 7: 9)
say on
speak
tell

ἐργάζομαι . 298
commit
do
labour for
minister about
trade
trade by
work

ἐργασία . . . 298
craft
diligence
gain
work (Eph. 4:19)

ἐργάτης . . . 298
labourer
worker
workman

ἔργον 298
deed
doing
labour
work

ἐρεθίζω . . . 300
provoke
provoke (to anger)

ἐρείδω 300
stick fast

ἐσεύγομαι . . 300
utter

ἐρευνάω . . . 300
search

ῥέω 300
call
say
speak
speak of
tell

ἐρημία . . . 300
desert
wilderness

ἔρημος, ἡ . . . 300
desert
wilderness

ἔρημος . . . 301
desert
desolate
solitary

ἐρημόω . . . 301
desolate
desolate, make
desolation, bring to
nought, come to

ἐρήμωσις . . . 301
desolation

ἐρίζω . . . 301
strive

ἐριθεία . . . 301
contention
contentious (Ro. 2:8)
strife

ἔριον . . . 301
wool

ἔρις . . . 301
contention
debate
strife
variance

ἐρίφιον . . . 301
goat

ἔριφος . . . 301
goat
kid

ἑρμηνεία . . . 301
interpretation

ἑρμηνεύω . . . 301
interpret
interpretation, be by

ἑρπετόν . . . 301
creeping things
serpent

ἔρχομαι . . 301
accompany
accompany (with συν, Acts 11:12)
appear
bring
come
come, shall (with μελλω)
enter
fall out
go
grow
light
next
pass
resort
set, be (Acts 19:27)
which was for to come (with μελλω, Mat.11: 14)

ἐρωτάω . . . 306
ask
beseech
desire
intreat
pray

ἔσεσθαι . . . 306
be
come, to
should be (Acts 11:28)

ἐσθής 307
apparel
clothing
raiment
robe

ἔσθησις . . . 307
garment

ἐσθίω 307
devour
devour, shall (with μελλω, Heb. 10:27)
eat
live

ἐσμέν . . . 307
are
be
being, have our
hope, have (with ελπι-ζω, 1 Cor. 15:19)
preached, unto us was the gospel (Heb. 4:2)

ἔσομαι . . . 308
come
fall (Mar. 13:25)
live long (Eph. 6:3)
may have
pass, shall come to
shall be
shall have
sojourn (Acts 7:6)

ἐσόμενος.. . . 309
follow, what would

ἔσοπτρον . . . 309
glass

ἑσπέρα . . . 309
evening
eventide

ἐστέ . . . 309
be
been, have
belong

ἐστί 310
are
be
belong
call
cannot (with ουκ, Heb. 9:5)
come
consisteth
dure for a while (Mat. 13:21)
follow (with μετα, Mat. 27:62)
followed (with μετα, Mat. 27:62)
have
is
make
meaneth
must needs
own (with ου Acts 21 11)

profit (with ωφελιμος, 1 Ti. 4:8)
remaineth, it (with το λοιπον)
say, is to
say, that is to (with ο, Mar. 7:11)
wrestle (with παλη, Eph. 6:12)

ἔστω, ἔστωσαν . 316
be

ἔσχατος . . . 317
ends of
last
latter end
lowest
uttermost

ἐσχάτως . . . 317
point of death

ἔσω . . . 317
in
inner
into
inward
within

ἔσωθεν . . . 317
inward
inwardly
within
within, from
without

ἐσώτερος . . . 317
inner
within

ἑταῖρος . . . 317
fellow
friend

ἑτερόγλωσσος . 317
tongues, (men of) other

ἑτεροδιδασκαλέω . 317
teach other doctrine
teach otherwise

ἑτεροζυγέω . . 318
yoke together with, unequally

ἕτερος 318
altered
another
else
next
next day
one
other
some
strange

ἑτέρως . . 318
otherwise

ἔτι 318
after that
also

any further
any longer
any more
even
further
henceforth
henceforth more
hereafter
longer
more
moreover
now
still
thenceforth
yet

ἑτοιμάζω . . . 319
prepare
provide
ready, make

ἑτοιμασία . . 320
preparation

ἕτοιμος . . . 320
prepared
readiness
ready
ready to our hand, made

τοίμως . . . 320
ready

ἔτος . . . 320
year

εὖ 320
good
well
well done

εὐαγγελίζω, -ομαι 320
declare
glad tidings, bring
glad tidings, declare
glad tidings, shew
good tidings, bring
gospel, preach the
gospel preached, have the
gospel to be preached, which by the
preach

εὐαγγέλιον . . 321
gospel

εὐαγγελιστής . 321
evangelist

εὐαρεστέω . 321
please
pleased, be well

εὐάρεστος . . 321
acceptable
accepted
wellpleasing

εὐαρέστως . . 322
acceptably

please...well (with εἰναι, Tit. 2:9)

εὐγενής . . . 322
noble, more
nobleman

εὐδία . . . 322
fair weather

εὐδοκέω . . . 322
good, think
please
pleased, be well
pleasure, be the good
pleasure, have
pleasure, take
willing, be

εὐδοκία . . . 322
desire
good pleasure
good will
seem good

εὐεργεσία . . 322
benefit
good deed done

εὐεργετέω . . 322
do good

εὐεργέτης . . 322
benefactor

εὔθετος . . . 322
fit
meet

εὐθέως . . . 322
anon
as soon as
by and by
forthwith
immediately
shortly
straightway

εὐθυδρομέω . . 323
straight course, come with a
straight course, with a

εὐθυμέω . . . 323
good cheer, be of
merry, be

εὔθυμος . . . 323
good cheer, of

εὐθυμότερον . . 323
cheerfully, more

εὐθύνω . . . 323
list (Jas. 3:4)
straight, make

εὐθύς . . . 323
right
straight

εὐθύς . . . 323
anon
by and by

forthwith
immediately
straightway

εὐθύτης . . . 323
righteousness

εὐκαιρέω . . . 323
convenient time, have
leisure, have
spend time

εὐκαιρία . . . 323
opportunity

εὔκαιρος . . . 323
convenient
time of need, in

εὐκαίρως . . . 323
conveniently
season, in

εὐκοπώτερος . . 323
easier

εὐλάβεια . . . 323
fear, godly
fear ['in that he feared']

εὐλαβέομαι . . 323
fear
fear, moved with

εὐλαβής . . . 324
devout

εὐλογέω . . . 324
bless
praise

εὐλογητός . . 324
blessed

εὐλογία . . . 324
blessing
bountifully
bounty
bounty, (a matter of)
speech, fair

εὐμετάδοτος . . 324
distribute, ready to

εὐνοέω . . . 324
agree

εὔνοια . . . 324
benevolence
good will

εὐνουχίζω . . 324
eunuchs, make

εὐνοῦχος . . . 324
eunuch

εὐοδόομαι . . 324
prosper
prosperous journey, have a

εὐπειθής . . . 324
intreated, easy to be

εὐπερίστατος . 324
beset, which doth so easily

εὐποιΐα . . . 325
good, to do

εὐπορέομαι . . 325
ability

εὐπορία . . . 325
wealth

εὐπρέπεια . . 325
grace

εὐπρόσδεκτος . 325
acceptable
accepted

εὐπρόσεδρος . . 325
attend upon (1 Co.7:35)

εὐπροσωπέω . . 325
fair shew, make a

εὑρίσκω . . . 325
find
get
obtain
perceive
see

εὐρύχωρος . . 326
broad

εὐσέβεια . . . 326
godliness
holiness

εὐσεβέω . . . 326
piety, shew
worship

εὐσεβής . . . 326
devout
godly

εὐσεβῶς . . . 327
godly

εὔσημος . . . 327
understood, easy to be

εὔσπλαγχνος . 327
pitiful
tenderhearted

εὐσχημόνως . . 327
decently
honestly

εὐσχημοσύνη . 327
comeliness

εὐσχήμων . . 327
comely
honourable

εὐτόνως . . . 327
mightily
vehemently

εὐτραπελία . . 327
jesting

ε.φημια . . . 327	ἐφικνέομαι . . 328	next	desire
report, good	reach	possessed with (be)	desire to have
		recover (with καλως)	envy
εὔφημος . . . 327	ἐφίστημι . 328	reign (with βασιλεια,	jealous over, be
report, of good	assault	Rev. 17:18)	move with envy
	come	rest (with αναπαυσις,	zealous, be
ευφορέω . . . 327	come in	Rev. 4:8)	zealously affect
bring forth plentifully	come to	retain	
	come unto	sick	ζηλωτής . . 337
εὐφραίνω -ομαι . 327	come upon	take for	zealous
fare	hand, be at	tremble (with τρομος,	
glad, make	instant, be	Mark 16:8)	ζημία . . . 337
merry, be	present	uncircumcised (with	damage
merry, make	stand	ακροβυστια, Acts	loss
rejoice	stand before	11:3)	
	stand by	use	ζημιόω . . . 337
εὐφροσύνη . . 327	stand over		cast away, be
gladness		ἕως . . . 334	lose
joy	ἐφοράω . . . 329	as far as	receive damage
	behold	even	suffer loss
εὐχαριστέω . . 327	look on	even until	
thank		even unto	ζητέω . . . 337
thankful, be	ἐφφαθά . . 329	far	about, be
thanks, give	Ephphatha	hitherto	desire
		how long	endeavour
εὐχαριστία . 327	ἔχθρα . . . 329	how long (with ποτε)	enquire
thankfulness	enmity	till	enquire for
thanks	hatred	to	go about
thanks, giving of		until	require
thanksgiving	ἐχθρός . . 329	unto	seek
	enemy	up to	seek after
εὐχάριστος . . 328	foe	while	seek for
thankful		whiles	seek means
	ἔχιδνα . . 329		seek, will (Mat. 2:13)
εὐχή . . . 328	viper		
prayer			ζήτημα . . . 338
vow	ἔχω . . . 329		question
	able, be	ζάω . . . 335	
εὔχομαι . . . 328	accompany	alive, be	ζήτησις . . . 338
pray	amend, began to (with	life	question
will	κομψοτερον)	lifetime	
wish	be	live	ζιζάνια . . . 338
	bold, be (John 8:57)	lively	tares
εὔχρηστος . 328	can	quick	
profitable	cannot (with ουκ)		ζόφος . . . 338
use, meet for	conceive (Ro. 9:10)	ζεστός . . . 337	blackness
	count	hot	darkness
εὐψυχέω . . . 328	diseased		mist
comfort, be of good	do	ζεῦγος . . . 337	
	eat (with νομη, 2 Tim.	pair	ζυγός . . . 338
εὐωδία . . 328	2:17)	yoke	balances, pair of
savour, sweet	enjoy (with απολαυσις,		yoke
smell, sweet	Heb. 11:25)	ζευκτηρία . . 337	
sweetsmelling	fear (with φοβος, 1 Tim.	band	ζύμη . . . 338
	5:20)		leaven
εὐώνυμος . 328	following	ζέω . . . 337	
left	following (Lu. 13:33)	fervent, be	ζυμόω . . 338
left, on the	have		leaven
	hold (h. fast)	ζῆλος . . . 337	
ἐφάλλομαι . . 328	keep	emulation	ζωγρέω . . 339
leap on	lack (with μη)	envy	captive, take
	law, go to (with κριμα,	envying	catch
ἐφάπαξ . . 328	1 Cor. 6:7)	fervent mind	
once	lie	indignation	ζωή . . . 339
once, at	must needs (with	jealousy	life
once (for all)	αναγκη)	zeal	lifetime
	necessity, of (with		
ἐφευρετής . . 328	αναγκη)	ζηλόω . . . 337	ζώνη . . . 340
inventor	need (with χρεια)	affect	girdle
		covet	purse
ἐφημερία . . . 328		covet earnestly	
course			ζωννύω . . . 340
			gird
ἐφήμερος . . 328			
daily			

ζωογονέω . . 340
live
preserve

ζῶον . . 340
beast

ζωοποιεω . . 340
alive, make
life, give
quicken

ἤ . . . 340
and
but
but either
either
except it be
neither
nor
or
or else
rather
save
than
that
what
yea

ἦ μήν . . . 342
surely

ἤπερ . . . 342
than

ἤτοι . . . 342
whether

ἡγεμονία . . 342
reign

ἡγεμονεύω . . 342
governor, be

ἡγεμών . . . 343
governor
prince
ruler

ἡγέομαι . . . 343
account
chief
chief(Acts 14:12; 15:
22)
chief, be
count
esteem
governor
judge
rule over, have the
suppose
think

ἡδέως, ἤδιστα . 343
gladly
gladly, most
gladly, very

ἤδη 343
already

even now
now
now already
time, by this
yet

ἡδονή . . . 343
lust
pleasure

ἡδύοσμον . . . 344
mint

ἦθος . . . 344
manners

ἤκω 344
come

Ἠλί . . . 344
Eli

ἡλικία. . . . 344
age
stature

ἡλίκος . . . 344
great, how
great, what

ἥλιος 344
east (with ανατολη)
sun

ἧλος . . . 344
nail

ἡμᾶς, from ἐγώ. 344
our
us
we

ἡμεῖς . . . 346
us
we
we ourselves

ἡμέρα . . . 347
age
age, be of a great (with
προβαινω, πολης,
Lu. 2:36)
alway (with πας)
daily
day
day by day
day time
ever, for (with αιων)
judgment
mid-day
mid-day
time
while
years

ἡμέτερος . . . 349
our
your [in some copies]

ἤμην . . . 350
be

ἡμιθανής . . . 350
half dead

ἡμῖν . . . 350
our
us
us, for
we

ἤμισυ . . . 351
half

ἡμιώριον . . 351
half an hour

ἡμῶν . . . 351
our
our (with μετα, 1 Joh.
4:17)
our company
us
us (with ψυχη, Joh.
10:24)
we

ἦν, ἦς, ἦσθα. 354
agree (with ισος)
be
charge of, have (with
επι, Acts 8:27)
have
hold
use

ἡνίκα . . . 357
when

ἤπιος . . . 357
gentle

ἤρεμος . . . 358
quiet

ἡσυχάζω . . 358
cease
peace, hold
quiet, be
rest

ἡσυχία . . . 358
quietness
silence

ἡσύχιος . . . 358
peaceable
quiet

ἡττάομαι . . 358
inferior, be
overcome

ἥττημα . . . 358
diminishing
fault

ἧττον 358
less
worse

ἤτω . . . 358
be

ἡχέω . . . 358
roar
sound

ἦχος 358
fame
sound

θάλασσα . . . 358
sea

θάλπω . . . 359
cherish

θαμβέομαι . . 359
amazed, be
astonished, be

θάμβος . . . 359
amazed (Lu. 4:36)
astonished (with πε-
ριεχω, Lu. 5:9)
wonder

θανάσιμος . . 359
deadly

θανατηφόρος . . 359
deadly

θάνατος . . . 359
deadly (Rev. 13:3, 12)
death
death, be—

θανατόω . . . 360
dead, become
death, cause to be put to
death, put to
killed, be
mortify

θάπτω . . . 360
bury

θαρρέω . . . 360
bold, be
boldly
confidence, have
confident, be

θαρσέω . . . 360
good cheer, be of
good comfort, be of

θάρσυς . . . 360
courage

θαῦμα . . . 360
admiration

θαυμάζω . . . 360
admiration, have in
admired, be
marvel
wonder

θαυμάσιος . . 361
wonderful

θαυμαστός . . 361
marvel
marvellous

Θεά . . . 361
goddess

θεάομαι . . . 361
behold
look
look upon
see

θεατρίζομαι . . 361
gazingstock, be made a

θέατρον . . . 361
spectacle
theatre

θεῖον . . . 361
brimstone

θεῖος . . . 361
divine
godhead

θειότης . . . 361
godhead

θειώδης . . . 361
brimstone

θέλημα . . . 361
desires
pleasure
will

θέλησις . . . 362
will

θέλω 362
desire
disposed, be
forward, be
intend
list
love
mean
please
rather, have
will
will have
willing, be
willingly

θεμέλιος . . . 363
foundation

θεμελιόω . . . 363
found
ground
lay the foundation
settle

θεοδίδακτος . . 364
God, taught of

θεομαχεω . . . 364
God, fight against

θεομάχος . . . 364
God, to fight against

θεόπνευστος . . 364
God, given by inspira-
tion of

Θεός 364
exceeding (Acts 7:20)

God
godly
God-ward

θεοσέβεια . . 373
godliness

θεοσεβής . . . 373
God, worshipper of

θεοστυγής . . 373
God, hater of

θεότης . . . 373
Godhead

θεραπεία . . . 373
healing
houshold

θεραπεύω . . . 373
cure
heal
worship

θεράπων . . . 374
servant

θερίζω . . . 374
reap

θερισμός . . . 374
harvest

θεριστής . . . 374
reaper

θερμαίνομαι . . 374
warm self
warmed, be

θέρμη . . . 374
heat

θέρος . . . 374
summer

θεωρέω . . . 374
behold
consider
look on
perceive
see
see, should (Acts 20:38)

θεωρία . . . 375
sight

θήκη . . . 375
sheath

θηλάζω . . . 375
suck
suck, give
sucklings

θήλεια . . . 375
woman

θῆλυ . . . 375
female

θήρα . . . 375
trap

θηρεύω . 375
catch

θηριομαχέω . . 375
beasts, fight with

θηρίον . . . 375
beast
beast, (venomous)
beast, wild

θησαυρίζω . . 375
heap treasure together
in store (1 Co. 16:2)
keep in store
lay up
lay up treasure
treasure up

θησαυρός . 375
treasure

θίγω . . . 376
handle
touch

θλίβω . . . 376
afflict
narrow
throng
tribulation, suffer
trouble

θλίψις . 376
afflicted, (be)
affliction
anguish
burdened (2 Co. 8:13)
persecution
tribulation
trouble

θνήσκω . . 376
dead, be
die

θνητός . . 376
mortal
mortality (2 Co. 5:4)

θορυβέομαι . . 376
ado, make
noise, make a
trouble self
uproar, set on an

θόρυβος . . 376
tumult
uproar

θραύω . . 376
bruise

θρέμμα . . 377
cattle

θρηνέω . . 377
lament
mourn

θρῆνος . . 377
lamentation

θρησκεία . . 377
religion
worshipping

θρῆσκος . . . 377
religious

θριαμβεύω . . 377
triumph, cause to
triumph over

θρίξ, τριχὸς . . 377
hair

θροέομαι . . 377
troubled, be

θρόμβος . . 377
great drops

θρόνος . . . 377
seat
throne

θυγάτηρ . . . 377
daughter

θυγάτριον . . 378
daughter, little
daughter, young

θύελλα . . . 378
tempest

θύϊνος . . . 378
thyine

θυμίαμα . . . 378
incense
odour

θυμιατήριον . . 378
censer

θυμιάω . . . 378
incense, burn

θυμομαχέω . . 378
displeased, be highly

θυμόομαι . . . 378
wroth, be

θυμός . . . 378
fierceness
indignation
wrath

θύρα . . . 378
door
gate

θυρεός . . . 378
shield

θυρίς . . . 378
window

θυρωρός . . . 379
door, that kept the
porter

θυσία . . . 379
sacrifice

θυσιαστήριον . . 379
altar

θύω . . . 379
kill
sacrifice

sacrifice, do	ἱεράτευμα . . 382	ἱλασμός . . . 384
slay	priesthood	propitiation
θώραξ 379	ἱερατεύω . . . 383	ἱλαστήριον . . 384
breastplate	priest's office, execute	mercy-seat
	the	propitiation
ἴαμα 379	ἱερεύς 383	ἵλεως . . . 384
healing	high priest	be it far
ἰάομαι . . . 379	priest	merciful
healed, be		
whole, make	ἱερόν . . . 383	ἱμάς 384
	temple	latchet
ἴασις . . . 379		thong
cure	ἱεροπρεπής . . 383	
heal	holiness, as becometh	ἱματίζομαι . . 384
healing		clothe
	ἱερός . . . 383	
ἴασπις . . . 380	holy	ἱμάτιον . . . 384
jasper		apparel
	ἱεροσυλέω . . 383	cloke
ἰατρός . . . 380	sacrilege, commit	clothes
physician		garment
	ἱερόσυλος . . 383	raiment
ἴδε 380	church, robber of	robe
behold		vesture
lo	ἱερουργέω . . 383	
see	minister	ἱματισμός . . 385
		apparel
ἰδέα . . . 380	ἱερωσύνη . . . 384	apparelled
countenance	priesthood	apparelled
		array
ἴδιος . . . 380	ἱκανός . . . 384	raiment
acquaintance, his	able	vesture
alone, when they were	content (with ποιεω,	
apart	Lu. 15:15)	ἱμείρομαι . . 385
aside	enough	affectionately desirous,
due	good	be
her own	great	
his	large	ἵνα . . . 385
his own	long	albeit
his proper	long while	because
his several	many	for to
home	meet	intent, to the
our own	much	intent that, to the
own	security	lest
private	sore	so as
privately	sufficient	so that
proper	worthy	that
severally		to
their	ἱκανότης . . . 384	
their own	sufficiency	ἱνατί or ἵνα τί . 390
thine own		wherefore
your own	ἱκανόω . . . 384	why
your own business	make able	
	make meet	ἰός . . . 390
ἰδιώτης . . . 381		poison
ignorant	ἱκετηρία . . . 384	rust
rude	supplication	
unlearned		ἰουδαΐζω . . . 390
	ἰκμάς . . . 384	Jews, live as the,— do
ἰδού . . . 381	moisture	
behold		ἰουδαϊσμός . . 390
lo	ἱλαρός . . . 384	Jews' religion
see	cheerful	
		ἱππεύς . . . 390
ἱδρώς . . . 382	ἱλαρότης . . . 384	horseman
sweat	cheerfulness	
		ἱππικόν . . . 390
ἱερατεία . . . 382	ἱλάσκομαι . . 384	horsemen
priesthood, office of the	merciful, be	
priest's office	reconciliation for, make	ἵππος . . . 390
		horse

Ἶρις 390
rainbow
ἰσάγγελος . . 390
angels, equal unto the
ἴσημι 390
know
ἴσθι . . . 390
be
give self wholly to (with
εν, 1 Ti. 4:15)
ἴσος or ἴσος . . 390
agree (with ην)
agree (Mark 14:56)
as much
equal
like
ἰσότης . . . 391
equal
equality
ἰσότιμος . . . 391
precious, like
ἰσόψυχος . . . 391
likeminded
ἵστημι . . . 391
abide
appoint
bring
continue
covenant
establish
hold up
lay
present
set
set up
stanch
stand
stand by
stand forth
stand still
stand up
ἱστορέω . . . 392
see
ἰσχυρός . . . 392
boisterous
mightier
mighty
powerful
strong
strong man
stronger
valiant
ἰσχύς . . . 392
ability
might
mightily
power
strength

ιτχυω . . . 392
able. be
avail
can do
cannot
cannot (with ουκ, Lu. 16:3)
could
good, be
might
prevail
strength, be of
whole, be
work, much (with μολις, Acts 27:16)

ἴσως 393
be, it may

ἰχθύδιον . . . 393
fish, little
fish, small

ἰχθύς 393
fish

ἴχνος 393
step

ἰῶτα 393
jot

κἀγώ, κἀμοί, κἀμέ 393
and I
both me
even I
even I also
even so I
even so I also
I
I also
I in like wise
me also
so I

καθά 393
as

καθαίρεσις . . 394
destruction
pulling down

καθαιρέω . . . 394
cast down
destroy
destroyed, should be
pull down
put down
take down

καθαίρω . . . 394
purge

καθάπερ . . . 394
as
as well as
even as

καθαπτω . . 394
fasten on

καθαρίζω . . . 394
clean
clean, make
cleanse
purge
purify

καθαρισμος . . 394
cleansing
purged, have (with ποιεω, Heb. 1:3)
purification
purifying

κάθαρμα . . . 394
filth

καθαρός . . . 394
clean
clear
pure

καθαρότης . . 394
purifying

καθέδρα . . . 394
seat

καθέζομαι . . 395
sit

καθεῖς or καθ' εἷς 395
every one

καθεξῆι . . . 395
after
afterward
order, by
order, in

καθεύδω . . . 395
asleep, be
sleep

καθηγητής . . 395
master

καθῆκον . . . 395
convenient
fit

κάθημαι . . . 395
dwell
sit
sit by
sit down

καθ' ἡμέραν . . 396
daily
day by day
every day

καθημερινός . . 396
daily

καθίζω . . . 396
continue
set
sit
sit down
tarry

καθίημι . . 396
let down

καθίστημι . . 396
appoint
be
conduct
make | make ruler
ordain
set

καθό . . . 396
according to that
as
inasmuch as

καθόλου . . . 396
at all

καθοπλίζομαι . 397
armed, be

καθοράω . . . 397
clearly see

καθότι . . . 397
according as
as
because
because that
forsomuch as

καθώς . . . 397
according as
according to
as
even as
how
when

καινός . . 398
new

καινότης . . . 398
newness

καίπερ . . . 398
and yet
though

καιρός . . 398
always
convenient season
due season
due time
opportunity
season
short time
time
while, a
while time

καίτοι, καί-τοιγε . 399
although
nevertheless
though

καίω 399
burn
light

κἀκεῖ . . . 399
and there
there also
thither also

κἀκεῖθεν . . 399
and afterward
and from thence
and thence
thence also

κἀκεῖνος . . . 399
and him
and other
and they
even he
him also
them
them also
them also; and them
they

κακία 400
evil
malice
maliciousness
naughtiness
wickedness

κακοήθεια . . 400
malignity

κακολογέω . . 400
curse
speak evil

κακοπάθεια . . 400
suffering affliction

κακοπαθέω . . 400
afflicted, be
endure afflictions
endure hardness
suffer trouble

κακοποιέω . . 400
evil, do
evil doing

κακοποιός . 400
evildoer
malefactor

κακὸς & τὸ κακὸν 400
bad
evil
harm
ill
noisome
wicked

κακοῦργος . . 400
evil doer
malefactor

κακουχούμενος . 400
adversity, which suffer
tormented

κακόω . . . 400
affected, make evil
entreat evil
harm
hurt
vex

κακῶς . . 401
amiss

diseased	κάμπτω . . . 403	covered (1 Cor. 11:4)
evil	bow	daily
grievously		down
miserably	κἄν . . . 403	even as
sick	also if	every
sore	and if	exceeding (Ro. 7:13)
	and if so much as	exceeding, far more
κάκωσις . . . 401	at the least	(with εις, 2 Co. 4:17)
affliction	if but	excellent, more (1 Co.
	though	12:31)
κάλαμη . . 401	yet	for
stubble		from...to [by]
	κανών . . . 404	godly
κάλαμος . . 401	line	in
pen	rule	in divers
reed		in every
	καπηλεύω . . 404	inasmuch
καλέω . . . 401	corrupt	into
bid		like as
call	καπνός . . . 404	like as (Heb. 4:15)
call forth	smoke	...ly
name was [called],		manner of, after the
whose	καρδία . . 404	means, by any (with
named, be	brokenhearted (with	τροπος, 2 Th. 2:3)
surname was, whose	συντριβω, Lu. 4:18)	measure, beyond
	heart	measure, out of
καλλιέλαιος . . 402	hearted	mightily (Acts 19:20)
olive tree, good		more
	καρδιογνώστης . 405	natural
καλοδιδάσκαλος . 402	hearts, which knowest	of
teacher of good things	the	on
		out...out of every
καλοποιῶν . . 402	καρπός . . . 405	over against
well doing	fruit	own [poets]
		part, on
καλός . . . 402	καρποφορέω . 405	particularly(with μερος,
better	fruit, bear	Heb. 9:5)
better (with μαλλον,	fruit, bring forth	privately
1 Cor. 9:15)	fruitful, be	respect of, in
fair		so
good	καρποφόρος . . 406	through
goodly	fruitful	throughout
honest		
meet	καρτερέω . . . 406	thus
well	endure	to
worthy		together
	κάρφος . . . 406	toward
κάλυμμα . . 403	mote	unto
vail		upon
	κατά . . . 406	uttermost (Acts 24:22)
καλύπτω . . 403	about	where
cover	according as	whereby
hide	according to	with
	after	your own (with υμας)
καλῶς & κάλλιον 403	against	
full well	alone [see lit.]	καταβαίνω . . 409
good	alone, when they were	come down
good place, in a	among	descend
honestly	and	fall
recover (with εχω)	apart [see lit.]	fall down
well	as	get down
well, very	as concerning	go down
	as pertaining to	step down
κάμηλος . . . 403	as touching	
camel	aside [see lit.]	καταβάλλω . . 410
	at	cast down
κάμινος . . 403	before	
furnace	beyond (Gal. 1:13)	
	by	
καμμύω . . . 403		
close	charitably	
	concerning	
κάμνω . . . 403		
faint		
sick		
wearied, be		

καταβαρέω . . 410
burden
κατάβασις . . 410
descent
καταβιβάζομαι . 410
brought down, be
thrust down, be
καταβολή . . . 410
conceive
foundation
καταβραβεύω . 410
beguile of reward
καταγγελεύς . 410
setter forth
καταγγέλλω . . 410
declare
preach
shew
should shew (Acts 26: 23)
speak of
teach
καταγελάω . . 410
laugh to scorn
καταγινώσκω . 411
blame
condemn
κατάγνυμι . . 411
break
κατάγω . . . 411
bring
bring down
bring forth
bring to land
land
touch
καταγωνίζομαι . 411
subdue
καταδέω . 411
bind up
κατάδηλος . . 411
evident,
καταδικάζω . . 411
condemn
καταδιώκω . 411
follow after
καταδουλόω . . 411
bondage, bring into
καταδυναστεύω . 411
oppress
καταισχύνω . 411
ashamed, be
ashamed, make
confound
dishonour
shame

κατακαίω . . . 411
burn
burn up
burn, utterly

κατακαλύπτομαι . 411
cover

κατακαυχάομαι . 411
boast
boast against
glory
rejoice against

κατάκειμαι . . 411
keep
lie
sit at meat
sit down

κατακλάω or κα-
τακλάζω . . 411
break

κατακλείω . . 412
shut up

κατακληροδοτέω . 412
divided by lot

κατακλίνω . . 412
sit at meat
sit down
sit down, make

κατακλύζομαι . 412
overflowed, be

κατακλυσμός . . 412
flood

κατακολουθέω . 412
follow
follow after

κατακόπτω . . 412
cut

κατακρημνίζω . 412
cast down headlong

κατάκριμα . . 412
condemnation

κατακρίνω . . 412
condemn
damned, be

κατάκρισις . 412
condemn
condemnation

κατακυριεύω . . 412
dominion over, exercise
lords over, be
lordship, exercise
overcame

καταλαλέω . . 412
speak against
speak evil of

καταλαλία . . 412
backbitings
speakings, evil

κατάλαλος . . 412
backbiter

καταλαμβάνω . 412
apprehend
attain
come upon
comprehend
find
obtain
overtake
perceive
take

καταλέγομαι . 412
number, take into the

κατάλειμμα . . 412
remnant

καταλείπω . . 413
forsake
leave
reserve

καταλιθάζω . . 413
stone

καταλλαγή . . 413
atonement
reconciliation
reconciling

καταλλάσσω . . 413
reconcile

κατάλοιπος . . 413
residue

κατάλυμα . . 413
guestchamber
inn

καταλύω . . . 413
come to nought
destroy
dissolve
guest, be
lodge
overthrow
throw down

καταμανθάνω 413
consider

καταμαρτυρέω . 413
witness against

καταμένω . . 413
abide

καταμόνας . . 413
alone

κατανάθεμα . 413
curse

καταναθεματίζω 413
curse

καταναλίσκω . 413
consuming

καταναρκέω . . 413
burdensome, be
chargeable, be

κατανεύω . . 413
beckon

κατανοέω . . . 414
behold
consider
discover
perceive

καταντάω . . 414
attain
come

κατάνυξις . . 414
slumber

κατανύσσω . . 414
prick

καταξιόομαι . . 414
worthy, account
worthy, count

καταπατέω . 414
trample
tread
tread down
tread underfoot

κατάπαυσις . . 414
rest

καταπαύω . . 414
cease
give rest
rest
restrain

καταπέτασμα . 414
veil

καταπίνω . . 414
devour
drowned, be
swallow
swallow up

καταπίπτω . . 414
fall
fall down

καταπλέω . . 414
arrive

καταπονέομαι . 414
oppressed, be
vexed, be

καταποντίζομαι 414
drowned, be
sink

κατάρα . . . 414
curse
cursed
cursing

καταράομαι . . 414
curse

καταργέω . 415
abolish
cease
cumber

deliver
destroy
done away, be
effect, become of no
effect, make of none
effect, make without
fail
loose
nought, bring to
nought, come to
put away
put down
vanish away
void, make

καταριθμέομαι . 415
numbered with, be

καταρτίζω . . 415
fit
frame
join together, perfectly
mend
perfect
perfect, make
prepare
restore

κατάρτισις . . 415
perfection

καταρτισμός . . 415
perfecting

κατασείω . . . 415
beckon

κατασκάπτω . . 415
dig down
ruins

κατασκευάζω . . 415
build
make
ordain
prepare

κατασκηνόω . . 415
lodge
rest

κατασκήνωσις . 415
nest

κατασκιάζω . . 415
shadow

κατασκοπέω . 415
spy out

κατάσκοπος . . 415
spy

κατασοφίζομαι 415
deal subtilly with

καταστέλλω . 415
appease
quiet

κατάστημα . . 415
behaviour

καταστολή apparel	416	καταψύχω cool	417	κατηχεω inform instruct seach	418	καύχησις boasting glory, whereof I may glorying rejoicing	419
καταστρέφω overthrow	416	κατείδωλος idolatry, wholly given to	417				
καταστρηνιάζω wax wanton against, begin to	416	κατέναντι before over against	417	κατιόομαι cankered, be κατισχύω prevail	418 418	κεῖμαι appointed, be be laid up, be lay	419
καταστροφή overthrow subverting	416	κατενώπιον before presence, before the sight of, in the	417	prevail against κατοικέω dwell dwellers	418	lay up lie made, be set, be	
καταστρώννυμι overthrown	416			inhabitants inhabiters			
κατασύρω hale	416	κατεξουσιάζω authority, exercise	417	κατοίκησις dwelling	418	κειρίαι graveclothes	420
κατασφάττω slay	416	κατεργάζομαι cause do	417	κατοικητήριον habitation	418	κείρω shear shearer	420
κατασφραγίζομαι sealed, be	416	do deed perform work		κατοικία habitation	418	κέλευσμα shout	420
κατάσχεσις possession	416	work out		κατοπτρίζομαι behold as in a glass	418		
κατατίθημι do lay shew	416	κατέρχομαι came come down depart descend go down land	417	κατόρθωμα deeds, very worthy	418	κελεύω bid command commandment. at commandment, give	420
κατατομή concision	416			κάτω, κατωτέρω beneath bottom	418	κενοδοξία vainglory	420
ιατατοξεύομαι thrust through	416	κατεσθίω devour	417	down under		κενόδοξος desirous of vain glory	420
κατατρέχω run down	416	κατευθύνω direct guide	417	κατώτερος lower	419	κενός empty in vain vain	420
καταφάγω devour devour up eat up	416	κατεφίστημι insurrection against, make	417	καῦμα heat	419	κενοφωνία vain babblings	420
				καυματίζω scorch	419		
καταφέρω fall give sink down	416	κατέχω have (Joh. 5:4) hold hold fast keep keep in memory let make toward possess retain seize on stay take withhold	417	καῦσις burned, be	419	κενόω effect, make of none reputation, make of no vain, be in void, make	420
				καυσόω heat, with fervent	419		
καταφεύγω flee	416			καύσων heat heat, burning	419		
καταφθείρω corrupt perish, utterly	416			καυτηριάζομαι seared with a hot iron	419	κέντρον pricks sting	420
καταφιλέω kiss	416			καυχάομαι boast boast, make glory joy rejoice	419	κεντυρίων centurion	420
καταφρονέω despise	416	κατηγορέω accuse object	417			κενῶς vain, in	420
καταφρονητής despiser	416	κατηγορία accusation accused (Tit. 1:6)	418	καύχημα boasting glory of, to glory, (whereof) to glorying rejoice rejoicing	419	κεραία tittle	420
καταχέω pour	416					κεραμεύς potter	420
ιαταχθόνιος earth, under the	416	κατήγορος accuser	418			κεραμικυς potter, of a	421
ιαταχράομαι abuse	416	κατήφεια heaviness	418			κεράμιον pitcher	421

ιέραμος . . . 421	κινάμωμον . . 423	κληρόομαι . . 425	κυινόω . . . 426
tiling	cinnamon	inheritance, obtain an	common, call
			defile
κεράννυμι, κεράω 421	κινδυνεύω . . 423	κλῆρος . . . 425	pollute
fill	danger, be in	heritage	unclean
pour out	jeopardy, be in	inheritance	
	jeopardy, stand in	lot	κοινωνέω . . . 426
ιέρας . . . 421	κίνδυνος . . . 423	part	communicate
horn	peril		distribute
		κλῆσις . . . 425	partaker, be
κεράτιον . . 421	κινέω 423	calling	
husk	move	vocation	κοινωνία . . . 427
	mover (Acts 24:5)		communicate, to
κερδαίνω . . . 421	remove	κλητός . . . 425	communication
gain	wag	called	communion
gain, get			contribution
win	κίνησις . . . 423	κλίβανος . . . 425	distribution
	moving	oven	fellowship
κέρδος . . . 421			
gain	κλάδος . . . 423	κλῖμα 425	κοινωνικός . . 427
lucre	branch	part	communicate, willing
		regions	to
κέρμα . . 421	κλάζω, κλάω . 423		
money	break	κλίνη 425	κοινωνός . . . 427
		bed	companion
κερματιστής . . 421	κλαίω 423	table	fellowship
changer of money	bewail		partaker
	weep	κλινίδιον . . . 426	partner
κεφάλαιον . . 421		couch	
sum	κλάσις . . . 424		κοίτη 427
	breaking	κλίνω 426	bed
κεφαλαιόω . . 421		bow	chambering
wound in the head	κλάσμα . . . 424	bow down	conceive
	broken	far spent, be	
ςεφιλή . . . 421	fragments	lay	κοιτών . . . 427
head		turn to flight	chamberlain
	κλανθμός . . . 424	wear away	
εφαλίς . . . 422	wailing		κόκκινος & τὸ κόκ-
volume	weeping	κλισία . . . 426	κινον . . . 427
	wept (Acts 20:37)	company	scarlet
κῆνσος . . . 422			scarlet colour
tribute	κλείς . . . 424	κλοπή . . . 426	scarlet coloured
	key	theft	
κῆπος . . . 422			κόκκος . . . 427
garden	κλείω 424	κλύδων . . . 426	corn
	shut	raging	grain
ιηπουρός . . . 422	shut up	wave	
gardener			κολάζομαι . . 427
	κλέμμα . . . 424	κλυδωνίζομαι . 426	punish
κηρίον . . . 422	theft	toss to and fro	
honeycomb			κολακεία . . . 427
	κλέος . . . 424	κνήθω 426	flattering
κήρυγμα . . . 422	glory	itching	
preaching			κόλασις . . . 427
	κλέπτης . . . 424	κοδράντης . . . 426	punishment
κήρυξ . . . 422	thief	farthing	torment
preacher			
	κλέπτω . . . 424	κοιλία 426	κολαφίζω . . . 427
τηρύσσω . . . 422	steal	belly	buffet
preach		womb	
preacher	κλῆμα . . . 424		κολλάω . . . 427
proclaim	branch	κοιμάομαι . . 426	cleave
publish		asleep, be	join
	κληρονομέω . . 425	asleep, fall	join self
κῆτος . . . 423	heir, be	dead, be	keep company
whale	heirs of. shall be (with	sleep	
	μελλω, Heb. 1:14)	sleep, fall on	κολλούριον . . 427
κιβωτός . . . 423	inherit		eyesalve
ark	inheritance, obtain by	κοίμησις . . . 426	
		rest, taking of	κολλυβιστής . 427
κιθάρα . . 423	κληρονομία . 425		changer
harp	inheritance	κοινός 426	moneychanger
		common	
ιθαρίζω . . . 423	κληρονόμος . 425	defiled	κολοβόω . . . 427
harp	heir	unclean	shorten
ιθαρῳδο- . . 423		unholy	
harper			

κυβερνητης . . 436	hinder	have	put forth
master	keep from	hold	say
shipmaster	let	obtain	say on (Acts 14:18)
κυκλόθεν . . 436	suffer, not	receive	sayings (Acts 14:18)
about	withstand	receive, should after	shew
round about	κώμη 442	(Heb. 11:8)	speak
κυκλόω . . . 436	town	take	tell
compass	village	take away	
compass about	κωμόπολις . . 442	take up	λεῖμμα . . . 458
round about, come	town	λαμπάς . . . 447	remnant
round about, stand	κῶμος . . . 442	lamp	λεῖος . . . 458
κύκλῳ . . . 436	revelling	light	smooth
round about | round	rioting	torch	λείπω . . . 458
κυλίομαι . . 436	κώνωψ . . . 442	λαμπρός . . 447	destitute, be
wallow	gnat	bright	lack
κύλισμα . . 436	κωφός . . . 442	clear	wanting, be
wallowing	deaf	gay	λειτουργέω . . 458
κυλλός . . . 436	dumb	goodly	minister
maimed	speechless	gorgeous	λειτουργία . . 458
κῦμα . . . 436		white	ministration
wave	λαγχάνω . . 442	λαμπρότης . . 447	ministry
κύμβαλον . . 436	lot be, his	brightness	service
cymbal	lots, cast	λαμπρῶς . 447	λειτουργικός . . 459
κύμινον . . 436	obtain	sumptuously	ministering
cummin	λάθρα . . . 443	λάμπω . . . 447	λειτουργός . . 459
κυνάριον . . 436	privily	give light	minister
dog	secretly	shine	ministered
κύπτω . . . 436	λαῖλαψ . . . 443	λανθάνω . . 447	λίντιον . . 459
stoop	storm	hid, be	towel
stoop down	tempest	ignorant of, be	λεπίς . . . 459
κυρία . . . 436	λακέω . . . 443	unawares	scale
lady	burst asunder	λαξευτός . . 447	λέπρα . . . 459
κυριακός . . 436	λακτίζω . . . 443	hewn in stone	leprosy
Lord's	kick	λαός . . . 447	λεπρός . 459
κυριεύω . . . 436	λαλέω . . . 443	people	leper
dominion over, have	preach	λάρυγξ . . 448	λεπτόν . . 459
lord	say	throat	mite
Lord of, be	speak	λατομέω . . 448	λευκαίνω . . 459
lordship over, exercise	speak after	hew	white, make
κύριος . . . 436	talk	λατρεία . . 448	whiten
God	tell	divine service	λευκός . . . 459
Lord	utter	service	white
master	λαλιά . . . 445	λατρεύω . . 449	λέων . . . 459
owner	saying	serve	lion
Sir	speech	service, do the	λήθη 459
κυριότης . . 442	λαμά or λαμμᾶ . 445	worship	forget (with λαμβανω,
dominion	lama	worshippers	2 Pet. 1:9)
government	λαμβάνω . . 445	λάχανον . . 449	λῆνός . . . 459
κυρόω . . . 442	accept	herb	winepress
confirm	amazed, be (with εκ-	λεγεών . . 449	winepress (with οινος)
κύων . . . 442	στασις)	legion	λῆρος . . . 459
dog	assay	λέγω . . . 449	idle tales
κῶλον . . . 442	attain	ask	λῃστής . . . 459
carcase	bring	bid	robber
	call, when I (2 Ti. 1:5)	boast	thief
	catch	call	
	come on	describe	λῆψις . . . 460
κωλύω . . 442	come unto (Acts 24:27)	give out	receiving
forbid	forget (with ληθη, 2 Pet.	name	
	1:9)		

λίαν . . . 460
chiefest, very (with
ὑ-ερ, 2 Cor. 11:5)
exceeding
great
greatly
sore
very

λίβανος . . . 460
frankincense

λιβανωτόν . . 460
censer

λιθάζω . . . 460
stone

λίθινος . . . 460
stone, of

λιθοβολέω . . 460
stone
stones, cast

λίθος 460
millstone
stone
stumblingstone
stumblingstone (with
προσκομμα)

λικμάω . . . 460
grind to powder

λιμήν 461
haven

λίμνη 461
lake

λιμός 461
dearth
famine
hunger

λίνον 461
flax
linen

λιπαρός . . . 461
dainty

λίτρα 461
pound

λίψ 461
south west

λογία 461
collection
gathering

λογίζομαι . . 461
account
account of
conclude
count
despise (with ουδεν,
Acts 19:27)
esteem
impute
imputed, shall be (with
μελλω, Ro. 4:24)

lay
number
reason
reckon
suppose
think
think on

λογικός . . . 461
reasonable
word, of the

λόγιον . . 461
oracle

λόγιος . . 461
eloquent

λογισμός . . . 461
imagination
thought

λογομαχέω . . 461
strive about words

λογομαχία . . 461
strife of words

λόγος . . . 462
account
cause
communication
concerning (Phi. 4:15)
doctrine
fame
have to do (Heb. 4:13)
intent
matter
mouth
none of these things
move me (with ποιεω,
ουδεις, Acts 20:24)
preaching
question
reason
reckon (with συναιρω,
Mat. 25:19)
rumour

saying
shew
speaker (Acts 14:12)
speech
talk
thing
tidings
treatise
utterance
word
work

λόγχη . . 464
spear

λοιδορέω . . 464
revile

λοιδορία . . 464
railing
reproachfully

λοίδορος . . . 464
railer
reviler

λοιμός . . . 464
pestilence
pestilent

το λοιπόν, ὁ λοι-
πόν, & λοιπόν 464
besides
finally
from henceforth
furthermore
henceforth
moreover
now
remaineth, it (with εστι)
then

λοιπός . . . 464
other
remain, which
remnant
residue
rest

τοῦ λοιποῦ . . 465
from henceforth

λουτρόν . . . 465
washing

λούω 465
wash

λύκος . . . 465
wolf

λυμαίνομαι . 465
havock, make

λυπέω . . 465
grief, cause
grieve
heaviness, be in
sorrow
sorrowful, be
sorry, be
sorry, make

λύπη . . . 465
grief
grievous (Heb. 12:11)
grudgingly (with εκ, 2
Cor. 9:7)
heaviness
sorrow

λύσις . . . 465
loosed, to be

λυσιτελεῖ . . 465
better, be

λύτρον . . . 465
ransom

λυτρόω . . . 465
redeem
redeemed, should have
(Lu. 24:31)

λύτρωσις . . 465
redeemed (with οιεω
Lu. 1:68)
redemption

λυτρωτής . . . 465
deliverer

λυχνία . . . 465
candlestick

λύχνος . . . 466
candle
light

λύω 466
break, break down
break up
destroy
dissolve
loose
melt
put off
unloose

μαγεία . . . 466
sorcery

μαγεύω . . . 466
sorcery, use

μάγος . . . 466
sorcerer
wise man

μαθητεύω . . . 466
disciple, be
instruct
teach

μαθητής . . 466
disciple

μαθήτρια . . 468
disciple

μαίνομαι . . . 468
beside self, be
mad, be

μακαρίζω . . 468
blessed, call
happy, count

μακάριος . . 468
blessed
happier
happy

μακαρισμός . . 469
blessedness

μάκελλον . . . 469
shambles

μακράν . . . 469
afar off
far
far off
good way off
great way off

μακρόθεν . . . 469
afar off
from far

ascend, shall (with ἀναβαίνω, Rev. 17: 8)	μεμβρανα . . 480 parchment	particular
be	μέμφομαι . . 480 find fault	particularly (with κατα, Heb. 9:5)
begin, shall		partly (with τις, 1 Cor. 11:18)
betrayed, shall be, and should betray (with παραδίδωμι, Joh. 6: 71)	μεμψίμοιρος . . 480 complainer	parts
		piece
	μέν . . . 480 even	portion
come, to	indeed	respect
come, shall (with ἐρχομαι)	so	side
come, that which is to	some	some sort
come, things to	truly	somewhat
come, which was for to (with ερχομαι, Mat. 11:14)	verily	μεσημβρία . . 483 noon
	μενοῦνγε . . . 481	south
delivered, shall be (with παραδίδωμι, Lu. 9: 44)	nay but yea doubtless	μεσιτεύω . . . 483 confirm
	yea rather	μεσίτης . . . 483
devour, shall (with εσθιω, Heb. 10:27)	yes verily	mediator
	μέντοι . . . 481	μεσονύκτιον . . 483
drink, shall (with πινω, Mat. 20:22)	but | howbeit likewise	midnight
fulfilled, shall be (with συντελεω, Mar. 13:4)	nevertheless yet	μέσος . . . . 483 among
hear, shall (with ακουω, Mat. 24:6)	μένω . . . . 481 abide	before them (Mat 14:6) between
heirs of, shall be (with κληρονομεω, Heb. 1. 14)	continue dwell	forth (with εις, Mar.3:3) midday
hereafter, which should imputed, shall be (with λογιζομαι, Ro. 4:24)	endure present, be remain	midnight midst
intend	stand	way
led into, was to be (with εισαγω, Acts 21:37)	tarry tarry for	μεσότοιχον . . 484 middle wall
mean	thine own (Acts 5:4)	μεσουράνημα . . 484
mind	μέριμνα . . . 482 care	midst of heaven
pass, shall come to (with γινομαι)	μεριμνάω . . 482	μεσόω . . . 484 about midst, be
pass, was to (with διερχομαι, Lu. 19:4)	care care, have	μεστός . . . 484 full
point, be at the	careful, be	μεστόω . . . 484
ready	take thought	fill
ready, be		μετά 484
return (with υποστρεφω, Acts 13:34)	μερίζω . . 482 deal	after
revealed, shall be (with αποκαλυπτω, Ro. 8: 18 ; 1 Pet. 5:1)	difference between, be distribute divide	afterward afterward (with ταυτα) again, that he (Lu.9:39)
shall	give part	against
should		among
smite, shall (with τυπτω, Acts 23:3)	μερίς . . . . 482 part	and (John 3:25)
suffer shall (with πασχω, Rev. 2:10)	partakers (Col. 1:12)	follow (with εστι, Mat. 27:62)
tarry	μερισμός . . . 483	follow (with ταυτα, 1 Pet. 1:11)
time to come	dividing asunder gift	followed (with εστι, Mat. 27:62)
which was for		hence
will	μεριστή, . . . 483 divider	hereafter
would		hereafter (with ταυτα)
yet, be	μέρος . . . 483 behalf	in
	coast	joyfully (with χαρα, Heb. 10:34)
μέλος . . . 479 member	course craft	...ly

of
on
ou. (with ἡμων, 1 Joh. 4:17)
setting, and (Mat. 27: 66)
since
to
together (with αλληλων, Lu. 23:12)
unto
upon
when
with
without (with ου, Acts 5:26)
μεταβαίνω . . 487 depart go pass remove
μεταβάλλομαι . 487 change mind
μετάγω . . . 487 turn about
μεταδίδωμι . . 487 give impart
μετάθεσις . . . 487 change removing translation
μεταίρω . . . 488 departed
μετακαλέομαι . 488 call call for call hither
μετακινέω . . 488 move away
μεταλαμβάνω . 488 eat have partaker, be receive take
μετάληψις . . 488 received (1 Ti. 4:3)
μεταλλάττω . . 488 change
μεταμέλομαι . . 488 repent repent self
μεταμορφόομαι . 488 changed, be transfigured, be transformed, be
μετανοέω . . 488 repent

μετάνοια . . 488
repentance

μεταξύ . . 488
between
mean while
next

μεταπέμπω . . 488
call for
send for

μεταστρέφω . . 489
pervert
turn

μετασχηματίζω . 489
change
transfer, in a figure
transform
transform self

μετατίθημι . . 489
carry over
change
remove
translate
turn

μετέπειτα . . 489
afterward

μετέχω . . 489
partaker, be
pertain
take part
use

μετεωρίζομαι . 489
doubtful mind, be of

μετοικεσία . 489
brought (Mat. 1:12)
carried away to (Mat. 1:11)
carrying away into

μετοικίζω . . 489
carry away
remove into

μετοχή . . 489
fellowship

μέτοχος . . 489
fellow
partaker
partner

μετρέω . . 489
measure
mete

μετρητής . . 489
firkin

μετριοπαθέω . . 489
compassion, have

μετρίως . . 489
little, a

μέτρον . . 489
measure

μέτωπον . . 489
forehead

μέχρι & μέχρις . 490
till
to
until
unto

μή 490
any
but
but that
cannot (with δύναμαι)
forbear (1 Cor. 9:6)
God forbid (with γίνομαι)
lack (with εχω)
lack (with πάρειμι, 2 Pet. 1:9)
lest
neither
never
no
no (with τις)
no wise, in (Lu. 13:11)
none
none (with τις)
nor
not
nothing
nothing (with τις)
that not
untaken
untaken away (with ανακαλυπτω)
without

ἐὰν μή . . 494
before (Joh. 7:51)
but
except
if no
if not
not
whosoever not
whosoever ... not (with ὁς)

ἵνα μή . . . 495
albeit not
lest
that no
that not
that nothing

μηδαμῶς . . 496
not so

μηδέ 496
neither
no not
nor
nor yet
not
not once
not so much as

μηδείς, μηδεμία,
μηδέν . . . 496
any
any man
any thing
no
no man
none
not
not a whit
not any
not at all
nothing
without any delay (with αναβολη, ποιεω, Acts 25:17)

μηδέποτε . . . 497
never

μηδέπω . . . 497
not yet

μηκέτι . . . 497
any longer
henceforth
hereafter
no henceforward
no longer
no more
no
not any more
not henceforth

μὴ οὐκ & οὐ μή . 497
neither...nor
never (with εις, αιων)
never (with πωποτε, Joh. 6:35)
never (with ποτε, 2 Pet. 1:10)
not

μήποτε or μή ποτε 497
if peradventure
lest
lest at any time
lest haply
no at all
whether or not

μήπω 497
not yet

μήπως or μή πως 497
lest by any means
lest by some means
lest haply
lest perhaps
lest [they]

μήτε 497
neither
nor
or
so much as

μήτι 498
how much more
not

μήτις or μή τις . 498
any
any man

οὐ μή . . . 498
any means, by
at all
neither
never
no
no at all
no case, in
no means, by
no wise, in
nor ever
not
not at all
not in any wise

μῆκος 499
length

μηκύνομαι . . 499
grow up

μηλωτή . . . 499
sheepskin

μήν 499
month

μηνύω . . . 499
shew
tell

μηρός 499
thigh

μήτηρ . . . 499
mother

μήτρα . . . 500
womb

μητραλῴης . . 500
murderer of mothers

μία, fem. to εἷς . 500
a
agree (with ποιεω, γνωμη, Rev 17:17)
certain, a
first
one
other (Mat. 24:41)

μιαίνω . . . 500
defile

μίασμα . . . 500
pollution

μιασμός . . . 500
uncleanness

μίγμα . . . 500
mixture

μίγνυμι . . . 500
mingle

μικρόν . . . 501
little, a

little while, a while, a		μνημονεύω	503	μονόομαι desolate, be	506	μύριοι ten thousand	511
μικρ-ός, -ότερος least less little small	501	mention, make mindful, be remember		μόνος alone only themselves, by	506	μύρον ointment	511
		μνημόσυνον memorial	503			μυστήριον mystery	511
μίλιον mile	501	μνηστεύομαι espouse	503	μονόφθαλμος eye, with one	506	μυωπάζω see afar off, cannot	512
μιμέομαι follow	501	μογιλάλος impediment in his speech, having an	503	μορφή form	506	μώλωψ stripe	512
μιμητής follower	501	μόγις hardly	503	μορφόομαι formed, be	506	μωμέομαι blame	512
μιμνήσκομαι mindful, be remember	501	μόδιος bushel	503	μόρφωσις form	506	μῶμος blemish	512
				μοσχοποίεω calf, make a	507	μωραίνω fool, become	512
μισέω hate hateful	501	μοί I me mine my	503	μόσχος calf	507	foolish, make savour, lose	
μισθαποδοσία recompence of reward	501			μόχθος painfulness travail	507	μωρία foolishness	512
μισθαποδότης rewarder	501	μοιχαλίς adulteress adulterous adultery	505	μοῦ I me	507	μωρολογία foolish talking	512
μίσθιος servant, hired	501	μοιχάομαι adultery, commit	505	mine mine own my		μωρός fool foolish foolishness (with ὁ, 1 Cor. 1:25)	512
μισθόομαι hire	502	μοιχεία adultery	505	μουσικός musician	511		
μισθός hire reward wages	502	μοιχεύω adultery, commit adultery, in	505	μυελός marrow	511	ναί even so surely truth	512
μίσθωμα hired house	502	μοιχός adulterer	505	μυέομαι instructed, be	511	verily yea yes	
μισθωτός hired servant hireling	502	μόλις hardly scarce scarcely work, much (with ἰσχύω, Acts 27:16)	505	μῦθος fable	511	ναός shrine temple	512
μνᾶ pound	502			μυκάομαι roar	511		
μνάομαι mindful, be remember remembrance (Lu. 1: 54) remembrance, come in remembrance, have in	502	μολύνω defile	505	μυκτηρίζομαι mocked, be	511	νάρδος spikenard	513
		μολυσμός filthiness	505	μυλικός millstone	511	ναυαγέω shipwreck, make shipwreck, suffer	513
				μύλος millstone	511		
μνεία mention remembrance	502	μομφή quarrel	505	μύλων mill	511	ναύκληρος ship, owner of a	513
		μονή abode mansion	505	μυριάς hundred thousand thou- sand (Rev. 9:16) innumerable company innumerable, innumerable multitude, innumerable ten thousand thousand, fifty (with πεντε) thousands	511	ναῦς ship	513
μνῆμα grave sepulchre tomb	502					ναύτης sailor shipman	513
		μονογενής only only begotten only child	505				
μνημεῖον grave sepulchre tomb	502					νεανίας young man	513
		μόνον alone but only	506			νεανίσκος young man	513
μνήμη remembrance	503			μυρίζω anoint	511	νεκρός dead	513

εκρόω . . . 514
dead, be
mortify

νεκρωσις . . 514
deadness
dying

νεος, νεώτερος . 514
new
young (man, woman)

νεοσσός . . . 514
young

νεότης . . . 514
youth

νεόφυτος . . 514
novice

νεύω 514
beckon

νεφέλη . . . 514
cloud

νέφος . . . 515
cloud

νερρύς . . . 515
reins

νεωκόρος . . 515
worshipper

νεωτερικός . 515
youthful

νή . . . 515
I protest bν

νήθω . . . 515
spin

νηπιάζω . . 515
child, be a

νήπιος . . . 515
babe
child
childish (with ὁς, 1 Cor. 13:11)

νησίον . . . 515
island

νῆσος . . . 515
island
isle

νηστεία . . 515
fast
fasting

νηστεύω . . . 515
fast

νῆστις . . . 515
fasting

νηφάλεος, & νεφά-
λιος . . . 515
sober
vigilant

νήφω . . . 515
sober, be
watch

νικάω . . . 515
conquer
overcome
prevail
victory, get the

νίκη . . . 516
victory

νῖκος . . . 516
victory

νιπτήρ . . . 516
bason

νίπτω . . . 516
wash

νοέω . . . 516
consider
perceive
think
understand

νόημα . . . 516
device
mind
thought

νόθος . . . 516
bastard

νομή . . . 516
eat (with εχω, 2 Tim. 2:17)
pasture

νομίζω . . . 516
suppose
think
wont, be

νομικός . . . 516
law, about the
lawyer

νομίμως . . . 516
lawfully

νόμισμα . . . 517
money

νομοδιδάσκαλος . 517
doctor of the law
teacher of the law

νομοθεσία . . 517
law, giving of the

νομοθετέω . . 517
establish
law, receive the

νομοθέτης . . 517
lawgiver

νομος . . . 517
law

νοσέω . . . 518
dote

νόσημα . . . 518
disease

νόσος . . . 518
disease
infirmity
sickness

νοσσιά . . . 518
brood

νοσσίον . . . 518
chicken

νοσφίζομαι . . 518
keep back
purloin

νότος . . . 518
south
south wind

νουθεσία . . . 518
admonition

νουθετέω . . . 519
admonish
warn

νουμηνία . . . 519
new moon

νουνεχῶς . . 519
discreetly

νοῦς . . . 519
mind
understanding

νύμφη . . . 519
bride
daughter in law

νυμφίος . . . 519
bridegroom

νυμφών . . . 519
bridechamber

νῦν . . . 519
henceforth
hence*forth*
hereafter (with ἀπὸ)
late, of
now
present
this
this time

τὰ νῦν or τανῦν 520
but now
now

νυνί . . . 520
now

νύξ . . . 520
midnight
night

νυστάζω . . . 521
slumber

νύττω . . . 521
pierce

νυχθήμερον . 521
night and a day

νωθρός . . . 52
dull
slothful

νῶτος . . . 52
back

ξενία . . . 52
lodging

ξενίζω . . . 521
entertain
lodge
strange
strange, think it

ξενοδοχέω . . 521
strangers, lodge

ξένος . . . 521
host
strange
stranger

ξέστης . . . 521
pot

ξηραίνω . . . 521
dry up
pine away
ripe, be
wither
wither away

ξηρός . . . 522
dry
land
withered

ξύλινος . . . 522
wood, of

ξύλον . . . 522
staff
stocks
tree
wood

ξυράω . . . 522
shave

ὅδε, ἥδε, τόδε . 522
he
she
such
these
thus

ὅ ἐστι 522
called
make, which
that is
that is to say
which is

ὁ ὢν καὶ ὁ ἦν καὶ
ὁ ἐρχόμενος 522
which art, and wast, and art to come
which art, and wast, and shalt be

which is, and which was,
and which is to come
which was, and is, and is
to come

ὀγδοήκοντα . . 522
fourscore

ὄγδοος . . . 522
eighth

ὄγκος . . . 522
weight

ὀδεύω . . . 523
journey

ὁδηγέω . . . 523
guide
lead

ὁδηγός . . . 523
guide
leader

ὁδοιπορέω . . . 523
go on a journey

ὁδοιπορία . . . 523
journey
journeying

ὁδός 523
highway
highway (Mat. 22:9)
journey
way

ὀδούς . . . 523
tooth

ὀδυνάομαι . . 524
sorrow
tormented, be

ὀδυνή 524
sorrow

ὀδυρμός . . . 524
mourning

ὄζω 524
stink

ὅθεν 524
thence, from
whence
whence, from
where
whereby
wherefore
whereupon

ὀθόνη 524
sheet

ὀθόνιον . . . 524
linen clothes

οἰκεῖος . . . 524
house, those of his own
houshold, of the

οἰκέτης . . . 524
servant
servant, houshold

οἰκέω . . . 524
dwell

οἴκημα . . . 524
prison

οἰκητήριον . . . 524
habitation
house

οἰκία 524
home
house
houshold

οἰκιακός . . . 525
houshold, them of
houshold, they of [his
own]

οἰκοδεσποτέω . . 525
house, guide the

οἰκοδεσπότης . . 525
goodman
house, goodman of the
house, master of the
housholder

οἰκοδομέω . . 525
build
build up
builder
building, be in
edify
embolden

οἰκοδομή . . . 525
building
edification
edify, wherewith one
may (Ro. 14:19)
edifying

οἰκονομέω . . 526
steward, be

οἰκονομία . . 526
dispensation
edifying
stewardship

οἰκονόμος . . 526
chamberlain
governor
steward

οἶκος 526
home
house
household
temple

οἰκουμένη . . . 527
earth
world

οἰκουρός . . 527
home, keeper at

οἰκτείρω, οἰκτειρέω 527
compassion on, have

οἰκτιρμός . . 527
mercy

οἰκτίρμων . . 527
merciful
mercy, of tender

οἶμαι 527
suppose

οἰνοπότης . . 527
winebibber

οἶνος 527
wine
winepress (with ληνος)

οἰνοφλυγία . . 527
wine, excess of

οἴομαι . . . 527
suppose
think

οἷος . . . 527
as
manner of, what
so as
such as
what
which

ὀκνέω 528
delay

ὀκνηρός . . . 528
grievous
slothful

ὀκταήμερος . . 528
eighth day

ὀκτώ 528
eight
eighteen (with δεκα)

ὄλεθρος . . . 528
destruction

ὀλιγόπιστος . . 528
little faith, of

ὀλίγος . . . 528
almost (with εν)
briefly
few
little
little, a
long (with ουκ)
season, a
short (s. space)
small
while, a

ὀλιγόψυχος . . 528
feebleminded

ὀλιγωρέω . . 528
despise

ὀλοθρευτής . . 528
destroyer

ὀλοθρεύω . . . 528
destroy

ὁλοκαύτωμα . . 528
burnt offering
burnt offering, whole

ὁλοκληρία . . 528
soundness, perfect

ὁλόκληρος . . 528
entire
whole

ὀλολύζω . . . 529
howl

ὅλος . . . 529
all
altogether
every whit
throughout
throughout (with δια,
Joh. 19:23)
whole

ὁλοτελής . . . 529
wholly

ὄλυνθος . . . 529
untimely fig

ὅλως . . . 529
at all
commonly
utterly

ὄμβρος . . . 529
shower

ὁμιλέω . . . 529
commune
talk

ὁμιλία . . . 530
communication

ὅμιλος . . . 530
company

ὄμμα 530
eye

ὄμνυμι, ὀμνύω . 530
swear

ὁμοθυμαδόν . . 530
accord, with one
mind, with one

ὁμοιάζω . . . 530
agree

ὁμοιοπαθής . . 530
passions, of like
passions, subject to like

ὅμοιος . . . 530
like
like manner (with
τροπος, Jude 7)

ὁμοιότης . . 530
like as
similitude

ὁμοιόω . . . 530
like, be
like, make
liken
likeness, in the
resemble

ὁμοίωμα . . . 531
  like to, made (Ro. 1:23)
  likeness
  shape
  similitude

ὁμοίως . . . 531
  likewise
  so

ὁμοίωσις . . . 531
  similitude

ὁμολογέω . . . 531
  confess
  confession is made
  give thanks
  profess
  promise

ὁμολογία . . . 531
  confession
  professed
  profession

ὁμολογουμένως . 531
  controversy, without

ὁμότεχνος . . 531
  craft, of the same

ὁμοῦ 531
  together

ὁμόφρων . . . 531
  mind, of one

ὅμως 531
  and even
  nevertheless
  though but

ὄναρ 531
  dream

ὀνάριον . . . 532
  ass, young

ὀνειδίζω . . . 532
  cast in teeth
  reproach
  reproach, suffer
  revile
  upbraid

ὀνειδισμός . . 532
  reproach

ὄνειδος . . . 532
  reproach

ὄνημι 532
  joy, have

ὀνικός 532
  millstone

ὄνομα 532
  called
  name
  named
  surname (with ἐπιτιθη-
  μι, Mar. 3:16, 17)

ὀνομάζω . . . 533
  call
  name

ὄνος 534
  ass

ὄντως 534
  certainly
  clean
  indeed
  truth, of a
  verily

ὄξος 534
  vinegar

ὀξύς 534
  sharp
  swift

ὀπή 534
  cave
  place

ὄπισθεν . . . 534
  after
  backside
  behind

ὀπίσω 534
  after
  back
  backward
  behind
  behind, get
  follow (with δεῦτε)

ὅπλα 534
  armour
  instruments
  weapon

ὁπλίζομαι . . 534
  arm self

ὁποῖος 534
  manner of, what
  sort, of what
  as
  whatsoever

ὁπότε 534
  when

ὅπου 535
  place, in what
  where
  whereas
  wheresoever
  wheresoever
  whither
  whithersoever

ὀπτάνομαι . . 535
  seen, be

ὀπτασία . . . 535
  vision

ὄπτομαι . . . 535
  appear
  look
  see
  shew himself

ὀπτός 536
  broiled

ὀπώρα 536
  fruit

ὅπως 536
  because
  how
  so that
  that
  to
  when

ὅραμα 536
  sight
  vision

ὅρασις 536
  look upon
  sight, in
  vision

ὁρατός 536
  visible

ὁράω 536
  behold
  perceive
  see
  take heed

ὀργή 537
  anger
  indignation
  vengeance
  wrath

ὀργίζομαι . . 537
  angry, be
  wroth, be

ὀργίλος . . . 537
  angry, soon

ὀργυιά 537
  fathom

ὀρέγομαι . . . 537
  covet after
  desire

ὀρεινός . . . 537
  hill

ὄρεξις 537
  lust

ὀρθοποδέω . . 537
  uprightly, walk

ὀρθός 537
  straight
  upright

ὀρθοτομέω . . 537
  divide, rightly

ὀρθρίζω . . . 538
  morning, come early in
  the

ὀρθρινός . . . 538
  morning

ὄρθριος . . . 538
  early

ὄρθρος 538
  morning, early in the

ὀρθῶς 538
  plain
  right
  rightly

ὅρια 538
  border
  coast

ὁρίζω 538
  declare
  determinate (Acts 2:23)
  determine
  limit
  ordain

ὁρκίζω 538
  adjure
  charge

ὅρκος 538
  oath

ὁρκωμοσία . . 538
  oath

ὁρμάω 538
  run
  run violently
  rush

ὁρμή 538
  assault

ὅρμημα . . . 538
  violence

ὄρνεον 538
  bird
  fowl

ὄρνις 538
  hen

ὁροθεσία . . . 538
  bound

ὄρος 538
  hill
  mount
  mountain

ὀρύσσω . . . 539
  dig

ὀρφανός . . . 539
  comfortless
  fatherless

ὀρχέομαι . . . 539
  dance

ὁσάκις 539
  as oft as
  as often as

ὅσιος 539
  holy
  mercies
  shalt be

ὁσιότης . . . 539	
holiness	
ὁσίως . . . 539	
holily	
ὀσμή . . . 539	
odour	
savour	
ὅσος . . . 539	
all	
all that	
as	
as long as	
as many as	
as much as	
how great	
how many	
how much	
*i*nasmuch as	
so many as	
that	
that ever	
the more	
those things	
what	
what great	
what ... soever	
whatsoever	
wherewith soever	
which	
while (Heb. 10:37)	
who	
whosoever	
ὀστέον . . . 540	
bone	
ὅστις . . . 540	
and	
and they	
as	
he that	
in that they	
such as	
that	
they that	
they which	
what	
whatsoever	
whereas ye	
which	
who	
whosoever	
ὀστράκινος . . 541	
earth, of	
earthen	
ὄσφρησις . . . 541	
smelling	
ὀσφύς . . . 541	
loin	
ὅταν . . . 541	
as long as	
as soon as	
that	

till (with εἰ μή. Mark 9:9)	
when	
whensoever	
while	
ὅτε . . 542	
after	
after that	
as soon as	
that	
when	
while	
ὅτι . . . 543	
as concerning that	
as though	
because	
because that	
for	
for that	
how	
how that	
in that	
that	
though	
why	
ὅτου, for οὗτινος 552	
whiles	
οὗ . . . 552	
where	
wherein	
whither	
whither*soever*	
οὐ, οὐκ, οὐχ . . 552	
cannot (with δυναμαι)	
cannot (with εστι, Heb. 9:5)	
cannot (with εχω)	
cannot (with ισχυω, Lu. 16:3)	
cannot be (with ενδεχεται, Lu. 13:33)	
cannot contain (with εγκρατευομαι)	
cannot tell (with ειδεω)	
long (with ολιγος)	
nay	
neither	
never	
no	
no (with πας)	
no man (2 Cor. 11:10)	
none	
none (with τις)	
nor	
not	
nothing	
nothing (with πας)	
nothing (with πας, ῥημα, Lu. 1:37)	
nothing (with τις)	
special (with τυγχανω, Acts 19:11)	
unworthy	
unworthy (with αξιος)	
when (Heb. 3:9)	

without (with μετα, Acts 5:26)	
yet but (with πλειων)	
οὐά or οὐαί . . 563	
all	
οὐαί . . . 563	
alas	
woe	
οὐδαμῶς . . 563	
not	
οὐδέ . . . 564	
also not	
even not	
neither	
neither	
never	
no	
no more	
no nor	
no not	
no so much as	
nor	
nor yet	
not	
not even	
nothing (with τις, 1 Tim. 6:7)	
so much as	
then not	
οὐδέποτε . 565	
neither at any time	
never	
no*thing* at any time	
nothing...at any time (with πας)	
οὐδέπω . . . 565	
as yet not	
never before	
never yet	
not yet	
yet	
οὐδείς . . 565	
any	
any man	
man	
neither any	
neither any thing	
never	
never man, yet (with πωποτε, Lu. 19:30)	
never...to any man (with πωποτε)	
no	
no man	
none	
none of these things move me (with ποιεω, λογος, Acts 20:24)	
not	
not any	
not at all	
nothing	
nought	
ought	

οὐκέτι or οὐκ ἔτι. 566	
after that	
after that not	
any more	
henceforth not	
hereafter not	
no longer	
no more	
not any more	
not as yet	
not now	
now no more	
now not	
yet	
yet not	
οὐκοῦν . . 567	
then	
οὖν . . 567	
and	
and so	
truly	
but	
now	
now then	
so	
likewise	
so then	
then	
therefore	
verily	
wherefore	
οὔπω . . . 571	
as yet	
hitherto not	
no as yet	
not yet	
οὐρά . . . 571	
tail	
οὐράνιος . . 571	
heavenly	
οὐρανόθεν . . 571	
heaven, from	
οὐρανός . . 571	
air	
heaven	
heaven*ly*	
sky	
οὖς . . . 573	
ear	
οὐσία . . 573	
goods	
substance	
οὔτε . . . 573	
neither	
no not	
none	
nor	
nor yet	
not	
nothing	
yet not	

οὗτος . . . 574	guilty, be	παγίς . . . 582	πάλαι . . . 583

οὗτος . . . 574
he
he it was that
it (Mat. 6:16)
the same
this
this man
this same
who

οὗτος, from οὗτος 575
such as
the same
these
they
this

αὕτη, fem. sing. of
οὗτος . . . 576
hereof
she
the same
this
this woman
which

αὗται, fem. plur. of
οὗτος . . . 576
these

οὕτω, οὕτως . . 576
after that
after this manner
as
even
even so
for all that
like [so]
likewise
manner, in this
no more
no more [so]
on this fashion
on this wise
so
so in like manner
thus
what

οὐχί 578
nay
not

ὀφειλέτης . . . 578
debtor
owed, which
sinner

ὀφειλή . . . 578
debt
due

ὀφείλημα . . 579
debt

ὀφείλω . . . 579
behove
bound, be
debt
debtor, be
due
duty, be

guilty, be
indebted, be
must needs
need
ought
owe
should

ὄφελον . . . 579
God, would to
would

ὄφελος . . . 579
advantageth
profit

ὀφθαλμοδουλεία . 579
eyeservice

ὀφθαλμός . . 579
eye
sight

ὄφις . . . 580
serpent

ὀφρύς . . . 580
brow

ὀχλέομαι . . 580
vexed, be

ὀχλοποιέω . . 580
gather a company

ὄχλος . . . 580
company
multitude
number
number of people
people
press

ὀχύρωμα . . . 581
strong hold

ὀψάριον . . 581
fish
small fish

ὀψέ 581
at even
even
in the end

ὀψία . . . 581
even
evening
eventide

ὄψιμος . . . 581
latter

ὄψις . . . 582
appearance
countenance
face

ὀψώνιον . . 582
charges
wages

παγιδεύω . . 582
entangle

παγίς . . . 582
snare

πάθημα . . . 582
affections
affliction
motion
suffering

παθητός . . . 582
suffer

πάθος . . . 582
affection
inordinate affection
lust

παιδαγωγός . 582
instructer
schoolmaster

παιδάριον . . 582
child
lad

παιδεία . . . 582
chastening
chastisement
instruction
nurture

παιδευτής . . 582
corrected, which
instructor

παιδεύω . . . 582
chasten
chastise
instruct
learn
teach

παιδιόθεν . . 582
child, of a

παιδίον . . . 582
child
child, little
child, young
damsel

παιδίσκη . . . 583
bondmaid
bondwoman
damsel
maid
maiden

παίζω . . . 583
play

παῖς . . . 583
child
maid
maiden
manservant
servant
son
young man

παίω 583
smite
strike

πάλαι . . . 583
any while
great while ago, a
long ago
old
old, of
time past, in

παλαιός . . 583
old

παλαιότης . . 583
oldness

παλαιόω . . 583
decay
old, make
wax old

πάλη 583
wrestle (with εστι, Eph.
6:12)

παλιγγενεσία . 583
regeneration

πάλιν . . . 583
again

παμπληθεί . . 584
all at once

πάμπολυς . . . 585
very great

πανδοχεῖον . . 585
inn

πανδοχεύς . . 585
host

πανήγυρις . . 585
general assembly

πανοικί . . . 585
with all house

πανοπλία . . 585
armour, all
armour, whole

πανουργία . . 585
craftiness
craftiness, cunning
subtilty

πανοῦργος . . 585
crafty

πανταχόθεν . . 585
every quarter, from

πανταχοῦ . . 585
places, in all
where, every

παντελές . . 585
in no wise [altogether]
uttermost

πάντη . . 585
always

πάντοθεν . . . 585
round about
side, on every

παντοκράτωρ . . 585
Almighty
Omnipotent

παντοτε . . . 585
alway
always
ever
evermore

πάντως . . . 585
all means, by
altogether
at all
needs
no doubt
no wise, in (lit. not at all)
surely

παρά 586
above
against
among
at
before
by
contrary to
friends, his (with αυτου, Mar. 3:21)
from
give, such things as they (with τα, αυτων, Lu. 10:7)
had, that she (with αυτου)
his (lit. of him)
in
more than
nigh unto
of
of
past
save
side,...by
sight of, in the
than
therefore
with

παραβαίνω . . 587
transgress
transgression, by

παραβάλλω . . 587
arrive
compare

παράβασις . . 587
breaking
transgression

παραβάτης . 587
breaker
transgress
transgressor

παραβιάζομαι . 587
constrain

παραβολή . . 587
comparison

figure
parable
proverb

παραβουλεύομαι. 588
regard, not to
regarding, not

παραγγελία . 588
charge
command

παραγγέλλω . . 588
charge
charge, give in
command
commandment, give
declare

παραγίνομαι. . 588
come
go
present, be

παράγω . . 588
depart
pass
pass away
pass by
pass forth

παραδειγματίζω . 588
example, make a public
shame, put to an open

παράδεισος . . 589
paradise

παραδέχομαι. . 589
receive

παραδιατριβή . 589
perverse disputing

παραδίδωμι . . 589
betray
betrayed, shall be, and should betray (with μελλω, Joh. 6:71)
bring forth
cast into prison
commit
deliver
deliver up
delivered, shall be (with μελλω, Lu. 9:44)
give
give over
give up
hazard
prison, put in
recommend

παράδοξος . . 590
strange

παράδοσις . . 590
ordinance
tradition

παραζηλόω . . 590
provoke to emulation
provoke to jealousy

παραθαλάσσιος . 590
sea coast, upon the

παραθεωρέω . . 590
neglect

παραθήκη . . 590
committed unto

παραινέω . . . 590
admonish
exhort

παραιτέομαι . 590
avoid
excuse
excuse, make
intreat
refuse
reject

παρακαθίζω . . 590
sit

παρακαλέω . . 590
beseech
call for
comfort
comfort, be of good
desire
exhort
exhortation
exhortation, give
intreat
pray

παρακαλύπτω . 591
hide

παρακαταθήκη . 591
committed to trust, that which is
committed unto, that thing which is

παράκειμαι . . 591
present, be

παράκλησις . . 591
comfort
consolation
exhortation
intreaty

παράκλητος . . 591
advocate
comforter

παρακοή . . . 591
disobedience

παρακολουθέω . 591
attain
follow
fully know
understanding, have

παρακούω . . . 591
neglect to hear

παρακύπτω . . 591
look
look
stoop down

παραλαμβάνω . 591
receive
take
take unto
take with | take up

παραλέγομαι. . 592
pass
sail by

παράλιος . . . 592
sea coast

παραλλαγή . . 592
variableness

παραλογίζομαι . 592
beguile
deceive

παραλύομαι . . 592
feeble
palsy, sick of the
palsy, taken with

παραλυτικός . . 592
palsy, sick of the
palsy, that had the

παραμένω. . . 592
abide
continue

παραμυθέομαι 592
comfort

παραμυθία 592
comfort

παραμύθιον . . 592
comfort

παρανομέω . . 592
contrary to the law

παρανομία . . 592
iniquity

παραπικραίνω . 592
provoke

παραπικρασμός 592
provocation

παραπίπτω . . 592
fall away

παραπλέω . . 592
sail by

παραπλήσιον. . 592
nigh unto

παραπλησίως . 593
likewise

παραπορεύομαι 593
go
pass
pass by

παράπτωμα 593
fall
fault
offence
sin
trespass

παμαρρύεω . . 593 let slip	παρείσακτος . . 594 brought in, unawares	prove provide shew	boldness boldness of speech confidence
παράσημος . . 593 whose sign was	παρεισδύνω . . 594 creep in unawares	stand stand before	freely openly
παρασκευάζω . 593 prepare self ready, be ready, make	παρεισέρχομαι 594 come in privily enter	stand by stand here stand up stand with	plainly plainness παρρησιάζομαι . 596
παρασκευή . . 593 preparation	παρεισφέρω . 594 give	yield παρίεμαι . . . 595	bold, be boldly freely
παρατείνω . 593 continue	παρεκτός . . 594 except saving	hang down πάροδος . . 595	preach boldly speak boldly wax bold
παρατηρέω . 593 observe watch	without παρεμβολή . . 594 army	way παροικέω . . . 595 sojourn in	πᾶς, πᾶσα, πᾶν . 597 all all manner of
παρατήρησις . . 593 observation	camp castle	stranger, be a παροικία . . 595	all means, by (with ἐν, 2 Th. 3:16) alway (with ἡμερι)
παρατίθημι . 593 allege commend commit commit the keeping of put forth set before	παρενοχλέω . . 594 trouble παρεπίδημος . . 594 pilgrim stranger παρέρχομαι . . 594	sojourning strangers, as (Acts 13: 17) πάροικος . . 595 foreigner sojourn stranger	always always (with δια) any any one as many as daily
παρατυγχάνω . 593 meet with	come come forth go	παροιμία . . . 596 parable	ever (with αιων, Jude 25) every
παραυτίκα . . 593 moment, but for a	pass pass away pass by	proverb παρομοιάζω . . 596 like unto, be	every one every way no (with ουκ)
ταραφέρω . . . 593 remove take away	pass over past transgress	παρόμοιος . . 596 like	nothing (with ουκ) nothing(with ουκ, ῥημα Lu. 1:37)
παραφρονέω . . 593 as a fool	πάρεσις . . . 595 remission	πάροινος . . . 596 given to wine	nothing...at any time (with ουδεποτε) throughly
παραφρονία . . 593 madness	παρέχω . . . 595 bring	παροίχομαι . . 596 past	whatsoever whole
παραχειμάζω . 593 winter	do give keep	παροξύνομαι . . 596 provoked, be easily stirred, be	whosoever πάσχα . . . 605 Easter
παραχειμασία . 594 winter in	minister offer	παροξυσμός . . 596 contention, a sharp	Passover πάσχω . . . 605
παραχρῆμα . 594 forthwith immediately presently straightway soon	shew trouble (with κοπος) παρηγορία . . 595 comfort	provoke unto παροργίζω . . 596 anger provoke to wrath	feel passion suffer suffer,shall(with μελλω, Rev. 2:10) vex
ἀρδαλις . . 594 leopard	παρθενία . . 595 virginity παρθένος . . . 595	παροργισμός . . 596 wrath	πατάσσω . . . 606 smite
ἱρειμι . . . 594 come have (Heb. 13:5) here, be lack (with μη, 2 Pet. 1:9) present present, be here	virgin παριστάνω . . 595 yield παρίστημι . 595 assist bring before come commend	παροτρύνω . . 596 stir up παρουσία . . . 596 coming presence πασοψίς . . . 596 platter	strike πατέω . . . . 606 tread tread down tread under foot πατήρ . . . 606 father parent
παρεισάγω . . 594 privily bring in	present presently give	ταιδησία . . 596 bold boldly	πατραλῴης 609 urderers of fathers

τατριά	. . .	609

family
kindred
lineage

πατριάρχη.   609
patriarch

πατοικός . . . 609
fathers, of

πατρίς . . . 609
country
own country

πατροπαράδοτος . 609
received by tradition
from father

πατρῷος . . . 609
father, of

παύομαι . . 609
cease
leave
refrain

παχύνομαι . . 609
wax gross

πέδη . . . 609
fetter

πεδινός . . . 609
plain

πεζεύω . . 609
go afoot

πεζῇ . . . 609
afoot
foot, on

πειθαρχέω . . 609
hearken
obey
obey magistrates

πειθός . . 609
enticing

πείθω πέποιθα . 609
agree
assuie
believe
confidence, have
confident, be
confident, wax
friend, make
obey
persuade
trust
yield

πεινάω . . . 610
hungred, be an
(hungry, hunger)

πεῖρα 610
assaying
trial

πειράζω . . . 610
assay
examine

---

go about
prove
tempt
tempter
try

πειρασμός . 610
temptation
try (1 Pet. 4:12)

πειράω . . 611
assay
go about

πεισμονή . . 611
persuasion

πέλαγος . . . 611
depth
sea

πελεκίζομαι . . 611
beheaded, be

πέμπτος . . . 611
fifth

πέμπω . . . 611
send
send again (with προσ-
τιθημι, Lu. 20:11, 12)
thrust in

πένης 611
poor

πενθερά . . . 611
mother in law
wife's mother

πενθερός . . . 612
father in law

πενθέω . . . 612
bewail
mourn
wail

πένθος . . . 612
mourning
sorrow

πενιχρός . . . 612
poor

πεντάκις . . . 612
five times

πεντακισχίλιοι . 612
five thousand

πεντακόσιοι . . 612
five hundred

πέντε 612
fifty thousand (with
μυριας)
five

πεντεκαιδέκατος . 612
fifteenth

πεντήκοντα . . 612
fifty

πεντηκοστη . . 612
Pentecost

πεποίθησις . . 612
confidence
trust

πέρ .   612
whomsoever
whomsoever (with ὁς,
Mark 15:6)

πέραν 613
beyond
farther side
other side
over

πέρας 613
end
utmost part
uttermost part

περί 613
about
above
against
as touching
at
behalf, on
company, and his (with
οἱ, Acts 13:13&21:8)
concern, which
concerning
concerning, as
estate (with τα, Col.
4:8)
for
how it will go with
(with τα, Phi. 2:23)
in
manner of, such (with
τουτου)
of
on
over
pertaining
pertaining to
sake, for
state (with τα, Phi. 2:
19, 20)
thereabout (with τουτ-
τον, Lu. 24:4)
thereof (Mat. 12:36)
touching
whereby (with ὁς, Acts
19:40)
wherein
whereof (with ἡς, Heb.
2:5)
whereof (with τις, 1 Tim.
1:7)
with

περιάγω . . . 615
compass
go about
lead about

περιαιρέω . . . 615
take away
take up

περιαστράπτω . 615
shine round
shine round about

περιβάλλω . . 615
array
cast about
clothe
clothed me
put on

περιβλέπω . . 616
look about on
look round about
look round about on

περιβόλαιον . . 616
covering
vesture

περιδέομαι . . 616
bound about, be

περιεργάζομαι . 616
busybody, be a

περίεργος . . . 616
busybody
curious

περιέρχομαι . . 616
fetch a compass
vagabond
wandering about

περιέχω . . . 616
astonished (with θαμ-
βος, Lu. 5:9)
contain
manner, after this (lit.
having this form)

περιζώννυμι . 616
gird
gird about
gird self

περίθεσις . . 616
wearing

περιΐστημι . . 616
avoid
shun
stand by
stand round about

περικάθαρμα . . 616
filth

περικαλύπτω . . 616
blindfold
cover
overlay

περίκειμαι . . 616
bound with, be
compassed with, be
hang about

περικεφαλαία . 616
helmet

περικρατής . . 616
come by

περικρύπτω . . 616
hide

περικυκλόω . . 616
compass round

περιλάμπω . . 616
shine round about

περιλείπομαι . 617
remain

περίλυπος . . 617
sorrowful, exceeding
sorrowful, very
sorry, exceeding

περιμένω . . . 617
wait for

πέριξ . . . 617
round about

περιοικέω . . . 617
round about, dwell

περίοικος . . 617
neighbour

περιούσιος . . 617
peculiar

περιοχή . . . 617
place

περιπατέω . . 617
go
occupied, be
walk
walk about

περιπείρω . . . 618
pierce through

περιπίπτω . . 618
fall among
fall into

περιποιέομαι . . 618
purchase

περιποίησις . . 618
obtain
obtaining
peculiar
purchased possession
saving

περιρρήγνυμι . 618
rend off

περισπάομαι . . 618
cumbered, be

περισσεία . . . 618
abundance
abundantly
abundantly (with εις,
2 Cor. 10: 15)
superfluity

περίσσευμα . . 618
abundance
left, that was
over and above

περισσεύω . . 618
abound
abound, make
abound, more
abundance
abundance, have
abundance, have more
abundant
abundant, be more
better, be the
enough and to spare,
have
exceed
exceed (with πλειων,
Mat. 5: 20)
excel
increase
left, be
redound
remain
remain over and above

περισσός & περισ-
σότερος . . 618
abundant, more
abundantly exceed-
ing
abundantly, more
advantage
exceedingly
greater
highly, very
measure, beyond
more
more, much
overmuch
superfluous
vehemently

περισσότερον . . 618
abundantly, more
great deal, a
more, far

περισσοτέρως . . 618
abundant, more
abundantly, more
earnest, the more (Heb.
2: 1)
exceedingly
exceedingly, more
frequent, more
more, much
rather, the

περισσῶς . . . 619
exceedingly
measure, out of
more, the

περιστερά . . . 619
dove
pigeon

περιτέμνω . . 619
circumcise

περιτίθημι . . 619
bestow, upon

put about
put on
put upon
round about, hedge
(with φραγμος)
set about

περιτομή . . . 619
circumcised (Phi. 3: 5)
circumcision

περιτρέπω . . 619
mad, make (with μανια,
Acts 26: 24)

περιτρέχω . . 619
run through

περιφέρω . . . 619
bear about
carry about

περιφρονέω . . 619
despise

περίχωρος . . 619
country about
country round about
region round about
region that lieth round
about

περίψημα . . . 620
offscouring

περπερεύομαι . 620
vaunt self

πέρυσι . . . 620
a year ago

πετάομαι . . . 620
fly
flying

πετεινόν . . . 620
bird
fowl

πέτομαι . . . 620
fly

πέτρα . . . 620
rock

πέτρος . . . 620
stone

πετρώδης . . . 620
stony

πήγανον . . . 620
rue

πηγή 620
fountain
well

πήγνυμι . . 620
pitch

πηδάλιον . . 620
helm
rudder

πηλίκος . . . 620
how great
how large

πηλός . . . 620
clay

πήρα 620
scrip

πῆχυς . . . 621
cubit

πιάζω . . . 621
apprehend
catch
lay hand on
take

πιέζω 621
press down

πιθανολογίς . 621
enticing words

πικραίνω . . . 621
bitter, be
bitter, make

πικρία . . . 621
bitterness

πικρός 621
bitter

πικρῶς . . . 621
bitterly

πίμπραμαι . . 621
swollen, be
swollen, should have
(Acts 28: 6)

πινακίδιον . . 621
writing table

πίναξ 621
charger
platter

πίνω, πίω, πίομαι 621
drink
drink, shall (with
μελλω, Mat. 20: 22)

πιότης . . . 622
fatness

πιπράσκω . . . 622
sell

πίπτω, έπεσον . 622
fail
fall
fall down
light on

πιστεύω . . . 622
believe
believer
commit
trust, commit to
trust with, be put in

πιστικος . . . 624
spikenard

πιστις. 624
  assurance
  belief
  believe
  faith
  fidelity

πιστός 626
  believe
  believer
  believing
  faithful
  faithfully
  sure
  true

πιστόω . . . 627
  assured of, be

πλανάω . . . 627
  astray, go
  deceive
  err
  out of the way, be
  seduce
  wander

πλάνη 627
  deceit
  deceive, to
  delusion
  error

πλανήτης . . 627
  wandering

πλάνος . . . 627
  deceiver
  seducing

πλάξ 627
  table

πλάσμα . . . 627
  thing formed

πλάσσω . . . 627
  form

πλαστός . . . 627
  feigned

πλατεῖα . . . 627
  street

πλάτος . . . 627
  breadth

πλατύνω . . . 627
  broad, make
  enlarge

πλατύς . . . 627
  wide

πλέγμα . . . 627
  broidered hair

πλείων, πλεῖον or
  πλέον, πλεῖστος 627
  above (lit. of more than)
  exceed (with περισ-
  σεύω, Mat. 5:20)
  excellent. more

further
great, very
greater
greater part
long
longer
many
many, very
more
most
part, more
yet but (with ου)

πλέκω 628
  plait

πλεονάζω . . 628
  abound
  abundant
  increase, make to
  over, have

πλεονεκτέω . . 628
  advantage of, get an
  defraud
  gain, make a

πλεονέκτης . . 628
  covetous

πλεονεξία . 628
  covetous practices
  covetousness
  greediness

πλευρα 628
  side

πλέω 628
  sail

πληγή 628
  plague
  stripe
  wound
  wounded

πλῆθος . . 629
  bundle
  company
  multitude

πληθύνω . . . 629
  abound
  multiply

πλήθω . . . 629
  accomplish
  fill
  full...came
  furnish

πλήκτης . . 629
  striker

πλημμύρα . 629
  flood

πλήν . . 629
  but
  but rather
  except
  nevertheless

notwithstanding
save
than

πλήρης . . . 629
  full

πληροφορέω . . 630
  believed, be most surely
  known, be fully
  persuaded, be fully
  proof of, make full

πληροφορία . . 630
  assurance
  assurance, full

πληρόω . . . 630
  accomplish
  accomplish, should (Lu.
    9:31)
  after (Acts 24:27)
  complete
  complete, be
  end
  expire
  fill
  fill up
  fulfil
  full
  full come, be
  full forty years old
    (with χρονος, τεσσα-
    ρακονταετης, Acts
    7:23)
  full make
  fully preach
  perfect
  supply

πλήρωμα . . . 630
  fill up, which is put in to
  filled up, piece that
  fulfilling
  full
  fulness

πλησίον . . . 631
  near

ὁ πλησίον . . 631
  neighbour

πλησμονή . . 631
  satisfying

πλήσσω . . . 631
  smite

πλοιάριον . . 631
  boat
  ship, little
  ship, small

πλοῖον . . . 631
  ship
  shipping

πλόος 631
  course
  sailing
  voyage

πλούσιος . . . 631
  rich

πλουσίως . . 632
  abundantly
  richly

πλουτέω . . . 632
  increased with goods,
    be
  rich
  rich, be made
  rich, wax

πλουτίζω . . 632
  enrich
  rich, make

πλοῦτος . . . 632
  riches

πλύνω . . . 632
  wash

πνεῦμα . . . 632
  ghost
  Holy Ghost (with
    αγιος)
  life
  spirit
  spiritual
  spiritually
  spiritually minded, be
    (with φρονημα. Ro.
    8:6)
  wind

πνευματικός . . 635
  spiritual

πνευματικῶς . . 635
  spiritually

πνέω 635
  blow
  wind

πνίγω 635
  choke
  throat, take by the

πνικτός . . . 635
  strangled

πνοή 635
  breath
  wind

ποδήρης . . . 635
  garment down to the
    foot

πόθεν 635
  whence
  whence, from

ποιέω . . . 636
  abide
  agree (with μια, γνωμη,
    Rev. 17:17)
  appoint
  avenge
  band together (with
    συστροφη, Acts 23
    12)

be	ποικίλος . . . 640	altogether (lit. in much)		go, will (Joh. 7:35)		
bear	divers	common		journey		
bewray (with δηλος,	manifold	far (lit. by much)		journey, make a		
Mat. 26:73)	ποιμαίνω . . . 640	far passed		journey, take a		
bring	feed	far spent		walk		
bring forth	feed cattle	great		πορθέω . . . 647		
cast out (lit. made cast	rule	great age, be of a (with		destroy		
out)		προβαινω, ἡμερα,		waste		
cause	ποιμήν . . . 640	Lu. 2:36)				
commit	pastor	great deal		πορισμός . . . 647		
content (with ἱκανος,	shepherd	great while		gain		
Lu. 15:15)		greatly				
continue	ποίμνη . . . 640	long		πορνεία . . . 647		
deal	flock	many		fornication		
delay, without any (with	fold	much		πορνεύω . . . 648		
αναβολη, μηδεις,	ποιμνιον . . . 640	oft		commit		
Acts 25:17)	flock	oftentimes		fornication, commit		
do		plenteous		πόρνη . . . 648		
do, would (Joh. 6:6)	ποῖος . . . 640	sore		harlot		
doing	what	straitly		whore		
execute	what manner of					
exercise	which	πολύσπλαγχνος . 645		πύρνος . . . 648		
fulfil		pitiful, very		fornicator		
gain	πολεμέω . . . 641	πολυτελής . . 645		whoremonger		
give	fight	costly				
have	make war	great price, of		πόρρω, πορρωτέρω 648		
hold	war	precious, very		far		
journeying (Lu. 13:22)	πόλεμος . . . 641			further		
keep	battle	πολύτιμος . . 645		great way off, a		
lay wait (with ενεδρα,	fight	costly, very		πόρρωθεν . . . 648		
Acts 25:3)	war	great price, of		afar off		
lighten the ship (with	πόλις . . . 641	πολυτρόπως . . 645		πορφύρα . . . 648		
εκβολη, Acts 27:18)	city	in divers manners		purple		
make						
mean (Acts 21:13)	πολιτάρχης . . 642	πόμα . . . 645		πορφύρεος, πορφυ-		
none of these things	rulers of the city	drink		ρούς . . . 648		
move me (with λογος,	πολιτεία . . 642	πονηρία . . 645		purple		
ουδεις, Acts 20:24)	commonwealth	niquity		πορφυρόπωλις . 648		
observe	freedom	wickedness		seller of purple, a		
ordain						
perform	πολίτευμα . . 642	πονηρός . . . 646		πυσάκις . . . 648		
provide	conversation	bad		how oft		
purged, have (with κα-		evil		how often		
θαρισμος, Heb. 1:3)	πολιτεύομαι . . 642	evil (with ρημα, Mat.				
purpose	conversation be, let	5:11)		πόσις . . . 648		
put	live	grievous		drink		
raising up (with επι-	πολίτης . . 642	harm		πόσος . . 648		
συστασις, Acts 24:12)	citizen	lewd		how great		
secure (Mat. 28:14)		malicious		how long		
shew	πολλάκις . . 642	wicked		how many		
shoot out	oft	wicked, more		how much		
spend	often	wickedness (1 Joh. 5:		what		
take	oftentimes	19)				
tarry	ofttimes	πόνος . . . 646		ποταμός . . . 649		
transgress the law (with	πολλαπλασίων . 643	pain		flood		
ανομια, 1 Joh. 3:4)	manifold more			river		
work		πορεία . . 646		stream		
yield	πολυλογία . . 643	journeying		water		
ποίημα . . . 640	much speaking	way		ποταμοφόρητος . 649		
thing that is made	πολυμερῶς . . 643	πορεύομαι . . 646		carried away of the flood		
workmanship	at sundry times	depart		ποταπός . . . 649		
ποίησις . . . 640	πολυποίκιλος . 643	go		what		
deed	manifold	go away		what manner of		
ποιητής . . 640	πολύς . . . 643	go forth		ποτέ . . . 649		
doer	abundant	go one's way		aforetime		
poet		go up				

any time
at length
at the last
ever
how long (with ἕως)
in the old time
in time past
once
sometime
when

πότε . . . 649
at any time
never (with ου μη, 2 Pet. 1:10)
sometimes
when

πότερον . . 649
whether

ποτηριον . . 649
cup

ποτίζω . . . 649
drink, give to
drink, make to
feed
water

πότος . . . 650
banqueting

του . . . 650
about
certain place, a—in

πού . . . 650
where
whither

πούς . . . 650
foot
footstool

πρᾶγμα . . . 651
business
matter
thing
work

πραγματεία . . 651
affair

πραγματεύομαι . 651
occupy

πραιτώριον . . 651
hall, common
hall, judgment
hall of judgment
palace
prætorium

πράκτωρ . . . 651
officer

πρᾶξις . . . 651
deed
office
work

πρᾷος . . . 651
meek

πραότης . . . 651
meekness

πρασιά . . . 651
ranks, in

πράσσω, πράττω 651
commit
deeds
do
exact
keep
require
should do (Lu. 22:23)
use arts

πραΰς . . . 652
meek

πραΰτης . . . 652
meekness

πρέπει. . . . 652
become
comely

πρεσβεία . . . 652
ambassage
message

πρεσβεύω . . . 652
ambassador, be an

πρεσβυτέριον . 652
elder
elders, estate of
presbytery

πρεσβύτερος, -τέρι 652
elder | elder women
eldest
old men

πρεσβύτης . . 652
aged
aged man
old man

πρεσβῦτις . . 652
aged women

πρηνής . . . 652
headlong

πρίζω . . . 653
saw asunder

πρίν, πρὶν . . 653
before
before that
ere

πρό . . . 653
above
ago
before
before (Acts 13:24)
ever, or

προάγω . . . 653
bring forth
bring
brought, would have (Acts 12:6)
go before

προαιρέομαι . . 653
purpose

προαιτιάομαι . 653
prove, before

προακούω . . . 653
hear before

προαμαρτάνω . 653
sin already
sinned, heretofore

προαύλιον . . 653
porch

προβαίνω . . 653
age, be of a great (with ἡμερα, πολυς, Lu. 2:36)
go farther
go on
stricken, be well

προβάλλω . . 653
put forward
shoot forth

προβατικός . . 654
sheep
sheep [market]

πρόβατον . . . 654
sheep
sheepfold (with αυλη, Joh. 10:1)

προβιβάζω . 654
draw
instruct, before

προβλέπω . . 654
provide

προγίνομαι . . 654
past, be

προγινώσκω . . 654
foreknow
foreordain
know
know before

πρόγνωσις . . 654
foreknowledge

πρόγονοι . . . 654
forefathers
parent

προγράφω . . 654
ordain, before
set forth, evidently
write
write afore
write aforetime

πρόδηλος . . . 654
evident
manifest beforehand
open beforehand

προδίδωμι . . 654
give, first

προδότης . . . 654
betrayer
traitor

πρόδρομος . . 654
forerunner

προειδέω . . . 654
foresee
see before

προελπίζω . . 654
trust, first

προέπω . . 654
forewarn
speak before
tell in time past

προενάρχομαι . 654
begin
begin before

προεπαγγέλλομαι 655
promise afore

προερέω . . . 655
foretel
say before
speak before
tell before

προέρχομαι 655
go before
go farther
go forward
outgo
pass on

προετοιμάζω . . 655
ordain, before
prepare, afore

προευαγγελίζομαι 655
preach before the gospel

προέχομαι . . 655
better, be

προηγέομαι . . 655
prefer

πρόθεσις . . . 655
purpose
shewbread

προθεσμία . . 655
time appointed

προθυμία . . . 655
forwardness of mind
readiness
readiness of mind
ready mind
willing mind

πρόθυμος . . . 655
ready
willing

προθύμως . . 655
of a ready mind

προΐστημι . . 655
maintain

over, be
rule

προκαλέομαι . . 655
provoke

προκαταγγέλλω . 655
foretell
notice before, have
shew, before

προκαταρτίζω . 655
beforehand, make up

πρόκειμαι . . 655
first, be
set before
set forth

προκηρύσσω . . 655
preach, before
preach, first

τροκοπή . . 655
furtherance
profiting

προκόπτω . . . 656
increase
proceed, shall
profit
spent, be far
wax

πρόκριμα . . . 656
prefer one before an-
other

προκυρόομαι . . 656
confirm before

προλαμβάνω . . 656
come aforehand
overtake
take before

προλέγω . . . 656
foretell
tell before

προμαρτύρομαι . 656
testify beforehand

προμελετάω . . 656
meditate before

προμεριμνάω . . 656
thought beforehand,
take

προνοέω . . . 656
provide
provide for

ποόνοια . . . 656
providence
provision

προοράω . . . 656
foresee
see before

προορίζω . . . 656
determine before
ordain
predestinate

προπάσχω . . 656
suffer before

προπέμπω . . 656
accompany
bring forward on jour-
ney
bring on journey
bring on way
conduct forth

προπετής . . . 656
heady
rashly

προπορεύομαι . 656
go before

πρός 656
about
according to
against
among
at
because of
before
between
by
for
house, at thy (Mat. 26:
18)
in
intent, for
nigh unto
of
pertain to, which
that
this end that, to
to
together (with αλλη-
λων, Lu. 24:14)
toward
unto
whereby (with o)
with
within
you-ward, to
you-ward, to (with
ὑμας)

προσάββατον . 661
day before the sabbath,
the

προσαγορεύομαι . 661
call

προσάγω . . . 661
bring
draw near

προσαγωγή . . 662
access

προσαιτέω . . 662
beg

προσαναβαίνω 662
go up

προσαναλίσκω 662
spend

προσαναπληρόω . 662
supply

προσανατίθημι . 662
add, in conference
confer

προσαπειλέομαι . 662
threaten, further

προσδαπανάω . 662
spend more

προσδέομαι . . 662
need

προσδέχομαι . . 662
accept
allow
look for
receive
take
wait for

προσδοκάω . . 662
expect
expectation, be in
look
look for
looked when
tarry
wait for

προσδοκία . 662
expectation
looking after

προσεάω . . . 662
suffer

προσεγγίζω . . 662
come nigh

προσεδρεύω . . 662
wait at

προσεργάζομαι . 662
gain

προσέρχομαι . . 662
as soon as come
come
come unto
comers thereunto (Heb.
10:1)
consent
draw near
go
go near
go to
go unto

προσευχή . . 663
pray earnestly (with
προσευχομαι, Jas. 5:
17)
prayer

προσεύχομαι . . 663
pray
pray earnestly (with
προσευχη, Jas. 5:17)
pray for
prayer, make

προσέχω . . . 664
attend unto
attendance at, give
attendance to, give
beware
given to, be
heed, give
heed, take
heed, to give
heed to, take
heed unto, give
regard, to have

προσηλόω . . 664
nail to

προσήλυτος . . 664
proselyte

πρόσκαιρος . . 664
dureth for a while
endure but for a time
season, for a
temporal

προσκαλέομαι . 664
call
call to
call unto
called for

προσκαρτερέω . 665
attend continually upon
continue
continue in
continue instant in
continue stedfastly
continue with
give selves continually
wait on
wait on continually

προσκαρτέρησις . 665
perseverance

προσκεφάλαιον . 665
pillow

προσκληρόομαι . 665
consort with

πρυσκλισις . . 665
partiality

προσκολλάομαι . 665
cleave to
join self
joined, be

πρόσκομμα . . 665
offence
stumbling
stumblingblock
stumblingstone
stumblingstone (with
λιθος)

προσκοπή . . 665
offence

προσκόπτω . . 665
beat upon
dash

stumble	increase	προτάσσομαι . . 668	morning
stumble at	lay	appoint, before	morning, in the
προσκυλίω . . 665	proceed further	προτείνω . . . 668	πρωΐα 670
roll	send again (with πεμ-	bind	early
roll to	πω, Lu. 20:11, 12)		morning
	speak to any more	πρότερον, τὸ πρό-	
προσκυνέω . . 665		τερον . . . 668	πρώϊμος . . . 670
worship	προστρέχω . . 667	before	early
	run	first	
προσκυνητής . 666	run thither to	first, at the	πρωινός . . . 670
worshipper	run to	former	morning
προσλαλέω . . 666	προσφάγιον . . 667	πρότερος . . . 668	πρῶρα . . . 670
speak to	meat	former	forepart
speak with			foreship
	πρόσφατος . . 667	προτίθημι . . 668	
προσλαμβάνω . 666	new	purpose	πρωτεύω . . . 670
receive		set forth	preeminence, have the
take	προσφάτως . . 667		
take unto	lately	προτρέπομαι . . 668	πρωτοκαθεδρία . 671
taken, having		exhort	seat, chief
πρόσληψις . . 666	προσφέρω, προσήν-	προτρέχω . . 668	seat, highest
receiving	εγκα . . . 667	outrun	seat, uppermost
	bring	run before	
προσμένω . . 666	bring to		πρωτοκλισία . . 671
abide still	bring unto	προϋπάρχω . . 668	room, chief
be with	deal with	before, be	room, highest
cleave unto	do	beforetime, be	rooms, uppermost
continue in	offer		
continue with	offer unto	πρόφασις . . . 668	πρῶτον & τὸ πρῶ-
tarry	offer up	cloke	τον 671
	present unto	colour	before
προσορμίζομαι . 666	put to	pretence	beginning, at the
draw to the shore		shew	chiefly
	προσφιλής . . 667		first
προσοφείλω . . 666	lovely	προφέρω . . . 668	first, at
owe besides		bring forth	first, at the
	προσφορά . . . 667	offer to	first of all
προσοχθίζω . . 666	offering		
grieved with, be	offering up	προφητεία . . 668	πρῶτος . . . 671
		prophecy	before
πρόσπεινος . . 666	προσφωνέω . . 667	prophesying	beginning
hungry, very	call unto		best
	speak to	προφητεύω . . 669	chief
προσπήγνυμι . 666	speak unto	prophesy	chiefest
crucify			first
	πρόσχυσις . . 667	προφήτης . . . 669	first of all
προσπίπτω . . 666	sprinkling	prophet	former
beat upon			
fall	προσψαύω . . 667	προφητικός . . 670	πρωτοστάτης . . 672
fall down at	touch	prophecy, of	ringleader
fall down before		prophets, of the	
	προσωπολημπτέω . 667		πρωτοτόκια . 672
προσποιέομαι . 668	respect to persons, have	προφῆτις . . 670	birthright
make as though		prophetess	
	προσωπολήπτης . 667		πρωτότοκος . . 672
προσπορεύομαι . 666	respecter of persons	προφθάνω . . 670	firstbegotten
come unto		prevent	firstborn
	προσωποληψία . 667		
προσρήγνυμι . 666	respect of persons	προχειρίζομαι . 670	πταίω 672
beat vehemently, a-		choose	full
gainst	πρόσωπον . . 667	make	offend
beat vehemently upon	appearance		stumble
	before	προχειροτονέομαι 670	
προστάσσω . . 666	before (2 Cor. 8:24)	choose before	πτέρνα . . . 672
bid	countenance		heel
command	face	πρύμνα . . . 670	
	fashion	hinder part (of the ship)	πτερύγιον . . 672
προστάτις . . 666	men's persons	stern	pinnacle
succourer	outward appearance		
	person	πρωΐ 670	πτέρυξ . . . 672
προστίθημι . . 666	presence	early	wing
add		early in the morning	
give, more			

πτηνόν	672	πυρέσσω	674	ῥάβδος	676	ῥίζα	678
bird		fever, be sick of a		rod		root	
				sceptre			
πτοέομαι	672	πυρετός	674	staff		ῥιζόομαι	678
terrify		fever				rooted, be	
				ῥαβδοῦχος	676		
πτόησις	672	πυρινός	674	serjeant		ῥιπή	678
amazement		fire, of				twinkling	
				ῥαδιούργημα	676		
πτύον	672	πυρόομαι	674	lewdness		ῥιπίζομαι	678
fan		burn				tossed, be	
		fiery		ῥαδιουργία	676		
πτύρομαι	672	fire, be on		mischief		ῥίπτω	678
terrify		try				cast	
				ῥακά	676	cast down	
πτύσμα	672			Raca		cast off	
spittle		πυρράζω	674			cast out	
		red, be		ῥάκος	676	scatter abroad	
πτύσσω	672			cloth		throw	
close		πυρρός	674				
		red		ῥαντίζω	676		
πτύω	672			sprinkle		ῥοιζηδόν	678
spit		πύρωσις	674			noise, with great	
		burning		ῥαντισμός	676		
πτῶμα	672	fiery trial		sprinkling		ῥομφαία	678
body, dead						sword	
carcase		πωλέω	674	ῥαπίζω	676		
corpse		sell		smite		ῥύμη	678
		sold, whatsoever is		smite with the palm of		lane	
πτῶσις	673			the hand		street	
fall		πῶλος	675	ῥάπισμα	677		
		colt		palm of the hand		ῥυπαρία	678
πτωχεία	673			smite with the hand		filthiness	
poverty		πώποτε	675	(with διδωμι)		ῥυπαρός	678
		at any time		strike with the palm of		vile	
πτωχεύω	673	never (with ου μη, Joh.		hand [see lit.]		ῥύπος	678
poor, become		6:35)				filth	
		never...to any man		ῥαφίς	677		
πτωχος	673	(with ουδεις)		needle		ῥυπόω	678
beggar		yet never man (with				filthy, be	
beggarly		ουδεις, Lu. 19:30)		ῥέδα	677		
poor				chariot		ῥύσις	678
		πωρόω	675			issue	
πυγμῇ	673	blinded, be		ῥέω	677		
oft		harden		flow		ῥυτίς	678
						wrinkle	
πυκνός	673	πώρωσις	675	ῥέω	677		
often		blindness		command		ῥύομαι	678
oftener		hardness		make		deliver	
				say		deliverer	
πυκτεύω	673	πώς	675	speak			
ught		haply		speak of		ῥώννυμαι	679
		means, by any				farewell	
πύλη	673	means, by some		ῥῆγμα	677		
gate		perhaps		ruin			
						σαβαχθανί	679
πυλών	673	πῶς	675	ῥήγνυμι, ῥήσσω	677	sabacthani	
gate		how		break			
porch		manner, after what		break forth		σαβαώθ	679
		means, by what		burst		sabaoth	
πυνθάνομαι	673	that		rend			
ask				tear ǀ throw down		σαββατισμός	679
demand						rest	
enquire				ῥῆμα	677		
enquire, would (Acts		ῥαββί	676	evil (with πονηρος, Mat.		σάββατον, σάβ-	
23:20)		Master		5:11)		βατα	679
understand		Rabbi		nothing		sabbath	
				nothing (with πας, ουκ,		sabbath day	
πῦρ	673	ῥαββονί, ῥαββουνί	676	Lu. 1:37)		week	
fiery		Lord		saying			
fire		Rabboni		word		σαγήνη	679
						net	
πυρά	674	ῥαββίζω	676	ῥήτωρ	678		
fire		beat		orator		σαίνω	679
		beat with rods				move	
πύργος	674			ῥητῶς	678		
tower				expressly		σάκκος	679
						sackcloth	

σαλεύω	. . .	679	thou	σηρικόν	. . .	685	offence	
move			thy house [see lit.]	silk			offend, things that	
shake			σεαυτοῦ, τῷ, τόν				stumblingblock	
shake together			also σαυτοῦ,	σῆς	. . .	685	σκάπτω	. . .	686
shaken, which cannot be			τῷ, τόν	. .	683	moth			dig	
stir up			thee	σητόβρωτος	. .	685	σκάφη	. . . .	686
σάλον	. . .	679	thine own self	motheaten			boat	
wave			thou thyself	σθενόω	.	685	σκέλος	.	686
σάλπιγξ	. . .	680	thy	strengthen			leg	
trump			thyself	σιαγών	. .	685	σκέπασμα	. .	686
trumpet			σεβάζομαι	. .	683	cheek			raiment	
σαλπίζω	. . .	680	worship	σιγάω	. .	685	σκευή	. . .	686
sound			σέβασμα	. . .	683	close, keep			tackling	
sound, which are yet to			devotion	peace, hold			σκεῦος	. .	686
(Rev. 8:13)			worshipped, that is	secret, keep			goods	
trumpet, sound a			σεβαστός	. . .	683	silence, keep			sail	
σαλπιστής	. .	680	Augustus'	σιγή	. .	685	stuff	
trumpeter			σέβομαι	. . .	683	silence			vessel	
σανδάλιον	. .	680	devout	σιδήρεος	. .	685	σκηνή	. . .	687
sandal			religious	iron			habitation	
σανίς	. . .	680	worship	iron, of			tabernacle	
board			σειρά	. . .	683	σίδηρος	. .	685	σκηνοπηγία	.	687
σαπρός	. . .	680	chain	iron			tabernacles	
bad			σεισμός	. . .	683	σικάριος	. .	685	σκηνοποιός	. .	687
corrupt			earthquake	murderer			tentmaker	
σάπφειρος	. .	680	tempest	σίκερα	. . .	685	σκῆνος	. .	687
sapphire			σείω	. . .	684	strong drink			tabernacle	
σαργάνη	. .	680	move	σιμικίνθιον	. .	685	σκηνόω	. . .	687
basket			quake	apron			dwell	
σάρδινος	. . .	680	shake	σίναπι	. . .	685	σκήνωμα	. .	687
sardine			σελήνη	. .	684	mustard seed			tabernacle	
σάρδιος	. . .	680	moon	σινδών	. .	685	σκιά	.	687
sardius			σεληνιάζομαι	. .	684	linen			shadow	
σαρδόνυξ	. . .	680	lunatic, be	linen cloth			σκιρτάω		687
sardonyx			σεμίδαλις	. .	684	linen, fine			leap	
σαρκικός	.	680	flour, fine	σινιάζω	. . .	685	leap for joy	
carnal			σεμνός	. . .	684	sift			σκληροκαρδία		687
fleshly			grave	σιτευτός	. . .	686	hardness of heart	
σάρκινος	. . .	680	honest	fatted			σκληρός		687
fleshy			σεμνότης	. .	684	σιτιστός	. .	686	fierce	
σάρξ	. . . .	680	gravity	fatling			hard	
carnal			honesty	σιτομέτριον	. .	686	σκληρότης	. .	687
carnally				portion of meat			hardness	
carnally minded, be			σημαίνω	. .	684	σῖτος	. . . .	686	σκληροτράχηλος	.	687
(with φρονημα, Ro.			signify	corn			stiffnecked	
8:6)			σημεῖον	. .	684	wheat			σκληρύνω	. . .	687
flesh			miracle	σιωπάω	. .	686	harden	
fleshly			sign	dumb			σκολιός	. . .	687
σαρόω	. . .	681	token	peace			crooked	
sweep			wonder	peace, hold			froward	
σάτον	. . .	681	σημειόομαι	. .	685	σκανδαλίζω	. .	686	untoward	
measure			note	offend			σκόλοψ	. . .	688
σβέννυμι	. .	681	σήμερον	. . .	685	offend, make to			thorn	
go out			day, this	σκάνδαλον	.	686	σκοπέω	. . .	688
quench			to-day	occasion of stumbling			consider	
σε	. . . . .	681	σήπω	. . .	685	occasion to fall			
thee			corrupted, be					

heed, take	thy	σπῖλος . . . 696	insurrection
look at	thy friends	spot	sedition
look on	σοῦ . . . 691	σπλάγχνα . . 696	standing (Heb. 9:8)
mark	home (Mark 5:19)	bowels	uproar
σκοπός . 688	thee	inward affection	στατήρ . . . 697
mark	thine	mercy, tender (with	money, piece of
σκορπίζω . . 688	thine own	ελεος, Lu. 1:78)	σταυρός . . . 697
disperse abroad	thou	σπλαγχνίζομαι . 696	cross
scatter	thy	compassion, have	σταυρόω . . . 697
scatter abroad	σουδάριον . . 694	compassion, be moved	crucify
σκορπίος . . 688	handkerchiefs	with	σταφυλή . . 698
scorpion	napkin	σπόγγος . . . 696	grapes
σκοτεινός . . 688	σοφία . . . 694	spunge	στάχυς . . 698
dark	wisdom	σποδός . . . 696	corn, ear of
darkness, full of	σοφίζω . . . 694	ashes	ear
σκοτία . . . 688	cunningly devised	σπορά . . . 696	στέγη . . 698
dark	make wise	seed	roof
darkness	σοφός . 694	σπόριμα . 696	στέγω . . 698
σκοτίζομαι . . 688	wise	corn	bear
darkened, be	σπαράσσω . . 695	corn field	forbear
σκοτόομαι . . 688	rend	σπόρος . . . 696	suffer
darkness, be full of	tear	seed	στεῖρα 698
σκότος 688	σπαργανόω . . 695	seed sown	barren
darkness	swaddling clothes,	σπουδάζω . . 696	στέλλομαι . . 698
σκύβαλον . . 688	wrap in	diligence, do	avoid
dung	σπάομαι . . . 695	diligence, give	withdraw self
σκυθρωπός . . 688	draw	diligent, be	στέμμα . . . 698
sad	draw out	endeavour	garland
sad countenance, of a	σπαταλάω . 695	forward, be	στεναγμός . . 698
σκύλλω . . . 688	pleasure, live in	labour	groaning
trouble	wanton, be	study	στενάζω . . . 698
trouble self	σπεῖρα . 695	σπουδαῖος . . 697	grief, with
σκῦλον . . . 688	band	diligent	groan
spoils	σπείρω . . . 695	diligent, more	grudge
	seed, receive	forward, more	sigh
σκωληκόβρωτος . 689	sow	σπουδαιότερον . 697	στενός . . . 698
eaten of worms	sower	diligently, very	strait
σκώληξ . . . 689	σπεκουλάτωρ . . 695	σπουδαίως,-οτέρως 697	στενοχωρέομαι . 698
worm	executioner	carefully, the more	distressed, be
σμαράγδινος . 689	σπένδομαι . 695	diligently	straitened, be
emerald	offered, be	instantly	στενοχωρία . . 698
σμάραγδος . 689	offered, be ready to be	σπουδή . . . 697	anguish
emerald	σπέρμα . . . 695	business	distress
σμύρνα . . . 689	issue	care	στερεός . . . 698
myrrh	seed	carefulness	stedfast
σμυρνίζομαι . . 689	σπερμολόγος . 696	diligence	strong
myrrh, be mingled with	babbler	earnest care	sure
σόι 689	σπεύδω . . . 696	forwardness	στερεόω . . . 698
thee	haste, make	haste	establish
thine own	haste unto	σπυρίς . . . 697	strength, receive
thou	haste, with	basket	strong, make
thy	σπήλαιον . . 696	στάδιος, στάδιον . 697	στερέωμα . . 698
σορός . . . 690	cave	furlong	stedfastness
bier	den	race	στέφανος . . 698
σός 690	σπιλάς . . . 696	στάμνος . 697	crown
thine	spot	pot	στεφανόω . . . 699
thine own	σπιλόω 696	στάσις 697	crown
	defile	dissension	
	spot		

στῆθος . . . 699	στρατολογέω . 701	συγκαλύπτομαι . 703	συζάω . . . 704
breast	soldier, choose to be a	cover	live with
στηκω . . . 699	στρατοπεδάρχης . 701	συγκάμπτω . . 703	συζευγνύω . . 704
stand	captain of the guard	bow down	join together
stand fast	στρατόπεδον . 701	συγκαταβαίνω . 703	συζητέω . . . 704
στηριγμός . 699	army	go down with	dispute
stedfastness	στρεβλόω . . 701	συγκατατίθεμαι . 703	dispute with
στηρίζω . . 699	wrest	consent	enquire
established	στρέφω . . 701	συγκατάθεσις . 703	question
fix	convert	agreement	question with
stablish	turn	συγκαταψηφίζομαι 703	reason
stedfastly set	turn again	numbered with, be	reason together
strengthen	turn back again	συγκεράννυμι . 703	συζήτησις . . 704
στίγμα . . . 699	turn self	mixed with, be	disputation
mark	turn self about	temper together	disputing
στιγμή . . . 699	στρηνιάω . . 701	συγκινέω . . . 703	reasoning
moment	live deliciously	stir up	συζητητής . . 704
στίλβω . . . 699	στρῆνος . . 701	συγκλείω . . 703	disputer
shining	delicacy	conclude	σύζυγος . . 704
στοά . . . 699	στρουθίον . 701	inclose	yokefellow
porch	sparrow	shut up	συζωοποιέω . . 704
στοιβάς . . 699	στρώννυμι, στρων-	συγκληρονόμος . 703	quicken together with
branch	νύω . . . 701	fellowheir	συκάμινος . . 704
στοιχεῖον . . 699	bed, make	heir together	sycamine tree
element	furnish	heir with	συκῆ . . 704
principle	spread	joint-heir	fig tree
rudiment	strew	συγκοινωνέω . 704	συκομωραία . . 705
στοιχέω . . 699	στυγητός . . 701	communicate with	sycomore tree
walk	hateful	fellowship with, have	σῦκον . . . 705
walk orderly	στυγνάζω . . 701	partaker of, be	fig
ρολή . . . 699	lower	συγκοινωνός . . 704	συκοφαντέω . 705
clothing, long	sad, be	companion	accusation, take by false
garment, long	στύλος . . 701	partake	accuse falsely
robe	pillar	partaker	συλαγωγέω . . 705
robe, long		partaker with	spoil
στόμα . . . 699	σύ . . . 701	συγκομίζω . . 704	συλάω . . . 705
edge	thou	carry	rob
face	συγγένεια . . 703	συγκρίνω . . 704	συλλαλέω . 705
mouth	kindred	compare among	commune with
στόμαχος . . 700	συγγενής . . 703	compare with	confer with
stomach	cousin	συγκύπτω . . 704	speak among
στρατεία . . 700	kin	bow together	talk with
warfare	kinsfolk	συγκυρία . . 704	συλλαμβάνω . 705
στράτευμα . . 700	kinsman	chance	catch
army	συγγνώμη . 703	συγχαίρω . . 704	conceive
soldier	permission	rejoice in	help
war, man of	συγκάθημαι . . 703	rejoice with	take
στρατεύομαι . . 700	sit with	συγχέω . . . 704	συλλέγω . . 705
soldiers	συγκαθίζω . . 703	stir up	gather
war	sit down together	συγχράομαι . . 704	gather together
warfare, go a	sit together, make	dealings with, have	gather up
στρατηγός . . 700	συγκακοπαθέω . 703	συγχύνω . . 704	συλλογίζομαι 705
captain	afflictions, be partaker	confound	reason with
magistrate	of	confuse	συλλυπέομαι . 705
στρατία . . 700	συγκακουχέομαι . 703	uproar, be in an	grieved, be
host	affliction with, suffer	σύγχυσις . . 704	συμβαίνω . 705
στρατιώτης . 700	συγκαλέω . 703	confusion	be
soldier	call together		

befall	συμπαρακαλέομαι 706	σύμφωνος . . 707
happen	comforted together, be	consent
happen, should (Mark	συμπαραλαμβάνω 706	συμψηφίζω . . 707
10:32)	take with	count
happen unto	συμπαραμένω . 706	σύμψυχος . . 707
συμβάλλω . . 705	continue with	of one accord
confer	συμπάρειμι . . 706	σύν . . . 707
encounter	present with, be here	beside
help		with
make	συμπάσχω . . 706	συνάγω . . . 708
meet with	suffer with	accompany (with ερχο-
ponder	συμπέμπω . . 706	μαι, Acts 11:12)
συμβασιλεύω . 705	send with	assemble
reign with		assemble selves
συμβιβάζω . . 705	συμπεριλαμβάνω 706	assemble together
compact	embrace	bestow
gather, assuredly	συμπίνω . . . 706	come together
instruct	drink with	gather
knit together		gather selves together
prove	συμπληρόω . . 706	gather up
συμβουλεύω . . 705	come	gathered together
consult	fill up	lead into
counsel	fully come	resort
counsel, give	συμπνίγω . . 706	take in
counsel, take	choke	συναγωγή . . 709
counsel together, take	throng	assembly
συμβούλιον . . 706	συμπολίτης . . 706	congregation
consultation	fellowcitizen	synagogue
council	συμπορεύομαι . 707	συναγωνίζομαι . 709
counsel	go with	strive together with
σύμβουλος . . 706	resort	συναθλέω . . . 709
counsellor	συμπόσιον . . 707	labour with
συμμαθητής . . 706	company	strive together for
fellowdisciple	συμπρεσβύτερος . 707	συναθροίζω . . 709
συμμαρτυρέω 706	elder, also an	call together
testify unto	συμφέρω . . . 707	gather together
witness, also bear	better for, be	συναίρω . . . 709
witness with, bear	bring together	reckon
συμμερίζομαι . 706	expedient, be	reckon (with λογος,
partaker with, be	expedient for, be	Mat. 25:19)
συμμέτοχος . . 706	good, be	take
partaker	profit	συναιχμάλωτος . 709
συμμιμητής . 706	profitable for, be	fellowprisoner
follower together	σύμφημι . . . 707	συνακολουθέω . 709
συμμορφόομαι . 706	consent unto	follow
conformable unto, be	συμφυλέτης . . 707	συναλίζομαι . . 709
made	countryman	assembled together, be
σύμμορφος . . 706	συμφύομαι . . 707	συναναβαίνω . 709
conformed to	spring up with	come up with
fashioned like unto	σύμφυτος . . . 707	συνανάκειμαι . 710
συμπαθέω . . 706	planted together	sit at the table with
compassion, have	συμφωνέω . . 707	sit down with
touched with a feeling	agree	sit together with
of, be	agree together	sit with
συμπαθής . . 706	agree with	sit with at meat
compassion one of ano-	συμφώνησις . 707	συναναμίγνυμι . 710
ther, having	concord	company, keep
συμπαραγίνομαι 706	συμφωνία . . 707	company with
come together	musick	company with, have
stand with		

συναναπαύομαι . 710
refreshed with, be
συναντάω . . 710
befall
meet
συνάντησις . . 710
meet
συναντιλαμβάνο-
μαι. . . . 710
help
συναπάγομαι . 710
carried away with, be
condescend
led away with, be
συναποθνήσκω . 710
dead with, be
die with
συναπόλλυμαι . 710
perish with
συναποστέλλω . 710
send, with
συναρμολογέομαι 710
framed together, be fitly
joined together, be fitly
συναρπάζω . . 710
catch
συναυξάνομαι . 710
grow together
συνδέομαι . . 710
bound with, be
σύνδεσμος . . 710
band
bond
συνδοξάζομαι . 710
glorified together, be
σύνδουλος . . 710
fellowservant
συνδρομή . . . 710
run together
συνεγείρω . . 710
raise up together
rise with
συνέδριον . . . 710
council
συνειδέω . . . 711
consider
know by
privy, be
ware of, be
συνείδησις . 711
conscience
σύνειμι . . . 711
with, be
σύνειμι . . 711
gathered together be

συνεισέρχομαι . 711
go in with
go with into

συνέκδημος . . 711
companion in travel
travel with

συνεκλεκτός . . 711
elected together with

συνελαύνω . . 711
set at one again (with
εις, ειρηνη, Acts 7:
26)

συνεπιμαρτυρέω . 711
witness, also bear

συνέπομαι . . 711
accompany

συνεργέω . . . 711
help with
work together
work with
workers together

συνεργός . . . 711
companion in labour
fellowhelper
fellowlabourer
fellowworker
helper
labourer together with
workfellow

συνέρχομαι . . 712
accompany
assemble
assembled with, be
come
come together
come with
company with
go with
resort

συνεσθίω . . . 712
eat with

σύνεσις . . . 712
knowledge
understanding

συνετός . . . 712
prudent

συνευδοκέω . 712
allow
consent
pleased, be
pleasure, have

συνευωχεομαι . 712
feast with

συνεφίστημι . 712
rise up together

συνεχω . . . 712
constrain
hold

keep in
sick of
press
stop
strait, be in a
straiten
taken with, be
throng

συνήδομαι . . 712
delight

συνήθεια . . . 712
custom

συνηλικιώτης . 712
equal

συνθάπτομαι . . 712
buried with, be

συνθλάομαι . . 712
broken, be

συνθλίβω . . 712
throng

συνθρύπτω . . 713
break

συνίημι . . . 713
consider
understand
wise, be

συνιστάνω . . 713
commend

συνιστάω, συνίσ-
τημι . . . 713
approve
commend
consist
make
stand
stand with

συνοδεύω . . 713
journey with

συνοδία . . . 713
company

συνοικέω . . . 713
dwell with

συννοικοδομέομαι . 713
builded together, be

συνομιλέω . . 713
talk with

συνομορέω . 713
join hard

συνοχή . . . 713
anguish
distress

συντάσσω . . 713
appoint

συντέλεια . . 713
end

συντελέω . . 713
end

finish
fulfil
fulfilled, shall be (with
μελλω, Mark 13:4)
make

συντέμνω . . . 713
cut short
short (Ro. 9:28)

συντηρέω . . . 713
keep
observe
preserve

συντίθημι . . 714
agree
assent
covenant

συντόμως . . 714
words, a few

συντρέχω . . . 714
run
run together
run with

συντρίβω . . . 714
break
break in pieces
broken to shivers, be
brokenhearted (with
καρδια, Lu. 4:18)
bruise

σύντριμμα . . 714
destruction

σύντροφος . . 714
brought up with

συντυγχάνω . . 714
come at

συνυποκρίνομαι . 714
dissemble with

συνυπουργέω . 714
help together

συνωδίνω . . . 714
travail in pain together

συνωμοσία . . 714
conspiracy

σύρτις . . . 714
quicksands

σύρω 714
drag
draw
hale

συσπαράσσω . 714
tear

σύσσημον . . 714
token

σύσσωμα . . . 714
of the same body

συστασιαστής . 714
insurrection with, make

συστατικός . . 714
commendation, of

συσταυρόω . 714
crucified with

συστέλλω . . 714
short
wind up [for burial]
wound up

συστενάζω . . 714
groan together

συστοιχέω . . 715
answer to

συστρατιώτης . 715
fellowsoldier

συστρέφω . . . 715
gather

συστροφή . . . 715
band together (with
ποιεω Acts 23:12)
concourse

συσχηματίζομαι . 715
conformed to
fashion self according
to

σφαγή . . . 715
slaughter

σφάγιον . . . 715
slain beast

σφάττω . . . 715
kill
slay
wound

σφόδρα . . . 715
exceeding
exceedingly
greatly
sore
very

σφοδρῶς . . . 715
exceedingly

σφραγίζω . . 715
seal
seal up
set a seal
set to seal
stop (2 Cor. 11:10)

σφραγίς . . . 715
seal

σφυρόν . . . 715
ancle bone

σχεδόν . . . 715
almost

σχῆμα . . . 716
fashion

σχίζω . . . 716
break

divide	σωφροσύνη . 719	ταραχος . . . 720
open	soberness	stir
rend	sobriety	ταρταρόω . . 720
rent, make a	σώφρων . . 719	hell, cast down to
σχίσμα . . . 716	discreet	τάσσω . . . 720
division	sober	addict
rent	temperate	appoint
schism		determined
σχοινίον . . 716	τάγμα . . . 719	ordained
cord, small	order	set
rope	τακτός . . . 719	ταῦρος . . . 720
σχολάζω . . 716	set	bull
empty		ox
give self	ταλαιπωρέω . 719	ταυτά, from ὁ αὐ-
σχολή . . . 716	afflicted, be	τος . . . 720
school	ταλαιπωρία . . 719	even thus
	misery	like
σώζω . . . 716	ταλαίπωρος . . 719	manner, like
heal	wretched	so
preserve		ταῦτα, from οὗτος 720
save	ταλαντιαῖος . . 719	afterward
save self	talent, weight of a	afterward (with μετα)
well, do	τάλαντον . . . 719	follow (with μετα, 1 Pet.
whole, be	talent	1:11)
whole, make		hereafter
	ταλιθά . . . 719	hereafter (with μετα)
σῶμα . . . 717	Talitha	him (Heb. 11:12)
bodily		so
body	ταμεῖον . . . 719	such
slave	chamber, secret	that
	closet	the
σωματικός . . 718	storehouse	the same
bodily		them
σωματικῶς . . 718	τάξις . . . 719	these
bodily	order	they
		this
σωρεύω . . 718	ταπεινός . . . 720	those
heap	base	thus
load	cast down	
	degree, of low	ταύταις, from οὑ-
σωτήρ . . . 718	estate, of low	τος 722
saviour	humble	that
	lowly	them
σωτηρία . . 718		these
deliver	ταπεινοφροσύνη . 720	those
health	humbleness of mind	
salvation	humility	ταύτας, from οὗτος 722
save	humility of mind	hence
saving	lowliness	these
	lowliness of mind	those
σωτήριον . . . 719		
salvation	ταπεινόω . . . 720	ταύτῃ, from οὗτος 722
	abase	it
σωτήριως . . . 719	bring low	same, the
salvation, that bringeth	humble	that
	humble self	this
σωφρονέω . . 719		this same
mind, be in right	ταπείνωσις . 720	
sober, be	estate, low	ταύτην, from οὗτος 723
sober minded, be	humiliation	her
soberly	made low, be	hereof
	vile	it
σωφρονίζω . . 719		same, the
sober, teach to be	ταράσσω . . . 720	that
	trouble	the
σωφρονισμός . . 719		this
sound mind	ταραχή . . . 720	
σωφρόνως . . 719	trouble	
soberly	troubling	

ταύτης, from οὗτος 723	
same, the	
thereby	
this	
ταφή 723	
bury (Mat. 27:7)	
τάφος 723	
sepulchre	
tomb	
τάχα 723	
peradventure	
perhaps	
ταχέως . . . 723	
hastily	
quickly	
shortly	
soon	
suddenly	
ταχινός . . . 724	
shortly	
swift	
τάχιον . . 724	
outrun	
quickly	
shortly	
sooner	
τάχιστα . . 724	
speed, with all	
τάχος 724	
quickly	
shortly	
speedily	
ταχύ . . . 724	
lightly	
quickly	
ταχύς . . . 724	
swift	
τε 724	
also	
and	
both	
even	
then	
whether	
τεῖχος . . . 726	
wall	
τεκμήριον . 726	
infallible proof	
τεκνίον . . . 726	
child, little	
τεκνογονέω . . 726	
children, bear	
τεκνογονία . . 726	
childbearing	
τέκνον . . . 726	
child	
daughter	
son	

τεκνοτροφέω . . 727	τεσσαρακυνταετής 729	reserve	certain
bring up children	forty years, of	watch	certain thing
	forty years old	τήρησις . . . 730	divers
τέκτων . . . 727	forty years old, full(with	hold	every man
carpenter	πληροω, χρονος, Acts	keeping	he
	7:23)	prison	man
τέλειος . . . 727			one
age, of full	τέσσαρες, -ρα . 729	τίθημι, ἔθηκα, ἐθέ-	one thing (Lu. 6:9)
man	four	μην, θῶ . . 731	ought
perfect		advise (with βουλη,	partly (with μερος, 1 Co.
	τεσσαρεσκαιδέκατος 729	Acts 27:12)	11:18)
τελειότης . . 727	fourteenth	appoint	some
perfection		bow	some man
perfectness	τεταρταῖος . . 729	commit	somebody
	four days	conceive	something
τελειόω . . . 727		give	somewhat
consecrate	τέταρτος . . . 729	kneel down	that nothing
finish	four	lay	thing
fulfil	fourth	lay aside	what
perfect		lay down	whatsoever
perfect, make	τετράγωνος . . 729	lay up	whatsoever (with εαν,
	foursquare	make	Eph. 6:8)
τελείως . . . 727		ordain	wherewith
end, to the	τετράδιον . . . 729	purpose	whomsoever
	quaternion	put	whose
τελείωσις . . 727		set	whosoever
perfection	τετρακισχίλιοι . 729	set forth	
performance	four thousand	settle	τίς 73ὸ
		sink down	every man
τελειωτής . . 727	τετρακόσιοι, -σια 729		how
finisher	four hundred	τίκτω, ἔτεκον . 731	how much
		bear	no (with μη)
τελεσφορέω . . 727	τετράμηνον . . 729	born, be	none (with μη)
perfection, bring fruit to	four months	bring forth	none (with ου)
		delivered, be(d.of a child)	nothing (with μη)
τελευτάω . . 727	τετραπλόος . . 729	travail, be in	nothing (with ου)
dead, be	fourfold		nothing (with ουδε, 1 Ti.
decease		τίλλω . . . 732	6:7)
die	τετράπους . . 729	pluck	
	fourfooted beasts		what
τελευτή . . . 727		τιμάω . . . 732	what manner
death	τετράρχης . . 730	honour	what thing
	tetrarch	value	where
τελέω . . . 727			whereby
accomplish	τετραρχέω . . 730	τιμή . . . 732	wherefore
end, make an	tetrarch	honour	wherefore (1 Joh. 3:12)
expire	tetrarch, be	precious	wherefore (with ενεκεν,
fill up		price	Acts 19:32)
finish	τεφρόω . . . 730	sum	whereof
fulfil	ashes, turn into		whereof (with περι, 1 Ti.
go over		τίμιος . . . 732	1:7)
pay	τέχνη . . . 730	dear	whereunto
perform	art	honourable	wherewith
	craft	precious	wherewithal
τέλος . . . 728	occupation	reputation, had in	whether
continual (with εις, Lu.			which
13:5)	τεχνίτης . . . 730	τιμιότης . . . 732	who
custom	builder	costliness	whom
end	craftsman		whose
ending		τιμωρέω . . . 732	why
finally	τήκομαι . . . 730	punish	
uttermost	melt		τίτλος . . . 740
		τιμωρία . . . 732	title
τελώνης . . . 728	τηλαυγῶς . . 730	punishment	
publican	clearly		τίω . . . 740
		τις 732	punished with, be
τελώνιον . . . 728	τηλικοῦτος . . 730	a	
custom, receipt of	so great	a kind of	τοι 740
	so mighty	any	nevertheless
τέρας . . . 728		any man	
wonder	τηρέω . . . 730	any thing	
	hold fast	any thing at all	
τεσσαράκοντα . 728	keep		
forty	keeper		
	observe		
	preserve		

ῥοιγαροῦν . . 740	τουτέστι, or τουτ'	these	τρίστεγον . . 750
therefore	ἔστι . . . 743	these things	third loft
wherefore	that is	they	τρισχίλιοι . . 750
	that is to say	this sort	three thousand
τοίνυν . . . 740	τοῦτο 743	those	τρίτος 750
then	hereunto	τράγος . . . 748	third
therefore	it	goat	thirdly
τοιόσδε . . . 740	mind, let this [be in	τράπεζα . . . 748	τρίχινος . . . 750
such	you] (with φρονεω,	bank	hair, of
τοιοῦτος . . . 740	Phi. 2:5)	meat	τρόμος . . . 750
like	partly	table	tremble (with εχω,
such	selfsame	τραπεζίτης . 748	Mark 16:8)
such an one	so	exchanger	trembling
τοῖχος . . . 740	that	τραῦμα . . . 748	τροπή 751
wall	the same	wound	turning
τόκος 740	therefore	τραυματίζω . . 748	τρόπος . . . 751
usury	thereunto	wound	as
τολμάω . . . 741	this	τραχηλίζομαι . 748	conversation
bold, be	thus	opened, be	even as
boldly	wherefore	τράχηλος . . 749	manner, like (with ἱς,
dare	τούτοις . . . 746	neck	Acts 1:11)
durst	such	τραχύς . . . 749	manner, like (with
τολμηρότερον . 741	them	rock (with τοπος, Acts	ὁμοιος, Jude 7)
boldly, the more	therein	27:29)	means
τολμητής . . . 741	therewith	rough	means, by any (with
presumptuous	these	τρεῖς, τρία . 749	κατα, 2 Th.2:3)
τομώτερος . . 741	this	three	way
sharper	those	τοῦτον . . 746	τρόμω . . . 749	τροποφορέω . . 751
τόξον . . . 741	him	afraid, be	manners, suffer the
bow	that	trembling	τροφή 751
τοπάζιον . . . 741	the same	τρέφω . . . 749	food
topaz	this	bring up	meat
τόπος . . . 741	τούτου . . . 746	feed	τροφός . . . 751
coasts	hereby	nourish	nurse
licence	him	τρέχω . . . 749	τροχία . . . 751
place	it	course, have	path
plain (Lu. 6:17)	such manner of (with	run	τροχός . . . 751
quarter	περι)	τριάκοντα . . 749	course
rock (with τραχυς, Acts	that	thirty	τρυβλίον . . . 751
27:29)	thenceforth	thirty fold	dish
room	thereabout	τριακόσιοι . . 750	τρυγάω . . . 751
where	thereabout (with περι,	three hundred	gather
τοσοῦτος . . . 742	Lu. 24:4)	τρίβολος . . . 750	τρυγών . . . 751
as large	this	brier	turtledove
so great	thus	thistle	τρυμαλιά . . 751
so long	τούτους . . . 747	τρίβος . . . 750	eye
so many	such	paths	τρύπημα . . . 751
so much	them	τριετία . . . 750	eye
these many	these	three years, space of	τρυφάω . . . 751
τότε . . . 742	this	τρίζω 750	pleasure, live in
that time	τούτῳ 747	gnash	τρυφή 751
then	hereby	τρίμηνον . . . 750	delicately
-οῦ, for τούτου . 743	herein	three months	riot
his	him	τρίς 750	τρώγω . . . 751
τοὐναντίον . . 743	one	three times	eat
contrariwise	the same	thrice	
τοὔνομα . . . 743	therein		
named (Mat. 27:57)	this		
	τούτων . . . 748		
	such		
	their		

τυγχάνω . . . 751
be
chance
enjoy
little
obtain
refresh...self (Acts 27: 3)
special (with ον, Acts 19:11)

υμπανίζομαι . 752
tortured, be

τύπος . . . 752
ensample
example
fashion
figure
form
manner
pattern
print

τύπτω . . . 752
beat
smite
smite, shall(with μελλω, Acts 23:3)
strike
wound

τυρβάζομαι . 752
troubled, be

τυφλός . . . 752
blind

τυφλόω . . . 752
blind

τύφομαι . . . 752
smoke

τυφόομαι . . . 752
highminded
pride, be lifted up with
proud, be

τυφωνικός . 752
tempestuous

τυχόν . . 752
be

ὑακίνθινος 752
jacinth

ὑάκινθος . . 753
jacinth

ὑάλινος . . 753
glass, of

ὕαλος . . . 753
glass

ὑβρίζω . . 753
despitefully, use
reproach
shamefully entreat
spitefully, entreat

ὕβρις 753
harm

hurt
reproach

ὑβριστής . . . 753
despiteful
injurious

ὑγιαίνω . . . 753
health, be in
safe and sound
sound
sound, be
whole
whole, be
wholesome

ὑγιής 753
sound
whole

ὑγρός 753
green

ὑδρία 753
waterpot

ὑδροποτέω . . 753
drink water

ὑδρωπικός . . 753
dropsy, having the

ὕδωρ 753
water

ὑετός 754
rain

υἱοθεσία . . . 754
adoption
adoption of children
adoption of sons

υἱός . . . 754
child
foal
son

ὕλη . . . 757
matter

ὑμᾶς 757
ye
you
you-ward, to (with προς)
your
your own (with κατα)

ὑμεῖς . . . 760
ye
ye yourselves
you

ὑμέτερος . . . 762
your
your own

ὑμῖν 762
ye
you
your
yourselves

ὑμνέω 767
hymn, sing an
praise unto, sing

ὕμνος 767
hymn

ὑμῶν 767
ye
you
you (with ψυχη, 2 Cor. 12:15)
your
your own
yourselves

ὑπάγω . . . 771
depart
get
get hence
go
go away
go way

ὑπακοή . . . 772
obedience
obedient
obedient, make (Ro. 5: 18)
obey
obeying (1 Pet. 1:22)

ὑπακούω . . . 772
hearken
obedient to, be
obey

ὕπανδρος . . . 772
husband, which hath an

ὑπαντάω . . . 772
go and meet
meet

ὑπάντησις . . 772
meet

ὕπαρξις . . . 772
goods
substance

ὑπάρχοντα . . 772
goods
has, that which one
possesseth,things which
possesseth,things which one
substance
that hast

ὑπάρχω . . 772
after
be
have
live

ὑπείκω . . . 773
submit self

ὑπεναντίος . . 773
adversary
contrary

ὑπέο 773
above
abundantly above, exceeding(with εκ, Eph 3:20)
behalf of, in
behalf of, on
beyond
by
chiefest, very (with λιαν, 2 Cor. 11:5)
concerning
exceeding
exceeding above
exceedingly
for
highly, very (with εκ, 1 Thes. 5:13)
more
more than
of
over
part of, on the
sake of, for
stead, in
than
to
toward
very

ὑπεραίρομαι . . 774
exalted above measure, be
exalted self

ὑπέρακμος . . 774
age,pass the flower of her (with ω, 1 Cor.7.36)
pass the flower of age (1 Cor. 7:36)

ὑπεράνω . . . 774
above, far
over

ὑπεραυξάνω . . 774
grow exceedingly

ὑπερβαίνω . . 774
go beyond

ὑπερβαλλόντως . 774
measure, above

ὑπερβάλλω . . 774
exceeding
excel
pass

ὑπερβολή . . . 774
abundance
exceeding
exceeding, far more
excellency
excellent, more
measure, beyond
measure, out of

ὑπερείδω . 775
wink at

ὑπερέκεινα .. 775
beyond

ὑπερεκτείνω .. 775
stretch beyond

ὑπερεκχύνομαι . 775
run over

ὑπερεντυγχάνω . 775
intercession for, make

ὑπερέχω ... 775
better
excellency
higher
pass
supreme

ὑπερηφανία .. 775
pride

ὑπερήφανος . 775
proud

ὑπερνικάω .. 775
more than conqueror, be

ὑπέρογκος .. 775
swelling, great

ὑπεροχή ... 775
authority
excellency

ὑπερπερισσεύω . 775
abound, much more
exceeding

ὑπερπερισσῶς . 775
measure, beyond

ὑπερπλεονάζω . 775
abundant, be exceeding

ὑπερυψόω.. 775
exalt, highly

ὑπερφρονέω . 775
think more highly

ὑπερῷον ... 775
chamber, upper
room, upper

ὑπέχω.. . 775
suffer

ὑπήκοος ... 775
obedient
obey (Acts 7:39)

ὑπηρετέω ... 775
minister
minister unto
serve

ὑπηρέτης .. 775
minister
officer
servant

ὕπνος . .. 776
sleep

ὑπό ... 776
among
by
from
in
in (Acts 5:21)
of
under
with

ὑποβάλλω .. 777
suborn

ὑπογραμμός . 778
example

ὑπόδειγμα .. 778
ensample
example
pattern

ὑποδείκνυμι .. 778
forewarn
shew
warn

ὑποδέομαι .. 778
bind on
shod, be

ὑποδέχομαι .. 778
receive

ὑπόδημα .. 778
shoe

ὑπόδικος .. 778
guilty

ὑποζύγιον 778
ass

ὑποζώννυμι .. 778
undergird

ὑποκάτω ... 778
under

ὑποκρίνομαι .. 778
feign

ὑπόκρισις. .. 778
condemnation
dissimulation
hypocrisy

ὑποκριτής . 778
hypocrite

ὑπολαμβάνω 778
answer
receive
suppose

ὑπολείπομαι .. 778
left, be

ὑπολήνιον . 779
winefat

ὑπολιμπάνω . 779
leave

ὑπομένω . 779
abide
endure
patient

patiently, take
suffer
tarry behind

ὑπομιμνήσκω . 779
mind, put in
remember
remembrance, bring to
remembrance, put in

ὑπόμνησις .. 779
remembrance (p. in. r.)

ὑπομονή ... 779
continuance, patient
enduring
patience
patient waiting

ὑπονοέω ... 779
deem
suppose
think

ὑπόνοια ... 779
surmising

ὑποπλέω .. 779
sail under

ὑποπνέω ... 779
blow softly

ὑποπόδιον .. 779
footstool

ὑπόστασις .. 779
confidence
confident
person
substance

ὑποστέλλω .. 779
draw back
keep back
shun
withdraw

ὑποστολή ... 780
draw back

ὑποστρέφω . 780
come again
return
return (with μελλω, Acts 13:34)
return again
return back again
turn back
turn back again

ὑποστρώννυμι . 780
spread

ὑποταγή .. 780
subjection

ὑποτάσσω . 780
obedience, be under
obedient to, be
put under
subdue unto
subject
subject, be

subject to, be
subject to, make
subject unto, be
subject unto, make
subjection, put in
subjection to, be in
subjection under, pr in
submit self unto

ὑποτίθημι .. 780
lay down
remembrance, put in

ὑποτρέχω. .. 780
run under

ὑποτύπωσις .. 780
form
pattern

ὑποφέρω ... 780
bear
endure

ὑποχωρέω .. 780
go aside
withdraw self

ὑπωπιάζω .. 781
keep under
weary

ὗς 781
sow

ὕσσωπος ... 781
hyssop

ὑστερέω ... 781
come behind
come short
destitute, be
fail
lack
suffer need
want
want, be in
worse, be the

ὑστέρημα ... 781
behind, that which is
lack
lacking, that which was
penury
want

ὑστέρησις. .. 781
want

ὕστερον ... 781
afterward
last
last, at the
last of all

ὕστερος ... 781
latter

ὑφαντός . .. 781
woven

ὑψηλός .. 781
esteemed highly

higher

ὑψηλοφρονέω . 781
highminded, be

ὕψιστος . . . 781
high, most
highcst

ὕψος . . . 781
exalted, be (Jas. 1:9)
height
high
high, on

ὑψόω . . . 781
exalt
lift up

ὕψωμα . . . 782
height
high thing

φάγος . . . 782
gluttonous

φάγω . . . 782
eat
meat

φαιλόνης . . . 782
cloke

φαίνω . . . 782
appear
seem
seen, be
shine
think (Mark 14:64)

φανερός . . . 783
abroad
appear (with ω, 1 Tim. 4:15)
known
manifest
openly
outward
outwardly

φανερόω . . . 783
appear
declare, manifestly
manifest
manifest forth
manifest, make
shew
shew self

φανερῶς . . 783
evidently
openly

φανέρωσις . . 783
manifestation

φανός . . . 783
lantern

φαντάζομαι . . 783
sight

φαντασία 783
pomp

φάντασμα . . 783
spirit

φάραγξ . . . 784
valley

φαρμακεία . . 784
sorcery
witchcraft

φαρμακεύς . . 784
sorcerer

φαρμακός . . 784
sorcerer

φάσις 784
tidings

φάσκω . . . 784
affirm
profess
say

φάτνη 784
manger
stall

φαῦλος . . . 784
evil

φέγγος . . . 784
light

φείδομαι . . . 784
forbear
spare

φειδομένως . . 784
sparingly

φέρω, οἴσω, ἤνεγκα 784
be
bear
bring
bring forth
carry
come
drive, let her (with ἐπιδίδωμι, Acts 27:15)
driven, be
endure
go on
lay
lead
move
reach
rushing
uphold

φεύγω 785
escape
flee
flee away

φήμη 785
fame

φημί 785
affirm
say

φθάνω . . . 785
attain
attain, already
come
prevent

φθαρτός . . . 785
corruptible

φθέγγομαι . . 786
speak

φθείρω . . . 786
corrupt
corrupt self
defile
destroy

φθινοπωρινός 786
fruit withereth, whose

φθόγγος . . . 786
sound

φθονέω . . . 786
envy

φθόνος . . . 786
envy

φθορά 786
corruption
destroy
perish

φιάλη 786
vial

φιλάγαθος . . 786
lover of good men

φιλαδελφία . . 786
kindness, brotherly
love, brotherly
love of the brethren

φιλάδελφος . . 786
love as brethren

φίλανδρος . . 786
love their husband

φιλανθρωπία . . 786
kindness
love toward man

φιλανθρώπως . 786
courteously

φιλαργυρία . . 786
love of money

φιλάργυρος . . 786
covetous

φίλαυτος . . . 786
lover of own self

φιλέω 786
kiss
love

φιληδονος . . . 787
lover of pleasure

φίλημα 787
kiss

φιλία 787
friendship

φιλόθεος . . . 787
lover of God

φιλονεικία . . 787
strife

φιλόνεικος . . 787
contentious

φιλοξενία . . . 787
entertain strangers
hospitality

φιλόξενος . . . 787
hospitality, given to
hospitality, lover of
hospitality, use

φιλοπρωτεύω . . 787
preeminence, love to have the

φίλος 787
friend

φιλοσοφία . . 787
philosophy

φιλόσοφος . . 787
philosopher

φιλόστοργος . . 787
kindly affectioned

φιλότεκνος . . 787
love their children

φιλοτιμέομαι . 787
labour
strive
study

φιλοφρόνως . . 788
courteously

φιλόφρων . . . 788
courteous

φιμόω 788
muzzle
peace, hold
silence, put to
speechless, be
still, be

φλογίζω . . . 788
fire, set on

φλόξ 788
flame
flaming

φλυαρέω . . 788
prate against

φλύαρος . . . 788
tattler

φοβέομαι . . . 788
afraid, be
afraid, be sore (with φόβος, μέγας, Lu. 8:9)

fear
fear exceedingly (Mar. 4:41)
reverence

φοβερός . 789
fearful
terrible

φόβητρον . . 789
fearful sight

φόβος . . . 789
afraid, be sore (with φοβέομαι, μεγας, Lu. 2:9)
exceedingly (with μεγας)
fear
fear (with εχω, 1 Ti. 5: 20)
fear exceedingly (with μεγας)
terror

φοῖνιξ . . . 789
palm
palm tree

φονεύς . . 789
murderer

φονεύω . . 789
kill
murder do
slay

φόνος . . . 789
murder
slain with, be (with αποθνησκω, Heb. 11: 37)
slaughter

φορέω . . . 789
bear
wear

φόρος . . 789
tribute

φορτίζω . . . 789
lade
laden, be heavy

φορτίον . . . 789
burden

φόρτος . . . 790
lading

ωραγέλλιον . . 790
scourge

φραγελλόω . . 790
scourge

φραγμός . . . 790
hedge
hedge round about (with περιτιθημι)
hedged
partition

φράζω . . . 790
declare

φράσσω . . . 790
stop

φρέαρ 790
pit
well

φρεναπατάω . . 790
deceive

φρεναπάτης . . 790
deceiver

φρένες . . . 790
understanding

φρίσσω . . . 790
tremble

φρονέω . . . 790
affection on, set the
care
careful, be
likeminded, be (with αυτο)
mind
mind, be of one or the same (with αυτος)
mind, let this [be in you] (with τουτο, Phi. 2:5)
mind, of one (with εις, Phi. 2:2)
regardeth
savour
think
understand

φρόνημα . . . 790
mind
minded, to be
minded, be carnally (with σαρξ, Ro. 8:6)
minded, be spiritually (with πνευμα, Ro. 8:6)

φρόνησις . . . 790
prudence
wisdom

φρόνιμος . . . 790
wise
wiser

φρονίμως . . . 791
wisely

φροντίζω . . . 791
careful, be

φρουρέω . . . 791
garrison, keep with a
keep

φρυάσσω . . . 791
rage

φρύγανον . . . 791
stick

φυγή . . . 791
flight

φυλακή . . . 791
cage
hold
imprisonment
prison
ward
watch

φυλακίζω . . . 791
imprison

φυλακτήριον . . 791
phylactery

φύλαξ . . . 791
keeper

φυλάσσω . . . 791
beware
keep
keep self
observe
save

φυλή . . . 791
kindred
tribe

φύλλον . . . 792
leaf

φύραμα . . . 792
lump

φυσικός . . . 792
natural

φυσικῶς . . . 792
naturally

φυσιόω . . . 792
puff up

φύσις . . . 792
kind
mankind (with ανθρωπινος)
natural
nature

φυσίωσις . . . 792
swellings

φυτεία . . . 792
plant

φυτεύω . . . 792
plant

φύω . . . 792
spring
spring up

φωλεός . . . 792
hole

φωνέω . . . 792
call
call for
crow
cry

φωνή 793
noise
noise (Acts 2:6)
sound
voice

φῶς 794
fire
light

φωστήρ . . . 794
light

φωσφόρος . . . 794
star, day

φωτεινός . . . 794
bright
light, full of

φωτίζω . . . 794
enlighten
illuminate
light
light, bring to
light, give (—lighten)
see, to make

φωτισμός . . . 795
light

χαίρω 795
farewell
glad, be
God speed
greeting
hail
joy
joyfully
rejoice

χάλαζα . . . 795
hail

χαλάω . . . 795
let down
strike

χαλεπός . . . 795
fierce
perilous

χαλιναγωγέω . 795
bridle

χαλινός . . . 795
bit
bridle

χάλκεος . . . 795
brass

χαλκεύς . . . 796
coppersmith

χαλκηδών . . 796
chalcedony

χαλκίον . . . 796
brasen vessel

χαλκολίβανον . 796
brass, fine

χαλκός brass money	796	χεῖλος lip shore	798	χοϊκός earthy	801	χρηματισμός God, answer of	803
χαμαί ground, on the ground, to the	796	χειμάζομαι tempest, be tossed with a	798	χοῖνιξ measure	801	χρήσιμος profit	803
χαρά gladness greatly joy joyful joyful, be exceeding joyfully (with μετα, Heb. 10:34) joyfulness joyous (Heb. 12:11)	796	χείμαρρος brook χειμών tempest weather, foul winter	798 798	χοῖρος swine χολάω angry, be χολή gall χόος dust	801 802 802 802	χρῆσις use χρηστεύομαι kind, be χρηστολογία good words χρηστός	803 803 803 803
χάραγμα grave mark	796	χείρ hand χειραγωγέω hand, lead by the	798 800	χορηγεω give minister	802	better easy good goodness gracious	
χαρακτήρ express image	796	χειραγωγός hand, some to lead by the	800	χορός dancing	802	kind χρηστότης	803
χάραξ trench	796	χειρόγραφον handwriting	800	χορτάζω feed fill satisfy	802	gentleness good goodness kindness	
χαρίζομαι deliver forgive frankly forgive give give, freely grant	796	χειροποίητος hands, made by hands, make with χειροτονέω choose ordain	800 800	χόρτασμα sustenance χόρτος blade grass hay	802 802	χρίω anoint χρίσμα anointing unction	803 803
χάριν because of cause of, for for sake of ...fore (Lu. 7:47) reproachfully wherefore	797	χείρων, χεῖρον sorer worse (and worse) χήρα widow χθές yesterday	800 800 800	χράομαι entreat use χραω lend χρεία business lack necessary necessity need need (with εχω) needful use want	802 802 802	χρονίζω delay tarry (t. so long) χρόνος oftentimes (Lu. 8:29) old, full forty years (with πληροω, τεσσαρακονταετης, Acts 7:23) season space time while while, a	803 804
χάρις acceptable benefit favour gift grace gracious joy liberality pleasure thank thanks thankworthy	797	χιλιάδες thousand χιλίαρχος captain captain, chief captain, high χίλιοι thousand χιτών clothes coat garment	800 801 801 801			χρονοτριβέω spend time	804
χάρισμα free gift gift	798	χιών snow χλαμύς robe	801 801	χρεωφειλέτης debtor χρή ought χρήζω need need, have	803 803 803	χρύσεος gold, of golden χρυσίον gold χρυσοδακτύλιος gold ring, with a	804 804 804
χαριτόω accepted, make favoured, be highly	798	χλευάζω mock χλιαρός lukewarm	801 801	χρῆμα money riches	803	χρυσολιθος chrysolite	804
χάρτης paper	798	χλωρός green pale	801	χρηματίζω called, be God, be admonished of God, be warned of reveal speak	803	χρυσόπρασος chrysoprasus χρυσός gold	804 804
χάσμα gulf	798					χρυσόω deck	804

χρώς . . .	805	ψεύδομαι . . .	806	ψύχος	808	season
body		falsely		cold		short
		lie				time
χω .ός . . .	805	ψευδομάρτυρ . .	806	ψυχρός . . .	808	time, high
cripple		witness, false		cold		
halt						ὡραῖος	812
lame		ψευδομαρτυρέω .	806	ψωμίζω . . .	808	beautiful
		witness, bear false		feed		ὠρύομαι . . .	812
χωρα	805			feed, bestow to		roar
coast		ψευδομαρτυρία .	806	ψωμίον . . .	808	ὡς	812
country		witness, false		sop		about
fields						according as
ground		ψευδοπροφήτης .	806	ψώχω . . .	808	after
land		prophet, false		rub		after that
region						as
		ψεῦδος . . .	806			as it had been
χωρέω . . .	805	lie		Ω	808	as it were
can receive		lying		Omega		as soon
come						as soon as
contain		ψευδόχριστος .	806	ὦ	808	even as
go		Christs, false		O		even like
place, have		ψευδώνυμος . .	806	ὦ, ἧς, ᾗ . . .	808	for
receive		falsely so called		appear (with φανερος,		greatly, how
receive, be room to				1 Tim. 4:15)		how
		ψεῦσμα . . .	807	be		like
χωρίζω . . .	805	lie		pass the flower of her		like as
depart				age (with ὑπερακμος,		like unto
put asunder		ψεύστης . . .	807	1 Cor. 7:36)		since
separate		liar		stand		so
						so that
χωρίον . . .	805	ψηλαφάω . . .	807	ὧδε	809	that
field		feel after		here		to wit
land		handle		hither		unto
parcel of ground		touch		place, in this		when
place				place, this		whensoever
possession		ψηφίζω . . .	807	there		while
		count				with all speed
χωρίς	805			ᾠδή . . .	809	ὡσαύτως & Ὡσαννά,
beside		ψῆφος . . .	807	song		see after ὥστε
by itself		stone				
without		voice		ὠδίν	809	ὡσεί . .	815
				pain		about
χῶρος	806	ψιθυρισμός . .	807	sorrow		as
north west		whispering		travail		as it had been
						as it were
		ψιθυριστής . .	807	ὠδίνω	809	like
		whisperer		birth, travail in		like as
ψάλλω . . .	806			travail		
melody, make		ψιχίον . . .	807			ὥσπερ	816
psalms, sing		crumb		ὦμος	809	as
sing				shoulders		even as
		ψυχή	807			like as
ψαλμός . . .	806	heart		ὤν, οὖσα, ὄν . .	810	ὡσπερεί . . .	816
psalms		heartily (with εκ, Col.		be		as
		3:23)		come		
ψευδάδελφος . .	806	heartily		have		ὥστε . . .	816
brethren, false		life				as
		mind		ὠνέομαι . . .	811	insomuch as
ψευδαπόστολος .	806	soul		buy		insomuch that
apostles, false		us (with ἡμων, John				so that
		10:24)		ὠόν . . .	811	so then
ψευδής . . .	806	you (with ἱμων, 2 Cor.		egg		that
false		12:15)				therefore
liar				ὥρα . . .	811	to
		ψυχικός . .	808	day		wherefore
ψευδοδιδάσκαλος	806	natural		eventide		
teacher, false		sensual		hour		ὡσαύτως . . .	817
				instant		even so
ψευδολόγος .	806	ψύχομαι . . .	808			
lies, speaking		wax cold				

| likewise
manner, after the same
manner, in like | ὠτίον 817
ear | ὠφελέω . . . 817
advantage | ὠφέλιμος . . . 817
profit |
| Ὡσαννά . . . 817
hosanna | ὠφέλεια . . . 817
advantage
profit | better
prevail
profit | profit (with εστι 1 Tim.
4:8)
profitable |

APPENDIX.

PART I.

Containing full lists of the references of ἀλλά, αὐτός, and γάρ, partially quoted in the Work.

'Αλλά.	Mar. 13:24	Joh. 7:12	Acts 1: 4	Ro. 10: 2	1Co. 11: 8	2Co. 9:12	1Th. 2: 4
	14:28	16	8	8	9	10: 4	—
Mat. 4: 4	29	22	2:16	16	17	12	7
5:15	36	24	4:17	18	12:14	13	8
17	—	27	32	19	22	18	13
39	49	28	5: 4	11: 4	24	11: 1	4: 7
6:13	16: 7	44	13	11	25	6	8
18	Lu. 1:60	49	7:39	18	14: 2	—	5: 6
7:21	4: 4	8:12	48	20	17	17	9
8: 4	5:14	16	10:20	12: 2	19	12:14	15
8	31	26	35	3	20	—	2Th. 2:12
9:12	32	28	41	16	22	16	3: 8
13	38	37	13:25	19	33	13: 3	9
17	6:27	42	15:11	21	34	4	11
18	7: 7	49	20	13: 3	15:10	—	15
24	25	55	16:37	5	—	7	1Ti. 1:13
10:20	26	9: 3	18: 9	14	35	8	16
34	8:16	31	21	14:13	37	Gal. 1: 1	2:10
11: 8	27	10: 1	19: 2	17	39	8	12
9	52	5	26	20	40	12	3: 3
13:21	9:56	8	27	15: 3	46	17	4:12
15:11	11: 4	18	20:24	21	—	2: 3	5: 1
16:12	33	26	21:13	16: 4	2Co. 1: 9	7	13
17	42	33	24	18	—	14	23
23	12: 7	11: 4	26:16	1Co. 1:17	12	3:12	6: 2
17:12	51	11	20	27	13	16	4
18:22	13: 3	15	25	2: 4	19	22	17
30	5	22	29	5	24	4: 2	2Ti. 1: 7
19: 6	14:10	30	27:10	7	2: 4	7	8
11	13	42	Ro. 1:21	9	5	8	9
20:23	16:21	51	32	12	13	14	12
26	30	52	2:13	13	17	17	17
28	17: 8	54	29	3: 1	3: 3	23	2: 9
21:21	18:13	12: 6	—	2	5	29	20
22:30	20:21	9	3:27	5	6	30	24
32	38	16	31	6	14	31	3: 9
24: 6	21: 9	27	4: 2	7	15	5: 6	4: 3
26:39	22:26	30	4	—	4: 2	13	8
27:24	36	42	10	4: 3	—	6:13	16
Mar. 1:44	42	44	12	4	5	15	Tit. 1: 8
45	53	47	13	14	8	Eph. 1:21	15
2:17	23:15	49	16	15	—	2:19	2:10
—	24. 6	13: 9	20	19	9	4:29	3: 5
22	21	10	24	20	16	5: 4	Philem. 14
3:26	22	—	5: 3	5: 8	—	15	16
29	Joh. 1: 8	18	11	6: 6	18	17	Heb. 2:16
4:17	13	14:24	14	8	5: 4	18	3:13
22	31	31	15	11	12	24	16
5:19	33	15:16	6: 5	—	15	27	4: 2
26	3: 8	19	13	12	16	29	5: 4
39	15	21	14	—	6: 4	6: 4	5
6: 9	16	25	15	13	7: 5	6	7:16
7: 5	17	16: 2	7: 7	7: 4	6	12	9:24
15	28	4	13	—	7	Phi. 1:18	10: 3
19	36	6	15	7	9	20	25
8:33	4: 2	7	17	10	11	29	39
9: 8	14	12	19	19	—	2: 3	11:13
13	23	13	20	20	—	4	12:11
22	5:18	20	8: 1	21	—	7	22
37	22	25	4	35	12	12	26
10: 8	24	—	9	8: 6	14	17	13:14
27	30	33	15	7	8: 5	27	Jas. 1:25
40	34	17: 9	20	9: 2	7	—	26
43	42	15	23	12	8	3: 7	2:18
45	6: 9	20	26	—	10	8	3:15
11:23	22	18:28	32	21	14	9	4:11
32	26	40	37	27	19	4: 6	1Pet. 1:15
12:14	27	19:21	9: 7	10: 5	21	17	19
25	32	24	8	13		Col. 2: 5	23
27	36	34	10	20		3:11	2:16
13: 7	38	20: 7	11	23		22	18
11	39	27	16	24		1Th. 1: 5	20
—	64	21: 8	24	29		8	25
20	7:10	23	32	33		2: 2	3: 4

1Pet. 3:14
21
4: 2
13
5: 2
—
3
2Pet. 1:16
21
2: 4
5
3: 9
—
1Joh. 2: 2
7
16
19
—
21
27
3:18
4: 1
10
18
5: 6
18
2Joh. 1
5
8
12
3Joh. 9
11
13
Jude 6
9
Rev. 2: 4
6
9
14
20
3: 9
9: 5
10: 7
9
17:12
20: 6
————

αὐτά.
Mat. 6:26
10: 1
11:25
13: 4
7
28
30
—
39
18: 8
19:14
23: 4
27: 6
10
Mar. 8: 7
10:14
16
—
15:24
Lu. 4:41
5: 7
10:21
14:19
17:31
18:16
Joh. 5:36
—
10: 3
12
27
28
13:17
14:11
15: 6
Acts 2:45

Rom. 1:32
2: 3
10: 5
Gal. 3:10
12
Eph. 6: 4
Heb. 9:23
1Pet. 1:12
Rev. 11: 6
18:14
————

αὐταῖς.
Mat. 28: 9
10
Mar. 16: 6
Lu. 8: 3
24: 1
4
10
11
Joh. 5:39
1Co. 14:34
Phil. 4: 3
1Tim. 1:18
5:16
Heb.10: 3
2Pet. 3:16
Rev. 9: 3
4
5
19
15: 1
————

αὐτάς.
Mar. 16: 8
Lu. 23:28
24: 4
5
Joh. 2: 7
11:19
14:21
Col. 3:19
Heb. 11:13
Jude 7
————

αὐτή.
Lu. 1:36
7:12
Rom. 8:21
1Cor. 7:12
11:14
Heb.11:11
Rev. 18: 6
————

αὐτῇ.
Mat. 1:20
5:31
10:11
12:39
14: 7
15:23
28
16: 4
20:21
21:19
22:39
Mar. 5:23
33
34
41

Mar. 5:43
6:23
7:27
29
11:13
14
14: 5
6
Lu. 1:30
35
36
45
56
58
2:38
7:12
13
—
21
48
8:48
55
10: 7
9
21
40
41
11:29
12:12
13: 6
12
13
31
19:41
20:19
23:12
24:13
18
33
Joh. 2: 4
4: 7
10
13
16
17
21
26
8: 7
10
11
11:23
25
31
33
40
20:13
15
16
17
18
Acts 1:20
5: 8
7: 5
9:38
41
16:18
20:22
22:13
Rom. 6: 2
12
9:12
16: 2
1Co. 11:15
—
Col. 2: 7
4: 2
Heb. 7:11
Jas. 3: 9
—
2Pet. 3:10
2Joh. 6
Rev. 1: 3
2:21
10: 6
—
13:12
16:19

Rev. 18: 6
—
—
7
9
11
24
19: 8
15
20:13
21:22
23
22: 3
————

αὐτήν.
Mat. 1:19
—
25
5:28
30
32
7:14
8:15
9:18
22
10:12
13
39
—
11:12
12:41
42
14: 4
15:23
16:25
—
19: 7
21:19
22:28
Mar. 1:31
—
4:30
6:17
26
28
—
8:35
—
9:43
10:11
15
11: 2
13
12:21
22
23
14: 6
Lu. 1:28
57
61
2: 6
4: 6
39
6:48
7:13
8:52
9:24
—
16:18
11:32
13: 7
8
—
9
12
18
16:16
17:33
—
—
13:28
14: 9
16:11
20:31
33

Lu. 21:21
Joh. 8: 3
10:17
18
—
—
11:31
33
12: 7
25
—
18:10
19:27
Acts 5: 9
10
7: 5
44
9:37
—
41
—
12:15
15:16
21: 3
27: 8
32
Ro. 7: 3
16: 2
1Co. 7:12
Gal. 1:13
Eph. 5:26
27
29
Col. 4:17
Heb. 4: 6
10: 1
12:17
1Pet. 3:11
1Joh. 2:21
Rev. 2:22
3: 8
11: 2
12: 6
17: 6
7
16
—
18: 8
9
20
21:23
24
26
27
————

αὐτῆς.
Mat. 1:19
2:16
5:28
6:34
7:13
27
8:15
9:25
10:35
—
15:28
16:18
21: 2
43
24:32
26:13
52
Mar. 1:30
31
5:29
6:22
7:25
—
13:28
14: 9
16:11
Lu. 1: 5
38

Lu. 1:41
58
—
2:35
4:38
39
7:47
8:44
54
55
56
10:10
42
21:20
21
Joh. 4:27
11: 1
4
5
16:21
Acts 5:10
8:27
13:17
15:16
16:15
18
19
19:27
27:14
Ro. 7:11
13: 3
1Co. 7:13
39
—
10:26
28
Gal. 4:30
Eph. 5:25
2Tim.3: 5
Heb. 6: 7
7:18
9: 5
11: 4
12:11
2Joh. 1
3Joh. 12
Rev. 2: 5
22
23
12: 1
—
4
5
17
14:18
21: 6
16:21
17: 2
16
18: 3

Rev. 21:24
25
22: 2
————

αὐτό.
Mat. 2:13
12:11
14:12
17:19
18: 2
13
26:29
27:59
60
Mar. 4: 4
7
37
6:29
9:18
28
36
—
50
14:25
Lu. 1:59
2:28
40
8: 5
7
9:40
45
47
11:14
14:35
15: 4
19:23
23:53
—
Joh. 1: 5
6:39
12: 7
14
14:17
15: 2
18:11
19:40
21: 6
Acts 5:39
7: 6
27: 6
Ro. 7:17
20
8:16
26
9:17
13: 6
2Co. 2: 3
3:14
5: 5
7:11
13:11
Gal. 1:12
2:10
22
Eph. 6:18
Phil. 1: 6
3:21
Col. 2:14
—
4: 4
8
1Th. 4:10
Heb. 9:19
1Pet. 4:10
2Pet. 1: 5
1Joh. 2:27
Rev. 5: 3
4

Rev. 8: 5
10: 9
10
—
————

αὐτοί.
Mat. 5: 4
5
6
7
8
9
12:27
20:10
25:44
Mar. 6:31
Lu. 2:50
6:11
9:36
11: 4
19
46
48
52
14: 1
12
16:28
17:13
18:34
22:23
71
24:14
35
52
Joh. 3:28
4:42
45
6:24
17: 8
19
21
18:28
Acts 2:22
13:14
15:32
16:37
18:15
20:34
22:19
24:15
20
27:36
28:28
Rom. 8:23
11:31
15:14
2Co. 1: 4
9
6:16
10:12
Gal. 2: 9
17
6:13
1Th. 1: 9
2: 1
14
3: 3
4: 9
5: 2
2Th. 3: 7
2Tim. 2:10
Heb. 1:11
3:10
8. 9
10
13: 3
17
Jas. 2: 6
7
1Pet. 1:15
2: 5
2Pet. 2:19

1Joh. 4: 5	Mat. 21:21	Mar. 8: 1	Lu. 7:22	Joh. 4:32	Joh. 20:23	Rom. 1:19	Mat. 8:34
Rev. 6:11	24	15	8:25	34	25	4:11	9:31
12:11	27	17	31	40	21: 3	9:26	10: 4
21: 3	31	21	32	5:11	5	10: 2	33
————	36	27	—	17	6	5	12:10
	42	29	36	19	10	11: 8	14
	22: 1	30	56	6: 7	12	9	16
αὐτοῖς.	20	34	9: 1	20	13	17	18
	21	9: 1	11	26	Acts 1: 3	27	22
Mat. 3: 7	29	4	13	29	4	15:27	13: 2
4:16	43	7	17	31	10	28	—
19	24: 2	9	20	32	2: 3	16:14	4
6: 1	4	12	21	35	4	15	20
8	45	14	46	43	14	1Co. 1:24	46
7:12	25:14	29	48	53	3: 5	7: 8	14: 3
23	16	31	55	61	8	11:13	5
8: 4	20	35	10: 9	70	4: 1	2Co. 2:13	—
15	22	36	18	7: 6	3	4: 4	22
26	40	10: 3	11: 2	9	14	5:19	26
32	45	5	17	16	17	6:16	35
9:12	26:10	11	12:37	21	18	8:22	36
15	19	14	13: 2	33	24	Gal. 2: 2	15:23
18	27	24	32	45	32	3:12	16: 1
24	31	27	15: 2	47	34	Eph. 2:10	21
28	38	32	6	8:12	5:13	4:18	22
30	45	36	12	14	25	Phil. 1:28	17:10
10: 1	48	38	16:15	21	6: 6	Col. 3: 7	12
5	27:17	39	28	23	7:25	1Th. 4:17	16
18	21	42	17:14	25	26	5: 3	—
11: 4	22	11: 2	20	27	43	2Th. 2:11	17
12: 3	26	5	37	28	60	1Ti. 4:16	23
11	65	6	18: 1	34	8: 5	2Ti. 2:25	25
16	28:16	17	7	39	18	4:16	18: 9
25	18	22	15	42	9:27	Tit. 3:13	15
39	Mar. 1:17	29	29	58	39	Heb. 6:16	25
13: 3	31	33	19:13	9:15	10: 8	8: 8	27
10	38	12: 1	32	16	20	10	28
11	44	15	40	20	23	11:16	29
13	2: 2	16	46	27	11: 3	12:19	30
14	8	17	20: 8	30	4	Jas. 2:16	32
24	17	24	15	41	12	—	34
28	19	28	17	10: 6	17	1Pet. 1:11	19: 3
29	25	38	25	—	12:10	2Pet. 2: 8	20:18
31	27	43	34	7	17	19	19
33	3: 4	44	21: 4	25	—	20	21:13
34	12	13: 5	10	28	13: 3	21	33
37	17	9	29	32	8	—	38
51	23	14:10	22: 4	34	19	22	39
52	33	13	6	11:11	21	Jude 11	44
57	4: 2	16	10	14	22	Rev. 5:13	46
14:16	9	20	13	44	43	6: 8	—
—	11	22	19	46	14:15	11	22:13
27	12	23	24	49	18	7: 2	15
15: 3	13	24	25	12:23	23	8: 2	22
10	21	27	35	35	15: 8	11:10	23
34	24	34	36	13:12	—	12	35
16: 1	33	41	38	15:22	20	12:12	43
2	34	44	40	24	38	13:16	45
6	35	48	46	16:19	16: 4	14: 9	46
8	40	15: 6	67	31	23	16: 6	23:15
15	5:13	8	23:17	17: 2	17: 2	20. 4	21
17: 3	16	9	25	8	18	11	24:47
9	19	11	34	10	34	13	51
11	39	12	35	14	18: 2	21:14	26:15
13	43	14	24:15	22	3		16
20	6: 4	15	19	23	11	————	25
22	7	16:14	27	26	20		48
27	8	15	29	—	21	αὐτόν.	—
18:19	10	19	30		19: 6		49
19: 4	11	Lu. 1: 7	33	18: 4	20: 7	Mat. 3: 5	50
8	31	22	35	5	18	14	56
11	34	34	36	6	36	15	59
13	37	—	38	21	21: 7	—	61
—	—	2: 7	40	31	24	16	67
15	—	9	41	38	—	4: 5	71
26	38	10	44	19: 4	26	—	—
28	39	17	46	5	22: 2	8	27: 1
20: 6	41	50	Joh. 1:12	6	23:21	11	2
7	46	51	26	15	31	5:15	—
8	48	3:11	38	16	24:21	29	3
17	50	4:39	39	20: 2	25: 6	6: 8	11
23	7: 6	5: 7	(Gr.40)	13	11	7:11	12
31	9	14	2: 7	17	26:11	24	18
21: 2	14	6: 2	8	19	30	8: 5	19
6	18	5	19	20	27:10	7	—
13	36	31	22	21	28:14	25	27
16	—	39	24	22	Rom. 1:19	31	28
		7: 6					

Mat. 27:30	Mar. 7:26	Mar. 14:69	Lu. 8: 9	Lu. 19: 9	Joh. 2:20	Joh. 10:24	Acts 6:15
31	32	15: 2	16	11	24	31	7: 2
—	33	4	19	14	3: 4	39	3
—	8:11	10	21	15	15	41	4
35	22	13	24	30	16	42	5
36	23	14	29	35	18	11: 3	8
39	—	16	30	39	26	11	10
43	25	17	—	46	36	15	—
—	26	18	31	47	4: 4	17	21
48	32	20	32	20: 2	10	29	—
49	38	—	37	9	15	32	—
64	9:11	—	38	10	23	34	—
28: 7	13	22	40	14	24	36	27
13	15	24	—	—	30	44	31
14	—	25	41	15	31	45	54
17	18	29	42	18	39	48	57
Mar. 1: 5	—	32	9: 9	19	40	—	8:20
10	19	36	18	20	—	53	32
12	20	—	29	21	45	57	38
26	—	44	39	27	47	12: 4	39
32	—	46	—	40	—	11	40
34	—	—	—	44	48	17	9: 3
36	22	16: 1	42	21: 7	49	18	—
37	—	6	—	38	52	21	6
40	25	7	45	22: 2	5:12	26	8
—	26	14	49	4	14	37	10
—	27	Lu. 1: 8	50	6	15	42	11
43	—	12	53	43	16	47	15
45	28	13	57	47	18	48	16
—	—	21	62	49	23	—	17
2: 3	31	50	10: 6	51	6: 6	13: 2	—
13	32	62	25	52	15	11	23
15	38	2: 4	26	54	—	16	24
16	39	7	30	—	21	32	25
23	45	—	31	56	25	—	26
3: 2	47	21	33	57	28	14: 7	27
—	10: 1	22	—	—	34	—	29
6	2	25	34	58	40	21	30
8	—	44	—	64	44	23	—
9	10	—	38	65	—	—	35
11	17	45	11: 1	66	54	16: 7	38
12	—	—	—	23: 1	64	19	43
13	21	46	5	3	71	18: 2	10: 3
19	33	48	13	7	7: 1	4	10
21	—	—	22	—	3	5	11
31	34	3:10	27	8	5	12	13
—	—	12	28	9	11	13	15
32	49	14	37	11	18	24	21
4: 1	11: 2	22	39	—	29	30	26
—	3	4: 4	53	—	30	31	35
10	4	5	54	15	—	—	38
—	17	9	12:44	16	31	19: 2	40
16	18	—	46	21	32	4	41
36	—	29	48	22	35	6	43
38	27	—	14: 1	23	39	—	48
5: 3	12: 1	35	—	26	43	12	11: 2
4	3	—	4	27	44	15	26
—	6	38	5	83	—	16	(Gr.25)
9	7	40	9	39	45	18	26
10	8	41	12	24:16	48	24	(Gr.25)
12	12	42	18	18	50	33	12: 4
17	—	—	31	20	8: 2	20: 2	—
18	13	5: 3	15:15	—	3	9	6
19	—	9	20	23	6	13	7
21	18	12	—	24	7	15	8
22	—	18	22	29	20	—	16
23	28	19	27	30	30	—	17
24	33	—	28	31	55	21:12	19
6:17	34	33	16: 2	51	—	22	20
19	—	6: 1	14	52	—	23	23
20	37	6	22	Joh. 1:10	—	25	13: 9
—	13: 3	7	27	11	57	Acts 1: 3	11
27	14: 1	7: 3	17:11	12	59	6	22
(Gr.28)	10	—	25	19	9: 2	9	28
33	11	4	18: 3	21	8	11	30
—	44	6	7	25	13	2:24	34
49	—	9	18	29	15	25	46
50	45	15	24	31	21	36	14:19
54	46	20	33	32	22	3: 4	20
56	—	36	35	33	23	7	15:21
7: 1	50	39	40	—	28	9	16: 3
5	51	40	—	42	34	10	9
12	55	42	19: 4	(Gr.43)	35	12	17:15
15	61	8: 4	5	2: 3	—	13	27
—	64	5	—	11	36	26	31
17	65		6	19	37	5: 6	18:12
18	—					6:12	26
							27

Acts 19: 2	Gal. 1:16	*αὐτός.*	Joh. 4: 2	Rev. 21: 3	Mat. 13.55	Mat. 27:53	Mar. 9: 7
4	18	Mat. 1:21	12	7	56	54	21
30	Eph. 1:20	3: 4	44		14:11	64	25
31	22	11	53	——————	12	28: 2	28
33	4:15	6: 4	5:20		15	3	42
20:14	21	8:17	37	*αὐτοῦ.*	31	—	10:10
18	Phi. 1:29	24	6: 6	Mat. 1: 2	36	4	—
37	2: 9	11:14	15	11	15:12	7	17
38	27	12: 3	7: 4	18	23	8	24
21:12	—	50	10	20	33	9	46
27	28	14: 2	9:21	21	16: 5	—	—
—	—	16:20	—	23	27	13	11: 3
30	29	21:27	12:24	25	—	Mar. 1: 3	14
31	3:10	25:17	49	2: 2	17: 1	5	18
34	21	26:48	14:10	3	2	7	27
35	Col. 1:16	27:57	16:27	11	—	16	12:19
36	2:12	Mar. 1: 8	18: 1	13	3	19	—
22:13	3:10	2:25	Acts 2:34	14	5	20	32
18	4:10	3:13	7:15	20	—	22	37
20	2Th. 2: 1	4:27	8:13	21	10	25	—
22	4	38	10:26	22	18	26	13: 1
24	6	42	14:12	3: 3	27	28	—
—	1Tim. 3: 7	6:16	16:33	4	18: 6	36	3
25	Philem. 12	17	17:25	6	15	41	14: 3
29	15	45	18:19	12	24	42	—
—	17	47	19:22	13	25	—	12
30	Heb. 2: 6	7:36	20:13	4:18	—	2:15	16
23: 3	7	8:29	35	21	29	—	21
10	—	12:21	21:24	24	—	16	23
15	—	36	22:20	5: 1	31	21	35
—	3: 2	37	24: 8	—	32	23	43
—	3	14:15	16	25	34	25	—
18	5: 5	44	25:22	35	19:10	3: 2	47
21	7	15:43	Ro. 7:25	41	25	5	56
—	7: 1	Lu. 1:17	9: 3	6:33	20:20	6	57
27	21	22	10:12	7: 9	21:10	10	58
28	24	2:28	15:14	28	34	14	65
30	9:24	3:15	1Co. 2:15	8: 3	35	21	15: 3
35	26	16	3:15	—	38	27	19
24:26	28	23	7:13	13	45	—	21
—	11: 5	4:15	9:27	14	22: 6	31	24
25: 2	6	30	15:28	21	13	4:25	26
3	19	5: 1	2Co. 10: 1	23	24	32	27
—	13:13	14	7	25	—	36	39
19	Jas. 1:12	16	11:14	9:10	33	5: 4	16: 7
21	2: 5	17	12:13	—	45	18	10
—	14	37	Eph. 2:14	11	23:18	—	Lu. 1: 5
24	5:14	6: 3	4:10	16	20	22	8
25	—	8	11	18	22	24	13
—	15	20	5:23	19	24: 1	27	14
26	19	35	Phi. 2:24	20	3	28	17
26:26	1Pet. 1:21	42	Col. 1:17	21	31	31	23
28: 6	3: 6	7: 5	18	24	45	35	24
—	5: 7	8: 1	—	10: 1	46	40	29
—	1Joh. 1:10	22	1Th. 3:11	2	51	6: 1	31
8	2: 3	37	4:16	—	25: 6	2	32
16	4	41	5:23	25	10	3	33
21	3: 1	54	2Th. 2:16	—	21	14	49
23	2	9:51	3:16	—	23	20	50
30	6	10: 1	Heb. 1: 5	35	26	—	55
Rom. 3:26	—	38	2:14	36	28	27	59
4:11	12	11:17	18	11:11	29	28	60
13	4:19	28	4:10	20	31	29	62
18	5:10	15:14	5: 2	12: 1	32	—	63
23	14	16:24	10:12	3	41	35	64
8:29	2Joh. 10	17:11	13: 5	4	—	56	—
32	Rev. 1: 7	16	Jas. 1:13	10	8	—	66
10: 9	—	18:39	1Pet. 2:24	14	24	7: 2	67
12	17	19: 2	5:10	19	27	15	75
11:36	—	9	1Joh. 1: 7	21	47	17	76
12:20	3:12	19	2: 2	26	—	19	77
—	—	20	6	29	51	25	80
14: 3	20	42	25	—	65	—	2:21
4	7: 9	22:41	3:24	33	67	33	27
15:11	9: 6	23: 9	4:10	—	27:19	—	33
1Co. 2: 9	11: 5	51	13	36	—	35	—
16	12:11	24:15	15	46	25	—	34
7:13	13:10	21	19	—	29	8: 4	38
8: 6	17:10	25	3Joh. 10	13:12	—	11	41
15:25	19: 5	28	Rev. 3:20	19	30	22	43
16:11	11	31	14:10	25	31	23	47
—	20: 2	36	17	32	32	25	—
12	3	39	17:11	36	35	26	48
2Cor. 2: 8	—	Joh. 1:27	19:12	41	37	27	51
7:15	22:18	2:12	15	44		30	3: 1
Gal. 1: 1		24	—	55		9: 3	4
		25		—			

Lu. 3: 7	Lu. 12:15	Joh. 2:12	Joh. 11:16	Acts 9: 2	Ro. 12:20	Heb. 3: 2	Rev. 1:16
16	—	17	32	18	15:10	5	17
17	43	22	44	10:38	21	7	2:18
19	46	23	12: 3	43	16: 2	15	3: 5
—	47	—	4	11:13	13	4: 1	—
4:13	48	3: 2	16	12: 5	15	7	—
14	58	8	17	7	1Co. 1: 9	10	20
22	13:17	17	19	10	29	13	21
32	—	20	37	15	30	—	5: 2
—	19	21	41	13: 8	7:12	6:10	5
35	14: 2	22	—	24	8: 3	7:25	9
—	8	29	50	29	6	10:13	6: 8
37	29	32	13: 1	31	10	—	—
42	32	33	23	16: 3	9: 7	11: 4	17
5:12	15: 1	35	15:10	32	23	5	7:15
13	14	4: 2	15	33	10:22	21	10: 1
—	20	8	16:17	17:16	14:25	12: 5	—
15	—	12	29	19	15:10	10	11:15
—	22	—	18: 1	18: 2	23	13:13	19
18	25	—	10	26	25	15	—
30	26	27	19	27	27	—	12: 4
6: 1	28	34	—	19:12	2Co. 2:11	21	5
3	16: 1	41	22	20:10	3: 7	Jas. 1:11	7
4	20	47	25	32	7: 7	—	—
6	21	51	26	38	13	2:22	9
7	23	—	19: 2	21:14	15	5:20	—
10	17: 2	53	18	19	8:18	1Pet. 1:21	10
14	12	5:28	23	33	19	24	13: 1
17	16	35	24	40	9: 9	2:14	—
—	31	37	25	22:14	15	21	2
19	18:40	—	—	20	11:15	22	—
—	19:14	38	29	22	33	24	3
40	—	6: 2	33	29	12:17	3:12	—
45	24	8	34	23: 2	Gal. 3:16	4:13	4
7: 6	26	16	35	7	Eph. 1: 4	2Pet. 1: 3	6
11	31	22	36	15	7	3: 4	—
15	33	—	20: 7	19	—	7	12
17	34	24	25	20	12	13	—
18	36	39	—	24: 2	14	1Joh. 1: 3	17
28	37	41	26	8	17	5	18
30	48	50	31	—	18	6	14: 1
36	20: 1	53	21: 2	23	—	7	—
38	20	60	20	24	19	10	7
—	26	61	24	25	—	2: 3	9
39	—	66	Acts 1:10	25: 3	22	4	10
8: 9	28	—	14	b	23	5	11
18	44	7: 3	18	7	2:10	11	—
19	21:38	5	20	8	18	12	15: 2
22	22:16	7	—	15	20	17	—
38	39	—	22	22	3: 5	27	8
44	44	10	2:22	25	6	28	—
45	47	12	24	27	7	—	16: 2
47	50	13	29	26:24	12	29	10
49	51	17	30	30	5:30	3: 9	12
53	59	29	—	28: 3	—	12	15
9: 7	60	30	31	4	6:10	—	17:14
29	64	32	—	29	—	17	18: 1
—	71	38	41	Ro. 1: 5	Phi. 1:29	19	19: 2
31	23: 2	51	3: 7	9	2:22	22	5
32	8	8: 6	16	20	3:10	—	7
33	—	20	—	—	—	—	10
34	10	26	—	2: 4	—	23	12
35	14	30	22	6	21	—	—
39	34	44	4:26	26	Col. 1: 9	24	13
42	49	55	5: 2	3: 7	11	4: 9	15
—	55	9: 2	7	20	14	12	19
51	24: 8	—	10	24	16	21	20
53	23	3	32	25	20	5: 1	—
54	47	14	41	26	—	2	21
10:34	Joh. 1: 3	17	6:11	4: 5	—	3	20: 3
—	7	18	14	13	24	—	4
35	10	—	15	5: 9	26	11	6
37	12	20	7: 4	—	29	14	11
39	14	21	5	10	3: 9	15	21: 3
11: 1	15	22	6	—	17	18	22: 3
8	16	23	9	6: 3	4:15	20	4
—	27	27	10	5	1Th. 1:10	2Joh. 6	—
16	35	31	23	9	2:19	11	12
18	37	40	25	12	3:13	3Joh. 7	14
21	48	10: 3	31	8: 9	2Th. 1: 9	10	19
22	2: 2	4	37	11	2Tim.1: 8	Jude 15	
—	5	5	8: 1	9:19	2:26	Rev. 1: 4	
—	11	20	30	11:33	4: 8	14	
53	12	11: 2	33	—	14	15	
54	—	12	—	34	Heb. 1: 3	16	
—		13	—	36	2: 6		
			—	—	8		

αὐτούς.

Mat. 1:18
2: 8
9

Mat. 4:21	Lu. 1:65	Joh. 8: 7	Acts 17: 5	αὐτῷ.	Mat. 16:22	Mat. 27:14	Mar. 10:48
24	2: 6	9:19	6	6	17:12	22	49
5: 2	9	12:40	9	9	14	28	51
7: 6	18	13: 1	16	Mat. 1:20	—	29	—
16	20	17: 6	18: 6	24	24	31	52
20	27	11	16	2: 2	18	34	11: 7
24	34	12	19: 2	5	26	38	—
26	43	14	3	8	—	42	21
29	46	15	6	11	18: 6	44	23
10:21	49	—	16	—	13	—	28
26	3:13	17	17	3:16	21	55	31
12:15	14	18	20: 2	4: 3	—	28: 9	12:14
13:15	4:21	23	6	6	22	17	16
42	23	18: 7	21:19	7	24	Mar. 1:13	17
50	31	29	21	8	26	18	26
54	40	Acts 1: 7	25	9	27	25	29
—	—	2:38	—	10	28	27	32
14:14	43	4: 2	32	—	32	30	34
18	5:17	7	22:30	11	34	37	13: 1
25	22	8	24:22	20	19: 2	40	2
15:14	31	13	26:11	22	3	41	14:11
30	34	15	18	24	—	43	12
—	36	18	27:43	25	7	44	13
32	6: 3	19	28:17	5: 1	10	2: 4	19
16: 4	9	21	23	39	13	14	21
17: 1	10	—	27	40	16	—	29
5	32	23	Ro. 1:20	7: 9	17	15	30
27	47	33	24	10	18	18	40
19: 2	8:21	5:13	26	8: 1	20	24	45
4	22	18	28	—	21	26	51
20: 2	9: 2	19	11:11	2	27	3: 7	53
12	3	21	23	4	20: 7	9	54
25	5	22	2Co. 8:24	5	20	10	61
32	10	26	9:13	7	21	11	65
21: 3	11	27	Gal. 4:17	16	22	32	—
14	13	—	6:16	19	29	33	67
17	14	33	Eph. 6: 9	20	33	38	72
37	16	35	Col. 2:15	21	34	41	15: 2
41	18	38	1Th. 2:16	22	21:14	5: 2	17
22:41	33	40	5:13	23	16	—	19
25:32	34	7:26	2Th. 1: 4	—	23	6	20
26:40	54	34	2:10	27	—	8	23
43	10: 1	36	11	28	25	19	27
44	2	42	Tit. 1:13	—	31	20	32
28:19	38	8: 6	3: 1	9: 2	32	24	41
20	11: 5	11	Heb. 1: 4	9	—	31	—
Mar. 1:19	31	14	12	—	33	33	Lu. 1:11
20	47	17	2:11	14	—	37	19
22	48	9:21	4: 8	18	41	6: 1	32
2:13	49	10: 8	8: 9	19	—	2	74
3: 5	53	20	10	27	22:12	3	2: 5
14	12:15	23	10:16	28	16	14	26
20	16	24	—	—	19	19	4: 3
23	24	28	11:16	32	21	30	5
4: 2	37	48	Jas. 3: 3	10:32	23	35	6
5:10	13: 4	11:15	1Pet. 4:14	11: 3	37	37	8
12	23	26	2Pet. 2: 1	12: 2	42	7:28	—
6: 7	14: 5	12:21	3: 5	4	46	32	9
33	7	13: 2	1Joh. 4: 4	15	23:20	—	12
—	25	15	Rev. 2: 2	22	21	34	16
34	15: 3	17	27	32	24: 1	8: 4	17
36	16:30	18	3: 9	—	3	11	20
48	17:14	43	7:15	46	25:21	19	22
—	18:31	50	16	47	23	22	35
—	19:11	51	17	48	26	23	5: 1
51	13	14: 1	—	13:10	37	29	5
8: 3	27	5	9: 5	12	44	32	9
5	33	23	11: 5	27	26: 7	9:13	11
9	20: 3	15: 2	—	28	15	19	14
13	19	5	7	36	17	21	20
31	23	7	11	51	18	23	27
9: 2	41	13	—	57	22	25	28
14	22:15	17	12	14: 2	24	38	29
33	45	27	12: 4	4	25	42	6:38
10: 1	70	39	13: 7	13	33	10:13	7: 2
6	23:14	16: 7	16:14	15	34	18	6
32	22	10	16	17	35	20	9
42	24:15	20	17:14	28	50	21	11
11: 6	17	23	19:15	31	52	—	43
12: 4	25	24	20: 4	33	62	28	8: 1
6	50	30	8	15:12	63	32	3
12	—	33	9	15	64	34	18
13:12	51	34	10	22	69	—	19
14: 7	Joh. 1:38	37	22: 5	25	75	35	20
37	6:17	39		30	27:11	37	25
40	7:50	40		33	13	39	
16:18	8: 2	17: 2		16:17			

Lu. 8:27	Lu. 19:31	Joh. 4:53	Joh. 14:8	Acts 10:25	Phi. 3:9	Rev. 7:15	Mat. 22:18
—	45	5:6	9	27	Col. 1:16	8:3	35
28	20:5	7	21	35	17	9:1	23:3
38	10	8	22	41	19	11	26
39	38	14	23	11:13	2:6	10:6	30
42	22:5	20	—	12:8	7	9	34
47	9	—	15:5	9	9	11:1	—
—	10	27	16:29	13:31	10	13:2	24:31
49	14	6:2	17:2	14:9	12	5	25:2
50	33	7	—	16:32	13	—	10
9:10	39	8	18:5	17:16	15	7	19
11	43	25	20	18	3:4	—	26:21
12	48	30	23	24	4:13	8	22
18	49	56	25	28	1Th. 4:14	14	26
30	56	65	30	34	5:10	15	36
32	—	68	31	18:18	2Th. 1:12	14:7	43
—	61	7:18	33	26	3:14	16:8	73
37	63	26	34	19:22	1Tim. 1:8	9	27:7
52	23:3	52	37	31	16	19:10	17
58	9	8:4	38	38	2Tim. 1:18	14	48
60	15	13	—	20:3	4:14	21:7	28:11
10:28	22	19	19:3	4	Heb. 1:5	22:3	Mar. 1:18
35	26	25	4	10	6	————	23
37	27	29	6	—	2:8		39
11:5	32	31	7	16	—		2:5
6	36	33	9	—	—	αὐτῶν.	19
8	—	39	10	21:8	10		20
—	38	41	32	20	13	Mat. 1:21	3:5
11	40	44	20:6	29	5:9	2:4	4:15
—	43	48	15	22:15	7:10	7	5:17
12	49	52	16	24	10:38	13	6:6
27	55	9:3	25	27	Jas. 1:5	4:8	50
37	24:19	7	28	23:9	2:3	21	52
45	42	9	29	11	23	23	54
12:8	Joh. 1:4	10	21:3	17	4:17	5:3	7:6
10	6	12	5	28	5:7	10	8:3
13	22	24	15	32	6:7	6:7	9:2
14	25	26	—	33	1Pet. 1:21	14	9
20	38	34	16	24:10	2:2	15	36
36	(Gr.39)	35	—	23	6	26	44
41	39	37	—	26	3:22	7:16	46
13:1	(Gr.40)	38	17	—	5:7	20	48
—	40	40	—	25:2	11	8:30	10:13
8	(Gr.41)	10:4	—	28:8	2Pet. 1:17	34	42
15	41	13	—	23	18	9:2	—
17	(Gr.42)	24	19	Ro. 1:17	3:14	4	11:12
23	42	33	22	24	15	15	12:15
31	(Gr.43)	38	23	4:3	18	—	23
14:6	43	11:8	Acts 2:30	22	1Joh. 1:5	29	28
15	(Gr.44)	10	3:10	23	2:5	30	14:18
16	45	20	16	6:4	6	32	22
18	(Gr.46)	24	4:32	8	8	35	40
25	46	27	37	8:32	10	36	52
29	—	30	5:17	9:33	15	10:29	59
15:1	(Gr.47)	32	21	10:11	27	11:1	69
16	(—)	34	32	11:4	28	12:9	70
18	48	(Gr.35)	36	35	3:2	25	16:12
21	—	38	37	—	3	13:54	14
27	(Gr.49)	39	40	36	5	58	Lu. 1:16
30	(—)	12:2	7:5	15:12	6	14:14	20
31	49	—	—	1Co. 1:5	9	32	51
16:1	(Gr.50)	6	8	2:11	15	15:8	77
2	50	13	10	14	17	17:2	2:15
6	(Gr.51)	16	23	11:14	24	7	22
7	51	—	30	15:27	—	9	42
29	(Gr.52)	18	33	28	4:13	12	46
31	2:10	29	35	—	15	14	51
17:2	18	34	38	38	16	22	4:2
3	3:1	13:3	40	2Co. 1:19	5:16	24	6
—	2	6	47	20	2Joh. 10	18:2	15
4	3	7	—	—	11	10	26
8	9	8	8:2	5:9	Rev. 1:1	12	27
9	10	—	11	21	6	17	29
12	26	9	31	7:14	2:7	20	30
16	27	10	35	13:4	17	35	40
19	4:9	25	9:7	—	—	20:13	42
37	11	27	12	Gal. 2:11	26	25	5:2
18:15	14	28	16	13	28	—	6
19	—	29	27	3:6	3:21	29	20
22	—	31	34	Eph. 1:4	6:2	34	22
37	19	32	39	10	—	—	25
39	25	36	10:3	2:16	4	21:3	29
42	33	—	4	3:21	—	7	30
43	50	37	—	4:21	—	—	34
19:17	—	38	7	6:9	5	41	34
22	51	14:5	19	20	8	45	35
25	52	6	23	Phil. 2:9	7:14	22:7	6:8

Lu.	Lu.	Joh.	Acts	Acts	1Co.	Heb.	Rev.
6:13	22:55	13:12	11:28	22:30	3:19	7:25	9: 8
17	58	15:25	29	23:10	5:13	8: 9	9
23	23: 1	16: 4	12:20	—	7:35	—	10
26	23	17: 9	13: 2	21	8: 7	—	—
7:42	24	12	13	27	12	10	16
—	25	—	19	28	10: 5	—	17
8:12	51	19	27	29	7	11	—
23	24: 5	20	32	25:17	8	—	18
37	11	18: 5	(Gr.33)	26:10	9	12	19
9:37	---	9	14: 3	18	10	—	—
45	13	18	5	27:21	12:18	—	—
46	16	19:31	13	28: 6	14:10	10:16	11: 5
47	30	20:24	27	17	15:10	17	—
57	31	26	15: 2	Ro. 1:21	16:19	—	6
10: 7	—	Acts 1: 9	4	24	2Co. 3:14	11:16	7
11:15	36	—	9	—	15	28	8
17	—	19	—	26	5:15	Jas. 1:27	9
48	41	26	12	2:15	19	3: 3	—
49	43	2: 3	22	3: 3	6:16	5: 3	12
12: 6	45	6	23	13	17	1Pet. 3:12	12: 8
13: 1	51	11	38	—	8: 2	14	10
15: 4	Joh. 3:19	3: 5	16:22	15	—	2Pet. 2: 2	13:16
12	22	—	—	16	—	3	14: 5
16: 4	4:38	5	24	18	9:14	11	11
29	52	16	25	10:18	11:15	1Joh. 4: 5	13
17:15	6: 7	29	17: 4	—	Gal. 2:13	3Joh. 9	—
18: 8	7:44	31	12	11: 9	Eph. 4:18	Jude. 15	17: 9
15	50	5:15	26	10	5: 7	12	17
34	8:59	24	33	—	12	16	18:11
19:11	10: 4	6: 1	18: 6	11	6: 9	Rev. 2:16	19:18
33	8	7:34	20	12	Phi. 3:19	6:11	19
20:23	20	8:15	19: 9	—	Col. 2: 2	—	21
33	32	16	12	—	1Th. 5:13	7: 3	20:12
21: 8	39	9:24	—	14	2Ti. 2:17	9	13
22:23	11:19	28	16	15	3: 9	17	21: 3
24	37	38	—	27	Tit. 1:12	8:12	4
25	46	39	19	15:27	—	9: 5	8
—	49	10:46	20:30	—	15	6	22: 4
41	12:36	11:20	21: 1	16: 5	Heb. 2:10	7	14
47	37	21	26	17	14	—	
50	40	22	22:23	1Co. 1: 2	7: 6		
55	—						

The following are given by Schmid as instances of the combination of the definite article with αὐτός. The list might be swelled greatly from the preceding.

ὁ αὐτός.	Lu.	1Co.	1Co.	2Co.	2Co.	Phi.	Heb.
Mat. 5:46	Lu. 17:35	1Co. 1:10	1Co. 12: 5	2Co. 1: 6	2Co. 12:18	Phi. 3:16	Heb. 11: 9
22:34	23:40	—	6	3:18	Eph. 6: 9	4: 2	13: 8
26:44	Acts 14: 1	—	8	4:13	Phi. 1:30	Heb. 1:12	Jas. 3:10
27:44	15:27	7: 5	9	6:13	2: 2	2:14	11
Mar. 14:39	Ro. 2: 1	10: 3	11	8:16	—	4:11	1Pet. 4: 1
Lu. 2: 8	9:21	4	25	12:18	18	6:11	4
6:33	12: 4	11: 5	15:39	—	3: 1	10: 1	5: 9
	16	20		—	16	11	1Joh. 2:27
	15: 5	12: 4					

Full list of the references in which γάρ, see p. 112 occurs.

γάρ.	Mat. 5:46	Mat. 10:19	Mat. 15:19	Mat. 22:30	Mat. 26: 9	Mar. 3:35	Mar. 7:28
Mat. 1:18	6: 7	20	27	23: 3	10	4:22	8: 3
20	8	23	16: 2	4	11	25	35
21	14	26	3	8	12	28	36
2: 2	16	35	25	9	28	5: 8	38
5	21	11:10	26	10	31	28	9: 6
6	24	13	27	13	43	42	—
13	32	18	17:15	(Gr.14)	52	6:14	31
20	—	30	20	17	73	17	34
3: 2	34	12: 8	18: 7	19	27: 1	18	39
3	7: 2	33	10	39	8	20	40
9	8	34	11	24: 5	19	31	41
15	12	37	20	6	23	36	49
4: 6	25	40	19:12	7	43	48	10:14
10	29	50	14	21	28: 2	50	22
17	8: 9	13:12	22	24	5	52	27
18	9: 5	15	20: 1	27	6	—	45
5:12	13	17	16	28	Mar. 1:16	7: 3	11:13
18	16	14: 3	21:26	25:14	22	8	18
20	21	4	32	29	38	10	23
29	24	24	22:14	35	2:15	21	32
30	10:10	15: 2	16	42	3:10	25	12:12
	17	4	28		21	27	14

Mar. 12:23	Lu. 19:5	Joh. 16:13	Acts 27:23	Ro. 8:38	1Co. 3:19	2Co. 1:13	Gal. 3:10
25	10	27	25	9:3	21	19	13
36	21	18:13	34	6	4:4	20	18
44	26	19:6	—	9	7	24	21
13:6	48	31	28:2	11	9	2:2	26
7	20:6	36	20	15	15	4	27
8	19	20:9	22	17	—	9	28
9	33	27	27	19	20	10	4:15
11	36	21:7	Ro. 1:9	28	5:3	11	22
19	—	8	11	32	7	17	24
22	38	Acts 1:20	16	10:2	12	3:6	25
33	21:4	2:15	—	3	6:16	9	27
35	8	—	17	4	20	10	30
14:5	9	25	18	5	7:7	11	5:5
7	15	34	19	10	9	14	6
40	23	39	20	11	14	4:5	13
56	26	3:22	26	12	16	11	14
70	35	4:3	2:1	—	22	15	17
15:10	22:2	12	—	13	31	17	6:3
14	16	16	11	16	8:5	18	5
16:4	18	20	12	11:1	8	5:1	7
8	27	22	13	13	10	2	9
Lu. 1:15	37	27	14	15	9:2	4	13
18	—	34	24	21	9	7	15
30	59	—	25	23	10	10	17
44	71	5:26	28	24	15	12	Eph. 2:8
48	23:8	36	3:2	25	16	13	10
76	12	6:14	3	29	—	14	14
2:10	15	7:33	7	30	17	21	5:5
3:8	22	40	9	32	19	6:2	6
4:8	34	8:7	20	34	10:4	14	8
10	41	16	23	12:3	5	16	9
5:9	Joh. 2:25	21	4:2	4	17	7:3	12
39	3:2	23	3	19	26	5	13
6:23	16	31	9	20	28	8	29
—	17	39	13	13:1	29	9	6:1
26	19	9:11	14	3	11:5	10	Phi. 1:8
32	20	14	15	4	6	12	18
33	24	15	—	—	7	13	19
34	34	10:46	5:6	6	8	8:9	21
38	—	13:8	7	—	9	10	23
43	4:8	27	10	8	12	12	2:5
44	9	36	13	9	18	13	13
—	18	47	15	11	19	9:1	20
45	23	15:21	16	14:3	21	2	21
48	37	28	17	4	22	7	27
7:5	42	16:3	19	6	23	10:3	3:3
6	44	28	20	7	26	4	18
8	45	37	21	8	29	8	20
28	47	17:20	23	9	31	12	4:11
33	5:4	23	6:5	10	12:8	14	Col. 2:1
8:17	13	28	7	11	12	—	5
18	19	—	10	17	13	18	3:3
29	20	18:3	14	18	14	11:2	20
—	21	15	19	15:2	13:9	—	24
40	22	18	20	3	12	4	4:13
46	26	28	21	4	14:2	5	1Th. 1:8
9:14	36	19:24	23	18	—	9	9
24	46	32	7:1	24	5	13	2:1
25	—	35	2	26	8	14	3
26	6:6	37	5	27	9	20	5
44	27	40	7	—	14	12:1	9
48	33	20:10	8	16:2	17	6	
50	55	13	11	18	31	—	14
56	64	16	14	19	33	9	19
10:7	71	—	15	—	34	10	20
24	7:1	27	—	1Co. 1:11	35	11	3:3
11:4	4	29	18	17	15:3	—	4
10	5	21:3	19	18	9	13	9
30	39	13	20	19	16	14	4:2
12:12	41	22	22	21	21	—	3
30	8:24	29	24	26	22	20	7
34	42	36	8:2	2:2	25	13:4	9
13:52	—	22:22	3	8	27	—	10
58	9:22	26	5	10	32	8	14
14:14	30	23:5	6	11	34	9	15
24	10:26	8	7	13	41	Gal. 1:10	5:2
28	11:39	11	11	14	52	12	3
16:2	12:8	17	13	16	53	13	7
13	43	21	14	3:2	16:5	2:6	18
28	47	24:5	15	3	7	8	2Th. 2:7
17:21	13:11	25:11	18	—	9	12	3:2
24	13	27	19	4	10	18	7
18:16	15	26:16	20	9	11	19	10
23	29	26	22	11	18	21	11
25	14:30	—	24	13	2Co. 1:8	3:10	1Ti. 2:3
32	16:7	—	—	17	12		5
		27:22	26	19			

1Ti. 2:13	2Ti. 4:15	Heb. 4: 4	Heb. 7:26	Heb.11: 2	Heb.13:16	1Pet. 2:25	1Joh. 5: 3
3:13	Tit. 1: 7	8	27	5	17	3: 5	2Joh. 11
4: 5	10	10	28	3	—	10	3Joh. 3
8	2:11	12	8: 3	10	18	17	Jude 4
10	3: 3	15	4	14	22	4: 3	Rev. 1: 3
16	9	5: 1	5	16	Jas. 1: 6	6	3: 2
5: 4	12	12	7	26	7	15	9:19
11	Philem. 7	13	8	27	11	2Pet. 1: 8	—
15	15	—	9: 2	32	13	9	13:18
18	22	6: 4	13	12: 3	20	10	14: 4
6: 7	Heb. 1: 5	7	16	6	24	11	5
10	2: 2	10	17	7	2: 2	16	16: 6
2Ti. 1: 7	5	13	19	10	10	17	14
12	8	16	24	17	11	21	17:17
2: 7	10	7: 1	10: 1	—	13	2: 4	19: 8
11	11	10	4	18	26	8	10
16	16	11	14	20	3: 2	18	21: 1
3: 2	18	12	15	25	7	19	22
6	3: 3	13	23	29	16	20	23
9	4	14	26	13: 2	4:14	21	25
4: 3	14	17	30	5	—	3: 4	22: 9
6	16	18	34	9	1Pet. 2:19	5	18
10	4: 2	19	36	11	20	1Joh. 2:19	
11	3	21	37	14	21	4:20	

APPENDIX. — PART II.

Containing a few Cursory Suggestions upon δὲ, καὶ, ὅ, and ὅς, the four words which Schmid passes by unnoticed on account of their too frequent occurrence.

Δέ, de,

Is used *adversatively*, as opposed to μέν, about 129 times in the New Testament. See Concordance, under μέν.

N. B.—Two or more δέ may thus follow one μέν.

Adversative or *distinctive*, without being preceded by μέν, although that particle is probably often implied but not expressed, as :—

Mar 5:33. *But* the woman fearing and
6: 4. *But* Jesus said unto them,
9:50. *but* if the salt have lost
Lu. 2:19. *But* Mary kept all these things,
6:49. *But* he that heareth, and doeth not,
11:20. *But* if I with the finger of God
21:33. *but* my words shall not
Joh. 1:12. *But* as many as received
14:10. *but* the Father that dwelleth
Acts 7:47. *But* Solomon built him an house.
19:15. Paul I know ; *but* who are ye ?
22:28. Paul said, *But* I was (free) born.
Ro. 2:10. *But* glory, honour, and peace, to
6:23. *but* the gift of God (is) eternal life
1Co. 1:23. *But* we preach Christ crucified,
1Ti. 6:11. *But* thou, O man of God, flee
Heb 10:27. *But* a certain fearful looking
Jude 10. *But* these speak evil of those things

Distributive : chiefly found in connexion with μέν.

Mat 21:35. *and* beat one, *and* killed another, *and* stoned another.
1Co.12: 8.)(to another the word of knowledge
9.)(To another faith by the same
—)(to another the gifts of healing,
10.)(to another prophecy ;)(to another

Frequently after γάρ, *for*, we find δέ, *but*.

2Co. 7:10. *but* the sorrow of the world worketh
Tit. 3: 4. *But* after that the kindness and love
Jas. 3: 8. *But* the tongue can no man tame ;

Δέ is never the first word in a sentence ; *generally* the second ; sometimes the third, as :—

Joh. 10:12. *But* he that is an hireling,
15:27. *And* ye also shall bear witness,
Acts 3:24. Yea, *and* all the prophets from
5:32. *And* (so is) also the Holy Ghost,
Jas. 5:12. *But* above all things, my brethren,

It may also be the fourth word, as :—

Acts 22:29. and the chief captain *also* was afraid,

Or even the fifth, as :—

Joh. 8:17.)(It is *also* written in your law,
1Joh. 2: 2. *and* not for our's only, but

Initiative, to mark the commencement of a subject.

Mat. 1:18. *Now* the birth of Jesus Christ
11: 2. *Now* when John had heard in the
1Co.15: 1. *Moreover,* brethren, I declare
1Ti. 4: 1. *Now* the Spirit speaketh expressly,

Continuative and Connective. This is by far the most frequent use of the particle δέ in the New Testament, with the exceptions of (perhaps) the Gospel of St. Mark, and the Revelation of St. John ; in the former of which καί is very frequently, in in the latter almost always, the connecting particle.

A few examples of the continuative and connective use of δέ :—

Mat. 1:—. *passim.*
3: 4. *And* the same John had his
4:18. *And* Jesus, walking by the sea of
10: 7. *And* as ye go, preach, saying,
14:15. *And* when it was evening, his
21:15. *And* when the chief priests and

Resumptive, of a narrative or argument interrupted for a time.

Mat 26:17. *Now* the first (day) of the (feast of)

Mar 13:32. *But* of that day and (that) hour
Lu. 4: 1. *And* Jesus being full of the Holy Ghost

Strongly Oppositive: (coming properly under the head of adversative).

Mat. 5:22. *But* I say unto you, That whosoever
12:28. *But* if I cast out devils by the Spirit
13:16. *But* blessed (are) your eyes, for they
Mar 7:11. *But* ye say, If a man shall say

Cautionary : accompanying a warning or admonition.

Mat.10:17. *But* beware of men for they
33. *But* whosoever shall deny me
12:36. *But* I say unto you, That every idle
Col. 2: 4. *And* this I say, lest any man
Jas. 5:12. *But* above all things, my brethren,

It is capable of an *Intensitive* or *Aggravating* force, as :—

Phi. 2: 8. unto death, even the death of the cross.
(q. d. *and that* death, the death, &c.)

Kaί, *kai.*

Generally simply connective or continuative *"and ;"* but its signification varies according to the character of the sentence, and the words or particles in connexion with which it is taken.
The following are some of the senses in which it occurs in the New Testament :—

καί, *also.*

Mat 12:45. Even so shall it be *also* unto this
13:26. then appeared the tares *also.*
15: 3. Why do ye *also* transgress the
24:39. so shall *also* the coming of the Son of
Mar 3:19. Iscariot, which *also* betrayed him:
12: 6. he sent him *also* last unto them,
Lu. 11:46. Woe unto you *also,* (ye) lawyers !
12:34. there will your heart be *also.*
Joh. 6:67. Will ye *also* go away ?
Acts 5: 2. his wife *also* being privy (to it),
&c. &c.

καί, *even.*

Mat 8:27. that *even* the winds and the sea
25:29. taken away *even* that which he hath.
Mar 6: 2. that *even* such mighty works are
Lu. 12: 7. But *even* the very hairs of your head
Acts 5:39. be found *even* to fight against God.
Ro. 5: 7. some would *even* dare to die.
Heb 11:19. raise (him) up, *even* from the dead ;
&c. &c.

καί, *both,* followed by καί, *and.*

Lu. 21:16. betrayed *both* by parents, and
Joh. 2: 2. And *both* Jesus was called, and
15:24. *both* seen and hated *both* me and
Acts 26:29. were *both* almost, and altogether
&c. &c. (constantly.)

καί, *but.*

Mat 11:19. *But* wisdom is justified of her
Mar 12:12. *but* feared the people: for
Lu. 2:51. *but* his mother kept all these

Lu. 4:26. *But* unto none of them was Elias
13:27. *But* he shall say, I tell you,
Joh. 7:30. *but* no man laid hands on him,
Acts 10:28. *but* God hath shewed me that I
Ro. 1:13. *but* was let hitherto, that I
1 Co.12: 5. administrations, *but* the same Lord.
&c. &c.

καί, *then.*

Mat 23:32. Fill ye up *then* the measure
Lu. 18:26. Who *then* can be saved ?
19:23. Wherefore *then* gavest not thou
20:44. how is he *then* his son ?
1 Co.15:29. why are they *then* baptized for
Jas. 2: 4. Are ye not *then* partial in
&c. &c.

καί is used *illatively* or *conclusively* :—

Heb 3:19. *So* we see that they could not

καί, *that.*

Mar 9:39. in my name, *that* can lightly
Lu. 5: 1. came to pass, *that,* as the
8: 1. came to pass afterward, *that* he
10:38. as they went, *that* he entered into
&c. &c.

καί, apparently *redundant.*

Mat 28: 9. his disciples,)(behold, Jesus

καί, joined with γάρ, usually is rendered simply *"for."*

Lu. 6:32. *for* sinners also love those that
&c. &c. (very frequent.)

καί, *and yet.*

Joh. 9:30. *and (yet)* he hath opened mine eyes.
16:32. *and yet* I am not alone, because
2 Co. 6: 9. unknown, *and (yet)* well known ;
10. having nothing, *and (yet)* possessing

καί, *yet.*

Mar 7:28. Yes, Lord : *yet* the dogs
1 Co. 5:10. *Yet* not altogether with the

καί, *for.*

Acts 23: 3. *for* sittest thou to judge me
1 Joh. 1: 2. *For* the life was manifested,
3: 4. *for* sin is the transgression of

καί, *or.*

Mat 7:10. *Or* if he ask a fish, will he
Jas. 4:13. To day *or* to morrow we will

καί, *when.*

Heb. 8: 8. saith the Lord, *when* I will

καί, *therefore.*

1 Co. 5:13. *Therefore* put away from among
(but the reading seems to be doubtful.)

καί, *if.*

Lu. 15: 4. *If* he lose one of them, (lit. *and* having lost one of them.)

καί, marking the union of two distinct quotations.

Mat 15: 4. and mother : *and,* He that
19:19. and (thy) mother : *and,* Thou shalt
Mar 7:10. mother ; *and,* Whoso curseth
Acts 1:20. dwell therein : *and* his bishoprick
1 Ti. 5:18. the corn. *And,* The labourer
Heb 10:16, 17. will I write them ; *And* their sins

'O, ἡ, τό, *ho*, mas., *hee*, fem., *to*, neut.

Commonly called the Prepositive Article. Its uses are various. The following are some of the most important.

The article usually indicates that the word to which it is joined is the *subject* of a proposition; that, namely, of which something is affirmed or denied, as :—

Joh. 1: 1. *the* Word was with God, and *the* Word [subject] was *God*. [predicate].
4:24. *God* [art.] (is) *a* Spirit : [no art.]
1Joh.4: 8. for *God* [art.] is *love*. [no art.]

The article, prefixed to *both* terms of a proposition, constitutes it a *reciprocating* or *convertible* proposition: i. e. one of which either term may be *equally* affirmed or denied of the other.

Lu. 11:34. *The* light of the body is *the* eye: (or, the eye is the light of the body:)
1Joh.3: 4. for sin is the transgression of the law. (rather, for)(sin is lawlessness; or, for)(lawlessness is sin.)

The article is used to mark *definiteness*.

Mat. 1:23. *a* [art.] virgin shall be with child, (*the one* prophesied of.)
4: 5. *a* [art.] pinnacle of the temple, (a well known part of it.)
24. throughout all)(Syria [art.] (lit. the Syrian [country.])
5: 5. *the* meek: (a class of persons.)
13:37. *the* Son of man ;
38. *The* field is *the* world ;
Lu. 12:54. *a* cloud [art.] rise (a well known phenomenon.—See 1Kings, 18:44.)
Joh.19: 5. *the* crown of thorns, and *the* purple
Acts24:23. *a* [art.] centurion to keep Paul, (*the one* who had charge of him.)
1Co. 5:13. *that* wicked person. (i. e. the incestuous person of whom he had spoken.)
2Th. 2: 3. come *a* [art.] falling away first, (rather, *the* apostasy.)
1Joh.5:19. world lieth in wickedness. [art.] (in *the* wicked one.)

Indefiniteness is generally marked by the *absence* of the article.

Mat 10: 8. Heal the sick, cleanse the lepers. [no art.] (i. e. sick, lepers, &c. generally.)
28:18. All power is given unto me (i. e. unlimited power.)
Ro. 3:20. by the deeds of the law there shall (i. e. deeds of law generally.)
1Co.15:16. For if the dead rise not, (i. e. dead generally.)
Rev. 2:22. I will cast her into a bed,

A similar omission takes place after the participle of existence.

Joh.10:12. and not the)(shepherd, whose own (i. e. not being, [no art.])
Acts 5:17. which is the)(sect of the Sadducces, (i. e. *being*, [no art.])
Heb 1: 3. Who being)(the brightness of [no art.]

Also frequently after a preposition.

Mar. 3:19. they went into an house. (or home.) [no art.]
Ro. 5:13. For until the law [no art.]
Gal. 2:16. not by the works of the law: [no art.]

The article is also sometimes used to mark either, first, *emphasis.*

Mar13:11. but *the* Holy Ghost. (lit. *the* Spirit *the* Holy.)
Joh. 1:21. Art thou *that* prophet ?
5:35. *a* burning and *a* shining light:
10:11. I am *the* good shepherd: (lit. *the* shepherd *the* good.)
2Th 2: 3. *that* man of sin be revealed,
Rev. 1: 3. the words of *this* prophecy,
4. *him* which is, and which was, (lit. from *the* " who is," &c.)

Or secondly, *hypothesis.*

Mat12:35. *A* good man out of the good (i. e. *any given* good man.)
18:17. as *an* heathen man and *a* publican. (i. e. *any.*)
Joh.12:24. Except *a* corn of wheat (i. e. *any.*)
1Co. 7:28. and if *a* virgin marry, (i. e. *any.*)

It is sometimes simply *descriptive*, or *designative.*

Mat. 3: 1. came John *the* Baptist,
Joh.13:13. Ye call me)(Master and)(Lord:
14:30. for *the* prince of this world cometh,
19:19. Jesus of Nazareth *the* King of
Ro. 10: 5. *the* man *that* doeth those things

The nominative with the article is sometimes used for the vocative.

Mat 11:26. Even so, Father: [nom. with art.]
Mar 10:47. Jesus, (thou) son of David, [nom. with art.]
Heb 1: 8. Thy throne, O God, [nom. with art.]
10: 9. I come to do thy will, O God. [nom. with art.]

Tὸ, the neuter, is prefixed to a clause, or sentence, or phrase.

Mar 9:23. Jesus said unto him,)(If thou canst believe,
Lu. 22: 2. sought)(how they might kill him ;
23. to enquire ...)(which of them it was
Ro. 9: 5.)(as concerning the flesh
16:19. I am glad therefore)(on your behalf:

It is prefixed also to the infinitive, when used substantively.

Ro. 7:18. [nom.] for)(to will is present
Acts 3:12. [gen.] made this man)(to walk ?
Lu. 5: 1. [dat.])(as the people pressed upon him
Mat13: 5. [acc.])(because they had no deepness of earth:

N. B. — The substantive with which the article agrees is often left out ; thus :—

Mat 21 :21. *this* (which is done) to the fig tree,
Mar 2:14. Levi *the* (son) of Alphæus

Mar 16: 1. Mary *the* (mother) of James,
Joh. 19:25. Mary *the* (wife) of Cleophas,
    21: 2. and *the* (sons) of Zebedee,
Acts 10:23. certain brethren)(from Joppa
Phi. 4:22. *they* that are of Cæsar's houshold.
Heb 13:24. *They* of Italy salute you.

In the Christian Witness, vol. i. p. 317, under "Scriptural Criticism," may be found some important remarks upon the article.

"Ος, ἥ, ὅ, *hos*, mas., *hee*, fem., *ho*, neut.

The *relative* (sometimes called the *subjunctive article*), answering to *who, which,* &c. in English. The following are a few of its less ordinary uses in the New Testament:—

Distributive (for the article ὁ, with *μέν*, and *δέ*).

Mat 13: 8. fruit, *some* an hundredfold, *some* sixtyfold, *some* thirtyfold.
    21:35. beat *one*, and killed *another*, and stoned *another*.
Mar 4: 4. *some* fell by the way side, and
Lu. 23:33. *one* on the right hand, and *the other*
Ro. 9:21. *one* vessel unto honour, *and another* unto
    14: 2. For *one* believeth that he may eat all
      5. *One* man esteemeth one day above another : *another* esteemeth
1Co. 7: 7. *one* after this manner, and *another* after
2Co. 2:16. To *the one* (we are) the savour of death unto death; and to *the other* the savour of life unto life.

For the interrogative *τίς, who?* or, *what?*
Mat 26:50. Friend, wherefore art thou come ? (i.e. for *what?*)

ἀνθ' ὧν, see under *ἀντί*, in Concordance.

Relative placed *before* the antecedent, in the order of *the Greek*.
Mat 26:48. *Whomsoever* I shall kiss, that same
Mar 6:16. It is John, *whom* I beheaded:

In conclusion, it may be asked, is there not a great and an important distinction to be noticed between the use of the article with the present participle, and the relative with the present tense indicative ; as, between ὁ ποιων, and ὃς ποιει ; ὁ σπειρων, and ὃς σπειρει.

The first seems to present office, or agency in the abstract ; the idea therefore conveyed to the mind is more indefinite.

Mat 7: 8. every one *that asketh* receiveth ; and he *that seeketh* findeth ; and to him *that knocketh* it shall be opened.
    13: 3. *a sower* went forth to sow ;
          &c. &c.

On the contrary perhaps, the relative with the present tense makes a more positive definite assertion of a specific action.
Lu. 2:11. a Saviour, *which is* Christ the Lord.
Ro. 4:16. *who is* the father of us all,
Jas. 4:12. who art thou *that judgest* another ?
          &c. &c.

A
CONCORDANCE

OF

VARIOUS READINGS

OCCURRING IN

THE GREEK NEW TESTAMENT,

AS ADOPTED BY

Griesbach, Lachmann, Tischendorf, Tregelles, Alford,
Wordsworth, Westcott and Hort, and "The Revisers:"

COMPARED

WITH THE TEXT OF STEPHENS 1550

AND THE

AUTHORISED VERSION OF 1611.

Multæ terricolis linguæ, cœlestibus una.

INTRODUCTION.

THIS Concordance of Various Readings is intended mainly as an Appendix to the ENGLISHMAN'S GREEK CONCORDANCE, but it can be used with any Greek Concordance, and is therefore sold separately. To this end the actual Greek words introduced by the various Editors are given, together with the change in English where needed.

It is imperative that every careful student of scripture should give attention to the various readings introduced by Editors of the Greek text. It is a matter of great thankfulness that these various readings do not touch any one of the fundamental doctrines of Christianity; but we want to know the actual words God caused to be written. For instance, all who have studied the subject acknowledge that there are words, &c., in the Authorised Version of 1611 that cannot be maintained, apart altogether from the question of translation. *What* is to be translated is the question raised where the Greek manuscripts differ. "Editors" are those who have devoted their time and energies to discover what the text was originally. We give the readings of several Editors, from Griesbach to the "Revisers" of 1881, and where they *all* agree, or all except Griesbach (seeing there has been so much additional valuable evidence since his day), we judge the reader will be safe in adopting that reading in preference to the one found in the Authorised Version, though of course some of the other well-accredited readings may be the true ones.

The following will explain the way in which the work has been carried out. Every person is supposed to have before him a copy of the Authorised English Version, and, if he wishes to refer to the Greek, a copy of the common Greek text.

Punctuation.—As the oldest Greek MSS have few or no points, Editors were compelled to punctuate for themselves: where they differ in this is more a matter of interpretation than a different reading. We therefore give only those where the Greek text is also altered.

Omissions.—Single words are recorded only under the word omitted. They are given in English where they affect the sense to an English reader. Where the word is required in English the omission is given in Greek.

Omissions of more than one word are recorded under every word omitted, except δέ, καί, τε. and ὁ, ἡ, τό, except Mark xvi. 9–20, and John vii. 53–viii. 11; these are recorded on the first page only, as "Lengthy Omissions."

Additions.—Single words are recorded only under the added word, English being given where needed.

Additions of more than one word are recorded under every word except δέ, καί, τε.

In all additions, the inflection used, and the place where the words are added, are pointed out.

New occurrences of words already in the common text are marked with a *.

New words introduced by the Editors are marked with a * in the heading.

Transpositions.—Transpositions which obviously affect the sense, or seem to give precedence to one word over another, are recorded under the words transposed— the new reading being given thus:

Luke 8:51 *trs* John and James
1 Co. 1: 1 *trs* Christ Jesus

Transpositions which do not obviously affect the sense are given in Greek under one of the principal words. Passages where an alteration occurs as well as the transposition are marked with a †.

Inflections.—These are marked under their respective roots. The actual word adopted by the Editors is given, and English added where, but only where, the sense is materially affected by the alteration.

Substitution.—Where one word is substituted for another, it is given under both headings, thus :

δεύτερος.

Mat. 21: 30 second—other, ἕτερος GTAW

ἕτερος.

Mat. 21:30*ἑτέρῳ *for* δευτέρῳ (-ρος) GTAW

Where δέ, καί, τε are interchanged, they are given only under the word that stands in the common text.

Where a pronoun is arranged under separate headings, immediately following one another, as αὐτά, αὐταῖς, αὐτή, &c., the interchange of such words is recorded only under the word in the common text.

The Article.—Changes in the article are recorded under the nouns, adjectives, infinitives and participles, with which they are connected. Other changes are under the heading ὁ, ἡ, τό.

Greek Text.—The Greek Text followed is that of Stephens 1550, but the differences between this and Elzevir 1624, are recorded.

Authorised Version.—The text of 1611 (but as at present printed) is taken, and where this differs materially from the text of Stephens 1550, it is recorded, and a text named which the Editors *probably* followed : in a few places a [?] is added where *no* authority can be traced. A † is added in a few cases where the A.V. as now printed differs from the version of 1611. Words in ( ) are those in italics in the A.V.

Editors.—The readings given (being variations from Stephens 1550) are those adopted by

Griesbach	G	1805
Lachmann	L	1842–50
Tischendorf	T	1865–72
Tregelles	Tr	1857–72
Alford	A	1862–71
Wordsworth	W	1870
Westcott & Hort	WH	1881
"The Revisers"	R	1881
Complutensian	C	1514
Erasmus	Er	1527
Beza	B	1598
Vulgate	Vul	592
Stephens	S	1550
Elzevir	E	1624

The marks [ ] imply that one or more Editors regard the reading as doubtful.

Readings marked doubtful by only *one* Editor are not recorded.

Readings adopted by G and L, unsupported by any of the more modern Editors, are not recorded.

Where all the Editors (except G) agree as to reading, it is marked Eds.

June, 1883.

—◦-◦—

VARIOUS READINGS.

LENGTHY OMISSIONS.

Mar. 16: 9-20 *omit the verses* T[A] [[WH]]
Joh. 7:53 to 8:11 placed by [A] at foot of page, by [[WH]] at end of Gospel ; *omit* [G]LTTr[E]

A, ἄλφα LTTrAWWH.

Rev. 1:11 *omit* I am Alpha and Omega, the first and the last : and GEds

Ἀαρών.

Heb. 5: 4 ὁ Ἀ.—*omit* ὁ GEds

ἀββᾶ, ἀββα WH.

Ἄβελ, Ἄ— WH.

Ἀβιληνή, Ἀβει— WH.

Ἀβραάμ, Ἀ— R.

Lu. 16:22 τοῦ Ἀ.—*omit* τοῦ GLTTrAWWH
23 τὸν Ἀ.—*omit* τὸν LTTrAWH
Heb. 7: 6 τὸν Ἀ.—*omit* τὸν LTTrAWH

* ἀγαθοεργέω, ἀγαθουργέω.

Acts 14:17*ἀγαθουργῶν for ἀγαθοποιῶν (-ιέω) Eds

ἀγαθοποιέω.

Mar. 3: 4 ἀγαθὸν ποιῆσαι T
Acts 14:17 ἀγαθουργέω Eds

ἀγαθοποιΐα.

1 Pet. 4:19 ἀγαθοποιΐαις LW

ἀγαθός.

Mat. 12:35 τὰ ἀ.—*omit* τὰ LTTrWWH
19:16 *omit* good¹ LTTrAWH
17 τί με ἐρωτᾷς περὶ τοῦ ἀγαθοῦ ; εἷς ἐστιν ὁ ἀγαθός (ὁ θεὸς God w), *read* Why askest thou me concerning the good ? One is good GEds

Mar. 3: 4*see ἀγαθοποιέω
Ro. 10:15 τὰ ἀ.—*omit* τὰ LTrAWWHR
13: 3 τῷ ἀγαθῷ ἔργῳ to the good work Eds

ἀγαθουργέω, see ἀγαθοεργέω.

ἀγαλλιάω.

Joh. 5:35 ἀγαλλιαθῆναι GLTTrAWWH
Acts 16:34 ἠγαλλιάτο A
1 Pet. 1: 8 ἀγαλλιᾶτε WH
Rev. 19: 7 ἀγαλλιῶμεν LTTrAWH

ἄγαμος.

1 Co. 7:34 see γυνή

ἀγαπάω.

Lu. 7:42 trs ἀγαπήσει αὐτόν LTTrAWH
Joh. 15: 9 trs ὑμᾶς ἠγάπησα LTrAWH
Ro. 13: 8 trs ἀλλήλους ἀ GLTTrAWWH
2 Co. 12:15 ἀ.¹—ἀγαπῶ TWHR
1 Joh. 4:10 ἀ.¹—ἠγαπήκαμεν WH
Jude 1*ἠγαπημένοις for ἡγιασμένοις (ἀγιάζω) Eds
Rev. 1: 5 ἀγαπῶντι loveth GEĉs

ἀγάπη.

Joh. 5:42 trs οὐκ ἔχετε τὴν ἀ. τοῦ θεοῦ T
1 Co.13: 4 *omit* charity³ [LTrA]WH
Eph. 1:15 *omit* love I.[A]WHR
Phil. 1:17 trs verses 16 and 17 except οἱ μὲν and οἱ δὲ Eds
1 Pet. 4: 8 ἀ.²—ἡ ἀγάπη EG
2 Pet. 2:13*ἀγάπαις for ἀπάταις (-τη) LTrR
Rev. 2:19 trs faith, and charity, and service Tr

ἀγαπητός.

Lu. 9:35 beloved—chosen, ἐκλέγω TTrAWHR
Philem. 2 beloved—sister, ἀδελφή LTTrAWHR
1 Joh. 2: 7*ἀγαπητύ for ἀδελφοί (-ός) GEds

Ἄγαρ, Ἄ— WH

Gal. 4:25 *omit* Agar LT[Tr]

ἀγγεῖον.

Mat. 13:48 ἄγγος TTrAWH

ἀγγελία.

1 Joh.1: 5*ἀγγελία for ἐπαγγελία A.V.Vul GEds

* ἀγγέλλω, bring word.

Joh. 4:51 ἤγγειλαν for ἀπήγγειλαν (ἀπαγγέλλω) T
20:18 ἀγγέλλουσα for ἀπαγγέλλουσα (-λω) LTTrAWHR

ἄγγελος.

Mar. 13:32 οἱ ἄ.—ἄγγελος an angel A
Lu. 1:28 *omit* the angel [T]AWHR: trs πρὸς αὐτὴν ὁ ἄ. T
22:43, 44 the verses [L] [[WH]]
Joh. 5: 4 *omit* waiting for(ver.3) to end of verse 4 [G]TTrAWH
Acts 27:23 trs ἄγγελος after λατρεύω Eds
Rev. 8: 7 *omit* angel GEds
13 angel—eagle, ἀετός GEds
9:11 τὸν ἄ.—*omit* τὸν A
10: 8 τοῦ ἀγγέλου A.V.C GEds
11: 1 ῥάβδῳ—add καὶ ὁ ἄγγελος εἱστήκει and the angel stood A.V.BE
14: 9 trs ἄγγελος τρίτος ᾽Εα.
16: 3 *omit* angel Eds
4, 8, 10, 12, 17 *omit* angel GEds

* ἄγγος, vessel, of various sorts.

Mat. 13·48 ἄγγη for ἀγγεῖα (-ῖον) TTrAWH

ἀγέλη.

Mat. 8:32 *omit* herd of¹ GLTTrWHR

ἁγιάζω.

Mat. 23:17 ἁγιάσας sanctified LTTrAWH
1 Co. 1: 2 trs ἡγιασμένοις ἐν χριστῷ ᾽Ιησοῦ τῇ οὔσῃ ἐν Κορίνθῳ LTrA
Jude 1 sanctified—beloved, ἀγαπάω Eds

ἅγιος, ἅγιον.

Mat. 25:31 *omit* holy GLTTrAWHR
Mar. 12:36 τῷ ἁ.—*omit* τῷ GW
Lu. 2:25 trs ἦν ἅγιον GEds
10:21*πνεύματι—add τῷ ἁγίῳ, read the Holy Spirit LTTrAWHR
Joh. 6:69*ὁ ἅγιος for ὁ χριστὸς ὁ υἱὸς GLTTrAWHR
7:39 *omit* Holy LT[TrA]WHR
Acts 3:21 τῶν ἁγίων GEds
4:25*add ἅ. LTTrAWHR, see πατήρ
31†trs τοῦ ἁ. πνεύματος Eds
6: 3 *omit* Holy GLTTrAWHR
8:18 *omit* Holy T[Tr]AWH
10:3 trs τοῖς ἁ. σου ἐποίησας LTTrAWH
Ro. 15:19*ἁγίου for θεοῦ (-ός) GLTr[A]W[WH]R
31 trs τοῖς ἁ. γένηται LTTrAWHR
1 Co. 2:13 *omit* Holy GEds
Eph. 3: 8 τῶν ἁ.—*omit* τῶν GEds
1 Th. 5:27 *omit* holy LTTrAWHR
Heb. 9: 2 ἅγια s—ἅγια A.V.B EGEds: ἅγια, ἁγίων. L (sic)
3 τὰ ἅγια τῶν ἁγίων Tr
24 trs εἰσῆλθεν ἅγια TTrAWH
2 Pet. 1:21 οἱ ἅ.—*omit* οἱ A.V.C GEds: holy men—*omit* holy TAWH
1 Joh. 5: 7 *omit* in heaven to in earth (ver. 8) GEds
Jude 14 trs ἁγίαις μυριάσιν GEds
20 trs ἐποικοδομοῦντες ἑαυτοὺς τῇ ἁγιωτάτῃ ὑμῶν πίστει GEds
Rev. 3: 7 trs he that is true, he that is holy A
13: 7 *omit* And it was to overcome them L[WH]
14:10†trs ἀγγέλων (omit τῶν) ἁγίων LTTrWHR: *omit* holy A

Rev. 15: 3 saints—nations ἔθνος GLTTrAW —ages, αἰών WHR
19: 8 trs τῶν ἁ. ἐστίν LTTrAWHR
22: G holy—spirits of the, πνεῦμα GEds
21°with (all GW)—add τῶν ἁγίων the saints GTrAWWHR

ἁγιότης.

2 Co. 1:12*ἁγιότητι for ἁπλότητι (-ης) LTTrAWHR

ἄγκυρα.

Acts 27:30 trs ἀγκύρας μελλόντων LTTrAWH

ἁγνεία, -νία . WH.

1 Co.14:38 ἀ.²—ἀγνοεῖται he is ignored LTWH

ἁγνότης.

2 Co. 11: 3*simplicity—add καὶ τῆς ἁγνότητος and purity LTrAW[WH]R

ἀγορά.

Mat. 11:16†trs καθημένοις ἐν ταῖς ἀ. TTrAWH

ἀγοράζω.

Mar. 11:15 τοὺς ἀγοράζοντας Eds
Lu. 19:45 *omit* therein and them that bought TTrAWH
Joh. 6: 5 ἀγοράσωμεν Eds

Ἀγρίππας.

Acts 26: 7 *omit* Agrippa Eds

ἀγρός.

Mar. 11: 8*ἀγρῶν for δένδρων (-ρον) TTrAWH
Lu. 9:12 τοὺς ἀ.—*omit* τοὺς T[Tr]AWH
12:28†trs (omit τῷ) ἐν ἀ. τὸν χόρτον ὄντα σήμερον TAWHR: τὸν χ. σ ἐν ἀ. ὄντα LTr
17:31 τῷ ἀ.—*omit* τῷ TTrAWH
36 add the verse A.V.B E, see ἀφίημι

ἄγω.

Mat. 14: 6 γίνομαι LTTrAWHR
21: 2 ἄγετε LTrA
Mar. 11: 2, 7 φέρω TTrAWH
13: 9 ἀχθήσεσθε for σταθήσεσθε (ἵστημι) A.V. Eʳ
11 ἄγωσιν GEds
Lu. 21:12 ἀπάγω TTrAWHR
23: 1 ἤγαγον GEds
Joh. 18:13*ἤγαγον LTTrₑWHR for ἀπήγαγον (ἀπάγω), [ἀπ]ήγαγον A
Acts 5:26 ἤγεν TWH
13:23*ἤγαγεν for ἤγειρεν(ἐγείρω) GEds
17: 5 προάγω LTTrAWH
22:24 εἰσάγω GLTTrAWWH

ἀγών.

2 Ti. 4: 7†trs τὸν καλὸν ἀγῶνα LTTrWH

ἀγωνία.

Lu. 22:43, 44 the verses [L] [[WH]]

ἀγωνίζομαι.

Joh.18:36 trs οἱ ἐμοὶ ἠγωνίζοντο ἂν Tr WH
1 Ti. 4:10*ἀγωνιζόμεθα for ὀνειδιζόμεθα (-ζω) LTTrWHR

Ἀδδί, Ἀδδεί TTrAWH.

ἀδελφή.

Mar. 3:32*σου²—add καὶ αἱ (omit αἱ W) ἀδελφαί σου and thy sisters LT[A]W
Philem. 2*ἀδελφῇ for ἀγαπητῇ (-τός) LTTrAWHR

ἀδελφός.

Mat. 12:47 *omit* the verse [T]WH

Mar. 3:31 *trs* his mother and his brethren GLTTᵣWWHR
Lu. 18:29 *trs* wife, or brethren, or
parents TAWHI
Acts 1:15*ἀδελφῶν for μαθητῶν (-τῆς) Eds
15:23 *omit* καὶ οἱ, *read* elder brethren LTTᵣAWHR
20:32 *omit* brethren LTTᵣAWHR
28:17 *trs* ἐγώ, ἄνδρες ἀδελ. LTTᵣAWHR
Ro. 15:15 *omit* brethren LTTᵣ[A]WHR
30 [brethren] AWH
1 Co. 7:14*ἀδελφῳ for ἀνδρί (ἀνήρ) Eds
8:11†*trs* ἐν τῇ σῇ γνώσει, ὁ ἀ. Eds
11: 2 *omit* brethren Eds
15:31*rejoicing—*add* ἀδελφοί brethren LTTᵣAWHR
2 Co. 8:18 *trs* τὸν ἀδελφὸν μετ᾿ αὐτοῦ TR
Eph. 6:10 *omit* my brethren LTTᵣAWHR
Jas. 5: 9 *trs* ἀδελ. κατ᾿ ἀλλήλων LTTᵣAWHR
10†*trs* ἀ. (*omit* μου Eds) τῆς κακο-
παθείας GEds
1 Joh. 2: 7 Brethren—Beloved, ἀγαπητός
GEds
3:14 *omit* (his) brother Eds

ᾅδης.

Lu. 10:15 τοῦ ᾅδου TᵣAWH
Acts 2:27 ᾅδην LTTᵣAWWH
31 ᾅδην TWH
1 Co. 15:55 O grave—O death, θανατός
LTTᵣAWH
Rev. 1:18 *trs* of death and of hell GEds

ἀδιαφθορία.

Tit. 2: 7 ἀφθορία Eds

ἀδικέω.

Lu. 10:19 ἀδικήσῃ S—ἀδικήσει ELTTᵣAWH
Acts 25:10 ἠδίκηκα TTᵣWH
2 Pet. 2:13 ...δικούμενοι for κομιούμενοι (κομίζω) WHR
Rev. 9: 4 ἀδικήσουσιν LTAWH

ἀδικία.

Mat. 23:25*ἀδικίας for ἀκρασίας (-ία) GW
Lu. 13:27 τῆς ἀ.—*omit* τῆς LTTᵣWHR
2 Th. 2:10 τῆς ἀ.—*omit* τῆς Eds
Heb. 1: 9*ἀδικίαν for ἀνομίαν (-ία) T

* Ἀδμείν, *see* Ἀράμ.

Ἀδραμυντηνός, Ἀδραμυντηνου WH.

Ἀδρίας, Ἀ— WH.

ἀδύνατος.

Acts 14: 8 *trs* ἀδύνατος ἐν Λύστροις TWH

ἀεί.

Mar. 15: 8 *omit* ever TWH
2 Pet. 1:12 *trs* ἀεὶ ὑμᾶς GTTᵣWWHR

ἀετός.

Rev. 8:13*ἀετοῦ for ἀγγέλου (-ος) GEds

ἀθετέω.

Mar. 6:26 *trs* ἀθετῆσαι αυτην TTᵣWH

* ἀθροίζω, to gather together.

Lu. 24:33 ἠθροισμενους for συνηθροισμέ-
νους (συναθροίζω) LTTᵣAWH

ἀθῶος, ἀθῷος LTAWH.

Mat. 27: 4 innocent—just, δίκαιος WH

αἴγειος, —γιος WH.

Αἴγυπτος.

Acts 7:11 γῆν Α.—Αἴγυπτον LTTᵣAWHR
12 Αἴγυπτον Eds
18*ἕτερος—*add* ἐπ᾿ Αἴγυπτον, *read*
arose over Egypt LTTᵣWHR
36 (τῇ LTᵣWHR) Αἰγύπτῳ GLTTᵣAWH
13:17 Αἰγύπτου LTᵣWHR   (E
Heb. 11:26 Αἰγύπτου GEds

αἰδώς

Heb. 12:28 *omit* α. *see* δέος

αἷμα.

Mat. 23:35 τοῦ α.¹—*omit* τοῦ W
Lu. 11:51 τοῦ α. *bis*—*omit* τοῦ LTTᵣAWH
22:43, 44 *the verses* [L] [[WH]]
Acts 17:26 *omit* blood LTT[A]WHR
20:28†*trs* τοῦ αἵματος τοῦ ἰδίου GEds
21:25 τὸ α.—*omit* τὸ LTTᵣ[A]WWHR

---

1 Co. 10:16 *trs* ἐστὶν τοῦ α. τοῦ χρ. TᵣWH
11:27 τοῦ αἵματος GEds
Col. 1:14 *omit* through his blood GEds
Heb. 2:14 *trs* of blood and flesh Eds
Rev. 16: 6 α.¹—αἵματα T
18:24 αἵματα GTWR

αἰνέω.

Lu. 24:53 *omit* praising and [TᵣA]WHR

αἱρέομαι.

2 Th. 2:13 εἵλατο GLTTᵣAWWH

αἱρετίζω.

Mat. 12:18 ἡρέτισα Tᵣ

αἴρω.

Mat. 22:13 *omit* take him away, and
LTTᵣAWH
Mar. 10:21 *omit* take up the cross
[LTTᵣWHR
13:15 *trs* τι ἆραι TᵣAWH
Joh. 10:18 ἦρεν took WH
16:22 ἀρεῖ shall take LTᵣAWH
19:38 ἦρεν—ἦραν T
1 Co. 5: 2*ἀρθῇ for ἐξαρθῇ (ἐξαίρω) GEds

αἰσχροκερδής.

1 Ti. 3: 3 *omit* not greedy of filthy lucre
GEds

αἰτέω.

Mat. 7: 9 ἐὰν α.—αἰτήσει, of *read* whom
his son shall ask LTTᵣAWHR
10 αἰτήσει LTTᵣAWH
Mar. 6:24 αἰτήσωμαι Eds
15: 6 παραιτέομαι TWH
Lu. 6:30 τῷ α.—*omit* τῷ [L]TWHR
11:12 αἰτήσῃ S—αἰτήσει JTTᵣAWHR
12:20*αἰτοῦσιν for ἀπαιτοῦσιν (-τεω)
TᵣAWH
Joh. 15: 7 αἰτήσασθε ask Eds

αἴτιαμα, αἰτίωμα GEds

Lu. 21:34 *trs* ἐπιστῇ ἐφ᾿ ὑμᾶς αἰφ. (ἐφ-WH)
TTᵣAWH

αἰφνίδιος.

Rev. 3:10 *omit* leadeth into captivity Tᵣ

αἰχμαλωσία.

2 Ti. 3: 6 αἰχμαλωτίζω GEds

αἰχμαλωτεύω.

2 Ti. 3: 6*αἰχμαλωτίζοντες for αἰχμα-
λω..ευοντες (-ύω) GEds

αἰχμαλωτίζω.

αἰών.

Mat. 6:13 *omit* For thine is *to end of
verse* GEds
13:39 τοῦ α.—*omit* τοῦ LTTᵣAWH
Mar. 11:14 *trs* εἰς τὸν αἰῶνα ἐκ σοῦ LTTᵣAWH
Lu. 1:70 τῶν ἀπ᾿ α.—*omit* τῶν TTᵣAWH
Ro. 16:27*αἰώνας—*add* τῶν αἰώνων, *read*
ever and ever LT
Gal. 1: 4†*trs* τοῦ αἰῶνος τοῦ ἐνεστῶτος
LTTᵣAWHR
Eph. 6:12 *omit* world, *read* this darkness GEds
Heb. 1: 2 *trs* ἐποίησεν τοὺς αἰῶνας Eds
1 Pet. 1:23 *omit* for ever GEds
5:11 *omit* and ever (τῶν α.) WH
2 Pet. 2:17 *omit* for ever LTTᵣAWHR
Jude 13 τὸν α.—*omit* τὸν GEds
25*power—*add* πρὸ παντὸς τοῦ
αἰῶνος before all time Eds
Rev. 1: 6 *omit* and ever (τῶν α.) AWH
5:14 *omit* him that liveth for ever
and ever GEds
14:11 *trs* εἰς αἰῶνας αἰώνων ἀναβαίνει
GEds
15: 3*αἰώνων for ἁγίων (ἅγιος) WHR

αἰώνιος.

1 Ti. 6:19 eternal—truly, ὄντως GEds

ἀκαθαρσία.

Eph. 5: 3 *trs* ἀκαθαρσία πᾶσα LTTᵣAWHR

ἀκαθάρτης.

Rev. 17: 4 filthiness—unclean things,
ἀκάθαρος GEds

ἀκάθαρτος.

Rev. 17: 4*τὰ ἀκάθαρτα for ἀκαθάρτητος
(-θαρτης) GEds

---

* ἀκατάπαυστος, insatiable.

2 Pet. 2:14 ἀκαταπάστους for ἀκαταπαύσ-
τους (ος) LWH

ἀκατάπαυστος.

2 Pet. 2:14 cannot cease—insatiable, ἀκα-
τάπαστος LWH

ἀκατάστατος.

Jas. 3: 8*ἀκατάστατον for ἀκατάσχετον
(-ος) Eds

ἀκατάσχετος.

Jas. 3: 8 unruly—restless, ἀκατάστατος
Eds

Ἀκελδαμά, -άχ LA, Ἀκ—άχ WH,
Ἀχ—άχ TTᵣ.

ἀκολουθέω.

Mat. 9: 9 ἀ.²—ἠκολούθει T
19 ἠκολούθει LTTᵣAWH
Mar. 2:15 ἠκολούθουν TᵣWHR
3: 7 *trs* ἠ. *after* Ἰουδαίας T: ἠκολού-
θησεν LTᵣAWH
8:34*ἀκολουθεῖν for ἐλθεῖν (ἔρχομαι)
GTTᵣAW
9:38 *omit* and he followeth not us
GWHR
38 ἀ.²—ἠκολούθει followed TWHR
10:28 ἠκολουθήκαμεν Eds
32 καὶ ἀ.—οἱ δὲ ἀ. TTᵣWH
14:51 followed—followed with, συν-
ακολουθέω LTTᵣAWHR: ἠκολού-
θησεν W
16:17*trs ἀκολουθήσει (*for* παρακο-
λουθήσει, -θέω) ταῦτα TᵣWH
Lu. 5:28 ἠκολούθει LTTᵣAWHR
Joh. 10: 5 ἀκολουθήσουσιν Eds
13:36 *trs* ἀ.² δὲ ὕστερον LTTᵣAWH
37 ἀκολουθεῖν TᵣWH
21:22 *trs* μοι ἀκολούθει LTTᵣAWWH
Rev. 6: 8 ἠκολούθει GEds
18: 5 followed—have reached, κολλάω A.V.C GEds

ἀκούω.

Mat. 11:15 *omit* to hear T[Tᵣ]AWH
13: 9 *omit* to hear T[Tᵣ]AWH
16 ἀκούουσιν LTTᵣAWH
43 *omit* to hear [L]T[Tᵣ]AWHR
17: 5 *trs* ἀκούετε αὐτοῦ LTTᵣAWH
22: 7 *omit* ἀ. *read* But the king
was wroth TᵣAWH
Mar. 3: 8 ἀκούοντες hearing LTTᵣAWHR
4:18 ἀκούσαντες heard TTᵣAWH
24 *omit* that hear GLTTᵣAWHR
5.36 heard—disregarded, παρακούω
TTᵣAWHR
7:14 ἀκούσατε LTTᵣAWH
16 *omit the verse* T[TᵣA]WHR
9: 7 *trs* ἀκούετε αὐτοῦ LTTᵣAWH
13: 7 ἀκούητε ye hear Tᵣ
Lu. 5: 1 τοῦ ἀ.—*omit* τοῦ TTᵣAWH
8:12 ἀκούσαντες heard TTᵣAWHR
14:35 *omit* to hear T
Joh. 5:25¹ 28 ἀκούσουσιν TTᵣWH
37 *trs* πώποτε ἀκηκόατε Eds
8:38*ἠκούσατε for ἑωράκατε (ὁράω)
LTTᵣAWHR
10:27 ἀκούουσιν TTᵣAWH
12:18 ἤκουσαν GEds
16:13 ἀκούσει TᵣAR: ἀκούει TWH
Acts 2: 6 ἤκουσεν WH
7:37 *omit* him shall ye hear LTTᵣA
9:13 ἤκουσα LTTᵣAWHR   (WHR
14: 9 ἤκουσεν LTTᵣ
24:22 *omit* when   heard these
things GEds
Ro. 10:14 ἀ.²—ἀκούσονται T: ἀκούσωσιν
LTᵣAWWHR
Phil. 1:27 ἀκούω TTᵣWH
2 Ti. 4:17 ἀκούσωσιν LTTᵣAWWH
Rev. 22: 8 *trs* ἀκούων καὶ βλέπων ταῦτα
GLTᵣAWHR: βλ. καὶ ἀ. ταῦ. T
18 τῷ ἀκούοντι GEds

ἀκρασία.

Mat. 23:25 excess—unrighteousness, ἀδικία GW

ἀκριβῶς.

Eph. 5:15 *trs* ἀκριβῶς πῶς TWHR

ἀκροατής.

Jas. 1:22 *trs* ἀκροαταὶ μόνον LT₊AWWH

ακροβυστία.
Ro. 4:12 τῇ ἀ.—omit τῇ GEds

ἄκρον.
Mat. 24:31 τῶν ἄκρων Tr, [τῶν] ἅ. WH

Ἀκύλας.
Acts 18:26 trs Priscilla and Aquila . LTTrAWH

* ἅλα, salt.
Mat. 5:13 ἅλα for ἅλας bis T (sic)
Mar. 9:50 ἅλα for ἅλας ter T
Lu. 14:34 ἅλα for ἅλας bis T

ἀλάβαστρον.
Mar.14: 3 τὸν ἀ.² LTW, τὴν ἀ. TrAWH

ἀλαζονεία, —νία TWH

ἄλαλος.
Mar. 7:37 τοὺς ἀ.—omit τοὺς TTrAWH

ἅλας.
Mat. 5:13 ἅλα bis T (sic)
Mar. 9:50 ἅλα ter T; ἅ.³—ἅλς LTrAWH
Lu. 14:34 ἅλα bis T

ἁλεεύς, see ἁλιεύς.

ἀλέκτωρ.
Mar.14:68 omit and the cock crew [L]WH
Lu. 22:60 ὁ ἀ.—omit ὁ GEds

Ἀλέξανδρος.
Acts 4: 6 Ἀλέξανδρος LTTrAWH

ἀλήθεια.
Joh. 16:13 trs εἰς τὴν ἀλήθειαν πᾶσαν LTrAWH, ἐν τῇ ἀληθείᾳ πάσῃ T
Gal. 3: 1 omit that ye should not obey the truth GEds
5: 7 τῇ ἀ.—omit τῇ TTr[A]WH
Jas. 3:14 trs glory not against the truth and lie T
3 Joh. 4 τῇ ἀληθείᾳ Eds

ἀληθής.
Joh. 6:55 ἀληθής for ἀληθῶς bis. LTTrAWH
8:16 ἀληθινός LTTrAWH

ἀληθινός.
Joh. 4:37 ὁ ἀ.—omit ὁ TTr[A]WH
8:16 ἀληθινή for ἀληθής LTTrAWH
Rev. 3: 7 trs he that is true, he that is holy A
6:10 ὁ ἀ.—omit ὁ GEds
19: 9 οἱ ἀληθινοί LAW
21: 5 trs faithful and true GEds

ἀληθῶς.
Joh. 6:55 ἀληθής bis LTTrAWH
7:26 omit very GEds
1 Th. 2:13 trs ἀληθῶς ἐστὶν WH

ἁλιεύς.
Mat. 4:18, 19 ἁλεεῖς WH
Mar. 1:16, 17 ἁλεεῖς TAWH
Lu. 5: 2 ἁλεεῖς TWH

ἁλίζω.
Mar. 9:49 omit and every sacrifice shall be salted with salt TTrWH

ἀλλά.
Mar. 2:22 omit but new to end of verse T[Tr]A[WH], see βλητέος
3:27 add at commencement ἀ. but TTrAWH
6:52 ἦν γὰρ—ἀ. ἦν TTrAWH
7:25 ἀκούσασα γὰρ—ἀλλ᾽ εὐθὺς ἀκ. TTrAWH
9: 8 εἰ μὴ LWH
Lu. 4: 4 omit but by every word of God T[Tr]AWH
9:56 omit For the Son to save (them) GLTTrAWH
11: 4 omit but deliver us from evil GTTrAWH
Joh. 3:15 omit should not perish, but [L]TTrAWH
6:23 for ἀλλα δὲ WH
9: 9 add ἀ. [L]TTrAWH, see λέγω
11:22 omit But [L]TTrAWH

Joh. 16:25 omit but¹ G[L]TTrAWHR A.V.†Er
Acts 9: 6 ἀλλὰ ἀνάστηθι but arise GEds
10:20 itaque A.V. Vul
Ro. 8: 1 omit who walk to end of ver. GEds
12:20 ἀ. ἐὰν for ἐὰν οὖν LTTrAWH
1 Co. 3: 5 omit but GEds
8: 6 [but] LWH
Phi. 3: 7 omit but [L]T[A]
1 Pet. 3:15 ἀλλὰ μετὰ but with Eds
Rev. 2: 9 πλούσιος δὲ—ἀ. πλ. GEds
3: 4 add at commencement ἀ. But GEds

ἀλλάττω, —άσσω.
Heb. 1:12 ἀλλάξεις for ἑλίξεις (—ίσσω) T

* ἀλλαχοῦ, elsewhere.
Mar. 1:38 let us go—add ἀλλαχοῦ elsewhere TTrAWH

ἀλληλούϊα, ἀλληλουϊά WH

ἀλλήλων.
Lu. 20:14 ἀλλήλους for ἑαυτούς TTrAWH
Acts 2: 7 omit one to another LTTrAWH
28: 4 trs πρὸς ἀ. ἔλεγον LTTrAWH
Gal. 5:17 trs ἀλλήλοις ἀντίκειται GEds

ἅλλομαι.
Acts 14:10 ἥλατο GEds

ἄλλος.
Mat. 10:23 another—the next, ἕτερος GLTTrWH
Mar. 3: 5 omit whole as the other GEds
4: 8 ἄλλα others TAWH
18 ἄλλοι for οὗτοι GEds
7: 8 omit (as) the washing to end of verse T[TrA]WH
10:12 γαμήσῃ ἄλλον LTTrAWH
14:19 omit and another (said, Is) it I? TTrWH
Lu. 6:10 om. as the other [L]T[Tr]AWH
7:19 ἕτερος TrWH
Joh. 6:23 ἀλλα δὲ—ἀλλά (om. other) WH
7:41 some (ἄ.²)—they, οἱ LTrAWH
18:15 ὁ ἀ.—om ὁ A.V.Er LT[Tr]WH
21:25 omit the verse T
Rev. 14: 9 καὶ—add ἄλλος, read another a third angel GEds
16: 7 omit another out of GEds
18: 1 I saw—add ἄλλον another A.V.C GEds

ἀλλοτριοεπίσκοπος, ἀλλοτριε— LTTrWH.

ἅλς.
Mar. 9:49 omit and every sacrifice shall be salted with salt T[Tr]WHR
50 ἅλα for ἅλας² LTrAWH

ἅλυσις.
Mar. 5: 3 ἁλύσει a chain LTTrAWH

ἄλφα, see A.

Ἀλφαῖος, Ἀλφαῖος WH.
Lu. 6:15 τὸν τοῦ Ἀ.—omit τὸν ἀ. TTrAWH

ἁμαρτάνω.
Lu. 17: 4 ἁμαρτήσῃ LTTrAWH
Ro. 6:15 ἁμαρτήσωμεν Eds

ἁμάρτημα.
Mar. 3:28 trs τοῖς υἱοῖς τῶν ἀνθ. τὰ ἁ. GEds
29 ἁμαρτήματος for κρίσεως (—σις) LTTrAWH
4:12 omit (their) sins, read it [L]TTrAWH
2 Pet. 1: 9 ἁμαρτημάτων for ἁμαρτιῶν (—ία) GTTr

ἁμαρτία.
Mat. 9: 2 trs σου αἱ ἁμαρτίαι LTTrAWH
Mar. 2: 5 trs σου αἱ ἁμαρτίαι GTTrAWH
10 trs ἁμαρτίας ἐπὶ τῆς γῆς WH
Lu. 5:20 trs ἁμαρτίας ἀφεῖναι LTTrAWH
7:47 trs αὑτῇ (αὐτῆς T) αἱ ἁμαρτίαι LT
Acts 2:38 τῶν ἁμαρτιῶν ὑμῶν LTTrWH
7:60 trs ταύτην τὴν ἁ. LTrAWH
Col. 2:11 omit of the sins GEds
2 Th. 2: 3 sin—lawlessness, ἀνομία TTrWH

Heb. 1: 3 trs τῶν ἁ. ποιησ. LTTrAWHR
9:26 τῆς ἁμαρτίας LTTrWH
13:11 omit for sin LA
Jas. 5:16 τὰς ἁμαρτίας for τὰ παραπτώματα (—α) LTTrWHR
1 Pet. 4: 1 ἁμαρτίαις WH
2 Pet. 1: 9 ἁμάρτημα GTTr

ἁμαρτωλός.
Mar. 2:16 trs sinners and publicans¹ LTrAWHR
16 trs (add τῶν) sinners and publicans¹ LTr
Lu. 5:30 omit and sinners A
6:34 οἱ ἀ.—omit οἱ LTTrAWHR
Joh. 9:31 trs ὁ θεὸς ἁμαρτωλῶν LTTrAWH
1 Pet. 4:18 ὁ ἁμαρτωλὸς T
Rev. 21: 8 unbelieving—add καὶ ἁμαρτωλοῖς and sinners W

ἀμελέω.
2 Pet. 1:12 I will not be negligent—I will take care, μέλλω Eds

ἀμήν.
Mat. 6:13 omit For thine to end of verse GEds
18:19 ἀμήν ([ἀ.] WH) λέγω verily I say LTTrAWH
28:20 omit Amen GLTTrAWH
Mar. 6:11 omit verily to end of verse G[L]TTrAWH
16:20 omit Amen EGLTTrAWWH
Lu. 13:35 omit Verily GEds
24:53 omit Amen G[L]TTrAWH
Joh. 21:25 omit the verse T: omit Amen GLTTrAWH
Ro. 15:33 [Amen] LTr
16:20 add Amen A.V.D B
24 omit the verse LTTr[A]WH
1 Co. 16:24 omit Amen [L]TT-[A]WH
2 Co. 13:14(13) omit Amen GEds
Eph. 6:24 om.Amen A.V.†LatGLTTrAWH
Phi. 4:23 omit Amen [L]TTr[A]WH
Col. 4:18 omit Amen GEds
1 Th. 3:13 add at end Amen [L]T
5:28 omit Amen GEds
2 Th. 3:18 omit Amen TTrAWH
1 Ti. 6:21 omit Amen GEds
2 Ti. 4:22 omit Amen GEds
Tit. 3:15 omit Amen G[L]TTrAWWH
Philem.25 omit Amen GLTTrAWWH
Heb.13:25 omit Amen TWH
1 Pet. 5:14 omit Amen GLTTrAWH
2 Pet. 3:18 omit Amen T[TrA]WH
1 Joh.5:21 omit Amen GEds
2 Joh. 13 omit Amen GEds
Rev. 1:18 omit Amen GEds
5:14 τὸ ἀμήν W
7:12 omit Amen† L[WH]
22:21 omit Amen GLTTrAWH

Ἀμιναδάβ, Ἀμει— A.
Lu. 3:33 omit of Aminadab WH

ἄμμος.
Heb.11:12 ἡ ἄμμος GEds

ἄμπελος.
Rev.14:18 clusters—add τῆς ἀμπέλου of the vine A.V.B BGEds

ἀμπελών.
Lu. 13: 6 trs πεφ. ἐν τῷ ἀ. αὐτοῦ LTTrAWH

Ἀμπλίας, —ιᾶτος TTrA, —ιᾶτος WHR.

* ἀμφιάζω, —έζω TTrA, to put on. clothe.
Lu. 12:28 ἀμφιά(έ)ζει for ἀμφιέννυσιν (—νμι) LTTrAWH

* ἀμφιβάλλω, to cast around.
Mar. 1:16 ἀμφιβάλλοντας for βάλλοντας (—λω) GEds

ἀμφίβληστρον.
Mar. 1:16 omit a net TTrAWH

ἀμφιέννυμι.
Lu. 12:28 ἀμφιέννυ(έ)ζω LTTrAWH

ἀμφότεροι.
Mat. 9:17 ἀμφότεροι GLTTrAWWH

Lu. 5:38 *omit* and both are preserved T[Tr]AWH
Acts 19:16*ἀμφοτέρων *for* αὐτῶν Eds

ἀμώμητος.
Phi. 2:15 ἄμωμος LTTrAWH

* ἄμωμον, an Indian spice plant.
Rev. 18:13 cinnamon—*add* καὶ ἄμωμον and amomum GEds

ἄμωμος.
Phi. 2:15*ἄμωμα *for* ἀμώμητα (-τος) LTTrAWH

Αμών, Ἀμώς LTTrAWH.

ἄν.
(for ὃς ἄν see ὅς.)
Mat. 6: 5*omit ἄν LTTrAWWH
7:12 ἐάν TWH
10:23 omit ἄν TAWH
33 omit ἄν LTTrAWH
12:32 ἄν¹—ἐάν LTTrAWWH
16:25 ἄν¹—ἐάν LTTrAWH
21:22 ἐάν Tr
44 omit the verse [L]T[WH]
22: 9 ἐάν LTTrAWWH
23: 3 ἐάν TWWH
26:48 ἐάν TA
Mar. 3:2* ἐάν TrAWH
4:25 ἄν ἔχῃ—ἔχει LTTrAWHR
6:56 ἄν¹—ἐάν T
8:35 ἄν¹—ἐάν TTrAWH
38 ἐάν LTTrAWH
9:18 ἐάν LTTrAWH
10:44 ἐάν GTrA
11:24 omit ἄν Eds
14: 9 ἐάν TAWH
Lu. 2:26*ᾖ—ἤ ἄν T, ἄν Tr, [ᾖ] ἄν WH
9:24 ἄν¹—ἐάν T
57 ἐάν LTrA
12:39 omit he would have watched, and T: omit ἄν² TrAWH
13:35 omit ἄν TTrAWH
15:26*ἄν εἴη TrWHR, [ἄν] εἴη LA
18:36*[ἄν] εἴη LT
Joh. 8:39 omit ἄν GTTrAWH
13:24 see λέγω
14: 7 omit ἄν T
16:13 omit ἄν LTTrAWH
Acts 2:12 omit ἄν LTTrWHR
21 ἐάν TrAWH
3:23 ἐάν TA
8:19 εων LGLTTrAWWH
17:20 omit ἄν LTTrWHR
21:33 omit ἄν LTTr[A]WWHR
1Co. 11:25 ἐάν LTTrAWH
26 ἄν¹—ἐάν LTTrAWH:
omit ἄν² GLTTrAWH
15:25 omit ἄν Eds
16: 2 ἐάν TrWH
2Co. 3:15*ἄν ἀναγινώσκηται LTTrAWHR
16 ἐάν TWH
Gal. 3:19*for οὗ (ὅς) WH
4:15 omit ἄν Eds
5:10 ἐάν TTrAWH
17 ἐάν [L]TTrAWH
Col. 3:17 ἐάν LTTrAWH
1Th. 2: 7 ἐάν LTTrAWH
Jas. 3: 4 omit ἄν TTrWHR
4: 4 ἐάν LTWH
5: 7 omit ἄν TTrAWH
1Joh.4:15 ἐάν WH
5:15 ἐάν TWH
Rev. 13:15 ἐάν LTTrAWH
See also ἐάν.

ἀνά, apiece.
Mat. 20:10†trs τὸ ([τὸ]AWH) ἀ. δηνάριον καὶ αὐτοί TTrAWH
Mar. 6:40 κατά bis LTTrAWH
Lu. 9: 3 omit apiece [TrA]WH

ἀναβαίνω.
Mat. 14:32*ἀναβάντων for ἐμβάντων (-αίνω) LTTrAWH
15:39*ἀνέβη f. ἐνέβη (ἐμβαίνω) GTrAW
20:17 καὶ ἀ.—μέλλων δὲ ἀναβαίνειν, read Jesus being about to go up WH
Mar. 15: 8*ἀναβὰς for ἀναβοήσας (-οάω) LTTrAWH
Lu. 2:42 ἀναβαινόντων LTTrAWH
Joh. 7:10 trs εἰς τὴν ἑορτήν, τότε καὶ αὐτὸς ἀ. LTTrAWH
21: 3 ἐμβαίνω GEds
Acts 1:13 trs εἰς τὸ ὑπερῷον ἀνέβησαν LTTrAWH

Acts 21: 4 ἐπιβαίνω LTTrAWHR
6*ἀνέβημεν for ἐπέβημεν (ἐπιβαίνω) TAW
Rev. 7: 2 ἀναβαίνοντα A.V.C GEds
11:12 ἀ.¹—ἀνάβατε Eds

ἀναβάλλομαι.
Acts 24:22†trs ἀ. δὲ αὐτοὺς ὁ Φηλιξ GEds

ἀναβλέπω.
Mar. 8:25 see διαβλέπω

ἀναβοάω.
Mat. 27:46 βοάω TrWH
Mar. 15: 8 crying aloud—coming up, ἀναβαίνω LTTrAWH
Lu. 9:38 βοάω LTTrAWH

*ἀνάγαιον, see ἀνώγεον.

ἀναγγέλλω.
Mat. 28:11*ἀνήγγειλαν for ἀπήγγειλαν (ἀπαγγέλλω) T
Mar. 5:14 ἀπαγγέλλω :Eds
19 ἀπαγγέλλω Eds
Joh. 5:15 εἶπον TWH
16:25 ἀπαγγέλλω Eds
Acts 14:27 ἀνήγγ-λλ ν LTTrAWHR
16:38 ἀπαγγέλλω Eds

ἀναγινώσκω.
2Co. 3:15 ἄν ἀναγινώσκηται LTTrAWHR
Rev. 5: 4 omit and to read GEds

ἀνάγκη.
Lu. 23:17 omit the verse [L]TTr[A]WHR
1Th. 3: 7 trs distress and affliction Eds

ἀναγνωρίζομαι.
Acts 7:13 γνωρίζω TrWH

ἀνάγω.
Lu. 22:66 led—led away, ἀπάγω TTrAWHR

ἀναζάω.
Lu. 15:32 is alive again—is alive, ζάω, TTrAWH
Ro. 14: 9 revived—lived, ζάω GEds
Rev. 20: 5 lived again—lived, ζάω GEds

ἀναζητέω.
Lu. 2:45*ἀναζητοῦντες for ζητοῦντες (ζητέω) LTTrAWH

ἀνάθεμα.
Lu. 21: 5*ἀναθέμασιν for ἀναθήμασιν (-μα) LT
Ro. 9: 3 trs ἀνάθεμα εἶναι αὐτὸς ἐγὼ Eds

ἀνάθημα.
Lu. 21: 5 ἀνάθεμα LT

ἀναιδεία, -δία TWH.

ἀναίρεσις.
Acts 22:20 omit unto his death GEds

ἀναιρέω.
Acts 2:23 ἀνείλατε GLTTrAWWH
7:21 ἀνείλατο GLTTrAWWH
9:29 trs ἀνελεῖν αὐτὸν LTTrAWH
10:39 ἀνεῖλαν LTTrAWH
2Th. 2: 8*ἀνελεῖ for ἀναλώσει (-λίσκω) LTTrAWHR

ἀνάκειμαι.
Mar. 5:40 omit lying G[L]TTrAWH
6:26*ἀνακειμένους for συνανακειμένους (-μαι) TTrAWH
Lu. 7:37 κατάκειμαι LTTrAWH
Joh. 12: 2*ἀνακειμένων σὺν for συνανακειμένων (-μαι) GEds

ἀνακλίνω.
Mar. 6:39 ἀνακλιθῆναι LWHR
Lu. 7:36 κατακλίνω LTTrAWH
9:15 κατακλίνω TTrWHR

ἀνακόπτω.
Gal. 5: 7 ἐγκόπτω GEds

ἀνακράζω.
Lu. 23:18 ἀνέκραγον TrAWH

ἀνακρίνω.
Acts 17:11 omit τὸ LTTr[WH]

* ἀνακυλίω, to roll up or away.
Mar. 16: 4 ἀνακεκύλισται for ἀποκεκύλισται (ἀποκυλίω) TTrAWHR

ἀνακύπτω.
Joh. 8: 7 ἀνέκυψεν καὶ WH

ἀναλαμβάνω.
ἀνελήμφθη for -λήφθη LTTrAWH
ἀναλημφθεὶς for -ηφθεὶς LTTrAWH

ἀνάληψις, -λημψις LTTrAWH.

ἀναλίσκω.
2Th. 2: 8 shall consume—will slay, ἀναιρέω LTTrAWH

ἀναλύω.
Lu. 12:36 ἀναλύσῃ LTTrAWH

Ἀνανίας, Ἀ— WH.
Acts 5: 5 ὁ Ἀνανίας GLTTrAWWH
9:12 trs Ἀνανίαν ὀνόματι LTTrAWH
13 ὁ Ἀ.—omit ὁ GLTTrAWWH

ἀναντιρρήτως, -τιρήτως WH.

ἀναξίως.
1Co. 11:29 omit unworthily LTTrAWH

ἀναπαύω.
Mar. 6:31 ἀναπαύσασθε TTrAWH
Rev. 6:11 ἀναπαύσονται WH
14:13 ἀναπαήσονται LTTrAWHR, ἀναπαύσονται W

ἀναπείθω.
Acts 18:13 trs ἀναπείθει οὗτος Eds

ἀνάπειρος, see ἀνάπηρος.

ἀναπέμπω.
Lu. 23:15†trs ἀνέπεμψεν γὰρ αὐτὸν πρὸς ἡμᾶς, for he sent him back to us TWH
Acts 25:21*ἀναπέμψω for πέμψω (-μπω) Eds

* ἀναπηδάω, to leap, spring up.
Mar. 10:50 ἀναπηδήσας for ἀναστὰς (ἀνίστημι) Eds

ἀνάπηρος, ἀνάπειρος LTrAWH.

ἀναπίπτω.
Mar. 6:40 ἀνέπεσαν TTrAWH
Lu. 14:10 ἀνάπεσε LTTrAWWH
17: 7 ἀνάπεσε Eds
Joh. 6:10 ἀ.²—ἀνέπεσαν LTTrAWH
13:12 ἀνέπεσεν TTrAWH
25*ἀναπεσὼν for ἐπιπεσὼν (-πίπτω) LTTrAWH

ἀναπληρόω.
Gal. 6: 2 ἀναπληρώσετε ye shall fulfil LT

ἀναπτύσσω.
Lu. 4:17 ἀνοίγω LTrWH

ἀνάπτω.
Acts 28: 2 ἅπτω LTTrAWWH

ἀνασπάω.
Acts 11:10 trs ἀνεσπάσθη πάλιν LTTrAWH

ἀνάστασις.
Mat. 22:28 trs ἀναστάσει οὖν LTTrAWH
2Ti. 2:18 τὴν ἀ.—omit τὴν TTr[A]WH

ἀναστρέφω.
Mat. 17:22 they abode—they abode together, συστρέφω LTTrWH
Joh. 2:15 ἀνατρέπω WH

ἀνατέλλω.
Mar. 4: 6 ἡλίου δὲ ἀνατείλαντος—καὶ ὅτε ἀνέτειλεν ὁ ἥλιος LTTrAWH

ἀνατολή.

Rev. 16:12 ἀνατολῆς TTrAWH
21:13 ἀνατολῶν GW

ἀνατρέπω.

Joh. 2:15*ἀνέτρεψεν for ἀνέστρεψεν (ἀνα-
στρέφω) WH

ἀνατρέφω.

Lu. 4:16*ἀνατεθραμμένος for τεθραμμένος
(τρέφω) T

ἀναφαίνομαι.

Acts 21: 3 ἀναφάναντες S—ἀναφανέντες
EGLTrAW

ἀναφέρω.

Lu. 24:51 omit and carried up into
heaven T[[WH]]
Heb. 7:27 offered up-offered, προσφέρω T

ἀναχωρέω.

Joh. 6:15 departed—escapeth, φεύγω T

ἀνεκτός, ἀνεκτότερος.

Mar. 6:11 omit Verily to end of verse
G[L]TTrAWH

ἀνέλεος, see ἀνίλεως.

ἄνεμος.

Jas. 3: 4 trsἀνέμων σκληρῶν LTTrAWWH
Rev. 6:13 trsἀνέμου μεγάλουGLTTrAWWH

ἀνεξερεύνητος, —ραύνητος TTrAWH.

ἀνεπίληπτος, —λημπτος LTTrAWH.

ἀνέρχομαι.

Gal. 1:17 went I up—went I, ἀπέρχομαι
LA

ἀνευρίσκω.

Lu. 2:16 ἀνεῦραν TTrWH

ἀνέχομαι.

Acts 18:14 ἀνεσχόμην LTTrWH
2Co. 11: 1 ἀνείχεσθε S—ἠνείχεσθε E
4 ἀνείχεσθε GTTrW, ἀνέχεσθε
LAWH

ἀνήκω.

Eph. 5: 4 τὰ οὐκ ἀ.—ἃ οὐκ ἀνῆκεν LTTrAWH

ἀνήρ.

Lu. 2:36 trs μετὰ ἀνδρὸς ἔτη LTTrWH
6: 8*ἀνδρὶ for ἀνθρώπῳ (—πος)
TTrAWH
24: 4 trs ἄνδρες δύο GLTTrAWWH
Joh. 4:16 trs σου τὸν ἄνδρα AWH
17 trsἄνδρα οὐκ ἔχω¹ T
Acts 10: 5 trs ἄνδρας εἰς Ἰόππην Eds
11:13 omit men Eds
13: 6*found—add ἄνδρα a man Eds
17: 5 trs ἄνδρας τινὰς LTrAWWH
1 Co. 7:13*τὸν ἄνδρα for αὐτόν Eds
14 husband²—brother, ἀδελφός
Eds
11:11 trs the woman without the
man, neither the man without the woman GEds
Eph. 5:23 ὁ ἀ.—omit ὁ GEds
28 trs οἱ ἄνδρες ὀφείλουσιν LW

ἀνθίστημι.

Lu. 21:15†trs LTTrAWHR, see ἀντέπω
2 Ti. 4:15 ἀντέστη Eds

ἀνθρώπινος.

Acts17:25*ἀνθρωπίνων for ἀνθρώπων
(—πος) LTTrAWH
1 Co. 2: 4 omit man's GEds

ἄνθρωπος.

Mat. 4: 4 ὁ ἄνθρωπος Eds
9:32 omit ἄνθρωπον L[TrA]WHR
12:31 omit unto men² LTT[A]WH
13:45 omit man WH
18:11 omit the verse LTT[A]WHR
19: 3 omit for a man LTAWH
25:13 omit wherein the Son of man
cometh GLTTrAWH
Mar. 7:15*trs ἐκ τοῦ ἀνθρώπου (for ἀπ'
αὐτοῦ)ἐκπορευόμενα LTTrAWHR

Mar. 8:36 τὸν ἄνθρωπον LTr[A]W
12: 1 trs ἄνθρωπος ἐφύτευσεν TWH
15:39 trs οὗτος ὁ ἄνθρωπος LTTrAWH
Lu. 2:15 omit καὶ οἱ ἄνθ. [L]T[TrA]WHR
25 trs ἄνθρωπος ἦν TWH
6: 6 trs ἄνθρωπος ἐκεῖ TTrAWHR
8 ἀνὴρ TTrAWH
10 unto the man—unto him,
αὐτῷ GEds
45 omit man² [L]TTrAWHR
9:56 omit For the Son to save
(them) GLTTrAWHR
13: 4 τοὺς ἀνθρώπους LTTrAWHR
Joh. 7:46 om. like this man (read thus)
L[TrA]WH
9:11 ὁ ἄνθρωπος TTrWH, [ὁ] ἄ. A
16 trs οὐκ ἔστιν οὗτος παρὰ θεοῦ ὁ ἄ.
LTTrAWHR
24 trs τὸν ἄ. ἐκ δευτέρου LTTrAWHR
24 trs οὗτος ὁ ἄνθρωπος LWH
35*ἀνθρώπου for θεοῦ (—ός) TWH
Acts 5:34*ἀνθρώπους for ἀποστόλους
(—λος) LTTrAWHR
17:25 men's—human, ἀνθρώπινος
LTTrAWH
19:16 trs ὁ ἄνθ. ἐπ' αὐτούς LTTrAWH
35 ἀνθρώπων, read who of men
LTTrAWH
1 Co. 3: 4*ἄνθρωποι for σαρκικοί (—ός) Eds
11:28 trs ἑαυτὸν ἄνθρωπος W
Gal. 3:12 omit the man, read he GEds
Jas. 3: 8 trs δαμάσαι δύναται ἀ. LTTrAWH
1 Pet. 1:24 of man—of it, αὐτῆς GEds
Rev. 4: 7 ἀνθρώπου of a man GEds
8:11 τῶν ἀνθρώπων GEds
16:18 ἄνθρωπος ἐγένετο man was
LTTrAW: omit οἱ Eds

ἀνθυπατεύω.

Acts18:12 ἀνθυπάτου (—ος) ὄντος LTTrAWH

ἀνθύπατος.

Acts18:12*see ἀνθυπατεύω

ἀνίλεως, ἀνέλεος LTTrAWWH.

ἄνιπτος.

Mar. 7: 5 unwashen—defiled, κοινός
GEds

ἀνίστημι.

Mat.17: 9 ἐγείρω LTTrAWH
20:19 ἐγείρω TTrAWH
Mar. 6:14*ἀνέστη for ἠγέρθη (ἐγείρω) A
10:50 rose—leaped up, ἀναπηδάωEds
12:23 omit when they shall rise
[L]TrWH
Lu. 6: 8 ὁ δὲ ἀ.—καὶ ἀ. LTTrAWHR
9:22*ἀναστῆναι for ἐγερθῆναι (ἐγείρω) LA
17:12*ἀνέστησαν for ἔστησαν (ἵστημι)
WH
24:12 omit the verse [L]T[Tr] [[WH]]
Acts 2:30 omit according to to Christ
GLTTrAWH
3:26 trs ἀναστήσας ὁ θεὸς TAWH
9:11 ἀνάστα TWH
10:23*ἀναστὰς ἐξῆλθεν having arisen
he went away GEds
Ro. 14: 9 omit rose and GEds

Ἄννα, Ἄ— WH.

Ἄννας, Ἄ— WH.

Acts 4:6 Ἄννας LTTrAWH

ἀνοίγω.

Mat. 3:16 ἠνεῴχθησαν LWH
7: 8 ἀνοίγεται it is opened LTr
9:30 ἠνεῴχθησαν LTrA
20:33 ἀνοίγωσιν LTTrAWH
Mar. 7:35*ἠνοίγησαν for διηνοίχθησαν
(διανοίγω) LTTrAWH
Lu. 4:17*ἀνοίξας for ἀναπτύξας (—ύσσω)
LTrWHR
11: 9 ἀνοιχθήσεται TA
10 ἀνοιχθήσεται LTAW
Joh. 9:10 ἠνεῴχθησαν LTTrAWH
17 ἠνέῳξεν TrAWH
30 ἠνέῳξεν LTTrWH
32 ἠνέῳξεν TrWH
10:21 ἀνοῖξαι TTrAWH
Acts 5:19 ἀνοίξας T
7:56 διανοίγω Eds
9: 8 ἠνεῳγμένων LA, ἠνοιγ— T
12:10 ἠνοίγη LTTrAWH
16:26 ἠνεῴχθησαν LTrAWH, ἠνοίχ— T
Rev. 3: 7 ἀ.²—ἀνοίξει shall open TTrAW

Rev. 3: 8 ἠνεῳγμένην TWH
4: 1 ἀνεῳγμένη GLW
10: 2 † 19:11 ἠνεῳγμένον LTTrAWH
20:12 ἀ.¹—ἠνοίχθησαν GEds
ἀ.²—ἠνοίχθη Eds

ἀνομία.

2 Th. 2: 3*ἀνομίας f. ἁμαρτίας (—ία) TTrWH
Heb. 1: 9 iniquity—unrighteousness,
ἀδικία T
8:12 omit and their iniquities
TTrAWHR

ἄνομος.

Mar. 15:28 omit the verse T[Tr]AWHR
1 Co. 9:21 ἀ.³—τοὺς ἀνόμους Eds

ἀνορθόω.

Lu. 13:13 ἀνορθώθη LTTrA

ἀνταπόδομα.

Lu. 14:12 trs ἀνταπόδομά σοι TTrAWH

ἀντέπω, ἀντεῖπον.

Lu. 21:15†trs to resist or (nor L) gainsay
([ἢ ἀ.] Tr) LTTrAWH

ἀντικαλέω.

Lu. 14:12 trs ἀντικαλέσωσίν σε LTTrAWH

ἀντικρύ, ἄντικρυς LTTrAWH.

ἀντιλέγω.

Lu. 20:27 λέγω, read which say there is
no resurrection TrWH
Acts 13:45 omit contradicting and
LTr[A]WH

ἀντίλημψις, —λημψις LTTrAWH.

ἀντιμετρέω.

Mat. 7: 2 μετρέω (omit again) GEds

Ἀντίπας, Ἀντεί— T.

ἀντιπέραν.

Lu. 8:26 ἀντιπέρα LTrAW, ἀντιπερα TWH

ἀντίχριστος.

1 Joh. 2:18 ὁ ἀ.—omit ὁ Eds

ἀνώγεον, ἀνάγαιον GLTTrAWWH.

ἄξιος.

Mat. 3: 8 καρπὸν ἄξιον fruit worthy
GEds
Acts 26:31 trs ἢ δεσμῶν ἄξιον LTTrWH
1 Co. 16: 4 trs ἄξιον ᾖ LTrAWH
Rev. 5:12 ἄξιος T

ἀπαγγέλλω.

Mat. 28: 9 omit and as they went to tell
his disciples LTTrAWHR
11 ἀναγγέλλω T
Mar. 5:14*ἀπήγγειλαν for ἀνήγγειλαν
(ἀναγγέλλω) GEds
19*ἀπάγγειλον for ἀνάγγειλον
(—έλλω) Eds
Joh. 4:51 ἀγγέλλω T: omit and told
(him) [TrA]WHR
16:25*ἀπαγγελῶ for ἀναγγελῶ (—λλω)
Eds
20:18 ἀγγέλλω LTTrAWH
Acts16:38*ἀπήγγειλαν for ἀνήγγειλαν
(ἀναγγέλλω) Eds
17:30*ἀπαγγέλλει for παραγγέλλει
(—λλω) TWH
22:26 trs τῷ χιλιάρχῳ ἀπήγγειλεν
GLTTrAWH
23:17 trs ἀπαγγεῖλαί τι LTTrAWH
26:20 ἀπαγγέλλων S—ἀπήγγελλον
A.V.C EGEds

ἀπάγω.

Mar. 14:44 ἀπάγετε LTTrAWH
Lu. 13:15 ἀπάγων WH
21:12*ἀπαγομένους for ἀγομένους
(ἄγω) TTrAWH
22:66*ἀπήγαγον for ἀνήγαγον (ἀνάγω)
TTrAWH
Joh. 18:13 ἄγω LTTrWHR, [ἀπ]άγω A
19:16 omit and led (him) away
Acts 23:17 ἄπαγε TTrWH
24: 7 omit and would (ver.6)to come
unto thee (ver. 8) LTTr[A]WHR

ἀπαιτέω.

Lu. 12:20 αἰτέω TrAWH

ἀπαντάω.

Mat. 28: 9 ὑπαντάω TTrWH
Mar. 5: 2 ὑπαντάω LTTrWH
Lu. 14:31 ὑπαντάω Eds
    17:12 ὑπαντάω T
Joh. 4:51 ὑπαντάω LTTrAWH
Acts 16:16 ὑπαντάω TTrAWH

ἀπάντησις.

Mat. 25: 1 ὑπάντησις LTTrAWH

ἅπαξ.

1 Pet. 3:20 omit once GEds
    See also ἐφάπαξ.

ἀπαρνέομαι.

Mar. 14:30 trs με ἀπαρνήσῃ LTTrAWWH
    31 ἀπαρνήσωμαι T
    72 trs τρίς με ἀπαρνήσῃ LTTrAWH
Lu. 9:23 ἀρνέομαι GLTTrAWH
    22:34 trs με ἀπαρνήσῃ εἰδέναι LTrWH
Joh. 13:38 ἀρνέομαι LTTrAWH

ἄπαρτι.

Joh. 13:19*for ἀπ' ἄρτι T
    14: 7*for ἀπ' ἄρτι T
Rev. 14:13 ἀπ' ἄρτι GLAWH

ἅπας.

Mar. 1:27*ἅπαντες for πάντες (πᾶς)TTrAWH
    5:40 πᾶς GEds
    8:25 ἅπαντα all things Eds
Lu. 2:39 πᾶς TTrWH
    3:16 πᾶς TWH
    4:40*ἅπαντες for πάντες (πᾶς) WH
    5:11 πᾶς LTTrWH
    28 πᾶς LTTrAWH
    7:16 πᾶς GTrAWH
    15:13 πᾶς LTrAWH
    17:27, 29 πᾶς LTrAWH
    19: 7 πᾶς Eds
    20: 6*ὁ λαὸς ἅπας for πᾶς ὁ λαὸς TTrAWH
    21: 4 ἅ.¹—πᾶς LWHR: ἅ.²—πᾶς LTrWIR
    12 πᾶς GEds
    15*ἅπαντες f. πάντες (πᾶς) TTrAWH
Joh. 4:25*ἅπαντα for πάντα(πᾶς) TTrAWH
Acts 2: 1 πᾶς LTTrAWH
    4 πᾶς LTTrWHR
    7*ἅπαντες for πάντες³(πᾶς) LTAR
    14 πᾶς LTTrWHR
    4:32 πᾶς LWH
    5:12 πᾶς LTrWH
    6:15 πᾶς LTTrWHR
    10: 8 trs ἅπαντα αὐτοῖς LTTrAWH
    13:29 πᾶς GEds
    16:33*ἅπαντες for πάντες (πᾶς) TWH
    25:24*ἅπαν for πᾶν (πᾶς) Eds
Gal. 3:28*ἅπαντες for πάντες (πᾶς) TTrA
2 Th. 2:12*ἅπαντες for πάντες (πᾶς) TTrA
1 Ti. 1:16*ἅπασαν for πᾶσαν (πᾶς) Eds

* ἀπασπάζομαι, to take leave of.

Acts 21: 6 ἀπησπασάμεθα for ἀσπασάμενοι (ἀσπάζομαι) Eds

ἀπατάω.

1 Ti. 2:14 ἅ.²—ἐξαπατάω Eds

ἀπάτη.

2 Pet. 2:13 deceivings—love feasts, ἀγάπη LTrR

ἀπεῖδον, see ἀφοράω.

ἀπείθεια, -θία WH.

Col. 3: 6 omit on the children of disobedience [L]TTrAWH

ἀπειθέω.

Acts 14: 2 ἀπειθήσαντες LTTrAWHR
    17: 5 omit which believed not GEds
Pet. 2: 7 unto them which be disobedient—unto the unbelieving, ἀπιστέω TTrWHR

ἀπειλή.

Acts 4:17 omit straitly LTTr[A]WH

ἀπεκδέχομαι.

Pet. 3:20*ἀπεξεδέχετο for ἅπαξ ἐξεδέχετο (ἐκδέχομαι) GEds

ἀπέναντι.

Mat. 21: 2 κατέναντι LTTrWH
    27:24 κατέναντι LTrWH
Mar. 12:41*ἀπέναντι for κατέναντι Tr

ἀπέρχομαι.

Mat. 5:30*εἰς γέενναν ἀπέλθῃ for βληθῇ (βάλλω) εἰς γ. LTTrAWH
    8:31 suffer us to go away—send us away, ἀποστέλλω GLTTrAWHR
    32 ἀπῆλθαν LTrWH
    14:25 ἔρχομαι LTTrWHR
    21:29, 30†I will not: afterward he repented and went trs with I (go) sir: and went not WH
    22:ἀπῆλθαν LTTrↄWH
    26:44 trs πάλιν ἀπελθών LTTrAWH
    28: 8*ἀπελθοῦσαι for ἐξελθοῦσαι (ἐξέρχομαι) TTrAWH
Mar. 6:27 (28) ὁ δὲ ἀ.—καὶ ἀ. LTTrAWH
    12:12 ἀπῆλθαν WH
Lu. 8:34 omit went and GEds
    9:12 πορεύομαι GLTTrAWH
    59 trs πρῶτον ἀπελθόντι(-θεῖν L) LTTrWH
    23:33 ἔρχομαι LTTrAWH
    24:12 omit the verse [L]T[Tr][[WH]]
    24 ἀπῆλθαν WH
Joh. 4:43 omit and went [L]TTrAWH
    18: 6 ἀπῆλθαν LTTrAWH
Acts 16:39*ἀπελθεῖν ἀπὸ for ἐξελθεῖν (ἐξέρχομαι) LTTrAWH
    23:32*ἀπέρχεσθαι for πορεύεσθαι (-νομαι) LTTrAWH
    28:29 omit the verse LTTrAWH
Gal. 1:17*ἀπῆλθον for ἀνῆλθον (ἀνέρχομαι) LA
Rev. 10: 9 ἀπῆλθα LTWH
    18:14 are departed¹—are destroyed, ἀπόλλυμι W
    14 are departed²—are destroyed, ἀπόλλυμι GEds
    21: 1*ἀπῆλθον GWR, -θαν LTTrAWH for παρῆλθεν (παρέρχομαι)
    4 ἀπῆλθαν LTTrAWH, -θεν W

ἀπέχω.

Mat. 14:24*add ἀ. TrWH, see στάδιον

ἀπιστέω.

1 Pet. 2: 7*ἀπιστοῦσιν for ἀπειθοῦσιν (-θέω) TTrWH

ἀπιστία.

Mat. 17:20 unbelief—little faith, ὀλιγοπιστία LTTrAWH

ἁπλότης.

2 Co. 1:12 simplicity—holiness, ἁγιότης LTTrAWH

ἀπό.

Mat. 7: 4 ἐκ LTTrWH
    13: 1 ἐκ LT: omit ἀ. TrWH
    14:24*add ἀ. TrWH, see στάδιον
    17: 9 ἐκ GEds
    20:20*for παρά LTrAWH
    24:29 ἐκ T
    25:29 ἀ. δὲ τοῦ—τοῦ δέ LTTrAWH
    26:42 omit from me [L]TTrAWH
    58 omit ἀ. T[WH]
    27:51 omit ἀ. T[WH]
    28: 2 omit from the door LTTrAWH
Mar. 1:10 ἐκ LTTrWH
    2:21*trs ἀπ' αὐτοῦ τὸ πλήρωμα A: τὸ πλ. ἀπ' αὐ. LTWH
    7:15 ἐκ LTTrAWH, see ἄνθρωπος
    8: 3*ἀ. μακρόθεν TTrAWH
    31 of—by, ὑπό Eds
    9: 9 ἐκ LWH
    11:13*ἀ. μακρόθεν Eds
    14:52 omit from them [L]TTrWHR
    16: 3*for ἐκ LTr
    9 παρά LTrWHR
Lu. 1:26*for ὑπό TTrAWHR
    2:37 omit ἀ. TTrAWH
    4:35*for ἐκ LTTrAWH
    38*for ἐκ TTrAWH
    5:36*piece¹—add ἀ. from [L]TTrAWH (E
    6:18*for ὑπό Eds
    7: 6 omit ἀ. T
    8: 3 ἐκ LTTrAWH
    29*for ὑπό WH
    43*for ὑπό LTTrAWH
    10:42 omit ἀ. [L]T[TrA]WH
    11: 4 omit but deliver us from evil GTTrAWH
    12:54 out of—πt. ἐπί TWH

Lu. 13: 7*ἔτη—add ἀφ' οὗ TTrAWH
    12*ἀπολέλυσαι—add ἀ. LT
    29 omit ἀ.² [L]T[TrA]
    15:16 ἐκ WH
    19:26 omit from him² [L]TAWH
    22:18*add ἀ. T[TrA]WHR, see νῦν
    43, 44 the verses [T.][[WH]]
    23:49*ἀ. μακρόθεν LTWH
    24:42 omit and of an honeycomb LT[TrA]WHR
Joh. 1:51 (52) omit hereafter LTTrↄWHR
    6:38*for ἐκ LTTrAWH
    8:11*ἀπὸ τοῦ νῦν for καί WHR
Acts 1:25*for ἐκ Eds
    4:36*for ὑπό Eds
    9: 3 ἐκ LTTrWWHR
    10:17 from—by, ὑπό TWHR
    21 omit which were sent unto him from Cornelius GEds
    33*for ὑπό LA
    15: 4*for ὑπό TrWH
    20 omit ἀ. LTTr[A]WH
    16:39*add ἀ. LTTrAWHR, see ἀπερχομαι
    40*for ἐκ TWH
    18: 2*for ἐκ Eds
    19:12 omit of them GEds
    13 καί, read certain also LTTrAWHR
    21:23*for ἐπί WH
    22:30 omit from (his) bands GEds
    26:22*for παρά Eds
    27:34*for ἐκ LTTrAWH
    28: 3*for ἐκ Eds
Ro. 13: 1 ὑπό LTTrWH
    15:15*for ὑπό TTrWH
    24*for ὑπό LA
2 Co. 10: 7 ἐπί TTrWH
1 Th. 1: 1 omit from God to end of verse [L]TTrAWH
    10 ἐκ TTrWH
1 Ti. 6: 5 omit from such withdraw thyself Eds
Jas. 1:14*for ὑπό A
2 Pet. 1:21*ἀπὸ θεοῦ from God TAWH
1 Joh. 2: 7 omit from the beginning² LTTrAWH
    3:22*for παρά LTTrAWH
    5:15*for παρά LTTrWH
Rev. 1: 5 ἀ.²—ἐκ LTTrAWHR
    2:17 omit to eat of GEds
    6: 4 ἐκ GLTTrAW[WH]R
    10 ἐκ Eds
    7:17 ἐκ GEds
    9:18*for ὑπό GEds
    16:17 ἀ.¹—ἐκ LTTrAWH
    19: 5*for ἐκ LTrAWWHR
    20: 9 omit from God LTAWWHR
    21: 4 ἐκ LTTrAWH
       See also ἄπαρτι.

ἀποβαίνω.

Lu. 5: 2 trs ἀπ' αὐτῶν ἀποβάντες TTrAWH

ἀπογραφή.

Lu. 2: 2 ἡ ἀ.—omit ἡ LTTrAWH

ἀποδείκνυμι.

Acts 2:22 approbatum A.V. Vul: trs ἀποδ. ἀπὸ τοῦ θεοῦ TTrWHR

* ἀποδεκατεύω, to tithe.

Lu. 18:12 ἀποδεκατεύω for ἀποδεκατῶ (-τάω) TWH

ἀποδεκατόω.

Lu. 18:12 ἀποδεκατεύω TWH
Heb. 7: 5 ἀποδεκατοῖν TTrAWH

ἀποδέχομαι.

Lu. 9:11*ἀποδεξάμενος for δεξάμενος (δέχομαι) LTTrAWH
Acts 15: 4 παραδέχομαι Eds
    21:17*ἀπεδέξαντο for ἐδέξαντο (δέχομαι) Eds

ἀποδίδωμι.

Mat. 18:26 trs ἀποδώσω σοι ([σοί] A) LTTrAWH
Lu. 20:25 trs τοίνυν ἀπόδοτε TTrAWHR
Ro. 14:12*ἀποδώσει for δώσει (δίδωμι) LTr, [ἀπο]δώσει A
1 Th. 5:15 ἀποδοῖ T
2 Ti. 4:14 ἀποδώσει shall reward Eds
Heb. 12: 16 ἀπέδετο LAWH
Rev. 22: 2 ἀποδιδοὺς TTrA

ἀποθνήσκω.

Lu. 20:28 die—be, ᾖ (ὢ) LTTrAWHR
30 *omit* took her to wife, and he died childless TTrAWHR
Joh. 11:21*trs* οὐκ ἄν (ἀπέθανεν *for* ἐτεθνήκει, θνήσκω LTTrWHR) ὁ ἀδελφός μου LTTrAWHR
32 *trs* μου ἀπέθανεν TTrAWHR
18:14*ἀποθανεῖν *for* ἀπολέσθαι (ἀπόλλυμι) LTTrAWHR
Ro. 7: 6 ἀποθανόντος that being dead A.V.B.E—ἀποθανόντες having died (in that) sGEds
1 Pet. 3:18*ἀπέθανεν *for* ἔπαθεν (πάσχω) LTTrWH

ἀποκαθίστωω. -άνω, -ημι.

Mat. 12:13 ἀπεκατεστάθη LTTrAWWH
Mar. 3: 5 ἀπεκατεστάθη GLTTrAWWH
8:25 ἀπεκατέστη TTrAWH
9:12 ἀποκαθιστάνει LTTrA, ἀποκατ— WH
Lu. 6:10 ἀπεκατεστάθη GLTTrAWH

ἀποκαλύπτω

1Co. 2:10 *trs* ἀπεκάλυψεν ὁ θεὸς Eds

ἀποκάλυψις.

1Co. 14:26 *trs* hath a revelation, hath a tongue Eds

ἀποκόπτω.

Acts 27:32 *trs* ἀπέκοψαν οἱ στρατιῶται LTTrAWH

ἀποκρίνομαι.

Mat. 22:46 *trs* ἀποκριθῆναι αὐτῷ LTTrAWH
24: 2*And—*add* ἀποκριθεὶς answering (*omit* Jesus) LTTrAWH
26:63 *omit* answered and TrWHR
Mar. 3:33 ἀποκριθεὶς αὐτοῖς λέγει TTrAWHR
5: 9 *omit* answered GEds, *see* λέγω
7: 6 *omit* answered and TTrAWHR
8:28 answered—spake, εἰπον TAWHR
9: 5*ἀποκριθῇ *for* λαλήσῃ (-λέω) TTrAWHR
12 *omit* answered and TTrAWHR
17 ἀπεκρίθη αὐτῷ answered him LTTrAWHR
38 answered—spake, φημί TTrAWHR
10: 5 καὶ ἁ. ὁ—ὁ δέ (*omit* answered and) TTrAWHR
20 *omit* answered and TWHR
29 *omit* answered and TWHR
11:29 *omit* answered and TTrAWHR
33 *omit* answering [L]TTrAWHR
12:17 *omit* answering LTTrAWHR
24 *omit* answering TTrAWHR
28 *trs* ἀπεκρίθη αὐτοῖς TTrAWH
13: 2, 5 *omit* answering TTrAWHR
14:20 *omit* answering and LTTrAWHR
40 *trs* ἀποκ. αὐτῷ LTTrAWWH
61†*trs* οὐκ ἀπεκ. οὐδέν TTrWHR
15: 3 *add* but he answered nothing A.V.C
12 *trs* πάλιν ἀποκριθεὶς LTTrAWHR
Lu. 5:22 *omit* answering L[Tr]
14: 5 *omit* answered, *read* he said to them LTTr[A]WHR
20:24 *omit* answered and TWHR
34 *omit* answering LTTrAWHR
Joh. 6: 7 ἀποκρίνεται answereth T
12:23 ἀποκρίνεται answereth TTr.WHR
13:38 ἀποκρίνεται answereth Eds
Acts 8:37 *omit the verse* GLTTrAWHR

ἀποκρύπτω.

Mat. 11:25 κρύπτω LTTrAWH
25:18 κρύπτω LTTrAWH

ἀποκτείνω, —ταίνω, —τέννω.

Mat. 10:28 ἀποκτεννόντων LTTrA
Mar. 12: 5 ἀποκτείνοντες GLTTrA, —νυντες WH
8 *trs* ἀπέκτειναν αὐτόν TTrAWHR
Lu. 6: 9*ἀποκτεῖναι *for* ἀπολέσαι (ἀπόλλυμι) GW
12: 4 ἀποκτεννόντων LTTrA
Joh. 5:16 *omit* and sought to slay him G[L]TTrAWHR
2Co. 3: 6 ἀποκτέννει TTrA
Rev. 6: 8 *trs* ἐπὶ τὸ τέτ. τῆς γῆς, ἀ. GEds
11 ἀποκτέννεσθαι GLTTrAWHR
13:10 ἀποκτανθῆναι (is) to be killed A

ἀποκυλίω.

Mar. 16: 4 ἀνακυλίω TTrAWHR

ἀπολαμβάνω.

Lu. 6:34 α¹.—λαμβάνω TTrAWHR
18:30 λαμβάνω LWH
Col. 3:24 ἀπολήμψεσθε LTTrAWH
2 Joh. 8 ἀπολάβητε ye receive Eds
3 Joh. 8 to receive—to sustain, ὑπολαμβάνω Eds

ἀπολείπω

2 Ti. 4:13, 20 ἀπέλειπον WH
Tit. 1: 5*ἀπέλιπον (-λειπον WH) *for* κατέλιπον (καταλείπω) Eds

ἀπολείχω.

Lu. 16:21 ἐπιλείχω LTTrAWHR

ἀπόλλυμι, —ολλύω.

Mat. 9:17 ἀπόλλυνται LTTrWHR
18:11 *omit the verse* LTTr[A]WHR
Mar. 2:22†*trs* ἀπόλλυται καὶ οἱ ἀσκοί. *read* the wine perisheth and the bottles. TTrAWHR
8:35 ἀ.²—ἀπολέσει TTrAWH
9:41 ἀπολέσῃ LTr
11:18 ἀπολέσωσιν LTTrAWWH
Lu. 6: 9 destroy—kill, ἀποκτείνω GW
9:56 *omit* for the Son of to save (them) GLTTrAWHR
15: 4 ἀ.¹—ἀπολέσῃ Tr
24 *trs* ἣν ἀπολωλὼς LTTrAWHR
17:33 ἀ.²—ἀπολέσει TWH
Joh. 3:15 *om.* not perish, but[L]TTrAWHR
12:25 ἀπολλύει loseth TTrWHR
18:14 ἀποθνήσκω LTTrAWHR
Acts 27:34*ἀπολεῖται *for* πεσεῖται (πίπτω) GEds
1 Co. 8:11 ἀπόλλυται perisheth Eds
10: 9 ἀπώλλυντο TTrWHR
2 Joh. 8 ἀπολέσητε ye lose Eds
Rev. 18:14*ἀπώλετο *for* ἀπῆλθεν¹ (ἀπέρχομαι) W
14*ἀπώλετο (-λοντο T) *for* ἀπῆλθεν² GEds

Ἀπολλωνία.

Acts 17: 1 τὴν Ἀπολλωνίαν LTTrWH

Ἀπολλώς.

1 Co. 3: 5 *trs* Apollos *and* Paul Eds
4: 6 Ἀπολλὼν TTrWH
Tit. 3:13 Ἀπολλὼν TWH

ἀπολογέομαι.

Acts 26: 1 *trs* ἀπελογεῖτο *after* χεῖρα Eds
2 *trs* ἐπὶ σοῦ μέλλων σημερον ἀ. GLTTrAWHR

ἀπολύω.

Mat. 5:32 ἀ.¹—ὁ ἀπολύων that putteth away LTTrAWHR
19: 9 *omit* and whoso to end of verse T[Tr]WH
Mat. 6:45 ἀπολύει sendeth away LTTrAWHR
10:12 γυνὴ ἀ.—αὐτὴ ἀπολύσασα she shall put away TTrAWHR
Lu. 22:68 *om.* nor let (me) go T[TrA]WHR
23:17 *omit the verse* [L]TTr[A]WHR
Joh. 18:39 *trs* ἀπολύσω ὑμῖν¹ LTTrWH
39 *trs* ἀπολύσω ὑμῖν² LTTrWWH
19:10 *trs* to release thee, and I have power to crucify thee LTTrAWHR

ἀποπίπτω.

Acts 9:18 ἀπέπεσαν LTTrAWH

ἀποπλύνω.

Lu. 5: 2 πλύνω LTTrAWHR

ἀποπνίγω.

Mat. 13: 7 πνίγω T

ἀπορέομαι, —ρέω.

Mar. 6:20*ἠπόρει *for* ἐποίει (ποιέω) TWHR
Lu. 24: *ἀπορεῖσθαι *for* διαπορεῖσθαι (-ρέω) LTTrAWHR

ἀπορρίπτω.

Acts 27:43 ἀπορίψαντας TWH

ἀποσκευάζομαι.

Acts 21:15 ἐπισκευάζομαι Eds

ἀποστέλλω.

Mat. 8:31*ἐπίτρεψον ἡμῖν ἀπελθεῖν—ἀπόστειλον ἡμᾶς GLTTrAWHR, *see* ἀπέρχομαι
Mar. 11: 3 ἀποστέλλει he sendeth GEds
12: 4 *om.* sent (him) awayLTTrAWHR
Lu. 4:43 ἀπεστάλην was I sent LTTrAWHR
7:20 ἀπέστειλεν WH
24:49 send—send out, ἐξαποστέλλω TTrAWHR
Joh. 1:24 οἱ ἀ.—*omit* οἱ TTrAWHR
4:38 ἀπέσταλκα T
7:29 ἀπέσταλκεν T
Acts 7:34 ἀποστείλω Eds
35 ἀπέσταλκεν Eds
10:21 *omit* which were sent unto him from Cornelius GEds
13:26 sent—sent forth, ἐξαποστέλλω Eds
15:33*ἀποστείλαντας αὐτοὺς *for* ἀποστόλους (-λος) GEds
16:36 ἀπέσταλκαν LTTrAWH
21:25*ἀπεστείλαμεν *for* ἐπεστείλαμεν (ἐπιστέλλω) LTrWH
26:17 *trs* ἀποστέλλω σε LTTrAWHR
Rev. 5: 6 *omit* τά LTTrAWHR : ἀπεσταλμένοι LTrWHR, ἀποστελλόμενα W

ἀποστερέω.

Jas. 5: 4 ἀφυστερέω TTrWH

ἀπόστολος.

Mar. 3:14*twelve—*add* οὓς καὶ ἀποστόλους ὠνόμασεν whom also he called apostles WH
Acts 5:34 apostles—men, ἄνθρωπος LTTrAWHR
15:33 the apostles—those who sent (ἀποστέλλω) them GEds
1 Co. 9: 1 *trs* am I not free? am I not an apostle? GEds
Rev. 2: 2 *trs* ἀποστόλους εἶναι GW
18:20 καὶ οἱ ἀ. *read* ye saints and ye apostles GEds

ἀποστρέφω.

Mat. 27: 3 στρέφω TTrAWHR

ἀποτάσσομαι.

Acts 18:21 ἀποταξάμενος καί taking leave and LTTrAWHR

ἀποτελέω.

Lu. 13:32*ἀποτελῶ *for* ἐπιτελῶ (-λεω) LTTrAWHR

ἀποτίθημι.

Mat. 14: 3†*trs* ἐν (*add* τῇ LTrA) φυλακῇ (ἀπέθετο *for* ἔθετο, τιθημι) LTTrAWH

ἀποτινάσσω.

Lu. 9: 5 ἀποτινάσσετε TAWH
Acts 28: 5 ἀποτιναξάμενος W

ἀποτομία.

Ro. 11:22 ἀ.²—ἀποτομία LTTrAWHR

ἀποφέρω.

Acts 19:12*ἀποφέρεσθαι *for* ἐπιφέρεσθαι (-ρω) LTTrAWHR

ἀποφεύγω.

2 Pet. 2:18 ἀποφεύγοντας are escaping from Eds

ἀποφθέγγομαι.

Acts 2: 4 *trs* ἀποφθέγγεσθαι αὐτοῖς Eds

ἀπροσωπολήπτως,—ήμπ— LTTrAWH.

ἅπτομαι, ἅπτω.

Mat. 17: 7 ἀψάμενος touching LTWH
Mar. 1:41 *trs* αὐτοῦ ἥψατο LTTrAWH
5:28 *trs* ἅψωμαι before κἂν TAWHR
6:56 ἀ.²—ἥψαντο LTTrAWHR
10:13 *trs* αὐτῶν ἅψηται WH
Lu. 8:45 *omit* and sayest thou, Who touched me? T[TrA]WHR
22:55 περιάπτω TTrAWHR
Acts 28: 2*ἅψαντες *for* ἀνάψαντες (ἀνάπτω) LTTrAWWH

ἀπώλεια.

Acts 25:16 *omit* to die GEds

2 Pet. 2: 2 pernicious ways—licentious-
ness, ἀσέλγεια GEds

ἄρα, ἄραγε, ἄρα γε.
Acts 7: 1 *omit* ἄρα LTTr[A]WHR
  11:18 ἄρα LTTrWHR, ἄρα [γε] A
Gal. 4:31 so then—wherefore, διό
  LTTrAWHR

ἀραβών, see ἀρραβών.

Ἀράμ.
Lu. 3:33 Ἀράμ—Ἀρνεί R: Ἀδμείν τοῦ
  Ἀρνεί TAWH

ἄραφος, see ἄρραφος.

ἀργός.
Mat. 20: 6 *omit* idle¹ GLTTrAWHR
Jas. 2:20*ἀργή *for* νεκρά(-ρός) LTTrAWHR

ἀργύριον.
Mat. 25:27 τὰ ἀργύρια TWH
  28:15 τὰ ἀ.—*omit* τὰ WH
Lu. 19:23 *trs* μου τὸ ἀργύριον LTTrAWH
1 Co. 3:12*ἀργύριον *for* ἄργυρον (-ος)
  TTrWH

ἄργυρος.
1 Co. 3:12 ἀργύριον TTrWH

Ἄρειος, Ἄριος T.

Ἀρεοπαγίτης, —γείτης T, Ἀρειο—W
Acts 17:34 ὁ Ἀ.—*omit* ὁ L[TrWH]

ἀρέσκεια, ἀρεσκία TWH.

ἀρέσκω.
Mar. 6:22 καὶ ἀ.—ἤρεσεν LTTrAWHR
1 Co. 7:32, 33, 34 ἀρέσῃ LTTrAWHR

Ἀρέτας, Ἀ— WH.

ἀρετή.
2 Pet. 1: 3 ἀρετῇ LTTrAWH, *see* ἴδιος

ἀριθμός.
Acts 4: 4 ὁ ἀ.—*omit* ὁ LT[Tr]AWHR
  5:36 *trs* ἀνδρῶν ἀριθμὸς Eds
Rev. 5:11 elders- -*add* καὶ ἦν ὁ ἀριθμὸς
  αὐτῶν μυριάδες μυριάδων and
  the number of them was ten
  thousand times ten thousand
  A.V.B EGEds

Ἀριμαθαία, Ἀ— WH.
Mat. 27:57 Ἀριμαθείας W

ἀριστερός.
Mar. 10:37*ἀριστερῶν *for* εὐωνύμων (-μος)
  TTrAWH

ἄρκτος, ἄρκος GEds.

**Ἀρμαγεδδών, Ἀρμαγεδών (Ἀρ M.
WH) GEds.**

* Ἀρνεί, see Ἀράμ.

ἀρνέομαι.
Lu. 9:23*ἀρνησάσθω *for* ἀπαρνησάσθω
  (-νέομαι) GLTTrAWHR
Joh. 13:38*ἀρνήσῃ *for* ἀπαρνήσῃ (-νέομαι)
  LTTrAWHR
Acts 4:16 ἀρνεῖσθαι LTTrAWHR
2 Ti. 2:12 ἀρνησόμεθα we shall deny
  LTTrAWHR

ἀρνίον.
Rev. 14: 1 τὸ ἀ. the Lamb GEds
  21: 9 *trs* τὴν γυναῖκα τοῦ ἀ. Eds

ἀρπάζω.
Mat. 12:29*ἀρπάσαι *for* διαρπάσαι (-άζω)
  LTTrAWH

ἀρραβών.
2 Co. 1:22 ἀραβῶνα LT
  5: 5 ἀραβῶνα T

ἄρραφος, ἄραφος TTrAWH.

ἄρρην.
Ro. 1:27 οἱ ἄρρενες S — οἱ ἄρσενες
  BLTrAWWH
  27*ἄρρενες *for* ἄρσενες (-σην) T
  27*ἄρρεσιν *for* ἄρσεσιν (-σην) T
Rev. 12: 5 ἄρσην Eds
  13 ἄρσην LTTrAWH

ἄρσην.
Ro. 1:27 *see* ἄρρην
Rev. 12: 5*ἄρσεν *for* ἄρρενα (-ρην) Eds
  13*ἄρσενα(ν L) *for* ἄρρενα (-ρην)
  LTTrAWH

ἀρτέμων.
Acts 27:40 ἀρτέμωνα LTTrAWWH

ἄρτι.
Mat. 26:53 *trs* ἄρτι *after* μοι, read now
  give TTrWH
Joh. 1:51(52) *omit* hereafter LTTrAWHR
  See also ἀπάρτι.

ἄρτος.
Mat. 16:11 ἄρτων loaves Eds
  12 τοῦ ἄ.—τῶν ἄρτων of the loaves
  LTrA[WH]R: τῶν Φαρισαίων καὶ
  Σαδδουκαίων of the Pharisees
  and Sadducees T
  26:26 τὸν ἄ.—*omit* τὸν LTTr[A]WHR
Mar. 6: 8 *trs* no bread, no scrip TTrAWHR
  36 *omit* ἄ. et γὰρ et οὐκ ἔχουσιν,
  read buy themselves somewhat to eat [L]TTrAWHR
  38 *trs* ἔχετε ἄρτους WH
  7: 2 τοὺς ἄρτους LTTrAWHR
Lu. 9:13 *trs* ἄρτοι πέντε TWH
  11:11 *omit* bread, will he give him
  a stone? or if (he ask) WH
Acts 20:11 τὸν ἄρτον Eds

ἀρχαῖος.
Mat. 5:27 *omit* by them of old time GEds
Rev. 20: 2 ὁ ὄφις ὁ ἀρχαῖος LTTrAWHR

ἀρχή.
Mar. 13: 8(9) ἀρχὴ a beginning LTTrWHR
Joh. 2:11 τὴν ἀ.—*omit* τὴν LTTrAWHR
1 Joh. 2: 7 *omit* from the beginning²
  LTTrAWHR
Rev. 1: 8 *omit* the beginning and the
  ending GEds
  22:13 ἡ ἀ. GLTTrAWHR: *trs* the first
  and the last, the beginning
  and the end GLTTrAWHR

ἀρχιερεύς.
Mar. 2:26 τοῦ ἀ.—*omit* τοῦ Eds
  8:31 τῶν ἀρχιερέων GEds
  11:18 *trs* chief priests and scribes
  Eds
Lu. 3: 2 ἀρχιερέως GEds
  20: 1 chief priests—priests, ἱερεύς
  TA
  19 *trs* the scribes and the chief
  priests LTTrAWHR
  22:50 *trs* τοῦ ἀρχιερέως τὸν δοῦλον
  TTrAWH
  23:23 *omit* and of the chief priests
  [L]T[TrA]WHR
Joh. 7:32 *trs* the chief priests and the
  Pharisees Eds: ὑπηρέτας be-
  fore οἱ ἀ. T
  18:16 τοῦ ἀρχιερέως TTrAWH
Acts 4: 1*ἀρχιερεῖς *for* ἱερεῖς (-εύς) WH
  6 ὁ ἀρχιερεὺς LTTrAWHR
  25: 2 οἱ ἀρχιερεῖς the chief priests
  LTTrAWHR
Heb. 10:11*ἀρχιερεὺς *for* ἱερεύς LA

ἄρχομαι, ἄρχω.
Mat. 16:22 *omit* began A, see λέγω
Mar. 14:69 *trs* and began again TWH
Lu. 3:23 *trs* ἀρ. ὡσεὶ ἐτῶν τριάκ. TTrWH
  24:47 ἀρξάμενοι TTrAWH
Acts 10:37 ἀρξάμενος TTrAWHR

ἄρχων.
Lu. 11:15 τῷ ἄρχοντι Eds

Ἀσά, Ἀσάφ LTTrAWHR.

ἄσβεστος.
Mar. 9:45 *omit* into the fire to end of
  verse [L]TTr[A]WHR

ἀσεβέω.
2 Pet. 2: 6 ἀσεβής WH

ἀσεβής.
Ro. 4: 5 ἀσεβῆν T
2 Pet. 2: 6*ἀσεβέσιν *for* ἀσεβεῖν (-βέω) WH

ἀσέλγεια.
2 Pet. 2: 2*ἀσελγείαις *for* ἀπωλείαις(-εια)
  GEds

ἀσθένεια.
Acts 28: 9 *trs* ἐν τῇ νήσῳ ἔχοντες ἀ.
  LTTrAWHR
Ro. 8:26 τῇ ἀσθενείᾳ infirmity Eds

ἀσθενέω.
Mat. 25:39*ἀσθενοῦντα *for* ἀσθενῆ (-ής)
  LTTrAWHR
Lu. 7:10 *omit* that had been sick
  LTTr[A]WHR
  9: 2 ἀσθενής L[Tr]: *omit* the sick
  TAWH
Joh. 5:13*ἀσθενῶν *for* ἰσθεὶς (ἰάομαι) T
Ro. 14:21 *omit* or is offended, or is made
  weak TWHR
1 Co. 8: 9 ἀσθενής Eds
2 Co. 11:21 ἠσθενήκαμεν LTTrWHR

ἀσθενής.
Mat. 25:39 ἀσθενῶ LTTrAWH
Lu. 9: 2*ἀσθενεῖς *for* ἀσθενοῦντας(-ενέω)
  L[Tr]
1 Co. 8: 9*ἀσθενέσιν *for* ἀσθενοῦσιν(-ενέω)
  Eds

Ἀσία.
Acts 19:27 [ἡ] Ἀ. TrWH
  20: 4 *omit* into Asia T[Tr]WH
Ro. 16: 5*Ἀσίας *for* Ἀχαΐας (-ία) GEds
Rev. 1:11 *omit* which are in Asia GEds

ἀσκός.
Mar. 2:22 *omit* but new to end of verse
  T[Tr]A[WH], see βλητέος

ἀσμένως.
Acts 2:41 *omit* gladly LTTrAWHR

ἀσπάζομαι.
Acts 21: 6 καὶ ἀσπ.—ἀπασπάζομαι, read
  having prayed (ver. 5) we
  took leave Eds
  25:13 ἀσπασάμενοι TTrAWHR
Ro. 16:21 ἀσπάζεται Eds
1 Co. 16:19 ἀ.²—ἀσπάζεται TAWH
Philem. 23 ἀσπάζεται GEds

ἀσπασμός.
Lu. 1:41 *trs* τὸν ἀ. τῆς Μαρίας ἡ Ἐ.
  LTTrAWH

ἄσπονδος.
Ro. 1:31 *omit* implacable Eds

Ἄσσος.
Acts 27:13 Ἄσσον S, ἆ-A.V.E: GEds, ἄ-B

ἀστραπή.
Rev. 16:18 *trs* lightnings, and voices, and
  thunders GEds

ἀστράπτω.
Lu. 17:24 ἡ ἀ.—*omit* ἡ T[TrA]WHR
  24: 4 ἀστραπτούσῃ LTTrAWHR

Ἀσύγκριτος, Ἀσύν— TWH.

ἀσφαλής.
Heb. 6:19 ἀσφαλήν LTr

ἀσφαλίζω.
Acts 16:24 *trs* ἠσφ. αὐτῶν LTTrAWH

ἄτεκνος.
Lu. 20:30 *omit* took her to wife, and he
  died childless TTrAWHR

* ἀτιμάω.
Mar. 12: 4 ἠτίμησαν LTr, ἠτίμασαν TAWHR,
  for ἠτιμωμένον (ἀτιμόω)

ἄτιμος.
1 Co. 12:23 ἀτιμότερα S—ἀτιμώτερα B

ἀτιμόω.

Mar. 12: 4 ἀτιμάω LTTrAWHR

ἄτοπος.

Acts 25: 5°ἄτοπον *for* τούτῳ LTTrAWHR

'Ατταλεια, –λία TAWH.

αὐξάνω, αὔξω.

Mat. 6:28 αὐξάνουσιν LTTrAWH
Mar. 4: 8 αὐξανόμενον LTTrAW, –μενα WHR
Lu. 12:27 *omit* they grow TA
2 Co. 9:10 αὐξήσει will increase GEds
Col. 1: 6°fruit—*add* καὶ αὐξανόμενον and groweth GEds

Acts 23:15 *omit* to-morrow GEds

αὐτός.

(αὐτοῦ, αὐτῆς, etc., are not distinguished from αὑτοῦ, αὑτῆς, etc.)

ὁ αὐτός, *etc.*

Mat. 5:46 the same—so, οὕτως LTrA
47°το αὐτὸ *for* οὕτως Eds
Mar. 10:10 the same—this, τούτου LTTrAWHR
Lu. 6:23, 26°τὰ αὐτά *f.* ταῦτα LTTrAWHR
38 *omit* same LTTrWHR
17:30°τὰ αὐτά (ταῦτά GLW) *for* ταῦτα GEds
Acts 3: 1 *trs* ἐπὶ τὸ αὐτὸ *after* ἡμέραν (2:47) *read* added together daily LTTrAWHR
1 Co. 12: 9 same[2]—one, εἰς LTTrAWHR
Phil. 3:16 *omit* rule, let us mind the same thing GLTTrAWHR
1 Th. 2:14°τὰ αὐτά *for* ταὐτά GEds
2 Pet. 3: 7 αὐτοῦ s—τῷ αὐτῷ A.V.B ELTWHR: τῷ αὐτοῦ GTrAW
1 Joh. 2:27 the same—his, αὐτοῦ TTrAWHR

αὐτά.

Mat. 18: 8 them[1]—it, αὐτόν LTTrAWHR
Mar. 10:16 *omit* a.[3] TTrAWHR
Joh. 15: 6 *omit* a.—it, αὐτό T
Ro. 10: 5 *omit* those things [L]TWHR
Rev. 10: 4°*for* ταῦτα Eds
22:18°*for* ταῦτα GEds

αὗται, *see under* οὗτος.

αὐταῖς.

Lu. 13:14°*for* ταύταις LTTrAWHR
24: 1 *omit* and certain (others) with them LTTrAWHR
Rev. 9: 3, 4 αὐτοῖς T
5 αὐτοῖς LT

αὐτή.

Mar. 10:12°*for* γυνή LTTrWHR, *see* ἀπολύω
Lu. 2:37°*for* αὕτη TTrAWHR
38°*for* αὕτη W
7:12°*for* αὕτη WWHR
8:42°*for* αὕτη WH
Ro. 7:10°*for* αὕτη GW
16: 2°*for* αὕτη GLTAWWHR
1 Co. 7:12 αὕτη LTAWWH

αὐτῇ.

Mat. 22:39 αὕτη WH
Mar. 12:31°*for* αὕτη LTr
Lu. 7:13 a.[1]—αὐτῆ T
21 ἐκεῖνος TTrAWHR
19:41 αὐτήν LTTrAWWH
Joh. 8: 7°*trs* ἐπ᾽ αὐτήν βαλέτω λίθον WH
11 *omit* unto her WHR
Acts 5: 8 πρὸς αὐτήν LTTrAWHR
Ro. 6:12 *omit* it in GEds
Col. 2: 7 *omit* therein TTr[A]WH]R
Heb. 7:11 αὐτῆς, *read* on the ground of it Eds
Rev. 10: 6 a.[2]—*see* θάλασσα
18: 6 *omit* unto her (a.[2]) Eds
9 αὐτήν TTrAWHR
11 αὐτήν TTrAWHR

αὕτη, *see under* οὗτος.

αὐτήν.

Mat. 13:48°they drew—*add* a. it L[A]
19: 7 *omit* her LTTrWH
Mar. 12:22 *omit* had her [L]TTrAWHR
Lu. 6:48°*add* a. TTrAWHR, *see* θεμελιόω
17:33 *omit* a.[2] [L]TTrAWHR

Acts 7: 5 *trs* αὐτήν and αὐτῷ W
9:37 *omit* a.[2] WH
Eph. 5:27 αὐτός (*omit* it) GEds
Heb. 5: 3°*for* ταύτην Eds
Rev. 2:20°*for* ἑαυτήν T
12:15°*for* ταύτην GEds
18: 7°*for* ἑαυτήν Eds
9 bewail her—*omit* her GEds
20 αὐτῇ GEds

αὐτῆς.

Mat. 1:25 *omit* her firstborn LTTrAWHR
5:28 *omit* a. T: αὐτήν LTrAW[WH]
6:34°*for* αὐτῆς AWH
23:37°*for* ἑαυτῆς T[Tr]AW[WH]
Mar. 1:31 *omit* a. LT[Tr]AWH
5:26°*for* ἑαυτῆς GLTrAWWH
6:22 αὐτοῦ WH
Lu. 2:22 αὐτῶν s—αὐτῆς her A.V.B R
10:38 om. a. *read* the house T[Tr]WH
12:53 om. her[1] T: om. her[2] TTrAWHR
Joh. 8: 5°sayest thou—*add* περὶ a. concerning her WR
1 Co. 7:39 *omit* a.[2] LTTrAWHR
10:28 *omit* GEds, *see* γῆ
11: 5°*for* ἑαυτῆς LTTrAWHR
Heb.12:15°*for* ταύτης LWH
1 Pet. 1:24°*for* ἀνθρώπου (-ος) GEds

αὐτό.

Mat. 14:12 it—him, αὐτόν TTrAWHR
Mar. 4:37 *omit* a. LTTrAWHR, *see* πλοῖον
6:29 it—him, αὐτόν T
Lu. 11:14 *omit* and it was [TrA]WHR
23:53 *omit* a.[1] LTTrAWHR
53 it[3]—him, αὐτόν LTTrAWHR
Joh. 14:17 *omit* a.[2] [L]WH
Acts 5:39 it[2]—them, αὐτούς GLTTrAWHR
1 Co. 5:13°fire[2]—*add* a. itself Eds
4:17°this—*add* a. very T
Phil. 3:21 *omit* that it may be GEds
Rev. 8: 5 αὐτόν EGLTTrAWWH

αὐτοί.

Mat. 5: 9 *omit* a. [L]T[TrAWH]
19:28°*for* ὑμεῖς[2] TTr
23: 4°τῷ δὲ—αὐτοὶ δὲ τῷ but they themselves LTTrAWHR
Mar. 2: 8°οὕτως—*add* a. G[A]W
7:36°αὐτοὶ μᾶλλον LTTrAWH
Lu. 13: 4°*for* οὗτοι LTTrAWHR
Joh. 17:11°*for* οὗτοι TWH
Acts 13: 4°*for* οὗτοι LTTrAWHR
1 Co. 16:17°*for* οὗτοι LAW

αὐτοῖς.

Mat. 8:15 unto them—unto him, αὐτῷ Eds
9:12, 24 *omit* unto them LTTrAWHR
13:11 *omit* unto them TWH
37 *omit* unto them LTTrAWHR
51 *omit* Jesus saith unto them LTTrAWHR
16: 8 *omit* unto them GLTTrAWHR
17:11 *omit* unto them LTTr[A]WHR
19: 4 *omit* unto them LTTrAWHR
14°said—*add* a. unto them T
20: 8 *omit* them T[TrA]WH
25:20, 22 *omit* beside them LTTrWHR
26:71°*for* τοῖς AW
Mar. 4: 9 *omit* unto them GEds
15°*see* καρδία
6:34 αὐτοῖς LTTrAWHR
8:29 αὐτούς LTTrAWHR, *see* ἐπερωτάω
9:14 πρὸς αὐτούς TTrAWHR
10:13°*for* τοῖς προσφέρουσιν (·ρω) WHR
11:17 *omit* unto them [L]AWH
12:17 *omit* unto them AWH
38 *omit* unto them TTrAWHR
Lu. 6: 2 *omit* unto them [L]TTrAWHR
19:40 *omit* unto them T[Tr]AWHR
20:25 πρὸς αὐτούς TTrAWHR
23:17 *omit* the verse [L]TTr[A]WHR
20°προσεφώνησεν—*add* a. LWHR
25. unto them G[L]TTrAWWHR
34 *see* λέγω
35 *omit* with them T[Tr]AWHR
24:36 *omit* and saith to end of verse T[[WH]]
40 *omit* the verse T[Tr][[WH]]
44 πρὸς αὐτούς TTrAWHR
Joh. 2:22 *omit* unto them GEds
7: 9 *omit* unto them T
33 *omit* unto them GEds
47 [them] TrWH
8:28 *omit* unto them LTTrAWHR
9:20 *omit* them [L]TTrAWHR
10: 7 *omit* unto them TAWH
25 *omit* them T
17:13 ἑαυτοῖς TTrAWHR
20:20 *trs* a. *after* πλευράν LTTrAWHR

Acts 4:18 *omit* a. LTTrAWHR
12:17 *omit* unto them[2] T[Tr]
13:19 *omit* to them TTr[A]WHR
15: 8 *omit* them[2] TTrAWHR
17:18 *omit* unto them TTr[A]WHR
18:20 *omit* with them LTTrAWHR
21 *omit* them LTTrAWHR
19:15°said—*add* a. unto them Eds
Ro. 1:21°*for* ἑαυτοῖς LTTrAWHR
27°*for* ἑαυτοῖς WH
9:26 *omit* unto them [L]Tr[WH]
10: 5 them—it, αὐτῇ LTTrAWHR
2 Co. 4: 4 *omit* unto them GEds
Col. 3: 7 them—these things, τούτοις Eds
1 Th. 5:13°*for* ἑαυτοῖς TTr
Heb. 8: 8 αὐτούς LTWH
Rev. 6:11°given—*add* a. unto them GEds
21:14 αὐτῶν GEds, *see* δώδεκα

αὐτόν.

Mat. 3:15 πρὸς a.—αὐτῷ LWH
7:24 *omit* a. LTTrWHR, *see* ὁμοιόω
14: 3 *omit* a. TWH
17: 8°*for* τὸν WH
21: 9°before—*add* a. him LTTr\WHR
44 *omit* the verse [L]T[WH]
22:13 *omit* take him away and LTTrAWHR
13°cast—*add* a. him LTTrAWHR
26:61 *omit* a. T
71 *omit* a.[1] [L]TrWH
27: 2 *omit* a.[2] LTTrAWH
43 *omit* him[1] T[Tr]WH
28:14 *omit* a. T[Tr]WH
Mar. 1:40 *omit* and kneeling down to him L[TrA]:*omit* to him[2] TWH
2:16 *omit* him LTTrWHR, *see* ἐσθίω
6:33 *omit* him[1] GLTrAWHR: them αὐτούς T
33 *omit* and came together unto him GEds
8:25 *omit* a. TTrAWHR, *see* διαβλέπω
9:18 *omit* a.[2] T
26 *omit* a. G[L]TTrAWHR
27 *omit* him[1] LTTrWHR
2: εἰσελθόντος αὐτοῦ LTTrWHR
10:26°*for* ἑαυτούς WHR
34 *omit* a.[2] [L]T[Tr]WHR
12: 8°cast—*add* a. him Eds
14:46 ἐπ᾽ a. τὰς χεῖρας αὐτῶν—τὰς χ. αὐτῷ TTrAWH
15:20 *omit* a.[1] T
Lu. 1:62 him—it, αὐτό LTTrAWH
2:21°*for* τὸ παιδίον GEds
45 *omit* a.[1] G[L]TTrAWHR
4: 9 *omit* a.[2] T[Tr]AWH
5:18°to lay—*add* a. him A[WH
6: 7 *omit* him[1] LTTrAW
12°ἐξῆλθεν—ἐξελθεῖν a. TTrAWHR
7: 6 *omit* to him (πρὸς a.) TWH
8:21 *omit* a. GLTTrAWHR
9:62 *omit* unto him A[WH]
10:33 *omit* a.[2] [L]T[Tr]AWHR
11:28 *omit* a. GLTTrAWHR
54 *omit* a. T
17:11 *omit* a. T[TrA]WHR
18: 7 πρὸς a.—αὐτῷ TTrAWHR
19: 5 *omit* saw him and TTr[A]WHR
22:43, 44 the verses [L][[WH]]
54 *omit* a.[2] LTTrAWH
57 *omit* him[1] LTr[A]WHR
63°*for* τὸν 'Ιησοῦν LTTrAWHR
64 *omit* a.[2] TTrAWH
23:11 *omit* a.[2] [L]T[Tr]AWHR
15 *see* ἀναπέμπω
24:12°*for* ἑαυτόν Tr: *omit* the verse [L]T[Tr][[WH]]
52 *omit* worshipped him and T[[WH]]
Joh. 1:19°sent—*add* πρὸς a. unto him LTrAWH
2:24°*for* ἑαυτόν LTTrAWHR
3: 2°*for* τὸν 'Ιησοῦν GEds
15 εἰς a.—ἐν αὐτῷ TTrAWHR
4:24 *omit* him[1] T
47 *omit* him[2] LTTrAWHR
5:16 *omit* and sought to slay him G[L]TTrAWH
6:15 *omit* a.[2] LTTrAWH
7:50 *omit* T, *see* ἔρχομαι
8: 3 *omit* unto him WH
11:44°ἄφετε—*add* a. T[Tr]AWHR
14: 7 *omit* him[2] [LTrA]WH
18:13 *omit* a. [L]TTrWHR
31 *omit* him[2] T
19: 3°*add* a. LTTrAWHR, *see* ἔρχομαι
6°crucify[2]—*add* a. him GLW
12 a.[2]—ἑαυτόν GEds
38°*for* τὸ σῶμα τοῦ 'Ιησοῦ[2] T
39°*for* τὸν 'Ιησοῦν Eds

Joh. 21:25 *omit the verse* T
Acts 3: 7*lifted up—*add a.* him
      LTTrAWHR
    13 *omit* him¹ LT[TrA]WHR
  7:21 *a.*¹—*αὐτοῦ* LTTrAWHR
    31 *omit* unto him LTTrAWHR
  9: 6 *omit* GEds, *see* κέντρον
    25 *omit a.* LTTrAWHR
    25**add a.* LTTrAWHR, *see* καθίημι
    43 *omit a.* TWH
  10:11 *omit* unto him GEds
    21 *omit* which were sent unto
      him from Cornelius GEds
  11:26(25) *omit a. bis* LTTrAWHR
  14:17*for ἑαυτόν LTTrWH
  17:15 *omit a.*¹ LTTrAWHR
  23:27 *omit a.* LTT[A]WWHR
    28 *omit a.* T[Tr]WH
    30 *omit* against him LT
    35 *trs a.* to end of verse
      LTTrAWHR
  24:23*for τὸν Παῦλον GEds
    26 *omit* that he might loose him
      Eds
  25: 7*round about—*add a.* him Eds
    25 *omit a.*² LTTrAWHR
  28:17*for τὸν Παῦλον GEds
1 Co. 7:13 him—the husband, ἀνήρ Eds
Eph. 1:20*ἐκάθισεν—καθίσας, set him T
1 Ti. 3: 7 *omit a.* LTTrAWHR
Heb. 2: 6 αὐτοῦ W
    7 *omit a.*³ G[L]T[Tr]A[WH], *see*
      χείρ
    12: 3 ἑαυτόν LTTrA, ἑαυτούς WHR
Jas.   5:14 *omit a.*² T
1 Joh.4:19 *omit* him Eds
    5:18*for ἑαυτόν TTrAWHR
Rev. 20: 3 *omit* him² GEds

αὐτός.

Mat. 6: 4 *omit* himself LTTrAWHR
    12: 3 *omit a.* GEds
    25:17 *omit* he also LTTr[A]WHR
Mar. 2:25 *omit a.*¹ [L]TTrWH
    4:38 *trs* αὐτός ἦν WH
    5:40*for ὁ LTTrWHR
    6:16 *omit* ἐστιν· a. G[L]TTrAWHR
    7:36 *omit a.* LTTrAWWH
    12:21 *om. a.* TTrAWHR, *see* καταλείπω
    15: 3 *add a.* A.V.C, *see* ἀποκρίνομαι
Lu.   8:41 οὗτος LTWH
    19: 2*for οὗτος LTrAWHR
    23:51 *omit* also himself LTTrAWHR
Joh. 1:27 *omit* he it is G[L]TTrAWHR
    5:37 ἐκεῖνος TTrAWHR
    7: 9*a. ἔμεινεν T
    9:21 *omit a.*¹ TTrAWHR *see* ἐρωτάω
    14:10 *omit a.* TTrAWHR
Acts 3:10*for οὗτος LT
    10:42 οὗτος LTrWH
1 Co. 7:13 οὗτος Eds
    9:20**add a.* GEds, *see* νόμος
Heb.10:12 οὗτος Eds
Rev. 17:11 οὗτος WH

αὐτοῦ.

Mat. 3: 7 *omit a.* read the baptism
      LT[TrA]WH
    12*ἀποθήκην a. his garner LTrW
  8: 5*for τῷ Ἰησοῦ LTTrAWHR
    13 *omit a. read* the servant
      LTTr[A]WHR
    21 *omit a. read* the disciples
      LTTrWHR
    25 *omit a.* GEds
  12:46 *omit a.*² [L]R
    49 *omit a.*¹ T[WH]
  13:57 *omit a.*¹ LTTrAWH, *see* ἴδιος
  14:15 *omit a. read* the disciples
      LTTrAWHR
    22 *omit a. read* the disciples
      GTTrAWWHR
  15: 6(5) *om.* or his mother L[A]WHR
    12 *omit a. read* the disciples
      LTAWHR
    30*for τοῦ Ἰησοῦ LTTrAWHR
    33, 36 *omit a. read* the disciples
      [L]T[Tr]AWHR
  16: 5, 20 *omit a. read* the disciples
      LTTrAWHR
  17:10 *omit a. read* the disciples
      LTTrWH
  18:25 *om. a.*² TTrAWH: *om. a.*³ T[A]WH
    29 *omit* at his feet GLTTrA[A]WHR
  19:10 *omit a. read* the disciples
      T[A]WHR
    25 *om. a. read* the disciples GEds
  24:45 *omit a.*¹ LTTrAWHR
    49*συνδούλους a. his fellow-ser-
      vants Eds
  25: 6 *omit a.* TAWH

Mat. 26: 8, 45 *omit a. read* the disciples
      LTTrAWHR
    36*μαθηταῖς a. his disciples LR
    65 *omit a.*² read the blasphemy
      [L]TTrAWHR
    27:64 *om. a. read* the disciples TWH
    28: 9 *omit* And. as they went to
      tell his disciples LTTrAWHR
Mar. 1:16 his—Simon's, Σίμωνος Eds
    42 *omit* as soon as he had spoken
      LTTrWHR
  3:31*ἀδελφοί a. GEds
  4:34 μαθηταῖς a.—ἰδίοις μ. TAWHR
  5:18 *trs* μετ' αὐτοῦ ᾖ LTTrAWH
  6: 4 a.¹—ἑαυτοῦ T
    4*συγγενέσιν a. [L]TTrAWH
    41 *omit a. read* the disciples
      TTrAWHR
  7:12 *omit a. bis* LTTrAWH
    15 him³—the man, ἄνθρωπος
      LTTrAWHR
    33 *omit a.*¹ T
  8: 1 *omit a. read* the disciples
      TTrWH
    35 ψυχὴν a.¹—ἑαυτοῦ ψ. WH
    35 ψυχήν a.²—ἑαυτοῦ ψ. GTrW
  9:18 *omit a.* [L]TTrAWH
    27*χειρὸς a. his hand LTTrWH
  10: 7*μητέρα a. his mother T
    7 *omit* and cleave to his wife
      TWH
    10 *omit a.*¹ read the disciples
      [L]TTr[A]WH
  12: 6 *omit* his LTTrAWH
    19 *omit a.*² read the wife TTrAWH
  13:27 *omit a. read* the angels
      [L]TTrAWH
    27 *om. a. read* the elect TTrA[WH]
  14:16 *omit a. read* the disciples
      T[Tr]WHR
    33*for ἑαυτοῦ LTTrAWH
  15:20**add a.* LTWHR, *see* ἴδιος
Lu.   1: 5 αὐτῷ LTTrAWHR
    29 *omit a. read* the saying
      GTTrAWHR
  2:28 *omit a.* [L]T[TrA]WH
    33**add a.* GTTrAWHR, *see* πατήρ
    33 *omit a.*¹ GTrAWH
  4:24 ἑαυτοῦ T
  5:15 *omit* by him LTTrAWHR
  6:40 *omit a.*¹ read the master
      LTTrAWHR
    45 *omit a.*¹ read the heart TWH
    45 *omit* treasure of his heart²
      [L]TTrAWH
  8:19*μήτηρ a. his mother T
    45 μετ' a.—σὺν αὐτῷ GLTTrAR:
      omit and they that were
      with him WH
  9: 1 *omit* his disciples (read the
      twelve) GTTrAWHR
    7 *omit* by him [L]TTrAWHR
    51 *omit a.*² [LTr]WH
    54 *omit a. read* the disciples
      T[TrA]WH
    62 *omit a.* [Tr]WH
  11:54 *omit* that they might accuse
      him T[Tr]AWHR
  12:15 a.²—αὐτῷ LTTrAWH
    22 [αὐτοῦ] WH
    31·*for* τοῦ θεοῦ (-ός) LTTrAWHR
    47*for ἑαυτοῦ LTTrAWHR
  14:26*for ἑαυτοῦ¹ LTTrA
    27 ἑαυτοῦ LTAWH
  15: 5*for ἑαυτοῦ TTrAWHR
    16 *omit* his belly WHR
    20*for ἑαυτοῦ LJTr
    26 *omit a. read* the servant
      A.V.B EGEds
    29*πατρὶ a. his father LTTrAWH
  16: 1 *omit a. read* the disciples
      TTrAWHR
  17: 1*μαθητὰς a. his disciples Eds
    24 *omit* in his day LWH
  18:13 ἑαυτοῦ TrAWH
  19:26 *omit* from him² (a.¹) [L]TAWH
    29 *omit a. read* the disciples
      T[Tr]AWHR
  20:26 a.¹—τοῦ AWHR
    45 *omit a. read* the disciples
      TTrWH, *see* μαθητής
  22:16 thereof—it, αὐτό LTTrAWHR
    39 *omit a. read* the disciples
      TTrAWHR
    43, 44 *the verses* [L][[WH]]
    45 μαθητὰς a. A.V.Er E
    51 *omit a.* TTrAWHR
    64 *omit* they struck him on the
      face, and [L]TTrAWHR
  23:49 αὐτῷ LTTrAWH
  24:27*for ἑαυτοῦ EGLTr
Joh.   2:12 *omit a.*² [L]Tr[A]WHR

Joh. 3:16 *om. a. read* the only begotten
      TWH
    17 *om. a. read* the Son T[TrA]WHR
  4:51 *omit a. read* the servants T
    51*for σοῦ LTTrAWHR
  5: 5*ἀσθενείᾳ a. his infirmity
      [L]TTrAWHR
  6: 2 *omit a. read* the miracles
      GEds
    22 *omit a.*¹ GLTTrAWHR, *see* ἐκεῖνος
    52*σάρκα a. his flesh L[WH]
  9: 6*τὸν—a. τὸν (read his eyes)
      LTTrAWHR
    21 a.²—ἑαυτοῦ TTrWH
  11:12 *omit a. read* the disciples
      LTTrAWHR
    54 *omit a. read* the disciples
      TTrAWHR
  14:10*add at end a. read his works
      [L]TTrAWHR
  19:17 τὸν σταυρὸν a.—αὐτῷ (ἑαυτῷ
      TR) τὸν στ. for himself the
      cross LTTrAWHR
    26 *omit a.* [L]TTr[A]WHR
    38*for τοῦ Ἰησοῦ³ LTrAWHR
  20:20 *omit a.* LTTrAWHR
    30 *omit a. read* the disciples
      LTTrAWHR
  21:14 *omit a. read* the disciples Eds
Acts 2:31 *omit* his soul GLTTrAWHR
  3:11*see ἰάομαι
    18 *omit a. read* the prophets
      LTTrAWHR
    18*χριστὸν a. his Christ Eds
  5: 2 *omit a.* LTTrAWHR
    32 *omit* his TTrWH
    41 *omit a. read* the name GEds
  7:13*for Ἰωσήφ² T
    14 *omit a.*² GLTTrAWHR
    20 *omit a.* GEds
    22*ἔργοις a. his deeds GEds
    25 *omit a.*¹ TTr[A]WHR
    37 *omit* him shall ye hear
      LTTrAWHR
  8:33 *omit a.*¹ read the humiliation
      LTTrWHR
  9:25*οἱ μαθηταὶ a. his disciples
      LTTrAWHR
  10: 7 *omit a. read* the household
      servants Eds
  12:13*for τοῦ Πέτρου GEds
  15:18 *omit* unto God are all his
      works GTTrAWHR
  16:34 *omit a. read* the house
      LT[Tr]AWHR
  21:11 ἑαυτοῦ Eds
    34*δέ²—*add a.* LTTrAWWH
  22:16*for τοῦ κυρίου (-ος) GEds
    20 *omit* unto his death GEds
  24: 8 *omit* LTTr[A]WHR, *see* κρίνω
    24 *omit a.*¹ GLTTrAWHR
  25: 8 *omit a.* LTTrAWHR, *see* Παῦλος
  26:30 *omit* and when he had thus
      spoken GEds
    28:29 *omit the verse* LTTrAWHR
Ro.   14:14*for ἑαυτοῦ GLTrW
    16: 2 *trs* ἐμοῦ αὐτοῦ LTTrAWHR
1 Co. 1:29 his—God's, θεοῦ GEds
    2:10 *omit a. read* the Spirit
      LTTr[A]WHR
    7:37*καρδίᾳ¹ a. LTTrAWHR
    37 *omit a.* LTTrAWHR, *see* ἴδιος
    9:10 *omit* of his hope GEds
2 Co. 3:13*for ἑαυτοῦ LTrAWWHR
    8:19 *omit* same LTrAWWHR
Eph. 3: 6 *omit a. read* the promise
      LTTrAWHR
    4:16*for ἑαυτοῦ T
    5:30 *omit a.* [A]WHR, *see* σάρξ
  31 his father—*omit* his LTTrAWHR
  31 his wife—*omit a.* T
Col.   1:14 *omit* through his blood GEds
    20 *omit* by him² LTr[WH]
    4:15 his—her, αὐτῆς LWH: their
      αὐτῶν TTrAR
2 Th.   2: 6*for ἑαυτοῦ TTrWHR
Heb. 1: 8*for σοῦ² WH
  11: 5 *omit a. read* the translation
      LTTrAWHR
  12:16 ἑαυτοῦ LTTrAWHR
Jas.   1:26 a.¹—ἑαυτοῦ WH: a.² ἑαυτοῦ
      LWH
    5:20*ψυχὴν a. his soul LTrWH
1 Pet. 1:24 *omit* thereof LTTr[A]WWHR
    2:24 *omit a.*² LTr[A]WHR
    3:10 *omit a. bis* LTTrAWHR
2 Pet. 3: 7 a. 8—τῷ a. GTrAW. Τῷ αὐτῷ
      A.V.B ELTWHR
3 Joh.   7 ὀνόματος 8—ὀνό. a. A.V.B E
Rev.   2:18 *omit* his¹ L[WH]
    6:17 his—their, αὐτῶν TTrWHR
    10: 1*τὴν κεφαλὴν—*add a.* GEds

Rev. 13: 8*add a. LTTrAWH, see ὄνομα
14: 1*add a. GEds, see ὄνομε
15: 2 omit over his mark (and) GEds
19:20*for τούτου GEds: trs ὁ μετ' a.
20:11 αὐτόν GT (GW
22:14 αὐτῶν LTTrAWH, see στολή

αὐτούς.

Mat. 14:14 omit τοῖς GLTTrAWWH
20:12 trs αὐτοὺς ἡμῖν LTWH
Mar. 1:27 ἑαυτούς LTTrAWR
4:15*see καρδία
5:10 αὐτά TTrWH
14*for τοὺς χοίρους (-ρος) GEds
9:16*for τοὺς γραμματεῖς (-τεύς)
GLTTrAWH
14: 7 αὐτοῖς LTTrAWH: omit a. T
Lu. ὁ:11 πρὸς a.—αὐτοῖς LTTrAWH
5:17 αὐτόν, read with him to heal
TAWH
9:34*ἐκείνους εἰσελθεῖν—εἰσ. αὐτούς
TTrAWH
11:53 omit a. TTrAWH, see ἐξέρχομαι
18: 1*προσεύχεσθαι—add a. Eds
19:27*slay—add a. them TTrAWH
20:45*see μαθητής
23:12*for ἑαυτούς TTrAWH
Joh. 6:17*add a. T, see ἤδη
18: 7 αὐτός W
20:10*for ἑαυτούς LTWH
Acts 2:40*exhort—add a. them Eds
4: 3*put—add a. them W
5:40 omit a. TTrAWH
10:48 αὐτοῖς T
11:26 αὐτοὺς καί LTTrAWH
15:33*add a. GEds, see ἀποστέλλω
16:40 omit a. LTTrAWH
19: 3 omit unto them Eds
21:25 omit LTTrWH, see μηδείς
23:30*λέγειν a. LT
2 Th. 1: 4 trs αὐτοὺς ἡμᾶς TTrAWH
Jas. 3: 3 trs ἡμῖν αὐτούς A
1 Pet. 4:14 omit on their part to end of
verse LTTrAWH
Jude 24 them—you, ὑμᾶς A.V.B
EGLTTrWWH
Rev. 5:10*for ἡμᾶς Eds
8: 6*for ἑαυτούς LTTrWH
11:11 ἐπ' a.—ἐν αὐτοῖς GEds
13: 7 omit L[WH], see δίδωμι

αὐτῷ.

Mat. 3:16 omit unto him [L]TWH
4: 3 omit to him TTrAWH
3*said—add a. to him Eds
5: 1 omit unto him L[WH]
8: 1 a.¹—αὐτοῦ LTrWH
5*for τῷ Ἰησοῦ GW
28 a.¹—αὐτοῦ LTTrWH, see ἔρχομαι
9:27 omit him L[Tr]WH
12:38*answered—add a. him
LTTrAWH
47 omit the verse [T]WH
15:22 omit unto him LTTrAWH
17:14 a.²—αὐτόν GEds
26 omit him¹ LTTrWH
18:34 omit unto him LTrAWH
19: 3 omit unto him² LTTrAWH
18 omit unto him T
21:23 a.¹—αὐτοῦ LTTrWH, see ἔρχομαι
31 omit unto him LTTrAWH
22:21 omit unto him T[A]WH
25:44 omit him GEds
26:17 omit unto him Eds
75 omit unto him [L]TTrAWH
27:11 omit unto him TWH
22 omit unto him LTTrAWH
42 ἐπ' αὐτόν TTrWH
44 a.²—αὐτόν GLTTrAWWH
28:17 omit him³ LTTrAWH
Mar. 1:41 omit unto him T
3: 7 omit him [L]TTrAWH
5: 2 a.¹—αὐτοῦ LTTrWH, see ἐξέρχομαι
6 αὐτόν AWH
9*add a. GEds, see λέγω
37 him—with him, μετ' αὐτοῦ
TTrAWH
6: 2 unto him—to this one, τούτῳ
TTrAWH
35 omit unto him T
8:20*add a. AWH, see λέγω
28*add a. LTTrAWH, see λέγω
9:17*answered—add a. him
LTTrAWH
19 him—them, αὐτοῖς GEds
10:35*saying—add a. to him
[L]TTrAWH
52*for τῷ Ἰησοῦ GEds
11: 7 a.²—αὐτόν LTTrAWH
12:29 omit him T[Tr]AWH

Mar. 14:53 omit with him TWH
Lu. 5: 5 omit unto him TWH
20 omit unto him GLTTrAWH
6:10*for τῷ ἀνθρώπῳ (-πος) GEds
7: 6 omit unto him T
8: 3 unto him—unto them, αὐτοῖς
TTrAWH
27 omit a.² T[TrA]WH
47 omit unto him LTTrAWH
49 omit to him T[Tr]WH
51*add a. LTTrAWH, see οὐδείς
10:35 omit unto him [L]TTr[A]WH
11:11 omit a.¹ WH see ἄρτος
12:17*for ἑαυτῷ WH
21*for ἑαυτῷ TWH
41 omit unto him LTr[A]WH
14: 6 omit him TTrAWH
16:29 omit unto him T[TrA]WH
17: 7*ἐρεῖ—add a. [L]TTrAWH
9 omit him GEds
12 omit a. L[TrA]WH
19:31 omit unto him L[TTr[A]WH
45 omit therein, and them that
bought TTrAWH
22:43, 44 the verses [L][[WH]]
49 omit unto him TTrAWH
Joh. 1:49(50) trs αὐτῷ after ἀπεκρίθη,
answered him TTrAWH:
ἀπ. [a.] L
4:17*said¹—add a. unto him
[L]A[WH]R
8:33 a.—πρὸς αὐτόν LTTrAWH
9:35 omit unto him T[TrA]WH
10:38 him—the Father, πατήρ
LTTrAWH
11:12*add a. after οὖν LTR, after
μαθηταί TrAWH, read said
unto him
12:13 him—them, αὐτῶν W
13:24*add a. LTTrAWH, see λέγω
26*add a. TTrAWH, see διδόναι
32 omit [LTrA]WH, see θεός
32*for ἑαυτῷ TTrWH
36 omit him² LTTrAWH
38 omit him Eds
16:29 omit unto him [L]TTrAH R
18:34 omit him Eds
19: 4 omit in him T
7 omit him T
11*answered—add a. him
[L]T[A]WH
Acts 7: 5†trs δοῦναι a. (αὐτήν) W
10: 7*for τῷ Κορνηλίῳ GEds
19 omit unto him WH
11:13 omit unto him LTTrWH
12: 9 omit unto him LTTrAWH
2 Co. 1:20 αὐτοῦ Eds, see ἐν
Eph. 2:15*for ἑαυτῷ LTTrAWH
Phi. 3:21*for ἑαυτῷ LTTrAWH
Heb. 2: 8 [under him¹] LWH
Jas. 2: 3 omit unto him GLTTrAWH
1 Joh. 3:15 ἑαυτῷ LT
5:10*for ἑαυτῷ TTrAWH
Rev. 6: 2 a.¹, 4 a.¹, 5 αὐτόν GEds
4 [αὐτῷ]² LWH
13: 7 omit L[WH], see δίδωμι
8 αὐτόν GEds
15 αὐτῇ LWHR
21: 6*δώσω—add a. T[A]W

αὐτῶν.

Mat. 6:15 omit their trespasses T[WH]
7:29*γραμματεῖς a. their scribes
LTTrAWH
11:16 omit a. LTT[A]WH
15: 2 omit a. T[Tr]WH
8 omit GLTTrAWH, see ἐγγίζω
17:14 omit a. LTTrAWH
18:31 omit a. LTTrAWH
35 omit their trespasses
GLTTrAWH
20:34 omit their eyes² LTTrAWH
21: 7 omit their [L]TTrAWH
23: 5 omit of their garments
LTTrAWH
26 of them—of it, αὐτοῦ LTTrAWH
25: 1 ἑαυτῶν LTTrAWH
3*for ἑαυτῶν¹ GLTTrAW[WH]
4 omit a.¹ read the vessels
LTTrAWH
4 a.²—ἑαυτῶν LTWH
7 ἑαυτῶν LTTrAWH
26:22 omit of them LTTrAWH, see
εἷς
Mar. 1:18 omit a. read the nets
LTT[A]WH
2:19*for ἑαυτῶν TTrAWH, see ἔχω
4:15 trs ἐν a. TTrAWH, see καρδία
9:44, 46 omit the verses T[Tr]WH
14:46 omit a. L: αὐτῷ TTrAWH

Mar. 14:52 omit from them [L]TTrWH
Lu. 2:22 a. their—her, αὐτῆς A.V.B. E
39 ἑαυτῶν LTTrAWH
11:48 omit their sepulchres
[L]TTrAWH
15: 4 trs ἐξ αὐτῶν ἕν TTrAWH
16: 4 ἑαυτῶν TTrAWH
19:35*for ἑαυτῶν LTTrAWH
36 ἑαυτῶν TrWH
22:47 αὐτούς GLTTrAWWH
55 omit a.¹ LTTrAWH
66*for ἑαυτῶν TTrAWWH
24:11 their—these, ταῦτα LTTrAWH
Joh. 6: 7 omit of them LTTrAWH
8:59 omit going through to end of
verse GLTTrAWH
11:19 omit a. TTrAWH
16: 4*ὥρα a. their time LTTrAWH
Acts 1:26 their lots—lots for them, αὐτοῖς LTTrAWH
5:18 omit their Eds
7:34 αὐτοῦ LTrWH
9:38 them—us, ἡμῶν Eds
10: 9*for ἐκείνων (-νος) Eds
10*for ἐκείνων (-νος) Eds
13:33(32) us their — our, ἡμῶν
LTTrWH
42*for τῶν Ἰουδαίων GEds
51 omit a. LTTrAWH
14:13 omit a. read the city GEds
14 ἑαυτῶν WH
19:12 omit of them GEds
16 them²—both, ἀμφότεροι
LTTrAWH
20:30 a.²—ἑαυτῶν TTrAWH
22:30 omit a. read the council GEds
23:30*ἐξ a. for ἐξαυτῆς LTTr, see
Ἰουδαίος
25:17 omit a. [A]WH
Ro. 10: 1*for τοῦ Ἰσραήλ GEds
15:27 trs εἰσὶν αὐτῶν Eds
1 Co. 14:10 omit of them A.V.TVul Eds
15:29*for τῶν νεκρῶν² (-ρός) GEds
2 Co. 3: 5*for ἑαυτῶν² LTrWH
Eph. 6: 9†trs καὶ a. καὶ ὑμῶν, read both
their Master and yours Eds
Heb. 8:11 omit a.¹ LTTrAWH
12 omit and their iniquities
TTrAWH
1 Pet. 4:19*for ἑαυτῶν LTTrAWH
Jude 15 omit among them LTTrAWH
Rev. 2:22 their—her, αὐτῆς GEds
4: 8*for ἑαυτό GLTTrAWH, see κατα
5:11 add A.V.B EGEds, see ἀριθμός
7:14 see στολή
9: 4 omit a. LTTr[A]WH
19 see ἐξουσία
19*add A.V.C GEds, see ἐξουσία
11: 8*for ἡμῶν GEds
12:10 αὐτούς LTAWH
17:13*for ἑαυτῶν Eds
19:18 αὐτῶν LTTrAWH
20: 4 omit a.¹ GEds
8*ἀριθμός—add a. GEds
21: 3 omit (and be) their God TTrWH

αὐτοῦ, adv.

Lu. 9:27*for ὧδε TTrAWH
Acts 15:34 omit the verse Eds

*αὐτόφωρος, see ἐπαυτοφώρῳ.

*αὐχέω, see μεγαλαυχέω.

ἀφαιρέω.

Rev. 22:19 ἀ.¹—ἀφέλῃ GEds
ἀ.²—ἀφελεῖ GEds

ἀφθαρσία.

1 Co. 15:54 omit WH, see φθαρτός
Tit. 2: 7 omit sincerity EGEds

ἄφθαρτος

1 Ti. 1:17 immortali A.V. Vul

*ἀφθορία, incorruption.

Tit. 2: 7 ἀφθορίαν for ἀδιαφθορίαν (-ία)
Eds

ἀφίημι, ἀφέω, ἀφίω.

Mat. 6:12 ἀφήκαμεν have forgiven
LTTrAWH
9: 2, 5 ἀφίενται Eds
18:12 ἀφήσει, read will he not
leave LTrWH
23:23 ἀ.³—ἀφεῖναι LTTrAWH
Mar. 2: 5, 9 ἀφίενται LTTrWH
10 trs εἰπὶ τῆς γῆς a. GLTTrWH
11:26 omit the verse TTrWH
12:21 see καταλείπω

Lu. 11: 4 α.²—ἀφίομεν LTTrAWH
42 to leave undone—to pass by
πάρειμι LTTrAWH
17:36 αdd δύο ἔσονται ἐν τῷ ἀγρῷ· ὁ
εἷς παραληφθήσεται, καὶ ὁ ἕτερος ἀφεθήσεται A.V.B E
18:2² ἀφέντες τὰ ἴδια, having left our
own LTTrAWH
23:34 [Then said *to* what they do]
L [[WH]]
Joh. 20:23 ἀφέωνται LTTrWH
Acts 5:38*ἄφετε *for* ἐάσατε (ἐάω)
LTTrAWH
Rev. 2: 4 ἀφῆκες TTrWH
20*ἀφεῖς *for* ἐᾷς (ἐάω) GEds
11: 9 ἀφίουσιν suffer LTTrAWH :
ἀφίουσιν W

ἀφίστημι.

1 Ti. 6: 5 omit from such withdraw
thyself Eds

ἀφοράω, ἀπεῖδον.

Phil. 2:23 ἀφίδω LTTrAWH

ἀφορίζω.

Mat. 25:32 ἀ.¹—ἀφορίσει TWH

ἀφροσύνη.

2 Co. 11: 1 τῇ ἀφροσύνῃ S—(τῆς E, omit τῇ
Eds) ἀφροσύνης EEds

ἄφρων.

Lu. 12:20 ἄφρον GW
1 Co. 15:36 ἄφρων LTTrAWH

*ἀφυστερέω, to come too late.

Jas. 5: 4 ἀφυστερημένος *for* ἀπεστερημέ-
νος (ἀποστερέω) TTrWH

Αχαΐα.

Ro. 16: 5 Achaia—Asia, Ασία GEds

Ἄχαζ, Ἄχας WH.

ἀχρειόομαι.

Ro. 3:12 ἠχρεώθησαν TTrWH

ἄχρι, ἄχρις.

Acts 1:22*for ἕως T
20: 4 omit into Asia T[Tr]WH
Gal. 4:19 μέχρις TTrWH
Rev. 20: 5*for ἕως GEds

Ἄψινθος.

Rev. 8:11 Ἀ.¹—ὁ Ἄψινθος GLTAWWH

*βαθέως, deeply.

Lu. 24: 1 for βαθέος (-ύς) LTTrAWWH

βάθος.

Eph. 3:18 trs height and depth LTTrAWHR
Rev. 2:24 βαθύς GEds

βαθύς.

Lu. 24: 1 βαθέως LTTrAWWH
Rev. 2:24*βαθέα for βάθη (-θος) GEds

Βαλάκ.

Rev. 2:14 ἐν τῷ Β.—τὸν Β. A.V.B H

βαλάντιον, βαλλ— LTTrAWH.

βάλλω.

Mat. 5:13 βληθέν LTTrAWHR
30 should be cast (β.²)—go, ἀπέρχομαι LTTrAWHR
27:35 βαλόντες LTA
35 omit that it might *to end of
verse* GLTTrAWHR
Mar. 1:16 ἀμφιβάλλω GEds
7:27 trs τοῖς κυναρίοις βαλεῖν TTrAWH
30 βεβλημένον LTTrAWHR, see παιδίον
12:43 β.¹—ἔβαλεν did cast LTrWH
43 β.²—βαλλόντων Eds
14:65 ἔβαλον W : λαμβάνω, *read*
received him with blows of
their hands LTTrAWHR
Lu. 12:58 βάλῃ GW, βαλεῖ LTTrAWHR
23:19 βληθεὶς TTr[A]WH
Joh. 5: 7 βάλῃ GEds
7:44*ἔβαλεν for ἐπέβαλεν (ἐπιβάλλω)
LTTrAWH
Acts 16:37 ἔβαλαν LTTrAWH

Rev. 2:10 βάλλειν LTTrAWH
24 βάλλω I put Eds
4:10 βάλλουσιν S—βαλοῦσιν shall
cast EGEds
6:13 βάλλουσα casting T
12:10*ἐβλήθη *for* κατεβλήθη (κατα-
βάλλω) LTTrAWH

βαπτίζω.

Mat. 3:11 β.¹—trs ὑμᾶς βαπτίζω LTTrWWH
20:22, 23 omit and be baptised *to*
baptised with GLTTrAWH
28:19 βαπτίσαντες having baptised
Mar. 1: 4 ὁ βαπτίζων T—(Tr
5 trs πάντες, καὶ ἐβ. GLTTrAWH
read all they of Jerusalem
6:24*βαπτίζοντος *for* βαπτιστοῦ
(-τῆς) TTrAWH
7: 4 β.¹—ῥαντίζω WH
1 Co. 1:15 ἐβ·πτίσθητε ye were baptised
Eds
10: 2 ἐβαπτίσθησαν LT

βάπτισμα.

Mat. 20:22, 23 omit GLTTrAWH, see
βαπτίζω
Col. 2:12 βαπτισμός TrA

βαπτισμός.

Mar. 7: 8 omit (as) the washing *to end
of verse* T[TrA]WHR
Col. 2:12*βαπτισμῷ *for* βαπτίσματι (-μα)
TrA

βαπτιστής.

Mar. 6:24 βαπτίζω TTrAWHR
Lu. 7:28 omit the Baptist TTrAWHR

βάπτω.

Joh. 13:26 βάψω shall dip TTrAWHR
26*βάψας οὖν *for* καὶ ἐμβάψας
(-βάπτω) TTrAWHR
Rev. 19:13 dipped in—sprinkled with,
περιρραίνω T, ῥαντίζω WHR

Βαραββᾶς.

Mat. 27:21 τὸν Βαραββᾶν TTrWH

Βαριω.

Mar. 14:40 καταβαρύνω Eds
Lu. 21:34*βαρηθῶσιν *for* βαρυνθῶσιν
(-νομαι) GEds
2 Co. 1: 8 trs ὑπὲρ δύναμιν ἐβαρήθημεν
LTTrAWH

Βαριησοῦς.

Acts 13: 6 Βαριησοῦ T

Βὰρ Ἰωνᾶ, Βαριωνᾶ LTAWH.

Βαρνάβας.

Acts 11:25 omit ὁ Β. read he LTTrAWH
13:50 τὸν Β.—omit τὸν LTTrAWH
Col. 4:10 Βαρνάβα A.V.B

Βαρσαβᾶς, —ββᾶς LTTrAWH.

βαρύνω.

Lu. 21:34 βαρέω GEds

βαρύτιμος.

Mat. 26: 7 πολύτιμος LT

βασανίζω.

Rev. 9: 5 βασανισθήσονται LTTrAWHR

βασιλεία.

Mat. 6:13 omit For thine *to end of verse*
GEds
13:52 τῇ βασιλείᾳ GLTTrAWHR
Mar. 1:14 omit of the kingdom
[L]TTrAWH
Lu. 9:62 εἰς τὴν β.—τῇ βασιλείᾳ LTTrAWH
23:42 εἰς τὴν βασιλείαν WH
1 Co. 6: 9 trs θεοῦ βασιλείαν GEds
Rev. 1: 6*βασιλείαν *for* βασιλεῖς (-εύς)
καί GEds
9 τῇ β.—omit τῇ GEds
5:10*βασιλείαν *for* βασιλεῖς (εὺς)
LTTrAWHR
11:15 ἡ βασιλεία the kingdom GEds

βασιλεύς.

Mat. 1: 6 omit the king² LTTrAWH
2: 3 trs ὁ βασιλεὺς Ἡρώδης LTTrAWH
22: 7 trs ὁ δὲ βασιλεὺς LTTrAWHR

Mat. 22:13 trs ὁ βασιλεὺς εἶπεν LTTrAWHR
27:29 ὁ β.—βασιλεῦ LTrWH
Mar. 6:22†trs ὁ δὲ βασιλεὺς εἶπεν TTrAWHR
15:12 τὸν βασιλέα Eds
18 ὁ βασιλεὺς GAW
Lu. 1: 5 τοῦ β.—omit τοῦ TTr[A]WHR
14:31 trs ἑτέρῳ β. συμβ. LTTrAWH
19:38 ὁ βασιλεὺς WH
23:38†trs ὁ β. τῶν Ἰουδαίων οὗτος
([οὗτος]L) LTTrAWHR
Joh. 1:50(49)†trs ὁ (om. ὁ TTrAWHR) β.
εἶ LTTrAWHR
Acts 12: 1 trs ὁ βασιλεὺς Ἡρώδης T
26: 7 trs βασιλεῦ *after* Ἰουδαίων
LTTrAWHR
Rev. 1: 6 kings and—a kingdom. βασιλεία GEds
5:10 kings—a kingdom, βασιλεία
LTTrAWHR

βασιλεύω.

Rev. 5:10 βασιλεύσουσιν they shall
reign GT, βασιλεύουσιν they
reign LTrAWWHR

βασίλισσα.

Acts 8:27 τῆς β.—omit τῆς Eds

βάσις.

Acts 3: 7 trs αἱ βάσεις αὐτοῦ LTTrAWH

βαστάζω.

Rev. 2: 3 trs hast patience, and hast
borne GEds

βάτος.

Mar. 12:26 τῆς β.—τοῦ β. GLTTrAWWH

βάτραχος.

Rev. 16:13 βάτραχοι GEds

βαττολογέω, βαττα— TAWH.

βέβαιος.

Heb. 3: 6 omit firm unto the end A[WH]

Βεελζεβούλ, —ύβ A.V.Vul, Βεεζ—WH

Βελίαρ, —αλ A.V.B ELR

Βενιαμίν, —μείν LTTrWH, at times A

*βελόνη, a needle.

Lu. 18:25 βελόνης *for* ῥαφίδος (-ις)
LTTrAWHR

*Βεώρ.

2 Pet. 2:15 *for* Βοσόρ WHR

Βηθαβαρά, —ρᾷ B

Joh. 1:28 Βηθανίᾳ GEds

Βηθανία.

Lu. 19:29 Βηθανιά AWH
Joh. 1:28*Βηθανίᾳ *for* Βηθαβαρᾶ GEds
11:18 ἡ Β.—omit ἡ TWH

Βηθεσδά, Βηθζαθά, TWH

Βηθσαϊδά.

Mat. 11:21 Βηθσαϊδά LTr

Βηθφαγή, —ῆ.

Mar. 11: 1 omit Bethphage LT

βῆμα.

Joh. 19:13 τοῦ β.—omit τοῦ Eds

βια.

Acts 24: 7 omit LTTr[A]WHR, see κρίνω

βιβλαρίδιον.

Rev. 10: 8 little book—book, βιβλίον
LTTrAWH

βιβλίον.

Joh. 21:25 omit the verse T
Rev. 5: 7 omit the book LTTrAWH
10: 8*βιβλίον *for* βιβλαρίδιον
LTrAWH
13: 8*τῷ βιβλίῳ *for* τῇ βίβλῳ (-λος)
GEds
20:12 trs ἄλλο βιβλίον GEds
22:18 β.²—τῷ βιβλίῳ GEds
19*τοῦ βιβλίου *for* βιβλον¹ (οε)
GEds
19 τῷ βιβλίῳ GEds

βίβλος.
Rev.13: 8 βιβλίον GEds
22.19 β.¹—βιβλίον GEds
19 book²—tree, ξύλον GEds

Βιθυνία.
Acts 16: 7 τὴν Β.—omit τὴν W

βίος.
Lu. 8:43 omit WH, see ἰατρός
1 Pet. 4: 3 omit of (our) life Eds

βλάπτω.
Mar. 16:18 βλάψῃ GLTrAWWH

βλαστάνω.
Mar. 4:27 βλαστᾷ LTTrAWH

βλασφημέω.
Mar. 2: 7*; βλασφημεῖ for βλασφημίας; (—μία) LTTrAWH
1 Cor. 4:13 δυσφημέω TAWH
1 Pet. 4:14 omit on their part to end of verse LTTrAWH

βλασφημία.
Mar. 2: 7 read thus speak? he blasphemeth, βλασφημέω LTTrAWH
3:28 αἱ βλασφημίαι GEds
Rev.13: 5 read great and blasphemous (βλάσφημος) things LA
6 βλασφημίας blasphemies Eds

βλάσφημος.
Acts 6:13 omit blasphemous GEds: trs λαλῶν ῥήματα TTrWH
Rev.13: 5* βλάσφημα for βλασφημίας (—ία) (LA

βλέπω.
Mar. 8:23 βλέπεις thou seest AWH
Lu. 7:21 τὸ β.—omit τὸ Eds
24:12 omit the verse [L]T[Tr][[WH]]
Joh. 9:19 trs βλέπει ἄρτι LTTrAWH
Acts 1:11* βλέποντες for ἐμβλέποντες (—πω) TTrWH
Heb.11: 3 τὸ βλεπόμενον that which is seen LTTrAWH
Rev. 6: 1 ἴδε GW: omit and see LTTrAWH
3 omit and see GEds
5,7 ἴδε GW: om.and see LTTrAWH
11: 9 βλέπουσιν see GEds
17: 8 βλεπόντων GEds
18:18* βλέποντες for ὁρῶντες (ὁράω) GEds
22: 8 β.²—ἔβλεπον W

βλητέος.
Mar. 2:22 omit but new wine to end of verse T[Tr]A[WH]: omit must be put WH

Βοανεργές, Βοανη— LTTrAWH.

βοάω.
Mat. 27:46* ἐβόησεν for ἀνεβόησεν (ἀναβοάω) TrWH
Lu. 9:38* ἰ³όησεν for ἀνεβόησεν (ἀναβοάω) LTTrAWH
Acts 21:34 ἐπιφωνέω Eds
25:24* βοῶντες for ἐπιβοῶντες (-οαω) LTTrWH: [ἐπι]β. A

βολίς.
Heb.12:20 omit or thrust through with a dart GEds

Βοόζ.
Mat. 1: 5 bis Βοός LTr: Βοές TAWH
Lu. 3:32 Βοός LTTrAWH

βόσκω.
Lu. 8:32 βοσκομένη LWHR

Βοσόρ.
2 Pet. 2:15 Βεώρ WHR

βουλεύομαι.
Lu. 14:31 βουλεύσεται will consult TWH
Joh. 11:53* ἐβουλεύσαντο for συνεβουλεύσαντο (συμβουλεύω) LTTrWH
Acts 5:33 took counsel—resolved, βούλομαι LTrWH
15:37 determined-was minded, βούλομαι Eds
27:39 ἐβουλεύοντο Eds
2 Co. 1:17 β.¹—βούλομαι Eds

βούλημα.
1 Pet. 4: 3* βούλημα for θέλημα Eds

βούλομαι.
Acts 5:33* βούλοντο for ἐβουλεύοντο (βουλεύομαι) LTrWH
15:37* ἐβούλετο for ἐβουλεύσατο (βουλεύομαι) Eds
2 Co. 1:17* βουλόμενος for βουλευόμενος (—μαι) Eds
Jas. 3: 4 βούλεται TTrWH
2 Joh. 12 ἐβουλήθην LTTrAWWH

βρέφος.
Lu. 1:44 trs τὸ β. ἐν ἀγαλλιάσει GW
Acts 7:19 trs τὰ βρέφη ἔκθετα LTTrAWH

βροντή.
Rev. 4: 5 trs voices and thunderings GEds
8: 5 trs thunderings and voices TTrAWH
16:18 trs lightnings, and voices, and thunders GEds

βύσσινος.
Rev. 18:12* βυσσίνου for βύσσου (-ος) GEds

βύσσος.
Rev. 18:12 βύσσινος GEds

Γαδαρηνός.
Mat. 8:28* Γαδαρηνῶν for Γεργεσηνῶν TTrAWH
Mar. 5: 1 Γερασηνός LTTrWHR: Γεργεσηνός A
Lu. 8:26, 37 Γερασηνός LTTrAWH: Γεργεσηνός T

γαζοφυλάκιον.
Lu. 21: 1 trs εἰς τὸ γ. τὰ δῶρα αὐτῶν TTrAWH

Γάϊος, Γαϊος (except 3 John 1) WH

Γαλατία.
2 Ti. 4:10 Γαλλία T

Γαλατικός.
Acts 16: 6 τὴν Γ.—omit τὴν LTTrAWH

Γαλιλαία.
Mat. 4:23 Γαλιλαίᾳ LTTrAWHR, see ὅλος
19: 1 τῆς Γ.—omit τῆς G
Lu. 4:44 Galilee—Judæa, Ἰουδαία AWH
23: 6 omit of Galilee T[A]WH
55 trs ἐκ τῆς Γ. αὐτῷ TAWH

* Γαλλία.
2 Ti. 4:10 Γαλλίαν for Γαλατίαν T

γαμέω, γάμω.
Mat. 19: 9 omit T[Tr]WH, see ἀπολύω
22:25 γήμας LTTrAWH
Mar. 10:12 γαμήσῃ ἄλλον marry another LTTrAWH
1 Co. 7: 9 γ.²—γαμεῖν TWH
28 γ.¹—γαμήσῃς LTTrAWH

* γαμίζω, to marry, to give in marriage.
Mat. 22:30 γαμίζονται for ἐκγαμίζονται (-ζω) LTTrAWH
24:38 γαμίζοντες for ἐκγαμίζοντες (-ζω) TWH
Mar. 12:25 γαμίζονται for γαμίσκονται (-κομαι) LTTrAWWH
Lu. 17:27 ἐγαμίζοντο for ἐξεγαμίζοντο (ἐκγαμίζω) LTTrAWH
20:35 γαμίζονται for ἐκγαμίσκονται (-κομαι) LTTrWH
1 Co. 7:38 see ἐκγαμίζω¹
38 γαμίζων for ἐκγαμίζων² (-ζω) GLTTrWH: [ἐκ]γ. A

γαμίσκομαι.
Mar. 12:25 γαμίζω LTTrAWWH
Lu. 20:34* γαμίσκονται for ἐκγαμίσκονται (-κομαι) LTTrAWH
35* γαμίσκονται for ἐκγαμίσκονται (-κομαι) T

γάμος.
Mat. 22:10 wedding — bride-chamber, νυμφών TWH
Joh. 2: 3* add γ. T, see οἶνος

γάρ.
Mat. 1:18 omit γ. LTTr[A]WH
11:10 omit for [L]T[Tr]WHR
13:17 omit for T
16: 2 see λέγω
18:11 omit the verse LTTr[A]WH
20:16 omit T[Tr]AWHR, see πολύς
23: 4 for—but, δέ LTTrAWH
5* for δέ² LTTrAWH
10 ὅτι LTTrAWH, see καθηγητής
24:28 omit for LTTrAWH
37* for δέ LTrWH
25: 3* αἵ γ. Tr, αἱ γ. TAWHR, for αἵτινες (ὅστις)
Mar. 3:35 omit for LT[Tr]AWH
4:28 omit for LTTrAWH
6:36 omit γ. [L]LTTrAWHR, see ἄρτος
52 for²—but, see ἀλλά TTrWHR
7: 8 omit for LTTrAWH
25 for—but, see ἀλλά TTrAWHR
28 omit γ. [L]TTrWHR
8: 3 for—and, see καί LTTrAWH
37* τί γ. for ἢ τί TTrWH
11:18* πᾶς γ. for ὅτι πᾶς TTrAWH
23 omit for [L]T[Tr]AWH
12:36 omit for [L]T[Tr]AWHR
13: 6 omit for TAWH
7 omit for T[Tr]AWH
9 omit for¹ T[Tr]AWH
22 for—and, δέ T
14: 2* for δέ LTTrAWH
16: 8* for δέ LTTrWHR
Lu. 1:66* and²—καί γ. for also LTTrAWH
4: 8 omit for GEds
6:33* καί¹—add γ. read for also T[WH]
33 omit for TWH
34 omit for T[Tr]AWH
48 see θεμελιόω
7:28 omit for TTrAWH
8:52* οὐκ—οὐ γ. read for she LTTrAWH
9:14 for—and, δέ T
56 omit GLTTrAWHR, see σώζω
10:42* for δέ TWH
12:23* ἡ—add γ. read for the life [LTTr]AWH
14:14 for²—but, δέ T
18:14* ἡ—add γ. GTW
19:26 omit for [L]T[Tr]AWH
20:40* for δέ TTrWH
42* αὐτὸς γ. for καὶ α. TWHR
22:37 [for²] LTr
23:34 see λέγω
Joh. 4: 9 omit T[WH], see συγχράομαι
5: 4 omit [G]TTrAWH, see ὕδωρ
6:40* for δέ GEds
10:26 οὐ γ.—ὅτι οὐκ TTrWH
Acts 3:22 omit for GEds
18:15 omit for Eds
20:29 omit for Eds
21:22* omit γ. TrWHR, see δεῖ
25:11 for—therefore, οὖν Eds
Ro. 2: 2* for δέ T
3: 2 omit γ. LTr[AWH]R
7 for—but, δέ TWH
28* for οὖν GLTTrAWH
4:15 for (γ.²)—but, δέ Eds
5: 6 ἔτι γ.—εἰ γε AWH
9:19 omit for E
32 omit for LTTrAWH
11:13 for—and, δέ LTTrAWH
14: 2 μὲν—add ἐπιτι A.V. Vul
5* μὲν—add γ. read For one [L]T[WH]
15* for δέ Eds
15: 2 omit γ. Eds
8* for δέ Eds
1 Co. 2:10* for δέ WH
7: 7 for—but, δέ Eds
40* for δέ³ WH
8: 8 omit for LTTrAWH
11* ἀπόλλυται γ. for καὶ ἀπολεῖται LTTrWH
9:16* for δέ GEds
10: 1* for δέ GEds
28 omit for the earth to end of verse GEds
11:31 for—but, δέ Eds
14: 5 for—and, δέ LTTrAWH
14 [for] LTrWH
16: 7* for δέ GEds
2 Co. 2: 1* for δέ WH
5:12, 21 omit for Eds
7: 8 for I—omit for [L]TrWH
8:21* add γ. GLTTrAWHR, see προνοέω
12: 1 for but, δέ LTTrWHR
Gal. 1:10 omit for² Eds
11* for δέ TrAWH
3:13 γέγραπται γ.—ὅτι γέγ. Eds
4:25 for—now, δέ WH
25* for δέ² GEds

Gal. 5:17*for δε² Eds
Phil. 1:23 for—but, δέ GEds
  23 πολλῶ—add γ. read for it is
    far EGEds
  2: 5 omit γ. LTTᵣAWHR
Col. 3:24 omit for Eds
  25*for δέ Eds
1 Th. 2: 9 omit for² GEds
  5: 3 omit for GTTᵣAWHR
  5*παντες γ. for ye are all GEds
1 Ti. 2: 3 omit for LTTᵣWHR
2 Ti. 2:13*γ. ἑαυτὸν, read for he Eds
Heb. 2: 8 trs τῷ γὰρ Eds
  8: 4 for if—if then, οὖν Eds
  11:32 trs με γὰρ LTTᵣAWHR
  13: 4*for δέ LTTᵣAWHR
Jas. 2:26 omit for WH
  4:14 omit for¹ [Tᵣ]WHR
1 Pet. 2:20*τοῦτο γ. for this Lᴬ
3 Joh. 3 omit for T[Tᵣ]
Rev. 14: 5 omit for LAWHR
  13*for δέ LTTᵣAWHR
  16: 6 omit for² GEds
  22: 9 omit for ςEds
  10*καιρος γ. Eds: omit ὅτι GEds
  18 omit for Eds

γέ.

Lu. 19:42 omit at least [L]T[ᵣA]WHR
  See also εἴγε, ἄραγε, καίγε and κοίτογε.

Γεθσημανῆ, —νεῖ LTTᵣAW —νεί TWH.

γέεννα

Mar. 9:47 τὴν γ. —omit τὴν WH

γείτων.

Lu. 15: 9 τὰς γ.—omit τὰς LTTᵣAWHR

γεμίζω.

Lu. 15:16 χορτάζω WHR

γέμω.

Rev. 4: 8 γέμουσιν are full GEds
  17: 3 γέμοντα LTAWHR
  4 γέμων T
  21: 9 τῶν γεμόντων, read who were
    full LTTᵣAWHR: omit τὰς W

γενεά.

Lu. 1:50*γ.² —καὶ γενεὰς, read generations and generations
  TTᵣAWHR
  11:29*this—add γενεὰ generation
  LTTᵣAWHR

γενέσια.

Mat. 14: 6 γενεσίοις LTTᵣAWHR

γένεσις.

Mat. 1:18*γένεσις for γέννησις GEds
Lu. 1:14*γενέσει for γεννήσει (-σις)
  GEds

* γένημα, see γέννημα.

γεννάω.

Mat. 1:12 bis, 13¹ γεννᾷ begetteth A
Lu. 1:35 nascetur A.V Vul
Joh. 3: 6 γεγεννημένον S, γεγενη—bis R
  8:41 ἐγεννήθημεν LTᵣAWHR
Gal. 4:23 γεγέννηται W
Heb. 11:12 ἐγεννήθησαν LA
2 Pet. 2:12 γεγεννημένα EGLTᵣAWHR for
  γεγεννημένα (γίνομαι) ST: trs
  γ. φυσικὰ Eds
1 Joh. 2:29 γεγέννηται S—γεγέννηται EGEds

γέννημα.

Mat. 26:29 γεννήματος LTTᵣAWHI
Mar. 14:25 γεννήματος TTᵣAWWH
Lu. 12:18 my fruits—the wheat, σῖτος
  TᵣWHR: γεννήματα S, γεννη- E
  22:18 γεννήματος LTTᵣAWHI
2 Co. 9:10 γεννήματα GLTTᵣAWWH

Γεννησαρέτ, Γενησαρέτ.

Mat. 14:34 Γεννησαρέθ LW

γέννησις.

Mat. 1:18 γένεσις GEds
Lu. 1:14 γένεσις GEds

γένος.

Mat. 17:21 omit the verse T[TᵣA]WHR

---

* ἱερασηνός.

Mar. 5: 1 Γερασηνῶν for ἱαδαρηνῶν
  LTTᵣWHR
Lu. 8:26. 87 Γερασηνῶν for Γαδαρηνῶν
  LTᵣAWHR

Γεργεσηνός.

Mat. 8:28 Γαδαρηνός TTᵣAWHR
Mat. 5: 1*Γεργεσηνῶν for Γαδαρηνῶν A
Lu. 8:26, 37*Γεργεσηνῶν f Γαδαρηνῶν T

γένομαι.

Lu. 9:27 γεύσωνται GLTTᵣAWWH
Joh. 8:52 γεύσηται GEds

γῆ.

Mat. 5:10 τῆς γ.—omit τῆς Eds
  13:23 trs την καλὴν γῆν LTTᵣAWH
  14:24*add γ. Tᵣ WH, see σταδίον
  25:18 ἐν τῇ γῇ —γῆν TTᵣAWH
  28:18 τῆς γῆς LTᵣA: [τῆς] γ. WH
Lu. 11: 2 omit as in heaven, so in earth
  G[L]TTᵣAWHR
  12:56 trs of the sky and of the
    earth A.V.C
  22:43, 44 the verses [L] [[WH]]
Joh. 6:21 τὴν γῆν T
  21:11 εἰς τὴν γῆν LTTᵣAWHR
Acts 7: 3 γ.³—τὴν γῆν Eds
  1 omit the land of LTTᵣAWHR
  36 omit the land of LTᵣWHR
  10:12 see ἑρπετόν
1 Co. 8: 5 trs γ.—omit the earth Eds
  10:28 omit for the earth to end of
    verse GEds
Heb. 11: 9 τὴν γ.—omit τὴν LTTᵣAWHR
  29*dry—add γῆς land Eds
  12:25 τῆς γ.—omit τῆς GEds
2 Pet. 3:13 trs καινὴν γῆν T
1 Joh. 5: 8 omit in heaven (ver. 7) to in
  earth (ver. 8) GEds
Rev. 5:13 ἐπὶ τῆς γῆς GEds
  8: 7*earth—add καὶ τὸ τρίτον τῆς
    γῆς κατεκάη and the third
    part of the earth was burnt
    up GEds
  10: 2 τῆς γῆς Eds
  12:12 τῇ γῇ GW
  13: 3 ᾗ γῆ EGLTAWWHR, see θαυμάζω
  16:14 omit of the earth and Eds
  17: 2 trs οἱ κατοικοῦντες τὴν γῆν ἐκ
    τοῦ οἴνου τῆς πορν. αὐτῆς GEds

γῆρας.

Lu. 1:36 γήρει (-ρος) GLTTᵣAWWH

* γῆρυς, see γῆρας.

γίνομαι.

Mat. 11:23 ἐγενήθησαν LTTᵣAWH
  14: 6*γενομένοις for ἀγομένων (ἄγω)
    LTTᵣAWHR
  16: 2 When it is to end of verse 3
    [TA][[WH]]
  18:31 γ.¹ —γινόμενα T
  24:21 γ.¹ —ἐγένετο T
  27:54 γινόμενα were happening
    LTTᵣAWH
  28: 4 ἐγενήθησαν LTTᵣAWH
Mar. 1:11 omit γ. T[WH]
  2:15 γίνεται it cometh to pass
    TTᵣAWH
  6: 2 γ.²—γινόμεναι TᵣWHR
  35 γινομένης T
  9: 3 ἐγένετο LTᵣAW
  6*trs ἔκφοβοι γὰρ (ἐγένοντο for
    ἦσαν) LTTᵣAWH
  7*ἐγένετο f. ἦλθεν (ἔρχομαι) TWHR
  10:44 εἶναι LTᵣWH
Lu. 2: 2 trs ἐγένετο πρώτη T
  8:34 γεγονὸς GEds
  40 omit it came to pass, that
    TᵣWHR
  9:57 omit it came to pass, that
    TᵣWHR
  10:13 γ.¹ —ἐγενήθησαν LTTᵣAWHR
  32 omit when he was TᵣWHR
  38 omit it came to pass TᵣWHR
  11: 2 omit Thy will be done
    GTTᵣAWHR
  18:23 ἐγενήθη TTᵣAWHR
  24 omit that he was very sorrow-
    ful (read saw him) T[Tᵣ]AWHR
  20:33 is she—shall she be, ἔσται R
  21: 9 trs γενέσθαι ταῦτα A
  22:26 γινέσθω TTᵣAWH
  42 γινέσθω TTᵣAWWHR
  43, 44 the verses [L] [[WH]]

Lu. 24:12 omit the verse [L]T[Tᵣ] [[WH]]
Joh. 1:27 omit is preferred before me
  G[L]TTᵣAWHR
  5: 4 omit waiting for (ver. 3) to
    end of verse 4 [G]TTᵣAWHR
  6:17 omit T, see ἤδη
  7:43 trs ἐγ. ἐν τῷ ὄχλῳ LTTᵣAWHR
  10:16 γενήσονται TᵣAWHR
  35 trs ἐγένετο τοῦ θεοῦ T
  13: 2 γινομένου TTᵣWHR
  15: 8 γένησθε LTᵣAWH
  21: 4 γινομένης coming TTᵣWWHR
Acts 1:22 trs σὺν ἡμῖν γενέσθαι Eds
  2:43 ἐγίνετο LTTᵣAWH
  4:22 γεγόνει LTTᵣAWH
  5:12 ἐγένετο 8—ἐγίνετο A.ᵛ B EGEds
  7:40 ἐγένετο LTTᵣAWHR
  52 ἐγένεσθε Eds
  8:13 γινόμενα GW
  10:10*ἐγένετο for ἐπέπεσεν (ἐπιπίπ-
    τω) Eds
  12:11 trs ἐν ἑαυτῷ γ. LTTᵣAWWH
  20:37 trs κλαυθμὸς ἐγέ. LTTᵣAWH
  21:14 γινέσθω LTTᵣAWWH
  22: 9 omit and were afraid
    LTTᵣ[A]WH
  23:10 γινομένης LTWHR
  24:25 see ἔμφοβος
  26:28 to be—to make, ποιέω
    LTTᵣAWHR, see πείθω
Ro. 7:13 γ.¹ —ἐγένετο Eds
  15: 8 γενέσθαι LTᵣ
  16: 7 γέγοναν LTTᵣAWG
1 Co. 10:32 trs καὶ Ἰουδαίοις γ. LTTᵣAWHR
  14:26 γινέσθω GEds
  15:20 omit (and) become Eds
2 Co. 1:18 was—is, ἐστίν Eds
  5:21 γενώμεθα Eds
Eph. 2:13 trs ἐγενήθητε ἐγγὺς LTTᵣAWHR
  3: 7 ἐγενήθην Eds
Phil. 3:21 omit that it may be GEds
1 Th. 2: 8 ἐγενήθητε Eds
Tit. 3: 7 γενηθῶμεν Eds
Heb. 3:14 trs τοῦ χριστοῦ γεγόναμε. GEds
  7:23 trs ἱερεῖς γεγονότες LAW
  9:11*γενομένων for μελλόντων (-ω)
    LWH
1 Pet. 1:16 be ye—ye shall be, ἔσεσθε Eds
2 Pet. 2:12 γεννάω EGLTᵣAWWHR, read
    brute beasts, naturally born
2 Joh. 12*γενέσθαι for ἐλθεῖν (ἔρχομαι)
    Eds
Rev. 1:19 γενέσθαι TA
  6:12 trs μέλας ἐγένετο GT
  8:11 ἐγένετο Eds
  11:15 γ.² —ἐγένετο GEds
  16:18 ἄνθρωπος ἐγένετο a man was
    LTTᵣAW
  21: 6 γέγοναν they are done
    LTTᵣWWHR: γέγονα[ν] ἐγώ A

γινώσκω.

Mat. 16: 3 When it is (ver. 2) to end of
  ver. 3 [TA][[WH]]
Mar. 4:11 om. to know LTTᵣAWHR: trs τὸ
  μυστήριον δέδοται TTᵣAWHR
  5:43 γνοῖ LTTᵣAWH
  6:33*ἔγνωσαν for ἐπέγνωσαν (ἐπι-
    γινώσκω) LTᵣAWH
  9:30 γνοῖ LTTᵣAWH
  13:29 γινώσκεται it is known ᴬ
Lu. 2:43 ἔγνωσαν LTTᵣAWHR, see γονεύς
  8:17 γνωσθῇ LTTᵣAWHR
  19:15 γνοῖ LTTᵣAWH
Joh. 10:14 γινώσκομαι ὑπὸ τῶν ἐμῶν—
  γινώσκουσίν με τὰ ἐμὰ mine
  own know me LTTᵣAWH
  38*γινώσκητε for πιστεύσητε²(-ῃε)
    LTTᵣAWHR
  14: 7 γ.¹ —ἐγνώκατε ye have known T
  7 γ.²—γνώσεσθε ye will know T:
    εἴδω TᵣAWH
  17: 3 γινώσκουσιν they know TTᵣ
Acts 21:24 γνώσονται will know GEds
  23:28 ἐπιγινώσκω Eds
  24:11 ἐπιγινώσκω LTTᵣAWHR
Ro. 10:19 trs Ἰσραὴλ οὐκ ἔγνω GEds
1 Co. 2:11*ἔγνωκεν for οὖδεν² (εἴδω) Eds
  8: 2*ἐγνωκέναι for εἰδέναι (εἴδω) Eds
  2 γ.¹ —ἔγνω LTTᵣAWH
Col. 4: 8 γνῶτε, read ye may know
    our LTTᵣWH
Jas. 5:20 γινώσκετε know ye AWH
1 Joh. 3:19 γνωσόμεθα we shall know Eds
  5:20 γινώσκομεν we know TTᵣAWHR
Rev. 2:17 εἴδω GEds
  3: 3 γνώσῃ TTᵣ

γλῶσσα.

1 Co. 14:18 γλώσσῃ a tongue LTTᵣA

1 Co. 14:23 *trs* λαλῶσιν γλ. LTTᵣAWH R
   26 *trs* hath a revelation, hath tongue Eds
   39†*trs* μὴ κωλύετε (*add* ἐν [L]A) γλώσσαις LTTᵣAWH R

1 Joh.3:18 τῇ γλώσσῃ with the tongue GEds

γνήσιος.

Phil. 4: 3 *trs* γνήσιε σύνζυγε LTTᵣAWH R

γνώμη.

Acts 20: 3 γνώμης TTᵣAWH R
Rev. 17:17 *trs* γνώμην μίαν G[A]

γνωρίζω.

Lu. 2:17*ἐγνώρισαν *for* διεγνωρισαν (διαγνωρίζω) LTTᵣAWH R
Acts 7:13*ἐγνωρίσθη *for* ἀνεγνωρίσθη (ἀναγνωρίζομαι) TᵣWH
Eph. 3: 3 ἐγνωρίσθη was made known GEds
   6:21 *trs* γνωρίσει ὑμῖν LTTᵣWH R
Col. 4: 9 γνωρίσουσιν LWH

γνῶσις.

Ro. 15:14 τῆς γνώσεως TWH. [τῆς] γ. A
Col. 2: 3 τῆς γ.—*omit* τῆς LTT.AWH R

γνωστός.

Joh. 18:16 ὃς ἦν γ.—ὁ γ. TTᵣAWH
Acts 15:18 γ. (γνωστὸν LW) *joined to* verse 17 GTTᵣAWH R

γογγυσμός.

1 Pet. 4: 9 γογγυσμοῦ Eds

Γολγοθᾶ, —ᾶ TᵣWH.

Mar. 15:22 τὸν (*omit* τὸν A[Tᵣ]) Γολγοθᾶν TAWH

Γόμορρα.

Mat. 10:15 Γομόρρας TᵣA
Mar. 6:11 *omit* verily *to end of verse* G[L]TTᵣAWH R

γονεύς.

Lu. 2:43*ἔγνω Ἰωσὴφ καὶ ἡ μήτηρ—ἔγνωσαν οἱ γονεῖς, *read* his parents knew it not LTTᵣAWH R
   18:29 *trs* wife, or brethren, or parents TAWH

γονυπετέω.

Mar. 1:40 *omit* and kneeling down L[TᵣAWH]

γράμμα.

Lu. 16: 6, 7 τὰ γράμματα bills LTTᵣAWH R
   23:38 *omit* in letters of Greek, and Latin, and Hebrew [L]TTᵣ[A]
2 Co. 3: 7 γράμματι LTᵣA   (WH R
2 Ti. 3:15 τὰ ἱερὰ γ. — *omit* τὰ [L]T[TᵣA]WH R

γραμματεύς.

Mat. 15: 1 *trs* Pharisees and scribes TTᵣWH R: *omit* οἱ LTTᵣWH R
   23:14(13) *omit the verse* LTTᵣAWH R, see κρίμα
   26: 3 *om.* and the scribes LTTᵣAWH R
Mar. 2:16 οἱ γ.—*omit* οἱ T
   8:31 τῶν γραμματέων GEds
   9:16 the scribes—them, αὐτούς GLTTᵣAWH R
   11:18 *trs* chief priests and scribes Eds
   15: 1 τῶν γραμματέων T
Lu. 5:30†*trs* Pharisees and their ([their] Tᵣ) scribes Eds
   11:44 *omit* scribes and Pharisees, hypocrites G[L]TTᵣAWH R
   20:19 *trs* scribes and the chief priests LTTᵣAWH R
Acts 4: 5 τοὺς γραμματεῖς LTTᵣAWH R
   23: 9 τινὲς τῶν γραμματέων some of the scribes TTᵣAWH R

γραφή.

Mar.15:28 *omit the verse* T[Tᵣ]AWH R
1 Pet. 2: 6 τῇ γ.—*omit* τῇ TTᵣAWH R

γράφω.

Lu. 10:20 ἐγράφη TTᵣAWH R
   23:38 ἐπιγράφω L[Tᵣ]: *omit* written TAWH R

Joh. 8: 6 καταγράφω WH R
   17 γεγραμμένον ἐστίν T
   15:25 *trs* ἐν τῷ νόμῳ αὐτῶν γ. LTTᵣWH
   21:24 ὁ γράψας LTᵣWH, [ὁ] γ. A
   25 *omit the verse* T
Acts 24:14 καὶ—*add* τοῖς ἐν GTTᵣ[A]WH R
   25:26 γ.²—γράψω Eds
Ro. 15: 4*ἐγράφη *for* προεγράφη² (προγράφω) Eds
2 Co. 13: 2 *omit* I write GEds
1 Joh.2:13 γ.³—ἔγραψα I have written Eds
2 Joh. 5 γράφω S—γράφων A.V.B E GEds: *trs* καινὴν γ. σοι LTTᵣ
3 Joh. 13 γ.¹—γράψαι σοι to write to thee Eds
   13 γ.²—γράφειν Eds

γρηγορέω.

Lu. 12:39 *om.* would have watched and T

γυμνητεύω, γυμνι— LTTᵣAWH.

γυναικάριον.

2 Ti. 3: 6 τὰ γ.—*omit* τὰ GEds

γυνή.

Mat.15:38 *trs* children and women T
   19:29 *omit* or wife LTTᵣAWH R
Mar. 7 :26 *trs* ἡ δὲ γ. ἦν LTAWH, ἡ γ. δὲ ἦν T
   10: 7 *omit* and cleave to his wife TWH
   12 a woman—she, αὐτή TTᵣAWH R
   29 *omit* or wife LTTᵣAWH R
   12:22 *trs* καὶ γ. ἀπέθανεν LTTᵣAWH R
Lu. 1: 5 ἡ γ. αὐτοῦ—γ. αὐτῷ LTTᵣAWH R
   28 *omit* blessed (art) thou among women T[Tᵣ]AWH R
   2: 5 *omit* wife LTTᵣAWH R
   11:27 *trs* φωνὴν γυνὴ LTAWH
   18:29 *trs* wife, or brethren, or parents TAWH R
   20:30 *omit* took her *to end of verse* TTᵣAWH R
   32 *trs* καὶ γ. ἀπέθανεν TTᵣAWH
   33*add at commencement* ἡ γυνὴ the woman TAWH
   23:55 αἱ γυναῖκες LTᵣWH R
Joh. 4: 9 *trs* γ. Σαμαρείτιδος οὔσης LTTᵣAWH
   11 *omit* ἡ γ. *read* she [A]WH
   8:10 *omit* and saw none but the woman WH R
   10 *omit* woman² W, γύναι WH
1 Co. 7:33, 34 γυναικί, καὶ μεμέρισται. καὶ ἡ γυνὴ ἡ ἄγαμος καὶ ἡ παρθένος ἡ ἄγαμος (*omit* ἡ ἄγ. TᵣWH) μεριμνᾷ LTᵣ, (his) wife, and is divided. And the woman that is unmarried and the (unmarried L) virgin careth for LTᵣWH
   11: 7 ἡ γυνα Eds
   11 see ἀνήρ
   14:35 γυναικί a woman LTTᵣAWH R
Eph. 5:31 τῇ γυναικί LTTᵣ
1 Ti. 2: 9 τὰς γ.—*omit* τὰς Eds
   12 τῆς διδάσκειν δὲ γ. LTTᵣAWH R
1 Pet.3: 1 αἱ γ.—*omit* αἱ LTTᵣ[A]WH R
Rev. 12:15 *trs* ἐκ τοῦ στόματος αὐτοῦ ὀπίσω τῆς γ. GEds

Δαβίδ, Δαυίδ GW, Δαυείδ LTTᵣAWH.

Mar. 12:35 *trs* Δαυείδ ἐστιν TTᵣAWH
Lu. 20:41 *trs* εἶναι Δαυείδ υἱὸν TAWH
Acts 13:22 *trs* ὃν Δ. αὐτοῖς LTTᵣAWH R
Rev. 3: 7 τοῦ Δ.—*omit* τοῦ LTᵣ[A]WH R
   22:16 τοῦ Δ.—*omit* τοῦ GEds

δαιμονίζομαι.

Mat.12:22 δαιμονιζόμενον LWH

δαιμόνιον.

Mar. 7:29 *trs* ἐκ τῆς θυγατρός σου τὸ δ. TAWH
Lu. 8:29*δαιμονίον *for* δαίμονος (-μων) LTTᵣAWH
   30 *trs* εἰσῆλθεν δα. πολλὰ LTWH
   9:49 τὰ δ.—*omit* τὰ Eds
Rev. 16:14*δαιμονίων *for* δαιμόνων (-μων) GEds
   18: 2*δαιμονίων *for* δαιμόνων (-μων) LTTᵣAWH R

δαίμων.

Mar. 5:12 *omit* all the devils TTᵣAWH R
Lu. 8:29 δαιμόνιον LTTᵣAWH R
Rev. 16:14 δαιμόνιον GEds
   18: 2 δαιμόνιον LTTᵣAWH R

δάκρυ, δάκρυον.

Mar. 9:24 *omit* with tears LTTᵣAWH R
Lu. 7:38 *trs* τοῖς δ. *before* ἤρξατο LTTᵣAWH

δάκτυλος.

Joh. 8: 8*κύψας—*add* τῷ δακτύλῳ, *read* with his finger wrote R
   20:25 *trs* μου τὸν δάκτυλον T

δανείζω, δανίζω TWH.

Lu. 6:34 δ.¹—δανίσητε TWH : δανείζετε TᵣA

Δάνειον, δάνιον WH.

δανειστής, δανιστής TWH.

Δανιήλ.

Mar. 13:14 *omit* spoken of by Daniel the prophet G[L]TTᵣAWH R

δέ.

Mat. 6: 1*προσέχετε δέ but take heed T, π. [δέ] AWH
   7:15 *omit* δέ¹ LT[TᵣA]WH R
   12:46 ¦ 13:1 *omit* δέ LTTᵣAWH R
   13:46*εὑρὼν δέ and having found GLTTᵣAWH R
   14: 9 *omit* nevertheless LTTᵣAWH
   16:11*add δέ LTTᵣAWH R, see προσέχω
   16 ἀποκριθεὶς δέ—καὶ ἀ. W
   17:26*add δέ LTTᵣWH R, see λέγω
   18:31 so—therefore, οὖν LTTᵣAWH R
   20: 5*πάλιν δέ and again TTᵣA, [δέ] WH
   10 ἐλθόντες δέ—καὶ ἐ. TᵣAWH R
   14 *omit* δέ W
   26 *omit* but¹ GLTTᵣAWH R
   21:24 *omit* and¹ L[WH]
   29 *omit* but [L]TWH
   22: 7 ἀκούσας δέ—καὶ ἀ. W
   37 *omit* δέ W
   39 *omit* and TWH
   23: 4*for γάρ LTTᵣAWH R
   5 δε²—γάρ, *read* for they make LTTᵣAWH R
   23*ταῦτα δέ but these GLTTᵣAW
   24:37 but—for, γάρ LTᵣWH   (WH R
   25: 9 *omit* but² GEds
   16 *omit* then [L]T[Tᵣ]WH R
   21 *omit* δέ GEds
   22 *omit* δέ TWH
   26·35*ὁμοίως δέ and likewise W
   27:41 *omit* δέ [L]T[TᵣA]WH R
   65 *omit* δέ GEds
Mar. 1: 6 ἦν δέ—καὶ ἦν LTTᵣAWH
   14 μετὰ δέ—καὶ μ. LTTᵣAWH
   28 ἐξῆλθεν δέ—καὶ ἐ. LTTᵣAWH
   2: 5 ἰδὼν δέ—καὶ ἰ. TWH R
   4: 5 ἄλλο δέ—καὶ ἄ. LTTᵣAWH R
   10 ὅτε δέ—καὶ ὁ. LTTᵣAWH
   36 *omit* and² LTᵣ[A]WH R
   37 τὰ δέ—καὶ τὰ LTTᵣAWH R
   5: 6 ἰδὼν δέ—καὶ ἰ. LTTᵣAWH R
   13 *omit* δέ [L]TTᵣAWH
   14 οἱ δέ—καὶ οἱ LTTᵣAWH
   19 howbeit—and, καί GEds
   6: 3 ἀδελφὸς δέ—καὶ ἀ. Eds
   4 ἔλεγεν δέ—καὶ ἐ. LTTᵣAWH
   15*ἄλλοι δέ but others Eds
   22*add δέ LTTᵣAWH R, see βασιλεύς
   24 ἡ δέ¹—καί TTᵣAWH
   27(28) ὁ δέ—καὶ LTTᵣAWH
   7:27 καί LTTᵣAWH
   8: 8 ἔφαγον δέ—καὶ ἔ. LTTᵣWH R
   20 *omit* and¹ [TᵣA]WI : καί T
   20 οἱ δέ—καί TAWH
   29 *omit* and² LTTᵣAWH
   9: 9 καταβαινόντων δέ—καί κ. LTTᵣWH
   38 *omit* and¹ [L]TTᵣWH
   10:27 *omit* and TTᵣAWH
   29 *omit* and¹ GEds
   42 καί LTTᵣAWH R, see Ἰησοῦς
   52 ὁ δέ—καὶ ὁ WH
   11: 4 ἀπῆλθον δέ—καὶ ἀ. LTTᵣAWH
   8 πολλοὶ δέ—καί π. TTᵣAWH
   12: 3, 14 οἱ δέ—καί LTTᵣAWH R
   29 *omit* and TTᵣAWH R, see Ἰησοῦς
   13:11 ὅταν δέ—καὶ ὅ. LTTᵣAWH R
   12 παραδώσει δέ—καί π. LTTᵣAWH R
   15 *omit* and L[Tᵣ]WH
   22*for γάρ T
   14: 2 but—for, γάρ LTTᵣAWH R
   9*ἀμὴν δέ and verily [L]TᵣAWH R
   19 *omit* and οἱ δέ TAWH
   15:31 *omit* δέ GEds
   33 γενομένης δέ—καὶ γ. LTTᵣAWH R
   16: 8 γάρ LTTᵣWH R

Mar.16:14*ὕστερον δέ and afterward LTᵣR, [δέ] WH
Lu. 1:76*σὺ δέ thou also TT,AWHR
2:35 omit also [LTᵣ]WH
6: 8 ὁ δέ—καί LTTᵣAWHR
9*for οὖν LTTᵣWHR
30 omit δέ [L]T[Tᵣ]WHR
7: 1 ἐπειδή (omit now) LTTᵣAWHR
21 omit and¹ LTTᵣAWHR
42 omit and [L]TTᵣAWHR
43 omit δέ [L]TTᵣAWHR
9:14*for γάρ T
57 καί TTᵣAWHR
10: 2*for οὖν LTTᵣAWHR
8 omit δέ LTTᵣAWHR
12 omit but G[L]TᵣAWWHR
30 omit and¹ TWHR
37*for οὖν GLTTᵣAWHR
42 and—for, γάρ TWHR,[δέ] A
11:33 omit δέ TTᵣAWHR
42*ταῦτα δέ now these [L]TᵣWHR
47 οἱ δέ—καί οἱ T
12:42 εἶπεν δέ—καί ε. TTᵣAWHR
13:15*for οὖν LTTᵣAWHR
18 then—therefore, οὖν TTᵣAWHR
35 omit and T[WH]: trs λέγω δέ GLTᵣAWWHR
14:14*for γάρ T
26 τε LTᵣAWH
15:28*for οὖν LTTᵣAWHR
16:29*λέγει—add δέ, read but Abraham Eds
17: 1 οὐαί δέ—πλὴν ο. LTᵣWHR
3 omit δέ LTTᵣAWHR
17 omit but LT[TᵣWH]
19:22 omit and¹ TTᵣAWHR
20:32 omit δέ A.V. E᷍ LTTᵣAWᵗHR
40 and—for, γάρ TTᵣAWHR
21:13 omit and T[TᵣA]WHR
23 omit but LTTᵣAWHR
36*for οὖν LTTᵣAWHR
22:36*ὁ δέ εἶπεν TR, ε. δέ TᵣWH, for ε. οὖν
44 ἐγένετο δέ—καί ε. TAWH
47 omit and¹ Eds
69*νυν—add δέ read but hereafter LTTᵣAWHR
23:20*for οὖν LTTᵣAWHR
24 καί LTTᵣAWHR
44 ἦν δε—καί ἦν LTTᵣAWHR
24:48 omit and TTᵣAWHR
Joh. 1:26 omit but TTᵣAWHR
38 omit then T
39(40) omit for GEds
42(43) omit and² GTTᵣAWWHR
2:17 omit and [L]TTᵣAWHR
3:18 omit but [L]T[Tᵣ]AWHR
36 omit and T
4:31 omit δέ [L]TTᵣAWHR
54*τοῦτο δέ now this Tᵣ, [δέ] AWH
5:11*add δέ LTᵣWHR, see ὅς
29 omit and² [L]T[Tᵣ]AWH
6:10 omit and [L]TTᵣAWHR
11 and¹—therefore, οὖν LTTᵣAWHR
23 omit howbeit TTᵣ[A]WHR
35 omit and¹ [L]TᵣAWHR, οὖν T
40 and¹—for, γάρ GEds
7: 9 omit δέ A.V. Vul GTTᵣ
12 omit δέ GTW[WH]
29 omit but GEds
41 omit but T
8:14 omit but T
46 omit and GLTTᵣAWHR
9: 9 omit δέ [L]TTᵣAWHR
11 and¹—therefore,οὖν LTTᵣAWHR
16*ἄλλοι δέ but others R, [δέ] WH
26 οὖν LTTᵣAWHR
28*οἱ δὲ ἐλοιδόρησαν but they railed Tᵣ
31 omit now LTTᵣAWHR
37 omit and¹ LTTᵣAWHR
10:12 omit but T[Tᵣ]WHR
20 and¹—then, οὖν T
22 τότε WH
11:29*δὲ ὡς and as soon TᵣWHR,[δέ] A
12: 4*for οὖν T[WH]R
16 omit δέ [L]TTᵣAWHR
23 omit now TTᵣAWHR
25 omit then TrAWHR, οὖν T
14:17 omit but [L]T[Tᵣ]AWHR
15:26 omit but T[TᵣA]WHR
16:20 omit and² LTTᵣAWHR
18: 4*for οὖν Tᵣ
19:14 omit and² Eds
15 omit οἱ δέ TTᵣAWHR, see ἐκεῖνος
16 and¹—therefore,οὖν LTTᵣAWHR
29 omit δέ LTTᵣAWHR. see πλήθω
21: 6 omit and¹ T
12 omit δέ [TᵣA]WH
20 omit then Eds
Acts 1: 7 omit and TTᵣWHR
4:14 τε LTTᵣAWHR

Acts 5:32 omit also LTTᵣ[A]WHR
6: 3*for οὖν TWH
7:15 κατέβη δέ—καί κ. LTTᵣAW
26 τε s—δέ EGW
49 ἡ δέ—καί ἡ WH
8:33 omit and LTTᵣ[A]WHR
11:17 omit and LTTᵣ[A]WHR
12:17 δέ²—τε LTTᵣAWHR
13:11 τε T
44 τε GA
46 δέ¹—τε LTTᵣAWHR
46 omit but LTTᵣWHR
52 τε LTᵣAWH
14:11 τε LTAWHR
13 ὁ δέ—ὅ τε LTTᵣAWHR
15: 2*for οὖν TTᵣWHR
6 τε TᵣAWH
32 τε s—δέ E
39*for οὖν LTTᵣAWHR
16: 7*ἐλθόντες δέ read and after Eds
11*for οὖν TA
38 τε T
17:14 δέ²—τε LTTᵣAWHR
18: 1 omit δέ LTTᵣ[A]WHR
21 omit but² LTTᵣAWHR
19:27 δέ² s—τε A.V.B EGLTTᵣAWHR
20: 5*οὗτοι δέ and these LTTᵣ[A]WHR
15*τῇ³—add δέ LTTᵣWHR
34 omit yea GEds
21:13 ἀπεκρίθη δέ—τότε ἀ. Eds
18 τε T
31 τε LTTᵣAWHR
22:23 τε LTᵣAWWH
23:28 τε LTTᵣAWH
24:10 τε LTTᵣAWHR
16 καί Eds
18 omit δέ A.V.B E
26 omit δέ GEds
25: 2 τε LTTᵣAWH
22 omit ὁ δέ LTTᵣAWHR
26:14|27:21|28: 2 τε Eds
28: 9*for οὖν LTTᵣAWHR
16 omit but LTTᵣAWHR
25 τε T
Ro. 2: 2 but—for, γάρ T
17*ei δέ for ἴδε GEds
3: 7*for γάρ TWH
29 omit δέ GLTTᵣAWHR
4:15*for γάρ² Eds
11:13*for γάρ LTTᵣAWHR
14 15 but—for, γάρ Eds
15: 8 now—for, γάρ Eds
1 Co. 2:10 γάρ WH
4: 2 ὁ δέ—ὧδε here LTTᵣAWHR
7: 7*for γάρ Eds
38 ὁ δέ—καί ὁ GEds
40 and—for, γάρ WH
8: 2 omit and Eds
9:16 yea—for, γάρ GEds
10: 1 moreover—for, γάρ GEds
27 omit δέ Eds
30 omit for¹ GEds
11:31*for γάρ Eds
34 omit and¹ GEds
12: 6 ὁ δέ—καί ὁ AWH
9 omit δέ¹ [L]TTᵣ[A]WHR
10 omit δέ² et δέ³ LT[ᵣWH]
10 omit δέ⁴ LTTᵣWHR
21 omit and G[LWH]
13:11 omit but LTTᵣAWHR
14: 5*for γάρ LTTᵣAWHR
15 omit and² L[TᵣWH]
40*πάντα δέ read but let all GEds
15:14 omit and² Eds
16: 7 but—for, γάρ GEds
2 Co. 2: 1 but—for, γάρ WH
5:16 omit δέ LTTᵣAWHR
6:14 τίς δέ—ἢ τίς, or what Eds
7:13 trs δέ after ἐπί¹ (commencing a sentence at ἐπί) Eds
8:13 omit and LTTᵣ[A]WHR
9:15 omit δέ LTTᵣAWHR
12: 1*for γάρ GEds
13: 9 omit and² Eds
Gal. 1:11 but—for, γάρ TᵣAWHR
2:16*εἰδότες δέ but knowing GEds
4:25*for γάρ WHR
25 and²—for, γάρ GEds
5:17 and²—for, γάρ Eds
Eph. 4:32 omit and L[WH]
Phil. 1:23*for γάρ GEds
4:12 καί A.V.C GLTTᵣAWHR
Col. 2: 4 omit and T[TᵣA]WHR
3:25 but—for, γάρ Eds
1 Th. 2:16 enim A.V. Vul
5:21*πάντα δέ, read but prove GLTTᵣAW, [δέ] WH
1 Ti. 5:20*τοὺς δὲ but them L, [δέ] AWH
25*ὡσαύτως δὲ but likewise LW
Philem.12 omit therefore LTTᵣAWHR
Heb.12:11 now—indeed, μέν TWHR
13: 4 but—for, γάρ LTTᵣAWHR

Jas. 1:19*ἔστω—add δέ LTTᵣAWHR, read but let, see ὥστε
2:15 omit δέ TTᵣWHR
3: 3*ei δέ for ἰδού Eds
4: 2 omit yet GLTTᵣAWHR
7*ἀντίστητε δέ but resist LTTᵣAWHR
12*σὺ δέ, read but who GLTTᵣAWHR
14 καί LTTᵣAWHR: omit and w
1 Pet. 3:11*ἐκκλινάτω δέ and let him eschew LTTᵣAWHR
15 omit and¹ LTTᵣ[A]WHR
4: 8 omit and TTᵣAWHR
2 Pet. 2:22 omit but LTTᵣAWHR
1 Joh.3: 2 omit but Eds
5: 5*add δέ after τίς [Tᵣ]R, after ἐστίν [WH], read and who
3 Joh. 11 omit but² GEds
Rev. 2: 9 πλούσιος δέ—ἀλλὰ π. GEds
14:13 and²—for, γάρ LTTᵣAWHR
20: 5 omit but LTAWWHR: καί οι Pᵣ
22:15 omit for GEds

δέησις.

Acts 1:14 omit and supplication GEds

δεῖ.

Mar.14:31 trs δέῃ με LTᵣWH
Lu. 24:46 omit and thus it behoved L[TTᵣAWHR]
Joh. 10:16 trs δεῖ με LTTᵣAWHR
Acts 10: 6 he shall tell to end of verse GEds
18:21 omit I must to Jerusalem LTTᵣAWHR
21:22 omit the multitude must come together TᵣWHR: trs δεῖ συνελθεῖν πλῆθος LTA
24:19 δεῖ s—ἔδει A.V.B EGEds
2 Co.12: 1*for δή LTTᵣWHR, see συμφέρω
Rev.13:10 omit must A

δειγματίζω.

Mat. 1:19*δειγματίσαι for παραδειγματίσαι (-τίζω) LTTᵣAWH

δεικνύω, -υμι.

Lu. 20:24*δείξατε for ἐπιδείξατε (-είχνυμι) GEds
24:40*ἔδειξεν for ἐπέδειξεν (ἐπιδείκνυμι) LTᵣWHR, [ἐπ]έ. A
Jas. 2:18 trs σοι δείξω TTᵣWH
Rev. 22: 8 δεικνύντος T

δειλός.

Rev.21: 8 τοῖς δὲ δ. A.V.C GEds

δεκαδύο.

Acts 19: 7 δώδεκα LTTᵣAWWH
24:11 δώδεκα LTTᵣAWH

* δεκαοκτώ, eighteen.

Lu. 13: 4, 11 for δέκα καὶ ὀκτώ T omit καὶ[LTᵣA]WH

δένδρον.

Mar.11: 8 trees—fields, ἀγρός TTᵣAWHR

δεξιός.

Mat.27:29 ἐν τῇ δεξιᾷ LTTᵣAWHR
Mar.10:37 trs σου ἐκ δεξιῶν TTᵣAWH
14:62 trs ἐκ δ. καθήμενον GLTTᵣAWWH
Rev.10: 5*αὐτοῦ—add τὴν δεξιάν, read his right hand GEds

δέομαι.

Lu. 8:38 ἐδεῖτο L, ἐδεῖτο TᵣAWH

* δέος, fear.

Heb.12:28 reverence and godly fear— εὐλαβείας καὶ δέους godly fear and awe LTTᵣAWHR

δεσμέω.

Lu. 8:29 ἐδεσμεύετο TTᵣWHR

δέσμιος.

Acts 28:16 omit the centurion to the guard: but LTTᵣAWHR
Heb.10:34*δεσμίοις for δεσμοῖς μου GEds

δεσμός.

Acts 22:30 omit from (his) bands GEds
Heb.10:34 me in my bonds—the prisoners, δέσμιος GEds

δεῦτε.

Lu. 20:14 *omit* como LTTᵣAWHR

δευτερόπρωτος.

La. 6: 1 *omit* second after the first [L]T[A]WHR

δεύτερος.

Mat. 21:30 second—other, ἕτερος GTAW
Acts 13:33 second—first, *see* πρῶτος GLTTᵣ
Rev. 6: 3 *trs* σφραγῖδα τὴν δ. GEds
11:14 ἡ δ.—*omit* ἢ W
14: 8*δεύτερος ἄγγελος ([ἄ.] WH) a second angel LTᵣAWWHR: ἄγ. δ. T.
21: 8 *trs* ὁ θάνατος ὁ δ. GEds

δέχομαι.

Mar. 6:11 ὃς ἂν τόπος μὴ δέξηται whatsoever place will not receive TTᵣAWHR
9:37 δ.³—δέχηται TTᵣAWHR
Lu. 9: 5 δέχωνται LTTᵣAWHR
11 received—welcomed, ἀποδέχομαι LTTᵣAWHR
Acts 21:17 received—welcomed, ἀποδέχομαι Eds
Co. 8: 4 *omit* that we would receive GEds

δέω.

Acts 10:11 *omit* δ. καί, *read* let down by four corners LTTᵣ[A]WHR
20:22 *trs* δεδεμένος ἐγὼ GLTTᵣAWWHR

δή.

2 Co.12: 1 δεῖ LTTᵣWHR, *see* συμφέρω
Rev. 2:10*ἰδού—*add* δὴ [A]W

* δηλαυγῶς, clearly.

Mar. 8:25 *for* τηλαυγῶς T

δῆλος.

1 Ti. 6: 7 *omit* (it is) certain LTTᵣAWHR

δηνάριον.

Mar. 6:37 *trs* δην. διακοσίων GLTTᵣAWWHR
14: 5 *trs* δην. τριακοσιων LTTᵣAWWHR

δήποτε.

Joh. 5: 4 *omit* waiting for (ver. 3) to end of verse 4 [G]TTᵣAWHR

δήπου, δὴ που WH.

διά.

Mat. 2:17* ι 3:3*for* ὑπό Eds
11: 2*for* δύο Eds
23:14(13) *omit the verse* LTTᵣAWHR, *see* κρίμα
Mar. 7:31*for* καί² LTTᵣAWHR, *see* ἔρχομαι
10: 1 by—and, καί LTTᵣAWHR
Lu. 5:19 *omit* by GEds
6:48*add* δ. TTᵣAWHR, *see* θεμελιόω
19: 4 *omit* δ. GEds
Joh. 7:22 *omit* therefore R
8:59 *omit* going through to end of verse GLTTᵣAWHR
Acts 13:49 κατά T
Ro. 15: 4*and—*add* δ. through Eds
1 Co.14:19 *omit* δ. Eds, *see* νοῦς
2 Co. 1:20*ἐν αὐτῷ³—δι' αὐτοῦ Eds
4:14 by—with, σύν Eds
Eph. 3: 9 *omit* by Jesus Christ GEds
Col. 1:14 *omit* through his blood GEds
20 *omit* by him (I say) LTᵣ[WH]
2 Th. 3:12 ἐν LTTᵣAWHR, *see* κύριος
Heb. 1: 3 *omit* by himself LTTᵣAWHR
1 Pet. 1:22 *omit* through the Spirit Eds
2 Pet. 1: 3 *omit* δ.² LTTᵣAWR, *see* ἴδιος
3: 9*for* εἰς¹ LT
Jude 25*add* δ. GEds, *see* κύριος
Rev. 1: 9 *omit* for² LTᵣ[A]WHR
6: 9 *omit* for² L[A]
21:24*for* ἐν GEds
See also διαπαντός

διαβλέπω.

Mar. 8:25*ἐποίησεν αὐτὸν ἀναβλε. made him look up—διεβλεψεν, he saw distinctly TTᵣAWHR

διάβολος.

Lu. 4: 5 *omit* the devil TTᵣAWHR
Rev. 2:10 *trs* ὁ δ. ἐξ ὑμῶν GEds
20: 2 ὁ διάβολος T

διαγνωρίζω.

Lu. 2:17 made known abroad—made known, γνωρίζω LTTᵣAWHR

διάδημα.

Rev. 12: 3 *trs* ἑπτὰ διαδήματα GEds

διαδίδωμι.

Joh. 6:11 δίδωμι T
Acts 4:35 διεδίδοτο LTTᵣAWH
Rev. 17:13 shall give—give, δίδωμι GEds

διακαθαρίζω.

Lu. 3:17 καὶ δ.—διακαθάραι to throughly purge TWHR

διακονέω.

Joh. 12:26 *trs* τις διακονῇ¹ LTTᵣAWHR
Philem. 13 *trs* μοι διακονῇ GEds

διακονία.

2 Co. 3: 9 ἡ δ.¹—τῇ διακονίᾳ with the ministration LTTᵣ
Rev. 2:19 *trs* GLTTᵣAWHR, *see* πίστις

διάκονος.

Mar. 10:43 *trs* ὑμῶν διάκονος GLTTᵣAWWHR
1 Th. 3: 2 minister of—fellow labourer with, συνεργός GLAW

διακόσιοι.

Acts 27:37 *omit* two hundred WH

διακρίνω.

Mat. 16: 3 When it is (ver. 2) to end of verse 3 [TA][[WH]]
Acts 11:12 *omit* nothing doubting A: διακρίναντα LTTᵣWHR
Jude 22 διακρινομένους Eds, *see* ἐλεέω

διάκρισις.

1 Co.12:10 διάκρισις T

διαλέγομαι.

Acts 17: 2 διελέξατο LTTᵣWHR
18:19 διελέξατο LTTᵣWH

διαλείπω.

Lu. 7:45 διέλειπεν T

διαλογίζομαι.

Mar. 11:31*διελογίζοντο *for* ἐλογίζοντο (λογίζομαι) Eds
Joh. 11:50 λογίζομαι Eds

διαλογισμός.

1 Ti. 2: 8 διαλογισμῶν WH

διαμαρτύρομαι.

Acts 2:40 διεμαρτύρατο Eds

διαμερίζω.

Mat. 27:35 *omit* that it might to end of verse GLTTᵣAWHR
Mar. 15:24 διαμερίζονται they part GEds
Lu. 11:17 *trs* δ. ἐφ' ἑαυτὴν T
12:53 διαμερισθήσονται LTTᵣAWHR: τρισίν (52) δ.' LTTᵣA

διάνοια.

Lu. 10:27 τῇ διανοίᾳ LTTᵣWHR, *see* ψυχή
Eph. 1:18 understanding—heart, καρδία GEds
Heb.10:16 τὴν διάνοιαν mind Eds

διανοίγω.

Mar. 7:35 ἀνοίγω LTTᵣAWH
Acts 7:56*διηνοιγμένους *for* ἀνεῳγμένους (ἀνοίγω) Eds

διαπαντός.

(*often* διὰ παντός *by* LTᵣAWH)
Acts 2:25*for* διὰ παντός GT

* διαπαρατριβή, violent contention.

1 Ti. 6: 5 διαπαρατριβαὶ *for* παραδιατριβαὶ (-βή) GEds

διαπορεύομαι.

Mar. 2:23*trs* αὐτὸν ἐν τοῖς σάββασιν (διαπορεύεσθαι f. παραπορεύεσθαι, -εύομαι LTᵣWHR) LTTᵣAWHR

διαπορέω.

Lu. 24: 4 ἀπορέω LTTᵣAWHR
Acts 2:12 διηπορούντο TTᵣAWHR

διαπραγματεύομαι.

Lu. 19:15 διεπραγματεύσαντο TᵣAWHR, *see* τίς

διαρπάζω.

Mat.12:29 δ.¹—ἁρπάζω LTTᵣAWH
29 δ.²—διαρπάσῃ T

διαρρήσσω, διαρρήγνυμι.

Mat. 26:65 διέρηξεν WH
Mar. 14:63 διαρήξας WH
Lu. 5: 6 διερήσσετο TTᵣAWH
8:29 διαρήσσων LTTᵣAWH

διασαφέω.

Mat.13:36*διασάφησον *for* φράσον (-αζω) LTᵣWHR

διασκορπίζω.

Mat. 26:31 διασκορπισθήσονται LTTᵣAWH
Mar. 14:27 διασκορπισθήσονται LTTᵣAWH: *trs* τὰ πρόβατα δ. TTᵣAWH

διαστέλλομαι.

Mat. 16:20 ἐπιτιμαω LWH

διατάσσω.

Acts 18: 2 τάσσω T
20:13 *trs* διατεταγμένος ἦν LTTᵣAWH

διατί, διὰ τί LTᵣAWH.

Lu. 5:33 *omit* why do TAWHR

διατρίβω.

Joh. 11:54 μένω TᵣAWH

* διαυγής, transparent.

Rev. 21:21 διαυγής *for* διαφανής GEds

διαφανής.

Rev. 21:21 διαυγής GEds

διαφεύγω.

Acts 27:42 διαφύγῃ GLTTᵣAWWH

διαφημίζω.

Mat. 28:15 is commonly reported—is reported, φημίζω T

διαφθείρω.

Rev. 8: 9 διεφθάρησαν LTTᵣAWHR

* διαχλευάζω, to scoff utterly.

Acts 2:13 διαχλευάζοντες *for* χλευάζοντες (-ζω) GEds

διδάσκαλος.

Mat. 23: 8*διδάσκαλος *for* καθηγητής Eds
Lu. 7:40 *trs* δ. εἰπέ, φησίν TTᵣAWH

διδάσκω.

Mar. 1:21 *trs* δ. εἰς τὴν συναγωγήν TA
6: 2 *trs* δ. ἐν τῇ συναγωγῇ TTᵣWH
Lu. 21:37 *trs* δ. ἐν τῷ ἱερῷ Tᵣ
Rev. 2:20 καὶ διδάσκει and she teacheth GEds, *see* πλανάω

διδαχή.

Mar. 1:27 *omit* ἡ LTTᵣAWHR, *see* καινός
12:38*trs* ἐν τῇ δ. αὐτοῦ ἔλεγεν TTᵣAWHR
Heb. 6: 2 διδαχήν LWH

δίδραχμον.

Mat. 17:24 τὰ δ.²—*omit* τὰ T

δίδωμι.

Mat. 5:42 δός LTTᵣAWH
15:36 ἐδίδου TTᵣWHR
24:45 δοῦναι GLTTᵣAWH
26:26 δοὺς having given LTTᵣWHR
Mar. 3: 6*ἐδίδουν *for* ἐποίουν (ποιέω) TᵣAWH
6:25 *trs* ἐξαυτῆς δῷς μοι LTTᵣAWHR
37 δ.³—δώσομεν LTTᵣAWH, δώσομεν T
8:37 [δώσει] A, δοῖ TTᵣWH
11:28 *trs* ἔδ. τὴν ἐξουσίαν ταύ. LTᵣWH
12:14 *trs* δ. κῆνσον Καίσαρι LTᵣWH

Mar. 13:22 shall shew—shall do, ποιέω TA
Lu. 10:19 δέδωκα I have given TTrAWHᴿ
  12:42 τοῦ δ.—omit τοῦ L[TrA]
  16:12 trs δώσει ὑμῖν TTrWHᴿ
  19:15 δεδώκει LTTrAWHR
  20:10 δώσουσιν LTTrAWHR
Joh. 5:26 trs καὶ τῷ υἱῷ ἔδωκεν TTrAWHᴿ
  36 δέδωκεν TTrAWHᴿ
  6:11*ἔδωκεν f. διέδωκεν (διαδίδωμι) T
  27 trs δίδωσιν ὑμῖν giveth you T
  32 δ.¹—ἔδωκεν LTrAWHR
  51 omit which I will give
        LTTrAWHᴿ
  7:19 ἔδωκεν LTrAWHᴿ
  10:28 trs δ. αὐτοῖς ζωὴν αἰω TT,AWH
  12:49 δέδωκεν Eds
  13: 3 ἔδωκεν TTrWHᴿ
  15 δέδωκα TR
  26*καὶ δώσω αὐτῷ and shall give
        to him for ἐπιδώσω (–δίδωμι)
        TTrAWHᴿ
  14:31*add δ. LTrWH, see ἐντολὴ
  16:23 trs the Father, he will give
        you in my name TTrAWHᴿ
  17: 2 δ.²—δώσει AWH
  6 ἔδωκας bis LTTrWHᴿ
  7 ἔδωκας LWH
  8 δ.¹—ἔδωκας LTTrAWHᴿ
  24 δ.²—δέδωκας Eds
  19: 3 ἐδίδοσαν LTTrAWH
  11 trs δεδομένον σοι LTTrAWH
Acts 5:31 τοῦ δοῦναι TR, [τοῦ] δ. WH
  11:18 trs εἰς ζωὴν ἔδωκεν Eds
  14: 3 διδόντος T
  20:35 trs μᾶλλον διδόναι GEds
Ro. 14:12 ἀποδώσει LTr, [ἀπο]δ. A
1 Co. 15:38 trs δίδωσιν αὐτῷ Eds
2 Co. 8:16 δόντι W
  13:10 trs ὁ κύριος ἔδωκέν μοι LTTrAWHᴿ
Eph. 3: 7 τῆς δοθείσης GLTTrAWHᴿ
  16 δῷ LTTrAWHᴿ
  6:19 δοθῇ GEds
1 Th. 4: 8 διδόντα giveth LTTrWHᴿ
2 Ti. 2: 7 δώσει will give Eds
  25 δῷη Eds
Jas. 5:18 trs ἔδωκεν ὑετὸν LTTr
2 Pet. 3:15 trs δοθεῖσαν αὐτῷ LTTrAWHᴿ
Rev. 1:19 διδῶ LTAWHᴿ, διδ. Tr
  6:11 ἐδόθη was given GEds
  8: 3 δ.²—δώσει LTTrAWHᴿ
  10: 9 δοῦναι to give GEds
  13: 7 omit and it was given unto
        to overcome them L[WH]
  15 trs πνεῦμα δοῦναι W
  16 δῶσιν they should give GEds
  16: 6 δέδωκας LTrAWWHᴿ
  17:13*ἐδίδοσαν for διαδιδώσουσιν
        (–δίδωμι) GEds
  19: 7 δώσομεν we will give LAWH

διεγείρω.

Mat. 1:24 ἐγείρω LTTrAWHᴿ
Mar. 4:38 ἐγείρω TTrAWHᴿ
Lu. 8:24*διεγερθεὶς for ἐγερθεὶς (ἐγείρω)
        TTrWHᴿ
Joh. 6:18 διεγείρετο TrAWH

* διενθυμέομαι, to consider, reflect.

Acts 10:19 διενθυμουμένου for ἐνθυμουμέ-
        νου (ἐνθυμέομαι) GEds

* διεξέρχομαι, to go through.

Acts 28: 3 διεξελθοῦσα for ἐξελθοῦσα (ἐξ-
        έρχομαι) AW

διερμηνευτής.

1 Co. 14:28 ἑρμηνευτής LTr

διερμηνεύω.

Lu. 24:27 διερμήνευσεν TTrAWHᴿ

διέρχομαι.

Mat. 19:24 to go through—to enter, εἰσέρ-
        χομαι) GTTrAWH
Mar. 10:25 διελθεῖν for εἰσελθεῖν¹ (εἰσέρ-
        χομαι) A.V.B EGEds
Joh. 4:15*διέρχωμαι for ἔρχωμαι TAWHᴿ
  8:59 omit going through to end of
        verse GLTTrAWHᴿ
Acts 11:22 om. that he should go LTT,WHᴿ
  16: 6 διῆλθον Eds

δίκαιος.

Mat. 20: 7 omit and whatsoever is right,
        (that) shall ye receive
        LTTrAWHᴿ
  27: 4*δίκαιον for ἀθῶον (ἀθῷος) WH
  24 omit just [L]T[Tr]AWH
2 Pet. 2: 8 ὁ δ.—omit ὁ LWH

δικαιοσύνη.

Mat. 5:20 trs ὑμῶν ἡ δικαιοσύνη TAWH
  6: 1*δικαιοσύνην for ἐλεημοσύνην
        (–νη) GEds
Ro. 4:11 τὴν δ.—omit τὴν T[WH]
  9:28 om. in righteousness: because
        a short work LTT₊[A]WHᴿ
  31 omit of righteousness² Eds
  10: 3 omit righteousness²
        GLT₊[A]WWHᴿ
Jas. 3:18 τῆς δ.—omit τῆς GLTTrAWWHᴿ
Rev. 22:11*δικαιοσύνην ποιησάτω f δι-
        καιωθήτω (–αιόω) GEds

δικαιόω.

Lu. 10:29 δικαιῶσαι LTTrAWHᴿ
Ro. 3:28 trs δ. πίστει GLTT₊AWHᴿ
Gal. 2:16 δ.³—trs ἐξ ἔργων νόμου οὐ δ.
        GLTTrAWWHᴿ
Rev. 22:11 let him be righteous—let him
        do righteousness, δικαιοσύνη
        et ποιέω GEds

δικαίωμα.

Heb. 9:10 δικαιώματα Eds

δικαστής

Lu. 12:14 κριτής LTTrAWHᴿ

δίκη.

Acts 25:15 καταδίκη Eds

δίκτυον.

Lu. 5: 5 τὰ δίκτυα the nets TT,WHᴿ
  6 τὰ δίκτυα the nets TT,AWHᴿ

διό.

Acts 13:35 διότι LTTrAWHᴿ
  20:26 διότι TAWHᴿ
1 Co. 14:13*for διόπερ LTTrAWHᴿ
2 Co. 1:20*add δ. Eds, see ἐν
  12: 7*revelations—add δ. therefore
        LTr[A]WH
Gal. 4:31*for ἄρα LTTrAWHᴿ
1 Th. 2:18 διότι Eds
1 Pet. 2: 6 wherefore — because, διότι
        GEds

διόπερ.

1 Co. 8:13 διό περ Tr
  14:13 διό LTTrAWHᴿ

* διόρθωμα, a making straight.

Acts 24: 2(3) διορθωμάτων for κατορθωμά-
        των (–μα) LTTrAWHᴿ

διορύσσω.

Mat. 24:43 διορυχθῆναι TTrWHᴿ
Lu. 12:39 διορυχθῆναι TAWH

διότι.

Acts 10:20 ὅτι GEds
  13:35*for διό LTTrAWHᴿ
  17:31 καθότι Eds
  20:26*for διό TAWHᴿ
Ro. 8:21*for ὅτι T
Gal. 2:16 ὅτι LTTrAWH
1 Th. 2:18*for διό Eds
1 Pet. 1:16*for ὅτι T
  2: 6*for διό GEds

Διοτρεφής, –έφης LAWH.

διπλοῦς.

Rev. 18: 6 δ.¹—τὰ διπλᾶ TTrR, [τὰ] δ. AWH

δίς.

Rev. 9:16*for δύο WH

* δισμυριάδες, see μυριάς.

διϋλίζω.

Mat. 23:24 οἱ δ.—omit οἱ LTrAWH

διχοστασία.

1 Co. 3: 3 omit and divisions LTTrAWHᴿ

διψάω.

Joh. 4:14 ⎰ 6:25 διψήσει LTTrAWHᴿ

διώκω.

Lu. 11:49*διώξουσιν for ἐκδιώξουσιν
        (–ώκω) WHᴿ, [ἐκ]δ. TrA
Ro. 14:19 διώκομεν we follow after T
Gal. 6:12 διώκονται T

δοκέω.

Mat. 24:44 trs οὐ δοκεῖτε ὥρᾳ LTTrAWHᴿ
Lu. 17: 9 omit I trow not [L]TTrAWHᴿ
Joh. 11:31*δόξαντες for λέγοντες (–γω)
        TTrAWHᴿ
Acts 15:34 omit the verse Eds

δοκιμάζω.

Lu. 12:56 οὐ δ.—οὐκ οἴδατε δοκιμάζειν ye
        know not how to discern
        TrWHᴿ
Heb. 3: 9 proved—by proving, δοκιμασία
        (Eds

* δοκιμασία, proof, trial.

Heb. 3: 9 ἐν δοκιμασίᾳ for ἐδοκίμασαν
        (δοκιμάζω) Eds

δόλος.

Mat. 26: 4 trs δ. κρατήσωσιν GLTTrAWWHᴿ
Rev. 14: 5 guile—falsehood, ψεῦδος GEds

δόμα.

Lu. 11:13 trs δόματα ἀγαθὰ GLTTrAWWHᴿ

δόξα.

Mat. 6:13 omit for thine to end of verse
        GEds
2 Co. 4: 4 τῆς δ. 8—τὸν δ. E
Eph. 1:12 trs δ.—omit τῆς Eds
Heb. 3: 3 trs οὗτος δόξης GEds
1 Pet. 1: 7 trs glory and honour Eds
  5:11 omit glory and LTT,AWHᴿ
2 Pet. 1: 3 δόξῃ LTTrAWHᴿ, see ἴδιος

δοξάζω.

Mat. 15:31 ἐδόξαζον T
Lu. 23:47 ἐδόξασεν LTTrAWHᴿ
Joh. 8:54 δ.¹—δοξάσω LTTrAWHᴿ
  13:32 omit if God be glorified in
        him [LTrA]WHᴿ
Acts 11:18 ἐδόξασαν LTT₊WHᴿ
1 Pet. 4:14 omit on their part to end of
        verse LTTrAWHᴿ
Rev. 15: 4 δοξάσει Eds

δουλεία, δουλία Tr.

δουλεύω.

Acts 7: 7 δουλεύσουσιν TTrAWHᴿ
Gal. 4: 9 δουλεῦσαι TTrWH

δοῦλος.

Mat. 13:28 omit servants AWH
Lu. 12:38 omit servants T[TrA]WHᴿ
1 Pet. 2:16 trs θεοῦ δοῦλοι TTrAWHᴿ
Rev. 2:20 τοὺς ἐμοὺς δούλους GEds
  10: 7 τοὺς ἑαυτοῦ δούλους GEds
  15: 3 τοῦ δούλου A.V.C LTTrAWHᴿ

δράκων.

Rev. 13: 4 τῷ δράκοντι GEds

δύναμαι.

Mat. 16: 3 When it is (ver. 2) to end of
        verse 3 [TA][[WH]]
  26: 9 ἐδύνατο TAWH
Mar. 3:25 δυνήσεται, read will not be
        able to TTrAWHᴿ
  27 trs οὐδεὶς δύναται GLTrW
  4:33 ἐδύναντο LT
  5: 3 ἐδύνατο LTTrAWH
  6: 5 ἐδύνατο TTrAWH
  7:24 ἠδυνάσθη TWH
  9:22, 23 δύνῃ LTTrAWH
Lu. 1:22 ἐδύνατο LTTrAWH
  16: 2 δύνῃ TTrAWHᴿ
Joh. 3: 2 trs δ. ταῦτα τὰ σημεῖα LTTrAWHᴿ
  11:37 ἐδύνατο LTTrAWH
  14: 5 omit δ. read how know we
        LTTrAWHᴿ
Acts 5:39 οὐ δυνήσεσθε ye will not be
        able to LTT₊WHᴿ
  10:47 trs δύναται κωλῦσαι LTTrAWHᴿ
  21:34 δυναμένου LTTrAWWHᴿ
  26:32 ἠδύνατο LW
1 Co. 3: 2 ἐδύνασθε GLTTrAWHᴿ
  15:50 δύναται TTrWH
1 Ti. 5:25 δύνανται LTTrAWWHᴿ
Heb. 10: 1 δύναται LTᵣWHᴿ
Rev. 3: 8 ἐδύνατο TWH
  7: 9 ἐδύνατο LTTrAWHᴿ
  9:20 ἐδύναται LTTrAWHᴿ
  14: 3 ⎰ 15:8 ἐδύνατο LTTrAWHᴿ

δύναμις.

Mat. 6:13 omit for thine to end of verse
        ⎰Eds

Mar. 6: 2 αἱ δυνάμεις WHR
    5 *trs* ποιῆσαι οὐδ. δ. LTTrAWH
Lu. 24:49 *trs* ἐξ ὕψους δύναμιν TTrAWHR
Acts 4:33 *trs* δυναμει μεγάλη LTTrAWH
    8:13 *trs* miracles and signs A.V.C
    GW
Ro. 8:38 *trs* nor powers *to end of verse*
    GEds

δυναμόω.

Heb.11:34*ἐδυναμώθησαν *for* ἐνεδυναμώθησαν (ἐνδυναμόω) LTTrWHR

δυνατέω.

Ro. 14: 4*δ. γάρ ἐστιν—δυνατεῖ γ. Eds
2Co. 9: 8*δυνατεῖ *for* δυνατός LTTrAWHR

δυνατός.

Mat. 19:26 *trs* δυνατά πάντα T
Acts 25: 5 *trs* ἐν ὑμῖν, φησίν. δ. GEds
Ro. 14: 4 δυνατέω Eds
2 Co. 9: 8 δυνατέω LTTrAWHR
Rev. 6:15 mighty men—strong, ιωχυρος
    GEds

δύνω.

Mar. 1:32 ἔδυσεν LTTrAWH

δύο.

Mat. 11: 2 two of—by, διά Eds
    27:51 *trs* εἰς δ. after κάτω TTrAWH.
Lu. 10: 1, 17*seventy—add [δ. two] LWH
    17:35 *trs* ἔσονται δύο LTTrAWHR
    36 add *the verse* A.V.B.E, *see*
    ἀφίημι
    21: 2 *trs* λεπτά δύο TrWH
Acts 10:19*for τρεῖς WH
    23:23 *trs* τινας δύο TTrWH
Gal. 4:24 αἱ δ.—omit αἱ GEds
Rev. 9:16 δίς WH; *see* μυριάς
    11: 4 δ.²—αἱ δύο A.V.C GEds
    12:14 αἱ δύο LTTrWWHR, [αἱ] δ. A

δυσβάστακτος.

Mat. 23: 4 omit and grievous to be borne
    T[Tr]AWH

δυσεντερία, —ιον LTTrAWWH.

* δυσφημέω, to defame.

1Co. 4:13 δυσφημούμενοι *for* βλασφημούμενοι (-φημίω) TAWHR

δώδεκα.

Mar. 3:16*add *at commencement* καὶ
    ἐποίησεν τοὺς δώδεκα and he
    appointed the twelve TWH
    5:25 *trs* δώδεκα ἔτη TWH
Lu. 22:14 omit twelve LTTrAWHR
Acts 19: 7*δώδεκα *for* δεκαδύο LTTrAWWH
    24:11*δώδεκα *for* δεκαδύο LTTrAWH
Rev. 7: 5, 6, 7, 8*δώδεκα *for* ιβ̄ LTTrAWWH
    21:14*in them—on them twelve, ἐπ'
    αὐτῶν δώδεκα GEds

δωρεά.

Ro. 5:17 [of the gift] LWı

ἐά.

Mar. 1:24 omit let us alone LTTrAWHR

ἐάν.

Mat. 7: 9, 10 omit ἐ. LTTrAWHR
    10:14 ἄν LTTrAWH
    42 ἄν LTTrWH
    11: 6 ἄν LTTrWH
    12:36 omit ἐ. LTTrAWH
    14: 7 ἄν LTrA
    16:19 ἐ.¹—ἄν LTrA: ἐ.² ἄν Tr
    18: 5 ἄν LTr
    18 ἐ.¹—ἄν LTrA
    20: 7 omit LTTrAWHR, *see* δίκαιος
    26 ἄν LTrWH
    27 ἄν LTTrAWH
    23:18 ἄν LTTrAWH
Mar. 4:26 omit ἐ. TTrAWHR
    5:28*ὅτι—add ἐ. TAWHR
    6:10 ἄν LTr
    8:36 omit ἐ. TAWHR, *see* κερδαίνω
    9:37 ἄν δίς LTTrAWH
    10:11, 15 ἄν LTTrAWH
    43 ἄν LTTrWH
    11:23 omit whatsoever he saith
    TTr[A]WHR
    32 omit ἐ. read shall we say Eds
    14:14 ἄν LTrA
Lu. 4: 6 ἄν LTrAWH
    9:48 ἐ.¹—ἄν LWH: ἐ.² ἄν TWH
    10:22 ἄν LTrAWH

Lu. 11:12 omit ἐ. TTr[A]WHR
    12:38 καὶ ἐ.—κἄν TTrAWHR
    17:33 ἐ.²—ἄν TrAWHR
    18:17 ἄν LTTrAWH
Joh. 5:19 ἄν TWH
    8:55 καὶ ἐ.—κἄν LTTrWH
    12:32 ἄν WH
    13:20 ἄν LTTrAWH
    21:25 omit the verse T
Acts 7: 7 ἄν LTrWH
    9: 2 ἄν T
Ro. 15:24 ἐ.¹—ἄν Eds
1Co. 13: 2 καὶ ἐ.¹—κἄν LAWH: κ. ἐ.² κἄν
    TrAWH
    3 καὶ ἐ.¹—κἄν LTrAWH: κ. ἐ.³ κἄν
    LAWH
    16: 3 ἄν LTr
2Co. 8:12 ἄν T
Gal. 6: 7 ἄν LTr
Eph. 6: 8 ἄν Tr
Heb. 3: 6*for ἐάνπερ TTrAWHR, ἐάν[περ] L
1Joh. 2:28*for ὅταν LTTrAWHR
    3:22 ἄν WH

See also ἄν.

ἐάνπερ.

Heb. 3: 6 ἐάν TTrAWHR
    14 ἐάν περ LTr
    6: 3 ἐάν περ LTrW

ἑαυτοῦ, —ῷ, —όν.

Mat. 6:34 αὑτῆς AWH
    18:31*ἑαυτῶν *for* αὐτῶν LTTrAWH
    23:37 αὑτῆς T[Tr]AW[WH]
    25: 1*ἑαυτῶν *for* αὐτῶν LTrAWH
    3 ἑ.¹—αὑτῶν GLTrAW[WH]: omit
    their T
    4*ἑαυτῶν *for* αὐτῶν² LTWH
    7*ἑαυτῶν *for* αὐτῶν LTTrAWH
    27:35 omit that it might *to end of*
    verse GLTTrAWH
Mar. 1:27*ἑαυτούς *for* αὐτούς LTrAWH
    2:19 αὑτῶν TTrAWH, *see* ἔχω
    5:26 αὑτῆς GLTrAWWH
    6: 4*αὑτοῦ *for* αὐτοῦ¹ T
    8:35*ψυχὴν αὑτοῦ¹—ἑαυτοῦ ψ. WH
    *ψυχὴν αὑτοῦ²—ἑαυτοῦ ψ. GTrW
    9:33 omit among yourselves
    LTTrAWH
    10:26 αὑτόν WHR
    14:33 αὑτοῦ LTTrAWH
Lu. 2: 3*ἑαυτοῦ *for* ἰδίαν (-ιος) LTTrWHR
    39*ἑαυτῶν *for* αὐτῶν LTTrAWWH
    4:24*ἑαυτοῦ *for* αὐτοῦ T
    12:17 αὑτῷ WH
    21 αὑτῷ TWH
    47 αὑτοῦ LTTrAWH
    14:26 ἑ.¹—αὑτοῦ LTTrA
    27*ἑαυτοῦ *for* αὐτοῦ LTrAWH
    15: 5 αὑτοῦ TTrAWH
    20 αὑτοῦ LTTr
    16: 4*ἑαυτόν *for* αὐτῶν TTrAWH
    18:11 *trs* ταῦτα πρὸς ἑ. TrWH: omit
    with himself T
    13*ἑαυτοῦ *for* αὐτοῦ TrAWH
    19:35 αὑτῶν LTTrAWH
    36*ἑαυτοῦ *for* αὐτοῦ TrWH
    20:14 themselves—one another,
    ἀλλήλων TTrAWH
    22:17 εἰς ἑαυτούς LTTrAWHR
    66 αὑτῶν LTTrAWHR
    23:12 αὑτούς TTrAWH
    48 omit ἑ. TTrAWH
    24:12 αὑτόν Tr: omit the verse
    [L]T[Tr][[WH]]
    27 ἑαυτοῦ 8—αὐτοῦ EGLTr
Joh. 2:24 αὑτόν LTTrAWHR
    9:21*ἑαυτοῦ *for* αὐτοῦ TTrWHR
    13:32 αὑτῷ TTrWH
    17:13*ἑαυτοῖς *for* αὐτοῖς TTrAWH
    18:34 σεαυτοῦ LTrAWH
    19:12*ἑαυτοῦ *for* αὐτόν² GEds
    17*see αὑτοῦ
    20:10 αὑτούς TTrWH
Acts 14:14*ἑαυτῶν *for* αὐτῶν WH
    17 αὑτοῦ LTTrWH
    20:30*ἑαυτῶν *for* αὐτῶν² TTrAWH
    21:11*ἑαυτοῦ *for* αὐτοῦ Eds
    28:29 omit the verse LTTrAW=
Ro. 1:24 αὑτοῖς LTTrAWH
    27 αὑτοῖς WH
    13: 9 σεαυτόν LTTrAWH
    14:14 αὑτοῦ GLTrW
1Co. 7:38*add ἑ. *see* ἐκγαμίζω
    11: 5 αὑτῆς LTTrAWH
2Co. 3: 5 ἑ.²—αὑτῶν LTrWH
    13 αὑτοῦ LTrAWWHL
Gal. 5:14 σεαυτόν GEds
Eph. 2:15 αὑτῷ LTTrAWH
    4:16 αὑτοῦ T
    5:25 omit ἑ.¹ LTTrAWHR

Phil. 3:21 αὑτῷ LTTrAWHR
1Th. 5:13 αὑτοῖς TTr
2Th. 2: 6 αὑτοῦ TTrWHR
Heb. 1: 3 omit by himself LTTrAWHR
    10:34 ἑαυτούς LTTrWHR
    12: 3*αὐτόν—ἑαυτόν LTTrA, ἑαυτους
    WHR
    16*ἑαυτοῦ *for* αὐτοῦ LTTrAWH
Jas. 1:26*ἑαυτοῦ f. αὐτοῦ¹ WH: *for* α.² LWH
1Pet. 4:19 αὑτῶν LTTrAWH: omit ἑ. WH
1Joh.3:15*ἑαυτῷ *for* αὐτῷ LT
    5:10 αὑτῷ TTrAWH
    18 αὑτόν TTrAWH
    21 ἑαυτά LTTrAWH
Jude 19 separate—add ἑαυτούς them-
    selves A.V.B EG
Rev. 2: 2*add ἑ. GEds, *see* λέγω
    20 αὑτήν T
    4: 8 αὑτῶν GLTTrAWHR, *see* κατά
    8: 6 αὑτούς LTTrWHR
    10: 4 omit their voices GEds
    17:13 αὑτῶν Eds
    18: 7 αὑτήν Eds

ἐάω.

Acts 5:38 ἀφίημι LTTrAWHR
Rev. 2:20 ἀφίημι GEds

ἑβδομηκονταέξ, —τα ἕξ GLTTrWWHR.

Ἐβέρ, Ἔβερ, Ἔβερ A.V.Vul TrA.

Ἐβραϊκός.

Lu. 23:38 omit in letters of Greek and
    Latin, and Hebrew
    [L]TTr[A]WHR

Ἐβραῖος et Ἐβραΐς, Ἐ— WH

Ἐβραϊστί, Ἐ— WH.

Joh. 20:16*him—add Ἐβραϊστί in He-
    brew [L]TTrAWHR

ἐγγίζω.

Mat. 15: 8 omit draweth nigh unto me
    with their mouth, and
    GLTTrAWHR
Mar. 14:42 ἤγγισεν T
Lu. 15: 1 *trs* αὐτῷ ἐγγίζοντες LTTrA W WH
Jas. 4: 8 ἐ.²—ἐγγίσει WH

ἐγγράφω, ἐνγ— TWH.

Lu. 10:20*ἐγγέγραπται f. ἐγράφη (γράφω)
    TTrAWHR

ἐγείρω.

Mat. 1:24*ἐγερθεὶς *for* διεγερθεὶς (-γείρω)
    LTTrAWHR
    9: 5 ἔγειρε LTTrAWH
    6 ἔγειρε LTrWH
    10: 8 *trs* raise the dead, cleanse
    the lepers GEds
    17: 9*ἐγερθῇ *for* ἀναστῇ (ἀνίστημι)
    LTTrAWH
    20:19*ἐγερθήσεται *for* ἀναστήσεται
    (ἀνίστημι) TTrAWH
    27:52 ἠγέρθησαν LTTrAWH
Mar. 2: 9 ἔγειρε GLTW, ἔγειρον TrAWH
    11 ἔγειρε GLTTrAWWH
    3: 3 ἔγειρε GLTTrAWH
    4:38*ἐγείρουσιν *for* διεγείρουσιν
    (-ρω) TrAWHR
    5:41 ἔγειρε GLTTrAWH
    6:14*trs* ἐγήγερται ἐκ νεκ. LTTrWHR:
    ἀνίστημι A
    10:49 ἔγειρε GLTTrAWWH
Lu. 5:23, 24 ἔγειρε GLTTrAWWH
    6: 8 ἔγειρε GLTTrAWH
    7:16 ἠγέρθη LTTrAWH
    8:24 arose—woke διεγείρω TTrWHR
    54 ἔγειρε LTTrAWH
    9: 7 ἠγέρθη LTTrWHR
    22 ἀνίστημι LA
Joh. 5: 8 ἔγειρε LTTrAWH
    7:52 ἐγείρεται LTTrAWH
    11:29 ἠγέρθη LTrAWH
Acts 3: 6 ἔγειρε καὶ L[Tr]: omit rise up
    and T[A]WH
    10:26 *trs* ἤγειρεν αὐτόν LTTrAWH
    13:23 raised—brought, ἄγω GEds
Eph. 5:14 ἔγειρε GLTTrAWH
Phil. 1:16*ἐγείρειν *for* ἐπιφέρειν (-ρω) Eds
Rev.11: 1 ἔγειρε LTTrAWWH

ἐγκάθετος, ἐνκ— TWH.

ἐγκαίνια, ἐνκ— TWH.

ἐγκαινίζω, ἐνκ— TWH.

* ἐγκακέω, δεε ἐκκακέω.

ἐγκαταλείπω.

Mar. 15:34 trs ἐγκατέλιπές με LTTrAWH
Acts 2:27 ἐνκ– TWH
     31*ἐγκατελείφθη (ἐνκ– TWH) for
      κατελείφθη (καταλείπω)
      LTTrAWH
Ro. 9:29 ἐνκ– T
2 Ti. 4:10 ἐγκατέλειπεν WH
     16 ἐγκατέλειπον WH
Heb. 13: 5 ἐγκαταλείπω TA

ἐγκατοικέω, ἐνκ– TWH.

* ἐγκαυχάομαι, to pride oneself in.

2 Th. 1: 4 ἐγκαυχᾶσθαι (ἐνκ– TWH) for
      καυχᾶσθαι(–χάομαι)LTTrAWH

ἐγκεντρίζω, ἐνκ– TWH.

ἐγκοπή, ἐκκ– T. ἐνκ– WH.

1 Co. 9:12 trs τινα ἑ. Eds

ἐγκόπτω, ἐνκ– TWH.

Gal. 5: 7*ἐνέκοψεν for ἀνέκοψεν (ἀνα-
      κόπτω) GEds
1 Pet. 3: 7*ἐγκόπτεσθαι for ἐκ⟨όπτεσθαι
      (–τω) Eds

ἐγκρίνω, ἐνκ– TWH.

ἐγκρύπτω.

Lu. 13:21 κρύπτω TTrAWH

ἔγκυος, ἐνκ– WH.

ἐγχρίω.

Rev. 3:18 ἐγχρῖσαι GW, –ῖσαι to anoint
      LAWH, ἐγχρισαι TTr

ἐγώ.

Mat. 12:28 trs ἐγὼ after θεοῦ GLTTrAWWH
     20:22, 23 omit GLTTrAWH, see βαπ-
      τίζω
Mar. 1: 2 omit ἑ. LTrAWH
     14:19 omit and another (said, Is) it
      I ? TTrWH
Lu. 7:27 omit ἑ. LTTrAWH
     9: 9 omit ἑ.² T[Tr]WH
     10: 3 omit ἑ. LTTrAWH
     11:20*ἑ. ἐκβάλλω R, [ἑ.] ἐκ. TrWH
     24:39 trs ἐγώ εἰμι αὐτός LTTrAWH
Joh. 1:20 trs ἐγὼ οὐκ εἰμὶ LTTrAWH
     27†trs οὐκ εἰμὶ ἑ. ([ἑ.] LTrWH)
      TTrA
     3:28*εἶπον [ἑ.] WH, trs ἑ. οὐκ εἰμὶ L
     4:14*ἑ. δώσω ² TR
     5:36 omit ἑ.² LTTrAWH
     6:51 omit which I will give
      LTTrAWH
     13:36*ἑ. ὑπάγω T
     14:14 ἑ.—τοῦτο, read that I will do
      WH
     26*add at end ἑ. WH
     15:10 I—I also, κἀγώ T
     16: 7*γὰρ—add ἑ. L[A]w
     16 om. because I go to the Father
      TTrAWH : omit ἑ. G[A]w
     17 omit ἑ. Eds
     17:19 omit ἑ.¹ [L]T[WH]
     18:37 omit ἑ.¹ TTr[A]WH
Acts 20:26 I (am)—I am, εἰμί LTTrAWH
     23: 6 omit ἑ.² WH
     26:17*οὓς—add ἑ. GEds
     27:23*εἰμι—add ἑ. LT[A]
Ro. 7:20 omit ἑ.¹ LTr[A]WWH
2 Ti. 4: 1 omit ἑ. LGEds
Rev. 1:11 omit GEds, see ἄλφα
     2:22 omit ἑ. GEds
     5: 4 omit ἑ. T[TrWH]
     21: 2 omit I John GEds
     22:18*add ἑ. GEds, see μαρτυρεω
      See also κἀγώ.

Ἐζεκίας, Ἐ– WH.

ἐθελοθρησκεία, –κία TWH.

ἐθέλω, see θέλω.

ἐθνικός.

Mat. 5:47*ἐθνικοὶ for τελῶναι (–νης) GEds
3 Joh. 7*ἐθνικῶν for ἐθνῶν (–νος) Eds

ἔθνος.

Mat. 24: 9 τῶν ἑ.—omit τῶν R
Lu. 21:24 trs τὰ ἔθνη πάντα LTTrAWH
Acts 9:15 τῶν ἐθνῶν LR, [τῶν] ἑ. WH
     13:42 omit the Gentiles GEds
Ro. 15:11 trs πάντα τὰ ἔθνη τὸν κύριον
      LTTrAWH
1 Co. 1:23*ἔθνεσιν for Ἕλλησιν (–ην) GEds
     10:20 omit the Gentiles LTA[WH]
2 Ti. 1:11 omit of the Gentiles TWH
3 Joh. 7 ἐθνικός Eds
Rev. 14: 8 τὰ ἔθνη Eds
     15: 3*ἐθνῶν f. ἁγίων (–ιος) GLTTrAW
     20: 3 trs ἔτι τὰ ἔθνη GLTTrAWH

εἰ.

Mat. 20:15 εἰ 8—ᾗ A.V.B BGEds
     27:42 omit if TTrAWH
Mar. 11:26 omit the verse TTrWH
     14:29 trs εἰ καὶ TTrAWH
Lu. 6: 9*for τί (τίς) LTTrAWH
     11:11 ᾗ GLTTrAWH: omit WH, see
      ἄρτος
     14: 3 omit WH
     23:39 οὐχί, read Art not thou the
      Christ ? TTrAWH
Joh. 13:32 omit [LTrA]WH, see δοξάζω
Acts 8:37 omit the verse GLTTrAWH
     22:27 omit εἰ Eds
Ro. 2:17*εἰ δέ for ἴδε GEds
     11: 6 omit But if to end of verse
      GLTT[A]WH
1 Co. 15:44*εἰ ἔστιν, read If there is Eds
2 Co. 5:14 omit if Eds
     13: 4 omit though [L]TTrAWH
Heb. 6:14*εἰ μὴν for ἦ μὴν LTTrAWH
     12: 7 εἰς (omit if) LTTrAWH
Jas. 3: 3*εἰ δέ for ἰδού Eds
1 Pet. 2: 3*for εἴπερ LTTrWH

εἰ καί.

Mat. 26:33 omit καί GEds
2 Co. 12:15 omit καί LTTrAWH

εἰ μή.

Mat. 17:21 omit the verse T[TrA]WH
     19: 9 omit εἰ GLTTrAWWH
     17 omit GEds, see ἀγαθός
Mar. 9: 8*for ἀλλὰ LWH
Joh. 13:10*for ἢ LTrA[WH]R
Acts 21:25 omit LTTrWHR, see μηδείς
2 Co. 3: 1 ἢ μή A.V.B GLTTrAEds

εἴ περ, εἴπερ.

Ro. 3:30*for ἐπείπερ LTTrAWH
2 Co. 5: 3*for εἴ γε LTr
1 Pet. 2: 3 εἰ LTTrWH

εἴτε.

1 Co. 12:26 whether—if anything, εἴ τι LTr

εἴ τις, εἴ τι.

Mat. 18:28*εἴ τι for ὅ τι (ὅστις) GEds
Mar. 7:16 omit the verse T[TrA]WH
     8:34*for ὅστις LTrWH
Acts 24:20 omit εἴ, read what evil GEds
1 Co. 7:13*for ἥτις (ὅστις) T
     12:26*for εἴτε LTr
Rev. 13:10 qui in A.V. Vul

εἰδέω, εἴδω, οἶδα.

Mat. 2:11*εἶδον for εὗρον (εὑρίσκω)
      A.V.C GEds
     9: 4 εἰδὼς LTTrAWH
     11: 9†trs ἐξῆλ. ; προφήτην ἰδεῖν;
      (i. πρ. R) read why went ye
      out ? to see a prophet ?
      TAWH
     13:17 εἶδον—εἶδαν LTrWH, ἴδαν T
     25:37 εἴδαμεν TrWH
     38 εἴδαμεν WH
Mar. 1:24 οἴδαμεν we know T
     2:12 εἴδαμεν LTTrAWH
     6:33 εἶδαν WH
     48 ἰδὼν seeing LTTrAWH
     50 εἶδαν TTrWH
     9: 9 trs ἃ εἶδ. διηγήσωνται LTTrAWH
     14 εἶδον they saw TTrR, εἶδαν WH
     15 ἰδόντες LTTrAWH
     38 εἴδαμεν WH
     12:15 εἰδὼς—ἰδὼν having known T
     28 ἰδὼν having perceived LTT
     13:29 trs ἴδητε ταῦτα LTT–WH

Lu. 1:29 omit when she saw (him)
      GTTrAWH
     2:20 ἴδον T
     5: 2 ἴδεν T
     26 εἴδαμεν WH
     9:32 εἶδαν TWH
     47 εἰδὼς TWH
     49 εἴδαμεν WH
     55 omit and said to end of verse
      LTTrAWH
     10:24 εἶδον—ἴδαν T, εἶδαν TrAWH
     12:56*add ο. TrWH, see δοκιμάζω
     13:35 trs ἴδητέ με LTTrAWH
     19: 5 omit saw him, and TTr[A]WH
     20:13 om. when they see TTr[A]WH
     22:57 trs οὐκ ο. αὐτόν, γυναι TTrAWH
     23:34 see λέγω
Joh. 1:39(40) see—ye shall see, ὄπτομαι
      TTrAWH : ἑ.² εἶδαν LTTrAWH
     5:32 οἴδατε ye know T
     6:22 εἶδον LTTrAWH
     8:19 trs ἂν ᾔδειτε LTTrAWH
     56 ἴδῃ—εἴδῃ T
     14: 4 omit ye know² [L]TTrAWH
     51†trs οἴδαμεν TTr[A]WH
     7*ἂν ᾔδειτε for ἐγνώκειτε (γινώ-
      σκω) ἂν TrAWH
     19: 6 ἴδον T
Acts 4:20 εἴδαμεν LTTrAWH
     6:15 εἶδαν TrWH
     8:18*ἰδὼν for θεασάμενος (θεάομαι)
      GEds
     9:35 | 12:16 εἶδαν LTTrAWH
     22:18 ἴδον T
     28: 4 εἶδαν TrWH
1 Co. 2: 2 trs (om. τοῦ GEds) τι εἰδέναι
      GLTTrAWWH
     11 οἶδεν²—γινώσκω Eds
     8: 2 γινώσκω Eds
2 Co. 12: 3 omit I cannot tell L[WH]
Eph. 5: 5*ἴστε for ἐστέ GEds
     6:21 trs καὶ ὑμεῖς εἰδῆτε LTTr
Phil. 1:30 εἴδετε A.V. CEds
     2:26*ὑμᾶς—add [ἰδεῖν], read to see
      you LWH
Jas. 1:19*ἴστε for ὥστε LTTrAWH
     5:11 ἴδετε see A
1 Pet. 1: 8 ἰδόντες A.V.B Eds
     3: 9 omit knowing (read because
      ye are) LTTrAWH
3 Joh. 12 οἶδας thou knowest LTTrAWH
     14 trs σε ἰδεῖν LTTrAWWH
Rev. 1: 2 ἴδεν T
     20 om. which thou sawest² GEds
     2:17*οἶδεν for ἔγνω (γινώσκω) GEds
     4: 1 ἴδον T
     4 omit I saw GEds
     6: 1, 2, 5, 8, 9, 12 ἴδον T
     7: 1, 2, 9 | 8:2, 13 | 9:1, 17 ἴδον T
     13: 3 omit I saw GEds
     14: 1, 14 | 15:1.5 | 16:13 ἴδον T
     17: 6 εἶδον—εἶδα LTTrA
     19:19 | 20:1, 4 ἴδον T
     21: 2 trs εἶδον after ἁγίαν A, after
      καινήν GLTTrWWHR

εἰδωλεῖον, –λῖον TWH.

εἰδωλόθυτον.

1 Co. 10:19 trs that which is offered in
      sacrifice to idols is anything,
      or that the idol Eds
     28 offered in sacrifice unto idols
      —offered in sacrifice, ἱερόθυ-
      τος LTTrAWH
Rev. 2:20 trs φαγεῖν εἰδωλόθυτα GEds

εἰδωλολατρεία, –ρια WH.

εἴδωλον.

1 Co. 8: 7 trs ἕως ἄρτι τοῦ ε. Eds
     10:19 trs Eds, see εἰδωλόθυτον
Rev. 9:20 τὰ εἴδωλα A.V.C GEds

εἴην, εἴης, εἴη, &c.

Joh. 13:24 see λέγω
Acts 20:16*εἴη for ἦν LTTrAWH
Rev. 3:15 εἴης—ἧς GEds

εἰκῆ, εἰκῇ LWH.

Mat. 5:22 omit without a cause
      LT[TrA]WH

εἴκοσι.

Acts 1:15 εἴκοσι LTAWH
Rev. 4: 4 τοὺς ε.—omit τοὺς GTTrWHR
      trs ε. τέσσαρας θρόνους LA
     5:14 omit four (and) twenty GEds
     11:16 οἱ ε.—omit οἱ L[A]

εἰκοσιτρεῖς, —τέσσαρες, —πεντε ε.

(in two words by most Editors)

εἰκών

Rev. 13:15 τὴν ε.—τῇ εἰκόνι GTT.WWIR
16: 2 *trs* προσκυ. τῇ ε. αὐτοῦ GEds
20· 4 τῇ εἰκονι EG

εἰλικρίνεια, —νία TWI.

εἰλίσσω, ἐλίσσω LTTrAWWH.

εἰμί.

Acts 20:26*for ἐγώ LTTrAWH
1 Pet. 1:16 omit ε. Eds
Rev. 1:11 omit GEds, see ἄλφα
21: 6 omit ε. T[A]WH
22:13 omit ε. GEds

εἶναι.

Mar. 6:49 ἐστίν TWIR
10:44*for γενέσθαι (γίνομαι) LTrWHR
Lu. 14:27 *trs* εἶναί μου TTrAWH
33 *trs* εἶναί μου LTTrWH
Acts 8:37 omit the verse GLTTrAWHR
18: 5*Ἰουδαίους—add ε. read Jesus was LTTrWH
28: 6 *trs* αὐτὸν εἶναι θεόν LTTrAWWH
Ro. 6:11 omit to be GL[Tr]AW: *trs* εἶναι νεκροὺς μὲν TTrWH
Phil. 3: 8 omit ε² LTTrWHR
Rev. 2: 2 omit ε. LTTrAWHR

εἵνεκεν, see ἕνεκα.

εἴπερ, see under εἰ.

εἶπον.

(LTTrAWH at times read εἶπαν for εἶπον.)
Mat. 4: 3 ε.²—εἰπόν WI
9*εἶπεν for λέγει (—γω) LTTrAWH
8:22 said—saith, λέγω Eds
9:11 λέγω LTTrWI
12:47 omit the verse T[WI]
48 ε.²—λέγω LTTrAWH
13:28 said²—say, λέγω LTTrAWH
15: 4*εἶπεν f. ἐνετείλατο (ἐντέλλομαι) λέγων (—γω) LTrWH
12 said—say. λέγω LTTrAWH
17:20 said—saith, λέγω LTTrAWH
26*see λέγω
18:17 : 22:17 εἰπόν TWI
19:16 *trs* αὐτῷ εἶπεν LTTrAWH
18 φημί WH
20:13 *trs* ἑνὶ αὐτῶν εἶπεν TWI
22:37 φημί GLTTrAWWH
24: 3 εἰπόν WI
27:49*εἶπαν for ἔλεγον (λέγω) LTrWH
Mar. 1:42 omit as soon as he had spoken LTTrWH
2: 8 said—saith, λέγω TTrAWH
3:32 said—say, λέγω Eds
5: 7 said—saith, λέγω Eds
6:16 λέγω TTrAWH
31 said—saith, λέγω TTrAWH
7:27 λέγω LTTrAWH
36 λέγω TTrAWH
8: 7 omit ε. TA, see παρατίθημι
20 said—say, λέγω TAWH
26 omit nor tell it to any in the town TWIR
28*εἰπον for ἀπεκρίθησαν (ἀποκρίνομαι) TAWH, see λέγω
9:12 φημί TTrAWH
17 omit and said LTTrAWH
18 εἴπω TTrAWH
10:20 φημί TTrAWH
29 φημί TAWH
51*trs αὐτῷ ὁ Ἰησοῦς (εἶπεν for λέγει, —γω) TTrAWH
11: 6*εἶπεν f. ἐνετείλατο (ἐντέλλομαι) LTTrAWH
23 omit whatsoever he saith TTr[A]WH
12: 7 *trs* πρὸς ἑαυτοὺς εἶπαν TTrAWH
24 φημί TTrAWH
32 ε.²—εἶπες TWI
36 said¹—saith, λέγω W
36 said²—saith, λέγω GTr
43*εἶπεν f. λέγει (—γω) GLTTrWHR
13: 4 εἰπόν LTTrAWH
15: 2 said—saith, λέγω TTrAWH
12 λέγω TTrAWH
Lu. 2:15 λαλέω TWI
5:13 λέγω TWI
6:26 *trs* εἴπωσιν ὑμᾶς T
7:31 omit and the Lord said GEds
42 omit tell me LTTr[A]WH
9:21 λέγω GLTTrAWHR

Lu. 9:55 omit and said *to end of verse* LTTrAWH
10:22 omit A.V.B EGTr[A]WH, see μαθητής
40 ε.²—εἰπόν TWI
14:10 ἐρέω TTrWH
15:17 φημί TWIR
18:16 λέγω TTrAWIR
19:30 λέγω LTrWH
20: 2 ε.²—εἰπόν TTrAWH
22:31 omit and the Lord said T[Tr]AWH
58 φημί LTTrAWH
67 ε.¹—εἰπόν TTrAWH
24:40 omit the verse T[Tr][[WH]]
Joh. 1:15 ὃν ε.—ὁ εἰπών WH
4:17 ε.²—εἶπες TWH
5:15*εἶπεν for ἀνήγγειλεν (ἀναγγέλλω) TWI
19 λέγω WH
7:20 omit and said LTTrAWH
8:23 λέγω LTTrAWH
9:11 omit and said¹ [L]TTrAWH
25 omit and said Eds
36 omit and said L[AWH]
10:24 εἰπόν TWI
26 omit as I said unto you [L]TTr[A]WH
11:28 ε.²—εἰπασα TrWH
12:30 *trs* καὶ εἰπεν Ἰησοῦς WH
13:24*see λέγω
14:28 omit I said² GEds
18: 4 said—saith, λέγω LTTrAWH
29 said—saith, φημί TTrAWH
34 *trs* εἰπόν σοι TAWH
21: 6 said—saith, λέγω T
17 said²—saith, λέγω T
Acts 4:19 *trs* εἰπον πρὸς αὐτοὺςLTTrAWWH
5: 9 omit ε. LTTrAWH
7: 7 *trs* ὁ θεὸς εἶπεν LTTrAWWH
37 εἶπας LTTrAWH
8:37 omit the verse GLTTrAWHR
9: 5 omit κύριος ε. Eds
6 omit GEds, see κέντρον
19: 2 omit ε.² Eds
21:13*Παῦλος—add καὶ εἶπεν, read answered and said T
22:24 εἶπας LTTrAWWH
23: 7*εἰπόντος for λαλήσαντος (λαλέω) LTrWH
24:22 εἶπας LTTrAWWH
26:15 ε.¹—εἶπα LTTrAWH
29 omit ε. LTTrAWH
30 omit and when he had thus spoken GEds
27:35 εἶπας LTTrAWH
28:26 εἰπόν GLTTrAWH
29 omit the verse LTTrAWH
1 Co. 11:22 *trs* εἰπω ὑμῖν Eds

εἴπως, see under εἰ.

εἰρήνη.

Lu. 19:38 *trs* ἐν οὐρανῷ ε. TTrAWH
24:36 omit and saith *to end of ver.* T[[WH]]
Ro. 10:15 omit that preach the gospel of peace, and LTTr[A]WH
Eph. 2:17*and³—add εἰρήνην peace Eds

εἴρω, see ἐρέω.

εἰς.

Mat. 5:39*for ἐπί LTTrAWH
6:13 omit ε.² GEds, see αἰών
9:13 omit to repentance GEds
12:18 ἐν Tr: omit ε. LAWH
13:30 omit ε.¹ [Tr]A[WH]
52 omit ε. GTTrAWHR, see βασιλεία
14:34 ἐπί TTrWHR
34*land—add ε. unto TTrWH
18: 6*for ἐπί A
15 omit against thee LT[A]WH
29 omit at his feet GLTTr[A]WHR
20:18*add ε. T, see θάνατος
21: 1*for πρός LTTrAWH
46*for ὡς LTTrAWH
22: 5 ε.²—ἐπί LTTrAWH
24:16*for ἐπί LTrWH
27: 5*for ἐν LTrWH
Mar. 1:10*for ἐπί LTTrAWH
39*for ἐν GEds
2: 1 ἐν οἴκῳ LT[Tr]WH
18*for παρά T
17 omit to repentance GEds
22 omit ε.²—T[Tr]A[WH], see νέος
3: 7*for πρός GLT
4: 8*for ἐν¹ (εἰς) TTrWHR: for ἐν²³ TTr
15*for ἐν TrAWH. see καρδία

Mar. 4.18 ἐπί T
6:55*ε. Γεννησαρετ unto Gennesaret TWH
55*or οἶς—add ε. into [L]LTrAWH
7:31*for πρός GLTTrAWH
8:13 omit T[Tr]AWH, see πλοῖον
9:42 omit in me TAWH
43 omit ε.³—L[TTr][A]WH,see πῦρ
10:10*for ἐν LTTrAWH
11: 8 omit and strawed (them) in the way TTrAWH
13:15 omit into the house [L]TWIR
14: 6 εἰς ἐμέ—ἐν ἐμοί GEds
Lu. 2:42 omit to Jerusalem T[Tr]AWH
4: 1 into—in ἐν LTTrAWH
5 omit into an high mountain [L]TTrAWH
23*for ἐν¹ GLTTrAWH
29 ε. τὸ—ὥστε GLTTrAWH
43 ἐπί LTTrAWH
44*for ἐν TTrAWH
6:29*for ἐπί T
8: 8*for ἐπί GEds
43 omit ε. GEds, see ἰατρός
9:62 omit ε.² LTTrAWH, see βασιλεία
10:11*add ε. LTTrAWH, see πους
12:49 ἐπί Eds
14:28*for πρός GEds
17: 3 omit against thee LTTrAWH
18:13 omit upon LTTr[A]WH
19: 4*ε. τὸ ἔμπροσθεν T[A]WH
20:20 ε. τὸ—ὥστε LTTrAWH
21:14 ἐν LTTrAWH
22:10*οὗ—ε. ἣν LTTrAWH
17*ἑαυτοῖς—ε. ἑαυτούς LTTrAWH
23:19 ἐν TTrAWH
42*for ἐν WH
24:47*for καί² TWI
50 πρός LTTrAWH
51 omit and carried up into heaven T[[WH]]
Joh. 3:15 ε. αὐτόν—ἐν αὐτῷ TTrAWH
6:22 omit ε.¹—GLTTrAWH, see ἐκεῖνος
47 omit on me T[Tr]AWH
11:32 πρός TTrAWH
15:21*ὑμῖν—ε. ὑμᾶς LTTrAWH
16:13 ἐν T
21: 4 ἐπί LT
11*for ἐπί LTTrAWH
Acts 2: 5*for ἐν T
3:19 πρός TWI
4: 6 (5) ἐν LTTrAWWH
5:15*καὶ ε. for κατά LTTrWH
16 omit unto LTTrAWH
7:12*for ἐν Eds
9:21*for ἐν T
28*for ἐν¹ Eds
12:25*for ἐξ WH
14:21*and³—add ε. to LTTrAWH
21*and¹—add ε. to LTTrA[WH]R
25*for ἐν T, see Πέργη
16: 1*and¹—add ε. to LTTrWHR
7*for κατά² EEds
40 πρός GEds
18:21 omit LTTrAWH, see δεῖ
20:13 ἐπί LTTrAWH
23:15*for πρός Eds
24:11*for ἐν Eds
15 πρός T
25: 4*for ἐν¹ Eds
16 omit to die GEds
20 omit ε.¹ TT[A]WH
26: 6*for πρός Eds
20 omit throughout LTTr[A]WH
27: 2*πλεῖν—add ε. LTTr[A]WH
29 upon—against, κατά Eds
1 Co. 12:13 omit ε.² read of one Spirit Eds
2 Co. 9: 5 πρός LTrW
13: 4 [toward you] AWH
Gal. 3:17 omit in Christ LTTrAWH
Eph. 5:32 [εἰς²] LAWH
Phil. 3:14*for ἐπί LTTrAWH
21 omit that it may be GEds
Col. 1:10 omit ε.² GEds, see ἐπίγνωσις
2 Ti. 2:14 ἐπί LTTrAWH
Philem. 5*for πρός LTTrAWH
Heb.12: 7*for εἰ LTTrAWH
Jas. 3: 3*for πρός LTTrAWH
5:12 omit ε. A.V.B EGEds. see ὑπόκρισις
1 Pet. 1:23 omit for ever GEds
2: 2*add ε. GEds, see σωτηρία
5*πνευματικός—add ε. read for an holy LTTrAWH
3: 5*for ἐπί Eds
2 Pet. 2:17 omit for ever LTTrAWH
3: 9 to us-ward—because of you, δι' ὑμᾶς LT
1 Joh.5:13 omit ε.¹ GEds, see ὄνομα
3 Joh. 5 to—that, τοῦτο Eds
Rev. 5:14 omit GEds, see ζάω
13:10*τις¹—add ε. LTAWWHR

Rev. 16: 2 *trs* εἰς *and* ἐπί Eds
4 *omit* ε.² LTTₜₐWHR
17 into—upon, ἐπί GEds

εἶς, ἕν.

Mat. 9:18*ἄρχων—add εἰς A.V.C
GLTₜ[WH]R
18:14 ἕν LTTₜWH
24 *trs* εἰς αὐτῷ TWH
19:17 *see* ἀγαθός
24:40 *omit* ὁ *bis. read* one is taken, and one LTTₜₐWHR
26:22*εἰς ἕκαστος LTTₜₐWHR
Mar. 4: 8 some ἕν—εἰς *ter* A, unto εἰς *ter* TTₜR: ἕν¹—εἰς WH: ἕν²³—ἕν WH
20 some¹—in, ἐν TTₜWHR
20 some²³—in, ἐν TTₜ[WH]R
8:28 ἕνα—ὅτι εἰς LTTₜₐWHR
14:10 ὁ εἰς the one TTₜₐWHR
51 *omit* ε. LTₜWHR
15:36 τις TTₜₐWHR
Lu. 9: 8 τῳ TAWHR, τίς Tₜ
12:25 *om.* ε̃. *read* a cubit T[Tₜ]AWHR
17:34 [one]¹ LWH
34 ὁ ε.—*omit* ὁ GLTTₜAW
35 ἡ μία A.V.Eₜ EGLT[Tₜ]AWHR
36 *add* the verse A.V.B E, *see* ἀφίημι
18:10 ὁ ε.—*omit* ὁ LTₜAWH
20: 3 *omit* ε̃ LTTₜAWHR
23:17 *omit* the verse [L]TTₜAWHR
24:18 ὁ ε.—*omit* ὁ LTTₜAWHR
Joh. 6: 9 *omit* ἕν [L]TTₜ[A]WHR
17:21 *omit* one² [L]TTₜAWHR
21:25 *omit* the verse T
Acts 4:32 καρδία—*add* unum A.V. Vul
1 Co. 6: 5 *omit* ε. LTTₜAWHR, *see* οὐδέ
12: 9*ἐνὶ *for* αὐτῷ² LTTₜAWHR
12 *omit* one² (τοῦ ἑνός) Eds
26 *omit* ἕν² *read* a member TTₜ[A]WHR
Jas. 4:13 *omit* ε̃. LTTₜWHR
1 Joh. 5: 7 *omit* GEds, *see* λόγος
Rev. 4: 8*add ἕν GLTAWHR, *see* κατά
22: 2 *omit* ε̃. GEds

εἰσάγω.

Acts 22:24*trs ὁ χιλίαρχος (εἰσάγεσθαι *for* ἄγεσθαι, ἄγω) αὐτὸν GLTTₜAWWH

εἰσέρχομαι.

Mat. 2:21*εἰσῆλθεν *for* ἦλθεν (ἔρχομαι) LTTₜAWH
7:13 ε.¹—εἰσέλθατε LTTₜAWH
8: 5 εἰσελθόντος LTTₜAWH
9:18*εἰσελθὼν *for* ἐλθὼν (ἔρχομαι) TAW
17:25 εἰσελθόντα LT, ἔρχομαι TₜAWH
19:24*εἰσελθεῖν *for* διελθεῖν (διέρχομαι) GTTₜAWH
24 *omit* to enter T[Tₜ]AWH: *trs* ε. *after* πλούσιον LTₜ
Mar. 1:21 *omit* ε. *read* he taught in the synagogue T[Tₜ]A
2: 1†*trs* ε. πάλιν LW: εἰσελθὼν π. TTₜAWHR
7:25*εἰσελθοῦσα *for* ἐλθοῦσα (ἔρχομαι) T
9:28 εἰσελθόντος αὐτοῦ LTTₜWHR
10:25 ε.¹—διέρχομαι A.V.B EGEds
13:15 εἰσελθάτω LTTₜWH
14:38 ἔρχομαι TAWH
16: 5 ἔρχομαι A
Lu. 8:33 εἰσῆλθον LTTₜAWWH
51 ε.¹—ἔρχομαι GLTTₜWWHR
10: 5†*trs* εἰσέλθητε οἰκίαν TTₜAWHR: οἰ. εἰσέλ. L
10 εἰσέλθητε LTTₜAWH
11:52 ε.¹—εἰσήλθατε GLTTₜAWH
18:24 εἰσπορεύομαι TTₜAWH
Acts 10:24 εἰσῆλθεν he entered LTₜWH, εἰσῆλθαν T
25 τοῦ εἰσελθεῖν GEds
11: 3†*trs* ε. (εἰσῆλθεν he went in TₜWH) *before* πρὸς LTTₜAWWH
20 ἔρχομαι GEds
13:14 ἔρχομαι TTₜWHR
18: 7*εἰσῆλθεν *for* ἦλθεν (ἔρχομαι) LT
28:16*εἰσήλθομεν LTAR, —θαμεν TₜWH, *for* ἤλθομεν (ἔρχομαι)
Jas. 5: 4 εἰσεληλύθαν LTTₜAWH
2 Joh. 7 are entered—are gone forth, ἐξέρχομαι Eds

εἰσίν.

Mat. 11: 8 *omit* ε. T[A]WH
20:16 *omit* T[TₜA]WHR, *see* πόλυς
Mar. 4:18 *omit* οὗτοί ε.² A.V.C
8: 3*for* ἥκασιν (ἥκω) AWH
Lu. 14:17*for* ἐστίν T

Joh. 10:12 ἐστίν LTTₜAWH
17: 7*for* ἐστίν TTₜAWH
Acts 23:21 *trs* εἰσὶν ἕτοιμοι LTTₜAWWH
1 Co. 14:10*for* ἐστίν Eds
37 ἐστίν Eds
Gal. 3: 7 *trs* υἱοί εἰσιν LTTₜWH
1 Ti. 5:25*for* ἐστίν W
1 Joh. 5: 7, 8 *omit* in heaven to in earth (ver. 8) GEds
Rev. 4:11 they are—they were, ἦσαν (ἦν) GEds
9:19 ἐστίν A.V.C GEds, *see* ἐξουσία
14: 4 *omit* ε.³ LTTₜAWH
17: 9 *trs* ἑπτὰ ὄρη ε. GLTTₜAWHR
19: 9 *trs* τοῦ θεοῦ ε. LTTₜAWHR

εἰσπηδάω.

Acts 14:14 ran in—sprang forth, ἐκπηδάω GEds

εἰσπορεύομαι.

Lu. 18:24*trs εἰσπορεύονται *for* εἰσελεύσονται (εἰσέρχομαι) *after* θεοῦ TTₜAWH

εἰσφέρω.

Lu. 12:11*εἰσφέρωσιν *for* προσφέρωσιν (-ρω) TTₜAWHR

εἶτα.

Mar. 4:28 εἶτεν *bis* TWH
Joh. 2: 3*add ε. T, *see* οἶνος
1 Co. 12:28 ἔπειτα LTTₜAWH
15: 5 ἔπειτα TT
7 ἔπειτα TA

εἴτε *see under* εἰ.

ἐκ, ἐξ.

Mat. 7: 4*for* ἀπό LTTₜWHR
10:14*dust—add ἐκ, read from your feet LT
13: 1*for* ἀπό LT
17: 9*for* ἀπό GEds
18:19*add ἐξ LTTₜAWH, *see* συμφωνέω
19:20 *om.* from my youth up LTTₜA
23:25 *omit* ἐξ L[Tₜ] (WH
24:29*for* ἀπό T
26:44 *omit* the third time [L]A
Mar. 1:10*for* ἀπό LTTₜAWHR
6:16 *omit* from the dead T[Tₜ]AWHR
51 *omit* beyond measure [Tₜ]WHR
7:15*for* ἀπό LTTₜAWHR, *see* ἄνθρωπος
9: 9*for* ἀπό LWH
21*ἐκ παιδιόθεν from a child Eds
12:33 *omit* and with all the soul [L]TWHR
13: 1*εἰς—add ἐκ Tₜ[A]
25*see ἐκπίπτω
14:20 *omit* ἐκ T[Tₜ]WH
31*see ἐκπερισσῶς
16: 3 ἀπό LTₜ
14*add ἐκ L[WH], *see* νεκρός
Lu. 1:35*born,—add ἐκ σοῦ A.V.B[L]
61*for* ἐν LTTₜAWH
4:35 ἀπό LTTₜAWH
38 out of—from, ἀπό TTₜAWHR
5: 3 out of—in, ἐν T
8: 3*for* ἀπό LTTₜAWH
27 *omit* ἐκ² TTₜWH, *see* χρόνος
10:27 ἐξ²³—ἐν LTTₜWH, *see* ψυχή
11:11*δέ—add ἐξ Eds
15:16*for* ἀπό WH
16: 4*μετασταθῶ—add ἐκ[L]TTₜAWH
22:16 thereof—it. αὐτό LTTₜAWH
Joh. 6:38 ἀπό LTTₜAWH
66*πολλοὶ—add ἐκ [L]Tₜ[A]WH
12: 3*ἦν—add ἐκ TAWH
4 *omit* ἐκ Tₜ WH
13:23*εἰς—add ἐκ GEds
16:28*for* παρά LTTₜAWH
18: 3*ἐκ ([ἐκ]WH) τῶν Φαρισαίων from the Pharisees TWH
Acts 1:25 ἀπό Eds
7: 3 *omit* ἐκ² [L]Tₜ[A]WH
8:37 *omit* the verse GLTTₜAWH
9: 3*for* ἀπό LTTₜAWH
12:25 from—to, εἰς WH
13:42 *om.* out of the synagogue GEds
16:40 ἀπό TWH
18: 2 ἀπό Eds
23:30*ἐξαυτῆς straightway—ἐξ αὐτῶν by them LTTₜ: ἐξ αὐτῆς A
24: 7 *omit* LTT[A]WHR, *see* κρίνω
26:17*ἐκ τῶν ἐθνῶν from the Gentiles LTTₜAWHR
27:34 ἀπό LTTₜAWH
28: 3 ἀπό Eds
Ro. 8:34*add ἐκ [WH]R, *see* νεκρός
11: 6 *omit* But if (it be) to end of verse GLTT₍[A]WHR

1 Co. 9: 7 *omit* of¹ Eds
2 Co. 2:16*ὀσμὴ bis—add ἐκ, read from death from life LTTₜAWHR
9: 2 *omit* ἐξ LTTₜ[A]WH
Gal. 3:21 ἐν WH, *see* νόμος
Eph. 5:30 *omit* ἐκ bis LTTₜ[A]WHR, *see* σάρξ
Phil. 3:11*τὴν ἐκ νεκρῶν from the dead Eds
1 Th. 1:10*for* ἀπό TTₜWHR
Jas. 2:18 ἐκ¹ by—χωρίς without A.V.B GEds
3 Joh. 10 *omit* ἐκ T
Rev. 1: 5 *omit* ἐκ GEds
5*for* ἀπό² LTTₜAWHR
2: 9*βλασφημίαν—add ἐκ GEds
6: 4*for* ἀπό GLTTₜAW[WH]R
10*for* ἀπό Eds
7:17*for* ἀπό GEds
9:18 *omit* ἐκ²³ GEds
13: 3*μίαν—add ἐκ GEds
15: 2 *om.* over his mark (and) GEds
16: 7 *omit* another out of GEds
11 *omit* ἐκ² A.V. Vul
17*for* ἀπό¹ LTTₜAWH
19: 5 out of—from, ἀπό LTTₜAWWHR
21: 4*for* ἀπό LTTₜAWH
9*εἰς—add ἐκ LTTₜAWH
22:19 *omit* out of ² L[Tₜ A]
See also ἐξαυτῆς.

ἕκαστος.

1 Co. 10:24 *omit* every man GEds
Eph. 6: 8†*trs* ἕκαστος ὃ (*omit* ὁ TAWH) ἐάν (ἄν Tₜ) τι (*om.* τι LTₜR) Eds
Phil. 2: 4 ε̃.¹—ἕκαστοι LTTₜAWHR: ε̃.²—ἕκαστοι GEds
Rev. 4: 8*see κατά
6:11 *omit* every one of GW: ἑκάστῳ LTTₜ[A]WHR

ἑκατόν.

Rev. 7: 4 *see* ρμδ´

ἑκατονταπλασίων.

Mat. 19:29 an hundredfold—many times more πολλαπλασίων LTTₜAWH

ἑκατοντάρχης, *see* ἑκατόνταρχος.

ἑκατόνταρχος.

Mat. 8: 5, 8 ἑκατοντάρχης T
13 —χη GLTTₜAWWH
27:54 —χης T
Lu. 7: 6 —χης TWH: *trs* φίλους ὁ ἑ. TTₜAWH
23:47 —χις TTₜWH
Acts 21:32 —χας LTTₜAWWH
22:26 —χης LTWH
23:23 —χων WH: 27: 6 —χης LTTₜAWH
27:11 —χης GLTTₜAWH
43 —χης LTTₜAWH
28:16 *omit* the centurion to of the guard: but LTTₜAWHR

* ἐκβαίνω, to go out.

Heb.11:15 ἐξέβησαν *for* ἐξῆλθον (ἐξέρχομαι) Eds

ἐκβάλλω.

Mat. 8:12 shall be cast out—shall go forth, ἐξέρχομαι T
25:30 ἐκβάλετε GLTTₜAWWH
Mar. 5:40 ὁ δὲ ε.—αὐτὸς δὲ ε. LTTₜAWH
7:26 ἐκβάλῃ GLTTₜAWWH
Lu. 6:42 *trs* ἐκβαλεῖν to end of verse TAWH
8:54 *omit* put them all out, and LTTₜAWH
9:40 ἐκβάλωσιν GEds
10: 2†*trs* ἐργάτας ἐκβάλῃ TTₜAWH, ἐκβάλῃ ἐρ. GLW

ἐκγαμίζω.

Mat. 22:30 γαμίζω LTTₜAWH
24:38 γαμίζω TWH
Lu. 17:27 γαμίζω LTTₜAWH
1 Co. 7:38 ε̃.¹—γαμίζων τὴν παρθένον ἑαυτοῦ (ἑα. πα. TWH) giveth his own virgin in marriage LTTₜ[A]WHR
38 ε̃.²—γαμίζω GLTTₜWHR, [ἐκ]γ. A

ἐκγαμίσκομαι.

Lu. 20:34 γαμίσκομαι LTTₜAWHR
35 γαμίζω LTTₜWHR, γαμίσκομαι A

ἐκδέχομαι.

Joh. 5: 3 *omit* waiting for to end of verse 4 [G]TTₜAWHR
1 Pet. 3:20 ἀπεκδέχομαι GEds

ἐκδίδωμι.
Mat.21:33 ἐξέδετο TAWH
41 ἐκδώσεται GLTTrAWWH
Mar.12: 1 ἐξέδετο TAWH
Lu. 20: 9 ἐξέδετο TAWH

ἐκδιώκω.
Lu. 11:49 διώκω WHR : [ἐκ]διώξουσιν TrA

ἐκδύω.
Mat.27:31 ἐκδύσαντες T

ἐκεῖ.
Mar. 1:13 omit there GEds
6:55 omit ἐ. LT[Tr]WHR
14:15 κἀκεῖ T καὶ ἐ. TrAWHR and there
Lu. 10: 6 trs ἐκεῖ ᾖ WH
17:23trs see there; or (omit or TTrR) see here TTrAWH
Acts14:28 omit there GEds
2 Co. 3:17 omit there Eds
Rev.12: 6*ἔχει—add ἐ. GTAWHR
22: 5 there—longer ἔτι GEds
See also κἀκεῖ.

ἐκεῖθεν.
Mar. 1:19 omit thence [L]LTTrAWHR
9:30 καὶ ἐ.—κἀκεῖθεν LTTrAWH
10: 1*καὶ ἐ. for κἀκεῖθεν LTT,AWH
Acts16:12 ἐ. τε—κἀκεῖθεν Eds
27:12*for κἀκεῖθεν LTTrAWHR
Rev. 22: 2*for ἐντεῦθεν² Eds

ἐκεῖνος.
Mat.18: 7 omit ἐ. read the man LTTrWH
26*δοῦλος ἐκεῖνος that servant T
27 om. ἐ. read the servant L[WH]
24:38*ἡμέραις—add ἐκείναις, read those days L[TrWH]R
48 om. ἐ. read the evil servant T
Mar. 2:20 ἐκείνῃ GEds, see ἡμέρα
4:20*ἐκεῖνοι for οὗτοι TTrAWH
6:11 omit verily to end of verse G[L]TTrAWH
7:15 omit those T[Tr]WH
Lu. 7:21*ἐκείνῃ for αὐτῇ TTrAWH
9:34 ἐ εἰσελθεῖν—εἰσ. αὐτούς TTrAWH
12:38 omit those servants T
14:21 17: 9 omit ἐ. read the servant LTTrAWH
18:14 ἢ ἐ.—παρ' ἐκεῖνον LTrAWH
19:27 those—these, τούτους TTrAWHR
20: 1 om. ἐ. read the days LTTrAWH
Joh. 5:37*ἐκεῖνος for αὐτός TTrAWH
6:22 omit that whereinto his disciples were entered GLTTrAWH
8:10 omit those thine accusers WH
13: 6 omit ἐκεῖνος LT[Tr]AWH
19:15*ἐκραύγασαν (om. οἱ δὲ)—add οὖν ἐκεῖνοι, read they therefore cried out TTrAWH
31 ἐκείνου ε—ἐκείνη B
Acts10: 9 αὐτῶν T
10 αὐτῶν Eds
Ro. 11:23 καὶ ἐ.—κἀκεῖνος GLTTrAWWH
Heb. 3:10 that—this, ταύτῃ Eds
Rev.16:14 omit ἐ. read the great LTTrAWHR
See also κἀκεῖνος.

ἐκζητέω.
Ro. 3:11 ὁ ἐ.—omit ὁ [L]WH

* ἐκζήτησις a seeking out.
1 Ti. 1: 4 ἐκζητήσεις for ζητήσεις (-ησις) TTrWHR

ἐκθαμβέω.
Mar. 9:15 ἐξεθαμβήθησαν LTTrAWH

* ἐκθαυμάζω, to marvel greatly.
Mar.12:17 ἐξεθαύμαζον for ἐθαύμασαν (θαυμάζω) TWHR

ἐκκακέω.
ἐγκακέω LTTrAWH, ἐγκ- or ἐνκ- TWH

ἐκκλάζω, ἐκκλάω.
Ro. 11:20 κλάζω LTr

ἐκκλησία.
Acts 2:47 omit to the church LTTrAWH
9:31 ἡμὲν οὖν ἐκκλησία the church Eds
Ro. 16:23 trs ὅλης τῆς ἐ. LTTrAWH

---

1 Co.11:18 the church—omit τῇ, read in assembly GEds
14:35 trs λαλεῖν ἐν ἐ. LTTrAWHR
Rev. 2: 1 τῷ ἐν Ἐφέσῳ ἐ. LTrWHR
8 τῆς—τῷ LWHR: trs ἐν Σμύρνῃ (Ζμ- T) ἐ. GEds
18 τῷ ἐν Θ. ἐ. LWH

ἐκκλίνω.
Ro. 16:17 ἐκκλίνετε TTrWH

ἐκκόπτω.
1 Pet. 3: 7 ἐγκόπτω GEds

* ἐκκράζω, to cry out.
Acts 24:21 ἐκέκραξα for ἔκραξα (κράζω) TTrAWH

ἐκκρέμαμαι.
Lu. 19:48 ἐξεκρέμετο TWH

ἐκλέγω.
Lu. 9:35*ἐκλελεγμένος for ἀγαπητός TTrAWH
Acts 1:24 trs ὃν ἐκ τούτων τῶν δύο ἕνα GEds
15: 7†trs ἐν ὑμῖν (ἡμῖν W) ἐ. ὁ θεὸς Eds
25 ἐκλεξαμένοις, read having chosen, to send men LTrWH

ἐκλείπω.
Lu. 16: 9 ἐκλίπῃ it shall fail LTTrAWHR
22:32 ἐκλίπῃ LTTrAWH
23:45*for σκοτίζομαι TWHR, see ἥλιος

ἐκλεκτός.
Mat. 20:16 omit T[TrA]WHR, see πολύς
1 Pet. 2: 6 trs ἐκλεκτὸν ἀκρογωνιαῖον WH
2 Joh. 1,13 Ἐκλεκτός (as a proper name)s

ἐκλύω.
Mat. 9:36 fainted—were harassed, σκύλλω GEds

ἐκμάσσω.
Lu. 7:38 ἐξέμαξεν TR

ἐκπειράζω.
1 Co.10: 9*ἐξεπείρασαν for ἐπείρασαν (πειράζω) T

* ἐκπερισσῶς, exceedingly.
Mar.14:31 for ἐκ περισσοῦ LTTrAWHR

* ἐκπηδάω, to leap forth.
Acts 14:14 ἐξεπήδησαν for εἰσεπήδησαν (εἰσπηδάω) GEds

ἐκπίπτω.
Mar. 13:25†trs ἔσονται ἐκ τοῦ οὐρανοῦ πίπτοντες (read from heaven) LTTrAWH
Acts 12: 7 ἐξέπεσαν LTTrAWH
27:29 ἐκπέσωμεν A.V.C GEds
1 Co.13: 8 πίπτω LTTrAWH
Rev. 2: 5 πίπτω GEds

ἐκπλήσσω, -ττω.
Mar.11:18 ἐξεπλήσσοντο T

ἐκπορεύομαι.
Mat. 17:21 omit the verse T[TrA]WHR
Mar. 11:19 ἐξεπορεύοντο they went LTrWH
Acts 19:12*ἐκπορεύεσθαι for ἐξέρχεσθαι (ἐξέρχομαι) GEds
Rev. 16:14 ἐκπορεύεσθαι s—ἃ (omit & L)
19:21 ἐξέρχομαι Eds

* ἐκσώζω, to preserve from danger.
Acts 27:39*ἐκσῶσαι for ἐξῶσαι (-ωθέω) WH

ἐκτεν ττερον.
Lu. 22:43, 44 the verses [L][[WH]]

ἐκτενής.
Acts 12: 5 ἐκτενῶς LTTrAWHR

ἐκτενῶς.
Acts 12: 5*for ἐκτενής LTTrAWHR

ἐκτίθημι.
Acts 7:? ἐκτεθέντος LTTrAWH

ἐκτός.
2 Co. 12: 3 out of—apart from, χωρίς LTTrAWHR

ἐκτρέφω.
Rev. 12: 6*ἐκτρέφωσιν for τρέφωσιν (-ω) W

ἐκφέρω.
Mar. 8:23*ἐξήνεγκεν for ἐξήγαγεν (ἐξάγω) TTrAWHR

ἐκφεύγω.
Heb.12:25*ἐξεφύγον for ἔφυγον (φεύγω) LTTrAWHR

ἐκφύω.
Mat. 24:32 ἐκφυῇ LTrA
Mar. 13:28 ἐκφυῇ s—ἐκφύῃ FGTWHR

ἐκχέω.
Mar. 2:22 omit ἐ. read the wine perisheth, and the bottles TTrAWH
Lu. 11:50*ἐκκεχυμένον for ἐκχυνόμενον (ἐκχύνω) TrWH
Acts 22:20 ἐκχυννω LTTrAWH
Rev. 16: 1 ἐκχέετε LTAWH

ἐκχύνω.
Mat. 23:35 26:28 ἐκχυννόμενον LTTrAWH
Mar. 14:24 ἐκχυννόμενον LTTrAWH: †trs ἐ. ὑπὲρ πολλῶν TTrA
Lu. 11:50 ἐκχυννόμενον LTA: ἐκχέω TrWH
22:20 ἐκχυννόμενον LTTrAWH
Acts 22:20*ἐξ-χυννετο for ἐξεχεῖτο (ἐκχέω) LTTrAWH

Ἐλαμίτης, —μείτην TWH.

ἐλεαω, see ἐλεεω.

* ἐλεγμός, a refuting, reproving
2 Ti. 3:16 ἐλεγμόν for ἔλεγχον (-χος) LTTrAWHR

ἔλεγχος.
2 Ti. 3:16 ἐλεγμός LTTrAWHR

ἐλέγχω.
Joh. 8: 9 omit being convicted by(their own) conscience WHR
Jude 15*ἐλέγξαι for ἐξελέγξαι (-γχω) LTTrAWHR
22*ἐλέγχετε for ἐλεεῖτε (ἐλεάω) LTTrAW

ἐλεεινός.
Rev. 3:17 ὁ ἐ. GL, [ὁ] ἐλεινός A

ἐλεέω, ἐλεάω.
Ro. 9:16 ἐλεῶντος LTTrAWH
Phil. 2:27 trs ἠλέησεν αὐτὸν LTTrAWWH
Jude 22 ἐλέγχετε (-χω) διακρινομενους. read and some convict, when contending LTTrAW:ἐλεᾶτε ὅ. WHR
23*add ἐ. Eds, see φόβος

ἐλεημοσυνη.
Mat. 6: 1 alms—righteousness, δικαιοσύνη GEds
4 trs ἡ σοῦ ἐ. ᾖ T

ἔλεος.
Mat. 9:13 12:7 ἔλεος LTTrAWH
23:23 τὸ ἔλεος LTTrAWH
Tit. 1: 4 omit mercy TTrAWWHR
3: 5 τὸ αὐτοῦ ἔλεος Eds
Heb. 4:16 ἔλεος Eds

ἐλεύθερος.
1 Co. 9: 1 trs Am I not free? am I not an apostle? GEds

* ἔλιγμα, anything tangled.
Joh. 19:39 for μίγμα WH

Ἐλισάβετ, Ἐλει- WH.
Lu. 1: 7 trs ἦν ἡ (omit ἡ L[TrWH]) Ἐ. LTTrAWHR

Ἐλισσαῖος, Ἐ- LT, —ισα- LTTrAWH.
Lu. 4:27 trs ἐν τῷ Ἰσραὴλ ἐπὶ Ἐ. τοῦ προφήτου LTTrAWHR

ἐλίσσω.
Heb. 1:12 shalt thou fold up—shalt thou change, ἀλλάσσω T

ἑλκύομαι.

Lu. 16:20 εἱλκωμένος LTTrAWWH

ἑλκύω.

Joh. 21: 6 ἑλκύσαι WHR

Ἕλλην.

Joh. 12:20 trs Ἕλληνές τινες LTTrAWH
Acts 11:20*Ἕλληνας for Ἑλληνιστάς GLTTrAR
18:17 omit the Greeks Eds
1 Co. 1:23 Greeks—Gentiles ἔθνος GEds

Ἑλληνικός

Lu. 23:38 omit in letters of Greek, and Latin, and Hebrew [L]TTr[A]WHR

Ἑλληνιστής.

Acts 11:20 Grecians—Greeks, Ἕλλην GLTTrAR

Ἑλληνιστί.

Joh. 19:20 trs Latin (and) Greek TTrAWHR

ἐλλογέω, -άω.

Ro. 5:13 ἐλλογᾶται WH
Philem. 18 ἐλλόγα LTTrAWH

Ἐλμωδάμ, Ἐ— L, —μαδάμ LTTrWHR.

ἐλπίζω.

1 Co. 15:19 trs ἐν χριστῷ ἠλ. ἐσμὲν Eds

ἐλπίς.

Acts 27:20 trs ἐλπὶς πᾶσα LTTrAWH
1 Co. 9:10 trs ὀφείλει ἐπ᾽ ἐ. LTTr WHR
10 omit of his hope GEds
10 trs ἐπ᾽ ἐ. τοῦ μετέχειν in hope of partaking GEds

Ἐλωΐ, -ί WH, Ἐλωΐ LTA.

Mat. 27:46*Ἐλωΐ for Ἠλί bis W

ἐμαυτοῦ.

2 Co. 11: 9 trs ἐμαυτὸν ὑμῖν LTTrAWHR

ἐμβαίνω.

Mat. 14:32 ἀναβαίνω LTTrAWHR
15:39 ἀναβαίνω GTrAW
Mar. 5:18 ἐμβαίνοντος, as he was coming Eds
8:13 trs πάλιν ἐμβὰς LTTrAWHR
Joh. 5: 4 omit waiting for (ver. 3) to end of verse 4 [G]TTrAWHR
6:22 omit that whereinto his disciples were entered GLTTrAWHR
21: 3*ἐνέβησαν for ἀνέβησαν (ἀναβαίνω) GEds
Acts 21: 6*ἐνέβημεν for ἐπέβημεν (ἐπιβαίνω) LTrWHR

ἐμβάπτω.

Joh. 13:26 βάπτω TTrAWHR

ἐμβλέπω.

Mar. 8:25 ἐνέβλεπεν LTTrAWHR
Acts 1:11 βλέπω TTrWHR

ἐμβριμάομαι.

Mat. 9:30 ἐνεβριμήθη LTTrAWH
Mar. 14: 5 ἐνεβριμοῦντο T
Joh. 11:38 ἐμβριμούμενος T

ἐμέ.

Mar. 9:42 omit in me TAWH
14: 6 εἰς ἐ.—ἐν ἐμοὶ GEds
Joh. 6:47 omit on me T[Tr]WHR
9: 4 I—we, ἡμᾶς TTrWHR
Philem. 17 ἐ.¹—μέ GEds
See also ἐμοί and μέ.

ἐμμένω.

Acts 28:30*ἐνέμεινεν for ἔμεινεν (μένω) TTrAWHR

Ἐμμόρ, Ἐ— WH, —μώρ LTTrAWWH.

Ἐμόρ A.V.†Er

ἐμοί.

Mat. 18:26 ἐμέ Tr
29 ἐμέ LTrA
Mar. 14:27 omit because of me TTrAWHR

Joh. 8:12 μοι LTrWH
Acts 24:20 omit in me LT[TrA]WHR
See also ἐμέ and μοι.

ἐμός.

Joh. 10:14 ἐμῶν—ἐμά LTTrAWHR, see γινώσκω
1 Co. 9: 2 τῆς ἐμῆς—μοῦ τῆς LTTrAWHR
2 Ti. 4: 6 ἐμῆς ἀναλύσεως—ἀ. μοῦ LTTrWH

ἐμοῦ.

Mat. 26:42 omit from me [L]TTrAWHR
Joh. 6:51*τοῦ ἐ. for τούτου τοῦ T
10: 8 trs ἦλθον πρὸ ἐ. GLTrAWHR: omit before me T
13:18 μετ᾽ ἐ.—μοῦ, read my bread TrAWHR
See also μοῦ.

* ἐμπαιγμονή, mockery.

2 Pet. 3: 3 ἡμερῶν—add ἐν ἐμπαιγμονῇ, read scoffers with scoffing GEds

ἐμπαίζω.

Mat. 27:29 ἐνέπαιξαν TWH
Lu. 14:29 trs αὐτῷ ἐμπαίζειν LTTrAWH
23:36 ἐνέπαιξαν TAWH

ἐμπεριπατέω, ἐνπ— TWH.

* ἐμπιπράω, to kindle.

Acts 28: 6 ἐμπιπρᾶσθαι for πίμπρασθαι (πίμπραμαι) T

ἐμπίπτω.

Lu. 6:39*ἐμπεσοῦνται for πεσοῦνται (πίπτω) LTTrAWHR
14: 5 πίπτω LTTrAWHR

ἐμπνέω, ἐνπ— TWH.

ἐμπορεύομαι.

Jas. 4:13 ἐμπορευσώμεθα S—ἐμπορευσόμεθα A.V.B EEds

ἔμπορος.

Rev. 18:23 οἱ ἐ.—omit οἱ L[WH]

ἔμπροσθεν.

Mar. 1: 2 omit before thee GEds
2:12*for ἐναντίον TWH
Lu. 19: 4 εἰς τὸ ἔμπροσθεν T[A]WHR
Joh. 1:27 omit is preferred before me G[L]TTrAWHR
Acts 10: 4*for ἐνώπιον LTTrAWHR
Rev. 4: 6 ἔντροσθεν T

ἐμπτύω.

Mar. 10:34 trs shall spit upon him, and shall scourge him LTTrAWHR

ἔμφοβος.

Acts 22: 9 omit and were afraid LTTr[A]WHR
24:25 tremefactus A.V. Vul

ἐν.

Mat. 4: 4*for ἐπί² LTrA
23*add ἐν TTrAWHR, see ὅλος
5:48 omit ἐν LTTrAWHR, see οὐρανός
6: 4 omit openly Eds
6 omit openly LTTrAWH
18 omit openly GEds
9:35 omit among the people GEds
12:18*for εἰς Tr
21 om. ἐν read on his name GEds
17:21 omit the verse T[TrA]WHR
20:26 ἐν ὑμῖν²—ὑμῶν A
21:25*for παρά LTrWH
23: 9 omit ἐν LTTrAWHR, see οὐρανός
24:20 omit on GEds
25:13 omit wherein the Son of man cometh GLTTrAWHR
18 omit ἐν TTrAWHR, see γῆ
27: 5 in—into, εἰς TTrWHR, see ναός
29*for ἐπί² LTTrAWHR, see δεξιός
59*ἐν σινδόνι TrA, [ἐν] σ. WH
Mar. 1: 8 omit ἐν T[Tr]AWH
8 omit ἐν² [LTr]AWH
39 εἰς GEds, see συναγωγή
45 ἐπί TTrAWH
2: 1*for εἰς² LTTrWH, see οἶκος
15 omit ἐν τῷ T[Tr]AWH
24 omit ἐν LTTrAWHR
3: 2*εἰ—add ἐν T
4: 8*for ἐν 2 3 WH
15 εἰς TrAWHR, see καρδία

Mar. 4:20*for ἐν¹ TTrWHR
20*for ἐν²³ TTr[WH]R
33*for ἐπί GEds
6:11 omit G[L]TTrAWHR, see κρίσις
32*ἀπῆλθον—add ἐν LWHR, see ἔρημος
8:26 omit nor tell (it) to any in the town TWHR
9:38 τινα—add ἐν A V.B EEds
10.10 εἰς LTTr AWHR, see οἰκία
44*ἐν ὑμῖν for ὑμῶν LWHR
11:10 omit in the name of the Lord GEds
26 omit the verse TTrWHR
14: 6*ἐν ἐμοί for εἰς ἐμέ GEds
27 omit because of me TTrAWHR
27 omit this night [L]TTrAWHR
30 omit in LTTrAWHR
15:29 omit ἐν LTTrA[WH]
16:18*add ἐν Tr[WH], see χείρ
Lu. 1:28 omit blessed (art) thou among women T[Tr]AWHR
61 ἐκ LTTrAWHR
2:38 omit ἐν LTTr[A]WHR
44 omit ἐν³ GEds
52 ἐν τῇ σοφίᾳ T
4: 1*for εἰς LTTrAWH
23 ἐν¹—εἰς GLTTrAWHR
44 εἰς TTrAWH
5: 3*for ἐκ T
6: 2 omit ἐν LTTrAWH
7:17 om. throughout² [L]T[Tr]AWHR
8:40 trs ἐν δὲ TrWH
9:37 omit ἐν T[Tr]AWH
49*for ἐπί WH
10:21 ἐν τῷ πνεύματι T
27*for ἐκ²³⁴ LTTrWHR, see ψυχή
38 trs ἐν δὲ TrWH
11: 2 omit which art in heaven GTTrAWHR
2 omit as in heaven, so in earth G[L]TTrAWHR
13: 4 omit ἐν² TrAWHR
14: 5 omit ἐν [L]Tr
16:26*for ἐπί TWHR
17:24 omit in his day LWH
36 add the verse A.V.B E, see ἀφίημι
19:13*ἐν ᾧ for ἕως LTTrAWH
45 omit therein, and them that bought TTrAWHR
20:10 omit ἐν TrAWHR
21:14*for εἰς LTTrAWH
23 omit ἐν², read to this people GEds
22: 7 omit ἐν TrA
55 omit ἐν² TTrAWH
23:19*for εἰς TTrAWHR
42 εἰς WH
24:18 omit ἐν¹ GTTrAWWHR
32 omit within us [TrA]WH
Joh. 2:19 [ἐν] TrWH
23 [ἐν]² LTr
3:13 omit which is in heaven WH
15*for εἰς TTrAWHR
4:53 omit ἐν¹ T[Tr]WHR
5: 4 omit waiting for (verse 3) to end of verse 4 [G]TTrAWHR
6:39 omit ἐν TrAWH
40*ἐγώ—add ἐν LT
44*αὐτόν²—add ἐν GEds
7:22 [ἐν] LWH
8: 3 ἐν¹—ἐπί WH
9:14*add ἐν LTTrAWHR, see ὅτε
12:35*with you—among you, ἐν ὑμῖν GLTTrAWH
13:32 omit If God be glorified in him [LTrA]WH
16:13*for εἰς T, see ἀλήθεια
20*for παρησία LTTrAWH
17:12 omit in the world LTTrAWHR
19: 4 omit in him T
40*αὐτό—add ἐν W
Acts 1: 8 omit ἐν² L[TrAWH]
17*for σύν GEds
21 omit ἐ¹ LTTrAWHR
2: 5 [ἐν] WH : εἰς T
38*for ἐπί LTrWHR
41*ἐν τῇ ἡμέρᾳ, read in the same day LTTr[A]WHR
43*add ἐν T, see φόβος
3:25*καί²—add ἐν GEds
4:6(5)*for εἰς LTrAWHR
27*add ἐν GEds, see πόλις
7:12 εἰς Eds
16*Συχέμ²—ἐν Σ. in Sychem LTTrWHR
22*Μωυσῆς—add ἐν TTrAW
22 omit in² LTTrAWH
33 ἐπί LTTrAWH
35 by—with, σύν Eds
39*ἐν ταῖς καρδίαις LTTrAWH
44 omit ἐν¹ A.V.Er LTTrAWHR

Acts 9:12 *omit* in a vision LT[Tr]A[Wн]R
  21 εἰς T
  28 ἐ.¹—εἰς Eds
10:39 *omit* ἐν² [L]TrWн
  40*ἐν τῇ τρίτῃ T
14:25 εἰς T, *see* Περγη
20:15 *omit* LTTrWH, *see* μένω
21:20*ὅσιν—add ἐν τοῖς, *read* among
  the Jews LTrAWWH
24:11 εἰς Eds
  14 καί—*add* ἐν ΕLW, *add* τοῖς
  ἐν GTT[A]WHR
  20 *omit* in me LT[TrA]WHR
25: 4 ἐν¹—εἰς Eds
26:10*ἐγώ—*add* ἐν GEds
28:29 *omit* the verse LTT-AWHR

Ro. 6:12 *omit* it in GEds
  7:23*με—*add* ἐν TT[AWH]R
  9:28 *omit* LTTr[A]WHR, *see* λόγος
10:20*εὑρέθην—*add* [ἐν], *read*
  amongst them LT-A
20*ἐγενόμην—*add* [ἐν], *read*
  amongst them LTr
11:25*for παρά TrAWH
13: 9 [ἐν τῷ] LTrAWH

1 Co. 6: 7 *omit* ἐν GEds
  20 *omit* and in your spirit, which
  are God's GEds
  8:11*for ἐπί Eds
  10: 8 *omit* ἐν LTTr[A]WH
  14: 6 *omit* by* T[Tr]
  39*add ἐν [L]A, *see* γλῶσσα

2 Co. 1:20 καὶ ἐν αὐτῷ—διὸ καὶ δι᾽ αὐτοῦ
  wherefore also through him
  Eds
  3: 7 *omit* ἐν² Eds
  9 *omit* ἐν LTTrAWHR
  5:12*μὴ ἐν *for* οὐ² LTTrWHR
  7.11 *omit* ἐν² [L]TTrAWWHR
  8.19*for σύν LTrAWHR
11:27 *omit* ἐν¹ Eds
12:10 ἐν²—and, καί TWH
  12 in signs—*omit* in Eds

Gal. 3: 1 *omit* among you LTTrAWHR
  omit ἐν¹ Tr-WH
  21*for ἐκ WH, *see* νόμος
  6:15 *omit* in Christ Jesus TTrAWHR

Eph. 1: 1 [in Ephesus] TAWH
  3 ἐν χριστῷ A.V.B EGEds
  6 ἐν ᾗ—ῆς, *read* grace which he
  freely bestowed on us LTTrA
  10 ἐν² *omit* LTTrAWHR   (WH
  2:12 *omit* ἐν¹ Eds
  3: 5 *omit* ἐν GEds
  8 *omit* ἐν, *read* to the Gentiles
  LTTrAWHR
  5:19*ἑαυτοῖς—*add* [ἐν] LA
  19 *omit* ἐν T[TrA]WHR
  6: 1 *omit* in the Lord L[TrAWH]
  16*for ἐπί LTTrWHR

Phil. 1: 7*καί¹—*add* ἐν [L]TTrAWWHR
  24 *omit* ἐν TWHR
  2:15 *omit* ἐν¹ Eds

Col. 2: 7 *omit* ἐν² LTT-[A]WHR
  7 *omit* therein TT-[AWH]R
  13 *omit* ἐν TTrWHR
  3:20*add ἐν GEds, *see* κύριος

1 Th. 1: 5 *omit* ἐν¹ T[Tr]WHR
  5 *omit* ἐν² [Tr]WHR
  7*and—*add* ἐν in Ed
  8*and—*add* ἐν in LT
  2: 5 *omit* ἐν² WH

2 Th. 2:10 *omit* ἐν² *read* to them Eds
  12 *omit* ἐν [L]TTr[A]WHR
  3:12*for διά LTTrAWHR, *see* κύριος

1 Ti. 2: 7 *omit* in Christ GEds
  3:14*τάχιον—*for* τάχει LTrWHR
  4:12 *omit* in spirit GEds
  15 *omit* ἐν² A.V.Vul Eds
  6:17 ἐν²—ἐπί LTTrWHR

Heb. 3: 9*add ἐν Eds, *see* δοκιμασία
  10:34 *omit* ἐν¹ GEds
  34 *omit* in heaven Eds
  11:26 *omit* ἐν, *read* of Egypt
  GTT-AWWHR
  38 ἐπί LTTrAWHR

Jas. 1:26 *omit* among you GEds
  5:10*ἐλάλησαν—*add* ἐν LTTrWHR

1 Pet. 1:12 *omit* ἐν LTrAWH
  4: 1 *omit* ἐν LTTrAWHR

2 Pet. 2:18 ἐν ἀσελγείαις E
  3:*add ἐν GEds, *see* ἐμπαιγμονή
  10 *omit* in the night GEds

1 Joh.2:24 *omit* in* L[WH]
  3:18*for ἔργῳ GEds
  4: 3 *omit* that Christ is come in
  the flesh GLTTrAWHR
  5: 6*ἐν τῷ αἵματι by blood Eds
  7, 8 *omit* in heaven (*verse* 7) *to*
  in earth (*verse* 8) GEds

Jude 18 ἐπί Eds, *see* χρόνος
Rev. 1: 9 *omit* in the[ ] GEds
  9*patience—*add* ἐν in Eds

Rev. 1:11 *omit* which are in Asia GEds
  2: 1*add ἐν GEds, *see* Ἔφεσος
  8*add ἐν GEds. *see* ἐκκλησία
  13 *omit* ἐν² Eds
  14 *omit* ἐν EGEds
  3:14*add ἐν GEds. *see* Λαοδικεία
  4: 4 *omit* ἐν LWH
  5: 2*ἐν φωνῇ GEds
  13 ἐν²—ἐπί GEds
  8: 7*ἐν αἵματι GEds
  9:19*add A.V.C GEds, *see* ἐξουσία
  11: 6 *omit* ἐν GEds
  6*ἐν πάσῃ GEds
  11*for ἐπί GLT[A]W[WH]R
  13: 3 *omit* ἐν, *see* θαυμάζω
  10 qui in A.V.Vul
  17:16 *omit* ἐν T[AWH]
  18:10 *omit* ἐν Eds
  16 *omit* ἐν LT-[AWH]R
  23 *omit* ἐν¹ L[A]
  19:17*ἐν φωνῇ T[AWH]
  21:14 *omit* ἐπί GEds, *see* δώδεκα
  23 om. ἐν, *read* shine for it GEds
  24 in—by, διά GEds

ἔναντι.
Acts 7:10*for ἐναντίον T
  8:21*for ἐνώπιον GEds

ἐναντίον.
Mar. 2:12 ἔμπροσθεν TWH
Lu. 1: 6*for ἐνώπιον TT-AWH
Acts 7:10 ἔναντι T

ἔνατος, *see* ἔννατος.

ἐνδείκνυμι.
2 Co. 8:24 ἐνδεικνύμενοι LTTrA

ἔνδειξις.
Ro. 8:26 τὴν ἔνδειξιν LTTrAWHR

ἐνδιδύσκω, —ομαι.
Mar. 15:17*ἐνδιδύσκουσιν *for* ἐνδύουσιν
  (ἐνδύω) LTTrAWH
Lu. 8:27 ἐνδύω TTrWHR, *see* χρόνος

ἐνδόμησις, ἐνδώμησις TTrWHR.

ἐνδυναμόω.
Heb.11:34 δυναμόω LTTrWHR

ἐνδύω.
Mar. 6: 9 ἐνδύσησθε s—ἐνδύσασθαι A.V.B
  EWH
  15:17 ἐνδιδύσκω LTTrAWH
Lu. 8:27*ἐνεδύσατο *for* ἐνεδιδύσκετο (ἐνδιδύσκω) TTrWHR, *see* χρόνος
1 Co. 15:54 *omit* ἐ.¹ WH, *see* φθαρτός

ἐνέγκω, *see* φέρω.

ἐνέδρα.
Acts 23:16 τὴν ἐνέδραν *for* τὸ ἔνεδρον
  EGLTTrAWH

ἔνεδρον.
Acts 23:16 ἐνέδρα EGLTTrAWH

ἕνεκα, ἕνεκεν, εἵνεκεν.
Mat. 19: 5 ἕνεκα LTTrAWH
  29 ἕνεκα T
Mar. 10:29*καί—*add* ἕνεκεν, *read* sake of
  the gospel G[L]TTrAW[WH]R
Lu. 4:18 εἵνεκεν GLTTrAWH
  18:29 εἵνεκεν TWH
Acts 19:32 ἕνεκα LTTrAWH
  28:20 εἵνεκεν TWH
Ro. 8:36 ἕνεκεν GLTTrAWWH
2 Co. 3:10 εἵνεκεν LTTrA
  7:12 ἕνεκεν ter LTTrAWH

ἐνενήκοντα, *see* ἐννενηκονταεννέα.

ἐνεός, *see* ἐννεός.

ἐνεργέω.
2 Co. 1: 6 *trs* τῆς ἐνεργουμένης τὸ πάσχο-
  μεν *after* παρακλήσεως GTWHR
Eph. 1:20 ἐνήργηκεν LTAWH

ἐνευλογέομαι.
Acts 3:25 εὐλογέω WH
Gal. 3: 8 εὐλογέω B

* ἔνθεν, thence.
Mat. 17:20 *for* ἐντεῦθεν LTTrAWH
Lu. 16:26 *for* ἐντεῦθεν GEds

ἐνθυμέομαι.

Acts 10:19 διενθυμέομαι GEds

ἔνι *for* ἔνεστι.
1 Co. 6: 5*for ἐστίν GEds

ἐνίστημι.
Ro. 8:38 *trs* GEds, *see* δύναμις

ἐνισχύω.
Lu. 22:43, 44 *the verses* [L][[WH]]
Acts 9:19 ἐνισχύθη WH

ἐνκακέω, *see* ἐκκακέω.

ἐνκόπτω, *see* ἐγκόπτω.

ἔννατος, ἔνατος.
Mar. 15:34 τῇ ἐνάτῃ ὥρᾳ LTTrAWH

ἐννενηκονταεννέα.
ἐνενήκοντα ἐννέα LTTrWH.

ἐννεός, ἐνεός LTTrAWWH.

ἔννυχον, ἔννυχα LTTrAWHR.

ἐνοικέω.
Ro. 7:17*ἐνοικοῦσα *for* οἰκοῦσα (-κέω)
  TWH
  8.11 διὰ τὸ ἐνοικοῦν αὐτοῦ πνεῦμα
  because of his Spirit that
  dwelleth s—διὰ τοῦ ἐνοικοῦν-
  τος αὐτοῦ πνεύματος by his
  Spirit, &c. A.V.B ETWHR

* ἐνορκίζω, to adjure.
1 Th. 5:27 ἐνορκίζω *for* ὁρκίζω Eds

ἐνοχλέω.
Lu. 6:18*ἐνοχλούμενοι *for* ὀχλούμενοι
  (-λέω) TTrAWH

ἔνοχος.
Mar. 14:64 *trs* ἔνοχον εἶναι TTrAWH

ἔνπροσθεν, *see* ἔμπροσθεν.

ἐντέλλομαι.
Mat. 15: 4 commanded, saying—said.
  εἶπον LTrWHR
Mar. 11: 6 had commanded—said, εἶπον
  LTTrAWH
Joh. 14:31 *see* ἐντολή

ἐντεῦθεν.
Mat. 17:20 ἔνθεν LTTrAWH
Lu. 16:26 ἔνθεν GEds
Rev. 22: 2 ἐ.²—ἐκεῖθεν Eds

ἐντολή.
Mat. 15: 6 commandment—word, λόγος
  LTrWHR: law, νόμος TA
Mar. 12:29 τῶν ἐ.—ἐντολή *read* commandment of all G[L]W: *omit* of
  all the commandments
  TTrAWHR
  30 *omit* this (is) the first commandment TAWHR
Joh. 11:57 ἐντολάς, commandments
  TTrAWHR
  14:31*ἐντολὴν ἔδωκεν *for* ἐνετείλατο
  (ἐντέλλομαι) LTrWH
1 Co. 14:37 *omit* the commandments T:
  ἐντολή commandment
  LTH[A]WWHR
2 Joh. 6 *trs* ἡ ἐντολή ἐστιν Eds
Rev. 22:14 *omit* ἐ. LTTrAWHR, *see* στολή

ἐντρέπομαι.
Heb.12: 9 ἐνετρεπόμεθα s—ἐντρεπόμεθα E

ἐντυγχάνω.
Acts 25:24 ἐνέτυχόν WH

ἐνύπνιον.
Acts 2:17 ἐνυπνίοις with dreams GEds

ἐνώπιον.
Lu. 1: 6 ἐναντίον TTrAWHR
  76*ἐ. *for* πρὸ προσώπου (-ον) WH
Acts 8:21 ἔναντι GEds
  10: 4 ἔμπροσθεν LTTrAWH
Rev. 14: 5 *omit* before the throne of
  God GEds

Ἐνώχ, Ἐ– wɪ.

ἕξ.

Rev. 13:18 *see* χξς

ἐξάγω.

Mar. 8:23 led out—brought out, ἐκφέρω
TTrAWH

ἐξαιρέω.

Acts 7:10 | 12:11 ἐξείλατο GLTTrAWWH
23:27 ἐξειλάμην LTTrAWWH

ἐξαίρω.

1Co. 5: 2 αἴρω GEds
13 ἐξάρατε GEds

ἐξαίφνης.

ἐξέφνης (except Acts 22:6) wɪ

ἐξακόσιοι.

Rev. 13:18 *see* χξς

ἐξαλείφω.

Acts 3:19 ἐξαλιφθῆναι WH

ἐξαπατάω.

2Co. 11: 3 *trs* ἐξηπάτησεν Εὔαν Eds
1Ti. 2:14*ἐξαπατηθεῖσα *for* ἀπατηθεῖσα
(–τάω) Eds

ἐξαποστέλλω.

Lu. 20:10 *trs* ἐξαπέστειλαν αὐτὸν δείραν-
τες TAWH
24:49*ἐξαποστέλλω *for* ἀποστέλλω
TTrAWHR
Acts 13:26*ἐξαπεστάλη *for* ἀπεστάλη (ἀποστέλλω) Eds

ἐξαρτίζω.

Acts 21: 5 *trs* ἐξαρτίσαι ἡμᾶς LTTrAWWH

ἐξαυτῆς.

Acts 10:33 | 11:11 | 21:32 ἐξ αὐτῆς A
23:39 straightway—by them, ἐξ
αὐτῶν LTTr, ἐξ αὐτῆς A

ἐξελέγχω.

Jude 15 ἐλέγχω LTTrAWHR

ἐξερευνάω, ἐξεραυνάω TTrAWH.

ἐξέρχομαι.

Mat. 8:12*ἐξελεύσονται *for* ἐκβληθήσονται
(–βάλλω) T
11: 7, 8, 9 ἐξήλθατε LTTrAWH
12:14 *trs* ἐξελθ. δὲ οἱ Φαρ. συμβ. ἔλα-
βον κατ᾽ αὐτοῦ LTTrWWHR
26:55 ἐξήλθατε LTTrAWH
28: 8 ἀπέρχομαι TTrAWH
Mar. 1:29 ἐξελθών, he was come out LTr
38 ἐξῆλθον TTrAWHR
5: 2 ἐξελθόντος αὐτοῦ LTTrWH
14 went out—went, ἔρχομαι Eds
14:48 ἐξήλθατε LTTrAWH
Lu. 4:41 ἐξήρχοντο T
6:12 ἐξελθεῖν αὐτὸν TTrAWHR
7:24, 25, 26 ἐξήλθατε LTrWH, –θετε R
8:35 ἐ.²–ἐξῆλθεν TWH
46 ἐξεληλυθυῖαν TTrAWH
10:35 omit when he departed
LTTr[A]WH
11:53*and as he said these things
unto them—and as he went
out thence, κἀκεῖθεν ἐξελθόντος αὐτοῦ TTrAWH
14:18 ἐξελθὼν having gone TTrAWH
22:52 ἐξήλθατε LTWH, –θετε R
Joh. 13:30 *trs* ἐξῆλθεν εὐθύς LTTrAWHR
18: 4 ἐξῆλθεν LTTrAWH
19:34 *trs* ἐξῆλθεν εὐθὺς TTrAWH
21: 3 ἐξῆλθαν WH
Acts 8: 7†*trs* φωνῇ μεγάλῃ ἐξήρχοντο Eds
15:24 omit which went out WH
16:39 ἀπέρχομαι LTTrAWH
40 ἐ.²–ἐξελθὼν TTrvWH
19:12 ἐκπορεύομαι GEds
28: 3 διεξέρχομαι AW
15 ἔρχομαι LTTrAWH
2Co. 6:17 ἐξέλθατε LTTrAWH
Heb.11:15 came out—went out, ἐκβαίνω
Eds
1Joh. 2 19 ἐξῆλθαν LTTrAWH
2Joh. ſ *ἐξῆλθαν LTrWH, –θον TAWHR *for*
εἰσῆλθον (εἰσέρχομαι)

3Joh. 7 ἐξῆλθαν LTTrWH
Rev. 14:18 omit came L[WH]
15: 6 ἐξῆλθαν WH
18: 4 ἐξέλθατε TTrAWWH
19:21*ἐξελθούσῃ *for* ἐκπορευομένῃ
(–μαι) GEds

ἔξεστιν.

Mat. 15:26*for ἔστιν καλόν (–ός) LTA
Acts 8:37 omit the verse GLTTrAWHR

ἐξετάζω.

Mat. 2: 8 *trs* ἐξετάσατε ἀκριβῶς LTTrAWH

ἐξήκοντα.

Rev. 13:18 see χξς

ἐξῆς.

Lu. 7:11 τῇ ἑ.–τῷ ἑ. TrWHR

ἐξίστημι, –τάω, –τανω.

Acts 8: 9 ἐξιστάνων LTTrAWH

ἐξολοθρεύομαι, ἐξολε– LTTrAWH.

ἐξομολογέομαι.

Ro. 14:11 *trs* ἐξομολογήσεται πᾶσα
γλῶσσα LTr
Phil. 2:11 ἐξομολογήσεται TAW
Rev. 3: 5 ὁμολογέω GEds

* ἐξουδενέω, to set at nought.

Mar. 9:12 ἐξουδενηθῇ *for* ἐξουδενωθῇ
(–νόω) LTTrAWH

ἐξουδενόω.

Mar. 9:12 ἐξουδενέω LTTrAWI, ἐξουθενόω T

* ἐξουθενόω, to set at nought.

Mar. 9:12 ἐξουθενωθῇ *for* ἐξουδενωθῇ
(–νόω) T

ἐξουσία.

Lu. 5:24 *trs* ὁ υἱὸς τοῦ ἀνθ. ἑ. ἔχει
TTrAWH
12: 5 *trs* ἔχοντα ἐξουσίαν LTTrAWH
Ro. 13: 1 omit ἐ.³ read those that be
GEds
1Co. 9:12 *trs* ἐξουσίας GEds
Rev. 9:19 ἡ γὰρ ἐξουσία τῶν ἵππων (τῶν ἵ.
for αὐτῶν GLTTrAWHR) ἐν τῷ
στόματι αὐτῶν ἐστιν καὶ ἐν
ταῖς οὐραῖς αὐτῶν. For the
power of the horses (of them
A.V.W) is in their mouth
and in their tails A.V.C GEds
11: 6 ἐ.¹–τὴν ἐξουσίαν LTr[A]WWHR
13: 4 τὴν ἐξουσίαν GEds
16: 9 τὴν ἐξουσίαν LTrWWHR
17:13 τὴν ἐ.–omit τὴν LTTrAWH

ἔξω.

Mat. 10:14*ἐξερχόμενοι—add ἕ. LTTrAWHR
12:47. omit the verse [T]WH
Lu. 8:54 omit put them all out, and
LTTrAWH
24:50 omit ἔξω [L]TTr[A]WHR
Joh. 18:29*Πιλᾶτος—add ἕ. LTTrAWHR
Acts 5:23 omit without GEds
16:13 omit ἑ. W
Rev. 11: 2 ἔξωθεν A.V.C LTTrWHR
14:20 ἔξωθεν Eds

ἔξωθεν.

Rev. 11: 2 ἔσωθεν within s—ἕ. without
A.V.B EGEds
2*for ἔξω A.V.C LTTrWHR
14:20*for ἔξω GEds

ἐξωθέω.

Acts 7:45 ἐξέωσεν T
27:39 ἐκσῴζω WH

ἑορτή.

Lu. 23:17 omit the verse [L]TTr[A]WHR
Joh. 5: 1 ἡ ἑορτῇ T
Acts 18:21 omit LTTrAWHR, see δεῖ

ἐπαγγελία.

Gal. 4:23 τῆς ἑ.–omit τῆς TrWHR
1Joh. 1: 5 ἀγγελία A.V.Vul GEds

ἐπάγγελμα.

2Pet. 3:13 τὰ ἐπαγγέλματα promises LT

ἐπαινέω.

Ro. 15:11 ἐπαινεσάτωσαν LTTrAWHR
1Co. 11:17 ἐπαινῶ LTrAW

ἐπαίρω.

Joh. 13:18 ἐπῆρκεν T
17: 1 ἐπάρας LTTrAWHR

ἐπαισχύνομαι.

2Ti. 1:16 ἐπαισχύνθη LTTrAWH

ἐπαιτέω.

Lu. 18:35*ἐπαιτῶν *for* προσαιτῶν (–τέω)
LTTrAWH

ἐπάναγκες.

Acts 15:28 *trs* τούτων τῶν ἐπάναγκες
LTTrWH

ἐπανάγω.

Mat. 21:18 ἐπαναγαγών LTAWH

ἐπαναπαύομαι.

Lu. 10: 6 ἐπαναπαήσεται TWH

ἐπάνω.

Mat. 21: 7 ἐ.¹–ἐπί LTTrAWH
Lu. 19:19 *trs* ἐπάνω γίνου TAWH
Joh. 3:31 omit is above all² T
Rev. 20:11*for ἐπί Tr

* ἐπάρατος, accursed.

Joh. 7:49 ἐπάρατοι *for* ἐπικατάρατοι(–τος)
LTTrAWHR

ἐπαρκέω.

1Ti. 5:16 ἐ.¹–ἐπαρκείσθω LTTr

ἐπαρχία –χεία TWH.

Acts 25: 1 ἐπαρχείῳ T

ἐπαυτοφώρῳ.

Joh. 8: 4 ἐπ᾽ αὐτοφώρῳ WWH

ἐπεί.

Mat. 21:46*for ἐπειδή TTrAWH
Lu. 7: 1 ἐπειδή LTTrAWH
Ro. 11: 6 omit but if (it be) to end of
verse GLTTr[A]WHR

ἐπειδή.

Mat. 21:46 ἐπεί TTrAWH
Lu. 7: 1*for ἐπεὶ δέ LTTrAWHR
2Co. 5: 4 ἐ. 8—ἐφ᾽ ᾧ A.V.B EGEds

ἐπείπερ.

Ro. 3:30 seeing—if indeed εἴ περ
LTTrAWHR

* ἐπεισέρχομαι, to come in upon.

Lu. 21:34, 35 ἐκείνη ὡς παγίς· ἐπεισελεύ-
σεται(ἐ. *for* ἐπελεύσεται, ἐπέρχομαι) γὰρ ἐπί, read unaware
as a snare: for it shall come
in upon LTTrAWH

ἔπειτα.

Mar. 7: 5 then—and, καὶ LTTrAWH
1Co. 12:28*for εἶτα LTTrAWH
15: 5*for εἶτα T
7*for εἶτα TA

ἐπέρχομαι.

Lu. 21:35 see ἐπεισέρχομαι
Acts 14:19 ἐπῆλθαν LTTrAWH

ἐπερωτάω.

Mat. 16: 1 ἐπηρώτων T
Mar. 8: 5 ἐρωτάω TTrAWH
29*ἐπηρώτα αὐτοὺς *for* λέγει (–γω)
αὐτοῖς LTTrAWHR
9:28 *trs* κατ᾽ ἰδίαν ἐπηρώτων αὐτὸν
LTTrAWHR
10: 2 | 12:18 ἐπηρώτων LTTrAWH
13: 3 ἐπηρώτα TTrAWH
15: 4 ἐπηρώτα TTrAWH
Lu. 6: 9 ἐπερωτῶ I ask TTrAWH
23: 3 ἐρωτάω TTrAWH
Joh. 9:23*ἐπηρώτησατε *for* ἐρωτήσατε
(–τάω) TWI
18: 7 *trs* ἐπηρώτησεν αὐτούς LTTrAWH

Joh. 18:21 ἐ.¹—ἐρωτάω Eds
21 ἐ.²—ἐρωτάω LTTrAWHB
Acts 1: 6 ἐρωτάω LTTrAWH

ἐπηρεάζω.

Mat. 5:44 omit despitefully use you,
and LTTrAWH

ἐπί.

Mat. 2:22 omit ἐ. LT[TrA]WH
4: 4 ἐ.²—ἐν LT.A
5:39 εἰς LTTrAWH
10:13*for πρός WH
13:14 omit ἐ. GEds
14:34*for εἰς TTrWH
18: 6 περί LTTrWH: εἰς to A
21: 5*ἐ. πῶλον upon a colt LTTrAWH
7*for ἐπάνω¹ LTTrAWH
44 omit the verse [L]T[WH]
22: 5*for εἰς² LTTrAWH
24:16 εἰς LTrWH
25:20, 22 omit beside them LTTrWHR
27:29 ἐ.³—ἐν LTTrAWHR, see δεξιος
35 omit that it might to end of
verse GLTTrAWH
42*αὐτῷ—ἐ. αὐτόν TTrWHR, ἐ. αὐτῷ
28:14 ὑπό LTr   (W
Mar. 1:10 εἰς LTTrAWH
45*for ἐν TTrAWH
2: 4 ᾧ· ᾧ wherein—where, ὅπου
LTTrAWH
4:18*for εἰς T
38 ἐ.¹—ἐν GEds
5:33 omit ἐ. read done to her
[L]TTrAWH
10:24 omit for them that trust in
riches TWH
14:46 omit ἐ. TTrAWH, see αὐτόν
15: 1 omit ἐ. τὸ LTT[A]WHR
Lu. 4: 4 omit but by every word of
God T[Tr]AWH
25 omit ἐ.² LTr[A]WH
43*for εἰς LTTrAWH
6:29 εἰς T
48 omit ἐ.² TTrAWHR, see θεμελιόω
8: 8 on—into, εἰς GEds
9:49 ἐν WH
10:11 omit unto you GLTTrAWH
11: 2 omit as in heaven so in earth
G[L]TTrAWH
12:49*for εἰς Eds
54*for ἀπό TWHR
16:26 beside—before, ἐν TWH
17: 4 προς Eds
22:52 ἐ.¹—πρός T
24:12 omit the verse [L]T[Tr][[WH]]
Joh. 8: 3*for ἐν¹ WH
21: 4*for εἰς LT
11 εἰς LTTrAWH, see γῆ
Acts 2:38 ἐν LTrWH
43*add ἐ. T, see φόβος
3:16 omit ἐ. WH
5:23*for πρό LTTrAWH
7:10*ἐ. ὅλον over all T
18*ἕτερος—add ἐπ' Αἴγυπτον, read
arose over Egypt LTTrWH
33*for ἐν LTTrAWH
10:11 omit unto him GEds
13:40 omit upon you LTTr[A]WH
14: 3*μαρτυροῦντι—add ἐ. T
15:14 omit ἐ. Eds
20:13*for εἰς LTTrAWH
21:23 ἀπό WH
24: 8 πρός A: omit LTTrWHR, see
κρινω
2]*for ὑπό Eds
28:14 παρά LTTrAWH
Ro. 3:22 omit and upon all LTTr[A]WH
1 Co. 8:11 ἐν Eds
2 Co. 5: 4 ἐφ' ᾧ for ἐπειδή A.V.B RGEds
10: 7*for ἀπό TTrWH
Eph. 1:10*for ἐν³ LTTrAWH
6:16 above—in, ἐν LTTrWH
Phi. 3:14 εἰς LTTrAWH
Col. 3: 6 omit on the children of disobedience [L]TTrAWH
1 Ti. 6:17*for ἐν² LTTrAWH
2 Ti. 2:14*for εἰς LTTrAWH
Heb. 2: 7 omit and didst set to end of
verse G[L]T[Tr]A[WH]
11:38*for ἐν LTTrAWH
1 Pet. 3: 5 εἰς Eds
Jude 18*for ἐν Eds, see χρόνος
Rev. 3: 3 omit on thee, ἐ. σε¹ LTTrAWH
5:13*for ἐν² GEds
10:11*and²—add ἐ. before T
11:11 ἐ.¹—ἐν GLT[A]W[WH]R: om. Tr
14: 6*εὐαγγελίσαι—add ἐ. LTTrAWH
6*καί—add ἐ. GEds
16: 2 trs εἰς and ἐπί Eds
17*for εἰς GEds

Rev. 17:16 upon—and, καί GEds
20:11 ἐπάνω Tr
21:14*for ἐν GEds, see δώδεκα
22: 5*ἐπ' αὐτούς GLTTrAWH: [ἐπ'] α.
16 omit ἐ. W   (WH
18*for πρός GEds

See also ἐφάπαξ.

ἐπιβαίνω.

Acts 21: 4*ἐπιβαίνειν for ἀναβαινειν
(-βαίνω) LTTrAWH
6 ἐμβαίνω LTrWHR, ἀναβαιν. IAW

ἐπιβάλλω.

Mar. 11: 7 ἐπιβάλλουσιν GEds
14:46 ἐπέβαλαν TWH
Joh. 7:44 βάλλω LTTrAWH
Acts 21:27 ἐπέβαλαν TTrWH

ἐπιβλέπω.

Lu. 9:38 ἐπιβλέψαι GTTrAWWHR

ἐπίβλημα.

Lu. 5:36 ἐ.²—τὸ ἐπίβλημα TTrAWH

ἐπιβοάω

Acts 25:24 βοάω LTTrWHR, [ἐπι. S A

ἐπιβουλή.

Acts 20: 3 trs ἐπιβουλῆς αὐτῷ LTTrWH

ἐπιγινώσκω.

Mar. 6:33 γινώσκω LT.AWH
Acts 19:34 ἐπιγνόντες GLTTrAWWH
23:28*ἐπιγνῶναι for γνῶναι (γινώσκω)
Eds
24:11*ἐπιγνῶναι for γνῶναι (γινώσκω)
LTTrAWH
28: 1 ἐπεγνωμεν we knew Eds

ἐπίγνωσις.

Col. 1:10 τῇ ἐπιγνώσει by the knowledge
GEds

ἐπιγράφω.

Lu. 23:38*ἐπιγεγραμμένη for γεγραμμένη
(γράφω) L[Tr]

ἐπιδείκνυμι.

Lu. 20:24 δείκνυμι GEds
24:40 δείκνυμι LTr[A]WH: omit the
verse T[Tr][[WH]]

ἐπιδίδωμι.

Lu. 11:11 omit ἐ.¹ WH, see ἄρτος
11 trs αὐτῷ ἐπιδώσει² TTrAWH
Joh. 13:26 δίδωμι TTrAWH

ἐπιείκεια, —κια WH.

ἐπιζητέω.

Mat. 6:32 ἐπιζητοῦσιν LTTrAWH
Mar. 8:12 ζητέω LTTrAWH
Lu. 4:42*ἐπιζήτουν for ἐζήτουν (ζητέω)
GEds
11:29 ζητέω TTrAWH
12:30 ἐπιζητοῦσιν TTrAWH

ἐπιθυμία.

2 Ti. 4: 3 omit τάς, see ἴδιος
2 Pet. 3: 3 trs ἐπιθυμίας αὐτῶν GLTTrAWH
Rev. 18:14 trs σου τῆς ἐ. τῆς ψυχῆς Eds

ἐπικαθίζω.

Mat. 21: 7 ἐπεκάθισεν he sat s—ἐπεκάθι-
σαν A.V.BR

ἐπικαλεω, —ομαι.

Mat. 10: 3 omit Lebbæus, whose surname was LTrWHR: omit
whose surname was Thad-
dæus TA
25*ἐπεκάλεσαν or ἐκαλεσαν (καλέω) GEds
Lu. 22: 3 surnamed—called, καλέω
Acts 15:22 surnamed—called, καλέω Eds
Ro. 10:14 ἐπικαλέσωνται Eds

ἐπικαταρατος.

Joh. 7:49 ἐπάρατος LTTrAWH

* ἐπικέλλω, to run aground.

Acts 27:41 ἐπέκειλαν for ἐπώκειλαν (ἐποκέλλω) LTTrAWH

Ἐπικούρειος, —ριος TWH.

ἐπιλέγω, —ομαι.

Joh. 5: 2 λέγω T

* ἐπιλείχω, to lick over.

Lu. 16:21 ἐπέλειχον for ἀπέλειχον (ἀπο-
λείχω) LTTrAWH

ἐπιμένω.

Acts 13:43 προσμένω GEds
15:34 omit the verse Eds
Ro. 6: 1 ἐπιμένωμεν GEds
11:22 ἐπιμένῃς TTrWH
23 ἐπιμένωσιν TTrWH

ἐπιπίπτω.

Jon. 13:25 ἀναπίπτω LTrAWH
Acts 10:10 γίνομαι Eds
13:11 πίπτω LTTrWH
19:17 πίπτω LTr
Ro. 15: 3 ἐπέπεσαν LTTrAWH
Rev. 11:11*ἐπέπεσεν for ἔπεσεν (πίπτω)
Eds

ἐπιποθία, —πόθεια WH.

ἐπιρράπτω.

Mar. 2:21 ἐπιράπτει TTrAWH

ἐπιρρίπτω.

Lu. 19:35 ἐπιρίψαντες LTTrAWH
1 Pet. 5: 7 ἐπιρίψαντες LTTrAWH

ἐπισκέπτομαι.

Lu. 1:78 ἐπισκέψεται WHR

* ἐπισκευάζομαι, to get ready.

Acts 21:15 ἐπισκευασάμενοι for ἀποσκευα-
σάμενοι (—σκευάζομαι) Eds

ἐπισκιάζω.

Lu. 9:34 ἐπεσκίαζεν TTrAWH
Acts 5:15 ἐπισκιάσει TrWH

ἐπισκοπέω.

1 Pet. 5: 2 omit taking the oversight
(thereof) T[A]WH

* ἐπισπείρω, to sow upon.

Mat. 13:25 ἐπέσπειρεν for ἔσπειρεν (σπείρω)
LTTrAWHR

ἐπίσταμαι.

1 Th. 5: 3*ἐπίσταται for ἐφίσταται (—στη-
μι) TTrWH

* ἐπίστασις, a stopping, checking.

Acts 24:12 ἐπίστασιν for ἐπισύστασιν
(—σις) LTTrAWH
2 Co. 11:28 ἐπίστασις for ἐπισύστασις Eds

ἐπιστέλλω.

Acts 21:25 have written—have sent.
ἀποστέλλω LTrWH

ἐπιστηρίζω.

Acts 18:23 στηρίζω LTTrAWH

ἐπιστολή.

2 Co. 10:10 trs ἐπιστολαὶ μέν LTTrWH
2 Pet. 3:16 ταῖς ἐ.—ταῖς LTrAWWHR

ἐπιστρέφω.

Mat. 9:22 στρέφω LTTrAWH
Lu. 2:20 ὑποστρέφω GEds
39*ἐπέστρεψαν for ὑπεστρεψαν
(ὑποστρέφω) TWH
Joh. 12:40 στρέφω LTTrAWH
Acts 26:18 τοῦ ἐ.—καὶ ἐ. A.V†B
2 Pet. 2:21 to turn—to turn back, ὑποστρέφω LTTrAWH

ἐπισυνάγω.

Mar. 1:33 trs ἦν ὅλη ἡ πόλις ἐ. LTTrAWH
Lu. 17:37*trs οἱ ἀετοὶ ἐπισυναχθήσονται
(ἐ. for συναχθήσονται, συνάγω)
TTrAWH

ἐπισυστασις.

Acts 24:12 ἐπίστασις LTTrAWHR
2 Co. 11:28 cometh upon—presseth upon.
ἐπίστασις Eds

ἐπιτάσσω.
Mar. 9:25 trs ἐπιτάσσω σοι TTrAWH

ἐπιτελέω.
Lu. 13:32 ἀποτελέω LTTrAWHR

ἐπιτίθημι.
Mar. 4:21 τίθημι Eds
8:25 τίθημι TrAWH
Lu. 4:40 ἐπιτιθεὶς LTTrAWH
8:16 τιθημι LTTrAWH
Joh. 9: 6*ἐπέθηκεν for ἐπέχρισεν (ἐπι-χρίω) WH
Acts 8:17 ἐπετίθεσαν LTTrAWH
Rev. 1:17 τίθημι GEds
22:18 ἐ.¹—ἐπιθῇ GEds

ἐπιτιμάω.
Mat. 16:20*ἐπετίμησεν for διεστείλατο (διαστέλλομαι) LWH
22 ἐπιτιμῶν Α, see λέγω
Mar.10:13 ἐπετίμησαν WH
Lu. 18:15 ἐπιτιμῶν LTTrAWH
23:40 ἐπιτιμῶν TTrAWH
2 Ti. 4: 2 trs exhort, rebuke T

ἐπιτρέπω.
Mat. 8:31 see ἀποστέλλω
Acts28:16†trs ἐ. τῷ Παύλῳ LTTrAWH
1 Co. 14:34 ἐπιτρέπεται Eds
16: 7 ἐπιτρέψῃ Eds

ἐπιφανής.
Acts 2:20 omit and notable T

ἐπιφέρω.
Acts19:12 ἀποφέρω LTTrAWH
25:18 φέρω Eds
Phil. 1:16 to add—to raise up, ἐγείρω Eds (verse 17 GEds)

ἐπιφωνέω.
Acts21:34*ἐπεφώνουν for ἐβόων (βοάω)Eds

ἐπιχρίω.
Joh. 9: 6 ἐπετίθημι WH

ἐποικοδομέω.
Acts 20:32 οἰκοδομέω Eds
1 Co. 3:14 ἐποικοδόμησεν TTrAWH
1 Pet. 2: 5*ἐποικοδομεῖσθε for οἰκοδομεῖσθε (-μέω) T

ἐποκέλλω.
Acts 27:41 ἐπικέλλω LTTrAWH

ἐποπτεύω.
1 Pet. 2:12 ἐποπτεύοντες behold Eds

ἐπουράνιος.
Mat. 18:35 οὐράνιος LTTrWH, |ἐπ|ᵤ. A

ἑπτά.
Lu. 11:26 trs ἑπτά after ἑαυτοῦ TTrₐWH
Rev. 1:11*ἐ. ἐκκλησίαις A.V.CGEds
13 omit seven LT[Tr A]WHR
3: 1 ἐ. πνεύματα A.V.B EGEds
5: 6 omit seven³ L[WH]
6: 1*ἐ. σφραγίδων seven seals GEds
16: 1*ἐ. φιάλας seven vials GEds

ἔπω, see εἶπον.

ἐραυνάω, see ἐρευνάω.

ἐργάζομαι.
Mat. 25:16 ἠργάσατο TAWH
26:10 ἠργάσατο TWH
Mar.14: 6 ἠργάσατο TWH
Acts 13:41 trs ἐργάζομαι ἐγώ Eds
3: 1 ἠργάζετο LTrA, ἠργάζοντο they wrought TWH
1 Co. 9: 6 τοῦ μὴ ἐ.—om. τοῦ LTTr[A]WHR
2 Co. 7:10*ἐργάζεται for κατεργάζεται (-ζομαι)Eds
Heb.11:33 ἠργάσαντο TTrWH
Jas. 1:20*ἐργάζεται for κατεργάζεται (-ζομαι) LTTrAWH
2 Joh. 8 εἰργάσασθε ye have wrought LTTrWH: ἠργασάμεθα WH

ἐργάτης.
Lu. 13:27 οἱ ἐ.—omit οἱ TTrAWH

ἔργον.
Mat. 11:19*ἔργων for τέκνων (-νον) TTrWH
Joh. 7: 3 trs σου τὰ ἔργα LWH
Acts 9:36 trs ἔργων ἀγαθῶν LTrWWH
15:18 omit unto God are all his works GTTrAWHR, see γνωστός
Ro. 11: 6 omit but if (it be) to end of verse GLTTr[A]WHR
13: 3 τῷ ἀγαθῷ ἔργῳ the good work Eds
2 Th. 2:17 trs work and word Eds
1 Ti. 5:25†trs τὰ ἔργα τὰ καλὰ Eds
Heb. 2: 7 omit and didst set to end of verse G[,]T[Tr,]A[WH]
13:21 omit work TWH
Jas. 2:17 trs ἔχῃ ἔργα GEds
26 τῶν ἐ.—omit τῶν T[Tr]WH
Rev. 2: 9 omit works, and LTTrAWH
13 om. thy works, and LTTrAWH
3: 2 τὰ ἔ.—omit τὰ L[TrA]WHR

ἐρευνάω, ἐραυνάω TTrWH, at times Α.

ἐρέω, see ἐρῶ.

ἔρημος, subst.
Lu. 4: 1 ἐν τῇ ἐρήμῳ LTTrAWH

ἔρημος, adj.
Mat. 23:38 omit desolate LWH
Mar. 6:32†trs ἐν τῷ πλοίῳ εἰς ἔ. τόπ. LWHR
Lu. 9:10 omit desert place belonging to TTrAWH
13:35 omit desolate GEds

ἐριθεία, -θια WH.
Phil. 1:16 trs verses 16 and 17 except οἱ μὲν and οἱ δὲ GEds

ἔρις.
2 Co. 12:20 ἔρις debate LTWH
Gal. 5:20 ἔρις Eds
Tit. 3: 9 ἔριν contention TWH

Ἑρμᾶς.
Ro. 16:14 trs Hermes, Patrobas, Hermas Eds

ἑρμηνεία, -νία WH.

* ἑρμηνευτής, interpreter.
1 Co. 14:28 ἑρμηνευτής for διερμηνευτής LT.

ἑρμηνεύω.
Joh. 1:38(39) μεθερμηνεύον LTrAWHR

Ἑρμῆς.
Ro. 16:14 trs Eds, see Ἑρμᾶς

Ἑρμογένης, Ἑ- T.

ἑρπετόν.
Acts10:12†trs καὶ τὰ (om. τὰ LTTrAWHR) ἐ. τῆς γῆς and creeping things of the earth Eds

ἔρχομαι.
Mat. 2:21 came—entered, εἰσέρχομαι LTTrAWH
6:10 ἐλθάτω TWH
7:25 ἦλθαν TrWH
27 ἦλθαν WH
8: 2 προσέρχομαι Eds
28 ἐλθόντος αὐτοῦ LTTrWH
9:18 came—entered, εἰσέρχομαι TAW: προσέρχομαι LWH
10:13 ἐλθάτω WH
13: 4 ἦλθον LTr, ἐλθόντα AWH
14:25*ἦλθεν for ἀπῆλθεν (ἀπέρχομαι) LTTrAWH
28 trs ἐλθεῖν πρός σε LTTrAWH
29 to go—καὶ ἦλθεν and went TWH
33 omit came and T[A]WHR
34 ἦλθαν WH
17:25*ἐλθόντα for ὅτε εἰσῆλθεν (εἰσέρχομαι) TrAWH
18:11 omit the verse LTTr[A]WH
21:23 ἐλθόντος αὐτοῦ LTTrWHR
24:48 omit his coming LTTrWHR
25: 6 omit cometh LTTrAWHR
13 omit wherein the Son of man cometh GLTTrAWHR
36 ἦλθατε LTTrAWH
Mar. 1:29 he entered LTr: ἦλθαν WH
39*ἦλθεν for ἦν TTrWWH
3: 8 ἦλθαν WH

Mar. 3:19 they went—ἔρχεται he cometh TWHR
31 ἐ. οὖν—καὶ ἔρχονταιLTTrAWWHR, καὶ ἔρχεται T
4:21 trs ἔρχεται ὁ λύχνος LTTrAWH
5:14*ἦλθον for ἐξῆλθον (ἐξέρχομαι) Eds
38 ἔρχονται they come Eds
6: 1 ἔρχεται cometh TTrAWWHR
29 ἦλθαν TTrAWH
53 trs ἐπὶ τὴν γῆν ἦλθον TWHR
7:25 εἰσέρχομαι T
31†trs ἦλθεν διὰ Σιδῶνος he came through Sidon LTTrAWH
8:22 ἔρχονται they come LTTrAWH
34 come—follow, ἀκολουθέω GTTrAW
9: 7 γίνομαι TWHR
14 ἐλθόντες they came TTrWH
33 ἦλθον they came LTTrAWH
12:14 οἱ δὲ ἐ.—καὶ ἐ. LTTrAWH
14:38*ἔλθητε for εἰσέλθητε (-έρχομαι) TAWH
40*ἐλθὼν for ὑποστρέψας(-στρέφω) LTrAWH
15:43 ἐλθὼν Eds
16: 5*ἐλθούσαι for εἰσελθούσαι (-έρχομαι) A
Lu. 1:59 ἦλθαν WH
2:16 ἦλθαν TTrAWH
5: 7 ἐ.²—ἦλθαν TWH
6:17 ἦλθαν WH
8:35 ἦλθαν TrWH
51*ἐλθὼν for εἰσελθὼν (-έρχομαι) GLTTrWWHR
9:23 ἔρχεσθαι GLTTrAWH
56 omit For the Son to to save (them) GLTTrAWH
11: 2 ἐλθάτω TTrWH
12:38 om.he shall come, ἐ.¹ TTrAWHR
17: 1 τοῦ μὴ ἐ.—omit τοῦ Ε: trs τὰ σκάνδαλα μὴ ἐλθεῖν TTrAWH
19:38 omit that cometh T
23:26 omit τοῦ GEds: ἐρχόμενον LTTrAWHR
33*ἦλθον (-θαν WH) for ἀπῆλθον (ἀπέρχομαι) LTTrAWH
24: 1 trs ἐπὶ τὸ μνῆμα ἦλθον (-θαν WH) TWH
23 ἦλθαν WH
Joh. 1:27 ὁ ὀπ. μου ἐ.—omit ὁ [TrA]WH
39(40) ἦλθαν TTrAWH
3:26 ἐ.¹—ἦλθαν TrAWH
4:15 ἔρχομαι Tr: διέρχομαι TAWHR
27 ἦλθαν TTrWH
6:14 trs εἰς τὸν κόσμον ἐρχόμενος T
23 ἦλθεν T
7:27 ἔρχηται S—ἔρχεται Ε
50 omit he that came to Jesus by night T
11:29 ἤρχετο TrAWH
12: 9 ἦλθαν WH
22*ἔρχεται f. καὶ πάλιν LTTrAWH
13: 1 ἦλθεν LTTrAWH
16: 7 ἔλθῃ T, WH
19: 3*add at commencement καὶ ἤρχοντο πρὸς αὐτὸν and came to him LTTrAWH
38 ἦλθον they came T
Acts 11:20*ἐλθόντες for εἰσελθόντες (-έρχομαι) GEds
12:10 ἦλθαν LTTrAWH
13:14*ἐλθόντες for εἰσελθόντες (-έρχομαι) TTrWH
44 ἔχω GLAW
14:24 ἦλθαν WH
15:30 κατέρχομαι LTTrAWH
18: 7 εἰσέρχομαι LT
21 omit I must to Jerusalem LTTrAWH
19: 1 κατέρχομαι T
21: 8 ἦλθον they came S—ἤλθομεν (-θαμεν TrWH) A.V.C EGEds
22:30 appear—come together, συνέρχομαι GEds
24: 8 omit and would have judged (ver. 6) to to come unto thee (ver. 8) LTTr[A]WHR
28:14 ἤλθαμεν LTTrAWH
15*ἦλθαν (-θον LR) for ἐξῆλθον (ἐξέρχομαι) TTrAWH
16 came—entered, εἰσέρχομαι LTTrAWH
23*ἦλθον (-θαν WH) for ἦκον (ἥκω) LTTrAWH
Ro. 15:24 omit I will come to you GEds
32 ἐλθὼν TWHR: trs ἐλ. ἐν χαρᾷ H
2 Co. 1:15 trs πρότερον πρὸς ὑμᾶς ἐ. (πρότ. ε. πρὸς υ. W) Eds
2: 1 trs ἐν λύπῃ πρὸς ὑμας ἐ. ᵤEds
12:21 ἐλθόντος μου Eds
Gal. 2:12 ἐ.²—ἦλθεν he came LTr
Heb. 6: 7 trs ἐρχόμενον πολλάκις Eds

1 Joh. **4: 3** *omit* that Christ is come in the flesh GLTTrAWHR
2 Joh. **12** γίνομαι Eds
Rev. **9:12** ἔρχεται LTTrAWHR
　　11:17 *omit* and art to come GEds
　　22:17 ἐ.¹ ² —ἔρχου GEds
　　17 ἐ.³—ἐρχέσθω GEds

ἐρῶ.

Lu. **14:10***ἐρεῖ *for* εἴπῃ (εἴπον) TTrWHR
　　22:13 εἴρηκει LTTrAWHR
Heb. **4: 7** it is said—it hath been said before, προερέω Eds
　　10:15*εἰρηκέναι *for* προειρηκέναι (προερέω) Eds
Rev. **17: 7** *trs* ἐρῶ σοι LTrAWHR

ἐρωτάω.

Mat. **15:23** ἠρώτουν LTTrAWH
　　19:17*for λέγω GEds, *see* ἀγαθός
Mar. **4:10** ἠρώτων LTrAWHR, ἠρώτουν T
　　8: 5*ἠρώτα *for* ἐπηρώτα (ἐπερωτάω) TTrAWH
Lu. **7: 4***ἠρώτων *for* παρεκάλουν (παρακαλέω) T
　　8:37 ἠρώτησεν LTrAWH
　　11:37 ἐρωτᾷ beseecheth LTAWHR, ἐρώτα Tr
　　23: 3*ἠρώτησεν *for* ἐπηρώτησεν (ἐπερωτάω) TTrAWH
Joh. **9:21**†*trs* αὐτὸν ἐ. αὐτὸς (*omit* αὐτὸς TTrAWHR) ἡλικίαν ἔχει LTTrAWHR
　　23 ἐπερωτᾶ TWH
　　18:21*ἐρωτᾷς *for* ἐπερωτᾷς (-τάω) Eds
　　21*ἐρώτησον *for* ἐπερώτησον (-τάω) LTTrAWHR
Acts **1: 6***ἠρώτων *for* ἐπηρώτων (ἐπερωτάω) LTTrAWH

ἔσεσθαι.

Acts **24:25** *omit* ἐ. GEds

ἐσθής.

Lu. **24: 4***ἐσθῆτι *for* ἐσθήσεσιν (-θησις) LTTrAWHR
Acts **1:10** ἐσθησις LTTrAWHR

ἔσθησις.

Lu. **24: 4** ἐσθής LTTrAWHR
Acts **1:10***ἐσθήσεσιν *for* ἐσθῆτι (-θής) LTTrAWHR

ἐσθίω, ἔσθω.

Mat. **24:49** ἐσθίῃ shall eat GEds
Mar. **1: 6** ἔσθων TTrAWH
　　2:16 αὐτὸν ἐ.—ὅτι ἤσθιεν that he did eat TTr; ὅτι ἐσθίει LWHR
　　7: 2 ἐσθίουσιν TTrWH
　　28 ἐσθίουσιν LTTrAWWH
Lu. **6: 1** *trs* and did eat the ears of corn TrAWH
　　7:33†*trs* ἔσθων ἄρτον LTrAWH, ἐσθίων ἄ. T
　　10: 7 ἔσθοντες LTTrAWH
　　22:30 ἔσθητε LTTrAWH

Ἐσλί, —λεί TTrAWH.

ἐσμέν.

Joh. **17:22** *omit* ἐ. TTrAWHR
Acts **10:39** *omit* ἐ. GEds
2 Co. **6:16***for ἐστέ LTTrWHR
Gal. **4: 28** ἐστέ TTrWH
1 Joh. **3: 1***κληθῶμεν—*add* καὶ ἐ. *read* sons of God, and we are (such) LTTrAWHR

ἔσομαι, ἔσῃ, ἔσται, ἐσόμεθα, ἔσεσθε, ἔσονται.

Mat. **5:37***ἔσται *for* ἔστω LA
　　6: 5 ἔσῃ—ἔσεσθε LTTrAWHR, *see* προσεύχομαι
　　12:11 *omit* shall there be TrA[WH]
　　17:17 *trs* μεθ' ὑμῶν ἔσομαι LTTrAWH
　　20:26 it shall be—it is, ἐστίν LTrWH
　　26*ἔσται *for* ἔστω LTTrAWH
　　27*ἔσται *for* ἔστω LTTrAWH
　　24:40 *trs* ἔσονται δύο LTWH
Mar. **3:29***ἔσται *for* ἐστίν Tr
　　6:11 *omit* verily to end of verse G[L]TTrAWH
　　10:43 shall it be—it is, ἐστίν LTTrAWHR
Lu. **9:48** shall be—is, ἐστίν LTTrAWHR
　　17:36 *add* the verse A.V.B E, *see* ἀφίημι

Lu. **19:46***καὶ ἔσται (*before* ὁ οἶκος) *for* ἐστίν TTrAWHR, *read* and my house shall be a house
　　20:33*ἔσται *for* γίνεται (γίνομαι) R
　　21:25 ἔσονται LTTrAWH
Joh. **14:17** shall be—is, ἐστίν LTrAWH
1 Pet. **1:16***ἔσεσθε *for* γένεσθε (γίνομαι) Eds
2 Joh. **3** ἔσται—sit A.V.Vul
Rev.10: **5** *trs* οὐκέτι ἔσται GEds
　　21: 3 *trs* μετ' αὐτῶν ἐ. GLTTrAWWHR
　　22:12 shall be—is, ἐστίν LTTrAWHR

ἐσόμενος.

Rev. 16: **5** ὅσιος holy one—ἐ. shalt be A.V.B

Ἐσρώμ, Ἐ— WH.

Lu. **3:33** Ἐσρών BLWHR

ἐστέ.

Mat. **23:28** *trs* ἐστε μεστοὶ LTTrAWH
Lu. **9:55** *omit* and said to end of verse LTTrAWH
　　11:48*add ἐ. TTrAWHR, *see* μάρτυς
　　24:17 *omit* ἐ. TTrAWHR, *see* ἵστημι
　　48 *omit* ἐ. T[Tr]AWH
Joh. **8:39***for ἦτε GLTTrAWHR
2 Co. **6:16** ἐσμέν LTTrWHR
Gal. **4:28***for ἐσμέν LTTrA
Eph. **2:19***but—*add* ἐ. ye are LTTrAWHR
　　5: 5 οἶδα GEds
Heb.12: **8** *trs* καὶ οὐχ υἱοί ἐ. LTTrAWHR
Jas. **4:14***for ἐστίν Eds

ἐστίν.

Mat. **6:13** *omit* GEds, *see* αἰών
　　7: 9 *omit* ἐ. LT·[A]WH
　　10:10 *omit* ἐ. LTTrAWH
　　11:11 *trs* ἐστὶν αὐτοῦ A
　　15:26 ἐ. καλόν—ἔξεστιν, *read* it is not allowed LTA
　　18: 7 *omit* ἐ. LT·AWH
　　19:17*add ἐ. GEds, *see* ἀγαθός
　　26 *omit* ἐ.² GLTTrAWWH
　　20:26*for ἔσται LTWH
Mar. **3:29** is—will be, ἔσται T
　　4:31 *omit* ἐ. LTTrAWHR, *see* μικρός
　　6:15 *omit* ἐ.² [L]TTrAWHR
　　16 *omit* ἐ. αὐτός G[L]TTrAWHR
　　49*for εἶναι TWH
　　10:27 *omit* ἐ. TTrWH
　　43*for ἔσται LTTrAWHR
　　12:29*first—*add* ἐ. is [L]TTrAWHR, *see* ἐντολή
Lu. **8:25** *omit* ἐ.¹ Eds
　　9:48*for ἔσται LTTrAWHR
　　10: 7 *omit* ἐ. LTTrAWH
　　14:17 εἰσίν T
　　16:15 *omit* ἐ. GEds
　　19: 9 *omit* ἐ. T[WH]
　　46 *see* ἔσται
　　23:38 *omit* ἐ. LTTrAWH
Joh. **1: 4***for ἦν LT
　　27 *omit* he it is Θ[L]TTrAWH
　　2: 3*for ἔχουσιν (ἔχω) T
　　3:31 *omit* is above all² Tr
　　8:17*add ἐ. T, *see* γράφω
　　10:12*for εἰσίν LTTrAWH
　　13:24*see λέγω
　　14:11 ἐμοί ἐ. B
　　17*for ἔσται LTTrAWH
　　17: 7 εἰσίν TTrAWH
　　21:25 *omit* the verse T
Acts **12:15** *trs* ἐστὶν αὐτοῦ LTTrAWH
　　15:18 *omit* LTTrAWHR, *see* ἔργον
　　28:22 *trs* ἡμῖν ἐστιν LTTrAWH
Ro. **10: 1** *omit* ἐ. GEds
　　11: 6 *omit* ἐ.¹ A: *omit* but if (it be) to end of verse GLTTr[A]WHR
　　14: *it omit* ἐ. Eds, *see* δυνατέω
1 Co. **1:25** *omit* ἐ.² TTrWH
　　3: *δὲ—*add* ἐ. LTTrAWHR
　　22 *omit* ἐ. LTTrAWH
　　6: 5 ἔνι GEds
　　20 *omit* GEds, *see* θεός
　　7: 8 *omit* ἐ. GEds
　　9 *omit* ἐ. W
　　29†*trs* ἐστὶν (΄ ΕΙΤWHR) τὸ λοιπόν Eds
　　9: 3 *trs* ἐστὶν αὕτη LTTrAWH
　　12: 6 *omit* it is GEds
　　14:10 εἰσίν Eds
　　37*for εἰσίν Eds
　　15:17*ὑμῶν—*add* [ἐ.] LWH
　　44 and there is—*trs* there is also Eds
2 Co. **1:18***for ἐγένετο (γίνομαι) Eds
　　2: 2 *omit* ἐ. Eds
　　18: 5 *omit* ἐ. [L]TTr[A]WH

Gal. **6:15***for ἰσχύει (-χύω) GEds
Eph. **5:23** *omit* ἐ.² Eds
Phil. **1: 8** *omit* ἐ. [L]TTrAWH
　　28†*trs* ἐστὶν αὐτοῖς GEds
Col. **3:20** *trs* εὐάρεστόν ἐστιν LTTrAWHR
1 Ti. **5:25** *omit* ἐ. LTTrAWH, εἰσίν W
Heb.12: **7** *omit* ἐ. LTT·[A]WHR
Jas. **4:14** it is—ye are, ἐστέ Eds
1 Pet. **1: 6** *omit* ἐ. TTrWH
1 Joh. **1: 5** *trs* ἐστὶν αὕτη TTrAWWH
　　5 *trs* οὐκ ἔστιν ἐν αὐτῷ TrWH
　　8 *trs* ἐν ἡμῖν οὐκ ἔστιν LT·W
　　2:10 *trs* οὐκ ἔστιν ἐν αὐτῷ LTA
　　4:12 *trs* ἐν ἡμῖν ἐστιν TTrAWH
Rev. **1: 4** *omit* ἐ. Eds
　　5: 2 *omit* ἐ. Eds
　　13 *omit* ἐ.¹ Eds
　　13 *omit* such as are TTr, [ἐ.] WH
　　9:19*for εἰσίν A.V.C GEds, *see* ἐξουσία
　　13:18*αὐτοῦ—*add* ἐ. Tr
　　17: 8 *omit* ἐ.³ GEds, *see* καίπερ
　　21:16 *omit* τοσοῦτόν ἐ. GEds
　　22:12*ἐ. αὐτοῦ *for* a. ἔσται LTTrAWH

ἔστω, ἔστωσαν.

Mat. **5:37** ἔσται, *read* your communication shall be LA
　　20:26 let him be—shall be, ἔσται LTTrAWH
　　27 let him be—shall be, ἔσται LTTrAWH
Acts **28:28** *trs* ὑμῖν ἔστω AWH

ἔσχατος.

Mar. **10:31** οἱ ἐ.—*omit* οἱ GLW[WH]
　　12: 6 *trs* ἐ. πρὸς αὐτούς LTTrAWHR
　　22 ἔσχατον LTTrAWH
Joh. **8: 9** *omit* (even) unto the last WH
Heb. **1: 2(1)** ἐσχάτου, *read* at the end of these days GEds
1 Pet. **1:20** ἐσχάτου, *read* the end of the times Eds
2 Pet. **3: 3** ἐσχάτων Eds
Jude **18** ἐσχάτου Eds, *see* χρόνος
Rev. **1:11** *omit* GEds, *see* ἄλφα
　　22:13 ὁ ἐ.—*omit* ὁ L[A]: *trs see* ἀρχή

ἔσω.

2 Co. **4:16***for ἔσωθεν LTTrAWHR

ἔσωθεν.

2 Co. **4:16** ἔσω ἡμῶν our inward LTTrWHR, ἔσω[θεν] ἡ. A
Rev. **11: 2** ἔ. within s—ἔξωθεν without A.V.B EGEds

ἑταῖρος.

Mat. **11:16** their fellows—the others, ἔτερος TTrWH

ἕτερος.

Mat. **10:23***ἑτέραν *f.* ἄλλην(-λος) GLTTrWHR
　　11:16*ἑτέροις *for* ἑταίροις(-ρος) TTrWH
　　21:30*ἑτέρῳ *for* δευτέρῳ (-ρος) GTAW
Lu. **7:19***ἕτερον *for* ἄλλον (-λος) Tr·WH
　　17:36 *add* the verse A.V.B E, *see* ἀφίημι
　　19:20 another—the other, ὁ ἐ. LTTrAWHR
Acts **19:39** *trs* περὶ ἐ. concerning other matters—περαιτέρω further LTrWH
1 Co. **8: 4** *omit* ἐ. read no God LTTrAWHR
　　14:21 ἑτέρων, *read* lips of others
Jas. **4:12** another — (thy) neighbour, πλησίον LTTrAWHR

ἔτι.

Mar. **8:17** *omit* yet² LTTrAWH
Lu. **22:37** *omit* yet LTTrAWH
Joh. **11:30***was²—*add* ἐ. still LTr[A]WHR
Ro. **5: 6** ἐ. γὰρ—εἴ γε AWH
　　6*ἀσθενῶν—*add* ἐ. GEds
1 Co. **3: 2** [yet] LWH
Rev. 10: **6** οὐκ ἔσται ἐ.—οὐκέτι ἐσ. GEds
　　22: 5*for ἔσται GEds

ἑτοιμάζω.

Mat. **22: 4** ἡτοίμακα LTTrAWHR
Mar. **15: 1***ἑτοιμάσαντες *for* ποιήσαντες (ποιέω) T

ἔτος.

Acts **13:19, 20** *trs* by lot about the space of four hundred and fifty years. And after these things he gave LTTrWWHR

Gal. 1:18 trs τρία ἔτη TWH
3:17 trs τετρακόσια καὶ τριάκοντα ἔτη GEds

εὖ.
Lu. 19:17 well—well done, εὖγε LTTrAWH

Εὖα, Εὖα, Εὖα—Εὖα WH.

εὐαγγελίζω.
Lu. 4:18 εὐαγγελίσασθαι GEds
Acts 8:25 εὐηγγελίζοντο Eds
14: 7 trs εὐαγ. ἦσαν LTTrAWH
21 εὐαγγελιζόμενοι preaching the gospel LT
17:18 trs εὐηγγ. αὐτοῖς ([α.]A) LA
Ro. 10:15 omit preach the gospel of peace and LTTr[A]WH
1 Co. 9:16 ε.² εὐαγγελίσωμαι LTrAWWH
Gal. 1: 8 ε.¹—εὐαγγελίσηται TWH

εὐαγγέλιον.
Ro. 15:29 omit of the gospel GEds
Eph. 6:19 [of the gospel] LWH

εὐαρεστέω.
Heb.11: 5 εὐαρεστηκέναι LAWH

* εὖγε, well done !
Lu. 19:17 for εὖ LTTrAWH

εὐδία.
Mat.16: 2 when it is evening to end of verse 3 [TA] [[WH]]

εὐδοκέω.
Mat. 3:17 ηὐδόκησα T
12:18 ηὐδόκησεν TTr
17: 5 ηὐδόκησα LTr
Lu. 3:22 εὐδόκησα LTTrAWH
Ro. 15:26, 27 ηὐδόκησαν TT,WH
1 Co.10: 5 ηὐδόκησεν LTTrAWH
1 Th. 2: 8 ηὐδοκοῦμεν WH
3: 1 ηὐδοκήσαμεν TTrWH
Heb.10: 6 ηὐδόκησας LTTr A
8 ηὐδόκησας LTTr

εὐδοκία.
Mat.11:26 trs εὐδοκία ἐγένετο LTWH
Lu. 2:14 εὐδοκίας, read among men of good pleasure LTTrAWH
10:21 trs εὐδοκία ἐγένετο LTrAWH

εὐθέως.
(Throughout Mark εὐθύς is read for ε. by most modern Editors.)
Mat.14:22 omit straightway T[WH]
27 εὐθὺς LTTrWH
21: 2 εὐθύς TWH
3 εὐθὺς TTrWH
26:74 εὐθὺς TrWH
Mar. 1:31 omit immediately TTrWH
2: 2 omit straightway [L]T[Tr]WH
12 trs καὶ ε. read he arose, and immediately TTrAWH
5: 2 omit immediately L[WH]
13 omit forthwith Jesus (read he gave) [L]TTr[A]WH
36 omit as soon as [L]TTr[A]WH
7:35 omit straightway [L]TTrAWH
Lu. 5:39 omit straightway TTrAWH
6:49 εὐθύς TTrAWH
Joh. 5: 9 omit immediately T
13:30 εὐθὺς LTTrAWH
See also εὐθύς.

εὐθυμότερον.
Acts 24:10 more cheerfully—cheerfully, εὐθύμως LTTrAWH

* εὐθύμως, cheerfully.
Acts 24:10 for εὐθυμότερον LTTrAWH

εὐθύς, adj.
Lu. 3: 5 εὐθείας LTTrAWH

εὐθύς, adv.
Mat. 3:16 trs εὐθὺς ἀνέβη LTTrWWH
Mar. 1:12 εὐθέως LW
23*and¹—add ε. straightway TAWH
5:42*astonished—add ε. straightway T[Tr]AWH
7:25*add ε. straightway TTrAWH, see ἀλλά
35*and²—add ε. straightway T

Mar.14:72*and¹—add ε. straightway LTTrWH
Joh. 21: 3 omit immediately LTTrAWH
Acts 10:16*for πάλιν Eds
See also εὐθέως.

εὐθύτης.
Heb. 1: 8 τῆς εὐθύτητος LTTrWHB

εὐκαιρέω.
Mar. 6:31 εὐκαίρουν LTTrAWH
Acts 17:21 εὐκαίρουν LTTrAWH

εὐλαβέομαι.
Acts 23:10 φοβέομαι LTTrAWH

εὐλαβής.
Acts 22:12*εὐλαβὴς for εὐσεβής LTTrAWH

εὐλογέω.
Mat. 5:44 omit bless them to hate you LTTrAWH
14:19 εὐλόγησεν LTrA
Mar.10:16 εὐλόγει blesseth LW: omit η. αὐτά, see κατευλογέω TTrAWH
Lu. 1:28 om. blessed (art) thou among women T[Tr]AWH
24:53 omit and blessing T
Acts 3:25*εὐλογηθήσονται for ἐνευλογηθήσονται (–γέομαι) WH
1 Co.14:16 εὐλογῆς LTTrAWH
Gal. 3: 8*εὐλογηθήσονται for ἐνευλογηθήσονται (–γέομαι)
Heb.11:20, 21 ηὐλόγησεν LA

Εὐνείκη, Εὐνί– EGEds.

εὔνοια.
1 Co. 7: 3 omit benevolence, read (her) due GEds

* εὐπάρεδρος, assiduous.
1 Co. 7:35 εὐπάρεδρος for εὐπρόσεδρον (–δρος) GEds

εὐπορέομαι.
Acts 11:29 εὐπορεῖτο LTTrAWH

εὐπρόσεδρος.
1 Co. 7:35 εὐπάρεδρος GEds

εὑρίσκω.
Mat. 2:11 found—saw, εἰδέω A.V.C GEds
26:43†trs πάλιν εὗρεν αὐτούς, read came again and found them LTTrAWH
60 omit (yet) found they none G[L]TTrAWH
Mar. 1:37 καὶ εὗρον αὐτὸν καὶ and they found him and TTrAWH
11:13 trs τι εὑρήσει LTTrAWWH
14:55 ηὕρισκον LTrAWH
Lu. 8:35 εὗραν TrWH
19:48 ηὕρισκον LTrWH
23: 2 εὕραμεν LTrWH
Joh.18:38 trs εὑ. ἐν αὐτῷ αἰτίαν LTTrAWH
19: 4†trs οὐδεμίαν αἰτίαν εὑρίσκω ἐν αὐτῷ LTrWH, αἰτ. ἐν αὐ. οὐ. εὑ. A, αἰτ. οὐχ εὑ. T
Acts 5:10 εὗραν Tr
7:11 ηὕρισκον TrAWH
19: 1 εὑρεῖν found LTTrAWH
Ro. 4: 1 trs εὑρηκέναι before Ἀβραάμ LTTrAB: omit hath found [A]WH
7:18 omit I find LTTrAWH
Heb. 9:12 εὑράμενος 8—εὑρόμενος B
11: 5 ηὑρίσκετο LTTrAWWH
2 Pet. 3:10*εὑρεθήσεται for κατακαήσεται (–καίω) TrWH
Rev. 9: 6 εὑρώσιν LE
18:14†trs αὐτὰ οὐ μὴ (οὐ μὴ αὐτὰ TTrWH) εὑρήσουσιν (they shall find) (εὕρῃς W) Eds

Εὐροκλύδων, Εὐρακύλων Eds.

εὐσεβής.
Acts 22:12 εὐλαβὴς LTTrAWH

εὐφραίνω, –ομαι.
Acts 2:26 ηὐφράνθη LTTrAWWH
Rev. 11:10 εὐφραίνονται Eds

Εὐφράτης.
Rev. 16:12 τὸν Ε.—omit τὸν GTTrWH]

εὐχαριστέω.
Joh. 6:11 εὐχαρίστησεν καὶ gave thanks and T
Ro. 1:21 ηὐχαρίστησαν GLTTrAWH
7:25 χάρις, read thanks (be) to God LTTrAWH

εὔχομαι.
Acts 26:29 εὐξάμην T
27:29 εὔχοντο TTrA
2 Co.13: 7 εὐχόμεθα we pray Edr
Jas. 5:16 προσεύχομαι LWH

εὐώνυμος.
Mar.10:37 ἀριστερός TTrAWH

ἐφάλλομαι.
Acts 19:16 ἐφαλόμενος LTTrAWH

ἐφάπαξ.
Heb. 7:27 | 9:12 | 10:10 ἐφ' ἅπαξ Tr

Ἐφεσῖνος.
Rev. 2: 1 in Ephesus, Ἐφεσος GEds

Ἔφεσος.
Eph. 1: 1 [at Ephesus] TAWH
Rev. 2: 1*ἐν Ἐφέσῳ for Ἐφεσίνης GEds

ἐφίστημι.
1 Th. 5: 3 ἐπίσταμαι TTrWH

* ἐφνίδιος, see αἰφνίδιος.

Ἐφραΐμ, –ίμ LTWH.

* ἐχθές for χθές Eds.

ἐχθρός.
Lu. 1:74 τῶν ἐ.—omit τῶν LTTrAWH

ἔχω.
Mat.16: 8*ἔχετε for ἐλάβετε (λαμβάνω) LWH
17:15*ἔχει for πάσχει (–χω) LTrWH
18:25 εἶχεν—ἔχει he hath LTrAWH
19:16 σχῷ LTTrAWH
21:38*σχῶμεν for κατάσχωμεν (κατέχω) LTTrAWH
26: 7 trs ἐ. ἀλάβαστρον μύρου LTTr,WH
Mar. 2:19†trs ἐ. τὸν νυμφίον μετ' αὐτῶν (μεθ' ἑαυτῶν L) LTTrAWH
4: 9 ὁ ἔχων—ὃς ἔχει Eds
25 ἂν ἔχῃ—ἔχει LTTrAWH
6:36 omit ε. [L]TTrAWH, see ἄρτος
7:16 omit the verse T[Tr A]WH
8: 7 εἶχαν LTTrAWH
16 ἔχουσιν they have LTTrAWH
9:42*add ἔχοντων A, see πίστις
12: 6†trs εἶχεν υἱὸν TTrAWH
14: 8 ἔσχεν GEds
Lu. 8:27 ὃς εἶχεν—ἔχων TWHR
17: 6' ἔχετε ye have TTrAWH
23:17 omit the verse [L]TTr[A]WH
Joh. 2: 3*add εἶχον T, see οἶνος
3 they have—there is, ἐστίν T
12: 6 ἔχων TTrAWH
15:22, 24 εἶχον—εἴχοσαν LTTrAWH
16:33 ἔχετε ye have s—ἕξετε ye shall have A.V.B EL
19:11 couldest have—hast, ἔχεις T
Acts 7: 1 omit ἔχει W
9:31 εἶχεν Eds
13:44†*ἐχομένῳ for ἐρχομένῳ (–μαι) GLAW
20:24 omit οὐδὲ ἔχω TTrAWH
23:25*ἔχουσαν for περιέχουσαν (–χω) LTTrWHR, [περι]έ. A
29 trs ἐ. ἔγκλημα LTTrAWWH
28:29 omit the verse LTTrAWH
Ro. 5: 1 ἔχωμεν let us have TTrAWH
1 Co. 7: 7 trs ἔχει χάρισμα GEds
29 οἱ ἔ.—omit οἱ E
12:12 trs πολλὰ ἔχει LTTrAWH
2 Co. 1:15 σχῆτε TTrAWH
2: 3 σχῶ TTrAWH
7: 5 ἔσχεν LTr
Gal. 6:10 ἔχωμεν TWH
Col. 1: 4*ἣν ἔχετε [WH] for τὴν ², rd. love which ye have A.V.†Vul Eds
1 Th. 1: 8 trs ἔχειν ἡμᾶς Eds
9 ἔχομεν A.V.C GEds
Philem. 7†trs πολλὴν ἔσχον I had great Eds
Heb. 9: 1 εἶχε TWH
1 Pet. 4: 5 omit ἔχοντι WH, see κρίνω

1 Joh. 2:23*add ἑ. A.V.B GEds. see ὁμολο-
 γεω
 28 σχῶμεν LTTᵣAWHR
2 Joh. 5 εἰχαμεν TTᵣWH
Rev. 2:10 ἔχητε LWH
 3: 4 trs ὀλίγα ἔχεις T
 4: 4 omit they had GEds
 7 ἔχων TTᵣAWHR
 8 εἴχου—ἔχον GLW. ἔχων
 TTᵣAWHR
 5: 6 ἔχων TTᵣAWHR
 8: 6 οἱ ἔχοντες A.V.C GEds
 9: 8 εἴχαν LTTᵣAWH
 9 εἰχαν WH
 14 ὁ ἔχων GEds
 10: 2 ἔχων GEds
 14:18 ἑ.—ὁ ἔχων LAWR, [ὁ] ἑ. WH
 15: 6 οἱ ἔχοντες GLTTᵣWR, [οἱ] ἑ AWH
 17: 3 ἔχοντα TA, ἔχων WH
 21:12 ἑ.—ἔχουσα GEds
 12 ἑ.²—ἔχουσα GLTTᵣAWHR
 14 ἔχων TTᵣAWHR
 22: 5†trs οὐχ ἔξουσιν (οὐκ ἔχουσιν
 TTᵣWH) χρείαν LTTᵣAWWH

 ἕως.

Mat. 13:30*for μέχρι LTTᵣAWH
Lu. 2:37*for ὡς LTTᵣAWHR
 16:16 μέχρι TTᵣAWHR
 19:13 ἔν ἡ LTTᵣAWHR
 22:34*for πριν ἡ LTTᵣAWHR
Joh. 8: 9 omit (even) unto the last WH
 12:35, 36 ὡς LTTᵣAWH
Acts 1:22 ἄχρι T
 17:14*for ὡς TTᵣWHR
Rev. 20: 5 ἄχρι GEds

 Ζαχαρίας.

Lu. 3: 2 τοῦ Ζ.—omit τοῦ GLTTᵣAWWH

 ζάω.

Mar. 5:23 ζήσῃ LTTᵣAWHR
Lu. 15:32*ἔζησεν for ἀνέζησεν (ἀναζάω)
 TTᵣAWHR
Joh. 5:25 ζήσουσιν LTTᵣAWH
 6:51 ζ.²—ζήσει TWH
 57 ζ.¹—ζήσει LTTᵣAWH
 58 ζήσει TTᵣAWH
 69 omit the living GLTTᵣAWH
 14:19 ζ.²—ζήσετε TTᵣA
Acts 14:15 τὸν ζ.—omit τὸν Eds
 25:24 trs αὐτὸν ζῆν LTTᵣAWWH
Ro. 14: 9*ἔζησεν for ἀνέζησεν (ἀναζάω)
 GEds
2 Co. 13: 4 ζ.²—ζήσομεν Eds
Gal. 2:14 trs καὶ οὐχ (οὐκ TᵣAWH) Ἰουδαι-
 κῶς ζῆς LTTᵣAWH
1 Ti. 6:17 omit the living LTTᵣAWHR
2 Ti. 3:12 trs ζῆν εὐσεβῶς TTᵣWH
Jas. 4:15 ζήσομεν A.V.B 1549 Eds
Rev. 5:14 omit him that liveth for ever
 and ever GEds
 7:17 ζωή, read fountains of waters
 of life GEds
 16: 3 ζωή GLTTᵣAWHR
 20: 5*ἔζησεν for ἀνέζησαν (ἀναζάω)
 GEds

 ζβέννυμι, see σβέννυμι.

 ζεστός.

Rev. 3:16 trs hot nor cold GTTᵣAWWHR

 * ζηλεύω, to be zealous.

Rev. 3:19 ζήλευε for ζήλωσον (-λόω) Eds

 ζῆλος.

2 Co. 9: 2 ὁ . . . ζ.—τὸ . . . ζ. TTᵣWH
 12:20 ζῆλος envying Eds
Gal. 5:20 ζῆλος emulation LTTᵣAWWH
Phil. 3: 6 ζῆλος Eds
Col. 4:13 zeal—labour, πόνος GEds

 ζηλόω.

Gal. 4:18 τὸ ζ.—omit τὸ LTTᵣAWHR
Rev. 3:19 ζηλεύω Eds

 ζηλωτής.

1 Pet. 3:13*ζηλωταὶ for μιμηταί (-τής) Eds

 ζημιόω.

Mar. 8:36 ζημιωθῆναι to lose TAWHR, see
 κερδαίνω

 ζητέω.

Mat. 12:47 omit the verse [T]WH
Mar. 1:37 trs σε ζητοῦσιν LW
 8:12*ζητεῖ σημεῖον for σ. ἐπιζητεῖ
 (-τέω) LTTᵣAWHR

Lu. 2:45 ἀναζητῶν LTTᵣAWHR
 4:42 ἐπιζητῶν GEds
 6:19 ἐζήτουν TTᵣAWH (WHR
 11:29*ζητεῖ for ἐπιζητεῖ (-τέω) TTᵣA
 54 omit seeking T[Tᵣ]AWHR
Joh. 5:16 omit and sought to slay him
 G[L]TTᵣAWH
 19·12 trs ὁ Πιλᾶτος ἐζήτει LTTᵣAWH
Acts 10:19 ζητοῦντες TAWH

 ζήτημα.

Acts 18:15 ζητήματα questions LTTᵣAWHR

 ζήτησιν.

Acts 15: 2*ζητήσεως for συζητήσεως
 (-τησις) GEds
 7*ζητήσεως for συζητήσεως
 (-τησις) TTᵣWHR
1 Ti. 1: 4 ἐκζήτησις TTᵣWHR

 ζιζάνια.

Mat. 13:27 τὰ ζ.—omit τα GEds

 * Ζμύρνα, see Σμύρνα.

 ζόφον.

Heb. 12·18*ζόφῳ for σκότῳ (-τος) Eds

 ζωή.

Mat. 19:17 trs εἰς τὴν ζ. εἰσελθ. LTTᵣAWWH
Mar. 9:43 trs εἰσελθ. εἰς τὴν ζ. LTTᵣAWWH
Lu. 1:75 omit της ζ. read all our days
 GEds
1 Joh. 5:20 ἡ ζ.—omit ἡ LTTᵣAWHR
Rev. 7:17*ζωῆς for ζώσας (ζάω) GEds
 16: 3*ζωῆς for ζώσα (ζάω)GLTTᵣAWHR

 ζωννύω, ζώννυμι.

Joh. 21:18 trs ζώσει σε TᵣAWH
Acts 12: 8*ζῶσαι for περίζωσαι (-ώννυμι)
 LTTᵣAWHR

 ζωογονέω.

1 Ti. 6:13*ζωογονοῦντος for ζωοποιοῦντος
 (-ποιέω) LTTᵣAWHR

 ζῷον, ζῶον LWH.

 ζωοποιέω.

1 Ti. 6:13 quickeneth—preserveth alive
 ζωογονεω LTTᵣAWHR

 ἤ.

Mat. 6:25*for καί¹ LTᵣ[WH]R
 7:10*καὶ ἐάν—ἢ καὶ LTTᵣAWHR
 15: 6(5) om. or his mother L[A]WHR
 19:29 omit or wife LTTᵣAWHR
 20:15 omit ἢ LTᵣ[A]WH
 15 for εἰ A.V.B EGEds
 26:53 omit ἢ² [L]TTᵣAWH
Mar. 3:33 or—and, καὶ LTTᵣAWH
 6:11 omit G[L]TTᵣAWH, see ἀμην
 15 omit or GEds
 8:37 ἢ τί—τί γάρ for what TTᵣAWH
 10:29 omit or wife LTTᵣAWH
 38*.40*for καί LTTᵣAWH
 11:28*for καί² TAWH
 13:21 omit or TᵣAWH
 32*for καί GEds
 35*ὀψὲ either at even TTᵣAWH
Lu. 2:26 omit ἢ Tᵣ[WH]
 6:42 omit either T[Tᵣ]AWH
 10:42*add ἢ WH, see ὀλίγος
 11:11*for εἰ GLTTᵣAWR
 12:11 [or what thing] TᵣAWH
 29 or—and, καὶ LTTᵣAWH
 47*for μηδέ TWHR
 14: 3*add at end ἢ οὐ or not ?
 [L]TTᵣAWH
 17:23 omit or TTᵣR
 18:14 παρά LTᵣAWH
 21:15*for οὐδὲ GT[Tᵣ]A[WH]
 22:34 see πριν
 68 omit me, nor let me go
 T[TᵣA]WHR
Joh. 6:34*for καί GTTᵣAWHR
 13:10 εἰ μή LTᵣA[WH]R, omit ἢ T
Acts 2:20 omit ἢ LTTᵣWHR
 10:14 or—and, καὶ LTTᵣAWH
 17:21*for καί² LTTᵣAWH
 24:11 omit ἢ GEds
 23 omit or come Eds
Ro. 14:21 omit TWHR, see ἀσθενέω
1 Co. 3: 5 omit ἀλλ' ἢ GEds
 5:10 or²—and, καὶ Eds
 11 ἢ¹ either 8—ἢ be A.V.B EGEds
 6: 2*add at commencement ἢ or
 GEds
 9: 7 omit or L[Tᵣ]AW[WH]
 11:14 omit ἢ Eds

2 Co. 3: 1*ἢ μή for εἰ μή A.V.B GLTTᵣAWHR
 6:14*τίς δέ—ἢ τίς Eds
Eph. 5: 4*for καί² LT
Phil. 2: 3 or—nor through, μηδὲ κατέ
 LTTᵣAWHR
Col. 2:16 or¹—and, καί AWH
1 Ti. 2: 9 or¹—and, καί LTTᵣAWH
 5:16 omit πιστὸς ἢ (omit man or)
 LTTᵣ[A]WHR
Heb. 12·20 omit or thrust through with
 a dart GEds
Jas. 11*for καί LTTᵣAWH
 13 καὶ and—ἢ or A.V.F FLTTᵣWHR
Rev. 13.17 omit or² GEds

 ἤ μήν.

Heb. 6:14 εἰ μήν LTTᵣAWHR

 ἡγεμών.

Mat. 27:23 omit ἢ. read he said TTᵣAWHR
Acts 23:34 omit ὁ ἢ. read he GEds

 ἤδη.

Mar.15:44*for παλαι LTᵣWH
Lu. 23:44*ἤδη ὡσεί now about LTWHR,
 [ἢ.] ὡσεί WH
 24:29*κεκλικεν—add ἢ. read already
 is far spent [L]TTᵣAWH
Joh. 6:17 καὶ σκοτία ἤδη ἐγεγόνει—κατέ-
 λαβεν δε αὐτοὺς ἡ σκοτία and
 darkness overtook them T
 11:17 omit already T: trs ἤδη ἡμέρας
 TᵣAWH
 19:28 trs ἤδη πάντα LTTᵣAWWH
 33 trs ἤδη αὐτον TTᵣAWH
Ro. 4:19 omit now [L]T[AWH]

 ἤκω.

Mar. 8: 3 came, ἥκασιν 8—ἥκουσιν EW:
 εἰσιν are AWH
Lu. 13.35 ἥξει LT[TᵣA]: omit (the time)
 come when WHR
Acts 28:23 ἐρχομαι LTTᵣAWH
Rev. 3: 9 ἥξουσιν LTTᵣAWHR

 Ἡλί.

Mat. 27:46 Ἡλὶ δια LA, Ἡλεί T, Ἐλωί WH

 Ἡλί, Ἡλεί TTᵣAWH.

 Ἡλίας, Ἡ-, Ἡλείας T. Ἡλείας WH.

Mat. 17: 4 trs Ἡλια μίαν LTTᵣAWHR
Lu. 9:54 omit even as Elias did
 TTᵣ[A]WHR

 ἡλικία.

Lu. 2:52 trs in stature and wisdom Tᵣ
 12:25 trs ἐπὶ τὴν ἡ. αὐτοῦ προσθ. AWH

 ἡλίκος.

Jas. 3: 5*ἡλίκον for ὀλίγον (·γος) Eds

 ἥλιος.

Mar. 4: 6 ὁ ἥλιος LTTᵣAWHR, see ἀνατέλλω
Lu. 23:45 and the sun was darkened—
 τοῦ ἡλίου ἐκλειπόντες (ἐκλί-
 ποντος T), read ninth hour,
 from the sun failing TWHR
Rev. 22: 5 omit of the sun W

 ἡμᾶς.

Mat. 8:25 omit us Eds
Lu. 11: 4 omit but deliver us from evil
 GTTᵣAWH
 23:15*for ὑμᾶς TWHR, see ἀναπεμ πω
Joh. 9: 4*for ἐμέ TTᵣWHR: for με T
Acts 7:27 ἡμῶν LTTᵣWWHR
Ro. 7: 6 [ὑμᾶς] LTTᵣAWH
 13:11†trs ἤδη ἡ. LTᵣW: ἤδη ὑμᾶς
 TAWH
 15: 7 us—you, ὑμᾶς GLTTᵣAWR
 16: 6 us—you, ὑμᾶς LTTᵣAWH
1 Co. 6:14 us 8—you, ὑμᾶς R
 7:15 us—you, ὑμᾶς TWH
2 Co. 8: 4 omit δέξασθαι ἡ. GEds
Gal. 4:17 for ὑμᾶς² E
Eph. 5: 2 us¹—you, ὑμᾶς TTᵣAWH
Col. 1:12 us¹—you, ὑμᾶς TWH
1 Th. 2:15 you 8—us A.V.B EGEds
 4 us—you, ὑμᾶς Eds
1 Pet. 1: 3 us 8—you, ὑμᾶς E
 4 us—you, ὑμᾶς A.V.B GEds
 3:18 us—you, ὑμᾶς WH
 21 us—you, ὑμᾶς LTTᵣAWH
 5:10 us—you, ὑμᾶς Eds
2 Pet. 3: 9 us—you, ὑμᾶς LTTᵣAWH
Rev. 1: 6 us—for us, ἡμῖν Tᵣ, ἡμῶν L
 5: 9 omit us LTAWWHR
 10 us—them, αὐτοὺς GEds

ἤμεθα, see ἤν.

ἡμεῖς.

Joh. 7:35 omit ἡ. T
Ro. 8:23 trs ἡμεῖς καὶ TAR, [ἡ. καὶ] LTᵣWH
2 Co. 6:16*for ὑμεῖς LTTᵣWH
Gal. 4:28 we—you, ὑμεῖς LTTᵣA
1 Joh.1: 4*for ὑμῖν TTᵣAWH

ἡμέρα.

Mat. 15:32 ἡμέραι GEds
24:42*ἡμέρᾳ for ὥρα LTTᵣAWH
28:15*σήμερον—add ἡμέρας LTᵣA[WH]
Mar. 1:13†trs τεσσεράκοντα ἡ. TTᵣWH
2:20 ἐκείνῃ τῇ ἡμέρᾳ (ἡ.²) that day GEds
6:11 omit verily to end of verse G[L]TTᵣAWH
8: 2 ἡμέραι GEds
9:31 † 10:34 μετὰ τρεῖς ἡμέρας after three days LTTᵣAWH
Lu. 1:59†trs τῇ ἡ. τῇ ὀγδόῃ LTTᵣWH
75 πάσαις ταῖς ἡμέραις WH
13:31 day—hour, ὥρα TAWH
14: 5 τῇ ἡ.—omit τῇ TWH
17: 4 omit in a day² LTTᵣAWH
24 omit in his day LWH
Joh. 2: 1†trs τῇ τρίτῃ ἡ. TrA
9:14*add ἡ. LTTᵣAWH, see ὅτε
Acts 2:20 τὴν ἡ.—omit τὴν LTTᵣAWH
9:43 trs αὐτὸν ἡμέρας ἱκανὰς μεῖναι LTᵣ
12: 3 οἱ ἡμέραι GLW, [αἱ] ἡ. A
28: 7 trs ἡμέρας τρεῖς AWH
Ro. 14: 6 omit and he that regardeth not the day, to the Lord he doth not regard (it) LTTᵣ[A]WH
1 Co.15: 4†trs τῇ ἡμέρᾳ τῇ τρίτῃ Eds
2 Co. 3:14*σήμερον—add ἡ. Eds
1 Th. 1: 2 ἡμέρα—omit ἡ LTTᵣ[A]WWH
4 trs ὑμᾶς ἡ ἡμέρα LW
2 Th. 3: 8 ἡμέρας LTTᵣWH
2 Pet. 3:10 ἡ ἡμέρα—omit ἡ Eds
Rev. 11: 6 τὰς ἡμέρας GEds

ἡμέτερος.

Lu. 16:12*for ὑμέτερος WH
Acts 24: 6 omit and would have judged to come unto thee (ver. 8) LTTᵣ[A]WH
Ro. 11:31 ὑμετέρῳ s—ἡμετέρῳ E
1 Co.15:31 our s—your, ὑμέτερος A.V.B EGEds
2 Co. 8: 8 ὑμετέρας s—ἡμετέρας E

ἤμην.

Acts 11:11 I was—we were, ἤμεν LTTᵣWH

ἡμῖν.

Mat. 8:31 ἡμᾶς GLTTᵣAWH, see ἀπο-στέλλω
Mar. 9:38 omit GWH, see ἀκολουθέω
Lu. 20:22 ἡμᾶς TTᵣAWH
24:32 omit within us [TᵣA]WH
Joh. 6:52 trs ἡμῖν οὗτος T
11:50 for us—for you, ὑμῖν TTᵣAWH
Acts 7:38 us—you, ὑμῖν WH
13:26*for ὑμῖν² TAWH
33(32) to us their—to our, ἡμῶν LTTᵣWH, αὐτῶν ἡμῶν W
14:17 us—you, ὑμῖν GLT[Tᵣ]AWH
15: 7 us—you, ὑμῖν LTTᵣWH
16:17 us² s—you, ὑμῖν ETTᵣWH
2 Co. 1: 8 omit to us Eds
8: 7 ἡμῶν ἐν ὑμῖν, read our love to you WH
10: 8 omit us LTTᵣAWH
Eph. 4: 6*for ὑμῖν GW
Col. 2:13 us s—you, ὑμῖν A.V.B☿
Philem. 6*for ὑμῖν GLTᵣAWWH
Heb.13:21*for ὑμῖν TWH
1 Pet. 1:12 us—you, ὑμῖν GEds
2:21 us² s—you, ὑμῖν EGEds
4: 3 omit us LTTᵣAWH
1 Joh.1: 9 us (our)—our, ἡμῶν W

ἤμισυ.

Lu. 19: 8 ἡμίσεια TTᵣA, -σεα L, -σια WH

ἡμιώριον, —ον LTTᵣAWH.

ἡμῶν.

Mar. 9:40 you is on your, ὑμῶν bis s—us is on our A.V.B ETTᵣAWWH
Lu. 1:74 omit our [L]TTᵣAWH
9:50 us bis—you ὑμῶν GLTTᵣAWH

Lu. 11: 2 omit our GTTᵣAWH
23: 2*ἔθνος ἡ. our nation LTTᵣ[A]W
Joh. 8:54*for ὑμῶν TTᵣAW (WH
19: 7 om. ἡ. read the law LTTᵣAWH
Acts 3:22*for ὑμῶν T
25 our—your, ὑμῶν TᵣAWH
4:25*add ἡ. LTTᵣAWH, see πατήρ
7:19 omit ἡ. read the fathers LTTᵣAWH
9:38*for αὐτῶν Eds
13:33(32)*for αὐτῶν ἡμῖν LTTᵣWH
14:17 our—your, ὑμῶν GLTTᵣAWH
15:36 omit ἡ. read the brethren GEds
19:25 ἡμῖν LTTᵣAWH
37*for ὑμῶν LTTᵣAWH
20: 7*for τῶν μαθητῶν (—τῆς) GEds
21:10 omit ἡ. A
24: 7 omit LTTᵣ[A]WH, see κρίνω
26: 6*πατέρας—add ἡ. A.V.Vul. Eds
28:25 our—your, ὑμῶν LTTᵣAWH
Ro. 6:11 omit our Lord GEds
8:26 omit for us Eds
16:24 omit the verse LTTᵣ[A]WH
1 Co. 5: 4 om. ἡ.¹ read the Lord [L]T[WH]
5*κυρίου—add ἡ. read our Lord [L]W
7 omit for us Eds
6:11*κυρίου—add [ἡ.] LWH
15:14*for ὑμῶν WH
16:23*κυρίου—add nostri A.V.Vul
2 Co. 1:14*κυρίου—add ἡ. read our Lord [L]TAWH
4:16*add ἡ. LTTᵣAWH, see ἔσωθεν
17 omit our WH
7:12 your care for us s—our care for you A.V.B EG
13*for ὑμῶν Eds
14 our—your, ὑμῶν LA
8: 7*for ὑμῶν WH, see ἡμῖν
19*for ὑμῶν GEds
11:31 omit ἡ. read the Lord Eds
Gal. 4: 6*for ὑμῶν Eds
Eph. 3:14 omit of our Lord Jesus Christ Eds
5: 2 us²—you, ὑμῶν AWH
Phil. 4:23 omit ἡ. read the Lord Eds
Col. 1: 3*for ὑμῶν LTTᵣAWH
3: 4 our—your, ὑμῶν TTᵣ
4: 8*for ὑμῶν¹ LTTᵣWH
1 Th. 1: 1 omit from God our to end of verse [L]TTᵣAWH
2: 4 our—your, ὑμῶν W
3: 2 omit and our fellow-labourer GEds
2 Th. 1: 2 omit ἡ. [LTᵣ]AWH
3: 6 omit ἡ. read the Lord [L]AWH
12 omit ἡ. LTTᵣAWH, see κύριος
1 Tj. 1: 2 omit ἡ.¹ Eds
Tit. 2: 8*for ὑμῶν GEds: trs λέγειν περὶ ἡ. LTTᵣAWH
10 *for ὑμῶν A.V.B EGEds
Philem.25 omit ἡ. read the Lord TWH
Heb. 1: 3 omit our Eds
9:14*for ὑμῶν LAWWH
13:23*ἀδελφὸν—add ἡ. read our brother Eds
1 Pet. 2:21 us¹ s—you, ἡμῶν EGLTTᵣAWH
1 omit for us LTTᵣAWH
2 Pet. 1: 1 σωτῆρος—add ἡ. E
2:20*κυρίου ἡ. our Lord LT
3: 2 us the—your, ὑμῶν Eds
1 Joh.1: 4 our s—your, ὑμῶν A.V.B EGW
3: 5 omit our LTTᵣAWH
21 om. our LTᵣ[A]WH: om. us WH
2 Joh. 3 us s—you, ὑμῶν A.V.B EGLW
12 our—your, ὑμῶν LTᵣAWH
Jude 3*κοινῆς—add ἡ. read our common LTTᵣAWH
25*add ἡ. GEds, see κύριος
Rev. 1: 5 [ἡμῶν] AWH
4:11*add ἡ. Eds, see κύριος
5:10 omit*unto our God A
11: 8 our—their, αὐτῶν GEds
19: 6*θεὸς—add ἡ. read our God GTTᵣW[WH]R
22:21 omit ἡ. read the Lord GEds

ἤν, ἤς (ἤσθα), ἤν·; ἤμεν, ἤτε, ἤσαν.

Mat. 3: 4 trs ἤν αὐτοῦ LTTᵣAWH
12:10 omit there was LTTᵣAWH
14:24 omit ἤν¹ TᵣWH, see στάδιον
23:30 ἤμεν bis—ἤμεθα GLTTᵣAWH
25: 2 trs ἐξ αὐτῶν ἤσαν LTTᵣAWH
Mar. 1:39 ἐρχόμενος, read went preaching TTᵣWHR
45 [ἤν] LWH
3: 1 omit ἤν L[Tᵣ]
4: 1 ἤσαν TTᵣWHR
36 ἤν²—ἤσαν T
5:13 omit they were [L]TTᵣAWH

Mar. 9: 6 were—became, see γίνομαι LTTᵣAWH
14:21 omit ἤν [L]T[Tᵣ]AWH
15:46 omit ἤν¹ T[TᵣA]WH
Lu. 7:12 omit ἤν EGW
12 ἱκανός—add ἤν EGT[TᵣA]WHR
11:14 omit and it was [TᵣA]WH
13:11 omit ἤν¹ LTTᵣAWH
15:32 omit ἤν² LTTᵣAWH
16:20 omit ἤν [L]TTᵣAWH
19: 2 omit ἤν² [L]TTᵣAWH
24:10 [ἤσαν δὲ] TrA
Joh. 1: 4 was¹—is, ἐστίν LT
8:39 were—are, ἐστέ GLTTᵣAWH
10: 8 ἤ (ᾖ) Tᵣ
11:41 omit where the dead was laid GLTTᵣAWH
18:16 ὃς ἤν—ὁ TTᵣAWH
19:14*δὲ ὡσεί—ἤν ὡς Eds
41*ἐτέθη ἤν τεθειμένος WH
Acts 2:43*add ἤν T, see φόβος
44 omit ἤσαν WH
4:34*ἤν for ὑπῆρχεν (ὑπάρχω) LTTᵣWH
10: 1 omit ἤν GEds
11:11*ἤμεν for ἤμην LTTᵣAWH
16: 9 trs Μακεδών τις ἤν Eds: omit ἤν A
20: 8 they were—we were, ἤμεν GEds
16 ἤν—εἴη LTTᵣAWH
22:29 trs αὐτὸν ἤν LTTᵣAWH
27:37 ἤμεθα LTTᵣAWWH
Gal. 4: 3 ἤμεν²—ἤμεθα TWH
15 omit ἤν Eds
Eph. 2: 3 ἤμεθα TTᵣAWH
1 Joh.2:19 trs ἐξ ἡμῶν ἤσαν² TᵣWH
Rev. 3:15*ἤς for εἴης GEds
4: 3 omit ἤν GEds
11*ἤσαν for εἰσίν GEds
5:11 add ἤν A.V.B EGEds, see ἀριθμός
9:10 ἤν - καί, read and stings; and in their tails is their power Eds
17: 4*ἤν for ἤ² A.V.CGEds
21:18 omit ἤν LTAWH

ἤπιος.

1 Th. 2: 7 νήπιος LWH

Ἡρῴδης, Ἡρῴδης WH.

Lu. 9: 9 ὁ Ἡ.—omit ὁ GLTTᵣAW[WH]
23:12 trs Herod and Pilate TTᵣAWH
Acts 12:20 omit ὁ Ἡ. read he GEds

Ἡρωδιανοί, Ἡρῳ— WH.

Ἡρωδιάς, Ἡρῳ— WH.

Mar. 6:22 τῆς Ἡ.—omit τῆς WH

Ἡσαΐας, Ἡσαΐας WH.

Mat.13:35*prophet—add Ἡσαΐου Isaiah T
Mar. 1: 2*ἐν—add Ἡ. Eds, see προφήτης
Lu. 4:17 trs τοῦ προφήτου Ἡ. LTTᵣAWH
Acts 8:28 trs Ἡ. τὸν προφήτην W
30 trs Ἡ. τὸν προφήτην LTTᵣAWH

ἡσύχιος.

1 Pet. 3: 4 trs quiet and meek LWH

ἡττάομαι.

2 Co.12:13 ἡσσώθητε LTTᵣAWH

ἤττον, ἥττων, ἤσσον LTTᵣAWH.

ἠχέω.

Lu. 21:25 ἤχος, read in perplexity at the noise of the sea GLTTᵣAR: ἠχοῦς (ἠχώ) WH

* ἤχον (neut.) a sound, noise.

Lu. 21:25 ἤχους for ἠχούσης (ἠχέω) GLTTᵣAR

* ἠχώ, an echo, see ἠχέω.

Θαδδαῖος.

Mat. 10: 3 omit whose surname was Thaddæus TA

θάλασσα.

Mat.14:24 omit θ. TᵣWH, see στάδιον
25 τὴν θάλασσαν LTTᵣAWH
26 τῆς θαλάσσης LTTᵣAWH
17:27 τὴν θ.—omit τὴν LTTᵣAWH
Rev. 10: 2 τῆς θαλάσσης GEds

Rev. 10: 6 [and the sea, and the things
which are therein] LWH
12:12 τῇ γῇ καὶ τῇ θαλάσσῃ GW
14: 7 τὴν θάλασσαν GTW

θαμβέω.

Acts 9: 6 *omit* (it is) hard (*ver.* 5) *to*
unto him (*ver.* 6) GEds

θάνατος.

Mat. 20:18 εἰς θάνατον T: [θανάτῳ] WH
Acts 25:25 *trs* αὐτὸν θανάτου LTTrAWWH
1 Co. 15:21 ὁ θ.—*omit* ὁ LTT[A]WWHR
55 θανάτε *for* ᾅδου (ᾅδης) LTTrAWHR
Phil. 2:27 θανάτου WH
Rev. 1:18 *trs* of death and of hell GEds
6: 8 ὁ θ.—*omit* ὁ T[AWH]
20: 6†trs ὁ δεύτερος (*omit* ὁ) θάνατος
GLTTrAWHR
14†trs ὁ θάνατος ὁ δεύτερός ἐστιν
GLTAWWHR, ὁ δεύτ. θ. ἐστιν Tr
21: 1 ὁ θ.—*omit* ὁ T
8†trs ὁ θάνατος ὁ δεύτερος GEds

θανατόω.

Mat. 26:59 *trs* θ. αὐτὸν W: αὐτὸν θανατώ-
σουσιν LTTrA

θαρσέω.

Lu. 8:48 *omit* be of good comfort
LTTrAWHR

θαῦμα.

2 Co. 11:14*θαῦμα *for* θαυμαστόν (-ός) Eds

θαυμάζω.

Mat. 9: 8 marvelled—were afraid, φοβέομαι LTTrAWHR
Mar. 6: 6 ἐθαύμασεν TWH
51 om.and wondered [L]TTrAWHR
12:17 ἐθαύμαζον LTrA, ἐκθαυμάζω
TWHR
15:44 ἐθαύμαζεν T
Lu. 24:12 *omit the verse* [L]T[Tr][[WH]]
Joh. 4:27 ἐθαύμαζον GEds
5:20 θαυμάζετε T
Acts 7:31 ἐθαύμασεν GTAW
Rev. 13: 3 ἐθαυμάσθη ἐν ὅλῃ τῇ γῇ there
was wonder in all the world
s—ἐθαύμασεν (-μάσθη LWH)
ὅλη ἡ γῇ all the world wondered A.V.BEGLTAWWHR
17: 8 θαυμασθήσονται LWH

θαυμαστος.

Joh. 9:30 τὸ θαυμαστόν TTrWHR
2 Co. 11:14 θαῦμα Eds

θεά, ἡ θεός.

Acts 19:35 *omit* goddess GEds
37 θεόν GEds

θεάομαι.

Joh. 8:10 *omit* and saw none but the
woman WHR
Acts 8:18 εἰδέω GEds

θεῖον.

Rev. 19:20 τῷ θ.—*omit* τῷ GEds
20:10 τοῦ θεῖον Tr

θέλημα.

Mar. 3:35 τὰ θελήματα A
Lu. 11: 2 *omit* thy will be done
GTTrAWHR
1 Pet. 4: 3 βούλημα Eds

θέλω.

Mat. 20:15 *trs* ὁ θέλω ποιῆσαι LTTrAWH
21:29 *trs* WH, οὐκ ἀπέρχομαι
27:34 ἐθέλησεν A, ἠθέλησεν LTTrWH
Mar. 7:24 ἠθέλησεν T
9:13 ἠθέλον TTrAWH
10:51 θέλεις ποιήσω; TWH
15:12 *omit* θ. read what then shall I
[Tr]WHR
Lu. 8:20 *trs* θελοντές σε TrWH
18: 4 ἠθέλεν Eds
Acts 2:12 θέλει *for* ἂν θέλοι LTTrWHR
9: 6 *omit* it is hard (*ver.* 5) *to*
unto him (*ver.* 6) GEds
17:20 τί ἂν θέλοι—τίνα θέλει LTTrWHR
24: 6 *omit* and would have *to* come
unto thee (*ver.* 8) LTTr[A]WH
25: 9 *trs* θέλων τοῖς Ἰουδαίοις
LTTrAWH
2 Co. 11:32 *omit* desirous LTTr[A]WWHR

---

1 Th. 4:13 θέλομεν we would GEds
Jas. 4:15 θέλῃ WH
1 Pet. 3:17 θέλοι GEds
Rev. 2:21*trs καὶ οὐ (add θέλει) μετανοῆ-
σαι ἐκ τῆς πορνείας αὐτῆς, read
to repent, and she willeth
not to repent of her fornication
GEds
11: 5 θ.¹—θέλει GEds
5 θ.²—θέλει GLAW, θελήσω
TTrWHR : *trs* θ. αὐτοὺς
LTAWWH
6†trs ὁσάκις ἐὰν θ. ἐν πάσῃ πλ. GW

θεμελιόω.

Lu. 6:48 for it was founded upon a
rock—because it was well
built, διὰ τὸ καλῶς οἰκοδο-
μεῖσθαι (-μῆσθαι TWHR) αὐτὴν
TTrAWHR
1 Pet. 5:10 θεμελιώσει will settle GTAW:
omit settle LTrWHR

θεομαχεω.

Acts 23: 9 *omit* let us not fight against
God (*leaving the sentence
incomplete*) GEds

θεός.

Mat. 3:16 τοῦ θ.—*omit* τοῦ T[A]WH
6:33 *omit* of God LT[A]WHR
19:17 *omit* GLTTrAWHR, *see* ἀγαθός
24 God—the heavens, οὐρανος
LTTrA
21:12 *omit* of God LTrWH
22:30 *omit* of God LT[A]WHR: *omit*
τοῦ TA
32 ὁ θ.⁴ θ.⁵—*omit* θ.⁵ read he is
not LTr[A]WHR, *omit* ὁ θ. T,
[ὁ] θ. WH
27:54 *trs* υἱὸς θεοῦ LTrA
Mar. 1: 1 *omit* the Son of God TWH:*omit*
τοῦ LTrA
10: 6 *omit* ὁ θ. read he[L]TTr[A]WHR
27 τῷ θ.¹—*omit* τῷ TTrAWWH
12:26 ὁ θ.³ ᵃ—*omit* ὁ LTrAWWHR
27 ὁ θ.—*omit* ὁ LTrAWWHR
27 *omit* the God² GEds
32 *omit* θ. read he is one GEds
15:39 *trs* θεοῦ ἦν WH
Lu. 1:37 τοῦ θεοῦ TTrAWH
2:38*θεῷ *for* κυρίῳ (-ριος) LTTrAWHR
4: 4 *omit* but by every word of
God T[Tr]AWH
12:31 τοῦ θ.—αὐτοῦ, read his kingdom LTTrAWHR
18:19 ὁ θ.—*omit* ὁ TA[WH]
27†trs παρὰ τῷ (*omit* τῷ L[Tr])
θεῷ ἐστιν LTTrAWH
20:36 τοῦ θ.—*omit* τοῦ TTrAWH
37 τοῦ θ.²³—*omit* τὸν LTTrAWHR
21: 4 *omit* of God T[Tr]AWHR
23:35 *trs* τοῦ θεοῦ ὁ, read Christ of
God, the chosen TAWHR
Joh. 1:18*θεὸς *for* υἱὸς TrWH
3: 5 God—the heavens, οὐρανός T
34 *omit* θ.³ read he[L]T[Tr]AWHR
5:44 [God] LWH
6:45 τοῦ θ.—*omit* τοῦ GLTTrAWWH
46*θεὸν *for* πατέρα² (-τήρ) T
7:17 τοῦ θ.—*omit* τοῦ T
9:35 of God—of man, ἄνθρωπος TWH
10:36 τοῦ θ.—*omit* τοῦ T
13:32 *omit* if God be glorified in
him [LTrA]WH
16:27 God—the Father, πατήρ
TrAWHR
19: 7 θεοῦ s—τοῦ θ. E
Acts 3:13*καὶ¹ ²—*add* (οT) θεός, read God
of Isaac and God of Jacob LT
25 *trs* ὁ θ.—διέθετο LWH
4:24 *omit* ὁ θ. read he LTTr[A]WHR
7:32 *omit* the God³ ⁴ LTTrAWHR
46 God²—house, οἶκος LT
8:22 *omit* the Lord, κυριος Eds
37 *omit* the verse GLTTrAWHR
10:2s *trs* δείξειεν ὁ θεὸς T
33 God²—the Lord, κύριος
LTTrAWH
12:24 of God—of the Lord, κύριος WH
13:44 of God—of the Lord, κυριος
LTTr
48*θεοῦ *for* κυρίου¹ WHR
14:15 τὸν θ.—*omit* τὸν Eds
15:18 *omit* unto God are all his
works GTTrAWHR
40 of God—of the Lord, κύριος
Eds
16:10*θεὸς *for* κύριος LTTrAWHR
32*θεὸν *for* κυρίου (-ος) WH
17:27*θεόν f. κύριον (-ος) GLTTrAWHR

Acts 18:26 *omit* of God A: *trs* ὁδὸν τοῦ
θεοῦ LTTrWH
19:11 *trs* ὁ θεὸς ἐποίει LTTrAWWH
20 *Dei for* κυρίου (-ος) A.V.Vul
20:21 τὸν θ.—*omit* τὸν TTrAWH
25 *omit* of God Eds
28 of God—of the Lord, κύριος
GLTTr
32 God—the Lord, κύριος WH
21:20*θεὸν *for* κυρίου (-ος) GEds
Ro. 1:19 *trs* θεὸς γὰρ GEds
2:13 τῷ θ.—*omit* τῷ [L]Tr[WH]
4: 2 τὸν θ.—*omit* τὸν LTTrAWWH
5: 8 *omit* ὁ θ. read he A
8:14 τοῦ υἱοὶ εἰσιν θ. LTTrA, υἱοὶ θ.
εἰσιν WH
28*συνεργεῖ—*add* ὁ θεός, read
God works together L[WH]
9:11 *trs* πρόθεσις τοῦ θεοῦ GEds
10:17 of God—of Christ, χριστός
LTTrAWHR
11:22*add v. LTTrAWHR,*see* χρηστότης
12: 1 *trs* τῷ θεῷ εὐάρεστον TWH
13: 1 τοῦ θ.—*omit* τοῦ GEds (WHR
14: 4 God—the Lord, κύριος LTTrA
10*θεοῦ *for* χριστοῦ (-τος) Eds
12 [τῷ θεῷ] LWH
15: 7 τοῦ θεοῦ LTTrAWH
17 τὸν θεὸν GEds
19 Spirit of God—Holy (ἅγιος)
Spirit GLT[A][WH]R
1 Co. 1:14 *omit* τῷ θ. read I give thanks
that TWH
29*τοῦ θεοῦ *for* αὐτοῦ GEds
2: 7 *trs* θεοῦ σοφίαν GEds
3:19 τῷ θ.—*omit* τῷ L[A]
6:20 *omit* and in your spirit,
which are God's GEds
7:17 *trs* the Lord and God GEds
24 τῷ θ.—*omit* τῷ GEds
9:21 θεοῦ Eds
14: 2 τῷ θ.—*omit* τῷ LTTr[A]WHR
25†trs ὄντως ὁ (*omit* ὁ T) θεὸς Eds
2 Co. 1: 2 *omit* God W
12 θ.¹—*omit* τοῦ LTTrAWWH
19 *trs* τοῦ θεοῦ γὰρ Eds
2:17 τοῦ θ.²—*omit* τοῦ LTTr[A]WHR
12:19 τοῦ θ.—*omit* τοῦ LTTrAWH
Gal. 1:15 *omit* θ. read him [L]TA[WH]
2: 6 ὁ θεός T, [ὁ] θ. WH
3:21 [of God] LWH
4: 7 *trs* διὰ θ. through God (*omit*
Christ) LTTrAWHR
Eph. 5:21 of God—of Christ, χριστός
GEds
Phil. 1:14*word—*add* τοῦ θεοῦ of God
LTTrAWHR
2:13 ὁ θ.—*omit* ὁ Eds
3: 3 θεοῦ, read by the Spirit of
God Eds
Col. 3:15 of God—of Christ, χριστός
GEds
16*θεῷ *for* κυρίῳ (-ριος) GEds
22 God—the Lord, κύριος GEds
1 Th. 1: 1 *omit* from God *to end of verse*
[L]TTrAWHR
4 τοῦ θεοῦ T, [τοῦ] θ. WH
4 τῷ θ.—*omit* τῷ [L]TTrAWHR
2 Th. 2: 4 *omit* as God GEds
16 ὁ θ.—*omit* ὁ [L]Tr[WH]
1 Ti. 3:16 God—who, ὅς GEds
5: 5 τὸν θ.—*omit* τὸν [L]T[WH]R
6:11 τοῦ θ.—*omit* τοῦ LTTr[A]WHR
13 τοῦ θ.—*omit* τοῦ T
17 τῷ θ.—*omit* τῷ TTrWHR
2 Ti. 2:14*θεοῦ *for* κυρίου (-ριος) LTrWH
Tit. 3: 8 τῷ θ.—*omit* τῷ Eds
Heb. 6:18 τὸν θεὸν T
10: 9 *omit* O God GEds
11: 4 τῷ θεῷ, read testifying by his
gifts to God LTr
6 τῷ θ.—*omit* τῷ T[TrWH]
Jas. 1:13 τοῦ θ.—*omit* τοῦ GLTTrAWWH
27 τῷ θ.—*omit* τῷ TW
2:19†trs εἷς ἐστιν ὁ θ. LTTrR, εἷς ὁ
(*omit* ὁ WH) θ. ἐστιν AWWH
3: 9 God²—the Lord, κυριος
LTTrAWH
4: 4†θ.¹—*trs* ἐστιν τῷ θεῷ T
1 Pet. 2: 5 τῷ θ.—*omit* τῷ LTTrAWHR
3: 5 τὸν θ.—*omit* τὸν Eds
15 God—Christ, χριστός Eds
18 τῷ θ.—*omit* τῷ W
22 τοῦ θ.—*omit* τοῦ TTr[A]WH
5: 2*willingly—*add* κατὰ θεον according to God LTTrR
1 Joh. 3:16 love—*add* τοῦ θεοῦ of God
A.V.†B
5:11 *trs* ὁ θεὸς ἡμῖν WH
13 *om.* that believe on the name
of the Son of God¹ GEds
Jude 4 *omit* God² GEds

Rev. 1: 8°ὁ κύριος—κ. ὁ θεός (the) Lord God GEds
4:11°add θ. Eds, see κύριος
5: 6 trs πνεύματα τοῦ θ. GLTTrAWBR
10 omit unto our God A
7:10 τῳ καθημενῳ ἐπὶ τοῦ θρόνου τοῦ θεοῦ ἡμῶν 8—τῳ θεῳ ἡμῶν τῳ κα. ἐπὶ τῳ θρόνῳ (τοῦ θρόνου BEG) A.V. B EGEds
11: 4 God—Lord, κυριος GEds
14: 5 omit before the throne of God GEds
19: 1 τοῦ θεου GEds
5 τῳ θεῳ Eds
17 τοῦ θ. GEds, see μέγας
20: 9 omit from God LTAWWHR
12 God—the throne, θρόνος GEds
21: 2 trs ἐκ τοῦ οὐρανοῦ ἀπὸ τοῦ θεοῦ GEds
3 omit (and be) their God TTrWH: trs αὐτῶν θ. LAW
4 omit God GTTr[A]WWHR
22 18 trs ἐπ' αὐτὸν ὁ θ. T

θεραπεια.

Mat. 24:45 οἰκετεία LTTrAWHR

θεραπεύω.

Mat. 12:10 θεραπεῦσαι T
Mar. 3: 2 θεραπεύει he healeth T
15 omit to heal sicknesses, and TTrAWHR
Lu. 4:40 ἐθεράπευεν TTrAWH
6: 7 θεραπεύει he healeth LTTrAWH
14: 3 θεραπεῦσαι LTTrAWHR

θερίζω.

Rev. 14:15 τοῦ θ.—omit τοῦ Eds

θεωρέω.

Mar. 3:11 ἐθεώρουν LTTrAWWH
Lu. 23:48 θεωρήσαντες having beheld LTTrAWHR
Joh. 6: 2°ἐθεώρουν for ἑώρων (ὁράω) LTTrAWHR
7: 3 θεωρήσουσιν TTrAWH
Acts 17:16 θεωροῦντος Eds

θηλάζω.

Lu. 23:29 gave suck—nourished, τρεφω LTTrAWHR

θηρίον.

Acts 10:12 omit and wild beasts Eds
Rev. 13: 4 τὸ θηρίον—τῳ θηρίῳ GEds
14: 9 trs προσκυνεῖ τὸ θ. GEds
17: 8 θ.¹—τὸ θηρίον A.V.C GEds
20: 4 τὸ θηρίον GEds

θησαυρός.

Lu. 6:45 omit treasure of his heart² [L]TTrAWHR

θλῖψις.

Acts 20:23 trs καὶ θλίψεις με LTTrAWH
1 Th. 3: 7 trs distress and affliction Eds

θνήσκω.

Joh. 11:21 ἀποθνήσκω LTTrWHR
39 τελευταω Eds
41 omit where the dead was laid GLTTrAWH
12: 1 omit which had been dead [L]T[TrA]WHR
Acts 14:19 τεθνηκέναι LTTrAWH

* θορυβάζω, to confuse by noise.

Lu. 10:41 θορυβάζῃ for τυρβάζῃ (-ζω) LTTrAWH

θόρυβος.

Mar. 14: 2 trs ἔσται θόρυβος TTrAWH

θρῆνος.

Mat. 2:18 omit lamentation, and LTTrAWH

θρησκεία, —κία T.

θρῆσκος, θρησκός TWH.

θρόμβος.

Lu. 22:43. 44 the verses [L][[WH]]

θρόνος.

Acts 2:30 τὸν θρόνον LTTrAWH
Rev. 4: 2 τοῦ θ.—τὸν θρόνον Eds

Rev. 4: 4 θ.²—θρόνους LT
9 τῳ θρόνῳ LTTrA
5:13 τῳ θρόνῳ LTA
6:16 τῳ θρόνῳ TA
7:10 τῳ θρόνῳ LTTrAWWH, see θρος
15 τοῦ θ.²—τῳ θρόνῳ T
14: 5 omit before the throne of God GEds
19: 4 τῳ θρόνῳ Eds
20:12°θρόνου for θεοῦ (-ός) GEds
21: 3°θρόνου for οὐρανου (-νος) LTAWHR
5 τῳ θρόνῳ GEds

Θυάτειρα.

Rev. 1:11 Θυάτειραν LAW

θυγάτηρ.

Mar. 5:34 θυγάτηρ LTrAWH
7:30 her daughter—the child, see παιδίον LTTrAWHR
Lu. 8:48 θυγάτηρ TrWH
12:53 θ.¹—θυγατέρα LTTrAWHR
Joh. 12.15 θυγάτηρ LTTrAWWH

θυμός.

Ro. 2: 8 trs wrath and indignation GEds

θύρα.

Mat. 28: 2 omit from the door LTTrAWHR
Mar. 11: 4 τὴν θ.—omit τὴν TrAWH
Lu. 13:24°θύρας f. πύλης (-λη)GLTTrAWHR

θυσία.

Mar. 9:49 omit and every sacrifice shall be salted with salt T[Tr]WHR
12:33 τῶν θ.—omit τῶν GLTTrAWH
Heb. 10: 5 trs offering and sacrifice w
8 θυσίας sacrifices Eds

θυσιαστήριον.

Rev. 8: 3 τὸ θ.¹—τοῦ θυσιαστηρίου TTrAWHR

θυω.

1 Co. 5: 7 ἐτύθη 8—ἐθύθη R
10:20 θ.¹—θυουσιν LTTrAWH
20 θ.²—θύουσιν trs after θεῳ LTTrAWH

Θωμας.

Joh. 20:28 ὁ Θ.—omit ὁ GLTTrAWWH
29 omit Thomas GEds

Ἰακώβ.

Acts 7: 8 ὁ Ἰ.—omit ὁ LTTrAWH

Ἰάκωβος.

Mar. 9: 2 τον Ἰ.—omit τὸν W
14:33 τον Ἰ.—omit τὸν GLTTrAW
15:40 τοῦ Ἰ—omit τοῦ LTTrAWH
16: 1 τοῦ Ἰ—omit τοῦ T[TrWH]
Lu. 8:51 trs John and James GEds
Acts 1:13 trs John and James Eds

Ἰαννα, —νναί LTTrAWHR.

ἰάομαι.

Mat. 13:15 ἰάσομαι LTTrAWHR
Lu. 4:18 omit to heal the broken-hearted G[L]TTrAWHR
7: 7 ἰαθήτω let he healed TTrAWH
5:13 was healed—was impotent, ἀσθενέω I
12:40 ἰάσομαι LTTrAWHR
Acts 3:11 τοῦ ἰ. χωλοῦ the lame man which was healed—αὐτοῦ he GEds
28:27 ἰάσομαι TTrAWHR

Ἰαρέδ, Ἰαρεθ L, —ρετ TWH.

Ἰάσων.

Acts 17: 6 τὸν Ἰ.—omit τὸν LTTr[A]WH

ἰατρος.

Lu. 8:43 εἰς ἰ.—ιατροῖς GLTTrAWR: omit had spent all her living upon physicians WH

ιβ', see δώδεκα.

ἰδε.

Mar. 13:21°for ἰδού¹ TTrAWH
21°for ἰδού² LTTrAWH
15:35°for ἰδού TTrAWH

Joh. 19: 5 ἰδού TTrAWH
26, 27°for ἰδ—¬ GLTTrAWH
Ro. 2:17 behold—but if, εἰ δέ GEds
Rev. 6: 1, 5, 7°for βλέπε (—πω) GW

ἰδέα—εἰδέα TTrWH.

ἴδιος.

Mat. 13:57°ἰδία πατρίδι T
Mar. 4:34°μαθηταῖς αὐτοῦ—ἰδίοις μ. his own disciples TAWHR
15:20 ἱμάτια τὰ ἰ.—ἱμ. αὐτοῦ LWHR
ἴδια ἱμάτια αὐτο
Lu. 2: 3 ἑαυτοῦ LTTrWHR
18:28°τὰ ἴδια for πάντα (πᾶς) LTTrAWHR
Acts 1:19 omit proper [TrA]WHR
24:24°ἰδίᾳ γυναικί LTTrWHR
1 Co. 7:37°καρδία αὐτοῦ—ἰδίᾳ κ. his own heart TTrAWH
15.38 τὸ ἴ.—omit τὸ LTTrAWH
Eph. 4:28°trs ταῖς (ἰδίαις his own LTTrW) χερσὶν τὸ ἀγαθόν LTTrAWWH
5:24 omit own LTTrAWH
Col. 3:18 omit own GEds
1 Th. 2:15 om. ἰ. read the prophets GEds
4:11 omit own² Eds
2 Ti. 4: 3†trs τάς ἰ. ἐπιθυμίας GLTTrAWWH
2 Pet. 1: 3°ἰδίᾳ δόξῃ καὶ ἀρετῇ by his own glory and virtue LTTrAWR

ἰδού.

Mat. 12:47 omit the verse [T]WH
Mar. 5:22 omit behold [L]TTrAWHR
13:21 ἰ.¹—ἴδε TTrAWH
21 ἰ.—ἴδε LTTrAWH
23 omit behold [L]TTrAWH
15:35 ἴδε TTrAWH
Lu. 2: 9 omit lo T[TrA]WHR
17:21 omit lo² TAWHR
24:49 omit behold T
Joh. 19: 5°for ἴδε TTrAWH
26, 27 ἴδε GLTTrAWH
Jas. 3: 3 behold—now if, εἰ δε Eds
Rev. 3.11 omit behold GEds
5: 6 omit lo GEds
6:12 omit lo Eds
15: 5 omit behold GEds

ἱδρώς.

Lu. 22:43, 44 the verses [L][[WH]]

Ἰεζαβήλ, —άβελ GTWHR, —cA TrAW.

Ἱεραπολις, Ἱερὰ Πόλις WH.

ἱερατεία, —τια WH.

ἱερεύς.

Mar. 2:26 τοὺς ἱερεῖς TWH
Lu. 20: 1°ἱερεῖς for ἀρχιερεῖς (με ς)TA
Acts 4: 1 priests—high priests, ἀρχιερεὺς WH
5:24 omit high priest and the LTTrAWH
Heb. 7:14°trs περὶ ἱερέων (ἰ. for ἱερωσύνης ιη) οὐδὲν Eds
8: 4 omit τῶν ἰ. read those that offer Eds
10:11 priest—high priest, ἀρχιερεύς LA

Ἱεριχώ, Ἱερει—τ, Ἱερει— WH.

* ἱερόθυτος, offered in sacrifice.

1 Co. 10:28 ἱερόθυτον for εἰδωλόθυτον LTTrAWH

ἱερόν.

Mat. 24: 1†trs ἀπὸ (ἐκ L) τοῦ ἰ. ἐπορεύετο LTTrAWH
26:55 trs ἐν τῳ ἰ. ἐκα. διδάσ. TTrAWHR
Acts 19:27 trs ἱερὸν Ἀρτεμιδος TA

ἱερος.

2 Ti. 3:15 τὰ ἰ.—omit τὰ [L]T[TrA]WHR

Ἱεροσόλυμα, Ἱ— WH.

Mat. 16:21 trs εἰς Ἰ. ἀπελθεῖν LTTrAWH
Lu. 2:42 omit to Jerusalem T[Tr]AWHR
18:31 Ἰερουσαλήμ TTrAWH
Joh. 2:23 τοῖς Ἱεροσολύμοις GLTTrAWH
10:22 τοῖς Ἰ.—omit τοῖς T
Acts 11: 2 Ἱερουσαλήμ LTTrAWH
22 Ἱερουσαλήμ LTTrAWWH
18:21 omit I must to Jerusalem LTTrAWHR

Acts 20:16 Ἱερουσαλήμ τ
   See also Ἱερουσαλήμ.

Ἱεροσολυμίτης, Ἱ– wh, –μείτης τwh.

Ἱερουσαλήμ, Ἱ– wh.

Mar 11: 1 Ἱεροσόλυμα LTTrA Wwh
Lu. 13:22 Ἱεροσόλυμα τwh
  19:11 *trs* εἶναι Ἱ. αὐτὸν TTrAwh
  21:20 τὴν Ἱ.–omit τὴν LTTrAwh
  24:49 omit of Jerusalem GLTTrAwhR
Acts 2:43*add* Ἱ. τ, *see* φόβος
  8:25 Ἱεροσόλυμα LTTrAwh
  15: 4 Ἱεροσόλυμα TrWh
  16: 4 Ἱεροσολύμοις (–μα) LTTrAWwh
  19:21 Ἱεροσόλυμα LTTrAWwh
  21: 4 Ἱεροσόλυμα GLTTrAwh
  15: 4 25:20 Ἱεροσόλυμα LTTrAWwh
   See also Ἱεροσόλυμα.

ἱερωσύνη.

Heb. 7:14 priesthood – priests, ἱερεύς:
  trs περὶ ἱ. οὐδὲν Eds

Ἰησοῦς.

Mat. 1:18 omit Jesus Tr[wh]
  4: 1 ὁ Ἱ.–omit ὁ A[wh]
  12 omit ὁ Ἱ. read he TTrAWhR
  18 omit ὁ Ἱ. read he GEds
  23 omit Jesus τ[Tr]Awh: *trs* ὁ Ἱ.
   after περιηχεν L[Tr]w
  8: 3 omit ὁ Ἱ. read he LTTrAwhR
  5 Jesus–he, αὐτῷ GW. αὐτοῦ
   LTTrAwhR
  7 omit ὁ Ἱ. read he LT[Tr]Awh R
  22 omit Ἱ. read he T
  29 omit Jesus GLTTrAwhR
  34 τοῦ Ἱησοῦ T
  9:12 omit Ἱ. read he LT[Tr]AwhR
  22 omit Ἱ. read he T
  12:25 13:36 omit ὁ Ἱ. read he
   LTTrAwh
  31:51 omit Jesus saith unto them
   LTTrAwh
  14:14 omit ὁ Ἱ. read he LTTrAwhR
  16 omit Ἱ. read he T
  22, 25 omit ὁ Ἱ. read he GEds
  27 omit ὁ Ἱ. read he T[Awh]: *trs*
   ὁ Ἱ. αὐτοῖς Lwh
  15:16 omit Ἱ. read he LTTrAwhR
  30 Jesus–his, αὐτῷ LTTrAwhR
  16:20 omit Jesus GEds
  21 ὁ Ἱ.–omit ὁ L[Tr]Awh
  17: 8 τὸν Ἱ.–αὐτὸν Ἱ. wh
  11, 20 omit Ἱ. read he LTTrAwhR
  18: 2 omit ὁ Ἱ. read he TTrAwh
  20:17 ὁ Ἱ.–omit ὁ wh
  21: 1 ὁ Ἱ.–omit ὁ Twh   (whR
  11 *trs* the prophet Jesus LTTrA
  12 ὁ Ἱ.–omit ὁ LTTrAwh
  22:20*αὐτοῖς–add ὁ Ἱησοῦς read
   Jesus saith LT
  37 omit Ἱ. read he LTTrAwhR:
   ttrs ἔφη αὐτῷ Ἱ. w
  24: 2 omit Ἱ. read he LTTrAwhR
  26:38*αὐτοῖς–add ὁ Ἱησοῦς, read
   Jesus saith W
  75 τοῦ Ἱ.–omit τοῦ LTTrAwh
  28: 9 ὁ Ἱ.–omit ὁ TAwh
Mar. 1:41 ὁ δὲ Ἱ.–καί, read he LTTrwhR
  5:13 omit forthwith Jesus, read
   he [L]TTr[A]wh
  19 ὁ δὲ Ἱ.–καί, read he GEds
  6:34 omit ὁ Ἱ. read he
   G[L]TTrAWwhR
  7:27 ὁ δὲ Ἱ. καί, read he
   LTTrAwh
  8: 1 omit ὁ Ἱ. read he GEds
  17 omit ὁ Ἱ. read he TT[Tr]Awh
  9: 8*trs* μεθ' ἑαυτῶν εἰ μὴ τὸν Ἱ.
   μόνον wh
  10:42*trs* καὶ προσκαλεσαμενος αὐτοὺς
   ὁ Ἱ. LTTrAwhR
  52 Jesus²–him, αὐτῷ GEds
  11:11 omit ὁ Ἱ. καί read he
   LTTrAwhR
  14, 15 omit ὁ Ἱ. read he GEds
  22 ὁ Ἱησοῦς GLTTrAwh
  33 *trs* τῷ Ἱ. λέγουσιν TTrAwhR
  12:29*trs* ἀπεκρίθη ὁ Ἱ. TTrAwhR
  41 omit he [L]TTrAwhR
  14:18 *trs* ὁ Ἱησοῦς εἶπεν TAwh
  22 om. ὁ Ἱ. read he[Ἱ]T[Tr]AwhR
  67*trs* ἦσθα τοῦ Ἱησοῦ LTTrAwhR
  16:19*Lord – add Ἱησοῦς Jesus
   LTr[wh]R
Lu. 3:23 ὁ Ἱ.–omit ὁ TTrAwh
  4:1*trs* πρὸς ἑαυτὸν ὁ Ἱ. LTTrAwh
  8 *trs* ὁ Ἱ. εἶπεν αὐτῷ Twh
  5: 8 τοῦ Ἱ.–omit τοῦ LTTrAWwh

Lu. 5:10 ὁ Ἱ.–omit ὁ [Tr]Awh
  34*ὁ δέ–add Ἱησοῦς, read Jesus
   said TTrAwhR
  6: 3 *trs* ὁ Ἱ. πρὸς αὐτοὺς εἶπεν T
  7 19 Jesus–the Lord, κύριος
   TTrAwhR
  22 8:38 omit ὁ Ἱ. read he
   [L]TTrAwhR
  8:41 τοῦ Ἱ.–omit τοῦ T[Tr]
  9:36 ὁ Ἱ.–omit ὁ LTTrAWwh
  43 omit ὁ Ἱ. read he TTrAwhR
  50 ὁ Ἱ.–omit ὁ T[A]wh
  60 omit ὁ Ἱ. read he [L]TTrAwhR
  62 *trs* ὁ Ἱ. πρὸς αὐτὸν LTr
  10:21 omit ὁ Ἱ. read he LTTrAwhR
  39 Jesus'–the Lord's, κύριος Eds
  41 Jesus–the Lord, κύριος TWhR
  13: 2 omit ὁ Ἱ. read he [L]TTrAwh
  18:40 ὁ Ἱ.–omit ὁ [Tr]Awh
  22:48*trs* Ἱησοῦς δὲ TTrAwh
  52 ὁ Ἱ.–omit ὁ LTTrAwhR
  63 Jesus–him, αὐτόν LTTrAwhR
  23:28 ὁ Ἱ.–omit ὁ TTrAwh
  34 *see* λέγω
  42 τῷ Ἱ.–omit τῷ (read said.
   Jesus, remember) TTrAwhR
  43 omit ὁ Ἱ. read he T[Tr]AwhR
  24:15 ὁ Ἱ.–omit ὁ TTrAwh
  36 omit Jesus GLTTrAwhR
Joh. 1:43(44) ὁ Ἱ.–omit ὁ GEds
  43(44)*αὐτῷ–add ὁ Ἱησοῦς, read
   Jesus findeth Eds
  47(48) ὁ Ἱ.–omit ὁ LTTrAWwh
  48(49) ὁ Ἱ.–omit ὁ GLTTrAWwh
  2:19 ὁ Ἱ.–omit ὁ LTTrAWwh
  24 ὁ Ἱ.–omit ὁ LTTrAwh
  3: 2 Jesus–him, αὐτόν GEds
  3 ὁ Ἱ.–omit ὁ GLTTrAWwh
  5 ὁ Ἱ.–omit ὁ LT[TrA]w[wh]
  10 ὁ Ἱ.–omit ὁ GLTTrAWwh
  4: 1*Ἱησοῦς for κύριος T
  13 44 ὁ Ἱ.–omit ὁ GLTTrAWwh
  16 om. ὁ Ἱ.–read he [L]Π[Tr]Awh
   omit ὁ L
  46 om.ὁ Ἱ.–read he GLTTrAwhR
   trs πάλιν ὁ Ἱ. w
  50 Ἱ.²–ὁ Ἱησοῦς LTTrAwh
  5: 1 ὁ Ἱ.–omit ὁ LTTrAwh
  17 omit Ἱ. read he Twh
  6: 3 ὁ Ἱ.–omit ὁ LTTrAwh
  5 *trs* τοὺς ὀφθαλμοὺς ὁ Ἱ.
   LTTrAWwh
  14 omit ὁ Ἱ.–read he TTrAwhR
  17*trs* (om. ὁ) Ἱ. πρὸς αὐτούς T
  29 ὁ Ἱ.–omit ὁ T
  43 ὁ Ἱ.–omit ὁ TTrwh
  7: 1 *trs* μετὰ ταῦτα πε. ὁ ([ὁ]T-wh)
   Ἱησοῦς Eds
  14 ὁ Ἱ.–omit ὁ LTTrAwh
  16 ὁ Ἱ.–omit ὁ TTrwh
  21 ὁ Ἱ.–omit ὁ TTrAwh
  39 ὁ Ἱ.–omit ὁ LTTrAWwh
  50 for αὐτὸν A.V. [?]
  8: 9 omit ὁ Ἱ. read he wh
  12 *trs* αὐτοῖς ἐλά. ὁ ([ὁ] Tr.wh) Ἱ.
   LTTrAwh
  19 ὁ Ἱ.–omit ὁ GLTTrAwh
  20 omit ὁ Ἱ. read he GEds
  21 omit ὁ Ἱ. read he Eds
  25, 39 [ὁ] Ἱ. TrWh
  34, 42 ὁ Ἱ.–omit ὁ L[Tr.wh]
  58 ὁ Ἱ.–omit ὁ TTrwh
  9: 3 ὁ Ἱ.–omit ὁ GLTTrAWwh
  35 ὁ Ἱ.–omit ὁ T[Tr]wh
  10:23, 25, 34 [ὁ] Ἱ. Trwh
  11: 9, 20 ὁ Ἱ.–omit ὁ GLTTrAW wh
  21 τὸν Ἱ.–omit τὸν T[Tr]wh
  32, 46 ὁ Ἱ.–omit ὁ LTTrAwh
  39 ὁ Ἱ.–omit ὁ LTTrAwh
  44*trs* [ὁ] Ἱ. αὐτοῖς wh
  45 omit ὁ Ἱ.–read he GEds
  51 ὁ Ἱ.–omit ὁ GLTTrAWwh
  54*trs* ὁ Ἱ.–omit ὁ Τr. TrAwh
  12: 1*add at end ὁ (omit ὁ TwhR)
   Ἱησοῦς, read Jesus raised
   Eds
  3 [τοῦ] Ἱ. Tr.wh
  12 ὁ Ἱ.–omit ὁ GLTT.Aw wh
  16 ὁ Ἱ.–omit ὁ TT.Awwh
  30 ὁ Ἱ.–omit ὁ LTTrAwh
  36 ὁ Ἱ.–omit ὁ LTT.Awh
  13: 3 omit ὁ Ἱ. read he[L]TTrAwhR
  8*trs* (omit ὁ) Ἱησοῦς αὐτῷ
   LTTrAwh
  10 ὁ Ἱ.–omit ὁ T[Tr]wh
  21, 27 ὁ Ἱ.–omit ὁ TTrAwh
  26 [ὁ] Ἱ. Tr.wh
  29 ὁ Ἱ.–omit ὁ TTrAwh
  31 ὁ Ἱ.–omit ὁ TTrAwh
  36 ὁ Ἱ.–omit ὁ LTTrAwhR
  38 ὁ Ἱ.–omit ὁ Eds
  14: 6 ὁ Ἱ.–omit ὁ Twh

Joh. 14:23 ὁ Ἱ.–omit ὁ GLTTrAWwh
  16:19 ὁ Ἱ.–omit ὁ TTrAwh
  31 ὁ Ἱ.–omit ὁ TTrAwh
  17: 1 ὁ Ἱ.–omit ὁ Twh
  18: 1, 2 ὁ Ἱ.–omit ὁ TTrAwh
  5 om. ὁ Ἱ. read he TrAwh: om. ὁ T
  8 ὁ Ἱ.–omit ὁ LTTrAWwh
  20 ὁ Ἱ.–omit ὁ TTrwh
  23 ὁ Ἱ.–omit ὁ LTTrAwh
  34 ὁ Ἱ.–omit ὁ LTTrAWwh
  36 ὁ Ἱ.–omit ὁ LTTrAWwh
  37 ὁ Ἱ.–omit ὁ [A]w[wh]
  19: 5 [ὁ] Ἱ. TrWh
  11 ὁ Ἱ.–omit ὁ GLTTrAWwh
  30 om. ὁ Ἱ. read he T: [ὁ] Ἱ. Trwh
  38 of Jesus³–of him, αὐτοῦ
   LTTrAwhR: him, αὐτόν T
  39 Jesus–him, αὐτόν Eds
  20:14 ὁ Ἱ.–omit ὁ GLTTrAWwh
  15 ὁ Ἱ.–omit ὁ LTTrAwh
  16, 17, 24 ὁ Ἱ.–omit ὁ LTTrAwh
  21 omit ὁ Ἱ. read he TTr[Awh]
  29 [ὁ] Ἱ. Twh
  31 ὁ Ἱ.–omit ὁ GLTTrAWwh
  21: 1 omit ὁ TTrwh: omit ὁ Ἱ. A
  4 ὁ Ἱ.–omit ὁ LTTrAwh
  5 ὁ Ἱ.–omit ὁ [Tr]Awh, [ὁ Ἱ.] L
  10, 12 [ὁ] Ἱ. Tr.wh
  13 ὁ Ἱ.–omit ὁ LTTrAwh
  14 ὁ Ἱ.–omit ὁ LTTrAwh
  17 ὁ Ἱ.–omit ὁ LTTrAwh: omit
   Ἱ. T[Tr]
  25 omit the verse T
Acts 1. 1 ὁ Ἱ.–omit ὁ LTTrAwh
  16 τὸν Ἱ.–omit τὸν LTTrAwh
  3:20 *trs* Christ Jesus LTT.AwhR
  26 omit Jesus GLTTrAwh
  5:42 *trs* Christ Jesus LTTrAwh
  8:12 τοῦ Ἱ.–omit τοῦ GLTTrAWwh
  37 omit the verse GLTTrAwhR
  9:20*Ἱησοῦν for χριστόν GEds
  27 τοῦ Ἱ.–omit τοῦ LTTrAwh
  29(28) omit Jesus Eds
  10:48*Ἱησοῦ χριστοῦ for τοῦ κυρίου
   (–ος) LTTrAwhR
  16: 7*Spirit–add Ἱησοῦ of Jesus
   GEds
  17: 3 ὁ Ἱησοῦς AwhR
  18:25*Ἱησοῦ for κυρίου² (–ος) Eds
  19:10 omit Jesus GEds
  24:24*Christ–add Ἱησοῦν Jesus
   LTwhR
Ro. 1: 1 *trs* Christ Jesus Tr
  2:16 *trs* Christ Jesus Twh
  6: 3, 11 *trs* Christ Jesus A.V.[?]
  8.11 τὸν Ἱησοῦν TT.[A]wh
  11*Christ–add Ἱησοῦν Jesus
   [L]TwhR: *trs* ἐκ νεκρῶν χρισ-
   τὸν Ἱ. TWh
  34*Christ–add Ἱησοῦς Jesus
   [L]T[Wh]R
  10: 9 κύριος Ἱησοῦς wh
  15: 5 *trs* Jesus Christ Tr
  8 omit Jesus LTTrAwhR
  16 *trs* Christ Jesus Eds
  16:18 omit Jesus GEds
  24 omit the verse LTTr[A]whR
1 Co. 1: 1 *trs* Christ Jesus LTTrAW
  4:17*Christ–add Ἱησοῦ Jesus
   LT[Wh]
  5: 5 omit Jesus Awh
  12: 3 Ἱησοῦς bis Eds
  16:22 omit Jesus Christ LTTrAWhR
2 Co. 1: 1 *trs* Christ Jesus TrAwhR
  19 *trs* Christ Jesus TwhR
  4: 6 omit Jesus LTTrAwh
  5:18 omit Jesus Eds
  13: 5 *trs* Christ Jesus TTr
Gal. 2 16 *trs* Christ Jesus¹ TTrwh
  16 *trs* Jesus Christ² A.V.[?]
  3:14 *trs* Jesus Christ A.V.[?]Tr.wh
  5:24*χριστοῦ Ἱησοῦ, read of Christ
   Jesus [L]TTrAwhR
  6:15 omit in Christ Jesus TTrAwh
Eph. 1; 1¹ 2:20 *trs* Christ Jesus
   LTTrAwhR
  3: 1 omit Jesus T[A]
  6*Christ–add Ἱησοῦ Jesus
   LTTrAwhR
  9 omit by Jesus Christ GEds
  14 omit of our Lord Jesus Christ
   Eds
Phil. 1: 1 *trs* Christ Jesus¹ Eds
  2 *trs* Christ Jesus w
  6 *trs* Christ Jesus LTTrAw
  8 *trs* Christ Jesus GEds
  2:21 *trs* Jesus Christ A.V.Vul
   GLTrAwhR
  3:12 omit Jesus GLTTrAwh [wh]
Col. 1; 1 *trs* Christ Jesus Eds
  2 omit and the Lord Jesus
   Christ G[L]TTrAWwhR

Col. 1:2⁸ *omit* Jesus GEds
    4:12°*Christ—add* 'Ιησοῦ Jesus
    LTTᵣAWH
1Th. 1: 1 *omit* from God *to end of*
    verse [L]TTᵣAWH
2Th. 2: 8°Lord—*add* 'Ιησοῦς Jesus
    GLTTᵣAW[WH]R
1Ti. 1: 1 *trs* Christ Jesus¹ TTᵣAWWH R
    1 *trs* Christ Jesus² GEds
    2 *trs* Jesus Christ A.V.Eᵣ
    16 *trs* Christ Jesus LTᵣAWH
    4: 6 *trs* Christ Jesus Eds
    5:21 *trs* Christ Jesus (*omit* Lord)
    Eds
2Ti. 1: 1 *trs* Christ Jesus¹ TTᵣAWWH R
    10 *trs* Christ Jesus LTTᵣWH
    2: 3 *trs* Christ Jesus Eds
    4: 1 *trs* Christ Jesus (*omit* Lord)
    Eds
    22 *omit* Jesus Christ TTᵣ[A]WHR
Tit. 1. 4 *trs* Christ Jesus (*omit* Lord)
    LTTᵣAWH
    2:13 *trs* Christ Jesus TTᵣWH
Philem. 6 *omit* Jesus LTTᵣ[A]WHR
    9 *trs* Christ Jesus LTTᵣAWHR
Heb.10:10 τοῦ 'I.—*omit* τοῦ GEds
1 Pet. 5:10 *omit* Jesus T[Tᵣ]WH
    14 *omit* Jesus LTTᵣAWH
Jude 5°'Ιησοῦς *for* κύριος LA
    25°*add* 'I. GEds, *see* κύριος
Rev. 1: 9 *trs* Christ Jesus¹ W
    12:17 τοῦ 'I.—*omit* τοῦ GEds
    19:10 τοῦ 'I. *bis*—*omit* τοῦ Eds

* 'Ιησοῦς, son of Eliezer.

Lu. 3:29 'Ιησοῦ *for* 'Ιωσῆ LTTᵣAWH

ἱκανός.

Lu. 7: 6 *trs* ἱκανός εἰμι TTᵣAWH
    11 *omit* many of [L]Tᵣ[A]WHR
    8:27 ἱκανῷ TTᵣWHR, *see* χρόνος
    23: 8 ἱκανῶν LTTᵣAWHR, *see* χρόνος
Acts 5:37 *omit* much LTTᵣAWH R
Ro. 15:23°ἱκανῶν *for* πολλῶν (-λυς) TᵣAWH

ἱμάτιον.

Mat.11: 8 *omit* i. [L]TTᵣAWH R   (WH
    23: 5 *omit* of their garments LTTᵣA
    24:18 τὸ ἱμάτιον garment LTTᵣAWHR
    27:35 *omit* that it might *to end of*
    verse GLTTᵣAWH
Mar. 2:21 ἱμάτιον παλαιόν LTTᵣAWH
Heb. 1:12°αὐτοὺς—*add* ὡς ἱμάτιον, *read*
    fold them up, as a garment,
    L[Tᵣ]WHR

ἱματισμός.

Mat. 27:35 *omit* that it might *to end of*
    verse GLTTᵣAWH

ἱμείρομαι.

1Th. 2: 8 ὑμείρομαι GEds

ἵνα.

Mat.12.17ª*for* ὅπως LTTᵣAWH
    20:32°θέλετε—*add* [ἵ.] LA
    27:35 *om*. GLTTᵣAWHR, *see* ἱματισμός
Mar. 4:22°μὴ—*add* ἵ. LT[A]WHR
    5:2¹*for* ὅπως LTTᵣAWHR
Lu. 11:54 *omit* that they might accuse
    him T[Tᵣ]AWHR
Joh. 12: 7ªαὐτήν—*add* ἵ. Eds
    18:28 *omit* ἵ.² LTTᵣAWHR
Acts 5:26 *omit* ἵ. LTTᵣ[A]WHR
Ro. 15:31 *omit* ἵ.² LTTᵣAWHR
1Co. 9:15 ἵ. τις—οὐδείς LTTᵣWHR
2Co. 12: 7 *omit* lest I should he exalted
    above measure² [L]Tᵣ[A]
1Th. 4: 1°'Ιησοῦ—*add* ἵ. A.V.Vul
    LTTᵣA[WH]R
1Joh.5:13 *omit* καὶ ἵ. GEds, *see* πιστεύω
2Joh. 6°ἵ. καθὼς T
Rev. 13:15°ποιήσῃ—*add* ἵ. LTᵣ[A]W[WH]R
    15 *omit* ἵ.² Eds

'Ιόππη.

Acts 9:42 τῆς 'I.—*omit* τῆς [Tᵣ]WH
    10:23 τῆς 'I.—*omit* τῆς GLTTᵣAWWH

'Ιορδάνης.

Mar. 1: 5 *trs* ὑπ' αὐτοῦ ἐν τῷ 'I. ποταμῷ
    TTᵣAWH
    9 *trs* εἰς τὸν 'I. ὑπὸ 'Ιωάννου
    LTTᵣAWH

'Ιουδαίω.

Lu. 4 14°'Ιουδαίας *for* Γαλιλαίας AWH
Acts 1: 8 τῇ 'I.—*omit* τῇ A

'Ιουδαῖος.

Joh. 3:25 'Ιουδαίου a Jew GEds
    4: 9 *omit* for the Jews have no
    dealings with the Samari-
    tans T[WH]
    5:16 *trs* οἱ 'I. τὸν 'Ιησοῦν LTTᵣAWH
    19:21 *trs* τῶν 'Ιουδαίων³ εἰμί TᵣAWH
Acts 9:22 τοὺς 'I.—*omit* τοὺς TWH
    13:42 the Jews—they, αὐτῶν GEds
    17:10 *trs* ἀπῄεσαν τῶν 'I A
    21:20 *omit* of Jews T: ἐν τοῖς 'Ιου-
    δαίοις among the Jews
    LTTᵣAWHR
    23:12†*trs* συστροφὴν οἱ 'Ιουδαῖοι GEds
    30 *omit* the Jews LTTᵣAWHR, *see*
    ἐξαυτῆς
    26: 4 οἱ 'I.—*omit* οἱ LTTᵣAWHR
    7 τῶν 'I.—*omit* τῶν GEds
    21 οἱ 'I.—*omit* οἱ TTᵣWHR
    28:29 *omit* the verse LTTᵣAWHR

'Ιούδας.

Mar. 14:10 ὁ 'I.—*omit* ὁ LTTᵣAWH
    43 ὁ 'Ιούδας LTᵣAW, [ὁ] 'I. WH
Lu. 3:26 'Ιωδά TTᵣAWHR
Joh. 13: 2†*trs* ἵνα παραδοῖ αὐτὸν 'Ιούδας
    Σίμωνος 'Ισκαριώτου TTᵣAWHR
    29 ὁ 'I.—*omit* ὁ LTTᵣAWH

ἵππος.

Rev. 9:19°*add* ἵ. GLTTᵣAWHR, *see* ἐξουσία

ἵρις.

Rev. 10: 1 ἡ ἵρις the rainbow GEds

'Ισαάκ.

Acts 7: 8 ὁ 'I.—*omit* ὁ LTTᵣAWH

'Ισαχάρ, 'Ισασχάρ E, 'Ισσάχαρ T,
'Ισσαχάρ TᵣAWHR.

'Ισκαριώτης.

Mat.10: 4 ὁ 'Ισκαριώτης EGLTAWWH
Mar. 3:19 'Ισκαριώθ LTTᵣAWWH
    14:10 'Ισκαριώθ TAWH: *omit* ὁ
    LTTᵣAWWH
    43°Judas—*add* ὁ 'Ισκαριώτης
    Iscariot LT[Tᵣ]A
Lu. 6:16 'Ισκαριώθ LTTᵣAWH
Joh. 6:71 'Ισκαριώτου, read Judas (son)
    of Simon Iscariot LTTᵣAWHR
    12: 4†*trs* 'Ιούδας ὁ 'I. εἷς ἐκ (*omit* ἐκ
    TᵣWHR) τῶν μαθητῶν αὐτοῦ
    TTᵣAWHR
    13. 2 'Ισκαριώτης TTᵣAWHR, *see* 'Ιού-
    δας
    26 'Ισκαριώτου, read Judas (son)
    of Simon Iscariot TTᵣAWHR

'Ισραήλ.

Mat. 10:23 τοῦ 'I.—*omit* τοῦ LTᵣA[WH]
Mar.15:32 τοῦ 'I.—*omit* τοῦ LTTᵣWH
Acts 4: 8 *omit* of Israel LTTᵣ[A]WHR
Ro. 10: 1 Israel—them, αὐτῶν GEds

'Ισραηλίτης, -λείτης TWH.

ἵστημι, ἱστάω, ἱστάνω.

(pluperf. ἱστήκειν WH)

Mat. 2: 9 ἐστάθη LTTᵣAWH
    4: 5 ἔστησεν set LTTᵣAWHR
    12:47 *omit the verse* [T]WH
    16 28 ἑστώτων GLTTᵣAWH: ἑστῶτες
    (*omit* τῶν) W
    24:15 ἑστός S—ἑστώς EG
    27:11 ἐστάθη LTTᵣAWH
    47 ἑστηκότων TTᵣWH
Mar. 3:25†*trs* ἡ οἰκία ἐκείνη σταθῆναι
    (στῆναι TᵣAWH) LTTᵣAWH
    26 στῆναι TTᵣAWH
    31 στήκω TTᵣWH
    13: 9 ἄγω A.V.Eᵣ
    14 ἑστός S—ἑστώς EG, ἑστηκότα
    TTᵣAWHR, ἑστώς L
Lu. 9:27 ἑστώτων GLTᵣAW
    17:12 ἀνέστημι WH
    24:17°; καὶ ἐστάθησαν ([; καὶ ἐ.] A)
    σκυθρωποί, read as ye walk?
    And they stood sad TTᵣAWHR
Joh. 1:26 στήκω TTᵣAWHR
    8: 9 standing—being, ὢν WWH
    44 ἔστηκεν WH
Acts 24:20 *trs* ἐν αὐτοῖς ἑστώς Eds
    25:10 *trs* ἑστώς *before* ἐπί TWH
Ro. 3:31 ἱστάνομεν LTTᵣAWH
Col. 4:12 σταθῆτε TTᵣWH
1Pet. 5:12 στῆτε stand ye LTTᵣAWHR

Rev. 5: 6 ἑστηκώς TTᵣ
    7: 9 ἑστῶτας AW
    11 εἱστήκεισαν LTTᵣA, ἑσ- W
    11: 1 *add* ἵ. A.V.B E, *see* ἄγγελος
    4 ἑστῶτες GEds
    12: 4 ἔστηκεν WHR
    13: 1(12:18) ἐστάθη it stood LTTᵣAWHR
    14: 1 ἑστός LTTᵣAWWH

ἰσχυρός.

Mat. 14:30 *omit* boisterous TWHR
Lu. 11:22 ὁ ἰ.—*omit* ὁ LTTᵣAWH
    15:14 ἰσχυρά LTTᵣAWWH
Rev. 6:15°ἰσχυροὶ *for* δυνατοί(-τός)GEds
    18: 2°ἰσχυρᾷ *for* ἰσχύι (-χύς) GEds

ἰσχύς.

Lu. 10:27 τῇ ἰσχύϊ LTTᵣWHR, *see* ψυχη
Rev. 18: 2 ἰσχυρός GEds

ἰσχύω.

Mar. 5: 4 *trs* ἴσχυεν αὐτόν LTTᵣAWH
Joh. 21: 6 ἴσχυον LTTᵣAWH
Acts 27:16 *trs* ἰσχύσαμεν μόλις Eds
Gal. 6:15 availeth—is, ἐστίν GEds
Rev. 12: 8 ἴσχυσεν he prevailed GWH

ἰχθύς.

Lu. 5: 6 *trs* πλῆθος ἰχθύων GTTᵣAWWH
    9:13 *trs* ἰχθύες δυο GLTTᵣAWH
1Co.15:39 *trs* of birds, (and) another of
    fishes Eds

'Ιωαννᾶς.

Lu. 3:27 'Ιωανάν LTTᵣAWHR

'Ιωάννης, 'Ιωάνης TᵣWH.

(Apostle.)

Mat. 9: 2 τὸν 'I.—*omit* τὸν GLTᵣAWH
    38 ὁ 'I.—*omit* ὁ GLW
    14:33 τον 'Ιωάνην WH
Lu. 8:51 *trs* John and James GEds
    9:49 ὁ 'I.—*omit* ὁ LTᵣAWH
Acts 1:13 *trs* John and James Eds
    3:11 τον 'Ιωάννην LTTᵣWH
Rev. 1: 1 'Ιωάνει WH
    21: 2 *omit* I John GEds

(Baptist.)

Mat. 3:14 *omit* 'I. read he LT[TᵣA]WWH
    11: 4 'Ιωάνει WH
    14: 4†*trs* ὁ (om. ὁ T) 'I. αὐτῷ°LTWH
    10 τὸν 'I.—*omit* τὸν LTTᵣAWH
    21:32 *trs* 'I. πρὸς ὑμᾶς LTTᵣAWH
Mar. 1: 6 ὁ 'Ιωάννης TTᵣAWH
Lu. 7:18, 22 'Ιωάννει T, 'Ιωάνει TᵣWH
Joh. 1:28 ὁ 'I. LTTᵣWH, [ὁ] 'I. A
    29 *omit* ὁ 'I. read he GEds
    35 ὁ 'I.—*omit* ὁ T[TᵣA]
    ·3:24 ὁ 'I.—*omit* ὁ T[TᵣA]
Acts 13:25 ὁ 'I.—*omit* ὁ LTTᵣAWH

(Chief Priest.)

Acts 4: 6 'Ιωάννης LTTᵣAWHR

(Mark.)

Acts 15:37 τὸν 'I.—*omit* τὸν GLAR

(Father of Peter), *see* 'Ιωνᾶς

* 'Ιωβήδ, *see* 'Ωβήδ.

'Ιωήλ.

Acts 2:16 *omit* Joel A

'Ιωνάν, 'Ιωνάμ TTᵣAWHR.

'Ιωνᾶς.

Mat. 16:17 *see* Βάρ 'Ιωνᾶ
Joh. 1:42(43) i 21:15,16,17 Jonas—John
    'Ιωάνου LTᵣWHR, 'Ιωάννου TA

'Ιωσῆς.

Mat. 13:55 Joses — Joseph, 'Ιωσήφ
    LTTᵣAWHR
    27:56 Joses—Joseph, 'Ιωσήφ TWH
Mar. 6: 3 15:40 'Ιωσῆτος LTTᵣAWH
    15:47 ἡ 'I. R: ὁ 'Ιωσῆτος LTTᵣAWH
Lu. 3:29 Jose—Jesus, 'Ιησοῦς LTTᵣAWHR
Acts 4:36 Joses—Joseph, 'Ιωσήφ Eds

'Ιωσήφ.

(all in one list.)

Mat. 1:24 ὁ 'I.—*omit* ὁ T[WH]
    13:55°'Ιωσήφ *for* 'Ιωσῆς LTTᵣAWHR
    27:56°'Ιωσήφ *for* 'Ιωσῆ TWH

Lu. 2:33 Joseph—his father, ὁ πατὴρ
αὐτοῦ GTTrAWHR
43 Joseph and his mother—his
parents, γονεύς LTTrAWHR
3:26 Joseph — Josech, Ἰωσήχ
TTrAWHR
Joh. 19:38 ὁ Ἰ.—omit ὁ LTTrAWHR
Acts 4:36* Ἰωσήφ for Ἰωσῆς Eds
7:13 Joseph's—his, αὐτοῦ T: τοῦ Ἰ.
—omit τοῦ LTTrAWHR

Ἰωσίας, Ἰωσείας LTTrAWH.

κἀγώ, κἀμοί, κἀμέ.

Mat. 10:33 trs κἀγὼ αὐτὸν LTTrAWH
18:33* for καὶ ἐγώ LTTrAWH
26:15 καὶ ἐγώ T
Mar. 11:29 omit also, κἀγώ TTrAWHR
Lu. 2:48 καὶ ἐγώ WH
16:9 κἀγὼ LTTrAWH
19:23* for καὶ ἐγώ LTTrAWH
21:49* for καὶ ἰδού ἐγώ T
Joh. 6:44*, 54* for καὶ ἐγώ LTTrAWH
14:16* for καὶ ἐγώ LTTrAWH
21* for καὶ ἐγώ LTTrAWH
15:10* for ἐγώ T
16:32* for καὶ ἐμὲ TTrAWH
17:6* for καὶ ἐμοί TrWH
11*, 22* for καὶ ἐγώ LTTrAWH
Acts 10:26 καὶ ἐγώ TTrAWH
28* for καὶ ἐμοί LTTrAWH
26:29 καὶ ἐγώ WH
1 Co. 2:3* for καὶ ἐγώ LTTrAWH
3:1* for καὶ ἐγώ GLTTrAWWH
16:10* for καὶ ἐγώ LTTrA
2 Co. 2:10* for καὶ ἐγώ LTTrAWH
Gal. 2:8* for καὶ ἐμοί LTrW
Rev. 22:8* for καὶ ἐγώ LTTrAWWH

καθαίρω.

Heb. 10:2 καθαρίζω Eds

καθάπερ.

Ro. 3:4* for καθώς TTrWH
9:13* 10:15* for καθώς WH
11:8* for καθώς TTrWH
1 Co. 10:10* for καθώς TTrWHR
Heb. 5:4 καθώσπερ TTrAWHR

καθαρίζω.

Mat. 8:3 ἐκαθερίσθη TWH
10:8 trs raise the dead, cleanse
the lepers GEds
Mar. 1:42 ἐκαθερίσθη TAWH
7:19 καθαρίζων LTTrAWHR
Acts 10:15 ἐκαθέρισεν Tr
11:9 ἐκαθέρισεν Tr
Heb. 10:2* κεκαθα(ε L)ρισμένους for κεκα-
θαρμένους (καθαίρω) Eds

καθαρός.

1 Pet. 1:22 omit pure, read from the
heart LTTrAWHR
Rev. 19:8 trs white clean GLTTrAWHR
22:1 omit pure GEds

καθέζομαι.

Joh. 6:3* ἐκαθέζετο for ἐκάθητο (κάθημαι) T
Acts 20:9* καθεζόμενος for καθήμενος
(-μαι) Eds

καθηγητής.

Mat. 23:8 διδάσκαλος Eds
10† trs ὅτι κ. ὑμῶν ἐστὶν εἷς for
your master is one LTTrAWH

καθήκω.

Acts 22:22 καθῆκεν GLTTrAWWH

καθημαι.

Mat. 19:28* καθήσεσθε for καθίσεσθε (-ίζω)
26:69 trs ἐκάθητο ἔξω LTTrAWH (WH
Mar. 12:36 καθίζω TrA
Lu. 10:13 καθήμενοι LTTrAWH
22:30* καθήσεσθε TTr, κάθησθε A, καθή-
σθε WH for καθίσησθε (-ίζω)
Joh. 6:3 κάθέζομαι T
Acts 20:9 καθέζομαι Eds
Jas. 2:3 trs ἦ κάθου ἐκεῖ WH
Rev. 11:16 omit οἱ Λ(ΛWH)R, οἱ (οἱ before
ἐνώπιον R) κάθηνται TTrR
14:6* καθήμενος for κατοικοῦντας
(-κέω) GEds
14 καθήμενον ὅμοιον GEds

καθίζω.

Mat. 19:28 κ.²—κάθημαι WH

Mar. 11:2 ἐκάθισεν WHR
12:36* κάθισον for κάθου (-θημαι) TrA
Lu. 22:30 καθίσεσθε GLWR: κάθημαι
TTrAWH
Eph. 1:20 καθίσας LTTrAWHR
Heb. 12:2 κεκάθικεν GEds

κάθημι.

Acts 9:25† trs διὰ τοῦ τείχους κ. αὐτόν
LTTrAWHR

καθίστημι.

Acts 6:3 καταστήσομεν S—καταστή-
σωμεν A.V. Vul RW
17:15 καθιστάνοντες LTTrAWH
Heb. 2:7 omit and didst set to end of
verse G[L]T[Tr]A[WH]

καθό.

1 Pet. 4:13 καθό S—καθώς R

καθότι.

Acts 17:31* for διότι Eds

καθώς.

Mar. 1:2* for ὡς TTrWH
Lu. 17:28* for καὶ ὡς TTrAWHR
Joh. 10:26 omit as I said unto you
[L]TTr[A]WH
Acts 10:47 ὡς LTTrAWH
Ro. 3:4 καθάπερ TTrWH
9:13 10:15 καθάπερ WH
11:8 καθάπερ TTrWH
1 Co. 10:10 καθάπερ TTrWHR
1 Th. 4:1* add κ. Eds, see περιπατέω
1 Pet. 4:13 καθό S—καθώς R

* καθώσπερ, even as, καθώς περ Tr.

Heb. 5:4 for καθάπερ TTrAWHR

καί.

Mat. 3:2 omit and LT[Tr]AWHR
10 omit also Eds
16 κ. βαπτισθείς—β. δέ LTTrAWWH
16 omit and¹ LT[TrA]WH
4:24 omit and¹ LTTrAWH
5:13 omit and LTTrAWHR
6:21 omit also L[WH]
25 κ.¹—ἤ LTr[WH]R: omit κ.¹ T
8:7 omit and¹ LT[Tr]AWH
8 κ. ἀποκριθείς—ἀ. δέ LTTrWH
13 omit and² LT[Tr]AWHR
9:10 omit κ.² T
10:2* κ. Ἰάκωβος and James LTWH
11:5 [and¹] LTr
5* κ. νεκροί and the dead
TTrAWHR, [κ.] ν. L
16 and—who, ὅς LTTrAWHR
17 omit and¹ LTTrAWHR
12:8 omit even GEds
22 omit both LTTrAWHR
44* empty—add κ. and (L)T[WH]
13:4 omit and³ AWH
14:13 κ. ἀκούσας—ἀ. δέ LTTrAWH
19 omit and² GLTTrAWWH
26 δέ LTWH, see μαθητής
15:5(5) omit and LTTr[A]WH
31* κ. χωλούς and the lame LTTrA
36 omit and¹ LTTrWHR (WHR
36* ἰχθύας—add κ. LTWHR
16:17 κ. ἀποκριθείς—ἀ. δέ LTTrAWH
19 omit and¹ T[A]WHR
17:7* Ἰησοῦς κ. LTTrWH: omit κ.²
LTWH
18:12* ὄρη—add κ. LTTrWH
15 omit and¹ GLTTrAWH
20:9 κ. ἐλθόντες—ἐ. δέ LWH
23 omit and¹ LTTrAWH
24 κ. ἀκούσαντες—ἀ. δέ TA
21:5 omit and¹ A
28 omit and¹ TWH
30 κ. προσελθών—π. δέ LTTrAWH
45 κ. ἀκούσαντες—ἀ. δέ T
22:27 omit also T[Tr]AWHR
23:34 omit and³ LTTrAWHR
24:27 omit also Eds
37 omit also LTTrAWHR
39 omit also LTTrAWHR
25:11 omit also L[Tr]
17 omit and [L]TWH
26:26 omit κ.³ LTTrWHR
27 omit κ.² [L] frWH]
33 omit κ. GEds
60 omit yea GLTTrWHR
71 omit also TWI
27:31 omit and² T
40* κ. κατάβηθι LT
41 omit also [L]T[WH]
35 .²* οὐρανοῦ—add κ. TTrWHR

Mar. 1:4 omit and [Tr]AWH (A
15 om. and saying T[WH], om. and
37* add κ. TTrAWHR, see εὑρίσκω
40 omit and³ T[A]WH
2:1 omit and² [L]TTrAWHR
9 omit and¹ G[Tr.]AW[WH]
11 omit and¹ G[LTTrA]WWHR
21 omit also GEds
27* ἐγένετο—add κ. TTrAWHR
3:31* for οὖν Eds, see ἔρχομαι
33* for ἤ LTTrAWHR
4:5* ground—add κ. and [LTr]A[WH]
5:15 omit and LTTrAWHR
38* θόρυβον—add κ. A.V.C GEds
6:22 omit and³ LTTrAWHR, see
ἀρέσκω
30 omit both Eds
38 omit and¹ [L]TTrAWHR
48 omit and² LTTrAWHR
50 κ.²—ὁ δέ TWHR
55* ἐκείνην—add κ. TTrWHR
7:5* for ἔπειτα LTTrAWHR
12 omit and LTTr[A]WHR
24 κ. ἐκεῖθεν—ἐ. δέ TAWHR
31 διά LTTrAWHR, see ἔρχομαι
32* κωφόν—add κ. LTTrAWHR
8:3* τινές γάρ—κ. τινες LTTrAWHR
19* κ. πόσους T
9:24 omit and¹ [L]T[Tr]AWHR
10:1* for διά LTTrAWH
5 δέ TTrAWHR, see ἀποκρίνομαι
12 omit κ.² TTrAWHR
14 omit and² GTTrAWWHR
28 omit then GEds
32 κ.³—οἱ δέ TTrAWHR
38, 40 and—or, ἤ LTTrAWHR
11:2* add κ. LTTrAWHR, see λύω
17* add κ. TTrAWHR, see λέγω
24* add κ. LTTrAWHR, see προσεύχομαι
28 and²—or, ἤ TAWHR
12:6 omit also [L]TTrAWHR
17 κ. ἀποκ. ὁ—ὁ δέ LTTrAWHR
22 omit and² TTrAWHR
31 omit and [L]TTrAWHR
32 omit and¹ WH
13:8 omit and TTrAB
8 omit and³ T[Tr]AWHR
22 omit even T[Tr]AWHR
32 and—or, ἤ GEds
34 omit and² LTTrAWHR
14:3 omit and² TAWHR
15* κ. ἐκεῖ and there TrAWHR,
κἀκεῖ T
15:24* αὐτόν—add κ. TTrAWHR
30 omit and LTTrAWHR
36 omit and² L[Tr]AWHR
41 omit also LT[Tr]WHR
46 omit and² Eds

7 a. 1:50* γενεῶν—κ. γενεάς TTrAWHR
2:12* κ. κείμενον and lying [L]TrAWH
3:17 omit and¹ TWHR (B
20 omit that T[A]WHR
4:3 κ. εἶπεν—ε. δέ LTTrAWHR
9 κ. ἠγαγεν—ἤ. δέ LTTrAWHR
5:1* him—add κ. also TTrAWHR
3 κ. καθίσας—καθίσας δέ TAWHR
12 κ. ἰδών—ἰ. δέ TWHR
39 omit κ. WH
6:4 ἔλαβεν κ.—λαβών LTTrAWHR
4 omit also LTTrAWH
5 omit also WHR
6 omit also LTTr[A]WHR
8 κ. εἶπεν—ε. δέ TTrAWHR
14* add κ. bis, read and James
. . . and Philip LTTrAWHR
15* add κ. bis, read and Matthew
LTTrAWHR, and James T[WH]R
16* add κ. read and Judas¹
LTTrAWHR
16 omit also LT[Tr]AWHR
18 omit and they² LTTrAWHR
28 omit and GEds
36 omit also [L]T[Tr]WHR
37 omit κ.¹ A.V.R
37* judged—add κ. and TAWHR
38 omit and¹³ LTTrAWHR
39* δε—add κ. read spake also
LTTrAWHR
7:22* κ. κωφοί and the deaf WH
32 omit and¹ LTTrAWHR
37* sinner—add κ. and Eds
8:20 κ. ἀπηγγέλη—ἀ. δέ LTTrAWHR
22 κ. ἐγένετο—ἐ. δέ LTTrAWHR
28 omit κ.¹ LTTrAWHR
36 omit also LTTr[A]WHR
9:5 omit very [L]TrAWHR
9 κ. εἶπεν—ε. δέ LTTrAWHR
28 omit κ.³ [L]WH
10:1 omit also [TrA]WHR
4 omit and T

Lu. 10:25 *omit* κ.² T[Tᵣ]ᴀWʜʀ
38 *omit that* [LTᵣ]Wʜʀ
11:54 *omit* and GEds
12:29*for* ἤ TTᵣWʜʀ
42 *omit and²* LTTᵣAWʜʀ
13:20 *omit* and W
14:18 *omit and³* TTᵣAWʜʀ
27 *omit and¹* TWʜʀ
34*ἐὰν δὲ κ. but if also* LTTᵣAWʜʀ
15:12 κ.²–ὁ δέ LTᵣAWʜʀ
19 *omit* and GEds
21 *omit and³* ᴸTTᵣAWʜʀ
24 *omit* κ.² Eds
32 *omit and³* T
16: 6 κ.¹–ὁ δέ LTTᵣAWʜʀ
7 *omit and³* TTᵣAWʜʀ
14 *omit also* TT[A]Wʜʀ
17:24 *omit also* G[L]TTᵣAWʜʀ
28 *omit also* TTᴀWʜʀ, *see* καθως
33 κ. ὃς ἐάν–ὃς δ' ἄν Wʜʀ
35 κ. ἤ–ἤ δέ TTᵣAWʜʀ
37*ἐκεῖ κ. thither also* TTᵣAWʜʀ
18: 1 *omit* κ.¹ LT[Tᵣ]WʜʀR
4 *omit* κ.² LTTᵣWʜʀ
13 κ. ὁ–ὁ δέ TTᵣWʜʀ
28 *omit and* LTTᵣAWʜʀ, *see* ἀφίημι
19:30*κ. λύσαντες* TTᵣAWʜ
42 *omit at least* [L]TT[Tᵣ]WʜʀR
46*add* κ. TTᵣAWʜʀ, *see* ἔσται
20:31 *ἀπά–add* κ. A.V.Eᵣ R
42 *and–for, see* γάρ TWʜʀ
21: 2 *omit also* [L]TT[Tᵣ]WʜʀR
22:22 *and–for, ὅτι* TTᵣAWʜʀ
68 *omit also* LTTᵣAWʜʀ
23: 2*κ. λεγόντα and saying
[L]TT[Tᵣ]WʜʀR
5*Jewry–add κ. and* TTᵣ[A]WʜʀR
11*κ. ὁ Ἡρώδης Herod also* T
27 *omit also* LTTᵣAWʜʀ
35 *omit also* LT
36 *omit and²* [L]TTᵣWʜʀR
45 *omit* κ.¹ TWʜʀ, *see* ἥλιος
45 κ. ἐσχίσθη–ἐ. δέ TWʜʀ
46 κ. ταῦτα–τοῦτο δέ TTᵣAWʜʀ
50*ἀνήρ²–κ. ἀνήρ T
51 *omit also* LTTᵣAWʜʀ
55 *omit also* Eds
24: 3 κ. εἰσελθοῦσαι–ε. δέ LTTᵣAWʜʀ
21*γε κ. read yea and beside
LTTᵣAWʜʀ
24 *omit even* LTᵣAWʜʀ
32 *omit and²* LTTᵣAWʜʀ
47 *and²–to, εἰς* TWʜ

Joh. 1:16 *and¹–for, ὅτι* GLTTᵣAWʜʀ
21 *omit and²* T
37 *omit and¹* T
42 (43) *omit and¹* [L]TTᵣAWʜʀ
46 (47) *omit and¹* T
2: 4*κ. λέγει, read and Jesus saith
[L]TᵣAWʜʀ
8 κ.³–οι δέ TTᵣAWʜʀ
3:32 *omit and¹* [L]TTᵣAWʜʀ
4:36 *omit and¹* G[L]TTᵣAWʜʀ
36 *omit both* Tᵣ[A]WʜʀR
46 κ. ἤν–ἤν δέ T
50 *omit and¹* [L]T[Tᵣ]AWʜʀR
52 *and–therefore, οὖν* TTᵣAWʜʀ
5:10*κ. οὐκ, read and it is not
[L]T[Tᵣ]AWʜʀR
27 *omit also* LTTᵣAWʜʀ
6: 2 κ. ἠκολούθει–η. δέ LTTᵣAWʜʀ
11*add κ. T, see εὐχαριστέω
24 *omit also* Eds
7: 1 *omit* κ. T
15 *and²–therefore, see* οὖν Eds
8:11 *and²–from henceforth, ἀπὸ
τοῦ νῦν* WʜʀR
14 *and¹–or, ἤ* GTTᵣAWʜʀR
25 *omit* and Eds
9:12*add at commencement κ. and
[Tᵣ]WʜʀR, see* οὖν
28*add at commencement κ. and
WʜʀR, see* οὖν
36*κ. τις and who* GTTᵣAWʜʀR
40 *omit and¹* TTᵣAWʜʀ
10: 4 *omit and¹* TTᵣAWʜʀ
22 *omit and²* TTᵣAWʜʀ
11:19 κ. πολλοί–π. δέ LTTᵣAWʜʀ
44 *omit and¹* GTTᵣAWʜʀ
57 *omit both* Eds
12: 6 *omit and²* TTᵣAWʜʀ
13*κύριον–add κ. read blessed
is he that cometh in the
name of the Lord, even the
King of Israel* TTᵣAWʜʀ
18 *omit also* Tᵣ
22*Philip²–add κ. and* LTTᵣAWʜʀ
26 *omit* κ.³ A.V.Vul GLTTᵣAWʜʀ
29 *omit* and W
13: 6 *omit and* TTᵣAWʜʀ
12*αὐτοῦ–add κ. TTᵣAWʜʀ
26 *see* βάπτω

Joh. 14: 4 *omit and²* [L]TTᵣAWʜʀ
5 *omit* and LTᵣWʜʀ
7 *omit and¹* LT[Tᵣ]WʜʀR
9 *omit and¹* LT[Tᵣ]WʜʀR
22*κύριε–add κ. GT[A]W   (Eds
17: 1 *om. and²* LTTᵣAWʜʀ: *om. also*
11*αs–add κ. also* Tᵣ
12*me–add κ. and* [L]TTᵣAWʜʀ
23 *omit and²* LTTᵣAWʜʀ
18: 4*add κ. LTTᵣAWʜʀ, see λέγω
18*ἤν δέ–add κ. read Peter also
LTTᵣAWʜʀ
19: 4*add at commencement κ. read
and Pilate* LTTᵣAWʜʀ
35*κ. ὑμεῖς ye also* GEds
20: 6*κ. Σίμων also Simon* TᵣAWʜʀ
13 *omit and¹* TR
14 *omit and¹* GLTTᵣAWʜʀ
20*shewed–add κ. both* LTTᵣAWʜʀ
28 *omit and¹* GEds
21:23 κ. οὐκ εἶπεν–ο. ε. δέ TᵣWʜʀ

Acts 2:17 *omit and¹* A
22 *omit also* LTTᵣAWʜʀ
33*ye–add κ. both* T[AWʜ]
36 *omit both* E
42 *omit and³* LTTᵣAWʜʀ
44*κ. πάντες δέ and all also* T
44 *omit were and and²* Wʜ
5:15*κ. εἰς for κατά* LTTᵣWʜʀ
7:35*θεός–add κ. read both a ruler
LT[Tᵣ]AWʜʀ
8: 8 κ. ἐγένετο–ἐ. δέ LTTᵣAWʜʀ
28 *omit* κ.³ A.V.C LT[Tᵣ]W
9: 3 κ. ἐξαίφνης–ἐ. τε Eds
24*δὲ κ. for τε LTTᵣAWʜʀ
29(28) *and he spake–omit and*
40*Πέτρος–add κ. Eds
10:14*for ἤ LTTᵣAWʜʀ
17 *omit* κ. LTTᵣ[A]WʜʀR
24 κ. τῇ–τῇ δέ Eds
39*whom–add κ. also* GEds
11: 2 κ. ὅτε–ὅ. δέ LTTᵣAWʜʀ
7*δέ–add κ. read heard also
LTTᵣAWʜʀ
20*spake–add κ. also* LTTᵣAWʜʀ
26*add κ. even* LTTᵣAWʜʀ, *see*
αὐτούς
28 *omit* κ. LTTᵣAWʜʀ
12: 3 κ. ἰδών–ἰ. δέ LTTᵣAWʜʀ
21 *omit* κ. [L]T[Tᵣ]WʜʀR
25 *omit and³* LTT[A]WʜʀR
13: 9 *omit* κ.² Eds
19 *omit* and Wʜ
39 *omit* and LT[Tᵣᴀ]
50 *omit and¹* GEds
14: 3 *omit and¹* GEds
15:23 *omit* κ. οι², *read elder brethren* LTTᵣAWʜʀ
37*with them–add κ. also
GLTTᵣAWʜʀ
16: 1*δέ–add κ. read also to Derbe
L[Tᵣ]WʜʀR
9*ἑστώς–add κ. LTTᵣWʜʀ
32 *and to all–with (σὺν) all* GEds
38 κ. ἐφοβήθησαν–ἐ. δέ LTTᵣAWʜʀ
17:18*τινές δέ κ. then certain also* Eds
21*κ.²–ἤ LTTᵣAWʜʀ
25 *see* κατά
32*add κ. LTTᵣAWʜʀ, see πάλιν
33 *omit* κ. LTTᵣAWʜʀ
18:21*add κ. LTTᵣAWʜʀ, see ἀποτασ-
σομαι
21 *omit and* LTTᵣAWʜʀ
19:13*for ἀπό LTTᵣAWʜʀ
16 *omit* κ.² Eds
21: 4 κ. ἀνευρόντες–ἀ. δέ Eds
25:25 *omit* κ. Eds
26:12 *omit* κ.¹ LTTᵣAWʜʀ
18 τοῦ ἐπιστρέψαι–κ. ἐ. A.V.†B
26 *omit* also Wʜ

Rᴀ. 1:24 *omit also* LTT[ᴀ]WʜʀR
4:11 *on it also* TTᵣ[A]WʜʀR
· 22 [a nd] LTᵣAWʜ
8:24 *omit yet* LT[Tᵣ]AWʜʀ
34 *omit* κ.¹ LTTᵣAWʜʀ
34 *omit even* [L]TWʜʀ
9:23 *omit* and Wʜ
11: 3 *omit and¹* Eds
17 *omit and¹* T[Tᵣ]AWʜʀ
26 *omit and², read he shall* Eds
30 *omit* κ.² GEds
12:15 *omit* and Eds
13:12 κ. ἐνδυσώμεθα–ἐ. ([δέ] Wʜ)Eds
14: 3 κ. ὁ–ὁ δέ LTTᵣAWʜʀ
6*regard (it)–add κ. and* GEds
9 *omit both¹* Eds
15:32 *omit and* LTTᵣAWʜʀ

1Co. 1:28 *omit and³* LTTᵣA[Wʜ]
3: 2 *omit* and Eds
5:10 *omit yet* Eds·*for ἤ² Eds
12 *omit also* LTTᵣAWʜʀ

1 Co. 5:13 *omit therefore* GEds
7:22 *omit also* Eds
34 [both] LTᵣWʜ
8:11 *and–for, see* γάρ LTTᵣWʜʀ
10: 9, 10 *omit also* Eds
11:19*ἵνα–add κ. read they also
[L]Tᵣ·Wʜ)
15: 6 *omit* κ. LTT[A]WʜʀR
14*ἄρα–add κ. read vain also
[L]TAW
28 *omit also* [L]Tᵣ[AWʜ]
16: 6 *omit* κ. Wʜ
10 *omit also* Wʜ
2 Co. 1:13 *omit even* LTTᵣAWʜʀ
4:13*therefore–add κ. also* T
5: 5 *omit also* Eds
8:24 *omit and¹ (κ.²) GEds
9: 5 *omit and²* T
10: 8 *omit* κ.¹ LTTᵣAWʜʀ
12:10*for ἐν² TWʜ
13: 4 *γάρ²–add* κ. E
Gal. 3:29 *omit and²* LTTᵣAWʜʀ
5:21 *omit also* [L]TTᵣWʜ
Eph. 1:18 *omit* and LTTᵣAWʜʀ   (R
3:21*church–add κ. and* LTT[A]Wʜ
4: 8 *omit* κ. LTW[Wʜ]
5: 4 *nor¹ (κ.²)–or, ἤ LT
23 *omit* and GEds
28*κ. οἱ, read so also* LTTᵣAWʜʀ,
[κ.] οἱ Wʜ
6: 9*add κ. Eds, see αὐτῶν
4: 3 *and¹–yea, ναι* GEds
Phil. 3:12 *omit that¹* T
Col. 1: 3 *omit* and LAWʜʀ
6 *omit and¹* Eds
7 *omit also* Eds
2:16*for ἤ¹ AWʜ
23 [and²] LWʜ
3:16 *omit and²³* Eds
17 *omit and²* Eds
23 *omit and¹* Eds
1 Th. 1: 8 *omit also* Eds
2: 2 *omit even* GEds
13*κ. διά, read and for this
LTTᵣAWʜʀ
4: 8 *omit also* LT[ᴀ]WʜʀR
5: 6 *omit* κ.¹ LTTᵣ[A]WʜʀR
15 *omit both* LTTᵣWʜʀ
25*pray–add [κ. also] LWʜ
2 Th. 2:14*whereunto–add κ. also* T
16 *omit even* LTTᵣAWʜʀ
3: 4 *omit both* [L]T[Tᵣ·Wʜ]
14 *omit and²* LTTᵣWʜʀ
1 Ti. 1:12 *omit* and LTTᵣAWʜʀ
2: 9 *omit also* LT[Tᵣ]WʜʀR
9*for ἤ¹ LTTᵣAWʜʀ
4:10 *omit both* LTTᵣ[A]WʜʀR
6:12 *omit also* GEds
2 Ti. 2:21 *omit and¹* LTTᵣAWʜʀ
4: 1*for κατά GEds
18 *omit and¹* LTTᵣAWʜʀ
Tit. 1: 4*grace–add κ. and* TTᵣAWʜʀR
10 *omit* κ.¹ LT[Tᵣ]AWʜʀ
3: 1 *omit and* LTTᵣAWʜʀ
Philem.11*δέ–add κ. read but now also* T
Heb. 1: 8*ever²–add κ. and* LTTᵣAWʜʀ
5:12 *omit and²* T[Tᵣ]Wʜ
7: 4 *omit even* LTᵣWʜʀ
22*so much–add κ. also* TAWʜʀ
26*ἡμῖν–add κ. read high priest
also* [L]TTᵣAW[Wʜ]
8: 2 *omit and²* Eds
9: 1 [also] TᵣWʜ
10 *omit and³* GLT[Tᵣ]AWWʜʀ
28*so–add κ. also* GEds
11:20*faith–add κ also* L[Tᵣ]AWWʜʀ
32*Γεδεών–add κ. W
32 *omit and³* LTTᵣWWʜʀ
32 *omit and¹* LTTᵣWʜʀ
13: 6 *omit* and [L]T[TᵣA]WʜʀR
Jas. 2: 3 κ. ἐπιβλέψητε–ἐ. δέ ᴀWʜ
4 *omit then* LTTᵣAWʜʀ
13 *omit* and GEds
3: 6 *omit and¹, read the tongue
kindleth* T
6*for ἤ³, read both defileth* T
12 *omit* κ. GEds, *see* οὐδείς (Wʜʀ
17 *and without–omit and* LTTᵣA
4: 2*πολεμεῖτε–add κ. (om. δέ) T
9 *omit and²* T
11 *and¹–or, ἤ LTTᵣAWʜʀ
13 κ.¹–ἤ A.V.B ELITᵣWʜʀ
1 Pet. 2: 6 *omit also* GEds
3: 1 *omit also* Wʜ
2 Pet. 2:12*add κ. Eds, see φθείρω
17*add κ. Eds, see νεφέλη
19 *omit* κ. T[Tᵣ]Wʜ
1 Joh.1: 3*declare we–add κ. also* Eds
2:20 *omit* and Wʜ
29*κ. πᾶς also everyone* TTᴀR
3:13*add at commencement κ.and* T
19 *omit and¹* L[Tᵣ·A]Wʜʀ

1 Joh. 5: 1 *omit* also [Lr.]WH
　13 *omit* and GEds
Jude　25 *omit* and[1] Eds
Rev. 1: 6 *omit* and GEds, *see* βασιλεύς
　9 *omit* also GEds
2: 3 *omit* and[3] GEds
　13 *omit* even T[Tr.A]
　19 *omit* κ.[a] *read* thy last works GEds
　20[a]*add* κ. GEds, *see* διδάσκω
　24 *omit* and *bis* GEds
3: 4 *omit* even GEds
　8 and[1]—which, ὅς GEds
　20[a]*door*[a]—*add* κ. *read* I will both τ[A]W
4: 2 *omit* and[1] Eds
　4 *omit* κ.[2] GEds
　10 *omit* κ.[1] GEds
5: 6 *omit* and. lo GTTrAWWHR
　13[a]κ. ἤκουσα heard I also T
7: 1 *omit* and L[Tr.A]WHR
9:10 *trs* κ.[3] Eds, *see* ἥν
　11 *omit* and GEds
　16 *omit* and[3] GEds
10: 7 *omit* κ. A.V.C
11: 2[a]κ. δύο LAW, [καί] ὁ. WH
　14 κ. ἰδού A.V.[b]B
　16 *omit* κ.[3] GEds
　17[a]κ. ὅτι and because T
12: 2[a]ἔχουσα—*add* κ. *read* was with child, and cried, LT[A]WHR
13: 4[a]τίς[a]—κ. τίς and who GEds
　5[a][κ.] δύο LWH
　6 *omit* and[3] GEds
　17 *omit* and LT[AWH]
15: 6 *omit* and[2] GEds
16: 5 *omit* and[2] GEds
17: 9 ὧδε—*et hic* A.V.Vul
　10 *omit* and[2] GEds
　16[a]*for* ἐπί GEds
18: 1, 16 *omit* and[1] Eds
　20[a]*add* κ. GEds. *see* ἀπόστολος
19: 1 *omit* and[1] GEds
　4 *omit* κ.[2] GEds
　5 *omit* and[2] T[Tr.A]WHR
　5 *omit* both GEds
　8 *omit* and[1] LTTrAWHR
　14 *omit* and[2] GLTrAWWHR
　15 *omit* and[a], *read* fierceness of the wrath GLTTrAWHR
　17 *omit* and[3] GEds
20: 3 *omit* and[a] Eds
　10[a]where—*add* κ. both GEds
21:11 *omit* and GEds
　13[a]*add* κ. *before* ἀπό[a3], *read* and on Eds: *before* ἀ.[a] A.V.C Eds
　16 *omit* κ.[3] TTr[A]WHR
　19 *omit* and LTAWHR
22: 7[a]κ. ἰδού and behold GEds
　12 *omit* and[1] GEds
　16 *omit* and[3] (κ.[2]) GTTrAWWHR
　17 *omit* and[3] GEds
　19 *omit* and[3] GEds

See also κἀγώ κἀκεῖ, κἀκεῖθεν, κἄν, &c.

Καϊάφας, Καιά— WH.
Acts 4: 6 Καϊάφας LTTrAWHR

καίγε.
Lu. 19:42[a]*for* καί γε GT
Acts 2:18[a]*for* καί γε GT
　17:27[a]*for* καίτοιγε TR

Κάϊν, Κάιν WH.

Καϊνάν, Και— WH.
Lu. 3:36 Καϊνάμ TAWH
　37 Καϊνάμ TWH

καινός.
Mat. 26:28 *omit* new T[A]WHR
Mar. 1:27 τίς ἡ διδαχὴ ἡ καινὴ αὕτη, ὅτι —διδαχὴ καινή, *read* a new doctrine! with authority he LTrWHR, a new doctrine with authority, he TA
　2:22 *omit* T[Tr.A[WH], *see* βλητέος
　14:24 *omit* new TTrAWH
　16:17 *omit* new TrWH

καίπερ.
Rev. 17: 8 κ. ἐστὶν and yet is—καὶ παρέσται.(-ειμι) and shall be present GEds

καιρός.
Mat. 13:30 τῷ κ.—*omit* τῷ GLTTrAWWH
　16: 3 when it is (ver. 2) to end of ver se 3 [TA][WH]]

Mar. 11:13†*trs* ὁ γὰρ κ. οὐκ ἦν TTrAWHR
Lu. 12:56 *trs* καιρὸν δὲ WH
Joh. 5: 4 *omit* waiting for (ver.3) to end of verse 4 [G]TTrAWHR
　7: 8†*trs* ὁ ἐμός κ. LTTrAWH
Ro. 12:11 τῷ καιρῷ in season s—τῷ κυρίω (-ριος) the Lord A.V.B REds

Καῖσαρ.
Mar. 12:17 *trs* τὰ Κ. ἀπόδοτε TTrAWHR
Lu. 20:25 Κ. τῷ Κ. Tr
　23: 2 *trs* φόρους Καίσαρι LTTrAWH
Acts 11:28 *omit* Caesar GEds

Καισάρεια, —ρια TWH.
Acts 12:19 τὴν Κ.—*omit* τὴν LTTrAWWH
　25: 4 εἰς Καισάρειαν Eds

καίτοι, καίτοιγε, καί τοι γε.
Acts 14:17 *omit* γε LTTrWHR
　17:27 καὶ γε LTrAWH, καίγε TR

καίω.
Mat. 13:40[a]καίεται *for* κατακαίεται (-καίω) GTrA
1Co. 13: 3 καυθήσομαι T: to be burned— that I may boast, καυχάομαι
Rev. 19:20 τῆς καιομένης LTTrAWH　(WH

κἀκεῖ.
Mat. 28:10 καὶ ἐκεῖ T
Mar. 1:38 καὶ ἐκεῖ GWWH
　14:15[a]*for* ἐκεῖ T, καὶ ἐκεῖ TrAWHR

κἀκεῖθεν.
Mar. 9:30[a]*for* καὶ ἐκεῖθεν LTTrAWH
　10: 1 καὶ ἐκεῖθεν LTTrAWWH
Lu. 11:53[a]*add* κ. TTrAWHR, *see* ἐξέρχομαι
Acts 16:12[a]*for* ἐκεῖθεν τε Eds
　27:12 ἐκεῖθεν (*omit* also) LTTrAWHR

κἀκεῖνος.
Mat. 20: 4 καὶ ἐκείνοις TAWH
Joh. 19:35 καὶ ἐκεῖνος LTrWH
Ro. 11:23[a]κἀκεῖνοι *for* καὶ ἐκεῖνοι (-νος) GLTTrAWWH

κακία.
Ro. 1:29 *trs* maliciousness, covetousness T

κακοήθεια, —θία WH.

κακοπαθέω.
2 Ti. 2: 3 συγκακοπαθέω, *read* endure hardness with (me) Eds

κακοπάθεια, —θία WH.

κακοποιός.
Joh. 18:30 κακὸν ποιῶν TTrAWH
1 Pet. 3:16 *omit* of you as of evildoers TAWHR

κακός, τὸ κακόν.
Joh. 18:30[a]κακὸν ποιῶν *for* κακοποιος TTrAWH
Ro. 9:11 φαῦλος LTTrAWHR
　13: 3 τῷ κακῷ Eds
2Co. 5:10 φαῦλος TTrWHR

κακοῦργος.
Lu. 23:32 *trs* κακοῦργοι δύο WH

καλέω.
Mat. 10:25 have called —have surnamed καλέω GEds
　22:43 *trs* κ. αὐτὸν κύριον LTrAWH, κ. κύριον αὐτόν T
Mar. 3:31[a]καλοῦντες *for* φωνοῦντες (φωνέω) LTTrAWH
Lu. 9:10 πόλιν καλουμένην TTrAWHR
　22: 3[a]καλούμενον *for* ἐπικαλούμενον (-λέω) TTrAWH
Joh. 10: 3 φωνέω LTTrAWHR
Acts 8:10[a]κ.[a2] *add* καλουμένη, *read* power of God which is called great GEds
　15:22[a]καλουμενον *for* ἐπικαλούμενον (-λέω) Eds
1Co. 7:18†*trs* κέκληται τις[a3] hath any been called Eds
1Th. 2:12 vocavit A.V.Vul
Heb. 5: 4 ὁ κ.—*omit* ὁ GEds
　11: 8 ὁ καλούμενος L, ὁ) κ. Tr

Rev. 19:11†*trs* πιστὸς κ. Tr, π. [κ.] WH, [κ.] π. A
　13 κέκληται Eds

κάλλιον, *see* καλῶν

καλός.
Mat. 15:26 ἔξεστιν LTA, *see* ἐστιν
Mar. 7:27 *trs* ἐστιν καλόν LTTrAWH
Lu. 3: 9 [good] LWH
Joh. 10:32 *trs* ἔργα καλὰ LT: καλά *after* ὑμῖν WH
1Ti. 5: 4 *omit* good and GEds
Tit. 3: 8 τὰ κ.—*omit* τὰ Eds

καλύπτω.
1Pet. 4: 8 καλύπτει covereth Eds

καλῶς, κάλλιον.
Mat. 5:44 *omit* LTTrAWHR, *see* μισέω
Lu. 6:48[a]*add* κ. TTrAWHR, *see* θεμελιόω

κἀμέ, κἀμοί, *see* κἀγώ.

κάμνω.
Rev. 2: 3 *omit* κ. GEds, *see* κοπιάω

κἄν.
Lu. 12:38[a]*for* καὶ ἐάν TTrAWH
　38[a]*for* καί[2] TTrAWH
Joh. 8:55[a]*for* καὶ ἐάν LTTrWH
1Co. 13: 2[a]*for* καὶ ἐάν[1] LAWH
　2[a]*for* καὶ ἐάν[2] TrAWH
　3[a]*for* καὶ ἐ.[1] LTTrAWH: *for*[a] LAWH

Κανὰ —ᾷ, —ά WH.

Κανναῖος, Cananaean, or Zealot, *see* Κανανίτης.

Κανανίτης.
Mat. 10: 4 Καναναῖος LTTrAWHR
Mar. 3:18 Καναναῖον (-ος) Eds

κανών.
Phi. 3:16 *omit* rule, let us mind the same thing GLTTrAWHR

Καπερναούμ, Καφαρ— LTTrAWWH.
Lu. 4:23 τὴν Κ. TAWH, *omit* τῇ GLTr

καρδία.
Mat. 12:35 *omit* of the heart GEds
　22:37 τῇ κ.—*omit* τῇ [A]WH
Mar. 4:15 in their hearts—in them, ἐν αὐτοῖς T, εἰς αὐτούς TrAWHR
　6:52 *trs* αὐτῶν ἡ κ. LTTrAWWH
　12:30, 33 τῆς κ.—*omit* τῆς WH
Lu. 4:18 *omit* to heal the broken-hearted G[L]TTrAWHR
　6:45 *omit* treasure of his heart[a] [L]TTrAWHR
　45 τῆς κ.[a]—*omit* τῆς LTTrAWH
　10:27 τῆς κ.—*omit* τῆς [Tr]WH
　21:14 ἐν ταῖς καρδίαις LTTrAWHR
　34 *trs* αἱ καρδίαι ὑμῶν LTrWH
　24:38 τῇ καρδίᾳ heart LTTrAWHR
Acts 2:26 *trs* μου ἡ κ. LTTrAWH
　37 τὴν καρδίαν LTTrAWH
　4:32 ἡ κ.—*omit* ἡ LTTrAWHR
　7:51 τῇ κ.—καρδίαις hearts LTTrWHR, ταῖς κ. W
　8:37 *omit* the verse GLTTrAWHR
Ro. 10: 6 τῇ κ.—*omit* τῇ E
2Co. 3: 3 καρδίαις, *read* tables, hearts of flesh LTTrAWHR
Eph. 1:18[a]καρδίας *for* διανοίας (-ια) GEds
　6: 5 τῆς κ.—*omit* τῆς T
Col. 3:16 ταῖς καρδίαις GEds
Heb. 8:10 καρδίαν heart T
Jas. 3:14 cordibus vestris A.V.Vul
1Joh. 3:19 τὴν καρδίαν WHR

καρπός.
Mat. 3: 8 καρπὸν ἄξιον fruit worthyG Eds
Mar.12: 2 τῶν καρπῶν the fruits TTrAWHR
Lu. 13: 6 εἰ τι ζητῶν καρπόν GEds
Joh. 15: 2 *trs* καρπὸν πλείονα LTTrAWH
Ro. 1:13 *trs* τινὰ καρπόν GEds
1Co. 9: 7 τὸν καρπόν Eds
Phi. 1:11 καρπόν fruit GEds

κατά.
Mar. 6:40[a]*for* ἀνὰ *bis* LTTrAWH
　14: 3 *omit* κ. LTTrAWHR
Lu. 23:17 *omit* the verse [L]TT[.[A]WHR
Joh. 5: 4 *omit* [G]TTrAWHR, *see* ὕδωρ
　18:29 *omit* κ. TWH

Joh. 21:25 *omit the verse* τ
Acts 2:30 *omit* GLTTᵣAWⱧR, *see* σάρξ
     5:15 into—even into, καὶ εἰς
        LTTᵣWⱧR
    13:49*for* διά T
     16: 7 κ.²—εἰς GEds
     17:25 κ. πάντα s—καὶ τὰ π. A.V.B
        E ·Eds
     24: 6 *omit* LTTᵣ[A]WⱧR, *see* κρίνω
     25: 7 *omit* against Paul LTTᵣAWⱧR
     27:29*for* εἰς Eds
Ro.   8: 1 *omit* who walk *to end of*
       verse GEds
1 Co.   7: 7 †*trs* ἐν τῇ κ. αὐτοῦ ἑδραῖος
       LTTᵣAWⱧR
Phi.   2: 3*μηδὲ κ. for ἤ LTTᵣAWⱧR
2 Ti.   4: 1 at—and (by), καί GEds
Heb. 7:21 *omit* after the order of Mel-
       chisedec TTᵣAWⱧR
Jas.   3:14 *omit* κ. T
1 Pet. 4:14 *omit* on their part *to end of*
       verse LTTᵣAWⱧR
     5: 2*add κ. LTTᵣR, *see* θεός
Rev.   4: 8 καθ᾽ ἑαυτό—κ. ἐν αὐτῶν
       GLTAWⱧR, ἕκαστον αὐτῶν Tᵣ
    12: 7 against—with, μετά GEds
     See also καταμόνας

καταβαίνω.

Mat. 8: 1 καταβάντος δὲ αὐτοῦ TᵣWⱧ
    11:23*καταβήσῃ for καταβιβασθήσῃ
       (-βιβάζω) LTᵣAWⱧR
    24:17 καταβᾶτω LTTᵣWⱧ
Mar. 15:30 καταβάς LTTᵣAWⱧR
Lu.   10:15*καταβήσῃ for καταβιβασθήσῃ
       (-βιβάζω) WⱧ
    22:43, 44 *the verses* [L] [[WⱧ]]
     44 καταβαίνοντος TA
Joh.   5: 4 *omit* waiting for (*ver.* 3) *to*
       end of ver. 4 [G]TTᵣAWⱧR
Rev.   3:12 ἡ καταβαίνουσα s—ἡ κατα-
       βαίνει E
    13:13†*trs* ἐκ τοῦ οὐρανοῦ καταβαίνειν
       (-βῇ G,-βαίνη W) GLTᵣAWWⱧR

καταβάλλω.

Rev. 12:10 βάλλω LTTᵣAWⱧR

* **καταβαρύνω**, to weigh down.

Mar. 14:40 καταβαρυνόμενοι for βεβαρη-
       μένοι (βαρέω) Eds

καταβιβάζω.

Mat. 11:23 shalt be brought down—shalt
       descend, καταβαίνω LTTᵣAWⱧR
Lu.   10:15 shalt be thrust down—shalt
       descend, καταβαίνω WⱧ

καταγγέλλω.

Acts 3:24*κατήγγειλαν for προκατήγγει-
       λαν (-ταγγέλλω) GEds

* **καταγράφω**, to delineate, write
    down.

Joh.   8: 6 κατέγραφεν for ἔγραφεν (γρά-
       φω) WⱧR

κατάγω.

Acts 24: 3 κατέρχομαι LTTᵣAWⱧR
    23:15 *trs* καταγάγῃ αὐτὸν Eds
     20 *trs* τὸν Παῦλον κ. εἰς τὸ συν-
       έδριον LTTᵣAWWⱧR

* **καταδίκη**, condemnation.

Acts 25:15 καταδίκην for δίκην (-κη) Eds

καταδιώκω.

Mar. 1:36 κατεδίωξεν TWⱧ

καταδουλόω.

Gal.   2: 4 καταδουλώσουσιν Eds

* **κατάθεμα**, an accursed thing.

Rev. 22: 3 κατάθεμα for κατανάθεμα GEds

* **καταθεματίζω**, to curse.

Mat. 26:74 καταθεματίζειν for καταναθε-
       ματίζειν (-ζω) GEds

καταισχύνω.

1 Co. 1:27 *trs* κ. τοὺς σοφοὺς [L]TTᵣAWⱧR

κατακαίω.

Mat. 13:40 καίω GTᵣA
2 Pet. 3:10 shall be burned up—shall be
       detected. εὑρίσκω TᵣWⱧ
Rev. 8: 7*add κ. GEds, *see* γῆ

κατάκειμαι.

Mar. 2:15 ἐν τῷ κ.—*omit* ἐν τῷ T[Tᵣ]WⱧR
Lu.   7:37*κατακειται for ἀνάκειται (-κει-
       μαι) LTTᵣAWⱧR

κατακληροδοτέω.

Acts 13:19 κατακληρονομέω GEds

* **κατακληρονομέω**, to allot.

Acts 13:19 κατεκληρονόμησεν for κατεκλη-
       ροδότησεν (κατακληροδοτέω)
       GEds

κατακλίνω.

Lu.   7:36*κατεκλίθη for ἀνεκλίθη (ἀνα-
       κλίνω) LTTᵣAWⱧR
    9:15*κατέκλιναν for ἀνέκλιναν (ἀνα-
       κλίνω) TTᵣWⱧR

κατακολουθέω.

Acts 16:17 κατακολουθοῦσα TTᵣWⱧ

κατακρημνίζω.

Lu.   4:29 τὸ κ.—*omit* τὸ GLTTᵣAWⱧR

κατακρίνω.

Jas.   5: 9 condemned—judged, κρίνω
       GEds

* **κατακύπτω**, to bend down.

Joh.   8: 8 κατακύψας for κάτω κύψας
       (κύπτω) WⱧ

καταλαλέω.

1 Pet. 3:16 καταλαλοῦσιν LTᵣW, -λαλεῖσθε
       ye are spoken evil of TAWⱧR

καταλαμβάνω.

Joh.   6:17*add κ. T, *see* ἤδη
     8: 4 κατείληπται WⱧR
Acts 25:25 κατελαβόμην Eds
Phi.   3:12 κατελήμφθην LTTᵣAWⱧ

κατάλειμμα.

Ro.   9:27 ὑπόλειμμα LTTᵣAWⱧR

καταλείπω.

Mar. 12:21*καὶ οὐδὲ αὐτὸς ἀφῆκεν neither
       left he any—μὴ καταλιπὼν
       leaving no TTᵣAWⱧR
Lu.   10:40 κατέλειπεν TᵣAWⱧ
Acts 2:31 ἐγκαταλείπω LTTᵣAWⱧR
Tit.   1: 5 ἀπολείπω Eds
2 Pet. 2:15 καταλείποντες forsaking TWⱧR

καταμαρτυρέω.

Mar. 15: 4 witness against—accuse, κα-
       τηγορέω LTTᵣAWⱧR

καταμόνας, κατὰ μόνας LTTᵣWⱧ.

καταναθεμα.

Rev. 22: 3 κατάθεμα GEds

καταναθεματίζω.

Mat. 26:74 καταθεματίζω GEds

καταντάω.

Acts 18:19 κατήντησαν they came LTTᵣA
1 Co. 10:11 κατήντηκεν Eds   (WⱧ

καταξιόομαι.

Lu.   20:35 habebuntur A.V. Vul
    21:36 may be accounted worthy—
       may prevail, κατισχύω
       TTᵣAWⱧ

καταπατέω.

Mat. 7: 6 καταπατήσουσιν LTTᵣAWⱧ

κατάπαυσις.

Heb. 4: 3 κ.¹—[τὴν] κ. TᵣWⱧ

καταπίνω.

1 Pet. 5: 8 καταπιεῖν to devour LTAWⱧR,
       καταπιειν Tᵣ

καταπίπτω.

Lu.   8: 6*κατέπεσεν for ἔπεσεν (πίπτω)
       TTᵣAWⱧR

καταράομαι.

Mat. 5:44 *omit* bless them *to* hate you
       LTTᵣAWⱧR
    25:41 οἱ κ.—*omit* οἱ TWⱧR

καταρτίζω.

1 Pet. 5:10 καταρτίσει will perfect Eds

κατασκάπτω.

Acts 15:16 καταστρέφω TTᵣWⱧR

κατασκηνόω.

Mat. 13:32 κατασκηνοῖν LTTᵣAWⱧ
Mar. 4:32 κατασκηνοῖν WⱧ

καταστρέφω.

Acts 15:16*κατεστραμμένα TWⱧR, -ρεμ- Tᵣ
       for κατεσκαμμένα(κατασκάπτω)

καταστρηνιάζω, -άω.

1 Ti.   5:11 καταστρηνιάσωσιν A

καταστροφή.

2 Pet. 2: 6 *omit* with an overthrow WⱧ

κατατίθημι.

Mar. 15:46 τίθημι LTᵣWⱧ

κατατοξεύω.

Heb. 12:20 *omit* or thrust through with
       a dart GEds

καταφάγω.

Joh.   2:17 καταφάγεται shall eat up GEds

καταφέρω.

Acts 25: 7*καταφέροντες for φέροντες
       (-ρω) LTTᵣAWⱧR

καταφθείρω.

2 Pet. 2:12 φθείρω Eds

κατέναντι.

Mat. 21: 2*for ἀπέναντι LTTᵣWⱧ
    27:24*for ἀπέναντι LTᵣWⱧ
Mar. 12:41 ἀπέναντι Tᵣ
2 Co. 2:17*for κατενώπιον LTTᵣAWⱧR
    12:19*for κατενώπιον Eds

κατενώπιον.

2 Co. 2:17 κατέναντι LTTᵣAWⱧR
    12:19 κατέναντι Eds

κατεργάζομαι.

Ro.   7: 8 κατηργάσατο TTᵣA
2 Co. 7:10 κ.¹—ἐργάζομαι Eds
       11 κατηργάσατο T
    12:12 κατηργάσθη T
Jas.   1:20 ἐργάζομαι LTTᵣAWⱧR
1 Pet. 4: 3 κατειργάσθαι Eds

κατέρχομαι.

Acts 15:30*κατῆλθον for ἦλθον (ἔρχομαι)
       LTTᵣAWⱧR
     19: 1*κατελθεῖν for ἐλθεῖν(ἔρχομαι)?
     21: 3*κατήλθομεν for κατήχθημεν
       (κατάγω) LTTᵣAWⱧR
     27: 5 κατήλθαμεν TTᵣWⱧ

κατεσθίω.

Mat. 23:14(13) *omit the verse* LTTᵣAWⱧR,
       see κρίμα
Mar. 12:40 κατέσθοντες TᵣAWⱧ

* **κατευλογέω**, to bless much.

Mar. 10:16 αὐτά¹—*add* κατευλόγει TTᵣAWⱧ,
       κατηυλόγει R, *see* εὐλογέω

κατέχω.

Mat. 21:38 let us seize on—let us possess,
       ἔχω LTTᵣAWⱧR
Joh.   5: 4 *omit* waiting for (*ver.* 3) *to*
       end of verse 4 [G]TTᵣAWⱧR

κατηγορέω.

Mar. 3: 2 κατηγορήσουσιν LTᵣ
     15: 4*κατηγοροῦσιν for καταμαρτυ-
       ροῦσιν (-τυρέω) LTTᵣAWⱧR
Lu.   6: 7*κατηγορεῖν for κατηγορίαν
       (-ρία) TTᵣAWⱧR
    11:54 *omit* that they might accuse
       him T[Tᵣ]AWⱧR
Acts 28:19 κατηγορεῖν LTTᵣAWⱧ

κατηγορία.
Lu. 6: 7 an accusation against—to accuse, κατηγορέω TTrAWHR

κατήγορος.
Joh. 8:10 omit those thine accusers WHR
Acts 24: 8 omit and would (ver. 6) to un-to thee (ver. 8) LTTr[A]WHR
Rev. 12:10 κατήγωρ GLTAWH

* κατήγωρ, an accuser.
Rev. 12:10 κατήγωρ for κατήγορος GLTAWH

κατισχύω.
Lu. 21:36*κατισχύσητε for καταξιωθῆτε (-ξιόομαι) TTrAWHR

κατοικέω.
Mat. 23:21 κατοικήσαντι dwelt GTrAW
Jas. 4: 5 dwelleth—he made to dwell, κατοικίζω LTTrAWHR
Rev. 2:13 trs ὁ σατανᾶς κατοικεῖ GEds
8:13 τοὺς κατοικοῦντας TTrAWHR
12:12 omit the inhabiters of GEds
13:12 trs ἐν αὐτῇ κ. GTTrAWHR
14: 6 dwell—sit, κάθημαι GEds

* κατοικίζω, to cause to dwell.
Jas. 4: 5 κατῴκισεν for κατῴκησεν (κατοικέω) LTTrAWHR

κατόρθωμα.
Acts 24: 2(3) very worthy deeds—re-forms, διόρθωμα LTTrAWHR

κάτω, κατωτέρω.
Mar. 14:66 trs κάτω ἐν τῇ αὐλῇ TTrAWHR
Joh. 8: 8 κατακύπτω WH

καυματίζω.
Mar. 4: 6 ἐκαυματίσθησαν they were scorched Tr

καυτηριάζομαι, καυστ— TTrWH.

καυχάομαι.
Ro. 5: 3 καυχώμενοι glorying TrA
1 Co. 1:29 καυχήσηται S—καυχήσεται E
13: 3*καυχήσωμαι for καυθήσωμαι (καίω) WH
2 Co. 10: 8 καυχήσομαι T
12:11 omit in glorying GEds
2 Th. 1: 4 ἐγκαυχάομαι LTTrAWHR

καύχησις.
Ro. 15:17 τὴν ([τὴν] WH) καύχησιν Eds
2 Co. 9: 4 omit τῆς κ. read same confidence GEds

Κεγχρεαί, Κενχ— TWH.

Κέδρος.
Joh. 18: 1 τοῦ Κεδρών GL, τοῦ κέδρου T

κεῖμαι.
Lu. 2:12 omit lying T
24:12 omit laid Tr[A]WHR: omit the verse [L]T[Tr][[WH]]
Joh. 2: 6 trs κ. after 'Ιουδαίων TTrAWHR
11:41 omit where the dead was laid GLTTrAWHR

κείρω.
Acts 8:32 κείραντος TA

κελεύω.
Mat. 15:35 παραγγέλλω LTTrWHR
Acts 23:35 κελεύσας LTTrAWHR
24: 8 omit and would (ver. 6) to come unto thee (ver. 8) LTTr[A]WHR

κενόω.
1 Co. 9:15 κενώσει LTTrAWHR

κέντρον.
Acts 9: 5 omit (it is) hard to (said) unto him (ver. 6) GEds
1 Co. 15:55 trs victory and sting LTTrWHR

κεραία, κερέα WH.

κέρας.
Rev. 13: 1 trs ten horns and seven heads GEds

κερδαίνω.
Mat. 25:16*ἐκέρδησεν for ἐποίησεν (ποιέω) LTrWH
Mar. 8:36 ἐὰν κ.—κερδῆσαι to gain TAWH
1 Co. 9:21 κερδάνω Eds
Jas. 4:13 κερδήσωμεν S— κερδήσομεν A.V.B EEds
1 Pet. 3: 1 ..ρδηθήσονται LTTrAWHR

κέρμα.
Joh. 2:15 τὰ κέρματα TrAWH

κεφαλαιόω.
Mar. 12: 4 ἐκεφαλίωσαν TWH

κεφαλή.
Mat. 26: 7 τῆς κεφαλῆς LTTrWHR
27:29 τῆς κεφαλῆς TTrAWHR
Lu. 7:44 omit τῆς κ. read with her hairs Eds
Acts 18:18 trs ἐν Κεγχρεαῖς τὴν κ. LTTrAWHR
Rev. 10: 1 τὴν κεφαλὴν Eds
13: 1 trs ten horns and seven heads GEds
14:14 τὴν κεφαλὴν LT

* κημόω, to muzzle.
1 Co. 9: 9 κημώσεις for φιμώσεις (-μόω) TTrA

κηρίον.
Lu. 24:42 omit and of an honeycomb LT[Tr]WHR

κῆρυξ, κῆρυξ WH.

κηρύσσω.
Mar. 6:12 ἐκήρυξαν TTrAWHR
Ro. 10:15 κηρύξωσιν Eds

Κηφᾶς.
Gal. 1:18*Κηφᾶν for Πέτρον Eds
2:11*Κηφᾶς for Πέτρος Eds
14*Κηφᾷ for Πέτρῳ Eds

κιθάρα.
Rev. 5: 8 κιθάραν a harp Eds

Κιλικία.
Acts 15:41 τὴν Κιλικίαν L, [τὴν] K. WH

κινάμωμον, κιννά— LTTrAWHR.

κίνησις.
Joh. 5: 3 omit waiting for to end of verse 4 GTTrAWHR

Κίς, Κείς LTTrAWH.

κλάδος.
Mar. 13:28 trs ἤδη ὁ κλάδος αὐτῆς LTrWH
Ro. 11:19 οἱ κ.—omit οἱ GEds

κλάζω, κλάω.
Acts 20: 7 τοῦ κ.—omit τοῦ GEds
Ro. 11:20*ἐκλάσθησαν for ἐξεκλάσθησαν (ἐκκλάω) LTr
1 Co. 11:24 omit broken LTTrAWHR

κλαίω.
Joh. 20:11 trs ἔξω κλαίουσα TTrAWHR
Rev. 18: 9 κλαύσουσιν TTrAWHR

κλάσμα.
Mar. 6:43 κλάσματα AWHR
8:19 trs κλασμ. πλήρεις LTTrAWWH

Κλαύδη.
Acts 27:16 Καῦδα LTrWHR, Κλαῦδα T, Κ[λ]αῦδα A

κλείς.
Mat. 16:19 κλεῖδας LTTrAWH
Rev. 1:18 κλεῖν GEds
20: 1 κλεῖν GEds

κλείω.
Rev. 3: 7 κ.¹—κλείσει shall shut Eds
7 κ.²—κλείων LTTrWHR

κλέπτης.
1 Th. 5: 2 κλέπτας thieves LWH

κληρονομέω.
Gal. 4:30 κληρονομήσει LTTrWH

κληρονομία.
Acts 20:32 τὴν κληρονομίαν TTrAWHR

κλῆρος.
Mat. 27:35 omit that it might to end of verse GLTTrAWHR
Lu. 23:34 κλήρους TA: sortes A.V.Vul
Acts 1:25 part—the place, τόπος LTTrAWHR

κλητός.
Mat. 20:16 omit for many be called, but few chosen T[TrA]WHR
1 Co. 1: 1 [called] LA

* κλινάριον, a small bed.
Acts 5:15 κλιναρίων for κλινῶν (-νη) LTTrAWHR

κλίνη.
Mar. 7: 4 omit and of tables TWHR
30 κλίνην LTTrAWHR, see παιδίον
Acts 5:15 κλινάριον LTTrAWHR

κλοπή.
Mar. 7:21, 22 trs fornications, thefts, murders, adulteries TTrAWHR

κοιλία.
Lu. 15:16 omit his belly WHR
23:29 αἱ κοιλίαι TTrAWHR

κοιμάομαι.
Lu. 22:45 trs κοιμωμένους αὐτοὺς TTrAWH
1 Th. 4:13 κοιμωμένων LTTrAWHR

κοινός.
Mar. 7: 5*κοιναῖς for ἀνίπτοις (-τος) GEds
Rev. 21:27*κοινόν for κοινοῦν (νόω) GEds

κοινόω.
Mar. 7:15 trs κοινῶσαι αὐτὸν TWH
Rev. 21:27 that defileth—common, κοινός GEds

κοινωνία.
Eph. 3: 9 fellowship—dispensation, οἰκονομία GEds
Phil. 3:10 τὴν κ.—omit τὴν LTTr[A]WHR

κοινωνός.
Mat. 23:30 trs αὐτῶν κοινωνοὶ LTrAWH

κόκκινος, τὸ κόκκινον.
Rev. 17: 4 κόκκινον GEds

κόκκος.
Mar. 4:31 κόκκον GLTrAW

κολακεία, —κία TWH.

Κολασσαί S—Κολοσσαί A.V.B EGTAWWHR.

κολλάω.
Mat. 19: 5*κολληθήσεται for προσκολληθή-σεται (-λάω) LTTrAWH
Rev. 18: 5*ἐκολλήθησαν for ἠκολούθησαν (ἀκολουθέω) A.V.CGEds

κολλούριον, κολλύριον TTrA.

κολυμβήθρα.
Joh. 5: 4 omit waiting for (ver. 3) to end of verse 4 [G]TTrAWHR
9:11 omit the pool of GLTTrAWHR

κομίζω.
Eph. 6: 8 κομίσεται LTTrAWH
Col. 3:25 κομίσεται TWH
Heb.11:13*κομισάμενοι for λαβόντες (λαμβάνω) TTrWHR
2 Pet.2:13 ἀδικέω, read suffering wrong as the hire of unrighteousness WH

κοπιάω.
Mat. 6:28 κοπιῶσιν LTWH, κοπιοῦσιν TrA

Lu. 12:27 οὐ κοπιᾷ, οὐδὲ νήθει they toil not, they spin not—οὔτε νήθει οὔτε ὑφαίνει (-νω) they neither spin nor weave TA

Rev. 2: 3 κ. καὶ οὐ κέκμηκας hast laboured, and hast not fainted —καὶ οὐ κεκοπίακες (-κας R) and hast not grown weary LTTrAWHR, καὶ οὐκ ἐκοπίασας GW

κόπος.
Heb. 6:10 omit τοῦ κ. read work and love GEds

κοπρία.
Lu. 13: 8 κοπρίαν 8-κόπριος EGLTTrAWH

* κόπριος, full of dung, filthy.
Lu. 13: 8 κόπρια for κοπρίαν (-ρια) EGLTTrAWWH

κόπτω.
Mar. 11: 8 κόψαντες TTrAWHR

Κορνήλιος.
Acts 10: 7 Cornelius—him. αὐτῷ GEds
21 omit which were sent unto him from Cornelius GEds

κόσμος.
Mat. 13:35 omit of the world LTTrAWH
Joh. 8:23 trs τούτου τοῦ κόσμου¹ LTrAWH
17:12 omit in the world LTTrAWH
16 trs οὐκ εἰμί ἐκ τοῦ κόσμου² LTTrAWWH
21:25 omit the verse T
Ro. 4:13 τοῦ κ.—omit τοῦ GEds
1 Co. 7:31 τῷ κ.—τὸν κόσμον LTTrAWH
Gal. 6:14 τῷ κ.—omit τῷ LTTrAWH
Jas. 2: 5 τῷ κόσμῳ as to the world Eds
1 Pet. 5: 9 τῷ κόσμῳ TTrWH
2 Pet.1: 4 τῷ κόσμῳ LTTrWH

κοῦμι, κούμ TWH, κοῦμ TrA.

κόφινος.
Mar. 6:43 κοφίνων TAWHR

κράββατος, κράβαττος LTTrAWWH.
Mar. 2: 9 trs τὸν κράβατ. σου LTTrAWH
Joh. 5:12 omit thy bed T[Tr]AWHR
Acts 9:33 κραβάττου Eds

κράζω.
Mat. 15:22*ἔκραζεν LTrWH. ἔκραξεν T for ἐκραύγασεν (κραυγάζω)
20:31 ἔκραξαν LTTrAWH
21:15 τοὺς κράζοντας LTTrAWHR
Mar. 1:26 φωνῶ TTrAWH
3:11 ἔκραζον LTTrAWH
9:26 κράξας GEds
15:39 om. cried out, and T[Tr]AWHR
Lu. 4:41 κραυγάζω LT
19:40 κράξουσιν TTrAWH
Joh. 7:37 ἔκραζεν T
12:13 κραυγάζω LTTrWH
19:12 κραυγάζω LTTrWH
Acts 19:34 κράζοντες T
21:36 ἔκραζοντες LTTrAWH
23: 6 ἔκραζεν TTrAWHR
24:21 ἔκκραζω LTTrAWH
Rev. 6:10 ἔκραξαν GEds
7:10 κράζουσιν they cry GEds
18:18 ἔκραξαν LTrAWHR
19 ἔκραξαν LAWHR

κραιπάλη, κρε— WH.

κραυγάζω.
Mat. 15:22 κράζω LTTrWH
Lu. 4:41*κραυγάζοντα for κράζοντα (-ζω) LT
Joh. 12:13*ἐκραύγαζον for ἔκραζον (κράζω) LTTrAWHR
19:12*ἐκραύγαζον LT, -σαν TrWH for ἔκραζον (κράζω)

κραυγή.
Lu. 1:42*κραυγῇ for φωνῇ TTrAWHR
Rev. 14:18 cry—voice, φωνῇ LTTrWHR

κρείσσων, κρείττων.
1 Co. 12:31 best — greater, μείζων LTTrAWHR
Heb.12:24 κρεῖττον a better thing GEds

κρέμαμαι, κρεμάννυμι, κρεμάω.
Mat. 22:40†trs κρέμαται καὶ οἱ προφῆται Eds

κριθή.
Rev. 6: 6 κριθῶν Eds

κρίμα, κρῖμα
Mat. 23:14(13) omit the verse LTTrAWHR, (it is ver. 13 in 8, and 14 in A.V.BE)

κρίνω.
Lu. 22:30 trs τὰς δώδεκα φυλὰς κ. WH
Joh. 7:24 κ.²—κρίνετε : TrAWH
Acts 20:16 κεκρίκει GEds
24: 6 κρῖναι A: omit and would have judged to to come unto thee (ver. 8) LTTr[A]WH
25: 9 κριθῆναι LTTrAWH
1 Co. 5:13 κρινεῖ will judge GLT
Heb.10:30 trs κρινεῖ κύριος Eds
Jas. 4:12 ὃς κ.—ὁ κρίνων LTTrAWH
5: 9*κριθῆτε for κατακριθῆτε (-κρίνω) GEds
1 Pet. 4: 5 ἔχοντι κ.—κρίνοντι WH
Rev. 18: 8 κρίνας judged GEds

κρίσις.
Mar. 3:29 ἁμάρτημα, read guilty of eternal sin LTTrAWHR
6:11 omit verily to end of verse G[L]TTrAWHR
Jas. 5:12 κρίσιν A.V.B EGEds, see ὑπόκρισις

κριτής.
Mat. 12:27 trs κριταὶ ἔσονται ὑμῶν LTTrAWH
Lu. 11:19 trs αὐτοὶ ὑμῶν κ. ἔσονται LAWH, α. κ. ἔσ. ὑ. T, α. κ. ὑ. ἔσ. Tr
12:14*κριτὴν for δικαστήν (-τής) LTTrAWH
Jas. 4:12*lawgiver—add καὶ κριτής and judge GLTTrAWH
5: 9 ὁ κριτής A.V.CGEds

* κρύπτη. a vault.
Lu. 11:33 κρυπτήν for κρυπτόν(-ος)EGEds

κρυπτός
Mat. 6:18 κρυφαῖος bis LTTrAWH
Lu. 11:33 κρυπτὸν 8—κρυπτήν(-τη)EGEds
Joh. 7: 4 trs τι ἐν κρυπτῷ LTTrAWH

κρύπτω.
Mat.11:25*ἔκρυψας for ἀπέκρυψας (ἀποκρύπτω) LTTrAWH
25:18*ἔκρυψεν for ἀπέκρυψεν (ἀποκρύπτω) LTTrAWH
Lu. 13:21*ἔκρυψεν for ἐνέκρυψεν (ἐγκρύπτω) TTrAWHR

*κρυφαῖος, secret, hidden.
Mat. 6:18 κρυφαίῳ bis for κρυπτῷ(-τός)

κρυφῇ, -φῆ LWH.

κτάομαι.
Lu. 21:19 κτήσεσθε ye shall possess LTrAWH

κτίζω.
Mat. 19: 4*κτίσας for ποιήσας (ποιέω)TrWH

κτίσις.
Col. 1:23 τῇ κ.—omit τῇ Eds

κυβεία, κυβία TWH.

* κυκλεύω, to encircle.
Rev. 20: 9 ἐκύκλευσαν for ἐκύκλωσαν (κυκλόω) LTAWWH

κυκλόθεν.
Rev. 5:11 κύκλῳ GLTTrAWWH

κυκλόω.
Rev. 20: 9 κυκλεύω LTAWWH

κύκλῳ.
Mar. 3:34 trs τοὺς περὶ αὐτὸν κύκλῳ LTTrWHR
Rev. 5:11*κύκλῳ f. κυκλόθεν GLTTrAWWH

κύλισμα.
2 Pet. 2:22 κυλισμος TTrAWH

* κυλισμός, a rolling.
2 Pet. 2:22 κυλισμόν for κύλισμα TTrAWH

κυλλός.
Mat. 15:30 trs κυλλούς,τυφλούς,κωφούς WH
31 om. the maimed to be whole WH
18: 8 trs maimed or halt LTWHR

κῦμα.
Acts 27:41 omit of the waves LT[TrA]WHR

Κύπρος.
Acts 13: 4 τὴν κ.—omit τὴν LTTrAWH

κύπτω.
Joh. 8: 8 κατακύπτω WH

Κυρηναῖος.
Lu. 23:26 Κυρηναῖον LTTrAWHR

κυρία—Κυρία (as a proper name) GLT.

κύριος.
Mat. 1:22 | 2:15 τοῦ κ.—omit τοῦ LTTrA
13:51 omit Lord LTTrAWHR (WWH
18:26 omit Lord LTTrAWH
20:30 omit O Lord T
30, 31 trs κ. ἐλέησον ἡμᾶς LTTrAWHL
21:30 trs WH, see ἀπέρχομαι
22:44 ὁ κ.—omit ὁ LTTrAWH
24:48 trs μου ὁ κύριος LTTrAWH
28: 6 omit ὁ κ. read he T[TrA]WH
Mar. 5:19 trs ὁ κύριός σοι TTrAWH
9:24 omit Lord GEds
11:10 omit in the name of the Lord GEds
12:36 ὁ κ.—omit ὁ LTrAWH
13:20 trs ἐκολόβωσεν κύριος TWH
Lu. 1:15 τοῦ κ.—omit τοῦ GT[Tr]WH
25 ὁ κ.—omit ὁ LTT[A]WH
2:38 the Lord—God, θεός LTTrAWH
4: 8 trs κύριον τὸν θεόν σου προσκυνήσεις LTTrWH
7:19*κύριον for Ἰησοῦν TTrAWHR
31 omit and the Lord said GEds
9:57 omit Lord LTTr[A]WH
59 omit Lord TWH
10:39*κύριον for Ἰησοῦ Eds
41*κύριος for Ἰησοῦς TWHR
12:37 trs ὁ κύριος ἐλθών R
13:25 omit κ.² [L]TTrAWHR
19:18 trs ἡ μνᾶ σου, κ. TTrAWHR
20:42 ὁ κ.—omit ὁ LTTrAWH
44 trs αὐτὸν κύριον TrAWH
22:31 omit and the Lord said T[Tr]AWHR
23:42 omit Lord [L]TTrAWHR
24:34 trs ὄντως ἠγέρθη ὁ κ. LTTrAWHR
Joh. 4: 1 the Lord—Jesus, Ἰησοῦ T
Acts 2:34 ὁ κ.—omit ὁ LTTrAWH
7:30 omit of the Lord LTTrAWHR
37 omit the Lord LTTrAWH
8:22*κύριον for θεοῦ (-ός) Eds
9: 5 omit κ. εἶπεν Eds
6 omit (it is) hard (ver. 5) to unto him (ver. 6) GEds
10 trs ἐν ὁράματι ὁ κύριος Eds
10:33*κύριον for θεοῦ² LTTrWHR
48†trs ἐν τῷ ὀνόματι (τοῦ κυρίου βαπτισθῆναι A) Ἰησοῦ χριστοῦ βαπ. LTTrWHR
11:16 τοῦ κυρίου GLTTrAWWH
12:11 ὁ κύριος WH
24*κύριου for θεοῦ WH
13:10 τοῦ κυρίου WH
11 τοῦ κ.—omit τοῦ GLTTrAWH
44*κύριου for θεοῦ LTTr
48 θεός, read word of God WH
15:11 τοῦ κυρίου LTrAWWH
40*κύριου for θεοῦ Eds
16:10 the Lord—God, θεός LTTrAWHR
32 the Lord—God, θεός WH
17:24 trs ὑπάρχων κύριος LTTrAWH
27 the Lord — God, θεός GLTTrAWH
18:25 the Lord²—Jesus Ἰησοῦ Eds
19:20 Dei A.V.Vul: trs τοῦ κ. ὁ λογος LTTrAWH
20:28*κύριου for θεοῦ GLTTr
32*κυρίῳ for θεῷ WH
21:14 trs τοῦ κ. τὸ θελημα LTTrAWWH
20 the Lord—God, θεός GEds
22:16 αὐτοῦ, read on his name GEds
26:15*δέ²—add κύριος read and the Lord said Eds

Ro. 6:11 *omit* our Lord GEds
  10: 9 κύριος Ἰησοῦς WH
  12:11 τῷ καιρῷ (-ρός) in season s—
    τῷ κυρίῳ the Lord A.V.B EEds
  14: 4*κύριος *for* θεός LTTrAWHR
    6 *omit* and he that regardeth
    not *to* regard (it) LTTr[A]WHR
  16:24 *omit the verse* LTTr[A]WH
1Co. 7:17 *trs* as the Lord hath distri-
    buted to every man, as God
    hath called GEds
  10: 9*κύριον *for* χριστόν LTTrAWHR
    26 *trs* κυρίου γάρ LTTrAWWH
    28 *omit* for the earth *to end of*
    verse GEds
  11:29 *omit* Lord's LTTrAWHR
    32 τοῦ κυρίου TTr[A]WWH
  12: 3 κύριος Ἰησοῦς EIs
  14:37 τοῦ κ.—*omit* τοῦ GEds
  15:47 *omit* the Lord LTTrAWHR
2 Co. 4:10 *omit* the Lord GEds
    14 [the Lord] TrAWH
  11:17 *trs* κατὰ κ. λαλῶ Eds
Gal. 1: 3 *trs* ἡμῶν καὶ κ. WH
    6:17 *omit* the Lord Eds
Eph. 3:14 *omit* of our Lord Jesus Christ
    Eds
    5:29 the Lord—Christ, χριστός
    Eds
    6: 1 *omit* in the Lord L[TrAWH]
    5 *trs* κατὰ σάρκα κ. LTTrWHR
    8 τοῦ κ.—*omit* τοῦ GEds
Phil. 2:30*κυρίου *for* χριστοῦ WH
Col. 1: 2 *omit* and the Lord Jesus
    Christ G[L]TTrAWWHR
    3:13*κυρίου *for* χριστός LTTrAWH
    16 the Lord—God, θεός GEds
    17 the Lord Jesus—Jesus Christ,
    χριστοῦ LW
    20 τῷ κ.—ἐν κ. in the Lord GEds
    22*κυρίου *for* θεοῦ GEds
1Th. 1: 1 *omit* from God our *to end of*
    verse [L]TTrAWHR
    4: 6 ὁ κ.—*omit* ὁ LTTrAWHR
Th. 2: 2*κυρίου *for* χριστοῦ GEds
    3:12 διὰ τοῦ κυρίου ἡμῶν Ἰησοῦ χρισ-
    τοῦ—ἐν κυρίῳ Ἰησοῦ χριστῷ
    in the Lord Jesus Christ
    LTTrAWHR
1Ti. 1: 1 *omit* Lord GEds
    5:21 *omit* the Lord Eds
2Ti. 2:14 the Lord—God, θεός WH
    19*κυρίου *for* χριστοῦ Eds
    4: 1 *omit* the Lord GEds
Tit. 1: 4 *omit* the Lord LTTrAWHR
Philem.20 the Lord²—Christ, χριστός
    GEds
Heb.10:30 *omit* saith the Lord TTrWHR
Jas. 1:12 *omit* the Lord Eds
    3: 9*κύριον *for* θεόν LTTrAWHR
    4:10 τοῦ κ.—*omit* τοῦ LTTrAWH
    5:14 τοῦ κ.—*omit* τοῦ L[Tr]A, [τοῦ
    κ.] WH
2Pet. 2:11 *omit* before the Lord L[TrWH]
    3: 9 ὁ κ.—*omit* ὁ LTTrAWWH
2Joh. 3 *omit* the Lord Eds
Jude 5 Ἰησοῦς LA: ὁ κ.—*om.* ὁ TTrAWH
    25*ἡμῶν—*add* διὰ Ἰησοῦ χριστοῦ
    τοῦ κυρίου ἡμῶν,*read* Saviour,
    through Jesus Christ our
    Lord GEds
Rev. 1: 8 ὁ κ.—κ. ὁ θεός GEds
    4:11 κυριε—ὁ κύριος καὶ ὁ θεός ἡμῶν
    our Lord and our God Eds
    11: 4*κύριον *for* θεοῦ GEds
    16: 5 *omit* Ο Lord GEds
    18: 8 [the Lord] AWH
    19: 1 *omit* the Lord GEds
    22: 6 ὁ κύριος LTTrAWHR

κωλύω.

Mar. 9:38 ἐκωλύομεν TTrAWHR
Lu. 9:49 ἐκωλύομεν WHR

κώμη.

Mar. 8:26 *omit* nor tell (it) to any in
    the town TWHR
Lu. 9:52 village—city, πόλις Τ

Κῶς.

Acts 21: 1 Κῶ GEds

κωφός.

Mat. 12:22 κ.¹—κωφόν LWH

λάθρα, -ρᾳ ᴛWH.

λακτίζω.

Acts 9: 5 *omit* (it is) hard *to* unto
    him (*ver.* 6) GEds

λαλέω.

Mar. 10:19 λ.²—λαλήσητε TTrAWH
    12:36 λαλησουσιν TTrAWH
    47 *omit the verse* [T]WH
Mar. 9: 6 say—answer, ἀποκρίνομαι
    TTrAWHR
    11:23*λαλεῖ *for* λέγει (-γω) LTTrAWHR
    12: 1*λαλεῖν *f.* λέγειν (-γω) LTTrAWHR
    14:31*ἐλάλει *for* ἔλεγεν (λέγω)
    LTTrAWHR
Lu. 2:15*ἐλάλουν *for* εἶπον TWH
Joh. 6:63 λελάληκα have spoken Eds
    7:46 *trs* ἐλάλησεν οὕτως LTTrAWHR
    46*οὗτος—*add* λαλεῖ, *read* this
    man speaketh T
    8:26*λαλῶ *for* λέγω LTTrAWHR
    12:50 *trs* ἐγὼ λαλῶ LTTrAWHR
    14:10 λ.¹—λέγω TTrAWHR
    18:20 λ.¹—λελάληκα have spoken Eds
Acts 7:44 ὁ λ.—*omit* ὁ A.V.Vul
    10: 6 *omit* he shall tell thee what
    thou oughtest to do GEds
    32 *omit* who, when he cometh,
    shall speak unto thee
    LTTr[A]WHR
    13:45*λαλουμένοις *for* λεγομενοις
    (-γω) LTTr.WHR
    17:19 ἡ ὑπὸ σοῦ λ.—*omit* ἡ L[TrWH]
    23: 7 εἶπον LTTrWHR, λαλουντος WH
    26:14 speaking — saying, λέγω
    LTTrAWHR
Ro. 15:18 *trs* τι λαλεῖν Eds
1Co. 13:11 *trs* ἐλάλουν ὡς νήπιος Eds
    14:18 λαλῶ LTTrAWHR
    15:34*λαλῶ *for* λέγω LTTrAWHR
Heb.11: 4 λαλεῖ A.V.Er. Eds
Rev. 1:12 ἐλάλει Eds
    10: 8 λαλοῦσαν Eds

λαλιά.

Mar. 14:70 *omit* and thy speech agreeth
    (thereto) LTTrAWHR

λουά, λαμμᾶ.

Mat. 27:46 λημά L, λεμά TTrAWH
Mar. 15:34 λεμά LT, λαμά TrAWWH

λαμβάνω.

(*Future* λήμψομαι, &c. LTTrAWH)

Mat. 15:36 καὶ λ.—ἔλαβεν LTTrWHR
    16: 8 have brought—have, ἔχω
    LWHR
    20: 7 *omit* and whatsoever is right
    (that) shall ye receive
    LTTrAWHR
    23:14(13) *omit the verse* LTTrAWHR,
    see κρίμα
    25:22 *omit* had received LTTrAWHR
Mar. 11:24 ἐλάβετε have received LTTrAWHR
    12: 3 οἱ δὲ λ.—καὶ λ. LTTrAR (R
    22 *omit* had her [L]TTrAWHR
    14:65*ἔλαβον *for* ἔβαλλον (βάλλω)
    LTTrAWHR
Lu. 6: 4 ἐ. καὶ—λαβών LTrAWHR
    34*λαβεῖν *for* ἀπολαβεῖν (-λαμ-
    βάνω) TTrAWHR
    18:30*λάβῃ *for* ἀπολάβῃ (-λαμβάνω)
    LWH
    20:30 *omit* took *to end of verse*
    TTrAWHR
Joh. 1:12 ἔλαβαν Tr
    13:26*σοῦ²—*add* λαμβάνει καί,*read*
    he taketh and giveth TTrAWHR
    16:15 λαμβάνει taketh GEds
Acts 1:20 λαβέτω Eds (WHR
    2:23 *omit* have taken, and LTTrA
    3: 3 *omit* λαβεῖν A.V.C
    16:24 εἰληφώς—λαβών Eds
1Co. 11:24 *omit* take, eat GEds
2Ti. 1: 5 λαβών LTTrAWHR
Heb.11:13 κομίζω TTrWHR
Rev. 11:17 εἰληφας WH
    18: 4 *trs* ἐκ τῶν πληγῶν αὐτῆς ἵνα
    μὴ λ. GEds
    22:17 λαβέτω Eds

λαμπρόν

Rev. 19: 8*trs* white, clean GLTTrAWHR

λάμπω.

2Co. 4: 6 λ.¹—λάμψει shall shine
    LTTrAWHR

Λαοδίκεια, -κια TWH.

Rev. 3:14*ἐν Λαοδικείᾳ ἐκκλησιας GEds

Λαοδικεύς.

Rev. 3:14 of the Laodiceans—in Laodi-
    cea. Λαοδίκεια GEds

λαός.

Mat. 9:35 *omit* among the people GEds
Mar. 11:32 ὄχλος WH
Lu. 1:10 *trs* ἦν τοῦ λαοῦ GLTTrAWWH
    20: 6†*trs* ὁ λαὸς ἅπας TTrAWH
Acts 3: 9 *trs* πᾶς ὁ λ. αὐτόν LTTrAWH
    11 *trs* πᾶς ὁ λ. πρὸς αὐτ. LTTrAWH
    5:12 *trs* πολλὰ ἐν τῷ λ. LTTrAWWH
Rev. 13: 7*kindreds—*add* καὶ λαὸν and
    people GEds
    18: 4 *trs* ὁ λ. μου ἐξ αὐτῆς TWHR
    21: 3 λαός GW

Λασαία, Λασέα TrAWH, Ἄλασσα L.

Λεββαῖος.

Mat. 10: 3 *omit* LTTrWHR, *see* ἐπικαλεω

λεγεών.

Mat. 26:53 λεγιώνων Τ, λεγιώνας WH
Mar. 5: 9 λεγιών LTTrAWH
    15 λεγιώνα LTTrAWH
Lu. 8:30 λεγιών TTrWH

λέγω.

Mat. 4: 9 saith—said, εἶπον LTTrAWHR
    8:22*λέγει *for* εἶπον (-πον) Eds
    9:11*ἔλεγον *for* εἶπον LTTrWHR
    24 λέγειν LTTrAWHR
    12:48*λέγοντι *for* εἰπόντι (-πον)
    LTTrAWHR
    13:2*λέγουσιν *for* εἶπον LTTrAWHR
    51 *omit* Jesus saith unto them
    LTTrAWHR
    15: 4 commanded, saying—said,
    εἶπον LTrWHR
    12*λέγουσιν *for* εἶπον LTTrAWH
    16: 2 when it is evening *to end of*
    verse 3 [TA] [[WH]]
    22 Πέτρος λέγει αὐτῷ ἐπιτιμῶν Pe-
    ter saith to him, rebuking A
    17:20*λέγει *for* εἶπεν (-πον) LTTrAWHR
    26 λέγει αὐτῷ ὁ Πέτρος—εἰπόντος
    δέ and when he said LTTrAWHR
    19:17 ἐρωτάω GEds, *see* αγαθός
    18 *see* φημί
    22:16 λέγοντας LTTrWHR
    23 οἱ λ.—*omit* οἱ LTTrAWHR
    35 *omit* and saying LTTrWHR
    27:33 *trs* κρανίου τόπος λ. LTTrAWHR
    49 εἶπον LTrWH
Mar. 1:15 *omit* and saying T[WH]
    25 *omit* saying T[WH]
    2: 8*λέγει *for* εἶπεν (-πον) TTrAWHR
    12 *omit* saying [L]A[WH]
    25 λέγει saith LTTrWHR
    3:11 λέγοντες Τ
    32 καὶ λέγουσιν *for* εἶπον δέ Eds
    33 ἀποκριθεὶς αὐτοῖς λέγει TTrAWHR
    5: 7*λέγει *for* εἶπεν (-πον) Eds
    9 answered, saying saith to
    him, λέγει αὐτῷ GEds
    6:11 *omit* verily *to end of verse*
    G[L]TTrAWHR
    14 ἔλεγον LWH
    16*ἔλεγεν *for* εἶπεν (-πον) TTrAWHR
    31*λέγει *f.* εἶπεν (-πον) TTrAWWHR
    35 ἔλεγον TTrAWHR
    7:27*λέγει *f.* εἶπεν (-πον) LTTrAWHR
    36*λέγωσιν *for* εἴπωσιν (-πον)
    TTrAWHR
    8:16 *omit* saying LTTrAWH
    20*καὶ λέγουσιν αὐτῷ (*om.* αὐτῷ Τ)
    for οἱ δὲ εἶπον TAWHR
    28*answered (spake TAWHR)—
    add αὐτῷ λέγοντες to him say-
    ing LTTrAWHR: *add* ὅτι TAWH
    29 saith unto¹—asked, ἐπερωτάω
    LTTrAWHR
    33 λέγων—καὶ λέγει and saith
    TTrAWHR
    9: 7 *omit* saying GTTrAWWHR
    38 *omit* saying TWHR
    10:51 εἶπον TTrAWHR
    11: 9 *omit* saying [L]TTrAWHR
    17 λέγων—καὶ ἔλεγεν and said
    TTrAWHR
    23 λ.²—λαλέω LTTrAWHR
    28 ἔλεγον said TTrAWHR
    12: 1 λαλέω LTTrAWHR
    36*λέγει *for* εἶπεν¹ W *for* ε.² GTr
    43 saith—said, εἶπον LTTrAWHR
    13: 5 *trs* began to say to them
    LTTrAWHR
    14: 4 *omit* and said T[Tr]AWHR

Mar. 14:31 λ.¹—λαλέω LTTrAWHR
15: 2*αὐτῷ λεγει *for* εἶπεν αὐτῷ TTrAWHR
  4 *omit saying* τ[ωι]
  12*ἔλεγεν *for* εἶπεν (-πον) TTrAWH
  12 *omit whom ye call* LTr
  28 *omit the verse* τ[Tr]AWHR
  34 *omit saying* TTrAWH
Lu. 3: 4 *omit saying* LTTrAWHR
  11 ἔλεγεν said LTTrAWHR
  22 *omit which said* LTTrAWHR
4: 4 *omit saying* LTTrAWHR
  34 *omit saying* τ[Tr]AWHR
5:13*λέγων *for* εἰπών (-πον) LTrWHR
7:32 λέγοντες TTrA, ἄ λέγει WHR
8: 9 *omit saying* LTT[A]WHR
  20 *omit which said* LTTr[A]WHR
  30 *omit saying* LWHR
  45 *omit and sayest thou,* Who touched me? τ[TrA]WHR
  50 *omit saying* LTT[A]WHR
9:21*λέγων *for* εἰπεῖν (-πον) GLTTrAWHR
11:53 *omit* λ. TTrAWHR, *see* ἐξέρχομαι
12:22 *trs* λεγω ὑμῖν TrAWHR
13:27 λέγων WH
18:16*λέγων *for* εἶπεν(-πον)TTrAWHR
  41 *omit saying* τ[Tr]AWHR
19:30*λέγων *for* εἰπών (-πον) LTrWH
20: 2 *omit saying* TrA: *trs* λέγοντες πρὸς αὐτὸν LTWHR
  27*λέγοντες *for* ἀντιλέγοντες (-γω) TrWHR
23:34 Then said Jesus *to* what they do [L][[WH]]
  39 *omit saying* τ[Tr]AWH
  40 φημί TTrAWH
  43 *trs* σοι λεγω TTrAWH
24:36 *omit and saith unto them,* Peace (be) unto you τ[[WH]]
Joh. 1:49(50) *om.* and saith [L]TTrAWHR
4:51 *omit saying* τ
5: 2*τὸ λεγόμενον *for* ἡ ἐπιλεγομένη (-γω) τ
  19*ἔλεγεν *for* εἶπεν (-πον) TWH
8:23*ἔλεγεν *for* εἶπεν (-πον) LTTrAWHR
  26 λαλέω LTTrAWHR
9: 9*δέ, ὅτι—ἔλεγον, Οὐχί, ἀλλά (οὐχί ἀ. L), *read* others said, No, but LTTrAWH
  11 ὁ λεγόμενος TTrWHR, [ὁ] λ. A
10:33 *omit saying* Eds
11:31 saying—thinking, δοκέω TTr
  56 ἔλεγαν τ   (WHR
12:34 *trs* λέγεις σύ TTrAWH
13:24*πυθέσθαι τίς ἂν εἴη that he should ask who-it should be —καὶ λέγει αὐτῷ, Εἰπὲ τίς ἐστιν and saith to him, Say who it is LTTrAWHR
14:10*λέγω *for* λαλῶ¹(-λέω) TTrAWH
15:15 *trs* λέγω ὑμᾶς LTTrAWH
16:12 *trs* ὑμῖν λεγειν TTrAWH
18: 4*καὶ λέγει *for* εἶπεν (-πον) LTTrAWHR
19: 6 *omit saying* τ
  24 *omit which saith* LTWH
21: 6*λέγει *for* ὁ δὲ εἶπεν (-πον) τ
  17*λέγει *for* εἶπεν² (-πον) τ
Acts 5:25 *omit saying* GEds
6: 9 τῶν λεγομένων τ
13:45 λαλέω LTTrWHR
15:24 *omit saying,* (Ye must) be circumcised, and keep the law LTTrAWHR
17: 7 *trs* ἕτερον λέγοντες LTTrWH
20:23 λέγων A
26:14*λέγουσαν *for* λαλοῦσαν (-λέω) LTTrAWHR
  14 *omit and saying* LTTrAWHR
28:26 λέγων TTrAWH
Ro. 11: 2 *omit saying* GEds
15:11*again—add λεγει he saith [L]A
1 Co. 7:12 *trs* λεγω ἐγώ Eds
15:34 λαλέω LTTrAWHR
Heb.10:30 *omit* saith the Lord TTrWHR
1 Joh. 11 *trs* λέγων γὰρ LTTrA
Rev. 2: 2*λέγοντας ἑαυτοὺς *for* φάσκοντας (-κω) GEds
  20 ἡ λέγουσα GEds
4: 1 λέγων GEds
  8 λέγοντες GEds
6: 7 λέγοντος GEds
9:14 λέγοντα Eds
16: 8 λέγουσαν Eds
  11 λέγουσιν they say LTTrAWHR
11:12 λεγούσης TrAWH
  15 λέγοντες GLTAWWHR
12:10 . *trs* ἐν τῷ οὐρανῷ λ. GEds
14: 7 λέγων GEds

Rev. 19: 1 λεγόντων Eds
  6 λέγοντας s—λέγοντες GA, λεγόντων ELTTrWWHR

λεῖμμα, λίμμα WH.

λείπω.

Tit. 3:13 λίπῃ τ

λεπρός.

Mat. 10: 8 *trs* raise the dead, cleanse the lepers GEds

Λευΐ, Λευεί TTrAWH.

Heb. 7: 9 Δευῒς L, Λευεῒς TTrAWH

Λευΐς, —εῖς —εῖς TTrAWH.

Lu. 5:29 ὁ Δ.—*omit* ὁ GLTTrAWWH

Λευΐτης, Λευείτης TTrAWH.

Λευϊτικός, Λευει— TAWH.

λευκός.

Acts 1:10 λευκαῖς LTTrAWH
Rev. 6:11 στολὴ λευκή a white robe GEds
20:11 *trs* μέγαν λευκόν GEds

λέων

Rev. 13: 2 λεόντων of lions τ

λῆψις, λῆμψις LTTrAWH.

λιβανωτός.

Rev. 8: 5 τὸ λ. s—τὸν λ. EGLTTrAWWH

λιθάζω.

Joh. 8: 5*λιθάζ ιν *for* λιθοβολεῖσθαι (-λεω) WWHR
10:32†*trs* ἐμὲ λιθάζετε TTrAWH

λιθοβολέω.

Mar. 12: 4 *omit* cast stones, and LTTrA
Joh. 8: 5 λιθάζω WWHR   (WHR

λίθος.

Mat. 21:44 *omit the verse* [L]T[WH]
Mar. 9:42 λίθος μυλικός—μύλος ὀνικός *lit.* a millstone turned by an ass LTTrAWH
13: 2 λ.²—λίθον TTrWH
Lu. 11:11 *omit* λ. WH, *see* ἄρτος
  17: 2*μυλος ὀνικός—λίθος μυλικός LTTrAWH
19:44†*trs* λίθον ἐπὶ λίθον (λίθῳ L) ἐν σοί LTTrAWHR
Joh. 8: 7 τὸν λ.—*om.* τὸν WHR, *see* αὐτῇ
1 Pet. 2: 7 λίθος LTrAWH
Rev.15: 6*λίθον *for* λίνον LTrWHR

λικμάω.

Mat. 21:44 *omit the verse* [L]T[WH]

λίμνη.

Rev. 20:14*add at end ἡ λίμνη τοῦ πυρός the lake of fire Eds

λιμός.

Lu. 21:11 *trs* pestilences and famines LTTrA

λίνον.

Rev. 15: 6 linen—stone, λίθος LTrWHR

Λίνος, Λίνος LTWWH.

λογίζομαι.

Mar. 11:31 διαλογίζομαι Eds
15:28 *omit the verse* τ[Tr]AWHR
Joh. 11:50*λογίζεσθε *for* διαλογίζεσθε (-ζομαι) Eds
1 Co. 13:11 *trs* ἐφρόνουν ὡς νήπιος ἐλογιζό— ὡς νήπιος LTTrAWH
2 Co. 3: 5†*trs* ἱκανοί ἐσμεν λογίζεσθαί (-σασθαι AW) τι ἀφ᾽ ἑαυτῶν LAW, ἀφ᾽ ἑα. ἱκ. ἐσ. λογισασθαί τι TTrWH

λόγος.

Mat. 8: 8 λόγῳ, *read* speak by a word GEds
15: 6*τὸν λογον *for* τὴν ἐντολήν (-λή) LTrWHR
19:22 *omit* that saying τ
25:19 *trs* λόγον μετ᾽ αὐτῶν LTTrAWH
Lu. 1:29†*trs* ἐπὶ τῷ λ. διετα. GTTrAWHR

Lu. 20:20 λόγον Tr
22:61 ῥῆμα WHR
Joh. 6:60 *trs* ὁ λόγος οὗτος LTTrAWH
7:40 τῶν λόγων τούτων these words (*omit* τούτων W) Eds
8:51 τὸν ἐμὸν λόγον LTTrAWH
19:13 τῶν λόγων ;τούτων these words Eds
21:23 *trs* οὗτος ὁ λόγος LTTrAWH
Acts 13:15 *trs* ἐν ὑμῖν λόγος LTTrWWH
  18: 5*λόγῳ *for* πνεύματι (-μα) GEds
19:38 *trs* ἔχουσιν πρός τινα A. GLTTr
20:24 λόγου TTrAWH   (AWWH
Ro. 9:28 *om.* in righteousness: because a short work LTTrAWH
13: 9 *trs* τῷ λόγῳ τούτῳ LTTrAWWH
2 Th. 2:17 *trs* work and word Eds
2 Pet. 3: 7 αὐτοῦ λ. s—τῷ αὐτῷ λ. ELTWHR, τῷ αὐτοῦ λ. GTrAW
1 Joh. 5: 7 *omit* in heaven *to* in earth (ver. 8) GEds
Jude 15*hard—add λόγων speeches τ
Rev. 1: 3 τὸν λόγον the word τ
17:17*οἱ λογοι *for* τὰ ῥήματα (-μα) GEds

λοιμός.

Mat. 24: 7 *om.* and pestilences LTTrAWHR
Lu. 21:11 *trs* pestilences and famines LTrAWH

λοιπόν, τὸ λοιπόν.

Mat. 26:45 τὸ λ.—*omit* τὸ [Tr]AWH
Mar. 14:41 τὸ λ.—*omit* τὸ LTrAW[WH]
Eph. 6:10 τοῦ λοιποῦ LTTrAWH
1 Th. 4: 1 τὸ λ.—*omit* τὸ GEds

λοιπός.

Eph. 4:17 *omit* other LTTrAWHR
Rev. 2:24 τοῖς (*omit* καί) λοιποῖς GEds

τοῦ λοιποῦ.

Eph. 6:10*see τὸ λοιπόν

λούω.

Heb.10:22(23) λελουσμένοι TWH   (WHR
Rev. 1: 5 washed—freed, λύω LTTr[A]

Λύδδα.

Acts 9:32, 35 Λύδδα LITrAWH
  38 Λύδδας TTrAWH

λυπέω.

Mat. 14: 9 λυπηθείς LTTrAWH
Mar. 14:19 οἱ δὲ ἤρξ. λ.—*omit* οἱ δὲ TAWH

λύπη.

Joh. 16:22 *trs* νῦν μὲν λύπην LTTrAWHR
Phil. 2:27 λύπην GEds

Λυσίας.

Acts 24: 7 *omit* LTTr[A]WHR, *see* κρίνω

λυχνία.

Rev. 1:20†*trs* αἱ (*omit* αἱ W) λυχνίαι αἱ ἑπτά GEds

λύω.

Mar. 11: 2 λύσατε αὐτὸν καί LTTrAWHR
Acts 24:26 *omit* that he might loose him Eds
2 Pet. 3:10 λυθήσεται LTTrWH
Rev. 1: 5*λύσαντι *for* λούσαντι (λούω) LTTrWHR, λ[ο]υ— A
5: 5 *omit* to loose GEds
20: 3 *trs* λυθῆναι αὐτὸν LAWHR

Λωΐς, Λωΐς WH.

* Μαγαδάν.

Mat. 15:39 *for* Μαγδαλά LTTrAWHR

Μαγδαλά.

Mat. 15:39 Μαγαδάν, Magadan LTTrAWHR

μαγεία, —γία TWH.

Μάγων.

Rev.20: 8 τὸν Μ.—*omit* τὸν LT[Tr]AWHR

μαθητεύω.

Mat. 27:57 ἐμαθητεύθη LTTrWH

μαθητής.

Mat. 8:25 *omit* disciples [L]TTrWHR
14:26 *omit* the disciples τ:†*trs* οἱ δὲ μ. ἰδόντες αὐτὸν LWH

Mat. 20:17 *omit* disciples TTr[WH]
26:20*twelve—*add* μαθητῶν disciples LT[WH]R
28: 9 *omit* and as they went to tell his disciples LTTrAWHR

Mar. 2:18*οἱ*—*add* μαθηταί, *read* the disciples of the Pharisees fast TTrAWH
23 *trs* οἱ μαθηταὶ αὐτοῦ ἤρξαντο LTTrAWH
3: 7 *trs* μετὰ τῶν μ. αὐτοῦ ἀνεχώρησεν GLTTrAWHR
8:14 *add* οἱ μαθηταί A.V.†B

Lu. 9: 1 *omit* his disciples GTTrAWWHR
10:22 at commencement καὶ στραφεὶς πρὸς τοὺς μαθητὰς εἶπεν and having turned to the disciples he said 8—*omit* A.V.B EGTr[A]WHR
t *trs* εἶναί μου μαθητῆς TTrAWH
20:45 unto his disciples—unto them, πρὸς αὐτοὺς A

Joh. 1:37 *trs* οἱ δύο μαθηταὶ αὐτοῦ TWIR
6:11 *omit* to the disciples, and the disciples GLTTrAWH
22 *om.* that whereinto his disciples were entered GLTTrAWH
66 *trs* τῶν μαθητῶν αὐτοῦ ἀπῆλθον LTTrAWH
9:28 *trs* μαθητής εἶ LTTrAWH
12:16 *trs* αὐτοῦ οἱ μαθηταὶ TWH
19:27 *trs* ὁ μαθητὴς αὐτὴν GTrAWWH

Acts 1:15 disciples—brethren, ἀδελφός Eds
14:20 *trs* τῶν μαθητῶν αὐτὸν LTTrAWH
20: 7 the disciples—we, ἡμῶν GEds
21: 4 τοὺς μ.—*omit* τοὺς A.V.C

Μαϊνάν, Μεννά [L]TTrAWH,
Μενάμ A.V.Br.

μακάριος.
Mat. 5: 4, 5 *trs* the verses LTTr

Μακεδονία.
Acts 16:10 τὴν Μ.—*omit* τὴν LTTrWH
12 τῆς Μ.—*omit* τῆς LTTrWHR
19:22 τὴν Μ.—*omit* τὴν T
20: 1 τὴν Μ.—*omit* τὴν LTTr[A]WH

μακροθυμέω.
Lu. 18: 7 μακροθυμεῖ LTTrAWHR

μακρός.
Mat. 23:14(13) *omit the verse* LTTrAWHR: *see* κρίμα

Μαλελεήλ, Με— T.

μᾶλλον.
Mar. 14:31 *omit* the more LTTrAWHR
Lu. 10:20 *omit* rather GEds
2 Co. 2: 7 *omit* rather [TrA]WH

μαμμωνᾶς.
Mat. 6:24 μαμωνᾷ GLTTrAWWH

Μανασσῆς.
Rev. 7: 6 Μανασσῆ Tr

μανθάνω.
1 Co. 14:35 μανθάνειν WH

μάννα.
Joh. 6:49 *trs* ἐν τῇ ἐρήμῳ τὸ μάννα LTTrAWHR
58 *omit* manna GTTrAWHR

μαργαρίτης.
Rev. 18:12 μαργαριτῶν TTrAWHR, —τας L
16 μαργαρίτῃ pearl LTTrAWHR
21:21 μ.¹—μαργαρίται LTAWWHR

Μάρθα.
Joh. 11:19 τὰς περὶ Μ.—τὴν Μ. LTrAWHR
24 ἡ Μάρθα LTTrAWH

Μαρία, Μαριάμ.
Mat. 1:20 Μαρίαν WH
27:61 Μ.¹—Μαριάμ TWH
28: 1 Μ.¹ Μαριάμ T
Mar. 6: 3 τῆς Μαρίας TTrAWH
15:40 Μ.¹—Μαριάμ WH
Lu. 2:19 Μαρία LTTrAWH
10:39 Μαριάμ TWH
42 Μαριάμ WH

Joh. 11: 1 τῆς Μαρίας T
2 Μαριάμ TrWH
19, 28, 31, 45 Μαριάμ LTTrAWH
20 Μαριάμ WH
32 Μαριάμ TTrAWH
12: 3 Μαριάμ TrWH
19:25 *bis* ¦ 20:1, 11 Μαριάμ T
20:16, 18 Μαριάμ TTrAWH
Acts 1:14 Μαριάμ TTrWH
12:12 τῆς Μαρίας LTTrAWWH
Ro. 16: 6 Μαρίαν LTrAWH

μάρτυρ, μάρτυς.
Lu. 11:48*μάρτυρές ἐστε *for* μαρτυρεῖτε (-ρέω) TTrAWH

μαρτυρέω.
Lu. 11:48 bear witness—are witnesses, μάρτυρ TTrAWH
Acts 26:22 μαρτύρομαι Eds
1 Th. 2:11(12) μαρτυρόμενος TTrAWWHR
Heb. 7:17 μαρτυρεῖται it is testified (of him) Eds
1 Joh. 5: 8 *omit* in heaven (*ver.* 7) to in earth (*ver.* 8) GEds
Rev. 22:18*μαρτυρῶ ἐγώ *for* συμμαρτυροῦμαι (-τυρέω) γάρ GEds

μαρτυρία.
Lu. 22:71 *trs* ἔχομεν μαρτ. χρείαν TTrAWH
Joh. 21:24 *trs* αὐτοῦ ἡ μαρτ. ἐστίν TTrAWH
Acts 22:18 τὴν μ.—*omit* τὴν LTTr[A]WH

μαρτύριον.
1 Co. 2: 1 testimony—mystery, μυστήριον WH

μαρτύρομαι.
Acts 26:22*μαρτυρόμενος *for* μαρτυρούμενος (-τυρέω) Eds
1 Th. 2:11(12)*μαρτυρούμενος *for* μαρτυρούμενοι (-τυρέω) TTrAWWH

μάρτυς, *see* μάρτυρ.

μασσάωμαι.
Rev. 16:10 ἐμασῶντο LTTrAWWH

μαστιγόω.
Mar. 10:34 *trs* shall spit upon him, and shall scourge him LTTrAWHR

μαστός.
Rev. 1:13 μαζοῖς L, μασθοῖς T

Ματθαῖος, Ματθ— LTTrAWH.

Ματθάν, Ματθ— LTTrAWH.

Ματθάτ.
Lu. 3:24 Ματθάθ T
29 Ματθάθ T, Μαθθάτ TrAWH

Ματταθίας, Lu. 3:25 Μαθθ— Tr.

μάχαιρα.
Mat. 26:52 *trs* τὴν μάχαιράν σου LTTrAWH
52 μ.³—μαχαίρῃ LTTrAWH
Lu. 21:24 μαχαίρης TTrAWH
22:49 μαχαίρῃ TTrAWH
Acts 12: 2 μαχαίρῃ TTrAWH
16:27 τὴν μάχαιραν LTTrAWH
Heb.11:34, 37 μαχαίρης LTTrAWH
Rev. 13:10 μαχαίρῃ *bis* LTTrAWH
14 μαχαίρης LTTrAWH

μέ.
Mat. 16:13 *omit* μέ, *read* that the Son of man is [L]TTrAWHR
19:14 μέ T
Mar. 10:36 *omit* με LTrWH, *see* ποιέω
Lu. 1:43 ἐμέ TWH
20:23 *omit* why tempt ye me TTrA
Joh. 6:35 ἐμέ TTrAWH (WHR
36 *omit* me [L]T[WH]
37 ἐμέ T
40 *omit* LTTrAWH, *see* πατήρ
44 μέ¹—ἐμέ TrA
45 ἐμέ TTrWWH
65 ἐμέ T
7:34*, 36*find—*add* μέ me LAWHR
37 *omit* unto me T
9: 4 me—us, ἡμᾶς T
10:14*add* μέ LTTrAWH, *see* γινώσκω
32 λιθάζετέ με—ἐμέ λ. TTrAWH
14: 7 ἐμέ T
14*ask—*add* μέ me [L]T[WH]R

Acts 9: 6 *omit* GEds, *see* κεν. ρορ
13:25 τίνα με—τί ἐμέ LTTrAWHR
18:21 *omit* LTTrAWHR, *see* δεῖ
22: 8, 13 ἐμέ LTTrWH
23:22 ἐμέ TTrWH
24:13 *omit* μέ A.V.B EGEds
19 ἐμέ LTTrAWH
26:16*εἶδές με WH, *read* wherein thou hast seen me
Ro. 8: 2 me—thee, σέ TWI
1 Co. 16:11 ἐμέ LTr
2 Co. 12:21 ἐλθόντος μου ταπ. με Eds
Heb. 3: 9 *omit* μέ bis Eds
Rev. 21: 9 *omit* unto me GEds
See also ἐμέ.

μεγαλαυχέω.
Jas. 3: 5 μεγάλα αὐχεῖ LTTrAWHR

μεγαλεῖα.
Lu. 1:49 μέγας LTTrWHR

μεγαλειότης.
Acts 19:27 τῆς μεγαλειότητος LTTrAWHR

μέγας.
Mat. 22:38 ἡ μεγάλη: *trs* the great and first Eds
Mar. 10:43 *trs* μέγας γενέσθαι TTrWH
Lu. 1:49*μεγάλα *for* μεγαλεῖα (-λεῖος) LTTrWHR
13:19 *omit* great [L]T[Tr]WHR
Acts 2:43*add μ. T, *see* φόβος
8: 8 πολὺς LTTrAWH
13 *omit* μεγάλας A.V.Er
11:28 μεγάλην LTTrAWH (WH
26:29*μεγάλῳ *for* πολλῷ(-λύς) LTTrA
Heb.10:35 *trs* μεγάλην μισθαποδοσίαν Eds
Jas. 3: 5*see μεγαλαυχέω
Rev. 11:12 φωνῆς μεγάλης TrAWHR
18 τοὺς μεγάλους LTrAWHR
12: 3 *trs* πυρρὸς μέγας LTTrAR
14:15 *trs* φωνῇ μεγάλῃ GLTTrAWWH
19 τὸν μέγαν GLTTrAWWH
16: 1 *trs* μεγάλης φωνῆς LTAWWH
17 *omit* great LA
18: 2 *omit* strong GEds, *see* ἰσχύς
19: 1 *trs* μ. ὄχλου πολλοῦ GLTTrAWHR
17 τὸ μέγα τοῦ, *read* great supper of God GEds
20:12 τοὺς μ.: *trs* the great and the small Eds
21:10 *omit* τὴν μ. *read* the holy city GEds

μέγιστος.
2 Pet. 1: 4 *trs* precious and exceeding great TWIR

μεθερμηνεύομαι.
Mar. 15:22 μεθερμηνευόμενος WH
Joh. 1:38(39)*μεθερμηνευόμενον *for* ἑρμηνευόμενον (-μηνεύω) LTrAWHR

μεθίστανται, -τημι.
1 Co. 13: 2 μεθιστάναι LTTr

μεθοδεία, -δία TWH.

μεθόρια.
Mar. 7:24 ὅρια LTTrWH

μείζων, μεῖζον.
Mat. 12: 6 μεῖζον Eds
Mar. 4:32 *trs* μείζων (μεῖζον TWHR) πάντων τῶν λαχ. LTTrAWHR
Joh. 5:36 μείζων LTrA
10:29 *trs* πάντων μεῖζον TTrAWH
1 Co. 12:31*μείζονα *for* κρείττονα (-των) LTTrAWH

Μελεᾶς, -άς TTrWH.

μελετάω.
Mar. 13:11 *omit* neither do ye premeditate [L]TT[A]WHR

μελίσσιος.
Lu. 24:42 *omit* and of an honeycomb LT[Tr]AWHR

Μελίτη, Μελιτήνη WH.

μέλλω.
Mat. 20:17*add μ. WH, *see* ἀναβαίνω
Lu. 9:31 ἤμελλεν TWH
10: 1 ἤμελλεν LTTrAWWH

Lu. 13: 9 *trs* καρπον εἰς τὸ μέλλον· εἰ δὲ
μήγε fruit hereafter; but if
not TTrAWHR
Joh. 6:71 ἔμελλεν LTTrAWH
7:35 *trs.* μέλλει οὗτος T
39 ἤμελλον T
'1:51 ἤμελλεν LTTrAW
Acts 12: 6 ἤμελλεν TTrAWH
16:27 ἤμελλεν LTTrAWH
23:20 they would—thou wouldest,
μέλλων Eds
30 *omit* μ. LTTrAWHR
27: 2 μελλοντι Eds
33 *trs* ἡμέρα ἤμελλεν (ἔμελλεν T)
LTTrAWi
Ro. 8:38 *trs* GEds, *see* δύναμις
Heb. 9:11 γίνομαι LWH
11: 8 ἔμελλεν LA
2 Pet. 1:12*μελλήσω for* οὐκ ἀμελήσω
(-λέω) Eds
Rev. 3: 2 are ready—were ready, ἔμελλον GEds
10: 4 ἤμελλον LTTrAWHi

μέλος.

Ro. 12: 4 *trs* πολλὰ μέλη Eds

Μελχί, -χεῖ TTrAWH.

Μελχισεδέκ.

Heb. 7:10 ὁ Μ.—*omit* ὁ LTTrAWHR
21 *omit* after the order of Melchisedec TTrAWHR

μέμφομαι.

Mar. 7: 2 *omit* they found fault GEds

μέν.

Mar. 1: 8 *omit* indeed [L]TTrAWHR
9:12 *omit* verily T[Tr]
10:39 *omit* indeed TTrAWHR
Lu. 10: 6 *omit* μ. Eds
11:28*μ. οὖν for* μενοῦνγε A
Acts 3:13*ye—add* μ. indeed GEds
5:23 *omit* truly Eds
14:12 *omit* μ. LTTrAWHR
19: 4 *omit* verily GLTTrAWH
22: 3 *omit* verily Eds
23: 8 *omit* μ. L[Tr]WH
Ro. 2: 8 *omit* μ. LTTrWHR
6:21*τὸ—add* μ. read for indeed LA
7:25 *omit* μ. T
16:19 *omit* μ. LTTrA[WH]
1 Co. 2:15 *omit* μ. T[TrA]
12:20 *omit* μ. [LTr]WH
15·51 *omit* μ. [L]TTrAWHR
2 Co. 4:12 *omit* μ. GEds
12: 1*for* μοὶ LTTrWHR, *see* συμφερω
Gal. 4:23 [μὲν] LWH
Phi. 1·29 *omit* μ. GEds
3: 3*μ. οὖν for* μενοῦνγε GLTrAW
Tit. 1:15 *omit* μ. Eds
Heb. 6:16 *omit* verily LTTr[A]WHR
12:11*for* δέ᾽ TWHR
1 Pet. 2:14 *omit* μ. GEds
4:14 LTTrAWHR, *see* κατα

* μενοῦν, *see* μενοῦνγε.

μενοῦνγε.

Lu. 11:28 μενοῦν TTrWHR, μὲν οὖν A
Ro. 9:20 *trs* ὦ ἄνθρωπε μ. (μενοῦν γε
LTr) LTTrAWH
10:18 μενοῦν γε LTrW
Phi. 3: 8 μὲν οὖν GLTrAW, μὲν οὖν γε WH

μέντοι.

2 Ti. 2:19 μέν τοι Tr

μένω.

Mat. 11:23 ἔμεινεν LTTrAWH
Joh. 5:38 *trs* ἐν ὑμῖν μ. TTrAWHR
10:40 ἔμενεν LWH
11:54*ἔμεινεν for* διέτριβεν (διατρίβω)
TrAWHR
14:10 ὁ ἐν ἐμοὶ μ.—*omit* ὁ [LT]A]WHR
16 may abide—may be, ᾖ LTTrAW
15: 4 μ.²—μένητε LTTrAWi   (WHR
4 μ.³—μένητε LTTrAWi
6 μένῃ LTTrAWH
11 might remain—might be, ᾖ
LTTrAWH
Acts 16:15 μένετε LTTrWWH
20:15 *omit* and tarried at Trogyllium LTTrAWH
28.30 ἔμεινεν TTrAWH
1 Co. 3:14 μενεῖ shall abide GLTAWHR
1 Joh. 2:27 *trs* μένει ἐν ὑμῖν LTTrAWH
27 μ.²—μένετε, abide ye Eds
4:16*αὐτῷ—add* μένει, read God
abideth in him [L]TA[W]HR

μερίζω.

Mar. 3:26 ἐμερίσθη, καί he is divided,
and T, καὶ ἑ. WHR
1 Co. 7:17 μεμέρικεν TTrWHR
34 *see* γυνη

μεριμνάω.

Mat. 6:34 μεριμνήσητε S, -σετε B
Lu. 12:11 μεριμνήσητε TTrWHR

μέρος.

Lu. 11:36 *trs* μέρος τι ([τι] A) TTrAWH
Eph. 4: 9 *omit* μ. W
1 Pet. 4:16 ὀνόμα, read in this name Eds

μεσονύκτιον.

Mar. 13:35 μεσονύκτιον TTrAWH

μέσος.

Mat. 14:24 *omit* TrWH, *see* σταδιον
Mar. 14:60 τὸ μ.—*omit* τὸ GLTTrAWH
Lu. 17:11 μέσον LTTrAWHR
22:27 ἐν μέσῳ ὑμῶν εἰμι TTrAWH
55 ἐν μ.²—μέσος TTrAWH
Joh. 8:59 *omit* going through to end of
verse GLTTrAWH
Acts 4: 7 τῷ μ.—*omit* τῷ G[A]
Phil. 2:15 ἐν μ.—μέσον Eds
Rev. 2: 7 *omit* the midst of GEds

μεστός.

Joh. 19:29*add* μ. LTTrAWHR, *see* πλήθω

μετά.

Mar. 5:37*αὐτῷ—μετ᾽ αὐτοῦ with him
TTrAWHR
9:24 *omit* with tears LTTrAWHR
31* | 10:34* *add* μ. LTTrAWHR, *see*
ἡμέρα
15:28 *omit the verse* T[Tr]AWHR
Lu. 8:45 σὺν GLTTrAR: *omit* and they
that were with him WH
Joh. 5: 4 *omit* [G]TTrAWHR, *see* ὕδωρ
12:35 ἐν ὑμῖν among you GLTTrAWH
13:18 μετ᾽ ἐμοῦ—μου, read my
bread TrAWH
Acts 13:20 *see* ἔτος
20:24 *omit* with joy LTTrAWHR
24: 7 *omit* LTTr[A]WHR, *see* κρίνω
Ro. 16:24 *omit the verse* LTTr[A]WHR
Rev. 12: 7*for* κατά GEds
13: 7 *omit* L[WH], *see* διδωμι

μεταβαίνω.

Mat. 17:20 μ.¹—μετάβα LTTrAWH

μεταβάλλομαι.

Acts 28: 6 μεταβαλόμενοι TrAWHR

μεταλαμβάνω.

Acts 27:34*μεταλαβεῖν for* προσλαβεῖν
(-λαμβάνω) GEds

μετάληψις, -λημψις LTTrAWH.

μεταμέλομαι.

Mat. 21:29 *trs* WH, *see* ἀπέρχομαι

μεταμορφόομαι.

Ro. 12: 2 μεταμορφοῦσθαι to be transformed LA

μετανοέω.

Mar. 6:12 μετανοῶσιν LTTrAWH
Lu. 13: 5 μετανοήσητε LTTrAWH
Rev. 2:21 μ.²—μετανοήσῃ GEds, *see* θέλω
22 μετανοήσουσιν TTrAWH

μετάνοια.

Mat. 9:13 *omit* to repentance GEds
Mar. 2:17 *omit* to repentance GEds

μεταπέμπω.

Acts 10:29 μ.³—μεταπέμψασθε A
20: 1*μεταπεμψάμενος for* προσκα-
λεσάμενος (-λέομαι) TTrWHR

μεταστρέφω.

Jas. 4: 9 μετατρέπω WH

* μετατρέπω, to turn back, change.

Jas. 4: 9 μετατραπήτω *for* μεταστρα-
φήτω (-τρέφω) WH

μετέχω.

1 Co. 9:10 τοῦ μετέχειν GEds, *see* ἐλπίς

μετρέω.

Mat. 7: 2*μετρηθήσεται for* ἀντιμετρη-
θήσεται (-μετρέω) GEds

μέτρον.

Lu. 6·38 τῷ γὰρ αὐτῷ μ. ᾧ—ᾧ γὰρ μ.
LTTrWHR
Rev. 21:15*had—add* μέτρον a measure
GLTTrAWHR

μέτωπον.

Rev. 13:16 τὸ μέτωπον forehead GEds

μέχρι, μέχρις.

Mat. 13:30 ἕως LTTrAWH
Lu. 16:16*for* ἕως TTrWHR
Gal. 4:19*for* ἄχρις TTrWHR
Heb. 3: 6 *omit* firm unto the end A[WH]

μή.

Mat. 11:23*for* ἡ LTTrAWHR, *see* ὑψόω
Mar. 8:26*for* μηδέ¹ T
12:21*for* οὐδέ TTrAWHR, *see* καταλειπω
Lu. 7:33*for* μήτε¹ TAWHR
8:49 not—no longer, μηκέτι LTTrWH
10: 4*for* μηδέ TrAWHR
15*for* ἡ LTTrAWHR, *see* ὑψόω
11:11 *omit* WH, *see* ἄρτος
12 *omit* μή WH
22:34 *omit* μή² LTr[A]WHR
Joh. 7:31*for* μήτε LTTrAWH
8: 6 *add* μή A.V.tC, *see* προσποιέω
Acts 23: 9 *omit* GEds, *see* θεομαχεω
Ro. 8: 1 *omit* who walk to end of
verse GEds
14: 6 *omit* LTTr[A]WHR, *see* κύριος
1 Co. 9:20*add* μή GEds, *see* νόμος
2 Co. 5:12*μὴ ἐν for* οὐ² LTTrWHR
Gal. 3: 1 *omit* that ye should not obey
the truth GEds
Col. 2:18 *omit* not [L]TTrAWHR
1 Ti. 3: 3 *omit* not greedy of filthy lucre
GEds
Tit. 2: 3 μ.²—μηδέ TTrAWHR
Heb. 9:17 μὴ τότε for μήποτε WH
12:19 *omit* μή WH
Rev. 2:10*for* μηδὲν LTrAWHR

ἵνα μή.

Joh. 3:15 *omit* not perish, but
[L]TTrAWHR
2 Co. 12: 7 *omit* lest I should be exalted
above measure² [L]Tr[A]
Gal. 6:12 *trs* μὴ after χριστοῦ LTTrAWHR
Col. 2: 4 ἵ. μὴ τις—ἵνα μηδεὶς Eds

μηδέ.

Mar. 3:20*for* μήτε LTTrAWWHR
8:26 neither—not, μή T
26 *omit* nor tell (it) to any in the
town TWHR
13:11 *omit* neither do ye premeditate [L]TTr[A]WHR
Lu. 3:14 neither—no one, μηδεὶς T
7:33*for* μήτε² T
10: 4 μή TTrAWHR
12·47 neither—or, ᾖ TWHR
Acts 23: 8 μήτε Eds
Eph. 4:27*for* μήτε Eds
Phil. 2: 3*μ. κατά LTTrAWHR
2 Th. 2: 2*for* μήτε¹ Eds
Tit. 2: 3*for* μή² TTrAWHR

μηδείς, μηδεμία, μηδέν.

Mar. 1:44 *omit* μηδέν, read tell no man
L[Tr]
11:14 μηδεὶς S—οὐδεὶς E
Lu. 3:14*μηδένα for* μηδέ T
6:35 μηδένα T
Joh. 8:10 *omit* and saw none but the
woman WH
Acts 11:12 *omit* nothing doubting A
21:25 *om.* that they observe no such
thing, save only LTTrWHR
23:14 μηδὲν WH
27:33 μηθέν LTTrAWH
Col. 2: 4*μηδεὶς for* μή τις Eds
Rev. 2:10 none of—not, μή LTrAWWHR

* μηθείς, μηθέν, no one, none.

Acts 23:14 μηθενός *for* μηδενός A
27:33 μηθέν *for* μηδέν LTTrAWH

μηκέτι.

Lu. 8:49*for* μή LTTrWH

μήποτε, μή ποτε.
Heb. 9:17 μὴ τότε WH

* μήπου, μή που. lest anywhere.
Acts 27:29 for μήπως TTrAWHR

μήπως, μή πως.
Acts 27:29 μήπω L, μηπου TTrAWHR
Ro. 11:21 omit μ. read neither will he
spare thee LTTr[A]WHR

μήτε.
Mar. 3:20 μηδέ LTrAWWHR
Lu. 7:33 μ.¹—μή TAWHR : μ.²—μηδέ T
Acts 23: 8*for μηδέ Eds
Eph. 4:27 μηδέ Eds
2Th. 2: 2 μ.¹—μηδέ Eds

μήτις, μή τι.
Mar. 14:19 omit and another (said, Is)
it I? TTrWH
Joh. 7:31 μή LTTrAWHR

οὐ μή.
Mat. 24: 2 οὐ μή²—omit μή GEds
25: 9*for οὐ LTrAWWHR
Mar. 13:31 omit μή TrAWH
Lu. 8:17*for οὐ³ LTTrAWHR
22:34 omit μή¹ TTrAWHR
Joh. 16: 7*for οὐ WH
Rev. 9: 6*for οὐ GEds

μήτηρ.
Mat. 12:47 omit the verse [T]WH
15: 6(5) omit or his mother L[A]WHR
Mar. 3:31 trs his mother and his brethren GLTTrWWHR   (WHR
10:29 trs or mother or father LTTrA
30 μητέρα mother LTr
Lu. 2:43 omit μ. LTTrAWHR, see γονεύς
48 trs εἶπεν πρὸς αὐτὸν η μ. αὐτοῦ
LTTrAWHR
12:53 μ.²—μητέρα T, τὴν μητέρα
LTrAWHR
Eph. 5:31 τὴν μ.—omit τὴν LTrA[WH]

μητραλῴης, μητρο— LTTrAWH.

μία fem. to εἷς.
Mar. 16: 2 τῆς μ.—μιᾷ LTr, τῇ ([τῇ] WH)
μιᾷ TWHR
Lu. 17:34 [μιᾶς] LWH
35 μία S—ἢ μ. EGLT[Tr]AWHR

μιαίνω.
Tit. 1:15 μ.¹—μεμιαμμένοις LTTrWH,
-αμέ- A

μίγμα.
Joh. 19:39 ἕλιγμα WH

μίγνυμι.
Rev. 8: 7 μεμιγμένον T

μικρόν.
Joh. 16:18 τὸ μ.—omit τὸ TrAWH
2Co. 11:16 trs κἀγὼ μικρόν τι GEds

μικρός.
Mar. 4:31 μικρότερον ὂν LTTrAWHR
Lu. 17: 2 trs τῶν μ. τούτων ἕνα TTrAWHR
Rev. 11:18 τοὺς μικροὺς LTTrAWHR
20:12 τοὺς μ. trs the great and the
small Eds

μιμητής.
1Pet. 3:13 followers—zealous, ζηλωτής
Eds

μιμνήσκομαι.
Heb. 10:17 μνησθήσομαι LTTrAWHR

μισέω.
Mat. 5:44 τοῖς μισοῦσιν ὑμᾶς GW: omit
bless to hate you LTTrAWHR
Rev. 2:15 which thing I hate—in like
manner, ὁμοίως GEds

μισθός.
Acts 1:18 τοῦ μ.—omit τοῦ GEds

μισθωτός.
Joh. 10:13 omit the hireling fleeth
LTTrAWHR

μνάομαι, see μιμνήσκομαι.

μνῆμα.
Mar. 5: 3*μνήμασιν for μνημείοις(-μείον)
GEds
5 trs tombs, and in the mountains GEds
15:46*μνήματι for μνημείῳ (-μεῖον)
TWH
16: 2*μνῆμα for μνημεῖον T
Rev. 11: 9 μνῆμα a grave GEds

μνημεῖον.
Mar. 5: 3 μνῆμα GEds
6:29 τῷ μ.—omit τῷ A.V.BEGEds
15:46 μ.¹—μνῆμα TWH
16: 2 μνῆμα T   (WHR
Lu. 11:48 omit their sepulchres [L]TTrA
24:12 omit the verse [L]T[Tr][[WH]]
Joh. 20:11 τὸ μ.¹—τῷ μνημείῳ GEds

μνημονεύω.
Heb. 11:15 μνημονεύουσιν TTr

μνηστεύομαι.
Lu. 1:27 ἐμνηστευμένῃ LTTrWH
2: 5 ἐμνηστευμένη LTTrAWH

* μογγιλάλος, speaking with hollow
voice.
Mar. 7:32 μογγιλάλον for μογιλάλον(-λος)
Tr

μογιλάλος.
Mar. 7:32 μογγιλάλος Tr

μόγις.
Lu. 9:39 μόλις WH

μοί.
Mat. 15: 8 omit GLTTrAWHR, see ἐγγίζω
18:28 omit me Eds
Mar. 8: 2 omit with me L[Tr]A
Lu. 9:38 trs μοι ἐστιν LTTrAWH
22:68 omit me, nor let (me) go
T[TrA]WHR
Joh. 13:36 omit me² LTTrAWHR
14:11 omit me³ T[Tr]WH
Acts 1: 8 μοῦ, read my witnesses Eds
9:15 trs ἐστίν μοι Eds
11: 9 omit me LTTrAWHR
20:22 ἐμοί TWH
23*witnesseth—add μ. to me
GEds
Ro. 9:19 trs μοι οὖν Eds
1Co. 7: 1 omit unto me T[Tr]AWHR
9:18 μοι TTrAWH
10:23 omit for me bis GEds
2Co. 6:16 μοῦ LTTrWH
12: 1 μέν LTTrWHR, see συμφέρω
2Ti. 1:18 ministered—add mihi A.V.Vul
Rev. 1:17 | 10: 4 omit unto me GEds
14:13 | 17: 1 omit unto me GEds
21: 5 omit unto me-LT[TrA]WWHR
See also ἐμοί.

μοιχάομαι.
Mat. 5:32 μ.¹—μοιχεύω LTTrAWHR
19: 9 omit T[Tr]WH, see ἀπολύω

μοιχεία.
Mar. 7:21, 22 trs fornications, thefts,
murders, adulteries TTrAWHR
Gal. 5:19 omit adultery GEds

μοιχεύω.
Mat. 5:32*μοιχευθῆναι for μοιχᾶσθαι
(-χάομαι) LTTrAWHR
Mar. 10:19 trs Do not kill, Do not com-
mit adultery LWHR
Jas. 2:11 μ.²—μοιχεύεις LTTrAWHR

μοιχός.
Jes. 4: 4 omit ye adulterers and Eds

μόλις.
Lu. 9:39*for μόγις WH

μόνας, see καταμόνας.

μονογενής.
Lu. 7:12 trs μονογενὴς υἱὸς TTrAWH
Joh. 1:18 ὁ μ.—omit ὁ TrWH

μόνος.
Lu. 24:12 [laid by themselves] A : omit
the verse [L]T[Tr][[WH]]
Rev. 9: 4 omit only GEds

μόσχος.
Lu. 15:30†trs τὸν σιτευτὸν μόσχον
TTrAWHR

μοῦ
Mat. 4:10*add μ.—G[L]W, see ὀπίσω
16:23 μ. εἶ—εἶ ἐμοῦ LTTrAWHR
18:14*for ὑμῶν LTrWH
19:20 omit from my youth up LTr
29 ἐμοῦ ὀνόματος TWH   (AWHR
20:23 omit μ.³ LTTrAWHR
21:28 omit μ. TTrAWH
24:36 omit μ. read the Father GLTTr
26:39 omit my T[Tr]   (A)WHR
27:35 omit that it might to —ad of
verse GLTTrAWHR
Mar. 3:33 omit my² Tr[A]WH
35 omit my² LTTrAWHR
9:41 omit μ. GLTrAWH
10:40 omit μ.² GEds
14:14*καταλυμα—add μ. read my
guestchamber [L]TTrAWHR
Lu. 4: 7 ἐμοῦ Eds
8 omit get thee behind me,
Satan, G[L]TTrAWHR
7: 6 trs μοῦ before ὑπό W
44 μ.¹—μοί TrAWH, see πούς
8:45 omit T[TrA]WHR, see λέγω
12:18 omit μ.² T[A]WH
18:21 omit my T[Tr]AWH
24:44*λόγοι—add μ. read my words
[L]TTrAWHR
Joh. 1:27 omit is preferred before me
G[L]TTrAWHR
6:40*see πατήρ
65 omit μ. read the Father
LTTrAWHR
8:28, 38 omit μ. read the Father
LTTrAWHR
10:29 omit μ.¹ read the Father's T
29 omit μ.² read the Father
T[Tr]AWHR
32 omit μ. read the Father
[L]T[Tr]AWHR
14:12 omit μ. read the Father
LTTrAWHR
28 omit μ.¹ read the Father
[L]TTrAWHR
15:10 om. μ.³ rd. the Father's LAWH
16:10 omit μ. read the Father
TTr[A]WH
20:17 omit μ.² read the Father
[L]TTrAWHR
Acts 2:25*κύριον—add μ. read my
Lord T
20:24 omit μ.¹ LTTrAWHR
1Co. 1: 4 omit my WH
9: 2*μ. τῆς for τῆς ἐμῆς LTTrAWHR
14:18 omit my GEds
39*ἀδελφοί μ.—add μ. read my
brethren [L]TTr[]WHR
2Co. 11:28 μοί Eds
12: 5 omit mine LT[A]WHR
9 omit my² LTTrAWHR
9 omit my³ T[]WH
Gal. 4:14 my¹—your, ὑμῶν Eds
Eph. 6:10 omit my brethren LTTrAWHR
Col. 1:24 omit μ.¹ GEds
Philem. 10 omit my² LTTrAWHR
Heb. 8: 9 omit μ.¹—E
10:34 omit μ. GEds, see δεσμός
38*δίκαιος—add μ. read my just
one LTTrA[WHR
Jas. 2:18 my faith—omit my TTrAWHR
5:10 omit my Eds   (WHR
19*ἀδελφοί μ. my brethren LTTrA
2Pet. 1:17*trs ὁ υἱός μου ὁ ἀγαπητός μου
οὗτός ἐστιν AWH
1Joh. 3:13, 18 omit my Eds
Rev. 2: 7*θεοῦ—add μ., read my God
G[A]W
13*πιστός—add μ. read my faithful one LT[TrA]W[WH]R
3: 2*θεοῦ—add μ. rd. my God GEds
7:14*κύριε—add μ. read my lord
G[L]TTrAWHR
See also ἐμοῦ.

μυλικός.
Mar. 9:42 see λίθος
Lu. 17: 2*see λίθος

* μύλινος of a mill (?)
Rev. 18:21 μύλινον for μύλον(-λος) LAWHR

μύλος.
Mat. 24:41*μύλῳ for μύλων (-ος)
LTTrAWHR
Mar. 9:42*see λίθος
Lu. 17: 2 see λίθος
Rev. 18:21 μύλινος LAWHR

μύλων.

Mat. 24:41 μύλος LTTrAWHR

Μύρα, Μύρρα LTTrAWH.

μυριάς.

Rev. 5-11 see ἀριθμός
9:16 δύο μυριάδες—δισμυριάδες LTA.
δίς μ. WH

μύρον.

Mat. 26: 9 omit ointment GEds
Mar. 14: 5°τοῦτο—add τὸ μύρον, read this
ointment GEds

μυστήριον.

1 Co. 2: 1°μυστήριον for μαρτύριον WHR

μωρός.

Mat 23:19 om. (ye) fools and [L]TTrAWHR
25: 2 trs foolish and wise LTT.AWHR
3 αἱ γὰρ (δὲ L) μ. for αἵτινες μ.
LTAWH

Μωσῆς, Μωϋσῆς LTTrAW, –υ– WH

Mat. 17: 4 Μωϋσεῖ LTTrAWH
Mar. 9: 4, 5 Μωϋσῆ TrA
10: 4 trs ἐπέτρεψεν M. LTT AWH
Lu. 9:33 trs μίαν M. GLTTrAWWH
Joh. 5:46 Μωϋσεῖ LTTrAWH
7:22 M.¹—ὁ M. T
8: 5†trs [ἡμῖν] Μωϋσῆς WH
9:29 Μωϋσεῖ LTTrAWH
Acts 15: 1 τῷ Μωϋσέως LTTrAWH
Ro. 9:15†trs M. γὰρ LAW, Μωϋσεῖ γ.
TTrWH

Ναζαρέθ, –ρέτ.

Mat. 4:13 Ναζαρά TTrAWH
Lu. 4:16 Ναζαρά TWH · om. τὴν LTTrAWH

Ναζαρηνός.

Mar. 10:47†for Ναζωραῖος LTTrAWHR
Lu. 24:19°Ναζαρηνοῦ for Ναζωραίου
TTrAWHR

Ναζωραῖος.

Mar. 10:47 Ναζαρηνός LTTrAWHR
Lu. 24:19 Ναζαρηνός TTrAWHR
Acts 9: 5°Jesus—add ὁ Ναζωραῖος the
Nazarene [L]W

Ναθάν, Ναθάμ TWH.

ναί.

Phil. 4: 3°for καί GEds
Rev. 22:20 omit even so (ν.²) GEds

* Ναιμάν, see Νεεμάν.

ναός.

Mat. 27: 5 εἰς τὸν ναόν TTrWHR
Lu. 1:21 trs ἐν τῷ ν. αὐτόν WH
Acts 7:48 omit temples GEds
Rev. 21:22 ν.²—ὁ ναός LW, [ὁ] ν. A

νεανίας.

Acts 23:18 νεανίσκος LTTrA
22 νεανίσκος LTTrAWH

νεανίσκος.

Mar. 14-51 trs νεανίσκος τις LTrWHR
51 om. the young men LTTrAWHR
Acts 23:18°νεανίσκον for νεανίαν (–νίας)
LTTrA
22°νεανίσκον for νεανίαν (–νίας)
LTTrAWH

Νεάπολις.

Acts 16:11 Νέαν Πόλιν TTrWHR

Νεεμάν, Ναιμάν LTTrAWH.

νεκρός.

Mat. 10: 8 trs raise the dead, cleanse the
lepers GEds
Mar. 6:16 om. from the dead T[Tr]AWHR
16:14°ἐγηγερμένον—add ἐκ νεκρῶν, rd.
risen from the dead L[WH]
Acts 24:15 omit of the dead LTTrAWHR
Ro. 8:34°risen—add ἐκ νεκρῶν from the
dead [WH]R
1 Co. 15:12 trs ἐκ νεκρῶν ὅτι A
29 the dead³—them, αὐτῶν GEds
Eph. 1:20 τῶν νεκρῶν W

Phil. 3:11 τῶν ν.—τὴν ἐκ ν. Eds
Col. 2:12 τῶν ν.—omit τῶν GT[A]WWH
1 Th. 1:10 τῶν νεκρῶν GLTTrAR, [τῶν] ν. WH
Jas. 2:20 dead—idle. ἀργός LTTrAWH
Rev. 20:13†trs τοὺς ν. τοὺς ἐν αὐτῇ GEds
13†trs τοὺς ν. τοὺς ἐν αὐτοῖς GEds

* νεομηνία, see νουμηνία.

νέος, νεώτερος.

Mar. 2:22 omit new² LTTrAWHR
22 omit but new wine to bottles
T[Tr]A[WH], see βλητέος

νεοσσός, νοσσός TAWH.

νεότης.

Mat. 19:20 omit from my youth up
LTTrAWH

νεφέλη.

Lu. 12:54 τὴν ν.—omit τὴν LTT.[A]WHR
2 Pet. 2:17 clouds—and mists, καὶ ὁμίχλαι
(–λη) GEds
Rev. 14:16 τῆς νεφέλης LTTrAWH

Νεφθαλείμ, Rev. 7: 6 λίμ AWH.

νήθω.

Mat. 6:28 νήθουσιν LTTrAWH

νήπιος.

1 Th. 2: 7°νήπιοι for ἤπιοι (–ιος) LWH

Νηρί, Νηρεί TTrAWH.

νηστεία.

Mat. 17:21 omit the verse T[Tr]A]WHR
Mar. 9:29 omit and fasting T[A]WH
1 Co. 7: 5 omit fasting and GEds

νηστεύω.

Lu. 5:34 νηστεῦσαι TTrAWH
Acts 10:30 omit fasting LTTr[A]WHR

νῆστις.

Mar. 8: 3 νήστις T

νηφάλεος, –λιος 1 Tim. GEds.

νικάω.

Ro. 3: 4 νικήσεις TWH
Rev. 2:17 νικοῦντι LTTr
13: 7 omit L[WH], see δίδωμι

Νικόδημος.

Joh. 3: 4 ὁ Ν.—omit ὁ Tr[WH]

Νικολαΐτης.

Rev. 2:15 τῶν Ν.—omit τῶν L[Tr]AWWHR

νῖκος.

1 Co. 15:55 trs victory and sting LTTrWHR

Νινευΐ.

Lu. 11:32 of Nineve—Ninevites, Νινευΐτης LTTrWWH, Νινευΐ A

Νινευΐτης.

Mat. 12:41 Νινευεῖται TTrAWH
Lu. 11:30 trs τοῖς Ν. σημείον TTrAWH
32°Νινευεῖται LTrW, Νινευεῖται TWH
for Νινευΐ

νομίζω.

Acts 14:19 νομίζοντες LTTrAWHR
16:13 ἐνομίζομεν προσευχήν, read
where we supposed was a
place for prayer LTTrWHR

νομοθετέω.

Heb. 7:11 νενομοθέτηται Eds

νομοθέτης.

Jas. 4:12 ὁ ν.—omit ὁ WH

νόμος.

Mat. 15: 6°τὸν νόμον for τὴν ἐντολήν TA
Lu. 2:24 τῷ νόμῳ LTTrWH
Acts 13:39 τοῦ ν.—omit τῷ LTTrAWH
15:24 omit saying, (Ye must) be
circumcised, and keep the
law LTTrAWHR
24: 6 omit LTTr[A]WHR, see κρίνω
Ro. 2:13 τοῦ ν.¹—omit τοῦ Eds
13 τοῦ ν.²—omit τοῦ LTTrAWH
17 τῷ ν.—omit τῷ Eds

Ro. 7: 2 omit τοῦ νόμου E
9:32 omit of the law LTTr[A]WWHR
10: 5 τοῦ ν.—omit τοῦ TTrAWH
1 Co. 7:39 omit by the law GEds
9:20°νόμου²—add μὴ ὢν αὐτὸς ὑπὸ
νόμον not being myself under
law GEds
Gal. 3:21†trs ἐκ νόμου (ἐν νόμῳ WH) ἂν
ἦν (ἦν ἂr T) LTTrAWH
Heb. 8: 4 τὸν ν.—omit τὸν LTTrAWHR
9:19 τὸν νόμον LTrAWWHR
10: 8 τὸν ν.—omit τὸν LTTr[A]WHR

νόσημα.

Joh. 5: 4 omit waiting for (ver. 3) to
end of verse 4 [G]TTrAWHR

νόσος.

Mar. 3:15 omit to heal sicknesses, and
TTrAWHR

νουθετέω.

1 Co. 4:14 νουθετῶν warning TWHR

νουμηνία, νεομηνία LTrWH.

νοῦς.

1 Co. 14:15 τῷ ν.²—omit τῷ E
19 διὰ τοῦ ν. τοῦ Eds
Rev. 13:18 τὸν ν.—omit τὸν GEds

Νυμφᾶν, Νύμφαν LWH.

νυμφών.

Mat. 22:10°νυμφών for γάμος TWH

νῦν.

Lu. 6:25°full—add ν. now T[Tr]AWHR
22:18°drink—add ἀπὸ τοῦ ν. henceforth T[Tr]AWH
Joh. 6:42°for οὖν TTrAWHR
8:11°add τοῦ ν. for καὶ WH
16:32 omit now LTTrAWHR
Acts 2:33 omit now GLTTrAWH
13:31°who—add ν. now LTTrAW[WH]
32°we—add ν. now W (R
22: 1 νυνὶ GLTTrAWWH
24:13 νυνὶ LTTrAWH
26:17 omit now GEds
Ro. 11:31°they—add ν. now [L]TWHR
1 Co. 5:11°for νυνὶ LTrAWH
12:18°for νυνὶ LTrAWHR
14: 6°for νυνὶ Eds
Col. 1:26°for νυνὶ LTTrAWHR
Heb. 8: 6°for νυνὶ LWH
9:26 νῦν LWH
11:16°for νυνὶ GEds

νυνί.

Acts 22: 1°for νῦν GLTTrAWWH
24:13°for νῦν LTTrAWH
1 Co. 5:11 νῦν LTrAWH
12:18 νῦν LTrAWHR
14: 6 νῦν Eds
Col. 1:26 νῦν LTTrAWHR
Heb. 8: 6 νῦν LWH
9:26°for νῦν LTTrAWHR
11:16 νῦν GEds

νύξ.

Mat. 27:64 omit by night GLTTrAWHR
Mar. 14:27 omit this night [L]TTrAWWHR
30 trs ταύτῃ τῇ ν. LTTrAWHR
Lu. 5: 5 τῆς ν.—omit τῆς LTTrAWHR
Joh. 7:50 omit by night LTTrAWHR
Acts 5:19 τῆς ν.—omit τῆς LTTr[A]WHR
16: 9 τῆς ν.—omit τῆς LTTr[A]WWHR
17:10 τῆς ν.—omit τῆς LTTrAWHR
18: 9 trs ἐν ν. δι' ὁράματος LTTrAWHR
23:31 τῆς ν.—omit τῆς Eds
27:23 trs ταύτῃ τῇ ν. GLTTrAWWH
2 Th. 3: 8 νυκτός LTTrWHR
2 Pet. 3:10 omit in the night GEds

Νῶε.

Lu. 17:26 τοῦ Ν.—omit τοῦ GLTTrAWWH

ξένος.

3 Joh. 5 εἰς τοὺς ξ.—τοῦτο ξ. Eds

ξέστης.

Mar. 7: 8 omit (as) the washing to end
of verse T[TrA]WHR

ξηραίνω.

Mar. 3: 3 ξηρὸς LTTrAWHR

ξηρός.

Mar. 3: 3³ *trs* τὴν χεῖρα ἔχοντι ξηράν (ξ.
for ἐξηραμμένην, ξηραίνω)
LTTrAWHR, τὴν ξηράν χ. ἐχ. T

ξύλον.

Rev. 22:19° τοῦ ξύλου *for* βίβλου² (-λος)
GEds

ξυράω.

Acts 21:24 ξυρήσονται TTrAWHR

ὁ, ἡ, τό.

(*In addition to those placed with nouns,
adjectives, participles, infinitives,
and proper names.*)

Mat. 6:34 *omit* the things of Eds
11:23 ἦ – ἦ (ὃς) W, μὴ LTTrAWHR
13:23 ὃ³ ⁶ – ὃ (ὃς) LTWH
21:25° βάπτισμα – *add* τό LTTrAWH
22: 5 ὁ – ὃς *bis* LTTrAWH
24:17° τά *for* τι (τις) GEds
38 *omit* ταῖς πρό, *read* days of
the flood A
26:28 *omit* τὸ² – LTTrAWH
71 τοῖς – αὐτοῖς AW
Mar. 3: 8 *omit* they¹ [L]TTr[A]WHR
5:27° τὰ περὶ the things concerning
TWHR, [τὰ] π. A
6:24 ἡ δε¹ – καὶ TTrAWHR
50° ὁ δε *for* καὶ TWHR
8:20° οἱ δε – καὶ TWHR
11:30° βάπτισμα – *add* τό Eds
12: 5 τούς – οὓς (ὃς) *bis* LTTrAWH
25 *omit* which are GLT[Tr]WWHR
13:32 *omit* which are TTrAWHR
14:24 *omit* τὸ² [L]TAWHR
15:23 ὁ – ὃς TTrWH
43 *omit* ὁ WH
Lu. 1:70 *omit* τῶν² TTrAWHR
2:39 *omit* τά T
5: 7 *omit* which were [L]TTrAWHR
6:15 *omit* τὸν τοῦ TTrAWHR
14:28 *omit* τά GTTrAWHR
32 *omit* τά WH
15:12° ὁ δε *for* καὶ² LTrAWHR
16: 6° ὁ δε *for* καὶ¹ LTTrAWHR
26 *omit* οἱ² L[A]WHR
20: 4° βάπτισμα – *add* τό T
24° οἱ δε TWHR
22:36° εἶπεν οὖν – ὁ δε ε. TR
37 τά – τό TTrAWHR
24:10° Μαρία² – *add* ἡ LTTr[A]WWHR
Joh. 2: 8° οἱ δε *for* καὶ³ TTrAWHR
6:33° ἄρτος – *add* ὁ T
7:23° νόμος – *add* ὁ T
41° οἱ *for* ἄλλοι² (-ος) LTTrAWHR
9:28° *add at commencement* οἱ δε Tr
11:19 τὰς περὶ – τὴν LTTrAWHR
19:15 *omit* οἱ δε TTrAWHR, *see* ἐκεῖνος
38 *omit* ὁ² LTTrAWH
21: 6 *omit* ὁ δε T
Acts 8:12 *omit* the things Eds
11:23° χάριν – *add* τὴν LTTrAWHR
19: 3° ὁ δε εἶπεν *for* ε. τε T
8 *omit* the things LTrWH
20:21 *omit* τὴν² LTTrAWHR
21: 8 *omit* τοῦ² GEds
23:15 *omit* τά A.V.Vul
30 *omit* τά LTTrWH
24:14° καὶ – *add* τοῖς ἐν GTTr[A]WHR
25:22 *omit* ὁ δε LTTrAWH
26: 4 *omit* τὴν² Tr[A]WH
12 *omit* τῆς L[T]rW
28:23 *omit* τά LTTrAWH
Ro. 6:10 ὁ ὃ – ὁ E *bis*
10: 1 *omit* ἡ³ Eds
12: 5 ὁ – τό Eds
13: 9 [namely] LTTrAWH
16.19 *omit* τό¹ Eds
1 Co. 7: 7° ὁ *for* ὃς *bis* Eds
9:13° τά ἐκ, *read* the things of the
temple TTrWHR, [τά] ἐκ A
21° ἁ. – τοὺς ἀνόμους Eds
15:10 *omit* ἡ' LTTrAWHR
2 Co. 7:14 *omit* which (I made) T[Tr]WH
Gal. 4:14 *omit* τοῦ² LTTrAWHR
Phil. 1:11 τῶν – τόν G[L]TTrAWWHR
Col. 1: 4 τήν³ – *see* ἔχω
16 *omit* that are¹ LTTrWHR
16 *omit* that are² [L]T[Tr]WHR
1 Th. 4:10 *omit* which are LT[T]rWH
Tit. 2:10° διδασκαλίαν – *add* τὴν Eds
Philem. 6 *omit* which is LTr[WH]
Heb.10:10 *omit* οἱ A.V.BEGEds
12:24 τὸ Ἄβελ A.V.TEr
25 τὸν *for after* παραιτησάμενοι
LTTrAWHR
Jas. 4:14 τό – τά L, *omit* WH
14 *omit* ἡ² WH

1 Pet. 5: 1 *omit* which are LTrAWHR
Rev. 1: 4 *omit* τοῦ¹ GEds
4° τῶν *for* ἅ (ὃς) Tr
11:19° θεοῦ – *add* ὁ LTTrWHR
16: 3° ἀπέθανεν – *add* τά LTTrAWWHR
17: 4 ἡ² – ἦν A.V.CGEds
19:14 armies – *add* τά which A.V.tc
EGL[A]WWHR
20:13° *add* τοὺς *bis* GEds, *see* νεκρός

ὅ, *see* ὅς.

ὅδε, ἥδε, τόδε.

Lu. 16:25 ὧδε, *read now here* Eds (WHR
Acts 15:23 *omit after* this manner LTTrA

ὁδηγέω.

Acts 8:31 ὁδηγήσει TTrWHR

ὁδός.

Mat. 5:25 *trs* μετ' αὐτοῦ ἐν τῇ ὁ. Eds
20:17 *trs* and in the way LTTrAWHR
Mar. 11: 8 *omit* and strawed (them) in
the way TTrAWHR
Acts 9: 2 *trs* ὄντας τῆς ὁδοῦ T
2 Pet. 2:15 τὴν εὐθεῖαν ὁ – *omit* τὴν GEds

Ὀζίας, Ὀζείας LTTrAWH.

ὀθόνιον.

Lu. 24:12 *omit the verse* [L]T[Tr][[WH]]

οἶδα, *see* εἰδέω.

οἰκεῖος.

1 Ti. 5: 8 τῶν ο. – *omit* τῶν LTTr[A]WHR

* οἰκετεία, a household,

Mat. 24:45 οἰκετείας *for* θεραπείας (-πεία)
LTTrAWHR

οἰκέω.

Ro. 7:17 ἐνοικέω TWH
1 Co. 3:16 *trs* ἐν ὑμῖν οἰκεῖ WH

οἰκία.

Mat. 7:24, 26 *trs* αὐτοῦ τὴν ο. LTTrAWH.
19:29 *trs* or houses *after* lands TTrA
23:14(13) *omit the verse* LTTr-AWHR,
see κρίμα
Mar. 3:27 *trs* εἰς τὴν ο. τοῦ ἰσχυροῦ εἰσελθὼν τὰ σκεύη αὐτοῦ TTrWH
7:24 τὴν ο. – *omit* τὴν A.V.BEds
10:10 εἰς τὴν οἰκίαν LTTrAWHR
13:15 *omit* into the house [L]TWH
Lu. 7:36 οἶκος LTTrAWH
10:38° τὴν οἰκίαν *for* τὸν οἶκον (-κος)
TWH
22:54° τὴν οἰκίαν *for* τὸν οἶκον (-κος)
TTrAWH

οἰκοδομέω.

Mat. 26:61 *trs* αὐτὸν οἰκοδομῆσαι T
Mar. 15:29† *trs* ο. (ἐν [WH]R) τρισὶν ἡμέραις
LTTrAWHR
Lu. 4:29 *trs* ᾠκοδόμητο αὐτῶν TTrAWH
6:48° *add* ο. TTrAWHR, *see* θεμελιόω
Joh. 2:20 οἰκοδομήθη TWH
Acts 4:11 οἰκοδόμος LTTrAWH
7:47 οἰκοδόμησεν TrWWH
9:31 οἰκοδομουμένη Eds
20:32° οἰκοδομῆσαι *for* ἐποικοδομῆσαι
(-μέω) Eds
1 Pet. 2: 5 ἐποικοδομεῖσθε T

οἰκοδομή.

Eph. 2:21 ἡ ο. – *omit* ἡ Eds

οἰκοδομία.

1 Ti. 1: 4 οἰκοδομίαν *for* οἰκονομίαν(-μία)
A.V.BE

* οἰκοδόμος, a builder.

Acts 4:11 οἰκοδόμων *for* οἰκοδομούντων
(-μέω) LTTrAWH

οἰκονομία.

Eph. 3: 9° οἰκονομία *for* κοινωνία GEds
1 Ti. 1: 4 οἰκονομίαν dispensation s–
οἰκοδομίαν edifying A.V.BE

οἶκος.

Mat. 12:44 *trs* εἰς τὸν ο. μου ἐπισ. LTTrAWH
Mar. 2: 1 ἐν οἴκῳ LTTrWH
7:17 τὸν οἶκον T
8:26 τὸν ο. – *omit* τὸν GEds

Lu. 1:69 τῷ ο. – *omit* τῷ LTTrAWH
7:36° τὸν οἶκον *for* τὴν οἰκίαν LTTrA
10:38 οἰκία TWH (WH
12:52 *trs* ἐνὶ οἴκῳ LTTrAWH
14:23 *trs* μου ὁ οἶκος TTrAWH
22:54 οἰκία TTrAWH
Acts 7:46° οἴκῳ *for* θεῷ (θεός) LT

* οἰκουργός, a worker at home.

Tit. 2: 5 οἰκουργούς *for* οἰκουρούς (-ρός)
LTTrAWHR

οἰκουρός.

Tit. 2: 5 keepers at home—workers at
home, οἰκουργός LTTrAWHR

οἰκτιρμός.

Col 3:12 οἰκτιρμοῦ of mercy GEds

οἶμαι.

Joh. 21:25 *omit the verse* T

οἶνος.

Mat. 27:34° οἶνον *for* ὄξος LTTrWHR
Mar. 2:22 *omit* but new wine *to* new
bottles T[Tr]A[WH]
Lu. 5:37† *trs* ῥήξει ὁ ο. ὁ νέος LTTrAWH
7:33 *trs* πίνων οἶνον LTTrAWH
Joh. 2: 3° ὑστερήσαντος ο. when they
wanted wine—οἶνον οὐκ εἶ-
χον, ὅτι συνετελέσθη ὁ οἶνος
τοῦ γάμου. εἶτα they had no
wine, for the wine of the
marriage-feast was finished.
Then T
3 ο. οὐκ ἔχουσιν they have no
wine—οἶνος οὐκ ἔστιν there
is no wine T
Rev. 18: 3 *omit* the wine L[Tr]A[WH]

οἶος.

Lu. 9:55 *omit* and said *to* end *of* verse
LTTrAWH

ὀκνέω.

Acts 9:38 ὀκνήσῃς, *read* Delay not Eds

ὀκτώ.

Lu. 13: 4, 11 *see* δεκαοκτώ
Acts 25: 6° more than—not more than
eight or, οὐ πλείους ὀκτὼ ἤ
GEds

ὀλεθρεύω, *see* ὀλοθρεύω.

* ὀλιγοπιστία, little faith.

Mat. 17:20 ὀλιγοπιστίαν *f.* ἀπιστίαν (-τία)
LTTrAWHR

ὀλίγος.

Mat. 20:16 *omit* for many be called, but
few chosen T[Tr]A]WHR
Lu. 10:42° *commence* ὀλίγων δέ ἐστιν χρεία
ἢ ἑνός but few things are
needful, or one WH
19:24 *trs* οὐκ ὁ. ἐργασίαν LTTrAWH
Jas. 3: 5 ἡλίκος Eds
1 Pet. 3:20 ὀλίγοι few (persons) Eds
Rev. 2:20 *omit* a few things GEds

* ὀλίγως, just.

2 Pet. 2:18 *for* ὄντως GEds

ὀλοθρεύω, ὀλεθρεύω LA.

ὅλος.

Mat. 4:23 ἐν (om. ἐν L) ὅλῃ τῇ Γαλιλαίᾳ
LTTrAWHR
21: 4 *omit* all LTTrAWHR
Mar. 12:33 *omit* and with all the soul
[L]TWHR
Lu. 8:43 *omit* WH, *see* ἰατρός
10:27 ὅλῃ *ter* LTTrWHR, *see* ψυχή
Acts 8:37 *omit the verse* GLTTrAWHR
13: 6° ὅλην τὴν νῆσον the whole island
GEds
19:29 *omit* whole LTTrAWHR
22:30 πᾶς GEds
Rev. 6:12° σελήνη ὅλη whole moon GEds
13: 3 *see* θαυμάζω

* ὀμείρομαι, to long for.

1 Th. 2: 8 ὀμειρόμενοι *for* ἱμειρόμενοι
(-μαι) GEds

ὅμιλος.

Rev. 18:17 omit the company GEds. see πλέω

✱ ὁμίχλη, ὁ–, a mist, for.

2 Pet. 2.17 καὶ ὁμίχλαι for νεφέλαι (-λη) GEds

ὄμμα.

Mat. 20:34*ὀμμάτων for ὀφθαλμῶν (-μός) LTTrAWH

ὄμνυμι, ὀμνύω.

Mar. 14:71 ὀμνύναι GLTTrAWWH
Acts 7:17 had sworn—vouchsafed, ὁμολογέω Eds

ὁμοθυμαδόν.

Acts 2: 1 with one accord—together, ὁμοῦ LTTrAWHR
18:12 trs οἱ Ἰουδαῖοι ὁ. WH

ὁμοιάζω.

Mat. 23:27*ὁμοιάζετε for παρομοιάζετε (-ζω) LTr
Mar. 14:70 omit and thy speech agreeth (thereto) LTTrAWHR

ὅμοιος.

Mar. 12:31 omit (is) like TAWH
Rev. 4: 3 ὅμοιος² δ—ὁμοία ℵ
9: 7 ὁ.¹—ὅμοιοι T
10 ὁμοίοις Tr
14:14 ὅμοιον GEds
16:13 like—as, ὡς GEds
21:18 ὅμοιον Eds

ὁμοιόω.

Mat. 7:24 ὁ. αὐτόν—ὁμοιωθήσεται he shall be likened LTTrWHR

ὁμοίως.

Mar. 4:16 trs ὁμοίως εἰσίν T
Lu. 13: 3*for ὡσαύτως LTTrAWH
5 ὡσαύτως TTrAWHR
Rev. 2:15*for ὁ μισῶ (-σέω) GEds

ὁμολογέω.

Lu. 12: 8 ὁ.¹—ὁμολογήσει WH
Acts 7:17*ὡμολόγησεν for ὤμοσεν (ὀμνυμι) Eds
1 Joh.2:23*add at end ὁ ὁμολογῶν τὸν υἱὸν καὶ τὸν πατέρα ἔχει he that acknowledgeth the Son hath the Father also A.V.B GEds
Rev. 3: 5*ὁμολογήσω for ἐξομολογήσομαι (-γέομαι) GEds

ὁμοῦ.

Acts 2: 1*for ὁμοθυμαδόν LTTrAWHR

ὀνειδίζω.

1 Ti. 4:10 suffer reproach—strive, ἀγωνίζομαι LTTrWHR

ὄνειδος.

Lu. 1:25 τὸ ὁ.—omit τὸ TTr[A]WH

ὀνικός.

Mar. 9:42*add ὁ. LTTrAWHR, see λίθος
Lu. 17: 2 omit ὁ. LTTrAWHR, see λίθος

ὄνομα.

Mar. 3:17 ὄνομα WH
5: 9 trs ὄνομά σοι LTTrAWH
9:41 τῷ ὁ.—omit τῷ GEds
11:10 omit in the name of the Lord GEds
Lu. 1:63 τὸ ὁ.—omit τὸ Tr[A]WH
8:30 trs ὄνομα ἐστίν LTTrWH
24:18 ᾧ ὁ.—ὀνόματι by name TrAWHR
Joh. 16:23 trs, see δίδωμι
Acts 5:41 trs κατηξιώθησαν ὑπὲρ τοῦ ὁ. LTTrAWHR
9:33 trs ὀνόματι Αἰνέαν LTTrAWWH
16:18 τῷ ὁ.—omit τῷ LTTrAWHR
Phil. 2: 9 τὸ ὄνομα LTTrWWHR, [τὸ] ὁ. A
1 Pet. 4:16*ὀνόματι for μέρει (-ρος) Eds
1 Joh. 5:13 om. that believe on the name of the Son of God¹ GEds
Rev. 3: 1*om.—omit τὸ GEds
13: 1 ὀνόματα names GLTTrWWHR
8 τὸ ὄνομα the name GW, τὸ ὁ.
αὐτοῦ his name LTTrAWHR

Rev. 14: 1*ὄνομα—add αὐτοῦ καὶ τὸ ὄνομα, read his name and his Father's name GEds
17: 3 (add τὰ Tr) ὀνόματα Eds
8 τὸ ὄνομα the name LTTrAWHR
19:16 τὸ ὁ. omit τὸ A.V.CGEds
21:12*which are—add τὰ ὀνόματα the names L[TrA]

ὀνομάζω.

Mar. 3:14*add ὁ. WH, see ἀπόστολος
1 Co. 5: 1 omit named GEds

ὄνος.

Lu. 14: 5 an ass—a son, υἱός LTTrAWWH

ὄντα, ὄντας. etc., see ὤν.

ὄντως.

Mar. 11:32 trs ὄντως ὅτι TTrAWHR
1 Ti. 6:19*for αἰωνίου (-νιος) GEds
2 Pet. 2:18 clean—just, ὀλίγως GEds

ὄξος.

Mat. 27:34 vinegar—wine, οἶνος LTTrWHR
Joh. 19:29 τοῦ ὄξους LTTrAWHR, see πλήθω

ὀπίσω.

Mat. 4:10*hence—add ὀπίσω μου behind me G[L]W
Lu. 4: 8 omit get thee behind me, Satan G[L]TTrAWHR

ὀπότε.

Lu. 6: 3 ὅτε LTTrWHR

ὅπου.

Mat. 2: 4*for ἐφ' ᾧ LTTrAWH
9:44, 46 omit the verses T[Tr]WHR
Acts 20: 6*for οὗ T

ὄπτομαι.

Mat. 17: 3 ὤφθη LTTrAWH
27: 4 ὄψῃ LTTrAWH
Lu. 13:28 ὄψεσθε TTr
22:43, 44 the verses [L][[WH]]
Joh. 1:39(40)*ὄψεσθε for ἴδετε (εἰδέω) TTrAWH
1:50(51) ὄψει—ὄψῃ GLTTrAWWH
11:40 ὄψῃ LTTrAWWH
Ro. 15:21 trs. ὄψονται before οἷς οὐκ WHR

ὅπως.

Mat. 12:17 ἵνα LTTrAWH
Mar. 5:23 ἵνα LTTrAWH
Acts 24:26 omit that he might loose him Eds

ὅραμα.

Acts 9:12 omit in a vision LTAℵ; trs ἄνδρα [ἐν ὁ.] TrWH

ὁράω.

Mar. 8:24 omit ὅτι and ὁρῶ A.V.BG
Lu. 9:36 ἑώρακαν TTrAWH
Joh. 6: 2 θεωρέω LTTrAWHR
46 trs ἑώρακέν τις LTTrAWWH
8:38 have seen²—have heard, ἀκούω LTTrAWHR
20:18 ἑώρακα I have seen TTrAWH
Acts 22:26 omit take heed, read what art thou about to do? GEds
1 Co. 9: 1 ἑώρακα TWH
Col. 2: 1 ἑώρακαν LTrAW, ἑόρακαν TWH
18 ἑόρακεν TAWH
Rev. 18:18 βλέπω GEds

ὀργή.

Ro. 2: 8 trs wrath and indignation GEds

ὀρεινός, ὀρι– WH.

ὀρθρινός.

Lu. 24:22*ὀρθριναί for ὄρθριαι (-ριος) Eds
Rev. 22:16 πρωϊνός GEds

ὄρθριος.

Lu. 24:22 ὀρθινός Eds

ὅρια.

Mar. 7:24*ὅρια for μεθόρια LTTrWH

ὁρκίζω.

Acts 19:13 ὁρκίζω I adjure GEds
1 Th. 5:27 ἐνορκίζω Eds

ὄρνις.

Mat. 23:37 trs ὄρνις ἐπισυνάγει LTTrAWH
Lu. 13:34 ὄρνιξ T

ὄρος.

Mar. 5: 5 trs tombs and mountain- GEds
11 τῷ ὄρει the mountain GEds
Lu. 4: 5 omit into an high mountain [L]TTrAWHR
Joh. 4:20 trs τῷ ὄρει τούτῳ GLTTrAWWH
Heb. 12:18 omit the mount LTTrAWHR
2 Pet. 1:18†trs τῷ ἁγίῳ ὄρει TrAWH

ὅς, ἥ, ὅ.

Mat. 5:32 ὃς ἄν—πᾶς ὁ LTTrAWH
11:16*ἅ for καί LTTrAWH
23*ᾗ for ᾗ W
12: 4 οὓς—ὃ LTTrAWH
18 εἰς ὅν—ἐν ᾧ Tr
13:23*ὃ ter for ὃ³** LTWH
46 omit who GLTTrAWHR, see δέ
18:30 omit οὗ LTTrAWH
34 omit οὗ L[WH]
19:29 ὅς—ὅστις LTTrAWWH
20: 7 omit LTTrAWHR, see δίκαιος
21:44 omit the verse [L]T[WH]
22: 5*ὃς bis for ὃ LTTrAWH
10*οὓς for ὅσους (ὅσος) WH
25: 3*αἱ γάρ for αἵτινες (ὅστις) Tr
13 omit GLTTrAWHR, see υἱός
26:50 ᾧ—ὃ GEds
27:33 ὅς—ὃ GLTTrAWWH (WHR
Mar. 1:11 in whom—in thee, σοί LTTrA
2: 4 ἐφ' ᾧ wherein—ὅπου where LTTrAWH
3:14*add οὓς WH, see ἀπόστολος
4: 9*ὅς for ὁ Eds, see ἔχω
22 omit ὁ LTTrAWH
6:11*ὅς for ὅσοι (-ος) TTrAWH
23 omit ὃ WH
9:38 omit GWHR, see ἀκολουθέω
11:23 ἅ—ὃ TTrAWHR
23 omit whatsoever he saith TTr[A]WH
12: 5*οὓς for τοὺς bis LTTrAWH
13:19 ἧς—ἣν LTTrWH
37 ἅ—ὃ LTTrAWHR, quod A.V.Vul
14:72 οὗ—ὃ W, ὡς how LTTrAWH
15: 6*ὃν for ὅνπερ (ὅσπερ) TWHR
12 omit whom ye call LTr, [ὃν] W
23*ὅς for ὁ TTrWH
Lu. 5: 9 ᾗ—ὧν TrWHR
25 ᾧ—ὃ TTrAWH
7:32*add ἅ WHR, see λέγω
8:18 trs ὃς ἂν γάρ TTrAWH
27 omit ὅς TWHR, see ἔχω
12:50 οὗ—ὅτου Eds
59 omit οὗ TTrWH
13: 7*ἣν—add ἀφ' οὗ TTrAWH
19 ὃν δ—ὃ ℵ
14:15 ὅστις TTrAWH
22*ᾧ for ὡς TTrAWH
15: 8*οὗ for ὅτου TrWH
16:20 omit ὅς [L]TTrAWHR
19:13*ἐν ᾧ for ἕως LTTrAWH
21:24*ἄχρι—add οὗ LTTrAWH
22:10 οὗ—εἰς ἣν LTTrAWH
18*οὗ for ὅτου TrAWH
24:10 omit which LTTr[A]WH
18 ᾧ ὄνομα—ὀνόματι TrAWH
Joh. 1:27 omit is preferred before m- G[L]TTrAWH
2:22 ᾧ—ὃν LTTrAWH
4:29*ἅ for ὅσα (ὅσος) TWHR
39*ἅ for ὅσα (ὅσος) TTrAWHR
45 ἅ—ὅσα (ὅσος) LTrAWHR
50 ᾧ—ὃν LTTrAWH
5: 4 omit [G]TTrAWHR, see ὕδωρ
11*ὅς δὲ ἀπεκρίθη but he answered LTTrAWH
6: 9 ὅ—ὅς LTTrAWWH
14 ὅ—ἅ WH
22 omit GLTTrAWHR, see ἐκεῖνος
51 omit which I will give LTTrAWHR
8:38 ἐγὼ ὅ—ἅ ἐγὼ LTTrWHR, ἐγὼ ℰ ℵ
38 ὅ—ἃ LTTrAWH
9:14*add ᾗ WHR, see ὅτε
10:29 ὅ—ὃ TTrAWH
11:45 ἅ—ὃ TrAWH
13:18 οὓς—τίς TTrAWH (WHR
15:14*ἅ (ὃ WH) for ὅσα (ὅσος) LTTrA
17:11 whom—which ᾧ GEds
12 οὓς—ᾧ, read in thy name which TTrAWH
24 οὓς—ὃ, read that which thou hast given WHR
18:16 ὃς ἦν—ὁ TTrAWH
19:17 ὅς—ὃ LTTrAWH

Joh. 21:25*ā for ὅσα (ὅσος) LTrAWHR
Acts 1:19*ὃ καί which also T
  7:16 ὅ—ῳ GLTTrAWWH
  8:27 omit ὅς² LT[TrWH]
  10:32 omit LTTr[A]WH, see λαλέω
    36 omit which L[Tr]WH
    45*οἱ for ὅσοι (ὅσος) LWH
  13:41 ῳ—ὃ LTTrAWWH
  17:23 whom—what, ὃ Eds
  20: 6 οὗ—ὅπου T
  24:18 οἷς—αἷς LTTrAWH
Ro. 2:16*ἡμέρα ᾗ LA, ᾗ ἥ. WH (omit ὅτε)
  4: 8 ῳ—οὗ, read whose sin the Lord will not impute TTrWH
  6:10 ὃ ὃ—ὃ bis E
  14:22*πίστιν—add ἥν, read the faith which thou hast, have LTTr[A]WH
  16:27 which ῳ A.V.C [WH] (WHR
1Co. 2: 9 which—whatsoever, ὅσος LTrA
  4: 2 ὃ δέ—ὧδε, read here moreover LTTrAWHR
    6 ὅ—ᾱ Eds
  7: 7 ὅς bis—ὃ Eds
2Co. 2:10 ῳ²—ὃ GEds
  5: 4 ἐφ᾽ ῳ for ἐπειδή A.V.BHGEds
Gal. 3:19 οὗ—ἄν WH
  5: 1 omit ᾗ LTTrAWH
Eph. 1: 6 ἐν ᾗ—ἧς LTTrAWH, see ἐν
    14 ὅς—ὃ LAWH
  5: 5 ὅ—ὅ LTTrAWH
  6: 8 omit ὃ TAWH
Col. 1: 4*see ἔχω
    24 ὅς (qui)—ὃ A.V.Vul
    27 ὅς—ὃ LTTrAWH
  2:17 ᾱ—ᾱ E
  3: 6 ᾱ—ᾱ A
    14*ὅ for ᾗτις (ὅστις) Eds
    23*ὃ for καὶ πᾶν ὅ τι Eds
1Ti. 3:16*ὅς for θεός GEds
2Ti. 2: 7 ᾱ—ὃ Eds
Tit. 3: 5 ὧν—ᾱ LTTrAWH
Philem.21 ὃ—ᾱ LTTrAWH
Heb. 7: 1*ὅς for ὁ LTrA
  9: 9 ὅν—ἥν, read according to which Eds
  10: 1 ᾱς—αἷς TA
Jas. 4:12 ὅς—ὃ LTTrAWH
1Pet. 3:21 ὃ ὃ—ῳ A.V.BE
2Pet. 3:16 οἷς—αἷς Eds
1Joh.5: 9 which—that, ὅτι Eds
Jude 23*add οὓς δέ LTTrAWR, see φόβος
Rev. 1: 4 ᾱ—τῶν Tr
    20 ὧν—οὓς LTTrAWH
    20 om. which thou sawest² GEds
  2:13 omit wherein LTTrWH, [αἷς]A
    15 see μισέω
  3: 8*ἣν for καί¹ GEds
    12 ἣ ὃ—ᾗ E
  4: 5 αἵ—ᾱ LTWH
  5: 6 οἵ—ᾱ W
    13 omit such as LTTrAWH
  6:11 omit οὗ GEds
  7: 3 omit οὗ LTTrAWH
  9:11*ὄνομα¹—ῳ ὄνομα T
    14 ὅς—ὃ GEds
  11:16*οἵ for οὗ² R
    16*θεοῦ—add οἵ TTr
  13: 4 ὅς—ὅτι, read because he gave GEds
    8 ὧν—οὗ LTTrAWH
    10 ὅς—ὅς who Eds
  14: 2*add ἥν GEds, see φωνή
    8*ἣ for ὅτι Eds
  16:14 see ἐκπορεύομαι
  20: 2 ὅς—ὃ T
  ὅ τι, see ὅστις

ὅσιος.
Rev. 16: 5 ὁ ὅ.—omit ὁ LTrAW[WH]:
  ἐσόμενος A.V.B

ὅσος.
Mat. 22:10 ὅς WH
Mar. 3:28 ὅσα LTTrAWH
  6:11 ὅς TTrAWH, see δέχομαι
    30 omit what² T
Joh. 4:29 ὅς TTrAWH
    39 ὅς TTrAWH
    45*ὅσα for ᾱ (ὅς) LTrAWHR
  15:14 whatsoever—what, ὅς LTTrAWH
  16:23 ὅσα ᾱν whatsoever—if anything, ᾱν τι LTTrAWH
  21:25 ὅς—ᾱ whatsoever: omit the verse T
Acts 10:45 as many as—who, οἵ (ὅς) LWH
1Co. 2: 9*ὅσα for ᾱ (ὅς) LTrAWH

ὅσπερ.
Mar.15: 6 ὅς TWHR

ὀστέον.
Eph. 5:30 omit of his flesh, and of his bones LTTr[A]WH

ὅστις, ἥτις, ὅ τι.
Mat. 18:28 that—if anything, εἴ τι GEds
  19:29*ὅστις for ὅς LTTrAWH
  25: 3 αἵτινες—αἱ γάρ, read for the foolish TAWH, αἵ γ. Tr, αἱ δέ L
Mar. 8:34 whosoever—if anyone, εἴ τις LTrWH
  9:11*28* ὅ τι for ὅτι LW
Lu. 10:35 ὅ τι—ὅτι WH
  14:15*ὅστις for ὅς TTrAWH (WH
Joh. 2: 5|8:25|14:13|15:16 ὅ τι—ὅτι
  21:25 omit the verse T
Acts 9: 6*ὅ τι for τί LTTrAR
  11:28 ἥτις LTTrAWWH
1Co. 6:20 omit GEds, see θεός
  7:13 which—if any, εἴ τις T
  2: 6 τι—ὅτι WH
2Co. 3:14 which (veil)—that (it), ὅτι LTTrAWWH
Col. 3:14, 23 ὅς Eds
  3:17 ὅ τι—ὅτι WH
1Joh.3:20*ὅ τι for ὅτι LR
Rev.17: 8 ὅ τι—ὅτι read that it was GEds

ὅταν.
Mar.11:19*for ὅτε TTrWHR
  12:23 when they shall rise L[Tr]WH
1Joh.2:28 when—if, ἐάν LTTrAWH
Rev. 8: 1*for ὅτε LTTrAWH

ὅτε.
Mat.17:25 omit ὅ. LTTrAWH, see εἰσέρχομαι
Mar. 4: 6*add ὅ LTTrAWH, see ἀνατέλλω
  11:19 ὅταν TTrWHR
Lu. 6: 3*for ὁπότε [Tr]WH
  13:35 omit when [TrA]WH
Joh. 4:45 ὡς T
  9:14 when—in the day that, ἐν ᾗ ἡμέρᾳ LTTrAWH
  12:17 when 8—because, ὅτι EGLTW
    41 when—because,ὅτι GLTTrAWH
Ro. 2:16 when—in which, ᾗ (ὅς) LAWH
1Co.12: 2*that—add ὁ. when[L]TTrAWH
Rev. 8: 1 ὅταν LTTrAWH

ὅτι.
Mat. 5:31 omit ὅ. LTTrAWH
  6: 5 omit ὅ.² LTTrAWH
    13 omit GEds, see αἰών
    16 omit ὅ. LTTrAWH
  7:14 because—how, τί GLTr
  9:18 omit ὅ. T
    33 omit ὅ. A.V.CGEds
  16:28*ὑμῖν—add ὅ. LTWH
  19: 9 omit ὅ. LTrA
    24*ὑμῖν—add ὅ. T
  20:12 omit ὅ. LTT[A]WH
  23:10*for γάρ LTTrAWH, see καθηγητής
    14(13) omit the verse LTTrAWH, see κρίμα
    36*ὑμῖν—add ὅ. G[A]W
  24:34*ὑμῖν—add ὅ. LTrWH
  26:29, 65 omit ὅ. LTTrAWH
Mar. 1:27 omit ὅ. LTTrAWH, see καινός
  2:16*add ὅ. LTTrWH, see ἐσθίω
  4:21*αὐτοῖς—add ὅ. TAWH
  6: 2 omit that GEds
    16 omit ὅ. LTTrAWH
    49*ἔδοξαν—add ὅ. TWH
  7: 2*αὐτοῦ—add ὅ. TTrWH
    6 omit [L]T[TrA]WH
    6*γέγραπται—add ὅ. TWH
  8: 4*αὐτοῦ—add ὅ. TTrAWH
    24 omit ὅ. and ὁρῶ A.V.BG
    28*add ὅ. TAWH, see λέγω
  9:11*, 28 ὅ τι LW
    41*ὑμῖν—add ὅ. [L]TTrAWH
  11: 3 omit that LTTrAWH
    18 ὅ. πᾶς—πᾶς γάρ TTrAWH
  14:21*add at commencement ὅ. read for the Son T[Tr]AWH
Lu. 4:25*ὑμῖν—add ὅ. T
  6: 5 omit ο. [Tr]WH
  7:22 omit how that L[Tr]WH
  8:20*ὅ. ἡ μήτηρ T
  10:35*for ὅ τι WH
  12:54*λέγετε—add ὅ. [L]TTrAWH
  13:14*ὅχλῳ—add ὅ. TAWH
    35 omit ὅ. L[TT[A]WH
  17:10 omit ὅ.² Eds
  18:29 omit ὅ. T

Lu. 19:34*ὅ. ὁ κύριος LTTrAWH
    40 omit ὅ. [Tr]WH
  21: 8 omit ὅ.[L]T[TrA]WH
  22:18 omit ὅ. TrAWH
    22*for καί TTrAWH
Joh. 1:16*for καί¹ GLTTrAWH
    50(51)*σοι—add ὅ. LTTrAWH
  2: 3*add ὅ. T, see οἶνος
    5*for ὃ τι WH
  4:42 [ὅτι] LWH
    53 omit ὅ.² LTTrAWH
  7:31 omit ὅ. LTTrAWH
    40*ἔλεγον—add [ὅτι] AWH
  8:25*for ὅ τι WH
  9: 9 omit ὅ.² LTTrAWHR, see λέγω
    11*μοι—add ὅ. TTrWH
  10: 7 omit ὅ. [L]T[TrA]WH
    26*οὐ γάρ—add ὅ. οὐκ LTTrAWH
    34*ὑμῶν—add ὅ. LTTrAWH
  12:17*for ὅτε EGLTW
    41*for ὅτε GLTTrAWH
  13:11*εἶπεν—add ὅ. LTTrAWH
  14: 2*ὑμῖν¹—add ὅ. read for I go Eds
    13*|15:16*for ὅτι WH
  16:16 omit because I go to the Father TTrAWH
    23 omit ὅ. LTTrAWH
  18: 6 omit ὅ. LTTrAWH
Acts 9: 6*for τί² WH
  10:20*for διότι GEds
  23: 5*γάρ—add ὅ. TT[A]WH
Ro. 9:12 omit that [L]TTrAWH
  8:21 διότι T
  9:28 omit LTTr[A]WH, see λόγος
  10: 5 trs ὅ. after γράφει TWHR
    9*σου¹—add ὅ. WH
1Co. 4: 9 omit that Eds
  7:29 ἀδελφοί add ὅ. B
  16: 2*for ὅ τι WH
2Co. 1:10 [that] LTrWH
  3:14*for ὅ τι GLTTrAWH
Gal. 2:16*for διότι LTTrAWH
  3:10*γάρ²—add ὅ. GEds
    13*ὅ. γέγραπται for γ. γάρ Eds
Eph. 3: 3 [ὅτι] LWH
Phil. 1:18*πλήν—add ὅ. read What then? only that LTTrAWH
Col. 3:17*for ὅ τι WH
1Pet. 1:16 διότι T
    16 omit because GEds
1Joh.2: 4*λέγων—add ὅ. [L]TTrAWH
  3:20 ὅ.¹—ὅ τι LR: omit ὅ.² A.V.Vul
  5: 9*for ἥν (ὅς) Eds
Jude 18 omit ὅ.² LT[Tr]WH
Rev. 3:17 omit ὅ.³ [A]W
  13: 4*for ὅς GEds
  14: 8 ὅς, read which hath made GEds
  17: 8*for ὅ τι GEds
  18: 7*λέγει—add ὅ. LTTrAWH
  21: 4 omit for L[TrA]WH
  22:10 ὅ. ὁ καιρός—ὃ κ. γάρ Eds

ὅτου.
Lu. 12:50*for οὗ (ὅς) Eds
  15: 8 ὅς TrWH
  22:18 ὅς TrAWH

οὗ, adv.
Lu. 22:10 where—in which εἰς ἥν LTTrAWH
Joh. 11:41 omit where the dead was laid GLTTrAWH
Acts 20: 6 ὅπου T

οὐ, οὐκ, οὐχ.
Mat. 13:34 not—nothing οὐδείς LTTrAWHR
    55*for οὐχί LTTrAWH
  15:17*for οὕτω LTTrWH
  16: 3 see λέγω
  17:21 omit the verse T[TrA]WH
  21:19*αὐτῆ²—add οὐ LT[A]WH
    29, 30 trs WH, see ἀπέρχομαι
    32 οὐ²—οὐδέ, read did not even repent LTTrWH, οὐ[δέ] A
  25: 9 οὐκ—οὐ μή LTrAWWH
  26:60 omit (yet) found they none G[L]TT.AWH
Mar. 3:27 omit οὐ GLT.W
  4:40 οὕτω; πῶς οὐκ—; οὕπω, read why are ye fearful? Have ye not yet faith? LTTrWH
  6:36 omit [L]TTrAWH, see ἄρτος
  8:21 not—not yet, οὕπω LTTrAWH
  9:38 omit GWHR, see ἀκολουθέω
    44, 46 omit the verses T[Tr]WHR
  11:26 omit the verse TTrWH
  14:61*καί—add οὐκ TTrWHR, see ἀποκρίνομαι
    68 οὔτε, read neither know, nor LTTrAWH

Lu. 4:22 οὐχί LTTrAWH
8:17 οὐ³—οὐ μή LTTrAWH
9:55 omit and said to end of verse LTTrAWH
56 omit for the Son to save (them) GLTTrAWH
12:24 οὐ¹—οὔτε TA
27 οὔτε TA, see κοπιάω (WH
14: 3*add at end ἢ οὗ or not [L]TTrA
17: 9 omit I trow not [L]TTrAWH
17*for οὐχί LTrWH
18: 4 καὶ ἄνθρωπον οὐκ—οὐδὲ ἅ. LTTrWH
30 οὐ μή—οὐχὶ μή TAWH
23:34 see λέγω

Joh. 2: 3*add οὐκ T, see οἶνος
4: 9 omit T[WH], see συγχράομαι
6:17 not—not yet, οὔπω LTTrAWH
42 οὐχί TrWH
7: 8*for οὔπω¹ GTTrA
42*for οὐχι LTrAWH
16: 7 οὐ μή TrWH
16 not—no longer, οὐκέτι LTTrAWH
19: 4*for οὐδεμίαν (–δεὶς) T (WH

Acts 2: 7 οὐχί TrAWH
31 οὔτε, read neither . . . nor Eds
5:28 omit οὐ, read we did straitly LTTrAWH
19:40*οὐ—add οὐ TT.[A]WHR
20: 6*add οὐ GEds, see ὀκτώ

Ro. 7:26*for οὐχί LTTrWH
4:19 omit not² LTTr.[A]WH
13: 9 omit thou shalt not bear false witness GEds
14: 6 omit LTTr.[A]WH R, see κύριος

1Co. 3: 4*for οὐχί LTTrAWH
6:10*for οὔτε³ TAWH
10 omit οὐ³ LTTrAWH
9: 8*οὐ after ταῦτα² for οὐχί Eds
15*add οὐ GEds, see χράομαι
10:18*for οὐχί LTAWWH

2Co. 3:10*for οὐδὲ GEds
5:12 οὐ²—μή LTTrWH
10:13*for οὐχί LTTrAWWH
12: 3 omit I cannot tell L[WH]

Phil. 3:13 not—not yet, οὔπω TWH
Heb. 10: 2 omit οὐκ, read they would E
Jas. 2: 6 οὐχί LW
2Pet. 1:12 omit οὐκ Eds, see ἀμελέω
1Joh. 4:20*for πῶς LTTrAWH
Rev. 7: 16*οὐδὲ²—οὐδ᾽ οὐ A
9: 6 οὐχ—οὐ μή GEds
20*for οὔτε¹ A.V.CGWWH
10: 6 see οὐκέτι

See also οὐ μή *after* μή.

οὐά, οὐᾶ T.

οὐαί.

Mat. 23:14(13) omit the verse LTTrAWH, see κρίμα

οὐδέ.

Mat. 8:10 no, not—with any one, παρ οὐδενί (–δεὶς) LTrAWH
21:32*for οὐ² LTrWH R, οὐδὲ] A
24:36*add o. LTWH R, see υἱός
Mar. 5: 3*for οὔτε Eds
11:26 omit the verse TTrWH
12:21 μή TTrAWH R, see καταλείπω
14:68 οὔτε Eds
Lu. 12:24 ο.¹—οὔτε TA
26*for οὔτε LTrWH
27 ο.¹—οὔτε TA, see κοπιάω
18: 4*καὶ ἄνθρωπον οὐκ—οὐδὲ ἄνθρωπον LTTrWH
20:36*for οὔτε LTrAWH
21:15 nor—or, ἤ GT[Tr]AWH
Joh. 1:25*for οὔτε bis LTTrAWH
21:25 omit the verse T
Acts 2:31 οὔτε Eds
4:12*for οὔτε LTTrWWH
20:24 omit neither count I TTrAWH
24:13*for οὔτε LTWH R
1Co. 3: 2*for οὔτε GEds
8: 5 σοφὸς οὐδὲ εἰς—οὐδεὶς σοφός LTTrAWH
2Co. 3:10 or -Eds
Gal. 1:12*for οὔτε LTr
1Th. 2: 3*) r οὔτε Eds
Rev. 5: 3 ο.¹²—οὔτε T: ο.³—οὔτε LTTrWH
9:20*for οὔτε¹ TA
12: 8*for οὔτε GEds
20: 4*for οὔτε Eds

οὐδείς, οὐδεμία, οὐδέν.

Mat. 8:10*οὐδενί for οὐδὲ LTrAWH
13:34*οὐδὲν for οὐ LTTrAWH
19:17 omit o. GEds, see ἀγαθός
Mar. 11:14 μηδεὶς, s—οὐδεὶς E
15: 3 add A.V.C, see ἀποκρίνομαι

Lu. 8:51 οὐδένα no man—τινὰ σὺν αὐτῷ, read no man to go in with him LTTrAWH
22:35 οὐθενός TT.AWH
23:14 οὐθέν TTrWH
Joh. 19: 4 οὐ T
11 trs κατ᾽ ἐμοῦ o. LTTrAWWH
Acts 9: 8 no man—nothing, οὐδέν LTTrWWH R
15: 9 οὐθὲν TTrAWH
19:27 οὐθὲν LTTrAWH
20:33 οὐθενός T
26:26 οὐθέν T[Tr]AWH, omit o. L
1Co. 6: 5*see οὐδέ
8: 2 omit LTTrAWH R, see οὐδέπω
9:15*οὐδεὶς for ἵνα τις LTTrWH R
13: 2 οὐθέν s—οὐδέν EGW
3 οὐθέν T
2Co. 11: 9 οὐθενός LTTrAWH
Jas. 3:12 οὐδεμία πηγὴ ἁλυκὸν καί—οὔτε ἁλυκόν, read neither (can) salt (water) yield fresh GEds
Rev. 3:17 οὐδέν LTTrAWH

οὐδέπω.

Lu. 23:53 οὔπω LTTrAWH R, trs οὐδεὶς o. T
Joh. 7:39 οὔπω LTTrAWH
Acts 8:16*for οὔπω Eds
1Co. 8: 2 οὐδέπω nothing yet—οὔπω not yet LTTrAWH

οὐθείς, οὐθέν, see under οὐδείς.

οὐκέτι, οὐκ ἔτι.

Mar. 5: 3*οὐκέτι οὐδείς, read bind him any longer Eds
Lu. 22:16 omit any more [LTr]AWH R
Joh. 16:16*for οὐ LTTrAWH R
Ro. 11: 6 om. o.³ GLTTr.[A]WH R, see ἔργον
Rev. 10: 6*οὐκ ἔσται ἔτι—οὐκέτι ἐσ. GEds
18:14 omit o. Tr

οὖν.

Mat. 6:22 omit therefore T
14:15*ἀπόλυσον—add o. read away therefore T[A]
18:31*for δέ LTTrAWH
28:19 omit therefore G[L]T[Tr]A
Mar. 3:31 καὶ Eds, see ἔρχομαι
11:31 omit then LTrAW[WH]
12: 6 omit therefore [L]TTrAWH
9 omit therefore TAWH
20 ἑπτά—add o. A.V.BEW
23 omit therefore TTr·\WH R
27 omit therefore T[Tr]AWH R
37 omit therefore [L]TTrAWH
Lu. 6: 9 then—and, δέ LTTrWH
36 omit therefore LTTrAWH
10: 2 therefore¹—and, δέ LTTrAWH
36 omit now [L]T[Tr]AWH
37 then—and, δέ GLTTrAWH
11:34 omit therefore LTTrAWH
12: 7 omit therefore L[L]TTrAWH
40 omit therefore LTTrAWH
13:15 then—but, δέ LTTrAWH
18*for δέ TTrAWH R (WH
14:34*good—add o. therefore T[Tr]A
15:28 therefore—but, δέ LTTrAWH
16:27 trs σε οὖν LTTrAWWH
20: 5 omit then [L]TTrAWH
33 trs οὖν ἐν τῇ TAWH, see γυνή
21: 8 omit therefore LTTrAWH
36 therefore—but, δέ LTTrAWH
22:36 then—but, δέ TTrWH
23:20 therefore—and, δέ LTTrAWH
Joh. 1:39(40)*came—add o. therefore [L]TTrAWH
4: 9, 11 omit then T
30 omit then GEds
33 omit therefore W
52*καὶ εἶπον—ε. οὖν LTTrAWH
5: 4 omit [G]TTrAWH, see ὕδωρ
12 omit then [L]T[Tr]AWH
18 omit o. T
6:11*for δέ LTTrAWH
35*for δέ T
42 then—now, νῦν TTrAWH
43 omit therefore G[L]TTrAWWH R
45 omit therefore GLTTrAWH
66*that (time)—add o. therefore T
68 omit then GLTTrAWH
7: 6 omit then T
15*καὶ ἐθαύμαζον—ἐ. οὖν Eds
16*ἀπεκρίθη—add o. read Jesus therefore Eds
47 omit then TA
8:41 omit then LTTrAWH
42 omit o. A.V.ErGLTTrAWH
48 omit then LTTrAWH
52 omit then LTTrAWH

Joh. 9:10*how—add o. then [L]T[AWH]R
11*for δέ LTTrAWH
12 omit then LTTrAWH R, see καί
17*say—add o. therefore Eds
20*answered—add o. therefore LTWH
26*for δέ LTTrAWH
28 omit then GEds, see δέ and καί
41 omit therefore [L]TTrAWH
10:19 omit therefore LTTrAWH
20*for δέ T
31 omit then T[Tr]WH
39 omit therefore [TrAWH]R
12: 4 then—but, δέ T[WH]R
29 [therefore] LTrWH
34*ἀπεκρίθη—add o. read the people therefore TAWH
13:22 omit then T[Tr]AWH
25*for δέ T
26*answered—add o. therefore [L]AWH R
26*add o. TTrAWH R, see βάπτω
31 ὅτε—add o. A.V.BELTTrAWH R
16:19 omit now GTTrAWWH R
18: 4 therefore—and, δέ Tr
24 ἀπέστειλεν—add o. A.V.B ELT[Tr]AWH R
31 omit therefore (o.²) LTrAWH
19: 4 omit therefore GLTTrAWH R, see καί
10 omit then T[A]
15*add o. TTrAWH R, see ἐκεῖνος
16*for δέ LTTrAWH
29 omit now Eds
29*for δέ LTTrAWH R, see πλήθω
21:11*went up—add o. therefore TrAWH
13 omit then GLTTrAWH
21*τοῦτον o. read Peter therefore LTTrAWH

Acts 6: 3 wherefore—but, δέ TWH, δή L
15: 2 therefore—but, δέ TTrWH
39 δέ LTTrAWH
16:11 therefore—and, δέ TA
18:14 omit o. LTTr.[A]WWH R
20:28 omit therefore [L]TTrAWH
25:11*for γάρ Eds
28: 9 so—and, δέ LTTrAWH
Ro. 3:28 therefore–for, γάρ GLTTrAWWH
9:19*why—add o. then L[A]W
11:13*μέν—add o. read inasmuch then LT[Tr]AWWH R
12:20 ἐὰν o.—ἀλλὰ ἐὰν but if LTTrA
13: 7 omit therefore Eds
14:12 omit then LTr[AWH]
1Co. 5: 7 omit therefore GEds
6: 7 omit therefore T[Tr]
2Co. 7:16 χαίρω—add o. A.V.BE
Gal. 5: 1 omit o. GEds: στήκετε—add o. Eds
Col. 2:20 omit wherefore GEds
1Th. 4: 1 omit then WH
2Ti. 2: 3 omit thou therefore Eds
4: 1 omit therefore GEds
Heb. 8: 4*for γάρ Eds
13:15 omit therefore [Tr]WH
Jas. 5:16*confess—add o. therefore LTTrAWH R
1Pet. 2:13 omit o. A.V.VulLTTrAWH
5: 1*elders—add o. therefore LTTrAWH
2Pet. 3:11 then—thus, οὕτως AWH
1Joh. 2:24 omit therefore LTTrAWH
Rev. 1:19*write—add o. therefore GEds
2:16*repent—add o. therefore GLT[A]WWH

οὔπω.

Mat. 15:17 not yet—not, οὐ LTTrWH R
Mar. 4:40*add o. LTrWH R, see οὐ
8:21*for οὐ LTTrAWH
11: 2*o. ἀνθρώπων LTrWH R, ἀνθ. o. T man yet
Lu. 23:53*οὐδεὶς o. for οὐδέπω οὐδείς LTrAWH R
Joh. 6:17*for οὐ LTTr.\WH R
7: 8 not yet¹—not, οὐ GTTrA
39*for οὐδέπω LTrAWH
Acts 8:16 οὐδέπω Eds
1Co. 8: 2*see οὐδέπω
Phil. 3:13*for οὐ TWH R

οὐρά.

Rev. 9:19*add o. A.V.C GEds, see ἐξουσία

οὐράνιος.

Mat. 5:48*ὁ οὐράνιος for ὁ ἐν τοῖς οὐρανοῖς (–νός) LTTrAWH R
18:35*οὐράνιος for ἐπουράνιος LTTrWH, [ἐπ]ο. A

Mat. 23: 9*ὁ οὐράνιος for ὁ ἐν τοῖς οὐρανοῖς (-νός) LTTrAWHR
Lu. 2:13 οὐρανός Tr

οὐρανός.

Mat. 5:48 ἐν τοῖς ο.—οὐράνιος, read your
heavenly Father LTTrAWHR
6: 1 τοῖς ο.—omit τοῖς T
7:21 ο.²—τοῖς οὐρανοῖς LTTrAWH
10:32, 33 τοῖς ο. LAWH, [τοῖς] ο. Tr
11:23 τοῦ ο.—omit τοῦ LTTrAWH
16: 2, 3 When it is evening to end
of verse 3 [TA][[WH]]
17 τοῖς ο.—omit τοῖς L[TrWH]
18:10 ἐν ο.¹—ἐν τῷ οὐρανῷ [L]A
18 τῷ ο.—omit τῷ bis LT[Tr]AWH
19:21 οὐρανοῖς TrAWH
24*τῶν οὐρανῶν for τοῦ θεοῦ (-ός)
LTTrA
22:30 τῷ οὐρανῷ LTTrAWH
23: 9 ἐν τοῖς ο.—οὐράνιος, read your
Father, the heavenly
LTTrAWH
24:30 τῷ ο.—omit τῷ LTTrAWH
Mar. 4: 4 omit of the air GEds
11:26 τοῖς ο.—omit τοῖς LA: omit the
verse TTrWH
Lu. 2:13*οὐρανοῦ for οὐρανίον (-νιος) Tr
10:15 τοῦ ο.—omit τοῦ LTTrWH
11: 2 omit which art in heaven
GTTrAWH
2 omit as in heaven, so in earth
G[L]TTrAWH
16 trs ἐξ ο. ἐζήτουν παρ' αὐτοῦ Eds
12:56 trs of the sky, and of the
earth A.V.C
15: 7 trs ἐν τῷ ο. ἔσται TAWH
17:24 ο.¹—τὸν οὐρανόν LTTrAWH
18:13 trs ἐπάραι εἰς τὸν ο. TTrAWH
22 τοῖς (omit τοῖς T[WH]) οὐρανοῖς LTTrAWH
22:43 τοῦ οὐρανοῦ LT,WH
43, 44 the verses [L][[WH]]
24:51 omit and carried up into
heaven T[[WH]]
Joh. 3: 5*τῶν οὐρανῶν for τοῦ θεοῦ(-ός) T
13 omit which is in heaven WH
6:58 τοῦ ο.—omit τοῦ LTTrAWH
Col. 4: 1 οὐρανῷ Eds
Heb.10:34 omit in heaven Eds
12:23 trs ἀπογεγραμμένων ἐν ο. GEds
2 Pet. 3:10 οἱ ο.—omit οἱ TA
1 Joh. 5: 7 omit in heaven to in earth
(verse 8) GEds
Rev. 6:14 ὁ οὐρανός A.V.CGEds
12:12 οἱ ο.—omit οἱ TTrAWH
16:17 omit of heaven Eds
21: 3 heaven—the throne, θρόνος
LTAWHR

οὖς.

Mar. 7:16 omit the verse T[TrA]WHR
Lu. 22:50 trs τὸ οὖς αὐτοῦ LTTrAWH

οὖσα, etc., see ὤν.

οὖτε.

Mar. 5: 3 οὐδέ Eds
14:68*for οὐ LTTrAWHR: for οὐδέ Eds
Lu. 12:24*for οὐ and οὐδέ TA
26 οὐδέ LTTrAWHR
27*see κοπιάω
20:36 οὐδέ LTrAWHR
Joh. 1:25 οὐδέ bis LTTrAWHR
Acts 2:31*for οὐ and οὐδέ Eds
4:12 οὐδέ LTTrWWHR
24:13 οὐδέ LTWHR
1 Co. 3: 2 οὐδέ GEds
6:10 ο.³—οὐ TAWHR
Gal. 1:12 οὐδέ LTr
6:15†trs ο. γάρ¹ TTrAWHR, see ἐν
1 Th. 2: 3 οὐδέ Eds
Jas. 3:12*see οὐδείς
Rev. 5: 3*for οὐδέ¹² T: for ο.³ LTTrWHR
9:20 ο.¹—οὐ A.V.CGWWHR, οὐδέ TA
12: 8 οὐδέ GEds
20: 4 οὐδέ Eds

οὗτος.

Mar. 8:35 omit the same GEds
Lu. 8:41*for αὐτός LT,WH
19: 2 αὐτός LTrAWHR, omit ο. T
20:30 omit took her to to end of
verse TTrAWH
Joh. 6:42 omit ο.² [L]TrAWH
7:46 omit ο. see ἄνθρωπος L[TrA]WHR
Acts 3:10 omit o. LT
10: 6 omit ο.² GEds, see ποιέω
42*for αὐτός LT,WHR
1 Co. 7:13*for αὐτός Eds

Heb.10:12*for αὐτός Eds
Jas. 1:25 omit he LTTrAWHR
Rev. 3: 5 the same—thus, οὕτως LTTrWH
17:11*for αὐτός T. (R

οὗτοι.

Mar. 4:18 these—others, ἄλλος GEds
18 omit ο. εἰσίν² A.V.C
20 these—those, ἐκεῖνος TTrAWHR
Lu. 13: 4 αὐτοί LTTrAWH
Joh. 17:11 αὐτοί TWH
Acts 13: 4 αὐτοί LTTrAWH
1 Co. 16:17 αὐτοί LAW
1 Joh.5: 7 omit in heaven to in earth
(verse 8) GEds
8 hi tres A.V.Vul

αὕτη.

Mat. 22:39*for αὐτῇ WH
Mar. 1:27 omit a. LTTrAWHR, see καινός
12:30 omit this (is) the first commandment TAWH
31 αὐτή LTr
14: 8 omit a. [L]T[Tr]AWHR
Lu. 2:37 αὐτή TTrAWH
38 αὐτή W, omit a. LTTrAWH
7:12 αὐτή WH
8:42 αὐτή WH
Ro. 7:10 αὐτή GW
16: 2 αὐτῇ GLTrAWWH
1 Co. 7:12*for αὐτῇ LTAWWH

οὕτω, οὕτως.

Mat. 5:46*for τὸ αὐτό LTrA
47 so—the same, τὸ αὐτό Eds
24:46 trs οὕτως ποιοῦντα LTTrAWH
Mar. 2: 8 omit so L[WH]
12 trs οὕτως οὐδέποτε TTrAWH
4:40 omit so LT,WHR, see οὐ
9: 3*can—add ο. thus TTrAWH
Lu. 6:10 omit so GTTrAWWHR
24:46 omit and thus it behoved
[L]TTrAWH
Joh. 8:59 omit going through to end of
verse GLTTrAWHR
13:25*ἐκεῖνος—add ο. read lying
thus T[Tr]AWWHR
1 Co. 14:25 omit and thus (καὶ ο.¹) GEds
2 Co. 11: 3 omit so LTTrAWH
Jas. 3: 6, 12 omit so Eds
2 Pet. 3:11*for οὖν AWHR
1 Joh. 2: 6 omit so LT,[A]WH
Rev. 3: 5*for οὗτος LTTrWHR

οὐχ, see οὐ.

οὐχί.

Mat. 13:55 οὐ LTTrAWH
Lu. 4:22*for οὐ LTTrAWH
17:17 οὐ LT,WH
18:30*for οὐ T,WH
23:39*for εἰ TTrAWHR
Joh. 6:42*for οὐ T,WH
7:42 οὐ LTrAWH
9: 9*add ο. [L]TTrAWHR, see λέγω
Acts 2: 7*for οὐ TrAWH
Ro. 2:26 οὐ LTTrWH
1 Co. 3: 4 οὐ LTTrAWHR
9: 8 οὐ Eds
10:18 οὐ LTAWWH
2 Co. 10:13 οὐ LTTrAWHR
Jas. 2: 6*for οὐ LW

ὀφειλή.

1 Co. 7: 3*ὀφειλήν for ὀφειλομένην (-λω)
εὔνοιαν GEds

ὀφείλημα.

Ro. 4: 4 τὸ ὀ.—omit τό GEds

ὀφείλω.

1 Co. 5:10 ὀφείλετε LTTrAWH
7: 3 due benevolence—(her) due,
ὀφειλήν GEds

ὄφελος.

Jas. 2:14, 16 τὸ ὀ.—omit τὸ LWH

ὀφθαλμοδουλεία, -λία TWH.

Col. 3:22 ὀφθαλμοδουλείᾳ LW

ὀφθαλμός.

Mat. 6:22 trs ᾖ ὁ ὀφ. σου ἁπλοῦς LTAWH
7: 5 trs ἐκ τοῦ ὀφ. σου τὴν δοκόν
LTTrAWH
20:33 trs οἱ ὀφθαλμοὶ ἡμῶν LTTrAWH
34 ὀ.¹—ὄμμα LTTrAWH
34 omit their eyes² LTTrAWH

Mar. 14:40 trs αὐτῶν οἱ ὀφθαλμοί TWH
Lu. 4:20 trs οἱ ὀφ. ἐν τῇ συναγωγῇ
TTrAWHR
Joh. 9:15 trs μου ἐπὶ τοὺς ὀφθ. GEds
Acts 9:18 trs αὐτοῦ ἀπὸ τῶν ὀφθ. LTTrAWH
1 Co. 12:21 ὁ ὀφθαλμός GEds
1 Pet. 3:12 οἱ ὀ.—omit οἱ LTTrAWH

ὄφις.

Rev. 20: 2 ὁ ὄφις ὁ ἀρχαῖος LTTrAWH

ὀφρύς.

Lu. 4:29 τῆς ὀ.—omit τῆς GTTrAWWHR

ὀχλέω.

Lu. 6:18 ἐνοχλέω TTrAWHR

ὄχλος.

Mat. 8:18 πολλοὺς ὀ.—ὄχλον a crowd LWH
12:15 omit ὀ. read many followed
LT[TrA]WHR
15:31 τὸν ὄχλον TAWHR
35 τῷ ὄχλῳ LTTrWHR (R
36 τοῖς ὄχλοις multitudes TTrAWH
Mar. 3:20 ὁ ὄχλος LTr,R, [ὁ] ὄχ. WH
32 trs περὶ αὐτὸν ὄχλος TTrAWH
6:33 omit οἱ ὀ. read they saw GEds
9:25 ὁ ὄχλος T
11:32*ὄχλον for λαόν (-ός) WH
Lu. 9:18 trs οἱ ὄχλοι λ-γουσιν TTrAWH
12:13 trs ἐκ τοῦ ὄχλου αὐτῷ TWH
22: 6 trs ἄτερ ὄχλου αὐτοῖς LTTrAWH
Joh. 7:12 ὀ.¹—τῷ ὄχλῳ T
40 trs ἐκ τοῦ ὄχλου οὖν LTTrAWH
12: 9 ὁ ὄχλος TWHR
12 ὁ ὄχλος WH
Acts 19:35 trs τὸν ὄχλον ὁ γραμματεύς WH

ὀψέ.

Mar. 11:11*for ὀψία TWH

ὄψιος, ὀψία.

Mat. 16: 2 when it is evening to end of
verse 3 [TA][[WH]]
Mar. 11:11 ὀψέ TWH

πάθημα.

Phil. 3:10 τῶν π.—omit τῶν TTrWH

παιδάριον.

Mat. 11:16 παιδίον GEds

παιδεία, παιδία (except Eph. 6:4) T.

παιδίον.

Mat. 11:16*παιδίοις for παιδαρίοις (-ριον)
GEds
15:38 trs children and women T
Mar. 7:30*trs τὸ παιδίον (π. for θυγατέρα
-τηρ) βεβλημένον ἐπὶ τὴν κλί-
νην καὶ τὸ δαι. ἐξε. LTTrAWH
Lu. 2:21 the child—him, αὐτόν GEds
9:47 παιδίον TrAWH

παῖς.

Lu. 1:69 τοῦ π.—omit τοῦ LTTrAWH
Acts 4:25 τοῦ π.—omit τοῦ GEds

πάλαι.

Mar. 15:44 any while—already, ἤδη LT,WH
2 Co.12:19*for πάλαι LTTrAWH

παλαιός.

Mar. 2:21 ἱμάτιον παλαιόν LTTrAWHR

παλιγγενεσία, παλινγ- TWH.

πάλιν.

Mat. 13:44 omit again [L]TTrAWH
26:44*saying—add π. again TWHR
Mar. 7:14*for πάντα (πᾶς) LTTrAWH
8: 1*add π. LTTrAWHR, see πάμπολυς
11: 3*π. ὧδε again hither TTrWHR
12: 5 omit again GLTTrAWH
14:40 trs π. after καὶ² LAWHR, omit
again Tr
69 omit again A, see ἄρχω
Lu. 6:43*neither—add π. again
[L]T[Tr]AWHR
Joh. 9:26 omit again LTTrAWH
10: 7 omit unto them again T
39 omit again T: trs αὐτόν π. WH
12:22 and again—cometh, ἔρχομαι
LTTrAWH
18:33 trs π. εἰς τὸ πραιτ. LT,TrAWHR

Acts 10:16 again–immediately, εὐθύς Eds
17:32† *trs* περὶ τούτου καὶ π. LTTrAWHR
2 Co. 12:19 again—πάλαι, *read* ye think
all this time LTTrAWHR

παμπληθεί, πανπ– TWH.

πάμπολυς.

Mar. 8: 1 very great—again great, πάλιν
πολλοῦ LTTrAWHR

Παμφυλία.

Acts 14:24 τὴν Παμφυλίαν TTrWH

πανδοχεῖον.

Lu. 10:34 πανδοκίον T

πανδοχεύς.

Lu. 10:35 πανδοκεί T

πανοικί.

Acts 16:34 πανοικει TAWI

* *πανταχῇ, –χῇ* LTrWH, everywhere.

Acts 21:28 *for* πανταχοῦ LTTrAWWH

πανταχόθεν.

Mar. 1:45 πάντοθεν Eds

πανταχοῦ.

Mar. 1:28* εὐθύς—*add* π. *read* abroad
everywher TrJAWHR
Acts 21:28 πανταχῆ LTTrAWWH

πάντῃ, –η TA.

πάντοθεν.

Mar. 1:45* *for* πανταχόθεν Eds
Joh. 18:20 *for* πάντοτε[2] B

πάντοτε.

Joh. 18:20 always (π.[2])—πάντοθεν R: all,
πᾶς GEds

πάντως.

Acts 18:21 *omit* LTTrAWHR, see δεῖ

παρά.

Mat. 8:10* *add* π. LTTrAWH, see οὐδέ
20:20 ἀπό LTrAWH
21:25 with—among, ἐν LTrWH
Mar. 2:13 by—to, εἰς T
16: 9* *for* ἀπό LTrWHR
Lu. 10:39 πρός TTrAWH
18:14* *for* ἢ LTrAWH
Joh. 16:28 ἐκ LTTrAWHR
Acts 4:37 πρός T
5:16 προς LTTrAWHR
18:20 *omit* with them LTTrAWHR
22:30 ὑπό Eds
26:12 *omit* π. LTTrWHR
22 ἀπό Eds
28:14* *for* ἐπί LTTrAWHR
Ro. 11:25 ἐν TrAWH
2 Co. 8: 3* *for* ὑπέρ Eds
2 Pet. 2:11 before the Lord L[TrWH]
1 Joh. 3:22 ἀπό LTTrAWHR
5:15 ἀπό LTTrWH

παραβαίνω.

2 Joh. 9 transgresseth—goeth for–
ward, προάγω Eds

παραβάλλω.

Mar. 4:30 compare—set forth, τίθημι
LTTrAWHR

* *παραβολεύομαι,* to venture.

Phil. 2:30 παραβολευσάμενος *for* παρα–
βουλευσάμενος (–λεύομαι)GEds

παραβολή.

Mat. 22: 1 *trs* ἐν π. αὐτοῖς LTTrAWHR
Mar. 4:10 τάς παραβολάς the parables
TTrAWHR
7:17 τὴν παραβολήν LTTrAWHR
Lu. 8: 9 *trs* αὐτη εἰη ἡ π. TWH
20:19 *trs* εἶπεν τὴν π. ταύτην LTTrAWH

παραβουλεύομαι.

Phil. 2:30 not regarding—hazarding,
παραβολεύομαι GEds

παραγγέλλω.

Mat. 15:35* παραγγείλας *for* ἐκέλευσεν
(κελεύω) LTTrWHR

Mar. 8: 6 παραγγέλλει commandeth
LTTr·WHR
Lu. 8:29 παρήγγελλεν 8 – παρήγγειλεν
A.V.BEG
Acts 1: 4 *trs* αὐτοῖς π. AW
17:30 commandeth—sendeth word
to, ἀπαγγέλλω TWH
1 Co. 11:17 παραγγέλλω LTrAW

παραγίνομαι.

Lu. 8:19 παρεγένετο TTrWH
Acts 5:22 *trs* π. ὑπηρέται LTTrAWH
10:32 *omit* who, when he cometh,
to end of verse LTTr·[A]WH
24:17 *trs* παρεγ. *after* μου LTTrAWH
2 Ti. 4:16* παρεγένετο *for* συμπαρεγένετο
(–ραγίνομαι) LTTrWHR

παράγω.

Mar. 1:16* καὶ παράγων *for* περιπατῶν
(–τέω) δέ LTTrAWHR
Joh. 8:59 *omit* going through to end of
verse GLTTrAWHR

παραδειγματίζω.

Mat. 1:19 δειγματίζω LTTrAWH

παράδεισος.

Rev. 2: 7 τῷ παραδείσῳ GEds

παραδέχομαι.

Acts 15: 4* παρεδέχθησαν *for* ἀπεδέχθησαν
(ἀποδ·χομαι) Eds

παραδιατριβή.

1 Ti. 6: 5 διαπαρατριβή GEds

παραδίδωμι.

Mat. 5:25 *omit* deliver thee[2] LT[Tr]WH
10:19 παραδῶσιν LTTr·WH
27: 3 παραδούς LTr·WH
Mar. 4:29 παραδοῖ LTTr·WH
14:10†trs αὐτὸν παραδοῖ TTrAWH, π.
α. L
11†trs αὐτὸν εὐκαίρως παραδοῖ
(–δῶ W) LTTrAWWH
Lu. 10:22 *trs* μοι παρεδόθη GLTTrAWWH
12:58 παραδώσει LTTrAWHR
20:20 εἰς τό π.—ὥστε π. LTTrAWH
22: 4 *trs* αὐτοῖς π. αὐτόν LTTrAWH
Joh. 6:71 *trs* παραδιδόναι αὐτόν LTTr·WH
13: 2 παραδοῖ LTTrAWHR, see Ἰούδας
19:11 παραδούς LTWHR
Acts 16: 4 παρεδίδοσαν LTTrAWWH
28:16 *omit* the centurion to the
guard: but LTTrAWH
1 Co. 11:23 π.[2]—παρέδιδετο LTTrAWH
15:24 παραδιδοῖ LTTrAR, –διδῷ WH

παραθήκη.

1 Ti. 6:20* παραθήκην *for* παρακαταθήκην
(–θήκη) GEds
2 Ti. 1:14* παραθήκην· *for* παρακαταθήκην
(–θήκη) GEds

παραιτέομαι.

Mar. 15: 6* παρητοῦντο *for* ᾐτοῦντο (αἰτέω)
TWH
Lu. 14:18 *trs* πάντες π. LTTrAWH

* *παρακαθέζομαι,* to sit down near.

Lu. 10:39 παρακαθεσθεῖσα *for* παρακα–
θίσασα (–τίζω) TTrA WH

παρακαθίζω.

Lu. 10:39 παρακαθέζομαι TTrAWHR

παρακαλέω.

Mar. 5:23 παρακαλεῖ beseecheth TTrAWH
Lu. 7: 4 besought—asked, ἐρωτάω T (R
8:31 παρεκάλουν A.V.Er LTTrAWH
32 παρεκάλεσαν LTTrAWH
Acts 16:40 *trs* π. τοὺς ἀδελφούς LTTrAWHR
20: 1* and[2]—*add* παρακαλέσας ex–
horted LTTrAWHR
2 Co. 1: 6 *trs* εἴτε παρακαλούμεθα τὸ σω–
τηρίας[2] *after* ὑπὲρ ὑμῶν LTrAW
2 Ti. 4: 2 *trs* exhort, rebuke T

παρακαταθήκη.

1 Ti. 6:20 παραθήκη GEds
2 Ti. 1:14 παραθήκη GEds

παρακολουθέω.

Mar. 16:17 ἀκολουθέω TrWH

---

2 Ti. 3:10 παρηκολούθησας didst fully
know (or follow) LTTrAWHR

παρακούω.

Mar. 5:36* παρακούσας *for* ἀκούσας (ἀκ–
ούω) TTrAWH

παρακύπτω.

Lu. 24:12 *omit the verse* [L]T[Tr][[WH]]

παραλαμβάνω.

Lu. 17:34, 35 παραλημφθήσεται LTTrAWH
36 *add the verse* A.V.BE, see
ἀφίημι
Joh. 14: 3 παραλήμψομαι LTTrAWH
2 Th. 3: 6 παρελάβοσαν they received
GATWR, –βετε ye received
LTrWH

παραμένω.

Phil. 1:25* παραμενῶ *for* συμπαραμενῶ
LTTrAWHR

παραπορεύομαι.

Mar. 2:23 διαπορεύομαι LTr·WHR
9:30 πορεύομαι LTr·WH
11:20 *trs* π. πρωΐ LTTrAWHR

παράπτωμα.

Mat. 6:15 *omit* their trespasses T[WH]
18:35 *omit* their trespasses GLTTr·A
Mar. 11:26 *omit the verse* TTr·WHR (WH
Jas. 5:16 faults–sins, ἁμαρτία LTTr·WHR

παραρρέω.

Heb. 2: 1 παραρυῶμεν LTTrAWH

παρασκευή.

Lu. 23:54 παρασκευῆς LTTrAWHR
Joh. 19:31 *trs* ἐπεὶ π. ἦν *after* Ἰουδαῖοι
A.V.Er TTrAWH

παρατηρέω, –ομαι.

Lu. 6: 7 παρετηροῦντο Eds
Acts 9:24 παρετηροῦντο Eds

παρατίθημι.

Mar. 6:41 παρατιθῶσιν TAWH
8: 6 π.[1]—παρατιθῶσιν TTrAWH
7†trs αὐτὰ εἶπεν καὶ ταῦτα παρα–
τιθέναι TrWHR: αὐτὰ παρέ–
θηκεν TA
Lu. 9:16 παραθεῖναι TTrAWH
23:46 παρατίθεμαι A.V.Vul Eds

παραφέρω.

Lu. 22:42 παρενέγκαι T, –ένεγκε A.V.Vul
LTrWHR
Heb.13: 9* παραφέρεσθε *for* περιφέρεσθε
(–φέρω) GEds
Jude 12* παραφερόμεναι *for* περιφερόμε–
ναι (–φέρω) GEds

παραχρῆμα.

Acts 9:18 *omit* forthwith GLTTrAWHR

* *παρεδρεύω,* to sit by, serve.

1 Co. 9:13 παρεδρεύοντες *for* προσεδρεύ–
οντες (–δρεύω) Eds

πάρειμι.

Lu. 11:42* παρεῖναι *for* ἀφιέναι (ἀφίημι)
LTTrAWH
Rev. 17: 8* *for* ἐστίν[3] GEds, see καίπερ

παρεισδύνω.

Jude 4 παρεισεδύησαν WH

* *παρεμβάλλω,* to put in beside.

Lu. 19:43 παρεμβαλοῦσιν *for* περιβαλοῦ–
σιν (–βάλλω) TWH

παρέρχομαι.

Mat. 14:15 *trs* παρῆλθεν ἤδη T
24:35 π.[1]—παρελεύσεται GLTTrAWH
26:39 παρελθάτω LTTrAWH
Mar. 13:31 π.[1]—παρελεύσεται GW
31 π.[2]—παρελεύσονται TTrAWH
Lu. 21:33 π.[2]—παρελεύσονται LTTrAWH
Acts 24: 7 *omit* and would have judged
(*verse* 6) to to come unto
thee (*verse* 8) LTTr·[A]WHR
Rev. 21: 1 ἀπέρχομαι GEds

παρέχω.

Lu. 7: 4 παρέξῃ LTTᵣAWH
Acts 28: 2 παρεῖχαν LTTᵣAWH

παρθενία, παρθενεία ᴀ.

παρθένος.

Acts 21: 9 trs τέσσαρες παρθ. LTTᵣAWH
1 Co. 7:28 [ἡ] π. LTᵣAWH
34 see γυνή
38*add π. LTTᵣ[A]WHR, see ἐκγαμίζω

παρίστημι.

Mar. 14:69 παρεστῶσιν TTᵣAWH
15:35 παρεἰστώτων T
Joh. 18:22 trs π. τῶν ὑπηρετῶν LTTᵣAWH
Acts 1:10 παριστήκεισαν WH
1 Co. 8: 8 παραστήσει, read will not commend us LTTᵣAWH

παρομοιάζω.

Mat. 23:27 ὁμοιάζω LTᵣ

παρόμοιος.

Mar. 7: 8 omit (as) the washing to end of verse T[TᵣA]WHR

παροργισμός.

Eph. 4:26 τῷ π.—omit τῷ LTTᵣ[A]WHR

παροψίς.

Mat. 23:26 omit and platter TA[WH]

πᾶς, πᾶσα, πᾶν.

Mat. 5:32*πᾶς ὁ for ὃς ἂν LTTᵣAWH
13:44 omit πάντα WH
18:29 omit all [L]TTᵣAWWH
19:20 trs ταῦτα πάντα LTᵣWH
23:36 trs πάντα ταῦτα LTᵣA
24: 2 trs ταῦτα πάντα LTTᵣAWH
6 omit all LTTᵣ[A]WH
33 trs ταῦτα πάντα TTᵣ
Mar. 1: 5 trs all they of Jerusalem, and were baptised GLTTᵣAWH
27 ἅπας TTᵣWH
4:11 τὰ π.—omit τὰ T
5:12 omit all G[L]TTᵣAWWH
40*πάντας for ἅπαντας (ἅπας) GEds
7:14 all—again πάλιν LTTᵣAWH
9:49 omit π.² T[Tᵣ]WHR, see ἅλς
12:28 πάντων GEds, †trs ἐντολή πρώτη π. TTᵣAWH
29 πάντων GLW: omit TTᵣAWH, see ἐντολή
13:30 trs ταῦτα πάντα TTᵣAWH
Lu. 1:75 πάσαις ταῖς ἡμέραις WH
2:39*πάντα for ἅπαντα (ἅπας) TTᵣWHR
3:16*πᾶσιν πᾶσιν ὁ ᾽Ιω. TWH
4: 4 omit but by every word of God T[Tᵣ]AWHR
7 πᾶσα GEds
40 ἅπαντα WH
5.⸵⸲*πάντα for ἅπαντα (ἅπας)LTTᵣAWH
28*πάντα for ἅπαντα LTTᵣAWH
7:16*πάντας for ἅπαντες GTᵣAWH
8:54 omit put them all out, and LTTᵣAWH
12:15*πάσης for τῆς, read all covetousness Eds
31 omit all [L]TTᵣAWH
14:10*ἐνώπιον—add πάντων, read presence of all LTTᵣAWH
17 omit π. [L]T[TᵣA]WHR
15:13*πάντα for ἅπαντα (ἅπας) LTᵣAWH
16:18 omit whosoever,² read he that LTTᵣAWH
17:27, 29*πάντας for ἅπαντας LTᵣAWH
18:28 all—our own, τὰ ἴδια LTTᵣAWH
19: 7*πάντες for ἅπαντες Eds
37 πάντων LTᵣ
20: 6 ἅπας TTᵣWH
32 omit of all LTTᵣAWH
21: 4*πάντα for ἅπαντα LWH
4*πάντα for ἅπαντα LTᵣWH
12*πάντων for ἁπάντων GEds
24 ἅπας TTᵣWH
24: 9 trs πάντα ταῦτα T
Joh. 3:31 omit what is above all² T
4:25 ἅπας TTᵣWH
10: 4*πάντα for πρόβατα¹ (—τον) LTTᵣAWH
16:13 πάσῃ T, see ἀλήθεια
18:20*πάντοτε for πάντοτε GEds
40 omit all TWH
21:17 trs πάντα σύ LTTᵣAWH
Acts 2: 1*πάντες for ἅπαντες LTTᵣAWH
4*πάντες for ἅπαντες LTTᵣWH

Acts 2: 7 omit all¹ L[Tᵣ]AWH
7 π.²—ἅπας LTAR
14*πάντες for ἅπαντες LTTᵣWHR
43*add π. T, see φόβος
3:21 omit all² GEds
4:32*πάντα for ἅπαντα LWH
5:12*πάντες for ἅπαντες LTᵣWH
6:15*πάντες for ἅπαντες LTTᵣWHR
11: 8 omit π. GEds
13:29*πάντα for ἅπαντα GEds
15:17 omit all² GEds
18 omit unto God are all his works GTTᵣAWH, om. all LW
16:33 ἅπας TWH
17:25 κατὰ πάντα 8—καὶ τὰ π. A.V.B EGEds
26 παντὸς προσώπου LTTᵣAWHR
30 πάντας LTTᵣAWH
21:21 omit all L[Tᵣ]
22:30*πᾶν for ὅλον (ὅλος) GEds
25:24 π.²—ἅπας Eds
Ro. 3:22 omit and upon all LTTᵣ[A]WHR
9:33 omit whosoever, read he that Eds
16:16*ἐκκλησίαι—add πᾶσαι, read all the churches GEds
24 omit the verse LTTᵣ[A]WHR
1 Co. 9:22 τὰ π.—omit τὰ Eds
23*πάντα for τοῦτο Eds
10:11 omit all [L]TTᵣ[A]WHR
12:19 [τὰ] π. LTᵣAWH
15:28 τὰ π.³—omit τὰ LTᵣAWH
2 Co. 5:17 omit all things LTTᵣAWH
Gal. 3:28 ἅπας TTᵣA
4:26 omit all G[L]TTᵣAWH
Eph. 1:22 π.¹—τὰ πάντα W
23 τὰ πάντα GEds
3: 9 omit all¹ [L]TWH
Phil. 4:23 you all—your spirit, τοῦ πνεύματος ὑμῶν Eds
Col. 2: 2 πᾶν Eds
3:11 τὰ π.—omit τὰ T'WH
23 omit π. Eds
2 Th. 2:12 ἅπας TTᵣA
1 Ti. 1:16 ἅπας Eds
6:17 trs π. πλουσίως GEds
Heb. 3: 4 τὰ π.—omit τὰ Eds
2 Pet. 1: 3 τὰ πάντα T
1 Joh. 2:20 ye know all things—ye all know, πάντες TWH
Jude 5*πάντα for τοῦτο Eds
25*add π. Eds, see αἰών
Rev. 5:13 π.²—πάντας W
6:15 omit every² Eds
7: 1 τις (τις) LT[A]WH
21: 5 trs ποιῶ πάντα Eds
7 all things—these things ταῦτα GEds
22:21 omit all TᵣAWH, see ἅγιος

πάσχω.

Mat. 17:15 ἔχω LTᵣWH
1 Pet. 3:18 suffered—died, ἀποθνήσκω LTTᵣWH

πιτάσσω.

Rev. 19:15 πατάξῃ GEds

πατήρ.

Mat. 2:22 trs τοῦ π. αὐτοῦ 'H. LTTᵣAWH
23: 9 trs ὑμῶν ὁ πατὴρ LTTᵣWH
Mar. 10:29 trs mother or father LTTᵣA
11:26 omit the verse TTᵣWH , (WH
Lu. 2:33*ὁ πατὴρ αὐτοῦ his father for Joseph GTTᵣAWH
23:34 see λέγω
Joh. 5:30 | 6:39 omit π. read the will of him that GEds
6:40*τοῦ πατρός μου for τοῦ πέμψαντός (πέμπω) με LTTᵣAWH
46 the Father²—God, θεός T
8:16 omit π. read he T[WH]
29 omit ὁ π. read he LTTᵣAWH
38 τῷ π. ὑμῶν—τοῦ πατρός LTTᵣAWH
44 π.¹—τοῦ πατρός GLTTᵣAWH
10:17 trs με ὁ πατὴρ LTTᵣAWH
38*τῷ πατρὶ for αὐτῷ LTTᵣAWH
15:10†trs τοῦ π. (μου T) τὰς ἐντολὰς TAWH
16:16 omit because I go to the Father LTTᵣAWH
27*πατρός for θεοῦ (—ός) TᵣAWH
17:21 πατὴρ TᵣWH
24, 25 πατήρ LTTᵣAWH (WH
Acts 3:22 omit unto the fathers GEds
4:25*ὁ πατρὸς ἡμῶν διὰ πνεύματος ἁγίου, read who by the Holy Spirit, (by) the mouth of our father LTTᵣAWH

Acts 7:14 trs 'Ιακωβ τον π. αὐτου Εas
16: 3†trs ὅτι ᾽Ελλην ὁ π. αὐτοῦ LTTᵣWH
Ro. 4: 1 father—forefather, προπάτωρ LTTᵣAWH
Eph. 5:31 τὸν π.—omit τὸν LTᵣA[WH]
Col. 2: 2 omit and of the Father, and of GEds
1 Th. 1: 1 omit from God our to end of verse [L]TTᵣAWH
2 Th. 2:16 ὁ πατὴρ LTTᵣAWH
1 Joh.2:23*add π. see ὁμολογέω A.V.B GEds
5: 7 omit in heaven to in earth (verse 8) GEds

πατραλῴης, πατρο- LTTᵣAWH.

Παῦλος.

Acts 13:13 τὸν Π.—omit τὸν LTTᵣAWWH
45 τοῦ Π.—omit τοῦ LTTᵣ[A]WH
14:11 ὁ Π.—omit ὁ LTTᵣAWWH
15:36 trs πρὸς Βαρνάβαν Π. LTTᵣWH
16: 9 trs τῷ Π. ὤφθη TTᵣAWH
14 τοῦ Π.—omit τοῦ TTᵣWH
18 ὁ Π.—omit ὁ TTᵣWH
28 ὁ Π.—omit ὁ LTTᵣWH: trs Π. μεγάλη φωνῇ WH, Π. φ. μ. L
17:22 ὁ Π.—omit ὁ LTTᵣWH
18: 1 omit ὁ Π. read he LTTᵣAWH
19:13 ὁ Π.—omit ὁ LTTᵣAWH
29 τοῦ Π.—omit τοῦ GLTTᵣAWH
30 τοῦ δὲ Π.—Π. δέ LTTᵣAWWH
21: 8 omit that were of Paul's company GEds
23: 1 trs τῷ συνε. ὁ Π. LTTᵣ: omit ὁ WH
11 omit Paul GEds
24:23 Paul—him, αὐτόν GEds
25: 7 omit against Paul LTTᵣAWH
8*ἀπολ. αὐτοῦ— τοῦ Παύλου ἀπολ. read Paul answered LTTᵣAWH
26:25*ὁ δέ—add Παῦλος, read but Paul said LTTᵣWWHR
27:11 τοῦ Π.—omit τοῦ LTTᵣ[A]WWH
28:17 Paul—he, αὐτόν GEds
30 omit ὁ Π. read he GEds
1 Co. 3: 5 trs Apollos and Paul Eds

πεζῇ, see πεζός.

* πεζός, on foot, walking.

Mat. 14:13 πεζοί for πεζῇ T

πειθός, πιθός WH.

πείθω, πέποιθα.

Mar. 10:24 omit for them that trust in riches TWH
Acts 26:28 πείθῃ χ. ποιῆσαι, read thou persuadest thyself to make me a Christian A
27:11 trs μᾶλλον ἐπείθετο LTTᵣAWH
Gal. 3: 1 omit that ye should not obey the truth GEds
Heb.11:13 omit and were persuaded of (them) GEds
13:18 we trust—πειθόμεθα we are persuaded Eds

πειράζω.

Lu. 20:23 omit why tempt ye me ? TTᵣAWH
Acts 9:26*ἐπείραζεν for ἐπειρᾶτο (πειράω) LTTᵣAWH
1 Co.10: 9 ἐκπειράζω T
Heb. 4:15 πεπειρασμένον for πεπειραμέ (πειράω) A.V.B EGEds
11:37 trs were tempted, were sawn asunder TWH
Rev. 2: 2 ἐπείρασας GEds

πειρασμός.

2 Pet. 2: 9 πειρασμῶν A.V.C T

πειράω.

Acts 9:26 πειράζω LTTᵣWH
Heb. 4:15 πειράζω A.V.B EGEds

πέμπω.

Lu. 7:10 trs εἰς τὸν οἶκον οἱ π. LTTᵣWH
20:11 trs ἕτερον πέμψαι LTTᵣAWH
12 trs τρίτον πέμψαι LTTᵣAWH
Joh. 6:40 him that sent me—my Father, πατὴρ LTTᵣAWH
Acts 25:21 ἀναπέμπω Eds
2 Th. 2:11 πέμπει sendeth Eds
Rev. 11:10 πέμπουσιν send T

πενθερά.

Lu. 4:38 ἡ π.—*omit* ἡ GEds

πέντε.

Mat. 25: 2 αἱ π.—*omit* αἱ EGEds

πεντήκοντα.

Acts 13:20 *see* ἔτος

* **περαιτέρω**, further, more.

Acts 19:3ᵇ ᵲ ιραιτέρω *for* περὶ ἐτέρων (-ρος) LTᵣWH

πέραν.

Mar. 5:21 *trs* εἰς τὸ πέραν πάλιν T
  10: 1 τοῦ π.—*omit* τοῦ LTTᵣAWHR

Πέργη.

Acts 14:25 εἰς τὴν Πέργην T

περί.

Mat. 18: 6*for ἐπί LTTᵣWHR
  19:17*add π. GEds, *see* ἀγαθός
Mar. 7:17 *omit* concerning LTTᵣAWHR
  14:24 ὑπέρ LTTᵣAWHR, *see* ἐκχύνω
Lu. 6:28*for ὑπέρ TAWH
Joh. 1:30 ὑπέρ LTTᵣAWHR
  8: 5*add π. WR, *see* αὑτῆς
  11:19 τὰς περὶ—τὴν LTᵣAWHR
Acts 10: 3*ὡσεί—*add* π. Eds
  12: 5*for ὑπέρ LTTᵣWHR
  19:39 concerning other matters—
   further, περαιτέρω LTᵣWH
  40*λόγον—*add* π. LTTᵣWHR
  21: 8 *omit* that were of Paul's
   company GEds
  26: 1*for ὑπέρ LTTᵣA
Ro. 1: 8*for ὑπέρ Eds
2 Co. 1: 8*for ὑπέρ LTTᵣR
Gal. 1: 4*for ὑπέρ GLTTᵣAW
Col. 1: 3 ὑπέρ LTᵣ
  2: 1 ὑπέρ LTTᵣAWHR
1 Th. 3: 2 ὑπέρ GEds
  5:10*for ὑπέρ TTᵣWH
Heb. 5: 3*for ὑπέρ Eds
  13:11 *omit* for sin A

περιαιρέω.

Acts 28:13*περιελόντες *for* περιελθόντες
  (-έρχομαι) WH

* **περιάπτω**, to fasten round.

Lu. 22:55 περιαψάντων *for* ἀψάντων
  (ἅπτω) TTᵣAWHR

περιαστράπτω.

Acts 9: 3 περιήστραψεν S, περιεσ—E

περιβάλλω.

Lu. 19:43 shall cast about—shall place
  near, παρεμβάλλω TWH
Rev. 7: 9 περιβεβλημένους GEds
  11: 3 περιβεβλημένοι TᵣWH
  17: 4 ἡ π.—ἦν π. A.V.C GEds

περιδρέμω, *see* περιτρέχω.

περιέρχομαι.

Acts 28:13 περιαιρέω WH

περιέχω.

Acts 23:25 ἔχω LTTᵣWHR, [περι]ἰ. A

περιζώννυμι.

Acts 12: 8 ζώννυμι LTTᵣAWHR

περίλυπος.

Lu. 18:24 *omit* that he was very sorrowful, *read* saw him T[Tᵣ]AWHR

περιπατέω.

Mar. 1:16 as he walked—as he passed
  along, παράγω LTTᵣAWHR
  2: 9 walk—go, ὑπάγω T
  6:49 *trs* ἐπὶ τῆς θαλάσσης π. TWH
  7: 5 *trs* οὐ π. οἱ μαθη. σου TTᵣAWH
Lu. 11:44 οἱ π.—*omit* οἱ L[A]W
Joh. 8:12 περιπατήσῃ Eds
Acts 14: 8 περιεπατηκει S—περιεπ. E,
  περιεπάτησεν LTTᵣAWHR
Ro. 8: 1 *omit* who walk *to end of*
  verse GEds
1 Th. 2:12 περιπατεῖν Eds

---

1 Th. 4: 1*God—*add* καθὼς καὶ περιπα-
  τεῖᵛε even as ye do walk Eds
Heb.13: 9 περιπατοῦντες are occupied
  LTTᵣWH

περιποιέομαι.

Lu. 17:33*περιποιήσασθαι *for* σῶσαι (σώζω) TTᵣAWHR

* **περιρραίνω**, to besprinkle.

Rev. 19:13 περιρεραμμένον *for* βεβαμμένον
  (βάπτω) T

περιρρήγνυμι.

Acts 16:22 περιρήξαντες LTTᵣAWH

περίσσευμα.

Lu. 6:45 τοῦ π.—*omit* τοῦ LTTᵣAWHR

περισσεύω.

Mat. 15:37 *trs* τὸ π. τῶν κλ. ἦραν LTTᵣAWH
Lu. 15:17 περισσεύονται TᵣAWH
Joh. 6:13 ἐπερίσσευσαν LTTᵣAWH
1 Co. 8: 8†*trs* μὴ φάγωμεν ὑστερούμεθα
  (περισσεύομεν L) οὔτε ἐὰν φάγωμεν περισσεύομεν (-νόμεθα
  TᵣR, ὑστερούμεθα L) LTᵣAWH

περισσός, περισσότερος.

Mat. 23:14(13) *omit the verse* LTTᵣAWHR,
  see κρίμα
Mar. 6:51 *omit* beyond measure[Tᵣ]WHR
  12:33*περισσότερον *for* πλεῖον TTᵣWHR
  14:31 ἐκ π.—ἐκπερισσῶς LTTᵣAWHR

περισσοτέρως.

Mar. 15:14 περισσῶς GEds
2 Co. 11:23 *trs* π. ἐν φυλακαῖς π. ἐν πληγαῖς
  ὑπερβ. LTᵣAWHR, π. ἐν πλ. π.
  ἐν φ. ὑπερβ. T

περισσῶς.

Mar. 15:14*for περισσοτέρως GEds

περιτέμνω.

Acts 15: 1 περιτμηθῆτε LTTᵣAWHR
  24 *omit* saying, (Ye must) be
  circumcised, and keep the
  law LTTᵣAWH

περιτίθημι.

Mat. 27:28 *trs* χλαμύδα κοκκίνην π. αὐτῷ
  LTTᵣAWH

περιτομή.

Phil. 3: 5 περιτομῇ GEds
Tit. 1:10 τῆς περιτομῆς TTᵣWH

περιτρέχω.

Mar. 6:55 περιέδραμον TTᵣWH

περιφέρω.

Heb.13: 9 carried about—carried away,
  παραφέρω GEds
Jude 12 carried about—carried along,
  παραφέρω GEds

περίχωρος.

Mar. 6:55 region round about—region,
  χώρα TTᵣAWH
Lu. 3: 3 τὴν π.—*omit* τὴν, *read* every
  country LTTᵣAWH

πετάομαι, πέτομαι GEds.

πετεινόν.

Acts 10:12 τὰ π.—*omit* τὰ LTTᵣAWHR

πέτρα.

Lu. 6:48 *omit* π.² TTᵣAWHR, *see* θεμελιόω
  8:13 τὴν πέτραν T
1 Co. 10: 4 *trs* δὲ LTTᵣAWH

Πέτρος.

Mat. 14:28 *trs* ὁ Π. εἶπεν αὐτῷ LWH
  29 ὁ Π.—*omit* ὁ LTTᵣAWH
  17:26 *omit* ὁ Π. LTTᵣAWHR, *see* λέγω
  18:21 *trs* ὁ Π. εἶπεν αὐτῷ LTTᵣAWHR
Mar. 5:37 τὸν Πέτρον TTᵣAWH
  8:32 *trs* ὁ Πέτρος αὐτὸν LTTᵣAWH
  33 τῷ Π.—*omit* τῷ LTTᵣAWH
  10:28 *trs* λέγειν ὁ Πέτρος TAWH
  13: 3 ὁ Πέτρος T

Lu. 9:20†*trs* (*cm.* ὁ) Π. δὲ ἀποκριθεὶς
  TTᵣAWH
  28 τὸν Π.—*omit* τὸν GLTTᵣAWWH
  18:28 ὁ Π.—*omit* ὁ T[A]W
  22:62 *omit* ὁ Π. *read* he GTTᵣ[A]WHR
  24:12 *omit the verse* [L]T[Tᵣ][[WH]]
Joh. 13:37 ὁ Π.—*omit* ὁ GLTTᵣAW[WH]
  18:17 *trs* τῷ Π. ἡ παιδίσκη ἡ θυρωρός
  LTTᵣA
  18 *trs* ὁ Π. μετ᾽ αὐτῶν LTTᵣAWHR
  27 ὁ Π.—*omit* ὁ LTTᵣAWWH
Acts 2:14 ὁ Πέτρος LTTᵣAWH
  3: 1 *trs* Πέτρος δὲ LTTᵣAWHR
  12 ὁ Πέτρος LTTᵣAWH
  5: 3 ὁ Πέτρος LTTᵣAWH
  8, 29 ὁ Π.—*omit* ὁ LTTᵣAWWH
  8:14 τὸν Π.—*omit* τὸν LTTᵣAWWH
  10:23 *omit* Peter GEds, *see* ἀνίστημι
  46 ὁ Π.—*omit* ὁ LTTᵣAWWH
  11: 4 ὁ Π.—*omit* ὁ LTTᵣAWWH
  12:13 Peter—he, αὐτοῦ GEds
Gal. 1:18 & 2:11, 14 Peter—Cephas,
  Κηφᾶς Eds

πηγή.

Jas. 3:12 *omit* π. GEds, *see* οὐδείς

πήρα.

Mar. 6: 8 *trs* no bread, no scrip
  TTᵣAWH

Πιλάτος, —ᾶτος LTTᵣWH, **Πει—** TWH.

Mar. 15: 1 τῷ Π.—*omit* τῷ LTTᵣAWH
  43 τὸν Πιλάτον TTᵣWH
Lu. 23:12 *trs* Herod and Pilate TTᵣAWH
  24 ὁ δὲ Π.—καὶ Π. LTTᵣAWH (E
Joh. 18:31 ὁ Π.—*omit* ὁ TᵣAWH
  19: 4 *trs* ὁ Πειλάτος ἔξω T

πίμπλημι, *see* πλήθω.

πίμπραμαι, —ρημι.

Acts 28: 6 ἐμπιπράω T

πίνω, πίω, πίομαι.

Mat. 6:25 *omit* or what ye shall drink
  24:49 πίνῃ GEds   (T[WH]
  27:34 πεῖν bis T
Mar. 2:16 *omit* and drinketh [L]WH
  15:23 *omit* to drink TTᵣAWHR
Joh. 4: 7, 9, 10 πεῖν TTᵣAWH
Acts 23:12, 21 πεῖν WH
Ro. 14:21 πεῖν WH
1 Co. 9: 4 & 10:7 πεῖν TAWH
  10: 4 *trs* πνευματικὸν ἔπιον πόμα
  LTTᵣAWWH
Rev. 16: 6 πεῖν TAWH, πῖν L
  18: 3 have drunk of—have fallen
  by, πίπτω TᵣWHR: πέπωκαν
  LTW, πέπ[τ]ωκαν A

πίπτω, ἔπεσον.

Mat. 17: 6 ἔπεσαν LTTᵣAWH
  21:44 *omit the verse* [L]T[WH]
Mar. 13:25*πίπτοντες *for* ἐκπίπτοντες
  (ἐκπίπτω) LTTᵣAWH
  14:35 ἔπιπτεν TAWH
Lu. 6: 39 ἐμπίπτω LTTᵣAWHR
  49 fell—fell together, συμπίπτω
  TTᵣAWH
  8: 6 fell—fell down, καταπίπτω
  TTᵣAWH
  14: 5*πεσεῖται *for* ἐμπεσεῖται (ἐμπίπτω) LTTᵣAWH
  23:30 πέσατε TTᵣAWH
Joh. 18: 6 ἔπεσαν LTTᵣAWH
Acts 13:11*ἔπεσεν *for* ἐπέπεσεν (ἐπιπίπτω)
  LTTᵣWHR
  19:17*ἔπεσεν *for* ἐπέπεσεν (ἐπιπίπτω)
  LTᵣ
  22: 7 ἔπεσα LTTᵣAWH
  27:34 shall fall—shall perish,
  ἀπόλλυμι GEds
1 Co. 10: 8 ἔπεσαν LTTᵣAWH
  13: 8*πίπτει *for* ἐκπίπτει (-τω)
  LTTᵣAWH
Heb. 11:30 ἔπεσαν LTTᵣAWH
Rev. 2: 5*πέπτωκας (-κες TWH) *for* ἐκ-
  πέπτωκας (ἐκπίπτω) GEds
  5: 8 & 7:11 ἔπεσαν LTTᵣAWWH
  6:16 πέσατε LAWWH
  11:11 ἐπιπίπτω Eds
  16:19 ἔπεσαν LTTᵣAWWH
  18: 2 *omit* is fallen² Tᵣ[A]
  3*πέπτωκαν TᵣWHR, πέπ[τ]ωκαν A
  for πέπωκεν (πίνω)
  19: 4 ἔπεσαν S, ἔπεσον EG
  10 ἔπεσα LTTᵣAWWH
  22: 8 ἔπεσα S—ἔπεσον BG

Πισιδία.

Acts 13:14 τὴν Πισιδίαν LTTrAWH

πιστεύω.

Mat. 27:42 πιστεύομεν L, πιστεύσωμεν T
Mar. 9:23 omit believe TTr[A]WH
     42 believe — have faith, πίστιν ἐχόντων A
  11:23 πιστεύῃ TAWH
  13:21 πιστεύετε GLTTrAWWH
Lu. 8:50 πιστεύσον TTrAWH
Joh. 4:21 trs πίστευέ μοι, γύναι TTrAWH, πίστευε L
  6:29 πιστεύητε TTrAWH
  7:31 trs ἐκ τοῦ ὄχλου δὲ πολ. ἐπίσ. LTTrAWH, π. δὲ ἐπ. ἐκ τοῦ ὄχ. T
  39 πιστεύσαντες believed LTTrAWH
 10:38 π.¹ — πιστεύετε T   (R
  38 π.² — πιστεύετε LTTrWH
  38 believe³ — understand, γινώσκω LTTrAWH
 12:47 believe — keep (them), φυλάσσω Eds
 13:19 trs πιστεύσητε (-εύητε TrWH) ὅταν γένηται TTrAWH
 17:20 πιστευόντων believe GEds
 21 πιστεύῃ TTrWH
 19:35 ; 20:31 πιστεύητε TWH
Acts 2:44 πιστεύσαντες TWH
 8:37 omit the verse GLTTrAWH
 9:42 trs ἐπίσ. πολλοὶ LTTrAWH
 11:21 ὁ πιστεύσας LTTrAWH
Ro. 10:14 π.² — πιστεύσωσιν Eds
2Th. 1:10 π.¹ — πιστεύσασιν believed GEds
1 Pet. 1:21 do believe — are believers, πιστός LTTrAWH
Joh. 3:23 πιστεύωμεν LTTr, -εύ[σ]ωμεν A
 5:13 om. that believe on the name of the Son of God¹ GEds
 13 and that ye may believe — οἱ πιστεύοντες who believe GLW, τοῖς πιστεύουσιν unto you that believe TTrAWH

πίστις.

Mar. 9:42 πίστιν ἐχόντων for πιστευόντων (-τεύω) A
Acts 6: 8 of faith — of grace, χάρις GEds
 14: 9 trs ἔχει πίστιν LTTrAWH
Ro. 3:25 τῆς π. LTTrAWH
 5: 2 omit by faith [LTr]A[WH]
Eph. 2: 8 τῆς π. — omit τῆς LTTr[A]WH
Tit. 2:10 trs πᾶσαν πίστιν LTTrAWH
Rev. 2:19 trs charity, and faith, and service GLTAWH: faith, and charity, and service Tr

πιστός.

1 Ti. 5:16 omit πιστὸς ἢ (omit man or) LTTr[A]WH
1 Pet. 1:21 πιστοὺς for πιστεύοντας (πιστεύω) LTTrAWH
Rev. 21: 5 trs faithful and true GEds

πλανάω.

Mat. 24:24 πλανηθῆναι T, πλανᾶσθαι TrWH
1 Pet. 2:25 πλανώμενοι LTTrAWH
Rev. 2:20 καὶ διδάσκει καὶ πλανᾷ and she teacheth and seduceth GEds

πλείων, πλεῖον or πλέον

πλεῖστος.

Mat. 20:10 πλεῖον LTrAWH
 26:53 πλείω LTTrAWH
Mar. 4: 1 πλεῖστος for πολὺς TTrAWWH
 12:33 more — much more, περισσότερος TTrAWH
Lu. 21: 3 πλείω LTA
Acts 27:12 πλείονες LTTrAWH
1 Co. 15: 6 πλείονες LTTrAWWH

πλεονεξία.

Lu. 12:15 τῆς π. — πάσης π. all covetousness Eds
Ro. 1:29 trs maliciousness, covetousness T
2 Pet. 2:14 πλεονεξίας GEds

πλέω.

Rev. 18:17 πᾶς ὁ ἐπὶ τόπον πλέων every one that saileth any whither GEds

πληγή.

2 Co. 11:23 trs in prisons more frequent, in stripes above measure LTrAWH

Rev. 9:18 three — add πληγῶν plagues GEds

πλῆθος.

Acts 17: 4 trs πλῆθος πολὺ LTTrAWH
 21:22 omit TrWH, see δεῖ

πληθύνω.

Acts 9:31 ἐπληθύνετο was multiplied Eds
2 Co. 9:10 πληθύνει shall multiply GLTAWWHE: πληθύνει Tr

πλήθω.

Lu. 21:22 πλησθῆναι for πληρωθῆναι (-ρόω) GEds
Joh. 19:29 οἱ δὲ πλήσαντες σπόγγον ὄξ. καὶ — σπ. οὖν μεστὸν τοῦ (om. τοῦ T) ὄξ. LTTrAWH

πλημμύρα.

Lu. 6:48 πλημμύρης TTrAWH

πλήν.

Lu. 17: 1 π. οὐαὶ for οὐαὶ δέ LTTrWH
Joh. 8:10 omit WH, see γυνή

πλήρης.

Mar. 4:28 πλήρης σῖτος LTTrA
 6:43 πλήρωμα TTrAWH

πληροφορέω.

Col. 4:12 πεπληροφορημένοι for πεπληρωμένοι (πληρόω) Eds

πληρόω.

Mat. 27:35 omit that it might to end of verse GLTTrAWH
Mar. 15:28 omit the verse T[Tr]AWH
Lu. 21:22 πλήθω GEds
Gal. 5:14 πεπλήρωται Eds
Col. 4:12 complete — fully assured, πληροφορέω Eds
2 Joh. 12 trs πεπληρωμένη ᾖ LTWH
Rev. 6:11 πληρωθῶσιν LWWHR, πληρώσωσιν GTTrA

πλήρωμα.

Mar. 6:43 πληρώματα for πλήρεις (-ρης) TTrAWH
1 Co. 10:28 omit for the earth (is) the Lord's, and the fulness thereof Eds

ὁ πλησίον.

Lu. 10:36 trs π. δοκεῖ σοι GTTrAWWH
Heb. 8:11 neighbour — fellow citizen, πολίτης GEds
Jas. 4:12 πλησίον for ἕτερον (-ρος) LTTrAWH

πλοιάριον.

Mar. 4:36 little ships — ships πλοῖον GLTTrAWH
Lu. 5: 2 πλοιάρια for πλοῖα (-οῖον) TA
Joh. 6:22 boat² — ship, πλοῖον GLTTrAWH
 23 boats — ships, πλοῖον LWH
 24 πλοιάρια for πλοῖα (-οῖον) LTTrAWH

πλοῖον.

Mat. 8:23 τὸ π. — omit τὸ LTTrAWH
 9: 1 τὸ π. — omit τὸ LTT[A]WH
 13: 2 τὸ π. — omit τὸ LTTrAWH
 14:22 τὸ π. — omit τὸ LTTrAWH
Mar. 4: 1 trs εἰς τὸ (om. τὸ TTrWWH) π. ἐμβάντα LTTrAWH
 36 πλοῖα for πλοιάρια (-ριον) GLTTrAWH
 37 ἤδη γεμίζεσθαι τὸ πλοῖον the ship was now filling LTTrAWH
 8:13 omit into the ship TAWH: omit τὸ LTrW: [εἰς π.] Tr
Lu. 5: 2 ships — boats, πλοιάριον TA: trs πλοῖα δύο WH
 3 trs ἐκ τοῦ π. ἐδίδασκεν AWH, ἐν τῷ πλοίῳ ἐδί. T
 8:37 τὸ π. — omit τὸ LTTrAWH
Joh. 6:17 τὸ π. — omit τὸ TTrAWH
 21 trs ἐγένετο τὸ πλοῖον LTTrAWH
 22 πλοῖον for πλοιάριον GLTTrAWH
 23 πλοῖα for πλοιάρια (-ριον) LWH
 24 πλοιάριον LTTrAWH
Acts 21: 3 τὸ πλοῖον ἦν LTTrAWH
 27:37 trs αἱ πᾶσαι ψυχαὶ ἐν τῷ π. LTTrAWWH
Rev. 18:17 omit π. GEds, see πλέω
 19 τὰ πλοῖα Eds

πλούσιος.

Mat. 19:23 trs πλούσιος δυσκόλως LTTrAWH
Rev. 6:15 trs chief captains and the rich men GEds

πλοῦτος.

2 Co. 8: 2 τὸ πλοῦτος LTTrAWH
Eph. 1: 7 τὸ πλοῦτος Eds
 2: 7 τὸ ὑπερβάλλον πλοῦτος Eds
 3: 8 ἀνεξ. πλοῦτος Eds
 16 τὸ πλοῦτος Eds
Phil. 4:19 τὸ πλοῦτος Eds
Col. 1:27 τὸ πλοῦτος Eds
 2: 2 πᾶν (τὸ L[Tr]WH) πλοῦτος Eds
Rev. 5:12 τὸν πλοῦτον W

πλύνω.

Lu. 5: 2 ἔπλυνον LTTrAWH, -ναν T for ἀπέπλυναν (ἀποπλύνω)
Rev. 22:14 add π. LTTrAWH, see στολή

πνεῦμα.

Mat. 3:16 τὸ π. — omit τὸ T[A]WH
Mar. 9:20 trs τὸ πνεῦμα εὐθὺς LTTrAWH
 25 trs ἄλαλον καὶ κωφ. π. LTTrAWH
 12:36 τῷ π. — omit τῷ GW
Lu. 2:40 omit in spirit LTTrAWH
 4: 1 trs πλήρης π. ἁγίου LTTrAWH
 9:55 omit and said to end of verse LTTrAWH
Acts 1: 5 trs ἐν π. βαπτισθ. LTTrAWH
 2:33 trs τοῦ π. τοῦ ἁγίου LTTrA
 4:25 add π. LTTrAWH, see πατήρ
 10:19 trs τὸ πνεῦμα αὐτῷ LTTrA
 45 trs τοῦ π. τοῦ ἁγίου LWH
 11:12 trs τὸ π. μοι LTTrAWH
 13: 4 trs τοῦ ἁγίου π. LTTrAWH
 15:28 trs τῷ π. τῷ ἁγίῳ TTrWWH
 18: 5 pressed in the spirit — constrained by the word, λόγος GEds
Ro. 8: 1 omit who walk to end of verse GEds
 11 see ἐνοικέω
1 Co. 6:20 omit and in your spirit, which are God's Eds
 7:34 τῷ πνεύματι LTTrAWH
 14:16 τῷ π. — omit τῷ LTTrAWH
Eph. 5: 9 spirit — light, φῶς GEds
Phil. 3: 3 see θεός
 4:23 add π. Eds, see πᾶς
1 Ti. 4:12 omit in spirit GEds
1 Pet. 1:22 omit through the Spirit Eds
 3:18 τῷ π. — omit τῷ GEds
1 Joh. 5: 7 omit in heaven to in earth (verse 8) GEds
Rev. 22: 6 πνευμάτων τῶν for ἁγίων (ἅγιος) GEds

πνευματικός.

1 Co. 10: 3 trs π. βρῶμα ἔφαγον TTrWH
Eph. 5:19 [spiritual] LA

πνίγω.

Mat. 13: 7 ἔπνιξαν for ἀπέπνιξαν (ἀποπνίγω) T

πνικτός.

Acts 15:20 τοῦ π. — omit τοῦ LTrWH
 29 πνικτῶν LTTrAWH

πόθεν.

Jas. 4: 1 π. μάχαι whence fightings Eds

ποιέω.

Mat. 5:36 trs π. ἢ μέλαιναν LTTrAWH
 44 omit LTTrAWH, see μισέω
 7:18 π.¹ — φέρω TWH: π.² — φέρῃ T
 12:50 ποιῇ A
 17: 4 ποιήσω I will make LTAWH
 19: 4 made¹ — created, κτίζω TrWH
 21:13 ποιεῖτε make LTTrAWH
 23: 3 trs do (ποιήσατε) and observe LTTrAWH
 25:16 made (them) — gained, κερδαίνω LTrWH
Mar. 3: 4 ἀγαθὸν ποιῆσαι T
 6 took — gave, δίδωμι TrAWH, ἐποίησαν T
 8 ποιεῖ is doing TrAWH
 12 ποιῶσιν TTrA
 16 add π. TWH, see δώδεκα
 5:19 πεποίηκεν GEds
 6:20 did many things — was much perplex'd, ἀπορέω TWH
 21 ἐποίησεν TTrAWH
 7: 8 omit (as) the washing to end of verse T[Tr]WH

Mar. 8:25 *omit* TTᵣAWᴴR, *see* διαβλεπω
10:36 **ποιησω** LTTᵣWʜ
11:17 πεποιηκατε TTᵣAWʜR
13:22°**ποιησουσιν** *for* δωσουσιν (δί-δωμι) TA
15: 1 held—prepared. ἑτοιμάζω T
14 *trs* ἐποιησεν κακόν TTᵣAWʜ
15 *trs* π. τὸ ἱκανόν τῷ ὄχλῳ T

Lu. 3:10, 12 **ποιήσωμεν Eds**
14*trs* τί ποιήσομεν (ποιήσωμεν TAWWʜR) καὶ ἡμεῖς LTTᵣAWʜ
6: 2 *omit* to do LTTᵣAWʜ
11 **ποιήσαιεν** LTTᵣAWʜ
8:39 *trs* σοι ἐποίησεν LTTᵣAWʜ
9:43 ἐποίει GLTTᵣAWʜR
54 *omit* even as Elias did TT₍A₎Wʜ R
14:13 *trs* δοχὴν ποιῇς Wʜ
16 ἐποίει TTᵣAWʜ R
16: 9 *trs* ἑαυτοῖς ποιήσατε TAWʜ
18: 7 **ποιήσῃ** LTTᵣAWʜ
23:34 *see* λεγω

Joh. 4:34 **ποιησω** LTᵣAWʜR
5:19 *trs* ποιεῖ ὁμοίως T
6:28 **ποιωμεν** 8—**ποιωμεν** A.V.B EGEds
38 **ποιησω** T
7:31 π.²—ποιεῖ doeth T
8:39 **ποιειτε** Wʜ
14:23 **ποιησομεθα** LTTᵣAWʜ
15:24 π.²—ἐποίησεν LTTᵣAWʜR
18:30°κακὸν ποιων TTᵣAWʜ
21:25 *omit the verse* T

Acts 2:36 *trs* ἐποίησεν ὁ θεός TWʜ
37 ι 4:16 **ποιησωμεν** TTᵣAWʜ
4: 7 *trs* τοῦτο ἐποιήσατε T
8: 2 ἐποίησαν Eds
9: 6 *omit* (it is) hard (*verse* 5) to unto him (*verse* 6) GEds
10: 6 *omit* he shall tell *to end of verse* GEds
15:17 ὁ π.—*omit* ὁ LTTᵣWʜ
18:21 *om.* I must *to* in Jerusalem LTTᵣAWʜ
19:14 οἱ τοῦτο π.—*om.* οἱ LTTᵣ₍A₎Wʜ
23:13 **ποιησάμενοι** Eds
26:28°**ποιῆσαι** *for* γενέσθαι (γίνομαι) LTTᵣAWʜR, *see* πειθω

Ro. 2:14 **ποιωσιν** LTTᵣAWʜR
3:12 ὁ ποιων T

1 Co. 5: 2 **πράσσω** TWʜ
7:37, 38² **ποιησει** shall do LTTᵣAWʜ

Heb. 8: 5 **ποιησεις** thou shalt make Eds
12:13 **ποιειτε** TTᵣWʜ

Jas. 4:13 **ποιήσωμεν** 8. **ποιήσομεν** A.V.B ELTAWʜ R
15 **ποιήσωμεν** 8.—**σομεν** A.V.B EEds

1 Joh. 5: 2°**ποιωμεν** *for* τηρῶμεν (τηρέω) Eds

Rev. 13: 7 *trs* π. LTTᵣAWʜR: *omit* L₍Wʜ₎, *see* διδωμι
13 *omit* he maketh GW
21:27 (add ὁ TTᵣ₍Wʜ₎R) ποιων Eds
21: 2 **ποιων** T
11°add π. GEds, *see* δικαιοσύνη
14 *omit* π. LTTᵣAWʜR, *see* στολη
15 *trs* maketh and loveth T

ποίμνη.

Joh. 10:16 ovile A.V.Vul

ποῖος

Mar. 4:30 τίς LTTᵣAWʜR, *see* τίθημι

πολεμέω.

Rev. 12: 7 π.¹—τοῦ (*om.* τοῦ T₍A₎) πολεμῆ-σαι GEds

πόλεμος.

Rev. 11: 7 *trs* μετ' αὐτῶν π. GEds
13: 5 to continue, ποιησαι 8—to make war, ποιησαι πολησαι E
7 *omit* L₍Wʜ₎, *see* διδωμι
16:14 τὸν πόλεμον A.V.C GEds
19:19 ι 20: 8 πόλεμον Eds

πολις

Mar. 1:45 *trs* εἰς π. φανερῶς T
6:11 *omit* verily *to end of verse* G₍L₎TTᵣAWʜ

Lu. 2:39 τὴν π.—*omit* τὴν LTTᵣAWʜ
7:37 *trs* ἥτις ἦν ἐν τῇ π. LTTᵣAWʜ
9:10 πόλιν καλουμένην TTᵣAWʜ
52°πόλιν *for* κώμην (-μη) T

Joh. 19:20 *trs* ὁ τόπος τῆς π. GEds

Acts 4:27°of a truth—*add* ἐν τῇ πόλει ταύτῃ in this city GEds
8: 5 τὴν πόλιν LTWʜ
15:36 *trs* πόλιν πᾶσαν LTTᵣAWʜ

Acts 16:13 city—gate, πύλη Eds
27: 8 *trs* πόλις ἦν T

2 Co. 11:32 *trs* π. Δαμασκηνῶν LTTᵣAWʜ

Rev. 11: 8 τῆς πόλεως A.V.C Eds
14: 8 *omit* ἡ π. *read* Babylon the great is fallen GEds

πολίτης.

Heb. 8:11°πολίτην *for* πλησίον GEds

πολλαπλασίων.

Mat. 19:29°πολλαπλασίονα *for* ἑκατοντα-πλασίονα (-σίων) LTTᵣAWʜ

πολυς

Mat. 8:18 *omit* great LWʜ
9:14 *omit* oft LTWʜ
14:24°*add* π. TᵣWʜ, *see* στάδιον
20:16 *omit* for many be called, but few chosen T₍TᵣA₎Wʜ
25:19 *trs* πολὺν χρόνον LTTᵣAWʜ

Mar. 4: 1 great—very great, πλεῖστος TTᵣAWWʜR
6: 2 οἱ πολλοί TWʜ, [οἱ] π. A
7: 8 *omit* (as) the washing *to end of verse* T₍TᵣA₎Wʜ
8: 1°*see* πάμπολυς
9:26 π.²—τοὺς πολλούς LTTᵣAWʜ
14:43 *omit* great ₍L₎TTᵣAWʜ

Lu. 6:17°ὄχλος πολὺς a great company TWʜR
23: 8 *omit* many things TTᵣAWʜ

Joh. 5: 3 *omit* great ₍L₎TTᵣAWʜ
7:12 *trs* περὶ αὐτοῦ ἦν π. LTTᵣAWʜ, ἦν περὶ α. π. T
40 *omit* many, · *read* (some) LTTᵣAWʜ
10:42 *trs* π. ἐπίσ. εἰς αὐτὸν ἐκεῖ LTTᵣAWʜ
21:25 *omit the verse* T

Acts 8: 7 π.¹—πολλοὶ LTTᵣAWʜR
8°χαρὰ μεγάλη (-γας)—πολλὴ χ. LTTᵣAWʜ
20:19 *omit* many GEds
24: 7 *omit* LTT₍A₎WʜR, *see* κρίνω
26:29 μέγας LTTᵣAWʜ
28:29 *omit the verse* LTTᵣAWʜ

Ro. 15:23 ἱκανός TᵣAWʜ

Heb. 12: 9. 25 πολύ LTTᵣAWʜ
15 οἱ πολλοὶ Eds

1 Pet. 1: 7 *see* πολύτιμος

Rev. 5: 4 πολύ Eds
17: 1 τῶν π.—*omit* τῶν LTTᵣ₍A₎Wʜ

πολύτιμος.

Mat. 26: 7°πολυτίμου *for* βαρυτίμου (-μος) LT

1 Pet. 1: 7°πολυτιμότερον *for* πολὺ τιμιώ-τερον (-μιος) GLTTᵣAWʜ

πονηρός

Lu. 11: 4 *omit* but deliver · us from evil GTTᵣAWʜ

Joh. 3:19 *trs* αὐτῶν πονηρά LTTᵣAWʜ

Acts 25:18°*add at end* πονηράν, *read* evil accusation LT₍A₎Wː πονη-ρῶν accusation of evil things TᵣWʜR

πόνος.

Col. 4:13°ζῆλον πολύν—πολὺν πόνον GLTTᵣAWʜR, π. πολὺν W

Πόντιος.

Mat. 27: 2 *omit* Pontius TTᵣWʜR

πορεύομαι.

Mat. 21: 2 πορεύεσθε LTTᵣAWʜ
28: 9 *omit* and as they went to tell his disciples LTTᵣAWʜR

Mar. 9:30°ἐπορεύοντο *for* παρεπορεύοντο (παραπορεύομαι) LTᵣWʜ

Lu. 7:11 ἐπορεύθη TWʜ
9:12°πορευθέντες *for* ἀπελθόντες (ἀπέρχομαι) GLTTᵣAWʜR
22:22 *trs* κατὰ τὸ ὡρισ. π. LTTᵣAWʜ
24:13 *trs* ἐν αὐτῇ τῇ ἡμ. ἦσαν π. TWʜ

Joh. 7:53 ἐπορεύθη WʜR   (E

Acts 9:31 πορευομένη Eds
16: 7 πορευθῆναι LTTᵣAWʜR
20: 1 πορεύεσθαι LTTᵣWʜR
23:32 ἀπέρχομαι LTTᵣAWʜR
27: 3 πορευθέντι LTTᵣAWʜ

Jas. 4:13 πορευσώμεθα 8. —σομεθα A.V.B EEds

πορνεία.

Mar. 7:21, 22 *trs* fornications, thefts, murders, adulteries TTᵣAWʜR

Ro. 1:29 *omit* fornication GEds

Rev. 17: 4 τῆς πορνείας GEds

πόρνη.

Lu. 15:30 τῶν πορνῶν LTᵣAWʜR

πόρρω, πορρωτέρω. -ρον.

Lu. 14:32 *trs* πόρρω αὐτοῦ w
14:28 πορρώτερον LTTᵣAWʜ

πορφύρα.

Rev. 17: 4 πορφύρεος GEds

πορφύρεος, -φυροῦς.

Rev. 17: 4°πορφυροῦν *for* πορφύρᾳ GEds

ποταμός.

Mat. 3: 6°Ἰορδάνῃ ποταμῷ the river Jordan LTTᵣAWʜ

ποτε.

Eph. 2:11 *trs* ποτὲ ὑμεῖς LTTᵣAWʜ

ποτήριον.

Mat. 26:27 τὸ π.—*omit* τὸ, *read* a cup TTᵣAWʜ
42 cup LTTᵣAWʜ

Mar. 7: 8 *omit* (as) the washing *to end of verse* T₍TᵣA₎Wʜ
14:23 τὸ π.—*omit* τὸ, *read* a cup LTTᵣAWʜ

Lu. 22:20 *trs* καὶ τὸ π. ὡσαύτως TTᵣAWʜ
42 *trs* τοῦτο τὸ ποτήριον TTᵣAWʜ

Rev. 17: 4 *trs* ποτήριον χρυσοῦν Eds

πού.

Gal. 4:15°*for* τίς A.V.Vul Eds

πούς.

Mat. 18:29 *omit* at his feet GLTTᵣ₍A₎Wʜ
Lu. 7:38 *trs* ὀπίσω παρὰ τοὺς π. αὐτοῦ GLTTᵣAWʜ
44†*trs* ὕδωρ μοι ἐπὶ π. TᵣAWʜ, ὕ. μου ἐπὶ τοὺς π. T
46 *trs* τοὺς πόδας μου GLTTᵣAWʜ
10:11°ὑμῶν—*add* εἰς τοὺς πόδας, *read* on us to the feet LTTᵣAWʜ
24:40 *omit the verse* T₍Tᵣ₎[₍Wʜ₎]

Joh. 13: 8 *trs* μου τοὺς πόδας LTTᵣAWʜ
10 *omit* save . . . (his) feet T₍Wʜ₎

Acts 21:11 *trs* feet and hands Eds

πραγματεία, -τία TWʜ.

πραγματεύομαι.

Lu. 19:13 πραγματεύσασθαι Wʜ

πρᾶος.

Mat. 11:29 πραΰς LTTᵣAWʜ

πραότης, by most editors πραΰτης.

1 Ti. 6:11 πραΰπάθεια Eds

πράσσω, πράττω.

Lu. 19:23 *trs* αὐτὸ ἔπραξα LTTᵣAWʜ
1 Co. 5: 2°πράξας *for* ποιήσας (-ιέω) TWʜ

* πραΰπάθεια, -θία TWʜ, gentleness.

1 Ti. 6:11 πραΰπάθειαν *for* πραοτητα (-ότης) Eds

πραΰς.

Mat. 11:29°πραΰς *for* πρᾶος LTTᵣAWʜ
1 Pet. 3: 4 πραέως TTᵣWʜ, πραεος LA

πρεσβύτερος, -τέρα.

Mat. 26:59 and elders LTTᵣAWʜ
27: 3 τοῖς π.—*omit* τοῖς LTTᵣAWʜ
12 τῶν π.—*omit* τῶν T₍A₎Wʜ
Mar. 14:43 τῶν π.—*omit* τῶν T
Acts 4: 5 τοὺς πρεσβυτέρους LTTᵣAWʜ
14:23 *trs* κατ' ἐκκλ. π. LTTᵣAWWʜ
16: 4 τῶν π.—*omit* τῶν Eds
24: 1 τῶν π.—π. τινῶν certain elders LTTᵣAWʜ

πρίζω, πρίω.

Heb. 11:37 *trs* were tempted. were κιωπ asunder TWʜ

πρίν, πρὶν ἤ.

Lu. 22:34 before that—until. ἕως LTTᵣAWʜR

Πρίσκα.

Ro. 16: 3ª Πρίσκαν for Πρίσκιλλαν GEds
1 Co. 16:19ª Πρισκα for Πρίσκιλλα TTrWHR

Πρίσκιλλα.

Acts 18:26 trs Priscilla and Aquila LTTrAWHR
Ro. 16: 3 Priscilla—Prisca, Πρίσκαν GEds
1 Co. 16:19 Priscilla—Prisca, Πρίσκα TTrWHR

πρό.

Mat. 24:38 omit ταῖς π. read days of the flood A
Lu. 1:76 π. προσώπου—ἐνώπιον WH
Joh. 10: 8 omit before me T
Acts 5:23 ἐπί LTTrAWHR
Jude 25ª add π. Eds, see αἰών

προάγω.

Acts 12: 6†trs π. αὐτὸν Tr, προαγαγεῖν a. LTA, προσαγαγεῖν (-άγω) a. WH
17: 5ª προαγαγεῖν for ἀγαγεῖν (ἄγω) LTTrAWHR
2 Joh. 9ª προάγων for παραβαίνων (-νω) Eds

προαιρέομαι.

2 Co. 9: 7 προῄρηται hath purposed Eds

προβάλλω.

Acts 19:33 προβαλόντων S, -λλόντων EGL

* προβάτιον, a little sheep.

Joh. 21:16 προβάτια f. πρόβατα (-τον) TWH
17 προβάτια for πρόβατα (-τον) TTrAWHR

πρόβατον.

Joh. 10: 4 sheep¹—all, τὰς, read all his own TTrA]WHR
12 omit the sheep³ [L]TTr[A]WHR
21:16 sheep—little sheep, προβάτιον TWH
17 sheep—little sheep, προβάτιον TTrAWHR

προβιβάζω.

Acts 19:33 drew—instructed, συμβιβάζω LTTrWHR

προγράφω.

Ro. 15: 4 π.²-γράφω Eds

προεπαγγέλλομαι.

2 Co. 9: 5ª προεπηγγελμένην for προκατηγγελμένην (-καταγγέλλω) Eds

προερέω.

Heb. 4: 7ª προείρηται for εἴρηται (ἐρῶ) Eds
10:15 had said before—had said, ἐρῶ Eds

προέρχομαι.

Mat. 26:39 προσέρχομαι TTr
Mar. 14:35 προσέρχομαι Tr
Acts 20: 5, 13 προσέρχομαι TrWH

πρόϊμος, see πρώϊμος.

προκαταγγέλλω.

Acts 3:24 have foretold—announced, καταγγέλλω GEds
2 Co. 9: 5 whereof ye had notice before —before promised προεπαγγέλλομαι Eds

προκηρύσσω, —ττω.

Acts 3:20 before was preached — was foreordained προχειρίζομαι GEds

προλαμβάνω.

Gal. 6: 1 προλημφθῇ LTTrAWHR

προνοέω.

2 Co. 8:21 προνοοῦμεν γάρ, for we provide LTTrAWHR
1 Ti. 5: 8 προνοεῖται TTr

προοράω.

Acts 2:25 προορώμην LTTrAWHR

* προπάτωρ, forefather.

Ro. 4: 1 προπάτορα for πατέρα (-τήρ) LTTrAWHR

πρός.

Mat. 3:15 π. αὐτόν—αὐτῷ LWH
10:13 ἐπί WH
21: 1 εἰς LTTrAWHR
26:55 omit with you T[Tr]AWHR
Mar. 1:27 omit π. TWH
3: 7 εἰς GLT
6:33 omit and came together unto him GEds
7:31 εἰς GLTTrAWHR
9:14ª αὐτούς—π. αὐτούς TTrWHR
33 omit among yourselves LTTrAWHR
10: 7 om. and cleave to his wife TWH
15:42ª see προσάββατον
Lu. 3:14 π. αὐτούς—αὐτοῖς LTTrAWHR
7: 6 omit to him TWH
9:62 omit unto him A[WH]
10:22 see μαθητής
39 for παρά TTrAWHR
11:53 omit TTrAWHR, see ἐξέρχομαι
14:28 εἰς GEds
17: 4ª for ἐπί Eds
18: 7 π. αὐτόν—αὐτῷ TTrAWHR
11 omit with himself T
20:25ª αὐτοῖς—π. αὐτούς TTrAWHR
45ª see μαθητής
22:52ª for ἐπί T
24:12 omit the verse [L]T[Tr][[WH]]
44ª αὐτοῖς—π. αὐτούς TTrAWHR
50ª for εἰς TTrWHR
Joh. 1:19ª sent—add πρὸς αὐτόν unto him LTTrAWHR
7:37 omit unto me T
50 omit π.² T, see ἔρχομαι
8: 3 omit unto him WHR
33ª π. αὐτόν for αὐτῷ LTTrAWHR
11:32ª πρὸς εἰς (πρός for εἰς TTrAWH) τοὺς πόδας GTTrAWHR
16:16 omit because I go to the Father WHR
19: 3ª add π. LTTrAWHR, see ἔρχομαι
21:23 omit what (is that) to thee T
Acts 2: 7 omit one to another LTTrAWHR
3:19ª for εἰς TWH
22 omit unto the fathers LTTrA
4:37ª for παρά T
5: 8ª π. αὐτήν for αὐτῇ LTTrAWHR [WHR
10ª for παρά LTTrAWHR
7:31 omit unto him LTTrAWHR
9: 5, 6 omit GEds, see κέντρον
10:21 omit GEds, see ἀποστέλλω
16:40ª for εἰς GEds
19: 3 omit unto them Eds
23:15 εἰς Eds
30 omit against him LT
24: 8ª for ἐπί A, see κρίνω
15ª for εἰς T
26: 6 εἰς Eds
Ro. 15:24 omit I will come to you GEds
2 Co. 9: 5ª for εἰς LTrW
Eph. 3:31 omit π. LTTr, see γυνή
Philem. 5 εἰς LTTrAWHR
Jas. 3: 3 εἰς LTTrAWHR
Rev. 12: 5ª God and—add π. to GEds
21: 9 omit unto me GEds
22:18 ἐπί GEds

προσάββατον, πρὸς σάββ. LTr.

προσάγω.

Mat. 18:24ª προσήχθη for προσηνέχθη (-σφέρω) LTrAWH
Acts 12: 6ª προσαγαγεῖν for προάγειν (-άγω) WH

προσαγωγή.

Eph. 3:12 τὴν π.—omit τὴν LTTr[A]WHR

προσαιτέω.

Mar. 10:46 omit begging TTrAWHR, see προσαίτης
Lu. 18:35 ἐπαιτέω LTTrAWH

* προσαίτης, a beggar.

Mar. 10:46 τυφλός—add προσαίτης, read a blind beggar TTrAWHR
Joh. 9: 8 προσαίτης for τυφλός GEds

προσαναλίσκω.

Lu. 8:43 omit π. WH, see ἰατρός

προσδέχομαι.

Ro. 16: 2 trs προσδ. αὐτήν LTTrAWHR

προσεγγίζω.

Mar. 2: 4 come nigh—bring nigh, προσφέρω TWH

προσεδρεύω.

1 Co. 9:13 παρεδρεύω Eds

προσεργάζομαι.

Lu. 19:16† trs δέκα προσηργάσατο LTAWH, δ. προσειρ- Tr

προσέρχομαι.

Mat. 5: 1 προσῆλθαν TTrWH
8: 2ª προσελθών for ἐλθών (ἔρχομαι) Eds
9:18ª προσελθών for ἐλθών (ἔρχομαι) LWH
28 : 13:36 : 14:15 προσῆλθαν LTr
17: 7 προσῆλθεν LTTrWH [WH
19: 3 : 21:23 προσῆλθαν WH
26:39ª προσελθών for προελθών (-ἔρχομαι) TTr
60 trs π. ψευδομαρτύρων LTTrAWHR
Mar. 14:35ª προσελθών for προ. ἐλθών (-ἔρχομαι) Tr
Lu. 13:31 προσῆλθαν TTrWH
Joh. 12:21 προσῆλθαν WH
Acts 20:1ª προσελθόντες for προελθόντες (-ἔρχομαι) TrWH
13ª προσελθόντες for προελθόντες (-ἔρχομαι) Tr
24:23 omit or come Eds
1 Ti. 6: 3 consent—cleaves, προσέχω Tr

προσευχή.

Mat. 17:21 omit the verse T[TrA]WHR
Acts 16:13 προσευχήν LTTrWHR, see νομίζω
16 τὴν προσευχήν, read the place of prayer Eds
1 Pet. 4: 7 τὰς π.—omit τὰς Eds

προσεύχομαι

Mat. 6: 5 προσεύχησθε, οὐκ ἔσεσθε ὡς read when ye pray, ye shall not be as LTTrAWHR
23:14(13) omit the verse LTTrAWHR, see κρίμα
26:36 trs ἐκεῖ προσεύξωμαι LTTrAWHR
Mar. 11:24 προσεύχεσθε καί, read whatsoever ye pray and ask for LTTrAWHR
13:33 omit and pray LT[Tr]AWH
Lu. 22:43, 44 the verses [L][[WH]]
Acts 21: 5 προσευξάμενοι Eds, see ἀσπάζομαι
Jas. 5:16ª προσεύχεσθε for εὔχεσθε (-χομαι) LWH

προσέχω.

Mat. 16:11 ὑμῖν; προσέχετε δέ (question ends at bread) read but beware LTTrAWHR
1 Ti. 6: 3ª προσέχεται for προσέρχεται (-χομαι) T
Heb. 2: 1 trs προσέχειν ἡμᾶς Eds

προσκαλέομαι.

Lu. 18:16 προσεκαλέσατο TTrAWHR
Acts 20: 1 called unto (him)—sent for μεταπέμπω TTrWHR

* προσκλίνω, to incline to.

Acts 5:36 προσεκλίθη for προσεκολλήθη (-σκολλάω) Eds

προσκολλάω.

Mat. 19: 5 κολλάω LTTrAWHR
Mar. 10: 7 om. and cleave to his wife TWH
Acts 5:36 προσκλίνω Eds

προσκυνέω.

Lu. 24:52 omit worshipped him, and T[[WH]]
Joh. 4:20 trs προσκυνεῖν δεῖ LTTrAWH
24 trs προσκυνεῖν δεῖ T
12:20 προσκυνήσουσιν LT·A
Rev. 5: 9 προσκυνήσουσιν LTTrAWHR
4:10 προσκυνοῦσιν S—προσκυνήσουσιν shall worship BGEds
9:20 προσκυνήσουσιν Eds
13:12 προσκυνήσουσιν LTTrAWHR
15 προσκυνήσουσιν T

προσλαμβάνω.

Acts 27:34 μεταλαμβάνω GEds
Philem. 12 omit thou therefore receive LTTrAWHR

πρόσληψις, –λημψις LTTrAWH.

προσμένω.

Acts 13:43*προσμένειν for ἐπιμένειν (-νω) GEds

προσπίπτω.

Mat. 7:25 προσέπεσαν TTrAWH, –παισαν L
Mar. 3:11 προσέπιπτον LTTrAWWH

προσποιέω.

Lu. 24:28 προσεποιησατο LTTrAWH
Joh. 8: 6 add at end μὴ προσποιούμενος A.V.†C

προσρήγνυμι.

Lu. 6:48, 49 προσέρηξεν TTrWH

προστάσσω

Mat. 21: 6 συντάσσω LTTrAWH
Acts 17:26*προστεταγμένους (πρὸς τ. L) for προτεταγμένους (-τάσσω) GEds

προσφέρω.

Mat. 8: 4 προσένεγκον LTTrAWWH
12:22 προσήνεγκαν LWH
18:24 προσαγω LTrAW
19:13 προσηνέχθησαν LTTrAWH
Mar. 2: 4*προσένεγκαι for προσεγγίσαι (-γίζω) TWH
10:13 those that brought (them)— them, αὐτοῖς WH
Lu. 12:11 εἰσφέρω TTrAWH
Heb. 7:27*προσενέγκας for ἀνενέγκας (ἀναφέρω) T

προσφορά.

Heb.10: 5 trs offering and sacrifice w
8 προσφοράς offerings Eds

προσφωνέω.

Mat. 11:16 προσφωνοῦντα LTTrAWH

προσωπολημπτέω, –λημπ– LTTrAWH.

προσωπολήμπτης, –λημπ– LTTrAWH.

προσωπολημψία, –λημψ– LTTrAWH.

πρόσωπον.

Mat. 16: 3 when it is (verse 2) to end of verse 3 [TA][[WH]]
Mar. 14:65 trs αὐτοῦ τὸ π. TTrAWH
Lu. 1:76 πρὸ π.–ἐνώπιον WH
22:64 omit struck him on the face, and [L]TTrAWH
24: 5 τὰ πρόσωπα TTrWH
Acts 17:26 παντὸς προσώπου LTTrAWH
2 Co. 11:20 trs εἰς πρόσωπον ὑμᾶς Eds
Rev. 7:11 τὰ πρόσωπα GEds
20:11 τοῦ προσώπου Eds

προτάσσω.

Acts 17:26 before appointed—appointed προστάσσω GEds

προτείνω.

Acts 22:25 προέτειναν A.V.BGEds

πρότερον, τὸ πρότερον.

Joh. 7:50*αὐτόν—add π. read came to him before LTTrAWH
51 πρῶτον LTTrAWH

πρόφασις.

Mat. 23:14(13) omit the verse LTTrAWH see κρίμα

προφητεία.

2 Pet. 1:21 trs προφ. ποτέ TrAWH
Rev. 11: 6 trs τῆς π. αὐτῶν GLTTrAWH

προφητεύω.

Mat. 7:22 ἐπροφητεύσαμεν LTTrAWH
11:13 ἐπροφήτευσαν LTTrAWH
15: 7 ἐπροφήτευσεν LTTrAWH
Mar. 7: 6 ἐπροφήτευσεν LTTrAWH
Lu. 1:67 ἐπροφήτευσεν LTTrAWH
Joh. 11:51 ἐπροφήτευσεν LTTrAWWH
Acts 19: 6 ἐπροφήτευον LTTrAWH
Jude 14 ἐπροφήτευσεν TTrWH

προφήτης.

Mat. 16: 4 omit the prophet LTTrAWH

Mat. 21:11 trs ὁ π. Ἰησοῦς LTTrAWH
26 trs ὡς π. ἔχ. τὸν Ἰω. LTTrAWH
27:35 omit that it might to end of verse GLTTrAWH
Mar. 1: 2 the prophets—τῷ (omit τῷ G[Tr]W) Ἡσαΐᾳ τῷ προφήτῃ Isaiah the prophet GEds
13:14 omit spoken of by Daniel the prophet G[L]TTrAWH
Lu. 7:28 omit prophet L[TrA]WH
11:29 omit the prophet GLTTrAWH
24:44 [τοῖς] π. Tr, τοῖς π. WH
Joh. 7:52 trs ἐκ τῆς Γαλ. π. LTTrAWH
Acts 3:21 trs ἀπ᾽ αἰῶνος αὐ. π. LTTrAWH
13:20 τοῦ π.—omit τοῦ TT[A]WH
Rev. 10: 7 τοὺς προφήτας GEds
22: 6 τῶν π. GEds, see ἅγιος

προχειρίζομαι.

Acts 3:20*προκεχειρισμένον for προκεκηρυγμένον (προκηρύσσω) GEds

πρωΐ, –ί WH.

Mat. 16: 3 When it is (verse 2) to end of verse 3 [TA][[WH]]
21:18*for πρωΐας TTrWH
Mar. 15: 1 τὸ π.—omit τὸ LTTr[A]WH
Joh. 18:28*for πρωΐα GLTTrAWWH

πρωΐα.

Mat. 21:18 πρωΐ TTrWH
Joh. 18:28 πρωΐ GLTTrAWWH

πρώϊμος, πρόϊμος TTrWH.

πρωϊνός.

Rev. 22:16*ὁ πρωϊνός for ὀρθρινός GEds

πρῷρα.

Acts 27:30 πρῴρης LTWH
41 πρῷρα LTWH, πρῶρα Tr

πρῶτον, τὸ πρῶτον.

Mat. 17:11 omit first LTTrAWH
Mar. 13:10 trs πρῶτον δεῖ LTTrAWH
Joh. 1:41(42)*for πρῶτος LTTrAWH
7:51*trs π. (for πρότερον) παρ᾽ αὐτοῦ LTTrAWH
Acts 11:26 πρώτως TTrAWH
Ro. 1:16 [first] LWH
Eph. 4: 9 omit first GEds

πρῶτος.

Mat. 21:31 first—latter, ὕστερος LTrWH (Tr refers 'the latter' to him who 'afterwards' repented: for WH see ἀπέρχομαι, verses 29, 30)
22:38 trs great and first Eds
Mar. 12:30 omit this (is) the first commandment TAWH
Joh. 1:41(42) πρῶτον LTTrAWH
5: 4 omit waiting for (verse 3) to end of verse 4 [G]TTrAWH
Acts 13:33*trs τῷ πρώτῳ (π. for δευτέρῳ, –ρος) ψα. γέγ. GTTr: τῷ ψ. γ. τῷ δ. (πρ. L) LAWWH
Phil. 1: 5 τῆς πρώτης LTTrAWH
Rev. 1:11 omit GEds, see ἄλφα
22:13 ὁ π.—omit ὁ L[A], see ἀρχή

πρωτότοκος.

Mat. 1:25 omit her firstborn LTTrAWH

* πρώτως, adv. first.

Acts 11:26 for πρῶτον TTrAWH

πταίω.

Jas. 2:10 πταίσῃ Eds

πτηνόν.

1 Co.15:39 trs birds, (and) another of fishes Eds

πτῶμα.

Mat. 14:12*πτῶμα for σωμα LTTrWH
Mar. 15:45*πτῶμα for σωμα LTTrAWH
Rev. 11: 8, 9¹ τὸ πτῶμα body GEds

πτωχός.

Mat. 19:21 τοῖς πτωχοῖς LTrAR, [τοῖς] π. WH
26: 9 τοῖς πτωχοῖς LW
Mar. 10:21 τοῖς π.—omit τοῖς LTrAW[WH]R
Lu. 19: 8 trs τοῖς π. δίδωμι TTrAWH
21: 3 trs αὕτη ἡ πτωχὴ LTrWH

πυγμῇ.

Mar. 7: 3 πυκνός T

Πύθων.

Acts 16:16 πύθωνα LTTrAWH

πυκνός.

Mar. 7: 3*πυκνά for πυγμῇ T

πύλη.

Mat. 7:13 omit (is) the gate L[T]WH
14 [the gate] LT
Lu. 13:24 gate—door, θύρα GLTTrAWH
Acts 16:13*πύλης for πόλεως (-λις) Eds

πυλών.

Rev. 21:12 τοὺς πυλῶνας Tr

πυνθάνομαι.

Joh. 13:24 see λέγω
Acts 10:18 ἐπύθοντο WH

πῦρ.

Mar. 9:22 trs καὶ εἰς π. αὐτὸν TAWH
44 omit the verse T[Tr]WH
45 omit into the fire that never shall be quenched [L]TT[A]
46 omit the verse T[Tr]WH (WH R
47 omit fire LTTrAWH
Joh. 15: 6 τὸ πῦρ TTrAWWH
2 Th. 1: 8†trs φλογὶ πυρός a flame of fire LTrW
Jude 23 τοῦ π.—omit τοῦ Eds, see φόβος
Rev. 13:13 trs καὶ πῦρ ἵνα GW
20:14*add π. Eds, see λίμνη

πυρόω.

Eph. 6:16 τὰ π.—omit τὰ L[TrAW]
Rev. 1:15 πεπυρωμένης (-ένῳ T) it burned LTTrAWH

πυρράζω.

Mat. 16: 2, 3 when it is evening (ver. 2) to end of verse 3 [TA][[WH]]

* Πύρρος.

Acts 20: 4 Sopater—add Πύρρου of Pyrrhus GEds

πωλέω.

Mat. 13:44 trs π. πάντα ὅσα ἔχει LTTrA, π. ὅσα ἔχει WH
Lu. 12: 6 πωλοῦνται TTrAWH

πῶλος.

Mar. 11: 4 τὸν π.—omit τὸν GLTTrAWWH

πωρόω.

Joh. 12:40 ἐπώρωσεν TTrAWH

πῶς.

Mar. 2:26 [how] TrAWH
4:30*for τίνι (τίς) TTrAWH
40 omit LT·WHR, see οὐ
8:21 omit how is it that TAWH
12:26*for ὡς TTrAWH
Gal. 2:14*for τί (τίς) GEds
1 Joh.4:20 οὐ, read he cannot love God, LTTrAWH

ῥαββί, ῥαββεί TWH, in Mark A.

Mat. 23: 7 omit Rabbi² LTTr[A]WH
Mar. 14:45 omit master² LTTr[A]WH

ῥαββουνί –ουνί, –ουνεί WH.

ῥαβδίζω.

2 Co. 11:25 ἐραβδίσθην LTTrAWH

ῥάβδος.

Mat. 10:10 ῥάβδον A.V.CW
Lu. 9: 3 ῥάβδον a stuff GLTTrAWH
Heb. 1: 8 ῥ.—ἡ ῥάβδος TTrAWH
8 ἡ ῥ.—omit ἡ LTTrWH

ῥακά, ῥαχά T.

Ῥαμᾶ, –ά WH.

ῥαντίζω.

Mar. 7: 4*ῥαντίσωνται for βαπτισωνται (-τίζω) WH
Heb. 9:19, 21 ἐράντισεν LTTrAWH

Heb.10:22 ῥεραντισμένοι LTTrAWH
Rev.19:13*ῥεραντισμένον for βεβαμμένον (βάπτω) WH

ῥαπίζω.

Mat. 5:39 ῥαπίζει smiteth LTTrAWH
26:67 ἐράπισαν LTTrAWH

ῥαφίς.

Mar.10:25 τῆς ῥ.—omit τῆς LTrWWH
Lu. 18:25 βελόνη LTTrAWH

Ῥεμφάν.

Acts 7:43 Ῥομφάν T, Ῥεφάν LTrAWH, Ῥομφά WH

ῥέω.

Mat. 5:21, 27, 31, 33, 38, 43 ἐρρήθη LTrAW
27:35 omit that it might to end of verse GLTTrAWH
Mar.13:14 omit spoken of by Daniel the prophet G[L]TTrAWH
Ro. 9:12, 26 ἐρρέθη LTTrAWH
Gal. 3:16 ἐρρέθησαν LTTrAWH

ῥήγνυμι, ῥήσσω.

Mar. 2:22 ῥήξει will burst LTTrAWH

ῥῆμα.

Mat. 5:11 omit ῥ. LTTrAWH
Mar.14:72 τὸ ῥῆμα Eds
Lu. 4: 4 omit but by every word of God T[Tr]AWH
20:26 αὐτοῦ ῥ.—τοῦ ῥ. AWH
22:61*ῥήματος for λόγου (-γος) WH
Ro. 10: 9*confess—add τὸ ῥῆμα the word WH
Rev.17:17 λόγος GEds

ῥίπτω.

Mat. 9:36 ἐριμμένοι TTrAWH, ῥεριμ– L
15:30 ἔριψαν TWH
Acts 27:19 ἔρριψαν (ἐρι– TWH) they cast out GEds

ῥμδ´.

Rev. 7: 4 ἑκατὸν τεσσεράκοντα (τεσσαρ– GW) τέσσαρες GLTTrAWWH

ῥύομαι.

Lu. 11: 4 omit but deliver us from evil GTTrAWH
2 Co. 1:10 ῥ.¹—ἐρύσατο TrWH
10 ῥ.²—ῥύσεται will deliver [L]TTrAWH
Col. 1:13 ἐρύσατο TTrWH
2 Ti. 3:11 ἐρύσατο TWH
4:17 ἐρύσθην LTTrAWH
2 Pet. 2: 7 ἐρύσατο TrAWH

* ῥυπαίνω, to make filthy.

Rev. 22:11 ῥυπανθήτω for ῥυπωσάτω (–πόω) LTTrAWH

* ῥυπαρεύομαι, to be filthy.

Rev. 22:11 ῥυπαρευθήτω for ῥυπωσάτω (–πόω) GW

ῥυπαρός.

Rev. 22:11*ῥυπαρός for ῥυπῶν (–πόω) GEds

ῥυπόω.

Rev. 22:11 ῥ.¹—ῥυπαρός GEds
11 ῥ.²—ῥυπαίνω LTTrAWH, ῥυπαρεύομαι GW

Ῥωμαϊκός.

Lu. 23:38 omit in letters of Greek, and Latin, and Hebrew [L]TTr[A]WH

Ῥωμαϊστί.

Joh. 19:20 trs Latin (and) Greek TTrAWH

Ῥώμη.

Acts 28:16 τὴν Ῥώμην T

ῥώννυμι.

Acts 23:30 omit farewell LTTrAWH

συβαχθανί, –νεί TTrWH.

σάββατον, σάββατα.

Mar. 16: 2 τῶν σαββάτων LTTrWHR

Lu. 6: 5 trs τοῦ σ. after ἐστιν WH
9 τῷ σαββάτῳ sabbath day LTTrAWH
Joh. 20:19 τῶν σ.—omit τῶν Eds
1 Co. 16: 2 σαββάτου Eds

Σαδδουκαῖος.

Mat. 16:12*add Σ. T, see ἄρτος
Acts 23: 7 τῶν Σ.—omit τῶν Eds

σαίνω, ἀσαίνω L.

1 Th. 3: 3 τῷ μηδ. σ.—τὸ μηδ. σ. Eds

Σαλά.

Lu. 3:32*for Σαλμών TWH

σαλεύω.

Heb.12:27 trs τὴν ([τὴν] WH) τῶν σ. LTTrAWH

Σαλμών.

Lu. 3:32 Salmon—Sala, Σαλά TWH

Σαμάρεια, –ρία TWH.

Σαμαρείτης, –ρίτης T.

Joh. 4: 9 omit for the Jews have no dealings with the Samaritans T[WH]

Σαμαρεῖτις, –ρῖτις T.

Σαπφείρη.

Acts 5: 1 Σαπφείρᾳ LTr

σάρδινος.

Rev. 4: 3 σάρδιος GEds

σάρδιος, –ον.

Rev. 4: 3*σάρδιον for σαρδίνῳ (–νος) GEds
21:20 σάρδιον Eds

Σάρεπτα, Σάρεφθα w.

Ro. 7:14 σάρκινος GEds
1 Co. 3: 1 σάρκινος GEds
4 carnal—men, ἄνθρωπος Eds
Heb. 7:16 σάρκινος Eds

σάρκινος.

Ro. 7:14*σάρκινος for σαρκικός GEds
1 Co. 3: 1*σαρκίνοις for σαρκικοῖς (–κός) GEds
Heb. 7:16*σαρκίνης f. σαρκικῆς (–κός) Eds

Σαρούχ, Σερούχ GLTTrAWWH.

σάρξ.

Lu. 24:39 σάρκας T
Joh. 6:51 trs ὑπὲρ τῆς τοῦ κόσμου ζωῆς, ἡ σ. μου ἐστίν T
Acts 2:30 omit according to the flesh, he would raise up Christ GLTTrAWH
Ro. 8: 1 omit who walk to end of verse GEds
1 Co.15:39 omit (kind of) flesh GEds
39*another²—add σάρξ flesh [L]TTrAWH, see ἰχθύς
2 Co. 1:18 τὴν σ.—omit τὴν TTr[WH]
Eph. 5:30 omit of his flesh, and of his bones LTTr[A]WH
Heb. 2:14 trs of blood and flesh Eds
1 Joh. 4: 3 omit that Christ is come in the flesh GLTTrAWH

Σαρών.

Acts 9:35 Σαρωνᾶ s, –ῶνα EGLTTrAWWH

Σατᾶν.

2 Co. 12: 7 Σατανᾶς LTTrAWH

Σατανᾶς.

Lu. 4: 8 omit get thee behind me, Satan G[L]TTrAWH
22: 3 ὁ Σ.—omit ὁ GLTTrAWWH
2 Co. 12: 7*Σατανᾶ for Σατᾶν LTTrAWH
Rev. 20: 2 ὁ Σατανᾶς Eds

Σαῦλος.

Acts 9: 8 ὁ Σ.—omit ὁ LTTrAWH
19, 26 omit ὁ Σ. read he GEds
13: 2 τὸν Σ.—omit τὸν LTTrAWWH

σαυτοῦ. see σεαυτοῦ.

σβέννυμι.

Mar. 9:44, 46 omit the verses T[Tr]WHR
1 Th. 5:19 ζβέννυτε T

σέ.

Mat. 5:25 omit deliver thee² LT[Tr]WH
18:15 omit against thee LT[A]WH
25:27 trs σε οὖν TTrAWH
Mar.10:35*desire—add σέ of thee Eds
Lu. 17: 3 omit against thee LTTrAWH
Joh. 21:23 omit what (is that) to thee? r
Acts 10: 6 omit GEds, see ποιέω
24: 8 omit LTTr[A]WH, see κρίνω
26: 3 trs σε ὄντα T
Ro. 8: 2*for μέ TWH
1 Co. 8:10 [thee] LWH
1 Ti. 3:15 δεῖ—add te A.V.Vul
Rev. 3: 3 omit on thee¹ LTTrAWH
15: 4 omit thee¹ LTTrAWH

σεαυτοῦ, σαυτοῦ, –τῷ, –τόν.

Mat. 18:16*σεαυτοῦ for σοῦ T
Joh. 18:34*σεαυτοῦ for σοῦ T
Ro. 13: 9*σεαυτόν for ἑαυτόν LTTrAWH
14:22 σαυτόν—σεαυτόν GLTTrAWWH
Gal. 5:14*σεαυτόν for ἑαυτόν GEds

σειρά.

2 Pet. 2: 4 chains—dens, σειρός TrAWH, σιρός LT

* σειρός, pit, cavern.

2 Pet. 2: 4 σειροῖς for σειραῖς (–ρά) TrAWH

σείω.

Heb.12:26 σείσω will shake LTTrAWH

Σελεύκεια, –κια TWH.

Acts 13: 4 τὴν Σ.—omit τὴν LTTrAWH

Σεμεΐ, Σεμεείν TTrAWH.

σημαίνω.

Acts 11:28 ἐσήμαινεν LWH

σημεῖον.

Mat. 16: 3 When it is (verse 2) to end of verse 3 [TA][[WH]]
Lu. 2:12 τὸ σ.—omit τὸ WH
21:11 trs ἀπ᾽ οὐρανοῦ σ. LWH
Joh. 6:14 σημεῖα WH
11:47 trs ποιεῖ σημεῖα LTTrAWH
Acts 8:13 trs miracles and signs A.V.C GW
1 Co. 1:22 σημεῖα signs GEds

σήμερον.

Mat. 16: 3 When it is (verse 2) to end of verse 3 [TA][[WH]]
Lu. 22:61*crow—add σ. to-day TTrAWH
24:21 omit to-day, read it is the third T[TrA]WH

σηρικόν, σιρικόν LTWHR.

σθενόω.

1 Pet. 5:10 σθενώσει will strengthen GEds

σιαγών.

Mat. 5:39 trs σ. σου LTrA, σ. [σου] WH

σιγάω.

Lu. 18:39*σιγήσῃ for σιωπήσῃ (–πάω) LTTrAWH

Σιδών.

Mar. 7:24 omit and Sidon TA[WH]
Lu. 4:26 Σιδωνία LTTrAWH

Σιδώνιος, –νία.

Lu. 4:26*Σιδωνίας for Σιδῶνος LTTrAWH

Σίλας.

Acts 15:34 omit the verse Eds
16:19 τὸν Σ.—omit τον A
29 τῷ Σ.—omit τῷ LTTrAWH

Σιλωάμ.

Joh. 9:11 τὸν Σ. read go to Siloam GLTTrAWH

Σίμων.

Mar. 1:16*(τοῦ LR) Σίμωνος for αὐτοῦ Eds
    36 ὁ Σ.—omit ὁ T[Tr]AWH
    3:16 trs ὄνομα τῷ Σ. TTrAWH
Lu. 5: 3 τοῦ Σ.—omit τοῦ LTTrAWH
    5 ὁ Σ.—omit ὁ TTrAWH
    7:43 ὁ Σ.—omit ὁ T[Tr]WH
    23:26 Σίμωνα LTTrAWHR
Joh. 12: 4 omit Simon's (son) TTrAWHR
Acts 10:17 τοῦ Σίμωνος LTTrAWWH
2 Pet.1: 1* for Συμεῶν A.V.C LWH

Σινά, -ά WH.

* σιρός, pit, cavern.

2 Pet. 2: 4 σιροῖς for σειραῖς (-ρά) LT

* σιτίον, grain, corn.

Acts 7:12 σιτία for σῖτα (-τος) Eds

σιτομέτριον.

Lu. 12:42 τὸ σ.—omit τὸ TrA[WH]

σῖτος.

Mar. 4:28 πλήρης σῖτος LTTrA
Lu. 12:18*τὸν σῖτον for τὰ γενήματα (-νημα) TrWHR
Acts 7:12 σιτίον Eds

Σιχάρ, see Συχάρ.

σιωπάω.

Lu. 18:39 σιγάω LTTrAWHR
    19:40 σιωπήσουσιν LTTrAWHR

σκανδαλίζω.

Mat. 17:27 σκανδαλίζωμεν T
Mar. 9:43 σκανδαλίσῃ TWHR
Ro. 14:21 om. or is offended, or is made weak TWHR

σκηνή.

Mar. 9: 5 trs τρεῖς σκηνάς LTTrAWH
Heb. 9: 1 omit σ. A.V.B GEds

σκληρός.

Acts 9: 5 omit (it is) hard to unto him (ver. 6) GEds

σκοπέω.

Phil. 2: 4 σκοποῦντες looking GEds

σκοτεινός, -τινόν WH.

σκοτία.

Mat. 4:16*†trs σκοτίᾳ (σκότει TW) φῶς εἶδεν LTTrAWWH
Joh. 6:17 ἡ σκοτία T, see ἤδη

σκοτίζομαι.

Lu. 23:45 ἐκλείπω TWHR, see ἥλιος
Eph. 4:18 σκοτόω LTTrAWH
Rev. 9: 2 σκοτόω LTAWH

σκότος.

Mat. 4:16 σκοτία LTrAWH
Heb.12:18 ζόφος Eds

σκοτόω, -τόομαι.

Eph. 4:18*ἐσκοτωμένοι for ἐσκοτισμένοι (σκοτίζομαι) LTTrAWH
Rev. 9: 2*ἐσκοτώθη for ἐσκοτίσθη (σκοτίζομαι) LTAWH

σκύλλω.

Mat. 9:36*ἐσκυλμένοι for ἐκλελυμένοι (ἐκλύω) GEds

σκώληξ.

Mar. 9:44, 46 omit the verses T[Tr]WHR

Σμύρνα, Ζμ- T.

Rev. 2: 8*ἐν Σμύρνῃ for Σμυρναίων GEds, see ἐκκλησία

Σμυρναῖος.

Rev. 2: 8 Σμύρνα GLTTrAWWHR, Ζμύρνα T

Σόδομα.

Mar. 6:11 omit verily to end of verse G[L]TTrAWHR

σοί.

Mat. 4: 9 trs ταῦτά σοι πάντα TTrAWH
9: 2 omit thee LTTrAWHR
    5 σοῦ (omit thee) GEds
12:47 omit the verse [T]WH
Mar. 1:11*for ᾧ (ὅς) LTTrAWH
2: 5 omit thee GTTrAWHR
    9 σοῦ (omit thee) GTTrAWWHR
9:43 σ. ἐστίν—ἐ. σε LTTrAWHR
    45 σέ Eds
    47 σέ TTrAWHR
10:21 σέ TAWHR
Joh. 5:14 trs σοί τι GEds
9:10 σοῦ s—σοί E
Acts 9: 5 omit GEds, see κύριος
10: 6 omit GEds, see ποιέω
    32 omit LTT[A]WHR, see λαλέω
24:13*δύνανται—add σ. read prove to thee Eds
1 Ti. 6:13 omit σ. T
Philem.12(11)*sent again—add σ. to thee Eds
3 Joh. 13*add σ. Eds, see γράφω
Rev. 14:15 omit for thee GEds

Σολομών, -ῶν.

Mat. 1: 6 Σολομῶνα GTTrAWWH
12:42 Σολομῶνος GLTTrAWWH
Lu. 11:31 Σολομῶνος bis GLTTrAWWH
Joh. 10:23 (τοῦ TrWH) Σολομῶνος GLTTrA
Acts 3:11 Σολομῶνος GTrW   (WWH
5:12 Σολομῶνος GTrAW
7:47 Σαλωμών T

σοῦ.

Mat. 5:39 omit σ. read the right cheek T[WH]
6:13 omit GEds, see αἰών
    21*for ὑμῶν bis LTTrAWH
9: 5*for σοί, read thy sins GEds
12:47 omit the verse [T]WH
15: 4 omit thy GEds
18:16 thee—thyself, σεαυτοῦ T, omit σ. L
19:19 omit thy¹ GLTTrAWWH
20:21 omit σ.¹ read the right hand LTWH
    21*εὐωνύμων σ. thy left GEds
Mar. 1: 2 omit before thee GEds
3: 5 omit σ. T[Tr]A
    32*add σ. LT[A]W, see ἀδελφή
10:19*μητέρα σ. thy mother LT
    37*εἰς²—add σ. T
    37 omit σ.² [L]TTrAWHR
14:70 omit and thy speech agreeth (thereto) LTTrAWH
Lu. 1:35*born—add ἐκ σ. A.V.B.[L]
11: 2 omit thy will be done GTTrAWHR
    34*ὀφθαλμός¹ σ. thine eye LTTrAWHR
18:20 omit σ.² LTrAWWHR
19:42 omit thy¹ LTr[A]WHR
    42 omit thy² [LTr\]WHR
Joh. 4:51 thy—his, αὐτοῦ LTTrAWHR
5:12 omit thy bed T[Tr]AWHR
8:10 omit those thine accusers WHR
9:10 σοῦ s—σοί E
17: 1 omit σ.² read the Son TT[A]WHR
    17 omit σ. read the truth LTTrAWHR
18:11 omit σ. read the sword GEds
Acts 4:28 omit thy² L[Tr]WH
    30 omit σ.¹ LTrWH
26: 3 omit σ. LTTrAWHR
1 Ti. 5:23 omit σ.¹ LTTrAWHR
6:21 thee—you, ὑμῶν LTTrWHR
Heb. 1: 8 thy²—his, αὐτοῦ WH
2: 7 omit and didst set to end of verse G[L]T[Tr]A[WH]
Jas. 2:18 omit thy² Eds
Rev. 2: 2 omit thy² LTTrAWHR
13 omit thy works, and LTTrAWHR
19 omit thy² Tr
20*γυναῖκα—add σ. read thy wife GL[A]W

σοφια.

Lu. 2:40 σοφίᾳ TrAWH
52 trs stature and wisdom Tr: τῇ σοφίᾳ TWH
1 Co. 1:30 trs σοφία ἡμῖν LTTrAWH

σοφός.

1 Ti. 1:17 omit wise GEds
Jude 25 omit wise GEds

Σπανία.

Ro. 15:28 τὴν Σ.—omit τὴν LTTrAWH

σπαράσσω, -ττω.

Mar. 9:20 συσπαράσσω LTWHR
26 σπαράξας GEds

σπείρω.

Mat. 13:18 σπείραντος LTTrAWH
24 σπείραντι A.V.C LTTrAWH
25 ἐπισπείρω LTTrAWH
27 ἔσπειρες Tr
Mar. 4: 3 τοῦ σ.—omit τοῦ LT[Tr]AWH

σπεκουλάτωρ, -τορ LTTrAWH.

σπέρμα.

2 Co. 9:10 σπόρος LTr

σπιλάς.

Jude 12 εἰσιν—add οἱ LTTrAWH

σπιλόω.

Jas. 3: 6 ἡ σ.—καὶ σ. T

σπόριμα.

Lu. 6: 1 τῶν σ.—omit τῶν LTTrAWH

σπόρος.

2 Co. 9:10*σπόρον for σπέρμα LTr

σπουδαιότερον.

2 Ti. 1:17 very diligently—diligently, σπουδαίως LTTrWHR

σπουδαίως, -οτέρως.

2 Ti. 1:17*for σπουδαιότερον LTTrWHR

σπυρίς, σφυρίς WH, L at times.

στάδιος, -ον.

Mar. 14:24*μέσον τῆς θαλάσσης ἦν was now in the midst of the sea—σταδίους πολλοὺς ἀπὸ τῆς γῆς ἀπεῖχεν was many furlongs distant from the land TrWH
Joh. 6:19 στάδια T
Rev. 21:16 σταδίων s—σταδίους EGLTrA

* στασιαστής, an insurgent.

Mar. 15: 7 στασιαστῶν for συστασιαστῶν (-τῆς) LTTrAWHR

στάσις.

Acts 24: 5 στάσεις seditions LTTrWWHR

σταυρός.

Mar.10:21 omit take up the cross [L]TTrWHR
Gal. 6:12 trs τῷ σ. τοῦ χριστοῦ μὴ LTTrAWHR

σταυρόω.

Mar.15:20 σταυρώσουσιν LTTrA
24 σταυροῦσιν TTrAWHR
Lu. 23:21 σταυρου, σταυρου LTTrAWH
Joh. 19:10 see ἀπολύω

σταφυλή.

Mat. 7:16 σταφυλάς LTTrAWH
Lu. 6:44 trs σταφυλὴν ῥυγῶσιν TTrAWH

στάχυς.

Lu. 6: 1 trs and did eat the ears of corn TrAWH

στήκω.

Mar. 3:31*στήκοντες for ἑστῶτες (ἵστημι) TTrAWH
11:25 στήκετε LTTrAWH
Joh. 1:26*στήκει for ἕστηκεν (ἵστημι) TTrAWH
1 Th. 3: 8 στήκετε TTrAWH

στηρίζω.

Lu. 9:51 ἐστήρισεν TTrAWH
22:32 στήρισον LTTrAWH
Acts 18:23*στηρίζων for ἐπιστηρίζων (-ζω) LTTrAWH
1 Pet. 5:10 στηρίξει will stablish GEds
Rev. 3: 2 στήρισον GLTTrAWWH

* στιβάς, bed of straw, twigs, &c.

Mar. 11: 8 στιβάδας *for* στοιβάδας (-βάς) LTTrAWHR

στοιβάς.

Mar. 11: 8 στιβάς LTTrAWHR

στολή.

Lu. 15:22 τὴν σ.—*omit* τὴν LTTrAWHR
Rev. 6:11 στολὴ λευκη᾽ a white robe GEds
7:14 στολὰς αὐτῶν²—αὐτάς ([a.]A) A.V.C GEds
22:14*ποιοῦντες τὰς ἐντολὰς αὐτοῦ do his commandments—πλύνοντες τὰς στολὰς αὐτῶν wash their robes LTTrAWHR

στόμα.

Mat. 15: 8 *omit* draweth nigh unto me with their mouth, and GLTTrAWHR

στρατεία.

2 Co. 10: 4 στρατιά T

στράτευμα.

Rev. 9:16 τῶν στρατευμάτων A.V.C GEds

στρατεύομαι.

1 Ti. 1:18 στρατεύσῃ TTr

στρατηγός.

Lu. 22: 4 τοῖς σ.—*omit* τοῖς TTrAWHR
Acts 5:24 ὁ σ.—*omit* ὁ LTTrAWHR

στρατιά.

2 Co. 10: 4*στρατιᾶς *for* στρατείας (-ία) T

στρατοπεδάρχης.

Acts 28:16 *omit* the centurion *to* the guard: but LTTrAWHR

στρέφω.

Mat. 9:22*στραφείς *for* ἐπιστραφείς (-στρέφω) LTTrAWHR
27: 3*ἔστρεψεν *for* ἀπέστρεψεν (ἀποστρέφω) TTrAWHR
Lu. 10:22 *see* μαθητής
Joh. 12:40*στραφῶσιν *for* ἐπιστραφῶσιν (-στρέφω) LTTrAWHR

στρώννυμι, -ύω.

Mat. 21: 8 σ.²—ἔστρωσαν T
Mar. 11: 8 *omit* and strawed (them) in the way TTrAWHR

στυγνάζω.

Mat. 16: 3 When it is (verse 2) to end of verse 3 [TA] [[WH]]

Στωϊκός, Στοϊ— LTA, Στωι— WH.

Acts 17:18 τῶν Σ.—*omit* τῶν LTTrAWHR

σύ.

Mar. 14:30*that—*add* σύ thou GEds
68 *trs* σὺ τί LTTrAWHR
Lu. 1:28 *om.* blessed (art) thou among women T[Tr]AWHR
16:25 *omit* σύ¹ GTTrAWHR
19:42 *trs* καὶ σύ after ταύτῃ WH
Joh. 1:21 *omit* σύ¹ T: *trs* σὺ ([σὺ]WH) Ἡλίας εἰ TrWH: σὺ οὖν τί; Ἡλ. εἶ A
8:53 *omit* σύ² GLTTrAWHR
9:1, *trs* τί σὺ TrAWH
2 Ti. 2 *omit* thou therefore Eds
Philem. 12 *omit* thou therefore receive LTTrAWHR

συγγένεια.

Lu. 1:61 ἐκ τῆς συγγενείας LTTrAWHR

συγγενής.

Mar. 6: 4 συγγενεῦσιν TTrWH
Lu. 1:36 συγγενίς LTWWHR
Ro. 16:11 συγγενῆν Tr

* συγγενίς, kinswoman.

Lu. 1:36 συγγενίς *for* συγγενής LTWWHR

συγκακοπαθέω.

2 Ti. 2: 3*συγκακοπάθησον *for* κακοπάθησον (-θέω) Eds

συγκαλέω.

Lu. 15: 9 συγκαλεῖ TWHR

συγκατατίθεμαι.

Lu. 23:51 συνκατατιθέμενος T

συγκεράννυμι.

Heb. 4: 2 συγκεκερασμένους LTrAWHR, -μένος T, συγκεκραμένους W

συγκλείω.

Gal. 3:23 συγκλειόμενοι LTTrAWHR

συγκληρονόμος.

1 Pet. 3: 7 συγκληρονόμοις TTrA

συγχράομαι.

Joh. 4: 9 *omit* for the Jews have no dealings with the Samaritans T[WH]

συγχύνω.

Acts 9:22 συνέχυννεν TAWH
21:31 συγχύννεται LTTrAWH, -ύνε- WR

σύγχυσις.

Acts 19:29 τῆς συγχύσεως GTTrAWWHR

συζήτησις.

Acts 15: 2 ζήτησις GEds
7 ζήτησις TTrWH
28:29 *omit the verse* LTTrAWHR

συζωοποιέω.

Col. 2:13 συνεζωοποίησεν GEds

συκομωραία B, —ρέα L, συκομορέα EGTTrAWWH.

συλλαλέω.

Mat. 17: 3 *trs* σ. μετ᾽ αὐτοῦ LTTrWH

συλλαμβάνω.

Lu. 1:31 συλλήμψῃ LTTrAWH
36 συνείληφεν TrWH
2:21 συλλημφθῆναι LTTrAWH
Acts 23:27 συλλημφθέντα LTTrAWH

συμβαίνω.

1 Co. 10:11 συνέβαινεν TTrWH

συμβάλλω.

Acts 4:15 συνέβαλλον LTTrAWH
20:14 συνέβαλλεν LTTrAWH

συμβιβάζω.

Acts 19:33*συνεβ.βασαν *for* προεβίβασαν (προβιβάζω) LTTrWH
Col. 2: 2 συμβιβασθέντες GEds

συμβουλεύω.

Joh. 11:53 took counsel together—took counsel, βουλεύομαι LTTrWHR

Συμεών.

2 Pet. 1: 1 Σίμων A.V.C LWHR

συμμαρτυρέω.

Rev. 22:18 μαρτυρέω GEds

* συμμορφίζω, to make conformable.

Phil. 3:10 συμμορφιζόμενος *for* συμμορφούμενος (-φόω) Eds

συμμορφόω.

Phil. 3:10 συμμορφίζω Eds

συμπαραγίνομαι.

2 Ti. 4:16 stood with—stood by, παραγίνομαι LTTrAWH

συμπαραλαμβάνω.

Acts 15:38 συμπαραλαμβάνειν LTTrAWHR

συμπαραμένω.

Phil. 1:25 παραμένω LTTrAWHR

* συμπίπτω, to fall together.

Lu. 6:49 συνέπεσεν *for* ἔπεσεν (πίπτω) TTrAWHR

συμφάγω, *see* συνεσθίω.

συμφέρω.

1 Co. 7:35 σύμφορος LTTrAWHR
10:33 σύμφορος LTTrAWH
2 Co. 12: 1 δεῖ, οὐ συμφέρον μέν, ἐλεύσομαι δέ I must glory, it is not expedient indeed, but I will come LTTrWHR

* σύμφορος, profitable.

1 Co. 7:35 σύμφορον *for* συμφέρον (-ρω) LTTrAWHR
10:33 σύμφορον *for* συμφέρον (-ρω) LTTrAWH

συμφωνέω.

Mat. 18:19*trs* συμφωνήσωσιν (-σουσιν TTrA) ἐξ ὑμῶν LTTrAWH
Lu. 5:36 οὐ συμφωνήσει will not agree LTTrAWH

σύν.

Mat. 27:44*συσταυρωθέντες—ad.σ.LTTrAWH
Mar. 15:32*συνεσταυρωμένοι—add σ. LTWH
Lu. 8:45*σ. αὐτῷ *for* μετ᾽ αὐτοῦ GLTTrAR
51*add σ. LTTrAWHR, *see* οὐδείς
23:35 *omit* with them [L]TTrAWHR
24: 1 *omit* and certain (others) with them LTTrAWH
Joh. 12: 2*add σ. GEds, *see* ἀνάκειμαι
Acts 1:14 *omit* σ.² LT[Tr]AW
17 with—among, ἐν GEds
7:35*for ἐν¹ Eds
16:32*for καὶ² GEds
2 Co. 4:14*for διά Eds
8:19 with²—in, ἐν LTTrAWWHR

συνάγω.

Mat. 13:30 συνάγετε LTrWH
25:32 συναχθήσονται LTTrAWH
Mar. 4: 1 συνάγεται is gathered Eds
Lu. 3:17 συναγαγεῖν to gather TWHR
17:37 ἐπισυναγω TTrAWHR
Joh. 20:19 *omit* assembled LTTrAWHR
Rev. 13:10 *omit* lendeth, *read* (is) for captivity Eds
19:17 συνάχθητε GEds

συναγωγή.

Mar. 1:21 τὴν σ.—*omit* τὴν B
39 εἰς τὰς συναγωγάς GEds
3: 1 τὴν σ.—*omit* τὴν T[Tr]AW
Lu. 4:44 εἰς τὰς συναγωγάς TTrAWHR
21:12 τὰς συναγωγάς TTrWHR, [τὰς σ. A
Joh. 18:20 τῇ σ.—*omit* τῇ GEds
Acts 13:42 *omit* of the synagogue GEds
17: 1 ἡ σ.—*omit* ἡ LTTr[A]WHR
Jas. 2: 2 τὴν σ.—*omit* τὴν LTTrAWHR

συναθροίζω.

Lu. 24:33 ἀθροίζω LTTrAWHR

συνακολουθέω.

Mar. 14:51*συνηκολούθει *for* ἠκολούθει (ἀκολουθεω) LTTrAWHR
Lu. 23:49 συνακολουθοῦσαι TTrAWHR

* συναλλάσσω, to commune with.

Acts 7:26 συνήλλασσεν *for* συνήλασεν (συνελαύνω) LTTrWWHR

συνανάκειμαι.

Mar. 6:26 ἀνάκειμαι (*omit* with him) TTrAWHR
Joh. 12: 2 ἀνάκειμαι σύν GEds

συναναμίγνυμι.

2 Th. 3:14 μὴ συναναμίγνυσθαι to have no company LTrAWHR

συναναπαύομαι.

Ro. 15:32 *omit* and may with you be refreshed L[A]

συναντάω.

Heb. 7: 1 ὁ σ.—ὃς σ. LTrA

συνάντησις.

Mat. 8:34 ὑπάντησιν LTTrWH

συνβ., συνγ., συνζ., etc.

☞ *In compounds of* συν *with words commencing with* β, γ, ζ, κ, λ, μ, π, σ *and* ψ, *the* ν *is mostly retained by* T *and at times by other Editors.*

συνειδέω, συνείδον.

Acts 5: 2 συνειδυίης LTTrAWH

συνείδησις.

Joh. 8: 9 *om.* being convicted by (their own) conscience WH
1 Co. 8: 7 with conscience of—being used to, συνήθεια LTTrWH

συνελαύνω.

Acts 7:26 συναλλάσσω LTTrWWH : *re-conciliabat* A.V.Vul

* συνεπιτίθημι to join in attack.

Acts 24: 9 συνεπέθεντο *for* συνέθεντο (συντίθημι) GEds

συνεργέω.

Jas. 2:22 συνεργεῖ worketh with TTr

συνεργός.

1 Th. 3: 2*om*συνεργὸν *for* διάκονον (-νος) GLAW
    2 *omit* and our fellow-labourer GEds

συνέρχομαι.

Mar. 6:33 *omit* and came together unto him GEds
Acts 10:23 συνῆλθαν WH
    45 συνῆλθαν TTrWH
    21:22 *omit* TrWH, *see* δεῖ
    22:30*συνελθεῖν *for* ἐλθεῖν (ἔρχομαι) GEds
1 Co. 7: 5 come—may be, ἦτε (ὦ) GEds: συνέρχησθε S, συνέρχεσθε B

συνεσθίω.

Acts 11: 3 συνέφαγεν did eat TrWH

συνήθεια.

1 Co. 8: 7*συνηθείᾳ *for* συνειδήσει (-σις) LTTrWH

συνθλάομαι.

Mat. 21:44 *omit the verse* [L]T[WH]

συνίημι.

Mat. 13:23 συνιείς LTTrWH
Mar. 7:14 σύνετε LTTrAWH
Ro. 3:11 ὁ σ.—*omit* ὁ L[TrWH]
2 Co. 10:12 συνιᾶσιν LTTrAWH
Eph. 5:17 συνίετε understand LTTrAWH

συνιστάνω, -άω, συνίστημι.

2 Co. 3: 1 συνιστᾶν LTr
    4: 2 | 6: 4 συνιστάντες LTTrAW, -τάνοντες WH
    10:18 σ.¹—συνιστάνων LTTrAWWH
Gal. 2:18 συνιστάνω GLTTrAWWH

συνοδία.

Lu. 2:44 *trs* εἶναι ἐν τῇ σ. LTTrAWH

συντάσσω.

Mat. 21: 6*συνέταξεν *for* προσέταξεν (προσ-τάσσω) LTrAWH

συντέλεια.

Mat. 24: 3 τῆς σ.—*omit* τῆς LTTrAWH

συντελέω.

Mat. 7:28 τελέω LTTrAWH
Mar. 13: 4 *trs* ταῦτα σ. πάντα TTrAWH
Joh. 2: 3*add σ. T, *see* οἶνος

συντέμνω.

Ro. 9:28 *omit* σ.² LTTr[A]WH, *see* λόγος

συντηρέω.

Lu. 5:38 *omit* and both are preserved T[Tr]AWH

συντίθημι.

Acts 24: 9 assented—joined in the charge, συνεπιτίθημι GEds

συντρίβω.

Lu. 4:18 *omit* to heal the broken-hearted G[L]TTrAWH

Συροφοίνισσα.

Mar. 7:26 Σύρα Φ. TrA: Συροφοινίκισσα LTWWH, Συραφ- G

σύρτις, σῦρτις L.

Acts 27:17 quicksand—Syrtis (as a pro-per name) EGTWWH

συσπαράσσω.

Mar. 9:20*συνεσπάραξεν *for* ἐσπάραξεν (σπαράσσω) LTWH

συστασιαστής.

Mar. 15: 7 στασιαστής LTTrAWH

συστατικός.

2 Co. 3: 1 *omit* of commendation² Eds

συστρέφω.

Mat. 17:22*συστρεφομένων *for* ἀναστρεφο-μένων (-φω) LTTrWH

συσχηματίζομαι.

Ro. 12: 2 μὴ συσχηματίζεσθαι not to be conformed LA

Συχάρ s, Σιχάρ B.

Συχέμ.

Acts 7:16 τοῦ Σ.—*omit* τοῦ TTrWH

σφάττω.

Rev. 6: 4 σφάξουσιν LTTrAWH
    13: 8 τοῦ ἐσφαγμένου A.V.C GEds

σφραγίζω.

2 Co. 1:22 ὁ καὶ σ.—*omit* ὁ [WH]R
    11:10 σφραγίσεται S—φράσσω A.V.B BGEds
Rev. 7: 3 σφραγίζωμεν S—σφραγίσωμεν A.V.BEGEds
    5³³, 6 *ter*, 7 *ter*, 8¹² *omit* (were) sealed Eds

σφραγίς.

Rev. 6: 3*trs* τὴν σ. τὴν δευτέραν GEds
    5*trs* τὴν σ. τὴν τρίτην GEds

* σφυδρόν, the ankle.

Acts 3: 7 σφυδρά *for* σφυρά (-ρόν) TWH

σφυρίς, *see* σπυρίς.

σφυρόν.

Acts 3: 7 σφυδρόν TWH

σχίζω.

Lu. 5:36*καινοῦ — add σχίσας, read rendeth a piece from a new garment TTrAWH
    36 maketh a rent—σχίσει he will rend LTTrAWH

σχίσμα.

1 Co. 12:25 σχίσματα schisms T

σχολάζω.

1 Co. 7: 5 σχολάσητε GEds

σώζω.

Mat. 18:11 *omit the verse* LTTr[A]WH
Lu. 9:56 *omit* for the Son *to* to save them GLTTrAWH
    17:33 to save—to gain, περιποιέομαι TTrAWH
Rev. 21:24 *omit* of them which are saved GEds

σῶμα.

Mat. 14:12 body—corpse, πτῶμα LTTrWH
    27:58 *omit the body*² [T|TrWH]
Mar. 14: 8 *trs* τὸ σῶμά μου LTrWH
    15:45 body-corpse,πτῶμα LTTrAWH
Joh. 19:38 *omit the body*² T
1 Co. 7:34 τῷ σώματι LTTrAWH
    15:38 τὸ ἴδιον σ.—*omit* τὸ LTTrAWH
    44 *omit* body⁴ Eds
2 Co. 4:10 τῷ σ.²—τοῖς σώμασιν bodies T

σωτηρία.

Acts 7:25 *trs* σωτηρίαν αὐτοῖς Eds
2 Co. 1: 6 *omit* and salvation² GTWH
1 Pet. 2: 2*add at end εἰς σωτηρίαν unto salvation GEds

σωτήριος.

Tit. 2:11 ἡ σ.—*omit* ἡ LTTrAWH

σωφρονίζω.

Tit. 2: 4 σωφρονίζουσιν TTrA

Ταβιθά, Ταβειθά WH.

τάλαντον.

Mat. 25:16 *omit* talents² LTr[A]WH

ταλιθά, ταλειθά WH.

ταμεῖον.

Mat. 6: 6 ταμεῖον TAWH

τάξις.

Heb. 7:21 *omit* after the order of Mel-chisedec TTrAWH

* ταπεινόφρων, lowly in mind.

1 Pet. 3: 8 ταπεινόφρονες *for* φιλόφρονες (-φρων) GEds

ταπεινόω.

Mat. 18: 4 ταπεινώσει LTTrAWWH
2 Co. 12:21 ταπεινώσει με LTTrA

ταράσσω.

Joh. 5: 4 *omit* waiting for (*ver.* 3) *to* end of verse 4 [G]TTrAWH
Acts 17:13*stirred up—*add* καὶ ταράσσον-τες and troubled LTTrAWH

ταραχή.

Mar. 13: 8 *omit* and troubles LTTr[A]WH
Joh. 5: 4 *omit* waiting for (*ver.* 3) *to* end of verse 4 [G]TTrAWH

τάσσω.

Mat. 8: 9*ἐξουσίαν—*add* τασσόμενος, read placed under L[WH]
Acts 18: 2*τεταχέναι *for* διατεταχέναι (διατάσσω) T

ταῦρος.

Heb. 9:13 *trs* of goats and of bulls Eds

ταῦτα, *see* ὁ αὐτός.

ταῦτα *from* οὗτος.

Mar. 8: 7*add* τ. TrWH, *see* παρατίθημι
Lu. 2:51 *omit* these [L|T[A]WH
    6:23, 26 τὰ αὐτά (ὁ αὐτός) LTTrAWH
    11:53 *omit* TTrAWH, *see* ἐξέρχομαι
    13: 2*for* τοιαῦτα (τοιοῦτος) TTrWH
    17:30 ταῦτα—ταῦτα GLW, τὰ αὐτά (ὁ αὐτός) LTTrAWH
    18: 4 *trs* ταῦτα δὲ TrAWH
    22 *omit* these things LTTrAWH
    23:46 τοῦτο LTTrAWH
    24:11*for* αὐτῶν¹ LTTrAWH
Joh. 9:40 *omit* these words T
    11:28 τοῦτο TTrAWH
Acts 5: 5 *omit* these things LTTrAWH
    24:22 *omit* when heard these things GEds
    26:30 *omit* and when he had thus spoken GEds
    28:29 *omit the verse* LTTrAWH
1 Co. 6: 8 τοῦτο Eds
Rev. 7: 1 these things—this, τοῦτο Eds
    10: 4 αὐτά Eds
    21: 7*for* πάντα (πᾶς) Eds
    22:18 these things—them αὐτά GEds

ταύταις.

Lu. 13:14 αὐταῖς LTTrAWH

ταύτη.

Mar. 14:27 *omit* this night [L]TTrAWWH
Acts 4:27*add* τ. GEds, *see* πόλις
Heb. 3:10*for* ἐκείνῃ (-νος) Eds

ταύτην.

Mat. 15:15 *omit* τ. read the parable LTTr[A]WH
Joh. 7: 8 *omit* τ.¹ read the feast Eds
Acts 1:16 *omit* τ. read the scripture LTTr[A]WWH

Heb. 5: 3 αὐτήν Eds
Rev. 12:15 αὐτήν GEds

ταύτης.
Acts 17:30 hujus ignorantiæ A.V.Vul
Heb.12:15 αὐτῆς LVH

τάχιον, —χειον WH.
1 Ti. 3:14 τάχος LTrWH

τάχος.
1 Ti. 3:14*ἐν τάχει for τάχιον LTrWH
Rev. 2: 5 τάχει s—ταχύ EGW, omit quickly LTTrAWH

ταχύ.
Mar.16: 8 omit quickly GEds
Lu. 15:22*τ. ἐξενέγκατε bring forth quickly L[Tr]WH
Rev. 2: 5 τάχος s—τ. EGW, omit quickly LTTrAWH

τε.
Mat. 23: 6 δέ LTTrAWH
Mar. 15:36 omit and³ LTTrAWH
Lu. 15: 2*οἱ—add τε, read both the Pharisees LTTrAWH
Acts 2: 3 ἐκάθισέν τε—καὶ ἐ. LTTrWH
3 τε TWH
43*add τε T, see φόβος
3:10 δέ LTTrAWH
7:26 τε s—δέ EGW
8: 1 δέ LTrA[WH]R, omit and³ T
6 δέ LTTrAWH
28 δέ WH
9: 6 omit GEds, see σκληρός
15*ἐθνῶν—add τε, read both Gentiles Eds
24 τε¹—δὲ καί and also LTTrAWH
10: 2 omit τε Eds
48 δέ TTrWH
11:13 δέ LTTrWH
12: 8 δέ LTrWH
13: 2 omit τε GEds
15: 3*τήν¹—add τε, read both Phenice LTTrAWH
9 omit τε W
32 τε s—δέ E
16:11 δέ LTTrAWH
12 ἐκεῖθέν τε—κἀκεῖθεν Eds
23 δέ WH
26 δέ LTTrAWH
17: 5 ἐπιστάντες τε—καὶ ἐ. LTTrAWH
19 δέ TrWH
18:11 δέ LTTrAWH
19: 2*εἶπεν—add τε, read and he said LTTrAWH
3 εἶπέν τε—ὁ δὲ ε. T
27 for δέ EGLTTrAWH
21:11 omit and² Eds
22:28 δέ LTTrWH, omit and¹ A
23:10 omit τε WH
35 omit τε LTTrAWH
24:23 omit and¹ Eds
26: 4*ἐν²—add τε. read and at Jerusalem Eds
10*many—add τε also LTTrAWH
20*πρῶτον—add τε, read both of Damascus LTTrAWH
23*τῷ—add τε,read both unto the people LTTrAWH
30*ἀνέστη—add τε, read and the king GEds
1 Co. 1: 2 omit both LTTr[A]WH
2 Co. 10: 8 omit τε [L]Tr[A]
12:12*σημείοις—add τε, read both in signs and TA[WH]R
Eph. 1:10 omit both GEds
Heb. 4:12 omit τε¹ Eds
5: 1 omit both L[TrWH]
6: 2 omit and² [Tr]WH
11:32 omit and³ LTTrWWH
Rev. 1: 2 omit and² GEds
19:18*ἐλευθέρων—add τε, read both free Λ.V.†GEds
18*μικρῶν—add τε W, read and both small
21:12 omit and¹ GEds
See also δέ and καί.

τεκνίον.
Gal. 4:19 little children—children, τέκνον LTTr

τέκνον.
Mat. 11:19 children—works, ἔργον TrWH
Mar. 12:19†trs μὴ ἀφῇ τέκνον leave no child TAWH

Lu. 7·35 trs πάντων τῶν τ. αὐτῆς LTTrAWH
1 Co. 4:17 trs μου τέκνον LTTrAWH
Gal. 4:19*τέκνα for τεκνία (-νίον) LTTr

Joh. 17: 4 τελειώσας having finished LTTrAWH
Acts 20:24 τελειῶσαι WH
2 Co. 12: 9 τελέω LTTrAWH

τελευταω.
Mar. 9:44, 46 omit the verses T[Tr]WH
Joh. 11:39*τετελευτηκότος for τεθνηκότος (θνήσκω) Eds

τελέω.
Mat. 7:28*ἐτέλεσεν for συνετέλεσεν (συντελέω) LTTrAWH
2 Co. 12: 9*τελεῖται for τελειοῦται (όω) LTTrAWH
Rev. 10: 7 ἐτελέσθη was finished GEds
17:17 τελεσθήσονται GEds

τέλος.
Heb. 3: 6 omit firm unto the end A[WH]
Rev. 1: 8 omit the beginning and the ending GEds
22:13 τὸ τ. GLTAWH, see ἀρχή

τελώνης.
Mat. 5:47 publicans—heathen, ἐθνικός GEds
Mar. 2:16 trs sinners and publicans¹ LTTrAWH
16 trs sinners and publicans² LTr
Lu. 5:29 trs πολὺς τελωνῶν LTTrAWH
30 τῶν τελωνῶν GEds
7:34 trs φίλος τελωνῶν GLTTrAWH

τεσσαράκοντα, τεσσε—
Mat. 4: 2 trs τ.² νύκτας T
Rev. 7: 4 see ρμδ²

τεσσαρακονταετής, τεσσε— TTrAWH.

τέσσαρες —ρα, τέσσε—
Rev. 4: 8 τὰ τ. GEds
5:14 omit four (and) twenty GEds
7: 4 see ρμδ²
9:13 omit four LTr[A]WH

τετρακόσιοι, —σω
Acts 13:20 see ἔτος

τετράμηνος, —νον
Joh. 4:35 τετράμηνος GEds

τετράρχης, τετραάρχης TWH.

τέχνη.
Acts 18: 3 τῇ τέχνῃ Eds

τηλαυγῶς.
Mar. 8:25 δηλαυγῶς T

τηρέω.
Mat. 19:17 τήρει LTrAWH
23: 3 omit observe¹ LTTrAWH
3 trs do and observe LTTrAWH
Joh. 12: 7 τηρήσῃ she might keep Eds
14:15 τηρήσετε ye will keep TTrWH
24 τετήρηκαν LTTrAWH
Acts 15:24 omit saying (Ye must) be to the law LTTrAWH
21:25 om. that they observe no such thing, save only LTTrWH
1 Co. 7:37 τοῦ τ.—omit τοῦ LTTrWH
Jas. 2:10 τηρήσῃ Eds
2 Pet. 2: 4 τηρουμένους GTTrAWH
1 Joh. 5: 2 keep—do, ποιέω Eds

τίθημι, ἔθηκα, ἐθέμην, θῶ, &c.
Mat. 14 3 put—put aside, ἀποτίθημι LTTrAWH
Mar. 4:21*τεθῇ for ἐπιτεθῇ (-τίθημι) Eds
30*ἐν τίνι αὐτὴν παραβολὴ θῶμεν; (θ. for παραβάλωμεν, -βάλλω) with what comparison shall we set it forth? LTTrAWH
6:56 ἐτίθεσαν TTrAWH
8:25*ἔθηκεν for ἐπέθηκεν (ἐπιτίθημι) LTrWH
15:46*ἔθηκεν for κατέθηκεν (κατατίθημι) LTrWH

Mar. 15:47 τέθειται LTTrAWH
Lu. 8:16*τίθησιν for ἐπιτίθησιν (-θημι) LTTrAWH
21:14 θέτε LTTrAWH
Joh. 19:41 ἐτέθη—ἦν τεθειμένος WH
20:15 trs ἔθηκας αὐτόν GLTTrAWH
Acts 9:37 trs ἔθηκαν αὐτήν TTr
1 Co. 3:10 ἔθηκα 1 laid LTTrAWH
1 Joh.3:16 τιθέναι—θεῖναι Eds
Rev. 1:17*ἔθηκεν for ἐπέθηκεν (ἐπιτίθημι) GEds

τίκτω, ἔτεκον.
Heb.11:11 omit was delivered of a child GLTTrAWH

τιμάω.
Mat. 15: 6(5) τιμήσει, read will not honour LTTrAWH

τιμή
1 Pet. 1: 7 trs glory and honour Eds
Rev. 19: 1 omit and honour GEds
21:24 omit and honour LTTrAWH, omit τήν W

τίμιος.
1 Pet. 1: 7 see πολύτιμος
2 Pet. 1: 4 trs precious and exceeding great TWH, καὶ τ. ἡμῖν LTrA. τ. ἡ. κ. μ. T, τ. κ. μ. ἡ. WH

Τιμόθεος.
Acts 17:15 τὸν Τιμόθεον TTrWH

τις, τι.
Mat. 12:47 omit the verse [T]WH
21:33 omit certain GEds
24:17 anything—the things, τά GEds
Mar. 4:22 omit τι [L]Tr[A]
5:25 omit certain LTTr[A]WH
7:16 omit the verse T[TrA]WH
8:26 omit TWH, see εἶπον
14:47 omit τις LTrAW[WH]
15:36*τις for εἰς TTrAWH
Lu. 8:51*add τινά LTTrAWH, see οὐδείς
9: 8*τις for εἰς TAWH, τίς Tr
11:37 omit certain TTrAWH
18: 3*δέ—add τις, read a certain widow E
20: 9 omit certain GEds
21: 2†trs τινα [καὶ] A
23:26 τινα LTTrAWH
24: 1 omit and certain (others) with them LTTrAWH
Joh. 6: 7 omit τι [L]Tr[A]WH
15:13 omit τις, read he lay T
16:23*ἄν τι for ὅσα ἄν LTTrAWH
Acts 5:34 omit τι Eds
10: 5*Σίμωνά τινα a certain Simon LTTrAWH
13: 1 omit certain LTTrAWH
15*εἰ—add τι A.V.Vul Eds
16: 1 omit certain² GEds
17:21*ἀκούειν—add τι LT[Tr]WH
19: 9 omit one LTTrAWH
14 τινος LTrWH
23: 9*add τ. LTTrAWH, see γραμματεύς
12 omit certain of GEds
24: 1*πρεσβυτέρων τινῶν certain elders LTTrAWH
25:26 τι²—τί (τίς) WH
26:26 omit τι WH
31*τι πράσσει T
28: 3*τι πλῆθος Eds
Ro. 8:24 τις τί—τι Eds
1 Co. 9:15 ἵνα τις—οὐδείς LTTrWH
2 Co. 8:12 omit τις, he hath Eds
11: 1*μικρόν τι some little EEds
12: 6 omit τι LTTr[A]WH
Eph. 6: 8 omit τι LTrR
Phil. 2: 1 τινα—τις GLTTrAWH
Col. 2: 4 μή τις—μηδείς Eds
Heb. 3:16 τινές—τίνες, read for who, when they heard, did provoke? GEds
1 Pet. 5: 8*τινά for τίνα (τίς) LR, omit τ. WH
3 Joh. 9*ἔγραψά τι I wrote somewhat Eds
Rev. 7: 1*τι for πᾶν LTr[A]WR
See also ὅ τι (ὅστις), εἴ τις, μή τι

τίς, τί.
Mat. 6:25 omit or what ye shall drink [T]WH
7:14*τί for ὅτι GLT
Mar. 1:27 omit LTTrAWH, see καινός
2:16 omit how is it TTrAWH (R
4:30 whereunto—how, πῶς TTrAWH

Mar. 4:30*τίνι *for* ποιῳ LTTrAWHR, *see*
τίθημι

Lu. 6: 9 εἰ (*omit* one thing) LTTrAWHR
8:45 *omit* τ[TrA]WHR, *see* λέγω
12:11 [or what thing] TrAWH
19:15 *omit* τίς, *read* they had
gained TrAWH
20:23 *omit* why tempt ye me
TTrAWH

Joh. 13:18*τίνας *for* οὕς (ὅς) TTrAWH
21:23 *omit* what (is that) to thee T

Acts 9: 6 *omit* GEds, *see* σκληρός
6 τί²—ὅ τι (ὅστις) LTTrAR, ὅτι WH
10: 6 *omit* GEds, *see* ποιέω
13:25 τίνα με—τί ἐμέ LTTrAWH
17:20 τί ἂν—τίνα LTTrWH
25:26*τί *for* τι² (τις) WH

Ro. 8:24 τις τί—τίς WH
1 Co. 3: 5 who *bis*—τί what LTTr[A]WH
Gal. 2:14 why—how, πῶς GEds
4:15 ποῦ Eds, *ubi* A.V.Vul
Col. 1:27 τίς ὁ—τί τό Eds
2 Ti. 3 τίνων LTTrAWH
Heb. 3:16*see τίς
1 Pet. 5: 8 τίνα τινά (τις) LR, *omit* τ.WH

* Τίτιος.

Acts 18: 7 ὀνόματι—*add* Τιτίου, *read* Ti-
tius Justus T[Tr]WH, Τίτου R

τοίνυν.

Jas. 2:24 *omit* then GEds

τοιοῦτος.

Mat. 18: 5*trs* ἓν παιδίον τοιοῦτον (—το
TWH) LTTrAWH
Mar. 7: 8 *omit* (as) the washing *to end*
of verse T[TrA]WHR
9:37 such—these, τούτων T
Lu. 13: 2 such—these, ταῦτα TTrWH
Acts 21:25 *omit* LTTrWHR, *see* μηδέν
1 Ti. 6: 5 *omit* from such withdraw
thyself Eds

τολμηρότερον.

Ro. 15:15 τολμηροτέρως Tr, —έρως WH

* τολμηροτέρως, more boldly.

Ro. 15:15 *for* τολμηρότερον TrWH

τόπος.

Mar. 6:11*add* τ. TTrAWHR, *see* δέχομαι
Lu. 4:17 τὸν τ.—*omit* τὸν T[WH]
9:10 *omit* desert place belonging
to the TTrAWHR, *see* πόλις
21:11 *trs* καὶ κατὰ τόπους TTrAWHR
Joh. 14: 3 *trs* τόπον ὑμῖν TTrAWH
20:25*τόπον *for* τύπον² (—πος) LT
Acts 1:25*τόπον *for* κλῆρον (—ρος)
LTTrAWHR
Heb.11: 8 τὸν τ.—*omit* τὸν LTTrAWHR
Rev. 18:17*add* τ. GEds, *see* πλέω

τοσοῦτος.

Mat. 8:10 *trs* τ. πίστιν ἐν τῷ Ἰσ. LTrAWH
Joh. 14: 9 τοσούτῳ χρόνῳ LT
Heb. 7:22 τοσούτο LTTrAWH
Rev. 21:16 *omit* τ. ἐστιν GEds

τότε.

Mat. 24:30 *omit* then² T
Lu. 11:24*[τ.] λέγει then he saith LWH
Joh. 2:10 *omit* then [L]T[TrA]WHR
10:22*for δέ WH
Acts 21:13*ἀπεκρίθη δέ—τότε ἁ. Eds
1 Co. 13:10 *omit* then Eds
Heb. 9:17*μὴ τ. *for* μήποτε WH

τοῦτο.

Mat. 17:21 *omit the verse* T[TrA]WHR
20:23*ἐμόν—*add* τ. *read* this is not
mine TA
23:14(13) *omit the verse* LTTrAWHR,
see κρίμα
Mar. 14: 9 *omit* τ. *read* the gospel
[L]TTrAWHR
36 *trs* τοῦτο ἀπ᾿ ἐμοῦ LTTrAWWH
Lu. 23:46*for ταῦτα Eds
24:40 *omit the verse* T[Tr][[WH]]
Joh. 3:32 *omit* that T
7:22 *omit* therefore T
11:28*for ταῦτα TTrAWH
14:14*for ἐγώ WH
16:18 *trs* τί ἐστιν τοῦτο LTrWH
Acts 20:29 *omit* this Eds
28:28*τ. τὸ σωτήριον this salvation
LTTrAWH
1 Co. 6: 8*for ταῦτα Eds
9:23 this—all things, πᾶς Eds

1 Co. 11:26 *omit* τ. *read* the cup Eds
15:54 *omit* WH, *see* φθαρτός
2 Co. 12:14*τρίτον—*add* τ. this third time
GLTTr[A]WWHR
Eph. 6:18 *omit* τ. LTTrAWHR
3 Joh. 5*for εἰς² Eds
Jude 5 this—all things, πᾶς Eds
Rev. 7: 1*for ταῦτα Eds

τούτοις.

Ro. 14:18 these things—this, τούτῳ GEds
Col. 3: 7*for αὐτοῖς Eds
Jude 7 *trs* τρόπον τούτοις Eds

τοῦτον.

Mat. 19:11 *omit* τ. *read* the saying [L]WH
22*λόγον—*add* [τ.], this saying
LAWH
21:44 *omit the verse* [L]T[WH]
Joh. 19:13 *τούτων Eds, *see* λόγος
Acts 17:23 him—this, τοῦτο Eds
1 Co. 3:12 *omit* τ. *read* the foundation
LTTr[A]WH
11:27 *omit* τ. *read* the bread GEds

τούτου.

Mat. 13:22 *omit* τ. *read* the world
LTTrAWH
40 *omit* τ. *read* the world
LTTr[A]WH
Mar. 4:19 *omit* τ. *read* the world
GLTTrAWH
10:10*for τοῦ αὐτοῦ LTTrAWH
Joh. 6:51 this—my, ἐμοῦ T
14:30 *omit* τ. *read* the world GEds
Acts 6:13 *omit* τ. *read* the holy
GLTTrAW[WH]
25:20 τούτων Eds
Ro. 11: 7 τοῦτο GEds
1 Co. 1:20 *omit* τ.² *read* the world Eds
Eph. 6:12 *omit* of this world w
Jas. 2: 5 *omit* τ. *read* the world GEds
Rev. 19:20 αὐτοῦ GEds

τούτους.

Mat. 7:24 [these] LTrWH
Lu. 19:27*for ἐκείνους (—νος) TTrAWH
Acts 16:36 *omit* τ. *read* the saying
LTrWHR

τούτῳ.

Mar. 6: 2*for αὐτῷ TTrAWH
Joh. 9:30 *trs* τ. γάρ TTrAWH
Acts 25: 5 ἄτοπος, *read* anything amiss
in the man LTTrAWHR : *omit*
τ. G
1 Co. 7:31 *omit* τ. *read* the world
LTTrAWH

τούτων.

Mar. 9:37*παιδίων τ. *for* τοιούτων π. T
42*μικρῶν—*add* τ. *read* these
little ones A.V.†C LTTr[A]WHR
Joh. 7:31 *omit* τ. Eds
40*add* τ. LTTrAWHR, *see* λόγος
Acts 15:28 *omit* these A

τράγος.

Heb. 9:13 *trs* of goats and of bulls Eds
19 τῶν τράγων Eds

τράπεζα.

Lu. 19:23 τὴν τ.—*omit* τὴν Eds

τραπεζίτης, —ζείτης TWH.

τράχηλος.

Ro. 16: 4 cervices A.V.Vul

τρεῖς, τρία.

Mar. 9:31* : 10:34*for τρίτῃ (—τος)
LTTrAWH, *see* ἡμέρα
Acts 10:19 *omit* three TA : two, δύο WH
1 Joh. 5: 7, 8 *omit* in heaven (*verse* 7)
to in earth (*verse* 8) GEds
8 *hi trs* A.V.Vul

τρέμω.

Acts 9: 6 *omit* (it is) hard (*verse* 5) *to*
unto him (*verse* 6) Eds
24:25 tremefactus A.V.Vul

τρέφω.

Lu. 4:16 ἀνατρέφω T
23:29*ἐθρέψαν *for* ἐθήλασαν (θηλάζω)
LTTrAWH
Rev. 12: 6 τρέφουσιν they feed TTr : ἐκ-
τρέφω W

τρέχω.

Lu. 24:12 *omit the verse* [L]T[Tr][[WH]]

* τρῆμα, a hole.

Mat. 19:24 τρήματος *for* τρυπήματος
(—μα) WH
Lu. 18:25 τρήματος *for* τρυμαλιᾶς (—λιά)
LTTrAWH

τριακοντοκτώ.

Joh. 5: 5 τριάκοντα καὶ (*omit* καὶ [L]Tr
[WH]) ὀκτώ GLTTrAWWH

τρίτος.

Mat. 20: 3 τὴν τ.—*omit* τὴν GLTTrAWWH
26:44 *omit* the third time [L]A
Mar. 9:31* : 10:34 τρεῖς LTTrAWHR, *see*
ἡμέρα
Rev. 8: 7*add* τ. GEds, *see* γῆ

τροποφορέω.

Acts 13:18 suffered he their manners—
he nourished them, τροφο-
φορέω GLTTAW

* τροφοφορέω, to bring nourishment

Acts 13:18 ἐτροφοφόρησεν *for* ἐτροποφό-
ρησεν (τροποφορέω) GLTAW

τρυμαλιά.

Mar. 10:25 τῆς τ.—*omit* τῆς LTrWWHR
Lu. 18:25 τρῆμα LTTrAWH

τρύπημα.

Mat. 19:24 τρῆμα WH

Τρωάς.

(Τρῳάς LTWH, except Acts 16:8, 11.)
Acts 16:11 τῆς τ.—*omit* τῆς LTTrAWH

Τρωγύλλιον

Acts 20:15 Τρωγυλίῳ A : *omit* and tarried
at Trogyllium LTTrWHR

τυγχάνω.

Lu. 13:30 *omit* τ. LTTr[A]WHR
Heb. 8: 6 τέτυχεν LTAWWHR

* τυπικῶς, typically.

1 Co. 10:11 *for* τύποι (—πος) Eds

τύπος.

Joh. 20:25 print*—place. τόπος LT
1 Co. 10:11 for ensamples—typically
τυπικῶς Eds
1 Th. 1: 7 τύπον an ensample Eds

τύπτω.

Lu. 22:64 *omit* they struck him on the
face, and [L]TTrAWHR

τυρβάζω.

Lu. 10:41 θορυβάζω LTTrAWHR

τυφλός.

Mat. 12:22 τ.¹—τυφλόν LWH
22 *omit* blind² and LTTrAWHR
15:14 *trs* τυφλοί εἰσιν ὁδηγοί LTrWH
14 *omit* of the blind WHR
Mar. 10:46 ὁ τ.—*omit* ὁ LTTrAWH
Lu. 14:21 *trs* the blind and the halt
LTTrAWH
Joh. 9: 6 *omit* of the blind man
[L]TTrAWH
8 blind—a beggar, προσαίτης
GEds
18 *trs* ἦν τυφλὸς TTrAWH

Τυχικός, Τύχικος, WH.

ὑγιής.

Mat. 15:31 *omit* the maimed to be
whole WH
Mar. 3: 5 *omit* whole as the other GEds
Lu. 6:10 *omit* whole GEds
Joh. 5: 4 *omit* waiting for (*ver.* 3) *to
end of verse* 4 [G]TTrAWH

ὑγρός.

Lu. 23:31 τῷ ὑ.—*omit* τῷ [Tr]WH

ὑδρία.

Joh. 2: 6 *trs* λίθιναι ὑδρίαι LTTrAWH

ὕδωρ.

Joh. 1.31 τῷ ὕ.—omit τῷ LTTr[A]WHR
    3: 3, 4 omit waiting for (ver. 3) to
        end of verse 4 [G]TTrAWHR
Rev. 8:10 τῶν ὑδάτων GEds
    11 τρίτον -add τῶν ὑδάτων A.V.B
        EGEds
    17: 1 τῶν ὕ.—omit τῶν LTTr[A]WHR
    22:17 τὸ ὕ.—omit τὸ GEds

ὑετός.

Jas. 5: 7 omit ὕ. LTTrAWH
Rev. 11: 6 trs ὑετὸς βρέχῃ ᾗ GEds

υἱός.

Mat. 1:25 τὸν υ.—omit τὸν LTTrAWH
    9:27 υἱός LTTrA
    15:22 υἱός LTTrAWH
    18:11 omit the verse LTTr[A]WHR
    20:30, 31 υἱὲ LT
    24:36*heaven—add οὐδὲ ὁ υἱός nor
        the Son LTWHR
    25:13 omit wherein the Son of man
        cometh GLTTrAWHR
Mar. 1: 1 omit the Son of God TWH
    10:35 οἱ υ.—omit οἱ A
    46 ὁ υἱός Eds
    47 ὁ υ.—υἱὲ LTTrWH
    12:37 trs αὐτοῦ ἐστιν υ. TTrAWH
Lu. 3:23 trs ὢν υ. ὡς ἐνομίζετο LTTrAWHR
    4. 9 ὁ υ.—omit ὁ GEds
    22†trs (omit ὁ T[Tr]AW) υ. ἐστιν
        Ἰωσὴφ οὗτος TAWH
    9:41 trs τὸν υἱόν σου ὧδε GW
    56 omit for the Son to save
        (them) GLTTrAWHR
    10: 6 υἱός A.V.BE
    14: 5 υἱός for ὄνος LTTrAWWH
    15-21 trs ὁ υἱὸς αὐτῷ AWH
    17:26 τοῦ υ.—omit τοῦ E
    20:44 trs αὐτοῦ υἱός TWH
    22:22 trs ὁ υἱὸς μέν TTrAWH
    24: 7 trs τὸν υ. τοῦ ἀνθρώπου ὅτι δεῖ
        TTrAWH
Joh. 1:18 Son—God, θεός TrWH
    45(46) τὸν υ.—om. τὸν LT[Tr]WHR
    6:69 that Christ the Son—the holy
        one ὁ ἅγιος GLTTrAWH
    19: 7 trs υ. θεοῦ ἑαυτὸν LTTrAWH
Acts 3:25 οἱ υἱοί GEds
    8:37 omit the verse GLTTrAWHR
    19:14 trs υἱοὶ after ἑπτὰ LTTrAWHR
Gal. 2:20 τοῦ υἱοῦ τοῦ θεοῦ—τοῦ θ. καὶ
        χριστοῦ of God and Christ
        LTr
Col. 3: 6 omit on the children of dis-
        obedience [L]TTrAWH
1 Joh.2·23†add υ. A.V.B GEds, see ὁμο-
        λογέω
    5:13 omit that believe on the name
        of the Son of God GEds
Rev. 1:13 υἱόν TWH
    14:14 υἱόν TWHR
    21: 7 ὁ υἱός—omit ὁ Eds
    12 τῶν υ.—omit τῶν Eds

ὑμᾶς.

Mat. 5:44 omit LTTrAWHR, see μισέω
    44 omit LTTrAWHR, see ἐπηρεάζω
    26:55 omit with you T[Tr]AWHR
Lu. 10:11 omit unto you GLTTrAWH
    13:27 omit you² [L]TrAWHR
    23:15 ὑμᾶς TWHR, see ἀναπέμπω
Acts 13:40 omit upon you LTTr[A]WHR
Ro. 12:14 omit you WH
    13:11*ἤδη υ. for ἡμᾶς ἤδη TAWHR
    15: 7*for ἡμᾶς GLTTrAWH
    24 omit I will come to you GEds
    16: 6*for ἡμᾶς LTTrAWHR
1 Co. 6:14 for ἡμᾶς E
    7:15*for ἡμᾶς TWH
    10:13 omit υ.³ GEds
2 Co. 7:11 omit υ. LTTr[A]WHR
    13: 4 [toward you] AWH
Gal. 4:17 you² s—us, ἡμᾶς E
Eph. 5: 2*for ἡμᾶς TTrAWHR
Col. 1:10 omit υ. read to walk GLTTrA
    12*for ἡμᾶς TWH   (WHR
    2:13*συνεζωοποίησεν υ. you hath
        he quickened Eds
1 Th. 2:15 ὑ. s—ἡμᾶς A.V.B EGEds
    3: 2 omit you² Eds
    4: 8*for ἡμᾶς Eds
2 Th. 2:17 omit υ. Eds
1 Pet. 1: 3 for ἡμᾶς E
    4 ἡμᾶς s—ὑ. A.V.B GEds
    3:18*for ἡμᾶς WH
    21*for ἡμᾶς LTTrAWHR
    4:14 omit on their part to end of
        verse LTTrAWHR

1 Pet. 5:10*for ἡμᾶς Eds
    10 omit υ. Eds, see καταρτίζω
2 Pet. 3: 9*for ἡμᾶς LTTrAWHR
Jude 5 omit ὑ.² Eds
    24 αὐτοὺς s—ὑμᾶς A.V.B
        EGLTTrWWHR

ὑμεῖς.

Mat. 9: 4 omit ὑ. LTTrAWHR
    19:28 ye²—yourselves, αὐτοί TTr
Mar. 11:26 omit the verse TTrWHR
    12:27 omit ὑ. οὖν T[Tr]AWHR
Lu. 6:31 omit ye also [L]WH
    9:55 omit and said to end of verse
        LTTrAWHR
Joh. 14:20 omit ὑ. ἔσεσθε TrAWH, [ὑ.] γ. L
Acts 7:26 omit ὑ. LTTr[A]WWHR
2 Co. 6:16 ye—we, ἡμεῖς LTTrWH
Gal. 4:28*for ἡμεῖς LTTrA

ὑμέτερος.

Lu. 16:12 your own—our own, ἡμέτερον
        (-ρος) WH
Ro. 11:31 your s - our, ἡμέτερος E
1 Co.15:31 ὑμετέραν for ἡμετέραν (-ρος)
        A.V.B EGEds
    16:17*ὑμέτερον for ὑμῶν LTTrAWWH
2 Co. 8: 8 your s—our, ἡμέτερος E

ὑμῖν.

Mat. 11:17 omit unto you² LTTrAWHR
    20:26 ἐν ὑ.²—ὑμῶν A
    23:14(13) omit the verse LTTrAWHR,
        see κρίμα
Mar. 6:11 omit verily to end of verse
        G[L]TTrAWHR
    8:12 omit unto you [A]WH
Lu. 6:25 omit υ.² TTrAWHR
    26 omit υ. GEds
    28 ὑμᾶς GLTTrA
    7:32 omit to you (υ.²) TTrWHR
    24:36 omit T[[WH]], see λέγω
Joh. 10:26 omit as I said unto you
        [L]TTr[A]WHR
    11:50*for ἡμῖν TTrAWH
    15:21 εἰς ὑμᾶς LTTrAWHR
    16: 3 omit unto you GEds
Acts 7:38*for ἡμῖν AWH
    13:26 to you²—to us, ἡμῖν TAWH
    14:17*for ἡμῖν GLT[Tr]AWHR
    15: 7*for ἡμῖν LTTrAWHR
    16:17 for ἡμῖν² ETTrWHR
    20:27 trs ὑ. after θεοῦ LTTrAWH
    32 omit you³ LTTrAWHR
Ro. 15:32 omit and may with you be
        refreshed L[A]
1 Co. 15:12 trs ἐν ὑμῖν τινες Eds
2 Co. 2: 3 omit unto you Eds
    8: 7*see ἡμῖν
Gal. 1: 8 omit unto you¹ T[WH]
    3: 1 omit among you LTTrAWHR
Eph. 4: 6 you—us, ἡμῖν GW, omit you
        LTTrAWHR
Phil. 1:28 ὑμῶν, read but of your salva-
        tion Eds
Col. 2:13 ἡμῖν s—ὑ. A.V.BE
2 Th. 3: 4 omit you² [L]TTrAWH
Philem. 6 you—us, ἡμῖν GLTrAWWH
Heb.13:21 you²—us, ἡμῖν TWHR
Jas. 1:26 omit among you GEds
1 Pet. 1:12*for ἡμῖν GEds
    2:21 for ἡμῖν EGEds
1 Joh.1· 4 ἡμεῖς (omit unto you)TTrAWHR
Jude 12 feast with—add ὑ. you A.V.C
Rev. 18: 6 omit you GEds

ὑμῶν.

Mat. 6:21 your bis—thy, σοῦ LTTrAWHR
    13:16 omit your² L[TrAWH]
    18:14 your—my, μοῦ LTrWH
Mar. 9:40 you, your s—us, our ἡμῶν bis
        A.V.B ETTrAWWHR
    10:44 υ.—ἐν ὑμῖν LWH
    11:26 omit the verse TTrWHR
    13:18 omit your flight, read it
        LTTrAWHR
Lu. 9:50*for ἡμῶν bis GLTTrAWHR
    12:22 omit υ. LTTrAWHR
    22*σώματι—add ὑ. read your
        body [LWH]R
    22:53 trs ἐστιν ὑμῶν LTTrAWHR
Joh. 6:58 omit υ. read the fathers
        LTTrAWHR
    8:38 omit ὑ. LTTrAWHR, see πατήρ
    54 your—our, ἡμῶν TTrAW
    55 ὑμῖν LTrWH
    12:35 μεθ´ ὑ.—ἐν ὑμῖν among you
        GLTTrAWH
    15:18 omit (it hated) you T

Acts 2:38*ἁμαρτιῶν—add ὑ. read your
        sins LTTrWHR
    3:22 your¹—our ἡμῶν T, omit your
        WHR
    25*for ἡμῶν TrAWHR
    26 αὐτῶν L [ὑμῶν] WH
    7:37 omit your¹ GLTTrAWHR
    43 omit ὑ. read the God
        LTTrAWHR
    14:17*for ἡμῶν GLTTrAWHR
    19:37 your—our, ἡμῶν LTTrAWHR
    25:25*for ἡμῶν LTTrAWHR
Ro. 12: 2 omit ὑ. Eds
    16:24 omit the verse LTTr[A]WHR
1 Co. 6:20 omit and in your spirit which
        are God's GEds
    14:26 omit of you LTTr[A]WH
    34 omit your LTTrAWH
    15:14 your—our, ἡμῶν WH
    16:17 ὑμέτερος LTTrAWH
2 Co. 7:12 your care for us s—our car
        for you A.V.B EG
    13 your—our, ἡμῶν Eds
    14*for ἡμῶν LA
    8: 7 ἡμῶν WH, see ἡμῖν
    19 your—our, ἡμῶν GEds
    12:14 omit to you² LTTrAWH
Gal. 4: 6 your—our, ἡμῶν GEds
    14*for ἡμῶn Eds
Eph. 1.16 omit of you LTTrAWHR
    2: 1*ἁμαρτίαις—add ὑ. read your
        trespasses LTTr[A]WHR
    5: 2*for ἡμῶν AWH
    6: 9 see αὐτῶν
Col. 1: 7 you—us, ἡμῶν LTrAWH
    3: 4*for ἡμῶν TTr
    5 omit ὑ. read the members
        TTrAWHR
    4: 8 your¹—our, ἡμῶν LTTrAWHR
1 Th. 1: 2 omit of you LTTr[A]WHR
    8 your—our, ἡμῶν W
1 Ti. 6:21*for σοῦ LTTrWH
Tit. 2: 8 you—us, ἡμῶν GEds
    10 ὑ. s—ἡμῶν A.V.B EGEds
Heb. 3:13 trs ἐξ ὑμῶν τις GLAW
    9:14 your—our, ἡμῶν LAWH
Jas. 2: 6 ὑμᾶς T
    3:14 cordibus vestris A.V.Vul
1 Pet. 1: 9 omit your WH
    2:21 for ἡμῶν EGLTTrAWHR
    3:16 omit of you, as of evildoers
        TAWHR
2 Pet. 3: 2*for ἡμῶν Eds
1 Joh. 1: 4 ἡμῶν s—ὑ. A.V.B EGW
2 Joh. 3 ἡμῶν s—ὑ. A.V.B EGLW
    12*for ἡμῶν LTrAWHR
Rev. 22:21 omit you GEds

ὑπάγω.

Mar. 2: 9*ὕπαγε for περιπάτει (-τέω) T
Lu. 4: 8 omit get thee behind me,
        Satan G[L]TTrAWHR
Joh. 13:33 trs ἐγὼ ὑπάγω GEds
    16:16 omit because I go to the
        Father TTrAWH
Rev. 13:10 vadet A.V.Vul
    14: 4 ὑπάγει LTTrAWH
    17: 8 ὑπάγει goeth LAWWH

ὑπακούω.

Mat. 8:27 trs αὐτῷ ὑπακ. LTTrAWH
Mar. 4:41 ὑπακούει TTrAWH; αὐτὸς ὑ. T
Heb. 5: 9 trs πᾶσιν τοῖς ὑ. αὐτῷ
        LTTrAWHR
1 Pet. 3: 6 ὑπήκουεν LWH

ὑπαντάω.

Mat. 28: 9*ὑπήντησεν for ἀπήντησεν
        (ἀπαντάω) TTrWH
Mar. 5: 2*ὑπήντησεν for ἀπήντησεν
        (ἀπαντάω)LTTrWH
Lu. 14:31*ὑπαντῆσαι for ἀπαντῆσαι
        (-τάω) Eds
    17:12*ὑπήντησαν for ἀπήντησαν
        (ἀπαντάω) T
Joh. 4:51*ὑπήντησαν for ἀπήντησαν
        (ἀπαντάω) LTTrAWHR
Acts 16:16*ὑπαντῆσαι for ἀπαντῆσαι
        (-τάω) TTrAWHR

ὑπάντησις.

Mat. 8:34*ὑπάντησιν for συνάντησιν
        (-σις) LTTrWH
    25: 1*ὑπάντησιν for ἀπάντησιν
        (-σις) LTTrAWH

ὑπάρχοντα.

Lu. 19: 8 trs μου τῶν ὑ. TTrAWH

ὑπάρχω.

Acts 4:34 ὁ.¹—ἦν LTTᵣWHR
  14: 8 *omit* being GEds

ὑπέρ.

Mar. 14:24*for* περί LTTᵣAWH
Lu. 6:28 περί TAWH
Joh. 1:30*for* περί LTTᵣAWH
Acts 12: 5 περί LTTᵣWH
  26: 1 περί LTTᵣA
Ro. 1: 8 περί Eds
  8:26 *omit* for us Eds
1Co. 5: 7 *omit* for us Eds
2Co. 1: 8 ὑ.¹—περί LTTᵣR
  8: 3 παρά Eds
  11: 5 | 12:11 *see* ὑπερλίαν
Gal. 1: 4 περί GLTTᵣAW
Col. 1: 3*for* περί LTᵣ
  2: 1*for* περί LTTᵣAWH
1 Th. 3: 2*for* περί GEds
  3:10 | 5:13 *see* ὑπερεκπερισσοῦ
  5:10 περί TTᵣWH
Heb. 5: 3 περί Eds
1 Pet. 4: 1 *omit* for us LTTᵣAWH

ὑπεραίρομαι.

2Co. 12: 7 *omit* lest I should be exalted
  above measure² [L]Tᵣ[A]

ὑπερβάλλω.

Eph. 2: 7 τὸ ὑπερβάλλον πλοῦτος Eds

* ὑπερεκπερισσοῦ, —σῶς.

Eph. 3:20 | 1 Th. 3:10 | 5:13 *for* ὑπὲρ
  ἐκ περισσοῦ GEds

ὑπερεκχύνομαι.

Lu. 6:38 ὑπερεκχυννόμενον LTTᵣAWH

* ὑπερλίαν.

2Co.11: 5 | 12:11 *for* ὑπὲρ λίαν
  GLTAWWHR

ὑπηρέτης.

Joh. 7:32 *trs* ὑ. οἱ ἀρχ. καὶ οἱ Φ. Τ

ὑπό.

Mat. 2:17 | 3: 3 διά Eds
  27:35 *omit* that it might *to end of
verse* GLTTᵣAWHR
  28:14*for* ἐπί LTᵣ
Mar. 8:31*for* ἀπό Eds
  13:14 *omit* spoken of by Daniel the
prophet G[L]TTᵣAWHR
Lu. 1:2ℓ ἀπό TTᵣAWHR
  5:15 *omit* by him LTTᵣAWH
  6:18 ἀπό GEds
  8:29 ἀπό WH
  43 ἀπό LTTᵣAWH
  9: 7 *omit* by him [L]TTᵣAWH
Joh. 8: 9 *omit* WHR, *see* ἐλέγχω
  10:14 *omit* ὑ. LTTᵣAWHR, *see* γινώσκω
Acts 4:36 ἀπό Eds
  10:17*for* ἀπό TWHR
  33 ἀπό LA
  15: 4 ἀπό TᵣWH
  22:30*for* παρά Eds
  23:30 *omit* ὑ. LTTᵣAWH
  24:21 ἐπι Eds
Ro. 13: 1*for* ἀπό LTTᵣWHR
  15:15 ἀπό TTᵣWHR
  24 ἀπό LA
1Co. 9:20*add* ὑ. GEds, *see* νόμος
Jas. 1:14 ἀπό A
  5:12 *for* εἰς A.V.B EGEds, *see* ὑπόκρισις
Rev. 9:18 by¹—from ἀπό GEds

ὑποκάτω.

Mat. 22:44*ὑποκάτω *for* ὑποπόδιον
  LTTᵣAWH
Mar. 12:36*ὑποκάτω *for* ὑποπόδιον AWH

ὑπόκρισις

Lu. 12: 1 *trs* ἥτις ἐστὶν ὑ. τῶν Φα. WH
Jas. 5:12 εἰς ὑπόκρισιν B—ὑπὸ κρίσιν
A.V.B EGEds
1 Pet. 2: 1 ὑπόκρισιν WH

ὑποκριτής.

Mat. 16: 3 *omit* O (ye) hypocrites
  23:14(13) *omit the verse* LTTᵣAWH,
see κρίμα
Lu. 11:44 *omit* scribes and Pharisees,
  hypocrites G[L]TTᵣAWHR
  13:15 ὑποκριται ye hypocrites Eds

---

3 Joh. 8*ὑπολαμβάνειν *for* ἀπολαμβά-
νειν (—νω) Eds

* ὑπόλειμμα, remainder.

Ro. 9:27 ὑπόλειμμα (—λιμμα WH) *for*
κατάλειμμα LTTᵣAWH

ὑπομένω.

Acts 17:14 ὑπέμεινεν LA, —αν TTᵣWH
Jas. 5:11 ὑπομείναντας endured
  LTTᵣAWH

ὑπομονή.

2 Th. 3: 5 τὴν ὑπομονήν A.V.CGEds
Rev. 2: 3 *trs* hast patience, and hast
  borne GEds
  14:12 ἡ ὑπομονή Eds

ὑπονοέω.

Acts 25:18 *trs* ἐγὼ ὑπενόουν Eds

ὑποπόδιον.

Mat. 22:44 ὑποκάτω, *read* enemies under
  thy feet LTTᵣAWH
Mar. 12:36 ὑποκάτω, *read* enemies under
  thy feet AWH

ὑποστρέφω.

Mar. 14:40 when he returned—he came,
  ἔρχομαι LTTᵣAWH
Lu. 2:20*ὑπέστρεψαν *for* ἐπέστρεψαν
  (ἐπιστρέφω) GEds
  39 ἐπιστρέφω TWH
  8:40 ὑποστρέφειν TWH
Acts 8:25 ὑπέστρεφον Eds
2 Pet. 2:21*ὑποστρέψαι *for* ἐπιστρέψαι
  (—στρέφω) LTTᵣAWH

ὑποτάσσω.

1Co.14:34 ὑποτασσέσθωσαν let them be
  under obedience LTTᵣWH
Eph. 5:22 *om* submit yourselves TAWHR:
  ὑποτασσέσθωσαν LTᵣ
1 Pet. 5: 5 *omit* be subject Eds

ὑστερέω.

Joh. 2: 3 *omit* ὑ. T, *see* οἶνος
1 Co. 12:24 ὑστερουμένῳ LTTᵣAWH

ὕστερον.

Mat. 21:29 *trs* WH, *see* ἀπερχομαι
Lu. 4: 2 *omit* afterward LTTᵣAWH

ὕστερος.

Mat. 21:31*for* πρῶτος LTᵣWH

* ὑφαίνω, to weave.

Lu. 12:27 ὑφαίνει *for* κοπιᾷ TA, *see*
κοπιάω

ὑψηλός.

Lu. 4: 5 *omit* into an high mountain
  [L]TTᵣAWH
  See also ὑψηλοφρονέω.

ὑψηλοφρονεω.

Ro. 11:20 ὑψηλὰ φρόνει TTᵣWH
1 Ti. 6:17 ὑψηλὰ φρονεῖν T

ὕψιστος.

Lu. 6:35 τοῦ ὑ.—*omit* τοῦ GLTTᵣAWH
Heb. 7: 1 τοῦ ὑ.—*omit* τοῦ A.V.CE

ὕψος.

Eph. 3:18 *trs* height and depth LTᵣAWH

ὑψόω.

Mat. 11:23 ἡ...ὑ.—μὴ...ὑψωθήσῃ; shalt
  thou be exalted ? LTTᵣAWH,
  ἡ (ὅς)...ὑψώθης W
Lu. 10:15 ἡ...ὑ.—μὴ...ὑψωθήσῃ; shalt
  thou be exalted ? LTTᵣAWH

φάγω.

Mat. 12: 4 ἔφαγεν—ἔφαγον LTWH
Mar. 8: 9 *om.* that had eaten T[Tᵣ]AWH
  14:22 *omit* eat GEds (R
Lu. 9:13 *trs* φαγεῖν ὑμεῖς LTAWH
1 Co. 11:24 *omit* take, eat GEds
Rev. 2:17 *omit* to eat of GEds

φαιλόνης, φελόνης EGLTTᵣAWWH.

φαίνω.

Mat. 2:13†*trs* κατ᾽ ὄναρ φ. (ἐφάνη L) LTᵣ
  19 *trs* φαίνεται κατ᾽ ὄναρ LTTᵣAWH
Rev. 8:12 φάνῃ LTWWHR, φανῇ TᵣA
  18:23 φάνῃ A.V.VᵤI LTWHR

Φαλέκ, Φάλεκ LTᵣWH.

νεφάλεος, —λιος, 1 Tim. EGEds.

φανερός.

Mat. 6: 4 *omit* openly Eds
  6 *omit* openly LTTᵣAWH
  18 *omit* openly GEds
Mar. 3:12 *trs* φανερὸν αὐτόν GW
  4:22 *trs* ἔλθῃ εἰς φανερόν TTᵣAWH

φανερόω.

2 Co. 11: 6 φανερώσαντες *read* we have
  made (it) manifest LTTᵣAWH

Φαρισαῖος.

Mat. 15: 1 *trs* Pharisees and scribes
  TTᵣWH, *omit* οἱ LTTᵣWH
  16:12*add* Φ. T, *see* ἄρτος
  19: 3 οἱ Φ.—*omit* οἱ LTTᵣAWH
  23:14(13) *omit the verse* LTTᵣAWH,
  see κρίμα
Mar. 2:16 καὶ οἱ Φ.—τῶν Φαρισαίων καὶ
  omit (καί WH), *read* scribes
  of the Pharisees TTᵣWH
  18 οἱ τῶν Φ.¹—οἱ Φαρισαῖοι (*omit*
  of) GEds
  9:11*say—add* οἱ Φαρισαῖοι καὶ
  the Pharisees and [L]T
  10: 2 οἱ Φ.—*omit* οἱ GLTᵣAWWH
Lu. 5:30 *trs* Pharisees and their
  scribes Eds
  11:44 *omit* scribes and Pharisees,
  hypocrites G[L]TTᵣAWHR
  14: 1 [τῶν] Φ. AWH
Joh. 7:32 *trs* the chief priests and the
  Pharisees Eds
  18: 3 τῶν Φαρισαίων LTTᵣWHR, [τῶν]
  Φ. A
Acts 23: 6 Φ.³—Φαρισαίων, *read* son of
  Pharisees Eds

φαρμακεία.

Gal. 5:20 φαρμακία WH
Rev. 9:21 φαρμακιῶν T, φαρμακός AWH
  18·23 φαρμακίᾳ TAWH

φαρμακεύς.

Rev. 21: 8 φαρμακεύς GEds

φαρμακός.

Rev. 9:21*φαρμάκων *for* φαρμακειῶν
  (—κεία) AWH
  21: 8*φαρμακοῖς *for* φαρμακεῦσιν
  (—κεύς) GEds

φάσκω.

Rev. 2: 2 λέγω GEds

φάτνη.

Lu. 2: 7 τῇ φ.—*omit* τῇ LTTᵣAWH
  12 τῇ φ.—*omit* τῇ GEds

φαῦλος.

Ro. 9:11*φαῦλον *for* κακόν (—κός)
  LTTᵣAWH
2 Co. 5:10*φαῦλον *for* κακόν (—κός)
  TTᵣWH

Lu. 11:33 φῶς LTᵣAWH

φείδομαι.

Ro. 11:21 φ.²—φείσεται, *read* neither
  will he spare GEds

φελόνης, *see* φαιλόνης.

φέρω, οἴσω, ἤνεγκα.

Mat. 7:18*ἐνεγκεῖν *for* ποιεῖν¹ (—έω) TWH
  for π.² T
Mar. 2: 3 *trs* πρὸς αὐτὸν φ. παραλ. LTᵣ
  φ. πρὸς αὐτὸν παραλ. TAWH
  6:27 ἐνέγκαι, *read* (him) to bring
  his head TTᵣAWH
  11: 2*φέρετε *for* ἀγάγετε (ἄγω)
  TTᵣAWH
  7*φέρουσιν *for* ἤγαγον (ἄγω)
  TTᵣAWH
Lu. 15:23 φέραντες—φέρετε TTᵣAWH
Acts 25: 7 καταφέρω LTTᵣAWH
  18*ἔφερον *for* ἐπίφερον (ἐπιφέρω)
  Eds

φεύγω.

Mar. 14:50 trs ἔφυγον πάντες TTrAWH
Joh. 6:15*φεύγει for ἀνεχώρησεν (ἀνα-
χωρέω) T
10:13 omit the hireling fleeth
[L]TTrAWH
Heb.12:25 ἐκφεύγω LTTrAWHR
Rev. 9: 6 φεύγει fleeth LTTrAWHR

φημί.

Mat. 13:29 φησίν saith LTTrAWHR
19:18*λέγει (ἔφη L) αὐτῷ, ποιας;—
ποίας; φησίν, which? saith
he T
18*ἔφη for εἶπεν (-πον) WH
22:37*ἔφη for εἶπεν GLTTrAWH
Mar. 9:12*ἔφη for εἶπεν (-πον) TTrAWH
38*ἔφη for ἀπεκρίθη (ἀποκρίνομαι)
TTrAWH
10:20*ἔφη for εἶπεν (-πον) TTrAWH
29*ἔφη ὁ Ἰησοῦς for ὁ Ἰ. εἶπεν
TAWH
12:24*trs ἔφη (ἔ. for εἶπεν) αὐτοῖς
ὁ Ἰησοῦς TTrAWH
Lu. 15:17*ἔφη for εἶπεν (-πον) TWH
22:58*ἔφη for εἶπεν (-πον) TTrAWH
23:40*ἔφη for λέγων (-γω) TWH
Joh. 18:29*φησίν for εἶπεν (-πον) TTrAWH
Acts 2:38 omit ἔφη LTTrAWHR
38*μετανοήσατε—add φησίν T
25:22 omit ἔφη LTTrAWHR
26:24 φησίν saith LTTrAWHR
28 omit ἔφη Eds

* **φημίζω, to speak, report.**

Mat. 28:15 ἐφημίσθη for διεφημίσθη (δια-
φημίζω) T

φθαρτός.

1 Co. 15:54 omit this corruptible shall
have put on incorruption,
and WH

φθέγγομαι.

Acts 4:18 τὸ...φ.—omit τὸ LTWH

φθείρω.

2 Pet. 2:12*καὶ φθαρήσονται for καταφθα-
ρήσονται (-θείρω) Eds

Φιλαδέλφεια, -φία TWH.

φιλέω.

Rev. 22:15 ὁ φ.—omit ὁ LTTrAWWH: trs
maketh and loveth T

Φίλητός, Φίλητος WH.

Φίλιππος.

Mat. 14: 3 omit Philip [T]A
Lu. 3:19 omit Philip GEds
Joh. 1:46(47) ὁ Φίλιππος LTTrAWH
6: 5 τὸν Φ.—omit τὸν LTTrAWH
7 ὁ Φίλιππος T
12:22 Φ.¹—ὁ Φίλιππος WH
Acts 8:37 omit the verse GLTTrAWH

φίλος.

Lu. 11: 8 trs φίλον αὐτοῦ TTrAWH
Acts 27: 3 τοὺς φίλους A.V.C GEds

Φιλοτιμέομαι.

Ro. 15:20 φιλοτιμούμαι LTr

φιλόφρων.

1 Pet. 3: 8 courteous—humble minded,
ταπεινόφρων GEds

φιμόω.

1 Co. 9: 9 κημόω TTrA
1 Pet. 2:15 φιμοῖν WH

φλόξ.

2 Th. 1: 8 φλογὶ πυρός a flame of fire
LTrW
Rev. 2:18 φλόξ T

φοβέομαι.

Mat. 9: 8*ἐφοβήθησαν for ἐθαυμασαν
(θαυμάζω) LTTrAWH
10:28 φ.¹—φοβεῖσθε GLTrW
28 φ.²—φοβεῖσθε TAWH
31 φοβεῖσθε LTTrAWH
Acts 23:10*φοβηθεὶς for εὐλαβηθεὶς (-βεό-
μαι) LTTrAWH

φόβητρον, -θρο- LTrAWH.

φόβος.

Acts 2:43*add at end ἐν Ἰερουσαλήμ,
φόβος τε ἦν μέγας ἐπὶ πάντας
in Jerusalem, and great fear
was upon all T
Jude 23 οὓς δὲ (omit οὓς δὲ WH) σώζετε
ἐκ πυρὸς ἁρπάζοντες, οὓς δὲ
ἐλεᾶτε (ἐλεεῖτε W) ἐν φόβῳ
and some save, snatching
(them) out of the fire; and
on some have mercy with
fear Eds

φοῖνιξ.

Rev. 7: 9 φοίνικας T

φονεύω.

Mar. 10:19 trs do not kill, do not commit adultery LWHR
Jas. 2:11 φ.²—φονεύεις LTTrAWH

φόνος.

Mar. 7:21, 22 trs fornications, thefts,
murders, adulteries TTrAWH
Gal. 5:21 omit murders [L]T[Tr]WHR

φορέω.

1 Co. 15:49 φ.² φορέσωμεν let us bear
LTTrW

φορτίον.

Acts 27:10*φορτίου for φόρτου (-τος) GEds

φόρτος.

Acts 27:10 φορτίον GEds

Φουρτουννάτος, Φορ- Eds.

φράζω.

Mat. 13:36 declare—explain, διασαφέω
LTrWH

φράσσω.

2 Co. 11:10 see σφραγίζω

φρεναπατάω.

Gal. 6: 3 trs φ. ἑαυτόν LTTrAWH

φρονέω.

Ro. 14: 6 omit LTT[r][A]WHR, see κύριος
1 Co. 4: 6 omit to think (of men) Eds
Phil. 2: 5 φρονεῖτε LTTrAWH
3:16 omit rule, let us mind the
same thing GLTTrAWHR
See also ὑψηλοφρονέω.

φρόνιμος.

Mat. 25: 2 trs foolish & wise LTTrAWHR
Lu. 12:42 ὁ φρόνιμος Eds

Φύγελλος, —ελος Eds.

φυγή.

Mar. 13:18 omit your flight LTTrAWH

φυλακή.

Mat. 14: 3 τῇ φυλακῇ LTrA
Mar. 6:17 τῇ φ.—omit τῇ GEds
Lu. 3:20 τῇ φ.—ἐν τῇ φυλακῇ LTTrA
12:38 omit watch? TTrAWH
23:19 εἰς φ.—ἐν τῇ φυλακῇ TTrAWH
25 τὴν φ.—omit τὴν LTTrAWH
2 Co. 11:23 trs in prisons more frequent,
in stripes above measure
LTrAWHR, see περισσοτέρως

φυλάσσω.

Mat. 19:20 ἐφύλαξα LTTrAWH
Lu. 18:21 ἐφύλαξα LTTrAWH
Joh. 12:47*φυλάξῃ for πιστεύσῃ (-τεύω)
Eds
Acts 21:24 trs φ. τὸν νόμον LTTrAWWH

φύσις.

1 Co. 11:14 trs ἡ φύσις αὐτὴ Eds
Gal. 4: 8 trs φύσει μὴ GEds

φωνέω.

Mar. 1:26*φωνῆσαν for κράξαν (κράζω)
TTrAWH
3:31 καλέω LTTrAWH
10:49 εἶπεν, φωνήσατε αὐτόν said,
Call ye him TTrAWH
14:68 omit and the cock crew [L]WH
72 trs δὶς φωνῆσαι LTTrAWH

Joh. 10: 3*φωνεῖ for καλεῖ (-λέω)
LTTrAWH
13:38 φωνήσῃ LTTrAWH

φωνή.

Mat. 24:31 omit φ. read with a great
trumpet TWH
Lu. 1:42 voice—cry, κραυγή TTrAWH
Joh. 12:30 trs ἡ φωνὴ αὕτη LTTrAWWH
Acts 11: 9 trs ἐκ δευτέρου φωνή WH
14:10 τῇ φ.—omit τῇ LTTrWH
1 Co. 14: 8 trs σάλπιγξ φωνὴν τῷ WH
Rev. 4: 5 trs voices and thunderings
GEds
6: 1 φωνῇ GLTTrAWH, φωνῇ WH
7 omit the voice of G[Tr]W
8: 5 trs thunderings and voices
TTrAWH
10: 4 omit their voices GEds
11:12 φωνῆς μεγάλης TrAWH
14: 2 φ. ἤκουσα—ἡ φωνὴ ἣν ἤκουσα
ὡς the voice which I heard
(was) as GEds
18*φωνῇ for κραυγή LTTrWH
16:18 trs lightnings and voices and
thunders GEds

φῶς.

Mar. 14:54 τὸ φ.—omit τὸ E
Lu. 11:33*φῶς for φέγγος LTTrAWH
Eph. 5: 9*φωτός for πνεύματος(-μα) GEds
Rev. 21:24†trs περιπατήσουσιν τὰ ἔθνη
διὰ τοῦ φωτὸς αὐτῆς GEds
22: 5*φωτὸς λύχνου light of a candle
LTTrAWH
5 φωτός—φῶς WH

φωτεινός, —τινός WH.

φωτίζω.

Rev. 22: 5 φωτιεῖ (-ίσει LWHR) ἐπ' ([ἐπ']
WH) shall give them light
GEds

χαίρω.

Lu. 6:23 χάρητε GEds
Ro. 16:19 trs ἐφ' ὑμῖν οὖν χ. Eds
Rev. 11:10 χαίρουσιν rejoice GEds

χαλκηδών, χαλκε— T.

χαρά.

Lu. 15:10 trs γίνεται χαρά TTrAWH
Acts 20·24 omit with joy LTTrAWH
2 Co. 1:15*χαρὰν for χάριν (-ρις) WH
Philem. 7 see χάρις
3 Joh. 4 joy—thankfulness, χάρις WH

χάραγμα.

Rev. 15: 2 omit over his mark (and)
GEds

χαρίζομαι.

2 Co. 2:10†trs ὧ κεχ. εἴ τι κεχ. GEds

χάρις.

Lu. 17: 9 trs ἔχει χάριν LTTrAWH
Acts 6: 8*χάριτος for πίστεως (-τις)GEds
24:27 χάριτα Eds
Ro. 7:25*χάρις for εὐχαριστῶ (-τέω)
LTTrAWH
11: 6 omit but if (it be) of works
to end of verse GLTT[A]WHR
16:24 omit the verse LTT[A]WHR
2 Co. 1:15 χαρά WH
Eph. 4: 7 ἡ χ.—omit ἡ LT[A]WH
Col. 3:16 τῇ χάριτι LTTrAWH
Philem. 7 χάριν 8—χαρὰν (-ρά) A.V.C
EGEds
3 Joh. 4*χάριν for χαράν (-ρά) WH
Jude 4 χάριτα LTTrAWWH

χειμών.

Mat. 16: 3 When it is (ver. 2) to end of
verse 3 [TA] [[WH]]

χείρ.

Mat. 12:10 τὴν χ.—omit τὴν LTTrAWH
13 trs σου τὴν χεῖρα LTTrAWH
19:15 trs τὰς χεῖρας αὐτοῖς LTTrAWH
26:23 trs τὴν χ. ἐν τῷ τρυ. LTTrAWH
Mar. 5:23 trs τὰς χεῖρας αὐτῇ LTTrAWH
9:27 trs χ. αὐτοῦ LTTrWHR
16:18*add at commencement καὶ ἐν
ταῖς χερσὶν and in (their)
hands Tr[WH]
Lu. 24:40 omit the verse T[Tr][[WH]]
Joh. 20:25 trs μου τὴν χεῖρα TTrAWH

Acts 2:23 χειρός, *read* the hand of lawless (men) LTTrAWHR
  9:12 (τὰς L[WH]R) χεῖρας hands
LTTrWHR
  19: 6 τὰς χ.—*omit* τὰς LTTrAWHR
  21:11 *trs* feet and hands Eds
    27 *trs* ἐπ᾽ αὐτὸν τὰς χ. GLTTrAWHR
  24: 7 *omit* LTTr[A]WHR, *see* κρίνω
Heb. 2: 7 *omit* and didst set *to end of*
verse G[L]T[Tr]A[WH]
1 Pet. 5: 6 χεῖραι T
Rev. 1:16 *trs* χειρὶ αὐτοῦ LTTrAWHR
    17 *omit* χ. GEds
  19: 2 τῆς χ.—*omit* τῆς GEds

Χερουβίμ, —βείν LTTrWH, —βίν A.

χήρα.

Mat. 23:14(13) *omit the verse* LTTrAWHR,
see κρίμα

χθές, ἐχθές Eds.

χιλίαρχος.

Acts 21:32 τὸν χ.—*omit* τὸν W
  24: 7 *omit* LTTr[A]WHR, *see* κρίνω
  25:23 τοῖς χ.—*omit* τοῖς LTTrAWHR
Rev. 6:15 *trs* chief captains, and the
rich men GEds

χίλιοι.

Rev. 20: 4 τὰ χ.—*omit* τὰ A.V.C Eds
    6 τὸ χίλια TTr [τὰ] χ. AWH

χιών.

Mar. 9: 3 *mit* as snow TTrAWHR

χλευάζω.

Acts 2:13 διαχλευάζω GEds

χξς'.

Rev. 13:18 ἑξακόσιοι ἑξήκοντα ἓξ LAWH

χοῖρος.

Mat. 8:32 τῶν χ.¹-τοὺς χοίρους GLTTrWHR
    32 *omit* of swine² GLTTr[A]WHR
Mar. 5:14 the swine—them, αὐτοὺς GEds

Χοραζίν, —ζείν TTrAWH.

Lu. 10:13 Χωραζίν S, Χο- EGLTTrAWWH

χορηγέω.

2Co. 9:10 χορηγήσει will minister GEds

χορτάζω.

Lu. 15:16*χορτασθῆναι *for* γεμίσαι (-μί-
ζω) WHR, *see* κοιλία

χόρτος.

Mat. 14:19 τοῦ χόρτου LTTrWH

χράομαι.

1Co. 9:15 οὐ κέχρημαι οὐδενί GEds

χρεία.

Joh. 13:10 οὐκ ἔχει χ. LTTrAWWH
Acts 28:10 τὴν χ.—τὰς χρείας Eds

χρεωφειλέτης, χρεοφ— LTTrA,
χρεοφιλ— WH.

χρῆμα.

Mar. 10:24 τοῖς χ.—*omit* τοῖς LTrAWR,
omit for them that trust in
riches TWH

χρηστός.

Lu. 5:39 better-good χρηστός TTrAWH
1Co. 15:33 χρηστά GTTrAWWH

χρηστότης.

Ro. 11:22 goodness²-χρηστότης θεοῦ
goodness of God LTTrAWHR

Χριστός.

Mat. 16:21*Ἰησοῦς—*add* χριστός WH
  23: 8 *omit* (even) Christ GEds
Lu. 4:41 *omit* Christ¹ GLTTrAWHR
  23:39*trs οὐχὶ (o. *for* εἰ) σὺ εἶ ὁ χ.
TTrAWHR
Joh. 1:41(42) ὁ χ.—*omit* ὁ GEds
  4:42 *omit* the Christ LTTrAWHR
  6:69 *omit* χ. GLTTrAWHR, *see* υἱός
  7:42 *trs* ἔρχεται ὁ χριστὸς LTrAWHR

Acts 2:30 *omit* according to the flesh,
he would raise up Christ
GLTTrAWHR
    36 *trs* αὐτὸν καὶ χ. GEds
  3:20 *trs* Christ Jesus LTTrAWHR
  4:33*Jesus—*add* χριστοῦ Christ,
[L]T, *trs* 'Ι. χ. τοῦ κυρίου T,
τοῦ κυρ. 'Ι. ([χ.]L)τῆς ἀν. LWH
  5:42 *trs* Christ Jesus LTTrAWHR
  8:37 *omit the verse* GTTrAWHR
  9:20 Christ—Jesus, Ἰησοῦς GEds
    34 ὁ χ.—*omit* ὁ LTTrAWHR
  10:48*'Ἰησοῦ χριστοῦ *for* τοῦ κυρίου
(-ος) LTTrWHR
  15:11 *omit* Christ GTTrAWHR
  16:31 *omit* Christ LTTrAWHR
  17: 3 ὁ χ.—*omit* ὁ LTTr
  19: 4 *omit* Christ GLTTrAWHR
  20:21 *omit* Christ L[Tr]AWH
  28:31 *omit* Christ T
Ro. 1: 1 *trs* Christ Jesus TTr
    16 *omit* of Christ GEds
  2:16 *trs* Christ Jesus TWH
  6: 3, 11 *trs* Jesus Christ A.V.[?]
  8:11 τὸν χ.—*omit* τὸν LTTrAWHR
  10:17*χριστοῦ *for* θεοῦ (-ός) LTTrA
  14:10 Christ—God, θεός Eds   (WHR
    18 τῷ χ.—*omit* τῷ L[Tr]
  15: 5 *trs* Jesus Christ Tr
    16 *trs* Christ Jesus Eds
    29 τοῦ χ.—*omit* τοῦ GEds
  16:20 *omit* Christ T[TrA]WH
    24 *omit the verse* LTTr[A]WHR
1Co. 1: 1 *trs* Christ Jesus LTTrAW
  3:11 ὁ χ.—*omit* ὁ GEds
  5: 4 *omit* Christ *bis* LTTrAWHR
  6:11*Jesus—*add* χριστοῦ Christ
LTTrWHR
  9: 1 *omit* Christ LTTrAWH
    18 *omit* of Christ Eds
    21 χριστοῦ of Christ Eds
  10: 9 Christ—the Lord κύριος
LTTrAWHR
  11: 3 χ.²—τοῦ χριστοῦ [L]TTrAWHR
  15:23 χ.²-τοῦ χριστοῦ GEds
  16:22 *omit* Jesus Christ LTTrAWHR
    23 *omit* Christ TTrAWH
2Co. 1: 1 *trs* Christ Jesus TTrAWHR
    5 χ.²-τοῦ χριστοῦ GEds
    19 *trs* Christ Jesus TWH
  6:15 χριστοῦ LTTrAWH
  10: 7 *omit* Christ³ GEds
  11: 3 τὸν χ.—*omit* τὸν T
    31 *omit* Christ LTTrAWHR
  13: 5 *trs* Christ Jesus TTr
Gal. 2:16 χ.¹—*trs* Christ Jesus TTrWH
    16 χ.²—*trs* Jesus Christ A.V.[?]
    20*add χ. LTr, *see* υἱός
  3:14 *trs* Jesus Christ A.V.[?] TrWH
    17 *omit* in Christ LTTrAWHR
  4: 7 *omit* χ. *read* heir through
God LTTrAWHR
  5: 1 *trs* ἡμᾶς χριστὸς GEds
    4 τοῦ χ.—*omit* τοῦ LTTr[A]WH
  6:15 *omit* in Christ LTTrAWHR
Eph. 1: 1 *trs* Christ Jesus¹ LTTrAWHR
  2:20 *trs* Christ Jesus LTTrAWHR
  3: 6 τῷ χ.—*omit* τῷ LTTrAWHR
    9 *omit* by Jesus Christ GEds
    11 τῷ χριστῷ LTTrAWHR
    14 *omit* of our Lord Jesus Christ
Eds
  4:15 ὁ χ.—*omit* ὁ Eds
  5:21*χριστοῦ *for* θεοῦ (-ός) GEds
    29*χριστός *for* κυρίου GEds
  6: 6 τοῦ χ.—*omit* τοῦ LTTrAWHR
Phil. 1: 1 *trs* Christ Jesus¹ Eds
    2 *trs* Christ Jesus W
    6 *trs* Christ Jesus LTTrAW
    8 *trs* Christ Jesus GEds
    16 [τὸν] χ. LTrA
  2:21 *trs* Jesus Christ A.V.Vul
GLTTrAWR:
omit τοῦ GLTTrAWWH
    30 *omit* of Christ A: of (the)
Lord, κύριος WH: *omit* τοῦ
LTTrAWHR
  3:12 τοῦ χ.—*omit* τοῦ GEds
  4:13 *omit* Christ GEds
Col. 1: 1 *trs* Christ Jesus Eds
    2 *omit* and the Lord Jesus
Christ G[L]TTrAWWHR
  2: 2 *omit* and of Christ GA· *omit*
τοῦ GEds
    17 τοῦ χ.—*omit* τοῦ GW
    20 τῷ χ.—*omit* τῷ GEds
  3:13 Christ—the Lord, κύριος
LTrAWHR
    15*χριστοῦ *for* θεοῦ (-ός) GEds
    16*κυρίου Ἰησοῦ—'Ι. χριστοῦ LW
1Th. 1. 1 *omit* from God *to end of*
verse [L]TTrAWH

1Th. 2:19·3:11 *omit* Christ LTTrAWH2
  3:13 *omit* Christ Eds
2Th. 1: 8 *omit* Christ [L]TTrAWHR
    12 *omit* Christ¹ [L]TTrAWHR
  2: 2 Christ—the Lord, κύριος GEd·
  3:12 χριστῷ LTTrAWHR, *see* κύριος
1Ti. 1: 1 *trs* Christ Jesus¹ TTrAWWHR
    1 *trs* Christ Jesus² GEds
    2 *trs* Jesus Christ A.V.F.
    16 *trs* Christ Jesus LTrAWH
  2: 7 *omit* in Christ GEds
  4: 6 *trs* Christ Jesus Eds
  5:21 *t.* Christ Jesus(om. Lord) Ed·
2Ti. 1: 1 *trs* Christ Jesus¹ TTrAWHR
    10 *trs* Christ Jesus LTTrAWH
  2: 3 *trs* Christ Jesus Eds
    19 Christ—(the) Lord, κύριος
GEds
  4: 1 *trs* Christ Jesus (omit Lord)
Eds
    22 *omit* Christ LTTr[A]WHR
Tit. 1: 4 *trs* Christ Jesus (omit Lord)
LTTrAWHR
  2:13 *trs* Christ Jesus TTrWH
Philem. 9 *trs* Christ Jesus LTTrAWHR
    20*χριστῷ *for* κυρίῳ² (-ριος) GEds
Heb. 3: 1 *omit* Christ GEds
  9:24 ὁ χ.—*omit* ὁ GEds
1Pet. 3:15*χριστόν *for* θεόν (-ός) Eds
1Joh. 1: 7 *omit* Christ LTTrAWH
  4: 3 *om.* Christ is come in the flesh
GLTTrAWHR, *omit* Christ W
  5: 6 ὁ χ.—*omit* ὁ TTrAWWHR
2Joh. 9 *omit* of Christ² Eds
Jude 25*add χ. GEds, *see* κύριος
Rev. 1: 9 *trs* Christ Jesus¹ W
    9 *omit* Christ *bis* LTTrAWHR
  12:17 *omit* Christ GLTTrAWHR
  20: 4 χριστοῦ 8-τοῦ χ. EGEds
  22:21 *omit* Christ LTTrA[WH]R

χρονίζω.

Heb.10:37 χρονίσει TTrWH

χρόνος.

Lu. 8:27 καὶ χρόνῳ ἱκανῷ οὐκ ἐνεδύσατο
ἱμάτιον and for a long time
had worn no clothes TTrWHR
  23: 8*θέλων ἐξ ἱκανοῦ—ἐξ ἱκανῶν
χρόνων θέλων of a long time
LTTrAWHR
Joh. 7:33 *trs* χρόνον μικρὸν LTTrAWH
  14: 9 τοσούτῳ χρόνῳ LT
Jude 18 ἐπ᾽ ἐσχάτου (add τοῦ LT[A])
χρόνου at the end of the
time Eds

χρύσεος, —σοῦς.

Rev. 1:13 χρυσᾶν LTTrAWH
  2: 1 χρυσέων LTrA
  4: 4 χρυσέους Tr
  5: 8 χρυσέας Tr

χρυσίον.

1Co. 3:12*χρυσίον f. χρυσόν (ός) ITTrWHR
1Ti. 2: 9*χρυσίῳ *for* χρυσῷ(-σός) LWHR
Rev.17: 4*χρυσίῳ *for* χρυσῷ (-σος)
GLAWWHR
  18:16*χρυσίῳ *for* χρυσῷ (-σός)
GLTTrAWWHR

χρυσός.

1Co. 3:12 χρυσίον TTrWHR
1Ti. 2: 9 χρυσίον LWHR
Rev.17: 4 χρυσίον GLAWWHR
  18:16 χρυσίον GLTTrAWWHR

χωλός.

Mat.18: 8 *trs* maimed or halt LTWHR
Lu. 14:21 *trs* the blind and the halt
LTTrAWHR
Acts 3:11 *omit* GEds, *see* ἰάομαι

χώρα.

Mat. 6:55*χώραν *for* περίχωρον (-ρος)
TTrAWHR

Χωραζίν, *see* Χοραζίν.

χωρέω.

Joh. 21:25 χωρήσειν TrWHR: *omit the*
verse T

χωρίς.

2Co. 12: 3*for ἐκτὸς LTTrAWHR
Jas. 2:18*for ἐκ¹ A.V.BGEds

ψαλμός.

Acts 13:33 *see* πρῶτος

ψεύδομαι.

Jas. 3:14†*trs* glory not against the truth, and lie T

ψευδομάρτυρ.

Mat. 26:60(61) two false witnesses—*omit* false witnesses TTₜAWHR

ψευδομαρτυρέω.

Ro. 13: 9 *omit* thou shalt not bear false witness GEds

ψεῦδος.

Rev. 14: 5*ψεῦδος *for* δόλος GEds

ψευδόχριστος.

Mar. 13:22 *omit* false Christs and ᴀ

ψιχίον.

Lu. 16:21 *om.* the crumbs [L]T[Tᵣ]AWHR

ψυχή.

Mar. 12:33 *omit* and with all the soul [L]TWHR

Lu. 9:56 *omit* for the Son *to* save (them) GLTTₜAWHR

10:27 ἐν ὅλῃ τῇ ψυχῇ σου καὶ ἐν ὅλῃ τῇ ἰσχύϊ σου, καὶ ἐν ὅλῃ τῇ διανοίᾳ LTTₜAWHR

14:26 *trs* ψυχὴν ἑαυτοῦ WH

Acts 2:31 *omit* his soul GLTTₜAWHR

4:32 ἡ ψ.—*omit* ἡ LTTₜAWHR

ψυχρός.

Rev. 3:16 *trs* hot nor cold GTTₜAWWHR

ψωμίζω.

1Co. 13: 3 ψωμίσω s—ψωμίζω ᴇ

Ω.

Rev. 1: 8 ὦ LAWH

11 *omit* GEds, *see* ᴀ

21: 6 : 22:13 ὦ LWH

ὦ, ἦς, ἦ, *etc.*

Mat. 20: 7 *omit* LTTₜAWHR, *see* δίκαιος

Lu. 20:28*ἦ *for* ἀποθάνῃ (-θνήσκω) LTTₜAWHR

Joh. 10: 6*ἦ *for* ἦν Tᵣ

14:16*ἦ (*after* αἰῶνα L, *after* ὑμῶν T) *for* μένῃ (-νω) LTTₜAWHR

15:11*ἦ *for* μείνῃ (μένω) LTTₜAWHR

17:19 *trs* ὦσιν καὶ αὐτοὶ Eds

1Co. 5:11 ἦ¹ s—ἦ A.V.ʙEGEds

7: 5*ἦτε *for* συνέρχησθε (-χομαι) GEds

Jas. 2:15 *omit* ὦσιν TTₜAWHR

Ὠβήδ.

Mat. 1: 5 Ἰωβήδ *bis* LTTₜAWH

Lu. 3:32 Ἰωβήδ LTTₜA, Ἰωβήλ WH

ὧδε.

Mat. 14:18 *trs* ὧδε αὐτούς LTTₜAWH

Mar. 9: 1 *trs* ὧδε τῶν TTₜAWHR

13: 2*be left—*add* ὦ. here LTₜWHR

Lu. 9:27 αὐτοῦ (*adv.*) TTₜAWH

15:17*ὦ. λιμῷ here with famine GTₜA, λιμῷ ὦ. LTWHR

16:25*for* ὧδε Eds

17:23 *trs* see there, or see here TTₜAWHR

21: 6*stone—*add* ὦ. here LWHR

1Co 4: 2*for* ὁ δέ LTTₜAWH

Jas. 2: 3 *omit* here² LTTₜAWHR

Rev. 14:12 *omit* here (are) GEds

ὤν, οὖσα, ὄν, *etc.*

Mar. 4:31*add* ὄν LTTₜAWHR, *see* μικρός

13:16 *omit* ὤν LTTₜWHR

14:43 *omit* ὤν A.V.Vul LTTₜ[A]WHR

Lu. 6: 3 *omit* ὄντες LTₜWH

Joh. 3:13 *omit* which is in heaven WH

6:71 *omit* being LTₜAWHR

8: 9*οὖσα *for* ἑστῶσα (ἵστημι) WWHR

9:40 *trs* μετ' αὐτοῦ ὄντες LTTₜAWHR

Acts 11:22*τῆς²—*add* οὔσης TTₜWHR

18:12*ἀνθυπάτου ὄντος *for* ἀνθυπατεύοντος (-πατεύω) LTTₜAWH

25:23 *omit* οὖσιν Eds

26:21*συλλαβόμενοι—*add* ὄντα T

1Co. 9:20*add* GEds, *see* νόμος

1Ti. 1:13 τὸν...ὄντα—τὸ...ὄ. LTTₜAWHR

Rev. 5: 5 *omit* ὤν GEds

ὠόν, ῳόν WH.

ὥρα.

Mat. 20: 6 *omit* hour LTTₜAWHR

24:36 τῆς ὥ.—*omit* τῆς GLTTₜAWHR

42 hour—day, ἡμέρα LTTₜAWHR

Mar. 15:34†*trs* τῇ ἐνάτῃ ὥρᾳ LTTₜAWHR

Lu. 13:31*ὥρᾳ *for* ἡμέρᾳ TAWHR

Joh. 4:52 *trs* τὴν ὥ. παρ' αὐτῶν LTTₜAWH

11: 9 *trs* ὥραί εἰσιν LTTₜAWWH

Acts 10:30 *omit* hour² LTTₜAWHR

ὥς.

Mat. 5:48* ¦ 6:5*16*for* ὥσπερ LTTₜAWHR

9:36*for* ὡσεί Tᵣ

21:46 εἰς LTTₜAWH

24:38*for* ὥσπερ LTAWH, ὥς Tᵣ

28: 3* 4*for* ὡσεί LTTₜAWH

9 *omit* LTTₜAWHR, *see* μαθητής

Mar. 1: 2 καθώς TTₜWHR

10*for* ὡσεί GEds

3: 5 *om.* whole as the other GEds

9: 3 *om.* as snow TTₜAWHR

12:26 πῶς TTₜAWH

14:72*for* οὗ LTTₜAWHR

Lu. 1:56*for* ὡσεί LTTₜWH

2:37 of about—up to. ἕως LTTₜAWH

3:22*for* ὡσεί LTTₜAWH

6: 4 [how] TₜWH, πῶς ʟ

10 *om.* as the other [L]T[Tᵣ]AWH

9:52*for* ὥστε WH

54 *omit* even as Elias did TTₜ[A]WH

11: 2 *omit* as in heaven so in earth G[L]TTₜAWH

14:22 as—which, ὅς TTₜAWH

17:28 also as—even as, καθώς TTₜAWH

18:11*ὥς *for* ὥσπερ LTₜ

Joh. 1:32*for* ὡσεί GEds

4: 6*for* ὡσεί Eds

45*for* ὅτε T

6:10*for* ὡσεί TTₜAWH

7:10 *omit* as it were T

46 *omit* L[Tₜ]AWH, *see* ἄνθρωπος

12:35* 36*for* ἕως LTTₜAWH

19:14*δὲ ὡσεί—ἦν ὡς Eds

39*for* ὡσεί GEds

Acts 1:15 ὡσεί T

4: 4*for* ὡσεί [LTₜA]WH

5:36*for* ὡσεί Eds

9:18*for* ὡσεί LTTₜWH

10:47*for* καθὼς LTTₜAWH

17:14 as it were—as far as, ἕως LTTₜWH

19:34 ὡσεί WH

27:37*ship—*add* ὡς about WH

Ro. 6:13 ὡσεί LTTₜAWH

1Co. 5: 3 *omit* as¹ Eds

9:22 *omit* as [L]TTₜAWWHR

10: 7 ὥσπερ LTTₜAWH

13: 1 γέγονα—*add* velut A.V.† Vul

2Co. 1: 7*for* ὥσπερ Eds

2Co. 9: 5*for* ὥσπερ GEds

Eph. 5:24*for* ὥσπερ LTTₜAWHR

6: 7*service—*add* ὡς A.V.ʙ GEds

1Th. 2:13 οὐ—*add* ut A.V.† Vul

2Th. 2: 4 *omit* as God GEds

Heb. 1:12*add* ὡς L[Tₜ]WHR, *see* ἱμάτιον

11:12*ὡς ἡ *for* ὡσεί GEds

Jas. 5: 5 *omit* as Eds

1Pet. 3:16 *omit* of you, as of evildoers TAWHR

4:19 *omit* as LTTₜAWHR

Rev. 1:14*for* ὡσεί GEds

4: 6*throne!—*add* ὡς as GEds

7 *omit* ὡς G[ᴀ]W

5:11*I heard—*add* ὡς as TTₜ[A]

6: 6*I heard—*add* ὡς as LTTₜAWHR

14: 2*add* ὡς GEds, *see* φωνή

3 *omit* as it were GT[TₜA]

16:13*for* ὅμοια (-ιος) GEds

19: 1*I heard—*add* ὡς as EGEds

12 *omit* as TTₜ[A]WHR

ὡσαννά, ὡ— LT.

ὡσαύτως.

Lu. 13: 3 ὁμοίως LTTₜAWHR

5*for* ὁμοίως TTₜAWHR

ὡσεί.

Mat. 9:36 ὡς Tᵣ

28: 3. 4 ὡς LTTₜAWH

Mar. 1:10 ὡς GEds

6:44 *omit* about GEds

Lu. 1:56 ὡς LTTₜWH

3:22 ὡς LTTₜAWH

9:14*κλισίας—*add* ὡ. read by about [LTᵣ]AWHR

Joh. 1:32 ὡς GEds

4: 6 ὡς Eds

6:10 ὡς TTₜAWH

19:14 δὲ ὡσεί—ἦν ὡς was about Eds

39 ὡς GEds

Acts 1:15*for* ὡς T

4: 4 ὡς [LTₜA]WH: *omit* about T

5:36 ὡς Eds

9:18 ὡς LTTₜWH

19:34*for* ὡς WH

Ro. 6:13*for* ὡς LTTₜAWH

Heb.11:12*for* ὡς ἡ GEds

Rev. 1:14 ὡς GEds

ὥσπερ.

Mat. 5:48 ¦ 6:5, 16 ὡς LTTₜAWH

24:38 ὡς LTTₜAWH

Lu. 18:11 ὡς (ὡς) LTₜ

1Co. 10: 7*for* ὡς LTTₜAWH

2Co. 1: 7 ὡς Eds

9: 5 ὡς GEds

Eph. 5:24 ὡς LTTₜAWH

ὥστε.

Lu. 4:29*for* εἰς τό GLTTₜAWH

9:52 ὡς WH

20:20*for* εἰς τό LTTₜAWH

Jas. 1:19 wherefore—ye know (this) εἰδέω LTTₜAWH

* ὠτάριον, a small ear.

Mar. 14:47 ὠτάριον *for* ὠτίον LTTₜAWH

Joh. 18:10 ὠτάριον *for* ὠτίον TTₜAWHR

ὠτίον.

Mar. 14:47 ὠτάριον LTTₜAWH

Joh. 18:10 ὠτάριον LTTₜAWHR

ὠφέλεια, λία WH.

ὠφελέω.

Mat. 16:26 ὠφεληθήσεται shall be profited LTTₜAWHR

Mar. 8:36 ὠφελεῖ doth it profit TAWHR